A ROLLING STONE PRESS BOOK

EDITOR
HOLLY GEORGE-WARREN

ASSOCIATE EDITOR
SHAWN DAHL

EDITORIAL ASSISTANT
GREG EMMANUEL

WRITERS
Paul Evans

Steve Futterman

Elysa Gardner

Mark Kemp

Evelyn McDonnell

Steven Mirkin

Michael Shore

(First edition contributors: Ken Braun, Jim Farber, Nelson George,

Jeff Howrey, Ira Kaplan, John Milward, Jon Pareles, Patricia Romanowski,

Mitchell Schneider, Michael Shore)

THE NEW

Rolling Stone

Encyclopedia of

Rock & Roll

Completely Revised and Updated

Edited by

Patricia Romanowski

and

Holly George-Warren

Consulting Editor

Jon Pareles

FIRESIDE

A ROLLING STONE PRESS BOOK

New York   London   Toronto   Sydney   Tokyo   Singapore

FIRESIDE

Rockefeller Center
1230 Avenue of the Americas
New York, NY 10020

Designed by Richard Oriolo

Manufactured in the United States of America

5   7   9   10   8   6   4

Library of Congress Cataloging-in-Publication Data
The new Rolling stone encyclopedia of rock & roll / edited by
Patricia Romanowski and Holly George-Warren ; consulting
editor, Jon Pareles.—Completely rev. and updated.
p. cm.
Rev. ed. of: The Rolling stone encyclopedia of rock & roll.
c1983.
"A Rolling Stone Press book."
Includes discographies.
1. Rock music—Bio-bibliography—Dictionaries.
I. Romanowski, Patricia.   II. George-Warren, Holly.
III. Pareles, Jon.   IV. Rolling stone (San Francisco, Calif.)
V. Rolling stone encyclopedia of rock & roll.
ML102.R6R64   1995
781.66'03—dc20
95-35045   CIP   MN

ISBN 0-684-81044-1

Acknowledgments

It took nearly an army of people and at least a trillion hours to complete this second edition of *The* ROLLING STONE *Encyclopedia of Rock & Roll*. There are countless people to thank for making it possible, so I'll limit it to those whom we absolutely couldn't have done it without. . . .

First, of course, our gratitude goes to the talented and hardworking writers who did such an amazing job: Paul Evans, Steve Futterman, Elysa Gardner, Mark Kemp, Evelyn McDonnell, Steven Mirkin, and Michael Shore (who also contributed to the first *Encyclopedia* and this time around, in addition to writing tons of new entries, revised and updated lots of old ones). Thanks also to the writers who contributed to the previous edition, from which this book was built: Ken Braun (who helped out again with his vast knowledge of African pop), Jim Farber, Nelson George, Jeff Howrey, Ira Kaplan, John Milward, and Mitchell Schneider.

My staff at Rolling Stone Press was relentless in the pursuit of *Encyclopedia* perfection: Editorial Assistant Greg "Trial by Fire" Emmanuel (who was lucky enough to join our staff four months before we finished the manuscript), Associate Editor Shawn "Cool, Calm, and Collected" Dahl and freelance assistant Ben "Mr. Exuberance" Hunter burned the midnight oil, pitched in and wrote or rewrote entries that had fallen through the cracks, helped with editing, fact-checking, proofreading, photo research, you name it . . . thank God for jacks of all trades! We got lots of help from two years' worth of Rolling Stone Press interns (who, we hope, got the education of their lives): Lora Corrado, Zev Borow, Jeff Jackson, Adam Sherwin, Mona Zutshi, Joshua J. Shoemaker, Heidi Schnorr, Carrie Klein, Laura Whiteley, Joseph Tristano, Mark Krzos, Anthony Bozza, Carrie Smith, Sidney Painter, Catherine Wallace, Kevin O'Dea, and Jamie Chesler. Thanks, also, to our crack team of fact-checkers: Andrea Odintz, David Cohen, Eric Berman, Tracie Matthews, Vanessa Baran, Emily Marcus, Kim Ahearn, Matt Birkbeck, and Joe Rosenthal. Special thanks go to Patricia Day Cobb, our ace-in-the-hole researcher extraordinaire, who single-handedly held down our London office.

The book could not have been completed without the guiding force of writer/editor/organizational queen Patricia Romanowski. (It was particularly gratifying for me to coedit this book with her, since she hired me back in 1982 as a fact-checker for the first edition of the *Encyclopedia*). Patty put together an excellent team at Rolling Stone Press East: Her husband, writer Philip Bashe, worked tirelessly on an enormous amount of the revisions. Andrea Dresdale did a super job updating, revising, and fact-checking. Computer whiz Danielle Karmel, Lisa LaRocco, Eve Yedziniak, Ariana Stritzl, and Jeremy Lehrman also assisted in many ways. Justin Eric Romanowski Bashe assisted by sleeping through the night.

Without the fine crew at Fireside/Simon & Schuster, we couldn't have created the monster book we envisioned. A thousand kudos to our very supportive editor, Dominick Anfuso, and his assistant, Casandra Jones, as well as for the editorial (and music trivia) expertise of Stephen Messina, John Paul Jones, Philip Metcalf, Sean Devlin, Will Rigby, Andy Hafitz, Jennifer Landau, and Tricia Wygal. We also appreciate the efforts of our agent, Sarah Lazin, and ROLLING STONE's Jann S. Wenner, Kent Brownridge, John Lagana, Fred Woodward, Geraldine Hessler, and Carolyn Horne.

We were very pleased (and surprised) by how helpful many musicians, their publicists and managers, and record company personnel were in ensuring that we got the facts straight. Above-and-beyond honors go to the following artists: Mitch Ryder, John Mayall, John Kay, Jeff Hanna, Otis Williams, Yoko Ono, Elliott Murphy, Ian Wallace, Richard Carpenter, Tonio K., Don Henley, Art Garfunkel, Mick Box, Barry Adamson, Jayne County, Handsome Dick Manitoba, Cedella Marley, Tony Levin, Sam Andrew, Ron Asheton, David Bowie, Bill Bruford, Fred Smith, Will Rigby, Kinky Friedman, Willie D, Corky Laing, Martin Price, Lene Lovich, Parrish Smith, Kangol, Ofra Haza, Alphonsus Cassel (Arrow), Swamp Dogg, Alejandro Escovedo, Franchesca Robi, Bo Diddley, Martin Phillipps, Jason Ringenberg, Steve Wynn, David Conley, and Gilbert O'Sullivan (NOT!). Also our undying gratitude to these music-biz honchos: Josh Grier; the indefatigable Rhino Guys: Gary Stewart, James Austin, David McLees, Ted Myers, Gary Peterson, Stephen Peeples, and David Dorn; Harry "Practically an RS Press Editor" Weinger; Andy Schwartz; Jennifer Gross; Bob Small; Steve Eggerton; Jennifer Graham; Steve Burton; Carrie Svingen; Michael Hill; and Doug Wygal. Others who went out of their way for us: Jim "the Hound" Marshall, David McGee, Jeff Tamarkin, Bonnie Miller, Anthony De-Curtis, David Fricke, Alan Light, Kevin O'Neil, Meredith Williams, Andrew List, Pete Howard and the *ICE* newsletter folks, Shane K. Bernard, B. George, Erik Sanko, Kelly Flynn, Robert Warren, Beth Cohen, Elizabeth McNamara, Sarah Hutt, and David Rees. And extra thanks to Jon Pareles for his guidance.

The *Encyclopedia* writers acknowledge the following:

PE: Thanks to Anthony DeCurtis and Susan Hayes.

MK: Thanks to Lorraine Ali, Scott Becker, Ernest Hardy, Sandy Masuo, Bob Merlis (Warner Bros.), Ron Coleman (SST), Mike D., Jason Fine, and Robb Moore (4AD).

EM: Thanks to Sara Valentine and Magenta.

SM would like to thank Holly, Shawn, and Patty for the chance, and for their patience and support. Thanks also to Richard Barone, Andy Schwartz (Epic), Carrie Svingen (Rykodisc), Kathie Gillis (Virgin), Jill Richmond (Bar/None), Stephen K. Peeples and everyone at Rhino, Lloyd Cole, Walter Salas-Humara, Steve Karas and Stacy Sanner (A&M), Susan Mainzer (Island), Jill Tomlinson (Island), John Otway, and Kris Needs.

MS acknowledges Patricia Romanowski, Holly George-Warren, and everyone at Rolling Stone Press for their assistance, and his wife, Susan, and daughter, Dara, for their love and support.

Finally, we thank all those readers who made the first *Encyclopedia* such a success. Here's to the next generation of ROLLING STONE *Encyclopedia of Rock & Roll* aficionados!

HOLLY GEORGE-WARREN
June 1995

Preface to the First Edition

by Jon Pareles

There's no stopping rock & roll. It is the most vital, unpredictable force in pop culture, and the exception to every rule. Like all important popular art, it can speak to and from the public's heart of hearts even if it has been crafted by the most knowing artisans. And even at its most elaborate it hints at a rebel spirit: the idea that an outsider with something important to say can broadcast it to the world. At its best, rock can be entertainment, good business, and catharsis all at once; at its worst, it's only rock & roll.

It is music that just can't be pinned down, a contradiction any old way you choose it. Rock can be both amateur and professional, innocent and slick, subtle and crass, sincere and contrived, smart and stupid. It is a happy bastard style, claiming a pedigree from jazz, blues, Tin Pan Alley, country, classical music, movies, television, sex, drugs, art, literature, electronics, and out-and-out noise. It is rooted in real emotion; it is also rooted in racism, cynicism, and greed.

Rock accepts everything its detractors say, only to laugh it off. Sure, its basics are stolen, and its ideas are often clichés. Yes, it tends to aim for a lowest common denominator and appeal to base, primal impulses. It is proud to be a commodity, one that brings in billions of dollars, with "artistic" success frequently measured in sales figures. It doesn't even have to be in tune. No matter—rock & roll moves people, in simple and sophisticated ways. And it never takes no for an answer.

The history of rock & roll is a wild tangle, affected by changes in technology, media, demographics, politics, and the economy as well as by the inspirations of packagers and musicians. Rock cheerfully accepts all its roles; it is product and spectacle and art, something for everybody, and its development and documentation are by no means orderly.

In the Fifties, pop was infiltrated by rockabilly from Memphis and blues from Chicago and rhythm & blues from New Orleans and doo-wop from city streetcorners, more like outbreaks of some mysterious contagion—rockin' pneumonia?—than a concerted artistic movement. The music business counterattacked with its own more malleable teen idols and girl groups, but by the early Sixties their records were rocking anyway. As baby-boom babies became America's largest population group, the Beatles and other British Invasion bands fed back Little Richard and Chuck Berry and teen-idol pop to an eager audience, and rock took over pop.

During the Sixties the music grouped and regrouped into an explosion of genres: folk rock, soul, Motown, psychedelic rock, hard rock, funk, blues rock, jazz rock, progressive rock, country rock, bubblegum. By the Seventies, a split had been established between singles buyers (who listened to bouncy AM pop) and album buyers, as genres solidified and subdivided; the early Seventies brought heavy metal, Southern rock, fusion, hard funk, singer/songwriters, and classical rock. As rock record buying peaked in the later Seventies, disco and punk and reggae arose to reemphasize rhythm and energy, and in the Eighties those styles—and all the rest—helped foster new wave, rap, and other genres yet unnamed. After all these years, rock is still wide open.

But one kind of tension shows up in every phase of rock. That's the tension between convention and rebellion—between familiarity and freedom. In the music itself, musicians forge personal statements from a common "commercial" language; imitators become innovators because they can't help leaving fingerprints on the formula. Periodically, when genres become too familiar, new generations of rockers arrive with something tougher and simpler, shaking down the current convention. That tension makes rock an eternal hybrid, testing and absorbing and mutating new ideas as the public listens.

The music business also sees battles between tradition and insurgency, between a pop-star careerism it understands and a rock-rebel goal it doesn't. Rock has always been a collision—and a marriage—of minority culture and majority tastes; new ideas pop out of unlikely places to threaten, then merge with, the mainstream. Virtually every rock genre has come out of nowhere—amateur musicians, independent record labels—to be taken up and marketed by major corporations when the coast is clear. As the music annexes ideas, the music business accepts new approaches.

Rock's most pervasive minority-to-majority connection has been to act out the tug-of-war between black and white culture in America. "If I could find a white man who had the Negro sound and the Negro feel," said Sam Phillips, who discovered Elvis Presley, "I could make a billion dollars." Rock has continually crisscrossed the color line, as each side borrowed the other's secrets and added a few tricks of its own, a constant process of thievery and homage and inexact imitation. In uncountable ways, rock is a metaphor for American culture—a vital, unpredictable mess of individualism and assimilation.

So much for my grand theories (which owe quite a bit to Greil Marcus, Ishmael Reed, Robert Palmer, Robert Christgau, and others). With the information in this encyclopedia, you are welcome to assemble your own thesis, and you'll be able to base it on accurate, objective, salient information. This encyclopedia was designed to tell, as clearly and concisely as possible, the stories of the people who made the music. As in the music, the category of "rock" is open-ended. We have included entries on country, blues, jazz, and even classical musicians who have left a mark on rock music. And since rock's commercial peaks don't always coincide with its artistic ones, we have included unsung (or perhaps unsold) innovators as well as hitmakers, Professor Longhair and Captain Beefheart along with Styx.

Why assemble another rock encyclopedia? Because, frankly, the others are inadequate. *The* ROLLING STONE *Encyclopedia of Rock & Roll* covers more musicians in more depth than any other rock encyclopedia. In particular, we have made efforts to cover more black music, and more new music, than earlier encyclopedias; and we have made every effort to cut through the inaccuracies—from public-relations mythmaking to moralistic scare tactics—that have surrounded rock from the start. . . . The facts are here.

So many people have been involved in rock that we were forced to make hard decisions about who was best to include in this encyclopedia. The criterion—which, like every critical standard in rock, is ultimately subjective—was that those people included had a direct impact on the music, through popularity or through influence on other musicians. . . . And since this is a biographical volume, not a critical one, the length of an entry is not directly related to a musician's worth. Someone who makes great records and does nothing else in public is likely to receive less space than a band that breaks up every two months; we have chosen to use as few or as many words as it takes to get the story straight. Musicians tend to lead complicated lives, and the entries make sense of them as economically as the facts allow.

Naturally, some bands and musicians are left out; given the inevitable limitations of space, we chose those whom we considered most important. We would appreciate hearing about any sins of omission, but we have tried to err on the permissive side, as rock always does.

To read about these thousands of musicians, finally, is to be astonished at the combinations of creativity, ambition, and recklessness it takes to make it in rock & roll. For every band in this encyclopedia, there are 20 whose records nobody heard, and hundreds that never recorded at all; there are musicians who practice in basements around the world trying to find that certain chemistry. As these entries show, a rock career can be as short as the trajectory of a single hit or as long as the reign of Chuck Berry or the Rolling Stones, and some factors are out of anyone's control. Still, musicians keep trying and keep breaking through—and the glory of rock & roll is that even now, anyone can try it.

Preface to the
Second Edition

by Jon Pareles

What a difference a decade makes! Little did we know, when the first ROLLING STONE *Encyclopedia of Rock & Roll* was compiled, that rock's ground rules were getting turned inside-out while we worked. This second edition—new! improved!—sorts out the results of changes small and large, while retaining its thorough documentation of rock from the beginning.

The tensions and frictions that put the heat in rock music have not gone away in a decade: tensions between races, between generations, between formula and innovation, between rebellion and acquiescence, between independence and the chance to reach the mass public. But in technology and aesthetics, the music has gone through startling transformations in a very short time.

Back when the first edition of this encyclopedia appeared, radio stations were the gatekeepers for new rock; the music-video alternative, inaugurated by the founding of MTV in 1981, was just gathering momentum. And recorded music was only on the verge of the digital era. In the early Eighties, few people anticipated that the time-honored carriers of rock music—the 45-r.p.m. single and the 33⅓-r.p.m. longplaying album—would be virtually swept away by cassettes and compact discs, turning vinyl into the province of disc jockeys, collectors, and diehards.

Most important, the two revolutionary styles that appeared in the mid-Seventies, hip-hop and punk rock, had just begun to infiltrate a generation of young musicians. Both hip-hop and punk were do-it-yourself efforts, created in home studios and local clubs by people without the inclination or the bankrolls to concoct slick, suave pop songs. They revived rock's grass-roots creativity one more time, and they were at home in an underground of low budgets and regional scenes.

Although they were initially spurned by mass media, they drew audiences of active, committed musicians and fans (who were often the same people).

In the early Eighties, skeptical observers feared that punk had run its course, promising an insurrection but merely supplying a few new costumes and postures for the same old rock. They were also convinced that rap was just a novelty, since listeners would be bound to tire of songs without melodies. As so often happens with rock, the experts were wrong. While pundits carped, some of the major performers of the Nineties were hanging out at all-ages hardcore matinees, slam dancing and thinking about maybe banging out a few chords themselves. Others were at hip-hop block parties, thinking of their first rhymes or checking out disc-jockey tricks. Hip-hop spread fast; punk's kin, new-wave rock, gradually dislodged or reconfigured the rock establishment.

By the early Nineties, punk and hip-hop had changed the listening reflexes of a generation. The noise of overdriven guitars, the jolts of sudden segues, the repetition of rhythm machines, and the atonal juxtapositions of sampled sounds have now been accepted as widely as the old I-IV-V chords of "Louie Louie." They don't just show up in music with cult followings; they thrive in the Top Ten.

Unexpectedly, many baby boomers who grew up with rock suddenly found there was a new youth music that drove *them* up the wall. They responded to Public Enemy or Nirvana as their parents had responded to Led Zeppelin or Little Richard. Younger fans, meanwhile, are anything but doctrinaire; they're still fascinated by the utopian Sixties mythos and delighted by the psychedelic improvisations of bands from the Grateful Dead to the Smashing Pumpkins.

Rock's new generation gap is just one of the fissures

that developed in the Eighties. The story of rock, and of all American popular music, is the story of subcultures—hillbilly cats, Southern soul belters, Mods, hippies, disco dancers, punks, rappers—breaking through to a general audience. Yet unlike many other American pop performers, rockers have grown increasingly leery of assimilation into the bland mainstream.

While rock has never exactly been united, recent years have brought an accelerating fragmentation, a profusion of genres and subgenres, each with its own rituals, fashions, and preferred range of beats per minute. There are still pop performers who want to reach everyone and who purposefully concoct hybrids and crossovers. But there are more and more purists who insist on being "real" or "alternative" or "independent," insisting on their subcultural credentials, determined not to sell out even if they sell millions of albums.

At the same time, over the last decade rock has hitched itself to the most mainstream of American media: television. When the Eighties began, fans had to go to clubs or concerts and wait on the whims of variety-show programmers to see musicians at work. But MTV and other music-video outlets brought current rock performance and fantasies to the furthest hinterlands, 24 hours a day, to all ages and all levels of hipness. Recording technology had long since separated the performer from the performance; music video symbolically reconnected them, even as it gave performers (and their directors) the chance to fabricate new, superhuman images, one more layer of studio gimmickry.

Of course, rock stars have always crafted their stage acts; early on, Elvis' pelvis drew as much attention as his voice. Yet full-time music video brought more musicians' faces (and bodies) into view; it raised the value of telegenic looks and spotlight-grabbing antics. Despite fuddy-duddies' fears, however, music video has not replaced songwriting with showmanship. Video did not kill the radio star, it only insisted that the star pay more attention to hair and wardrobe. For all its far-reaching effects, video has just thrown one more giant variable into the marketing, and the cultural clout, available to rockers who are willing to fully exploit it.

When the first edition of this encyclopedia appeared, Michael Jackson had just released *Thriller,* which combined remarkable music with cunning video image-mongering to become the best-selling album of all time. Madonna was just getting her first singles played in dance clubs. A decade later, some rockers thrive on music video; some distrust it. But now, every performer has to at least consider his or her attitude toward the camera, which has become nearly as important a tool as a guitar or an amplifier.

Even live concerts have been overhauled, often turned into spectacles, so that people who got acquainted with musicians on television won't be underwhelmed by their actual physical presence. Oddly enough, the fact that it's possible to see music performances on television, in private and in comfort, hasn't by any means eliminated the ritual of the rock concert, with all its communal messiness and tribal exhilaration.

Another transformation was well under way a decade ago: the computerization of popular music. Synthesizers were coming into their own, and digital recording was making inroads. Sampling and other digital wizardry have gradually blurred boundaries between handmade and machine-made sounds; since all but the most high-tech electronics are cheap and plentiful, nobody cares any more where any given noise came from.

But only gradually have most musicians and marketers begun to think of their calling as the creation of information, to be manipulated, processed, and recombined with other information, including but not limited to visuals. As this encyclopedia goes to press, musicians have begun linking their music not just to movie soundtracks and video clips, but to multimedia games that allow users to edit and remix the music at will. Fans have always been collaborators with popular musicians, lending the power of their desires to their favorite songs. Now, fans are able to join in the creation of the music itself, so there will be no such thing as the final or definitive version of a song—just whatever sounds right at the moment.

As information ricochets all over the place, faster and faster, the music business is looking forward, with fear and trepidation, to a time when it will no longer be manufacturing tapes or discs, but simply making music and graphics available to be downloaded from central data banks. More anarchistic types, meanwhile, are preparing to bypass the business entirely and beam their own tunes to anyone who wants to plug in. I can't help looking forward to the inevitable chaos.

Amid all these tectonic shifts, the music will still be made by individual musicians, chasing inspiration with any tool at hand: pen and paper, a cheap guitar, a computer, a set of drums, a microphone. They're in bedrooms and basements and garages and studios, alone and in groups, studied or self-taught, guided by ambition and hope and raw instinct. This encyclopedia tells many of their stories, in full knowledge that music still unheard will continue to surprise and delight the world.

Introduction

by Patricia Romanowski

The first revision of *The* ROLLING STONE *Encyclopedia of Rock & Roll* continues on the slightly overgrown path we first cleared back in 1980, when the editors of Rolling Stone Press began putting together an accurate guide to the people and phenomena of rock & roll. Each of the alphabetically arranged entries provides basic biographical information and, where appropriate, a selective or full discography plus group personnel chronology showing as clearly as can be determined the history of personnel changes. This is followed by an essay that not only sums up the subjects' lives and careers but attempts to place their work in critical and historical perspective. Throughout the book also appear definitions of musical styles and trends, as well as alphabetically placed boxes listing the Grammy Awards won by the artists covered herein and a box on Rock and Roll Hall of Fame inductees.

Approach and Content. In compiling this second edition we took a hard look at the 1300-plus extant entries and determined that the new edition could accommodate approximately 500 new entries. To create the additional space necessary to make room for this many, we opted to delete most entries on nonperformers (such as songwriters, record producers, disc jockeys).

We have consolidated some artists who were originally listed as solo artists back into the groups with which they came to fame. So, for example, Eddie Kendricks and David Ruffin are back in the Temptations entry, and Ronnie Spector's solo career is traced in the Ronettes. We also consolidated groups that share many of the same members (The Babys/John Waite/Bad English). Extensive cross-referencing throughout the *Encyclopedia* will guide readers to the correct entry.

It was only with great regret and hard consideration that we cut a handful of entries (listed in the appendix). These were cut either because they were marginal artists at the time of the first edition (for example, Alessi) or because their then-tangential connection to rock & roll grew even weaker (for example, Tim Curry).

Choosing which new artists to include was a difficult decision that involved not only Holly George-Warren, Jon Pareles, and me, but our writers and countless other acquaintances. Not surprisingly, each person we consulted—actually everyone we knew—had an opinion and a short list of favorites: hot new bands they were sure would make a big splash and older, unfairly neglected artists. While a third of our choices were obvious (Nirvana, k. d. lang) and a second third very nearly indisputable, a good third fell onto a list for which any of a number of other acts could have been chosen. Generally, however, artists who were critically or commercially successful, influential, or otherwise interesting for other, even nonmusical, reasons fared better than those who were not. Conversely, a few artists were so little-known or so unique they could not be ignored. Other times the inclusion of a given artist in the original edition dictated making room for a newer artist in the same vein. Or the original edition's subtle overemphasis on certain types of artists and genres at the expense of others demanded correction in this edition. For that reason there are more new country and rap entries than new reggae or singer/songwriter entries.

As for the length of any given entry, this really is one place—maybe the only place—where size does not matter. There is no reason for John Lennon's entry to be longer than any of his fellow former Beatles' except that it took more words to tell his and Yoko Ono's story, not necessarily that there was "more to say," or that their contributions were more "valuable." While the writers of new pieces were asked to write within five basic sets of word-length parameters, the subject's so-called "importance" was considered with the same weight we gave other criteria: length of career, influence on other artists and listeners, uniqueness, newsworthy extra-music activities (lawsuits, arrests, benefit work, acting and writing credits, etc.), and the degree to which the subject was representative of a given style, period, or issue.

Our Sources. Jon Pareles has addressed in his new preface some of the cataclysmic changes within music and the music business over the past decade. Concurrently, there have been a series of rapidly evolving changes in how we learn about and document music.

First, the media provide more and, in some cases, better coverage of music today than they did then. Not only are there more publications devoted to music, but most of them are increasingly specialized, which, at least theoretically, should result in more accurate reporting. At the other end of the spectrum, mainstream publications have expanded their coverage of persons and events that a decade ago would not have been documented anywhere but in ROLLING STONE and a few other magazines. While neither development guarantees against factual inaccuracies (or the ever-present PR concerns of artists and their employers), taken together they give researchers and writers something that's almost as valuable as the information itself: the ability to judge an item's veracity. For example, while a string of reviews from local newspapers across the country can provide invaluable insight into a group's concert tour, revealing everything from lineup and playlist to audience response, for the correct spellings of musicians' names or the financial nuts and bolts of the Jacksons' Victory Tour we would favor accounts from respected, fact-checked national publications. Conversely, obituaries from local newspapers and specialized magazines are generally more complete and accurate than the "abridged" accounts that appear in larger publications. This is particularly true when the artist is less well known or past his or her career peak.

Second, our first edition was published on the eve of what became "the rock-book boom." Suddenly the history of rock & roll was being rewritten through serious studies, autobiographies, and biographies of groups and individual artists. And while few of these proved error-free, they made great contributions, if not to setting the record straight, at least to broadening our understanding of the subjects. In our first edition, we included a list of rock stars who had written books; it took up half a page. Today, a great percentage of the artists covered here have written their own stories—not to mention the large number who have had books written about them. In the case of Elvis Presley, for example, the number ranges up somewhere near 300. Because so much of what passes for rock history is gossip, we recalled every mother's favorite adage and always considered the source. While there are many books and writers that rewarded our faith time and again, there are also those whose flaws, prejudices, and errors were well known.

On the book publishing front, however, the most heartening development is the rise of specialized publishing companies. Their dedication to producing a range of invaluable reference works and collectors' magazines for a limited market is to be commended and supported. As mainstream book publishers' commitment to popular music and culture waxes and wanes, it's nice to know that highly reliable, invaluable reference works, like the Motown Records discography *Heat Wave*, or small but important autobiographies and biographies (like John Swenson's *Bill Haley*), will not cease being published simply because they stand no chance of hitting the best-seller list.

Third, and perhaps most important, is the CD-driven "anthologization" of rock's recorded history. Thanks to anthologies and historic compilations, artists who hung up their rock & roll shoes decades ago are suddenly back in the studio and on the stage. While we have done our best to track every act still working, we cannot possibly document every one-off reunion or every version of a group that boasts a latterday member and takes the stage at your local motel lounge or releases a tribute to the hometown's pro football team.

Searchin'. These new waves of information have rendered the history of rock, some parts of which might have seemed as immutable as if they'd been chiseled in stone, as ephemeral as scratches in the sand. There is probably no artist's story that could not, with the next wave—the next book, the next interview, the next record, the next day—be suddenly recast and rewritten in triumph or in tragedy. The twists and turns of any artist's life can rarely be foreseen: just ask Tom Jones or Tina Turner. A decade ago, it would have been hard to imagine looking for Flo and Eddie on a Care Bears soundtrack, Little Richard on a Disney roster, Sonny Bono in the U.S. Congress, or Lisa Marie Presley on the Jackson family tree. And yet there they are.

We noticed some interesting and unexpected trends, such as the beginnings of what may prove to be music-family dynasties as rock stars' children follow in their parents' footsteps and the increasing viability of recording careers in the absence of hit records. Another emerging trend—a surprising number of recent deaths—may simply be a statistical consequence of so many subjects entering middle age. Nonetheless, it is sobering to realize what a disproportionate number died too young, and how many of them died by their own hands or as a result of violence.

Our Method. As we did in the first edition, we collected information from a broad range of sources in all media: print (newspapers, magazines, books), video (documentaries as well as commercial releases), and CDs, LPs, and singles (as well as their accompanying liner notes). We made several attempts at contacting each and every artist or group and/or their appointed press representative or manager. We invited those who were included in our first edition to submit corrections of factual errors to their existing entry and to provide current information.

We were very encouraged and happily surprised at the number of responses we received. For the most part, artists who took the time to answer us personally, via post, fax, or phone, graciously pointed out errors and offered verifiable corrections. We have thanked in the Acknowledgments section many of the artists who helped us set the record straight, even when the facts of the original entry presented a much rosier picture. (We apologize to anyone we may have overlooked.) It is important to note, however, that we refused to disclose the full contents of entries and did not offer artists the chance to review or approve their entries before publication. While fact-checkers, researchers, writers, and editors may have contacted an artist with specific questions, we never submitted to any artist or artist's representative the full, completed text of his or her entry for further comment. The only exception to this policy was made for John Mayall's Bluesbreakers, because usually reliable sources and current documentation proved maddeningly contradictory or unavailable. Mr. Mayall kindly devoted hours to correcting and documenting the full discography/chronology of his various groups and limited his corrections to those portions of the text that concerned these changes.

Any artist or group that could not be traced through a computer search of national newspapers and a thorough review of current record charts and record catalogues, or that was not listed in any industry directory as having a manager, an agent, or other means of contact, and/or whose death could not be verified was considered as having retired. Early on, we decided that this could not become a "where are they now?" collection. However, through dogged persistence and some nice strokes of luck, we managed to track down a surprising number of artists. The temptation to add what we learned of their recent, nonmusical pursuits proved irresistible. For a small minority, however, an artist's name returned to the news only through tragedy or death.

For the artists covered in the new entries, we used these research hunts to collect all the information we needed. These facts were corroborated by other independent sources. In many ways these new entries show the benefit of documenting a piece of history as it happens, while the records are still available, the artists still

living (and talking), and the trail still too hot to be overgrown with legend, hype, and rumor.

We kept all of the letters we received from readers after the first edition was published. In every instance, we researched readers' corrections and considered their comments. As it turned out, not all "corrections" were correct, but the approximately 20 percent that were proved invaluable. Despite the decade-plus lapse between these two editions, we like to think of *The* ROLLING STONE *Encyclopedia of Rock & Roll* as a living reference work. We remain open to and welcome all comments, suggestions, information, and corrections. Please address them to: Rolling Stone Press, *Encyclopedia of Rock & Roll,* 1290 Avenue of the Americas, New York City, NY 10104.

What makes the history of rock & roll so fascinating—and frustrating—is the fact that when all is said is done, this is show business. Over the course of a career, which might span the proverbial 15 minutes or 50 years, six different interviews usually yield six different versions of the same story, all from the horse's mouth. When there are artists retracting and/or denouncing their own autobiographies, writers who conduct lengthy interviews without pad or tape recorder, and so-called reputable publications that exempt their "arts" sections from the rigorous fact-checking standards they routinely apply to the front page, the results can be baffling. While in some areas, no source is as valuable as the subject, we made it a rule to approach "official" information with a healthy skepticism (which, by the way, has been generously rewarded).

For example, despite the fact that there is an established industry procedure for verifying record sales and certifying gold and platinum records, press releases overflow with references to "triple platinum" releases that were not certified even gold. There are "hits" that never charted, and "sold-out tours" that played to half-empty halls. This time out, we also noticed a rash of people claiming to be the first Western, or American, or British rock act to play behind the Iron Curtain, and the peculiar tendency for press releases to refer to Grammy nominations by the more flattering (and totally false) term "awards." True, not every writer at a magazine or newspaper has at his or her fingertips the National Academy of Recording Arts and Sciences' official list of Grammy winners, so "errors" that may not have first been put forth in total innocence are innocently repeated.

In every case, we weighed our sources and our standard references (see later), taking into consideration the reliability of all. In many instances, the truth is quite clear: For our purposes, a chart position is a *Billboard* chart position or, for British charts, those listed in Guinness' *British Hit Singles* and *British Hit Albums;* a gold or platinum record is one so certified by the Recording Industry Association of America; an award is really an award if the organization bestowing it says so in its official publications or press releases. Record release dates are based on the copyright date on the actual record or CD, or, if that is not available, the date the record entered the charts, the dates of contemporaneous reviews and feature stories about it (usually from ROLLING STONE), or discographies that appear in reputable publications (such as *Goldmine*), reliable reference works (*The ROLLING STONE Album Guide*, for example, and *The Trouser Press Record Guide*), and books (such as label histories, autobiographies, biographies). Accounts of other important events are based on a wide range of sources, and each source is almost always corroborated by at least two other reliable sources.

The trail begins to wind and sometimes disappear when it comes to another type of information, namely accurate birthdates. The first time out, about 75 percent of our requests for a performer's date of birth were either refused, answered incompletely (day and month but no year), or answered in a way that proved misleading. We are very pleased to report that many artists whose birthdates were not entirely accurate in the first edition volunteered corrections. (How interesting to note that they all "became" older.) Others, however, persist in denying the truth, and in cases where we have sufficient documentation to support another year, we have used it. Where the artist has either refused to offer any date or has given one that stretches credulity, we have calculated it from published accounts that mention the artist's age (adding "circa" before the date) or omitted the year altogether; feel free to draw your own conclusions.

Discographies and Chronologies. Generally speaking, most of our discographies are selective, which is to say that we have edited them to give the reader a general picture of an artist or group's recorded history through the inclusion of important releases of original material (as opposed to greatest-hits packages); releases that have special critical, commercial, or historical significance; and releases that have been deemed to be representative of the entire oeuvre. Most of the new artists have released so few albums that their discographies are complete (except, of course, for those records released after this book goes to press).

For artists and groups whose careers are considerably longer, the selective discography is almost a given. Before the late Sixties, careers were based on singles, not albums. Ironically, however, many popular artists then released two, three, four, maybe even five albums a year. It's interesting to note that in 1963 and 1964 alone the Beatles released more albums than Madonna did in a decade; Johnny Cash had eight charting LPs out (including some greatest-hits and repackages) in 1969, exactly double the four upon which Michael Jackson built his entire post-Motown solo career over 12 years.

Decisions on what to keep and what to cut were made on a case-by-case basis. To cite one example, it was absolutely necessary that we list every single Beatles album of new original material, though we have not included most of the repackaged greatest-hits releases. In contrast, space alone prohibits listing the full discography of Johnny Cash, while lack of critical, historical, and commercial importance eliminated most of Chubby Checker's, and a paucity of verifiable information and/or product has rendered most doo-wop groups' discographies misleadingly short. Among those releases we have routinely omitted are soundtracks where the artist's input is minimal or not historically significant, Christmas albums, and those that did not chart within the Top 100 albums, as determined by *Billboard*. We omitted most of Elvis Presley's soundtrack releases (due to space considerations and because there was such a wealth of other significant albums to choose from), but we included a handful of extremely successful Christmas albums in other artists' discographies and included soundtracks where they are a crucial part of the artist's work (e.g., Quincy Jones, Curtis Mayfield, Ry Cooder). Some discographies end up being more complete than necessary because group personnel and lineup shifts occur around them, and it's simply easier to fix these changes to records than to provide a longer, more complicated explanation in the text.

Rather than be limited by hard-and-fast restrictions, we chose instead to try to craft for each entry a discography that worked with the narrative text to give a full picture of the artist or group, musically, historically, commercially, and critically. To that end, we have also not indicated differences in content between formats except where they are of interest beyond their existence, and then only in the text. Nor have we routinely included alternate foreign releases or alternate titles or information regarding dates and labels of reissued product except when the record was too important to cut and information regarding the original release was unavailable or seemed unreliable.

Although these discographies are based on LPs or their equivalents (we refer to both vinyl records and CDs as "albums" and "LPs"), where appropriate, we have also included a limited number of EPs (extended-play recordings), foreign releases (particularly British), and cassette-only releases. Because the *Encyclopedia* is concerned primarily with history, wherever possible, the record label given is the one that the work was first released on in the U.S. (unless it was released a year or more previously in another country). In the interest of saving space, record labels are noted in parentheses following the album title of the first release on that label listed. Thereafter, each album can be assumed to have been released on the same label until indicated otherwise by a new label name following a title. In those instances where foreign releases are included, the label is followed by an abbreviation for the country of release. Alternate formats (EP- and cassette-only releases) are noted following the title, as is the word "soundtrack" where applicable. An "N.A." in the place of the release date or the label signifies that the information was "not available" or impossible to verify with a reasonable degree of certainty.

How to Read These Entries. The artists' entries come in two basic forms: that for a solo artist and that for a group. The solo artist's entry begins with his or her name, followed by his or her given name (if appreciably different from his or her stage name), date of birth, place of birth, date of death, and place of death. Only in cases where there are discrepancies among highly reliable sources are two possibilities offered. This is followed by a discography.

The group entry begins with the group's date and place of formation, followed by a personnel chronology/discography that sets forth for each group member the same basic biographical information provided for solo artists, followed by that member's role in the band. Except for original lineups, all personnel shifts are listed as they occur chronologically in parentheses, with a plus sign (+) indicating an addition to the group and a minus (–) a departure.

The personnel chronology lists only those musicians who have recorded with the group or whose membership is clearly documented in published articles or press releases. Thus most guest musicians are not listed, although major ones are mentioned in the entry text. Where the discography is complete, the chronology indicates the approximate order of two main recurrent events in the life of a band: personnel changes and record releases. Generally speaking, the chronology of a successful, well-documented band that began recording in the late Sixties will reveal which musicians appeared on a given album. Bearing in mind that there are exceptions to every rule, this same claim probably cannot be made as readily for less thoroughly covered acts, such as R&B and disco groups.

While we use album credits as a source of information, there are a number of compelling reasons why following these credits strictly and exclusively would distort the order of events. For one thing, there are many groups for whom personnel listings are incomplete or nonexistent. Second, the nature of the music business is such that months, even years, may elapse between the recording of a given song and its release as a single or on an album (a common situation with Motown artists, for example). During that time, key personnel events, including deaths, may have occurred. Third, it is more common now than ever to repackage recordings, so that a single album may contain songs recorded by any number of previous lineup configurations.

How the chronologies were handled was largely determined by the amount and quality of information available and the group itself. It is an arduous but relatively simple task to construct a chronology for, say, Fleetwood Mac, a group with many widely documented changes over the course of relatively few albums. It is as good as impossible, however, to accurately and fully list the name of every singer who ever appeared with the Drifters. Some groups have endured for decades, yet their true historical significance is restricted to a finite period in time. For these, we have indicated "original lineup" or "best-known lineup." In cases where the space necessary to recount a group's complete chronology was in inverse proportion to its significance, or where a group has developed into the musical equivalent of a temporary employment agency, we have indicated "numerous personnel changes follow," or words to that effect. There are also a handful of cases where only one or several versions of a long-lived group could be determined; there we indicate "lineup circa late Sixties" or "lineup circa 1994." Regardless of how complete the discography/chronology section is, it is not intended to replace the discussion of these events in the body of the text. We use this abbreviated format simply because it provides a great amount of information in a small amount of space, makes it easy to see at a glance the basic order of events, saves the basic biographical information from being buried in the text, and gives the writer the option of not having to list in the text releases and personnel changes about which there may not be too much to say at the expense of other, more important occurrences. Virtually all discography and personnel listings are current through the end of 1994, though we have continued to include major updates for selected entries through summer 1995.

The Charts. As in the *Encyclopedia*'s first edition, chart positions are based on those published weekly in *Billboard* and compiled and published in Joel Whitburn's series of Record Research books. Record Research books are the Bible of U.S. chart, label, and title information, and no serious rock fan (especially anyone prone to making bets on these matters) should be without at least one of these scrupulously researched and dependable tomes. Fortunately, many of these are now available to the general public in bookstores. A wider variety of more specialized titles is available from Record Research, Inc., P.O. Box 200, Menomonee Falls, WI 53052-0200; 414-251-5408.

One of the most profound changes in popular music has been the continuing "subgenre-fication" of styles. Today *Billboard* tracks record sales, radio airplay, and club play through over 30 different charts. For our purposes, we are concerned with the singles and LP charts in three different categories: pop, R&B (rhythm & blues), and C&W (country & western). Through the years, *Billboard* has refined its methods of compiling its charts, most notably in 1991 when it incorporated actual record sales figures and changed the charts' titles to best reflect the current market.

Unless indicated otherwise, every chart position included here should be assumed to be U.S. pop, derived from the "Hot 100" (established in August 1958) for singles, and the "Billboard 200" for albums. "R&B" and "C&W" follow positions from the rhythm & blues and country & western charts or their equivalents. The official chart titles in all three genres, and on all six charts, have changed periodically. For example, through the years the official title of what we consider the R&B singles chart has evolved from "Race Records" in 1945, to "Rhythm & Blues Records" in 1949, to "Hot Soul Singles" in 1973 and "Hot Black Singles" in 1981 before reverting to "Hot R&B Singles" in 1990. (In fact, for a period between November 1963 and January 1965, there were no R&B singles charts, and from August to early October 1972, no R&B LPs chart.) In this book, however, all of these positions are categorized as R&B. In our discussions of music, however, we do make stylistic distinctions between R&B, soul, rap, hip-hop, and black music, although any charting records within these genres would be charted under "R&B." The country charts, which debuted in 1944, contained "C&W" in their titles only between 1949 and 1962; since then, it's been just country, and we use the terms "country" and "C&W" interchangeably. (For a clearer understanding of our use of genre terms, please see the alphabetically listed definitions that appear throughout the book.)

Discussions of a record's showing on other charts, such as jazz, modern rock, world music, or new age, is limited. Where necessary, we have included some British chart positions. These are denoted by "U.K." and apply to pop singles or albums only.

In every instance, the chart position shown is the highest attained by that recording. The year that follows the position is, in almost all cases, the year it debuted on the chart. Discrepancies may arise for those singles for which Record Research's *Top Pop Artists & Singles, 1955–1978* was the main source. For that book, the year given was that in which the record reached its peak, or highest, position. Then it is only a problem in those instances where a record was released at year's end but did not chart until early the next year. In updating the material carried over from the first edition, we have made every effort to revise the chart positions to reflect the "debut" as opposed to the "peak" year. Because a record's natural commercial life cycle is pretty short and

its fate rendered in mere weeks, the year of debut and the year of peak are usually the same.

Perspective. All that explains how we traced, collected, sifted, and verified our information. Here I'll try to give some idea of how we determined what to do with it.

The Rolling Stone *Encyclopedia of Rock & Roll* is a reference work—not a history, not a consumer guide, not an alphabetized collection of critics' musings. It's hard to resist your own opinion about anything you love, including rock & roll. Perhaps the hardest part of this job for all of us was not only consciously putting aside our personal opinions but deliberately separating the prevailing critical line from the facts. For better or worse, however, sometimes it's the historical backdrop and the facts that dictate the critical line, and not the other way around.

As the deservedly esteemed music historian Peter Guralnick advised me over a decade ago, "It isn't necessary to have an opinion about everything." And he's right. History is not a story that has been told but a story that bears retelling. Incumbent on anyone who tackles this job is the willingness to suspend the writer's and editor's reflexive need to be "right" (although we strive to always be accurate) and to allow even the most familiar stories to tell us how to tell them. That has meant allowing for possibilities and improbabilities, and seeing every artist and every record not as we might see them today but within their original contexts, on their own terms. In a field where great music, even whole careers, were sparked by hearing a single two-minute-long recording—perhaps even one made a half-century before by someone from the other side of the world—nothing can be discounted. Every entry, whether the subject is Abba or Frank Zappa, demands and deserves attention and respect.

What we offer here is not opinion but perspective, and the difference is important. We seek to tell the stories of some fascinating people, their work, and their times. By the self-imposed editorial parameters of this project we have been spared the obligation to speculate or theorize. We cannot determine whether Kiss "deserved" to be heard; we can only tell you what happened once they were. At the same time, no history can ignore the tide of public and critical opinion, and neither can we. But there is a crucial difference between our reporting prevailing critical opinion of a given artist and presenting our own. We have sought to tread that line very carefully, taking liberties only when dealing with an artist or group whose work is less well known or has been, in our judgment, overlooked.

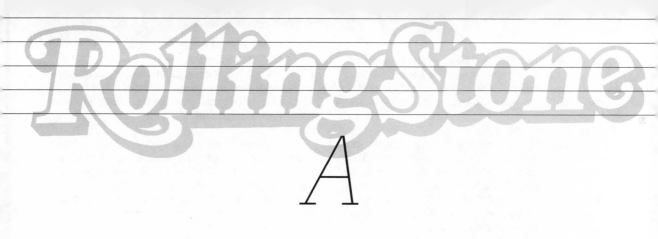

A

Abba

Formed 1971, Sweden
Benny Andersson (b. Dec. 16, 1946, Stockholm,
Swed.), kybds., synth., voc.; Bjorn Ulvaeus (b. Apr.
25, 1945, Gothenburg, Swed.), gtr., voc.; Agnetha
"Anna" Fältskog (previously Ulvaeus; b. Apr. 5,
1950, Jönköping, Swed.), voc.; Anni-Frid "Frida"
Synni-Lyngstad-Fredriksson-Andersson (b. Nov. 15,
1945, Narvik, Nor.), voc.

1974—*Waterloo* (Atlantic)   1975—*Abba*   1976—
Greatest Hits, vol. 1; Arrival   1977—*The Album*
1979—*Voulez-Vous; Greatest Hits, vol. 2*   1980—
Super Trouper   1981—*The Visitors*   1982—*Abba,
The Singles, The First Ten Years*   1984—*I Love
Abba*   1986—*Abba Live*   1995—*Thank You for the
Music* (A&M).
Anni-Frid "Frida" Lyngstad-Fredriksson-Andersson
solo: 1982—*Something's Going On* (Atlantic)
1984—*Shine.*
Agnetha Fältskog solo: 1983—*Wrap Your Arms
Around Me* (Atlantic)   1985—*Eyes of a Woman*
(Epic)   1987—*I Stand Alone* (Atlantic).

Easily the most commercially successful group of the
Seventies, Abba became the focus of a revival in the
early Nineties, when their *Abba Gold* topped charts
around the world. Their wholesome image and buoyant,
catchy records made the group international pop stars
(Nelson Mandela once declared Abba his favorite pop
group) and the second most profitable corporation on
the Stockholm stock exchange. Ironically, it was their
massive financial success that, according to group members, led to the death and kidnapping threats that
prompted their disbanding in 1982.

Though Bjorn Ulvaeus and Benny Andersson's hook-
laden singles ("Fernando" and "Money, Money, Money,"
1976; "Knowing Me, Knowing You," 1977) often topped
European charts, U.S. success was limited to several hit
albums and three Top Ten singles: "Waterloo" (#6, 1974),
"Dancing Queen" (#1, 1977), and "Take a Chance on Me"
(#3, 1978).

Each member was a solo star in Sweden before Abba
(an acronym of their first initials) coalesced in 1973. "Waterloo" won the prestigious Eurovision Song Contest in
1974, a year after they began recording in English. Abba
tours were limited initially because of the difficulty of re-
creating their densely layered, richly produced sound live.
Nevertheless, they mounted their first international tour in
1977 and appeared in the U.S. two years later. Longtime
live-in lovers Benny and Anni-Frid (who both have children from teenage marriages) were wed in 1978; they divorced in 1981. Two years earlier, Bjorn and Agnetha's
marriage of six years had also ended in divorce. Abba's
public image, however, remained harmonious. By then
they had sold an estimated 100 million records worldwide.

In 1982 Phil Collins produced Frida's post-Abba solo
debut, *Something's Going On,* which featured "I Know
There's Something Going On," a Top Twenty hit. In 1985

her duet with B. A. Robertson, "Time," was a minor U.K. hit. Andersson and Ulvaeus cowrote with British lyricist Tim Rice the London and Broadway musical *Chess,* from which "One Night in Bangkok" became a #3 hit for Murray Head in 1985. Agnetha "Anna" Fältskog has also released solo albums and had several minor U.K. hits; her "Can't Shake Loose" hit #29 in 1983.

Abba's enduring—and most U.S. critics might claim, inexplicable—appeal manifested in the Australian Abba impersonators Bjorn Again, Erasure's #1 U.K. cover EP *Abba-esque,* and Roxette's adding "Money Money Money" to their live set. U2 performed "Dancing Queen" on their Zoo Tour, with Bjorn Ulvaeus and Benny Andersson joining them onstage in Stockholm in 1993.

ABC

Formed 1980, Sheffield, England
Martin Fry (b. Mar. 9, 1958, Manchester, Eng.), voc.;
Mark White (b. Apr. 1, 1961, Sheffield), gtr., kybds.;
Mark Lickley, bass; David Robinson, drums;
Stephen Singleton (b. Apr. 17, 1959, Sheffield), saxophone.
1980—(– Lickley; – Robinson; + David Palmer
[b. May 29, 1961, Chesterfield, Eng.], drums)   1982—
The Lexicon of Love* (Mercury)   1983—*Beauty Stab
(– Singleton; – Palmer; + Eden, voc., perc.; + David
Yarritu, kybds., synth.)   1985—*How to be a . . . Zillionaire!* 1987—*Alphabet City* 1989—*Up* 1990—
Absolutely.

Hailed by the British music press as "purveyors of perfect pop," ABC was actually a highly self-conscious white neosoul group that articulated singer Martin Fry's grandiloquent vision. His mannered vocals recall "Thin White Duke"–era David Bowie, and his songs of romance revisit the worldly fatalism of Roxy Music's Bryan Ferry.

Fry was writing and editing his own music fanzine, *Modern Drugs,* when he interviewed White and Singleton about their electric rock band, Vice Versa. They asked Fry to join them, and he did—changing the group's name to ABC and its direction toward pop. Completed by a rhythm section, the group recorded "Tears Are Not Enough" and released it on their own Neutron Records. A British Top Twenty in 1981, it was followed over the next six months by three more crafty, melodramatic Top Ten hits, with "Poison Arrow," "The Look of Love," and "All of My Heart," all from the lavish Trevor Horn–produced *Lexicon of Love.* Released stateside, the album garnered rave reviews and sold well (#24, 1982); bolstered by lush, evocative videos, "The Look of Love" (#18, 1982) and "Poison Arrow" (#25, 1983) were hit singles, too.

ABC lost most of its U.S. fans with *Beauty Stab* (#69, 1983), a harsher, harder-rocking, guitar-based collection that contained only one charting single: "That Was Then but This Is Now" (#89, 1984). With female percussionist Eden and American keyboardist David Yarritu replacing David Palmer and Stephen Singleton, ABC adopted a cartoonish image and rebounded with *Zillionaire* (#30, 1985), which yielded the yearning pop ballad "Be Near Me" (#9, 1985) and another hit in "(How to Be a) Millionaire" (#20, 1986).

Shortly thereafter, Fry was diagnosed with Hodgkin's disease, an often curable form of cancer. ABC was off the scene until *Alphabet City* (#48, 1987), which featured the group's biggest hit to date, the Motown tribute "When Smokey Sings" (#5, 1987). As of this writing, Fry's illness has continued to keep the group sidelined.

Paula Abdul

Born June 19, 1962, Los Angeles, California
1988—*Forever Your Girl* (Virgin)   1990—*Shut Up*
and Dance (The Dance Mixes)* 1991—*Spellbound
1995—*Head over Heels.*

A true MTV-era success story, Paula Abdul choreographed videos for several popular artists, then became a pop star herself. Trained as a dancer, Abdul had had little singing experience before recording 1988's *Forever Your Girl,* and her vocals were widely panned. Nonetheless, the album sold seven million copies domestically, thanks to catchy hooks, perky bubblegum-funk arrangements, and glossy videos that displayed Abdul's true strengths: her stylish, high-energy dance technique and plucky girl-next-door charm.

The second daughter of a French-Canadian mother and a father of Syrian and Brazilian extraction, Abdul began taking dance lessons when she was seven; at ten, she won a scholarship to study tap and jazz dancing. She captained her high school cheerleading squad, and after graduating, she attended college at California State, Northridge, and successfully auditioned for the Los Angeles Lakers' cheerleaders. Abdul eventually became head Laker girl, and her work was spotted by Jackie Jackson (with whom she later became romantically involved), who asked her to choreograph the Jacksons' "Torture" video. She also befriended sister Janet Jackson and choreographed all of her *Control* videos (she makes a cameo as Janet's girlfriend in "Nasty"). Abdul's other clients include the Pointer Sisters, ZZ Top, and Duran Duran, and she has worked on network television (*The Tracey Ullman Show*) and in films.

In the late Eighties Abdul signed to Virgin Records. The release of her debut album followed auspiciously on the heels of "Knocked Out," a single that Abdul recorded for a Virgin sampler. That song became popular on R&B radio, but with *Forever Your Girl,* Abdul immediately crossed over into the pop stratosphere, topping the albums chart and producing four #1 singles: 1988's "Straight Up" and, in 1989, "Forever Your Girl," "Cold

Hearted," and "Opposites Attract." Another track, "(It's Just) the Way That You Love Me," went to #3.

Virgin capitalized on Abdul's success by releasing an album of dance remixes of her hit songs in 1990. In 1991 she released *Spellbound,* an LP of new songs—some of them cowritten by Abdul, many written and produced by the New York–based R&B trio the Family Stand. (Other contributors included John Hiatt and Prince.) The album peaked at #1 and spawned the #1 singles "Rush, Rush" (Abdul's first hit ballad) and "The Promise of a New Day," "Blowing Kisses in the Wind" (#6, 1991), "Vibeology" (#16, 1992), and "Will You Marry Me" (#19, 1992). But legal troubles ensued when Yvette Marine, credited as a backup singer on *Forever Your Girl,* sued Virgin, alleging that her voice had been overdubbed on some of the album's lead vocals. In 1993, after a series of disputes, a jury ruled in Virgin's favor. In 1992 Abdul married actor Emilio Estevez; they split up in 1994.

A-Bones: See the Cramps

A Cappella

Generally believed to mean "voices singing without instrumental accompaniment." While that is how the term is used today, a cappella is derived from the Italian, which translates literally as "in the chapel style." In its original usage, a cappella referred to the singing done in church without instrumental accompaniment. Modern a cappella is generally associated with the doo-wop R&B groups of the late Fifties and early Sixties, among them hundreds of young, predominantly urban black and white male singers who perfected their vocal technique and harmony without instrumental accompaniment, often outdoors. Virtually every popular vocal group of the Fifties and Sixties—from Dion and the Belmonts to the Temptations—began this way.

The first a cappella/doo-wop hits were recorded by a New Haven–based group, the Nutmegs, in 1955: "Story Untold" and "Ship of Love." Since the genre's heyday, pure a cappella has become the almost exclusive province of a handful of groups, among them the Persuasions, 14 Karat Soul, and Take 6. Despite the respect good a cappella singing commands, few pop groups have made a cappella recordings, and surprisingly few women outside gospel have essayed the style. Among the notable exceptions are Sweet Honey in the Rock and the Roches.

AC/DC

Formed 1973, Sydney, Australia
Angus Young (b. Mar. 31, 1955, Glasgow, Scot.), gtr.; Malcolm Young (b. Jan. 6, 1953, Glasgow, Scot.), gtr.; Bon Scott (b. Ronald Belford, July 9, 1946, Kirriemuir, Scot.; d. Feb. 19, 1980, London, Eng.), voc.; 1974—(+ Phillip Rudd [b. May 19, 1946, Melbourne, Austral.], drums; Mark Evans [b. Melbourne, Austral.], bass). 1976—*High Voltage* (Atlantic) 1977—*Let There Be Rock* (– Evans; + Cliff Williams [b. Dec. 14, 1949, Rumford, Eng.], bass) 1978—*Powerage; If You Want Blood, You've Got It* 1979—*Highway to Hell* 1980—(– Scott; + Brian Johnson [b. 1948], voc.) *Back in Black* 1981—*Dirty Deeds Done Dirt Cheap; For Those About to Rock We Salute You* 1983—*Flick of the Switch* (– Rudd; + Simon Wright, drums) 1984—*'74 Jailbreak* 1985—*Fly on the Wall* 1986—*Who Made Who* 1988—*Blow Up Your Video* 1989—(– Wright; + Chris Slade, drums) 1990—*The Razors Edge* (Atco) 1992—*Live (Special Collector's Edition); Live.*

Australian heavy-metal band AC/DC features knickers-clad guitarist Angus Young, who became as famous for mooning audiences regularly as for his gritty blues-based lead guitar, and songs about sex, drinking, and damnation. Their raucous image, constant touring, and raw, juvenile yet amusing lyrics in songs like "Big Balls" and "The Jack" helped make them one of the top hard-rock bands of the Eighties and Nineties. The group has remained a top concert draw, and its albums consistently go platinum despite its never having had a Top Twenty single in the U.S.

The Young brothers moved with their family from Scotland to Sydney in 1963. In 1973 they formed the first version of AC/DC with Bon Scott. After a year of working with temporary bassists and drummers they settled on drummer Phillip Rudd and bassist Mark Evans in 1974. Their first four albums were produced by ex-Easybeats Harry Vanda and George Young, Angus' older brother. The group had gained a solid reputation in their homeland early on, but it wasn't until 1979 with the platinum *Highway to Hell* (#17, 1979) that they became a presence on the American charts.

Within months of AC/DC's American success, vocalist Scott died from choking on his own vomit after an all-night drinking binge. Two months later he was replaced by ex-Geordie vocalist Brian Johnson, and less than four months after that, *Back in Black* began a year-long run on the U.S. chart, peaking at #4 (1980), selling over 10 million copies, and featuring the double-entendre-ridden "You Shook Me All Night Long." *Dirty Deeds Done Dirt Cheap,* a 1981 reissue of a 1976 Australian LP, went to #3 in the U.S., followed by *For Those About to Rock We Salute You,* the group's first and, to date, only U.S. #1 LP, in late 1981.

The relatively disappointing showings of the gold albums *Flick of the Switch* (#15, 1983) and *Fly on the Wall* (#32, 1985) gave way to the multiplatinum *Who Made Who* (the soundtrack to *Maximum Overdrive*) and *The*

Razors Edge (#2, 1990). The latter contains the group's closest thing to a hit single, "Moneytalks" (#23, 1991). In January 1991 three fans were crushed to death at an AC/DC show in Salt Lake City, Utah. In late 1992 the group paid the families of the three deceased teenagers an undisclosed sum, following an out-of-court settlement. Other parties to the settlement included the convention center, the concert's promoter, and the company in charge of security.

Johnny Ace

Born John Alexander Jr., June 29, 1929, Memphis, Tennessee; died December 24, 1954, Houston, Texas
1974—*Johnny Ace Memorial Album* (MCA).

Johnny Ace was one of the most popular balladeers of the early Fifties but is perhaps most famous for the way he died: He allegedly shot himself while playing Russian roulette. Ace served in the navy during World War II. After his discharge he joined Adolph Duncan's Band as a pianist; he often jammed with B. B. King and Bobby "Blue" Bland in Memphis' famed Beale Streeters. In 1953 he released his first single, "My Song," which became a big R&B hit. Like his subsequent releases, it featured his soothing baritone in a subdued arrangement similar to the style of Nat "King" Cole.

On Christmas Eve 1954 Ace died backstage at Houston's City Auditorium. In recent years some familiar with the details of Ace's death have questioned whether it might have been a murder. One of his biggest pop successes came with the posthumously released Top Twenty hit "Pledging My Love" in early 1955. In 1983 Paul Simon invoked the singer's name in "The Late Great Johnny Ace," a song about the murder of John Lennon.

Ace

Formed 1972, London, England
Alan "Bam" King (b. Sep. 1946, London), gtr., voc.; Phil Harris (b. July 1948, London), gtr.; Paul Carrack (b. Apr. 1951, Sheffield, Eng.), kybds., voc.; Terry "Tex" Comer (b. Feb. 1949, Burnley, Eng.), bass; Steve Witherington, drums.
1974—(– Witherington; + Chico Greenwood, drums; – Greenwood; + Fran Byrne [b. Mar. 1948, Dublin, Ire.], drums) *Five-A-Side* (Anchor)   1975—*Time for Another*   1976—(– Harris; + Jon Woodhead [b. San Francisco, Calif.], gtr., voc.)   1977—*No Strings*.
Paul Carrack solo: 1980—*Nightbird* (Vertigo, U.K.)   1982—*Suburban Voodoo* (Epic)   1987—*One Good Reason* (Chrysalis)   1988—*The Carrack Collection*   1989—*Groove Approved*.

Ace became the best known of London's pub-rock bands when "How Long," written and sung by Paul Carrack, became a #3 U.S. hit in 1975. The group had been founded by Alan King and Phil Harris, and "How Long"

was a product of their first recording session. What many listeners believed was a love song actually concerned Terry Comer's temporary departure from the band to work with the Sutherland Brothers and Quiver and his return to Ace. The rest of the group's material failed to match the success of their debut single, and after a 1976 tour with Yes, they resettled in Los Angeles and in 1977 disbanded. Carrack, Byrne, and Comer joined Frankie Miller.

Carrack later recorded with Roxy Music, Squeeze (he sings lead on its 1981 hit "Tempted") [see Squeeze entry], and a short-lived backup band for Carlene Carter. In 1982 he joined Nick Lowe's Noise to Go, and in 1985, Mike + the Mechanics, for which he sang lead on the latter group's Top Ten "Silent Running (On Dangerous Ground)" and the Number One "Living Years" [see Genesis entry]. In 1987 Carrack's "Don't Shed a Tear" went Top Ten. He rejoined Squeeze for their 1993 album, *Some Fantastic Place*, then returned to Mike + the Mechanics for 1995's *Beggar on a Beach of Gold*.

Will Ackerman

Born November 1949, Germany
1976—*In Search of the Turtle's Navel* (Windham Hill)   1977—*It Takes a Year*   1979—*Childhood and Memory*   1981—*Passage*   1983—*Past Light*   1986—*Conferring with the Moon*   1988—*Imaginary Roads*   1992—*The Opening of Doors*.

Guitarist/record company impresario Will Ackerman used his entrepreneurial skills in service of his affinity for mellow, meditative instrumental music, founding Windham Hill Records, the world's first and foremost New Age label.

The German-born Ackerman grew up in California and New England (Windham refers to a county in Vermont) and began playing the guitar at age 12. Influenced by acoustic artists like Leo Kottke and John Fahey—creator of the "American primitive" technique—Ackerman developed an open-tuned, modal style. After a stint studying English and history at Stanford University, Ackerman dropped out and went into business as a builder and carpenter, working for several small record companies. Eventually, he recorded what became his first album, *In Search of the Turtle's Navel*. He initially pressed 500 copies and gave a large number of those to a bookstore run by his companion Anne Robinson. Ackerman and Robinson, who later married, started Windham Hill in 1976 with the intent of distributing the guitarist's efforts and the work of similar artists.

As the label grew slowly, Ackerman's own recordings got airplay on radio stations in a number of states. In 1980 Ackerman and Robinson scored a distribution deal with the independent company Pickwick Records and also signed a fledgling New Age icon, pianist George

Winston. Windham Hill soon became an icon itself, symbolizing soft, soothing tones and pastoral album covers to both a growing contingent of young adult fans and detractors.

By the time Pickwick folded in 1983, Windham Hill had acquired enough commercial cachet to secure a new contract with a major label, A&M Records. The terms allowed Ackerman and Robinson to launch new labels on their own, allowing for the eventual creation of Open Air (for light rock), Magenta (for jazz), Legacy (for folk), and Gang of Seven (for recorded monologues). Meanwhile, Windham Hill continued to thrive ($30 million in sales in 1990) with an increasingly diverse roster of artists, among them singer/songwriter Cliff Eberhardt, husband-and-wife duo Tuck & Patti, and of course Ackerman himself.

Barbara Acklin

Born February 28, 1943, Chicago, Illinois
1968—*Love Makes a Woman* (Brunswick)   1969—
Seven Days of Night*   1970—*I Did It*; *Someone
***Else's Arms*   1971—*I Call It Trouble*.**

Barbara Acklin is an R&B singer/songwriter whose late-Sixties hits include "Love Makes a Woman." After singing with a gospel choir during her teens, Acklin began her professional career as a background vocalist for St. Lawrence Records in 1964. She sang lead on a handful of singles under the pseudonym Barbara Allen and wrote songs (including Jackie Wilson's 1966 hit "Whispers [Gettin' Louder]") before signing with Brunswick around 1967.

There she recorded a string of duets with Gene Chandler [see entry] (including "From the Teacher to the Preacher," #57, 1968), as well as solo sessions, writing much of her material herself or with her producer and husband, Eugene Record of the Chi-Lites. An Acklin–Record composition, "Love Makes a Woman," reached #15 on the pop chart and #3 R&B in 1968. Her other R&B Top Forty hits include "Am I the Same Girl," "Just Ain't No Love" (1968), and "I Did It" (1970). During the late Seventies she toured with Tyrone Davis, and by 1981 she was recording with producer Gene Chandler. "Have You Seen Her," the 1971 Chi-Lites hit she cowrote with Record, was covered by Hammer on his 1990 LP, *Please Hammer Don't Hurt 'Em.*

Roy Acuff

Born Roy Claxton Acuff, September 15, 1903, Maynardsville, Tennessee; died November 23, 1992, Nashville, Tennessee
1966—*Roy Acuff Sings Hank Williams* (Hickory)
1970—*Best of Roy Acuff* (Capitol); *The Great Roy Acuff*; *Songs of the Smoky Mountains*; *The Voice of Country Music*   1985—*Roy Acuff: Columbia*

Historic Edition (Columbia)   1989—*The Best of Roy Acuff* (orig. 1963; Capitol)   1992—*The Essential Roy Acuff 1936–1949* (Legacy).

Singer, songwriter, fiddler, bandleader, music publisher, show-business booster, Roy Acuff was the "King of Country Music" for more than 50 years, and continued to perform regularly at the Grand Ole Opry until shortly before his death at the age of 89.

As a teenager he suffered a sunstroke, which prevented him from realizing his ambition to play pro baseball. He took up the fiddle and later joined a traveling medicine show that was passing through his Tennessee mountain hometown—only after he had been assured that he'd work only after sundown. In medicine and tent shows traversing the South he perfected an act that included oldtime string-band music, hymns, a few popular contemporary songs, and comedy routines (he was known for the yo-yo he played with onstage). In 1933 he formed the Tennessee Crackerjacks, with whom he performed on Knoxville radio. The next year, the group became the Crazy Tennesseans, and in 1936 they began recording. That same year Acuff recorded his two best-known hits, "Great Speckled Bird" (a million-selling record in 1943) and "Wabash Cannonball."

In 1938 he changed the group's name to the Smoky Mountain Boys. Acuff and the Boys began appearing regularly at Nashville's Grand Ole Opry, and Acuff became one of the Opry's first solo stars. His dry, high-pitched voice became familiar on such hits as "Night Train to Memphis," "Fire Ball Mail," and "Wreck on the Highway." His career sales total exceeds 25 million records. He also appeared in several feature films through the Forties, including *The Grand Ole Opry.*

In 1942 Acuff formed the Acuff-Rose Music Publishing Company with songwriter Fred Rose. Though Acuff continued to record, his success as a music publisher eclipsed that of his later recording career. Acuff-Rose eventually became one of the biggest country music publishing companies in the world, and Acuff and Rose were mentors to many of Nashville's most successful songwriters and performers (Hank Williams, Marty Robbins, Boudleaux Bryant, and others). Such was Acuff's popularity and influence that in 1944 and 1948 he ran for the governorship of Tennessee. He continued to appear at the Opry and traveled the world to entertain troops during both World War II and the Vietnam War.

In 1962 he became the first living musician elected to the Country Music Hall of Fame. Among his many honors were the Grammy Lifetime Achievement Award (1987) and the National Medal of Art and the Kennedy Lifetime Achievement Award (both 1991). He recorded his last single in 1974. In 1971 his version of "I Saw the Light" from the Nitty Gritty Dirt Band's *Will the Circle Be Unbroken* became his last charting single. In 1983 he moved into a home that was especially constructed for him on the grounds of the Opryland USA amusement park. He died of congestive heart failure.

Adam and the Ants/Adam Ant

Formed 1977, London, England
1978—First solid formation: Adam Ant (b. Stuart Leslie Goddard, Nov. 3, 1954, London), voc., gtr., piano; David Barbe (a.k.a. Barbarossa, b. Eng.), drums, perc.; Matthew Ashman (b. London), gtr., piano; Andrew Warren (b. Eng.), bass   1979—*Dirk Wears White Sox* (Do-It Records, U.K.) (– Warren; + Leigh Gorman, bass)   1980—(– Ashman; + Marco Pirroni [b. Apr. 27, 1959, London], gtr.; – Barbe; + Terry Lee Miall [b. Nov. 8, 1958, London], drums; + Merrick [b. Chris Hughes, Mar. 3, 1954, London], drums; – Gorman; + Kevin Mooney [b. Eng.], bass) *Kings of the Wild Frontier* (Epic)   1981— (– Mooney; + Gary Tibbs [b. Jan. 25, 1958, London], bass) *Prince Charming*   1983—*Dirk Wears White Sox*   1990—*Antics in the Forbidden Zone.*
Adam Ant solo: 1982—*Friend or Foe* (Epic)   1983— *Strip*   1985—*Vive Le Rock*   1988—*Manners & Physique* (MCA)   1995—*Wonderful* (Capitol).

The undisputed leaders of Britain's short-lived fantasy-oriented New Romantic movement of the early Eighties, Adam and the Ants were less well appreciated Stateside. Using its music as only one facet of a fantasy world complete with self-promoting mottoes like "Antmusic for Sexpeople" and its own vocabulary (fans were Antpeople), Adam and the Ants took England by storm. Starting in late 1980 Adam's fashion sense (which combined hero images of pirates, Western men, and cartoonish imitations of Native American Indians) was widely imitated. His unusual music, which featured double-drum rhythms from Burundi and yodeling vocals, produced several British pop singles, including "Antmusic" (#2) and "Dog Eat Dog" (#4), and a #1 LP, *Kings of the Wild Frontier.*

Ant, who had worked in various British bands since 1976, first came to national attention under the auspices of ex–Sex Pistols' manager Malcolm McLaren, who worked with the band on their debut LP, *Dirk Wears White Sox* (initially released in England only). McLaren left in 1980, taking with him Gorman, Barbe, and Ashman to form Bow Wow Wow [see entry]. Ant then joined with ex–Rema Rema guitarist Marco Pirroni and the pair developed the Antpeople image and wrote the songs for *Kings of the Wild Frontier,* the group's U.S. debut. Despite extensive media coverage and a well-publicized tour in the U.S., the album sold a disappointing 300,000 copies. In November 1981 *Prince Charming,* recorded with ex–Roxy Music bassist Gary Tibbs, spent over six months on the British charts, but failed to hit in the U.S.

Adam Ant

In 1982 the Ants disbanded, and Adam's debut solo effort, a single entitled "Goody Two Shoes," was #1 in England and #12 in the U.S., making *Friend or Foe* a Top Twenty album. But none of his succeeding LPs has fared nearly as well, although *Manners & Physique,* produced by former Prince cohort André Cymone, boasted "Room at the Top" (#17, 1990). Adam has also pursued acting; his credits include *World Gone Wild, Slam Dance,* and television's *The Equalizer.* His early 1993 "comeback" tour (with Pirroni) got a lukewarm reception. Adam returned the next year, making a couple of guest appearances onstage with Nine Inch Nails, and he released *Wonderful* in 1995.

Bryan Adams

Born Bryan Guy Adams, November 5, 1959, Kingston, Canada
1980—*Bryan Adams* (A&M)   1981—*You Want It, You Got It*   1983—*Cuts Like a Knife*   1984—*Reckless*   1986—*Live! Live! Live!*   1987—*Into the Fire*   1991—*Waking Up the Neighbours*   1993—*So Far So Good.*

With his trademark white T-shirt and blue jeans, Bryan Adams may have looked like a regular guy. But his unerring gift for radio-friendly pop hooks made him the most successful artist exported from Canada in the Eighties, even as critics dismissed his straightforward, anthemic rock as a shallow formularization of Bruce Springsteen.

Adams' father was a Canadian diplomat, and Adams attended military schools in England, Austria, Portugal, and Israel. When he was 12 his parents separated, and he lived with his mother in Vancouver, British Columbia. By then he had taught himself to play guitar and decided to make music his career. At 16, he quit school, bought a grand piano with money from his college fund, and joined bands. At age 17 he befriended Jim Vallance, who had written songs for the Canadian band Prism. After two years of writing and recording demo tapes, their partnership produced the 1979 disco-styled Canadian single "Let Me Take You Dancing." The pair sold songs to Bachman-Turner Overdrive, Joe Cocker, and Juice Newton, then landed a publishing deal with A&M Records, which led to Adams' recording contract.

Adams' eponymous debut album stiffed, but the followup, *You Want It, You Got It* (#118, 1982) did better, and Adams opened shows for such bands as the Kinks, Foreigner, and Loverboy. *Cuts Like a Knife* (#8, 1983) was Adams' U.S. breakthrough, producing hits in "Straight from the Heart" (#10, 1983), the title cut (#15, 1983), and "This Time" (#24, 1983); the latter two were accompanied by popular eye-catching videos. *Reckless* (#1, 1984) was even bigger, selling over five million copies and yielding such hits as "Run to You" (#6, 1984), "Somebody" (#11, 1985), and "Summer of '69" (#5, 1985), Adams' first hit ballad in "Heaven" (#1, 1985), and "It's Only Love" (#15, 1985), a duet with Tina Turner (with whom Adams toured, and for whom he produced a track on her 1986 *Break Every Rule*). Adams appeared at Live Aid in Philadelphia in 1985, and in 1986 performed on Amnesty International's Conspiracy of Hope Tour with Sting and U2.

His *Into the Fire* yielded hits in "Heat of the Night" (#6, 1987), "Hearts of Fire" (#26, 1987), and "Victim of Love" (#32, 1987). Adams refused to allow the use of the album's "Only the Strong Survive" in the Tom Cruise film *Top Gun,* because he felt the movie glorified war.

After performing at the 1988 Freedomfest in London to honor freed South African apartheid fighter Nelson Mandela, Adams began work on *Waking Up the Neighbours.* Meantime, Joe Cocker recorded Adams' "When the Night Comes," and Dion recorded his "Drive All Night"; Adams had a quick cameo in the 1989 Clint Eastwood film *Pink Cadillac* and performed at Roger Waters' 1990 Berlin production of *The Wall.* The release of *Neighbours* (#6, 1992) was preceded by the appearance of "(Everything I Do) I Do It for You" under the credits of the Kevin Costner film *Robin Hood—Prince of Thieves.* The ballad was an instant smash, topping the U.S. pop chart for seven weeks, and the U.K. chart for a record-breaking 16 weeks. In February 1992 Adams took issue with his homeland's "Canadian Content" regulations, which restricted airplay of *Neighbours* because Adams cowrote and coproduced the record with an Englishman, Mutt Lange. Adams briefly threatened to boycott the annual Juno Awards, Canada's version of the Grammys, where he ended up winning Entertainer and Producer of the Year awards. A hits collection, *So Far So Good* (#6, 1993), proved his continuing appeal in the Nineties.

Faye Adams
Born Faye Scruggs
1980—*Faye Adams* (Savoy).

Faye Adams was a blues shouter in the tradition of Big Maybelle and was best known for her 1953 hit "Shake a Hand." She joined Joe Morris' Blues Cavalcade in the early Fifties, shortly before Herb Abramson signed the group to Atlantic Records. Abramson left to join the army before the group had a chance to record, and the Cavalcade soon disbanded. Adams was then signed by Herald Records. "I'll Be True" (#1 R&B, 1953) and "Hurts Me to My Heart" (#1 R&B, 1954) followed "Shake a Hand" (#1 R&B, #22 pop, 1953).

Adams recorded over thirty tracks for Herald before moving to Imperial in 1957. From there her career faded, although she continued to record for Lido, Warwick, Savoy, and Prestige, until her retirement in 1963.

Johnny Adams
Born Lathan John Adams, January 5, 1932, New Orleans, Louisiana
1970—*Heart and Soul* (SSS Int'l)   1984—*From the Heart* (Rounder)   1986—*After Dark*   1988—*Room with a View of the Blues*   1989—*Walking on a Tightrope*   1991—*Johnny Adams Sings Doc Pomus: The Real Me*   1992—*I Won't Cry: From the Vaults of Ric and Ron Records*   1993—*Good Morning Heartache.*

Johnny Adams is a New Orleans–based R&B vocalist. Although his early style, which couched his big soulful croon in plush orchestral and choral arrangements (he was known as "the Tan Canary"), was much closer to pop than to late-Fifties New Orleans R&B, his early records on the Ric label, "Come On" and "A Losing Battle" (both 1960), were big local hits, and the latter made the R&B Top Thirty. Little is known of Adams' early life. In 1963 he changed labels (to Watch), but he had no hits until 1969, when he made his comeback with four consecutive hits on the SSS International label: "Release Me" (#34 R&B), "Reconsider Me" (#28 pop, #8 R&B), "I Can't Be All Bad" (#45 R&B), and "I Won't Cry" (#41 R&B, 1970). Without the strings and choirs, his later style is earthier, drawing on country music and the blues. He continues to work and record in New Orleans.

Marie Adams
Born Lyndon, Texas

R&B vocalist Marie Adams has been successful both as a solo act and in collaborations with other performers. A gospel singer before she signed with Peacock Records in 1952, Adams had an R&B Top Ten hit with her first release, the very secular "I'm Gonna Play the Honky Tonks." That led to jobs with some of the biggest bandleaders of the Fifties—Cherokee Conyer, Pluma Davis, and Johnny Otis (as a star of the Johnny Otis Show). One Otis group in which she took part was the Three Tons of Joy (Adams weighed over 260 pounds), a vocal trio with Sadie and Francine McKinley. The Three Tons' recording of "Ma, He's Making Eyes at Me" topped the British pop charts in 1957. A duet with Otis, "Bye Bye Baby," was a Top Twenty hit the following year.

Adams left the Johnny Otis group around 1960 and recorded as a solo act on the Sure Play and Encore labels. She rejoined the Three Tons of Joy for an album and a world tour with Johnny Otis in 1972.

Barry Adamson: See Magazine

King Sunny Ade
Born Sunday Francis Adeniyi, September 1, 1946, Ondo, Nigeria
1968—*The Master Guitarist* (African Songs/Serengeti, U.K.) 1976—*The Late General Muritala Mohammed* (Decca); *Sunny Ade Live Play* (Sunny Alade) 1978—*Festac 77* 1980—*Check "E"* 1981—*The Message* 1982—*Ariya Special*; *Juju Music* (Mango) 1983—*Synchro System*; *Ajoo* (Makossa) 1984—*Aura* (Island) 1985—*Otito* (Sunny Alade) 1986—*Saviour* 1987—*Return of the Juju King* (Mercury) 1988—*Live! Live Juju!* (Rykodisc) 1989—*Funmilayo* (Sunny Alade).

A superstar in his native Nigeria since the late Sixties, *juju* bandleader King Sunny Ade was hailed by American critics in 1982 as "the next Bob Marley." While Ade, who sings in his native Yoruba tongue, never achieved that level of popularity in the U.S., he and his 20-piece African Beats band did whet American and European appetites for world music. In addition, Ade helped open the door for other Afro-pop artists, among them fellow Nigerian *juju* stars Ebenezer Obey and Dele Abiodun, Zaire's Tabu Ley Rochereau and Papa Wemba, Senegal's Youssou N'Dour, South Africa's Mahlathini and the Mahotella Queens, and Madagascar's Rossy and Tarika Sammy.

Born into the royal family of Ondo, the youthful Ade horrified his parents by pursuing music, which was considered a profession for commoners. He dropped out of school in 1963 to join semipro bands in the capital of Lagos, playing *juju*—a popular Nigerian guitar music style since the Twenties, which had been radically altered by the infusion of electric guitars and Western rock influences. Within a year Ade was a guitarist with a top *juju* outfit, Moses Olaiya's Rhythm Dandies. By 1967 he had formed his own band, the Green Spots (taking off on the name of longtime *juju* king I. K. Dairo's Blue Spots

King Sunny Ade

band), and recorded his first single, "Challenge Cup," which celebrated a local soccer team's championship and became a national hit.

By the early Seventies Ade's Green Spots had grown into the African Beats, an orchestral ensemble with four or five vocalists, just as many guitarists, a Hawaiian guitarist (inspired by the pedal-steel heard on records by Ade's favorite country singer, Jim Reeves), keyboards or vibraphone (in the Eighties, he added synthesizers), bass, trap drums, and a half-dozen or so percussionists, including the talking drum players so central to the distinctive *juju* sound. ("Talking drums" are small hand drums with variable pitch.) Ade's style of *juju* music is a gently hypnotic, polyrhythmic mesh of burbling guitars, sweet harmony vocals, swooping Hawaiian guitar, and throbbing talking drums.

By 1975 Ade was a certified superstar in his homeland; by decade's end, he'd released a half-dozen albums a year, selling around 200,000 copies of each.

He set up his own Sunny Alade record label and Ariya nightclub in Lagos. The early Eighties found Ade building a substantial European cult following, leading Island Records to sign him for both Europe and North

Aerosmith: Tom Hamilton,
Joey Kramer, Joe Perry,
Steven Tyler, Brad Whitford

America, where his influence had already been felt on such albums as Talking Heads' *Remain in Light* (1980) and King Crimson's *Discipline* (1981). *Juju Music,* featuring new recordings of tunes from Ade's vast repertoire, got universal rave reviews, as did his first of many U.S. tours; the album sold well enough to graze the bottom of the pop chart (#111, 1983). *Synchro System,* with a harder rhythmic edge and more prominent synthesizers, sold slightly better (#91, 1983), but when *Aura* failed to chart, despite a guest appearance by Stevie Wonder, Island dropped Ade. The African Beats then broke up, amidst dissension and claims of being underpaid (though Ade was reportedly losing money on tours, supporting his large band while playing undersized venues). Back in Lagos, Ade formed a new band, Golden Mercury, retaining his trademark sound and continuing to record and tour internationally, periodically returning to the U.S.

Aerosmith

Formed 1970, Sunapee, New Hampshire
Steven Tyler (b. Steve Tallarico, Mar. 26, 1948, New York City, N.Y.), voc.; Joe Perry (b. Sep. 10, 1950, Lawrence, Mass.), gtr.; Brad Whitford (b. Feb. 23, 1952, Winchester, Mass.), gtr.; Tom Hamilton (b. Dec. 31, 1951, Colorado Springs, Colo.), bass; Joey Kramer (b. June 21, 1950, New York City), drums.
1973—*Aerosmith* (Columbia)   1974—*Get Your Wings*   1975—*Toys in the Attic*   1976—*Rocks*   1977—*Draw the Line*   1978—*Live Bootleg*   1979—*A Night in the Ruts* (– Perry; + Jim Crespo, gtr.)   1980—*Aerosmith's Greatest Hits* (– Whitford; + Rick Dufay, gtr., voc.)   1982—*Rock in a Hard*

Place   1984—(– Crespo; – Dufay; + Perry; + Whitford)   1985—*Done with Mirrors* (Geffen); *Classics Live!* (Columbia)   1987—*Classics Live II*; *Permanent Vacation* (Geffen)   1988—*Gems* (Columbia)   1989—*Pump* (Geffen)   1991—*Pandora's Box* (Columbia)   1993—*Get a Grip* (Geffen)   1994—*Big Ones*; *Box of Fire* (Columbia).
The Joe Perry Project: 1980—*Let the Music Do the Talking* (Columbia)   1981—*I've Got the Rock 'n' Rolls Again*   1984—*Once a Rocker Always a Rocker.*
The Whitford St. Holmes Band: 1981—*Whitford St. Holmes* (Columbia).

Fronted by Mick Jagger lookalike Steve Tyler and known for its aggressive blues-based style, Aerosmith was the top American hard-rock band of the mid-Seventies, despite endless attacks from critics who considered them a poor man's Rolling Stones. But the members' growing drug problems and internal dissension contributed to a commercial decline that began with 1977's *Draw the Line.* Two crucial lineup changes and a few poorly received albums preceded a 1984 reunion of the original lineup and the multiplatinum *Permanent Vacation,* which signaled one of the most spectacular comebacks in rock history. Though now vociferous adherents of the sober lifestyle and pushing past forty, Aerosmith forfeited none of their bad-boy image, and their live shows were among the best of their long career. Even critics liked them better the second time around.

The group was formed in 1970 by Joe Perry, Tom Hamilton, and Tyler, who was then a drummer. The group was completed with drummer Joey Kramer and

Brad Whitford; Tyler became lead singer. For the next two years all five members shared a small apartment in Boston and played almost nightly throughout the area, occasionally venturing to New York. Clive Davis saw them perform at Max's Kansas City in New York and signed them to Columbia. A minor hit and future FM-radio staple from their debut, "Dream On," strengthened their regional following.

Meanwhile, Aerosmith began to tour widely. By 1976 "Dream On" recharted, rising to #6 and spawning innumerable power-ballad imitations. And by the time of "Walk This Way" (#10, 1977), the band had become headliners. Its phenomenal success was short-lived, however. A series of sold-out tours and platinum albums (including *Aerosmith, Get Your Wings, Toys in the Attic*) peaked in 1976.

By 1977 the group's constant touring and the band members' heavy drug use (Perry and Tyler were nicknamed "the Toxic Twins" for their heroin habits) had begun to take their toll. After months of rest, Aerosmith recorded *Draw the Line* and appeared as the villains in Robert Stigwood's movie *Sgt. Pepper's Lonely Hearts Club Band;* their version of Lennon and McCartney's "Come Together" from the soundtrack was a minor hit. But Aerosmith was unraveling: In 1979 Perry quit, admitting to long-standing personality and musical conflicts with Tyler, his songwriting partner. Jim Crespo took his place. The next year Whitford departed to form the Whitford St. Holmes Band with ex–Ted Nugent sidekick Derek St. Holmes and was replaced by Rick Dufay. Neither Perry's nor Whitford's outside records did particularly well.

Rock in a Hard Place, Aerosmith's first new recording in almost three years and the first without Perry, peaked at #32, as the band was eclipsed by a new breed of young hard-rockers. In early 1984 the five original members met backstage at an Aerosmith concert and decided to re-form. *Done with Mirrors*, their first "comeback" LP, sold moderately. The group's reascendance began in earnest when Perry and Tyler appeared with rap duo Run-D.M.C. in a video for the latter's version of the 1977 Aerosmith warhorse "Walk This Way" (#4, 1986). That fall, just as "Walk This Way" was peaking on the chart, *Permanent Vacation* (#11, 1987) was released, with three hit singles and their accompanying videos— "Dude (Looks Like a Lady)" (#14, 1987), "Angel" (#3, 1988), and "Rag Doll" (#17, 1988)—introducing Aerosmith to a new generation.

Aerosmith further consolidated its success with the quadruple-platinum *Pump* (#5, 1989), which boasted "Love in an Elevator" (#5, 1989), "Janie's Got a Gun" (#4, 1989)—the song about incest won 1990's Grammy for Best Rock Performance by a Duo or Group—"What It Takes" (#9, 1990), and "The Other Side" (#22, 1990).

In 1991 the group signed a record deal with Sony worth a reported $30 million for four albums and including provisions for 22 percent royalties. Three years later, in summer 1994, the group landed a seven-figure deal from G. P. Putnam's Sons for its group autobiography. With the hit singles "Living on the Edge" (#18, 1993), "Cryin" (#12, 1993), and "Crazy" (#7, 1993), *Get a Grip* hit #1, followed by 1994's double-platinum #6 greatest-hits package, *Big Ones*, continuing Aerosmith's run at the top. *Box of Fire*, a 12-CD compilation of Aerosmith's Columbia output, went gold in early 1995.

African Music

"Jungle music" is an epithet that has been applied to rock & roll since its beginnings, and though usually meant derisively, there is considerable truth in it: Rock's pounding drums, jangling guitars, call-and-response vocals, and sensual communal dance all bear more than incidental resemblance to tribal music and dance of tropical Africa. Rock & roll's roots extend firmly into Africa via its origins in the blues and in black gospel music, and musicians from Bo Diddley, to James Brown, to the Rolling Stones, Santana, Talking Heads, and rappers such as Arrested Development have drawn from those roots to reinforce the African presence in Western pop.

Since the Second World War, the intercontinental connection has gone full circle. Many of the styles popular in modern urban Africa are hybrids of traditional African elements and African-American elements. In the Fifties Ghanaian bandleaders such as guitarist E. K. Nyama and trumpeter E. T. Mensah developed *highlife*, a nightclub dance music influenced by calypso. At the same time, South African pennywhistle bands like the Solven Whistlers used swing jazz tunes and arrangements. In the Sixties the Congolese *kasongo* and *kiri-kiri* of "jazz orchestras" like l'O.K. and Afrisan Internationale reflected the African taste for the Cuban rhumba, while the Kenyan *sukuma* of Nashil Pichen and Peter Tsotsi combined Congolese guitar styles with Arabian influences. South African 'smodern groups like the Dark City Sisters and Mahlathini and the Mahotella Queens forged a female vocal group style from Zulu polyphonic singing and Motown-like pop.

In the Seventies Nigerian *juju* musicians Ebenezer Obey, Prince Nico Mbarga, and King Sunny Ade, among others, added multiple electric guitars to the ancient interplay of multiple drums, while saxophonist/keyboardist/orator Fela Anikulapo Kuti re-Africanized James Brown funk arrangements in a style known as *afro-beat*. These particular Nigerians—immensely popular in their country—attracted considerable attention in Europe and America.

Contemporary African musicians have, from time to time, been accepted into the American mainstream. South African singer Miriam Makeba and trumpeter

Hugh Masekela put "Pata Pata" and "Grazing in the Grass," respectively, on AM radio in the mid-Sixties. Osibisa, a predominantly Ghanaian band, sold around 100,000 copies each of their first two albums to Americans in the early Seventies. A couple of years later, Cameroonian saxophonist Manu Dibango made a prototypical disco hit with "Soul Makossa."

Since the early Eighties, African musicians have performed fairly frequently in the more cosmopolitan American cities. African music also gained an immense amount of attention due to pop advocates like Paul Simon, Peter Gabriel (who started the RealWorld label to give attention to African and other world artists), and David Byrne (who started another world music label, Luaka Bop). In 1988 the public radio show *Afropop* debuted on 60 stations and had reached 200 by 1990, when it became *Afropop Worldwide*, expanding its purview to include styles from the Middle East, the Caribbean, Spain, North and South America, and other areas within the African diaspora.

Some styles from around the world that are derived from African sources are *afoxé*, a Bahian dance-music form based on Congo-Angolan rituals; *cumbia*, a Colombian dance-music hybrid; *juju*, modern Nigerian pop music; *mbaqanga*, a South African form developed in the Sixties; *merengue*, from the Dominican Republic; *palmwine*, acoustic-based music from Ghana and Sierra Leone; *rai*, Algerian electronic dance-music; *rara*, percussive Haitian festival music; *soukous*, modern Congolese or Zairean dance music; and *zouk*, modern dance music produced in Paris and based on music from Martinique and Guadeloupe.

a-ha

Formed 1982, Oslo, Norway
Morten Harket (b. Sep. 14, 1959, Kongsberg, Nor.), voc.; Magne "Mags" Furuholmen (b. Nov. 1, 1962, Oslo), kybds.; Pål Waaktaar (b. Sep. 6, 1961, Oslo), gtr.
1985—*Hunting High and Low* (Warner Bros.)
1986—*Scoundrel Days*   1988—*Stay on These Roads*
1990—*East of the Sun, West of the Moon*   1991—*Headlines and Deadlines: The Hits of a-ha*   1993—*Memorial Beach*.

With chiseled Scandinavian good looks and a few pop hooks, a-ha are a Norwegian electropop answer to Duran Duran, as mid-Eighties teen idols of the music-video age. It might be argued that Steve Barron, who directed the video for the trio's "Take On Me," and Michael Patterson and Candace Reckinger, who animated the clip, were as important to a-ha's American success as the band members themselves.

A-ha's three members had played in such Scandinavian bands as Spider Empire, Soldier Blue, and Bridges before coming together in the early Eighties and moving together to London. Their first single, "Take On Me" (#1, 1985), got heavy MTV play with its video clip, which blended live action and animation in a romantic adventure starring the handsome Harket as a comic-book hero who comes to life and pulls an unsuspecting young woman into the action. The song propelled *Hunting High and Low* to #15. A-ha would score a few more hits—"The Sun Always Shines on TV" (#20, 1985) and "Cry Wolf" (#50, 1987)—but its album sales steadily decreased, and *East of the Sun* and *Memorial Beach* failed to chart at all. A-ha remained a steady draw internationally, however, especially in Latin America, where it topped the singles charts no fewer than 14 times, and in 1991 played for record-breaking crowds at Brazil's "Rock in Rio" concert. In 1987 a-ha wrote and recorded the theme song for the James Bond film *The Living Daylights*.

Air Supply

Formed 1976, Melbourne, Australia
1978—Graham Russell (b. June 1, 1950, Nottingham, Eng.), voc., gtr.; Russell Hitchcock (b. June 15, 1949, Melbourne), voc.; Ralph Cooper (b. April 6, 1951, Coffs Harbour, Austral.), drums; David Moyse (b. Nov. 5, 1957, Adelaide, Austral.), gtr.; David Green (b. Oct. 30, 1949, Melbourne), bass; Rex Goh (b. May 5, 1951, Singapore), gtr.; Frank Esler-Smith (b. June 5, 1948, London, Eng.), kybds.
1980—*Lost in Love* (Arista)   1981—*The One That You Love*   1982—*Now and Forever*   1983—*Greatest Hits*   1985—*Air Supply*   1986—*Hearts in Motion*   1988—(Group disbands)   1991—(Group re-forms: Russell; Hitchcock; Cooper) *The Earth Is* (Giant)   1993—*The Vanishing Race*.

Air Supply is an Australian group based around the duo of Graham Russell (the main songwriter) and Russell Hitchcock. Their light pop-rock hits have earned Air Supply several platinum LPs and gold singles worldwide; *Greatest Hits* was quadruple platinum in the U.S., and *The Earth Is*, which failed to chart here, went gold in more than 20 countries.

The group originally consisted of lead vocalists Hitchcock and Russell, backed by studio musicians. As such, they had several hit singles in Australia, including "Love and Other Bruises" (1976), "Empty Pages," and "Do What You Do" (both 1977), and two gold albums. After forming a band to record their third LP, they came up with one of the U.S.'s biggest hits in 1979, "Lost in Love" (#3, 1979). A string of Top Ten hits followed: "Every Woman to Me" (#5, 1980), "The One That You Love" (#1, 1981), "Even the Nights Are Better" (#6, 1982), and "Making Love Out of Nothing at All" (#2, 1983). To date, the group has sold over 15 million records worldwide.

The group first disbanded in 1988, but Russell and Hitchcock re-formed Air Supply in 1991, including only Cooper from the old lineup. The pair has continued to tour with various backing configurations.

Laurel Aitken
Born 1928, Cuba
1993—*Rasta Man Power* cassette (ROIR).

Laurel Aitken emigrated to Jamaica in the early Fifties and began recording in the incipient local record industry. His records were popular throughout the West Indies and eventually reached Britain when his 1953 single "Little Sheila" (on Melodisc Records) became the first Jamaican record issued in the U.K. Subsequent releases in a variety of styles (the bluebeat of "Bartender," the old-fashioned gospel of "Daniel Saw the Stone") were popular among England's West Indian immigrants, and in the early Sixties Aitken moved to London.

As one of the stars of Melodisc's Bluebeat label (a specialty line catering to the transplanted West Indian population), Aitken—along with Prince Buster, Derrick Morgan, and other Bluebeat artists—pioneered ska in England. Songs such as "Bugaboo," "You Was Up," "Fire in Your Wire," and "The Rise and Fall of Laurel Aitken"—distinguished by Aitken's low, gruff voice and unabashed sexual humor—popularized ska with British white youth while fomenting a subgenre of ska called "rude" songs, with lyrics as brash and raucous as the music. Occasional tracks in a serious vein, such as "Lion of Judah," "Judgment Day," and "Landlords and Tenants," proved Aitken could appeal to other than prurient interests, but one of his biggest hits, "Pussy Price" in 1968, was as rude a song as has ever been recorded.

In 1980 Aitken had a minor U.K. pop hit with "Rudi Got Married," an "answer" record to the Specials' "Message to You Rudy." Later in the decade he recorded with Floyd Lloyd and the Potato 5.

Alabama
Formed 1969 (as Young Country), Fort Payne, Alabama
Jeff Cook (b. Aug. 27, 1949, Fort Payne), gtr., fiddle, voc.; Randy Owen (b. Dec. 13, 1949, Fort Payne), gtr., voc.; Teddy Gentry (b. Jan. 22, 1952, Fort Payne), bass, voc.
N.A.—*Wild Country* (LSI); *Deuces Wild*; *Alabama 3* 1973—(+ Rich Scott, drums) 1979—(– Scott; + Mark Herndon [b. May 11, 1955, Springfield, Mass.], drums) 1980—*My Home's in Alabama* (RCA) 1981—*Feels So Right* 1982—*Mountain Music* 1983—*The Closer You Get* 1984—*Roll On* 1985—*40 Hr. Week*; *Alabama Christmas* 1986—

Greatest Hits; The Touch 1987—Just Us 1988— Alabama Live 1989—Southern Star 1990—Pass It On Down 1991—Greatest Hits II 1992—American Pride 1993—Cheap Seats 1994—Greatest Hits, vol. III.

The biggest-selling country group of the Eighties, Alabama began in 1969 as a trio of cousins: Jeff Cook, Randy Owen, and Teddy Gentry. Then known as Young Country, they performed on weekends at a local amusement park, Canyonland. In 1973 they moved to Myrtle Beach, South Carolina, and there, with drummer Rich Scott, began playing their own songs in clubs. By this time they had changed their name to Alabama.

After a few self-produced singles, the group signed with GRT Records in 1977. Its first release, "I Want to Be with You," made the country Top 100, but subsequent releases failed to match even that standing. In 1979 Alabama went to MDJ Records of Dallas, and its first single on the independent label, "I Wanna Come Over," reached #32 on the country chart in 1980, and the followup, "My Home's in Alabama," #17. Alabama's first RCA single, "Tennessee River," hit #1 in 1980. It was the first of 37 country chart-toppers. To date the group has sold over 50 million records worldwide of its country-pop sound. Of its 16 albums on RCA through 1993, only that year's *Cheap Seats* failed to go gold or platinum—an indication that after nearly 15 years, Alabama's thunder had been stolen by Garth Brooks, Travis Tritt, and other contemporary country acts. Nevertheless, 1993 did see the quartet win the People's Choice award for favorite musical group.

The Alarm
Formed 1978 (as Seventeen), Rhyl, Wales
Eddie McDonald (b. Nov. 1, 1959), bass; Mike Peters (b. Michael Peters, Feb. 25, 1959), voc., gtr.; Dave Sharp (b. David Sharp, Jan. 28, 1959), gtr., voc.; Nigel Twist (b. July 18, 1958), drums.
1983—*The Alarm* EP (I.R.S.) 1984—*Declaration* 1985—*Strength* 1987—*Eye of the Hurricane* 1988—*Electric Folklore Live* 1989—*Change* 1990—*Standards* 1991—*Raw.*

The earnest guitar-dominated band the Alarm first came to the attention of American audiences when it opened U2's 1983 tour. Like U2, the Alarm sought to forge a new, idealistic arena rock, one marked by a sense of band-audience communion and punk's galvanizing spirit. Eschewing electronic effects, the Alarm's Mike Peters and Dave Sharp strummed acoustic guitars.

The quartet came together in their native Wales while all were in their teens. Peters and Nigel Twist were part of the Toilets when Eddie MacDonald and Sharp joined them in 1978. Inspired by the Sex Pistols, for a while they called themselves Seventeen. In 1981 they relocated to London where, after gigging steadily in clubs, they were signed by I.R.S. Records. The following year they became the Alarm. Despite scoring hits on rock-oriented radio with such songs as "Strength" (#61, 1985) and "Rain in the Summertime" (#71, 1987), only one album broke the Top Forty, *Strength* (#39, 1985). Sharp released a solo album, *Hard Travellin'*, in late 1991; since then, the band's future has been uncertain.

Al B. Sure!
Born Albert Brown, Boston, Massachusetts
1988—*In Effect Mode* (Warner Bros.)   1990—*Private Times . . . and the Whole 9*   1992—*Sexy Versus*.

In the late Eighties, as rap was working its way into popular culture, Al B. Sure! was among a handful of young black artists who traded on old-fashioned R&B crooning and old-fashioned sex appeal. The handsome singer had been the star quarterback on his football team in Mount Vernon, New York, but he turned down an athletic college scholarship and instead attended Manhattan's Center for the Media Arts, where he studied various aspects of music making. In Manhattan, Sure! and his cousin made a series of demo tapes; through the support of their friend Eddie F, a member of the rap group Heavy D. and the Boyz, the tapes came to the attention of manager Andre Harrell, who helped land Sure! a contract with Warner Bros. Shortly after being signed, the singer won the 1987 Sony Innovator Talent Search, whose deciding judge was Quincy Jones.

Sure!'s debut album, *In Effect Mode*, sold two million copies and spawned the #1 R&B (#7 pop) single "Nite and Day." The album's melodic dance tracks and romantic ballads also earned Sure! a Grammy nomination for Best R&B Male Vocal Performance. The singer released more albums, but none matched the success of his debut.

Arthur Alexander
Born Arthur Bernard Alexander Jr., May 10, 1940, Florence, Alabama; died June 9, 1993, Nashville, Tennessee
1962—*You Better Move On* (Dot)   1972—*Arthur Alexander* (Warner Bros.)   1993—*Lonely Just Like Me* (Elektra Nonesuch); *The Ultimate Arthur Alexander* (Razor & Tie).

Country-soul vocalist Arthur Alexander wrote and recorded the 1962 hit "You Better Move On." He began singing in church as a child, and during his teens belonged to an a cappella group called the Heartstrings. In 1961 he was working a day job as a bellhop and recording occasionally. Early the next year, his song "You Better Move On" hit #24 on the pop charts. It was not only

Alexander's first and most successful single, but the first hit to come out of Rick Hall's Muscle Shoals studios. Dot Records unwisely attempted to market Alexander as a pop singer, and such followup releases as the Barry Mann–Cynthia Weil composition "Where Have You Been (All My Life)" and his own "Anna (Go to Him)" (both 1962) were well sung but commercially unsuccessful.

His records had more impact in England, and his songs were later recorded by the Beatles ("Anna"), the Rolling Stones ("You Better Move On"), Bob Dylan ("Sally Sue Brown"), Elvis Presley ("Burning Love"), and Otis Redding ("Johnny Heartbreak"). In 1972 Alexander's eponymous album on Warner Bros. drew critical kudos but low sales. A few years later he reentered the pop chart with "Every Day I Have to Cry" (#45, 1975), but then quit the music business, tired, as he said, of "the rip-offs." After 1981 he drove a bus for a Cleveland social-services agency. He remained popular in England where three of his albums (*Shot of Rhythm and Soul, Soldiers of Love*, and *Arthur Alexander*) were reissued through the Eighties. Following the 1991 murder of his eldest son, he returned to music.

Alexander was on the verge of a commercial comeback in 1993, with the release of his first LP in two decades, *Lonely Just Like Me*. Unanimously praised by critics, the album featured backing by such Muscle Shoals mainstays as guitarist Dan Penn and keyboardist Spooner Oldham. Sadly, just a few months after its release and on the eve of a summer tour, Alexander died of heart failure.

Alice in Chains
Formed 1987, Seattle, Washington
Jerry Cantrell (b. Mar. 18, 1966, Tacoma, Wash.), gtr.; Layne Staley (b. Aug. 22, 1967, Bellevue, Wash.), voc.; Sean Kinney (b. May 27, 1966, Seattle), drums; Mike Starr (b. Apr. 4, 1966, Honolulu, Hawaii), bass.
1990—*We Die Young* promotional EP (Columbia); *Face Lift*   1991—*Sap* EP   1992—*Dirt* (– Starr; + Mike Inez [b. May 14, 1966, San Fernando, Calif.], bass)   1993—*Jar of Flies* EP.

A metal band with an alternative rock edge, Alice in Chains was among the biggest to emerge from the grunge scene that spawned Nirvana, Pearl Jam, and Soundgarden. The group's dark, bitter songs, laden with references to drug addiction and death, occupy a musical landscape somewhere between Metallica's dense head bangers and Pearl Jam's grinding anthems.

Layne Staley formed Alice N' Chains with an earlier lineup while still in high school. In 1987 he met Jerry Cantrell at the Music Bank, a notorious Seattle warehouse rehearsal space, and the two put together the newly christened Alice in Chains along with Cantrell cohorts Kinney and Starr. By 1989 the group had signed to Columbia Records, where it became the beneficiary of an aggressive promotion campaign that saw the release of a five-song promotional EP, *We Die Young*, and had the group opening for a range of disparate acts, including Iggy Pop and Poison. As a result, by September 1991, *Face Lift* (#42) had sold a half-million copies and featured the Grammy-nominated "Man in the Box." A low-key EP, *Sap*, and a track in the Seattle youth culture movie, *Singles*, kept the band in the public eye between albums.

The group's thematically bleaker sophomore effort, *Dirt* (#6), went platinum in 1992 (eventually selling three million copies), and the group's appearance on the following summer's Lollapalooza Tour confirmed its popularity. Reports of drug abuse, however, had begun to plague Staley and the band; a couple of songs from *Dirt*—"Junkhead" and "Angry Chair"—had hinted at mental fatigue and self-destruction. Yet Alice in Chains' success was at an all-time high: In late 1993 *Dirt* went double-platinum, and the following year the acoustic *Jar of Flies* rocketed to #1, the first EP to ever top the *Billboard* album charts. In 1994 Staley hooked up with fellow Seattleites Mike McCready (Pearl Jam), Barrett Martin (Screaming Trees), and John Baker Saunders to play a few gigs under the name Gacy Bunch; the next year they changed their name to Mad Season and released *Above* (#24).

Lee Allen

Born July 2, 1927, Pittsburg, Kansas; died October 18, 1994, Los Angeles, California
1958—*Walkin' with Mr. Lee* (Ember).

Although the closest Lee Allen ever came to getting a hit for himself was "Walkin' with Mr. Lee" (#54, 1958), his tenor saxophone session performances and arrangements were integral to numerous hits by Fats Domino, Little Richard, and others who recorded in New Orleans in the Fifties and early Sixties. He moved to New Orleans in 1944, where he attended Xavier University on a music and athletic scholarship. By 1948 he was performing professionally with Paul Gayten's band, one of the pioneer New Orleans R&B bands. In 1956 he joined Dave Bartholomew's band, which recorded and toured with Fats Domino during Domino's peak years. At that time Allen also worked as a session musician and arranger; he and baritone saxophonist Alvin "Red" Tyler led New Orleans' most in-demand session ensemble, the Studio Band, which included drummers Earl Palmer and Charles "Hungry" Williams, guitarists Ernest McLean and Justin Adams, pianists Salvador Doucette, Edward Frank, and Allen Toussaint, bassist Frank "Dude" Fields, and trumpeter Melvin Lastie.

Bumps Blackwell hired the Studio Band to back

Little Richard on some of his hit records: "Tutti Frutti," "Long Tall Sally," "The Girl Can't Help It," and others. Allen also played behind Shirley and Lee ("Let the Good Times Roll"), Huey Smith and the Clowns ("Rockin' Pneumonia and the Boogie Woogie Flu"), Sam Cooke, Lowell Fulson, Charles Brown, and Jimmy Clanton.

In 1957 Allen signed a solo contract with Herald Records. His first single was "Walkin' with Mr. Lee," a #1 hit in New Orleans, followed by "Tic Toc" and a tour of the U.S. in the late Fifties. He then returned to the New Orleans studios to work for $42 per session on hit records that sold millions of copies. He retired in the early Sixties but returned in 1981 to record and tour with the Blasters; he also guested on some of the Alvins' solo albums.

In 1994 Allen contributed tenor saxophone and vocals to *Crescent City Gold*, an album featuring an aggregation of New Orleans jazz and R&B greats. Later that year he died of cancer at age 67.

Peter Allen

Born Peter Allen Woolnough, February 10, 1944, Tenterfield, Australia; died June 18, 1992, San Diego, California
1971—*Peter Allen* (Metromedia)   1972—*Tenterfield Saddler*   1974—*Continental American* (A&M) 1976—*Taught by Experts*   1977—*It's Time for Peter Allen*   1979—*I Could Have Been a Sailor*   1980— *Bi-Coastal*   1982—*The Best*   1983—*Not the Boy Next Door* (Arista)   1985—*Captured Live at Carnegie Hall*   1990—*Making Every Moment Count* (RCA)   1993—*Peter Allen at His Best* (A&M)

Singer/songwriter/pianist Peter Allen became a popular cabaret-style performer in the late Seventies. He began playing piano and singing in local clubs at age 11; within three years he was performing the day's rock hits in hotels. By his 18th birthday he'd left school for Sydney, where he met Chris Bell (who changed his last name to Allen). Together the duo toured the world as Chris and Peter Allen. Judy Garland saw them perform in Hong Kong and hired them as her opening act. The duo made twenty appearances on *The Tonight Show* and toured the U.S. In 1964 Allen and Garland's daughter, Liza Minnelli, were engaged; they married in 1967. In 1970 the couple separated on the same day that Allen broke up his partnership with Chris Bell. Allen and Minnelli divorced in 1973 but remained friends until his death.

Allen's first two albums, *Peter Allen* and *Tenterfield Saddler*, attracted favorable reviews but sold poorly. His big break came in 1974, when a song he cowrote, "I Honestly Love You," became a #1 hit for Olivia Newton-John and later won a Grammy for Record of the Year. Subsequent hits included "I Go to Rio" (a minor U.S. hit, but #1 in France and Australia) and "Six-Thirty Sunday Morning." In 1981 Allen was one of four cowriters (including

Burt Bacharach and Carole Bayer Sager) of the Oscar-winning theme song from the movie *Arthur*, "Arthur's Theme (The Best That You Can Do)," a #1 hit for Christopher Cross. He also cowrote (with Bayer Sager) Melissa Manchester's "Don't Cry Out Loud," among other hits.

Allen's own chart appearances were spotty, although critics compared him favorably to such modern classic songwriters as Jerome Kern. His forte was live performance, where his campy, outrageous, show-bizzy style alternated with a more sedate, serious persona. His sequined costumes, Hawaiian-print shirts, and trademark humor made him a concert staple. Ironically, the biggest commercial disappointment of his career was the 1988 Broadway musical *Legs Diamond*, which he wrote and starred in; it closed after 64 performances. A waltz he wrote, "I Call Australia Home," is popular in his homeland and the signature song of Qantas Airways. He died of AIDS-related causes just months after diagnosis.

Luther Allison
Born August 17, 1939, Mayflower, Arkansas
1969—*Love Me Mama* (Delmark)   1972—*Bad News Is Coming* (Gordy)   1974—*Luther's Blues*   1976— *Night Life*   1979—*Gonna Be a Live One Here Tonight* (Rumble)   1993—*Hand Me Down My Moonshine* (Inak, Ger.)   1994—*Soul Fixin' Man* (Alligator); *Serious* (Blind Pig).

Blues guitarist Luther Allison is part of the generation of electric blues guitarists that came of age in the Sixties and was able to appeal both to old-line blues audiences and to younger, white rock audiences. Born on a cotton plantation, Allison was one of 15 children. Before he was ten years old, he sang with a gospel group, the Southern Travellers, on tours through the South. He moved with his family to Chicago around 1951 and took up guitar. There he befriended a neighborhood boy whose father was Muddy Waters. He first performed as a blues guitarist with his elder brother's band, which played Chicago clubs between 1954 and 1957, then formed his own, the Rolling Stones, later renamed the Four Jivers, which lasted a year.

For the next decade Allison was a mainstay of the Chicago blues scene, often playing in the bands of Freddie King and Magic Sam. He made his first records for Delmark in 1967, the same year he took to the road with his group, the Tornados. In 1968 he toured and recorded for World Pacific with Shakey Jake and began making annual appearances at the Ann Arbor Blues and Jazz Festival. Hoping to find success in the music business, he moved to California in the late Sixties and soon began playing such rock venues as the Fillmore West and in New York City, the Fillmore East and Max's Kansas City. Dispirited, he returned to Chicago and recorded three al-

bums for Motown's Gordy subsidiary label and the soundtrack to *Cooley High*.

He began touring Europe in the Seventies, and through the Eighties and early Nineties performed in Japan, the former Soviet Union, Poland, Scandinavia, and Western Europe—while making his home near Paris, France.

Mose Allison
Born Mose John Allison Jr., November 11, 1927, Tippo, Mississippi
1957—*Back Country Suite* (Prestige)   1983— *Lessons in Living* (Elektra/Musician)   1988—*Ever Since the World Ended* (Blue Note); *Greatest Hits* (Fantasy)   1990—*My Backyard* (Blue Note)   1993— *I Don't Worry About a Thing* (Rhino)   1994—*The Earth Wants You* (Blue Note); *Allison Wonderland— The Mose Allison Anthology* (Rhino); *High Jinks!: The Mose Allison Trilogy* (Columbia).

Singer/pianist Mose Allison has been popular in jazz circles for over 35 years, and he is known in rock for his songs—which have been covered by the Who ("A Young Man Blues"), Bonnie Raitt ("Everybody's Cryin' Mercy"), John Mayall ("Parchman Farm"), Van Morrison ("If You Only Knew"), the Clash ("Look Here"), and the Yardbirds ("I'm Not Talking"), among others—and a sardonic sense of humor, as evidenced in his "Your Mind Is on Vacation (But Your Mouth Is Working Overtime)."

The son of a stride jazz pianist, Allison began playing piano at age six and later took up the trumpet. He absorbed both jazz and country blues, and when he arrived in New York City in 1956 he played piano with "cool" jazzmen Al Cohn, Stan Getz, Gerry Mulligan, and Zoot Sims, blending the simplicity of the blues with modernist harmonies. He began to sing in 1957, when he formed his own trio, and his understated and laconically cynical songs have been periodically rediscovered by the rock audience. As of 1993, Allison, in his mid-sixties, was still performing over 100 nights a year.

The Allman Brothers Band
Formed 1968, Macon, Georgia
Duane Allman (b. Nov. 20, 1946, Nashville, Tenn.; d. Oct. 29, 1971, Macon), gtr.; Gregg Allman (b. Dec. 8, 1947, Nashville, Tenn.), kybds., gtr., voc.; Berry Oakley (b. Apr. 4, 1948, Chicago, Ill.; d. Nov. 11, 1972, Macon), bass; Dickey Betts (b. Dec. 12, 1943, West Palm Beach, Fla.), gtr., voc.; Jai Johanny Johanson, a.k.a. Jaimoe (b. John Lee Johnson, July 8, 1944, Ocean Springs, Miss.), drums; Butch Trucks (b. Jacksonville, Fla.), drums.
1969—*The Allman Brothers Band* (Capricorn) 1970—*Idlewild South*   1971—*At Fillmore East*

The Allman Brothers Band: Butch Trucks, Dickey Betts, Berry Oakley, Duane Allman, Gregg Allman, Jai Johanny Johanson

(– D. Allman) 1972—*Eat a Peach* (+ Chuck Leavell, kybds.; – Oakley; + Lamar Williams [b. 1947; d. Jan. 25, 1983, Los Angeles, Calif.], bass) 1973—*Brothers and Sisters* 1974—*Beginnings* 1975—*Win, Lose or Draw*; *The Road Goes on Forever* 1976—*Wipe the Windows, Check the Oil, Dollar Gas* 1978— (– Leavell; – Williams; + Dan Toler, gtr.; + Rook Goldflies, bass) 1979—*Enlightened Rogues* 1980—*Reach for the Sky* (Arista) 1981—*Brothers of the Road*; *The Best of the Allman Brothers Band* (Polydor) 1982—(+ Leavell; – Johanson; group disbands) 1989—(Group re-forms: Gregg Allman; Dickey Betts; Jaimoe; Butch Trucks; + Warren Haynes, gtr.; + Allen Woody, bass; + Johnny Neel, kybds.) *Dreams* 1990—*Live at Ludlow's Garage, 1970*; *Seven Turns* (Epic) (– Neel) 1991—*Shades of Two Worlds*; *Decade of Hits (1969–79)* (Polydor) 1992—*An Evening with the Allman Brothers Band* (Epic) 1994—*Where It All Begins* 1995—*2nd Set*. Duane Allman solo: 1972—*An Anthology* (Capricorn) 1974—*An Anthology, vol. 2*.
Gregg Allman solo: 1974—*Laid Back* (Capricorn); *The Gregg Allman Tour*.
The Gregg Allman Band: 1977—*Playin' Up a Storm* 1987—*I'm No Angel* (Epic) 1988—*Just Before the Bullets Fly*.
Dickey Betts solo: 1974—*Highway Call* (Capricorn).
Dickey Betts and Great Southern: 1977—*Dickey Betts and Great Southern* (Arista) 1978—*Atlanta's Burning Down*.
The Dickey Betts Band: 1988—*Pattern Disruptive* (Epic).
Sea Level (Leavell; Jaimoe; Williams): 1977—*Sea Level* (Capricorn) 1978—*Cats on the Coast*; *On the Edge* 1979—*Long Walk on a Short Pier* 1980—*Ball Room* (Arista).

The Allman Brothers Band blended strains of Southern music—blues, R&B, country, and gospel—into a flexible, jam-oriented style that reflected the emergence of the "New South" and set the style for Lynyrd Skynyrd, the Marshall Tucker Band, and countless other Southern rockers. Oddly—or eerily, some would say—the band's unusual string of untimely deaths has been repeated in other Southern-rock bands. Through personal tragedy and turmoil, the Allman Brothers Band has endured, and while it lacks the commercial clout of its early-Seventies heyday, remains well respected and well received by legions of fans.

Brothers Gregg and Duane Allman formed the Kings in Daytona Beach, Florida, in 1960 and played in various bands until 1965, when they formed the Allman Joys. After their version of Willie Dixon's "Spoonful" failed as a single, the two brothers and two other band members went to Los Angeles, where they signed with Liberty Records as the Hourglass. They recorded two albums of outside material (*Hourglass*, 1967, and *Power of Love*, 1968) before moving to Muscle Shoals, Alabama, to record at Fame Studios. Liberty rejected the resulting tapes, and Duane and Gregg returned to Florida.

Soon after, the brothers joined the 31st of February, whose drummer was Butch Trucks. While preparing to record an album, Gregg was called back to Los Angeles to make good on the Liberty contract. (A 1973 Polydor album called *Duane and Gregg* consisted of demos made by the 31st of February.) While Duane stayed in Jacksonville, Gregg began playing with the Second Coming, which included Dickey Betts and Berry Oakley, veterans of Tommy Roe and the Romans. But before Duane became an established member of the Second Coming, Fame Studios owner Rick Hall asked him to return to Muscle Shoals to play lead guitar for a Wilson Pickett session. At Duane's suggestion, Pickett recorded Lennon and McCartney's "Hey Jude." Duane became Fame's primary session guitarist, recording over the next year with Aretha Franklin, King Curtis, Percy Sledge, Clarence Carter, and Arthur Conley.

Atlantic Records vice president Jerry Wexler signed Duane to a solo agreement, and Allman assembled a group. He hired Jai Johanny Johanson, a Muscle Shoals drummer who had worked with Otis Redding, Percy Sledge, Joe Tex, and Clifton Chenier. He went back to Florida and reconvened Trucks, Oakley, Betts, and Gregg. Once assembled, the Allman Brothers Band moved to Macon, Georgia, where Phil Walden was setting up Capricorn Records. (In 1991 Trucks said of the group's long tenure with the label: "We had grossed $40 million and woke up one day to realize our own manager [Phil Walden] had cheated us out of every cent.")

The Allman Brothers Band, their debut LP, was well received only in the South. After its release, Duane continued to play on sessions with Boz Scaggs, Laura Nyro, Otis Rush, Delaney and Bonnie, Ronnie Hawkins, and

American Music Club: Bruce Kaphan,
Mark Eitzel, Dan Pearson, Tim Mooney

Scheff, drums) *Engine* (Grifter/Frontier)   1988—
(– Scheff) *California*   1989—(– Mallon; + Mike
Simms, drums) *United Kingdom* (Demon, U.K.)
1991—(+ Bruce Kaphan [b. Jan. 7, 1955, San Fran-
cisco], pedal steel gtr., kybds.) *Everclear* (Alias)
1993—(– Simms; + Tim Mooney [b. Oct. 6, 1958, Las
Vegas, Nev.], drums) *Mercury* (Reprise)   1994—*San
Francisco*.

Led by the charismatic songwriter Mark Eitzel, American Music Club became one of the most important U.S.
underground bands of the Eighties.

In 1980 Eitzel moved to San Francisco from Columbus, Ohio, with his band Naked Skinnies. After that group
dissolved, he formed American Music Club, going through
various lineups and becoming infamous for his desperate
attempts to either entertain or terrify the audience. Tom
Mallon produced and released the band's debut on his
Grifter label; later he joined the group. *The Restless
Stranger* introduced Eitzel's songs of loneliness and
decay, set to AMC's postpunk honky-tonk. *Engine*, featuring such classic downers as "Gary's Song," "Nightwatch-
man," and "Outside This Bar," revealed a band with great
emotional and musical depth. *California* confirmed the
band as an underground favorite and garnered international attention.

When the band's label, Frontier, signed a licensing
deal with BMG it financed what would have been AMC's
major-label debut. Bruce Kaphan, who had been playing
as a sideman for the band, joined full-time and produced
Everclear, but the BMG deal collapsed, and AMC parted
company with both Frontier and Mallon. While in limbo,
the band recorded the partially live *United Kingdom*,
named after the only country in which the album was re-

leased and where AMC had developed a strong following. In 1991 Eitzel released a solo live record, *Songs of
Love*, on the same U.K. label.

Everclear was eventually released by the indie Alias
to much fanfare (ROLLING STONE critics dubbed it album
of the year in 1991) but negligible sales. Eitzel's alienation from religion—as a teen, he was born again—fueled songs like "What the Pillar of Salt Held Up" and
"Jesus' Hands." Notorious for his often alcohol-fueled
rages and depressions, the singer became sober around
this time. He subsequently returned to drinking, although not to the onstage abuses of yore.

In 1991 AMC's revolving door of drummers settled
on the Toiling Midgets' Tim Mooney, who had also
played with the band in the mid-Eighties (Eitzel moonlighted in the Midgets for a while and sang on their
1992 Matador release *Son*). The band signed with
Reprise/Warner Bros. in 1992 after a bidding war. *Mercury*, produced by Mitchell Froom, was a strange major-
label debut, full of lush, discordant music and obtuse
musings with titles like "What Godzilla Said to God
When His Name Wasn't Found in the Book of Life" and
"Johnny Mathis' Feet." The critically acclaimed *San
Francisco* (1994) featured a cover of the Mamas and the
Papas' 1966 hit "California Dreamin'" as a hidden track.

Tori Amos

**Born Myra Ellen Amos, August 22, 1963, Newton,
North Carolina**
**1992—*Little Earthquakes* (Atlantic); *Crucify* EP
1994—*Under the Pink*.**

After she spent her youth studying classical piano, child
prodigy Tori Amos' first foray into rock—with her band, Y

The Grammy Awards

Presented by the National Academy of Recording Arts and Sciences, the Grammy Awards are as unpredictable as the Academy Awards for movies, and even less reliable as a guide to quality. Winners are chosen based on votes cast by the members of the Academy. The decisions appear to be influenced, though not guided exclusively, by sales. As is the case with almost everything about the awards, there are so many exceptions to every rule (Madonna has earned only one Grammy to date) that only a handful of generalizations might apply. The Song of the Year is always a top-selling single, but not necessarily the year's biggest or best hit. While many Grammy choices are downright baffling (A Taste of Honey's winning Best New Artist of the Year for their 1978 one-shot "Boogie Oogie Oogie"), they often reflect a pop sensibility.

In some instances, an artist or group's Grammy history provides an important part of their story: Michael Jackson's sweep of the 1983 awards with *Thriller* and the domination of certain categories year after year by Aretha Franklin, Quincy Jones, Ray Charles, the Manhattan Transfer, and Stevie Wonder, most would agree, were deserved. Equally interesting are those performers whose Grammy history tells us more about the awards than about the artist. For example, Elvis Presley received just three performance awards, all in gospel-related categories; the Rolling Stones didn't win a performance award until 1995, when *Voodoo Lounge* won Rock Album of 1994 (earlier they did receive a Life-time Achievement Award). Harder rock, funk, rap, and other subgenres were all but ignored until the late Eighties, when the NARAS unveiled a series of new categories designed to recognize artists in those fields. In the years since the first Grammy Awards were presented in May 1959, the NARAS has constantly expanded and revised the winning categories from the original 28 to 1995's 87. It's impossible to note the dozens of changes that have occurred in that time, although interesting to note that, for example, there was no separate category for blues recordings until 1982, and the Best Rock & Roll Recording category came and went a few times. In 1967 *Sgt. Pepper's Lonely Hearts Club Band* won for Best Contemporary Album; the rock category was missing that year.

One might also ponder, fruitlessly, we're sorry to add, why certain artists and recordings are categorized as they are. Where does one draw the line between hard rock and heavy metal? A pop performance and a rock performance? Gospel and soul gospel? It's also difficult to ascertain exactly how many Grammy Awards are given in certain categories. Through the Seventies, artists who also produced their records were awarded two separate Grammys: one as the artist of the work, the second as the producer. Inexplicably, while George Harrison performed on and produced *The Concert for Bangla Desh,* he received only one award, while Fleetwood Mac and Stevie Wonder (to name just two) were awarded dual awards in several instances. In later years it appears that artist–producers receive one, not two, Grammy Awards.

The Grammys we are concerned with fall into two categories: performer and nonperformer awards. Rather than limit our listings to specific categories, we have chosen to base the listing of awards on the artist or group. So, for example, while we have no reason to include classical recording awards per se, we do list Branford and Wynton Marsalis'. While there are exceptions, the awards recognize the following participants for their respective contributions to a given record:

Album of the Year, Record of the Year: producer and artist
Song of the Year: songwriter
Best Performance: artist

In addition, there are Grammy Awards for Producer of the Year, Video of the Year, and four special awards: the Bing Crosby Award (first given in 1962), the Special Trustees Award (first given in 1967), the Lifetime Achievement Award (first given in 1962), and the Grammy Legend Award (first given in 1989). While the Grammy Awards are presented early in the year following the eligibility period (in other words, awards given at the 1994 ceremony cover records released in 1993), the special awards are listed by the year they are presented, the NARAS' reasoning being that these artists are not given awards for any single year's work but for that of a lifetime.

What follows in the boxes

The Animals: John Steel, Dave Rowberry, Eric Burdon, Chas Chandler, Hilton Valentine

The Animals

Formed 1962, Newcastle upon Tyne, England
Alan Price (b. Apr. 19, 1942, County Durham, Eng.),
kybds.; Eric Burdon (b. May 11, 1941, Newcastle
upon Tyne), voc.; Bryan "Chas" Chandler (b. Dec.
18, 1938, Newcastle upon Tyne), bass; John Steel
(b. Feb. 4, 1941, Gateshead, Eng.), drums; Hilton
Valentine (b. May 21, 1943, North Shields, Eng.), gtr.
1964—*The Animals* (MGM)   1965—*The Animals on
Tour*; *Animal Tracks* (– Price; + Dave Rowberry
[b. Dec. 27, 1943, Newcastle upon Tyne], kybds.)
1966—*The Best of the Animals*; *Animalization*; *Ani-
malism* (– Steel; + Barry Jenkins [b. Dec. 22, 1944,
Leicester, Eng.], drums)   late 1966—(Group disbands)   1968—(Burdon forms Eric Burdon and the
New Animals: Burdon, voc.; Barry Jenkins, drums;
+ Johnny Weider [b. Apr. 21, 1947, Shepherd's Bush,
Eng.], gtr.; + Vic Briggs [b. Feb. 14, 1945, Twicken-
ham, Eng.], gtr.; + Danny McCulloch [b. July 18,
1945, London, Eng.], gtr.; + Zoot Money, keybds.,
voc.)   1967—*Eric Is Here*; *Best of Eric Burdon and
the Animals, vol. 2*; *Winds of Change*   1968—*The
Twain Shall Meet*; *Every One of Us* (– McCulloch;
– Briggs; + Andrew Somers [a.k.a. Andy Summers,
b. Dec. 31, 1942, Blackpool, Eng.], gtr.)   1969—*Love
Is*; *The Greatest Hits of Eric Burdon and the Animals* (group disbands)   1977—(Original lineup re-
forms: Burdon; Price; Chandler; Valentine; Steel)
Before We Were So Rudely Interrupted (United
Artists)   1983—*Ark* (I.R.S.)   1984—*Rip It to Shreds:
Greatest Hits Live*.

Of the original British Invasion bands, the Animals were
the most clearly influenced by black American R&B
rather than blues. Originally the Alan Price Combo
(formed in 1958), they became the Animals shortly after

the addition of lead vocalist Eric Burdon in 1962. By
1964, under the wing of U.K. producer Mickie Most, they
had recorded their second single, "House of the Rising
Sun," a #1 hit on both sides of the Atlantic in summer
1964.

More hits followed through 1966: "Don't Let Me Be
Misunderstood" (#15, 1965), "We Gotta Get Out of This
Place" (#13, 1965), "It's My Life" (#23, 1965). In late 1965
Price left the band (the result of tension between him
and Burdon) for a solo career [see entry]. That, and frequent drug use by members, shook up the band somewhat, but Price was replaced by Dave Rowberry, and the
Animals had another hit ("Inside-Looking Out," #34,
1966) before John Steel left. With Barry Jenkins (formerly
of the Nashville Teens) replacing Steel, the group had
several more hits ("Don't Bring Me Down," #12, 1966;
"See See Rider," #10, 1966), but by the end of the year
Hilton Valentine left to pursue a solo career, and Chas
Chandler became the Animals' and Jimi Hendrix's manager. Steel became Chandler's assistant.

Now billed Eric Burdon and the Animals, the band
endorsed psychedelia with "San Franciscan Nights" (#9,
1967), "Monterey" (#15, 1968), and "Sky Pilot" (#14, 1968).
The Animals fell apart, but a year and a half later Burdon
formed Eric Burdon and the New Animals, with a lineup
that briefly included future Police guitarist Andy Summers, before embarking on an intermittently successful
solo career [see Eric Burdon entry].

The original Animals reunited for a Christmas show
at City Hall in Newcastle in 1968. In 1969 Valentine
recorded a solo album entitled *All in Your Head*. The
original band reunited in 1976 to record a one-shot LP,
Before We Were So Rudely Interrupted. In 1983 they reunited once more. The Animals recorded *Ark* and
mounted a tour (captured on *Rip It to Shreds*) before the
band members again went their separate ways. In 1992

an Animals lineup that included Vic Briggs (who had become a Sikh and recorded under the name Vikram S. Khalsa) and Barry Jenkins performed in Moscow's Red Square. In 1994 the Animals were inducted into the Rock and Roll Hall of Fame.

Paul Anka

Born July 30, 1941, Ottawa, Canada
1960—Paul Anka Sings His Big 15 (ABC); Paul Anka Sings His Big 15, vol. 2   1961—Anka at the Copa 1962—Young, Alive and in Love (RCA); Let's Sit This One Out   1963—Diana and Other Hits; Paul Anka's 21 Golden Hits   1969—Goodnight My Love; Life Goes On   1971—Paul Anka (Buddah)   1972—Jubilation   1974—Anka (United Artists)   1975—Feelings; Times of Your Life   1976—The Painter 1977—The Music Man   1978—Listen to Your Heart (RCA); Paul Anka—His Best   1981—Both Sides of Love   1983—Walk a Fine Line (Columbia)   1989— 30th Anniversary Collection (Rhino).

Disparaged by many critics for his often overwrought vocal style on songs such as "Puppy Love," Paul Anka was unique among late-Fifties teen idols in that he was also a successful songwriter. After his string of early hits tapered off in 1962, Anka concentrated on composing film scores (*The Longest Day*) and writing and performing more adult-oriented works, like the English lyrics to the French song that became Frank Sinatra's theme song, "My Way."

The son of a Lebanese restaurateur, Anka began performing at age ten, singing and doing impersonations. Four years later Anka's father paid for a trip to Hollywood, where, in September 1956, the 15-year-old recorded "I Confess" (backed by the Cadets) for Modern. Anka returned to Canada and later, though underage, worked a nightclub in Gloucester, Massachusetts. In 1957 he won a contest for saving soup-can labels. First prize was a trip to New York City, and in May of that year Anka auditioned for ABC with "Diana," a song he had written about a girl he knew. Within a year, "Diana" was a #1 hit.

Throughout his career, Anka composed many of his hits, including "You Are My Destiny" (#7, 1958), "Crazy Love" (#15, 1958), "Lonely Boy" (#1, 1959), "Hello Young Lovers" (#23, 1960), "Put Your Head on My Shoulder" (#2, 1959), and "Puppy Love" (#2, 1960), the last two about his relationship with Annette Funicello. Although his Top Twenty hits ended temporarily in 1962, he continued to write and record in French, German, and Italian and remained a top concert draw around the globe. Like many of his teen-idol contemporaries, Anka briefly essayed an acting career; his film credits include *Girls Town* (1959), *Look in Any Window* (1961), and *The Longest Day* (1962), for which he also wrote the theme song.

In 1974 Anka's controversial "(You're) Having My Baby," a duet with his protégée Odia Coates, became his first #1 since 1959. Due in part to outcry against the song's seemingly sexist tone, Anka substitutes "our baby" for "my baby" in concert. In 1983 he made his last foray into the Top Forty with "Hold Me 'Til the Mornin' Comes." He has become a fixture on the Las Vegas–Lake Tahoe circuit, where he is extremely successful.

Over 400 of his compositions have been recorded, including "It Don't Matter Anymore" (Buddy Holly), the lyrics to "My Way" (Frank Sinatra), and "She's a Lady" (Tom Jones). He wrote the *Tonight Show* theme (originally entitled "It's Really Love," and written for and recorded by Funicello). His "Times of Your Life" became the signature song for Kodak films in the mid-Seventies. He has amassed worldwide record sales in excess of 100 million copies.

Annette: See Annette Funicello

Anthrax

Formed 1981, New York City, New York
Scott Ian (b. Dec. 31, 1963, Queens, N.Y.), gtr.; Dan Spitz (b. Jan. 28, 1963, Queens), gtr.; Dan Lilker (b. Oct. 18, 1964, Queens), bass; Charles Benante (b. Nov. 27, 1962, Bronx, N.Y.), drums; Neil Turbin, voc. 1984—Fistful of Metal (Caroline/Megaforce) (– Turbin; – Lilker; + Joey BellaDonna [b. Oct. 30, 1960, Oswego, N.Y.], voc.; + Frank Bello [b. Sep. 7, 1965, Bronx], bass)   1985—Armed and Dangerous; Spreading the Disease (Island)   1987—Among the Living; I'm the Man EP   1988—State of Euphoria 1990—Persistence of Time   1991—Attack of the Killer B's   1992—(– BellaDonna; + John Bush [b. Aug. 24, 1963, Los Angeles, Calif.], voc.)   1993— Sound of White Noise (Elektra).

Anthrax began as an average posthardcore thrash band, but eventually developed its own distinct sound by blending rap's street sense with heavy metal's brute force. The band hit a career height in 1991 when it joined forces with rap group Public Enemy for a recording and video of the latter's rallying cry, "Bring the Noise." Two years later the band inked a reported $10 million, five-album deal with Elektra.

Anthrax hit New York City's postpunk metal scene in 1981 when Bayside, Queens, native Scott Ian, still in his teens, formed the band along with friends Neil Turbin and former Overkill guitarist Dan Spitz. The group literally began following managers Johnny and Marsha Zazula, heads of the independent metal label Megaforce Records, around the city. Eventually the couple signed the band and began directing its career. By album num-

Anthrax: Dan Spitz, Frankie Bello, Scott Ian, Charlie Benante, John Bush

ber three, Anthrax had landed on Island, and its cult following had begun to expand. The group's 1987 EP, *I'm the Man,* sold platinum and hinted at Anthrax's growing social consciousness in songs such as "Indians" and "One World."

One of the few heavy metal–oriented bands to get consistently high critical marks, Anthrax—along with Metallica and Megadeth—redefined the metal genre in the Eighties, stressing anger, speed, and emotional intensity over big hair and power ballads. Anthrax altered that style somewhat after replacing longtime lead singer Joey BellaDonna with L.A. native and ex–Armored Saint singer John Bush in 1992. Bush, a more traditional, smooth-voiced vocalist, gave the group a slicker sound, though the basic speed-metal foundation remained.

AOR

This abbreviation stands for both "album-oriented rock" and "album-oriented radio." The terms are interchangeable, which in itself explains the peculiar marketing effect of a broadcasting format that fostered a rigidly codified musical genre, and vice versa. AOR music, which is now termed "classic rock," is played all the time because it's popular; it remains popular because it's played all the time. Although in recent years playlists are beefed up with "undiscovered classics" (i.e., new releases of older material or album cuts that were not overplayed before), the same acts—Led Zeppelin, the Who, Eric Clapton, Yes, and their various solo projects and offshoots—reign.

AOR and classic rock grew out of the ashes of once "progressive free-form" FM radio. By the early Seventies, FM had garnered enough of an audience that it could no longer be considered "underground." It maintained commercial status by limiting the choice of music to a prescribed playlist. Through AOR, FM radio became almost as, and some would argue substantially more, conservative than the AM radio of the Sixties to which FM had been an alternative. For example, Sixties AM radio offered a broad mix of styles, many of which featured black artists. Because AOR focused on hard and blues-based rock, however, its playlist (with exceptions such as Jimi Hendrix and Stevie Wonder) were predominantly white. An AOR radio station plays album cuts rather than commercially released singles; it ultimately renders the LP an extended single-style marketing device, since in most cases AOR stations play only certain album cuts in an AM-style playlist rotation.

Stylistically, AOR bands derive from the musical genres that had found success on pre-AOR FM radio. Classic AOR stars like Styx, Kansas, and Foreigner incorporate the high-harmony vocals, instrumental virtuosity, pseudoclassical keyboard orchestrations, and epic themes of British progressive rock; REO Speedwagon trades on heavy-metal mixes; .38 Special is based in guitar-heavy Southern boogie-rock; Toto refers to laid-back California studio rock; and Journey to San Francisco rock. Like a sponge, the AOR format can easily include everyone from onetime new-wave artists like Blondie and the Go-Go's to straight rock artists, such as John Mellencamp and Bruce Springsteen.

Usually scorned by music critics, AOR has remained a successful sales institution; in the form of MTV—especially in its early years—AOR even took over "rock video." AOR stations showed flagging ratings in the

Eighties, and AOR developer/consultant Lee Abrams admitted his format had become "boring," but it ultimately proved as timeless and enduring as air guitar and "Stairway to Heaven."

April Wine
Formed 1969, Halifax, Nova Scotia, Canada
David Henman, gtr.; Ritchie Henman, drums; Jimmy Henman, bass; Myles Goodwyn (b. June 23, 1948, Woodstock, Can.), piano, gtr., voc.
1970—*April Wine* (Big Tree) (– J. Henman; + Jimmy Clench, bass)   1971—*On Record* (– D. Henman; – R. Henman; + Gary Moffet [b. June 22, 1949, Ottawa, Can.], gtr.; + Jerry Mercer [b. Apr. 27, 1939, Montreal, Can.], drums)   1973—*Electric Jewels* (Aquarius)   1974—*Live*   1975—*Stand Back* (Big Tree) (– Clench; + Steve Lang [b. Mar. 24, 1949, Montreal, Can.], bass)   1976—*The Whole World's Goin' Crazy* (London); *Forever for Now* (Aquarius)   1977—*April Wine Live at the El Mocambo* (London) (+ Brian Greenway [b. Oct. 1, 1951, Ontario, Can.], gtr., voc., kybds.)   1979—*First Glance* (Capitol)   1980— *Harder . . . Faster*   1981—*The Nature of the Beast* 1982—*Power Play*   1984—*Animal Grace*   1985— *Walking Through Fire* (– Lang; – Moffet; – Mercer; + Daniel Barbe, kybds.; + Jean Pellerin, bass; + Marty Simon, drums) (group disbands)   1991—(Group reforms: Goodwyn; Mercer; Greenway; Clench; + Steve Segal, gtr.)   1993—*Attitude* (Fre/EMI).

April Wine became one of the top Canadian heavy-metal bands of the Seventies through frequent touring and a basic hard-rock sound. They earned ten gold LPs in Canada and are one of the few acts ever to have a Canadian release, *The Whole World's Goin' Crazy,* shipped platinum. In the U.S., after attracting attention with *First Glance,* they earned their first American gold LP with *The Nature of the Beast* (#26, 1981), which featured 11 originals by leader Myles Goodwyn, including "Just Between You and Me" (#21, 1981).

In 1984 Goodwyn, the sole remaining original member since 1978, left to pursue his solo career, which he later described as "disappointing" (he only released one album, *Serious Business*). He moved to the Bahamas, but returned to Montreal, where, in 1991, he, Greenway, Mercer, and Clench re-formed the group with Steve Segal. A 1992 reunion tour of Canada and the U.S. was welcomed by fans of the first Canadian group in history to sell 100,000 copies of an English-language album.

Arc Angels: See Charlie Sexton

Arcadia: See Duran Duran

The Archies
Formed 1968, Riverdale, New York
"Archie" (Ron Dante, b. Carmine Granito, Aug. 22, 1945, Staten Island, N.Y.), voc.; Toni Wine, voc.; Ellie Greenwich (b. 1940, Brooklyn, N.Y.), voc.; Andy Kim (b. Andrew Joachim, Dec. 5, 1946, Montreal, Can.), voc.; Tony Passalacqua, voc.
1968—*The Archies* (Calendar)   1969—*Everything's Archie* (RCA); *Jingle Jangle*   1970—*Sunshine* (Kirshner); *The Archies Greatest Hits*   1993—*The Archies* (Sony).

The Archies were a make-believe group based on the comic book and mid-Sixties cartoon series of the same name. "Sugar, Sugar," cowritten by Jeff Barry and Andy Kim, was a #1 hit and the biggest-selling single of 1969, with six million copies sold worldwide. Songwriter Barry produced the Archies: studio musicians (among them Hugh McCracken, Dave Appell, and Bobby Bloom) were hired to provide the cartoon series' soundtrack. The singing Archie, voiced by Ron Dante, led his group, which included songwriters Ellie Greenwich and Andy Kim, through a number of hits, including "Bang-Shang-a-Lang" (#2, 1968), "Jingle Jangle" (#10, 1969), and "Who's Your Baby" (#40, 1970).

Dante later produced several Barry Manilow hits and records by Cher and Pat Benatar. In 1971 he became editor of the literary magazine *Paris Review.* He continued to work as a composer into the Nineties. Among his most familiar later "performances" is the "you deserve a break today" theme from McDonald's commercials. Andy Kim went on to a successful pop career, with a number of Top Forty singles, among them "Baby I Love You" (#9, 1969) and "Rock Me Gently" (#1, 1974).

Argent
Formed 1969, England
Rod Argent (b. June 14, 1941, St. Albans, Eng.), kybds., voc.; Jim Rodford (b. July 7, 1941, Eng.), bass; Robert Henrit (b. May 2, 1944, Broxbourne, Eng.), drums; Russ Ballard (b. Oct. 31, 1945, Waltham Cross, Eng.), gtr., voc.
1970—*Argent* (Epic)   1971—*Ring of Hands*   1972— *All Together Now*   1973—*In Deep*   1974—*Nexus* (– Ballard; + John Grimaldi [b. May 25, 1955, St. Albans, Eng.], gtr., cello, mandolin, violin; + John Verity [b. July 3, 1949, Bradford, Eng.], gtr., voc., bass); *Encore*   1975—*Circus*   1976—*Counterpoint; Anthology: A Collection of Greatest Hits.*
Russ Ballard solo: 1974—*Russ Ballard* (Epic)
1976—*Winning*   1978—*At the Third Stroke*   1980— *Barnet Dogs*   1981—*Into the Fire*   1984—*Russ Ballard* (EMI)   1985—*The Fire Still Burns.*
Rod Argent solo: 1991—*Red House* (Relativity).

After the Zombies [see entry] broke up in 1967, keyboardist Rod Argent started his own band just in time to capitalize on the Zombies' postmortem hit, "Time of the Season" (#3, 1969). Argent had heavier rhythms than the Zombies, while continuing that band's penchant for minor keys and obscure lyrics. Although their debut album was their most consistent, the group peaked commercially with "Hold Your Head Up" (#5, 1972), and "Liar" and "God Gave Rock & Roll to You" became FM-radio staples. In 1974 songwriter Ballard left, and after expanding to a quintet, Argent folded in mid-1976.

Ballard and Argent went on to solo careers, although Ballard was more successful as a songwriter (Redbone's "Come and Get Your Love," Three Dog Night's "Liar," Rainbow's "Since You've Been Gone," Ace Frehley's "New York Groove," Santana's "Winning," Hot Chocolate's "So You Win Again") and producer (Roger Daltrey, Leo Sayer) than as a performer. John Verity, Jim Rodford, and Robert Henrit formed Phoenix, which recorded briefly for Columbia. By 1978 Rodford had joined the Kinks; six years later Henrit joined him as Mick Avory's replacement.

Through the years Rod Argent has worked as a pianist, composer, record producer, and arranger. He played piano on the Who's "Who Are You," coproduced Nanci Griffith's *Late Night Grand Hotel,* and has scored music for BBC Television. His musical *Masquerade* was staged in London in 1982, and he was the keyboardist for the London productions of two Andrew Lloyd Webber musicals, *Cats* and *Starlight Express.* He released a series of U.K. solo albums in the late Seventies and Eighties: *Moving Home, Siren Songs,* and *Red House* (which was released in the U.S. as well). In 1994 Argent coproduced and played keyboards on Jules Shear's *Healing Bones.*

Armageddon: See Renaissance; the Yardbirds

Joan Armatrading
Born December 9, 1950, St. Kitts, West Indies
1974—Whatever's for Us (A&M) 1975—Back to the Night 1976—Joan Armatrading 1977—Show Some Emotion 1978—To the Limit 1979—How Cruel; Steppin' Out 1980—Me, Myself, I 1981—Walk Under Ladders 1983—The Key; Track Record 1985—Secret Secrets 1986—Sleight of Hand; Classics Volume 21 1988—The Shouting Stage 1990—Heart and Flowers 1991—The Very Best of Joan Armatrading 1992—Square the Circle.

Joan Armatrading's synthesis of folk, reggae, soul, and rock has made her a critical and cult favorite in America, where *Me, Myself, I* (#28, 1980) and *The Key* (#32, 1980) were successful. In Europe, particularly in the U.K., she is

a major star. She left the West Indies and moved to England with her family while still a child. She began her professional career in 1972 in collaboration with lyricist Pam Nestor (born April 28, 1948, Guyana), but by the mid-Seventies the two had parted.

A distinctive vocalist and lyricist, Armatrading has worked with producers Gus Dudgeon, Glyn Johns, Richard Gottehrer, and Steve Lillywhite, but generally does her own arranging; she produced *Heart and Flowers.* Her backup bands have included alumni of Fairport Convention and Little Feat, and guitarist Albert Lee. Except for a sole charting single, "Drop the Pilot" (#78, 1983), from *The Key,* Armatrading has had relatively little commercial success in the States. In comparison, her albums have consistently charted in the U.K. Top Thirty, with *Show Some Emotion, Me, Myself, I, Walk Under Ladders,* and *The Key* going Top Ten.

Arrested Development
Formed 1988, Atlanta, Georgia
Speech (b. Todd Thomas, Oct. 25, 1968, Milwaukee, Wis.), voc.; Headliner (b. Tim Barnwell, July 26, 1967, N.J.), DJ; Rasa Don (b. Donald Jones, Nov. 22, 1968, N.J.), voc., drums; Aerle Taree (b. Jan. 10, 1973, Wis.), voc., dancer, stylist; Montsho Eshe (b. Dec. 23, 1974, Ga.), dancer, choreographer; Baba Oje (b. May 15, 1932, Laurie, Miss.), spiritual adviser. 1992—3 Years, 5 Months & 2 Days in the Life of . . . (Chrysalis) 1993—Unplugged 1994—(– Taree; + Ajile, voc., dancer; + Kwesi, DJ, voc.; + Nadirah, voc.) Zingalamaduni.

Arrested Development took the light, funky sound of the Native Tongues school of hip-hop (De La Soul, Queen Latifah), blended in the folk-blues instrumentation of their native South (harmonica, acoustic guitars), added uplifting, gospel-tinged lyrics, and became one of the most successful crossover acts in rap. On the strength of its first single, "Tennessee" (#6 pop, #1 R&B), the group's 1992 debut album shot to #13 (#3 R&B).

Born in Milwaukee and raised part-time in Ripley, Tennessee, Todd Thomas moved to Georgia in 1987 to study at the Art Institute of Atlanta. There he met Tim Barnwell, a New Jersey native raised in the coastal Georgia town of Savannah. After an initial, unsuccessful attempt at gangsta rap under the name Disciples of a Lyrical Rebellion, Thomas and Barnwell, who started going by the names Speech and DJ Headliner, reexamined their motives for wanting to make music. In 1988 they discovered the political fire-and-brimstone sound of Public Enemy and decided to change direction. Rejecting gangsta-rap expressions like "nigga," "bitch," and "ho," the two incorporate their Christian values into politically and philosophically charged songs that celebrate African-American culture and history. Inspired by Speech's belief that the black community needed spiritual rebirth, they renamed the group Arrested Development.

With the addition of drummer Rasa Don, the group's music became softer and funkier. By the time of its 1992 signing to Chrysalis, Arrested Development had expanded into a coed and multigenerational group, including "extended family" members Aerle Taree, Speech's cousin and designer of the group's clothing; dancer/choreographer Montsho Eshe; and elder spiritual advisor Baba Oje.

The group's platinum-selling debut was a critical as well as commercial success. The album produced two other hits: "People Everyday" (#8 pop, #2 R&B, 1992) and "Mr. Wendal" (#6, 1992). "Tennessee" featured the singer Dionne Farris, who had her own Top Ten single, "I Know," in 1995. The non-LP single "Revolution," recorded for Spike Lee's film *Malcolm X*, reached #90 (#49 R&B, 1992). In 1993 Arrested Development's performance on MTV's *Unplugged* (#38 R&B) was issued on CD, and the group participated in the third annual Lollapalooza tour. Taree departed and three new members joined for the summer 1994 release, *Zingalamaduni*, which means "beehive of culture" in Swahili.

Arrow

Born Alphonsus Cassel, November 16, 1954,
Montserrat, West Indies
1974—*On Target* (Arrow)   1977—*Positively Jumpy*
1983—*Hot Hot Hot*   1985—*Soca Savage* (London)
1987—*Best of Arrow, Vol. 1* (Arrow)   1988—*Knock Dem Dead* (Mango)   1989—*Massive* (Arrow); *Ola Soca* (Mango)   1990—*Soca Dance Party*   1991—*Zombie Soca* (Arrow)   1992—*Best of Arrow, vol. 2*; *Model De Bam Bam*   1993—*Outrageous*.

A founding father and leading purveyor of soca, a Trinidad-based blend of soul music and calypso, Arrow is best known in the U.S. for having written "Hot, Hot, Hot"—an international hit for the singer in 1983, but an American hit only as it was covered in 1987 by Buster Poindexter (David Johansen's lounge-lizard alter ego).

While growing up in Montserrat, West Indies, the youngest of nine children, Arrow listened to American R&B on the radio; meanwhile, he began composing calypso songs at a young age, earning the island-wide title of "calypso king" in a 1971 competition. He retained the title for four years and in 1974 started releasing albums on his own label, while supporting himself by selling insurance and running a men's clothing store.

In 1983, with numerous LPs already to his credit, Arrow signed with Chrysalis Records. Subsequent singles such as 1984's "Long Time" and 1988's "Groove Master" proved popular in British and American dance clubs, but the singer's ebullient melodies and seductive rhythms never made him a big star outside the Caribbean. Having switched labels repeatedly throughout the Eighties, Arrow returned to releasing his own albums in 1991. He continues to draw crowds at calypso and reggae festivals.

Art Ensemble of Chicago

Formed 1969, Paris, France
Roscoe Mitchell (b. 1940, Chicago, Ill.), saxes, flutes, reeds, misc.; Lester Bowie (b. 1941, Frederick, Md.), trumpet, misc.; Malachi Favors, a.k.a. Magoustous (b. 1937, Lexington, Miss.), bass, perc., misc.; Joseph Jarman (b. 1941, Pine Bluff, Ark.), saxes, flute, reeds, misc.
1969—*People in Sorrow* (Nessa); *Reese and the Smooth Ones* (BYG); *A Jackson in Your House*; *Message to Our Folks* (Polydor); *Tutankhamun* (Freedom)   1970—(+ Don Moye, a.k.a. Dougoufana Famoudou [b. 1946, Rochester, N.Y.], drums, perc.) *Certain Blacks* (America)   1971—*Home* (Galloway); *Art Ensemble with Fontella Bass* (America); *Phase One*; *Chi-Congo*   1972—*Baptizum* (Atlantic); *Live at Mandel Hall* (Delmark/Trio)   1973—*Fanfare for the Warriors* (Atlantic)   1978—*Nice Guys* (ECM); *Kabala* (AECO)   1980—*Full Force* (ECM); *Urban Bushmen*   1981—*Among the People*   1985—*The Third Decade*   1991—*Dreaming of the Masters* (DIW/Columbia)   1992—*America–South Africa* (as the Art Ensemble of Soweto); *Thelonious Sphere Monk*.

The Art Ensemble of Chicago was the most innovative jazz group to emerge in the Seventies. Their compositions and collective improvisations draw from all sorts of world musics, traditional and avant-garde jazz, rhythm & blues, African music, twentieth-century European art music, even rock & roll, gospel, martial music, jug-band music, and the natural sounds of human and animal voices. The quintet has been known to employ 500 instruments in a concert, which might also include a slide show, dance, or vaudeville shtick.

The Ensemble evolved from collective jazz experiments in Chicago in the early and mid-Sixties. Roscoe Mitchell and Malachi Favors first played together in Muhal Richard Abrams Experimental Band in 1961. Along with Abrams, the two were charter members of the Association for the Advancement of Creative Music, founded in 1965 with such jazz experimentalists as Anthony Braxton and the future members of Air. Lester Bowie (who had played R&B with Little Milton and Albert King) was also an AACM member. In 1968 the Roscoe Mitchell Art Ensemble (including Mitchell, Bowie, Favors, and drummer Phillip Wilson) began gigging and earned a local reputation for both their music and their integration of music and conceptual theater.

Before the end of 1968, Wilson had joined the Paul Butterfield Blues Band. The Ensemble continued without a drummer, but the addition of Joseph Jarman (who had studied under John Cage and Indian classical musicians) kept them a quartet. In 1969 they moved to Paris, and over the next two years they recorded 11 albums and three film scores, performed hundreds of concerts, and met Don Moye. They returned to the U.S. in 1971 to tour. Atlantic signed the Art Ensemble in 1972, but it took a grant from the National Endowment for the Arts to finance their second Atlantic album. Since then they have recorded for large and small labels including their own AECO Records.

Each of the members has recorded solo and with other musicians, including Anthony Braxton, Henry Threadgill (of Air), and Jack DeJohnette. Abrams and singer Fontella Bass (who had a #1 soul hit with "Rescue Me" in 1965; Bowie and Bass were married at this time) have performed frequently with the Art Ensemble. From the late Seventies onward, the Art Ensemble members have spent six months each year on solo projects and six months as a group.

Although the late Eighties and Nineties saw the band recording in a variety of different settings (*Dreaming of the Masters* is a collaboration with pianist Cecil Taylor; *America–South Africa* has them joined by an African vocal choir), band members' side projects cut into the Ensemble's visibility. Bowie led the popular Brass Fantasy, Mitchell composed and played with his own new music groups, and Moye played in the all-star Leaders band with Lester Bowie.

The Art of Noise
Formed 1983, London, England
Anne Dudley (b. May 7, 1956), kybds.; Jonathan "J. J." Jeczalik (b. May 11, 1955), kybds.; Gary Langan, various instruments.
1985—(Who's Afraid of) The Art of Noise (Island) 1986— In Visible Silence (Chrysalis) 1987—In-No-Sense? Nonsense!

With its name culled from an Italian Futurist manifesto, the Art of Noise approached pop from a distinctly postmodern slant. Using the studio as their tool, these three producers-programmers-arrangers were virtually anonymous; star power, when called for, was imported.

Dudley, Jeczalik, and Langan met as part of Trevor Horn's innovative production team in the early Eighties. Under Horn's auspices, Art of Noise was formed to fash-

ion state-of-the-art dance instrumentals. "Beat Box" and "Close (to the Edit)"—with their audacious and influential mixture of treated musical textures, found sounds, and overdriven disco rhythms—became popular on both sides of the Atlantic.

Breaking away from Horn, the Art of Noise recruited rock & roll guitar pioneer Duane Eddy to update his 1960 hit "Peter Gunn" (#50, 1986); the song was later nominated for a 1986 Grammy for Best Rock Instrumental Performance. The video for "Paranoimia" (#34, 1986) incorporated computer-generated TV character Max Headroom; Art of Noise also contributed to the *Headroom* television series. Eschewing any pretense of aesthetic purity, the group began doing considerable advertising work for Revlon, Swatch, and Barclays' Bank, among others. In July 1986 the Art of Noise toured for the first time, appearing in the U.S., Japan, and at a solitary British performance. The next year the group worked on the soundtrack to the film adaptation of *Dragnet*.

A remake of Prince's "Kiss" (#31, 1988) featuring Sixties pop icon Tom Jones helped revive Jones' career. Other left-of-center recordings followed, including "Yebo" (#63 U.K., 1989), which featured South African singers Mahlathini and the Mahotella Queens. By the turn of the decade the three were concentrating on individual projects, and the Art of Noise dissolved.

Peter Asher: See Peter and Gordon

Ashford and Simpson
Nickolas Ashford (b. May 4, 1943, Fairfield, S.C.); Valerie Simpson (b. Aug. 26, 1948, Bronx, N.Y.)
1973—Keep It Comin' (Tamla); Gimme Something Real (Warner Bros.) 1974—I Wanna Be Selfish 1976—Come As You Are 1977—Send It 1978—Is It Still Good to Ya? 1979—Stay Free 1980—Musical Affair 1981—Performance 1982—Street Opera 1983—High-Rise (Capitol) 1984—Solid 1986—Real Love 1989—Love or Physical.
Valerie Simpson solo: 1971—Exposed (Tamla) 1972—Valerie Simpson.

During the late Sixties, writers, performers, and producers Nickolas Ashford and Valerie Simpson wrote and produced some of Motown's greatest hits, and since the early Seventies they've also become successful performers. The son of a construction worker, Ashford grew up in Willow Run, Michigan, where he sang in the church choir as a child. He spent one semester at Eastern Michigan College before dropping out. Against his parents' wishes, he left home and moved to Harlem with only $57. He worked as a busboy and began attending the White Rock Baptist Church in Harlem, where in 1964 he

Nickolas Ashford and Valerie Simpson

met Simpson, then 17 years old. She had recently graduated high school and was studying music at Chatham Square School.

They began writing songs together (the first bunch of which they sold for $64). Two years later, when Ray Charles had a hit with their "Let's Go Get Stoned," they signed on with Berry Gordy's Motown organization as staff writers and producers. They created a series of romantic duets, including Marvin Gaye and Tammi Terrell's "Ain't No Mountain High Enough" and "You're All I Need to Get By," and Diana Ross' "Reach Out and Touch (Somebody's Hand)." While neither of Simpson's Ashford-produced solo albums sold well, the pair were anxious to concentrate on performing (which Gordy discouraged) and recorded *Keep It Comin'* just before leaving Motown in 1973 for Warner Bros. They married in 1974.

Their early R&B hit singles included "So, So Satisfied" (#27, 1977) and "Is It Still Good to Ya?" (#12, 1978), and 1979's "Found a Cure" was their first 45 to make the pop Top Forty. They had to wait six years for their next one, "Solid," which reached #12 in 1985 and topped the R&B chart. Two other R&B hits followed: "Outta the World" (#4, 1985) and "Count Your Blessings" (#4, 1986). *Send It, Is It Still*, and *Stay Free* have been certified gold.

Ashford and Simpson continue to tour and work frequently as independent writers and producers; their clients include Diana Ross (*The Boss*), Gladys Knight and the Pips (*About Love*), and Whitney Houston ("I'm Every Woman"). The last song, contained on *The Bodyguard* soundtrack, hit #5 in 1993. Simpson's brother, Ray Simpson, is a lead vocalist for the Village People.

Asia

Formed 1981, Los Angeles, California
Carl Palmer (b. Mar. 20, 1947, Birmingham, Eng.), drums; John Wetton (b. July 12, 1949, Derby, Eng.), bass, voc.; Steve Howe (b. Apr. 8, 1947, London, Eng.), gtr.; Geoffrey Downes (b. Eng.), kybds.
1982—*Asia* (Geffen)   1983—*Alpha* (– Wetton; + Greg Lake [b. Nov. 10, 1948, Bournemouth, Eng.], bass, voc.)   1985—(– Howe; + Mandy Meyer, gtr.; – Lake; + Wetton) *Astra*   1986—(Group disbands) 1990—(Group re-forms: Palmer; Welton; Downes; + Pat Thrall [b. San Francisco, Calif.], gtr.) *Then & Now*   1992—*Asia: Live in Moscow* (Rhino) (– Thrall; + Howe; + John Payne, voc., bass; + Al Pitrelli, gtr.); *Aqua* (JRS).

The first supergroup of the Eighties, Asia was composed of famous musicians whose earlier work in major rock groups virtually guaranteed their success. Carl Palmer had been a member of Emerson, Lake and Palmer; Steve Howe and Geoffrey Downes had both belonged to Yes, and Downes had worked with the Buggles; John Wetton had been bassist for King Crimson, U.K., Family, and Roxy Music. Greg Lake, who briefly replaced Wetton, was also an ELP alumnus. Despite widespread critical revulsion and a cool reception in its native U.K., the group was embraced by AOR radio programmers and bombastic-rock fans.

The group's debut LP, *Asia*, held the #1 spot for over two months in 1982, sold over three million copies, and launched two hits: "Heat of the Moment" (#4, 1982) and "Only Time Will Tell" (#17, 1982). *Alpha*, with the #10 1983 hit "Don't Cry," was also certified platinum. At its commercial peak, Asia performed live from the Budokan Theatre in Tokyo, Japan, in a satellite telecast, *Asia in Asia*, that was seen by 20 million viewers. But *Astra* proved markedly less popular than its predecessors. Howe was replaced by ex-Krokus guitarist Meyer, and in 1986 Asia disbanded until 1990, when it re-formed with guitarist Pat Thrall (formerly of Automatic Man and the Pat Travers band) in the spot originally held by Howe. By 1992 Howe was back in with Downes, Palmer, John Payne, and Al Pitrelli to record *Aqua* (Simon Phillips, Anthony Glynne, and Nigel Glockler also contributed).

Asleep at the Wheel

Formed 1970, Paw Paw, West Virginia
Original lineup: Ray Benson (b. Ray Benson Seifert, Mar. 16, 1951, Philadelphia, Pa.), gtr., voc.; Leroy Preston, drums, gtr.; Lucky Oceans (b. Reuben Gosfield), pedal steel gtr.
1973—*Comin' Right at Ya* (United Artists)   1974—*Asleep at the Wheel* (Epic)   1975—*Fathers and Sons; Texas Gold* (Capitol)   1976—*Wheelin' and

Dealin'; Texas Country (United Artists) 1977—*The Wheel* (Capitol) 1978—*Collision Course* 1979—*Served Live* 1980—*Framed* (MCA) 1981—*American Band 3* (Capitol) 1985—*Asleep at the Wheel* (MCA) 1987—*Asleep at the Wheel: 10* (Epic) 1988—*Western Standard Time* 1990—*Keepin' Me Up Nights* (Arista) 1992—*Route 66* (Liberty); *Greatest Hits (Live and Kickin')* (Arista); *The Swingin' Best of Asleep at the Wheel* (Epic) 1993— (Lineup: Benson, gtr., voc.; Tim Alexander, piano, accordion, voc; Cindy Cashdollar, Hawaiian steel gtr.; Mike Francis [b. June 25, 1951, Yuma, Ariz.], sax; Ricky Turpin, fiddle, electric mandolin, voc.; David Earl Miller, bass; Tommy Beavers, drums) *Asleep at the Wheel Tribute to the Music of Bob Wills and the Texas Playboys* (Liberty).

For over two decades Asleep at the Wheel has been steadfastly dedicated to reviving, with slight modernization, the Western swing pioneered by Bob Wills in the Thirties and Forties, a hybrid of country, big-band jazz, Cajun fiddling, and bebop. With frequent personnel changes (there were over 55 lineup changes between the group's inception and 1983 alone), Asleep at the Wheel has become a dependable attraction in country circles, skirting the rock mainstream. The group was founded by three Easterners: lead guitarist/vocalist Ray Benson, rhythm guitarist, vocalist, and songwriter Leroy Preston, and pedal steel guitarist Lucky Oceans; female singer Chris O'Connell joined for their debut album. At first they mixed satiric originals with Western swing standards, to the incomprehension of their early record companies.

After a few years in San Francisco, they resettled in Austin, Texas, in 1974. The following year Asleep at the Wheel signed with Capitol and began to reach the country market with such deadpan songs as "The Letter That Johnny Walker Read" (#10 C&W, 1975) and versions of "Bump Bounce Boogie" (#31 C&W, 1975) and "Nothin' Takes the Place of You" (#35 C&W, 1976). Most of its releases since 1976 have garnered at least one Grammy nomination; in 1978 the group won the first of several when its version of Count Basie's "One O'Clock Jump" won for Best Country Instrumental Performance.

Though the group's LPs are not huge sellers, it has retained a strong live following. For the critically acclaimed 1993 Bob Wills tribute album, Benson—the group's sole remaining founding member and leader—assembled such artists as Dolly Parton, Vince Gill, Chet Atkins, Marty Stuart, Garth Brooks, Huey Lewis, Lyle Lovett, and Merle Haggard, who were joined by Texas Playboys Eldon Shamblin and Johnny Gimble and Asleep alumni Lucky Oceans, Chris O'Connell, and Floyd Domino. Two singles from the Wills tribute album have won Grammys: In 1993 "Red Wing" earned Best

Country Instrumental Performance and in 1994 "Blues for Dixie," with a vocal by Lyle Lovett, garnered Best Country Performance by a Duo or Group with Vocal.

The Association

Formed 1965, Los Angeles, California
Jules Alexander (b. Sep. 25, 1943, Chattanooga, Tenn.), gtr., voc.; Terry Kirkman (b. Dec. 12, 1941, Salinas, Kan.), kybds., voc.; Brian Cole (b. Sep. 8, 1942, Tacoma, Wash.; d. Aug. 2, 1972, Los Angeles), bass, voc.; Ted Bluechel Jr. (b. Dec. 2, 1942, San Pedro, Calif.), drums; Jim Yester (b. Nov. 24, 1939, Birmingham, Ala.), gtr., voc.; Russ Giguere (b. Oct. 18, 1943, Portsmouth, N.H.), gtr., voc.
1966—*And Then . . . Along Comes the Association* (Valiant) 1967—*Renaissance* (– Alexander; + Larry Ramos [b. Apr. 19, 1942, Kauai, Hawaii], gtr., voc., harm.); *Insight Out* (Warner Bros.) 1968—*Birthday*; *Greatest Hits* 1969 (+ Alexander) *Goodbye Columbus* soundtrack; *The Association* 1970—*"Live"* (– Giguere; + Richard Thompson [b. San Diego, Calif.], gtr., voc.) 1971—*Stop Your Motor* 1972—*Waterbeds in Trinidad!* (CBS) 1981—(Group reforms with surviving original members) 1986—*Songs That Made Them Famous* (Pair).

A primarily soft-rock and ballad band, the Association sold over 15 million records in the Sixties. The group first formed when Terry Kirkman, who had played in several bands, including a brief stint in Frank Zappa's Mothers of Invention, and Jules Alexander recruited Brian Cole and Jim Yester (whose brother Jerry was a member of the Lovin' Spoonful). Russ Giguere and Ted Bluechel joined soon after, and following six months of rehearsal the band debuted in Pasadena.

The hits, most written by various group members, began in 1966 with the group's first single, "Along Comes Mary" (which some listeners believed was an ode to marijuana) and continued with the more romantic songs for which the Association is best remembered: "Cherish" (#1, 1966), "Windy" (#1, 1967), "Never My Love" (#2, 1967), and "Everything That Touches You" (#10, 1968). Its singles, including the theme song from the movie *Goodbye Columbus* (1969), continued to chart but never again reached the Top Thirty. After an unsuccessful try at progressive rock from 1969 through 1973, the group faded from the charts and began working nightclubs.

Several members (Ramos, Bluechel, Yester) released a single in 1975, but the Association attracted no further notice until early 1981, when all of the band's original surviving members (Cole died in 1972 of a heroin overdose) made a comeback attempt. Giguere and Ramos continued to tour with other musicians under the Association name into the Nineties. In 1990 BMI designated "Never My Love" (along with the Beatles' "Yesterday") one of the most often played songs in history.

Chet Atkins

Born June 20, 1924, Luttrell, Tennessee
1951—*Chet Atkins Plays Guitar* (RCA)   1958—*Chet Atkins at Home*   1960—*Mister Guitar*   1962—*Back Home Hymns*   1963—*The Pops Goes Country* 1964—*Best of Chet Atkins*   1965—*My Favorite Guitars*   1966—*Chet Atkins Picks on the Beatles* 1969—*Solid Gold '69*   1970—*Me and Jerry* (with Jerry Reed)   1971—*For the Good Times*   1974— *The Atkins-Travis Travelin' Show* (with Merle Travis)   1976—*Chester and Lester* (with Les Paul) 1985—*Stay Tuned* (Columbia)   1989—*Chet Atkins, C.G.P.*   1990—*Neck and Neck* (with Mark Knopfler) 1992—*Sneakin' Around* (with Jerry Reed); *The RCA Years: 1947–1981*   1994—*Read My Licks.*

With more than 35 million copies of his 75-plus original releases sold, Grammy Lifetime Achievement Award–winner Chet Atkins is one of the most successful guitarists in history; as a country music producer, he was largely responsible for the pop-oriented "Nashville Sound" of the Sixties.

Raised in poverty, Atkins received musical training from his evangelical-singer father and an older half-brother. He took up the guitar at age nine, and counted among his influences Les Paul, Django Reinhardt, and Merle Travis (Atkins' finger-picking style is a modification of Travis' technique). Beginning professionally in his teens playing fiddle for Archie Campbell, by the late Forties he had switched exclusively to guitar, performed at the Grand Ole Opry, and recorded as a sessionman and a solo artist. In the late Fifties he became vice president in charge of RCA's Nashville operations and as such was involved as both a player and producer in the development of Eddy Arnold, Perry Como, Elvis Presley, and Roy Orbison. Later he expanded country music's horizons by helping introduce black country singer Charley Pride and encouraging the "outlaw" movement of Waylon Jennings and Willie Nelson.

As a producer at RCA from 1957 through the mid-Seventies, Atkins established the Nashville Sound, string-laden and embellished with pop-style backup choruses. Traditionalists balked, but Atkins insisted that the style, augmented by his use of innovative studio technique (echo, reverb, tremolo guitars), brought country music into the pop mainstream.

Admired by such diverse musicians as Paul McCartney, Leo Kottke, Earl Klugh, and George Benson, Atkins' guitar style is characterized by versatility. He has recorded 12 duet albums featuring the likes of Les Paul,

Chet Atkins

Doc Watson, Jerry Reed, and Mark Knopfler. He has also performed with sitar player Ravi Shankar, the Atlanta Symphony, and Arthur Fiedler and the Boston Pops. As designer of a series of Chet Atkins Signature Guitars, he has consistently maintained an interest in the technical side of guitar-playing.

In 1973 Atkins became, at 49, the youngest inductee into the Country Music Hall of Fame; a year later, he released an autobiography, *Country Gentleman*, its title Atkins' longtime nickname. In the Eighties, backing off from producing, the guitarist enjoyed a performing renaissance: He toured with folksy pundit Garrison Keillor and continued to put out critically acclaimed albums with other guitarists.

Atlanta Rhythm Section/ARS

Formed 1971, Doraville, Georgia
Barry Bailey (b. June 12, 1948, Decatur, Ga.), gtr.; Rodney Justo, voc.; Paul Goddard (b. June 23, 1945, Rome, Ga.), bass; Robert Nix, drums; J. R. Cobb (b. Feb. 5, 1944, Birmingham, Ala.), gtr.; Dean Daughtry (b. Sep. 8, 1946, Kinston, Ala.), kybds.
1972—*Atlanta Rhythm Section* (MCA) (– Justo; + Ronnie Hammond [b. Macon, Ga.], voc.)   1973— *Back Up Against the Wall*   1974—*Third Annual Pipe Dream* (Polydor)   1975—*Dog Days*   1976— *Red Tape*   1977—*A Rock and Roll Alternative; Atlanta Rhythm Section* (MCA)   1978—*Champagne Jam* (– Nix; + Roy Yeager [b. Feb. 4, 1946, Greenwood, Miss.], drums)   1979—*Are You Ready!; Underdog*   1980—*The Boys from Doraville* 1981—*Quinella* (Columbia) (group disbands) 1989—(Group re-forms as ARS: Buie; Hammond; Bailey; Daughtry; + Steve Stone, gtr.; + Sean Burke, drums; + J. E. Garnett, bass; – Garnett; + Justin

Senker, bass) *Truth in a Structured Form* (Imagine/CBS) 1991—*The Best of ARS* (Polydor).

Composed of former sessionmen, the Atlanta Rhythm Section smoothed out Southern rock's rough edges with studio sophistication. J. R. Cobb, Dean Daughtry, and producer/manager Buddy Buie had been members of the Classics IV [see entry]. Daughtry, Rodney Justo, and Robert Nix had also been in the Candymen, a group that at one time included Bobby Goldsboro, had backed Roy Orbison, and recorded two LPs (*The Candymen*, 1967, and *Bring You Candypower*, 1968). They met the other Section members while working together on a Roy Orbison session in 1970.

Soon after they formed the group, adding lead vocalist Justo for their debut LP. He was soon replaced by Ronnie Hammond, a former recording engineer. Though hampered by the lack of a distinctive frontman or a group identity and only moderate sales, the Atlanta Rhythm Section became established through frequent touring in the late Seventies. Beginning in 1977 the group had a string of hit singles that included "So in to You" (#7, 1977), "Imaginary Lover" (#7, 1978), "I'm Not Gonna Let It Bother Me Tonight" (#14, 1978), "Do It or Die" (#19, 1979), and a remake of the Classics IV hit "Spooky" (#17, 1979). *A Rock and Roll Alternative* and *Underdog* have been certified gold; *Champagne Jam*, platinum, but after *Quinella* peaked at #70 with only one charting single ("Alien" [#29, 1981]), the band members drifted apart.

Four original members, with three new musicians, re-formed as ARS, but *Truth in a Structured Form*, an attempt to update the band's trademark sound, flopped. As of late 1993 Buie and Cobb, who are active as songwriters, were seeking a record deal for a revamped Atlanta Rhythm Section.

Atlantic Starr

Formed 1976, White Plains, New York
Sharon Bryant (b. Aug. 14, 1956, Westchester County, N.Y.), voc.; Wayne Lewis (b. Apr. 13, 1957, White Plains), voc., kybds.; David Lewis (b. Sep. 8, 1958, White Plains), voc., gtr.; Jonathan Lewis (b. White Plains), kybds., trombone, voc.; William Sudderth, trumpet; Koran Daniels, sax; Clifford Archer, bass; Porter Carroll, drums, voc.; Joseph Phillips, perc.
1978—*Atlantic Starr* (A&M)   1979—*Straight to the Point*   1980—(– Daniels; + Damon Rentie, sax)   1981—*Radiant*   1982—*Brilliance*   1983—*Yours Forever*   1984—(– Bryant; – Sudderth; – Archer; – Carroll; – Rentie; + Barbara Weathers [b. Dec. 7, 1963, Greensboro, N.C.], voc.)   1985—*As the Band Turns*   1987—*All in the Name of Love* (Warner Bros.)   1989—(– Weathers; – Phillips; + Porscha Martin, voc.) *We're Movin' Up*   1992—(– Martin; + Rachel

Oliver, voc.) *Love Crazy* (Reprise)   1994—(– Oliver; + Aisha Tanner [b. July 27, 1973, Oakland, Calif.], voc.) *Time* (Arista).

Atlantic Starr's low-key soul balladry never received the attention of more flamboyant outfits like Earth, Wind and Fire or P-Funk, but they were staples on the R&B charts from the late Seventies through the Eighties, racking up over 20 chart singles, 13 in the Top Twenty. Three songs, "Secret Lovers" (#3 pop, #4 R&B, 1985), "Always" (#1 pop, #1 R&B, 1987), and "Masterpiece" (#3 pop, 1992), crossed over onto the upper echelons of the pop charts.

Formed by the Lewis brothers along with polished vocalist Sharon Bryant, the early Atlantic Starr was a nine-piece outfit. Signed by A&M in 1978, they hit the chart that year with "Stand Up" (#16); "When Love Calls" (#101 pop, #5 R&B, 1982) was their first R&B Top Ten.

In the mid-Eighties the band had its greatest success with the more upbeat *As the Band Turns* (#17 pop, 1985) and a dance track, "Freak-a-Ristic" (#90 pop, #6 R&B, 1985). The album's title reflects the soap-opera-like internal feuding that occurred during the recording of their 1983 LP *Yours Forever*. Bryant and four other bandmembers attempted a coup d'état over songwriting and the band's direction. The album was recorded under such tense conditions that the band's longtime producer, James Anthony Carmichael, quit, and A&M dropped the band.

Atlantic Starr reemerged in 1985 as a quintet, with a new female vocalist, Barbara Weathers. This lineup recorded *As the Band Turns*, which featured the hit "Secret Lovers." The next album, *All in the Name of Love*, reached #18 on the pop charts in 1987 and spawned the #1 single "Always." After Weathers left in 1989 a series of female vocalists followed. The 1992 hit song "Masterpiece," from *Love Crazy*, featured Rachel Oliver. Atlantic Starr's next album—on another label—also had another female singer, but the group was unable to realize its earlier achievements.

Brian Auger

Born July 18, 1939, London, England
1967—*Open* (Marmalade)   1968—*Definitely What*   1969—*Streetnoise*   1970—*Befour* (RCA)   1971—*Brian Auger's Oblivion Express*; *A Better Land*   1972—*Second Wind*   1974—*Closer to It*   1975—*Straight Ahead*; *Live Oblivion, volumes 1 and 2*   1975—*Genesis* (Polydor) (early Steampacket recordings); *This Is* (Metronome); *Reinforcements* (RCA)   1977—*Happiness Heartaches* (Warner Bros.); *Best of Brian Auger* (RCA)   1978—*Encore*   1987—*Here and Now* (Grudge)   1989—*Planet Earth Calling* (Dunhill/Garland)   1991—*Streetnoise* (Polygram).

British keyboardist Brian Auger helped lay the groundwork for fusion with his jazz-rock hybrids in the Sixties and early Seventies. In 1964 he abandoned pure jazz and upright piano for R&B and a Hammond organ. He soon formed the Brian Auger Trinity with bassist Rick Brown and drummer Mickey Waller. Within a few months he was asked to join a new group, Steampacket, which included vocalists Long John Baldry, Rod Stewart, and ex-model Julie Driscoll. In mid-1966 Auger left, and the group dissolved.

Auger then reorganized Trinity with bassist Dave Ambrose (b. Dec. 11, 1946, London), drummer Clive Thacker (b. Feb. 13, 1940, Enfield, Eng.), guitarist Gary Boyle (b. Bihar, India), and Driscoll. In 1969 the band had hits in Europe ("Save Me") and England (a cover of Dylan's "This Wheel's on Fire"). Subsequent singles floundered, however, and during a 1969 U.S. tour Driscoll quit the group. She later married pianist Keith Tippetts and continued to record occasionally under the name Julie Tippetts. Further hampered by contractual and management problems, Trinity broke up in mid-1970 after releasing *Befour*.

Auger reemerged late in the year with the four-piece Oblivion Express (at one time including drummer Robbie McIntosh, who went on to play with the Average White Band before his 1977 death), a jazz-rock combo that released several influential albums but failed to crack the U.S. market in a big way. The group's latter-day vocalist was Alex Ligertwood, later of Santana and Average White Band. By 1977 Auger was playing synthesizers as well, and the following year he did a reunion album with Julie Driscoll Tippets, *Encore*. As the Seventies closed, Auger, who'd moved to California, was without a recording contract. He wrote "Happiness Is Just Around the Bend," a minor 1974 hit for the Main Ingredient.

Since then Auger has remained active, releasing albums in Europe and, to a lesser extent, America. In 1990 he teamed up with singer Eric Burdon and continues to tour the globe. A live CD recorded in California, *Access All Areas*, was issued in Europe in 1993.

Frankie Avalon

Born Francis Avallone, September 18, 1939, Philadelphia, Pennsylvania
1959—*Swingin' on a Rainbow* (Chancellor).

Teen idol Frankie Avalon was originally a trumpet-playing prodigy when, at age 18, he joined a group called Rocco and the Saints (which then included neighbor Bobby Rydell). He began making appearances on local television, and in 1958 his debut single, "DeDe Dinah," was #7. Through the late Fifties and up until 1960, Avalon had six Top Ten hits: "Ginger Bread" (#9, 1958), "Bobby Sox to Stockings" (#8, 1959), "A Boy Without a Girl" (#10, 1959), "Just Ask Your Heart" (#7, 1959), "Venus" (#1, 1959), and "Why" (#1, 1960). He was a regular on Dick

Clark's *American Bandstand*, appeared in several beach-party movies with Annette Funicello (including 1965's *Beach Blanket Bingo*), and also appeared in *Disc Jockey Jamboree* (1957), *Guns of the Timberland* (1960), and *The Carpetbaggers* (1962).

By the Seventies he was appearing regularly on the resort club circuit and occasionally had TV roles in such shows as *Love, American Style*. His 1976 disco remake of "Venus" peaked at #46. In 1987 he and Funicello coproduced and costarred in *Back to the Beach;* the pair's Back to the Beach concert tour (1989/90) was well received. They also released a Christmas single, "Together We Can Make a Merry Christmas," and made a number of guest appearances, including on Pee Wee Herman's *Pee Wee's Playhouse*. Avalon continues to tour solo and with Bobby Rydell and Fabian as one of the "Boys of Bandstand."

Average White Band/AWB

Formed 1972, Scotland
Alan Gorrie (b. July 19, 1946, Perth, Scot.), bass, voc.; Onnie McIntyre (b. Sep. 25, 1945, Lennox Town, Scot.), gtr., voc.; Roger Ball (b. June 4, 1944, Dundee, Scot.), kybds., saxes; Malcolm "Molly" Duncan (b. Aug. 24, 1945, Montrose, Scot.), tenor sax; Robbie McIntosh (b. 1950, Scot.; d. Sep. 23, 1974, Los Angeles, Calif.), drums; Hamish Stuart (b. Oct. 8, 1949, Glasgow, Scot.), gtr., voc.
1973—*Show Your Hand* (MCA) 1974—*AWB* (Atlantic) (– McIntosh; + Steve Ferrone [b. Apr. 25, 1950, Brighton, Eng.], drums) 1975—*Cut the Cake*; *Put It Where You Want It* (MCA) 1976—*Soul Searching* (Atlantic); *Person to Person* 1977—*Benny and Us* 1978—*Warmer Communications* 1979—*Feel No Fret* 1980—*Shine* (Arista); *Volume VIII* (Atlantic) 1989—(Group re-forms: Gorrie; McIntyre; Ball; + Alex Ligertwood, voc.) *Aftershock* (Trk).

The Average White Band's derivative but convincing funk crossed the Atlantic and the color line, heralding the arrival of disco in the mid-Seventies. Each of the members had been active in various English and Scottish bands before Alan Gorrie founded the group. Robbie McIntosh had been with Brian Auger's Oblivion Express (as had latter-day vocalist Alex Ligertwood); Roger Ball and Malcolm Duncan had been members of the Dundee Horns.

After opening for Eric Clapton at his January 1973 Rainbow Theatre comeback concert, they released an unnoticed debut album. The next year they began abbreviating the band name as AWB, and a 1974 album produced by Arif Mardin yielded a Grammy Award–winning disco hit, "Pick Up the Pieces" (#1, 1975). The group was shaken by drummer McIntosh's death of accidental heroin poisoning at a Hollywood party but regrouped for a second gold album, *Cut the Cake* (which it dedicated to McIntosh). *Put It Where You Want It* is a rerelease of their debut album. *Benny and Us* featured soul singer Ben E. King.

In 1975 AWB began recording together less often as its members worked as sidemen, including backup work for Chaka Khan in 1978. Gorrie, Ferrone, and Stuart recorded as Easy Pieces, with Renee Geyer. Ferrone later played drums for Duran Duran, and Stuart joined Paul McCartney's band for *Flowers in the Dirt* and his subsequent tour. In 1989 Gorrie, McIntyre, and Ball enlisted vocalist Alex Ligertwood and re-formed the AWB. The group has continued to perform into the Nineties.

Hoyt Axton

Born March 25, 1938, Duncan, Oklahoma
1962—*The Balladeer* (Horizon)   1963—*Thunder 'n' Lightnin'*; *Saturday's Child*   1964—*Hoyt Axton Explodes* (Vee Jay); *The Best of Hoyt Axton*; *Hoyt Axton Sings Bessie Smith* (Exodus); *Bessie Smith . . . My Way* (Vee Jay)   1965—*Mr. Greenback Dollar Man* (Surrey)   1969—*My Griffin Is Gone* (CBS)   1971—*Joy to the World* (Capitol); *Country Anthem*   1973—*Less Than a Song* (A&M)   1974— *Life Machine*   1975—*Southbound*   1976—*Fearless* 1977—*Road Songs*   1977—*Snowblind Friend* (MCA); *Free Sailin'*   1979—*A Rusty Old Halo* (Jeremiah)   1980—*Where Did the Money Go*   1982— *Everybody's Going on the Road*; *Pistol Packin' Mama*   1986—*Hoyt Axton's Greatest Hits*   1990— *Spin of the Wheel* (DPI).

Singer/songwriter Hoyt Axton's most famous songs— "Joy to the World," "Greenback Dollar," and "The Pusher"— were made hits by other artists. The son of Mae Axton, who worked as Hank Snow's publicist and wrote "Heartbreak Hotel," and a blues-singer father, Axton moved frequently during his childhood. While country music was the sound he grew up on, he began performing in West Coast folk clubs in the late Fifties. In 1962 he signed with Horizon Records and recorded his debut, *The Balladeer*, featuring future Byrd Roger McGuinn on guitar, live at Los Angeles' Troubadour folk club; later that year, the Kingston Trio's version of "Greenback Dollar" became the first of his hit credits (Axton maintains that, due to his own business naiveté, he ended up making only $800 for the song). Other covers include Steppenwolf's "The Pusher" (1968), Three Dog Night's "Joy to the World" (#1, 1971), and Ringo Starr's "No No Song" (#3, 1975).

Axton acquired and eventually kicked a ten-year cocaine habit. In 1979 he appeared in the movie *The Black Stallion* and founded a record label, Jeremiah. Axton's

acting, in fact, became nearly as much a signature as his music; after debuting in 1962 in the TV series *Bonanza*, the eventual father of five children went on to land paternal character roles in films including *E.T.*, *Gremlins*, and *We're No Angels*.

In the late Seventies Axton released his strongest solo work (*Road Songs* featured backup by James Burton on guitar and Linda Ronstadt on duet vocals) and established himself as a country artist, gaining Top Twenty country records with "Della and the Dealer" and "A Rusty Old Halo." He maintained a relentless concert schedule that found him on the road 300 days a year. He continues to tour and record.

Kevin Ayers

Born August 16, 1945, Herne Bay, England
1970—*Joy of a Toy* (Harvest)   1971—*Shooting at the Moon*   1972—*Whatevershebringswesing* 1973—*Bananamour*   1974—*Confessions of Dr. Dream* (Island); *June 1, 1974* (with John Cale, Brian Eno, and Nico)   1975—*Sweet Deceiver*; *Joy of a Toy/Shooting at the Moon* (Harvest)   1976—*Old Ditties*   1977—*Yes, We Have No Mañanas*   1978— *Rainbow Takeaway*.

Cheerfully eccentric Kevin Ayers first became active in British progressive rock in 1963, when he and some friends from Canterbury founded the Wilde Flowers. In 1966 Ayers and drummer Robert Wyatt left to start Soft Machine [see entry]. He played bass with the group until 1968, then began his ongoing solo career. Singing in a deep bass voice and making quiet jokes about moons and bananas—his specialty is pataphysical humor, the British equivalent of Zen koans—Ayers has played alongside Mike Oldfield (who first recorded on Ayers' albums), Steve Hillage, John Cale, Brian Eno, and Andy Summers. In 1980 Ayers made some concert appearances in the U.S. He spends most of his time at his estate on the island of Ibiza and continues to release albums in Britain every few years.

Roy Ayers

Born September 10, 1940, Los Angeles, California
1967—*Virgo Vibes* (Atlantic)   1968—*Stone Soul Picnic*   1969—*Daddy Bug*   1971—*Roy Ayers: Ubiquity* (Polydor)   1972—*He's Coming*   1973—*Virgo Red* 1974—*Change Up the Groove*   1975—*A Tear to a Smile*; *Red, Black and Green*   1976—*Mystic Voyage*; *Vibrations*; *Everybody Loves the Sunshine* 1977—*Lifeline*   1978—*Let's Do It*; *You Send Me*; *Step into Our Life*   1979—*Fever*   1980—*No Stranger to Love*   1981—*Africa, Center of the World*; *Love Fantasy*   1982—*Feeling Good*   1984—

In the Dark (Columbia)   1985—*You Might Be Surprised*   1987—*I'm the One (for Your Love Tonight)*   1989—*Wake Up* (Ichiban)   1992—*Double Trouble*   1995—*Evolution: The Polydor Anthology* (Polydor).

Vibraphonist Roy Ayers crossed over from jazz to funk and found commercial success in the mid-Seventies with what he called "disco jazz." He learned to play piano at an early age; at five, his playing impressed Lionel Hampton, who gave him a pair of mallets. Ayers began playing vibes professionally with West Coast bands in the late Fifties. In 1965 he formed his own quartet but disbanded it when Herbie Mann invited him to join his band. He recorded and toured with Mann from 1966 to 1970, and Mann produced Ayers' first three solo albums.

Around 1970 Ayers began experimenting with electronics and rock rhythms. He was probably the first vibraphonist to electrify his instrument and certainly the first to employ such devices as the wah-wah pedal and effects like fuzztone. In 1970 he formed Roy Ayers Ubiquity, a fully electrified ensemble that fused jazz, rock, Latin pop, and R&B. Guest soloists with Ubiquity have included drummer Billy Cobham, flutist Hubert Laws, guitarist George Benson, trombonist Wayne Henderson of the Crusaders, vocalist Dee Dee Bridgewater, R&B composer and vocalist Edwin Birdsong, and Nigerian saxophonist Fela Anikulapo Kuti, with whom he toured Nigeria in 1979, resulting in the 1981 LP *Africa, Center of the World*. His albums from this period earned him a loyal audience among jazz and R&B fans.

Beginning in 1976, Ayers' records hit the charts after receiving radio and disco play; "Running Away," which became a dance-club classic, made the R&B Top Twenty in 1977. "The Freaky Deaky" inspired a dance step of the same name in 1978. Ayers broke up Ubiquity that year and formed a recording partnership with Henderson on the album *Step into Our Life;* they had a minor hit with "Heat of the Beat" (#59 R&B, 1978).

In 1981 Ayers formed his own label, Uno Melodic, upon which to release other artists' work that he produced. Throughout the next decade Ayers continued to have hits, including "In the Dark" (#35 R&B, 1984), "Slip 'n Slide" (#49 R&B, 1985), and "Hot" (#20 R&B, 1986), and remained popular in Great Britain. In 1987 Ayers recorded with Whitney Houston on her "Love Will Save the Day."

By the Nineties, Ayers had become a seminal influence on the burgeoning acid-jazz scene, particularly in the U.K. Such hip-hop artists as Big Daddy Kane, A Tribe Called Quest, Brand Nubian, and Monie Love sampled Ayers' Seventies recordings. This brought him even more visibility, as did his appearance on *Jazzmatazz*, the hip-hop–jazz project produced by Guru of Gang Starr.

Aztec Camera

Formed 1980, East Kilbride, Scotland
Roddy Frame (b. Jan. 29, 1964, East Kilbride), voc., gtr., most other instruments in studio.
1983—*High Land, Hard Rain* (Sire)   1984—*Oblivious* EP; *Knife*; *Still On Fire* EP (WEA)   1985—*Backwards and Forwards* EP (Sire)   1987—*Love*   1988—*Somewhere in My Heart* EP (WEA)   1990—*Stray* (Sire)   1993—*Dreamland.*

This one-man band arrived on the heels of punk. Roddy Frame had started writing songs at 15. He formed Aztec Camera a year later as a vehicle for his highly individual style of folky pop.

Initially signed to the Glasgow independent label Postcard, Aztec Camera soon moved to the much higher-profile English indie Rough Trade. A flurry of attention in Great Britain piqued Sire's interest. Before the release of *High Land, Hard Rain*, however, the group's original bassist, Campbell Owens, and drummer, Dave Mulholland, departed. Aztec Camera has since consisted of Frame with various backup musicians.

Frame's songs never charted well in the U.S., but his penchant for hook-drenched melodies and clever wordplay made him a critic's darling. Aztec Camera's debut fared better in Britain, with modest hits including "Oblivious" and "Walk Out to Winter." The second album, produced by Dire Straits' Mark Knopfler, offered more of the same. Frame fell out of critical favor with 1987's *Love*, an ill-conceived attempt to marry his singer/songwriter pop with Philadelphia soul. He reclaimed his critical reputation with *Stray*.

Babes in Toyland

Formed 1987, Minneapolis, Minnesota
Michelle Leon, bass; Katherine "Kat" Bjelland
(b. Dec. 9, 1963, Salem, Ore.), voc., gtr.; Lori Barbero
(b. Nov. 27, 1960, Minneapolis), drums.
1990—*Spanking Machine* (Twin/Tone)   **1991**—*To*
Mother   **1992**—(– Leon; + Maureen Herman
[b. July 25, 1966, Philadelphia, Pa.], bass) *Fontanelle*
(Reprise)   **1993**—*Painkillers* EP   **1995**—*Neme-*
sisters.

Babes in Toyland, one of the first all-female bands to
come out of the early-Nineties grunge scene, featured
Kat Bjelland's distinctive and demanding vocals. Defying expectations by wearing baby-doll dresses while
venting a deep rage, Bjelland and her band opened doors
for such groups as Hole and Bikini Kill.

In 1987 Bjelland moved from San Francisco, where
she had played with L7's Jennifer Finch and Hole's
Courtney Love in a band called Sugar Baby Doll, to Minneapolis, then an indie-rock hotbed. Babes' original all-
girl lineup included Barbero, who had never drummed
before, bassist Chris Holetz, and singer Cindy Russell;
Holetz and Russell left after one year and Leon joined.

Babes released its first single on an independent
label in 1989 and already had a following by the time
Spanking Machine was released a year later. They toured

**Babes in Toyland: Kat Bjelland, Lori Barbero, Maureen
Herman**

Europe that fall with Sonic Youth. Originally released only in Europe, *To Mother*, a seven-song disc, spent 12 weeks on top of the U.K. indie charts. That and frequent touring, including the Reading Festival, secured Babes in Toyland's European following.

Leon left Babes in early 1992 after her boyfriend, roadie Joe Cole, was shot and killed when he and his roommate Henry Rollins were attacked by burglars. She was replaced by Maureen Herman. Babes' major-label debut, *Fontanelle*, was produced by Sonic Youth's Lee Ranaldo and featured a cover photo by noted artist Cindy Sherman. In 1993 Babes first broke through to American audiences, after being the only female-led band on that summer's Lollapalooza Tour and having their video for "Bruised Violet" plugged by MTV's *Beavis and Butt-head. Painkillers* featured that track and a live CBGB performance.

Babyface: See L.A. Reid and Babyface

The Babys/John Waite/Bad English

Formed 1976, London, England
John Waite (b. July 4, 1955, Lancashire, Eng.), bass, voc.; Wally Stocker (b. Mar. 17, 1954, London), gtr., voc.; Mike Corby (b. July 3, 1955, Eng.), voc., kybds., gtr.; Tony Brock (b. Mar. 31, 1954, Bournemouth, Eng.), drums, voc.
1976—*The Babys* (Chrysalis)   1977—*Broken Heart* (– Corby)   1978—*Head First* (+ Jonathan Cain, kybds.; + Ricky Phillips, bass)   1980—*Union Jacks* 1981—*On the Edge* (– Cain); *Anthology.*
John Waite solo: 1982—*Ignition* (Chrysalis)   1984— *No Brakes* (EMI)   1985—*Mask of Smiles*   1987— *Rover's Return*   1992—*Essential John Waite* (Chrysalis)   1995—*Temple Bar* (Imago).
Bad English, formed c. 1988: Waite; Cain; Phillips; + Neal Schon (b. Feb. 27, 1954, San Mateo, Calif.), gtr.; + Deen Castronovo, drums.
1989—*Bad English* (Epic)   1991—*Backlash* (– Schon; – Castronovo).

Power pop with a veneer of youthful vibrancy made the Babys a hot act on FM rock radio in the late Seventies. Formed in London as a teen-oriented act, the group signed with Chrysalis in late 1976 on the strength of one of the first video demos. Conceived by producer Mike Mansfield, it showed off their looks. Aided by massive promotion, the group had such hits as "Isn't It Time" (#13, 1977). As the Seventies drew to a close, the Babys experimented with a more synthesizer-oriented style on *Head First* and 1980's *Union Jacks,* which bore two moderate hits, "Back on My Feet Again" (#33, 1980) and "Turn and Walk Away" (#42, 1980). Jonathan Cain joined Journey in early 1981, and the Babys disbanded.

Chrysalis released lead singer John Waite's solo

debut, *Ignition,* in 1982, and the album's "Change" went to #54. *No Brakes* became a Top Ten LP on the strength of "Missing You" (#1, 1984). "Every Step of the Way" (#25, 1985) was Waite's last Top Thirty single; his fourth album, *Rover's Return,* stalled at #77. Two years later Waite reemerged, fronting Bad English, which featured two ex-Babys, Jonathan Cain and Ricky Phillips, and included Cain's ex–Journey mate, Neal Schon, and drummer Deen Castronovo. The group's eponymously titled debut struck platinum, peaking at #21 in 1989 and boasting two Top Ten hits: "When I See You Smile" (#1) and "Price of Love" (#5). After the group's second album Schon quit the group; he and Castronovo joined Hardline, and Castronovo later joined Paul Rodgers for his Muddy Waters tribute record. Cain began pursuing a solo career while John Waite continued his with 1995's *Temple Bar.*

Bachman-Turner Overdrive/BTO

Formed 1972, Winnipeg, Canada
Randy Bachman (b. Sep. 27, 1943, Winnipeg), gtr., voc.; Tim Bachman (b. Winnipeg), gtr.; Robbie Bachman (b. Feb. 18, 1953, Winnipeg), drums; C. F. (Fred) Turner (b. Oct. 16, 1943, Winnipeg), bass, voc.
1973—*Bachman-Turner Overdrive* (Mercury); *Bachman-Turner Overdrive 2* (– Tim Bachman; + Blair Thornton [b. July 23, 1950], gtr.)   1974—*Not Fragile* 1975—*Four Wheel Drive; Head On*   1976—*Best of Bachman-Turner Overdrive (So Far)*   1977—*Freeways* (– Randy Bachman; + Jim Clench, bass, voc.) 1978—*Street Action; Rock 'n' Roll Nights*   1984— *Bachman-Turner Overdrive* (Compleat)   1993— *Bachman-Turner Overdrive: The Anthology* (PolyGram).

Bachman-Turner Overdrive parlayed workmanlike heavy metal, a blue-collar image, and nonstop touring into over seven million records sold in the U.S. by 1977. The group—in various personnel combinations—has retained an impressive following in its homeland, where Randy Bachman is a respected guitar hero and successful solo artist.

Guess Who founders Chad Allan and Randy Bachman had left that group in 1966 and 1970 respectively [see entry]. After Bachman made a solo album (*Axe*, 1970), he teamed up with Allan and younger brother Robbie Bachman in Brave Belt. After two albums (*Brave Belt I* and *Brave Belt II*), Tim Bachman and vocalist/bassist Fred Turner—both Mormons like Randy—replaced Allan, and Brave Belt became Bachman-Turner Overdrive, named in part after the truckers' magazine *Overdrive.*

Twenty-five record companies rejected the band before Mercury released its 1973 debut album, but extensive touring netted BTO several hit singles, including "Taking Care of Business" (#12, 1974) and "You Ain't

Seen Nothin' Yet" (#1, 1974). In 1975 Tim Bachman left to become a producer. That year Warner Bros. rereleased *Brave Belt II* under the title *As Brave Belt.* With Randy Bachman's departure in 1977 for a solo career (he released *Survivor* and later formed Ironhorse, which recorded two LPs, *Ironhorse* and *Everything Is Grey*), BTO's momentum slowed considerably, although the group did release two more LPs.

The group disbanded for the first time in 1979 or 1980, but has regrouped several times since to tour under the names Bachman-Turner Overdrive and BTO. Randy Bachman toured as Bachman-Turner Overdrive (sometimes with Turner, sometimes without) while brother Robbie Bachman performed under the BTO moniker (again, not always with Turner along). The ensuing confusion caused Randy to file suit against his ex-bandmates brother Robbie, Turner, and Thornton for rights to the band's logo. As of 1994, the case was not settled. Randy Bachman also records as a solo artist and tours occasionally with the reconstituted Guess Who. Nineteen-ninety-three's *Any Road* (Sony, Canada), his first solo album of the decade, features the guitarist's protégé from their early days in Winnipeg, Neil Young, on "Prairie Town."

Bad Brains

Formed 1979, Washington, D.C.
H.R. (b. Paul D. Hudson, Feb. 11, 1956, London, Eng.), voc.; Dr. Know (b. Gary Wayne Miller, Sep. 15, 1958, Washington), gtr.; Darryl Aaron Jenifer (b. Oct. 22, 1960, Washington), bass; Earl Hudson (b. Dec. 17, 1957, Ala.), drums.
1982—*Bad Brains* cassette (ROIR); *Bad Brains* EP (Alternative Tentacles); *I and I Survive/Destroy Babylon* EP (Important) 1983—*Rock for Light* (PVC) 1986—*I Against I* (SST) 1988—*Live* 1989—*Attitude: The ROIR Session* (ROIR/Important); *Quickness* (Caroline) 1990—*The Youth Are Getting Restless* 1991—*Spirit Electricity* (SST) (– H.R.; – E. Hudson; + Israel Joseph-I [b. Dexter Pinto, Feb. 6, 1971, Trinidad], voc.; + Mackie Jayson [b. May 27, 1963, New York City, N.Y.], drums) 1993—*Rise* (Epic) (– Joseph-I; – Jayson; + H.R.; + E. Hudson) 1995—*God of Love* (Maverick).

The members of Bad Brains started out playing Seventies jazz-rock fusion, but took a sharp turn when they began breaking up their live sets into reggae and punk. Together with Black Flag and Dead Kennedys, the band became pioneers of punk's hardcore fringe, influencing nearly every subsequent hardcore or quasi-hardcore outfit. As an all-black rock band, they also inspired Living Colour and the entire New York City Black Rock Coalition of the Eighties.

By 1977 guitarist Gary Miller (a.k.a. Dr. Know) had grown tired of his fusion noodling and looked to the Sex Pistols and Bob Marley for fresh inspiration. He and his mates viewed punk and reggae as complementary (both musically and politically) and believed that if punk and reggae acts could share the same stages in the U.K., they could share one band's set list in the U.S.

Bad Brains' single "Pay to Cum" remains a classic of the hardcore genre. Unfortunately, the band's music was never well documented on record; "Pay to Cum" was available only in its rare single form and on the band's self-titled ROIR cassette (reissued in 1991 on LP and CD by Dutch East Wax). Ric Ocasek produced 1983's *Rock for Light,* which delivered one side each of reggae and hardcore.

The long-awaited *I Against I* was an all-rock explosion, leaning more toward heavy metal than punk. It left the band fragmented, with H.R. and Earl Hudson wanting to do more reggae, and Dr. Know and Darryl Jenifer preferring the new hard-rock direction. After years of coming and going, both H.R. and Hudson left again in 1989 (the two have recorded several reggae albums under H.R.'s name since 1985's *It's About Luv* on Olive Tree). Bad Brains recruited Trinidadian-born singer Israel Joseph-I to replace H.R. and released *Rise.* In 1995 H.R. and Hudson returned and the band released *God of Love.*

Bad Company

Formed 1973, England
Paul Rodgers (b. Dec. 12, 1949, Middlesbrough, Eng.), voc.; Mick Ralphs (b. March 31, 1948, Hereford, Eng.), gtr.; Simon Kirke (b. July 28, 1949, Shrewsbury, Eng.), drums; Boz Burrell (b. Raymond Burrell, 1946, Lincoln, Eng.), bass.
1974—*Bad Company* (Swan Song) 1975—*Straight Shooter* 1976—*Run with the Pack* 1977—*Burnin' Sky* 1979—*Desolation Angels* 1982—*Rough Diamonds* 1982—(Group disbands) 1986—(Group reforms: Ralphs; Kirke; + Brian Howe, voc.) *10 from 6* (Atlantic); *Fame and Fortune* 1988—*Dangerous Age* 1990—*Holy Water* (Atco) 1992—*Here Comes Trouble* 1993—(+ Rick Wills, bass; + Dave Colwell, gtr.) *The Best of Bad Company Live . . . What You Hear Is What You Get.*
Paul Rodgers solo: 1983—*Cut Loose* (Atlantic) 1993—*Muddy Waters Blues* (Victory) 1993—*The Hendrix Set.*
Rodgers with the Firm: 1985—*The Firm* (Atlantic) 1986—*Mean Business.*
Rodgers with the Law: 1991—*The Law* (Atlantic).

The members of Bad Company were stars before their first concert in March 1974. Paul Rodgers and Simon Kirke had been members of Free, Mick Ralphs had been Ian Hunter's main sidekick in Mott the Hoople, and Boz Burrell had played with King Crimson [see entries]. Their self-titled debut album, recorded in only ten days with a minimum of overdubs in Ronnie Lane's mobile studio, eclipsed all that by going #1 worldwide with the single "Can't Get Enough." The album from which it came also hit #1 and to date has sold more than four million copies.

Playing sparse, elemental hard rock dominated by Rodgers' husky vocals and Ralphs' power chords, the original Bad Company sold more than 12 million records worldwide. Its 1975 release, *Straight Shooter,* yielded the Top Ten single "Feel Like Makin' Love" (#10, 1975), while *Run with the Pack* was the group's third consecutive album to go platinum.

On *Desolation Angels* (which included the Rodgers-penned hit "Rock and Roll Fantasy," #13, 1979), Bad Company added synthesizers and strings. Indicative of its increasingly sporadic activities, three years elapsed between *Angels* and *Rough Diamonds,* which seemed an anachronism upon its 1982 release. The group disbanded that year, with Rodgers releasing a solo LP in 1983, then forming yet another supergroup, the Firm, with Jimmy Page, bassist/keyboardist Tony Franklin, and drummer Chris Slade.

The Firm never came close to matching the level of success its two principals had enjoyed with their previous groups. After two LPs, the quartet broke up in 1986, just as Ralphs and Kirke were putting Bad Company back together. Former Ted Nugent vocalist Brian Howe stood in for Rodgers. The group stuck closely to the original lineup's riffy blues-rock formula, but its first album, *Fame and Fortune,* disappeared from the chart after just nine weeks. However, *Dangerous Age* eventually went gold, while *Holy Water* went platinum and produced a Top Twenty hit, the power ballad "If You Needed Somebody." *Here Comes Trouble* also sold in excess of one million copies and gave the group two more Top Forty hits. In 1993 Bad Company expanded into a quintet, adding journeyman bassist Rick Wills (Frampton's Camel, Roxy Music, Foreigner) and rhythm guitarist Dave Colwell, and celebrated its 20th anniversary with a live greatest-hits album.

Rodgers, meanwhile, has struggled to find musical direction. The Law, a hard-rock duo with drummer Kenney Jones, couldn't get arrested. Since then the singer has released two curious tribute albums, one interpreting the music of Muddy Waters, the other a live set of Jimi Hendrix tunes, featuring Neal Schon on guitar.

Bad English: See the Babys

Badfinger

Formed 1968, England
Peter Ham (b. Apr. 27, 1947, Swansea, Wales; d. Apr. 23, 1975, Weybridge, Eng.), voc., gtr., piano; Tom Evans (b. June 5, 1947, Liverpool, Eng.; d. Nov. 23, 1983), voc., gtr.; Mike Gibbins (b. Mar. 12, 1949, Swansea), drums; Ron Griffiths, bass.

1968—(– Griffiths; + Joey Molland [b. June 21, 1947, Liverpool, Eng.], voc., gtr., kybds.; Evans switches to bass) 1970—*Magic Christian Music* (Apple); *No Dice* 1971—*Straight Up* 1973—*Ass* 1974—*Badfinger* (Warner Bros.); *Wish You Were Here* (– Molland; + Bob Jackson, kybds.) 1975—(– Ham; group disbands) 1978—(Group reforms: Molland; Evans; + Joe Tanzin, gtr.; + Kenny Harck, drums; – Tanzin; – Harck) 1979—*Airwaves* (Elektra) 1981—(+ Tony Kaye, kybds.; + Glenn Sherba, gtr.; + Richard Bryans, drums) *Say No More* (Radio) 1989—*The Best of Badfinger, vol. 2* (Rhino) 1990—*Day After Day* (Rykodisc) 1995—*Come and Get It: The Best of Badfinger* (Capitol).
Joey Molland solo: 1983—*After the Pearl* (Earthtone) 1992—*The Pilgrim* (Rykodisc).

Badfinger was a popular British pop-rock band of the early Seventies. Originally called the Iveys, the group signed with Apple Records in late 1968 after its demo tape found its way into Paul McCartney's hands. In 1969 McCartney supervised the quartet's soundtrack work on the Ringo Starr–Peter Sellers film *The Magic Christian,* for which he wrote "Come and Get It," Badfinger's first hit (#7, 1970).

During the early Seventies Badfinger had three more hit singles: "No Matter What" (#8, 1970), "Day After Day" (#4, 1972), and "Baby Blue" (#14, 1972). Peter Ham and Tom Evans' "Without You," covered by Harry Nilsson on *Nilsson Schmilsson,* became a #1 single in February 1972; in 1994 it was a hit again, this time for Mariah Carey. The group frequently backed the ex-Beatles on tours and records, appearing at George Harrison's 1971 benefit concert for Bangladesh and on *All Things Must Pass,* on John Lennon's *Imagine,* and on Ringo Starr's "It Don't Come Easy."

After its fourth album, 1973's *Ass,* sold disappointingly, Badfinger moved to Warner Bros. the following year for a reported $3 million advance. It proved a disastrous relationship. The group's second album for its new label, *Wish You Were Here,* was selling a brisk 25,000 copies a week when Warner Bros., claiming (erroneously, it would turn out) that $600,000 in a band escrow account was missing, pulled the album from stores. In frustration over management problems, Molland quit. A despondent Ham, the leader and chief songwriter, hanged himself in his London home on April 23, 1975. Badfinger collapsed. A third album, recorded before his suicide, was never released.

Soon thereafter, Molland formed a group called Natural Gas in Los Angeles with former Humble Pie drummer Jerry Shirley; Evans returned to England to join the Dodgers. By 1978 Molland was installing carpets for a living, while Evans was a pipefitter. Together they revived Badfinger, releasing *Airwaves* in 1979 and *Say No More* in

1981. Each produced a minor hit in "Love Is Gonna Come at Last" and "Hold On," respectively.

Business problems continued to haunt the group, which didn't see royalties from its days with Apple Records until 1985. Unfortunately by then Evans had committed suicide—eerily, in the same manner as Ham. Molland and drummer Gibbins (the latter played on Bonnie Tyler's 1978 smash "It's a Heartache"), now both living in America, still tour as Badfinger; Molland has also recorded two solo albums.

Joan Baez

Born January 9, 1941, Staten Island, New York
1960—*Joan Baez* (Vanguard)   1961—*Joan Baez 2*
1962—*In Concert*   1963—*In Concert 2*   1964—*Joan Baez 5*   1965—*Farewell Angelina*   1966—*Noel*;
Portrait*   1967—*Joan*   1968—*Baptism*; *Any Day Now*   1969—*David's Album*   1970—*One Day at a Time*; *The First Ten Years*   1971—*Blessed Are
1972—*Carry It On*; *Come from the Shadows* (A&M);
The Ballad Book* (Vanguard)   1973—*Where Are You Now, My Son?*; *Hits, the Greatest and Others
1974—*Gracias a la Vida (Here's to Life)* (A&M)
1975—*Diamonds and Rust*; *Live in Japan* (Vanguard)   1976—*Love Song Album*; *From Every Stage* (A&M); *Gulf Winds*   1977—*Blowing Away* (Portrait); *Best of Joan Baez* (A&M)   1979—*Honest Lullaby* (Portrait); *Country Music* (Vanguard)
1993—*Rare, Live and Classic*.

Singer/songwriter Joan Baez was the perfect symbol of the early-Sixties folk revival: young, sincere, technically gifted, and equally committed to traditional songs and social action. In the Seventies she found it increasingly difficult to be both commercial and socially conscious, and by the early Eighties she all but ceased recording, concentrating instead on her political, humanitarian activities.

Baez became involved with political issues while attending Boston University in the mid-Fifties. Baez emerged from the 1959 Newport Folk Festival acclaimed for the purity of her voice. In the early Sixties, she released several influential albums of sparsely arranged traditional folk material and—largely through her association with the anthemic "We Shall Overcome"—she became a voice of the early Sixties civil rights movement.

Baez also played an important role in the rise of Bob Dylan by recording his songs and sharing concert bills with him in the early Sixties. From 1963 through 1965, they were virtually inseparable. Nearly a decade later their romance provided the subject matter for Baez's hit "Diamonds and Rust." By 1975 the two were reconciled, and they sang duets in Dylan's Rolling Thunder Revue, captured on the fall 1976 TV special "Hard Rain." Baez also appeared in Dylan's 1978 feature film, *Renaldo and Clara*.

Joan Baez

By 1965 politics had become Baez's main concern. In that year, she founded in Carmel, California, the Institute for the Study of Nonviolence, signaling her increasing preoccupation with U.S. involvement in Vietnam. She later founded the Humanitas International Human Rights Committee. In 1968 she married student protest leader David Harris, who was jailed for draft evasion a year later, fueling Baez's antiwar fervor (reflected in *David's Album* and *One Day at a Time*). The marriage ended in 1974, five years after the birth of their son, Gabriel.

Baez's career suffered under the burden of her political commitment. At the height of her antiwar activities, she devoted the second side of *Where Are You Now, My Son?* to a quasi-documentary account of a U.S. bombing raid of Hanoi. But in the early Seventies, she also made some of the most commercial music of her career, including her #3 rendition of the Band's "The Night They Drove Old Dixie Down" (a gold single in 1971) and *Diamonds and Rust*. Her voice had become lower and richer than in her folk phase.

Baez has remained politically active. In 1973 she was a vocal opponent of the coup in Chile and the assassination of Socialist president Salvador Allende. In August 1981 Baez toured Latin America and was met with bomb threats and harassment. Later in the year, she met with U.S. government officials in Washington, D.C., to discuss human rights in South America. A 90-minute TV special on the tour was scheduled for 1982, but was not shown. She has toured on behalf of Amnesty International and appeared at the Live Aid concert in 1985. In 1968 Baez published a slim autobiography, *Daybreak*, and in 1987, another, *And a Voice to Sing With*, a personal, impressionistic account of her life. Her sister Mimi is the widow of novelist and songwriter Richard Fariña.

Dan Baird: See Georgia Satellites

Anita Baker

Born December 20, 1957, Detroit, Michigan
1983—*The Songstress* (Beverly Glen) 1986—*Rapture* (Elektra) 1988—*Giving You the Best That I've Got* 1990—*Compositions* 1994—*Rhythm of Love*.

With the success of singer Anita Baker's *Rapture,* a new musical appellation came into being: "Quiet Storm." Baker's elegant, smoldering approach to R&B was a marked return to traditional vocalizing. In the controlled passion of her approach, Baker was reminiscent of one of her idols, jazz-pop singer Nancy Wilson.

Baker began her singing career with the Detroit band Chapter 8, which released an eponymously titled album on Ariola in 1980. After moving to Los Angeles she recorded her first solo album, *The Songstress,* which yielded the R&B hit "Angel" (#5 R&B). Despite legal difficulties from her former record label, Baker moved on to Elektra. *Rapture,* with its single "Sweet Love" (#8), was an immediate and influential hit, ultimately selling more than four million copies. Baker helped write some of *Rapture's* most popular tunes, including "Sweet Love" and "Watch Your Step." Her next album, *Giving You the Best That I've Got,* went to #1, its title track single climbing to #3. *Compositions,* recorded live in the studio and featuring Baker's own songs, played up her jazz sensibilities. Despite producing no hit singles, it still went platinum. In the years between *Compositions* and *Rhythm of Love* (#3 pop, #1 R&B, 1994), Baker gave birth to two sons.

Ginger Baker

Born Peter Baker, August 19, 1939, Lewisham, England
Ginger Baker's Air Force: 1970—*Air Force* (Atco); *Air Force 2*.
Ginger Baker solo: 1972—*Fela Ransome-Kuti and Africa '70 with Ginger Baker* (Signpost); *Stratavarious* (Polydor); *Ginger Baker at His Best* 1977—*Eleven Sides of Baker* (Sire) 1980—*Kuti and Africa* 1986—*Horses and Trees* (Celluloid) 1990—*Middle Passage* (Island/Axiom) 1992—*Unseen Rain* (Day Eight Music).
Baker-Gurvitz Army: 1975—*Baker-Gurvitz Army* (Janus); *Elysian Encounter* (Atco) 1976—*Hearts on Fire*.
With Masters of Reality: 1990—*Masters of Reality* (Delicious Vinyl/Island) 1993—*Sunrise on the Sufferbus* (Chrysalis).
BBM: (Baker, drums, perc.; + Jack Bruce, bass, cello, voc.; + Gary Moore, gtr., voc.) 1994—*Around the Next Dream* (Virgin).
The Ginger Baker Trio: 1994—*Going Back Home* (Atlantic).

In the adulation that outlasted Cream [see entry], Ginger Baker was touted as a great drummer. "Toad," his lengthy live showcase, paved the way for a decade of heavy-metal drum solos, and he was one of the first rock drummers to incorporate third world rhythms into his style.

As a teenager Baker played with traditional jazz bands, but he got his first taste of R&B with Alexis Korner's Blues Incorporated when Charlie Watts left the group to join the fledgling Rolling Stones in 1962. A year later Baker and two other group members, singer Graham Bond and bassist Jack Bruce, formed the Graham Bond Organisation. He and Bruce remained until forming Cream with Eric Clapton in mid-1966. Over the course of two-plus years, Cream became a supergroup [see entry]. After Cream split up in November 1968, Baker joined the short-lived Blind Faith [see entry].

Ginger Baker's Air Force debuted in January 1970. The percussion-dominated group was loosely structured, both in arrangements and personnel, which in various permutations included Stevie Winwood, Rick Grech, Bond, Denny Laine, and Remi Kabaka, one of three full-time drummers. Another drummer, Phil Seaman, and the members of Air Force encouraged Baker's growing interest in African music, and in 1971 he moved to Lagos, Nigeria, to build the first 16-track studio in West Africa. For the next few years he played with local talent, formed the group Salt, and ran his recording studio. Paul McCartney recorded *Band on the Run* there in 1973, by which time Baker had been musically inactive for many months. In 1974 he reemerged with the Baker-Gurvitz Army, which recorded three jazz-rock albums before disbanding in the late Seventies. By then Baker was reportedly spending a lot of his time playing polo.

In the early Eighties he moved to Milan, Italy, where he signed with CGD Records, formed a band with American musicians, and set up a drum school in a small mountain village. But mostly Baker ran an olive farm and tended to his health, for he'd only recently kicked a 21-year heroin addiction. In 1986 producer Bill Laswell coaxed the drummer to play on Public Image Ltd.'s *Album.* Since then Baker has relocated to California and recorded several LPs with Laswell behind the board and occasionally on bass. He has also teamed up with Masters of Reality for, to date, two albums. In 1994 Baker joined Bruce and Gary Moore (Thin Lizzy) for *Around the Next Dream.*

LaVern Baker

Born November 11, 1929, Chicago, Illinois
1958—*LaVern Baker Sings Bessie Smith* (Atlantic) 1970—*Let Me Belong to You* (Brunswick) 1971—*LaVern Baker: Her Greatest Recordings* (Atco) 1991—*LaVern Baker: Soul on Fire* (Rhino); *LaVern Baker: Live in Hollywood '91* 1992—*Woke Up This Morning* (DRG).

A major R&B vocalist during the Fifties, LaVern Baker saw her career decline in the early Sixties before she essentially retired. Her triumphant return to recording and performing in the late Eighties is one of the rare happy endings in the history of early R&B.

Baker first sang gospel as a little girl but was familiar with more secular styles; her aunt, Merline Baker, was better known as Memphis Minnie, a blues singer and guitarist. The singer got her first professional experience working at Chicago's Club De Lisa, where she appeared in the mid-Forties as Little Miss Sharecropper. She was soon signed by Columbia, but her recordings for that label were unsuccessful, as were her efforts for King beginning in 1952. Her luck changed with the emerging Atlantic label in 1953, where she cut tunes like "Tweedle Dee," "Bop-Ting-a-Ling," and "Play It Fair."

Ahmet Ertegun and Herb Abramson, who produced most of her sessions, started getting her stronger material in 1956. Rocking items like "Jim Dandy," "Jim Dandy Got Married," and "Voodoo Voodoo" established her as a major international R&B star in the late Fifties, although her sales were perpetually hampered by white acts' cover versions. (At one point, the competition was so fierce that Baker fired off a letter to her Detroit congressman. All she got back was publicity.) Her only big pop hit came in 1959 with the ballad "I Cried a Tear" (#6), which featured King Curtis on sax. The followup, "I Waited Too Long," only reached #33. Although continuing to score minor hits through the early Sixties ("Tiny Tim," "Shake a Hand," "Bumble Bee," "You're the Boss," "Saved," "See See Rider"), by the time she switched to Brunswick in 1963, her career was waning.

In 1969 a case of pneumonia she developed during a tour entertaining troops in Vietnam forced Baker to seek treatment in the Philippines. Nearly two decades passed before she journeyed back to the States from Subic Bay, where she had run a nightclub. The occasion was Atlantic Records' 40th-anniversary celebration in New York City in 1988. Shortly thereafter, she replaced Ruth Brown on Broadway in *Black and Blue,* and in 1990 she was given the Rhythm & Blues Foundation's Career Achievement Award. In 1990 she was inducted into the Rock and Roll Hall of Fame. Well past 60, Baker still commands rave reviews.

Long John Baldry

Born January 12, 1941, East Maddon, England
1966—*Looking for Long John* (United Artists)
1971—*It Ain't Easy* (Warner Bros.); *Long John's*
Blues 1972—*Everything Stops for Tea* 1974—
Heartaches (Golden Hour) (Pye) 1976—*Baldry's*
Out (EMI); *Welcome to Club Casablanca*
(Casablanca) 1977—*Good to Be Alive* 1980—
Long John Baldry 1981—*Rock with the Best*
(Capitol, Can.) 1982—*Best of Long John*
Baldry* (EMI) 1991—*It Still Ain't Easy* (Stony
Plain, Can.).

Although sustained commercial success has eluded him, blues vocalist John Baldry's influence in the Sixties on future British superstars was considerable. He played in Dixieland bands before becoming a solo performer on the English folk-club circuit. After touring Europe with Ramblin' Jack Elliott [see entry] between 1957 and 1961, he turned to the blues and R&B.

Baldry (nicknamed Long John because of his six-foot-seven frame) came to prominence in Britain's early-Sixties blues-rock scene. He played in Alexis Korner's Blues Incorporated [see entry] (which at times included Jack Bruce, Ginger Baker, Mick Jagger, and Charlie Watts) until 1962, when he toured Germany with a jazz band for a few months.

Upon his return to England, he joined the Cyril Davies R&B All-Stars [see entry], and when Davies died in January 1964 from leukemia, Baldry recruited some of the All-Stars to start his own band, the Hoochie Coochie Men, which included Rod Stewart. The following year Baldry formed Steampacket with Stewart, Brian Auger, Julie Driscoll, drummer Mickey Waller (later with Jeff Beck), and guitarist Vic Briggs (later with the Animals). In 1966 he formed Bluesology; its roster included keyboardist Reg Dwight, who would later change his name to Elton John.

Beginning in 1967 Baldry had several hit pop ballads in the U.K. ("Let the Heartaches Begin," #1, 1967, "Mexico," #15, 1968), but he turned to blues and rock in 1971 and recorded *It Ain't Easy.* Former protegés John and Stewart each produced one side of the disc, which yielded a U.S. Top 100 single, "Don't Try to Lay No Boogie-Woogie on the King of Rock 'n' Roll." After spending a couple of months in a mental institution in 1976, Baldry released an LP titled *Baldry's Out.* Through the late Seventies, Baldry toured the U.S. and Canada. He became a Canadian citizen in 1980, and resides in Vancouver. Baldry still tours on occasion, is often heard on commercial voiceovers, and has become something of a star to the kiddie set as the voice of Captain Robotnick, sworn enemy of the popular cartoon hero Sonic the Hedgehog.

Marty Balin: See the Jefferson Airplane

Hank Ballard

Born November 18, 1936, Detroit, Michigan
1992—*Naked in the Rain* (After Hours) 1993—*Sexy*
Ways: The Best of Hank Ballard and the Mid-
nighters (Rhino).

Hank Ballard earned distinction as a rock pioneer by laying sexually explicit lyrics over raw gospel-derived rhythms. With his backup group the Midnighters, he recorded several successful sides for the King label in the early Fifties. In his best year, 1954, he had three R&B Top Ten hits with the "Annie" trilogy—"Work with Me, Annie," "Annie Had a Baby," and "Annie's Aunt Fanny"— each of which sold over a million copies internationally despite being widely banned from the airwaves. They made Ballard a top draw on the R&B circuit, although he did not have another major hit until "Teardrops on My Letter" in 1958.

While recording "Teardrops," he quickly composed a B-side novelty dance tune called "The Twist." Chubby Checker's slicker version, released in 1960, became one of early rock's best-selling singles. Ballard and the Midnighters had two hits in 1960, "Finger Poppin' Time" (#7) and "Let's Go, Let's Go, Let's Go" (#6). In 1963 he embarked on a solo career. By then his fortunes had waned, and he returned to playing soul clubs. Befitting a man whose biggest successes were risqué records, Ballard tried to promote his 1974 song "Let's Go Streaking" by recording it in the nude.

Ballard, who still performs in clubs, was inducted into the Rock & Roll Hall of Fame in 1990, three months after his wife and manager, Theresa McNeil, was killed in a hit-and-run accident.

Russ Ballard: See Argent

Afrika Bambaataa

Born Kevin Donovan, April 10, 1960, Bronx, New York
1983—*Don't Stop . . . Planet Rock (The Remix EP)*
(Tommy Boy)   1988—*The Light* (EMI)   1991—
1990–2000 The Decade of Darkness*   1993—*Time
***Zone* (Planet Rock).**

Afrika Bambaataa was an important rap-music pioneer who, much like Grandmaster Flash, became a forgotten elder statesman as rap evolved. Bambaataa, who took his name (which means "affectionate leader") from a movie about Zulu warriors, quit the notorious Black Spades street gang in the mid-Seventies and formed Zulu Nation, a music-oriented "youth organization." Among the members who became minor rap luminaries were DJs Red Alert, Jazzy Jay, and Whiz Kid, as well as Afrika Islam, who went on to work with Ice-T.

Bambaataa became a popular DJ on the nascent South Bronx rap scene, where his encyclopedic knowledge of funk grooves earned him the nickname "Master of Records." He formed two rap crews, the Jazzy 5 (with MCs Ice, Freeze, Dee, and AJ Les) and SoulSonic Force (Mr. Biggs [Ellis Williams], Pow Wow [Robert Darrell Allen], and Emcee G.L.O.B.E. [John Miller]). Each made its debut 12-inch single in 1980: Jazzy 5's "Jazzy Sensation" and SoulSonic Force's "Zulu Nation Throwdown,"

both classic proto-hip-hop party anthems, with round-robin rapping backed by live bands playing slinky funk vamps.

In 1982 Bambaataa and SoulSonic Force dropped the live band to go high-tech. Producer Arthur Baker (who had worked on "Jazzy Sensation") and synthesizer player John Robie provided electronic "beat-box" rhythm and an eerie keyboard hook modeled on "Trans-Europe Express," by Kraftwerk [see entry], whose robotic trance music had long been popular with inner-city youth. The result was "Planet Rock," a pop hit (#48, 1982) that went gold and spawned an entire school of "electro-boogie" rap and dance music.

While Bambaataa would continue to exert some influence on rap music, "Planet Rock" turned out to be his only hit. Bambaataa's groundbreaking tracks that failed to chart include 1982's "Looking for the Perfect Beat" (sampled in Duice's 1993 rap-dance hit "Dazzey Duks" [#12 pop]); 1983's "Renegades of Funk" (on which G.L.O.B.E. pioneered the rapid-fire "poppin'" style of rap later popularized by Big Daddy Kane and Das EFX); 1984's "World Destruction" by Time Zone, a rap-rock fusion unit featuring Bambaataa, ex–Sex Pistol John Lydon, and bassist/producer Bill Laswell; and 1984's "Unity," which Bambaataa recorded with rap forebear James Brown. Even Bambaataa's and SoulSonic Force's appearance in the 1984 rap movie *Beat Street* brought problems: Emcee G.L.O.B.E. and Pow Wow were arrested for their roles in a 1979 Manhattan bank holdup, when a policeman watching the movie recognized Pow Wow from the bank surveillance video. G.L.O.B.E. and Pow Wow later got probation and community service sentences for convictions on conspiracy to commit bank robbery.

Bambaataa has remained active if not commercially successful. *The Light* featured guests George Clinton, Sly and Robbie, Boy George, and UB40; *Decade of Darkness* collected dance-oriented tracks produced for an Italian label. Bambaataa formed his own label to release the *Time Zone* compilation.

Bananarama/Shakespear's Sister

Formed late 1981, London, England
Sarah Dallin (b. Dec. 17, 1960, Bristol, Eng.), voc.;
Keren Woodward (b. Apr. 2, 1961, Bristol, Eng.),
voc.; Siobhan Fahey (b. Sep. 10, 1960, Ireland), voc.
1983—*Deep Sea Skiving* (London)   1984—*Bana-*
narama*   1986—*True Confessions*   1987—*Wow!
1988—(– Fahey; + Jacqui O'Sullivan) *The Greatest*
Hits Collection*   1991—*Pop Life*   1992—(– O'Sulli-
van) *Please Yourself.*
Shakespear's Sister: Fahey, voc.; Marcella Detroit
(b. Marcella Levy, June 21, ca. 1954, Detroit, Mich.),
voc., gtr.

1989—*Sacred Heart* (ffrr-PolyGram) 1992—*Hormonally Yours* (London).

Bananarama is the most successful British girl group in pop history despite the original trio's inability to play instruments and refusal to do concert tours. Musically, Bananarama (the name combines the late Sixties kids' show *The Banana Splits* and Roxy Music's "Pyjama-rama") presented fluffy pop tunes and a girly image that won fans and sold records.

Woodward and Dallin were childhood friends. Dallin met Fahey at the London College of Fashion, and the three began singing at friends' parties. Bananarama's first single was produced by ex–Sex Pistols drummer Paul Cook. The trio sang backup on Fun Boy Three's "It Ain't What You Do, It's the Way That You Do It," and the guys returned the favor on Bananarama's first U.K. hit, "He Was Really Sayin' Somethin'," which was a minor 1965 hit for Motown's Velvelettes.

Deep Sea Skiving collected Bananarama's earliest singles. *Bananarama* was produced and cowritten by Swain and Jolley (Spandau Ballet, Alison Moyet) and gave the group their first U.S. hit, "Cruel Summer" (#9, 1984). The song was big in England a year before it broke in the U.S.; the band always had greater success at home (although the British press hated them). "Robert De Niro's Waiting," Bananarama's second single, got little airplay in the States.

Bananarama switched producers to Stock/Aitken/Waterman (Kylie Minogue, Rick Astley) while recording *True Confessions* (#15, 1986), and the team (who produced two of the album's tracks) delivered the smash cover of Shocking Blue's 1970 #1 hit "Venus" (#1, 1986). S/A/W produced *Wow!,* which featured "Love in the First Degree" and "I Heard a Rumour" (#4, 1987) (used in the Fat Boys movie *Disorderlies*).

In 1987 Fahey married the Eurythmics' Dave Stewart and a few months later left Bananarama. She was replaced on *Pop Life* by Jacqui O'Sullivan, formerly of the Shilelagh Sisters. That album was produced primarily by ex–Killing Joke bassist Youth and included a cover of the Doobie Brothers' "Long Train Running." O'Sullivan left the group in mid-1991, and Bananarama continued as a duo, releasing 1992's *Please Yourself,* before being dropped from their record label the following year.

Fahey formed Shakespear's Sister with Marcella Detroit, who in the Seventies toured with Eric Clapton and cowrote "Lay Down Sally." From their first single, "You're History," Fahey was eager to leave Bananarama behind. The band's name came from a Smiths song, which was itself inspired by a Virginia Woolf essay lamenting the lack of credit given women artists. Although their records have been self-consciously artsy and strange, Shakespear's Sister had a major pop hit with a song from their second album, the ballad "Stay" (#4, 1992).

The Band

Formed 1967, Woodstock, New York
James Robbie Robertson (b. July 5, 1944, Toronto, Can.), gtr.; Richard Manuel (b. Apr. 3, 1945, Stratford, Can.; d. Mar. 4, 1986, Winter Park, Fla.), piano, voc.; Garth Hudson (b. Aug. 2, ca. 1943, London, Can.), organ, sax; Rick Danko (b. Dec. 9, 1943, Simcoe, Can.), bass, viola, voc.; Levon Helm (b. May 26, 1940, Marvell, Ark.), drums, voc., mandolin.
1968—*Music from Big Pink* (Capitol) 1969—*The Band* 1970—*Stage Fright* 1971—*Cahoots* 1972—*Rock of Ages* 1973—*Moondog Matinee* 1975—*Northern Lights—Southern Cross* 1976—*The Best of the Band* 1977—*Islands* 1978—*The Last Waltz* (Warner Bros.); *Anthology* (Capitol) 1993—*Jericho* (Pyramid) 1994—*Across the Great Divide* (Capitol) 1995—*Live at Watkins Glen.*
Robbie Robertson solo: 1987—*Robbie Robertson* (Geffen) 1991—*Storyville.*
Robbie Robertson and the Red Road Ensemble: 1994—*Music for "The Native Americans"* (Capitol).
Levon Helm solo: 1977—*Levon Helm and the RCO All-Stars* (ABC) 1978—*Levon Helm* 1980—*American Son* (MCA) 1982—*Levon Helm* (Capitol).
Rick Danko: 1977—*Rick Danko* (Arista) 1993—*Danko/Fjeld/Andersen* (Rykodisc).

With its rock-ribbed, austerely precise arrangements and a catalogue of songs that link American folklore to primal myths, the Band—four Canadians and a Southerner—made music that was both earthy and mystical, still unsurpassed in its depth and originality. The group had been playing together for most of a decade before it recorded its first album in 1968. Beginning with Levon Helm, the five members joined rockabilly singer Ronnie Hawkins' Hawks one by one, and by 1960 the future Band had all been with Hawkins on and off, an association that continued until 1963. They then began working on their own, variously as Levon and the Hawks, or the Crackers, or the Canadian Squires. Singer John Hammond Jr. (John Paul Hammond) heard them in a Canadian club in 1964 and asked them to perform and record with him in New York City, Chicago, and Texas.

Once active in Greenwich Village they attracted Bob Dylan's attention. Helm and Robbie Robertson were in the electrified backup band at Dylan's controversial Forest Hills concert of August 28, 1965. Despite a falling out between Dylan and Helm, Dylan hired the Hawks—with drummer Mickey Jones in lieu of Helm—for his 1965–66 world tour, inaugurating a longtime collaboration.

After Dylan's 1966 motorcycle accident, the group settled near the suddenly reclusive star in the Woodstock, New York, area. Helm rejoined, and while recording extensively with Dylan (the much-bootlegged

The Band: Rick Danko, Levon Helm, Richard Manuel, Garth Hudson, Robbie Robertson

sessions were released in 1975 as *The Basement Tapes*), they began working on their own material, most of it written by Robertson and Richard Manuel. Recorded in a basement studio in their house (Big Pink) in West Saugerties, the material made up the Band's debut album. With its unflashy sound and enigmatic lyrics, *Music from Big Pink* was a revolutionary album; although its long-term influence was enormous, it has yet to be certified gold.

The group moved to Hollywood, but its second album, *The Band,* was a celebration of rural life and the past. It was the group's masterpiece and commercial breakthrough, and the quintet undertook its first head-lining tour to support it. Robertson was emerging as chief songwriter as well as producer, and his impressions of the road inspired the Band's third album, *Stage Fright.* After 1971's *Cahoots* (with an appearance by Van Morrison) the Band recorded a double live LP, *Rock of Ages,* followed in 1973 by a tribute to early rock & roll (*Moondog Matinee,* named after Alan Freed's radio show).

With the exception of a joint appearance in 1969 at the Isle of Wight Festival in Britain, the Band rarely worked with Dylan in the early Seventies. But shortly after the group played at the Watkins Glen concert in July 1973 (documented on a 1995 live album), it joined Dylan in the studio for his *Planet Waves.* The next year, they toured together and did the live album *Before the Flood.* The Band's output continued to slow through the Seventies. In November 1975 the group released its first new material in four years, *Northern Lights—Southern Cross,* followed two years later by *Islands.* Robertson

produced an album for Neil Diamond, *Beautiful Noise,* in 1976. After 16 years together, the Band called it quits with a gala concert on Thanksgiving Day 1976. The Band and guests (including Dylan, Morrison, Neil Young, Muddy Waters, Joni Mitchell, and Neil Diamond) performed at San Francisco's Winterland (the site of its first concert as the Band in 1969) for *The Last Waltz,* filmed by Martin Scorsese.

After the breakup, Helm continued to record and tour, with the RCO All-Stars, an aggregation that included Dr. John, Paul Butterfield, Steve Cropper, Duck Dunn, and Booker T. Jones; the Cate Brothers; and Danko. He made his acting debut in 1980 in *Coal Miner's Daughter* and has since appeared in several other films. Robertson starred in and composed part of the score for 1980's *Carny* and wrote music for Scorsese's *The King of Comedy* before releasing his first solo album in 1987. *Robbie Robertson,* produced by Daniel Lanois, received tremendous media attention and went gold; 1991's *Storyville,* however, fared poorly. In 1994 Robertson, whose mother was of Mohawk Indian descent, composed the soundtrack to a six-hour television documentary, *The Native Americans,* which featured Native American musicians collectively dubbed the Red Road Ensemble. Danko, too, recorded on his own.

The Band regrouped in 1983 with guitarist Jimmy Weider replacing Robertson, who'd declined an invitation to join. On March 4, 1986, following an appearance at the Cheek to Cheek Lounge in Winter Park, Florida, Manuel returned to his room and hanged himself with a belt. His body contained traces of cocaine and alcohol. The three remaining originals carried on with a variety of backing musicians. In 1993 they released the Band's first album of new material in 16 years, *Jericho*, which included interpretations of Bruce Springsteen's "Atlantic City" and Bob Dylan's "Blind Willie McTell," as well as their own compositions.

In 1994 the Band was inducted into the Rock and Roll Hall of Fame. Robertson turned out for the ceremony, but Helm stayed home. As he made abundantly clear in his 1993 autobiography, *This Wheel's on Fire*, the drummer bitterly resented Robertson for allegedly having claimed sole writing credit for collaborative efforts.

The Bangles

Formed 1981, Los Angeles, California
Susanna Hoffs (b. Jan. 17, 1957, Newport Beach, Calif.), gtr., voc.; Debbi Peterson (b. Aug. 22, 1961, Los Angeles), drums, voc.; Vicki Peterson (b. Jan. 11, 1958, Los Angeles), gtr., voc.; Annette Zilinskas (b. Nov. 6, 1964, Van Nuys, Calif.), bass, voc.
1982—*Bangles* EP (Faulty Products)   1984— (– Zilinskas; + Michael Steele [b. June 2, 1954], bass, voc.) *All Over the Place* (Columbia)   1985—*Different Light*   1988—*Everything*   1990—*Greatest Hits*.
Susanna Hoffs solo: 1991—*When You're a Boy* (Columbia).

The Bangles wanted to be an all-girl Beatles from California: four pop stars who played competently, wrote good songs, and had distinct personalities. The group formed when a "band members wanted" ad in an L.A. newspaper led Hoffs to the Peterson sisters. The group first called themselves the Colours, followed by the Supersonic Bangs, which they shortened to the Bangs. When a group with prior claim to that moniker showed up, they became the Bangles.

As the Bangs, the group was heralded as part of L.A.'s "paisley underground," a constellation of folky psychedelic bands that included the Rain Parade and Dream Syndicate. After establishing a reputation through a self-released single and live shows, the band signed a management deal with I.R.S. Records head Miles Copeland. By the time their debut EP was released the group was renamed the Bangles.

In 1983 the band signed to Columbia. Bass player Zilinskas quit and joined Blood on the Saddle; she was replaced by Michael Steele, who had once sung for the Runaways. Veteran power-pop producer David Kahne produced *All Over the Place*, which featured such classic Bangles songs as "Hero Takes a Fall" and Kimberley Rew's (Soft Boys, Katrina and the Waves) "Going Down to Liverpool." The record initially sold a respectable 150,000 copies and earned critical praise.

After seeing the video for "Hero Takes a Fall," Prince became a fan of the Bangles, particularly of Hoffs. He gave them the song "Manic Monday" (#2, 1986), written under the pseudonym Christopher; the single paved the way for the breakthrough success of *Different Light* (#2, 1986). The Kahne-produced album included "Walk Like an Egyptian" (#1, 1986); Jules Shear's "If She Knew What She Wants" (#29, 1986); "Walking Down Your Street" (#11, 1987); and a cover of Alex Chilton's "September Gurls." In 1987 the Bangles' version of Paul Simon's "Hazy Shade of Winter" from the *Less Than Zero* soundtrack became their second #1.

Everything (#15, 1988), yielded the hits "In Your Room" (#5, 1988) and "Eternal Flame" (#1, 1989). The group's plan to share songwriting, vocals, and fame had been steadily eroded by the media's focus on Hoffs, especially in light of her feature role in the largely forgotten 1987 film *The Allnighter*, which her mother, Tamar Hoffs, cowrote, directed, and produced. The other Bangles resented the star treatment and the musical direction in which it pushed the band. In late 1989 the group broke up.

Hoffs' solo album (produced by Kahne) featured songs by or cowritten with such diverse figures as Diane Warren, Cyndi Lauper, and Juliana Hatfield. A version of David Bowie's "Boys Keep Swinging" (with the Who's John Entwistle on bass) gave the album its title. Vicki Peterson began collaborating with Susan Cowsill; they billed themselves as the Psycho Sisters and played clubs backed by the Continental Drifters (which the two eventually joined), and also sang backup for Giant Sand. Peterson sang and played guitar on the Continental Drifters' self-titled 1994 album, which included her composition "Mixed Messages." In 1994 she joined the Go-Go's' reunion tour, filling in for Charlotte Caffey, who was pregnant. Debbie Peterson formed the band Kindred Spirits, which released a self-titled album on I.R.S. in 1994.

Tony Banks: See Genesis

The Barbarians

Formed circa 1965, Boston, Massachusetts
Jerry Causi, bass; Jeff Morris, gtr.; Bruce Benson, gtr.; Moulty (b. Victor Moulton), drums.
N.A.—*The Barbarians* (Laurie)   1979—*The Barbarians* (Rhino)   1994—*Are You a Boy or Are You a Girl* (One Way).

A classic mid-Sixties protopunk garage band, the Barbarians boasted a drummer named Moulty who had a hook for a left hand. He sang many of the band's songs, including the autobiographical "Moulty" (#90, 1966), in which he implored, "Don't turn away" and spoke of meeting "a girl, a real girl." The group had a minor hit with "Are You a Boy or Are You a Girl" (#55, 1965), a reference to the band's prepsychedelic long hair. The Barbarians appeared in the mid-Sixties documentary *The T.A.M.I. Show.* Moulty now operates a cleaning service in Massachusetts.

Barclay James Harvest

Formed 1967, Oldham, England
Stewart "Woolly" Wolstenholme (b. Apr. 15, 1947, Oldham), kybds., voc.; Melvyn John Pritchard (b. Jan. 20, 1948, Oldham), drums; John Lees (b. Jan. 13, 1947, Oldham), gtr., voc.; Les Holroyd (b. Mar. 12, 1948, Bolton, Eng.), bass, voc.
1970—*Barclay James Harvest* (Capitol) 1971—*Once Again* (Sire) 1972—*Early Morning Onward* (EMI); *Barclay James Harvest* (Sire) 1973—*Baby James Harvest* (Capitol) 1974—*Live* (Polydor); *Everyone Is Everybody Else* 1975—*Time Honoured Ghosts* 1976—*Octoberon* (MCA) 1977—*Gone to Earth* 1978—*Live Tapes* (Polydor); *XII* 1979—*Best of, vol. 2* (Harvest) (– Wolstenholme) 1980—*Eyes of the Universe* (Polydor) 1992—*Best of Barclay James Harvest* 1993—*Caught in the Light.*

This English art-rock band has developed a loyal cult following in its homeland, though only one album, 1976's *Octoberon,* has ever charted in the U.S. With a remarkably consistent personnel record for a veteran band that's never been financially successful, BJH has carried on for more than 25 years. Like the nascent Pink Floyd, with whom it is often compared, BJH was a hard-rock group with classical overtones when it signed to EMI/Parlophone in 1968. The group turned a frequently heard criticism—"poor man's Moody Blues"—into a song title on its 1977 LP *Gone to Earth.*

Barclay James Harvest was formed by art-school classmates John Lees and Stewart "Woolly" Wolstenholme. Beginning in 1970 EMI released its albums on a subsidiary label, Harvest, which was named after the promising BJH. But the promise never panned out, leaving BJH as a minor British attraction supported by an enthusiastic but limited cult. They released a number of albums in the Eighties, but none in the U.S. Cofounder Wolstenholme left the group in 1979 and recorded a 1980 solo album, *Maestro.*

The Bar-Kays

Formed mid-Sixties, Memphis, Tennessee
Jimmy King (b. 1949; d. Dec. 10, 1967, Wis.), gtr.; Ron Caldwell (b. 1948; d. Dec. 10, 1967, Wis.), organ; Phalin Jones (b. 1949; d. Dec. 10, 1967, Wis.), sax; Carl Cunningham (b. 1949; d. Dec. 10, 1967, Wis.), drums; Ben Cauley, trumpet; James Alexander, bass.

1967—*Soul Finger* (Volt) 1969—*Gotta Groove* (Stax) 1982—*Night Cruisin'* (Mercury) 1984—*Dangerous* 1985—*Banging the Wall* 1987—*Contagious* 1989—*Bar-Kays: Animal* 1993—*Ghetto Styles* (Zoo).

The Bar-Kays were part of the Stax-Volt roster in the mid-Sixties and had one big hit, "Soul Finger" (#17), in 1967. Their career seemed finished when four members died in the icy plane crash that also killed Otis Redding in 1967. Bassist James Alexander, who'd missed the flight, and trumpeter Ben Cauley, the only passenger to survive the accident, re-formed the group in late 1968, although Cauley quit soon after. Since then Alexander and a changing roster of Bar-Kays have consistently placed singles on the R&B chart and enjoyed the occasional pop hit, such as "Shake Your Rump to the Funk" (#23, 1976). The Eighties saw five R&B Top Tens for the group: "Boogie Body Land" (#7, 1980), "Hit and Run" (#5, 1981), "Do It (Let Me See You Shake)" (#9, 1982), "Freakshow on the Dance Floor" (#2, 1984) (from the hip-hop film *Breakin'*), and "Certified True" (#9, 1987).

Still regarded as one of soul's premier backing bands, the Bar-Kays worked in the early Seventies with such artists as the Staple Singers, Albert King, Carla Thomas, Johnnie Taylor, and Isaac Hayes. They backed Hayes on his Grammy Award–winning *Shaft* soundtrack in 1971. Several excellent R&B musicians have passed through the Bar-Kays' ranks, including vocalist Vernon Burch and drummer Willie Hall, who went on to play in Hayes' band for several years and then joined the revamped Booker T. and the MG's in 1975. Since 1987 the Bar-Kays lineup has remained fairly stable, including vocalist Larry Dodson, keyboardist Winston Stewart, and saxist Harvey Henderson, with Alexander still at the helm.

Richard Barone: See the Bongos

Syd Barrett

Born Roger Keith Barrett, January 6, 1946, Cambridge, England
1970—*The Madcap Laughs* (Harvest); *Barrett* 1989—*Opel* (Capitol/EMI) 1994—*Crazy Diamond—The Complete Syd Barrett* (Harvest/Capitol); *Octopus* (Cleopatra).

British singer/songwriter/guitarist Syd Barrett was an art-school student in London when he founded and named Pink Floyd [see entry] in 1964. He wrote "See Emily Play" and "Piper at the Gates of Dawn" for the group, and his acid-inspired lyrics were the quintessence of London's 1967 Summer of Love. Barrett was dismissed from the band in April 1968 because of his drug-induced personality problems; David Gilmour re-

Syd Barrett

placed him. Barrett has subsequently spent time in a mental ward and lived as a recluse in his hometown. As of this writing, he remains in seclusion. He released two 1970 solo albums, assisted by members of Pink Floyd, who dedicated a popular 1975 song, "Shine On, You Crazy Diamond," to the group's eccentric founder. Both 1994 releases are anthologies.

Len Barry: See the Dovells

Basehead
Formed April 1990, Washington, D.C.
Michael Ivey (b. Feb. 5, 1968, Pittsburgh, Pa.), voc., gtr., kybds., bass, perc.; Brian Hendrix (b. July 29, 1968, Pittsburgh, Pa.), drums, perc.; DJ Unique (b. Paul Howard), DJ.
1991—Play with Toys (Emigre) (– Howard; + Keith Lofton [b. May 9, 1967, Washington], gtr.; + Bill Conway [b. Nov. 29, 1967, Washington], bass; + Clarence "Citizen Cope" Greenwood [b. May 20, 1965, Washington], DJ) 1992—Not in Kansas Anymore (Imago).

Featuring a scratching DJ and spoken-sung vocals by group leader Michael Ivey, Basehead defied simple cate-gorization. Ivey mumbled or sleepily crooned his wryly ironic lyrics over quirky, quietly rockish arrangements in a hip-hop–college rock hybrid critics have termed "slacker rap," while comparing Ivey to Lou Reed, Tom Waits, and Sly Stone.

A middle-class black who grew up learning guitar, Ivey formed high school bands with fellow Pittsburgh native Brian Hendrix, then complained about the lack of guitar parts in their keyboard-dominated R&B covers. While studying film at Howard University, D.C., Ivey (who made his directing debut with the video "Do You Wanna Fuck [or What]?" from *Not in Kansas Anymore*) recorded *Play with Toys* almost exclusively himself. The album signaled its offbeat genre crossing by opening with Ivey, as "Jethro and the Graham Crackers," per-forming a hillbilly version of James Brown's "Sex Ma-chine" to the sound of audience catcalls.

The tiny West Coast label Emigre released 3,000 copies of *Play with Toys* to considerable college-radio play and rave reviews. Ivey recruited friends from Howard U. for a 1991 tour with "alternative rap" acts Me Phi Me, Disposable Heroes of Hiphoprisy, and Divine Styler. The Basehead band also played on three tracks of the *Kansas* album, which backed Ivey's deadpan takes on racial and sexual politics with a somewhat harder sound.

Bash & Pop: See the Replacements

Basia
Born Basia Trzetrzelewska, September 30, 1956, Ja-worzno, Poland
1987—Time and Tide (Epic) 1989—London War-saw New York 1991—Brave New Hope EP 1994—The Sweetest Illusion.

The Polish-born Basia crossed the Iron Curtain in the Eighties to become an international pop singer and fix-ture on "jazz-lite" stations everywhere. Born in the in-dustrial city of Jaworzno, she first performed with the all-female group Alibabki in 1975, touring the Soviet bloc for two years. In 1979 she moved to Chicago to sing with a cover band in a Polish-American club. Two years later she was in London, singing for the jazz-funk group Bronze, then joined Matt Bianco, a threesome whose hit record, *Whose Side Are You On?*, featured a smooth pop blend of jazz and Latin styles.

In 1985 Basia left Matt Bianco to go solo, taking key-boardist Danny White with her as cowriter. Her first album, the platinum *Time and Tide* (#36, 1988), yielded the pop hits "Time and Tide" (#26, 1988) and "New Day for You" (#53, 1989). She continued to explore soul, samba, swing, and bossa nova on *London Warsaw New York* (#20, 1990), a platinum album that featured the single "Cruising for Bruising" (#29, 1990). *The Sweetest Illusion* (1994) included more Latin-tinged material, including the salsa-styled "An Olive Tree."

Bauhaus/Peter Murphy/ Love and Rockets

Formed 1979, Northampton, England
Peter Murphy (b. July 11, 1957, Northampton), voc.; Daniel Ash (b. July 31, 1957, Northampton), gtr., voc.; David J (b. David J. Haskins, Apr. 24, 1957, Northampton), bass, voc.; Kevin Haskins (b. July 19, 1960, Northampton), drums.
1980—*In the Flat Field* (4AD, U.K.) 1981—*Mask* (Beggars Banquet, U.K.) 1982—*The Sky's Gone Out* (A&M) 1983—*Burning from the Inside* (group disbands) 1989—*Swing the Heartache: The BBC Sessions* (Beggars Banquet).
Peter Murphy solo: 1988—*Love Hysteria* (Beggars Banquet) 1990—*Deep* 1992—*Holy Smoke* 1995—*Cascade* (Atlantic).
Tones on Tail (Formed 1982, Eng.; Ash; Kevin Haskins; Glenn Campling, bass): 1986—*'Pop'* (Beggars Banquet) 1987—*Night Music* 1990—*Tones on Tail* (Beggars Banquet).
Love and Rockets (Ash; Haskins; J): 1985—*Seventh Dream of Teenage Heaven* (Beggars Banquet, U.K.) 1986—*Express* (Beggars Banquet) 1987—*Earth-Sun-Moon* 1989—*Love and Rockets* 1994—*Hot Trip to Heaven* (American).
David J solo: 1990—*Songs from Another Season* (Beggars Banquet) 1992—*Urban Urbane* (MCA).
Daniel Ash solo: 1991—*Coming Down* (Beggars Banquet) 1992—*Foolish Thing Desire*.

Resembling a convention of the undead and playing songs distinguished by spare, atmospheric guitars, sonorous, death-rattle vocals, and deliberate tempos, Bauhaus was the progenitor of gothic rock.

In 1978 brothers David and Kevin Haskins formed the Craze with Daniel Ash, an old school friend. With the addition of vocalist Peter Murphy they became Bauhaus 1919, named after the German architectural group whose credo was "less is more." The "1919" was dropped for their 1979 debut single, "Bela Lugosi's Dead," an eight-minute epic later heard in the 1983 David Bowie film, *The Hunger.*

An appearance on BBC radio DJ John Peel's show led to a record contract. While Bauhaus became an underground success in Britain, and made the U.K. chart with "Kick in the Eye" (#59, 1981) and *Mask* (#30, 1981), 1982's *The Sky's Gone Out* was its American debut. That year the band released its biggest U.K. hit, a cover of David Bowie's "Ziggy Stardust" (#15). Bauhaus' influence was also felt in the Batcave, a popular London club

that took its musical and sartorial cues from the band. *Burning from the Inside*, more a compilation of solo songs than a band project (Murphy was ill and missed most of the sessions), foreshadowed Bauhaus' breakup later that year.

Murphy joined Japan's Mick Karn in the experimental Dali's Car; they recorded one album in 1984. In 1988 he started his solo career. Collaborating with keyboardist/producer Paul Stratham, Murphy toned down the more excessive, arty elements of Bauhaus and emphasized his Bowie-esque vocals. He had a minor hit with 1990's "Cuts You Up" (#55), from the album *Deep* (#44, 1990).

Ash, along with Bauhaus roadie Glenn Campling, originally began Tones on Tail as a side project in 1982. When Bauhaus split, Kevin Haskins signed on. After a 1984 U.S. tour, Ash and Haskins dissolved the band. David J joined the Jazz Butcher, but left after one album, *A Scandal in Bohemia* (1984). With their solo careers stalled, the members of Bauhaus planned to reunite in 1985. When Murphy demurred at the last minute, the other three decided to re-form as Love and Rockets (the name comes from the underground comic book series by Los Angelenos Gilbert and Jaime Hernandez). A more danceable version of Bauhaus' atmospherics, their initial release, 1985's *Seventh Dream of Teenage Heaven*, went unreleased in the U.S. until 1988, but their U.K. hit cover of the Temptations' "Ball of Confusion" was included in their U.S. debut, *Express* (#72, 1986); they broke into the mainstream in 1989 with *Love and Rockets* (#14) and the Top Ten single "So Alive" (#3).

In the early Nineties, Ash and J each cut a pair of solo albums. Love and Rockets came under the sway of the acid house/techno sound rampant in England and returned to the studio in 1994. This new inspiration is evident on the resultant *Hot Trip to Heaven*, especially the 14-minute ambient "Body and Soul" and "Ugly," featuring Middle Eastern–inflected vocals by Natacha Atlas of Trans-Global Underground.

Bay City Rollers

Formed 1970, Edinburgh, Scotland
Alan Longmuir (b. June 20, 1953, Edinburgh), bass; Eric Faulkner (b. Oct. 21, 1955, Edinburgh), gtr.; Derek Longmuir (b. Mar. 19, 1955, Edinburgh), drums; Leslie McKeown (b. Nov. 12, 1955, Edinburgh), voc.; Stuart "Woody" Wood (b. Feb. 25, 1957, Edinburgh), gtr.
1975—*Bay City Rollers* (Arista) 1976—*Rock 'n' Roll Love Letter; Dedication* (– A. Longmuir; + Ian Mitchell [b. Aug. 22, 1958], gtr.; Wood switches to bass; – Mitchell; + Pat McGlynn [b. Mar. 31, 1958, Edinburgh], gtr.) 1977—*Greatest Hits* (– McGlynn) 1978—*Strangers in the Wild* (– McKeown; + Duncan

Faure, voc.) 1993—(Lineup for 1993 U.S. tour: A. Longmuir; Faulkner; Wood; + Kass, voc., drums).

The Bay City Rollers were touted as the "new Beatles." Actually, the Rollers were cute, young musicians who were vigorously promoted to a market of teenagers. Probably the most successful act ever to emerge from Scotland, they scored their first English hit in 1971. Through the next few years, under the guidance of mentor/manager Tam Paton (who named the group by arbitrarily sticking a pin in a U.S. map and hitting Bay City, Michigan), they slowly expanded their predominantly female audience. Clad in tartan uniforms highlighted by knicker-length pants, they eventually inspired a genuine outbreak of teenage frenzy reminiscent of Beatlemania in the early Sixties. Rollermania spread to the U.S. briefly in early 1976 with the group's first Stateside concerts and a late 1975 #1 single, "Saturday Night." Their closeknit, wholesome image was tarnished somewhat in the late Seventies with the disclosures that they had all regularly taken Valium to help them cope with the rigors of superstardom and life on the road and that Faulkner and Mitchell had been treated for overdoses.

By the early Eighties they were a quartet playing bars in the U.S., still wearing their tartan plaid. As with so many revived groups, there are several acts touring under the Rollers name, among them ex-vocalist Les McKeown's Bay City Rollers; for a while Faulkner toured with an outfit called the New Rollers.

The Beach Boys
Formed 1961, Hawthorne, California
Brian Wilson (b. June 20, 1942, Hawthorne), voc., bass, piano; Dennis Wilson (b. Dec. 4, 1944, Hawthorne; d. Dec. 28, 1983, Marina del Rey, Calif.), voc., drums; Carl Wilson (b. Dec. 21, 1946, Hawthorne), voc., gtr.; Mike Love (b. Mar. 15, 1941, Los Angeles, Calif.), voc., misc., perc.; Al (Alan) Jardine (b. Sep. 3, 1942, Lima, Ohio), voc., gtr.
1962—(– Jardine; + David Marks [b. Newcastle, Pa.], gtr.) Surfin' Safari (Capitol) 1963—Surfin' USA (– Marks; + Jardine); Surfer Girl; Shut Down; Little Deuce Coupe 1964—Shut Down, vol. 2; All Summer Long; The Beach Boys' Christmas Album; Beach Boys Concert 1965—(+ Bruce Johnston [b. June 24, 1944, Chicago, Ill.], gtr., voc.) The Beach Boys Today; Summer Days (and Summer Nights!!); The Beach Boys' Party! 1966—Pet Sounds; Best of the Beach Boys, vol. 1 1967—Best of the Beach Boys, vol. 2; Smiley Smile; The Beach Boys Deluxe Set; Wild Honey 1968—Friends; Best of the Beach Boys, vol. 3; Stack o' Tracks 1969—20/20; Close Up 1970—Sunflower (Brother) 1971—Surf's Up; (+ Blondie Chaplin [b. S.A.], gtr., voc.) 1972— (– Johnston; + Ricky Fataar [b. S.A.], drums., voc.)

Carl and the Passions/So Tough; Holland 1973—The Beach Boys in Concert 1974—(– Fataar; – Chaplin) Endless Summer (Capitol) 1975—Spirit of America; Good Vibrations: Best of the Beach Boys 1976—15 Big Ones; Beach Boys '69 (The Beach Boys Live in London) (Capitol) 1977—The Beach Boys Love You (Brother) 1978—M.I.U. Album (+ Johnston) 1979—L.A. (Light Album) (Caribou) 1980—Keepin' the Summer Alive 1981—Ten Years of Harmony (– C. Wilson) 1982— (+ C. Wilson) Sunshine Dream (Capitol) (– B. Wilson) 1983—(– D. Wilson) 1985—(+ B. Wilson) The Beach Boys '85 (Caribou) 1986—Made in U.S.A. (Capitol) 1988—(– B. Wilson) 1989—Still Cruisin' (Capitol) 1992—Summer in Paradise (Brother) 1993—Good Vibrations: Thirty Years of the Beach Boys (Capitol) 1995—The "Smile" Era.
Mike Love solo: 1981—Looking Back with Love (Boardwalk).
Brian Wilson solo: 1988—Brian Wilson (Sire).
Carl Wilson solo: 1981—Carl Wilson (Caribou) 1983—What You Do to Me.
Dennis Wilson solo: 1977—Pacific Ocean Blue (Caribou).

In their early-Sixties hits the Beach Boys virtually invented California rock. Brian Wilson's songs celebrated an idealized California teenhood—surfing, driving, dating—and his productions were a glossy, perfectionistic,

The Beach Boys: Al Jardine, Dennis Wilson, Brian Wilson, Carl Wilson, Mike Love

ultra-smooth blend of guitars and vocal harmonies, with their experiments concealed. While the Beach Boys attempted more grown-up topics and more obvious progressivism in the late Sixties, they survived into the Nineties as America's premier nostalgia act. They have sold well over 65 million records worldwide.

The three Wilson brothers were encouraged by their parents, Murry and Audree, to try music and sports. Brian was a varsity baseball player at suburban Hawthorne High when he began to work seriously on music. His first band included brothers Dennis and Carl (who got expelled from Hawthorne High for going to the bathroom without permission), cousin Mike Love, and friend Al Jardine. As the Pendletones, Kenny and the Cadets (Brian was "Kenny"), or Carl and the Passions, the group played local gigs. On Dennis' suggestion, Love and Brian wrote "Surfin'," which became a regional hit on the soon defunct Candix label in December 1961 while the group was calling itself the Beach Boys. Like most of their early songs, "Surfin'" used Chuck Berry guitar licks with vocal harmonies (arranged by Brian) recalling Fifties pop groups like the Four Freshmen.

Murry Wilson, who was later revealed to have been psychologically and physically abusive to his sons, managed their band and got them a contract with Capitol. The hits began: "Surfin' Safari" (#14, 1962); "Surfin' U.S.A." (#3, 1963), a note-for-note copy of Berry's "Sweet Little Sixteen" with new lyrics; and "Surfer Girl" (#7, 1963), all of which launched and capitalized on the "surf music" fad, although only Dennis surfed regularly. "Surfer Girl" marked Brian's emergence as a producer, with its complex vocal harmonies and sophisticated pop chords.

The next two years established the Beach Boys' legacy: "I Get Around" (#1, 1964); "Fun, Fun, Fun" (#5, 1964), written by Brian and Love in a taxi to the Salt Lake City airport; "Help Me, Rhonda" (#1, 1965); "California Girls" (#3, 1965); and such ballads as "In My Room" (#23, 1963), and "Don't Worry, Baby" (#24, 1964). Early in 1965 Brian Wilson suffered a nervous breakdown and decided to quit touring. *Pet Sounds* was released in March 1966. It included "Wouldn't It Be Nice" and "God Only Knows," but sold comparatively poorly; it ushered in the era of studio experimentation, predating the Beatles' *Sgt. Pepper's Lonely Hearts Club Band*. The highlight of the Beach Boys' borderline psychedelic period was "Good Vibrations" (#1, 1966), Wilson's production masterpiece. It took six months and cost $16,000 to make, with several distinct sections and such exotic instruments as Jew's harp, sleighbells, harpsichord, and theremin.

Brian's ambitions, neuroses, and drug intake were increasing. He and Van Dyke Parks began collaborating on *Smile* in late 1966, but after a mysterious fire at the studio where they were working, Wilson reportedly destroyed most of the tapes in a fit of paranoia. Several *Smile* songs have surfaced since; the Wilson–Parks "He-roes and Villains" (#12, 1967) appeared on *Smiley Smile*, and the title cut of 1971's *Surf's Up* was also a *Smile* composition. The *Smile* debacle, and *Smiley Smile*, marked the end of Brian's reign as the Beach Boys' sole producer.

On *Wild Honey, Sunflower,* and *Holland,* other group members shared writing and production, along with Bruce Johnston, who had joined the touring Beach Boys after Brian retired from the road in late 1964. (Johnston replaced Glen Campbell after a brief stint.) Johnston has been associated on and off with the Beach Boys, primarily as producer, ever since. The Beach Boys' late-Sixties touring band also included Daryl Dragon (later the Captain of the Captain and Tennille) on keyboards, Blondie Chaplin (later with Rick Danko and others) on guitar, bass, and vocals, and Ricky Fataar (later of Joe Walsh's band) on drums (the latter two were members in the early Seventies). In 1968 the Beach Boys became the first major American rock band to play behind the Iron Curtain when they performed in Czechoslovakia.

The Beach Boys got a custom label, Brother Records, with Reprise: Their first album under the deal, *Sunflower,* inaugurated a five-year hiatus for Brian, although he tried one live show in early 1970 at the Whisky-a-Go-Go in Los Angeles. While the band continued to release new material, the bulk of its live repertoire from the early Seventies onward has been its mid-Sixties hits, which went platinum in the repackages *Endless Summer* and *Spirit of America. Holland,* recorded during a six-month stay in Amsterdam, returned the Beach Boys to the charts with "Sail On Sailor" (#79, 1973).

Meanwhile, efforts continued to coax Brian out of his Bel Air mansion, which included a sandbox as well as a recording studio. In the late Sixties he had briefly run a West Hollywood health food store, the Radiant Radish, and in 1972 he produced an album by his wife, Marilyn, and her sister Diane Rovell, as Spring (later American Spring). In 1976, after a much-publicized rehabilitation, Brian rejoined the band for *15 Big Ones,* which included oldie remakes (Chuck Berry's "Rock and Roll Music," which went to #5) and Brian Wilson originals such as "It's O.K." (#29).

In 1977 open personality clashes (primarily between Dennis Wilson and Mike Love) jeopardized the band's future as it switched labels; eventually Love's brothers Stan and Steve were removed from Beach Boys management. Steve Love was later sentenced to five years of probation for embezzling nearly $1 million from the group. For the Beach Boys' first Caribou album, *L.A. (Light Album),* Johnston was back as coproducer; in the mid-Seventies he had left the band to write songs (including Barry Manilow's hit "I Write the Songs") and make a solo album, *Going Public* (1977). Early in 1982 the Beach Boys were back in the Top Twenty with a remake of the Del-Vikings' "Come Go with Me."

In Brian's absence the other Beach Boys gained some prominence. Dennis Wilson's writing and singing surfaced on *20/20* in 1969, while he was friendly with Charles Manson. In 1971 Dennis appeared in *Two-Lane Blacktop* with James Taylor, and in 1977 he released a solo album, *Pacific Ocean Blue*. By 1979 he was romantically involved with Fleetwood Mac's Christine McVie. Carl Wilson has had a songwriting credit on nearly every Beach Boys album since 1967 and did a solo tour in support of 1981's *Carl Wilson*. Mike Love was featured on Celebration's "Almost Summer" (#28, 1978). Al Jardine, who along with Love has practiced transcendental meditation since 1967, has supplied several Beach Boys songs, including "Lady Lynda," a tribute to his wife.

The Eighties proved a tumultuous decade for the group. Carl Wilson quit in 1981 to concentrate on his solo career. He, more than the others, seemed to resist the band's increasingly nostalgic appeal. But since his return the following year, the Beach Boys have been predominantly an oldies-but-goodies act, albeit an extraordinarily successful one. In 1983 they unwittingly became the center of controversy when Secretary of the Interior James Watt banned them from performing a Fourth of July concert at the Washington Monument. Public opinion was solidly against Watt, who later resigned, and the group was personally invited to play the Washington Monument the next summer by First Lady Nancy Reagan. Nineteen-eighty-three marked Brian's return to the stage with the group, but also the death of Dennis. On December 28 the hard-living drummer drowned while swimming off his boat in Marina Del Rey, California. With the help of President Ronald Reagan, special permission was granted so that Dennis' body could be buried at sea.

Brian has since come and gone from the group. The Beach Boys enjoyed their fourth #1 hit, "Kokomo" (1988), from the film *Cocktail*, without him. Brian's long-awaited first solo album came out that year. Coproduced by his longtime therapist, Dr. Eugene Landy (who later surrendered his license to practice therapy after an investigation by the California State Board of Medical Quality for alleged improprieties), *Brian Wilson* elicited glowing reviews but sold poorly. As of 1993 Brian was a touring Beach Boy again. Later Mike Love sued Brian, his cowriter Todd Gold, and Landy, claiming he had been defamed in Wilson's autobiography, *Wouldn't It Be Nice?: My Own Story*. The case was settled out of court in early 1994. Later, in 1995, Love prevailed in a royalty dispute with Brian Wilson. A jury found that Brian Wilson had failed to honor a 1969 agreement under which Love was to have received 30 percent of the $10 million Wilson received from the sale of the group's song catalog.

In 1994 Brian Wilson and his estranged daughter Carnie reconciled their differences and contributed "Fantasy Is Reality/Bells of Madness" to Rob Wasser-man's *Trios* LP. The Beach Boys were inducted into the Rock and Roll Hall of Fame in 1988.

The Beastie Boys

Formed 1981, New York City, New York
MCA (b. Adam Yauch, Aug. 5, 1965, New York City), voc., bass; Mike D (b. Michael Diamond, Nov. 20, 1966, New York City), voc., drums; John Berry, gtr.; Kate Schellenbach (b. Jan. 5, 1966, New York City), drums.
1982—*Polly Wog Stew* EP (Rat Cage) (– Berry; – Schellenbach; + King Ad-Rock [b. Adam Horovitz, Oct. 31, 1967, New York City], voc., gtr.) 1984—*Rock Hard* EP (Def Jam) 1986—*Licensed to Ill* (Def Jam–Columbia) 1989—*Paul's Boutique* (Capitol) 1992—*Check Your Head* 1994—*Some Old Bullshit* EP; *Ill Communication*.
Kate Schellenbach with Luscious Jackson: 1994—*Natural Ingredients* (Capitol).

The Beastie Boys were the first white group to offer a successful sendup of rap. After emerging from New York's hardcore punk underground of the early Eighties, the group crossed over into the mainstream with its first full-length album, *Licensed to Ill* (#1, 1986). Featuring "(You Gotta) Fight for Your Right (to Party)" (#7), the album sold 720,000 copies in six weeks, becoming Columbia's fastest-selling debut ever. By the late Eighties, the Beastie Boys' sound had begun to mature, expanding into spaced-out funk and psychedelia, yet retaining its adolescent charm and hit-making sensibility.

At 14, Adam Horovitz, son of playwright Israel

The Beastie Boys: Mike D, Ad-Rock, MCA

Horovitz, joined the hardcore band the Young and the Useless. His friends Adam Yauch and Mike Diamond, children of wealthy New York families, had formed the four-piece hardcore band the Beastie Boys along with Kate Schellenbach, later of the group Luscious Jackson, and John Berry, later of Thwig. By 1982 the Beasties had released a seven-inch EP, *Polly Wog Stew,* on the independent label Rat Cage. Horovitz joined shortly thereafter.

The Beasties' first attempt at rap came with the 1983 12-inch spoof, "Cookie Puss," based on a crank call they made to the Carvel ice cream company. It wasn't until the trio teamed up with friend Rick Rubin—who would start the Def Jam label in his college dorm room the next year—that the Beasties began taking rap seriously. The marriage was perfect, producer Rubin working into the group's bratty raps samples with appropriately white, upper-middle-class references: Led Zeppelin, heavy metal guitar, and the theme to TV's *Mr. Ed.*

With thumbs-up from Rubin's then-partner, Russell Simmons, head of Rush Productions and manager of Run-D.M.C., the Beasties were signed to Def Jam in 1985. That same year they appeared in one of rap's first movies, *Krush Groove,* with the single "She's on It." They also opened for Madonna's Virgin Tour, during which they shouted obscenities to the audiences and got booed in return. In 1986 the trio toured with Run-D.M.C.'s violence-plagued Raisin' Hell Tour.

Nineteen-eighty-seven was a watershed year for the Beasties. The success of "Fight for Your Right" led to the trio headlining their own tour, which was plagued by lawsuits, arrests, blame for violence and vandalism, and accusations of sexism and obscenity. In 1988 they appeared in Run-D.M.C.'s movie, *Tougher Than Leather.*

Partially due to a bitter legal dispute with Rubin, three years elapsed before the release of their second album, *Paul's Boutique* (#14, 1989), on Capitol. The band made an artistic leap on the record, turning their obnoxious, white, bourgeois take on rap into a funky, album-long sound collage. The record produced the Top Forty song "Hey Ladies" (#36).

It would be another three years until their third LP, *Check Your Head* (#10, 1992), an eclectic album on which the Beastie Boys picked up their instruments again, was released on their own Capitol-distributed Grand Royal label. The record broke the Top Ten in a week, even though it jumps stylistically from funk to rap to hardcore. In 1994 the Beasties released a compilation of their early hardcore singles and EPs as *Some Old Bullshit,* followed by a new album, *Ill Communication* (#1, 1994), which continued in the eclectic (and successful) vein of *Check Your Head* and debuted at the top of the albums chart. That summer, the Beastie Boys joined Smashing Pumpkins, the Breeders, George Clinton, and other big names for Lollapalooza '94 (Luscious Jackson played on the second stage).

The Beat/The Nerves

The Beat, formed 1979, Los Angeles, California
Paul Collins (b. New York City, N.Y.), gtr., voc.; Steve Huff, bass; Mike Ruiz, drums; Larry Whitman, gtr. 1979—*The Beat* (Columbia)   1982—*The Kids Are the Same*   1983—(– Whitman; – Ruiz; + Jay Dee Daugherty, drums; + Jimmy Ripp, gtr.) *To Beat or Not To Beat* EP (Passport).
The Nerves, formed 1976, San Francisco, California: Collins, drums; Peter Case (b. Apr. 5, 1954, Buffalo, N.Y.), bass; Jack Lee, gtr., voc. 1976—*Nerves* EP (Nerves).

The power pop Paul Collins produced with the Nerves and his own band, the Beat, has been compared to the music of the Hollies and the Byrds for its soaring harmonies and spare, gritty guitars.

The Nerves were part of the early San Francisco new-wave scene; they are best known for the original version of "Hangin' on the Telephone," covered by Blondie in 1978. They broke up in 1978; bassist Peter Case [see entry] went on to form the Plimsouls, songwriter Jack Lee attempted a solo career, and Collins moved to Los Angeles. There he met bassist Steve Huff through a classified ad; the two began to write songs and record them at Huff's home studio. The resulting tape attracted drummer Mike Ruiz, who brought in Larry Whitman.

In 1979 the new band opened for Eddie Money at Bill Graham's Kabuki Theater in San Francisco. Graham became their manager and secured a contract with Columbia later that year. While the Beat's energetic, concise songs were popular on college radio, they never had a national hit. Columbia dropped them in 1982. The next year, Collins returned with a new Beat, backed by former members of the Patti Smith Group and Tom Verlaine's solo band. In the early Nineties, Collins, now living in New York, began recording and touring with his Paul Collins Band.

The Beat (English): See the English Beat; Fine Young Cannibals

The Beatles

Formed 1959, Liverpool, England
John Lennon (b. John Winston Lennon, Oct. 9, 1940, Liverpool; d. Dec. 8, 1980, New York City, N.Y.), gtr., voc., harmonica, kybds.; Paul McCartney (b. James Paul McCartney, June 18, 1942, Liverpool), bass, voc., gtr., kybds.; George Harrison (b. Feb. 25, 1943, Liverpool), gtr., voc., sitar; Stu Sutcliffe (b. Stuart Fergusson Victor Sutcliffe, June 23, 1940, Edinburgh, Scot.; d. Apr. 10, 1962, Hamburg, Ger.), bass; Pete Best (b. 1941, Eng.), drums.

*1962—(– Best; + Ringo Starr [b. Richard Starkey Jr., July 7, 1940, Liverpool], drums, perc. voc., misc.) 1963—*Please Please Me* (Parlophone, U.K.); *With the Beatles*; *Introducing . . . The Beatles* (Vee-Jay) 1964—*Meet the Beatles* (Capitol); *The Beatles' Second Album*; *A Hard Day's Night* (United Artists); *Something New* (Capitol); *The Beatles' Story*; *Beatles '65* 1965—*The Early Beatles*; *Beatles VI*; *Help!*; *Rubber Soul* 1966—*Yesterday . . . and Today*; *Revolver* 1967—*Sgt. Pepper's Lonely Hearts Club Band*; *Magical Mystery Tour* 1968—*The Beatles* (Apple) 1969—*Yellow Submarine* (Capitol); *Abbey Road* 1970—*Hey Jude*; *Let It Be* (Apple) 1973—*The Beatles 1962–1966* (Capitol); *The Beatles 1967–1970* 1976—*Rock 'N' Roll Music* 1977—*Love Songs*; *Live at the Hollywood Bowl*; *Live at the Star Club in Hamburg, Germany, 1962* (Atlantic) 1980—*Rarities* (Capitol) 1982—*Reel Music*; *20 Greatest Hits* 1988—*Past Masters, vol. 1*; *Past Masters, vol. 2* 1994—*Live at the BBC* (EMI).

The impact of the Beatles—not only on rock & roll but on all of Western culture—is simply incalculable. As musicians they proved that rock & roll could embrace a limitless variety of harmonies, structures, and sounds; virtually every rock experiment has some precedent on Beatles records. As a unit they were a musically synergistic combination: Paul McCartney's melodic bass lines, Ringo Starr's slaphappy no-rolls drumming, George Harrison's rockabilly-style guitar leads, John Lennon's assertive rhythm guitar—and their four fervent voices. One of the first rock groups to write most of its material, they inaugurated the era of self-contained bands and forever centralized pop. And as personalities, they defined and incarnated Sixties style: smart, idealistic, playful, irreverent, eclectic. Their music, from the not-so-simple love songs they started with to their later perfectionistic studio extravaganzas, set new standards for both commercial and artistic success in pop. Although many of their sales and attendance records have since been surpassed, no group has so radically transformed the sound and meaning of rock & roll.

* Discography reflects original U.S. album releases.

The Beatles: (top) Paul McCartney, Ringo Starr, (bottom) George Harrison, John Lennon

Lennon was performing with his amateur skiffle group the Quarrymen at a church picnic on July 6, 1957, in the Liverpool suburb of Woolton when he met McCartney, whom he later invited to join his group; soon they were writing songs together, such as "The One After 909." By the year's end McCartney had convinced Lennon to let Harrison join their group, the name of which was changed to Johnny and the Moondogs in 1958. In 1960 an art-school friend of Lennon's, Stu Sutcliffe, became their bassist. Sutcliffe couldn't play a note but had recently sold one of his paintings for a considerable sum, which the group, now rechristened the Silver Beetles (from which "Silver" was dropped a few months later, and "Beetles" amended to "Beatles"), used to upgrade its equipment. Tommy Moore was their drummer until Pete Best replaced him in August 1960.

Once Best had joined, the band made its first of four trips to Hamburg, Germany. In December Harrison was deported back to England for being underage and lacking a work permit, but by then their 30-set weeks on the stages of Hamburg beerhouses had honed and strengthened their repertoire (mostly Chuck Berry, Little Richard, Carl Perkins, and Buddy Holly covers), and on February 21, 1961, they debuted at the Cavern club on Mathew Street in Liverpool, beginning a string of nearly 300 performances there over the next couple of years.

In April 1961 they again went to Hamburg, where Sutcliffe (the first of the Beatles to wear his hair in the long, shaggy style that came to be known as the Beatle haircut) left the group to become a painter, while McCartney switched from rhythm guitar to bass. The Beatles returned to Liverpool as a quartet in July. Sutcliffe died from a brain hemorrhage in Hamburg less than a year later.

The Beatles had been playing regularly to packed houses at the Cavern when they were spotted on November 9 by Brian Epstein (b. Sep. 19, 1934, Liverpool). After being discharged from the British Army on medical grounds, Epstein had attended the Royal Academy of

Dramatic Art in London for a year before returning to Liverpool to manage his father's record store.

The request he received for a German import single entitled "My Bonnie" (which the Beatles had recorded a few months earlier in Hamburg, backing singer Tony Sheridan and billed as the Beat Boys) convinced him to check out the group. Epstein was surprised to discover not only that the Beatles weren't German but that they were one of the most popular local bands in Liverpool. Within two months he became their manager. Epstein cleaned up their act, eventually replacing black leather jackets, tight jeans, and pompadours with collarless gray Pierre Cardin suits and mildly androgynous haircuts.

Epstein tried landing the Beatles a record contract, but nearly every label in Europe rejected the group. In May 1962, however, producer George Martin (b. Jan. 3, 1926, North London, Eng.) grew interested in the quartet and signed it to EMI's Parlophone subsidiary. Pete Best, then considered the group's undisputed sex symbol, was asked to leave the group on August 16, 1962, and Ringo Starr, drummer with a popular Liverpool group, Rory Storme and the Hurricanes, was added, just in time for the group's first recording session. On September 11 the Beatles cut two originals, "Love Me Do" b/w "P.S. I Love You," which became their first U.K. Top Twenty hit in October. In early 1963 "Please Please Me" went to #2, and they recorded an album of the same name in one 10-hour session on February 11, 1963. With the success of their third English single, "From Me to You" (#1), the British record industry coined the term "Merseybeat" for groups like Gerry and the Pacemakers, Billy J. Kramer and the Dakotas, and the Searchers, who also hailed from Liverpool on the Mersey River. By midyear the Beatles were given billing over Roy Orbison on a national tour, and the hysterical outbreaks of "Beatlemania" had begun. Following their first tour of Europe in October, they moved to London with Epstein. Constantly mobbed by screaming fans, the Beatles required police protection almost any time they were seen in public. Late in the year "She Loves You" became the biggest-selling single in British history. In November 1963 the group performed before the Queen Mother at the Royal Command Variety Performance.

EMI's American label, Capitol, had not released the group's 1963 records (which Martin licensed to independents like Vee-Jay and Swan with little success) but was finally persuaded to release its fourth single, "I Want to Hold Your Hand" and *Meet the Beatles* in January 1964 and to invest $50,000 in promotion for the then unknown British act. The album and the single became the Beatles first U.S. chart-toppers. On February 7 screaming mobs met them at New York's Kennedy Airport, and more than 70 million people watched each of their appearances on *The Ed Sullivan Show* on February 9 and 16. In April 1964 "Can't Buy Me Love" became the first record to top American and British charts simultaneously, and that same month the Beatles held the top five positions on *Billboard*'s singles chart ("Can't Buy Me Love," "Twist and Shout," "She Loves You," "I Want to Hold Your Hand," "Please Please Me").

Their first movie, *A Hard Day's Night* (directed by Richard Lester), opened in America in August; it grossed $1.3 million in its first week. The band was aggressively merchandised—Beatle wigs, Beatle clothes, Beatle dolls, junk food, lunch pails, a cartoon series—from which, because of Epstein's ineptitude, it made surprisingly little. The Beatles also opened the American market to such British Invasion groups as the Dave Clark Five, the Rolling Stones, and the Kinks.

By 1965 Lennon and McCartney rarely wrote songs together, although by contractual and personal agreement songs by either of them were credited to both. The Beatles toured Europe, North America, the Far East, and Australia that year. Their second movie, *Help!* (again directed by Lester), was filmed in England, Austria, and the Bahamas in the spring and opened in the U.S. in August. On August 15 they performed to 55,600 fans at New York's Shea Stadium, setting a record for largest concert audience. McCartney's "Yesterday" (#1, 1965) would become one of the most often covered songs ever written. In June the Queen had announced that the Beatles would be awarded the MBE (Member of the Order of the British Empire). The announcement sparked some controversy—some MBE holders returned their medals—but on October 26, 1965, the ceremony took place at Buckingham Palace. (Lennon returned his medal in 1969.)

With 1965's *Rubber Soul*, the Beatles' ambitions began to extend beyond love songs and pop formulas. Their success led adults to consider them, along with Bob Dylan, spokesmen for youth culture; and their lyrics grew more poetic and somewhat more political. In summer 1966 controversy erupted when a remark Lennon had made to a British newspaper reporter months before was widely reported in the U.S. Lennon said, "Christianity will go. It will vanish and shrink. I needn't argue about that, I'm right and will be proved right. We're more popular than Jesus Christ right now." The remark incited denunciations and Beatles record bonfires. Lennon later apologized.

The Beatles gave up touring after an August 29, 1966, concert at San Francisco's Candlestick Park and made the rest of their music in the studio, where they had begun to experiment with exotic instrumentation ("Norwegian Wood," 1965, had featured sitar) and tape abstractions such as the reversed vocal tracks on "Rain." "Strawberry Fields Forever," part of a double-sided single released in February 1967 to fill the unusually long gap between albums, featured an astonishing display of electronically altered sounds and hinted at what was to come. With "Taxman" and "Love You To" on *Revolver,* Harrison began to emerge as a songwriter.

It took four months and $75,000 to record *Sgt. Pepper's Lonely Hearts Club Band* using a then-state-of-the-art four-track tape recorder and building each cut layer by layer. Released in June 1967, it was hailed as serious art for its "concept" and its range of styles and sounds, a lexicon of pop and electronic noises; such songs as "Lucy in the Sky with Diamonds" and "A Day in the Life" were carefully examined for hidden meanings. The album spent 15 weeks at #1 (longer than any of their others) and has sold over eight million copies. On June 25, 1967, the Beatles recorded their new single, "All You Need Is Love," before an international television audience of 400 million, as part of a broadcast called *Our World.*

On August 27, 1967—while the four were in Wales beginning their six-month involvement with transcendental meditation and the Maharishi Mahesh Yogi (which took them to India for two months in early 1968)—Epstein died alone in his London flat from an overdose of sleeping pills, later ruled accidental. Shaken by Epstein's death, the Beatles retrenched under McCartney's leadership in the fall and filmed *Magical Mystery Tour,* which was aired by BBC-TV on December 26, 1967, and later released in the U.S. as a feature film. Although the telefilm was panned by British critics, fans, and Queen Elizabeth herself, the soundtrack album contained their most cryptic work yet in "I Am the Walrus," a Lennon composition.

As the Beatles' late-1967 single "Hello Goodbye" went to #1 in both the U.S. and Britain, the group launched the Apple clothes boutique in London. McCartney called the retail effort "Western communism," but the boutique closed in July 1968. Like their next effort, Apple Corps Ltd. (formed in January 1968 and including Apple Records, which signed James Taylor, Mary Hopkin, and Badfinger), it was plagued by mismanagement. In July the group faced its last hysterical crowds at the premiere of *Yellow Submarine,* an animated film by German poster artist Heinz Edelmann featuring four new Beatles songs.

In August they released McCartney's "Hey Jude" (#1), backed by Lennon's "Revolution" (#12), which sold over six million copies before the end of 1968—their most popular single. Meanwhile, the group had been working on the double album *The Beatles* (frequently called the White Album), which showed their divergent directions. The rifts were artistic—Lennon moving toward brutal confessionals, McCartney leaning toward pop melodies, Harrison immersed in Eastern spirituality—and personal, as Lennon drew closer to his wife-to-be, Yoko Ono. Lennon and Ono's *Two Virgins* (with its full frontal and back nude cover photos) was released the same month as *The Beatles* and stirred so much outrage

that the LP had to be sold wrapped in brown paper bags. (*The Beatles* went to #1, *Two Virgins* peaked at #124.)

The Beatles attempted to smooth over their differences in early 1969 at filmed recording sessions. When the project fell apart hundreds of hours of studio time later, no one could face editing the tapes (a project that eventually fell to Phil Spector), and "Get Back" (#1, 1969) was the only immediate release. Released in spring 1970, *Let It Be* is essentially a documentary of their breakup, including an impromptu January 30, 1969, rooftop concert at Apple Corps headquarters, their last public performance.

By spring 1969 Apple was losing thousands of pounds each week. Over McCartney's objections, the other three brought in manager Allen Klein to straighten things out; one of his first actions was to package nonalbum singles as *Hey Jude.* With money matters temporarily out of mind, the four joined forces in July and August 1969 to record *Abbey Road,* featuring an extended suite as well as more hits, including Harrison's much-covered "Something" (#3, 1969). While its release that fall spurred a "Paul Is Dead" rumor based on clues supposedly left throughout their work, *Abbey Road* became the Beatles' best-selling album, at nine million copies. Meanwhile, internal bickering persisted. In September Lennon told the others, "I'm leaving the group. I've had enough. I want a divorce." But he was persuaded to keep quiet while their business affairs were untangled. On April 10, 1970, McCartney released his first solo album and publicly announced the end of the Beatles. At the same time, *Let It Be* finally surfaced, becoming the group's 14th #1 album (a postbreakup compilation would become their 15th in 1973) and yielding the Beatles' 18th and 19th chart-topping singles, "Let It Be" and "The Long and Winding Road."

Throughout the Seventies, as repackages of Beatles music continued to sell, the four were hounded by bids and pleas for a reunion. Lennon's murder by a mentally disturbed fan on December 8, 1980, ended those speculations.

In 1988 the Beatles were inducted into the Rock and Roll Hall of Fame. McCartney, citing business conflicts with the two other surviving members, did not attend. Relations between him and Harrison, in particular, had been strained for some time. But in January 1994 *Goldmine* magazine reported that McCartney, Harrison, and Starr had begun recording music for a long-rumored Beatles documentary the previous August, with more secret sessions scheduled. George Martin was said to be the producer. Later that year *Live at the BBC* was released, featuring 56 songs the Beatles performed on British radio between 1962 and 1965. It debuted at #1 in the U.K.; in the U.S., it debuted and peaked at #3. In March 1995 McCartney confirmed that he, Harrison, and Starr were recording new songs. When released, they will be the first new Beatles songs since 1969.

[See also: George Harrison; John Lennon and Yoko Ono; Julian Lennon; Paul McCartney; Ringo Starr.]

Beats International: See Housemartins

The Beau Brummels

Formed 1964, San Francisco, California
Sal Valentino (b. Sal Spampinato, Sep. 8, 1942, San Francisco), voc.; Ron Elliott (b. Oct. 21, 1943, Healdsburg, Calif.), gtr., voc.; Declan Mulligan (b. County Tipperary, Ire.), bass; John Petersen (b. Jan. 8, 1942, Rudyard, Mich.), drums; Ron Meagher (b. Oct. 2, 1941, Oakland, Calif.), gtr.
1965—(– Mulligan; Meagher switches to bass) *Introducing the Beau Brummels* (Autumn) (– Petersen)   1966—*Beau Brummels '66* (Warner Bros.)   1967—*Triangle*   1968—*Bradley's Barn* (group disbands)   1974—(Group re-forms: Valentino, Elliott, Meagher, Petersen; + Dan Levitt, gtr.)   1975—*The Beau Brummels*   1987—*The Best of the Beau Brummels* (Rhino)   1994—*Autumn of Their Years.*

The Beau Brummels were the first nationally successful rock act to emerge from San Francisco; they were also the first American rock band influenced by the Beatles to have a hit. With the exception of their Irish-born bassist, Declan Mulligan (who quit the group before their hits began), all the members were Bay Area high school graduates. Their early performances featured covers of Beatles and Rolling Stones songs as well as Ron Elliott's originals. San Francisco disc jockey Tom Donahue signed them to his Autumn Records. Their first release, "Laugh, Laugh" (produced by Sylvester Stewart, who later reached fame as Sly Stone), went to #15 in 1965, only a few months after they had played their first live show together. Their next single, "Just a Little" (#8), was their only Top Ten hit. None of their subsequent releases—"You Tell Me Why," "Don't Talk to Strangers," "Good Time Music" (1965), and "One Too Many Mornings" (1966)—entered the Top Thirty.

In 1965 Autumn went out of business, and the group's contract was sold to Warner Bros. It failed to regain commercial favor, but produced interesting failures, including 1967's progressive *Triangle* (recorded after Petersen had left to join Harper's Bizarre [see entry]) and one of the first country-rock albums, *Bradley's Barn* (recorded in Nashville in 1968 by Valentino and Elliott). Neither LP sold well, and by the end of 1968 the Beau Brummels moniker was retired. Valentino then recorded a couple of singles for Warner Bros. before assembling Stoneground. Elliott released a solo album called *The Candlestick Maker* in 1969 and then took a lengthy sabbatical before resurfacing with a group called Pan in the early Seventies. In 1974 the original Beau Brummels re-

grouped, augmented by guitarist Dan Levitt. They released *The Beau Brummels*, but the LP met with little success, and the group disbanded. In the years since, versions of the Beau Brummels have included Valentino, Elliott, and Mulligan, in various combinations. Nineteen-ninety-four's *Autumn of Their Years* includes material recorded from 1964 to 1966.

Beausoleil

Formed 1976, Louisiana
Tommy Alesi (b. July 15, 1951, San Diego, Calif.), drums; Jimmy Breaux (b. Nov. 18, 1967, Breaux Bridge, La.), accordion; David Doucet (b. July 6, 1957, Lafayette, La.), gtr., voc.; Michael Doucet (b. Feb. 14, 1951, Lafayette, La.), fiddle, voc.; Al Tharp (b. Feb. 8, 1950, Indianapolis, Ind.), bass, banjo, voc.; Billy Ware (b. John William Ware, Apr. 26, 1954, Mobile, Ala.), perc.
1977—*The Spirit of Cajun Music* (Rounder)   1980—*Zydeco Gris Gris*   1981—*Parlez-Nous à Boire* (Arhoolie)   1986—*Bayou Boogie* (Rounder); *Belizaire the Cajun* (Arhoolie); *Allons à Lafayette*   1987—*Hot Chili Mama*   1989—*Live! From the Left Coast* (Rounder); *Bayou Cadillac*   1990—*Déjà Vu*   1991—*Cajun Conja* (RNA/Rhino)   1992—*Bayou Deluxe: The Best of Michael Doucet & Beausoleil* (Forward/Rhino)   1993—*La Danse de la Vie*   1994—*L'echo.*

The premier Cajun band, Beausoleil has moved comfortably between traditional Cajun music and rock and jazz influences. They are best known for their work on two 1986 soundtracks, *The Big Easy* and *Belizaire the Cajun.*

In the mid-Seventies Beausoleil's founder, Michael Doucet, fronted Coteau, known as the "Cajun Grateful Dead." Meanwhile, funded by an NEA grant, he tracked down early Cajun music. The original Beausoleil (the name of an Acadian settlement in Nova Scotia) was a trio: Doucet, mandolin/guitar player Kenneth Richard, and Coteau member Bessyl Duhon on accordion and fiddle. But Doucet employed French folk musicians on Beausoleil's 1976 debut, recorded and released in France. In 1977 a new Beausoleil included his brother David on guitar and Duhon on accordion (later replaced by Pat Breaux, who was then replaced by his brother, Jimmy) and signed with Arhoolie Records. *The Spirit of Cajun Music,* their American debut, is an eclectic mix of blues, ballads, standards, and traditional music.

Beausoleil are regulars on the folk festival circuit and *The Prairie Home Companion* National Public Radio show. They shared the stage with the Grateful Dead in 1990 and backed Mary Chapin Carpenter on the Grammy-winning "Down at the Twist and Shout" (1991). For their 1991 album *Cajun Conja,* they were joined by guitarist Richard Thompson.

The Beautiful South: See Housemartins

Be-Bop Deluxe
Formed 1972, England
Bill Nelson (b. Wakefield, Eng.), gtr., voc., kybds.;
Robert Bryan (b. Eng.), bass; Nicholas Chatterton-
Dew (b. Eng.), drums; Ian Parking (b. Eng.), gtr.;
Richard Brown (b. Eng.), kybds.
1974—(Group disbands; re-forms: Nelson; + Milton
Reame-James, kybds.; + Paul Jeffreys, bass;
+ Simon Fox, drums) *Axe Victim* (Harvest)
(– Reame-James; – Jeffreys; + Charles Tumahai,
bass) 1975—*Futurama* (+ Andrew Clark, kybds.)
1976—*Sunburst Finish*; *Modern Music* 1977—*Live
in the Air Age* 1978—*Drastic Plastic* 1979—*The
Best and the Rest of Be-Bop Deluxe.*
Bill Nelson solo: 1982—*The Love That Whirls (Diary
of a Thinking Heart)* (PVC); *La Belle et la Bête*;
Flaming Desire and Other Passions EP 1984—*Vis-
tamix* (Portrait) 1986—*On a Blue Wing* 1989—
The Strangest Things Sampler (Cocteau/Enigma);
Pavillions of the Heart and Soul; *Simplex*; *Quit
Dreaming and Get on the Beam*; *Sounding the
Ritual Echo*; *Savage Gestures for Charms Sake*;
A Catalogue of Obsessions; *The Summer of God's
Piano*; *2fold Aspect of Everything*; *Das Kabinett/La
Belle et la Bête*; *Chamber of Dreams*; *Map of
Dreams*; *Chance Encounters in the Garden of
Lights.*
Bill Nelson's Red Noise: 1979—*Sound-on-Sound*
(Harvest).
Bill Nelson's Orchestra Arcana: 1988—*Optimism*
(Cocteau/Enigma) 1989—*Iconography.*

Bill Nelson was an accomplished guitarist by his late
teens and began his professional career in his early
twenties. With a Yorkshire-based group, Gentle Revolution, he recorded two locally distributed albums. On his
own he recorded a home-produced LP entitled *Northern
Dream* in 1971. He put together Be-Bop Deluxe, styled
after David Bowie's science-fiction rock efforts, in early
1972. Though a modest success in England, the band
failed to attract large audiences in America, and Nelson
retired its name in 1979.

His next group, Bill Nelson's Red Noise, produced a
1979 LP entitled *Sound-on-Sound.* Since then Nelson
has recorded prolifically as a soloist, though until 1989
only a handful of his records—some all-instrumental,
some with vocals—have been released in the U.S., although one to eight years after their release in the
U.K. *Quit Dreaming and Get on the Beam,* a 1981 double
LP, hit the English Top Ten. He also produced A Flock of
Seagulls' "Telecommunication."

Beck
Born Beck Hansen, July 8, 1970, Los Angeles, Cali-
fornia
1993—*Golden Feelings* (Sonic Enemy Records)
1994—*A Western Harvest Field by Moonlight* EP
(Finger Paint Records); *Mellow Gold* (DGC); *One
Foot in the Grave* (K); *Stereopathetic Soul Manure*
(Flipside).

Beck took the lo-fi sound of DIY indie rock to the top of
the charts in 1994 with his oddball folk-rap hit, "Loser."
But his avant-pop musical palette extends well beyond
the beats and samples of that hit, including everything
from feedback and other sources of noise to toy instruments and found instruments. His disjointed, surreal
lyrics have often been compared to *Highway 61 Revisited*–era Bob Dylan.

Beck was born to bohemian parents. His mother,
Bibbe, was raised amid New York's Andy Warhol Factory
art scene of the Sixties and in the Nineties played in the
underground Los Angeles punk-drag band Black Fag.
His father was a bluegrass street musician. During his
teens he discovered the music of Sonic Youth and Pussy
Galore. After hearing a record by Mississippi John Hurt,
however, he began playing his own postpunk brand of
acoustic country blues.

In 1989 Beck took a bus to New York City, where he
caught the tail end of the ill-fated East Village antifolk
scene. After running out of money, Beck moved back to
Los Angeles, where he started performing in arty Silver-
lake coffeeshops along with other underground acts
such as Ethyl Meatplow and That Dog. He was approached during this period by Bong Load Records
owner Tom Rothrock, whose casual recording sessions
with Beck produced "Loser." The single became so popular on L.A.'s alternative radio station KROQ that it led to
a bidding war among the major labels. DGC signed Beck
to an unusual deal whereby the songwriter could continue recording for small indie labels. "Loser" reached
#10 and its album, the critically acclaimed *Mellow Gold*
(#13, 1994), sold 500,000 copies. A second single, "Beer-
can," reached only #27 on *Billboard*'s Modern Rock Chart.

Beck followed up with *Stereopathetic Soul Manure,*
another critical success that failed to sell well. *One Foot
in the Grave* was released on the Olympia, Washington,
label K.

Jeff Beck
Born June 24, 1944, Surrey, England
Jeff Beck Group: (Formed 1967, England: Beck, gtr.;
Rod Stewart (b. Jan. 10, 1945, London, Eng.), voc.;
Ron Wood (b. June 1, 1947, Hillingdon, Eng.), bass;
Aynsley Dunbar (b. 1946, Liverpool, Eng.), drums.
1967—(– Dunbar; + Mickey Waller, drums) 1968—

(+ Nicky Hopkins, kybds.) *Truth* (Epic) (– Waller; + Tony Newman, drums) 1969—*Beck-Ola* 1971— (New group: Max Middleton, kybds.; Cozy Powell [b. Dec. 29, 1947, Cirencester, Eng.], drums; Clive Chaman, bass; Bobby Tench, voc.) *Rough and Ready* 1972—*The Jeff Beck Group* (new lineup: Tim Bogert, bass; Carmine Appice, drums) 1973— *Beck, Bogert and Appice* 1975—*Blow by Blow*; *Truth/Beck-Ola* 1976—*Wired* 1977—*Jeff Beck with the Jan Hammer Group—Live* 1980—*There and Back* 1985—*Flash* 1989—*Jeff Beck's Guitar Shop with Terry Bozzio and Tony Hymas* 1991— *Beckology* 1993—*Crazy Legs* (with the Big Town Playboys).

One of the most influential lead guitarists in rock, Jeff Beck has helped shape blues rock, psychedelia, and heavy metal. Beck's groups have been short-lived, but his aggressive style—encompassing screaming, bent sustained notes, distortion and feedback, and crisply articulated fast passagework—has been more important than his material.

After attending Wimbledon Art College in London, Beck backed Lord Sutch before replacing Eric Clapton in the Yardbirds [see entry]. He established his reputation with that band, but he left in late 1966 and after a short sabbatical released a version of "Love Is Blue," played deliberately out of tune because he loathed the song. In 1967 he founded the Jeff Beck Group with Ron Wood and Rod Stewart; the band's reworkings of blues-based material laid the groundwork for Seventies heavy metal. Clashing temperaments broke up the group after two acclaimed LPs and several U.S. tours. Stewart and Wood went on to join the Faces [see the Small Faces/the Faces entry], and Stewart continued to use drummer Mickey Waller on his solo albums until 1974.

Beck was planning to form a band with Vanilla Fudge members Tim Bogert and Carmine Appice when he was sidelined for 18 months with a fractured skull he sustained in a car crash. (A car aficionado, Beck has been in three crashes and was once sidelined for months after getting his thumb trapped under a car.) When he recovered, Bogert and Appice were busy in Cactus, so Beck assembled a second Jeff Beck Group and put out two albums of Memphis funk laced with heavy metal. When Cactus broke up in late 1972, Beck, Bogert and Appice returned Beck to a power trio format, but weak vocals hampered the band, and it dissolved in early 1974.

Beck went into the first of many periods of hibernation. In 1975 he reemerged in an all-instrumental format, playing jazzy tunes. He toured as coheadliner with the Mahavishnu Orchestra and started an on-again, off-again collaboration with former Mahavishnu keyboardist Jan Hammer in 1976 with *Wired* (#16). During the later Seventies Beck reportedly spent most of his time on his 70-acre estate outside London. He and Hammer worked together on the 1980 album *There and Back,* but Hammer did not join Beck for his 1980 tour, the guitarist's first in over four years.

In 1981 Beck appeared at Amnesty International's Secret Policeman's Ball, and in 1985 toured Japan, but his concert tours occur even less frequently than his album releases. *Flash,* which includes Beck's sole charting single, "People Get Ready" (#48, 1985), with Rod Stewart on vocals, and the Grammy-winning "Escape," written by Hammer, peaked at #39. Four years later *Jeff Beck's Guitar Shop with Terry Bozzio and Tony Hymas* (#49, 1989) garnered the Grammy for Best Rock Instrumental Performance. *Crazy Legs,* an homage to Gene Vincent's Blue Caps and rockabilly guitar legend Cliff Gallup, met with mixed reviews. Through the Eighties Beck turned up on recordings by artists including Mick Jagger, Malcolm McLaren, and Roger Waters.

The Bee Gees

Formed 1958, Brisbane, Australia
Barry Gibb (b. Sep. 1, 1947, Manchester, Eng.), voc., gtr.; Robin Gibb (b. Dec. 22, 1949, Isle of Man, Eng.), voc.; Maurice Gibb (b. Dec. 22, 1949, Isle of Man, Eng.), voc., bass, kybds.
1967—*Bee Gees First* (Atco) 1968—*Horizontal*; *Rare Precious and Beautiful*; *Rare Precious and Beautiful, vol. 2*; *Idea* 1969—*Odessa*; *Best of Bee Gees* 1970—*Cucumber Castle* (Barry and Maurice as a duo) (Atco); *Sound of Love* (Polydor) 1971—*2 Years On* (Atco); *Trafalgar* 1972—*To Whom It May Concern* 1973—*Life in a Tin Can* (RSO); *The Best of the Bee Gees, vol. 2* 1974—*Mr. Natural* 1975— *Main Course* 1976—*Children of the World*; *Bee Gees Gold* 1977—*Here At Last . . . Live*; *Saturday Night Fever* soundtrack 1979—*Spirits Having Flown*; *Bee Gees Greatest* 1981—*Living Eyes* 1983—*Staying Alive* 1987—*E-S-P* (Warner Bros.) 1989—*One* 1990—*Tales from the Brothers Gibb: A History in Song, 1967–1990* (Polydor) 1991—*High Civilization* (Warner Bros.) 1993—*Size Isn't Everything* (Polydor).

In over 30 years of latching on to trends, the Bee Gees became one of the wealthiest groups in pop. The three Gibb brothers, sons of English bandleader Hugh Gibb, started performing in 1955, going under such names as the Rattlesnakes and Wee Johnny Hays and the Bluecats. They moved with their parents to Brisbane in 1958 and worked talent shows and other amateur outlets, singing sets of Everly Brothers songs and an occasional Barry Gibb composition, by this time calling themselves the Bee Gees. They signed with Australia's Festival Records in 1962 and released a dozen singles and two al-

The Bee Gees: Maurice Gibb, Barry Gibb, Robin Gibb

bums in the next five years. Then as now, close high harmonies were the Bee Gees' trademark, and the Gibbs wrote their own material.

They hosted a weekly Australian TV show, but their records went unnoticed until 1967, when "Spicks and Specks" hit #1 after the Bee Gees had relocated to England. There they expanded to a quintet with drummer Colin Peterson and bassist Vince Melouney (both Australians) and found themselves a new manager, Robert Stigwood, then employed by the Beatles' NEMS Enterprises. Their first Northern Hemisphere single, "New York Mining Disaster 1941," was a hit in both the U.K. and the U.S. (#14, 1967) and was followed by a string of equally popular ballads: "To Love Somebody" (#17, 1967), "Holiday" (#16, 1967), "Massachusetts" (#11, 1967), "Words" (#15, 1968), "I've Got to Get a Message to You" (#8, 1968), and "I Started a Joke" (#6, 1969). Their cleancut neo-Edwardian image and English-accented harmonies were a variation on the Beatles' approach, although the Bee Gees leaned toward ornate orchestration and sentimentality.

Cracks in their toothsome facade began to show in 1969, when the nonfamily members left the group (Peterson claiming the Bee Gees name for himself) and reports of excessive lifestyles and fighting among the brothers surfaced. From mid-1969 to late 1970 Robin tried a solo career and had a #2 U.K. hit, "Saved by the Bell." Meanwhile, Barry and Maurice (then married to singer Lulu) recorded *Cucumber Castle* as a duo and cut some singles individually. The trio reunited for two more hit ballads—the million sellers "Lonely Days" (#3, 1970) and "How Can You Mend a Broken Heart" (#1, 1971)—before bottoming out with a string of flops between 1971 and 1975. Stigwood effected a turnabout by recruiting producer Arif Mardin, who steered them toward R&B and brought them to Miami to work out the funk-plus-falsetto combination that brought them their third round of hits. *Main Course* (#14, 1976), including "Jive Talkin'" (#1, 1975) and "Nights on Broadway" (#7, 1975), caught disco on the upswing and gave the Bee Gees their first platinum album.

In 1976 Stigwood's RSO label broke away from its parent company, Atlantic, rendering Mardin unavailable to the Bee Gees. Engineer Karl Richardson and arranger Albhy Galuten took over as producers, and the group continued to record with Miami rhythm sections for hits like "You Should Be Dancing" (#1, 1976) and a ballad, "Love So Right" (#3, 1976), which recalled such black vocal groups as the Spinners and the Stylistics rather than the Beatles. Stigwood, meanwhile, had produced the films *Jesus Christ Superstar* and *Tommy,* and asked the Bee Gees for four or five songs he could use in the soundtrack of *Saturday Night Fever.* The soundtrack album, a virtual best-of-disco, included Bee Gees chart-toppers "Stayin' Alive," "Night Fever," and "How Deep Is Your Love," and eventually sold 30 million copies worldwide. Barry, with Galuten and Richardson, also wrote and produced hits for Yvonne Elliman, Samantha Sang, Tavares, Frankie Valli, and younger brother Andy Gibb [see entry] as well as the title tune for *Grease.*

In 1978, with *Saturday Night Fever* still high on the charts, the Bee Gees started Music for UNICEF, donating the royalties from a new song and recruiting other hitmakers to do the same. They also appeared in Stigwood's movie fiasco *Sgt. Pepper's Lonely Hearts Club Band* and continued to record. After *Saturday Night Fever,* even the platinum *Spirits Having Flown,* with three #1 hits—"Too Much Heaven," "Tragedy," and "Love You Inside Out"—seemed anticlimactic. As of 1979, the Bee Gees had made five platinum albums and more than 20 hit singles.

Their career then entered another dry season. In October 1980 the Bee Gees filed a $200-million suit against Stigwood, claiming mismanagement. Meanwhile, Barry produced and sang duets with Barbra Streisand on *Guilty* (1980). The lawsuit was settled out of court, with mutual public apologies, in May 1981. *Living Eyes* was the Bee Gees' last album for RSO. They composed the soundtrack to *Saturday Night Fever*'s critically dismissed sequel, *Stayin' Alive;* the soundtrack went to #6 and platinum and included "Woman in You" (#24, 1983). Barry has also written and produced an album for

Dionne Warwick, *Heartbreaker*. With his brothers he cowrote Diana Ross's "Chain Reaction" and the Kenny Rogers–Dolly Parton hit, "Islands in the Stream."

In 1987 the Brothers Gibb again joined forces and again refired their singing career with *E-S-P*, which included "You Win Again" (#75, 1987). While these records appeared commercial disappointments in comparison to previous chart showings, in fact this was the case only in the U.S. *E-S-P* went to #1 in Germany and the Top Five in the U.K. Thus began a third phase of the Bee Gees' history, in which records (such as "You Win Again") would top the charts practically everywhere but in America.

Shattered by the death of their younger brother Andy Gibb in March 1988, the Bee Gees retired for a time, and Maurice suffered a brief relapse of his alcoholism. The group's most recent work continues to fare far better outside the States. *High Civilization,* which did not even chart in the U.S., hit #2 in Germany and the U.K. Top Thirty; *One* (German Top Five, U.K. Top Thirty) featured the trio's highest-charting single of the Eighties, "One" (#7, 1989).

Bees Make Honey

Formed 1972, England
Ruan O'Lochlainn, gtr., piano, sax; Deke O'Brien, gtr., voc.; Bob Cee Benberg, drums; Barry Richardson, bass, voc.; Mick Molloy, gtr., voc.
1973—(– O'Lochlainn; + Malcom Morley, kybds.; – Benberg; + Fran Byrne, drums; – O'Brien; Richardson moved to sax; + Rod Demick, bass, voc.) *Music Every Night* **(EMI) 1974—(+ Kevin McAlea, piano; + Ed Dean, gtr.; + Willie Finlayson, gtr., voc.).**

A pioneering U.K. pub-rock band alongside Brinsley Schwarz and Ducks Deluxe, Bees Make Honey's main claims to fame are its two top-notch drummers. Bob Cee Benberg graduated to the big time with Supertramp, while his replacement, Fran Byrne, had a momentary taste of glory with Ace. The group recorded several albums, but only one was released. Bees Make Honey disbanded in autumn 1974, a few months after the pub-rock scene ground to a halt.

Adrian Belew

Born Robert Steven Belew, December 23, 1949, Covington, Kentucky
1982—*Lone Rhino* (Island) 1983—*Twang Bar King* 1986—*Desire Caught by the Tail* 1989—*Mr. Music Head* (Atlantic) 1990—*Young Lions* 1991—*Desire of the Rhino King* 1992—*Inner Revolution* 1994—*Here* (Caroline).
With the Bears: 1987—*The Bears* (Primitive Man) 1988—*Rise and Shine.*

Always the bridesmaid but never the bride, guitarist Adrian Belew has had notable success as a supporting musician but limited popularity as a solo artist. A wizard of sonic manipulation and texture, Belew has been the guitarist of choice for the art-rock crowd, playing with Frank Zappa, Talking Heads, David Bowie, Laurie Anderson, and King Crimson [see entries].

In his hometown of Cincinnati, Belew was originally a rock drummer before developing his guitar-playing prowess. He was working the mid-American club circuit with his band Sweetheart when Zappa happened to attend a Nashville performance and tapped Belew for his band. Belew toured and recorded with Zappa (*Sheik Yerbouti,* 1979). After touring with David Bowie (captured on 1978's *Stage;* he also appears on 1979's *Lodger*), Belew recorded with Talking Heads (*Remain in Light,* 1980). Belew's startling work—his careening solo on "The Great Curve"—immediately established him as a sought-after player. Belew toured briefly with the first expanded edition of Talking Heads and can be heard on their live 1982 album *The Name of This Band Is Talking Heads.* Belew later worked with Talking Heads Chris Frantz and Tina Weymouth on the first album by their band Tom Tom Club.

In 1981 Belew joined Robert Fripp, Bill Bruford, and Tony Levin in a latter-day King Crimson. Belew's virtuosic playing—which by now included a whole lexicon of electronically produced animal sounds—as well as his urgent singing of his own caustic lyrics helped make this one of the most popular and respected Crimson lineups. Belew recorded *Discipline* (1981), *Beat* (1982), and *Three of a Perfect Pair* (1984) with the band before they broke up in 1984. He also made guest appearances on Laurie Anderson's *Mister Heartbreak* (1984) and *Home of the Brave* (1986) and Paul Simon's *Graceland* (1986).

With the Bears—a short-lived band he helped form in 1985—and in his subsequent career as a solo artist, Belew displayed his ease with pop songwriting and singing. *Mr. Music Head* yielded the minor hit "Oh Daddy" (#58, 1989), a humorous look at the vicissitudes of a middle-aged rocker, which Belew sang with his 11-year-old daughter, Audie. He joined David Bowie on his 1989 "Sound + Vision" career retrospective tour. In 1994 Belew's guitar playing was featured on the industrial band Nine Inch Nails' album *The Downward Spiral.* Belew's own album of that year, *Here,* recorded at his home in Cincinnati, showcased his vocals and multi-instrumental expertise; Belew played all the instruments and produced the album.

Archie Bell and the Drells

Formed mid-Sixties, Houston, Texas
Archie Bell (b. Sep. 1, 1944, Henderson, Tex.); Huey "Billy" Butler; Joe Cross; James Wise.

1968—*Tighten Up* (Atlantic)   1969—(– Butler;
– Cross; + Willie Parnell; + Lee Bell) *There's Gonna
Be a Showdown*   1977—*Dance Your Troubles Away*
(Philadelphia International); *Hard Not to Like It.*
Archie Bell solo: 1981—*I Never Had It So Good*
(Becket).

Archie Bell and his group had the nation dancing in 1968
with the strutting "Tighten Up" (#1 pop, #1 R&B), which
featured a choked guitar phrase. The Drells were frequently produced by noted Philadelphia soul stylist
Bunny Sigler, although their followup hit, the Top Ten "I
Can't Stop Dancing" in late 1968, was produced by the
then-emerging black music titans Kenny Gamble and
Leon Huff. They scored another Top Thirty success in
early 1969, "There's Gonna Be a Showdown," but have
since reached only a loyal black audience; in 1970 they
released a #33 R&B version of "Wrap It Up," a minor hit
for the Fabulous Thunderbirds in 1986. "Let's Groove
(Part 1)" was a Top Ten R&B hit in 1976. In the late Seventies Archie Bell and the Drells recorded extensively for
the Philadelphia International label, releasing a discofied
version of "Tighten Up." By 1981 Bell was recording solo
for the Becket label.

William Bell

**Born William Yarborough, July 16, 1939, Memphis,
Tennessee**
1967—*The Soul of a Bell* (Stax)   1968—*Tribute to a
King*   1969—*Bound to Happen*   1971—
Wow . . . William Bell   1973—*Phases of Reality*
1974—*Relating*   1977—*Coming Back for More* (Mer-
cury); *It's Time You Took Another Listen*   1983—
Survivor (Kat Family)   1985—*Passion* (Wilbe)
1989—*On a Roll*   1990—*The Best of William Bell*
(Stax)   1992—*A Little Something Extra.*

A soul singer of great subtlety, William Bell was one of
the principal architects of the Memphis Sound. Starting
off with Rufus Thomas' band in 1953 and recording with
the Del Rios vocal quartet in 1957, Bell became an early
writer and performer for the Stax/Volt label. Going solo
in 1961, the next year he released "You Don't Miss Your
Water," its stark power exemplifying the Stax style that
provided counterpoint to Motown's pop approach. Sidelined by two years in the army, Bell reemerged in the
mid-Sixties with songs that fared respectably on the
R&B charts: "Everybody Loves a Winner" (#18, 1967) and
"A Tribute to a King" (#16, 1968). The latter, an homage to
Otis Redding, made clear, however, that Bell had been
eclipsed commercially by such other Stax talents as
Redding, Sam and Dave, and Wilson Pickett.

A 1968 R&B Top Ten, "I Forgot to Be Your Lover," and
duets with Judy Clay ("Private Number," "My Baby Specializes") highlighted Bell's skills as a balladeer, and the

singer worked at crafting sophisticated soul into the
Seventies. (In 1986, Billy Idol released "To Be a Lover," a
Top Ten cover of Bell's "I Forgot to Be Your Lover.") In
1969 Bell moved to Atlanta and founded his own
Peachtree label; with 1976 and his signing to Mercury
came the refreshing success of "Trying to Love Two," a
#1 R&B hit.

Throughout the Eighties, on the Kat Family and
Wilbe labels, Bell continued a low-profile career. As a
writer ("Born Under a Bad Sign") and as an elegant
singer of romantic tumult, his work is seminal.

Bell Biv DeVoe

Formed 1988, Boston, Massachusetts
Michael Bivins (b. Aug. 10, 1968, Boston), voc.;
Ricky Bell (b. Sep. 18, 1967, Boston), voc.; Ronnie
DeVoe (b. Nov. 17, 1967, Boston), voc.
1990—*Poison* (MCA)   1991—*WBBD-Bootcity! The
Remix Album*   1993—*Hootie Mack.*

As members of the teenage R&B vocal group New Edition [see entry], Ricky Bell, Michael Bivins, and Ronnie
DeVoe kept fairly low profiles, leaving the limelight to
singers Ralph Tresvant and Bobby Brown, and later
Johnny Gill. But when Brown went solo in 1986, Bell,
Bivins, and DeVoe began thinking about pursuing their
own separate paths together. Two years later—with
some prodding from prominent hip-hop producers
Jimmy Jam and Terry Lewis—Bell Biv DeVoe was born,
and the fierce, provocative pop funk it eventually unleashed on the charts marked a dramatic departure from
New Edition's wholesome image.

On New Edition's last studio album, 1988's *Heart
Break*, Bell, Bivins, and DeVoe had worked with Jam and
Lewis, who had crafted for them a harder-edged, more
urban sound. As a subsequent tour wrapped, the producers approached the three singers with the idea for
Bell Biv DeVoe. The trio then enlisted various hip-hop sa-
vants—including Public Enemy producers Hank and
Keith Shocklee—to write and produce material for its
debut album. Released in 1990, *Poison* featured street-
smart, rap-tinged arrangements and sexually suggestive
lyrics. Its title track, a slamming slice of misogyny,
topped the R&B chart, and became a #3 pop hit. The
album itself shot to #5 pop and #1 R&B that year and included "Do Me!" (#3 pop, #4 R&B), "B.B.D. (I Thought It
Was Me)" (#1 R&B), and "When Will I See You Smile
Again?" (#3 R&B).

In 1991 the group had a #9 R&B single, "She's Dope!"
Later that year Bell Biv DeVoe released *WBBD-Bootcity!
The Remix Album* (#18 pop and R&B). In 1992 the trio
reappeared on the singles chart with "Gangsta" (#21
pop, #22 R&B, 1993), an unlikely collaboration with
smooth soul singer Luther Vandross. In 1993 Bell Biv
DeVoe released its third album, *Hootie Mack* (#19 pop, #6

R&B), which yielded the single "Something in Your Eyes" (#38 pop, #6 R&B, 1993).

Regina Belle

Born Regina Edna Belle, July 15, 1963, Englewood, New Jersey
1987—*All By Myself* (Columbia)   1989—*Stay with Me*   1993—*Passion*.

A contemporary soul singer with roots in gospel and jazz, Regina Belle had several R&B hits in the late Eighties before her #1 pop 1992 duet with Peabo Bryson, "A Whole New World (Aladdin's Theme)"—the theme song from the Walt Disney animated film *Aladdin*. Born to a gospel-loving mother and a father who was an R&B enthusiast, Belle began singing in church as a child and was influenced early on by the jazz of Billie Holiday and Nancy Wilson and the pop soul of Phyllis Hyman. During high school, Belle studied opera at the Manhattan School of Music. Then, while majoring in accounting and history at Rutgers University, she sang with a jazz ensemble.

In 1985 she began singing backup for the Manhattans and was soon signed to Columbia. Belle's debut album, *All By Myself,* yielded the #2 R&B hit "Show Me the Way," as well as favorable comparisons to Anita Baker and Sade. *Stay with Me* became a #1 R&B album and topped the singles chart for that genre with "Baby Come to Me" and "Make It Like It Was." Also in 1989, Belle teamed up with ex–Kool and the Gang singer James "J.T." Taylor on "All I Want Is Forever," a #2 R&B hit featured in the movie *Tap.*

Jesse Belvin

Born December 15, 1933, Texarkana, Arkansas; died February 6, 1960, Los Angeles, California
1975—*Yesterdays* (RCA)   1990—*Jesse Belvin: The Blues Balladeer* (Specialty)   1991—*Goodnight, My Love* (Flair/Virgin).

Jesse Belvin's untimely death came just as the singer was achieving success commensurate with his influence on West Coast black vocal music in the Fifties. He began his career as a 16-year-old vocalist for Big Jay McNeely's band. After a stint in the army, he formed a vocal duo with Marvin Phillips—Jesse & Marvin—and scored an R&B Top Ten hit with "Dream Girl" in 1953. Over the next eight years, he served as unofficial leader of L.A.'s doo-wop groups, coaching them, writing, and arranging their material, and using his influence with the city's independent companies to get them recorded. His biggest songwriting success was with "Earth Angel," a million-seller for the Penguins in 1955. He also sang with the Cliques, the Sharptones, Three Dots and a Dash, and the Sheiks. The Cliques had a 1956 hit with his "The Girl in My Dreams."

Belvin recorded as a solo artist for numerous labels, including Specialty, Knight, and Modern/Kent, but not until the mid-Fifties did his soft, careful enunciation and tasteful ballads enjoy some success. "Goodnight My Love" hit the R&B Top Ten in 1956. In 1958 Belvin was signed to RCA; in 1959 "Guess Who" went #7 R&B. Nine months later he died in an auto accident.

Belly: See Throwing Muses/Belly

Pat Benatar

Born Patricia Andrzejewski, January 10, 1953, Brooklyn, New York
1979—*In the Heat of the Night* (Chrysalis)   1980—*Crimes of Passion*   1981—*Precious Time*   1982—*Get Nervous*   1983—*Live from Earth*   1984—*Tropico*   1985—*Seven the Hard Way*   1988—*Wide Awake in Dreamland*   1989—*Best Shots*   1991—*True Love*   1993—*Gravity's Rainbow*.

Pat Benatar was the most successful female hard-rock singer of the Eighties. She grew up on Long Island, where at age 17 she began vocal training in preparation for study at the Juilliard School of Music. She soon rebelled against the rigorous training and ended her studies. After turning 18, she married Dennis Benatar, a GI stationed in Richmond, Virginia. There she worked as a bank clerk before taking a job as a singing waitress. In 1975 the couple returned to New York; they were later divorced.

Benatar began working Manhattan's cabaret circuit in 1975 with a chanteuse style derived from Barbra Streisand and Diana Ross. At Catch a Rising Star, she attracted the attention of club owner Rick Newman, who became her manager. By 1978 she had switched to a more aggressive rock approach, and after being rejected by several labels was signed to Chrysalis.

Benatar's debut went platinum (the first of six) on the strength of the #23 single "Heartbreaker." Her followup, *Crimes of Passion,* sold over four million copies in late 1980, yielding two hit singles, "Hit Me with Your Best Shot" (#9, 1980) and "Treat Me Right" (#18, 1981). *Precious Time* (also multiplatinum) boasted "Promises in the Dark" (#38, 1981) and "Fire and Ice" (#17, 1981).

Benatar's early sex-kitten image—which she later stated had been thrust upon her—belied the singer's control over her career and her material. In 1982 she married her guitarist and musical director, Neil Giraldo, with whom she writes most of her songs. Her streak of hits continued with "Shadows of the Night" (#13, 1982), "Little Too Late" (#20, 1983), "Love Is a Battlefield" (#5, 1983), and "We Belong" (#5, 1984). She returned to recording after the birth of her daughter with "Invincible" (#10, 1985), "Sex as a Weapon" (#28, 1985), and "All Fired Up" (#19, 1988). Something of a stylistic departure,

True Love, a collection of blues recordings, produced no hits. Two years later, Benatar was back with *Gravity's Rainbow.*

Tony Bennett
Born Anthony Dominick Benedetto, August 13, 1926, Queens, New York
1957—*The Beat of My Heart* (Columbia) 1959—*Basie Swings, Bennett Sings* (Roulette) 1962—*I Left My Heart in San Francisco* (Columbia); *Tony Bennett at Carnegie Hall* 1964—*When Lights Are Low* 1966—*The Movie Song Album* 1975—*The Tony Bennett/Bill Evans Album* (Fantasy) 1976—*The Rodgers and Hart Songbook* (DRG) 1977—*Together Again: Tony Bennett and Bill Evans* 1986—*The Art of Excellence* (Columbia) 1987—*Tony Bennett Jazz; Bennett/Berlin* 1990—*Astoria: Portrait of the Artist* 1991—*Forty Years: The Artistry of Tony Bennett* 1992—*Perfectly Frank* 1993—*Steppin' Out* 1994—*Tony Bennett—MTV Unplugged.*

The epitome of cool, Tony Bennett is second only to Frank Sinatra as an interpreter of classic jazz-inflected American song. Careful articulation, a sure sense of swing, and an air of restrained bemusement characterize his style. Originally popular in the late Fifties, Bennett enjoyed a remarkable resurgence in the early Nineties.

His mother American, his father an Italian grocer, Benedetto worked as a singing waiter in his teens. After performing with the U.S. Army's entertainment corps in World War II and then appearing on the Arthur Godfrey talent show, he was discovered, under the stage name Joe Bari, while performing with Pearl Bailey in 1949. Bob Hope then enlisted him to open shows at New York's Paramount Theater, and changed his name to Tony Bennett. In 1950 he was signed to Columbia Records. His first hit, "Because of You" (#1, 1951), remained on the charts for 32 weeks. His next single, Hank Williams' "Cold, Cold Heart," was the first notable pop cover of a country tune. Both featured the Percy Faith Orchestra, which provided the lush backdrop for most of the 24 Top Forty charters he earned before 1964. Among those hits were "Rags to Riches" (#1, 1953), "Stranger in Paradise" (#2, 1953), and "There'll Be No Teardrops Tonight" (#7, 1954). During that period, his *Basie Swings, Bennett Sings* served as a blueprint for later forays into jazz singing; in 1956 he formed an alliance with Ralph Sharon, the pianist and musical director who would become Bennett's lifelong collaborator. In 1962 Bennett sold out Carnegie Hall and recorded his first Grammy Award winner and subsequent trademark, "I Left My Heart in San Francisco" (#19, 1962).

But Bennett was primarily an album artist. Given occasionally to the experimental—1957's *The Beat of My Heart* highlighted percussion as the primary instrumentation—he achieved equal aesthetic triumphs with the polished pop of *The Movie Song Album* (1966) and the straight-ahead jazz of *When Lights Are Low* (1964), a tribute to the King Cole Trio. Critics reserved especial praise for his work with Bill Evans, a pianist whose elegant minimalism matched Bennett's own.

Yet after his Sixties heyday came a fallow spell. Bennett continued to appear in concert but, from 1978 to 1985, didn't record. In the late Seventies, he'd formed an independent label, which fared poorly commercially, and his contract with Columbia was not renewed. While other vocalists of the prerock era had expanded their repertoire to include songs by younger composers, Bennett adamantly refused such a manuever, continuing to reword material by the Gershwins, Rodgers and Hart, Cole Porter, and the like. And his career stalled. He concentrated instead on painting and began exhibiting in Paris, London, and New York.

The late Eighties, however, marked Bennett's return to the studio. *Bennett/Berlin* was a critically lauded set of Irving Berlin standards performed with Dizzy Gillespie, Dexter Gordon, and George Benson; *The Art of Excellence* featured "Everybody Has the Blues," a duet with Ray Charles. But it was with 1992's *Perfectly Frank,* a homage to Bennett's favorite singer, Frank Sinatra, that his revival began in earnest. The album won a Grammy, as did *Steppin' Out,* a collection of songs made famous by Fred Astaire. The singer's son, Danny Bennett, who had managed his father since 1979, capitalized on the newfound popularity, engineering a campaign that saw Bennett appearing in a cameo role on television's youth-oriented *The Simpsons* in 1991. Paul Shaffer, musical director for *Late Night with David Letterman,* became Bennett's champion; by appearing on that television show, the singer furthered his exposure to a younger demographic. With the release of *Forty Years: The Artistry of Tony Bennett,* a four-CD retrospective, Bennett's stature was confirmed, while his hipness quotient intensified with his appearance, alongside Flea and Anthony Kiedis of the Red Hot Chili Peppers, as a presenter at the 1993 MTV Music Video Awards. In 1995 *Tony Bennett—MTV Unplugged,* including duets with k. d. lang and Elvis Costello, gained Bennett two more Grammy Awards.

George Benson
Born March 22, 1943, Pittsburgh, Pennsylvania
1965—*It's Uptown* (Columbia) 1966—*The George Benson Cookbook* 1967—*Giblet Gravy* (Verve/MGM) 1968—*Shape of Things to Come* (A&M) 1969—*The Other Side of Abbey Road* 1971—*Beyond the Blue Horizon* (CTI) 1972—*White Rabbit* 1973—*Body Talk* 1974—*Bad Benson*

1976—*Benson and Farrell* (with Joe Farrell); *Breezin'* (Warner Bros.) 1977—*In Flight* 1978— *Weekend in L.A.* 1979—*Livin' Inside Your Love* 1980—*Give Me the Night* 1981—*The George Benson Collection* 1983—*In Your Eyes* 1984—*20-20* 1987—*Collaboration* (with Earl Klugh) 1988— *Twice the Love* 1989—*Tenderly* 1990—*Big Boss Band Featuring the Count Basie Orchestra* 1991— *Midnight Moods* (Telstar) 1993—*Love Remembers*.

Jazz guitarist/vocalist George Benson's breakthrough came in 1976 when *Breezin'* brought him into the pop mainstream. His jazz-pop formula has been updated by the likes of Earl Klugh and Kenny G.

Benson won a singing contest when he was four years old and later performed on radio as Little Georgie Benson. He took up the guitar at age eight, but he worked as a vocalist with numerous Pittsburgh R&B bands before playing guitar in public at age 15. Soon after, he began playing sessions outside Pittsburgh. With his groups the Altairs and George Benson and His All-Stars, he recorded for Amy Records. By the late Fifties he had given up singing to concentrate solely on the guitar. In 1965 he moved to New York and met his main influence, Wes Montgomery; John Hammond signed him to Columbia. Though his mainstream jazz albums on Columbia, A&M, and CTI helped him establish a reputation, sales were never outstanding.

In late 1975 Benson signed with Warner Bros., where for the first time in his recording career, he was encouraged to sing. *Breezin'*, winner of three Grammy awards in 1976, featured Leon Russell's "This Masquerade," the first song in history to reach Number One on the jazz, R&B, and pop charts. His success continued throughout the late Seventies and early Eighties (all six Warner albums of the period are gold; four of those are platinum). Understated pop funk with vocals modeled on Stevie Wonder and Donny Hathaway, his hits included "On Broadway" (#7, 1978), "Give Me the Night" (#4, 1980), and "Turn Your Love Around" (#5, 1981).

Benson's sales have remained consistent, but his life hasn't been without tumult. Becoming a Jehovah's Witness in the early Eighties, he credited his conversion for his good fortune. However, his son was killed in a 1991 bar fight. In 1988 CTI Records was awarded $3.2 million in a judgment against Warner Bros. Records; Warners, a jury ruled, owed the money in damages for breaching an agreement with Benson. During this period, Benson reaffirmed his jazz roots with live work with Dizzy Gillespie, Freddie Hubbard, and Lionel Hampton. In 1989 *Tenderly*, with pianist McCoy Tyner, reached the #1 jazz spot; in 1993 Benson again proved his hit-making currency when his *Love Remembers* supplanted Kenny G's *Breathless* as #1 Contemporary Jazz album.

Brook Benton

Born Benjamin Franklin Peay, September 19, 1931, Lugoff, South Carolina; died April 9, 1988, New York City, New York
1960—*The Two of Us* (with Dinah Washington) (Mercury) 1961—*Brook Benton's Golden Hits; The Boll Weevil Song and 11 Other Great Hits; If You Believe* 1962—*Singin' the Blues* 1963—*Brook Benton's Golden Hits, vol. 2* 1967—*Laura, What's He Got That I Ain't Got* (Reprise) 1969—*Do Your Own Thing* (Cotillion) 1970—*Brook Benton Today; Home Style* 1971—*The Gospel Truth* 1973— *Something for Everyone* (MGM) 1975—*Brook Benton Sings a Love Story* (RCA) 1976—*This Is Brook Benton* (All Platinum) 1977—*Making Love Is Good for You* (Olde Worlde) 1986—*The Brook Benton Anthology* (Rhino).

One of a handful of black singers who wrote their own material in the early Sixties, Brook Benton had four gold records and 16 Top Twenty hits over a lengthy and resilient career. Benton's hits feature his smooth baritone (in a style he learned from Nat "King" Cole and Billy Eckstine) and lush string backing. In the early Fifties he sang with Bill Landford and the Golden Gate gospel quartets. By the middle of the Fifties Benton had begun recording pop songs for Epic and then Vik Records, for which he had a minor 1958 hit, "A Million Miles from Nowhere."

Collaborations with songwriter Clyde Otis and arranger Belford Hendricks produced 1958 hits for Nat "King" Cole ("Looking Back") and Clyde McPhatter ("A Lover's Question"). In 1959 Otis helped get Benton a contract with Mercury, and Benton began four years of success for the label, beginning with four Benton/ Otis/Hendricks compositions: "It's Just a Matter of Time" (#3), "Endlessly" (#12), "Thank You Pretty Baby" (#16), and "So Many Ways" (#6).

Benton's early-Sixties hits included two duets with Dinah Washington, "Baby (You've Got What It Takes)" (#5, 1960) and "A Rockin' Good Way" (#7, 1960), as well as the folk-tinged "The Boll Weevil Song" (#2, 1961) and "Frankie and Johnny" (#20, 1961). Other hits included more standard soul-pop fare like "Think Twice" (#11, 1961), "Revenge" (#15, 1961), "Lie to Me" (#13, 1962), "Shadrack" (#19, 1962), and "Hotel Happiness" (#3, 1963). Thereafter his Mercury releases fared noticeably worse on the charts. He recorded for RCA (1965–67) and Reprise (1967–68) with meager results.

In 1970 he had one more big pop hit with a stirring version of Tony Joe White's "Rainy Night in Georgia" (#4 pop, #1 R&B, 1970) on Cotillion. As the decade progressed, he recorded for MGM, Brut, Stax, All Platinum, and Olde Worlde. He died at age fifty-six from pneumonia.

Berlin

Formed 1979, Los Angeles, California
John Crawford (b. Jan. 17, 1957, Palo Alto, Calif.),
bass, voc.; Rob Brill (b. Jan. 21, 1956, Babylon, N.Y.),
drums; Terri Nunn (b. June 26, 1959, Baldwin Hills,
Calif.), voc.
1983—*Pleasure Victim* (Geffen)   1984—*Love Life*
1986—*Count Three & Pray*   1989—*Best of Berlin
1979–1988.*

While best known for the Giorgio Moroder–produced
"Take My Breath Away" (#1, 1986) from the *Top Gun*
soundtrack, Berlin's real raison d'être is probably better
divined from the title of its panting, quasipornographic
song "Sex (I'm a . . .)" (#62, 1983).

A vehicle for teen actress (in *Lou Grant*) turned
singer Terri Nunn, Berlin combined her moaning boy-toy
image with the rhythm section of John Crawford and
Rob Brill (three different groups of musicians backed
them on album). The resulting slick synth pop and a
steamy video brought *Pleasure Victim* (#30, 1983) some
commercial success. *Love Life* (#28, 1984) successfully
repeated the debut album's formula. *Count Three & Pray*
(#61, 1986) featured cameos by Ted Nugent, David
Gilmour, and Elliot Easton. While the *Top Gun* track
soared, the rest of the album sputtered, and when Nunn
left in 1987, Berlin called it quits. Crawford went on to
form the Big F in 1989.

Chuck Berry

Born Charles Edward Anderson Berry, October 18,
1926, San Jose, California
1958—*After School Sessions* (Chess); *One Dozen
Berrys*   1959—*Chuck Berry Is on Top*   1960—*New
Juke Box Hits*   1964—*Chuck Berry Greatest Hits*
1965—*Chuck Berry in London*   1967—*Golden Hits*
(Mercury); *Chuck Berry's Golden Decade* (Chess)
1972—*The London Sessions*   1973—*Golden Decade,
vol. 2*   1974—*Golden Decade, vol. 3*   1975—*Chuck
Berry '75*   1979—*Motorvatin'* (Atlantic); *Rockit*
(Atco)   1982—*The Great Twenty-eight* (Chess)
1986—*Rock 'n' Roll Rarities* (Chess/MCA)   1987—
Hail! Hail! Rock 'n' Roll (MCA)   1988—*The Chess
Box* (Chess/MCA)   1990—*Missing Berries: Rarities,
vol. 3.*

The archetypal rock & roller, Chuck Berry melded the
blues, country, and a witty, defiant teen outlook into
songs that have influenced virtually every rock musician
in his wake. In his best work—about 40 songs (including
"Round and Round," "Carol," "Brown-Eyed Handsome
Man," "Roll Over Beethoven," "Back in the U.S.A.," "Little
Queenie"), recorded mostly in the mid- and late Fifties—
Berry matched some of the most resonant and witty
lyrics in pop to music with a blues bottom and a country

Chuck Berry

top, trademarking the results with his signature double-
string guitar lick.

Berry learned guitar as a teenager. From 1944 to 1947
he was in reform school for attempted robbery; upon release he worked on the assembly line at a General Motors Fisher Body plant and studied hairdressing and
cosmetology at night school. In 1952 he formed a trio
with drummer Ebby Harding and pianist Johnnie Johnson, his keyboardist on and off for the next three
decades. By 1955 the trio had become a top St.
Louis–area club band, and Berry was supplementing his
salary as a beautician with regular gigs. He met Muddy
Waters in Chicago in May 1955, and Waters introduced
him to Leonard Chess. Berry played Chess a demo tape
that included "Ida Red"; Chess renamed it "Maybellene,"
and sent it to disc jockey Alan Freed (who got a cowriting credit in the deal), and Berry had his first Top Ten hit.

Through 1958 Berry had a string of hits. "School
Day" (#3 pop, #1 R&B, 1957), "Rock & Roll Music" (#8
pop, #6 R&B, 1957), "Sweet Little Sixteen" (#2 pop, #1
R&B, 1958), and "Johnny B. Goode" (#8 pop, #5 R&B,
1958) were the biggest. With his famous "duckwalk,"
Berry was a mainstay on the mid-Fifties concert circuit.
He also appeared in such films as *Rock, Rock, Rock*
(1956), *Mister Rock and Roll* (1957), and *Go, Johnny, Go*
(1959).

Late in 1959 Berry was charged with violating the
Mann Act: He had brought a 14-year-old Spanish-speak-
ing Apache prostitute from Texas to check hats in his St.

Louis nightclub, and after he fired her she complained to the police. After a blatantly racist first trial was disallowed, he was found guilty at a second. Berry spent two years in federal prison in Indiana, leaving him embittered.

By the time he was released in 1964, the British Invasion was under way, replete with Berry's songs on early albums by the Beatles and Rolling Stones. He recorded a few more classics—"Nadine," "No Particular Place to Go"—although it has been speculated that they were written before his jail term. Since then he has written and recorded only sporadically, although he had a million seller with "My Ding-a-Ling" (#1, 1972), and 1979's *Rockit* was a creditable effort. Berry still plays concerts, often with pickup bands, and he appeared in the 1979 film *American Hot Wax.*

In January 1986 Berry was among the first round of inductees into the Rock and Roll Hall of Fame. The following year he published the at-times sexually and scatologically explicit *Chuck Berry: The Autobiography,* and was the subject of a documentary/tribute film, *Hail! Hail! Rock 'n' Roll,* for which his best-known disciple, Keith Richards of the Rolling Stones, organized a backing band.

When not on the road, Berry lives in Wentzville, Missouri, where he owns the amusement complex Berry Park. Problems with the law and the Internal Revenue Service have continued to plague him. Shortly before a June 1979 performance for Jimmy Carter at the White House, the IRS charged Berry with income tax evasion, and he served a 100-day prison term in 1979. In 1988 in New York City, he paid a $250 fine to settle a $5 million lawsuit from a woman he allegedly punched in the mouth. In 1990 police raided his home and, finding 62 grams of marijuana and a number of videotapes of women—one of whom was apparently a minor—using the restroom in a Berry Park restaurant, filed felony drug and child-abuse charges against Berry. In order to have the child-abuse charges dropped, Berry agreed to drop a misconduct suit against the prosecuting attorney and to plead guilty to one misdemeanor count of marijuana possession. Berry was given a six-month suspended jail sentenced, placed on two years' unsupervised probation, and ordered to donate $5,000 to a local hospital.

Jello Biafra: See the Dead Kennedys

The B-52's

Formed 1976, Athens, Georgia
Cindy Wilson (b. Feb. 28, 1957, Athens), voc., perc., gtr.; Keith Strickland (b. Oct. 26, 1953, Athens), drums; Fred Schneider III (b. July 1, 1956, Newark, N.J.), voc.; Ricky Wilson (b. Mar. 19, 1953, Athens, d. Oct. 12, 1985), gtr.; Kate Pierson (b. April 27, 1948, Weehawken, N.J.), voc.

The B-52's: Keith Strickland, Cindy Wilson, Ricky Wilson, Kate Pierson, Fred Schneider

1979—*The B-52's* (Warner Bros.) **1980**—*Wild Planet* **1981**—*Party Mix* EP **1982**—*Mesopotamia* EP **1983**—*Whammy!* **1985**—(– R. Wilson) **1986**— *Bouncing off the Satellites* (Strickland switches to guitar) **1989**—*Cosmic Thing* (Reprise) **1990**— (– C. Wilson) **1991**—*Party Mix/Mesopotamia* cassette **1992**—*Good Stuff.*
Fred Schneider and the Shake Society: 1991—*Fred Schneider and the Shake Society* (Reprise).

Initially, the gleefully eccentric party music of the B-52's —stripped-down, off-kilter funk, topped by chirpy vocals and lyrics crammed with Fifties and Sixties trivia—garnered such a large following at dance clubs and colleges that their debut album sold 500,000 copies despite minimal airplay. Named for the tall bouffant hairdos worn on stage by the two female 52's, the band claims it originated in a jam session under the influence of tropical drinks. Fred Schneider, Kate Pierson, and Keith Strickland had had a little performing experience; the Wilson siblings had none. The B-52's debuted at a Valentine's Day party in 1977 in the college town of Athens, Georgia; they originally performed with taped guitar and drum parts, but preferred the sound when someone accidentally pulled the plug on the tape recorder.

Their first gig was at Max's Kansas City, and they soon attracted a New York cult, partly thanks to their stage image: miniskirts, go-go boots, toy instruments, and demonstrations of such dance steps as the Camel Walk and the Shy Tuna. They pressed 2,000 copies of the single "Rock Lobster," which sold out rapidly, before signing in early 1979 to Warner Bros. Their debut album sold steadily as the band toured the U.S. and Europe. *Wild Planet,* which hit #18 in 1980, was even more successful, and songs from it reappeared in remixed, more danceable versions on the *Party Mix* EP. For 1982's *Mesopotamia,* the B-52's collaborated with producer David Byrne of Talking Heads, who brought in backup musicians to broaden the sound.

Whammy! was a Top Thirty LP, boosted by the singles "Legal Tender" and "Song for a Future Generation" and their accompanying videos that captured the group's trademark retro American style. Guitarist Ricky Wilson's death from AIDS in 1985 made it impossible for the group to tour or promote *Bouncing off the Satellites.* Nearly four years passed before they returned with their most successful release, *Cosmic Thing.* With Keith Strickland moving from drums to lead guitar, the B-52's seemed to strike the perfect balance between their stylistic idiosyncrasies and a four-on-the-floor drive with "Love Shack" (#3, 1990); other hit singles from the LP, produced by Don Was and Nile Rodgers, were "Roam" (#3, 1990) and "Deadbeat Club" (#30, 1990). In 1990 Cindy Wilson retired from the group, which continued as a trio on *Good Stuff* (#16, 1992). Kate Pierson appears on Iggy Pop's hit single "Candy (1990)." Calling themselves the BC-52's, the band recorded "Meet the Flintstones" for the 1994 film version of *The Flintstones.* Cindy Wilson briefly rejoined the band for the group's ensuing appearances.

Big Audio Dynamite/B.A.D. II/Big Audio

Formed 1984, London, England
Mick Jones (b. Michael Jones, June 26, 1955, London), voc., gtr.; Don Letts, kybds.; Leo "E-Zee Kill" Williams, bass; Greg Roberts, drums; Dan Donovan, kybds.
1985—*This Is Big Audio Dynamite* (Columbia)
1986—*No. 10 Upping St.*   1988—*Tighten Up Vol. 88*
1989—*Megatop Phoenix.*
As B.A.D. II: 1991—(– Letts; – Williams; – Roberts; – Donovan; + Gary Stonadge [b. Nov. 24, 1962, Southampton, Eng.], bass; Nick Hawkins [b. Feb. 3, 1965, Luton, Eng.], gtr.; Chris Kavanagh [b. June 4, 1964, Woolwich, Eng.], drums; DJ Zonka [b. Michael Custance, July 4, 1962, London], DJ) *The Globe.*
As Big Audio: 1994—(+ Andre Shapps, kybds.) *Higher Power.*

With Big Audio Dynamite, Mick Jones took the mixing of styles he had experimented with in the Clash to adventurous extremes, creating a rock-reggae-house-hip-hop fusion ahead of its time. B.A.D. was one of the first British bands to sample and mix club and rock music, prefiguring such groups as EMF and the Farm.

Just over a year after he was kicked out of the Clash by Joe Strummer and Paul Simonon [see the Clash entry], who wanted the band to return to its "punk roots," Jones bounced back with an unlikely combo featuring filmmaker/DJ Don Letts and former Basement 5 bassist Leo Williams. The group played a series of dates in 1984 in France, opening for U2 and the Alarm, before adding keyboardist Dan Donovan. On *This Is Big Audio Dynamite,* B.A.D. programmed a swirl of sound effects and audio verité collage, including a running motif of dialogue from such movies as *A Fistful of Dollars.* Jones sang about the kind of political issues he had in the Clash on such songs as "Medicine Show," "E=MC2," and "The Bottom Line," but the emphasis was on dancing and rocking. B.A.D. polished their hybrid further on *No. 10 Upping St.,* which was produced and written by Jones with his old Clash-mate Joe Strummer and featured the college radio hit "C'mon Every Beatbox."

Tighten Up Vol. 88, featuring the single "Just Play Music," had barely been released when Jones caught chicken pox in 1988 from his daughter and nearly died. He spent nine months recuperating. The acid-house–inspired *Megatop Phoenix* was a spiritual rebirth for Jones; the album was dedicated to his grandmother, whose death in 1989 was even more traumatic to the singer than his own brush with mortality. Jones had found in the rave scene a musical movement whose energy reminded him of punk. Unfortunately, the rest of the band wasn't as interested in the new style, and they and Jones subsequently parted ways. Letts, Williams, and Roberts formed Screaming Target, while Donovan joined Sisters of Mercy.

Jones formed B.A.D. II in 1990 with three young musicians who shared his passion for raves and soccer, including former Sigue Sigue Sputnik drummer Chris Kavanagh. (Though DJ Zonka guested on 1991's *The Globe,* he didn't become an official member of the group until after its release.) In England they released an eight-song disc called *Kool-Aid,* as well as a live album, *Ally Pally Paradise,* that was packaged like a bootleg DJ record, white label and all.

On *The Globe* B.A.D. II explored systems, techno, and ambient music. The album also featured an acoustic ballad, an orchestral reprise, and the single "Rush" (#32), a techno rocker that samples the Who's "Baba O'Riley." The song was released as a B side to "Should I Stay or Should I Go?" when the Jones-penned Clash tune became a #1 U.K. single in 1991 after being used in a Levi's ad. Touring heavily behind the album, including opening for U2 on the U.S. Zoo TV Tour and playing with PiL on the 1992 MTV 120 Minutes Tour, B.A.D. II mixed rock-concert staging with a clubby environment, playing extended versions of songs and highlighting DJ Zonka's role. With the same lineup (plus keyboardist/coproducer Andre Shapps), the band returned as Big Audio in 1994, releasing *Higher Power*.

The Big Bopper

Born Jiles Perry "J. P." Richardson, October 24, 1930, Sabine Pass, Texas; died February 3, 1959, Iowa
1989—*Helloo Baby!: The Best of the Big Bopper, 1954–1959* (Rhino).

The Big Bopper, a disc jockey moonlighting as a pop star, was killed in a plane crash with Buddy Holly and Ritchie Valens, leaving as his legacy the line, "Oh baby that's-a what I like!"

Richardson began working as a disc jockey at KTRM, Beaumont, Texas, while still attending high school, calling himself the "Big Bopper." Except for a two-year hitch in the army he worked at KTRM the rest of his life. He began writing songs during his army years, and in 1957 he sent a demo of original material to a Houston record producer, who brought him to the attention of Mercury Records. He cut two country & western singles for Mercury under his real name and a novelty record called "The Purple People Eater Meets the Witch-Doctor" as the Big Bopper. The flip side was a rockabilly original called "Chantilly Lace," which became the international hit of 1958.

He followed "Chantilly Lace" with two modest singles, "Little Red Riding Hood" and "The Big Bopper's Wedding," and developed a stage show based on his radio persona. Buddy Holly, a longtime West Texas friend, invited him to accompany a Midwestern tour in the winter of 1959. On February 3, 1959, between concert stops in Mason City, Iowa, and Fargo, North Dakota, the tour plane flew into a snowstorm and crashed, killing all on board.

Richardson left little in the way of recordings. As a songwriter, however, he returned to the charts a year after his death with "Running Bear," which he'd written for Johnny Preston.

Big Brother and the Holding Company

Formed 1965, San Francisco, California
Peter Albin (b. June 6, 1944, San Francisco), bass, gtr., voc.; Sam Andrew (b. Dec. 18, 1941, Taft, Calif.), gtr., piano, sax, voc.; James Gurley (b. Dec. 22, 1939, Detroit, Mich.), gtr.; David Getz (b. Jan. 24, 1940, Brooklyn, N.Y.), drums, piano, voc.; Janis Joplin (b. Jan. 19, 1943, Port Arthur, Tex.; d. Oct. 4, 1970, Hollywood, Calif.), voc.

1967—*Big Brother and the Holding Company* (Mainstream); 1968—*Cheap Thrills* (Columbia) (– Joplin; – Andrew) 1970—(+ David Shallock, bass; + Nick Gravenites [b. Chicago, Ill.], voc.) *Be a Brother* (– Gurley; – Shallock; – Gravenites; + Andrew; + Michael Pendergrass, gtr.; + Kathy McDonald, voc.; + Mike Finnigan, kybds.) 1971—*How Hard It Is* 1973—*Joplin's Greatest Hits* 1982—*Farewell Song* 1984—*Cheaper Thrills* (Edsel) 1985—*Big Brother and the Holding Company Live* (Capitol) 1986—*Joseph's Coat* (Edsel) 1993—*Janis* (Sony).

While Big Brother and the Holding Company are remembered as Janis Joplin's band, they were active before Joplin joined them and after she left. Leader Peter Albin (a country-blues guitarist who had played with future founders of the Grateful Dead Jerry Garcia and Ron McKernan) met Sam Andrew, Big Brother's musical director, who had a jazz and classical background and had played rock & roll professionally; they approached James Gurley (who had taught himself to play guitar on hallucinogenic sojourns through the California desert) and the three began playing open jam sessions hosted by entrepreneur Chet Helms in 1965. Helms encouraged them to form a group, found them a drummer, and set up their first gig, at the Trips Festival of January 1966. In the Festival audience was art historian and amateur musician David Getz, who soon replaced the original drummer. Big Brother and the Holding Company became the house band at the Avalon Ballroom, playing a progressive style of instrumental rock. Feeling a need for a strong vocalist, Helms recalled having heard Joplin before, and contacted her in Austin, Texas. She returned to San Francisco to join the band in June 1966.

The Holding Company was clearly blues-influenced, and Joplin had listened intensively to Bessie Smith, Ma Rainey, and Big Mama Thornton. Joplin's voice and presence, and the band's devil-may-care intensity, made them a whole greater than the sum of its parts—and a Bay Area sensation. Their debut album spread their reputation, and their appearance at the Monterey Pop Festival in June 1967 thrust them into the national spotlight. New manager Albert Grossman brought them to Columbia Records, which issued their legacy, *Cheap Thrills*.

Cheap Thrills went to #1 with the help of "Piece of My Heart" (#12, 1968). Numerous observers convinced Joplin that she could use a more precise backing band, and at the end of 1968 she and Andrew left the group [see Janis Joplin entry]. After a year, Big Brother returned as a loose assemblage of four to eight musicians, which might include Gravenites (ex–Electric Flag), McDonald (a backup vocalist for Ike and Tina Turner, Joe Cocker, and Leon Russell), or no lead singer at all. Albin and Andrew were the only regular members (at times only Andrew). In 1972 Big Brother disbanded; the group re-formed in 1986. By the early Nineties they were recording and performing in Europe and on the West Coast; Andrew was also reported forming a band with ex-Monkee Peter Tork and saxophonist Snooky Flowers, formerly with the Kozmic Blues Band, the group that had succeeded Big Brother in backing Joplin.

Big Country

Formed 1982, Dunfermline, Scotland
Stuart Adamson (b. Apr. 11, 1958, Manchester, Eng.), voc., gtr.; Mark Brzezicki (b. June 21, 1957, Slough, Eng.), drums; Tony Butler (b. Feb. 2, 1957, London, Eng.), bass; Bruce Watson (b. Mar. 11, 1961, Timmins, Ontario, Can.), gtr.
1983—*The Crossing* (Mercury)   1984—*Wonderland* EP; *Steeltown*   1986—*The Seer*   1988—*Peace in Our Time* (Reprise)   1990—*Through a Big Country: Greatest Hits* (Mercury, U.K.)   1991—*No Place Like Home* (Vertigo, U.K.)   1993—*The Buffalo Skinners* (Fox/RCA)   1994—*The Best of Big Country* (Mercury).

In the early Eighties Big Country was among a sprinkling of bands that favored guitars over synthesizers and earnest idealism over irony. Like their contemporaries in U2 and the Alarm, the members of Big Country were inspired by punk's energy and its emphasis on connecting with the audience.

Lead singer Stuart Adamson launched his rock career by playing guitar in a self-styled punk quartet called the Skids, who released three albums between 1977 and 1980 and had a #10 hit in England with the 1979 single "Into the Valley." Believing that the band was not living up to its initial ideals of professional and artistic integrity, Adamson decided to form his own band in Scotland. Big Country's first incarnation featured Adamson on vocals and guitar, plus four local Scottish musicians, among them guitarist Bruce Watson. Adamson and Watson eventually parted company with the other three and hooked up with London sessionmen Mark Brzezicki and Tony Butler, who had previously played in a trio with Pete Townshend's brother Simon, a childhood friend of Butler's.

After a series of sessions with producer Chris Thomas, Big Country decided to enlist U2 producer Steve Lillywhite for its debut album. The resulting effort, 1983's *The Crossing,* emphasized the young band's penchant for passionate, often anthemic songs and Celtic-flavored arrangements that were at once fierce and folky. ROLLING STONE made note of Adamson's "unconventional guitar playing, which at times recalls such traditional instruments as bagpipes or fiddles"—a feature that was a highlight of Big Country's first and thus far biggest hit, "In a Big Country" (#17, 1983). The following year the EP *Wonderland* and the album *Steeltown* were also well received. Since then, the band's recordings have faltered critically and commercially in the U.S., though still consistently reaching the Top Thirty in the U.K.

Big Daddy Kane

Born Antonio M. Hardy, September 10, 1968, Brooklyn, New York
1988—*Long Live the Kane* (Cold Chillin')   1989—*It's a Big Daddy Thing*   1990—*Taste of Chocolate*   1991—*Prince of Darkness*   1993—*Looks Like a Job for Big Daddy Kane*   1994—*Daddy's Home.*

With his suave good looks and hard, smooth vocal delivery, Big Daddy Kane became rap's first niche-marketed sex symbol. In addition to his own albums, videos, and performances, he has written hits for other artists and posed nude in *Playgirl* magazine (June 1991) and for Madonna's 1992 book, *Sex.* He has been described as the Barry White of rap.

Kane grew up in the tough Bedford-Stuyvesant neighborhood of Brooklyn. As a child, he listened to his mother's records by artists such as Evelyn "Champagne" King; later, he discovered his own favorites in White and Otis Redding. In junior high Kane was introduced to the two worlds he would soon join: the rap world and the Five Percent Nation, an elitist black Muslim sect popular among the hip-hop community. By high school, he had begun writing poetry and looking up to the pioneering rap of Melle Mel, Grandmaster Caz, and Kool Moe Dee.

As his wordplay improved, Kane was asked to write material for the Juice Crew and Kurtis Blow. By 1988 his songs had been covered by Biz Markie ("Vapors" [#80 R&B, 1988] and the notorious "Pickin' Boogers") and Roxanne Shanté ("Have a Nice Day" and "Go On Girl"). After touring as Shanté's DJ, Kane decided to try rapping.

For his first album, produced by Marley Marl, the songs Kane wrote for himself proved as wide-ranging as those he'd written for others. The macho posturing on "Raw" became his calling card, with the rest of the album ranging from the romantic ("The Day You're Mine") to the cool and funky ("Ain't No Half-Steppin'"). Kane's subsequent albums relied on a similar recipe. Although he has received consistent critical kudos, Kane has also been criticized for promoting homophobia and sexism. In the Nineties he has acted in movies, appearing in *Posse* and *Meteor Man.*

Big Star/Alex Chilton

Formed 1971, Memphis, Tennessee
Alex Chilton (b. Dec. 28, 1950, Memphis), voc., gtr.; Chris Bell (b. Jan. 12, 1951, Memphis; d. Dec. 27, 1978, Memphis), voc., gtr.; Andy Hummel (b. Jan. 26, 1951, Memphis), bass; Jody Stephens (b. Oct. 4, 1952, Memphis), drums.
1972—*#1 Record* (Ardent)   1973—(– Bell)   1974—*Radio City* (– Hummel)   1978—*Third* (a.k.a. *Sister Lovers* [Rykodisc, 1992]) (PVC)   1992—*Big Star Live* (Rykodisc)   1993—(+ Jonathan Auer, gtr, voc.;

+ Ken Stringfellow, gtr., bass) *Columbia: Live at Missouri University* (Zoo).
Alex Chilton solo: 1977—*Singer Not the Song* EP (Ork)   1979—*Like Flies on Sherbert* (Peabody)   1985—*Feudalist Tarts* EP (Big Time)   1986—*No Sex* EP   1987—*High Priest*   1991—*19 Years: A Collection of Alex Chilton* (Rhino)   1994—*Clichés* (Ardent)   1995—*A Man Called Destruction.*
Chris Bell solo: 1992—*I Am the Cosmos* (Rykodisc).

Big Star's combination of Beatles-style melody, Who-like punch, and Byrdsy harmonies defined power pop before the term (or an audience for it) existed. Though the group lasted less than four years, it has had an enduring effect, particularly on a new generation of alternative rockers. A commercial failure, Big Star has acquired near mythic status via such songs as "September Gurls," as well as through the continuing solo work and mystique of its chief singer/songwriter, Alex Chilton. Paid homage to by the Replacements ("Alex Chilton" from 1987's *Pleased to Meet Me*), Big Star has influenced a number of artists, ranging from Georgia's R.E.M. to Scotland's Teenage Fanclub to New Zealand's Chills.

The band was formed in Memphis by singer/songwriter Chris Bell; Alex Chilton, who'd been a hitmaker in the Box Tops [see entry], was recruited soon after. Following the release of the band's richly textured debut, *#1 Record,* Bell left the group. Drummer Jody Stephens and bassist Andy Hummel stayed on, and, with Chilton at the helm, the band recorded the more stripped-down *Radio City.* (Chilton's "September Gurls," from *Radio City,* was later covered by the Bangles on their platinum album *Different Light.*) Though both albums garnered critical raves, neither sold well and the band fizzled. The dark and haunting *Third* (a.k.a. *Sister Lovers;* the LP was never titled at its completion), more of a Chilton solo effort, was not officially issued in the U.S. for years.

Bell, whose solo recordings were posthumously released in 1992, was killed in a car accident in 1978. Chilton moved to New York, formed a band that included future dB Chris Stamey, and recorded an EP. He made the adventurous *Like Flies on Sherbert* in Memphis with *Third's* producer Jim Dickinson. Then after producing recordings by the Cramps [see entry] and swampabilly band Panther Burns, Chilton disappeared from the scene. He reemerged in New Orleans in the mid-Eighties, playing mostly cover songs in clubs. His music of this period, recorded on *Feudalist Tarts, No Sex,* and *High Priest,* veered more toward R&B. Usually with a trio, he continued to tour the U.S. and European club circuit into the Nineties, mixing his original songs with an eclectic selection of covers. He recorded several of the jazz songs and standards of his live shows on *Clichés. A Man Called Destruction* consists of Chilton originals and R&B-tinged obscurities.

In 1993 students at the University of Missouri coaxed Chilton and drummer Jody Stephens (by then projects director at Ardent Records, Big Star's Seventies label) to reunite for a campus concert. With bassist Andy Hummel long retired from music, Jon Auer and Ken Stringfellow of the Posies were recruited to round out the quartet. *Columbia* chronicles the sloppy but spirited set that draws from all three Big Star LPs. Big Star sporadically performed together through the following year.

Big Youth
Born Manley Buchanan, circa 1949, Kingston, Jamaica
1973—*Screaming Target* (Trojan, U.K.)   1976—*Natty Cultural Dread; Hit the Road Jack*   1977—*Reggae Phenomenon* (Big Youth, U.K.)
1978—*Dreadlocks Dread* (Klik, U.K.); *Isaiah, First Prophet of Old*   1979—*Everyday Skank (Best of)* (Trojan, U.K.)   1982—*Some Great Big Youth* (Heartbeat)   1983—*The Chanting Dread Inna Fine Style*   1984—*Live at Reggae Sunsplash* (Sunsplash)   1985—*A Luta Continua* (Heartbeat)   1988—*Manifestation*   1990—*Jamming in the House of Dread* cassette (ROIR).

A cabbie turned disc jockey, Big Youth was Jamaica's most popular "toaster" (a disc jockey who ad libs over instrumental tracks) in the Seventies. His early records featured rhymes, doggerel, and scat singing over previously released tunes by other artists remixed to cut out the original vocals and bring out the bass and drums. His style influenced the early rappers, who adapted his Caribbean methods to the inner city. Like his first hit, "Ace 90 Skank" (1972), his songs frequently dealt with current events: When a heavyweight boxing championship was fought in Kingston in 1973, Youth took to the airwaves with "George Foreman" and "Foreman and Frazier."

Big Youth later adopted Rastafarianism as his religion, and his songs took on weightier topics, as in "House of Dreadlocks" and "Natty Cultural Dread." He also began writing his own music, recording with a band and singing in a high, breathy croon rather than toasting. "When Revolution Come," produced by Prince Buster, was his first of many Jamaican chart-toppers in the mid-Seventies. He performs periodically in the U.S. and Great Britain and appears at the annual Reggae Sunsplash festival.

Bikini Kill
Formed October 1990, Olympia, Washington
Tobi Vail (b. July 20, 1969, Auburn, Wash.), drums; Kathleen Hanna (b. Kathleen Hanna-Dando, June 9, 1969, Portland, Ore.), voc.; Billy Boredom (b. William F. Karren, Mar. 10, 1965, Memphis,

Tenn.), gtr.; Kathi Wilcox (b. Nov. 19, 1969, Vancouver, Wash.), bass.
1992—*Bikini Kill* EP (Kill Rock Stars)   1993—*Yeah Yeah Yeah Yeah* (split album with Huggy Bear's *Our Troubled Youth*); *Pussy Whipped*.

Proclaiming themselves riot grrrls and calling for "Revolution Girl Style Now," Bikini Kill pioneered both a musical and a feminist movement in the early Nineties. Hanna, Vail, and Wilcox met at Evergreen College in Olympia. In their feminist fanzine *Bikini Kill* they articulated an agenda for young women in and outside of music; the band put those ideas to practice. Bikini Kill soon earned a reputation in the punk underground for confronting certain standards of that genre; for example, asking people to slam at the side of the stage, so that women would not get pushed out of the front, and inviting women to take the mic and talk about sexual abuse. A former stripper, Hanna (who inspired Nirvana's first hit by spraypainting "Smells Like Teen Spirit" on Kurt Cobain's house) challenges the sexual expectations of her audience by pulling her shirt off or writing "Kill Me" across her stomach or chest.

In 1991 Bikini Kill circulated a tape, *Revolution Girl Style Now,* that introduced their fiery style. Some of the same songs appear in new versions, produced by Fugazi's Ian Mackaye, on their debut EP, which features the call-to-arms "Double Dare Ya" and the wrenching "Feels Blind." The Olympia-based indie Kill Rock Stars (Bikini Kill refuses to work with majors) released *Yeah Yeah Yeah Yeah,* an album backed with British riot grrrl band Huggy Bear's *Our Troubled Youth,* in a joint venture with the U.K. label Catcall on International Women's Day.

Huggy Bear and Bikini Kill toured England together in the spring of 1993, generating a wave of international interest in riot grrrl and a storm of controversy in the British press. That fall, Joan Jett produced a Bikini Kill single featuring the anthem "Rebel Girl"; Jett and the band toured together the next year. On *Pussy Whipped* Bikini Kill returned to a rawer sound; the album included songs by Vail and Wilcox as well as Hanna.

Birdsongs of the Mesozoic: See Mission of Burma

The Birthday Party/Nick Cave and the Bad Seeds
Formed 1977 (as the Boys Next Door), Melbourne, Australia; as the Birthday Party, 1980, London, England
Nick Cave (b. Nicholas Edward Cave, Sep. 22, 1957, Warracknabeal, Austral.), voc.; Rowland S. Howard (b. Oct. 24, 1959, Melbourne), gtr.; Mick Harvey

(b. Sep. 29, 1958, Rochester, Austral.), gtr., kybds., bass, drums; Tracy Pew (d. 1986), bass; Phil Calvert, drums.
1981—*Prayers on Fire* (Thermidor, U.K.)   1982—*Junkyard* (4AD, U.K.) (– Calvert)   1983—*The Bad Seed* EP; *Mutiny!* EP (Mute) (group disbands) 1985—*A Collection . . .* (Missing Link, U.K.)   1991—*Peel Session Album* (Strange Fruit).
Nick Cave and the Bad Seeds, formed September 1983, London, England: Cave, voc.; Harvey, drums, bass, gtr., kybds.; Barry Adamson (b. June 1, 1958, Manchester, Eng.), bass; Blixa Bargeld (b. Jan. 12, 1959, Berlin, Ger.), gtr.
1984—*From Her to Eternity* (Mute)   1985—*The Firstborn Is Dead*   1986—(+ Thomas Wydler [b. Oct. 9, 1959, Zurich, Switz.]), drums) *Kicking Against the Pricks*; *Your Funeral . . . My Trial* 1987—(– Adamson)   1988—(+ Roland Wolf, kybds.; + Kid Congo Powers [b. Brian Tristan, March 27, 1961, La Puente, Calif.], gtr.) *Tender Prey* 1990—(– Wolf) *The Good Son*   1992—(– Powers; + Conway Savage [b. July 27, 1960, Foster, Austral.], kybds.; + Martyn P. Casey [b. July 10, 1960, Chesterfield, Eng.], bass) *Henry's Dream*   1993—*Live Seeds* 1994—*Let Love In.*
Crime and the City Solution, formed 1984, Melbourne, Australia: Simon Bonney (b. June 3, 1961, Sydney, Austral.), voc.; Bronwyn Adams (b. July 31, 1961, Melbourne), violin; Rowland S. Howard, gtr.; Harry Howard (b. Oct. 10, 1961, Melbourne), bass; Mick Harvey, drums. 1986—(+ Epic Soundtracks [b. Paul Godley], drums) *Room of Lights* (Mute) 1987—(– Soundtracks; – R. Howard; – H. Howard; + Alexander Hacke [b. Oct. 11, 1965, Berlin, Ger.], gtr.) *Shine*   1989—*The Bride Ship*   1990—*Paradise Discotheque*   1992—*The Dolphins and the Sharks* 1993—*The Adversary Live.*
These Immortal Souls, formed 1987, London, England: R. Howard; H. Howard; Soundtracks; Genevieve McGuckin, kybds.
1987—*Get Lost (Don't Lie!)* (SST)   1992—*I'm Never Gonna Die Again* (Mute).
Cave/Bargeld/Harvey: 1989—*Ghosts . . . of the Civil Dead* soundtrack (Mute).

The Birthday Party's combination of cacophonous, feverish, overdriven postpunk guitar with Delta blues and Nick Cave's alternately morose and ranting vocals set loose an entire generation of Australian and English noisemongers upon the earth. Since the Birthday Party imploded in 1983, its members, led by singer/songwriter Nick Cave, have formed an orbit of bands that share members and a dramatically gothic sensibility.

The Birthday Party had its beginnings in Melbourne, Australia, where the teenaged Nick Cave, sent to boarding school after a series of petty thieveries and mischief in his hometown, met Mick Harvey. They started writing songs and put together their first band in the mid-Seventies. Originally called the Boys Next Door, in 1979 they released *Door Door* and *Hee Haw* in Australia.

Feeling constrained by the provincial Melbourne scene, the band set off for England in 1980, changing its name to the Birthday Party en route. An Australian album was released that year under both names. Their intense, assaultive live act and appearances on early supporter John Peel's BBC-1 radio program led to a contract with 4AD and the recording of their signature album, *Junkyard*. Bassist Tracy Pew was arrested on drug charges in 1981 (he died from epilepsy in 1986); former Magazine [see entry] bassist Barry Adamson guested on *Junkyard*. Phil Calvert left to join the Psychedelic Furs.

Because of their violent and sacrilegious subject matter ("Dead Joe," "Big-Jesus-Trash-Can," "The Six Strings That Drew Blood") and dark, brooding attitude, the Birthday Party found themselves lumped with "goth" bands like Bauhaus. They moved to Berlin in 1982 and recorded another EP, *The Bad Seed*, but drug problems and personal pressures were too much to deal with, and the band split while recording their final EP, *Mutiny!*, in 1983.

Cave, with Adamson and Harvey, returned to London. They formed the Bad Seeds, adding Einstürzende Neubauten [see entry] guitarist Blixa Bargeld. A more refined, controlled version of the Birthday Party, the Bad Seeds retained the earlier band's intensity, but Cave added a Leonard Cohen–style romantic gloom. He also unveiled an Elvis obsession, with a cover of "In the Ghetto" on *Eternity*; both *The Firstborn Is Dead* and its initial single "Tupelo" (1985) directly concern Presley. Cave showed his range on 1986's *Kicking Against the Pricks*, covering Leadbelly, gospel, Hendrix, and "By the Time I Get to Phoenix" with conviction. The same year, the group released a double EP of original material, *Your Funeral . . . My Trial*. After a two-year break, the Bad Seeds came back, adding Cramps guitarist Kid Congo Powers, who filled out the band's sound on *Tender Prey*.

Cave then took time off from rock to pursue his literary ambitions. *King Ink*, a collection of song lyrics, plays, and prose pieces, was published in England in 1988; a novel, *And the Ass Saw the Angel*, was published the next year. The Southern Gothic fable, filled with Cave's scatologically religious imagery, received generally favorable notices.

He returned to music in 1990 with *The Good Son*. Recorded in Brazil with a mostly acoustic band, the album has a quiet, mournful intensity. The Bad Seeds' next two albums, *Henry's Dream* and *Let Love In*, in-creasingly focused on Cave's richly narrative compositions.

Simon Bonney, a friend of the Birthday Party's in Melbourne, began playing with ex-members once the band broke up in 1983. Bonney had led several versions of Crime and the City Solution, but until ex–Birthday Party members Rowland S. and Harry Howard and Mick Harvey joined in 1984, he was unable to get signed. Former Swell Maps drummer Epic Soundtracks was enlisted in time for *Room of Lights*; in 1987, the Howards and Soundtracks left to form These Immortal Souls. Bonney followed the Melbourne–Berlin axis, using Neubauten guitarist Alexander Hacke and German session musicians on later albums (after that band fizzled, Bonney began a solo career, as did Soundtracks).

The music of these bands is so dramatic, it is no surprise that most of the musicians have been drawn to cinema. Cave appeared, as himself, in Wim Wenders' 1988 film *Wings of Desire* (as did Crime and the City Solution); a part in *Johnny Suede* (with Brad Pitt) followed in 1991. Collaborating with Bargeld and Rowland S. Howard, Cave wrote and performed the soundtrack for *Ghosts . . . of the Civil Dead*. Both Cave and Crime and the City Solution appeared on the soundtrack of Wenders' 1990 film *Until the End of the World*; Bonney and Cave each contributed two songs to the director's 1993 *Faraway, So Close*.

Elvin Bishop

Born October 21, 1942, Tulsa, Oklahoma
1969—*Elvin Bishop* (Fillmore)   1970—*Feel It* (Epic)
1971—*Rock My Soul*; *Applejack*   1972—*Crabshaw Rising: The Best of Elvin Bishop*   1974—*Let It Flow* (Capricorn)   1975—*Juke Joint Jump*   1976—*Struttin' My Stuff*; *Hometown Boy Makes Good*   1977— *Live! Raisin' Hell*   1978—*Hog Heaven*   1979—*The Best of Elvin Bishop*   1988—*Big Fun* (Alligator) 1991—*Don't Let the Bossman Get You Down!* 1994—*Tulsa Shuffle: The Best of Elvin Bishop* (Legacy).

Although Elvin Bishop's good-humored blues rock was well-received live, the ex–Paul Butterfield guitarist didn't establish his solo recording career until his 1976 smash hit single "Fooled Around and Fell in Love"— sung by Mickey Thomas, who went on to join Jefferson Starship.

Bishop met Paul Butterfield at the University of Chicago. Though Bishop had just started playing guitar, he and Butterfield began jamming together at parties; Bishop also played the Chicago folk circuit by himself. Eventually he and Butterfield jammed with Muddy Waters, Howlin' Wolf, and other leading South Side bluesmen.

He moved to New York, where he worked breaking

toys (for manufacturers' discounts) at a department store, but returned to Chicago to join the first Paul Butterfield Blues Band [see entry]. After *The Resurrection of Pigboy Crabshaw*, Bishop left the Blues Band to form his own group, settling in Mill Valley, California. He brought with him a Boston folk trio: Jo, Janice and Mary. Jo Baker was the only one to remain with the group. Bishop also jammed with Al Kooper at the Fillmore when Mike Bloomfield was ill. Bishop signed with Bill Graham's Fillmore Records and made several albums.

Dickey Betts of the Allman Brothers Band persuaded Capricorn's Phil Walden to sign Bishop. His first few Capricorn LPs sold fairly well, yielding near-hits in "Travelin' Shoes" and "Sure Feels Good." His breakthrough finally came with *Struttin' My Stuff* and its #3 single "Fooled Around and Fell in Love." Bishop hasn't had a real hit since, but continues to tour and record every so often. Nineteen-eighty-eight's *Big Fun* was his first U.S. release in nearly ten years (a 1981 LP, *Is You Is or Is You Ain't My Baby*, came out in Germany); *Don't Let the Bossman Get You Down!*, a mix of Bishop originals and old blues, was hailed as a delightful return to form.

Biz Markie

Born Marcel Hall, April 8, 1964, New York City, New York
1988—*Goin' Off* (Cold Chillin') 1989—*The Biz Never Sleeps* 1991—*I Need a Haircut* 1993—*All Samples Cleared!*

The class clown of New York hip-hop, Biz Markie proved himself as adept at goofily sincere crooning and low-brow comedy as rapping. A rap link to the Coasters of "Charlie Brown" and "Yakety Yak," he is also known for losing the first rap-sampling lawsuit to be decided by a judge.

Born in Harlem and reared on Long Island, Biz got his start on the early-Eighties downtown–Manhattan rap scene in such clubs as the Roxy and the Funhouse. In 1985 he met producer Marley Marl (L.L. Cool J, Big Daddy Kane) and made his first demo recordings. His debut album, *Goin' Off* (#90 pop, #19 R&B, 1988), had such club hits as "Vapors" (#80 R&B, 1988), "Make the Music with Your Mouth, Biz" (a showcase for his human beat-box skills), and the gross-out comedy classic "Pickin' Boogers."

Biz Markie's triumph came with *The Biz Never Sleeps* (#66 pop, #9 R&B, 1989), which featured a Top Ten pop crossover hit in "Just a Friend" (#9, 1990)—a disarmingly abject expression of romantic betrayal in which Biz rapped the verses and sang the pleading chorus in passionate, off-key fashion.

But his next album brought disaster: *Haircut* (with a cover showing a chainsaw being put to Biz's head) included "Alone Again"—built on an unauthorized sample of the piano figure underpinning Gilbert O'Sullivan's 1972 #1 pop hit, "Alone Again (Naturally)." O'Sullivan sued, and in a landmark court case, the presiding judge ruled against Biz Markie, ordering Warner Bros. to remove all copies of *Haircut* worldwide. The album (#113 pop, #44 R&B, 1991) quickly went out of print and labels made greater efforts to clear permission before using copyrighted material. Markie covered himself, and kept his sense of humor, with *All Samples Cleared!*—appearing on the cover as an angry judge handing down a sentence on himself.

Björk: See the Sugarcubes

Bill Black Combo

Formed 1959, Memphis, Tennessee
Bill Black (b. William Patton Black, Sep. 17, 1926, Memphis; d. Oct. 21, 1965, Memphis), bass; Carl McAvoy, piano; Martin Wills, saxophone; Reggie Young, gtr.; Jerry Arnold, drums.
1960—*Solid and Raunchy* (Hi); *Saxy Jazz* 1961—*That Wonderful Feeling* (Circa 1961: + Bobby Emmons, piano; + Bob Tucker, gtr.) 1962—*Let's Twist Her*; *Record Hop* (– Black) 1963—*Untouchable Sound*; *Greatest Hits* 1964—*Bill Black's Combo Plays the Blues*; *Tunes by Chuck Berry*; *Goes West*; *Goes Big Band* 1965—*More Solid and Raunchy*; *Mr. Beat* 1966—*All-Timers* 1967—*Black Lace*; *King of the Road* 1969—*Solid and Raunchy the Third* 1972—*Juke Box Favorites* 1973—*Rock 'n' Roll Forever* 1974—*Bill Black Is Back* 1975—*Solid and Country*; *World's Greatest Honky-Tonk Band*. Circa 1981: Bob Tucker, gtr.; Gil Michael, pedal steel gtr., fiddle; Bill Compton, drums; Robert Gladney, sax; Phil Munsey, bass.

In 1954 in Memphis, Bill Black, a neighbor of guitarist Scotty Moore, happened to visit Moore's home one day when he and a young truck driver named Elvis Presley were playing together for the first time. Soon thereafter Sam Phillips, founder of Sun Records, hired both Black and Moore to rehearse with Presley. Their first recording, "That's All Right," was Presley's first hit.

Black toured and recorded with Presley until 1959, when he formed the Bill Black Combo, an instrumental group. The Top Twenty hit "Smokie (Part 2)" sold over a million copies in 1959, as did "Josephine," "White Silver Sands," and "Don't Be Cruel" in 1960. During this time Black became particularly popular in Europe. He retired from the band in 1962 and died three years later from a brain tumor. The Bill Black Combo continued working and recording.

Clint Black

Born February 4, 1962, Long Branch, New Jersey
1989—*Killin' Time* (RCA)   1990—*Put Yourself in My Shoes*   1992—*The Hard Way*   1993—*No Time to Kill*   1994—*One Emotion*.

With his husky, expressive voice and matinee-idol looks, Clint Black is one of the dominant forces in Nineties country music. Between 1989 and late 1994, he sold over eight million albums and had 12 #1 C&W singles, including "A Better Man" (1989) and "Loving Blind" (1991).

Born in New Jersey (where his father was working on a pipeline), Black grew up near Houston. His father, a Cole Porter fan, originally wanted to name his son after the songwriter. He resisted the urge, and Clint was spared the name "Cole Black." Part of a musical family, Black started playing harmonica at 13; by 15 he had taught himself guitar, had started writing songs, and was performing everything from Merle Haggard to Yes with one of his three brothers in the Full House Band. He dropped out of high school in 1979 and spent the next eight years working in construction, writing songs, and playing clubs.

Black met Hayden Nicholas, his main songwriting collaborator, at a club in 1987. Nicholas joined Black's band, and the two soon began work on a demo. Their break came later that year when ZZ Top producer and manager Bill Ham met Black, was impressed, and got him a deal with RCA.

"A Better Man" was the first C&W debut single to top the charts in 14 years. *Killin' Time* (#31 pop, #1 C&W, 1989) contained three other #1 C&W singles: "Killin' Time" (1989), "Nobody's Home" (1989), and "Walkin' Away" (1990). It held the #1 spot on the C&W chart for eight months, sold over three million copies, and won four Academy of Country Music awards. Black, who, unlike other country acts, toured with his studio band, also became a major concert attraction.

Put Yourself in My Shoes (#18 pop, #1 C&W, 1990) proved that Black was no fluke, with two #1 C&W hits, "Where Are You Now" (1991) and "Loving Blind" (1991). Black was named best male vocalist of 1990 by the Country Music Association. He recorded a duet with legendary King of the Cowboys Roy Rogers, "Hold On Partner" (#42 C&W, 1991).

Black's marriage to *Knots Landing* star Lisa Hartman in 1991 and his messy break with manager Bill Ham in 1992 led to some speculation that Black was losing touch with his "roots." But the rueful, melancholy album *The Hard Way* (#8 pop, #2 C&W, 1992) proved otherwise.

The following year's *No Time to Kill* included a hit duet with Wynonna Judd, "A Bad Goodbye" (#2 C&W, 1993), and backing vocals from Kenny Loggins and former Eagle Timothy B. Schmit. In 1994 Black released his fifth album, *One Emotion* (#8 C&W), which yielded several C&W Top Ten singles, including the #1 "A Good Run of Bad Luck."

Frank Black: See Pixies

Blackbird: See Rank and File

The Black Crowes

Formed 1988, Atlanta, Georgia
Chris Robinson (b. Dec. 20, 1966, Atlanta), voc.; Rich Robinson (b. May 24, 1969, Atlanta), gtr.; Jeff Cease, gtr.; Johnny Colt (b. May 1, 1968, Cherry Point, N.C.), bass; Steve Gorman (b. Aug. 17, 1965, Hopkinsville, Ky.), drums.
1990—*Shake Your Moneymaker* (Def American) (– Cease; + Marc Ford [b. April 13, 1966, Los Angeles, Calif.], gtr.)   1992—*The Southern Harmony and Musical Companion*   1994—(+ Eddie Harsch [b. May 27, 1957, Toronto, Ont.], kybds.) *Amorica* (American).

With members not much older than the trends they revived, the Black Crowes had the look (long hair, velvet flares, fur-trimmed vests, impossibly skinny physiques) and the bluesy, boozy, two-guitar rock sound of the early-Seventies Rolling Stones and Faces.

The Robinson brothers' father Stan was a onetime singer who had a pop hit in 1959 with "Boom-a-Dip-Dip." He discouraged his sons from becoming professional musicians, but by 1984 they had formed the band Mr. Crowe's Garden (named for a favorite childhood fairy tale), which evolved into the Black Crowes, with Chris dropping out of college along the way. Their debut album, *Shake Your Moneymaker* (#4, 1990) sold a million copies and won them Best New American Band in the ROLLING STONE readers and critics polls. In true album-rock throwback fashion, its singles were only minor hits: "Jealous Again" (#75, 1990), "She Talks to Angels" (#30, 1991), and a cover of Otis Redding's "Hard to Handle" (#26, 1991).

In March 1991 the Black Crowes were fired from their opening-act slot on ZZ Top's Miller Beer–sponsored tour after Chris Robinson, onstage in Atlanta, made sarcastic remarks about commercialism. That May the Crowes launched their own tour and—three shows in—fired opening act Maggie's Dream, after hearing that band in a Miller Beer radio ad. Also in May, Chris Robinson was arrested for assault and disturbing the peace after a post-show argument with a female customer at a Denver convenience store. Before pleading no contest three months later (he got six months' probation and a $53 fine), he collapsed of malnutrition and exhaustion during a British tour. Upon his recovery the Crowes played Moscow on the Monsters of Rock Tour of the Soviet Union.

With new guitarist Marc Ford (from Los Angeles band Burning Tree), the Crowes acted on their pro-marijuana rhetoric by playing the April 1992 Great Atlanta Pot Festival, staged by the National Organization to Reform Marijuana Laws. Two months later the band's second album (named for an antebellum hymnal) entered the *Billboard* pop albums chart at #1; again its singles were only minor hits: "Remedy" (#48, 1992) and "Thorn in My Pride" (#80, 1992). In February 1993 the band played a free show in Houston, with its own hand-picked security, to make up for a show the previous October, at which, the band felt, security guards had roughed up fans. The next month the band ended a Louisville, Kentucky, show after one song, ostensibly because of a backstage fracas between its road crew and plainclothes narcotics officers. The band's security chief and merchandising supervisor were charged with assault and resisting arrest. The band's 1994 album, *Amorica*, reached #11, but again yielded no hit singles. *Amorica*'s original cover, depicting a closeup of a woman's bikini underwear with pubic hair showing, was changed after some chains refused to carry the album.

Black Flag/Henry Rollins/ Greg Ginn

Formed 1977, Hermosa Beach, California
Greg Ginn (b. ca. 1953), gtr.; Charles Dukowski, bass; Keith Morris, voc.; Brian Migdol, drums.
1978—*Nervous Breakdown* EP (SST) (– Morris; – Migdol; + Chavo Pederast, voc.; + Robo, drums)
1980—*Jealous Again*   1981—(– Pederast; + Dez Cadena, gtr.; + Henry Rollins [b. Henry Garfield, Feb. 13, 1961, Washington, D.C.], voc.) *Damaged*   1983—*Everything Went Black*   1984—*The First Four Years* (– Robo; – Cadena; – Dukowski; + Bill Stevenson [b. ca. 1964], drums; + Dale Nixon [Ginn's bass-playing pseudonym], bass) *My War; Family Man* (– Nixon; + Kira Roessler, bass) *Slip It In*
1985—*Loose Nut; The Process of Weeding Out* EP; *In My Head*   1986—(– Stevenson; + Anthony Martinez, drums) *Who's Got the 10 1/2?*   1987—*Wasted . . . Again.*
Henry Rollins solo: 1987—*Hot Animal Machine* (Texas Hotel); *Big Ugly Mouth*   1989—*Sweat Box*   1991—*Human Butt* (1/4 Stick)   1993—*The Boxed Life* (Imago).
With Henrietta Collins and the Wifebeating Childhaters: 1987—*Drive By Shooting* EP (Texas Hotel).
With Rollins Band: 1988—*Life Time* (Texas Hotel); *Do It*   1989—*Hard Volume*   1990—*Turned On* (1/4 Stick)   1992—*The End of Silence* (Imago)   1994—*Weight.*
With Wartime: 1990—*Fast Food for Thought* EP (Chrysalis).

Greg Ginn solo: 1993—*Getting Even* (Cruz); *Dick*   1994—*Let It Burn (Because I Don't Live There Anymore).*
With Gone: 1986— *"Let's Get Real, Real Gone for a Change"* (SST); *Gone II—But Never Too Gone!*   1994—*The Criminal Mind.*
As Poindexter Stewart: 1993—*College Rock* EP (SST).

Black Flag became America's premier hardcore punk band in the early Eighties. With its uncompromising DIY ethic, constant low-budget touring, and angry, driving songs, the group provided the blueprint for subsequent postpunk bands.

Guitarist Greg Ginn formed the group in 1977, two years after he graduated from UCLA with a degree in economics. He and bassist Chuck Dukowski cofounded SST Records so they could get the group's music into the hands of its small but rabid audience. (With its roster of other critically acclaimed bands, including Minutemen, Hüsker Dü, Sonic Youth, and Meat Puppets, SST became the most respected American indie of the Eighties.)

Black Flag's early songs were marked by Ginn's scorching rhythm and tangled lead guitar work, Dukowski's guttural bass playing, and a succession of wailing vocalists. The band's first single, "Wasted," reflected the nihilistic angst of Black Flag's suburban, middle-class, "party-hearty" surroundings, with a theme that popped up repeatedly in later songs such as "T.V. Party" (from *Damaged*) and "Annihilate This Week" (*Loose Nut*).

When singer Keith Morris left to form the Circle Jerks, Black Flag went through several vocalists before locking in with Henry Rollins, a Washington, D.C., skinhead who had jumped onstage with the band during a New York performance. MCA refused to release the group's first full-length album, *Damaged*, but after Ginn released it himself on SST—to overwhelmingly favorable critical response—a bitter legal dispute ensued with MCA-distributed Unicorn Records. For two years Black Flag was forbidden to use its name or logo. When Unicorn went bankrupt, Ginn came out of the struggle vowing never to deal with other labels, especially the majors.

Nineteen-eighty-four to 1986 was Black Flag's most prolific period, with more than one recording coming out per year, in addition to its continuous touring. In 1986 Ginn formed a side band, Gone (which released several albums) and dissolved Black Flag. He has since focused on running SST, although he returned to music in 1993, releasing solo albums under his own name and the pseudonym Poindexter Stewart.

Rollins formed his own Rollins Band, which has recorded seven albums and gained a wide following after appearing on the 1991 Lollapalooza tour. He has also toured as a spoken-word artist, released numerous spoken-word recordings, and written a number of books published by his own vanity press, 2.13.61.

Blackfoot

Formed Jacksonville, Florida
Rick Medlocke, voc., gtr.; Jakson Spires, drums, voc.; Greg T. Walker, bass, voc.; Charlie Hargrett, gtr.
1975—*No Reservations* (Island)   1976—*Flyin' High* (Epic)   1979—*Strikes* (Atco)   1980—*Tomcattin'* 1981—*Marauder*   1983—*Siogo*   1984—*Vertical Smiles*   1994—*After the Reign* (Wildcat).

The Southern-rock band Blackfoot came out of the Jacksonville, Florida, bar circuit that nourished the Allman Brothers Band and Lynyrd Skynyrd. For most of the Seventies, Blackfoot followed in Skynyrd's footsteps before moving toward British-style heavy metal.

Rick Medlocke, who was raised by his Sioux grandfather, folk musician and songwriter Shorty Medlocke, formed his first group with Jakson Spires and Greg T. Walker (both of Indian extraction) when he was ten. The group was joined by transplanted New Yorker Charlie Hargrett in the late Sixties. Calling themselves Fresh Garbage, they became regulars on the North Florida bar circuit. Not long after changing their name to Blackfoot, the group broke up to allow Medlocke and Walker to join Lynyrd Skynyrd as substitutes for departed members in 1971, Medlocke as second drummer. After a year with Skynyrd, Medlocke reunited the original Blackfoot. "Highway Song" and "Train, Train," from 1979's platinum *Strikes,* both made the Top Forty, but Blackfoot has yet to come close to attaining such record sales again.

Ritchie Blackmore/Rainbow

Formed 1975, Los Angeles, California
Ritchie Blackmore (b. Apr. 14, 1945, Weston-super-Mare, Eng.), gtr.; Ronnie James Dio (b. ca. 1950, Cortland, N.Y.), voc.; Gary Driscoll, drums; Craig Gruber, bass; Mickey Lee Soule, kybds.
1975—*Ritchie Blackmore's Rainbow* (Polydor) (– Driscoll; – Gruber; – Soule; + Cozy Powell [b. Dec. 29, 1947, Cirencester, Eng.], drums; + Tony Carey [b. Oct. 16, 1953], kybds.; + Jim Bain, bass)   1976— *Rainbow Rising*   1977—*Onstage* (– Carey; – Bain; + Bob Daisley, bass; + David Stone, kybds.)   1978— *Long Live Rock 'n' Roll* (– Dio; – Daisley; – Stone) 1979—(+ Roger Glover [b. Nov. 30, 1945, Brecon, Wales], bass; + Don Airey, kybds.; + Graham Bonnet, voc.) *Down to Earth*   1980—(– Bonnet; – Powell; + Joe Lynn Turner, voc.; + Bob Rondinelli, drums)   1981—*Difficult to Cure* (– Airey; + David Rosenthal, kybds.); *Jealous Lover*   1982—*Straight Between the Eyes* (Mercury)   1983—*Bent out of Shape*   1986—*Finyl Vinyl.*

Hard-rock guitarist Ritchie Blackmore began studying classical guitar at age 11, then switched to rock in his teens. He became a session player and worked with Screaming Lord Sutch before cofounding Deep Purple in 1968 [see entry]. Associates claim that Blackmore is often arrogant and belligerent, and after Purple had peaked, he left in 1975 amid rumors of dissension. He founded his own band, made up mostly of members of the upstate New York band Elf, and it was billed alternately as Rainbow or Ritchie Blackmore's Rainbow.

The frequently changing lineup included vocalists Ronnie James Dio (who later replaced Ozzy Osbourne in Black Sabbath and found success on his own) and Graham Bonnet (briefly a member of Deep Purple after singer Ian Gillan split in 1973), keyboardist Tony Carey (marginally successful in the mid-Eighties both under his own name and as Planet P), and drummer Cozy Powell (formerly of the Jeff Beck Group and later with Sabbath, the Michael Schenker Band, and others). Ex–Deep Purple bassist Roger Glover joined Blackmore in 1979, and with vocalist Joe Lynn Turner and Blackmore he cowrote Rainbow's Top Forty 1982 hit "Stone Cold."

Rainbow dissolved two years later when Blackmore, Glover, and the other three members of the "classic" Purple lineup got back together. Turner, after releasing a solo album in 1985, joined Purple in 1990 but was replaced (by Ian Gillan, whom he'd replaced) in 1993.

Black Oak Arkansas

Formed 1969, Los Angeles, California
Jim Dandy Mangrum (b. Mar. 30, 1948, Black Oak, Ark.), voc.; Ricky Reynolds (b. Oct. 29, 1948, Manilan, Ark.), gtr.; Jimmy Henderson (b. May 20, 1954, Jackson, Miss.), gtr.; Stan Knight (b. Feb. 12, 1949, Little Rock, Ark.), gtr.; Pat Daugherty (b. Nov. 11, 1947, Jonesboro, Ark.), bass; Wayne Evans, drums.
1969—*The Knowbody Else* (Stax)   1970—*Black Oak Arkansas* (Atco)   1972—*Keep the Faith; If an Angel Came to See You*   1973—*High on a Hog* (Atlantic) 1974—*Street Party; Hot and Nasty*   1975—*Raunch and Roll Live; Ain't Life Grand; X-Rated* (MCA) 1976—*Balls of Fire; Live Mutha* (Atco); *10 Year Overnight Success* (MCA)   1977—*Race with the Devil* (Capricorn); *Best of; I'd Rather Be Sailing* 1993—*Hot & Nasty: The Best of Black Oak Arkansas* (Rhino)   1994—(Band re-forms: Mangrum and Reynolds; + Johnny Roth, gtr.; + Buddy Church, gtr.; + Artie Wilson, bass; + Johnny Courville III, drums).

Black Oak Arkansas was a Southern heavy-metal group whose boogie philosophy and long-haired, bare-chested frontman, Jim Dandy Mangrum, were briefly popular in the early to mid-Seventies. All of the band's original members grew up in rural Arkansas near the small town of Black Oak. They were in a juvenile gang before becoming a band. (In a 1976 press release they boast of having stolen a P.A. system.) They toured the South as Knowbody Else and released one album on Stax before moving to Los Angeles in 1969 and changing their name to Black Oak Arkansas.

With almost constant touring, they eventually built up an enthusiastic following, composed mainly of young fans who appreciated the group's down-home Dixie boogie and quasi-mystical lyrics. In 1970 they made their national debut, but big-time success eluded them until *High on a Hog* and *Raunch and Roll* went gold. They also had a #25 hit with "Jim Dandy" which featured Dandy exchanging double entendres with female singer/sometime group member Ruby Starr (died 1995). By the mid-Seventies the group was a huge draw on the U.S. concert circuit. The group sustained numerous personnel changes, and by 1977 Mangrum was the only original member of the band left. Mangrum and original guitarist Ricky Reynolds formed a new Black Oak Arkansas for the Nineties, on the heels of a Rhino Records compilation.

Black Sabbath

Formed 1967, Birmingham, England
Ozzy Osbourne (b. Dec. 3, 1948, Birmingham), voc.;
Terry "Geezer" Butler (b. July 17, 1949, Birmingham), bass; Tony Iommi (b. Feb. 19, 1948, Birmingham), gtr.; Bill Ward (b. May 5, 1948, Birmingham), drums.
1970—*Black Sabbath* (Warner Bros.) 1971—*Paranoid*; *Master of Reality* 1972—*Volume 4* 1973—*Sabbath, Bloody Sabbath* 1975—*Sabotage* 1976—*We Sold Our Soul for Rock 'n' Roll*; *Technical Ecstasy* 1978—*Never Say Die* 1979—(– Osbourne; + Ronnie James Dio [b. circa 1950, Cortland, N.Y.], voc.) 1980—*Heaven and Hell* 1981—(– Ward; + Vinnie Appice [b. Staten Island, N.Y.], drums) *Mob Rules* 1982—(– Dio; – Appice; + Dave Donato, voc.; + Ward, drums) 1983—*Live Evil* (– Donato; + Ian Gillan [b. Aug. 19, 1945, Hounslow, Eng.]; *Born Again* 1984—(– Gillan) 1985—(– Ward; – Butler; + Glenn Hughes [b. Penkridge, Eng.], vocals; + Geoff Nichols [b. Birmingham], kybds.; + Dave Spitz [b. New York City, N.Y.], bass; + Eric Singer [b. Cleveland, Ohio], drums) *Seventh Star* 1987—(– Spitz; – Hughes; + Bob Daisley, bass; + Tony Martin, voc.; – Singer; + Bev Bevan [b. Nov. 25, 1946, Birmingham], drums) *The Eternal Idol* (– Bevan; – Daisley) 1989—(+ Cozy Powell [b. Dec. 29, 1947, Cirencester, Eng.], drums; + Spitz) *The Headless Cross* (I.R.S.) (– Nichols; + Lawrence Cottle, bass; – Cottle) 1990—(+ Neil Murray, bass; – Murray; + Nichols) *TYR* 1991—(– Powell; – Martin; + Appice, drums; + Butler, bass; + Dio, voc.)

1992—*Dehumanizer* (Reprise) 1993—(– Dio; – Appice; + Butler; + Martin; + Bob Rondinelli, drums).

Mixing equal parts of bone-crushing volume, catatonic tempos, and ominous pronouncements of gloom and doom delivered in Ozzy Osbourne's keening voice, Black Sabbath was the heavy-metal king of the Seventies. Despised by rock critics and ignored by radio programmers, the group sold over eight million albums before Osbourne departed for a solo career in 1979 [see entry].

The four original members, schoolmates from a working-class district of industrial Birmingham, first joined forces as Polka Tulk, a blues band. They quickly changed their name to Earth, then, in 1969, to Black Sabbath; the name came from the title of a song written by bassist Geezer Butler, a fan of occult novelist Dennis Wheatley. The quartet's eponymously titled 1970 debut, recorded in two days, went to #8 in England and #23 in the U.S. A single, "Paranoid," released in advance of the album of the same name, reached #4 in the U.K. later that year; it was the group's only Top Twenty hit.

The single didn't make the U.S. Top Forty, but the *Paranoid* LP, issued in early 1971, eventually sold four million copies despite virtually no airplay. Beginning in December 1970 Sabbath toured the States relentlessly. The constant road work paid off, and by 1974 Black Sabbath was considered peerless among heavy-metal acts, its first five LPs all having sold at least a million copies apiece in America alone.

In spite of its name, the crosses erected onstage, and songs dealing with apocalypse, death, and destruction, the band members insisted their interest in the black arts was nothing more than innocuous curiosity (the sort that led Ozzy Osbourne to sit through *eight* showings of *The Exorcist*), and in time Black Sabbath's princes-of-darkness image faded.

Eventually, so did its record sales. Aside from a platinum best-of, *We Sold Our Soul for Rock 'n' Roll* (1976), not one of three LPs from 1975 to 1978 went gold. Osbourne, racked by drug use and excessive drinking, quit the band briefly in late 1977 (former Savoy Brown–Fleetwood Mac vocalist Dave Walker filled his shoes for some live dates). In January 1979 he left again, this time for good. Ronnie James Dio, formerly of Ritchie Blackmore's Rainbow, replaced Osbourne.

Although Dio could belt with the best of them, Sabbath would never be the same. Its first album with Dio, *Heaven and Hell* (1980), went platinum; its second, *Mob Rules* (1981), gold. But thereafter, the group's LPs sold fewer and fewer copies, as Black Sabbath went through one personnel change after another. Ill health forced Bill Ward out of the band in 1981; Carmine Appice's brother Vinnie took his place. Friction between Iommi and Dio led the singer to quit angrily in 1982; he took Appice with him to start his own band, Dio. Vocalists over the years have included Dave Donato; Deep Purple singer Ian Gillan; Glenn Hughes, another ex-member of Purple; Tony Martin; and Dio again.

By 1986's *Seventh Star,* only Iommi remained from the original lineup. He had to wince when Geezer Butler teamed up with the phenomenally successful Osbourne in 1988, though the bassist did return to the fold three years later. Despite bitterness expressed in the press between Osbourne and Iommi, the original foursome reunited in 1985 at the Live-Aid concert in Philadelphia, and again in 1992, at the end of what was supposedly Osbourne's last tour. Throughout 1993 word had it that Osbourne, Iommi, Butler, and Ward would tour, but by year's end Osbourne had backed out, allegedly over money. The indefatigable Tony Iommi went right back to work with Butler, rehiring vocalist Tony Martin and adding former Rainbow drummer Rob Rondinelli.

Black Sheep
Formed 1983, North Carolina
Dres (b. Andres Titus, March 18, 1967, New York City, N.Y.), voc.; Mista Lawnge (b. William McLean, Dec. 11, 1970, New York City, N.Y.), voc.
1991—*A Wolf in Sheep's Clothing* (Mercury)
1994—*Non-Fiction.*

Black Sheep's Andres "Dres" Titus and William "Mista Lawnge" McLean met in North Carolina, where both sets of parents had relocated from New York City. At an early-Eighties Sparkie Dee show there, McLean was introduced to DJ Red Alert, a key figure on the early New York hip-hop scene, who told the aspiring rapper to look him up if he ever made it back to the Big Apple. McLean did so in 1985, without Titus, and started hanging out with Native Tongues groups such as the Jungle Brothers and A Tribe Called Quest. In 1989 McLean persuaded Titus to move up from North Carolina, and the two started working on the debut album, *A Wolf in Sheep's Clothing,* released in 1991. Heralded for its smart blend of guitars, bass, horns, playful melodies, and humorous lyrics, particularly the track "Flavor of the Month," the album peaked at #30. Three years later they released their sophomore effort *Non-Fiction.*

Black Uhuru
Formed 1974, Kingston, Jamaica
Don Carlos (b. Euvin Spencer, June 29, 1952, Kingston), voc.; Rudolph "Garth" Dennis (b. Dec. 2, 1949, Kingston), voc.; Derrick "Duckie" Simpson (b. June 24, 1950, Kingston), voc.
1977—(– Carlos; – Dennis; + Errol Nelson, voc.; + Michael Rose [b. July 11, 1957, Kingston], voc.)
***Love Crisis* (Prince Jammy's) (– Nelson)   1978—**
(+ Sandra "Puma" Jones [b. October 5, 1953, S.C.;
d. Jan 28, 1990], voc.)   1979—*Showcase* (Taxi)
1980—*Sinsemilla* (Mango)   1981—*Red*   1982—*Tear It Up*; *Chill Out*   1983—*The Dub Factor*; *Anthem*
1985—*Reggae Greats* (– Rose; + Delroy "Junior" Reid, voc.)   1986—*Brutal* (RAS); *Brutal Dub*
1987—(– Jones; + Olafunke [b. Janet Reid, Jam.], voc.) *Positive*   1988—*Positive Dub*   1990—(– Olafunke; – Reid; + Carlos; + Dennis) *Now* (Mesa); *Now Dub*   1991—*Iron Storm*   1992—*Iron Storm Dub*
1993—*Mystical Truth*; *Mystical Truth Dub*; *Liberation: The Island Anthology* (Island).

Over the course of a long career that has come full circle back to its original lineup, Black Uhuru has remained true to its fierce Rastafarian politics and haunting vocal harmonies. The group's most popular period coincided with Michael Rose's membership, when the vocal group was backed by Jamaica's finest instrumentalists, with songs made distinctive by "Puma" Jones' descant and melodies that suggest Hebrew cantillation.

The original (and mid-Nineties) Uhuru (Swahili for "freedom") was formed by "Duckie" Simpson with Garth Dennis and Don Carlos. They played clubs around Jamaica but failed to attract much local attention despite their Top Cat single "Folk Songs." Dennis and Carlos quit soon after (Dennis to join the Wailing Souls), and Simpson brought Errol Nelson and Rose to Uhuru. Their next singles, "Natural Mystic" and "King Selassie," found their way to England in 1977, and U.K. distributor Count Shelly issued their first album there.

Nelson left the group to join the Jayes, and Simpson and Rose recorded some singles as a duo. After cutting a couple of songs with producer Lee "Scratch" Perry, they teamed with drummer Sly Dunbar (an old friend of Rose's) and his partner Robbie Shakespeare. Uhuru's "Observe Life" was the first single Sly and Robbie produced and the first issued on their Taxi label.

Simpson and Rose were then joined by Sandra "Puma" Jones, a Southern-born American with a master's degree from Columbia University who had come to Jamaica as a social worker. Her only professional experience had been as a dancer and backup singer with Ras Michael and the Sons of Negus. With Sly and Robbie the trio recorded its best-known singles, "General Penitentiary," "Guess Who's Coming to Dinner," "Plastic Smile," "Abortion" (which was anti-, and was banned in Jamaica), and "Shine Eye Gal." *Showcase* followed. After its release, New York City radio station WLIB sponsored Uhuru's first appearance outside Jamaica, a concert at New York City's Hunter College, and Island Records signed the group to its Mango subsidiary. *Sinsemilla* (Black Uhuru's American debut) and *Red* were recorded in Jamaica with Sly and Robbie and their Taxi All-Stars (Keith Richards added his guitar to the former).

Rose's move to New York at the time of 1982's *Chill*

Out was reflected in the album's urban subject matter. Island tried to build on its success by remixing *Anthem* for American listeners. Although it won a Grammy for Best Reggae Album, Rose was unhappy with the band's direction and left soon afterward; he released in Jamaica a couple of singles and an album, *Proud* (1990).

Junior Reid replaced Rose on *Brutal,* and dance-music specialist Arthur Baker joined Sly and Robbie in the production booth. Jones left before the recording of *Positive* (she died of cancer in 1990) and was briefly replaced by Janet Reid.

In late 1987 original members Dennis and Carlos joined Simpson onstage during a Jamaican awards show. They decided to make this impromptu reunion permanent, recording the Grammy-nominated *Now.* Ice-T added contemporary hip-hop elements to "Tip of the Iceberg" on 1992's *Iron Storm.*

Rubén Blades
Born July 16, 1948, Panama City, Panama
1979—*Bohemio y Poeta* (Fania)   1980—*Maestra Vida, Primera Parte*; *Maestra Vida, Segunda Parte* 1982—*El Que la Hace la Paga*   1984—*Mucho Mejor* 1984—*Buscando America* (Elektra)   1985—*Escenas* 1986—*Crossover Dreams*; *Doble Filo* (Fania) 1987—*Agua De Luna* (Elektra)   1988— *Antecedente*; *Nothing But the Truth*   1990—*Y Son del Solar . . . Live!*   1991—*Caminando* (Sony Discos International).

Panamanian singer Rubén Blades is as much a political activist as he is a singer and actor. As one of the premier performers of salsa music, he is an innovator who has broadened the genre's appeal far beyond its Latin American base.

Son of a police officer and an actress mother, Blades was influenced as a child by his maternal grandmother, a Rosicrucian vegetarian who exposed him early to American films. Rock & roll also affected him; when he joined his brother's band in 1963, he sang in English. The Canal Zone riots of 1964, however, checked his romance with stateside culture, and he began delving into salsa, the Afro-Cuban music powered by horns and percussion. While playing with local bands, he worked on a law degree at the University of Panama; he took time off to make an album in New York City with Latin musician Pete Rodriguez but returned to finish his studies.

In 1974, after a stint as an attorney for the Bank of Panama, Blades moved to New York. Two years later he became the songwriter/vocalist for the Willie Colon Combo. The pair released *Siembra,* one of salsa's top-selling albums, and for Fania, the major salsa label, Colon produced Blades' first records. In 1982 Blades formed his own band, Seis del Solar. Signing him as its first Latin artist, Elektra released *Buscando America,* an album that stirred controversy among salsa purists for its use of synthesizers and rock-inflected instrumentation. In addition, its lyrics, inspired by Blades' friend, Colombian author Gabriel García Márquez (*One Hundred Years of Solitude*), were somber, poetic, and political, a sharp departure from salsa's traditionally escapist themes. With 1985 came *Escenas,* featuring a duet with Linda Ronstadt; throughout the Eighties Blades continued to record for both Fania and Elektra, for the latter releasing *Nothing but the Truth,* his English-language singing debut.

Blades had also been busy at other pursuits. Immediately after his Elektra debut, Blades enrolled at Harvard, where he earned a master's degree in international law. In 1985 he starred in the salsa film *Crossover Dreams,* drawing notice for his acting and, in the process, helping to raise the profile of salsa. Subsequent roles in forgettable fare (*Critical Condition, Fatal Beauty*) didn't seem to affect his acting career, and he regained credibility with television roles and parts in such films as *Waiting for Salazar, The Milagro Beanfield War, Mo' Better Blues,* and *The Two Jakes.* For the movies *When the Mountains Tremble, Caminos Verdes,* and *Q&A,* Blades composed scores.

All along, Blades remained active in politics. In 1992 he launched Papa Egoro, a Panamanian political party dedicated to social justice. The next year, he announced his temporary retirement from music and acting in order to pursue the Panamanian presidency in 1994; he lost that race.

Blake Babies: See Juliana Hatfield

Bobby "Blue" Bland
Born January 27, 1930, Rosemark, Tennessee
1960—*Barefoot Rock and You Got Me* (Duke) 1961—*Two Steps from the Blues*   1962—*Here's the Man*   1963—*Call On Me*   1964—*Ain't Nothing You Can Do*   1968—*Touch of the Blues*   1972—*The Best of Bobby Bland* (MCA)   1973—*His California Album* (ABC)   1974—*Dreamer*; *B. B. King and Bobby Bland/Together for the First Time . . . Live* (with B. B. King); *Ain't Nothing You Can Do* (MCA); *Here's the Man*; *The Soul of the Man*; *The Best of Bobby Bland, vol. 2*   1975—*Get On Down with Bobby Bland*   1976—*Bobby Bland and B. B. King/Together Again . . . Live* (with B. B. King)   1977—*Reflections in Blue*   1978—*Come Fly with Me*   1979—*I Feel Good, I Feel Fine* (MCA)   1980—*Sweet Vibrations* 1981—*Try Me, I'm Real*   1982—*Here We Go Again*; *Introspective Early Years*   1985—*Members Only* (Malaco)   1986—*After All*   1987—*Blues You Can Use*; *First Class Blues*   1989—*Midnight Run* 1991—*Portrait of the Blues*   1992—*I Pity the*

Fool/The Duke Recordings, vol. 1 1993—*Years of Tears* 1994—*Turn On Your Love Light/The Duke Recordings, vol. 2* (MCA).

One of the patriarchs of modern soul singing, Bobby "Blue" Bland's distinctively grainy vocal style draws on gospel and blues. Raised in Memphis, he joined a gospel ensemble, the Miniatures, in the late Forties. He later met guitarist B. B. King and joined the Beale Streeters, an informal group of Memphis blues musicians that included King, Johnny Ace, Roscoe Gordon, and Willie Nix. But not until 1954 (after working as King's chauffeur) did he land his first recording contract, when an executive of Duke Records heard him sing at a Houston talent show.

His first successful single, "It's My Life, Baby," was released in 1955. He played one-nighters around the country accompanied by his band, led by tenor saxophonist Bill Harvey and trumpeter/arranger Joe Scott. Members of the band, under the pseudonym Deadric Malone, wrote or cowrote most of Bland's material. His band was bigger and brassier than most current blues bands and anticipated the rich sound of Sixties soul music while harking back to big-band jazz.

Since 1957, when "Farther Up the Road" was a #5 R&B hit, Bland has had over 30 R&B Top Twenty singles, including "I'll Take Care of You" (#2, 1959), "I Pity the Fool" (#1, 1961), "Don't Cry No More" (#2, 1961), "Turn On Your Love Light" (#2, 1961), and "That's the Way Love Is" (#1, 1963).

Most of Bland's records enjoyed only modest success in the pop market; only three singles ever made the pop Top Thirty. In the mid-Sixties Bland adopted a slicker, more upbeat style, but his career stalled until Duke Records was taken over by ABC-Dunhill in 1972. Dunhill paired him with producer Steve Barri (the Four Tops), who guided Bland back to a bluesier vocal style while giving him contemporary material by Leon Russell and Gerry Goffin, as well as new material by Deadric Malone. *His California Album* and *Dreamer* introduced him to white audiences and proved to be the most popular LPs of his career.

While he never achieved the wide recognition of B. B. King (with whom he toured and collaborated on two LPs, *Together* and *Together Again*), he had a considerable influence on modern soul music. He continues to record and tour internationally. In 1992 he was inducted into the Rock and Roll Hall of Fame.

The Blasters

Formed 1979, Los Angeles, California
Phil Alvin (b. Mar. 6, 1953, Los Angeles), gtr., voc.;
Dave Alvin (b. Nov. 11, 1955, Los Angeles), gtr.;
John Bazz (b. July 6, 1952), bass; Bill Bateman
(b. Dec. 16, 1951, Orange, Calif.), drums; Gene
Taylor (b. July 2, 1952, Tyler, Tex.), piano.

1980—*American Music* (Rollin' Rock) 1981—*The Blasters* (Slash) 1982—*Over There: Live at the Venue, London* EP 1983—*Non Fiction* 1985—*Hard Line* 1990—*The Blasters Collection.*
Phil Alvin solo: 1986—*Un "Sung Stories"* (Slash) 1994—*County Fair 2000* (HighTone).
Dave Alvin solo: 1987—*Romeo's Escape* (Epic) 1991—*Blue Blvd* (HighTone) 1993—*Museum of Heart* 1994—*King of California.*

The Blasters led the early-Eighties American roots music revival, performing styles from rockabilly and country to blues and R&B. Brothers Phil and Dave Alvin (whose father was a labor organizer) grew up in the Los Angeles suburb of Downey listening to the music of Big Joe Turner, T-Bone Walker, Jimmy Reed, and Elvis Presley. The brothers played in various bands and in 1979 they formed the Blasters, named after bluesman Jimmy McCracklin's Blues Blasters.

The group struggled for gigs around L.A. until X's John Doe took them under his wing in 1980. When the Blasters' first album, *American Music*, caused a buzz on the underground scene, the punk label Slash signed the band. *The Blasters* came out the following year, reaching #36 on the album chart and getting generally positive notices. The Alvins' longtime hero, New Orleans R&B saxophonist Lee Allen, guested on the album.

After a live EP in 1982, the Blasters tried to branch out on *Non Fiction*, with songs that broke from the rockabilly mold. For *Hard Line* the Blasters attempted a commercial crossover, enlisting John Mellencamp, who wrote and produced one song ("Colored Lights"), and Elvis Presley's former backup singers, the Jordanaires. The band broke up shortly thereafter, with Dave Alvin joining X [see entry] (he had already appeared on an album by X's acoustic-country alter ego, the Knitters) and Phil Alvin returning to graduate school, where he got a master's degree in mathematics and artificial intelligence, later pursuing a Ph.D. in these subjects at UCLA.

By the mid-Eighties, both Alvin brothers had become active in Los Angeles' burgeoning spoken-word performance scene, with Dave appearing on three spoken-word compilation albums and eventually having published two books of his poetry. For Alison Anders' (*Gas, Food, Lodging*) first film, *Border Radio*, Dave made a cameo appearance and composed the soundtrack music, released by Enigma Records in 1987.

The Alvin brothers have each pursued solo projects. Phil Alvin's *Un "Sung Stories"* is a traditionalist album that features the very *un*traditionalist Sun Ra's Arkestra on three songs. With original bassist John Bazz, Phil put together a new version of the Blasters for some tracks on his 1994 solo album and ensuing performances. (The entire original lineup did one reunion show at an L.A. benefit in the early Nineties.)

In addition to releasing several solo albums, Dave formed the Pleasure Barons in 1991, which has featured a Who's Who of roots-oriented members from John Doe to Mojo Nixon to postpunk country singer Rosie Flores. He also has produced several albums, among them rockabilly legend Sonny Burgess' *Tennessee Border* (1992) and a 1994 Merle Haggard tribute, *Tulare Dust,* to which he also contributed a track.

Carla Bley

Born Carla Borg, May 11, 1938, Oakland, California
1972—*Escalator Over the Hill* (JCOA)   1974—
***Tropic Appetites* (Watt)   1975—*13 and 3/4*   1977—**
Dinner Music*   1978—*European Tour 1977
1979—*Musique Mechanique*   1981—*Social Studies*
(ECM)   1982—*Carla Bley Live!*   1984—*Heavy*
Heart* (Watt)   1985—*I Hate to Sing*; *Night Glo
1988—*Duets*   1989—*Fleur Carnivore*   1991—*The*
Very Big Carla Bley Band*   1993—*Go Together
1994—*Big Band Theory.*

Composer Carla Bley has experimented with free jazz, punk rock, big bands, orchestras, and forms and groupings of her own. But while many of her pieces are tricky and eccentric, they are rarely less than tuneful, and her gift for bittersweet parody has earned her comparisons with Kurt Weill. Bley plays keyboards and sax, but she is best known for her tunes, her arrangements, and the bands she has conducted.

The daughter of a piano teacher and choir director, she began composing at age nine. After she moved to New York in the late Fifties, her works were performed by pianists George Russell and Paul Bley (whom she married) and later by vibraphonist Gary Burton (who has done an entire album of Bley's pieces entitled *Dreams So Real*) and Charlie Haden's Liberation Music Orchestra (which reunited in 1982). She began performing in 1964, when she and her second husband, trumpeter Michael Mantler, formed the Jazz Composers Orchestra, which featured Cecil Taylor, Pharoah Sanders, and others.

With lyricist Paul Haines, she began working on *Escalator Over the Hill* in 1968. To record it she assembled an unlikely assortment of musicians including Linda Ronstadt, Jack Bruce, John McLaughlin, Gato Barbieri, and Don Cherry and Charlie Haden from Ornette Coleman's quartet. Since then she has continued to use both jazz and rock musicians. *Tropic Appetites* featured singer Julie Tippets (who as Julie Driscoll was part of Brian Auger's Trinity). *Dinner Music* used R&B session players Stuff, and *Nick Mason's Fictitious Sports* (1981), which was released under Pink Floyd drummer Mason's name, used her band along with British progressive rockers.

In 1977 she formed the Carla Bley Band, which has included NRBQ pianist Terry Adams, Soft Machine bassist Hugh Hopper, Mothers of Invention keyboardist Don Preston, and Modern Lovers drummer D. Sharpe. Bley has been active in the dissemination of new music, beginning in 1964, when she was a charter member of the Jazz Composers Guild (with Cecil Taylor, Sun Ra, and others), a cooperative to promote avant-garde music. In 1966 Bley and Mantler founded JCOA (Jazz Composers Orchestra Association) Records. Six years later, they began the New Music Distribution Service, which (until its demise in 1990) handled hundreds of small independent jazz, classical, and rock labels, including Bley and Mantler's own Watt Records. Mantler moved back to Europe in 1991, divesting himself of Watt Records; his daughter with Bley, Karen Mantler—a Watt recording artist who also plays organ in her mother's band—took over operations.

Bley's output and workload increased during the Eighties and Nineties. She contributed arrangements to *Ballad of the Fallen* and *Dreamkeeper* by Charlie Haden's Liberation Orchestra and three Hal Willner projects: *Lost in the Stars*, *That's the Way I Feel Now*, and *Amarcord Nino Rota*. She also played on the Golden Palominos' *Drunk with Passion* and *Visions of Excess* in addition to continuing her work for bands of varying size and making duet recordings with bassist Steve Swallow (*Duets, Go Together*).

Mary J. Blige

Born Mary Jane Blige, January 11, 1971, Bronx, New York
1992—*What's the 411?* (Uptown/MCA)   1993—
What's the 411? The Remixes*   1994—*My Life.

In 1992 Mary J. Blige became a top pop diva by appealing to older fans with her soul sensibility and maintaining youthful credibility with her hip-hop savvy. Blige was born in the Bronx but spent her early years in Savannah, Georgia, where she sang at a Pentecostal church. Her family moved to Yonkers, New York, where Blige continued to sing. Her first demo (recorded at a karaoke studio in a shopping mall) was a version of Anita Baker's "Caught Up in the Rapture," which eventually got her signed by Andre Harrell to Uptown Records.

Blige's debut, *What's the 411?* (#6 pop, #1 R&B, 1992), mixed Blige's affinity for classic soul (she covered Chaka Khan's "Sweet Thing") with a contemporary urban edge: The album includes cameos by rappers Grand Puba, Heavy D., C. L. Smooth, De La Soul's P. A. Pasemaster Mase, and EPMD's Erick Sermon. Blige first charted with "You Remind Me" (#29 pop, #1 R&B, 1992), from the film *Strictly Business*, but her debut album's single "Real Love" (#7 pop, #1 R&B, 1992) made Blige one of the biggest crossover artists of the year. In 1993 a remix album of *What's the 411?* was released and the "Sweet Thing" single peaked at #28 on the pop charts.

Blige's 1994 album, *My Life*, reached #7 (#1 R&B) and yielded a #7 single, "Be Happy."

Blind Faith

Formed 1969, London, England
Steve Winwood (b. May 12, 1948, Birmingham, Eng.), kybds., gtr., voc.; Eric Clapton (b. Mar. 30, 1945, Ripley, Eng.), gtr., voc.; Ginger Baker (b. Aug. 19, 1939, Lewisham, Eng.), drums; Rick Grech (b. Nov. 1, 1946, Bordeaux, Fr.; d. Mar. 17, 1990), bass, violin.
1969—*Blind Faith* (Atco).

Blind Faith's already famous personnel stayed together for one album and one arena-circuit tour before splitting up. Eric Clapton and Baker had been two thirds of Cream, and Steve Winwood had led (and would return to) Traffic [see entry]. Rick Grech was from Family [see entry], which had been considerably more popular in Britain than in the U.S.

The first rock "supergroup" debuted before 100,000 fans in London's Hyde Park on June 7, 1969, and began a sold-out American tour in July before its one and only album had been released. The LP was recorded in such haste that side two consisted of just two songs, one of them a 15-minute jam entitled "Do What You Like." Nevertheless, *Blind Faith* did include two classics: Winwood's "Can't Find My Way Home" and Clapton's "Presence of the Lord." Its jacket, featuring a prepubescent nude girl, was deemed controversial in the U.S. and was replaced by a photograph of the band. (A later U.S. reissue bore the original cover.)

Clapton and Winwood went on to highly successful solo careers. Grech's post–Blind Faith résumé included Baker's Air Force, Traffic, the Crickets, and KGB, a mid-Seventies "supergroup" (far less super than Blind Faith, however) that included Mike Bloomfield, Carmine Appice, and Barry Goldberg. Grech died in 1990.

Blind Melon

Formed 1990, Los Angeles, California
Shannon Hoon (b. Sep. 26, 1967, Lafayette, Ind.), voc.; Rogers Stevens (b. Oct. 31, 1970, West Point, Miss.), gtr.; Christopher Thorn (b. Dec. 16, 1968, Dover, Pa.), gtr.; Brad Smith (b. Sep. 29, 1968, West Point, Miss.), bass; Glen Graham (b. Dec. 5, 1968, Columbus, Miss.), drums.
1992—*Blind Melon* (Capitol).

Blind Melon play folk rock influenced by Seventies AOR and the Grateful Dead's spacious jams. In 1989 Brad Smith and Rogers Stevens moved from the small town of West Point, Mississippi, to Los Angeles, where they met Shannon Hoon and ex–heavy-metal guitarist Christopher Thorn. After only a week together, the band recorded a demo that sparked label interest, and they eventually signed with Capitol. While preparing for their debut, Hoon sang backup with fellow Hoosier Axl Rose on Guns n' Roses' *Use Your Illusion* albums.

The video for its second single, "No Rain" (featuring the band's "Bee Girl" mascot), played frequently by MTV, *Blind Melon* (#3, 1992) went platinum, and "No Rain" reached #1 on the AOR, modern rock, and metal charts.

Blodwyn Pig

Formed 1968, England
Original lineup: Mick Abrahams (b. Apr. 7, 1943, Luton, Eng.), gtr., voc.; Jack Lancaster, saxes, flute; Andy Pyle, bass; Ron Berg, drums.
1969—*Ahead Rings Out* (A&M)   1970—*Getting to This*   1993—(Lineup: Abrahams; Dave Lennox, kybds.; Graham Walker, drums; Mike Summerland, bass) *Lies* (Viceroy).

Mick Abrahams quit Jethro Tull [see entry] after one album to form Blodwyn Pig. A blues guitarist in the British style of Eric Clapton and Peter Green, he made Blodwyn Pig more blues-based than Jethro Tull. Like Ian Anderson, Jack Lancaster was influenced by Rahsaan Roland Kirk and played alto and soprano sax simultaneously a la Rahsaan. Pig's debut album was a distinctly British meeting of rock, blues, and jazz.

Abrahams left the group after recording the second album (another U.K. Top Ten), while the remaining members of Pig enlisted guitarist Peter Banks (formerly of Yes) and guitarist/vocalist Larry Wallis (later of UFO) to take his place. The second lineup never recorded and disbanded in December 1970.

In 1970 Abrahams formed Womnet, which never recorded; the following year he formed the Mick Abrahams band, which continued in a blues vein with a hint of country. This group issued LPs in 1971 and 1972. Disillusioned with the music business, Abrahams quit and drove a truck, all the while playing sessions and recording an instructional guitar record, *Have Fun Learning Guitar with Mick Abrahams* (1974). In 1974 Abrahams, Lancaster, and Pyle hooked up with former Jethro Tull drummer Clive Bunker in place of Ron Berg, but nothing came of it, and Blodwyn Pig broke up again. Lancaster went on to become a producer.

In 1988 Abrahams, also a financial consultant, once again re-formed Blodwyn Pig, with Bunker, Pyle, and Bruce Boardman, Bernie Hetherington, and Dick Heckstall-Smith (Graham Bond, John Mayall, Colosseum). This group, with a few changes, continued into the Nineties playing other clubs. They recorded *All Said and Done*, which was released only in Europe in 1991. Blodwyn Pig saw its next U.S. release in 1993. Pyle has put in time with Savoy Brown, the Kinks, and Chicken; Berg, too, was a member of Savoy Brown, as well as Network.

Blondie

Formed 1975, New York City, New York
Deborah Harry (b. July 1, 1945, Miami, Fla.), voc.;
Chris Stein (b. Jan. 5, 1950, Brooklyn, N.Y.), gtr.,
voc.; Clem Burke (b. Nov. 24, 1955, New York City),
drums; Gary Valentine, bass; Jimmy Destri (b. Apr.
13, 1954, Brooklyn), kybds.
1976—*Blondie* (Private Stock) (– Valentine; + Frank
Infante, bass)   1977—*Plastic Letters* (Chrysalis)
(+ Nigel Harrison [b. April 24, 1951, Stockport, Eng.],
bass; Infante switched to guitar)   1978—*Parallel
Lines*   1979—*Eat to the Beat*   1980—*Autoamerican*
1981—*The Best of Blondie*   1982—*The Hunter*
1994—*The Platinum Collection* (Chrysalis).
Deborah Harry and Blondie: 1988—*Once More into
the Bleach* (Chrysalis).
Deborah Harry solo: 1981—*KooKoo* (Chrysalis)
1986—*Rockbird* (Geffen)   1989—*Def, Dumb &
Blonde* (Sire)   1993—*Debravation*.
Jimmy Destri solo: 1982—*Heart on a Wall*
(Chrysalis).
Checquered Past (Burke and Harrison with Steve
Jones, others):   1984—*Checquered Past* (EMI).

Blondie: Chris Stein, Frank Infante, Deborah Harry, Nigel
Harrison, Jimmy Destri, Clem Burke

Blondie started as an ironic update of trashy Sixties pop. By the end of the Seventies it was far and away the most adventurous and commercially successful survivor of the New York punk scene, with three platinum albums (*Parallel Lines, Eat to the Beat,* and *Autoamerican*) and an international recognition factor for bleached-blond lead singer Deborah Harry, new wave's answer to Marilyn Monroe. Blondie's repertoire, most of it written by Harry and boyfriend Chris Stein, was always on the melodic side of punk, and soon grew increasingly eclectic, trademarked mostly by Harry's deadpan delivery.

Born in Miami, Harry was adopted at age three months by Richard and Catherine Harry. She grew up in Hawthorne, New Jersey, and after graduating from high school moved to Manhattan. Harry joined a folk-rock band, the Wind in the Willows, which released one album for Capitol in 1968; she worked as a beautician, a Playboy bunny, and a barmaid at Max's Kansas City. In the mid-Seventies she became the third lead singer of a glitter-rock band, the Stilettoes, which also included future Television bassist Fred Smith. Stein, a graduate of New York's School of Visual Arts, joined the band in October 1973, and he and Harry reshaped it, first as Angel and the Snakes, then as Blondie.

By 1975 the band was appearing regularly at CBGB, home of the burgeoning punk underground. Its first single, "X Offender," was independently produced by Richard Gottehrer and Marty Thau, who sold it to Private Stock. The label released Blondie's debut, also produced by Gottehrer, in December 1976. The group expanded its cult following to the West Coast with shows at Los Angeles' Whisky-a-Go-Go in February 1977 and opened for Iggy Pop on a national tour. A few months later, they made their British concert debut. In July Gary Valentine (who wrote "[I'm Always Touched by Your] Presence Dear") left the band to form his own trio, Gary Valentine and the Know, which broke up in spring 1980.

After one album for Private Stock and some legal wrangling, Blondie signed with Chrysalis in October 1977. Mike Chapman, a veteran of glitter pop, produced *Parallel Lines,* which slowly made its way into the Top Five, breaking first in markets outside the U.S. Blondie's third single, the disco-style "Heart of Glass," hit #1 in April 1979 and established the group with a platinum album. Blondie maintained its popularity and dabbled in black-originated styles, collaborating with Eurodisco producer Giorgio Moroder for the *American Gigolo* soundtrack ("Call Me," #1, 1980), covering a reggae tune "The Tide Is High" (#1, 1980), and writing a rap song, "Rapture" (#1, 1981), on *Autoamerican.* Harry also did the rounds as a celebrity, including an endorsement of Gloria Vanderbilt designer jeans in 1980.

As the group's success continued, there were reports that Stein and Harry were asserting more control; by 1981 some Blondie backing tracks were played by session musicians under Stein's direction. Burke produced the New York band Colors, and Destri released a solo album, *Heart on the Wall,* in 1982. In 1981 Harry released her solo *KooKoo.* Produced under the direction of Chic's Bernard Edwards and Nile Rodgers, *KooKoo* went gold.

Harry also began acting, appearing Off-Broadway in *Teaneck Tanzi: The Venus Flytrap* (1983), in the films *Union City* (1979), *Videodrome* (1982), and John Waters' *Hairspray* (1988), in the television series *Wiseguy,* and in Showtime's *Body Bags.*

Early in 1982 Infante brought suit against the group, claiming they were out to destroy his career by excluding him from group meetings, rehearsals, and recording sessions. The suit was settled out of court and Infante remained in the band. However, by late 1982, following a disastrous tour (Blondie was never known as a great live act), the group quietly disbanded.

Harry and Stein's planned vacation from the music business stretched to a couple of years after he was felled by a rare genetic illness called pemphigus. Harry's comeback momentum was again stalled in the mid-Eighties by legal problems with the group's label, Chrysalis. *Rockbird* drew critical raves, but neither it nor her subsequent releases have approached Blondie's in sales or acclaim, although she has had major hits in the U.K. ("French Kissin' in the U.S.A.," #8, 1986, and "I Want That Man," #13, 1989). She sang a duet with Iggy Pop, "Well, Did You Evah!," on the AIDS benefit album *Red Hot + Blue.*

Harrison and Burke joined a group called Checquered Past, which included ex–Sex Pistol Steve Jones. Later Harrison supervised the music for several feature films, including *Repo Man,* before becoming an A&R man for Capitol and Interscope. In the early Nineties Burke became one of the Romantics. Stein continued producing acts for his Animal Records label, and Destri began producing.

Bloodstone

Formed 1962, Kansas City, Missouri
Willis Draffen Jr. (b. Kansas City), voc., gtr.; Charles Love, voc., gtr.; Charles McCormick, bass, voc.; Harry Williams Jr. (b. Tupelo, Miss.), perc., voc.; Roger Durham (b. 1946; d. 1973), perc., voc.
1973—*Natural High* (London); *Unreal* (– Durham) 1974—*I Need Time*; *Riddle of the Sphinx* 1975— *Train Ride to Hollywood* 1976—*Do You Wanna Do a Thing?*; *Lullaby of Broadway* (Decca) 1979— *Don't Stop* (Tamla) 1981—(– McCormick; + Ron Wilson [b. Los Angeles, Calif.], kybds., voc.; + Ronald Bell [b. Calif.] perc., voc.) 1982—*We Go a Long Way Back* (T-Neck) 1985—*Greatest Hits* (CBS).

Bloodstone's pop music blended soul vocal harmonies with funk and Hendrix-inspired guitar flash. The five original members were high school classmates in Kansas City, where they formed an a cappella group, the Sinceres, in 1962. In 1968 they spent a year as a nightclub act in Las Vegas, then moved on to Los Angeles. There they decided to learn to play instruments. They

reappeared as Bloodstone in 1971, with a succession of drummers (including Edward Summers, Darryl Clifton, and Melvin Webb) as associate members. On the advice of their manager, they moved to England, where in 1972 they teamed up with English producer Mike Vernon (John Mayall, Ten Years After, Savoy Brown) for their first five albums.

Bloodstone's first single, "Natural High," went gold, reaching #4 on the R&B chart and #10 pop in 1973. The group followed it with a series of soul hits, including "Never Let You Go" (#7 R&B, 1973), "Outside Woman" (#34 pop, #2 R&B, 1974), "That's Not How It Goes" (#22 R&B, 1974), "My Little Lady" (#4 R&B, 1975), "Give Me Your Heart" (#18 R&B, 1975), and "Do You Wanna Do a Thing" (#19 R&B, 1976).

In 1975 Bloodstone produced and appeared in a feature movie entitled *Train Ride to Hollywood,* for which it also wrote the soundtrack. Among the songs covered in this musical comedy were "Toot Toot Tootsie" and "As Time Goes By," and like all of the band's albums since *Unreal,* the soundtrack also contained versions of oldies like "Sh-Boom" and "Yakety Yak."

Blood, Sweat and Tears

Formed 1967, New York City, New York
Al Kooper (b. Feb. 5, 1944, Brooklyn, N.Y.), kybds., voc.; Steve Katz (b. May 9, 1945, New York City), gtr., voc.; Fred Lipsius (b. Nov. 19, 1944, New York City), alto sax, piano; Jim Fielder (b. Oct. 4, 1947, Denton, Tex.), bass; Bobby Colomby (b. Dec. 20, 1944, New York City), drums; Dick Halligan (b. Aug. 29, 1943, Troy, N.Y.), kybds., trombone, flute; Randy Brecker (b. Nov. 27, 1945, Philadelphia, Pa.), trumpet, flugelhorn; Jerry Weiss (b. May 1, 1946, New York City), trumpet, flugelhorn.
1968—*Child Is Father to the Man* (Columbia) (– Kooper; – Brecker; – Weiss; + Chuck Winfield [b. Feb. 5, 1943, Monessen, Pa.], trumpet, flugelhorn; + Lew Soloff [b. Feb. 20, 1944, Brooklyn, N.Y.], trumpet, flugelhorn; + Jerry Hyman [b. May 19, 1947, New York City], trombone; + David Clayton-Thomas [b. Sep. 13, 1941, Surrey, Eng.], voc.) *Blood, Sweat and Tears* 1970—*Blood, Sweat & Tears 3* (– Hyman; + Dave Bargeron [b. Sep. 6, 1942, Mass.], trombone, tuba, trumpet) 1971—*B, S & T; 4* 1972—*Greatest Hits* (– Lipsius; – Halligan; – Clayton-Thomas; + Bobby Doyle [b. Houston, Tex.], voc; + Lou Marini Jr. [b. Charleston, S.C.], saxes, flute; + Georg Wadenius [b. Sweden], gtr.; + Larry Willis [b. New York City], kybds.; – Doyle; + Jerry Fisher [b. 1943, Dekalb, Tex.], voc.); *New Blood* (– Katz; – Winfield; + Tom Malone, trumpet, flugelhorn, trombone, saxes) 1973—*No Sweat* (– Fielder; – Soloff; – Marini; – Malone; + Ron McClure, bass; + Tony Klatka, trumpet; + Bill Tillman, saxes, flute,

clarinet; + Jerry LaCroix, voc., sax, flute, harmonica) 1974—*Mirror Image* (– LaCroix; – Fisher; + Clayton-Thomas; + Joe Giorgianni, trumpet, flugelhorn) 1975—*New City* (– Wadenius; – McClure; – Giorgianni; + Danny Trifan, bass; + Mike Stern, gtr.; + Forrest Buchtell, trumpet; + Don Alias, perc.) 1976—*More Than Ever* (– Colomby; – Alias; + Roy McCurdy, drums) 1977—*Brand New Day* (ABC) 1980—(Lineup continues to fluctuate, with only Clayton-Thomas remaining) *Nuclear Blues* 1991—*Live & Improvised* (Columbia).

Founder Al Kooper conceived Blood, Sweat and Tears as an experiment in expanding the size and scope of the rock band with touches of jazz, blues, classical, and folk music. When Kooper [see entry] was forced out of the band soon after its eclectic debut, *Child Is Father to the Man*, BS&T became increasingly identified as a "jazz-rock" group, although its music was essentially easy-listening R&B or rock with the addition of brass.

Kooper formed BS&T after leaving the Blues Project [see entry] in 1967. The nucleus of the original band was Steve Katz, also of the Blues Project; Jim Fielder, who had played with the Mothers of Invention and the Buffalo Springfield; and Bobby Colomby, who had drummed behind folksingers Odetta and Eric Andersen. The horn players were recruited from New York jazz and studio bands. *Child Is Father* featured songs by Harry Nilsson, Tim Buckley, Randy Newman, and Gerry Goffin and Carole King, along with Kooper originals and arrangements by Fred Lipsius for brass, strings, and studio effects. The band nearly broke up when Kooper, Randy Brecker, and Jerry Weiss left (Brecker to join the Thad Jones–Mel Lewis Band). Regrouping under Katz and Colomby, and fronted by David Clayton-Thomas (who had sung with a Canadian blues band, the Bossmen), BS&T entered a period of immense popularity. *Blood, Sweat and Tears* featured arrangements of music by French composer Erik Satie and jazz singer Billie Holiday, as well as by Laura Nyro, Steve Winwood, and others. It was the #1 album for seven weeks in 1969, sold over three million copies, and spawned three gold singles: "You've Made Me So Very Happy," "Spinning Wheel," and "And When I Die," all of which hit #2 in 1969.

In 1970 the U.S. State Department sent the band on a goodwill tour of Yugoslavia, Romania, and Poland. The album *3* duplicated the *Blood, Sweat and Tears* mix of styles and was almost as popular. The album went to #1, and two singles, "Hi-De-Ho" and "Lucretia MacEvil," hit the Top Thirty. But interest in the group began to wane. *4*, which contained almost all original material, barely made the Top Ten. In 1971 "Go Down Gamblin'" was its last hit. By the time Clayton-Thomas left for a solo career in 1972, BS&T's place on the charts had been filled by similarly styled bands such as Chicago, Chase, and Ides of March. Katz left the next year, first to join the short-

lived American Flyer and then to an A&R position at Mercury Records.

BS&T became regulars in Las Vegas, with ever-changing personnel recruited largely from big bands like Maynard Ferguson's, Woody Herman's, and Doc Severinsen's. Vocalist Jerry LaCroix appeared between his tenures with Edgar Winter's White Trash and Rare Earth, while guitarist Mike Stern later played with Miles Davis' early-Eighties band. Clayton-Thomas' return in 1974 briefly boosted BS&T's popularity. Columbia dropped it, and Colomby, the last original member, left in 1976. Colomby continued to influence BS&T as producer of *Brand New Day*, and, with Clayton-Thomas, as co-owner of the band's name and catalogue. He then moved on to a career in A&R for several labels, as well as TV reporting. Since 1975 the act has been billed as Blood, Sweat and Tears Featuring David Clayton-Thomas, and it continues to perform live.

Luka Bloom

Born Barry Moore, May 23, 1955, Newbridge, Ireland
1990—*Riverside* (Reprise)   1992—*The Acoustic Motorbike*   1994—*Turf*.

The kid brother of Irish folk star Christy Moore, Barry Moore chose a professional alias that combined the surname of a character from James Joyce's *Ulysses* with a

Luka Bloom

reference to the protagonist of a Suzanne Vega song. Likewise, the themes addressed in Luka Bloom's music, a Celtic-flavored folk-rock hybrid driven by the singer's vigorous "electro-acoustic" guitar work, have revealed a fascination with both Irish and American culture.

The youngest of six children, Bloom began touring European folk clubs in the mid-Seventies. Chronic tendinitis eventually forced him to develop a guitar style that relied more on strumming than finger-picking. After recording three albums (now out of print) as Barry Moore, playing briefly in a rock band called Red Square, and spending time in New York City, the singer moved to Washington, D.C., having renamed himself Luka Bloom. In 1987 Bloom landed a regular gig at a Manhattan pub and spent several months commuting to New York once a week. That experience, and subsequent stints opening for Hothouse Flowers and the Pogues on their American tours, influenced the writing on his sparsely produced debut album. *Riverside* featured song titles like "Dreams in America" and "An Irishman in Chinatown." Bloom returned to his native country, where he wrote and recorded *The Acoustic Motorbike,* which includes a lyrical cover of New York–based rapper L. L. Cool J's "I Need Love." For *Turf* Bloom re-created the sound of his live performances by recording the album in a studio set up with a stage, P.A., and lights, and for four songs, even an audience (although no one was allowed to clap).

Michael Bloomfield

Born July 28, 1944, Chicago, Illinois; died February 15, 1981, San Francisco, California
**1968—*Super Session* (Columbia) (with Al Kooper, Stephen Stills)   1969—*It's Not Killing Me; The Live Adventures of Mike Bloomfield and Al Kooper*
1973—*Try It Before You Buy It; Triumvirate*   1976—*Mill Valley Session* (Polydor)   1977—*If You Love These Blues, Play 'Em As You Please* (Guitar Player); *Analine* (Takoma); *Count Talent and the Originals* (Clouds); *Michael Bloomfield* (Takoma)
1980—*Between the Hard Place and the Ground*
1981—*Cruisin' for a Bruisin'; Living in the Fast Lane* (Waterhouse)   1983—*Bloomfield* (Columbia)
1994—*"Don't Say That I Ain't Your Man!": Essential Blues, 1964–1969* (Legacy).**

As a teenager living on Chicago's North Shore, Michael Bloomfield ventured downtown to seek out the patriarchs of Chicago blues—Muddy Waters, Albert King, and others—and learned their guitar techniques firsthand. Playing Chicago blues and folk clubs with singer Nick Gravenites and harmonica player Charlie Musselwhite in the early Sixties, he attracted the attention of Paul Butterfield, whose band he joined in 1965 [see entry]. Bloomfield played electric guitar on Dylan's "Like a Rolling Stone" and later that year on *Highway 61 Revisited.*

Michael Bloomfield

He left the Butterfield band after recording a second album with them and formed the Electric Flag with Gravenites, but quit after their first album [see entry]. Thereafter he devoted himself mainly to studio work and solo ventures, including *Super Session* with Al Kooper and *Triumvirate* with John Hammond Jr. (John Paul Hammond) and Dr. John (Mac Rebennack).

Bloomfield's last shot at stardom came in 1975 with KGB, an attempt by MCA Records to create a supergroup with Bloomfield, keyboardist Barry Goldberg, bassist Rick Grech, drummer Carmine Appice, and singer Ray Kennedy. After one album, Bloomfield abandoned the group and the corporate music world. He supported himself by scoring pornographic movies. His previous movie soundtrack credits included *Medium Cool, Steelyard Blues,* and *Andy Warhol's Bad.* In 1975 he returned to recording solo albums, releasing eight in the six years before his death from an accidental drug overdose. *If You Love These Blues, Play 'Em As You Please*, a blues guitar "sampler" produced by *Guitar Player* magazine, was nominated for a Grammy Award in 1977.

Kurtis Blow
Born Kurt Walker, August 9, 1959, New York City, New York

1980—*Kurtis Blow* (Mercury)   1981—*Deuce*
1982—*Tough*   1983—*Party Time?*   1984—*Ego Trip*
1985—*America*   1986—*Kingdom Blow*   1988—
Back by Popular Demand   1994—*The Best of Kurtis Blow.*

Kurtis Blow's "The Breaks" (#87 pop, #4 R&B, 1980) was one of the first records to popularize rap outside the form's native New York City. A graduate of New York City's High School of Music and Art, Blow was a disco DJ before he made records. He started out working at a Harlem disco in 1976, blatantly copping rhymed lines from an originator of rap, DJ Hollywood (Anthony Holloway). Later he worked with one of the masters of instrumental track editing, Grandmaster Flash (Joseph Saddler). In 1979, while he was working on his first single, "Christmas Rappin'," the Sugar Hill Gang's "Rapper's Delight" rocketed up the charts; a Mercury A&R rep heard what Blow was up to and signed him to an initial two-single deal. "Christmas Rappin'" was released at the end of the year and became—with "Rapper's Delight" and the Fatback Band's "King Tim III"—one of the first rap records on the market. It sold almost 400,000 copies; "The Breaks" sold over 600,000 copies nationwide. By the end of 1980, Blow was performing around the country with his partner Davy D (David Reeves) at the turntables. In 1981 he toured Europe.

Blow's subsequent albums varied little. He was admired by a number of younger rappers, including Run (Joe Simmons) of Run-D.M.C., who as a teenager had worked for Blow. Run-D.M.C. repaid him by doing a guest rap on *Ego Trip*'s "8 Million Stories." By the time of 1988's *Back by Popular Demand*, Blow's lighthearted style was passé. In the early Nineties, Blow began promoting and performing at rap shows featuring the genre's pioneers.

David Blue
Born S. David Cohen, February 18, 1941, Providence, Rhode Island; died December 2, 1982, New York City, New York
1966—*David Blue* (Elektra)   1967—*These 23 Days in September* (Reprise)   1970—*Me* (as S. David Cohen)   1972—*Stories* (Asylum)   1973—*Nice Baby and the Angel*   1975—*Comin' Back for More*   1976—*Cupid's Arrow.*

David Blue was better known for his friendship with Bob Dylan than for his own Dylan-influenced songs and recordings. He met Dylan and others—Phil Ochs, Fred Neil, Eric Andersen—on the Greenwich Village folk music scene after arriving in New York around 1960. By his own estimation a songwriter rather than a musician, he began writing songs in the Greenwich Village folk style but did not perform them publicly until after he had recorded his first album. He had cut several songs the year before for an Elektra compilation album called *Singer/Songwriter Project,* which also included Richard Fariña. At that point he changed his name from Cohen to Blue.

He moved to Los Angeles, where he formed a rock band, and in 1968 he recorded his first Reprise album. His second Reprise album was cut in Nashville with session musicians. *Nice Baby* was produced by Graham Nash and featured Dave Mason, Glenn Frey, Chris Ethridge (Flying Burrito Bros.), and John Barbata (Turtles, Jefferson Starship); the Eagles recorded Blue's "Outlaw Man" on *Desperado.* In 1975 Blue joined Dylan on the Rolling Thunder Revue and appeared in the resulting film, *Renaldo and Clara* (1978). He died while jogging in Greenwich Village.

Blue Cheer
Formed 1967, Boston, Massachusetts
Dickie Peterson (b. 1948, Grand Forks, N. Dak.), voc., bass; Paul Whaley, drums; Bruce "Leigh" Stephens, gtr.
1968—*Vincebus Eruptum* (Philips); *Outside Inside* (– L. Stephens; + Randy Holden, gtr.)   1969—*New! Improved!* (– Whaley; – Holden; + Norman Mayell [b. 1942, Chicago, Ill.], drums; + Bruce Stephens [b. 1946], voc., gtr.; + Ralph Burns Kellogg, kybds.); *Blue Cheer*   1970—(– B. Stephens; + Gary Yoder, gtr.) *The Original Human Beings*   1971—*Oh! Pleasant Hope* (group disbands)   1985—(Group re-forms: Peterson; Whaley; + Tony Rainier, gtr.)   1989—*The Beast Is Back* (Megaforce) (– Whaley)   1986—*Louder Than God: The Best of Blue Cheer* (Rhino).

Blue Cheer appeared in spring 1968 with a thunderously loud remake of Eddie Cochran's "Summertime Blues" that many regard as the first true heavy-metal record. One of the first hard-rock power trios, the group was named for an especially high-quality strain of LSD. Its manager, Gut, was a former Hell's Angel.

After moving to San Francisco, the band was taken under the wing of an enthusiastic DJ, Abe "Voco" Kesh of underground KMPX-FM. He aired a three-song tape of Blue Cheer, leading to a contract with Philips Records. "Summertime Blues" reached #14, while the trio's first album, *Vincebus Eruptum,* hit #11 and remains something of a heavy-metal landmark. None of the group's subsequent five albums had nearly the same impact, however, and in 1971 Peterson, the lone original member left, broke up the band.

Leigh Stephens, who now raises thoroughbreds in California, recorded two solo albums, another with the band Silver Metre, and two more with Bruce Stephens; he too has released a solo album, 1982's *Watch That First Step.* Peterson has twice put together new versions of

Blue Cheer, in 1979 and 1985. The second attempt, which included Whaley and guitarist Tony Rainier, son of an original Blue Cheer roadie, produced an album, *The Beast Is Back*. With Peterson still at the helm, but Whaley gone, Blue Cheer has put out two more LPs in Europe.

Bluegrass

A subgenre of country music, bluegrass shed its formative skin and forged a separate identity in the mid-Forties when bandleader Bill Monroe [see entry] altered the complexion of "hillbilly" music. Flanked by his legendary band, the Blue Grass Boys, Monroe devised a theretofore unseemly consolidation of musical styles that fused country, jazz, blues, gospel, and Celtic folk into a unified sound. Monroe's inventive spirit lives on through a new generation of virtuosos eager to push bluegrass into the 21st century.

The seeds of bluegrass were planted in the Twenties with the advent of commercial country music, which had already been influenced by disparate sources such as deep-rooted folk and blues traditions. Reflecting many rural Americans' lot—hard work, low wages, and limited opportunity—the musical focal point of this straightforward "backwoods" fare was the fiddle, whose timbre reinforced the music's frequently melancholy subject matter. When Monroe arrived on the scene in the Thirties, he brought his mandolin to the fore, replacing the fiddle as lead instrument. He also introduced songs that featured uptempo rhythms and passionate intertwining vocal harmonies. This evolution, however, did not fully come to fruition until 1945, when two innovators in their own right, Lester Flatt and Earl Scruggs, joined Monroe. Flatt, on guitar, had developed an immediately recognizable bass string run in the key of G, and Scruggs had perfected a syncopated three-finger roll on banjo that enabled him to play clusters of notes with speed and clarity. These revolutionary and often imitated techniques took Monroe's string-driven sound—the sound of bluegrass—to new heights.

Bluegrass waned in popularity during the late Fifties but resurged with the Sixties folk boom. Since then, bluegrass has remained vibrant thanks to a new generation of musicians who have incorporated different musical styles, such as pop, into the already diverse bluegrass melange. This "new grass" attitude was pioneered by the Country Gentlemen, one of the first progressive bluegrass bands, which covered songs by Bob Dylan, Lefty Frizzell, Paul Simon, and Arlo Guthrie. Other important contemporary practitioners include the Seldom Scene, who perform contemporary country, folk, pop, and bluegrass standards with taste and alacrity; Béla Fleck and the Flecktones [see entry], whose records feature complex arrangements and liberal helpings of funk; and the Tony Rice Unit's "spacegrass," which incorporates jazz and traditional bluegrass. One musician who particularly defines the many facets of bluegrass is Mark O'Connor, a multi-instrumentalist who is most renowned for his fiddling. Having appeared on nearly 500 records during his nine-year tenure in Nashville, O'Connor has played bluegrass as well as jazz, country, pop, fusion, and various combinations of all of these styles.

Blue Öyster Cult

Formed 1969, Long Island, New York
Eric Bloom, gtr., voc.; Albert Bouchard (b. May 24, 1947, Watertown, N.Y.), drums, voc.; Joe Bouchard (b. Nov. 9, 1948, Watertown), bass, voc.; Allen Lanier, kybds., synth., gtr.; Donald "Buck Dharma" Roeser, lead gtr.
1972—*Blue Öyster Cult* (Columbia)   1973—*Tyranny and Mutation*   1974—*Secret Treaties*   1975—*On Your Feet or on Your Knees*   1976—*Agents of Fortune*   1977—*Spectres*   1978—*Some Enchanted Evening*   1979—*Mirrors*   1980—*Cultosaurus Erectus*   1981—*Fire of Unknown Origin* (– A. Bouchard; + Rick Downey, drums)   1982—*Extraterrestrial Live*   1983—*Revolution by Night*   1985— (– Downey; + Jimmy Wilcox, drums)   1986—*Club Ninja* (– Lanier; + Tommy Zvoncheck, kybds.)   1987—(– Zvoncheck; + Lanier; – Wilcox; + A. Bouchard)   1988—*Imaginos*   1990—*Career of Evil: The Metal Years*   1992—(+ Jon Rogers, bass; + Chuck Bürgi, drums)   1994—*Cult Classic* (Herald).   Buck Dharma solo: 1982—*Flat Out* (Portrait).

Semisatiric exponents of the high-decibel apocalypse, Blue Öyster Cult forged an unlikely alliance between teen tastes and critical appeal and were a major heavy-metal band from the mid-Seventies through the Eighties. The group goes back to 1967, when future rock critic R. Meltzer and future Cult producer Sandy Pearlman decided to organize a band. Along with fellow Stony Brook University students Allen Lanier, Donald Roeser, and Albert Bouchard, they formed Soft White Underbelly (a name the Cult still uses for club dates). Vocalist Meltzer was replaced by Les Bronstein, with whom they recorded one unreleased LP for Elektra, and several vocalists followed before Eric Bloom joined in 1969. With Bloom, the group's name changed to Oaxaca. By then, Bouchard's brother Joe had joined the band. They recorded another unreleased LP before changing the group's name from the Stalk-Forrest Group to Blue Öyster Cult.

They signed with Columbia in late 1971, and their debut album was released a few months later. There followed several years of extensive touring as Alice Cooper's opening act. Their show—featuring lasers and flash pots and Buck Dharma's guitar solos—built a small but loyal following that paved the way for their 1976 commercial breakthrough with the platinum LP *Agents of Fortune* and its #12 hit single "(Don't Fear) the Reaper," a Buck Dharma composition. *Agents* also featured vocals and songwriting from Patti Smith, who was then Lanier's girlfriend. The Cult's performances have been captured on three live LPs: *On Your Feet or on Your Knees*, their second gold album, *Some Enchanted Evening*, and *Extraterrestrial Live*.

The band's dark imagery is symbolized by its logo, the ancient symbol of Cronos, the Titan god who ate his son the Grim Reaper. A good deal of BÖC's success and image can be credited to their longtime manager and occasional songwriter and producer Pearlman. The group has also enjoyed the support of rock writers like Meltzer, who has also written songs for the band. In 1980 it coheadlined with Black Sabbath on the Black and Blue Tour.

Although "Burnin' for You" was a Top Forty hit and frequently aired video clip, the album it came from, *Fire of Unknown Origin*, was the group's last gold record. Subsequent studio albums—*Revolution by Night, Club Ninja*, and *Imaginos*—came less frequently and had decreasing commercial impact. The original lineup regrouped in 1988, but by *Cult Classics* (which featured rerecorded versions of BÖC chestnuts) the Bouchard brothers had left the band.

Blue Ridge Rangers: See Creedence Clearwater Revival

The Blues

The basic vocabulary of rock is the blues. The 12-bar song form, the bent notes, and the basic attitude of the blues—that joyful music can come out of real pain—have filtered into rock directly, via the blues songs in the rock repertoire ("I'm So Glad," "Love in Vain," "Rollin' and Tumblin'," "Dust My Broom," "Hootchie Koochie Man"), and indirectly, as a way of approaching a song.

The blues arose sometime after the Civil War as a distillate of the African music brought over by slaves. From field hollers, ballads, church music, and rhythmic dance tunes called jump-ups evolved a music for a singer who would engage in call-and-response with his guitar; he would sing a line, and the guitar would answer. The early blues were irregular and followed speech rhythms, as can be heard in the recordings made in the Twenties and Thirties by Charley Patton, Blind Lemon Jefferson, Robert Johnson, and Lightnin' Hopkins. Radio broadcasts and records spread the blues across the South, and they became more regular, settling into a form in which one line of lyrics was repeated, then answered—AAB—over a chord progression of four bars of tonic, two of subdominant, two of tonic, one of dominant, one of subdominant, and two of tonic.

In the Thirties and Forties the blues spread northward with the black migration from the predominantly rural South and filtered into big-band jazz; they also became electrified as the electric guitar became popular. In Northern cities like Chicago and Detroit in the later Forties and early Fifties, Muddy Waters, John Lee Hooker, Howlin' Wolf, and Elmore James amplified basic Mississippi Delta blues, built backing bands with bass, drums, piano, and amplified harmonica, and began scoring national hits with songs based on simple but powerful repeated riffs. In the same period, T-Bone Walker in Houston and B. B. King in Memphis were perfecting a style of lead guitar playing that used the smoothness of jazz technique on the moaning, crying phrases of blues singing. Blues lyrics continued to evolve as a colloquial, poetic form—frank, autobiographical, and reflecting the full range of life's sorrows and joys. Blues singers, rarely sacrificing emotion to technique, tended to reach their peak in their mature years, reflecting the premium the blues places on experience.

The urban bluesmen were "discovered" in the early Sixties by young white musicians in America and Europe; and their bands—the Paul Butterfield Blues Band, the Rolling Stones, the Yardbirds, John Mayall's Bluesbreakers, Canned Heat, the original Fleetwood Mac—brought the blues to young white audiences. Since the Sixties, rock has undergone periodic blues revivals, while rock guitarists from Eric Clapton and Jimi Hendrix to Bonnie Raitt and Eddie Van Halen have used the blues as a foundation for their unique styles. Originators like John Lee Hooker and B. B. King—and their heirs Buddy Guy and Otis Rush in Chicago, Johnny Copeland in Texas—continue to make music in the blues traditions.

The mainstream popularity of younger players in the Eighties, particularly guitarists Robert Cray and Stevie Ray Vaughan, helped keep the blues vital, especially as these musicians adopted styles that incorporated the volume and bravado of rock. And, during the decade, more blues clubs sprang up in major cities, with factors as various as CD reissues of blues classics and a general interest in "roots music" of every kind boosting interest in the blues.

The Blues Brothers
Formed 1977, New York City, New York
Jake Blues (b. John Belushi, Jan. 24, 1949, Chicago, Ill.; d. Mar. 5, 1982, Los Angeles, Calif.), voc.; Elwood Blues (b. Dan Aykroyd, July 1, Ottawa, Can.), harmonica, voc.

1978—*Briefcase Full of Blues* (Atlantic) 1980—*Made in America*; The Blues Brothers soundtrack 1981—*The Best of the Blues Brothers* 1992—*The Definitive Collection*.

Grammy Awards

Anita Baker
1986 Best R&B Song: "Sweet Love" (with Gary Bias and Louis Johnson)
1986 Best R&B Vocal Performance, Female: *Rapture*
1987 Best Soul Gospel Performance by a Duo or Group, Choir or Chorus: "Ain't No Need to Worry" (with the Winans)
1988 Best R&B Song: "Giving You the Best That I've Got" (with Randy Holland and Skip Scarborough)
1988 Best R&B Vocal Performance, Female: "Giving You the Best That I've Got"
1989 Best R&B Vocal Performance, Female: *Giving You the Best That I've Got*
1990 Best R&B Vocal Performance, Female: *Compositions*

The Beatles
1964 Best New Group
1964 Best Performance by a Vocal Group: *A Hard Day's Night*
1967 Album of the Year: *Sgt. Pepper's Lonely Hearts Club Band* (with George Martin)
1967 Best Contemporary Album: *Sgt. Pepper's Lonely Hearts Club Band* (with George Martin)
1972 Trustees Award

Jeff Beck
1985 Best Rock Instrumental Performance: "Escape"
1989 Best Rock Instrumental Performance: *Jeff Beck's Guitar Shop with Terry Bozzio and Tony Hymas* (with Terry Bozzio and Tony Hymas)

The Bee Gees
1977 Best Pop Vocal Performance, Group: "How Deep Is Your Love"
1978 Album of the Year: *Saturday Night Fever* (with others)
1978 Best Pop Vocal Performance by a Duo, Group or Chorus: *Satur-*

day Night Fever
1978 Best Arrangement for Voices: "Stayin' Alive"
1978 Best Producer of 1978 (with Albhy Galuten and Karl Richardson)

Barry Gibb (the Bee Gees)
1980 Best Pop Performance by a Duo or Group with Vocal: "Guilty" (with Barbra Streisand)

Regina Belle
1993 Best Pop Performance by a Duo or Group with Vocal: "A Whole New World (Aladdin's Theme)" (with Peabo Bryson)

Pat Benatar
1980 Best Rock Vocal Performance, Female: *Crimes of Passion*
1981 Best Rock Vocal Performance, Female: "Fire and Ice"
1982 Best Rock Vocal Performance, Female: "Shadows of the Night"
1983 Best Rock Vocal Performance, Female: "Love Is a Battlefield"

Tony Bennett
1962 Record of the Year: "I Left My Heart in San Francisco"
1962 Best Solo Vocal Performance, Male: *I Left My Heart in San Francisco*
1994 Album of the Year: *MTV Unplugged*
1994 Best Traditional Pop Vocal Performance: *MTV Unplugged*

George Benson
1976 Best Pop Instrumental Performance: *Breezin'*
1976 Best R&B Instrumental Performance: "Theme from Good King Bad"
1976 Record of the Year: "This Masquerade" (with Tommy LiPuma)
1978 Best R&B Vocal Perfor-

mance, Male: "On Broadway"
1980 Best Jazz Vocal Performance, Male: "Moody's Mood"
1980 Best R&B Instrumental Performance: "Off Broadway"
1980 Best R&B Vocal Performance, Male: *Give Me the Night*
1983 Best Pop Instrumental Performance: "Being with You"

Chuck Berry
1984 Lifetime Achievement Award

Big Daddy Kane
1990 Best Rap Performance by a Duo or Group: "Back on the Block" (with Quincy Jones and others)

Henry Rollins (Black Flag)
1994 Best Spoken Word or Nonmusical Album: *Get in the Van: On the Road with Black Flag*

Black Uhuru
1984 Best Reggae Recording: *Anthem*

Rubén Blades
1986 Best Tropical Latin Performance: *Escenas*
1988 Best Tropical Latin Performance: *Antecedente*

Blood, Sweat and Tears
1969 Album of the Year: *Blood, Sweat and Tears*
1969 Best Contemporary Instrumental Performance: "Variations on a Theme by Erik Satie"

Michael Bolton
1989 Best Pop Vocal Performance, Male: "How Am I Supposed to Live Without You"
1991 Best Pop Vocal Performance, Male: "When a Man Loves a Woman"

Booker T. and the MG's
1994 Best Pop Instrumental Performance: "Cruisin'"

Steve Cropper (Booker T. and the MG's)
1968 Best R&B Song: "(Sittin' On) The Dock of the Bay" (with Otis Redding)

Debby Boone
1977 Best New Artist
1980 Best Inspirational Performance: *With My Song I Will Praise Him*
1984 Best Gospel Performance by a Duo or Group: "Keep the Flame Burning" (with Phil Driscoll)

David Bowie
1984 Best Video, Short Form: *David Bowie*

Boyz II Men
1991 Best R&B Performance by a Duo or Group with Vocal: *Cooleyhighharmony*
1992 Best R&B Performance by a Duo or Group with Vocal: "End of the Road"

1994 Best R&B Performance by a Duo or Group with Vocal: "I'll Make Love to You"
1994 Best R&B Album: *II*

Garth Brooks
1991 Best Country Vocal Performance, Male: *Ropin' the Wind*

Brothers Johnson
1977 Best R&B Instrumental Performance: "Q"

Bobby Brown
1989 Best R&B Vocal Performance, Male: "Every Little Step"

Clarence "Gatemouth" Brown
1982 Best Traditional Blues Recording: *Alright Again*

James Brown
1965 Best R&B Recording: "Papa's Got a Brand New Bag"
1986 Best R&B Recording, Male: "Living in America"

1992 Lifetime Achievement Award

Ruth Brown
1989 Best Jazz Vocal Performance, Female: *Blues on Broadway*

Peabo Bryson
1992 Best Pop Performance by a Duo or Group with Vocal: "Beauty and the Beast" (with Celine Dion)
1993 Best Pop Performance by a Duo or Group with Vocal: "A Whole New World (Aladdin's Theme)" (with Regina Belle)

David Byrne
1988 Best Album of Original Instrumental Background Score Written for a Motion Picture or Television: *The Last Emperor* (with Ryuichi Sakamoto and Cong Su)

What started as a joke on *Saturday Night Live* turned into million-selling records and a movie featuring comedians John Belushi (Jake Blues) and Dan Aykroyd (Elwood Blues). In fall 1977 Belushi and Aykroyd concocted the Blues Brothers as a preshow warmup act for *SNL* studio audiences. Dressed in baggy Fifties-style suits, narrow ties, fedoras, and Ray-Ban sunglasses, Belushi sang Sixties soul songs and Aykroyd played middling harmonica.

Their top-notch backing band included such Memphis session musicians as guitarist Steve Cropper and bassist Donald "Duck" Dunn (members of Booker T. and the MG's), who'd performed on some of the original hits the Blues Brothers covered (Sam and Dave's "Soul Man" and "Hold On, I'm Comin'"). During a September 1978 engagement opening for comedian Steve Martin in Los Angeles, they recorded *Briefcase Full of Blues* live. With two hit singles—"Soul Man" (#14) and "Rubber Biscuit" (#37)—the album was platinum by 1979. They toured occasionally, particularly to promote their 1980 film "biography," *The Blues Brothers,* which grossed over $32 million in its first two months of release. They had further hits with covers of the Spencer Davis Group's "Gimme Some Lovin'" (#18, 1980) and Johnnie Taylor's "Who's Making Love" (#39, 1980). Belushi died in Hollywood of an accidental drug overdose.

In 1988 the Blues Brothers Band (Steve Cropper, Duck Dunn, Matt Murphy, Alan Rubin, and Lou Marini) reunited and began touring the world, often with soul singer Eddie ("Knock on Wood") Floyd. The lineup has expanded to include keyboardist Leon Pendarvis, trombonist Birch Johnson, drummer Steve Potts, and vocalist Larry Thurston. In 1992 this group released *Red, White & Blues,* on which Aykroyd made a guest appearance.

Blues Image
Formed 1966, Tampa, Florida
Malcolm Jones (b. Cardiff, Wales), bass; Mike Pinera (b. Sep. 29, 1948, Tampa), gtr.; Joe Lala (b. Tampa), drums, perc.; Manuel Bertematti, drums.
1968—(+ Frank "Skip" Konte [b. Canon City, Okla.], kybds.) 1969—*Blues Image* (Atco) 1970—*Open; Red, White, and Blues Image.*

Tampa-based Blues Image was one of the first groups to experiment with Latin-tinged rock and is best remembered for its 1970 #4 hit, "Ride Captain Ride." *Open* contained Blues Image's lone smash hit. The quintet disbanded two years later, with some of the members joining Manna in 1972. Lead guitarist Mike Pinera's career itinerary took him to Iron Butterfly [see entry], Ramatam, the New Cactus Band, and Thee Image. After releasing solo albums in 1978 and 1979, *Isla* and *Forever*, he played behind Alice Cooper [see entry]. Conga player Joe Lala became an in-demand session player; among those he's backed are Stephen Stills in Manassas, Crosby, Stills, Nash and Young, Jackson Browne, Joe Walsh, and the Souther-Hillman-Furay Band.

Blues Incorporated: See Alexis Korner

Blues Magoos

Formed 1964, Bronx, New York
Ralph Scala (b. Dec. 12, 1947, Bronx), kybds., voc.;
Ronnie Gilbert (b. Apr. 25, 1946, Bronx), bass, voc.;
Peppy Castro (b. Emil Thielhelm, June 16, 1949),
gtr., voc.; Geoff Daking (b. Dec. 8, 1947, Del.),
drums; Mike Esposito (b. 1943, Del.), gtr.
1966—*Psychedelic Lollipop* (Mercury)   1967—*Elec-*
***tric Comic Book*   1968—*Basic Blues Magoos* (group**
disbands)   1969—(Group re-forms: Castro; + Eric
Kaz [b. 1946, Brooklyn, N.Y.], kybds.; + Roger Eaton,
bass; + Richie Dickon, per.) *Never Goin' Back to*
Georgia* (ABC)   1970—(– Eaton; + various) *Gulf
Coast Bound*   1992—*Kaleidoscope Compendium:
***The Best of the Blues Magoos* (Mercury).**

A lightweight blues-rock band known to wear bell-bottoms trimmed with neon-filled plastic tubes, the Blues Magoos were popular at the height of psychedelia. They signed with Mercury in mid-1966 and released *Psychedelic Lollipop* (#21), which featured the gold single "(We Ain't Got) Nothin' Yet" (#5, 1967). The band played the Fillmores and opened tours for Herman's Hermits and the Who. In 1969, a few months after the group disbanded, Castro put together a halfhearted new version of the band (which included Eric Kaz) before joining the Broadway cast of *Hair*. He later played in the soft-rock group Barnaby Bye with brothers Billy and Bobby Alessi, as well as Wiggy Bits and Balance. The latter band had a #22 hit in 1981, "Breaking Away."

The Blues Project

Formed 1965, New York City, New York
Danny Kalb (b. Sep. 19, 1942, Brooklyn, N.Y.), gtr.,
voc.; Roy Blumenfeld, drums; Andy Kulberg
(b. 1944, Buffalo, N.Y.), bass, flute; Steve Katz
(b. May 9, 1945, New York City), gtr., harmonica,
voc.; Tommy Flanders, voc.; Al Kooper (b. Feb. 5,
1944, Brooklyn, N.Y.), kybds., voc.
1966—*Live at the Cafe Au Go Go* (Verve/Forecast)
(– Flanders); *Projections*   1967—*Live at Town Hall*
(group disbands)   1968—*Planned Obsolescence*
1969—*Best of the Blues Project*   1971—(Group re-
forms: Kalb; Blumenfeld; + Don Kretmar, bass, sax)

Lazarus **(Capitol)   1972—(+ Flanders; + David**
Cohen [b. 1942, Brooklyn], piano; + Bill Lussenden,
gtr.) *Blues Project* (group disbands)   1973—(Group
re-forms: Kalb; Blumenfeld; Kulberg; Katz; Kooper)
Reunion in Central Park* (MCA)   1989—*The Best of
the Blues Project: "No Time Like the Right Time"
(Rhino).

The Blues Project, along with the Paul Butterfield Blues Band, helped start the blues revival of the late Sixties. The group was formed with folk, bluegrass, and pop musicians. Danny Kalb, formerly one of Dave Van Ronk's Ragtime Jug Stompers, and Roy Blumenfeld, a jazz fan, had discussed playing folk and country blues on electric instruments and drums. Blumenfeld brought in Andy Kulberg, who had studied modern jazz theory at the NYU School of Music, and Kalb rounded up guitarist Artie Traum and folksinger Tommy Flanders. Traum dropped out during rehearsals, and Steve Katz, who had played with the Ragtime Jug Stompers and Jim Kweskin's Even Dozen Jug Band, replaced him. The final addition was keyboardist Al Kooper (one of the Royal Teens), fresh from Bob Dylan's *Highway 61 Revisited* sessions. The group made its debut at Greenwich Village's Cafe Au Go Go in summer 1965, toured the East Coast, traveled to San Francisco in spring 1966, then played campus shows all the way back to New York.

They made their debut album in May 1966. Flanders then left for a solo career, and recorded *Moonstone* for Verve in 1969. The Project continued as a quintet, which did three open-air concerts in Central Park in the summer of 1966 and gigs as backup band for Chuck Berry.

Projections yielded the FM standbys "I Can't Keep from Crying" and the instrumental "Flute Thing," but the Blues Project's popularity was limited to New York and scattered college towns. Chief arranger and songwriter Kooper left the group after a second live album had been recorded in the summer of 1967, Kalb mysteriously disappeared, and the group soon disbanded. Katz joined Kooper in Blood, Sweat and Tears [see entry]; Kalb later returned to session work; and Kulberg and Blumenfeld went to California to form Seatrain. *Planned Obsolescence* was pieced together from recordings the Project had made as a quintet in 1967.

Kalb revived the Blues Project in 1971. Blumenfeld joined him and brought in Seatrain alumnus Kretmar. *Lazarus* sold no better than previous Project releases. The eponymously titled followup found Flanders again singing with the group, which now included pianist David Cohen, once of Country Joe and the Fish, and guitarist Bill Lussenden. The next year, Kooper reunited the original lineup—minus Flanders—for a concert in Central Park, documented on the live *Reunion*.

There have been periodic reunion concerts ever since, continuing up into the early Nineties. Kulberg and guitarist Chris Michie collaborated on soundtrack music for PBS documentaries, independent feature films, TV commercials, and such shows as *Starsky and Hutch*. Kulberg, who settled in San Francisco, also won a local drama critics' award for his 1985 stage musical, *The Dead End Kid*. Kalb continues to live in New York City, where he performs sporadically and teaches guitar.

The Bobbettes
Formed 1956, New York City, New York
Helen Gathers (b. 1944), voc.; Laura Webb (b. 1943), voc.; Reather Dixon (b. 1945), voc.; Emma Pought (b. 1944), voc.; Janice Pought (b. 1945), voc.
1961—(– Gathers).

Conspicuously absent from many histories of rock & roll are the Bobbettes, the first female vocal group to have a #1 R&B hit and a pop Top Ten hit (#6), 1957's "Mr. Lee." The young women, all between the ages of 11 and 14, not only sang but wrote it as well, along with ten other songs they recorded.

The girls began singing together at Harlem amateur nights (including the famed Apollo Theatre) with three other girls under the name the Harlem Queens in 1955. Within two years, they had three fewer members, a new name, and their first hit. The song was written about one of their fifth-grade schoolteachers, Mr. Lee, whom they did not like, a fact made quite clear by their 1960 hit "I Shot Mr. Lee." They continued to record consistently through 1966 and sporadically through 1974. They also provided backup vocals for Clyde McPhatter, the Five Keys, and Ivory Joe Hunter. Several later singles grazed the lower reaches of the chart—"Have Mercy, Baby" and "Dance with Me, Georgie" (both 1960) and "I Don't Like It Like That, Part 1" (1961). They sang backup on Johnny Thunder's #4 1962 hit "Loop De Loop" and on "Love That Bomb" for the film *Dr. Strangelove*.

The BoDeans
Formed 1985, Waukesha, Wisconsin
Guy Hoffman (b. May 20, 1954), drums; Sam Llanas (b. Feb. 8, 1961, Waukesha), voc., gtr.; Kurt Neumann (b. Oct. 9, 1961, Waukesha), gtr., voc., mandolin.
1986—(+ Bob Griffin [b. Dec. 4, 1959, Waukesha], bass) *Love & Hope & Sex & Dreams* (Slash)   1988—(– Hoffman) *Outside Looking In*   1989—(+ Michael Ramos [b. Nov. 18, 1958, Houston, Tex.], kybds.) *Home*   1991—(+ Rafael "Danny" Gayol, drums) *Black and White*   1993—(– Gayol) *Go Slow Down*.

The title of the BoDeans' debut album, *Love & Hope & Sex & Dreams,* alludes to the Rolling Stones song "Shattered," and to promote it, Llanas, Neumann, Griffin, and Hoffman went by the stage names Sammy, Beau, Bob, and Guy BoDean, a la the Ramones. Both bands have strongly influenced the BoDeans' bracing guitar rock; the band's wistful pop sensibility, however, is evocative of Buddy Holly and the Everly Brothers.

Chief songwriters Sam Llanas and Kurt Neumann, whose plangent harmonies are a key feature of the band's sound, met in high school in Waukesha, Wisconsin. In Milwaukee they hooked up with drummer Guy Hoffman, who left the band in 1988. Subsequent drummers have included Bo Conlon (on the road), Danny Gayol (on *Black and White*), and honorary BoDean Kenny Aronoff, of John Mellencamp fame (on *Home, Go Slow Down,* and on the road). Keyboardist Susan Julian also toured with the band briefly and appeared on *Home.* To date, the BoDeans have won critical praise and amassed a loyal cult following.

Body Count: See Ice-T

Angela Bofill
Born 1954, New York City, New York
1978—*Angie* (GRP)   1979—*Angel of the Night*   1981—*Something About You* (Arista)   1983—*Too Tough; Teaser*   1988—*Intuition* (Capitol)   1993—*I Wanna Love Somebody* (Jive).

Pop-jazz singer Angela Bofill grew up in the Bronx, the daughter of a French-Cuban father (a former bandleader) and a Puerto Rican mother. At age ten she began studying piano and viola, and a few years later began writing her own songs. In high school she sang in the All-City Chorus and after hours with a group called the Puerto Rican Supremes. By graduation day she was singing on the Latino club circuit with the Group, Ricardo Morrero's popular salsa band. Meanwhile she studied voice (she has a four-octave range) at the Hartford Conservatory and the Manhattan School of Music. She developed an interest in jazz through friendships with Herbie Hancock, Joe Zawinul, and Flora Purim. After earning her music degree she was hired by the Dance Theater of Harlem as a singer, dancer, composer, and arranger. She also wrote and performed a jazz suite premiered at the Brooklyn Academy of Music and sang with jazz masters Dizzy Gillespie and Cannonball Adderley and with the reggae group Inner Circle.

Through flutist Dave Valentin of the Group, she met Dave Grusin and Larry Rosen of GRP Records, who signed her to a seven-year contract in 1978. Her debut was a best-selling jazz album and a promising soul and pop debut. "This Time I'll Be Sweeter" made #23 on the R&B singles charts. Her second album moved her closer to widespread popularity, charting at #10 R&B.

It was two years before she made another record. In

the interim she settled a royalty dispute with GRP by transferring her contract to Arista. She also toured North America, South America, and the Orient. Her 1981 album was produced by Narada Michael Walden. She produced half of *Too Tough* herself.

Marc Bolan: See T. Rex

Tommy Bolin

Born 1951, Sioux City, Iowa; died December 4, 1976, Miami, Florida
1975—*Teaser* (Nemperor)   1976—*Private Eyes* (Columbia)   1989—*The Ultimate . . .* (Geffen).

Guitarist/songwriter Tommy Bolin played in several hard-rock bands before dying of a drug overdose in 1976. Bolin dropped out of high school in Sioux City in 1968 and drifted to Denver. There he joined Zephyr, a quintet fronted by a woman singer named Candy Givens. Its eponymously titled debut album cracked the Top Fifty in 1969. Next Bolin played in a group called Energy.

In 1971 Joe Walsh left the James Gang [see entry]. Two years later, when his replacement, Dominic Troiano, quit the band, Walsh recommended Bolin. In addition to playing guitar, Bolin wrote much of the material on *Bang* (1973) and *Miami* (1974). Though best known for hard rock, he was a versatile musician, playing jazz-rock fusion on Billy Cobham's 1973 LP *Spectrum.*

Bolin went from the James Gang to filling Ritchie Blackmore's shoes in Deep Purple in 1975 [see entry]. For the next two years he recorded both with that group (*Come Taste the Band* contained seven of his songs) and on his own: His first solo album, *Teaser,* came out in 1975. Bolin also appears on Deep Purple's *Last Concert in Japan* (a 1977 U.K. release) and *When We Rock We Rock, and When We Roll, We Roll* (1978). After Purple disbanded in summer 1976, the guitarist returned to his solo career. *Private Eyes* came out shortly before Bolin's death; his body was found in a Miami hotel room.

Michael Bolton

Born Michael Bolotin, February 26, 1953, New Haven, Connecticut
1983—*Michael Bolton* (Columbia)   1987—*The Hunger*   1989—*Soul Provider*   1991—*Time, Love and Tenderness*   1992—*Timeless (The Classics)*   1993—*The One Thing.*

Not since Barry Manilow has a singer/songwriter at once inspired such enduring enthusiasm among fans and such chronic irritation among critics as Michael Bolton.

Bolton became infatuated with soul music at an early age, listening to records by Ray Charles and Marvin Gaye. He took up the saxophone at seven, began playing

Michael Bolton

guitar at 11, and by his early teens was singing with the Nomads, a local bar band. The Nomads were signed to Epic Records when Bolton was 15, but were dropped after two singles. Two more record deals later—one as a solo artist, one with a hard-rock outfit called Blackjack—Bolton was still struggling, now with a wife and three children to support.

In 1982 he signed a solo deal with Columbia. Bolton's eponymous first album for the label peaked at #89 in 1983; that same year, though, Laura Branigan took his song "How Am I Supposed to Live Without You" to #12. Soon afterward, superstars as diverse as Barbra Streisand, Kenny Rogers, and Kiss recorded Bolton's tunes, while he established relationships with such successful songwriters as Diane Warren, Eric Kaz, and Barry Mann and Cynthia Weil, who would later contribute and collaborate on material for Bolton's own albums. In 1987 the singer cracked pop's Top Twenty with "That's What Love Is All About" (#19), cowritten by Kaz. The following year, Bolton reached #11 with a cover of Otis Redding's "(Sittin' on) The Dock of the Bay," which Redding's widow pronounced her favorite rendition of the song.

Bolton's next album, *Soul Provider,* shot to #3, and included Bolton's own #1 version of Branigan's hit. In 1990, two other tracks, "How Can We Be Lovers" and "When I'm Back On My Feet Again," made #3 and #7 respectively. The next year's *Time, Love and Tenderness* topped the charts, and generated the singles "Time, Love and Tenderness" (#7) and a #1 rendering of Percy

Sledge's "When a Man Loves a Woman." The album's #4 single "Love Is a Wonderful Thing," which Bolton cowrote with Andrew Goldmark, caused some trouble for the singer. In 1994 a federal jury found that his song borrowed significantly from the Isley Brothers' 1966 composition of the same name, and ordered that the Isleys receive 66 percent of all the single's royalties (an amount that could reach $15 million).

In 1992 Bolton released an album of covers, *Timeless (The Classics)*, which followed its predecessor to #1 and produced a #11 single with the Bee Gees' "To Love Somebody." (Also in 1992 the singer scored a #12 duet with saxophonist Kenny G, "Missing You Now.") *The One Thing* peaked at #3 and yielded the #6 hit "Said I Loved You . . . But I Lied."

Graham Bond

Born October 28, 1937, Romford, England; died May 8, 1974, London, England
1965—*The Sound of '65* (Columbia, U.K.)   1966—*There's a Bond Between Us*   1968—*Mighty Graham Bond* (Pulsar, U.K.); *Love Is the Law*   1970—*Solid Bond* (Warner Bros.)   1971—*Holy Magick* (Vertigo, U.K.)   1972—*This Is Graham Bond* (Philips, U.K.)   1974—*We Put Our Magick on You* (Mercury).

Along with Alexis Korner and John Mayall, Graham Bond was a pioneer of British R&B. Initially a jazz musician, Bond earned his early reputation in the late Fifties playing alto sax with the Don Rendell Quintet. He left Rendell in 1962 to join Korner's R&B-rock band, Blues Incorporated. His discovery of the electric organ as a blues instrument led him to quit the group in 1963 and, with drummer Ginger Baker and bass player Jack Bruce, to form the Graham Bond Organisation, to which guitarist John McLaughlin was later added. When McLaughlin left the band in 1964 to join Brian Auger's Trinity, Bond replaced him with saxophonist Dick Heckstall-Smith, also late of Blues Incorporated. After Bruce's 1965 departure for Mayall's Bluesbreakers, Bond employed a succession of bassists. In late summer Baker left, emerging three months later with Bruce (and Eric Clapton) in Cream. Shortly thereafter the Graham Bond Organisation collapsed. An album of the group's work was released in the U.K. in 1984.

Bond tried working as a solo act but was forced to take on session work. After reuniting with Ginger Baker in 1970 in Baker's shortlived supergroup Air Force, Bond collaborated with lyricist Pete Brown on *Two Heads Are Better Than One* (1972).

He married British singer Diane Stewart, with whom he shared a fascination for the occult (he claimed to be the son of renowned Satanist Aleister Crowley). Together they formed Holy Magick. After that marriage failed, Bond formed Magus in 1973 with British folksinger

Carolanne Pegg. The group broke up within the year because of Bond's financial mismanagement. He also had drug problems. After suffering a nervous breakdown, Bond spent a month in the hospital in 1973. At the time that he died, he had been trying to revive his career. His body was discovered under the wheels of a stationary train.

Gary "U.S." Bonds

Born Gary Anderson, June 6, 1939, Jacksonville, Florida
1960—*Dance Till Quarter to Three* (Legrand); *Twist Up Calypso*   1961—*Greatest Hits of Gary U.S. Bonds*   1981—*Dedication* (EMI)   1982—*On the Line; Certified Soul* (Rhino)   1990—*Best of Gary U.S. Bonds*.

An early-Sixties hitmaker with a rough, expressive voice, Gary "U.S." Bonds had his career revived in 1981 by fan Bruce Springsteen. As a young streetcorner doo-wop singer named Gary Anderson, Bonds caught the attention of Norfolk, Virginia, music business jack-of-all-trades Frank Guida, who signed him to his Legrand Records. With Guida as producer, they released some of the most exuberant R&B singles of the day. Their first national release in late 1960, "New Orleans," was credited by Guida to one "Gary U.S. Bonds"; Anderson was not consulted. When the single became a hit, Anderson found himself with a new identity. For the next two years Bonds had a string of hits—"School Is Out" (#5, 1961), "Dear Lady Twist" (#9, 1962), "Twist, Twist Senora" (#9, 1962)—which peaked with the May 1961 release of his #1 hit "Quarter to Three." Though Bonds recorded for Legrand through the mid-Sixties, his last chart single of the decade was "Copy Cat" in 1962.

Bonds doggedly continued playing one-nighters as a lounge act until 1978, when Bruce Springsteen—of whom Bonds had never heard—showed up and jammed with him. Springsteen (who often climaxed his concerts with "Quarter to Three") later proposed making a comeback album. *Dedication*, produced by Springsteen's guitarist Steve Van Zandt, was a hit in 1981, and the Springsteen-penned "This Little Girl" was a #11 single that same year—Bonds' first hit in nearly 20 years. A 45 produced by Springsteen and Van Zandt, "Out of Work," hit #21 in 1982. Bonds remains active on the touring circuit.

The Bongos

Formed 1980, Hoboken, New Jersey
Richard Barone (b. Oct. 1, 1960, Tampa, Fla.), gtr., voc.; Frank Giannini (b. Aug 6, 1959, Morristown, N.J.), drums, voc.; Rob Norris (b. Apr. 1, 1955, New York City, N.Y.), bass, voc.

The Bongos: Richard Barone, James Mastro, Rob Norris, Frank Giannini

1982—*Drums Along the Hudson* (PVC) (+ James Mastro [b. James Mastrodimus, Dec. 9, 1960, Springfield, Ohio], gtr., voc.)   1983—*Numbers with Wings* EP (RCA)   1985—*Beat Hotel*.
Richard Barone/James Mastro: 1983—*Nuts and Bolts* (Passport).
Richard Barone solo: 1987—*Cool Blue Halo* (Passport)   1990—*Primal Dream*   1993—*Clouds over Eden* (Mesa).
James Mastro with the Health and Happiness Show: 1993—*Tonic* (Bar/None).

Hoboken, formerly a sleepy Hudson port town best known as Frank Sinatra's birthplace, became a major pop center in the early Eighties, spurred by the fresh, literate, guitar-based pop of the Bongos.

Although they were formed after the breakup of an early Hoboken band, the Bongos were initially popular in England, where they released several singles and took part in a "New York in London" concert with the Bush Tetras, Raybeats, Fleshtones, and dB's, recorded and later released as *Start Swimming*.

Drums Along the Hudson, a compilation of their British singles, was released to rapturous reviews. James Mastro, who had played in Richard Lloyd's post-Television band, was added to flesh out the live sound and stayed on. A 1982 tour with the B-52's brought them to the attention of RCA, which released an EP, *Numbers with Wings*, and *Beat Hotel*, but the records fizzled commercially. Mastro departed and was briefly replaced by ex-Voidoid Ivan Julian before the band called it quits.

Barone recorded the live *Cool Blue Halo,* trying out a cello-based chamber-pop sound. In *Primal Dream* and *Clouds over Eden* he expanded that sound in a studio context. James Mastro also used strings in his first solo project, Strange Cave. In 1991, he formed the Health and Happiness Show (named after a Hank Williams radio program) with former Feelie and Richard Lloyd drummer Vincent Denunzio. The group released *Tonic* in 1993. In 1992 Razor & Tie reissued The Bongos' catalog.

Bon Jovi

Formed 1983, New Jersey
Jon Bon Jovi (b. John Francis Bongiovi Jr., Mar. 2, 1962, Sayreville, N.J.), voc.; Richie Sambora (b. July 11, 1959, Woodbridge, N.J.), gtr.; David Bryan (b. David Bryan Rashbaum, Feb. 7, 1962, New York City, N.Y.), kybds.; Alec John Such (b. Nov. 14, 1956, Yonkers, N.Y.), bass; Tico Torres (b. Hector Torres, Oct. 7, 1953, New York City, N.Y.), drums.
1984—*Bon Jovi* (Mercury)   1985—*7800° Fahrenheit* 1986—*Slippery When Wet*   1988—*New Jersey* 1992—*Keep the Faith* (Jambco)   1994—*Cross Road: 14 Classic Grooves*.
Jon Bon Jovi solo: 1990—*Blaze of Glory (Young Guns II)* (Mercury).
Richie Sambora solo: 1991—*Stranger in This Town* (Jambco).
David Bryan solo: 1992—*Netherworld* (Moonstone).

Like an American Def Leppard, Bon Jovi used good looks and good hooks, toned-down aggression and pumped-up production, to forge the pop-metal alloy that made it one of the dominant mainstream rock bands of the latter Eighties.

As a working-class teenager John Bongiovi showed little interest in school, preferring to sing with his friend David Rashbaum in local bands. Cousin Tony Bongiovi, owner of New York City's Power Station recording studio, let John sweep floors there and record demos with such musicians as Aldo Nova and members of Bruce Springsteen's E Street Band. The nucleus of the Bon Jovi band played clubs to support local radio play for one demo, "Runaway." PolyGram won a record label bidding war (reportedly signing only John Bongiovi, with the rest of the band as his employees) and had Bongiovi de-ethnicize the spelling of his first and last names (Rashbaum dropped his surname, too). After seeing Bon Jovi at a New Jersey club, Sambora auditioned and replaced Dave Sabo (later of Skid Row).

Bon Jovi's self-titled debut album (#43, 1984) yielded hits in "Runaway" (#39, 1984) and "She Don't Know Me" (#48, 1984). Tony Bongiovi then sued the band, claiming he had helped develop its sound; Jon called his cousin's influence "slim to none" but settled out of court. *Fahren-*

heit (#37, 1985) went gold, with minor hit singles in "Only Lonely" (#54, 1985) and "In and Out of Love" (#69, 1985).

Bon Jovi then made two crucial marketing moves: bringing in composer Desmond Child (former leader of the Seventies New York club band Rouge, who also wrote for Aerosmith, Cher, and Kiss) as a song doctor, and basing the next album's content on the opinions of New York and New Jersey teenagers for whom they played tapes of over 30 possible songs. The resulting selections formed *Slippery When Wet* (#1, 1986), which sold over nine million copies, with the help of straightforward performance videos that showcased the videogenic band. Hit singles included "You Give Love a Bad Name" (#1, 1986), the anthemic "Livin' on a Prayer" (#1, 1986)— both of which Child cowrote—and "Wanted Dead or Alive" (#7, 1987).

The *Slippery* formula was followed for *New Jersey* (#1, 1988), which sold over five million copies and contained the hits "Bad Medicine" (#1, 1988), "Born to Be My Baby" (#3, 1988), "I'll Be There for You" (#1, 1989), "Lay Your Hands on Me" (#7, 1989), and "Living in Sin" (#9, 1989). In the midst of a 1989 tour Jon Bon Jovi—who had had a brief fling with actress Diane Lane (Sambora went out with Cher for a while, too, and Bon Jovi backed her on some tracks of her 1989 *Heart of Stone* album)—married his high school sweetheart Dorothea Hurley in Las Vegas (they had a daughter in May 1993). Later that year Bon Jovi played the Soviet Union in the Moscow Music Peace Festival—arranged as part of a community-service sentence on Bon Jovi's manager Doc McGhee, who in 1988 had pleaded guilty to drug-smuggling charges from a 1982 arrest.

After 18 months of touring, the band members went separate ways. Jon Bon Jovi's *Blaze of Glory* (#3, 1990)— for the movie soundtrack of the Western *Young Guns II* (in which he had a bit part), recorded with Jeff Beck, Elton John, Little Richard and others—yielded hits in the title track (#1, 1990) and "Miracle" (#12, 1990) and earned Oscar and Grammy nominations. Bon Jovi ended a year of breakup rumors with a Tokyo concert on December 31, 1991; the band then recorded *Keep the Faith* (#5, 1992), which had hit singles in the title track (#27, 1993) and "Bed of Roses" (#10, 1993). Bon Jovi's 1994 anthology, *Cross Road* (#8), yielded the hit single "Always" (#4, 1994).

Simon Bonney: See the Birthday Party

Karla Bonoff
Born December 27, 1952, Los Angeles, California
1977—*Karla Bonoff* (Columbia) 1979—*Restless Nights* 1981—*Wild Heart of the Young* 1988— *New World* (Gold Castle).

Songwriter Karla Bonoff has written some of Linda Ronstadt's most effective ballads, including "Someone to Lay Down Beside Me." She began playing Monday-night hoots at the Troubadour folk club near her family's West L.A. home when she was 16. After briefly attending UCLA in the late Sixties, she was part of Bryndle, a short-lived group that included Wendy Waldman and Andrew Gold and recorded an unreleased album for A&M. Ronstadt included "Lose Again," "Someone to Lay Down Beside Me," and "If He's Ever Near" on her *Hasten Down the Wind*. Bonoff's first solo album was released in late 1977. It sold respectably, but she was mercilessly compared to Ronstadt, and she took two years to assemble a second album.

Wild Heart of the Young yielded a Top Twenty hit in "Personally" (#19, 1982), but Bonoff then retreated behind the scenes and focused on composing. Her songs were recorded by Bonnie Raitt and Nicolette Larson; Bonoff briefly returned to recording to contribute tracks for the Eighties films *About Last Night . . .* and *Footloose*. In 1990 Bonoff wrote three songs for Ronstadt's album *Cry Like a Rainstorm, Howl Like the Wind;* one of them, "All My Life," won Ronstadt and Aaron Neville a Best Pop Vocal Duo Grammy. In 1993 Wynonna (Judd) topped the country charts with a recording of Bonoff's "Tell Me Why" (Bonoff played guitar and sang backup vocals on it). The following year she contributed two songs to the soundtrack of the film *8 Seconds,* and announced that she, Waldman, Gold, and Edwards would re-form Bryndle.

The Bonzo Dog Band
Formed 1965, London, England
Roger Ruskin Spear (b. June 29, 1943, Wormwood Scrubbs, Eng.), kazoos, Jew's harp, various other musical and nonmusical toys; Rodney Slater (b. Nov. 8, 1944, Lincolnshire, Eng.), saxes; Vivian Stanshall (b. Mar. 21, 1943, Shillingford, Eng.; d. Mar. 3, 1995, London), voc., trumpet, ukulele; Neil Innes (b. Dec. 9, 1944, Essex, Eng.), voc., gtr., kybds.; Vernon Dudley Bohay-Nowell (b. July 29, 1932, Plymouth, Eng., d. Mar. 5, 1995, London), gtr.; "Legs" Larry Smith (b. Jan. 18, 1944, Oxford, Eng.), drums; Sam Spoons (b. Martin Stafford Ash, Feb. 8, 1942, Bridgewater, Eng.), perc.
1967—*Gorilla* (Liberty) 1968—(– Bohay-Nowell; – Spoons; + Dennis Cowan [b. May 6, 1947, London], bass) *Urban Spaceman* 1969—*Tadpoles* 1970— *Keynsham* (United Artists) (group disbands) 1971—(group re-forms: Stanshall; Innes; Cowan; + Bubs White, gtr.; + Andy Roberts, gtr., fiddle; + Dave Richards, bass; + Dick Parry, flute; + Hughie Flint [b. Mar. 15, 1942, Eng.], drums) 1972—*Let's Make Up and Be Friendly* 1990—*Best of the Bonzo Dog Band* (Rhino); *Bestiality of the Bonzo Dog Doo Dah Band* (Liberty).

Originally the Bonzo Dog Dada Band, the group was the brainchild of art-college classmates Roger Spear and Rodney Slater, and its express purpose was to do to music—especially the jazz and popular music of the Twenties and Thirties—what Dadaists Marcel Duchamp and Tristan Tzara had done to art and poetry: give it a good kick in the pants. Early versions of the group contained about 30 members, mostly fellow art students. By the time they began performing in pubs in 1965—the Dada in their name changed to Doo-Dah—they had been reduced to fewer than a dozen. Within a year they were playing clubs and had broadened their act to include parodies of musical styles, surrealistic sight gags, and comic skits in the punning, non-sequitur style of the popular British *Goon Show.* Their stage setup was cluttered with Spear's collection of useless gadgets, machines, mannequins, and robots.

They cut two singles for Parlophone before signing with Liberty in 1967. *Gorilla* included gag advertisements and radio interviews sandwiched between parodies of Prohibition-era jazz, Tony Bennett, Rodgers and Hammerstein, and Elvis Presley (most of the material written by Viv Stanshall or Neil Innes). It was Innes' interest in electronic music, rock, and drugs that lent subsequent LPs the psychedelic touches epitomized by "I'm the Urban Spaceman," a Top Five 1968 British hit written by Innes and produced by one Apollo C. Vermouth, a.k.a. Paul McCartney. The Bonzos appeared in *Magical Mystery Tour,* singing a Presley takeoff titled "Death Cab for Cutie."

Despite growing popularity, the Bonzos broke up in 1970. Larry Smith, Vernon Bohay-Nowell, and Sam Spoons joined Bob Kerr's Whoopee Band, an outfit similar to the early Bonzos. Slater quit show business to become a government social worker. Innes and Cowan formed a group called World and made an album called *Lucky Planet* before Innes briefly joined McGuinness Flint. Stanshall, with Dennis Cowan, Spear, and former Bonzo roadie "Borneo" Fred Munt (as percussionist and saxophonist) formed the Big Grunt. Spear left to put together the Kinetic Wardrobe, in which he was backed by a band of robots. He toured Britain and the Continent opening for the Who in the early Seventies. Stanshall led several other groups—the Human Beans, Gerry Atric and His Aging Orchestra, Viv and His Gargantuan Chums—boasting Eric Clapton and Keith Moon and John Entwistle of the Who as sidemen on occasional singles.

In 1971 Stanshall, Innes, and Cowan revived the Bonzo Dog Band—or at least the name—for one album, *Let's Make Up and Be Friendly.* In spite of contributions from Smith and Spear, old Bonzo fans did not take well to the new band, and there were no further revival attempts. Spear returned to his Kinetic Wardrobe. Smith toured twice in 1974, supporting Elton John and Eric Clapton. Innes has released solo albums (including 1973's *How Sweet to Be an Idiot*) and worked primarily as a composer for British television, most notably *Monty Python's Flying Circus* and *Rutland Weekend Television* with Python's Eric Idle. In 1977 he and Idle wrote, directed, and performed in *The Rutles,* a television special spoofing the Beatles. Innes played the John Lennon character, Ron Nasty.

Stanshall, whose voice graces a number of commercials, announced on Mike Oldfield's *Tubular Bells* and David Bowie's *Peter and the Wolf* as well as on his own BBC show, *Viv Stanshall's Radio Flashes.* He released several solo albums and contributed lyrics to Steve Winwood's first two solo LPs. In 1991 he staged a show, *Rawlinson Dogends,* at London's Bloomsbury Theatre. Included in the backing band were ex-Bonzos Spear and Slater. Stanshall died in a fire at his apartment in London on March 5, 1995.

Boogie

This term derives from the jazz-based "boogie-woogie," which generally referred to a style of piano playing that featured a "hot" rhythm based on eight-to-the-bar figures with the left hand. Boogie-woogie style is believed to have originated in Kansas City with such pianists as Pete Johnson and Joe Turner; other leading boogie-woogie pianists were Albert Ammons, Meade Lux Lewis, James P. Johnson, and Fats Waller early in his career. The term "boogie-woogie" itself probably found its first expression in the phrase "booger-rooger," for a "hot" party or musical good time, used by Twenties Texas country bluesman Blind Lemon Jefferson. Through such blues guitarists as Albert Smith (with his post–World War II hit "Guitar Boogie") and John Lee Hooker (with his "Boogie Chillun") the phrase came to refer to guitar playing as well.

Although in the Seventies the Allman Brothers' expanded "boogie" jams incorporated blues, gospel, country, and R&B, the term came to refer to the simple, unadorned blues/R&B-based rock of white bands like Britain's Foghat and latter-day Southern rock groups like .38 Special. It also means a form of dancing in which one stands before a bandstand and moves one's hips to the beat. As an extension from the white heavy post–blues-rock application of the term, "to boogie" can also mean for a musician to play with enough rhythm to make an audience boogie.

Boogie Down Productions/KRS-One
Formed 1986, Bronx, New York
KRS-One (b. Lawrence "Kris" Parker, 1966, Bronx), voc.; Scott LaRock (b. Scott Sterling, Bronx; d. Aug. 25, 1987, Bronx), DJ.
1987—*Criminal Minded* (B Boy) (– LaRock; + Kenny

Parker [b. Bronx], DJ)   1988—*By All Means Necessary* (Jive)   1989—*Ghetto Music: The Blueprint of Hip Hop*   1990—*Edutainment*   1991—*Ya Know the Rules* EP; *Live Hardcore Worldwide: Paris, London, & NYC*   1992—*Sex and Violence.*
KRS-One solo: 1993—*Return of the Boom Bap* (Jive).

Beginning as a pioneering gangsta rap group, Boogie Down Productions had become the hip-hop vehicle for rapper Kris "KRS-One" Parker's philosophical proselytizing by the time of 1990's *Edutainment*. Parker had embarked on an ambitious antiviolence crusade after his partner, DJ Scott LaRock, was gunned down in 1987 while trying to break up a street fight. Still, it is Boogie Down Production's blend of hip-hop with reggae dancehall and rock influences that sets the group apart from other message-oriented rappers.

Growing up on welfare in Brooklyn and the Bronx, Kris Parker was introduced to rap music through his mother's collection of discs, including some by the Treacherous Three and Grandmaster Flash. Parker ran away from home at 13 and began living on the streets. During the day he would read about philosophy and religion at the library, and at night he'd practice his rapping at the homeless shelters where he lived. At 17 he got his GED.

While staying at the Franklin Armory Shelter in the Bronx, Parker met social worker Scott Sterling, known on weekends as DJ Scott LaRock. The two formed BDP and released *Criminal Minded* on the independent B Boy record label in 1987. The album's smooth grooves and hard rhymes foreshadowed gangsta rap. In August that year LaRock was killed.

Parker kept going with his brother Kenny, releasing *By All Means Necessary* (#75 pop, #18 R&B, 1988) the following year. The album introduced the rapper's "edutainment" style of rap in songs such as "My Philosophy" and "Stop the Violence," the latter of which Parker turned into a movement in 1989 to help curb black-on-black violence. BDP's albums sold relatively well. Both *Ghetto Music* (#36 pop, #7 R&B, 1989) and *Edutainment* (#32 pop, #9 R&B, 1990) went gold and continued Parker's message of antiviolence. Although *Live Hardcore Worldwide* failed to make it onto the pop chart, *Sex and Violence* reached #42 (#20 R&B, 1992). *Return of the Boom Bap* reached #37 (#5 R&B, 1993).

By the late Eighties Parker had begun doing college lecture tours wherein he would touch on a range of topics including Afrocentrism, religion, politics, violence, and his own revisionist views of American history. In 1991 he organized a group of artists including Chuck D., L. L. Cool J, Queen Latifah, British folkie Billy Bragg, and R.E.M.'s Michael Stipe for the consciousness-raising compilation, *H.E.A.L. [Human Education Against Lies]: Civilization Vs. Technology.* Ironically, Parker himself became the subject of a violent episode in 1992 when he jumped onstage at a show by the rap duo P.M. Dawn and pushed leader Prince Be off the stage for earlier questioning the legitimacy of Parker's teachings.

James Booker

Born December 17, 1939, New Orleans, Louisiana; died November 8, 1983, New Orleans
1976—*Junco Partners* (Island, U.K.)   1981—*New Orleans Piano Wizard: Live!* (Rounder)   1982—*Classified*   1993—*Resurrection of the Bayou Maharajah*; *Spiders on the Keys.*

Although James Booker had only one hit, his keyboards on hits by Joe Tex, Fats Domino, Bobby Bland, Lloyd Price, and Junior Parker and his unpredictable temperament made him a New Orleans legend. A child piano prodigy, the son of a minister and brother of gospel singer Betty Jean Booker, he made his first recordings for Imperial Records, working with Dave Bartholomew, when he was 14. He also recorded for the Ace and Duke labels and toured with Joe Tex, Shirley and Lee, Huey Smith's Clowns (impersonating the road-weary Smith), and the Dovells.

In the late Fifties Booker's already high value as a session musician rose when he became the first notable New Orleans R&B musician to play the organ. His R&B organ instrumental "Gonzo" (on Peacock Records) hit #3 on the national R&B chart and made the pop Top Fifty in 1960. He continued to work as a session musician and sideman with B. B. King, Little Richard, and Wilson Pickett, among others, into the mid-Sixties, when he was sidelined by drug problems and a jail term. He began working again around 1968, most notably with Fats Domino, Dr. John, Ringo Starr, and the Doobie Brothers. He toured Europe in 1977 (the Rounder live album was recorded in Zurich that year), then returned to regular engagements in New Orleans. The Clash covered his "Junco Partner" on its 1981 album *Sandinista!* In 1983 Booker died from a heart attack.

Booker T. and the MG's

Formed 1961, Memphis, Tennessee
Booker T. Jones (b. Nov. 12, 1944, Memphis), organ; Lewis Steinberg (b. Sep. 13, 1933), bass; Al Jackson (b. Nov. 27, 1935, Memphis; d. Oct. 1, 1975, Memphis), drums; Steve Cropper (b. Oct. 21, 1941, Willow Springs, Mo.), gtr.
1962—*Green Onions* (Stax)   1963—(– Steinberg; + Donald "Duck" Dunn [b. Nov. 24, 1941, Memphis], bass)   1966—*And Now, Booker T. and the MG's*   1967—*Hip Hug-Her; Back to Back*   1968—*The Best of Booker T. and the MG's* (Atlantic); *Doin' Our Thing* (Stax); *Soul Limbo; Uptight* soundtrack   1969—*The Booker T. Set*   1970—*McLemore Avenue*

1971—*Melting Pot* 1973—*Star Collection* (Warner Bros.) 1974—*Greatest Hits* 1975—*Memphis Sound* (– Jackson) 1976—*Union Extended*; *Time Is Tight* (+ Willie Hall [b. Aug. 8, 1950], drums) 1977—*Universal Language* (Asylum) 1992—(Lineup: Dunn; Cropper; Jones; Steve Jordan, drums) 1994—(+ James Gadson, drums) *That's the Way It Should Be* (Columbia) (– Jordan; – Gadson; + Steve Potts [b. Nov. 12, 1953, Memphis, Tenn.], drums).
Steve Cropper solo: 1969—*Jammed Together* (Stax) 1970—*With a Little Help from My Friends* (Volt) 1982—*Night After Night* (MCA).

As the rhythm section of the Stax Records house band, Booker T. and the MG's were principal architects of the lean, punchy Stax sound. Though they had some instrumental hits on their own, they did invaluable backup work on hits by other Stax and Atlantic performers like Otis Redding, Sam and Dave, Wilson Pickett, Albert King, Eddie Floyd, and Rufus and Carla Thomas.

Booker T. Jones was a teenage multi-instrumental prodigy who joined the Stax organization in 1960 as a saxophonist. Jamming with Mar-Keys guitarist Steve Cropper led to the formation of the MG's (Memphis Group) and to the recording of "Green Onions." The single went to #3 and gold in 1962 and was followed by several minor hits, including "My Sweet Potato" (1966), then "Hip Hug-Her" (#37, 1967), a cover version of the Rascals' "Groovin'" (#21, 1968), "Soul-Limbo," (#17, 1968), and two film soundtrack hits in 1969, "Hang 'Em High" (#9) and "Time Is Tight" (#6).

The best-known version of the band was composed of Jones, Cropper, Jackson, and Dunn. Along with much of the MG's material, Cropper has writing credits on Wilson Pickett's "In the Midnight Hour," Eddie Floyd's "Knock on Wood," Sam and Dave's "Soul Man," Otis Redding's "(Sittin' on) The Dock of the Bay," and at least 20 other Stax-Volt hits. He produced, among others, Redding. In 1969 Cropper opened his own Memphis studio, TMI. Among his extra-MG's projects were *Jammed Together* with Albert King and Roebuck Staples, and a solo album, *With a Little Help from My Friends*, with Leon Russell, Buddy Miles, Jim Keltner, Carl Radle, the Bar-Kays, the Memphis Horns, and the MG's.

In 1975, with the MG's disbanded, Cropper moved to Los Angeles, where he resumed his session career by playing with Rod Stewart, Art Garfunkel, and Sammy Hagar. They toured sporadically as part of the Stax/Volt Revue. The MG's proper were a very informal assemblage and played together only intermittently, partly due to Jones' frequent absences while completing his music major at Indiana University. Often limited to working only when Jones was available on weekends and vacations, the group eventually broke up in 1971.

Soon afterward Jones began working as a producer (for Rita Coolidge, Bill Withers, and Willie Nelson [on *Stardust*], among others), as a session player, and as a solo vocal performer. Jackson also returned to session work, notably for Al Green. In 1973 he joined Dunn in a short-lived MG's reunion. A reunion album was in the planning stages two years later when Jackson was shot and killed in his home by a burglar. Former Bar-Kays drummer Willie Hall took his place in reunion sessions with Jones, Cropper, and Dunn between 1975 and 1978. In 1977 Jones, Cropper, and Dunn toured with Levon Helm's RCO All Stars. Since then Cropper and Dunn have been active as freelance musicians and producers, joining the Blues Brothers in 1978, while Jones has worked on his solo career. He had a disco dance hit with his 1982 A&M single "Don't Stop Your Love."

Through the Eighties the members were actively involved in dozens of projects. Cropper continued producing such artists as John Prine, Poco, Jeff Beck, Tower of Power, and Jose Feliciano. Through the late Eighties and early Nineties, Cropper, Dunn, and Potts also worked a side job as the Blues Brothers Band [see the Blues Brothers entry].

The MG's reunited for a 1990 tour, with session drummer Anton Fig (Paul Shaffer's band on David Letterman's late-night TV talk show). The group was inducted into the Rock and Roll Hall of Fame in 1992. That year they were the house band for the Bob Dylan tribute show at Madison Square Garden. In 1993 they played backup for Neil Young's tour. Following their induction, the members began playing together, and finding an enthusiastic audience, decided to reconvene on a more permanent basis. In 1994 they released their first album in 17 years, *That's The Way It Should Be,* with Steve Jordan (who'd preceded Fig in the Letterman band and had played with Keith Richards) on drums; the band also planned to tour with the late Al Jackson's nephew, Steve Potts, on drums.

The Boomtown Rats/Bob Geldof
Formed 1975, Dun Laoghaire, Ireland
Bob Geldof (b. Oct. 5, 1954, Dublin, Ire.), voc.; Johnny Fingers (b. Ire.), kybds.; Pete Briquette (b. Ire.), bass; Simon Crowe (b. Ire.), drums; Gerry Cott (b. Ire.), gtr.; Garry Roberts (b. Ire.), gtr.
1977—*The Boomtown Rats* (Mercury) 1979—*A Tonic for the Troops* (Columbia); *The Fine Art of Surfacing* 1981—(– Cott) *Mondo Bongo* 1983—*Ratrospective* 1985—*In the Long Grass.*
Bob Geldof solo: 1986—*Deep in the Heart of Nowhere* (Atlantic) 1988—*The Vegetarians of Love* 1993—*The Happy Club* (Polydor).

Irish new wavers, the Boomtown Rats were full-fledged pop stars in Britain and Europe while being virtually ignored in the U.S., where none of their four albums even cracked the Top 100. By the mid-Eighties, the group was overshadowed by the high-profile humanitarian activities of its lead singer, Bob Geldof, who was nominated for a Nobel Peace Prize.

Originally called the Nightlife Thugs, they changed their name to the Boomtown Rats after a gang in Woody Guthrie's *Bound for Glory*. They moved to London (and into a communal house in Chessington) in 1976. Their stage show attracted attention for Johnny Fingers, who was known for wearing pajamas, and the Mick Jagger–David Bowie posturings of frontman Bob Geldof (who had previously worked as a meat worker, bulldozer operator, photographer, and *Melody Maker* correspondent).

While most of London's punk bands were sneering at rich, selfish rock stars, Geldof announced his ambition to become one. The first Rats single, "Looking After No. 1," hit #11 in England in August 1977 (the first new-wave single to be playlisted by the BBC), and the media discovered Geldof's willingness to utter controversial opinions on virtually any subject. The Rats' first album (recorded in Germany and released in England in late 1977) did well in the U.K. With *A Tonic for the Troops* ("She's So Modern") the group established a pattern of critical raves but poor sales in the U.S. In Britain its success continued; by early 1981 the Rats had nine consecutive Top Fifteen singles, among them two Number Ones: "Rat Trap" (1978) and "I Don't Like Mondays" (1979). The latter became a controversial, minor U.S. hit (#73, 1980). It was based on the case of a 17-year-old San Diego girl named Brenda Spencer, who randomly shot 11 passersby (killing two) on Monday, January 29, 1979, and explained her actions by saying, "I don't like Mondays." The single was banned by some radio stations and prompted a lawsuit by the girl's parents, who claimed it created adverse pretrial publicity.

The Eighties found the Rats continuing to tour internationally and release records, such as 1981's *Mondo Bongo* and the reggae single "Banana Republic." It was their last British Top Ten single, although through 1984 a number of records charted, including "The Elephant's Graveyard," "Never in a Million Years," "House on Fire," "Tonight," and "Drag Me Down."

In 1982 Geldof played the lead role of Pink in a film of Pink Floyd's *The Wall*. Moved by news coverage of the Ethiopian famine, Geldof and Ultravox's Midge Ure cowrote "Do They Know It's Christmas," which was recorded in a single 24-hour session by an ad hoc group that included Boy George, Paul McCartney, George Michael, Phil Collins, Paul Young, Sting, and members of Duran Duran, Spandau Ballet, U2, and Kool and the Gang. Within 10 days the song sold over 2 million copies, hitting #1 on the U.K. chart in 1984. (It went to #3 in December of the following year and remains the biggest-selling single in the history of British pop.) All proceeds went directly to famine relief, and in January 1985 Geldof toured Africa to see for himself that the food was being distributed. Later that month, he addressed the group of American performers gathered by Michael Jackson, Quincy Jones, and Lionel Richie to record a similar benefit record, "We Are the World," under the group name U.S.A. for Africa. U.S.A. for Africa—which included Bob Dylan, Bruce Springsteen, Ray Charles, Tina Turner, Diana Ross, the Jacksons, Cyndi Lauper, Paul Simon, Lionel Richie, Michael Jackson, Stevie Wonder, Willie Nelson, Huey Lewis, and Geldof—raised $40 million. Geldof later remarked, "'We Are the World' sounds too much like the Pepsi generation." In a characteristically blunt appraisal of the resulting rash of benefit records, Geldof described them as artistically "awful."

On July 13, 1985, over 1.5 billion people tuned in to watch Live Aid, a 16-hour-long star-studded concert that was broadcast via satellite from London's Wembley Stadium and Philadelphia's JFK Stadium. Among the performers were Madonna, Paul McCartney, Queen, Phil Collins, David Bowie, Led Zeppelin (with Phil Collins and Tony Thompson sitting in for the deceased John Bonham), Power Station (with Michael des Barres), Duran Duran, U2, Judas Priest, Black Sabbath, and the Boomtown Rats. All told, the shows and the resulting album raised about $120 million. In November of that year, Columbia Records canceled the Boomtown Rats' U.S. record deal. The group broke up in 1986.

Geldof went on to become a familiar face, pictured with Mother Teresa and other world leaders. In June 1986 Queen Elizabeth II awarded him with an honorary knighthood, making him Bob Geldof, KBE (Knight Commander of the British Empire); because he is an Irish citizen he is not, as has been published, referred to as Sir Bob. That year saw the publication of his critically well received best-selling autobiography, *Is That It?* Geldof, who often admitted that becoming an institution overnight has at times overwhelmed him, stated in 1990, "I never said we were going to stop world poverty or world hunger. [The function] was to raise the issue to the top of the political agenda, and we did that."

In the meantime, Geldof's recording career went on hold. He said that he accepted the offer to write his book only because the advance covered his debts. As a recording artist, wide commercial appeal still eludes him. Geldof is a director of Planet 24 Productions, which produces the popular U.K. morning television program *The Big Breakfast*.

Debby Boone

Born September 22, 1956, Hackensack, New Jersey
1977—*You Light Up My Life* (Curb/Warner Bros.)
1978—*Midstream* 1979—*The Promise* 1980—
***Love Has No Reason* 1990—*The Best of* (Curb).**

Debby Boone had one of the longest-running #1 hit singles—ten weeks—with "You Light Up My Life" in 1977. One of singer Pat Boone's four daughters, Debby began performing with her sisters in 1969 as the Boone Girls. They toured with their father and recorded for the Lamb & Lion label. In 1977 producer Mike Curb persuaded Debby to record solo. The song he chose for her, "You Light Up My Life," the theme song from a movie, won an Oscar for Best Song and resulted in Boone winning three Grammy Awards, including that year's Best New Artist.

Boone retired to start a family; she married Gabriel, the son of singer Rosemary Clooney and actor Jose Ferrer. She wrote an autobiography that chronicled her teenage "rebelliousness" and her life with Christ, entitled *Debby Boone . . . So Far.* She returned to performing in 1982, when she starred in the play *Seven Brides for Seven Brothers,* a hit around the country, which closed within weeks of its Broadway debut. Boone's recent work is in the contemporary Christian vein. In 1990 she played a lead in a revival of *The Sound of Music.*

Pat Boone

Born Charles Eugene Boone, June 1, 1934, Jacksonville, Florida
1962—*Pat Boone's Golden Hits* (Dot)   1990—*Greatest Hits* (Curb).

Singer Pat Boone was easily the most commercially successful of the white Fifties teen idols, with a string of 38 Top Forty hits, among them several cleaned-up hit cover versions that outsold the arguably superior versions by the original artists: Little Richard's "Tutti Frutti" (#12, 1956) and "Long Tall Sally" (#8, 1956), Ivory Joe Hunter's "I Almost Lost My Mind" (#1, 1956), the Five Keys' "Gee Whittakers!" (#19, 1955), and Joe Turner's "Chains of Love" (#10, 1956).

Boone claims to be a descendant of early American frontier hero Daniel Boone. He attended high school in Nashville, where he lettered in three varsity sports as well as serving as student body president. Following his graduation, he married country & western star Red Foley's daughter, Shirley. In the early Fifties he attended David Lipscomb College in Nashville before transferring to North Texas State. There he won a local talent show, which led to an appearance on the Ted Mack program and then Arthur Godfrey's amateur hour, where Boone became a regular for a year.

By mid-decade he had begun recording with some mildly successful singles for Nashville's Republic Records. In February 1955 he released his first single for Dot Records, "Two Hearts, Two Kisses." By the end of the year he had his first of dozens of hits for the label, a relaxed cover of Fats Domino's "Ain't That a Shame," which hit #1.

Over the next seven years Boone made 54 chart appearances, including many two-sided hits, and became one of the all-time biggest-selling pop singers. His Top Ten hits for Dot included "At My Front Door (Crazy Little Mama)" (#7, 1955), "I'll Be Home" (#4, 1956), "Friendly Persuasion" (#5, 1956), "Don't Forbid Me" (#1, 1957), "Why Baby Why" (#5, 1957), "Love Letters in the Sand" (#1, 1957), "April Love" (#1, 1957), "A Wonderful Time Up There" (#4, 1958), "Moody River" (#1, 1961), and "Speedy Gonzales" (#6, 1962). He starred in 15 films, including *Bernadine* and *April Love* (both 1957) and *State Fair* (1962). From 1957 to 1960 he had his own television series, *The Pat Boone–Chevy Showroom,* on ABC.

Boone did not have another Top Forty single after 1962, but he continued to record for Dot through the late Sixties, then for a series of other labels until the early Eighties. He still records special projects, such as his "Let Me Live," which has become an anthem for the antichoice movement.

At the height of his popularity, he became an author, penning a series of tomes full of wholesome teen advice: *Twixt Twelve and Twenty, Between You, Me and the Gatepost,* and *The Care and Feeding of Parents.* In 1981 he published *Pray to Win.*

From the Sixties, Pat, with Shirley and their four daughters—Cherry, Lindy, Debby, and Laury—performed together. In 1977 his daughter Debby Boone became a star in her own right; later daughter Cherry revealed her problems with an eating disorder and wrote a book about it entitled *Starving for Attention.* Since 1983 Boone has hosted a contemporary Christian radio show that is heard on over 185 stations across the country. In 1994 he appeared in the title role of a Branson, Missouri, production of *The Will Rogers Follies.*

Earl Bostic

Born April 25, 1913, Tulsa, Oklahoma; died October 28, 1965

Earl Bostic's alto sax propelled Lionel Hampton's big band into R&B in the late Forties and gave his own band a #1 R&B hit in 1951; his style was the cornerstone of rock and soul sax playing.

Bostic began playing clarinet and tenor saxophone in high school. He studied music at universities in Omaha and New Orleans and, after receiving his degree, remained in New Orleans to play with Fate Marable's band. He moved to New York in the early Forties and played with Don Redman and Cab Calloway before joining Hampton. In 1945 he formed his own nine-piece band, which recorded on the Majestic, Gotham, and King labels. He had his biggest hit with "Flamingo" (#1 R&B, 1951), following it the same year with "Sleep," a #9 R&B hit. He was active in jazz and R&B until he died of a heart attack in 1965.

Boston

Formed 1975, Boston, Massachusetts
Tom Scholz (b. Mar. 10, 1947, Toledo, Ohio), gtr.,
kybds.; Brad Delp (b. June 12, 1951, Boston), voc.,
gtr.; Barry Goudreau (b. Nov. 29, 1951, Boston), gtr.;
Fran Sheehan (b. Mar. 26, 1949, Boston), bass; Sib
Hashian (b. Aug. 17, 1949, Boston), drums.
1976—*Boston* (Epic)   1978—*Don't Look Back*
Early 1980s—(– Goudreau; – Sheehan; – Hashian)
1986—*Third Stage* (MCA) (group disbands, Scholz
remains)   1994—*Walk On.*
Barry Goudreau solo: 1980—*Barry Goudreau* (Por-
trait)   1984—(with Orion the Hunter) *Orion the
Hunter.*
RTZ (Goudreau and Brad Delp): 1992—*Return to
Zero* (Giant).

In 1976 sonic-rock group Boston had the fastest-selling
debut album in rock. *Boston* was a slightly altered version of tapes guitarist Tom Scholz had made in his 12-
track basement studio, characterized by what he calls
"power guitars, harmony vocals, and double-guitar
leads." Scholz had a master's degree in mechanical engineering from MIT and was a senior product designer for
Polaroid Corporation who made music in his off-hours.
Eventually the tapes attracted the interest of Epic
Records, which signed Scholz and a band of local musicians, Boston. Upon signing, the band recut some tracks
on the West Coast with producer John Boylan, but its
1976 debut was essentially Scholz's basement tapes. It
sold 11 million copies and spawned three Top Forty singles—"More Than a Feeling" (#5, 1976), "Long Time"
(#22, 1977), and "Peace of Mind" (#38, 1977). Boston went
almost directly to the arena circuit on tour. In early 1995
Billboard ranked *Boston* the third-best-selling album of
all time, behind Michael Jackson's *Thriller* and Fleetwood Mac's *Rumours.*

Two years later *Don't Look Back* (#1, 1978) presented
the Boston formula virtually unchanged and sold a comparatively disappointing six million copies, while less-
than-sellout concert crowds suggested that audience
interest was flagging. This time the group took eight
years to record a followup. Barry Goudreau, who'd released a solo album in 1980, quit in 1982 to form Orion
the Hunter, which issued a Top Sixty LP in 1984.

By the time *Third Stage* appeared in 1986, only
Scholz and singer Brad Delp remained. The loss of the
others hardly mattered, as Delp's soaring vocals and
Scholz's guitar define the Boston sound. The album
lodged at #1 for four weeks and produced hit singles in
"Amanda" (#1, 1986), "We're Ready" (#9, 1986), and
"Can'tcha Say (You Believe in Me)/Still in Love" (#20,
1987).

And then: another long wait, during which Scholz
fended off lawsuits. In 1989 Goudreau sued Scholz for allegedly damaging his musical career; the two reached
an out-of-court settlement. The following year Scholz
won his seven-year legal battle against CBS, which had
sued him for allegedly reneging on his contract with the
label. Scholz countersued, claiming the company owed
him millions in back royalties. A jury sided with the guitarist, and CBS was ordered to release his money.

In addition to selling millions of records, Scholz invented the Rockman, a paperback-sized guitar amplifier
with headphones that is hugely popular with musicians.
Shortly after winning the CBS suit, he built a new studio
and began work on Boston's fourth album. Released in
1994, *Walk On* included only Scholz from the original
lineup. Delp formed a band called RTZ in 1991 with
Goudreau and released *Return to Zero,* featuring "Until
Your Love Comes Back Around" (#26, 1992).

David Bowie

Born David Robert Jones, January 8, 1947, London,
England
1967—*The World of David Bowie* (Deram, U.K.)
1970—*Man of Words, Man of Music* (Mercury); *The
Man Who Sold the World*   1971—*Hunky Dory* (RCA)
1972—*The Rise and Fall of Ziggy Stardust and the
Spiders from Mars*   1973—*Aladdin Sane*; *Pin Ups*;
Images 1966–67 (London)   1974—*Diamond Dogs*
(RCA); *David Live*   1975—*Young Americans*
1976—*Station to Station*; *ChangesOneBowie*
1977—*Low*; *"Heroes"*   1978—*Stage*   1979—*Lodger*
1980—*Scary Monsters*   1981—*ChangesTwoBowie*;
Christiane F soundtrack   1982—*Cat People* sound-
track; *Baal*   1983—*Let's Dance* (EMI); *Golden Years*
(RCA); *Ziggy Stardust/The Motion Picture*   1984—
Fame and Fashion; *Tonight* (EMI)   1987—*Never Let
Me Down*   1989—*Sound + Vision* (Rykodisc)
1990—*ChangesBowie*   1993—*Black Tie White
Noise* (Savage)   1994—*Sound + Vision* with CD-
ROM (Rykodisc).
Tin Machine: (Formed 1989, Switzerland: Bowie;
Reeves Gabrels [b. June 4, 1956, Staten Island, N.Y.],
gtr.; Hunt Sales [b. Mar. 2, 1954, Detroit, Mich.],
drums; Tony Sales [b. Sep. 26, 1951, Cleveland,
Ohio], bass)   1989—*Tin Machine* (EMI)   1991—*Tin
Machine II* (Victory).

A consummate musical chameleon, David Bowie created a career in the Sixties and Seventies that featured
his many guises: folksinger, androgyne, alien, decadent,
blue-eyed soul man, modern rock star—each one
spawning a league of imitators. His late-Seventies collaborations with Brian Eno made Bowie one of the few
older stars to be taken seriously by the new wave. In the
Eighties, *Let's Dance* (#1, 1983), his entree into the mainstream, was followed by attempts to keep up with current trends.

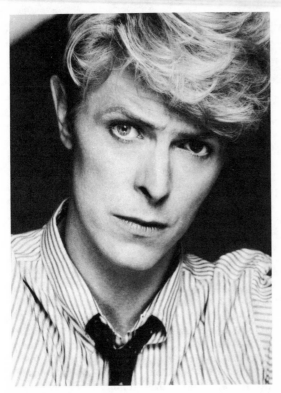

David Bowie

David Jones took up the saxophone at age 13, and when he left Bromley Technical High School (where a friend permanently paralyzed Jones' left pupil in a fight) to work as a commercial artist three years later, he had started playing in bands (the Konrads, the King Bees, David Jones and the Buzz). Three of Jones' early bands—the King Bees, the Manish Boys (featuring session guitarist Jimmy Page), and Davey Jones and the Lower Third—each recorded a single. In 1966, after changing his name to David Bowie (after the knife) to avoid confusion with the Monkees' Davy Jones, he recorded three singles for Pye Records, then signed in 1967 with Deram, issuing several singles and *The World of David Bowie* (most of the songs from that album, and others from that time, are collected on *Images*).

On these early records, Bowie appears in the singer/songwriter mold; rock star seemed to be just another role for him. In 1967 he spent a few weeks at a Buddhist monastery in Scotland, then apprenticed in Lindsay Kemp's mime troupe. He started his own troupe, Feathers, in 1968. American-born Angela Barnett met Bowie in London's Speakeasy and married him on March 20, 1970. Son Zowie (now Joey) was born in June 1971; the couple divorced acrimoniously in 1980. After Feathers broke up, Bowie helped start the experimental Beck-

enham Arts Lab in 1969. To finance the project, he signed with Mercury. *Man of Words, Man of Music* included "Space Oddity," its release timed for the U.S. moon landing. It became a European hit that year but did not make the U.S. charts until its rerelease in 1973, when it reached #15.

Marc Bolan, an old friend, was beginning his rise as a glitter-rocker in T. Rex and introduced Bowie to his producer, Tony Visconti. Bowie mimed at some T. Rex concerts, and Bolan played guitar on Bowie's "Karma Man" and "The Prettiest Star." Bowie, Visconti, guitarist Mick Ronson, and drummer John Cambridge toured briefly as Hype. Ronson eventually recruited drummer Michael "Woody" Woodmansey, and with Visconti on bass they recorded *The Man Who Sold the World,* which included "All the Madmen," inspired by Bowie's institutionalized brother, Terry. *Hunky Dory* (#93, 1972), Bowie's tribute to the New York City of Andy Warhol, the Velvet Underground, and Bob Dylan, included his ostensible theme song, "Changes" (#66, 1972, rereleased 1974, #41).

Bowie started changing his image in late 1971. He told *Melody Maker* he was gay in January 1972 and started work on a new, theatrical production. Enter Ziggy Stardust, Bowie's projection of a doomed messianic rock star. Bowie became Ziggy; Ronson, Woodmansey, and bassist Trevor Bolder became Ziggy's band, the Spiders from Mars. *The Rise and Fall of Ziggy Stardust and the Spiders from Mars* (#75, 1972) and the rerelease of *Man of Words* as *Space Oddity* (#16, 1972) made Bowie the star he was portraying. The live show, with Bowie wearing futuristic costumes, makeup, and bright orange hair (at a time when the rock-star uniform was jeans), was a sensation in London and New York. It took *Aladdin Sane* (#17, 1973) to break Bowie in the U.S. Bolan and other British glitter-rock performers barely made the Atlantic crossing, but Bowie emerged a star. He produced albums for Lou Reed (*Transformer* and its hit "Walk on the Wild Side") and Iggy and the Stooges (*Raw Power*) and wrote and produced Mott the Hoople's glitter anthem "All the Young Dudes."

In 1973 Bowie announced his retirement from live performing, disbanded the Spiders, and sailed to Paris to record *Pin Ups* (#23, 1973), a collection of covers of mid-Sixties British rock. That same year, the 1980 Floor Show, an invitation-only concert with Bowie and guests Marianne Faithfull and the Troggs, was taped for broadcast on the TV program *The Midnight Special.*

Meanwhile, Bowie worked on a musical adaptation of George Orwell's *1984,* but was denied the rights by Orwell's widow. He rewrote the material as *Diamond Dogs* (#5, 1974) and returned to the stage with an extravagant American tour. Midway though the tour, Bowie entered Philadelphia's Sigma Sound Studios (the then-current capital of black music) and recorded the tracks that would become *Young Americans* (#9, 1975). The session had a major effect on Bowie, as his sound and show were revised. Bowie scrapped the dancers, sets, and costumes for a spare stage and baggy Oxford trousers; he cut his hair and colored it a more natural blond. His new band, led by former James Brown sideman Carlos Alomar, added soul standards (e.g., Eddie Floyd's "Knock on Wood") to his repertoire. *David Live* (#8, 1974), also recorded in Philadelphia, chronicles this incarnation.

"Fame," cowritten by Bowie, John Lennon, and Alomar, was Bowie's first American #1 (1975). Bowie moved to Los Angeles and became a fixture of American pop culture. He also played the title role in Nicolas Roeg's *The Man Who Fell to Earth* (1976). *Station to Station* (#3, 1976), another album of "plastic soul" recorded with the *Young Americans* band, portrayed Bowie as the Thin White Duke (also the title of his unpublished autobiography). His highest charting album, it contained his second Top Ten single, "Golden Years" (#10, 1975). Bowie complained life had become predictable and left Los Angeles. He returned to the U.K. for the first time in three years before settling in Berlin. He lived there in semiseclusion, painting, studying art, and recording with Brian Eno. His work with Eno—*Low* (#11, 1977), *"Heroes"* (#35, 1977), *Lodger* (#20, 1979)—was distinguished by its appropriation of avant-garde electronic music and the "cut-up" technique made famous by William Burroughs. Composer Philip Glass wrote a symphony incorporating music from *Low* in 1993.

Bowie revitalized Iggy Pop's career by producing *The Idiot* and *Lust for Life* (both 1977) and toured Europe and America unannounced as Pop's pianist. He narrated Eugene Ormandy and the Philadelphia Orchestra's recording of Prokofiev's *Peter and the Wolf* and spent the rest of 1977 acting with Marlene Dietrich and Kim Novak in *Just a Gigolo*. The next year, he embarked on a massive world tour. A second live album, *Stage* (#44, 1978), was recorded on the U.S. leg of the tour. Work on *Lodger* was begun in New York, continued in Switzerland, and completed in Berlin.

Bowie settled in New York to record the paranoiac *Scary Monsters* (#12, 1980), updating "Space Oddity" in "Ashes to Ashes." One of the first stars to understand the potential of video, he produced some innovative clips for songs from *Lodger* and *Scary Monsters*.

After *Scary Monsters,* Bowie turned his attention away from his recording career. In 1980 he played the title role in *The Elephant Man,* appearing in Denver, in Chicago, and on Broadway. He collaborated with Queen in 1981's "Under Pressure" and provided lyrics and vocals for "Cat People (Putting Out Fire)" (#67, 1982), Giorgio Moroder's title tune for the soundtrack of Paul Schrader's remake of *Cat People.* His music was used on the soundtrack of *Christiane F* (1982) (he also appeared in the film). Also that year, Bowie starred in the BBC-TV production of Brecht's *Baal,* and as a 150-year-old vampire in the movie *The Hunger.*

In 1983 Bowie signed one of the most lucrative contracts in history, and moved from RCA to EMI. *Let's Dance* (#4, 1983), his first album in three years, returned him to the top of the charts. Produced by Nile Rodgers with Stevie Ray Vaughan on guitar, the album was a slick revision of Bowie's soul-man posture. It contained three Top Twenty singles—"Let's Dance" (#1, 1983), "China Girl" (#10, 1983), and "Modern Love (#14, 1983)—which were supported with another set of innovative videos; the sold-out Serious Moonlight Tour followed. Bowie's career seemed to be revitalized.

What first seemed like a return to form actually ushered in a period of mediocrity. Without Nile Rodgers' production savvy, Bowie's material sounded increasingly forced and hollow; his attention alternated between albums and film roles. *Tonight* (#11, 1984) had only one hit, "Blue Jean" (#8, 1984). Bowie and Mick Jagger dueted on a cover of Martha and the Vandellas' "Dancing in the Street"(#7, 1985) for Live Aid. Although *Never Let Me Down* (#34, 1987), with Peter Frampton on guitar, was roundly criticized, it made the charts with "Day In, Day Out" (#21, 1987) and the title song (#27, 1987). Bowie hit the road with another stadium extravaganza, the Glass Spiders tour; it was recorded for an ABC-TV special.

Bowie had scarcely better luck in his acting career: *Into the Night* (1985), *Absolute Beginners* (1986) (a Julien Temple musical featuring some Bowie songs), *Labyrinth* (1986), *The Linguini Incident* (1992), and *Twin Peaks—Fire Walk with Me* (1992) were neither critical nor commercial successes.

Bowie set about reissuing his earlier albums on CD. *Sound + Vision* (#97, 1989), a greatest-hits collection, revived interest in Bowie's career; the set list for the accompanying tour was partially based on fan response to special phone lines requesting favorite Bowie songs. Bowie claimed it would be the last time he performed those songs live. Later reissues, with previously unreleased bonus tracks, brought the Ziggy-era Bowie back onto the charts.

Bowie formed Tin Machine in 1989. The band included Bowie discovery Reeves Gabrels on guitar and Hunt and Tony Sales, who had worked with Bowie on Iggy Pop's *Lust for Life* album and tour in the Seventies. Although Bowie claimed that the band was a democracy, Tin Machine was perceived as Bowie's next project. The group debuted with a series of club dates in New York and Los Angeles. Their eponymous album (#28, 1989), a rougher, more guitar-oriented collection than Bowie's previous albums, received better reviews than Bowie's last few recordings. A second album, *Tin Machine II* (#126, 1991), lacked the novelty of the debut and was quickly forgotten.

In 1992 Bowie married Somalian supermodel Iman. *Black Tie White Noise* (#39, 1993), which Bowie called his wedding present to his wife, received generally positive reviews, but failed to excite the public.

Bow Wow Wow

Formed 1980, London, England
Annabella Lwin (b. Myant Myant Aye, ca. 1966, Rangoon, Burma), voc.; Matthew Ashman (b. London), gtr.; Dave Barbarossa (b. Eng.), drums; Leigh Gorman (b. Eng.), bass.
1981—*See Jungle! See Jungle! Go Join Your Gang Yeah! City All Over! Go Ape Crazy!* (RCA)   1982—*The Last of the Mohicans; I Want Candy; 12 Original Recordings* (Capitol)   1983—*When the Going Gets Tough, the Tough Get Going* (RCA).
Annabella Lwin solo: 1986—*Fever* (RCA).

After manager/entrepreneur Malcolm McLaren assembled the Sex Pistols, he followed up with Bow Wow Wow. He discovered Annabella Lwin (from a reportedly aristocratic Burmese family, who arrived in England a refugee at the age of five) working in a dry cleaner's when she was 14. Although she didn't sing, she had the look, and he installed her in front of Matthew Ashman, Dave Barbarossa, and Leigh Gorman, whom he had separated from Adam and the Ants. The key to the group's sound was Barbarossa's percussion, a pounding tom-tom beat derived from Burundi ritual music. With Annabella's girlish squeal, Bow Wow Wow's songs (mostly written by

Bow Wow Wow: (top) Matthew Ashman, Leroy Gorman, (bottom) Annabella Lwin, Dave Barbarossa

McLaren and the instrumentalists) were a heady concoction of African rhythms, Balinese chants, surf instrumentals, and New Romantic pop melodies.

EMI released "C30, C60, C90 Go!" in fall 1980, and the song entered the U.K. Top Thirty despite EMI's refusal to promote it because it allegedly advocated home taping. The group's next release was one of the first commercial recordings to be released on tape but not on vinyl. *Your Cassette Pet* was a 20-minute, eight-song cassette packaged to resemble a pack of Marlboro cigarettes and became the first tape to place on the British singles chart. Songs like "Sexy Eiffel Tower" helped to win headlines suggesting that McLaren was promoting child pornography. EMI dropped Bow Wow Wow after issuing its second single, "W.O.R.K.," in 1981.

"W.O.R.K." became a best-selling import single in the U.S., and Bow Wow Wow signed with RCA. Just before a planned U.S. tour, Annabella's mother instigated a Scotland Yard investigation of alleged exploitation of a minor for immoral purposes. A magistrate granted permission to leave England only when McLaren and RCA promised not to publish a photograph of Annabella as the nude woman of Manet's painting *Déjeuner sur l'Herbe* or to promote her as "a sex kitten."

A 1982 EP, containing the minor hit "I Want Candy," produced by Joan Jett's producer/manager, Kenny Laguna, used the *Déjeuner sur l'Herbe* photo on its jacket after all. Later albums moved away from the Burundi beat and toward heavy metal. Bow Wow Wow eventually booted Lwin from the group; she recorded one solo LP that went nowhere in the mid-Eighties. After a hiatus from show business, she returned in summer 1994 with a single, "Car Sex." Guitarist Matthew Ashman surfaced in 1988 with the Chiefs of Relief, a band that included former Sex Pistols drummer Paul Cook.

The Box Tops

Formed 1967, Memphis, Tennessee
Alex Chilton (b. Dec. 28, 1950, Memphis), voc.; Bill Cunningham (b. Jan. 23, 1950, Memphis), kybds., bass; Gary Talley (b. Aug. 17, 1947), gtr., bass; John Evans, organ; Danny Smythe, drums.
1967—*The Box Tops "The Letter"/"Neon Rainbow"* (Bell)   1968—*Cry Like a Baby* (– Evans; – Smythe; + Tom Boggs [b. July 16, 1947, Wynn, Ark.], drums; + Rick Allen [b. Jan. 28, 1946, Little Rock, Ark.], organ, bass); *Super Hits; Non-Stop*   1969—*Dimensions*   1970—(– Cunningham; + Swain Scharfer, piano; + Harold Cloud, bass) (group disbands)   1982—*Greatest Hits* (Rhino).

The Box Tops came out of Memphis in the late Sixties with a string of blue-eyed-soul hits. Young Alex Chilton's raw lead vocals sparked million-selling singles "The Letter" (#1, 1967) and "Cry Like a Baby" (#2, 1968). Their success was partially due to producer/writer Dan Penn, who later released a solo album that was a Box Tops sounda-like. As was later evidenced by Chilton's recordings with Big Star [see entry], the gravelly delivery Penn had him employ on Box Tops records was not Chilton's natural voice. (Chilton later attributed the sound to lack of sleep and too much booze.)

The band toured infrequently, and its lineup was unstable: John Evans and Danny Smythe quit the group at the height of its success to return to college. After several albums for Bell and minor hits like "Sweet Cream Ladies" (#28, 1969), the Box Tops disbanded in 1970, and Chilton soon joined Big Star. Guitarist Talley has remained in music as a country and R&B sessionman in Memphis. Into the Nineties, Chilton occasionally performs with the Box Tops for oldies shows.

Tommy Boyce and Bobby Hart

Formed 1964, Los Angeles, California
Tommy Boyce (b. Sidney Thomas Boyce, Sep. 29, 1939, Charlottesville, Va.; d. Nov. 23, 1994, Nashville, Tenn.); Bobby Hart (b. Feb. 18, 1939, Phoenix, Ariz.).
1967—Test Patterns (A&M)   1968—I Wonder What She's Doing Tonite; Which One's Boyce and Which One's Hart?; It's All Happening on the Inside.

One of the top songwriting teams of the mid-Sixties, Boyce and Hart teamed up to write "Last Train to Clarksville," "Valleri," and "(I'm Not Your) Steppin' Stone" for groups like the Monkees and Paul Revere and the Raiders. They began working together in the early Sixties and their "Come a Little Bit Closer," a hit in 1964 for Jay and the Americans, led to a songwriting contract with Screen Gems. They wrote most of the material for the made-for-TV Monkees. In May 1967 they began recording as a duo and a few months later enjoyed pop success with "I Wonder What She's Doing Tonite" (#8, 1967) and "Alice Long (You're Still My Favorite Girlfriend)" (#27, 1968). They toured nightclubs through the late Sixties. In 1975 they teamed up with ex-Monkees Davy Jones and Mickey Dolenz for an album and tour.

In the late Seventies Boyce moved to London for a while and produced hits for British Fifties revivalist bands Showaddywaddy and Darts. He also worked with Meat Loaf and Iggy Pop. On November 23, 1994, Boyce shot himself to death at his Nashville, Tennessee, home.

Hart, with Austin Roberts, wrote the country hit "Over You" by Lane Brody (it was heard in the film *Tender Mercies,* and was nominated for an Academy Award in 1983); in 1985 he cowrote New Edition's R&B hit "My Secret," and in 1988 he cowrote Robbie Nevil's hit "Dominoes." The duo has to its credit more than 300 compositions and sales of more than 42 million records.

Eddie Boyd

Born November 25, 1914, Coahoma County, Mississippi; died July 13, 1994, Helsinki, Finland
1967—Eddie Boyd and His Blues Band (Decca)
1968—7936 South Rhodes (Epic); Eddie Boyd Live (Storyville)   1974—Legacy of the Blues, vol. 10 (GNP).

Guitarist, keyboardist, and singer Eddie Boyd was responsible for the 1952 #1 R&B hit "Five Long Years." Half-brother of Memphis Slim and first cousin of Muddy Waters, Boyd was born on a plantation in Coahoma County, Mississippi, where he worked until he ran away from home in 1928. He taught himself to play guitar and keyboards and began touring the Mississippi bar and juke joint circuit during the early Thirties. In 1936 he moved to Memphis, where he worked in Beale Street bars.

In 1937 he formed his first group, the Dixie Rhythm Boys, with whom he toured Tennessee and Arkansas before moving to Chicago in 1941. Quickly embraced by the Southside blues circles, he worked through the mid-Forties with Memphis Slim, Sonny Boy Williamson, and his cousin Waters. He made his first recordings (with Williamson) for the Victor/Bluebird label around 1943 and has recorded for several labels over the years, including Chess Records from 1952 to 1957. He gave Chess two R&B Top Ten hits—"24 Hours" and "Third Degree"—in 1953.

By the start of the Sixties Boyd was recording for small independent labels, but a blues and R&B resurgence led him to Decca in 1965. From mid-decade on he frequently toured Europe and England with rock artists like John Mayall and recorded for various European labels. He lived in London, Paris, Finland, and other foreign locations. By 1971 he had made Helsinki his permanent home. He remained active both in recording and club work (which included occasional trips back to the U.S.) until shortly before his death.

Boy George: See Culture Club

Boyz II Men

Formed 1988, Philadelphia, Pennsylvania
Wanya "Squirt" Morris (b. July 29, 1974), voc.;
Michael "Bass" McCary (b. Dec. 16, 1972), voc.;
Shawn "Slim" Stockman (b. Sep. 26, 1973), voc.;
Nathan "Alex Vanderpool" Morris (b. June 18, 1972), voc.
1991—Cooleyhighharmony (Motown)   1994—II.

The teenaged hip-hop/harmony quartet Boyz II Men became an overnight sensation in 1991 upon release of its three-million-selling debut album. With nostalgic nods to Fifties, Sixties, and Seventies vocal groups—from the

Blue Notes to the O'Jays—the Boyz' first hit, "Motown-philly," climbed to #3 on the pop charts (#4 R&B). The group's musical and visual style was described by ROLLING STONE as "distinctive, nonthreatening, and video friendly."

The group met and began singing their sugary sweet harmonies together at the High School for the Creative and Performing Arts in Philadelphia. In 1989 they gained an important fan in Michael Bivins (of New Edition and Bell Biv DeVoe), who helped them land their record deal. The quartet's massive success in turn helped breathe new life into Motown Records, which had fared poorly through the Eighties.

Cooleyhighharmony is divided into a dance side and a ballads side. Followup singles from the album included "It's So Hard to Say Goodbye to Yesterday" (#2 pop, #1 R&B, 1991) and "Uhh Ahh" (#16 pop, #1 R&B, 1991). In 1992 the group toured with Hammer. The group returned in 1994 with the seven-million-selling smash *II* (#1 pop, 1994) and became the third act in the rock era to succeed itself on the singles chart at #1 (after Elvis Presley and the Beatles), with the hits "I'll Make Love to You" and "On Bended Knee."

Billy Bragg

Born Steven William Bragg, December 20, 1957, Barking, Essex, England
1986—*Talking with the Taxman About Poetry* (Elektra)   1987—*Back to Basics*   1988—*Help Save the Youth of America*; *Workers Playtime*   1990—*The Internationale* EP   1991—*Don't Try This at Home*.

Billy Bragg is a true working-class hero: an irrepressible socialist troubadour whose anthems of love and politics have transcended the usual ghettoizations of folk and punk troublemakers. The singer, songwriter, and guitarist got his inimitable cockney accent growing up in an industrial suburb of London. He left school at 16 and became a punk rocker, forming his first band, Riff Raff, with childhood friend Wiggy in 1977. They released a few singles and one EP before disbanding in 1981. Discouraged, Bragg joined the army, but bought his way out after three months.

He began playing solo gigs around England before signing with a British indie. Bragg's debut, *Life's a Riot with Spy vs. Spy* (his first three British records were compiled for U.S. release on *Back to Basics*), went to #30 on the U.K. charts in 1984. It featured "A New England," whose chorus of "I don't want to change the world . . . I'm just looking for another girl" introduced Bragg's continuing effort to balance a political call-to-arms with the search for loving arms. (In 1985 Kirsty MacColl made "A New England" a #7 U.K. hit.) Bragg has called Thatcherism in general and the British miners'

strike in particular the catalyst for his political conversion; he played several benefits for miners in 1984–85.

With *Brewing Up with Billy Bragg,* the "Big-Nosed Bard of Barking" began to reach college-radio audiences in the U.S. and garner international press. *Talking with the Taxman About Poetry,* featuring such classic tunes as "Levi Stubbs' Tears," solidified his standing as a moving and witty songwriter. In 1986 Bragg helped found Red Wedge, a collective of musicians that toured the U.K. to promote the British Labour party. He has also toured extensively in the U.S., as well as the Soviet bloc and Latin America, supporting the causes of such political groups as ACT UP, Committee in Solidarity with the People of El Salvador, and Democratic Socialists of America. Live, Bragg is both an endearing entertainer and an effective speech maker.

In 1988 Bragg had a #1 U.K. hit with "She's Leaving Home," a duet he recorded with Cara Tivey for a benefit album (although it was probably airplay of "With a Little Help From My Friends" by Wet Wet Wet, the other side of the single, that propelled sales). In 1989 he reactivated the label Utility to nurture new acts and released *The Internationale,* a seven-track disc whose liberation songs showed that the singer didn't consider leftist politics buried beneath the Berlin Wall's rubble. Bragg also began pursuing more commercial musical directions, releasing a dance track ("Won't Talk About It") with Beats International on the 1990 album *Let Them Eat Bingo,* and recording *Don't Try This at Home* with a band, full production, and such guests as Kirsty MacColl, R.E.M.'s Peter Buck, and ex-Smiths guitarist Johnny Marr. The track "Sexuality," a dance hit in England, was a celebration of active and diverse lovemaking in the age of AIDS.

Brand Nubian/Grand Puba

Formed 1990, New Rochelle, New York
Lord Jamar (b. Lorenzo DeChalus, Sep. 17, 1968, Bronx, N.Y.), voc.; Sadat X (b. Derek Murphy, Dec. 29, 1968, New York City, N.Y.), voc.; Grand Puba Maxwell (b. Maxwell Dixon, Mar. 4, 1966, Bronx, N.Y.), voc.; DJ Alamo, DJ.
1990—*One for All* (Elektra) (– Maxwell; – Alamo; + Sincere Allah [b. Terence Perry, June 5, 1970, New Rochelle], voc.)   1992—*In God We Trust* (– Perry)   1994—*Everything Is Everything*.
Grand Puba solo: 1992—*Reel to Reel* (Elektra).

Brand Nubian arrived on the hip-hop scene of the early Nineties as one of the more outspoken advocates of the Five Percent Nation, an Islamic offshoot that considers whites "devils" and maintains that only 5 percent of the black population will serve as enlightened spiritual leaders. The group's didactic lyrics mostly center on Islamic themes.

Founded by Grand Puba Maxwell, who had rapped

with the nonreligious group Masters of Ceremony in the late Eighties, Brand Nubian mixes supple, laid-back rhythms with the singsong delivery of Puba and Lord Jamar. When the former departed in the fall of 1991 for a solo career—taking DJ Alamo with him—Jamar took over as lead rapper.

Aside from receiving positive critical notice, *One for All* reached #34 on the R&B charts (#130 pop, 1991), and produced the minor R&B hit singles "Wake Up" (#92, 1991) and "Slow Down" (#63, 1991), the latter of which borrowed a sample from Edie Brickell and New Bohemians' "What I Am." *In God We Trust* (#12 pop, #4 R&B, 1993) fared much better, including the hit "Punks Jump Up to Get Beat Down" (#42 R&B, 1992), which reached #2 on *Billboard*'s rap singles chart.

Grand Puba's solo debut *Reel to Reel* (#28 pop, #14 R&B, 1992), though stylistically similar to Brand Nubian's music, featured less of the Five Percenter doctrine. Puba's single "360° (What Goes Around)" (#68 pop, #30 R&B, 1992) took its main sample from Gladys Knight and the Pips' "Don't Burn Down the Bridge."

Laura Branigan

Born July 3, 1957, Brewster, New York
1982—*Branigan* (Atlantic)   1983—*Branigan 2*
1984—*Self Control*   1985—*Hold Me*   1987—*Touch*
1990—*Laura Branigan*   1994—*Over My Heart*.

In 1982 Laura Branigan's "Gloria" peaked at #2 on the pop chart and began a run of hits that, for a few years at least, made Branigan's plaintive alto belt a radio staple. After singing in her choir and performing in high school musical productions, Branigan attended the American Academy of Dramatic Arts in Manhattan, then found work touring Europe as a backup singer in Leonard Cohen's band. Eventually, she came to the attention of promoter Sid Bernstein, who helped land Branigan a record deal.

Branigan, her debut album, featured "Gloria"; the following year, *Branigan 2* solidified her success with two more hit singles: "Solitaire" (#7, 1983) and the Michael Bolton–penned "How Am I Supposed to Live Without You" (#12, 1983). In 1984 the title track to a third album, *Self Control,* gave Branigan her last Top Ten song to date (#4). On her 1994 album, *Over My Heart,* Branigan sings some of the songs' lyrics in Spanish and in a South African dialect.

Brass Construction

Formed 1968, Brooklyn, New York
Randy Muller, voc., kybds., flute, perc.; Wade Williamston, bass; Joseph Arthur Wong, gtr.; Morris Price, trumpet, voc., perc.; Wayne Parris, trumpet, voc.; Larry Payton, drums; Sandy Billups, voc., con-
gas; Jesse Ward Jr., sax, voc.; Michael Grudge, sax, voc.
**1975—*Brass Construction* (United Artists)   1976—*II*
1977—*III*   1978—*IV*   1979—*5*   1980—*6*   1982—*Attitudes* (EMI/Liberty)   1983—*Conversations* (Capitol)   1993—*Movin' & Changin': The Best of Brass Construction* (EMI).**

Brass Construction was one of the horn-dominated big bands that ushered in the disco era of the mid-Seventies. Formed by Randy Muller, Brass Construction's cosmopolitan sound—a mix of Sly and the Family Stone funk, big-band jazz, Latin salsa, and Caribbean upbeats—was underscored by its makeup: Muller was from Guyana, Joseph Wong from Trinidad, and Wayne Parris and Michael Grudge from Jamaica. By 1975, when United Artists signed them, their nine-man lineup was firm and remained consistent through their recording career.

With Muller as writer and arranger, the first album was mainly instrumental, with vocals used as choral embellishments. Their first single, "Movin'," hit #1 on the R&B charts in 1976 (pop #14). "Changin'" followed it at #24 R&B, and the album went platinum. The second album, which included "Ha Cha Cha (Function)" (#8 R&B, 1977) and brought the vocals into the foreground, sold gold. *III*'s single, "L-O-V-E-U," made only #18, but the album went gold. Their subsequent releases included no more hit singles, although their albums continued to regularly place in the Top Forty.

After 1979 Muller divided his attentions between Brass Construction and another New York dance band, Skyy, for whom he is producer and songwriter. Of their seven albums, *Skyy Line* (#18 pop, 1981) was the most successful, featuring "Call Me" (#26 pop, #1 R&B, 1981).

Brave Combo

Formed 1979, Denton, Texas
Lyle Atkinson, bass and tuba; Dave Cameron, drums; Carl Finch (b. Nov 29, 1951, Texarkana, Ark.), gtr., kybds., accordion; Tim Walsh, saxophone, clarinet, flute.
**1981—*Music for Squares* (Four Dots)   1982—*Originals* cassette; *Urban Grown-ups*   1983—
(– Cameron; – Walsh; + Mitch Marine, drums;
+ Jeffrey Barnes [b. July 27, 1951, Fremont, Ohio], horns) *World Dance Music*   1985—(– Atkinson,
+ Bubba Hernandez [b. Cenobio Xaxier Hernandez, Nov 28, 1958, San Antonio, Tex.], bass)   1986—
Polkatharsis (Rounder)   1987—*Musical Varieties*
1989—*Humansville*   1990—*A Night on Earth*
1991—*Eejhanaika*   1992—(– Marine; + Phil Hernandez [b. Feb 5, 1971, Buffalo, N.Y.], drums; + Joe Cripps [b. Jan. 5, 1965, Little Rock, Ark.], perc.) *It's Christmastime, Man*   1993—(+ Danny O'Brien**

[b. July 12, 1966, Lakenheath, Eng.], trumpet) *No, No, No, Cha Cha Cha.*

The brainchild of University of North Texas art student and accordionist Carl Finch, Brave Combo was formed with a singular purpose—to destroy people's misconceptions about what's cool to like in music. A potent mixture of polka and other genres—conjunto, salsa, merengue, cha cha, ska, zydeco, and rumba, among others—played with superior musicianship, Brave Combo's witty, adventurous albums have made them critical and cult heroes, influencing bands including 3 Mustaphas 3 and Camper Van Beethoven.

Originally releasing albums on its own Four Dots label, the band forged an alliance with Rounder Records in 1986 to widen its audience. After an initial tour of mental institutions, Brave Combo's music has since been heard on the National Public Radio shows *Prairie Home Companion* and *Fresh Air,* in the movie *True Stories* (directed by David Byrne), at the Macy's Thanksgiving Day Parade, and at festivals around the world. Finch has also produced the recordings of other artists, ranging from conjunto legend Santiago Jimenez to singer/songwriter Sara Hickman.

Bread
Formed 1969, Los Angeles, California
David Gates (b. Dec. 11, 1940, Tulsa, Okla.), voc., gtr., kybds.; James Griffin (b. Memphis, Tenn.), voc., gtr.; Robb Royer, kybds.
1969—*Bread* (Elektra) (+ Mike Botts [b. Sacramento, Calif.], drums)   1970—*On the Waters*   1971—*Manna* (– Royer; + Larry Knechtel [b. Bell, Calif.] kybds.)   1972—*Baby I'm-a Want You; Guitar Man*   1973—*The Best of Bread*   1974—*The Best of Bread, vol. 2*   1977—*Lost Without Your Love.*
David Gates solo: 1973—*First* (Elektra)   1975—*Never Let Her Go*   1979—*Goodbye Girl*   1994—*Love Is Always Seventeen* (Discovery).

Bread's mellow pop rock was an early-Seventies model for the "adult contemporary" sound. Led by guitarist and songwriter David Gates, the nucleus of Bread was made up of studio players who had been working as Pleasure Faire before they made their first album for Elektra in 1969. Their second album gained them the first of several gold singles, "Make It with You," a #1 hit in the summer of 1970. Buoyed by its success, they permanently added drummer Mike Botts (studio musician Jim Gordon had handled percussion on their first album) to play live concerts. Hits like "It Don't Matter to Me" (#10, 1970), "If" (#4, 1971), "Baby, I'm-A Want You" (#3, 1971), "Everything I Own" (#5, 1972), and "Guitar Man" (#11, 1972) continued until the group broke up in 1973. After three years together Bread had earned six gold albums. Thereafter,

Gates had hit singles with "Never Let Her Go" (#29, 1975) and "Goodbye Girl" (#15, 1978). Bread re-formed in late 1976 to release its seventh gold album and a single, "Lost Without Your Love" (#9, 1977), and disbanded once again. In 1994 Gates released his first album in over 13 years.

Gates and Griffin's legal battle over the rights to the Bread name dragged on from the late Seventies to 1984, during which time a judge prohibited the group from recording, performing, or collecting royalties until the case was resolved. Griffin remains active in the music business. Knechtel retired from music but returned to recording (including a New Age album, *Mountain Moods*) and touring (with Elvis Costello). Botts has written commercial jingles and children's music.

The Breeders: See Pixies

Brewer and Shipley
Formed 1968, Los Angeles, California
Mike Brewer (b. 1944, Oklahoma City, Okla.), gtr., voc.; Tom Shipley (b. 1942, Mineral Ridge, Ohio), gtr., voc.
1968—*Brewer and Shipley Down in L.A.* (A&M)
1969—*Weeds* (Kama Sutra)   1970—*Tarkio*   1971—*Shake Off the Demon*   1972—*Rural Space*   1974—*Brewer and Shipley (ST-11261)* (Capitol)
1975—*Welcome to Riddle Bridge*   1976—*Best of Brewer and Shipley* (Kama Sutra)   1978—*Not Far from Free* (Mercury).

Folk rockers Mike Brewer and Tom Shipley grew up in the Midwest and met in L.A. They signed songwriting contracts with A&M in 1965. Without the duo's approval, A&M released some of their demos as an album entitled *Down in L.A.* To counter that album, the pair, who had moved to a communal 20-acre farm outside Kansas City, Missouri, released the first of several increasingly successful country-style albums for Kama Sutra. *Tarkio* contained the 1971 hit "One Toke over the Line," which was the subject of some controversy when the FCC—then intent on banishing drug references from the airwaves—discovered the meaning of toke. Although informally banned, the song was a #10 hit that year. The duo switched to Capitol in 1974 but has had only marginal success since. Brewer released a solo LP in 1983; Shipley has worked as a recording engineer for Joni Mitchell, among others.

Edie Brickell and New Bohemians
Formed 1985, Dallas, Texas
Edie Brickell (b. Mar. 10, 1966, Oak Cliff, Tex.), voc., gtr.; Kenny Withrow (b. Apr. 13, 1965), gtr.; Brad Houser (b. Sep. 7, 1960), bass; Wes Burt-Martin (b. May 28, 1964), gtr.; Matt Chamberlain (b. Apr. 17,

1967), drums; John Bush, perc.
1988—*Shooting Rubberbands at the Stars* (Geffen)
1990—*Ghost of a Dog.*
Edie Brickell solo: 1994—*Picture Perfect Morning*
(Geffen).

Edie Brickell and New Bohemians' relaxed, improvisational blend of rock, jazz, folk, and reggae suited its bohemian image. Frontwoman Brickell made a reluctant star, shy and a bit awkward, especially onstage; but her endearingly offbeat soprano, with its subtle jazz inflections, charmed critics and fans alike. So did the trippy ingenuity of her lyrics, which drew on subjects ranging from the tragic Andy Warhol protégée Edie Sedgwick to the need for simplicity in expression addressed by the group's first single "What I Am."

Brickell joined the New Bohemians in 1985, after catching the band's gig in a Dallas bar. An art student at the city's Southern Methodist University, Brickell had dabbled in songwriting but was intimidated by the prospect of singing live. That night, though, a shot of Jack Daniel's gave her the courage to join the band onstage for an improvised jam. A couple of weeks later, Brickell and local guitarist Kenny Withrow were enlisted as full-time band members.

The group quickly developed a strong following and was signed to Geffen Records in late 1986. Recording sessions were plagued by delays and tensions between the band and producer Pat Moran. *Shooting Rubberbands at the Stars* was finally released in fall of 1988. Supported by the success of "What I Am" (#7, 1988) the album reached #4. A second effort, *Ghost of a Dog,* peaked at #32 and yielded no major hit singles, but a romantic relationship with Paul Simon kept Brickell's name in the press. Brickell married Simon in June 1992 and gave birth to their son in December. In 1991 the band had dissolved. Brickell went solo, writing and performing acoustic guitar on all the songs for *Picture Perfect Morning*, which was produced by her husband and Roy Halee, and featured such guests as Dr. John, Barry White, and Art and Cyril Neville).

Brinsley Schwarz
Formed 1970, England
Brinsley Schwarz, gtr., voc., sax; Nick Lowe (b. Mar. 25, 1949, Woodbridge, Eng.), bass, voc., gtr.; Billy Rankin, drums; Bob Andrews (b. June 20, 1949), kybds., bass, voc.
1970—*Brinsley Schwarz* (Capitol); *Despite It All* (Liberty, U.K.) (+ Ian Gomm [b. Mar. 17, 1947, London, Eng.], gtr.)   1972—*Silver Pistol* (United Artists, U.K.); *Nervous on the Road*   1973—*Please Don't Ever Change*   1974—*New Favourites*; *Original Golden Greats*   1978—*15 Thoughts of Brinsley Schwarz*   1979—*Brinsley Schwarz* (Capitol).

Brinsley Schwarz was not successful outside the early-Seventies English pub circuit, but the later successes of its members have given the group semilegendary status.

Overzealous promotion almost nipped the band in the bud when a planeload of U.K. journalists was flown to the States to witness its Fillmore East debut and returned with tales of overpromotion that hounded the band until its death. Brinsley Schwarz's good-time aura and country-flavored rock—a back-to-basics attitude in the wake of psychedelia—attracted ardent followers in England, but major success eluded it. The group's last album, *New Favourites,* was produced in 1974 by Dave Edmunds. After its release, Nick Lowe teamed up with Edmunds to form Rockpile [see entry], but not before he and Ian Gomm cowrote "Cruel to Be Kind," which eventually became Lowe's biggest U.S. hit (#12, 1979) [see entry]. Gomm himself scored an American hit in 1979 with "Hold On" (#18). Bob Andrews and Brinsley Schwarz earned subsequent kudos in the Rumour [see entry], primarily backing Graham Parker and later Garland Jeffreys. In 1979 Capitol released a Brinsley Schwarz double-album compilation.

British Invasion
Between 1964 and 1966—after the dominance of girl groups and doo-wop R&B, and just before the advent of psychedelia—British rock bands dominated the pop charts in both their homeland and the U.S. British Invasion bands included the Beatles, Rolling Stones, Yardbirds, Kinks, Animals, and Manfred Mann, as well as "Merseybeat" (so named because the Mersey River runs through Liverpool) bands like Gerry and the Pacemakers (one of whose hits was "Ferry Cross the Mersey"), Billy J. Kramer and the Dakotas, Wayne Fontana and the Mindbenders, and Herman's Hermits, who further exploited the Liverpool-based softer pop rock the Beatles had first purveyed. The hallmarks of British Invasion and Merseybeat rock—jangly guitars, pleasant melodies, immaculate vocal harmonies, and a general air of teenage romantic innocence—were later a direct influence on mid- and late-Seventies power-pop groups like the Raspberries, Big Star, XTC, and the Knack.

David Bromberg
Born September 19, 1945, Philadelphia, Pennsylvania
1972—*David Bromberg* (Columbia); *Demon in Disguise*   1974—*Wanted Dead or Alive*   1975—*Midnight on the Water*   1976—*How Late'll Ya Play 'Til?* (Fantasy)   1977—*Best: Out of the Blues* (Columbia); *Reckless Abandon* (Fantasy)   1978—*Bandit in a Bathing Suit*; *My Own House*   1980—*You Should See the Rest of the Band*   1989—*Sideman Serenade* (Rounder).

As a virtuoso on guitar, mandolin, fiddle, and other stringed instruments, David Bromberg was a folk-rock mainstay through the Seventies. He grew up in Tarrytown, New York, and studied at Columbia University before becoming part of the mid-Sixties Greenwich Village folk scene. He began playing sessions regularly in the late Sixties and has since appeared on over 90 albums, including ones by Bob Dylan, Ringo Starr, Tom Paxton, Chubby Checker, Sha Na Na, Carly Simon, and Phoebe Snow. Bromberg's eclecticism embraces blues, jazz, rock, bluegrass, country, and old-timey traditional music. He began releasing solo albums in 1972 and by 1976 had formed the David Bromberg Band and toured extensively worldwide. In 1978 and 1979 he toured with fellow Fantasy Records artist Ralph McTell. But in mid-1980, following the accidental death of a bandmember, and wishing to spend more time with his family, Bromberg announced his retirement from performing and began studying the craft of violin making in Chicago. Nonetheless, he continued to perform occasionally, including annual concerts at New York's Bottom Line until 1992. He has since become a leading collector, and international dealer, of violins.

The Brooklyn Bridge

Formed 1968, Long Island, New York
Johnny Maestro (b. John Mastrangelo, May 7, 1939, Brooklyn, N.Y.), voc.; Fred Ferrara (b. 1945), voc.; Mike Gregorio (b. 1947), voc.; Les Cauchi (b. 1945), voc.; Tom Sullivan (b. 1946), musical director; Carolyn Woods (b. 1947), organ; Jim Rosica (b. 1947), bass; Jim Macioce (b. 1947), gtr.; Artie Cantanzarita (b. 1949), drums; Shelly Davis (b. 1950), trumpet, kybds.; Joe Ruvio (b. 1947), sax.
1969—Brooklyn Bridge (Buddah); The Second Brooklyn Bridge.

The Del-Satins, a longstanding vocal quartet with which Johnny Maestro (formerly of the Crests) sang, and the Rhythm Method, a seven-piece band led by Tom Sullivan, joined forces to become the Brooklyn Bridge when they found themselves rivals at a Long Island talent contest in 1968. They had their first hit with a Jim Webb song originally recorded by the Fifth Dimension, "Worst That Could Happen" (#3, 1969). "Blessed Is the Rain," "Your Husband—My Wife," and "Welcome Me Love" (all 1969) grazed the Top Forty. The group charted its last single in 1970 but continued to record. By 1975, when they signed with Private Stock, the group had been trimmed to a quintet, with Maestro still leading. They continued playing throughout the New York–New Jersey metropolitan area and appearing at nostalgia shows, and in 1988 released a Christmas record, "Christmas Is."

In the early Nineties, Maestro and Ferrara (an ex–Del Satin) continued to live on Long Island and play 120 to 130 shows a year with a Brooklyn Bridge lineup.

Garth Brooks

Born Troyal Garth Brooks, February 7, 1962, Yukon, Oklahoma
1989—Garth Brooks (Capitol)   1990—No Fences
1991—Ropin' the Wind   1992—Beyond the Season (Liberty); The Chase   1993—In Pieces   1994—The Hits.

The most stunning success story of the early Nineties contemporary country music boom was that of Garth Brooks. Blending rock and country influences, he is a singer/songwriter whose style owes as much to the influence of James Taylor as it does to George Jones. In performance, Brooks' high-energy stage show reflects his admiration for theatrical rock bands such as Queen and Kiss. Having sold more than 40 million albums since 1989, Brooks has easily outdistanced his competition. By 1992 a household name, Brooks also presented a new breed of wholesome, all-American country music hero—one who defended homosexuals in a song ("We Shall Be Free," from 1992's The Chase) and talked to Barbara Walters on national television about his past marital infidelity.

Brooks' mother had herself been a singer before marrying his father, a working-class draftsman. Both parents had children by former spouses; Brooks was the younger of two they had together. Brooks learned to play guitar and sing with his mother and joined a band during high school. His primary interest was sports, though, and he attended the state university on a track scholarship. Only after graduating did Brooks devote himself to music. He moved to Nashville in 1985, but found little luck there. After moving back to Oklahoma, marrying, and saving some money, Brooks decided to give Nashville another try. His persistence paid off when a Capitol Records talent scout spotted the singer in a club and signed him.

Released in 1989, Brooks' self-titled debut album peaked at #2 on the country albums chart and spawned four Top Ten country singles: "Much Too Young (to Feel This Damn Old)" (#8 C&W, 1989), "If Tomorrow Never Comes" (#1 C&W, 1989), "Not Counting You" (#2 C&W, 1990), and "The Dance" (#1 C&W, 1990). No Fences outdid its predecessor, reaching #1 on the country chart and #3 on pop, and generating four #1 country hits: "Friends in Low Places" (1990), "Unanswered Prayers" (1990), "Two of a Kind, Workin' on a Full House" (1991), and "The Thunder Rolls" (1991). The video for the last single got flak from Country Music Television and the Nashville Network for its graphic depiction of domestic violence, a subject Brooks addressed in the song. But VH-1 supported Brooks, thus heightening his crossover appeal to pop audiences.

Brooks' winning streak continued with 1991's Ropin' the Wind, the first album in history to enter both Billboard's pop and country albums charts at #1. This time, there were three chart-topping country singles in

"Shameless" (1991) and 1992's "What's She Doing Now" and "The River," as well as "Rodeo" (#3 C&W, 1991) and "Papa Loved Mama" (#3 C&W, 1992). Later in 1992 a Christmas album, *Beyond the Season,* shot to #2 on the pop and country albums charts. Before the year was out, the singer topped both those charts again, with *The Chase,* which yielded "We Shall Be Free" (#12 C&W, 1992), "Somewhere Other Than the Night" (#1 C&W, 1992), "Learning to Live Again" (#4 C&W, 1993), and "That Summer" (#1 C&W, 1993).

Brooks' *In Pieces* surprised no one by debuting at #1 on the pop and country charts, and producing two #1 country singles: "Ain't Going Down (Til the Sun Comes Up)" (#1 C&W, 1993) and "American Honky-Tonk Bar Association" (#1 C&W, 1993). *The Hits* peaked at #1 on both pop and country charts in 1994. Hit singles of 1994 included "Standing Outside the Fire" (#3 C&W) and "One Night a Day" (#7 C&W).

The Brothers Johnson
George Johnson (b. May 17, 1953, Los Angeles, Calif.), gtr., voc.; Louis Johnson (b. Apr. 13, 1955, Los Angeles), bass, voc.
1976—*Look Out for #1* (A&M)   1977—*Right on Time* 1978—*Blam!*   1980—*Light Up the Night*   1981— *Winners*   1982—*Blast! (The Latest and the Greatest)*   1984—*Out of Control*   1988—*Kick It to the Curb*
Louis Johnson solo: 1981—*Passage* (A&M).

George and Louis Johnson have been playing music together since they were seven and eight years old. They put together their first group, the Johnson Three + 1, with older brother Tommy on drums and cousin Alex Weir (later a member of the Brothers Johnson Band) on rhythm guitar. They worked their way up from school dances to opening L.A. shows for such acts as the Dells, David Ruffin, and Bill Medley. Bobby Womack produced their first single, "Testify."

George had just graduated from high school when Billy Preston invited him to join his band, the God Squad, as lead guitarist. When Preston's bass player abruptly left in the middle of a tour, George persuaded Preston to hire Louis. In their two years with Preston, the Johnsons contributed several songs to his albums, including his 1974 single "Struttin'" (#22 pop, #11 R&B).

The brothers left Preston in 1975 and spent almost a year writing songs, rehearsing, and recording demo tapes. That same year Quincy Jones hired the Johnsons for a tour of Japan. He later recorded four Johnson compositions on his *Mellow Madness* (#16, 1975) and, having signed the duo to an A&M recording contract of their own, produced their first four albums.

Look Out for #1 sold over a million copies, with two hit singles, "I'll Be Good to You" (#3 pop, #1 R&B, 1976) and "Get the Funk Out Ma Face" (#30 pop, #4 R&B, 1976).

Right on Time went gold three days after its release and platinum three months later. "Strawberry Letter 23" (a Shuggie Otis song) was a hit single (#5 pop, #1 R&B, 1977) and "Q," the Brothers' tribute to Jones, was awarded the 1977 Grammy for Best Instrumental. With the eight-piece Brothers Johnson Band, George and Louis toured the U.S., Europe, and Japan in 1977.

A departure from the nonstop dance format of their first two albums, *Blam!* contained the Johnsons' first ballad and "Ride-O-Rocket," a song written for them by Ashford and Simpson. The U.S. tour in support of that album took them to 80 cities. After a year's vacation, they returned to the charts in 1980 with *Light Up the Night* (#5 pop, #1 R&B) and its hit single "Stomp!" (#7 pop, #1 R&B). Their first self-produced album, 1981's *Winners,* was their first LP to sell fewer than a million copies, but it did deliver a #11 R&B single, "The Real Thing."

After that, the Brothers Johnson's A&M contract was satisfied with the release of the greatest-hits package *Blast!, Out of Control,* and *Kick It to the Curb.* Their last R&B Top Twenty hits were "Welcome to the Club" (1982) and "You Keep Me Coming Back" (1984). In 1989 the Brothers Johnson appealed to A&M principals Jerry Moss and Herb Alpert to release them from their deal, which they did. Louis now resides in Osaka, Japan, and George in Pasadena, California, where he develops talent. In 1994 they reunited and toured for the first time in 11 years.

Arthur Brown
Born June 24, 1942, Whitby, England
1968—*The Crazy World of Arthur Brown* (Track) 1972—*Galactic Zoo Dossier* (Polydor)   1973—*Kingdom Come* (Track, U.K.); *The Journey* (Polydor) 1975—*Dance with Arthur Brown* (Gull).

The eccentric Arthur Brown had one U.S. hit, "Fire" (#2, 1968). A trailblazer of theatrical rock, he capped his performances by igniting what appeared to be his hair (actually a metal helmet), and so became the rage in London during the summer of 1967. Pete Townshend gave him a record deal with the Who's Track label, but Brown proved unable to repeat his initial success, and by 1969 his band, the Crazy World of Arthur Brown (which included drummer Carl Palmer, later of Emerson, Lake and Palmer and Asia, and keyboardist Vincent Crane of Atomic Rooster), had broken up.

Brown has made several comeback attempts since. From 1970 to 1974 he fronted Kingdom Come, an electronic rock band (and one of the first to employ a drum machine). After departing that group he toured the Middle East, and upon returning to England he studied meditation. He played a small role in the Who's *Tommy* movie in 1975. The Who connection continues to this day: In 1989 Pete Townshend convened the Who to cut "Fire" for his *The Iron Man* solo LP.

Brown moved to Austin, Texas, in 1980 and now tours occasionally with a group he calls the Even Crazier World of Arthur Brown. He's recorded a number of albums for small labels, including *Brown, Black, and Blues* (Blue Wave Records), with former Mothers of Invention drummer Jimmy Carl Black, then Brown's partner in a housepainting company.

Bobby Brown

Born Robert Baresford Brown, February 5, 1969, Boston, Massachusetts
**1986—*King of Stage* (MCA)   1988—*Don't Be Cruel*
1989—*Dance! . . . Ya Know It!*   1992—*Bobby*
1993—*Remixes in the Key of B.***

After leaving the popular kiddie-funk vocal group New Edition in 1986, Bobby Brown found even greater success as a solo artist. The singer's bad-boy charisma and sexually charged dance moves thrilled female fans, and the hook-ridden songs and buoyant New Jack Swing arrangements on his albums suited his breezily confident delivery to a tee.

Brown's first solo album, 1986's *King of Stage*, produced the #1 R&B hit "Girlfriend," but his pop crossover came with 1988's *Don't Be Cruel*. Brown enlisted the fledgling writer/producers who would soon emerge as giants in the hip-hop and R&B communities: Antonio "L.A." Reid and Kenny "Babyface" Edmonds helped craft most of the album's material, and Teddy Riley collaborated with Brown on the singer's first #1 pop single, "My Prerogative" (1988). The album also topped the pop chart, and Brown enjoyed five more Top Ten pop hits in 1988 and 1989: "Don't Be Cruel" (#8 pop, #1 R&B, 1988), "Roni" (#3 pop, 1989), "Every Little Step" (#3 pop, #1 R&B, 1989), "On Our Own" (#2 pop, #12 R&B, 1989), and "Rock Wit'cha" (#7 pop, #3 R&B, 1989). A remix album, *Dance! . . . Ya Know It!,* reached #9 (#7 R&B). In 1990 Brown had another #1 pop single, a duet with Glenn Medeiros called "She Ain't Worth It."

Meanwhile, unsubstantiated rumors of drug abuse were tainting Brown's good fortune. When he married wholesome pop superstar Whitney Houston in 1992, cynics assumed that both singers were trying to alleviate image problems. Houston appeared on Brown's 1992 album, *Bobby*, on the duet "Something in Common." *Bobby* became a #2 pop album and topped the R&B chart; it also spawned the hits "Humpin' Around" (#3 pop, #1 R&B, 1992) and "Good Enough" (#7 pop, #5 R&B, 1992). In 1993 Houston and Brown—who had fathered three children with a previous girlfriend—welcomed a daughter, Bobbi.

Charles Brown

Born 1922, Texas City, Texas
1971—*Blues n' Brown* (Jewel)   1986—*One More for the Road* (Blueside)   1989—*Driftin' Blues* (DCC)
1990—*All My Life* (Bullseye Blues)   1992—*Driftin' Blues: The Best of Charles Brown* (EMI); *Someone to Love* (Bullseye Blues)   1994—*Just a Lucky So and So*; *These Blues* (Verve).

A highly influential black singer of the prerock era, Charles Brown is a master of "ballad blues," the smooth, jazz-inflected vocal music whose better-known exponent was Nat "King" Cole. While Brown's hits ended in the early Fifties, he continues to tour and record.

Prompted by his uncle and grandmother to study both the raw blues of Big Maceo and Leroy Carr and the sophisticated style of Art Tatum, Brown learned piano as a child, but his first job was teaching chemistry. His musical career began with a move to Los Angeles in 1943, when he filled the pianist's spot in Johnny Moore's Three Blazers. He first recorded in 1945, when after winning a talent contest for playing Rachmaninoff, he was given studio time by Philo Records. His "Drifting Blues," released as a single by the Three Blazers, introduced his sound—so smoky and smoothly elegant that it became known as "cocktail blues," despite its bleak undercurrents. Its vocals also revealed Brown's influences, Robert Johnson and Louis Jordan among them.

In 1948 Brown left the Three Blazers and throughout the early Fifties penned wistful R&B chart-toppers that have become blues classics: "Trouble Blues" (#1, 1949), "Black Night" (#1, 1951), "Seven Long Days" (#2, 1951), "Hard Times" (#7, 1952). He first recorded his classic "Merry Christmas Baby" (covered in the Sixties by Otis Redding and in the Eighties by Bruce Springsteen) in 1947, and in 1961 he released "Please Come Home for Christmas," later recorded by the Eagles; these two holiday songs are perhaps his best-known numbers (the latter entered the Christmas charts for ten consecutive seasons). In 1962 Sam Cooke refashioned Brown's "I Want to Go Home" into "Bring It On Home to Me," one of Cooke's biggest hits.

While Brown continued to write and perform (in 1990 he toured with Bonnie Raitt), he remains best known as a songwriter, whose compositions have been recorded by B. B. King, Fats Domino, and Bruce Springsteen, and as a stylist upon whom the early Ray Charles, among many others, patterned his singing technique.

Clarence "Gatemouth" Brown

Born April 18, 1924, Vinton, Louisiana
1974—*Clarence "Gatemouth" Brown Sings Louis Jordan* (Black and Blue)   1975—*Gate's on the Heat* (Barclay); *Down South in Bayou Country*   1976—*Bogalusa Boogie Man*   1978—*Blackjack* (Music is Medicine)   1979—*San Antonio Ballbuster* (Charly)   1982—*Alright Again!* (Rounder)   1983—*One More Mile; The Original Peacock Recordings*   1986—*Real Life; Pressure Cooker* (Alligator)   1989—*Standing My Ground*   1991—*No Looking Back*

1993—*Just Got Lucky* (Evidence)   1995—*The Man* (Verve).

Although blues singer/guitarist Clarence "Gatemouth" Brown has had only one chart single during his career, his mix of blues and country marks him as a Texas original. Born in Louisiana, he grew up in Orange, Texas. His father was a musician who taught him to play guitar when he was five; by age ten he could play fiddle and mandolin as well, and in ensuing years he picked up drums, bass, and harmonica. Nicknamed by a teacher for his big voice, "Gatemouth" Brown began singing at an early age.

In the early Forties he was a drummer for the Brown Skin Models. After serving in the Army Corps of Engineers, he returned to show business after World War II, working in big bands in San Antonio. He made his solo debut in 1945 when he sat in for an ill T-Bone Walker. That show introduced him to club owner Don Robey, who signed him to a management contract that bound him for the next 20 years. Robey sent Brown to Los Angeles in 1947 to record for Aladdin Records. In 1949 Brown was the first to record for Robey's own company, Peacock Records; that same year he cut "Mary Is Fine," his only hit. Either under his own name or as D. Malone, Robey took songwriter's credit on many of Brown's compositions; Brown's bitter "You Got Money" was written about Robey. Between 1947 and 1960 Brown recorded over 50 sides for Peacock, including "Pale Dry Boogie" and "Okie Dokie Stomp."

He spent most of the Fifties leading two bands, a 23-piece black orchestra and a smaller group of white musicians. This arrangement allowed him to play both all-black clubs and white establishments where blacks were usually not allowed. His style combined elements of country, jazz, blues, and Cajun music, and has influenced guitarists as diverse as Albert Collins, Frank Zappa, Roy Buchanan, and Guitar Slim.

Brown broke free of Robey sometime between 1959 and 1964. He continued touring and recording and worked for a while as a deputy sheriff in New Mexico. By 1971 he was performing again and building a following in Europe, especially in France, where he enjoyed a strong following and recorded for French companies. His half-brother, James "Widemouth" Brown, was also a singer until his death in 1971.

Brown settled in New Orleans and recorded his first domestically released album, *Blackjack*. In 1979 he recorded *Makin' Music* with country star Roy Clark. *Alright Again!* won a Best Blues Grammy in 1982. Brown continued touring extensively. He later appeared on Michelle Shocked's *Arkansas Traveler* album.

Dennis Brown

Born February 1, 1957, Kingston, Jamaica
1972—*Super Reggae and Soul Hits* (Trojan)   1975—
Just Dennis   1978—*Visions of Dennis Brown*

Dennis Brown

(Lightning); *Westbound Train* (Third World)
1979—*Words of Wisdom* (Laser); *Live at Montreux*;
Wolf and Leopards   1980—*Spellbound*   1981—*Foul Play* (A&M)   1982—*Love Has Found a Way*   1989—
Visions (Shanachie); *Words of Wisdom*   1990—*Slow Down*   1991—*Over Proof*; *Victory Is Mine* (RAS).
With Gregory Isaacs: 1984—*Judge Not* (Shanachie)
1989—*No Contest* (Music Works).

The most prominent exponent of the romantic style of reggae known as "lovers rock," singer Dennis Brown began his career in Jamaican and other West Indian tourist clubs when he was nine. In his teen years, he became a protégé of Jamaican bandleader and producer Bryon Lee, and by the mid-Sixties he was recording regularly for such producers as Coxsone Dodd, Derrick Harriot, and Joe Gibbs. He had a string of Jamaican hits in the late Sixties and Seventies, including "No Man Is an Island" (1968), "Silhouettes" (1968), "Baby Don't Do It" (1971), "Look of Love" (1971), "Things in Life" (1972), and "Money in My Pocket" (1972)—mostly conventional pop love songs set to reggae rhythms.

In 1979 he rerecorded "Money in My Pocket" for issue in the U.K.; it reached #14 on the British charts and launched Brown's international popularity. That year he toured Europe, and in 1980 he signed with A&M, his first major label. He toured North America, poised to reach the pop market with such derooted numbers as "Foul Play" and "If I Ruled the World," both of which were given some airplay on black stations. This period also yielded two modest pop chart hits in the U.K., "Love Has

Found Its Way" (#47, 1982) and "Halfway Up Halfway Down" (#56, 1982).

In 1983 Brown tried to expand his American following by recording with K.C. and the Sunshine Band but ended up alienating the fans he had. His collaborations with Gregory Isaacs (*Judge Not* and *No Contest*), however, reestablished his credibility. He has remained popular in Jamaica, working with producers King Jammy and Gussie Clark. In America, Brown signed with the world music specialist Shanachie in 1987 and appeared on the Reggae Sunsplash Tour in 1991.

James Brown

Born May 3, 1933, Barnwell, South Carolina
1959—*Please Please Please* (King); *Try Me*   1960—
Think*   1963—*The James Brown Show Live at the
Apollo*   1964—*Pure Dynamite!*   1965—*Papa's Got
a Brand New Bag*   1966—*I Got You (I Feel Good)
1967—Raw Soul*   1968—*"Live" at the Apollo, vol. 2
1969—Say It Loud, I'm Black and I'm Proud*   1970—
It's a New Day—Let a Man Come In; Sex Machine
1971—Hot Pants* (Polydor); *Revolution of the Mind
1972—There It Is*   1974—*The Payback; Hell; Real-
ity*   1976—*Body Heat*   1979—*The Original Disco
Man*   1983—*Bring It On!* (Augusta Sound)   1986—
***Gravity* (Scotti Bros.); *In the Jungle Groove* (Poly-**
dor)   1989—*Roots of a Revolution*   1990—*Messing*
with the Blues*   1991—*Star Time; Love Over-Due
(Scotti Bros.)   1992—*The Greatest Hits of the*
Fourth Decade*   1993—*Soul Pride: The Instrumen-
***tals (1960–1969)* (Polydor); *Universal James* (Scotti**
Bros.).

"Soul Brother Number One," James Brown was perhaps the best known and clearly the most successful black artist of the Sixties and early Seventies; his polyrhythmic funk vamps virtually reshaped dance music. With some 800 songs in his repertoire, the astonishingly prolific Brown has from the Sixties into the Nineties influenced a wide range of artists, from Michael Jackson to Prince to Public Enemy. And his adamant refusal to conform to anyone's vision other than his own bolstered his epic status.

Brown was born into poverty in the rural South around the time of the Depression (some records give his birthdate as 1928; he claims it is 1933). As a child, he picked cotton, shined shoes, danced for pennies in the streets of Augusta, Georgia—and stole. Convicted of armed robbery at age 16, he spent three years in a juvenile detention institution. While incarcerated, Brown made the acquaintance of Bobby Byrd, who with his family gospel group visited the institution to perform. Byrd's family eventually helped obtain Brown's release by taking the youngster in and getting him a job. Brown tried semiprofessional sports, first as a boxer, then as a

James Brown

baseball pitcher, but a leg injury ruined his chances of going pro. In the meantime, Byrd and Brown had put together a gospel group, which performed under a succession of different names at the Mt. Zion Baptist Church, in Toccoa, Georgia, and at auditoriums in the area. Byrd and Brown sang duets, with three or four other members singing background vocals and harmonies. After seeing a rock & roll show featuring Hank Ballard and the Midnighters, Fats Domino, and others, Brown and Byrd left gospel music behind, transforming the group (Johnny Terry, Sylvester Keels, and Floyd Scott) into the Flames. Each Flame sang, danced, and played an instrument or two—Brown's were piano and drums. Byrd also played keyboards and shared vocals; he would remain Brown's sideman off and on over the next three-plus decades.

From a base in Macon, Georgia, the Flames had been touring the South for two years when Ralph Bass, head of Federal Records, signed them in 1956. Their first single, "Please, Please, Please," was a big hit in Georgia and adjacent states, and eventually sold a million copies. Subsequent releases in the same gospel-influenced yet distinctly rougher R&B style made Brown a regional star until "Try Me" became a national hit in 1958, charting #1 in R&B, #48 in pop.

By this time, Brown had become de facto leader of the group, by now called the Famous Flames. Guided by Universal Attractions director Ben Bart, Brown created the James Brown Revue, complete with opening acts, his own emcee and a stage band—the James Brown Band.

The show was precisely choreographed, with Brown pumping his hips, twisting on one foot, and splitting to the floor as the troupe executed their own intricate steps; night after night, he would feign heart failure before returning for an encore with a sweep of his cape. Sweating off a purported seven pounds a night, and breaking box-office records in every major black venue in America, Brown earned the nickname "Mr. Dynamite" and the title "The Hardest Working Man in Show Business."

As Brown's band became one of the tightest in the field, Brown wanted to showcase them on his recordings. Federal, however, refused to let him use them in the studio, so he arranged for the band to record for another company as Nat Kendrick and the Swans. The resulting instrumental hit, "Mashed Potatoes," persuaded Federal's parent company, King, to take over Brown's contract and to sign up the James Brown Band both for Brown's sessions and as a separate act. From then on, Brown concentrated on pared-down, jump-and-shout dance music ("Think," "Night Train"). If a new song made the concert crowd dance, he would record it that night, often in one take. Simultaneously, Brown was sending such raw, emotive R&B ballads as "Bewildered" (#8 R&B, #40 pop, 1961), "I Don't Mind" (#4 R&B, #47 pop, 1961), and "Lost Someone" (#2 R&B, #48 pop, 1961) up the charts.

Brown's *Live at the Apollo,* recorded in Harlem in 1962 and patterned after Ray Charles' live *In Person,* sold a million copies, unprecedented for a black music album. In 1963, frustrated by King's failure to reach into the white market, Brown and Bart formed Fair Deal Productions. "Out of Sight," which Fair Deal released through Smash Records, hit #1 R&B, #24 pop.

Brown's revised contract with King in 1965 gave him complete artistic control. He revamped his band under the leadership of Nat Jones, and with his "Papa's Got a Brand New Bag," he became a world-class force in popular music. Disposing of the conventional verse and chorus structure, eliminating even chord progressions, he distilled his sound to its essence: rhythm. "Brand New Bag" topped the R&B charts, as did "I Got You (I Feel Good)" and "It's a Man's, Man's, Man's World." After Alfred "Pee Wee" Ellis replaced Jones as bandleader, James continued to score with "Cold Sweat," "I Got the Feelin'," "Say It Loud, I'm Black and I'm Proud," "Give It Up or Turn It A-Loose," and "Mother Popcorn"—which were also Top Twenty (many of them Top Ten) pop hits. Concurrently, he recorded instrumental albums (a total of 11 between 1961 and 1971) that never attained great commercial success, but, featuring his organ and piano work, continued his rhythmic explorations (tracks from the best of these can be found on the 1993 anthology, *Soul Pride*).

The latter Sixties found James Brown a cultural hero, "Soul Brother Number One." As a black man of wealth, independence, and influence, he was a symbol of self-de-

termination and triumph over racism. He took that responsibility seriously. Songs such as "Say It Loud," "Don't Be a Drop-Out," and "I Don't Want Nobody to Give Me Nothing (Open Up the Door I'll Get it Myself)" contained direct social messages. He sponsored programs for ghetto youth, spoke at high schools, invested in black businesses, performed for troops in Vietnam, and went on television after the assassination of Martin Luther King to plead for calm—a service for which he was ceremoniously thanked by Vice President Hubert Humphrey.

In late 1969 Brown faced the mutiny of his celebrated Sixties band, which included saxophonist Maceo Parker and trombonist Fred Wesley. Brown enlisted hot young instrumentalists who, with his nurturing, continued to develop the sound that would be called funk. The youngbloods, who as the new band were dubbed the J.B.'s, included brothers William "Bootsy" and Phelps "Catfish" Collins, whose distinctive bass and lead guitar playing, respectively, ushered in a new sound in soul music. The Collinses left after a year, later joining George Clinton's Parliament/Funkadelic organization. Key Sixties band members saxophonist St. Clair Pinckney and guitarist Jimmy Nolan, as well as Parker and Wesley, eventually returned, but the only consistent member was drummer John "Jabo" Starks, who originally joined in 1965.

The J.B.'s were then led by Wesley, who with Brown began creating music that was even less formal than before; as the instrumental sections dug into funk grooves, Brown, dubbing himself "Minister of New New Super Heavy Funk," mixed sociopolitical messages and stream-of-consciousness phrasing with an undeniable beat.

Brown had been managing himself since the death of his manager in the late Sixties, and in 1971 he had signed with an international record company, Polydor, and sold it his entire back catalogue. His records—"Hot Pants" (#15, 1971), "Make It Funky" (#68, 1971), "Talking Loud and Saying Nothing" (#27, 1972), "Get on the Good Foot" (#18, 1972), "The Payback" (#26, 1974), "My Thang" (#29, 1974), and "Papa Don't Take No Mess" (#31, 1974)—continued to sell by the millions. Though R&B chart-toppers, they increasingly failed to crack the pop Top Twenty.

Around 1975 Brown's popularity began to wane. Because of financial difficulties, Brown was forced to sell his three black radio stations and his jet. The U.S. government claimed he owed $4.5 million in back taxes, a manager said Brown was part of a payola scandal, Brown's son Teddy had died in a car crash in 1973, and his second marriage ended. Young record buyers favored heirs like the Ohio Players, Kool and the Gang, and the Parliafunkadelicment Thang (which now employed Wesley and Parker).

He was welcomed to Africa and Japan as a star, and at home he continued to work. When disco peaked in the late Seventies, he promoted himself as "The Original Disco Man," which he was. When "It's Too Funky in Here" reached #15, it was called a "comeback." With a cameo role in the 1980 movie *The Blues Brothers,* Brown introduced his soul-church preaching to a new generation. Returning to American stages that year, he drew much of his audience from the white punk-funk faction, for whom he was the essence of polyrhythmic minimalism. In 1980 he recorded "Rapp Payback (Where Iz Moses?)," a homage to his earlier singles "Brother Rapp" and "The Payback," which prefigured the enormous influence he would come to have on the incipient rap scene. The single, a British dance hit (#39 U.K., 1981), helped activate a James Brown resurgence there. Finding himself label-less in the early Eighties, Brown recorded the album *Bring It On!* for his own Augusta Sound label.

In 1984 Brown joined with rapper Afrika Bambaataa on "Unity," released on New York rap label Tommy Boy. By this time, his music had been claimed as the virtual basis for hip-hop beats; among others, Kool Moe Dee and Eric B. & Rakim scored hits by sampling Brown's rhythms, and his 1969 recording "Funky Drummer" (featuring drummer Clyde Stubblefield) began appearing in myriad versions on rap and pop records. The rappers also borrowed poses from Brown's persona—street-savvy, self-contained, defiant. With Brown inducted as a charter member into the Rock and Roll Hall of Fame in 1986, his revival was bolstered by "Living in America," the theme song to *Rocky IV.* Recorded at the request of director Sylvester Stallone, the single (#4, 1986), included on the album *Gravity* (with guest stars Alison Moyet and Steve Winwood), won a Grammy in 1987 for Best R&B Performance. In 1989 Brown (with writer Bruce Tucker) published an autobiography, *James Brown: The Godfather of Soul.*

In 1988, however, Brown's career ground to a halt. When his fourth wife, Adrienne, reported beatings, Brown was charged with assault with intent to murder and aggravated assault and battery. Surrendering to Aiken County, South Carolina, authorities near his 60-acre home in May, he was released on bond. Then followed a year of bizarre legal troubles during which Adrienne, after her own arrest for alleged possession of PCP, first announced that she would file for legal separation, then relented and also withdrew the assault charges. Then Adrienne was arrested again for PCP possession and for arson. In September, as rumors circulated about his own PCP abuse and problems with the IRS, he allegedly threatened a group of people with a shotgun and then engaged in an interstate car chase with police that ended with his receiving a six-year sentence in a work-release program.

Paroled in 1991 after serving two years of his sentence—during which he was visited by the Reverend Al Sharpton, Jesse Jackson, and Republican stalwart Lee Atwater but ignored by the music industry and most of his old friends—Brown returned to work with a pay-per-view television concert and a new album. With *Star Time*, a four-CD retrospective (later chosen by ROLLING STONE as Reissue of the Year) just released, the best of Brown's catalogue was freshly available, and the singer's critical stature was unassailable.

Roy Brown

Born September 10, 1925, New Orleans, Louisiana; died May 25, 1981, Los Angeles, California
N.A.—*The Blues Are All Brown* (Bluesday); *Roy Brown Sings 24 Hits* (King); *Roy Brown and Wynonie Harris*   1973—*Hard Times* (Bluesway)   1976—*Hard Luck Blues* (King)   1978—*Good Rocking Tonight* (Route 66); *Laughing but Crying*   1979—*Cheapest Price in Town* (Faith)   1982—*Good Rockin' Tonight* (Quicksilver).

Blues shouter Roy Brown had a major impact on early rock & roll. He wrote and recorded the jump-blues "Good Rocking Tonight" in 1947, and it became a #13 R&B hit the following year; Elvis Presley recorded it at one of his 1954 Sun Records sessions and also had a hit. Throughout the late Forties and Fifties, Brown enjoyed over a dozen Top Ten R&B hits, including " 'Long About Midnight" (#1, 1948), "Boogie at Midnight" (#3, 1949), "Cadillac Baby" (#6, 1950), and "Hard Luck Blues" (#1, 1950).

Brown's big-band backups helped shape the New Orleans sound (Fats Domino, Allen Toussaint); his stage shows with his band, the Mighty Men, foreshadowed modern rock theatrics. B. B. King, Bobby "Blue" Bland, and others have cited Brown's singing as an influence. Brown was still playing frequent club dates when he died of a heart attack in 1981. Three years later Robert Plant and the Honeydrippers had a Top Twenty-five hit with Brown's "Rockin' at Midnight."

Ruth Brown

Born January 30, 1928, Portsmouth, Virginia
1959—*Late Date with Ruth Brown* (Atlantic); *Miss Rhythm*   1962—*Along Comes Ruth* (Philips); *Gospel Time* (Lection)   1976—*Sugar Babe* (President)   1982—*The Soul Survives* (Flair)   1988—*Have a Good Time* (Fantasy)   1989—*Blues on Broadway*; *Miss Rhythm (Greatest Hits and More)* (Rhino)   1993—*The Songs of My Life* (Fantasy).

Known as "Miss Rhythm," Ruth Brown was perhaps the biggest female R&B star of the Fifties, briefly rivaling Dinah Washington as the era's leading black woman singer. In its early days, her label Atlantic Records was known as "the House that Ruth Built."

As a teenager she sang in her church choir, then

worked with jazz big bands in the Forties. She signed with the fledgling Atlantic in 1948 and recorded over 80 songs for the label before 1962, making her its most prolific and best-selling act of that period. At first her hits were confined to the R&B charts, which she topped with "Teardrops from My Eyes" (1950), "5-10-15 Hours" (1952), "(Mama) He Treats Your Daughter Mean" (1953, recorded with a band led by Ray Charles), "Oh What a Dream" and "Mambo Baby" (both 1954). In 1956 she began performing in disc jockey Alan Freed's rock & roll shows and attracting a white youth audience. "Lucky Lips"—written by Jerry Leiber and Mike Stoller—made #25 on the pop chart in 1957, followed the next year by "This Little Girl's Gone Rockin'" (#24 pop). Her last R&B Top Ten hit, "Don't Deceive Me," appeared in early 1960.

In 1961 Brown left Atlantic for Philips. She had a couple of minor hits on that label, then retired. In the Seventies she reemerged to record for Cobblestone and President, and later, Fantasy, where her records featured jazz and blues stylings. Brown costarred in the 1986 Off-Broadway musical *Staggerlee*, and in 1989 earned a Tony Award for her role in Broadway's *Black and Blue*. She appeared in the John Waters film *Hairspray* (1988). Brown continues to perform and record.

Jackson Browne

Jackson Browne

Born October 9, 1948, Heidelberg, West Germany
1972—*Jackson Browne* (Asylum)   1973—*For Everyman*   1974—*Late for the Sky*   1976—*The Pretender*
1978—*Running on Empty*   1980—*Hold Out*   1983—*Lawyers in Love*   1986—*Lives in the Balance*
1989—*World in Motion*   1993—*I'm Alive.*

Siner/songwriter Jackson Browne's introverted, finely observed songs made him one of the West Coast's most influential songwriters. Browne's first songs infused domestic sagas with a sense of romantic doom, making lovers into heroes. In the Eighties Browne focused more sharply on the sociopolitical, but in 1993 he returned to more personal themes with *I'm Alive*.

Browne's family moved to Southern California when he was young, and in his late teens he played guitar with an embryonic version of the Nitty Gritty Dirt Band, which later performed his songs. He spent the winters of 1967 and 1968 in Greenwich Village, where he backed Tim Buckley and Nico; she did an early cover of Browne's "These Days." By 1969 he had begun to establish a reputation as a songwriter, and in the next few years Tom Rush, the Byrds, Bonnie Raitt, Linda Ronstadt, and others performed his songs, and he toured as an opening act for Laura Nyro and Joni Mitchell. Browne's solo debut produced a hit with "Doctor My Eyes" (#8, 1972) and eventually went gold. He cowrote the Eagles' first hit, "Take It Easy."

With each album his following grew, and *The Pre-* *tender* became his first platinum album; its sense of despair derived in part from the suicide of Browne's first wife, Phyllis, in 1976, two and a half years after the birth of their son, Ethan. A 1977 tour produced *Running on Empty*, a live concept album about touring featuring new material recorded onstage, in hotel rooms, and on the tour bus, including hits in the title track and a remake of "Stay" (#20, 1978). Nineteen-eighty's *Hold Out* went to #1 in its first week of release. Browne's 1983 album *Lawyers in Love* introduced many of the sociopolitical themes he would continue to explore in such later albums as *Lives in the Balance* and *World in Motion*. Though *Lawyers*, boosted by the Top Twenty title track, hit #8, fans were less enthusiastic about the latter two albums, the first Browne LPs since *The Pretender* that did not go platinum.

In 1993 Browne returned to matters of the heart with *I'm Alive*, on which he worked with longtime collaborator and coproducer Scott Thurston (Don Was also produced two tracks). The album generated unusually careful media scrutiny, coming as it did after Browne's highly publicized breakup with actress Daryl Hannah.

Browne continues to tour internationally and has been active in numerous organizations devoted to social change, including MUSE (Musicians United for Safe Energy), Amnesty International, and the Christic Institute. He has produced albums for Warren Zevon, his former guitarist David Lindley, Native American poet John

Trudell, and high school friend Greg Copeland, as well as Nicaraguan group Guardabarranco. He has collaborated with fellow West Coast songwriters, including J. D. Souther, Lowell George, Valerie Carter, and the Eagles.

Brownsville Station
Formed 1969, Ann Arbor, Michigan
Cub Koda (b. Michael Koda, Oct. 1, 1948, Detroit, Mich.), gtr., voc.; Michael Lutz, gtr., voc.; T. J. Cronley, drums; Tony Driggins, bass.
1970—*No B.S.* (Warner Bros.) 1972—(– Cronley; + Henry Weck, drums) *A Night on the Town* (Big Tree) 1973—(– Driggins; Lutz switches to bass) *Yeah* 1974—*School Punks* 1975—(+ Bruce Nazarian, gtr., bass, voc.) *Motor City Connection* 1977— *Brownsville Station* (Private Stock) 1979—*Air Special* (Epic) 1993—*Smokin' in the Boys' Room: The Best of Brownsville Station* (Rhino).
Cub Koda solo: 1993—*Welcome to My Job—The Cub Koda Collection, 1963–1993* (Blue Wave) 1994— *Abba Dabba Dabba—A Bananza of Hits* (Schoolkids').

Brownsville Station was formed by Michael Lutz and Cub Koda through a chance meeting at a local music store. A rock act, Brownsville spent most of its ten years together earning a reputation as an energetic live act on the arena circuit. The band's 1973 hit single "Smokin' in the Boys' Room" reached #3 in January 1974. Like much of their material, "Smokin' " was written by Koda. After the group disbanded in June 1979, Koda began a solo career; he has recorded ten LPs. He has also written for numerous publications, including *Goldmine.* Lutz teaches and writes music; Weck co-owns a recording studio. In 1985 Mötley Crüe made its commercial breakthrough with a Top Twenty cover of "Smokin' in the Boys' Room."

Jack Bruce
Born John Symon Asher Bruce, May 14, 1943, Glasgow, Scotland
1969—*Songs for a Tailor* (Atco) 1970—*Things We Like* 1971—*Harmony Row* 1972—*Jack Bruce at His Best* (Polydor) 1974—*Out of the Storm* (RSO) 1977—*How's Tricks* 1980—*I've Always Wanted to Do This* (Epic) 1982—*Truce* (Chrysalis) 1989— *Willpower* (Polydor); *A Question of Time* (Epic) 1993—*Somethinels* (CMP) 1994—*Cities of the Heart.*
With BBM: (Bruce, bass, cello, voc.; Ginger Baker, drums, perc.; Gary Moore, gtr. voc.) 1994—*Around the Next Dream* (Virgin).

The punchy bass riffs and urgent tenor vocals Jack Bruce lent to Cream were widely imitated by the heavy-metal bands that followed. Although Bruce's virtuosity and arty inclinations led him to make jazzy, complex music after he left Cream, he has returned periodically to hard rock.

At age 17 he won a scholarship to the Royal Scottish Academy of Music for cello and composition but dropped out after three months to play jazz in Glasgow. He moved to London in his late teens and played with British R&B pioneers Alexis Korner and Graham Bond. In 1965 he left the Graham Bond Organisation, whose drummer was Ginger Baker, for John Mayall's Bluesbreakers, a band that included guitarist Eric Clapton.

After a brief stint in Manfred Mann, Bruce joined Clapton and Baker in forming Cream in 1966 [see entries]. The three virtually invented a hard-rock trio style—complete with extended improvisations in which Bruce's bass chased Clapton's guitar—before breaking up in 1968. Most of Cream's hit singles were written by Bruce and lyricist Pete Brown.

Since Cream's breakup Bruce has divided his efforts between fusion, hard rock, and an ambitious, eccentric folk-rock–classical hybrid style of songwriting he tried on *Songs for a Tailor, Harmony Row,* and *Out of the Storm.* Of those songs, "Theme for an Imaginary Western" became a hit for Mountain. Bruce's first post-Cream group, Jack Bruce and Friends, included jazz guitarist Larry Coryell and Jimi Hendrix Experience drummer Mitch Mitchell. In 1970 and 1971 Bruce was a member of the Tony Williams Lifetime [see entry], the pioneering fusion band that also included guitarist John McLaughlin. Bruce's *Things We Like* was a jam session with McLaughlin, Dick Heckstall-Smith, and other British progressive jazzmen; Bruce also appeared (as vocalist) with McLaughlin on Carla Bley's 1972 *Escalator over the Hill,* and in 1979 he toured with McLaughlin and Mahavishnu Orchestra alumni Billy Cobham and Stu Goldberg.

On the hard-rock side, Bruce put together a power trio with Mountain's Leslie West and Corky Laing, which released albums in 1972, '73, and '74 [see Mountain entry]. He appeared on Frank Zappa's *Apostrophe* in 1974, and in 1975 he fronted the Jack Bruce Band, with keyboardist Bley and former Rolling Stones guitarist Mick Taylor, on a tour of Europe; they did not record. The 1980 version of Jack Bruce and Friends included drummer Cobham, ex–Humble Pie guitarist Clem Clempson, and erstwhile Bruce Springsteen pianist David Sancious. In 1981 Bruce joined another power trio, B.L.T., led by Robin Trower, and in 1982 Bruce and Trower collaborated on *Truce.* Bruce kept a low profile through the rest of the Eighties, reportedly battling drug and alcohol problems.

Following a European tour with a 13-piece Latin-jazz-rock orchestra, Bruce recorded *A Question of Time,* which mirrored his growing interest in world music and reunited him with Cream drummer Ginger Baker. *Somethinels* (with lyrics by Peter Brown) featured Eric Clapton, Dick Heckstall-Smith, and Clem Clempson, while

Cities of the Heart, recorded live at a 1993 show, featured Baker, Clempson, and ex–P-Funk/Talking Heads keyboardist Bernie Worrell. In 1994 Bruce and Gary Moore (who was a replacement guitarist on a Bruce tour) recorded *Around the Next Dream* with Baker.

Bill Bruford

**Born William Scott Bruford, May 17, 1949,
Sevenoaks, Kent, England
1978—Feels Good to Me (Polydor) 1979—One of a
Kind 1980—The Bruford Tapes; Gradually Going
Tornado 1986—Master Strokes.
Earthworks, formed 1986: Bruford, drums, electronic drums, perc., kybds.; Iain Ballamy, sax,
kybds.; Django Bates, kybds., trumpet, E-flat tenor
horn; Mick Hutton, bass. 1987—Earthworks (EG)
(–Hutton; + Tim Harries, bass) 1989—Dig?
1991—All Heaven Broke Loose.**

After distinguishing himself with Yes, King Crimson, and Genesis, Bill Bruford became a jazz-rock bandleader and made fusion music with the same crisp angularity and tasteful smarts that marked his drumming. Bruford supported his more adventurous work by returning periodically to the big-rock arena, with U.K. in 1979, a re-formed Crimson in 1981, fellow ex–Yes-men Jon Anderson, Rick Wakeman, and Steve Howe in 1989, and a full Yes reunion in 1991 [see entries].

After Crimson disbanded in 1974 Bruford took sundry odd jobs: on the obscure 1975 all-star album *Flash Fearless Vs. the Zorg Women* (with Alice Cooper, the Who's John Entwistle, and Jim Dandy Mangrum of Black Oak Arkansas, among others); on 1975 albums by Yes's Chris Squire (*Fish Out of Water*) and Steve Howe (*Beginnings*) and British folk rocker Roy Harper (*HQ*); and 1976 albums by American progressive rockers Pavlov's Dog (*At the Sound of the Bell*) and space rockers Absolute Elsewhere (*In Search of Ancient Gods*). In 1976 Bruford toured with Genesis—at the request of drummer Phil Collins, who was replacing departed frontman/vocalist Peter Gabriel—then formed the British jazz-rock band National Health with ex–Hatfield and the North keyboardist Dave Stewart. In 1977 Bruford recruited Stewart, ex–Soft Machine/Tony Williams Lifetime/Gong guitarist Alan Holdsworth (a major influence on Eddie Van Halen), and Americans Jeff Berlin (bass) and Annette Peacock (vocals) to record *Feels Good to Me.* Rather than play drum solos, Bruford, who wrote all the songs, played the serpentine melodies on vibes.

After guesting on Peacock's 1978 album *X-Dreams,* Bruford formed U.K. Bruford left after one album and tour (he was replaced by ex–Missing Persons Terry Bozzio) to form his eponymous jazz-rock band, dissolving it only when Fripp re-formed King Crimson in 1981. In that band Bruford played electronic drum pads, made by English inventor Dave Simmons, which were fed with sampled or synthesized sounds. When Crimson disbanded again, the Simmons drums keyed the approach of Earthworks—in which Bruford tapped out repeated keyboardlike melodies and chordal harmonies, to back the boppish lines of Iain Ballamy and Django Bates, two rising stars of the British jazz scene who were half Bruford's age. In between Crimson and Earthworks, Bruford recorded two solo albums with ex–Yes/Moody Blues keyboardist Patrick Moraz (1983's *Music for Piano and Drums,* 1985's *Flags*); in 1987 he recorded (*Clouds About Mercury*) and toured with ECM guitarist David Torn, and played drums and percussion with the New Percussion Group of Amsterdam on the album *Go Between.*

Peabo Bryson

**Born April 13, 1951, Greenville, South Carolina
1976—Peabo (Bang) 1977—Reaching for the Sky
(Capitol) 1978—Crosswinds 1979—We're the
Best of Friends (with Natalie Cole) 1980—Paradise;
Live and More (with Roberta Flack) (Atlantic)
1981—I Am Love (Capitol); Turn the Hands of Time
1982—Don't Play with Fire 1983—Born to Love
(with Roberta Flack) 1984—Straight from the
Heart (Elektra) 1984—The Peabo Bryson Collection (Capitol) 1985—Take No Prisoners (Elektra)
1988—Positive 1991—Can You Stop the Rain (Columbia) 1994—Peabo Bryson.**

Peabo Bryson grew up on a farm in South Carolina, sang in a rural church, and joined his first group, Al Freeman and the Upsetters, as a harmony singer at age 14. His first professional group was Mose Dillard and the Tex-Town Display, with whom he sang from 1968 to 1973, touring the U.S., the Caribbean, and Vietnam. The group recorded on the Curtom and Bang labels. Bang president Eddie Biscoe encouraged Bryson to write and sing his own material, and in 1970 he signed a solo contract with Bang and moved to Atlanta, where he worked as a staff producer before recording his solo debut album. He had his first hit as guest vocalist with Michael Zager's Moon Band, whose "Do It with Feeling" made the R&B Top Thirty in 1976. On his own he placed three singles in the R&B Top Thirty: "Underground Music" (1976), "Just Another Day" (1977), and "I Can Make It Better" (1977).

He signed with Capitol in 1977, and his label debut included R&B hit singles in the title song, "Reaching for the Sky" (#6, 1978), and "Feel the Fire" (#13, 1978). *Crosswinds* boasted a #2 R&B single, "I'm So into You." In 1979 Bryson toured with Natalie Cole; their studio collaborations yielded an album, *We're the Best of Friends,* and two R&B hit singles: "Gimme Some Time" (#8 R&B, 1979) and "What You Won't Do for Love" (#16 R&B, 1980). Later in 1980, after charting R&B Top Twenty with Michael McDonald's "Minute by Minute," he joined Roberta

Flack for a concert tour and a live album that gave the duo a hit R&B single, "Make the World Stand Still" (#13 R&B, 1981). In 1983 the pair had a bigger hit with "Tonight, I Celebrate My Love" from *Born to Love* (#16 pop, #5 R&B).

The next year Bryson's "If Ever You're in My Arms Again" (#6 pop, #10 R&B, 1984) became the first of a series of crossover hits, culminating in two hit duets from Disney animated films *Beauty and the Beast* ("Beauty and the Beast" with Celine Dion, #9, 1992) and *Aladdin* ("A Whole New World [Aladdin's Theme]" with Regina Belle, #1, 1993); both earned Oscars for best song. Bryson's recordings have appeared on the classical (*The King and I,* with Lea Salonga) and contemporary jazz (Kenny G's *Breathless,* featuring Bryson singing "By the Time This Night Is Over") charts.

Roy Buchanan

Born September 23, 1939, Ozark, Arkansas; died August 14, 1988, Fairfax, Virginia
1972—*Roy Buchanan* **(Polydor)   1973—***Roy Buchanan Second Album* **   1974—***That's What I Am Here For***;** *In the Beginning* **   1975—***Rescue Me***;** *Live Stock* **   1976—***A Street Called Straight* **(Atlantic) 1977—***Loading Zone* **   1978—***You're Not Alone* **1980—***My Babe* **(Waterhouse)   1985—***When a Guitar Plays the Blues* **(Alligator)   1986—***Dancing on the Edge* **   1988—***Hot Wires* **   1992—***Sweet Dreams: The Anthology* **(Polydor)   1993—***Guitar on Fire: The Atlantic Sessions* **(Rhino).**

Blues guitarist Roy Buchanan was considered a musician's musician in the Seventies for his impeccable Telecaster leads. Among his fans were Jeff Beck, Eric Clapton, and Robbie Robertson. The son of a Pentecostal preacher, Buchanan grew up in Pixley, California, and was a proficient guitarist by age nine. At 15 he ran away to Los Angeles and came under the tutelage of R&B great Johnny Otis. The guitarist toured and recorded with rockabilly star Dale Hawkins ("Suzy Q") for three years before joining Ronnie Hawkins. He moved to the Washington, D.C., area, and in the mid-Sixties did East Coast session work. In 1968 he formed the Soundmasters and worked clubs on the Eastern Seaboard regularly for the next several years.

A 1971 ROLLING STONE article inspired some interest in Buchanan, as did a PBS documentary called *The Best Unknown Guitarist in the World.* He claimed the Rolling Stones had asked him to replace Brian Jones in 1969, but he turned them down. In 1972 Buchanan signed his first solo recording contract. He toured and released albums steadily to a cult audience throughout his life, which ended in a Virginia jail cell. An intoxicated Buchanan was arrested on the street by police responding to a phone call from his wife. When deputies went to check on him an hour later, they found the 48-year-old father of seven hanging by his own shirt.

Lindsey Buckingham: See Fleetwood Mac

The Buckinghams

Formed 1965, Chicago, Illinois
Carl Giammarese (b. Aug. 21, 1947, Chicago), gtr.; Dennis Tufano (b. Sep. 11, 1946, Chicago), gtr., harmonica; Nick Fortune (b. Nicholas Fortuna, May 1, 1946, Chicago), bass; Jon-Jon Poulos (b. Mar. 31, 1947, Chicago; d. Mar. 26, 1980), drums; Dennis Miccolis, kybds.
1967—*Kind of a Drag* **(U.S.A.) (– Miccolis; + Marty Grebb [b. Sep. 2, 1946, Chicago], kybds.);** *Time and Charges* **(Columbia)   1968—***Portraits***;** *In One Ear and Gone Tomorrow* **   1969—***Greatest Hits* **(– Grebb; + John Turner, kybds.)   1970—(Group disbands)   1980—(Group re-forms: Tufano; Giammarese; Fortuna; – Tufano; + John Cammelot, kybds.; + Tom Scheckel [b. Nov. 19, 1954, Chicago], drums)   1985—***A Matter of Time* **(Red)   1991—***Mercy, Mercy, Mercy: A Collection* **(Legacy).**

In 1967 the Buckinghams' rock-with-horns sound made them a staple of Top Forty radio, with five Top Twenty hits. The group came together in 1965 when Carl Giammarese and Nick Fortune of the Centuries teamed up with Dennis Tufano and Jon-Jon Poulos of the Pulsations. Adding Dennis Miccolis on keyboards, the new Pulsations auditioned for a Chicago variety show, *All Time Hits.* Informed that the program's producers were looking for a British-style group, they changed their name to the Buckinghams—and passed the audition.

Four singles on two local labels failed to chart, but "Kind of a Drag"—with its polite horns and cheesy organ—rocketed to #1 in February 1967. The group signed with Columbia Records, which paired it with producer/manager James Guercio. Through the end of the year, the Buckinghams monopolized the airwaves with "Don't You Care" (#6), "Mercy, Mercy, Mercy" (#5), "Hey Baby (They're Playing Our Song)" (#12), and "Susan" (#11). But as per the title of a 1968 Buckinghams LP, *In One Ear and Gone Tomorrow,* the quintet's appeal mysteriously vanished. It broke up in 1970, by which time producer Guercio was perfecting the brass-rock sound with the group Chicago.

Tufano and Giammarese recorded as a duet for Ode Records in 1973, while keyboardist Marty Grebb formed the Fabulous Rhinestones. Poulos, who went into management, died of a drug overdose in 1980 at age 32. That year Tufano, Giammarese, and Fortune revived the band, and they have continued to play the oldies circuit. By 1985, Tufano had departed to pursue acting.

Jeff Buckley: See Tim Buckley

Tim Buckley

Born February 14, 1947, Washington, D.C.; died
June 29, 1975, Santa Monica, California
1967—*Tim Buckley* (Elektra); *Goodbye and Hello*
1969—*Happy Sad*   1970—*Blue Afternoon* (Straight);
Lorca (Elektra)   1971—*Starsailor* (Warner Bros.)
1972—*Greetings from L.A.*   1974—*Look at the Fool*
(DiscReet); *Sefronia*   1990—*Dream Letter (Live in
London, 1968)* (Retro).

Tim Buckley was a highly respected singer/songwriter
through the late Sixties. His professional career began in
the early Sixties when he played frequently with bassist
Jim Fielder (later of Buffalo Springfield and Blood, Sweat
and Tears) and attracted the attention of Frank Zappa's
manager Herb Cohen, who got him a deal with Elektra in
1966. (Buckley later signed with Cohen's Straight
Records.) His second album, *Goodbye and Hello*, was
produced by the Lovin' Spoonful's Jerry Yester.

   Buckley soon began exploring avant-garde jazz and
later recorded in Swahili. After several label switches, he
tried funky, danceable material in the mid-Seventies, but
without success. On June 29, 1975, Buckley died of a
heroin and morphine overdose; according to coroner's
inquest testimony, he had snorted what he believed was
cocaine. The man who owned the house where he died
was later convicted of involuntary manslaughter. Buckley's son Jeff, who barely knew his father, launched his
own career in 1994 with an EP titled *Live at Sin-é* and an
LP, *Grace.*

Buckwheat Zydeco

Born Stanley Dural Jr., November 14, 1947,
Lafayette, Louisiana
1980—*Take It Easy Baby* (Blues Unlimited)   1983—
100% Fortified Zydeco (Black Top)   1984—*Turning
Point* (Rounder)   1985—*Waitin' for My Ya Ya*
1987—*Zydeco Party*; *On a Night Like This* (Island)
1988—*Taking It Home*   1990—*Where There's
Smoke There's Fire*   1992—*On Track* (Charisma)
1993—*Menagerie: The Essential Zydeco Collection*
(Island)   1995—*Five Card Stud*

Born in the heart of the bayou, Buckwheat Zydeco blends
a love for Creole culture with an ability to rock out, a combination that has made him a popular exponent of zydeco. Playing organ and piano since the age of nine (he
was nicknamed after a Little Rascals character—a
moniker he considers racist but has stuck with), he led his
own R&B band, Buckwheat and the Hitchhikers, in 1971.
From 1976 to 1978 he played keyboards with zydeco master Clifton Chenier; this inspired a newfound appreciation
of his ethnic roots and led him to play the accordion.

Buckwheat Zydeco

   In 1979 Buckwheat formed Ils Sont Partis and released a string of well-received independent releases.
On a Night Like This, which featured Buckwheat's interpretations of songs by Bob Dylan, the Blasters, and
Booker T. and the MG's, as well as his own compositions,
was embraced by critics and nominated for a Grammy.
Further widening his popularity, Buckwheat has opened
shows for U2 and Robert Cray, toured with Eric Clapton
(who played on *Taking It Home*), and worked with Keith
Richards (he appears on the Stone's *Talk Is Cheap*) and
Los Lobos' David Hidalgo (who produced *Where There's
Smoke There's Fire*). Buckwheat's music has been featured in the films *The Big Easy* and *Casual Sex?* True to
his heritage, he forbids his music to be classified as
"Cajun" and speaks frequently about the racism that
kept zydeco music off the air for years while its white
counterpart (Cajun) was popularized.

Buffalo Springfield

Formed 1966, Los Angeles, California
Neil Young (b. Nov. 12, 1945, Toronto, Can.), voc.,
gtr.; Stephen Stills (b. Jan. 3, 1945, Dallas, Tex.),
voc., gtr.; Richie Furay (b. May 9, 1944, Dayton,
Ohio), voc., gtr.; Dewey Martin (b. Sep. 30, 1942,
Chesterville, Can.), voc., drums; Bruce Palmer
(b. 1946, Liverpool, Can.), bass.
1967—*Buffalo Springfield* (Atco); *Stampede* (unreleased) (– Palmer; + Ken Koblun, bass; – Koblun;
+ Jim Fielder [b. Oct. 4, 1947, Denton, Tex.], bass;
– Young; + Doug Hastings, gtr.) *Buffalo Springfield*

Buffalo Springfield: Richie Furay, Dewey Martin, Neil Young, Stephen Stills, Bruce Palmer

Again (Atco) (– Palmer; – Fielder; – Hastings; + Young; + Jim Messina [b. Dec. 5, 1947, Maywood, Calif.], bass) **1968—*Last Time Around* 1969—*Retrospective* 1973—*Buffalo Springfield.***

During its brief and stormy lifetime, the Buffalo Springfield broke ground for what became country rock. After the band's dissolution, several members found success in Poco; Crosby, Stills, Nash and Young; Loggins and Messina; and as solo artists.

Furay and Stills had played together, as had Canadians Young and Palmer, before the four hooked up in Los Angeles in 1966 to form Buffalo Springfield (named after a steamroller). Originally called the Herd (not to be confused with Peter Frampton's first group), they added Martin on drums and vocals.

After a stint as the house band at the Whisky-a-Go-Go and touring with the Byrds, the Springfield inked a deal with Atlantic and released its first album in 1967. Stills' "For What It's Worth" (#7, 1967) gave the group its biggest hit. By the time of its second album, the Springfield was a major group coming apart at the seams. After Palmer was deported (following a drug bust) and producer Jim Messina was added on bass, and amid persistent squabbling between Stills and Young (who quit in May 1967, only to rejoin four months later), the group disbanded in May 1968.

When *Last Time Around* was released later that year, all of the Springfields were on their own. Martin kept the

band's name alive with some hired musicians and then had an abortive solo career. Stills and Young were successful in the Seventies with CSN&Y [see entry] and solo work. Short-term bassist Jim Fielder joined Blood, Sweat and Tears [see entry], while Messina and Furay formed Poco [see entry] with pedal-steel guitarist Rusty Young, who had played on the Springfield's final album. Loggins went on to the duo Loggins and Messina [see entry].

Jimmy Buffett

Born December 25, 1946, Pascagoula, Mississippi
1970—*Down to Earth* (Barnaby) 1973—*A White Sport Coat and a Pink Crustacean* (Dunhill) 1974— *Living and Dying in 3/4 Time; A1A* 1975—*Rancho Deluxe* (United Artists) 1976—*Havana Daydreamin'* (ABC) 1976—*High Cumberland Jubilee* (Barnaby) 1977—*Changes in Latitudes, Changes in Attitudes* (ABC) 1978—*Live; Son of a Son of a Sailor; You Had to Be There* 1979—*Volcano* (MCA); *Before the Salt* (Barnaby) 1981—*Coconut Telegraph* (MCA); *Somewhere over China* 1983—*One Particular Harbour* 1984—*Riddles in the Sand* 1985—*Last Mango in Paris; Songs You Know by Heart—Jimmy Buffett's Greatest Hit(s)* 1986— *Floridays* 1988—*Hot Water* 1989—*Off to See the Lizard* 1990—*Feeding Frenzy* 1992—*Boats Beaches Bars & Ballads* (Margaritaville) 1993—*Before the Beach; Margaritaville Cafe Late Night Menu* 1994—*Fruitcakes.*

Singer/songwriter Jimmy Buffett is known for humorous chronicles of a laid-back seafaring life; his philosophical outlook is encapsulated in tunes like "Why Don't We Get Drunk (and Screw)" and "My Head Hurts, My Feet Stink and I Don't Love Jesus." He has since built a small Key West–based financial empire, written several best-selling books, and become a leading environmentalist.

Raised in the Deep South, Buffett attended Auburn University and then the University of Southern Mississippi, majoring in journalism (he later worked as a *Billboard* reporter). He moved to Nashville in the late Sixties, intent on becoming a country singer. His first album, 1970's *Down to Earth,* sold 324 copies. Barnaby Records then temporarily misplaced the master tape of his second album before its release. By 1972 Buffett had left both Nashville and a failed marriage, moving to Key West. There he helped to support himself by smuggling a little marijuana from the Caribbean. He signed to ABC-Dunhill, and his 1973 release, *A White Sport Coat and a Pink Crustacean,* found Buffett developing his drunken-sailor persona. Buffett's commercial breakthrough came in 1977 with the platinum *Changes in Latitudes, Changes in Attitudes* (#12) and its hit single, "Margaritaville" (#8).

During that period Buffett toured infrequently, spending most of his time living on his 50-foot ketch *Eu-*

phoria II. He frequently docked at Montserrat, where his 1979 LP *Volcano* was recorded. He formed the first version of his Coral Reefer Band in 1975. Buffett scored and acted in the 1974 film *Rancho Deluxe,* and appeared in the 1977 movie *FM.* His 1981 *Coconut Telegraph* album inspired a fan-club newsletter of the same name, which has maintained a worldwide subscriber base of "Parrot Heads."

The 1985 compilation *Songs You Know By Heart* (subtitled *Jimmy Buffett's Greatest Hit[s]* in self-mocking reference to the fact that "Margaritaville" was his only major pop hit) sold two million copies; 1992's *Boats Beaches Bars & Ballads* also went platinum. By that time Buffett had established a Margaritaville empire, including a record label and Margaritaville Store and Cafe outlets in Key West and New Orleans. He also wrote two best-selling books, *Tales from Margaritaville,* a collection of short stories, and the novel *Where Is Joe Merchant?,* as well as two children's books, *The Jolly Man* and *Trouble Dolls,* both coauthored with his daughter, Savannah Jane. He continues performing to sell-out crowds and crusades on behalf of Florida's endangered manatees. In 1993 *Forbes* magazine listed Buffett as the 40th richest entertainer in the world, with an estimated 1992–93 income of $20 million.

The Buggles
Formed 1979, England
Trevor Horn (b. July 15, 1949, Hertfordshire, Eng.), bass, voc.; Geoffrey Downes (b. Eng.), kybds.
1980—*Age of Plastic* (Island)   1982—*Adventures in Modern Recording* (Epic).

The electro-pop "Video Killed the Radio Star," written by Horn, Downes, and Bruce Wooley, was a huge international hit in 1979, #1 in the U.K. and Top Forty here. On August 1, 1981, it was the first video ever aired by MTV and soon proved itself a piece of musical prophecy.

Keyboardist Downes and vocalist Horn viewed themselves more as producers than as rock stars. Following "Video Killed the Radio Star," the duo had three more U.K. hits, including "The Plastic Age" in 1980. After producing Yes' *Tormato,* they shocked the music world by joining the band in March 1980 [see entry]. They appeared on *Drama* and Yes' 1980–81 tour. Following Yes' 1981 breakup, Downes joined Asia [see entry]. Horn went on to become a successful producer for many hit groups, including Frankie Goes to Hollywood and ABC, as well as Band Aid's "Do They Know It's Christmas."

Eric Burdon
Born May 11, 1941, Newcastle upon Tyne, England
Eric Burdon and War: 1970—*Eric Burdon Declares War* (Polydor)   1971—*The Black Man's Burdon* (MGM)   1976—*Love Is All Around* (ABC).
Eric Burdon solo: 1971—*Guilty* (MGM)   1974—*Ring of Fire* (Capitol); *Sun Secrets*   1975—*Stop*   1978—*Survivor* (Polydor)   1988—*Wicked Man* (GNP).
Eric Burdon/Brian Auger Band: 1993—*Access All Areas* (SPV, Eur.).

Eric Burdon's rudely emotive vocals kept him on the charts through the British Invasion (as frontman for the Animals), psychedelia (as a solo act), and early-Seventies funk (with War). He grew up in working-class Newcastle and went to art school, where he studied graphics and photography and was introduced to blues records. Unable to find a job, he became a musician and in 1962 joined the Alan Price Combo, which became the Animals [see entry]. With their success, Burdon took to drinking, womanizing, and shooting his mouth off, experiences that no doubt shaped a later song entitled "Good Times."

By 1967 a post-Animal Burdon had been converted to flower power. He traded his denims for a Nehru jacket and moved to California. After the 1969 double album, *Love Is,* Burdon announced his retirement. In late 1969 Burdon heard a funk band called Night Shift; they became War and backed him on his 1970 hit "Spill the Wine" (#3) and their debut album, *Eric Burdon Declares War.* After a second album together, Burdon became exhausted on a 1971 European tour, and War went on without him [see War entry].

Since then Burdon has remained active, recording solo albums, making an album with blues legend Jimmy Witherspoon (*Guilty*) in 1971 and an Animals reunion album, *Before We Were So Rudely Interrupted,* in 1977. ABC put out material recorded in 1970 by Burdon and War on a 1976 album, *Love Is All Around.* During the late Seventies Burdon appeared in several European movies, and in 1981 he starred in and composed the soundtrack for a German film entitled *Come Back.* In 1983 the original Animals lineup re-formed for an album and tour, and three years later Burdon published his autobiography, *I Used To Be An Animal, But I'm All Right Now.*

In 1990 Burdon formed a touring band with ex-Doors guitarist Robbie Krieger and appeared in the TV show *China Beach.* In 1991 Burdon formed a band with veteran British jazz-rock keyboardist Brian Auger; they released a 1993 album, *Access All Areas,* recorded live in California and released only in Europe. Burdon's name turned up in the press that year after his repeated requests that his friend Jimi Hendrix's death be reinvestigated by Scotland Yard. It was announced that Scotland Yard might reopen its investigation, but this did not occur.

Solomon Burke
Born 1936, Philadelphia, Pennsylvania
1962—*Solomon Burke* (Apollo); *Solomon Burke's Greatest Hits* (Atlantic)   1963—*If You Need Me*   1964—*Rock 'n Soul*   1965—*The Best of Solomon

Burke 1967—*King Solomon* 1968—*I Wish I Knew* 1969—*Proud Mary* (Bell) 1971—*Electronic Magnetism* (MGM) 1972—*Cool Breeze* soundtrack; *We're Almost Home* 1973—*Get Up and Do Something* 1974—*I Have a Dream* (Dunhill) 1975—*Music to Make Love By* (Chess) 1977—*Back to My Roots*; *Greatest Hits* (Atlantic) 1981—*Take Me, Shake Me* (Savoy); *Sidewalks, Fences and Walls* (Infinity) 1984—*Soul Alive!* (Rounder) 1986—*A Change Is Gonna Come* 1989—*The Best of Solomon Burke* (Atlantic) 1992—*Home in Your Heart: The Best of Solomon Burke* (Rhino) 1993—*Soul of the Blues* (Black Top) 1994—*Solomon Burke Live at the House of Blues.*

With his big, powerful voice and fervent-but-controlled emotionality, Solomon Burke was a pioneer of soul music in the early Sixties. By the age of nine he was a preacher and choir soloist for his family's Philadelphia church, the House of God for All People. At 12 he began hosting his own gospel radio show, *Solomon's Temple*, and touring the gospel circuits billed as the "Wonder Boy Preacher." In 1955 he began recording both religious and secular music for Apollo and Singular before signing with Atlantic in 1960.

At Atlantic Burke made some of the first soul records by setting his gospel "preaching" style in song forms borrowed from R&B, rock & roll, and other secular music. His second Atlantic release, "Just Out of Reach (of My Two Open Arms)," was a country & western song, and it became his first hit when it reached #7 on the R&B charts in 1961. Burke called his big-beat dance songs "rock 'n soul music" and won crossover popularity with "Cry to Me" (#44 pop, #5 R&B, 1962), "If You Need Me" (#37 pop, #2 R&B, 1963), "You're Good for Me" (#49 pop, #8 R&B, 1963), "Got to Get You off My Mind" (#22 pop, #1 R&B, 1965), and "Tonight's the Night" (#28 pop, #2 R&B, 1965). He had two more R&B Top Twenty records on Atlantic, including "Keep a Light in the Window" and "Take Me (Just as I Am)" in 1967. He was a primary influence on Mick Jagger, who covered Burke's "You Can Make It If You Try," "Everybody Needs Somebody to Love," and "Cry to Me" on early Rolling Stones albums. Burke was also covered by Otis Redding ("Down in the Valley").

In 1969 he moved to Bell and hit with a cover of John Fogerty's "Proud Mary" (#45 pop, #15 R&B, 1969). In the Seventies Burke recorded with uneven results for MGM, Dunhill, and Chess, but did enjoy a couple of R&B hits, including "Midnight and You" (#14 R&B, 1974) and "You and Your Baby Blues" (#19 R&B, 1975). In 1981 he toured with the Soul Clan, which included Don Covay, Wilson Pickett, Ben E. King, and Joe Tex. That year he also returned to his gospel roots, releasing the Grammy-nominated *Take Me, Shake Me*. He made his film debut in *The Big Easy* (1987). As of 1994 Burke was living in Beverly Hills (he owns a chain of West Coast mortuaries). He is the father of 21 children and a great-grandfather. He continues to tour and record.

T Bone Burnett

Born John Henry Burnett, January 14, 1948, St. Louis, Missouri
1972—*The B-52 Band & the Fabulous Skylarks* (UNI) 1980—*Truth Decay* (Takoma) 1982—*Trap Door* EP (Warner) 1983—*Proof Through the Night* 1984—*Behind the Trap Door* EP (Demon, U.K.) 1986—*T Bone Burnett* 1988—*The Talking Animals* (Columbia) 1992—*The Criminal Under My Own Hat.*

T Bone Burnett is a critically acclaimed singer/songwriter whose own projects have been eclipsed by his work as a producer for such artists as Elvis Costello, Roy Orbison, the BoDeans, Los Lobos, and Counting Crows.

Burnett grew up in Fort Worth, Texas, where he absorbed the area's rich tradition of blues, Tex-Mex, and R&B music. Foreshadowing his later fame, Burnett opened his own studio and opted for producing blues records over attending college. By the early Seventies Burnett had relocated to Los Angeles, where he produced a record for Delbert McClinton and Glen Clark and recorded his first solo album.

After teaming up with singer, songwriter, and Dylan crony Bob Neuwirth and moving to the East Coast, Burnett found himself in the right place at the right time. Recruiting musicians for his Rolling Thunder Revue in 1975, Dylan tapped Burnett to be one of his guitarists. When the tour ended, Burnett and two other Rolling Thunder members, Dave Mansfield and Steve Soles, formed the Alpha Band. After three eccentric, eclectic, but unsuccessful albums (1977's *Alpha Band* and *Spark in the Dark* and 1978's *Statue Makers of Hollywood*), the Alpha Band split up and Burnett went solo.

Burnett, who reportedly influenced Dylan's conversion to Christianity, wove themes of personal religiousness throughout his work. His nimble wordplay and highly crafted songwriting caught the attention of the rock community if not the public; Pete Townshend and Richard Thompson were among the guest musicians on *Proof Through the Night*. Despite critical kudos and vocal support from rock heavyweights—Mark Knopfler and Bono are avid Burnett admirers—Burnett has remained more a cult figure. None of his own albums has ever gone gold.

As a producer, though, Burnett is responsible for some of the most highly regarded albums of the late Eighties and Nineties. Burnett's flair for roots rock comes through on Los Lobos' albums . . . *And a Time to Dance* and *How Will the Wolf Survive?*, the BoDeans' debut, *Love & Hope & Sex & Dreams*, and Marshall Crenshaw's *Downtown*. On Elvis Costello's *King of America*, Burnett revamped Costello's sound by mating him with American musicians and emphasizing an earthier approach. During this period, Burnett also produced a contemporary Christian singer named Leslie Phillips, who soon after changed her name to Sam Phillips and turned to secular music making. Burnett continued producing her and, in 1989, became her husband.

Two years before Roy Orbison's death, Burnett produced the music for the all-star collaborative video that featured Orbison with Bruce Springsteen, Jackson Browne, Tom Waits, and a host of acolytes. His other production credits include Costello's *Spike*, Counting Crows' 1993 debut, *August and Everything After*, Sam Phillips' *Martinis & Bikinis*, and Bruce Cockburn's *Dart to the Heart*.

Billy Burnette
Born May 8, 1953, Memphis, Tennessee
1971—*Billy Burnette* (Columbia/Entrance)   1979—
***Billy Burnette* (Polydor); *Between Friends*   1980—**
Billy Burnette* (Columbia)   1981—*Gimme You
1993—*Coming Home* (Capricorn).

Son of Dorsey Burnette, nephew of Johnny Burnette, and cousin of Rocky Burnette, Billy Burnette moved from Memphis to Los Angeles, where he made his recording debut at age seven with "Hey Daddy." His second record, "Just Because We're Kids," was written by Dr. Seuss (Theodor Seuss Geisel), produced by Herb Alpert, and released on A&M Records when he was 11 years old. During his early teen years he recorded for Warner Bros., made TV appearances, and—at age 13—toured the Far East with the Brenda Lee show. He moved to Memphis in 1972, where he started playing guitar and writing songs at age 16; the next year he began an apprenticeship with producer Chips Moman (Elvis Presley, Aretha Franklin), who produced his first solo album. He also toured with Roger Miller.

Burnette spent most of the Seventies leading his father's band, playing guitar, and singing with Delaney Bramlett. His songs have been recorded by Charlie Rich, Loretta Lynn, Conway Twitty, Irma Thomas, Ray Charles, Jerry Lee Lewis, the Everly Brothers, Charley Pride, Glen Campbell, Gary Stewart, Tammy Wynette, and Levon Helm. He made two country albums in 1979, but it was not until after his father died that year that he began playing rock & roll. His first Columbia album contained remakes of "Tear It Up" and "Honey Hush," two rockers made famous by his father's Rock 'n' Roll Trio.

In 1987 Burnette joined Fleetwood Mac, replacing Lindsey Buckingham; he appears on their *Behind the Mask*. He left the group in January 1993, shortly before the release of his Capricorn debut, *Coming Home*, but returned to Fleetwood Mac for its 1994 tour.

Dorsey Burnette
Born December 28, 1932, Memphis, Tennessee; died August 19, 1979, Canoga Park, California
1963—*Dorsey Burnette* (Capitol)   N.A.—*Dorsey Burnette* (Dot); *Dorsey Burnette's Greatest Hits* (Era); *Tall Oak Tree*   1977—*Things I Treasure* (Calliope).

Dorsey played bass in brother Johnny Burnette's pioneering rockabilly group, the Rock 'n' Roll Trio. Following their brief fling with stardom in 1955–56, he moved with his brother from Memphis to Los Angeles. They wrote a number of successful tunes for Rick Nelson ("Believe What You Say," "It's Late"), and each enjoyed moderate solo success in the early Sixties. Dorsey's hits on Era Records included "Tall Oak Tree" (#23, 1960) and "Hey Little One." From 1968 until his death in 1979 from a heart attack, he was a popular mainstream country artist, charting ten C&W singles. In 1973, after some 20 years in the music business, he was named the year's most promising newcomer by the Academy of Country Music. He died six years later.

Johnny Burnette
Born March 25, 1934, Memphis, Tennessee; died August 1, 1964, Clear Lake, California
1975—*The Very Best of Johnny Burnette* (United Artists)   1976—*Tear It Up* (Solid Smoke)   1979—*Stars of Rock 'n' Roll, vol. 1* (MCA)   1981—*Johnny Burnette's Rock and Roll Trio and Their Rockin' Friends from Memphis* (Rock-a-billy).

With his brother Dorsey, Johnny was a mid-Fifties rockabilly pioneer and had some solo success in the early Sixties. A guitarist, singer, and songwriter, with Dorsey he put together the Rock 'n' Roll Trio along with guitarist Paul Burlison (who released his first solo album in 1981 on a small Memphis label). They had a couple of minor hits like "Train Kept a-Rollin'," distinguished by Burlison's breakthrough fuzz guitar riff, but disbanded in late 1957.

Johnny and Dorsey moved to Los Angeles, where they cowrote several hits for Rick Nelson, among others. In 1958 Johnny got a solo contract with Liberty Records, for which he cleaned up his sound and image. He had the biggest hit of his career in November 1960 as a teen idol with the million-selling "You're Sixteen" (#8). With a couple of lesser hits in 1961, Johnny had his last taste of rock glory. He was plotting a comeback when he drowned in a boating accident in 1964.

Rocky Burnette
Born June 12, 1953, Memphis, Tennessee
1979—*The Son of Rock 'n' Roll* (EMI)   1980—*Rocky Burnette*.

After 26 years in the shadow of his father, Johnny, and uncle Dorsey Burnette, Rocky—the self-proclaimed "Son of Rock 'n' Roll"—came into his own with a #8 hit single, "Tired of Toein' the Line." He began writing songs in his early teens and at age 14, three years after his father's death, became a songwriter with the Acuff-Rose publishing company. His songs were recorded by several minor country singers. After finishing college, where he studied film and the Bible, Rocky made some unreleased recordings for Curb Records. In January 1979, broke after leaving Curb, he traded the rights to a couple of his songs for the studio time to record "Clowns from Outer Space," which he sent to EMI in London. EMI released it as a single. Its B side, "Tired of Toein' the Line," was written in less than half an hour. EMI put it on the A side. It hit first in Europe and Australia, making the British chart in 1979, before crossing to America the following year. To date, that was his first—and last—hit, although he had a single, "Three Flags," that appeared on the lower reaches of the country chart in 1990.

Burning Spear

Born Winston Rodney, March 1, 1945, St. Ann's Parish, Jamaica
1975—*Marcus Garvey* (Island)   1976—*Garvey's Ghost* (Mango); *Man in the Hills*   1977—*Dry and Heavy*; *Live* (Island)   1979—*Harder than the Best*   1980—*Hail H.I.M.* (Tammi)   1981—*Social Living*   1982—*Farover* (Heartbeat)   1983—*Fittest of the Fittest*   1984—*Resistance*; *Reggae Greats* (Mango)   1986—*People of the World* (Slash)   1988—*Mistress Music*   1989—*Live in Paris: Zenith '88*   1990—*Mek We Dweet* (Mango); *100th Anniversary*   1993—*The World Should Know* (Heartbeat).

In a career remarkable for its consistency of both quality and subject matter, Winston Rodney, a.k.a. Burning Spear, concerns himself with oppression—black Jamaicans' heritage of slavery—and mystical transcendence through Rastafarianism. His stark, hypnotic reggae is for the most part far removed from thoughts of love or sex or marijuana, the staples of pop reggae.

Rodney, Burning Spear's sole member since 1977, was born in the same neighborhood as Bob Marley and Thirties black leader Marcus Garvey, St. Ann's Parish, and continues to live in the northern hill region of Jamaica. He formed Burning Spear with bass vocalist Rupert Willington in the late Sixties. (Burning Spear was the name given to Kenyan leader Jomo Kenyatta.) In 1969 the two cut their first singles for Clement "Sir Coxsone" Dodd. Second tenor Delroy Hines joined soon after, and Spear became a vocal trio in the popular Jamaican style, with a repertoire based on traditional songs and chants, dating from slave times. They were not particularly popular, and between 1971 and 1974 the group virtually disappeared.

Burning Spear

In 1974, however, a runaway hit single on Lawrence "Jack Ruby" Lindo's Fox label, "Marcus Garvey" (about a black nationalist), was heard all over Jamaica, followed by "Slavery Days." Dodd released three five-year-old singles—"Swell Headed," "Foggy Road," and "Ethiopians Live It Out"—and Britons as well as Jamaicans snapped them up, along with other singles and two import albums, *Burning Spear* and *Rocking Time*.

Marcus Garvey and its dub remix, *Garvey's Ghost* (which featured guitarist Earl "Chinna" Smith, bassist Robbie Shakespeare, drummer Leroy "Horsemouth" Wallace, and keyboardist Tyrone Downie), were released in the U.S. When Willington and Hines left Burning Spear in 1977, Rodney continued to record solo. He appeared in the film *Rockers* (made in 1977, released in the U.S. in 1980) in concert footage, and in an interview in the documentary *Reggae Sunsplash* (1980). While Rodney's brand of traditional reggae has fallen out of favor in his homeland, he tours the U.S. regularly with his own highly regarded band. In Jamaica he teaches cultural history at the Marcus Garvey Youth Club, which he founded.

Kate Bush

Born July 30, 1958, Bexleyheath, England
1978—*The Kick Inside* (EMI America); *On Stage*; *Lionheart*   1980—*Never for Ever*   1982—*The Dreaming*   1983—*Kate Bush EP*   1985—*Hounds of Love*

1986—*The Whole Story*   1989—*The Sensual World*
(Columbia)   1990—*This Woman's Work* (EMI, U.K.)
1993—*The Red Shoes* (Columbia)

British singer/songwriter Kate Bush's idiosyncratic style
has proved immensely popular in her homeland and
elsewhere in the world. Her debut single, "Wuthering
Heights," hit #1 in the U.K. a month after its release in
January 1978 and went on to become the year's best-
selling single there and in Australia (only Abba was more
popular in Western Europe). But except for "Running Up
That Hill" (#30, 1985), Bush has yet to achieve the same
broad popularity here in the U.S., where her albums, particularly her later, more mature works, have been critically well received. Nonetheless, she has proven a major
influence on artists such as Sinéad O'Connor, Jane
Siberry, Björk, Tori Amos, and Dolores O'Riordan of the
Cranberries.

Bush was something of an art-rock prodigy. The
daughter of a British physician, Bush began playing
piano at the age of 11. She had been writing songs for
two years when family friends told Dave Gilmour of Pink
Floyd about the 16-year-old's four-octave range and interest in the supernatural. Gilmour financed the demo
tape that got her signed to EMI. Because of her age and
developing talent, she spent the next two years studying
music, dance, and mime and writing the songs for her
first album, recorded in 1977 under the supervision of
Gilmour and producer Andrew Powell (Pink Floyd, Alan
Parsons, Cockney Rebel). The album was preceded by
the release of "Wuthering Heights." The song's runaway
success also spurred sales of the Emily Brontë novel. Pat
Benatar covered the song on *Crimes of Passion*.

The Kick Inside went Top Ten in the U.K., and two
singles—"The Man with the Child in His Eyes" (#85 U.S.,
1987) and "Wow," from *Lionheart*—made the Top
Twenty. Bush's double EP of concert recordings also
cracked the Top Ten. She sang on Peter Gabriel's eponymous 1980 album, and her elaborately theatrical self-
produced *The Dreaming*, which entered the U.K. chart at
#3, shows his influence. Soon thereafter she constructed
a state-of-the-art studio in her home, where she records.
A known perfectionist, Bush uses the studio as an instrument, much the way Brian Wilson did, and her
recordings evince a range of influences and styles, from
Celtic to Middle Eastern musics, and a mastery of rock
and pop idioms, from lavish ballads to hard rockers.

Her next release, *Hounds of Love* (#30 U.S., #1 U.K.,
1985), featured her biggest U.S. single, "Running Up That
Hill," as well as two other U.K. Top Twenty singles,
"Cloudbusting" and the title track. Her 1986 retrospective album and video, *The Whole Story*, was another U.K.
#1 hit. With *The Sensual World*, Bush returned to litera-
ture for her inspiration, namely to James Joyce's Molly
Bloom, on whose soliloquies in *Ulysses* Bush based the

title track's concept. *This Woman's Work* is a box set.

After a four-year hiatus, Bush returned with the ambitious (some critics thought confused) *The Red Shoes*,
its title taken from the 1948 Michael Powell film (which
was based on a Hans Christian Andersen tale) about a
young ballerina. Bush, who had long been directing her
own evocative videos, wrote, directed, and costarred
(with performance artist–mime master Lindsay Kemp and
actress Miranda Richardson) in her own 50-minute film.

The Bush Tetras
Formed 1979, New York City, New York
Pat Place (b. 1954, Chicago, Ill.), gtr.; Laura Kennedy
(b. May 30, 1957, Cleveland, Ohio), bass; Dee Pop
(b. Dimitri Papadopoulous, March 14, 1956, Queens,
N.Y.), drums; Cynthia Sley (b. May 3, 1957, Cleve-
land, Ohio), voc., percussion.
1980—*Too Many Creeps* EP (99)   1981—*Rituals* EP
(Stiff)   1983—*Wild Things* cassette (ROIR)
(– Kennedy; – Dee Pop)   1989—*Better Late Than*
***Never* cassette.**

Emerging from Cleveland's "new-wave" and New York's
"no-wave" scenes, the Bush Tetras mixed funk, noise,
and no-nonsense urban-jungle lyrics. In 1977 James
Chance [see entry] enlisted Pat Place for his incipient
Contortions. Although she had no musical experience,
she played bass, then slide guitar (as a Contortion and
sometime member of James White and the Blacks)
and developed her atonal slide style. Laura Kennedy and
Cynthia Sley, classmates at the Cleveland Institute of
Art, were in a performing art group associated with Pere
Ubu, Johnny and the Dicks. Kennedy moved to New York
in 1977 to make films. Through a Cleveland acquaintance, Contortion Adele Bertei, she also worked as a
roadie for the Contortions. When that band broke up in
1979, she joined rehearsals with Bertei, Place, Dee Pop,
and guitarist Jimmy Uliano. Bertei and Uliano dropped
out after several months (Bertei went on to form the
Bloods) and were replaced by lyricist and intoner Sley,
who had been in New York since 1979 designing clothes
for Lydia Lunch and Judy Nylon.

The Bush Tetras debuted in New York in early 1980.
Their first record, a three-song EP, featured the club hit
"Too Many Creeps." It was followed by a four-song EP,
Rituals, produced by Topper Headon of the Clash; it appeared on national disco charts early in 1982. (The
band's other releases include a 1983 live cassette and a
1989 anthology.)

In 1983 the band lost momentum as members began
dropping out. By the mid-Eighties, Sley had formed a
new band, Mad Orphan (the name later changed to the
Lovelies), with her husband, ex-Voidoid Ivan Julian (the
couple later split). In the Nineties Sley started the all-
women band 1-800-BOXX, before calling it quits. Pop

formed the group Floor Kiss with his then-wife, ex–John Cale vocalist Deerfrance, later playing drums with a succession of outfits. Kennedy left the music business, and Place turned up in the Nineties, playing guitar behind spoken-word artist Maggie Estep. The Bush Tetras briefly reunited in 1992 to play a handful of shows.

Bushwick Bill: See Geto Boys

Jerry Butler

Born December 8, 1939, Sunflower, Mississippi
1964—*Delicious Together* (with Betty Everett) (Vee-Jay)   1967—*Mr. Dream Merchant* (Mercury)
1968—*Golden Hits Live; The Soul Goes On*   1969—*The Ice Man Cometh; Ice on Ice*   1970—*You and Me; The Best of Jerry Butler*   1971—*Jerry Butler Sings Assorted Sounds; Gene & Jerry—One & One* (with Gene Chandler); *Sagittarius Movement*
1972—*The Spice of Life*   1973—*The Power of Love*
1974—*Sweet Sixteen*   1976—*Love's on the Menu* (Motown)   1977—*Suite for the Single Girl; Thelma and Jerry* (with Thelma Houston); *It All Comes Out in My Song*   1978—*The Soul Goes On* (Mercury)
1979—*Nothing Says I Love You Like I Love You* (Philadelphia International)   1980—*The Best Love I Ever Had*   1982—*Ice and Hot* (Fountain)   1987—*The Best of Jerry Butler* (Rhino)   1993—*Time and Faith* (Ichiban).

A distinctive soul singer for nearly four decades, Jerry Butler and childhood friend Curtis Mayfield defined Chicago soul with the Impressions. Butler, who had a gospel background, moved with his family from Mississippi to Chicago in 1942. By the time he and Mayfield put together Jerry Butler and the Impressions in 1957 [see entry], Butler was perfecting a delicate, hesitant delivery. The Impressions had their first hit with "For Your Precious Love" (#11, 1958), cowritten by Butler. Butler went solo shortly thereafter but worked with Mayfield as songwriter and producer for several more years. The team scored its first post-Impressions hit in 1960 with Mayfield's "He Will Break Your Heart" (#7). Specializing in mellow ballads, Butler continued to score occasional hits until he moved to Philadelphia in 1967 and shifted gears with Gamble and Huff.

Butler's two albums with that production team, *The Ice Man Cometh* and *Ice on Ice,* were among the most highly acclaimed soul works of the early Seventies. Hits of this collaboration include "Never Give You Up" (#20, 1968), "Hey, Western Union Man" (#16, 1968), and "Only the Strong Survive" (#4, 1969). In 1971 Butler and Gene Chandler recorded together, and later in the decade he teamed up with Thelma Houston. Butler remained active on the lounge circuit, and in 1979 he reunited with Gam-

ble and Huff for *Nothing Says I Love You Like I Love You* and its followup, *The Best Love I Ever Had.* In 1980 he founded Fountain Records.

He was inducted with the Impressions into the Rock and Roll Hall of Fame in 1991. Shortly thereafter he was elected to public office in Chicago, and has since served as Cook County commissioner while continuing to record.

Paul Butterfield Blues Band/Paul Butterfield

Formed 1963, Chicago, Illinois
Paul Butterfield (b. Dec. 17, 1942, Chicago; d. May 4, 1987, North Hollywood, California), voc., harmonica; Jerome Arnold, bass; Sam Lay, drums; Elvin Bishop (b. Oct. 21, 1942, Tulsa, Okla.), gtr; Mark Naftalin, kybds.; Mike Bloomfield (b. July 28, 1944, Chicago; d. Feb. 15, 1981, San Francisco, Calif.), gtr.
1965—*The Paul Butterfield Blues Band* (Elektra) (– Lay; + Billy Davenport, drums)   1966—*East-West* (– Bloomfield)   1967—*The Resurrection of Pigboy Crabshaw* (– Bishop; + various members)
1968—*In My Own Dream*   1969—*Keep On Moving*
1971—*Sometimes I Just Feel Like Smilin'; Live*
1972—(Group disbands) *Golden Butter—The Best of the Paul Butterfield Blues Band; Offer You Can't Refuse* (Red Lightnin').
Paul Butterfield's Better Days, formed 1972, Woodstock, N.Y. (original lineup: Butterfield; Billy Rich, bass; Amos Garrett, gtr.; Geoff Muldaur, voc.; Christopher Parker, drums; Ronnie Barron, kybds.):
1973—*Better Days* (Bearsville); *It All Comes Back*
1976—*Put It in Your Ear*   1981—*North-South.*
Paul Butterfield solo: 1986—*The Legendary Paul Butterfield Rides Again* (Amherst).

Paul Butterfield, a white singer and harmonica player who apprenticed with black bluesmen, helped spur the American blues revival of the Sixties. The teenage Butterfield ventured into Chicago's South Side clubs, eventually working his way into onstage jams with Howlin' Wolf, Buddy Guy, Otis Rush, Little Walter, Magic Sam, and other blues legends. Butterfield played with University of Chicago classmate Elvin Bishop in bar bands named the Salt and Pepper Shakers and the South Side Olympic Blues Team. In 1963 he formed the Paul Butterfield Blues Band with two former members of Howlin' Wolf's band, Jerome Arnold and Sam Lay, later adding Bishop, Mark Naftalin, and lead guitarist Mike Bloomfield. The group built a strong local following, and its debut album was released in 1965. At that year's Newport Folk Festival, after playing its own set, the Butterfield band backed Bob Dylan for his controversial premiere electric performance. East-West featured extended jams and showed the influences of jazz and In-

Butthole Surfers: King Coffey, Paul Leary, Jeff Pinkus, Gibby Haynes, Theresa Nervosa

dian music. Bloomfield left to form Electric Flag, Bishop moved to lead guitar.

By 1967 Butterfield had begun the first of many experiments, adding a brass section (including David Sanborn on alto saxophone) and changing his orientation from blues to R&B. He played on Muddy Waters' 1969 album *Fathers and Sons* and, after disbanding the Blues Band in 1972, moved to Woodstock, New York. There he formed Butterfield's Better Days with Amos Garrett, Geoff Muldaur, and Ronnie Barron.

Butterfield made an appearance at the Band's *Last Waltz* concert in 1976, and during the late Seventies he toured with Levon Helm's RCO All Stars and with ex-Band bassist Rick Danko in the Danko-Butterfield Band. In early 1980, while recording *North-South* in Memphis, Butterfield was stricken with a perforated intestine and peritonitis, which forced him to undergo four major operations over the next several years. Butterfield's next—and last—album, *The Legendary Paul Butterfield Rides Again,* came out in 1986, one year before the 44-year-old musician, an alcoholic, was found dead in his apartment.

Butthole Surfers

Formed 1981, San Antonio, Texas
Gibby Haynes (b. Gibson Haynes, ca. 1957), voc.;
Paul Leary (b. ca. 1958), gtr.   1983—*Butthole*
***Surfers* (Alternative Tentacles) (+ King Coffey,**
drums; + Theresa Nervosa, drums)   1984—*Live*
PCPPEP*   1985—*Psychic . . . Powerless . . . Another
Man's Sac* (Touch and Go); *Cream Corn from the
Socket of Davis* EP   1986—*Rembrandt Pussyhorse

(+ Jeff Pinkus, bass)   1987—*Locust Abortion Technician*   1988—*Hairway to Steven*   1989—*Double Live* (Latino Bugger Veil); *Widowermaker!* (Touch and Go) (– Nervosa)   1990—*"The Hurdy Gurdy Man"* EP (Rough Trade)   1991—*Piouhgd*   1993—*Independent Worm Saloon* (Capitol)   1995—*The Hole Truth and Nothing Butt.*

Butthole Surfers are perhaps the most perversely confrontational and calculatedly outrageous American postpunk band. Their stage shows have included everything from backdrop projections of auto accidents and sex-change operations to androgynous nude dancers, crude pyrotechnics, and the incessant gross-out shenanigans of singer Gibby Haynes. (At an early show he removed the dress he was wearing during a performance and—depending on who tells the story—either simulated sex or had sex with one of the band's dancers.) Though the Butthole Surfers' music combines the noisy, avant-garde tendencies of late-Seventies no wave with the throbbing, distorted drive of hardcore, much of it is informed by classic, psychedelic rock.

Haynes, whose father hosted a children's TV show in Dallas under the name Mr. Peppermint, met Paul Leary in 1977 while attending San Antonio's Trinity College. Four years later, Haynes, then doing graduate work in accounting, and Leary, son of the business school's dean, formed a band. They became Butthole Surfers when an announcer mistook one of their song titles for their band name. In San Francisco in 1981, the Surfers met the Dead Kennedys' Jello Biafra, who signed them to his Alternative Tentacles label. The band's self-titled first album contained the legendary dada-hardcore anthem, "The Shah Sleeps in Lee Harvey's Grave."

Between 1982 and 1985 the Surfers went through a succession of bass players and drummers. They toured constantly, perfecting their bizarre show by adding dancers, sometimes two drummers, and cultivating a hard-core cultish Deadhead-style following. Membership stabilized with the addition of King Coffey on drums in 1983. In 1985 the group signed with Touch and Go, and its music got even weirder and more depraved. Haynes' gut-wrenching sleaze and pseudo-Satanic ranting hit an all-time low on such songs as "Lady Sniff" (Psychic . . . Powerless . . .) and "Sweet Loaf" (Locust Abortion Technician's spoof of Black Sabbath's "Sweet Leaf"), while Leary's inventive lead guitar chugged and meandered around newly added instrumentation such as acoustic guitars, piano, organ, violin, and strange effects, like speeded-up and slowed-down vocals, and tape manipulations. Rembrandt Pussyhorse stands as one of the most "out" psychedelic albums of the post-punk era, featuring snaky, Middle Eastern–like instrumentation and drones, twisted folk melodies, avant-garde improvisation, industrial noise and feedback, and gastrointestinal sounds. Haynes' attempts to shock include deranged laughter, Exorcist-like growls, and lyrics such as "There's a creep in the cellar that I'm gonna let in . . . and he really freaks me out when he peels off his skin." After appearing on the first Lollapalooza Tour in 1991, the Surfers signed with Capitol. Two years later the band released its major-label debut, the slightly more accessible Independent Worm Saloon, produced by former Led Zeppelin bassist John Paul Jones. In 1993 Haynes also formed a side band with actor Johnny Depp called P.

The Butthole Surfers' music has received radically mixed reviews, with underground observers generally applauding the envelope-pushing experimentations, and many mainstream rock critics put off by the band's constant arty attempts to shock. Through it all, the group is among the few Eighties fringe acts to rise from independent to major-label status with its core audience and sound intact.

Buzzcocks

Formed 1975, Manchester, England
Howard Devoto (b. Howard Trafford), voc.; Steve Diggle, gtr., bass; John Maher, drums; Pete Shelley (b. Peter McNeish, Apr. 17, 1955), voc., gtr.
1977—(– Devoto; + Garth Smith, bass) 1978—(– Smith; + Steve Garvey, bass) Another Music in a Different Kitchen (UA/I.R.S.); Love Bites 1979—Singles Going Steady (I.R.S.) 1981—A Different Kind of Tension (group disbands) 1993—(Group reforms: Shelley; Diggle; + Tony Barber, bass; + Phil Barker, drums) Trade Test Transmissions (Caroline).

The Buzzcocks were a successful U.K. new-wave singles band during the late Seventies, combining Beatlesque romance and melodicism with a buzzsaw guitar attack and blistering punk-rock tempos. They came together at Manchester University in 1975 and made frequent London club appearances the following year. Their first recordings, including the four-song EP called Spiral Scratch (widely credited as Britain's first independent-label punk recording), were made with visionary early group leader Howard Devoto. When Devoto left the group in 1977 to form Magazine [see entry], Diggle switched from bass to guitar, and Garth Smith joined. Pete Shelley (who himself left the group in February 1981) became chief vocalist and songwriter. During their second U.S. tour in 1980, they picked up an enthusiastic coterie of followers, but their record sales were disappointing. In mid-1980, displeased with its lack of international success, the group disbanded. Shelley had a British hit on his own with "Homosapien," a sharp turn from the trademark Buzzcocks sound to synth-and-sequencer dance music.

In 1989 Shelley, Diggle, Garvey, and Maher reunited for a U.S. tour. Four years later, with a new rhythm section—and with Nirvana's Kurt Cobain having told the rock press they were an inspiration—Buzzcocks recorded a well-received comeback album, Trade Test Transmissions, and toured the U.S.

The Byrds

Formed 1964, Los Angeles, California
Roger McGuinn (b. James Joseph McGuinn III, July 13, 1942, Chicago, Ill.), gtr., voc.; Chris Hillman (b. Dec. 4, 1942, Los Angeles), bass, voc.; Gene Clark (b. Harold Eugene Clark, Nov. 17, 1941, Tipton, Mo.; d. May 24, 1991, Sherman Oaks, Calif.), voc., tambourine, gtr.; David Crosby (b. David Van Cortland, Aug. 14, 1941, Los Angeles), gtr., voc.; Michael Clarke (b. June 3, 1944, New York City, N.Y.; d. Dec. 19, 1993, Treasure Island, Fla.), drums.
1965—Mr. Tambourine Man (Columbia) 1966—Turn! Turn! Turn! (– Clark); Fifth Dimension 1967—Younger Than Yesterday (– Crosby; – Clarke) 1968—(+ Kevin Kelley [b. 1945, Calif.], drums; + Gram Parsons [b. Ingram Cecil Connor III, Nov. 5, 1946, Winter Haven, Fla.; d. Sep. 19, 1973, Yucca Valley, Calif.], gtr., voc.) Notorious Byrd Brothers; Sweetheart of the Rodeo (– Hillman; – Parsons; – Kelley; + Clarence White [b. June 6, 1944, Lewiston, Maine; d. July 14, 1973, Palmdale, Calif.], gtr., voc.; + Gene Parsons [b. Apr. 9, 1944], drums; + John York, bass) 1969—Dr. Byrds and Mr. Hyde (– York; + Skip Battin [b. Feb. 2, 1934, Gallipolis, Ohio], bass, voc.); The Ballad of Easy Rider 1970—The Byrds

(*Untitled*) 1971—*Byrdmaniax* 1972—*Farther Along* (– Gene Parsons; – Battin; + John Guerin, bass; + temporary drummers Daryl Dragon [b. Aug. 27, 1942, Los Angeles], Jim Moon); *Best of the Byrds—Greatest Hits, vol. 2* 1973—(Group disbands; original group reunites for one-shot album) *The Byrds* (Asylum); *Preflyte* (Columbia) 1980—*Singles 1965–67* 1990—*The Byrds*.
Roger (Jim) McGuinn solo: 1973—*Roger McGuinn* (Columbia) 1974—*Peace on You* 1975—*Roger McGuinn and Band* 1976—*Cardiff Rose* 1977—*Thunderbyrd* 1991—*Back from Rio* (Arista).
McGuinn, Clark and Hillman: 1979—*McGuinn, Clark and Hillman* (Capitol).
McGuinn and Hillman: 1980—*City*.
Gene Clark (solo): 1977—*Two Sides to Every Story* (Polydor) 1991—*Echoes* (Legacy) 1994—*Looking for a Connection* (Dos).

The Byrds, led by Roger McGuinn, pioneered folk rock and later country rock. With their high harmonies, ringing guitars (especially McGuinn's electric Rickenbacker 12-string), and obsession with studio technique, they also became a sonic model for many rock bands, including the Eagles, Tom Petty, the latter-day Fleetwood Mac, and R.E.M.

The band was formed in summer 1964 as the Jet Set (McGuinn was fascinated by airplanes) and toyed with the name Beefeaters before settling on the Byrds, misspelled a la the Beatles. McGuinn had been a member of the Limeliters and the Chad Mitchell Trio and had backed Judy Collins until he went solo in 1964. Hillman had worked in the Hillmen and the Green Grass Group. Gene Clark was a member of the New Christy Minstrels. He and Crosby met at L.A.'s Troubadour on a hootenanny night. A few months after their formation, with Beatles publicist Derek Taylor on the payroll, the Byrds were touted as "L.A.'s answer to London." After signing with Columbia in November 1964 (jazz trumpeter Miles Davis had recommended them to the record company) they recorded demos released years later as *Preflyte*. In January 1965 they met Bob Dylan, who publicly endorsed them and, more important, provided their first hit, the #1 "Mr. Tambourine Man." The single, cut by studio musicians, with McGuinn on guitar and the group singing, had Dylan's lyrics, a guitar hook, chorus harmonies, and a rock rhythm section: folk rock. *Mr. Tambourine Man*, released in June 1965, went to #6.

In 1966 the Byrds had a major hit with the anthemic "Turn! Turn! Turn!"—a Bible passage set to music by Pete Seeger. But the album of the same name suffered a dearth of new material, and the Byrds were less commercial for the rest of their existence. By the time *Fifth Dimension* was released in summer 1966, Gene Clark had left. He had frequently argued with McGuinn, and

he suffered from a fear of flying that made touring difficult. His departure, plus their somewhat avant-garde LP, marked the start of the Byrds' "space rock" phase. The hit single "Eight Miles High" (#14, 1966) from *Fifth Dimension* solidified their new style, sporting a thunderous bass line, free-form guitar lines, and a corps of otherworldly harmonies. It was also one of the first records to be widely banned because of supposedly drug-oriented lyrics.

As McGuinn's technocratic grip on the Byrds began to tighten, internal tensions increased and occasionally erupted into onstage fisticuffs. After 1967's *Younger Than Yesterday*, Crosby was gone, bound for superstardom with Stills, Nash and Young [see entry]. McGuinn and the two remaining Byrds—bassist Hillman and drummer Michael Clarke—added studio players for 1968's countryish *The Notorious Byrd Brothers*. Praised by some critics as a conceptual masterpiece, it fared less well with the record-buying public. By fall 1968's *Sweetheart of the Rodeo*, Clarke had left to join the Dillard and Clark group. *Sweetheart*, recorded in Nashville with newcomers Gram Parsons and Kevin Kelley, mixed country and rock as they had mixed folk and rock, anticipating groups from the Eagles to Firefall.

By October McGuinn was the only original Byrd remaining, as Parsons and Hillman left to continue their country experiments with the Flying Burrito Brothers [see entry]. He kept the patchwork Byrds alive through 1973 with a series of partners who were occasionally brilliant (like former bluegrass guitarist Clarence White) but more often merely functional. The various combos toured steadily and put out a series of mildly successful albums, including *Untitled*, which contained McGuinn's "Chestnut Mare" (cowritten with Jacques Levy, a later collaborator with Dylan), one of his signature tunes. Despite the regrouping of the original lineup for a one-shot album in 1973 (which, despite dubious quality—Hillman later called the disc "embarrassing"—reached the Top Twenty), the Byrds were finally put to rest.

McGuinn subsequently embarked on a low-key solo career. In late 1975 and early 1976 he was prominently featured in Dylan's Rolling Thunder Revue. With fellow Revue trouper Mick Ronson producing, he recorded *Cardiff Rose*. In early 1977 he assembled a new band, wryly dubbed Thunderbyrd, and recorded an album of the same name. By late in the year he was playing occasional dates in tandem with Clark, and the alliance soon expanded to include Hillman as well. In 1979 the three recorded their self-titled debut disc and enjoyed some pop success with "Don't You Write Her Off" (#33, 1979). In 1980 McGuinn and Hillman returned with *City*, before the band gradually fragmented, and McGuinn took up his solo career again. It was more than ten years before he released another LP. *Back from Rio*, with assistance from admirers such as Tom Petty and Elvis Costello, reached #44.

The same month the LP charted, January 1991, the Byrds were inducted into the Rock and Roll Hall of Fame. McGuinn, Hillman, and Crosby had been at odds with Michael Clarke and Gene Clark for touring using the Byrds name. To prevent them from doing so, in 1989 McGuinn, Hillman, and Crosby had played three dates to establish their legal right to the name. A year later they recorded four songs for inclusion on the four-CD *The Byrds* anthology.

Just four months after the Hall of Fame ceremonies, Gene Clark died at age 46; in 1993 Michael Clarke (who, undeterred, continued to play clubs billed as Michael Clarke's Byrds) died of liver failure.

David Byrne

Born May 14, 1952, Dumbarton, Scotland
1981—*The Complete Score from the Broadway Production of "The Catherine Wheel"* (Sire)   1985—*Music for "The Knee Plays"* (ECM)   1986—*Sounds from True Stories* (Sire)   1988—*Married to the Mob* soundtrack (Reprise)   1989—*Rei Momo* (Luaka Bop/Sire)   1991—*The Forest*   1992—*Uh-Oh* 1994—*David Byrne*.
With Brian Eno: 1981—*My Life in the Bush of Ghosts* (Sire).
With Ryuichi Sakamoto and Cong Su: 1988—*The Last Emperor* soundtrack (Virgin Movie Music).

In his work outside Talking Heads [see entry], David Byrne has explored electronics, performance art, and world music. Byrne was born in Scotland but raised in Baltimore, Maryland, where his father was an electronics engineer. Coming from a working-class environment, Byrne felt alienated from the many wealthy students he encountered as an art student at the Rhode Island School of Design. He dropped out after one year but stayed in Providence, playing one-man shows with a ukulele and eventually forming the Artistics (a.k.a. the Autistics), and then Talking Heads.

Byrne's first project outside the Heads, *My Life in the Bush of Ghosts,* was a collaboration with Heads producer Brian Eno. The resulting collage of electronic music, vocal tapes, and African and other third world rhythms was widely acclaimed as groundbreaking. It ran into controversy when Moslems objected to the track "Qu'ran" for its use of religious text; it was replaced with "Very Very Hungry." This was the first of many times Byrne has been accused by detractors of colonialist appropriation.

Byrne next turned to theatrical collaborations, writing music for the Twyla Tharp dance piece *The Catherine Wheel.* For *Knee Plays,* a section of Robert Wilson's epic *CIVIL warS,* Byrne incorporated text and music based on New Orleans brass bands. In 1986 he wrote, directed, and starred in the film *True Stories,* a series of vignettes about American eccentrics. He produced and wrote the majority of songs for the film soundtrack (not the same as the Talking Heads album) and performed two of them. He also composed the soundtrack for the Jonathan Demme film *Married to the Mob.* With Ryuichi Sakamoto and Cong Su, he won an Oscar for the soundtrack to *The Last Emperor.* Byrne has also written soundtracks for two movies by Philip Haas.

In 1988 Byrne's conversion to world music led him to form Luaka Bop Records, which has released, along with Byrne's records, music by Brazilian, Cuban, and Asian artists, as well as the U.K. avant-dance band A. R. Kane and the Los Angeles rockers Geggy Tah. He also made Cuban records available in the U.S. for the first time since the 1961 boycott. Byrne collaborated with a number of Latin musicians on the Steve Lillywhite–produced *Rei Momo,* particularly percussionist Milton Cardona, arranger Angel Fernandez, and songwriters Willie Colon and Johnny Pacheco. He again ran into accusations of white privilege when Colon said in *Billboard* that Byrne had exploited musicians starved for validation. Byrne included many of the album's performers in his 14-piece band on the *Rei Momo* world tour.

Byrne's film *Ilé Aiyé (The House of Life),* a documentary about Yoruban dance-music rituals, kicked off the *Alive from Off Center* series on PBS in summer 1989. He worked with Robert Wilson again on 1991's *The Forest,* a composition for a full orchestra.

Uh-Oh featured more conventional rock songs, with Byrne using the same band on every track—although that band included Meters bassist George Porter Jr., Latin percussionists Hector Rosado and Cafe, and Miami drummer Oscar Salas. Byrne formed an all-new band with a more stripped-down sound (Todd Turkisher on drums, Paul Socolow on bass, and Mauro Refosco on mallet instruments and percussion) for *David Byrne,* which marked a return to the wry, affectless writing style he perfected with Talking Heads.

Byrne, whom *Time* dubbed "Rock's Renaissance Man" in a 1986 cover story, produced an EP, *Mesopotamia,* for the B-52's, and in 1983 produced *Waiting* for Fun Boy Three. His photographs have been featured in *Interview, Artforum,* and several exhibits.

C

Roy C

Born Roy Charles Hammond, 1943, New York City, New York
1973—*Sex and Soul* (Mercury)   1975—*Something Nice*   1977—*More Sex and More Soul*.

Roy C's songs about love and infidelity were rarely real hits—he made the R&B Top Twenty only once—but their consistency earned him respect within his profession. After changing his name from Roy Charles Hammond to avoid being mistaken for either Ray Charles or Roy Hamilton, he joined the Long Beach, Long Island–based vocal group the Genies as lead singer in 1956. In 1959 the Genies had a minor R&B hit entitled "Who's That Knockin'" before breaking up later that year.

   C began his solo career with his biggest success: a Black Hawk single, "Shotgun Wedding" (#14 R&B, 1965). Subsequent recordings for Black Hawk and Shout (where he was produced by Bert Berns) fared less well. In 1969 he formed his own record company, Alaga, and returned to the charts in 1971 with "Got to Get Enough." After writing and producing the Mark IV's 1972 single "Honey I Still Love You," C signed with Mercury. The label repackaged his early singles in album form and released "Don't Blame the Man" (1973), "Loneliness Had Got a Hold of Me" (1974), and "Love Me Till Tomorrow Comes" (1975), among others. Meanwhile, former Genie Claude Johnson teamed up with Roland Trone (d. 1983) and became Don (Trone) and Juan, today best remembered for "What's Your Name" (1962).

Cabaret Voltaire

Formed 1973, Sheffield, England
Stephen Mallinder (b. Sheffield), voc., bass, perc.; Richard H. Kirk (b. Sheffield), gtr., kybds., wind instruments; Christopher R. Watson, kybds., tape machines.
1978—*Extended Play* EP (Rough Trade, U.K.)
1979—*Mix Up*   1980—*Live at the YMCA 27-10-79*; *Three Mantras*; *The Voice of America*; *1974–1976* cassette (Industrial, U.K.)   1981—*3 Crépuscule Tracks* EP (Rough Trade, U.K.); *Live at the Lyceum* cassette; *Red Mecca* (– Watson)   1982—*2 × 45*; *Hail! Live in Japan*   1983—*The Crackdown* (Some Bizarre, U.K.); *Johnny YesNo* (Doublevision, U.K.)   1984—*Micro-Phonies* (Some Bizarre-Virgin, U.K.)   1985—*Drinking Gasoline* (Caroline); *The Arm of the Lord*   1986—*The Drain Train* EP (Mute)   1987—*The Golden Moments of Cabaret Voltaire* (Rough Trade, U.K.); *Code* (EMI Manhattan)   1988—*Eight Crépuscule Tracks* (Giant)   1990—*Listen Up with Cabaret Voltaire* (Mute); *The Living Legends*; *Groovy, Laidback and Nasty* (Parlophone, U.K.)   1992—*Plasticity* (Instinct, U.K.); "*International Language*"

1994—*The Conversation*.
Richard H. Kirk solo: 1980—*Disposable Half-Truths* cassette (Industrial, U.K.)   1983—*Time High Fiction* (Doublevision, U.K.)   1986—*Black Jesus Voice* (Rough Trade, U.K.); *Ugly Spirit*.
Peter Hope and Richard Kirk: 1987—*Hoodoo Talk* (Native-Wax Trax!).
Stephen Mallinder solo: 1982—*Pow-Wow* (Fetish, U.K.)   1985—*Pow-Wow Plus* (Doublevision, U.K.).

Cabaret Voltaire was one of the earliest electronic industrial-dance groups. Along with Throbbing Gristle and Psychic TV, the trio had a profound influence on the techno, ambient, and industrial styles that came to prominence in the late Eighties and early Nineties.

Little is known about the members of Cabaret Voltaire, except that in the early Seventies, seven teenagers came together in the industrial city of Sheffield and began making tapes of noises to play at parties for laughs. The group was soon whittled down to just Stephen Mallinder, Richard Kirk, and Christopher Watson, who hooked up with the music department at Sheffield Haddam University and gained access to a synthesizer, tape recorders, and other instruments.

Inspired by the dada art movement, the ambient work of Brian Eno, and their industrial environment, Cabaret Voltaire blended the sounds of everyday objects with the textures of musical instruments to create aural collages of noise, beats, and disembodied vocals. They named themselves after the dadaist club formed in Zurich in 1917 by Hugo Ball. Though Cabaret Voltaire adopted punk's anti–rock-star attitude, it was not a punk band, and in fact was bottled off stage by punks during its first London show at the Lyceum in April 1978.

Cabaret Voltaire's early recordings are harsh and abrasive; their first EP contains a distorted version of Lou Reed's "Here She Comes Now." As the group matured during its prolific early-Eighties period, it became increasingly interested in Middle Eastern sounds and more accessible dance music; it hit an artistic peak with 1982's *2 × 45*.

Watson left the group in 1981 to work in television and later showed up with the avant-garde Hafler Trio. By the mid-Eighties Cabaret Voltaire's music had become slicker, though the group never scored a major hit. In the late Eighties it had begun flirting with house music, releasing 12 different mixes of the 1989 single "Hypnotized." By the Nineties Cabaret Voltaire had returned to the more ambient sounds of its earlier days.

Cactus: See Vanilla Fudge

The Cadets
Formed 1954, Los Angeles, California
Original lineup: Ted Taylor (d. Oct. 22, 1988, Louisiana), tenor voc.; William "Dub" Jones, bass voc.; Aaron Collins, voc.; Willie Davis, voc.; Lloyd McCraw, voc.
1957—*Rockin' 'n' Reelin'* (Modern).

This Los Angeles vocal quintet was actually two groups in one. As the Jacks, they sang soul ballads for RPM, scoring their biggest hit with a cover of the Feathers' "Why Don't You Write Me" (#4 R&B) in 1955. As the Cadets, they sang rock & roll and R&B jump songs for the Modern label. Their cover of the Jayhawks' "Stranded in the Jungle" reached #4 on the R&B chart and #15 pop in 1956. An interesting footnote: Aaron Collins' sisters Rosie and Betty became the Teen Queens, famous today for their hit "Eddie My Love" (#14, pop, #2 R&B, 1956), which Collins penned with Willie Davis.

When the Cadets broke up in the late Fifties, Davis and Collins continued with a revamped lineup; William Jones joined the Coasters. With his gospel-style wail, Ted Taylor opted for a solo career, which began promisingly in 1965 with "Stay Away from My Baby" (#14, 1965), followed by "It's Too Late" (#30, 1969), "Something Strange Is Goin' On in My House" (#26, 1970), and "How's Your Love Life, Baby" (#44 R&B, 1971). He was killed with his wife in a car accident while on tour. Jones has sung with a latter-day version of the Coasters, while Collins and Davis have retired from the business.

The Cadillacs
Formed 1953, New York City, New York
Lineup circa 1954: Earl Carroll (b. Nov. 2, 1937, New York City), lead voc.; Robert Phillips (b. 1935, New York City), voc.; La Verne Drake (b. 1938, New York City), voc.; Johnny "Gus" Willingham (b. 1937, New York City), voc.; James "Poppa" Clark, voc.
1990—*The Best of the Cadillacs* (Rhino).

A distinguished Fifties R&B group whose legend has grown appreciably over the years, the Cadillacs considered uptempo numbers like "Speedo" (sometimes spelled "Speedoo") (#17 pop, 1956; #3 R&B, 1955) their forte, although latter-day fans often prefer their slow ballads. Originally called the Carnations, the Cadillacs came together in 1953 after a series of informal sing-along sessions in Harlem. A short time later they met manager Esther Navaroo, who persuaded them to change their name to the Cadillacs and helped them record "Gloria," a song she had written. (Navaroo received writer's credit for many of the group's releases, although it was later revealed that some songs had been written by the group members.) Their stage show included flamboyant attire and tight choreography, a precursor of and influence on the Motown style, not surprising since the Temptations and the Four Tops fell under the tutelage of the Cadillacs' choreographer, Cholly Atkins.

In late 1955 the group released "Speedo," about its happy-go-lucky singer Earl Carroll. The record employed fast scat harmonies and became one of the Cadillacs' few hits, along with "Peek-a-Boo" (#28, 1959) and "What You Bet" (#30 R&B, 1961). Other releases included "Zoom," "Woe Is Me," and "Rudolph the Red-Nosed Reindeer" (1956). In 1957 the group splintered into two singing groups, both calling themselves the Cadillacs. The group that included Carroll released "Jay Walker," "Please Mr. Johnson" (both 1959), and several other singles through 1961. Through 1963 both groups of Cadillacs released records to dwindling public interest.

In 1961 Earl Carroll left to replace Cornell Gunter in the Coasters. Three years later Carroll's new group released "Speedo's Back in Town," a tribute to Speedo recorded live at the Apollo. The Cadillacs continued to run through the Sixties. In the early Eighties the group re-formed with original members Carroll and Phillips. Carroll is now on the custodial staff of Public School 87 in New York City, where he remains a local celebrity.

J. J. Cale

Born Jean Jacques Cale, December 5, 1938, Oklahoma City, Oklahoma
1972—Naturally (Shelter); Really   1974—Okie
1976—Troubadour   1979—Number 5   1981—
Shades   1982—Grasshopper (Mercury)   1983—#8
1990—Travelog (Silvertone)   1992—Number 10
1994—Closer to You (Virgin).

The essentials of self-described "semiretired," reclusive singer/songwriter J. J. Cale's style—sinuous, bluesy guitar lines and mumbly, near-whispered vocals—have been popularized by Eric Clapton and Dire Straits. Cale's songs have been hits for other artists; most well-known are Clapton's versions of "After Midnight" and "Cocaine."

Cale took up guitar at age ten. After playing in a succession of Tulsa, Oklahoma, bands (one group included Leon Russell) during high school, he went on the road in 1959 and played in the Grand Ole Opry road company. By the early Sixties, he was back in Tulsa playing with Russell, and in 1964 the two moved to Los Angeles with fellow Oklahoma native Carl Radle (later of Derek and the Dominos). Cale hooked up with Delaney and Bonnie, and by 1965 he was recording on his own, including the first release of "After Midnight." He left Delaney and Bonnie and in 1967 returned to Tulsa.

Radle passed on some of Cale's homemade demo tapes to Denny Cordell, and Cale became one of the first signings of Cordell and Russell's Shelter Records in 1969. Following Clapton's 1970 success with "After Midnight"

(#18), Cale recorded Naturally in 1972, from which "Crazy Mama" went to #22. "Magnolia," also on that album, was later covered by Poco and José Feliciano. Throughout the Seventies, Cale recorded and toured at a leisurely pace.

Cale moved to Mercury Records in 1982, releasing two albums, Grasshopper (#149, 1982) and #8 (1983). Disappointed by their sales, he asked to be released from his contract. He spent the next six years living in a mobile home outside Los Angeles, emerging only for an annual tour.

Cale released two albums on Silvertone, a U.K.–based independent label, Travelog (#131, 1990), and Number 10 (1992). He also produced John (Paul) Hammond's Got Love If You Want It (1992) and Trouble No More (1994). Closer to You continued Cale's trademark laidback bluesy songwriting.

John Cale

Born March 9, 1942, Cwmamman, South Wales
1969—Vintage Violence (Columbia)   1971—Church of Anthrax   1972—The Academy in Peril (Reprise)
1973—Paris 1919   1974—Fear (Island); June 1, 1974
1975—Slow Dazzle; Helen of Troy   1977—Guts
1980—Sabotage/Live (IRS)   1981—Honi Soit (A&M)
1982—Music for a New Society (Ze)   1984—
Caribbean Sunset; John Cale Comes Alive   1985—
Black Rose (Island); Artificial Intelligence
1989—Land; Words for the Dying (Warner Bros.)
1990—Songs for Drella (with Lou Reed) (Sire);
Wrong Way Up   1991—Even Cowgirls Get the Blues (ROIR)   1992—Fragments of a Rainy Season (Rykodisc)   1994—Seducing Down the Door: A John Cale Collection (Rhino).

John Cale has brought an avant-garde ear to rock & roll ever since he founded the Velvet Underground with Lou Reed in 1966. His work shows a fascination with opposites: lyricism and noise, subtlety and bluntness, hypnotic repetition and sudden change. Even as a student of classical music, he was an extremist: During a recital at the Guildhall School of Music, London, where he was studying theory and composition, he demolished a piano. Cale studied in Britain with composer Humphrey Searle, came to America in 1963 to work with Iannis Xenakis and Aaron Copland under the auspices of a Leonard Bernstein Fellowship, then settled in New York with such radical composers as John Cage and La Monte Young. That year Cale was one of a group of pianists to perform Erik Satie's nearly 19-hour-long "Vexations." Through his association with the Lower Manhattan art community, Cale met Reed, who directed him toward electric instruments and rock & roll and helped conceive the Velvet Underground [see entry], for which Cale played keyboards, bass, and electric viola.

John Cale

After two Velvets albums, Cale left in 1968 for a solo career. In the early Seventies he worked as an A&R man for Warner Bros. and Elektra, and as a consultant for Columbia, remixing albums by Barbra Streisand and Paul Revere and the Raiders in quadrophonic sound. On his solo albums of the decade, he used elegant pop (*Paris 1919,* with Little Feat's Lowell George), hard rock (*Fear*), Phil Spector/Brian Wilson gloss (*Slow Dazzle*), minimalism (*Church of Anthrax,* with fellow La Monte Young pupil Terry Riley), full orchestra (*The Academy in Peril*), and punk (*Sabotage*). Lyrically, he displayed equal daring; delivered in a strong baritone, his work ranged from musings about terrorism, espionage, and states of psychological extremity to love songs. His Seventies tours, generally featuring guitarist Chris Spedding, were often acts of disturbing theater (recorded at New York's CBGB, *Even Cowgirls Get the Blues* captured the punk ambience of the period); at one point Cale chopped up a chicken onstage, causing his band members to walk out.

By the next decade Cale had established himself as a producer/collaborator on some 80 albums, ranging from the debut efforts of Iggy Pop and the Stooges, Patti Smith, Jonathan Richman's Modern Lovers, and Squeeze to four albums by former Velvets' singer Nico; he also had worked with Brian Eno, Kevin Ayers, Kate and Anna McGarrigle, Nick Drake, and Mike Heron and scored soundtracks for Andy Warhol's *Heat* and Roger Corman's *Caged Heat.* While commercial success continued to elude him, he was lauded as one of punk's godfathers, a status he contended against with characteristic irony: His primary interest remained classical music. As the Eighties waned he continued producing (Happy Mondays), scoring (the soundtrack for Jonathan Demme's *Something Wild*), and releasing solo work as various as the almost-pop of *Wrong Way Up* to "The Falklands Suite," an orchestration of Dylan Thomas poetry that highlighted *Words for the Dying.*

By 1993 Cale had come full circle: Having, two years earlier, collaborated with Lou Reed on *Songs for Drella,* a tribute to Velvet Underground mentor Andy Warhol, he teamed with the Velvets on a brief reunion tour, an event that all four original members had for years dismissed as a possibility. The reunion fizzled after Cale and Reed disagreed over who would produce the group's planned MTV *Unplugged* appearance and recording. In 1995 Cale began making plans to record an album with ex-Velvets Maureen Tucker and Sterling Morrison.

Cameo

Formed 1974, New York City, New York
Larry Blackmon (b. New York City), drums, bass, voc.; Tomi Jenkins, voc.; Nathan Leftenant, trumpet, voc.
1977—*Cardiac Arrest* (Chocolate City)   1978—*We All Know Who We Are*   1979—*Ugly Ego; Secret Omen*   1980—*Cameosis; Feel Me*   1981—*Knights of the Sound Table*   1982—*Alligator Woman* (Atlanta Artists)   1983—*Style*   1984—*She's Strange*   1985—*Single Life*   1986—*Word Up!*   1988—*Machismo*   1990—*Real Men . . . Wear Black*   1992—*Emotional Violence* (Reprise)   1993—*The Best of Cameo* (Mercury)   1994—*In the Face of Funk* (Way 2 Funky).

The brainchild of multi-instrumentalist and songwriter Larry Blackmon, the group Cameo is a confusingly complex net of personal and financial entanglements. Originally the New York City Players, by the early Seventies the Juilliard-trained Blackmon became leader of the dozen or so musicians and in 1974 changed their name to Cameo. Viewed as a minor-league Funkadelic (with whom Cameo shared a label and for whom they frequently opened), they were moderately successful, with three Top Ten R&B hits: "I Just Want to Be" (#3 R&B, 1979), "Sparkle" (#10 R&B, 1979), and "Shake Your Pants" (#8 R&B, 1980).

Unhappy with how the band was being treated, and

finding the North inhospitable to African Americans, in 1981 Blackmon moved operations to Atlanta, where he started his Atlanta Artists label. The early albums were unsuccessful, and to save money, the personnel of the band was reduced to a core band of Blackmon, Tomi Jenkins, and Nathan Leftenant. This version of the band produced the spare, ominous, stalking funk of "She's Strange" (#47 pop, #1 R&B, 1984), "Word Up" (#6 pop, #1 R&B, 1986), "Candy" (#21 pop, #1 R&B, 1986), and "Back and Forth" (#50 pop, #3 R&B, 1987).

Stardom gave the always voluble Blackmon license to make outrageous statements, dismissing Steve Winwood and Peter Gabriel as false funk, calling Kool and the Gang plagiarists, and chastising rap musicians for irresponsible attitudes. Cameo also made a striking visual impression, with geometric haircuts and Jean-Paul Gaultier–designed clothes (with Blackmon's oversized red leather codpiece the center of attention). In 1987 Cameo collaborated with Miles Davis on "In the Night."

Blackmon has made a name for himself as producer; his credits include Bobby Brown's debut. In 1991 he was named vice president of A&R at Warner-Reprise Records, though by 1994 that relationship had ended. Later that year Blackmon released *In the Face of Funk* on his own label Way 2 Funky and toured with Teena Marie and the Gap Band.

Glen Campbell

Born April 22, 1936, Billstown, Arkansas
1967—*Gentle on My Mind* (Capitol); *By the Time I Get to Phoenix*   1968—*Hey Little One*; *A New Place in the Sun*; *Bobbie Gentry and Glen Campbell* (with Bobbie Gentry); *Wichita Lineman*   1969—*Galveston*; *Glen Campbell Live*   1970—*Try a Little Kindness*   1971—*Glen Campbell's Greatest Hits*; *The Last Time I Saw Her*   1975—*Arkansas*; *Rhinestone Cowboy*   1976—*The Best of Glen Campbell*; *Bloodline*   1977—*Southern Nights*   1978—*Basic*   1979—*Highwayman*   1980—*Somethin' 'Bout You Baby I Like*   1981—*It's the World Gone Crazy*   1984—*Old Home Town* (Atlantic America)   1987—*Still Within the Sound of My Voice* (MCA); *The Very Best of Glen Campbell* (Capitol)   1988—*Light Years* (MCA)   1990—*Walkin' in the Sun* (Capitol Nashville); *Greatest Country Hits* (Curb); *Classics Collection* (Capitol Nashville)   1991—*Unconditional Love*; *Show Me Your Way*   1992—*Wings of Victory*   1993—*Somebody Like That* (Liberty).

Glen Campbell has been a critically respected mainstream country-pop star for more than two decades. A subtle, adept interpreter (as evidenced in such Jimmy Webb compositions as "Wichita Lineman"), Campbell has also been well received by contemporary Christian audiences.

Campbell was one of 12 children in a family where everyone played guitar and sang. He got his first guitar at age four and left home as a teenager to tour with an uncle, a musician named Dick Bill. In 1960 Campbell moved to Los Angeles, where he became known in country and rock circles and supported himself with session work for Frank Sinatra, Rick Nelson, Johnny Cash, Dean Martin, the Mamas and the Papas, Gene Clark, and several of Phil Spector's groups. In 1965 he played bass or guitar (sources differ) with the Beach Boys for eight months following Brian Wilson's decision not to appear with the band.

Campbell signed with Capitol in 1962 and recorded with occasional and minor success; his 1965 cover of Donovan's "Universal Soldier" entered the Top Fifty. In 1967 he hit with John Hartford's "Gentle on My Mind" (#39) and became a regular guest on the Smothers Brothers' variety program. His other Sixties hits included the Jimmy Webb compositions "By the Time I Get to Phoenix" (#11, 1967), "Wichita Lineman" (#3, 1968), and "Galveston" (#4, 1969). From January 1969 to June 1972 Campbell hosted his own variety show, *The Glen Campbell Goodtime Hour.* His later hits include "Rhinestone Cowboy" (#1, 1975), Allen Toussaint's "Southern Nights" (#1, 1977), and "Country Boy (You Got Your Feet in L.A.)" (#11, 1976). Over the years, he has also worked in movies (*True Grit* with John Wayne; *Norwood*) and has made countless appearances on television, including the syndicated series *The Glen Campbell Music Show* (1982–83).

Though Campbell's appearances in the pop Top Forty are rare these days, he remains a strong presence on the country and gospel charts. He has spoken freely in recent interviews about his 1981 baptism. In 1991 he launched a long-running tour that featured John Hartford, Jim Stafford, and Nicolette Larson. He tours approximately 200 days a year. In 1992 he voiced Chanticleer the Rooster in the animated feature film *Rock-a-Doodle.* In 1994 his autobiography, *Rhinestone Cowboy: An Autobiography,* appeared.

Milton Campbell: See Little Milton

Camper Van Beethoven/Cracker

Formed in 1984, Santa Cruz, California
David Lowery (b. Sep. 10, 1960, San Antonio, Tex.), gtr., voc., drums; Victor Krummenacher (b. Apr. 7, 1965, Riverside, Calif.), bass, voc.; Chris Molla, gtr., voc., drums; Jonathan Segal (b. Sep. 3, 1963, Marseilles, France), violin, kybds., mandolin, noise, voc.; Greg Lisher (b. Nov. 29, 1963, Santa Cruz), gtr. 1985—*Telephone Free Landslide Victory* (Independent Project)   1986—*Camper Van Beethoven II & III* (Pitch a Tent); *Camper Van Beethoven* (+ Chris Pedersen [b. Aug. 16, 1960, San Diego, Calif.], drums;

– Molla)   1987—*Vampire Can Mating Oven* EP
1988—*Our Beloved Revolutionary Sweetheart* (Virgin)   1989—*Key Lime Pie* (– Segal; + Morgan Fichter, violin).
Cracker, formed 1992, California (Lowery; Johnny Hickman, voc., gtr.; Davey Faragher, voc., bass; Michael Urbano, drums; Phil Jones, drums, perc.):
1992—*Cracker* (Virgin)   1993—*Kerosene Hat.*

Camper Van Beethoven introduced an eclectic, often humorous blend of hippie psychedelia, avant-garde improvisation, country-western shadings, pseudo-ethnic sounds, and a hardcore punch to the mid-Eighties postpunk scene. What saved the group from novelty status was its genuine talent for making interesting, adventurous music. After its breakup, David Lowery went on to greater commercial success in his band, Cracker.

Born in San Antonio, Texas, and raised in L.A.'s San Fernando Valley, CVB leader Lowery's first band, Sitting Duck, experimented with ethnic sounds by way of TV shows and advertisements, and played alongside thrashy punk and psychedelic rock & roll. The earliest version of Camper Van Beethoven grew out of Sitting Duck in 1983 and included Lowery, Victor Krummenacher, Chris Molla, and guitarist David McDaniel (the short-lived member who actually named the band). It wasn't until the next year, however, that the Campers began following their eclectic muse in earnest. Lowery had returned to college in Santa Cruz and was soon followed by Krummenacher and Molla. There they met local guitarist Greg Lisher and composition student Jonathan Segal.

The band's first album, *Telephone Free Landslide Victory,* on the arty L.A.-based label Independent Projects, produced the humorous "Take the Skinheads Bowling," which became a cult favorite among college students. The album also featured a slowed-down, violin-drenched version of Black Flag's first single, "Wasted." The album was followed by a string of equally offbeat collections of songs—which featured titles like "ZZ Top Goes to Egypt" and "Joe Stalin's Cadillac"—on which the Campers experimented with everything from Beatlesque tape manipulation and Arabic-like drones to absurdist lyrics and offbeat covers (such as Ringo Starr's "Photograph" and Pink Floyd's "Interstellar Overdrive"). In 1987, with the eccentric guitarist Eugene Chadbourne, the group recorded *Camper Van Chadbourne* for the tiny indie label Fundamentalist Records. Virgin signed the band in 1988, releasing the more accessible (yet still very offbeat) *Our Beloved Revolutionary Sweetheart* and *Key Lime Pie.*

In 1988 Krummenacher, Lisher, and Pedersen took the band's arty quality to their side project, Monks of Doom, and Segal recorded a solo album. Camper Van Beethoven parted ways in 1989, and Lowery took the hooky pop side of the band into his group Cracker. After the first, self-titled album won airplay on college radio, Cracker's followup, *Kerosene Hat* (#59, 1993), yielded the modern-rock radio hit "Low."

Can

Formed 1968, Cologne, West Germany
Irmin Schmidt (b. May 29, 1937, Berlin, Ger.), kybds., voc.; Michael Karoli (b. Apr. 29, 1948, Straubing, W. Ger.), gtr., violin, voc.; Holger Czukay (b. Mar. 24, 1938, Danzig, Ger.), bass, voc., electronics; Jaki Liebezeit (b. May 26, 1938, Dresden, Ger.), drums, reeds, voc.; Malcolm Mooney, voc.; David Johnson, flute, electronics (– Johnson)
1969—*Monster Movie* (United Artists, U.K.)
(– Mooney; + Kenji "Damo" Suzuki [b. Jan. 16, 1950, Jap.], voc.)   1970—*Soundtracks*   1971—*Tago Mago*   1972—*Ege Bamyasi*   1973—*Future Days* (– Suzuki)   1974—*Limited Edition; Soon Over Babaluma*   1975—*Landed* (Virgin, U.K.)   1976—*Unlimited Edition* (Caroline, U.K.); *Flow Motion* (Virgin, U.K.); *Opener: 1971–1974* (Sunset, U.K.)   1977—(+ Rosko Gee, bass; + Reebop Kwaku Baah [b. Konongo, Ghana; d. ca. mid-1980s], perc.) *Saw Delight* (Virgin, U.K.) (– Czukay)   1978—*Cannibalism* (United Artists, U.K.); *Out of Reach* (Peters Int'l)   1979— (+ Czukay) *Can* (Laser, U.K.) (Group disbands)   1980—*Cannibalism 1* (Spoon, Ger.)   1981—*Incandescence 1969–1977* (Virgin, U.K.); *Delay 1968* (Spoon, Ger.)   1986—(Original lineup re-forms: Schmidt; Karoli; Czukay; Liebezeit; Mooney)   1989—*Rite Time* (Mercury, U.K.)   1990—*Cannibalism 2* (Spoon-Mute); *Cannibalism 3.*

European art-rock band Can was one of the first groups to use electronic "treatments" of instruments, and it pioneered an exploratory postpsychedelic rock style that would later influence Amon Duul, Ash Ra Temple, and the waves of technopop artists, including Pete Shelley, that followed. Can's sound was based on repetitive, trance-inducing rhythms overlaid with atmospheric noise and sudden bursts of distorted electronic effects, with instruments often unrecognizable in the mix.

The group's debut, *Monster Movie,* showed a rather primitive approach. But with Malcolm Mooney taken ill and replaced by Kenji "Damo" Suzuki—discovered by the band singing on the streets of Munich—Irmin Schmidt and Holger Czukay made fuller use of their studies with German avant-garde composer Karlheinz Stockhausen. The band expanded frontiers and sounded more assured on *Tago Mago, Ege Bamyasi, Future Days,* and *Babaluma.* Can music was a natural for film soundtracks, and the group scored part of Jerzy Skolimowski's *Deep End;* its film scores are collected on *Soundtracks.*

Can enjoyed a couple of hit singles abroad with

David Gilmour's "I Want More" and a version of "Silent Night" in 1976. With the addition of ex–Traffic members Rosko Gee and Reebop Kwaku Baah, Can's sound got funkier on the well-received *Saw Delight*.

But then the band entered limbo, with various members splitting off for solo and collaboration LPs. The most prolific was Czukay, whose solo endeavors include *Movies* (1980), a Brian Eno–style tape-loop and *musique concrète* montage, *On the Way to the Peak of Normal* (1982), *Der Osten Ist Rot* (1984), *Rome Remains Rome* (1987), and *Radio Wave Surfer* (1991). Czukay has also worked with Rolf Dammers (*Canaxis,* 1982), Eurythmics, David Sylvian (1988's *Plight and Premonition* and 1989's *Flux + Mutability*), and Jah Wobble (1981's *How Much Are They* EP with Liebezeit and 1983's *Snake Charmer* with the Edge). As of 1994, these are all foreign releases, with the exception of *Snake Charmer.* In the late Eighties the original lineup reunited to record *Rite Time*.

C+C Music Factory

Formed October 1990, New York City, New York
Robert Clivillés (b. Aug. 30, 1964, New York City), drums, perc., bass; David Cole (b. June 3, 1962, Johnson City, Tenn.; d. Jan. 24, 1995, New York City), kybds., bass, voc.; Zelma Davis (b. Aug. 2, 1970, Republic of Liberia), voc.; Freedom Williams (b. Feb. 13, 1966, Brooklyn, N.Y.), voc.
1991—*Gonna Make You Sweat* (Columbia)   1994— *Anything Goes.*
Clivillés and Cole: 1992—*Greatest Remixes Vol. 1* (Columbia).
Freedom Williams solo: 1993—*Freedom* (Columbia).

In the early Nineties, as the creative team guiding C+C Music Factory, Robert Clivillés and David Cole personified the reemergence of the producer/songwriter as star in pop music. They also endured clashes with artists who felt that their work within this dance-pop collective hadn't been properly acknowledged.

Clivillés and Cole met in the mid-Eighties at a Manhattan nightclub where Clivillés DJ'ed while Cole played live keyboards. Before long, they were remixing club hits for the likes of Janet Jackson ("Pleasure Principle"), Natalie Cole ("Pink Cadillac"), and Fleetwood Mac ("Big Love"). The duo next set its sights on making original recordings, using keyboards and a computer to write and arrange material, then recruiting performers to lay down vocals. Their breakthrough came when they assembled the R&B trio Seduction, whose debut album, *Nothing Matters Without Love* (#36, 1989), produced several hit singles, including "You're My One and Only (True Love)" (#23 pop, #56 R&B, 1989) and "Two to Make It Right" (#2 R&B, 1989).

With C+C Music Factory, Clivillés and Cole brought their own involvement to the fore. The outfit's 1991 debut album, *Gonna Make You Sweat,* which that year hit #2 on the pop chart and yielded a #1 title track (on the pop and R&B charts) and the #3 single "Here We Go" (#7 R&B), featured singers Martha Wash and Deborah Cooper and rapper Freedom Williams; but these vocalists were only briefly mentioned in the LP's production notes and liner material. Furthermore, Wash, whose booming soprano had also been the uncredited voice of Seduction and the dance group Black Box (she sang with the Weather Girls [see entry] and Two Tons O'Fun, as well) was conspicuously absent in C+C's popular videos, in which the more lithe, attractive Davis lip-synched to her vocals.

In 1991, Wash filed two lawsuits against Clivillés and Cole, one charging that she hadn't received ample credit for *Sweat,* the other protesting her deceptive exclusion from the videos. In 1992, while still hashing it out with her lawyers, the producers released a follow-up album, as Clivillés and Cole. *Greatest Remixes Vol. 1* (#87, 1992) spawned the #4 single, "Things That Make You Go Hmmm. . . ." Later that year, Williams also sued the team, claiming they had misled him about solo opportunities and withheld royalties (part of Wash's claim, too).

Williams did strike out on his own, releasing *Freedom* in 1993. Wash settled her differences with Clivillés and Cole, though, and in 1994 C+C Music Factory resurfaced with *Anything Goes,* featuring Wash, Davis, and the Latin hip-hop/R&B threesome Trilogy. That same year, Clivillés and Cole won a Grammy for their production work with Whitney Houston on the soundtrack to *The Bodyguard.* In early 1995 Cole died of complications from spinal meningitis.

Canned Heat

Formed 1966, Los Angeles, California
Bob "Bear" Hite (b. Feb. 26, 1945, Torrance, Calif.; d. Apr. 5, 1981, Venice, Calif.), voc., harmonica; Alan "Blind Owl" Wilson (b. July 4, 1943, Boston, Mass.; d. Sep. 3, 1970, Topanga, Calif.), gtr., harmonica, voc.; Henry Vestine (b. Dec. 24, 1944, Washington, D.C.), gtr.; Frank Cook, drums; Larry Taylor (b. Samuel Taylor, June 26, 1942, Brooklyn, N.Y.), bass.
1967—*Canned Heat* (Liberty)   1968—(– Cook; + Adolpho "Fito" de la Parra [b. Feb. 8, 1946, Mexico City, Mex.], drums) *Boogie with Canned Heat*; *Living the Blues*   1969—(– Vestine; + Harvey Mandel [b. Mar. 11, 1945, Detroit, Mich.], gtr.) *Hallelujah*   1970—*Vintage Heat* (Janus); *The Canned Heat Cookbook/Best Of* (Liberty); *Hooker 'n' Heat* (with John Lee Hooker); *Live in Europe* (– Wilson; – Taylor; – Mandel; + Vestine, gtr.; + Antonio de la Barreda, bass) *Future Blues*   1971—*Live at the Topanga Corral* (Wand)   1972—*Historical Figures and Ancient Heads* (United Artists) (– Barreda;

+ Richard Hite, bass) 1973—*New Age* 1974—*One More River to Cross* (Atlantic) 1975—*The Very Best of Canned Heat* (United Artists) 1978—*Human Condition* (Takoma) 1981—(– B. Hite) *Hooker 'n' Heat Live* (Rhino) 1984—(+ James Thornbury, slide gtr., harmonica, voc.) 1987—*The Best of Canned Heat* (EMI) 1990—*Reheated* (Chameleon) 1992—*Burnin' Live* (Aim) 1994—(Lineup: de la Parra; Vestine; Thornbury; + Junior Watson, gtr., voc.; + Ron Shumake, bass, voc.) *Uncanned (The Best of Canned Heat)* (EMI) (+ Taylor; + Mandel); *Internal Combustion* (River Road/Two Goats).

Blues-rockers Canned Heat were rare among the American white blues–loving bands of the late Sixties and early Seventies in that they had a couple of hit records. As one critic noted, they were more popularizers than purists, and one might argue that the 1981 death of cofounder Bob Hite essentially ended the band. In fact, since Al Wilson's death in 1970 dozens of personnel shifts have occurred (the above chronology lists only the most important), but the band has continued under the leadership of Fito de la Parra, and as of 1994 also includes Henry Vestine.

The original Canned Heat evolved out of a jug band that was formed in 1965. Blues fanatics Alan Wilson and Bob Hite (nicknamed the "Bear" because of his 300-pound frame) changed the group's focus to electric boogie. Though their debut, *Canned Heat,* sold respectably, their appearance at the Monterey Pop Festival that year attracted more attention. Their second album spawned a #16 hit, Wilson's "On the Road Again," and they toured Europe. "Going Up the Country" gave them a #11 hit in 1969, and they played the Woodstock Festival in August.

The following year was a watershed, with a worldwide hit cover of Wilbert Harrison's "Let's Work Together" and an appearance at the Isle of Wight Festival in England. But the drug overdose death of Wilson (who was partly blind and subject to severe depression) in late 1970 proved to be a setback from which the band never fully recovered. Taylor and guitarist Harvey Mandel joined John Mayall's band. (Later Mandel would be considered to replace Mick Taylor in the Rolling Stones and record a number of albums, as both an artist and a session musician.) The remaining members, with replacements, soldiered on. They backed bluesman John Lee Hooker on *Hooker 'n' Heat* that year; in 1989 a latter-day version of the band backed him again on *The Healer.* In 1973 the band backed Clarence "Gatemouth" Brown and Memphis Slim on French albums released on the Barclay label.

Canned Heat's electric blues fell out of fashion, and by the early Eighties it was playing the California bar circuit. Sometime after Hite's death (he suffered a fatal heart attack) the group drifted, and while 1990's *Reheated* revived interest, Canned Heat has not made a commercial comeback, though it remains a steadily working band. In the early Nineties guitarist Mandel rejoined the group for some live dates, and original members Larry Taylor, Mandel, and Vestine appear on 1994's *Internal Combustion.*

Freddy Cannon

Born Frederick Anthony Picariello, December 4, 1939, Lynn, Massachusetts
1961—*The Explosive Freddy Cannon* (Swan) 1962—*Freddy Cannon Sings Happy Shades of Blue*; *Freddy Cannon's Solid Gold Hits*; *Freddy Cannon at Palisades Park* 1964—*Freddy Cannon Steps Out* 1965—*Freddy Cannon* (Warner Bros.) 1966—*Freddy Cannon's Greatest Hits*; *Action!* 1982—*14 Booming Hits* (Rhino).

A major star in the early Sixties, singer, guitarist, and songwriter Freddy Cannon broke big with two million-sellers: "Tallahassee Lassie" (#6, 1959) and an updated version of a 1922 jazz hit, "Way Down Yonder in New Orleans" (#3, 1960). Cannon was discovered in 1957 by a Boston disc jockey; two years later he recorded "Tallahassee Lassie," a song his mother had written.

He toured internationally during the mid-Sixties, scoring minor hits regularly. His only other big hit, the Chuck Barris–penned "Palisades Park," was #3 in 1962. That same year, he was featured in the British film *Just for Fun.* In 1965 he had a Top Twenty hit with "Action," the theme song from the TV series *Where the Action Is.* He remained a major performer in the U.K. years after his star had faded in America. In 1960 *The Explosive Freddy Cannon* became the first LP by an American artist to go to #1 in England. In the Seventies he became a promotion man for Buddah Records, but he returned to the charts in 1981 with "Let's Put the Fun Back in Rock 'n' Roll," backed by the Belmonts.

The Capris

Formed 1957, New York City, New York
Original lineup: Nick Santo (b. Nick Santa Maria, 1941), voc.; Mike Mincelli (b. 1941), voc.; Frank Reina (b. 1940), voc.; John Cassese (b. 1941), voc.; Vinnie Narcardo (b. 1941), voc.
1981—*There's a Moon Out Again* (Ambient Sound/Epic).

The Capris were a one-hit vocal group of the late Fifties who were rediscovered and temporarily revived in 1980 on the Ambient Sound label. The five original members, then just teenagers, had been singing in subway stations and on streetcorners in Queens, New York, before they were discovered by independent record producers in

1958. A song written by lead singer Nick Santo, "There's a Moon Out Tonight," was recorded in 1958 and released twice but went nowhere, and the group soon disbanded.

Two years later WINS disc jockey Murray the K used the song in a contest, and soon afterward "There's a Moon Out Tonight" hit #3 (1961). The group re-formed and continued to perform. In 1963 Santo quit to join the New York City Police Department; in the ensuing years members have come and gone. In 1981 three original Capris (Santo, Mike Mincelli, and Frank Reina), former Del-Satin Tommy Ferrara, and ex-Emotion Tony Dano came together to record the Ambient Sound LP that was released in 1981.

Captain and Tennille

Daryl Dragon (a.k.a. the "Captain," b. Aug. 27, 1942, Los Angeles, Calif.), kybds.; Toni Tennille (b. Catheryn Antoinette Tennille, May 8, 1943, Montgomery, Ala.), voc.
1975—*Love Will Keep Us Together* (A&M)   1976—*Song of Joy*   1977—*Come in from the Rain; The Captain and Tennille's Greatest Hits*   1978—*Dream*   1979—*Make Your Move* (Casablanca)   1980—*Keeping Our Love Warm.*
Toni Tennille solo: 1984—*More Than You Know* (Mirage)   1987—*All of Me* (Gaia)   1992—*Never Let Me Go* (Bay Cities).

The Captain and Tennille are a husband-and-wife pop duo who debuted on the pop charts with the top-selling single of 1975, a bouncy version of Neil Sedaka's "Love Will Keep Us Together." The single sold over 2½ million copies and was awarded a Grammy for Record of the Year.

Toni Tennille began singing with her three sisters in their hometown of Montgomery. Her father had sung professionally in the Thirties, and her mother was a local television talk-show host. Tennille studied classical piano for nine years, and in 1964 she moved with her family to Los Angeles, where she joined the South Coast Repertory Theater. There she cowrote a rock musical entitled *Mother Earth,* and during the play's run she met Daryl Dragon, a keyboard player in the house band. The son of conductor Carmen Dragon, Daryl plays clarinet, keyboards, guitar, and bass. Before he met Tennille, he had also worked with the Beach Boys, and when Tennille's play closed in 1971, after three performances, he invited her to come with him on a Beach Boys tour. They were married on Valentine's Day, 1975.

In 1974 the two financed and produced a single, "The Way I Want to Touch You," which was first a regional hit. "Love Will Keep Us Together" followed, and upon its rerelease in 1975, "The Way I Want to Touch You" went to #4. Other hit singles included "Lonely Night (Angel Face)" (#3, 1976), "Muskrat Love" (#4, 1976), a cover version of Smokey Robinson's "Shop Around" (#4, 1976), "Can't Stop Dancin'" (#13, 1977), "You Never Done It Like That" (#10, 1978), and "Do That to Me One More Time" (#1, 1979). From mid-1977 on, the duo's misses outnumbered their hits; still they managed to sell over 23 million records throughout their career. During that time Tennille provided backup vocals for Pink Floyd's *The Wall* and Elton John's "Don't Let the Sun Go Down on Me."

They hosted their own prime-time series on ABC in 1976/1977, and in the early Eighties Tennille hosted a daytime talk show (with Daryl as musical director). The couple moved to Nevada, where Dragon set up a studio and produces records and scores films. Tennille recorded four albums of standards, made guest appearances on television, and has performed on the musical stage. The duo occasionally performs as Captain and Tennille.

Captain Beefheart and the Magic Band

Formed 1964, California
Captain Beefheart (b. Don Van Vliet, Jan. 15, 1941, Glendale, Calif.), voc., harmonica, saxes, bass clarinet, musette; Alex St. Clair, gtr.; Doug Moon, gtr.; Jerry Handley, bass; Paul Blakely, drums.
1966—(– Moon; – Blakely; + Jeff Cotton [a.k.a. Antennae Jimmy Semens], gtr.; + John French [a.k.a. Drumbo], drums)   1967—(+ Ry Cooder [b. Mar. 15, 1947, Los Angeles], gtr.) *Safe As Milk* (Buddah) (– Cooder)   1968—*Strictly Personal* (Blue Thumb)   1969—(– St. Clair; – Handley; + Zoot Horn Rollo [b. Bill Harkleroad], gtr., flute; + Rockette Morton [b. Mark Boston], bass; + the Mascara Snake [b. Victor Fleming], bass clarinet) *Trout Mask Replica* (Straight)   1970—(– Cotton; + Ed Marimba [b. Art Tripp III], drums, marimba, perc.) *Lick My Decals Off, Baby*   1971—*Mirror Man* (Buddah)   1972—(+ Winged Eel Fingerling [b. Eliot Ingber], gtr.) *The Spotlight Kid* (Reprise) (– French; – Ingber; + Orejon [b. Roy Estrada], bass; + Milt Holland, perc.); *Clear Spot*   1974—(– Estrada; + St. Clair, gtr.; + Mark Marcellino, kybds.) *Unconditionally Guaranteed* (Mercury) (all new lineup: Van Vliet; + Dean Smith, gtr.; + Ira Ingber, bass; + Gene Pello, drums; + Ty Grimes, perc.; + Michael Smotherman, kybds.; + Jimmy Caravan, kybds.; + Mark Gibbons, kybds.; + Bob West, bass); *Bluejeans and Moonbeams*   1978—(all new lineup: Van Vliet; Tripp; + Bruce Lambourne Fowler, trombone; + Richard Redus, gtr., bass, accordion; + Robert Arthur Williams, drums, perc.; + Jeff Morris Tepper, gtr.; + Eric Drew Feldman, kybds., bass, synth.) *Shiny Beast (Bat Chain Puller)* (Warner Bros.)   1980—(– Redus; + Gary Lucas, gtr., French horn; + French, gtr., bass, drums, marimba, perc.) *Doc at the Radar Station*

Captain Beefheart

(Virgin) 1982—(– French; – Williams; + Cliff Martinez, drums, perc.; + Richard Midnight Hatsize Snyder, bass, marimba, viola) *Ice Cream for Crow* (Epic; Virgin, U.K.) 1984—*The Legendary A&M Sessions* (A&M).

The irregular rhythms, grating harmonies, and earthy, surreal lyrics of Captain Beefheart's songs and his blues-inflected 7½-octave vocals suggest a near-chaotic improvised blend of Delta blues, avant-garde jazz, Twentieth-Century classical music, and rock & roll. Actually, Beefheart's repertoire is a sort of modern chamber music for rock band, since he plans every note and teaches the band their parts by ear. Because it breaks so many of rock's conventions at once, Beefheart's music has always been more influential than popular, leaving its mark on such groups as Devo, Pere Ubu, Public Image Ltd., the Contortions, and Talking Heads.

A child-prodigy sculptor, Don Van Vliet was noticed at age four by Portuguese sculptor Augustinio Rodriguez, who featured Van Vliet and his clay animals on his weekly television show for the next eight years. When Van Vliet was 13, his parents declined their son's scholarship to study art in Europe and moved the family to Lancaster, California, in the Mojave Desert, where Van Vliet met the young Frank Zappa. Van Vliet taught himself to play harmonica and saxophone and played with local R&B bands the Omens and the Blackouts before enrolling in Antelope Valley College in 1959. After one semester, he dropped out and went to Cucamonga, California, with Zappa, intending to form a band, the Soots, and make a film, *Captain Beefheart Meets the Grunt People.* Both projects fell through, and while Zappa went to Los Angeles to form the Mothers of Invention, Van Vliet returned to Lancaster and, adopting the Beefheart stage name, formed the first Magic Band in 1964.

A&M signed the group in 1964 and released its version of "Diddy Wah Diddy," which sold enough locally for A&M to commission an album. Label president Jerry Moss rejected the tapes of Van Vliet's originals as "too negative," and the band broke up (the album was released in 1984). With a new band, Beefheart redid the songs as *Safe As Milk,* which attracted enough interest for the band to tour Europe. Shortly before a scheduled appearance at the 1967 Monterey Pop Festival, guitarist Ry Cooder's abrupt departure forced the group to cancel.

Strictly Personal was radically remixed by producer Bob Krasnow and released on his own Blue Thumb label as the band toured Europe. Van Vliet, disgusted, retired to the San Fernando Valley until Zappa, now in charge of his own Straight Records, promised him complete artistic control over his next recordings. After composing 28 songs in 8½ hours, Beefheart formed a new Magic Band and recorded *Trout Mask Replica* over the next year. That album and 1970's *Lick My Decals Off, Baby* brought Beefheart critical acclaim, and along with his appearance on Zappa's *Hot Rats* (1969), enough interest for a national tour. The next two albums, marginally more commercial-sounding, reached the lower echelons of the pop charts. *Mirror Man* was recorded in late 1968, but Buddah didn't release it until 1971, after Beefheart had left the label.

After a two-year hiatus, Van Vliet signed with Mercury and released two openly conventional pop-blues albums, then toured with and dissolved another Magic Band. For a short time, he appeared as a vocalist with Zappa and the Mothers of Invention, including songs on 1975's *Bongo Fury.* In 1978 Warner Bros. re-signed him and released *Shiny Beast (Bat Chain Puller),* hailed by critics as a return to *Trout Mask* form; Beefheart toured a somewhat more receptive new-wave circuit. Virgin sued to keep Beefheart on its roster (it had British rights to Beefheart since his Mercury period) and won ownership of *Doc at the Radar Station* and *Ice Cream for Crow.*

Beefheart's 1980 American and European tours, including a November 1980 appearance on *Saturday Night Live,* were his most successful to date. But after the release of *Ice Cream for Crow,* Van Vliet left the music business and retired to a trailer in the Mojave where he lives with his wife, Jan, and devotes himself to painting. In 1985, with the help of New York postmodern painter and Beefheart fan Julian Schnabel, Van Vliet began exhibiting his semi-abstract, primitivist canvases (some of which have adorned his album covers) at galleries in America and Europe, some of them selling for as much $25,000. By the mid-Nineties, it was widely rumored that Van Vliet suffered from an undisclosed, chronic illness.

Captain Sensible: See the Damned

Mariah Carey

Born March 27, 1970, Long Island, New York
1990—*Mariah Carey* (Columbia)   1991—*Emotions*
1992—*MTV Unplugged* EP   1993—*Music Box*
1994—*Merry Christmas.*

With a stunning seven-octave voice that she put through stratospheric gymnastics, Mariah Carey became an overnight star. Her vocal prowess and range drew comparisons to Minnie Riperton and Yma Sumac, but most often to her contemporary, Whitney Houston. Yet unlike Houston, Carey cowrote or coproduced her own gospel-inflected, dance-pop songs and ardent ballads.

Carey was born to a black Venezuelan aeronautics engineer father and an Irish-American opera singer mother who also worked as a voice coach. The couple divorced when Mariah was three, and she moved with her mother to a succession of different towns in Long Island, New York. At 17 she moved to New York City and pursued a career in music while supporting herself as the self-professed "world's worst waitress."

Carey befriended keyboardist Ben Margulies, with whom she began writing songs, and landed backup singing jobs. One, with minor late-Eighties dance-music singer Brenda K. Starr, proved crucial when Starr met Columbia Records chief Tommy Mottola at a party and gave him a demo tape of Carey's songs. Mottola reportedly played the tape in his car on his way home and doubled back to the party to seek out Carey. He signed her and made her career development a top priority. Carey's debut album (#1, 1990) yielded #1 hit singles in "Vision of Love" (1990), "Love Takes Time" (1990), "Someday" (1991), and "I Don't Wanna Cry" (1991), and brought her Grammy awards in 1991 for Best New Artist and Best Female Vocalist. *Emotions* (#1, 1991) continued Carey's roll, with such hits as the title track (#1, 1991), "Can't Let Go" (#2, 1991), and "Make It Happen" (#5, 1992). *Unplugged* produced a hit cover of the Jackson 5's "I'll Be There" (#1, 1992), which also led to a solo recording deal for Trey Lorenz, the backup singer featured on the single with Carey.

In June 1993 Carey married Mottola, a man 20 years her senior. She then released the eight-million-selling *Music Box* (#1, 1993), which promptly yielded the #1 hits "Dreamlover" and "Hero." In fall 1993 she embarked on her first-ever tour, for which she received mixed reviews. Her 1994 Christmas album spawned the hit "All I Want for Christmas Is You."

Belinda Carlisle: See the Go-Go's

Carl Carlton

Born 1952, Detroit, Michigan
N.A.—*You Can't Stop a Man in Love* (Backbeat)
1974—*Everlasting Love* (ABC)   1975—*I Wanna Be with You*   1981—*Carl Carlton* (20th Century-Fox)
1982—*The Bad C.C.* (RCA).

Carl Carlton's career, modeled on that of fellow Detroit native Little Stevie Wonder, began when he was 14. He had been singing since he was nine, first in churches, then for local talent shows, where he was discovered by scouts from Lando Records, a gospel label. When his contract was bought by Back Beat in 1968, he became a child star. Billed as Little Carl Carlton, he had a hit with "Competition Ain't Nuthin'" (#36 R&B, 1968). His followup, "46 Drums, 1 Guitar," made the R&B Top Twenty in 1968. He sustained his career after his voice matured, placing such singles on the charts as "Don't Walk Away" (#38 R&B, 1969) and "Drop By My Place" (#12 R&B, 1970).

He recorded "Everlasting Love" (a 1967 hit for Robert Knight) in 1972, just before Duke-Peacock was incorporated into ABC Records. ABC shelved the master and forgot about it until 1974, by which time Carlton was contemplating a factory job. It was released and rose to #11 R&B, and by the end of 1974 had crossed over to the pop market and reached #6. After he acquired a band, Mixed Company, "Smokin' Room" (#13 R&B, 1975) kept him on the charts. After that, though, Carlton's career waned. ABC dropped him, and he didn't find a new label until 1980. He returned on 20th Century-Fox with racier material: "This Feeling's Rated X-Tra" (#57 R&B, 1980). Then "She's a Bad Mama Jama (She's Built, She's Stacked)" gave him the biggest hit of his career (#22 pop, #2 R&B, 1981). Carlton had a few more R&B hits—"Baby I Need Your Loving" (1982) and "Private Property" (1985).

Eric Carmen: See the Raspberries

Kim Carnes

Born July 20, 1945, Los Angeles, California
1972—*Rest on Me* (A&M)   1975—*Kim Carnes*
1976—*Sailin'*   1979—*St. Vincent's Court* (EMI)
1980—*Romance Dance*   1981—*Mistaken Identity*
1982—*Voyeur; The Best of You* (A&M)   1983—*Cafe Racers* (EMI)   1985—*Barking at Airplanes*   1986—*Light House*   1988—*A View from the House* (MCA)
1993—*Gypsy Honeymoon: The Best of Kim Carnes* (EMI).

Singer/songwriter Kim Carnes recorded the top-selling single of 1981, "Bette Davis Eyes." Carnes grew up in suburban Los Angeles. By her early twenties she was working the city's nightclubs, singing mainly ballads; she was also a member of the New Christy Minstrels. Ballads composed the bulk of her several albums (including *Sailin'*, produced by Jerry Wexler) through the Seventies. Her songs, some of which were cowritten with her husband, Dave Ellingson (who is also a member of her backup band), have been covered by Frank Sinatra, Rita Coolidge, Anne Murray, and Barbra Streisand. The couple's biggest break came when Kenny Rogers recorded their songs on 1980's *Gideon*. That same year Carnes duetted with Rogers on his hit "Don't Fall in Love with a Dreamer."

In 1978 she signed with EMI and gradually began recording rock-oriented material. She had a #10 hit in 1980 with a cover of Smokey Robinson's "More Love." But album sales remained sluggish until 1981's *Mistaken Identity* and its single, a Donna Weiss–Jackie DeShannon composition, "Bette Davis Eyes" (#1, 1981), which won a Grammy for Record of the Year. Later hits include "Draw of the Cards" (#28, 1981), "Voyeur" (#29, 1982), "What About Me?"—with Kenny Rogers and James Ingram (#15, 1984)—and "Crazy in the Night (Barking at Airplanes)" (#15, 1985).

Mary Chapin Carpenter

Born February 21, 1958, Princeton, New Jersey
1988—*Hometown Girl* (Columbia)   1989—*State of the Heart*   1990—*Shooting Straight in the Dark*   1992—*Come On Come On*   1994—*Stones in the Road*.

An Ivy League–educated singer/songwriter with a preference for plain clothes and a reflective, literate style of lyric writing, Mary Chapin Carpenter has always stopped short of mocking the sequined outfits, big hair, and simple romanticism often associated with country divas. Accordingly, Carpenter's music—which incorporates folk and rock textures as well as country—has been embraced by both Nashville and fans of progressive pop.

Carpenter grew up listening to records by Woody Guthrie, the Beatles, and Judy Collins. After she graduated high school, her father, a publishing executive, encouraged her to attend an open-mike session at a local bar. Though reluctant at first, the singer soon began performing live on a regular basis; while studying at Brown University, where she earned a degree in American civilization, Carpenter spent weekends and summers performing a mixture of radio hits and rootsy standards in bars. She next decided to focus on her own material and moved to Washington, D.C., where she won several local music awards and became a favorite on the local club circuit. In the mid-Eighties Carpenter landed a deal with Columbia Records.

Carpenter's debut album, recorded in 1987, was released on Columbia the following year. The articulate

country-folk songs on *Hometown Girl* impressed critics, but it was a sophomore album, 1989's *State of the Heart*, that proved Carpenter's commercial potential, spawning two Top Ten country hits: "Never Had It So Good" (#8) and, in 1990, "Quittin' Time" (#7). The Academy of Country Music named Carpenter 1989's Best New Female Vocalist.

The Nineties have seen Carpenter's star rise yet further. Her 1990 album, *Shooting Straight in the Dark*, yielded the #2 country single "Down at the Twist and Shout," a hit that won her a 1992 Grammy for Best Vocal Performance, Female Country. *Come On Come On* (1992) reached #6 on the country albums charts, producing seven hit singles and earning the singer another Grammy, for a cheekily sexy track called "I Feel Lucky." That single peaked at #4 on the C&W chart, as did "Passionate Kisses" (written by Lucinda Williams). "He Thinks He'll Keep Her" reached #1 C&W. Carpenter's *Stones in the Road* (1994) featured such guest musicians as country artists Lee Roy Parnell and Trisha Yearwood, folkie Shawn Colvin, Heartbreaker Benmont Tench, saxophonist Branford Marsalis, ex-R.E.M. producer Don Dixon (on bass), and drummer Kenny Aronoff. The album continued Carpenter's Grammy streak, netting her 1994's Best Country Vocalist, Female, award for "Shut Up and Kiss Me" and that year's Best Country Album award for *Stones in the Road*.

The Carpenters

Richard Carpenter (b. Oct. 15, 1946, New Haven, Conn.), voc., kybds.; Karen Carpenter (b. Mar. 2, 1950, New Haven, Conn.; d. Feb. 4, 1983, Los Angeles, Calif.), voc., drums.
1969—*Ticket to Ride* (A&M)   1970—*Close to You*   1971—*Carpenters*   1972—*A Song for You*   1973—*Now and Then; The Singles 1969–1973*   1975—*Horizon*   1976—*A Kind of Hush*   1977—*Passage*   1978—*Christmas Portrait*   1981—*Made in America*   1983—*Voice of the Heart*   1985—*Yesterday Once More*   1989—*Lovelines*   1991—*Once from the Top*. Richard Carpenter solo: 1987—*Time* (A&M)

A popular brother-and-sister team, the Carpenters sold millions of hit records in the early Seventies. Richard started piano lessons at age 12 and studied classical piano at Yale before the family relocated to Downey, California, in 1963. Richard studied at USC and Cal State at Long Beach. He formed his first group in 1965, a jazz-pop instrumental trio that included younger sister Karen on drums and their friend Wes Jacobs (who later abandoned pop for a seat in the Detroit Symphony) on bass and tuba. The group won a battle of the bands at the Hollywood Bowl and subsequently signed with RCA. Four sides were recorded, but after label executives deemed them not commercially viable, they were never released.

In late 1966 the trio broke up. Richard and Karen recruited four Cal State students into the vocal harmony-oriented band Spectrum. They played various Southern California venues to less than ecstatic response and disbanded.

The Carpenter siblings' densely layered, pop-oriented demo tapes eventually caught the attention of Herb Alpert, who signed them to A&M in 1969. They released their first album that November. Originally titled *Offering*, it was ignored until repackaged as *Ticket to Ride*, on the strength of the moderate success of their Beatles cover single. *Close to You*'s title track, a Burt Bacharach tune, sold more than a million copies and went to #1 in the U.S. and several other countries. Their hits continued: "We've Only Just Begun" (#2, 1970), "For All We Know" (#3, 1971; it won an Oscar as Best Song of the Year in 1970), "Rainy Days and Mondays" (#2, 1971), "Superstar" (#2, 1971, written by Leon Russell), "It's Going to Take Some Time" (#12, 1972), "Hurting Each Other" (#2, 1972), "Goodbye to Love" (#7, 1972), "Sing" (#3, 1973), "Yesterday Once More" (#2, 1973), "Top of the World" (#1, 1973), "I Won't Last a Day Without You" (#11, 1974), "Please Mr. Postman" (#1, 1975), and "Only Yesterday" (#4, 1975).

The 1973 LP *The Singles 1969–1973* was a best seller, and the Carpenters were three-time Grammy winners. They hosted a short-lived variety series on NBC, *Make Your Own Kind of Music*, in 1971. At the request of President Nixon, they performed at a White House state dinner honoring West German chancellor Willy Brandt, May 1, 1973. They toured internationally through the mid-Seventies. Their 1976 tour of Japan was, at the time, the biggest-grossing concert ever in that country. From 1976 to 1980 the pair hosted five ABC television specials. Through the late Seventies the Carpenters were noticeably absent from the charts, but returned to the Top Twenty in 1981 with "Touch Me When We're Dancing."

On February 4, 1983, Karen Carpenter died in her parents' home of cardiac arrest, resulting from her long struggle with anorexia nervosa. Her story was presented in the highly rated made-for-television movie *The Karen Carpenter Story* in 1988. During the writing of that film, on which Richard was an advisor, he admitted to the producers that in the late Seventies he had been addicted to Quaaludes. The posthumous LP *Lovelines* drew critical notice for its inclusion of four tracks Karen had recorded for an unreleased 1980 solo album. Richard's solo effort, *Time*, featured duets with Dionne Warwick and Dusty Springfield yet failed to chart. With time, the duo's saccharine image has receded somewhat, and Karen Carpenter is acknowledged by women rock musicians, including Chrissie Hynde and Madonna, as a pioneer. Sonic Youth, Sheryl Crow, Matthew Sweet, Cracker, and the Cranberries were among the 14 acts that contributed to the 1994 Carpenters tribute album *If*

I Were a Carpenter. Around the same time that fall, the Karen and Richard Carpenter Performing Arts Center at Cal State University in Long Beach opened.

Paul Carrack: See Ace; Squeeze; Mike + the Mechanics in Genesis entry

Joe "King" Carrasco and the Crowns

Formed 1979, Texas
Joe "King" Carrasco (b. Joseph Teutsch, Dumas, Tex.), gtr., voc.
1980—*Joe "King" Carrasco and the Crowns* (Hannibal) 1981—*Party Safari* 1982—*Synapse Gap (Mundo Total)* (MCA) 1983—*Party Weekend* 1984—*Tales from the Crypt (The Basement Tapes 1979)* tape (ROIR) 1989—*Tex-Mex Rock-Roll* 1990—*Royal, Loyal & Live* (Rio's Royal Texacali). Joe King Carrasco y Las Coronas: 1987—*Bandido Rock* (Rounder).

Calling his music "nuevo wavo," Joe Carrasco blends garage rock (Sam the Sham), Tex-Mex (Doug Sahm), Chicano polkas, and new-wavish intensity into speedy, good-humored party music. Carrasco started playing in West Texas rock & roll bands before he was a teenager. By 1973, when he settled in Austin, he had played with bands such as Salaman, a mariachi outfit, and Shorty y los Corvettes, which had a couple of local Spanish hits. His Chicano colleagues dubbed him "King" Carrasco.

In 1976 he formed his own band, El Molino, with local trumpeter Charlie McBurney, keyboardist Augie Meyers (of the Sir Douglas Quintet), and saxophonist Rocky Morales. El Molino was popular in Austin and San Antonio, where it recorded *Tex-Mex Rock-Roll* on Carrasco's Lisa label in 1978 (it was reissued by ROIR in 1989). The album found a cult audience in New York and London (Elvis Costello was an early admirer). Carrasco had no takers when he took the album to L.A. in search of a distribution deal, but he moved to the city's Mexican barrio and wrote songs with Sir Douglas Quintet drummer Johnny Perez.

Returning to Austin in 1979, he met Kris Cummings. Mike Navarro, and bassist Brad Kizer. Cummings had studied piano in New Orleans with Huey "Piano" Smith and Professor Longhair, but Carrasco gave her the Farfisa organ that defined the Crowns' trashy sound. They went to New York in late 1979, where their partylike shows, bolstered by Carrasco's antics (cape and crown, leaping from the stage during guitar solos, and wandering as far as his 60-foot cord allowed), won the enthusiastic support of clubgoers and the music press.

They returned to Austin heroes in the spring of 1980

and later that year signed to Stiff Records. Despite some critical kudos, a small loyal following, and a reputation as an exciting live act, Carrasco never achieved widespread popularity. He continued to perform into the Nineties.

Jim Carroll

Born 1950, New York City, New York
1980—*Catholic Boy* (Atco)   1982—*Dry Dreams*
1984—*I Write Your Name* (Atlantic)   1991—*Praying Mantis* (Giant)   1993—*A World Without Gravity: The Best of the Jim Carroll Band* (Rhino).

Poet, novelist, and former heroin addict Jim Carroll followed his friend Patti Smith into rock & roll with unexpected results: an almost-charting single, "People Who Died." After two more albums of music, he resumed publishing books of his poetry, and his first album of the Nineties, *Praying Mantis*, is one of the earliest full-length spoken-word releases.

Carroll was a prodigy. His first collection of poetry was published when he was 16, followed in 1970 by *The Basketball Diaries*, his teenage journal of high school, hustling, and heroin. A later poetry collection, *Living at the Movies*, was rumored to have been nominated for a Pulitzer (it was not); his writings have also appeared in the *Paris Review*. In 1974 Carroll moved to Northern California, where he kicked his drug habit and, along with a San Francisco band, began performing his version of rock & roll in area clubs.

On a visit to New York he played his demo tape for Earl McGrath, then president of Rolling Stones Records, who arranged a record deal with Atco and produced *Catholic Boy*. The album featured "People Who Died," a powerful invocation of friends fallen victim to drugs and street life, and drew critical raves. His next two albums were not as well received, and Carroll dismissed his band (which, for *Dry Dreams*, had included Lenny Kaye) to concentrate on his writing.

Since then he has published three additional books (*The Book of Nods*, 1986; *Forced Entries: The Downtown Diaries, 1971–1973*, 1987; *Fear of Dreaming: The Selected Poems of Jim Carroll*, 1993), written lyrics for Blue Öyster Cult and Boz Scaggs, and acted (he appeared in the 1985 film *Tuff Turf*). His singing appearances are rare, and he most often appears publicly to read from his work. *The Basketball Diaries* became a 1995 feature film, with Leonardo DiCaprio starring as Carroll, who makes a cameo appearance.

The Cars

Formed 1976, Boston, Massachusetts
Ric Ocasek (b. Richard Otcasek, Mar. 23, 1949, Baltimore, Md.), voc., gtr.; Ben Orr (b. Benjamin Orzechowski, Cleveland, Ohio), bass, voc.; Elliot Easton (b. Elliot Steinberg, Dec. 18, 1953, Brooklyn, N.Y.), gtr.; Greg Hawkes, kybds.; David Robinson, drums.
1978—*The Cars* (Elektra)   1979—*Candy-O*   1980— Panorama   1981—*Shake It Up*   1984—*Heartbeat City*   1985—*Greatest Hits*   1987—*Door to Door*. Ric Ocasek solo: 1983—*Beatitude* (Geffen)   1986— *This Side of Paradise*   1991—*Fireball Zone* (Reprise)   1993—*Quick Change World*. Ben Orr solo: 1986—*The Lace* (Elektra). Greg Hawkes solo: 1983—*Niagara Falls* (Passport). Elliot Easton solo: 1985—*Change No Change* (Elektra).

Ric Ocasek's artful pop songs drove the Cars, new wave's fastest, most consistent success. Their debut and second albums sold more than six million copies worldwide, and each album since (except their final group effort, *Door to Door*) sold over a million. Although the group initially got the critics' nod for Ocasek's coolly detached stance and the smoothly burnished keyboard-and guitar-laced hooks, in retrospect the Cars were essentially the new-wave model of a Top Forty hit machine. That their off-center pop sensibility found expression in a series of original and frequently aired music videos (especially "You Might Think") made them, for a time, one of America's top bands.

Ocasek and Ben Orr had been partners for nearly a decade before starting the Cars. Ocasek took up guitar at ten and immediately began to write songs. He started working as a musician after he'd dropped out of Antioch College and Bowling Green State University. He met Orr—who as a teenager had fronted the house band on a TV rock show, *Upbeat*—in Cleveland, where Orr worked in a studio as a producer and session musician. After working together in various bands in Cleveland, New York City, Woodstock, and Ann Arbor, they settled in Cambridge, Massachusetts, in the late Seventies.

As part of a folk trio, Milkwood, they released an album on Paramount in 1972, with Hawkes as session keyboardist. Ocasek and Orr continued to form bands, while Hawkes worked with Martin Mull and the Boston group Orphan, and wrote music with progressive rockers Happy the Man. In 1974 Easton joined Cap'n Swing, Ocasek and Orr's current band, which became popular in Boston but broke up when no recording contract was forthcoming. Hawkes rejoined, and Robinson, formerly of Jonathan Richman's Modern Lovers, DMZ, and Los Angeles' the Pop, completed the Cars in late 1976.

After intensive rehearsals in Ocasek's basement, the Cars made some demo tapes, including "Just What I Needed," which became a top-requested song on Boston radio station WBCN. Recorded in just two weeks, *The Cars* yielded three chart singles—"Just What I Needed"

The Cars: Greg Hawkes, Elliot Easton, Ben Orr, Ric Ocasek, David Robinson

(#27, 1978), "My Best Friend's Girl" (#35, 1978), and "Good Times Roll" (#41, 1979)—and went platinum, staying on the charts so persistently that the release of *Candy-O,* recorded early in 1979, was delayed. By 1979 the Cars were on the arena circuit; with "Let's Go" (#14, 1979) and "It's All I Can Do" (#41, 1979), *Candy-O* went platinum in two months. On *Panorama,* the Cars toyed with dissonance and odd meters; it went platinum with "Touch and Go" (#37, 1980), while *The Cars* remained on the charts.

In 1981 Ocasek produced Suicide's Alan Vega and Martin Rev, a single for Boston's New Models, and EPs for the Peter Dayton Band, Bebe Buell, and Romeo Void. Robinson produced singles for the Vinny Band and Boy's Life; Easton produced the Dawgs. The Cars also bought Intermedia Studios in Boston and remodeled it as Syncro Sound, where they recorded parts of *Shake It Up.* That album, with singles "Shake It Up" (#4, 1981) and "Since You're Gone" (#41, 1981), also went platinum. Ocasek, Orr, and Hawkes started solo albums in 1982; Robinson sat in on percussion with the Boston band Ooh Ah Ah, and Easton produced Peter Bond Set and Jules Shear. Ocasek also did production for Bad Brains, and the whole band contributed to the soundtrack of the 30-minute film *Chapter-X.*

Three years later *Heartbeat City* launched the hit singles "You Might Think" (#7, 1984), "Magic" (#12, 1984), "Drive" (#3, 1984), and "Hello Again" (#20, 1984). "Drive," which was used as background music to film clips documenting the famine stricken of Africa during the Live Aid concert and telecast, recharted in the U.K.; Ocasek donated the resulting royalties to the Band Aid Trust. The video for the song starred model Paulina Porizkova, whom Ocasek would wed in 1989.

The Cars' last Top Twenty hits were "Tonight She Comes" (#7, 1985) and "You Are the Girl" (#17, 1987). The latter comes from *Door to Door,* an album recorded as the group was unraveling due to personal conflicts; Ocasek later described it as "a substandard album." Fans agreed; it peaked at #26. Throughout the Cars' career Ocasek and Orr shared lead vocals, with Orr singing "My Best Friend's Girl," "Just What I Needed," "Drive," "Let's Go," and "Candy-O." Of the group members' solo efforts, theirs were by far the most popular. Each had a hit single: Ocasek, "Emotions in Motion" (#15, 1986), and Orr, "Stay the Night" (#24, 1987). Ocasek produced Weezer's eponymous 1994 debut album.

Carlene Carter

Born Rebecca Carlene Smith, September 26, 1955, Nashville, Tennessee
1978—*Carlene Carter* (Warner Bros.) 1979—*Two Sides to Every Woman* 1980—*Musical Shapes* 1981—*Blue Nun* 1983—*C'est C Bon* (Epic) 1990—*I Fell in Love* (Reprise) 1993—*Little Love Letters* (Giant).

A third-generation member of America's preeminent country music family, Carlene Carter is the granddaughter of Mother Maybelle Carter, of the Carter Family, and daughter of June Carter Cash and Fifties country star Carl Smith. Since she began recording in the late Seventies, Carlene Carter has evolved from an unfocused twangy rocker to a successful country singer/songwriter.

Carter spent her early years in Nashville; her parents divorced and her mother remarried Johnny Cash when

Carlene was 12. As a child, she often traveled with her mother, aunts, and grandmother, who toured as Mother Maybelle and the Carter Sisters. Learning piano at six and guitar at ten, Carter began singing onstage during her family's shows. After two brief teenage marriages, during which she had two children, Carter appeared sporadically as a member of the Carter Family revue.

In 1978 Carter recorded her first, self-titled album in England, backed by Graham Parker's band, the Rumour. A collection of upbeat, piano-based pop songs, *Carlene Carter* received some favorable notices but flopped. Her second album, *Two Sides to Every Woman,* recorded with New York session players, rocked harder, but lacked personality—though Carter herself certainly did not. At a performance in a New York club to support the album, she introduced one of its racier songs with the comment, "If this song doesn't put the cunt back in country, nothing will." Unbeknownst to her, her stepfather and mother were in the audience. The comment briefly caused a family rift, and earned Carter a *Playboy* award, "Quote of the Year."

In the late Seventies Carter married her third husband, British singer, songwriter, and producer Nick Lowe [see entry], whose bandmates in Rockpile, Dave Edmunds and Billy Bremner, joined him in backing her on her raucous country-rock breakthrough album, *Musical Shapes* (#139, 1980). Though still far from a commercial success, the album won critical raves and broadened Carter's audience.

Disappointing followup albums, *Blue Nun* and *C'est C Bon,* as well as personal problems (an ectopic pregnancy that almost killed her and the breakup of her marriage to Lowe), put Carter out of commission in the mid-Eighties. The party lifestyle had also taken its toll, and Carter temporarily quit the music business. In 1986 she began performing with the Johnny Cash and June Carter Cash family revue. Stating, "It was time to learn about my heritage," Carter dug into her country roots wholeheartedly for the first time, and after two years of touring with her family, she returned to Nashville drug- and alcohol-free and eager to commence her solo career.

In 1990 Carter hit country chart paydirt with *I Fell in Love* (#19 C&W), an album ranging from progressive country rock to traditional Appalachian folk and produced by Tom Petty bassist Howie Epstein. The album yielded several C&W hit singles: the title track (#3 C&W, 1990), "Come On Back" (#3 C&W, 1990), "The Sweetest Thing" (#25 C&W, 1991), and "One Love" (#33 C&W, 1991). *Little Love Letters* (#35 C&W, 1993), again produced by Epstein, with whom Carter was living, featured Heartbreaker keyboardist Benmont Tench, as well as guitarists John Jorgenson, Albert Lee, and NRBQ's Al Anderson, who toured with Carter. Anderson and Carter cowrote the album's #3 C&W hit, "Every Little Thing."

Clarence Carter

Born January 14, 1936, Montgomery, Alabama
1968—*This Is Clarence Carter* (Atlantic); *The Dynamic Clarence Carter* **1969—***Testifyin'* **1970—***Patches* **1971—***The Best of Clarence Carter* **1973—***Sixty Minutes with Clarence Carter* (Fame); *Real* (ABC) **1975—***Loneliness and Temptation* **1976—***Heart Full of Song* **1981—***Let's Burn* (Venture) **1985—***Messin' with My Mind* (Ichiban) **1986—***Dr. CC* **1987—***Hooked on Love* **1988—***Touch of Blues* **1990—***Between a Rock and Hard Place* **1992—***Snatching It Back: The Best of Clarence Carter* (Rhino).

Blind singer/guitarist Clarence Carter is best known for his late-Sixties hit singles "Slip Away" and "Patches." His career began as part of Clarence and Calvin and the C and C Boys on the Duke label. In 1965 they joined Rick Hall's Fame Records. Calvin Scott had a car accident shortly afterward and retired, but Carter stayed with Fame, recording solo and playing on sessions. As guitarist of the Mellow Men, he backed Otis Redding, Joe Tex, Solomon Burke, and Gene Chandler. In 1968 he met Candi Staton, whom he later married. Staton had hits as a soul ballad singer in the early Seventies and as a disco star in the late Seventies. (They divorced after a few years.) Carter had nine R&B hits before he crossed over to the pop chart with 1968's "Slip Away" (#6 pop, #2 R&B) and "Too Weak to Fight" (#13 pop, #3 R&B). He followed up in 1969 with "Snatching It Back" (#4 R&B), "The Feeling Is Right" (#9 R&B), and "Doin' Our Thing" (#9 R&B). His 1970 story song "Patches" (#4 pop, #2 R&B) was hailed as an instant classic. Carter signed with ABC in the mid-Seventies, but the hits stopped coming for a while. Carter continued to tour and record, releasing albums regularly through the Eighties. His last hit was from *Dr. CC,* "Strokin'," a song sufficiently ribald to preclude radio play. Nonetheless, it sold 1.5 million copies.

The Carter Family

Formed 1926, Maces Spring, Virginia
Alvin Pleasant Carter (b. Apr. 15, 1891, Maces Spring; d. Nov. 7, 1960, Maces Spring), voc.; Sara Dougherty Carter (b. July 21, 1898, Wise County, Va.; d. Jan. 9, 1979), voc., gtr., autoharp, banjo; Maybelle Addington Carter (b. May 10, 1909, Nickelsville, Va.; d. Oct. 23, 1978), voc., gtr., autoharp, banjo.
1961—*The Famous Carter Family* (Harmony) **1963—***Great Original Recordings by the Carter Family* **1964—***Keep on the Sunny Side* (Columbia) **1965—***The Best of the Carter Family* **1967—***An Historic Reunion* **1991—***The Carter Family* (MCA) **1993—***Anchored in Love: Their Complete Victor Recordings 1927–1928* (Rounder); *My Clinch Moun-*

The Carter Family pioneered modern country music by setting folk songs to string-band backup and were one of the most popular groups in America from 1926 until they disbanded in 1943. After that, Maybelle and A.P. continued to perform separately with their children through the Fifties and Sixties. Their songs, which included such standards as "Wildwood Flower," "Wabash Cannonball," "I'm Thinking Tonight of My Blue Eyes," "Will the Circle Be Unbroken," and their radio program theme song, "Keep on the Sunny Side," were immensely popular; the 78-r.p.m. version of "Wildwood Flower" sold over a million copies.

The group formed in 1926 when A.P. Carter and his wife, Sara Dougherty, were joined by A.P.'s brother Ezra's wife (and Sara's cousin), Maybelle. Each had performed with friends and neighbors and as a group for about a year before A.P. had them record for Ralph Peer, who had been sent by RCA Victor to record local musicians (Jimmie Rodgers was recorded on the same day). The Carter Family was soon recording quite frequently, although it wasn't until they had left Virginia some years later that any of them could stop working day jobs. In 1928 they recorded their biggest hit, "Wildwood Flower." Their success was considerable despite the fact that the group never ventured more than a few hundred miles from home to perform.

In 1936 A.P. and Sara were divorced, but the group continued to perform and record, and in 1938 moved to Del Rio, Texas, where for the next three years they were regulars on radio station XERA. They next moved to Charlotte, North Carolina, to work for WBT, but shortly after their arrival, A.P. and Sara decided to retire. The original Carter Family had their last radio shows around 1939. The next year, Maybelle began working with her daughters June, Helen, and Anita as Maybelle Carter and the Carter Sisters. Meanwhile A.P. and several of his children had formed another group, with whom he performed until his death in 1960. After A.P. died, Maybelle and her daughters adopted the Carter Family name.

The family's influence on latter-day singers and songwriters derives not only from their songs and recordings but also from Maybelle Carter's unique acoustic guitar–strumming techniques, particularly what has become known as the "chicken-scratch," or the "Carter" style, which is widely imitated by folksingers. Maybelle and Sara reunited at the 1967 Newport Folk Festival to record *An Historic Reunion.* Throughout the Sixties, Maybelle performed with her daughters in her son-in-law Johnny Cash's revue and later on his television program. She sang the title track on the Nitty Gritty Dirt Band's *Will the Circle Be Unbroken* in 1971. With the exception of Maybelle's three daughters and of June's daughter, Carlene Carter [see entry], none of the second- and third-generation Carters have achieved wide recognition, although many of them are active in country music as performers and session musicians. June, Helen, and Anita Carter are sometimes joined by their children to sing Carter Family songs during concert performances.

Peter Case

Born April 5, 1954, Buffalo, New York
With the Plimsouls (Lou Ramirez, drums; Dave Pahoa, bass; Eddie Munoz, gtr.): 1980—*Zero Hour* EP (Beat)   1981—*The Plimsouls* (Planet)   1983—*Everywhere at Once* (Geffen)   1992—*The Plimsouls . . . Plus* (Rhino).
Peter Case solo: 1986—*Peter Case* (Geffen)   1989—*The Man with the Blue Postmodern Fragmented Neo-traditionalist Guitar*   1992—*Six Pack of Love* 1994—*Peter Case Sings Like Hell* (Vanguard) 1995—*Torn Again.*

Singer/songwriter Peter Case began his career in punk-rock bands, but in the mid-Eighties went solo and became a folk-rock troubadour. The son of two teachers, Case dropped out of school in tenth grade, got his GED, and studied at State University of New York at Buffalo. One winter he boarded a Greyhound bus, eventually winding up in San Francisco, where he busked on street corners and in coffeehouses, sometimes accompanying poet Allen Ginsberg.

In 1976 Case cofounded seminal West Coast punk band the Nerves with Paul Collins (later of the Beat), for whom he played bass. By 1978 he had moved to L.A. and formed the Plimsouls, a power-pop band popular in the local club scene. After a successful indie EP, Elektra subsidiary Planet signed the group, but when *The Plimsouls* stiffed, dropped them. The band then released the independent 12-inch "A Million Miles Away," a college-radio hit that brought the band its second major-label deal. *Everywhere at Once* included that single and a number of other catchy tunes but failed to deliver on sales, despite the band's cameo in the teen flick *Valley Girl.*

In 1984 Case dissolved the Plimsouls, became a born-again Christian, and started playing solo shows. One night he saw singer/songwriter Victoria Williams performing in a restaurant; the two formed the Incredibly Strung Out Band and married in April 1985 (they divorced in 1989). The critically praised *Peter Case,* produced by T Bone Burnett and Mitchell Froom, included the college-radio hit "Steel Strings."

Case's second album also pleased critics with its strong melodies and writerly lyrics. It included contributions from David Lindley, Jim Keltner, and Los Lobos' David Hidalgo. *Six Pack of Love* saw Case return to his more rocking roots. In 1993 he formed a band including

ex-Plimsoul Eddie Munoz. The following year, Case released on Vanguard a collection of folk blues songs,
which he recorded live to two-track in a living-room studio set up by producer Marvin Etzioni (Lone Justice).

Johnny Cash

Born February 26, 1932, Kingsland, Arkansas
1957—*With His Hot and Blue Guitar* (Sun)   1958—
Songs That Made Him Famous*   1959—*Fabulous
Johnny Cash* (Columbia)   1960—*Ride This Train
1962—*Sound of Johnny Cash*   1963—*Ring of Fire*
1964—*Keep on the Sunny Side; I Walk the Line*
1965—*Orange Blossom Special*   1968—*The Holy*
Land; At Folsom Prison*   1969—*Jackson; At San
Quentin*   1970—*Johnny Cash Show*   1971—*A Man
in Black*   1973—*Gospel Road; Sunday Morning
Coming Down; America*   1974—*Five Feet High and
Rising; Ragged Old Flag*   1975—*Look at Them
Beans*   1977—*Last Gunfighter Ballad*   1980—*Rock-
***abilly Blues*   1982—*The Survivors* (with Jerry Lee**
Lewis, Carl Perkins); *The Adventures of Johnny*
Cash*   1985—*Rainbow*   1986—*Believe in Him
(Word)   1987—*Johnny Cash Is Coming to Town*
(Mercury); *The Vintage Years (1955–1963)* (Rhino)
1988—*Water from the Wells of Home* (Mercury)
1990—*The Sun Years* (Rhino)   1991—*The Mystery*
of Life* (Mercury)   1992—*The Essential Johnny
***Cash (1955–1983)* (Columbia Legacy)   1994—**
***American Recordings* (American).**
With Willie Nelson, Kris Kristofferson, and Waylon
Jennings: 1985—*Highwayman* (Columbia); *Despera-*
does Waiting for a Train*   1987—*They Killed Him
(Mercury)   1990—*Highwayman 2*   1995—*The Road*
***Goes On Forever* (Liberty).**

Country music patriarch Johnny Cash, the "Man in
Black," has walked the line between rock and country
since his early days as a rockabilly singer. His songs' characteristic marching bass lines have influenced Waylon
Jennings, among others, while his deep, quavery baritone
growl has become a trademark. A preeminent songwriter,
Cash has been courted over the years by rock's elite, beginning with Dylan in the 1960s. In 1994 Cash returned
to the spotlight, boosted by the support of a whole new
generation of fans, with the release of the stark (just vocals and acoustic guitar) *American Recordings.*

The son of Southern Baptist sharecroppers, Cash
began playing guitar and writing songs at age 12. During
high school, he performed frequently on radio station
KLCN in Blytheville, Arkansas. Cash moved to Detroit in
his late teens and worked there until he joined the Air
Force as a radio operator in Germany. He left the Air
Force and married Vivian Liberto in 1954; the couple settled in Memphis, where Cash worked as an appliance
salesman and attended radio announcers' school.

Johnny Cash

With the Tennessee Two—guitarist Luther Perkins
and bassist Marshall Grant—he began recording for Sam
Phillips' Sun Records in 1955. The trio recorded "Cry, Cry,
Cry" (#14 C&W, 1955), and followed it with "Folsom
Prison Blues" (#5 C&W, 1956). Later in 1956 came Cash's
most enduring hit, the million-seller "I Walk the Line"
(#17, 1956).

Cash moved near Ventura, California, in 1958, signed
with Columbia, and began a nine-year period of alcohol
and drug abuse. He released a number of successful
country and pop hits, among them "Ring of Fire" (#1 pop,
#1 C&W, 1963), written by June Carter of the Carter Fam-
ily and Merle Kilgore. By then, he had left his family and
moved to New York's Greenwich Village. Late in 1965,
Cash was arrested by Customs officials for trying to
smuggle amphetamines in his guitar case across the
Mexican border. He got a suspended sentence and was
fined. After a serious auto accident and a near fatal overdose, his wife divorced him. By then Cash had moved to
Nashville, where he became friends with Waylon Jennings. Together they spent what both have described as
a drug-crazed year and a half.

But in Nashville, Cash began a liaison with June
Carter, who helped him get rid of his drug habit by 1967
and reconverted him to fundamentalist Christianity. By
the time Cash and Carter married in early 1968, they had
begun working together regularly. They had hit duets
with "Jackson" (#2 C&W, 1967), "Long-Legged Guitar
Pickin' Man" (#6 C&W, 1967), and versions of Bob Dylan's
"It Ain't Me, Babe" (#58 pop, #4 C&W, 1964) and Tim
Hardin's "If I Were a Carpenter" (#36 pop, #2 C&W, 1970).

Cash's 1968 live album, *At Folsom Prison* (#13), became a million-seller in 1968. Bob Dylan invited him to sing a duet ("Girl from the North Country") and write liner notes for *Nashville Skyline,* and Dylan appeared in the first segment of ABC-TV's *The Johnny Cash Show* in June 1969. The highly rated series, which lasted two years, developed a reputation as an eclectic showcase of contemporary American music, with guests ranging from Louis Armstrong to Carl Perkins to Bob Dylan. Cash had a 1969 hit with Shel Silverstein's "A Boy Named Sue" (#2), a track from *Johnny Cash at San Quentin;* his best-selling album, the live LP was #1 for four weeks.

In 1970 Cash performed at the Nixon White House. He and June Carter traveled to Israel in 1971 to make a documentary, *Gospel Road.* Cash continued to tour and make hits through the Seventies, including "A Thing Called Love" (#2 C&W, 1972) and "One Piece at a Time" (#1 C&W, 1976). He also became active in benefit work, particularly on behalf of prisoners, Native American rights, and evangelist Billy Graham's organization.

In 1982 Cash regrouped with Sun Records label mates Carl Perkins and Jerry Lee Lewis to record *The Survivors.* Three years later Cash hooked up with three other compadres—Kris Kristofferson, Waylon Jennings, and Willie Nelson—to form the Highwaymen, releasing *Highwayman* in 1985. The Highwaymen performed together sporadically throughout the late Eighties and Nineties, recording *Highwayman 2* in 1990. They released *The Road Goes On Forever,* produced by Don Was, in 1995.

Cash's long relationship with Columbia Records ended in the mid-Eighties, and in 1986 he began a somewhat desultory liaison with Nashville's branch of Mercury Records. By the late Eighties, his long streak of country hits had ended, and Cash complained to an interviewer that he'd been "purged" from Nashville, replaced by contemporary "hat acts." He continued to perform constantly, however, usually with a package tour that included his wife and her sisters Helen and Anita Carter, as well as Johnny and June's son, John Carter Cash (other Cash and Carter siblings would sometimes show up too). Throughout these years, Cash turned to acting, in a slew of Western-themed movies and TV shows. He also suffered from health problems, and underwent heart surgery and drug treatment for an addiction to painkillers.

Already a member of the Nashville Songwriter's Hall of Fame (Cash has more than 400 songs to his credit) and the Country Music Hall of Fame, Cash was inducted into the Rock and Roll Hall of Fame in 1992. Also that year came the release of the critically acclaimed boxed set, *The Essential Johnny Cash.* In 1993, he began his return to the forefront with a guest vocal turn on U2's *Zooropa;* he sang lead vocals on the darkly haunting track "The Wanderer." The following year, Cash was toasted by alt-rock audiences with the release of *American Record-*

ings, on the label by the same name, known for its rap and rock artists. Label chief Rick Rubin's production emphasized Cash's brooding, deep vocals, backed by his own simple, but rhythmic acoustic guitar. Featuring, among Cash's own compositions, covers of such artists as Nick Lowe, Leonard Cohen, and Tom Waits, the album's songs veered from Cash's "Redemption" to satanic-rocker Glenn Danzig's "Thirteen." Appearing solo or backed by guitar, bass, and drums, Cash performed in several intimate venues crawling with such hipsters as actor Johnny Depp and his gal-pal model Kate Moss, who starred in the video for the album's "Delia's Gone," frequently shown on MTV. Though the album only reached #110 on the pop charts (#29 C&W), it received airplay on alternative-rock and college radio stations, garnering critical raves and the 1994 Grammy for Best Contemporary Folk Album.

Rosanne Cash

Born May 24, 1955, Memphis, Tennessee
1980—*Right or Wrong* (Columbia)   1981—*Seven Year Ache*   1982—*Somewhere in the Stars*   1985— Rhythm and Romance*   1987—*King's Record Shop* 1989—*Hits 1979–1989*   1990—*Interiors*   1993—*The Wheel.*

The oldest daughter of country music star Johnny Cash and Vivian Liberto, Rosanne Cash began her recording career with a sound that blended Nashville C&W and California country rock. By the Nineties, she had developed into an eloquent and introspective singer/songwriter.

Though born in Memphis, Cash grew up in Ventura, California, where her parents had moved in 1958. The two divorced in 1966. The day after graduating from high school, she joined her father's touring revue as a wardrobe assistant and later became a backup singer. After three years with the Johnny Cash show, she moved to London in 1976, returning home in 1977 to attend Vanderbilt University in Nashville. Then she moved to Hollywood and enrolled in the Lee Strasberg Theater Institute the next year. She took time off in January 1978 to record a demo produced by Rodney Crowell [see entry], attracting the attention of the German-based Ariola label. She went to Munich to record an album, and although it was never released in the U.S. it persuaded the Nashville branch of Columbia Records to sign her.

Cash and Crowell married in 1979. For a while she played with Crowell's band, the Cherry Bombs, before Columbia released her debut U.S. album, *Right or Wrong,* which sold surprisingly well despite her inability to tour; she was pregnant. Her 1981 followup, *Seven Year Ache,* drew critical raves and solid sales and yielded a #1 country hit with the title tune (two other tracks from the LP hit #1 as well).

Cash continued to score on the country charts: "Ain't No Money" (#4 C&W, 1982), "I Don't Know Why You Don't Want Me" (#1 C&W, 1985), "Never Be You" (#1 C&W, 1985), "Hold On" (#5 C&W, 1986), "Second to No One" (#5 C&W, 1986). By the mid-Eighties, though, childbearing had curtailed her touring (she and Crowell have three daughters), and a cocaine dependence landed her in rehab. She sprang back, however, with the eclectic *King's Record Shop* (#6 C&W, 1987), which featured a remake of her father's "Tennessee Flat Top Box" (#1 C&W, 1987) and marked a healing of a strained relationship with her dad. The album also yielded #1 C&W hits in John Hiatt's "The Way We Make a Broken Heart," "If You Change Your Mind," and "Runaway Train." A longtime Beatles fan, Cash took the group's "I Don't Want to Spoil the Party" to the top of the country charts in 1989.

Self-produced, *Interiors* (#23 C&W, 1990) was Cash's first album without Crowell at the helm. Her brutally dark take on intimate relationships was reflected throughout and made clear the marital problems that had been hinted at on earlier albums, both in her own songs and in those contributed by her husband. Cash began touring the singer/songwriter circuit in the Nineties, and as her songs became more personal and her music's sound more stripped down, her country hits stopped coming. In 1992 her marriage ended in divorce. Its painful aftermath and her own self-actualization were the themes of her critically acclaimed album *The Wheel* (#37 C&W, 1993). Cash's interest in Jungian psychology was apparent in her compositions as well. Always highly critical of the Nashville country star lifestyle, Cash relocated to New York City and began a relationship with guitarist, songwriter, and producer John Leventhal (Shawn Colvin), with whom she began collaborating and touring. (Cash and Leventhal married in 1995.)

David Cassidy

Born April 12, 1950, New York City, New York
1972—*Cherish* (Bell); *Rock Me Baby* 1974—*Cassidy Live* 1975—*The Higher They Climb* (RCA) 1976—*Home Is Where the Heart Is* 1990—*David Cassidy* (Enigma) 1992—*Didn't You Used to Be* (Scotti Bros.).

Early-Seventies teen idol and actor David Cassidy is the son of actor Jack Cassidy and actress Evelyn Ward. He moved to Hollywood in 1957 with his mother when his parents divorced. (His father then married actress Shirley Jones, who played Cassidy's mother in the television series *The Partridge Family*.) During his teens, he played guitar and drums, wrote songs, and acted. His credits include Allan Sherman's Broadway production *Fig Leaves Are Falling* and guest shots on television's *Bonanza* and *Marcus Welby, M.D.*

In fall 1970 he began a four-year run as Keith Partridge on *The Partridge Family* (inspired by the Cowsills).

The Partridge Family's premiere single, "I Think I Love You" (released before the TV series debuted), sold nearly six million copies. Several hits followed. Cassidy received royalties from the sales of Partridge Family coloring books, lunch boxes, dolls, comic books, postcards, clothes, books, records, and the show itself [see entry].

His solo recording career began in 1971 with a Top Ten remake of the Association's "Cherish." His several world tours inspired mass hysteria. Cassidy began to disclaim the teen-idol role after a 14-year-old fan named Bernadette Wheeler suffered a fatal heart attack at a London show in May 1974. That year he quit the TV series, and in 1975 he signed a long-term contract with RCA.

Cassidy's subsequent efforts did little to establish credibility with more mature listeners in the United States. Across the Atlantic, in the U.K., it was quite a different story, with Cassidy claiming ten Top Twenty singles there between 1972 and 1985, including two chart-toppers ("How Can I Be Sure," "Daydreamer" b/w "The Puppy Song"). In 1976 he and Mick Ronson cut a single entitled "Gettin' It On in the Streets" and were supposed to record an album and form a band; none of it ever came to pass.

During 1978–79 he returned to television in a police drama, *David Cassidy—Man Undercover*, but he never abandoned music. He starred in *Joseph and the Amazing Technicolor Dreamcoat* on Broadway, and in 1987 he took over Cliff Richard's role in Dave Clark's London musical *Time*. In 1990 he launched a comeback effort that resulted in his first U.S. Top Thirty appearance since 1972, "Lyin' to Myself" (#27, 1990). Seemingly resigned to the *Partridge Family* legacy (the show found new audiences in syndication and on Nick at Nite), he entitled a recent effort *Didn't You Used to Be* and had another ex-Partridge, comedian/disk jockey Danny Bonaduce, open some of his shows. In 1993 he opened in the New York production of *Blood Brothers*, a dramatic musical costarring Petula Clark and his half-brother Shaun Cassidy. His autobiography, *Come On, Get Happy*, was published in 1994.

Shaun Cassidy

Born September 27, 1959, Hollywood, California
1977—*Shaun Cassidy* (Curb); *Born Late* 1978—*Under Wraps* 1979—*Room Service; That's Rock 'n' Roll—Shaun Cassidy Live* 1980—*Wasp.*

Following in the footsteps of his half-brother David Cassidy, Shaun Cassidy was a teen idol in the late Seventies. The son of actor Jack Cassidy and actress Shirley Jones, he grew up in Beverly Hills and formed his first rock band at age 11, just after he began writing his own songs. Signed by Mike Curb to the Warner Bros./Curb label in 1975, Cassidy had his first success in Europe, where his photos saturated the teen magazines. His debut single—"Morning Girl," released in January 1976—went Top

Twenty in most of Europe. His second single, a cover of Eric Carmen's "That's Rock 'n' Roll," expanded his appeal to Australia, and later went gold in the U.S. in a 1977 release.

He starred in *The Hardy Boys Mysteries* TV series from 1977 to 1979. His first U.S. single, a cover of the Crystals' 1963 hit "Da Doo Ron Ron," was released in May 1977 and hit #1; his simultaneously released debut album, *Shaun Cassidy,* went platinum. "Hey Deanie," another Carmen song, hit #7 in 1978, but followups sank. Like half-brother David before him, Shaun tried with little success to make the transition to a serious rocker; his 1980 *Wasp* was produced by Todd Rundgren and featured versions of songs by David Bowie, Ian Hunter, Pete Townshend, and David Byrne.

He concentrated on acting. Among his television credits are the 1979 television movie *Like Normal People,* the 1980 series *Breaking Away,* and, later in the decade, the soap *General Hospital.* In 1993 he played David Cassidy's twin in the Broadway production of *Blood Brothers.*

Jimmy Castor
Born June 22, 1943, New York City, New York
N.A.—*Hey Leroy* (Smash)   1972—*It's Just Begun* (RCA); *Phase Two*   1973—*Dimension 3*   1974—*The Everything Man* (Atlantic)   1975—*Super Sound* (Atco); *Butt of Course*   1976—*E Man Groovin'.*

Singer, songwriter, and saxophonist Jimmy Castor is best known for "Troglodyte (Cave Man)," a 1972 funk novelty hit, but his career stretches back to the Fifties. He assembled his first group, Jimmy Castor and the Juniors (Johnny Williams, Orton Graves, Al Casey Jr.), around 1955. Their "I Promise to Remember" (a Castor original) was a modest New York hit in 1956, but later that year Frankie Lymon and the Teenagers' cover version was a national hit. Castor, a friend of the Teenagers, was asked to sub for Lymon on occasion.

After graduating from New York's High School of Music and Art, Castor dropped out of the music business to study accounting at City College of New York. He reentered the music business in 1962, when he played the sax on Dave "Baby" Cortez's Top Ten hit "Rinky Dink." He then recorded solo for the Winley, Clown, Jet-Set, and Decca labels before forming the Jimmy Castor Bunch (percussionist Leonard Fridie Jr., bassist Douglas Gibson, guitarist Harry Jensen, drummer Robert Manigault, and keyboardist Gerry Thomas) in the mid-Sixties. The Bunch recorded for Compass and Capitol before "Hey, Leroy, Your Mama's Callin' You" hit (#31 pop, 1967; #16 R&B, 1966) on Smash. "Troglodyte" (#6 pop, #4 R&B, 1972) is Castor's biggest hit to date. Castor left RCA for Atlantic and returned to the Top Twenty with a sequel to "Troglodyte," "The Bertha Butt Boogie" (#16 pop, #22 R&B, 1975). His other hits on Atlantic were "Potential"

(#25 R&B, 1975), "King Kong, Part 1" (#23 R&B, 1975), and "Space Age" (#28 R&B, 1977).

Through the early Eighties, Castor continued to record solo, his singles peaking at the nether points of the R&B chart. In 1988 he had an R&B Top Thirty hit in a duet with Joyce Sims, "Love Makes a Woman." In the early Nineties Castor became a Teenager when he joined the two surviving group members and two other singers in a re-formed lineup of that group.

Nick Cave and the Bad Seeds: See the Birthday Party

Cerrone
Born 1952, St. Michel, France
1976—*Love in C Minor* (Cotillion)   1977—*Cerrone's Paradise; Cerrone 3: Supernature*   1978—*Cerrone IV: The Golden Touch; Brigade Mondaine* (Malligator)   1979—*Cerrone V: Angelina* (Atlantic)   1982—*Back Track* (Pavillion).

Composer, producer, and drummer Jean-Marc Cerrone was one of the principal architects of the late-Seventies synthesizer-dominated "Euro-disco" sound. After training to be a hairdresser, he began his musical career in the early Seventies working as a session drummer until he was able to open a chain of record stores in the suburbs of Paris. In 1976 he went to London, where he tried and failed to get a recording contract. He financed the production of his first album himself, recording *Love in C Minor* with English session musicians and singers Stephanie de Sykes and Madeline Bell. The album was rejected by every major French company, so Cerrone formed his own Malligator label and marketed it himself. As soon as it was given disco play in France, a commercial demand arose and the album was on the way to gold sales in France. The LP-side-long title track was edited to single-side length, and as such became a stateside disco hit (#36 pop, #29 R&B, 1977).

After that Cerrone had little impact in the U.S. In Europe, however, he was a major star of the late Seventies, selling over ten million records. He continued to base his operations in France, where he has published at least one best-selling novel. In the mid-Eighties he moved to Los Angeles, where he worked as a session musician. In 1994 he released the single "Love and Be Loved."

Peter Cetera: See Chicago

Chad and Jeremy
Formed circa 1963, London, England
Chad Stuart (b. Dec. 10, 1943, Eng.), voc., gtr., piano, sitar, tamboura, tablas, banjo, flute; Jeremy Clyde (b. Mar. 22, 1944, Eng.), voc., gtr.

1964—*Yesterday's Gone* (World Artists)   1965—
Chad and Jeremy Sing for You; Before and After
(Columbia); *I Don't Want to Lose You Baby*   1966—
The Best of Chad and Jeremy (Capitol); *More Chad
and Jeremy; Distant Shores* (Columbia)   1967—*Of
Cabbages and Kings*   1968—*The Ark*   1992—
Painted Dayglow Smile (Legacy)   1993—*Yester-
day's Gone—A Golden Classics Collection*
(Collectables).

Chad and Jeremy's innocuous soft-rock hits kept them
on the charts from 1964 through 1966. Sons of affluent
British families, both were well educated (Eton, the Sor-
bonne). They met while studying at the Central School of
Drama in London, where they began singing folk-based
material. In 1964 one of their first singles, "Yesterday's
Gone," went to #21 in the U.S.

The pair soon moved to Hollywood and began to
rival Peter and Gordon as the world's top folk-rock duo.
Chart hits like "A Summer Song" (#7, 1964) and "Distant
Shores" (#30, 1966) combined with frequent television
appearances (*Hullabaloo, The Hollywood Palace*) kept
them in the public eye. They broke up in late 1966, when
Jeremy departed to act in a London stage musical.

The two later regrouped and recorded *Of Cabbages
and Kings,* one of the first "concept albums," and *The
Ark.* They ended their partnership in November 1967.
Thereafter Clyde resumed his acting career: He has appeared on the London stage, in movies, and in a television miniseries. Stuart served as musical director for *The
Smothers Brothers Comedy Hour,* tried as a duet with his
wife, Jill, and worked as a musical-comedy composer. In
1985 the pair appeared together in a West End production of *Pump Boys and Dinettes.*

Eugene Chadbourne: See Camper Van Beethoven

Chairmen of the Board
Formed 1969, Detroit, Michigan
**Original lineup: General Norman Johnson (b. May
23, 1943), voc.; Danny Woods (b. Apr. 10, 1944), voc.;
Harrison Kennedy (b. Ontario, Can.), voc.; Eddie
Curtis, voc.**
**1970—*Give Me Just a Little More Time* (Invictus); *In
Session*   1972—*Bittersweet*   1973—*Greatest Hits*
1990—*Greatest Hits* (HDH/Fantasy)**

The Chairmen of the Board is a soul vocal group whose
biggest hit was the Holland-Dozier-Holland–produced
"Give Me Just a Little More Time" (#3, 1970). The group's
leader and main songwriter, General Norman Johnson,
grew up in Norfolk, Virginia, where he sang in church
choirs as a child. By age 12 he had formed his first group,

the Humdingers. During his senior year of high school
(1961), Johnson and his group the Showmen recorded
his salute to rock & roll, "It Will Stand," for Minit Records.

After several more singles for Minit and later Swan,
Johnson left the group to sign with ex-Motown producers Holland-Dozier-Holland's Invictus label. There the
Chairmen of the Board was formed, with Johnson; another Showman, Danny Woods; Harrison Kennedy of the
Canadian group Stone Soul Children; and Eddie Curtis,
an alumnus of Lee Andrews and the Hearts and Huey
Smith and the Clowns. Their debut single, "Give Me Just
a Little More Time," was followed by several minor hits
and "Pay to the Piper" (#13) in 1970. They briefly disbanded the next year but regrouped in 1972. They continue to tour and have had local hits in the Southeast.
Several of Johnson's songs have been hits for other performers, including Honey Cone ("Want Ads," "Stick Up,"
"One Monkey Don't Stop No Show"), Freda Payne
("Bring the Boys Home"), and Clarence Carter
("Patches"). In 1994 Johnson duetted with Joey Ramone
on "Rockaway Beach" for the album *Godchildren of Soul.*

The Chambers Brothers
Formed circa 1961, Los Angeles, California
**George E. Chambers (b. Sep. 26, 1931, Flora, Miss.),
voc., bass; Willie Chambers (b. Mar. 3, 1938, Miss.),
voc., gtr.; Lester Chambers (b. Apr. 13, 1940,
Miss.), voc., harmonica; Joe Chambers (b. Aug. 24,
1942, Scott County, Miss.), voc., gtr.**
**1965—(+ Brian Keenan [b. Jan. 28, ca. 1944, New
York City, N.Y.; d. ca. mid-1980s], drums) *People Get
Ready* (Vault)   1966—*Chambers Brothers Now*
1968—*Shout!; The Time Has Come* (Columbia); *A
New Time, a New Day*   1969—*Love, Peace and
Happiness*   1970—*Chambers Brothers Live at Fill-
more East; Feelin' the Blues* (Vault)   1971—*A New
Generation* (Columbia); *The Chambers Brothers'
Greatest Hits*   1972—*Oh My God!*   1973—*Best of
the Chambers Brothers* (Fantasy)   1974—*Unbonded*
(Avco)   1975—*Right Move.***

Black gospel, funk, and psychedelic innovators, the
Chambers Brothers had an enthusiastic following in the
late Sixties. The four brothers grew up in a poverty-
stricken Mississippi sharecropping family and first sang
together at the Mount Calvary Baptist Church in Lee
County. George, the eldest, was drafted into the army in
1952. Once discharged, he gravitated to south Los Angeles and was eventually joined by his brothers. They
began performing around Southern California as a
gospel and folk quartet in 1961.

After their first New York dates in 1965, they became
an interracial group with the addition of drummer Brian
Keenan and moved toward rock. The group attracted national attention at the 1965 Newport Folk Festival and

worked both the psychedelic ballrooms (the Fillmores, Electric Circus) and soul venues like New York's Apollo Theatre. They signed with Columbia in 1967, and the title track from their first album for that label, "Time Has Come Today," became a major hit (#11, 1968) and was later used to great effect in the 1978 antiwar film *Coming Home*. They charted with several more singles, including "I Can't Turn You Loose" (#37, 1968), and LPs (*A New Time, a New Day* and *Love, Peace and Happiness*) over the next few years.

The original group broke up in early 1972, with drummer Keenan joining Genya Ravan's band. The Chambers Brothers reunited in 1974 for *Unbonded*. They continue an on-again, off-again career. In 1980 they supported Maria Muldaur on her *Gospel Nights* and made commercials for Levi Strauss. Early in 1980 Lester relocated to New York (where he formed a band with ex–Electric Flag bassist Harvey Brooks), and several of the brothers worked on solo careers. Willie and Joe became session players, George sang gospel, and all the brothers belong to an extended-family gospel choir called the Chambers Family Singers. Keenan went on to run his own Connecticut recording studio; in the mid-1980's, he died of an apparent heart attack.

The Champs

Formed 1957, Los Angeles, California
Original lineup: Dave Burgess (b. Lancaster, Calif.), gtr.; Dale Norris (b. Springfield, Mass.), gtr.; Chuck Rio (b. Rankin, Tex.), sax; Gen Alden (b. Cisco, Tex.), drums; Bobby Morris (b. Tulsa, Okla.), bass.
1960—*Everybody's Rockin'* (Challenge)   1994—*Greatest Hits—Tequila* (Curb).

The Champs were West Coast sessionmen whose first single, the instrumental "Tequila" (written by Rio), stayed on the charts 19 weeks, reached #1, eventually sold more than six million worldwide, and won a Grammy Award for the best R&B record of 1958. Subsequent hits—"Too Much Tequila" (#30, 1960), "Limbo Rock" (#40, 1962), and "Tequila Twist" (#99, 1962)—failed to match the success of "Tequila." Over the years the group underwent numerous personnel changes, including a brief membership by guitarist/vocalist Delaney Bramlett (later of Delaney and Bonnie), before disbanding in 1965. Two other ex-Champs, Jimmy Seals and Dash Crofts, went on to form the Dawnbreakers before they reemerged in 1970 as Seals and Crofts [see entry].

James Chance

Born James Siegfried, April 20, 1953, Milwaukee, Wisconsin
1979—*Buy the Contortions* (with the Contortions) (Ze); *Grutzi Elvis* soundtrack; *Off-White* (with

James White and the Blacks)   1980—*Live aux Bains Douches* (with the Contortions) (Invisible, Fr.)   1981—*Live in New York* (with the Contortions) (ROIR); *Sax Maniac* (with James White and the Blacks) (Animal/Chrysalis)   1982—*James White Presents the Flaming Demonics* (Ze)   1991—*Soul Exorcism* cassette (with the Contortions) (ROIR).

James Chance's music is an edgy, atonal fusion incorporating funk, free-form jazz, and punk aggression. His "punk funk" has been a pervasive influence in New York City dance music, and former bandmates show up in many New York dance groups.

Growing up in suburban Milwaukee, Siegfried started studying piano in the first grade. In high school he became interested in jazz and at age 19 took up the alto sax. He attended the Wisconsin Conservatory of Music but dropped out less than a semester short of receiving his degree. He went to New York in 1976 and studied for a short time with avant-garde saxophonist David Murray.

In 1977 Chance formed the original Contortions with organist Adele Bertei, guitarist Jody Harris, bassist George Scott III, slide guitarist Pat Place, and drummer Don Christensen. Like Captain Beefheart, he arranged and demonstrated to his musicians the instrumental parts of every song. Contortions concerts—the first of which were given in fall 1977—could be violent experiences: Chance was notorious for diving from the stage and engaging in fisticuffs with spectators.

The first Contortions recordings were the four tracks they contributed to a Brian Eno–produced *No New York* anthology (Antilles/Island). In 1979 Chance dissolved the Contortions and regrouped as James White and the Blacks. At the recording of *Off-White*, the Blacks included all the original Contortions except Bertei, who occasionally performed with them as a guest, along with Lydia Lunch and Voidoid Robert Quine. That group also dissolved; Bertei formed the Bloods and Place the Bush Tetras (in the Nineties, Place backed spoken-word artist Maggie Estep), while Scott joined Lunch in 8 Eyed Spy, later reuniting with Harris and Christensen in the Raybeats. Chance collaborated with Arto Lindsay (DNA, Lounge Lizards), Bradley Field (Teenage Jesus and the Jerks), and George Scott on a Diego Cortez film soundtrack, *Grutzi Elvis*. (Scott died in 1980 of a heroin overdose.) Chance continued to perform in New York, backed by pickup bands, until he relocated in 1980 to Paris, the base from which he toured Europe. The reception and respect accorded him there far exceeded what he received in America. Throughout the Eighties, Chance returned periodically to New York, where he played with musicians like trombonist Joseph Bowie (of the Black Arts Group, later founder of Defunkt), reedman Henry Threadgill (of the experimental jazz group Air), and guitarists

Bern Nix (Ornette Coleman) and Tomas Donker (the Dance).

In 1987 Chance led the horn section on the False Prophets' *Implosion;* in 1991, along with Adele Bertei and Alex Chilton, he contributed vocals to the Chet Baker tribute album, *Imagination* (Rough Trade). By late 1994, plans were made to release *Buy the Contortions* on Henry Rollins' reissue label, Infinite Zero, in conjunction with a return to live performance by a regrouped Contortions, led by Chance, who had moved back to New York.

Gene Chandler

Born Eugene Dixon, July 6, 1937, Chicago, Illinois
1962—*Duke of Earl* (Vee Jay)   1964—*Just Be True* (Constellation); *Greatest Hits*   1965—*Live! On Stage*   1966—*The Duke of Soul* (Checker)   1967— *The Girl Don't Care* (Brunswick)   1968—*There Was a Time*   1969—*The Two Sides of Gene Chandler* 1970—*The Gene Chandler Situation* (Mercury) 1971—*One & One* (with Jerry Butler)   1978—*Get Down* (Chi-Sound)   1979—*When You're #1* (20th Century)   1980—*Gene Chandler '80*   1981—*Here's to Love* (Chi-Sound)   1982—*I'll Make the Living If You Make the Loving Worthwhile*   1984—*Stroll on with the Duke* (Solid Smoke); *The Duke of Soul* (Chess)   1985—*Your Love Looks Good on Me* (Fastfire).

A fixture in Chicago soul for over 30 years, balladeer Gene Chandler was raised on the tough South Side and sang doo-wop in streetcorner groups before joining the army in 1957. After his discharge in 1960 he joined Chicago's Dukays, who had a minor hit late in 1961 with "The Girl Is a Devil." A&R man Carl Davis, who had discovered the Dukays, renamed Eugene Dixon after Davis' favorite actor, Jeff Chandler, and produced his solo debut, a backward glance at doo-wop style called "Duke of Earl" (#1 pop, #1 R&B, 1962). The single sold a million copies within a month of its November 1961 release.

Chandler's string of hits lasted until the early Seventies. The best of them were written and arranged by Curtis Mayfield, including "Just Be True" (#19, 1964), "You Can't Hurt Me No More" (#92, 1965), "Nothing Can Stop Me" (#18, 1965), and "What Now" (#40, 1965). The hits slowed after that, though he made several memorable records, including his 1968 collaboration with Barbara Acklin, "From the Teacher to the Preacher" (#57) followed by "Groovy Situation" (#12, 1970).

Chandler gave up touring to concentrate on songwriting and production, bought Bamboo Records, and moved it to Chicago. There he produced hits, including Mel and Tim's 1969 "Backfield in Motion," and continued to record throughout the Seventies, including a soul hit with Jerry Butler. He also founded Mr. Chand Records and worked for A&M as a producer from 1974 to 1977. In 1976 Chandler was convicted of selling 388 grams of heroin; he served a four-month sentence. A #53 disco hit, "Get Down," returned Chandler to the pop chart in 1979; it went to #11 in the U.K. Similarly, "Does She Have a Friend for Me" attracted scant interest stateside but became a Top Thirty hit in England. Among his industry positions is executive vice president of Chi-Sound Records.

The Chantels

Formed 1956, New York City, New York
Arlene Smith (b. Oct. 5, 1941, New York City), voc.; Lois Harris, voc.; Sonia Goring, voc.; Jackie Landry, voc.; Rene Minus, voc.
1958—*We Are the Chantels* (End) 1959—(– Smith; – Harris; + Annette Smith, voc.)   1990—*The Best of the Chantels* (Rhino).

The Chantels were one of the first and most popular of the girl groups. The five girls (all between 14 and 17) had been singing together in their Bronx parochial school choir since childhood. Led by Arlene Smith, the group was named after Saint Francis de Chantelle School, the rival school of their own alma mater, Saint Anthony of Padua. Richard Barrett of the Valentines produced their first singles ("He's Gone," "The Plea"), both Smith compositions that failed to hit. However, in 1958 the Chantels had their biggest success with another Smith song, "Maybe" (#15 pop, #2 R&B, 1958), which sold over a million copies. The Chantels' version hit #116 when rereleased in 1969; Janis Joplin covered it that year.

After several more singles—none of them major hits—End dropped them in 1959 and they moved to Carlton Records. By then Smith had quit to pursue a solo career, Harris was in college, and the following Chantels records were often recorded using other singers, including producer Barrett. Nonetheless, "Look in My Eyes" (#14 pop, #6 R&B, 1961) and "Well, I Told You" (#29, 1961) were hits before the group disbanded in 1970.

Smith later attended the Juilliard School of Music. In the early Seventies she re-formed the Chantels with new members. The other four original Chantels retired from show business. A schoolteacher, Smith continues to perform with the Chantels.

Harry Chapin

Born December 7, 1942, New York City, New York; died July 16, 1981, Jericho, New York
1972—*Heads and Tales* (Elektra); *Sniper and Other Love Songs*   1973—*Short Stories*   1974—*Verities and Balderdash*   1975—*Portrait Gallery*   1976—*On the Road to Kingdom Come; Harry Chapin's Greatest Stories Live*   1977—*Dance Band on the Titanic* 1978—*Living Room Suite*   1979—*Legends of the*

Lost and Found 1980—*Sequel* (Boardwalk)
1985—*Anthology of Harry Chapin* (Elektra).

Although singer/songwriter Harry Chapin initially came to fame with his folkish story songs, his true legacy is that of an antihunger activist who, years before such public activism became common, was performing over half of his 200 concert dates each year for charitable causes.

The son of a jazz drummer, Chapin sang in the Brooklyn Heights Boys Choir, and in his teens he played guitar, banjo, and trumpet in a band with his brothers. After a stint at the Air Force Academy, Chapin spent a semester at Cornell University. He and his brothers began working in Greenwich Village clubs and making documentary films. (A documentary he made with Jim Jacobs in the late Sixties called *Legendary Champions* was nominated for an Academy Award.) His brothers left the country in 1964 to escape the draft, and Chapin continued in filmmaking.

He formed his own band, including a cello player, in 1971. Chapin's debut album, *Heads and Tales,* was released in February 1972 and stayed on the charts for over half a year, peaking at #60 when "Taxi" became a Top Twenty single. His 1973 album, *Short Stories,* produced another solid hit with "W.O.L.D." (#36). *Verities and Balderdash* became Chapin's first gold album in 1974 on the strength of his #1 "Cat's in the Cradle" (a hit cover in the early Nineties by Ugly Kid Joe). His subsequent albums sold respectably through the end of the Seventies. His *The Night That Made America Famous* ran on Broadway for 75 performances and was nominated for two Tony Awards.

Chapin's later backup band included his brother Steve (piano and vocals), who also produced Harry's 1977 LP *Dance Band on the Titanic.* Another Chapin brother, Tom, has carried on a career of his own in recent years and is among the most popular artists recording for children. Besides frequent appearances with Harry, Tom released an album on Fantasy Records in 1976 and hosted the children's television series *Make a Wish* (for which Harry wrote the music) for five years.

Chapin was an active lobbyist for various causes and a benefactor of Long Island arts organizations. In 1975 he founded World Hunger Year (WHY) and became a familiar figure on Capitol Hill and other centers of government as he worked tirelessly against hunger. The next year he served as a delegate to the Democratic National Convention and was named one of the Jaycees' Ten Most Outstanding Young Men in America.

Chapin died in a car crash on the Long Island Expressway while driving to a benefit performance. By then he had raised over $5 million for charity. In 1987 he was honored at an all-star Carnegie Hall tribute during which his widow, Sandy (who continues his work), accepted a posthumously awarded Special Congressional Gold Medal on his behalf. An album documenting the event—with performers including Bruce Springsteen, Richie Havens, and Judy Collins—entitled *Tribute* was released in 1990.

Marshall Chapman
Born January 7, 1949, Spartanburg, South Carolina
1977—*Me, I'm Feeling Free* (Epic) 1978—*Jaded Virgin* 1979—*Marshall* 1982—*Take It On Home* (Rounder) 1987—*Dirty Linen* (Tall Girl) 1991—*Inside Job* 1995—*It's About Time*.

Singer, songwriter, and guitarist Marshall Chapman, of an aristocratic Southern family, was schooled at Nashville's Vanderbilt University, where she studied French and fine arts and started jamming with country, blues, and rock musicians. Around 1973, after living in France and Boston, she moved back to Nashville. There she waited tables and wrote songs, waiting for the opportunity to sing in local bars. She won the admiration of country stars like Tompall Glaser, Linda Hargrove, Jessi Colter, and Waylon Jennings.

In 1976 she went to Los Angeles, where she was signed by Columbia. Her debut album consisted predominantly of country-flavored songs. "Somewhere South of Macon" got airplay on country stations before it was decided that some of its lines were suggestive. Other songs—most often "A Woman's Heart (Is a Handy Place to Be)"—were covered by performers such as Colter, Crystal Gayle, Glaser, Olivia Newton-John, and the Earl Scruggs Revue. In concert, however, she fronted a rock & roll trio and drew rock crowds. Despite critical praise, Chapman's records did not sell, and once her third one was released, Epic dropped her.

Since then, she has continued to perform and record with her band, the Love Slaves. More recently her material has been covered by Emmylou Harris, Ronnie Milsap, Conway Twitty, and Jimmy Buffett, among others.

Tracy Chapman
Born March 20, 1964, Cleveland, Ohio
1988—*Tracy Chapman* (Elektra) 1989—*Crossroads* 1992—*Matters of the Heart*.

Quiet and publicity shy, Tracy Chapman at first seemed an unlikely candidate for stardom. Add to that the fact that singer/songwriter Chapman delivered spare, sobering folk-rock songs, and you have perhaps the most astonishing pop music success story of the late Eighties. With her 1988 self-titled debut album, Chapman topped the album charts and entered the ranks of rock's most popular and respected live performers.

Growing up in a predominantly black working-class neighborhood, Chapman was close to her older sister and single mother and shared their love of music, ranging from Mahalia Jackson to Neil Diamond. At an early age, the singer began writing songs and teaching herself guitar. A minority placement scholarship enabled Chapman to attend Wooster, a prestigious prep school; there she became interested in folk-influenced rock music. She then attended Tufts University, majoring in anthropology and African studies while singing and playing guitar at coffeehouses, and recording demos at the campus radio station. After hearing her play, Chapman's classmate Brian Koppelman, the son of music industry honcho Charles Koppelman, recommended her to his father. In 1986 Chapman signed a management deal with Koppelman's SBK Publishing; in addition to hooking her up with manager Elliot Roberts (Joni Mitchell, Neil Young), Koppelman helped secure her a contract with Elektra Records.

Produced by David Kershenbaum (Joan Baez, Joe Jackson), Chapman's Elektra debut set her socially conscious songs and rich, emotive alto against sparse acoustic arrangements. Released in spring of 1988, the album was critically praised, and Chapman began opening shows for 10,000 Maniacs to support it. But that summer, after a stunning solo performance at a star-studded Nelson Mandela tribute at England's Wembley Stadium, Chapman earned herself headliner stature. The album's sales soared, and a single, "Fast Car," reached #6. In September Chapman began a six-week international tour with Bruce Springsteen, Sting, Peter Gabriel, and Youssou N'Dour on behalf of Amnesty International.

After capping off the year with four Grammys, including Best New Artist, Chapman released *Crossroads*. Dealing with topics ranging from spirituality to racism in a bluntly realistic manner, the album was hardly a departure; but despite reaching #9, it proved less commercially successful than its predecessor. Infamous by now for her shyness and reluctance to deal with reporters, Chapman withdrew for a few years, returning in 1992 with *Matters of the Heart,* which got mixed reviews and peaked at #53.

The Charlatans

Formed 1964, San Francisco, California
George Hunter, voc.; Mike Wilhelm, gtr.; Richard Olson, bass; Michael Ferguson, piano; Sam Linde, drums (– Linde; + Dan Hicks [b. Dec. 9, 1941, Little Rock, Ark.], drums).
1967—(– Ferguson; + Patrick Gogerty, piano; + Terry Wilson, drums; Hicks switches to gtr.)
1968—(– Hicks; – Hunter; – Gogerty; + Darrel De- Vore, piano; + Terry Wilson, drums) 1969—*The Charlatans* (Philips).

As the original Haight-Ashbury band, the Charlatans remained true to the area's bohemian ethic. They were an amateur group, conceived by draftsman/designer George Hunter, whose main talent was a sense of rock's visual possibilities. Outfitted in Victorian and Old West costumes, they first played for three months at the Red Dog Saloon in Virginia City, Nevada, in the summer of 1965, before returning to the Haight. For this show, Ferguson designed what is generally considered to be the first rock poster ever. Soon they were sharing bills with the Jefferson Airplane and the Grateful Dead (then called the Warlocks) at the Fillmore, Avalon, and other Bay Area venues.

The Charlatans' repertoire remained essentially unchanged throughout their brief career: folk, blues, ballads, and jug-band tunes. MGM signed them, then sold the group to Kama Sutra. They recorded one unreleased album for that label (Kama Sutra did release an unsuccessful single over the group's objections). Reduced to a quartet (Hunter departed in early 1968, as did Dan Hicks to form his Hot Licks [see entry]), the Charlatans finally released their first album in 1969 before disbanding.

Bobby Charles

Born Robert Charles Guidry, February 21, 1938, Abbeville, Louisiana
1971—*Bobby Charles* (Bearsville) 1995—*Wish You Were Here Right Now* (Stony Plain).

Bobby Charles, discovered by Leonard Chess during a mid-Fifties talent search, contributed to the creation of South Louisiana swamp-pop music, a mixture of traditional Cajun, Creole, C&W, and New Orleans R&B. He recorded several sides in New Orleans that garnered some attention when Chess released them in the late Fifties. Their impact with other artists was more substantial. Several of the songs (among them "See You Later Alligator," "I Don't Know Why I Love You But I Do") were covered by Bill Haley and Clarence "Frogman" Henry. With Fats Domino and Dave Bartholomew, Charles wrote Domino's classic hit "Walkin' to New Orleans."

Charles toured with the Platters, Little Richard, Chuck Berry, and B. B. King before retiring from personal appearances in the early Sixties. Throughout the decade, though, he recorded for several labels and did promotional work for Chess Records. By the early Seventies he was living in Woodstock, New York, where Albert Grossman signed him to Bearsville Records. His much-ballyhooed comeback album, *Bobby Charles,* included guest appearances by the Band, Dr. John, and other notables, but despite an excellent single—"Small Town Talk" (later covered by Rick Danko of the Band)—the LP failed to find a market, and Charles was soon dropped. He appeared on two Paul Butterfield albums (including *Better Days,* from 1973) and made a rare live appearance at the Band's *Last Waltz* concert, Thanksgiving Day 1976. That same year, two of his compositions were covered on Joe

Cocker's *Sting Ray. Wish You Were Here Right Now* (1995) was Charles' first album released in North America in 24 years.

Ray Charles

Born Ray Charles Robinson, September 23, 1930, Albany, Georgia
1957—*Ray Charles* (Atlantic)   1958—*The Great Ray Charles*   1959—*What'd I Say; Genius of Ray Charles*   1962—*Story, vol. 1; Story, vol. 2; Modern Sounds in Country and Western Music* (ABC); *Modern Sounds in Country and Western Music 2*   1963—*Story, vol. 3* (Atlantic); *The Greatest Ray Charles*   1964—*Have a Smile with Me* (HMV); *Great Hits* (Atlantic)   1966—*Crying Time* (ABC-Paramount)   1967—*A Man and His Soul*   1973—*Ray Charles Live* (Atlantic)   1977—*True to Life*   1983—*Wish You Were Here Tonight* (Columbia)   1984—*Do I Ever Cross Your Mind; Friendship*   1985—*The Spirit of Christmas*   1986—*From the Pages of My Mind*   1987—*Ray Charles Live (1958–59); His Greatest Hits, vol. 1 (1960–1971)* (DCC); *His Greatest Hits, vol. 2 (1960–72)*   1988—*Greatest Country & Western Hits (1962–65); Greatest Hits, vol. 1 (1960–67)* (Rhino); *Greatest Hits, vol. 2 (1960–72); Just Between Us* (Columbia)   1989—*Anthology* (Rhino); *Seven Spanish Angels and Other Hits* (Columbia)   1990—*Would You Believe?* (Warner Bros.)   1991—*Ray Charles 1954–1966* (Time Life Music); *The Birth of Soul—The Complete Atlantic Rhythm & Blues Recordings, 1952–59* (Atlantic)   1993—*My World* (Warner Bros.)   1994—*Blues + Jazz* (Rhino).
With Milt Jackson: 1958—*Soul Brothers* (Atlantic)   1962—*Soul Meeting*   1989—*Soul Brothers/Soul Meeting*.
With Cleo Laine: 1976—*Porgy and Bess* (RCA).

Singer, composer, and pianist Ray Charles virtually invented soul music by bringing together the fervor of gospel, the secular lyrics and narratives of blues and country, the big-band arrangements of jazz, and rhythms and improvisational possibilities from all of them, making music that was both sophisticated and spontaneous.

He was raised in Greenville, Florida, and started playing piano before he was five; at six he contracted glaucoma, which went untreated and eventually left him blind. He studied composition (writing music in Braille) and learned to play alto saxophone, clarinet, trumpet, and organ while attending the St. Augustine School for the Deaf and the Blind from 1937 to 1945. His father died when he was ten, his mother five years later, and he left school to work in dance bands around Florida, dropping his last name to avoid confusion with boxer Sugar Ray

Ray Charles

Robinson. In 1947, with $600 worth of savings, he moved to Seattle and worked as a Nat King Cole–style crooner.

Charles made his first single, "Confession Blues," in Los Angeles and recorded for several independent West Coast labels until he scored a Top Ten R&B hit in 1951 with "Baby Let Me Hold Your Hand" and began a national tour with blues singer Lowell Fulson. Late in 1953 he went to New Orleans and became pianist and arranger for Guitar Slim (Eddie Jones). Guitar Slim's "The Things That I Used to Do," arranged by Charles and featuring him on piano, sold a million copies, and when Charles returned to recording—leading and arranging for his own band—the earthier style carried over to his own work. Atlantic signed him in 1954, and he made a few conventional recordings in New York; he also assembled a band for labelmate Ruth Brown.

"I've Got a Woman," with a seven-piece band, fronted by Charles' pounding gospel piano and a new raspy, exuberant vocal sound, became his first national hit (#2 R&B, 1955). Through the decade he appeared regularly on the charts as he synthesized more and more styles and was nicknamed the "Genius." He recorded with Milt Jackson of the Modern Jazz Quartet, sang standards with strings and expanded his band to a full-scale revue, complete with horns and gospel-style backup singers, the Raelettes.

"What'd I Say" (#6 pop, #1 R&B, 1959), a wild blues, gospel, and Latin mix, became Charles' first million-seller. In late 1959 he signed to ABC-Paramount Records and moved into the pop market with "Georgia on My Mind" (#1, 1960) and "Hit the Road, Jack" (#1, 1961).

Modern Sounds in Country and Western (1962), which included Charles' versions of songs by Hank Williams, Floyd Tillman, and other country songwriters, sold over a million copies, as did its single, "I Can't Stop Loving You" (#1, 1962).

In 1965 Charles was arrested for possession of heroin and revealed that he had been using it since he was 16. He cleaned up in a California sanatorium and spent a year away from performing. In 1966 he made his motion-picture debut in Ballad in Blue (also known as Blues for Lovers). In it, Charles (playing himself) befriends a blind boy in London; he also performed two of his best-known songs, "What'd I Say" and "I Got a Woman." While his singing remained influential through the Sixties (especially on Steve Winwood and Joe Cocker) and he kept making hits—including Ashford and Simpson's "Let's Go Get Stoned" (#31, 1966)—his taste was moving away from rock, although he did appear on Aretha Franklin's Live at Fillmore West (1971).

His albums from the mid-Sixties onward have down-played gospel and blues in favor of jazz standards, pop songs, and show tunes, although his singing remains distinctive. Charles made custom-label deals with ABC (Tangerine Records) and later Atlantic (Crossover), for which he recorded an album a year. In 1978 he published his autobiography (cowritten with David Ritz), Brother Ray; it became a national bestseller. The following year, his version of "Georgia on My Mind" was named "the official song of the State of Georgia." It was later used as the theme song for the hit television series Designing Women. Charles also appeared in the movie The Blues Brothers (1980); he subsequently made guest appearances on the television series St. Elsewhere and Who's the Boss.

In 1983 he recorded another country album, Wish You Were Here Tonight; one year later, he released Friendship, which included duets with ten country artists, including Hank Williams Jr., the Oak Ridge Boys, Mickey Gilley, Merle Haggard, Johnny Cash, and Willie Nelson. As of the mid-Nineties, that was the last album of new material to make the pop albums chart. Ironically, Charles has become best known to younger listeners through a series of Diet Pepsi ads ("You Got the Right One, Baby, Uh-huh!"), which began airing in 1990. He was also featured prominently on USA for Africa's 1985 hit, "We Are the World," in which his vocal interplay with Bruce Springsteen was a prime example of his trade-mark call-and-response style. In 1990 he won his tenth performance Grammy (not counting his 1987 Lifetime Achievement Award) for his duet with Chaka Khan, "I'll Be Good to You," from Quincy Jones' Back on the Block. In 1986 Charles was not only a recipient of the Kennedy Center Honors but one of the first inductees into the Rock and Roll Hall of Fame. The recipient of numerous Grammys, Charles won his most recent in 1993 for "A

Song for You," named by President Clinton as his favorite song. In 1993 President Clinton presented Charles with a National Medal of the Arts. Charles has received similar national awards from countries around the world.

Throughout his career, Charles has been active in a range of political and humanitarian causes. He provided financial support for the Reverend Martin Luther King Jr. and the civil rights movement; he is also a staunch supporter of Israel. In 1984 he performed his version of "America the Beautiful" at the Republican National Convention. Three years later, he formed the (Ray Charles) Robinson Foundation for Hearing Disorders, with a $1 million personal endowment.

Chase

Formed 1970, Las Vegas, Nevada
Bill Chase (b. 1935, Chicago, Ill.; d. Aug. 9, 1974, Jackson, Minn.), trumpet; Alan Ware, trumpet; Jerry Van Blair, trumpet; Ted Piercefield, trumpet; Jay Burrid (b. Jay Mitthauer), drums; Terry Richards, voc.; Angel South, gtr.; Dennis Johnson, bass.
1971—Chase (Epic) (– Burrid; – South)   1972—Ennea (+ John Emma [b. 1952, Geneva, Ill.; d. Aug. 9, 1974, Jackson, Minn.], gtr.; + Wallace Yohn [b. 1947, Scottsdale, Ariz.; d. Aug. 9, 1974, Jackson, Minn.], kybds.; + Walter Clark [b. 1949; d. Aug. 9, 1974, Jackson, Minn.], drums)   1974—Pure Music (entire group disbands and re-forms: Tom Gordon, drums; Dartanyan Brown, bass, voc.; Joe Morrissey, trumpet; Jay Sollenberger, trumpet; Jim Oatts, trumpet; Jim Peterik, voc.) Get It On.

Inspired by the success of horn bands like Blood, Sweat and Tears and Chicago, big-band trumpeter Bill Chase (who had worked with Woody Herman, Maynard Ferguson, and Stan Kenton) assembled this jazz-rock group. Unlike other brass rock groups, Chase used four trumpets. Their debut album spawned the hit single "Get It On" (#24, 1971) and was voted the #1 LP in that year's down beat readers' poll. The group toured internationally and released two more LPs and then disbanded. Chase had just reorganized an almost entirely new group and was on a comeback tour when the small airplane he was traveling in crashed near Jackson, Minnesota, killing him, Clark, Emma, and Yohn. Vocalist Jim Peterik had sung with the Ides of March ("Vehicle") and later joined Survivor ("Eye of the Tiger").

Cheap Trick

Formed 1974, Rockford, Illinois
Robin Zander (b. Jan. 23, 1953, Loves Park, Ill.), voc.; Tom Petersson (b. Tom Peterson, May 9, 1950, Rockford), bass; Rick Nielsen (b. Dec. 22, 1946, Rockford),

Cheap Trick: Robin Zander, Tom Petersson, Rick Nielsen, Bun E. Carlos

gtr.; Bun E. Carlos (b. Brad Carlson, June 12, 1951, Rockford), drums.
1977—*Cheap Trick* (Epic); *In Color* 1978—*Heaven Tonight* 1979—*Live at Budokan*; *Dream Police* 1980—*Found All the Parts* EP; *All Shook Up* (– Petersson; + Pete Comita [b. Italy], bass) 1981— (– Comita; + Jon Brant [b. Feb. 20, 1954], bass) 1982—*One on One* 1983—*Next Position Please* 1985—*Standing on the Edge* 1986—*The Doctor* (– Brant; + Petersson) 1988—*Lap of Luxury* 1990—*Busted* 1991—*The Greatest Hits* 1994— *Woke Up with a Monster* (Warner Bros.); *Budokan II (Live)* (Epic).
Robin Zander solo: 1993—*Robin Zander* (Interscope).

The aggressively marketed, hard-touring, self-caricaturing rock group Cheap Trick worked its way up to platinum sales with a blend of Beatles-style pop and a cartoonish stage act, which played Rick Nielsen's exaggerated mugging and guitar gymnastics against Robin Zander's teen-idol looks and rich, powerful voice.

In 1961 Nielsen, then in his teens, began playing locally in Rockford, Illinois, using his ever-increasing collection of rare and valuable guitars. His band, the Phaetons, became the Boyz, then the Grim Reapers, and finally Fuse in 1967, with the addition of bassist Tom Petersson. One album for Epic in 1968 was generally ignored. Frustrated, Fuse, which by then included college dropout Bun E. Carlos on drums, moved to Philadelphia in 1971. As Sick Man of Europe, they enlisted ex-Nazz vocalist Robert "Stewkey" Antoni, but the group soon

disbanded. After a year in Europe, Nielsen and Petersson returned to Rockford, reunited with Carlos, and a few months later asked folkie vocalist Zander to join the group they named Cheap Trick. Midwestern booking agent Ken Adamany, who'd played in one of Steve Miller's high school bands, became their manager. Adamany encouraged them to develop their stage show, and Cheap Trick toured incessantly over the next several years, playing an average of 250 shows a year, opening for Kiss, the Kinks, Santana, Boston, and others.

Cheap Trick's early releases were only moderately successful in the U.S.; its 1977 debut sold 150,000 copies, while *In Color* and *Heaven Tonight* barely reached the Top Forty. In Japan, however, all three had gone gold, and the group's initial tour there in early 1978 met with hysteria reminiscent of Beatlemania. During that visit Cheap Trick recorded *Live at Budokan*, which went triple platinum in the States largely on the strength of their single "I Want You to Want Me" (#7, 1979), a song that had originally appeared on *In Color*.

By the time *Dream Police* (#6) was released in fall 1979, the band was headlining arenas and stadiums. *All Shook Up*, produced by George Martin, went gold in late 1980 but was considered a disappointment, producing no Top Forty singles. The band contributed "Everything Works If You Let It" to the *Roadie* soundtrack that year, and Nielsen, Zander, and Carlos played on John Lennon and Yoko Ono's recording sessions for *Double Fantasy*. Since they are not credited, it is unclear whether those tracks have been released. ,

As the Eighties began, the group's activities slowed considerably. In 1981 Epic rejected an LP, and after a flurry of lawsuits and countersuits, Cheap Trick began recording *One on One*. Petersson departed in 1980 to form a group with his wife, Dagmar, as vocalist. He recorded an LP in 1982, but Epic refused to release it. Pete Comita replaced him but was himself replaced by Jon Brant before the recording of *One on One*, which included two minor hits, "If You Want My Love" and "She's Tight," and eventually went platinum.

Cheap Trick's fortunes began to sag with the release of *Next Position Please*, produced by Todd Rundgren. Neither it nor the group's next two albums went gold, although 1985's *Standing on the Edge* contained its strongest material since *Heaven Tonight*. *The Doctor* didn't even crack the Top 100, and the quartet's future seemed in jeopardy.

Then came *Lap of Luxury*, one of the surprise hits of 1988. The hard-rock ballad "The Flame" gave the group its first #1 single, a version of "Don't Be Cruel" became the first Elvis Presley cover to hit the Top Ten since the singer's death, and "Ghost Town" reached #33. Just as inexplicably, the band's next album, *Busted*, stiffed. One single, "Can't Stop Fallin' into Love," did go Top Twenty. Aside from a solo album from Zander, and a duet he recorded with Heart's Ann Wilson, "Surrender to Me" (#6, 1989), Cheap Trick maintained a low profile until 1994's *Woke Up with a Monster,* its first album for Warner Bros.

Chubby Checker

Born Ernest Evans, October 3, 1941, Andrews, South Carolina
1960—*Twist with Chubby Checker* (Cameo/Parkway) 1961—*For Twisters Only; Let's Twist Again; Your Twist Party* 1962—*Teen Twisters Only; All the Hits* 1982—*The Change Has Come* (MCA). With the Fat Boys: 1988—*Coming Back Hard Again* (Tin Pan Apple).

Although Chubby Checker didn't invent the Twist, the dance craze was his ticket to stardom. Written and recorded as a B side by R&B singer Hank Ballard, Checker's version of "The Twist" went to #1 in September 1960, stayed on the chart for four months, dropped off, and returned to #1 early in 1962. It is the only rock & roll record to enjoy two stays at #1 more than a year apart.

The young Ernest Evans worked as a chicken plucker in a local poultry shop while in high school. On the job he would frequently entertain customers by singing songs and telling jokes. Evans' boss put him in touch with Philadelphia's Cameo-Parkway label, which signed him in 1959. Shortly thereafter—at the suggestion of Dick Clark's wife—he became "Chubby Checker" (in emulation of the similarly built Fats Domino). His first single, "The Class," released in the summer of 1959, featured Checker doing vocal impersonations, but it was only a minor hit, and subsequent singles were even less successful.

Then "The Twist" hit. After it, Checker promoted several less successful dance crazes: the Hucklebuck, the Fly, the Mess Around, the Pony, the Limbo—even Freddie and the Dreamers' the Freddie. His Top Ten hits included "Pony Time" (#1, 1961), "Let's Twist Again" (#8, 1961), "The Fly" (#7, 1961), "Slow Twistin'" (#3, 1962), "Limbo Rock" (#2, 1962), and "Popeye the Hitchhiker" (#10, 1962). In December 1963 Checker married Dutch-born Catharina Lodders, Miss World 1962; he wrote "Loddy Lo" for her. His hits ended in 1965, and Checker became a mainstay on the nightclub circuit. He recorded for Buddah in 1969 and for Chalmac in 1971, with regular appearances as part of rock revival shows and a featured spot in the film *Let the Good Times Roll.* His early-Eighties work for MCA moved toward disco, with some success ("Running," #91, 1982; "Harder Than Diamond," #104, 1982), but in 1988 Checker hit the Top Forty for the first time in 25 years with a rap version of "The Twist," featuring the Fat Boys. The song went to #2 in the U.K. He continues to tour 250 nights a year.

Clifton Chenier

Born June 25, 1925, Opelousas, Louisiana; died December 12, 1987, Lafayette, Louisiana
1965—*Louisiana Blues & Zydeco* (Arhoolie) 1966—*Bon Ton Roulet* 1967—*Black Snake Blues* 1970—*King of the Bayous* 1971—*Bayou Blues* (Specialty) 1972—*Live* (Arhoolie) 1974—*Out West* 1976—*Bogalusa Boogie* 1978—*And His Red Hot Louisiana Band; Cajun Swamp Music Live* (Tomato) 1980—*Classic Clifton* (Arhoolie) 1983—*I'm Here!* (Alligator) 1993—*Zydeco Dynamite: The Clifton Chenier Anthology* (Rhino).

Clifton Chenier was the undisputed king of zydeco music, the rousing black Creole party music that, influenced by Cajun music, mixes blues, French folk tunes, country, New Orleans R&B, and rock & roll. Wearing a jeweled crown and flashing his gold tooth onstage, Chenier pumped his chrome-studded accordion and sang in Creole French as well as English; he also played harmonica, piano, and organ.

He grew up as a sugar cane cutter and weekend musician in such places as New Iberia, Louisiana, where he met his wife, Margaret, in 1945. In 1946 he followed his brother Cleveland to Lake Charles, Louisiana, for a job at an oil refinery, where he worked until 1954. The brothers began playing at parties as a duet, with Clifton on accordion and Cleveland on "rub board," a piece of corrugated steel played with beer-can openers like a washboard. In 1954 Chenier made his first recordings at radio station KAOK in Lake Charles for Elko Records, and a year later recorded his more R&B-style material at Specialty, including the R&B hit "Ay 'Tit Fille (Hey Little Girl)" (originally "Ay Tete Fee") and "Boppin' the Rock."

Chenier became a full-time musician, performed on both coasts, and in 1958 moved to Houston. In 1964 he began to record for the folk-oriented Arhoolie label and had a number of regional Gulf Coast hits, including "Louisiana Blues" and "Black Gal." He appeared in 1966 at the Berkeley Blues Festival, and continued to appear regularly on the West Coast and more infrequently in the East. He earned a Grammy Award for *I'm Here!* in 1983.

He was featured in the 1974 documentary *Hot Pepper* by Les Blank and inspired a generation of zydeco accordionists, including Rockin' Dopsie, Rockin' Sidney, Queen Ida, and Buckwheat Zydeco. Chenier had suffered from diabetes since 1979, one reason his recorded output slowed during his last decade. Upon his death, son C.J., who has come into his own as a zydeco singer and musician, took over the Red Hot Louisiana Band.

Cher

Born Cherilyn Sarkasian LaPier, May 20, 1946, El Centro, California
1965—*All I Really Want to Do* (Imperial) 1966—

Cher 1967—*With Love, Cher* 1968—*Backstage* 1969—*3614 Jackson Highway* (Atco) 1971—*Cher* (Kapp) 1972—*Foxy Lady* 1973—*Half-Breed* (MCA) 1974—*Dark Lady* 1975—*Stars* (Warner Bros.) 1976—*I'd Rather Believe in You* 1977—*Allman and Woman: Two the Hard Way* (with Gregg Allman) (Warner Bros.) 1979—*Take Me Home* (Casablanca) 1980—*Black Rose* 1982—*I Paralyze* (Columbia) 1987—*Cher* (Geffen) 1989—*Heart of Stone* 1991—*Love Hurts.*

In a long career on the brink of its fourth decade, Cher has reinvented herself a number of times, first as hippie rock singer, then as wisecracking TV comedienne, and finally as a forthright film star, middle-aged sex symbol, and fitness guru. Cher dropped out of school and left home at 16, moving to Hollywood to be an actress. In 1963 she sang in sessions for producer Phil Spector and met Sonny Bono. Her musical and romantic partnership with Bono lasted until 1975. [See Sonny and Cher entry.]

After their bitter split Cher hosted her own TV variety show, which lasted one year. She had been having an affair with record producer David Geffen, but married guitarist Gregg Allman five days after her divorce from Bono. That 1975 marriage produced a son, Elijah Blue, and an album, the critically reviled *Allman and Woman: Two the Hard Way.* The couple divorced in 1979. Cher became famous for her relationships with younger rockers, including a late-Seventies romance with Kiss' Gene Simmons and an early-Nineties relationship with Bon Jovi guitarist Richie Sambora.

In 1979 Cher had her first hit since her breakup with Bono with the disco *Take Me Home* (#25, 1979) and its title track (#8, 1979). In 1980 she formed the hard-rock band Black Rose with her boyfriend Les Dudek (who had previously played with Steve Miller and Boz Scaggs), but critics buried them. Cher returned to playing Las Vegas and Atlantic City, where she has always been popular; her casino stints also led her to the infamous Sun City resort in South Africa.

Cher made her Broadway debut in Robert Altman's *Come Back to the 5 and Dime, Jimmy Dean, Jimmy Dean* in 1982. She starred in the movie of the play also, a role that finally broke down the Hollywood doors she had been knocking on for years. In the next decade she landed featured roles in *Silkwood, Mask, The Witches of Eastwick, Suspect, Moonstruck,* and *Mermaids;* she won an Oscar for best actress for her performance in *Moonstruck.*

In 1987 Cher returned to recording and had a gold record with *Cher* (#32, 1987), which featured the singles "I Found Someone" (#10, 1987) and "We All Sleep Alone" (#14, 1988). Sonny and Cher reunited for a performance on *Late Night with David Letterman* in February 1988. In 1989 her duet with Peter Cetera from the *Chances Are* soundtrack, "After All" (#6, 1989), became a hit. *Heart of Stone* (#10, 1989) went double platinum with the singles "If I Could Turn Back Time" (#3, 1989), "Just Like Jesse James" (#8, 1989), and "Heart of Stone" (#20, 1989). Cher's cover of Betty Everett's "The Shoop Shoop Song (It's in His Kiss)" (#33, 1990) was featured in *Mermaids.* In 1993 Cher recorded "I Got You Babe," her 1965 hit with Sonny, backed by MTV cartoon characters Beavis and Butt-head for *The Beavis and Butt-head Experience* album.

Always obsessed with her appearance, Cher has released exercise videos, a diet guide, perfume, and a line of skin-care products. (She has denied reports that she has had numerous cosmetic surgical procedures.) Since playing the mother of a physically deformed child in *Mask,* Cher has been active in a charity benefiting children with craniofacial problems.

Neneh Cherry

Born Neneh Mariann Karlsson, March 10, 1964, Stockholm, Sweden
1989—*Raw Like Sushi* (Virgin) 1992—*Homebrew.*

Throwing punches like a tomboy homegirl, dropping beats and wisdom like a cosmo boho, or prancing like an African queen, Neneh Cherry plays an intelligently crafted version of postrap dance pop. The daughter of artist Moki Cherry and West African percussionist Amadu Jah, Cherry was raised by her mother and stepfather Don Cherry, a pioneering jazz trumpeter, and grew up shuttling between Stockholm and New York. Her early memories include falling asleep in jazz clubs while her stepfather played in Ornette Coleman's band and sitting on Miles Davis' lap.

Cherry dropped out of school at 14. The following year she went to Africa with her biological father. In 1980 she joined the Cherries in London, where she found through the burgeoning punk scene a new, tough identity. She sang backup for ska band the Nails and briefly performed with seminal all-girl group the Slits. After being raped on a street late one night, Cherry moved back to New York. But friends convinced her to return to London to sing and play percussion with Rip Rig + Panic, a group whose mixture of punk, funk, jazz, and soul coincided with her own musical interests.

Cherry recorded three albums with Rip Rig + Panic (*God,* 1981; *I Am Cold,* 1982; *Attitude,* 1983). At 18 she married drummer Bruce Smith and had her first child. The couple split within three years, and Cherry began singing with RR+P spinoff Float Up C.P. She also started rapping at a London club, where she was spotted by a talent scout. Her first single, "Stop the War," was about the Falkland Islands.

Cherry began dating and working with composer and musician Cameron McVey, who cowrote *Raw Like*

Neneh Cherry

Sushi (#40, 1989) and, under the name Booga Bear, co-produced several songs. The album received critical accolades for its pop melodies, positive messages, and fusion of hip-hop with jazz and rock stylings; in retrospect, *Raw* was probably the first "alternative rap" album. The hit "Buffalo Stance" (#3, 1989) introduced Cherry's tough street smarts, followed by "Kisses on the Wind" (#8, 1989). The birth of Cherry's second baby shortly before the album's release added to her image as a strong, mature sex symbol; she memorably appeared shimmying and fully pregnant on the British TV show *Top of the Pops.*

A few months after the album's release, Cherry collapsed backstage at the MTV Music Awards, possibly with Lyme disease. For the next few years, her only artistic foray was recording "I've Got You Under My Skin" for the *Red Hot + Blue* AIDS benefit album. She and McVey married and moved to a converted schoolhouse in Sweden in which Cherry had grown up. There they began writing and recording *Homebrew.* The album was more thoughtful, less in-your-face, than Cherry's debut, although the opening track, "Sassy" (featuring Gang Starr rapper Guru), showed the singer's braggadocio was intact. *Homebrew* prospered mostly on alternative and college radio, where the Michael Stipe duet "Trout" was

popular. The "Buddy X" video became a staple on MTV; its multicultural cast of defiant and dancing individuals vividly illustrated Cherry's unique pop sensibilities. In 1994 she recorded a duet with Youssou N'Dour, "7 Seconds."

Chic/Nile Rodgers/Bernard Edwards

Formed 1976, Bronx, New York
Bernard Edwards (b. Oct. 31, 1952), bass; Nile Rodgers (b. Sep. 19, 1952), gtr.; Norma Jean Wright, voc.; Tony Thompson, drums; Alfa Anderson (b. Sep. 7, 1946), voc.
1977—*Chic* (Atlantic) (– Wright; + Luci Martin [b. Jan 10, 1955], voc.)   1978—*C'est Chic*   1979—*Risque*; *Greatest Hits*   1980—*Real People*   1981—*Take It Off*   1982—*Tongue in Chic*   1983—*Believer*   1991—*Dance Dance Dance: The Best of Chic* (Atlantic/Rhino) (group re-forms)   1992—*The Best of Chic, vol. 2* (– Thompson; + Sterling Campbell, drums; + Sylver Logan Sharp, voc.; + Jenn Thomas, voc.); *Chic-ism* (Warner Bros.).
Bernard Edwards solo: 1983—*Glad to Be Here* (Warner Bros.).
Nile Rodgers solo: 1983—*Adventures in the Land of the Good Groove* (Warner Bros.)   1985—*B-Movie Matinee*   1986—(as Outloud) *Out Loud.*

Boasting a series of gold and platinum hit singles that began with 1977's #1 "Dance, Dance, Dance (Yowsah, Yowsah, Yowsah)," Chic's stripped-down, not-quite-mechanical groove made them the premier black disco group of the late Seventies and early Eighties. In addition, cofounders Nile Rodgers and Bernard Edwards have produced, written, or played on records by many other performers and become two of the most influential contemporary black writers and producers.

Edwards and Rodgers met in the Bronx while working at various gigs around New York in 1970. Over the next six years, they worked in soul and R&B groups; Rodgers played for the Apollo Theatre's house band. Soon after meeting former Patti LaBelle drummer Tony Thompson, they formed a rock-fusion power trio called Big Apple Band, but changed their name to Chic in the wake of Walter Murphy and the Big Apple Band's disco hit "A Fifth of Beethoven."

Frustrated by its inability to land a record deal, the band teamed with vocalists Alfa Anderson (who had sung on *The Wiz* soundtrack) and Norma Jean Wright to make disco records. Several record companies rejected the original demo tape of "Dance, Dance, Dance" before Atlantic took it in late 1977. In less than a month the single, powered by Rodgers' distinctive rhythm guitar, sold a million copies and reached #6. Their second album, *C'est Chic* (with the five-million-selling #1 song, "Le

Freak," the all-time top-selling single for Warner/Elektra/Asylum), and its followup, *Risque,* were both certified platinum. "Dance, Dance, Dance" (#1, 1977), "I Want Your Love" (#7, 1979), and "Good Times" (#1, 1979) were gold singles. "Good Times" inspired two hits: the Sugar Hill Gang's "Rapper's Delight," based on the instrumental track, and Queen's "Another One Bites the Dust."

In 1983, after releasing *Believer,* Chic disbanded. The band's influence remained, however, with covers or adaptations appearing by musicians as various as Andrew Ridgely and Monie Love. In 1992, with Rodgers and Edwards at their core but with a new drummer and new singers, Chic re-formed and signed to Warner Bros.

Rodgers released two solo albums; Edwards, one (none was a hit). In 1989, with Tony Thompson, Edwards formed the band the Distance and recorded their album. But it was as producers, both as a team and individually, that the two made the greatest impact. Sister Sledge's *We Are Family* (1979) established them as studio purveyors of a streamlined sound; they went on to collaborate on albums including Diana Ross' highly successful *Diana,* Debbie Harry's *KooKoo,* Sheila and B. Devotion's self-titled LP, and a soundtrack, *Soup for One.*

On his own, Edwards produced such artists as Power Station (with Robert Palmer and Tony Thompson), ABC, Jody Watley, Rod Stewart, Gladys Knight, and Kenny Loggins, his most noteworthy effort being Robert Palmer's *Riptide* and its 1985 #1 single "Addicted to Love." Rodgers has been even more prolific, producing more than 50 records in a period from 1981 to 1993. He, too, has worked with a tremendous variety of musicians, among them Southside Johnny, Peter Gabriel, the Thompson Twins, Eric Clapton, Kim Carnes, the Stray Cats, Ric Ocasek, Duran Duran, and David Lee Roth. Especially with his more notable productions—David Bowie's *Let's Dance* and *Black Tie White Noise,* Madonna's *Like a Virgin,* Mick Jagger's *She's the Boss,* and the B-52's' *Cosmic Thing*— he lent a new sonic clarity to contemporary music, without sacrificing any of its power.

Chicago/Peter Cetera

Formed 1967, Chicago, Illinois
Terry Kath (b. Jan. 31, 1946, Chicago; d. Jan. 28, 1978, Los Angeles, Calif.), gtr., vocs.; Peter Cetera (b. Sep. 13, 1944, Chicago), bass, voc.; Robert Lamm (b. Oct. 13, 1944, Brooklyn, N.Y.), kybds., voc.; Walter Parazaider (b. Mar. 14, 1945, Chicago), saxes, clarinet; Danny Seraphine (b. Aug. 28, 1948, Chicago), drums; James Pankow (b. Aug. 20, 1947, Chicago), trombone; Lee Loughnane (b. Oct. 21, 1946, Chicago), trumpet.
1969—*Chicago Transit Authority* (Columbia) 1970—*Chicago II* 1971—*Chicago III*; *Chicago at*
Carnegie Hall* 1972—*Chicago V* 1973—*Chicago VI* 1974—*Chicago VII* (+ Laudir De Oliveira [b. Brazil], perc.) 1975—*Chicago VIII*; *Chicago IX* 1976—*Chicago X* 1977—*Chicago XI* 1978— (– Kath; + Donnie Dacus, gtr.) *Hot Streets* 1979— *Chicago XIII* (– Dacus; + Chris Pinnick, gtr.) 1980—*Chicago XIV* 1981—*Chicago's Greatest Hits, vol. 2* (– Pinnick; + Bill Champlin, voc., kybds., gtr.) 1982—*Chicago 16* (Warner Bros.) 1983—*If You Leave Me Now* (Columbia) 1984—*Chicago 17* (Warner Bros.) (– Cetera; + Jason Scheff, bass, voc.) 1986—*Chicago 18* 1988—(+ DaWayne Bailey, gtr.) *Chicago 19* (Reprise) 1989—*Chicago's Greatest Hits 1982–89* (– Seraphine; + Tris Imboden, drums) 1991—*Twenty 1*; *Group Portrait* (Columbia). Peter Cetera solo: 1981—*Peter Cetera* (Warner Bros.) 1986—*Solitude/Solitaire* 1988—*One More Story* 1992—*World Falling Down.*

Chicago followed the lead of Blood, Sweat and Tears and the Electric Flag by grafting a horn section onto a rock band. Over a quarter of a century, Chicago has produced 20 Top Ten hits and 15 platinum or multiplatinum albums and sold over 100 million records.

School friends Terry Kath and Walter Parazaider formed the band in 1967 and named it the Big Thing. After they were joined by James William Guercio, who had worked with the Buckinghams and Blood, Sweat and Tears as a Columbia staff producer, they changed their name to the Chicago Transit Authority. The band's 1969 debut, *Chicago Transit Authority,* like BS&T's, was an ambitious jumble of jazz and rock, including protesters' chants from the 1968 Chicago Democratic convention.

Under Guercio's guidance and pressure from the city of Chicago, Chicago shortened its name and moved toward MOR pop with a string of hits ("Does Anybody Really Know What Time It Is?" #7, 1970; "Colour My World," #75, 1971; "Saturday in the Park," #3, 1972; "Feeling Stronger Every Day," #10, 1973; "Wishing You Were Here," #11, 1974, and many others) that made the group a constant presence on AM radio and kept its albums in the gold and platinum range. Several band members made cameo appearances in the Guercio-produced-and-directed 1973 film *Electra Glide in Blue.*

In 1974 the group's unofficial leader, keyboardist Robert Lamm, made a solo album, *Skinny Boy.* Despite its moniker, Chicago worked out of Los Angeles (Guercio's base) from the late Sixties on. In the later Seventies the group's appeal began to flag. In 1977 they left Guercio, who had founded his own Caribou studio. Kath died of an accidental self-inflicted gun wound (some sources claim he was playing Russian roulette) in 1978: He was replaced by Donnie Dacus, formerly with Stephen Stills and Boz Scaggs. In 1979 Chicago played several benefits for presidential candidate Jerry Brown. Columbia, which had sold millions of Chicago records, dropped the group from its roster in 1981; ironically, with Warners, the group started a second-phase streak of hits: "Hard to Say I'm Sorry" (#1, 1982), "Hard Habit to Break" (#3, 1984), "You're the Inspiration" (#3, 1984), "Will You Still Love Me?" (#3, 1986), "I Don't Wanna Live Without Your Love" (# 3, 1988), "Look Away" (#1, 1988), "You're Not Alone" (#10, 1989), "What Kind of Man Would I Be?" (#5, 1989). In 1992 the group commemorated its silver anniversary with a controversial concert tour during which only its hits were performed.

Cetera released a self-titled solo album in 1981. He left the group in 1985 (and was replaced by Jason Scheff, son of longtime Elvis Presley bassist Jerry Scheff) for what began as a promising solo career with "Glory of Love" (#1, 1986), "The Next Time I Fall" (a duet with Amy Grant, #1, 1986), "One Good Woman" (#4, 1988), and "After All" (a duet with Cher, #6, 1989). Nonetheless, none of his albums went Top Twenty, only one, *Solitude/Solitaire*, was certified gold, and *World Falling Down* peaked at #163. In 1987 Cetera produced ex-Abba vocalist Agnetha Fältskog's solo album *I Stand Alone* and duetted with her on "I Wasn't the One (Who Said Goodbye)."

Chicken Shack

Formed 1967, London, England
Stan Webb, gtr., voc.; Andy Sylvester, bass; Christine Perfect (b. July 12, 1943, Birmingham, Eng.), piano, voc.; Dave Bidwell, drums.
1968—*Forty Blue Fingers, Freshly Packed and Ready to Serve* (Blue Horizon); *OK, Ken?* 1969—(– Perfect; + Paul Raymond, kybds.) *Hundred Ton Chicken*; *Accept* 1970—(– Sylvester; – Bidwell; – Raymond; + Hughie Flint, drums; + John Glascock, bass) 1971—(– Flint; + Paul Hancox, drums) 1972—*Imagination Lady* (London) (– Glascock; + Bob Daisley, bass; + Chris Mercer, reeds; + Tony Ashton, piano) 1973—*Unlucky Boy* (group disbands) 1974—*Goodbye* (Nova) 1978—(– Webb; + Robbie Blunt, gtr.; + Ed Spevock, drums; + Dave Winthrop, sax; + Paul Martinez, bass) *The Creeper* (Ariola).

Chicken Shack was a leading band of the late-Sixties British blues revival but is best remembered for pianist/singer Christine Perfect, who later became better known as Christine McVie of Fleetwood Mac. Stan Webb, Andy Sylvester, and Perfect played together in a Birmingham band, the Shades of Blue, in 1965. That band broke up when Perfect completed art college and moved to London. She later met up with Webb and Sylvester, and they regrouped as Chicken Shack, adding Bidwell. They made their U.K. debut at the Windsor Blues Festival

in August 1967. There Perfect met her future husband, John McVie of Fleetwood Mac.

Chicken Shack's rendition of the Etta James blues "I'd Rather Go Blind" reached the U.K. Top Twenty in May 1969, but in August Perfect left the group. A year later, after recording a solo album, she joined Fleetwood Mac [see entry]. Chicken Shack had a U.K. Top Thirty hit with "Tears in the Wind" before Sylvester, Dave Bidwell, and Paul Raymond dropped out, later to join Savoy Brown.

Subsequent personnel under Webb's leadership included Hughie Flint (cofounder of McGuinness Flint), Paul Hancox (formerly of Wayne Fontana and the Mindbenders), Chris Mercer (veteran of numerous British blues sessions), Tony Ashton (of Family and Paice, Ashton and Lord), Bob Daisley (who later joined Ritchie Blackmore's Rainbow and Ozzy Osbourne). Webb disbanded Chicken Shack in 1973. After brief stints with Savoy Brown and his own Broken Glass (which cut one album for Capitol in 1975), he revived Chicken Shack with Robbie Blunt and Paul Martinez, who went on to play with Robert Plant after the demise of Led Zeppelin.

The Chieftains

Formed 1963, Dublin, Ireland
Paddy Moloney (b. 1938, Donnycarney, Dublin), uilleann pipes, tin whistle; Sean Potts (b. 1930), tin whistle, bodhran; Michael Tubridy (b. 1935), flute, concertina, whistle; Martin Fay (b. 1936, Dublin), fiddle; David Fallon, bodhran.
1964—*Chieftains 1* (Claddagh) 1969—(– Fallon; + Peadar Mercier [b. 1914], bodhran, bones; + Sean Keane [b. 1946, Dublin], fiddle, whistle) *Chieftains 2* 1971—(+ Derek Bell [b. 1935, Belfast, N. Ire.], harp, dulcimer, oboe) *Chieftains 3* 1973—*Chieftains 4* 1975—(+ Ronnie McShane, bones) *Chieftains 5* 1976—(– Mercier; + Kevin Conneff [b. Dublin], bodhran) *6 Bonaparte's Retreat* 1977—*Chieftains Live* (Island) 1978—*7* (Columbia); *8* 1980—(– Tubridy; – Potts; + Matt Molloy [b. Ballaghadereen, Co. Roscommon, Ire.], flute) *9 Boil the Breakfast Early* 1981—*10 Cotton Eyed Joe* (Shanachie) 1985—*In China* 1987—*Celtic Wedding* (BMG Classics/RCA) 1989—*A Chieftains Celebration* 1991—*"Reel Music"/The Filmscores* (RCA Victor); *The Bells of Dublin* 1992—*An Irish Evening: Live at the Grand Opera House, Belfast*; *Another Country* 1993—*The Celtic Harp*.
With James Galway: 1987—*In Ireland* (RCA) 1991—*Over the Sea to Skye* 1995—*The Long Black Veil*.
With Van Morrison: 1988—*Irish Heartbeat* (Mercury).

The Chieftains are indisputably the world's leading proponents of traditional Irish music. As such, their appeal has extended well beyond Ireland's folk community, engendering international praise and collaborations with leading symphony orchestras and major rock artists. The five original Chieftains—including current members Paddy Moloney, initially the group's sole producer/arranger and still its leader, and fiddler Martin Fay—met in the late Fifties while playing in Ceoltoiri Chaulann, a folk ensemble. As the Chieftains, they aimed to lend their classical training to skilled interpretations of Celtic music, using traditional instruments like tin whistle, uilleann pipes, and bodhran drum. In the decade following the group's 1964 debut, it put out albums sporadically—*Chieftains 2* didn't materialize until 1969—and made some personnel changes as its members tried to maintain their day jobs.

The Chieftains finally became a full-time act in 1975, and commemorated by selling out London's Royal Albert Hall and providing the Oscar-winning soundtrack for Stanley Kubrick's film *Barry Lyndon*. In 1979 they played before 1.3 million people at an outdoor Mass in Dublin, as supporting act for Pope John Paul II. The following year, they released their ninth studio album, *9 Boil the Breakfast Early,* which introduced vocals to their music, courtesy of bodhran player Kevin Conneff. *Cotton Eyed Joe* found the Chieftains diversifying further, experimenting with American country textures. In 1983 they were among the first Western acts to play China, performing with a Chinese folk orchestra. Appearances with prominent North American symphonies, including the Boston Pops, followed.

In 1987 the group recorded the first of two traditional albums with Irish classical flutist James Galway. The following year saw a similar collaboration with Van Morrison. Morrison also appeared, alongside singer/songwriter Nanci Griffith and others, on *A Chieftains Celebration*. That year the Irish government made the Chieftains national musical ambassadors. The group's 1990s accomplishments include *The Bells of Dublin* (1991), featuring such folk and rock luminaries as Griffith, Elvis Costello, Jackson Browne, and Rickie Lee Jones; *An Irish Evening* (1992), recorded live at Belfast's Grand Opera House with Griffith and Roger Daltrey; and *Another Country* (1992), a collaboration with C&W stars including Willie Nelson and Emmylou Harris. The latter recordings won Grammys, for Best Traditional Folk Album and Best Contemporary Folk Album, respectively. *The Long Black Veil* includes collaborations with Sinéad O'Connor, Sting and the Rolling Stones.

The Chiffons
Formed 1960, Bronx, New York
Barbara Lee (b. May 16, 1947, Bronx), voc.; Patricia
Bennett (b. Apr. 7, 1947, Bronx), voc.; Judy Craig (b. 1946, Bronx), lead voc.
1962—(+ Sylvia Peterson [b. Sep. 30, 1946, Bronx], voc.) 1963—*He's So Fine* (Laurie) 1966—*Sweet Talkin' Guy.*

A black female vocal group, the Chiffons had several international hits in the early Sixties. Barbara Lee, Patricia Bennett, and Judy Craig met and began singing together in high school. In 1960 manager/songwriter Ronald Mack got them a contract with Big Deal Records. After one small hit that year, a cover of the Shirelles' "Tonight's the Night," they were not heard from again until 1962, when fourth member Sylvia Peterson joined. Their three-year string of hits included the Mack-penned "He's So Fine" (#1, 1963), which George Harrison was found to have unintentionally plagiarized in 1976 with his 1970 hit "My Sweet Lord." (In 1975 the Chiffons recorded their version of "My Sweet Lord.")

Other hits for the Chiffons included "One Fine Day" (#5, 1963), "Nobody Knows What's Going On" (#49, 1965), and "Sweet Talkin' Guy" (#10, 1966). In 1963 the group also recorded two songs as the Four Pennies ("My Block" and "When the Boy's Happy"). After 1966 the group ceased to appear on the charts in the U.S., but a 1972 rerelease of "Sweet Talkin' Guy" went to #4 in the U.K. They continued to perform into the Eighties.

The Chi-Lites
Formed 1960, Chicago, Illinois
Marshall Thompson (b. Apr. 1941, Chicago), voc.; Creadel Jones (b. 1939, St. Louis, Mo.), voc.; Robert Lester (b. 1942, McComb, Miss.), voc.; Eugene Record (b. Dec. 23, 1940, Chicago), voc.; Clarence Johnson, voc. (– Johnson).
1968—*Give It Away* (Brunswick) 1971—*Give More Power to the People* 1972—*A Lonely Man* 1973—*A Letter to Myself; The Chi-Lites* (– Jones; + Stan Anderson, voc.) 1974—*Toby* 1975—*Half a Love; Chi-Lites Greatest Hits, vol. 2* (– Record; + David Scott, voc.; + Danny Johnson, voc.) 1976—*Happy Being Lonely* 1977—*The Fantastic Chi-Lites* (Mercury) (– Johnson; + Vandy Hampton, voc.) 1980—(Original lineup re-forms: Thompson; Lester; Jones; Record) *Heavenly Body* (Chi-Sound) 1981—*Me and You* 1983—*Bottom's Up* (Larc) (– Jones) 1990—*Just Say You Love Me* (Ichiban) 1992—*The Chi-Lites Greatest Hits* (Rhino).

The Chi-Lites' yearning ballads, featuring falsetto vocals and close harmonies, made them a leading soul vocal group of the early Seventies. Originally known as Marshall and the Hi-Lites (later Chi-Lites), the quintet performed around Chicago and recorded for local labels. Former cab driver Eugene Record became lead singer and eventually their songwriter and producer as well. The Chi-Lites signed with Chicago-based, nationally distributed Brunswick in 1968 and had a few soul hits before Record's "Have You Seen Her" (#3, 1971), cowritten with Barbara Acklin, became a pop hit. "Oh Girl" (#1, 1972) also sold in the millions and was later covered by Paul Young. The Chi-Lites had 11 Top Twenty R&B hits between 1969 and 1974. In 1976 they were embroiled in the Brunswick label's tax evasion problems. Record went solo, recording for Warner Bros., while the Chi-Lites switched to Mercury, with meager results. Record returned in 1980, and with the group recording on his own Chi-Sound label, the Chi-Lites hit the R&B Top Twenty with "Hot on a Thing" in 1982 and "Bottom's Up" in 1983. Creadel Jones retired, not permanently, however, in 1983. Record has been in and out of the group several times, and there have been several personnel changes that are not included in the chronology above. A core of the original members—Lester, Thompson, and Jones—were still performing as of mid-1993.

The Chills

Formed October 1980, Dunedin, New Zealand
Martin Phillipps (b. July 2, 1963, N.Z.), gtr., voc.;
Peter Gutteridge (b. May 19, 1961, N.Z.), gtr., voc.;
Alan Haig (b. Aug. 5, 1961, N.Z.), drums; Jane Dodd
(b. Sep. 9, 1962, N.Z.), bass; Rachel Phillipps (b. June
17, 1965, N.Z.), kybds.
1981—(– Gutteridge; – Dodd; – Rachel Phillipps;
+ Fraser Batts [b. Apr. 14, 1964, N.Z.], kybds, gtr.;
+ Terry Moore [b. Oct. 27, 1961, Eng.], bass) 1982—
***Dunedin Double* EP (Flying Nun, N.Z.) (– Batts;**
– Haig; + Martyn Bull [b. Mar. 6, 1961, N.Z.; d. July
18, 1983, N.Z.], drums) 1983—(+ Peter Allison
[b. June 7, 1960, N.Z.], kybds.; + David Kilgour
[b. Sep. 6, 1961, N.Z.], gtr., voc.) June 1983—
(– Bull; – Kilgour; + Haig, drums) November 1983—
(– Moore; + Martin Kean [b. June 17, 1961], bass)
1984—(– Kean; + Moore, bass) 1985—*The Lost EP*
1986—(– Moore; – Allison; – Haig; + Caroline East-
her [b. Nov. 30, 1958, N.Z.], drums; + Andrew Todd
[b. Dec. 15, 1958, N.Z.], kybds.; + Justin Harwood
[b. July 6, 1965, N.Z.], bass) *Kaleidoscope World*
(Creation, U.K.) 1987—*Brave Words* (Flying Nun)
1988—(– Easther; + James Stephenson [b. May 17,
1970], drums) 1990—*Submarine Bells* (Slash)
(– Todd; – Harwood; + Moore; + Gillian Dempster
[b. Apr. 26, 1970, N.Z.], kybds.) 1992—(– Stephen-
son; – Dempster; + Steven Schayer [b. Feb. 12, 1965,
U.S.], gtr.; + Earl Robertson [b. Apr. 15, 1962, U.S.],
drums; + Lisa Mednick [b. June 27, 1957, U.S.],
kybds.) *Soft Bomb* (– Robertson; + Craig Mason
[b. July 28, 1961, N.Z.], drums).

Antipodean isolation bred a unique musical scene in New Zealand in the Eighties, when bands like the Clean, Tall Dwarfs, the Bats, Straitjacket Fits, the Verlaines, and the Jean Paul Sartre Experience created postpunk singer/songwriter music. The Chills were the first of several kiwi bands to be signed by American labels; in 1992 the band, always a volatile unit, exploded under the pressure of being an international act.

Martin Phillipps began playing music at age 15 when he joined the Same, one of the town of Dunedin's first punk bands. He started the Chills in 1980 with ex–Clean guitarist Peter Gutteridge (later of Snapper). Gutteridge soon left the group, thus starting the endless cycle of personnel changes that saw 14 Chills lineups in 12 years. In March 1982 the band recorded three songs for the *Dunedin Double* EP, the debut compilation from Flying Nun, the record company that soon became synonymous with the sound of the South Island.

In May the Chills recorded their first single, "Rolling Moon," and the following month drummer Martyn Bull was diagnosed with leukemia. The band took a brief hiatus then resumed under the moniker Time Flies, with the Clean's David Kilgour. That lineup lasted only a few months. In July 1983 Bull died, a traumatic event in Phillipps' life, which he later commemorated on the single "I Love My Leather Jacket."

Phillipps re-formed the band with an eighth lineup and the name a Wrinkle in Time in 1983, but soon reverted to the Chills. In 1984 the band released its second and third singles, "Pink Frost" and "Doledrums," and recorded *The Lost EP.* The next year, the Chills' ninth lineup made its first overseas trip, to England. They were well received by the press there and promoted by influential disc jockey John Peel. On returning to New Zealand, however, the band broke up again.

In 1986 the British label Creation issued *Kaleidoscope World,* a collection of singles. The Chills finally released their first album, *Brave Words,* the following year. They played the New Music Seminar in New York that summer and spent the fall in Europe negotiating a record deal and touring. In 1988, after performing throughout Australia and New Zealand, drummer Caroline Easther left due to ear problems, and the 11th version of the Chills toured the U.S., then relocated to Europe.

The Chills signed to Slash and recorded *Submarine Bells* in 1989. The album was released in 1990 to critical acclaim, but the single "Heavenly Pop Hit" failed to live up to its title. The band collapsed again that summer, and after going through several more lineups, Phillipps recorded *Soft Bomb* as basically a solo effort, accompanied by longtime Chill Terry Moore. The album was wanly received, and at the end of a bitter U.S. tour, Phillipps announced at a New York show the Chills' demise. As of fall 1993 Phillipps was in New Zealand writing material and hoping to pursue a solo career, with the Chills number 15 also a possibility.

Alex Chilton: See Big Star

The Chipmunks
Formed mid-Fifties
Alvin Chipmunk, lead voc., harmonica; Simon Chipmunk, voc., perc.; Theodore Chipmunk, voc., kybds.
1959—*Let's All Sing with the Chipmunks* (Liberty) 1960—*Sing Again with the Chipmunks* 1962—*Christmas with the Chipmunks* 1964—*The Chipmunks Sing the Beatles* 1980—*Chipmunk Punk* (Excelsior) 1981—*Urban Chipmunk* (RCA); *Christmas with the Chipmunks* 1982—*Chipmunk Rock*; *The Chipmunks Go Hollywood* 1992—*Chipmunks in Low Places* (Sony Kids' Music) 1994—*Here's Looking at Me! Greatest Hits of the Past 35 Years* (Sony Wonder).

The Chipmunks were one of the very biggest acts of the Golden Era of rock & roll, selling over 30 million records before being forced into hibernation by the British Invasion. In 1980 the trio revived its career with a comeback album that was more successful than anything attempted by their peers like Bill Haley and Pat Boone—more successful, in fact, than most of the punk albums that precipitated the Chipmunks' triumphant return.

The Chipmunk brothers began singing together at home, imitating the popular harmony groups of the time: the Drifters, the Clovers, and especially the Coasters, with their penchant for novelty songs. They performed at nut-gathering parties until they were discovered by songwriter/producer Ross Bagdasarian, a.k.a. David Seville (born January 27, 1919, Fresno, Calif.). With his cousin William Saroyan, Bagdasarian had written "Come on a My House," a hit for Rosemary Clooney in 1951, and on his own had written and produced "Witch Doctor," a 1½-million-seller for David Seville and His Orchestra in 1958. With "Witch Doctor" he had devised a studio technique that involved synchronizing tracks recorded at different speeds. This technique suited the Chipmunks' high-pitched, cheeky voices perfectly.

Their first collaboration was "The Chipmunk Song." Released just before Christmas 1958, it hit #1 before the end of the year, sold 3½ million copies in five weeks (setting a new record for fast-selling discs), and eventually sold seven million. It also won three Grammys. While they never equaled that success, they followed it with a string of hits: "Alvin's Harmonica" (#3, 1959, another gold record), "Ragtime Cowboy Joe" (#16, 1959, gold), "Alvin's Orchestra" (#33, 1960), "Rudolph the Red-Nosed Reindeer" (#21, 1960), and "The Alvin Twist" (#40, 1962). All

these records, singles as well as albums, were among the first stereo releases.

In the 1961–62 TV season, the Chipmunks starred in their own CBS series, *The Alvin Show,* which Bagdasarian wrote and produced. The Chipmunks often sang their records on the show in what historians cite as an early form of music video.

When Bagdasarian died in 1972, the Chipmunks' career seemed over forever. Their names appeared occasionally in the news: Simon was arrested in 1974 and charged with possession of poppy seeds, Theodore was hit with a paternity suit in 1976, and later that year Alvin, with much attendant publicity, was converted to a fundamentalist Christian sect, only to renounce it several months later.

The new wave shook them out of their idleness, and they turned to their original mentor's son, Ross Bagdasarian Jr., to produce their first album in over a decade, *Chipmunk Punk.* On it they chewed their way through songs by Blondie, the Cars, Tom Petty, and the Knack, showing themselves able if predictable interpreters. Even without singles, it sold over 750,000 copies. It was followed by *Urban Chipmunk* and *Chipmunk Rock,* and it was Chipmunkmania all over again. By 1983 they were primed for a triumphant return to the small screen in a new Saturday-morning series. Their band was expanded to include backing vocalists the Chipettes—Brittany, Jeanette, and Eleanor—who, along with Theodore, are voiced by Bagdasarian's wife Janice Karman. *Chipmunks in Low Places,* featuring C&W stars Billy Ray Cyrus, Tammy Wynette, and Waylon Jennings, among others, peaked at #21 and was nominated for the 1992 Grammy for Best Album for Children.

Charlie Christian
Born 1919, Dallas, Texas; died March 2, 1942, New York City, New York
1972—*Solo Flight—The Genius of Charlie Christian* (Columbia) 1987—*The Genius of the Electric Guitar.*

As the musician who took the guitar out of the rhythm section and made it a lead instrument, Charlie Christian had a profound influence on both jazz and rock & roll.

Christian's recording career spanned only three years. He was discovered playing in a jazz band in Oklahoma City by John Hammond in 1939. Benny Goodman brought him to New York to play with his sextet and his orchestra, and it was with Goodman that he revolutionized jazz guitar. The newly introduced electrified guitar gave the instrument an authoritative volume and tonal range it had never had, and Christian's innovative single-string picking technique made the guitar a solo voice equal to the trumpet and the saxophone. Additionally, as one of the participants in after-hours jam sessions with Thelonious Monk, Dizzy Gillespie, and Kenny

Grammy Awards

Glen Campbell

1967 Best Contemporary Male Solo Vocal Performance: "By the Time I Get to Phoenix"

1967 Best Country & Western Recording: "Gentle on My Mind" (with Al De Lory)

1967 Best Country & Western Solo Vocal Performance, Male: "Gentle on My Mind"

1967 Best Vocal Performance, Male: "By the Time I Get to Phoenix"

1968 Album of the Year: *By the Time I Get to Phoenix* (with Al De Lory)

Captain and Tennille

1975 Record of the Year: "Love Will Keep Us Together"

Daryl Dragon (Captain and Tennille)

1975 Record of the Year: "Love Will Keep Us Together"

Mariah Carey

1990 Best New Artist

1990 Best Pop Vocal Performance, Female: "Vision of Love"

Larry Carlton (the Crusaders)

1981 Best Pop Instrumental Performance: "The Theme from *Hill Street Blues*"

1987 Best Pop Instrumental Performance (Orchestra, Group or Soloist): "Minute by Minute"

Kim Carnes

1981 Record of the Year: "Bette Davis Eyes"

1983 Best Album of Original Score Written for a Motion Picture or Television Special: *Flashdance* (with others)

Mary Chapin Carpenter

1991 Best Country Vocal Performance, Female: "Down at the Twist and Shout"

1992 Best Country Vocal Performance, Female: "I Feel Lucky"

1993 Best Country Vocal Performance, Female: "Passionate Kisses"

1994 Best Country Vocal Performance, Female: "Shut Up and Kiss Me"

1994 Best Country Album: *Stones in the Road*

The Carpenters

1970 Best New Artist

1970 Best Contemporary Vocal Performance by a Group: "Close to You"

1971 Best Pop Vocal Performance by a Group: *Carpenters*

June Carter (the Carter Family)

1967 Best Country & Western Performance, Duet, Trio, or Group (Vocal or Instrumental): "Jackson" (with Johnny Cash)

1970 Best Country Vocal Performance by a Duo or Group: "If I Were a Carpenter" (with Johnny Cash)

Johnny Cash

1967 Best Country & Western Performance, Duet, Trio, or Group (Vocal or Instrumental): "Jackson" (with June Carter Cash)

1968 Best Country Vocal Performance, Male: "Folsom Prison Blues"

1969 Best Country Vocal Performance, Male: "A Boy Named Sue"

1970 Best Country Vocal Performance by a Duo or Group: "If I Were a Carpenter" (with June Carter Cash)

1986 Best Spoken Word or Nonmusical Recording: *Interviews from the Class of '55 Recording Sessions* (with others)

1991 Grammy Legend Award

1994 Best Contemporary Folk Album: *American Recordings*

Rosanne Cash

1985 Best Country Vocal Performance, Female: "I Don't Know Why You Don't Want Me"

General Johnson (Chairmen of the Board)

1970 Best R&B Song: "Patches" (with Ronald Dunbar)

The Champs

1958 Best R&B Performance: "Tequila"

Tracy Chapman

1988 Best Contemporary Folk Recording: *Tracy Chapman*

1988 Best New Artist

1988 Best Pop Vocal Performance, Female: "Fast Car"

Ray Charles

1960 Best Performance by a Pop Single Artist: "Georgia on My Mind"

1960 Best R&B Performance: "Let the Good Times Roll"

1960 Best Vocal Performance, Single Record or Track, Male: "Georgia on My Mind"

1960 Best Vocal Performance, Album, Male: *The Genius of Ray Charles*

1961 Best R&B Recording: "Hit the Road Jack"

1962 Best R&B Recording: "I Can't Stop Loving You"

1963 Best R&B Recording: "Busted"

1966 Best R&B Recording: "Crying Time"

1966 Best R&B Solo Vocal Performance, Male or Female: "Crying Time"

1975 Best R&B Vocal Performance, Male: "Living for the City"

1987 Lifetime Achievement Award

1990 Best R&B Performance by a Duo or Group with Vocal: "I'll Be Good to You" (with Chaka Khan)

1993 Best R&B Vocal Performance, Male: "A Song for You"

Chubby Checker

1961 Best Rock & Roll Recording: "Let's Twist Again"

Clifton Chenier

1983 Best Ethnic or Traditional Recording: *I'm Here*

Chicago
1976 Best Pop Vocal Performance by a Duo, Group or Chorus: "If You Leave Me Now"

The Chieftains
1992 Best Traditional Folk Album: *An Irish Evening Live at The Grand Opera House, Belfast*
1992 Best Contemporary Folk Album: *Another Country*
1993 Best Traditional Folk Album: *The Celtic Harp*

The Chipmunks (Ross Bagdasarian)
1958 Best Comedy Performance: "The Chipmunk Song"
1958 Best Recording for Children: "The Chipmunk Song"
1960 Best Album Created for Children: *Let's All Sing with the Chipmunks*

Eric Clapton
1972 Album of the Year: *The Concert for Bangla Desh* (with others)
1990 Best Rock Vocal Performance, Male: "Bad Love"
1992 Record of the Year: "Tears in Heaven" (with Russ Titelman)
1992 Album of the Year: *Unplugged* (with Russ Titelman)
1992 Song of the Year: "Tears in Heaven" (with Will Jennings)
1992 Best Pop Vocal Performance, Male: "Tears in Heaven"
1992 Best Rock Song: "Layla" (with Jim Gordon)
1994 Best Traditional Blues Album: *From the Cradle*

Petula Clark
1964 Best Rock & Roll Recording: "Downtown"
1965 Best Contemporary Rock & Roll Vocal Performance, Female: "I Know a Place"

The Reverend James Cleveland
1974 Best Soul Gospel Performance: *In the Ghetto*
1977 Best Soul Gospel Performance, Traditional: *James Cleveland Live at Carnegie Hall*

1980 Best Soul Gospel Performance, Traditional: *Lord, Let Me Be an Instrument* (with the Charles Ford Singers)
1990 Best Gospel Album by a Choir or Chorus: *Having Church*

Jimmy Cliff
1985 Best Reggae Recording: *Cliff Hanger*

Joe Cocker
1982 Best Pop Vocal Performance by a Duo or Group with Vocal: "Up Where We Belong" (with Jennifer Warnes)

Marc Cohn
1991 Best New Artist

Natalie Cole
1975 Best New Artist
1975 Best R&B Vocal Performance, Female: "This Will Be"
1976 Best R&B Vocal Peformance, Female: "Sophisticated Lady (She's a Different Lady)"
1991 Album of the Year: *Unforgettable with Love* (with Andre Fischer, David Foster, and Tommy LiPuma)
1991 Best Traditional Pop Performance: "Unforgettable"
1991 Record of the Year: "Unforgettable" (with David Foster)
1993 Best Jazz Vocal Performance: "Take a Look"

Albert Collins
1986 Best Traditional Blues Recording: *Showdown!* (with Johnny Copeland and Robert Cray)

Judy Collins
1968 Best Folk Performance: "Both Sides Now"

Shawn Colvin
1990 Best Contemporary Folk Recording: *Steady On*

The Commodores
1985 Best R&B Performance by a Duo or Group with Vocal: "Nightshift"

Lionel Richie
1982 Best Pop Vocal Performance, Male: "Truly"
1984 Album of the Year: *Can't Slow Down*
1984 Producer of the Year (with James Anthony Carmichael [tie with David Foster])
1985 Song of the Year: "We Are the World" (with Michael Jackson)

Harry Connick Jr.
1989 Best Jazz Vocal Performance, Male: *When Harry Met Sally*
1990 Best Jazz Vocal Performance, Male: *We Are in Love*

Ry Cooder
1988 Best Recording for Children: *Pecos Bill* (with Robin Williams and Mark Sottnick)
1993 Best World-Music Album: *A Meeting by the River* (with V. M. Bhatt)
1994 Best World Music Album: *Talking Timbuktu* (with Ali Farka Touré)

Rita Coolidge
1973 Best Country Vocal Performance by a Duo or Group: "From the Bottle to the Bottom" (with Kris Kristofferson)
1975 Best Country Vocal Performance by a Duo or Group: "Lover Please" (with Kris Kristofferson)

Chick Corea
1975 Best Jazz Performance by a Group: *No Mystery* (with Return to Forever)
1976 Best Jazz Performance by a Group: *The Leprechaun*
1976 Best Instrumental Arrangement: "Leprechaun's Dream"
1978 Best Jazz Instrumental Performance, Group: *Friends*
1979 Best Jazz Instrumental Performance, Group: *Duet* (with Gary Burton)
1981 Best Jazz Instrumental Performance, Group: *Chick Corea and Gary Burton in Concert, Zurich, October 28, 1979* (with Gary Burton)
1988 Best R&B Instrumental Performance (Orchestra, Group, or Soloist): "Light Years"

Chick Corea Akoustic Band
1989 Best Jazz Instrumental Performance, Group: *Chick Corea Akoustic Band* (with John Patitucci and Dave Weckl)

Robert Cray
1986 Best Traditional Blues Recording: *Showdown!* (with Albert Collins and Johnny Copeland)
1987 Best Contemporary Blues Recording: *Strong Persuader* (with the Robert Cray Band)
1988 Best Contemporary Blues Recording: "Don't Be Afraid of the Dark" (with the Robert Cray Band)

Crosby, Stills and Nash
1969 Best New Artist

Christopher Cross
1980 Record of the Year: "Sailing" (with Michael Omartian)
1980 Album of the Year: *Christopher Cross* (with Michael Omartian)
1980 Best New Artist
1980 Song of the Year: "Sailing"
1980 Best Arrangement Accompanying Vocalists: "Sailing"

Sheryl Crow
1994 Record of the Year: "All I Wanna Do"

1994 Best New Artist
1994 Best Female Pop Vocal Performance: "All I Wanna Do"

Rodney Crowell
1989 Best Country Song: "After All This Time"

Culture Club
1983 Best New Artist

Clarke, he was one of the originators of be-bop, which became the dominant force in jazz after his death. Christian developed tuberculosis in 1940. He was hospitalized in the summer of 1941 and spent the last six months of his life in the hospital.

Christian Rock

Christian rock is not traditional gospel music, but rather pop or rock with a specifically Christian, oftentimes conservative message. Within the genre are artists whose identification with the term range from the doggedly rigid underground (Petra, Carman, Phil Keaggy, Sandi Patti), to the mainstream crossovers (Amy Grant, Stryper, King's X), to the secular pop artists who express their Christian faith in more universal terms (U2, Van Morrison, Bruce Cockburn, T Bone Burnett). While such rock & roll antecedents as the blues and traditional country music are rife with Christian and Biblical imagery, few self-identified rockers have embraced the more fundamentalist views. Among the secular artists who have flirted with Christian rock are Jewish-born Bob Dylan, whose born-again Christian phase of the late Seventies/early Eighties spawned *Slow Train Coming, Saved,* and *Shot of Love;* the Byrds, with "Jesus Is Just Alright" (later a Doobie Brothers Top Forty hit); and Seals and Crofts, whose title track to the 1974 album *Unborn Child* expressed an antichoice sentiment that would later become a predominant theme of fundamentalist Christianity.

The most fiercely independent Christian rockers are of the born-again variety. Like the DIY postpunk movement of the early Eighties, this group of musicians has forged its own nonmainstream movement represented by an array of independent labels bankrolled by likeminded believers, including the umbrella label Word, as well as Myrrh, Benson, Sparrow, and Frontline. The Christian-rock arena encompasses nearly every pop music style, from heavy metal (Stryper), alternative rock (Alter Boys, Adam Again), and rap (D.C. Talk), to adult contemporary (Steven Curtis Chapman, Margaret Becker, Michael English). Some Christian rockers are former mainstream artists who changed their lives and retreated from the limelight, Mylon LeFevre, ex-cohort of Ten Years After guitarist Alvin Lee, and Mark Farner, formerly of Grand Funk Railroad, among them.

Lou Christie

Born Lugee Alfredo Giovanni Sacco, February 19, 1943, Glen Willard, Pennsylvania
1963—*Lou Christie* (Roulette)   1966—*Lightnin' Strikes* (MGM); *Lou Christie Painter of Hits; Lou Christie Strikes Again*   1969—*I'm Gonna Make You Mine* (Buddah); *This Is Lou Christie* (Marble Arch)   1971—*Paint America Love* (Buddah)   1974—*Lou Christie* (Three Brothers)   1988—*EnLightn'ment Strikes: The Best of Lou Christie* (Rhino)   1989—*Rhapsody in the Rain* (Polygram).

Singer Lou Christie had two big hits in 1963—"The Gypsy Cried" (#24) and "Two Faces Have I" (#6)—in the quavery falsetto style popularized by Del Shannon and Frankie Valli. Three years later he returned to the charts with "Lightnin' Strikes" (#1, 1966).

In Pennsylvania the young singer had won a scholarship to Moon Township High School, where he studied classical music and vocal technique and also sang with a group called the Classics. From 1959 to 1962 he recorded with various local acts for several small Pittsburgh labels, adopted the stage name of Lou Christie, and in October 1962 recorded "The Gypsy Cried." The first of several songs cowritten with Twyla Herbert (a mystic 20 years Christie's senior who claimed she could foresee his future and predict his hits), it was a big local hit and was subsequently picked up for national distribution by Roulette Records. By then Christie had moved to New York, where he found frequent session work as a background vocalist. Shortly after the release of "Two

Faces Have I" (#6, 1963), he served two years in the army. After his discharge in 1966 he signed with MGM and returned with the lushly produced "Lightnin' Strikes," which sold over two million copies.

His followups included "Rhapsody in the Rain" (#16, 1966), a fairly sexually explicit song for its time. Christie subsequently recorded for Colpix and Columbia before signing to Buddah in 1969. "I'm Gonna Make You Mine" (#10, 1969) was a hit in the U.S., Europe, and the U.K. Christie experienced problems with drugs in the early Seventies, and after cleaning up in London, he held a range of jobs, including offshore oil driller, ranch hand, and carnival barker. In the late Seventies he returned to New York, where he has done background vocal work. He continues to tour.

The Church

Formed 1980, Sydney, Australia
Steven Kilbey (b. Sep. 13, ca. 1959, Welwyn
Garden City, Eng.), bass, voc.; Marty Willson-
Piper (b. May 7, ca. 1959, Stockport, Cheshire, Eng.),
gtr., voc.; Peter Koppes (b. ca. 1959, Austral.),
gtr., voc.; Richard Ploog (b. ca. 1959, Austral.),
drums.
1981—*Of Skin and Heart* (Parlophone, Austral.)
1982—*The Blurred Crusade* (Carrere, Austral.)
1983—*Seance*   1984—*Remote Luxury* (Warner
Bros.)   1985—*Heyday*   1988—*Starfish* (Arista)
1990—*Gold Afternoon Fix* (– Ploog; + Jay Dee
Daugherty [b. March 22, 1956, Santa Barbara, Calif.],
drums)   1992—*Priest = Aura* (– Daugherty;
– Koppes)   1994—*Sometime Anywhere*.

This Australian quartet initially rehashed the jangly, psychedelic side of the Byrds, though by mid-decade the Church had forged its own style of guitar pop with willfully obscure lyrics. Principal songwriter Steven Kilbey is a private man who grew up consumed by rock music, listening to rare, import-only albums alone in his bedroom. In 1980 Kilbey formed the Church with friends Marty Willson-Piper and Peter Koppes, who shared his passion for music. Drummer Richard Ploog was added a year later. After much success among underground and alternative-rock audiences in Australia and abroad, the Church gained a larger, AOR-oriented audience when Arista signed the band to a U.S. deal in 1987. Often lumped together with R.E.M., the group finally reached the pop charts with its first Arista release, 1988's *Starfish* (#41), and subsequent single, "Under the Milky Way" (#24).

Ploog left after 1990's *Gold Afternoon Fix*, replaced by former Patti Smith Group drummer Jay Dee Daugherty for 1992's *Priest = Aura*. By 1993 only Kilbey, who still lives in Australia, and Willson-Piper, who lives in Sweden with his wife and daughter, remained. Since 1987 Kilbey, Willson-Piper, and Koppes have each released several solo albums; Kilbey also collaborated with Go-Between G. W. McLennan for the 1991 album *Jack Frost*.

Ciccone Youth: See Sonic Youth

Cinderella

Formed 1983, Philadelphia, Pennsylvania
Eric Brittingham (b. May 8), bass; Tom Keifer
(b. Jan. 26), gtr., kybds., voc.; Jeff LeBar (b. Mar. 18),
gtr.; Tony Destra, drums.
1986—(– Destra; + Jody Cortez, drums) *Night Songs*
(Mercury) (– Cortez; + Fred Coury, drums)   1988—
Long Cold Winter*   1990—*Heartbreak Station
(– Coury)   1994—*Still Climbing*.

In 1986 Cinderella was a heavy-metal band when heavy metal was not cool. Their teased coiffures, leather 'n' lace costumes, and thudding blues-based music heard on the multiplatinum albums *Night Songs* (#3, 1986) and *Long Cold Winter* (#10, 1988) and Top Twenty singles "Nobody's Fool" (#13, 1986), "Don't Know What You Got (Till It's Gone)" (#12, 1988) and "Coming Home" (#20, 1989) can be seen as the advance wave of the metallic invasion that produced Guns n' Roses, Poison, et al.

Cinderella was formed by Philadelphia bar-band veterans Tom Keifer and Eric Brittingham. Jeff LeBar, who sometimes played the same clubs as the nascent band, thought they needed a guitarist and volunteered. They chose the name Cinderella for its lack of heavy-metal connotations, but the band did have a Prince Charming, in the form of Jon Bon Jovi. He saw them in a club in 1985 and recommended them to his label, Mercury, which signed them the next year. Drummer Fred Coury joined while they recorded *Night Songs*. Produced by Andy Johns, the album has a slick, aggressive sound, topped off by Keifer's throat-shredding vocals. The band supported it and their followup, the bluesy, ballad-laden *Long Cold Winter*, with near-constant touring, opening for Bon Jovi, David Lee Roth, Judas Priest, and AC/DC and playing before a crowd of over 100,000 at England's Castle Donnington festival in 1987.

Heartbreak Station (#19, 1990), led by the ballad "Shelter Me" (#38, 1990), was a surprising turn toward a softer sound. Embellished with horns, gospel singers, and strings arranged by ex–Led Zeppelin John Paul Jones, it gave the band entrée to MTV and classic-rock formats and secured their headliner status.

Circle Jerks

Formed 1980, Los Angeles, California
Keith Morris, voc.; Greg Hetson, gtr.; Roger (Dowding) Rogerson, bass; Lucky Lehrer, drums.
1980—*Group Sex* (Frontier)   1982—*Wild in the*
***Streets* (Faulty Products) (– Lehrer; + John Ingram,**
drums)   1983—*Golden Shower of Hits* (LAX)
(– Rogerson; – Ingram; + Zander Schloss, bass;
+ Keith Clark, drums)   1985—*Wönderful* (Combat

Core) 1987—*VI* (Relativity) 1992—*Gig* 1995—
Oddities, Abnormalities and Curiosities (Mercury).

This unruly L.A. hardcore band became a popular live attraction particularly among skateboarders and slam dancers. Lead singer Keith Morris had the whine and scowl of Johnny Rotten, and the group's music was basic loud, speedy, three-chord punk.

When Morris left Black Flag after that group's first EP (*Nervous Breakdown,* 1978), he teamed up with former Redd Kross guitarist Greg Hetson in a garage in Hawthorne and formed the Circle Jerks. The group recorded its first album in 1980 and the next year appeared in the L.A. punk documentary, *Decline of Western Civilization.*

Wild in the Streets was originally released on Faulty Products, the label of Police manager Miles Copeland. *Golden Shower of Hits* contains a humorous hardcore medley in which the group desecrates Seventies AM pop gems like "Afternoon Delight," "Having My Baby," and "Love Will Keep Us Together." The group changed rhythm sections for *Wönderful,* which was marked by a more heavy-metal sound. *VI* continued in the direction of its predecessor. The Circle Jerks performed into the Nineties, releasing *Gig,* an anthology of live recordings, in 1992, and the band's major-label debut, *Oddities, Abnormalities and Curiosities,* in 1995.

Eric Clapton

**Born Eric Clapp, March 30, 1945, Ripley, England
1970—*Eric Clapton* (Atco)   1972—*History of Eric Clapton; Eric Clapton at His Best* (Polydor)   1973—*Eric Clapton's Rainbow Concert* (RSO)   1974—*461 Ocean Boulevard*   1975—*There's One in Every Crowd*; *E. C. Was Here*; *The Best of E. C.* (Polydor)   1976—*No Reason to Cry* (RSO)   1977—*Slowhand*   1978—*Backless*   1980—*Just One Night*   1981—*Another Ticket*   1982—*Time Pieces I* (RSO)   1983—*Money and Cigarettes* (Duck/Warner Bros.); *Time Pieces II*   1985—*Behind the Sun*   1986—*August*   1988—*Crossroads* (Polydor)   1989—*Homeboy* soundtrack (Virgin); *Journeyman* (Duck/Warner Bros.)   1991—*24 Nights*   1992—*Rush* soundtrack (Reprise); *Unplugged* (Duck/Warner Bros.)   1994—*From the Cradle* (Reprise)   1995—*The Cream of Clapton* (Polydor).
With Derek and the Dominos: 1970—*Layla and Other Assorted Love Songs* (Atco)   1973—*Derek and the Dominos in Concert* (RSO)   1990—*The Layla Sessions—20th Anniversary Edition* (Polydor)   1994—*Live at the Fillmore.***

In the Yardbirds, Cream, Derek and the Dominos, and his own bands, guitarist Eric Clapton has continually redefined his own version of the blues. Raised by his grand-

Eric Clapton

parents after his mother abandoned him at an early age, Clapton grew up a self-confessed "nasty kid." He studied stained-glass design at Kingston Art School and started playing guitar at 15 and joining groups two years later. He stayed with his first band, the early British R&B outfit the Roosters (which included Tom McGuinness, later of Manfred Mann and McGuinness Flint), from January to August 1963 and frequently jammed in London clubs with, among others, future members of the Rolling Stones. The guitarist put in a seven-gig stint with a Top Forty band, Casey Jones and the Engineers, in September 1963. He joined the Yardbirds in late 1963 and stayed with them until March 1965, when they began to leave behind power blues for psychedelic pop [see entry].

Upon leaving the Yardbirds, Clapton did construction work until John Mayall asked him to join his Bluesbreakers in spring 1965. With Mayall, he contributed to several LPs while perfecting the blues runs that drew a cult of worshipers (the slogan "Clapton Is God" became a popular graffito in London). Also with Mayall he participated in a studio band called Powerhouse (which included Jack Bruce and Steve Winwood); they contributed three cuts to a 1966 Elektra anthology, *What's Shakin'.* Clapton left the Bluesbreakers in July 1966 and cut a few tracks with Jimmy Page, then with bassist Jack Bruce and drummer Ginger Baker he formed Cream [see entry].

Clapton perfected his virtuoso style, and Cream's concerts featured lengthy solo excursions, which Clapton often performed with his back to the crowd. During his tenure with Cream, Clapton contributed lead fills to the Beatles' "While My Guitar Gently Weeps" and appeared on Frank Zappa's *We're Only in It for the Money.*

When Cream broke up in November 1968, Clapton formed the short-lived supergroup Blind Faith with Baker, Winwood, and Rick Grech [see entry]. During their only U.S. tour, Clapton embraced Christianity, which he has given up and reaffirmed periodically ever since. As a corrective to Blind Faith's fan worship, Clapton began jamming with tour openers Delaney and Bonnie, then joined their band as an unbilled (but hardly unnoticed) sideman. Clapton's 1969 activities also included a brief fling with John Lennon's Plastic Ono Band (*Live Peace in Toronto*).

He moved to New York in late 1969 and continued to work with Delaney and Bonnie through early 1970. With several members of the Bramletts' band, and friends like Leon Russell and Stephen Stills, whose solo albums Clapton played on, he recorded his first solo album, *Eric Clapton,* which yielded a U.S. #18 hit, the J. J. Cale song "After Midnight."

The album marked Clapton's emergence as a strong lead vocalist, a role he continued to fill after forming Derek and the Dominos with bassist Carl Radle, drummer Jim Gordon, and keyboardist Bobby Whitlock, all former Delaney and Bonnie sidemen. The Dominos' only studio album, the two-record *Layla* (#16, 1970), was a guitar tour de force sparked by the contributions of guest artist Duane Allman. The title track, an instant FM standard (and a Top Ten hit two years later), was a tale of unrequited love inspired by Pattie Boyd Harrison (wife of ex–Beatle George), whom Clapton eventually married in 1979; they divorced in 1989. Clapton toured on and off with the Dominos through late 1971, but the group collapsed due to personal conflicts, most, Clapton later claimed, drug- or alcohol-induced. Over the following two decades, Derek and the Dominos would prove one of the most star-crossed groups in rock: Allman died in a motorcycle crash in October 1971; Radle died of alcohol poisoning in 1981; Gordon was convicted of murdering his mother and imprisoned in 1984.

Clapton sat in on albums by Dr. John and Harrison, who enticed Clapton to play at the benefit concert for Bangladesh in August 1971. Depressed and burdened by a heroin habit, Clapton retreated to the isolation of his Surrey, England, home for most of 1971 and 1972. With the aid of Pete Townshend, he began his comeback with a concert at London's Rainbow Theatre in January 1973. Supported by Townshend, Winwood, Ron Wood, Jim Capaldi, and others, Clapton released tapes from the ragged concert in a September 1973 LP. By the time *461 Ocean Boulevard* (#1, 1974) was released, he had kicked heroin for good.

In the Seventies Clapton became a dependable hitmaker with the easygoing, more commercial style he introduced on *461*—a relaxed shuffle that, like J. J. Cale's, hinted at gospel, honky-tonk, and reggae; retaining a blues feeling but not necessarily the blues structure. Playing fewer and shorter guitar solos, he emphasized his vocals—often paired with harmonies by Yvonne Elliman or Marcy Levy—over his guitar virtuosity. He had hits with his cover of Bob Marley's "I Shot the Sheriff" (#1, 1974) and originals "Lay Down Sally" (#3, 1978) and "Promises" (#9, 1979). His albums regularly sold in gold quantities; *Slowhand* and *Backless* were certified platinum.

He had a Top Ten hit in 1981 with "I Can't Stand It," from *Another Ticket* (#7), and later that year formed his own label, Duck Records. During the early Eighties he made frequent appearances at major benefit concerts. In that decade Clapton's singles veered closer to balladry than blues, producing a string of hits, including "I've Got a Rock 'n' Roll Heart" (#18, 1983) and "Forever Man" (#26, 1985).

In 1985 he separated from his wife Pattie and went into rehabilitation to overcome the alcoholism that had replaced his heroin addiction over a decade before. The next year Italian actress Lori Del Santo gave birth to Clapton's only child, Conor.

Clapton continued to tour and record. *24 Nights* captured Clapton's 1990–91 concert series at London's Royal Albert Hall, which since 1987 has become an annual event. Guests on the album include Jimmie Vaughan, Phil Collins, Buddy Guy, Albert Collins, and Robert Cray. He had spent the better part of the past two years on the road, and in August 1990 his agent and two members of his road crew died in the same helicopter crash that claimed Stevie Ray Vaughan. On March 20, 1991, his four-and-a-half-year-old son, Conor, died after falling over 50 stories through a window in his mother's Manhattan apartment. A maintenance worker had left it open by mistake. Clapton was staying in a hotel just blocks from the apartment when the tragedy occurred. The following year Clapton made public service announcements warning parents to protect their children by installing gates over windows and staircases.

After a period of seclusion, Clapton began work again, writing music for *Rush,* a film about drug addiction. In March 1992, almost a year after Conor's death, Clapton taped a segment for MTV's *Unplugged* series, the soundtrack of which peaked at #2 in 1992 and included a reworking of "Layla" (#12, 1993) and "Tears in Heaven" (#2, 1993), the latter written for his son. That year he was nominated for nine Grammy awards and won six, including Record of the Year, Song of the Year, and Best Pop Vocal Performance, Male, for "Tears in Heaven." In early 1993 Clapton and his former cohorts in Cream, Jack Bruce and Ginger Baker, reunited to perform three songs at the group's Rock and Roll Hall of Fame induction. In 1994 Clapton released an album of remakes of acoustic and electric blues, *From the Cradle,* which topped the charts and won a Grammy for Best Traditional Blues Album. The double-platinum album became the best-selling traditional blues recording in history. In early 1995 Clapton was honored with an M.B.E. (Member of the British Empire).

The Dave Clark Five
Formed 1961, Tottenham, England
Dave Clark (b. Dec. 15, 1942, Tottenham), drums, voc.; Mike Smith (b. Dec. 6, 1943, London, Eng.), piano, voc.; Rick Huxley (b. Aug. 5, 1942, Dartford, Eng.), gtr.; Lenny Davidson (b. May 30, 1944, Enfield, Eng.), gtr.; Denis Payton (b. Aug. 11, 1943, London, Eng.), sax.
1964—*Glad All Over* (Epic); *American Tour; The Dave Clark Five Return* 1965—*Coast to Coast; Having a Wild Weekend; I Like It Like That* 1966—*The Dave Clark Five's Greatest Hits; Try Too Hard; Satisfied with You; More Greatest Hits* 1967—*5 by 5; You Got What It Takes* 1968—*Everybody Knows* (Columbia); *Weekend in London* (Epic) 1971—*Good Old Rock 'n' Roll* 1993—*The History of the Dave Clark Five* (Hollywood).

The Dave Clark Five, a British Invasion phenomenon, was formed by members of the Tottenham Hotspurs soccer team in suburban London because they needed to raise funds to travel to Holland for a match. Photogenic leader Dave Clark, a former film stuntman, had never played drums but quickly learned; he soon became the group's chief songwriter, producer, and manager as well.

The quintet's sound differed strikingly from those of its British Invasion counterparts. On songs like "Glad All Over" and especially "Anyway You Want It," the DC5 was probably the *loudest* U.K. act until the arrival of the Who. Denis Payton's sax underpinned a dense, churning rhythm section, while Clark's crackling snare-drum triplets punctuated the mix. And in Mike Smith the DC5 possessed a truly outstanding (and greatly overlooked) soul shouter.

"Glad All Over" (#6, 1964) was the first in a string of 17 Top Forty hits in just three years. The group's Top Tens included "Bits and Pieces" (#4), "Can't You See That She's Mine" (#4), and the ballad "Because" (#3) in 1964; "I Like It Like That" (#7), "Catch Us If You Can" (#4), and "Over and Over" (#1) in 1965; and "You Got What It Takes" (#7) in 1967. The DC5 was the second British act (after the Beatles) to appear on the *Ed Sullivan Show;* its 18 appearances on that show eclipsed both the Fab Four

and the Rolling Stones. Clark and company also followed the Beatles into film, appearing (with the Animals) in *Get Yourself a College Girl* (1964) and *Having a Wild Weekend* (1965).

By 1968 the group's U.S. hits had dried up, although the Dave Clark Five continued to score hits in Britain through 1970, the year the band split up. Smith and Clark continued to put out records under the name Dave Clark and Friends for another three years. Smith then made an album with onetime Manfred Mann vocalist Mike D'Abo in 1975. He later got into commercial jingle writing and session work, and appeared on the original album to *Evita.* In 1990 he recorded an album of Fifties American rock standards as well as originals.

Clark wrote and produced the 1986 musical *Time,* which starred Cliff Richard, and later, David Cassidy. An accompanying album of music from the stage production featured Richard, Freddie Mercury, Stevie Wonder, and others. Clark, a savvy businessman, has owned the DC5's original masters from the beginning. When he put together the 1993 double-CD retrospective, it marked the first time the DC5 catalogue was made available in twenty years. Over its career, the Dave Clark Five has sold over 50 million records worldwide.

Petula Clark
Born November 15, 1932, Epsom, England
1965—*Downtown* (Warner Bros.) 1967—*These Are My Songs* 1968—*Petula Clark's Greatest Hits, vol. 1.*

British pop singer Petula Clark is best known in America for mid-Sixties hits such as "Downtown" and "Don't Sleep in the Subway," but has also carried on a varied career in Europe. She began singing professionally at age eight; by nine she was a regular on radio shows; at 11, she hosted her own radio show, *Pet's Parlour.* Along with other child stars Julie Andrews and Anthony Newley, she performed for British troops during World War II.

She was 12 when she made her film debut in *A Medal for the General.* By the early Fifties she was a major star in the U.K., with over 20 movie credits. In 1954 "The Little Shoemaker" (#12, U.K.) became her first hit, followed by "Majorca" and others. She got her first #1 in the U.K. with 1961's "Sailor," followed by her first million-seller, "Romeo" (#3, 1961, U.K.). That same year she married Vogue Records publicity director Claud Wolff, who became her manager. As of 1994, they are still married. They moved to France and she became popular there with such hits as "Chariot" and "Monsieur," also a big seller in Germany. Her string of English hits continued throughout the early Sixties—"My Friend the Sea," "Ya Ya Twist," "Casanova"—and she cracked the American market with "Downtown" (#1, 1964), which won a Grammy Award in 1964.

Clark toured U.S. nightclubs for the next few years and managed follow-up hits like "I Know a Place" (#3, 1965), "My Love" (#1, 1966), and "I Couldn't Live Without Your Love" (#9, 1966). Although she cut down her personal appearances to raise her family, there were a few more hits, like "Don't Sleep in the Subway" (#5, 1967), "The Other Man's Grass Is Always Greener" (#31, 1967), and "Kiss Me Goodbye" (#15, 1968). She also revived her film career in the late Sixties, starring in *Goodbye, Mr. Chips* and *Finian's Rainbow*. She has also performed on the British stage, in *The Sound of Music* (1981), *Candida*, and *Someone Like You* (1990), which she cowrote with Fay Weldon. She made her Broadway debut in 1993 in *Blood Brothers*, costarring David Cassidy and his half-brother Shaun Cassidy. Clark continues to perform and record. In late 1988 a remix of "Downtown" entitled "Downtown '88" was a Top Ten U.K. hit.

Stanley Clarke

Born June 30, 1951, Philadelphia, Pennsylvania
1973—*Children of Forever* (Polydor)   1974—*Stanley Clarke* (Nemperor)   1975—*Journey to Love*   1976—*School Days*   1978—*Modern Man*   1979—*I Wanna Play for You* (Epic)   1980—*Rock, Pebbles and Sand*   1981—*The Clarke/Duke Project* (with George Duke)   1982—*Let Me Know You*   1983—*The Clarke/Duke Project II* (with George Duke)   1984—*Time Exposure*   1988—*If This Bass Could Talk*   1990—*3* (with George Duke)   1993—*East River Drive*   1994—*Live at the Greek* (with Larry Carlton, Billy Cobham, Najee, and others) (Slamm Dunk).

Stanley Clarke earned a considerable reputation as a jazz bassist before entering the rock market with Return to Forever and switching to electric bass. His trademark on acoustic bass is precise upper register vamping; on the electric, a metallic plunk.

Clarke studied at the Philadelphia Academy of Music before moving to New York City in 1970. He soon worked with Art Blakey, Gil Evans, the Thad Jones–Mel Lewis Orchestra, and Chick Corea [see entry], whom he met in Philadelphia in 1971. Clarke also played in a group led by saxophonist Stan Getz; the vaguely Brazilian-styled material Corea furnished for Getz became the repertoire for a Corea quintet with Clarke, reedman Joe Farrell, singer Flora Purim, and percussionist Airto Moreira on the Corea albums *Return to Forever* (1972) and *Light as a Feather* (1973).

Corea and Clarke, both Scientologists, kept the name Return to Forever for their group. They formed an electrified band with drummer Lenny White and guitarist Bill Connors—soon replaced by Al DiMeola—which grew increasingly bombastic and popular. In 1976 Clarke and DiMeola both left to pursue their solo careers. Clarke had already begun releasing his own fusion albums, including 1975's *Journey to Love* with guest Jeff Beck.

In spring 1979 he joined Rolling Stones Ron Wood and Keith Richards for a North American tour as the New Barbarians, then followed the tour with a half-studio, half-live double album *I Wanna Play for You*. He teamed up with keyboardist George Duke (who had appeared on previous Clarke LPs) as the Clarke/Duke Project in 1981 and had a hit with the ballad "Sweet Baby." He also recorded with Corea, White, and Chaka Khan on the acoustic jazz session *Echoes of an Era*. In 1983, Clarke joined Corea, White, and DiMeola on a Return to Forever reunion tour.

Clarke has worked as a producer, and has played on albums by Santana, Aretha Franklin, and Quincy Jones, among others; he also appeared on Paul McCartney's *Tug of War* (1982). In the late Eighties Clarke turned to composing for television and films. He began by writing for TV pilots, movies of the week, and even *Pee-wee's Playhouse;* by the Nineties he graduated to feature films scoring, among others, the Tina Turner bio-pic, *What's Love Got to Do with It,* and John Singleton's *Boyz N the Hood* and *Poetic Justice.* In 1989 Clarke played in the band Animal Logic with former Police drummer Stewart Copeland.

The Clash

Formed 1976, London, England
Mick Jones (b. Michael Jones, June 26, 1955, London), gtr., voc.; Paul Simonon (b. Dec. 15, 1955, London), bass; Tory Crimes (b. Terry Chimes, London), drums; Joe Strummer (b. John Graham Mellor, Aug. 21, 1952, Ankara, Turkey), voc., gtr.
1977—*The Clash* (CBS, U.K.) (– Crimes; + Nicky "Topper" Headon [b. May 30, 1955, Bromley, Eng.], drums)   1978—*Give 'Em Enough Rope* (Epic)   1979—*The Clash; London Calling*   1980—*Black Market Clash* EP; *Sandinista!*   1982—*Combat Rock* (– Headon; + Crimes, drums)   1985—(– Jones; – Crimes; + Vince White [b. ca. 1961], gtr.; + Nick Sheppard [b. ca. 1961], gtr.; + Pete Howard, drums) *Cut the Crap*   1988—*The Story of the Clash, vol. 1*   1991—*Clash on Broadway*   1994—*Super Black Market Clash.*
Havana 3 A.M. (Simonon, bass.; Gary Myrick, gtr.; Nigel Dixon, voc.): 1991—*Havana 3 A.M.* (I.R.S.).
Joe Strummer solo: 1987—*Walker* (Virgin Movie Music)   1989—*Earthquake Weather* (Epic).

The Clash took the raw anger of British punk and worked it into a political and aesthetic agenda. Outstripping all of their peers in terms of length and depth of career, they were rebels with a cause—with many causes, from anti-Thatcherism, to racial unity, to the Sandinistas. Their music was roots-based but future-visionary; their experiments with funk, reggae, and rap never took them far from a three-minute pop song. Hyped as "the only band that matters," the Clash fell apart just as they broke through to a wide American audience. By then, they had shown that punk was not just a flash in the pan and had delivered an arsenal of unforgettable rock songs.

The Clash were very much dependent on the band chemistry between its four longest-time members, Strummer, Jones, Simonon, and Headon. Primary songwriter Strummer, the son of a British diplomat, grew up in a boarding school. He quit school while still in his teens and in 1974 formed the 101ers, a pub-rock band named either for the address of the building where they squatted or for the number of the torture room in the George Orwell novel *1984.*

Jones and Simonon are both from working-class Brixton. The gangling, handsome Simonon was attending art school when he met Jones. He had never played an instrument until he heard the Sex Pistols; he then acquired a bass and joined Jones' band, the London SS, which in its 11-month existence included Tory Crimes and Topper Headon (as well as future Generation X/Sigue Sigue Sputnik bassist Tony James). Seeing the Pistols induced Strummer (a name he got when he strummed "Johnny B. Goode" on a ukulele as a busker in London subway stations) to leave the 101ers, which included guitarist Keith Levene, soon after they recorded a single, "Keys to Your Heart." Strummer and Levene then joined Jones, Simonon, and Crimes in their new group, named the Clash by Jones because that was the word that seemed to appear most often in newspaper headlines.

The Clash played their first, unannounced gig opening for the Sex Pistols in summer 1976 as a quintet. They opened for the Pistols on their Anarchy in the U.K. Tour after Levene quit. (He eventually joined Public Image

Ltd.) The Clash was managed by Malcolm McLaren associate Bernard Rhodes, who helped the band articulate its political mission. Where the Sex Pistols were nihilists, the Clash were protesters, with songs about racism, police brutality, and disenfranchisement. They mixed rock with reggae, the music of Britain's oppressed Jamaicans; one of their early singles was a cover of Junior Murvin's "Police and Thieves." Over the years, the Clash has been active in several political causes and has performed benefit concerts for Rock Against Racism.

In February 1977 British CBS Records signed the Clash for a reported $200,000 advance. Their debut album was released that spring and entered the British charts at #12. Columbia considered the album too crude for American release (although the import sold 100,000 copies, making it the biggest-selling import album of that time). In response, the Clash recorded "Complete Control" with Jamaican producer Lee "Scratch" Perry.

Crimes quit the group in late 1976. Headon, who had been drumming with Pat Travers in Europe since his stint in the London SS, accompanied the group on its first national headlining tour. The White Riot Tour, named after the current Clash single, ended at a London concert where the audience ripped the seats out of the floor. It was the first in a series of confrontations between the Clash and the police, especially in Britain, where the group members were arrested on charges ranging from petty theft to illegal possession of firearms (for shooting prize pigeons).

In October 1978 the Clash's stormy relationship with Rhodes took a turn for the worse and the band fired the manager, only to rehire him years later. They worked with journalist Caroline Coon and Kosmo Vinyl, among others, in between times.

One of the four songs on an EP entitled *Cost of Living,* a cover of the Bobby Fuller–Sonny Curtis "I Fought the Law," was the first Clash record released in the U.S. At Columbia's behest, American producer Sandy Pearlman, best known for his work with Blue Öyster Cult, produced *Give 'Em Enough Rope,* which reached #2 on the British charts but failed to reach the American Top 200.

The Clash launched their Pearl Harbour Tour of America in February 1979. They also persuaded Columbia to release their first album, which in its American version contained only ten of the original 14 tracks. A bonus 45 and EP selections dating as far back as two years made up the rest. The album eventually went gold. The Clash toured the U.S. again that fall, with Mickey Gallagher, of Ian Dury's Blockheads, on keyboards.

London Calling (#27, 1980), with its eclectic collection of pop styles, was both an artistic and a commercial breakthrough. Produced by Guy Stevens (who had worked with Mott the Hoople) and supplemented by a brass section and Gallagher, the album went gold thanks to a hit single penned by Jones, "Train in Vain (Stand by Me)" (#23, 1980). Beginning with *London Calling,* the Clash insisted that their records sell at lower than standard prices, a laudable position, considering that album prices were rising sharply then, due in part to the oil crisis.

In 1980 the semidocumentary film *Rude Boy* was released. It wove a fictional story about a fan (played by Ray Gange) around actual footage of Clash shows and backstage scenes, filmed during the previous 18 months. That year Jones also produced an album by his then-girlfriend, singer Ellen Foley.

The Clash recorded *Sandinista!* in New York, producing it themselves. The triple-LP package was a deliberately anticommercial gesture. It sold for less than most double albums, and Columbia took the lost profits out of the group's royalties and tour support funds. The sprawling, often-experimental album was chosen by a poll of *Village Voice* critics as album of the year, and *Sandinista!* (#24, 1981) was the first Clash album to sell more copies in the U.S. than in the U.K.

In December 1981, as the band was beginning to record their next album, Headon was arrested for heroin possession. In April 1982, just as *Combat Rock* was about to be released, Strummer disappeared, to be found a month later in Paris. (Some accounts say the vanishing act was a publicity stunt engineered by Rhodes.) Upon Strummer's return, Headon left the group, reputedly because of "political differences," although Strummer later revealed the problem was the drummer's drug use; he was replaced by Crimes for the Clash's U.K. tour. Ironically, Headon wrote "Rock the Casbah" (#8, 1982), which became an early MTV staple and the Clash's biggest hit. In July that year Headon was arrested in London for receiving stolen property.

Combat Rock (#7, 1982), produced by Glyn Johns, continued the Clash's forays into funk and rap. One song featured poet Allen Ginsberg. The album went platinum; the single "Should I Stay or Should I Go" was a Top Fifty hit that summer. In fall of 1982 the Clash toured the U.S. with the Who, playing for their biggest audiences yet. In spring 1983 they headlined at the US Festival in California, with Pete Howard now on drums.

That fall Simonon and Strummer kicked Jones out of the band, replacing him with two guitarists, Vince White and Nick Sheppard. Jones went on to form Big Audio Dynamite [see entry]. *Cut the Crap* was poorly received by critics and fans; the new Clash was a feeble imitation of its old self, and the band soon called it quits.

Strummer briefly reunited with Jones to work on B.A.D.'s second album. He pursued film work with director Alex Cox, writing "Love Kills," the theme song for *Sid & Nancy;* starring in *Straight to Hell* and contributing to the soundtrack; and scoring *Walker.* Forming the short-lived combo Latino Rockabilly War (including ex–Circle Jerk guitarist Zander Schloss), Strummer recorded the B side of the soundtrack for *Permanent Record,* a 1988 film about teen suicide. In 1988 Strummer toured as the rhythm guitarist for the Pogues [see entry]; he later produced their 1990 album, *Hell's Ditch,* and filled in for erstwhile frontman Shane MacGowan following its release. In 1989 he appeared in Jim Jarmusch's film *Mystery Train,* and released the poorly received solo album *Earthquake Weather.*

Simonon formed the roots-oriented Havana 3 A.M. with longtime L.A. scenester Gary Myrick; they recorded one album. Headon released a solo album in England in 1987, but later that year was sentenced by a London court to 15 months in jail for supplying heroin to a friend who died of an overdose.

The Story of the Clash, vol. 1 and *Clash on Broadway* compiled Clash songs. In 1991 the Clash had their biggest British hit ever when "Should I Stay or Should I Go" was rereleased, after being featured in a Levi's commercial. It went to #1 in the U.K.

The Classics IV

Formed mid-1960s, Jacksonville, Florida
J. R. Cobb (b. Feb. 5, 1944, Birmingham, Ala.), gtr.; Dennis Yost, voc.; Kim Venable, drums; Joe Wilson, bass; Wally Eaton, gtr. (– Wilson; + Dean Daughtry [b. Sep. 8, 1946, Kinston, Ala.], bass).
1975—*The Very Best of the Classics IV* (United Artists).

The Classics IV made several major soft-pop hits, including "Spooky" (#3, 1968), "Stormy" (#5, 1968), and "Traces" (#2, 1969), featuring lead vocalist Dennis Yost. J. R. Cobb, producer/writer Buddy Buie, and Dean Daughtry went on to studio work and in 1974 formed the Atlanta Rhythm Section [see entry].

Johnny Clegg

Born October 31, 1953, Rochdale, England
With Juluka, formed 1976, Johannesburg, South
Africa (Clegg, gtr., voc.; Sipho Mchunu [b. 1951,
Kuanskop, South Africa], voc., gtr., perc.): 1979—
Universal Men (Priority) 1981—*African Litany*
(+ Gary Van Zyl [b. Riversdale, South Africa], bass;
+ Scorpion Madondo [b. South Africa], sax., flute)
1982—*Ubhule Bemvelo* 1983—*Scatterlings*
(Warner Bros.) (+ Derek De Beer [b. South Africa],
drums; + Cyril Mnculwane [b. South Africa], kybds.;
+ Glenda Millar, kybds.); *Work for All* 1984—*Musa
Ukungilandela; The International Tracks; Stand
Your Ground* 1986—*The Good Hope Concerts*
1991—*The Best of Juluka* (Rhythm Safari).
With Savuka, formed 1986, Johannesburg, South
Africa (Clegg, gtr., voc.; Dudu Zulu [b. Mntowazi-
wayo Ndlovu, Dec. 25, 1957, South Africa; d. May 4,
1992, South Africa], voc., perc.; + De Beer, drums;
Keith Hutchinson [b. South Africa], kybds., sax,
voc.; Solly Letwaba [b. South Africa], bass; Steve
Mavuso [b. South Africa], kybds., voc.; Mandisa
Dlanga [b. South Africa], voc.): 1987—*Third World
Child* (Capitol) 1988—*Shadow Man* 1990—*Cruel,
Crazy, Beautiful World* (– Zulu; – Dlanga) 1993—
Heat, Dust & Dreams 1994—*In My African Dream*
(Rhythm Safari).

One of the most politically charged "world music" artists
to emerge from Africa in the Eighties, Johnny Clegg fell
so deeply in love with Zulu tribal culture that he not only
fused it with Western-based music, he actually became
an honorary Zulu tribesman. He was arrested and otherwise harassed for flouting South Africa's apartheid system to play with blacks, yet managed to garner
international acclaim.

Clegg took after both of his parents: His mother was
a cabaret singer, and his father, a journalist who admired
black culture and abhorred apartheid. Born in England,
he moved with his family to South Africa at the age of
six. As a teenager, Clegg was arrested frequently for
hanging out in Zulu bars, listening to the music he preferred. He later lectured on Zulu anthropology at the University of the Witwatersrand in Johannesburg.

He left academic life in the mid-Seventies to pursue
a career in music. In Johannesburg he befriended migrant gardener/street musician Sipho Mchunu, who
taught him traditional Zulu music. The two formed a duo,
Johnny and Sipho, which was renamed Juluka (Zulu for
"sweat") and played *mbaqanga* music with political
lyrics, gradually integrating Western funk, soul, and reggae elements. Juluka gained a large, interracial South
African audience, and found some success internationally, especially with 1983's *Scatterlings*. After Mchunu
returned to his family's farm in Zululand in 1985, Clegg

formed a fully electric, more rock-oriented update of Juluka, called Savuka (Zulu for "we have arisen"), which included Juluka drummer Derek De Beer. Ironically, Clegg
was expelled from the Musicians Union in his native
Britain, for performing in South Africa. Despite its never
having had a U.S. hit single, Savuka enjoyed a high
enough international profile to be invited on the 1988
Amnesty International Conspiracy of Hope Tour, with
Bruce Springsteen, Sting, Peter Gabriel, and others.
Cruel, Crazy, Beautiful World (1990) included songs inspired by the assassination of Clegg's friend, antiapartheid activist David Webster. In 1992 Savuka
percussionist Dudu Zulu—with whom Clegg performed
the acrobatic, crowd-pleasing Zulu dances known as
Indlamu—was murdered during factional warfare between different Zulu tribes. Clegg's next album, *Heat,
Dust & Dreams*, featuring many non–South African
guest musicians, included "The Crossing," a tribute to
Dudu Zulu.

The Reverend James Cleveland

Born December 23, 1932, Chicago, Illinois; died February 9, 1991, Los Angeles, California
1961—*This Sunday in Person: James Cleveland
with the Angelic Gospel Choir* (Savoy) 1962—*Rev.
James Cleveland with the Angelic Choir, vol. 2*
1963—*Peace Be Still: Rev. James Cleveland and the
Angelic Choir, vol. 3* 1968—*Songs of Dedication*
1970—*I Stood on the Banks of Jordan: Rev. James
Cleveland with the Angelic Choir, vol. 4* 1973—*In
the Ghetto: Rev. James Cleveland and the Southern
California Community Choir; Give It to Me: Rev.
James Cleveland and the Southern California Com-
munity Choir* 1978—*Tomorrow* (with the Charles
Fold Singers) 1979—*Lord Let Me Be an Instru-
ment: James Cleveland with the Charles Fold
Singers, vol. 4* (with the Charles Fold Singers)
1980—*James Cleveland Sings with the World's
Greatest Choirs* 1982—*It's a New Day; 20th An-
niversary Album; Where Is Your Faith* 1983—*This
Too Will Pass: James Cleveland, Charles Fold and
the Charles Fold Singers* 1990—*Jesus Is the Best
Thing That Ever Happened to Me* (with the Charles
Fold Singers); *Touch Me* (with the Charles Fold
Singers).

The Reverend Cleveland was a dominant force in gospel
music, and through numerous releases and the work of
the Gospel Music Workshop Convention, continues as
such today. As the leader of the Southern California
Community Choir, Cleveland has been a leader in expanding the musical base of gospel music and integrating jazz and pop rhythms and arrangements into
spiritual material. The pop gospel of Andrae Crouch and
Edwin Hawkins are offshoots of Cleveland's pioneering

efforts. His vocal style, ridiculed by some when he started singing in the Fifties, earned Cleveland the title "Gospel's Louis Armstrong."

His recordings of "Peace Be Still," "Lord Remember Me," "Father, I Stretch My Hands to Thee," and "The Love of God" are gospel standards. His 1972 double-platinum album with Aretha Franklin, *Amazing Grace*, is interesting not just because of the music, but for the fact that Franklin's father, the Reverend C. L. Franklin, gave the Reverend Cleveland the opportunity to arrange for Detroit's New Bethel Baptist Church choir when Cleveland was only 26. Cleveland also appeared on Elton John's *Blue Moves* LP in 1976.

In 1968 Cleveland organized the interdenominational Gospel Music Workshop Convention, which brings together top gospel musicians with churchgoers annually and showcases new artists. In the early Eighties the organization boasted over 25,000 members and 250 chapters; a decade later the membership has more than doubled. The GMWC has played an important role in gaining exposure for gospel music outside churches.

Jimmy Cliff

Jimmy Cliff

Born James Chambers, April 1, 1948, St. James, Jamaica
1967—*Hard Road to Travel* (Island, U.K.)   1968—*Jimmy Cliff*   1970—*Wonderful World, Beautiful People* (A&M)   1971—*Another Cycle* (Island, U.K.)   1972—*The Harder They Come* soundtrack (with various artists) (Mango)   1973—*Unlimited* (Warner Bros.)   1974—*Struggling Man* (Island); *House of Exile* (EMI, U.K.); *Music Maker* (Warner Bros.)   1975—*Brave Warrior* (EMI, U.K.); *Follow My Mind* (Warner Bros.)   1976—*In Concert—The Best of Jimmy Cliff*   1978—*Give Thanx*   1980—*I Am the Living*   1981—*Give the People What They Want*   1982—*Special* (Columbia)   1984—*The Power and the Glory*   1985—*Cliff Hanger*   1988—*Hanging Fire; The Best of Jimmy Cliff* (Mango)   1990—*Images* (Cliff Sounds and Films).

As the star of the groundbreaking film *The Harder They Come* and its soundtrack album, Jimmy Cliff was one of the first reggae stars to be heard outside Jamaica. Although he remains active and is popular in Europe and Africa, he never achieved the international stardom of Bob Marley. Like Ivan, the character he plays in *The Harder They Come*, he left his country home for the city when he was barely a teenager. He arrived in Kingston in 1962; within the year he had recorded his first record, a single called "Daisy Got Me Crazy." In the following months he cut a half-dozen tracks for various disc jockeys to play over their "sound systems." In 1962 he had a hit produced by Leslie Kong, "Dearest Beverly." Cliff's second collaboration with Kong, "Hurricane Hattie,"

went to #1 on the island, followed by "My Lucky Day," "King of Kings," and "Miss Jamaica." As a vocalist for Byron Lee's Dragonaires, he toured the Americas in 1964; at the New York World's Fair, Cliff met Chris Blackwell of Island Records, who signed him and enticed him to move to London in 1965.

Cliff worked at first as a backup singer. By divesting himself of his Jamaican patois, assuming the style of a cosmopolitan and the repertoire of a jet-setting troubadour, he developed a following in France and Scandinavia, and in 1967, "Give and Take" hit the British charts. The following year, he traveled to Brazil as Jamaica's representative at an international music festival. His song "Waterfall" won a festival prize and became a South American hit. "Wonderful World, Beautiful People" was an international best-seller in 1969, a Top Ten hit in the U.K., and one of the first reggae tunes widely heard outside Jamaica.

In 1969 Desmond Dekker recorded Cliff's "The Song We Used to Sing." Cliff was best known at this time as a songwriter. (Bob Dylan described his "Vietnam" as "the best protest song ever written.") He wrote "You Can Get It If You Really Want" for Dekker, and the Pioneers had a hit with his "Let Your Yeah Be Yeah." Cliff returned to Jamaica at the end of 1969 and recorded "Many Rivers to Cross," which inspired Jamaican filmmaker Percy Henzell to offer him the lead in *The Harder They Come*.

After the film, Cliff became a major star in Europe, Africa, and Latin America. "Under the Sun, Moon and Stars," "Struggling Man," and "House of Exile" were international hits between 1973 and 1975. In the attempt to expand his following, he left Island in 1973, signing with EMI in the U.K. and Warner Bros. in the U.S. But instead of reaching new fans, he almost lost those he had. In Jamaica he was denounced for abandoning his musical, religious, and national roots.

A Muslim—Cliff converted from Rastafarianism in 1973—he is welcomed in Africa and the Middle East. African religion, culture, history, and music became recurrent themes in his songs and were the focus of a film he made in 1980, *Bongo Man.*

In 1982 Cliff switched labels (moving to Columbia) and returned to Jamaica. There, he recorded *Special* (#186, 1982) and coheadlined the World Music Festival in an effort to win back his Jamaican fans. Cliff recorded parts of two albums, *The Power and the Glory* and *Cliff Hanger,* with Kool and the Gang, the latter winning the Grammy for Best Reggae Recording in 1985. That year, Bruce Springsteen covered his song "Trapped" on the *USA for Africa* benefit album.

An appearance in the 1986 movie *Club Paradise,* with Robin Williams and Peter O'Toole, was accompanied by seven songs on the soundtrack, including "Seven Day Weekend," a duet with Elvis Costello. None of the above helped Cliff gain American listeners. He formed his own production company, Cliff Sounds and Films, in 1990, and released *Images* that year.

Climax Blues Band

Formed 1968, Stafford, England
Original lineup: Colin Richard Francis Cooper
(b. Oct. 7, 1939, Stafford), sax, harmonica, clarinet, gtr., voc.; Peter John Haycock (b. Apr. 4, 1952, Stafford), gtr., voc.; Arthur Wood (b. Stafford), kybds.; Derek Holt (b. Jan. 26, 1949, Stafford), bass, gtr., kybds., voc.; George Newsome (b. Aug. 14, 1947, Stafford), drums, harmonica.
1968—*Climax Chicago Blues Band* (Sire, U.K.); *The Climax Blues Band Plays On* (Sire)   1970—*A Lot of Bottle*   1972—*Tightly Knit*; *Rich Man*   1973—*FM Live*   1974—*Sense of Direction*   1975—*Stamp Album*   1976—*Gold Plated*   1978—*Shine On*   1979—*Real to Reel*   1980—*Flying the Flag* (Warner Bros.)   1981—*Lucky for Some*   1983—*Sample and Hold* (Virgin).

While its name reveals its British blues revival beginnings, the Climax Blues Band became a dependable AOR outfit that reached the Top Forty every few years, with a sound trademarked by shared lead vocals from Peter Haycock and Colin Cooper, and Cooper's saxophone playing. The group toured Europe and America frequently through the Seventies. Since then it has released albums—mostly on small European or U.K. labels—with decreasing frequency.

CBB recorded each of its first two albums in less than three days. At first, it was a derivative blues band distinguished mainly by its youthful lineup; Haycock was only 16 when the band got started. By 1973, when the group first received extensive FM radio airplay in the U.S. with "Rich Man," it had already moved toward pop songwriting and production. Climax's first U.S. tour that same year yielded *FM Live* (#37, 1973), recorded in New York City during an Academy of Music concert broadcast over WNEW-FM. Its first self-produced album, *Gold Plated,* became CBB's biggest seller on the strength of "Couldn't Get It Right" (#3, 1977), and 1980's *Flying the Flag* featured the MOR ballad "I Love You" (#12, 1981). By the time of 1983's *Sample and Hold,* the group's name was carried by Haycock, Cooper, and keyboardist George Glover, along with studio musicians.

Through its lengthy tenure, the group has kept a low profile and a reputation for professionalism. The group records occasionally and tours with shifting lineups. In 1988 the group released *Drastic Steps* on a British label. Still very popular throughout Europe, the Climax Blues Band released a European double-CD retrospective in late 1994.

Patsy Cline

Born Virginia Patterson Hensley, September 8, 1932, Winchester, Virginia; died March 5, 1963, Camden, Tennessee
1989—*Walkin' Dreams: Her First Recordings, vol. 1* (Rhino); *Hungry for Love: Her First Recordings, vol. 2*; *Rockin' Side: Her First Recordings, vol. 3*   1991—*The Patsy Cline Collection* (MCA)   1994—*The Patsy Cline Classics Collection* (Curb).

Country singer Patsy Cline's career was in full swing, with pop Top Forty hits and national concert tours, when she was killed in a plane crash at the age of 30. Her honeyed soprano has been emulated not only by country singers like Loretta Lynn and Dolly Parton, but also by pop singers like Linda Ronstadt.

Cline took up piano at age eight but didn't begin singing until her teens. In 1948 she won a trip to Nashville through an audition; nine years later she appeared on TV on *Arthur Godfrey's Talent Scouts* and was spotted by Owen Bradley of Decca Records. Her first record, "Walkin' After Midnight," was both a country hit (#3) and a pop hit (#12) in 1957.

She was soon one of country music's biggest stars. Despite her numerous country hits, she sought a broader audience and refused to be saddled with a hillbilly or cowgirl image. Under Bradley's direction she came to embody the smooth, sophisticated new Nashville sound. "I Fall to Pieces" was a pop hit (#12) in 1961, followed later that year by "Crazy" (#9 pop, #2 C&W), a song written by a then little-known writer named Willie Nelson.

She had another pop Top Twenty hit with "She's Got You" (#14) in 1962.

On March 5, 1963, Cline was returning from a Kansas City, Missouri, show, when the single-engine plane her manager was piloting crashed. Over 25,000 attended her funeral. In 1973 Cline became the first woman solo artist elected to the Country Music Hall of Fame. Actress Jessica Lange played the singer in the 1985 bio-pic *Sweet Dreams;* its soundtrack climbed to #29 on the U.S. LP chart.

George Clinton/ Parliament/Funkadelic

**Born July 22, 1940, Kannapolis, North Carolina
1982—*Computer Games* (Capitol)   1983—*You Shouldn't-Nuf Bit Fish*   1985—*Some of My Best Jokes Are Friends*   1986—*R&B Skeletons in the Closet*; *The Best of George Clinton*   1986—*The Mothership Connection (Live from Houston)*
1989—*The Cinderella Theory* (Paisley Park/Warner Bros.)   1993—*Hey Man . . . Smell My Finger.*
Parliament (Clinton, voc.; Bernie Worrell [b. Apr. 19, 1944, N.J.], kyds.; Bootsy Collins [b. William Collins, Oct. 26, 1951, Cincinnati], bass; Eddie Hazel [b. Apr. 10, 1950], gtr.; Raymond "Tiki" Fulwood [b. May 23, 1944], drums; Gary Shider, gtr.; "Junie" Morrison, kybds.): 1970—*Osmium* (Invictus)   1974—*Up for the Down Stroke* (Casablanca)   1975—*Chocolate City*   1976—*Mothership Connection*; *The Clones of Dr. Funkenstein*   1977—*Parliament Live—P. Funk Earth Tour*; *Funkentelechy vs. the Placebo System*
1978—*Motor-Booty Affair*   1979—*Gloryhallastoopid—or Pin the Tale on the Funky*   1981—*Trombipulation*   1984—*Parliament's Greatest Hits.*
Funkadelic: 1970—*Funkadelic* (Westbound); *Free Your Mind and Your Ass Will Follow*   1971—*Maggot Brain*   1972—*America Eats Its Young*   1973—*Cosmic Slop*   1974—*Standing on the Verge of Getting It On*   1975—*Let's Take It to the Stage*; *Funkadelic's Greatest Hits*   1976—*Tales of Kidd Funkadelic*; *Hardcore Jollies* (Warner Bros.)
1977—*The Best of the Funkadelic Early Years* (Westbound)   1978—*One Nation Under a Groove* (Warner Bros.)   1979—*Uncle Jam Wants You*   1981—*Connections and Disconnections* (LAX); *The Electric Spanking of War Babies* (Warner Bros.).
P-Funk All-Stars: 1983—*Urban Dancefloor Guerrillas* (Uncle Jam/CBS Associated).
Incorporated Thang Band: 1988—*Lifestyles of the Roach and Famous* (Warner Bros.).**

Since 1955 George Clinton (a.k.a. Dr. Funkenstein, a.k.a. the Maggot Overlord, a.k.a. Uncle Jam) has headed a loose aggregation of musicians known variously as "The Mothership Connection," his "Parliafunkadelicment Thang," or "P-Funk All-Stars." Composed of members of two main groups, Parliament and Funkadelic, and various offshoot bands, the organization made some of black pop's most adventurous—and often popular—music of the Seventies. By the Eighties and Nineties, Clinton's zany presence was being felt in the music of a wide range of postdisco and postpunk artists, from Prince to Public Enemy, Dr. Dre, and the Red Hot Chili Peppers. Clinton's music mixes funk polyrhythms, psychedelic guitar, jazzy horns, vocal-group harmonies, and often scatological imagery. His lengthy concerts are unpredictable, characterized by extended, improvised jams, and sometimes compared in scope to those of the Grateful Dead. One of his many quotable mottoes is: "Free your mind and your ass will follow."

As a teenager in Plainfield, New Jersey, Clinton straightened hair working in a local barbershop, where he also founded a vocal group called the Parliaments. They struggled through the Fifties and most of the Sixties, by which time Clinton had moved to Detroit to work as a staff writer for Motown. In 1967 the Parliaments had a major hit with Clinton's "(I Wanna) Testify" (#20 pop, #3 R&B), a straight love song. The Parliaments' next charted single, "All Your Goodies Are Gone" (#21 R&B), suggested Clinton's future direction. Hanging out with Detroit hippies and listening to local hard-rock bands like the MC5 and the Stooges influenced Clinton's approach to music, and he began to contemplate making a radical change in the Parliaments' sound.

At the same time in 1967, a legal battle over the Parliament name ensued, so Clinton and the group's singers began recording with their backup band as Funkadelic

George Clinton

for Westbound Records in 1968. After winning the lawsuit, Clinton would record Parliament (the "s" was dropped) and Funkadelic separately. Initially Parliament was more commercially oriented and Funkadelic more experimental and gritty, though as time went on these distinctions blurred.

Early Funkadelic albums built a cult audience. Parliament/Funkadelic concert appearances featured Clinton jumping out of a coffin, musicians running around in diapers, smoking marijuana, and simulating sex acts. On both Parliament and Funkadelic albums, Clinton wrote about the dark realities of funk—which he had elevated to a philosophy—using negative imagery from the Process Church of Final Judgment and clear-eyed wit; he wrote for denizens of "Chocolate City" surrounded by "vanilla suburbs."

Parliament's 1974 hit on Casablanca, "Up for the Down Stroke" (#63 pop, #10 R&B), introduced Clinton's concepts to a wider audience and helped Funkadelic get signed to Warner Bros. Over the years, the group attracted top R&B instrumentalists, including bassist Bootsy Collins (ex–James Brown), guitarists Eddie Hazel and Gary Shider, keyboardist Bernie Worrell, keyboardist Junie Morrison (ex–Ohio Players), and reedmen Fred Wesley and Maceo Parker (ex–James Brown). Parliament's *Mothership Connection* and gold single "Tear the Roof Off the Sucker" (#15 pop, #5 R&B) made Clinton and company a major concert attraction. With a weird, lengthy stage show that included a spaceship descending on stage from a huge denim cap, the P-Funk crew rivaled Earth, Wind and Fire as black America's favorite band. From 1976 to 1981, Clinton's salesmanship and success landed recording contracts for many P-Funk offshoots: Bootsy's (Collins) Rubber Band [see Bootsy Collins entry], Eddie Hazel, the Horny Horns, Parlet, Bernie Worrell, the Brides of Funkenstein, Phillippe Wynne, Junie Morrison, and Zapp [see entry].

Parliament's "Flash Light" (#16 pop, #1 R&B)—in which Worrell introduced the synthesized bass lines later imitated by many funk and new-wave bands—and the platinum *Funkentelechy vs. the Placebo Syndrome* in 1977; "Aqua Boogie" (#1 R&B) in 1979; and Funkadelic's funk anthem "One Nation Under a Groove" (#28 pop, #1 R&B) in 1978, were Clinton's commercial peaks in the Seventies.

Beginning in 1980, internal strife and legal problems temporarily sapped Clinton's P-Funk tribe of its energy and key performers. And while P-Funk's sound got absorbed into mainstream funk and hip-hop, Clinton's many projects became entangled. Drummer Jerome Brailey left P-Funk to start his own group, Mutiny, which pointedly devoted its first album to imprecations against the "Mamaship." Other ex-sidemen actually recorded as Funkadelic, although their album (the poorly received *Connections and Disconnections*) carried a sticker to the

effect that Clinton was not involved. After Warner Bros. refused to release *The Electric Spanking of War Babies* (with guest Sly Stone) as a double album, Clinton cut it to a single LP and began proceedings to end his Warners contract. He recorded two singles, "Hydraulic Pump" and "One of Those Summers," with the P-Funk All-Stars on an independent label, Hump Records. Then he reemerged with a name that was not in litigation—his own—on a George Clinton solo album, *Computer Games* (1982), which included P-Funk's core members and the hit single, "Atomic Dog" (#1 R&B, 1982).

In 1983 Clinton began a six-year sabbatical from the pop limelight, during which time his music showed up (both in spirit and as samples) in rap and hip-hop (as well as on albums of Clinton's collected works); "Atomic Dog" became one of the most-requested dancefloor songs. In 1985 he produced the Red Hot Chili Peppers' second album, *Freaky Styley.* Clinton returned to music making in 1989 with *The Cinderella Theory* (featuring guests Chuck D and Flavor Flav) on Prince's Paisley Park label, and regrouped the P-Funk All-Stars for concerts. In 1993 he and P-Funk performed at President Clinton's Youth Inaugural Ball. Later that year, he released *Hey Man . . . Smell My Finger* (with an all-star lineup of guests including rappers Ice Cube and Yo-Yo, and members of the Chili Peppers), and though the album was not a commercial smash (peaking at #145), it appeared that Clinton's career was back on the upswing. In the summer of 1994, he appeared on the Lollapalooza tour.

The Clovers
Formed 1946, Washington, D.C.
Lineup circa 1950: John "Buddy" Bailey (b. ca. 1930, Washington), voc.; Matthew McQuater, voc.; Harold "Hal" Lucas Jr. (b. ca. 1923; d. Jan. 6, 1994, Washington), voc.; Harold Winley, bass voc.; Bill Harris, gtr.
1953—(– Bailey; + Charlie White [b. ca. 1930, Washington], voc.) 1954—(– White; + Billy Mitchell, voc.) 1975—*Their Greatest Recordings—The Early Years* (Atco) 1991—*Down in the Alley* (Rhino); *The Best of the Clovers—Love Potion No. 9* (EMI).

Emerging out of the Washington, D.C., area, the Clovers were the most successful R&B group of the Fifties. They were an important force in the fusion of big-beat R&B with gospel-style vocals, which laid the groundwork for soul music a decade later. With the Top Thirty success of "Love, Love, Love" in 1956, the Clovers became one of the first black vocal groups to chart on the pop chart.

The group was formed in a Washington, D.C., high school by Harold Lucas in the late Forties. Then known as the Four Clovers, they were singing at a local nightspot, the Rose Club, when they were discovered by record store owner Lou Krefetz, who became their manager and got them a contract with Atlantic Records in 1950. By then the group's lineup had settled into that outlined above. Label president Ahmet Ertegun wrote their first of many R&B hits in 1951, including two R&B #1s, "Don't You Know I Love You" and "Fool, Fool, Fool." Through 1952 they continued their hitting streak with "One Mint Julep," "Ting-A-Ling," "Hey Miss Fannie," and "I Played the Fool." They were also a top draw at black nightclubs.

Their string of R&B hits continued through the early Fifties with "Crawlin'," "Good Lovin'" (1953), "Lovey Dovey," "I've Got My Eyes on You," "Your Cash Ain't Nothing but Trash" (1954), "Blue Velvet" (later covered by Bobby Vinton), "Devil or Angel" (later covered by Bobby Vee), and "Nip Jip" (1955). In late 1952, Bailey joined the army; his replacement, Charles White, had sung with the Dominoes and the Checkers. In April 1954 he left for the Playboys, and Billy Mitchell replaced him. In 1956 the Clovers had another R&B hit with "From the Bottom of My Heart." Ironically, however, "Love, Love, Love"'s historic appearance in the pop listings marked the beginning of the Clovers' commercial decline. After moving to United Artists in 1959, they had their last major hit with Leiber and Stoller's "Love Potion No. 9" (#23 R&B). In 1961 the group disbanded, and two groups of Clovers (one led by Bailey and Winley, another by Lucas) and their innumerable variations performed and recorded through the years. Lucas had only stopped touring approximately two years before he died in early 1994. In 1988 he and the other founding members received the Rhythm and Blues Foundation's Pioneer Award.

The Coasters/The Robins

Formed 1955, Los Angeles, California
Carl Gardner (b. Apr. 29, 1928, Tyler, Tex.), tenor voc.; Leon Hughes, tenor; Billy Guy (b. June 20, 1936, Ittasca, Tex.), baritone voc.; Bobby Nunn (d. Nov. 5, 1986, Los Angeles), bass voc.
1956—*The Coasters* (Atco) (– Nunn; – Hughes; + Will "Dub" Jones [b. Los Angeles], bass voc.; + Cornell, or Cornelius, Gunter [b. Nov. 14, 1938, Los Angeles; d. Feb. 26, 1990, Las Vegas, Nev.], tenor voc.) 1958—*Greatest Hits* 1959—*One by One* 1960—*Coast Along* 1961—(– Gunter; + Earl "Speedo" [also spelled "Speedoo"] Carroll [b. Nov. 2, 1937, New York City, N.Y.], tenor voc.) 1962—*Greatest Recordings* 1965—(– Jones; + Ronnie Bright [b. Oct. 18, 1938], tenor voc.; – Guy; + Jimmy Norman, baritone) 1971—*Their Greatest Recordings—The Early Years* 1974—*On Broadway* (King) 1978—*20 Great Originals* (Atlantic) 1992—*50 Coastin' Classics: The Coasters Anthology* (Rhino/Atlantic) 1994—*The Very Best of the Coasters* (Rhino).

The Coasters' comic vocals plus the writing and production of Jerry Leiber and Mike Stoller resulted in a string of wisecracking doo-wop hits in the late Fifties. They were among the first black singing groups to truly cross over and be considered a rock & roll act, and their catalogue includes not only their famous humorous hit singles but social protest (1959's "What About Us"), one of the first great rock anthems ("That Is Rock and Roll"), and a wealth of future cover hits for artists ranging from Elvis Presley ("Girls, Girls, Girls") to Leon Russell ("Young Blood").

The group originated in the late Forties as a Los Angeles vocal quartet, the Robins. Protégés of Johnny Otis, they recorded for Savoy Records, hitting #1 on the R&B chart in 1950 with "Double Crossing Blues," which featured Little Esther Phillips. They began their association with Leiber and Stoller when they moved from Crown Records to RCA in 1953. When Leiber and Stoller founded Spark Records in 1954, the Robins became the label's most successful act, hitting on the West Coast with "Riot in Cell Block No. 9," "Framed," "The Hatchet Man," and "Smokey Joe's Cafe." The last song attracted Atlantic Records, which bought the Robins' catalogue in 1955 and contracted Leiber and Stoller as independent producers.

At that point the Robins split into two groups: Carl Gardner and Bobby Nunn stayed with Leiber and Stoller, while the other Robins went on to record for Whippet Records. Billy Guy and Leon Hughes joined Gardner and Nunn to become the Coasters (so named because of their West Coast origins). Their first single, "Down in Mexico," made the R&B Top Ten in 1956. Its double-sided followup, "Searchin'" b/w "Young Blood," went to #1 on the R&B chart and #3 on the pop chart in 1957; it was the first of the Coasters' four gold records. The group, together with Leiber and Stoller, moved to New York. After yet another personnel change—the addition of Cornell (a.k.a. Cornelius) Gunter from the Flairs—the Coasters returned to the charts with "Yakety Yak" (#1, 1958), "Charlie Brown" (#2, 1959), "Along Came Jones" (#9, 1959), and "Poison Ivy" (#7, 1959). Their backup group often featured King Curtis on sax and Mickey Baker or Adolph Jacobs on guitar. By decade's end, the Coasters were America's most popular black rock & roll group.

Four more Coasters records made the Top Forty in 1960 and 1961, and (joined by Earl "Speedo" Carroll, formerly of the Cadillacs, and Ronnie Bright, the featured vocalist on Johnny Cymbal's "Mr. Bass Man") they continued to record for Atco until 1966. Their last chart appearance was in 1971, with a Leiber-and-Stoller re-produced "Love Potion No. 9" (#76). They last worked with Leiber and Stoller in 1973, and in 1976 they released their last single, a version of "If I Had a Hammer." Since then, Nunn, Gardner, and Hughes individually, and Guy and Jones together, at one time or another all led groups billed as the Coasters.

In 1988 Gardner, Guy, Jones, and Gunter (with Tom Palmer) performed at the Atlantic Records' 40th-anniversary concert in New York City. In 1987 the Coasters were inducted into the Rock and Roll Hall of Fame. Gunter was murdered in Las Vegas in early 1990. Ten years earlier, latter-day member Nathaniel Wilson had disappeared from Las Vegas; his dismembered body was recovered in California a month later. Nunn died in 1986 of a heart attack.

Billy Cobham

Born May 16, 1944, Panama
1973—*Spectrum* (Atlantic)   1974—*Crosswinds*; *Total Eclipse*   1975—*Shabazz; A Funky Thide of Sings*   1976—*Life and Times; "Live"—On Tour in Europe*   1978—*Inner Conflicts; Simplicity of Expression* (Columbia); *A Live Mutha for Ya*   1979— *B.C.*   1980—*The Best of Billy Cobham* 1981—*Stratus* (Iankustic)   1982—*Observations* (Elektra)   1983—*Smokin'*   1985—*Warning* (GRP); *Power Play*   1987—*Picture This*   1988—*Billy's Best Hits.*

Recording with Miles Davis and then starring with the Mahavishnu Orchestra in the Seventies, drummer Billy Cobham was a key figure in the development of jazz-rock fusion.

Learning to play timbales by age three, Cobham moved with his mother from Panama to New York when he was about seven to join his pianist father. In 1959 he enrolled at the High School of Music and Art. After serving in the armed forces, he worked in the city's jazz circles, playing with the Billy Taylor Trio and the New York Jazz Sextet in the late Sixties. In 1968 he earned his first session credit, George Benson's *Giblet Gravy,* followed by two albums with Horace Silver. He has since played on numerous recordings, backing James Brown, Quincy Jones, Carlos Santana, Carly Simon, Sam and Dave, and Larry Coryell, among others. In 1969, after stints with Stanley Turrentine and Kenny Burrell, he joined the Miles Davis band that virtually invented jazz rock; ultimately, he played on eight Davis albums, including the landmark *Bitches Brew.* Concurrently, with Michael and Randy Brecker, he founded the jazz-rock group Dreams, which recorded two albums before disbanding in 1970.

In 1971 Cobham joined fellow Davis alumnus John McLaughlin in his Mahavishnu Orchestra, staying with the pioneering fusion group until the end of 1973 [see entry]. He then went solo, recording *Spectrum* with such guests as jazz bassist Ron Carter and saxophonist Joe Farrell, and rock guitarist Tommy Bolin; the album and its two successors made the pop Top Forty. In 1974 Cobham assembled a band called Spectrum including keyboardist George Duke, guitarist John Scofield (who later joined Miles Davis), and ex–Santana bassist Doug Rauch

(later replaced by Alphonso Johnson). By 1976 the group had become the Billy Cobham–George Duke Band.

In 1979 and 1980 he worked extensively as part of Jack Bruce's band, followed by a year's stint with Grateful Dead guitarist Bob Weir's Midnites. In the mid-Seventies he produced albums for Airto and pianist David Sancious. Throughout the decade Cobham's solo albums, either in a small-group format or with more extensive lineups, continued to mine the jazz-rock vein.

Cobham settled ultimately in Zurich, Switzerland, continuing to record solo projects during the Eighties. Still an influential percussionist, Cobham found a new forum in the drum clinic. By the start of the Nineties Cobham was without a record deal but had begun touring with ex–Dixie Dregs keyboardist T. Lavitz and former Toto bassist Jeff Berlin, as well as with jazz all-star ensembles.

Eddie Cochran

Born October 3, 1938, Oklahoma City, Oklahoma; died April 17, 1960, London, England
1960—*Eddie Cochran* (Liberty)   1962—*Cherished Memories; Memorial Album; Singing to My Baby* 1963—*Never to Be Forgotten*   1964—*My Way* 1970—*C'mon Everybody* (Sunset); *10th Anniversary Album* (Liberty)   1972—*Legendary Masters* (United Artists)   1990—*Greatest Hits* (Curb).

In his brief career Eddie Cochran made a lasting imprint on rock with songs like "Summertime Blues." Born in Oklahoma, he was raised in Minnesota until 1949, when he moved with his family to Bell Gardens, California. By then he had taught himself to play blues guitar. He and guitarist Hank Cochran (no relation) began recording as the Cochran Brothers in 1955.

The following year, Eddie and Hank split up, and Cochran began writing songs with Jerry Capeheart, whom he'd met while buying guitar strings at a local music shop. While the two were recording background music for a low-budget film, the producer, Boris Petroff, enlisted him to sing his song "Twenty Flight Rock" in another movie he was making: *The Girl Can't Help It,* with Jayne Mansfield. Liberty Records signed him soon after.

His first hit was 1957's "Sittin' in the Balcony" (#18). A year later Cochran and Capehart's good-humored anthem of teen boredom, "Summertime Blues," made the Top Ten. It has since revisited the charts in versions by the Who and Blue Cheer. Two more hits, "C'mon Everybody" (#35, 1958) and "Somethin' Else" (#58, 1959), established him as a star, especially in England.

Cochran toured steadily, backed by the Kelly Four (bassist Connie Smith, who was later replaced by Dave Schrieber; drummer Gene Ridgio; and a series of pianists and saxophonists). He was an exceptionally talented guitarist, an energetic stage performer, and an early master of studio overdubbing; he played and sang all the parts on both "C'mon Everybody" and "Summertime Blues." Cochran was 21 when he died on April 17, 1960, in an auto accident en route to the London airport. His hit single at the time was "Three Steps to Heaven," which went to #1 in the U.K. Injured in the crash were Gene Vincent and Cochran's fiancée, Sharon Sheeley, cowriter of "Somethin' Else" and composer of Ricky Nelson's 1958 #1 smash "Poor Little Fool." Cochran and Nelson both entered the Rock and Roll Hall of Fame posthumously in 1987.

Bruce Cockburn

Born May 27, 1945, Ottawa, Canada
1970—*Bruce Cockburn* (True North, Can.)   1971— *High Winds, White Sky*   1972—*Sunwheel Dance* 1973—*Night Vision*   1974—*Salt, Sun & Time* 1975—*Joy Will Find a Way*   1976—*In the Falling Dark* (Island)   1977—*Circles in the Storm*   1978— *Further Adventures Of*   1979—*Dancing in the Dragon's Jaws* (Millennium)   1980—*Humans* 1981—*Inner City Front; Mummy Dust* (or *Resumé*) (True North, Can.)   1983—*The Trouble with Normal* (Columbia)   1984—*Stealing Fire* (Gold Mountain) 1986—*World of Wonders* (MCA)   1987—*Waiting for a Miracle* (True North, Can.)   1989—*Big Circumstance* (Gold Castle)   1990—*Bruce Cockburn Live* (True North, Can.)   1991—*Nothing but a Burning Light* (Columbia)   1993—*Christmas*   1994—*Dart to the Heart* (Columbia).

Singer/songwriter Bruce Cockburn has been a major star in his homeland since his album debut in 1970, garnering 10 Juno awards, two Canadian platinum records, and 13 gold. A virtuoso guitarist, Cockburn has progressed from folk-style songs to his own blend of jazz, reggae, and rock, and most recently Latin and Afropop. His lyrics have ranged from hippie-ish mysticism to openly fundamentalist Christianity, although Cockburn told *Musician* magazine in 1986: "Personally, I think the whole moral majority, hard-right, virulent anticommunist thinking that's centered around America First is pathological and dangerous. . . . [O]ne of the reasons I stopped making such a public issue of being a Christian has to do with not wanting to be identified with that version of fundamentalism." Since the mid-Eighties, his work has become increasingly political.

In his late teens Cockburn traveled through Europe as a street musician, then studied at Boston's Berklee School of Music for three years before returning to Ottawa to play organ in a Top Forty cover band and harmonica in a blues band. He made his recording debut in 1970 as a soloist; his first two albums, *Bruce Cockburn* and *High Winds, White Sky,* were released in Canada on True North and appeared in the U.S. on Epic, but his next

four appeared only in Canada. There he began to win wide acclaim. In 1976 he signed with Island and made forays into the U.S.; his first Millennium album included his first and, to date, only U.S. hit, "Wondering Where the Lions Are" (#21, 1980).

With 1980's *Humans,* Cockburn's work began focusing on political and humanitarian issues, inspired not only by his religious beliefs but by fact-finding trips to strife-torn areas around the globe. He is perhaps best known to U.S. audiences through his 1984 single "If I Had a Rocket Launcher," which, although it peaked at #88, was an oft-seen video on MTV. *Mummy Dust,* alternately titled *Resumé,* summed up his first ten albums. While critics applaud Cockburn's eclecticism and craft, his albums have only rarely broken into the Top 100 here. He performed at President Clinton's inauguration in 1993.

Joe Cocker

Born John Robert Cocker, May 20, 1944, Sheffield, England
1969—*With a Little Help from My Friends* (A&M); *Joe Cocker!*   1970—*Mad Dogs and Englishmen* 1972—*Joe Cocker*   1974—*I Can Stand a Little Rain* 1975—*Jamaica Say You Will*   1976—*Sting Ray; Live in L.A.*   1977—*Greatest Hits*   1978—*Luxury You Can Afford*   1982—*Sheffield Steel* (Island)   1984— *Civilized Man* (Capitol)   1986—*Cocker*   1987—*Unchain My Heart; Classics Volume 4* (A&M) 1989—*One Night of Sin* (Capitol)   1990—*Joe Cocker Live*   1992—*Night Calls*   1993—*The Best of Joe Cocker*   1994—*Have a Little Faith* (550).

British white-soul singer Joe Cocker parlayed Ray Charles-ish vocals and an eccentric stage presence into a string of late-Sixties hits only to suffer from his excesses in drugs and alcohol by the mid-Seventies. In the Eighties and Nineties, however, he has gone from tragic figure to well-respected interpreter, and his gritty, powerful voice remains one of the most distinctive in rock & roll.

Cocker attended Sheffield Central Technical School and worked as a gas fitter for the East Midlands Gas Board. In 1959 he joined his first group, the Cavaliers, playing drums and harmonica. He moved to lead vocals in 1961, and the band changed its name to Vance Arnold (Cocker) and the Avengers. They released regional singles and toured locally with the Hollies and the Rolling Stones. Decca offered Cocker a contract in 1964, and he took a six-month leave of absence from the gas company. Cocker's version of the Beatles' "I'll Cry Instead" (which he hated so much that he refused to sing it onstage) and an English tour opening for Manfred Mann were ignored, and he went back to his day job.

The following year, Cocker and keyboardist Chris Stainton assembled the Grease Band with guitarists

Henry McCullough and Alan Spenner, and two other musicians. They played Motown covers in northern England pubs until 1967, when producer Denny Cordell became Cocker's manager and persuaded him and the band to move to London. A Cocker-Stainton song, "Marjorine," became a minor British hit, and after some exposure in London, Cocker and the Grease Band recorded *With a Little Help from My Friends* in 1968 with guests Jimmy Page, Steve Winwood, and others. The title track, one of many cover versions Cocker would record over his career, went to #1 in England and #68 in the U.S. His explosive performance of the song at the Woodstock Festival was a festival highlight, and his habit of wildly flailing his arms as he sang became as much a rock archetype as Pete Townshend's windmill. When Cocker sang Traffic's "Feelin' Alright" on *The Ed Sullivan Show* in 1969, the program's producer hid him behind a group of dancers—shades of Elvis Presley and his wiggling hips.

During the U.S. tour, Cocker met Leon Russell, who wrote "Delta Lady" and coproduced *Joe Cocker!,* the Grease Band's swan song. Russell also pulled together the assemblage of musicians, animals, and hangers-on for the boisterous Mad Dogs and Englishmen Tour Cocker made in 1970, resulting in a film and a #2 double live album that yielded a pair of hits—"The Letter" (#7, 1970) and "Cry Me a River" (#11, 1970)—and a film. But the tour left Cocker broke and ill. On a 1972 tour, with Stainton again leading the band, Cocker was often too drunk to remember lyrics and hold down food, although material from that tour was released in 1976 as *Live in L.A.* Cocker toured Britain and then Australia, where he was arrested for possession of marijuana.

At the height of his troubles, Cocker had one of the biggest hits of his career, the achingly tender "You Are So Beautiful" (#5, 1975), cowritten by Billy Preston. (The song has become a modern standard and was used recently in the 1993 film *Carlito's Way*.) He recorded regularly throughout the Seventies, but without much success. In 1976 he sang on TV's *Saturday Night Live,* with comedian John Belushi doing a deadly accurate parody behind him. Given Cocker's state at the time, it seemed more cruel than funny.

Nineteen eighty-two turned Cocker's career around. A duet with Jennifer Warnes, "Up Where We Belong," from the movie *An Officer and a Gentleman,* hit #1. Since then, nine other Cocker songs have graced films, from "You Can Leave Your Hat On" (*9½ Weeks,* 1986) to "When the Night Comes" (*An Innocent Man,* 1990). The latter, a dramatic hard-rock ballad cowritten by Bryan Adams, hit #11 in 1990. The singer continues to tour, sometimes accompanied by old friend Chris Stainton.

Cocteau Twins
Formed 1981, Grangemouth, Scotland
Robin Guthrie (b. Jan. 4, 1962, Grangemouth), gtr.,
various instr.; Elizabeth Fraser (b. Aug. 29, 1963, Grangemouth), voc.; Will Heggie, bass.
1982—*Garlands* (4AD); *Lullabies* EP 1983—(– Heggie) *Head over Heels*; *Peppermint Pig* EP; *Sunburst and Snowblind* EP 1984—(+ Simon Raymonde [b. April 3, 1962, London, Eng.], bass, kybds.) *Pearly-Dewdrops' Drops* EP; *Treasure* 1985—*Aikea-Guinea* EP; *Tiny Dynamite* EP; *Echoes in a Shallow Bay* EP 1986—(– Raymonde) *Victorialand* (+ Raymonde); *Love's Easy Tears* EP; *The Moon and the Melodies*; *The Pink Opaque* 1988—*Blue Bell Knoll* (4AD/Capitol) 1990—*Iceblink Luck* EP; *Heaven or Las Vegas* 1993—*Four-Calendar Café* (Capitol).

One of contemporary pop's more distinctive and prolific acts, Cocteau Twins have maintained an avid cult following since the early Eighties. While their singles have only occasionally entered the Top Forty in England (though they've topped the U.K.'s independent charts without fail), and have never done so in the U.S., the band is appreciated by many critics and progressive pop fans for its lush, dreamy sound, which centers on Elizabeth Fraser's ethereal vocals and composer, producer, and multi-instrumentalist Robin Guthrie's inventive use of modern musical devices like tape loops, echo boxes, and drum machines. Fraser and Guthrie are partners outside the studio as well; longtime lovers, they had a daughter together in 1989.

The couple met in 1979, when Guthrie spotted Fraser dancing in a pub. At the time, he and bassist Will Heggie were forming a band, and after hearing Fraser sing, they recruited her, completing the Cocteaus' original lineup. In 1982, the trio signed with the British label 4AD and released its debut album, *Garlands,* which drew wide praise and attracted the interest of influential BBC Radio 1 DJ John Peel. Heggie quit the band soon afterward, though, leaving Fraser and Guthrie to record their second album, *Head over Heels* (1983), as a duo.

The Twins became a threesome again later that year, with the addition of bassist Simon Raymonde, who would eventually play an active role in writing, arranging, and producing the band's songs. (Fraser also emerged as more of a creative contributor as time went on.) In the years that followed, Cocteau Twins put out several albums and/or EPs a year. They moved to Capitol for the 1993 release, *Four-Calendar Café,* which they supported in 1994 with their first world tour in four years. The group used a four-piece backing band for the first time and also made their debut appearance on U.S. television, performing on *The Tonight Show With Jay Leno.*

David Allan Coe
Born September 6, 1939, Akron, Ohio
1970—*Penitentiary Blues* (SSS) 1974—*Mysterious Rhinestone Cowboy* (Columbia); *Mysterious Rhine-*

stone Cowboy Rides Again 1976—*Once upon a Rhyme; Long-Haired Redneck* 1977—*David Allan Coe Rides Again; Tattoo* 1978—*The Family Album* 1979—*Human Emotions* 1980—*I've Got Something to Say* 1981—*Invictus Means Unconquered* 1982—*D.A.C.* 1983—*Castles in the Sand* 1984—*For the Record: The First 10 Years* 1989—*Crazy Daddy.*

Singer/songwriter David Allan Coe is the composer of country hits like Tanya Tucker's "Would You Lay with Me (in a Field of Stone)" and Johnny Paycheck's "Take This Job and Shove It." Coe's life is the stuff of outlaw legends. Orphaned at age nine, he was arrested the next year for stealing a car. After spending several years in an Ohio reformatory, he was released on parole, only to be arrested again for possession of obscene material (a comic book). He was sentenced to the Ohio State Correctional Facility, where he claimed to have fatally stabbed a fellow convict who made homosexual advances to him. According to Coe, he was convicted of murder and spent three months on death row before Ohio's abolition of the death penalty. It was later revealed that Coe lied about the murder—it never happened. In the early Nineties, without a record label, Coe admitted some regret over his past image.

By the time he was finally released in 1967, he had been writing songs for 14 years. Encouraged by fellow prisoner Screamin' Jay Hawkins, Coe pursued his music career and with singer Hugh X. Lewis' help met music publisher Audie Ashworth and producer Shelby Singleton, who helped get Coe a contract with his Plantation label; Coe later signed with Columbia. Coe's albums have sold respectably through the Seventies and early Eighties, though his greatest success has been as a songwriter of hits for other artists. In 1976 he was featured in a PBS documentary, *The Mysterious Rhinestone Cowboy,* so titled because of the mask Coe wore onstage in his early days. Only his 1983 album, *Castles in the Sand,* hit the pop chart, at #183, but he scored a #1 country hit with "The Ride" (about a singer's encounter with Hank Williams' ghost) and "Mona Lisa Lost Her Smile." He has also appeared in several films, among them *The Last Days of Frank and Jesse James* (with Willie Nelson, Waylon Jennings, Johnny Cash, and Kris Kristofferson).

Leonard Cohen
Born September 21, 1934, Montreal, Canada
1967—*Songs of Leonard Cohen* (Columbia) 1969—*Songs from a Room* 1971—*Songs of Love and Hate* 1972—*Live Songs* 1973—*New Skin for the Old Ceremony* 1975—*Best of Leonard Cohen* 1977—*Death of a Ladies' Man* 1979—*Recent Songs* 1984—*Various Positions* (PVC) 1988—*I'm Your*

Leonard Cohen

Man (Columbia) 1992—*The Future* 1994—*Cohen Live.*

Singer/songwriter Leonard Cohen was a noted poet and novelist before turning to music in the Sixties. His songs have been widely covered, by Judy Collins ("Suzanne," "Famous Blue Raincoat") and Aaron Neville ("Bird on a Wire"), among others, and in Europe his aura of quasi-suicidal romantic despair has won him acclaim as an heir of Jacques Brel.

Cohen studied English literature at Montreal's McGill University and later at Columbia University in New York, and published his first book of poems, *Let Us Compare Mythologies,* in 1956. In 1957 he recited his poetry to jazz piano backup, beat-style. Cohen tried and failed to sell songs in the late Fifties and continued to write poems as well as two novels, *The Favorite Game* (1963) and *Beautiful Losers* (1966).

He set some poems from his 1966 collection, *Parasites of Heaven,* to simple chord progressions; Judy Collins recorded one of them, "Suzanne," for her album *In My Life,* and she brought Cohen onstage at a 1967 Central Park concert. Cohen performed at the 1967 Newport Folk Festival, and his debut album came out early in 1968. Songs from that album later appeared on the soundtrack of Robert Altman's *McCabe and Mrs. Miller.*

After his second album, which included "Bird on a Wire" and "Famous Blue Raincoat," Cohen began extensive touring of the U.S. and Europe and appeared in 1970 at the Isle of Wight festival. But he cut back on touring after *Songs of Love and Hate;* although he entertained Israeli troops in 1973, his *Live Songs* was recorded around 1970. Cohen lived on a Greek island in the mid-Seventies and continued to write poems, prose, and songs. In 1976 he resumed touring, and in 1977 he collaborated with Sixties pop producer Phil Spector on *Death of a Ladies' Man,* which also included backing vocals by Bob Dylan. He pronounced the finished album mix a "catastrophe," and on *Recent Songs* he returned to a more conventional folk-pop style. *Various Positions* evinced Cohen's fascination with religious themes.

With Cohen's dry, flat baritone intoning his hard-bitten, topical poems over sleek, modern-sounding tracks, *I'm Your Man* suddenly made him hip, and prompted a 1991 tribute album, *I'm Your Fan,* with Cohen songs recorded by such college-radio stars as R.E.M., Nick Cave, Pixies, Ian McCulloch of Echo and the Bunnymen, Lloyd Cole, and others. *The Future* has been Cohen's best-seller to date; its anthemic "Democracy" was performed by Don Henley at MTV's January 1993 Inaugural Ball for President Bill Clinton.

He has published many other books, including *The Spice-Box of Earth* (1961), *Flowers for Hitler* (1964), *Selected Poems, 1956–1968* (1968), *The Energy of Slaves* (1972), *Death of a Lady's Man* (1978), *Book of Mercy* (1984), and *Stranger Music* (1993).

Marc Cohn

Born July 5, 1959, Cleveland, Ohio
1991—*Marc Cohn* (Atlantic)   1993—*The Rainy Season.*

Singer/keyboardist Marc Cohn writes songs that fuse the influences of Sixties soul music and Seventies singer/songwriter pop. On the strength of his self-titled debut album, he earned the 1991 Grammy for Best New Artist.

Cohn grew up Cleveland, where he listened to Van Morrison, Jackson Browne, James Taylor, and the Band. He taught himself to play piano while attending Oberlin College and performed solo in Los Angeles clubs before moving to New York City in the Eighties and founding a 14-piece band, the Supreme Court. Discovered by Carly Simon, the blues-based outfit played at Caroline Kennedy's 1986 wedding but broke up after only five performances. Cohn then began concentrating on songwriting, eventually landing a contract with Atlantic. Producing his own debut, he scored a #13 hit in 1991 with "Walking in Memphis," a homage to that city's blues players and its most famous former resident, Elvis

Presley. The song was covered by numerous performers, among them Tom Jones. *The Rainy Season,* bluesier and more somber than its predecessor, featured David Crosby, Graham Nash, Bonnie Raitt, and Heartbreaker Benmont Tench.

Lloyd Cole

Born January 31, 1961, Buxton, England
With the Commotions, formed 1982, Glasgow, Scotland (Cole, voc., gtr.; Blair Cowan, kybds.; Neil Clark, gtr.; Lawrence Donegan, bass; Stephen Irvine, drums): 1984—*Rattlesnakes* (Polydor, U.K.) 1985—*Easy Pieces* (Geffen)   1988—*Mainstream* (Capitol)   1989—*1984–1989.*
Lloyd Cole solo: 1990—*Lloyd Cole* (Capitol)   1991—*Don't Get Weird on Me, Babe*   1993—*Bad Vibes* (Fontana, U.K.).

Lloyd Cole's literate, knowing songs about modern love have a sharp wit and fluid imagery that recalls the mid-Sixties' Dylan. The English-born Cole entered the University of Glasgow in 1981 to study philosophy. The following year, he met keyboard player Blair Cowan, who introduced him to guitarist Neil Clark. Deciding

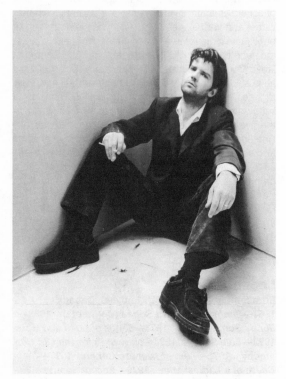

Lloyd Cole

they had the core for a band, the trio called themselves the Commotions. At first a large soul band—with two female singers—inspired by the Staple Singers, the Commotions were quickly pared to a quintet of Cole, Cowan, Clark, bassist Lawrence Donegan, and drummer Stephen Irvine. Cole soon became the band's main songwriter; they were signed to British Polydor on the strength of his material. The label released the single "Perfect Skin" (#26 U.K.) and debut LP *Rattlesnakes* (#13 U.K.) in England in 1984. (Geffen issued the LP in the U.S. in 1985.) Though the Commotions' next two albums made the U.K. Top Ten, Cole left the band in 1988, following a tour supporting *Mainstream* (#9 U.K., 1987).

After the breakup, Cole relocated to New York City and began working as a solo artist. His debut album was produced by Lou Reed drummer Fred Maher, with ex-Voidoid Robert Quine on guitar and singer/songwriter Matthew Sweet on bass. *Don't Get Weird on Me, Babe* was divided: one-half rockers and the other string-laden ballads. As with the Commotions, Lloyd failed to garner much U.S. commercial success. After he was dropped by Capitol in 1992, Cole's *Bad Vibes* was released in England by Fontana, without making much of a stir. The following year, in 1994, independent Rykodisc issued the album in the U.S.

Natalie Cole

Born February 6, 1950, Los Angeles, California
1975—*Inseparable* (Capitol)   1976—*Natalie*
1977—*Thankful*   1978—*Natalie . . . Live!*   1979—
We're the Best of Friends (with Peabo Bryson)
1980—*Don't Look Back*   1981—*Happy Love*
1983—*I'm Ready* (Epic)   1984—*The Natalie Cole*
Collection (Capitol)   1985—*Dangerous* (Modern)
1987—*Everlasting* (Manhattan)   1989—*Good to Be*
Back (EMI)   1991—*Unforgettable with Love* (Elektra)   1993—*Take a Look*.

When Natalie Cole debuted in 1975, she was hailed as the next Aretha Franklin, and Inseparable brought her a gold record and two Grammies, including that year's Best New Artist. But by 1983 a decade-long drug problem that began in the early Seventies had forced her career into a downward spiral from which she did not reemerge commercially until 1987.

The second of Nat "King" Cole's five children, Natalie grew up in the exclusive Hollywood enclave known as Hancock Park. Her father died of lung cancer when she was 15, and she moved east several years later to attend the University of Massachusetts at Amherst, where she began singing in local clubs with a group called Black Magic and earned a degree in child psychology. Although she was arrested for possession of heroin in Canada in 1973 and continued to have problems with al-

cohol and cocaine through the following decade, Cole launched an initially dazzling career. She met her first husband, songwriter Marvin Yancy (they married in 1976), when he and his partner Chuck Jackson coproduced *Inseparable*. Her critically acclaimed debut included "This Will Be" (#6 pop, #1 R&B, 1975) and "Inseparable" (#32 pop, #1 R&B, 1976).

She subsequently released a top-selling album nearly every year throughout the Seventies and made consistent appearances on the singles chart: "Sophisticated Lady" (#25 pop, #1 R&B, 1976), "I've Got Love on My Mind" (#5 pop, #1 R&B, 1977), "Our Love" (#10 pop, #1 R&B, 1978). In 1978 she hosted *The Natalie Cole Special* on prime-time TV. The next year, she teamed up with Peabo Bryson for an album and two R&B Top Twenty singles—"Gimme Some Time" and "What You Won't Do for Love." None of her solo releases penetrated the pop Top Twenty until 1987's "Jump Start" (#13 pop, #2 R&B) and "I Live for Your Love" (#13 pop, #4 R&B), and a cover of Springsteen's "Pink Cadillac" (#5 pop, #9 R&B, 1988) from her first commercial comeback, *Everlasting*. Two duets with Ray Parker Jr., "I Don't Think That a Man Should Sleep Alone" (#5 R&B) and "Over You" (#5 pop, #10 R&B), were also released in 1987. In 1989 she scored another hit with "Miss You Like Crazy" (#7) and married her second husband, Andre Fischer, a producer and former member of the group Rufus.

Cole, who spoke openly of growing up in her father's shadow and in 1983 appeared on Johnny Mathis' Cole tribute album (*Unforgettable—A Tribute to Nat "King" Cole*), swept the 1991 Grammy awards with her quintuple-platinum #1 album *Unforgettable with Love*, a tribute to her father. On it she not only recorded a number of his best-known songs, but in a feat of technical wizardry, produced a duet and video of her "singing with" him on the title track. (Hank Williams Jr. did the same thing in 1992 using old recordings of his father for "There's a Tear in My Beer.") That album garnered six Grammys, including Record of the Year, Album of the Year, and Song of the Year (for "Unforgettable").

In 1993 she made her acting debut in the acclaimed TV series *I'll Fly Away* and released *Take a Look*, another collection of pop standards from a range of artists, among them Billie Holiday, Carmen McRae, and her father. "Take a Look" from that album reached #68 in 1993 and earned her yet another Grammy, for Best Jazz Vocal Performance.

Ornette Coleman

Born March 19, 1930, Fort Worth, Texas
1958—*Something Else!* (Contemporary); *Tomorrow*
Is the Question   1959—*The Shape of Jazz to Come*
(Atlantic)   1960—*Change of the Century*; *This Is*
Our Music; Free Jazz   1962—*Ornette on Tenor*

1965—*At the Golden Circle, vol. 1 and 2* (Blue Note)
1968—*New York Is Now!*; *Love Call* (Blue Note)
1969—*Crisis* (Impulse)   1971—*Science Fiction* (Columbia)   1972—*Skies of America*   1977—*Dancing
in Your Head* (Horizon)   1979—*Body Meta* (Artist's
House)   1980—*Soapsuds, Soapsuds*   1982—*Of
Human Feelings* (Antilles); *Broken Shadows* (Columbia)   1986—*Song X* (with Pat Metheny) (Geffen); *Opening the Caravan of Dreams* (Caravan of
Dreams)   1987—*In All Languages*; *Prime
Design/Time Design*   1988—*Virgin Beauty* (CBS
Portrait)   1993—*Beauty Is a Rare Thing: The Complete Atlantic Recordings* (Rhino).

Ornette Coleman's bluesy, playful music revolutionized
jazz in the Sixties by ignoring regular harmonies and
rhythms. In the Seventies he formalized his "harmolodic"
theory and applied it to rock instrumentation with his
group, Prime Time, pioneering a powerful and increasingly influential jazz-rock-funk-ethnic-music fusion.

Coleman taught himself to play alto sax in his early
teens. At age 16, he switched to tenor sax and began
playing in R&B and jazz bands around the South. His unorthodox notions of music were already meeting resistance (he switched back to alto sax when three
members of the audience in Baton Rouge threw his
tenor sax over a cliff), and he got used to getting fired. In
1950 he wrote an unpublished book in which he theo-
rized that melody "has nothing to do with harmony or
chords or key centers."

He went to Los Angeles in 1952 with the Pee Wee
Crayton Band. He returned to Fort Worth after Crayton
fired him, then returned to Los Angeles in 1954. The L.A.
jazz community ignored him for the most of the decade.
In 1958 he formed his first band with trumpeter Don
Cherry, bassist Charlie Haden, and drummer Billy Higgins, and established a mode of playing in which, as he
explained, "no one player has the lead; anyone can come
out with it at anytime."

In 1959 the Coleman quartet went to New York,
where their engagements and recordings developed the
concept of "free jazz." For *Free Jazz*, a collective improvisation, Coleman employed a "double quartet" (drummers
Higgins and Ed Blackwell, trumpeters Cherry and Freddie Hubbard, bassists Haden and Scott LaFaro, and reedmen Coleman and Eric Dolphy).

Coleman withdrew from public appearance between 1962 and 1965, during which time he taught himself to play trumpet and violin. When he resumed
performing, he introduced compositions for these instruments and for wind quintets, larger chamber orchestras,
and vocalists. He rarely performed with a regular band,
although he continued to collaborate with Haden,
Cherry, Higgins, Blackwell, and tenor saxophonist
Dewey Redman. (In the late Seventies Cherry, Haden,

Redman, and Blackwell formed Old and New Dreams,
playing their own music and occasional new Coleman
tunes.) He also played with saxophonist Pharoah
Sanders, drummer Elvin Jones, and Yoko Ono, whose
1968 performance with Coleman's band is documented
on her 1970 *Yoko Ono/Plastic Ono Band*).

A Guggenheim fellowship allowed him to compose
Skies of America, a long work for orchestra that he debuted at 1972's Newport in New York Festival and
recorded later that year with the London Symphony Orchestra. *Skies of America* introduced his theory of har-
molodics, in which harmonies, rhythms, and melodies
function independently.

Coleman went to Morocco in 1973 to record with the
Master Musicians of Joujouka (a short selection was included on *Dancing in Your Head*), and in New York and
Paris he became interested in the guitar and electrified
instruments and started working with guitarist James
"Blood" Ulmer. He rehearsed a new band, Prime Time—
electric guitarists Bern Nix and Charles Ellerbee, electric
bassist Rudy MacDaniel, and drummers Ronald Shannon Jackson and his son Denardo Coleman—for two
years before recording *Dancing in Your Head* in Paris and
introducing them at the 1977 Newport in New York Festival.

Prime Time's music incorporated rock and funk
rhythms and melodic fragments that recall Joujouka and
R&B among its harmolodic possibilities; Coleman stated
that he considered it dance music. The band's instrumentation—especially in latterday lineups—suggested
a double rock band version of Coleman's double quintets. In the early Eighties ex–Prime Time members Ulmer
and Jackson started their own harmolodic rock-funk
bands, and Coleman returned to public performance,
touring the U.S. and Europe in 1982.

Song X, a 1986 collaboration with guitarist Pat
Metheny (who had covered Coleman tunes on his own
recordings) was a critical success; later that year the two
men toured together with a band that included Charlie
Haden, Jack DeJohnette, and Denardo Coleman.
Denardo, who had made his recording debut with his father at ten years of age, was now both a drummer in Ornette's bands and his business manager.

In 1987—to celebrate the 30th anniversary of the formation of the original quartet—Coleman released *In All
Languages,* pairing a reunited version of the 1957
acoustic group and a 1987 electric band both covering
the same material. *Virgin Beauty* featured a guest appearance by Grateful Dead guitarist Jerry Garcia, a longtime Coleman admirer. Coleman participated in the
formation of the Caravan of Dreams, an arts center that
opened in his hometown of Fort Worth, Texas. An affiliated record label released Coleman's next few recordings.

Coleman continued writing for all manner of instrumentation and size; later editions of Prime Time mixed acoustic and electric instruments. In 1993 Coleman's monumental Atlantic recordings were released in an acclaimed CD boxed set, *Beauty Is a Rare Thing.*

Albert Collins

Born October 1, 1932, Leona, Texas; died November 24, 1993, Las Vegas, Nevada
1965—*The Cool Sound of Albert Collins* (TCF Hall) 1969—*Truckin' with Albert Collins* (Blue Thumb); *Love Can Be Found Anywhere (Even in a Guitar)* (Imperial); *Trash Talkin'* 1970—*The Complete Albert Collins* 1972—*There's Gotta Be a Change* (Tumbleweed) 1978—*Ice Pickin'* (Alligator) 1980—*Frostbite* 1981—*Frozen Alive!* 1983—*Don't Lose Your Cool* 1984—*Live in Japan* 1985— *Showdown!* (with Robert Cray and Johnny Copeland) 1986—*Cold Snap* 1991—*Iceman* (Pointblank/Charisma); *The Complete Imperial Recordings* (EMI) 1992—*Truckin' with Albert Collins* (MCA) 1993—*Collins Mix* (Pointblank/Charisma).

Guitarist, singer, and songwriter Albert Collins' hard-rocking Texas shuffle blues and his gregarious showmanship made him one of the most popular contemporary bluesmen. Jimi Hendrix once called him "one of the best guitarists in the world," and six of his albums were nominated for Grammy awards. In 1986

Albert Collins

Showdown, recorded with Robert Cray (who had played in Collins' backing band) and Johnny Copeland, won for Best Traditional Blues Recording.

The son of sharecroppers, he grew up in rural Texas before moving to Houston's Third Ward ghetto at age nine. He studied piano in school, and a cousin gave him a cheap electric guitar and taught him the unusual minor-key tuning that remains a distinctive aspect of his sound. Another cousin, Sam "Lightnin'" Hopkins, was a primary influence on his single-string guitar technique.

Collins began working the Houston blues-club circuit in 1948, playing with Clarence "Gatemouth" Brown. The following year he formed his own band, the Rhythm Rockers, and fronted them until 1951, when he joined Piney Brown's band. After leaving Brown in 1954 he became a pickup guitarist, performing and occasionally recording with Johnny "Guitar" Watson, Little Richard, and Willie Mae Thornton, among others. A 1958 session resulted in his first record, "The Freeze," an instrumental that introduced Collins' "cool sound"—the highly amplified, sustained treble notes of his guitar set against three horns, keyboard (piano or, more often, organ), bass, and drums. Over the next five years he recorded more than a dozen such instrumentals, including "Defrost," "Thaw-Out," "Sno-Cone," and "Hot 'n' Cold." Several were regional hits. "Frosty" reportedly sold a million copies in 1962 without placing on national charts.

Sometime around 1968 blues scholar Bob Hite of Canned Heat discovered Collins playing in a Houston lounge and brought him to the attention of Imperial Records, which awarded him a contract. Collins moved to Los Angeles, where for the next two years he recorded three albums, produced by members of Canned Heat. These were also the first on which he sang. The Canned Heat connection attracted young, white blues fans, and Collins frequently played West Coast rock venues, including the Fillmore West.

In 1971 Collins was the first artist signed to producer Bill Szymczyk's Tumbleweed label, and there he recorded his sole charting R&B single, "Get Your Business Straight" (#46, 1972). But Tumbleweed folded two years later, and he did not record again until 1978. With his band the Icebreakers, he recorded *Ice Pickin'*, which was named Best Blues Album of 1979 by several American and European journals and nominated for a Grammy Award. From then on, through a series of releases on Alligator, he continued to rack up Grammy nominations and solidify his reputation as "the Master of the Telecaster." In the late Eighties, he appeared to be on the verge of a mainstream breakthrough. At the insistence of George Thorogood, Collins appeared at Live Aid in Philadelphia in 1985. He appeared in a wine-cooler ad with blues-singing wannabe Bruce Willis and had a cameo in the film *Adventures in Babysitting.*

Throughout his career Collins guested on albums by

artists as diverse as David Bowie (*Labyrinth*), John Lee Hooker (*Mr. Lucky, Boom, Boom*), Branford Marsalis (*Super Models in Deep Conversation*), and John Zorn (*Spillane*). He received several W. C. Handy Awards as well. Collins died at his home of cancer; he was 61. In 1994 he was posthumously honored with three W. C. Handy awards, including Entertainer of the Year.

Bootsy Collins

Born William Collins, October 26, 1951, Cincinnati, Ohio
1976—*Stretchin' Out in Bootsy's Rubber Band* (Warner Bros.)   1977—*Ahh . . . the Name Is Bootsy, Baby!*   1978—*Bootsy? Player of the Year*   1979— *This Boot Is Made for Fonk-N*   1980—*Ultra Wave* 1982—*The One Giveth and the Count Taketh Away* 1988—*What's Bootsy Doin'?* (Columbia)   1990— *Jungle Bass* (Zillitron)   1994—*Back in the Day: The Best of Bootsy* (Warner Bros.); *Blasters of the Universe* (Rykodisc).
With Zillatron (Collins; Bernie Worrell, kybds.; Buckethead, gtr.): 1994—*Zillatron: Lord of the Harvest* (Rykodisc).

As Parliament-Funkadelic bassist and songwriter, Collins has attracted a personal following to challenge George Clinton's. Already given to spontaneous reproduction, it was natural for P-Funk to spawn Bootsy's

Bootsy Collins

Rubber Band. While Bootsy's records have sold better than the parent group's, Collins continues to play with P-Funk on occasion in addition to his work with other musicians [see George Clinton entry].

Collins worked as a session musician for King Records in his hometown of Cincinnati until James Brown recruited the 16-year-old and his group, the Pacemakers, into his J.B.s in 1969. Two years later Collins left Brown, and after doing sessions with the Spinners and Johnnie Taylor—and turning down the Spinners' invitation to join them—he joined P-Funk. He became Clinton's right-hand man, contributing music and lyrics to many of P-Funk's best-known songs and helping to formulate the band's doctrine of "silly seriousness." When Clinton negotiated Funkadelic's contract with Warner Bros. in 1976, a solo contract for Collins was part of the deal.

Collins put together Bootsy's Rubber Band from musicians outside the P-Funk family. Guitarist Phelps "Catfish" Collins (Bootsy's elder brother) and drummer Frankie "Kash" Waddy had been Pacemakers and J.B.s; saxophonist Maceo Parker and trombonist Fred Wesley had been J.B. stalwarts until Collins lured them to the Rubber Band. Others had been members of the Complete Strangers, a Cincinnati band Collins had sponsored: singers Gary "Mudbone" Cooper, Leslyn Bailey, and Robert "Peanuts" Johnson; keyboardist Frederick "Flintstone" Allen (later replaced by Joel "Razor Sharp" Johnson); and trumpeters Rick Gardner and Richard "Kush" Griffith. The Rubber Band became part of P-Funk; its horn section, the Horny Horns, became an integral part of every P-Funk session; and Clinton brainchildren like the Brides of Funkenstein sang with the Rubber Band.

With Clinton collaborating with Collins on material and production, Bootsy's albums were very much in the P-Funk mold: irrepressibly rhythmic, ironic, at once earthy and spacy. The ostensible difference was in their intended audiences. While P-Funk was aimed at teenaged older American youth, Bootsy wrote for the "geepies"—kids six to 12 years old who could respond to songs of Collins' alter egos like Caspar the Friendly Ghost and Bootzilla. He advocated abstinence from drugs and liquor (if not prepubertal sex) and projected an aura of childlike optimism.

His second and third albums went gold (*Player of the Year* went to #1 R&B), and he had 10 R&B Top Thirty singles in five years: "Stretchin' Out" (#18, 1976), "I'd Rather Be with You" (#25, 1976), "The Pinocchio Theory" (#6, 1977), "Can't Stay Away" (#19, 1977), "Bootzilla" (#1, 1978), "Hollywood Squares" (#17, 1978), "Jam Fan (Hot)" (#13, 1979), "Mug Push" (#25, 1980), "Take a Lickin' and Keep On Kickin'" (#29, 1982), and "Body Slam!" (#12, 1982).

Aside from his work with the Rubber Band and P-Funk, Collins has produced, arranged, and written songs for other acts. He arranged Johnnie Taylor's 1976 gold hit, "Disco Lady." He produced albums by Zapp and the Sweat Band in 1980 and by Godmoma in 1981. He has also collaborated on songs with Sly Stewart and James Brown. After *The One Giveth and the Count Taketh Away* (1982), Collins was not heard from again for six years, until *What's Bootsy Doin'?* In the interim he had recorded with an array of artists, including Keith Richards, Bill Laswell, the Last Poets, Buddy Miles, and Wilbert Longmire. He recorded and performed with Deee-Lite, and appeared on the record and in the video for their hit "Groove Is in the Heart." In 1994 he appeared in Ice Cube's video for "Bop Gun."

Nineteen-ninety-four also saw the release of three Bootsy albums (one a best-of) and what appeared to be a resurgence. Resplendent in his freaky wardrobe, Bootsy talked openly about the toll performing and drugs had taken before his hiatus. "I got so tired of living up to that Bootsy character," he told ROLLING STONE in 1994. "I'd become a so-called star, and I just didn't know how to handle it."

Judy Collins

Born May 1, 1939, Seattle, Washington
1961—A Maid of Constant Sorrow (Elektra)   1962—
Golden Apples of the Sun   1964—Judy Collins #3;
The Judy Collins Concert   1965—Judy Collins'
Fifth Album   1966—In My Life   1967—Wildflowers
1968—Who Knows Where the Time Goes   1969—
Recollections   1970—Whales and Nightingales;
Living   1972—Colours of the Day/The Best of Judy
Collins   1973—True Stories and Other Dreams
1975—Judith   1976—Bread and Roses   1977—So
Early in Spring: The First Fifteen Years   1979—
Hard Times for Lovers   1980—Running for My Life
1982—Times of Our Lives   1984—Home Again
1985—Amazing Grace (Telstar)   1987—Trust Your
Heart (Gold Castle)   1989—Sanity and Grace; In-
nervoices (with Richard Stolzman) (RCA)   1990—
Fires of Eden (Columbia)   1993—Judy Sings
Dylan . . . Just Like a Woman (Geffen).

Judy Collins, who describes herself as an "interpretive singer," was a major force in Sixties folk rock, and her cover versions provided exposure for then-unknown songwriters such as Joni Mitchell, Leonard Cohen, Sandy Denny, and Randy Newman. Her later repertoire incorporated show tunes, pop standards, and cabaret material. Collins' clear, unwavering soprano has been equally effective on "Both Sides Now" (#8, 1968) and "Send in the Clowns" (#36, 1975; #18, 1977).

Inspired by her blind father, Chuck Collins, a bandleader and radio personality in the Rocky Mountain area,

she began classical piano training at five and made her public debut at 13 with the Denver Symphony. Collins attended college in Jacksonville, Illinois, and then the University of Colorado. She had become interested in traditional folk music and began playing regularly in local coffeehouses before moving to Chicago around 1960. By then she had married college lecturer Peter Taylor (they were divorced in 1966). Shortly after she moved to Chicago, her debut album, *A Maid of Constant Sorrow*, was released.

She began steady club work and met politically conscious folksinger/songwriters with whom she frequently performed at civil rights rallies. Her later political concerns would include ecology, endangered species, and abortion rights. *Judy Collins #3* and *The Judy Collins Concert* found her moving away from traditional ballads and focusing on protest material by Bob Dylan, Tom Paxton, and Phil Ochs.

With *In My Life*, she abandoned the sparse production of her early folk-oriented efforts for the often idiosyncratic experiments of producer Joshua Rifkin, who later spurred the Scott Joplin revival with his piano rag recordings. On *Wildflowers*, she debuted as a songwriter. For the gold *Who Knows Where the Time Goes*, her backing ensemble included Stephen Stills on guitar. The alliance prompted a short affair, which Stills later documented in the Crosby, Stills and Nash hit "Suite: Judy Blue Eyes."

In 1969 she played Solveig in the New York Shakespeare Festival's production of Ibsen's *Peer Gynt*. Two years later, *Whales and Nightingales* went gold with a #15 single: an unaccompanied choral version of "Amazing Grace." In 1974 Collins codirected the documentary *Antonia: A Portrait of the Woman*, about a former music teacher turned conductor; it was nominated for an Academy Award.

In 1975 she released one of her best-selling LPs, *Judith*, which produced a major European hit, "Send in the Clowns" (from Stephen Sondheim's *A Little Night Music*). Despite the help of veteran producer Jerry Wexler, *Bread and Roses* did not go gold, and she maintained a very low profile for the next two and a half years. The title track of *Hard Times for Lovers* would be her last U.S. hit single (#66, 1979).

Collins published her autobiography, *Trust Your Heart*, in 1987, wherein she detailed her battle with alcoholism. Her previous book, *Amazing Grace*, concerned her experiences with spirituality. In 1995 she published a novel, *Shameless*. She recorded 1989's *Innervoices* with classical clarinetist Richard Stolzman. In 1992 presidential candidate Bill Clinton revealed that his daughter Chelsea was named for Collins' recording "Chelsea Morning," and that her *Colours of the Day* was his favorite album of all time. Collins released an album of Bob Dylan songs in 1993.

Paul Collins: See the Beat

Phil Collins: See Genesis

Color Me Badd

Formed in 1987, Oklahoma City, Oklahoma
Bryan Abrams (b. Nov. 16, 1969, Oklahoma City),
voc.; Mark Calderon (b. Sep. 27, 1970, Oklahoma
City), voc.; Sam Watters (b. July 23, 1970, Oklahoma
City), voc.; Kevin "KT" Thornton (b. June 17, 1969,
Oklahoma City), voc.
1991—C.M.B. (Giant)   1993—Time and Chance.

Color Me Badd was part of an early-Nineties revival of
R&B vocal groups that also included Boyz II Men and En
Vogue. The multiracial quartet's 1991 debut sold four
million copies and spawned the racy hip-hop doo-wop
hit "I Wanna Sex You Up" (#2).

All four members attended Northwest Classen High
School in Oklahoma City, where they would sing the
doo-wop featured in Levi's 501 Blues commercials in the
hallways between classes. In time, the group discovered
the Sixties R&B vocal harmonies of the Dells, the Temptations, and the Four Tops.

In 1987 Kool and the Gang's Robert Bell heard Color
Me Badd and helped the group relocate to New York City
and find a manager. The quartet landed a deal with Giant
Records in 1991 and released C.M.B., which peaked at #3
and produced four additional hits: "I Adore Mi Amor" (#1,
1991), "All 4 Love" (#1, 1991), "Thinkin' Back" (#16, 1992),
and "Slow Motion" (#18, 1992).

Their sophomore release, Time and Chance (#56
pop, #20 R&B, 1993), produced by Jimmy Jam and Terry
Lewis and DJ Pooh (Ice Cube), didn't produce the hits,
with only the title track charting (#24 pop, #9 R&B, 1993).

Jessi Colter

Born Miriam Johnson, May 25, 1947, Phoenix, Ari-
zona
1970—A Country Star Is Born (RCA)   1975—I'm
Jessi Colter (Capitol)   1976—Jessi; Diamond in the
Rough   1977—Mirriam   1978—That's the Way a
Cowboy Rocks and Rolls   1980—Leather and Lace
(with Waylon Jennings)   1981—Ridin' Shotgun.

Country-pop singer Jessi Colter adopted her stage name
from one of Jesse James' gang of outlaw rogues, an outlaw and counterfeiter of whom, according to the singer,
she is a great-great-great-grand-niece. She began performing as a child, playing piano in her minister mother's
church. At age 16 she married guitarist Duane Eddy, who
produced her first record for Jamie and took her on the
road with him. Despite these early efforts, she did not
break through as a singer then.

She and Eddy divorced in 1968, and in 1969 she married Waylon Jennings. She first gained prominence by
writing songs for Dottie West, Don Gibson, Nancy Sinatra, and others. I'm Jessi Colter gave her a pop hit with
"I'm Not Lisa" (#4, 1975). She has since released several
more country-pop albums and appeared on the Outlaws
compilation with her husband and Willie Nelson. She
continues to tour frequently with Jennings, who has
contributed background vocals and guitar to many of
her albums. In the Nineties, she began working predominantly in children's music.

Shawn Colvin

Born Shanna Colvin, January 10, 1958, Vermillion,
South Dakota
1989—Steady On (Columbia)   1992—Fat City
1994—Cover Girl.

When folk-pop artist Shawn Colvin made her recording
debut in the late Eighties, her graceful melodies, reflective lyrics, and achingly pure soprano led some critics to
compare the singer/songwriter to her idol, Joni Mitchell.
Fittingly, it was through the help of Suzanne Vega—another heir to Mitchell's delicate, cerebral tradition—that
Colvin finally landed a major-label contract, after years of
impressing audiences on the Northeast U.S. club circuit.

One of four children, Colvin taught herself to play her
brother's guitar when she was ten. Though her inclination was toward folk music, the aspiring singer found
herself dabbling in various genres as her family moved
around. She played with a rock band in Illinois and a
country-swing outfit in Texas, and did Springsteen covers in California. Eventually, Colvin decided to follow her
own muse. Settling in New York, she began performing
in Greenwich Village, at first covering the work of other
local folk artists. Then one of Colvin's own compositions,
"I Don't Know Why," earned her an appearance at a folk
revue at the legendary Bottom Line, where Vega was
also on the bill. The song proved popular with college
radio stations in Boston. Meanwhile, Colvin collaborated
on material with songwriter/guitarist John Leventhal,
who became her romantic partner as well.

In the late Eighties Vega enlisted Colvin for backup
vocals on the single "Luka," which became Vega's breakthrough hit. Colvin toured Europe with Vega, and secured her own deal with Columbia Records. Her debut,
Steady On, was produced and cowritten by Leventhal
and included a support vocal from Vega. Despite peaking
at #111 on the pop chart, the album won Colvin a
Grammy for Best Contemporary Folk Recording. Her
second effort, Fat City, was recorded in the wake of a
personal and professional estrangement from Leventhal.
Produced by Larry Klein, the album featured guest appearances by such noted artists as Richard Thompson
(with whom Colvin has frequently toured in recent

years), Bruce Hornsby, and Klein's then-wife, Joni Mitchell. In 1993 Colvin married Thompson's tour manager, Simon Tassano. For 1994's *Cover Girl* Colvin performed songs by Tom Waits, Bob Dylan, Sting, and others.

Commander Cody and His Lost Planet Airmen

Formed 1967, Ann Arbor, Michigan
Commander Cody (b. George Frayne, Boise, Idaho), voc., piano; John Tichy (b. St. Louis, Mo.), gtr., voc.; Andy Stein (b. New York City, N.Y.), fiddle, sax, trombone; Billy C. Farlow (b. Decatur, Ala.), voc., gtr.; Rick Higginbotham, gtr.; Stan Davis, pedal steel gtr.; Bill Kirchen (b. Ann Arbor), gtr., voc.
1971—(+ Lance Dickerson, drums; + Bruce Barlow, bass) *Lost in the Ozone* **(Paramount) 1972—***Hot Licks, Cold Steel and Trucker's Favorites* **1973—***Country Casanova* **1974—***Live from Deep in the Heart of Texas* **1975—***Commander Cody and His Lost Planet Airmen* **(Warner Bros.);** *Tales from the Ozone* **1976—***We've Got a Live One Here!* **1977—***Rock 'n' Roll Again* **(Arista) 1978—***Flying Dreams* **1980—***Lose It Tonite* **(Peter Pan) 1986—***Let's Rock* **(Blind Pig) 1988—***Commander Cody Returns from Outer Space* **(Edsel);** *Sleazy Roadside Stories* **(Relix Indie C&W) 1990—***Aces High*; *Too Much Fun—The Best of Commander Cody* **(MCA) 1993—***Lost in Space* **(Relix) 1994—***Worst Case Scenario* **(Rounder).**

Behind their hard-drinking, deep-toking image, Commander Cody's various bands have always played a virtuosic, revved-up assortment of boogie-woogie, Western swing, country, and rockabilly. Frayne grew up in Brooklyn and studied sculpture and painting at the University of Michigan; during summers he was a lifeguard at Long Island's Jones Beach, where he performed with an all-lifeguard band, Lorenzo Lightfoot A. C. and Blues Band. After graduating, Frayne and some college friends formed the Lost Planet Airmen, which played around the Michigan and Wisconsin area while Frayne taught art for a year at Wisconsin State University. Frayne christened his onstage persona after Commando Cody, Skymarshall of the Universe, from a 1952 film, *The Lost Planet Airmen*.

When the band lineup stabilized, they moved to San Francisco in 1969 and earned a local following. Their debut album, *Lost in the Ozone*, mixed originals like "Seeds and Stems" and oldies, notably a hit remake of Tex Ritter's "Hot Rod Lincoln" (#9, 1972). The followup, *Hot Licks, Cold Steel and Trucker's Favorites,* was recorded on four tracks for a mere $5,000. They toured through the early Seventies and had two more minor novelty hits—"Beat Me Daddy Eight to the Bar," and Rit-

ter's "Smoke Smoke Smoke"—before leaving Paramount to sign with Warner Bros.

The making of the band's Warner debut album was chronicled in Geoffrey Stokes' book *Starmaking Machinery*. The album included Cody's last U.S. hit, "Don't Let Go." After a 1976 European tour, the Airmen disbanded. The rhythm section of Lance Dickerson and Bruce Barlow joined Roger McGuinn's Thunderbyrd. Cody recorded two albums with singer Nicolette Larson, then toured backed by former bandmate Bill Kirchen and his group the Moonlighters in 1979. Kirchen went on to gain a cult following for his solo endeavors. He appeared on Nick Lowe's *The Impossible Bird* album and toured with Lowe in 1995.

Commander Cody and His Lost Planet Airmen have continued to record and tour with an ever-changing lineup. As of 1994, Frayne's group consisted of Glen Sherba, Peter Walsh, Al Kash, and Dave Tolmie. Meanwhile, he has found acclaim as a painter. The Commander's art has been exhibited in galleries around the world, and he published some of his paintings in the 1979 book *StarArt*.

The Commodores/Lionel Richie

Formed 1968, Tuskegee, Alabama
Lionel Richie Jr. (b. 1950, Tuskegee Institute, Ala.), voc., piano; Milan Williams (b. 1949, Miss.), kybds., trombone, gtr.; Ronald LaPread (b. 1950, Ala.), bass, trumpet; Walter "Clyde" Orange (b. Dec. 9, 1946, Fla.), drums; William King Jr. (b. Jan. 29, 1949, Ala.),

The Commodores: Thomas McClary, Walter Orange, Ronald LaPread, Milan Williams, William King, Lionel Richie

horns; Thomas McClary (b. 1950, Fla.), gtr.
1974—*Machine Gun* (Motown) 1975—*Caught in the Act; Movin' On* 1976—*Hot on the Tracks* 1977—*Commodores; Commodores Live* 1978—*Natural High; Greatest Hits; Platinum Tour* 1979—*Midnight Magic* 1980—*Heroes* 1981—*In the Pocket* 1982—*All the Great Hits* (– Richie) 1983—*Commodores Anthology* (+ James Dean "J.D." Nicholas [b. Apr. 11, 1952, Paddington, Eng.], voc., kybds.; – McClary); *Commodores 13* 1985—*Nightshift* 1986—(– LaPread) *United* (Polydor) 1988—*Rock Solid* (– Williams) 1992—*Commodores Hits, vol. 1* (Commodore Records); *Commodores Hits, vol. 2* 1993—*Commodores XX—No Tricks* 1995—*The Anthology Series* (Motown).
Lionel Richie solo: 1982—*Lionel Richie* (Motown) 1983—*Can't Slow Down* 1986—*Dancing on the Ceiling* 1992—*Back to Front.*

The Commodores began as a pop-and-funk sextet, a funky party band, whose music was heavily influenced by Sly and the Family Stone and the Bar-Kays. During their second, most commercially successful phase, the Commodores became a popular ballad group led by singer/songwriter Lionel Richie. Following Richie's departure, the group began a third phase, marked by the Grammy-winning memorial tribute "Nightshift." In its latest incarnation, the Commodores is a trio based on cofounders Walter Orange and William King and latter-day member James Dean "J.D." Nicholas.

The six original group members met at a Tuskegee Institute talent show when they were all freshmen. With drummer Walter Orange, the only one with professional experience, handling vocals, the group began performing as the Mystics. They later picked the name Commodores out of a dictionary by placing a finger on the page. In the summer of 1969 they traveled via van to Harlem, seeking summer employment. Soon after their arrival, their equipment was stolen, then sold back to them. Undaunted, they landed a gig at Small's Paradise, where they met a local businessman they knew, Benny Ashburn, who became their manager. They signed to Atlantic Records and released one single produced by Jerry "Swamp Dogg" Williams, which did not chart.

In 1971 the group signed to Motown, and for the first two years worked as the opening act for the Jackson 5. Because the group refused to conform to the polished Motown style, the Commodores did not record until 1974, when they were teamed up with producer/arranger James Carmichael, who produced all their albums until 1983.

On their first three albums, the Commodores' sound was dominated by a hard funk, which inspired one reviewer to describe them as "black music's answer to heavy metal." The group had several early hits, including "Machine Gun" (#22, 1974), "I Feel Sanctified" (#75, 1974), "Slippery When Wet" (#19, 1975), and "Fancy Dancer" (#39, 1977). Although each of the group members writes, Richie eventually became the Commodores' main songwriter, and by 1977 his ballads were taking center stage. "Just to Be Close to You," "Sweet Love," and "Easy" were all Top Ten hits.

By 1978 when the group appeared in the disco movie *Thank God It's Friday,* the Commodores were moving swiftly toward crossover pop stardom, largely on the strength of Richie tunes like "Three Times a Lady" (#1, 1978), a platinum single that firmly established the Commodores as the premier black pop group. "Sail On" and "Still" were Top Five ballads in 1979.

Richie began to pursue outside projects. He wrote the #1 "Lady" and produced "Share Your Love" for Kenny Rogers. He also wrote and performed a duet with Diana Ross on another #1 hit, the title theme song from the movie *Endless Love.* In 1982 Richie released his solo debut, *Lionel Richie* (Motown), featuring his Top Five hit "Truly." Earlier that year Ashburn died of a heart attack in New Jersey, and Richie departed for a solo career. He was followed a year later by McClary. In the meantime James Dean "J.D." Nicholas came aboard, and two years later the group had a #3 pop, #1 R&B hit with Orange's tribute to Marvin Gaye and Jackie Wilson, "Nightshift." The song won a Grammy, but the Top Fifteen album of the same title was their last for Motown.

They moved to Polydor for two albums, but by then LaPread and Williams had departed, leaving the present core membership of Orange, King, and Nicholas. The three cofounded Commodore Records and began releasing greatest-hits packages that featured Orange and Nicholas on all lead vocals. In the U.S. to date, the group has been awarded three platinum albums. Worldwide, the Commodores have sold over 40 million records.

In the meantime, Lionel Richie's spectacular solo success eclipsed even the Commodores at their commercial peak. His self-titled debut peaked at #3, followed a year later by the #1 *Can't Slow Down,* which won the 1984 Grammy for Album of the Year and contained the hit singles "All Night Long (All Night)" (#1, 1983), "Running with the Night" (#7, 1983), "Hello" (#1, 1984), "Stuck on You" (#3, 1984), and "Penny Lover" (#8, 1984). It was said to be the biggest-selling album in the history of Motown Records.

In 1985, with Michael Jackson, he cowrote "We Are the World," which was recorded for the benefit project USA for Africa, and the next year Richie won an Oscar for the #1 song "Say You, Say Me" from the film *White Nights.* The streak continued with his third solo effort, *Dancing on the Ceiling* (#1, 1986), which featured the #2 title track, "Love Will Conquer All" (#9, 1986), "Ballerina Girl" (#7, 1987), and "Se La" (#20, 1987). Those three albums alone were certified for U.S. sales of over 16 million copies. In addition, Richie has strong followings in the U.K., Canada, and throughout Europe.

Following nearly six years' hiatus, Richie returned with *Back to Front,* a greatest-hits package that included some of his work with the Commodores as well as three brand-new songs. His latest singles to date were "Do It to Me" (#1, 1992) and "My Destiny" (#56, 1992). He has won a number of awards, including the Oscar and five Grammies.

The Commotions: See Lloyd Cole

Concrete Blonde

Formed 1981, Los Angeles, California
Johnette Napolitano (b. Sep. 22, 1957, Hollywood, Calif.), voc., bass; Jim Mankey (b. May 23, 1955, Penn.), gtr.; Harry Rushakoff (b. Nov. 17, 1959, Chicago), drums.
1987—*Concrete Blonde* (I.R.S.)   1989— (– Rushakoff; + Paul Thompson, drums; + Alan Bloch, bass); *Free*   1990—(– Bloch) *Bloodletting* 1992—(– Thompson; + Rushakoff) *Walking in London*   1993—(+ Thompson) *Mexican Moon*   1994— *Still in Hollywood.*

Concrete Blonde got its start playing the same early-Eighties Los Angeles club circuit that spawned bands like X, Wall of Voodoo, and the Go-Go's. It's ultimately proved among the most resilient bands to emerge from that L.A. scene. The lean rock textures and dark, edgy lyricism of Concrete Blonde's music may not have made its members household names, but it has earned the band an enduring level of credibility and respect.

Singer Johnette Napolitano met guitarist Jim Mankey while both were working at Leon Russell's Los Angeles studio. After Russell relocated to Nashville, Napolitano and Mankey began working on their own songs in a studio owned by Mankey's brother Earle (a founding member of the band Sparks, with whom Jim also played). Calling itself the Dreamers, the duo set out in search of a drummer and bassist. By 1984 Napolitano herself had assumed bass duties. As Dream 6, the band released an EP on a French independent label that year (Capitol reissued the EP in 1993). Dream 6 was courted by several major labels, but its demands for complete artistic control put off many record company executives. Finally, in 1987, after signing to I.R.S. Records, Concrete Blonde—a name suggested by a fellow I.R.S. artist, R.E.M.'s Michael Stipe—released its debut album, with Harry Rushakoff on drums.

Ex–Roxy Music drummer Paul Thompson took over for Rushakoff on the band's sophomore album and on its third LP, 1990's *Bloodletting* (#49), which yielded a Top Twenty hit with the lovelorn "Joey." Rushakoff reap-

peared on a less commercially successful fourth album, 1992's *Walking in London* (#73), and he and Thompson both played on 1993's *Mexican Moon* (#67). The album's "Heal It Up" became popular on "modern rock" radio formats. In 1995 Napolitano teamed with fellow punk veteran Holly Vincent to record an album titled *Vowel Movement,* on which both women played all instruments and sang.

Con Funk Shun

Formed 1968, Vallejo, California
Michael Cooper, gtrs., perc., synth, voc.; Karl Fuller, trumpet, voc.; Paul Harrell, saxes, flute, voc.; Cedric Martin, bass, voc.; Louis McCall, drums, voc.; Felton Pilate, trombone, gtr., synth, voc.; Danny Thomas, kybds., voc.
1976—*Con Funk Shun* (Mercury)   1977—*Secrets* 1978—*Loveshine*   1979—*Candy*   1980—*Spirit of Love; Touch*   1981—*Con Funk Shun 7*   1982—*To the Max*   1983—*Fever*   1985—*Electric Lady* 1986—*Burnin' Love*   1992—*The Best of Con Funk Shun* (Mercury).

This Memphis soul band had been together almost ten years when it placed "Ffun" at the top of the national R&B chart in 1977. In 1968 high school classmates Michael Cooper and Louis McCall formed the group, calling it Project Soul, and established its current lineup within a year. In the early Seventies Project Soul relocated to Memphis, backed the Stax Records group the Soul Children (and in that capacity appeared in the 1973 movie *Wattstax*), and contributed to other Stax sessions. In 1972 the group changed its name to Con Funk Shun. After several local hits on Memphis labels, Mercury signed it in 1976. Con Funk Shun made its first appearance on the R&B chart with "Sho Feels Good to Me" (#66) the following year.

The success of "Ffun" (#23) made *Secrets* the first of four gold albums. It was followed by the Top Twenty R&B hits "Shake and Dance with Me" (#5 R&B, 1978), "Chase Me" (#4 R&B, 1979), "Got to Be Enough" (#8 R&B, 1980), "Too Tight" (#8 R&B, 1980), "Bad Lady" (#19 R&B, 1981), "Ms. Got-the-Body" (#15 R&B, 1983), "Baby I'm Hooked (Right into Your Love)" (#5 R&B, 1983), "Electric Lady" (#4 R&B, 1985), "I'm Leaving Baby" (#12 R&B, 1985), and "Burnin' Love" (#8 R&B, 1986). In 1987, after the release of *Burnin' Love,* Con Funk Shun disbanded. Cooper went on to a solo career, while Felton Pilate has worked with M.C. Hammer.

Arthur Conley

Born April 1, 1946, Atlanta, Georgia
1967—*Sweet Soul Music* (Atco); *Shake, Rattle & Roll* 1968—*Soul Directions*   1969—*More Sweet Soul.*

Arthur Conley was a minor soul star when his "Sweet Soul Music" hit #2 in 1967. Conley had been discovered by Otis Redding around 1965. He became Redding's protégé and was signed to Stax-Volt, later touring internationally with that label's revue. With Redding as producer, Conley recorded "Sweet Soul Music," a Conley-Cooke-Redding litany of tribute to the black male soul stars of the era that used the melody of a Sam Cooke tune entitled "Yeah Man." His next pop-chart entry was a cover of Big Joe Turner's hit "Shake, Rattle, and Roll" (#31, 1967). As the Sixties closed, Conley had several other hits, including "Funky Street" (#14, 1968) and a cover of the Beatles' "Ob-la-di, Ob-la-da" (#51, 1969). According to Peter Guralnick, in his *Sweet Soul Music,* Conley depended on Redding, and in the wake of his mentor's death, the singer's career foundered. He also sang with the Soul Clan (Solomon Burke, Ben E. King, Joe Tex, Don Covay, and Wilson Pickett) on two singles, "Soul Meeting" (#91, 1968) and the unreleased "That's How It Feels," supposedly recorded shortly after Redding's death. By the Seventies he had faded from sight, reportedly having moved to France. As of the mid-Eighties, he was still living in Europe.

Harry Connick Jr.

Born September 11, 1967, New Orleans, Louisiana
1987—Harry Connick Jr. (Columbia) 1988—20
1989—When Harry Met Sally 1990—We Are in
Love; Lofty's Roach Soufflé 1991—Blue Light, Red
Light 1992—25 1993—11 1994—She.

Singer/pianist Harry Connick Jr. built a career on his retro taste for Tin Pan Alley–style show business and jazz piano exotica.

The son of New Orleans' chief district attorney, five-year-old Harry played "The Star Spangled Banner" at his father's inauguration. Due to his father's clout, Harry Jr. was able to attend nightclub performances while still a child. He became friendly with the legendary New Orleans pianist James Booker, who gave the boy lessons at home. As an adolescent Connick studied at the New Orleans Center for the Creative Arts with Branford and Wynton Marsalis' father Ellis. At 18, Connick headed for New York, where he actively campaigned for a contract with Columbia Records, the home of his idol Wynton Marsalis.

Connick's eponymous debut was an instrumental project that showcased his facility as a jazz and New Orleans–style pianist. *20,* named for his age at the time of its release, featured Connick's vocals on a few tracks. His amiable performance style, clean-cut looks, and reverence for Forties-era show biz attracted media attention and fostered a growing cult following. Full-fledged stardom followed Connick's appearance on the soundtrack to the hit film *When Harry Met Sally. . . .* From this point

on, Connick the singer and Connick the jazz pianist would be compartmentalized, with singing getting the lion's share of attention.

Mounting an extravagant tour in 1990, which saw him fronting a big band, Connick struck some as an incarnation of the young Sinatra, albeit without the undercurrent of arrogant menace. Singing in a light, self-consciously off-the-cuff manner reminiscent of Sinatra and Bobby Darin, playing ersatz New Orleans piano, and bounding about the stage and through the audience with tireless enthusiasm, Connick drew raves from critics and fans apparently starved for old-fashioned entertainment. But Connick wasn't peddling a nostalgia act. On *We Are in Love* Connick wrote original songs; *Lofty's Roach Soufflé,* a jazz piano trio recording, contained Connick's instrumental compositions. For a nonrock act Connick's sales are staggering: Three of his albums have gone platinum, two others are gold.

Unsurprisingly, Connick began appearing in films, acquitting himself in featured roles (*Memphis Belle* and *Little Man Tate*). He also appeared on the 1990 Academy Awards telecast to sing the nominated theme from *The Godfather, Part III.* In 1993 his wholesome image was barely scratched after he was arrested at New York's Kennedy International Airport for trying to bring a gun onto a plane; charges were later dismissed. That same year saw the release of *11* (recorded in 1979), which captured the piano-pounding prodigy in all his precociousness.

The Contours

Formed 1958, Detroit, Michigan
Billy Gordon, voc.; Billy Hoggs, voc.; Joe Billingslea, voc.; Sylvester Potts, voc.; Hubert Johnson (d. July 11, 1981), voc.; Huey Davis, voc., gtr.
1981—Do You Love Me? (Motown).

Hoarse screams over feverish dance beats characterized the Contours' string of hits in the mid-Sixties. Originally a quartet formed in 1958 by Billy Gordon, Billy Hoggs, Joe Billingslea, and Sylvester Potts, the Contours were unknown even in their hometown of Detroit until joined by Hubert Johnson. He had them sing for his cousin Jackie Wilson, and in turn Wilson presented them to Motown owner Berry Gordy Jr. They cut their first record, "Whole Lotta Woman," in 1961; when it flopped, Gordy prepared to drop them. Wilson persuaded Gordy to give them another chance. That chance was a Gordy composition, "Do You Love Me?"—originally intended for the Temptations—which the Contours took to the top of the R&B chart in 1962 (#3 pop). The song was later covered many times, notably by the Dave Clark Five.

While the Contours never repeated the success of the million-selling "Do You Love Me?" they did follow it with five more clear-the-floor-'cause-I-gotta-dance numbers: "Shake Sherry" (#21 R&B, 1963), "Can You Jerk

Like Me?" (#15 R&B, 1965), "The Day When She Needed Me" (#37 R&B, 1965), "First I Look at the Purse" (#12 R&B, 1965), and "Just a Little Misunderstanding" (#18 R&B, 1966). Their last chart hit, "It's So Hard Being a Loser" (#35 R&B, 1967), was a ballad. One later member of the Contours was future Temptation Dennis Edwards.

In 1988 "Do You Love Me?" reached #11 after being featured in the film *Dirty Dancing*. The Contours, who include original members Billingslea and Potts (Johnson committed suicide in 1981), joined the subsequent *Dirty Dancing* tour, and they continue to perform.

Ry Cooder

Born Ryland Peter Cooder, March 15, 1947, Los Angeles, California
1970—*Ry Cooder* (Reprise)   1972—*Into the Purple Valley*; *Boomer's Story*   1974—*Paradise and Lunch* 1976—*Chicken Skin Music*   1977—*Showtime* (Warner Bros.)   1978—*Jazz*   1979—*Bop Till You Drop*   1980—*The Long Riders* soundtrack; *Borderline*   1981—*The Border* soundtrack (Backstreet) 1982—*The Slide Area* (Warner Bros.)   1984—*Paris, Texas* soundtrack   1985—*Alamo Bay* (Slash) 1986—*Blue City* (Warner Bros.); *Crossroads*   1987— *Get Rhythm*   1989—*Johnny Handsome*   1993—*A Meeting by the River* (with V. M. Bhatt); (Water Lily Acoustics); *Geronimo* soundtrack (Columbia) 1994—*Trespass* soundtrack (Sire); *Talking Timbuktu* (with Ali Farka Touré) (Hannibal).

Ry Cooder is a virtuoso on fretted instruments—slide guitar, mandolin, Mexican tiple, banjo, Middle Eastern saz—who crossbreeds his own sense of syncopation with vernacular musics. As a fan/musicologist, he has sought out local styles such as calypso, Hawaiian "slack-key" guitar, Tex-Mex, gospel, country, and vaudeville "coon songs." He records with L.A. session players and various "ethnic" musicians in and out of their own contexts.

Cooder began playing guitar when he was three years old. He has had a glass eye since he was four, when he accidentally stuck a knife in his left eye. In the early Sixties Cooder became active in Southern California blues and folk circles, and in 1963 he played in an unsuccessful group with vocalist Jackie DeShannon. With Taj Mahal, another musical archivist, he started the Rising Sons in 1966. He also appears on Mahal's debut album. Cooder was a busy session player in the late Sixties, working for Gordon Lightfoot and on numerous commercials. He was a member of Captain Beefheart's Magic Band and appeared on Beefheart's *Safe as Milk* (1967), although he quit just before Beefheart was scheduled to play the Monterey Pop Festival. He also sat in on Little Feat's 1971 debut LP.

Cooder appeared on the soundtracks of *Candy* (1968) and *Performance* (1970; with Mick Jagger), and claims to have recorded extensively on the Rolling Stones' *Let It Bleed*. Although he is credited only for the mandolin on "Love in Vain," he claims to have provided the main riff for the Stones' "Honky Tonk Women."

Since 1969, when he got a solo contract, Cooder has cut down on session work to concentrate on his yearly albums. His general strategy is to rework obscure songs (mostly pre-Sixties) in his own lunging, syncopated style laced with elements from outside rock. He has championed the music of Bahamian guitarist Joseph Spence (a major influence), and he later produced an album by the Gabby Pahinui Hawaiian Band. On 1974's *Paradise and Lunch* he recorded a duet with jazz pianist Earl "Fatha" Hines, and following *Chicken Skin Music* (1976), he toured with a band that included Mexican accordionist Flaco Jimenez and a Tex-Mex rhythm section alongside gospel-style singers Bobby King, Eldridge King, and Terry Evans, which appears on the live *Showtime*.

Jazz actually contained early-jazz ragtime and vaudeville songs. Cooder played a one-time concert at Carnegie Hall with an orchestral group and tap dancers for its unveiling. *Bop Till You Drop, Borderline*, and *The Slide Area* turned toward Fifties and Sixties R&B. *Bop* was the first major-label digitally recorded album; the next two albums (and attendant tours) featured songwriter John Hiatt. Cooder also provided soundtracks for *Blue Collar* (1979), *The Long Riders* (1980), *Southern Comfort* (1981), *The Border* (1981), *Paris, Texas* (1984), *Streets of Fire* (1984), *Cocktail* (1988), *Steel Magnolias* (1989), and *Geronimo* (1993). Cooder played only a few session dates in the Seventies, behind Randy Newman (*Good Old Boys* and *Sail Away*), Arlo Guthrie, and Van Dyke Parks. He joined Nick Lowe, Jim Keltner, and John Hiatt in Little Village, a group whose self-titled debut appeared in early 1992. He recorded with V. M. Bhatt, an Indian musician whom he had not met before recording the critically acclaimed *A Meeting by the River*. Cooder's critically acclaimed and commercially successful *Talking Timbuktu* featured Ali Farka Touré, a West African guitar master, and hit #1 on the world-music chart and remained there 25 weeks straight, setting a record for that chart. It earned Cooder and Touré 1994's Best World Music Grammy.

Sam Cooke

Born January 22, 1935, Chicago, Illinois; died December 11, 1964, Los Angeles, California
1960—*Cookes Tour* (RCA); *Hits of the 50's*; *Sam Cooke*   1961—*My Kind of Blues*; *Twistin' the Night Away*   1962—*Best of Sam Cooke, vol. 1*; *Mr. Soul* 1963—*Night Beat*   1964—*Soul Stirrers* (London); *Ain't That Good News* (RCA); *At the Copa*   1965— *Shake*; *Best of Sam Cooke, vol. 2*; *Try a Little Love* 1966—*Unforgettable Sam Cooke*   1968—*Man Who*

Sam Cooke

Invented Soul 1969—***The Gospel Soul of Sam Cooke with the Soul Stirrers, vol. 1*** (Specialty) 1975—***Sam Cooke Interprets Billie Holiday*** (RCA) 1976—***Forever*** 1985—***One Night Stand: Sam Cooke Live at the Harlem Square Club, 1963*** 1986—***The Man and His Music*** 1991—***Sam Cooke with the Soul Stirrers*** (Specialty).

Songwriter and performer Sam Cooke merged gospel music and secular themes and provided the early foundation of soul music. Cooke's pure, clear vocals were widely imitated, and his suave, sophisticated image set the style of soul crooners for the next decades.

One of eight sons of a Baptist minister, Cooke grew up in Chicago and was a top gospel artist by 1951. As a teenager he became lead vocalist of the Soul Stirrers (which later included Johnnie Taylor), with whom he toured and recorded for nearly six years. Cooke's phrasing and urban enunciation were distinctive from the start. Hoping not to offend his gospel fans, he released his pop debut, "Lovable" (1956), as Dale Cooke, but Specialty dropped him for deserting the Soul Stirrers. He released his own "You Send Me" the following year, and the 1.7-million-selling #1 song was the first of many hits. In the next two years his several hits—"Only Sixteen" (#28, 1959), "Everybody Likes to Cha Cha" (#31, 1959)—

concentrated on light ballads and novelty items. He signed to RCA in 1960 and began writing bluesier, gospel-inflected tunes.

Beginning with his reworking of "Chain Gang" (#2) in August 1960, Cooke was a mainstay in the Top Forty through 1965, with "Sad Mood" (#29, 1961), "Wonderful World" (#12, 1960), "Twistin' the Night Away" (#9, 1962), "Bring It On Home to Me" (#13, 1962), "Another Saturday Night" (#10, 1963), and "Shake" (#7, 1965).

His shooting death on December 11, 1964, tarnished his image. Bertha Franklin, manager of the Hacienda motel in Los Angeles, claimed she killed the singer in self-defense after he'd tried to rape a 22-year-woman and then turned on Franklin. Justifiable homicide, ruled the coroner. Nearly thirty years later there remain questions about the circumstances surrounding Cooke's murder, and there has been talk of reopening the investigation.

Two months later his song "Shake" peaked at #7 on the singles chart. Cooke's hits have been covered widely by rock and soul singers: "Shake," for instance, was interpreted by Otis Redding and Rod Stewart. The posthumously released "A Change Is Gonna Come" hit #31 in 1965. It represented a return to Cooke's roots, placing him back in the spiritual setting from which he had first emerged just nine years before.

Cooke was also a groundbreaking independent black music capitalist. He owned his own record label (SAR/Derby), music publishing concern (Kags Music), and management firm. His influence can be heard in the work of artists as varied as Michael Jackson and the Heptones, but is most profoundly felt in the singing of Redding, Stewart, and Al Green. (The 1994 compilation *Sam Cooke's SAR Records Story, 1959–1965* suggests that his impact as a producer, though less widely recognized, was no less important.) Cooke was one of the first inductees into the Rock and Roll Hall of Fame, in 1986; three years later the Soul Stirrers entered separately [see Rock and Roll Hall of Fame box].

Rita Coolidge

Born May 1, 1944, Lafayette, Tennessee
1971—***Rita Coolidge*** (A&M); ***Nice Feelin'*** 1972—***Lady's Not for Sale*** 1974—***Fall into Spring*** 1975—***It's Only Love*** 1977—***Anytime . . . Anywhere*** 1978—***Love Me Again*** 1979—***Natural Act*** (with Kris Kristofferson); ***Satisfied*** 1981—***Greatest Hits***; ***Heartbreak Radio*** (with Kris Kristofferson) 1992—***Love Lessons*** (Caliber).

Former backup singer Rita Coolidge became a hitmaking soloist in the late Seventies and early Eighties. The daughter of a Baptist minister and a Cherokee Indian, she sang in church choirs as a child. In her late teens she briefly attended Florida State University before moving to Memphis, where she did radio jingles. She cut a locally successful hit single, then moved to Los Angeles.

By 1969 she was recording and touring regularly as part of Delaney and Bonnie and Friends, and she joined much of that same troupe on Joe Cocker's "Mad Dogs and Englishmen" tour, where her featured rendition of "Superstar" was a highlight. (Leon Russell wrote Cocker's "Delta Lady" about Coolidge.) She continued backup work in the early Seventies for Eric Clapton, Stephen Stills, Boz Scaggs, Graham Nash, Marc Benno (who later joined Coolidge's backup band, the Dixie Flyers), and Dave Mason. (Her sister Priscilla recorded with her husband and producer, Booker T. Jones of Booker T. and the MG's.)

In 1971 Coolidge met Kris Kristofferson [see entry], whom she married two years later. By then her first solo albums had been released to little response. In 1977 *Anytime . . . Anywhere* went platinum on the strength of three hit singles: Jackie Wilson's "Higher and Higher" (#2, 1977), Boz Scaggs's "We're All Alone" (#7, 1977), and the Temptations' "The Way You Do the Things You Do" (#20, 1978). She frequently toured with Kristofferson, whose growing movie career provided her cameo roles in *Pat Garrett and Billy the Kid, Convoy,* and *A Star Is Born.* They also collaborated on 1979's *Natural Act,* released shortly before their divorce in 1980, and collected two Grammys for Best Country Duo.

In the Eighties Coolidge scored with "All Time High" (#36, 1983) from the soundtrack to the James Bond thriller *Octopussy.* Although she hasn't enjoyed any hits since, the singer remains visible. She was one of the original veejays on the video music channel VH-1, duetted with former Pink Floyd leader Roger Waters on his *Amused to Death* solo album, and continues to record and perform. *Love Lessons* featured duets with country star Lee Greenwood, her sister Priscilla, and Bonnie Bramlett (now Bonnie Sheridan).

Alice Cooper

Born Vincent Furnier, February 4, 1948, Detroit, Michigan
Group formed in the mid-Sixties in Phoenix, Arizona: Glen Buxton (b. Nov. 10, 1947, Akron, Ohio), gtr.; Michael Bruce (b. Mar. 16, 1948), gtr., kybds.; Dennis Dunaway (b. Dec. 9, 1948, Cottage Grove, Ore.), bass; Neal Smith (b. Sep. 23, 1947, Akron, Ohio), drums.
1969—*Pretties for You* (Straight)   1970—*Easy Action*   1971—*Love It to Death* (Warner Bros.); *Killer*   1972—*School's Out*   1973—*Billion Dollar Babies*   1974—*Muscle of Love; Alice Cooper's Greatest Hits* (group disbands; Cooper goes solo)   1975—*Welcome to My Nightmare*   1976—*Alice Cooper Goes to Hell*   1977—*Lace and Whiskey; The Alice Cooper

Alice Cooper

Show   1978—*From the Inside*   1980—*Flush the Fashion*   1981—*Special Forces*   1982—*Zipper Catches Skin*   1983—*DaDa*   1986—*Constrictor* (MCA)   1987—*Raise Your Fist and Yell*   1989—*Trash* (Epic)   1991—*Hey Stoopid*   1994—*The Last Temptation.*

Before Kiss' Gene Simmons spat "blood" and belched fire, or Iron Maiden's corpse-mascot Eddie graced the concert stage, Alice Cooper pioneered shock-rock theatrics—simulated executions, the chopping up of baby dolls, and Alice draping himself with a live boa constrictor—and explicit lyrics to become a controversial yet hugely popular figure in the early and mid-Seventies. After a decade of fluctuating record sales, Alice returned to platinum with the #20 1989 LP *Trash.* Vincent Furnier, son of a preacher, assembled his hard-rocking band in Phoenix. They were first known as the Earwigs, then the Spiders, and finally the Nazz (not to be confused with Todd Rundgren's band). They moved en masse to Los Angeles in 1968. Billing themselves as Alice Cooper (who, according to a Ouija board, was a Seventeenth Century witch reincarnated as Furnier), they established themselves on the Southern California bar circuit with a bizarre stage show and a reputation as the worst band in Los Angeles. Frank Zappa's Straight Records released their first two albums, which sold poorly and, with tour costs, left them $100,000 in debt.

The band members moved to Detroit, where they lived for several months in a single hotel room before the release of their major-label debut and breakthrough album, *Love It to Death*. Joining Cooper's taboo-defying lyrics to powerful hard rock, the album became the first in a string of gold and platinum releases and included "Eighteen" (#21, 1971). Subsequent hit singles included "School's Out" (#7, 1972), "Elected" (#26, 1972), "Hello, Hooray" (#35, 1973), and "No More Mr. Nice Guy" (#25, 1973). *Killer* (#21, 1971), *School's Out* (#2, 1972), and *Billion Dollar Babies* (#1, 1973) are all platinum.

In 1973 Surrealist master Salvador Dali filmed the singer, wearing diamond necklaces and tiara, as he bit the head off a small replica of the Venus de Milo for a holographic work. With such widespread success, even amid the gruesome stage sets and macabre makeup, Cooper seemed less threatening. He formed a new band in 1974, featuring ex–Lou Reed guitarists Dick Wagner and Steve Hunter. (In 1977 former band members Bruce, Dunaway, and Smith formed Billion Dollar Babies and recorded one unsuccessful album.) An April 1975 prime-time TV special, *Alice Cooper—The Nightmare*, seemed to indicate Cooper's acceptance as a mainstream entertainer, as did a handful of appearances on *The Hollywood Squares* game show. His then-current hit, "Only Women Bleed" (#12, 1975), was a ballad, as were two subsequent hits: "I Never Cry" (#12, 1976) and "You and Me" (#9, 1977).

In 1978 Cooper committed himself to a psychiatric hospital for treatment of alcoholism, an experience chronicled on *From the Inside*, which includes some lyrics by Elton John's partner Bernie Taupin, and the hit "How You Gonna See Me Now" (#12, 1978). Neither the hard-rocking *Flush the Fashion* nor *Special Forces* was especially successful, and Cooper took a hiatus. He returned in 1986 with *Constrictor*, followed by *Raise Your Fist and Yell*, both deep in the heavy-metal vein. The Nightmare Returns Tour and MTV Halloween special brought Cooper's violent, twisted onstage fantasies to a new generation, and he closed the Eighties with the platinum *Trash* and "Poison" (#7, 1989), his first Top Twenty single in over a decade.

Cooper has appeared in several films: *Prince of Darkness* (1988), *Freddy's Dead: The Final Nightmare* (1991), and *Wayne's World* (1992). For *The Decline of Western Civilization, Part II—The Metal Years*, he rerecorded "Under My Wheels" with Guns n' Roses' Axl Rose, Slash, and Izzy Stradlin. Prominent among Cooper's legion of second-generation fans are Steve Vai, Nikki Sixx, Joe Satriani, and Slash, all of whom guested on *Hey Stoopid*.

Julian Cope/The Teardrop Explodes

Born October 21, 1957, Deri, Mid Glamorgan, Wales, U.K.
The Teardrop Explodes, formed 1978, Liverpool, England: Cope, voc., bass; Michael Finkler, gtr.; Paul Simpson, kybds.; Gary Dwyer, drums.
1979—(– Simpson; + Dave Balfe, kybds.; – Finkler; + Alan Gill, gtr.).   1980—*Kilimanjaro* (Mercury) 1981—*Wilder*.
Julian Cope solo: 1983—*World Shut Your Mouth* (Mercury)   1984—*Fried*   1986—*Julian Cope* EP (Island)   1987—*Saint Julian*; *Eve's Volcano* EP 1988—*My Nation Underground*   1989—*Skellington* (CopeCo-Zippo)   1990—*Droolian* (MoFoCo-Zippo) 1991—*Peggy Suicide*   1992—*Floored Genius: The Best of Julian Cope and the Teardrop Explodes 1979–91*; *Jehovah Kill*   1994—*Autogeddon* (American).

As singer of the neopsychedelic Liverpool band the Teardrop Explodes, Julian Cope was a wildly eccentric frontman whose lyrics were often maddeningly inscrutable and whose stage manner was unpredictable. When he left the Teardrops in 1983—during the recording sessions for what would have been the group's third album—Cope continued on an even more bizarre career path.

Before the Teardrops, Cope had played in two short-lived bands with future Echo and the Bunnymen singer Ian McCulloch. Shortly after the Teardrops imploded, his solo career began on a rough note when he intentionally jabbed himself in the stomach with a microphone stand onstage at London's Hammersmith Palais. Cope soon became well known for his experimentation with psychedelic drugs, which led some observers to liken him to two of his musical heroes, the acid casualties Syd Barrett and Roky Erickson. Mercury dropped Cope after his second album and refused to release his completed third one, *Skellington* (which later came out independently).

In 1987, after moving to Island Records, Cope got his first slight crack at mainstream acceptance with "World Shut Your Mouth" (#84), from his most critically acclaimed album, *Saint Julian* (#105, 1987). Henceforth, each of his Island records has made it into the Top 200, though barely.

Cope's mental state continued to be an issue. In 1990, during a three-year hiatus from music, he appeared at London's anti–Poll Tax demonstration disguised as an alien named Mr. Sqwubbsy. His next release, the oddball double-length album *Peggy Suicide*, was a resounding artistic success, though its theme—an ambitious but confused political/environmental statement—was as convoluted as anything the singer had previously done. By 1992 it appeared that Cope's fans had grown weary of his eccentricities. Following a compilation of solo and

Julian Cope

Teardrops material, Cope released *Jehovah Kill* to critical indifference and much less media attention. *Autogeddon* completed Cope's musical triology that began with *Peggy Suicide* and *Jehovah Kill*—this time with a theme of the evils of the automobile. In 1994 Cope's memoir, *Head On,* was published in England.

Stewart Copeland: See the Police

Chick Corea

Born Armando Anthony Corea, June 12, 1941, Chelsea, Massachusetts
1966—*Tones for Jones Bones* (Vortex)   1968—*Now He Sings, Now He Sobs* (Solid State)   1969—*Is* 1970—*Song of Singing* (Blue Note); *Piano Improvisations, vol. 1 and vol. 2* (ECM); *Circling In* (Blue Note) 1971—*A.R.C.* (ECM); *Circle, Paris Concert*   1972— *Inner Space* (Atlantic); *Crystal Silence* (ECM); *Return to Forever*   1973—*Light as a Feather* (with Return to Forever) (Polydor); *Hymn of the Seventh Galaxy* (with Return to Forever)   1974—*Where Have I Known You Before* (with Return to Forever) 1975—*Chick Corea* (Blue Note); *No Mystery* (with Return to Forever) (Polydor)   1976—*The Romantic Warrior* (with Return to Forever) (Columbia); *The Leprechaun* (Polydor); *My Spanish Heart*   1977—

Musicmagic (Columbia)   1978—*Mad Hatter* (Polydor); *Friends; Circulus* (Blue Note); *Secret Agent* (Polydor)   1979—*Delphi 1* (Blue Note)   1980—*Tap Step* (Warner)   1981—*Three Quartets*   1982—*Trio Music* (ECM); *Touchstone* (Warner Bros.)   1983— *Again and Again* (Elektra/Musician)   1984—*Children's Songs* (ECM)   1985—*Chick Corea Works, Voyage, Septet*   1986—*The Chick Corea Elektric Band* (GRP)   1987—*Trio Music Live in Europe* (ECM); *Light Years* (GRP)   1988—*Eye of the Beholder*   1989—*Chick Corea Akoustic Band*   1990— *Inside Out*   1991—*Alive, Beneath the Mask* 1992—*Play* (with Bobby McFerrin) (Blue Note) 1993—*Paint the World* (GRP).

Chick Corea established himself as a major jazz keyboardist, including a three-year stint with Miles Davis, before turning to rock fusion with Return to Forever. In the late Seventies he returned to acoustic piano. Corea's tone on piano is distinctively brittle and precise and has been widely imitated.

The son of a musician, Corea began studying classical piano at four and played with his father's band. As a teenager he also played with a Latin band. He briefly attended Columbia University and the Juilliard School, but quit to go professional. Corea's first major job was with Mongo Santamaria in 1962, followed by work with Blue Mitchell, Stan Getz (for two years), Herbie Mann, and Sarah Vaughan. In 1968 Miles Davis Quintet drummer Tony Williams invited him to sit in for an ailing Herbie Hancock, and Corea wound up working for Davis for three years; at Davis' behest he began playing the electric Fender Rhodes piano, appearing on *Filles de Kilimanjaro,* and the landmark jazz-rock albums *In a Silent Way* and *Bitches Brew.*

Corea formed the avant-garde Circle with bassist Dave Holland, drummer Barry Atschul, and reedman Anthony Braxton in 1971. Circle recorded three albums, while Corea recorded two solo sessions. Corea was introduced to Scientology, which led him to adopt the idea of "communication"—in practice, playing simpler music. He formed Return to Forever.

Fellow Scientologist Stanley Clarke [see entry], whom Corea met during a brief stint with saxophonist Joe Henderson, cofounded Return to Forever. Corea had written some of the group's initial material for a Stan Getz band (on Getz's album *Captain Marvel*) including Clarke, percussionist Airto Moreira, and drummer Tony Williams. When Corea recorded the material on his own, Joe Farrell replaced Getz, Moreira played both drums and percussion, and Moreira's wife, Flora Purim, sang. The result was a Corea album called *Return to Forever,* followed by *Light as a Feather.* The two albums contained melodic pop jazz, full of buoyant melodies and quasi-Latin rhythms.

When Moreira and Purim left to start their own group, Fingers, in 1973, Farrell went back to session work and Corea and Clarke revamped Return to Forever with drummer Lenny White and guitarist Bill Connors. Openly modeled on the Mahavishnu Orchestra (Corea had performed with Mahavishnu John McLaughlin in Davis' band), the new group made bombastic use of electric instruments, including Corea's synthesizers. After guitarist Al DiMeola replaced Connors, Return to Forever reached a peak of popularity on the rock circuit. Clarke and DiMeola went solo in 1976, and Corea briefly expanded Return to Forever to a 13-piece ensemble before retiring the group name. Corea, Clarke, White, and DiMeola did a reunion tour in 1983.

During the late Seventies and Eighties, Corea played mostly acoustic piano as half of a duet with fellow pop refugee Herbie Hancock [see entry] and with various acoustic groups that have included drummer Steve Gadd, bassist Eddie Gomez, Henderson, Farrell, vocalist Gayle Moran (Corea's wife), and others, including a trio reuniting him with bassist Miroslav Vitous and drummer Roy Haynes, who had recorded earlier on *Now He Sings, Now He Sobs*. He also recorded solo albums and duets with vibraharpist Gary Burton and wrote a monthly column for *Contemporary Keyboard* magazine.

The Chick Corea Elektric Band formed in 1985 with two top-rated L.A. musicians, bassist John Patitucci and drummer Dave Weckl; guitarist Frank Gambale and others have joined over the years. In order to accommodate his fusion/traditional jazz mind-split, Corea formed the Akoustic Band in 1989 with Patitucci and Weckl. This trio performed jazz standards as well as Corea originals, including a reworking of his classic, "Spain." Patitucci and Weckl left the Elektric Band in 1993, replaced by bassist Jimmy Earl and drummer Gary Novak.

Corea started his own label, Stretch Records (a subsidiary of GRP) in 1992 to record like-minded musicians, including Patitucci and guitarist Robben Ford.

The Cornelius Brothers and Sister Rose

Formed circa 1970, Miami, Florida
Eddie Cornelius (b. 1943), voc.; Carter Cornelius (b. 1948, d. Nov. 7, 1991, Dania, Fla.), voc.; Rose Cornelius (b. 1947), voc.
1972—*Cornelius Brothers and Sister Rose* (United Artists)   1973—*Big Time Lover*   1976—*Greatest Hits*.

The Cornelius family enjoyed a major pop hit in 1971 with "Treat Her Like a Lady," which featured brother Eddie's lead vocals. The two brothers and sister Rose began working in the Sixties as a gospel act called the Split Tones. Just after they hit with their first secular release, "Lady," the group suffered a car crash that put it

out of action for several months. The trio came back with the Top Five "Too Late to Turn Back Now" (#2, 1972) and followed up with lesser hits like "Don't Ever Be Lonely" (#23, 1972). By 1974 the Corneliuses were no longer a pop-chart presence.

Hugh Cornwell: See the Stranglers

Larry Coryell

Born April 2, 1943, Galveston, Texas
1967—*Out of Sight & Sound* (as Free Spirits) (ABC)
1968—*Lady Coryell* (Vanguard)   1969—*Coryell*; Spaces   1971—*Live at the Village Gate; Barefoot Boy* (Flying Dutchman)   1972—*Offering* (Vanguard)   1973—*The Real Great Escape*   1974—*Introducing the 11th House*   1975—*Level One* (as Eleventh House) (Arista); *Restful Mind* (Vanguard); *Planet End*   1977—*Lion and the Ram* (Arista); *Twin House* (with Philip Catherine) (Atlantic); *Back Together Again* (with Alphonse Mouzon); *Two for the Road* (with Steve Kahn) (MCA)   1978—*Splendid* (with Philip Catherine) (Elektra); *Larry Coryell and Eleventh House at Montreux* (Vanguard)   1984—*Comin' Home* (Muse)   1986—*Equipoise*   1989—*The Dragon Gate* (Shanachie)   1991—*12 Frets to the Octave*   1992—*Live From Bahia* (CTI)   1993—*Fallen Angel*.

Guitarist Larry Coryell's penchant for high volume and fast fingerwork led him to jazz rock early. Coryell played piano as a child, switching to guitar in his teens. After studying journalism at the University of Washington, he moved to New York City in 1965, where he worked with drummer Chico Hamilton in 1966 and cofounded an early jazz-rock band, the Free Spirits. In 1967 he joined vibraphonist Gary Burton's band; two years later he recorded "Memphis Underground" with flutist Herbie Mann.

Coryell began leading his own bands in 1969. He toured Europe and the U.S. that year with a band that included ex-Cream bassist Jack Bruce, ex–Jimi Hendrix Experience drummer Mitch Mitchell, and Coryell's longtime keyboardist Mike Mandel. In 1970 he joined John McLaughlin, Billy Cobham, Chick Corea, and future Weather Report bassist Miroslav Vitous on *Spaces*. *Barefoot Boy* (1971) was a virtual tribute to Hendrix.

Coryell formed a variety of bands in the Seventies, including the Mahavishnu Orchestra–styled Eleventh House, and later toured playing solo acoustic guitar and in a duo with ex-Focus guitarist Philip Catherine or session guitarist Steve Kahn. Although he returned briefly to the electric fusion format, Coryell mainly concentrated on acoustic guitar. Aside from continued duets with Catherine, Coryell played in tandem with Al DiMeola, John McLaughlin, John Scofield, and others.

Coryell's leanings toward traditional jazz surfaced during the late Eighties and Nineties. Coryell toured and recorded in acoustic quartet settings with such jazz heavyweights as bassists Buster Williams and George Mraz, pianists Stanley Cowell and Kenny Barron, and drummers Beaver Harris and Billy Hart. He recorded *Live From Bahia* in Brazil with drummer Billy Cobham, saxophonist Donald Harrison, trumpeter Marcio Montarroyos, and vocalist Dori Caymmi. The album was a blend of samba, rhumba, rock, and funk, with African and Caribbean rhythms. In 1993 Coryell shifted direction once again, forming the Fallen Angels band, which recorded with horns and synthesizers.

Elvis Costello

Born Declan Patrick McManus, August 25, 1954, London, England
1977—*My Aim Is True* (Columbia)   1978—*This Year's Model*   1979—*Armed Forces*   1980—*Get Happy!!*; *Taking Liberties*   1981—*Trust*; *Almost Blue*   1982—*Imperial Bedroom*   1983—*Punch the Clock*   1984—*Goodbye Cruel World*   1985—*The Best of Elvis Costello and the Attractions*   1986—*King of America*; *Blood and Chocolate*   1989—*Spike* (Warner Bros.)   1990—*Girls Girls Girls* (Columbia)   1991—*Mighty Like a Rose* (Warner Bros.)   1993—*The Juliet Letters*; *2½ Years* (Rykodisc)   1994—*Brutal Youth* (Warner Bros.); *The Very Best of Elvis Costello and the Attractions* (Rykodisc)   1995—*Kojak Variety* (Warner Bros.).

In the late Seventies, Elvis Costello arrived as part of a new wave of singer/songwriters who reinvigorated the literate, lyrical traditions of Bob Dylan and Van Morrison with the raw energy and sass that were principal ethics of punk. Early in his career, Costello listed "revenge and guilt" as his primary motivations, but what really counted was the construction of his songs, which set densely layered wordplay in an ever-expanding repertoire of styles. Since Costello's melodic instincts were as sure as his gifts as a lyricist, his musical experiments generally drew kudos, enhancing his reputation as a quintessential critics' favorite. (Rock singer David Lee Roth once remarked that critics liked the bespectacled, nerdy Costello so much because they all looked liked him.) Granted, some members of the pop intelligentsia never forgave Costello for moving beyond the brash minimalist urgency of his first few albums; but it's just this progress that has allowed the singer to remain a relevant, respected artist into the Eighties and Nineties.

Costello's father was a successful big-band singer and trumpet player. While attending Catholic school in working-class London, Costello tried playing violin and several other instruments before discovering the guitar at 15, at which point he was already interested in song-

Elvis Costello

writing. Soon after, he moved to Liverpool to live with his mother, who'd divorced his father. In the early Seventies, he and his high school sweetheart married and had a son, settling in London. There, Costello continued to write, record demos, and perform (sometimes under the name D. C. Costello, his mother's maiden name), while supporting his family as a computer operator. In 1975 he quit his job, became a roadie for Brinsley Schwarz, and got friendly with their bass player, Nick Lowe. Stiff Records signed Costello in 1976 on the advice of staff producer Lowe; one of the label's owners, Jake Riviera, became his manager and rechristened him Elvis Costello.

Costello's debut single, "Less Than Zero," was released in April 1977 and was included on *My Aim Is True*, which Lowe produced. Soon Top Twenty in England, *Aim* (#32 U.S.) made Costello a major British cult star and attracted critical kudos in the U.S. Costello then assembled the Attractions: keyboardist Steve "Nieve" Nason, drummer Pete Thomas, and bassist Bruce Thomas. Bolstered by his new cohorts on *This Year's Model* (#30, 1978), he rocked harder, while maintaining his distinctively wounded, clipped vocal delivery; meanwhile, his image was amplified by punk-friendly habits like onstage rudeness, brief sets, and an aversion to the press. In late 1978 Costello left his wife and young son, only to return to them a year later. His next release, the Top Ten *Armed Forces* (originally titled *Emotional Fascism*), repeatedly equated love affairs with military maneuvers ("Oliver's Army"). By then Costello's style encompassed lush, Beatlesque arrangements and more diverse influences.

While he toured the U.S. to promote *Armed Forces* in 1979, Costello's onstage contrariness and dark moods —

sometimes induced by drinking—reached alarming proportions. In Columbus, Ohio, that March, a minor but much-publicized conflict with American singers Bonnie Bramlett and Stephen Stills occurred in a hotel bar after Costello reportedly referred to Ray Charles as a "blind, ignorant nigger." Besides tainting his work with the Rock Against Racism organization, this outburst brought the wrath of the previously supportive press. Costello lay low for a while, producing the Specials' 1979 debut and appearing at the Concert for Kampuchea. *Taking Liberties* consisted of previously released English material and studio outtakes.

Trust (#28, 1981) brought Costello back to frontline duty, and his subsequent American tour revealed an uncharacteristically polite and reserved stage manner, as if experience had mellowed the performer, who was still in his mid-20s. His touring partners were Squeeze, a critically acclaimed pop band whose 1981 LP *East Side Story* Costello coproduced. Later that same year Costello released *Almost Blue*, an album of country & western covers recorded in Nashville that got mixed reviews. (A C&W aficionado, Costello later re-covered a version of his "Stranger in the House" with George Jones, while Costello's own songs have been covered by Dave Edmunds and Linda Ronstadt.)

Imperial Bedroom (#30, 1982), in contrast, earned raves. Full of wry, elegant, haunted ballads, the album marked Costello's most sophisticated pop craftsmanship yet, garnering comparisons to such prerock bards as Cole Porter and Rodgers and Hart. With 1983's *Punch the Clock* (#24), Costello continued to move beyond the punk minimalism of his early work, serving up soulful, accessible pop ("Everyday I Write the Book," a Top Forty U.S. hit) and serious balladry (the politically astute "Shipbuilding"). While less consistent, 1984's *Goodbye Cruel World* (#35) also found him diversifying in this vein.

Costello's personal life was also undergoing changes. Estranged again from his wife, he struck up a relationship with the Pogues' bassist Caitlin O'Riordan while the Irish band toured with him in the fall of 1984. (Costello also produced the Pogues' 1985 album, *Rum Sodomy & the Lash*.) Costello divorced his wife in 1985 and married O'Riordan in 1986. Also in 1986, Costello temporarily traded in the Attractions for a pickup band he called the Confederates—former Elvis Presley guitarist James Burton, Ronnie Tutt, and Jerry Scheff—who appeared with him on all but one cut (on which the Attractions appeared) on the lushly melodic *King of America* (#39). Later that year, Costello re-enlisted the Attractions for the more raucous *Blood and Chocolate* (#84). The tour to promote both these albums alternated between sets featuring the Attractions, the Confederates, and Costello performing solo, acoustically. In addition, Costello designed the Spinning Songbook, a device through which audience members could "choose,"

by luck of the draw, songs from his vast repertoire.

In 1987 Costello cowrote a bunch of songs with Paul McCartney, several of which materialized two years later on *Spike* (#32). Costello's 1989 album—which also included support from Roger McGuinn, Chrissie Hynde, and the Dirty Dozen Brass Band—produced a Top Twenty hit in the McCartney-Costello collaboration "Veronica" (#19, 1989) and went gold. Some critics found *Spike* inconsistent, though, preferring the subsequent collection *Girls Girls Girls*, on which Costello chronicled his career thus far with his own favorite material.

Like *Spike*, 1991's *Mighty Like a Rose* (#55) was made without the Attractions, and was perceived as lacking focus. In 1993, though, Costello found a new sense of direction in perhaps his most ambitious project yet: *The Juliet Letters*, a song cycle he wrote and performed with the string players in England's Brodsky Quartet, inspired by an article about letters sent to Shakespeare's character Juliet Capulet, received by a Veronese academic. The album and subsequent tour drew wild praise from some, while baffling or putting off others. In 1994 Costello reunited with the Attractions for *Brutal Youth* (which also featured Nick Lowe); the maturely rocking results garnered almost unanimous acclaim. That summer, Costello began touring with the Attractions, marking a reconciliation between Costello and bassist Bruce Thomas, whose published memoirs had enraged the singer. In the 1990s, Rykodisc began releasing the early Costello albums on compact disc, with extra tracks consisting of live and previously unreleased recordings.

James Cotton
Born July 1, 1935, Tunica, Mississippi
1967—*James Cotton Blues Band* (Verve)   1968—*Pure Cotton*; *Cotton in Your Ears*; *Cut You Loose!* (Vanguard)   1971—*Taking Care of Business* 1974—*100% Cotton* (Buddah)   1975—*High Energy* 1975—*Superharp Live and on the Move*   1980—*Take Me Back* (Blind Pig)   1984—*High Compression* (Alligator)   1986—*Live from Chicago* 1987—*Live at Antone's* (Antone's)   1990—*Mighty Long Time*   1994—*Living the Blues* (PolyGram/Verve).

A blues harmonica player, Cotton has played for years with Muddy Waters and frequently contributed to the records of rockers such as Johnny Winter. He has also led his own band, supporting himself on club dates and recording sporadically.

Cotton began playing blues harmonica after meeting Sonny Boy Williamson (Aleck "Rice" Miller). He left home at nine to seek out Williamson, whom he had heard on radio station KFFA in West Helena, Arkansas; he spent the next six years playing with him. For two years after that he was with Howlin' Wolf and then formed his own band with Willie Nix before joining Muddy Waters, with whom he worked for 12 years. In 1966 he left Waters to form his own band. Over the next few years he worked with several rock acts, including Paul Butterfield, Janis Joplin, Steve Miller, Boz Scaggs, Johnny Winter, Edgar Winter, Elvin Bishop, and the J. Geils Band's Peter Wolf. He has also recorded with Howlin' Wolf, Otis Spann, Big Mama Thornton, and Muddy Waters (he appeared on Waters' Hard Again tour in the late Seventies).

In the Eighties Cotton was nominated for three Grammy awards and won several W. C. Handy International Blues awards. He has continued to tour and record in the Nineties, appearing with numerous rock acts, including the Grateful Dead. *Living the Blues* features Dr. John and Jerry Garcia, along with blues artists Lucky Peterson and John Primer.

John Cougar: See John Mellencamp

The Count Five
Formed circa 1965, San Jose, California
Ken Ellner (b. 1948, Brooklyn, N.Y.), voc.; John "Mouse" Michalski (b. 1948, Cleveland, Ohio), gtr.; Sean Byrne (b. 1947, Dublin, Ire.), gtr.; Roy Chaney (b. 1948, Indianapolis, Ind.), bass; Craig "Butch" Atkinson (b. 1947), drums.
1966—*Psychotic Reaction* (Double Shot) 1993— *Psychotic Reunion Live!* (Performance) 1994—*Psychotic Reaction: The Complete Count Five.*

A psychedelic garage band, the Count Five scored one major hit, "Psychotic Reaction" (#5, 1966). They emerged from the same California Bay Area bar circuit that spawned the Syndicate of Sound ("Little Girl") and the Golliwogs (later Creedence Clearwater Revival). In 1966 they signed with the Los Angeles–based Double Shot label. Followups to "Psychotic Reaction" failed to make national impact, although the band remained popular for a while regionally. Byrne continued his music career in his homeland, joining two fairly obscure groups, Public Foot the Roman and later Legover.

Counting Crows
Formed August 1991, San Francisco, California
Adam Duritz (b. Aug. 1, 1964, Baltimore, Md.), voc., piano, harmonica; David Bryson (b. Nov. 5, 1961), gtr., voc.; Dan Vickrey (b. Aug. 26, 1966, Walnut Creek, Calif.), gtr.; Matt Malley (b. July 4, 1963), bass, voc.; Charlie Gillingham (b. Jan. 12, 1960, Torrance, Calif.), kybds., voc; Steve Bowman (b. Jan. 14, 1967), drums.
1993—*August and Everything After* (DGC) 1994— (– Bowman; + Ben Mize [b. Feb. 2, 1971], drums).

Vocalist/songwriter Adam Duritz's Northern California band is an early-Nineties graduate of MTV's school of heavy rotation. The group scored a multiplatinum hit with its rootsy first album *August and Everything After*.

In 1991 Duritz first played acoustic shows with guitarist David Bryson in the San Francisco area. After honing a folk-based sound—comparable to that of early recordings by Van Morrison—the duo recruited bassist Matt Malley, guitarist Dan Vickrey, keyboardist Charlie Gillingham, and drummer Steve Bowman (later replaced by Ben Mize). As the Counting Crows, the group recorded *August and Everything After* (#4, 1994) under the production tutelage of T Bone Burnett, an idol of Duritz's, in the Big Pink–like atmosphere of a Los Angeles mansion.

In the midst of the alternative-rock boom, the group sold over five million copies of their more traditional-rock-sounding album without ever releasing a U.S. single. MTV and radio's incessant playing of "Mr. Jones," a song about a singer grasping for rock stardom, helped vault the album 40 notches on the pop album chart in one week. "Round Here" was a second semiautobiographical song; its video also proved popular on MTV.

Country
Country, the music of America's heartland, can be traced back to British immigrants who brought with them a tradition of storytelling Celtic ballads and string-instrument playing, especially fiddling. The tradition survived in isolated rural communities but developed an American accent as music for square dances and hoedowns.

By the early 1900s "mountain music" had separated into string-band music—the beginnings of bluegrass—and vocal-harmony music derived from church music. But as recordings and radio began to disseminate pop, other influences crept in. Nashville, Tennessee, with its weekly Grand Ole Opry radio broadcasts, became the center of country music by the Thirties, and has been a battleground between traditionalists and modernizers ever since.

In the late Thirties Roy Acuff and others began to shift toward a poplike solo singer-plus-band setup, while Western swing bands in Texas began to borrow from blues, jazz, even polkas. In the Forties and Fifties country came to accept some improvisational elements and became country & western music; but long after blues and rock & roll had appeared, drums were barred from the Opry stage.

The tremendously popular postwar "honky-tonk" style—the music of Hank Williams, Hank Thompson, Lefty Frizzell, Webb Pierce, George Jones, Loretta Lynn, and Merle Haggard—predominated into the Sixties.

In the latter Sixties, while rockabilly singers like Jerry Lee Lewis and Johnny Cash were returning to country roots, rockers like Bob Dylan, Gram Parsons, and the

Byrds rediscovered country and brought it to a younger, longhaired audience. Meanwhile, country songwriters like Kris Kristofferson and C&W mavericks like Willie Nelson and Waylon Jennings began to forge non-Nashville alliances with rockers.

By the mid-Seventies country rock (played by rock musicians) and outlaw country (played by country musicians) were becoming virtually indistinguishable. But although country had borrowed numerous pop trappings and recording techniques, there was still a strain of mainstream country music that told simple stories with unobtrusive backing, with the twang of Southern accents echoed by the twang of steel guitars.

Country crossed over further into the pop realm in the late Seventies, when longtime country stars, such as Dolly Parton, began not only placing hits on the pop chart but becoming media personalities. An "Urban Cowboy" phase of quick rise-and-fall country stars followed, and by the mid-Eighties, a subgenre consisting of artists dubbed "new traditionalists" began to proliferate. Ricky Skaggs, John Anderson, and Randy Travis were among those who followed in the footsteps of earlier country stylists like Frizzell and Jones.

By the early Nineties, country music was huge. With a greatly expanded audience (many of them ex-rock fans) and with dozens of new young stars—some collectively known as "hat acts"—country was a bigger business than ever. Led by Garth Brooks, many country artists shot straight to the top of the pop album charts, beating out rock, rap, and dance music artists. Country record labels began snapping up as much new talent as they could get. The result: By 1993, of the 200 artists signed to country label rosters, only 40 had been recording before 1985. (So much for country music's tradition of sticking with its oldtimers!) The new breed of country star—Brooks, Clint Black, Reba McEntire, Trisha Yearwood, Billy Ray Cyrus, and Travis Tritt, among others—drew on virtually all the genre's antecedents as well as rock's past, including Southern rock, country rock, and singer/songwriter balladry.

At the same time, a folkier, more roots-based genre of country flourished outside the Nashville mainstream. Called "Western beat," this subgenre consisted of artists with a more purist C&W sensibility (often with twangier vocal styles than mainstream country) and frequently an "outsider" perspective within the lyrics. Western beat practitioners include Lucinda Williams, Jimmie Dale Gilmore, Joe Ely, and Townes Van Zandt, among others.

Country Joe and the Fish

Formed 1965, San Francisco, California
Country Joe McDonald (b. Jan. 1, 1942, Washington, D.C.), voc., gtr.; Chicken Hirsch (b. 1940, Calif.), drums; Bruce Barthol (b. 1947, Berkeley, Calif.), bass; Barry Melton (b. 1947, Brooklyn, N.Y.), gtr.; David Cohen (b. 1942, Brooklyn, N.Y.), gtr., kybds.
1967—*Electric Music for the Mind and Body* (Vanguard); *I-Feel-Like-I'm-Fixin'-to-Die* 1968—*Together* 1969—*Here We Go Again; Greatest Hits* 1970—*C. J. Fish* 1971—*Life and Times of Country Joe and the Fish (From Haight-Ashbury to Woodstock)* 1973—*The Best of Country Joe McDonald and the Fish* 1976—*The Essential Country Joe McDonald* 1977—*Reunion* (Fantasy) 1980—*Collector's Items: The First 3 EP's* (Rag Baby) 1987—*The Collected Country Joe and the Fish* (Vanguard).
Country Joe McDonald solo: 1969—*Thinking of Woody Guthrie* (Vanguard); *Tonight I'm Singing Just for You* 1970—*Hold On, It's Coming; Quiet Days at Clichy* 1971—*War, War, War* 1972—*Incredible! Live!* 1973—*The Paris Sessions* 1974—*Country Joe* 1975—*Essential Country Joe; Paradise with an Ocean View* (Fantasy) 1976—*Love Is a Fire* (Fantasy) 1977—*Goodbye Blues* 1978—*Rock and Roll Music from the Planet Earth* 1979—*Leisure Suite* 1981—*On My Own* (Rag Baby); *Into the Fray* 1982—*Animal Tracks* 1983—*Child's Play* 1984—*Peace on Earth* 1986—*Vietnam Experience* 1991—*Superstitious Blues* (Rykodisc).

Country Joe and the Fish were one of the most overtly political bands to emerge from San Francisco's late-Sixties folk-turned-psychedelic scene. Joe McDonald (named after Stalin by left-leaning parents) wrote his first song, "I Seen a Rocket," as a campaign song for a friend's high school class presidency attempt. At age 17 he joined the navy for three years. After a year at Los Angeles City College he moved to Berkeley and wrote protest songs while occasionally publishing a magazine, *Et Tu, Brute.*

McDonald made his first record, *The Goodbye Blues*, in 1964 with Blair Hardman. He then joined the Berkeley String Quartet and the Instant Action Jug Band, which included Barry Melton. The two started Country Joe and the Fish in 1965 to make a series of political EPs for Takoma, including the first appearance of the notorious "F-U-C-K" cheer ("Gimme an F!" etc.).

The group started as a loose-knit jug band but switched to electric instruments late in 1966. As the Summer of Love loomed, the Fish were signed to Vanguard and settled into a stable lineup for two years. The "Feel-Like-I'm Fixin'-to-Die Rag," a black-humored electric shuffle about the Vietnam War, brought them notoriety with their second album; the "F-U-C-K" cheer was changed to "F-I-S-H."

The band appeared at the Monterey Pop Festival (and in the film of it), and at Woodstock, McDonald, solo, led nearly 500,000 people in the cheer. The Fish continued to tour and record, but by 1969 they were getting fewer bookings after their arrest in Worcester, Massachusetts, for inciting an audience to lewd behavior (the cheer). The group began to unravel, although McDonald and Melton (who also had a 1969 marijuana bust) kept a lineup together to appear in the 1971 film *Zachariah*. The Fish disbanded in 1970. McDonald tried some film scores (including a Dutch version of Henry Miller's *Quiet Days in Clichy* and a Chilean political film, *Qué Hacer* (in which he also appeared) and continued his solo career, sometimes in tandem with Melton, who released his own solo album in 1971, *Bright Sun Is Shining*. McDonald continued to tour, and he has a strong European following. He joined Jane Fonda and Donald Sutherland in the FTA (Free/Fuck the Army) Revue, a non-USO show, and has been active in the causes of Vietnam veterans and saving whales.

While on tour in Europe in 1973 McDonald sat on a hot stove and had to be hospitalized for three months. His second wife, actress Robin Menken, filed for divorce and got an injunction to prevent him from visiting their daughter, Seven. With his debts mounting, he signed with Fantasy in late 1975 and recorded *Paradise with an Ocean View*. He married a third wife, Janice, and logged over 100,000 miles touring the U.S. The Fish regrouped for 1977's *Reunion*, but McDonald was solo again for *Rock and Roll Music from the Planet Earth*. In the Eighties McDonald began releasing albums on his own Rag Baby label. Melton is now a public defender in Mendocino County, north of San Francisco. He ran unsuccessfully for a city judgeship in Mendocino in 1992.

Wayne/Jayne County

Born Wayne County, Georgia
1976—*Max's Kansas City* (Ram)   1978—*The Electric Chairs* (Safari)   1980—*Rock 'n' Roll Resurrection* (Attic)   1993—*Goddess of Wet Dreams* (ESP).

Rock & roll's most famous transsexual, Jayne County started out as rock & roll's most famous transvestite, Wayne County. His life in the spotlight began when he moved to New York from his native Georgia in the late Sixties. County appeared playing a female role opposite Patti Smith in an Off Broadway production of *Femme Fatale* before tackling the role of Florence Nightingale in *World—Birth of a Nation*. In 1970 Andy Warhol cast County in his show *Pork*, with which County traveled to England. David Bowie was impressed and signed County to his Mainman management company.

On returning to New York, County's first band, Queen Elizabeth, began performing in lower Manhattan clubs like Max's Kansas City, where groups like the New York Dolls were forging a new union between camp and rock & roll. Queen Elizabeth's drummer, Jerry Nolan, was a late addition to the Dolls' lineup and later joined Johnny Thunders' Heartbreakers [see entry]. County's stage wardrobe consisted of skimpy pink dresses, fishnet stockings, heavy makeup, and a platinum-blond wig, but in spite of the sexual spoofs, County's performances were more rock & roll show than drag show.

In 1975, after being dropped by Mainman, County cut an album for ESP-Disk; its release was delayed, and then the tracks were lost in a fire. His vinyl debut was three tracks on the double-album compilation *Max's Kansas City*. He formed the Electric Chairs in 1977 and toured Britain that year. In 1978 the Electric Chairs were signed up by a German label, Safari, and released their first album. County disappeared for some time after that, reemerging in 1980 after starting the hormone treatment for a sex-change operation (County never had the final operation). *Rock 'n' Roll Resurrection* was a live set that included "Cream in My Jeans," "If You Don't Want to Fuck, Fuck Off," and "Bad in Bed." By the late Eighties County was living in London, England, and planning to forsake music for a religious college, to study Biblical archaeology. But 1993 saw the release of her first U.S. record in a decade and a half, *Goddess of Wet Dreams*. County's autobiography, *Man Enough to Be a Woman*, was published in England in 1995.

Don Covay

Born March 1938, Orangeburg, South Carolina
1964—*Mercy* (Atlantic)   1966—*Seesaw*   1969—*The House of Blue Lights* (with the Jefferson Lemon Blues Band)   1970—*Different Strokes for Different Folks* (Janus) (with the Jefferson Lemon Blues Band)   1973— *Super Dude I* (Mercury)   1974—*Hot Blood*   1976—*Travelin' in Heavy Traffic* (Philadelphia International)   1992—*Checkin' in with Don Covay* (Mercury)   1994—*Mercy, Mercy: The Definitive Don Covay* (Razor & Tie).

As a soul singer with a high gospel-inspired voice, Covay had a handful of hits in the Sixties and Seventies, but is best known for a songwriting catalogue that includes Aretha Franklin's "See Saw" and "Chain of Fools." The son of a Baptist minister who moved the family to Washington when Covay was a child, he sang with the family gospel quartet the Cherry-Keys. When he was 17, he joined the Rainbows, who had already had a local hit, "Mary Lee." His solo career got under way two years later when he opened a Washington concert for Little Richard, who named him Pretty Boy and took him to Atlantic Records. Atlantic issued Covay's first Pretty Boy disc, "Bip Bop Bip," in 1957.

Covay recorded under his own name and with his group, the Goodtimers, for Sue, Columbia, Epic, RCA, Arnold, Cameo, Parkway, Landa, and Rosemart, placing two singles on the pop chart—"Pony Time" (#60, 1961) and "Mercy Mercy" (#35, 1964)—before Atlantic reacquired him in 1965. With Atlantic he scored his first soul hit, "Please Do Something" (#21 R&B, 1965). "See Saw" was both an R&B hit (#5, 1965) and a pop hit (#44). Covay continued to record for Atlantic until 1971, when he signed with Janus. In 1972 he joined Mercury, both as an artist and as an A&R director. He returned to the charts in 1973 with "I Was Checkin' Out, She Was Checkin' In" (#29 pop, #6 R&B) and followed it the next year with "It's Better to Have (and Don't Need)" (#21 R&B). In 1981 he toured with Wilson Pickett and Solomon Burke in a package called the Soul Clan. Covay was the subject of a critically acclaimed tribute album, *Back to the Streets: Celebrating the Music of Don Covay,* in 1993.

Cover

The term "cover" refers to the second version, and all subsequent versions, of a song, performed either by another act than the one that originally recorded it or by anyone except its writer. In the prerock era, most hits were covers. Then, as now, the lion's share of the money in music derived from song publishing, so it made economic sense to have many artists record the material in the publisher's catalogue. This explains why in 1957 there were four Top Twenty versions of "The Banana Boat Song," recorded by the Tarriers, the Fontane Sisters, Steve Lawrence, and Sarah Vaughan.

In the early days of rock & roll, the term assumed an unsavory connotation because white vocal groups and singers often rushed to cover black doo-wop hits, and because they had more access to airplay, cover versions outsold the original recordings. Thus, the Crew-Cuts charted higher with their version of the Penguins' "Earth Angel" than did the original group, and Bill Haley's somewhat "cleaner" version of "Shake, Rattle, and Roll" fared better commercially than Big Joe Turner's randier original.

Interestingly, while the British Invasion is credited with changing the economics of rock music by introducing self-contained groups that wrote their own songs as opposed to relying on professional songwriters, the catalogues of the Beatles, the Animals, and the Rolling Stones, among others, are full of American covers. In the Stones' and the Animals' early days, it was Chicago blues tunes; for the Beatles, Carl Perkins covers. Later the Stones covered a large number of Motown hits: "Just My Imagination," "Ain't Too Proud to Beg," and "Going to a Go-Go." With Peter Tosh, Mick Jagger did the Temptations' "Don't Look Back"; with David Bowie, Martha and the Vandellas' "Dancing in the Street" (which was also a hit for Van Halen).

In the Sixties, as singer/songwriters came into their own, an established cover singer like Judy Collins or Linda Ronstadt would give unknown songwriters (such as Joni Mitchell or Leonard Cohen) exposure by covering new songs; although they were the first recordings, they were cover versions. The Sixties also saw a proliferation of truly bizarre cover versions, as singers from other genres and actors attempted to "get hip" by recording rock & roll songs. Examples of this misguided trend probably run in the thousands, but the best/worst (including Bill Shatner's paranoid reading of "Mr. Tambourine Man" and Sebastian Cabot intoning "It Ain't Me Babe") of them have been anthologized by Rhino Records in its *Golden Throats* series.

Beginning in the Seventies covers became, if not more respectable, certainly more lucrative, especially for contemporary teen idols (Donny Osmond doing Paul Anka's "Puppy Love," Shaun Cassidy with the Ronettes' "Da Doo Ron Ron," and Leif Garrett's cover of "Runaround Sue") and rock groups (Van Halen with Roy Orbison's "Pretty Woman," David Lee Roth with the Beach Boys' "California Girls," Mötley Crüe with Brownsville Station's "Smoking in the Boys Room"). Other artists, Linda Ronstadt foremost among them, breathed new life—and had huge hits—covering Buddy Holly's "That'll Be the Day," Chuck Berry's "Back in the U.S.A.," and Smokey Robinson's "Ooo Baby Baby," in addition to her California folk-rock repertoire.

Among more adventurous artists, such as Bryan Ferry, covers were given a whole new spin, as in his distraught reworking of Lesley Gore's "It's My Party" or his manic version of the Everly Brothers' "The Price of Love." Generally speaking, covers rarely deviate that significantly in style or feel from the original. Perhaps that is why recordings that turn the original version inside out, such as Sid Vicious' sneering version of Frank Sinatra's theme, "My Way," are so compelling.

Beginning in the Eighties, however, the term *cover* became nearly synonymous with "tribute." Not only was the market deluged with note-perfect copy covers (such as Mariah Carey's take on the Jackson 5's "I'll Be There," Hall and Oates' remake of the Righteous Brothers' "You've Lost That Lovin' Feelin'," Phil Collins' multitracked Supremes chestnut "You Can't Hurry Love"), but tribute albums, compiling various artists' interpretations of a single artist's or group's work, became popular. Perhaps the single biggest factor in the Eagles' 1994 reunion was the success of the tribute album *Common Thread.*

Although occasionally a hit cover brought a fresh interpretation (Talking Heads' version of Al Green's "Take Me to the River," Billy Idol's charged reading of William Bell's "I Forgot to Be Your Lover"), most sounded very much like their originals, certainly no mistake in a competitive radio market. Some songs have taken on a life of their own, returning several times: "Daddy's Home" has been a hit three times, in 1961 originally for Shep and the Limelites, in 1973 for Jermaine Jackson, and in 1982 for

Cliff Richard; "Cupid," in 1961 originally for Sam Cooke, in 1970 for Johnny Nash, in 1976 for Dawn, and in 1980 for the Spinners. Only rarely are there three hit versions of the same song presented as differently as "Fever," in its 1956 version by Willie John, redone in 1958 by Peggy Lee, and again in 1965 by the McCoys. A 1992 version by Madonna simply copied Lee's. Even when cover records fail to breathe new life into the songs themselves, they do fatten the purses of artists, publishers, and songwriters: In 1987 Billy Idol scored his first U.S. #1 single with a cover of Tommy James' "Mony Mony"; he was preceded by Tiffany's version of James' "I Think We're Alone Now."

Coverdale/Page: See Jimmy Page; Whitesnake

Cowboy Junkies

Formed 1985, Toronto, Canada
Michael Timmins (b. Apr. 21, 1959, Montreal, Can.), gtr.; Alan Anton (b. Alan Alizojvodic, June 22, 1959, Montreal, Can.), bass; Margo Timmins (b. Jan. 27, 1961, Montreal, Can.), voc.; Peter Timmins (b. Oct. 29, 1965, Montreal, Can.) drums.
1986—*Whites off Earth Now!* (Latent)   1988—*The Trinity Session* (RCA)   1990—*The Caution Horses* 1992—*Black-Eyed Man*   1993—*Pale Sun Crescent Moon.*

The Cowboy Junkies play slow, pensive country- and blues-based songs rendered unearthly by Margo Timmins' angelic drawl. The band is based on its sibling trio and an old musical partnership between Michael Timmins and Alan Anton, childhood friends who moved to New York and then London to play in punk bands in the early Eighties. When neither situation worked out, Michael moved back to Toronto and began jamming with his brother; soon they were joined by Anton and Margo. They chose their name and the title of their first album specifically to provoke attention. It worked; the self-released debut and the band's local following won them a deal with RCA.

The Trinity Session, recorded in a 14-hour session in an old church on a shoestring budget, became a sensation on college radio, helped by some video play and Lou Reed's endorsement of their version of the Velvet Underground's "Sweet Jane." The album also included covers of Hank Williams' "I'm So Lonesome I Could Cry," Patsy Cline's "Walking After Midnight," and a reworking of "Blue Moon."

On *The Caution Horses* Michael wrote more songs and proved that his obsession with country music had trained his ear for lyric twists and simple melodies. The album was recorded live, but in a professional studio.

On *Black-Eyed Man,* Michael continued to develop his narrative style in a country vein, writing about

"Southern Rain" and murder in a trailer park. Townes Van Zandt wrote two songs for the album, and "Crescent Moon," the opening track of the band's 1993 album, was dedicated to the Texas singer/songwriter. That album's literary pretensions—two tracks quoted William Faulkner and Gabriel García Márquez—were balanced by a cover of Dinosaur Jr's "The Post."

The Cowsills

Formed mid-Sixties, Newport, Rhode Island
Barbara Cowsill (b. 1929; d. Jan. 31, 1985), voc.; William "Bud" Cowsill (b. Jan. 9, 1948, Newport), gtr., voc.; Bob Cowsill (b. Aug. 26, 1950, Newport), gtr., voc.; Dick Cowsill (b. Aug. 26, 1950, Newport), voc.; Paul Cowsill (b. Nov. 11, 1952, Newport), kybds., voc.; Barry Cowsill (b. Sep. 14, 1954, Newport), bass, voc.; John Cowsill (b. Mar. 2, 1956, Newport), drums; Susan Cowsill (b. May 20, 1960, Newport), voc.
1967—*The Cowsills* (MGM)   1968—*We Can Fly; Captain Sad and His Ship of Fools*   1969—*The Best of the Cowsills; The Cowsills in Concert*   1971—*On My Side* (London).

This musical family from Rhode Island provided the inspiration for TV's *The Partridge Family* [see David Cassidy; Partridge Family]. Under father William "Bud" Cowsill's direction, the Cowsill kids and mom played the New York City clubs regularly in the mid-Sixties, attracting the attention of MGM, which released their debut album in November 1967. By early 1968 they had had their first hit single, "The Rain, the Park, and Other Things" (#2). Lots of touring, network TV appearances, and a few more hits, including the theme from the rock musical *Hair* (#2, 1969), preceded their disbandment in early 1970. Mother Barbara died in 1985; three of the brothers and Susan reunited to tour and record demos five years later.

In the Nineties Barry Cowsill worked as a solo artist, and Bill Cowsill formed the band Blue Shadows, which released an album in Canada in 1994. In 1991 Susan Cowsill joined forces with ex-Bangle Vicki Peterson to form the L.A.-based Psycho Sisters. The duo performed together and did vocals with such artists as Giant Sand, Steve Wynn, and the Continental Drifters, the group the two joined. The Drifters released a self-titled album in 1994, and Susan Cowsill married fellow Drifter Peter Holsapple (ex-dB's).

Kevin Coyne

Born January 21, 1944, Derby, England
1972—*Case History* (Dandelion, U.K.)   1973—*Marjory Razorblade* (Virgin)   1974—*Blame It on the Night*   1975—*Matching Head and Feet*   1976— *Heartburn; In Living Black and White*   1978—*Dy-*

namite Daze; Millionaires and Teddy Bears; Beautiful Extremes 1979—Babble (with Dagmar Krause) 1980—Bursting Bubbles 1982—Pointing the Finger; Politicz; Dandelion Years 1983—Beautiful Extremes Etcetera; Legless in Manila (Rough Trade) 1990—Peel Sessions (Strange Fruit).

British songwriter Kevin Coyne released several albums in the Seventies, but his unconventional song formats and abrasive vocal style have proven commercially unsuccessful. Born and raised in England, he attended art school in the early Sixties. In 1965 he began working as a social therapist in a psychiatric hospital in Preston, England, and his experiences were the subject of several of his songs. After appearing sporadically in Preston clubs, he moved to London in 1969.

In 1972 Coyne abandoned social work for a musical career. He was already known as lead vocalist with the group Siren, which recorded two albums for Dandelion. His first solo effort, Case History, was released on Dandelion in the U.K. and has since become a collector's item. He signed with Virgin in 1973 and drew critical kudos for his double set Marjory Razorblade, which was reduced to a single disc for U.S. release. Throughout the mid-Seventies he continued to record regularly and generally kept his own band together. His strongest backing aggregation played on 1976's Heartburn and the double live set In Living Black and White. Group personnel included Zoot Money (keyboards and vocals) and Andy Summers (guitar), who joined the Police shortly thereafter. Coyne has written and appeared in several theatrical productions. He is also a painter and artist.

Cracker: See Camper Van Beethoven

Floyd Cramer
Born November 27, 1933, Huttig, Arkanasas
1961—On the Rebound (RCA)   1962—I Remember Hank Williams   1965—Hits from the Country Hall of Fame   1968—The Best of Floyd Cramer, vol. 2 1970—This Is Floyd Cramer   1971—Sounds of Sunday   1979—Super Hits   1980—Dallas   1981— Great Country Hits.

A Nashville session veteran, Cramer is credited with inventing the delicately ornamented style of piano playing that characterized the Nashville sound. According to the pianist, the style derived from his applying the fiddle and steel guitar technique of note bending to the piano, resulting in the "slip note," which produces the blurred, almost melancholy sound Cramer has become known for.

Cramer played piano by ear from a very early age, and after graduating high school in 1951, headed for Shreveport, Louisiana, where he joined the band of the influential country radio program The Louisiana Hayride.

Soon he was backing such artists as Elvis Presley, Faron Young, and Webb Pierce, both on the road and in the studio. At the urging of Chet Atkins, Cramer moved to Nashville in the mid-Fifties, at a time when Atkins, Patsy Cline, and other artists were forging the modern, smoother Nashville sound. There he played on sessions with Cline, Jim Reeves, Don Gibson, Roy Orbison, Brenda Lee, and the Everly Brothers.

In 1959 he was awarded a solo recording contract, and in 1960 his "Last Date" (#2, 1960) sold over a million copies, followed by "On the Rebound" (#4, 1961), "San Antonio Rose" (#8, 1961), and "Chattanooga Choo Choo" (#36, 1962). He has since recorded over 50 albums for RCA. "Last Date" has had several hit reincarnations: with lyrics by Skeeter Davis and Boudleaux Bryant, it became "Last Date with You," a Top Thirty pop and Top Five C&W hit for Davis; with other lyrics by Conway Twitty, entitled "Lost Her Love on Our Last Date," Twitty had a #1 C&W hit in 1973; a decade later Emmylou Harris went to #1 on the C&W chart with the same song but with the title "Lost His Love on Our Last Date." Cramer continues to tour and record.

The Cramps
Formed 1975, New York City, New York
Lux Interior (b. Erick Lee Purkhiser, c. 1948, Akron, Ohio), voc.; Poison Ivy Rorschach (b. Christine Marlana Wallace, c. 1954, Sacramento, Calif.), gtr.; Bryan Gregory (b. Detroit, Mich.), gtr.; Pam "Balam" Gregory (b. Detroit, Mich.), drums.
1975—(– Pam Gregory; + Miriam Linna [b. October 16, 1955, Sudbury, Canada], drums)   1977— (– Linna; + Nick Knox [b. Nicholas George Stephanoff], drums)   1980—Songs the Lord Taught Us (I.R.S.)   1981—(– Gregory; + Kid Congo Powers [b. Brian Tristan, March 27, 1961, La Puente, Calif.], gtr.) Psychedelic Jungle   1983—Smell of Female EP (Enigma)   1984—Bad Music for Bad People (I.R.S.) 1986—A Date with Elvis (Big Beat)   1987—Rockin' n' Reelin' in Auckland New Zealand (Vengeance) 1990—(+ Candy Del Mar, bass) Stay Sick! (Restless) 1991—Look Mom, No Head!   1994—Flame Job (Medicine).

The Cramps combine rockabilly, psychedelia, sex, and B-movie sleaze into a thick, swampy stew. They were conceived in Cleveland, by Erick Purkhiser (who took the name Lux Interior) and Christine Wallace (Poison Ivy Rorschach), who had met in Sacramento and moved together to Lux's native Ohio. Lux and Ivy moved to New York in 1975 and started the Cramps after enlisting brother and sister Bryan and Pam "Balam" Gregory the following year. Aspiring journalist Miriam Linna, who'd known Lux and Ivy in Ohio, replaced Balam on drums after a few months. With their energetic two-guitar, no-

The Cramps: Harry Drumdini, Poison Ivy, Slim Chance, Lux Interior

bass attack and Lux's energetic, slightly deranged stage presence, the Cramps quickly became mainstays of the CBGB scene. Linna left in 1977 to join Nervus Rex (she has since played with the Zantees and the A-Bones, and founded *Kicks* magazine and Norton Records with fellow A-Bone Billy Miller) and was replaced by drummer Nick Knox.

With this lineup, the band went to Ardent studios in Memphis to record its Alex Chilton–produced 1977 singles "Surfin' Bird" b/w "The Way I Walk" and "Human Fly" b/w "Domino." In 1979 they combined them, along with "Lonesome Town," also from the Chilton sessions, for an EP, *Gravest Hits*. Signed to I.R.S., with Chilton again producing, they released *Songs the Lord Taught Us*, its echoey psychobilly powering originals ("T.V. Set"), Fifties classics (Johnny Burnette's "Tear It Up"), and oddities ("Strychnine"). These recordings, as well as the band's wild performances, earned them a rabid cult following, including a fan club, Legion of the Cramped (one of its founders was future Smiths frontman Morrissey).

In May 1980 Bryan Gregory left the band under mysterious circumstances; soon after, he released a single with Beast and unsuccessfully sought to become an actor. (Reportedly, his post-Cramps occupations have ranged from coven warlock to sex-shop entrepreneur to tattoo artist.) After the Cramps relocated to Los Angeles, Gregory was replaced by then–Gun Club guitarist and founding member Kid Congo Powers, who played on the aptly named, self-produced *Psychedelic Jungle* (1981).

In late 1981 the band filed a $1.1 million suit against I.R.S. charging the company and its owner, Miles Copeland, with thwarting their industry growth. The case was settled out of court, details untold, but effectively releasing the band from the label. With the exception of the 1983 live EP, *Smell of Female* (released within a week after the case was settled), and the *Bad Music for Bad People* compilation, the Cramps were missing in action in American record stores for the rest of the decade. With only Lux and Ivy remaining, the Cramps toured extensively, using a revolving cast of (usually female) guitarists and, in later years, bass players. *A Date with Elvis*, released in Britain in 1986, did not come out in the U.S. until 1990. For *Stay Sick!*, Ivy became the producer, and bassist Candy Del Mar joined the band. Both albums emphasized the band's sexual obsessions, with songs that could be offensive were it not for their good-humored tastelessness.

In the early Nineties, drummer Nick Knox departed and was briefly replaced by Nickey Alexander. In 1991, Lux and Ivy, with help from Iggy Pop, released *Look Mom, No Head!*, and toured Europe and the States, with bassist Slim Chance, who took Del Mar's place, and drummer Jim Sclavunos.

The Cranberries

Formed 1990, Limerick, Ireland
Dolores O'Riordan (b. Sept. 6, 1971, Limerick), voc.; Noel Hogan (b. Dec. 25, 1971, Limerick), gtr.; Mike Hogan (b. Apr. 29, 1973, Limerick), bass; Fergal Lawler (b. Mar. 4, 1971, Limerick), drums
1993—*Everybody Else Is Doing It, So Why Can't We?* (Island)   1994—*No Need to Argue*.

The Celtic-tinged music of the Cranberries combines the vocal strength of their chanteuse, Dolores O'Riordan, with a simple acoustic-guitar-driven sound.

In 1990 brothers Mike and Noel Hogan formed a band with drummer Fergal Lawler called the Cranberry Saw Us. They soon recruited O'Riordan, who had been writing songs since she was 12. After listening to guitarist Noel Hogan's instrumental demos, O'Riordan quickly composed the lyrics and melody to "Linger."

Following their signing with Island Records, the Cranberries had a falling-out with their original manager/producer, Pearse Gilmore, who had struck a separate, secretive deal with the record company to upgrade his own studios. In 1992, replacing Gilmore with a new manager and a new producer, they recorded their debut album, *Everybody Else Is Doing It, So Why Can't We?*

(#18, 1993). The Cranberries' U.S. tour included an appearance at Woodstock '94; that performance and heavy MTV rotation of the "Linger" video helped propel the atmospheric single to #8. *No Need to Argue* (#6, 1995) produced more hit singles, including "Zombie" and "Ode to My Family."

Robert Cray

Born August 1, 1953, Columbus, Georgia
1980—*Who's Been Talking* (Tomato)   1983—*Bad Influence* (HighTone)   1985—*False Accusations*
1986—*Strong Persuader* (Mercury)   1988—*Don't Be Afraid of the Dark*   1990—*Midnight Stroll*   1992—*I Was Warned*   1994—*Shame + Sin*   1995—*Some Rainy Morning.*
With Albert Collins and Johnny Copeland: 1985—*Showdown!* (Alligator).

Guitarist and singer Robert Cray revitalized the audience for the blues in the Eighties. With a lean style owing much to Albert Collins, Cray is also capable of Jimi Hendrix–like pyrotechnics; a player of unarguable conviction, he has managed to evade the myopia of the "blues purist" by incorporating funk, R&B, and jazz touches. His lyrics also introduce an emotion that was rare in the blues: remorse.

Of middle-class background, Cray learned the blues secondhand, through his parents' collection of Otis Rush, Buddy Guy, and Chicago blues records. By 1974 the Robert Cray Band (then featuring bassist Richard Cousins and drummer Tom Murphy) had established itself on the Pacific Northwest blues scene; in 1978 Cray appeared in *Animal House*, playing in the movie's fictional band. Also that year, he signed with Tomato, which released his debut two years later.

Who's Been Talking died commercially, but *Bad Influence* and *False Accusations* brought Cray a growing following among musicians (Eric Clapton later covered "Bad Influence"). The latter album was Cray's breakthrough, a Top 200 release. *Strong Persuader* fared even better, entering the Top Twenty and winning a Grammy. With David Sanborn on saxophone, 1988's *Don't Be Afraid of the Dark* confirmed Cray's maturity.

While hailed as a songwriter of emotionally complex material, Cray continued to draw notice chiefly for his guitar work: He played with Clapton and Keith Richards in the Chuck Berry documentary *Hail! Hail! Rock 'n' Roll*, and with Steve Cropper at a 1992 Guitar Legends concert in Spain. Backed by the Memphis Horns, *Midnight Stroll* and *I Was Warned* showed the guitarist and a new lineup of players moving even farther from their blues base. While writing songs with Boz Scaggs, and trying out gospel- and Stax-inflected numbers, Cray ensured nonetheless that the music retained its grit.

Cream

Formed 1966, England
Eric Clapton (b. Mar. 30, 1945, Ripley, Eng.), gtr., voc.; Jack Bruce (b. May 14, 1943, Glasgow, Scot.), bass, harmonica, voc.; Ginger Baker (b. Aug. 19, 1939, Lewisham, Eng.), drums, voc.
1966—*Fresh Cream* (Atco)   1967—*Disraeli Gears*
1968—*Wheels of Fire*   1969—*Goodbye; The Best of Cream*   1970—*Live Cream*   1972—*Live Cream, vol. 2; Off the Top* (Polydor)   1975—*The Best of Cream Live*   1983—*Strange Brew: The Very Best of Cream*
1995—*The Very Best of Cream.*

Cream was the prototypical blues-rock power trio. In a mere three years it sold 15 million records, played to SRO crowds throughout the U.S. and Europe, and redefined the instrumentalist's role in rock. Cream formed in mid-1966 when drummer Ginger Baker left Graham Bond's Organisation, bassist Jack Bruce (formerly of Bond's band) left Manfred Mann, and Eric Clapton, already a famous guitarist in the U.K., left John Mayall's Bluesbreakers.

Debuting at the 1966 Windsor Jazz and Blues Festival, Cream established its enduring legend on the high-volume blues jamming and extended solos of its live shows. Its studio work, however, tended toward more sophisticated original rock material, most of it written by Bruce with lyricist Pete Brown. Cream's U.S. hit singles included "Sunshine of Your Love" (#5, 1968), "White Room" (#6, 1968), and a live version of the Robert Johnson country blues "Crossroads" (#28, 1969). *Wheels of Fire*, made up of a live LP and a studio LP (both recorded

Cream: Ginger Baker, Eric Clapton, Jack Bruce

in the U.S.), was #1 for four weeks in summer 1968, just as the group was coming apart.

Tension within the band led to a quick breakup. Cream gave its farewell concert, which was filmed as *Goodbye Cream,* on November 26, 1968, at London's Royal Albert Hall. After patching together the *Goodbye* LP—which featured "Badge," cowritten by Clapton and George Harrison—Clapton and Baker subsequently formed Blind Faith [see entry], and Bruce went solo [see entry]. Clapton and Baker soon also went on to solo careers [see entries]. In 1993 the trio was inducted into the Rock and Roll Hall of Fame; Clapton, Baker and Bruce reunited to perform three songs at the ceremonies.

Creedence Clearwater Revival/John Fogerty/Tom Fogerty

Formed 1959, El Cerrito, California
John Fogerty (b. May 28, 1945, Berkeley, Calif.), gtr., voc., harmonica, sax, piano; Tom Fogerty (b. Nov. 9, 1941, Berkeley, Calif.; d. Sep. 6, 1990, Scottsdale, Ariz.), gtr.; Stu Cook (b. Apr. 25, 1945, Oakland, Calif.), bass; Doug "Cosmo" Clifford (b. Apr. 24, 1945, Palo Alto, Calif.), drums.
1968—*Creedence Clearwater Revival* (Fantasy) 1969—*Bayou Country*; *Green River*; *Willie and the Poor Boys* 1970—*Cosmo's Factory*; *Pendulum* 1971—(– Tom Fogerty) 1972—*Mardi Gras*; *Creedence Gold* 1973—*More Creedence Gold*; *Live in Europe* 1976—*Chronicle* 1980—*Live at Albert Hall.*
John Fogerty solo: 1973—*The Blue Ridge Rangers* (Fantasy) 1975—*John Fogerty* (Asylum) 1985—*Centerfield* (Warner Bros.) 1986—*Eye of the Zombie.*
Tom Fogerty solo: 1972—*Tom Fogerty* (Fantasy) 1973—*Excalibur* 1974—*Zephyr National* 1975—*Myopia* 1981—*Deal It Out.*
Tom Fogerty with Ruby: 1976—*Ruby* (Alchemy) 1977—*Rock and Roll Madness* 1985—*Precious Gems* (Fantasy).
Sidekicks (Tom Fogerty with Randy Oda): 1991—*Rainbow Carousel* (Fantasy).

John Fogerty's fervent vocals and modernized rockabilly songs built on his classic guitar riffs made Creedence Clearwater Revival the preeminent American singles band of the late Sixties and early Seventies. The Fogerty brothers were raised in Berkeley, where John studied piano and at the age of 12 got his first guitar. He met Cook and Clifford at the El Cerrito junior high school they all attended. They began playing together, and by 1959 were performing at local dances as Tommy Fogerty and the Blue Velvets. In 1964 the quartet signed to San Francisco–based Fantasy Records, where Tom had been

Creedence Clearwater Revival: Tom Fogerty, Doug Clifford, Stu Cook, John Fogerty

working as a packing and shipping clerk. The label renamed them the Golliwogs and began putting out singles. "Brown-Eyed Girl" sold 10,000 copies in 1965, but the followups were flops. Greater success came after they adopted the CCR moniker in 1967.

Several Fogerty compositions appeared on *Creedence Clearwater Revival,* but cover versions of Dale Hawkins' "Suzie Q" and Screamin' Jay Hawkins' "I Put a Spell on You" were the group's first hit singles. With the release of *Bayou Country* it became the most popular rock band in America. Beginning with the two-sided gold hit "Proud Mary" (#2, 1969) b/w "Born on the Bayou," Creedence dominated Top Forty radio for two years without disappointing the anticommercial element of the rock audience.

CCR's rough-hewn rockers often dealt with political and cultural issues, and the quartet appeared at the Woodstock Festival. Creedence had seven major hit singles in 1969 and 1970, including "Bad Moon Rising" (#2, 1969), "Green River" (#2, 1969), "Fortunate Son" (#14, 1969), "Down on the Corner" (#3, 1969), "Travelin' Band" (#2, 1970), "Up Around the Bend" (#4, 1970), and "Lookin' Out My Back Door" (#2, 1970).

Although Creedence's success continued after *Cosmo's Factory,* it was the group's artistic peak. Internal dissension, primarily the result of John Fogerty's dominant role, began to pull the band apart in the early Seventies. Tom left in January 1971, one month after the release of the pivotal *Pendulum,* which became the group's fifth platinum album. It carried on as a trio, touring worldwide; *Live in Europe* was the recorded result. CCR's final album, *Mardi Gras,* gave Cook and Clifford an equal share of the songwriting and lead vocals. Not coincidentally, it was the band's first not to go platinum. Creedence disbanded in October 1972, and Fantasy has subsequently released a number of albums, including a live recording of a 1970 Oakland concert, which upon original release was erroneously titled *Live at Albert Hall* (it was later retitled *The Concert*).

Tom Fogerty released a number of albums on his own and with his band Ruby and worked occasionally in the early Seventies with organist Merl Saunders and Grateful Dead guitarist Jerry Garcia. He moved to Arizona in the mid-Eighties and died there from respiratory failure brought on by tuberculosis in 1990 at age 48. Clifford released a solo album in 1972 of Fifties-style rock & roll. Thereafter, he and Cook provided the rhythm sections for Doug Sahm on his 1974 LP and the Don Harrison Band after 1976. In the mid-Eighties Cook joined country group Southern Pacific, which had several hits.

Not surprisingly, John Fogerty's solo pursuits have attracted the greatest attention. Immediately after the breakup he released a bluegrass/country album, *The Blue Ridge Rangers,* on which he played all the instruments. Two songs, the Hank Williams classic "Jambalaya (On the Bayou)" and "Hearts of Stone," made the Top Forty. Nearly three years passed before his next LP, another one-man show titled *John Fogerty.* It sold poorly, and his next album, to be called *Hoodoo,* was rejected by Asylum Records. Unhappy with the music business, Fogerty and his family retired to a farm in rural Oregon. Except for two brief Creedence reunions—at Tom Fogerty's 1980 wedding and at a school reunion three years later—he was not heard from for ten years.

He emerged with *Centerfield* (#1, 1985), a typically simple, tuneful collection that sold two million copies and produced hit singles in "The Old Man Down the Road" (#10, 1985), "Rock and Roll Girls" (#20, 1985), and "Centerfield" (#44, 1985). "Old Man" and another song from the album, "Zanz Kant Danz," landed Fogerty in legal trouble, however. The latter, a thinly veiled attack against Fantasy owner Saul Zaentz ("Zanz can't dance but he'll steal your money"), led Zaentz to sue for $142 million, not only over that song, but over "Old Man": Fantasy claimed the song plagiarized the music of the 1970 CCR B side "Run Through the Jungle." In 1988 a jury ruled in Fogerty's favor; six years later the Supreme Court ordered Fantasy to reimburse Fogerty for over $1 million in lawyers' fees.

For years Fogerty refused to perform CCR songs live; he'd had to surrender his artist's royalties on them to get out of his Fantasy contract in the Seventies. But during a July 4, 1987, concert for Vietnam veterans in Washington, D.C., he broke his boycott, singing eight Creedence classics. Since then, he has once again dropped largely out of sight, surfacing only for the annual Rock and Roll Hall of Fame induction ceremonies; in 1993 his own turn came when CCR were inducted into the hall. As of 1994, Fogerty was rumored to be working on a new LP; but then, the same has been said every year since 1986's gold *Eye of the Zombie.*

Marshall Crenshaw

Born Marshall Howard Crenshaw, November 11, 1953, Detroit, Michigan
1982—*Marshall Crenshaw* (Warner Bros.)   1983— *Field Day*   1985—*Downtown*   1987—*Mary Jean & 9 Others*   1989—*Good Evening*   1991—*Life's Too Short* (Paradox/MCA)   1994—*My Truck Is My Home* (Razor & Tie).

From his portrayal of John Lennon in the traveling Seventies stage show Beatlemania to his role as Buddy Holly in the 1987 film La Bamba, Marshall Crenshaw has breathed new life into old forms. His solidly crafted rootsy pop albums have been praised for their tunefulness, spirit, and romantic lyrics.

Crenshaw grew up in a musical family—his brother, Robert Crenshaw, has drummed in his band—in suburban Detroit, where he listened to Sixties pop/AM radio and rockabilly. He began playing guitar when he was six. After high school he performed in oldies bands until he moved to Los Angeles and got the role in *Beatlemania.* He quit after two years and in 1980 moved to New York City, where he gigged around town and won praise for his original tunes and solid musicianship. His debut, released to much acclaim, contains his biggest hit to date, "Someday Someway" (#36).

Crenshaw's songs have been covered by Bette Midler, the Nitty Gritty Dirt Band, and Robert Gordon. In the U.K. Owen Paul took the Crenshaw B side "My Favorite Waste of Time" to #3. A musical aficionado, Crenshaw has recorded songs by Richard Thompson, John Hiatt, Bobby Fuller, the Isley Brothers, and Chris Knox. By *Good Evening,* his lack of success had eaten away at his relationship with Warners, and he was barely writing songs; in one last (unsuccessful) bid for stardom, he recorded a Diane Warren tune, then moved to MCA.

Crenshaw's acting career includes an appearance in *Peggy Sue Got Married.* He turned down the lead in the London stage production of *Buddy,* however, because he considered the show blindly nostalgic. Enlisting fellow pop-culture trivia buffs, Crenshaw oversaw and wrote reviews for *Hollywood Rock: A Guide to Rock 'n' Roll in the Movies* in 1994.

The Crests

Formed 1956, New York City, New York
Johnny Maestro (b. John Mastrangelo, May 7, 1939, Brooklyn, N.Y.), voc.; Tommy Gough, voc.; Jay Carter, voc.; Harold Torres, voc.; Patricia Van Dross or Vandross, voc.
1960—*The Crests' Biggest Hits* (Coed); *The Crests Sing All the Biggies*   1990—*Best of the Crests* (Rhino).

A rare doo-wop group—its lineup included two black men, a black woman, an Italian, and a Puerto Rican—the

Crests recorded a few popular doo-wop sides (including "My Juanita," "No One to Love") in 1957 before signing to Coed Records. Forbidden to go on tour by her mother, Patricia Vandross quit the group (her younger brother is Luther Vandross). The remaining quartet went on to record a series of hits, including "16 Candles" (#2, 1959) and "Step by Step" (#14, 1960). Maestro went solo in 1960, with initially disappointing results, and James Ancrum replaced him, but the Crests' headlining days were finished. In 1968 Maestro began singing with the Del-Satins, which later evolved into the Brooklyn Bridge [see entry].

Crime and the City Solution: See the Birthday Party

The Critters
Formed circa early 1960s, New Jersey
Don Ciccone (b. Feb. 26, 1946, New York, N.Y.), gtr., voc.; James Ryan (b. 1947, Plainfield, N.J.), gtr.; Kenneth Gorka (b. 1947, East Orange, N.J.), bass; Christopher Daraway (b. 1947, Brooklyn, N.Y.), organ; Jack Decker (b. 1947, Newark, N.J.), drums.
1966—*The Critters* (Project 3); *Younger Girl* (Kapp); *Touch 'n' Go with the Critters* (Project 3) 1994— *Anthology: The Complete Kapp Recordings, 1965–1967* (Taragon).

With a mellow pop style similar to the Association's, the Critters had three minor pop hits in 1966 on Kapp Records, including a cover of the Lovin' Spoonful's "Younger Girl" and their only Top Twenty entry, the gentle "Mr. Dieingly Sad." They had one minor followup in 1967, "Don't Let the Rain Fall Down on Me." Originally called the Vibratones, they were formed by guitarist/vocalist Don Ciccone, who later joined the Four Seasons [see entry] and was instrumental in the latter's substantial mid-Seventies comeback.

Jim Croce
Born January 10, 1943, Philadelphia, Pennsylvania; died September 20, 1973, Natchitoches, Louisiana
1969—*Approaching Day* (Capitol); *Croce* 1972— *You Don't Mess Around with Jim* (ABC) 1973—*Life and Times*; *I Got a Name* 1974—*Photographs and Memories: His Greatest Hits* (ABC); *The Faces I've Been* (Lifesong) 1977—*Time in a Bottle: Jim Croce's Greatest Love Songs* (21 Records/Atlantic).

Singer/songwriter Croce had several early-Seventies hits before he died in a plane crash. Croce began playing guitar professionally at 18, when he entered Villanova University. There he hosted a folk and blues show on campus radio and played in local bands. After graduation he did construction work and had to alter his guitar

technique after breaking a finger with a sledge hammer. By 1967 he was living in New York City and playing the coffeehouse circuit. He and his wife, Ingrid, released *Approaching Day* on Capitol that year. When it failed to chart he returned to club work and drove trucks.

In 1971 he submitted some songs to producer Tommy West, an old college chum. With partner Terry Cashman, West helped Croce cut *You Don't Mess Around with Jim*. Released in early 1972, it produced two hit singles, "Operator" (#17, 1972) and the title track (#8, 1972). *Life and Times* and "Bad, Bad Leroy Brown" (#1, 1973) followed. He was killed when his chartered plane crashed into a tree soon after takeoff on September 20, 1973, in Louisiana. Among the five other victims of the crash was his longtime guitarist Maury Muehleisen. (Croce, in fact, had supported Muehleisen on his own Capitol album, *Gingerbread*.)

I Got a Name, completed before Croce's death and released in late 1973, went gold, as did its #10 title track and "Time in a Bottle" (#1, 1973). Within months of Croce's death, three of his LPs were in the Top Twenty: *Life and Times*, *I Got a Name*, and *You Don't Mess Around with Jim*. The last reigned at #1 for five weeks in early 1974. In 1984 the singer's widow Ingrid opened a San Diego club called Croce's, where his son, A.J., performs.

Steve Cropper: See Booker T. and the MG's; Blues Brothers

Crosby, Stills, Nash and Young
Formed 1968, Los Angeles, California
David Crosby (b. David Van Cortland, Aug. 14, 1941, Los Angeles), gtr., voc.; Stephen Stills (b. Jan. 3, 1945, Dallas, Tex.), gtr., kybds., bass, voc.; Graham Nash (b. Feb. 2, 1942, Blackpool, Eng.), gtr., kybds., voc.; Neil Young (b. Nov. 12, 1945, Toronto, Can.), gtr., voc.
Crosby, Stills and Nash: 1969—*Crosby, Stills and Nash* (Atlantic) 1977—*CSN* 1980—*Replay* 1982—*Daylight Again* 1983—*Allies* 1990—*Live It Up* 1991—*CSN* 1994—*After the Storm*.
Crosby, Stills, Nash and Young: 1970—*Déjà Vu* (Atlantic) 1971—*Four Way Street* 1974—*So Far* 1988—*American Dream*.
Crosby and Nash: 1972—*Graham Nash/David Crosby* (Atlantic) 1975—*Wind on the Water* (ABC) 1976—*Whistling Down the Wire* 1977—*Crosby-Nash Live* 1978—*Crosby & Nash Greatest Hits*.
David Crosby solo: 1971—*If I Could Only Remember My Name* (Atlantic) 1989—*Oh Yes I Can* (A&M) 1993—*Thousand Roads* (Atlantic) 1994—*It's All Coming Back to Me Now*.
Graham Nash solo: 1971—*Songs for Beginners* (At-

lantic) 1973—*Wild Tales* 1980—*Earth and Sky*
(EMI) 1986—*Innocent Eyes* (Atlantic).
Stephen Stills solo: 1970—*Stephen Stills* (Atlantic)
1971—*Stephen Stills 2* 1972—*Manassas* (with
Manassas) 1973—*Manassas Down the Road* (with
Manassas) 1975—*Stills* (Columbia); *Stephen Stills*
Live (Atlantic) 1976—*Illegal Stills* (Columbia); *Still*
Stills: The Best of Stephen Stills (Atlantic) 1978—
Thoroughfare Gap (Columbia) 1984—*Right by You*
(Atlantic) 1991—*Stills Alone* (Vision).
The Stills-Young Band: 1976—*Long May You Run*
(Reprise).

The close high harmonies and soft-rock songs of David
Crosby, Stephen Stills, and Graham Nash, sometimes
joined by Neil Young, sold millions of albums and were
widely imitated throughout the Seventies. The members
were as volatile as their songs were dulcet, and since
1970 have continually split up and regrouped. Crosby,
Stills and Nash—all singers, songwriters, and guitarists—had already recorded before their debut LP,
Crosby, Stills and Nash, was released in 1969: Crosby
with the Byrds [see entry], Stills and Young with Buffalo
Springfield [see entry], and Nash with the Hollies [see
entry].

Crosby had worked as a solo performer before joining the Byrds in 1964. In 1967 he quit because of differences with leader Roger McGuinn, among them
McGuinn's refusal to record Crosby's "Triad," a song
about a menage à trois that the Jefferson Airplane
recorded on *Crown of Creation;* Crosby sang it on *Four
Way Street.* After leaving the Byrds, Crosby began preparation for a solo album, which eventually appeared in
1971 as *If I Could Only Remember My Name.* He also
produced Joni Mitchell's debut album in 1968; Mitchell's
"Woodstock" later became a hit for Crosby, Stills, Nash
and Young.

Young had quit Buffalo Springfield on the eve of the
1967 Monterey Pop Festival, and Crosby sat in for him at
that concert. After the Springfield broke up in May 1968,
Stills and Crosby began jamming together and were
soon joined by Nash. Nash, who had been dissatisfied
with the Hollies—they had refused to record "Marrakesh
Express" and "Lady of the Island"—joined Crosby and
Stills.

Recorded early in 1969, *Crosby, Stills and Nash* was
an immediate hit, with singles "Marrakesh Express"
(#28) and Stills' "Suite: Judy Blue Eyes" (#21) (about Judy
Collins). Although their harmonies were less than perfect
outside the recording studio, Crosby, Stills, Nash and
Young (who joined them in summer 1969) began touring
in midyear. Their second live appearance was before half
a million people at the Woodstock Festival in August
1969.

The quartet's first album, *Déjà Vu,* took two months

to make, but had advance orders for two million copies
and included three hit singles: "Woodstock" (#11, 1970),
"Teach Your Children" (#16, 1970), and "Our House" (#30,
1970). A few weeks after *Déjà Vu* was released, the National Guard shot and killed four students in an antiwar
demonstration at Kent State University, and Young wrote
"Ohio," which the group recorded and released as a single (#14, 1970). They toured that summer, but by the time
the live album *Four Way Street* was released, they had
disbanded.

Crosby and Nash released solo and duo albums in
the early Seventies and toured together, while Young returned to his solo career [see entry], and Stills started his.
Stills' solo debut, which included "Love the One You're
With" (#4, 1971), featured guest guitarists Eric Clapton
and Jimi Hendrix. In 1974 the quartet toured together for
the last time; Young traveled separately. Stills and Young
made a duet album, *Long May You Run,* in 1976, but
Young suddenly left Stills midtour.

In 1977 Crosby, Stills and Nash regrouped for the
quadruple-platinum *CSN,* which included "Just a Song
Before I Go" (#7, 1977). The next summer they toured as
an acoustic trio, and in the fall of 1979 they performed at
the antinuclear benefit concerts sponsored by Musicians
United for Safe Energy. In 1980 Nash was granted American citizenship. In 1982 the trio released *Daylight
Again,* for which Stills wrote most of the songs, and
toured arenas once more. *Daylight* was a Top Ten LP and
boasted two Top Twenty singles, "Wasted on the Way"
(#9) and "Southern Cross" (#18).

In 1985 Crosby—who'd had a number of run-ins
with the law and been charged with drug and weapons
possession before—was sentenced to prison after leaving the drug rehabilitation program he was allowed to
enter in lieu of serving a five-year prison sentence for
possessing cocaine and carrying a gun. He appeared
with Crosby, Stills, Nash and Young at Live Aid while out
on appeal bond. Shortly after his release from prison in
1986, he wrote a compelling account of his long-term
drug abuse entitled *Long Time Gone,* which was published in 1990. The four reunited to record the last quartet album to date, *American Dream* (#16, 1989), after
which Young refused to tour with his ex-bandmates. The
trio's next album, *CSN,* did not crack the Top 100. Yet the
group maintains a large and loyal following, and their
concerts continue to draw fans. Crosby and Nash have
worked in television; Crosby on *Shannon's Deal* and
Roseanne, and Nash with his own cable-television talk
show. Shortly after the release of *After the Storm* in 1994,
Crosby received a liver transplant.

Christopher Cross

Born Christopher Geppert, circa 1951, San Antonio,
Texas
1980—*Christopher Cross* (Warner Bros.) 1983—*An-*

other Page 1985—*Every Turn of the World*
1988—*Back of My Mind* (Reprise).

By his late teens Christopher Cross was fronting a copy band in Texas clubs that, in 1972, was ranked Austin's leading cover band. Cross kept writing his own songs as well, and was finally signed by Warner Bros. in fall 1978. When his debut LP was released two years later, it went quadruple platinum and yielded four Top Twenty hits: "Sailing" (#1); "Ride Like the Wind" (#2), which featured backing vocals by Michael McDonald; "Never Be the Same" (#15); and "Say You'll Be Mine" (#20).

In 1980 Cross won five Grammy Awards, including Record of the Year, Album of the Year, and Song of the Year. His debut LP was still going strong on the chart in late 1981. In the fall of that year Cross had another massive hit with "Arthur's Theme (The Best That You Can Do)" (from the hit film *Arthur*), a song cowritten by Cross, Peter Allen, Burt Bacharach, and Carole Bayer Sager. It received an Academy Award for Best Original Song. His star soon faded: *Every Turn of the World* (#127, 1985) met mediocre sales, and yielded only a minor hit single in "Charm the Snake" (#68, 1985); his final album, *Back of My Mind*, featured McDonald on backing vocals again, but still flopped.

Sheryl Crow
Born February 11, 1962, Kennett, Missouri
1993—*Tuesday Night Music Club* (A&M).

Once a backup singer for Michael Jackson and Don Henley, Sheryl Crow gained mass popularity as a solo artist almost a year after the release of her 1993 debut album, *Tuesday Night Music Club*, which rose up the charts after Crow's appearance at Woodstock '94.

Crow grew up in a rural farming community in Missouri. Exposed to music all her life—her parents were amateur musicians who often played in big bands in Memphis, Tennessee—she started singing in rock groups at 16. After receiving a degree in classical piano from the University of Missouri, Crow taught music at a St. Louis elementary school. Then, in 1986, the aspiring singer/songwriter moved to Los Angeles to pursue a career in the music business. Her first big gig was singing backup on Michael Jackson's 1987–88 *Bad* Tour. She was also a backup singer for Don Henley, George Harrison, Joe Cocker, Stevie Wonder, and Rod Stewart.

In 1991 Crow signed with A&M. She recorded a self-titled debut album the next year, but then convinced the record company to scrap it because of its slick production. She replaced it with the rawer *Tuesday Night Music Club* (#3, 1994), which was recorded with a loose-knit group of musicians who gathered on Tuesday nights at producer Bill Bottrell's Los Angeles studio. The supportive atmosphere encouraged Crow to focus her writing on her personal experiences: The album's "What I Can Do for You" discusses sexual harassment and "No One Said It Would Be Easy" deals with a relationship's dissolution. The often boozy evenings also produced more lighthearted songs, including "Leaving Las Vegas," a group collaboration written on the first Tuesday get-together, and "All I Wanna Do" (#2, 1994); the latter received a Grammy as 1994's Record of the Year.

Crowded House
Formed July 1985, Melbourne, Australia
Neil Finn (b. May 27, 1958, Te Awamutu, New Zealand), voc., gtr.; Paul Hester (b. Jan. 8, 1959, Melbourne), drums; Nick Seymour (b. Dec. 9, 1958, Benella, Austral.), bass.
1986—*Crowded House* (Capitol) 1988—*Temple of Low Men* 1989—*I Feel Possessed* EP 1991—(+ Tim Finn [b. June 25, 1952, Te Awamutu, N.Z.], kybds., voc.) *Woodface* 1993—(– Tim Finn; + Mark Hart [b. July 2, 1953, Fort Scott, Kan.], kybds.) *Together Alone*.

Formed by two ex-members of the eccentric, cult-favored pop outfit Split Enz, Crowded House quickly eclipsed that band's popularity, thanks to a debut album of buoyant, impeccably crafted guitar pop. With their radiant melodies and breezy wit, the songs written by Crowded House's singer/guitarist Neil Finn invited references to the work of such smart pop icons as Squeeze, the Kinks, and the Beatles.

Finn got his start playing in Split Enz [see entry], which was fronted by his big brother Tim, as a teenager. After the group's demise—precipitated by Tim's decision to pursue a solo career—Neil decided to form a band with Paul Hester, a drummer who had joined the latterday Enz. After enlisting bassist Nick Seymour, the trio Crowded House released its eponymous debut album in 1986, to widespread acclaim. Commercial success wasn't immediate, but the album spawned two Top Ten hits in 1987, the wistful ballad "Don't Dream It's Over" (#2) and the more upbeat "Something So Strong" (#7). A moodier sophomore album, 1988's *Temple of Low Men* (#40), got some good notices but sold poorly.

In 1991 Crowded House resurfaced as a quartet: Tim Finn joined as keyboardist and vocalist/songwriter for *Woodface*. The album did well on the modern-rock charts, but again yielded no pop hits; after touring with the group that year, the elder Finn returned to his critically praised (but commercially less distinguished) solo career. Crowded House remained a four-piece band, though, replacing Tim with American musician Mark Hart for 1993's *Together Alone*.

Rodney Crowell
Born August 7, 1950, Houston, Texas
1978—*Ain't Living Long Like This* (Warner Bros.)

1980—*But What Will the Neighbors Think*   1981—
Rodney Crowell   1986—*Street Language* (Colum-
bia)   1988—*Diamonds & Dirt*   1989—*Keys to the
Highway; The Rodney Crowell Collection* (Warner
Bros.)   1992—*Life Is Messy* (Columbia)   1993—
Greatest Hits   1994—*Let the Picture Paint Itself*
(MCA)   1995—*Jewel of the South.*

Rodney Crowell is a country-rock singer/songwriter best
known for his production work and his compositions
performed by other singers, particularly Rosanne Cash,
to whom he was married for 13 years. Crowell's performance of his own confessional songs, many of which
were inspired by his rocky marrige to Cash, have earned
him more critical acclaim than country or pop chart success.

He began drumming in his father's Houston rockabilly band when he was 11 years old, and he played with
garage rock & roll bands in his high school and college
years before moving to Nashville in the early Seventies.
Jerry Reed got him a staff songwriting job and recorded
several of his songs.

In 1975 Crowell joined Emmylou Harris' Hot Band as
backup singer and guitarist, and Harris subsequently
recorded more than a dozen Crowell originals ("Leaving
Louisiana in the Broad Daylight," "Amarillo"). In 1978
Crowell left the Hot Band to make his recording debut,
produced by Harris' then-husband, Brian Ahern; guest
musicians included Willie Nelson, Ry Cooder, and Mac
Rebennack (Dr. John). The album sold fewer than 20,000
copies, but two years later the title song hit #1 on the
country charts twice, in separate versions by Waylon
Jennings and the Oak Ridge Boys. Other Crowell interpreters have included Carlene Carter, Willie Nelson, the
Dirt Band, Bob Seger, Alan Jackson, Trisha Yearwood,
Jimmy Buffett, and Foghat.

In 1979 Crowell began producing Rosanne Cash [see
entry], whom he married later that year. He had a hit of
his own in 1980 with "Ashes by Now," which made the
pop Top Forty. In addition to his own albums and his
wife's Eighties LPs, he has produced albums by Guy
Clark, Bobby Bare, Carl Perkins, Johnny Cash, Jerry Lee
Lewis, and Jim Lauderdale, among others. In 1985, along
with his wife, he ended a cocaine dependence.

Crowell finally attained country chart success with
1988's *Diamonds & Dirt,* which netted him five #1 C&W
singles, including a duet with Rosanne Cash, "It's Such a
Small World" (his first-ever Top Ten country single).
Crowell became the first country artist to have five self-
penned #1 C&W hits from one album. His increasingly
confessional songs, many of whose lyrics reflected the
tumultuous state of his marriage, turned up on his wife's
albums as well as his own. *Keys to the Highway* (1989)
was a moving testament to his father, who had died just
before the album's recording.

In 1992 Crowell and Cash divorced, resulting in
many of the songs on *Life Is Messy.* The album featured
such guest artists as Linda Ronstadt and Steve Winwood. Crowell left Columbia for MCA in 1994, releasing
the more upbeat *Let the Picture Paint Itself.*

The Crows

Formed circa 1951, New York City, New York
Daniel "Sonny" Norton (d. 1972), lead voc.; William
Davis, baritone voc.; Harold Major, tenor voc.; Jerry
Wittick, tenor voc.; Gerald Hamilton (d. ca. Sixties),
bass voc.
1952—(– Wittick; + Mark Jackson, gtr., tenor voc.).

The Crows' 1954 pop hit "Gee" (#14 pop, #6 R&B) was
one of the first records by a black group to cross over into
the pop market. The group, which perfected its sound on
Harlem streetcorners, released two flop sides with singer
Viola Watkins ("Seven Lonely Days" b/w "No Help
Wanted") for the newly formed Rama Records in 1953.
Under the guidance of label head George Goldner the
group next recorded William Davis' "Gee," the Crows'
only pop hit. Its success prompted Goldner to launch a
subsidiary label, Gee, in 1956 (its roster included Frankie
Lymon and the Cleftones). The flip side of "Gee," "I Love
You So," was a Top Fifty hit for the Chantels in 1958. After
a quick succession of failed singles (including 1954's
"Mambo Shevitz"), Davis joined the Continentals, and
the Crows disbanded.

Arthur "Big Boy" Crudup

Born 1905, Forrest, Mississippi; died March 28, 1974,
Nassawadox, Virginia
1968—*Look on Yonder's Wall* (Delmark)   1969—
***Mean Ole Frisco* (Trip)   1970—*Crudup's Mood* (Del-**
mark)   1971—*Father of Rock 'n' Roll* (RCA)
1974—*Roebuck Man* (Liberty).

Bluesman Arthur "Big Boy" Crudup wrote "That's All
Right, Mama"—one of the first songs Elvis Presley
recorded and his first hit—and other rock standards, including "My Baby Left Me" and "Rock Me Mama."
Crudup grew up in the Deep South, where he sang in
church as a child. In the late Thirties he joined a gospel
group called the Harmonizing Four and moved with
them to Chicago. In 1939 he began playing the guitar
and the blues. A year later he was discovered by Okeh
and Bluebird Records talent scout Lester Melrose, who
helped Crudup get a record deal, but also took advantage of his client's naiveté and never paid him royalties.
Crudup stayed with Melrose until 1947, when he realized
that he was being cheated. Melrose sold Crudup's contract to RCA, but Crudup recorded only sporadically, and
often on other labels under the name Elmore Jones or
Percy Crudup (his son's name).

Crudup recorded through the mid-Fifties until he quit in disgust. "I just give it up," he said later. He was retired from music, digging and selling sweet potatoes, when, during the Sixties, Philadelphia blues promoter Dick Waterman took an interest in him and his business problems. Waterman began working with the American Guild of Artists and Composers in an attempt to collect some of the royalties Melrose (by then deceased) had withheld from Crudup. Waterman eventually collected $60,000 from BMI and reached a settlement with the music publisher Hill and Range.

Crudup resumed his music career in 1968 and toured the U.S. and Europe until his death from a heart attack in 1974. During his lifetime he had supported a family of 13 children, only four of whom were actually his.

Julee Cruise

Born December 1, 1956, Creston, Iowa
1990—*Floating into the Night* (Warner Bros.)
1993—*The Voice of Love*.

Julee Cruise was already a veteran of the musical stage and an accomplished French hornist by the time she lent her breathy, ethereal vocals to David Lynch's bizarre 1986 film *Blue Velvet*. Cruise earned a degree in French horn at Iowa's Drake University, apprenticed with the Chicago Symphony, and acted at Minneapolis' Guthrie Theater and the award-winning Margo Jones Children's Theater. She also acted and sang off-Broadway, and in TV and radio ads.

Her soft, dreamily atmospheric debut album was produced by David Lynch (who also wrote the lyrics) and Angelo Badalamenti, who scored *Blue Velvet* and Lynch's TV series *Twin Peaks* (and, coincidentally, is a French hornist himself). Cruise also sang—while hanging on wires over a stage full of cars, dolls, and writhing dancers—in Lynch and Badalamenti's 1989 performance piece "Industrial Symphony #1," staged at the Brooklyn Academy of Music. In 1992 Cruise toured with the B-52's, replacing Cindy Wilson.

Cruise's 1993 release, *The Voice of Love,* was another lush, narcotic Lynch-Badalamenti collaboration, which featured her songwriting debut, "In My Other World." Cruise is married to Edward Grinnan, an editor for Norman Vincent Peale's *Guidepost* magazine.

The Crusaders/Joe Sample

Formed 1954, Houston, Texas
Wilton Felder (b. Aug. 31, 1940, Houston), tenor sax, bass; Joe Sample (b. Feb. 1, 1939, Houston), kybds.; Nesbert "Stix" Hooper (b. Aug. 15, 1938, Houston), drums; Wayne Henderson (b. Sept. 24, 1939, Houston), trombone.
1971—*Pass the Plate* (Chisa)   1972—*Crusaders 1* (Blue Thumb)   1973—*The 2nd Crusade*; *Unsung*

Heroes; *The Crusaders at Their Best* (Motown) **1974—*Scratch* (Blue Thumb) (+ Larry Carlton [b. Mar. 2, 1948, Torrance, Calif.], gtr.); *Southern Comfort*   1975—*Chain Reaction*   1976—(+ Robert "Pops" Popwell [b. Atlanta, Ga.], bass) *Those Southern Knights*; *The Best of the Crusaders*   1977— (– Henderson) *Free As the Wind* (– Carlton) 1978—*Images* (– Popwell)   1979—*Street Life* (MCA)   1980— *Rhapsody and Blues*   1981—*Standing Tall*   1982—*Royal Jam*   1983—(– Hooper; + Leon "Ndugu" Chancler, drums) *Ghetto Blaster* 1986—*The Good and Bad Times*; *Life in the Modern World*   1987—*The Vocal Album*   1991—(+ Marcus Miller, bass, synth.) *Healing the Wounds* (GRP) 1992—*The Golden Years*.**
Wilton Felder solo: 1978—*We All Have a Star* (ABC) 1980—*Inherit the Wind* (MCA)   1985—*Secrets* 1991—*Nocturnal Moods* (Par).
Nesbert Hooper solo (as Stix Hooper): 1979—*The World Within* (MCA).
Joe Sample solo: 1978—*Rainbow Seeker* (MCA); *Carmel* (ABC/Blue Thumb)   1981—*Voices in the Rain* (MCA)   1983—*The Hunter*   1985—*Oasis* 1986—*Swing Street Cafe*   1987—*Roles*   1989— *Spellbound* (Warner Bros.)   1990—*Ashes to Ashes* 1991—*Collection* (GRP)   1993—*Invitation* (Warner Bros.)   1994—*Did You Feel That?*

After ten years of playing under the name of the Jazz Crusaders and being overlooked by pop, jazz, and soul audiences, the Crusaders became one of popular music's hottest instrumental bands in the Seventies. As session players, they are the world's most successful outfit, having worked on more than 200 gold albums.

Wilton Felder, Joe Sample, and Nesbert Hooper first played together in their Houston high school marching band. They then formed the Swingsters, a bebop jazz and Texas-style R&B group. While attending Texas Southern University, they met Wayne Henderson and, with two other students, formed the Modern Jazz Sextet (a tuxedoed outfit modeled on the Modern Jazz Quartet). In 1958 the four future Crusaders dropped out of college and moved to Los Angeles, where as the Nighthawks, they backed Jackie DeShannon at one point and played dance clubs as far away as Las Vegas until 1961, when they returned to jazz. As the Jazz Crusaders, they landed a record contract from World Pacific Jazz and during the next decade built a modest following. In 1969, frustrated by lack of recognition, the quartet took a year off.

When they reemerged as the Crusaders, their music had changed to a blend of funk vamps and riffs, terse solos, and dance rhythms. Their singles began placing in the R&B Top Forty—"Put It Where You Want It" (#39, 1972), "Don't Let It Get You Down" (#31, 1973), "Keep That Same Old Feeling" (#21, 1976), and "Street Life"

(#17, 1979), sung by Randy Crawford—and the pop Top 100. Most of their Seventies albums went gold, and in 1975 they became the only instrumental band chosen by the Rolling Stones as an opening act. As studio players, the Crusaders backed Steely Dan, Curtis Mayfield, Joni Mitchell, Ray Charles, Van Morrison, Joan Baez, B. B. King, and Barry White, among others.

In 1974 Carlton became the first new full-fledged member in almost 20 years. Felder played both bass and sax in recording sessions until Popwell's induction in 1976. The next year both Henderson and Carlton left, Henderson to go into production work, Carlton to begin his successful solo career. With Popwell's departure, the band was back to the three who had met in their high school band room; this core remained constant until Hooper's departure in 1983, when Leon "Ndugu" Chancler joined as drummer. In 1986 the Crusaders celebrated their 30th anniversary with *The Good and Bad Times*. For 1991's *Healing the Wounds* the group included Sample, Felder, and Marcus Miller on bass and synthesizer. The Crusaders dissolved soon after; Felder and Sample continued to record solo albums. Sample put together a group called the Soul Committee for 1994's *Did You Feel That?*

The Crystals

Formed 1961, Brooklyn, New York
Original lineup: Dee Dee Kennibrew (b. Delores Henry, 1945, Brooklyn), voc.; Dolores "La La" Brooks (b. 1946, Brooklyn), voc.; Mary Thomas (b. 1946, Brooklyn), voc.; Barbara Alston (b. 1945, Brooklyn), voc.; Patricia Wright (b. 1945, Brooklyn), voc.
1963—*He's a Rebel* (Philles).

One of producer Phil Spector's first successful groups, the Crystals had a sultry image. The group was formed by Brooklyn schoolgirls. In 1961 they met Spector while auditioning in New York, and they became the first act signed to his Philles Records. Their first two releases— "There's No Other (Like My Baby)" (#20, 1961) (the B side of "Oh Yeah Maybe Baby") and Barry Mann and Cynthia Weil's "Uptown" (#13, 1962)—were hits, but their third, "He Hit Me (And It Felt Like a Kiss)," was denied airplay when radio programmers objected to the violent implications of its title and lyrics ("He hit me and I was glad . . .").

The group's only #1 hit, Gene Pitney's "He's a Rebel," was not recorded by the Crystals but by a group of L.A. session singers, the Blossoms, fronted by Darlene Love [see entry], who also sang on the followup, "He's Sure the Boy I Love" (#11, 1963). The original Crystals were featured on the 1963 hits "Da Doo Ron Ron" (#3) and "Then He Kissed Me" (#6). But their 1964 releases— "Little Boy" and "All Grown Up"—were unsuccessful, and Spector lost interest in them. They bought their contract back from him and signed with United Artists, but their Motown-influenced singles also failed to hit.

Kennibrew has kept the Crystals active, and since 1986 she—along with Marilyn Byers and Gretchen Gale—have toured consistently.

The Cult

Formed 1983, Brixton, London, England
Ian Astbury (b. Ian Lindsay, May 14, 1962, Heswell, Merseyside, Eng.), voc.; Billy Duffy (b. William H. Duffy, May 12, 1959, Manchester, Eng.), gtr.; Jamie Stewart, bass; Les Warner (b. Feb. 13, 1961), drums.
1984—*Dreamtime* (Beggars Banquet)   1985—*Love* (Sire)   1987—*Electric*   1989—*Sonic Temple* (– Stewart; – Warner)   1991—*Ceremony* (+ Craig Adams [b. Apr. 4, 1962, Otley, Yorkshire, Eng.], bass; + Scott Garrett [b. March 14, 1966, Washington, D.C.], drums)   1994—*The Cult*.

When the Cult first surfaced on the British indie label Beggars Banquet in the early Eighties, its music attempted to bridge the gap between heavy metal and goth-style punk. It wasn't until the group decided to claim the heavy-metal tag in earnest, however, that it finally found its signature sound, which combines the pseudomysticism of the Doors and Led Zeppelin with the hard-rock crunch of AC/DC. For some listeners, the Cult is a brilliant parody; for others, it is the real thing.

Ian Astbury, son of a merchant navy man, formed Southern Death Cult in Bradford, England, in 1981. Two years later he recruited ex–Theatre of Hate guitarist Billy Duffy, a Manchester native who had played in a pre-Smiths combo with Morrissey, and changed the group's name to simply the Cult.

Although the lineup was rounded out on *Dreamtime* by bassist Jamie Stewart and drummer Les Warner, the group's roster was never etched in stone: After that album's release in 1984, the Cult had a succession of drummers, both onstage and in the studio, including Mickey Curry, Big Country's Mark Brzezicki, and future Guns n' Roses drummer Matt Sorum. Over the years, Warner would resurface now and again. By *Ceremony*, both Stewart and Warner were gone for good, and the band's official lineup was back down to original members Astbury and Duffy, soon joined by Craig Adams and Scott Garrett.

The dreamy, layered, almost experimental music on the Cult's 1984 debut kept the band obscure. The group's 1985 major-label debut, *Love*, however, reached #87 and spawned two U.K. Top Twenty singles, "She Sells Sanctuary" and "Rain." With producer Rick Rubin (Beastie Boys, Run-D.M.C.) behind the mixing board for *Electric* (#38, 1987), the Cult was propelled out of cultdom and into the more lucrative heavy-metal arena. The band's subsequent albums fared much better: The platinum-selling *Sonic Temple* reached #10 in 1989, with the singles "Edie (Ciao Baby)" (#93, 1989), a tribute to the late Andy Warhol star/model Edie Sedgwick, and "Fire Woman" (#46, 1989). On *Ceremony* (#25, 1991) Astbury continued his Native American/Robert Bly bonding philosophy in songs such as "Wild Hearted Son" (containing an Indian dance chant), the environmentalist "Earth Mofo," and "Indian."

After a three-year hiatus Astbury and company returned with *The Cult* (#69, 1994), an album closer in sound and spirit to *Love*, but interest in the band had diminished.

Culture Club/Boy George

Formed 1981, London, England
Boy George (b. George O'Dowd, June 14, 1961, Eltham, Kent, Eng.), voc.; Roy Hay (b. Aug. 12, 1961, Southend-on-Sea, Essex, Eng.), gtr., kybds.; Mikey Craig (b. Feb. 15, 1960, London), bass; Jon Moss (b. Sep. 11, 1957, London), drums.
1982—*Kissing to Be Clever* (Virgin) 1983—*Colour by Numbers* 1984—*Waking Up with the House On Fire* 1986— *From Luxury to Heartache* (Virgin/Epic) 1993—*At Worst . . . The Best of Boy George and Culture Club* (SBK).
Boy George solo: 1987—*Sold* (Virgin) 1989—*High Hat* 1991—*The Martyr Mantras* 1995—*Cheapness & Beauty* (EMI).

Led by soulful tenor and ever quotable androgyne Boy George, Culture Club took its blue-eyed soul to the top of the charts. An exponent of London's postpunk New Romantic club scene, which saw disaffected youths sporting flamboyant clothes and makeup, Boy George charmed with his disarming playfulness and basically wholesome wit. Culture Club's music, ridden with sensual rhythms and irresistible hooks, proved equally accessible. George's decidedly feminine makeup, long braided locks, and penchant for long, dresslike tunics clearly stood out amid the other acts in heavy rotation on the then-nascent MTV, where for a time Culture Club was a staple. But after two huge albums, the band and its frontman began a downward spiral that culminated in the Eighties' biggest pop star drug scandal.

George appeared briefly in the Malcolm McLaren–managed pop outfit Bow Wow Wow before meeting bassist Mikey Craig. The two enlisted drummer Jon Moss, who had played with Adam and the Ants and the Damned, and guitarist/keyboardist Roy Hay. Culture Club had its first major hit with the reggae-laced 1982 single "Do You Really Want to Hurt Me," which went to #1 in England and #2 in the U.S. The group's debut album reached America in early 1983, yielding two more Top Ten singles that year, "Time (Clock of the Heart)" (#2, 1983) and "I'll Tumble 4 Ya" (#9, 1983). A second album,

1983's *Colour by Numbers,* shot to #2 and spawned the hits "Church of the Poison Mind" (#10, 1983), "Karma Chameleon" (#1, 1983), "Miss Me Blind" (#5, 1984), and "It's a Miracle" (#13, 1984). Culture Club won the 1983 Grammy for Best New Artist.

A disappointing third album followed, though, and before long rumors were circulating that George was addicted to heroin. Pressured by police raids, the singer publicly revealed his drug habit in July 1986, months after the release of Culture Club's fourth and final album. George was arrested on possession charges and sought treatment with Dr. Meg Patterson, who had helped Eric Clapton and Pete Townshend overcome dependencies. Once weaned off heroin, however, George turned to prescription narcotics. Later that year two of his friends died of drug overdoses—one, musician Michael Rudetsky, at George's home.

After being cleared of charges implicating him in Rudetsky's death, George successfully completed another drug rehabilitation program. Several solo albums followed, producing dance hits in Europe, but George failed to reemerge significantly on the U.S. pop charts until his cover of Dave Berry's 1964 British hit "The Crying Game" was featured in the 1992 film of the same name. Buoyed by the movie's success, the single reached #15. In 1995 George released a new solo album and a telling autobiography, *Take It Like a Man.*

The Cure

Formed 1976, Crawley, England
Robert Smith (b. Apr. 21, 1959, Blackpool, Eng.), gtr., voc.; Michael Dempsey, bass, voc.; Laurence "Lol" Tolhurst (b. Feb. 3, 1959), drums.
1979—*Three Imaginary Boys* (Fiction, U.K.) 1980—*Boys Don't Cry* (– Dempsey; + Simon Gallup [b. June 1, 1960, Surrey, Eng.], bass; + Mathieu Hartley, kybds.); *Seventeen Seconds* (– Hartley) 1981—*Faith; Carnage Visors* cassette (Fiction); . . . *Happily Ever After* 1982—*Pornography* 1983—*The Walk* EP; *Japanese Whispers* 1984—*The Top; Concert: The Cure Live* (Fiction) (+ Porl Thompson [b. Nov. 8, 1957, London, Eng.], gtr.; + Boris Williams [b. Apr. 24, 1957, Versailles, Fr.], drums) 1985—*The Head on the Door* (Elektra) 1986—*Quadpus* EP; *Standing on a Beach: The Singles; Staring at the Sea: The Singles* 1987—*Kiss Me, Kiss Me, Kiss Me* 1988—*The Peel Sessions* EP (Strange Fruit) (+ Roger O'Donnell, kybds.) 1989—*Disintegration* (Elektra) 1990—*Pictures of You* EP; *Integration; All Mixed Up* 1991—*Entreat* (Fiction) (– Tolhurst; – O'Donnell; + Perry Bamonte [b. Sep. 6, 1960, London, Eng.], kybds.) 1992—*Wish* (Elektra) 1993—*Show; Paris.*

Dubbed the "masters of mope rock," the Cure rose from Britain's late-Seventies punk scene to become one of the

The Cure: Simon Gallup, Perry Bamonte, Boris Williams, Robert Smith

biggest-selling "underground" acts of the Eighties. Frontman Robert Smith, who has been described as the "messiah of melancholy" and the "guru of gloom," is known for wearing death-white facial makeup, crimson lipstick, and teased black hair; he is rivaled only by Morrissey as a heartthrob for the discontented. The Cure's goth-pop style is characterized by self-obsessed lyrics, minor-key melodies, and Smith's vexatious whine.

Robert Smith grew up in working-class Crawley, Sussex, a suburb of London. He recalls his childhood years as difficult, a time of run-ins with his parents and the law. At 17 he formed the Easy Cure with childhood friends Laurence Tolhurst and Michael Dempsey as a sort of catharsis for his feelings of frustration. The group's music has remained therapeutic for Smith.

The Cure made its initial splash in the U.K. with the 1979 single "Killing an Arab," which stirred controversy when it reappeared on the mid-Eighties retrospective, *Standing on a Beach: The Singles.* Some U.S. radio DJs used the song, which was inspired by Albert Camus' *The Stranger,* to advance anti-Arab sentiments; the group included a disclaimer with subsequent pressings stating that the song "decries the existence of all prejudice and consequent violence." The Cure's music evolved from

the sparse punk pop of that song and other early singles, including "Boys Don't Cry" and "Jumping Someone Else's Train," to the dirgy, moody music of *Faith* and *Seventeen Seconds,* to the more focused hits on the later albums *Kiss Me, Kiss Me, Kiss Me, Disintegration,* and *Wish.*

While the Cure had been a top hitmaking indie band in the U.K. since the early Eighties, it wasn't until the release of *Standing on a Beach* (and its CD-only counterpart, *Staring at the Sea*) (#48, 1986) that the band moved beyond its cult status in the U.S. *Kiss Me, Kiss Me, Kiss Me* (#35) debuted in June 1987, spawning the minor hits "Why Can't I Be You?" (#54, 1987), "Just Like Heaven" (#40, 1987), and "Hot Hot Hot!!!" (#65, 1988). In 1989 *Disintegration* reached #12 and included the group's biggest hit yet, "Love Song" (#2). *Wish* is the band's most successful album to date, reaching #2 and including the surprisingly upbeat "Friday I'm in Love" (#18).

Curved Air

Formed 1970, England
Sonja Kristina (b. Apr. 14, 1949, Brentwood, Eng.), voc.; Darryl Way, violin, kybds.; Florian Pilkington-Miksa, drums; Ian Eyre, bass; Francis Monkman, synth.
1970—*Air Conditioning* (Warner Bros.)   1971—*Second Album* (– Eyre; + Mike Wedgwood, bass) 1972—*Phantasmagoria* (– Way; – Pilkington-Miksa; – Monkman; + Jim Russell, drums; + Kirby, gtr.; + Eddie Jobson [b. Apr. 28, 1955, Billingham, Eng.], violin, synth.)   1973—*AirCut* (group disbands) 1974—(+ Kristina; + Way; + Pilkington-Miksa; + Monkman; + Phil Kohn, bass)   1975—*Live* (London) (– Pilkington-Miksa; – Monkman; – Kohn; + Tony Reeves, bass; + Mick Jacques, gtr.; + Stewart Copeland [b. July 16, 1952, Va.], drums); *Midnight Wire* (RCA)   1976—*Airborne* (BTM).

Curved Air appeared in 1970 with a female vocalist, classically trained musicians playing electric violins and synthesizers, novel record packaging (their debut was pressed on colored vinyl and enclosed in a transparent cover), and much record company promotion. They attracted an ardent though limited British following that put "Back Street Luv" (from *Second Album*) into the U.K. Top Five.

The group broke up once in mid-career when Eddie Jobson replaced Brian Eno in Roxy Music, Mike Wedgwood joined Caravan, and Kirby was recruited to play with an ersatz Fleetwood Mac. Sonja Kristina, who was by that time the only remaining original member, attempted a solo career before rejoining the London cast of *Hair,* of which she had been a part in the late Sixties. Curved Air was reunited several months later by the original members (Kohn substituting for Eyre) for a once-only British tour in the fall of 1974. That tour resulted in a live album, but prior commitments precluded a permanent regrouping. With new members (most notable of them Stewart Copeland, later of the Police), Kristina and Way maintained the group until its final breakup in 1977. Copeland married Kristina; they have since divorced.

Johnny Cymbal
Born February 3, 1945, Cleveland, Ohio; died March 15, 1993

Johnny Cymbal had two hits: one under his own name, one under the pseudonym of Derek. The first was "Hey Mr. Bassman" (#16, 1963), a self-penned tribute to the bass vocalists on doo-wop records; the prominent bass part was sung by Ronald Bright, who had also appeared on recordings by the Valentines and the Coasters. Cymbal's followups, "Teenage Heaven" and "Dum Dum De Dum," failed to crack the Top Forty. As Derek he hit #11 in 1969 with "Cinnamon." After his followup, "Back Door Man," failed to dent the Top Forty, he returned to his original name. In the Seventies he produced David Cassidy, the Partridge Family, and Gene Pitney; in 1980 he relocated to Nashville and wrote country songs that were recorded by Glen Campbell and the Flying Burrito Brothers, among others. He died of a heart attack at age 48.

Cypress Hill
Formed 1988, Los Angeles, California
B-Real (b. Louis Freese, June 2, 1970, Los Angeles), voc.; Sen Dog (b. Senen Reyes, Nov. 20, 1965, Cuba), voc.; DJ Muggs (b. Lawrence Muggerud, Jan. 28, 1968, Queens, N.Y.), DJ.
1991—*Cypress Hill* (Ruffhouse/Columbia)   1993—*Black Sunday*.

A Latino rap trio based near South-Central Los Angeles, Cypress Hill made a controversial name for itself in the early Nineties by speaking out in favor of marijuana legalization. The trio's songs—characterized by smooth, funky, bass-heavy rhythms, a nasal vocal delivery reminiscent of the Beastie Boys, and hard-hitting musical mixes filled with screaming sirens and car alarms—feature constant references to pot ("cheeba," "blunts," "buddha") and guns.

In 1986 Cuban-born Sen Dog and his younger brother, rapper Mellow Man Ace, formed a group called DVX, which included homeboys B-Real and Muggs. Pioneers of the Latin lingo style, "Spanglish," they became a trio and renamed the group for a neighborhood street when Ace departed for a solo career.

Cypress Hill's self-titled debut reached #31 in 1992

Cypress Hill: DJ Muggs, B-Real, Sen Dog

and remained on the charts for 88 weeks. It contained the controversial single "How I Could Just Kill a Man" (#77, 1992) b/w "The Phuncky Feel One" (#94, 1992). In 1993 the trio released a highly successful followup, the pessimistic *Black Sunday* (#1 pop, #1 R&B, 1993), which gave the group a Top Twenty single via "Insane in the Brain" (#19, 1993).

Cyrkle

Formed 1961, Easton, Pennsylvania
Don Dannemann (b. May 9, 1944, Brooklyn, N.Y.), voc., gtr.; Tom Dawes (b. July 25, 1944, Albany, N.Y.), bass; Marty Fried (b. 1944, Wayside, N.J.), drums.
1966—*Red Rubber Ball* (Columbia) (+ Mike Losekamp [b. 1947, Dayton, Ohio], organ, bass, harmonica) 1967—*Neon*.

Cyrkle had some pop-rock hits in the mid-Sixties, including Paul Simon's "Red Rubber Ball." Don Dannemann, Tom Dawes, and Marty Fried met at Lafayette College in Easton in the early Sixties and formed a trio, the Rhondells, to play at frat parties. By 1963 they were regulars at Eastern Seaboard clubs. In early 1966 Beatles manager Brian Epstein signed the Rhondells, got them a contract with Columbia, and renamed them the Cyrkle—a moniker coined by none other than John Lennon.

Epstein had the group open on the Beatles' summer 1966 U.S. tour. The exposure sent their debut single, "Red Rubber Ball" (written by Paul Simon) to #2. They followed up with "Turndown Day" (#16, 1966), toured steadily through 1967 (including Europe), then broke up the following year. Dannemann has since become a prolific and highly successful composer and singer of commercial jingles.

Billy Ray Cyrus

Born August 25, 1961, Flatwoods, Kentucky
1992—*Some Gave All* (Mercury) 1993—*It Won't Be the Last* 1994—*Storm in the Heartland*.

Not since Vanilla Ice has an entertainer become so hot so fast, or inspired as much derisive backlash, as country singer Billy Ray Cyrus did in 1992. Cyrus' ticket to superstardom was a catchy #1 country single called "Achy Breaky Heart," (#4 pop, 1992) penned by Don Von Tress, which propelled the singer's debut album *Some Gave All* to the top of both pop and country charts. The album sold over nine million copies, and Cyrus eclipsed Garth Brooks—for a while, anyway—as contemporary country's biggest crossover star.

Cyrus began playing guitar at 20, forming a band called Sly Dog. He moved to Los Angeles soon afterward to pursue a recording contract. He wound up selling cars instead, and eventually moved back East to Huntington, West Virginia. Cyrus was signed to Mercury in 1990, and recorded *Some Gave All* with the members of a reformed Sly Dog. The "Achy Breaky Heart" single and video premiered in early 1992, and Mercury promoted them with dance-club contests that made "the Achy-Breaky" a national dance craze. But Cyrus' music, much of which he wrote, was dismissed as fluff by critics and by several of his Nashville peers. The singer's combination of good ole boy simplicity and fussy machismo earned him an unfortunate reputation as a dumb hunk. In a nod to his skeptics, Cyrus called his 1993 sophomore album *It Won't Be the Last* (and it wasn't). The album was actually better received than its predecessor had been, but it didn't spawn any monster hits on the order of "Achy Breaky."

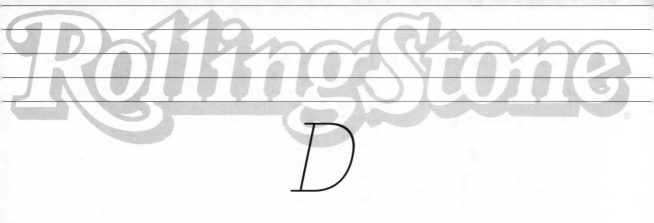

Michael D'Abo: See Manfred Mann

Dick Dale

Born Richard Anthony Monsour, May 4, 1937, Boston, Massachusetts
1962—*Surfer's Choice* (Deltone)   1963—*King of the Surf Guitar* (Capitol); *Checkered Flag*   1964—*Mr. Eliminator*; *Summer Surf*   1984—*The Tigers Loose* (Balboa)   1986—*Greatest Hits* (Crescendo)   1989—*King of the Surf Guitar: The Best of Dick Dale and His Del-tones* (Rhino)   1993—*Tribal Thunder* (Hightone)   1994—*Unknown Territory*.

Guitarist Dick Dale's 1961 West Coast hit "Let's Go Trippin'" (#60 pop), released two months before the Beach Boys' "Surfin'," is considered the harbinger of the Sixties surf-music craze. Billed as the "King of the Surf Guitar," Dale pioneered a musical genre that Beach Boy Brian Wilson and others would later bring to fruition. His twangy, heavily reverbed tone on the 1962 "Misirlou" (which, like "Trippin'," the Beach Boys covered on their early LPs) influenced Beach Boy Carl Wilson and many other California guitarists; his signature staccato slide down the strings was copied by the Chantays to open their classic "Pipeline." Dale said he created this style to mirror the feeling of surfing, which he'd first discovered as a teenager, when his family moved from Boston to Southern California.

"Misirlou" had originally been a Greek pop standard in the Forties; Dale, whose father was Lebanese, often worked Middle Eastern melodies into his music (even recording "Have Nagila" on the flip side of one early single), translating mandolin-style rapid double-picking to his highly amplified Fender Stratocaster. The left-handed Dale played his Strat upside down; he later claimed the young Jimi Hendrix often came to see him perform at the Rendezvous Ballroom in Balboa. Dale developed a close relationship with the Fender company: He was the first to road-test its portable reverb unit, and he designed the Showman amplifier with Leo Fender.

Dale and his band the Del-tones were so popular in Southern California's Huntington Beach/Balboa area that he felt no need to tour nationally. Though he appeared on TV's *Ed Sullivan Show* in 1963, Dale never reaped the commercial rewards of the surf boom; his only other appearance on the chart came in 1963 with "The Scavenger." In 1965, disillusioned with the music business, he retired. The following year doctors found six cancerous tumors in his intestines; he was told he had only months to live, but survived surgery. He re-formed the Del-tones in 1970 and continued performing around Southern California with different versions of the group (ranging from seven to 12 pieces) through the Eighties. Dale rerecorded many of his best-known tunes on the 1986 *Greatest Hits* and recorded *The Tigers Loose* live in Huntington Beach.

Dale's comeback began with a guest appearance in the 1987 Frankie Avalon–Annette Funicello movie *Back to the Beach* (he had appeared in several of their Sixties beach-party epics), in which he and Stevie Ray Vaughan performed "Pipeline." Their version was nominated for a Best Rock Instrumental Grammy. He returned in earnest in 1993, with critics acclaiming the speed-metal ferocity of *Tribal Thunder*, which added a Native American feel to Dale's Bedouin-surf mix, prompted the first nationwide tour of his career, and even brought him to MTV with his first music video, "Nitro." Dale continues to perform as of the mid-Nineties; he gained more prominence via his "Misirlou," which opened the hit film *Pulp Fiction* (1994).

Roger Daltrey: See the Who

The Damned/Captain Sensible

Formed 1976, England

Brian James (b. Brian Robertson), gtr.; Captain Sensible (b. Ray Burns, Apr. 23, 1955, Eng.), bass; Rat Scabies (b. Chris Miller, July 30, 1957, Surrey, Eng.), drums; Dave Vanian (b. David Letts), voc.

1977—*Damned, Damned, Damned* (Stiff) (+ Lu [Robert Edmunds], gtr.; – Scabies; + Jon Moss [b. Sep. 11, 1957, London, Eng.], drums); *Music for Pleasure* 1979—(– James; – Lu; + Alistair Ward [a.k.a. Algy], bass) *Machine Gun Etiquette* (Chiswick) 1980—(– Ward; + Paul Grey, bass) *The Black Album* (I.R.S.) 1981—(+ Roman Jugg, kybds., gtr.) 1982—*Strawberries* (Bronze) 1983— (– Grey) 1984—(– Sensible; + Bryn Merrick, bass) 1985—*Phantasmagoria* (MCA) (– Merrick) 1986— *Anything* 1987—*The Light at the End of the Tunnel* 1989—*Final Damnation* (Restless) 1991—*The Best of the Damned* (Emergo) 1993—*Tales from the Damned* (Cleopatra).
Captain Sensible solo: 1984—*A Day in the Life of Captain Sensible* (A&M).

The Damned were the first British punk band to record, to chart, and to tour America. Their history goes back to early 1975, when Brian James joined Mick Jones in the London S.S., a punk group whose members included Paul Simonon and Terry Chimes (a.k.a. Tory Crimes), who later formed the Clash with Jones; Tony James, who went on to Chelsea and Generation X; and Rat Scabies, with whom Brian James joined Nick Kent's Subterraneans. When Kent returned to writing for the *New Musical Express*, James, Sensible, and Scabies stayed together as the Masters of the Backside. They were managed by Malcolm McLaren (who later managed the Sex Pistols), and their singer was Chrissie Hynde, who later formed the Pretenders [see entry]. Scabies enlisted Vanian, a gravedigger, into the group after overhearing him sing "I Love the Dead" at his sister's funeral.

The four first performed in London in July 1976. They were notorious for their stage act, with Sensible dressed in a tutu and prodding front-row spectators with his bass, Scabies bounding from behind his drums to exchange blows with onlookers, and Vanian as Dracula in a black cape. Stiff Records signed them in September, and in October they released a single, "New Rose," one month before the Sex Pistols' first record. Early in 1977 they released their first album (produced by Nick Lowe, as was "New Rose") and played clubs in New York, Los Angeles, and San Francisco.

Their second album (produced by Nick Mason of Pink Floyd) got a poor reception. Scabies had left to form a group with Patti Smith pianist Richard Sohl and former Clash/future Public Image Ltd. guitarist Keith Levene. He was replaced by Jon Moss for a tour of Britain with the Dead Boys, but by April 1978 the Damned had fallen apart. James formed Tanz der Youth, Moss and second guitarist Lu went to the Edge, and Sensible formed King.

In early 1979 Scabies, Sensible, and Vanian got together again. With bassist Henry Badowski of King they toured Britain as the Doomed—James owned the name "the Damned" and only later relinquished it. Their new records were the most popular of their four years: "Love Song" hit #20 on the U.K. singles chart, and "Smash It Up" made the Top Forty. Later in the year, they returned to the U.S., and in 1980, after Ward had been replaced by Paul Grey, formerly of Eddie and the Hot Rods, they cut their first American-released album. In 1982 Captain Sensible released a solo album in the U.K., *Women and Captains First* (A&M), which included the hit single "Wot" (#26 U.K.). His U.S. solo debut album, *A Day in the Life of Captain Sensible*, contained tracks from his first two albums, which were not released here. James and Dead Boys vocalist Stiv Bators formed the Lords of the New Church [see Dead Boys entry].

In 1984 Captain Sensible left the band, and Bryn Merrick joined. The group's next few singles went Top Forty in the U.K.: "Grimly Fiendish," "The Shadow of Love," and "Is It a Dream" (1985); "Anything" (1986); "Gigolo" and a cover of Love's "Alone Again Or" (1987). The biggest single of the Damned's career was 1986's "Eloise," which went to #3 in their homeland. In the summer of 1989 the group made its farewell concert tour.

Damn Yankees

Formed April 1989, New York City, New York
Ted Nugent (b. Dec. 13, 1948, Detroit, Mich.), gtr., voc.; Jack Blades (b. Apr. 24, 1954, Palm, Calif.), bass, voc.; Tommy Shaw (b. Sept. 11, 1953, Montgomery, Ala.), gtr., voc.; Michael Cartellone (b. June 7, 1962, Cleveland, Ohio), drums.
1990—*Damn Yankees* (Warner Bros.) 1992—*Don't Tread.*

Damn Yankees was the most successful of a spate of late-Eighties groups formed by aging corporate-rock stars—such as Bad English (vocalist John Waite with ex–Journey guitarist Neal Schon) and the Firm (ex–Led Zeppelin guitarist Jimmy Page with ex–Bad Company vocalist Paul Rodgers). Damn Yankees added Ted Nugent's trademark metallic crunch to the polished AOR melodicism of Styx and Night Ranger, the respective former bands of Tommy Shaw and Jack Blades.

Nugent and Shaw met at a record-label convention in 1988, began casually jamming and composing together, then recruited Blades. They later maintained that Damn Yankees was not the record-company-boardroom product it seemed—and in fact, they were turned down by every major label at their first New York City audition.

They finally landed a deal with Warner Bros., and the group's debut album (#13, 1990) went platinum, thanks largely to the anthemic power-ballad "High Enough" (#3, 1990). *Don't Tread* (#22, 1992) yielded the chart single "Where You Goin' Now" (#20, 1992). Nugent, meanwhile, became famous—or infamous—for his outspoken espousal of bow-hunting (which he practiced himself to feed his family) and his verbal attacks on such animal-rights advocates as k.d. lang and Chrissie Hynde [see Ted Nugent entry]. During the band's one-year hiatus in the mid-Nineties, Shaw and Blades collaborated on an album, *Hallucination* (1995).

Dancehall

Dancehall is a precursor to American rap and hip-hop. In Jamaican nightclubs of the Seventies, DJs started talking, or "toasting," over prerecorded tracks that they would manipulate by adjusting the sound system's playback controls. In fact, early rap was an Americanized version of toasting, which itself was a descendent of an African-American tradition of playfully trading insults called "the dozens."

The dancehall that came to prominence in the U.S. in the early Nineties was developed by younger Jamaican artists who borrowed back from rap and hip-hop, incorporating computerized drum tracks and samples into their mixes.

A forerunner of dancehall is the dub-toasting DJ, U-Roy (Ewart Beckford), one of the first Jamaican sound-system DJs to have chart success in the late Sixties. Toasting DJs—including I-Roy, Big Youth, and Dennis Alcapone—proliferated during the Seventies. Modern-day dancehall was born in 1985 when Jamaican producer/label executive King Jammy started using a Casio keyboard to produce computerized reggae. Yellowman (Winston Foster), Jamaica's biggest-selling artist since Bob Marley, gained a worldwide following during the Eighties and is sometimes considered the King of Dancehall. One of the first dancehall club hits in the U.S.

was "Sorry," in 1990, an altered version of Tracy Chapman's "Baby Can I Hold You" sung by Foxy Brown. The song was produced by the team of Steely and Clevie, who took over as Jamaica's hottest backing duo since the legendary reggae rhythm section of Sly and Robbie.

Other modern dancehall artists include the London-based Frighty and Colonel Mite, Super Cat, Shabba Ranks, Ninjaman, Cobra, and the chart-topping Ini Kamoze. Like rap, techno, and house music, dancehall is largely a producer's medium.

The Charlie Daniels Band

Charlie Daniels, born 1937, Wilmington, North Carolina
1970—*Charlie Daniels* (Capitol); *Te John, Grease, and Wolfman* (Kama Sutra) 1972—*Honey in the Rock* 1974—*Way Down Yonder* (reissued as *Whiskey* on Epic, 1977); *Fire on the Mountain* 1975—*Nightrider* 1976—*Saddle Tramp* (Epic); *Volunteer Jam* (Capricorn) 1977—*High Lonesome*; *Midnight Wind* (Epic) 1978—*Volunteer Jam III and IV* 1979—*Million Mile Reflections* 1980—*Full Moon*; *Volunteer Jam VI* 1981—*Volunteer Jam VII* 1982—*Windows* 1983—*A Decade of Hits* 1985— *Me and the Boys* 1987—*Powder Keg* 1988— *Homesick Heroes* 1990—*Simple Man*; *Christmas Time Down South* 1991—*Renegade* 1993—*All-Time Greatest Hits*; *America, I Believe in You* (Liberty) 1994—*The Door* (Sparrow).

Sessionman-turned-bandleader Charlie Daniels worked his way up to platinum sales with heavy touring, an instinct for quasi-political novelty singles and an eclectic repertoire that touched on boogie, bluegrass, country, blues, hard rock, and a bit of Tex-Mex.

The son of a North Carolina lumberman, guitarist and fiddler Daniels turned pro at 21 when he formed the Jaguars. For the next decade (except for five weeks when he worked in a Denver junkyard), he played in Southern bars and roadhouses. In 1964 a song he cowrote, "It Hurts Me," became the B side of Elvis Presley's double-sided hit "Kissin' Cousins." It went Top Thirty. Daniels disbanded the Jaguars and in 1967 settled in Nashville, where he became a session musician, playing guitar, fiddle, bass, and banjo on albums by Bob Dylan, Ringo Starr, Leonard Cohen, and Pete Seeger, and on numerous country sessions. His songs were covered by Tammy Wynette, Gary Stewart, and others. He also worked as a producer, most notably on four albums by the Youngbloods.

In 1971 he started the Charlie Daniels Band, modeled after the Allman Brothers Band, with two drummers and twin lead guitars. *Honey in the Rock* included the talking-bluegrass novelty "Uneasy Rider," a Top Ten hit in 1973. The band played nearly 200 shows a year and built

Charlie Daniels

a loyal following in the South and West. *Nightrider* included the definitive rebel rouser "The South's Gonna Do It" (#29, 1975). Daniels began his annual Volunteer Jam concerts in 1974 in Nashville, and several have been recorded for live albums.

In 1975 Daniels moved to Epic for a reported $3 million contract, recorded *Saddle Tramp,* then realigned his band with three new members. He continued a grueling tour schedule (including benefits in 1976 for presidential candidate Jimmy Carter; he later performed at Carter's inaugural ball) and recorded albums. His multimillion-selling breakthrough, *Million Mile Reflections,* yielded "The Devil Went Down to Georgia" (#3, 1979), for which Daniels received the Best Country Vocal Grammy Award.

Daniels' music often has a political edge. During the Iranian hostage crisis, he had a hit with "In America" (#11, 1980); two years later his version of Dan Daley's "Still in Saigon," concerning the traumas of a Vietnam vet, was a Top Twenty-five hit. The title cut of Daniels' 1990 *Simple Man* called for the lynching of drug dealers, and for rapists and child abusers to be left in swamps, where alligators and snakes could gnaw them to death. In 1993 Daniels switched to Nashville's Liberty Records, with another patriotic anthem in the title cut of *America, I Believe in You.* The following year, Daniels released his first gospel recording. Entitled *The Door,* it featured a songwriting collaboration between Daniels and Steven Curtis Chapman.

Danny and the Juniors

Formed 1957, Philadelphia, Pennsylvania
Danny Rapp (b. May 10, 1941; d. Apr. 5, 1983, Ariz.), lead voc.; Joe Terranova (b. Jan. 30, 1941), baritone; Frank Maffei, second tenor; Dave White (b. David White Tricker), first tenor.
1958—*Rock and Roll Is Here to Stay* (Singular).

Danny and the Juniors are best remembered for their 1958 #1 hit "At the Hop." The foursome, all born in Philadelphia, came together in high school as Juvenairs and were subsequently discovered by music entrepreneur Artie Singer, who became their manager. Together they wrote "At the Hop" and recorded it for the local Singular label (Leon Huff helped with the production). ABC-Paramount picked it up, and it went gold on both sides of the Atlantic. The group toured frequently over the next few years (often as part of disc jockey Alan Freed's revue) and scored a few minor hits, notably the Top Twenty followup "Rock and Roll Is Here to Stay" (1958). By the beginning of the Sixties they'd switched to the Swan label, where they last charted in early 1963. David White Tricker released a solo album on Bell Records in 1971 under his full name. The Juniors' saxophonist, Lenny Baker, cofounded Sha Na Na in the late Sixties. Rapp committed suicide in 1983.

Dante and the Evergreens

Formed late Fifties, Los Angeles, California
Dante Drowty (b. Sep. 8, 1941), lead voc.; Tony Moon (b. Sep. 21, 1941), first tenor; Frank Rosenthal (b. Nov. 12, 1941), bass; Bill Young (b. May 25, 1942), second tenor.

A short-lived novelty act of the early Sixties, Dante and the Evergreens had a big hit with the lighthearted "Alley Oop" (#13, 1960). A competing version by the Hollywood Argyles hit the top of the chart that year. The Evergreens were supposedly formed by high school friends in the Los Angeles area. They cut a demo that struggling producers Lou Adler and Herb Alpert liked, leading to their production of "Alley Oop" and the group's only other chart single, "Time Machine" (1960). Years later Alpert claimed that Dante and the Evergreens were actually himself and Adler.

Danzig

Formed 1986, Los Angeles, California
Glenn Danzig (b. June 23, 1955, Lodi, N.J.), voc.; John Christ (b. Feb. 19, 1965, Baltimore, Md.), gtr.; Eerie Von (b. Aug. 25, 1964, Lodi, N.J.), bass; Chuck Biscuits (b. Apr. 17, Calif.), drums.
1988—*Danzig* (Def American)   1990—*Danzig II—Lucifuge*   1992—*Danzig III: How the Gods Kill*   1993—*Thralldemonsweatlive* EP   1994—*Danzig 4* (American) (– Biscuits; + Joey Castillo [b. Mar. 30, 1966, Gardenia, Calif.], drums).

Danzig is everything about heavy metal parents fear: Satanic, profane, antiauthoritarian, and no doubt proud of its "cult" status. Stentorian, muscular, multitattooed vocalist Glenn Danzig was a member of the Misfits, part of the late-Seventies New York punk scene. Though now cited as an influence by many metal bands, the Misfits never escaped the hardcore ghetto and dissolved. In 1982 Danzig formed Samhain, recruiting Eerie Von, a drummer turned bassist. The addition four years later of Chuck Biscuits and John Christ completed the quartet.

In 1986, Rick Rubin signed Danzig to his Def American label. While critics consider Danzig's music more muscular, varied, and compelling than other metal, stardom eluded the band, although their third LP, *Danzig III—How the Gods Kill,* peaked at #24 in 1992.

In 1994, Danzig garnered attention via *Thralldemonsweatlive's* live version of "Mother" (from *Danzig*), which got a thumbs up from MTV's Beavis and Butthead (#43, 1994). That same year, a song penned by Danzig, "Thirteen," was featured on Johnny Cash's *American Recordings.* Near the year's end, the band's new album, *Danzig 4,* entered the charts at #29.

Terence Trent D'Arby

Born Terence Trent Darby, March 15, 1962, New York City, New York
1987—*Introducing the Hardline According to Terence Trent D'Arby* (Columbia)   1989—*Terence Trent D'Arby's Neither Fish nor Flesh*   1993—*Terence Trent D'Arby's Symphony or Damn (Exploring the Tension Inside the Sweetness)*   1995—*Terence Trent D'Arby's Vibrator* (Work).

American-born, British-based rock & soul singer Terence Trent D'Arby has a voice so flexible that he has been compared to Sam Cooke, Smokey Robinson, Al Green, even Roberta Flack. A media manipulator from day one, in 1987 D'Arby proclaimed his first album among "the most brilliant debuts from any artist in the past ten years" before its release. Reaction to D'Arby's braggadocio and widely publicized "discrepancies" in his early bio was cool. Yet few critics or R&B aficionados failed to note the encyclopedic references to Sixties rock and soul in his style.

Born into a musical Manhattan family—his father played guitar and was a rock & roll fan before becoming a Pentecostal minister—D'Arby (then known as Terry Darby) spent his teen years in DeLand, Florida, where he sang with the DeLand High School Modernaires. He also was an avid boxer.

After studying journalism at the University of Central Florida for a year, he quit to join the Army in 1980 so he could continue boxing. When he refused paratrooper training, the Army assigned Darby to a supply clerk post

Terence Trent D'Arby

in the Third Armored Division in Germany (Elvis Presley's old unit). His interest in Frankfurt's nightlife and renewed desire to sing coincided with an increasing frustration with military life. Shortly after joining the nine-piece, pop-soul combo Touch (in 1989 IMP-Polydor released an album of the group's music, *The Touch with Terence Trent D'Arby: Early Works*), Darby went AWOL. He turned himself in just before his solo signing to Columbia.

In October 1987 D'Arby (with new spelling) released his first single from *Hardline* (#4, 1987), "If You Let Me Stay" (#68); it wasn't until the following January that the handsome, androgynous singer hit #1 with "Wishing Well," whose blend of rock and funk drew comparisons to Prince. His subsequent hit was the romantic "Sign Your Name" (#4, 1988), released in May.

Two years after D'Arby's debut the more experimental *Neither Fish nor Flesh* met with critical kudos but was a commercial flop, yielding no hit singles and reaching only #61. Four years later D'Arby returned with 1993's *Symphony or Damn* (#119), which fared even worse, though it did manage to score a Top 100 single, "Delicate" (#74).

Bobby Darin

Born Walden Robert Cassotto, May 14, 1936, Bronx, New York; died December 20, 1973, Los Angeles, California
1959—*That's All* (Atco)   1960—*This Is Darin*; *Darin at the Copa*   1961—*The Bobby Darin Story*; *Two of a Kind: Bobby Darin with Johnny Mercer*   1967—*If I Were a Carpenter* (Atlantic)   1972—*Bobby Darin* (Motown)   1974—*Darin 1936–1974*   1989—*Capitol Collector's Series* (Capitol)   1991—*Splish Splash: The Best of Bobby Darin, vol. 1* (Atco); *Mack the Knife: The Best of Bobby Darin, vol. 2.*

Although Bobby Darin began his career as one of the most popular Fifties teen idols, he viewed himself as a serious singer, musician, and songwriter. Darin briefly attended Manhattan's Hunter College before dropping out to pursue a music career. He wrote some songs for Don Kirshner's Aldon Music and landed an Atco recording contract in 1957. His records met with little success until label president Ahmet Ertegun produced "Splish Splash," a song that Darin had written in 12 minutes. (He eventually wrote over 75 songs.) Reaching #3 in 1958, it sold over 100,000 copies in less than a month. Three more gold singles followed: "Queen of the Hop" (#9, 1958), his own "Dream Lover" (#2, 1959), and "Mack the Knife" (#15, 1959), for which Darin won two Grammy Awards. Darin was also extremely successful in the U.K., where "Dream Lover" went to #1.

"Beyond the Sea," a remake of a 1945 French hit, "La Mer," clearly indicated the direction Darin was headed. Its swinging, big-band-style arrangements sounded more at home in Vegas than on *American Bandstand,* and in fact, Darin moved quickly onto the nightclub circuit, with appearances at the Copacabana in New York City and the Sahara and Flamingo hotels in Las Vegas. Nineteen-sixty's "Clementine" (#21), "Won't You Come Home Bill Bailey" (#19), and "Artificial Flowers" (#20) were all in this more "adult" vein.

Brash, outspoken, and ambitious (he said he wanted to be "bigger than Sinatra"), Darin was, by many accounts, a man in a hurry. He suggested that this was because he was certain he would die at an early age from a congenital heart defect. He went to Hollywood and made several movies, beginning in 1960 with *Come September* (he later married his leading lady, Sandra Dee) and 1963's *Capt. Newman, M.D.,* for which he received an Oscar nomination. He appeared in approximately eight more films, including *State Fair* (1962).

Darin scored hits with "You Must Have Been a Beautiful Baby" (#5, 1961), "Irresistible You" (#15, 1961), "What'd I Say" (#24, 1962), his own "Things" (#3, 1962), "You're the Reason I'm Living" (#3, 1963), and "18 Yellow Roses" (#10, 1963). A string of nonhit singles led to Darin's 1965 move to folk-rock material by writers like Randy Newman and Tim Hardin, whose "If I Were a Carpenter" (#8, 1966) provided Darin with his first Top Ten single since 1961 and last major hit. (Ironically, Hardin's sole, albeit minor, hit single, "Simple Song of Freedom," was written by Darin.)

He continued to appear in Las Vegas and on TV through the mid-Sixties and worked extensively for Robert Kennedy during his 1968 presidential campaign. Darin claimed to have had a mystical-religious experience at Kennedy's funeral service that prompted him to stop working, sell his possessions, and retreat to a mobile home at Big Sur, California. After more than a year of contemplation he reemerged, bluejeaned and mustachioed, to start his own short-lived label, Direction Records.

Working in a soft-rock vein, he cut an unsuccessful politically oriented album called *Born Walden Robert Cassotto.* The early Seventies found Darin signed to Motown and playing Las Vegas again. His Motown releases were commercially unsuccessful (allegedly, the label still has a number of unreleased tracks), and critics consider them the nadir of his career. He married legal secretary Andrea Joy Yeager in June 1972 (he had divorced Dee in 1967). He died during heart surgery to repair a faulty heart valve in 1973. He was inducted into the Rock and Roll Hall of Fame in 1990.

Das Fürlines

Formed 1985, Black Forest, Germany
Wendy Wild (b. Aug. 31, 1956), voc., banjo, gtr.; Holly Hemlock (b. Oct. 10, 1956), gtr., voc.; Liz Luv (b. Aug. 24, 1960), bass; Deb O'Nair (b. May 7, 1957), kybds., voc.; Rachel Schnitzel (b. Mar. 11, 1958), drums., voc.
1985—*Das Fürlines Go Hog Wild* (Palooka)   1986—*Lost in the Translation*   1987—*Das Fürlines Live at Paddles*   1988—*The Angry Years*   1992—*Bratwurst, Bierhalls & Bustiers: The Box Set.*

One of the most compelling and sensually alluring live bands on the New York postpunk scene, the five-girl Das Fürlines pioneered the punk-polka genre, making their initial splash with *Go Hog Wild,* a sloppy but inspired set of the sort of adrenalized polka that would become the group's signature.

Not much is known about the quintet's early days in its homeland, the Black Forest region of Germany. Soon after its formation, though, the band relocated to New York City and quickly assimilated into the East Village postpunk music scene. The fetching fivesome—Wendy Wild, Holly Hemlock, Liz Luv, Deb O'Nair, and Rachel Schnitzel—became renowned for their elaborate costumes and frenetic performances, which included a storytelling segment and chicken-polka-dancing contests. Though the group seemed the toast of the town—they were featured on such TV shows as *Entertainment Tonight* and *Andy Warhol's 15 Minutes*—a record deal eluded them. Impatiently, they released their debut, *Das Fürlines Go Hog Wild*, on their own vanity label. The promise suggested by such *Hog Wild* cuts as "Polka Palooka" and "Honk 'n' Holler" was more than realized on the frankly sexual second LP, *Lost in the Translation*, on which the comely lasses did breathy polka versions of "Funkytown" ("Polkatown"), "The Immigrant Song," and "Magic Carpet Ride" ("Hofbrau Haus"). With 1987's *Live at Paddles*, the Fürlines transferred the musky heat of their infamous live performances to vinyl. *The Angry Years*, an ambitious concept album based on the self-help classic *Women Who Love Too Much*, sums up the group's erotic command, personal exhaustion, and gluttony in a brilliant rock & roll statement.

The group split up after a 1988 U.S. tour (each Fürline had been horribly betrayed by her mate while on the road, causing irreparable rifts among them). Das Fürlines' contribution to Twentieth-Century American culture is expertly documented on *Bratwurst, Bierhalls & Bustiers*, a four-CD collection of B sides, rare singles, G-strings, outtakes, and spoken-word recipes. The carefully annotated track listings and liner notes—written by their fan-club president, Bebe Dahl—provide each band member's vital statistics and preferences of all sorts.

Cyril Davies
Born 1932, England; died January 7, 1964, England
1970—*The Legendary Cyril Davies* (Folklore, U.K.).

Cyril Davies was a catalyst of the early-Sixties British R&B scene. He began his professional career in the early Fifties as a banjoist in traditional jazz bands and later moved into skiffle, which led him to blues and R&B in the late Fifties. By then Davies was concentrating on singing and playing blues harmonica. He and Alexis Korner opened a series of blues clubs in London's Soho district and jammed with visiting blues performers like Sonny Terry, Brownie McGhee, Memphis Slim, and Muddy Waters.

In the early Sixties Korner and Davies went electric and in 1961 cofounded Blues Incorporated [see Alexis Korner entry], which proved an important breeding ground for future stars like Mick Jagger, Charlie Watts, and Brian Jones (Rolling Stones), and Jack Bruce and Ginger Baker (Cream). Blues Incorporated were the house favorites at London's Marquee Club by the end of 1962, but Davies left the group to form his Cyril Davies All-Stars. Guitarist Jeff Beck, keyboardist Nicky Hopkins, and drummer Mickey Waller were all, at some time, members of the All-Stars, and the group's live performances and recordings inspired a cult following. After Davies died of leukemia, All-Stars vocalist Long John

Baldry shaped his Hoochie Coochie Men from the remains of Davies' band.

Dave and Ray Davies: See the Kinks

The Reverend Gary Davis
Born April 30, 1896, Laurens, South Carolina; died May 5, 1972, Hammonton, New Jersey
N.A.—*Pure Religion* (Prestige, recorded 1960); *The Guitar and Banjo of Rev. Gary Davis* (recorded 1964) 1972—*When I Die I'll Live Again* (Fantasy)   1973—*O, Glory* (Adelphi); *A Little More Faith* (Prestige) 1990—*Reverend Gary Davis at Newport* (Vanguard) 1992—*From Blues to Gospel* (Biograph)   1993—*Blues and Ragtime* (Shanachie).

Influential in both blues and folk, the Reverend Gary Davis' percussive finger-picked guitar style lives through the work of Ry Cooder, Taj Mahal, and Jorma Kaukonen. Davis was born into a poor family. He suffered from ulcerated eyes and was partially blind throughout his youth and totally blind by age 30. When he was five, he taught himself to play the harmonica, and during the next two years he learned banjo and guitar. At 19 Davis enrolled in a school for the blind in Spartanburg, South Carolina.

He jammed the blues with Sonny Terry, Blind Boy Fuller, Big Red, and others, spending the Twenties as an itinerant musician in the Carolinas. By the close of that decade, though, Davis had decided the blues was the "devil's music." He was ordained in 1933 at the Free Baptist Connection Church in Washington, North Carolina, and soon became a popular gospel singer on the revival circuit. In 1935 he was discovered by a talent scout for the New York "race" label Perfect Records, for whom he recorded religious songs. He lived as a street singer for the next three decades in Harlem, recording occasionally (the most noteworthy sessions in 1956 and 1957), and subsisting off his small royalties, music lessons, and passing the plate whenever he had a congregation. He emerged in 1959 at the Newport Folk Festival, then toured America and England and moved his family to Jamaica, Queens. Davis died of a heart attack in 1972.

Mac Davis
Born January 21, 1942, Lubbock, Texas
1971—*I Believe in Music* (Columbia)   1972—*Baby Don't Get Hooked on Me*   1973—*Mac Davis* 1974—*Song Painter; Stop and Smell the Roses* (reissue of *I Believe in Music*)   1975—*All the Love in the World; Burnin' Thing*   1976—*Forever Lovers* 1977—*Thunder in the Afternoon*   1978—*Fantasy* 1979—*Greatest Hits*   1980—*It's Hard to Be Humble* 1981—*Midnight Crazy* (Casablanca)   1982—*Forty*

1984—*Soft Talk*   1985—*Till I Made It with You*
1994—*Will Write Songs for Food* (Columbia).

Mac Davis is a country-pop singer/songwriter whose songs, recorded by himself and by others, have sold millions of records. His father bought him his first guitar at age nine, but it wasn't until after a year at Emory University in Atlanta and after working in Atlanta's probation department that he formed his first rock band.

In the early Sixties Davis became Vee Jay Records' Southern regional sales manager; four and a half years later he worked for Liberty Records. Liberty later sent him to Hollywood to work in its music publishing division. There he sold several of his tunes to major artists: "In the Ghetto," "Memories," and "Don't Cry Daddy" (Elvis Presley); "Friend, Lover, Woman, Wife" (O.C. Smith); "Watching Scotty Grow" (Bobby Goldsboro); "Something's Burning" (Kenny Rogers and the First Edition).

Since he first recorded it, "I Believe in Music" has sold millions of copies in cover versions by over 50 artists. In 1972 a #1 hit, "Baby Don't Get Hooked on Me," started a streak that continued through the mid-Seventies with "Rock and Roll (I Gave You the Best Years of My Life)" (#15, 1975), "One Hell of a Woman" (#11, 1974), and "Stop and Smell the Roses" (#9, 1974). In December 1974 he began hosting his own television variety program, *The Mac Davis Show*.

Later recordings—"Burnin' Thing" (1975), "Forever Lovers" (1976), "It's Hard to Be Humble," "Texas in My Rear View Mirror" (1980)—were less successful. Davis made his film debut in 1979, costarring with Nick Nolte as a quarterback in *North Dallas Forty*. He later starred in the romantic comedy *Cheaper to Keep Her*. In 1981 he signed a personal performance contract at the MGM Grand Hotel in Las Vegas. While he put recordings on hold for the latter half of the Eighties, Davis became a fixture on TV talk shows. In 1992 he made his Broadway debut playing the title character in *Will Rogers Follies*. The following year Dolly Parton recorded Davis' "Slow Dancing with the Moon" as the title track of a new album, which also included another Davis composition, "Full Circle." In 1994 Davis signed a new recording deal with Columbia Nashville and released *Will Write Songs for Food*.

Miles Davis
Born Miles Dewey Davis, May 25, 1926, Alton, Illinois; died September 28, 1991, Santa Monica, California
**1968—*Miles in the Sky* (Columbia); *Filles de Kilimanjaro*   1969—*In a Silent Way*; *Bitches Brew*
1970— *Live at the Fillmore*   1971—*A Tribute to Jack Johnson*; *Live/Evil*   1972—*On the Corner*
1974—*Big Fun*; *Get Up with It*   1976—*Agharta*
1981—*The Man with the Horn*   1982—*We Want Miles*   1983—*Star People*   1984—*Aura; Decoy*
1985—*You're Under Arrest*   1986—*Tutu* (Warner Bros.)   1989—*Amandla*   1992—*Doo-Bop*   1993—*Miles & Quincy Live at Montreux* (with Quincy Jones)   1994—*Live at Newport, 1958 and 1963* (with Thelonious Monk) (Legacy).**

Miles Davis played a crucial and inevitably controversial role in every major development in jazz since the mid-Forties, and no other jazz musician has had so profound an effect on rock. He was the most widely recognized jazz musician of his era, an outspoken social critic and an arbiter of style—in attitude and fashion—as well as music.

Davis was raised in an upper-middle-class black home. In 1941 he began playing semiprofessionally with St. Louis jazz bands. Four years later, his father sent him to study at New York's Juilliard School. Immediately upon arriving in New York City, Davis sought out alto saxophonist Charlie Parker, whom he had met the year before in St. Louis. He became Parker's roommate and protégé, playing in his quintet on the 1945 Savoy sessions, the definitive recordings of the bebop movement. He dropped out of Juilliard and played with Benny Carter, Billy Eckstine, Charles Mingus, and Oscar Pettiford as well as with Parker.

As a trumpeter he was far from virtuosic, but he more than made up for his limitations by emphasizing his strengths: his ear for ensemble sound, his unique phrasing, and a distinctive haunted tone. He started moving away from speedy bop and toward something more introspective. His direction was defined by his collaboration with Gil Evans on the *Birth of the Cool* sessions in 1949 and early '50, playing with a nine-piece band that included Max Roach, John Lewis, Lee Konitz, and Gerry Mulligan using meticulous arrangements by Evans, Mulligan, Lewis, Davis, and Johnny Carisi.

By 1949 Davis had become a heroin addict. He continued to perform and record over the next four years, but his addiction kept his career in low gear until he cleaned up in 1954. The following year, he formed a group with drummer Philly Joe Jones, bassist Paul Chambers, pianist Red Garland and, in his first major exposure, tenor saxophonist John Coltrane. The Miles Davis Quintet quickly established itself as the premier jazz group of the decade.

Between 1958 and 1963 the personnel in Davis' groups—quintets, sextets, and small orchestras—shifted constantly and included pianists Bill Evans and Wynton Kelly, saxophonists Cannonball Adderley, Sonny Stitt, and Hank Mobley, and drummer Jimmy Cobb. Continuing the experiments begun with *Birth of the Cool*, Davis' work moved toward greater complexity—as on his orchestral collaborations with Gil Evans (*Miles Ahead*, 1957; *Porgy and Bess*, 1958; *Sketches of Spain*,

1959; *Quiet Nights,* 1962)—and greater simplicity, as on *Kind of Blue* (1959), where he dispensed with chords as the basis for improvisation in favor of modal scales and tone centers.

In 1963 Davis formed a quintet with bassist Ron Carter, pianist Herbie Hancock [see entry], drummer Tony Williams [see entry], and saxophonist George Coleman, who was replaced by Wayne Shorter in 1965. This group stayed together until 1968. In that time, it exerted as much influence on the jazz of the Sixties as the first Davis quintet had on the jazz of the Fifties. Davis and his sidemen—especially Shorter—wrote a body of original material for the quintet.

In 1968 Davis began the process that eventually brought him to a fusion of jazz and rock. With *Miles in the Sky,* the quintet introduced electric instruments (piano, bass, and George Benson's guitar on one piece) and the steady beat of rock drumming to their sound. With *Filles de Kilimanjaro,* on which Chick Corea [see entry] substituted on some tracks for Hancock, and Dave Holland replaced Carter, the rock influence became more pronounced. *In a Silent Way* featured three keyboardists—Hancock, Corea, and composer Joe Zawinul, on electric pianos and organs—and guitarist John McLaughlin [see entry] in addition to Williams, Shorter, Holland, and Davis. For his next recording sessions he put together what he called "the best damn rock & roll band in the world"—Shorter, McLaughlin, Holland, Corea, and Zawinul, plus organist Larry Young, bassist Harvey Brooks, bass clarinetist Bennie Maupin, and percussionists Jack DeJohnette, Lenny White, Charles Alias, and Jim Riley—and, with no rehearsals and virtually no instructions, let them jam. The result was the historic *Bitches Brew,* a two-LP set that sold over 400,000 copies.

In the three years following *Brew's* release, Davis amassed a rock-star-level following and performed in packed concert halls in America, Europe, and Japan. As his sidemen (who in the early Seventies included pianist Keith Jarrett and percussionists Billy Cobham and Airto Moreira) ventured out on their own, in such bands as Weather Report [see entry] and the Mahavishnu Orchestra [see entry], jazz-rock fusion became one of the dominant new forms.

A car crash that broke both his legs in 1972 put a temporary stop to Davis' activity and marked the beginning of his growing reclusiveness. The recordings he made between 1972 and 1975 advanced the ideas presented on *Bitches Brew,* extracting the percussive qualities of tuned instruments, making greater use of electronics and high-powered amplification, and deemphasizing solos in favor of ensemble funk. His sidemen in the mid-Seventies included bassist Michael Henderson, guitarists Reggie Lucas and Pete Cosey, drummers Al Foster and Mtume, and saxophonists Sonny Fortune and Dave Liebman. *Agharta,* recorded live in Japan in

1975, was his last album of new material for five years. He spent much of that time recuperating from a hip ailment. With the encouragement of his new wife, actress Cicely Tyson, he reemerged in 1981 with a new album and concert appearances. While many old supporters were disappointed by his newly acquired pop clichés (including some vocals), *The Man with the Horn* was his most popular release since *Bitches Brew* and marked his return to live concerts. *We Want Miles* was a live set; *Star People* reenlisted Gil Evans as arranger along with Davis' Eighties sextet: Mike Stern or John Scofield on guitar, Marcus Miller or Tom Barney on electric bass, Bill Evans on saxophone, Al Foster on drums, and Mino Cinelu on percussion.

Davis' music took increasingly commercial turns; he recorded material by Cyndi Lauper and the rock band Scritti Politti (Davis guested on the group's *Provision*), later experimenting with hip-hop and go go music rhythms. Critics generally lambasted the lukewarm funk of Davis' new music, but the trumpeter had reached new heights of popularity, his concerts selling out all over the world and his recordings even making dents in the pop charts. Davis continued to surround himself with young musicians, among them, saxophonists Kenny Garrett and Bob Berg and keyboardist Joey DeFrancesco.

Tutu, Davis' first recording for Warner Bros. after ending his 30-year tenure with Columbia, was a purely studio-created project with Davis' horn the only "live" instrument. *Aura* (recorded in 1985) had Davis in front of Danish arranger Palle Mikkelborg's big band for pieces that harkened back to the protofusion experiments of the late Sixties.

In 1985 Davis contributed to the antiapartheid *Sun City* recording, and the next year he and his band appeared at the televised Amnesty International Concert at Giants Stadium. Davis devoted increasing time to visual art—his paintings were exhibited in galleries and a book devoted to them was published. In 1988 Davis' marriage to Tyson ended, and Gil Evans, his close friend and musical associate, died; the long-rumored adaptation of *Tosca* that the two had been discussing for years never came to fruition.

Davis' quest for increased public recognition led him to TV and film. He appeared on *Miami Vice,* made commercials for a New York jazz radio station, and had a featured role in the 1990 film *Dingo.* Davis also worked on the soundtracks for *Siesta, The Hot Spot,* and *Scrooged.* In 1989, Davis' controversial autobiography (cowritten with poet Quincy Troupe) was published. While detailing Davis' drug problem and romantic involvements, the book was noticeably skimpy in its praise for important Davis collaborators.

In failing health, Davis began to look backward for the first time in his career. (On a 1986 public television special devoted to him, Davis claimed about his past music, "If I had to go back and play like that, I'd have a heart attack or something.") He provided trumpet obbligato on the title track of pianist/vocalist Shirley Horn's *You Won't Forget Me.* (Davis had championed Horn's career back in the early Sixties.)

The summer before his death Davis participated in a career retrospective—something he had always studiously avoided—held at La Villette in Paris. Joining Davis and his current band were important Davis-associated instrumentalists including Jackie McLean, John McLaughlin, Chick Corea, Herbie Hancock, and Wayne Shorter. Shortly after that concert, Davis performed at the Montreux Jazz Festival with a big band led by Quincy Jones, re-creating the legendary Davis–Gil Evans collaborations. In 1990 Davis received the Grammy Award for Lifetime Achievement.

Davis died in September 1991, reportedly suffering from pneumonia, respiratory failure, and a stroke. The posthumously released *Doo-Bop,* a jazz/hip-hop collaborative project with rapper Easy Mo Bee, proved that Davis continued experimenting to the end.

Spencer Davis Group

Formed 1963, Birmingham, England
Original lineup: Spencer Davis (b. July 17, 1942, Swansea, Wales), voc., gtr., harmonica; Pete York (b. Aug. 15, 1942, Middlesborough, Eng.), drums; Steve Winwood (b. May 12, 1948, Birmingham), voc., gtr., kybds.; Muff Winwood (b. Mervyn Winwood, June 14, 1943, Birmingham), bass.
1965—*1st Album* (Sonet, U.K.) 1966—*Second Album* (Fontana, U.K.); *Autumn '66* 1967—*Gimme Some Lovin'* (United Artists); *I'm a Man* (– S. Winwood; – M. Winwood; + Eddie Hardin, drums, voc.; + Phil Sawyer, gtr.; – York; + Nigel Olsson, drums; – Hardin; + Dee Murray [d. Jan. 14, 1992, Atlanta, Ga.], bass) 1968—*The Very Best of the Spencer Davis Group; Spencer Davis Greatest Hits; With Their New Face On* 1969—*Heavies* 1973—*Gluggo* (Vertigo) 1974—*Living on a Back Street* (Mercury) 1987—*The Best of the Spencer Davis Group* (Rhino).
Spencer Davis solo: 1972—*Mousetrap* (United Artists) 1984—*Crossfire* (Allegiance).

The Spencer Davis group was a British R&B-influenced rock band best known for introducing Stevie Winwood [see entry] to the pop audience with "Gimme Some Lovin'" and "I'm a Man." Various Spencer Davis groups continued to record into the Seventies.

Davis was a lecturer on German at the University of Birmingham who moonlighted as a musician. In 1963 he met drummer Pete York and persuaded brothers Steve and Muff Winwood to leave their trad-jazz band. They toured England and parts of the Continent, then moved to London and released "Keep On Running" in 1965. "Gimme Some Lovin'" (written by Davis and the Winwood brothers) went to #7 in early 1967; two months later "I'm a Man" (by Steve Winwood, Davis, and J. Miller) went to #10. Both were driving, repetitive songs that featured young Steve Winwood's lead vocals.

In 1967 Steve Winwood had left to form Traffic [see entry]; his brother Muff moved into producing and A&R work. His credits include producing Dire Straits, Sparks, Squeeze, and the Bay City Rollers. After a few personnel changes, Davis was joined by Nigel Olsson and Dee Murray, who in 1969 went on to join Elton John's band. At that point, Davis ended the group.

From 1969 to 1972 Davis performed in acoustic duos with Alun Davies (later with Cat Stevens) and Peter Jameson, with whom he recorded two bluegrass-influenced albums. He re-formed the Spencer Davis Group with York in 1972, but their albums were ignored. By the late Seventies Davis was working as an independent producer and as a publicist for Island Records. In 1970 he moved to the United States, where he has worked in various capacities in the record business. His solo album *Crossfire* featured such guests as Dusty Springfield and Booker T. Jones. In 1984 he toured the world with his own band, then with Brian Auger and Chris Farlowe. Later in the decade he opened shows for Hall and Oates, among others, and he guested on the television series *Married with Children.*

In the Nineties he is touring with Mike Pinera, Peter Rivera, and Jerry Corbetta in a group called the Classic Rock Allstars. Though he heads his own management firm in Los Angeles, he finds time to perform over 200 dates a year.

Tyrone Davis

Born May 4, 1938, Greenville, Mississippi
1969—*Can I Change My Mind* (Dakar) 1970—*Turn Back the Hands of Time* 1972—*I Had It All the Time; It's All in the Game; Tyrone Davis' Greatest Hits* 1973—*Without You in My Life* 1976—*Love and Touch* (Columbia) 1977—*Let's Be Closer Together* 1978—*I Can't Go On This Way* 1979—*In the Mood with Tyrone Davis* 1980—*I Just Can't Keep On Going* 1981—*Everything in Place* 1982—*The Best of Tyrone Davis; Tyrone Davis* (Highrise) 1991—*I'll Always Love You* (Ichiban) 1992—*The Best of Tyrone Davis* (Rhino); *Something's Mighty Wrong; The Best of the Future Years* 1994—*You Stay on My Mind.*

Romantic mid-tempo ballads like 1969's "Can I Change My Mind" made Davis one of the top black singers of the Seventies. He spent his early years in Mississippi, then at age 14 moved with his family to Saginaw, Michigan. Five years later he went to work in a Chicago steel factory, and there he began to get involved with the local music scene, making friends with Otis Rush, Freddie King, Mighty Joe Young, and Otis Clay. Through Clay he met producer Howard Burrage, who named him Tyrone the Wonder Boy and recorded him for the Four Brothers and Hit Sound labels.

After Burrage died, Davis continued to record but without major success until 1969's "Can I Change My Mind" (#5). Its brassy flourishes, relaxed rhythms, and aggressive horns perfectly complemented Davis' style. More hits followed: "Is It Something You've Got" in spring 1969, and his biggest song, "Turn Back the Hands of Time" (#3, 1970). Davis' later releases ("I'll Be Right Here," "Let Me Back In," "Could I Forget You") were essentially MOR soul. In the mid-Seventies he left Dakar for Columbia Records, where he enjoyed a number of R&B hits, including "In the Mood," "Give It Up (Turn It Loose)," and "Get On Up (Disco)."

Davis continues to record and tour; a 1992 profile states that he has had the same band for 12 years. In the view of many critics, Davis remains a rare and underappreciated talent.

Bobby Day

Born Robert Byrd, July 1, 1930, Fort Worth, Texas; died July 27, 1990, Los Angeles, California
N.A.—*Rockin' with Robin* (Class); *Golden Classics* (Collectables).

Singer Bobby Day is best known for recording bright, driving pop like "Rockin' Robin." As a child, Day moved to L.A. with his family and later met and worked with Johnny Otis. He recorded his own "Little Bitty Pretty One" in late 1957, but Thurston Harris' more rousing version became the hit. Between solo sides, Day was lead vocalist with the Day Birds and then with the Hollywood Flames, whose "Buzz Buzz Buzz" made the Top Twenty in 1957. He released more singles for Class Records, peaking at #2 in 1958 with "Rockin' Robin," replete with bird sounds. Despite stints at several labels (RCA, Rendezvous, Sureshot), Day never again cracked the Top Ten, although "Over and Over," the "Robin" B side, was a #1 hit for the Dave Clark Five in 1965, while a 13-year-old Michael Jackson turned "Rockin' Robin" into a #2 hit in 1972. Shortly before his death from cancer at age 60, Day had appeared on a national oldies tour with Tiny Tim and Donnie Brooks.

Morris Day: See the Time

Taylor Dayne

Born Leslie Wunderman, March 7, 1963, Baldwin, New York
1988—*Tell It to My Heart* (Arista)   1989—*Can't Fight Fate*   1993—*Soul Dancing*.

Unlike most female dance-pop divas, big-voiced Taylor Dayne is a white Jewish girl from Long Island. In 1985 fellow Baldwinian Dee Snider of Twisted Sister suggested that Leslie Wunderman change her name to something more glamorous. By that time, she had sung with various high school and local bands, and recorded two unsuccessful singles under the name "Leslee."

As Taylor Dayne, she was discovered singing in Russian-American clubs in the Brighton Beach section of Brooklyn; her debut album hit #21, thanks to its title track (#7, 1987). The album yielded such other disco-ish hits as "Prove Your Love" (#7, 1988), "I'll Always Love You" (#3, 1988), and "Don't Rush Me" (#2, 1988). *Can't Fight Fate* (#25, 1989), on which Dayne tried to sound more mature, included "With Every Beat of My Heart" (#5, 1989), "Love Will Lead You Back" (#1, 1990), "I'll Be Your Shelter" (#4, 1990), and "Heart of Stone" (#12, 1990). Dayne wrote much of the music herself for 1993's *Soul Dancing* (#51), which also contained a remake of disco heavyweight Barry White's "Can't Get Enough of Your Love" (#20).

The dB's

Formed 1978, New York City, New York
Will Rigby (b. Mar. 17, 1956, Winston-Salem, N.C.), drums, voc.; Peter Holsapple (b. Feb. 19, 1956, Greenwich, Conn.), gtr., organ, voc.; Gene Holder (b. July 10, 1954, Philadelphia, Pa.), bass, gtr.; Chris Stamey (b. Dec. 6, 1954, Chapel Hill, N.C.), gtr., organ, voc.
1981—*Stands for Decibels* (Albion, U.K.); *Repercussions* 1983—(– Stamey)   1984—(+ Rick Wagner, bass) *Like This* (Bearsville) (– Wagner; + Jeff Beninato, bass)   1987—*The Sound of Music* (I.R.S.) (– Holder; + Harold Kelt, kybds., gtr.; + Eric Peterson, gtr.)   1993—*Ride the Wild TomTom* (Rhino) 1994—*Paris Avenue* (Monkey Hill).
Chris Stamey solo: 1983—*It's a Wonderful Life* (dB) 1984—*Instant Excitement* EP (Coyote)   1986— *Christmas Time*   1987—*It's Alright*   1991—*Fireworks* (Rhino)   1995—*The Robust Beauty of Improper Linear Models in Decision Making: Compositions and Improvisations for Guitar* (with Kirk Russ) (ESD).
Peter Holsapple and Chris Stamey: 1991—*Mavericks* (Rhino).
Peter Holsapple with Continental Drifters: 1994— *Continental Drifters* (Monkey Hill).
Will Rigby solo: 1985—*Sidekick Phenomenon* (Egon).

Ironic pop-rockers, the dB's met at elementary school in Winston-Salem, North Carolina. Peter Holsapple and Chris Stamey brought their first group together in 1972, and as members of Rittenhouse Square they recorded an album for an independent label the next year. In 1975 Will Rigby joined a group that Stamey formed at the University of North Carolina, Chapel Hill, called Sneakers. They released an EP, Mitch Easter (later of Let's Active) joined on guitar, and the group traveled to New York to play Max's Kansas City in 1976 before breaking up. (A Sneakers LP, *In the Red,* came out posthumously in 1978; in 1992 a Sneakers anthology, *Racket,* was released.)

In early 1977 Stamey moved to New York, where he played with Alex Chilton's band, and did a one-off project with Television guitarist Richard Lloyd. He recorded a Chilton-produced single for Ork Records and set up his own label, Car Records. Rigby and Gene Holder moved to New York, and as Chris Stamey and the dB's, the trio began playing locally in June 1978 and released a single, "If and When"; Holsapple joined the group that fall.

The dB's were favorites of the New York club scene and rock press, but U.S. record companies shied away. Their first two albums were originally released only in Britain by the U.K. label Albion. Stamey left to pursue a solo career in 1983. Finally, the band scored a deal with a U.S. label, Bearsville, but their recording career was legally halted for four years after label chief Albert Grossman died suddenly, not long after the release of *Like This.* In the meantime, Holder moved from bass to guitar, and a succession of new players began coming in. The band opened for R.E.M. on their 1984 and 1987 U.S. tours. Eventually, the dB's signed to I.R.S., releasing *The Sound of Music* (#171, 1987). The band toured from fall 1977 to spring 1978, but fizzled out by the end of that year.

Holsapple then played keyboards and guitar on R.E.M.'s *Green* tour, and also guested on *Out of Time.* He later recorded *Mavericks* with Chris Stamey, and joined the Continental Drifters, marrying fellow Drifter Susan Cowsill [see Cowsills entry]. Stamey released several solo albums and toured sporadically. He also guested on recordings by the Golden Palominos and Freedy Johnston, among others. Rigby went on to make a solo album and to play drums with such artists as Matthew Sweet and Murray Attaway. Holder worked mainly as a producer for the Individuals (with whom he played), the Wygals, Freedy Johnston, and others.

The Dead Boys
Formed 1976, Cleveland, Ohio
Cheetah Chrome (b. Gene Connor), gtr.; Stiv Bators (b. Stivin Bator, Oct. 22, 1949, Cleveland; d. June 4, 1990, Paris, Fr.), voc.; Jimmy Zero, gtr.; Jeff Magnum, bass; Johnny Blitz, drums.
1977—*Young, Loud and Snotty* (Sire)   1978—*We Have Come for Your Children*   1981—*Night of the Living Dead Boys* (Bomp).
Stiv Bators solo: 1980—*Disconnected* (Bomp).
Lords of the New Church, formed early Eighties

(Stiv Bator, voc.; Brian James, gtr.; Dave Tregunna, bass; Nick Turner, drums): 1982—*Lords of the New Church* (I.R.S.) 1983—*Is Nothing Sacred?*   1984—*The Method to Our Madness*   1985—*Killer Lords* 1988—*Live at the Spit* (Illegal).

The Dead Boys, Cleveland natives (Chrome and Blitz had played in the seminal Rocket from the Tombs), emigrated to New York when the Bowery scene first gained national attention in 1976. Managed by CBGB's owner Hilly Kristal, they were adopted by scenemakers for their raucous, impish brand of punk, fully captured by the title of their debut album if not exactly by the music on it. Genya Ravan's production couldn't hide the fact that, for all their highjinks, the Boys had little to offer musically, making them the American counterparts to England's the Damned.

After Johnny Blitz was seriously injured in a mugging, the band regrouped for the Felix Pappalardi–produced *We Have Come for Your Children,* then dissolved. Bators, who released several solo singles on Bomp and had an album released on Lolita in France in 1983 (*The Church and the New Creatures*), did an album with Sham 69 members as the Wanderers. By the time he hooked up with ex-Damned Brian James, Bator had dropped the "s" in his name. Calling themselves the Lords of the New Church they combined Seventies punk with Eighties apocalyptics to create a postpunk sound. The band fell apart in the mid-Eighties. On June 4, 1990, Bators died in his sleep from injuries he sustained when he was was struck by a car on a Paris street. He'd been recording there with a new band featuring ex-members of Hanoi Rocks, Sigue Sigue Sputnik and other groups, and had reportedly planned to include Cheetah Chrome in the sessions and on a subsequent U.S. tour.

The Dead Kennedys
Formed 1978, San Francisco, California
Jello Biafra (b. Eric Boucher, ca. 1959, Boulder, Colo.), voc.; East Bay Ray, gtr.; Klaus Fluoride, bass; J. H. Pelligro, drums.
1980—*Fresh Fruit for Rotting Vegetables* (I.R.S.) 1981—*In God We Trust, Inc.* EP (Alternative Tentacles)   1982—*Plastic Surgery Disasters*   1985—*Frankenchrist*   1986—*Bedtime for Democracy* 1987—*Give Me Convenience or Give Me Death.*
Jello Biafra solo: 1987—*No More Cocoons* (Alternative Tentacles)   1989—*High Priest of Harmful Matter—Tales from the Trial*   1991—*I Blow Minds for a Living.*
Jello Biafra with D.O.A.: 1989—*Last Scream of the Missing Neighbors* EP (Alternative Tentacles).
Jello Biafra with NOMEANSNO: 1991—*The Sky Is Falling and I Want My Mommy* (Alternative Tentacles).

Jello Biafra with Mojo Nixon: 1994—*Prairie Home Invasion* (Alternative Tentacles).

Formed in the volatile San Francisco punk scene of the late Seventies, the Dead Kennedys became one of the West Coast's most visible punk bands, pioneering hardcore. Fueled by a cutting political preoccupation, lead singer Jello Biafra's quavering vocals conveyed the excess that marked such songs as "Drug Me" and "California Über Alles." Biafra and company directed diatribes against the Moral Majority, creeping U.S. imperialism and fascism, and their perceptions of a plastic suburban lifestyle. The band's rapid-fire instrumental overkill attracted punk fans in the U.S. and abroad; they even matched the Sex Pistols on their home turf, going Top Five in England with the airplay-banned "Too Drunk to Fuck." Biafra ran for mayor of San Francisco in 1979; one of his campaign planks was that businessmen wear clown suits downtown.

The Dead Kennedys formed their own record label, Alternative Tentacles, which in 1982 released a compilation album, *Let Them Eat Jellybeans,* consisting of tracks by various unsigned American bands. The DKs' *Frankenchrist* album made free-speech history when, in 1986, Biafra and others associated with Alternative Tentacles were charged with distributing pornography to minors under the nation's revised obscenity laws; the album included the H.R. Giger painting *Landscape #XX,* which featured genitalia and sex acts in a surreal, assembly-line setting. The case ended in a hung jury and was dismissed, but the drawn-out legal battle put such a strain on the Kennedys that they split up after *Bedtime for Democracy. Give Me Convenience or Give Me Death* collects the band's more accessible material. The Dead Kennedys made the news again in 1993 when a box of reissues of their first album were mixed up with a package of Christian radio broadcast CDs and inadvertently shipped to Christian stations around the country.

Biafra has persisted with his political ranting—which often revolves around free speech issues—on his spoken-word albums, college-lecture tours, and occasional collaborations with other artists. Mostly, he tends to the business of running Alternative Tentacles, which continues to put out music by button-pushing rock bands. Klaus Fluoride formed the politically charged acoustic band Five Year Plan, and East Bay Ray plays with hard rockers Skrapyard.

Death Metal: See Thrash

DeBarge/El DeBarge

Formed 1978, Grand Rapids, Michigan
Bunny DeBarge (b. Mar. 15, 1955, Grand Rapids),

El DeBarge

voc.; El DeBarge (b. Eldra DeBarge, June 4, 1961, Grand Rapids), voc., kybds.; Marty DeBarge (b. Mark DeBarge, June 19, 1959, Grand Rapids), voc.; Randy DeBarge (b. Aug. 6, 1958, Grand Rapids), voc.
1981—*The DeBarges* (Gordy)   1982—(+ James DeBarge [b. Aug. 22, 1963, Grand Rapids], voc.) *All This Love*   1983—*In a Special Way*   1985—*Rhythm of the Night*   1986—*Greatest Hits* (Motown) 1988—(– El DeBarge; – Bunny DeBarge) *Bad Boys* (Striped Horse).
Bunny DeBarge solo: 1987—*In Love* (Motown).
El DeBarge solo: 1986—*El DeBarge* (Gordy)   1989— *Gemini* (Motown)   1992—*In the Storm* (Warner Bros.)   1994—*Heart, Mind and Soul* (Reprise).
Chico DeBarge (b. Jonathan "Chico" DeBarge, 1966, Grand Rapids):   1986—*Chico DeBarge* (Motown).

At its peak in the mid-Eighties, the family act DeBarge was touted as a fledgling pop-soul dynasty whose legacy might someday rival that of the Jacksons. El DeBarge was singled out a la Michael Jackson for his superb singing and dancing skills. The Jackson association continued; Jermaine was instrumental in the group's signing to Motown's Gordy Records subsidiary, and in 1984 James DeBarge and Janet Jackson eloped (within seven months they filed for an annulment). In the early Nineties, though, the group's collective star, and El's individual one, had fallen, thanks to legal problems and what was generally perceived as a lack of creative progress. By late 1994, though, El DeBarge showed signs of a comeback with the Babyface production Heart, Mind and Soul.

DeBarge landed its first record deal as a quartet, four of ten siblings raised by a black mother and a white father. The family was religious, and the group members began singing in church. In the late Seventies their sights shifted from gospel to pop, and they moved to Hollywood in pursuit of a contract with Motown Records. (Two older brothers, Bobby and Tommy DeBarge, already played in a Motown band called Switch.) In 1979 brothers El, Marty, and Randy DeBarge and sister Bunny were signed to the Motown subsidiary Gordy. The vocal group released its debut, *The DeBarges*, in 1981, establishing its penchant for creamy love songs. Two gold albums followed, 1982's *All This Love* (with brother James added to the lineup) and 1983's *In a Special Way*.

DeBarge's most successful album was 1985's *Rhythm of the Night*. The catchy title track became a #3 single, and "Who's Holding Donna Now" went to #6. El then left DeBarge; his biggest solo hit as such was 1986's "Who's Johnny" (#3), from the *Short Circuit* soundtrack. Meanwhile, El's brothers switched to Striped Horse Records, while Bunny stayed on at Motown, releasing the solo album *In Love*. Another brother, Chico, joined Motown in 1986 and released a harder-edged funk album, featuring "Talk to Me" (#21 pop, #7 R&B, 1986).

Before long, unfortunately, Chico got press for more dubious accomplishments: He and brother Bobby were arrested and convicted on cocaine-trafficking charges in 1988. El himself served jail time in 1987, after failing to complete a sentence he'd received after allegedly hitting a woman who had rejected his advances. The sentence involved performing a benefit concert. El enlisted hot producer/songwriter Babyface for his 1994 recording, *Heart, Mind and Soul,* which received critical praise.

Joey Dee and the Starliters

Formed 1958, Passaic, New Jersey
Joey Dee (b. Joseph DiNicola, June 11, 1940, Passaic), voc.; Carlton Latimor, organ; Willie Davis, drums; Larry Vernieri, voc., dancer; David Brigati, voc., dancer.
1961—*Doin' the Twist at the Peppermint Lounge* (Roulette)   1962—*Hey, Let's Twist!*
Joey Dee solo: N.A.—*Joey Dee* (Roulette); *Dance, Dance, Dance.*

In 1960 Joey Dee and the Starliters (sometimes misspelled "Starlighters") were the house band at New York's famed Peppermint Lounge. When Dee noticed that everyone there was gyrating to Chubby Checker's "The Twist," he and R&B producer Henry Glover decided to personalize the dance fad, and they came up with the "Peppermint Twist." Released in late 1961, the song was

a #1 smash and landed the group cameo roles in two quickie fad films, *Hey Let's Twist* and *Two Tickets to Paris*. The group scored a few more hits ("Hey Let's Twist," "Shout," "What Kind of Love Is This," "Hot Pastrami with Mashed Potatoes") before sinking back into lounge-band anonymity in late 1963.

By then, however, the Starliters featured three of the four future Young Rascals: Felix Cavaliere, Gene Cornish, and Eddie Brigati (whose brother David had been with Dee from the beginning). A psychedelic twist: In 1966 the group included Jimi Hendrix. And a showbiz twist: An earlier version of the group had actor-to-be Joe Pesci on guitar and backing vocals. In 1987 Dee established the Foundation for the Love of Rock 'n' Roll—later renamed the National Music Foundation—which tried to find health insurance and a retirement community for needy musicians. Dee continues to perform. By the Nineties, Dee's act included his wife Lois and son Ronnie and played cruise liners and Atlantic City resorts.

Deee-Lite

Formed 1986, New York City, New York
Lady Miss Kier (b. Kier Kirby, Youngstown, Ohio), voc.; Super DJ Dmitry (b. Dmitry Brill, ca. 1964, Kirovograd, Ukraine), DJ; Jungle DJ Towa Towa (b. Towa Tei, Tokyo, Jap.), DJ.
1990—*World Clique* (Elektra)   1992—*Infinity Within*   1994—(– DJ Towa Towa; + DJ Ani, DJ, bass) *Dewdrops in the Garden*.
Towa Tei solo: 1995—*Future Listening!* (Elektra).

Deee-Lite combines techno, ambient, house, rap, and funk with a sense of style that borrows equally from Sixties psychedelia and Seventies kitsch. After four years of notoriety on New York's hip underground club scene, the trio scored mainstream success with its infectious dance hit "Groove Is in the Heart" (#4, 1990).

Kier Kirby and her three sisters and brother were raised in various spots across the eastern U.S., including Pittsburgh. At 18 Kier moved to New York to study textile design at the Fashion Institute of Technology, but dropped out after becoming disillusioned with the program. In 1982 she met Dmitry Brill, a classically trained Ukrainian émigré who had discovered pop music early on, learning "Stairway to Heaven" on guitar at age 12. With a mutual interest in dance music, the two began writing songs together and formed Deee-Lite, named for Cole Porter's "It's De-lovely," in 1986. One year later, they added Towa Tei, a club DJ who had recently moved from Japan.

Deee-Lite became a hot ticket among New York's club culture, attracting large, multiracial, pansexual crowds to shows in which the trio would dress outrageously and throw flowers from the stage. Elektra signed the group and released *World Clique* in 1990 to commercial and critical success; the album reached #20 and sold a half-million copies. In addition to "Groove Is in the Heart," *World Clique* contained the minor hit "Power of Love" (#47). Deee-Lite's visual style and sex appeal won the group plenty of photo spreads in music and fashion magazines. The trio followed up two years later with *Infinity Within* (#67, 1992), whose songs carried more obvious political messages—touching on the environment, voting, and safe sex. The 1994 album *Dewdrops in the Garden* was coproduced by a new collaborator, DJ Ani (DJ Towa Towa went on sabbatical). At this point, Deee-Lite wholeheartedly embraced rave culture, headlining Ravestock (Friday night to early Saturday morning) at Woodstock '94 (the Orb, Aphex Twin and Orbital also performed).

Deep Purple

Formed 1968, Hertford, England
Rod Evans (b. 1945, Edinburgh, Scot.), voc.; Nick Simper (b. 1946, London, Eng.), bass; Jon Lord (b. June 9, 1941, Leicester, Eng.), kybds.; Ritchie Blackmore (b. Apr. 14, 1945, Weston-super-Mare, Eng.), gtr.; Ian Paice (b. June 29, 1948, Nottingham, Eng.), drums.
1968—Shades of Deep Purple (Tetragrammaton); Book of Taliesyn 1969—Deep Purple (– Evans; + Ian Gillan [b. Aug. 19, 1945, London, Eng.], voc.; – Simper; + Roger Glover [b. Nov. 30, 1945, Brecon, S. Wales], bass); Powerhouse (released 1978) (Purple, Europe) 1970—Concerto for Group and Orchestra (Warner Bros.); Deep Purple in Rock 1971—Fireball 1972—Machine Head; Purple Passages; Made in Japan 1973—Who Do We Think We Are! (– Glover; + Glenn Hughes [b. Penkridge, Eng.], bass; – Gillan; + David Coverdale [b. Sep. 22, 1949, Saltburn, Eng.], voc.) 1974—Burn; Stormbringer 1975—(– Blackmore; + Tommy Bolin [b. 1951, Sioux City, Ia.; d. Dec. 4, 1976, Miami, Fla.], gtr.) Come Taste the Band (– Bolin); 24 Carat Purple 1976—Made in Europe 1978—When We Rock, We Rock and When We Roll, We Roll 1980—Deepest Purple 1982—In Concert (Portrait) 1984—(Group re-forms: Blackmore; Gillan; Glover; Lord; Paice) Perfect Strangers (Mercury) 1986—Nobody's Perfect 1989—(– Gillan; + Joe Lynn Turner, voc.) 1990—Slaves and Masters (RCA) 1992—Knocking at Your Back Door: The Best of Deep Purple in the '80s (Mercury) 1993—(– Turner; + Gillan, voc.) The Battle Rages On (Giant).
Roger Glover solo: 1974—The Butterfly Ball and the Grasshopper's Feast (Oyster).

Deep Purple shifted halfway through its career from rock with pseudo-classical keyboard flourishes to guitar-dominated heavy metal; in the latter, vastly popular phase, it was listed as loudest rock band by the Guinness Book of World Records. In the wake of a highly publicized regrouping of the classic lineup, Deep Purple has emerged as one of the longest-lived (with a few interruptions) U.K. hard-rock/metal outfits and a showcase for some of the most successful hard-rock stars of the Seventies, Eighties, and Nineties, including guitarist Ritchie Blackmore and singer David Coverdale.

After woodshedding in Hertfordshire, England, Deep Purple had its first success with an American hit, a version of Joe South's "Hush" (#4, 1968), followed by Neil Diamond's "Kentucky Woman" (#38, 1968). The group's popularity couldn't keep its label, Tetragrammaton, from going under after the band's 1968 tour. In 1969, with a new lineup including Ian Gillan, who had sung in *Jesus Christ Superstar*, Deep Purple recorded Lord's *Concerto for Group and Orchestra*, but after it failed to sell Ritchie Blackmore began to dominate the band. His simple repeated guitar riffs helped make Deep Purple one of the most successful groups of the early Seventies, but his personality clashes with other band members, particularly Gillan, precipitated several personnel shifts in between.

In Rock and *Fireball* attracted attention, and *Machine Head* made the U.S. Top Ten (#7), thus adding to the band's success in England, Europe, Japan, and Australia. One year after *Machine Head* was released, "Smoke on the Water"—about the band's near-disastrous Montreux concert with Frank Zappa—became a #4 hit single, and the album returned to the Top Ten, eventually selling over two million copies. By late 1974, Deep Purple had sold nearly 15 million albums. But the band had begun to fall apart. Gillan left for a solo career in 1973. He released a number of albums in the U.K. In 1975 he formed the Ian Gillan Band and after it dissolved in 1983, joined Black Sabbath [see entry]. Roger Glover followed Gillan, moving on to session and production work (for Judas Priest, Elf, Nazareth, Ian Gillan, Spencer Davis, Michael Schenker of UFO, Barbi Benton, and Blackmore's Rainbow). Gillan's replacement, David Coverdale, sang on *Burn* and *Stormbringer*. He would find greater fame, however, in the Eighties with Whitesnake [see entry] and his collaboration with Jimmy Page. Jon Lord recorded a British solo album, *Gemini Suite* (1974). Blackmore left in 1975 to form Ritchie Blackmore's Rainbow [see entry]. He was replaced by Tommy Bolin, with whom the group recorded one LP, *Come Taste the Band*, before announcing their retirement in 1976. In 1980 a bogus reincarnation of Deep Purple led by original vocalist Evans popped up on the West Coast bar circuit. Blackmore and Glover took legal action to prohibit Evans from using the name. In 1984 they reclaimed the name for themselves, reuniting for their first new LP since 1976, the Top Twenty, platinum *Perfect Strangers*, which included "Knocking at Your Back Door." Despite being welcomed warmly by its fans, Deep Purple was plagued by personal tensions, and Gillan again departed in 1989. He pursued a solo career, only to return again for 1994's *The Battle Rages On*, but left again shortly thereafter.

Def Leppard

Formed 1977, Sheffield, England
Joe Elliott (b. Aug. 1, 1959, Eng.), voc.; Pete Willis (b. Feb. 16, 1960, Eng.), gtr.; Rick Savage (b. Dec. 2, 1960, Eng.), bass; Rick Allen (b. Nov. 1, 1963, Eng.), drums; Steve Clark (b. Apr. 23, 1960, Eng.; d. Jan. 8, 1991, London, Eng.), gtr.
1980—*On Through the Night* (Mercury)   1981—*High 'n' Dry* (– Willis; + Phil Collen ([b. Dec. 8, 1957], gtr.)   1983—*Pyromania*   1987—*Hysteria*   1991—(– Clark)   1992—*Adrenalize* (+ Vivian Campbell [b. Aug. 25, 1962, Belfast, N. Ire.], gtr.)   1993—*Retro Active*.

In the beginning a chartbreaking debut album, tours with more established heavy-metal bands, and pinup good looks made Def Leppard one of the leaders of the Eighties British heavy-metal renaissance. The members, barely out of their teens when their first album debuted, soon became one of the most consistently successful pop metal groups of the decade and beyond, becoming, as one *Goldmine* article put it, "The Heavy Metal Band You Can Bring Home to Mother."

Pete Willis and Rick Savage started the group in Sheffield in 1977. Joe Elliott had coined the name Deaf Leopard before joining them; Willis and Savage changed the spelling. As a quartet with a since-forgotten drummer, they built a local pub following, and in 1978, after being joined by Steve Clark and hiring a temporary drummer, they produced their first record, an EP called *Getcha Rocks Off*, released on their own Bludgeon Riffola label. The record got airplay on the BBC and sold 24,000 copies.

Their self-made success and precociousness (Elliott, the group's eldest member, was 19, and Rick Allen, who became their permanent drummer after playing with several professional Sheffield bands, was 15) brought them the attention of the British rock press. AC/DC manager Peter Mensch added them to his roster and got them a contract with Mercury. Their first album was a hit in the U.K. and reached #51 in the U.S. The group toured Britain with Sammy Hagar and AC/DC; played the 1980 Reading Festival; first toured the U.S. opening for Ted Nugent, Pat Travers, Judas Priest, and AC/DC. A second U.S. tour, with Blackfoot, Ozzy Osbourne, and Rainbow, got heavy coverage in the U.S. metal press and created a growing American audience.

The group's second album, *High 'n' Dry*, was the first of a string of platinum and multiplatinum LPs, hitting #38 in 1981 and selling over two million copies. (It was remixed and rereleased in 1984 with two more tracks, a remixed "Bringin' on the Heartbreak" and "Me and My Wine.") MTV, undeniably a factor in the band's U.S. success, began airing "Bringin' on the Heartbreak," and within the next few years virtually all the band's videos (beginning with *Pyromania*'s "Rock of Ages," "Photograph," and "Foolin'") would go into heavy rotation. By early 1982 the group had reentered the studio to record *Pyromania*, which would eventually sell a phenomenal ten million copies. Midway through the recording, founding guitarist Pete Willis was fired for alcoholism and replaced by Phil Collen, formerly of Girl. At the same time co–lead guitarist Steve Clark was beginning a slide into extreme alcohol addiction that would eventually prove fatal.

Shortly after *Pyromania*'s release, the band embarked on its first world tour. When producer Mutt Lange, with whom the group had recorded since its major-label debut, was unavailable to work on their next album, Def Leppard turned to Jim Steinman, most famous for his work with Meat Loaf. When Steinman proved incompatible, *High 'n' Dry* engineer Nigel Green stepped in. Just one month later, drummer Rick Allen lost his left arm in a New Year's Eve car accident after he attempted to pass another driver at high speed. Surgeons reattached the limb, but after infection set in, it was amputated. Def Leppard's future was in doubt, but by the spring of 1985 Allen was learning to play drums again with the help of a specially adapted Simmons kit. (He now performs with special equipment, using prerecorded tapes of his drumming for some parts.) The band continued recording, but when Lange heard the tapes, he suggested the band scrap them and start again. In August 1986 Allen performed for the first time since his accident on the European Monsters of Rock Tour.

In early 1987 the band finally completed work on the long-awaited *Hysteria*, which spun off six Top Twenty singles: "Animal" (#19, 1987; and their first Top Forty hit in the U.K.), "Hysteria" (#10, 1988), "Pour Some Sugar on Me" (#2, 1988), "Love Bites" (#1, 1988), "Armageddon It" (#3, 1988), and "Rocket" (#12, 1989). Though longtime fans and some critics found it disappointingly poppish on the verge of bubblegum, that change in direction no doubt contributed to its selling over 14 million copies and topping the U.S. LPs chart for six weeks.

Tragedy struck the group again when on January 8, 1991, guitarist Steve Clark died of a fatal mixture of drugs and alcohol. Beginning in 1982, he had undergone treatment for his alcoholism several times. His addiction was so disabling that Phil Collen had done most of the leads on *Hysteria*, and later the group forced Clark to take a lengthy sabbatical. Once in 1989, after being found comatose in a gutter, he was admitted to a psychiatric hospital, but he seemed beyond help. The group continued recording and even made the video for "Let's Get Rocked" as a foursome.

Clark's replacement, Vivian Campbell, who had previously played with Ronnie James Dio and Whitesnake, joined in 1992, weeks after the release of *Adrenalize*. Another #1 LP, *Adrenalize* spawned a flurry of hit singles: "Have You Ever Needed Someone So Bad" (#12, 1992), "Let's Get Rocked" (#15, 1992), "Make Love Like a Man" (#36, 1992), and "Stand Up (Kick Love into Motion)" (#34, 1992). *Retro Active* (#9, 1993) is a platinum collection of B sides, rarities, and covers, which yielded the hit singles "Two Steps Behind" (#32, 1994) (also on the *Last Action Hero* soundtrack) and "Miss You in a Heartbeat" (#39, 1994). The album also includes one Mick Ronson song, "Only After Dark."

The DeFranco Family
Formed 1973, Port Colborne, Canada
Benny DeFranco (b. July 11, 1954, Port Colborne);
Nino DeFranco (b. Oct. 19, 1956, Port Colborne);
Marisa DeFranco (b. July 23, 1955, Port Colborne);
Merlina DeFranco (b. July 20, 1957, Port Colborne);
Tony DeFranco (b. Aug. 31, 1959, Port Colborne).
1973—*Heartbeat—It's a Lovebeat* (20th Century-Fox)   1974—*Save the Last Dance for Me*.

Modeled after wholesome family acts like the Osmonds, the Cowsills, the Jackson 5, and TV's Partridge Family (David Cassidy), the Canadian-born DeFranco Family were sponsored by Laufer Publications (publishers of *Tiger Beat* and *Fave* magazines), which managed the group and distributed fan-club material featuring 13-year-old lead singer Tony DeFranco. "Heartbeat—It's a Lovebeat" sold 2½ million copies in 1973, becoming the year's top single. The next year, the family charted two more singles: "Abra-Ca-Dabra" (#32) and a remake of the Drifters' classic "Save the Last Dance for Me" (#18). But their career was ultimately distinguished by its brevity.

Derek and the Dominos: See Eric Clapton

Desmond Dekker
Born Desmond Dacres, July 16, 1941, Kingston, Jamaica
1969—*The Israelites* (Uni)   1970—*You Can Get It* (Trojan)   1974—*Double Dekker*   1978—*Sweet 16 Hits*   1980—*Black and Dekker* (Stiff)   1981—*Compass Point*   1992—*Rockin' Steady: The Best of Desmond Dekker* (Rhino).

Desmond Dekker was one of the pioneers of reggae and the creator of one of the genre's best-known songs, "The Israelites." As a teenager in Jamaica, he worked in the same welding shop as Bob Marley, who encouraged him to audition for producer Leslie "King" Kong. Kong helped Dekker put together a group, the Aces, and produced

their first record, "Honour Thy Father and Mother," in 1963. Eventually a #1 hit in Jamaica, it was followed by a score of Caribbean hits that won Dekker the title "King of the Bluebeat" and the annual Golden Trophy (awarded to Jamaica's top singer) five times between 1963 and 1969.

In 1964 Chris Blackwell released "Honour Thy Father and Mother" in Britain on his Island label. Dekker's first U.K. Top Twenty hit was a 1967 single on Pyramid, "007 (Shanty Town)," later featured on the soundtrack of *The Harder They Come* (1972). Dekker's only U.S. hit, "The Israelites" (#9, 1969), personalized imagery from the Biblical Exodus story. It sold over a million copies worldwide, reaching #1 in Britain.

A handful of British hits followed "The Israelites," including "It Miek" (#7, 1969) and "You Can Get It If You Really Want" (#2, 1970), written for him by Jimmy Cliff. A reissue of "The Israelites" returned him to the British Top Ten in 1975. "Sing a Little Song" made the Top Twenty later that year. Dekker didn't record again until 1980, when Stiff Records signed him at the height of the ska and rock-steady revival. His comeback album, *Black and Dekker*, featured one of the original rock-steady groups, the Pioneers, and Graham Parker's band the Rumour in supporting roles. Its followup, *Compass Point*, was produced by singer Robert Palmer.

In 1984 Dekker was declared bankrupt by a British court. He claimed that his former manager had withheld funds. Things looked up for Dekker, however, when a 1990 British TV ad for Maxell Tapes used the melody of "The Israelites" for its jingle, and the song was reissued once again.

Delaney and Bonnie
Bonnie Bramlett, born November 8, 1944, Acton, Illinois; Delaney Bramlett, born July 1, 1939, Pontotoc County, Mississippi
1969—*Accept No Substitute: The Original Delaney and Bonnie* (Elektra); *Home* (Stax)   1970—*On Tour with Eric Clapton* (Atco); *To Bonnie from Delaney* 1971—*Motel Shot*; *Genesis* (GNP-Crescendo) 1972—*D and B Together* (Columbia)   1973—*The Best of Delaney and Bonnie* (Atco)   1990—*The Best of Delaney and Bonnie* (Rhino).
Bonnie Bramlett solo: 1973—*Sweet Bonnie Bramlett* (Columbia)   1975—*It's Time* (Capricorn) 1976—*Lady's Choice*   1978—*Memories*.
Delaney Bramlett solo: 1972—*Something's Coming* (Columbia)   1977—*Delaney and Friends—Class Reunion* (Prodigal); *Mobius Strip* (Columbia); *Giving Birth to a Song* (MGM).

This husband-and-wife duo's best songs fused gospel, country, funk, and rock, but they were overshadowed by their Friends, a backup crew that occasionally included

Eric Clapton, Leon Russell, Dave Mason, and George Harrison. The couple met in Los Angeles in 1967. Bonnie Lynn had worked as a bewigged, blackfaced Ikette with Ike and Tina Turner in the mid-Sixties; Delaney had fallen in with a group of Southwestern musicians, including Russell and J. J. Cale, contacts that netted him a brief stint with the Champs and then a steady job with the Shindogs, house band for ABC's *Shindig.* The Shindogs were moonlighting at a Los Angeles bowling alley when Bramlett met Lynn; a week later they married.

Although the group's first album went largely unnoticed, Blind Faith offered Delaney and Bonnie an opening slot on its 1969 tour. Clapton began riding in the couple's tour bus, which turned into a rolling jam session. After Blind Faith disbanded, Clapton began to perform regularly with the duo, assuming a low-key, sideman-only stance.

Clapton brought them to England, where Harrison, Mason, and others came onstage for shows that resulted in Delaney and Bonnie's best-selling album, *On Tour with Eric Clapton* (#29, 1970). The entourage briefly participated in John Lennon's Plastic Ono Band in late 1969 and toured Europe with Clapton. They returned to America as headliners in 1970, but their drawing power plummeted when Clapton left, and Leon Russell then hired most of the Friends to tour with Joe Cocker's Mad Dogs and Englishmen. The Bramletts canceled their tour. They appeared on Clapton's solo debut in 1970, produced by Delaney, and continued to record their own albums, which included two major hits, "Never Ending Song of Love" (#13, 1971) and Dave Mason's "Only You Know and I Know" (#20, 1971).

In 1972 they signed with Columbia and made their last album, *Together,* before their marriage dissolved. Delaney made two solo LPs for Columbia to fulfill contractual obligations (*Something's Coming* and *Mobius Strip*) as well as 1977's *Giving Birth to a Song* on MGM and *Class Reunion* for Motown's Prodigal label. Bonnie, backed by the uncredited Average White Band, made one album for Columbia (*Sweet Bonnie Bramlett*) before signing with Capricorn. While touring with Stephen Stills in 1979, she punched Elvis Costello in a Columbus, Ohio, bar when he called Ray Charles "a blind, ignorant nigger." She later had a recurrent acting role in the hit Nineties TV sitcom *Roseanne.* She had by then changed her surname to Sheridan. Delaney overcame alcoholism at his Rock and Roll Ranch in Shadow Hills, California, became a born-again Christian, and recorded commercial jingles. In 1993 Delaney and Bonnie's daughter Bekka Bramlett replaced Stevie Nicks in Fleetwood Mac.

De La Soul

Formed 1985, Amityville, New York
Posdnuos (b. Kelvin Mercer, Aug. 17, 1969, Bronx,
N.Y.), voc.; **Trugoy the Dove (b. David Jolicoeur, Sep. 21, 1968, Brooklyn, N.Y.), voc.; P. A. Pasemaster Mase (b. Vincent Mason, March 24, 1970, Brooklyn, N.Y.), voc.**
1989—*3 Feet High and Rising* (Tommy Boy) 1991—*De La Soul Is Dead* 1993—*Buhlōōne Mind State.*

De La Soul made rap history as the first group to go against the hip-hop grain of macho braggadocio, hectoring social comment, and mammoth beats. With its light rhythms, laid-back raps, thoughtfully irreverent lyrics, esoteric sampling, and quasi-hippie attitude, De La Soul paved the way for a steady stream of gently adventurous "alternative" rap groups (A Tribe Called Quest, PM Dawn, Basehead, and Digable Planets).

De La Soul began as three high school friends whose stage names reflected their sense of whimsical in-jokery: through backward spelling David Jolicoeur became "Trugoy [his favorite food, yogurt] the Dove"; Kelvin Mercer derived "Posdnuos" (his nickname as a high school DJ, "Sound-Sop"). Their first demo, "Plug Tunin'," attracted the attention of Paul "Prince Paul" Houston, of local rap group Stetsasonic. He played the tape for colleagues on New York's rap scene, and soon De La Soul signed with Tommy Boy. Houston produced the group's debut album, a mock–game show soundtrack that introduced such De La terms as "the D.A.I.S.Y. Age (Da Inner Sound, Y'all)." De La Soul were labeled "hippies"—a term at which the group bridled—but also hailed as ingenious revolutionaries. The album brimmed with off-center inventiveness, its samples taken not from the usual James Brown rhythm tracks but from TV shows and obscure recordings, many from De La Soul's parents' collections. "Transmitting Live from Mars" set a sample from a French-lesson record atop a sample from the 1968 Turtles hit "You Showed Me." The former Turtles filed a $1.7-million lawsuit, charging their music was sampled without their permission: The case was settled out of court for an undisclosed sum. *3 Feet* (#24 pop, #1 R&B, 1989) yielded a hit single in "Me Myself and I" (#34 pop, #1 R&B, 1989), set to a sample of Funkadelic's 1979 "(not just) Knee Deep." De La Soul then formed "Native Tongues," a loose alliance with A Tribe Called Quest, the Jungle Brothers, Queen Latifah, Monie Love, and Black Sheep.

De La Soul's second album was an obvious reaction to the perception that its debut, however innovative, was "soft." Titled *De La Soul Is Dead* (#26 pop, #24 R&B, 1991), it took a darker, more serious tone with songs about drug abuse ("My Brother's a Basehead"), incest ("Millie Pulled a Pistol on Santa"), and the vicissitudes of fame ("Ring Ring Ring [Ha Ha Hey]") (#22 R&B, 1991). Critical and commercial reaction to the album was mixed. De La Soul came back strong in late 1993, however, with *Buhlōōne Mind State* (#40 pop, #9 R&B), hailed as a return to the group's quirky, ground-breaking form.

The Delfonics

Formed 1964, Philadelphia, Pennsylvania
William Hart (b. Jan. 17, 1945, Washington, D.C.),
lead voc.; Wilbert Hart (b. Oct. 19, 1947, Philadelphia), baritone voc.; Ricky Johnson, bass voc.;
Richard Daniels, tenor voc.
1965—(– Daniels; – Johnson; + Randy Cain III
[b. Herbert Randal, May 2, 1945, Philadelphia], tenor
voc.)   1968—*La La Means I Love You* (Philly
Groove)   1969—*The Sound of Sexy Soul*; *The Delfonics Super Hits*   1970—*The Delfonics*   1972—*Tell
Me This Is a Dream*   1973—(– Cain; + Major Harris
[b. Richmond, Va.], tenor voc.)   1974—*Alive and
Kicking* (– Harris; + John Johnson, voc.)   1975—*Let
It Be Me* (Sounds Superb)   1985—*Best of the Delfonics* (Arista).

The Delfonics' late-Sixties MOR soul hits were among
producer Thom Bell's earliest works and set standards
for elegant black pop. Originally the Orphonics, the
group formed in the mid-Sixties around chief songwriter
William Hart in a Philadelphia high school. Their high-
pitched harmony style shone on medium-tempo ballads
like "He Don't Really Love You," a local hit in 1967,
shortly after they'd signed with manager Stan Watson,
who persuaded them to call themselves the Delfonics.
They worked East Coast clubs until early 1968, when
Watson formed the Philly Groove label and brought in
budding producer Thom Bell.

   Their first collaboration with Bell, "La La Means I
Love You" (a phrase Hart picked up from his young son),
was an instant #4 smash in spring 1968. Bell also worked
on subsequent Delfonics hits ("I'm Sorry," "Break Your
Promise," "Ready or Not, Here I Come," "You Get Yours
and I'll Get Mine" and their 1970 Top Ten landmark "Did-
n't I [Blow Your Mind This Time]").

   R&B veteran Major Harris ("One Monkey Don't Stop
No Show") joined the group in 1973, when Cain retired
due to illness; he left the following year. In 1975 Harris
had a solo hit with "Love Won't Let Me Wait" (#5 pop, #1
R&B, 1975). Although no charting singles followed 1974's
"Lying to Myself," the group continued to perform. As of
the early Nineties, Harris, the Hart brothers, and Cain
had regrouped.

The Del-Lords: See the Dictators

The Dells

Formed 1953, Harvey, Illinois
Marvin Junior, first tenor voc.; Michael "Mickey"
McGill, baritone voc.; Johnny Funches, lead voc.;
Chuck Barksdale, bass voc.; Vern Allison, tenor voc.
1959—(– Funches; + Johnny Carter)   1968—*There
Is* (Cadet)   1969—*The Dells Greatest Hits*   1970—

Like It Is   1972—*Freedom Means*   1973—*Give
Your Baby a Standing Ovation*   1974—*The Mighty
Mighty Dells*; *The Dells vs. the Dramatics*
(Chess/MCA)   1975—*No Way Back* (Mercury); *The
Dells Greatest Hits, vol. 2* (Cadet)   1976—*They Said
It Couldn't Be Done* (Mercury)   1977—*Love Connec-
tion*   1980—*I Touched a Dream* (20th Century-Fox)
1981—*Whatever Turns You On*   1984—*One Step
Closer*; *The Dells* (Chess)   1988—*The Second Time*
(Urgent/Ichiban)   1992—*On Their Corner: Best of
the Dells* (MCA); *I Salute You* (Philadelphia Interna-
tional)   1994—*You Gotta Have Soul: vol. 2* (Vee-Jay).

The Dells are a black vocal group that has been together
more than forty years and whose story and perseverance
inspired filmmaker Robert Townshend's *The Five Heartbeats*. The original members began singing together as
freshmen at Thornton Township High School in the
Chicago suburb of Harvey. A streetcorner a cappella
doo-wop group, they called themselves the El Rays and
picked up their style from records by the Clovers and the
Dominoes. Harvey Fuqua of the Moonglows took them
as protégés, and within months the El Rays were including Michael McGill's and Marvin Junior's originals in
their club sets.

   In late 1953 they recorded their first single for Chess,
the a cappella "Darling Dear, I Know" b/w "Christine."
The resulting $36 in royalties sent the group back to the
streetcorners, but the quintet continued to record for
Chess until 1955, when, billing itself as the Dells, it
switched to Vee Jay Records. Their second release for
that label, "Oh What a Night," became a Top Ten R&B hit.
Barksdale did not sing on this single, since he had left the
group to join Otis Williams and the Charms; he soon rejoined the Dells.

   En route to a gig in 1958, the group had an auto accident that left McGill in the hospital for six months,
forced Funches to retire, and put the band out of commission for nearly two years. In 1959 Funches was replaced by ex-Flamingo falsetto Johnny Carter.

   The early Sixties found the Dells slowly regrouping
and label-hopping between Vee Jay and Chess. By mid-
decade they had become a contemporary soul group a la
the Temptations and the Impressions; they hit the pop
chart in 1968 with three Top Twenty hits ("There Is," #20;
"Always Together," #18; and their biggest hit, "Stay in My
Corner," #10 pop, #1 R&B), and in 1969 with a medley of
"I Can Sing a Rainbow"/"Love Is Blue" (#22) and a Top
Ten remake of "Oh What a Night." They hit occasionally
in the early Seventies ("Give Your Baby a Standing Ovation," "The Love We Had [Stays on My Mind]"). All told,
the Dells have had 30 R&B Top Forty and eight pop Top
Forty hits.

   Through the years the group has backed countless
singers, including Jerry Butler, Dinah Washington, and

Barbara Lewis (they sang on her 1963 hit "Hello Stranger"). Although pop hits have eluded the group in the past two decades, the Dells have recorded consistently and remain a live attraction. Their 1992 LP, *I Salute You*, was produced by Kenny Gamble and Leon Huff. "The Heart Is the House of Love" (#13 R&B, 1991) was included on the *Five Heartbeats* soundtrack.

The Del-Vikings/Dell Vikings

Formed 1956, Pittsburgh, Pennsylvania
Clarence Quick (b. Brooklyn, N.Y.), voc.; Dave Lerchey (b. New Albany, Ind.), voc.; Norman Wright (b. Oct. 21, 1937, Philadelphia, Penn.), voc.; Don Jackson, voc.; Corinthian "Kripp" Johnson [b. Cambridge, Mass.; d. June 22, 1990], voc.
1957—(– Jackson; + Donald "Gus" Backus [b. Southampton, N.Y.], voc.) (numerous personnel changes follow).

One of rock's first racially integrated groups, the Del-Vikings were a vocal quintet that came together at a Pittsburgh Air Force base and scored two Top Ten hits in 1957, "Come Go with Me" (#5) and "Whispering Bells" (#9). The group first recorded for Luniverse (owned by Dickie Goodman of the "Flying Saucer" novelty hits) in 1956 with little success. The following year, after adding Kripp Johnson, they recorded the R&B-tinged million-seller "Come Go with Me." The group toured widely, and in mid-1957 scored again with "Whispering Bells."

But after that ex–Del-Viking Kripp Johnson formed his own group of Del-Vikings and added a second "l" to their name, thus sparking confusion that has plagued rock historians ever since. Among these new Dell Vikings was Chuck Jackson, who had soul hits in the Sixties ("I Don't Want to Cry," "Any Day Now," "Tell Him I'm Not Home") and Seventies ("Needing You"). This group then recorded as the Versatiles. The first group, with some personnel shifts, continued to tour and record, breaking up in the mid-Sixties, then regrouping in 1970. In the Seventies Johnson, Lerchey, Wright, and others were touring internationally. Despite a dizzying sequence of personnel changes, the Del-Vikings continue and as late as 1991 had released a new single, "My Heart" b/w "Rock & Roll Remembered."

Sandy Denny

Born January 6, 1947, Wimbledon, England; died April 21, 1978, London, England
1968—*All Our Own Work* (Pickwick) 1970—*Fotheringay* (A&M); *Sandy Denny* (Saga) 1971—*The Northstar Grassman and the Ravens* (A&M) 1972—*Sandy*; *Rock On* 1973—*Like an Old Fashioned Waltz* (Island) 1977—*Sandy Denny* (Nova); *Rendezvous* (Island) 1985—*Who Knows Where the Time Goes?* (Hannibal) 1987—*The Best of Sandy*

Denny **1991—*Sandy Denny and the Strawbs* (Rykodisc).**

Sandy Denny's smoky alto made her one of England's most popular singer/songwriters of the early Seventies, both as a member of the electric folk group Fairport Convention and on her own. She studied classical piano, and while working as a nurse after graduating high school, she learned guitar. She later enrolled in Kensington Art School (classmates included Jimmy Page, Eric Clapton, and John Renbourn) and began frequenting London's folk pubs and coffeehouses. Denny jammed with the then-struggling Simon and Garfunkel, who encouraged her to start performing regularly.

By the mid-Sixties she was playing London folk clubs and had recorded one privately distributed LP. During 1967, she belonged to the nascent Strawbs [see entry] for six months, recording one unreleased album (issued years later by Rykodisc). She also wrote "Who Knows Where the Time Goes?," the title track of a gold album by Judy Collins. In May 1968 Denny joined Fairport Convention [see entry], with whom she recorded three albums. She quit the group in December 1969, following the release of its landmark *Liege and Lief*.

Denny hesitantly announced a solo career and formed Fotheringay (named after a song on *Fairport Convention*) with American guitarist Jerry Donahue, bassist Pat Donaldson, guitarist Trevor Lucas (whom she married in 1973), and drummer Gerry Conway. Though Fotheringay was moderately successful, the group disbanded late in 1970 before completing a second album.

Denny, voted top British female vocalist in the 1970 and 1971 *Melody Maker* polls, started her solo career in earnest, touring Europe, the U.S., and Britain frequently over the next few years, usually backed by Fairport and Fotheringay alumni. In 1972 she joined the Bunch, a casual aggregation of electrified folkies (including Richard Thompson and Fairport percussionist Dave Mattacks), and recorded an album of rock oldies, *Rock On*. She also contributed vocals to Led Zeppelin's "The Battle of Evermore."

Around the time of *Like an Old Fashioned Waltz*, Denny rejoined Fairport Convention, although she had already played a low-key support role in the group's 1973 tour. (Lucas and Donahue had preceded her into the group.) Though she contributed to 1975's *Rising for the Moon*, the reunion never quite clicked, and Denny and Lucas left Fairport in February 1976. She released *Rendezvous* in May 1977 and died the next year from head injuries sustained in a fall down a flight of stairs in her home. In 1989 Lucas died of a heart attack.

John Denver

Born John Henry Deutschendorf, December 31, 1943, Roswell, New Mexico

1969—*Rhymes and Reasons* (RCA)   1970—*Whose Garden Was This; Take Me to Tomorrow*   1971—*Poems, Prayers and Promises; Aerie*   1972—*Rocky Mountain High*   1973—*John Denver's Greatest Hits; Farewell Andromeda*   1974—*Back Home Again; A John Denver Songbook; Beginnings with the Mitchell Trio* (Mercury)   1975—*An Evening with John Denver* (RCA); *Windsong*   1976—*Spirit*   1977—*I Want to Live; John Denver's Greatest Hits, vol. 2*   1980—*Autograph*   1981—*Some Days Are Diamonds*   1982—*Seasons of the Heart*   1983—*It's About Time*   1985—*Dreamland Express*   1986—*One World*   1990—*The Flower That Shattered the Stone* (Windstar)   1991—*Different Directions.*

Through the Seventies, country-pop singer/songwriter John Denver was one of the most successful recording artists in the world. Of his albums, 12 are gold and four are platinum, and in the mid-Seventies he had a string of gold singles.

Denver was raised in an Air Force family and lived in various Southern and Southwestern towns. In his early teens his grandmother gave him a 1910 Gibson acoustic guitar. He enrolled at Texas Tech in 1961, majoring in architecture and playing in local clubs. In 1964 he dropped out of college and moved to Los Angeles, and after he adopted Denver as his stage name, he replaced Chad Mitchell in the Chad Mitchell Trio in 1965. The Trio, a major draw on the early-Sixties hootenanny circuit, was $40,000 in debt upon Denver's arrival, which he later helped it pay back. They recorded for Mercury (which later repackaged the results under Denver's name as *Beginnings*) and toured widely. At a 1966 Trio concert at Gustavus Adolphus College in Minnesota, Denver met sophomore Ann Martell, who married him the next year.

Rhymes and Reasons included Denver's "Leaving on a Jet Plane," a #1 hit that year for Peter, Paul and Mary; Denver shared their producer, Milt Okun. His own rise began with the million-selling "Take Me Home, Country Roads" (#2, 1971). After he had moved to Aspen, Colorado, *Rocky Mountain High* went platinum in 1972. The #1s "Annie's Song" (written for his wife), "Sunshine on My Shoulders," plus "Back Home Again" (#5) made Denver the best-selling pop musician of 1974. *Greatest Hits* sold over ten million copies worldwide and stayed in the Top 100 for two years. The governor of Colorado proclaimed John Denver the state's poet laureate.

While the hits continued—"Thank God I'm a Country Boy" (#1, 1975), "I'm Sorry" (#1, 1975)—Denver tried TV and film appearances, with variety specials, dramatic roles, and a screen debut in 1977's *Oh, God!* He started Windsong Records (distributed by RCA) in 1976, and signed the Starland Vocal Band ("Afternoon Delight," #1, 1976), whose Bill and Taffy Danoff had written "Take Me Home . . ." with Denver.

Denver has done volunteer work for ecological causes, the ERA, and space exploration (he's a board member of the National Space Institute) and against nuclear power. In 1984 he made the first of several tours of the then–Soviet Union; he recorded a special version of "Let Us Begin (What Are We Making Weapons For?)," from *One World*, in Moscow with Soviet singer Alexandre Gradsky. In 1987 he returned to the USSR, where he performed a benefit concert for victims of the Chernobyl power plant disaster.

Through the Eighties and into the Nineties, Denver's commercial star faded (1985's *Dreamland Express* reached only #90, 1990's *The Flower That Shattered the Stone*, only #185); he had a brief return to prominence in late summer 1993, when he was arrested for drunk driving in Aspen, Colorado. That same year he became the first nonclassical musician given the Albert Schweitzer Music Award, for lifetime humanitarianism. In 1994 he published *Take Me Home: An Autobiography*.

Depeche Mode

Formed 1980, Basildon, England
Vince Clarke (b. July 3, 1960, South Woodford, Eng.), kybds.; Andrew Fletcher (b. July 8, 1961, Nottingham, Eng.), kybds.; Dave Gahan (b. David Gahan, May 9, 1962, Epping, Eng.), voc.; Martin Gore (b. July 23, 1961, Basildon, Eng.), gtr., kybds.
1981—*Speak and Spell* (Mute) (– Clarke)   1982—*A Broken Frame* (+ Alan Wilder [b. June 1, 1959, London, Eng.], drums, kybds., voc.)   1983—*Construction Time Again*   1984—*People Are People*   1985—*Some Great Reward; Catching Up with Depeche Mode*   1986—*Black Celebration*   1987—*Music for the Masses*   1989—*101*   1990—*Violator*   1993—*Songs of Faith and Devotion*   1995—(– Wilder).

Perhaps the quintessential Eighties electropop band, Depeche Mode—the name was inspired by a French fashion magazine—parlayed a fascination with synthesizers into huge success in the British charts (all the band's albums have been in the U.K. Top Ten) and eventually on the U.S. pop charts. Whereas a more traditional four-piece rock band might feature three members playing instruments and the fourth singing and perhaps playing guitar or bass, the lineup of this British group was thus described in a 1993 press release: "Dave (Gahan) is the singer, Martin (Gore) the songwriter, Alan (Wilder) the musician, and Andrew (Fletcher) the coordinator." Though Depeche Mode's stark, synthetic sound and often moody or provocative lyrics buck classic pop convention, the hooks that distinguish its most popular songs are among postmodern rock's most ingratiating.

When the group's original members united in 1980,

in a working-class suburb of London called Basildon, they gravitated toward synthesizers and drum machines in part because of their convenience—they were easy to carry around and didn't require amplifiers. In fact, they took the train to their early gigs in local pubs. The group's recording career began auspiciously: 1981's dance-beat-ridden *Speak and Spell* (#10, U.K.) became one of the year's best-selling albums in England. Shortly after its release, though, principal songwriter Vince Clarke left. He eventually formed the techno-driven bands Yazoo and, later, Erasure [see entry].

But Depeche Mode bounced right back with 1982's *A Broken Frame* (#8, U.K.), on which Gore assumed chief songwriting duties; soon after, Alan Wilder, who had toured with the band earlier, joined as a full-time member. Two years later the band released the critically and commercially groundbreaking *Some Great Reward* (#5, U.K.), whose content ranged from the bitter and shocking "Blasphemous Rumours" to "People Are People," a catchy plea for tolerance that went to #13 in the U.S., where Depeche Mode had previously been considered an obscure alternative act.

In spite of its success on the American tour circuit, selling out arenas, Depeche Mode didn't have another U.S. hit until "Personal Jesus" (#28, 1990), its first gold single. *Violator* (#7, 1990), the album that single introduced, yielded the group's first Top Ten single, "Enjoy the Silence" (#8, 1990). *Songs of Faith and Devotion* (1993) was heralded by critics as a bold foray into warmer musical textures and more spiritual imagery. It also entered the American albums charts at #1, boding well for Depeche Mode's future on both sides of the Atlantic.

Rick Derringer

Born Rick Zehringer, August 5, 1947, Union City, Indiana

With the McCoys: 1965—*Hang On Sloopy* (Bang) 1966—*You Make Me Feel So Good* 1968—*Infinite McCoys* (Mercury); *Human Ball* 1970—*Outside Stuff* 1974—*Rick Derringer and the McCoys.* Solo: 1973—*All American Boy* (Blue Sky) 1975—*Spring Fever* 1976—*Derringer* 1977—*Sweet Evil*; *Live* 1978—*If I Weren't So Romantic, I'd Shoot You* 1979—*Guitars and Women* 1980—*Face to Face* 1983—*Good Dirty Fun* (Passport) 1993—*Back to the Blues* (BluesBureau Int'l).

A teen star with the Sixties prototype garage band, the McCoys ("Hang On Sloopy"), singer/guitarist Rick Derringer joined Johnny and Edgar Winter for several successful albums in the early Seventies. He has conducted an uneven solo career since.

Rick Zehringer formed the McCoys at age 13 after he and his younger brother, drummer Randy, persuaded the kid next door to buy a bass. Producer/songwriter Bert

Berns brought them to New York, where they recorded "Hang On Sloopy." In mid-1965 that song became the McCoys' only #1 hit. "Fever" hit #7 later that year.

A few minor hits followed, and in the late Sixties Zehringer produced a couple of psychedelic blues-rock albums for the group. By 1969 the McCoys were the house band at Steve Paul's club, the Scene, in New York. Paul soon became their manager and introduced them to Johnny Winter. After changing his name to Derringer, Rick produced and played on several Winter albums (including *Johnny Winter And* and the gold *Live Johnny Winter And*). When Johnny quit touring to kick a heroin habit in late 1971, Derringer joined Johnny's brother Edgar Winter and his band White Trash for a seven-month tour (he appears on *Roadwork*). Derringer then produced Edgar's *They Only Come Out at Night* and the #1 instrumental single "Frankenstein." By December 1973 he was back on the road with Edgar and cobilled as a feature attraction.

Derringer's first solo album, *All American Boy* (#25, 1973), featured his best-known composition, "Rock and Roll Hoochie Coo" (previously recorded by both Winters), which went to #15 as a single. In 1973 he produced Johnny Winter's "comeback" LP, *Still Alive and Well*. He continued studio work with Johnny (*Saints and Sinners*) and Edgar throughout the Seventies. In addition, he played guitar on sessions with Steely Dan, Alice Cooper, Bette Midler, Todd Rundgren, and many others.

Derringer's unsuccessful second solo album prompted the 1976 formation of a group called Derringer. The group produced four albums (*Derringer, Sweet Evil, If I Weren't So Romantic, I'd Shoot You,* and *Live*) and toured constantly through the late Seventies. But the group never clicked, and Rick ended the decade playing East Coast clubs with makeshift pickup bands that for a while included guitarist Neil Giraldo and drummer Myron Grombacher, who later joined Pat Benatar's band. After *Good Dirty Fun,* Derringer would not release another album for ten years.

Behind the scenes through the Eighties, Derringer produced demos for Cyndi Lauper's first solo album; produced and played on singles and albums by "Weird" Al Yankovic (from 1983's "I Love Rocky Road" to 1990's *UHF*); and sang on and produced a single for professional wrestler Hulk Hogan ("Real American") and a version of "Rock and Roll Hoochie Koo" by Wrestlemania. Derringer returned in 1993 with *Back to the Blues*.

Desert Rose Band: See Flying Burrito Brothers

Jackie DeShannon

Born August 21, 1944, Hazel, Kentucky
1968—*Laurel Canyon* (Imperial) 1969—*Put a Little*

Love in Your Heart   1972—*Jackie* (Atlantic)
1974—*Your Baby Is a Lady*   1975—*New Arrangement* (Columbia)   1978—*You're the Only Dancer* (Amherst); *Songs* (Capitol)   1991—*The Best of Jackie DeShannon* (Rhino).

Singer/songwriter Jackie DeShannon is one of the most important songwriters of her time, and many of her songs, made hits by other artists, are classics: Brenda Lee's "Dum Dum" (1961), the Byrds' "Don't Doubt Yourself, Babe" (1965), the Searchers' "Needles and Pins" and "When You Walk in the Room" (both 1964), and Kim Carnes' "Bette Davis Eyes" (1981). In the course of a career that has spanned more than four decades, DeShannon has recorded in a wide range of pop styles, from folk to standards.

Born into a musical Kentucky family, she had her own local radio show by age 11 and scored a regional hit when she moved with her family to Chicago. She landed on the West Coast in 1960. There she sang backed by a group called the Nighthawks, which eventually evolved into the Crusaders.

DeShannon's first songwriting success came in the early Sixties with hits for Brenda Lee (including "Dum Dum," #4, 1961) and the Searchers ("When You Walk in the Room," #35, 1964; a minor hit for DeShannon as well). In 1965 the Byrds included her "Don't Doubt Yourself, Babe" on *Mr. Tambourine Man.* DeShannon began recording in 1960, though, as she later remarked, her record company tolerated rather than encouraged her. In 1963 she and Ry Cooder formed a short-lived and unrecorded band. In 1964 she opened for the Beatles during their first American tour. Later that year, she met Jimmy Page in England, and they wrote several songs in early 1965 that were recorded by Marianne Faithfull (for whom Jackie penned the British hit "Come Stay with Me"). Page plays on her "Don't Turn Your Back on Me." DeShannon's single of Burt Bacharach's "What the World Needs Now Is Love" was a #7 hit in 1965 and earned four Grammy nominations. Her next hit was the four-million-selling "Put a Little Love in Your Heart" (#4) in 1969.

In the early Seventies DeShannon recorded *Your Baby Is a Lady* and *Jackie* in a slick country-soul style, but neither LP sold well. She also sang background vocals on some Van Morrison sessions; Morrison later produced some of her own sessions. She switched to Columbia in 1975 for *New Arrangement,* which also sold poorly. In 1977 DeShannon released an album on the small Amherst label. Her songwriting prowess was still being recognized into the Eighties: Bruce Springsteen has performed "When You Walk in the Room" in concert, and DeShannon and Donna Weiss cowrote Kim Carnes' 1981 international hit, "Bette Davis Eyes," which won a Grammy for Song of the Year. She currently heads Raider Music and Film, a production company.

Devo: Bob Mothersbaugh, Bob Casale, Mark Mothersbaugh, Alan Myers, Jerry Casale

Devo
Formed 1972, Akron, Ohio
Jerry Casale, bass, voc.; Mark Mothersbaugh, voc., kybds., gtr.; Bob "Bob I" Mothersbaugh, gtr., voc.; Bob "Bob II" Casale, kybds. gtr., voc.; Alan Myers, drums.
1978—*Q: Are We Not Men? A: We Are Devo!* (Warner Bros.)   1979—*Duty Now for the Future* 1980—*Freedom of Choice*   1981—*Devo Live* EP; *New Traditionalists*   1982—*Oh No! It's Devo* 1984—*Shout* (– Myers; + David Kendrick, drums) 1987—*Now It Can Be Told* (Enigma); *Devo E-Z Listening Disc* (Rykodisc)   1988—*Total Devo* (Enigma) 1989—*Smooth Noodle Maps*   1990—*Hardcore, vol. 1* (Rykodisc)   1991—*Hardcore, vol. 2*   1992—*Live: The Mongoloid Years.*

Sporting an original tongue-in-cheek world view proclaiming man to be in a state of genetic and cultural "de-evolution," Devo made the unlikely step from novelty act to real contender—an ironic new-wave version of Kiss, whose marketing was as important as its music. The group exploited film and video from the beginning of its career, yet was never sufficiently pop-oriented to earn much play on MTV. Indeed, when Devo proved unable to follow up its one big hit, 1980's "Whip It," the group faded from view, and its smart-alecky view of America as a happy-faced toxic-waste dump found expression in *The Simpsons.*

The details of the members' pre-Devo existence were intentionally obscured as part of their automaton-like image (they always performed in uniform, favoring futuristic yet sturdy ensembles that featured yellow reactor-attendant suits, upturned red flowerpots for hats, and roller-derby-style protective gear). Mark Mothersbaugh and Jerry Casale met while studying art at

Kent State University. Neither was musical, so to build their band, the two recruited their "Bob I" and "Bob II" brothers and drummer Alan Myers and produced a ten-minute video clip entitled *The Truth About De-Evolution,* which won a prize at the Ann Arbor Film Festival in 1975. They followed up with club dates. In summer 1977 Devo released its first single, "Jocko Homo" b/w "Mongoloid," on its own Booji Boy Records (the infantile robot Booji was the group's corporate mascot and was often featured in videos and concerts). Devo's cutting-edge status was confirmed when David Bowie introduced the band at its New York City debut, at Max's Kansas City. In early 1978 its second single, a syncopated version of the Rolling Stones' "Satisfaction," increased the band's growing cult and garnered the group a record deal with Warner Bros.

Q: Are We Not Men? A: We Are Devo!, produced by Brian Eno, was released in fall 1978, and the group hit the road in earnest. *Freedom of Choice* provided their 1980 commercial breakthrough by eventually going platinum with the million-selling single "Whip It." Devo continued to revive rock chestnuts with noteworthy success. The group covered Johnny Rivers' "Secret Agent Man" in 1980 and received substantial airplay in mid-1981 with a hiccupy rendition of Lee Dorsey's "Working in a Coalmine." The group also changed its identity: Clad in leisure suits and crooning born-again lounge music, Devo occasionally opened its own concerts disguised as "Dove, the Band of Love."

Neither *New Traditionalists* nor *Oh No! It's Devo* produced a hit single. (Devo's last charting single was "Theme from *Dr. Detroit*" [#59, 1983], for the Dan Aykroyd comedy film). The band lost its Warner Bros. contract and disappeared for four years. Mark Mothersbaugh began composing and producing music for commercials and television shows, including CBS' *Pee Wee's Playhouse,* Nickelodeon's *Rugrats,* and MTV's *Liquid Television.*

With Alan Myers replaced by David Kendrick, Devo re-formed for *Total Devo* (1988), which barely charted. A subsequent tour of small halls and large clubs, with no expensive high-tech theatrics, yielded the live album *Now It Can Be Told.* Devo's next studio album, *Smooth Noodle Maps,* failed to chart at all, and the band once again vanished—just as its songs began being covered by alternative-rock bands (Nirvana with "Turnaround"; Soundgarden and Superchunk with "Girl U Want"). In 1992 two bands—Los Angeles' Clawhammer and Chicago's Honeywagon—emerged, playing nothing but Devo songs (echoing the 1980 Rhino collection *KROQ Devotees Album*). By then Rykodisc had begun issuing archival live and studio Devo tracks, including the *E-Z Listening Disc* (originally available only through Devo's fan club), on which the band recorded Muzak versions of its own songs. Devo reunited in 1991 for a 30-city European tour. In 1995 Devo wrote and recorded a new song for the soundtrack to the movie *Mighty Morphin Power Rangers.*

Neil Diamond

Born January 24, 1941, Brooklyn, New York
1966—*The Feel of Neil Diamond* (Bang)   1967—*Just for You*   1968—*Neil Diamond's Greatest Hits; Velvet Gloves and Spit* (Uni)   1969—*Brother Love's Traveling Salvation Show; Touching You, Touching Me*   1970—*Neil Diamond Gold; Tap Root Manuscript; Shilo* (Bang)   1971—*Do It!; Stones* (Uni)   1972—*Moods; Hot August Night* (MCA)   1973—*Double Gold* (Bang); *Rainbow* (MCA); *Jonathan Livingston Seagull* soundtrack (Columbia)   1974—*His 12 Greatest Hits* (MCA); *Serenade* (Columbia)   1976—*Beautiful Noise; And the Singer Sings His Song* (MCA)   1977—*Love at the Greek* (Columbia); *I'm Glad You're Here with Me Tonight*   1978—*You Don't Bring Me Flowers*   1979—*September Morn*   1980—*The Jazz Singer* soundtrack (Capitol)   1981—*On the Way to the Sky* (Columbia)   1982—*12 Greatest Hits, vol. 2; Heartlight*   1983—*Classics—The Early Years*   1984—*Primitive*   1985—*Love Songs* (MCA)   1986—*Headed for the Future* (Columbia)   1987—*Hot August Night II*   1988—*The Best Years of Our Lives*   1991—*Lovescape*   1992—*The Greatest Hits 1966–1992; Glory Road—1968 to 1972* (MCA); *The Christmas Album* (Columbia)   1993—*Up on the Roof—Songs from the Brill Building*   1994—*Live in America.*

Pop songwriter Neil Diamond, a veteran of the Brill Building song factory, became one of the best-selling MOR performers of the Seventies. Singing his own melodramatic quasi-gospel songs in a portentous baritone, he has sold over 92 million records worldwide, amassing over 35 Top Forty singles and 18 platinum albums.

Diamond recorded his first single soon after graduating from Brooklyn's Erasmus Hall High School. He attended NYU as a premedical student on a fencing scholarship until 1962, when he dropped out and began hawking songs to Broadway publishers, one of whom soon hired him as a $50-a-week staff songwriter. Diamond worked for various publishers, including Don Kirshner's Aldon Music, where he wrote the Monkees' #1 1967 hit "I'm a Believer." Fellow songwriters Jeff Barry and Ellie Greenwich helped him sign in 1965 with Bang Records, for which he recorded a string of Top Twenty hits: "Cherry, Cherry" (#6, 1966), "I Got the Feeling" (#16, 1966), "You Got to Me" (#18, 1967), "Girl, You'll Be a Woman Soon" (#10, 1967), "Thank the Lord for the Night Time" (#13, 1967), and "Kentucky Woman" (#22, 1967). Bang lost interest after Diamond began looking for significance with songs like "Shilo." He moved to California in 1966, where Uni Records promised him full artistic control. His Uni (later MCA) debut, *Velvet Gloves and Spit,* sold poorly, but subsequent singles—"Brother Love's Traveling Salvation Show" (#22, 1969), "Sweet Caroline" (#4, 1969), "Cracklin' Rosie" (#1, 1970), and "Song Sung Blue" (#1, 1972)—established Diamond as a major star. He toured the U.S., Europe, and Australia in 1972 and placed two albums in the U.S. Top Five: *Moods* and the live *Hot August Night* (which also became Australia's best-selling album; three million sales in a country of 14 million people). He also played a 20-performance one-man show on Broadway in 1972.

The following year Diamond signed with Columbia for a record-breaking $5 million; his first album for his new label, the soundtrack to *Jonathan Livingston Seagull,* grossed more money than the film itself. He returned to touring in February 1976 and appeared in the Band's *Last Waltz* concert on Thanksgiving Day. Band guitarist Robbie Robertson produced Diamond's *Beautiful Noise,* a tribute to Diamond's Sixties songwriting days. It was his 11th album in a row to go gold.

NBC aired a TV special of Diamond in concert on February 24, 1977; since then his television specials have proved popular with viewers. In 1980 he starred in a poorly received remake of *The Jazz Singer.* Nonetheless, his soundtrack LP for that film went platinum five times over, yielding Top Ten singles in "Love on the Rocks," "America," and "Hello Again." *Heartlight* was another Top Five album, and the title track (#5, 1982) became a long-running staple of "Lite FM" adult-contemporary radio. *Primitive* (#35, 1984), *Headed for the Future* (#20, 1986), *Hot August Night II* (#59, 1987), and *The Best Years of Our Lives* (#46, 1989) all went gold. *Lovescape* (#44, 1991) included a duet with Kim Carnes, "Hooked on the Memory of You," Diamond's first duet since his chart-topping 1978 "You Don't Bring Me Flowers" with Barbra Streisand. *Up on the Roof* found Diamond singing the Brill Building pop of his early days. Critics panned the album, but gave glowing reviews to Diamond's subsequent tour, which as always was attended by intensely devoted throngs. Meanwhile, Diamond continues to collect royalties for the many cover versions of his songs, including Deep Purple's "Kentucky Woman" and UB40's chart-topping Eighties version of "Red, Red Wine," and Urge Overkill's "Girl, You'll Be a Woman Soon," from the 1994 *Pulp Fiction* soundtrack.

The Diamonds
Formed 1954, Toronto, Canada
Stan Fisher, lead voc.; Ted Kowalski, tenor; Phil Leavitt, baritone; Bill Reed, bass.
1958—(– Kowalski; – Reed; + John Felton [d. May 18, 1982, Mount Shasta, Calif.]; + Evan Fisher), various personnel changes through the years.   1984—*Best of the Diamonds* (Rhino).

The Diamonds were a clean-cut white vocal group that had 16 hits between 1956 and 1961, ten of which were covers of songs recorded by black R&B artists. Their first was a rendition of Frankie Lymon and the Teenagers' "Why Do Fools Fall in Love?" The Teenagers' version was the bigger hit: #7 as compared to #16 for the Diamonds. From that point on, however, the Diamonds' copies outsold and sometimes totally eclipsed the originals.

Their biggest hit, "Little Darlin'" (originally by the Gladiolas), was #2 in the U.S. in 1957 and became a big hit in the U.K. and Europe as well. Later that year they had a Top Five smash with "The Stroll," which briefly popularized the dance of the same name. The Diamonds played many package tours in the late Fifties and appeared frequently on TV variety shows. After several minor hits as the decade closed—"High Sign," "Kathy-O," "Walking Along," "She Say (Oom Dooby Doom)"—the Diamonds, by then plagued by frequent personnel changes, were reduced to a lounge act. Their last hit was 1961's "One Summer Night."

In 1974 the original lineup reunited for an oldies show in New York City. A group working under the name the Diamonds recorded a country album in 1987; this lineup contained no members from the group's golden era.

Manu Dibango
Born February 10, 1934, Douala, Cameroon
1972—*Soul Makossa* (Atlantic)   1973—*Makossa Man*; *O Boso* (London)   1975—*Makossa Music* (Creole)   1976—*Manu '76* (Decca); *Super Kumba* 1978—*Afrovision* (Island); *Sin Explosion* (Decca) 1980—*Gone Clear* (Island); *Reggae Makossa* 1981—*Ambassador* (Mango)   1983—*Melodies Africanes, vols. 1 & 2* (Sonodisc)   1984—*Deadline* (RCA)   1985—*Electric Africa* (Celluloid)   1986—*Afrijazzy*   1990—*Trois Kilos de Cafe*   1992—*Polysonik* (Soundwave).

Manu Dibango's "Soul Makossa" was one of the first African pop songs to catch on in America. Dibango moved from Cameroon to Europe at age 15 and studied piano and music theory in Paris and Brussels. At age 20 he took up the saxophone and over the next 15 years maintained a career as a jazz and R&B musician in Europe. In the late Sixties Dibango returned to Africa, settling in Kinshasa, Zaire. There he assembled a band composed of African, European, and Caribbean musicians to play an array of Western instruments (horns, keyboards, electric guitars, and basses) and traditional African instruments on music that drew on jazz, R&B, calypso, Cuban, rock, and traditional and modern African forms.

Beginning in the early Seventies, he and his bands toured and recorded in Europe and Africa. "Soul Makossa," recorded in France by La Société Française du Son in 1972 and released in the U.S. the following year, reached #35 pop and #21 R&B on the American singles chart. In 1974 Dibango toured the U.S. He traveled to the West Indies in 1980 and 1981, and there recorded with reggae musicians Sly Dunbar and Robbie Shakespeare.

Dibango returned to France in 1983 and recorded the solo piano compositions released as *Melodies Africanes, vols. 1 & 2*. He collaborated with Herbie Hancock and New York avant-funk producer/bassist Bill Laswell on *Deadline* and *Electric Africa*. Laswell also produced a remake of "Soul Makossa" on *Afrijazzy*.

Trois Kilos de Cafe, Dibango's autobiography, was published in 1990, the same year he also released an identically titled retrospective album containing rerecorded versions of his past work. In 1991, leading the Soul Makossa Gang, Dibango continued to keep his sound contemporary. Adding to the African music sung in what Dibango calls the "Negropolitan" languages, the band included the English raps of MC Mello.

Dick and Deedee
Formed 1961, Santa Monica, California
Dick St. John Gosting, b. 1944, Santa Monica; Deedee Sperling, b. 1945, Santa Monica.
N.A.—*Songs We've Sung on Shindig* (Warner Bros.); *Tell Me the Mountain's High* (Liberty); *Thou Shalt Not Steal* (Warner Bros.); *Turn Around; Young and in Love*.

A popular duo of the early Sixties, Dick and Dee Dee dressed the part of clean-cut preppies—he in conservative dark suits and she in chiffon. Friends since grammar school, they were both students at Santa Monica High School when Liberty Records (for whom Dick had previously recorded on his own) contracted them to cut a single in 1961. Their first release was "I Want Someone," backed by "The Mountain's High." The B side became the duo's biggest hit, peaking at #2 in mid-1961.

In 1962 Dick and Deedee left Liberty for Warner Bros., where they had a few successful chart records beginning with "Young and in Love" (#17, 1963), continuing through "Turn Around" (#27, 1963), and the Top Fifteen lesson in morality "Thou Shalt Not Steal" (#13) in late 1964. They toured on and off, but continued to devote the bulk of their time to school, even at the height of their career. By the mid-Sixties they had retired from pop music. As Dick and Sandy St. John they published *Rock & Roll Cookbook*, with recipes collected from artists as diverse as Bobby Lewis and Kurt Cobain, in 1993.

The Dickies
Formed 1977, Los Angeles, California
Chuck Wagon (d. 1981), kybds.; Stan Lee (b. Sept. 24, 1956), gtr.; Billy Club, bass; Leonard Graves Phillips, voc.; Karlos Kabellero, drums; John Melvoin, drums; Enoch Hain, gtr.; Charlie Alexander, bass; Lorenzo Buhne, bass; Cliff Martinez, drums.
1979—*The Incredible Shrinking Dickies* (A&M); *Dawn of the Dickies* 1983—(– Wagon) *Stukas over Disneyland* (PVC) 1986—*We Aren't the World!* (ROIR) 1988—*Killer Klowns* EP (Enigma) 1989—*Great Dictations* (A&M); *Second Coming* (Enigma) 1994—*Idjit Savant* (Triple X).

The Dickies are best known for their covers of "classic" rock tunes, which they speed up to comic proportions. Their repertoire includes "Nights in White Satin," "Eve of Destruction," the Banana Splits television cartoon theme song, "Communication Breakdown," "Hair," and Black Sabbath's "Paranoid." The San Fernando Valley group was one of L.A.'s most popular punk bands in the late Seventies, although A&M was undoubtedly disappointed that their local following never expanded nationally. Alongside their twisted covers, they have penned such originals as "(I'm Stuck in a Pagoda) with Tricia Toyota" and "Rondo (The Midget's Revenge)"; tunes like "I'm a Chollo" and "Goin' Homo" proved that there were no limits to how low the Dickies would sink for a laugh. In 1988 their perennial B-movie sensibility landed one of their tracks in the movie *Killer Klowns from Outer Space*. The band has gone through a number of personnel changes, including the 1981 suicide of keyboardist Chuck Wagon, with Lee and Phillips remaining the band's core. The Dickies continued to perform and record into the Nineties.

The Dictators
Formed 1974, Bronx, New York
Handsome Dick Manitoba (b. Richard Blum, Jan. 29, 1954), voc.; Ross the Boss Funicello (b. Jan. 3, 1954, Bronx), gtr., voc.; Scott "Top Ten" Kempner (b. Feb. 6, 1954, Bronx), gtr., voc.; Adny Shernoff (b. Andy Shernoff, Apr. 19, 1952, Bronx), kybds., bass, voc.; Stu Boy King, drums.
1975—*Go Girl Crazy* (Epic) (– King; + Ritchie Teeter [b. Mar. 16, 1951, Long Island, N.Y.], drums; + Mark Mendoza [b. July 13, 1956, Long Island, N.Y.], bass) 1977—*Manifest Destiny* (Elektra) (– Mendoza) 1978—*Bloodbrothers* (Asylum) 1981—*Fuck 'Em If They Can't Take a Joke* cassette (ROIR) 1994—(Lineup: Manitoba; Funicello; Kempner; Shernoff; + Frank Funaro, drums).
Del-Lords: 1984—*Frontier Days* (Enigma) 1986—*Johnny Comes Marching Home* 1988—*Based on a True Story* 1989—*Howlin' at the Halloween Moon* (Restless) 1990—*Lovers Who Wander* (Enigma).
Manitoba's Wild Kingdom: 1990— . . . *And You?* (Popular Metaphysics/MCA).

Loved by some, hated by many more, and misunderstood or ignored by the rest, the Dictators straddled heavy metal and punk rock with a slapstick sense of humor. In the early Seventies Andy "Adny" Shernoff was editing a mimeographed rock fanzine, *Teenage Wasteland Gazette,* an influence on *Creem* and a forerunner of *Punk* magazine. With virtually no musical experience, he gave up writing to form the Dictators with Scott Kempner and Ross the Boss Funicello. The latter had been in a unit called Total Crud. Manitoba, who began as their roadie, soon became their vocalist and front man.

Though their music was much closer to brazenly amateurish heavy metal than punk, the Dictators were mainstays in the early days at Manhattan's CBGB. In 1976 Manitoba was nearly killed when, after he heckled transvestite (now transsexual) rocker Wayne/Jayne County at CBGB, County hit him over the head with a microphone stand. Despite, or because of, such antics, their debut was a critical success, but sold only 6,000 copies.

They broke up in late 1978, Teeter resurfacing in a New York band called VHF a year later. Ross the Boss went to San Francisco in 1979 and formed Shakin' Street, which released one LP for Columbia in 1980; in 1982 he formed a heavy-metal band called Manowar. Mendoza joined the briefly incredibly popular Twisted Sister, as did Teeter at one point. Shernoff has been involved in Off Broadway theatrical productions and has produced many records for New York bands. Kempner formed the Del-Lords, and Manitoba and Shernoff belonged to Manitoba's Wild Kingdom, which by 1990 also included Ross the Boss Funicello. The Dictators played several reunion shows in 1980, 1981, 1986, and 1987. They performed as part of CBGB's 20th-anniversary celebration in 1994, which precipitated a full-scale reformation.

Bo Diddley

Born Ellas Bates, December 30, 1928, McComb, Mississippi
1962—*Bo Diddley* (Checker)   1963—*Is a Gunslinger*; *Bo Diddley Rides Again* (Pye, U.K.) 1964—*Two Great Guitars* (with Chuck Berry) (Chess); *Hey Good Looking*   1965—*Let Me Pass* 1974—*Big Bad Bo* (Checker)   1975—*Another Dimension*   1976—*20th Anniversary* (RCA)   1986— *Superblues: Bo Diddley, Muddy Waters, and Little Walter* (Chess/MCA)   1989—*Breaking Through the B.S.* (Triple X)   1990—*The Chess Box* (Chess/MCA) 1993—*This Should Not Be* (Triple X); *Live*   1994— *Promises* EP   1995—*The Mighty Bo Diddley.*

Bo Diddley's syncopated "hambone" beat—CHINK-a-CHINK-a-CHINK, a-CHINK-CHINK—is a cornerstone of rock & roll songs, from Diddley's own "Who Do You Love," "Mona," "Bo Diddley," and "I'm a Man" to the Who's "Magic Bus," Bruce Springsteen's "She's the One," and the Pretenders' "Cuban Slide." Dressed in black and sporting a low-slung rectangular guitar and thick horn-rimmed glasses, Diddley has been on the road for over four decades.

Adopted by a Mississippi sharecropping family who changed his last name to McDaniel, he moved with them to the South Side of Chicago. As a child he began studying violin under Professor O. W. Frederick at the Ebenezer Baptist Church. In grammar school he acquired the Bo Diddley nickname, given to him by classmates. By the time he entered Foster Vocational School in his early teens, he had switched to the guitar and regularly played on Chicago's Maxwell Street when he wasn't in school, where he learned to make violins and guitars. After several years of performing on streetcorners, he played at the 708 Club in 1951 and became a regular South Side performer for the next four years.

In July 1955 Leonard Chess signed Diddley to his Checker label. Diddley's first single, "Bo Diddley," was an immediate #1 R&B success. "I'm a Man" (1955, later recorded by the Yardbirds and others) also fared well on the R&B chart. His biggest pop success came in 1959, when "Say Man" (#3 R&B) hit the Top Twenty late in the year. He had a lesser hit in 1962 with the rollicking "You Can't Judge a Book by the Cover" (#48 pop, #21 R&B). According to Diddley, he never received royalties during those years.

Diddley toured steadily through the late Fifties and early Sixties, playing rock package tours and one-nighters at R&B venues. The band that recorded with him in the mid-Fifties included drummers Clifton James and Frank Kirkland, pianist Otis Spann, Bo's half-sister "The Duchess" on guitar and vocals, and Diddley's eternal sidekick, bassist and maracas shaker Jerome Green (who also provided call-and-response repartee on "Hey Bo Diddley" and "Bring It to Jerome").

Diddley's legacy was enhanced considerably during the mid-Sixties, when many of his songs were covered by British Invasion groups like the Rolling Stones. Through the years, his material has also been recorded by the Doors, Tom Rush, Quicksilver Messenger Service, and Ronnie Hawkins, among many others.

Diddley has recorded erratically over the past three decades. In the early Sixties he even recorded surfing albums (*Surfin' with Bo Diddley*). In the mid-Sixties he recorded traditional blues with Little Walter and Muddy Waters on *Superblues* (reissued in 1986). In the early Seventies Diddley continued to tour frequently, concentrating on Europe. One such outing was documented in *Let the Good Times Roll.* Around the same time, he also appeared in D. A. Pennebaker's *Keep On Rockin'.* In 1976 RCA released *20th Anniversary of Rock 'n' Roll,* a tribute to Diddley that featured over 20 artists. Diddley opened several dates for the Clash on their 1979 U.S. tour. He

Digable Planets: Doodlebug, Ladybug, Butterfly

made cameo appearances in George Thorogood's video "Bad to the Bone" (1982) and the Dan Aykroyd–Eddie Murphy movie *Trading Places*. He tried recording over electro-funk grooves on 1993's *This Should Not Be*; critics agreed with the album's title. As of the mid-Nineties, Diddley continues to write and perform.

Digable Planets

Formed 1989, New York City, New York
Butterfly (b. Ishmael Butler, July 3, 1969, Seattle, Wash.), voc.; Ladybug (Katrina Lust), voc.; Squibble the Termite (Michael Gabredikan), DJ.
1992—(– Lust; – Gabredikan; + Doodlebug [b. Craig Irving, Feb. 20, 1967, Philadelphia, Pa.], voc.; + Ladybug, a.k.a. Mecca, [b. Mary Ann Vieira, July 25, 1973, Washington, D.C.], voc.) 1993—*Reachin' (a new refutation of time and space)* (Elektra) 1994—*Blowout Comb*.

Digable Planets were the most successful group to emerge from the 1993 "jazz rap" movement—in which middle-class black bohemians, acutely aware of their cultural heritage and far less angry-sounding than inner-city hard-core rappers, revived a style that went back to the late Sixties' Last Poets. Digable Planets briefly crossed over to the pop charts in spring 1993 with the single "Rebirth of Slick (Cool Like Dat)" (#15 pop, #8 R&B), which featured sampled horn riffs from a record by hard-bop jazz great Art Blakey and his Jazz Messengers.

The first version of the group met at City College of New York; according to founder Butterfly, the group name came from the belief that "each person is a planet," and the individual members' names from admiration for the selfless, community orientation of some insect species. Butterfly recruited Doodlebug from the New York City rap/poetry collective Dread Poets Society; Doodlebug brought along his friend, Mecca, who became the second Ladybug. Butterfly's father had exposed him to Blue Note jazz as a youth; Doodlebug's father had been a member of the Black Panthers; Ladybug's parents were Brazilian.

Digable Planets emerged from a "hip bop" scene that had been fermenting since at least 1989, when Spike Lee had recruited Gang Starr, which was already mixing jazz samples into its records, to record "Jazz Thing" for his film *Mo' Better Blues*. Following such jazz-rap hybrids as A Tribe Called Quest and Us3, Digable Planets released the mellow *Reachin'* (#15 pop, #5 R&B, 1993). In addition to the Blakey horns in "Rebirth of Slick," the album included samples from Sonny Rollins, Eddie Harris, the Last Poets, and the Crusaders (as well as K.C. and the Sunshine Band and Curtis Mayfield), and lyrics saluting jazz legends, existentialist authors, Nikki Giovanni, and Jimi Hendrix.

Digital Underground

Formed 1988, Oakland, California
Shock-G (b. Greg Jacobs, Aug. 25, 1963, Queens, N.Y.), voc.; Humpty Hump (b. Edward Ellington Humphrey, May 25, 1966, Tampa, Fla.), voc.; Money

Grammy Awards

Charlie Daniels Band
1979 Best Country Vocal Performance by a Duo or Group: "The Devil Went Down to Georgia"

Terence Trent D'Arby
1988 Best R&B Vocal Performance, Male: *Introducing the Hardline According to Terence Trent D'Arby*

Bobby Darin
1959 Best New Artist of 1959
1959 Record of the Year: "Mack the Knife"

Miles Davis
1960 Best Jazz Composition of More Than Five Minutes: "Sketches of Spain" (with Gil Evans)
1970 Best Jazz Performance, Large Group or Soloist with Large Group: *Bitches Brew*
1982 Best Jazz Instrumental Performance, Soloist: *We Want Miles*
1986 Best Jazz Instrumental Performance, Soloist: *Tutu*
1989 Best Jazz Instrumental Performance, Big Band: *Aura*
1989 Best Jazz Instrumental Performance, Soloist (on a Jazz Recording): *Aura*
1990 Lifetime Achievement Award
1992 Best R&B Instrumental Performance: *Doo-Bop*
1993 Best Large Jazz Ensemble Performance: *Miles & Quincy Live at Montreux* (with Quincy Jones)

The Delfonics
1970 Best R&B Vocal Performance by a Duo or Group: "Didn't I (Blow Your Mind This Time)"

Jackie DeShannon
1981 Song of the Year: "Bette Davis Eyes" (with Donna Weiss)

Neil Diamond
1973 Album of Best Original Score Written for a Motion Picture: *Jonathan Livingston Seagull*

Digable Planets
1993 Best Rap Performance by a Duo or Group: "Rebirth of Slick (Cool Like Dat)"

Dire Straits
1985 Best Rock Performance by a Duo or Group with Vocal: "Money for Nothing"
1986 Best Music Video, Short Form: *Dire Straits: Brothers in Arms*

Mark Knopfler (Dire Straits)
1985 Best Country Instrumental Performance: "Cosmic Square Dance" (with Chet Atkins)
1990 Best Country Instrumental Performance: "So Soft, Your Goodbye" (with Chet Atkins)
1990 Best Country Vocal Collaboration: "Poor Boy Blues" (with Chet Atkins)

The Dixie Hummingbirds
1973 Best Soul Gospel Performance: "Loves Me Like a Rock"

Willie Dixon
1988 Best Traditional Blues Recording: *Hidden Charms*

Dr. John
1989 Best Jazz Vocal Performance, Duo or Group: "Makin' Whoopee" (with Rickie Lee Jones)
1992 Best Traditional Blues Album: *Goin' Back to New Orleans*

Fats Domino
1987 Lifetime Achievement Award

The Doobie Brothers
1979 Record of the Year: "What a Fool Believes"
1979 Best Pop Vocal Performance by a Duo, Group or Chorus: *Minute by Minute*

Duran Duran
1983 Best Video Album: *Duran Duran*
1983 Best Video, Short Form: "Girls on Film"/"Hungry Like the Wolf"

Bob Dylan
[See also: Traveling Wilburys]
1972 Album of the Year: *The Concert for Bangla Desh* (with others)
1979 Best Rock Vocal Performance, Male: "Gotta Serve Somebody"
1991 Lifetime Achievement Award
1994 Best Traditional Folk Album: *World Gone Wrong*

B. (b. Ronald Brooks, Sep. 22, 1969, Oakland), voc.; DJ Fuze (b. David Scott, Syracuse, N.Y.), DJ. 1990—*Sex Packets* (Tommy Boy); *This Is an E.P. Release* EP 1991—*Sons of the P* 1993—*The Body-Hat Syndrome*.
Raw Fusion (Money B. and DJ Fuze): 1991—*Live From the Styleetron* (Hollywood) 1994—*Hoochiefied Funk*.

Digital Underground strives to be the Parliament/Funkadelic of rap. Like P-Funk's George Clinton, D.U. mastermind Shock-G wears colorful costumes onstage and assumes a variety of zany alter egos in the music. Also like P-Funk, the group is an umbrella organization: With its core membership based in the Bay Area, Digital Underground uses a revolving-door crew of musicians from around the country, some of whom are pseudonymously credited.

Shock-G is the child of a television producer mother and computer executive father. As a boy, he was shuttled between Florida, New York, Pennsylvania, and California. In the late Seventies he dropped out of high school and got involved in street life—pimping, selling drugs, and stealing cars. He eventually returned to school, earning his high school diploma and taking college courses in music. In 1987 he put together the first version of Digital Underground in Oakland and scored a #1 hit in the Netherlands with his self-released single, "Underwater Rimes."

In 1990 the current lineup released its debut album, *Sex Packets* (#24 pop, #8 R&B, 1990), which sold a million copies on the strength of a #11 pop single, "Humpty Dance," rapped by Shock-G's alter ego, Humpty Hump. The album was praised for its clever lyrics and inventive mixes. The gold followup, *This Is an E.P. Release*, reached #29 on the pop charts, and featured rapper 2Pac [see entry].

D.U.'s *Sons of the P* (#44 pop, #23 R&B, 1991) (P standing for P-Funk) featured George Clinton and included the single "Kiss You Back," which barely made the Top Forty. *The Body-Hat Syndrome* (#79 pop, #16 R&B) continued their sociopolitical commentary of previous albums (proposing the use of a mind condom—a Body Hat—for protection from the power structure).

The Dillards

Formed 1962, Salem, Missouri
Rodney Dillard (b. May 18, 1942, Salem), voc., gtr., synth., dobro; Doug Dillard (b. Mar. 6, 1937, Salem), banjo; Mitchell Jayne (b. May 7, 1930, Salem), bass; Dean Webb (b. Mar. 28, 1937, Independence, Mo.), mandolin.
1963—*Back Porch Bluegrass* (Elektra) 1964— *Live . . . Almost!* (+ Byron Berline [b. July 6, 1944, Caldwell, Kan.], fiddle) 1965—*Pickin' and Fiddlin'* (– D. Dillard; + Herb Pederson, banjo; – Berline) 1968—*Wheatstraw Suite* 1970—(+ Paul York, drums) *Copperfields* 1972—(– Pederson; + Billy Ray Latham, banjo) *Roots and Branches* (Anthem) 1973—*Tribute to the American Duck* (Poppy) 1974—(– Jayne; + Jeff Gilkinson, bass) 1976—*Best of the Dillards* 1977—*The Dillards Versus Incredible L.A. Time Machine* (Flying Fish) 1979—*Mountain Rock* (Crystal Clear); *Decade Waltz* (Flying Fish) 1980—*Homecoming and Family Reunion* 1985—*Rodney Dillard at Silver Dollar City* 1988— (– R. Dillard; group disbands) 1990—(Group reforms: R. Dillard; D. Dillard; Jayne; Webb) *Let It Fly* (Vanguard).
Dillard and Clark (Doug Dillard; Gene Clark; others): 1969—*Fantastic Expedition* (A&M) 1970— *Through the Morning, Through the Night.*
Doug Dillard and Band: 1968—*The Banjo Album* (Together) 1973—*Dueling Banjos; You Don't Need a Reason to Sing* 1976—*Heaven* (Flying Fish) 1979—*Jack Rabbit!* 1986—*What's That?* 1989— *Heartbreak Hotel.*
Dillard-Hartford-Dillard (Dillard brothers with John Hartford): 1976—*Glitter Grass from the Nashwood Hollyville Strings* (Flying Fish) 1980—*Permanent Wave.*
Herb Pederson solo: 1976—*Southwest* (Epic) 1977—*Sandman* 1984—*Lonesome Feeling* (Sugar Hill).

A bluegrass band from the Ozarks that went electric, the Dillards helped pave the way for country rock, the bluegrass revival, and newgrass. The original quartet left Missouri for Hollywood in 1962. They were cast to play a hillbilly band, the Darling Family, on *The Andy Griffith Show* and were signed by Elektra. Their 1963 debut, *Back Porch Bluegrass,* included "Duelin' Banjos," which Eric Weissberg later popularized in the 1972 film *Deliverance.* Their repertoire grew to include Bob Dylan songs as well as traditional bluegrass, and on a 1965 tour with the Byrds the Dillards reportedly helped Roger McGuinn arrange vocal harmonies on *Mr. Tambourine Man.* By then their lineup included national fiddling champion Byron Berline.

In 1965 Doug Dillard left the Dillards; he played on *Gene Clark with the Gosdin Brothers* and in 1968 formed the Dillard-Clark Expedition. The Expedition's first album lineup included Bernie Leadon, later of the Flying Burrito Brothers and the Eagles; they toured with another ex-Byrd, drummer Michael Clarke, who then joined the Burrito Brothers. Berline joined the group for its second album, but the Expedition disbanded in 1969. Doug Dillard recorded solo albums in the early Seventies and has continued to work as a studio musician. In 1976 the Dillard brothers recorded the first of two albums with their former neighbor John Hartford, and Doug continued to record with his band through the late Eighties.

Meanwhile, Rodney maintained the Dillards band name and released increasingly electric albums with a shifting band through the Seventies and Eighties. By 1987, he was the sole remaining original member, and the next year, the group broke up, but not for long. In 1989 the original quartet reunited, an event captured on the video *A Night in the Ozarks.* Pederson produced their reunion effort, *Let It Fly.*

Dino, Desi and Billy

Formed circa 1964, Los Angeles, California
Dino Martin Jr. (b. Nov. 17, 1953, Los Angeles; d. Mar. 21, 1987, near Riverside, Calif.), bass; Desi Arnaz Jr. (b. Jan. 19, 1953, Los Angeles), drums; Billy Hinsche (b. June 29, 1953), gtr.
1965—*I'm a Fool* (Reprise) 1966—*Our Time's Coming.*

Teenybopper favorites Dino, Desi and Billy consisted of Dean Martin's son, the son of Desi Arnaz and Lucille Ball,

Dinosaur Jr: Murph, J Mascis, Mike Johnson

and the son of a real-estate broker who'd sold houses to both Martin and Arnaz Sr. Frank Sinatra heard them playing at Dino Sr.'s home and helped them get a contract with Reprise. The trio hit the pop chart in 1965 with "I'm a Fool" (#17) and "Not the Lovin' Kind" (#25). Though presented as basically cuddly and cute, DD&B were also hip and later tackled heavier fare like Dylan's "Chimes of Freedom." By 1966 they were eclipsed by psychedelia. Hinsche later became a regular in the Beach Boys' touring troupe. Martin was a moderately successful tennis professional and married actress Olivia Hussey and then skating star Dorothy Hamill (he had remarried at the time of his death). In March 1987 Martin, a member of the California Air National Guard, died on a routine exercise flight, when his F-4C Phantom jet crashed into California's San Bernardino Mountains. Arnaz has pursued an acting career.

Dinosaur Jr

Formed 1984, Amherst, Massachusetts
J Mascis (b. Joseph D. Mascis, Dec. 10, 1965), gtr., voc.; Lou Barlow (b. July 17, 1966, Northampton, Mass.), bass; Murph (b. Emmett "Patrick" J. Murphy, Dec. 21, 1964), drums.

1985—*Dinosaur* (Homestead)   1987—*You're Living All Over Me* (SST)   1988—*Bug* (– Barlow; + various guests)   1989—*Just Like Heaven* EP   1991—*The Wagon* EP (Blanco y Negro)   1991—*Green Mind* (Sire)   1992—(+ Mike Johnson [b. Michael Allen Johnson, Aug. 27, 1965], bass) *Whatever's Cool with Me* EP   1993—*Where You Been*   1994—(– Murph) *Without a Sound*.
Lou Barlow with Sebadoh: 1989—*Freed Weed* (Homestead)   1991—*III*   1992—*Smash Your Head on the Punk Rock* (Sub Pop)   1993—*Bubble & Scrape*   1994—*Bakesale*.

Dinosaur Jr is the vehicle for J Mascis' grungy lead guitar style, ragged vocals, and inward-looking song lyrics—a combination owing as much to Neil Young as to the postpunk fury of such early-Eighties alternative pioneers as Hüsker Dü.

From early on, Mascis was known for his lethargic, nontalkative demeanor and reclusive lifestyle, and he has often been described as a "slacker." After his hardcore band Deep Wound broke up in 1983, Mascis and bassist Lou Barlow formed Dinosaur in the liberal environment of their hometown, the five-college city of Amherst, Massachusetts. At the time, Mascis played drums. When former All White Jury drummer Patrick "Murph" Murphy joined, Mascis moved to guitar. The band recorded one album for the East Coast independent label Homestead before signing to the West Coast independent SST in 1987. Meanwhile, the attention the band received for its growing cult status got them into legal hot water with another group that called itself the Dinosaurs. When that group (consisting of former members of such Sixties bands as Jefferson Airplane and Country Joe and the Fish) sued, Mascis and company were forced to change the name; they chose to simply add "Jr."

After the release of the underground smash single "Freak Scene," followed by *Bug*, Barlow quit to form Sebadoh (which later recorded on Sub Pop). Dinosaur went through a revolving-door period upon landing its Sire contract, with temporary members including the Screaming Trees' Van Connor and Gumball's Don Fleming; Mascis, meanwhile, also sat in on drums with other bands, including hometown buddies Gobblehoof. On *Green Mind* Mascis played nearly everything himself, the guitar with the most success. After new bassist Mike Johnson joined, the band put out an EP, *Whatever's Cool with Me*, and followed up with the full-length *Where You Been* (#50, 1993). That album was greeted with massive critical success. In 1993 Dinosaur Jr appeared on the summer's Lollapalooza Tour. Murph left in 1994, so Mascis was back to playing the drums, etc., himself on *Without a Sound* (#44, 1994), seemingly concentrating on his singing rather than his fretboard.

Dion and the Belmonts/Dion DiMucci

Formed 1958, Bronx, New York
Dion (b. Dion DiMucci, July 18, 1939, Bronx), lead voc.; Fred Milano (b. Aug. 22, 1939, Bronx), second tenor voc.; Carlo Mastrangelo (b. Oct. 5, 1938, Bronx), baritone voc.; Angelo D'Aleo (b. Feb. 3, 1940, Bronx), first tenor voc.
1959—*Presenting Dion and the Belmonts* (Laurie). Dion DiMucci solo: 1961—*Runaround Sue* (Laurie) 1962—*Lovers Who Wander* 1963—*Ruby Baby* (Columbia); *Dion Sings to Sandy (and All His Other Girls)* (Laurie) 1968—*Dion* 1969—*Sit Down Old Friend* (Warner Bros.) 1971—*You're Not Alone*; *Sanctuary* 1972—*Suite for Late Summer* 1973— *Reunion* 1976—*Streetheart* 1977—*Dion's Greatest Hits* (Columbia) 1978—*Return of the Wanderer* (Lifesong) 1984—*24 Original Classics* (Arista) 1989—*Yo Frankie* 1992—*Dream on Fire*.

Perhaps the suavest of New York City's late-Fifties white teen idols, Dion DiMucci broke from that clean-cut pack with an engagingly cool, streetwise swagger epitomized by "The Wanderer." Through the years, he has boldly essayed new musical directions with mixed results, yet endured as an influence on rock singers ranging from Billy Joel to Lou Reed.

He started singing at age five and picked up a guitar a few years later. As a teenager he began singing on streetcorners. He also began dabbling in drugs and eventually acquired a heroin habit that he didn't kick until 1968. Shortly after dropping out of high school, Dion recorded a demo as a Valentine's Day present for his mother. It reached the producers of the *Teen Club* TV show out of Philadelphia, where Dion made his performing debut in 1954.

Recording his vocals separately over those of a backing group called the Timberlanes, he released "The Chosen Few," and in early 1958 Dion rounded up some neighborhood friends and dubbed them the Belmonts after Belmont Avenue, a street near the Bronx's Italian Arthur Avenue area. Their second single, "I Wonder Why," skirted the Top Twenty. "No One Knows" and "Don't Pity Me" followed, but the big break came in the spring of 1959, when "A Teenager in Love" (#5) became an international hit. The next year "Where or When" climbed to #3.

The group toured frequently, often on package tours with other stars; in February 1959 Dion passed up a ride on a chartered plane that later crashed, killing Buddy Holly, Ritchie Valens, and the Big Bopper. But soon Dion felt confined, and his drug dependency worsened. (When "Where or When" peaked, he was in a hospital detoxifying.)

By early 1960 Dion was recording solo, backed by the uncredited Del-Satins. He hit the Top Ten with "Runaround Sue" (#1), "The Wanderer" (#2), "Lovers Who Wander" (#3), and "Little Diane" (#8) in 1962, and "Ruby Baby" (#2), "Drip Drop" (#6), and "Donna the Prima Donna" (#6) in 1963. By then he was recording for Columbia.

In 1964 Dion went into near seclusion, releasing a string of unsuccessful covers ("Johnny B. Goode," "Spoonful"). He reappeared in 1965 for another round with the Belmonts (who'd remained active after 1960, achieving moderate success with "Tell Me Why" and "Come on Little Angel"). Together they released "Mr. Movin' Man" and "Berimbau" and an album for ABC. In early 1968 he moved with his wife, Susan (the real "Runaround Sue," whom he married in 1963), and their daughter to Miami, where, with the help of his father-in-law, he finally kicked heroin. (The couple had two more daughters.) Later that year he recorded "Abraham, Martin and John," a #4 hit ballad tribute to Lincoln, King, and Kennedy; the flop followup was a cover of Jimi Hendrix's "Purple Haze."

Dion spent the next few years on the coffeehouse circuit. His Warner Bros. debut, *Sit Down Old Friend,* featured just his voice and acoustic guitar on eight songs. He also released a nonalbum single, the antidrug "Your Own Backyard." Both that folky album and the lusher *Suite for Late Summer* failed to sell, and Dion reunited with the Belmonts. The group played Madison Square Garden in mid-1972, as documented on the *Reunion* LP. Dion then briefly reentered the show-biz mainstream, frequently guesting on TV variety shows like *Cher.* The transfusion also helped the Belmonts, whose *Cigars Acapella Candy* sold respectably. In the mid-Seventies Dion recorded with Phil Spector, but their collaboration, *Born to Be with You,* was released only in the U.K.

Dion attempted to update with *Streetheart* in 1976. He recorded five albums of Christian music; in 1988 he published his candid autobiography *The Wanderer: Dion's Story.* The next year he was inducted into the Rock and Roll Hall of Fame and recorded *Yo Frankie,* produced by Dave Edmunds and featuring such guests as Lou Reed, in whose songs Dion's influence had long been apparent.

Dire Straits

Formed 1977, London, England
Mark Knopfler (b. Aug. 12, 1949, Glasgow, Scot.), gtr., voc.; David Knopfler (b. 1951, Glasgow, Scot.), gtr.; John Illsley (b. June 24, 1949, Leicester, Eng.), bass; Pick Withers, drums.
1978—*Dire Straits* (Warner Bros.) 1979—*Communiqué* 1980—(– D. Knopfler; + Hal Lindes, gtr.) *Making Movies* 1982—(+ Alan Clark, kybds.) *Love over Gold* (– Withers; + Terry Williams, drums; + Tommy Mandel, kybds.) 1983—*Twisting by the*

Pool EP   1984—*Alchemy* (– Mandel)   1985—
(+ Guy Fletcher, kybds.) *Brothers in Arms* (– Lindes; – Clark)   1988—(Group disbands) *Money for Nothing*   1991—(Group re-forms: M. Knopfler; Illsley; Fletcher; Clark; other musicians) *On Every Street*.
The Notting Hillbillies: 1990—*Missing . . . Presumed Having a Good Time* (Warner Bros.).
Mark Knopfler and Chet Atkins: 1990—*Neck and Neck* (Columbia).

British songwriter, vocalist, and guitarist Mark Knopfler led Dire Straits to international success with a series of albums full of virtuoso-caliber musicianship and the finely developed songcraft that made some of his best story-songs (such as "Romeo and Juliet") irresistible. A touch of wry humor ("Money for Nothing"), a lack of pretentiousness, and a knack for creating groove-driven songs also helped make Dire Straits one of the most successful groups of the mid- to late Eighties.

The group's debut album introduced Knopfler's minor-key Dylanesque songs and his limpid mixture of J.J. Cale's and Albert King's guitar styles; the Dire Straits trademark is a dialogue between Knopfler's vocals and guitar lines, as heard in the group's first hit, "Sultans of Swing" (#4, 1979).

Mark and David Knopfler, sons of an architect, both learned guitar in their teens. Mark became a rock critic at the *Yorkshire Evening Post* while working for an English degree. He then taught problem students at Loughton College and an adult extension course, worked in South London pub bands, and wrote some songs.

By early 1977 Mark was teaching literature part-time and jamming with David (then a social worker) and David's roommate, John Illsley, a timber broker who was pursuing a sociology degree at the University of London. In July 1977, after rehearsing with studio drummer Pick Withers, the group made a five-track demo tape that included "Sultans of Swing." Critic and DJ Charlie Gillett played "Sultans" on his BBC radio show, *Honky Tonkin'*, and listeners and record companies responded.

After opening for Talking Heads on a 1978 European tour, the group spent 12 days and about $25,000 to record *Dire Straits* (#2, 1979), which eventually sold over two million copies worldwide as "Sultans of Swing" became a hit (#4, 1979). Jerry Wexler and Barry Beckett produced the gold *Communiqué* (#11, 1979).

During sessions for *Making Movies* in July 1980, David Knopfler left, and Bruce Springsteen's E Street Band pianist Roy Bittan sat in. For the ensuing tour, Dire Straits added Hal Lindes and Alan Clark to play the longer selections from *Making Movies* (#19, 1980), which also went gold. It included the minor hit and MTV favorite "Skateaway" (#58, 1980). *Love over Gold* (#19, 1982), with no singles-length cuts, went gold and topped the U.K. chart. Later, Withers departed and was replaced by ex-Rockpile drummer Terry Williams. Tommy Mandel also joined.

Following an EP (*Twisting by the Pool,* whose title track went to #14 U.K.) and a live collection (*Alchemy,* #3 U.K.) came the group's biggest commercial success: the six-million-selling *Brothers in Arms* (#1 pop, #1 U.K., 1985). It featured three hit singles: "Money for Nothing" (#1, 1985)—on which Sting makes a cameo appearance and sings "I want my MTV"—"Walk of Life" (#7, 1985), and "So Far Away" (#19, 1986). In 1987 *Brothers in Arms* passed the three-million sales mark in the U.K., becoming the best-selling LP in that nation's history. By then, Mark Knopfler had had his hand in a number of extra-group projects, including producing Aztec Camera's *Knife* and Bob Dylan's *Infidels,* writing one of Tina Turner's comeback hits, "Private Dancer," and scoring a couple of films (*Local Hero* [1983], *Cal* [1984], *The Princess Bride* [1987]), the soundtracks of which fared well in the U.K. Knopfler also composed soundtracks for *Comfort and Joy* (1987) and *Last Exit to Brooklyn* (1989).

With *Brothers* still riding the charts on both sides of the Atlantic, Knopfler continued pursuing his own projects, appearing on Joan Armatrading's *The Shouting Stage,* coproducing Randy Newman's *Land of Dreams,* and recording with his idol, country guitar master Chet Atkins. (To date, Knopfler and Atkins have won three Grammys for their duet recordings.) In 1988, following appearances at Nelson Mandela's 70th Birthday Party concert at Wembley and Knopfler's touring with Eric Clapton, he announced the group's dissolution.

Knopfler returned to recording with Guy Fletcher and the Notting Hillbillies, a side project with Brendan Croker, Paul Franklin, Ed Bicknell, and Steve Phillips. The group's debut album, *Missing . . . Presumed Having a Good Time,* was a phenomenal hit in the U.K., where it entered the chart at #2. It was not nearly as successful in the U.S., peaking at #52, despite an appearance on *Saturday Night Live* and a tour. *Money for Nothing,* a greatest-hits compilation, went gold, peaking at #62.

Given the group's high profile in the mid-Eighties and the six years that had elapsed between new albums, the platinum *On Every Street* (#12, 1991) was expected to generate great interest. That was not the case in the U.S., where their tour was not a hot ticket and no hit single emerged. As critics have pointed out, however, *Brothers in Arms* was perhaps a fluke, a departure from the group's usual more laid-back style.

Disco

Disco reigned as the most popular dance music of the Seventies, and in every aspect from the way it was produced and consumed to its emphasis on a club-based communal culture, it set the stage for a number of later developments, including hip-hop, rap, ballroom, house, acid jazz, and techno. Disco is music geared for just one purpose—to get people on a dance floor moving—and at its peak, it existed primarily on records rather than in live performances. Almost all disco features the genre's characteristic rhythm, with a solid thump on each beat, and its vocals are often simple exhortations to dance, party, or boogie. But the many variations within the style—from the plush orchestrations of Kenny Gamble and Leon Huff to the skeletal *charanga*-derived groove of Chic and the loping beat of the Bee Gees to the mechanical synthesizer patterns of Eurodisco—assured its continuing vitality into the Eighties.

Although discotheques, clubs where the main entertainment was dancing to recorded music, had existed since the Sixties (and before them, juke joints served the same purpose more informally), the disco beat arose in the mid-Seventies. Like punk, which followed soon thereafter, disco was a reaction to the extended dance-resistant FM rock of the early Seventies. It first surfaced from New York's gay male subculture, whose disc jockeys searched among obscure black pop records for the most danceable cuts.

Word of mouth made some of those songs into underground hits—such as Manu Dibango's "Soul Makossa"—and within a short time record companies began to look toward the disco scene as an incubator for hits, and to make records with instrumental breaks and novelty effects that disc jockeys could mix and match on their own. By the late Seventies disco records were often marked with bpm—beats per minute—to make segues easier.

Disco became a fad in the mid-Seventies as all sorts of pop practitioners rushed to apply the latest beat to their own material. Because disco depended more on its instrumental groove than its vocals, and because recorded performances were far more important than live ones, disco became a producer's music. There were numerous one-shots, and a specific producer or studio—like the T.K. studio in Florida, home of George McCrae and KC and the Sunshine Band, or Giorgio Moroder in Munich, who produced Donna Summer's first hits—would be hot for a while before the vogue moved on. But disco was still stigmatized as music for blacks and gays until 1977, when the soundtrack for *Saturday Night Fever*, featuring the Bee Gees, the Trammps, and other groups, sold 20 million copies. The movie convinced a mass audience that disco was theirs to enjoy, and the album provided a handle on the proliferation of anonymous disco acts; along with new material by the Bee Gees, it featured a selection of established disco hits.

In the years before and after *Saturday Night Fever* the pop market was flooded with disco; even the Rolling Stones ("Miss You") and Rod Stewart ("Da Ya Think I'm Sexy?") tried the beat. There was also a flood of records featuring the music of everyone from Beethoven to the Beach Boys and the Beatles, remixed and "disco-ized," and a number of older acts, such as the Four Seasons, that jump-started their flagging careers with disco-style hits. All-disco radio stations began earning top ratings in urban areas, and disco-derived fashions (spandex, lamé) were everywhere. But disco peaked as a commercial force by 1980; sales declined as consumers realized it was easier to listen to this week's disco hit on the radio than to buy it, and they rarely made a long-term identification with disco's biggest stars, an often ephemeral group that could also claim among its number a diverse array of established artists that included (however briefly) Kraftwerk *and* Ethel Merman. Before rap music was recognized as a separate genre, artists such as Afrika Bambaataa, Grandmaster Flash, and the Sugar Hill Gang got their first exposure on the dance floor.

Musicians, however, were still intrigued. By the early Eighties disco rhythms had filtered into new wave, and there was a subgenre of danceable rock-disco records, among them Blondie's "Heart of Glass." Meanwhile, pure disco had returned to independent labels and reverted to its hard-core subculture of fans—still going regularly to clubs and still dancing. While it is difficult to argue disco's importance on the basis of enduring stars, it did change the face of popular music in several important ways. It brought to prominence the producer as *auteur,* paving the way for such latterday artist-producers as Jellybean and Arthur Baker and powerhouse teams such as C+C Music Factory; Stock, Aitken, and Waterman; and L.A. Reid and Babyface. It also reestablished black music as a stylistically distinct commercial category, and high R&B chart standings would not necessarily be reflected on the pop chart, as they had been during the Motown/Stax era of the Sixties and early Seventies. Disco marked the end of the broad audience consensus in pop music tastes that typified Sixties AM radio. From that point on, popular music would continue to splinter into countless stylistic and marketing categories and subcategories.

Disposable Heroes of HipHoprisy
Formed 1990, Oakland, California
Michael Franti (b. Apr. 21, 1967, Oakland), voc.; Rono Tse (b. Dec. 8, 1966, Hong Kong), perc., electronics.
1992—*Hypocrisy Is the Greatest Luxury* (Island). Michael Franti with Spearhead: 1994—*Home* (Capitol).

This highly political rap group was formed by two ex-members of the Bay Area interracial punk-rock band the Beatnigs, who'd recorded for Dead Kennedys front man Jello Biafra's Alternative Tentacles label. Rapper Michael Franti, who stands six-feet-six, had been a University of San Francisco basketball star; percussionist Rono Tse played his own homemade instruments (made from tire rims, grinders, chains, and fire extinguishers, as well as electronic drums) and danced during shows.

The Disposable Heroes formed after the 1989 Persian Gulf War, debuting on Island with the double-A-sided single "Television Is the Drug of the Nation" b/w "Winter of the Long Hot Summer." Their next single, "Language of Violence," was the first significant rap track to attack homophobia and set Franti apart from the mainstream of rappers, who either condemned homosexuality or let gay-bashing pass unremarked.

On its critically acclaimed debut album the group preached tolerance and attacked prejudice amidst a wide variety of musical settings, ranging from the jazzy to the industrial. The Disposable Heroes opened tours for U2, Public Enemy, and Arrested Development, and in summer 1991 they landed a spot on the first Lollapalooza package tour of alternative rock and rap groups. In 1993 the duo appeared with author William S. Burroughs on an album of his readings called *Spare Ass Annie and Other Tales.* At the end of the year the group announced an indefinite hiatus, with Franti to record a solo album, and Tse to produce Asian-flavored hip-hop through his Vitamin C production company. In 1994, Franti's new group Spearhead released *Home,* coproduced by Joe "The Butcher" Nicolo (Schoolly D, Kris Kross).

Divinyls

Formed 1980, Sydney, Australia
Christina Amphlett (b. Oct. 25, ca. 1960, Geelong, Victoria, Austral.), voc.; Mark McEntee (b. July 16, ca. 1961, Perth, Austral.), gtr.; Bjarre Ohlin, gtr., kybds.; Rick Grossman, bass; Richard Harvey, drums.
1982—*Monkey Grip* EP (WEA, Austral.)   1983—*Desperate* (Chrysalis)   1985—*What a Life!*   1988—*Temperamental* (– Ohlin; – Grossman; – Harvey) 1991—*Divinyls* (Virgin); *Essential Divinyls* (Chrysalis).

Critically acclaimed upon their emergence as a sort of Australian answer to the Pretenders, Divinyls never hit it big in the U.S. until a decade later. By then the band consisted solely of the singer, Christina Amphlett, and her cowriter, guitarist Mark McEntee.

Amphlett left school at age 17 to travel alone to Europe, spending time in Paris and, in Barcelona, Spain, getting jailed for street singing. Back in Sydney, she joined a church choir (purely "to develop the top range of my voice," she later said). During one choir performance her stool fell over and got tangled in her microphone cord, so she dragged the stool across the stage while singing. McEntee, who was in the audience that night, introduced himself, and the pair began writing songs together and soon formed a band. Amphlett gained instant notoriety with her snarling, nasal voice and trashy onstage look—dumpy schoolgirl uniforms worn over torn fishnet stockings—and her pouty-lipped, heavy-lidded makeup.

Monkey Grip contained several songs from a film of the same name in which Amphlett had a costarring role. Three songs from that EP—"Boys in Town," "Only Lonely," and "Elsie"—turned up on *Desperate.* Despite critical acclaim for *Desperate,* the band did not catch on commercially, finding the most success with *What a Life!* (#91, 1985), which yielded a minor hit single in "Pleasure and Pain" (#76, 1986).

Chrysalis dropped Divinyls after *Temperamental,* the band dissolved, and Amphlett and McEntee—who say their relationship has always been purely professional and platonic—moved to Paris, where they lived in the sleazy Pigalle area and wrote songs. Their demo tapes eventually led to the eponymous album (#15, 1991) that was their biggest hit yet, thanks to "I Touch Myself" (#4, 1991), a slick double-entendre ode to masturbation and/or romance. Amphlett and McEntee toured using hired musicians as backup.

The Dixie Cups
Formed 1964, New Orleans, Louisiana
Barbara Ann Hawkins (b. 1943, New Orleans), voc.;
Rosa Lee Hawkins (b. 1946, New Orleans), voc.;
Joan Marie Johnson (b. 1945, New Orleans), voc.
1964—*Chapel of Love* (Red Bird).

The Dixie Cups were a black girl group that hit the top of the chart in 1964 with "Chapel of Love," a song that producer Phil Spector (with Jeff Barry and Ellie Greenwich) had originally written for the Ronettes. The trio—the Hawkins sisters and their cousin—first sang together in the grade school chorus. By 1963 the three had decided to pursue a career in music, and they began singing locally as the Meltones. Within a year, Joe Jones, a successful singer in his own right (notably, the Top Five 1960 release "You Talk Too Much"), became their manager. He groomed them for five months and then took them to New York, where producers/songwriters Jerry Leiber and Mike Stoller signed them to their fledgling Red Bird Records.

Their initial release, "Chapel of Love," proved to be their biggest hit, although they enjoyed subsequent success with such efforts as "People Say" (#12, 1964), "You Should Have Seen the Way He Looked at Me" (#39, 1964), "Iko Iko" (#20, 1965; later a minor hit for Dr. John and the Belle Stars), and "Little Bell" (#51, 1965), the last of their hits. Red Bird Records went under in 1966; the Dixie Cups then switched to ABC-Paramount and later temporarily retired from show business.

In 1974 the Hawkins sisters moved from New York back to New Orleans, where they pursued successful modeling careers. They resumed touring (with Dale Mickle replacing Johnson).

Dixie Dregs

Formed 1973, Florida

Steve Morse (b. July 28, 1954, Hamilton, Ohio), gtr.; Andy West (b. Feb. 6, 1954, Newport, R.I.), bass; Rod Morgenstein (b. Apr. 19, 1957, New York City, N.Y.), drums; Steve Davidowski, kybds.; Allen Sloan (b. Miami Beach, Fla.), electric violin.

1977—*Free Fall* (Capricorn) (– Davidowski; + Mark Parrish, kybds.)   1978—*What If* (– Parrish; + T Lavitz, kybds.)   1979—*Night of the Living Dregs*   1980—*Dregs of the Earth* (Arista) (– Sloan; + Mark O'Conner [b. Aug. 4, 1962, Seattle, Wash.], violin, gtr.)   1981—*Unsung Heroes*   1982—*Industry Standard* (group disbands)   1992—(Group reforms: Morse; Morgenstein; Lavitz; Sloan; + David LaRue, bass) *Bring 'Em Back Alive* (Capricorn) (– Sloan; + Jerry Goodman, violin)   1994—*Full Circle.*

Steve Morse solo: 1984—*The Introduction* (as the Steve Morse Band) (Elektra/Musician)   1989—*High Tension Wires* (MCA)   1991—*Southern Steel* (as the Steve Morse Band)   1992—*Coast to Coast.*

T Lavitz solo: 1991—*Mood Swing* (Nova); *T Lavitz and His Band Habitz* (Enigma Classics).

A strictly instrumental band of virtuosi, the Dixie Dregs began as a jazz-rock fusion band modeled after the Mahavishnu Orchestra. They have since forged their own unique style of fusion, one that combines stunning technical prowess with flash, wit, and soul. A highlight of their 1992 live album, for example, found them sandwiching a history-of-rock medley that ranged from "Free Bird" to "My Sharona" into their own "Take It Off the Top." They have been nominated for five Grammy awards.

Steve Morse and Andy West had played together since they were tenth-grade classmates in Augusta, Georgia, putting together a conventional rock & roll band called Dixie Grit. Dixie Grit broke up when Morse was accepted into the University of Miami's School of Music, although he didn't have a high school diploma (having been expelled after refusing to cut his hair). At Miami, he studied in the jazz department with Jaco Pastorius, Pat Metheny, and Narada Michael Walden. There he met Allen Sloan and Rod Morgenstein. Sloan was a classically trained violinist who had played with the Miami Philharmonic and only recently had become interested in pop music. Morgenstein was a jazz drummer. Morse, Sloan, and Morgenstein began playing together, and at Morse's urging West enrolled at the university and joined the group. Their first album, *The Great Spectacular,* was recorded and produced as a course project. Upon graduation in 1975, they moved to Augusta, and began their professional careers.

After the Dregs opened a Nashville show for Sea Level in 1976, Chuck Leavell persuaded Capricorn Records to sign them. Before the end of the year, Mark Parrish—an original member of Dixie Grit—replaced Steve Davidowski. In turn he was replaced by T Lavitz in time for the Dregs' appearance at the 1978 Montreux Jazz Festival in Switzerland. Morse let the group's style become increasingly eclectic; Mark O'Conner (a three-time national champion fiddler) brought a more traditional old-time playing style. *Industry Standard* was the first Dregs (the group dropped the "Dixie" for *Unsung Heroes*) album to feature vocal performances; guest vocalists included Alex Ligertwood (Santana, Average White Band) and Doobie Brother Patrick Simmons.

After *Industry Standard,* the group members went their separate ways. Morse, acknowledged as one of the most important guitarists of the past two decades, formed the Steve Morse Band and released a series of solo albums. He also played with Kansas, appearing on *Power* (1986) and *In the Spirit of Things* (1988). He has been named Best Overall Guitarist five times in *Guitar Player* magazine's readers' poll. Morgenstein, who was a member of Morse's band, went on to join Winger [see entry]. Lavitz released his own solo albums and worked with a number of other groups, including Widespread Panic, the Bluesbusters, the Aquarium Rescue Unit, and Billy Cobham's band.

The group reunited in 1992 for a series of shows that produced the acclaimed *Bring 'Em Back Alive.* West, who was a computer programmer, did not join the reunion, and shortly after it began Sloan returned to his work as an anesthesiologist. His replacement, Jerry Goodman, had belonged to the Mahavishnu Orchestra. West's replacement, Dave LaRue, is also a member of Morse's band. *Full Circle* and the Dixie Dregs' supporting tour met with critical acclaim.

The Dixie Hummingbirds

Formed 1928, Greenville, South Carolina

James L. Davis, tenor voc.; Barney Gipson, lead tenor voc.; Barney Parks, baritone voc.; J. B. Matterson, bass voc.

1929—(– Matterson; + Fred Owens, bass voc.)   Thirties—(– Owens; + various bass singers)   1939—(+ Jimmy Bryant, bass voc.; – Gipson; + Ira Tucker, lead tenor voc.; – Bryant; + William Bobo [d. 1976], bass voc.)   1944—(– Parks; + Beachy Thompson, baritone voc.)   Early Fifties—(+ James Walker [b. ca. 1926, Mileston, Miss.; d. Oct. 30, 1992, Philadelphia, Pa.], second lead tenor voc.; + Howard Carroll, gtr.)   1977—*Dixie Hummingbirds Live* (Peacock)   1979—*Golden Flight; Gospel at Its Best; We Love You Like a Rock*   1984—(– Davis)   1987—(+ Paul Owen, voc.)   1992—(– Walker).

The Dixie Hummingbirds were the leading Southern black gospel quartet for over 50 years, a seminal force in

The Dixie Hummingbirds

Folk Festival in 1966. The Seventies found them embracing contemporary pop styles with mixed results. They backed Paul Simon in the studio, and on their *We Love You Like a Rock* covered Simon's "Loves Me Like a Rock" and Stevie Wonder's "Jesus Children of America" (which featured Wonder's keyboards). "Loves Me Like a Rock" was awarded a Grammy for Best Gospel Performance in 1973. While William Bobo had died in 1976, and James L. Davis finally retired in 1984, Tucker and Walker kept the group going into the late Eighties.

Willie Dixon
Born July 1, 1915, Vicksburg, Mississippi; died January 29, 1992, Burbank, California
1973—*Willie Dixon—Catalyst* (Ovation)   1970—*I Am the Blues* (Columbia)   1988—*The Chess Box* (Chess/MCA); *Hidden Charms* (Bug/Capitol)   1990—*The Big Three Trio* (Columbia).

Willie Dixon was an important link between the blues and rock & roll, and he wrote scores of blues classics in the Fifties. Growing up in Mississippi, he composed poetry and sang in church before moving with his family to Chicago permanently in 1937. A big man (often weighing 250 pounds), the young Dixon won the city's Golden Gloves championship for his weight class in 1938. But his interest switched to music soon after, when he was introduced to the washtub bass. Dixon soon graduated to a four-string upright and later to a Fender electric. His walking bass lines played a major role in defining the postwar urban blues.

By the early Fifties Dixon was selling his songs for $30 apiece and was thus cheated out of thousands of dollars in royalties. He is a prolific composer, and his catalogue includes "You Shook Me," "Little Red Rooster," "Back Door Man," "Bring It On Home," "I'm Your Hoochie Coochie Man," "The Seventh Son," "I Just Wanna Make Love to You," "Wang Dang Doodle," "You Can't Judge a Book by Its Cover," "Spoonful," and "I Can't Quit You Baby." They were covered by such rock bands as Led Zeppelin, the Doors, Foghat, Cream, and the Allman Brothers.

Dixon's own recording career, which began in the early Fifties, was relatively unsuccessful. For a while he was the bass player in the house band at Chess Records and regularly backed Chuck Berry, Bo Diddley, Muddy Waters, and others, arranging and later producing them, in addition to Howlin' Wolf, Elmore James, and Otis Rush, to name a few. In between takes he'd sell his own songs and act as the business intermediary between black artists and the Polish-born Chess brothers.

Dixon remained sporadically active, touring Europe (where he was revered) almost annually after 1960. He played some U.S. dates in 1975 and 1976 with his tour band the Chicago Blues All-Stars. The 1987 settlement of

the development of that genre and in the parallel development of soul music. Clyde McPhatter, Bobby Bland, and Jackie Wilson are only some of the singers influenced by lead Hummingbird Ira Tucker. Even James Brown's sex-machine calisthenics have some precedent in the Hummingbirds' fervid performances.

The quartet was founded by James Davis and became prominent in the Carolinas during the Thirties, making its first record for Decca in 1939. That same year they were joined by two singers from Spartanburg, South Carolina—Tucker, formerly of the Gospel Carriers, and William Bobo, a member of the Heavenly Gospel Singers—when the Hummingbirds bettered the Carriers and the Heavenlies in a singing competition.

In 1942 the quartet moved to Philadelphia and began broadcasting regularly on radio and touring the Northeast gospel circuit. John Hammond began to book them into New York cafes and nightclubs beginning in 1942. In 1945 they began recording for the Apollo and Gotham labels, and in 1952 they signed with Peacock, recording such gospel classics as "Jesus Walked the Water," "In the Morning," and "I Just Can't Help It."

In the early Fifties, the Hummingbirds became a sextet with the additions of second lead tenor James Walker and guitarist Howard Carroll; the great Claude Jeter of the Swan Silvertones also joined the group briefly during the Fifties.

The Dixie Hummingbirds performed at the Newport

a long-running dispute with Led Zeppelin over the group's failure to credit Dixon as writer of "Whole Lotta Love" (which was largely based on his "You Need Love") led to his forming the Blues Heaven Foundation, a preservation society for blues music and culture that also worked to secure copyrights and royalties for other artists. His final recording, "Dustin' Off the Bass," was included on Rob Wasserman's GRP album *Trios* (1994), and teamed him with Wasserman and former Chuck Berry drummer Al Duncan.

One year after Dixon's death (he'd earlier lost part of his right leg to diabetes) Blues Heaven, with the help of John Mellencamp, managed to buy the original Chess Records studios in Chicago. "Time makes everything change," Dixon once said, "but the blues are basically about the facts of life. This is why they hang around so long, because everybody practically faces the same things in life sooner or later anyway."

DNA/Arto Lindsay

DNA formed 1977, New York City, New York (Arto Lindsay [b. May 28, 1953, Richmond, Va.], gtr., voc.; Ikue Ile Mori [b. Dec. 17, 1953, Tokyo, Jap.], drums; Robin Crutchfield, kybds.)
1978—(– Crutchfield; + Tim Wright, bass, gtr.)
1980—*A Taste of DNA* (American Clave).
Ambitious Lovers (Arto Lindsay, gtr., voc; Peter Scherer, kybds.): 1984—*Envy* (Editions EG)   1988—*Greed* (Virgin)   1991—*Lust* (Elektra).

DNA was a leader in New York's no wave movement. Radically challenging rock conventions, its tightly structured songs, some of them under 30 seconds long, used neither fixed rhythms nor standard harmonies, and the three instrumental parts were usually independent and clashing. Chief writer Arto Lindsay's untuned guitar was emblematic both of the band's aesthetic adventurousness and of the "downtown" sensibility Lindsay carried on in his work after DNA's demise.

Lindsay arrived in New York in 1975, having spent most of his life in a Brazilian village where his missionary father had built a school. While working as a messenger for the *Village Voice*, he played guitar for the first time when he jammed with James Chance and other no wave pioneers in 1977. Out of those sessions emerged the Contortions (Chance's group), Teenage Jesus and the Jerks (Lydia Lunch), and Mars. Lindsay wrote lyrics for Mars and would have joined them as drummer had he not decided to form a band with Ikue Ile Mori and Robin Crutchfield. Mori had just that year arrived from Tokyo. Through Teenage Jesus she met Lindsay, whose unorthodox guitar playing inspired her to try the drums.

DNA debuted with a 1978 single, "Little Ants" b/w "You and You" on the Lust/Unlust label, shortly before contributing four tracks to the no wave compilation *No*

New York produced by Brian Eno. At the end of 1978 Crutchfield left to form Dark Day and was replaced by Tim Wright, previously a member of Cleveland's Pere Ubu. Under his influence, DNA's music became even more turbulent and concise before the band broke up in 1981.

In addition to playing with DNA, each member worked with other musicians. Mori played violin, viola, and cello on Mars' *John Gavanti*, an inversion of Mozart's *Don Giovanni*. Wright played bass on David Byrne and Brian Eno's *My Life in the Bush of Ghosts* (1981).

Lindsay has achieved the largest measure of success. A founder of the "fake jazz" group the Lounge Lizards [see entry], he played with them until 1981. He also recorded with James Chance, Kip Hanrahan, and Seth Tillet. He has worked with the Toykillers and Ambitious Lovers; the latter, a duo with keyboardist Peter Scherer, released three albums titled after mortal sins and scored a minor dance hit with a 1991 cover of Jorge Ben's "Umbabarauma."

Mainly, Lindsay's role has been that of an avant-garde presence. He played on *Better an Old Demon Than a New God,* a 1984 album presented by poet John Giorno that showcased musicians with literary leanings. In the late Eighties, as curator of the Kitchen, a New York haven for experimentalism, he hosted a new-music series that featured jazz, rap, Latin, and industrial sounds. In 1992 he introduced a new band, Arto. With Melvin Gibbs on bass, Marc Ribot on guitar, Bernie Worrell on keyboards, and Lindsay on vocals and guitar, their sound ranged from psychedelic to Brazilian to funk to noise.

Dr. Buzzard's Original Savannah Band: See Kid Creole and the Coconuts

Dr. Dre: See N.W.A

Dr. Feelgood

Formed 1971, Canvey Island, England
Lee Brilleaux (b. Lee Green, 1953, Durban, S.A.; d. Apr. 7, 1994, Canvey Island), voc., harmonica, slide gtr.; John B. Sparks, bass; Wilko Johnson (b. John Wilkinson, 1947), gtr.; John "the Figure" Martin (b. 1947), drums.
1975—*Malpractice* (Columbia)   1977—*Sneakin' Suspicion* (– Johnson; + John Mayo, gtr.)   1981—(– Mayo; + Johnny Guitar, gtr.)   1982—(– Sparks; – Martin; + Buzz Barwell, drums; + Pat McMullen, bass)   1983—(– McMullen; + Paul Mitchell, bass; – Guitar; + Gordon Russell, gtr.; numerous personnel changes follow over the years).

British R&B revivalists Dr. Feelgood were one of the leading bands of the British back-to-basics movement of the mid-Seventies. Lee Brilleaux, John B. Sparks, and Wilko Johnson hailed from Canvey Island. They drifted around England and made the rounds of pub bands together and separately before forming Dr. Feelgood in 1971. Johnson brought in John Martin, previously a member of Finian's Rainbow. They took their name from a minor early-Sixties British hit by Johnny Kidd and the Pirates (not the Aretha Franklin song of the same title) and assembled a repertoire of Johnson originals and standards by Willie Dixon, Bo Diddley, Huey "Piano" Smith, Leiber and Stoller, and other (mostly black) R&B and rock & roll patriarchs.

Dr. Feelgood signed a United Artists (U.K.) contract in 1974. Its acclaimed debut album, *Down by the Jetty,* was recorded in mono, most of it in one take, with piano and saxes courtesy of Brinsley Schwarz and Bob Andrews of the Schwarz group. A growing concert following and enthusiastic support from people like Pete Townshend boosted its second album, *Malpractice,* into the U.K. Top Twenty and a single, "She's a Wind Up," into the Top Forty. Its 1976 U.K. release *stupidity* topped the charts, and although Dr. Feelgood toured the United States that year, it never found a foothold Stateside. *Malpractice* and *Sneakin' Suspicion* were its only albums released in the U.S.

In 1977 Johnson left to form the Solid Senders; he later joined Ian Dury and the Blockheads. Henry McCullough stepped in for him on Dr. Feelgood's 1977 British tour, but John Mayo had replaced him by the time the group recorded *Be Seeing You* with producer Nick Lowe. "Milk and Alcohol" hit the British Top Ten in 1979, and "As Long as the Price Is Right" reached #40 later in the year. Dr. Feelgood released six more albums for United Artists.

By 1982 Brilleaux was the only original member left. He continued recording and touring with a succession of musicians. With his death from cancer at age 41, Dr. Feelgood was no more. Its last album, *Down at the Doctor's,* was recorded at Brilleaux's Dr. Feelgood Music Bar in Canvey Island, three months before he died.

Dr. Feelgood and the Interns
Formed 1962, Atlanta, Georgia

Dr. Feelgood and the Interns was not really a group but a nom-de-disc for noted bluesman Willie Perryman (born c. 1912; died July 25, 1985, Atlanta, Georgia), son of a sharecropper. Dr. Feelgood and the Interns had two moderate pop hits in 1962: "Dr. Feel-Good" and "Right String but the Wrong Yo Yo." The latter was recorded in 1930 by Perryman's brother Rufus under his alias Speckled Red. It had been revived in the Fifties by Perryman when he recorded under the alias of Piano Red ("Rockin' with Red," "Red's Boogie") for such labels as RCA, Jax, Checker, and Arhoolie. "Rockin' with Red (Rock, Rock,

Rock)" sold one million copies in 1950. Perryman, who'd honed his style in Atlanta honky-tonks, was with the Okeh label when he enjoyed his biggest pop success in 1962 as Dr. Feelgood. The Beatles covered the flip side of "Dr. Feelgood," "Mr. Moonlight," on *Beatles '65.* He died of cancer at age 73.

Dr. Hook (and the Medicine Show)
Formed 1968, Union City, New Jersey
Ray Sawyer (b. Feb. 1, 1937, Chickasaw, Ala.), voc., gtr.; Dennis Locorriere (b. June 13, 1949, Union City), voc., gtr.; William Francis (b. Jan. 16, 1942, Mobile, Ala.), kybds., perc.; George Cummings (b. July 28, 1938, Meridian, Miss.), pedal steel gtr.; John "Jay" David (b. Aug. 8, 1942, Union City), drums.
1971—*Dr. Hook and the Medicine Show* (Columbia) (+ Richard Elswit [b. July 6, 1945, New York City, N.Y.], gtr.; + Jance Garfat [b. Mar. 3, 1944, Calif.], bass) 1972—*Sloppy Seconds* 1973—*Belly Up* (– David; + John Wolters, drums) 1974—*Fried Face* 1975—*Ballad of Lucy Jordan; Bankrupt* (Capitol) (– Cummings) 1976—*A Little Bit More* (+ Bob "Willard" Henke, gtr.) 1977—*Makin' Love and Music; Street People* (Columbia); *Revisited* 1978—*Pleasure and Pain* (Capitol) 1979—*Sometimes You Win* 1980—*Greatest Hits; Rising* (Casablanca) 1982—*Players in the Dark.*

Dr. Hook and the Medicine Show are slapstick purveyors of parody rock, whose "Sylvia's Mother" was taken straight by Top Forty listeners and became the first of ten Top Forty hits in the Seventies and Eighties. The group began performing professionally in New Jersey, doing cover versions. During those years, the two front men—ex-Jersey folkie Dennis Locorriere and Ray Sawyer, who wears an eyepatch (hence, Dr. Hook) since having lost an eye after a 1967 car crash—developed a repertoire spiced with off-color material.

Their manager, Ron Haffkine, discovered them while looking for backup musicians to perform *Playboy* cartoonist humorist/songwriter Shel Silverstein's material in the movie *Who Is Harry Kellerman and Why Is He Saying All Those Terrible Things About Me?* (1971). The group played "Last Morning" on the soundtrack and also appeared in the movie. After several months of rehearsal Dr. Hook went to California to record another batch of Silverstein's tunes. The group's debut LP featured "Sylvia's Mother" (#5, 1972), which sold 3½ million copies worldwide but proved to be a mixed blessing. Its lilting style, a too-subtle parody of pop, left the public ill-prepared for the manic, unkempt group behind it. *Sloppy Seconds* was also written by Silverstein and gave the group another Top Ten hit, "The Cover of Rolling Stone" (#6, 1973), which took a satirical look at the rock culture—and landed Dr. Hook on the cover of ROLLING STONE. By the time of *Belly Up,* the band members were writing their own material, but with less success. By 1974 Dr. Hook had filed for bankruptcy and switched to Capitol. The group had hit in 1976 with Sam Cooke's "Only Sixteen" (#6) and "A Little Bit More" (#11). The next few years brought several more hits: "Sharing the Night Together" (#6, 1978), "When You're in Love with a Beautiful Woman" (#6, 1979), "Better Love Next Time" (#12, 1979), "Sexy Eyes" (#5, 1980), and "Baby Makes Her Blue Jeans Talk" (#25, 1982).

By late 1979 Dr. Hook had amassed 35 gold and platinum albums in Australia and Scandinavia, where the group remained a popular attraction until its breakup in 1985. Three years later Sawyer (who'd recorded a solo country album in 1977) revived the name and has been touring the U.S. and overseas ever since. Locorriere retired from music but resurfaced in the late Eighties as a backup singer on Randy Travis' *Always and Forever.*

Dr. John

Born Malcolm "Mac" Rebennack, November 20, 1942, New Orleans, Louisiana
1968—*Gris-Gris* (Atco)   1969—*Babylon*   1970— *Remedies*   1971—*The Sun, Moon & Herbs*   1972— *Dr. John's Gumbo*   1973—*In the Right Place*; *Triumvirate* (with Mike Bloomfield and John Paul Hammond) (Columbia)   1974—*Desitively Bonnaroo* 1975—*Cut Me While I'm Hot* (DJM); *Hollywood Be Thy Name* (United Artists)   1978—*Tango Palace* 1979—*City Lights* (Horizon)   1980—*Take Me Back to New Orleans* (with Chris Barber) (Black Lion) 1981—*Dr. John Plays Mac Rebennack* (Clean Cuts) 1983—*The Brightest Smile in Town*   1987—*The Ultimate Dr. John* (Warner Bros.)   1989—*In a Sentimental Mood*   1990—*Bluesiana Triangle* 1991—*Bluesiana 2* (Windham Hill); *On a Mardi Gras Day* (with Chris Barber) (Great Southern)   1992— *Goin' Back to New Orleans*   1993—*Mos' Scocious: The Dr. John Anthology* (Rhino)   1994—*Television* (GRP/MCA).

Combining funky New Orleans roots, glitter, and voodoo charm, pianist Dr. John was an energetic front man in the early Seventies ("Right Place, Wrong Time") and a behind-the-scenes mover before and since.

Rebennack got his first taste of show biz through his mother, a model who got young Malcolm's face on Ivory Soap boxes; his father ran a record store. By his early teens he was an accomplished pianist and guitarist. From hanging around his dad's store and at Cosimo Matassa's studio, he got to know local musicians. By the mid-Fifties he was doing session work with Professor Longhair, Frankie Ford, and Joe Tex. He also helped form the black artists' cooperative AFO (All for One) Records,

and he was the first white man on the roster. By the start of the Sixties he had graduated to producing and arranging sessions for others (Lee Allen, Red Tyler, Earl Palmer) and recording some on his own (notably 1959's "Storm Warning" on Rex Records). Rebennack's reputation was based on his guitar and keyboard playing, but a 1961 gunshot wound to his hand briefly forced him to take up bass with a Dixieland band.

In the mid-Sixties Rebennack moved to L.A. and became a session regular, notably for producer Phil Spector. He played in various unsuccessful, wildly named bands like the Zu Zu Band (with Jessie Hill) and Morgus and the Three Ghouls. He also developed an interest in voodoo, to which he had been introduced by a mystical voodoo artist named Prince Lala in the Fifties at AFO. In 1968 Rebennack unveiled his new public persona of Dr. John Creaux the Night Tripper (later shortened to Dr. John) after a New Orleans crony, Ronnie Barron, decided not to front the act. With New Orleans associates (Hill as Dr. Poo Pah Doo and Harold Battiste as Dr. Battiste of Scorpio of bass clef), he recorded *Gris-Gris* for Atlantic in 1968. As indicated by the song titles—"I Walk on Gilded Splinters," "Gris Gris Gumbo Ya Ya," "Croker Courtbouillion"—it was a brew of traditional Creole chants, mystical imagery, and traces of psychedelia, which merged with Mardi Gras finery in Rebennack's onstage wardrobe (brightly colored robes, feathered headdresses) and his retinue of dancers and singers.

Dr. John slowly acquired a loyal cult following, including Eric Clapton and Mick Jagger, who played on *The Sun, Moon & Herbs.* He moved to the more accessible regions of funk (backed by the Meters) on *In the Right Place* (#24, 1973). Produced by Allen Toussaint (who also played in Dr. John's band on a 1973 tour and who produced *Desitively Bonnaroo*) "Right Place, Wrong Time" (#9) was his biggest hit, followed a few months later by "Such a Night" (#42). In 1973 Dr. John also worked in Triumvirate, a short-lived trio with Mike Bloomfield and John Hammond Jr. (John Paul Hammond). He appeared in the Band's 1978 farewell concert film, *The Last Waltz.* In 1981 he released the first of several solo-piano LPs, *Dr. John Plays Mac Rebennack.*

In the late Eighties, Dr. John began reaching back to his New Orleans roots—while also subtly mainstreaming his appeal. His 1989 *In a Sentimental Mood* collected old blues and saloon standards and earned him his first Grammy, for his duet with Rickie Lee Jones on "Makin' Whoopee." *Bluesiana Triangle* detoured into jazz, with drummer Art Blakey and saxophonist David "Fathead" Newman, while *Goin' Back to New Orleans*—with a cast of New Orleans all-stars featuring Al Hirt, Pete Fountain, Danny Barker, Alvin "Red" Tyler, and the Neville Brothers—won him another Grammy. By that time his gruff baritone voice had become familiar to millions through a succession of TV commercial jingles. In 1991 rap group

PM Dawn sampled Dr. John's "I Walk on Gilded Splinters"; two years later Beck sampled the same track for his folk-rap slacker anthem, "Loser." In 1993 Dr. John published his autobiography, *Under a Hoodoo Moon* (cowritten with Jack Rummel). In 1994 he appeared on the Windham Hill album *Crescent City Gold,* along with fellow New Orleans veterans Allen Toussaint, Earl Palmer, Alvin Tyler, Lee Allen, and Edward Frank.

Bill Doggett
Born February 6, 1916, Philadelphia, Pennsylvania
N.A.—*Everybody Dance to the Honky Tonk* (King);
***Hot Doggett*; *A Salute to Ellington*.**

Pianist/organist Bill Doggett had a #2 hit in 1956 with the instrumental "Honky Tonk." He recorded for King beginning in 1952 and toured roadhouses throughout the decade with a band (including guitarist Billy Butler and saxophonist Clifford Scott, who later enjoyed moderate success as a solo act) that was renowned for its boogie-woogie groove.

Doggett had worked with several jazz bands in the Thirties and Forties, including a stint with Louis Jordan's Tympany 5. He followed up "Honky Tonk" with "Slow Walk," which nearly cracked the Top Twenty in late 1956 after Doggett's appearance on *American Bandstand.* Doggett continued to place singles on both the pop and R&B charts over the next five years and to record jazz with artists such as Illinois Jacquet.

Thomas Dolby
Born Thomas Morgan Robertson, October 14, 1958,
Cairo, Egypt
1982—*The Golden Age of Wireless* (Capitol)
1983—*Blinded by Science* EP (Harvest)   1984—*The
***Flat Earth*   1988—*Aliens Ate My Buick* (EMI-**
Manhattan)   1992—*Astronauts & Heretics* (Giant)
1994—*Retrospectacle* (Capitol); *The Gate to the
***Mind's Eye* soundtrack.**

Best known for his first hit, "She Blinded Me with Science," Thomas Robertson is the son of a prominent British archaeologist. He got his "Dolby" nickname (after the British laboratory that created the noise-reduction system for audiotapes) from schoolmates impressed by his avid interest in electronics.

After teaching himself guitar, piano, and computer programming and singing in Parisian subways and playing cocktail piano in London clubs, Dolby built his own synthesizers and P.A. systems, which he used while working as a sound man for such British postpunk bands as the Fall and the Members. In 1979 he cofounded the Camera Club with Bruce Woolley; a year later he joined Lene Lovich's band and wrote her 1981 hit "New Toy." Dolby then played keyboards and synthesizer on For-

eigner's *4,* Joan Armatrading's *Walk Under Ladders,* Def Leppard's *Pyromania,* and Malcolm McLaren's *Duck Rock.* He also wrote and produced Whodini's "Magic's Wand," one of the first million-selling 12-inch rap singles.

Dolby's debut, *The Golden Age of Wireless* (#13, 1982), yielded a minor hit in "Europa and the Pirate Twins" (#67, 1983). The followup EP (#20, 1983) featured the comical synth-dance hit "She Blinded Me with Science" (#5, 1983), with guest vocals by British eccentric Magnus Pike, who also starred in the song's Dolby-directed video. In addition, Dolby directed *Live Wireless,* a long-form tour document, and the video for the manically funky "Hyperactive" (#62, 1984), from *The Flat Earth* (#35, 1984)—which also included a reverently gentle cover of Dan Hicks and His Hot Licks' "I Scare Myself."

As a producer, Dolby worked on George Clinton's *Some of My Best Jokes Are Friends* (1985), Joni Mitchell's *Dog Eat Dog* (1985), three albums for British band Prefab Sprout, and two tracks on Israeli singer Ofra Haza's *Wind* (1989). Dolby also composed and recorded film scores for *Fever Pitch* (1985), *Gothic* (1986), and *Howard the Duck* (1986). In 1986 Dolby Labs sued him for copyright infringement, eventually letting him use "Dolby" only with "Thomas."

In 1988 Dolby—living in Los Angeles, married to actress Kathleen Beller (Kirby Colby of *Dynasty*), and backed by a full band—released *Aliens Ate My Buick* (#70, 1988), for which George Clinton cowrote the track "Hot Sauce." It failed to produce a hit single, as did 1992's *Astronauts & Heretics,* which featured such guests as Jerry Garcia and Bob Weir of the Grateful Dead, Eddie Van Halen, and Ofra Haza. Dolby formed the high-tech firm Headspace, which in 1993 introduced the interactive virtual-reality music program, *The Virtual String Quartet. The Gate to the Mind's Eye* is the soundtrack to a *Mind's Eye* home video game.

Fats Domino
Born Antoine Domino, May 10, 1929, New Orleans,
Louisiana
1956—*Fats Domino—Rock and Rollin'* (Imperial);
***This Is Fats Domino*   1957—*Here Stands Fats**
***Domino*   1958—*Fabulous Mr. D*   1959—*Let's Play**
***Fats Domino*   1960—*Fats Domino Sings*   1961—*I**
***Miss You So*   1962—*Twistin' the Stomp*   1963—**
***Just Domino*   1966—*Getaway with Fats Domino**
(ABC)   1968—*Fats Is Back* (Reprise)   1970—*Fats
1972—*Legendary Masters Series* (United Artists)
1990—*They Call Me the Fat Man—Antoine "Fats"
***Domino: The Legendary Imperial Recordings* (EMI)**
1993—*Christmas Is a Special Day* (Right Stuff/EMI).

With 65 million record sales to his credit, New Orleans singer and pianist Fats Domino outsold every Fifties rock & roll pioneer except Elvis Presley. Born into a musical

Fats Domino

Richard, all of whom recorded Domino material. Domino's big breakthrough came in mid-1955, when the Top Ten "Ain't That a Shame" (quickly covered by Pat Boone and revived in the late Seventies by Cheap Trick) established his identity with white teenagers. For the next five years Domino struck solid gold with "I'm in Love Again" (#3), "Blueberry Hill" (#2), and "Blue Monday" (#5) in 1956; "I'm Walkin'" (#4, 1957); "Whole Lotta Loving" (#6, 1958); and many others. He eventually collected 23 gold singles. His last million-seller came in 1960 with "Walkin' to New Orleans." He left Imperial for ABC in 1963 and recorded for a number of labels, all with less success.

In 1968 Domino revived public interest in his career with his rollicking cover of the Beatles' "Lady Madonna." The Beatles consistently sang the Fat Man's praises, noting that "Birthday" on *The Beatles* did little more than sort through the old Domino-Bartholomew bag of riffs and tricks. Through the mid-Seventies Fats played six to eight months a year. In 1980 he performed at the Montreux Jazz Festival. Domino continues to record and tour periodically. In 1993, he released his first major-label album in 25 years, *Christmas Is a Special Day*, to critical acclaim but only middling sales. He has lived for many years in a palatial home in New Orleans with his wife and eight children, all of whom have first names beginning with the letter A.

Lonnie Donegan
Born Anthony Donegan, April 29, 1931, Glasgow, Scotland
1961—*More Tops with Lonnie* (Pye, U.K.)   1962—*Golden Age of Donegan* (Golden Guinea, U.K.)   1968—*Showcase* (Marble Arch, U.K.)   1969—*Lonnie Donegan Rides Again*   1978—*Puttin' on the Style* (United Artists, U.K.)   1989—*Lonnie Donegan* (LaserLight)   1994—*More Than Pie in the Sky* (Bear Family, Ger.).

Banjoist Lonnie Donegan was one of the first British artists to enter the American Top Twenty, and his 1956 success with "Rock Island Line" inspired a generation of young Britons in the late-Fifties English skiffle craze.

Anthony Donegan's father was a violinist in the National Scottish Orchestra, and by the age of 13 Donegan was playing the drums. At 17 he became a Dixieland jazz convert, switched to the guitar, and played in an amateur jazz band before entering Britain's National Service. He picked up the banjo while working as a drummer with the Wolverines Jazz Band. Once discharged he moved to London and became banjoist and guitarist with the Ken Colyer Jazz Band, which in 1952 recorded one of the first jazz discs cut in England. By then Donegan had adopted the name Lonnie, in honor of his idol Lonnie Johnson.

In 1953 Colyer's band was renamed Chris Barber's band; the following year they recorded *New Orleans*

family, Antoine Domino began playing piano at nine and a year later was playing for pennies in honky-tonks like the Hideaway Club, where bandleader Bill Diamond accurately nicknamed him Fats. At 14 Domino quit school to work in a bedspring factory so he could play the bars at night. Soon he was playing alongside such New Orleans legends as Professor Longhair and Amos Milburn. He also heard the stride and boogie-woogie piano techniques of Fats Waller and Albert Ammons. He mastered the classic New Orleans R&B piano style—easy-rolling left-hand patterns anchoring right-hand arpeggios. By the age of 20 he was married and a father, had survived a near-fatal car crash, and had almost lost his hand in a factory accident.

In the mid-Forties Domino joined trumpeter Dave Bartholomew's band. It was soon apparent, however, that Domino was more than a sideman, and Bartholomew helped arrange his contract with Imperial and became his producer. Their first session in 1949 produced "The Fat Man," which eventually sold a million and whetted the national appetite for the "New Orleans sound." Domino and Bartholomew cowrote most of Domino's material.

By the time the rock & roll boom began in the mid-Fifties, Fats was already an established R&B hitmaker ("Goin' Home," 1952; "Going to the River," 1953), his records regularly selling between half a million and a million copies apiece. His pounding piano style was easily adapted to the nascent rock sound, although he proved less personally magnetic than contemporaries like Elvis Presley, Chuck Berry, Jerry Lee Lewis, or Little

Joys, which contained a version of "Rock Island Line" featuring Donegan's vocals. It became an international sensation, selling three million and launching Donegan's solo career as the "King of Skiffle" and one of England's top entertainers of the late Fifties. Donegan's followup, "Lost John," didn't crack the American Top Twenty; his only other U.S. hit was "Does Your Chewing Gum Lose Its Flavor (on the Bedpost Overnight)" in 1961. "Lost John" went to #2 on the U.K. chart, beginning Donegan's six-year domination of the English hit parade, during which he enjoyed 17 Top Ten hits. In lieu of a fan club he formed a folk music appreciation society. Adam Faith (who later produced some of Donegan's sessions) and the nascent Beatles played at one of the society's 1958 membership drives in Liverpool. By 1963 Beatlemania had eclipsed skiffle, although Donegan continued to tour.

In 1974 Donegan toured the U.S. as an opening act for Tom Jones. He began hanging out on the fringe of the rock crowd. At a backstage party following a Wings concert in 1976, an impromptu jam with Faith, Elton John, Ringo Starr, and Leo Sayer led to the idea of an all-star Donegan reunion LP—*Puttin' on the Style*—which also featured Ron Wood, Rory Gallagher, Brian May of Queen, Albert Lee, Gary Brooker (Procol Harum), Mick Ralphs (Mott the Hoople, Bad Company), and other Donegan fans.

Donegan subsequently recorded two countryish albums, including one with Doug Kershaw. In 1981, the year he celebrated the silver anniversary of "Rock Island Line," he underwent heart surgery for chronic cardiac problems.

Ral Donner

Born February 10, 1945, Chicago, Illinois; died April 6, 1984, Chicago
N.A.—*Takin' Care of Business* (Gone); *Takin' Care of Business, vol. 2* (Rondo) 1977—*Elvis Scrapbook* (Gone) 1978—*You Don't Know What You've Got* (Pye, U.K.); *Ral Donner, Ray Smith and Bobby Dale* (Crown).

After Elvis Presley came out of the army, Ral Donner became the most successful imitator of Presley's earlier style. Donner cut his first sides for Scotty Records in 1958, then was spotted playing at the Medina Temple by Sammy Davis Jr. Davis arranged for Donner to perform at New York's Apollo Theatre, which resulted in a deal with Gone Records. In mid-1961 "Girl of My Best Friend" (previously recorded by Elvis on *Elvis Is Back*) became the first of four Donner singles ("Please Don't Go," "She's Everything," and his biggest hit, the #4 "You Don't Know What You've Got") to reach the Top Forty. Donner recorded extensively but unsuccessfully through the early Seventies for a plethora of labels. Because of his similarity to Presley, he was asked to narrate the 1981 documentary-style motion picture *This Is Elvis*. Like The King, Donner died young, but of cancer.

Donovan

Donovan

Born Donovan Leitch, May 10, 1946, Glasgow, Scotland
1965—*Catch the Wind* (Hickory); *Fairytale* 1966—*Sunshine Superman* (Epic) 1967—*Mellow Yellow*; *For Little Ones*; *Wear Your Love Like Heaven*; *A Gift from a Flower to a Garden* 1968—*Donovan in Concert*; *The Hurdy Gurdy Man* 1969—*Donovan's Greatest Hits*; *Barabajagal* 1970—*Open Road* 1973—*Cosmic Wheels*; *Essence to Essence* 1974—*7-Tease* 1976—*Slow Down World* 1977—*Donovan* (Arista) 1991—*The Classics Live* (Great Northern Arts) 1992—*Troubadour: The Definitive Collection, 1964–1976* (Epic/Legacy).

Though for many years in the Seventies and Eighties, Donovan's flowery philosophy was considered passé, his compositions ("Catch the Wind," "Sunshine Superman," "Season of the Witch," "Mellow Yellow") still stand as novel examples of folk-rock hippie mysticism.

Donovan Leitch grew up in the Gorbals section of Glasgow. His family moved to the outskirts of London when he was ten; at 15 he completed the British equivalent of secondary school and enrolled in college, but stayed only a year. At age 18 he began recording his songs. Talent scouts from the British rock TV program *Ready Steady Go* heard the demos, and in early 1965 Donovan became a regular on the show. His debut single, "Catch the Wind," hit the Top Twenty-five in mid-1965; like its followups—"Colours" and "Universal Soldier"—the song was almost entirely acoustic. Donovan's U.S. performing debut was at the 1965 Newport Folk Festival.

With producer Mickie Most (with whom he worked until 1969), he left Hickory for Epic. Folklike refrains and

The Doobie Brothers: Cornelius Bumpus, Patrick Simmons, Tiran Porter, Michael McDonald, John McFee, Keith Knudsen, Chet McCracken

exotic instrumentation (sitars, flutes, cellos, harps) kept Donovan's singles in the Top Forty. His biggest hit, "Sunshine Superman," hit #1 in 1966 on both sides of the Atlantic. "Mellow Yellow" quickly reached #2 later that year. Some claimed its lyrics referred to smoking banana peels, but Donovan later claimed the song's subject was an electric dildo. Subsequent hits included 1967's "Epistle to Dippy" (#19) and "There Is a Mountain" (#11). By the time of 1968's "Wear Your Love Like Heaven" (#23, later the ad jingle for Love cosmetics) and "Jennifer Juniper" (#26, written for Jenny—sister of Pattie Boyd Harrison Clapton—Boyd, the future Mrs. Mick Fleetwood), Leitch's wardrobe had changed to love beads and flowing robes.

In 1967 Donovan traveled to India to study with the Maharishi Mahesh Yogi. Shortly thereafter he publicly renounced all drug use and requested that his followers substitute meditation for getting stoned. A few more hits followed—"Hurdy Gurdy Man" (#5, 1968), "Atlantis" (#7, 1969), and "Goo Goo Barabajagal (Love Is Hot)" with the Jeff Beck Group (#36, 1969)—but after 1970 no one paid much attention.

After a period of seclusion in Ireland, Donovan starred in and wrote the music for the 1972 German film *The Pied Piper*. He also scored *If It's Tuesday This Must Be Belgium,* then a full-length animation feature, *Tangled Details,* and Franco Zeffirelli's *Brother Sun, Sister Moon* in 1973. Following his sparsely attended 1971 U.S. tour, Donovan didn't perform in public until 1974, when he completed *7-Tease,* a conceptual LP about a young hippie and his search for inner peace.

The next year, *7-Tease* toured as a theatrical stage revue. In 1976 Donovan toured U.S. clubs in support of *Slow Down World.* He has published one book of poetry, *Dry Songs and Scribbles.* He essentially retired from recording, though he did release two albums in Germany. In 1983 Jerry Wexler produced *Lady of the Stars.*

Though Donovan sporadically performed in U.S. clubs beginning in the late Eighties, his name seemed to appear most often in the U.S. press as a footnote in items about his children. Daughter Ione Skye became an actress; her film credits include *River's Edge.* Son Donovan Leitch Jr. was the "it" boy of 1993–94, a model, actor, and singer in his group Nancy Boy. In the early Nineties, Happy Mondays helped rekindle a U.K. Donovan revival of sorts, and he toured there with them in 1992. Two years later he appeared at a memorial concert in England commemorating the 25th anniversary of Rolling Stone Brian Jones' death. (Donovan is married to one of Jones' former girlfriends, Linda Lawrence, and raised Jones' son Julian.) In 1995 Donovan was recording a new album with producer Rick Rubin, for American Records.

The Doobie Brothers

Formed 1970, San Jose, California
Tom Johnston (b. Visalia, Calif.), gtr., voc.; John Hartman (b. Mar. 18, 1950, Falls Church, Va.), drums; Patrick Simmons (b. Jan. 23, 1950, Aberdeen, Wash.), gtr., voc.; Dave Shogren (b. San Francisco, Calif.), bass.
1971—*The Doobie Brothers* (Warner Bros.)
(– Shogren; + Tiran Porter [b. Los Angeles, Calif.], bass; + Michael Hossack [b. Sep. 18, 1950, Paterson, N.J.], drums)   1972—*Toulouse Street*   1973—*The Captain and Me* (– Hossack; + Keith Knudsen [b. Oct. 18, 1952, Ames, Iowa], drums)   1974—*What Once Were Vices Are Now Habits* (+ Jeff "Skunk" Baxter [b. Dec. 13, 1948, Washington, D.C.], gtr.)   1975—*Stampede* (+ Michael McDonald [b. Feb. 12, 1952, St. Louis, Mo.], kybds., voc.)   1976—*Takin' It to the Streets*; *The Best of the Doobie Brothers* 1977—*Livin' on the Fault Line* (– Johnston)   1978— *Minute by Minute*   1979—(– Hartman; – Baxter; + John McFee [b. Nov. 18, 1953, Santa Cruz, Calif.],

gtr.; + Chet McCracken [b. July 17, 1952, Seattle, Wash.], drums; + Cornelius Bumpus [b. Jan. 13, 1952], sax, kybds.) 1980—*One Step Closer* 1981—*The Best of the Doobies, vol. 2* 1982—(Group disbands) 1983—*The Doobie Brothers Farewell Tour* 1988—(Group re-forms: Johnston; Simmons; Hartman; Porter; Hossack; + Bobby LaKind [b. 1945; d. Dec. 24, 1992], perc.) 1989—*Cycles* (Capitol) 1991—*Brotherhood.*
Tom Johnston solo: 1979—*Everything You've Heard Is True* (Warner Bros.) 1981—*Still Feels Good.*
Pat Simmons solo: 1983—*Arcade* (Elektra).
Michael McDonald solo: See entry.

Fans of the Doobie Brothers' first incarnation as a California country-boogie band had little use for the band's second, even more popular sound: an intricate jazz-inflected white funk. Tom Johnston, who fronted the early Doobies, met John Hartman through Skip Spence of Moby Grape, a group Johnston and Hartman hoped to emulate. They first played together in the short-lived group Pud with bassist Gregg Murphy. When Pud disbanded in 1969, Hartman and Johnston began jamming with local semipro musician Dave Shogren and later with Pat Simmons. They built up an avid following among California Hell's Angels by playing open jam sessions on Sunday afternoons and dubbed themselves the Doobie Brothers ("doobie" was then popular California slang for a marijuana cigarette).

Warner Bros. A&R man Ted Templeman signed them and produced all their albums through 1980. Their debut LP failed to expand their audience much beyond their local following. With the addition of Michael Hossack and Tiran Porter, the group recorded *Toulouse Street,* which established the formula for its first hits: a strong beat, high harmonies, and repetition of a single phrase like "Listen to the music." The second and third Doobies albums were both million-sellers, the latter certified double platinum and containing such hits as "Long Train Runnin'" (#8, 1973) and "China Grove" (#15, 1973).

The transformation of Steely Dan [see entry] into a studio-based duo sent Jeff "Skunk" Baxter, who'd done session work on *What Were Once Vices . . . ,* into the Doobies full-time. "Black Water," originally a B side, became the group's first #1 in 1975. Johnston quit touring because of a stomach ailment and was replaced by another Steely Dan alumnus, Michael McDonald. Baxter and McDonald revamped the Doobies' old songs in concert, and McDonald wrote most of their new material, shifting the group toward its later amalgam of funk and pop. McDonald's burry tenor replaced high harmonies as the band's trademark. Johnston rejoined in 1976, but left permanently the next year to try a solo career; he has made two solo albums.

The multimillion sales of *Minute by Minute* (#1, 1978) established McDonald as the clear leader of the band. He sang lead on the Doobies' other #1, "What a Fool Believes." After a 1978 tour of Japan, Baxter left to do session work; he has also produced albums by Livingston Taylor and Carla Thomas. Hartman quit the music business to tend to his California horse ranch. More than a year of auditions enlisted ex-Clover guitarist John McFee and former session drummer (America, Hank Williams Jr., Helen Reddy) Chet McCracken. Sax player/vocalist Cornelius Bumpus, who'd been in a late version of Moby Grape, also joined. For a 1980 tour, the Doobies were clearly McDonald's backup band; that lineup included session drummer Andy Newmark. The group disbanded in fall 1982 after a farewell tour. Soon afterward McDonald (*If That's What It Takes*) and Simmons (*Arcade*) released their first solo LPs. Not surprisingly, McDonald's distinctive voice made him an instant star on his own [see entry].

In 1987 the Doobies reunited around Johnston for a series of concerts; two years later he, Simmons, Hartman, Porter, Hossack, and percussionist Bobby LaKind (formerly a Doobies lighting man) returned to the band's original sound with the gold *Cycles* (#17) and the Top Ten single "The Doctor." A 1991 release, *Brotherhood,* didn't fare nearly as well, and after a tour, the group claimed to have called it a day. But in 1994, it undertook a major summer tour with a lineup of Johnston, Simmons, Hossack, Knudsen, and McFee; LaKind died of cancer in 1992. McFee joined the popular country group Southern Pacific, which included Stu Cook of Creedence Clearwater Revival.

The Doors
Formed 1965, Los Angeles, California
Jim Morrison (b. Dec. 8, 1943, Melbourne, Fla.; d. July 3, 1971, Paris, Fr.), voc.; Ray Manzarek (b. Feb. 12, 1935, Chicago, Ill.), kybds.; Robby Krieger (b. Jan. 8, 1946, Los Angeles), gtr.; John Densmore (b. Dec. 1, 1944, Los Angeles), drums.
1967—*The Doors* (Elektra); *Strange Days* 1968—*Waiting for the Sun* 1969—*The Soft Parade* 1970—*Morrison Hotel/Hard Rock Cafe*; *Absolutely Live*; *13* 1971—*L.A. Woman* (– Morrison) 1972—*Weird Scenes Inside the Gold Mine* 1973—*The Best of the Doors* 1978—*An American Prayer—Jim Morrison* 1980—*The Doors Greatest Hits* 1983—*Alive, She Cried* 1985—*Classics* 1991—*Greatest Hits*; *The Doors/An Oliver Stone Film* soundtrack; *In Concert* 1995—*An American Prayer* (reissue with new material).
Without Morrison: 1971—*Other Voices* 1972—*Full Circle.*
Robby Krieger solo: 1981—*Robby Krieger and Friends* (Capitol) 1983—*Versions* (Passport) 1988—*No Habla* (IRS).
Robby Krieger Organization: 1995—*RKO Live* (One Way).

The Doors: John Densmore, Robby Krieger, Ray Manzarek, Jim Morrison

Ray Manzarek solo: 1975—*The Whole Thing Started with Rock & Roll Now It's Out of Control* (Mercury); *The Golden Scarab*.

Sex, death, reptiles, charisma, and a unique variant of the electric blues gave the Doors an aura of profundity that not only survived but has grown during the two decades plus since Jim Morrison's death. By themselves, Morrison's lyrics read like adolescent posturings, but with his sexually charged delivery, Ray Manzarek's dry organ, and Robby Krieger's jazzy guitar, they became eerie, powerful, almost shamanistic invocations that hinted at a familiarity with darker forces, and, in Morrison's case, an obsession with excess and death. At its best, the Doors' music—"Light My Fire," "L.A. Woman"—has come to evoke a noirish view of Sixties California that contrasts sharply with the era's prevailing folky, trippy style.

Morrison and Manzarek, acquaintances from the UCLA Graduate School of Film, conceived the group at a 1965 meeting on a Southern California beach. After Morrison recited one of his poems, "Moonlight Drive," Manzarek—who had studied classical piano as a child and played in Rick and the Ravens, a UCLA blues band—suggested they collaborate on songs. Manzarek's brothers, Rick and Jim, served as guitarists until Manzarek met John Densmore, who brought in Robby Krieger; both had been members of the Psychedelic Rangers. Morrison christened the band the Doors, from William Blake via Aldous Huxley's book on mescaline, *The Doors of Perception.*

The Doors soon recorded a demo tape, and in the summer of 1966 they began working as the house band at the Whisky-A-Go-Go, a gig that ended four months

later when they were fired for performing the explicitly Oedipal "The End," one of Morrison's many songs that included dramatic recitations. By then Jac Holzman of Elektra Records had been convinced by Arthur Lee of Love to sign the band.

An edited version of Krieger's "Light My Fire" from the Doors' debut album became a #1 hit in 1967, as did the album, while "progressive" FM radio played (and analyzed) "The End." Morrison's image as the embodiment of dark psychological impulses was established quickly, even as he was being featured in such teen magazines as *16. Strange Days* (#3, 1967) and *Waiting for the Sun* (#1, 1968) both included hit singles and became best-selling albums. *Waiting for the Sun* also marked the first appearance of Morrison's mythic alter ego, the Lizard King, in a poem printed inside the record jacket entitled "The Celebration of the Lizard King." Though part of the poem was used as lyrics for "Not to Touch the Earth," a complete "Celebration" didn't appear on record until *Absolutely Live* (#8, 1970).

It was impossible to tell whether Morrison's Lizard King persona was a parody of a pop star or simply inspired exhibitionism, but it earned him considerable notoriety. In December 1967 he was arrested for public obscenity at a concert in New Haven, and in August 1968 he was arrested for disorderly conduct aboard an airplane en route to Phoenix. Not until his March 1969 arrest in Miami for exhibiting "lewd and lascivious behavior by exposing his private parts and by simulating masturbation and oral copulation" onstage did Morrison's behavior adversely affect the band. Court proceedings kept the singer in Miami most of the year, although the prosecution could produce neither eyewitnesses nor photos of Morrison performing the acts. Charges were dropped, but public furor (which inspired a short-lived Rally for Decency movement), concert promoters' fear of similar incidents, and Morrison's own mixed feelings about celebrity resulted in erratic concert schedules thereafter.

The Soft Parade (#6, 1969), far more elaborately produced than the Doors' other albums, met with a mixed reception from fans, but it too had a #3 hit single, "Touch Me." Morrison began to devote more attention to projects outside the band: writing poetry, collaborating on a screenplay with poet Michael McClure, and directing a film, *A Feast of Friends* (he had also made films to accompany "Break On Through" and the 1968 single "The Unknown Soldier"). Simon and Schuster published *The Lords and the New Creatures* in 1971; an earlier book, *An American Prayer*, was privately printed in 1970 but not made widely available until 1978, when the surviving Doors regrouped and set Morrison's recitation of the poem to music. In 1989 *Wilderness: The Lost Writings of Jim Morrison* was published. Although Morrison expressed to friends and associates his wish to be remembered as a poet, overall his writings have found few fans among critics. By then some felt, especially after "Touch Me," that the band had sold out, and Morrison's dangerous persona was more often ridiculed than not. Critic Lester Bangs once tagged him "Bozo Dionysus."

Soon after *L.A. Woman* (#9, 1971) was recorded, Morrison took an extended leave of absence from the group. Obviously physically and emotionally drained, he moved to Paris, where he hoped to write and where he and his wife, Pamela Courson Morrison, lived in seclusion. He died of heart failure in his bathtub in 1971 at age 27. Partly because news of his death was not made public until days after his burial in Paris' Père-Lachaise cemetery, some still refuse to believe Morrison is dead. His wife, one of the few people who saw Morrison's corpse, died in Hollywood of a heroin overdose on April 25, 1974.

The Doors continued to record throughout 1973 as a trio, but after two albums it seemed they had exhausted the possibilities of a band without a commanding lead singer. Manzarek had hoped to reconstitute the group with Iggy Pop, whose avowed chief influence was Morrison, but plans fell through. After the Doors broke up, Manzarek recorded two solo albums, and one with a short-lived group called Nite City. He produced the first three albums by Los Angeles' X, and in 1983 he collaborated with composer Philip Glass on a rock version of Carl Orff's modern cantata, *Carmina Burana*. Krieger and Densmore formed the Butts Band, which lasted three years and recorded two albums. In 1972 a Doors greatest-hits collection, *Weird Scenes Inside the Gold Mine*, was released, hit #55, and went gold. Krieger released his first solo album in 1981 and toured in 1982.

Ironically, the group's best years began in 1980, nine years after Morrison's death. With the release of the Danny Sugerman–Jerry Hopkins biography of Morrison, *No One Here Gets Out Alive*, sales of the Doors' music and the already large Jim Morrison cult—spurred by his many admirers and imitators in new-wave bands—grew even more. Record sales for 1980 alone topped all previous figures; as one ROLLING STONE magazine cover line put it: "He's Hot, He's Sexy, He's Dead." And that was just the beginning. The 1983 release of *Alive, She Cried*, followed by MTV's airing of Doors videos, introduced Morrison and the band to a new generation, and Oliver Stone's 1991 film biography of the group, starring Val Kilmer as Morrison, was a critical and commercial success. Of the 12 Doors albums, all are gold, and seven are platinum. The 1995 reissue of *An American Prayer* features "The Ghost Song," a new track on which the surviving Doors provided musical backing to an old recording of Morrison reading from his work.

In 1990 his graffiti-covered headstone was stolen; in 1993, on what would have been his 50th birthday, hundreds of mourners—many not even born before he died—traveled from around the world to pay tribute. The group was inducted into the Rock and Roll Hall of Fame in 1993.

Doo-wop

A form of R&B-based harmony vocalizing using phonetic or nonsense syllables (like a repeated "doo-wop") for rhythm and intricate harmonic arrangements. Doo-wop began with black urban vocal groups but was soon picked up by white hopefuls in New York and Philadelphia. The ornate vocal arrangements of doo-wop were based in a cappella vocalizing; their musical accompaniment was often muted and softly swinging for maximum moody romantic effect, with Latin rhythms very popular.

Classic doo-wop singles include "Sh-Boom" by the Chords, "Earth Angel" by the Penguins, "In the Still of the Nite" by the Five Satins, "Little Darlin'" by Maurice Williams and the Gladiolas, and two of the few hard-rocking examples of the genre, "Book of Love" by the Monotones and "Get a Job" by the Silhouettes. Other important doo-wop groups are the Clovers, the "5" Royales, the Turbans, the Cadillacs, and the Flamingos. Doo-wop's influence spread throughout rock & roll, and many songs that are not strictly of the genre brim with doo-wop–style backing vocals, especially those by early rock performers such as Frankie Lymon and the Teenagers and Dion and the Belmonts.

Though now considered a nostalgic form, doo-wop had a burgeoning revival with the early-Seventies rock revival shows. In the early Eighties the Ambient Sound label released new recordings by the Harptones, the Moonglows, and the Capris. Since then, doo-wop has retained a loyal following, and thanks in part to countless CD reissues, a number of classic doo-wop groups have returned to performing, joining the many who never quit.

Lee Dorsey

Born December 24, 1924, New Orleans, Louisiana; died December 1, 1986, New Orleans
1966—*The New Lee Dorsey* (Amy) 1970—*Yes We Can* (Polydor) 1978—*Night People* (ABC) 1985—*Holy Cow!* (Arista).

New Orleans singer Lee Dorsey's dry voice fronted Allen Toussaint's songs ("Working in a Coal Mine," "Holy Cow") for over a decade. Dorsey had been a boxer and a Marine before signing with the Fury label at the start of the Sixties. In late 1961 "Ya Ya" (later covered by John Lennon and others) hit #7. "Do Re Mi" did well (#27) three months later, but Dorsey's promising start was cut short by the collapse of his record company. He met Toussaint, who put him back on the charts in late 1965 with "Ride Your Pony," a moderate hit. The next year marked the zenith of Dorsey's career. His Amy Records releases included "Get Out of My Life Woman"; the loping Top Ten smash "Working in a Coal Mine" (a minor hit for

Devo in 1981); and "Holy Cow" (later covered by the Band on *Moondog Matinee*), which rose to #23. Dorsey had two minor hits in 1967 ("My Old Car," "Go Go Girl"), then faded from view.

In 1969 he had another minor hit, "Everything I Do Gonna Be Funky." The following year Dorsey and Toussaint recorded *Yes We Can* (the title track was later a hit for the Pointer Sisters) for Polydor Records. Dorsey remained active—mostly in New Orleans—throughout the Seventies and made a guest appearance on the debut album by Southside Johnny and the Asbury Jukes. He signed with ABC Records in December 1977, and Toussaint wrote and produced all the songs on 1978's *Night People*. But ABC was sold, and Dorsey again found himself professionally adrift. In 1980 the Clash hired him to open a U.S. tour, and in 1985—and despite failing health—he performed at the annual Jazz and Heritage Festival in New Orleans. He died approximately a year and a half later after a battle with emphysema.

Doug E. Fresh

Born Douglas Davis, September 17, 1966, New York City, New York
1986—*Oh, My God!* (Reality)   1988—*The World's Greatest Entertainer*.

Doug E. Fresh's claim to fame as the "original human beat box" precedes his musical reputation. His vocal simulation of drums, computer blips, and telephone ringing briefly encouraged a few other rappers in the mid-Eighties; by the Nineties the technique had become a dated novelty.

Doug Davis' initial version of Doug E. Fresh and the Get Fresh Crew consisted of Ricky D. (who soon left to chart his own career as Slick Rick [see entry]) and the double-DJ team of Barry Bee and Chill Will. The group delivered its first smash single, "The Show" (#4 R&B), in 1985, before the debut album was released. By the time *Oh, My God!* came out the next year, Davis had found religion. Subsequent singles failed to catch fire as "The Show" had, although "All the Way to Heaven" went to #19 R&B. "Lovin' Ev'ry Minute of It" reached only #38, and "Play This Only at Night" failed even to make it into the Top Forty. Doug E. Fresh scored a minor comeback in 1988 with "Keep Risin' to the Top" (#17 R&B), from *The World's Greatest Entertainer*. In 1994 Fresh had a small comeback with the dance single "I-ight (Alright)."

Carl Douglas

Born Jamaica
1974—*Kung Fu Fighting* (20th Century-Fox).

A 4,000-year-old Chinese martial art and a reggae-tinged disco beat provided Carl Douglas the inspiration for his gold hit record, "Kung Fu Fighting." Douglas, a Ja-

maican raised in the United States and England, got into the record business while studying engineering in London in the early Sixties. His British-based career as a singer and composer was undistinguished (the soundtrack to the 1972 movie *Embassy* was his major accomplishment) until he cut "Kung Fu Fighting." The song hit first in England, where it made #1 in August 1974. By October it had reached that position on American R&B charts, soon hitting #1 on the pop charts too. It inspired a dance step, the Kung Fu. Douglas appeared only once more on American charts—with a followup, "Dance the Kung Fu," in 1975 (#48 pop, #8 R&B)—but he continued to have hits in England, where "Run Back" made the Top Thirty in 1977. Since then, little has been heard from Douglas. "Kung Fu Fighting" was covered in concert by Robyn Hitchcock and the Egyptians in 1993.

The Dovells

Formed 1959, Philadelphia, Pennsylvania
Original lineup: Len Barry (b. Leonard Borisoff, Dec. 6, 1942, Philadelphia), lead voc.; Arnie Satin (b. Arnie Silver, May 11, 1943), baritone voc.; Jerry Summers (b. Jerry Gross, Dec. 29, 1942), first tenor voc.; Mike Dennis (b. Mike Freda, June 3, 1943), second tenor voc.; Danny Brooks (b. John Meely, Apr. 1, 1942; d. early 1970s), bass voc.; Mark Stevens.
1961—*Bristol Stomp* (Parkway)   1962—*All the Hits for Your Hully Gully Party*   1963—*You Can't Sit Down*; *Biggest Hits* (Wyncote).

The Dovells were an early-Sixties white doo-wop group, all born in Philadelphia. The group's string of dance hits began in late 1961 with the #2 hit "Bristol Stomp." Their 1962 hits included "Do the New Continental" (#37), "Bristol Twistin' Annie" (#27), and "Hully Gully Baby" (#25). They reached #3 in 1963 with "You Can't Sit Down." But subsequent releases on Cameo Parkway went nowhere. In their heyday, the Dovells frequently toured as part of Dick Clark's road revue.

In 1965 lead singer Len Barry had several hits, the biggest being "1-2-3," which was produced by Leon Huff. Barry was known for his wild, manic stage manner, modeled after James Brown's. When the hits stopped coming, he toned down his style and hit the supper-club circuit. The Dovells continued to tour and record through 1974. Mark Stevens and Summers, with other singers, continue to perform as the Dovells.

Nick Drake

Born June 18, 1948, Burma; died November 25, 1974, Birmingham, England
1969—*Five Leaves Left* (Island)   1970—*Bryter Layter*   1972—*Pink Moon*   1979—*Fruit Tree: The Complete Works of Nick Drake*   1994—*Way to Blue* (Rykodisc).

Nick Drake

Since Nick Drake's death, his eerie, jazz-tinged folk music has had an ever-growing cult following. Born to British parents, Drake spent his first two years on the Indian subcontinent before moving to the English village of Tamworth-in-Arden. He played saxophone and clarinet in school but turned to the guitar at age 16. Two years later he began writing his own songs. He was a student at Cambridge University in 1968, when Ashley Hutchings of Fairport Convention heard him performing at London's Roundhouse. Hutchings introduced him to Joe Boyd, who managed Fairport, John Martyn, and other leaders of the British folk revival. Boyd immediately signed Drake to Island Records and booked him on concert bills.

Drake was a shy, awkward performer and remained aloof from the public and press. By all accounts his isolation and confusion, results of severe mental illness that at times would leave him catatonic and requiring hospitalizations, grew more severe. By the end of 1970 he had stopped doing concerts. He lived for a short while in Paris at the behest of Françoise Hardy (who never released the recordings she made of his songs) and then settled in Hampstead, where he became increasingly

reclusive, allowing the company of only his close friends John and Beverly Martyn. He recorded *Pink Moon* totally unaccompanied, submitted the tapes to Island by mail, and entered a psychiatric rest home. When he left the home months later, vowing never to sing another song, he got a job as a computer programmer. In 1973 he began writing songs again. Drake had recorded four when he died in bed at his parents' home in 1974, the victim of an overdose of antidepressant medication. Suicide was considered probable by the coroner, but Drake's friends and family disagreed. *Fruit Tree* is a box set containing his three albums plus the four songs recorded in 1973; *Way to Blue* is dubbed an "introduction to Nick Drake."

The Dream Academy
Formed 1983, London, England
Gilbert Gabriel (b. Nov. 16, 1956, Paddington, London), kybds.; Nick Laird-Clowes (b. Feb. 5, 1957, London), voc., gtr.; Kate St. John (b. Oct. 2, 1957, London), voc., oboe, sax.
1985—*The Dream Academy* (Warner Bros.)   1987—*Remembrance Days* (Reprise)   1990—*A Different Kind of Weather*.

In the mid-Eighties the Dream Academy was among a wave of British acts whose elegant, arty reexamination of psychedelic textures foreshadowed the retro-mania that would consume guitar rock a few years later. In fact, the Academy's self-titled debut album was produced by Pink Floyd's David Gilmour. That album's hit single, 1985's "Life in a Northern Town" (#7), was an unabashedly nostalgic ballad, littered with references to John F. Kennedy and the Beatles. The three members were all children of the Sixties, and had been inspired by what they viewed as pop music's textural eclecticism and daring during the latter part of that decade. But even as he dressed in velvet suits with Nehru collars, Academy singer/guitarist Nick Laird-Clowes—who shared songwriting duties with keyboardist Gilbert Gabriel—insisted that the band's delicate, diversely textured songs were more contemporary than some of its critics maintained. In any case, the trio released two more albums that generally echoed the first in terms of their arrangements and production values, but neither was commercially successful. St. John later joined Van Morrison's touring revue and married American singer/songwriter Sid Griffin (ex–Long Ryders).

Dream Pop
Also known as shoegazing music, this swirling, airy psychedelic-tinged pop style came out of London in the late Eighties from a collective of self-promoting, self-consciously arty bands that the British music press dubbed

the "scene that celebrates itself." Included among its ranks were My Bloody Valentine, Pale Saints, Lush, Ride, Blur, Bleach, Moose, and many other bands influenced by the melodic, atmospheric pop of the Cocteau Twins and the textured, feedback-drenched guitars of the Jesus and Mary Chain. After an initial deluge of bands with one-syllable names, dream pop had played itself out by 1994, with only the most distinctive of the lot (My Bloody Valentine, Lush) remaining of interest to fans and critics. Aside from the music of Los Angeles' Medicine, the style has remained primarily a British import.

The Dream Syndicate/Steve Wynn

Formed 1981, Los Angeles, California
Steve Wynn (b. Feb. 21, 1960, Santa Monica, Calif.), gtr., voc.; Karl Precoda (b. ca. 1961), gtr.; Kendra Smith (b. Mar. 14, 1960, San Diego, Calif.), bass; Dennis Duck (b. Mar. 25, 1953), drums.
1982—*The Dream Syndicate* EP (Down There); *The Days of Wine and Roses* (Ruby)   1983—*Tell Me When It's Over* EP (Rough Trade) (– Smith; + Dave Provost, bass)   1984—*Medicine Show* (A&M); *This Is Not the New Dream Syndicate Album . . . Live!* EP (– Precoda; + Paul Cutler [b. Aug. 5, 1954, Phoenix, Ariz.], gtr.; – Provost; + Mark Walton [b. Aug. 9, 1959, Fairfield, Calif.], bass)   1986—*Out of the Grey* (Big Time)   1987—*50 in a 25 Zone* EP   1988—*Ghost Stories* (Enigma)   1989—*Live at Raji's* (Restless)   1992—*Tell Me When It's Over: The Best of Dream Syndicate (1982–1988)* (Rhino).
Steve Wynn solo: 1990—*Kerosene Man* (RNA/Rhino)   1992—*Dazzling Display*   1994—*Fluorescent*.
Steve Wynn with Gutterball: 1993—*Gutterball* (Mute)   1995—*Weasel* (Breakout/Enemy).
Kendra Smith solo: 1992—*Kendra Smith Presents the Guild of Temporal Adventures* (Fiasco)   1995—*Five Ways of Disappearing* (4AD).
Kendra Smith with Opal: 1985—*Northern Line* EP (One Big Guitar)   1987—*Happy Nightmare Baby* (SST)   1989—*Early Recordings* (Rough Trade).

The Dream Syndicate put L.A.'s early-Eighties "paisley underground" on the national music map. The group blended Steve Wynn's Dylanesque poetizing with a potpourri of Sixties instrumental influences, including feedback-drenched psychedelia, a Velvet Underground drone, and flat-out, Stooges-like rock attacks.

Steve Wynn met Kendra Smith at the University of California's Davis campus in 1981. Within a year, the two moved to Los Angeles and formed the Dream Syndicate with Karl Precoda and Dennis Duck. The group's self-released debut EP attracted the attention of L.A.'s thriving underground music scene, but it was the full-length *The Days of Wine and Roses* that earned the Syndicate a national following. When *Medicine Show* appeared on A&M in 1984, the group's hometown supporters cried

"sellout," but otherwise the album was highly praised for its continued commitment to rock & roll.

The Dream Syndicate regrouped for its 1986 comeback, *Out of the Grey*, which moved closer to a Neil Young–inspired cow-punk sound. Wynn and company went so far as to recruit former Young producer Elliot Mazer for their bare-bones followup, *Ghost Stories. Live at Raji's*, which was recorded in early 1989 at a favorite L.A. punk-rock dive, spelled the end of the Dream Syndicate.

Wynn immediately embarked on a solo career, recruiting a host of musicians to help out on his highly personal *Kerosene Man*, followed by the critically acclaimed *Dazzling Display*. In 1993 Wynn's garagey supergroup Gutterball (also featuring Johnny Hott and Bryan Harvey, formerly of House of Freaks, and Stephen McCarthy, ex–Long Ryders) released its self-titled debut; Wynn also continued as a solo artist. Meanwhile, Kendra Smith has performed with Opal, as well as released solo albums.

The Drifters/Clyde McPhatter

Formed 1953, New York City, New York
Clyde McPhatter (b. Clyde Lensley McPhatter, Nov. 15, 1931, Durham, N.C.; d. June 13, 1972, Teaneck, N.J.), lead voc.; David "Little David" Baughan (b. New York City; d. 1970), tenor voc.; William Anderson, tenor voc.; David Baldwin, baritone voc.; James Johnson, bass voc.
1953—(– Baughan; – Anderson; – Baldwin; – Johnson; + Billy Pinckney [sometimes spelled Pinkney, b. Aug. 15, 1925, Sumter, S.C.], tenor voc.; + Andrew "Bubba" Thrasher (b. Wetumpka, Ala.), baritone voc.; + Gerhart "Gay" Thrasher (b. Wetumpka, Ala.), tenor voc.; + Willie Ferbee, bass voc.; – Ferbee; Pinckney moves to bass)   1954—(– McPhatter; + Baughan, lead voc.; + Johnny Moore [b. 1934, Selma, Ala.], tenor voc.)   1955—(– Baughan; Moore moves to lead voc.)   1956—(– A. Thrasher; – Pinckney; + "Carnation" Charlie Hughes, baritone voc.; + Tommy Evans, bass voc.)   1957—(– Moore; – Hughes; + Bobby Hendricks [b. 1937, Columbus, Ohio], lead voc.; + Jimmy Millinder, baritone voc.)   1958—(Group disbands; new lineup: Charlie Thomas, tenor voc.; Ben E. King [b. Benjamin Earl Nelson, Sep. 23, 1938, Henderson, N.C.], tenor voc.; Dock [a.k.a. Doc] Green [b. Oct. 8, 1934; d. Mar. 10, 1989, N.Y.], baritone voc.; Elsbeary Hobbs, bass)   1959—(+ Johnny Lee Williams, tenor voc.)   1960—(– King; + James Poindexter, tenor voc; – Poindexter; + Rudy Lewis [d. 1964], tenor voc.; – Hobbs; + William Van Dyke, bass voc.; – Van Dyke; + George Grant, bass voc.; – Grant; + Tommy Evans, bass voc.)   1962—(– Green; + Gene Pearson, baritone voc.)   1963—(– Evans; + Johnny Terry, bass voc.; + J. Moore)   1964—(– Lewis)   1966—

(– Terry; + Dan Danbridge, bass voc.; – Danbridge; + William Brent, bass voc.; – Pearson; + Rick Sheppard, baritone voc.)   1967 on—(Numerous additional personnel changes throughout the years) 1968—*The Drifters' Golden Hits* (Atlantic)   1988—*Let the Boogie Woogie Roll: Greatest Hits 1953–1958*; *1959–1965 All-Time Greatest Hits and More*   1994—(Lineup: Charlie Thomas, lead voc.; Barry Hobb, bass voc.; Terry King, voc.). Clyde McPhatter solo: 1991—*Deep Sea Ball: The Best of Clyde McPhatter* (Atlantic).

The Drifters helped create soul music by bringing gospel-styled vocals to secular material. Literally scores of singers (like Clyde McPhatter and Ben E. King) worked with this durable institution. After McPhatter left Billy Ward and His Dominoes [see entry], Atlantic Records' Ahmet Ertegun encouraged the singer to put together his own vocal group. According to an early press release and rock lore, their name came from the fact that the original members had drifted from one group to another. The truth is that all the members of the first lineup were discovered by McPhatter singing with the Mount Lebanon Singers at the Mount Lebanon Church in Harlem. In fact, they chose to name themselves after a bird called the drifter. Clyde McPhatter, already known to the record-buying public, propelled the group to immediate success. He was among the first to apply the emotional fervency of gospel to pop songs about romance, a stylistic keystone in the creation of modern R&B and soul. At its peak, the first set of Drifters was an extremely popular and influential live act, not only for their stellar vocals but also for their flashy choreography. After a string of hits—"Money Honey" (#1 R&B, 1953), later covered by Elvis Presley; "Such a Night" (#2 R&B, 1954); "Honey Love" (#21 pop, #1 R&B, 1954); "White Christmas" (#80 pop, #2 R&B, 1954); "Whatcha Gonna Do" (#2 R&B, 1955), all Top Ten R&B—McPhatter was drafted into the army in late 1954.

Following McPhatter's departure, lead vocals fell briefly to "Little David" Baughan before Bill Pinckney discovered Johnny Moore. Although McPhatter and Ben E. King are most often recalled as the group's important lead singers, Moore would prove the longest-lasting and enduring of the three vocalists. Moore-led singles of this period include "Hypnotized" and "Fools Fall in Love," but they were not enough to buoy the flagging group. Other personnel changes occurred, hits became rarer, Moore and Hughes were drafted in 1957, and the Drifters were occasionally reduced to posing as other groups, such as the Coasters and the Ravens. Group morale was at an all-time low, so when manager George Treadwell, who owned the group's name, heard a young, new group called the Crowns at the Apollo Theatre one night, he fired the entire Drifters lineup and christened his discoveries the new Drifters.

This lineup, which featured three lead tenors and included Ben E. King, proved even more successful than the original group. They were assigned to producers/writers Mike Leiber and Jerry Stoller, and their first release, "There Goes My Baby," was a #2 hit in 1959. The lushly produced song's style—incorporating orchestral strings, a gentle Latin rhythm, and King's yearning, romantic lead—became the Drifters' calling card. King was featured on "This Magic Moment" (#16 pop, #4 R&B, 1960), "Save the Last Dance for Me" (#1 pop, #1 R&B, 1960), and "I Count the Tears" (#17 pop, #6 R&B, 1961), but shortly after "Save the Last Dance for Me" hit in October 1960, he left for a solo career [see entry].

Over the next two years, leads on Drifters hits would be split among Rudy Lewis ("Some Kind of Wonderful" [#32 pop, #6 R&B, 1961], "Please Stay" [#14 pop, #13 R&B, 1961], "Up on the Roof" [#5 pop, #4 R&B, 1962], and "On Broadway" [#9 pop, #7 R&B, 1963]), Charlie Thomas ("Sweets for My Sweet" [#16 pop, #10 R&B, 1961]), and Johnny Moore ("I'll Take You Home" [#25 pop, #24 R&B, 1963] and "Under the Boardwalk" [#4 pop, #4 R&B, 1964]). Lewis died suddenly in 1964; his last-released single was "Vaya con Dios." From 1964 on, Moore dominated the Drifters' hits, which although produced by Bert Berns (as was "Under the Boardwalk") retained the sound of the Leiber and Stoller hits and gave the group consistency regardless of who was in the lineup. The Drifters kept placing R&B chart hits ("I've Got Sand in My Shoes," "Saturday Night at the Movies") through the Sixties while playing the club circuit. Although the group never had another major U.S. hit after that, a reissue of their 1965 single "Come On Over to My Place" went to #9 in the U.K., where the group has enjoyed a large, loyal following since 1960 when "Dance with Me" went to #17 there.

When the Drifters' Atlantic contract expired in 1972, Moore, with a new lineup, moved to England, where they signed with the Bell label and released a string of U.K. Top Ten hits: "Like Sister and Brother" (#7, 1973), "Kissin' in the Back Row of the Movies" (#2, 1974), "Down on the Beach Tonight" (#7, 1974), "There Goes My First Love" (#3, 1975), "Can I Take You Home Little Girl" (#10, 1975), and "You're More Than a Number in My Little Red Book" (#5, 1976).

At the same time, here in America and elsewhere in the world, any number of Drifters aggregations could be found performing in nightclubs. Among the group's many members, the Drifters have included at least one past or future Swallow, Carol, Raven, Diamond, DuDropper, Turban, Ink Spot, Cadillac, Cleftone, Domino, Royal Joker, or Temptation. Another interesting footnote: During the two years following the recording of 1961's "Some Kind of Wonderful," additional backing vocals on record were provided by a quartet consisting of Dionne and Dede Warwick, their aunt, Cissy Houston (mother of Whitney), and Doris Troy (of "Just One Look" fame).

McPhatter emerged from his two years in the service in 1955 to relaunch his solo career. With Atlantic Records' full support, he quickly charted with a duet with Ruth Brown ("Love Has Joined Us Together" [#8, 1955]). His other hits included "Treasure of Love" (#16 pop, #1 R&B, 1956), "Without Love (There Is Nothing)" (#19 pop, #4 R&B, 1957), "Just to Hold My Hand" (#26 pop, #6 R&B, 1957), "A Lover's Question" (#6 pop, #1 R&B, 1958), "Come What May" (#3 R&B, 1958), "Since You've Been Gone" (#38 pop, #14 R&B, 1959), "Ta Ta" (#23 pop, #7 R&B, 1960), "Lover Please" (#7 pop, 1962), and the #1 R&B hit "Long Lonely Nights" (1957).

Although McPhatter had a few more hits after leaving Atlantic, he never regained a commercial foothold after the mid-Sixties. He lived in England for a couple of years in the late Sixties, but in 1972 succumbed to a heart attack after years of alcoholism. He was inducted into the Rock and Roll Hall of Fame in 1987.

Ducks Deluxe

Formed 1972, London, England
Sean Tyla, gtr., kybds., voc.; Martin Belmont, gtr., voc.; Nick Garvey, bass, voc.; Tim Roper, drums.
1974—*Ducks Deluxe* (RCA) (+ Andy McMasters, organ)   1975—*Taxi to the Terminal Zone* (RCA, U.K.) (– Garvey; – McMasters; – Roper; + Mick Groom, bass, voc.; + Billy Rankin, drums) (group disbands)   1978—*Don't Mind Rockin' Tonite* 1981—*Last Night of a Pub Rock Band* (Blue Moon, U.K.).

Ducks Deluxe were part of Britain's back-to-the-roots pub-rock movement in the early Seventies, attracting a cult following before they disbanded and went on to more successful projects. They played London pubs, including the Music Bar in Kensington and the Tally Ho in Kentish Town, with a repertoire of Fifties songs by Eddie Cochran, Chuck Berry, Little Richard, and others, and originals by Tyla, Belmont, and Garvey. Their second album, *Taxi to the Terminal Zone* (produced by Dave Edmunds), wasn't released in America. Their last performance took place on July 1, 1975 (where they were joined by pub-rock stalwart Brinsley Schwarz); it was later released as *Last Night of a Pub Rock Band* in Britain. Tyla formed the Tyla Gang; Belmont eventually joined the Rumour [see entry], and later Nick Lowe's band; Garvey and McMasters founded the Motors [see entry].

Slim Dunlap: See the Replacements

Duran Duran

Formed 1978, Birmingham, England
Simon Le Bon (b. Oct. 27, 1958, Bushey, Eng.), voc.; Andy Taylor (b. Feb. 16, 1961, Dolver-Hampton,

Eng.), gtr., synth.; Nick Rhodes (b. Nicholas Bates, June 8, 1962, Birmingham), kybds.; John Taylor (b. June 20, 1960, Birmingham), bass; Roger Taylor (b. Apr. 26, 1960, Birmingham), drums.
1981—*Duran Duran* (Harvest)   1982—*Rio; Carnival EP*   1983—*Seven and the Ragged Tiger* (Capitol) 1984—*Arena* (– R. Taylor; – A. Taylor)   1986—*Notorious*   1988—*Big Thing*   1989—*Decade* (+ Warren Cuccurullo [b. Dec. 8, 1956], gtr.)   1990—*Liberty* 1993—*Duran Duran (The Wedding Album)*   1995— *Thank You*.
Arcadia (Le Bon; Rhodes; R. Taylor): 1985—*So Red the Rose* (Capitol).
Andy Taylor solo: 1987—*Thunder* (MCA)   1990— *Dangerous* (A&M, U.K.).
The Power Station (A. Taylor; J. Taylor; Robert Palmer, voc.; Tony Thompson, drums): 1985—*The Power Station* (Capitol).

Duran Duran was one of several British New Romantic bands—that being a fashion-conscious merger of new wave and disco. Although the New Romantic trend never really caught on in the U.S., thanks in part to provocative videos that soon became MTV staples, Duran Duran quickly became one of the biggest acts of the mid-Eighties, with nine Top Ten hits, three platinum albums, and a string of sold-out concert tours.

Named after a character in Roger Vadim's sex-kitten sci-fi movie *Barbarella*, Duran Duran began as Nick Rhodes and John Taylor. Andy Taylor (none of the Taylors in the band are related), answering an ad in *Melody Maker*, joined later. Simon Le Bon met the group through a friend of his who worked at the Rum Runner, a club the group frequented and at which Rhodes had been a DJ. They had a hit single in Europe in 1981 with "Planet Earth" and broke in the U.S. in 1983 with "Hungry Like the Wolf" (#3), "Rio" (#14), "Is There Something I Should Know" (#4), and "Union of the Snake" (#3). Lead singer Simon Le Bon became a popular pinup boy among British and U.S. teens, and the group achieved notoriety for its videos, particularly Godley and Creme's "Girls on Film," which featured female models in various stages of undress. (Andy Warhol once remarked that he masturbated to the group's videos.) The clip was banned by BBC-TV and, in the U.S., by MTV. *Seven and the Ragged Tiger*, which included the hits "New Moon on Monday" (#10, 1984) and "The Reflex" (#1, 1984) and went to #1 in the U.K., hit #4 Stateside and was later certified double platinum.

The next album, *Arena*, another #4 on the album chart, included "The Wild Boys" (#2, 1984) and "Save a Prayer" (#16, 1985). In spring 1985 the group's title theme song to the James Bond film *A View to a Kill* became its second #1 hit. By then the group members had become almost as familiar to readers of fashion magazines and society columns as to rock fans. Both Nick Rhodes (in 1984) and Simon Le Bon (in 1985) married models, and in 1985 Le Bon made international news when his racing boat capsized and he had to be rescued. In interviews to promote their 1993 release, band members spoke frankly of their glory years' being a time of emotional turmoil, drug abuse, and a general loss of creative and financial control.

The strain took its toll, as over the next year and a half following "A View to a Kill," John Taylor and Andy Taylor joined with singer Robert Palmer and drummer Tony Thompson to form the Power Station. A one-shot enterprise, the Power Station had two of the biggest hits of spring 1985: "Some Like It Hot" (#6) and "Get It On" (#9), the latter a retread of the T. Rex classic "Bang a Gong (Get It On)." Meanwhile, Rhodes, Le Bon, and Roger Taylor formed Arcadia, and in late 1985 had a #6 hit with "Election Day," which included narration by Grace Jones. The followup single, "Goodbye Is Forever," peaked at #33, and the album, So Red the Rose (#23), was certified platinum.

That summer the group had appeared together at the U.S. Live Aid concert, but did not release a new studio album until Notorious (#120, which was released late in 1986. Earlier that year, Roger Taylor announced he was taking a year off from the group; he never returned. That spring Andy Taylor left to pursue a solo career; he had a Top Thirty hit earlier that year with "Take It Easy." And although John Taylor also had a Top Thirty single with "I Do What I Do," in 1986, he remained with the group. As Duran Duran, the group had two hits from the Notorious album: "Notorious" (#2, 1987) and "Skin Trade" (#39, 1987). Big Thing featured "I Don't Want Your Love" (#4, 1988) and "All She Wants Is" (#22, 1989).

Although the group continued to make interesting videos, its commercial hold started to slip. The greatest-hits Decade peaked at #67, and Liberty did not enter the Top Forty and contained no hits. With the next album, guitarist Warren Cuccurullo, formerly of Missing Persons, joined the group, which for a while at this point was spelling its name Duranduran. With 1993's Duran Duran (#7, 1993), the group delivered the hit singles "Ordinary World" (#3, 1993) and "Come Undone" (#7). To date, the group has sold over 20 million albums worldwide. In early 1995 the group released an album of covers.

Ian Dury

Born May 12, 1942, Upminster, England
1975—Handsome (Dawn, U.K.) 1977—New Boots and Panties!! (Stiff) 1978—Wotabunch (Warner Bros.) 1979—Do It Yourself (Stiff) 1980—Laughter 1981—Lord Upminster (Polydor); Juke Box Dury (Stiff) 1992—Sex & Drugs & Rock & Roll: The Best of Ian Dury and the Blockheads (Rhino).

While his Cockney accent eluded American audiences, Ian Dury became a superstar in Great Britain with a good-natured mix of pop, funk, reggae, music hall, and general boisterousness.

Stricken by polio at the age of seven, Dury spent two years in the hospital and several more in a school for the physically handicapped. He studied at the Royal College of Art and taught painting at the Canterbury Art College. In 1970 he formed his first group, Kilburn and the High Roads, a band specializing in Fifties rock & roll spiced with bebop jazz. The High Roads established themselves on the pub circuit, and in 1973 Dury quit teaching.

The group's songs won the support of some influential British critics, among them Charlie Gillett, who became their manager. They cut an album for Raft Records, a subsidiary of Warner Bros., but Warners blocked its release until 1978. They released an album on Dawn, a Pye label, before disbanding in 1975.

Dury and High Roads pianist/guitarist Chaz Jankel continued to write songs together. Under Dury's name they recorded New Boots and Panties!! with session musicians and former High Roaders like saxophonist Davey Payne. Then, invited to join the Live Stiffs package tour of Britain in the fall of 1977, Dury and Jankel assembled the Blockheads: Payne, bassist Norman Watt Roy, drummer Charley Charles, pianist Mickey Gallagher, and guitarist John Turnbull. New Boots stayed on the British charts for almost two years, eventually selling over a million copies worldwide. "What a Waste," a single from the album, reached #9 (U.K.) in 1978, and a later single, "Hit Me with Your Rhythm Stick," hit #1 (U.K.).

In 1978 Arista bought American distribution rights to Dury's Stiff catalogue and released New Boots. Sales were unimpressive, and Arista dropped the contract. Back home, Do It Yourself entered the charts at #2 on its mid-1979 release, and "Reasons to Be Cheerful (Part 3)" went to #3. The Blockheads' 1979 tour of Britain included an appearance at the People of Kampuchea concert. When the tour ended, Jankel left the band; he was replaced by Wilko Johnson, formerly of Dr. Feelgood. After signing with Polydor, Dury reunited with Jankel, who traveled with him to the Bahamas to record Lord Upminster with Sly Dunbar and Robbie Shakespeare. Included on that album was a single, "Spasticus Autisticus," which was written for the United Nations Year of the Disabled, but rejected.

Dury recorded less frequently, turning his attention to acting and writing music for British television programs and commercials. He has acted on stage, on television, and in film (including in The Cook, the Thief, His Wife and Her Lover, 1989). With Gallagher he wrote Apples, a musical in which he also starred. Most recently he has hosted a U.K. late-night program, Metro.

Bob Dylan

Bob Dylan

Born Robert Allen Zimmerman, May 24, 1941, Duluth, Minnesota
1962—*Bob Dylan* (Columbia) 1963—*The Freewheelin' Bob Dylan* 1964—*The Times They Are a-Changin'*; *Another Side of Bob Dylan* 1965—*Bringing It All Back Home*; *Highway 61 Revisited* 1966—*Blonde on Blonde* 1967—*Bob Dylan's Greatest Hits*; *John Wesley Harding* 1969—*Nashville Skyline* 1970—*Self Portrait*; *New Morning* 1971—*Bob Dylan's Greatest Hits, vol. 2* 1973—*Pat Garrett and Billy the Kid*; *Dylan* 1974— *Planet Waves* (Asylum); *Before the Flood* 1975— *Blood on the Tracks* (Columbia); *The Basement Tapes* 1976—*Desire*; *Hard Rain* 1978—*Bob Dylan at Budokan*; *Street Legal* 1979—*Slow Train Coming* 1980—*Saved* 1981—*Shot of Love* 1983—*Infidels* 1984—*Real Live* 1985—*Empire Burlesque*; *Biograph* 1986—*Knocked Out Loaded* 1988— *Down in the Groove* 1989—*Oh Mercy*; *Dylan & the Dead* (with the Grateful Dead) 1990—*Under the Red Sky* 1991—*The Bootleg Series, vol. 1–3 (Rare & Unreleased) 1961–1991* 1992—*Good As I Been to You* 1993—*The 30th Anniversary Concert Celebration* (with other artists); *World Gone Wrong* 1994—*Bob Dylan's Greatest Hits, vol. 3* 1995—*Unplugged.*

Now in the fourth decade of his career, Bob Dylan has been the most inscrutable and unpredictable figure in rock. In both his stance and his music, he was the most influential American pop musician of the Sixties, and the repercussions of his many styles are still widespread. Dylan was deified and denounced for every shift of interest, while whole schools of musicians took up his ideas, and his lyrics became so well known that politicians from Jimmy Carter to Václav Havel have cited them. By personalizing folk songs, Dylan reinvented the singer/songwriter genre; by performing his allusive, poetic songs in his nasal, spontaneous vocal style with an electric band, he enlarged pop's range and vocabulary while creating a widely imitated sound. By recording with Nashville veterans, he reconnected rock and country, hinting at the country-rock of the Seventies. In the Eighties and Nineties, although he has at times seemed to flounder, he still has the ability to challenge, infuriate, and surprise listeners.

Robert Zimmerman's family moved to Hibbing, Minnesota, from Duluth when he was six. After taking up guitar and harmonica, he formed the Golden Chords while he was a freshman in high school. He enrolled at the arts college of the University of Minnesota in 1959; during his three semesters there, he began to perform solo at coffeehouses as Bob Dylan (after Dylan Thomas; he legally changed his name in August 1962).

Dylan moved to New York City in January 1961, saying he wanted to meet Woody Guthrie, who was by then hospitalized with Huntington's chorea. Dylan visited his idol frequently. That April he played New York's Gerde's Folk City as the opener for John Lee Hooker, with a set of Guthrie-style ballads and his own lyrics to traditional tunes. A *New York Times* review by Robert Shelton alerted A&R man John Hammond, who signed Dylan to Columbia and produced his first album.

Although *Bob Dylan* included only two originals, "Talking New York" and "Song to Woody," Dylan stirred up the Greenwich Village folk scene with his caustic humor and gift for giving topical songs deep resonances. *The Freewheelin' Bob Dylan* (#22, 1963) included "Blowin' in the Wind" (a hit for Peter, Paul and Mary), "A Hard Rain's a-Gonna Fall," and "Masters of War," protest songs on a par with Guthrie's and Pete Seeger's. Joan Baez, already established as a "protest singer," recorded Dylan's songs and brought him on tour; in summer 1963 they became lovers.

By 1964 Dylan was playing 200 concerts a year. *The Times They Are a-Changin'* (#20, 1964) mixed protest songs ("With God on Our Side") and more personal lyrics ("One Too Many Mornings"). He met the Beatles at Kennedy Airport and reportedly introduced them to marijuana. *Another Side of Bob Dylan* (#43, 1964), recorded in summer 1964, concentrated on personal songs and imagistic free associations such as "Chimes of Freedom"; Dylan repudiated his protest phase with "My Back Pages." In late 1964 Columbia A&R man Jim Dickson introduced Dylan to Jim (later Roger) McGuinn, to whom Dylan gave "Mr. Tambourine Man," which became the Byrds' first hit in 1965, kicking off folk rock. Meanwhile, the Dylan-Baez liaison fell apart, and Dylan met 25-year-old ex-model Shirley Noznisky, a.k.a. Sara Lowndes, whom he married in 1965.

With *Bringing It All Back Home* (#6), released early in 1965, Dylan turned his back on folk purism; for half the album he was backed by a rock & roll band. On July 25, 1965, he played the Newport Folk Festival (where two years earlier he had been the cynosure of the folksingers) backed by the Paul Butterfield Blues Band, and was booed. The next month, he played the Forest Hills tennis stadium with a band that included Levon Helm and Robbie Robertson, which accompanied him on a tour and later became the Band [see entry]. "Like a Rolling Stone" (#2, 1965) became Dylan's first major hit.

The music Dylan made in 1965 and 1966 revolutionized rock. The intensity of his performances and his live-in-the-studio albums—*Highway 61 Revisited* (#3, 1965), *Blonde on Blonde* (#9, 1966)—were a revelation, and his lyrics were analyzed, debated, and quoted like no pop before them. With rage and slangy playfulness, Dylan chewed up and spat out literary and folk traditions in a wild, inspired doggerel. He didn't explain; he gave off-the-wall interviews and press conferences in which he'd spin contradictory fables about his background and intentions. D. A. Pennebaker's documentary of Dylan's British tour, *Don't Look Back,* shows some of the hysteria. As "Rainy Day Women #12 & 35" went to #2 in April 1966, Dylan's worldwide record sales topped ten million, and more than 150 other groups or artists had recorded at least one of his songs.

On July 29, 1966, Dylan smashed up his Triumph 55 motorcycle while riding near his Woodstock, New York, home. With several broken neck vertebrae, a concussion, and lacerations of the face and scalp, he was reportedly in critical condition for a week and bedridden for a month, with aftereffects including amnesia and mild paralysis. Though the extent of Dylan's injuries was later questioned by biographers, he did spend nine months in seclusion. As he recovered, he and the Band recorded the songs that were widely bootlegged—and legitimately released in 1975—as *The Basement Tapes* (#7), whose droll, enigmatic, steeped-in-Americana sound would be continued by the Band on their own.

In 1968 Dylan made his public reentry with the quiet *John Wesley Harding* (#2), which ignored the baroque psychedelia in vogue since the Beatles' 1967 *Sgt. Pepper;* Dylan wrote new enigmas into such folkish ballads as "All Along the Watchtower." On January 20, 1968, he returned to the stage, performing three songs at a Woody Guthrie memorial concert, and in May 1969 he revealed a new, more mellow voice on the overtly countryish *Nashville Skyline* (#3), featuring "Lay Lady Lay" (#7, 1969) and "Girl from the North Country," with a guest vocal by Johnny Cash.

Dylan's early Seventies acts seemed less portentous. His 1970 *Self Portrait* (#4) included songs by other writers and live takes from a 1969 Isle of Wight concert with the Band. Widely criticized, Dylan went back into the studio and rush-released the mild, countryish *New Morning* (#7, 1970). By mid-1970 Dylan had moved to 94 MacDougal Street in Greenwich Village; on June 9, he received an honorary doctorate in music from Princeton.

George Harrison, with whom Dylan cowrote "I'd Have You Anytime," "If Not for You," and a few other songs that summer, persuaded Dylan to appear at the Concert for Bangla Desh; Leon Russell, who also performed, produced Dylan's single "Watching the River Flow." That year he also released his first protest song since the mid-Sixties, "George Jackson." In 1971 *Tarantula,* a collection of writings from the mid-Sixties, was published to an unenthusiastic reception.

Dylan sang at the Band concert that resulted in *Rock of Ages* (1972) but didn't appear on the album; he sat in on albums by Doug Sahm, Steve Goodman, McGuinn, and others. Late in 1972 he played Alias and wrote a score for Sam Peckinpah's *Pat Garrett and Billy the Kid* (#16, 1973), including "Knockin' on Heaven's Door" (#12, 1973). *Writings and Drawings by Bob Dylan,* a collection of lyrics and liner notes up to *New Morning,* was published in 1973. Between Columbia contracts, Dylan moved to Malibu in 1973 and made a handshake deal with David Geffen's Asylum label, which released *Planet Waves* (#1, 1974); Columbia retaliated with *Dylan* (#17, 1973), embarrassing outtakes from *Self Portrait.* Dylan and the Band played 39 shows in 21 cities, selling out 651,000 seats for a 1974 tour; the last three dates in L.A. were recorded for *Before the Flood.*

Dylan scrapped an early version of *Blood on the Tracks* and recut the songs with local musicians in Minneapolis. He cowrote some of the songs on *Desire* (#1, 1976) with producer Jacques Levy; before making that LP, Dylan had returned to some Greenwich Village hangouts. A series of jams at the Other End led to the notion of a communal tour, and in October bassist Rob Stoner began rehearsing the large, shifting entourage (including Baez and such Village regulars as Ramblin' Jack Elliott and Bobby Neuwirth) that became the Rolling Thunder Revue, which toured on and off—with guests including Allen Ginsberg, Joni Mitchell, Mick Ronson, McGuinn, and Arlo Guthrie—until spring 1976. The Revue started with surprise concerts at small halls (the first in Plymouth, Massachusetts, for an audience of 200) and worked up to outdoor stadiums like the one in Fort Collins, Colorado, where NBC-TV filmed *Hard Rain.* The troupe played two benefits for convicted murderer Rubin

"Hurricane" Carter (subject of Dylan's "Hurricane"), which, after expenses, raised no money. Dylan's efforts helped Carter get a retrial, but he was convicted and one of the witnesses, Patty Valentine, sued Dylan over his use of her name in "Hurricane."

In 1976 Dylan appeared in the Band's farewell concert, *The Last Waltz*, which was filmed by Martin Scorsese. His wife, Sara Lowndes, filed for divorce in March 1977. She received custody of their five children: Maria (Sara's daughter by a previous marriage whom Dylan had adopted), Jesse, Anna, Samuel, and Jakob. Dylan took a $2-million loss on *Renaldo and Clara*, a four-hour film released early in 1978 including footage of the Rolling Thunder Tour and starring himself and Joan Baez. He embarked on an extensive tour (New Zealand, Australia, Europe, the U.S., and Japan, where he recorded *Bob Dylan at Budokan*), redoing his old songs with some of the trappings of a Las Vegas lounge act.

Dylan announced in 1979 that he was a born-again Christian. McGuinn, the Alpha Band (an outgrowth of Rolling Thunder), and Debby Boone had introduced him to fundamentalist teachings. *Slow Train Coming*, overtly God-fearing, rose to #3; "Gotta Serve Somebody" (#24, 1979) netted Dylan his first Grammy (for Best Rock Vocal Performance, Male). His West Coast tour late in 1979 featured only his born-again material; *Saved* and *Shot of Love* continued that message. In late 1981 he embarked on a 22-city U.S. tour; in 1982 amid rumors he had repudiated his born-again Christianity, Dylan traveled to Israel. *Infidels* (#20, 1983), recorded with a band that included Mark Knopfler, Mick Taylor, and reggae greats Sly and Robbie, answered no questions. Despite its title, the album was more churlish than religious, although Dylan did admit that "Neighborhood Bully" was about Arab-Israeli relations.

Biograph (#33, 1985), a five-disc retrospective with 18 previously unreleased tracks, helped put Dylan's long career in perspective, but *Empire Burlesque* (#33), released the same year, puzzled listeners with its backup singers and cluttered production by dance-music specialist Arthur Baker. A tour with Tom Petty and the Heartbreakers in 1986 supported the sloppy, cryptic *Knocked Out Loaded* (#53).

Dylan further confounded fans with a 1987 tour double-billed with the Grateful Dead, who also backed him. The shows yielded a concert album, *Dylan & the Dead* (#37, 1989). He appeared in the film *Hearts of Fire* with the singer Fiona. Although both Dylan and the movie were ravaged by the critics, Dylan's role as a burnt-out middle-aged rock star struck some as coming too close to the truth.

Dylan delayed the release of *Down in the Groove* (#61, 1988) twice in six months. The final product, with guests including Eric Clapton, Steve Jones (Sex Pistols), rappers Full Force, and members of the Dead, sounded tentative and unfocused. But as "Lucky," one-fifth of the Traveling Wilburys, Dylan appeared to enjoy participating in a group project.

Dylan was inducted into the Rock and Roll Hall of Fame in 1989 and later that year released his best-received album of the Eighties, *Oh Mercy* (#30). Produced by Daniel Lanois (U2, Robbie Robertson) in New Orleans, it was a coherent collection of songs, and Dylan sounded reenergized and engaged. But as he had throughout his career, Dylan defied expectations. On his Never Ending Tour, started in 1988, Dylan recast his songs, at times throwing them away with offhand performances. His appearance on the *L'Chaim—To Life* telethon led to rumors he had joined a Hasidic sect. *Under the Red Sky* (#38, 1990), the followup to *Oh Mercy*, was almost universally panned.

In 1990 Dylan was named a *Commandeur dans l'Ordre des Arts et des Lettres*, France's highest cultural honor. At the Grammy Awards in 1991, where he was given a Lifetime Achievement Award, Dylan's whimsical acceptance "speech" and sloppy, almost unintelligible performance of "Masters of War" (the Gulf War had recently raged) left some fans scratching their heads, while others applauded his pugnacious attitude. For *The Bootleg Series, vol. 1–3 (Rare & Unreleased)* (#49, 1991), Dylan opened up the vaults; its 58 outtakes, live tracks, and demos proving Dylan's prolific virtuosity.

Columbia Records marked the 30th anniversary of Dylan's first album with an all-star concert at New York's Madison Square Garden. More than 30 stars, including Neil Young, Pearl Jam's Eddie Vedder, Tom Petty, George Harrison, Eric Clapton, Johnny Cash, Lou Reed, and Dylan himself, participated in the October 16, 1992, show, dubbed the "Bobfest" by Young. Broadcast live on pay-per-view, it was released as an album and video the next year. As if to bring his career full circle, Dylan recorded two folkish solo guitar and vocal albums of traditional songs: *Good As I Been to You* (#51, 1992) and *World Gone Wrong* (#70, 1993). The latter earned Dylan the 1994 Grammy for Best Traditional Folk Album.

In the mid-1990s Dylan's live concerts revived. Assembling one of the best bands of his career, he stopped throwing away his songs, instead playing both countryish rock and acoustic string-band versions of his best compositions. He made a triumphant appearance at Woodstock '94, though he had snubbed the original 1969 festival. In late 1994 Dylan performed on *MTV Unplugged*, with his new band augmented by Pearl Jam's producer Brendan O'Brien on keyboards (highlights were released on the 1995 *Bob Dylan Unplugged* album).

E

Sheila E.

Born Sheila Escovedo, December 12, 1957, Oakland, California
1984—*The Glamorous Life* (Warner Bros.)   1985—
Sheila E. in Romance 1600   1987—Sheila E.
1991—*Sex Cymbal.*

A gifted drummer and percussionist, Sheila E. also proved herself at home fronting a band, once her friendship with Prince gave her the chance to do so. In fact, she became the only one of his many protégées to find anything more than the most fleeting musical success.

Sheila's father, Pete Escovedo, was a popular Bay Area Latin percussionist, who played with Santana and his own Latin band, Azteca. She picked up percussion herself as a child, but with several brothers also following their father's footsteps (one of whom, Peto, would play with Seventies funk band Con Funk Shun), she did not get to perform with her father's band until she was a teenager. An immediate hit with Azteca, she soon quit high school to join the band full-time, also recording two mid-Seventies albums with her father. She became an in-demand studio percussionist, recording and touring with Diana Ross, Herbie Hancock, Lionel Richie, and Marvin Gaye in the late Seventies and early Eighties. In 1978, while touring with jazz-fusion keyboardist George Duke, she met Prince, who had just recorded his first album. They became fast friends (though never lovers, she would later insist), but did not work together until 1984, when she sang a duet with him on "Erotic City," the B side of his #1 pop hit "Let's Go Crazy." Prince convinced her to become a solo act, renaming her and restyling her in his typical scanty-paisley fashion.

Her debut album, *The Glamorous Life* (#28, 1984) yielded a #7 pop hit in the title track, a Latin take on Prince's pop-savvy funk rock; the poppier "Belle of St. Mark" reached #34. *Sheila E. in Romance 1600* (#50, 1985) contained "A Love Bizarre," a duet with Prince (#11, 1985), also heard in the rap movie *Krush Groove*. Her third album (#56, 1987), which featured many family members, yielded only a minor hit single in "Hold Me" (#68, 1987); Sheila put her solo career on hold to join Prince's band, the Revolution, on drums, for the world tour documented in his *Sign 'O' the Times* album and film. A collapsed lung suffered after recording 1991's *Sex Cymbal* kept her from touring to support it; the album, topping at #146, flopped.

The Eagles

Formed 1971, Los Angeles, California
Don Henley (b. July 22, 1947, Gilmer, Tex.), drums, voc.; Glenn Frey (b. Nov. 6, 1948, Detroit, Mich.), gtr., piano, voc.; Bernie Leadon (b. July 19, 1947, Minneapolis, Minn.), gtr., banjo, mandolin, voc.; Randy Meisner (b. Mar. 8, 1946, Scottsbluff, Neb.), bass, gtr., voc.

The Eagles: Glenn Frey, Don Henley, Timothy B. Schmit, Don Felder, Joe Walsh

1972—*Eagles* (Asylum) 1973—*Desperado* 1974—
(+ Don Felder [b. Sep. 21, 1947, Gainesville, Fla.],
gtr., voc.) *On the Border* 1975—*One of These
Nights*; *Eagles: Their Greatest Hits, 1971–1975*
1976—(– Leadon; + Joe Walsh [b. Nov. 20, 1947, Wichita, Kan.], gtr., voc.) *Hotel California* 1977—
(– Meisner; + Timothy B. Schmit [b. Oct. 30, 1947,
Sacramento, Calif.], bass, voc.) 1979—*The Long
Run* 1980—*Live* 1982—*Eagles Greatest Hits, vol.
2* 1994—*The Very Best of the Eagles* (Elektra)
(Band re-forms: Frey; Henley; Walsh; Felder;
Schmit) *Hell Freezes Over* (Geffen).
Don Henley solo: 1982—*I Can't Stand Still* (Asylum)
1984—*Building the Perfect Beast* (Geffen) 1989—
The End of the Innocence.
Glenn Frey solo: 1982—*No Fun Aloud* (Asylum)
1984—*The Allnighter* (MCA) 1988—*Soul Searchin'*
1992—*Strange Weather* 1994—*No Fun Aloud*
(Elektra).
Joe Walsh solo: See entry.
Timothy B. Schmit solo: 1984—*Playin' It Cool* (Asylum) 1987—*Timothy B* (MCA) 1990—*Tell Me the
Truth*.
Don Felder solo: 1983—*Airborne* (Elektra).
Randy Meisner solo: 1980—*One More Song* (Epic)
1982—*Randy Meisner*.

The Eagles epitomized commercial Southern California
rock in the Seventies. Their well-crafted songs merged
countryish vocal harmonies with hard-rock guitars, and
lyrics that were alternately yearning ("One of These

Nights," "Best of My Love") and jaded ("Life in the Fast
Lane," "Hotel California"). During the band's hugely successful career, they had an increasingly indolent recording schedule until their breakup in the fall of 1980.
Subsequently, each of its members pursued a solo career, with Henley's the most successful commercially
and critically. In the Nineties the band's sound was frequently cited as an influence by young country stars,
many of whom contributed tracks to the album *Common
Thread: The Songs of the Eagles* (#3, 1993), which won
Album of the Year at the 1994 Country Music Awards.
That same year, the Eagles revival culminated in the
band's reunion tour and album.

The group originally coalesced from Los Angeles'
country-rock community. Before producer John Boylan
assembled them as Linda Ronstadt's backup band on
her album *Silk Purse* (1970), the four original Eagles were
already experienced professionals. Leadon had played in
the Dillard-Clark Expedition and the Flying Burrito
Brothers [see entry]; Meisner, with Poco [see entry] and
Rick Nelson's Stone Canyon Band. Frey had played with
various Detroit rock bands (including Bob Seger's) and
Longbranch Pennywhistle (with J. D. Souther, a sometime songwriting partner), and Henley had been with a
transplanted Texas group, Shiloh. After working with
Ronstadt, Henley and Frey decided to form the Eagles,
recruiting Leadon and Meisner.

Intending to take the country rock of the Byrds and
Burritos a step further toward hard rock, the Eagles
recorded their first album with producer Glyn Johns in
England. "Take It Easy" (#12, 1972), written by Frey and
Jackson Browne, went gold shortly after its release, as
did their debut album. (Another single, "Witchy Woman,"
reached #9 that year.) *Desperado* was a concept album
with enough of a plot line to encourage rumors of a
movie version. The LP yielded no major pop hits, but its
title track, a ballad penned by Henley, has become a
classic rock standard, covered by Linda Ronstadt, among
others. With *On the Border,* the Eagles changed producers, bringing in Bill Szymczyk (who worked on all subsequent albums) and adding Felder, who had recorded
with Flow in Gainesville, Florida, then became a session
guitarist and studio engineer in New York, Boston, and
Los Angeles.

The increased emphasis on rock attracted more listeners—mid-Seventies hits included "Best of My Love"
(#1, 1975), "One of These Nights" (#1, 1975), "Lyin' Eyes"
(#2, 1975), and "Take It to the Limit" (#4, 1976)—but
alienated Leadon. After *One of These Nights,* Leadon left
to form the Bernie Leadon–Michael Georgiades Band,
which released *Natural Progressions* in 1977. (Leadon
went on to become a Nashville session musician, and in
the Nineties formed Run-C&W, a jokester group who
played a blend of country and R&B.)

Leadon was replaced by Joe Walsh, who had established himself with the James Gang [see entry] and on his own. His Eagles debut, *Hotel California,* was their third consecutive #1 album (the second was their 1975 greatest-hits compilation, which is the second-biggest-selling LP in the U.S. to date). "New Kid in Town" (#1, 1977), the title cut (#1, 1977), and "Life in the Fast Lane" (#11, 1977) spurred sales of more than 15 million copies worldwide.

Meisner left in 1977, replaced by Schmit, who had similarly replaced him in Poco. Meisner has released two solo albums, *Randy Meisner* (1982) and *One More Song* (1980). (In 1981, he toured with the Silveradoes; later, in 1990, Meisner reemerged in the group Black Tie, alongside Billy Swan and Bread's James Griffin.) Henley and Frey sang backup on *One More Song,* and in the late Seventies they also appeared on albums by Bob Seger and Randy Newman. In 1981 Henley duetted with Stevie Nicks on the #6 single "Leather and Lace."

Between outside projects and legal entanglements, it took the Eagles two years and $1 million to make the multiplatinum LP *The Long Run,* their last album of all-new material. Parting hit singles included "Heartache Tonight" (#1, 1979), "The Long Run" (#8, 1980), and "I Can't Tell You Why" (#8, 1980).

Walsh continued to release solo albums [see entry], though his biggest single to date has been 1978's cheeky "Life's Been Good" (#12). Felder and Schmit also put out their own albums and contributed songs to film soundtracks. Schmit's second LP, *Timothy B,* included the Top Thirty single, "Boys Night Out" (#25, 1987).

In 1982 Don Henley and Glenn Frey both embarked on solo careers. Frey charted with "The One You Love" (#15, 1982) and "Sexy Girl" (#20, 1984) before a movie proved his ticket into the Top Ten: "The Heat Is On," featured in *Beverly Hills Cop,* shot to #2 in 1985. Frey followed this success by becoming an actor, making a guest appearance as a drug dealer on the popular TV series *Miami Vice.* The episode was based on a track from his album *The Allnighter,* "Smuggler's Blues," which consequently reached #12 (1985). Later in 1985, Frey's "You Belong to the City" hit #2.

Ultimately, though, Henley was the ex-Eagle who garnered the greatest chart success. His "Dirty Laundry" (from his first solo effort, *I Can't Stand Still*) made it to #3, but the 1984 album *Building the Perfect Beast* was to be his true arrival as solo hitmaker and respected singer/songwriter. The kickoff single, "The Boys of Summer," went to #5—supported by an evocative black-and-white video that fast became an MTV favorite—and earned Henley a Grammy for Best Rock Vocal Performance, Male. The hits "All She Wants to Do Is Dance" (#9, 1985) and "Sunset Grill" (#22, 1985) followed. A third album, *The End of the Innocence,* produced a #8 title track, and the additional singles "The Last Worthless Evening" and "The Heart of the Matter," which both hit

#21. The LP won Henley another Grammy, in the same category as before. (Henley has not released another album since; in the early Nineties, he sought release from his Geffen Records contract, initiating a long and bitter legal dispute that as of the mid-Nineties has not been resolved.)

In 1990 Henley founded the Walden Woods Project, dedicated to preserving historic lands around Walden Pond in Concord, Massachusetts (where Henry David Thoreau and others reflected and wrote), from corporate development. Among the singer's various fund-raising means were holding charity concerts, featuring other top rock artists, and donating proceeds from some of his own recordings, including a reggae version of the *Guys And Dolls* standard "Sit Down You're Rocking the Boat" (1993). In 1993 the Walden Woods Project got a big boost from *Common Thread: The Songs of the Eagles,* co-organized by Henley and featuring Clint Black, Trisha Yearwood, Travis Tritt, and others.

In 1994, after years of fending off reunion rumors, Henley, Frey, Walsh, Felder, and Schmit—who had appeared together in the video for Tritt's version of "Take It Easy"—hit the road for a massively successful tour (which was eventually curtailed due to Frey's gastrointestinal troubles). In November the band released *Hell Freezes Over* (#1, 1994), which featured four new songs, including the single "Get Over It," and 11 of the old hits culled from the band's 1994 live appearance on MTV. Within months the reunion LP had sold over four million copies. In the 20 years since its release, the group's *Greatest Hits* has sold 14 million copies.

Snooks Eaglin

Born Fird Eaglin, January 21, 1936, New Orleans, Louisiana
1958—*Blues from New Orleans, vol. 1* (Storyville); *Country Boy in New Orleans* (Folkways); *New Orleans Street Singer* 1961—*That's All Right* (Bluesville) 1971—*Possum up a Simmon Tree* (Arhoolie) 1978—*Down Yonder* (GNP/Crescendo) 1987—*Baby, You Can Get Your Gun!* (Black Top) 1988—*Out of Nowhere* 1989—*Snooks Eaglin* 1992—*Teasin' You* 1995—*Soul's Edge.*

Blind blues guitarist/singer Snooks Eaglin has long been a fixture on the New Orleans R&B circuit. He was blinded by complications from brain tumor surgery when he was 19 months old. A Crescent City street singer in the Fifties who also played clubs with Sugar Boy Crawford, Allen Toussaint, and Dave Bartholomew, Eaglin began recording country blues for Folkways in 1958. In the Sixties he backed up Professor Longhair. While largely unknown outside Louisiana, Eaglin's virtuosic guitar work, huge repertoire (he reportedly knows over 2,500 songs), and often humorous versions of New

Orleans standards, have gained him a cult following. Fats Domino's rhythm section has appeared on his Black Top albums and bassist George Porter Jr. (the Meters) has played with Eaglin in the Nineties. Eaglin performed on Earl King's *Hard River to Cross* (1994).

Steve Earle

Born January 17, 1955, Fort Monroe, Virginia
1986—*Guitar Town* (MCA)   1987—*Exit 0*   1988—
Copperhead Road*   1990—*Shut Up and Die Like an
Aviator*   1991—*The Hard Way*   1993—*Essential
***Steve Earle*   1995—*Train a Comin'* (Winter Harvest).**

At the start of his career as an opening act for both George Jones and the Replacements, and through his songs—which incorporate the populism of Hank Williams and Bruce Springsteen—Steve Earle bridged country and rock.

Son of an air traffic controller, Earle was raised in South Texas, where he spent a rebellious adolescence as a long-haired Vietnam War opponent with country music sympathies. Leaving home at 16, he married at 19 the first of his five wives, and moved, nearly penniless, to Nashville. Befriending such older proponents of country's "outlaw" movement as Townes Van Zandt and Guy Clark, he wrote songs for Johnny Lee and Patty Loveless and almost managed to place one of his songs on an Elvis Presley album. At age 31 Earle released his critically acclaimed debut, *Guitar Town*. With his backup band the Dukes recalling the twangy style of Duane Eddy, he assailed Reaganomics and championed society's outsiders, appearing at Farm Aid II and allying himself with Fearless Hearts, a relief group for homeless children. *Exit 0* was also well received; *Copperhead Road* scored #56 on the pop chart, but that year Earle, as a result of an altercation with a Dallas security guard, was made to pay a $500 fine and given a one-year unsupervised probation. The tougher guitar sound and darker lyrics of *The Hard Way* reflected his legal problems; again critics lauded his work, but it fared considerably less well than its predecessor.

In 1994 Earle was arrested in Nashville for crack possession and sentenced to almost a year in jail; he served 45 days in a rehabilitation facility in the end. In the meantime, Earle's version of "What's Your Name" appeared on the 1994 Lynyrd Skynyrd tribute LP, *Skynyrd Frynds*. After a four-and-a-half-year hiatus from the studio, Earle released the acoustic *Train a Comin'* on the Nashville indie label Winter Harvest.

Earth, Wind and Fire

Formed 1969, Chicago, Illinois
Maurice White (b. Dec. 19, 1941, Memphis, Tenn.),

Earth, Wind and Fire: Larry Dunn, Ralph Johnson, Philip Bailey, Maurice White, Al McKay, Fred White, Verdine White, Johnny Graham, Andrew Woolfolk

voc., kalimba, drums; Verdine White (b. July 25, 1951), bass; Donald Whitehead, kybds.; Wade Flemons, electric piano; Michael Beale, gtr.; Phillard Williams, perc.; Chester Washington, horns; Leslie Drayton, horns; Alex Thomas, horns; Sherry Scott, voc.
1970—*Earth, Wind and Fire* (Warner Bros.)   1972—
***The Need of Love* (group disbands; new lineup:**
M. White; V. White; + Philip Bailey [b. May 8, 1951, Denver, Colo.], voc., perc.; + Larry Dunn [b. June 19, 1953, Colo.], kybds., synth.; + Jessica Cleaves [b. 1943], voc.; + Roland Bautista, gtr.; + Roland Laws, reeds); *Last Days and Time* (Columbia) (– Laws; – Bautista; – Cleaves; + Johnny Graham [b. Aug. 3, 1951, Ky.], gtr.; + Al McKay [b. Feb. 2, 1948, La.], gtr., perc.; + Andrew Woolfolk [b. Oct. 11, 1950, Tex.], sax, flute; + Ralph Johnson [b. July 4, 1951, Calif.], drums)   1973—*Head to the Sky*   1974—*Open Our Eyes; Another Time* (Warner Bros.) (+ Freddie White [b. Jan. 13, 1955, Chicago], drums)   1975—*That's the Way of the World; Gratitude* (– Freddie White)   1976—*Spirit*   1977—*All 'n All*   1978—*The Best of Earth, Wind and Fire, vol. 1* (ARC)   1979—*I Am*   1980—*Faces* (– McKay; + Bautista, gtr.)   1981—*Raise*   1983—*Powerlight* (Columbia); *Electric Universe* (– Bautista; + Sheldon Reynolds, gtr., kybds., voc.)   1987—*Touch the World*   1988—*The Best of Earth, Wind and Fire, vol. 2*   1990—*Heritage*   1993—(+ Gary Bias, sax; + Ray Brown, trumpet; + Reggie Young, trombone) *Millennium* (Warner Bros.).

Innovative yet popular, precise yet sensual, calculated yet galvanizing, Earth, Wind and Fire changed the sound of black pop in the Seventies. Their encyclopedic sound tops Latin-funk rhythms with gospel harmonies, unerring horns, Philip Bailey's sweet falsetto, and various exotic ingredients chosen by leader and producer Maurice White. Unlike their ideological rivals, the down and dirty but equally eclectic Parliament/Funkadelic, EW&F have always preached clean, uplifting messages.

Maurice White is the son of a doctor and the grandson of a New Orleans honky-tonk pianist. After attending the Chicago Conservatory, between 1963 and 1967 he was a studio drummer at Chess Records, where he recorded with the Impressions, Muddy Waters, Billy Stewart ("Summertime"), and Fontella Bass ("Rescue Me"), among others. From 1967 to 1969 he worked with the Ramsey Lewis Trio ("Wade in the Water"); he later wrote and produced Lewis' 1975 hit "Sun Goddess." While with the trio, he took up kalimba, the African thumb piano, which became an EW&F trademark. White moved to Los Angeles in late 1969 and formed the first Earth, Wind and Fire (White's astrological chart has no water signs), which recorded for Capitol as the Salty Peppers. Warners signed the group for two moderately successful albums, but after 18 months, White hired a new, younger band, retaining only his brother Verdine on bass.

The band's second Columbia LP, *Head to the Sky*, went to #15 in 1974, starting a string of gold and, later, platinum albums. In 1975 *That's the Way of the World* (a soundtrack) yielded the Grammy-winning "Shining Star" (#1, 1975). The band moved up to the arena circuit with elaborate stage shows that included such mystical trappings as pyramids and disappearing acts. (Effects for the 1978 national tour were designed by magician Doug Henning.) Although White's longtime coproducer Charles Stepney died in 1976, EW&F continued to sell. *All 'n All* became their fourth platinum album, and they won two Grammies in 1978. They were a high point of Robert Stigwood's 1978 movie *Sgt. Pepper's Lonely Hearts Club Band*, and their version of the Beatles' "Got to Get You into My Life" went to #9.

White began to do outside production in 1975 and worked on albums by the Emotions (*Rejoice*, 1977), Ramsey Lewis (*Sun Goddess*, 1975), and Deniece Williams (*This Is Niecy*, 1976). He did composing and production work on Valerie Carter's *Just a Stone's Throw Away* (1977). EW&F's 1979 album, *I Am*, featured the Emotions on "Boogie Wonderland" (#6, 1979). In 1980 the group toured Europe and South America; 1981's *Raise* featured the Top Five hit "Let's Groove." While *Touch the World* went gold, *Powerlight* (#12, 1983) yielded their last major hit single, "Fall in Love with Me" (#17, 1983). Singer Philip Bailey also enjoyed success with his solo career, including a hit duet with Phil Collins, "Easy Lover" (#2, 1985), and a Grammy-winning gospel LP, *Triumph!* (1986).

In 1990 *Heritage* featured guest rapper M.C. Hammer. Since their inception, Earth, Wind and Fire have sold over 19 million albums. For *Millennium*, the group returned to Warner Bros. Records. According to White, "We came out here to try to render a service to mankind, not to be stars. We are actually being used as tools by the Creator."

Earthworks: See Bill Bruford

Elliott Easton: See the Cars

Sheena Easton
Born April 27, 1959, Bellshill, Scotland
1981—*Sheena Easton* (EMI); *You Could Have Been with Me*   1982—*Madness, Money and Music*   1983—*Best Kept Secret*   1984—*A Private Heaven*   1985—*Do You*   1987—*No Sound but a Heart*   1988—*The Lover in Me* (MCA)   1989—*The Best of Sheena Easton* (EMI)   1991—*What Comes Naturally* (MCA)   1993—*No Strings.*

Sheena Easton became a pop star in 1981 with a vocal style and image suggesting a new-wave version of easy-rock singers Marie Osmond and Olivia Newton-John. Easton attended the Royal Scottish Academy of Drama and Art and graduated in June 1979 qualified to teach, but instead she began a singing career. (While in school, she had frequently moonlighted in local nightclubs and pubs.) She successfully auditioned for EMI Records in May 1979 and received national exposure when the BBC-TV show *Big Time* documented her grooming for stardom. Her first single, "Modern Girl," was released in February 1980 and hit the Top Ten in England; that November she performed for Queen Elizabeth at the Royal Variety Show.

Easton's American breakthrough came in the spring of 1981, when "Morning Train" stayed at #1 on the U.S. singles chart for two weeks. Its success propelled the reissued "Modern Girl" up to #18, and at one point Easton had the distinction of having two singles in the Top Ten. Her hits continued with the theme song from the James Bond film *For Your Eyes Only* (#4, 1981) and "When He Shines" (#30, 1982) from her second album, *You Could Have Been with Me*. She has also received gold records in Japan and Canada, and a Grammy in 1981 for Best New Artist. In 1984 she won a second Grammy, Best Mexican/American Performance, for a duet with Luis Miguel, "Me Gustas Tal Como Eres"; the year before she had released the Spanish-only album *Todo Me Recuerda a Ti*.

Easton revamped her wholesome image with *A Private Heaven* (#15, 1984), which included the tough-talking hit single "Strut" (#7, 1984) and "Sugar Walls" (#9, 1984), a highly suggestive track written for her by Prince. She would duet with Prince on his 1987 hit "U Got the

Look." She played Don Johnson's wife in several episodes of *Miami Vice* (1987). In the Nineties she appeared in movies (*Indecent Proposal*), on Broadway (*The Man of La Mancha*), and on television (*Jack's Place, Body Bags,* and *The Highlander*).

The Easybeats

Formed 1963, Sydney, Australia
George Young (b. Nov. 6, 1947, Glasgow, Scot.), gtr.; Gordon Fleet (b. Aug. 16, 1945, Bootle, Eng.), drums; Dick Diamonde (b. Dec. 28, 1947, Hilversum, Neth.), bass; Harry Vanda (b. Harry Vandenberg, Mar. 22, 1947, The Hague, Neth.), gtr.; Stevie Wright (b. Dec. 20, 1948, Leeds, Eng.), voc.
1967—*Friday on My Mind* (United Artists); *Good Friday* 1968—*Falling Off the Edge of the World*; *Vigil* 1970—*Friends* 1985—*The Best of the Easybeats* (Rhino).
Flash and the Pan: 1979—*Flash and the Pan* (Epic) 1980—*Lights in the Night* 1982—*Headlines.*

The Easybeats, whose members all emigrated to Australia with their families, were the Sixties Australian rock band that launched producers/songwriters Harry Vanda and George Young. The group established itself as Australia's leading pop band in 1965 with "She's So Fine," the first of four chart-toppers Down Under. In 1966 the Easybeats returned to England and began recording with producer Shel Talmy (the Kinks, the Who), an association that resulted in the worldwide hit "Friday on My Mind" (#16, 1967). After their initial success, Vanda and Young kept the Easybeats name for a few years and had some moderately successful U.K. hits before officially disbanding in 1969 and forming a production company back in Australia. As Happy's Whiskey Sour they had a British hit with "Shot in the Head," and as the Marcus Hook Roll Band they recorded "Natural Man" in 1972. They produced Stevie Wright's solo debut, *Hard Road,* and oversaw the early career of Young's brothers Angus and Malcolm's band, AC/DC. Vanda and Young also concocted three studio albums that enjoyed some European success as Flash and the Pan. In 1988 the pair produced AC/DC's *Blow Up Your Video.*

Eazy-E: See N.W.A

Echo and the Bunnymen

Formed 1978, Liverpool, England
Pete De Freitas (b. Aug. 2, 1961, Port of Spain, Trinidad; d. June 15, 1989, Liverpool), drums; Ian McCulloch (b. May 5, 1959, Liverpool), voc.; Les Pattinson (b. Apr. 18, 1958, Merseyside, Eng.), bass; Will Sergeant (b. Apr. 12, 1958, Liverpool), gtr.

1980—*Crocodiles* (Sire) 1981—*Heaven Up Here* 1983—*Porcupine* 1984—*Ocean Rain* 1986—*Songs to Learn and Sing* (– De Freitas; + Blair Cunningham [b. Oct. 11, 1957, New York City, N.Y., drums]; – Cunningham; + De Freitas) 1987—*Echo and the Bunnymen* 1989—(– McCulloch; + Noel Burke [b. Belfast, N. Ire., voc.]; – De Freitas; + Damon Reece, drums) 1990—*Reverberation.*
Ian McCulloch solo: 1989—*Candleland* (Sire) 1992—*Mysterio.*

The standard-bearers of Liverpool's neopsychedelic movement, Echo and the Bunnymen's moody, atmospheric music combined punk's energy and edge with the Doors' poetic theatricality. Self-consciously literary, outspoken, and sometimes arrogant (singer Ian McCulloch was known as "Mac the Mouth"), they never matched their popularity in Europe in the United States. Their influence can be seen in the attitudes and guitar textures of such Nineties English bands as Suede.

The Bunnymen were formed when McCulloch was kicked out of an early version of the Teardrop Explodes. (He had earlier played with Teardrop leader Julian Cope [see entry] in the seminal Liverpool punk band the Crucial Three.) Recruiting fellow Doors fan Will Sergeant and Sergeant's friend, Les Pattinson, they were originally a trio backed by Echo, a drum machine. An independently released 1979 single, "Pictures on My Wall" b/w "Read It in Books" led to a contract with Sire. Before going into the studio to record "Rescue," Echo was replaced with the flesh-and-blood drummer Pete De Freitas. This all-human version of the band released *Crocodiles* (#17 U.K., 1980). Early press focused on the strength of the band's songwriting, its unadorned sound, and McCulloch's teased, nearly vertical nest of hair.

Heaven Up Here (#10 U.K., 1981) was a darker album, more interested in textures than songs. It reached the bottom of the U.S. charts (#184) but was again widely praised in the press and topped many British polls. *Porcupine* (#137, 1983), which hit #2 in the U.K., signaled a new direction for the band, as did the singles "The Back of Love" (#19 U.K., 1982) and "The Cutter" (#8 U.K., 1983). Augmented by sitarist/violinist Shankar, the music took on an Eastern tint, with modal strings and droning bagpipes. *Ocean Rain* (#87, 1984), the band's first entry into the U.S. Top 100 album chart, continued this direction, with a full string section in evidence on the quieter, melodic "The Killing Moon" (#9 U.K., 1984).

The band toured during most of 1985, but tensions arose the following year while they prepared to record *Echo and the Bunnymen* (#4 U.K., 1987). De Freitas left the band, only to return later (Haircut 100 drummer Blair Cunningham filled in during his absence). The band also had to rerecord the album. A quieter, reflective work, it was their U.S. best-seller, peaking at #51 in 1987. That year, working with Doors keyboardist Ray Manzarek, Echo recorded a cover of "People Are Strange" for the 1987 movie *The Lost Boys*. In 1988 following a tour with New Order, McCulloch left to pursue a solo career, releasing *Candleland* (#18 U.K., 1989) and *Mysterio* (#46 U.K., 1992), neither of which matched the group's earlier success.

The band soldiered on, choosing St. Vitas Dance singer Noel Burke from thousands of audition tapes. In June 1989, during rehearsals for their first post-McCulloch album, De Freitas was killed in a motorcycle accident. He was replaced by Damon Reece on the Geoff Emerick–produced *Reverberation* (1990), which failed to make the U.K. or U.S. charts. Bunnymen II fizzled soon after, and Sergeant rejoined McCulloch to form Electrafixion in 1994. With drummer Tony Mack and bassist Leon De Sylva, the group recorded an EP, *Zephyr*.

Duane Eddy

Born April 26, 1938, Corning, New York
1958—*Have "Twangy" Guitar Will Travel* (Jamie)
1959—*Especially for You*; *The Twang's the Thing*
1960—*$1,000,000 Dollars Worth of Twang*   1962—
$1,000,000 Dollars Worth of Twang, vol. 2*; *Twistin'
and *Twangin'* (RCA)   1965—*The Best of Duane*
Eddy   1970—*Twangy Guitar* (London)   1987—
Duane Eddy* (Capitol)   1993—*Twang Thang: The
Duane Eddy Anthology* (Rhino).

Guitarist Duane Eddy had a string of instrumental hits ("Rebel Rouser," #6, 1958; "Peter Gunn," #27, 1960) that invariably featured a staccato signature riff labeled the "twangy" guitar sound. His work has influenced numerous guitarists (the Ventures, Shadows, George Harrison), especially in England.

Eddy began playing the guitar at age five. In 1951 he moved with his family to Phoenix. Shortly after dropping out of Coolidge High School at 16, he got a series of steady jobs working with local dance groups, and he acquired the custom-made Chet Atkins–model Gretsch guitar he still plays. In 1957 Phoenix DJ, producer, and entrepreneur Lee Hazlewood became his mentor, and Eddy started touring with Dick Clark's Caravan of Stars. The Hazlewood-produced "Rebel Rouser" (on Clark's Jamie label) began a six-year streak of nearly 20 hits, among them "Ramrod" (#27, 1958), "Cannonball" (#15, 1958), and "Forty Miles of Bad Road" (#9, 1959). Though Eddy and Hazlewood parted company in 1961, they have gotten back together for comeback attempts.

Eddy switched to RCA in 1962 and had a hit with "Dance with the Guitar Man" (#12, 1962), followed by "Deep in the Heart of Texas" and "The Ballad of Palladin" (#33, 1962). He signed with Colpix in 1965 and released LPs like *Duane Does Dylan* and *Duane a Go-Go*. The various back-to-the-roots movements of the Seventies (es-

pecially the rockabilly revival) rekindled interest in Eddy, who occasionally performs at oldies shows in the U.S. but concentrates primarily on the U.K., where he had a #9 hit in 1975, "Play Me Like You Play Your Guitar."

Eddy's early backup group, the Rebels, included guitarist Al Casey, saxophonist Steve Douglas, and pianist Larry Knechtel, later with Bread. At the height of his success, Eddy made his film debut in *Because They're Young* (1960), scoring a #4 hit with the theme song. He occasionally worked as a producer in the Seventies, including a solo LP by Phil Everly (*Star Spangled Springer*, 1973). Eddy moved to California in the late Sixties and then to Lake Tahoe, Nevada, in 1976. His 1977 comeback single on Asylum, "You Are My Sunshine," was produced by Hazlewood and included vocals by Willie Nelson and Waylon Jennings. Jennings' wife, Jessi Colter, was married to Eddy from 1966 to 1969.

In 1986 Eddy was introduced to a new generation of fans through British avant-dance group Art of Noise, which enlisted him to play on its industrial-disco version of "Peter Gunn" (#50, 1986). The following year, *Duane Eddy*—his first major-label album in over 15 years—was released; Jeff Lynne, Paul McCartney, George Harrison, and Ry Cooder all helped produce it. In 1994, a year after Rhino released the box-set collection *Twang Thang*, Eddy was inducted into the Rock and Roll Hall of Fame.

Dave Edmunds

Born April 15, 1944, Cardiff, Wales
1972—*Rockpile* (MAM)   1975—*Subtle as a Flying*
Mallet* (RCA)   1977—*Get It* (Swan Song)   1978—
Tracks on Wax 4*   1979—*Repeat When Necessary
1981—*Twangin'*; *The Best of Dave Edmunds*
1982—*D.E. 7th* (Columbia)   1983—*Information*
1984—*Riff Raff*   1987—*I Hear You Rockin'*   1990—
Closer to the Flame* (Capitol)   1993—*The Dave Ed-
munds Anthology 1968–90* (Rhino)   1994—*Plugged*
In* (Pyramid).

Guitarist, singer, producer, and songwriter Dave Edmunds, an active fan of American rockabilly, spurred Britain's pub-rock movement, cofounded Rockpile, and has sustained a solo career for more than two decades.

Like many of his contemporaries, Edmunds was a rock & roll fan and soon found himself picking out the guitar parts played by James Burton on Rick Nelson's records, Chet Atkins on Everly Brothers hits, and Scotty Moore on early Elvis sides. During the early Sixties he played in several British blues-rock bands before forming Love Sculpture in 1967 with bassist John Williams and drummer Bob Jones (the group later included drummer Terry Williams, also of Rockpile and, later, Dire Straits). They played rocked-up versions of light-classical pieces by Bizet and Khachaturian, whose "Sabre Dance" gave them a Top Five U.K. hit in 1968. They toured the U.S. for six weeks before disbanding the next year.

Back in his native Wales, Edmunds built the eight-track Rockfield Studio in Monmouthshire and taught himself how to re-create Sam Phillips' Sun Records slap echo and Phil Spector's Wall of Sound. He spent the early Seventies in the studio producing himself (including a 1971 hit remake of Smiley Lewis' 1955 hit "I Hear You Knockin'" and an album called *Rockpile*) and others, including the Flamin' Groovies, Del Shannon, and pub-rockers Deke Leonard, Ducks Deluxe, and, later, Brinsley Schwarz and Graham Parker. When he produced Brinsley Schwarz's last LP in 1974, he met bassist Nick Lowe, later of Rockpile, the fiercely rocking band the two shared and led for their own albums.

In 1975 Edmunds costarred in and scored most of the film *Stardust,* and he also released *Subtle as a Flying Mallet,* for which Lowe wrote songs and played bass. After 1977's *Get It,* Edmunds toured regularly with Rockpile. Most of his albums have consisted primarily of covers. *Repeat When Necessary* premiered songs by Elvis Costello ("Girls Talk," a minor hit in America, but a gold U.K. hit) and Graham Parker ("Crawling from the Wreckage"), and contained the uptempo "Queen of Hearts." Though it was a Top Twenty British hit, he could not get Atlantic to release it in the States. Two years later country-pop vocalist Juice Newton took the song to #2 in a near-identical version.

Rockpile broke up acrimoniously in 1981, shortly after releasing its only album under the Rockpile moniker, *Seconds of Pleasure* [see entry]. Edmunds resumed his solo career. (Williams later drummed on some of his records, and guitarist Billy Bremner, the fourth member of Rockpile, joined Edmunds' 1983 touring band.) *Twangin'* produced a minor hit single with a cover of John Fogerty's "Almost Saturday Night," and "The Race Is On" introduced the Stray Cats, a Long Island neo-rockabilly group for whom Edmunds later produced multimillion-selling albums.

D.E. 7th, his first Columbia release, included the rave-up "From Small Things (Big Things One Day Come)," written for Edmunds by Bruce Springsteen. *Information,* one of Edmunds' most successful U.S. LPs, featured two songs written and produced by the Electric Light Orchestra's Jeff Lynne. One of them, "Slipping Away," paired Edmunds' traditional sound with synthesizers, electronically processed vocals, and a drum machine, and became a Top Forty hit in 1983. Lynne stayed on to produce all of the unsuccessful *Riff Raff,* after which Edmunds returned to his roots-rock bent. He has continued to work as a producer, with the Everly Brothers and the reunited Stray Cats, and played guitar on the three tracks of the soundtrack to Paul McCartney's 1984 film *Give My Regards to Broad Street*. His other production credits include the Fabulous Thunderbirds (*Tuff*

Enuff), k.d. lang (*Angel with a Lariat*), and Dion DiMucci (*Yo Frankie*).

Bernard Edwards: See Chic

808 State
Formed 1988, Manchester, England
Graham Massey (b. Aug. 4, 1960, Eng.), programmer, engineer, kybds.; Andrew Barker (b. Mar. 9, 1968, Eng.), DJ; Darren Partington (b. Nov. 1, 1969, Eng.), DJ; Martin Price (b. Mar. 26, 1955, Farnworth, Lancaster, Eng.), programmer, engineer, kybds.; Gerald Simpson (b. Feb. 16, 1964, Manchester), programmer, engineer, kybds.
1988—*Newbuild* EP (Creed)   1989—*Quadrastate* EP (– Simpson); *808:90* (ZTT); *The EP of Dance* EP 1990—*Utd. State 90* (Tommy Boy)   1991—*Ex:el* 1993—(– Price) *Gorgeous.*

Of the many techno-dance outfits to spring from Manchester in the late Eighties, 808 State was the one most committed to emphasizing the "groove" over technical expertise. The group played a major role in developing the techno-rave sound.

808 State grew out of Manchester's legendary Eastern Bloc record shop, where store owner Martin Price also operated his independent label, Creed. It was there that Graham Massey met the local DJ duo of Darren Partington and Andrew Barker, who were trying to land a deal with Price's label. The four men, along with another local musician, Gerald Simpson, wound up recording together. In 1989 they produced the British club smash "Pacific State"; Simpson left soon after to form his own project, A Guy Called Gerald.

The next year 808 State released its U.S. debut, *Utd. State 90,* which included "Pacific State" and another dance club favorite, "Cubik." The critically acclaimed followup, *Ex:el,* featured guest vocalists Bernard Sumner of New Order ("Spanish Heart") and Björk Gudmundsdóttir of the Sugarcubes ("Oops" and "Qmart"). 808 State's subsequent U.S. tour consisted of a handful of rave appearances.

In 1992 Price left to produce a succession of British rap acts and form the label Sun Text. Later that year, 808 State released *Gorgeous,* and it has since produced dance remixes for other artists, including David Bowie and the British rapper MC Tunes.

Einstürzende Neubauten
Formed April 1, 1980, Berlin, Germany
Blixa Bargeld (b. Jan. 12, 1959, Berlin), voc., gtr., perc., industrial perc.; N. U. Unruh (b. June 9, 1957, New York City, N.Y.), voc., bass, perc., industrial

perc.; Beate Bartel, industrial perc.; Gudrun Gut, industrial perc.
1980—(– Bartel; – Gut; + F. M. Einheit [b. Dec. 18, 1958, Dortmund, Ger.], industrial perc.)   1983—*Drawings of Patient O.T.* (ZE/PVC)   1984—*80–83 Strategies Against Architecture* (Homestead)
(+ Alexander Hacke [b. Oct. 11, 1965, Berlin], gtr., electronics; + Mark Chung [b. June 3, 1957, Leeds, Eng.], bass); *2 × 4* cassette (ROIR)   1985—*½ Mensch* (Some Bizarre)   1987—*Fuenf auf der Nach Oben Offenen Richterskala*   1989—*Haus der Luege*   1991—*Strategies Against Architecture II* (Mute)
1993—*Interim EP; Tabula Rasa.*

Generally acknowledged as the world's first "industrial" band, Germany's Einstürzende Neubauten—which translates to "collapsing new buildings"—is essentially an avant-garde conceptual/performance-art collective. These hard-hat Dadaists make their postmodern, neotribal statement with howling vocals and "instruments" that include power tools and large metal industrial objects beaten with hammers, chains, and pipes.

Neubauten's earliest manifestations were in such hit-and-run art statements as Blixa Bargeld and expatriate American N. U. Unruh appearing half-naked, beating on the sides of a hole in a Berlin Autobahn overpass. The Neubauten name took on chillingly prophetic overtones when, a few months after its formation, Berlin's newly constructed, American-built congress hall caved in. The group's earliest, largely free-form recordings—German-issued singles and EPs compiled on *80–83*—mixed atavistic, guttural vocals with distorted guitar and bass drones, and thunderous metal percussion.

With the addition of F. M. Einheit—who brought in power drills, jackhammers, amplified air-conditioning ducts, and giant industrial springs—and guitarist Alexander Hacke and bassist Mark Chung, Einstürzende Neubauten expanded its sonic range, exerted ever-finer control over its noise elements, and gradually grew closer to conventional rock-band approaches. The group integrated its first actual chord progression into the title track of *Drawings of Patient O.T.;* the cassette-only live album *2 × 4* found Bargeld at times singing plaintively in a near–Middle Eastern style; *½ Mensch* ("Half-Man") ranged from Bargeld's multitracked a cappella vocal workouts, to soft balladlike interludes and even some off-kilter dance beats; *Fuenf auf der Nach Oben Offenen Richterskala* ("Five on the Open-Ended Richter Scale"), recorded after a brief breakup, was uncharacteristically quiet and restrained. In 1993 Neubauten released its most accessible album to date, *Tabula Rasa,* recorded during the Persian Gulf War and including the crackling sounds of burning oil (taped before Iraqis ignited the Kuwaiti oil fields).

Outside the group Bargeld has worked with Nick Cave and the Bad Seeds [see entry], and Hacke with Crime and the City Solution; Einheit formed Berlin's experimental theater-music outfit Stein (Stone), using the sonic properties of friction between rocks and concrete.

The Electric Flag

Formed 1967, San Francisco, California
Michael Bloomfield (b. July 28, 1944, Chicago, Ill.; d. February 15, 1981, San Francisco), gtr.; Buddy Miles (b. Sep. 5, 1946, Omaha, Neb.), drums, voc.; Barry Goldberg, kybds.; Nick Gravenites (b. Chicago, Ill.), voc.; Harvey Brooks, bass; Peter Strazza, tenor sax; Marcus Doubleday, trumpet; Herbie Rich, baritone sax.
1968—*A Long Time Comin'* (Columbia) (– Bloomfield)   1969—*The Electric Flag*   1974—(Lineup: Bloomfield; Miles; Goldberg; Gravenites; + Roger "Jellyroll" Troy, bass, voc.) *The Band Kept Playing* (Atlantic).

The short-lived Electric Flag intended to combine blues, rock, soul, jazz, and country; they ended up sparking the rock-with-brass trend of Blood, Sweat and Tears and Chicago. Michael Bloomfield [see entry] started the band in 1967 after leaving the Paul Butterfield Blues Band, and he brought Nick Gravenites with him. Goldberg had played with Mitch Ryder and came to the Flag after the breakup of the Goldberg-Miller Blues Band (with Steve Miller), bringing Strazza with him. The rest had session backgrounds: Buddy Miles [see entry] in R&B, drumming for Otis Redding and Wilson Pickett; Harvey Brooks as the folk-rockers' bassist with Bob Dylan, Judy Collins, Phil Ochs, and Eric Andersen, as well as the Doors; Marcus Doubleday from early-Sixties work with the Drifters, Jan and Dean, and Bobby Vinton.

Based in San Francisco, the Electric Flag debuted at the Monterey Pop Festival in June 1967, and their first album made the Top Forty. But ego conflicts among the members soon undermined them, and the band lasted only 18 months. Bloomfield quit after the debut album, leaving Miles as leader for the Flag's remaining months. Before the breakup, they'd recorded enough material for a second album. The Buddy Miles Express was modeled after the Flag, but Miles left it to join Jimi Hendrix's Band of Gypsys. Gravenites turned to songwriting, then joined Big Brother and the Holding Company [see entry]. The rest returned to work as sidemen.

In 1974 Bloomfield, Miles, Gravenites, and Goldberg (joined by Roger "Jellyroll" Troy) reunited for a two-album deal. The first, produced by Jerry Wexler, re-created the old sound with Dr. John's Bonaroo Brass and the Muscle Shoals Horns. But the band's third incarnation broke up before recording a second album.

The Electric Light Orchestra

Formed 1971, Birmingham, England

**Roy Wood (b. Nov. 8, 1946, Birmingham), gtr., voc.;
Jeff Lynne (b. Dec. 30, 1947, Birmingham), gtr., voc.,
synth.; Bev Bevan (b. Nov. 25, 1944, Birmingham),
drums; Rick Price (b. Birmingham), bass.
1972—No Answer/ELO (United Artists) (– Wood;
– Price; + Richard Tandy [b. Mar. 26, 1948, Birmingham], kybds., gtr.; + Michael D' Albuquerque, bass;
+ Mike Edwards, cello; + Colin Walker, cello; + Wilf
Gibson, violin) 1973—ELO II (– Walker; – Gibson;
+ Hugh McDowell [b. July 31, 1953, London, Eng.],
cello; + Mik Kaminsky [b. Sep. 2, 1951, Harrogate,
Eng.], violin); On the Third Day 1974—(– D'Albuquerque; – Edwards; + Kelly Groucutt [b. Sep. 8,
1945, Coseley, Eng.], bass, voc.; + Melvyn Gale
[b. Jan. 15, 1952, London, Eng.], cello; – Groucutt)
Eldorado 1975—Face the Music 1976—Olé ELO;
A New World Record (Jet) 1977—Out of the Blue
(– Gale; – Kaminski; – McDowell) 1979—
Discovery; Greatest Hits 1981—Time 1983—Secret Messages (– Bevan) 1985—(+ Bevan)
1986—Balance of Power (CBS Associated) 1990—
(New lineup as ELO II: Bevan; Groucutt; Kaminski;
+ Eric Troyer, kybds., voc.; + Phil Bates, gtr., voc.)
Afterglow (Epic); ELO Classics (Sony Music Special
Products) 1991—Part Two (Scotti Bros.) 1992—
Performing ELO's Greatest Hits Live (with the
Moscow Symphony Orchestra).
Jeff Lynne solo: 1990—Armchair Theatre (Reprise).**

The Electric Light Orchestra became a major arena and stadium draw in the mid- and late Seventies on the strength of Beatles-like orchestral pop—"Can't Get It Out of My Head" (#9, 1975), "Telephone Line" (#7, 1977), "Evil Woman" (#10, 1976)—and elaborate staging. Formed in 1971 as an offshoot of the Move by leader Roy Wood (who left after ELO's first LP to form Wizzard), drummer Bev Bevan, guitarist/songwriter Jeff Lynne, and bassist Rick Price, ELO initially sought to explore classically tinged orchestral rock. The band has fashioned a series of multimillion-selling LPs and radio hits by sweetening futuristic electronic effects with rich strings, synthesizers, keyboards, and occasional horns. They remain based in England, although their greatest success has been in America.

The Electric Light Orchestra has a history of facelessness. Even the most ardent fans generally can't name more than one or two band members (up until 1986 or so original members Lynne and Bevan were the backbone, with studio assistance from longtime member and multi-instrumentalist Richard Tandy). Wood left the group in 1972, before their first hit, a version of Chuck Berry's "Roll Over Beethoven," complete with chugging cellos sending up the opening strains of the Fifth Symphony (they occasionally use fragments of Grieg and others as well).

After Wood quit, Lynne brought the band to the U.S. in 1973 for a 40-date debut tour that was marred by technical problems in miking the cellos (a radical addition to the live rock format). On the Third Day (#52, 1973) produced a moderate hit with "Showdown" (#53, 1974). Eldorado (#16, 1974), a pseudo-concept album, gave ELO a major hit with "Can't Get It Out of My Head" (#9, 1975). Face the Music (#8, 1975) went gold on the strength of "Evil Woman" (#10, 1976) and "Strange Magic" (#14, 1976). Each subsequent album, including Xanadu, went at least gold, and five (A New World Record, Out of the Blue, Discovery, Greatest Hits, and the Xanadu soundtrack) are platinum. In 1977 ELO's records and tours grossed over $10 million, and A New World Record (#5, 1976) eventually sold five million copies worldwide.

By the late Seventies ELO were recording for their own label, Jet, whose distribution switch to CBS led ELO to sue the old distributor, United Artists, claiming they had flooded the market with millions of defective copies of the platinum double LP Out of the Blue (#4, 1977). ELO's most elaborate tour was in 1978, when they traveled with a laser-equipped "spaceship" (some said it looked like a giant glowing hamburger) that opened with the group playing inside. The Orchestra's live shows were also enhanced by taped backing tracks, and they were accused on more than one occasion of lip-synching the supposed "live parts." (Interestingly, in another decade this practice would be very common, though hardly accepted.) In 1979 they stayed off the road completely (the first time they hadn't toured since 1972). Discovery (#5, 1979) went platinum nonetheless, yielding two hits with "Don't Bring Me Down" (#15) and "Shine a Little Love" (#15). In 1980 Lynne contributed an album side's worth of songs to the Olivia Newton-John movie Xanadu soundtrack (#4, 1980). Three of those songs, "All Over the World" (#13, 1980), "I'm Alive" (#16, 1980), and "Xanadu" (#8, 1980), were hits.

ELO toured the U.S. in late 1981 to promote their latest album, Time. Certified gold, Time (#16, 1981) featured the hit single "Hold On Tight" (#10, 1981). Still, it marked the start of ELO's commercial decline. Although it hit #1 in the U.K., Time didn't help draw U.S. fans to concert halls. Although each boasted a Top Twenty single, neither Secret Messages (#36, 1983, contains "Rock 'n' Roll Is King") nor Balance of Power (#49, 1986, contains "Calling America") revived mass interest. Between the releases of these two, Bevan briefly joined Black Sabbath. By 1986 ELO was essentially the trio of Lynne, Bevan, and Tandy.

In the meantime, Lynne had become a sought-after record producer (Dave Edmunds' Information) and over the next few years would amass some impressive credits: George Harrison's Cloud Nine, Roy Orbison's Mystery Girl, and Tom Petty's *Full Moon Fever*, among others. In 1988 he joined Harrison, Petty, Orbison, and Bob Dylan in the Traveling Wilburys [see entry]. His 1990 solo album was a U.K. Top Thirty hit, but barely scraped onto the U.S. albums chart.

In 1991 a new, Bevan-led, Lynne-less version of the group (now known as ELO II or Electric Light Orchestra, Part II) released an eponymously titled album. The following year that group recorded a live greatest-hits album with the Moscow Symphony Orchestra.

The Electric Prunes

Formed 1965, Los Angeles, California
James Lowe, autoharp, harmonica, voc.; Mark Tulin, bass, kybds.; Ken Williams, gtr.; Preston Ritter, drums; Weasel Spagnola, gtr., voc.
1967—*Electric Prunes* (Reprise) (– Ritter; + Quint, drums); *Underground* (group disbands; new lineup: John Herren [b. Elk City, Okla.], kybds.; Mark Kincaid [b. Topeka, Kan.], gtr., voc.; Ron Morgan, gtr.; Brett Wade [b. Vancouver, Can.], bass, flute, voc.; Richard Whetstone [b. Hutchinson, Kan.], drums, voc.); *Mass in F Minor*   1968—*Release of an Oath: The Kol Nidre* (– Herren)   1969—*Just Good Old Rock 'n' Roll*.

The Electric Prunes were actually two separate groups. The original was one of the first psychedelic bands from Los Angeles. They signed to Reprise in 1966 and had a national hit with the reverb-heavy "I Had Too Much to Dream (Last Night)" (#11, 1966). They followed up with "Get Me to the World on Time" (#27) in 1967. For reasons unknown, the group disbanded, and a totally new band calling itself the Electric Prunes emerged in 1967 with *Mass in F Minor* and *Release of an Oath* in 1968, both the creations of writer/arranger David Axelrod. Their fifth LP, *Just Good Old Rock 'n' Roll*, was an attempt to return to roots music but was unsuccessful. The Electric Prunes again disbanded, this time for good.

Electronic: See Joy Division

Elephant's Memory

Formed 1967, New York City, New York
Rick Frank (b. Feb. 12, 1942, New York City), drums; Stan Bronstein (b. July 17, 1938, Brooklyn, N.Y.), voc., sax, clarinet.
1969—(+ Richard Sussman [b. Mar. 28, 1946, Philadelphia, Penn.], kybds.; + Myron Yules [b. Mar. 6, 1935, Brooklyn, N.Y.], bass, trombone; + John Ward [b. Feb. 12, 1949, Philadelphia, Penn.], gtr.; + Chester Ayres [b. Richard Ayres, Sep. 5, 1942, Neptune, N.J.], gtr.; + Michal [b. Apr. 20, 1949, Israel], voc.) *Elephant's Memory* (Buddah)

(+ Chris Robison, gtr., kybds., voc.; – Robison; – Sussman; – Yules; – Ward; – Ayres; – Michal; + Wayne "Tex" Gabriel, gtr.; + Adam Ippolito, kybds., voc.; + Gary Van Scyoc, bass, voc.)   1970— *Take It to the Streets* (Metromedia)   1972—*Elephant's Memory* (Apple)   1973—(– Ippolito; – Gabriel; + Robison; + John Sachs, gtr., voc.) 1974—*Angels Forever* (RCA).

Elephant's Memory, remembered for its street-band reputation and association with John Lennon, was formed in New York City's East Village by drummer Rick Frank and Stan Bronstein, a veteran of the strip-tease circuit. They started out as an eclectic seven-piece outfit playing brassy jazz-flavored rock and funk and earned a reputation for outrageous live spectacles featuring bizarre costumes, light shows, and the destruction of plastic sculptures.

Around the time they got a contract with Buddah, Carly Simon was briefly a member but left the group; she was replaced by an Israeli woman identified only as "Michal." Buddah pigeonholed them as a bubblegum act and, after working on the soundtrack for the film *Midnight Cowboy*, the group changed labels. In 1970 it dropped the horns, and Bronstein and Frank added new hard-rocking sidemen. They had a minor hit, "Mongoose," in 1970. Their LP *Take It to the Streets* added to their cult following.

When John Lennon was looking for a band in 1972, Jerry Rubin suggested Elephant's Memory. After a jam at Max's Kansas City, Lennon signed them up. Over the next two years, the group recorded with Lennon and his wife, Yoko Ono (*Some Time in New York City*, 1972; Ono's *Approximately Infinite Universe*, 1973). During the same period, they also released an LP on Apple and backed Chuck Berry and Bo Diddley, and the group appeared with John and Yoko at the One to One benefit concert at Madison Square Garden; recordings of that event were released as *John Lennon Live in New York City* in 1986. *Angels Forever* was recorded in Wales. In early 1981 ex-Elephant guitarist Tex Gabriel was active on the New York club scene with his band, Limozine. Bronstein has appeared on records by a number of other acts, including David Johansen.

Eleventh Dream Day

Formed 1983, Chicago, Illinois
Janet Beveridge Bean (b. Feb. 10, 1964, Louisville, Ky.), drums, voc.; Rick Rizzo (b. July 4, 1957), gtr., voc.; Shu Shubat, bass.
1985—(– Shubat; + Douglas McCombs [b. Jan. 9, 1962], bass; + Baird Figi, gtr.)   1987—*Eleventh Dream Day* EP (Amoeba)   1988—*Prairie School Freakout*   1989—*Beet* (Atlantic)   1991—*Lived to Tell* (– Figi; + Matthew "Wink" O'Bannon [b. July

22, 1956], gtr.) 1993—*El Moodio.*
Freakwater, formed 1983, Louisville, Ky. (Bean, gtr., voc.; Catherine Ann Irwin, gtr., voc.; Dave Gay, bass): 1989—*Freakwater* (Amoeba) 1991—*Dancing Underwater* 1993—*Feels Like the Third Time* (Thrill Jockey).

Eleventh Dream Day is one of the Midwest's most enduring alternative bands, having latched on to Neil Young's mordant guitar aesthetic years before it was hip. Janet Beveridge Bean and Rick Rizzo met in 1981 when he was a student at the University of Kentucky at Lexington and she was a teenaged drummer. Rizzo had just discovered punk rock and taught himself to play guitar via the songbook of Young's album *Zuma.*

The couple (who married in the fall of 1988) moved to Chicago and formed Eleventh Dream Day with bassist Shu Shubat. In spring 1985 Shubat left and was replaced by Douglas McCombs; guitarist/songwriter Baird Figi also joined around this time, giving the band its Television-style twin-guitar sound. The band's first, independent records introduced their flat, Americanist narratives (mostly penned by Rizzo) shot through with twisted guitar and an earnest country twang. *Prairie School Freakout,* recorded in one night with a worn-out, buzzing amp, caught the attention of Atlantic, which signed the band.

Beet, produced by Gary Waleik of Boston alt-rock band Big Dipper, was a modest major-label debut that spent five months on the college-radio charts. On *Lived to Tell,* Bean wrote and sang several of the best tracks. It was a solid, well-received album, but the band suffered a setback when, while touring to promote it, Figi quit the band. He was replaced by Matthew O'Bannon, Eleventh Dream Day's roadie and an old friend. The Jim Rondinelli–produced *El Moodio* featured the Rizzo-Bean duet "Makin' Like a Rug" and a cameo by guitarist Tara Key, of punk-pop combo Antietam. (Rizzo and Bean guested on Key's 1993 album *Bourbon County.*)

Before Bean moved to Chicago, she had been playing country songs with her friend Catherine Ann Irwin. The two have continued to collaborate as Freakwater, with Chicagoan Dave Gay on bass.

Ramblin' Jack Elliott

Born Elliott Charles Adnopoz, August 1, 1931, Brooklyn, New York
1962—*Ramblin' Jack Elliott Sings Woody Guthrie and Jimmie Rodgers* (Monitor) **1968**—*Young Brigham* (Reprise) **1976**—*The Essential Ramblin' Jack Elliott* (Vanguard) **1989**—*Hard Travelin'* (Fantasy).

A Jew from Brooklyn, Ramblin' Jack Elliott is one of the last roaming cowboy-troubadours, a distinction he earned by wandering in the West with Woody Guthrie shortly before the latter was hospitalized with terminal Huntington's chorea.

Elliott left home in 1946 to join the rodeo in Chicago, beginning years of traveling that provided the stories he told on stage. As early as 1953 Elliott was performing regularly in Greenwich Village's Washington Square Park, helping to lay the groundwork for the early-Sixties folk boom. In the late Fifties he settled on the moniker "Ramblin' Jack" (after calling himself Buck Elliott for a while). He toured England and Europe for several years, jamming with traditional folk artists like Peggy Seeger and Ewan McColl and with British R&B stalwart Long John Baldry. He often performed Guthrie compositions ("Pretty Boy Floyd") and such flat-picking showcases as "Black Snake Moan."

Upon returning to the U.S. in 1961 Elliott found himself an old hand in the burgeoning folk renaissance, and his Vanguard debut album was received enthusiastically. Bob Dylan, also a Guthrie fan, was heavily influenced by Elliott, who recorded several Dylan songs in the Sixties (claiming once that Dylan wrote "Don't Think Twice, It's All Right" for him). He was also part of Dylan's 1975 Rolling Thunder entourage.

Elliott recorded consistently through the Sixties and Seventies. In 1968 he performed at a star-studded memorial concert for Guthrie at Carnegie Hall. His best work can be found on compilations like Vanguard's *Essential Jack Elliott* and Folkways' *Songs to Grow On* (all Guthrie material). As of spring 1994, Elliott was still touring, living out of his mobile home, and planning to release his first new studio album in two decades.

Shirley Ellis

Born 1941, Bronx, New York
N.A.—*The Name Game* (Congress); ***Sugar, Let's Shing a Ling*** (Columbia).

Soul singer Shirley Ellis had three Top Ten novelty hits in the mid-Sixties: "The Nitty Gritty" (#8, 1964), "The Clapping Song" (#8, 1965), and her signature song, "The Name Game" (#3, 1965). In the Fifties Ellis wrote "One, Two, I Love You" for the Heartbreakers. She started working with writer Lincoln Chase, whom she later married. Chase's previous hits included "Such a Night" for the Drifters and "Jim Dandy" for LaVern Baker. Before marrying Ellis, Chase had recorded for several labels (Decca, Liberty, Splash, Dawn, Columbia, RCA Victor, Swan) with minimal success. Chase wrote all of Ellis' hits, including lesser successes like "That's What the Nitty Gritty Is" (1964) and "The Puzzle Song" (1965). Ellis' pop success was fleeting. As the Sixties progressed, she switched to Columbia, had one minor hit, "Soul Time" (1967), then retired.

Joe Ely

Born February 9, 1947, Amarillo, Texas
1977—*Joe Ely* (MCA)   1978—*Honky Tonk Masquerade*   1979—*Down on the Drag*   1981—*Musta Notta Gotta Lotta; Live Shots*   1984—*High Res*   1987—*Lord of the Highway* (Hightone)   1988—*Dig All Night*   1990—*Live at Liberty Lunch* (MCA)   1992—*Love and Danger*   1995—*Letter to Laredo.*
With the Flatlanders: 1990—*More a Legend Than a Band* (Rounder).

Joe Ely's band and his songs are rooted in the traditions of his native West Texas—honky-tonk, C&W, R&B, rockabilly, Western swing, and Tex-Mex. Outside the Lubbock and Austin, Texas, club circuit, most of his early support came from the rock press until the Clash introduced him to their fans in 1980.

Ely began playing in rock & roll bands in his hometown of Lubbock at age 13. When he was 16, he dropped out of school to wander from Texas to California, Tennessee, New York, Europe, New Mexico, and back to Texas. He worked as a fruit picker, a circus hand, a janitor, a dishwasher, and an itinerant musician. On return trips to Lubbock, he played in bands with Jimmie Dale Gilmore [see entry], with whom he would collaborate off and on for three decades. Their best-known group effort, the Flatlanders, played old-timey country music and recorded an album in 1972, which was not widely released until 1990.

Once again in Lubbock in 1974, he decided to stay and form his own band with guitarist Jesse Taylor, steel guitarist Lloyd Manes, bassist Gregg Wright, and drummer Steve Keeton. They became local favorites, then began traveling the state honky-tonk circuit.

In 1977 MCA signed Ely, and producer Chip Young took him and his band to Nashville to cut his first album. By that time, he had assembled a repertoire of 300 songs, most of them his own or written by Gilmore or fellow-Lubbock songwriter (ex-Flatlander) Butch Hancock.

Ely's second album, the critically acclaimed *Honky Tonk Masquerade*, featured accordionist Ponty Bone and was even more multifarious than the first. *Down on the Drag*, produced by Bob Johnston (Bob Dylan, Aretha Franklin, Johnny Cash), focused his image as a toughskinned-but-gentlehearted singer/songwriter, but made him no more appealing to radio programmers.

Ely picked up some valuable fans among musicians, however. Merle Haggard took him on a tour of Britain in 1979, and the next year the Clash asked him to open their Texas shows. The Clash's Joe Strummer invited him along for the rest of their American tour and back to England with them: *Live Shots* was recorded at Clash concerts in England. Due to low sales, Ely was dropped by MCA in the mid-Eighties and began recording for independent Hightone. His relationship with MCA re-

sumed in 1990, however. *Live at Liberty Lunch* (#57 C&W, 1990) documented an Ely performance at one of Austin's best clubs. With *Love and Danger*, Ely continued to forge his own sound from Texan raw materials, recording his own material as well as two songs by fellow Lone Star State songwriter Robert Earl Keen and a contribution from ex-Blaster Dave Alvin.

Emerson, Lake and Palmer

Formed 1970, England
Keith Emerson (b. Nov. 1, 1944, Todmorden, Eng.), kybds.; Greg Lake (b. Nov. 10, 1948, Bournemouth, Eng.), bass, gtr., voc.; Carl Palmer (b. Mar. 20, 1947, Birmingham, Eng.), drums, perc.
1970—*Emerson, Lake and Palmer* (Cotillion)
1971—*Tarkus; Pictures at an Exhibition*   1972—*Trilogy*   1973—*Brain Salad Surgery* (Manticore)
1974—*Welcome Back, My Friends, to the Show That Never Ends—Ladies and Gentlemen, Emerson, Lake and Palmer*   1977—*Works, vol. 1* (Atlantic); *Works, vol. 2*   1978—*Love Beach*   1979—*Emerson, Lake and Palmer in Concert*   1980—*Best of Emerson, Lake and Palmer*   1986—(Group re-forms: Emerson; Lake; + Cozy Powell [b. Dec. 29, 1947, Cirencester, Eng.], drums) *Emerson, Lake and Powell* (Polydor) (– Powell)   1987—(+ Palmer; – Palmer)   1988—(+ Robert Barry, gtr.) *To the Power of Three* (as "3") (Geffen) (– Barry)   1992—(+ Palmer) *Black Moon* (Victory)   1993—*The Return of the Manticore.*
Greg Lake solo: 1981—*Greg Lake* (Chrysalis).

Emerson, Lake and Palmer ushered in the classical-flavored progressive rock of the early Seventies. With Greg Lake's predominantly acoustic ballads becoming hit singles and Keith Emerson's keyboard excesses supplying pretensions, the trio was enormously popular in the early Seventies, although it never regained its full momentum after a 1975–77 hiatus.

The group was formed after Emerson, then leading the Nice [see entry], and Lake, formerly of King Crimson, jammed at the Fillmore West in 1969 while both were touring with their respective bands. Emerson had studied classical piano and later dabbled in jazz; he made his professional debut at 19 with British R&B singer Gary Farr and the T-Bones. Two years later he joined the VIPs, some of whose members later surfaced in Spooky Tooth; and in early 1967 he joined American soul singer P. P. Arnold's band, then headquartered in Europe.

After plans to work with Jimi Hendrix Experience drummer Mitch Mitchell fell through, in June 1970 Emerson and Lake decided on Carl Palmer, a veteran of Chris Farlowe, Arthur Brown, and Atomic Rooster. ELP debuted on August 25; just four days later the trio appeared at the 1970 Isle of Wight Festival, playing Emerson's transcription of Mussorgsky's *Pictures at an Exhibition*,

Grammy Awards

The Eagles
1975 Best Pop Vocal Performance by a Duo, Group or Chorus: "Lyin' Eyes"
1977 Record of the Year: "Hotel California"
1977 Best Arrangement for Voices: "New Kid in Town"
1979 Best Rock Vocal Performance by a Duo or Group: "Heartache Tonight"

Don Henley (Eagles)
1985 Best Rock Vocal Performance, Male: "The Boys of Summer"
1989 Best Rock Vocal Performance, Male: *The End of the Innocence*

Earth, Wind and Fire
1975 Best Vocal Performance by a Group: "Shining Star"
1978 Best R&B Instrumental Performance: "Runnin' "
1978 Best R&B Vocal Performance by a Duo, Group or Chorus: *All 'n All*
1979 Best R&B Instrumental Performance: "Boogie Wonderland"
1979 Best R&B Vocal Performance by a Duo, Group or Chorus: "After the Love Has Gone"
1982 Best R&B Performance by a Duo or Group with Vocal: "Wanna Be with You"

Sheena Easton
1981 Best New Artist
1984 Best Mexican/American Performance: "Me Gustas Tal Como Eres" (with Luis Miguel)

Duane Eddy
1986 Best Rock Instrumental Performance (Orchestra, Group or Soloist): "Peter Gunn" (with the Art of Noise)

Jeff Lynne (Electric Light Orchestra) [See Traveling Wilburys]

The Emotions
1977 Best R&B Vocal Performance by a Duo, Group or Chorus: "Best of My Love"

Brian Eno
1987 Album of the Year: *The Joshua Tree* (with U2 and Daniel Lanois)
1992 Producer of the Year (with Daniel Lanois) (tie with L.A. Reid and Babyface)

Enya
1992 Best New Age Album: *Shepherd Moons*

Gloria Estefan
1993 Best Tropical Latin Album: *Mi Tierra*

Melissa Etheridge
1992 Best Rock Vocal Performance, Female: "Ain't It Heavy"
1994 Best Rock Vocalist, Female: "Come to My Window"

Eurythmics
1986 Best Rock Performance by a Duo or Group with Vocal: "Missionary Man"

Annie Lennox (Eurythmics)
1992 Best Music Video, Long Form: *Diva* (with Sophie Muller and Rob Small)

---

which later became the band's third album. Its debut LP, recorded in October 1970, went gold on the strength of Lake's "Lucky Man" (#48, 1971). FM radio play and flamboyantly bombastic concerts—with Emerson's electric keyboards flashing lights and whirling around, Palmer's $25,000 percussion set including xylophone, tympani, and gong as well as an elevator platform, and the usual lights and smoke—cemented the group's following.

Each of ELP's first nine albums went gold. *Trilogy,* which reached #5, contained the trio's highest-charting single, Lake's gentle "From the Beginning" (#39, 1972). In 1973 the group formed its own Manticore Records, which released albums by Italy's Premiata Forneria Marconi (P.F.M.) and sometime Lake lyricist Pete Sinfield, along with ELP's *Brain Salad Surgery.* ELP's 1973–74 world tour required 36 tons of equipment, including a quadraphonic sound system, lasers, and other paraphernalia, and was documented on the triple live set *Welcome Back, My Friends, to the Show That Never Ends.*

With six million in sales behind them, ELP took a two-year break, ending it in 1977 with the release of *Works, vol. 1* and, later that same year, *vol. 2.* Though advertised as ELP albums, both albums consisted largely of solo pieces, such as Lake's "C'est La Vie" and "I Believe in Father Christmas." A 1977 world tour called for an entourage of 115 people, including full orchestra and choir, but had to be drastically reduced when ticket sales didn't materialize. Shortly after the late-1978 release of *Love Beach,* the group's only LP to that point not to make the Top Forty, ELP announced its breakup.

Of the three, Palmer enjoyed the most successful post-ELP career, joining the progressive-pop supergroup Asia in 1981 [see entry]. Emerson was sporadically active; he scored the 1981 thriller film *Nighthawks* and issued a little-heard album of Christmas music in 1988, while Lake revived the solo career begun during the group's hiatus. He released an eponymously titled album in 1981, toured the U.S., and briefly took John Wetton's spot in Asia for a Far East tour.

Having witnessed Yes' mid-Eighties commercial revival, Emerson and Lake put ELP back together in 1985—only the *P* stood for veteran drummer Cozy Powell; Palmer wasn't interested in rejoining at the time. This lineup's lone album produced one memorable song, the single "Touch & Go" (#60, 1986). Following a U.S. tour, Powell left. This time when asked, Palmer agreed, but when rehearsals for a new ELP album proved unproductive, Emerson and Lake recorded instead as "3" with a California guitarist named Robert Barry. This configuration's 1988 LP, *To the Power of Three,* attracted little attention.

Emerson, Lake and Palmer tried once again, and came up with *Black Moon,* released in 1992 on the Victory label. Despite dismal sales, ELP discovered a vast audience for its live show: A nine-month 1992–93 world tour took the group to North America, Europe, and South America. *The Return of the Manticore* box set featured new studio recordings of "Pictures at an Exhibition" as well as tracks from each member's pre-ELP days: the Nice's "Hang On to a Dream," King Crimson's "21st Century Schizoid Man," and Arthur Brown's "Fire." As of 1994, a new album was underway, with Keith Olsen (Fleetwood Mac, Pat Benatar) producing.

EMF

Formed October 1989, Cinderford, England
James Atkin (b. Mar. 28, 1967, Cinderford), voc.; **Ian Dench** (b. Aug. 7, 1964, Cinderford), gtr.; **Derran "Derry" Brownson** (b. Nov. 10, 1970, Cinderford), kybds.; **Zachary Foley** (b. Dec. 9, 1970, Cinderford), bass; **Mark Decloedt** (b. June 26, 1967, Cinderford), drums.
1991—*Schubert Dip* (EMI) **1992**—*Unexplained* EP; *Stigma.*

EMF emerged from the sleepy, rural Gloucester area in the west of England in spring 1991 with "Unbelievable," an international rock-dance smash that leapt to the top of the charts. All five members had played in local bands before meeting at keyboardist Derry Brownson's Cinderford clothing store, Kix. Two months after forming, EMF played its first gig; band members later claimed the name stood for "Epsom Mad Funkers," not the oft-speculated "Ecstasy Mother Fuckers" which gave the mistaken impression the group was part of England's rave scene. The group added techno elements to its rock sound only after discovering a cheap Casio sampler/sequencer in a local store.

EMF gradually built a reputation in England, busing in fans from its native Forest of Dean area to London for club gigs. EMI signed the group in spring 1990; by the end of the year "Unbelievable" was a smash British hit, and it later went to #1 on the American pop charts, while EMF's debut album (#12, 1991)—titled with a pun on the classical composer and on the British candy sherbet dip—also yielded a lesser hit in "Lies" (#18, 1991). While Tom Jones added "Unbelievable" to his stage show, *Stigma* failed to chart or yield a hit single.

An Emotional Fish

Formed 1988, Dublin, Ireland
Gerard Whelan (b. July 14, 1964, Dublin), voc.; **David Frew** (b. Apr. 30, 1962, Dublin), gtr.; **Martin Murphy** (b. Nov. 9, 1967, Dublin), drums; **Enda Wyatt** (b. June 13, 1960, Dublin), bass.
1990—*An Emotional Fish* (Atlantic) **1993**—*Junk Puppets.*

An Emotional Fish was among a number of Irish acts that got their start by recording on Mother Records, a label that U2 launched to encourage aspiring talent. Also like other Irish acts that cropped up in the Eighties and early Nineties, Fish garnered the inevitable U2 comparisons for its grandly passionate guitar rock. Singer Gerard Whelan and guitarist David Frew were raised in London by Irish parents, but met only after returning to their native Dublin. There, the musicians hooked up with bassist Enda Wyatt and drummer Martin Murphy. By 1989 the four had a local following. They rejected offers from major labels, however, to record their first single, the anthemlike "Celebrate," on Mother. After "Celebrate" entered the Irish Top Ten, the majors came courting again; this time Fish bit, signing with Atlantic. The group's eponymous debut album garnered mixed reviews—some critics found it moving, others bombastic—but appealed to college-rock fans in the U.S. The band's 1993 followup, *Junk Puppets,* inspired a similar response.

The Emotions

Formed 1968, Chicago, Illinois
Wanda Hutchinson (b. Dec. 17, 1951, Chicago), voc.; **Sheila Hutchinson** (b. Jan. 17, 1953, voc.); **Jeanette Hutchinson** (b. 1951, Chicago), voc.
1970—(+ Theresa Davis [b. Aug. 22, 1950, Chicago], voc.) *Untouched* (Stax); *So I Can Love You* **1976**—*Flowers* (Columbia) **1977**—(– J. Hutchinson; + Pamela Hutchinson [b. 1958, Chicago], voc.) *Sunshine* (Stax); (+ J. Hutchinson) *Rejoice* (Columbia) **1979**—*Come into Our World* **1981**—*New Affair.*

A gospel-turned-soul family group in the Staples tradition, the Emotions have been entertaining black audiences since they could walk. Their biggest successes (like the #1 "Best of My Love") came in the late Seventies under the guidance of Maurice White of Earth, Wind and Fire (with whom they recorded EW&F's 1979 hit "Boogie Wonderland").

Father/manager (and occasional guitarist and vocalist) Joe had his three oldest daughters performing in church as tots. Beginning in 1961 they traveled the gospel circuit as the Heavenly (later the Hutchinson) Sunbeams and occasionally toured with Mahalia Jackson. While attending Chicago's Parker High School in the mid-Sixties, they became the Three Ribbons and a Bow (Papa Joe was the "beau") and began concentrating on more secular material, cutting an unsuccessful series of singles for several Midwestern labels, including Vee Jay. While touring, they met the Staples, who helped them acquire a contract with Stax-Volt in 1968.

Rechristened the Emotions, the group enjoyed substantial R&B success and made occasional modest pop inroads—"So I Can Love You" (#39 pop, #3 R&B, 1969), "Show Me How" (#52 pop, #13 R&B, 1971)—through the early Seventies. They appeared in the 1973 film *Wattstax* and toured with the Jackson 5, Sly and the Family Stone, B. B. King, Stevie Wonder, Bobby "Blue" Bland, and others.

When Stax folded in 1975, the Emotions signed with Maurice White's Kalimba Productions and thus got on the Columbia roster. White wrote the title track and produced their gold debut for the label, *Flowers* (which prominently featured Wanda's material and lead vocals), as well as the platinum followup, *Rejoice* (#7, 1977). They enjoyed hit singles with "I Don't Wanna Lose Your Love" (#51 pop, #13 R&B, 1976) and the Grammy-winning disco favorite "Best of My Love" and toured with Earth, Wind and Fire in 1976. Other hits were "Don't Ask My Neighbors" (#44 pop, #7 R&B, 1977) and "Smile" (#6 R&B, 1978). By the late Seventies they were writing the bulk of their material themselves. In the mid-Eighties they retired from recording.

The English Beat

Formed 1978, Birmingham, England
Andy Cox (b. Jan. 25, 1956, Birmingham), gtr.;
Everett Morton (b. Apr. 5, 1951, St. Kitts, W. Indies), drums; David Steele (b. Sep. 8, 1960, Isle of Wight, Eng.), bass; Dave Wakeling (b. Feb. 19, 1956, Birmingham), gtr., voc.
1979—(+ Ranking Roger [b. Roger Charlery, Feb. 21, 1961, Birmingham], voc.; + Saxa [b. ca. 1930, Jam.], sax) 1980—*I Just Can't Stop It* (Sire) 1981—
Wha'ppen 1982—*Special Beat Service* (I.R.S.)
1983—*What Is Beat?*
General Public (Wakeling; Roger; others): 1984—
... *All the Rage* (I.R.S.) 1986—*Hand to Mouth*
1995—*Rub It Better* (Epic).
Ranking Roger solo: 1988—*Radical Departure* (I.R.S.).
Dave Wakeling solo: 1991—*No Warning* (I.R.S.).

The English Beat (known simply as the Beat everywhere except the U.S., where a Los Angeles power-pop band also went by that name) originated in the British ska revival of the late Seventies. Since the band's breakup in 1983, members of the group have gone on to fame as founders of Fine Young Cannibals and General Public.

The three white members of the multiracial Beat, Dave Wakeling, Andy Cox, and David Steele, began playing together in 1978. Reggae and other Jamaican rhythms tempered their punk-rock repertoire when they were joined by Everett Morton, a black West Indian who had drummed for Joan Armatrading. The quartet played its first gig at a Birmingham club in March 1979, opening for a punk group whose black drummer was Ranking Roger; soon after Roger began "toasting" (chanting over the songs) at its gigs and later joined the Beat as second vocalist.

The Specials released the Beat's debut record, a cover of Smokey Robinson's "Tears of a Clown," on their 2-Tone label in late 1979. For that recording session, the group enlisted Saxa, a 50-year-old Jamaican saxophonist who had played with the Beatles in their Liverpool years and with such ska stars as Prince Buster, Desmond Dekker, and Laurel Aitken. When the single went to #6 in the U.K., Saxa joined the Beat.

The group formed its own label, Go Feet. Its first two releases, "Hands Off . . . She's Mine" and "Mirror in the Bathroom," made the U.K. Top Ten, and the third, "Best Friend," made the Top Thirty. After recording a debut album, the Beat toured Europe accompanied by David "Blockhead" Wright, who became an unofficial member. The group returned to Birmingham to find *I Just Can't Stop It* at #3, U.K. Billed as the English Beat, it toured the U.S. in fall 1980, opening for the Pretenders and Talking Heads, and returned to tour as headliners in 1981 and '82. In Britain *Wha'ppen* (1981) went to #2, and "Too Nice to Talk To" hit #7, while "Drowning" and "Doors to Your Heart" made the Top Forty.

Special Beat Service (#39 pop, 1982) was the English Beat's first album to sell well in America, with the track "Save It for Later" receiving FM airplay. Shortly after its release, Saxa announced that he would no longer tour with the group. The remainder of the band split acrimoniously a year later. Cox and Steele went on to form Fine Young Cannibals [see entry], while Wakeling and Roger became General Public.

General Public recorded two albums, . . . *All the Rage* (1984) and *Hand to Mouth* (1986), which, even with the help of the Clash's Mick Jones (on *Rage*) and Saxa (on *Hand*), failed to make the U.K. or U.S. charts. The group disbanded in 1988. Roger released a solo LP, *Radical Departure*, that year, and with the Specials' Neville Staples toured as Special Beat in 1990. Wakeling left the music business in 1989 after sessions for an album, *The Happiest Man in the World*, fell apart (an album, *No Warning*, was released in 1991). He moved to Los Angeles, where he works for Greenpeace; in 1993 Wakeling organized a benefit album titled *Alternative NRG*, which was recorded using solar power. Later that year a reformed General Public recorded a Staple Singers song,

"I'll Take You There" (#22, 1994), that was featured in the 1994 film *Threesome;* the next year GP released *Rub It Better.*

Brian Eno

Born Brian Peter George St. John le Baptiste de la Salle Eno, May 15, 1948, Woodbridge, England
1973—*No Pussyfooting* (with Robert Fripp) (Antilles); *Here Come the Warm Jets* 1974—*June 1, 1974* (with John Cale, Nico, and Kevin Ayers) (Island); *Taking Tiger Mountain (By Strategy)* (Antilles) 1975—*Another Green World; Evening Star* (with Robert Fripp); *Discreet Music* (Obscure) 1977—*Before and After Science* (Island); *Cluster and Eno* 1978—*Music for Films* (Polydor); *After the Heat* (with Moebius and Rodelius) (Sky); *Music for Airports* (Editions EG) 1980—*Possible Musics* (with Jon Hassell); *The Plateaux of Mirror* (with Roger Eno and Harold Budd) 1981—*Days of Radiance* (with Laraaji); *My Life in the Bush of Ghosts* (with David Byrne) (Sire); *Music for Airplay* (Editions EG) 1982—*Ambient 4: On Land* 1983—*Apollo: Atmospheres & Soundtracks* (with Daniel Lanois and Roger Eno) 1984—*The Pearl* (with Daniel Lanois and Harold Budd) 1985—*Hybrid* (with Michael Brook and Daniel Lanois); *Voices* (with Roger Eno); *Thursday Afternoon* 1986—*More Blank Than Frank* (Polydor); *Desert Island Selection* 1990—*Wrong Way Up* (with John Cale) (Opal/Warner Bros.) 1991—*My Squelchy Life* 1992—*Nerve Net* (Warner Bros.); *The Shutov Assembly* (Opal) 1993—*Neroli* (Gyroscope/Caroline); *Brian Eno II* (Virgin) 1994—*Brian Eno I.*

Self-described "nonmusician" and studio experimentalist Brian Eno has greatly influenced an encyclopedia of styles—from art rock to punk to world music to techno. A founding member of Roxy Music, he went on to work as a solo artist and a producer/collaborator with U2, Talking Heads, David Bowie, Robert Fripp, and others. His series of ambient music records (by himself and with such composers as Jon Hassell, Harold Budd, and Laraaji) feature an atmospheric instrumental sound that found expression in both New Age and minimalist work. An aesthetic breakthrough, his tape-delay system, developed for Robert Fripp as "Frippertronics," insisted on the conscious use of recording technology as a method of composition and paved the way for the "sampling" used extensively in rap and techno.

An art-school alumnus, Eno was influenced by contemporary composers John Tilbury and Cornelius Cardew and such minimalists as La Monte Young and Terry Riley; he also participated occasionally in a rock band called Maxwell's Demon. In 1971 he helped start Roxy Music [see entry]. Their synthesizer player and ec-

centric visual centerpiece, he electronically "treated" the band's other instruments. After working on *Roxy Music* and *For Your Pleasure,* he departed in 1973 due to friction with songwriter Bryan Ferry.

After *No Pussyfooting* (with Robert Fripp), Eno put out two records of free-associative, noisily inventive songs—*Here Come the Warm Jets* and *Taking Tiger Mountain (By Strategy)*—and produced the Portsmouth Sinfonia, an orchestra of quasi-competent musicians playing discordant versions of light classics. His 1974 solo tour ended when he was hospitalized for a collapsed lung, although he appeared on two concert albums: *June 1, 1974* (with Kevin Ayers, John Cale, and Nico) and *801 Live* (801 was a group led by Roxy Music guitarist Phil Manzanera).

Although Eno dabbles on all sorts of instruments, he is most accomplished on tape recorder, of which he owns dozens, and is fascinated by the happy accidents of the recording process. He created a deck of tarotlike cards called Oblique Strategies ("Emphasize the flaws"; "Use another color"), and has used them to make artistic decisions.

In 1975 Eno started Obscure Records to release his tapes and works by other composers. His many collaborations of the decade included *Evening Star* with Robert Fripp; an album by Robert Calvert of Hawkwind; a David Bowie trilogy (*Low, "Heroes,"* and *Lodger*); and albums with the German synthesizer band Cluster. His concurrent production work included the Talking Heads (*More Songs about Buildings and Food; Fear of Music; Remain in Light*); debuts for Ultravox (*Ultravox!*) and Devo (*Q: Are We Not Men? A: We Are Devo!*); and a no-wave compilation featuring DNA, the Contortions, and Teenage Jesus and the Jerks, entitled *No New York.*

Under his own name, Eno has recorded ambient music albums (*Discreet Music, Music for Films,* and *Music for Airports,* which was broadcast for a while at New York's LaGuardia Airport); pop albums (*Before and After Science* and with John Cale, *Wrong Way Up*); and a Top 30 album (*My Life in the Bush of Ghosts,* which lent a techno edge to the fast-developing genre of world music).

In 1980 Eno began a partnership with producer Daniel Lanois that proved as fruitful as his alliances with Fripp and Talking Heads. Working on *Voices* with Eno's brother, Roger, and *The Plateaux of Mirror* with minimalist composer Harold Budd, the pair forged a path into unexplored sonic territory. They went on to craft a new sound for U2, producing the Irish quartet's albums *The Unforgettable Fire* and *The Joshua Tree.* For Eno, long regarded as a cult figure, this was an uncharacteristically high-profile enterprise; his collaboration on U2's *Achtung Baby* and *Zooropa* saw him moving the rock band in a quasi-ambient direction and also employing industrial noise touches.

By the Nineties, Eno was an established voice in a range of contemporary musics. In *Low Symphony*, composer Philip Glass spun off themes and variations of Bowie's *Low*, a work indelibly stamped by Eno; the ambient techno bands like the Orb and Irresistible Force owed an obvious debt to Eno. As composer, producer, keyboardist, and singer, he is responsible less for a new sound in pop than for a new way of thinking about music—as an atmosphere, rather than a statement, an experiment in sound, rather than a virtuosic expression. Combining the cerebral qualities of European high culture with the technological outlook of a futurist, he has also been responsible for an aesthetic movement that incorporates both Western and third world sounds.

John Entwistle: See the Who

En Vogue

Formed July 18, 1988, Oakland, California
Cindy Herron (b. Sep. 26, 1965, San Francisco, Calif.), voc.; Maxine Jones (b. Jan. 16, 1966, Paterson, N.J.), voc.; Terry Ellis (b. Sep. 5, 1966, Houston, Tex.), voc.; Dawn Robinson (b. Nov. 28, 1968, New London, Conn.), voc.
1990—*Born to Sing* (Atlantic)   1991—*Remix to Sing* (EastWest)   1992—*Funky Divas*   1993—*Runaway Love* EP.

With their tight four-part harmonies, provocative choreography, shared leads, and retro glamour, En Vogue revived the R&B girl-group tradition. Cindy Herron, Maxine Jones, Terry Ellis, and Dawn Robinson barely knew each other before auditioning for a group being assembled by Bay Area producers Denzil Foster and Thomas McElroy, whose previous credits included Timex Social Club ("Rumors"), Club Nouveau ("Lean on Me"), and Tony! Toni! Toné!. They envisioned rejuvenating R&B with hip-hop rhythms, and their New Jack Swing grooves raised En Vogue above the slew of contemporary girl groups (e.g., Sweet Sensation, Exposé).

En Vogue, then just Vogue, sang two songs on *FM²*, Foster and McElroy's Quincy Jones–styled concept album. The quartet recorded *Born to Sing* (#21) in fall 1989. After its release the following spring, the album went platinum, led by the single "Hold On" (#2). En Vogue was nominated for a Grammy and toured with Freddie Jackson and Hammer.

That was just a prelude to En Vogue's stunning success with the multiplatinum *Funky Divas* (#8, 1992), whose Foster and McElroy–produced mix of pop, R&B, rock, rap, and reggae included the hit singles "My Lovin' (You're Never Gonna Get It)" (#2, 1992) and "Free Your Mind" (#8, 1992). The music and vocals were widely praised by critics, but En Vogue's visual style also played a role. Like their stylistic predecessors, the Supremes, En Vogue performed in chic designer costumes connoting a sexy elegance.

Part of En Vogue's image is their unity: They trade off star vocal turns and cultivate a mystique of separate-but-equal personalities. They profess sisterlike affection, and although Cindy Herron, a former Miss Black California, has acted since age 11, including a role in the film *Juice*, none has pursued a solo career since En Vogue's formation. (Their producers do include solo albums in the band's seven-year contract.)

Runaway Love (#49 pop, #16 R&B, 1993) featured new versions of tracks from *Funky Divas*, as well as "Whatta Man," where the women provided the chorus to raps by Salt-n-Pepa.

Enya

Born Eithne Ni Bhraonain, May 17, 1961, Gweedore, Ireland
1986—*Enya* (Atlantic)   1988—*Watermark* (Geffen)   1991—*Shepherd Moons* (Reprise).

Enya began her professional career playing keyboards in the successful Irish family act Clannad but eventually achieved greater fame as a solo artist. Combining elements of classical, New Age, and traditional Irish folk music, and lending her ethereal voice to lyrics that incorporated both English and Gaelic (and sometimes Latin), Enya has produced melodic, gently haunting material that has been better received by New Age–disdaining critics and pop fans than anyone could have expected.

One of nine children born to a couple of musicians (her father led the Slieve Foy Band, a noted Irish show band), Enya received classical piano training during her youth. She joined the group Clannad (Gaelic for "family") in 1979, three years after it was formed by a few of her brothers, sisters, and uncles. In 1982 Enya quit the band—whose theme music for a variety of television shows had by then landed it on the pop charts—in hopes of pursuing what she saw as a more personal, less conventional musical vision. Enya's 1986 debut, composed of music she had originally written for a BBC-TV series, *The Celts*, garnered little attention, but its texturally similar successor, 1988's *Watermark*, yielded a #1 single in the U.K., "Orinoco Flow," and sold three million copies worldwide. Enya wrote the melodies and played most of the instruments on her songs, while former Clannad manager Nicky Ryan served as her producer/arranger, and his wife Roma Ryan contributed lyrics. In 1991 Enya topped the success of *Watermark* with her third album, *Shepherd Moons*, which went to #17 on the U.S. pop chart.

EPMD

Formed 1986, Brentwood, New York
Erick Sermon (a.k.a. E Double E, b. Nov. 25, 1968,

Bayshore, N.Y.), voc.; Parrish Smith (a.k.a. PMD, b. May 13, 1968, Smithtown, N.Y.), voc., programmer. 1988—*Strictly Business* (Fresh) 1989—*Unfinished Business* 1991—*Business as Usual* (Def Jam) 1992—*Business Never Personal.*
Erick Sermon solo: 1993—*No Pressure* (Def Jam).
PMD (Parrish Smith) solo: 1994—*Shadé Business* (Def Jam).

Once described as "the rap equivalent of a rock & roll garage band," EPMD (stands for "Erick and Parrish Making Dollars") got into the hip-hop business not to spout their political agenda, but to have fun and get paid. Erick Sermon and Parrish Smith grew up together on Long Island, home to rappers Eric B. and Rakim, De La Soul, and Public Enemy's Flavor Flav. In 1987, while on a college break, Smith (who played tight end for Southern Connecticut State University's football team) recorded with Sermon the duo's raps, which they had first performed together the previous year. EPMD immediately released the songs as a 12-inch single on Sleeping Bag (a subsidiary of independent Fresh Records) ("It's My Thing" b/w "You're a Customer"), which sold 500,000 copies. Within six weeks of its release, *Strictly Business* had topped the R&B LPs chart and gone gold. Hits included "You Gots to Chill" (#22 R&B, 1988) and "Strictly Business" (#25 R&B, 1988).

EPMD's initial sound blended suburban angst with the hard-core edge of their inner-city rap brethren. The group's self-produced raw, bass-heavy rhythm tracks were fortified liberally by sampled loops (Steve Miller's "Fly Like an Eagle," Bob Marley's "I Shot the Sheriff"). Critics pegged Sermon's slurred vocal delivery as everything from "cotton-mouthed" to sounding like he was "rapping through a mouthful of marbles."

As its title suggests, *Unfinished Business* offered more of the same. By the early Nineties, with the vast popularity of gangsta rap, EPMD acknowledged the style by injecting *Business as Usual* with a harder edge, and it paid off. The album went to #36 on the pop chart and scored hits with "Gold Digger" (#14 R&B, 1991) and "Rampage" (#30 R&B, 1992), the latter a collaboration with L. L. Cool J. In 1992 the duo released *Business Never Personal* (#14 pop, #5 R&B), which contained the hit "Crossover" (#42 pop, #14 R&B, 1992). Sermon and Smith formed a production team, working with K-Solo, Das EFX, and Redman, and put together the "Hit Squad" package tour.

In early 1993, EPMD called it quits, and both Sermon and Smith released solo albums. Sermon's *No Pressure* (#16 pop, #2 R&B, 1993) had one single, "Stay Real" (#92 pop, #52 R&B). Smith (now just PMD after his moniker, Parrish Mad Deep) continued to stay in the business with *Shadé Business* (#12 R&B, 1994).

Erasure

Formed 1985, London, England
Vince Clarke (b. July 3, 1960, South Woodford, Eng.), synth.; Andy Bell (b. Apr. 25, 1964, Peterborough, Eng.), voc.
1986—*Wonderland* (Sire) 1987—*The Circus; The Two Ring Circus* 1988—*The Innocents; Crackers International* EP 1989—*Wild!* 1991—*Chorus* 1992—*Abba-esque* (Mute); *Pop!—The First 20 Hits* (Sire).

After rising to prominence in England as one half of the technopop duo Yazoo, songwriter and synthesizer ace Vince Clarke formed Erasure, another two-man electronic music outfit that found Clarke paired with a distinctive, charismatic singer. As the voice of Erasure, Andy Bell became the flamboyant foil to Clarke's shy-wizard persona. Bell was one of the first openly gay pop entertainers, and his gender-bending theatricality has defined Erasure's live performances as much as his high-pitched voice and the danceable, synth-drunk songs that he and Clarke have collaborated on have established the band's overall sound.

An original member of Depeche Mode, Clarke left that group early on to form Yazoo (known as Yaz in the U.S.) with vocalist Alison Moyet [see entry]. Yazoo released two critically acclaimed albums, 1982's *Upstairs at Eric's* (#2 U.K.) and 1983's *You and Me Both* (#1 U.K.), which were successful in England but never surpassed cult-favorite status in America. When Moyet decided to embark on a solo career, Clarke teamed up briefly with Irish singer Feargal Sharkey in the Assembly. Then, in 1985, Clarke placed a blind ad for a vocalist in a British music paper; Bell responded and was selected from over 40 applicants.

Erasure's first album, 1986's *Wonderland* (#71 U.K.), was a commercial failure that led some critics and Yazoo fans to compare Bell's voice unfavorably with Moyet's warm, husky alto. *The Circus* was better received and reached #6 on the English charts—thus vindicating Bell, whose creative input was greater on the sophomore effort. The following year, a third album, *The Innocents,* hit the top of the U.K. charts (as did the next three LPs), and two of its singles—"Chains of Love" and "A Little Respect"—almost entered the U.S. Top Ten, peaking at #12 and #14, respectively.

To date, Erasure hasn't produced any more Top Forty singles in America (although its sixth album, 1991's *Chorus,* peaked at #29), but the band continued to attract attention into the early Nineties for its outrageous stage shows, which have featured Bell in gaudy drag costumes, paying homage to everyone from Tammy Wynette to Judy Garland. In 1992 Erasure paid tribute to a couple of Swedish songbirds with *Abba-esque,* an Abba tribute album. Later that year, Clarke and Bell released a compilation of their "first 20 hits," most of which deserved to be classified as such in England more than the States.

Eric B. and Rakim

Formed 1985, New York City, New York
Eric B. (b. Eric Barrier, Nov. 8, ca. 1965, Elmhurst, N.Y.), DJ; Rakim (b. William Griffin Jr., Jan. 28, ca. 1968, Long Island, N.Y.), voc.
1987—*Paid in Full* (4th & Broadway)   1988—*Follow the Leader* (Uni)   1990—*Let the Rhythm Hit 'Em* (MCA)   1992—*Don't Sweat the Technique*.

Rappers Eric B. and Rakim's first single, "Eric B. Is President" (#48, 1986), sparked early debate on the legality of unauthorized, uncredited sampling when James Brown sued to prevent the duo's use of a fragment of his music. With Rakim's relaxed vocal delivery ("Microphone Fiend," "Paid in Full") and rhymes that have been described as "existential," together with Eric B.'s deft turntable manipulation, the duo became one of the most acclaimed hip-hop acts of the late Eighties. The two met in 1985 when Eric Barrier was working as a DJ at New York City radio station WBLS and looking for an MC to rap over his turntable work. A year later they released "Eric B. Is President" on the independent Harlem label Zakia.

Paid in Full (#58 pop, #8 R&B) appeared in 1987 with a new mix of the single, as well as songs such as "I Know You Got Soul" (#64 R&B, 1987) and "I Ain't No Joke" (#38 R&B, 1987). The duo's subsequent three albums reached the Top Forty, with *Follow the Leader* peaking at #22, *Let the Rhythm Hit 'Em* at #32, and *Don't Sweat the Technique* at #22. In 1991 Eric B. and Rakim scored another hit with the theme to *House Party 2*, "What's on Your Mind" (#34 R&B). The duo parted ways after *Don't Sweat the Technique*, but not before running into another legal dispute over their sampling of Funkadelic's "No Head, No Backstage Pass," from *Follow the Leader*'s "Lyrics of Fury."

Roky Erickson/13th Floor Elevators

Born Roger Kynard Erickson, July 15, 1947, Dallas, Texas
1980—*Roky Erickson and the Aliens* (CBS, U.K.)   1981—*The Evil One* (415)   1985—*Fire in My Bones* (Texas Archive Recordings)   1986—*Don't Slander Me* (Pink Dust); *Gremlins Have Pictures*   1987—*I Think of Demons* (Edsel, U.K.)   1990—*Reverend of Karmic Youth* (Skyclad)   1991—*You're Gonna Miss Me: The Best of Roky Erickson* (Restless)   1992—*Love to See You Bleed* (Swordfish); *Mad Dog*   1995—*All That May Do My Rhyme* (Trance Syndicate).
With the 13th Floor Elevators, formed 1965, Austin,

Tex. **(Erickson, voc., gtr.; Tommy Hall, jug; Benny Thurman, bass; John Ike Walton, drums; Stacy Sutherland [d. 1977, Tex.], gtr.): 1967—*The Psychedelic Sounds of the 13th Floor Elevators* (International Artists) (– Thurman; – Walton; + Danny Thomas, drums; + Danny Galindo, bass)   1967—*Easter Everywhere*   1968—*Thirteenth Floor Elevators Live*; *Bull of the Woods*   1987—*Elevator Tracks* (Texas Archive Recordings).**

Roky Erickson made his mark in the 1960s Texas-based psychedelic band the 13th Floor Elevators, whose garage classic "You're Gonna Miss Me" (#56, 1966) was the closest the group got to a hit single. The Elevators disbanded in 1969 after Erickson was arrested on charges of marijuana possession, and spent three years in Rusk State Hospital for the criminally insane. Since the Seventies, Erickson, who sings in a high, soaring tenor voice, has had an erratic solo career, and fluctuating mental impairment.

The son of an architect and amateur opera singer, Erickson took up piano at five and guitar at 12. Not long after quitting Travis High School, he wrote "You're Gonna Miss Me," the protopunk tune that was originally recorded by Erickson's combo, the Spades, in 1965. The song caught the attention of jug player/lyricist Tommy Hall, who asked Erickson to join the 13th Floor Elevators, the band Hall had founded with the purpose of spreading psychedelia. After the Elevators re-recorded and released "You're Gonna Miss Me," they got a deal with International Artists; their debut album, *Psychedelic Sounds*, sold 140,000 copies. The band released other singles and albums, but had started getting harassed by police for their heavy marijuana and LSD experimentation. In 1969 Erickson was busted for possession of one joint, pleaded not guilty by reason of insanity, and was sentenced to Rusk, where he was diagnosed as schizophrenic, subjected to electroshock therapy, and treated with Thorazine and other powerful psychoactive drugs.

By 1973 Erickson was out of the hospital and performing again. He wrote the first in a series of songs based on horror themes, including "I Walk with a Zombie," and recorded "Red Temple Prayer (Two-Headed Dog)," which had a profound influence on punk but did not chart. Due to ill-advised management, publishing, and legal decisions, numerous unauthorized releases of his music, from which he has not received royalties, have circulated since the early Eighties. In 1982 Erickson signed an affidavit proclaiming himself "inhabited" by a Martian; two years later he stopped recording, and in 1987 he ceased performing.

By the early Nineties Erickson was living on $200 monthly social security checks and help from friends. In January 1990 he was arrested on mail theft charges, which were later dropped. Also in 1990 a group of high-profile bands including R.E.M., ZZ Top, and the Butthole Surfers appeared on the album *Where the Pyramid Meets the Eye: A Tribute to Roky Erickson* (Sire). Three years later, in 1993, Erickson reemerged in a brief performance at the Austin Music Awards, and reentered the studio later that year, recording six new songs, with assistance from Austin guitarists Charlie Sexton and Paul Leary (Butthole Surfers). In 1995 Erickson's *All That May Do My Rhyme*, a folky collection of songs, was released on Trance Syndicate, the label owned by Butthole Surfer King Coffey.

Alejandro Escovedo: See Rank and File

Esquerita
Born Eskew Reeder Jr., or Esquerita Milochi, New Orleans, Louisiana; died 1986, New York City, New York
1987—*Vintage Voola* (Norton)   1990—*Esquerita* (Capitol).

Esquerita is one of the most original, colorful, and mysterious figures in rock & roll, a pianist and singer whose look and style most likely influenced Little Richard's. Little is known of Esquerita's life, and the veracity of some of his claims is hard to establish. Still, there is no denying that he was among, if not the first to combine a pumping piano style, falsetto screams and whoops, and racy lyrics into some very wild early rock & roll records. Visually as well, it would seem that Esquerita originated the flamboyant mannerisms and piled-high pompadour later adopted by Little Richard, who was still recording gospel records when his and Esquerita's paths first crossed. Among his releases—all of which have become highly valued collector's items—were "Oh Baby," "Rockin' the Joint," "I Need You," "Batty over Hattie," and "Esquerita Voola." He wrote Jim Lowe's 1956 #1 hit "The Green Door," but Esquerita himself never even made the Top 100 singles chart. Esquerita eventually moved to New York City, where he performed on occasion. He died of AIDS.

David Essex
Born David Albert Cook, July 23, 1947, London, England
1973—*Rock On* (Columbia)   1974—*David Essex* 1975—*All the Fun of the Fair*   1976—*Out on the Street*   1979—*Imperial Wizard* (Mercury)   1980— *Hot Love*   1981—*Be-Bop the Future.*

In the mid-Seventies English pop star David Essex inspired teenybopper hysteria in his homeland. While he was able to overcome that image there and establish himself as an actor while continuing to chart singles, here in America, he is best known for his 1974 gold single, "Rock On."

Essex grew up in London's East End, and at 14 he started playing the drums with a succession of amateur bands; by the time he graduated from high school he had become a lead singer. In the late Sixties theater columnist Derek Bowman put Essex through voice and dance training and then helped him land a role in the London production of *The Fantasticks*. He moved on to rave reviews as Jesus Christ in *Godspell*, which opened in November 1971 in London. Soon he was a teen pop idol. Essex had a hand in writing most of his U.K. hits ("Lamplight," "Gonna Make You a Star," "Hold Me Close," and "Rock On"). Most were produced by former commercial jingles writer Jeff Wayne.

In late 1974 Essex toured Britain, where young fans greeted him with hysteria. Essex made two films based on the rags-to-riches-to-rags theme of rock stardom: *That'll Be the Day* (1973), in which he costarred with Ringo Starr and Keith Moon, and *Stardust* (1975), in which he shared billing with Starr and Dave Edmunds. He sang Paul McCartney's "Yesterday" in *All This and World War II*, but was forced to turn down a role in the Who's *Tommy* because of shooting conflicts with *Stardust*. None of these films had much impact in the U.S., but "Rock On" garnered a Grammy nomination.

His reputation as a teenybopper singer proved unshakable in the late Seventies despite attempts to attract a more mature audience (e.g., *Out on the Street*). He played Che Guevara in the British stage production of *Evita* in 1978 and has since had several more hit singles in Britain. He starred in the film *Silver Dream Machine*, appeared in *Childe Byron*, and starred in the musical *Mutiny*, based on *Mutiny on the Bounty*. Among his U.K. Top Ten hits are "Rollin' Stone" (1975), "Oh What a Circus" (1978), "Silver Dream Machine (Part 1)" (1980), "A Winter's Tale" (1982), and "Tahiti" (1983). In 1989 "Rock On" was revived in current teen idol Michael Damian's #1 cover version.

Gloria Estefan
Born Gloria Fajardo, September 1, 1957, Havana, Cuba
With Miami Sound Machine, formed 1975, Miami, Fla.: (Estefan, voc.; Enrique "Kiki" Garcia, drums; Juan Marcos Avila, bass; Emilio Estefan Jr., kybds., perc.; Raul Murciano, sax, kybds.; Merci Murciano, voc.): 1982—(– Merci Murciano)   1984—*Eyes of Innocence* (Epic)   1985—*Primitive Love*   1987—*Let It Loose.*
Gloria Estefan solo: 1989—*Cuts Both Ways* (Epic) 1991—*Into the Light*   1992—*Greatest Hits*   1993— *Mi Tierra*   1994—*Hold Me, Thrill Me, Kiss Me.*

Gloria Estefan

Gloria Estefan rose out of Miami's Cuban community to become a top-selling international pop star, first with the dance band Miami Sound Machine and then with her own ballads. She moved to Miami in 1959 when her father, a bodyguard to Cuban president Fulgencio Batista, fled the revolution. She spent her early life nursing her father, who was diagnosed with multiple sclerosis after serving in Vietnam; she sang for hours in her bedroom to release her emotions.

In October 1975 Gloria Fajardo and her cousin Merci Murciano auditioned for keyboardist Emilio Estefan's wedding band, the Miami Latin Boys. They passed, and the rechristened Miami Sound Machine became one of the most popular groups in Miami, playing a mix of disco-pop and salsa. (Merci left the band in a dispute in 1982.) In 1978 Emilio and Gloria married, and the following year Miami Sound Machine released the first of several Spanish-language albums for CBS's Hispanic label. They became popular in Latin markets in the U.S. and overseas, but the band didn't cross over until Estefan sang in English on *Eyes of Innocence;* in 1984 "Dr. Beat" became a top dance hit in Europe.

In 1985 Miami Sound Machine released its first all-English album. *Primitive Love* (#21, 1985) went double platinum, with three Top Ten hits: "Conga" (#10, 1986), "Bad Boy" (#8, 1986), and "Words Get in the Way" (#5, 1986). Most of the songs were written, arranged, and performed by "the Three Jerks," Joe Galdo, Rafael Vigil, and Lawrence Dermer. At this point Miami Sound Machine became two bands: the studio group and the touring band, which included original members Kiki Garcia and Marcos Avila. Gloria was the common denominator. (Emilio had moved from keyboards to management.)

The band was billed as Gloria Estefan and the Miami Sound Machine on their triple-platinum *Let It Loose* (#6, 1987), which included the hits "Rhythm Is Gonna Get You" (#5, 1987), "Can't Stay Away from You" (#6, 1988), "Anything for You" (#1, 1988), and "1-2-3" (#3, 1988). It was Estefan's last record with the Miami Sound Machine; remaining original member Garcia left after the band's 1988 tour. She wrote most of the lyrics and some of the music on her solo debut, *Cuts Both Ways* (#8, 1989), which yielded Estefan's second #1 hit, "Don't Wanna Lose You" (1989), as well as "Here We Are" (#6, 1989).

On March 20, 1990, while traveling between shows on a snowy Pennsylvania highway, Estefan's tour bus was hit by a tractor-trailer. Her husband and son were slightly injured, but one of Estefan's vertebrae was broken. She recovered from surgery that included inserting eight-inch metal rods in her back. In 1991 her song about the accident, "Coming Out of the Dark," went #1; the platinum *Into the Light* (#5) also yielded the hits "Can't Forget You" (#43, 1991) and "Live for Loving You" (#22, 1991), which were especially popular on adult-contemporary radio formats. In 1993 Estefan paid tribute to her Latin roots with her first solo all-Spanish album, *Mi Tierra* (#27), which features cameos from such stars of Cuban music as Nestor Torres, Luis Enrique, Israel (Cachao) Lopez, Paquito D'Rivera, Arturo Sandoval, and Tito Puente. In 1994 *Hold Me, Thrill Me, Kiss Me* yielded the #13 hit single "Turn the Beat Around."

Sleepy John Estes

Born January 25, 1903, Ripley, Tennessee; died June 5, 1977, Brownsville, Tennessee
1963—*The Legend of Sleepy John Estes* (Delmark) 1967—*1929–40* (Folkways) 1974—*Down South Blues, 1935–1940* (MCA).

An important first-generation bluesman, Sleepy John Estes lost the sight of one eye as a child and became completely blind by 1950. When Estes was 12 his sharecropper father gave him his first guitar. By the time he was 20 he was playing local house parties. Shortly thereafter he moved to Memphis, where he performed on Beale Street with mandolinist Yank Rachell. He supported himself by working the late shift at a trainyard, where his tendency to doze off (later discovered to be a result of blood-pressure problems) earned him his nickname. In the Thirties Estes moved to Chicago with harmonica player Hammie Nixon. Over the next few years he worked as a street musician and occasionally as a medicine-show barker, hawking swamp root for Dr. Grimm's Traveling Menagerie.

In 1941 Estes and Nixon recorded blues for Bluebird: "Someday, Baby" and "Drop Down, Mama." He subsequently returned to Brownsville, Tennessee, and remained an obscure performer until the late Fifties, when filmmaker Ralph Blumenthal (who was making a documentary on black migration to the North) rediscovered him. The new attention got Estes a contract with the Chicago-based Delmark label. By 1964 he had gone on his first European tour and appeared at the Newport Folk Festival. Estes' LP *Broke and Hungry* included a guest spot by guitarist Mike Bloomfield, and Estes later played and sang on Ry Cooder's LP *Boomer's Story*. Around the same time, Joy of Cooking had a minor pop hit with the Estes-penned "Going to Brownsville" (1971). Estes died of a stroke in 1977 while preparing to embark on a European tour.

Melissa Etheridge
Born May 29, 1961, Leavenworth, Kansas
1988—*Melissa Etheridge* (Island)   1989—*Brave and Crazy*   1992—*Never Enough*   1993—*Yes I Am*.

Melissa Etheridge's raw, raspy voice and gritty delivery have inspired comparisons to everyone from Kim Carnes to Janis Joplin to Bruce Springsteen. Her fervid, percussive guitar work drives the confrontational and often hard-bitten love songs that earned the singer/songwriter a solid core following encompassing fans of both alternative and album-oriented rock. She broke through to mass popularity with her 1994 album, *Yes I Am.*

A self-taught musician, Etheridge got her first guitar when she was eight and began writing songs shortly afterward. She started performing at 12, in a country group, and played in various bar bands through her teens. After attending Boston's Berklee College of Music, Etheridge moved to the Los Angeles area, where she performed in clubs. In 1987 Island Records founder Chris Blackwell spotted her and offered her a contract. Etheridge's first recording gig involved contributing songs to the soundtrack of a film called *Weeds.* Then, working with drummer Craig Krampf, who was eventually replaced by Fritz Lewak, and bassist Kevin McCormick (both Lewak and McCormick have remained in her band), the singer released her eponymous debut album in 1988. *Melissa Etheridge* spawned a pair of singles, "Bring Me Some Water" and "Like the Way I Do." Though neither entered the Top Forty, both were well-received by album-oriented rock radio. The album went gold, as did its successor, 1989's *Brave and Crazy.*

Melissa Etheridge

Etheridge's third LP, 1992's gold *Never Enough,* yielded the song "Ain't It Heavy," which failed to chart significantly but earned the singer a Grammy (on her fourth nomination) for Best Rock Vocal Performance, Female. In 1993 Etheridge publicly declared that she was a lesbian; that same year, she released a fourth album, the triple-platinum *Yes I Am* (#16). That album produced several hits, including "Come to My Window" (#25, 1994), "I'm the Only One" (#11, 1994), and "If I Wanted To" b/w "Like the Way I Do" (#16, 1995).

Eurythmics
Formed 1980, London, England
Annie Lennox (b. Dec. 25, 1954, Aberdeen, Scotland), voc., flute; Dave Stewart (b. David A. Stewart, Sep. 9, 1952, Sunderland, Eng.), gtr., kybds.
1981—*In the Garden* (RCA, U.K.)   1983—*Sweet Dreams (Are Made of This)* (RCA); *Touch*   1984—*1984: For the Love of Big Brother* soundtrack   1985—*Be Yourself Tonight*   1986—*Revenge*   1987—*Savage*   1989—*We Too Are One* (Arista)   1991—*Greatest Hits*   1993—*Live 1983–1989*.
Dave Stewart solo: 1990—*Lily Was Here* soundtrack (Arista); *Dave Stewart and the Spiritual Cowboys*   1995—*Greetings from the Gutter* (EastWest)
Annie Lennox solo: 1992—*Diva* (Arista)   1995—*Medusa*.

The Eurythmics were perhaps the greatest of the early-Eighties British synth-pop bands, mixing a cynically business- and image-conscious approach with a sometimes soulful, mournful sound. Although Dave Stewart's studio wizardry provided the band's foundation, Annie Lennox's theatrical appearance and beautiful, icy wail ultimately were the duo's calling cards.

Lennox grew up in Aberdeen, Scotland, the only daughter of a bagpipe-playing shipyard worker. Her piano- and flute-playing skills won her a scholarship to the Royal Academy of Music in London, but she quit on the eve of finals, disgusted with the school's pretensions. She spent three years working odd jobs in London and playing with a folk-rock band, a jazz-rock group, and a cabaret duo. A friend introduced her to Dave Stewart.

Stewart came from an upper-middle-class family in Northern England. By the early Seventies his band Long-dancer was signed to Elton John's Rocket Records, but it never accomplished anything. He then played in a variety of groups, which ranged from soul to medieval music. When he met Lennox he was writing music with a recluse named Peet Coombes.

Lennox and Stewart immediately began a musical and romantic partnership. With Coombes they formed a band called Catch, which shortly became the Tourists. The Tourists' three albums (*The Tourists*, 1979; *Reality Effect*, 1979; *Luminous Basement*, 1980) mixed folk, psychedelia, and new wave. A cover of the Dusty Springfield hit "I Only Want to Be with You" was a big hit in England (#4, 1979) but barely made it into the U.S. Hot 100 (#83, 1980).

When the band disintegrated in late 1980, so did Lennox and Stewart's romance. They continued to work together, however, and named their partnership after Eurythmics, a system of music instruction developed in the 1890s that emphasizes physical response. Their debut was recorded in Germany and featured Blondie drummer Clem Burke, members of Can and DAF, and Marcus Stockhausen, son of the avant-garde composer. Despite good reviews, it was weakly supported by their label.

Lennox and Stewart were committed to making the Eurythmics a solid business and artistic venture, however. In a makeshift studio that Stewart set up, they recorded *Sweet Dreams (Are Made of This)* (#15, 1983), using an eight-track recorder and synthesizers. Though the first British single, "Love Is a Stranger," attracted some attention in clubs, it was the title track (#1) that propelled the band to stardom.

As the singer for the Tourists, Lennox was a platinum blonde often called the British Blondie. Sick of that dolly image, Lennox wore an orange crewcut and a man's suit in the Eurythmics' early work. When the band performed at the 1984 Grammys, she dressed like Elvis. In the video for "Who's That Girl?" she plays a chanteuse who leaves a club with her butch alter ego; at the end, she-Annie kisses he-Annie.

Touch (#7, 1983) yielded "Here Comes the Rain Again" (#4, 1984), but their next release, the soundtrack for *1984* (the film based on George Orwell's novel), was a disappointment. The film's director complained on a televised awards show that he had been forced to use the band's music, and the single "Sexcrime (Nineteen Eighty-Four)" was widely misinterpreted. Lennox suffered another public humiliation when she married a Hare Krishna and divorced him a year later. But *Be Yourself Tonight* (#9, 1985) returned the band to the public grace, showcasing Lennox's soulful vocals in a duet with Aretha Franklin, "Sisters Are Doin' It for Themselves" (#18, 1985). The album also yielded the hit single "Would I Lie to You" (#5, 1985). On *Revenge* (#12, 1986), the Eurythmics went for an arena-rock sound and produced their last Top Twenty single, "Missionary Man" (#14, 1986).

In 1987 Stewart married singer Siobhan Fahey, formerly of Bananarama and more recently in Shakespear's Sister. Many critics considered the Eurythmics to have run out of steam on *We Too Are One* (#34, 1989), so it was not surprising when Lennox announced that she was taking a couple years off from music to work for a homeless charity. She had delivered a stillborn baby in 1988 and wanted to devote time to her family (she is married to filmmaker Uri Fruchtman, with whom she's since had two children). In 1992 she released *Diva* (#23, 1992), a double-platinum-selling solo album that received three Grammy nominations. *Medusa* (#11, 1995) is a collection of covers. Stewart, meanwhile, had already released one soundtrack album, *Lily Was Here*, and put together the band Spiritual Cowboys, which included drummer Martin Chambers (Pretenders). He has also produced records for Daryl Hall, Tom Petty, Mick Jagger, and Bob Dylan. In 1995 Stewart released his first real solo album, *Greetings from the Gutter*, a modern Ziggy Stardust–like opus with a funky backing band (Bootsy Collins is on bass).

Betty Everett

Born November 23, 1939, Greenwood, Mississippi 1964—*Delicious Together* (with Jerry Butler) (Vee-Jay) 1974—*Love Rhymes* (Fantasy); *There'll Come a Time* (MCA) 1975—*Happy Endings* (Fantasy) 1976—*It's in His Kiss* (DJM).

Soul vocalist Betty Everett had a decade's worth of hits in the Sixties and Seventies. She played piano and sang in church as a child before moving with her family to Chicago at age 17. Everett's career peaked with the pop novelty "The Shoop Shoop Song (It's in His Kiss)" (#6, 1964) and a duet with Jerry Butler, "Let It Be Me" (#5, 1964), the Everly Brothers hit. Lesser hits included

"You're No Good," "I Can't Hear You," and "Getting Mighty Crowded." A minor 1964 hit, "Smile," was a duet with Jerry Butler.

Vee Jay's mid-Sixties collapse brought her to a change in labels. After a hitless tenure with ABC-Paramount, Everett made a modest 1969 comeback on Uni with "There'll Come a Time," "I Can't Say No to You," and "It's Been a Long Time." By 1970 she was recording for Fantasy ("I Got to Tell Somebody," 1971). Everett achieved respectable soul sales over the next couple of years with albums like *Love Rhymes* and *Happy Endings*. By then she was taking advantage of her prestigious standing in Europe with regular continental tours.

Everly Brothers

Don Everly (b. Feb. 1, 1937, Brownie, Ky.), gtr., voc.; Phil Everly (b. Jan. 19, 1939, Brownie, Ky.), gtr., voc. 1958—The Everly Brothers (Cadence); Songs Our Daddy Taught Us 1960—The Fabulous Style of the Everly Brothers; It's Everly Time (Warner Bros.); A Date with the Everly Brothers 1963—Sing Great Country Hits 1964—The Very Best of the Everly Brothers 1967—The Everly Brothers Sing 1968— Roots 1972—Stories We Could Tell (RCA) 1973— Pass the Chicken and Listen 1984—Reunion Concert (Passport); EB 84 (Mercury) 1985—Cadence Classics (Their 20 Greatest Hits) (Rhino); All They Had to Do Is Dream 1988—Some Hearts (Mercury) 1990—All-Time Greatest Hits (Curb); The Best of the Everly Brothers: Rare Solo Classics 1994—Walk Right Back: The Everly Brothers on Warner Bros., 1960–63 (Warner Bros.); The Mercury Years (Mercury); Heartaches and Harmonies (Rhino).
Don Everly solo: 1970—Don Everly (Ode) 1974— Sunset Towers 1976—Brother Juke Box (Hickory). Phil Everly solo: 1973—Star Spangled Springer (RCA) 1975—Phil's Diner (Pye) 1976—Mystic Line 1979—Phil Everly (Elektra).

The Everly Brothers are the most important vocal duo in rock. The enduring influence of the brothers' close, understated, yet expressive harmonies is evident in the work of such British Invasion bands as the Beatles and the Hollies and folk-oriented acts, such as Simon and Garfunkel, not to mention countless solo artists, among them Dave Edmunds, Gram Parsons, Emmylou Harris, and Linda Ronstadt. Most of the Everlys' hit singles, which merged Nashville's clean instrumental country style with innocuous teenage themes, cut a course to the right of contemporary country-rock hybrids like rockabilly. Their indisputable mastery is revealed in their ballads, among them "Let It Be Me."

They were the children of Midwestern country stars Ike and Margaret Everly. They toured with their parents around the South and Midwest and performed on the family radio show (a taped sample of which appears on *Roots*) throughout their childhoods. In the summer of 1955, still teenagers, they left for Nashville, where they were soon hired by Roy Acuff's publishing company as songwriters. Don had a minor success when his "Thou Shalt Not Steal" became a hit for Kitty Wells. The brothers also recorded a country single entitled "Keep On Loving Me" for Columbia before signing with Cadence in 1957. Songwriters Felice and Boudleaux Bryant gave them "Bye Bye Love," which 30 acts had previously rejected. It was an international hit (#2 U.S., 1957), topped the country chart, and established an Everlys style with close country harmonies over a rocking beat.

The Everlys toured internationally with a small combo over the next few years, sporting matching suits and haircuts and leaving fans to identify each brother by the color of his hair (Don's was darker). Their heyday lasted through 1962, by which time they were at Warner Bros., with cumulative record sales of $35 million. In their three years with Cadence (which they left in a dispute over royalties) they averaged a Top Ten hit every four months, including four #1 hits: "Wake Up Little Susie," "All I Have to Do Is Dream," "Cathy's Clown," and "Bird Dog."

Some of their most successful records—"Till I Kissed You" (#4, 1959), "When Will I Be Loved" (#8, 1960)—were written by Don or Phil Everly. Their best-selling single, "Cathy's Clown" (sales of which exceeded two million), came after their switch to Warner Bros., but their success with the new label was short-lived. In June 1962 their string of hits ended with "That's Old-Fashioned" (#9, 1962). They remained major stars in England, but their careers slowed markedly in the U.S. despite continued releases on Warner Bros. ("Bowling Green," #40, 1967) and, beginning in 1972, RCA (where they moved shortly after hosting a summer TV series on CBS). Their latter-day backup band was led by keyboardist Warren Zevon and included future Los Angeles studio guitarist Waddy Wachtel.

By then the brothers' personal lives had gone through serious upheavals. Both were addicted to speed for a while, and Don was hospitalized for a nervous breakdown. Their relationship became increasingly acrimonious until it blew up at the John Wayne Theater at Knott's Berry Farm in Buena Park, California, on July 14, 1973. Phil smashed his guitar and stalked off stage, leaving Don to announce the duo's obvious breakup. Subsequent solo attempts by both were largely unsuccessful.

Nineteen eighty-three returned the Everlys to the spotlight. Phil's duet with Cliff Richard, "She Means Nothing to Me," reached the British Top Ten in the spring. That September the brothers reunited onstage at London's Royal Albert Hall for a triumphant concert that was chronicled on *Reunion Concert* and in a video documentary that was widely aired. In 1984 they released *EB 84* (#38, 1984), produced by longtime fan Dave Edmunds. "On the Wings of a Nightingale," penned by another admirer, Paul McCartney (who'd mentioned the pair in his "Let 'Em In"), went to #50 in the U.S. and #41 in England. Edmunds also produced 1986's *Born Yesterday,* which came out the same month the duo was inducted into the Rock and Roll Hall of Fame. The Everlys were without a label in the mid-Nineties but still performing together live. Don Everly's daughter Erin was briefly married to singer Axl Rose of Guns n' Roses.

Everything But the Girl

Formed 1981, England
Tracey Thorn (b. Sep. 26, 1962, Hertfordshire, Eng.), voc.; Ben Watt (b. Dec. 6, 1962, London, Eng.), gtr., kybds.
1984—*Eden* (Blanco y Negro); *Everything But the Girl* 1985—*Love Not Money* 1986—*Baby, the Stars Shine Bright* 1988—*Idlewild* 1990—*The Language of Life* (Atlantic) 1991—*Worldwide* 1992—*Acoustic* 1994—*Amplified Heart.*

Everything But the Girl makes melodic, literate, and scrupulously crafted pop that often draws on prerock traditions, incorporating elements of jazz, theatrical music, and early-Sixties rock & roll.

Watt (who is the chief composer) and vocalist Thorn first met at Hull University. Before joining with Watt, Thorn made two albums as a member of the Marine Girls. In 1982 the duo (who took their name from a local store whose slogan claimed they could supply "everything but the girl") recorded a version of Cole Porter's "Night and Day." Thorn then cut a minialbum, *A Distant Shore,* and Watt released his, *North Marine Drive.*

Everything But the Girl first charted in Britain with "Each and Everyone" (#28 U.K., 1984); a cover of "I Don't Want to Talk About It" by Danny Whitten (Crazy Horse guitarist who died in 1972) became their biggest hit (#3 U.K.) in 1988.

Signing with Atlantic, Everything But the Girl went for the full L.A. studio treatment on 1990's *The Language of Life.* With Tommy LiPuma producing, a host of first-call session musicians, and a guest appearance by jazz saxophonist Stan Getz, *The Language of Life* made the U.S. charts (#77, 1990) and a popular single, "Driving," was culled from it.

Despite its accomplishments, the group found itself stranded by a sound that was too light for rock airplay yet too sophisticated for "lite" airplay. Neither the followup album, *Worldwide,* nor *Acoustic* (an "unplugged" project that concentrated on covers, including Thorn's rendition of Springsteen's "Tougher Than the Rest") had the commercial impact of *Language of Life. Amplified Heart* (1994) also received little airplay.

Exposé

Formed 1986, Miami, Florida
Jeanette Jurado (b. Nov. 14, 1966, Los Angeles, Calif.), voc.; Ann Curless (b. Oct. 7, 1965, New York City, N.Y.), voc.; Gioia Carmen Bruno (b. Italy, June 11, 1965), voc.
1987—*Exposure* (Arista) 1989—*What You Don't Know* 1992—(– Bruno; + Kelly Moneymaker [b. June 4, 1965, Fairbanks, Alaska], voc.) *Exposé.*

Exposé began as a project of Miami pop svengali Lewis Martinee. But by their third album, the three women were trying to assert themselves as artists. Martinee wrote and recorded the single "Point of No Return" with Ale Lorenzo, Laurie Miller, and Sandee Casanas, whom he dubbed Exposé in 1985. The song became a dance hit, followed by 1986's "Exposed to Love," and the group began work on an album. Before its completion, Martinee replaced all three members—reports conflict about whether the women quit or were fired (perhaps, it has been suggested, for not looking the part). Martinee hired Jeanette Jurado, Ann Curless, and Gioia Carmen Bruno to be the new Exposé.

With its Latin-tinged dance grooves, the multiplatinum *Exposure* (#16, 1987) broke the Beatles' record for most Top Ten hits from a debut album with "Come Go with Me" (#5 pop, #14 R&B, 1987), a rerecorded "Point of No Return" (#5, 1987), "Let Me Be the One" (#7 pop, #29 R&B, 1987), and the ballad "Seasons Change" (#1 pop, #27 R&B, 1987). The gold *What You Don't Know* (#33, 1989) followed this success with the singles "What You Don't Know" (#8, 1989), "Tell Me Why" (#9, 1989), "When I Looked at Him" (#10, 1989), and "Your Baby Never Looked Good in Blue" (#17, 1990).

On their third album, Exposé replaced Bruno, who was having throat problems, with the L.A.-based Kelly Moneymaker, who had performed with Todd Rundgren and Wayne Newton. The trio branched away from Martinee on *Exposé,* using four songs written by hitmaker Diane Warren (including "As Long As I Can Dream," written with Roy Orbison) and working with producers Steve Thompson and Michael Barbiero (Madonna, Guns n' Roses) on several tracks. That album includes the hit "I'll Never Get Over You (Getting Over Me)" (#8, 1993).

Extreme

Formed 1985, Boston, Massachusetts
Pat Badger (b. July 22, 1967, Boston), bass; Nuno Bettencourt (b. Sep. 20, 1966, Azores, Portugal), gtr.; Gary Cherone (b. July 26, 1961, Malden, Mass.), voc.; Paul Geary (b. July 24, 1961, Medford, Mass.), drums.
1989—*Extreme* (A&M) 1990—*Extreme II: Pornograffitti* 1992—*III Sides to Every Story* 1995—*Waiting for the Punchline.*

Extreme's metal funk is more in line with fellow Bostonians Aerosmith, and Nuno Bettencourt is considered one of the premier hard-rock guitarists, but the group is best known for the acoustic ballad "More Than Words" (#1, 1991). That uncharacteristically soft single made their second album, *Pornograffitti* (#10, 1990), a Top Ten, double-platinum hit.

Gary Cherone and Paul Geary were part of the Dream, an early-Eighties Boston band. When they broke up, Cherone began writing songs with Bettencourt, a Portuguese-born guitarist who had lived in Boston since he was four. Bettencourt brought in Badger, and the new band began to build a strong local following. A&M Records signed the band in 1987; in 1989 they released their self-titled debut (#80).

That album stalled at the low end of the Hot 100, and *Pornograffitti* threatened to do the same until "More Than Words" attracted a mainstream audience. The band kept its metal credentials by touring with ZZ Top, while a second ballad, "Hole Hearted" (#4, 1991), returned the band to the Top Ten. Seemingly unwilling to give up either style, the band released *III Sides* (#10, 1992), an ambitious project divided into three suites: the aggressive "Yours," the introspective "Mine," and a 22-minute orchestral piece, "The Truth." The album, particularly the final three songs, recorded at Abbey Road Studios with a 70-piece orchestra, demonstrated the band's eclecticism and willingess to experiment.

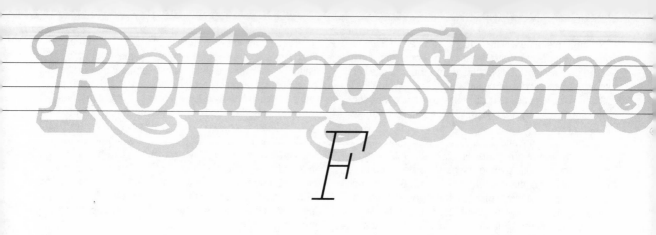

Fabian

Born Fabiano Forte, February 6, 1943, Philadelphia, Pennsylvania
1959—*Hold That Tiger!* (Chancellor); *Fabulous Fabian* N.A.—*16 Greatest Hits* (ABC); *The Very Best of Fabian* (United Artists).

Fabian was marketed alongside several other late-Fifties Philadelphia teen idols, including Frankie Avalon and Bobby Rydell. From 1959 to 1960 his Top Ten hits included "Turn Me Loose" (#9, 1959), his signature song, "Tiger" (#3, 1959), and an Elvis Presley imitation, "Hound Dog Man" (#9, 1959), the theme from his first feature film in 1959.

He then turned to acting. In 1960 he starred with John Wayne in *North to Alaska* and in 1966 was featured in *Fireball 500.* Since the early Seventies, Fabian has occasionally appeared on TV sitcoms such as *Laverne and Shirley* and *Blossom.* In 1974, before Fifties acts were in great demand on the oldies circuit, Fabian posed nude for a woman's magazine, a move that he publicly regretted; he claimed he looked "fat and stupid." In 1977 he was involved in a program under the auspices of California governor Jerry Brown to encourage citizen volunteers to work with mental patients.

Besides touring on his own, Fabian tours as part of a package, the Golden Boys (or the Boys of Bandstand) with Avalon and Rydell. The 1980 film *The Idolmaker* is said to have been based on Fabian's first manager, Bob Marcucci, who discovered the teenager and manufactured him in the image of Ricky Nelson. He is also a television producer.

The Fabulous Thunderbirds

Formed 1974, Austin, Texas
Jimmie Vaughan (b. Mar. 20, 1951, Dallas, Tex.), gtr.; Kim Wilson (b. Jan. 6, 1951, Detroit, Mich.), voc., harmonica; Keith Ferguson (b. July 23, 1946, Houston, Tex.), bass; Mike Buck (b. June 1, 1952), drums.
1979—*The Fabulous Thunderbirds* (Takoma)
1980—(– Buck; + Fran Christina [b. Feb. 1, 1951, Westerly, R.I.], drums) *What's the Word?* (Chrysalis)
1981—*Butt Rockin'* 1982—*T-Bird Rhythm* 1986—(– Ferguson; + Preston Hubbard [b. Mar. 15, 1953, Providence, R.I.], bass) *Tuff Enuff* (Columbia)
1987—*Hot Number* (Epic) 1989—*Powerful Stuff* 1990—(– Vaughan; + Michael "Duke" Robillard, gtr.; + Doug "the Kid" Bangham, gtr.) 1991—*Walk That Walk, Talk That Talk; The Essential Fabulous Thunderbirds Collection* (Chrysalis).
The Vaughan Brothers (Jimmie Vaughan; Stevie Ray Vaughan): 1990—*Family Style* (Epic).
Kim Wilson solo: 1993—*Tigerman* (Antone's)
1994—*That's Life.*

Blues stalwarts the Fabulous Thunderbirds hit their commercial peak in the mid-Eighties. Known for their relentless touring, its members were archetypal roots musicians, lean and energetic in style.

Starting in 1963, guitarist Jimmie Vaughan, older brother of Stevie Ray Vaughan, played Hendrix and Clapton covers in Dallas bands such as the Swinging Pendulums and the Chessmen before founding the Fabulous Thunderbirds. With vocalist Lou Ann Barton and drummer Otis Lewis departing shortly after the band's 1974 beginning, Vaughan solidified the lineup with bassist Keith Ferguson (who'd declined an offer to join ZZ Top), drummer Mike Buck, and singer/harmonica player Kim Wilson, with Wilson becoming chief songwriter.

With a self-titled debut blueprinting their no-frills approach, the Fabulous Thunderbirds went on to gain overseas exposure and a new-wave following by opening for Rockpile in 1980 (Rockpile bassist Nick Lowe produced the T-Birds' fourth album). Replacing Buck with Roomful of Blues drummer Fran Christina, they continued live work, but spent the next four years without a record contract. In 1986 came their big break: Signed to Columbia, the Fabulous Thunderbirds opened shows for the Rolling Stones and Santana, and with the Top Ten "Tuff Enuff" (produced by Dave Edmunds, Lowe's former partner in Rockpile), gained a mainstream audience. *Hot Number* (#49, 1987) also fared well; by then, however, only Vaughan and Wilson remained of the original members.

In 1990 Vaughan left to record with his brother, effectively ending the original Thunderbirds. With Wilson at the helm, a reconstituted outfit carried on, featuring New England–based guitarists Duke Robillard, a jazz and blues player who'd founded Roomful of Blues, and the more rock-oriented Kid Bangham. The group finally fizzled, with Kim Wilson going solo. His albums *Tiger Man* (1993) and *That's Life* (1994) were very much in the T-Birds' vein.

Donald Fagen: See Steely Dan

Fairport Convention/Fairport

Formed 1967, London, England
Judy Dyble, piano, voc.; Richard Thompson (b. Apr. 3, 1949, London), gtr., voc.; Simon Nicol (b. London), gtr., banjo, dulcimer, bass, viola, voc.; Ashley "Tyger" Hutchings (b. Jan. 1945, London), bass, voc., gtr.; Martin Lamble (b. 1950, Eng.; d. Aug. 1969, London), drums; Iain Matthews (b. Ian Matthew MacDonald, June 1946, Lincolnshire, Eng.), voc., perc., gtr.
1968—*Fairport Convention* (Polydor) (– Dyble; + Sandy Denny [b. Jan. 6, 1947, London; d. Apr. 21, 1978, London], gtr., voc., kybds.); *What We Did on Our Holidays* (Island) (– Matthews); *Heyday* 1969—(– Lamble; + Dave Swarbrick [b. Apr. 5, 1947, London], voc., violin, mandolin) *Unhalfbricking* (+ Dave Mattacks [b. 1948, London], drums, voc., kybds.); *Liege and Lief* (– Denny; – Hutchings; + Dave Pegg [b. Nov. 2, 1947, Eng.], gtr., viola, voc.) 1970—*Full House* 1971—*Angel Delight* (A&M) (– Thompson; – Nicol; + Roger Hill [b. Eng.], gtr., mandolin) 1972—*Babbacombe Lee* (– Hill; – Mattacks; + Tom Farnell, drums; + David Rea, gtr.; – Farnell; – Rea; + Trevor Lucas [b. Dec. 25, 1943, Bungaree, Austral.; d. Feb. 4, 1989, Sydney, Austral.], gtr.; + Jerry Donahue [b. Sep. 24, 1946, New York City, N.Y.], gtr., voc.; + Mattacks); *The History of Fairport Convention* (Island) 1973—*Rosie* 1974—*Nine* (A&M) (+ Denny); *Live Convention (A Moveable Feast)* (Island) (– Mattacks; + Paul Warren, drums; – Warren; + Bruce Rowland [b. Eng.], drums) 1975—*Rising for the Moon* 1976—(– Denny; – Lucas; – Donahue; – Mattacks) *Fairport Chronicles* (A&M); *Live at the L.A. Troubadour; Gottle o' Geer* 1985—(Group re-forms: Pegg; Nicol; Mattacks; + Martin Allcock, bass, gtr., bouzouki; + Ric Sanders, electric violin) 1986—*Gladys' Leap* (Varrick) 1987—*Expletive Delighted; In Real Time* (Island) 1989—*Red & Gold* (Rough Trade) 1995—*Jewel in the Crown* (Green Linnet).

Fairport Convention seeded Britain's folk-rock movement, and most British musicians who've tried to play Celtic folk material on modern instruments have some connection with Fairport or its many offshoots. The group's repertoire included traditional British songs rearranged for electric instruments, songs by Bob Dylan and other current songwriters, and originals by Richard Thompson and Iain Matthews (both founders) and Sandy Denny. As the Bunch, Fairport and friends also recorded an album of Fifties and Sixties rock classics entitled *Rock On*. Their eclecticism inspired their imitators and descendants.

The original Fairport Convention—at first called the Ethnic Shuffle Orchestra—included folk-club veterans who were also Byrds fans and was named after Simon Nicol's house in Muswell Hill, London. From the beginning, the lineup was unstable. Judy Dyble left in 1968 to form Trader Horne and later Penguin Dust; her replacement, Sandy Denny, had sung with the Strawbs before their first album. Matthews left after *What We Did on Our Holidays* (in the U.S., *Fairport Convention*) to form the country-pop band Matthews Southern Comfort ("Woodstock," 1971) and to record solo and with the short-lived Plainsong [see Iain Matthews entry]. Lamble was killed in an equipment-van crash right before *Unhalfbricking*'s release.

Fairport had its first European hit with *Unhalfbricking*'s "Si Tu Dois Partir," a French translation of Dylan's "If You Gotta Go, Go Now." Denny, whose song "Who Knows Where the Time Goes" was covered by Judy Collins, left to form Fotheringay with husband Trevor Lucas and Jerry Donahue [see Sandy Denny entry]; in 1973 the three rejoined Fairport. *A Moveable Feast* was a live set from Denny's second stint with the band.

By then Thompson had started a solo career [see entry], and fiddler Dave Swarbrick had joined Fairport. Swarbrick led the group in its later years, and it toured internationally. By 1976 the band had dropped "Convention" from its name; and by 1979 Fairport had given up, due to financial problems, constantly shifting lineup, and Swarbrick's hearing impairment. Pegg joined Jethro Tull; Swarbrick recorded solo albums. Nicol and Mattacks toured with Richard and Linda Thompson (who had sung with the Bunch as Linda Peters) in 1982. Mattacks became a respected session drummer (for, among others, Paul McCartney, Elton John, and Mark Knopfler); he appeared most recently on XTC's *Nonesuch* and played with Richard Thompson on a recent world tour.

Group members have reunited at various times, but because Fairport Convention has never been a financially lucrative proposition, each member has continued to hold down his "day job," with Pegg in Tull and running Woodworm Records and Studio, Mattacks doing sessions, and the other members working with other acts as well. Since renewing the band in the Eighties, the members have chosen not to include another female singer, feeling that Denny was "irreplaceable," although they do perform with guest singers sometimes. Ric Sanders' previous bands include Soft Machine, and he had done sessions with Jethro Tull and Gerry Rafferty, among others. Martin Allcock belonged to a number of other British bands.

Red & Gold is the new lineup's first album of new material; it includes a title song written by Ralph McTell. By then Allcock had joined Pegg in Jethro Tull. Most of Fairport's tangled career up until the Eighties is documented on *Fairport Chronicles*. Fairport (Mattacks, Pegg, Nicol, Allcock, and Sanders) toured the U.S. in summer 1994.

Andy Fairweather-Low: See Amen Corner

Adam Faith
Born Terry Nelhams, June 23, 1940, London, England
1974—*I Survive* (Warner Bros.).

A pop idol in pre-Beatlemania England, Adam Faith had over a dozen major hits there in the early Sixties. He formed a teenage skiffle group called the Worried Men

with fellow messenger boys at Rank Screen Services. By 1958 he was recording solo as Adam Faith. In 1959 he recorded "What Do You Want," which climbed to #1 and became Britain's best-selling record of 1960. More U.K. hits followed, among them: "Poor Me" (#1, 1960), "Someone Else's Baby" (#2, 1960), and "Lonely Pup" (#4, 1960).

Faith became interested in acting during the Sixties, appearing in *Beat Girl* (1962) and several other English films, as well as TV series like *Drumbeat* (1959) and *Budgie* in the early Seventies. In 1972, at the urging of David Courtney, the drummer from his backup band of the Sixties (another stalwart in that band was guitarist Russ Ballard, later of Argent), he eased back into music by becoming Leo Sayer's manager and producer (along with Courtney). He and Courtney also teamed up to produce Roger Daltrey's debut solo LP, *Daltrey*. Years later Sayer successfully sued him for withholding royalties and won 650,000 pounds.

The early Seventies also found Faith appearing in *Stardust* with David Essex and *McVicar* with Roger Daltrey. After recovering from a severe car accident in 1973, Faith released an unsuccessful comeback record, *I Survive*. In 1977 he produced a star-studded comeback LP, *Puttin' On the Style*, for British skiffle king Lonnie Donegan. He has since become a financial consultant (his advice column runs in a London daily), but has returned to show business, as an actor. His autobiography is entitled *Poor Me*.

Marianne Faithfull
Born December 29, 1946, London, England
1965—*Come My Way* (Decca)   1966—*Faithful Forever* (London)   1978—*Faithless* (NEMS)   1979—*Broken English* (Island)   1981—*Dangerous Acquaintances*   1983—*A Child's Adventure* 1987—*Strange Weather*   1990—*Blazing Away* 1994—*Faithfull: A Collection of Her Best*   1995—*A Secret Life*.

Marianne Faithfull first appeared on the British pop scene as the angel-faced, sweet-voiced singer of "As Tears Go By" (#22 U.S., #9 U.K.) in 1964, when she was 17. The song was written for her by Rolling Stones Mick Jagger and Keith Richards, and although she had three more hits independently of the Stones—"Come and Stay with Me" (#26 U.S., #4 U.K.), "This Little Bird" (#32 U.S., #6 U.K.), and "Summer Nights" (#24 U.S., #10 U.K.), all in 1965—she became better known as Jagger's girlfriend than as a singer.

Faithfull is the daughter of a London University lecturer in Renaissance studies and an Austrian baroness descended from Leopold von Sacher-Masoch (from whose name "masochism" is derived). She attended St. Joseph's Convent School in Reading until she was 17. At 18 she married London art dealer John Dunbar, through

Marianne Faithfull

whom she met Jagger. She and Dunbar were separated after the birth of their son, Nicholas, in 1965, and divorced in 1970.

During the late Sixties Faithfull became pregnant by Jagger (she miscarried) and was later heavily involved in drug use (she was hospitalized following an overdose on the Australian movie set of *Ned Kelly*, in which she was to costar with Jagger). Although she abandoned her recording career after 1966, she contributed lyrics (uncredited) to the Rolling Stones' "Sister Morphine." Her major activity after 1966 was acting: with Alain Delon in a 1968 French film, *The Girl on the Motorcycle*; in Chekhov's *Three Sisters* at the Royal Court Theatre, London, in 1969; and as Ophelia opposite Nicol Williamson in a 1970 film production of *Hamlet*.

Following her breakup with Jagger in 1970 and her widely publicized eight-month commitment to a hospital to cure her heroin addiction, Faithfull withdrew from public life, reappearing only briefly in 1974 on a David Bowie television special. In 1977 she recorded her first album in over ten years, and although it received little notice, it led to her signing with Island Records in 1979. Her Island debut, *Broken English*—marked by stark instrumentation, venomous lyrics, and Faithfull's raspy vocals—was barely recognizable as the work of the woman who sang "As Tears Go By." It was followed by several more critically acclaimed albums for Island. *Strange Weather* occasioned Faithfull's limited return to live performance; on *Blazing Away*, she was backed by Dr. John, Band member Garth Hudson, along with her guitarist and co-composer, Barry Reynolds. She also acted in the films *Turn of the Screw* (1992) and *Shopping* (1993), and onstage in a 1989 production of Kurt Weill's *Seven*

Deadly Sins in New York, Chicago, and Berlin, and in the Brecht-Weill *Threepenny Opera* in Dublin in 1991. Her autobiography, entitled *Faithfull* (cowritten with David Dalton), was published in 1994.

Faith No More

Formed 1982, San Francisco, California
Chuck Mosely, voc.; James "Jim" Martin (b. July 21, 1961, Oakland, Calif.), gtr.; Roddy Bottum (b. July 1, 1963, Los Angeles, Calif.), kybds.; Billy Gould (b. April 23, 1963, Los Angeles, Calif.), bass; Michael "Mike" Bordin (b. November 27, 1962, San Francisco), drums.
1985—*We Care a Lot* (Mordam)   1987—*Introduce Yourself* (Slash)   1988—(– Mosely)   1989—(+ Michael "Mike" Patton [b. Jan. 27, 1968, Eureka, Calif.], voc.) *The Real Thing*   1990—*You Fat Bastard: Live at Brixton Academy*   1992—*Angel Dust*   1993—*Songs to Make Love To* EP   1994—(– Martin; + Dean Menta, gtr.)   1995—*King for a Day, Fool for a Lifetime.*

Most fans who bought Faith No More's 1990 hit single "Epic" had no idea the group had been around for eight years and had begun life as a postpunk hardcore-thrash band. Bassist Billy Gould and keyboardist Roddy Bottum had both played on the Los Angeles punk-rock scene of the late Seventies, before moving to San Francisco to attend college. Through a classified ad placed by drummer Mike Bordin, they formed Faith No More, recruiting guitarist Jim Martin from a local thrash band with future Metallica bassist Cliff Burton. At club gigs they let audience members be vocalists; Chuck Mosely, who often wore a dress, was among the most frequent volunteers, and eventually joined the band (Courtney Love, later of Hole, was also a volunteer). "We Care a Lot"—a sardonic thrash-funk answer to "We Are the World"—got college-radio play, and some MTV play for its video, leading to a deal with Warner Bros.–distributed Slash Records. Mosely was kicked out after two albums and two European tours, for "unpredictable behavior."

With an album's worth of new music written, Faith No More auditioned new vocalists and quickly selected Mike Patton, from the bizarrely theatrical Mr. Bungle. Patton wrote lyrics to match Faith No More's new tunes for *The Real Thing* (#11, 1990), which sold over a million copies, thanks largely to "Epic" (#9, 1990), an anthemic mix of funk-rap verses and hard-rock choruses. On tour, Patton sometimes wore leisure suits or monster masks, while the band played surprising, but seemingly sincere, covers of Madonna's "Vogue," New Kids on the Block's "You Got It (the Right Stuff)," and the Commodores' easy-listening classic "Easy."

In 1991 Patton recorded an album with Mr. Bungle, and Faith No More contributed "The Perfect Crime" to the soundtrack of the film sequel *Bill & Ted's Bogus Journey,* in which Jim Martin had a bit part. *Angel Dust* (#10, 1992) failed to yield a hit single, while *Songs to Make Love To* included the band's covers of "Easy" and the Dead Kennedys' "Let's Lynch the Landlord." Martin left the group in January 1994. Trey Spruance from Mr. Bungle recorded all the guitar parts for *King for a Day, Fool For a Lifetime,* although Dean Menta officially joined the band.

Falco

Born Johann Holzel, February 19, 1957, Vienna, Austria
1982—*Einzelhaft* (A&M) 1984—*Junger Roemer* 1986—*Falco 3*; *Emotional* (Sire) 1988—*Wiener Blut* 1992—*The Remix Hit Collection*.

Falco stands as Austria's most successful international pop artist on the basis of two unlikely singles: 1983's "Der Kommissar," a driving technopop ditty on which he rapped in German, and the #1 camp classic "Rock Me Amadeus," from his 1986 album *Falco 3*.

Young Johann Holzel's parents had wanted him to become a doctor, but he dashed those hopes when, after graduating school, he moved to West Berlin and began singing in a jazz-rock outfit. Taking the moniker Falco from East German ski jumper Falko Weissflog, he returned to Vienna in the late Seventies, where he played bass guitar in a punk band called Drahdiwaberl before landing a contract as a solo artist.

While Falco's version of "Der Kommissar" was a dance-club favorite in the U.S., it was an English-language cover by After the Fire that became the hit, topping at #5 in 1983. Though best known for his cheekier material—and for prancing around dressed as a punk Mozart on MTV, in the popular video for "Rock Me Amadeus"—Falco has also addressed serious matters in his songs. "Jeanny," also from *Falco 3*, was a controversial tale of prostitution that narrowly escaped censorship in Germany, and "The Sound of Musik" took aim at Austria's president Kurt Waldheim. Despite these respectable efforts, his last two releases failed to break the Top 100.

The Fall

Formed 1977, Manchester, England
Mark E. Smith (b. Mark Edward Smith, Mar. 5, 1957, Manchester), voc., kybds., harmonica; Martin Bramah, gtr.; Una Baines, kybds.; Tony Friel, bass; Karl Burns, drums.
1978—(– Friel; – Baines; + Marc Riley, bass, gtr., kybds.; + Yvonne Pawlett, kybds.) 1979—*Live at the Witch Trials* (Step Forward, U.K.) (– Bramah; – Pawlett; – Burns; + Craig Scanlon [b. Dec. 7, 1960, Manchester], gtr.; + Stephen Patrick Hanley [b. May 20, 1959, Ire.], bass; + Mike Leigh, drums) 1979— *Dragnet* 1980—*Totale's Turns (It's Now or Never)* (Rough Trade, U.K.) (– Leigh; + Paul Hanley [b. Manchester], drums, gtr., kybds.); *Grotesque (After the Gramme)* 1981—*Slates* EP; *Early Years* (Step Forward, U.K.) (– Paul Hanley; + Karl Burns; *A Part of America Therein* (Cottage) (+ Paul Hanley) 1982—*Room to Live* (Kamera, U.K.); *Hex Enduction Hour* (– Riley) 1983—(+ Brix Smith [b. Laura Elise Smith, Calif.], gtr., voc.) *Perverted by Language* (Rough Trade, U.K.) 1984—*The Wonderful and Frightening World of . . .* (Beggars Banquet, U.K.); *Call for Escape Route* EP (– Paul Hanley; + Simon Rogers, kybds., bass) 1985—*Hip Priests and Kamerads* (Situation Two, U.K.) 1986—*The Fall* EP (Beggars Banquet); *This Nation's Saving Grace* (– Burns; + Simon Wolstencroft [b. Jan. 19, 1963, Altrincham, Eng.], drums); *Bend Sinister* (+ Marcia Schofield [b. 1963, Brooklyn, N.Y.], kybds.) 1987—*The Fall In: Palace of Swords Revisited* (Rough Trade, U.K.) 1988—*The Frenz Experiment* (Beggars Banquet); *I am Kurious Oranj* 1989— *Seminal Live* (– Brix Smith; – Rogers; + Martin Bramah) 1990—*Extricate* (Cog Sinister, U.K.); *458489 A-Sides* (Beggars Banquet); *458489 B-Sides* (– Schofield; + Dave Bush [b. June 4, 1959, Taplow, Eng.], kybds.) 1991—*Shiftwork* (Cog Sinister, U.K.) 1992—*Code: Selfish* (+ Burns) 1993—*The Infotainment Scan* (Matador).

Through ongoing personnel and label shifts, and with an audience that's international in scope yet cultish in size, the Fall has held fast to a dour, distinctive sound, becoming the longest-lived and most prolific band to emerge from England's late-Seventies punk-rock movement. Sole constant Mark E. Smith is a white-rap progenitor who delivers caustic commentary on British life in a distinctively accented, sneering sing-speech (sometimes turning his back on audiences to read handwritten lyric sheets). The Fall's music, rooted in rockabilly and skiffle, hinges on abrasive, twangy guitars and nagging, rackety rhythms.

Named after the Camus novel, the Fall followed the Buzzcocks out of the grimy Northern England industrial city of Manchester, recording *Live at the Witch Trials* in one day. By *Grotesque* and *Slates,* the Fall's scraggly dissonance had grown thicker and, at times, more bright and tuneful. The hooky 1981 single "Totally Wired" became something of a new-wave anthem.

On a 1983 tour Mark E. Smith met Brix Smith at a Chicago show; she married him and replaced Marc Riley as second guitarist (she also led her own band, the Adult Net), moving the Fall's sound in a poppier direction. Mark E. Smith, a frequent critic of clerical hypocrisy (going back to *Dragnet*'s "Spectre vs. Rector"), wrote a musical play about papal politics called *Hey! Luciani,* which was mounted in London in 1985–86; the Fall recorded the title song as a single.

The Frenz Experiment's faithful cover of the Kinks' "Victoria" was a hit single in the U.K. and got some video play on MTV in America; the disco-influenced "Hit the North" seemed to presage the imminent explosion of Manchester's "rave" scene (of which inveterate antitrendy Smith wanted no part). *I am Kurious Oranj,* based on a Smith fantasy about William of Orange, was the score for a ballet by avant-garde choreographer Michael Clark. Brix Smith dissolved her marriage to Mark E. Smith and left the Fall in 1990. New keyboardist Dave Bush pushed the group's sound toward dub-reggae and techno-dance styles.

Georgie Fame

Born Clive Powell, June 26, 1943, Lancashire, England
1965—*Yeh Yeh* (Imperial)   1966—*Get Away*
1968—*The Ballad of Bonnie and Clyde* (Epic)
1971—*Fame and Price* (with Alan Price) (Columbia).

Georgie Fame is best known in the U.S. for his 1968 novelty hit "The Ballad of Bonnie and Clyde," and as an R&B/jazz singer and keyboardist in Britain. Clive Powell played keyboards in Eddie Cochran's band during his last tour, before English impresario Larry Parnes steered him to a 1960 job with Billy Fury's band, the Blue Flames. Parnes also suggested the name change to Georgie Fame.

In 1962 Fame left Fury and took along the Blue Flames. By the mid-Sixties Fame was playing jazzy R&B; guitarist John McLaughlin was in the band for a short time. In late 1963 his expanded group (including Cream's Ginger Baker) released two instrumental singles followed by its influential 1964 set, *Rhythm and Blues at the Flamingo.*

In 1965 Fame had a #1 U.K. hit, "Yeh Yeh," which also slipped into the U.S. Top Thirty. He had another U.K. #1 in 1966 with "Get Away." When Fame disbanded the Blue Flames later that year, the lineup included future Jimi Hendrix Experience drummer Mitch Mitchell. Fame's first solo LP, *Sound Venture* (Columbia), was MOR jazz; the next year he played an Albert Hall concert with Count Basie. His ragtime novelty hit, 1968's "Bonnie and Clyde," hit #7 in the U.S. From 1971 to 1973 he teamed up with former Animals keyboardist Alan Price; they had a #11 U.K. hit in 1971, "Rosetta." Fame also recorded an LP, *Shorty,* in the early Seventies with his group. In 1974 Fame reincarnated the Blue Flames (including Colin Green) and released an album of R&B ballads, *Georgie Fame.* In the Eighties he turned to writing for the stage and produced musical tributes to Hoagy Carmichael (1981) and George Gershwin (1986). In 1989 he toured with Van Morrison, on whose *Avalon Sunset* he appears.

Family

Formed 1967, Leicester, England
Roger Chapman (b. Apr. 8, 1944, Leicester), voc.;
Rob Townsend (b. July 7, 1947, Leicester), drums;
Rick Grech (b. Nov. 1, 1946, Bordeaux, Fr.; d. Mar. 17, 1990), bass, violin, voc.; Jim King (b. ca. 1945, Eng.), sax, flute; Charlie Whitney (b. June 4, 1944, Eng.), gtr., voc.
1968—*Music in a Doll's House* (Reprise)   1969—*Family Entertainment* (– Grech; – King; + John "Poli" Palmer [b. May 25, 1943, Eng.], perc., flute, piano; + John Weider [b. Apr. 21, 1947, Eng.], bass, violin)   1970—*A Song for Me; Anyway* (United Artists) (– Weider; + John Wetton [b. July 12, 1949, Derby, Eng.], bass, voc.)   1971—*Fearless* (– Wetton; + Jim Cregan, bass, gtr.)   1972—*Band Stand* (– Palmer; + Tony Ashton, kybds., voc.)   1973—*It's Only a Movie* (– Townsend)   1974—*Best of Family* (Reprise).

Although Family's wildly eclectic progressive rock made it a hitmaker in England, the group remained relatively unknown in the U.S. Family featured the often grating, goatish vibrato singing of Roger Chapman and a repertoire by Chapman and Charlie Whitney, tempered in later years by the jazzy flute and vibraphone of John "Poli" Palmer. The group started in Leicester in 1962 as the Farinas, which included Chapman, Whitney, King, and, later, Grech. They turned into the pinstripe-suited Roaring Sixties, and finally settled on the Family name at the suggestion of Kim Fowley.

Traffic's Dave Mason (with Jimmy Miller) coproduced its debut. The group's harder-rocking followup, *Family Entertainment,* prompted a U.S. tour. Unfortunately, the day before it was to start, Rick Grech quit to join Blind Faith [see entry], and Family's debut performance at the Fillmore East ended in a fistfight between Chapman and promoter Bill Graham. A few days later Chapman lost both his voice and his visa, and Family returned to England. The band's appearance at the 1970 Rotterdam Festival was filmed in *Stomping Ground,* and it was featured in Jenny Fabian's novel *Groupie.* Family's reputation continued to grow at home, with hit singles in *Anyway*'s "In My Own Time" (#4 U.K., 1971) and *Band Stand*'s "Burlesque" (#13 U.K., 1972).

Family opened for Elton John in 1972, but never found a U.S. audience despite FM airplay for *Fearless* and *Band Stand. It's Only a Movie,* the group's final album, was released in Britain on its own Raft label in 1973. That fall, Family played a farewell tour of England, including a final gig in Leicester. Chapman and Whitney founded Streetwalkers; Chapman recorded some solo albums and appears on Mike Oldfield's *Islands.* Cregan later joined Rod Stewart's band, and Palmer went into session work, appearing on albums by Pete Townshend of the

Who. Ashton and Townsend joined the U.K. group Medicine Head, then Townsend drummed for Kevin Ayers' band in the Seventies, and Dave Kelly's group in the early Eighties.

Fanny

Formed 1970, California

June Millington (b. 1949, Manila, Philippines), gtr., voc.; Alice de Buhr (b. 1950, Mason City, Iowa), drums; Addie Clement, lead gtr.; Jean Millington (b. 1950, Manila, Philippines), bass, voc.
1970—(– Clement; + Nicole "Nicky" Barclay [b. Apr. 21, 1951, Washington, D.C.], kybds.) *Fanny* **(Reprise) 1971—***Charity Ball* **1972—***Fanny Hill* **1973— *Mother's Pride* 1974—(– June Millington; – de Buhr; + Patti Quatro [b. Detroit, Mich.], bass; + Brie Brandt-Howard, drums) 1975—***Rock and Roll Survivors* **(Casablanca) (group disbands).**
Nickey Barclay: 1976—*Diamond in a Junkyard* **(Ariola).**
Jean Millington and June Millington: 1978—*Ladies on the Stage* **(United Artists).**
June Millington: 1981—*Heartsong* **(Olivia).**

The members of Fanny were true rock & roll pioneers, forming one of the first all-female hard-rock groups. The band's nucleus was the Philippine-born Millington sisters, who moved to Sacramento, California, when their father, a navy man, was transferred in 1961. They formed their first quartet, the Sveltes, with girlfriends in high school. They played in a series of local bands for five years, under different names, and were performing at the Troubadour in Los Angeles when record producer Richard Perry's secretary discovered them.

After her boss got them signed to Warner Bros., the group changed its name to Fanny. According to June Millington, "We didn't really think of it [the name] as a butt, a sexual term. We felt it was like a woman's spirit watching over us." Nonetheless, the group's record company launched promotional campaigns that exploited the sexual aspect, including bumper stickers urging people to "Get Behind Fanny" and ads that showed the women from the back.

Perry produced the group's first three albums, and Fanny also backed up Barbra Streisand on her 1970 LP *Stoney End. Charity Ball* yielded their first chart single with its title cut. Perhaps their most fully realized effort was *Fanny Hill,* recorded at the Beatles' Apple studios in London. The group's hardest-rocking release, 1973's *Mother's Pride,* was produced by Todd Rundgren.

Around the same time, Fanny toured extensively (including several dates with Jethro Tull), performing its rock opera, *Rock and Roll Survivors.* Bassist Patti Quatro, Suzy Quatro's elder sister, replaced June Millington, and original Svelte Brie Howard joined. Ironically the group

broke up shortly after scoring their highest-charting single, "Butter Boy," from the last album. Later that year Jean convinced June to return to music, and together they formed the L.A. All-Stars. They were on the verge of signing a record contract but refused when they learned that one of its conditions was that they be called Fanny again.

June became deeply involved in the women's music movement, producing records for Cris Williamson and Holly Near, among others. She recorded with another all-female rock group, Isis, in the mid-Seventies, and she has recorded solo. By 1979 Jean Millington was married to ex–David Bowie guitarist Earl Slick, playing club dates, and recording and producing for Olivia Records.

Keyboardist and chief songwriter Nickey Barclay, who had been included in Joe Cocker's Mad Dogs and Englishmen, went on to form her own group called Good News in 1976 and released an Ariola-America LP, *Diamond in a Junk Yard.* She also played on Keith Moon's solo album *Two Sides of the Moon.*

Richard and Mimi Fariña

Richard Fariña (b. 1937, Brooklyn, N.Y.; d. Apr. 30, 1966, Carmel, Calif.), dulcimer, voc.; Mimi Fariña (b. Mimi Baez, Apr. 30, 1945, New York City, N.Y.), gtr., voc.
1965—*Celebrations for a Grey Day* **(Vanguard) 1966—***Reflections in a Crystal Wind* **1968— *Richard Fariña; Memories* 1971—***The Best of Richard and Mimi Fariña; Mimi Fariña and Tom Jans* **(A&M).**

The Fariñas were an American husband-and-wife folk duo whose promising career ended with Richard's death in 1966. Richard was born to Irish and Cuban parents. Although his parents had immigrated to the United States in the Twenties, Fariña spent extended periods during his youth in Cuba as well as in Brooklyn and Northern Ireland. While living in Northern Ireland in the mid-Fifties, he became actively involved with the IRA, and the British government had him deported. He later moved to Cuba and supported Castro. In 1959 he moved to Greenwich Village and began performing; he was briefly married to folksinger Carolyn Hester.

In 1963 he wed Joan Baez's younger sister, Mimi, in Paris. The couple moved to California, where they began working as a duo. They recorded three albums for Vanguard in the mid-Sixties. The second, *Reflections in a Crystal Wind,* was one of the earliest fusions of folk material with a rock rhythm section. Material from all three was later included on Vanguard's *Best of Richard and Mimi Fariña.* Throughout, Fariña maintained his literary career, writing plays, magazine articles, and *Been Down So Long It Looks Like Up to Me,* a novel concerned with the cultural transition from the beatniks to the hippies.

He was returning home from a promotional party for the book when he died in a motorcycle crash in 1966 on his wife's 21st birthday. The book was subsequently reprinted.

Mimi withdrew from the public eye for a few years, but has subsequently worked as both a singer and an actress (notably as a member of the Committee). As the Sixties closed, she performed and recorded occasionally, often with other partners (including Tom Jans), and occasionally shared the stage with her sister, Joan. In the early Seventies she helped establish Bread and Roses, a charitable organization that provides entertainment for prisoners, hospital patients, and other institutionalized people.

Chris Farlowe

Born John Henry Deighton, October 13, 1940, Essex, England
1967—*The Fabulous Chris Farlowe* (CBS, U.K.)
1968—*Paint It Farlowe* (Immediate, U.K.)   1970—
From Here to Mama Rosa (with the Hill) (Polydor)
1985—*Out of the Blue* (Polydor, U.K.)   1988—*Born*
Again   1991—*The Soulful Chris Farlowe* (Sony).

A minor English R&B figure in the early Sixties, vocalist Chris Farlowe's records sold poorly until mid-decade, when Mick Jagger gave him his first major U.K. hit with a Jagger-Richards composition, "Out of Time."

John Deighton began playing the guitar at age 13 and soon formed the John Henry Skiffle Group, which won the All-English Skiffle Championship. By 1962 he was calling himself Chris Farlowe and singing R&B at London's Flamingo Club with his Thunderbirds. Their early recordings included "Buzz with the Fuzz" and "Stormy Monday Blues" (which Farlowe released under the alias Little Joe Cook).

But it was only after Jagger (who sang occasional backup vocals on Farlowe's records) became his patron that the Thunderbirds sustained any serious impact. "Out of Time" hit #1 in July 1966, but later that year Farlowe disbanded the Thunderbirds, only to re-form the group the following year (with Carl Palmer on drums). Other band members included guitarist Albert Lee, keyboardist Pete Solley, and keyboardist Dave Greenslade, later of Colosseum. In 1970 Farlowe formed a new group, the Hill, which recorded one album. That same year he joined Greenslade in Colosseum. When that group broke up in November 1971, Farlowe lent his services to Atomic Rooster for two LPs.

Concurrently he worked on various solo projects. In 1972 Farlowe retired from music to run his Nazi war memorabilia shop in North London. In 1975 he attempted a last-ditch comeback by reissuing "Out of Time" and an LP, *The Chris Farlowe Band Live*. He again retired, but resurfaced in 1985 with *Out of the Blue*. Three

years later Farlowe came out with *Born Again* and sang on Jimmy Page's first solo album, *Outrider*.

Charlie Feathers

Born June 12, 1932, Holly Springs, Mississippi
1973—*Good Rockin' Tonight/Live in Memphis*
(Edsel, U.K.)   1991—*Charlie Feathers*
(Elektra/Nonesuch)   1993—*Uh Huh Honey* (Norton).

Although rockabilly pioneer Charlie Feathers never achieved commercial success, he was present at the creation of the form. Feathers himself hints that a mysterious, undisclosed "conspiracy" denied him mainstream fame; today he is a cult legend.

Raised on a farm, Feathers quit school after the third grade, learned guitar from a black sharecropper, and worked on oil pipelines in Illinois and Texas as a teen. Moving to Memphis at 18, he contracted spinal meningitis and spent months bedridden, listening to the radio. Upon recuperating he concentrated on music. Feathers later claimed that he spent a great deal of time in the mid-Fifties at Sam Phillips' Sun studios, arranging some of Elvis Presley's early material. Though most of Feathers' assertions have been unsubstantiated, he did cowrite Presley's "I Forgot to Remember to Forget" (#1 C&W, 1955). That year, his own debut single on Flip, "I've Been Deceived," showed the influence of Hank Williams, and from then until 1959, he recorded for Sun and smaller labels (King, Kay, and Walmay among them). Such singles as "Tongue-Tied Jill" and "Get with It" did little on the charts, but Feathers persevered, playing local roadhouses until gaining, in 1977, a gig at London's Rainbow Theatre that drew raves from rockabilly revivalists.

In the late Seventies Feathers got the financial backing to start his own short-lived record label, Feathers, upon which he released a couple of albums and several singles. Frequently comic in tone, his work was often straightforwardly country, but with 1991's *Charlie Feathers* (his only major label release) and the critical praise it provoked, it seemed apparent that Feathers will be remembered essentially as a great, early, if not widely known, rocker.

The Feelies

Formed 1976, Haledon, New Jersey
Bill Million (b. William Clayton, ca. 1953, Haledon), gtr., voc.; Glenn Mercer (b. ca. 1955, Haledon), gtr., voc.; John J., bass; Dave Weckerman (b. ca. 1950), drums.
1977—(– J.; – Weckerman; + Keith Clayton [b. Keith DeNunzio, Apr. 27, 1958, Reading, Pa.], bass; + Vinny D. [b. Vincent DeNunzio, Aug. 15, 1956, Reading, Pa.], drums)   1978—(– Vinny D.; + Anton Fier [a.k.a. Andy Fisher] [b. June 20, 1956, Cleveland, Ohio], drums)   1980—*Crazy Rhythms* (Stiff)

1986—(– Fier; + Stanley Demeski [b. ca. 1960], drums; + Brenda Sauter [b. ca. 1959], bass, violin; + Weckerman, perc.) *The Good Earth* (Coyote) 1988—*Only Life* 1991—*Time for a Witness* (A&M).

With their quirky rhythms, frantically strummed guitars, pop melodies, and enigmatic lyrics, the Feelies epitomized New York's postpunk bands. They stubbornly rejected a commercial recording career after one album and disappeared for several years, reappearing in the late Eighties with their twin-guitar sound intact and gaining a stronghold in the American indie-rock scene.

Glenn Mercer and Bill Million, the group's songwriters, met at high school in Haledon, New Jersey, where several years later the Feelies made their live debut. After a lineup change, they began playing New York's new-wave venues and quickly earned a place in the vanguard of that city's rock experimentalists; in 1978 the *Village Voice* named them the best underground band in New York. That fall, Vinny D. left to play with Richard Lloyd (Television) and was replaced by Anton Fier.

Adamant about producing their own records, the Feelies did not sign a long-term recording contract until 1980, although they did record a single, "Fa Ce La," for the English independent label Rough Trade in 1979. *Crazy Rhythms* introduced the band as four nerds making intricate and intense white noise; songs included "The Boy with the Perpetual Nervousness" and a cover of the Beatles' "Everybody's Got Something to Hide (Except Me and My Monkey)."

Frustrated and disappointed by Stiff's demands for a hit single, the band fizzled. Fier went on to work with Pere Ubu and form the Golden Palominos [see entries]. Mercer and Million wrote the soundtrack for *Smithereens* in 1982. They played in several different New Jersey bands, including the Weckerman-led Yung Wu (who released an album in 1987), the Trypes (who released a 1984 EP), and Beatles and Velvet Underground cover bands. It was the instrumental group the Willies, with Weckerman, Brenda Sauter, and Stan Demeski, that led to the reactivation of the Feelies in 1983. As in the past, the Feelies played sporadically, mostly on holidays.

Their second album, *The Good Earth* (coproduced by R.E.M.'s Peter Buck), introduced a kinder, gentler group, with a more reflective, acoustic tone. Live, the Feelies built their songs into a frenzied crescendo culminating in the album track "Slipping (into Something)," with Mercer shaking feedback out of his electric guitar, Million strumming his acoustic at a breakneck pace, and the two percussionists egging the whole thing on. That fall the Feelies appeared as the band playing the high school reunion in Jonathan Demme's *Something Wild*.

The Feelies' subsequent albums echoed the progression of their live shows, each more manic than the next, with Mercer increasingly taking a leading role. On *Only Life*, their major-label debut, they finally gave in to their longtime Velvets fetish with a cover of "What Goes On." The Feelies have never been musical innovators as much as performance perfectionists, wearing their influences on their sleeves with their frequent covers of Neil Young, Patti Smith, the Monkees, and Modern Lovers, among others. On *Time for a Witness*, those borrowings were dramatically overstated, each song sounding like someone else's, culminating in a cover of the Stooges' "Real Cool Time."

The Feelies broke up shortly after their last album. Demeski went on to play with Luna, while Mercer and Weckerman formed the group Wake Ooloo.

José Feliciano

Born September 10, 1945, Lares, Puerto Rico
1968—*Feliciano!* (RCA); *Souled* 1969—*Feliciano/10 to 23*; *Alive, Alive-O!* 1970—*Fireworks* 1971—*Encore! Jose Feliciano's Finest Performances*; *Jose Feliciano* 1972—*Jose Feliciano Sings* 1973—*Compartments* 1974—*And the Feeling's Good* 1975—*Just Wanna Rock 'n' Roll* 1976—*Sweet Soul Music* (Private Stock) 1981—*Jose Feliciano* (Motown) 1983—*Romance in the Night* 1988—*All Time Greatest Hits* (RCA) 1989—*I'm Never Gonna Change* (EMI) 1992—*Latin Street '92* (Capitol/EMI Latin).

José Feliciano reached worldwide popularity with his obsessive flamenco-flavored versions of pop hits such as "Light My Fire" (#3, 1968). Born blind, Feliciano was the second of 12 children of a poor Puerto Rican farmer; he grew up in New York's Spanish Harlem. Feliciano was introduced to the accordion and the guitar as a child. He first performed at the Bronx's El Teatro Puerto Rico. At 17 he dropped out of high school and began playing Greenwich Village clubs and coffeehouses like the Cafe Id (where he met his first wife and manager, Hilda Perez) and Gerde's Folk City (where he was discovered).

The next year, he released his first single, "Everybody Do the Click," and album, *The Voice and Guitar of Jose Feliciano*, and appeared at the Newport Folk Festival. Initially most of his releases were in Spanish, intended for the Latin market (in 1966, he played before 100,000 in Buenos Aires). In 1968 his cover of the Doors' "Light My Fire" hit the Top Five, nearly equaling the success of the original version. It went gold, as did *Feliciano!* (#2, 1968). He followed up with minor hits ("Hi Heel Sneakers") and released a controversial rendition of "The Star Spangled Banner," recorded live at the fifth game of the 1968 World Series.

Feliciano has toured frequently each year for almost

two decades, including Communist Eastern Europe. Besides guitar, Feliciano also plays bass, banjo, keyboards, timbales, mandolin, and harmonica. His occasional compositions ("Rain," "Destiny") have been covered by Anne Murray and Blue Swede. He frequently appeared on television shows, including dramatic roles on *Kung Fu* and *McMillan and Wife*. Feliciano contributed to the soundtrack of the early-Seventies film *MacKenna's Gold*. He signed with Motown in 1980, and his label debut, *Jose Feliciano*, was produced by Berry Gordy Jr. and Suzee Ikeda. He recorded two more LPs for Motown, both for its Spanish-language division.

Subsequent U.S. success has been meager, although in the early Seventies he recorded with Joni Mitchell ("Free Man in Paris"). His last charting English-language single was the theme song to the television series *Chico and the Man* (#96, 1974). Nevertheless, he has three gold albums in the U.S., and over 40 gold and platinum citations from around the world. He has recorded nearly as many Spanish-language records as English, and he has won Grammys in both language categories. An East Harlem public school was renamed The José Feliciano Performing Arts School in his honor.

Freddy Fender
Born Baldemar Huerta, June 4, 1937, San Benito, Texas
1974—*Before the Next Teardrop Falls* (ABC/Dot) 1975—*Are You Ready for Freddy* 1976—*Rock 'n' Country*; *If You're Ever in Texas* 1977—*Best of Freddy Fender* 1991—*The Freddy Fender Collection* (Reprise) 1993—*Canciones de Mi Barrio* (Arhoolie).

Freddy Fender is a Tex-Mex country rocker who specializes in the polka-waltz style called *conjunto* and is known for his tearful, choked-up singing in Spanish and English. Most recently he has found a new audience as lead singer of the all-star Texas Tornados [see entry]. Fender began playing the guitar as a child and started performing professionally in the late Fifties. At one Corpus Christi nightclub he was the victim of an after-hours fight that left his nose permanently crooked and a deep knife scar in his neck.

In 1957 two early recordings—Spanish versions of English-language hits first recorded by Elvis Presley ("Don't Be Cruel") and Harry Belafonte ("Jamaica Farewell")—became big sellers in Mexico and South America. In 1959 he signed to Imperial, changed his surname to Fender (inspired by the guitar), and cut "Holy One" and the original version of "Wasted Days and Wasted Nights," which sold 100,000 copies. On Friday, May 13, 1960, shortly after the release of yet another moderate hit, "Crazy, Crazy, Baby," Fender was arrested for possession of two marijuana cigarettes in Baton Rouge, Louisiana. He subsequently served three years in the Angola State Prison.

Upon his release he played bars in New Orleans and in San Benito, Texas, from 1963 until 1968. By 1975 he had released more than 100 records on regional labels, and in early 1974 he met producer Huey Meaux, who masterminded Fender's 1975 national pop breakthrough, "Before the Next Teardrop Falls" (#1). Before the end of the year he'd placed two more 45s in the Top Twenty: "Wasted Days and Wasted Nights" (#8) and "Secret Love" (#20). Fender's subsequent releases have kept him before country audiences.

His acting credits include the films *Short Eyes* (1977) and *The Milagro Beanfield War* (1987). In the mid-Eighties Fender, who holds a degree in sociology, completed treatment for drug and alcohol dependency.

Jay Ferguson: See Jo Jo Gunne; Spirit

Bryan Ferry: See Roxy Music

The Fifth Dimension
Formed 1966, Los Angeles, California
LaMonte McLemore (b. Sep. 17, 1940, St. Louis, Mo.), voc.; Marilyn McCoo (b. Sep. 30, 1943, Jersey City, N.J.), voc.; Ron Townson (b. Jan. 20, 1941, St. Louis, Mo.), voc.; Florence LaRue Gordon (b. Feb. 4, 1944, Philadelphia, Pa.), voc.; Billy Davis Jr. (b. June 26, 1940, St. Louis, Mo.), voc.
1967—*Up, Up and Away* (Soul City) 1968—*The Magic Garden*; *Stoned Soul Picnic* 1969—*The Age of Aquarius* 1970—*Portrait* (Bell) 1971—*Love's Lines, Angles and Rhymes*; *The Fifth Dimension Live*; *Reflections* 1972—*Greatest Hits on Earth* 1975—*Earthbound* (ABC) 1986—*Anthology* (Rhino).
Marilyn McCoo and Billy Davis Jr.: 1976—*I Hope We Get to Love in Time* (ABC) 1977—*The Two of Us* 1978—*Marilyn and Billy* (Columbia).

The Fifth Dimension had a string of pop-soul hits in the late Sixties and early Seventies (seven gold LPs, five gold singles), and they introduced songs by Laura Nyro and Jim Webb. Both the Fifth Dimension and the Friends of Distinction were offshoots of a vocal group, the Hi-Fi's, formed by Marilyn McCoo and LaMonte McLemore. McCoo, who had won the Grand Talent Award in the Miss Bronze California pageant, was working as a fashion model, and McLemore (a onetime minor-league baseball player) was photographing her when they decided to start the Hi-Fi's with Floyd Butler and Harry Elston, who later formed the Friends of Distinction. The Hi-Fi's toured with Ray Charles' revue before breaking up. McCoo then recruited Florence LaRue, who had also won a Grand Talent Award, and they brought in McLemore's fellow St. Louis–born Angeleno, Ron Townson. Billy Davis Jr. was singing with his own group, the Saint Gospel Singers, when McLemore, his cousin, invited him to join.

As the Versatiles, they signed with Johnny Rivers' Soul City label. After a minor West Coast hit, "I'll Be Loving You Forever," Rivers persuaded them to change their name. Their manager suggested the Fifth Dimension. The quintet's first hit was a cover of the Mamas and the Papas' "Go Where You Wanna Go" (#16, 1967), but its pop dominance began with its first Jim Webb song, "Up, Up and Away" (#7, 1967), which received four Grammys. In 1968 the Fifth Dimension made hits of Laura Nyro's "Stoned Soul Picnic" (#3) and "Sweet Blindness" (#13); in 1969 the group had its biggest seller with a medley from *Hair*, "Aquarius/Let the Sunshine In" (#1, 1969), which sold nearly two million copies. Another Nyro composition, "Wedding Bell Blues," topped the chart later that year. The group apparently took the song to heart, for McCoo and Davis married, as did LaRue and manager Marc Gordon.

In the early Seventies the Fifth Dimension moved toward easy-listening ballads, with occasional hits, including "(Last Night) I Didn't Get to Sleep at All" (#8, 1972). The act began to play the nightclub and television circuits; it also appeared at the Nixon White House. McCoo and Davis left to work as a duo in late 1975; their 1976 album *I Hope We Get to Love in Time* included the #1 hit "You Don't Have to Be a Star." By 1980 McCoo and Davis had split up, and she was cohosting the TV show *Solid Gold*. The remains of the Fifth Dimension, meanwhile, reunited with Webb in 1975 for the unsuccessful *Earthbound;* LaRue, McLemore, and Townson continue to tour, with Greg Walker and Phyllis Battle. In the Nineties the group starred in a national tour of the popular Fats Waller musical *Ain't Misbehavin'.*

Fine Young Cannibals
Formed 1983, Birmingham, England
Andy Cox (b. Jan. 25, 1956, Birmingham), gtr.; David Steele (b. Sep. 8, 1960, Isle of Wight, Eng.), bass, kybds; Roland Gift (b. Apr. 28, 1961, Birmingham), voc.
1985—*Fine Young Cannibals* (I.R.S.)   1989—*The Raw and the Cooked*   1990—*The Raw and the Remix.*

When the English Beat broke up in 1983, two of the group's founders, Andy Cox and David Steele, continued as Fine Young Cannibals, recruiting the handsome, half-white, half-Caribbean actor/singer Roland Gift as front man. With Cox and Steele's market-tested blend of ska rhythms, dance beats, and pop hooks, and Gift's quaver-

ing, American soul-influenced falsetto and striking, video-friendly face, the Cannibals attained the chart success their predecessor never knew.

Taking the name from an obscure 1960 film, *All the Fine Young Cannibals,* the trio released its first album in 1985 and became familiar to MTV viewers through "Johnny Come Home" and a humorous, overstated remake of Elvis Presley's "Suspicious Minds." The Cannibals gained even more visibility with their updated version of the Buzzcocks' "Ever Fallen in Love," done for the Jonathan Demme film *Something Wild.* When director Barry Levinson heard the music, he asked the group to write some material for his film *Tin Men,* and the resulting tunes made up most of the "raw" side of the group's follow-up, *The Raw and the Cooked.*

That album shot to #1 and remained there for most of the summer of 1989. It ultimately sold more than two million copies, producing two #1 hits ("Good Thing" and "She Drives Me Crazy"); a third single, "Don't Look Back," reached #11, and two others made it into the Top 100.

Throughout, Gift was getting film offers. After the entire band appeared in *Tin Men,* the singer landed roles in *Sammy and Rosie Get Laid* and *Scandal;* he also appeared in a stage performance of *Romeo and Juliet.* With Gift becoming increasingly involved with his acting, Cox and Steele did a remixed version of *The Raw and the Cooked.*

Tim Finn: See Crowded House; Split Enz

The Fireballs
Formed 1957, Raton, New Mexico
Chuck Tharp (b. Feb. 3, 1941), voc.; Stan Lark (b. July 27, 1940), bass; Eric Budd (b. Oct. 23, 1938), drums; George Tomsco (b. Apr. 24, 1940), gtr.; Dan Trammell (b. July 14, 1940), gtr.
1959—(– Trammell)   1960—(– Tharp; + Jimmy Gilmer [b. 1940, LaGrange, Ill.], voc., piano)   1962— (– Budd; + Doug Roberts [d. Nov. 18, 1981], drums) 1963—*Sugar Shack* (Dot).

Jimmy Gilmer and the Fireballs had the biggest hit of 1963 with the million-selling "Sugar Shack." Gilmer began singing as a youngster, and in 1951 he moved with his family to Amarillo, Texas, where he studied piano for four years at the Musical Arts Conservatory. While studying engineering at Amarillo College in 1957, he formed his first pop band. In 1960 he replaced Chuck Tharp as singer of the Fireballs, a group of high school friends that had placed two instrumentals in the Top Forty, "Torquay" (#39, 1959) and "Bulldog" (#24, 1960). Gilmer was introduced to the band by Buddy Holly's producer Norman Petty at his Clovis, New Mexico, recording studio.

With Gilmer on piano and vocals, their first release, "Quite a Party," made the Top Thirty. "Sugar Shack," credited to Jimmy Gilmer and the Fireballs, and featuring a distinctive-sounding keyboard called a Solovox, held the #1 spot on the chart for over a month. Another 1963 single, "Daisy Petal Pickin'," hit #15. By mid-decade, however, Gilmer and the Fireballs had gone their separate ways. Gilmer had little subsequent success, while the Fireballs returned to the chart in 1968 with a rocked-up version of a Tom Paxton song, "Bottle of Wine" (#9).

Firefall

Formed circa 1974, Boulder, Colorado
Rick Roberts (b. 1950, Fla.), gtr., voc.; Jock Bartley (b. Kan.), gtr., voc.; Mark Andes (b. Feb. 19, 1948, Philadelphia, Pa.), bass; Larry Burnett (b. Washington, D.C.). gtr., voc.; Michael Clarke (b. June 3, 1944, New York City, N.Y.; d. Dec. 19, 1993, Treasure Island, Fla.), drums.
1976—Firefall (Atlantic)   1977—Luna Sea   1978—Élan   1980—Undertow; Clouds Across the Sun   1983—Break of Dawn   1984—Mirror of the World   1992—Firefall's Greatest Hits (Rhino)   1994—Messenger (Redstone).

With its lightweight blend of acoustic guitars, high harmonies, and pop-flavored country rock, Firefall jumped onto the national scene with one of 1976's biggest hits, "You Are the Woman" (#9, 1976). The band's chief writer and leader, guitarist Rick Roberts, sang on the Byrds' (Untitled) before joining the Burrito Brothers (which then included another ex-Byrd, drummer Michael Clarke), where he stayed until 1972. Roberts then released a couple of solo albums (Windmills, 1972, and She Is a Song, 1973) while trying to establish himself in L.A. music circles.

He eventually retreated to Boulder, where he formed Firefall in mid-decade, recruiting ex-Spirit and Jo Jo Gunne bassist Mark Andes. With Washington, D.C., singer/songwriter Larry Burnett, he wrote most of the material for the group's gold debut, Firefall. Its second LP, which also went gold, contained "Just Remember I Love You" (#11, 1977). The following year's Élan continued Firefall's streak, going platinum, thanks to Roberts' "Strange Way" (#11, 1978). Two more Top Forty hits followed in the early Eighties, "Headed for a Fall" (#35, 1980) and "Staying with It" (#37, 1981), but thereafter Firefall faded from the airwaves. The group's 1984 album, Mirror of the World, failed to even chart. Ten years later a new Firefall, led by original guitarist/singer Jock Bartley, released Messenger on the independent Redstone label.

fIREHOSE: See Minutemen

The Firm: See Jimmy Page

First Edition: See Kenny Rogers

Wild Man Fischer

Born 1945, Los Angeles, California
1969—An Evening with Wild Man Fischer (Bizarre)
1977—Wildmania (Rhino)   1981—Pronounced Normal   1984—Nothing Crazy.

A man who got his start on streetcorners singing made-to-order compositions for a dime, Larry "Wild Man" Fischer was a well-known eccentric on the Los Angeles rock fringe in the late Sixties. A former mental patient, he met Frank Zappa, who produced An Evening with Wild Man Fischer for Bizarre Records in 1969. Fischer spent a good deal of the early Seventies roaming the country, singing for his widely scattered band of cult followers.

In 1975 he released his first record in six years, a single promoting a record store, "Go to Rhino Records." He came to record the song because, according to store owner Richard Foos, the Rhino Records store was the only one Fischer could hang around in without being thrown out. When the single sold 2,000 copies, Foos and Harold Bronson decided to start Rhino Records, which has since grown to become a major source of reissues and obscurities. The label's first LP release was Fischer's Wildmania, which reconfirmed the singer's out-to-lunch status. Little is known of Fischer's current whereabouts; he told a Los Angeles Times reporter that he lives "all over." On August 3, 1982, Wild Man Fischer "quit" show business. The next day he was "back in" show business.

Fishbone

Formed Los Angeles, California
John "Norwood" Fisher (b. Sep. 12, 1965, Los Angeles), bass, voc.; Phillip Dwight "Fish" Fisher (b. July 16, 1967, Los Angeles), drums; Kendall Rey Jones (b. Sep. 9, 1965, Los Angeles), gtr., voc.; Angelo Christopher Moore (b. Nov. 5, 1965, Los Angeles), voc., saxophone; Christopher Gordon Dowd (b. Sep. 20, 1965, Las Vegas, Nev.), trombone, kybds., voc.; Walter Adam Kibby II (b. Nov. 13, 1964, Columbus, Ohio), trumpet.
1985—Fishbone EP (Columbia)   1986—In Your Face 1987—It's a Wonderful Life (Gonna Have a Good Time) EP   1988—Truth and Soul   1990—Bonin' in the Boneyard EP (+ John Bigham [b. March 3, 1959, Chicago, Ill.], gtr., kybds.)   1991—The Reality of My Surroundings   1993—Give a Monkey a Brain and He'll Swear He's the Center of the Universe (– Jones).

Fishbone's mélange of ska, funk, punk, and metal was born when residents of South Central L.A. were bussed to the San Fernando Valley for junior high school. Dropped into foreign territory, the Fisher brothers, Jones, Dowd, and Kibby banded together with Valley resident Moore and expressed the tensions of integration through music. Combining homeboy and Valley boy tastes (they cite Funkadelic and Rush as equal influences), Fishbone confront and transcend racial barriers.

Fishbone played under a variety of names, including Hot Ice, Megatron, and Counterattack, before recording their debut EP. *Fishbone* is a fierce, hardcore record on which the band flexes its credentials as both able social commentators and avid partiers. Producer David Kahne slicked up Fishbone's sound on *In Your Face*, but the record still lives up to its title. Kahne also produced *It's a Wonderful Life*, a collection of twisted Christmas carols, and *Truth and Soul*, which featured a metallic version of "Freddie's Dead." In 1988 Fishbone backed Little Richard on "Rock Island Line," a track on the Woody Guthrie and Leadbelly tribute *Folkways: A Vision Shared*. In an odder pairing yet, they backed Annette Funicello singing the Sixties hit "Jamaican Ska" in the film *Back to the Beach*.

Bonin', a collection of studio tomfoolery, including an X-rated version of the title track, was produced by the Jungle Brothers. Fishbone spent more than a year making *The Reality of My Surroundings*, producing it mostly themselves, with assistance from Kahne. (They reportedly fought with Columbia for their independence and were resentful of Kahne's control.) The album was the band's biggest, featuring "Everyday Sunshine" and "Sunless Saturday," both favored by the alt-rock crowd. The video for "Sunless Saturday" was directed by Spike Lee. Having never received much radio play, Fishbone has relied on critical acceptance and infamous live shows, where they thrash and mosh like hyperkinetic punks, to build their following.

The concurrent release of Fishbone's fourth album and their slot on the main stage of Lollapalooza '93 boded well for the band's future (*Give a Monkey a Brain* broke the Top 100). This breakthrough was marred, however, when Norwood Fisher was arrested with four others for trying to kidnap ex-Fishbone guitarist Kendall Jones off a California street in April 1993. Jones had left the band in March, reportedly obsessed with the apocalypse and denouncing Fishbone as "demonic." Fisher said he was trying to take Jones to psychiatric experts. Jones claimed he left the band over philosophical differences. Fisher was later acquitted of the kidnaping charges, and in early 1994 the band (minus Jones) began touring again.

The "5" Royales
Formed late 1940s, Winston-Salem, North Carolina
Johnny Tanner (b. ca. 1927), tenor voc.; Lowman

Pauling (b. ca. 1927; d. 1974), baritone and bass voc., gtr.; Clarence Pauling (a.k.a. Clarence Paul), voc.; Otto Jeffries, bass voc.; William Samuels, voc. Circa 1950—(– C. Pauling; + Obadiah Carter, tenor and baritone voc.; + Jimmy Moore, tenor and baritone voc.; + Johnny Holmes) 1953—(– Jeffries; + Eugene Tanner, voc.) 1960—(– L. Pauling) 1994—*Monkey Hips and Rice: The "5" Royales Anthology* (Rhino).

The "5" Royales were originally a gospel group called the Royal Sons Gospel Group (then Quintet). They emerged in 1953 with two R&B #1 hits on the Apollo label, "Baby Don't Do It" and "Help Me Somebody," both of which were written by lead guitarist Lowman Pauling. Inexplicably, there were at times six members of the "5" Royales.

They enjoyed their first pop success in 1957, when "Think" hit #66. Their most famous song, "Dedicated to the One I Love," another Pauling original, peaked at #81 in 1961 (it had been released with even less success in 1957). "Dedicated to the One I Love" would hit the Top Five twice in cover versions by the Shirelles (1961) and the Mamas and the Papas (1967). Later releases (with little mass-market impact) came out on ABC, Home of the Blues, Vee Jay, and Smash, through 1965, and the group broke up.

Original Royal Son Clarence Pauling, going under the name Clarence Paul, became an influential writer, producer, and A&R man for Motown, working with, among others, Stevie Wonder and Marvin Gaye. All the other members have since retired; Lowman Pauling died in 1974. The "5" Royales are among the few groups of their era who have yet to reunite.

The Five Satins
Formed 1955, New Haven, Connecticut
Original lineup: Fred Parris (b. Mar. 26, 1936), lead voc.; Lou Peebles, voc.; Ed Martin, voc.; Stanley Dortch, voc.; Jim Freeman, voc. (– Peebles; – Dortch; + Al Denby, voc.) (numerous personnel shifts throughout the years).
1981—(As Freddie Parris and the Satins: Freddie Parris, lead voc.; Dennis Ray; Bernard Jones; Larry DeSalvi) 1982—*The Five Satins Sing* (Collectables).

The Five Satins were one of the best-known doo-wop vocal groups of the Fifties. They evolved from lead singer Freddie Parris' high school group called the Scarlets. By 1956 he'd organized a new group, christened it the Five Satins, and recorded his "In the Still of the Night" in the basement of an East Haven Catholic church on a two-track machine. Originally released in 1956 on the Standard label, it was later leased to Ember Records and became a #24 hit that October. (The song had some chart success when reissued in 1960 and 1961 and has become an R&B ballad standard. It has been estimated to have sold 15 to 20 million copies and is a perennial winner in oldies-station listeners' polls.)

Soon after the single's release, Parris returned to the army. The Satins had recorded while he was on leave and continued to record with sporadic success. "To the Aisle" (with Bill Baker on lead vocals) hit #25 in 1957. Out of the Satins' many releases, only "Shadows" and "I'll Be Seeing You" reached the lower rungs of the Hot 100 as 1960 began. They re-created the latter tune and "In the Still of the Night" a cappella in the 1973 film *Let the Good Times Roll*. Upon his discharge in 1958, Parris re-formed the group.

The Five Satins were featured on Dick Clark's *American Bandstand* and many of his road revues in the late Fifties. They also toured Europe, where they built up a following. In 1970 the group appeared in the film *Been Down So Long It Looks Like Up to Me*. By the early Seventies they were a staple item on rock revival shows. In 1974, with Parris still underpinning the harmonies, they signed with Kirshner Records and released "Two Different Worlds." The group had an R&B Top Forty hit, "Everybody Stand Up and Clap Your Hands," in 1976 under the name Black Satin. The following year the group appeared on Southside Johnny and the Asbury Jukes' "First Night" from *This Time It's for Real*.

Onetime member Willie Wright went on to become a successful disc jockey in Connecticut. The many labels for which the Five Satins have recorded include Red Bird, Cub, Chancellor, Warner Bros., Roulette, and Mama Sadie. By 1982 the group was recording for Elektra and experiencing limited success on the pop chart (#71) with "Memories of Days Gone By," a medley of classic doo-wop hits. Parris and company continue to perform into the Nineties.

Roberta Flack

**Born February 10, 1939, Asheville, North Carolina
1969—*First Take* (Atlantic)   1970—*Chapter Two*
1971—*Quiet Fire*   1972—*Roberta Flack and Donny Hathaway*   1973—*Killing Me Softly*   1975—*Feel Like Makin' Love*   1977—*Blue Lights in the Basement*   1978—*Roberta Flack*   1980—*Featuring Donny Hathaway; Live and More* (with Peabo Bryson)   1982—*I'm the One*   1983—*Born to Love* (with Peabo Bryson) (Capitol)   1989—*Oasis* (Atlantic)   1991—*Set the Night to Music*   1993—*Softly with These Songs: The Best of Roberta Flack*
1994—*Roberta*.**

Roberta Flack's clear, reserved vocals have given her a string of ballad hits. The daughter of a church organist, she entered Howard University in Washington, D.C., on a full music scholarship at age 15. While working toward her degree in music, she was the first black student teacher at an all-white school in Chevy Chase, Maryland, then after graduation taught at another all-white school in Farmville, North Carolina. Eventually she returned to Washington, where she taught in several junior high schools and began singing in local clubs. Four years later, she left teaching for good.

In 1968 she was discovered by musician Les McCann. That November she signed with Atlantic, and a few months later recorded her entire debut album in less than ten hours. Entitled *First Take*, it sold well; by 1971 Flack had toured Europe and Ghana, as well as the U.S. Her first hit single was a duet with Donny Hathaway, "You've Got a Friend" (#29, 1971), which she followed with a Carole King–Gerry Goffin composition, "Will You Love Me Tomorrow." Meanwhile, the Clint Eastwood movie *Play Misty for Me* was released with a song from Flack's debut album, "The First Time Ever I Saw Your Face," on the soundtrack. It became a #1 hit in 1972, and returned the three-year-old *First Take* to the LP chart; it reigned at #1 for five weeks that spring. Another Flack-Hathaway duet, "Where Is the Love" (#5, 1972), followed. After two more #1 hits, "Killing Me Softly with His Song" (1973) and "Feel Like Makin' Love" (1974), Flack cut back her performing to concentrate on recording and to pursue outside interests, including educational programs for disadvantaged youth.

She reemerged in late 1977 with *Blue Lights in the Basement*, which contained "The Closer I Get to You" (#2, 1978); by then she had been awarded four gold records in three years. Hathaway's death in 1979 interrupted the recording of *Roberta Flack Featuring Donny Hathaway;* the album included "You Are My Heaven" and "Back Together Again." In 1980 Flack toured and recorded a live album with vocalist Peabo Bryson (*Live and More*); they collaborated again in 1983 with *Born to Love*, which featured "Tonight, I Celebrate My Love" (#16). In 1981 she composed and produced her first soundtrack, for *Bustin' Loose*. The following year, Flack charted one of her last pop hit singles of the decade, "Making Love" (#13, 1982); "Oasis," a #1 R&B hit from the album of the same name, did not chart on pop. But in 1991 Flack returned to the pop charts when the title track to *Set the Night to Music*, a duet with Maxi Priest, went to #6.

Throughout the Eighties she performed around the world, including many dates with symphony orchestras and several shows with Miles Davis. She contributed "Goodbye Sadness" to Yoko Ono's tribute album to her late husband, John Lennon, *Every Man Has a Woman Who Loves Him*.

The Flamingos

**Formed 1951, Chicago, Illinois
Original lineup: Earl Lewis, voc.; Zeke Carey**

(b. Jan. 24, 1933, Bluefield, Va.), voc.; Jake Carey (b. Sep. 9, 1926, Pulaski, Va.), voc.; Johnny Carter (b. June 2, 1934, Chicago), voc.; Sollie McElroy (b. July 16, 1933, Gulfport, Miss.; d. Jan. 15, 1995), voc.; Paul Wilson (b. Jan. 6, 1935, Chicago; d. May 1988), voc.
1954—(– McElroy; + Nate Nelson [b. Apr. 10, 1932, Chicago; d. Apr. 10, 1984], voc.) 1956—(– Carter; – Z. Carey) (group disbands) 1957—(Group reforms: + Tommy Hunt [b. June 18, 1933, Pittsburgh, Pa.], voc.) 1958—(+ Z. Carey, voc.; + Terry Johnson [b. Nov. 12, 1935, Baltimore, Md.], voc.) 1961—(– Hunt) 1984—*Flamingos* (Chess) 1990—*Best of the Flamingos* (Rhino).

Vocal-group aficionados consider the Flamingos one of the best, if not the best, of their era. Their cool yet dramatic vocals and elegant harmonies were unparalleled, and this smooth, mature style influenced later groups such as the Four Tops and the Temptations. They are also remembered for their one major pop success (1959's "I Only Have Eyes for You") and contributions of talent to other noted black acts. The group began singing on Chicago's South Side. Early recordings on the Chance label revealed influences ranging from Christian gospel and Jewish hymns to the clean harmonies of the Four Freshmen on such releases as Johnny Carter's "Golden Teardrops." Lead vocalist Sollie McElroy was replaced by Nate Nelson, who subsequently joined the Platters. McElroy joined the Moroccos, another Chicago group, in 1955. McElroy died of complications due to cancer in early 1995.

The Flamingos (who were also known as the Five Flamingos) followed with a variety of sentimental songs aimed at the white market. They remained also-rans until 1956, when "I'll Be Home" hit the R&B Top Ten. (Although the song was credited to Fats Washington and New Orleans record distributor Stan Lewis, Nate Nelson subsequently claimed to have written all but the opening line.) Typical of the times, a white artist—Pat Boone—had a bigger pop hit with his cover version. Their crossover break came in 1959 with the languid "I Only Have Eyes for You" (#11 pop, #3 R&B).

For the next two years, the Flamingos had several minor hits on the End label, among them "I Was Such a Fool" and "Nobody Loves Me Like You" in 1960, and "Time Was" in 1961. They scored occasional soul hits through the early Seventies with such releases as "Boogaloo Party" (#22 R&B, 1966) and "Buffalo Soldier" (#28 R&B, 1970). Other labels with which the group has been associated include Parrot, Decca, and, beginning in 1972, Ronze. Onetime member Johnny Carter joined the Dells, while another, Tommy Hunt, became a minor soul star ("Human," #48, 1961). In the early Nineties cousins Zeke and Jake Carey were still leading a group of Flamingos.

The Flamin' Groovies

Formed 1965, San Francisco, California
Cyril Jordan (b. 1948, San Francisco), gtr., Mellotron, voc.; Roy Loney (b. Apr. 13, 1946, San Francisco), voc., gtr.; George Alexander (b. May 18, 1946, San Mateo, Calif.), bass, voc., harmonica; Tim Lynch (b. July 18, 1946, San Francisco), gtr.
1966—(+ Ron Greco, drums; – Greco; + Danny Mihm [b. San Francisco], drums) 1969—*Supersnazz* (Epic) 1970—*Flamingo* (Kama Sutra) 1971—*Teenage Head* (– Lynch; + James Farrell, gtr., voc.; – Loney; + Chris Wilson, voc., gtr., harmonica) 1973—(– Mihm; + Terry Rae, drums; – Rae; + David Wright, drums) 1976—*Shake Some Action* (Sire); *Still Shakin'* (Buddah) (– Farrell; + Mike Wilhelm, gtr.) 1978—*The Flamin' Groovies Now* (Sire) 1979—*Jumping in the Night* 1983—*Bucketful of Brains* (Voxx) (– Wilson; – Wilhelm; – Wright; + Jack Johnson, gtr.; + Paul Zahl, drums) 1986—*One Night Stand* (ABC, U.K.) 1989—*Groovies' Greatest Grooves* (Sire).

While the three-minute pop-rock song has gone in and out of fashion, the Flamin' Groovies have stuck to the form since the mid-Sixties despite marginal commercial success. They formed in the Bay Area during the tail end of the British Invasion, but were overshadowed by psychedelic jam bands on the San Francisco scene. The group was briefly known as the Chosen Few and then the Lost and Found before becoming the Flamin' Groovies.

In 1969 the group made its own album, *Sneakers*, which sold 2,000 copies and was bought by Epic. Rereleased as *Supersnazz*, it was popular only in the Midwest. The Groovies toured the Midwest, then returned to San Francisco, where they booked concerts at what had been Bill Graham's Fillmore West. That venture ended when their business manager disappeared with the receipts.

The band moved to New York and made *Flamingo* and *Teenage Head,* but in 1971 founding member Tim Lynch was arrested for drug offenses and draft evasion. Roy Loney, the group's main songwriter, quit; he reemerged in the late Seventies with his own group, the Phantom Movers. The group moved to England in 1972, released two singles, and returned to San Francisco.

Greg Shaw, editor of *Bomp* magazine, helped finance a single, "You Tore Me Down," and in 1976 pop revivalist Dave Edmunds (whom the band had met in Britain) produced the Groovies' major-label comeback, *Shake Some Action*. While the band toured Europe with the Ramones, Buddah released old tapes as *Still Shakin'*. Edmunds also produced *Now,* and the band continued to tour as the Eighties began, though they did the bulk of their performing and recording in Europe, Australia, and New Zealand. They were particularly popular in France.

Flash and the Pan: See the Easybeats

The Flatlanders: See Joe Ely; Jimmie Dale Gilmore

Béla Fleck/the Flecktones

Béla Fleck, born July 10, 1958, New York City, New York
1980—*Crossing the Tracks* (Rounder)   1981—*Fiddle Tunes for Banjo*   1982—*Natural Bridge*   1984—*Double Time; Deviation* (with New Grass Revival)
1986—*In Roads*   1987—*Daybreak; Places*   1988—*Drive*   1995—*Tales from the Acoustic Planet.*
With the Flecktones, formed 1990, Nashville, Tenn.
(Fleck, banjo; Howard Levy, harmonica, kybds.; Victor Lemonte Wooten, bass; Roy "Future Man" Wooten, Synth-axe Drumitar):   1990—*Béla Fleck and the Flecktones* (Warner Bros.)   1991—*Flight of the Cosmic Hippo*   1992—*UFO TOFU*   1993—(– Levy) *Three Flew Over the Cuckoo's Nest.*

While he has yet to spur a full-scale revival of the instrument, Béla Fleck nevertheless played the key role in modernizing the five-string banjo. In his hands the instrument rises out of its traditional bluegrass context to enter the world of contemporary fusion music.

Named for Hungarian composer Béla Bartók, Fleck was turned on to the banjo the way any New Yorker growing up in the rock era might have been—through TV's *Beverly Hillbillies* theme and the 1972 hit single "Dueling Banjos." At age 14 Fleck began playing the banjo while studying guitar and music theory at the New York High School of Music and Art. Fleck's private banjo teachers included renowned players Erik Darling and Tony Trischka.

After graduation Fleck relocated to Boston to join the bluegrass band Tasty Licks. He moved to Kentucky in 1979 and helped form the group Spectrum; Fleck's first solo album, *Crossing the Tracks,* was released a year later. In 1982 Fleck joined the New Grass Revival, a forward-thinking outfit whose eclecticism expanded and subverted bluegrass music. "Seven by Seven" a Fleck composition from the 1986 album *New Grass Revival* (Capitol) was nominated for a Grammy. By the time New Grass Revival split, Fleck's reputation as the banjo's most daring practitioner was widespread.

In 1989 Fleck participated in a sort of bluegrass supergroup, composed of New Grass Revival mandolinist Sam Bush, Mark O'Connor on fiddle, Edgar Meyer on bass, and Jerry Douglas on dobro, releasing *Strength in Numbers* (MCA). A stylistically diverse amalgamation of musical concepts, the album relied heavily on classical compositions as well as traditional bluegrass ideas.

Pulling together three musicians whose unconven-tional approach to their instruments matched his own, Fleck formed the Flecktones in 1990. The virtuosic playing of Howard Levy on harmonica, Victor Wooten on bass, and his brother Roy "Future Man" on his invention, the Drumitar, a guitar-shaped drum synthesizer, garnered as much attention as Fleck's technically flawless, wildly imaginative picking. With a sound that drew upon jazz, funk, world music, and rock while hinting at country roots, the Flecktones became popular with both jazz and rock audiences. After Levy left the band in 1993, the Flecktones carried on as a trio. Bruce Hornsby and Branford Marsalis were among the guests who performed on 1993's *Three Flew Over the Cuckoo's Nest.*

Fleetwood Mac

Formed 1967, London, England
Peter Green (b. Peter Greenbaum, Oct. 29, 1946, London), gtr., voc.; Mick Fleetwood (b. June 24, 1947, Redruth, Eng.), drums; John McVie (b. Nov. 26, 1945, London), bass; Jeremy Spencer (b. July 4, 1948, West Hartlepool, Eng.), gtr., voc.
1968—*Fleetwood Mac* (Blue Horizon) (+ Danny Kirwan [b. May 13, 1950, London], gtr., voc.)
1969—*English Rose* (Warner Bros.); *Then Play On* (Reprise)   1970—(– Green) *Kiln House* (– Spencer; + Christine Perfect/McVie [b. July 12, 1943, Birmingham, Eng.], kybds., voc.)   1971—*Fleetwood Mac in Chicago* (Blue Horizon); *Future Games* (+ Bob Welch [b. July 31, 1946, Los Angeles, Calif.], gtr., voc.)   1972—*Bare Trees* (– Kirwan; + Bob Weston, gtr.; + Dave Walker, voc., gtr.)   1973—*Penguin* (– Walker); *Mystery to Me* (– Weston) 1974—*Heroes Are Hard to Find* (– Welch; + Lindsey Buckingham [b. Oct. 3, 1947, Palo Alto, Calif.], gtr., voc.; + Stevie Nicks [b. Stephanie Nicks, May 26, 1948, Phoenix, Ariz.], voc.)   1975—*Fleetwood Mac* 1977—*Rumours* (Warner Bros.)   1979—*Tusk* 1980—*Live*   1982—*Mirage*   1987—*Tango in the Night* (– Buckingham; + Billy Burnette [b. May 8, 1953, Memphis, Tenn.], gtr., voc.; + Rick Vito [b. Oct. 13, 1949, Darby, Penn.], gtr., voc.)   1988—*Greatest Hits*   1990—*Behind the Mask*   1991—(– Vito) 1992—*25 Years . . . The Chain*   1993—(– Burnette; – Nicks; + Bekka Bramlett [b. Apr. 19, 1968, Westwood, Calif.], voc.; + Dave Mason [b. May 10, 1946, Worcester, Eng.], gtr., voc.   1994—(+ Burnette; – C. McVie).
Mick Fleetwood solo: 1981—*The Visitor* (RCA).
Mick Fleetwood's Zoo: 1992—*Shakin' the Cage* (Warner Bros.).
Christine McVie solo: 1976—*The Legendary Christine Perfect Album* (recorded in 1969) (Sire)   1984—*Christine McVie* (Warner Bros.).
Stevie Nicks solo: 1981—*Bella Donna* (Modern) 1983—*The Wild Heart*   1985—*Rock a Little*   1989—

Fleetwood Mac: Lindsey Buckingham, John McVie,
Christine McVie, Stevie Nicks, Mick Fleetwood

The Other Side of the Mirror 1991—*Time Space—
The Best of Stevie Nicks* 1994—*Street Angel.*
Lindsay Buckingham solo: 1981—*Law and Order*
(Asylum) 1984—*Go Insane* (Elektra) 1992—*Out
of the Cradle* (Reprise).
Bob Welch solo: 1977—*French Kiss* (Capitol)
1979—*Three Hearts*; *The Other One* 1980—*Man
Overboard.*
Bob Welch with Paris: 1975—*Paris* (Capitol)
1976—*Big Towne, 2061.*
Peter Green solo: 1970—*In the End of the Game*
(Reprise) 1980—*Little Dreamer* (Sail).
Jeremy Spencer solo: 1973—*Jeremy Spencer and
the Children of God* (CBS) 1979—*Flee* (Atlantic).

Whoever named Fleetwood Mac was either lucky or prescient. The only thing about the group that hasn't
changed since it formed in 1967 is the rhythm section of
Mick Fleetwood and John McVie. Through the Seventies, the band's personnel and style shifted with nearly
every recording as Fleetwood Mac metamorphosed from
a traditionalist British blues band to the makers of one of
the best-selling pop albums ever, *Rumours*. From that
album's release in 1977 to the present, Fleetwood Mac
has survived additional, theoretically key, personnel
changes and remained a dominant commercial force.

Peter Green's Fleetwood Mac was formed by
ex–John Mayall's Bluesbreakers Green, McVie, and
Fleetwood along with Elmore James enthusiast Jeremy
Spencer. McVie had been a charter member of the Blues-
breakers in 1963, Fleetwood had joined in 1965, and
Green had replaced Eric Clapton in 1966. With its reper-

toire of blues classics and Green's blues-style originals,
the group's debut at the British Jazz and Blues Festival
in August 1967 netted it a record contract. Fleetwood
Mac was popular in Britain immediately, and its debut
album stayed near the top of the British chart for 13
months. The quartet had hits in the U.K. through 1970,
including "Black Magic Woman" and the instrumental
"Albatross" (which was #1 in 1968 and reached #4 when
rereleased in 1973). America, however, largely ignored
Fleetwood Mac; its first U.S. tour had the group third-
billed behind Jethro Tull and Joe Cocker, neither of
whom was as popular in Britain.

Green and Spencer recorded *Fleetwood Mac in
Chicago* with Willie Dixon, Otis Spann, and other blues
patriarchs in 1969 (the LP wasn't released until 1971), yet
the group was already moving away from the all-blues
format. In May 1970 Green abruptly left the group to follow his ascetic religious beliefs. He stayed out of the
music business until the mid-Seventies, when he made
two solo LPs. His departure put an end to Fleetwood
Mac's blues leanings; Danny Kirwan and Christine Perfect moved the band toward leaner, more melodic rock.
Perfect, who had sung with Spencer Davis in folk and
jazz outfits before joining British blues-rockers Chicken
Shack in 1968, had performed uncredited on parts of
Then Play On, but contractual obligations to Chicken
Shack kept her from joining Fleetwood Mac officially
until 1971; by then she had married McVie.

Early in 1971 Spencer disappeared in Los Angeles
and turned up as a member of a religious cult, the Children of God (later the title of a Spencer solo effort). Fleetwood Mac went through a confused period. Bob Welch
joined, supplementing Kirwan's and Christine McVie's
songwriting. Next Kirwan was fired and replaced by Bob
Weston and Dave Walker, both of whom soon departed.
Manager Clifford Davis then formed a group around
Weston and Walker, called it Fleetwood Mac, and sent it
on a U.S. tour. An injunction filed by the real Fleetwood
Mac forced the bogus band to desist (they then formed
the group Stretch), but protracted legal complications
kept Fleetwood Mac from touring for most of 1974. From
then until around the time of the *Tusk* tour in 1979/80,
the band managed itself, with Mick Fleetwood taking
most of the responsibility.

The group relocated to California in 1974. After
Welch left to form the power trio Paris in 1975, Fleetwood
Mac finally found its best-selling lineup. Producer Keith
Olsen played an album he'd engineered, *Buckingham-
Nicks* (Polydor), for Fleetwood and the McVies as a demo
for his studio; Fleetwood Mac hired not only Olsen but
the duo of Lindsey Buckingham and Stevie Nicks, who
had played together in the Bay Area acid-rock group
Fritz from 1968 until 1972, before recording with Olsen.
Fleetwood Mac now had three songwriters, Bucking-
ham's studio craft, and an onstage focal point in Nicks,

who became a late-Seventies sex symbol as *Fleetwood Mac* (#1, 1975) racked up five million in sales. The McVies divorced in 1976, and Buckingham and Nicks, who were romantically linked, separated soon after, but the tensions of the two years between albums helped shape the songs on *Rumours* (#1, 1977), which eventually sold over 17 million copies, won the Grammy for Album of the Year, and contained the 1977 hits "Go Your Own Way" (#10), "Dreams" (#1), "Don't Stop" (#3), and "You Make Loving Fun" (#9). In early 1995 the R.I.A.A. listed it as the second-best-selling album of all time.

After touring the biggest venues around the world—with Nicks, who was prone to throat nodes, always in danger of losing her voice—Fleetwood Mac took another two years and approximately $1 million to make *Tusk* (#4, 1979), an ambitious, frequently experimental project that couldn't match its predecessors' popularity, although it still turned a modest profit and spun off a couple of hits: "Tusk" (#8, 1979) and "Sara" (#7, 1979). Buckingham and Mac engineer Richard Dashut also produced hit singles for John Stewart and Bob Welch. Like many bands who've overspent in the studio, Fleetwood Mac's next effort was a live double album (#14, 1980).

In 1980 Fleetwood and Dashut visited Ghana to record *The Visitor* with African musicians, and Nicks began work on her first solo LP, *Bella Donna,* which hit #1 and went quadruple platinum with three Top Twenty singles: "Stop Draggin' My Heart Around" (a duet with Tom Petty), "Leather and Lace" (a duet with Don Henley), and "Edge of Seventeen (Just Like the White Winged Dove)." Late 1981 saw the release of Buckingham's solo LP, *Law and Order* (#32, 1981) and his Top Ten single "Trouble."

Fleetwood Mac's first collection of new material in three years, *Mirage* (#1), was less overtly experimental and featured the 1982 hit singles "Hold Me" (written by Christine McVie about her relationship with Beach Boy Dennis Wilson) (#4), "Gypsy" (#12), and "Love in Store" (#22). The following year Nicks released her second solo effort, *The Wild Heart,* which contained "Stand Back" (#5). Unlike Buckingham's critically lauded but only moderately popular solo releases, Nicks' were hugely popular, with her third release, *Rock a Little* ("Talk to Me"), charting at #12. In 1984 Christine McVie released two hit singles, "Got a Hold on Me" (#10) and "Love Will Show Us How" (#30), and Buckingham released his critically acclaimed *Go Insane.* Under stress for several reasons—among them each member having his or her own management team, Buckingham's increasing authority in the studio, Nicks' ascent to solo stardom and chemical dependency (treated during a 1987 stint at the Betty Ford Clinic), and Fleetwood's bankruptcy—the group took a hiatus, not coming back together again until 1985, when they began work on *Tango in the Night.* Clearly, given Buckingham's long dissatisfaction with his position in the group, it would be his last Fleetwood Mac project. He officially left the group after deciding not to tour with them to support the album. His replacements, Billy Burnette [see entry], who was a member of Fleetwood's informal side group Zoo, and Rick Vito, toured instead. While the group was at work on *Tango,* Nicks was also recording, working, and touring behind *Rock a Little.* Released in the spring in 1987, *Tango* quickly moved into the Top Ten, bolstered by the Top Twenty hits "Little Lies," "Seven Wonders," and "Everywhere."

Behind the Mask (#18, 1990), Fleetwood Mac's first studio album not to go platinum since 1975, came out in 1990, around which time Christine McVie and Nicks both announced they would remain in the group but no longer tour. Later that year the drummer's memoirs, *Fleetwood: My Life and Adventures in Fleetwood Mac,* was published.

In early 1991 Vito left the group, followed two years later by Burnette. In January 1993 Buckingham joined Fleetwood, the McVies, and Nicks to perform Bill Clinton's campaign anthem, "Don't Stop" at his presidential inaugural gala. The next month Nicks announced her departure from the group; in 1994 she released *Street Angel,* her first album of new material in four years.

Two new members joined Fleetwood Mac in fall 1993: Dave Mason [see entry] and Bekka Bramlett (the daughter of Delaney and Bonnie Bramlett, with whom Mason had toured before Bekka was born). Bramlett had also sung with the Zoo. Christine McVie declined to tour with the band during the summer of 1994; Burnette rejoined for performances in the U.S. and the U.K. As of 1995, the band's albums have been certified for sales exceeding 31 million copies in the U.S.

The Fleetwoods

Formed 1958, Olympia, Washington
Gary Troxel (b. Nov. 28, 1939, Centralia, Wash.),
voc.; Barbara Laine Ellis (b. Feb. 20, 1940, Olympia),
voc.; Gretchen Diane Christopher (b. Feb. 29, 1940,
Olympia), voc.
1990—*Best of the Fleetwoods* (Rhino).

The Fleetwoods were unique among vocal groups in that their angelic, mellow style proved popular not only with the predominantly white pop audience but with R&B fans as well. Their debut single, "Come Softly to Me," hit #1 on the pop chart, then crossed over to #5 R&B in 1959. The three high school friends were known originally as Two Girls and a Guy. They had several other hits, including "Tragedy" (#12, 1959), and a second #1 hit, the DeWayne Blackwell composition "Mr. Blue," in 1959, but broke up in 1963 after releasing a cover of Jesse Belvin's "Goodnight My Love" (#32, 1963). The trio reunited occasionally through the years, and in the wake of the Rhino anthology, Christopher and Troxel, with Cheryl Huggins in Ellis' place, toured.

The Fleshtones

Formed 1976, Queens, New York
Peter Zaremba (b. Sep. 16, 1954, Queens), voc.,
organ, harmonica, perc.; Keith Streng (b. Sep. 18,
1955, Queens), gtr.; Jan Marek Pakulski (b. Aug. 22,
1956, Lewiston, Maine), bass; Lenny Calderone
(b. ca. 1955, New York, N.Y.), drums.
1979—(– Calderone; + Bill Milhizer [b. Sep. 21, ca.
1948, Troy, N.Y.], drums)   1980—*Up Front* EP (I.R.S.)
1982— *Roman Gods*; *Blast Off* (ROIR) (+ Gordon
Spaeth [b. Sep. 21, ca. 1950, New York City, N.Y.],
sax, organ, harmonica)   1983—*Hexbreaker* (I.R.S.)
(– Pakulski; + Robert Burke Warren [b. Mar. 29,
1965, Quantico, Vir.], bass)   1987—*Fleshtones Vs.
Reality* (Emergo)   1988—(– Warren; + Fred Smith,
bass)   1989—(– Smith; + Andy Shernoff [b. Apr. 19,
1952, Bronx, N.Y.], bass)   1990—(– Shernoff; + Ken
Fox [b. Feb. 19, 1965, Toronto, Can.], bass)   1992—
Powerstance (Ichiban)   1994—*The Angry Years*
(Impossible); *Beautiful Light* (Ichiban).

Pigeonholed as garage-rock revivalists, the Fleshtones
mix the hallmarks of that genre—fuzz-guitar and fuzz-
bass riffs, Farfisa organ, "sha-la-la" backing vocals—with
elements of rockabilly, surf rock, and Stax-Volt soul into
their exuberant retro-raveup rock.

Shortly after forming in 1976, the Fleshtones began
playing at CBGB and Max's Kansas City, winning fans on
Manhattan's burgeoning punk-rock scene with their
spirited shows. Their 1979 debut single, "American Beat"
b/w "Critical List," on New York independent label Red
Star Records (home of Suicide, among other acts), led to
a deal with I.R.S. Records, which released the group's
debut EP, *Up Front*. The Fleshtones' first full-length
album, *Roman Gods*, was well received by critics but
sold in only cult-sized numbers. *Blast Off* collected
earlier tracks recorded with original drummer Lenny
Calderone.

While their audience never grew beyond cult status,
the Fleshtones kept recording and touring, gaining
enough of an international profile to inspire Spain's Impossible Records label to release the 1994 compilation
The Angry Years. Fleshtones spin-offs included Peter
Zaremba's Love Delegation and Keith Streng's Full-Time
Men.

Flipper

Formed 1979, San Francisco, California
Will Shatter (b. Russell Wilkinson, 1956; d. Dec. 9,
1987, San Francisco), voc., bass; Bruce Loose
(b. Bruce Calderwood, June 6, 1959, Fresno, Calif.),
bass, voc.; Ted Falconi (b. Laurence Falconi, Sep. 2,
1947, Bryn Mawr, Pa.), gtr.; Steve DePace (b. Jan. 29,
1957, San Francisco), drums.
1982—*Album—Generic Flipper* (Subterranean)

1984—*Gone Fishin'*; *Blow'n Chunks* (ROIR)   1986—
Public Flipper Ltd. (Subterranean)   1987—*Sex
Bomb Baby* (– Shatter)   1992—(+ John Dougherty
[b. Apr. 20, 1961, Oakland, Calif.], bass) *American
Grafishy* (Def American).

Flipper emerged from San Francisco in the early Eighties
as one of America's most powerful and distinctive postpunk bands. Opting for slow-paced noise dirges that, despite their tempo and volume, could never be mistaken
for heavy metal, Flipper influenced many Seattle
"grunge" bands, including Nirvana. Flipper's sometimes
topical ("Love Canal") or philosophical ("Life" rejected
nihilism by declaring "Life's the only thing worth living
for!") lyrics also set it apart.

Will Shatter and Steve DePace had played together
in the Bay Area punk band Negative Trend before forming Flipper with guitarist Ted Falconi and Bruce Loose
(sometimes spelled "Lose"), who traded bass and lead
vocals onstage with Shatter and wrote songs with him
offstage. Loose was already notorious in local punk clubs
for inventing the Worm, a postpogo dance in which he
threw himself on the floor and flailed about, trying to
knock people over. With a sardonic onstage attitude,
Flipper quickly drew a large cult following, and recorded
its first single, "Love Canal" b/w "Ha Ha Ha," in 1980.
Flipper's debut album included "Life," and the seven-
minute classic "Sex Bomb"—in which Shatter periodically screamed a single line ("She's a sex bomb, baby,
yeah!") while the band ground out one monolithic, bass-
heavy riff.

Flipper carried on in this fashion until December 9,
1987, when Shatter died of an accidental heroin overdose. Three years later Flipper regrouped, with Falconi's
old friend John Dougherty on bass; soon after American
Records' Rick Rubin—who had once covered Flipper
songs in the New York City band Hose—called seeking a
demo of new songs. He not only signed Flipper but reissued its first album. The band toured Europe and the U.S.
after the 1992 release of *American Grafishy*.

Flo and Eddie: See the Turtles

A Flock of Seagulls

Formed 1980, Liverpool, England
Mike Score (b. Nov. 5, 1957, Liverpool), voc., kybds.;
Ali Score (b. Alistair Score, Aug. 8, 1956, Liverpool),
drums; Paul Reynolds (b. Aug. 4, 1962, Liverpool),
gtr.; Frank Maudsley (b. Nov. 10, 1959, Liverpool),
bass.
1982—*A Flock of Seagulls* (Jive)   1983—*Listen*
1984—*The Story of a Young Heart* (– Reynolds;
+ Gary Steadnin [b. U.S.], gtr.; + Chris Chryssaphis
[b. U.S.], kybds.)   1986—*Dream Come True*.

One of the first post–new-wave pop bands of the MTV era, A Flock of Seagulls crafted a few techno-rock hits, but is perhaps better-remembered for frontman Mike Score's bizarre "waterfall" haircut—an exaggerated pompadour that cascaded his peroxide-blond locks forward in a long, thin point hanging down to his nose.

Score, in fact, was a former hairdresser with no real musical training when he, salon assistant Frank Maudsley, and Score's brother Ali first formed the band. They made their recording debut with a British EP on Bebop Deluxe guitarist Bill Nelson's Cocteau label; the jet-paced single "Telecommunication" failed to chart in America, but its mix of Eurodisco sequencer beats and sleek dance-rock rhythms found a home in new-wave rock-disco dance clubs. The band's self-titled debut album (#10, 1982) yielded hits in the upbeat "I Ran (So Far Away)" (#9, 1982) and "Space Age Love Song" (#30, 1982), which codified A Flock of Seagulls' ballad technique—wrapping simple, yearning love songs in pillowy, billowy layers of string synthesizers and plangent guitar chords that seemed to zoom off into infinity. The group, which got constant MTV play, tried to affect a half-baked sci-fi aura in its videos.

Listen (#16, 1983) yielded only one hit single, the lovely ballad "Wishing" (#26, 1983), while Story of a Young Heart peaked at #66 (1984), with its single "The More You Live, The More You Love" hitting only #56 (1984). The band eventually replaced departed guitarist Paul Reynolds with a pair of American musicians, and gave it one last try with Dream Come True, which failed to chart at all.

Eddie Floyd

Born June 25, 1935, Montgomery, Alabama
1967—Knock on Wood (Stax)   1968—I've Never Found a Girl   1970—California Girl   1973—Baby Lay Your Head Down (Gently on My Bed)   1974—Soul Street   1977—Experience (Malaco)   1986—Try Me (Seasaint)   1988—Flashback (Wilbe)   1993—Rare Stamps (Stax).

R&B singer and songwriter Eddie Floyd was in his teens when he moved to Detroit, where his uncle Robert West founded the Lupine and Flick labels, two early rivals of Berry Gordy Jr.'s fledgling Motown empire. He had sung in a number of vocal harmony groups before cofounding the Falcons, initially a racially integrated group, in 1956. West arranged the group's deal with Mercury, but they recorded without success, and in 1957, a personnel shuffle resulted in their gaining a new lead singer, Joe (brother of the Four Tops' Levi) Stubbs. Their 1959 hit "You're So Fine" was a Top Twenty pop hit.

Following a few less successful singles, Stubbs left and was replaced by Wilson Pickett, with whom the Falcons recorded "I Found a Love" (complete with backing vocals by another LuPine group, the Primettes, which included future Supremes Mary Wilson and Diana Ross). This version of the Falcons disbanded in 1963, although other groups of singers going under the Falcons name continued to record.

Over the next few years, Floyd released singles on Lupine, Atlantic, and Safice, which he partly owned, before he moved to Washington, D.C., and began commuting to Memphis, where he wrote songs for Stax. He cowrote "Knock on Wood" with Steve Cropper for Otis Redding, but when the label released Floyd's demo version, it went to #28 in 1966. (According to Floyd, the song has been covered over 60 times, including a #1 hit disco version by Amii Stewart in 1979.) Later hits included 1967's "Raise Your Hand," 1968's "I've Never Found a Girl," and "Bring It On Home to Me" (#17) and "California Girl" in 1970. He also wrote songs for others, including "Comfort Me" for Carla Thomas, whom he also produced; "Don't Mess with Cupid" for Otis Redding; "Someone's Watching Over You" for Solomon Burke; and "634-5789" for Wilson Pickett.

Floyd occasionally toured the U.S. and Europe as part of the Stax Revue, but the financially beleaguered label took his career under with it. In 1977 he put out a disco record on Malaco called Experience, but he, like so many other singers of his generation, was displaced on the charts by disco. In 1989 he reunited with several Stax/Atlantic artists for President Bush's inaugural ball. The next month he joined Steve Cropper as a special guest on the Blues Brothers Band world tour. He continues to perform around the world.

The Flying Burrito Brothers

Formed 1968, Los Angeles, California
Gram Parsons (b. Ingram Cecil Connor III, Nov. 5, 1946, Winter Haven, Fla.; d. Sep. 19, 1973, Yucca Valley, Calif.), gtr., voc., kybds.; Chris Hillman (b. Dec. 4, 1942, Los Angeles), bass, gtr., voc.; Sneaky Pete Kleinow (b. ca. 1935, South Bend, Ind.), pedal steel gtr.; Chris Ethridge, bass.
1969—The Gilded Palace of Sin (A&M) (+ Michael Clarke [b. June 3, 1944, New York City; d. Dec. 19, 1993, Treasure Island, Fla.], drums, harmonica; – Ethridge [Hillman moves to bass]; + Bernie Leadon [b. July 19, 1947, Minneapolis, Minn.], gtr., voc., banjo, dobro)   1970—Burrito Deluxe (– Parsons; + Rick Roberts [b. 1950, Fla.], gtr., voc.)   1971—Flying Burrito Brothers (– Kleinow; + Al Perkins, pedal steel gtr.; – Leadon); Last of the Red Hot Burritos (+ Byron Berline, fiddle; + Roger Bush, bass; + Kenny Wertz, gtr.)   1972—(– Hillman; – Perkins; – Clarke; + Alan Munde, banjo, gtr.; + Don Beck, pedal steel gtr.; + Erik Dalton, drums)

1974—*Close Up the Honky Tonks* (group re-forms: Kleinow; Ethridge; + Floyd "Gib" Gilbeau, voc., gtr., fiddle; + Joel Scott Hill, bass, voc.; + Gene Parsons, drums)   1975–*Hot Burrito* (Arista); *Flying Again* (Columbia) (– Ethridge)   1976–(+ Skip Battin [b. Feb. 2, 1934, Gallipolis, Ohio], bass) *Sleepless Nights* (A&M); *Airborne* (Columbia)   1988—*Farther Along: The Best of the Flying Burrito Brothers* (A&M).
Gram Parsons solo: See entry.
Chris Hillman solo: 1982—*Morning Sky* (Sugar Hill) 1984—*Desert Rose.*
Chris Hillman with the Desert Rose Band: 1987— *The Desert Rose Band* (Curb)   1988—*Running* 1990—*Pages of Life*   1991—*A Dozen Roses*; *True Love.*

When Gram Parsons led the Flying Burrito Brothers, his emotive, haunting songs and the band's classic C&W-based virtuosity set the standard for California country rock. After he left, followed by cofounder Chris Hillman, the band quickly devolved into uninspired followers of the style they'd started. Eventually, ex-Burritos went on to greater commercial success in the Eagles, Firefall, and the Desert Rose Band.

Parsons had joined Chris Hillman in the Byrds [see entry] for *Sweetheart of the Rodeo* before the two started the Burritos in Los Angeles. As the lineup gelled (four different drummers played on the band's first album), they recruited ex-Byrd Michael Clarke as drummer. The first album, *The Gilded Palace of Sin* (#164, 1969) only sold about 40,000 copies. The band developed a rabid local following, however, including members of the Rolling Stones (recording in L.A. at the time), who arranged for the group to play at Altamont.

Parsons, who began spending most of his time with Keith Richards, had already lost interest in the Burritos by the recording of the second album. In 1970 Parsons left the band for a solo career [see entry] and was replaced by Rick Roberts, who'd recorded with the Byrds. When Bernie Leadon left to join the nascent Eagles [see entry] and Hillman and Al Perkins were recruited by Stephen Stills for Manassas, Roberts became de facto leader. After Manassas, Hillman joined the Souther-Hillman-Furay Band for two LPs, released a couple of solo albums, and started his own group, the Desert Rose Band, which scored several C&W hits.

Roberts recruited members of bluegrass-rockers Country Gazette for a 1973 European tour, but disbanded the Burritos late in 1973. Roberts then left to form Firefall [see entry]. In 1975 Kleinow and Ethridge revived the name with ex–Canned Heat bassist Joel Scott Hill and fiddler "Gib" Gilbeau, but Ethridge left in 1976. Various aggregations of Burritos have periodically hit the honky-tonk club circuit into the Nineties.

The Flying Lizards
Formed 1978, Ireland
David Cunningham, kybds.; Deborah Evans, voc.
1980—*Flying Lizards* (Virgin).

As the Flying Lizards, conceptual artist David Cunningham and session vocalist Deborah Evans enjoyed novelty hits with their radically rearranged, disinterested versions of Barrett Strong's "Money" and Eddie Cochran's "Summertime Blues."

Irish art-school student Cunningham performed with a 13-piece band, Les Cochons Chic. He made a minimalist solo album, *Grey Scale,* in the late Seventies. In 1978 he conceived the Flying Lizards and put out "Summertime Blues," which attracted some attention in Britain. The followup, "Money," had its signature riff played on an upright piano with rubber toys, sheet music, cassettes, and telephone directories inside. The song was recorded for approximately $14 in a home studio. "Money" (#50, U.S., #5 U.K., 1979) picked up substantial U.S. airplay and prompted Virgin to ask for an album, which also included a Brecht-Weill song and more Cunningham instrumentals.

Cunningham later worked with the Pop Group, the Modettes, the Electric Chairs, and This Heat. He returned to experimental music and work in theater and film. In 1984 the Flying Lizards regrouped to issue *Top Ten* (not released stateside), which dismantled songs by Jimi Hendrix, Little Richard, and Leonard Cohen, among others.

Focus
Formed 1969, Amsterdam, Netherlands
Thijs Van Leer (b. Mar. 31, 1948, Amsterdam), organ, flute, voc.; Martin Dresden, bass; Hans Cleuver, drums.
1970—(+ Jan Akkerman [b. Dec. 24, 1946, Amsterdam], gtr.)   1971—*In and Out of Focus* (Sire) (– Cleuver; + Pierre Van der Linden [b. Feb. 19, 1946, Neth.], drums; – Dresden; + Cyril Havermanns, bass); *Moving Waves* (– Havermanns; + Bert Ruiter [b. Nov. 26, 1946], bass)   1972—*Focus III*   1973—*Live at Rainbow* (– Van der Linden; + Colin Allen, drums, perc.)   1974—*Hamburger Concerto* (Atco); *Ship of Memories* (Harvest) 1975—*Mother Focus* (– Allen); *Dutch Masters* 1976—(+ Van der Linden, drums; – Akkerman; – Van der Linden; + Philip Catherine [b. London, Eng.], gtr.; + Steve Smith, drums; + Eef Albers, gtr.) 1978—*Focus Con Proby* (with P. J. Proby) (Harvest). Jan Akkerman solo: 1973—*Profile* (Sire)   1974— *Tabernakel* (Atco)   1977—*Eli*   1978—*Jan Akkerman* (Atlantic).

The progressive-rock band Focus became a major draw in Europe playing extended songs with tinges of classical melody from flutist Thijs Van Leer and pyrotechnical solos by guitarist Jan Akkerman. In the U.S. Focus is remembered for a yodeling novelty single, "Hocus Pocus" (#9, 1973).

Classically trained Jan Akkerman became known in the Netherlands as a member of Brainbox, which also included drummer Pierre Van der Linden. Meanwhile, Thijs Van Leer, a classically trained keyboardist and flutist, formed Focus in 1969 as a trio; its first gig was as a pit band for the Dutch production of *Hair*. In 1970 Akkerman joined in order to try making more complex music than Brainbox's. Focus' debut album was modestly successful in Europe, and the followup included "Hocus Pocus," which became an international hit. The band considered it a joke but wound up stuck with it as a signature song.

Focus had their second and last U.S. chart showing with "Sylvia" (1973), then returned to more ambitious compositions on *Focus III*, which went gold, as had *Moving Waves*. In the early Seventies Focus was a headlining band in the U.S. and Europe. After 1974's *Hamburger Concerto*, the group turned to more concise four-minute pop songs on 1975's *Mother Focus*. Akkerman left in 1976 to continue his concurrent solo career; he was replaced by guitarist Philip Catherine in the group's waning years. *Focus Con Proby* featured British pop star P. J. Proby. After Focus' peak, Akkerman released a string of solo albums, and Van Leer released the three-volume *Introspection, Nice to Have Met You,* and *O My Love*. Future Journey drummer Steve Smith was briefly a member in 1978. The group re-formed for a Dutch television special around 1990.

Dan Fogelberg

Born August 13, 1951, Peoria, Illinois
1972—*Home Free* (Columbia)   1974—*Souvenirs*
(Full Moon/Epic)   1975—*Captured Angel*   1977—
Nether Lands   1978—Twin Sons of Different
Mothers* (with Tim Weisberg)   1979—*Phoenix
1981—*The Innocent Age*   1982—*Greatest Hits*
1984—*Windows and Walls*   1985—*High Country*
Snows*   1987—*Exiles*   1990—*The Wild Places
1991—*Dan Fogelberg Live—Greetings from the*
***West*   1993—*River of Souls*.**

Singer/songwriter Dan Fogelberg studied piano for a few years, began playing the guitar, and was composing at age 14. During the two years he studied art at the University of Illinois in Champaign, he also played campus coffeehouses, where he met Irving Azoff, ex-student and manager of local bands like REO Speedwagon. In 1971 Fogelberg dropped out of school, moved to Los Angeles, and signed with Columbia. *Home Free* went largely unnoticed, but his second album, *Souvenirs* (produced by Joe Walsh), went double platinum on the strength of "Part of the Plan" (#31, 1975).

In the early Seventies Fogelberg was very active in West Coast music circles, guesting on LPs by Jackson Browne, Roger McGuinn, and Randy Newman. Uncomfortable with the starmaker lifestyle, he left California in late 1974. In 1976 his backup group, Fool's Gold, released a self-titled LP that featured its own single, "Rain, Oh Rain."

Eventually settling in Boulder, Colorado, Fogelberg continued his string of platinum albums with *Captured Angel* (#23, 1975); *Nether Lands* (#13, 1977); *Twin Sons of Different Mothers* (#8, 1978), a collaboration with jazz-pop flutist Tim Weisberg; *Phoenix* (#3, 1979); and *The Innocent Age* (#6, 1981), a double-album song cycle.

Although the singer/songwriter genre was in noticeable decline by the early Eighties, Fogelberg bucked the trend with *The Innocent Age*. Four singles from that album, "Hard to Say," "Leader of the Band," "Run for the Roses," and "Same Old Lang Syne," reached the Top Twenty. His last big hit was 1984's "Language of Love" (#13, 1984), an uncharacteristically hard rocker. From there, however, Fogelberg changed gear, recording bluegrass with guest stars Doc Watson, Ricky Skaggs, and David Grisman on *High Country Snows*. It was his first album in more than a decade to sell fewer than 500,000 copies. None of his four subsequent albums has matched his former sales, but Fogelberg still commands an audience. *River of Souls* marked another departure, incorporating South African singers, Brazilian rhythms, and other world-music elements.

John Fogerty: See Creedence Clearwater Revival

Foghat

Formed 1971, London, England
"Lonesome" Dave Peverett (b. 1950, Eng.), gtr., voc.;
Roger Earl (b. 1949, Eng.), drums; Rod Price
(b. Eng.), gtr.; Tony Stevens (b. Sept. 12, 1949, Eng.),
bass.
1972—*Foghat* (Bearsville)   1973—*Foghat*   1974—
***Energized; Rock and Roll Outlaws* (– Stevens;**
+ Nick Jameson [b. Mo.], bass, kybds., synth.)
1975—*Fool for the City* (– Jameson; + Craig Mac-
Gregor [b. Conn.], bass)   1976—*Night Shift*   1977—
Live*   1978—*Stone Blue*   1979—*Boogie Motel
1980—*Tight Shoes* (– Price; + Erik Cartwright, gtr.)
1981—*Girls to Chat and Boys to Bounce*   1982—*In*
the Mood for Something Rude*   1983—*Zig-Zag Walk
1988—*Best of Foghat* (Rhino)   1992—*Best of*
Foghat, vol. 2.

Foghat's basic blues-based boogie and extensive U.S. touring brought it a loyal audience and gold and platinum albums (*Rock and Roll Outlaws, Fool for the City,*

Grammy Awards

José Feliciano

1968 Best Contemporary Pop Vocal Performance, Male: "Light My Fire"
1968 Best New Artist
1983 Best Latin Pop Performance: *Me Enamore*
1986 Best Latin Pop Performance: "Lelolai"
1989 Best Latin Pop Performance: "Cielito Lindo"
1990 Best Latin Pop Performance: "Por Que te Tengo Que Olvidar?"

Fifth Dimension

1967 Best Contemporary Group Performance (Vocal or Instrumental): "Up, Up and Away"
1967 Best Contemporary Single: "Up, Up and Away"
1967 Best Performance by a Vocal Group: "Up, Up and Away"
1967 Record of the Year: "Up, Up and Away" (with Marc Gordon and Johnny Rivers)
1969 Best Contemporary Vocal Performance by a Group: "Aquarius/Let the Sunshine In"
1969 Record of the Year: "Aquarius/Let the Sunshine In" (with Bones Howe)

Billy Davis Jr. (Fifth Dimension)

1976 Best R&B Performance by a Duo, Group or Chorus: "You Don't Have to Be a Star (to Be in My Show)" (with Marilyn McCoo)

Marilyn McCoo (Fifth Dimension)

1976 Best R&B Performance by a Duo, Group or Chorus: "You Don't Have to Be a Star (to Be in My Show)" (with Billy Davis Jr.)

Roberta Flack

1972 Record of the Year: "The First Time Ever I Saw Your Face"
1972 Best Pop Vocal Performance by a Duo, Group or Chorus: "Where Is the Love" (with Donny Hathaway)
1973 Best Pop Vocal Performance, Female: "Killing Me Softly with His Song"
1973 Record of the Year: "Killing Me Softly with His Song"

Fleetwood Mac

1977 Album of the Year: *Rumours* (with Richard Dashut and Ken Caillat)

A Flock of Seagulls

1982 Best Rock Instrumental Performance: "D.N.A."

Aretha Franklin

1967 Best R&B Recording: "Respect" (with Jerry Wexler)
1967 Best R&B Solo Vocal Performance, Female: "Respect"
1968 Best R&B Vocal Performance, Female: "Chain of Fools"
1969 Best R&B Vocal Performance, Female: "Share Your Love with Me"
1970 Best R&B Vocal Performance, Female: "Don't Play That Song"
1971 Best R&B Vocal Performance, Female: "Bridge over Troubled Water"
1972 Best R&B Vocal Performance, Female: *Young, Gifted and Black*
1972 Best Soul Gospel Performance: *Amazing Grace*
1973 Best R&B Vocal Performance, Female: "Master of Eyes"
1974 Best R&B Vocal Performance, Female: "Ain't Nothing Like the Real Thing"
1981 Best R&B Vocal Performance, Female: "Hold On, I'm Comin' "
1985 Best R&B Vocal Performance, Female: "Freeway of Love"
1987 Best R&B Performance by a Duo or Group with Vocal: "I Knew You Were Waiting (for Me)" (with George Michael)
1987 Best R&B Vocal Performance, Female: *Aretha*
1988 Best Soul Gospel Performance, Female: *One Lord, One Faith, One Baptism*
1991 Grammy Legend Award
1994 Lifetime Achievement Award

Night Shift, plus four others) in the mid-Seventies. "Lonesome" Dave Peverett founded Foghat along the lines of Savoy Brown, his previous band [see entry]. (Tony Stevens and Roger Earl had also been in Savoy Brown.) After three years of heavy touring—throughout the Seventies the group averaged eight months per year on the road—cofounder Stevens was replaced by Nick Jameson, who had helped mix Foghat's first albums. While he was in the band, Jameson was also producer, and he oversaw its first hit single, "Slow Ride" (#20, 1976).

Jameson left in 1976 for a solo career and other production work. By then the band was based on Long Island and recruited replacements in the U.S. In 1977 Foghat hosted a benefit concert for the New York Public Library's blues collection, with guests Muddy Waters and John Lee Hooker. Their late-Seventies albums yielded three hits: "Stone Blue" (#36, 1978), "Third-Time Lucky" (#23, 1979), and a live version of "I Just Want to Make Love to You" (#33, 1977).

In 1993 Peverett, Price, Stevens, and Earl re-formed the original Foghat lineup for a U.S. tour.

Folk Revival

As the Fifties ended and the Sixties began, students and city dwellers became interested in folk music—authentic rural performers like Leadbelly and Woody Guthrie, and collectors and re-creators like the Weavers, the Kingston Trio, Josh White, and Burl Ives. Guthrie had spread the idea of the topical protest song, and during the McCarthy era it was taken up by the American left. The Weavers' Pete Seeger had an international repertoire that included children's songs, spirituals, organizing songs, and foreign pop.

As McCarthyism wound down, folk music and pop for acoustic guitars spread in mainstream popularity, and the folk revival encouraged amateur strummers to try it themselves. There was even a folk-oriented prime-time television series called *Hootenanny,* which ran from April 1963 to September 1964, and featured artists ranging from the commercial (such as the Chad Mitchell Trio) to the authentic (the Carter Family).

Folk music's legacy to rock & roll appears in an array of forms, from Bob Dylan's incalculably influential work to the more mainstream Top Forty hits of Peter, Paul and Mary. One result was folk rock and the creation of a subset of rock artists referred to as singer/songwriters. Even though there were plenty of rock, R&B, and country artists writing their own material before that, the singer/songwriter subgenre became synonymous with "folky," and in the folk tradition of straightforward lyrics came the more personal, introspective, confessional songs associated with the genre. Periodically, there appears to be another folk revival on the horizon, but more often than not, it's simply the emergence of one or several important folk-styled singer/songwriters, such as Tracy Chapman and Suzanne Vega in the Eighties, rather than a widespread movement.

Folk Rock

Folk rock, a hybrid that sprung up in 1965, contained borrowings from two seemingly contradictory genres. The idea was to set the folk songs of the hootenanny era, especially those of Bob Dylan and his many disciples (and to a degree the work of their predecessors, such as Woody Guthrie), to a rock & roll beat. In practice, it generally meant that strumming guitars were augmented by a rhythm section, as in Simon and Garfunkel's "The Sounds of Silence" or in the Byrds' version of Dylan's "Mr. Tambourine Man." Another genre that folk rock borrowed from was traditional country music.

With an importance placed on lyrics by folk singers, folk rockers followed suit, and in so doing gave rock songwriters the impetus to try unconventional lyrics. When Dylan himself went electric, he created a more muscular, blues-tinged brand of folk rock, whereas the meticulous pop of the Byrds helped to lay the groundwork for the California rock of the Seventies. Other practitioners of folk rock included the Lovin' Spoonful, Donovan, the Turtles, the Mamas and the Papas, and—leaning more toward the country element the Buffalo Springfield.

Wayne Fontana and the Mindbenders

Formed 1963, Manchester, England
Wayne Fontana (b. Glynn Geoffrey Ellis, Oct. 28, 1945, Manchester), voc.; Bob Lang (b. Jan. 10, 1946, Manchester), bass; Eric Stewart (b. Jan. 20, 1945, Manchester), gtr.; Ric Rothwell (b. Mar. 11, 1944, Manchester), drums.
1965—*Wayne Fontana and the Mindbenders* (Fontana); *The Game of Love* 1966—*Eric, Rick, Wayne, Bob* (– Fontana; + Graham Gouldman [b. May 10, 1946, Manchester], bass); *The Mindbenders* 1967—*With Woman in Mind; A Groovy Kind of Love.*
Wayne Fontana solo: 1966—*Wayne One* (Fontana).

Wayne Fontana and the Mindbenders' contribution to the British Invasion was "Game of Love" (#1, 1965), and the Mindbenders minus Fontana followed up with "A Groovy Kind of Love" (#2, 1966).

Glynn Ellis started out in a school skiffle group, the Velfins. By 1963 he was playing in a Manchester pub band, the Jets, while working as an apprentice telephone engineer. Ellis arranged to have the Jets play for a Fontana Records talent scout at Manchester's Oasis Club, but only Ellis and bassist Bob Lang showed up for the audition. They recruited some musician friends from the audience and landed a contract, with Ellis becoming Wayne Fontana at a Philips/Fontana Records executive's behest. They started recording R&B covers in 1963 and began to score British hits in 1964 with a version of Major Lance's "Um, Um, Um, Um, Um, Um."

In 1965 "Game of Love" became an international hit, but after one more hit, "It's Just a Little Bit Too Late" (#45, 1965), Fontana decided on a solo career. He had a few U.K. hits—"Pamela, Pamela" and "Come On Home"—before moving into cabaret and nostalgia-rock revues, including a major English tour in 1979.

The Mindbenders had two U.S. hits on their own, "A Groovy Kind of Love" and "Ashes to Ashes," and they appeared in *To Sir with Love* before breaking up in the late Sixties. Gouldman—whose songs were British Invasion hits for Herman's Hermits, the Yardbirds, and others—and Stewart founded a group called Hotlegs, and then 10cc [see entry] in the Seventies. A version of Wayne Fontana and the Mindbenders continues to perform.

Steve Forbert

Born 1955, Meridian, Mississippi
1978—*Alive on Arrival* (Nemperor) 1979—*Jackrabbit Slim* 1980—*Little Stevie Orbit* 1982—*Steve Forbert* 1988—*Streets of This Town* (Geffen)

1992—*The American in Me*   **1993**—*What Kinda Guy? The Best of Steve Forbert* (Columbia/Legacy) **1995**—*Mission of the Crossroad Palms* (Cantador).

Folk-rock singer/songwriter Steve Forbert learned guitar at age 11 and later played in a variety of semipro rock bands on through college. At age 21, he quit his job as a truckdriver and moved to New York, where he began singing for spare change in Grand Central Station. Forbert worked his way up through the Manhattan clubs before landing a contract with Nemperor in 1978. His debut album, *Alive on Arrival*, was well received, and its followup, *Jackrabbit Slim* (#20, 1979), yielded a #11 single, "Romeo's Tune" (allegedly dedicated to the late Supreme Florence Ballard).

Little Stevie Orbit and *Steve Forbert* were neither critical nor commercial hits. In 1985 Forbert moved to Nashville and has continued to perform. His 1988 album, *Streets of This Town*, was produced by Garry Tallent, as was *Mission of the Crossroad Palms*. Forbert retains a sizable following and the respect of many critics for his finely crafted songs. To MTV viewers, however, he is probably best known for his cameo role as Cyndi Lauper's tuxedoed boyfriend in the "Girls Just Wanna Have Fun" video.

Force M.D.'s
Formed 1979 as Dr. Rock and the M.C.'s, Staten Island, New York
Stevie D. (b. Steve Lundy, Dec. 15, 1965, New York City, N.Y.), voc.; T.C.D. (b. Antoine Maurice Lundy, Feb. 3, 1965, New York City, N.Y.), voc.; Jesse Lee Daniels (b. July 4, 1963, N.C.), voc.; Trisco Pearson (b. ca. 1963, New York City, N.Y.), voc.; Mercury (b. Charles Richard Nelson, (1965, New York City, N.Y.), voc.
1984—*Love Letters* (Tommy Boy)   **1986**—*Chillin'* **1987**—*Touch and Go* (– Daniels)   **1990**—*Step to Me* (– Pearson; – Nelson; + Khalil [b. Rodney Lundy, Aug. 9, 1968, New York City, N.Y.], voc.; + Shaun Waters [b. July 11, 1965, Portland, Ore.], voc.) **1992**—*For Lovers and Others* (+ Daniels)   **1994**— *Get Ready* (THG/PolyGram).

Nearly a decade before Color Me Badd and Boyz II Men took hip-hop doo-wop to the top of the charts, Force M.D.'s crossed romantic R&B harmonies with a rap attitude. The Lundy brothers (T.C.D. and Stevie D.), along with their uncle Jesse Lee Daniels and friends Trisco and Mercury, began their career in the late Seventies, singing hip-hop–inspired doo-wop songs on the Staten Island Ferry and Greenwich Village streetcorners. On a good day, they would bring home $400. Then calling themselves Dr. Rock and the M.C.'s, they began appearing at such hip-hop venues as the Roxy, in New York.

After the group was signed to Tommy Boy in 1984,

the renamed Force M.D.'s began churning out R&B hits. The group's first single from *Love Letters*, "Let Me Love You," only reached #49 R&B, but its second, "Tears," went to #5 R&B. Followup hits from the debut album included "Forgive Me Girl" (#49 R&B, 1985) and "Itchin' for a Scratch" (#13 R&B, 1985).

The Jimmy Jam–Terry Lewis ballad "Tender Love" (#10 pop, #4 R&B, 1986), from the rap movie *Krush Groove*, introduced Force M.D.'s to the larger pop audience. Other singles that year were "Here I Go Again" (#18 R&B, 1986), "One Plus One" (#29 R&B, 1986), and "I Wanna Know Your Name" (#21 R&B, 1986). In 1987 the quartet scored its first #1 R&B single, "Love Is a House," with the followup hit "Touch and Go" (#10 R&B, 1987). The group's star began fading by 1988, its only hit single that year being "Couldn't Care Less" (#23 R&B). Force M.D.'s teamed up with the rap group Stetsasonic in 1988 for a hip-hop remake of the Floaters' "Float On" (#56 R&B).

By the early Nineties, Mercury and Trisco had departed to pursue solo careers; a third Lundy brother, Khalil, joined the group, along with Shaun Waters. After working with other artists as producers, Force M.D.'s returned in 1994 with *Get Ready*.

Emile Ford and the Checkmates
Born Emile Sweetman, October 16, 1937, St. Lucia, West Indies

This shy West Indian became the first nonwhite to hit the British pop chart when "What Do You Want to Make Those Eyes at Me For?" sold a million copies in 1959. Ford, who was discovered singing in London coffeehouses, was heavily influenced by Fats Domino. He was backed by a group called the Checkmates, whose original members included his stepbrothers George and Dave Sweetman, John Cuffley, Ken Street, Les Hart, Peter Carter, and Alan Hawkshaw. After his gold disc in 1959, Ford's followups flopped. He moved into record production and then relocated to the Continent, where he played on and off for the next several years, sometimes returning to Britain in rock revival shows. The Checkmates later backed singer P. J. Proby.

Frankie Ford
Born August 4, 1939, Gretna, Louisiana
N.A.—*Best of Frankie Ford* (Ace).

Frankie Ford was a white singer and pianist whose "Sea Cruise" (#14, 1959) remains one of the best New Orleans rockers of all time. To date the record has sold more than 30 million copies worldwide.

Ford, who appeared on *Ted Mack's Amateur Hour* at age eight, was marketed in the late Fifties as Ace Records' attempt at a teen idol. The "Sea Cruise" track was made by Huey "Piano" Smith and the Clowns; Smith's vocals were erased and Ford's overdubbed, as was the case with the less popular followup, "Alimony." Ford's touring band included Mac Rebennack, later better known as Dr. John, on guitar. The singer had minor hits in 1960 ("You Talk Too Much" and "Time After Time") and 1961 ("Seventeen"). He was drafted in 1962. After his discharge, he returned to recording—with the Paula and ABC labels, as well as his own, Briarmeade— but he has supported himself primarily by performing in oldies package shows. Ford also comanages several other oldies acts, including the Dixie Cups and Johnny Preston.

Lita Ford

Born Rosanna Ford, September 23, 1959, London, England
1983—*Out for Blood* (Mercury)   1984—*Dancin' on the Edge*   1988—*Lita* (RCA)   1990—*Stiletto*   1991—*Dangerous Curves*   1992—*The Best of Lita Ford*   1995—*Black* (ZYX).

After the Runaways [see entry] broke up, guitarist and singer Lita Ford pursued a solo career as a hard-rock artist, counterbalancing her blond bombshell image by flexing her metal muscularity. She has found rare acceptance in that male world: She was the first woman in 20 years to be inducted into *Circus* magazine's Hall of Fame and was the first woman ever on the cover of *Hit Parader*.

Inspired by Jimi Hendrix, Ford led a power trio on her first two albums. Neither did well, and in 1986 she changed labels, managers, and producers. Ford hit it big with the platinum pop metal of *Lita* (#29, 1988), which was produced by glam master Mike Chapman and featured "Kiss Me Deadly" (#12, 1988), "Can't Catch Me" (cowritten with Motörhead's Lemmy), and "Close My Eyes Forever" (#8, 1989), a duet with Ozzy Osbourne. Sales were helped by her videos, in which she looked like a gas-station calendar girl come to life. Ford's subsequent records failed to sell as well. In 1992 she was a member of the house band for Howie Mandel's CBS show *Howie*. In 1995 Ford released *Black*, a less hard-rocking album produced by the Robb Brothers (Lemonheads, Buffalo Tom).

Julia Fordham

Born August 10, 1962, Portsmouth, England
1988—*Julia Fordham* (Virgin)   1989—*Porcelain*   1991—*Swept*   1994—*Falling Forward*.

In the late Eighties Julia Fordham was among a new crop of female singer/songwriters whose folk-influenced, intellectually ambitious pop traced its lineage to the earlier work of Joni Mitchell and Joan Armatrading. Her sultry alto and delicate, jazz-inflected songs about love and other social dilemmas have endeared her to fans of both alternative pop and adult contemporary music.

Fordham grew up on the southern coast of England, got her first guitar at six, and eventually began performing in local pubs with her older brother. In her late teens, Fordham moved to London, where she hooked up with pop singer Mari Wilson and recorded an album as part of a beehive-hairdo-sporting group called Mari Wilson and the Wilsations. After two years as a Wilsation, Fordham found work backing singer Kim Wilde, then decided to parlay the songwriting she'd been doing since early adolescence into more serious artistic pursuits. Fordham released a self-titled solo album in 1988. A sophomore album, 1989's *Porcelain*, reached the top of the adult-contemporary chart, and Fordham became a familiar presence on VH-1. Like its predecessor, *Porcelain* embellished a mellow pop-jazz with touches of African folk and Brazilian samba. A third album, *Swept*, proved less successful. Fordham returned in 1994 with a less controlled delivery on *Falling Forward*, singing with abandon on "Caged Bird" and the gospel-tinged "Hope, Prayer & Time."

Foreigner

Formed 1976, New York City, New York
Mick Jones (b. Dec. 27, 1944, London, Eng.), gtr., voc.; Ian McDonald (b. June 25, 1946, London), flute, kybds., reeds, gtr., voc.; Al Greenwood (b. New York City), kybds., synth.; Lou Gramm (b. May 2, 1950, Rochester, N.Y.), voc.; Ed Gagliardi, bass; Dennis Elliott (b. Eng.), drums.
1977—*Foreigner* (Atlantic)   1978—*Double Vision*   1979—(– Gagliardi; + Rick Wills, bass) *Head Games*   1980—(– McDonald; – Greenwood)   1981—*4*   1982—*Records*   1984—*Agent Provocateur*   1987— *Inside Information*   1991—(– Gramm; + Johnny Edwards, voc.) *Unusual Heat*   1992—*The Very Best . . . and Beyond* (– Wills; – Elliott; + Gramm)   1993—*Classic Hits Live* (Atlantic)   1994—(Lineup: Jones; Gramm; + Mark Schulman, drums; + Jeff Jacobs, kybds.; + Bruce Turgon, bass) *Mr. Moonlight* (Rhythm Safari).
Lou Gramm solo: 1987—*Ready or Not* (Atlantic)   1989—*Long Hard Look*.
Mick Jones solo: 1989—*Mick Jones* (Atlantic).

Despite accusations of formulaic commercialism, Foreigner's heavy metal with keyboard flourishes has racked up sales of over 30 million records worldwide to date.

The band is led by British journeyman rocker Mick Jones, who played in the Sixties with Nero and the Gladiators, a Shadows-like group that had several hits in England, including "Hall of the Mountain King." He worked with French rock singer Johnny Hallyday, then

Foreigner: (top) Lou Gramm, Mick Jones, (bottom) Rick Wills, Dennis Elliott

with a latter-day version of Spooky Tooth. Jones had worked as an A&R man in New York before joining the Leslie West Band. A year later he decided to form his own band. In early 1976 he met ex–King Crimson [see entry] multi-instrumentalist Ian McDonald at recording sessions for Ian Lloyd, former lead singer of Stories. A few months later Jones and McDonald formed Foreigner with four unknown musicians, including lead vocalist Lou Gramm, founder and lead singer of Black Sheep, a Free and Bad Company cover band in upstate New York.

The group's 1977 debut sold more than four million copies in the U.S. and stayed in the Top Twenty for a year, on the strength of "Feels Like the First Time" (#4, 1977), "Cold as Ice" (#6, 1977), and "Long, Long Way From Home" (#20, 1978). *Double Vision* (#3, 1978), which sold five million records, spawned "Hot Blooded" (#3, 1978) and a #2 hit with the title track. Late in the year Foreigner headlined the Reading, England, music festival. "Dirty White Boy" (#12) and "Head Games" (#14) hit in 1979. Several personnel changes occurred, so that by late 1980 the group was a quartet, with Rick Wills (formerly of Frampton's Camel, Small Faces, and Roxy Music) on bass. Gagliardi and Greenwood went on to form the much-ignored Spys.

Foreigner's next album, *4* (#1, 1981), was its biggest ever, racking up six million in sales. It provided two Top Ten singles: a rare ballad, "Waiting for a Girl Like You" (#2), and "Urgent" (#4), which featured Junior Walker on sax. *Agent Provocateur* (#4, 1984) went platinum, yielding the #1 pop hit "I Want to Know What Love Is," an epic piece of AOR-gospel on which Gramm was backed by

the New Jersey Mass Choir. The album spawned another hit in "That Was Yesterday" (#12, 1984). *Inside Information* (#15, 1987) also went platinum, featuring the hit "Say You Will" (#6, 1987). Gramm then went solo, and scored with "Midnight Blue" (#5, 1987) and "Just Between You and Me" (#6, 1989). Jones' solo album reached only #184 and had no hit singles. In 1989 Jones and Billy Joel coproduced the latter's *Stormfront*. In late summer 1993, Jones and Gramm announced that they were re-forming Foreigner, with an entirely new backing band. This band released *Mr. Moonlight*.

Robert Forster: See the Go-Betweens

The Foundations
Formed 1967, London, England
Peter Macbeth (b. Feb. 2, 1943, London), bass; Alan Warner (b. Apr. 21, 1947, London), gtr.; Clem Curtis (b. Nov. 28, 1940, Trinidad), voc.; Eric Allan Dale (b. Mar. 4, 1936, West Indies), trombone; Tony Gomez (b. Dec. 13, 1948, Ceylon), organ; Pat Burke (b. Oct. 9, 1937, Jam.), sax, flute; Mike Elliot (b. Aug. 6, 1929, Jam.), sax; Tim Harris (b. Jan. 14, 1948, London), drums.
1967—*Baby Now That I've Found You* (Uni)   1968— (– Curtis; + Colin Young [b. Sep. 12, 1944, Barbados], voc.)   1969—*Build Me Up Buttercup*; *Digging the Foundations*.

The Foundations were a mid-Sixties pop band that had two major hits: the Motown-ish "Baby Now That I've Found You" and "Build Me Up Buttercup." In London the group became the house band at the Butterfly Club in Westbourne Grove. Record store owner Barry Class became the Foundations' manager and introduced them to songwriter Tony Macauley, who got them a record deal and then wrote and produced their hits.

Their debut single, "Baby Now That I've Found You" (#11, 1968), went gold. A minor hit, "Back on My Feet Again," followed before "Build Me Up Buttercup" (cowritten by Macauley and former Manfred Mann vocalist Mike d'Abo) hit #3 in early 1969. Followups like "In the Bad, Bad Old Days" and "My Little Chickadee" failed to hit, and the group split up in 1970, although the name was used by a British cabaret act (with little relation to the original group) for several years in the early Seventies.

The Four Seasons
Formed 1956, Newark, New Jersey
Original lineup: Frankie Valli (b. Francis Casteluccio, May 3, 1937, Newark), voc.; Tommy DeVito (b. June 19, 1936, Belleville, N.J.), gtr.; Nick DeVito, gtr.; Hank Majewski (d. 1969), bass.

1960—(– N. DeVito; + Bob Gaudio [b. Nov. 17, 1942, Bronx, N.Y.], kybds.; – Majewski; + Nick Massi [b. Sep. 19, 1935, Newark], bass) 1963—*Sherry* (Vee Jay); *Greetings*; *Big Girls Don't Cry*; *Ain't That a Shame* 1964—*Stay*; *Dawn* (Philips); *Rag Doll* 1965—(– Massi; + Joe Long, bass; numerous personnel changes follow) *Entertain You*; *Gold Vault Hits*; *Working My Way Back to You* 1966—*Second Vault*; *Looking Back* 1968—*Seasoned Hits* (Fontana) 1969—*Genuine Imitation Life Gazette*; *Big Ones* 1970—(– T. DeVito) 1972—*Chameleon* (Mowest) 1974—(– Gaudio) 1975—*Who Loves You* (Warner Bros.) 1977—*Helicon* 1980—(Group re-forms: Valli; Gaudio; Gerry Polci [b. 1954, Passaic, N.J.], drums, voc.; + Don Ciccone [b. Feb. 28, 1946, N.Y.], gtr.; + Jerry Corbetta [b. Sep. 23, 1947, Denver, Colo.], kybds.; + Larry Lingle [b. Apr. 4, 1949, Kans.], gtr.) 1981—*Reunited Live* 1985—*Streetfighter* 1987—*Frankie Valli and the Four Seasons—25th Anniversary Collection* 1988—*Anthology* (Rhino) 1990—*Rarities, vol. 1*; *Rarities, vol. 2*; *20 Greatest Hits: Live* (Curb); *Greatest Hits, vol. 1*; *Greatest Hits, vol. 2* (Rhino) 1992—*Hope + Glory* (Curb) 1995—*Oh What a Night*. Frankie Valli solo: 1975—*Inside You* (Motown); *Close Up* (Private Stock) 1976—*Story* 1978—*Frankie Valli Is the Word* (Warner Bros.) 1979—*Very Best of Frankie Valli* (MCA) 1981—*Heaven Above Me*; *The Very Best of Frankie Valli* (Warner Bros.).

During their nearly 40-year career, Frankie Valli and the Four Seasons have sold over 100 million records, making them the most long-lived and successful white doo-wop group. Lead singer Valli (whose three-octave range and falsetto are the group's trademark) has also maintained a successful solo career.

Valli, sometimes billed under his real name and later as Valley (after Texas Jean Valley, a country singer who had encouraged him as a child), began singing in his mid-teens with the Newark vocal groups the Romans and the Varietones. The Varietones, which included Hank Majewski and the DeVito brothers, eventually became the Four Lovers. The Lovers' "You're the Apple of My Eye," a tune songwriter Otis Blackwell gave them in exchange for their not recording his "Don't Be Cruel" (which he then gave to Elvis Presley), was a hit in 1956, and they appeared on *The Ed Sullivan Show*.

The Four Lovers became the Four Seasons (named after a Jersey cocktail lounge) with the addition of Bob Gaudio, formerly of the Royal Teens and composer of their hit "Short Shorts." As the group's chief songwriter, Gaudio changed their repertoire and sound, which were later refined by producer Bob Crewe. After a single, "Bermuda," flopped, they again became the Four Lovers

and returned to the clubs. They also served as Crewe's production group, arranging, performing and providing instrumental and vocal backing in singles Crewe produced for other singers. This arrangement continued until 1962, when Valli, desperate over the group's lack of success, nearly quit the band. Then they recorded a song by Gaudio, "Sherry." After the song was featured on *American Bandstand*, the Four Lovers became the Four Seasons once again, and within months "Sherry" hit #1.

The followup, "Big Girls Don't Cry," also went to #1, and over the next five years (until Valli's first solo hit, "I Can't Take My Eyes Off You" in 1967), the Four Seasons had 50 hits, including "Santa Claus Is Coming to Town" (in an arrangement later imitated by Bruce Springsteen) (#23, 1962); "Walk Like a Man" (#1), "Ain't That a Shame" (#22), and "Candy Girl" (#3) in 1963; "Dawn" (#3), "Girl Come Running" (#30), "Let's Hang On" (#3), and "Working My Way Back to You" (#9) in 1965; "Opus 17 (Don't Worry 'bout Me)" (#12), "I've Got You Under My Skin" (#9), and "Tell It to the Rain" (#10) in 1966; "Beggin'" (#16), "C'mon Marianne" (#9), and "Watch the Flowers Grow" (#30) in 1967.

The group left Vee Jay over a royalty dispute in 1964, and by 1965 were recording for Philips, continuing their string of hits, which ended abruptly with their excursion into psychedelia, *Genuine Imitation Life Gazette*. (They had also recorded several singles, including a cover of Dylan's "Don't Think Twice" in 1965 under the pseudonym the Wonder Who.) As the Sixties closed, the group's popularity waned. By the time they signed to Motown's Mowest subsidiary, in 1971, Valli and Gaudio were the only original members left, and a $1.4 million debt had taken its toll.

In 1972 Crewe, whose independent label had folded, joined the group at Mowest. But even with the Crewe-Gaudio-Valli team intact, none of their singles hit. The release of a 1972 LP, *The Night*, was canceled, and the group toured supporting the Four Tops and the Vandellas. Valli's ten-year-old hearing problem (diagnosed as otosclerosis, excessive calcium deposits in the ear) became critical. (Faced with the possibility of going deaf, Valli underwent surgery in 1976.) Meanwhile, Gaudio retired from performing to concentrate on writing and producing. In 1973 one Gerald Zelmanowitz testified before a Senate subcommittee that the Four Seasons had ties to organized crime, a charge he later retracted.

Valli signed a solo contract with Private Stock in 1974 and soon had several hits, including "My Eyes Adored You" (#1, 1975), "Swearin' to God" (#6, 1975), and a cover of Ruby and the Romantics' "Our Day Will Come" (#11, 1975). The Four Seasons had almost ceased to exist, but in 1975 they made a comeback with one of their biggest-selling singles, "Who Loves You" (#3), followed the next year by "December 1963 (Oh What a Night)" (#1, 1976). Shortly before a 1977 tour, Valli announced—with some bitterness—that he would never work with the Four Seasons again, although he and Gaudio have retained co-ownership of the group and its name. But despite Valli's solo success ("Grease" hit #1 and sold over seven million copies), the Four Seasons re-formed in 1980 with Gaudio, Valli, guitarist Don Ciccone (former lead singer of the Critters and a Season since 1974), keyboardist Jerry Corbetta (ex–lead singer of Sugarloaf), guitarist Larry Lingle, and drummer Gerry Polci (who had been doing vocals with the group since 1973).

In 1984 Valli and Gaudio formed FBI Records, and the Four Seasons teamed with the Beach Boys for the single "East Meets West." More recent incarnations of the group boast six Four Seasons or more. Valli has appeared in the films *Eternity* and *Modern Love*. In 1990 the original members were inducted into the Rock & Roll Hall of Fame. Thanks to the 1994 film *Forrest Gump*, the Four Seasons' "December 1963 (Oh What a Night)" reentered the Hot 100, becoming the longest-running single in the chart's history, with over 50 weeks total.

The Four Tops

Formed 1954, Detroit, Michigan
Levi Stubbs (b. Levi Stubbles, Detroit), voc.; Renaldo "Obie" Benson (b. Detroit), voc.; Lawrence Payton (b. Detroit), voc.; Abdul "Duke" Fakir (b. Dec. 26, 1935, Detroit), voc.
1965—*Four Tops* (Motown); *Second Album* **1966**—*On Top*; *Live* **1967**—*Reach Out*; *On Broadway*; *Greatest Hits* **1968**—*Yesterday's Dreams* **1969**—*Four Tops Now*; *Soul Spin* **1970**—*Still Waters Run Deep*; *Changing Times*; *The Magnificent Seven* (with the Supremes) **1971**—*Greatest Hits, vol. 2*; *The Return of the Magnificent Seven* (with the Supremes) **1972**—*Dynamite* (with the Supremes); *Nature Planned It*; *Keeper of the Castle* (Dunhill) **1973**—*Four Tops Story* (Motown); *Main Street People* (Dunhill) **1981**—*Tonight* (Casablanca) **1982**—*One More Mountain* **1983**—*Back Where I Belong* (Motown) **1985**—*Magic* **1988**—*Indestructible* (Arista) **1989**—*Anthology* (Motown) **1993**—*Until You Love Someone: More of the Best (1965–1970)* (Rhino).

One of Motown's most consistent hitmakers and its longest-lived lineup, the Four Tops have charted with scores of upbeat love songs featuring Levi Stubbs' rough-hewn lead vocals. (In 1994 they celebrated four decades together, without a single change in personnel.) The four members met at a party in Detroit and soon began calling themselves the Four Aims. They were signed to Chess Records in 1956 and soon changed their name to the Four Tops to avoid confusion with the Ames Brothers. The single "Kiss Me Baby" b/w "Could It Be You" was the first of a string of supper-club–style flops

The Four Tops: (top) Lawrence Payton, Renaldo Benson, (bottom) Levi Stubbs, Abdul Fakir

that lasted for seven years on a series of labels (Red Top, Riverside, and Columbia). All the while, the group performed in top clubs.

By 1964 they had joined up with old friend Berry Gordy Jr., the founder of Motown Records. Gordy had them cut the unreleased *Breaking Through* for his experimental Workshop Jazz subsidiary. Later that year they were finally directed toward contemporary soul. Under the wing of Motown's top production and writing team, Holland-Dozier-Holland, the Four Tops were launched with "Baby I Need Your Loving," which went to #11 in 1964. Over the next eight years they made almost 30 appearances on the chart, and Levi Stubbs (whose brother Joe sang in the Falcons) became an international star and a major influence on other singers from the Sixties to the present (in 1986 Billy Bragg had a U.K. hit with "Levi Stubbs Tears").

The group's 1965 hits included "Ask the Lonely" (#24), "Same Old Song" (#5), and "I Can't Help Myself (Sugar Pie, Honey Bunch)," which was #1. "Reach Out I'll Be There" hit the top of the pop chart in October 1966. They followed up with "Standing in the Shadows of Love" (#6, 1967).

Like other top Motown acts, the Four Tops also became popular in major nightclubs around the world. Even in their hit-making prime, the Tops had less athletic choreography than the Temptations, for example, and the group was equally comfortable handling standards, show tunes, and big ballads. Like virtually all of Motown's first-tier acts, the Tops sought the longevity and stability of a career built equally on live appearances and records. In 1967 they scaled the charts with "Bernadette" (#4) and "Seven Rooms of Gloom" (#14); but when Holland-Dozier-Holland left Motown in 1967 to form their own label, the group's chart successes dwindled. In fact, two of the Four Tops' bigger hits from 1968 were covers: the Left Banke's "Walk Away Renee" (#14) and Tim Hardin's "If I Were a Carpenter" (#20). While many historians view HDH's departure as an irreparable blow to the group, in fact, the Tops cut a number of adventurous and successful singles under the guidance of other Motown staff producers, including "River Deep, Mountain High," with the Jean Terrell–led Supremes (#14 pop, #7 R&B, 1970) and "Still Water (Love)" (#11 pop, #4 R&B, 1970). In addition, Obie Benson cowrote Marvin Gaye's "What's Goin' On."

In 1972 the group left Motown for ABC/Dunhill, where it quickly recorded a couple of million-sellers: "Keeper of the Castle" (#10) and in 1973 "Ain't No Woman (Like the One I've Got)" (#4). It proved to be only a brief pop chart resurgence, though the group continued to hit the R&B Top Twenty, with "Seven Lonely Nights" and "Catfish." The Tops continued to tour the world, performing to packed houses. In 1981 the group moved to Casablanca Records, and released the comeback hit "When She Was My Girl" (#11 pop, #1 R&B). Two years later they were back at Motown, and after performing in a "battle of the bands" with the Temptations on the Motown twenty-fifth-anniversary television special, embarked on the first of several coheadlining tours with that group, billed as T'n'T. The first tour ran nearly three years, went around the world, and included a sold-out stint on Broadway.

In 1986 Stubbs provided the voice for the man-eating plant Audrey II in the film *Little Shop of Horrors;* in 1985 the group had its last Motown hit: "Sexy Ways" (#21 R&B). Like many older Motown artists, the Four Tops sought another label, and in 1988 they signed with Arista. "Indestructible" (#35 pop, #66 R&B) marked another resurgence in the band's career, especially in the U.K., where their "Loco in Acapulco" from the soundtrack of the Phil Collins film *Buster,* was a Top Ten hit. Chartwise, the Four Tops remain one of the most popular American acts in the U.K., where a remix of "Reach Out I'll Be There" hit #11 in 1988, and the saloon standard "It's All in the Game" went to #5 in 1970.

In 1989 the group appeared on Aretha Franklin's *Through the Storm,* and in 1990 Stevie Wonder inducted them into the Rock and Roll Hall of Fame. They continue to tour and record.

Kim Fowley

Born July 21, 1939, Los Angeles, California
1967—*Love Is Alive and Well* (Tower/Capitol)
1968—*Born to Be Wild* (Imperial)   1969—*Outrageous; Good Clean Fun*   1972—*I'm Bad* (Capitol)
1973—*International Heroes*   1975—*The Incredible Kim Fowley* (Original Sound)   1977—*Living in the Streets* (Sonet)   1978—*Visions of the Future* (Capitol); *Sunset Boulevard* (PVC)   1979—*Animal God of the Streets; Snake Document Masquerade* (Island) 1980—*Hollywood Confidential*   1981—*Son of Frankenstein* (a.k.a. *Bad News from the Underworld*) (Moxie)   1988—*Automatic* (Secret) 1992—*Hotel Insomnia* (Marilyn)   1993—*White Negroes in Deutschland*   1995—*Kings of Saturday Night* (with Ben Vaughn) (Sector 2).

Songwriter, producer, writer, manager, publisher, consultant, and general scenemaker and rock & roll Renaissance man Kim Fowley is the son of actor Douglas Fowley (Doc on *Wyatt Earp*) and step-grandson of composer Rudolf Friml. In 1957 he met Brian Wilson and began writing songs; he made local news by singing with three members of a black vocal group, the Jay-hawks. Since then Fowley has demonstrated an ear for new talent and a knack for gimmicky novelty singles.

In 1959, working as a disc jockey in Boise, Idaho, he produced the first sessions for Paul Revere and the Raiders ("Like, Long Hair" on Gardena). In the early Sixties he assembled the Murmaids and produced their version of David Gates' "Popsicles and Icicles" (#3, 1964). He also produced the Hollywood Argyles' "Alley Oop" (#1, 1960); "Nutrocker," based on Tchaikovsky's music, for B. Bumble and the Stingers (#23, 1962); and the Rivingtons' "Papa-Oom-Mow-Mow" (#48, 1962).

In London in the mid-Sixties, Fowley appeared on the TV show *Ready, Steady, Go.* He also produced sessions for Slade, Family, Dave Mason and Jim Capaldi of Traffic, and Soft Machine. Back in Los Angeles, he sang on the Mothers of Invention's *Freak Out.* He also produced records by the Seeds and the Fraternity of Man ("Don't Bogart That Joint"). Fowley then produced Gene Vincent's 1969 comeback, *I'm Back and I'm Proud;* part of Warren Zevon's 1969 *Wanted Dead or Alive;* two albums for Helen Reddy; and Jonathan Richman and the Modern Lovers. Fowley also wrote or cowrote songs recorded by the Beach Boys, the Byrds, Doug Sahm's Sir Douglas Quintet, Them, Leo Kottke, and Cat Stevens. In addition, he has published countless rock songs. Fowley has also recorded sporadically on his own, both under his own name and as "groups" including the Renegades ("Charge!").

In the late Seventies Fowley formed the Runaways [see entry], who included Joan Jett and Lita Ford; he cowrote their "Cherry Bomb." In 1987, long after the original group had come apart, Fowley unsuccessfully launched another group with the same name (which he owns), and he later assembled a similar all-female rock band, the Orchids. He has had two books of poetry published.

Inez and Charlie Foxx

Inez Foxx, born September 9, 1942, Greensboro, North Carolina; Charlie Foxx, born October 23, 1939, Greensboro, North Carolina
1964—*Mockingbird* (Sue)   1973—*Inez at Memphis* (Volt).

Inez and Charlie Foxx were a brother-and-sister vocal duo who are best known for such novelty hits as "Mockingbird" (#7, 1963). The pair started recording around 1957 on the Sue label. Their sporadic success throughout the early Sixties peaked with "Mockingbird" (later covered by James Taylor and wife Carly Simon). The Foxxes tried to repeat that hit with several subsequent releases (some credited only to Inez, although Charlie usually supplied background vocals), like "Hi Diddle Diddle" (1963), "Hurt by Love" (1964), "I Stand Accused—Guilty" (1967), and "(1-2-3-4-5-6-7) Count the Days" (1968). By the late Sixties they were recording for Musicor/Dynamo; in 1969 Inez began releasing solo records on Stax-Volt. Charlie, or Charles, as he was billed, released an album in the U.K. in 1981.

Peter Frampton

Born April 22, 1950, Beckenham, England
1972—*Wind of Change* (A&M)   1973—*Frampton's Camel*   1974—*Something's Happening*   1975—*Frampton*   1976—*Frampton Comes Alive!*   1977—*I'm in You*   1979—*Where I Should Be*   1981—*Breaking All the Rules*   1982—*The Art of Control*   1986—*Premonition* (Atlantic)   1989—*When All the Pieces Fit*   1992—*Shine On: A Collection* (A&M)   1994—*Peter Frampton* (Relativity).

After years as the moderately successful lead guitarist and singer in a string of British bands—the Herd, Humble Pie, and his own Frampton's Camel—Peter Frampton's nearly continuous U.S. touring paid off in 1976 when his live set *Frampton Comes Alive!* sold over six million copies and was briefly ranked among the ten best-selling albums ever.

Frampton made his professional debut at age ten and joined the Herd at 16. The band had several U.K. teenybopper hits, including "From the Underworld" and "Paradise Lost" in 1967, and "I Don't Want Our Loving to Die" in 1968. Frampton was named "Face of 1968" by several British magazines. He left the Herd in 1969 to establish a reputation as a more serious musician, and formed Humble Pie [see entry] with ex–Small Face Steve Marriott and ex–Spooky Tooth bassist Greg Ridley. He wrote and sang part of Humble Pie's early repertoire but left in 1971 to pursue his own career.

After a stint of session work (George Harrison's *All Things Must Pass*, Harry Nilsson's *Son of Schmilsson*), Frampton recorded a solo debut with assistance from

Peter Frampton

Ringo Starr, Billy Preston, and others. He formed Frampton's Camel with ex–Spooky Tooth Mike Kellie, Rick Wills (later of Roxy Music, the reunited Small Faces, Foreigner, and Bad Company), and Mike Gallagher in 1973 in order to tour the U.S. Frampton released an album a year and continued touring, making some inroads on FM radio, until the double-record *Frampton Comes Alive!* (#1, 1976), recorded at Winterland in San Francisco with a band composed of guitarist/keyboardist Bob Mayo, bassist Stanley Sheldon, and drummer John Siomos. The album included the best of Frampton's solo compositions and yielded three 1976 hit singles: "Show Me the Way" (#6), "Baby I Love Your Way" (#12), and "Do You Feel Like We Do" (#10). By year's end Frampton had grossed nearly $70 million in concert fees and royalties.

The followup album, *I'm in You* (#2, 1977), had a #2 hit with the title cut, a gushy ballad, although its other singles didn't reach the Top Ten. Frampton made his movie debut in Robert Stigwood's 1978 debacle, *Sgt. Pepper's Lonely Hearts Club Band*, but even before the movie was released there were rumors that he had succumbed to depression and heavy drinking. In June 1978 he suffered a concussion, muscle damage, and broken bones in a car crash in the Bahamas. Later that year his relationship with longtime girlfriend Penny McCall ended. By the late Seventies, Frampton had returned to touring 10,000-seaters, although *Where I Should Be* went gold and produced a Top Twenty hit, "I Can't Stand It No More" (#14, 1979).

Four albums in the Eighties on A&M and Atlantic failed to catch fire; Frampton began playing on others' records again. David Bowie, once a student of Frampton's art-teacher father, asked the guitarist to play on his 1987 *Never Let Me Down* LP and subsequent Glass Spider tour. Next Frampton started collaborating with his former Humble Pie cohort Steve Marriott, but their plans died in the house fire that claimed Marriott's life in 1991. *Peter Frampton*, his first album of new songs in five years, was a typically tuneful collection that showcased his lyrical guitar solos.

Connie Francis

Born Concetta Maria Franconero, December 12, 1938, Newark, New Jersey
1958—*Who's Sorry Now* (MGM) 1986—*The Very Best of Connie Francis* (Polydor) 1987—*The Very Best of Connie Francis, vol. 2* 1993—*White Sox, Pink Lipsticks . . . and Stupid Cupid* (Bear Family, Ger.).

During the period between 1958 and the emergence of the Beatles in spring 1964, singer Connie Francis had 35 Top Forty hits, including three #1s: "Everybody's Somebody's Fool" and "My Heart Has a Mind of Its Own" in 1960, and "Don't Break the Heart That Loves You" in 1962. Popular in Italy, Germany, Japan, France, and Spain, where she records in the native languages, Francis has had over 50 U.S. chart singles (and 25 in the U.K.), more hits than any other female vocalist except Aretha Franklin. Although she came up with, performed with, and got lumped in with the late-Fifties teen idols, her international success and a catalogue that ranges from country music (1964's *Connie Sings Great Country Favorites* with Hank Williams Jr.) to Jewish, Irish, Spanish, Italian, and Latin compilations, places her in a class by herself.

Concetta Franconero debuted at age four playing "Anchors Aweigh" on accordion; by age ten she began appearing on a local television show. By 11 she had appeared on several New York children's programs, and shortly after her 12th birthday sang "Daddy's Little Girl" on Arthur Godfrey's TV talent show. It was Godfrey who suggested that she change her name, which she did, though never legally. While still in her teens she recorded many demos, finally landing a deal with MGM in 1955. After a year and a half of releasing flop singles, and with her contract in jeopardy, her father, a former dock worker, suggested she record an uptempo version of one of his favorites, a 1923 tune called "Who's Sorry Now." It was a #4 hit in early 1958, and she later had hits with other oldies like "Among My Souvenirs" (#7, 1960) and "Together" (#6, 1961), both of which were written in 1928.

Over the next five years, Francis had 25 records in the Top 100. Some of her best sellers were "Stupid Cupid" (#14, 1958), "My Happiness" (#2, 1959), "Lipstick on Your Collar" (#5, 1959), "Mama" (#8, 1960), and "Vacation" (#9, 1962), the last of which she cowrote. Francis appeared in four films: *Where the Boys Are, Follow the Boys, Looking for Love,* and *When the Boys Meet the Girls.* She also sang the theme for *Where the Boys Are* (#4, 1961) and appeared in Brylcreem hair-cream commercials: "A little dab'll do ya!"

Francis' big hits ended with the beginning of Beatlemania, though she had several minor successes through the end of the decade and continued to perform to sell-out crowds around the world. In December 1960, she became the youngest performer to ever headline at the Copacabana. Surgery to correct a problem with her nose resulted in her inability to sing in air-conditioned rooms, and she sang with great difficulty. She made her return to live performing in November 1974 at the Westbury Music Fair on Long Island. After the performance, a man entered her hotel room and beat and raped her. She later sued the Howard Johnson's motel for negligence and was awarded $3,055,000 in damages.

It would be several more years before she recovered from the traumatic assault. She stopped performing and underwent 2½ years of psychiatric treatment. There were frequent reports in the press of battles between her and her father, who had long been instrumental in her career. Her only brother, George, was murdered in 1981. She underwent three additional operations on her nose, and approximately seven years after her last live performance Francis made a triumphant return to the Westbury Music Fair. In 1984 she published her autobiography, *Who's Sorry Now?*, a revealing account of the early rock & roll scene, including her romance with singer Bobby Darin.

Christopher Franke: See Tangerine Dream

Frankie Goes to Hollywood

Formed 1980, Liverpool, England
Holly Johnson (b. William Johnson, Feb. 19, 1960, Khartoum, Sudan), voc.; Paul Rutherford (b. Dec. 8, 1959, Liverpool), voc.; Nasher Nash (b. Brian Nash, May 20, 1963), gtr.; Mark O'Toole (b. Jan. 6, 1964, Liverpool), bass; Peter Gill (b. Mar. 8, 1964, Liverpool), drums.
1984—*Welcome to the Pleasuredome* (ZTT/Island) 1986—*Liverpool* 1994—*Bang! . . . The Greatest Hits of Frankie Goes to Hollywood* (Atlantic).
Holly Johnson solo: 1989—*Blast* (Uni) 1990—*Hallelujah* EP (MCA) 1991—*Dreams That Money Can't Buy.*

In pop music, controversy can be the mother of ascension. After Frankie Goes to Hollywood's sexually suggestive debut single, 1984's "Relax," was banned by the BBC—along with its accompanying video, set in a gay bar—it shot to the top of the British charts, where it remained for five weeks. And just as producer Trevor Horn's techno-savvy ingenuity had parlayed the mediocre hook propelling "Relax" into an insidious dance track, a promotion blitz engineered by ex-journalist Paul Morley turned the Liverpudlian quintet into an omnipresent phenomenon. Most memorable were the "Frankie Say . . ." T-shirts, as cheekily unabashed in their admonitions on sex and politics as singer Holly Johnson was about his homosexuality.

Frankiemania seemed destined to cross the Atlantic, but the amused fascination with which Americans observed the hoopla didn't translate into huge sales. The group's second smash U.K. single, "Two Tribes," a tepid but danceable anti–Cold War chant, peaked just outside the Top Forty here, despite a popular video in which Reagan and Chernenko look-alikes duked it out in a boxing ring. "Relax" reemerged as a U.S. single, hitting #10 in early 1985. After that, though, Frankie's 1984 debut album, *Welcome to the Pleasuredome*, spawned no more megahits at home or abroad. A subsequent album flopped, as did Johnson's brief solo career. Johnson discovered in the early Nineties that he was HIV-positive, and became a spokesman for AIDS awareness. In 1994 he published a frank and catty autobiography, *A Bone in My Flute*, and released a single, "Legendary Children."

Aretha Franklin

Born March 25, 1942, Memphis, Tennessee
1956—The Gospel Sound of Aretha Franklin (Checker) 1961—Aretha (Columbia) 1962—The Electrifying Aretha Franklin; The Tender, Moving, Swinging Aretha Franklin 1963—Laughing on the Outside 1964—Unforgettable: A Tribute to Dinah Washington; Running Out of Fools 1965—Yeah! Aretha Franklin in Person 1966—Soul Sister 1967—Take It Like You Give It; Greatest Hits, vol. 1; I Never Loved a Man the Way I Love You (Atlantic); Take a Look (Columbia); Aretha Arrives (Atlantic) 1968—Lady Soul; Aretha Now; Aretha in Paris; Greatest Hits, vol. 2 (Columbia) 1969—Soul '69 (Atlantic); Aretha's Gold 1970—This Girl's in Love with You; Spirit in the Dark 1971—Live at Fillmore West; Greatest Hits 1972—Young, Gifted and Black; Amazing Grace 1973—Hey Now Hey (The Other Side of the Sky); The First Twelve Sides (Columbia); The Best of Aretha Franklin (Atlantic) 1974—Let Me in Your Life; With Everything I Feel in Me 1975—You 1976—Sparkle; Ten Years of Gold 1977—Sweet Passion 1978—Almighty Fire 1979—La Diva 1980—Aretha (Arista) 1981—Love All the Hurt Away 1982—Jump to It 1983—Get It Right 1984—Aretha's Jazz (Atlantic) 1985—Who's Zoomin' Who (Arista); 30 Greatest Hits (Atlantic); Aretha Franklin Sings the Blues (Columbia)

Aretha Franklin

1986—Aretha (Arista) 1987—Aretha After Hours (Columbia); One Lord, One Faith, One Baptism (Arista) 1989—Through the Storm 1991—What You See Is What You Sweat 1992—The Queen of Soul (Rhino); Jazz to Soul (Columbia/Legacy) 1994—Aretha's Greatest Hits (1980–1994) (Arista).

Aretha Franklin is not only the definitive female soul singer of the Sixties, but one of the most influential and important voices in the history of popular music. She fused the unpredictable leaps and swoops of the gospel music she grew up on with the sensuality of R&B, the innovation of jazz, and the precision of pop. After she hit her artistic and commercial stride in 1967, she made over a dozen million-selling singles, and since then has recorded 20 #1 R&B hits. She moved toward the pop mainstream with fitful success in the Seventies, but in the late Eighties experienced a resurgence in popularity, and continues to record in a less ecstatic, perhaps more mature style.

Franklin's father, the Reverend C. L. Franklin, was the pastor of Detroit's 4,500-member New Bethel Baptist Church and a nationally known gospel singer ("the Man with the Million-Dollar Voice"). Her mother, Barbara, who was also a gospel singer, deserted the family (which included her son Vaughan from a previous marriage) when Aretha was six and died four years later. Aretha and her sisters, Carolyn and Erma, sang regularly at her father's church, and Aretha's first recordings were made there when she was 14. The Franklins were among the most prominent black families in Detroit. Many future stars, including Smokey Robinson, knew the family, and in the Fifties Berry Gordy Jr. tried to sign Aretha to his fledgling Motown label. Reverend Franklin refused.

The teenaged Aretha toured the gospel circuit with her father, and she was befriended by Clara Ward, Mahalia Jackson, James Cleveland, and Sam Cooke. Cooke, who had only recently crossed over from recording gospel to pop, was an inspiration to the young singer, encouraging her to sign with the label he recorded for, RCA. In fact, Aretha nearly did, until she was heard and signed by legendary talent scout John Hammond to Columbia. She moved to New York City, and at first found acceptance in the R&B market with "Today I Sing the Blues" (#10 R&B, 1960), "Won't Be Long" (#7 R&B, 1961), and "Operation Heartbreak" (#6 R&B, 1961), but in six years and ten albums, she had only one pop hit: "Rock-a-bye Your Baby with a Dixie Melody" (#37 pop, 1961). As reissues have focused new attention on Franklin's Columbia years, they have proven not to have been wasted entirely. She recorded several original songs ("Without the One You Love," "I'll Keep On Smiling," "Land of Dreams," "I Still Can't Forget") and a critically lauded tribute to her late friend Dinah Washington, as well as a 1962 version of "Try a Little Tenderness" that is said to have inspired Otis Redding to record it.

In 1966 she and Columbia parted, and she signed with Atlantic. With the help of producer Jerry Wexler, arranger Arif Mardin, and engineer Tom Dowd, Franklin began to make the records that would reshape soul music. Her first session (and the only one recorded at Muscle Shoals) yielded "I Never Loved a Man (the Way I Love You)" (#9 pop, #1 R&B, 1967) and heralded a phenomenal three years in which she sold in the millions with "Respect" (#1 pop and R&B, 1967), "Baby I Love You" (#4 pop, #1 R&B, 1967), "Chain of Fools" (#2 pop, #1 R&B, 1968), "Since You've Been Gone" (#5 pop, #1 R&B, 1968), "Think" (#7 pop, #1 R&B, 1968), "The House That Jack Built" (#6 pop, #2 R&B, 1968), "I Say a Little Prayer" (#10 pop, #3 R&B, 1968), "See Saw" (#14 pop, #9 R&B, 1968), "The Weight" (#19 pop, #3 R&B, 1969), "Share Your Love with Me" (#13 pop, #1 R&B, 1969), "Eleanor Rigby" (#17 pop, #5 R&B, 1969), "Call Me" (#13 pop, #1 R&B, 1970), and "Spirit in the Dark" (#23 pop, #3 R&B, 1970).

Franklin's material ranged from R&B numbers by Otis Redding ("Respect"), Don Covay ("See Saw" [with Steve Cropper], "Chain of Fools"), and Ronnie Shannon ("I Never Loved a Man") to pop fare by Carole King and Gerry Goffin ("[You Make Me Feel Like] a Natural Woman"), Lennon and McCartney ("Eleanor Rigby"), and Burt Bacharach and Hal David ("I Say a Little Prayer"). She also recorded many of her own songs, cowritten with her first husband and then-manager Ted White ("Dr. Feelgood," "Since You've Been Gone [Sweet Baby]," "Think"), or her sister Carolyn ("Save Me" [with King Curtis]), who received solo songwriting credit for "Ain't No Way." Most of Franklin's Sixties sessions were recorded with the Muscle Shoals Sound Rhythm Section, who, after the first session, were imported to New York City, or with a band led by saxophonist King Curtis. Franklin herself was responsible for the vocal arrangements, whose gospel-style call-and-response choruses often featured her sister Carolyn as well as the Sweet Inspirations [see entry].

By 1968 Franklin reigned throughout America and Europe as "Lady Soul"—a symbol of black pride. She was presented an award by Martin Luther King Jr. (to whose cause her father had been a major financial supporter) and appeared on the cover of *Time*, the accompanying profile of which would be her last major interview for many years. As *Time* reported (and other sources have since concurred), Franklin's personal life was quite turbulent. Throughout her career, Franklin has remained an enigmatic figure, alternately outspoken and reclusive, and much of her personal life has been shrouded in secrecy. She had married White in 1961. She already had two sons, Clarence and Edward, born before her 17th birthday; she has never publicly identified either boy's father. With White, she gave birth to Teddy Jr., since the Eighties a guitarist in her band. Her marriage to White ended in 1969, by which time he had struck her in public on one occasion and shot her new production manager on another. Franklin herself was arrested in 1968 for reckless driving and again in 1969 for disorderly conduct. Also in 1969 her father was arrested for possession of marijuana. He hosted a controversial conference for black separatist groups that ended in a violent confrontation with Detroit police that left one officer dead and several other people wounded. During this time his daughter Aretha was rumored to be drinking heavily.

The hits continued (giving her more million-sellers than any other woman in recording history)—"Don't Play That Song" (#11 pop, #1 R&B, 1970), "Bridge over Troubled Water" (#6 pop, #1 R&B, 1971), "Spanish Harlem" (#2 pop, #1 R&B, 1971), "Rock Steady" (#9 pop, #2 R&B, 1971), "Day Dreaming" (#5 pop, #1 R&B, 1972), and "Until You Come Back to Me (That's What I'm Gonna Do)" (#3 pop, #1 R&B, 1973). In the early Seventies she gave birth to her fourth son, Kecalf, and in 1978 she married actor Glynn Turman. During this time Franklin seemed to be searching, sometimes aimlessly, for direction. But this period was not without its high points: *Spirit in the Dark, Live at Fillmore West,* and *Young, Gifted and Black* were all critically acclaimed. The pure gospel *Amazing Grace* (recorded live in Los Angeles with her father officiating and the Reverend James Cleveland at the piano and conducting the choir) would be her last album with Wexler. During her last years with Atlantic she moved from producer to producer: Quincy

Jones (*Hey Now Hey*), Curtis Mayfield (*Sparkle,* which included "Something He Can Feel," a 1992 Top Ten hit for En Vogue and Franklin's last Top Forty pop hit for nearly six years), Lamont Dozier (*Sweet Passion*), Van McCoy (*La Diva*). Her concerts became Las Vegas–style costume extravaganzas, and she soon established a reputation for her idiosyncratic (some would say ill-advised) costume choices. She also began showing signs of the unpredictability that would dog her career, particularly after a bad experience while flying resulted in a phobia that curtailed her touring.

In 1980 Franklin left Atlantic, signed with Arista, and positioned herself as the grande dame of pop. Her cameo appearance (she sang "Respect" and "Think") in *The Blues Brothers* movie that year has been cited as the beginning of a new phase. Her first two Arista albums were produced by Arif Mardin, and each included an old soul standard as well as glossier MOR material. "Love All the Hurt Away," a collaboration with George Benson, went to #6 on the R&B chart in 1981. Her version of Sam and Dave's "Hold On, I'm Comin'" earned a Grammy for Best R&B Vocal Performance, Female. With the Luther Vandross–produced *Jump to It,* she reestablished herself as a hitmaker when the title tune hit #1 R&B and #24 pop in 1982. Vandross was also behind the board for *Get It Right.*

But the momentum of her commercial comeback was halted by a series of personal tragedies, beginning with a 1979 attack on her father, in which he was shot by burglars in his Detroit home. He began to recover from his injuries but then lapsed into a coma from which he did not emerge before his death in 1984. In 1982 Franklin moved back to the Detroit area, where she still lives. Two years later, she and Turman divorced. The year after her father's death, Franklin came fully back into the public eye with *Who's Zoomin' Who* (#13, 1985), a Narada Michael Walden–produced work that spun off three hit singles: the Grammy-winning "Freeway of Love" (#3 pop, #1 R&B, 1985), the title track (#7 pop, #2 R&B, 1985), and a Top Twenty duet with the Eurythmics, "Sisters Are Doin' It for Themselves." The album, which included guest performances by Clarence Clemons, Dizzy Gillespie, Carlos Santana, Peter Wolf, and most of Tom Petty's Heartbreakers, as well as backing vocals by sister Carolyn and Sylvester, among others, became her highest-charting album since 1972. The hits' accompanying videos were heavily played on MTV, and Franklin once again found the pop crossover success that had eluded her. Its followup, *Aretha,* included the Top Thirty "Jimmy Lee" (#2 R&B, 1986) and a version of "Jumpin' Jack Flash," produced by and featuring Keith Richards, as well as her Grammy-winning #1 duet with George Michael, "I Knew You Were Waiting (for Me)" (1987).

Subsequent albums were less popular. Her critically acclaimed *One Lord, One Faith, One Baptism* marked a return to gospel and featured Mavis Staples and the Reverend Jesse Jackson. It earned Franklin her 15th Grammy, for Best Soul Gospel Performance, Female. Despite its hit title track (a duet with Elton John; #16 pop, #17 R&B, 1989), *Through the Storm* peaked at #55, and 1991's *What You See Is What You Sweat* made the lowest showing of any new LP in her career. It contained a #13 R&B cover of Sly and the Family Stone's "Everyday People."

In 1988 Franklin's sister Carolyn died of cancer; around the same period her brother and manager Cecil also died. Since 1986 Franklin has made several highly publicized starts at writing her autobiography. In 1987 Franklin became the first woman inducted into the Rock and Roll Hall of Fame. She appeared with Frank Sinatra on his *Duets* album and (coincidentally; they are in no way related) in 1993 starred in her own television special, *Duets,* which featured her singing with a number of current pop stars, including Bonnie Raitt, Elton John, Smokey Robinson, George Michael, and Rod Stewart. She appeared at the inaugural celebration for President Bill Clinton, where her rendition of "I Dreamed a Dream" (from *Les Miserables*) barely got more attention than her wearing a fur coat (for which she offered no apologies). Nineteen-ninety-four's "A Deeper Love" (#63 pop, #30 R&B, 1994), from the *Sister Act 2* soundtrack, was written and produced by Robert Clivillés and David Cole of C+C Music Factory. "Willing to Forgive" was another Top Twenty R&B hit that year.

Erma Franklin (born 1939) and Carolyn Franklin (born 1945; died April 25, 1988, Bloomfield Hills, Michigan) were professional singers for as long as their better-known sister. After many years on the gospel circuit, Erma began recording soul and pop material in the mid-Sixties. Her 1967 Shout release, "Piece of My Heart" (#10, R&B), preceded Janis Joplin's version by several months. She recorded for the Brunswick label in the late Sixties and early Seventies. Carolyn sang backup for many of Atlantic's stars in the Sixties. She later recorded as a solo artist for RCA.

Michael Franks

Born September 18, 1944, La Jolla, California
1973—*Michael Franks* (Brut)   1976—*The Art of Tea* (Reprise)   1977—*Sleeping Gypsy* (Warner Bros.)
1978—*Birchfield Nines*   1979—*Tiger in the Rain*
1980—*One Bad Habit*   1982—*Objects of Desire*
1983—*Passionfruit*   1985—*Skin Dive*   1987—*The Camera Never Lies*   1989—*Previously Unavailable* (DRG)   1990—*Blue Pacific* (Reprise)   1993—*Dragonfly Summer.*

Songwriter Michael Franks has been recording his own droll, laid-back pop-jazz tunes since 1973, with occasional pop recognition. His songs have been covered by

Melissa Manchester, Manhattan Transfer, and the Carpenters, and he has written for Rod Stewart and Barbra Streisand.

Franks played folk and rock in high school in La Jolla, and he majored in contemporary literature at UCLA while working part-time as a musician. In the late Sixties he completed a master's in contemporary culture at the University of Montreal. While in Canada he opened shows for Gordon Lightfoot and worked with Carnival, later Lighthouse.

In the early Seventies Franks taught undergraduate music courses and worked toward a Ph.D. at UCLA and Berkeley. His doctoral dissertation was entitled "Contemporary Songwriting and How It Relates to Society." He scored two films in 1971, *Count Your Bullets* and *Zandy's Bride.* In 1972 Sonny Terry and Brownie McGhee recorded three of his songs, with Franks backing them on mandolin and banjo, on their *Sonny & Brownie.* Buddah/Brut signed him in 1972, and his "Can't Seem to Shake This Rock 'n' Roll" received some airplay. He toured the U.S. opening for comedian Robert Klein in 1973.

After scoring another film in England, Franks returned to California and took on a research project for Warner Bros. Pictures that led to his Reprise signing. His albums have featured well-known backing musicians—the Crusaders on *The Art of Tea,* which included the minor hit "Popsicle Toes" (#43, 1976); Brazilian musicians on *Sleeping Gypsy*—and have earned him a cult following.

In the Eighties, Franks adopted a cooler sound, which eventually found favor in the rising "light jazz" and adult contemporary radio formats. "Your Secret's Safe with Me" got some exposure via its video on VH-1. Franks is known for the varied and respected company he keeps on his records, which have featured Astrud Gilberto (on *Passionfruit*), Patti Austin, Flora Purim, the Brecker Brothers, David Sanborn, Joe Sample, Larry Carlton, Luther Vandross, Art Garfunkel, Earl Klugh, and Steve Jordan, among many others. *Dragonfly Summer* includes guest appearances by Dan Hicks and Peggy Lee.

Freakwater: See Eleventh Dream Day

John Fred and His Playboy Band
Formed late Fifties, Baton Rouge, Louisiana
John Fred (b. May 8, 1941, Baton Rouge), voc., harmonica; Charlie Spinosa (b. Dec. 29, 1948, Baton Rouge), trumpet; Ronnie Goodson (b. Feb. 2, 1945, Miami, Fla.), trumpet; Andrew Bernard (b. 1945, New Orleans, La.), sax; James O'Rourke (b. Mar. 14, 1947, Fall River, Mass.), gtr.; Harold Cowart (b. June 12, 1944, Baton Rouge), bass; Joe Micelli (b. July 9, 1946, Baton Rouge), drums; Tommy Dee (b. Thomas De Generes, Nov. 3, 1946, Baton Rouge), organ.
1965—*John Fred and His Playboys* (Paula)   1966— *34:40 of John Fred and His Playboys*   1967—*Agnes English*   1969—*Permanently Stated*   1970—*Love in My Soul* (Uni).

John Fred and His Playboy Band were an R&B-inspired rock band best known for its 1968 hit, the three-million-seller "Judy in Disguise (with Glasses)." Led by John Fred, a former all-American basketball player at Louisiana State University, who began recording in 1958 with "Shirley" on Montel Records, the group established itself in Louisiana and Texas clubs in the early Sixties. Its lone hit (which was also the group's 16th single), "Judy in Disguise" (a wordplay on the Beatles' "Lucy in the Sky"), hit #1 in January 1968; the 45's success propelled *Agnes English* to the lower rungs of the album chart. But followups like "Hey Hey Bunny" (#57, 1968) didn't come close to matching "Judy," and the group broke up the next year. Fred formed another Playboy Band in the mid-Seventies before going to work for R.C.S. Records in Baton Rouge, where he coproduced a 1979 LP for Irma Thomas. In the late Eighties Fred found a second career singing commercial jingles (winning a Clio Award for one of them), and later revived the Playboy Band to play the oldies circuit.

Freddie and the Dreamers
Formed 1960, Manchester, England
Freddie Garrity (b. Nov. 14, 1936), voc., gtr.; Derek Quinn (b. May 24, 1942), gtr., harmonica; Roy Crewsdon (b. May 29, 1941), gtr., piano, drums; Pete Birrell (b. May 9, 1941), bass; Bernie Dwyer (b. Sep. 11, 1940), drums.
1964—*You Were Made for Me*   1965—*Freddie and the Dreamers* (Mercury); *Do the Freddie*   1966— *Freddie and the Dreamers*   1992—*The Best of Freddie and the Dreamers* (EMI).

Freddie and the Dreamers, all born in Manchester, were the buffoons of the British Invasion. The group was formed by ex-milkman Freddie Garrity, who had previously worked in a Fifties skiffle band. A bespectacled young man with a slight resemblance to Buddy Holly, Freddie looked silly and nerdish, and—while the band played deadpan foils—gave forth with a cackling laugh and exaggerated dancing that included fairly acrobatic midair splits. In 1962, after successfully auditioning for the BBC, they rose to prominence in England and signed with Columbia. Their first single, a cover of James Ray's "If You've Gotta Make a Fool of Somebody," hit the British Top Five. Over the next few years they enjoyed a half-dozen U.K. hits, including "You Were Made for Me" (#3, U.K.) and "I Understand" (#5, U.K.).

"I'm Telling You Now," originally released in England in 1963, went to #1 in the U.S. in spring 1965, spurred by the group's touring and appearances on the *Shindig!* and *Hulabaloo* television shows. Another American hit, "Do the Freddie" (#18, 1965), sparked a momentary dance craze in emulation of Freddie's arm and leg waving. The group was featured in such films as *Seaside Swingers, Just For You,* and *Cuckoo Patrol.* Their U.S. hits ended in 1966. The band played cabarets and clubs until breaking up in 1968. Garrity and Pete Birrell thereafter hosted their own children's TV series in England called *The Little Big Time.* The Dreamers re-formed in 1976, with only Garrity remaining from the original lineup, and they remained active in supper clubs and cabarets into the Nineties.

Free

Formed 1968, London, England
Paul Rodgers (b. Dec. 12, 1949, Middlesbrough, Eng.), voc.; Paul Kossoff (b. Sep. 14, 1950, London; d. March 19, 1976, New York City, N.Y.), gtr.; Andy Fraser (b. Aug. 7, 1952, London), bass; Simon Kirke (b. July 28, 1949, Shrewsbury, Eng.), drums.
1969—*Tons of Sobs* (A&M) 1970—*Free; Fire and Water; Highway* 1971—(Group disbands) *Free Live* 1972—(Group re-forms) *Free at Last* (– Kossoff; – Fraser; + Tetsu Yamauchi [b. Oct. 21, 1947, Fukuoka, Jap.], bass; + John "Rabbit" Bundrick, kybds.; + Kossoff; – Kossoff) 1973—*Heartbreaker* (group disbands) 1975—*Best of Free* 1993—*Molten Gold: The Anthology.*

Free distilled British blues down to riffs, silences, and Paul Rodgers' ornately anguished vocals—most memorably in "All Right Now" (#4, 1970). The style the group established was made more ponderous and commercially successful by Bad Company, Foreigner, and other Seventies hard-rock bands.

Free started in the London pubs when Simon Kirke and Paul Kossoff, then in the blues band Black Cat Bones, heard Rodgers singing with Brown Sugar. The three enlisted 16-year-old Andy Fraser from John Mayall's Bluesbreakers, and they got the name Free from Alexis Korner. The quartet failed to make inroads with its first two albums and a U.S. tour opening for Blind Faith in 1969, but *Fire and Water,* which included "All Right Now," signaled that Free had honed its approach.

Yet just months after "All Right Now"'s success, in mid-1971, the group split up. Kossoff and Kirke joined bassist Tetsu Yamauchi (later with the Faces) and session keyboardist John "Rabbit" Bundrick for one album, *Kossoff, Kirke, Tetsu and Rabbit;* Rodgers formed a group called Peace; and Fraser started Toby. By 1972 the original Free had re-formed for *Free at Last.* Personal problems and drug use—especially Kossoff's—took a toll on the band, and it broke up for good in early 1973. Fraser joined guitarist Chris Spedding in Sharks for one album; Kossoff started Back Street Crawler (later Crawler), but died of a drug-induced heart attack in 1976 on an airplane en route to New York. Rodgers and Kirke were joined by Yamauchi and Bundrick for 1973's *Heartbreaker,* then retired the Free name to start Bad Company [see entry]. Yamauchi replaced Ronnie Lane in the Faces, while Bundrick has added keyboards to the Who.

Bobby Freeman

Born June 13, 1940, San Francisco, California
1958—*Do You Wanna Dance* (Jubilee) 1959—*Get in the Swim* (Josie) 1960—*Loveable Style of Bobby Freeman* (King) 1964—*C'mon and Swim* (Autumn).

A journeyman R&B singer, Bobby Freeman is best known for "Do You Wanna Dance," which became a #5 hit for him in 1958 and was later covered by several artists, including the Beach Boys (1965), Bette Midler (1973), and the Ramones (1978). A pianist as well as a singer, by age 14 Freeman was working with a San Francisco group called the Romancers, which recorded briefly for the Dootone label. He was 17 when he recorded his "Do You Wanna Dance." He followed up with lesser hits ("Betty Lou Got a New Pair of Shoes" and "Need Your Love") and made sporadic appearances on the pop chart through the late Fifties and mid-Sixties with "Mary Ann Thomas" (1959), "Ebb Tide," (1959), "(I Do the) Shimmy Shimmy" (1960), and "The Mess Around" (1961).

In 1964 Freeman enjoyed a brief resurgence with some Sly Stone–produced sides on Autumn Records, most notably the dance-craze–inspired "C'mon and Swim," which hit the Top Five. He tried to milk the brief dance craze with the followup "S-W-I-M," but by then the public had cooled, although he continued to tour widely over the next couple of years. By the late Sixties he was supporting himself primarily as a singer in strip bars. By 1974 he was signed by Touch Records, a small Los Angeles–based label that released a single, "Everything's Love," with little success. He continues to perform.

Glenn Frey: See the Eagles

Kinky Friedman

Born Richard Friedman, October 31, 1944, Rio Ducksworth, Texas
1973—*Sold American* (Vanguard) 1975—*Kinky Friedman* (ABC) 1976—*Lasso from El Paso* (Epic) 1983—*Under the Double Ego* (Sunrise) 1993—*Old Testaments and New Revelations* (Fruit of the Tune).

Kinky Friedman

Country songwriter and sometime leader of the Texas Jewboys, Kinky Friedman drawls his way through tunes like "High on Jesus," "Asshole from El Paso," "Ride 'em Jewboy," and "Get Your Biscuits in the Oven and Your Buns in Bed." Richard Friedman studied psychology at the University of Texas, then joined the Peace Corps; he claims to have instructed Borneo natives in throwing the Frisbee. Back in Texas, at a farm called Rio Duckworth, he started King Arthur and the Carrots, whose songs like "Beach Party Boo" and "Schwinn Twenty-four," and Friedman's penchant for gaudy stage outfits, attracted the attention of Austin patrons like Kris Kristofferson and Commander Cody.

Friedman began making albums in 1973, with the support over the years of Waylon Jennings (who produced "Carryin' the Torch"), Ringo Starr, Billy Swan, and Bob Dylan, who invited Kinky to appear with the Rolling Thunder Revue, which provided some live cuts for Friedman's *Lasso from El Paso*. Friedman has appeared at Nashville's Grand Ole Opry but is apparently too vulgar for the mainstream country audience.

Friedman moved to New York City in 1979 and frequently headlined at the Lone Star Cafe. In 1986 he published his first mystery novel: *Greenwich Killing Time*. He has since written seven others: *A Case of Lone Star* (1987), *When the Cat's Away* (1989), *Frequent Flyer* (1990), *Musical Chairs* (1991), *Elvis, Jesus & Coca-Cola* (1993), *Armadillos & Old Lace* (1994), and *God Bless John Wayne* (1995). Friedman is not only the author of his books, but their protagonist as well. His books are best-sellers in England, Australia, and Germany. In 1986 he made an unsuccessful bid for Kerrville, Texas, justice of the peace. During the campaign, Friedman revealed that he had harbored his friend Abbie Hoffman at his ranch when the radical was being sought as a fugitive from justice in the mid-Seventies.

The compilation *Old Testaments and New Revelations* sold more than 100,000 copies, and Friedman continues to perform, although he considers himself primarily a novelist today. As he wrote in response to our researcher: "I've finally found a lifestyle that doesn't require my presence."

The Friends of Distinction
Formed 1967, Los Angeles, California
Harry Elston (b. Nov. 4, 1938, Dallas, Tex.); Floyd Butler (b. June 5, 1941, San Diego, Calif.); Jessica Cleaves (b. Dec. 10, 1948, Beverly Hills, Calif.); Barbara Love (b. July 24, 1941, Los Angeles).
1969—*Grazin'* (RCA); *Highly Distinct* 1970—*Real Friends*; *Whatever* 1971—*Friends and People*.

Black MOR pop vocal group the Friends of Distinction are best remembered for their 1969 "Grazin' in the Grass" (#3). The group was formed around chief composer Harry Elston, who had worked with Ray Charles, as did Floyd Butler and future Fifth Dimension members Marilyn McCoo and LaMonte McLemore under the name the Hi-Fi's. That group disbanded after a short tour with Charles, and after the Friends of Distinction came together, ex-football-star-turned-Hollywood-actor Jim Brown became the group's financial backer. It signed with RCA in 1968.

By early 1969 "Grazin'" had hit the Top Five. Lesser hits—"Going in Circles" (#15, 1969) and "Let Yourself Go" (#63, 1969)—followed. "Love or Let Me Be Lonely" was their last big hit (#6, 1970). In 1971 Barbara Love (daughter of West Coast disc jockey Reuben Brown) left the group, which soon disbanded. Jessica Cleaves went on to join Earth, Wind and Fire.

Robert Fripp
Born May 16, 1946, Wimbourne, England
1973—*No Pussyfooting* (with Brian Eno) (Island, U.K.) 1975—*Evening Star* (with Brian Eno) 1979—*Exposure* (Polydor, U.K.) 1980—*God Save the Queen/Under Heavy Manners* 1981—*Let the Power Fall*; *The League of Gentlemen* 1982—*I Advance Masked* (with Andy Summers) (A&M) 1984—*Bewitched* (with Andy Summers) 1985—

God Save the King (Polydor)   1986— *Robert Fripp and the League of Crafty Guitarists Live!*; *The Lady or the Tiger* (with Toyah Wilcox) (Editions EG)   1987—*Network* (Polydor)   1991—*Show of Hands* (Editions EG); *Kneeling at the Shrine* (EG)   1993— *The First Day* (with David Sylvian) (Virgin).

Guitarist, composer, and producer Robert Fripp has been at the forefront of progressive rock and new wave, and his pioneering use of electronics helped usher in ambient music. Founder of King Crimson [see entry], solo artist, and musical theoretician, he grounds his conceptual approach on a highly distinctive blend of rigorous technique and metaphysical discipline.

Starting off with the League of Gentlemen, a band of accompanists for visiting American singers, Fripp first recorded with Giles, Giles and Fripp. Their one album, *The Cheerful Insanity of Giles, Giles and Fripp* (1968), set forth the experimental approach King Crimson would expand from 1969 to 1975. Along with those of Yes and Emerson, Lake and Palmer, the band's eight albums, featuring a variety of highly technical players, typified the fusion of classical music elements and theatrical attack that was the hallmark of progressive rock.

Concurrently, Fripp teamed up with Brian Eno (for *No Pussyfooting* and *Evening Star*) and developed "Frippertronics," a method of tape-looped solo guitar improvisation that produces layers of sound. In 1974 Fripp also took up the teachings of J. G. Bennett, a proponent of the mystical philosophers Gurdjieff and P. D. Ouspensky. The result was an intensification of Fripp's conviction that music is an expression of spiritual aspiration, a link between the human and the divine.

Disbanding King Crimson before their final, live album came out, Fripp produced jazz records for a group called Centipede. He then briefly retired, declaring his intention to act henceforth as "a small, self-sufficient, mobile, intelligent unit." Lending his signature guitar to David Bowie's *"Heroes,"* he returned to performance in 1977 and went on to produce Peter Gabriel's second album and Daryl Hall's 1980 solo LP, *Sacred Songs*.

Exposure was Fripp's solo debut. With vocals by Hall, Gabriel, Terre Roche, and Peter Hammill, it showed him working relatively closely within the pop-song format. Re-forming King Crimson in 1981 and releasing three albums with them, he also collaborated in the early Eighties with Police guitarist Andy Summers on *I Advance Masked* and *Bewitched*. As the decade progressed, either under his own name or as the League of Gentlemen, Fripp continued innovating—from the "Frippertronics"-driven *Let the Power Fall* to the Crimsonlike *The League of Gentlemen*.

Furthering his theoretical interests, Fripp founded Guitar Craft in the mid-Eighties. A tutorial in his world view, it offered guitar instruction and philosophical discussion. *The League of Crafty Guitarists Live!* and *Show of Hands,* featuring his students' acoustic playing, showcased the school's approach. With his wife, singer/actress Toyah Wilcox, in 1986 Fripp put out *The Lady or the Tiger,* a spoken-word album with musical backing; *Kneeling at the Shrine,* with Toyah fronting a new Fripp outfit, Sunday All Over the World, followed in 1991. Two years later, *The First Day* found Fripp pairing with David Sylvian. One of his more orthodox song-oriented outings, it made clear that his guitar style, for all its electronic modification, remained irrevocably melodic.

Bill Frisell

Born William Frisell, March 18, 1951, Baltimore, Maryland
1983—*In Line* (ECM)   1985—*Rambler*   1988—*Lookout for Hope*; *Works*   1989—*Before We Were Born* (Elektra/Musician)   1990—*Is That You?*   1991— *Where in the World?*   1993—*Have a Little Faith* (Elektra/Nonesuch)   1994—*This Land.* With Vernon Reid: 1986—*Smash & Scatteration* (Rykodisc).

Bill Frisell is one of rock's leading experimental guitar players, a trained jazz musician who has played primarily with the downtown New York avant-garde scene (although he is now based in Seattle). Frisell grew up in Denver, the son of a tuba- and bass-playing father. He initially played clarinet and saxophone, but switched to guitar while studying music at North Colorado University. He also plays banjo, bass, and ukulele. In 1977 he got a degree in arranging and composition from Berklee College of Music; the next year he moved to New York.

Counting Jimi Hendrix and jazz guitarists Wes Montgomery and Jim Hall among his influences, Frisell has played in a number of collaborative ensembles, including Power Tools with Ronald Shannon Jackson and Melvin Gibbs, Naked City with John Zorn, the Paul Bley Quartet, and the Paul Motian Trio. He has played on nearly 50 albums, including Hal Wilner's tributes to Nino Rota, Charles Mingus, and Walt Disney. He has also worked with Marianne Faithfull, Jan Garbarek, John Scofield, Marc Johnson's Bass Desires, and Don Byron.

Frisell's first album, *In Line,* showcases solo work and duets with bassist Arild Andersen. On *Rambler,* he plays with such out-jazz musicians as trumpeter Kenny Wheeler and Motian. On *Lookout for Hope,* Frisell debuted the Bill Frisell Band, featuring cellist Hank Roberts, bassist Kermit Driscoll, and drummer Joey Baron; the quartet also plays on *Where in the World? Is That You?* was recorded with Wayne Horvitz. *Have a Little Faith* is a collection of covers that includes songs by John Philip Sousa, Sonny Rollins, Charles Ives, Bob Dylan, and Madonna.

Fred Frith: See Henry Cow

Lefty Frizzell

Born William Orville Frizzell, March 21, 1928, Corsicana, Texas; died July 19, 1975, Nashville, Tennessee
1966—*Lefty Frizzell's Greatest Hits* (Columbia)
1982—*Columbia Historic Edition* 1984—*Lefty Frizzell: His Life—His Music* (Down Home Music)
1991—*The Best of Lefty Frizzell* (Rhino).

Singer Lefty Frizzell was one of the legends of honky-tonk country music; his original vocal style and literate songwriting influenced such C&W artists as Merle Haggard, Willie Nelson, Randy Travis, and Dwight Yoakam.

At age 12, Frizzell had a spot on a children's radio program, and by 16 he was a professional musician. His main musical model was the plaintive vocal style of Jimmie Rodgers, "the Singing Brakeman"; Frizzell's own nickname came from his abilities as a fighter. A demo of Frizzell's song "If You've Got the Money I've Got the Time" brought him to the attention of Columbia Records, which signed him in the early Fifties. In the years 1950–54, Frizzell had 15 Top Ten country hits, including the classics "Always Late (with Your Kisses)" (#1, 1951), "Mom and Dad's Waltz" (#2, 1951), "I Want to Be with You Always" (#1, 1951), "Travellin' Blues" (#6, 1951), and "Run 'Em Off" (#8, 1954). Top Nashville piano session man Floyd Cramer was a mainstay in Frizzell's band.

Frizzell became disillusioned by the music industry, however, and was plagued by a drinking problem that would continue until his death. By the late Fifties, his hits were scarce (his classic 1959 version of "The Long Black Veil" hit #6 on the C&W chart), and by the early Sixties he was all but forgotten. "Saginaw, Michigan" (#1 C&W, 1964) was Frizzell's last major hit. He was in the midst of a comeback when he died from a stroke at age 47. Two years after his death in 1975, a Frizzell tribute album, *To Lefty from Willie*, was released by Willie Nelson. Dwight Yoakam, one of many New Traditionalist Frizzell fans, recorded "Always Late (with Your Kisses)" on his 1987 album *Hillbilly Deluxe*.

Edgar Froese: See Tangerine Dream

Front 242

Formed 1981, Belgium
Daniel .B. (b. Daniel Bressanutti, Aug. 27, 1954, Genk, Belgium), prod.; Patrick Codenys (b. Nov. 16, 1958, Brussels, Belgium), kybds.; Jean-Luc De Meyer (b. Nov. 18, 1957, Brussels, Belgium), voc.
1982—*Geography* (New Dance) 1983—(+ Richard 23; a.k.a. Richard JK [b. Richard Jonckheere, Jan. 20, 1963, Brussels, Belgium], drums, voc.) 1985—*No Comment EP* (Wax Trax!) 1987—*Official Version*; *Back Catalogue* 1988—*Front by Front* 1991—*Tyranny for You* (MCA) 1993—*06:21:03:11 Up Evil*; *05:22:09:12 Off*.

Front 242 helped pioneer the techno-industrial sound, which is characterized by massive electronic beats, foreboding samples, minimal keyboard lines, and growled vocals. Though the group never enjoyed chart success in the U.S., it influenced a generation of like-minded groups, including Ministry and Nine Inch Nails.

Formed by Daniel Bressanutti (a.k.a. Daniel .B.), who never performs live with the group, Front 242 soon came to include Bressanutti's fellow design student Patrick Codenys; neither had any previous musical experience. Vocalist Jean-Luc De Meyer came aboard shortly after. Drawing equally from Kraftwerk, Devo, and the do-it-yourself ethos of punk rock, the duo hoped to bring their avant-garde ideas about mixed-media art into the music world. Using early, rudimentary synthesizers, they began looping recorded voice fragments and other found sounds and laying them over minimal drum-machine beats and keyboards. Critics of traditional rock generally dismissed the sound as cold and impersonal, though many among the post–baby boom generation responded favorably.

The group's first album, *Geography*, attracted the attention of the American independent label Wax Trax!, which became a haven for industrial-dance outfits. By 1983 Bressanutti and Codenys were joined by vocalist Jean-Luc De Meyer and drummer Richard Jonckheere. Front 242 signed to Epic in 1990, releasing *Tyranny for You* the following year; the album barely cracked the Top 100 (#95). In 1993 Epic reissued the band's back catalogue.

Throughout the Eighties Front 242 had released a number of underground dance-club singles, including "Quite Unusual," from 1985's *No Comment*, and the club smash "Headhunter," from 1988's *Front by Front*. Understanding the limitations of techno-industrial live shows, the band began using video images, dramatic lighting, and stage plots, calling the concept "electronic body music."

Off (1993) included guest vocals by members of New York City's Spill, Eran Westwood and 99 Kowalski. After a decade of making underground music, Front 242's biggest break came in 1993, when the group played on the summer's Lollapalooza Tour.

Fugazi

Formed 1987, Arlington, Virginia
Ian MacKaye (b. ca. 1963), gtr., voc.; Guy Picciotto (b. ca. 1966), gtr., voc.; Joe Lally (b. ca. 1964), bass; Brendan Canty (b. ca. 1967), drums.

1988—*Fugazi* EP (Dischord)   1989—*Margin Walker* EP   1990—*Repeater*   1991—*Steady Diet of Nothing* 1993—*In On the Kill Taker.*

Of all the bands to rise from the Eighties American independent hardcore punk scene, Fugazi has remained truest to the do-it-yourself ethos, releasing albums on its own successful Dischord label. The band also steadfastly shuns mainstream attention and offers from major record labels. Fugazi's sound is a progression on the loud-fast aesthetic practiced by founding member Ian Mackaye's former bands, Embrace and the legendary Minor Threat.

Ian MacKaye started Dischord in the Arlington, Virginia, house he moved into after graduating from Washington, D.C.'s Wilson High School in 1980. He formed the label to put out records by his first band, the Teen Idles, followed by his next group, Minor Threat, which, along with Black Flag, was one of the most highly regarded hardcore punk bands. When Minor Threat broke up in 1983, MacKaye moved on to the short-lived Embrace before teaming up with Happy Go Licky members Guy Picciotto and Brendan Canty in 1987 to form Fugazi. Joe Lally, a native of Rockville, Maryland, had worked as a roadie for one of the Dischord bands before joining Fugazi on bass.

Despite the quartet's firm status as an independent entity, with relatively little promotion Fugazi has managed to amass a huge following, consistently packing large venues and selling about 150,000 copies of each album. Fugazi takes a decidedly pragmatic approach to rock & roll, eschewing the excessive rock-star lifestyle. The band keeps its album and concert prices low (for years, their CDs were priced at eight dollars each and admission to their all-ages shows was five dollars), renounces drugs and alcohol (Minor Threat inadvertently spawned the "straight-edge" hardcore movement of the mid-Eighties via the lyrics to such songs as "Out of Step" and "Straight Edge"), refuses extravagant catering spreads backstage, uses only reputable, "alternative" promoters, and discourages the hardcore rituals of slam dancing and stage diving at shows. On album, Fugazi retains the attitude and angst inherent in the hardcore punk rock of their predecessors, but has slowed down the tempos and added dense, metal-like instrumental foundations and the precise syncopations of reggae and the Police. *In On the Kill Taker* was Fugazi's first album to appear on the charts, peaking at #153 in 1993.

The Fugs

Formed 1965, New York City, New York
Ed Sanders (b. Kansas City, Mo.), voc., gtr.; Tuli Kupferberg (b. New York City), voc.; Ken Weaver (b. Galveston, Tex.), voc., drums.
1965—*First Album* (ESP)   1966—*The Fugs (Kill for*

Peace)   1968—*Tenderness Junction* (Reprise); *It Crawled into My Hand, Honest*   1969—*The Belle of Avenue A* (group disbands)   1970—*Golden Filth* 1983—*Proto-punk* (PVC)   1984—(Group re-forms: Sanders; Kupferberg; Weaver; with others) *Refuse to Be Burnt-Out*   1986—*No More Slavery*   1987— *Star Peace*   1991—*Songs from a Portable Forest* (Gazell)   1994—(Current lineup: Sanders; Kupferberg; + Steve Taylor, gtr., voc.; + Coby Batty, voc., perc.; + Scott Petito, bass, synth.) *Fugs Finale* (Fantasy); *Fantasy.*
Ed Sanders solo: 1969—*Sanders' Truckstop* (Reprise)   1972—*Beer Cans on the Moon.*
Tuli Kupferberg solo: 1989—*Tuli and Friends* (Shimmy Disc).

These perverse post-Beatnik poets were too pointedly topical and obscene for mass consumption, but the Fugs were the most relentless comic satirists of the hippie era. Their targets included sexual repression, rock, politics, and the foibles of humanity in general.

Ed Sanders had graduated from New York University in 1960 with a BA in ancient Greek; in 1961 he marched on the Pentagon. He was a published poet who briefly ran the Peace Eye bookstore and published the literary magazine *Fuck You.* Tuli Kupferberg, a lanky, hirsute, perennially bedraggled-looking figure whom Beat poet Allen Ginsberg immortalized in *Howl* as "the person who jumped off the Brooklyn Bridge and survived," was also a published poet and a graduate of Brooklyn College.

With Ken Weaver and an ever-changing roster of backing musicians—including Peter Stampfel and Steve Weber of the Holy Modal Rounders, guitarists Vinny Leary, Pete Kearney, and Ken Pine, bassists John Anderson and Charles Larkey, and drummer Bob Mason—they became a long-running off-off Broadway rock-theater phenomenon in Greenwich Village, with audiences often walking out on their scathingly profane, put-down-riddled theater-of-outrageous-absurdity performances.

After more than 900 shows at the Players Theater and the Bridge Theater, they embarked on a cross-country tour in a borrowed Volkswagen van. In late 1968 they toured Europe, at one point trying unsuccessfully to get into then-troubled Czechoslovakia in order to masturbate in front of invading Russian tanks.

In the late Sixties Sanders released solo albums on Reprise, *Sanders' Truckstop* and *Beer Cans on the Moon,* and reported on the Charles Manson trial for the underground press; he later wrote a best-selling book about the murder case and the trial, *The Family.* A collection of his poems, *Thirsting for Peace in a Raging Century,* won an American Book Award in 1988. In mid-1979 Sanders presented a two-hour rock-theater extravaganza in Woodstock. Kupferberg went on to publish books (including *1001 Ways to Make Love* and *1001 Ways to Beat* the Draft) and to publish cartoons. He has published in more than 100 publications. From the mid-Seventies to 1982 he worked as a production assistant for the now-defunct *SoHo Weekly News*. He became the Director of Revolting Theater and continues to perform at colleges and at New York venues, reading poetry or playing with his band, Tuli and the Fuxxons.

The band regrouped in 1984 for a reunion concert and continued to stage annual reunions and release records through the end of the decade. The band reformed to play in Woodstock, N.Y., upon the occasion of Woodstock '94, held in nearby Saugerties.

The Bobby Fuller Four

Formed mid-1960s, El Paso, Texas
Bobby Fuller (b. Oct. 22, 1943, Baytown, Tex.;
d. July 18, 1966, Los Angeles, Calif.), gtr., voc.;
Randy Fuller, bass; DeWayne Quirico, drums; Jim
Reese, gtr.
1965—The Bobby Fuller Four (Mustang)   1966—
KRLA King of the Wheels   1987—The Best of the
Bobby Fuller Four (1965–1966) (Rhino).

"I Fought the Law" established the Bobby Fuller Four for a half-year of stardom in 1966. The group, all Texans, established a reputation in El Paso, then moved to Los Angeles. "Let Her Dance" became popular in the Southwest in 1965, and "I Fought the Law"—written by a member of Buddy Holly's Crickets, Sonny Curtis— reached #9 in 1966. (The Clash later covered it.) A Buddy Holly cover, "Love's Made a Fool of You" (#26, 1966), was a follow-up hit.

In July 1966 Bobby Fuller died under mysterious circumstances in his car parked in front of his Hollywood home. The fact that he had been beaten up and had ingested gasoline was not released to the public at the time. Although the police ruled his death a suicide, friends speculated that he was murdered, possibly by mobsters. Afterward, the Randy Fuller Four continued, but without success.

Jesse "Lone Cat" Fuller

Born March 12, 1896, Jonesboro, Georgia; died January 29, 1976, Oakland, California
1963—San Francisco Bay Blues (Prestige)   1993—
Jazz, Folk Songs, Spirituals & Blues (Fantasy).

Jesse Fuller was a country-bluesman, a one-man band, and the composer of "San Francisco Bay Blues." Fuller never knew his father, and the man his mother lived with often brutally mistreated him. By age five Fuller had learned to play a homemade stringed mouth bow. After living with his mother's relatives a few years, he left home at ten and began traveling around the South and Midwest, working odd jobs and playing the blues.

In the early Twenties Fuller was discovered outside Universal Film Studios shining shoes. He was given bit parts in *The Thief of Bagdad, East of Suez,* and other movies, for which he was paid $7.50 a day. During his middle age, he worked a succession of jobs, including cowherding, broom making, and car washing. He remained committed to music, however, and in the late Thirties debuted on radio station KNX (Oakland) singing "John Henry."

In 1951 Fuller decided to devote himself entirely to his music, and over the next decade he built a small cult following. He often used a one-man band setup he had devised that allowed him to play guitar, harmonica, hi-hat with castanets, and his own invention, the footdella (a piano–string bass operated with a foot pedal). He wrote "San Francisco Bay Blues" in 1954, and five years later appeared at the Monterey Jazz Festival. Fuller became popular in Europe and England, and toured the U.S. regularly throughout the Sixties. It wasn't until the mid-Fifties that he began recording, cutting his early tracks for Prestige (later reissued on Fantasy). In 1976 he died of heart disease.

Lowell Fulson

Born March 31, 1921, Choctaw Indian territory, Oklahoma
1966—Tramp (Kent)   1969—Now (United)   1972—
On a Heavy Bag (Jewel)   1973—I've Got the Blues
1975—Lowell Fulson (Arhoolie); The Ol' Blues
Singer (Granite)   1977—Hung Down Head (Chess);
Blues Masters   1978—Lovemaker (Big Town)
1983—One More Blues (Evidence)   1988—It's a
Good Day (Rounder)   1992—Hold On (Bullseye
Blues).

A journeyman R&B performer whose recording career spans four decades, Fulson hit the pop chart in the mid-Sixties. He is best known, however, for several songs he wrote that have become modern blues classics.

Of Native American and African descent, Fulson (not Fulsom, as is often written) grew up in Tulsa, where many of his relatives played stringed instruments. He left home around age 17 to join a traveling country & western string band. In 1940 Fulson moved to Texas, where he played with the popular Texas Alexander. Shortly thereafter he was drafted and served in the Pacific, where he often entertained fellow soldiers.

A few months after his discharge in late 1945, Fulson moved to California, where he began recording in Oakland, California, in 1946, concentrating on dance-hall blues numbers he had learned during his time with Alexander. His R&B hits began in 1948 with "Three O'Clock Blues" (a.k.a. "Three O'Clock in the Morning"), "You Know That I Love You," and "Come Back Baby" for Downbeat. They continued on the Swingtime label in

1950 and 1951 with "Every Day I Have the Blues" (#5 R&B, 1950), "Blue Shadows" (#1 R&B, 1950), and "Lonesome Christmas" (#7 R&B, 1950).

By the mid-Fifties Fulson was recording for Chess/Checker, notably "Reconsider Baby" (#3 R&B, 1954), now a blues standard. His brief pop success began in 1965, when "Black Nights" (#11 R&B, 1965), on the Kent label, became a minor hit, followed two years later by "Make a Little Love" (#20 R&B, 1967), and his most successful release, "Tramp" (#5 R&B, 1967), which almost cracked the pop Top Fifty. Later Otis Redding and Carla Thomas had hits with his songs. In 1960 Fulson married Guitar Slim's widow, Sadie; she died in 1992. From the Seventies on, Fulson continued to tour and perform around the world. In 1993 he was inducted into the Rhythm and Blues Hall of Fame; he is the recipient of five W. C. Handy Awards.

Fun Boy Three: See the Specials

Annette Funicello
Born October 22, 1942, Utica, New York
1959—*Annette* (Buena Vista)   1960—*Annette Sings Anka*; *Hawaiiannette (Annette Sings Songs of Hawaii)*; *Italianette (Annette Sings Songs with an Italian Flavor)*   1961—*Dance Annette*   1962—*Annette Funicello*; *Annette—The Story of My Teens . . . and Sixteen Songs That Tell It*   1993—*Annette: A Musical Reunion with America's Girl Next Door* (Walt Disney Records).

Annette Funicello was the first female rock singer who needed only one name, for she was indeed America's girl next door. Funicello experienced something of a revival in the Eighties when Los Angeles disc jockey Rodney Bingenheimer began playing her old records, and since then an array of rockers, from the B-52's Fred Schneider to Redd Kross, have noted her influence.

Walt Disney discovered and cast her as the last of 24 children for his new kids' TV show, *The Mickey Mouse Club*. Early in the show's original run, from fall 1955 to early 1959, Annette emerged as the most popular Mouseketeer, and when the show was canceled she alone remained under contract to Disney. There she costarred in such films as *Babes in Toyland* (1961) and *The Monkey's Uncle* (1965), the title theme of which she recorded with the Beach Boys.

Pairing Annette with songwriters Richard and Robert Sherman, Disney launched her recording career with a series of catchy but innocent hits, "Tall Paul" (#7, 1959), "First Name Initial" (#20, 1959), and "Pineapple Princess" (#11, 1960). She became a regular on Dick Clark's shows and soon befriended other teen idols, including Paul Anka, with whom she fell in love. He wrote "Puppy Love" and "Put Your Head on My Shoulder" for her. Annette made her biggest contribution to teen culture, however, in a series of beach-party films costarring Frankie Avalon: *Beach Party* (1963), *Muscle Beach Party, Bikini Beach, Pajama Party* (all 1964), and *Beach Blanket Bingo* (1965).

She retired from show business after marrying in 1965, although she made rare television appearances (and in 1968 had a cameo role in the Monkees' surrealistic *Head*) and in the mid-Seventies was the spokesperson for Skippy peanut butter. In 1987, while filming *Back to the Beach* with Avalon, Funicello noticed the first symptoms of multiple sclerosis. She and Avalon toured the country through 1988, and in 1992 she publicly announced that she was suffering from MS. She has since become a spokesperson for others with the illness, and in 1994 she published her well-received autobiography, *A Dream Is a Wish Your Heart Makes: My Story.*

Funk
In its narrowest sense, funk is bass-driven, percussive, polyrhythmic black dance music, with minimal melody and maximum syncopation. Its lineage can be traced from James Brown's one-chord workouts of the Sixties on through Booker T. and the MGs, the Bar-Kays, Sly and the Family Stone, the Ohio Players, Con Funk Shun, Parliament/Funkadelic, New Orleans' the Meters, and various other bands. With some simplification of its rhythms, funk provided the basis for disco and became a cornerstone of hip-hop, rap, and virtually every other black-inspired and dance genre to emerge since.

In the late Seventies funk became a much-abused term of praise, along with "funky." Originally, "funky" meant dirty and sexy, as in "funky drawers," and before it was stretched entirely out of shape, as a description of music it implied something more urgent and repetitive than "swinging."

Funkadelic: See George Clinton

Richie Furay: See Poco

Billy Fury
Born Ronald Wycherly, April 17, 1941, Liverpool, England; died January 28, 1983, London, England
1960—*The Sound of Fury* (Decca, U.K.); *Billy Fury* (Ace of Clubs, U.K.)   1961—*Halfway to Paradise* 1963—*Billy* (Decca, U.K.); *We Want Billy*   1967—*Best of* (Ace of Clubs, U.K.)   1977—*The Billy Fury Story* (Decca, U.K.).

Billy Fury was one of England's major pre-Beatles pop stars. In late 1958 he was writing songs while working on a Mersey tugboat. Impresario Larry Parnes, impressed by the young singer, gave him his stage name and sent him touring through the U.K.

Fury's first British hit came in spring 1959 with "Maybe Tomorrow" (#18, U.K.), followed in 1960 by two of his own songs: "Colette" (#9, U.K.) and "That's Love" (#19, U.K.). Around the same time, he released a rockabilly album, *The Sound of Fury*. Shortly thereafter, keyboardist Georgie Fame led a defection of Fury's entire band (including guitarist Colin Green, bassist Tony Makins, and drummer Red Reece) in 1962. They then backed Fame on his own successful solo career.

Fury gradually abandoned rock & roll for MOR covers of American hits, which provided mid-decade successes like "Halfway to Paradise" (#3, U.K.), "Jealousy" (#2, U.K.), and "I'd Never Find Another You" (#5, U.K.). By the time his chart records ended in 1965, he had nearly 20 English hits. He was featured in David Essex's film *That'll Be the Day* in 1973. Ill health had been a persistent problem, and Fury worked when he could while retaining hopes of someday retiring to open a bird sanctuary. He died of heart disease in 1983.

Fusion

Almost any genre that merges musical forms can be considered "fusion" (for instance, British progressive rock, which fused rock instrumentation with classical motifs). But most bands categorized as fusion groups derive from jazz-rock fusion, pioneered by jazz trumpeter Miles Davis, who in the mid-Sixties used electric instruments and rock rhythms in extended improvisatory jazz suites.

Various Davis alumni—John McLaughlin and Billy Cobham with the Mahavishnu Orchestra, Chick Corea with Return to Forever, Joseph Zawinul and Wayne Shorter with Weather Report, Tony Williams (and McLaughlin) with Lifetime—codified jazz-rock fusion into a commercially successful format, featuring complicated riffs and flashy virtuoso solos in bands led by Jean-Luc Ponty, Stanley Clarke, Al DiMeola, and others.

The term "jazz rock" was also applied to such brass-dominated pop bands as Chicago and Blood, Sweat and Tears, but in these cases both "jazz" and "rock" seemed incidental at best. Since the first jazz-rock fusions, other variants have sprung up: In the late Seventies, free-jazz saxophonist Ornette Coleman revolutionized the genre with the more dense and inventive "harmolodic fusion."

From its Seventies heyday, jazz-rock fusion of a complex variety was largely subsumed in the Eighties by the easy-listening "jazz lite" of such commercial stars as saxophonist Kenny G. The start of the Nineties, however, suggested the resurgence of more challenging fare via experimentation with punk, world-music forms, and hip-hop sounds by players as varied as Arto Lindsay, Herbie Hancock, Guru, Digable Planets, and Sonny Sharrock. Fittingly, it was Miles Davis' last album, the hip-hop-inflected *Doo-Bop* (1992), that showcased the latest revival.

Kenny G

Born Kenneth Gorelick, June 5, 1956, Seattle, Washington
1982—*Kenny G* (Arista)   1984—*G Force*   1985—*Gravity*   1986—*Duotones*   1988—*Silhouette*   1989—*Live*   1992—*Breathless*.

President Bill Clinton spoke for a lot of Americans in the early Nineties when he called Kenny G one of his favorite jazz musicians. Most jazz purists have dismissed the saxophonist—Kenny G, that is—as a purveyor of soulless fluff. Nonetheless, Kenny G's smooth, mellow "contemporary jazz" style has made him one of the most commercially successful instrumental recording artists in history.

Gorelick took up the saxophone as a child, after seeing the instrument played by a soloist on *The Ed Sullivan Show*. Although he started on alto sax and learned to play tenor as well, the soprano sax eventually became his signature instrument. At 17, he played in Barry White's Love Unlimited Orchestra, and in the mid-Seventies he became the only white musician in a Seattle-based funk outfit called Cold, Bold, and Together. After graduating magna cum laude from the University of Washington, with a degree in accounting, Kenny G spent a few years playing in Oregon's Jeff Lorber Fusion Band, then signed with Arista Records as a solo act in the early Eighties.

G's first three albums sold respectably for instrumentals, but it was his fourth, *Duotones,* that proved the charm, reaching #6 on the pop chart and spawning the #4 single "Songbird." *Silhouette* followed its predecessor into the Top Ten (#8, 1988), and includes a couple of singles that did well on the R&B and adult-contemporary charts, notably "We've Saved the Best for Last," on which Smokey Robinson sang. *Breathless* (#2 pop, #2 R&B, 1992) featured vocals by Peabo Bryson and Aaron Neville. G has also recorded with R&B divas Aretha Franklin, Whitney Houston, Dionne Warwick, and Natalie Cole. In 1993 the saxophonist was the only nonsinging pop star to appear on Frank Sinatra's *Duets* album.

Peter Gabriel

Born February 13, 1950, London, England
1977—*Peter Gabriel* (Atco)   1978—*Peter Gabriel* (Atlantic)   1980—*Peter Gabriel*   1982—*Peter Gabriel (Security)* (Geffen)   1983—*Peter Gabriel Plays Live*   1985—*Birdy* soundtrack   1986—*So*   1989—*Passion: Music for "The Last Temptation of Christ"* soundtrack   1990—*Shaking the Tree: Sixteen Golden Greats*   1992—*Us*   1994—*Secret World Live*.

As frontman for the British progressive-rock band Genesis, Peter Gabriel cowrote, sang, and acted out elaborate story songs, wearing masks and costumes. Since leaving

Peter Gabriel

Genesis [see entry] in 1975 to begin a solo career, Gabriel has revealed a new array of guises, including soundtrack composer, social activist, world-music aficionado, and music-video innovator.

Gabriel's first solo album was an eponymously titled effort, as were his next three. (The idea, he once explained, was to suggest issues, as one would for a magazine.) The first and second LPs drew attention for the respective singles "Solsbury Hill" and "D.I.Y." The third, produced by Steve Lillywhite, yielded "Games Without Frontiers" (#48, 1980) and showed Gabriel striving to break rock conventions; for instance, drummers Jerry Marotta and Phil Collins (Gabriel's former Genesis bandmate) were prohibited from using cymbals.

Gabriel's fourth album, subtitled *Security* (1982), was the singer's first to go gold; it also gave him his first Top Forty single with "Shock the Monkey." That same year Gabriel financed the World of Music, Arts, and Dance (WOMAD) Festival, designed to bring African and Far Eastern music—which had increasingly influenced his work—to Western ears. To offset the festival's debt, he staged a Genesis reunion concert and released a WOMAD album, featuring cuts by himself, Robert Fripp (the producer of his second LP), and Pete Townshend alongside ethnic-music sources. The WOMAD Festival became an annual event, and the organization eventually spawned an education program and record label.

In 1984 Gabriel was tapped to score Alan Parker's film *Birdy*; the singer consequently won the Grand Jury Prize at Cannes. In 1985 he founded Real World Inc., aimed at developing cross-cultural projects in technology and the arts. The following year, he started the United Nations University for Peace, intended to fund an international human-rights computer network, and set up Real World Studios, a recording complex near Bath, England, where artists including Van Morrison and New Order have since worked. (A Real World record label, dedicated to exposing ethnic music from around the world, was established in 1989.)

Nineteen eight-six also saw Gabriel's commercial breakthrough. *So,* coproduced with Daniel Lanois, reached #2 and produced the funky chart-topping "Sledgehammer," which Gabriel accompanied with a groundbreaking video full of provocative live-action-animation images. A video for "Big Time" (#8, 1987) followed suit. Other singles included "In Your Eyes" (#26, 1986) and "Don't Give Up" (#72, 1987), a duet with Kate Bush.

Gabriel joined U2, Sting, and others for a 1986 tour on behalf of Amnesty International. A 1988 Amnesty Tour followed, with Gabriel, Sting, Bruce Springsteen, Tracy Chapman, and Youssou N'Dour (who had sung on *So*). Also in 1988, Gabriel performed "Biko," his tribute to South African civil-rights martyr Steven Biko (from 1980's *Peter Gabriel*) at a Nelson Mandela tribute at London's Wembley Stadium, and composed music for Martin Scorsese's controversial adaptation of *The Last Temptation of Christ*. The 1989 soundtrack album won a Grammy for Best New Age Performance.

Gabriel's next studio album, 1992's *Us,* was inspired by his mid-Eighties divorce from childhood sweetheart Jill Moore and the breakup of a subsequent relationship with actress Rosanna Arquette. The album reached #2 and generated "Digging in the Dirt" (#52, 1992) and "Steam" (#32, 1992). In 1993 Gabriel enlisted an international roster including Sinéad O'Connor, Crowded House, James, and PM Dawn for a WOMAD tour. The 1994 double CD *Secret World Live* was recorded during two Italian concerts in 1993.

Rory Gallagher

Born March 2, 1949, Ballyshannon, Ireland; died June 14, 1995, London, England
1971—*Rory Gallagher* (Atco) 1972—*Deuce* (Polydor); *Live!* 1973—*Blueprint*; *Tattoo* 1974—*Irish Tour '74*; *In the Beginning* (Emerald Gem) 1975—*Against the Grain* (Chrysalis); *Sinner . . . and Saint* (Polydor) 1976—*The Story So Far*; *Calling Card* (Chrysalis); *The Best Years* (Polydor) 1978—*Photo Finish* (Chrysalis) 1979—*Top Priority* 1980—*Stage Struck* 1982—*Jinx* 1987—*Defender* (I.R.S.) 1990—*Fresh Evidence.*
With Taste: 1969—*Taste* (Atco)

Blues guitarist Rory Gallagher grew up in Cork, Ireland, and got his first guitar at age nine. He played in pickup bands until leaving school at 15 and toured in the early Sixties with the Fontana Showband. By the time the group broke up in 1965, it was called the Impact. Gallagher then began working regularly in Hamburg, Germany, and in Ireland with bassist Charlie McCracken and ex-Them drummer John Wilson in a power trio he called Taste. They moved to London in 1969 and released the first of several guitar showcase LPs, which met with some enthusiasm in the U.K. and Europe. Taste specialized in hard-rocking versions of blues and country chestnuts like "Sugar Mama." The group broke up in 1971, and Gallagher began leading small bands under his own name.

Bucking all trends, he subsequently conducted a moderately successful solo career, with increasing emphasis on his own blues-rock material. Gallagher played on Muddy Waters' *The London Sessions* (1972) and on the star-studded 1978 comeback LP by English skiffle star Lonnie Donegan. He regularly toured in the U.S., Britain, and Europe; a 1974 Irish tour was the subject of a documentary by director Tony Palmer. In June 1995, Gallagher died from complications following a liver transplant.

Gang of Four

Formed 1977, Leeds, England
Jon King (b. June 8, 1955, London, Eng.), voc., melodica; Hugo Burnham (b. March 25, 1956, London), drums; Andy Gill (b. Jan. 1, 1956, Manchester, Eng.), gtr.; Dave Allen (b. Dec. 23, 1955, Cambria, Eng.), bass.
1978—*Damaged Goods* EP (Fast Product, U.K.) 1980—*Entertainment!* (Warner Bros.) 1981—*Solid Gold* (– Allen; + Sara Lee, bass) 1982—*Another Day, Another Dollar* EP; *Songs of the Free* (– Burnham) 1983—*Hard* 1984—*At the Palace* (Phonogram, U.K.) (group disbands) 1990—*A Brief History of the 20th Century* (Warner Bros.) (group reforms: King; Gill) 1991—*Mall* (Polydor).

The English-born Gang of Four played dissonant, dub-reggae-influenced, atonal funk with political lyrics. They were extremely influential in the U.K. and a solid concert draw in the U.S. The group started at art school in Leeds in 1977, naming itself after a Chinese Communist political faction associated with Mao Tse-Tung's widow. Gang of Four released its debut EP, *Damaged Goods*, on the independent Fast Product label. Touring and the record, which became a hit at rock discos, brought them a contract with EMI in Britain and, after a self-financed tour, with Warner Bros. in the U.S., which began a jumbled release schedule. (*Entertainment!* was released in Britain in October 1979 and in the U.S. in May 1980, for example.)

In the middle of the U.S. tour supporting *Solid Gold*, bassist Dave Allen quit; he was replaced on tour by Busta "Cherry" Jones, who had performed with Talking Heads and Chris Spedding. Later in 1981 bassist Sara Lee, who had been a member of the League of Gentlemen with Robert Fripp, joined the Gang of Four as a full-time member. On their 1982 tour the Gang of Four appeared as a five-piece group with vocalist Edi Reader. Although their music had apparently been too raw for U.S. radio, they received extensive play in clubs for such danceable British hits as "At Home, He's a Tourist," "Damaged Goods," and "I Love a Man in Uniform."

In 1983 King and Gill fired Burnham and used a drum machine on *Hard*, ironically attacked by critics as sounding too soft. Drummer Stephen Goulding of Graham Parker and the Rumour was added for a tour, while Burnham became a record industry A&R executive (after stints at Island and Imago, he landed at Quincy Jones' Qwest label). Citing musical differences, King and Gill disbanded Gang of Four in 1984; Allen and Burnham played an encore at a London farewell show.

Dave Allen went on to form Shriekback (with ex-XTC and League of Gentlemen keyboardist Barry Andrews) [see entry], King Swamp, and Low Pop Suicide. In addition, Allen founded the independent label World Domination; in 1994, that label released Allen's first solo album, *The Elastic Purejoy*.

Andy Gill produced the Red Hot Chili Peppers' debut album and worked on film soundtracks. (Allen and Jon King cowrote the music for 1984's *The Karate Kid*.) King formed two bands, Mechanic Preachers and King Butcher, before he and Gill re-formed Gang of Four for the critically well-received *Mall*.

Gangsta Rap

Gangsta is a rap subgenre characterized by violent, hard-hitting, often gang-related themes delivered in an angry, forceful vocal style and often set in an urban sonic collage of siren and gunshot effects. Pioneered by Philadelphia rapper Schoolly D on his 1986 song "PSK — What Does It Mean?" (about the Philly gang Parkside Killers), gangsta rap was popularized by the South-Central Los Angeles group N.W.A on the group's controversial, politically charged second album, *Straight Outta Compton*. The most extreme gangsta rap group was the Geto Boys, whose grisly, pornographic depictions of rape and murder ignited a storm of protest from citizens' groups and only grudging support from even the most ardent First Amendment champions.

After initially being defended for their musical *vérité* style, by the early- to mid-Nineties gangsta rappers were increasingly criticized for their preoccupation with guns, misogyny, antihomosexuality, and use of abusive terms such as "bitch" and "ho." Despite a growing number of rap and hip-hop artists stridently rejecting gangsta values, by 1994 it had become the dominant rap and hip-hop style, with some of the biggest-selling pop artists—Ice Cube, Ice-T, Dr. Dre, Snoop Doggy Dogg, Naughty by Nature, Cypress Hill, Scarface—performing at least some gangsta rap material. The style has had its share of controversy, from the 1992 Ice-T/"Cop Killer" ordeal (which, ironically, involved the gangsta rapper's nonrap, heavy-metal side project, Body Count) to the arrests of Snoop Doggy Dogg on a murder charge and Tupac Shakur on a sexual assault charge.

A mid-Nineties gangsta rap backlash found one California state assemblyman worrying in the *New York Times* that, "for years, these rappers have been preaching drug culture and violence. But now they are openly living that lifestyle." Meanwhile, some school systems had begun banning what they considered gangsta rap fashions such as baggy clothing and head bandannas. In 1995 former education secretary William Bennett joined forces with the National Political Congress of Black Women to make antirap TV commercials aimed at bringing public pressure to bear on Time Warner and its Warner Music Division for distributing albums by such artists as Snoop Doggy Dogg and Dr. Dre.

Gang Starr

Formed 1988, Brooklyn, New York
The Guru Keith E. (b. Keith Elam, July 18, 1966, Boston, Mass.), voc.; DJ Premier (b. Chris Martin, May 3, 1969, Brooklyn), DJ.
1989—*No More Mr. Nice Guy* (Wild Pitch) 1991—*Step in the Arena* (Chrysalis) 1992—*A Daily Operation* 1994—*Hard to Earn*.

Gang Starr's music honors hip-hop's jazz roots. Indeed, the duo's biggest break came when director Spike Lee brought them together with saxophonist Branford Marsalis to collaborate on a piece for the film *Mo' Better Blues*.

Keith Elam (his Guru moniker stands for "Gifted Unlimited Rhymes Universal") formed the initial version of Gang Starr in his native Boston, where his father was the city's first black judge. Elam rebelled against his upbringing and moved to New York City in 1983 to seek a career in music, but not before studying business at Morehouse College in Atlanta. In the mid-Eighties Elam heard a demo tape by Chris Martin, a DJ from Brooklyn who was then studying computer science at Prairie View A&M University in Texas. When Martin returned to New York, the two moved into a Brooklyn apartment and began jamming.

Gang Starr's first album featured the songs "Positivity" and "Jazz Music," which pointed in the direction the duo would explore further on later albums. Gang Starr's major-label debut, *Step in the Arena*, reached #19 on the

Gang Starr: Guru, DJ Premier

R&B charts. After the release of *A Daily Operation*, Elam announced plans to do a solo project of jazz/hip-hop fusion music, featuring noted jazzmen Courtney Pine, Marsalis, and others. The resulting album, *Jazzmatazz*, came out in 1993.

The Gap Band

Formed early 1970s, Los Angeles, California
Ronnie Wilson, voc., trumpet, kybds.; Charles Wilson, lead voc., kybds.; Robert Wilson, bass, voc.; plus other musicians.
1974—*Magician's Holiday* (Shelter) 1977—*The Gap Band* (Tattoo) 1979—*The Gap Band II* (Mercury) 1980—*The Gap Band III* 1982—*Gap Band IV* (Total Experience) 1983—*Gap Band V—Jammin'* 1985—*Gap Gold/Best of the Gap Band*; *Gap Band VI* 1986—*Gap Band VII*; *The 12" Collection* (Mercury) 1987—*Straight from the Heart* (Total Experience) 1989—*Round Trip* (Capitol) 1994—*Best Of* (Mercury); *Testimony* (Rhino) 1995—*Ain't Nothin' but a Party*.
Charlie Wilson solo: 1992—*You Turn My Life Around* (Bon Ami).

As the Gap Band, the three Wilson brothers, natives of Tulsa, Oklahoma, became one of the most popular funk bands of the Eighties. Their father was a Pentecostal minister and their mother a pianist, and every Sunday the boys sang before their father's sermon. When they started the band in the early Seventies, they named themselves using the first initials of three neighborhood streets—Greenwood, Archer, and Pine—to form Gap.

By 1974 they had met Leon Russell, who signed them to his Shelter Records, where they cut one album. They also performed as Russell's backup band for several years. In the mid-Seventies the Wilsons moved to Los Angeles, where they recorded one gospel-styled single, "This Place Called Heaven," for A&M. They then moved to RCA-distributed Tattoo Records and cut a self-titled album that attracted some attention.

The Gap Band signed to Mercury Records, and "Shake," "Steppin' (Out)," and "I Don't Believe You Want to Get Up and Dance (Oops, Up Side Your Head)," all R&B Top Ten hits, brought them to national prominence. Then "Burn Rubber (Why You Wanna Hurt Me)" (#1 R&B, 1980) and "Yearning for Your Love" (#5 R&B, 1981) from the platinum *III* (#16, 1981) established them as a major act. Another platinum album, *Gap Band IV* (#14) contained two 1982 #1 R&B singles: "Early in the Morning" (#24 pop) and "Outstanding"; "You Dropped a Bomb on Me" peaked at #2 (#31 pop).

The Gap Band continued with more R&B hits, including "Party Train" (#3 R&B, 1983), "Jam the Motha'" (#16 R&B, 1983), "Beep a Freak" (#2, 1984), "I Found My Baby" (#8, 1985), "Going in Circles" (#2 R&B, 1986), "Big Fun" (#8 R&B, 1986), "I'm Gonna Git You Sucka" (#14, 1988), "All of My Love" (#1 R&B, 1989), "Addicted to Your Love" (#8 R&B, 1990), and "We Can Make It Alright" (#18 R&B, 1990). The group's only other album to enter the Top Forty was the gold *Gap Band V—Jammin'* (#28, 1983). *The Gap Band II* has also been certified gold.

In 1990 Charles worked with Dave Stewart on the soundtrack *Rooftops;* the film was a box-office flop. Later he toured with Eurythmics and cowrote two songs on that group's *We Too Are One* ("Revival" and "Your Love Is Precious"). He later released his solo debut album, *You Turn My Life Around* (#42 R&B, 1992). He never left the group, however, and the Gap Band continues to tour and record in the early-Nineties.

Jerry Garcia: See the Grateful Dead

Art Garfunkel
Born November 5, 1941, New York City, New York
1973—*Angel Clare* (Columbia)   1975—*Breakaway*
1977—*Watermark*   1979—*Fate for Breakfast*
1981—*Scissors Cut*   1988—*Garfunkel*; *Lefty*
1993—*Up 'Til Now* (Sony).

Art Garfunkel contributed high harmonies and arranging ideas to Simon and Garfunkel's string of folk-pop hits in the late Sixties [see entry]. When that duo disbanded in 1970, part of the reason was Garfunkel's growing interest in film, although he has released occasional solo albums

since. The two reunited to sing for half a million fans at a September 1981 concert in New York's Central Park and have played together onstage several times in the Nineties.

Garfunkel met Paul Simon in grade school in Queens. The two had a teenybopper hit record, "Hey Schoolgirl" (#49, 1958), as Tom and Jerry. Garfunkel also recorded a few unsuccessful sides on his own as "Arty Garr" for the Octavia and Warwick labels in the early Sixties. But he had been seriously studying architecture and mathematics at Columbia University before deciding to join Simon in a professional music career.

Garfunkel's first film, *Catch-22*, was shot in 1969 as he and Simon drifted apart, and Garfunkel appeared in *Carnal Knowledge* (1971) and in Nicolas Roeg's *Bad Timing/A Sensual Obsession* (1980). He didn't revive his recording career until 1973, with the lavishly orchestrated *Angel Clare* (#5), which included the first of his solo hit singles, Jimmy Webb's "All I Know" (#9, 1973). His other appearances in the Top Forty in the Seventies included "I Only Have Eyes for You" (#18, 1975) and "Breakaway" (#39, 1976). Garfunkel is particularly fond of moody, romantic ballads. His 1975 LP, *Breakaway*, included a studio reunion with Simon for "My Little Town," which became a Top Ten hit. In 1978 Garfunkel teamed with Simon and James Taylor for a Top Twenty version of Sam Cooke's "(What a) Wonderful World"; he also undertook his first U.S. solo tour.

Garfunkel seemed to fade from view in the Eighties, but 1993 saw the release of *Up 'Til Now*, which hit the stores around the same time as Garfunkel's acclaimed onstage reunion with his former partner at Carnegie Hall for a series of concerts billed as a Paul Simon career retrospective. Garfunkel also returned to the big screen that year, costarring in director Jennifer Lynch's controversial film *Boxing Helena*. In addition to touring, since the mid-Eighties the singer has been walking across America. He heads west a week at a time, flies home, then picks up where he left off. As of late 1993 the singer was nearing Butte, Montana.

Leif Garrett
Born November 8, 1961, Hollywood, California
1977—*Leif Garrett* (Atlantic)   1978—*Feel the Need* (Scotti Brothers)   1979—*Same Goes for You*
1980—*Can't Explain*   1981—*My Movie of You*.

Leif Garrett was a mid-Seventies television teen idol. He began his recording career at age 16 with a self-titled collection of rock oldies that included "Surfin' U.S.A." (#20, 1977). It became the first of several moderate hits, followed by remakes of "Runaround Sue" (#13, 1978) and "The Wanderer" (#49, 1978). He made his film debut as a child in the 1969 film *Bob and Carol and Ted and Alice*. Among his other film credits are the *Walking Tall* movies;

he briefly had his own television series, *Three for the Road* (1975). The biggest hit of Garrett's career came in 1979, when "I Was Made for Dancin'" hit the Top Ten in both the U.S. and the U.K. After appearing in a few little-noticed films, Garrett largely faded from view.

Marvin Gaye

Born Marvin Pentz Gay Jr., April 2, 1939, Washington, D.C.; died April 1, 1984, Los Angeles, California
1961—*Soulful Mood* (Tamla)   1963—*That Stubborn Kinda Fellow*   1964—*Together* (with Mary Wells)
1965—*How Sweet It Is*   1966—*Greatest Hits*; United (with Tammi Terrell)   1967—*Greatest Hits, vol. 2*   1968—*You're All I Need to Get By*; Marvin Gaye and His Girls (with Terrell, Wells, Kim Weston)   1969—*M.P.G.*   1970—*Superhits*   1971—*What's Going On*   1972—*Hits of Marvin Gaye*; Trouble Man soundtrack   1973—*Let's Get It On*; Diana and Marvin (with Diana Ross)   1974—*Anthology*; Live   1976—*The Best of Marvin Gaye* 1978—*Here, My Dear*   1981—*In Our Lifetime* 1982—*Midnight Love* (Columbia)   1985—*Romantically Yours*; Dream of a Lifetime   1990—*The Marvin Gaye Collection* (Tamla/Motown)   1991—*The Last Concert Tour* (Giant)   1993—*Seek and You Shall Find: More of the Best (1963–1981)* (Rhino) 1994—*The Marvin Gaye Classics Collection* (Motown); The Norman Whitfield Sessions   1995—*The Master: 1971–1984*.

With a career that exemplified the maturation of romantic black pop into a sophisticated form spanning social and sexual politics, Marvin Gaye was one of the most consistent and enigmatic of the Motown hitmakers. Certainly among the most gifted composers and singers, with a mellifluous tenor and a three-octave vocal range, he was also moody—avoiding TV, rarely performing live, and sometimes not showing up for the few concerts he did schedule. From "How Sweet It Is (To Be Loved By You)" to "I Heard It Through the Grapevine," from "What's Going On" to "Sexual Healing," Gaye sang some of the most memorable black pop of the Sixties, Seventies, and Eighties. He was nominated for eight Grammys before winning two in 1983. His life ended tragically one year later—and one day before his 45th birthday—when he was shot to death by his father, an Apostolic preacher, after a violent argument. In many respects, Gaye was, as author David Ritz titled his biography of him, a divided soul.

Gaye started singing at age three in church and was soon playing the organ as well. After a stint in the air force, he returned to D.C. and started singing in street-corner doo-wop groups, including a top local group, the Rainbows. He formed his own group, the Marquees, in 1957. Under the auspices of supporter Bo Diddley, they

Marvin Gaye

cut "Wyatt Earp" for the Okeh label. In 1958 Harvey Fuqua heard the group and enlisted it to become the latest version of his ever-changing backing ensemble, the Moonglows. As such, Gaye was heard on "Mama Loocie" and other songs for the Chess label in 1959.

By the early Sixties the group was touring widely. While playing a club in Detroit, it was heard by local impresario Berry Gordy Jr., who quickly signed Gaye to his fledgling Motown organization in 1961. Soon after, Gaye married Gordy's sister Anna. Gaye's first duties with the label were as a session drummer (he played on all the early hits by Smokey Robinson and the Miracles).

Gaye got his first hit with his fourth release, "Stubborn Kind of Fellow," in 1962. Over the next ten years, working with nearly every producer at Motown (including Holland-Dozier-Holland, Smokey Robinson, and Norman Whitfield), he enjoyed over 20 big hits. Although he specialized in mid-tempo ballads, he also had dance hits: "Hitch Hike" (#30, 1963), "Can I Get a Witness" (#22, 1963, which became a virtual anthem among the British mods), and "Baby Don't You Do It" (#27, 1964).

But by and large he favored romantic, sometimes sensual ballads. He felt that his desire to move into a more mainstream, sophisticated style was hindered by Motown's emphasis on hits. For a performer as unenthusiastic about some of his material as Gaye later claimed to be, he gave almost every song he ever recorded an inspired reading. His Top Ten hits included "Pride and Joy" (#10, 1963), "I'll Be Doggone" (#8, 1965), "Ain't That Peculiar" (#8, 1965), and "How Sweet It Is to Be Loved by You" (#6, 1965). Among his 39 Top Forty singles of the period were also such unlikely hits as "Try It Baby" (#15, 1964, with background vocals by the Temptations), "You're a

Wonderful One" (#15, 1964, with backing vocals by the Supremes), "One More Heartache" (#29, 1966), "Chained" (#32, 1968), and "You" (#34, 1968).

Beginning in 1964 Gaye was teamed with Mary Wells for a couple of hits, "Once Upon a Time" (#19, 1964) and "What's the Matter with You" (#17, 1964), and with Kim Weston for "It Takes Two" (#17, 1967). But his greatest duets were with Tammi Terrell: "Ain't No Mountain High Enough" (#19, 1967), "Your Precious Love" (#5, 1967), "Ain't Nothing Like the Real Thing" (#8, 1968), and "You're All I Need to Get By" (#7, 1968), all penned and produced by Ashford and Simpson. In a 1967 concert Terrell collapsed into his arms onstage, the first sign of the brain tumor that killed her three years later. Although, contrary to popular belief, Gaye and Terrell were not romantically involved, he was deeply affected by her illness and death. Shortly thereafter Gaye had his biggest solo hit of the Sixties with "I Heard It Through the Grapevine" (#1, 1968), a song that had already been recorded by another Motown act, Gladys Knight and the Pips.

The second, quite distinct phase of Gaye's career began in 1971 with *What's Going On.* Along with Stevie Wonder, Gaye was one of the first Motown artists to gain complete artistic control of his records. *What's Going On* was a self-composed-and-produced song cycle that could rightfully be called a concept album. Berry Gordy Jr., who still maintains that he didn't understand the record, was reluctant to release it. Gaye was vindicated when the album hit #6 and spun off three Top Ten singles: "What's Going On" (#2, 1971), "Inner City Blues (Make Me Wanna Holler)" (#9, 1971), and "Mercy Mercy Me (the Ecology)" (#4, 1971) were impassioned, timeless statements on Vietnam, civil rights, and the state of the world. "What's Going On" has been covered many times in the ensuing years, including a Top Twenty version by Cyndi Lauper in 1986.

In 1972 Gaye scored the 20th Century–Fox film *Trouble Man,* and the dark, minimalist title track gave him yet another Top Ten hit (#7, 1973). By 1973 he had shifted his attention to pure eroticism with *Let's Get It On,* the title track of which went to #1. His late-1973 album with Diana Ross, *Diana and Marvin,* produced three fairly successful singles: "You're a Special Part of Me" (#12, 1973), "Don't Knock My Love" (#46, 1974), and "My Mistake (Was to Love You)" (#19, 1974), but this project was one of many things Gaye did with Motown that he felt were forced upon him.

Gaye's rocky marriage of 14 years to Anna Gordy Gaye was the subject of *Here, My Dear* as the Seventies closed, with Gaye still reeling from the divorce settlement; he filed for bankruptcy, and his ex-wife later considered suing him for invasion of privacy over the content of *Here, My Dear.* (The album had been precipitated by court hearings in 1976, when a judge instructed Gaye to make good on overdue alimony payments by recording an album and giving his wife $600,000 in royalties.) With Gordy he fathered a son, Marvin Gaye III. He married his second wife, Janice, in 1977 and that year had a #1 hit, "Got to Give It Up, Pt. 1." They had two children: Nona, who has since become a recording artist in her own right, and Frankie.

Under pressure from the Internal Revenue Service, Gaye moved to Europe to record his 1981 release, *In Our Lifetime,* which concentrated on his philosophies of love, art, and death. The next year, he left Motown for Columbia. His first album for the label, *Midnight Love,* sold two million copies and included the hit "Sexual Healing," which won a Grammy for Best R&B Vocal Performance, Male. He sang live on the Grammy broadcast and, in 1983, in concert at Radio City Music Hall. Also in 1983 he appeared in one of the more memorable segments of Motown's 25th-anniversary television special, obviously somewhat disoriented but riveting nonetheless. His a cappella version of "The Star-Spangled Banner," performed before the 1983 NBA All-Star game that year, became an instant bootlegged classic and is included on *The Marvin Gaye Anthology.*

Despite his success, Gaye was depressed, and his cocaine abuse was escalating. He returned to the U.S. and moved into his parents' home—where he often quarreled with his father, with whom he'd been at odds since his teenage years. As Gaye later confessed to the cowriter of what was to have been his autobiography, David Ritz's *Divided Soul,* his internal life was marked by what Gaye believed was an irreconcilable conflict between good (as represented by his strict religious upbringing) and evil (sex, drugs). In early 1984 Gaye reportedly threatened suicide several times, before his father shot him to death at point-blank range, following a Sunday morning shouting match. After his death Motown and Columbia collaborated to produce *Dream of a Lifetime* and *Romantically Yours,* both based on unfinished recordings from the *Sexual Healing* sessions; among the tracks on the first album were the ribald "Savage in the Sack" and "Masochistic Beauty," and some questioned whether Gaye had intended to release them at all. In 1987 Gaye was inducted into the Rock and Roll Hall of Fame.

Gloria Gaynor

Born September 7, 1949, Newark, New Jersey
1975—*Never Can Say Goodbye* (MGM); *Experience Gloria Gaynor*   1976—*I've Got You* (Polydor) 1977—*Glorious*   1978—*Gloria Gaynor's Park Avenue Sound*   1979—*Love Tracks*; *I Have a Right* 1982—*Gloria Gaynor* (Atlantic)   1984—*I Am What I Am* (CBS)   1986—*The Power* (Stylus, U.K.)   1988— *Gloria Gaynor's Greatest Hits* (Polydor)   1990—*Glo-

ria Gaynor 90 (New Music, It.) 1992—*Love Affair* (Polydor).

Gloria Gaynor is a singer who is best known for her anthemic late-Seventies disco hit "I Will Survive." One of six children, she grew up listening to records by Nat King Cole and Sarah Vaughan. Following high school, she worked as an accountant but quit to join a band in Canada. She soon found herself back in Jersey, however, working day jobs until one night at a club a friend persuaded her to sing with the band. The group, the Soul Satisfiers, took her on tour for a year and a half. She then formed her own band and went to New York, where she was discovered by Columbia Records.

Gaynor's first single, "Honey Bee," was a disco hit in 1973, but Columbia soon lost interest. She signed to MGM, and *Never Can Say Goodbye* was a hit in early 1975. One of the first LPs specifically programmed for dancing, the title cut (an earlier hit for the Jackson 5 and then Isaac Hayes) hit #9. She followed up with a less successful cover of another Motown hit, the Four Tops' "Reach Out I'll Be There," before a string of less popular singles. But five years later "I Will Survive" hit #1 on the pop chart (#4 R&B); *Love Tracks* went platinum.

Gaynor's last big hit was "I Am What I Am" (from the play *La Cage Aux Folles*), which hit #13 in the U.K. but made it only to #82 here. She continues to tour the U.S. and Europe, where she has been especially popular in Italy. In recent years she has also been writing her own material, some of it in a gospel vein.

J. Geils Band

Formed 1967, Boston, Massachusetts
Jerome Geils (b. Feb. 20, 1946, New York City, N.Y.),
gtr.; Peter Wolf (b. Peter Blankfield, Mar. 7, 1946,
Bronx, N.Y.), voc.; Magic Dick (b. Dick Salwitz, May
13, 1945, New London, Conn.), harmonica; Danny
Klein (b. May 13, 1946, New York City, N.Y.), bass;
Stephen Jo Bladd (b. July 13, 1942, Boston), drums.
1968—(+ Seth Justman [b. Jan. 27, 1951, Washington, D.C.], kybds.) 1971—*The J. Geils Band* (Atlantic) 1972—*The Morning After; Full House* 1973—*Bloodshot; Ladies Invited* 1974—*Nightmares (and Other Tales from the Vinyl Jungle)* 1975—*Hot Line* 1976—*Blow Your Face Out* 1977—*Monkey Island* 1978—*Sanctuary* (EMI America) 1980—*Love Stinks* 1981—*Freeze-Frame* 1982—*Showtime!* 1983—(– Wolf) 1984—*You're Gettin' Even While I'm Gettin' Odd* 1985—*Flashback: Best of the J. Geils Band* (EMI America) 1993—*The J. Geils Band Anthology: Houseparty* (Rhino).
Bluestime (Jay Geils; Magic Dick; + Michael "Mudcat" Ward, bass; + Steve Ramsay, drums; + Jerry Miller, gtr): 1994—*Bluestime* (Rounder).

Peter Wolf solo: 1984—*Lights Out* (EMI America) 1987—*Come as You Are* 1990—*Up to No Good* (MCA).

The J. Geils Band merged its collectors' dedication to blues, doo-wop, and R&B with enough pop know-how to keep the group contemporary. The band was named after guitarist J. (Jerome) Geils, but its lyricist and onstage focus was singer Peter Wolf. A high school dropout who learned to jive-talk on Bronx streetcorners, Wolf moved to Boston before he was 20 and earned a passable reputation as a painter before becoming a disc jockey on Boston's WBCN-FM, where he called himself Woofuh Goofuh. He joined the Hallucinations, which included drummer and fellow doo-wop collector Stephen Jo Bladd, and by 1967 the group was playing covers of R&B, blues, and Fifties rock & roll, from John Lee Hooker to the Miracles. Meanwhile, Geils, bassist Klein, and harpist Magic Dick were working as an acoustic trio called the J. Geils Blues Band. After the Hallucinations broke up in 1967, Bladd and Wolf joined the J. Geils Band, which by then had gone electric.

While other fledgling bands were going psychedelic, this group acted like greasers, and its showmanship and taste in obscure covers earned it a following in New England. Justman, who later became the band's producer and composer, was an organist who had moved north from Atlantic City to attend Boston University; he joined in 1968.

The band toured almost constantly in the early Seventies, while occasionally reaching the Top Forty with such songs as "Looking for a Love" (#39, 1971), the reggae-style "Give It to Me" (#30, 1973, making its album, *Bloodshot,* gold), and "Must of Got Lost" (#12, 1974). In 1977 the Geils band briefly called itself Geils and released *Monkey Island,* the group's first self-produced effort. In 1979 Wolf's five-year marriage to actress Faye Dunaway ended in divorce.

After nine LPs with Atlantic, the band switched to EMI America in 1978 for *Sanctuary,* its first gold disc in five years. In 1980 the J. Geils Band conducted its most extensive tour ever (U.S., Japan, Europe) to support *Love Stinks.* The album introduced Justman's synthesizer work and went gold. *Freeze-Frame* (#1, 1981), with the hits "Centerfold" (#1, 1981), "Freeze-Frame" (#4, 1982), and "Angel in Blue" (#40, 1982), was the band's best-selling album to date.

But tension had been brewing between the songwriting team of Wolf and Justman. When the group turned down material the singer had been writing with R&B legend Don Covay and Michael Jonzun of the Jonzun Crew, Wolf left—reluctantly—for a solo career in 1983. His *Lights Out,* coproduced by Jonzun, produced two Top Forty hits the following year, "Lights Out" (#12) and "I Need You Tonight" (#36), and the title track to

1987's *Come As You Are* reached #15. A third LP, in 1990, disappeared, and Wolf along with it. He resurfaced in 1993 and began to play his first live shows. As for Wolf's former bandmates, they broke up after releasing one unsuccessful album with Justman on lead vocals, 1984's *You're Gettin' Even While I'm Gettin' Odd*. In 1993 Magic Dick and Geils, now calling himself Jay, put together a new band, Bluestime, and released an album of blues covers and originals the following year.

Bob Geldof: See Boomtown Rats

Gene Loves Jezebel

Formed 1981, London, England
Jay Aston (b. Porthcawl, Wales), voc, gtr.; Michael Aston (b. Porthcawl), gtr., voc.; Ian Hudson, gtr.; Peter Rizzo, bass; Chris Bell, drums.
1983—*Promise* (Situation Two, U.K.)   1985— (– Hudson; + James Stevenson, gtr.) *Immigrant* (Relativity); *Desire* EP   1986—*Discover* (Geffen) 1988—*The House of Dolls* (– M. Aston)   1990— (+ Robert Adam, gtr.) *Kiss of Life*   1993—*Heavenly Bodies* (Savage).

Led by the heavily made-up and elaborately coifed twins Jay and Michael Aston, Gene Loves Jezebel's mid-Eighties New Romantic–style pop was powered by wailing guitars, tribal drums, and Michael Aston's willfully off-key vocals.

Formed when the Astons moved to London with guitarist Ian Hudson, the early version of the band featured bassist Julianne Regan and drummer Dick Hawkins. By the time Gene Loves Jezebel released its 1983 U.K. debut album, *Promise* (Geffen released it in the States in 1987), the band had gone through several personnel changes, with Hudson leaving and coming back. The Astons traveled to the U.S. to record with fellow Welshman John Cale in 1984. *Immigrant* put the band on the U.K. independent chart, and in 1986, helped by the vogue for "haircut" bands, Gene Loves Jezebel was signed by Geffen.

Discover (#155, 1986), the group's major-label debut, featured former Generation X guitarist James Stevenson. *The House of Dolls* (#108, 1987) saw the Astons moving to a more conventional style of hard rock and contained their first Hot 100 single, "Motion of Love" (#87, 1988). Michael quit the band and moved to Los Angeles in 1989. Jay remained in London and, keeping the band together, recorded *Kiss of Life* (#123, 1990) and 1993's *Heavenly Bodies*. When that album fizzled, so did the group, with Aston going solo and Stevenson joining the Cult.

General Public: See the English Beat

Generation X: See Billy Idol

Genesis

Formed 1966, Godalming, England
Tony Banks (b. Mar. 27, 1950, East Hoathly, Eng.), kybds.; Michael Rutherford (b. Oct. 2, 1950, Guildford, Eng.), gtr., bass, voc.; Peter Gabriel (b. February 13, 1950, London, Eng.), voc.; Anthony Phillips (b. December 1951, Putney, Eng.), gtr.; Chris Stewart, drums.
1968—(– Stewart; + John Silver, drums)   1969— *From Genesis to Revelation* (Decca, U.K.) (– Silver; + John Mayhew, drums)   1970—*Trespass* (Charisma, U.K.) (– Phillips; – Mayhew; + Phil Collins [b. Jan. 31, 1951, London], drums, voc.; + Steve Hackett [b. Feb. 12, 1950, London], gtr.) 1971—*Nursery Cryme*   1972—*Foxtrot*   1973— *Genesis Live*; *Selling England by the Pound* 1974—*The Lamb Lies Down on Broadway* (Atco) 1975—(– Gabriel)   1976—*A Trick of the Tail*; *The Best of Genesis* (Buddah)   1977—*Wind & Wuthering* (Atco); *Seconds Out* (Atlantic) (– Hackett) 1978—. . . And Then There Were Three . . .   1980— *Duke*   1981—*Abacab*   1982—*Three Sides Live* 1983—*Genesis*   1986—*Invisible Touch*   1991—*We Can't Dance*   1992—*Live/The Way We Walk, vol. 1: The Shorts*   1993—*Live/The Way We Walk, vol. 2: The Longs*.
Phil Collins solo: 1981—*Face Value* (Atlantic) 1982—*Hello, I Must Be Going!*   1985—*No Jacket Required*   1989—. . . But Seriously   1990—*Serious Hits Live!*   1993—*Both Sides*.
Tony Banks solo: 1979—*A Curious Feeling* (Charisma)   1983—*The Fugitive*; *The Wicked Lady* (Atlantic)   1986—*Quicksilver*   1989—*Bankstatement*.
Mike Rutherford solo: 1979—*Smallcreep's Day* (Atlantic)   1982—*Acting Very Strange*.
Mike + the Mechanics (Rutherford, gtr., bass; + Paul Carrack [b. April 22, 1951, Sheffield, Eng.], voc., kybds.; + Paul Young [b. June 17, 1947, Manchester, Eng.], voc.; + Adrian Lee [b. Sep. 9, 1947, London], kybds.; + Peter Van Hook [b. June 4, 1950, London], drums): 1985—*Mike + the Mechanics* (Atlantic) 1988—*The Living Years*   1991—*Word of Mouth* 1995—*Beggar on a Beach of Gold*.
Steve Hackett solo: 1976—*Voyage of the Acolyte* (Chrysalis)   1978—*Please Don't Touch*   1979— *Spectral Mornings* (Charisma, U.K.)   1980— *Defector*   1981—*Cured* (Virgin/Epic).
Peter Gabriel solo: See entry.

The long career of Genesis breaks down neatly into two contrasting eras: For the first half Genesis was a cult band fronted by theatrical vocalist Peter Gabriel, playing majestic art rock that set the style for such American acts as Kansas and Styx—story songs set to complex, richly textured music with hints of classical pomp. After Gabriel left [see entry], drummer Phil Collins took over as lead singer—proving himself a more down-to-earth frontman—and the band's audience expanded exponentially, as Genesis streamlined its music into romantic pop songs and abandoned costume drama for laser lightshows. By the mid-Eighties Genesis was one of the world's most popular bands.

After Gabriel and Tony Banks played together in a band called Garden Wall, they formed a "songwriters' collective" with Mike Rutherford and Anthony Phillips while all four were students at Charterhouse, an exclusive British secondary school. In late 1967 British record mogul Jonathan King suggested the name Genesis and got the group a contract that resulted in the poppish 13-song *From Genesis to Revelation* (1968), which was released in the U.S. as *In the Beginning* in 1974.

On graduation, the four members lived together in an English country cottage and rehearsed for several months before playing their first gig in September 1969. They developed an elaborate stage show—Gabriel had a series of costume changes, including a bat and a flower—and with the adroit drumming of Phil Collins (formerly with Flaming Youth), their songs grew into extended suites on *Nursery Cryme, Foxtrot,* and *Selling England by the Pound.* They gained a large following in England and a dedicated cult in the United States. In 1974 Genesis' theatricality peaked with a two-LP set and attendant live show, *The Lamb Lies Down on Broadway,* in which Gabriel played Rael, who suffered various metamorphoses in a surreal Manhattan.

Gabriel left Genesis after *Lamb* for a solo career, and the group took 18 months to adjust. They auditioned over 400 singers before deciding Collins could take over; on tour, they employ a second drummer so that Collins can roam the stage (Bill Bruford was the first, for the 1976 tour, and Chester Thompson for the rest). Genesis dispensed with costumes and continued to perform older material, which was credited to the whole group. *A Trick of the Tail* and *Wind & Wuthering* expanded their cult (the latter included their first hit single, "Your Own Special Way" [#62, 1977]), and . . . *And Then There Were Three . . .,* with somewhat shorter songs, became their first gold album in 1978 (the LP later went platinum).

Genesis began to score U.S. Top Forty hit singles with "Follow You, Follow Me" (#23, 1978) from . . . *And Then There Were Three . . .* and "Misunderstanding" (#14, 1980) from *Duke,* in which they turned their narrative skills to love songs. For *Abacab,* they incorporated some new-wave concision; the album (#7, 1981) sold two million copies, and the title song (#26, 1981) and "No Reply at All" (#29, 1981) were hits. The latter featured the

Earth, Wind and Fire horn section, which also appeared on Collins' two-million-selling solo debut, *Face Value* (#7, 1981). That album yielded the Top Twenty hits "I Missed Again" (#19, 1981) and "In the Air Tonight" (#19, 1981).

Since then, Genesis has remained intact despite each member's solo projects. Collins' second solo album, *Hello, I Must Be Going!* (1982), was a Top Ten hit and featured a cover of the Supremes' "You Can't Hurry Love" (#10, 1982). The group's *Genesis* (#9, 1983) spawned "That's All" (#6, 1983) and "Illegal Alien" (#44, 1984). In 1984 Collins produced ex–Earth, Wind and Fire vocalist Philip Bailey's *Chinese Wall* album and dueted with him on the hit single "Easy Lover" (#2, 1984). The next year Collins earned an Oscar nomination and won a Grammy for his movie love theme "Against All Odds (Take a Look at Me Now)" (#1, 1984), and hit #1 with "Separate Lives" (a duet with Marilyn Martin) from the film *White Nights.* His own 1985 album *No Jacket Required* hit #1 faster than Michael Jackson's *Thriller* had, with such hits as "One More Night" (#1, 1985), "Sussudio" (#1, 1985), "Don't Lose My Number" (#4, 1985), and "Take Me Home" (#7, 1986). For the July 13, 1985, Live Aid concert, Collins performed on his own in London that morning, then flew via Concorde to the Philadelphia show to perform there solo later that day, as well as play drums in the "Led Zeppelin Reunion" with Robert Plant and Jimmy Page. Also in 1985, Mike Rutherford launched Mike + the Mechanics, whose debut album (#26, 1985) produced hit singles with "Silent Running" (#6, 1985) and "All I Need Is a Miracle" (#5, 1986). *The Living Years* (#13, 1988) yielded a #1 hit in the title track, which was inspired by the death of Rutherford's father.

Genesis returned to the charts with *Invisible Touch* (#3, 1986), containing the title track (#1, 1986), "Throwing It All Away" (#4, 1986), and "Land of Confusion" (#4, 1986). The viciously satirical video for the last featured England's *Spitting Image* puppets of Ronald Reagan, Margaret Thatcher, and others. "Tonight, Tonight, Tonight" (#3, 1987) was featured in TV commercials for Michelob beer, which also sponsored Genesis' 1987 tour (the Michelob campaign, which also used Eric Clapton's "After Midnight," was later satirized in Neil Young's "This Note's for You" video).

In 1988 Collins, who had acted professionally as a child, starred in the movie *Buster* (he'd made his big-screen debut as an extra in the Beatles' *A Hard Day's Night*); the soundtrack produced #1 hits for Collins in a cover of the Mindbenders' 1966 hit "Groovy Kind of Love" and "Two Hearts," cowritten with Lamont Dozier of the famed Holland-Dozier-Holland Motown team. His . . . *But Seriously* (#1, 1989), an attempt to confront social issues, certified Collins as an "adult contemporary" superstar, with "Another Day in Paradise" (#1,

1989), "I Wish It Would Rain Down" (#3, 1990), "Do You Remember?" (#4, 1990), and "Something Happened on the Way to Heaven" (#4, 1990).

The hits continued for Genesis into the Nineties, as *We Can't Dance* (#4, 1991) produced "No Son of Mine" (#12, 1991), "Hold On My Heart" (#12, 1992), and "I Can't Dance" (#7, 1992).

Gentle Giant

Formed 1970, England
Derek Shulman (b. Feb. 2, 1947, Glasgow, Scot.), voc., sax; Ray Shulman (b. Dec. 8, 1949, Glasgow), voc., bass, violin, perc.; Phil Shulman (b. Aug. 27, 1937, Glasgow), sax; Kerry Minnear (b. Apr. 2, 1948), voc., kybds.; Gary Green (b. Nov. 20, 1950), voc., gtr.; Martin Smith, drums; Malcolm Mortimer, drums.
1970—*Gentle Giant* (Vertigo) 1971—(– Mortimer) *Acquiring the Taste* 1972—(– Smith; + John Weathers, drums, voc.) *Three Friends* (Columbia) 1973—*Octopus* (– P. Shulman); *In a Glass House* (WWA, U.K.) 1974—*The Power and the Glory* (Capitol) 1975—*Free Hand; A Giant Step* (Vertigo, U.K.) 1976—*Interview* (Capitol); *Playing the Fool* 1977—*The Missing Piece; Pretentious* 1978—*Giant for a Day* 1980—*Civilian* (Columbia).

Merging medieval madrigals and Béla Bartók's dissonances with rock dynamics, Gentle Giant was one of the most dauntingly complex of Seventies British progressive-rock bands. It formed from the remains of an obscure late-Sixties British pop band called Simon Dupree and the Big Sound, which included all three Shulman brothers (Derek was Simon Dupree). The Big Sound had one U.K. Top Ten hit, "Kites," in 1967.

John Weathers had been with Graham Bond and the Grease Band before joining the Shulmans; Gary Green had played with blues and jazz bands; and Kerry Minnear had studied at the Royal Academy of Music. With Gentle Giant the Shulmans moved in the direction of King Crimson and Jethro Tull, though they often used dissonant counterpoint far more intricate than either of them. At first they had only a small European cult following. The political concept album *The Power and the Glory* finally broke them in America. *The Missing Piece* flirted with shorter, harder-rocking song structures, and the group simplified its music, to little commercial avail, in the late Seventies. For a short time the group was managed by radio consultant Lee Abrams, who produced its final LP, *Civilian*.

After the band's breakup, Derek Shulman moved to New York City and became an A&R executive with Polygram Records (it was he who signed Bon Jovi to that label). He has since worked for Atco Records and Giant Records.

Bobbie Gentry

Born Roberta Lee Street, July 27, 1944, Chickasaw County, Mississippi
1967—*Ode to Billie Joe* (Capitol) 1968—*The Delta Sweete; Bobbie Gentry and Glen Campbell* (with Glen Campbell) 1969—*Touch 'Em with Love; Bobbie Gentry's Greatest* 1970—*Fancy* 1990—*Greatest Hits* (Curb).

Bobbie Gentry came to national prominence in 1967 with the first—and biggest—hit of her career, the enigmatic ballad "Ode to Billie Joe." From childhood, Gentry was determined to be a music star, and she wrote her first song at age seven on a piano. By her teens she had moved to California, where she attended UCLA (majoring in philosophy) and the L.A. Conservatory of Music. She worked as a secretary, occasionally performing in clubs at night, and then briefly as a Las Vegas showgirl before cutting her debut disc in 1967. "Ode to Billie Joe" hit #1, as did the album of the same name that year. A triple Grammy winner, "Ode" went on to sell three million copies internationally. The ballad provided the groundwork for a movie of the same title in 1976.

Gentry's later career never matched the success of her debut, although she was a star in England and hosted a British TV series, *The Bobbie Gentry Show*, in the early Seventies. In America her late-Sixties releases generally stalled in the middle rungs of the pop chart, except for a 1970 duet with Glen Campbell on the Everly Brothers' "All I Have to Do Is Dream" (#27). By the mid-Seventies she was a staple on the Vegas-Reno circuit. In 1978 she married country singer Jim Stafford and has since retired from show business.

The Gentrys

Formed 1963, Memphis, Tennessee
Larry Raspberry, gtr., voc.; Larry Wall, drums; Jimmy Johnson, trumpet, organ; Bobby Fisher, sax, gtr., piano; Pat Neal, bass; Bruce Bowles, voc.; Jimmy Hart, voc.
1965—*Keep On Dancing* (MGM) 1970—*The Gentrys* (Sun).

The Gentrys were a Memphis garage band whose biggest hit was 1965's "Keep On Dancing." They formed in 1963 to play sock hops and were soon winning local talent contests and battles of the bands. In 1964, after appearing on *Ted Mack's Original Amateur Hour*, they were signed to the local Youngstown label, and their first release, "Sometimes," was a regional hit. Their followup, "Keep On Dancing" (allegedly cut in an amazing 35 minutes), was leased to MGM and hit #4 in October 1965. Their 1966 releases, "Spread It On Thick" and "Everyday I Have to Cry," failed to crack the Top Forty.

The group broke up in 1970, but Hart took over

singing lead, and with a new group of musicians recorded three minor hits: "Why Should I Cry," "Cinnamon Girl," and "Wild World" on Sun. In 1973 group leader Larry Raspberry started Alamo, which recorded one album, then the Highsteppers, who recorded for Stax. In the early Seventies the Bay City Rollers revived "Keep On Dancing." Jimmy Hart now works as a professional-wrestling manager for, among others, Hulk Hogan; Wall worked in record promotion. In 1995 Hart and Hogan announced that they had written a song about James Bulger, the two-year-old Liverpool toddler who was abducted and murdered by two ten-year-olds, entitled "Another Hulkmaniac in Heaven." It was included on Hogan's 1995 recording debut, *American Made.*

Georgia Satellites

Formed 1979, as Keith and the Satellites; lineup solidified in 1983, Atlanta, Georgia
Dan Baird (b. Dec. 12, 1953, Calif.), gtr., voc.; Mauro Megellan, drums; Rick Price (b. Aug. 15, 1951, Atlanta), bass; Rick Richards (b. Mar. 30, 1954, Jasper, Ga.), gtr.
1986—*The Georgia Satellites* (Elektra) 1988—*Open All Night* 1989—*In the Land of Salvation and Sin* 1991—(Group disbands) 1993—(Group re-forms: Richards; Price; + Joey Huffman, kybds.; + Billy Pitts, drums) *Let It Rock.*
Dan Baird solo: 1992—*Love Songs for the Hearing Impaired* (American).

A latter-day boogie band, the Georgia Satellites proffer bare-bones, full-tilt rock & roll, served up with a silly grin and lust in their hearts. They had a Top Ten single and album with "Keep Your Hands to Yourself" (#2, 1986) from their eponymous debut (#5, 1986).

Formed in Atlanta in 1979 as Keith and the Satellites with Richards and Baird along with Keith Christopher from local new-wave unit the Brains ("Money Changes Everything"), they honed their sound (called "hick AC/DC" by some record execs) during a residency at Hedgen's Rock 'n' Roll Tavern. In 1983, now known as the Satellites (Christopher left early on), the band shopped around a six-song demo with no success and called it quits the following year.

Making Waves, a British indie label, heard the tape and offered to finance a U.K. tour, releasing the tape as *Keeping the Faith* (1985). Richards and Baird recruited two other former Brains, Magellan and Price, and took the label up on its offer. The tour fell through, but the band persevered, moving to Nashville where it was discovered by Elektra.

Unable to match their debut single and album's success (a cover of "Hippy Hippy Shake" included on the soundtrack of *Cocktail* [1988] hit #45), the Georgia Satellites split again in 1991. After the breakup, Price played

on Paul Westerberg's *14 Songs* (1993); Baird released a 1992 solo album, *Love Songs for the Hearing Impaired.*

After a 1992 reunion show, Richards and Price decided to give the Satellites another try, releasing *Let It Rock* in 1993.

Gerardo

Born Gerardo Mejia III, April 16, 1965, Guayaquil, Ecuador
1991—*Mo' Ritmo* (Interscope) 1992—*Dos.*

Perpetually sporting ripped jeans, a trademark bandanna, and little else, Gerardo was the first Latino rapper to become a pop star. He burst onto MTV and into the mass consciousness in 1991 with the #7 pop single "Rico Suave," on which he rapped, in Spanish and English, lyrics that exploited the Latin lover stereotype (cheekily, he insisted).

Having moved to Los Angeles when he was 12, Gerardo developed a keen interest in the sultry dancing style favored in local nightclubs. Discovered at such an establishment in the late Eighties, Gerardo was cast as a gang member in the 1988 Robert Duvall–Sean Penn vehicle *Colors.* "Rico Suave" was the first single from Gerardo's 1991 debut album, *Mo' Ritmo*, a critically maligned effort that fused Latin rhythms with funk textures. The followup single, "We Want the Funk" (#16, 1991), sampled a Parliament song, and Gerardo persuaded George Clinton to make a cameo in the accompanying video. The young rapper seemed omnipresent for a few months, but by the time his sophomore album was released in 1992, it seemed safe to assume that Gerardo's fifteen minutes of fame were up. *Dos* was a commercial dud, and the suave one has not been heard from since.

Gerry and the Pacemakers

Formed 1959, Liverpool, England
Gerry Marsden (b. Sep. 24, 1942, Liverpool), voc., gtr.; Les Maguire (b. Dec. 27, 1941, Wallasey, Eng.), piano; John Chadwick (b. May 11, 1943, Liverpool), bass; Freddie Marsden (b. Oct. 23, 1940, Liverpool), drums.
1964—*Don't Let the Sun Catch You Crying* (Laurie); *Gerry and the Pacemakers' Second Album* 1965—*Ferry Cross the Mersey* (United Artists) 1991—*The Best of Gerry and the Pacemakers, the Definitive Collection* (EMI America).

Gerry and the Pacemakers were on the pop end of Liverpool's mid-Sixties Merseybeat trend. They built up a following in Liverpool clubs like the Cavern and in the Hamburg, Germany, clubs. In 1962 they became the second group—after the Beatles—to be signed by manager Brian Epstein. Produced by George Martin, their first three records hit #1 on the British chart: "How Do You Do It?" (which the Beatles had also recorded), "I Like It," and "You'll Never Walk Alone." "How Do You Do It?" was one of their biggest U.S. hits (#9) in 1964. They scored Top Ten successes in the U.S. that year with the ballad "Don't Let the Sun Catch You Crying" and in 1965 with "Ferry Cross the Mersey." That year they starred in a movie of the same name, which featured nine original songs by leader Gerry Marsden.

By 1966, however, their releases ceased having much impact on U.S. charts, and the group disbanded a year later. Marsden began a successful cabaret career, scoring minor U.K. hits like "Please Let Them Be" and "Gilbert Green" and acting on stage and TV, where he hosted a children's show, *The Sooty and Sweep Show*, for several years. In 1973 he re-formed the Pacemakers for a nostalgia tour of America, and ever since has performed all over the world.

In 1985 Marsden sang lead on a new version of "You'll Never Walk Alone," credited to "Crowd," intended to raise money for victims of a fire at a British soccer stadium. It went to #1, making him the only British artist ever to top the chart twice with different renditions of the same song. He nearly repeated that feat four years later with a new "Ferry 'Cross the Mersey" that included Paul McCartney and Frankie Goes to Hollywood's Holly Johnson. Once again the cause was soccer related: Proceeds from the record benefited families of fans who'd been crushed to death by unruly crowds during a match. It, too, made #1, seven spots higher than the original 1964 version.

The Geto Boys

Formed as the Ghetto Boys, 1986, Houston, Texas
Scarface (b. Brad Jordan, Nov. 9, 1969, Houston), voc.; Willie D (b. Willie Dennis, Nov. 1, 1966, Houston), voc.; Bushwick Bill (b. Richard Shaw, Dec. 8, 1966, Kingston, Jam.), voc.; Ready Red (b. Collins Lyaseth), DJ.
1988—*Making Trouble* (Rap-a-Lot); *Grip It! On That Other Level*   1990—*Geto Boys* (Def American) 1991—*We Can't Be Stopped* (Rap-a-Lot)   1992— (– Willie D; + Big Mike [b. Mike Barnett, Sep. 27, 1971, New Orleans, La.], voc.) *Uncut Dope*   1993— *Till Death Do Us Part*.
Scarface solo: 1991—*Mr. Scarface Is Back* (Rap-a-Lot)   1993—*The World Is Yours*   1994—*The Diary*.
Bushwick Bill solo: 1992—*Little Big Man* (Rap-a-Lot).
Willie D solo: 1989—*Controversy* (Rap-a-Lot) 1992—*I'm Goin' Out Lika Soldier*   1994—*Play Wicha Mama* (Wize Up/Wrap)
Willie D with Sho: 1993—*Trouble Man* (Wize Up/Wrap).

The Geto Boys ignited a firestorm of controversy with their first major-label release, a gangsta rap album containing an unprecedented level of explicit violence and pathology. When Geffen, then-distributor of Def American releases, refused to handle the record, it started a fierce debate within the music industry about whether record companies should refuse certain albums.

At 22, James "Li'l J" Smith brought together the members of the Geto Boys for his new label, Rap-a-Lot Records. Smith wanted to kick off his label with a group that would represent his old neighborhood, the Fifth Ward, a violent Houston, Texas, ghetto. Smith hand-picked the members: Willie D, a Fifth Ward native who once served time for robbing a Texaco station; Scarface, a multi-instrumentalist (piano, violin, guitar, drums) raised in a more middle-class section of Houston on as much rock & roll (Led Zeppelin, Blue Öyster Cult) as R&B; and Bushwick Bill, a 4-foot-6 dwarf born in Jamaica and raised in the Bushwick section of Brooklyn, New York.

After two albums for Rap-a-Lot, the group signed with Def American (which later became American Recordings), the label of death-metal band Slayer and shock comic Andrew "Dice" Clay. Geffen's refusal to distribute the Geto Boys' album led to accusations that the company operated under a double standard, profiting from the homophobia, racism, and misogyny of white artists such as Clay, while refusing to release similar material by an African-American rap group. Virgin agreed to distribute the album, but the Geto Boys, disgruntled by the ordeal, returned to Rap-a-Lot. Their post-controversy album, *We Can't Be Stopped*, shot to #24, higher than any previous release. Its single, "Mind Playing Tricks on Me" (#23 pop, #10 R&B, 1991), was based on the childhood feelings of Scarface, a suicide-prone manic-depressive who spent two of his teenage years in a mental ward.

Outside of the Geto Boys, the members are not friends. Indeed, each of the original rappers has done his own albums, and Willie D left the group permanently in 1992. Still, that same year the Geto Boys returned with *Uncut Dope*, with Big Mike Barnett replacing Willie D. In 1993 *Till Death Do Us Part* reached #1 on the R&B chart.

The Geto Boys have had several brushes with tragedy. In May 1991 Bushwick Bill lost his eye when his 17-year-old girlfriend shot him; drunk and depressed, he had talked her into shooting him by threatening to kill the couple's child if she didn't. In January 1993 Scarface was wounded and a friend of his killed by an off-duty cop during a gang-related fight outside a Shreveport, Louisiana, Waffle House.

Andy Gibb

Born March 5, 1958, Brisbane, Australia; died March 10, 1988, Oxford, England

1977—*Flowing Rivers* (RSO)   **1978**—*Shadow Dancing*   **1980**—*Andy Gibb's Greatest Hits; After Dark.*

Pop singer Andy Gibb was the younger brother of the Bee Gees (who often contributed songs, harmonies, and production to his albums). He began a successful solo career in the late Seventies with three #1 hits: "I Just Want to Be Your Everything" and "(Love Is) Thicker Than Water" in 1977, and "Shadow Dancing" in 1978.

By the time the elder Gibb brothers were getting their international career rolling in the late Sixties, young Andy was already playing in amateur bands of his own. Following his brothers, he first established himself in Australia in the mid-Seventies with tours and singles like "Words and Music." He then signed with Bee Gees manager Robert Stigwood, on whose RSO Records his first album was recorded under the tutelage of brother Barry. Brother Maurice supervised the platinum *Shadow Dancing,* which in addition to the title cut contained the hits "An Everlasting Love" (#5, 1978) and "(Our Love) Don't Throw It All Away."

Three Top Twenty hits followed in 1980, but Gibb's sales began to slack off the following year. His personal life, too, took a nosedive. In 1982 he was fired as host of the popular syndicated TV show *Solid Gold* after one year and was let go from Broadway's *Joseph and the Amazing Technicolor Dreamcoat* for missing performances. By 1985 Gibb was at the Betty Ford Clinic undergoing treatment for substance abuse, and two years later he filed for bankruptcy. The singer's fortunes began to look up somewhat when he signed with Island Records in January 1988, but while recording the album in England, Gibb died suddenly of a viral heart inflammation.

Debbie Gibson

Born Deborah Gibson, August 31, 1970, Merrick, New York
1987—*Out of the Blue* (Atlantic)   **1989**—*Electric Youth*   **1990**—*Anything Is Possible*   **1993**—*Body Mind Soul.*

Fresh-faced teenager Debbie Gibson emerged from her suburban Long Island home studio with a wholesome image and a knack for writing innocent poppy tunes young music fans could relate to. Having begun piano studies as a toddler, Gibson won a local songwriting contest at 12 and was signed to Atlantic Records four years later on the basis of her demo. Although categorized as bubblegum, the singles "Only in My Dreams" and "Shake Your Love"—both from *Out of the Blue,* which went to #7—boasted hooks that suggested a savvy songwriter in the making. Both songs peaked at #4 in 1987, and they were followed into the Top Ten by the album's title track (#3) and the #1 ballad "Foolish Beat" in

1988. Because she wrote and played on her records, Gibson benefited from comparisons to her contemporary Tiffany.

Electric Youth did well initially, reaching #1 and charting two Top Forty singles (the title track at #11, "No More Rhyme" at #17), but by then, even fans seemed to have tired of Gibson the goody-goody wunderkind, who lived at home, was managed by her mom, and preached against sexual promiscuity and drug use. (In 1989 rock satirist Mojo Nixon released "Debbie Gibson Is Pregnant with My Two-Headed Love Child.") *Anything Is Possible* (#41, 1990) went gold but didn't make the Top Forty. After a sabbatical, during which she appeared as Eponine in the Broadway company of *Les Miserables,* Gibson attempted a comeback with *Body Mind Soul.* The 1993 LP tried to present the 22-year-old singer in a more mature, even sensual light. The video for the single "Losin' Myself" (#86, 1993) featured her in slinky lingerie, while the song "Shock Your Mama" slyly poked fun at her squeaky clean image. The album only reached #109, though, and the following year Gibson lost her record contract. In July 1993 she played Sandy in the London stage production of *Grease.*

Jimmy Gilmer and the Fireballs: See the Fireballs

Jimmie Dale Gilmore

Born May 6, 1945, Amarillo, Texas
1988—*Fair and Square* (Hightone)   **1989**—*Jimmie Dale Gilmore*   **1991**—*After Awhile* (American Explorer/Elektra Nonesuch)   **1993**—*Spinning Around the Sun* (Elektra).
With the Flatlanders: 1990—*More a Legend Than a Band* (Rounder).
With Butch Hancock: 1993—*Two Roads* (Caroline).

Texas singer/songwriter Jimmie Dale Gilmore's distinctive high, plaintive voice, intriguing, esoteric lyrics, and traditional country & western sound have put him in the forefront of a looseknit group of mavericks who play a roots-based music that's been dubbed "western beat." Having recorded his first album in 1972 as a member of a Lubbock, Texas, country group, the Flatlanders, Gilmore has continuously collaborated over the years with ex-bandmates Butch Hancock and Joe Ely [see Joe Ely entry]. Several of Gilmore's songs, including "Dallas" and "Tonight I Think I'm Gonna Go Downtown," have been covered by such artists as David Byrne, 10,000 Maniacs, and Nanci Griffith.

Gilmore, who was named after "Singing Brakeman" Jimmie Rodgers, took up guitar as a teen, after first playing fiddle and trombone. Developing a repertoire of traditional country songs, he began providing music at poker

Jimmie Dale Gilmore

1993) earned Gilmore rave reviews, including twice being chosen "Best Country Artist" in ROLLING STONE's annual critics' poll. In 1994 Gilmore recorded two songs with Mudhoney for a Sub Pop single and duetted with Willie Nelson on the benefit album *Red Hot + Country.*

David Gilmour: See Pink Floyd

Greg Ginn: See Black Flag

Gipsy Kings
Formed 1976 as Los Reyes, Arles, France
Nicolas Reyes, voc., gtr.; Andre Reyes, gtr.; Tonino Baliardo, gtr.; Diego Baliardo, gtr.; Paco Baliardo, gtr.; Jahloul "Chico" Bouchikhi, gtr.
1979—(– Bouchikhi; + Canut Reyes, gtr.)   1982—
Allegria* (CBS, France)   1983—*Luna de Fuego
1987—*Gipsy Kings* (Elektra)   1989—*Mosaique*
1991—*Este Mundo*   1992—*Live*   1994—*Love & Lib-erté*   1995—Best of the Gipsy Kings (Nonesuch).

Among the more unlikely sounds to emanate from the airwaves in 1989 were the frenetic flamenco chords and *gitane* shouts of the Gipsy Kings. One of the first real manifestations of the new interest in world music, this group of actual French Gypsies caused a brief sensation blending exotica with familiar European MOR like "Volare" and "My Way."

The Gipsy Kings grew out of the family group Los

parties in his hometown of Lubbock. His first demo recordings were financed in 1965 by Buddy Holly's father. By then a budding songwriter, Gilmore began forming bands: first, the T. Nickel House Band, which included Joe Ely on bass, then the Hub City Movers.

After a stint living in Austin, Gilmore returned to Lubbock in 1972 and formed the Flatlanders with Ely, Hancock, mandolinist Tony Pearson, fiddler Tommy Hancock, and musical-saw player Steve Wesson. That March the group was invited to record an album in Nashville for a small label, which released the recordings only on eight-track. The Flatlanders fizzled soon after (though there have been occasional reunions ever since), and Gilmore, who'd been a philosophy student at Texas Tech, moved to Denver and joined a spiritual sect headed by Indian guru Maharaji Ji. After five years, Gilmore left the group and returned in 1980 to Austin, where he began performing his own material, as well as songs written by Butch Hancock, with whom he frequently played. After eight years, he recorded his first solo album, 1988's *Fair and Square. Jimmie Dale Gilmore* followed the next year. He was "discovered" playing at a 1989 folk festival in Cambridge, England, by 10,000 Maniacs' singer/songwriter Natalie Merchant and Elektra executive David Bither, who signed Gilmore to the label. Both 1991's *After Awhile* and *Spinning Around the Sun* (#62 C&W,

Gipsy Kings: Paco Baliardo, Andre Reyes, Diego Baliardo, Canut Reyes, Nicolas Reyes, Tonino Baliardo

Reyes, led by father Jose—a renowned flamenco singer—with sons Andre and Nicolas and brother-in-law Bouchikhi. When Jose Reyes died, flamenco guitar virtuoso Tonino Baliardo joined, and the group changed its name to the Gipsy Kings. Sticking to a traditional Gypsy sound on early recordings, the acoustic-based unit gained attention only after modernizing its sound at the behest of producer and manager Claude Martinez. (The group continued to sing in *gitane,* a dialect mixing French, Spanish, and Catalan.)

Their 1987 album *Gipsy Kings* became a hit throughout Europe and yielded two hit singles, "Bamboleo" and "Djobi Djoba." After its U.S. release, *Gipsy Kings* (#57)—helped by the fern bar ubiquity of "Bamboleo"—stayed 42 weeks on the *Billboard* charts, going gold. (The Gipsy Kings have 15 international gold and platinum records.) While neither *Mosaique* nor *Este Mundo* achieved the American recognition of their predecessor, the Gipsy Kings remain a popular international live act.

Girl Groups

In the early Sixties, individually faceless and collectively appealing female vocal groups like the Shangri-Las, the Ronettes, the Crystals, and the Shirelles produced one of rock's most charmingly "innocent" styles. The "girl-group sound" was designed to capture a yearning adolescent romanticism, and it contained enough intrinsic moral tension to keep sociologists occupied for some time. With a highly theatrical style based partly on doo-wop vocalizing (e.g., the Crystals' "Da Doo Ron Ron"), the girl groups were hugely successful for several years before being largely swept away by the British Invasion, psychedelic rock, and the singer/songwriter trend.

Girl groups provided platforms for such auteur producers as Phil Spector and George "Shadow" Morton, who created dense, ornate "walls of sound" around the pristine adolescent harmonizing of the vocal groups and crafted girl-group records as mini-melodramas or, as Spector put it, "little symphonies for the kids." The first girl-group hit was probably the Shirelles' 1961 "Will You Love Me Tomorrow," a surprisingly mature Carole King song about premarital sex. Girl groups provided a top-selling forum for the best of New York's Brill Building songwriting teams, such as King and Gerry Goffin, Doc Pomus and Mort Shuman, and Barry Mann and Cynthia Weil.

The girl-group formation carried over into the Motown sound of the later Sixties via the Supremes and Martha Reeves and the Vandellas, but by then the sound had changed significantly. With Motown's promotional savvy behind them, the Supremes, to name just one group, became anything but faceless. While members of most groups never received recognition of their talents outside the old girl-group genre, several made impres-

sive returns to the charts. A classic R&B girl group in its first incarnation, Patti LaBelle and the Bluebelles returned as Labelle with the provocative "Lady Marmalade" in 1975. All three members—LaBelle, Sara Dash, and Nona Hendryx—found success as stylistically divergent solo artists. (The fourth Bluebelle, Cindy Birdsong, had replaced Florence Ballard in the Supremes.) Ronnie Spector, former lead singer of the Ronettes, enjoyed a measure of success in the late Eighties when fans such as Bruce Springsteen and Eddie Money acknowledged her influence and involved her in recording projects. And Darlene Love, whose voice led the Spector groups the Blossoms and the Crystals, is widely regarded as one of the best singers in pop music today.

While there are always a few girl groups on the charts—the Mary Jane Girls and En Vogue come to mind—the sense of innocent, romantic yearning that so richly colored and, it might be said, dated the genre seems impossible to recapture. Latter-day attempts by acts like Bananarama pale in comparison, for while the original girl groups could be sweet or surly, they were never goofy. The genre's influence endures, if only for the fact that most of the first women in rock were "girls."

Philip Glass

Born January 31, 1937, Baltimore, Maryland
1972—*Music with Changing Parts* (Chatham Square); *Solo Music* (Shandar)   1973—*Music in Similar Motion/Music in Fifths* (Chatham Square) 1974—*Music in Twelve Parts—Parts 1 & 2* (Elektra); *Strung Out for Amplified Violin* (Music Observations)   1975—*North Star* (Virgin); *Mad Rush/Dressed Like an Egg* (Soho News)   1976— *Einstein on the Beach* (CBS Masterworks); *Dance Nos. 1 & 5* (Tomato)   1982—*Glassworks* (Columbia) 1983—*The Photographer* (CBS Masterworks); *Koyaanisqatsi* (Antilles)   1985—*Satyagraha* (CBS Masterworks); *Mishima* (Nonesuch)   1986—*Songs from Liquid Days* (Columbia); *The Olympian* 1987—*Akhnaten* (CBS Masterworks)   1988— *Powaqqatsi* (Nonesuch)   1989—*Solo Piano; Mad Rush/Metamorphosis/Wichita/Vortex/Sutra* (all one record) (CBS Masterworks)   1993—*The Low Symphony* (Point); *Hydrogen Jukebox* (with Allen Ginsberg) (Nonesuch).

With his operas, orchestral works, dance pieces, and film scores, Philip Glass is the quintessential postmodernist composer. Bridging high and popular art, he uses Western and world-music elements, minimalism and high-volume amplification, and has influenced both ambient and New Age music.

Glass studied flute as a child and piano at the University of Chicago, where he also studied philosophy and mathematics. In the late Fifties he earned a master's degree in composition at New York's Juilliard School of Music. A 1964 Fulbright grant sent him to Paris to study with Nadia Boulanger. There, a job transcribing Indian music with Ravi Shankar and a growing fascination with Eastern structures led him to repudiate his earlier work and the 12-tone music of purist contemporary classical composers.

After hitchhiking through Africa and India, Glass returned to New York in 1967 and began composing according to principles soon termed minimalist: The music involved repeated rhythmic cycles of notes and, over the years, incorporated counterpoint and harmony. To play it, Glass formed the Philip Glass Ensemble, which toured art galleries and, as early as 1974, rock clubs, including Max's Kansas City. He supported himself as a carpenter, furniture mover, and taxi driver. While initially refusing to publish his music so that the Ensemble could get more jobs playing live, Glass formed Chatham Square Productions in 1971 to record his works. He made substantial impact overseas—David Bowie and Brian Eno were among his early fans—and Virgin U.K. signed him in 1974.

Glass and scenarist Robert Wilson collaborated in 1976 on the first of his "portrait operas," *Einstein on the Beach*, a four-and-a-half-hour opera that toured Europe and played the Metropolitan Opera House. After Virgin released an album of short pieces, *North Star*, in 1975, Glass began gigging at both Carnegie Hall and rock clubs.

From the late Seventies onward, much of Glass' energy went into theater works, including *Satyagraha* (its Sanskrit libretto was taken from the *Bhagavad Gita*) and *Akhnaten* (examining the myth of a pharaoh). He collaborated again with Wilson on *the CIVIL WarS*, whose intended 1984 performance was canceled due to lack of funds. In 1984 as well, he collaborated on *The Juniper Tree*, an opera based on a Grimms fairy tale, and music for the 23rd Olympics. In the mid- and late Eighties, among his other stage works were *A Descent into the Maelstrom* with choreographer Molissa Finley, and the operas *The Fall of the House of Usher, 1000 Airplanes on the Roof*, and *The Making of the Representative for Planet 8*. He also scored two documentaries, *Koyaanisqatsi* and *Powaqqatsi*, the feature film *Mishima*, and plays for the Mabou Mines company.

For his recordings, Glass signed in 1981 the first exclusive composer's contract with CBS Masterworks since Aaron Copland and released his most popular instrumental album, *Glassworks*, a collection of orchestral and ensemble pieces. *The Photographer*, a music-theater work, included a song with lyrics by David Byrne of Talking Heads. In 1983 Glass collaborated with ex-Doors keyboardist Ray Manzarek on a version of Carl Orff's *Carmina Burana. Songs from Liquid Days* (1986), with

lyrics by Paul Simon, Laurie Anderson, Suzanne Vega, and David Byrne, became his best-selling album. In 1990 Glass collaborated with poet Allen Ginsberg on *Hydrogen Jukebox*, an interpretation of Ginsberg's poems. In 1993 the composer released *The Low Symphony*, based on David Bowie's 1977 *Low* album, formed a new record label, Point, and signed an agreement with Elektra Nonesuch that would allow the company to record Glass' new material, remake several of his classics, and release CDs of his earliest pieces.

Glitter

Also known as "glam," glitter rock sprang out of an early-Seventies backlash against the late-Sixties sexual revolution and revolved around a glorified sexual ambiguity and androgyny as practiced by performers like David Bowie and Marc Bolan of T. Rex, and a fashion consciousness best expressed by British proto-art-rockers Roxy Music. Self-consciously decadent, glitter-rockers adorned themselves with foppish and/or futuristic clothing, lots of makeup, and the glitter dust that gave the genre its name and that subsequently became a debased code that could even apply to such performers as British pop star Gary Glitter.

Glitter-rock music was usually a slicker form of hard rock, and included everything from British pop-rockers Sweet to New York "glitter punks" the New York Dolls, who in many senses apotheosized glitter even as they signaled its decline. The genre influenced such rockers as Joan Jett; to a limited extent, early Kiss and Queen; and, in its emphasis on visual style, the more androgynous wing of new wave.

Gary Glitter

Born Paul Francis Gadd, May 8, 1940, Banbury, England
1972—*Glitter* (Bell)   1991—*Greatest Hits* (Rhino).

Gary Glitter was at the forefront of the English glam-rock phase, along with David Bowie, T. Rex, and Slade. He had several hits in Britain with a distinctive sound (later revived by Adam and the Ants), featuring heavy drumming, handclaps, echo guitar, and football-cheer choruses, but only minor success in America.

In 1960 Paul Gadd began releasing ballads as Paul Raven. He toured with Cliff Richard, Tommy Steele, and Billy Fury. His "Paul Raven" rendition of Burt Bacharach's "Walk On By" became a big hit in the Middle East in 1961. He began working with writer/producer Mike Leander in 1965; the association continued into the Seventies.

Gadd sang on the soundtrack to *Jesus Christ Superstar* in 1970 and, under the name Paul Monday, recorded a version of the Beatles' "Here Comes the Sun." But like his earlier records, it went nowhere. After considering such monikers as Terry Tinsel and Horace Hydrogen, he and Leander settled on the Gary Glitter identity in 1971.

Unashamedly climbing onto the glitter-rock bandwagon, Gary Glitter burst onto the English scene in 1972 and by midyear was inspiring regular crowd hysteria. "Rock and Roll Part II" hit #2 in England and became his only U.S. Top Ten entry. Over the next two years he reeled off a string of hits, many of which topped the U.K. chart: "I Didn't Know I Loved You (Till I Saw You Rock 'n' Roll)," "Do You Wanna Touch Me?" (later a #20 hit for Joan Jett), "Hello, Hello, I'm Back Again," "I'm the Leader of the Gang," and "I Love You Love Me" in 1973, and "Always Yours," "Oh Yes You're Beautiful," "Love Like You and Me," and "Remember Me This Way" in 1974.

As the decade progressed, Glitter moved further and further into self-parody. By the first of his highly publicized and short-lived "retirements" in 1976, he could boast 13 consecutive English hits. Through his glory years he was perpetually backed by the Glitter Band wearing stacked heels and playing bejeweled, oddly shaped guitars. Led by Peter Oxendale (piano) and Gerry Shephard (guitar), the Glitter Band began making records on its own in the mid-Seventies, including some disco-ish U.K. hits and a 1979 Oxendale and Shephard album, *Put Your Money Where Your Mouth Is* (Nemperor).

In October 1980 Glitter was in London bankruptcy court trying to work out a deal to pay off his nearly half-million pounds in back taxes. Not coincidentally, he returned to the road the following month. He also tried to raise some of the money by auctioning off his extravagant stage wardrobe.

Since then Glitter has turned up in the news (an accidental overdose of sleeping pills in 1986), on British TV (a talk segment on a late-night program called *Night Network*), and occasionally on the U.K. chart. "Another Rock and Roll Christmas" (#7, 1984) went gold, and the singer's annual Christmas tours still draw crowds.

The Go-Betweens
Formed Brisbane, Australia, 1977
Robert Forster (b. June 29, 1957, Brisbane), voc., gtr.; Grant McLennan (b. Feb. 12, 1958, Rock Hampton, Austral.), voc., gtr., bass; Lindy Morrison (b. Nov. 2, 1951, Austral.), drums.
1982—*Send Me a Lullabye* (Rough Trade, U.K.) 1983—*Before Hollywood* 1984—(+ Robert Vickers [b. Nov. 25, 1959, Austral.], bass) *Spring Hill Fair* (Sire, U.K.) 1985—*Metals and Shells* (PVC) 1986—*Liberty Belle and the Black Diamond Express* (Big Time) 1987—(+ Amanda Brown [b. Nov. 17, 1965, Austral.], violin, oboe, voc., kybds.) *Tallulah* (Beggars Banquet) 1988—(– Vickers, + John Willsteed [b. Feb. 13, 1957, Austral.], bass) *16 Lovers Lane*

(Beggars Banquet/Capitol) 1990—*1978–1990*.
Robert Forster solo: 1990—*Danger in the Past* (Beggars Banquet, U.K.) 1993—*Calling from a Country Phone* 1994—*I Had a New York Girlfriend*.
G. W. McLennan solo: 1991—*Watershed* (Beggars Banquet, U.K.) 1993—*Fireboy* 1995—*Horsebreaker Star* (Beggars Banquet/Atlantic).

During their 12 years together, the Go-Betweens released a string of exquisitely crafted, heady pop albums that received cult and critical acclaim but never broke through commercially. The band was formed by Brisbane University students McLennan and Forster, who were inspired by Sixties folk and Seventies punk. The two developed complementary songwriting and singing styles, with McLennan's extroverted minstrelsy balancing Forster's poetic odes. Both wrote about strange people, strange situations, and strange love, loading gentle, moody melodies with intense emotion.

After a string of Australian and British singles, the Go-Betweens moved to London in 1982. With the 1983 addition of bassist Robert Vickers, McLennan moved from bass to guitar. Despite successful tours, laudatory reviews and at last, a major U.S. record company, success eluded the band. In 1987 they returned to Australia, leaving Vickers in New York. The rich pop album *16 Lovers Lane* was the band's swansong. Returning to Australia, Morrison and Brown formed the group Cleopatra Wong. Forster and McLennan have released solo albums, with McLennan gaining some radio airplay with his Atlantic release, *Horsebreaker Star*. McLennan also recorded with the Church's Steve Kilbey, calling themselves Jack Frost.

Godley and Creme: See 10cc

The Go-Go's
Formed 1978, Hollywood, California
Belinda Carlisle (b. Aug. 17, 1958, Hollywood), voc.; Charlotte Caffey (b. Oct. 21, 1953, Santa Monica, Calif.), gtr.; Jane Wiedlin (b. May 20, 1958, Oconomowoc, Wis.), gtr.; Margot Olaverra, bass; Elissa Bello, drums.
1979—(– Bello; + Gina Schock [b. Aug. 31, 1957, Baltimore, Md.], drums) 1980—(– Olaverra; + Kathy Valentine [b. Jan. 7, 1959, Austin, Tex.], bass) 1981—*Beauty and the Beat* (I.R.S.) 1982—*Vacation* 1984—*Talk Show* (– Wiedlin; group disbands) 1990—*Greatest* (group re-forms: Carlisle; Wiedlin; Caffey; Schock; Valentine) 1994—*Return to the Valley of the Go-Go's*.
Belinda Carlisle solo: 1986—*Belinda* (I.R.S.) 1987—*Heaven on Earth* (MCA) 1989—*Runaway Horses*

The Go-Go's: Kathy Valentine, Jane Wiedlin, Gina Schock, Charlotte Caffey, Belinda Carlisle

1991—*Live Your Life Be Free*   1993—*Real* (Virgin). Jane Wiedlin solo: 1985—*Jane Wiedlin* (I.R.S.). 1988—*Fur* (EMI Manhattan)   1990—*Tangled* (EMI). The Graces: 1989—*Perfect View* (A&M). House of Schock: 1988—*House of Schock* (Capitol).

The Go-Go's began as a comically inept all-girl punk novelty act, but within a few years they had made a #1 debut album that yielded two Top Twenty hit singles ("Our Lips Are Sealed" and the gold "We Got the Beat") and were selling out arenas on tour.

Belinda Carlisle, who had been a cheerleader in high school, nearly became a member of the seminal L.A. punk band the Germs. With Jane Wiedlin, another L.A. punk-scene regular, she began playing guitar. They were soon joined by a more experienced guitarist, Charlotte Caffey, and they recruited a rhythm section in the inexperienced Olaverra and Bello.

The group debuted as the Go-Go's at Hollywood's punk club the Masque, with a 1½-song set. Though onlookers considered them another hilariously daring bunch of amateurs, they began rehearsing in earnest and soon recruited Gina Schock, a serious and adept drummer who'd toured briefly with cult-film star Edie Massey and her Eggs. By that time the Go-Go's had been playing the punk circuit for nearly a year, their sound gradually growing from punk to a Blondie-ish bouncy pop rock.

They went to England, where they attracted the attention of British ska-rockers Madness, who had the Go-Go's open a tour there. The British independent label Stiff recorded a Go-Go's single, and "We Got the Beat" became a minor hit in new-wave dance clubs in Britain and America. In early 1980 Olaverra became ill and was eventually replaced by Kathy Valentine. Valentine had played briefly with British all-female heavy-metal band Girlschool on a trip to England, later joined L.A. punk band the Textones, and joined the Go-Go's after a four-day crash course in bass and the band's repertoire.

The first Go-Go's album was produced by girl-group veteran Richard Gottehrer, who'd also produced Blondie's first albums. By spring 1982 *Beauty and the Beat* was #1, and "We Got the Beat" and "Our Lips Are Sealed" (the latter cowritten with Terry Hall of Britain's Specials and Fun Boy Three) were long-running hits. *Vacation* (#8, 1982) was slightly less popular but yielded a summertime Top Ten single in the title cut. *Talk Show* was less successful (#18, 1984) but spawned hit singles in "Head Over Heels" (#11, 1984) and "Turn to You" (#32, 1984). Wiedlin left the group soon after, prompting its dissolution.

Carlisle launched a successful post–Go-Go's solo career with *Belinda* (#13, 1986), on which Caffey and Wiedlin also appeared. It went gold and yielded a hit single in "Mad About You" (#3, 1986). *Heaven on Earth* (#13, 1987) went platinum, yielding Carlisle's biggest hits, "Heaven Is a Place on Earth" (#1, 1987) and "I Get Weak" (#2, 1987), plus another Top Ten hit in "Circle in the Sand" (#7, 1987). *Live Your Life Be Free*, however, flopped, as did the first two albums by Wiedlin (*Fur* produced a hit single in "Rush Hour," #9, 1988), who became an ardent animal rights activist. Caffey, with Merideth Brooks and Gia Ciambotti, recorded one album as the Graces, before the Go-Go's reunited for a tour to promote a 1990 best-of collection. Four years later, they reunited once again, this time to record new material for *Return to the Valley of* the Go-Go's. After the album's release, the band embarked on a lengthy tour, with ex-Bangles guitarist Vicki Peterson subbing for the pregnant Caffey.

Andrew Gold
Born August 2, 1951, Burbank, California
1975—*Andrew Gold* (Asylum)   1977—*What's Wrong with This Picture?* (Elektra/Asylum)   1978—*All This and Heaven Too*   1980—*Whirlwind.*
Wax (with Graham Gouldman): 1986—*Magnetic Heaven* (RCA)   1992—*What Else Can We Do?* (Caroline).

A studio musician, guitarist, and arranger who was instrumental in Linda Ronstadt's pop breakthrough, Andrew Gold went solo and had a hit of his own with "Lonely Boy" (#7, 1977). Gold is the son of soundtrack composer Ernest Gold (*Exodus*) and singer Marni Nixon, who dubbed vocals for nonsinging stars in *West Side Story, My Fair Lady,* and other Hollywood musicals. In the late Sixties Andrew cofounded Bryndle with Karla Bonoff, Wendy Waldman, and ex–Stone Poney Kenny Edwards. The group recorded one unreleased album for A&M.

When Bryndle broke up, Gold and Edwards started the Rangers. A demo tape reached Edwards' former employer Linda Ronstadt, who hired them both for her backing band. Gold became her arranger through 1977 and worked on albums including *Heart Like a Wheel* and its hit single "You're No Good," on which Gold played most of the instruments. He made his first solo album in 1975 and opened shows for Ronstadt while continuing to play in her backup band. In 1977 *What's Wrong with This Picture?* yielded "Lonely Boy." *All This and Heaven Too* included "Thank You for Being a Friend" (#25, 1978), which later became the theme song of the popular TV series *The Golden Girls.*

Gold's songs have been covered by Leo Sayer, Judy Collins, the James Gang, Cliff Richard, and Ronstadt; he has played sessions for Wendy Waldman, Carly Simon, Art Garfunkel, Loudon Wainwright III, James Taylor, Maria Muldaur, Karla Bonoff, John David Souther, and Eric Carmen. He has produced Bonoff, Nicolette Larson, Rita Coolidge, Moon Martin, and others. He and 10cc's Graham Gouldman made four albums under the name Wax (two were not released in the U.S.: *American English* and *A Hundred Thousand in Fresh Notes*). *Magnetic Heaven* included a hit single, "Right Between the Eyes" (#43, 1986). A followup, "Bridge to Your Heart," went to #12 in the U.K. In the mid-Nineties Bryndle re-formed.

Golden Earring
Formed 1961, The Hague, Netherlands
Lineup circa 1968: George Kooymans (b. Mar. 11, 1948, The Hague), gtr., voc.; Rinus Gerritsen (b. Aug. 9, 1946, The Hague), bass, kybds., harmonica; Barry Hay (b. Aug. 16, 1948, Saizabad, Neth.), voc., flute, sax; Cesar Zuiderwijk (b. July 18, 1950, The Hague), drums.
1964—*Just Earring* (Polydor)   1972—*Together*   1973—*Hearing Earring* (Track)   1974—*Moontan* (MCA)   1975—*Switch*   1976—*To the Hilt*   1977—*Golden Earring Live*   1979—*Grab It for a Second; No Promises, No Debts* (Polydor)   1980—*Long Blond Animal*   1982—*Cut* (21 Records)   1984—*N.E.W.S.; Something Heavy Going Down—Live from the Twilight Zone*   1986—*The Hole.*

A Dutch group that was formed in 1961, Golden Earring were superstars in their homeland and a minor act everywhere else until "Radar Love" hit #13 in 1974. By then the band had experimented with a range of styles before settling on the hard-rock approach that's brought them into the U.S. Top Forty only twice in their career. Nonetheless, Golden Earring remains the Netherlands' most successful and longest-lived rock export.

The group's original lineup in the mid-Sixties included longtime mainstays George Kooymans and Rinus Gerritsen. As schoolboys, they had their first hit in 1964 with the bubblegum-ish "Please Go." It was the first of nearly 20 Dutch hits. By 1968 the maturing band had tired of the pop format and shifted to hard rock. Attempts to break into the U.S. and U.K. markets were largely unsuccessful, and its first U.S. tour in 1968 went unnoticed. In 1972, shortly after the group enjoyed a big hit in Europe with "Back Home," the Who (whose live histrionics the group openly imitated during its concerts) hired Golden Earring to open for a European tour and signed the group to its Track label. *Hearing Earring* (1973) was a compilation of previous Dutch releases and preceded their breakthrough tour of British college campuses.

Moontan spawned "Radar Love," and Golden Earring briefly became widely known in the U.S., where it opened stadium shows for the Doobie Brothers and Santana. But immediate followup success to "Radar" proved elusive, and through the decade, later LPs never reached the U.S. Top 100, although the group continued to score European hits. In addition to his activities with Earring, Kooymans produced records by other artists, including the 1979 European hit remake of "Come On" by the young Dutch group New Adventures.

In 1982 Golden Earring returned to the U.S. chart with the hit single and stylish video "Twilight Zone" (#10) from *Cut* (#24), but the group's three mid-Eighties LPs that followed never made the Top 100. Each member has released solo LPs, all European.

The Golden Palominos
Formed 1981, New York City, New York
Anton Fier (b. June 20, 1956, Cleveland, Ohio), drums, programming.

1981—*The Golden Palominos* (Celluloid) 1985—*Visions of Excess* 1986—*Blast of Silence* 1989—*A Dead Horse* 1991—*Drunk with Passion* (Charisma) 1993—*This Is How It Feels* (Restless) 1994—*Pure.*

Depending on how you look at it, the Golden Palominos have had several dozen members, or only one—Anton Fier. The former Feelies, Pere Ubu, and Lounge Lizards [see entries] drummer assembles various players for his downtown New York supergroup, whose eclectic outings are invariably grandiose and somewhat arty. As a Palomino, Fier first performed around New York with drummer David Moss, guitarist Arto Lindsay, saxman John Zorn, bassist Bill Laswell, and bassist Jamaaladeen Tacuma. The funky, avant-garde *Golden Palominos* featured that lineup plus Mark Miller, Fred Frith, and Nicky Skopelitis.

On *Visions of Excess*, Fier extended his scope beyond Manhattan's experimental fringe, drawing in R.E.M.'s Michael Stipe, former Cream bassist Jack Bruce, guitarist Richard Thompson, ex-Pistol John Lydon, former dB Chris Stamey, P-Funk's guitarist Mike Hampton and keyboardist Bernie Worrell, keyboardist Carla Bley, and guitarist Henry Kaiser, and introducing singer Syd Straw. No more than two band members were ever in the studio at the same time during the album's recording. *Visions'* music was composed by Fier and former Raybeats guitarist Jody Harris, with the lyrics handled mostly by the vocalists. The tracks include a cover of Moby Grape's "Omaha."

The countryish *Blast of Silence* features much the same lineup, minus Stipe and Lydon, and adding Numbers Band singer/guitarist Robert Kidney; singer/songwriter Peter Blegvad; singer, songwriter, and producer Don Dixon; singer, songwriter, and producer T Bone Burnett; and others. On *A Dead Horse*, Fier aimed less for big names and more for a stable lineup, including Laswell, Skopelitis, Kidney, singer Amanda Kramer (ex–Information Society), and such guests as Worrell and ex-Stone Mick Taylor. *Drunk with Passion* features a few star cameos again, including Stipe, Thompson, and Bob Mould (Sugar, Hüsker Dü). *This Is How It Feels* is a concept album based on the Graham Greene novel *The End of the Affair*. Personnel are Fier, Laswell, bassist Bootsy Collins, Skopelitis, Worrell, programmer Matt Stein, Kramer, singers Lori Carson and Lydia Kavanaugh, and keyboardist Jeff Bova. Laswell, Collins, Skopelitis, Kramer, Carson, and Kavanaugh rejoined Fier for 1994's *Pure*, which also featured guitarist Knox Chandler.

Bobby Goldsboro

Born January 18, 1941, Marianna, Florida
1968—*Honey* (United Artists) 1990—*All-time Greatest Hits* (Curb).

Singer/songwriter Bobby Goldsboro had over 25 charting singles between 1962 and 1973. Two of his biggest,

"Honey" and "Watching Scotty Grow," were sentimental MOR hits. Goldsboro moved to Dothan, Alabama, with his family in his teens. He later studied at Auburn University, but left after two years and began playing the guitar with various local groups before joining Roy Orbison, with whom he cowrote some songs. He worked in Orbison's backup band from 1962 to 1964, then started a solo career.

His first major hit was "See the Funny Little Clown" (#9, 1964), followed in 1965 by "Little Things" (#13), and the year after, "It's Too Late" (#23). With 1968's gold "Honey" (#1), about the death of a young bride, Goldsboro became a major star. He became a regular on TV talk shows and in supper-club venues. Subsequent hits included "Autumn of My Life" (#19, 1968) and "Watching Scotty Grow" (#11, 1971).

In the Seventies Goldsboro hosted his own nationally syndicated TV show for three seasons and formed a successful music-publishing company in Nashville. A decade later he began creating children's stories. His first, *Easter Egg Mornin'*, was turned into an animated special that originally aired on the Disney Channel in 1991; it and three others have been released on Rhino Records' children's label. In addition to performing live, Goldsboro served as musical director for the TV series *Evening Shade*.

Gong

Formed 1970, Paris, France
Daevid Allen (b. Austral.), gtr., voc.; Gilli Smyth (b. Fr.), voc.; Christian Tritsch, bass, gtr.; Didier Malherbe, sax, flute; Pip Pyle (b. Eng.), drums.
1970—(– Pyle; + Laurie Allen [b. Eng.], drums)
1971—*Continental Circus* soundtrack (Philips); *Camembert Electrique* (Caroline) (+ Steve Hillage [b. Aug. 2, 1951, Eng.], gtr.; + Tim Blake [b. Eng.], synth.) 1973—*Radio Gnome Invisible: The Flying Teapot* (Virgin) (– Tritsch; – L. Allen; + Mike Howlett [b. Eng.], bass; + Pierre Moerlen [b. Colmar, Fr.], drums, perc.; + Mirielle Bauer [b. Fr.], perc.); *Radio Gnome Invisible Part II: Angel's Egg* 1974—*You* (– D. Allen; – Hillage; – Blake; + Benoit Moerlen [b. Colmar], kybds., perc.) 1976—*Shamal* (+ Allan Holdsworth [b. Eng.], gtr.; + Patrice Lemoine, kybds.; + Francis Mose, bass) 1977—(+ Mino Cinelou, perc.) *Gazeuse!* (Polydor); *Live Etc.* (– Holdsworth; + D. Allen); *Gong Est Mort* (Tapioca) (– D. Allen) 1978—*Expresso II* (Polydor) 1979—*Downwind* (Arista); *Time Is the Key* (Arista, U.K.); *Pierre Moerlen's Gong Live*; *Expresso* (Arista) 1981—*Leave It Open* 1987—*Breakthrough.*

Gong started out as a European posthippie band with its own mythology of Pothead Pixies and UFOs and an unpredictable, punning mixture of rock and folk and jazz and synthesizers. Eventually, after numerous personnel changes and offshoots (some called Gong), the band moved into more conventional jazz rock.

The group's founder and leader was Daevid Allen, who had arrived in England from Australia in 1961. While attending Canterbury College of Art in 1966, he joined the original Soft Machine. Following the group's first European tour, Allen was refused reentry to the U.K. He then returned to France, where he lived and wrote poetry through 1969. By then he was playing regularly with vocalist Gilli Smyth, with whom he cut two LPs in 1969, *Magick Brother, Mystick Sister* and *Banana Moon*.

By 1970 the duo had expanded into the group Gong; original drummer Pip Pyle quickly returned to England to join Canterbury jazz-rock group Hatfield and the North (and, later, National Health) and was replaced by Laurie Allen (no relation to Daevid). Band members took fanciful stage names, such as Dingo Virgin (for Allen), Shakti Yoni (Smyth), Bloomdido Bad de Grasse (saxman Didier Malherbe), and Hi T. Moonweed (synthesizer player Tim Blake). Daevid Allen began dropping in and out of the group in 1972, but after his departure in 1974 he contributed to *You*, which, coupled with earlier releases *Flying Teapot* and *Angel's Egg*, completed his "Radio Gnome Invisible" trilogy about the imaginary planet Gong. Allen later recorded several LPs for Virgin and occasionally performed, sometimes billed as Gong. His 1976 LP *Good Morning* featured backup from the Spanish group Euterpe. By 1977 he was working with the New York avant-garde outfit Material [see Bill Laswell/Material entry] for *About Time*. In 1979 Allen released *N'existe Pas* and then led the first Gong-related group to play the United States. During the late Seventies he lived in Woodstock, New York, and did solo tours (backed by tape collages), billed as the Divided Alien Clockwork Band.

Following Allen's exit from Gong proper, the leadership was assumed by percussionist Pierre Moerlen, who had joined the group in 1973 for *Angel's Egg*. Moerlen's father was the Strasbourg Cathedral organist and taught at the Strasbourg Conservatory, where Pierre studied from 1967 until 1972. Under Moerlen's influence, the group began to specialize in percussion-heavy jazz rock. His rotating cast of sidemen included such guitarists as Steve Hillage (who had departed by 1976 for a fairly successful solo career that included *L*, produced by Todd Rundgren and, in the Eighties, production work with such artists as Simple Minds and Robyn Hitchcock), ex–Rolling Stone Mick Taylor (on whose 1979 solo debut Moerlen guested), and Allan Holdsworth (Tony Williams' Lifetime, Bill Bruford, and his own solo ventures), as well as keyboardists Mike Oldfield and Moerlen's brother Benoit. Of the original group, Didier Malherbe remained.

In 1977 Moerlen's group reunited with Allen to record *Gong Est Mort*. Afterward, Allen went back to his solo work; in 1993 he recorded with New York postpunk artist/producer Kramer the album *Who's Afraid,* which was released on Kramer's Shimmy Disc label. In 1980 Moerlen finally led his version of Gong stateside for some concerts. In subsequent years he had to compete with other Gong incarnations led by numerous band alumni before his own edition of the group finally drifted apart.

Steve Goodman
Born July 25, 1948, Chicago, Illinois; died September 20, 1984, Seattle, Washington
1971—*Steve Goodman* (Buddah)   1973—*Somebody Else's Troubles*   1975—*Jessie's Jig and Other Favorites* (Asylum)   1976—*Words We Can Dance To* 1978—*Say It in Private*   1979—*High and Outside* 1980—*Hot Spot*   1982—*Artistic Hair* (Red Pajamas) 1983—*Affordable Art*   1984—*Santa Ana Winds* 1995—*No Big Surprise: The Steve Goodman Anthology*.

Singer/songwriter Steve Goodman is best remembered as the author of Arlo Guthrie's 1972 hit "The City of New Orleans," a modern train song. Through the Seventies he released a series of folk albums.

Goodman enrolled in 1964 at the University of Illinois to study political science; in summer 1967 he went to New York City and played in the parks for spare change for several months until he moved back to Chicago, where he began attending Lake Forest College. In 1969 he gave up academics for music and started performing in Chicago folk clubs.

Despite critical acclaim, Goodman's recordings never sold particularly well, and by 1973 he was still living in a $145-a-month apartment several blocks from Wrigley Field. *Somebody Else's Troubles* featured Bob Dylan (as Robert Milkwood Thomas) on piano on the title track. Goodman toured through the early Seventies, but was mostly known for his "City of New Orleans," which he wrote about his experiences while campaigning for Edmund Muskie. His songs have since been covered by David Allan Coe, John Denver, Joan Baez, and others.

Goodman, who'd been suffering from leukemia since the early Seventies, succumbed to kidney and liver failure in 1984 at age 36 after undergoing a bone-marrow transplant. A year later, a *Tribute to Steve Goodman* came out on Red Pajamas, the label he had founded shortly before his death. Among the performers on the two-disc set were longtime friends John Prine, Arlo Guthrie, and Bonnie Raitt.

The Good Rats
Formed 1965, Long Island, New York
Peppi Marchello (b. Brooklyn, N.Y.), voc.; Mickey Marchello (b. Brooklyn), gtr.; Joe Franco, drums;

Grammy Awards

Peter Gabriel
1989 Best New Age Performance: *Passion: Music for "The Last Temptation of Christ"*
1992 Best Music Video, Short Form: "Digging in the Dirt" (with John Downer)
1993 Best Music Video, Short Form: "Steam" (with Stephen R. Johnson)

Art Garfunkel [See also: Simon and Garfunkel]
1968 Best Contemporary Pop Performance, Vocal, Duo or Group: "Mrs. Robinson" (with Paul Simon)
1968 Record of the Year: "Mrs. Robinson" (with Paul Simon and Roy Halee)
1970 Record of the Year: "Bridge over Troubled Water" (with Paul Simon and Roy Halee)
1970 Album of the Year: *Bridge over Troubled Water* (with Paul Simon and Roy Halee)
1970 Best Arrangement Accompanying Vocalists: "Bridge over Troubled Water" (with others)

Marvin Gaye
1982 Best R&B Vocal Performance, Male: "Sexual Healing"
1982 Best R&B Instrumental Performance: "Sexual Healing"

Gloria Gaynor
1979 Best Disco Recording: "I Will Survive"

Genesis
1987 Best Concept Music Video: "Land of Confusion" (with Jon Blair, John Lloyd, and Jim Yukich)

Phil Collins (Genesis)
1984 Best Pop Vocal Performance, Male: "Against All Odds (Take a Look at Me Now)"
1985 Album of the Year: *No Jacket Required* (with Hugh Padgham)
1985 Best Pop Vocal Performance, Male: *No Jacket Required*
1985 Producer of the Year, Nonclassical (with Hugh Padgham)
1988 Best Song Written Specifically for a Motion Picture or Television: "Two Hearts" (with Lamont Dozier)
1990 Record of the Year: "Another Day in Paradise" (with Hugh Padgham)

Bobbie Gentry
1967 Best New Artist
1967 Best Vocal Performance, Female: *Ode to Billie Joe*
1967 Best Contemporary Female Solo Vocal Performance: *Ode to Billie Joe*

Steve Goodman
1984 Best Country Song: "City of New Orleans"
1987 Best Contemporary Folk Recording: *Unfinished Business*

Amy Grant
1982 Best Gospel Performance, Contemporary: *Age to Age*
1983 Best Gospel Performance, Female: "Ageless Medley"
1984 Best Gospel Performance, Female: "Angels"
1985 Best Gospel Performance, Female: *Unguarded*
1988 Best Gospel Performance, Female: *Lead Me On*

Mickey Hart (Grateful Dead)
1991 Best World Music Album: *Planet Drum*

Al Green
1981 Best Soul Gospel Performance, Traditional: *The Lord Will Make a Way*
1982 Best Soul Gospel Performance, Contemporary: *Higher Plane*
1982 Best Soul Gospel Performance, Traditional: *Precious Lord*
1983 Best Soul Gospel Performance, Male: *I'll Rise Again*
1984 Best Soul Gospel Performance by a Duo or Group: "Sailin' on the Sea of Your Love" (with Shirley Caesar)
1986 Best Soul Gospel Performance, Male: "Going Away"
1987 Best Soul Gospel Performance, Male: "Everything's Gonna Be Alright"
1989 Best Soul Gospel Performance, Male or Female: "As Long as We're Together"
1994 Best Pop Vocal Collaboration (with Lyle Lovett): "Funny How Time Slips Away"

Green Day
1994 Best Alternative Music Performance: *Dookie*

Nanci Griffith
1993 Best Contemporary Folk Album: *Other Voices, Other Rooms*

Buddy Guy
1991 Best Contemporary Blues Album: *Damn Right, I've Got the Blues*

John "the Cat" Gatto, gtr.; Lenny Koe, bass.
1969—*Good Rats* (Kapp) 1974—*Tasty* (Warner Bros.) 1976—*Rat City in Blue* (Rat City) 1978—*From Rats to Riches* (Passport); *Birth Comes to Us All* 1981—*Great American Music* (Great American).

The Good Rats were regulars on the Long Island bar circuit from 1965 until they disbanded in the early Eighties. What distinguished them from their garage-band brethren was that for years they appeared on the brink of wider success. Beyond a hardcore following, greater renown eluded them.

Founded by brothers Peppi and Mickey Marchello, the group originally played crude garage rock. Peppi Marchello was known to pelt the audience with rubber rats and carry a baseball bat onstage. They cut their self-titled debut for Kapp Records in 1969, but little came of it. In August 1972 they temporarily disbanded. In January 1973 the brothers re-formed the group with new musicians recruited from New York–area bar bands. In 1974 Warner Bros. signed them, but their label debut, *Tasty,* sold poorly.

By the mid-Seventies the group was still toiling in the bars. In 1976 it released *Rat City in Blue* on its own Rat City Records, and in late 1978 the Rats signed with Passport. *From Rats to Riches* was produced by anarchic kindred spirits Flo and Eddie. *Birth Comes to Us All* was recorded at the Who's Ramport studio in England and included guest appearances by keyboardist Manfred Mann.

Professionally, the group endured a series of bad breaks the band members referred to as "the curse of the Rat." But through the early Eighties, they made a respectable living working New York–area and East Coast clubs. The band has reunited on various occasions. Drummer Joe Franco went on to join a latterday version of Twisted Sister and has worked with such artists as Mariah Carey, Taylor Dayne, Hall and Oates, and Natalie Cole. He is also a popular sessionman for commercials and wrote a best-selling book on drumming that is used as a text in leading music schools. John Gatto works in a Long Island music store as a guitar technician, and Lenny Koe works in another Long Island music store and as a sound technician. Peppi Marchello continues to perform. His son, Gene, also a guitarist, has a group called Marchello.

Robert Gordon

Born 1947, Washington, D.C.
1977—*Robert Gordon with Link Wray* (Private Stock) 1978—*Fresh Fish Special* 1979—*Rock Billy Boogie* (RCA) 1980—*Bad Boy* 1981—*Are You Gonna Be the One* 1982—*Too Fast to Live, Too Young to Die* 1994—*All for the Love of Rock & Roll* (Viceroy).

Singer Robert Gordon emerged from the New York new-wave scene in 1976 looking and sounding every bit the rockabilly revivalist he has always claimed not to be.

Gordon grew up in the D.C. suburb of Bethesda, Maryland, where he began singing at an early age; at 14 he joined his first band, the Confidentials (which, with some personnel changes, became the Newports). By age 17, Gordon was appearing in nightclubs. After a stint in the service, he moved to New York City, where, around 1976/77, he formed Tuff Darts. He appeared with that group on *Live at CBGB's,* but departed the band soon after.

Gordon's debut album, *Robert Gordon with Link Wray,* featured his childhood hero Link Wray on guitar. "Red Hot" was a minor hit in 1977, and Gordon and Wray toured Europe and the U.S. that year. *Fresh Fish Special* featured Bruce Springsteen's "Fire," which was written especially for Gordon and later became a hit for the Pointer Sisters. In December 1978 Gordon signed with RCA, and in 1979 he released *Rock Billy Boogie.* In 1980 Gordon's fifth album, featuring three songs by Marshall Crenshaw, was released. With its emphasis on a more contemporary pop sound, the LP was a decisive change from the rockabilly of his previous albums. Gordon had a minor hit with Crenshaw's "Someday, Someway" in 1981. Gordon has continued to record, including a French release entitled *Live from New York City,* and still tours in the United States, Europe, and Japan.

Lesley Gore

Born May 2, 1946, New York City, New York
1963—*I'll Cry if I Want To* (Mercury) 1964—*Lesley Gore Sings of Mixed-up Hearts*; *Boys, Boys, Boys*; *Girl Talk* 1965—*Golden Hits of Lesley Gore* 1966—*Lesley Gore Sings All About Love* 1967—*California Nights* 1968—*Lesley Gore Golden Hits, vol. 2* 1972—*Someplace Else Now* (Mowest) 1976—*Love Me by Name* (A&M) 1986—*The Lesley Gore Anthology* (Rhino).

As a teenager, Lesley Gore wrote and sang a series of pop weepers; after her hits ended, she moved into acting and songwriting. Gore's father was a swimsuit manufacturer who sent her to the Dwight Preparatory School for Girls in Englewood, New Jersey. In her senior year, she was discovered by Quincy Jones, who got her a deal with Mercury and produced her recordings through 1967. As she turned 17, they released her song "It's My Party," which went to #1 in June 1963.

At year's end, she had three more Top Five smashes—"Judy's Turn to Cry," "She's a Fool," and the ballad she performed in the filmed T.A.M.I. Show, "You Don't Own Me" (later recorded by Joan Jett). The latter title expressed an undeniably feminist viewpoint virtually unheard before on the pop chart. Subsequent hits included "That's the Way Boys Are" (#12, 1964), "Maybe I Know" (#12, 1964), "Sunshine, Lollipops and Rainbows" (#13, 1965), and "California Nights" (#16, 1967).

Throughout her peak years, Gore studied at least part-time at Sarah Lawrence College, and she graduated in 1968 after her hits had stopped in 1967 (her last chart record was 1967's "Brink of Disaster"). Moving to California, she worked with independent producer Bob Crewe on a series of unsuccessful releases. She tried acting—in films like *Girls on the Beach* and *Ski Party* and TV fare like *Batman.* Largely out of sight for several years, Gore made some club appearances in 1970 and 1971, and in

1972 she signed with Motown subsidiary Mowest, but 1972's *Someplace Else Now* sold poorly. In late 1974 she switched to A&M and was reunited with Quincy Jones for *Love Me by Name*. Again, sales were disappointing here, but the album was well received in England.

In 1980 Gore contributed lyrics to the Oscar-nominated "Out Here on My Own" from the *Fame* soundtrack, which featured music by her brother, Michael. She continues to write and perform. In the latter Eighties she recorded "Since I Don't Have You" b/w "It's Only Make Believe" with Lou Christie.

Gospel

The term "gospel music" was probably coined in the Twenties by Thomas A. Dorsey, a Georgia blues singer who was converted and began composing religious songs in popular styles. The music was initially denounced, but it caught on in the black sanctified church, and has since evolved alongside black secular music, although it is somewhat more conservative and serves different functions. Gospel singing is rooted in the ornate vocal style of old spirituals and in the impassioned "testifying" declamation of Baptist preachers.

The close-harmony group vocals of late Forties and Fifties gospel—with the group responding to and urging on a soaring, improvising lead singer—had many links to the a cappella and doo-wop pop of the Fifties, and such church-trained singers as Sam Cooke and Clyde McPhatter moved from gospel groups into pop. In the Sixties, soul music was spearheaded by gospel-turned-pop singers like Aretha Franklin, Wilson Pickett, and Solomon Burke.

The characteristic gospel sound—shouted responses from the congregation and bluesy rolling keyboard riffs (on piano or church organ) that could be repeated rhythmically to build excitement—has shown up in the music of performers ranging from Ray Charles to James Brown to Mavis Staples.

Goth

Goth musicians and fans wear lots of black clothing, black makeup, and dyed black hair to mirror their chosen musical style's dark, brooding lyrics and mopey, often minor-key melodies. With roots in late-Seventies punk-era bands such as Joy Division, Bauhaus, the Cure, and Siouxsie and the Banshees, goth has maintained a strong cult following through the years, with the Cure and Nick Cave prevailing as the genre's godfathers.

In its early-Eighties heyday, the goth scene revolved around the London club Batcave and bands such as Alien Sex Fiend, Sex Gang Children, Sisters of Mercy, and the L.A. group Christian Death. Interestingly (perhaps appropriately, given the music's themes of alienation, suicide, death, and depression), goth, like heavy metal, gets little attention from the music press, even though the Cure's music has maintained a steady following.

Larry Graham/Graham Central Station

Born August 14, 1946, Beaumont, Texas
1974—*Graham Central Station* (Warner Bros.);
Release Yourself* 1975—*Ain't No Bout-A-Doubt It
1976—*Mirror* 1977—*Now Do U Wanta Dance*
1978—*My Radio Sure Sounds Good to Me* 1979—
Star Walk.
Larry Graham solo: 1980—*One in a Million You*
(Warner Bros.) 1981—*Just Be My Lady* 1982—
Sooner or Later* 1983—*Victory.

As bassist for Sly and the Family Stone, Larry Graham updated James Brown's percussive bass lines into a style that set the groove for the progressive funk of the Seventies. After leaving Sly, he led Graham Central Station and developed a new image as a ballad singer.

Graham moved with his family to Oakland, California, at age two. By his teens he could play guitar, bass, harmonica, and drums; he also had a three-octave-plus vocal range. At 15 he began playing guitar with his cocktail lounge singer/pianist mother in her Dell Graham Trio. When they were reduced to a duo, Graham switched to bass. After four years, he quit to attend college for a year and a half, while working as a backup musician for John Lee Hooker, Jimmy Reed, the Drifters, and Jackie Wilson.

In 1967 Graham joined Sly and the Family Stone and stayed with the group until late 1972 [see entry]. He then took a local group called Hot Chocolate (not the Hot Chocolate of "Emma" and "You Sexy Thing" fame) and, with the addition of ex–Billy Preston keyboardist Robert Sam, formed the original Graham Central Station. Its debut album, *Graham Central Station,* sold over a quarter-million copies and yielded a minor pop hit, "Can You Handle It," in 1974. *Release Yourself* featured another small hit, "Feel the Need." GCS's third LP, *Ain't No Bout-A-Doubt It* went gold four months after its release, with "Your Love" reaching the Top Forty.

Graham wrote every selection on the group's fourth release, *Mirror,* a progressive funk outing. In early 1977 the group released *Now Do U Wanta Dance* (with its Top Ten R&B title track), but neither it nor *My Radio Sure Sounds Good to Me* (which marked the addition of Graham's wife, Tina, as vocalist) attracted the hoped-for pop crossover success. *Star Walk* was the last group effort.

By the end of 1980 Graham was billed on his own and singing ballads. *One in a Million You* hit #26 on the pop chart, and the title track was a #9 single. In 1981 Graham produced and played nearly all the instruments on *Just Be My Lady,* which included a #4 R&B title track.

Later R&B Top Thirty singles include "Don't Stop When You're Hot" and "Sooner or Later" (both 1982), and a mildly successful duet with Aretha Franklin, "If You Need My Love Tonight" (1987).

In 1993 Graham led a nine-piece band, Psychedelic Psoul, which backed comedian (and guitar player) Eddie Murphy for a series of live shows (including one at the Montreux Jazz Festival) featuring Murphy's original material. Also that year Graham Central Station, with Graham at the helm, embarked on a national tour.

Grand Funk Railroad

Formed 1968, Flint, Michigan
Mark Farner (b. Sep. 29, 1948, Flint), gtr., voc.; Mel Schacher (b. Apr. 3, 1951, Owosso, Mich.), bass; Don Brewer (b. Sep. 3, 1948, Flint), drums.
1969—On Time (Capitol) 1970—Grand Funk; Closer to Home; Live Album 1971—Survival; E Pluribus Funk 1972—Mark, Don and Mel, 1966–1971 (+ Craig Frost [b. Apr. 20, 1948, Flint], kybds.); Phoenix 1973—We're an American Band 1974—(as Grand Funk) Shinin' On; All the Girls in the World—Beware!! 1975—Caught in the Act; (as Grand Funk Railroad) Born to Die 1976—Good Singin', Good Playin' (MCA); Grand Funk Hits (Capitol) (group disbands) 1981—(Group re-forms: Farner; Brewer; + Dennis Bellinger [b. Flint], bass) Grand Funk Lives (Full Moon/Warner Bros.) 1983— What's Funk 1991—Grand Funk Railroad (Capitol); More of the Best (Rhino).
Mark Farner solo: 1977—Mark Farner (Atlantic) 1978—No Frills.

Grand Funk Railroad (a.k.a. Grand Funk), the most commercially successful American heavy-metal band from 1970 until it disbanded in 1976, established the Seventies success formula: continuous touring. Unanimously reviled or ignored by critics and initially by radio programmers, Grand Funk (Railroad) nonetheless amassed 11 gold or platinum albums, sold over 20 million LPs overall, and regularly set attendance records at arenas and stadiums. A prototypical "people's band," Grand Funk was a simplified model of blues-rock power trios like Cream and the Jimi Hendrix Experience. The members were all millionaires within two years of their debut.

Mark Farner began playing guitar at age 15 after a broken finger and bad knees ended his football career. After his high school expelled him in his senior year, he started playing full-time in semipro bands and, briefly, with Terry Knight and the Pack, a group that had a minor hit with "I (Who Have Nothing)" in 1966. The group also included drummer Don Brewer.

In late 1968 Farner and Brewer hooked up with bassist Mel Schacher, ex–? and the Mysterians; they made Terry Knight, a former Detroit radio DJ, their man-

Grand Funk Railroad: Mel Schacher, Don Brewer, Mark Farner, Craig Frost

ager and gave him complete business and artistic control. His first order of business was to name the trio Grand Funk Railroad. The band's first date was in Buffalo, New York, in March 1969; the following July it played (for free) for 125,000 people at the Atlanta Pop Festival. While the music consisted mostly of power chords, the group's onstage writhing and sweating made up in energy what it lacked in finesse. Capitol Records witnessed the group's set and signed it immediately.

With Knight producing, Grand Funk released its debut, On Time, that fall. Two years later the trio had one gold and five platinum LPs. Farner wrote and sang most of the early material, though Brewer later took the lead vocals on a few tunes. In Grand Funk's best year, 1970, it supposedly sold more than any other group in America. The next year, the band broke the Beatles' ticket sales record at New York's Shea Stadium, selling out a two-day stand in 72 hours and grossing over $300,000.

An undeniably triumphant moment, it marked the end of the honeymoon between Knight and the band. On March 27, 1972, Grand Funk terminated its relationship with Knight; he responded with $60 million in lawsuits. The band lost momentum while courts straightened out the mess, but with attorney John Eastman (Linda McCartney's father) handling its affairs, GFR eventually ditched Knight by buying him out.

Grand Funk's first post-Knight LP, Phoenix, introduced a fourth member, organist Craig Frost (who later joined Bob Seger's Silver Bullet Band). In 1973 Todd Rundgren produced the platinum We're an American Band, the title track of which was the group's first big

AM hit (#1). Rundgren also produced Grand Funk's tenth LP, *Shinin' On*, which yielded another #1 single, a remake of Little Eva's "The Locomotion." The band continued to tour in 1975, as documented in *Caught in the Act*, but interest within the group was lagging. It scored two more pop hits that year: "Some Kind of Wonderful" (#3) and "Bad Time" (#4). The 1976 LP *Born to Die* was to be Grand Funk's last, but when Frank Zappa agreed to produce, the four members stayed together for *Good Singin', Good Playin'*.

The group broke up in 1976 and returned to Michigan. Brewer and Schacher formed Flint, which released one album locally before disbanding. By the late Seventies Brewer had moved to Boca Raton, Florida. Farner spent his time with his wife and two children on his 1,500-acre farm in upstate Michigan and opened an alternative-energy store. He released two solo LPs—*Mark Farner* in 1977 and *No Frills* in 1978—and toured on occasion. In 1981 Farner and Brewer reunited for *Grand Funk Lives*, which picked up some AOR airplay with a remake of the Animals' "We Gotta Get Out of This Place." After a second album, *What's Funk*, in 1983, Grand Funk split up for good, with Brewer joining former bandmate Craig Frost in Bob Seger's Silver Bullet Band. Farner, meanwhile, had become a born-again Christian. In 1988 a song of his, "Isn't It Amazing," hit #2 on the Inspirational chart.

Grandmaster Flash and the Furious Five

Formed 1977, Bronx, New York
Grandmaster Flash (b. Joseph Saddler, Jan. 1, 1958, Barbados), turntables; Cowboy (b. Keith Wiggins, Sep. 20, 1960; d. Sep. 8, 1989), voc.; Melle Mel (b. Melvin Glover), voc.; Kid Creole (b. Nathaniel Glover), voc.; Mr. Ness (b. Eddie Morris), voc.; Rahiem (b. Guy Williams), voc.
1982—*The Message* (Sugarhill) 1983—*Greatest Messages* 1988—*On the Strength* (Elektra).
Grandmaster Melle Mel and the Furious Five:
1984—*Work Party* (Sugarhill) 1985—*Stepping Off*.
Grandmaster Flash solo: 1985—*They Said It Couldn't Be Done* (Elektra) 1986—*The Source* 1987—*Ba-Dop-Boom-Bang*.
Grandmaster Flash/The Furious Five/Grandmaster Melle Mel: 1989—*The Greatest Hits* (Sugarhill) 1994—*Message from Beat Street: The Best of Grandmaster Flash, Melle Mel, & the Furious Five* (Rhino).

Disco DJ Grandmaster Flash and his rap group, the Furious Five, were the premier DJ-rap team of the early Eighties. Flash began spinning records at Bronx block parties, gym dances, and parks when he was 18. Within a year, he was working at local discos while studying electronics at technical school by day. He developed an idiosyncratic style that involved "cutting" (segueing between tracks precisely on the beat), "back-spinning" (turning records manually to make the needle repeat brief lengths of groove), and "phasing" (manipulating turntable speeds) to create aural montages. Strictly a spinner, he began working with rappers around 1977, first with Kurtis Blow [see entry] and then with the Furious Five, who had mastered a routine of trading and blending lines and had introduced choreography to their act.

Flash and the Five were popular throughout New York by 1978, but they did not record until the Sugar Hill Gang's "Rapper's Delight" showed that rap records could be hits in 1979. Flash and the Five recorded "Superrappin'" for Harlem-based Enjoy Records in 1979, before signing with Sugarhill Records the next year. Their first Sugarhill release, "Freedom" (#19 R&B, 1980), sold over 50,000 copies; it was followed by "Birthday Party" (#36 R&B, 1981).

These records' appeal was not limited to New York, and in 1980 Flash and the Five toured the nation. "The Adventures of Grandmaster Flash on the Wheels of Steel" (#55 R&B, 1981) was the first record to capture the urban "cutting" technique pioneered by Flash; it incorporated snatches of Chic's "Good Times," Blondie's "Rapture," and Queen's "Another One Bites the Dust." "The Message" (#4 R&B, 1982), a groundbreaking rap in its haunting depiction of ghetto life, was one of the most powerful and controversial songs of 1982, although it sounds tame compared to the gangsta rap that would follow.

During recording of the group's anticocaine single, "White Lines," in 1983, Flash and Melle Mel had a falling-out. The next year there were two Furious Fives performing, though both had lost the power and dazzle of the original group. Flash eventually dropped the Furious Five from his name but continued making solo albums through the Eighties. In 1987 Melle Mel, Flash, and the Furious Five reunited for a charity concert hosted by Paul Simon at Madison Square Garden; the result was another album, 1988's *On the Strength*. The group reunited again in 1994 for a rap oldies package show that also included Kurtis Blow, Whodini, and Run-D.M.C. Flash and Melle Mel guested on Duran Duran's 1995 album of covers, *Thank You*, which included "White Lines."

Grand Puba: See Brand Nubian

Amy Grant

Born November 25, 1960, Augusta, Georgia
1976—*Amy Grant* (Word) 1979—*My Father's Eyes* 1980—*Never Alone* 1981—*Amy Grant in Concert*; *Amy Grant in Concert, vol. 2* 1982—*Age to Age*

1983—*A Christmas Album*   1984—*Straight Ahead* (A&M)   1985—*Unguarded*   1986—*The Collection* 1988—*Lead Me On*   1991—*Heart in Motion*   1992— *Home for Christmas*   1994—*House of Love.*

Singer/songwriter Amy Grant charted an ascent to pop stardom in the Eighties and early Nineties that would make her one of the most successful crossover artists in Christian music. With bouncy, hummable songs that became less overtly spiritual on each new album, and with videos that emphasized her wholesome good looks, Grant communicated the message that, as she told a reporter in 1991, "Christians can be sexy."

Grant grew up in Nashville and began playing the guitar while in summer camp, inspired by a friend who played John Denver songs. As a high school freshman, Grant was lured to a Bible-study meeting by her older sister's boyfriend; not long afterward, at 15, she landed a deal with Word Records, a Christian label. For a while, the young singer balanced studies at prep school and then Vanderbilt University with making records for Word's Myrrh label. By the time Word signed a distribution deal with A&M Records in the mid-Eighties, Grant's star had already risen on the Christian-music circuit. Nineteen-eighty-five's *Unguarded* marked her official arrival as a pop artist, cracking the Top Forty on the album charts and going platinum. Grant showed up at the Grammys that year—to accept one of five awards she's won in the gospel category—wearing a leopard-skin-print jacket and no shoes. In 1986 she recorded a duet with Chicago's Peter Cetera, the very secular #1 love song "The Next Time I Fall." The video also became popular on MTV, which had previously dismissed Grant.

As Grant's visibility increased, so did skepticism among the more conservative in the Christian music community. But accusations of "selling out" to pop trends didn't faze the singer, who maintained that her songs had never been spiritually didactic and her music had always drawn on accessible pop textures. *Heart in Motion* (#10, 1991) included the #1 single, "Baby Baby." Although the song's accompanying video showed Grant frolicking chastely with a male model, she and songwriter husband Gary Chapman cowrote the song for Millie, the second of their three children. "Every Heartbeat" and "That's What Love Is For," also from *Motion,* went to #2 and #7, respectively. In 1992 Grant's *Home for Christmas* peaked at #2. *House of Love* (#13, 1994) was certified double platinum in 1995, with its title track charting at #37.

Eddy Grant
Born Edmond Montague Grant, March 5, 1948, Plaisance, Guyana, West Indies
1979—*Living on the Front Line* (Epic); *Walking on Sunshine*   1982—*Killer on the Rampage*   1984—
Going for Broke   1986—*Born Tough*   1990—*File Under Rock* (Enigma); *Barefoot Soldier.*

With his dreadlocks and gravelly voice, Eddy Grant may have looked like a Rastafarian reggae artist, but in fact he was a pop-savvy, business-conscious straight arrow and something of a one-man music industry.

Grant's family moved to Britain while he was a youngster. By age 19, he was fronting an interracial British pop-rock band, the Equals, who scored a minor trans-Atlantic hit in 1968 with "Baby, Come Back" (#32). In 1972 Grant left the Equals to form a production company and open a recording studio. He released his debut album on his own Ice Records label, setting his career pattern by playing every instrument himself, and merging reggae, funk, soul, rock, and pop elements. *Walking on Sunshine* (#20 U.K., 1979) hit big in England with the danceable title track, and "Living on the Frontline," (#11 U.K., 1979), a protest song about South Africa. In 1982 Grant moved back to the Caribbean, relocating his home and studio to Barbados, and found massive U.S. success with *Killer on the Rampage* (#10, 1983), which contained a #2 smash hit in the funk-rock anthem "Electric Avenue." The reggae-rock ballad "I Don't Wanna Dance" was a minor followup hit (#53, 1983). *Going for Broke* (#64, 1984) yielded his last U.S. hit, "Romancing the Stone" (#26, 1984), written for but not included in the hit film of the same name. By the early Nineties Grant was still reportedly wealthy enough to bid unsuccessfully for control of the late Bob Marley's $16-million estate.

The Grass Roots
Formed 1966, Los Angeles, California
Warren Entner (b. July 7, 1944, Boston, Mass.), gtr., voc., kybds.; Creed Bratton (b. Feb. 8, 1943, Sacramento, Calif.), gtr., banjo, sitar; Ricky Coonce (b. Aug. 1, 1947, Los Angeles), drums; Rob Grill (b. Nov. 30, 1944, Los Angeles), bass, voc.
1967—*Let's Live for Today* (Dunhill)   1969—*Lovin' Thing* (– Bratton; + Dennis Provisor [b. Nov. 5, ca. 1950, Los Angeles], organ); *Leaving It All Behind* 1971—*Their 16 Greatest Hits*   1972—(– Coonce; – Provisor; + Reed Kailing, gtr.; + Virgil Webber, gtr.; + Joel Larson, drums)   1975—*The Grass Roots* (Haven) (– Grill)   1982—*Powers of the Night* (MCA).

The Grass Roots were a major American singles band during the late Sixties and early Seventies. The group was formed when pop producer/writers P. F. Sloan and Steve Barri, who had recorded the 1966 hit "Where Were You When I Needed You" (#28) under the name the Grass Roots, decided to continue recording and drafted a Los Angeles bar band, the Thirteenth Floor, to play on the records. Barri and Sloan continued to work together. The group that recorded the 1967 hits "Let's Live for Today" (#12) (a remake of an Italian hit by the Rokes) and "Things I Should Have Said" (#23) became the Grass Roots.

The group had several major hits, including the gold "Midnight Confessions" (#5, 1968), "I'd Wait a Million Years" (#15, 1969), "Heaven Knows" (#24, 1969), "The River Is Wide" (#31, 1969), "Temptation Eyes" (#15, 1971), "Sooner or Later" (#9, 1971), and "Two Divided by Love" (#16, 1971). After 1972's "The Runway" (#39), the hits dried up, and the Grass Roots returned to small clubs. By the mid-Seventies, the band was recording for the small Haven Records, where it managed one moderate comeback hit, "Mamacita" (#71, 1975).

Bassist/vocalist Rob Grill's 1980 solo LP, *Uprooted*, featured Mick Fleetwood and Lindsey Buckingham of Fleetwood Mac. He began touring as Rob Grill and the Grass Roots in 1981 before releasing *Powers of the Night* the following year. He and the "group" make the rounds of the oldies circuit to this day. Guitarist Warren Entner, meanwhile, got into the business end of the entertainment industry, managing the heavy-metal acts Quiet Riot, Faith No More, L7, and Rage Against the Machine. He also was the executive producer of the 1983 film *Pirates of Penzance*.

The Grateful Dead

Formed 1965, San Francisco, California
Jerry Garcia (b. Jerome John Garcia, Aug. 1, 1942, San Francisco; d. Aug. 9, 1995, Forest Knolls, Calif.), gtr., voc.; Bob Weir (b. Robert Hall Weir, Oct. 16, 1947, San Francisco), gtr., voc.; Ron "Pigpen" Mc-Kernan (b. Sep. 8, 1945, San Bruno, Calif.; d. Mar. 8, 1973, San Francisco), kybds., harmonica, voc.; Phil Lesh (b. Philip Chapman Lesh, Mar. 15, 1940, Berkeley, Calif.), bass, voc.; Bill Kreutzmann, a.k.a. Bill Sommers (b. Apr. 7, 1946, Palo Alto, Calif.), drums. 1967—*The Grateful Dead* (Warner Bros.) (+ Mickey Hart [b. ca. 1950, Long Island, N.Y.], drums, perc.) 1968—*Anthem of the Sun* (+ Tom Constanten, kybds.) 1969—*Aoxomoxoa* 1970—*Live Dead* (– Constanten); *Workingman's Dead*; *American Beauty* (– Hart) 1971—*Grateful Dead* (+ Keith Godchaux [b. July 14, 1948, San Francisco; d. July 23, 1980, Marin County, Calif.], kybds.; + Donna Godchaux [b. Aug. 22, 1947, San Francisco], voc.) 1972—*Europe '72* 1973—*History of the Grateful Dead, vol. 1* (MGM); *Wake of the Flood* (Grateful Dead) 1974—*Grateful Dead from the Mars Hotel*; *Skeletons from the Closet* (Warner Bros.) (+ Hart) 1975—*Blues for Allah* (Grateful Dead) 1976—*Steal Your Face* 1977—*Terrapin Station* (Arista); *What a Long Strange Trip It's Been: The Best of the Grateful Dead* (Warner Bros.) 1978—*Shakedown Street*

The Grateful Dead: Mickey Hart, Phil Lesh, Jerry Garcia, Brent Mydland, Bill Kreutzmann, Bob Weir

(Arista) 1979—(– K. Godchaux; – D. Godchaux; + Brent Mydland [b. 1953, Munich, Ger.; d. July 26, 1990, Lafayette, Calif.], kybds.) 1980—*Go to Heaven* 1981—*Reckoning*; *Dead Set* 1987—*In the Dark* 1989—*Built to Last*; *Dylan and the Dead* (Columbia) 1990—*Without a Net* (Arista) (+ Vince Welnick [b. Feb. 22, 1952, Phoenix, Ariz.], kybds.) 1991—*One from the Vault* (Grateful Dead); *Infrared Roses* 1992—*Two from the Vault* 1993—*Dick's Picks*.
Jerry Garcia solo: 1972—*Garcia* (Warner Bros.); *Hooteroll* (Douglas) 1973—*Live at the Keystone* (Fantasy) 1974—*(Compliments of) Garcia* (Round) 1975—*Old and in the Way* 1976—*Reflections* 1978—*Cats Under the Stars* (Arista) 1982—*Run for the Roses* 1988—*Almost Acoustic* (Consensus Reality/Grateful Dead); *Keystone Encores, vols. 1 and 2* (Fantasy) 1991—*Jerry Garcia/David Grisman* (with David Grisman) (Acoustic Disc); *Jerry Garcia Band* (Arista) 1993—*Not for Kids Only* (with David Grisman) (Acoustic Disc).
Bob Weir solo: 1972—*Ace* (Warner Bros.) 1976—*Kingfish* (Round) 1977—*Kingfish Live n' Kickin'* (Jet) 1978—*Heaven Help the Fool* (Arista) 1981—*Bobby and the Midnites* 1984—*Where the Beat Meets the Street* (Columbia).
Mickey Hart solo: 1972—*Rolling Thunder* (Warner Bros.) 1976—*Diga Rhythm Band* (Round) 1987—*Apocalypse Now Sessions: The Rhythm Devils Play River Music* (Passport) 1989—*Music to Be Born By* (Rykodisc) 1990—*At the Edge* 1991—*Planet Drum*.
Phil Lesh (with Ned Lagin): 1975—*Seastones* (Round).

The Grateful Dead were the longest-lasting psychedelic band and probably the most improvisatory major rock group. Beginning in the late Sixties, they played long, freeform concerts that touched down on their own country-, blues-, and folk-tinged rock songs, and on a wide range of country, blues, and rock cover versions. Although Grateful Dead albums usually sold in the range of 250,000 copies, the group had but one Top Ten single: "Touch of Grey" (#9, 1987). They concentrated on live shows rather than the recording process, and by the Nineties were consistently among the top-grossing tour attractions in all of rock. Nearly as famous as the band itself are the legions of "Deadheads"—predominantly white 18- to 24-year-olds who have lovingly preserved the Sixties by emulating their Summer of Love predecessors' philosophy and that period's accoutrements: tie-dyed clothing, hallucinogenic drugs, and the Dead's music. The death of founding guitarist, singer, and songwriter Jerry Garcia in August 1995, however, seemed to spell the end of an era.

Garcia took up guitar at 15, spent nine months in the army in 1959, then moved to Palo Alto, where he began his long-standing friendship with Robert Hunter, who later became the Dead's lyricist. In 1962 he bought a banjo and began playing in folk and bluegrass bands, and by 1964 he was a member of Mother McCree's Uptown Jug Champions, along with Bob Weir, Pigpen, and longtime associates Bob Matthews (who engineered Dead albums and formed the Alembic Electronics equipment company) and John Dawson (later of New Riders of the Purple Sage).

In 1965 the band became the Warlocks: Garcia, Weir, Pigpen, Bill Kreutzmann, and Phil Lesh, a former electronic-music composer. With electric instruments, the Warlocks debuted in July 1965 and soon became the house band at Ken Kesey's Acid Tests, a series of public LSD parties and multimedia events held before the drug had been outlawed. LSD chemist Owsley Stanley bankrolled the Grateful Dead—a name from an Egyptian prayer that Garcia spotted in a dictionary—and later supervised construction of the band's massive, state-of-the-art sound system. The Dead lived communally at 710 Ashbury Street in San Francisco in 1966-67 and played numerous free concerts; by 1967's Summer of Love, they were regulars at the Avalon and Carousel ballrooms and the Fillmore West.

MGM signed the band in 1966, and they made some mediocre recordings that were eventually released in 1973. Their legitimate recording career began when Warner Bros. signed them. While their 1967 debut album featured zippy three-minute songs, *Anthem of the Sun* and *Aoxomoxoa* featured extended suites and studio experiments that left the band $100,000 in debt to Warner Bros., mostly for studio time, by the end of the Sixties. Meanwhile, the Dead's reputation had spread, and they appeared at the Monterey Pop Festival in 1967 and Woodstock in 1969.

As the Seventies began, the Dead recouped their Warner debt with three comparatively inexpensive albums—*Live Dead* (recorded in concert), *Workingman's Dead*, and *American Beauty*. *Live Dead* featured extended psychedelic explorations, such as the classic "Dark Star," while in sharp contrast the latter two found the Dead writing concise countryish songs and working out clear-cut, well-rehearsed arrangements. *Workingman's Dead* (including "Uncle John's Band" and "Casey Jones") and *American Beauty* (including "Truckin'," "Ripple," and "Box of Rain") received considerable FM radio airplay, sold respectably, and provided much of the Dead's concert repertoire into the Nineties.

With a nationwide following, the Dead expanded their touring schedule and started various solo and side projects (aside from the band members' own works, many Dead members also appeared on the half-dozen-plus albums Dead lyricist Robert Hunter began releasing in 1973). They worked their way up to a 23-ton sound system and a large traveling entourage of road crew, family, friends, and hangers-on—most of whom would later become staff employees complete with health insurance and other benefits, as the band evolved into an efficient and highly profitable corporation, which eventually drew admiring profiles in the financial and mainstream press. The Dead finished out their Warners contract with a string of live albums, including 1971's *Grateful Dead* (which introduced more concert staples such as "Bertha" and "Wharf Rat"). In 1973 they played for over half a million people in Watkins Glen, New York, on a bill with the Band and the Allman Brothers. By then they had formed their own Grateful Dead Records and a subsidiary, Round, for nonband efforts.

Europe '72 was the last album to feature keyboardist Pigpen, a heavy drinker who died in 1973 of liver disease. Keith Godchaux, who had played piano with Dave Mason, joined the band and brought along his wife, Donna, as background vocalist. The pair toured and recorded with the Dead until 1979, when they were asked to leave and were replaced by pianist Brent Mydland. The following year, Keith Godchaux was killed in a car crash in Marin County.

In 1974 the Dead temporarily disbanded while members pursued outside projects, but they resumed touring in 1976. After signing with Arista, they began to use non-Dead producers for the first time: Keith Olsen (Fleetwood Mac) for *Terrapin Station* and Little Feat's Lowell George for *Shakedown Street*. In 1978 the band played three concerts at the foot of the Great Pyramid in Egypt, which were recorded but not released. *Go to Heaven* yielded "Alabama Getaway" (#68, 1980), like "Truckin'" and "Uncle John's Band" a minor hit single. The Dead's main support continued to be their touring six months each year. They celebrated their 15th anniversary with the release of two more live albums, including the mostly acoustic *Reckoning*.

The band took a hiatus from recording until 1987, during which time the Dead toured with Bob Dylan (one tour was recorded for the album *Dylan and the Dead*), while Garcia's health and personal habits made disturbing headlines: In January 1985 he was arrested for heroin possession in San Francisco's Golden Gate Park; in July 1986, 15 months after being in a drug treatment program and while touring with Dylan, Garcia collapsed into a five-day, near-fatal diabetic coma brought on by drug use. Once he recovered, the Dead made a triumphant return with *In the Dark*, their first Top Ten album (#6, 1987), yielding "Touch of Grey" (#9, 1987). Two years later, however, trouble suddenly began following the Dead and its normally mellow army of Deadheads on tour. In April 1989 there were 55 arrests (mostly for drugs and disturbing the peace) and violent encounters with police at two Pittsburgh shows; and 70 arrests and reports of vandalism by Dead fans at three Irvine, California, shows. In October 1989 a college student died of a broken neck outside a Dead show at the New Jersey Meadowlands (his death was never explained, but an investigation cleared security guards of guilt); in December of that year a 19-year-old fan high on LSD died while in police custody for public intoxication at the Los Angeles Forum (the autopsy reported neck compression during restraint, but police were cleared of any wrongdoing). As a result, the Dead recorded public service announcements imploring fans to act responsibly.

In July 1990 Mydland died of an overdose of injected cocaine and morphine. He was replaced by Vince Welnick, formerly of San Francisco's Tubes; Bruce Hornsby, a Dead fan, sometimes sat in on piano during concerts as well. Welnick was not on the two *From the Vault* albums, which issued old tapes of legendary Dead shows (from 1968 in Los Angeles and San Francisco, and from the latter in 1974). In September 1992 the bearish, chain-smoking Garcia was hospitalized with diabetes, an enlarged heart, and fluid in the lungs. The Dead were forced to postpone a tour until the end of the year; doctors put Garcia on a strict diet, exercise, and no-smoking regimen. The Dead returned to the road with a slimmer, more fit Garcia in mid-December 1992 with a series of Bay Area concerts.

That same year Garcia—whose paintings, often pastel watercolors, had been exhibited internationally—unveiled a line of designer silk neckties bearing his artwork. By then the massive catalogue of Dead merchandise also included skis and snowboards as well as T-shirts and even a line of toddler wear.

Weir's first solo effort was 1972's *Ace*, which featured most of the Dead backing him. During the Dead's sabbatical he formed Kingfish with ex–New Rider Dave Torbert; in the early Eighties Weir toured and recorded with Bobby and the Midnites, including drummer Billy Cobham (Mahavishnu Orchestra), bassist Alphonso Johnson (Weather Report), and guitarist Bobby Cochran (Steppenwolf). In 1991 Weir and his sister Wendy published *Panther Dream*, a children's book and companion audiocassette aimed at raising awareness of endangered rain forests—a cause the Dead had been supporting for several years through its Rex Foundation.

Phil Lesh teamed with electronic music composer Ned Lagin to record the atonal, aleatoric *Seastones*. The Godchauxs recorded as a duo, backed by Garcia and friends. Dead drummer Mickey Hart has explored world music through his solo albums, with the Diga Rhythm Band, the Rhythm Devils (Hart and Kreutzmann composed incidental percussion music for the soundtrack of the film *Apocalypse Now*), and by producing albums by musicians from Africa, Asia, and South and Central America on Rykodisc. In 1991 Hart helped arrange a U.S. tour by the Gyuto Monks of Tibet.

Garcia's outside projects included session work with Jefferson Airplane and Crosby, Stills, Nash and Young. He formed New Riders of the Purple Sage in 1969 as a side project [see entry]. From 1970 to 1973 he played occasional gigs with Bay Area keyboardist Merl Saunders (captured on the Keystone albums), and he kept up his bluegrass banjo skills with *Old and in the Way*, which also featured Peter Rowan (Seatrain), Vassar Clements, and David Grisman. Garcia recorded his first solo album, *Garcia*, in 1972; the cover shows his right hand, which had been missing its third finger since a childhood accident. Garcia joined organist Howard Wales on *Hooteroll*, and he toured and recorded with various Jerry Garcia bands in the Seventies and Eighties, before recording with David Grisman (who'd played mandolin on *American Beauty*) for two acoustic albums. Just a week after his 53rd birthday, on the morning of August 9, 1995, Garcia was found dead in his room at Serenity Knolls, a treatment facility in Forest Knolls, California, where he had reportedly gone to battle a heroin dependency. A spokesman for the band announced that Garcia had died of a heart attack.

Dobie Gray

Born Leonard Victor Ainsworth, July 26, 1942, Brookshire, Texas
1973—*Drift Away* (Decca)   1975—*New Ray of Sunshine* (Capricorn)   1978—*Midnight Diamond* (Infinity)   1979—*Dobie Gray*   1981—*Welcome Home* (Robox).

Following a brief but successful mid-Sixties pop career, singer Dobie Gray turned to country soul. Gray was born to sharecroppers with eight children. By the early Sixties he had moved to the West Coast to become a singer. Through a radio ad, he met Sonny Bono, who helped him get started. Gray had a minor hit, "Look at Me" (1963), but his next single, "The 'In' Crowd," was the biggest hit of his early period (#13, 1965) and a gold record. "See You at the 'Go-Go,'" which followed, stalled on the lower rungs of the chart.

By the late Sixties Gray had enrolled in prelaw classes and started acting. He appeared in a New York production of *The Beard,* Jean Genet's *The Balcony,* and the L.A. production of *Hair.* Despite his success in theater, Gray returned to music and through 1969 and 1970 he worked with the group Pollution. While cutting demos for songwriter Paul Williams, he met Williams' brother, Mentor, with whom he worked as staff writer for A&M Records.

In 1973 Gray released *Drift Away,* the first of three MCA albums produced by Mentor Williams. The title track (written by Williams and later covered by Rod Stewart, among others) sold 1½ million copies and hit #5. Late that summer Gray followed up with "Loving Arms," which sold over 100,000 copies. In 1975 (the same year he signed with Capricorn for the disco-tinged New Ray of Sunshine), Gray began playing benefit concerts for presidential candidate Jimmy Carter; in January 1977 he sang at Carter's inaugural-eve ceremonies. Gray became a regular guest at the Charlie Daniels Band's annual Volunteer Jam in Nashville. As of this writing, he continues to perform in and around Nashville.

Great Southern: See the Allman Brothers Band

Great White

Formed 1981, Los Angeles, California
Lorne Black, bass; Garry Holland, drums; Mark Kendall (b. Apr. 29, 1957, Calif.), gtr.; Jack Russell (b. Dec. 5, 1960, Calif.), voc.
1982—*Out of the Night* EP (EMI)   1984—*Great White*   1986—(– Holland; + Audie Desbrow [b. May 17, 1957, Calif.], drums) *Shot in the Dark* (Enigma) 1987—(+ Michael Lardie [b. Sept. 8, 1958, Alaska], kybds.) *Once Bitten* (Capitol)   1988—*Recovery: Live!* (Enigma) (– Black; + Tony Montana, bass) 1989—*Twice Shy* (Capitol)   1991—*Hooked*   1992— (– Montana; + Dave Spitz, bass) *Psycho City* (– Spitz; + Teddy Cook [b. Aug. 5, 1965, Long Island, N.Y.], bass).

Great White, a no-frills blues/metal band, hit the Top Ten in 1989 with a cover of ex–Mott the Hoople frontman Ian Hunter's "Once Bitten Twice Shy" (#5). Founded by friends Mark Kendall and Jack Russell, Great White eschewed the glitter and makeup that characterized the

L.A. scene, concentrating on raunch and straightahead rock. They recorded a self-financed EP, *Out of the Night,* produced by Don Dokken, that caught the attention of EMI, which released it and an album, *Great White.* They sold poorly, resulting in EMI's dropping the band.

Their pal Audie Desbrow joined in 1986, just before the recording of *Shot in the Dark* (#82, 1986), released by Enigma, an independent label distributed by Capitol, which then signed the band. Engineer/keyboardist Michael Lardie and bassist Tony Montana were added before the recording of *Once Bitten* (#23, 1987).

The double-platinum *Twice Shy* (#9, 1989) broke the band worldwide and was followed by *Hooked* (#18, 1991), but success and endless touring took its toll: Kendall sat out most of the *Hooked* tour after suffering a hemorrhage due to alcohol abuse, and bassist Tony Montana left before recording *Psycho City* (#107, 1992). Dave Spitz sat in for the album, and Teddy Cook, who subbed for the tour, joined the band.

Boris Grebenshikov
Born November 27, 1953, Leningrad (St. Petersburg), U.S.S.R.
1989—*Radio Silence* (Columbia).

As the singer/songwriter for the band Aquarium, Boris Grebenshikov was one of the leaders of the Soviet musical underground in the Eighties. Ironically, though freed by perestroika, Grebenshikov failed to find an audience outside his homeland.

Grebenshikov trained to be a computer engineer at the University of Leningrad before forming Aquarium in 1972. Because Grebenshikov refused to submit his lyrics for state censorship, Aquarium circulated tapes through an underground network of music fans. Banned from official venues, the Sixties-influenced band played gigs in people's apartments. After perestroika opened Soviet culture, the authorities embraced Aquarium, encouraging Grebenshikov's international career as a symbol of the new Russia. When the official Soviet record company, Melodiya, finally released Aquarium's records in 1987, they formally became the country's biggest band.

That year Grebenshikov met Kenny Schaffer and Marina Albee, the founders of Belka International, a company promoting American-Soviet relations. Schaffer brought the singer to New York, where Columbia Records beat out four other labels to sign the so-called Russian Dylan. Grebenshikov recorded *Radio Silence* in New York under intense pressure to adjust to a new city, studio, language, and culture. British filmmaker Michael Apted captured the recording sessions for the documentary *The Long Way Home,* on Britain's Granada television. Produced by Eurythmics' Dave Stewart and featuring cameos by Chrissie Hynde and Annie Lennox, the album sank under Grebenshikov's hippie idealism and rudimentary English. Despite its large investment in him, Columbia dropped Grebenshikov, and he returned to St. Petersburg, where he rejoined Aquarium.

Al Green

Born April 13, 1946, Forrest City, Arkansas
1970—*Green Is Blues* (Hi); *Gets Next to You*   1972—
Let's Stay Together*; *I'm Still in Love with You
1973—*Call Me*   1974—*Living for You*; *Explores*
Your Mind*   1975—*Al Green Is Love*; *Greatest Hits
1976—*Full of Fire*; *Have a Good Time*   1977—*The*
Belle Album*; *Greatest Hits, vol. 2*   1978—*Love Rit-
ual*   1979—*Truth and Time*   1980—*The Lord Will
***Make a Way* (Myrrh)   1981—*Higher Plane*   1982—**
Precious Lord*   1983—*I'll Rise Again*; *Al Green
Sings the Gospel* (Motown)   1984—*Trust in God
1985—*He Is the Light* (A&M)   1987—*Soul Survivor*
1989—*Love Ritual: Rare and Previously Unreleased*
1968–76* (MCA); *I Get Joy* (A&M)   1991—*One in a
***Million* (Word).**

Al Green

To a greater extent than even his predecessors Sam Cooke and Otis Redding, Al Green embodies both the sacred and the profane in soul music. He was one of the most popular vocalists in the Seventies, selling over 20 million records. His wildly improvisational, ecstatic cries and moans came directly from gospel music, and in the late Seventies he returned to the Baptist church as a preacher. He continues to record albums in a pop-gospel style (to date he has earned eight gospel Grammys) with close ties to the Memphis soul music that made him famous.

Green was born to a large family of sharecroppers. When he was nine, he and his brothers formed a gospel quartet, the Green Brothers. They toured the gospel circuits in the South and after the family moved to Grand Rapids, Michigan, three years later. Green's father dismissed him from the quartet after he caught him listening to the "profane music" of Jackie Wilson. At 16 he formed a pop group, Al Green and the Creations, with high school friends. Two members of the Creations, Palmer James and Curtis Rogers, founded a record company, Hot Line Music Journal, for which the group—renamed Al Green and the Soul Mates—cut "Back Up Train" in 1967. The single went to #5 on the national R&B chart. Followups failed, however, and the group broke up.

Green met Willie Mitchell in Midland, Texas, in 1969. Mitchell was a bandleader, a producer, and a vice president of Hi Records of Memphis, to which he signed Green. He also became Green's producer and songwriting partner for the next eight years. *Green Is Blues* introduced the sound that would distinguish all the records Green made with Mitchell: simple but emphatic backbeats riding subdued horns and strings, and Green's voice floating untethered over the instruments.

His second album contained Green's first solo hits—"You Say It" (#28 R&B, 1970), "Right Now, Right Now" (#23 R&B, 1970), and "I Can't Get Next to You" (#11 R&B, 1970)—and his first gold single, "Tired of Being Alone" (#11 pop, #7 R&B, 1971), which he wrote. That began a three-year string of gold singles, most of them written by Green, Mitchell, and Jackson: "Let's Stay Together" (#1 pop, #1 R&B, 1971), "Look What You Done for Me" (#4 pop, #2 R&B, 1972), "I'm Still in Love with You" (#3 pop, #1 R&B, 1972), "You Ought to Be with Me" (#3 pop, #1 R&B, 1972), "Call Me (Come Back Home)" (#10 pop, #2 R&B, 1973), "Here I Am (Come and Take Me)" (#10 pop, #2 R&B, 1973), "Sha La La (Make Me Happy)" (#7 pop, #2 R&B, 1974), "L-O-V-E (Love)" (#13 pop, #1 R&B, 1975).

In October 1974 Green was hospitalized with second-degree burns on his back, arm, and stomach. A former girlfriend, Mrs. Mary Woodson of New Jersey, had poured boiling grits on him while he was bathing in his Memphis home and then killed herself with his gun. The incident apparently triggered a spiritual crisis in Green, and he announced his intention to go into the ministry. In 1976 he purchased a church building in Memphis and was ordained pastor of the Full Gospel Tabernacle.

He did not, however, give up his pop career, and he preached at his church only when he was not on tour. His records continued to place regularly on the R&B chart and occasionally on the pop chart. In 1977 he built himself a studio and, with *Belle*, began producing his own records, maintaining the style and standards he had set with Mitchell. But during a 1979 concert in Cincinnati, he fell off the stage and narrowly escaped serious injury. He considered the incident a warning from God. For a time thereafter, his public appearances were limited to religious services in churches around the country, where he both sings and preaches.

His records of the Eighties, distributed by Myrrh, a gospel label, contain only religious songs, both standard hymns and Green's originals, in a style that mixes Memphis soul with gospel. In 1982 he did a stint on Broadway, costarring with Patti LaBelle in Vinnette Carroll's gospel musical *Your Arms Too Short to Box with God.* Talking Heads scored one of their biggest pop hits with a cover of Green's "Take Me to the River," and Green himself duetted with Annie Lennox of Eurythmics on "Put a Little Love in Your Heart," for the soundtrack of the 1988 film *Scrooged.* In 1992 Green signed a new deal with BMG Records and returned to the Memphis soul sound of his roots with *Don't Look Back* (as yet unreleased in the U.S.), which featured production help from David Steele and Andy Cox (Fine Young Cannibals) and Arthur Baker (Afrika Bambaataa's "Planet Rock" and other early-Eighties dance hits). In 1994 Green duetted with Lyle Lovett on the Grammy-winning "Funny How Time Slips Away" for *Rhythm, Country, and Blues,* a collection of duets that teamed up well-known artists in each of these fields.

Norman Greenbaum

Born November 20, 1942, Malden, Massachusetts
1969—*Spirit in the Sky* (Reprise)   1970—*Back Home Again*   1972—*Petaluma.*

In 1970 folksinger/songwriter Norman Greenbaum's electrified jug-band stomp "Spirit in the Sky" sold two million copies. After playing local coffeehouses while attending Boston University, he had moved to the West Coast in the mid-Sixties and formed Dr. West's Medicine Show and Junk Band, a psychedelic jug band that had a minor hit, "The Eggplant That Ate Chicago" (#52, 1966), before disbanding in 1967. Greenbaum then formed several other unsuccessful groups before embarking on his solo career in 1968. Working with producer and cowriter Eric Jacobson, he released a couple of unsuccessful singles from his Reprise debut, *Spirit in the Sky,* before the title track hit #3 on the American chart. Greenbaum's followups ("Canned Ham," 1970; "California Earthquake," 1971) never hit.

When *Petaluma* was released in 1972, he was largely out of the public eye, spending most of his time running a goat dairy on a farm near Petaluma, California. Since 1983 the singer has also dabbled in management and concert production; as of 1994 he was writing new songs for a demo. In 1986 British glam-rock band Doctor and the Medics recorded a hit cover of "Spirit in the Sky."

Green Day

Formed 1989, Berkeley, California
Billie Joe Armstrong (b. Feb. 17, 1972, San Pablo, Calif.), voc., gtr.; Mike Dirnt (b. Mike Pritchard, May 4, 1972, Calif.), bass; Al Sobrante, drums.
1990—(– Sobrante; + John Kiftmeyer, drums)
***39/Smooth* (Lookout) (– Kiftmeyer; + Tré Cool [b. Frank Edwin Wright III, Dec. 9, 1972, Ger.], drums)   1992—*Kerplunk*   1994—*Dookie* (Reprise).**

Punk revivalists in style, the raucous trio from California sold more than six million copies of their major-label debut, *Dookie.* Although Green Day's taut, three-minute, guitar-driven songs ably revive the fierceness of the group's stylistic progenitors (the Clash, the Sex Pistols, the Buzzcocks), punk's original aim—to annoy, outrage, shock—is not Green Day's thing.

Friends since age ten, Billie Joe Armstrong and Mike Dirnt grew up in Rodeo, California. They formed their first real band, Sweet Children, at 14. Tré Cool grew up in remote Mendocino County, California. When they were 17, Green Day recorded their first EP, *1,000 Hours.* After winning fans via a nurturing, all-ages hardcore scene in Berkeley and two albums on Lookout, Green Day signed with Reprise in April 1993. Their 1994 release, *Dookie,* proclaimed the next generation of punk, hitting #2 on the album chart, buoyed by the band's effervescent presence on MTV and at Lollapalooza and Woodstock '94. The band also won the 1994 Best Alternative Music Performance Grammy.

Green River: See Mudhoney; Pearl Jam

Professor Griff: See Public Enemy

Nanci Griffith

Born Nanci Caroline Griffith, July 6, 1953, Austin, Texas
1978—*There's a Light Beyond These Woods* (B.F. Deal Records)   1982—*Poet in My Window* (Featherbed Records)   1985—*Once in a Very Blue Moon* (Philo/Rounder)   1986—*Last of the True Believers* 1987—*Lone Star State of Mind* (MCA)   1988—*Little Love Affairs*; *One Fair Summer Evening*   1989—*Storms*   1991—*Late Night Grande Hotel*   1993—*Other Voices, Other Rooms* (Elektra)   1994—*Flyer.*

Chronicling the lives of everyday people in a sweet voice and a direct, realistic style, singer/songwriter Nanci Griffith's brand of contemporary folk music—"folkabilly," she calls it—draws on both country textures and Southern literary tradition. (She has written short stories and man-

Nanci Griffith

uscripts for novels.) Griffith is equally well regarded for her covers of songs by a range of artists, from Woody Guthrie to Lyle Lovett.

As a child, Griffith was exposed to a variety of jazz, country, and folk records; folksinger Carolyn Hester was a particular favorite. Griffith began playing guitar and singing in bars when she was 14 and continued while studying at the University of Texas. After graduating and working briefly as a teacher, she began recording for independent labels. By the mid-Eighties her graceful soprano had attracted the attention of MCA Records.

Her MCA debut, *Lone Star State of Mind,* included a rendition of Julie Gold's "From a Distance," which Griffith wanted to release as a single; MCA refused, and in 1990 Bette Midler had a smash hit with the song. (Griffith's version did become a #1 single in Ireland, where she's enormously popular.) Griffith's frustration with MCA worsened, and she eventually defected to Elektra Records. *Other Voices, Other Rooms* (the title of Truman Capote's first book), an assortment of songs by influential folk and rock artists, featured guest musicians Bob Dylan, John Prine, and Emmylou Harris, and peaked on the charts at #54 in 1993. Despite widespread support from fans and peers, to date Griffith has not carved out a niche on commercial radio.

Grin: See Nils Lofgren

Stefan Grossman
Born April 16, 1945, New York City, New York
1966—*How to Play Blues Guitar* (with Rory Block)

(Kicking Mule) 1969—*Crosscurrents* (with Danny Kalb) (Cotillion) 1970—*Ragtime Cowboy Jew* (Transatlantic); *Yazoo Basin Boogie* (Kicking Mule) 1971—*Those Pleasant Days* (Transatlantic) 1972—*Hot Dogs!* (Kicking Mule) 1973—*Stefan Grossman Live!* (Transatlantic) 1973—*Memphis Jelly Roll* (Kicking Mule) 1975—*Bottleneck Serenade; How to Play Ragtime Guitar* (with Tom Van Bergeyk) 1976—*My Creole Belle* (Transatlantic) 1977—*Fingerpicking Guitar Techniques* (Kicking Mule) 1988—*Shining Shadows* (Shanachie) 1990—*Guitar Landscapes.*
With John Renbourn: 1966—*How to Play Blues Guitar* (Kicking Mule) 1978—*How to Play Blues Guitar, vol. II; Stefan Grossman and John Renbourn* 1980—*Thunder on the Run; Under the Volcano* 1986—*Live in Concert* 1987—*The Three Kingdoms* (Shanachie) 1989—*Love, Devils & the Blues; Snap a Little Owl.*

A patron and champion of country blues, Stefan Grossman has been a peripheral figure on the international music scene for nearly two decades. He first gathered attention in 1965 and 1966 in New York when he played with the Even Dozen Jug Band and on occasion with the anarchic Fugs. He attempted to spread the word about such stalwart genuine articles as the Reverend Gary Davis, one of Grossman's heroes. By 1967 he had moved to England, where he lived for a while with Eric Clapton, and was prominent in the blues revival there. By the start of the Seventies he had relocated to Rome and issued a number of instructional books and records (mostly on the Transatlantic label) on blues guitar technique. In 1972 Grossman formed his own Kicking Mule label to gain a wider hearing for budding folk and blues talent. (That label folded in the late Seventies.)

He has toured and recorded with John Renbourn, formerly of Pentangle, as well as other noted guitarists. Grossman continues to produce instructional albums for the Shanachie label, where, as a label executive in the late Eighties and early Nineties, he oversaw its blues releases. As of this writing, he was beginning work on archival video projects.

The Groundhogs
Formed 1963, England
T. S. "Tony" McPhee (b. Mar. 22, 1944, Lincolnshire, Eng.), gtr., voc.; Pete Cruikshank (b. July 2, 1945), bass; Ken Pustelnik, drums; Steve Rye, harmonica.
1968—*Scratching the Surface* (Liberty) 1969—*Blues Obituary* (Imperial) (– Rye) 1970—*Thank Christ for the Bomb* (Liberty) 1971—*Split* (United Artists) 1972—*Who Will Save the World?* 1973—*Hogwash; The Groundhogs with John Lee Hooker and John Mayall* (Cleveland) 1974—*Best of*

Groundhogs 1969–1972 (United Artists) 1976—
(– Cruikshank; – Pustelnik; + Rick Adams, gtr.;
+ Martin Kent, bass; + Mick Cook, drums) *Black Diamond; Crosscut Saw.*

Tony McPhee's Groundhogs shifted slowly from blues to heavy metal and established a sizable cult following in Britain by the early Seventies. McPhee, who had worked for the post office, established the first Groundhogs in 1963; they backed up visiting U.S. blues musicians, including Little Walter and John Lee Hooker. The group recorded a single ("Shake It") and an album with Hooker for Britain's Xtra label. The original band broke up in 1965, but McPhee re-formed the group in 1968, and the Groundhogs put out a pair of blues albums.

In 1970 the Groundhogs moved into heavy metal with *Thank Christ for the Bomb*, their first substantial British success, and played that year's Isle of Wight Festival. *Split* hit the British Top Ten in 1971, as did 1972's *Who Will Save the World?* The Groundhogs continued to tour the U.K. extensively. Their only U.S. tour ended prematurely in 1972, when McPhee was injured while horseback riding in the Pocono Mountains.

The Groundhogs recorded *Hogwash* and *Solid* (released only in the U.K.) in 1973 and 1974, but McPhee had begun solo activities, including a 1973 album, *The Two Sides of T. S. McPhee*, and collaborations with blues-folksinger Jo Ann Kelly (born January 5, 1944, London, England; died October 21, 1990). McPhee also produced an album for blues singer Big Joe Williams, and in early 1976 he revived the Groundhogs once more.

Grunge

A postpunk hard-rock subgenre of the "alternative" movement that dominated Nineties rock, grunge emerged from Seattle and entered the American lexicon with Nirvana's surprise 1992 chart-topper, "Smells Like Teen Spirit." Grunge had already been going for several years before that, with such other Seattle groups as Soundgarden, Mudhoney, Alice in Chains, Tad, and what is generally believed to have been the city's first grunge band, the Melvins—an outfit from nearby Aberdeen that played a slow, sludgy punk metal that smacked of Flipper (later cited as an influence by Nirvana). Grunge bands were influenced equally by punk and by such Seventies hard-rock bands as Led Zeppelin, Black Sabbath, AC/DC, and Kiss. They were preceded, and no doubt influenced, by such mid-Eighties American postpunk bands as Minneapolis' Replacements and Hüsker Dü and New York noise rockers Sonic Youth. Many grunge bands recorded for Seattle's Sub Pop label, founded by men who'd worked day jobs at the Seattle headquarters of Muzak.

Also identified with the grunge scene were such non-Seattle bands as Dinosaur Jr (from Amherst, Massa-chusetts) and San Diego's Stone Temple Pilots; such female hardcore punk, or "foxcore," bands as L7, Hole (whose frontwoman, Courtney Love, married Nirvana's Kurt Cobain), Babes in Toyland, and Scrawl; and—because they emerged from Seattle as Nirvana found mass success—Pearl Jam, which in fact sounded slicker than any true grunge band, and were dismissed as "fake grunge" by Cobain (who later admitted admiration for Pearl Jam frontman Eddie Vedder).

There was also a brief, early-Nineties fashion craze for the grunge "look"—characterized by untucked plaid-flannel shirts, stocking caps, and moth-eaten sweaters.

The Guess Who

Formed 1962, Winnipeg, Canada
Chad Allan (b. Allan Kobel, ca. 1945), voc., gtr.; Bob Ashley, piano; Randy Bachman (b. Sep. 27, 1943, Winnipeg), gtr., voc.; Garry Peterson (b. May 26, 1945), drums; Jim Kale (b. Aug. 11, 1943, Winnipeg), bass.
1965—(– Ashley; + Burton Cummings [b. Dec. 31, 1947, Winnipeg], kybds., voc.) *Shakin' All Over* (Scepter) 1966—(– Allan; + Bruce Dekker, voc.; – Dekker) 1969—*Wheatfield Soul* (RCA); *Canned Wheat Packed by the Guess Who* 1970—*American Woman* (– Bachman; + Greg Leskiw [b. Aug. 5, 1947], gtr.; + Kurt Winter [b. Apr. 2, 1946], gtr.); *Share the Land* 1971—*So Long, Bannatyne; Best of* 1972—*Rockin'* (– Leskiw; + Don McDougall [b. Nov. 5, 1947], gtr.); *Live at the Paramount* (– Kale; + Bill Wallace [b. May 18, 1949], bass, voc.) 1973—*#10; Best of, vol. 2* 1974—*Artificial Paradise; Road Food* (– Winter; – McDougall; + Dominic Troiano, gtr., voc.); *Flavours* 1975—*Power in the Music; Born in Canada* (group disbands) 1977—*The Greatest of the Guess Who* (RCA) 1979—(Group re-forms: Kale; McDougall; + Allan McDougall, voc.; + Vince Masters, drums; + David Inglis, gtr.; + David Parasz, horns) *All This for a Song* (Hilltak) (numerous personnel changes since).
Burton Cummings solo: 1976—*Burton Cummings* (Portrait) 1977—*My Own Way to Rock* 1981—*Sweet Sweet* (Alfa).

The Guess Who was Canada's premier singles band through the early Seventies. The group, its original members all born in Winnipeg, dates back to 1962, when buddies Chad Allan and Randy Bachman formed Allan and the Silvertones, later the Reflections, and then (to avoid confusion with a Detroit group) Chad Allan and the Expression. In 1965 the group changed its name to the Guess Who and had a surprise hit with a cover of Johnny Kidd and the Pirates' "Shakin' All Over" (#22, 1965). Its record company saw in the Guess Who's name an opportunity to imply that the band was actually a famous

British group incognito. The group toured the United States as part of Dick Clark's Caravan of Stars Revue. That summer Burton Cummings joined, and when Allan left in 1966, he became the band's lead vocalist and focal point.

In 1968 the Guess Who landed a regular spot on the CBC-TV show *Where It's At,* hosted by ex-leader Allan. The group had minor success in Canada, but was unable to crack the U.S. market until producer Jack Richardson mortgaged his house to pay for the quartet to record in New York in September 1968. Richardson produced the first gold Guess Who single in the U.S., "These Eyes" (#6, 1969). The band's second RCA LP, *Canned Wheat,* boasted two hits—"Laughing" (#10, 1969) and "Undun" (#22, 1969).

In 1970 the Guess Who's record sales totaled $5 million, largely on the strength of its third RCA album, *American Woman.* The fuzz guitar–propelled title track (#1) and "No Time" (#5) were U.S. hits. The Guess Who performed at the White House with Prince Charles and Princess Anne in attendance; First Lady Pat Nixon, undoubtedly briefed as to the scathing anti-U.S. sentiment of "American Woman," requested that the band delete the song from its set.

While at the height of success, Cummings and Bachman were feuding bitterly; the guitarist, having recently converted to the Mormon faith, found the band's hedonistic lifestyle offensive. In July 1970 he departed, first for a brief collaboration with Allan as Brave Belt, then without Allan as Bachman-Turner Overdrive [see entry]. The Guess Who replaced him with two guitarists and continued its singles success with "Share the Land" (#10, 1970), "Hand Me Down World" (#17, 1970), "Rain Dance" (#19, 1971), and "Albert Flasher" (#29, 1971). But two years passed before the band's next Top Forty hit, by which time former James Gang guitarist Dominic Troiano was a member. A novelty tribute to disc jockey Wolfman Jack, "Clap for the Wolfman," made the Top Ten, and another single, "Dancin' Fool" (not the Frank Zappa song), cracked the Top Thirty. Nevertheless, the group disbanded the next year.

Cummings had a hit on his first solo album with "Stand Tall" (#10, 1976) and recorded into the early Eighties. His 1981 album *Sweet Sweet* included a Top Forty hit, "You Saved My Soul." He and Randy Bachman eventually made peace, and in 1983 the original group got back together for an album and concert video. Four years later the two toured together. Meanwhile, an ever-changing lineup has continued to tour as the Guess Who ever since 1979. Aside from Jim Kale, sometimes not a single original or early-era member would be onstage, although as of 1989 he and drummer Garry Peterson were on the payroll. The Kale-led Guess Who has released several marginal albums on small labels such as Hilltak and El Mocambo.

Guitar Slim

Born Eddie Jones, December 10, 1926, Greenwood, Mississippi; died February 7, 1959, New York City, New York
1954—*Things That I Used to Do* (Specialty)   1987— *The Atco Sessions* (Atlantic)   1991—*Sufferin' Mind* (Speciality).

Blues guitarist/singer Eddie "Guitar Slim" Jones' "Things That I Used to Do" was one of the top R&B records of 1954, selling a million copies. The song (now a blues standard) fused gospel and the blues, and featured Jones' electric guitar as well as the piano of a then largely unknown Ray Charles.

Jones began singing in church choirs as a child. While still in his teens, he formed a trio with pianist Huey "Piano" Smith and later began working solo. He recorded for Imperial and JB between 1951 and 1952. He may have served in the U.S. Army in Korea in the early Fifties. An electric guitar pioneer, Jones was also a flashy dresser and a famed showman, known for playing hot in-concert solos while wandering as far as his 200-foot extension cord would allow. He died of pneumonia at the age of 32 and is buried (with his gold-top Gibson Les Paul guitar) in Thibodaux, Louisiana. His son has performed under the name Guitar Slim Jr.

The first known "Guitar Slim," incidentally, was a blues musician from Texas, Norman Green (born July 25, 1907; died September 28, 1975), who had minor hits, including "Fifth Street Alley Blues" and "Old Folks Boogie."

Guns n' Roses

Formed 1985, Los Angeles, California
Axl Rose (b. William Bailey, Feb. 6, 1962, Lafayette, Ind.), voc.; Slash (b. Saul Hudson, July 23, 1965, Stoke-on-Trent, Eng.), gtr.; Duff McKagan (b. Michael McKagan, Feb. 5, 1964, Seattle, Wash.), bass; Steve Adler (b. 1965, Ohio), drums; Izzy Stradlin (b. Jeff Isbell, Apr. 8, 1962, Lafayette, Ind.) gtr.
1986—*Live?! *@ Like a Suicide* EP (Uzi/Suicide) 1987—*Appetite for Destruction* (Geffen)   1988— *GN'R Lies*   1990—(– Adler; + Matt Sorum [b. Nov. 19, 1960, Long Beach, Calif.], drums; + Dizzy Reed [b. Darren Reed, June 18, 1963, Hinsdale, Ill.], kybds.)   1991—*Use Your Illusion I*; *Use Your Illusion II* (– Stradlin; + Gilby Clarke [b. Aug. 17, 1962, Cleveland, Ohio], gtr.)   1993—*The Spaghetti Incident?.*
Izzy Stradlin with the JuJu Hounds (Stradlin, gtr., voc.; Jimmy Ashhurst, bass; Charlie "Chalo" Quintana, drums; Rick Richards, gtr.): 1992—*Izzy Stradlin & the JuJu Hounds* (Geffen).
Duff McKagan solo: 1993—*Believe in Me* (Geffen).
Gilby Clarke solo: 1994—*Pawn Shop Guitars* (Virgin).

Guns n' Roses: Axl Rose,
Duff McKagan, Matt Sorum,
Slash

Slash with Snakepit (Slash, gtr.; Sorum, drums; Clarke, gtr.; Mike Inez, bass; Eric Dover, voc.): 1995—*It's Five O'Clock Somewhere* (Geffen).

With *Appetite for Destruction* the biggest-selling debut in history, Guns n' Roses gained stardom in the late Eighties with Seventies-derived hard rock and a hedonistic rebelliousness that recalled the early Rolling Stones. Combining heavy-metal technique with punk attitude, they provoked charges of multifarious bigotry but leavened their outrage with songs that bespoke the inchoate emotions of hard rock's primarily young white male audience.

Raised in a working-class Indiana family, high school dropout Axl Rose had, by age 20, compiled a police record that included charges for public intoxication, criminal trespass, and contributing to the delinquency of a minor. An ELO and Queen fan, the singer became friends with guitarist Izzy Stradlin, and the two joined forces in Los Angeles in the early Eighties to form a band. Crafting their name from those of two groups they'd played in, Hollywood Roses and L.A. Guns, they formed Guns n' Roses with English-born biracial guitarist Slash, whose parents, both in the music industry, had moved to Los Angeles when he was 11. With bassist Duff McKagan, whose own past included stealing a rumored 133 automobiles, and drummer Steve Adler, the Gunners accrued notoriety (alluding to the band's heroin and alcohol abuse, their posters featured the legend "Addicted: Only the Strong Survive").

After independently releasing an EP, Guns n' Roses signed with Geffen in 1986, and, with producer Mike Clink (Heart, Eddie Money), put out *Appetite for Destruction*. Opening for Aerosmith, they built a live follow-

ing, and in September 1988, with wide MTV exposure given "Sweet Child o' Mine" (#1, 1988) and "Welcome to the Jungle" (#7, 1988), the album reached #1; it stayed there for five weeks and on the charts for nearly three years. By 1995 it had sold 13 million copies.

Next came *GN'R Lies,* a Top Five album that combined tracks from the EP with new songs, notably "Used to Love Her," with its chorus of ". . . but I had to kill her," and "One in a Million," its lyrics disparaging "faggots," "immigrants," and "niggers." Controversy ensued and would not let up. In 1988, two fans died in crowd disturbances at England's Monster of Rock Festival, and while opening for the Rolling Stones' 1989 tour garnered Gn'R a larger audience, Slash shocked television viewers with an obscenity-laden speech at the American Music Awards the following year. Concurrently, reports surfaced of heroin use by Rose, Stradlin, and Adler, and Adler was fired for not straightening out.

In 1990 the band performed at Farm Aid IV and contributed a cover of Bob Dylan's "Knockin' on Heaven's Door" to the *Days of Thunder* soundtrack and an original, "Civil War," to *Nobody's Child,* a project to benefit Romanian orphans; Slash and McKagan played on Iggy Pop's *Brick by Brick* and Slash recorded with Dylan, Michael Jackson, and Lenny Kravitz, and on a tribute album for Les Paul. But with Matt Sorum, formerly of the Cult, brought in on drums and with new keyboardist Dizzy Reed, 1990 was a year of regrouping.

The following year brought even greater success if no less turmoil. Gn'R embarked on its first headlining world tour and released "You Could Be Mine" (#29, 1991) from the *Terminator 2* soundtrack. But Rose's marriage to Erin Everly, daughter of Don Everly of the Everly Brothers, ended after three weeks amidst allegations of physical abuse, and Rose, after allegedly attacking a camera-wielding fan at a St. Louis concert, was charged with four misdemeanor counts of assault and one of property damage. Rose pleaded not guilty and remained unrepentant about an ensuing riot that left 60 people hospitalized, the band's equipment destroyed or stolen, and the hall sustaining over $200,000 in damages.

With Rose embarked on psychotherapy (during which he maintained discovery of sexual abuse at age two by his father), 1991 saw the simultaneous release of *Use Your Illusion I* and *Use Your Illusion II,* both shipping platinum. Due to tension with Rose, Stradlin then left and formed the JuJu Hounds with bassist Jimmy Ashhurst, drummer Charlie "Chalo" Quintana, and ex–Georgia Satellites guitarist Rick Richards (Stradlin's replacement was Gilby Clarke of Candy and Kills for Thrills). The band then set off on a 28-month tour, the longest in rock history. Among 1992's highlights were an MTV Vanguard award for the group's body of work and an appearance in April at the Freddie Mercury Tribute, an AIDS benefit that via satellite drew the largest concert audience in history. In 1993 Gn'R released *The Spaghetti Incident?,* an album of covers that paid homage to the band's punk roots. Among the tracks was one penned by Charles Manson, for which the band was heavily criticized. By 1994, rumors were proliferating that the band had broken up. Clarke released a solo album, *Pawn Shop Guitars,* and at the year's end Slash recorded a solo album with Snakepit, *It's Five O'Clock Somewhere* (#70, 1995), featuring Sorum and Clarke, Mike Inez of Alice in Chains, and Jellyfish guitarist Eric Dover on lead vocals.

Guru: See Gang Starr

Arlo Guthrie
Born July 10, 1947, Coney Island, New York
1967—*Alice's Restaurant* (Reprise)   1968—*Arlo*
1969—*Running Down the Road*; *Alice's Restaurant* soundtrack (United Artists)   1970—*Washington County*   1972—*Hobo's Lullaby* (Reprise)   1973—Last of the Brooklyn Cowboys   1974—Arlo Guthrie 1975—Pete Seeger/Arlo Guthrie Together in Concert 1976—Amigo   1977—The Best of (Warner Bros.) 1978—One Night   1979—Outlasting the Blues 1981—Power of Love   1986—Someday (Rising Son) 1991—All Over the World   1992—Son of the Wind.

Folksinger Arlo Guthrie became popular in the late Sixties when his tall-tale "Alice's Restaurant" became an underground favorite and later a movie in which he appeared. His biggest pop hit was Steve Goodman's "City of New Orleans," and he is still a regular attraction on the folk circuit.

One of several children born to folksinger Woody and

Marjorie Guthrie, Arlo grew up among musicians. At age three he danced and played the harmonica for Leadbelly. Pete Seeger was also a frequent guest. His mother taught him guitar at age six. Guthrie attended private schools in Brooklyn and then in Stockbridge, Massachusetts, the setting of "Alice's Restaurant." He attended college in Billings, Montana, but soon returned to New York to pursue a music career.

By late 1965 Guthrie was a regular on the East Coast coffeehouse circuit, and in 1967 he toured Japan with Judy Collins. Shortly after his appearance at the Newport Folk Festival, he released his debut LP, which included the 18-minute "Alice's Restaurant." As the Sixties closed, he continued to build a following, and he appeared at Woodstock in August 1969.

Guthrie's career picked up noticeably in the early Seventies with *Washington County* and *Hobo's Lullaby,* which included the #18 hit, "The City of New Orleans" (1972). Subsequent LPs have been well received, although his record sales have dropped off; he has been less interested in elaborate pop productions.

In 1977 Guthrie converted to Catholicism. During the late Seventies he regularly toured the U.S. and Europe backed by Shenandoah, with whom he also recorded. Throughout the Seventies he often performed and recorded with Pete Seeger (*Together in Concert,* among others), and he was an activist for numerous causes, including the antinuclear and ecological movements. In the late Eighties, Guthrie began acquiring his entire recording catalogue from Warner Bros. and reissuing it on his own Rising Son label. In 1992 his label produced the Grammy-nominated Woody's *20 Grow Big Songs,* an album of his father's children's songs recorded by Arlo, his brother Joady, his sister Nora, and all their children. That same year, Arlo also bought the Trinity Church in Great Barrington, Massachusetts, which had been prominent in the "Alice's Restaurant" story; he converted the church into the home of Rising Son Records and the Guthrie Center, a nonprofit community service charity. In 1994 Guthrie appeared as an aging hippie in the short-lived network TV show, *Byrds of Paradise.*

Woody Guthrie
Born Woodrow Wilson Guthrie, July 14, 1912, Okemah, Oklahoma; died October 3, 1967, Queens, New York
1967—*This Land Is Your Land* (Folkways)   1977—*A Legendary Performer* (RCA)   1988—*The Greatest Songs of Woody Guthrie* (Vanguard)   1993—*Songs to Grow on for Mother and Child* (Smithsonian Folkways).

In the Thirties and Forties, Woody Guthrie reinvented the American folk ballad as a vehicle for social comment and

Woody Guthrie

protest, laying the groundwork for Bob Dylan and numerous other rock singer/songwriters with such neotraditional songs as "This Land Is Your Land," "Pastures of Plenty," "So Long, It's Been Good to Know You," and nearly a thousand others.

Guthrie's father was a singer, banjo player, and sometime professional boxer. Woody left home at 16 and roamed through Texas and Louisiana, working as a newsboy, sign painter, spittoon washer, and farm laborer, and at other menial jobs; he also sang in the streets. While visiting his uncle Jeff Guthrie in Pampa, Texas, in 1929, he learned to play guitar. During the Depression, Guthrie rode the rails as a hobo until around 1937, when he settled in Los Angeles and hosted a radio show on KFVD for a dollar a day.

Guthrie's politics moved leftward, and at the start of World War II he relocated to New York. There he met the Weavers and Pete Seeger. He briefly embraced communism, although he was denied membership in the U.S. Communist Party because he refused to renounce his religion, but he did write a column for a communist newspaper, *The People's Daily World*.

Although these leanings did not endear Guthrie to the U.S. government, his anti-Hitler songs did; his guitar had a sign on it saying "This Machine Kills Fascists." From 1943 to 1945 Guthrie was with the U.S. merchant marine in the U.K., Italy, and Africa. In 1945 he married Marjorie Greenblatt Mazia, and together they had four children: Cathy (who was killed in a fire at age four), Nora, Joady, and Arlo.

Although Guthrie's songs traveled widely, he didn't record until 1940, when Alan Lomax taped several hours of talking and singing for the Library of Congress. Those sessions were later released on commercial labels, including RCA (*Woody Guthrie—A Legendary Performer* and *Dust Bowl Ballads*) and Elektra. He also recorded with Leadbelly and Sonny Terry, but his recordings had little impact by themselves.

During his years of riding the rails, Guthrie developed a drinking problem. In 1952 he was diagnosed as alcoholic and confined to a mental institution before his problem was correctly diagnosed as Huntington's chorea, a genetically transmitted degenerative disorder of the nervous system from which Guthrie's mother had died. The disease kept him largely inactive and hospitalized during the last decade of his life.

Guthrie's fame has steadily increased over the years. Bob Dylan, who had traveled to New York to visit Guthrie in the hospital, sang his idol's praises early on, and Guthrie's son, Arlo, has also carried on the family name as a singer/songwriter. Pete Seeger, whose relationship with Woody dates back to the Thirties, organized a series of memorial concerts for the singer in the late Sixties. Two of those concerts—at Carnegie Hall in 1968 and the Hollywood Bowl in 1970—were recorded and released as albums featuring Dylan, Tom Paxton, Joan Baez, Judy Collins, Richie Havens, and Country Joe McDonald. In 1976 Guthrie's autobiography, *Bound for Glory* (published in 1943), was made into a motion picture with David Carradine playing Guthrie. That same year, Guthrie's previously unpublished prose work, *Seeds of Man,* was published. In 1988 he was inducted into the Rock and Roll Hall of Fame.

Gutterball: See Dream Syndicate; Long Ryders

Buddy Guy
Born George Guy, July 30, 1936, Lettsworth, Louisiana
1967—*Left My Blues in San Francisco* (Chess) 1968—*A Man and the Blues* (Vanguard); *This Is Buddy Guy* 1970—*I Was Walking Through the Woods* (Chess) (with Junior Wells) 1972—*Hold That Plane* (Vanguard); *Buddy Guy & Junior Wells Play the Blues* (with Junior Wells) (Atlantic) 1981—*Stone Crazy!* (Alligator); *Drinkin' TNT 'n' Smokin' Dynamite* (Blind Pig) (with Junior Wells) 1991—*Alone & Acoustic* (Alligator) (with Junior Wells); *Damn Right, I've Got the Blues* (Silvertone) 1992—*Live in Montreux* (with Junior Wells) (Evidence); *The Very Best of Buddy Guy* (Rhino); *The Complete Chess Studio Recordings* (Chess/MCA); *My Time After Awhile* (Vanguard) 1993—*Feels Like Rain* (Silvertone) 1994—*Slippin' In.*

Eric Clapton once described Buddy Guy as the best guitar player alive. In fact, it's been through the support of

Buddy Guy

his many famous and respected admirers that blues master Guy has come to the attention of rock audiences, from touring with the Rolling Stones in 1970 to soliciting guest appearances from Clapton, Jeff Beck, and Mark Knopfler for *Damn Right, I've Got the Blues,* the Grammy-winning 1991 album that both reestablished his stature in the music community and marked his greatest commercial success yet.

Guy began playing his instrument as a teenager, inspired by such Southern blues greats as Lightnin' Slim and Guitar Slim. The young guitarist left Baton Rouge in 1957 to test his chops in Chicago, the urban capital of the electric blues. Guy was on the verge of starving when a merciful stranger led him to the 708 Club and persuaded that evening's performer, Otis Rush, to allow him to sit in. Guy's impromptu performance earned him a steady gig at the club, and he was soon playing regularly at other local venues. His fierce, visceral style caught the ear of venerable composer/bassist Willie Dixon, who helped Guy land a contract with the noted blues label Chess Records. Though Guy was originally signed by Leonard Chess as a singer, he became a house guitarist for the company, playing on records by such legendary artists as Muddy Waters and Howlin' Wolf in addition to making radiant recordings on his own. (Waters was an early Guy supporter, having caught his show at the 708 Club.)

Since Guy's arrangement with Chess prevented him

from getting credit for his work with artists on other labels, he eventually switched to Vanguard. Some of his most memorable work on Vanguard was done in collaboration with the great harmonica player Junior Wells [see entry], who Guy first met in a Chicago club and with whom he still maintains a close association. Some of Guy's most acclaimed solo albums have been recorded live.

Indeed, in spite of the success Guy has had in recent years with star-studded albums like *Damn Right, I've Got the Blues* and its successors, 1993's *Feels Like Rain* (featuring Bonnie Raitt, Paul Rodgers, John Mayall, and Travis Tritt) and 1994's *Slipping In* (with the Double Trouble rhythm section, pianist Johnnie Johnson, and guitarist David Grissom), many of his fans insist that he is best appreciated in concert. He tours constantly, appearing at blues clubs and festivals around the world. Guy owns two Chicago clubs, the Checkerboard Lounge and Legends.

Guy/Teddy Riley

Formed 1985, New York City, New York
Teddy Riley (b. Oct. 8, 1966, Harlem, N.Y.), various instr.; Aaron Hall (b. Aug. 10, 1964, Bronx, N.Y.), voc.; Timmy Gatling, voc., dancer.
1987—*Guy* (Uptown) 1990—(– Gatling; + Damion Hall [b. Albert Damion Hall, June 6, 1968, Brooklyn, N.Y.], voc., choreography) *The Future* (MCA).
Aaron Hall solo: 1993—*The Truth* (Silas).
Damion Hall solo: 1994—*Straight to the Point* (Silas).
Teddy Riley with Blackstreet: 1994—*Blackstreet* (Interscope).

In the late Eighties, while barely out of his teens, Teddy Riley fathered New Jack Swing, a contemporary strain of R&B that married traditional soul singing to the hip-hop beats that drove rap music. Though Riley first became recognized for his work with Guy, a trio he formed with friends, the wunderkind quickly became one of the most sought-after writer/producers in the R&B community, lending his distinctive talents to hot young artists like Keith Sweat and Bobby Brown and established stars such as James Ingram and Michael Jackson.

Riley took up keyboards and percussion as a young child and was playing piano in Harlem clubs by age ten. He began jamming with local funk musicians at 12 and performed with a couple of bands before putting together Guy with Aaron Hall, a church-trained singer, and Timmy Gatling. The group's eponymous debut generated the R&B hit "Groove Me" (#4, 1988). Gatling quit shortly after its release and was replaced by Hall's brother Damion, a singer, dancer, and choreographer. Riley scored Guy singles for the film soundtracks to *Do the Right Thing* ("Mr. Fantasy") and *New Jack City*

("New Jack City"). The group's sophomore LP, *The Future* (#16 pop, #1 R&B, 1990), yielded three R&B Top Ten singles in 1991: "Let's Chill" (#3), "Do Me Right" (#2), and "D-O-G Me Out" (#8).

Guy split up soon afterward, with the Hall brothers pursuing solo careers and Riley developing his own production company and continuing his collaborations with major artists. He worked extensively on Michael Jackson's *Dangerous* album, and with the hip-hop acts Wreckx-N-Effect, Kool Moe Dee, and SWV. In 1994 Riley formed Blackstreet with Chauncey "Black" Hannibal, Dave Hollister, and Levi Little; as a pledge of allegiance to the group, each member had the band's name tattooed on his arm. Blackstreet's self-titled album was a Top Ten R&B hit and spawned the single "Before I Let You Go" (#2 R&B, 1995).

GWAR
Formed 1985, Richmond, Virginia
Odorus Urungus (b. David Brockie, Aug. 30, 1963, Oshawa, Ontario, Can.), voc.; Balsac the Jaws of Death (b. Michael Derks, June 28, 1968, Va.), gtr.; Flattus Maximus (b. Peter Lee, Dec. 20, 1967, Tex.), gtr.; Beefcake the Mighty (b. Michael Bishop, Sep. 7, 1968, Hawaii), bass; Jizmak the Gusha (b. Brad Roberts, Nov. 6, 1967, Mich.), drums; Slymenstra Hymen (b. Danyelle Stampe, Nov. 27, 1967, Calif.), whips; Sexicutioner (b. Charles Varga, May 21, 1958, Va.), chains; Sampler Sound-EFX (b. David Musel, Jan. 23, 1962, Iowa), tapes, electronics;
Techno-Destructo (b. Hunter Jackson, Sep. 15, 1959, Va.), voc.; Sleazy P. Martini (b. Don Drakulich, Oct. 9, 1960, Washington, D.C.), mgr.
1988—*Hell-o* (Shimmy Disc) 1990—*Scumdogs of the Universe* (Metal Blade) 1992—*America Must Be Destroyed* 1994—*This Toilet Earth.*

The alleged spawn of aliens from Uranus stranded in Antarctica (actually musicians, dancers, and art students at Virginia Commonwealth University), GWAR—an acronym for "God What an Awful Racket"—is in fact a theatrical speed-metal shock-rock troupe from Virginia, which draws on Alice Cooper, professional wrestling, and splatter films.

GWAR's members perform such songs as "Vlad the Impaler" and "Maggots Are Falling Like Rain" in grotesque, outsized masks and costumes, while enacting mock-pagan rituals, with fake (and washable) bodily fluids spewing over the audience from decapitated limbs and impaled bodies. Some say that without the onstage spectacle, GWAR's albums are beside the point; for them, there's GWAR's long-form home video, *Phallus in Wonderland,* which was nominated for a 1993 Grammy.

GWAR has had some shows canceled by fearful authorities in England. After a 1990 performance in Charlotte, North Carolina, GWAR was banned from playing there for a year, and David Brockie was fined for disseminating obscenity. In 1993, police in Athens, Georgia, shut down a GWAR show; the band, backed by the American Civil Liberties Union, sued the city, which settled out of court; the band donated its winnings to charity.

Sammy Hagar

Born October 13, 1947, Monterey, California
1976—*Nine on a Ten Scale* (Capitol)   1977—*Sammy*
Hagar*   1978—*Musical Chairs*; *All Night Long
1979—*Street Machine*   1980—*Danger Zone*; *Loud*
***and Clear*   1982—*Standing Hampton* (Geffen);**
Three Lock Box*; *Rematch* (Capitol)   1984—*VOA
(Geffen)   1987—*Sammy Hagar*   1994—*Unboxed.*

Best known as the successor to Van Halen frontman
David Lee Roth, whom he replaced in 1985, Sammy
Hagar entered the rock market as lead vocalist with
Montrose [see entry], and he went solo in 1975. Years
of touring as an arena-show opening act made him a
middle-level star, and in certain areas—St. Louis, Washington, Detroit—he became a headliner.

As a teenager, Hagar considered following his father
into the boxing ring, but by age 19 he was supporting
himself as a musician in Southern California bar bands.
After seven years of beer-joint one-nighters, he began a
two-year stint with Montrose in 1973. His first solo disc
picked up some AOR airplay with a cover of Van Morrison's "Flamingos Fly," but it wasn't until 1977, when he
formed his own band, that his career gained momentum.

Hagar gathered three Montrose alumni: bassist Bill
Church, keyboardist Alan Fitzgerald, and drummer Den-
nis Carmasi (who replaced original drummer Scott
Matthews and was later replaced by Chuck Ruff), and
guitarist David Lewark (later replaced by Gary Pihl). The
Sammy Hagar Band began touring widely in the late
Seventies, opening for Boston, Electric Light Orchestra,
Kansas, Foghat, Kiss, and other high-volume bands. His
late-Seventies releases all sold in the 100,000-to-200,000
range. Hagar had a Top Twenty hit with "Your Love Is
Driving Me Crazy" from *Three Lock Box*. *VOA* (#32, 1984)
went platinum and yielded a hit in "I Can't Drive 55"
(#26, 1984), an anthemic protest against the lowering of
highway speed limits. Two years after joining Van Halen
[see entry], Hagar released an eponymous solo album
(#14, 1987) which produced the hit single "Give to Live"
(#23, 1987).

Nina Hagen

Born Katherina Hagen, March 11, 1955, East Berlin,
Germany
1980—*Nina Hagen Band* EP (Columbia)   1982—
Nunsexmonkrock*   1983—*Fearless*   1985—*Nina
***Hagen in Ekstasy*   1988—*Punk Wedding* EP (Amok,**
Can.)   1989—*Nina Hagen* (Mercury, Ger.).

Singing about God and flying saucers in an operatic
punk howl, Nina Hagen is one of the most eccentric
artists rock has known and a vital link in the chain connecting prepunk conceptual artist Yoko Ono with postpunk performance artist Diamanda Galas. Hagen was
born into an artistic family in Communist Germany. She

sang for her first band in 1972, performing blues and Janis Joplin and Tina Turner covers—an emotive vocal training that shaped her own work. She studied music in school in 1973. One of her early bands, Automobil, did performances that combined the formats of a rock concert and a dance-music club, long before British raves.

Hagen renounced her Eastern bloc citizenship and moved to West Berlin in 1976, when her stepfather, a dissident songwriter, was exiled. Already known west of the Berlin Wall, Hagen immediately signed with CBS in Germany. She spent time in London, working with the Slits and discovering punk. She formed a band with other Germans, and their first album, *Nina Hagen Band,* became a European smash. Hagen ignored her success and moved to Holland to hang with Herman Brood, with whom she appeared in the film *Cha Cha,* along with singer Lene Lovich. She became infamous for such antics as demonstrating masturbation techniques on Austrian TV. In 1979 she was contractually obligated to rejoin her band, and *Unbehagen,* their second album, immediately went gold in Germany.

Hagen's debut American release featured two tracks each from her first two albums, including "African Reggae" and German versions of the Tubes' "White Punks on Dope" and Lovich's "Lucky Number." She recorded *Nunsexmonkrock* in New York with a band including Paul Shaffer and Chris Spedding; she sang in English but, with her voice wildly changing pitches and tone, she evoked Babylon. Hagen's religious interests took on a new thematic twist after she claimed to have seen a UFO in Malibu in 1981: The deities in her songs rode in flying saucers on *Fearless.* The dance-music album was produced by Giorgio Moroder and Keith Forsey and featured the club hit "New York New York" and the Red Hot Chili Peppers rapping on "What It Is."

Nina Hagen in Ekstasy mixed dance, punk, and metal sounds; the album included covers of "My Way" and Norman Greenbaum's "Spirit in the Sky." Unable to land even a novelty hit, Hagen stopped recording for CBS. In 1987 the singer's marriage to a teenage fan became a cause célèbre, something she celebrated on her Canadian EP *Punk Wedding. Nina Hagen* featured "Viva Las Vegas," a cover of Joplin's "Move Over," and "Ave Maria."

Merle Haggard

Born April 6, 1937, Bakersfield, California
1969—*Okie from Muskogee* (Capitol) 1970—*The Fightin' Side of Me* 1972—*The Best of Merle Haggard* 1976—*Songs I'll Always Sing* 1977—*A Working Man Can't Get Anywhere Today* 1981—*Songs for the Mama Who Tried* (MCA) 1982—*Big City* (Epic); *Poncho and Lefty* (with Willie Nelson); *Going Where the Lonely Go* 1985—*Kern River* 1986—*A Friend in California* 1987—*Walking the

Line **(with George Jones and Willie Nelson);** *Seashores of Old Mexico* **(with Willie Nelson)** **1990—*Blue Jungle* (Curb) 1994—*Merle Haggard 1994* 1995—*The Lonesome Fugitive: The Merle Haggard Anthology (1963–1977)* (Razor & Tie).**

One of country music's most gifted and prolific songwriters, Merle Haggard symbolizes the American workingman—dignified, downtrodden, and not unlikely to visit the neighborhood bar—of whom he often sings. He is also a staunch upholder of musical traditions, particularly Western swing, and he leads one of country music's most improvisatory bands. Though an outspoken critic of the Nashville star system, Haggard was inducted into the Country Music Hall of Fame in 1994; that same year he was feted with two simultaneous tribute albums, one consisting of country superstars, the other a group of rootsy country mavericks. Haggard himself fits equally into both camps.

Haggard was born to a family of transplanted Oklahomans who were living in a converted boxcar in California. When he was nine, his father died of a brain tumor. He quit school in the eighth grade and hopped a freight train at age 14. Through the end of his teens, he mostly roamed the Southwest. Haggard had been in and out of reformatories—from which he frequently escaped—by the age of 14 for such petty crimes as car theft. A 20-year-old married father, he was arrested for breaking into a cafe (drunk, he thought the booming business was closed) and spent nearly three years in San Quentin. He was paroled in 1960. (In 1972 then–California governor Ronald Reagan expunged Haggard's criminal record, granting him a full pardon.)

After prison, Haggard went back to Bakersfield and worked for his brother digging ditches. He started playing lead guitar in a local country band, and by 1962, when he went to Las Vegas to back singer Wynn Stewart, Haggard had decided to make music his career. In 1963 he formed an enduring partnership with Lewis Talley and Fuzzy Owen, the owners of Tally Records, an independent label in the Bakersfield area for which Haggard made his early recordings. In 1963, Haggard's first release sold only 200 copies, but his second, "Sing a Sad Song," made #19 on the *Billboard* country chart. He recorded with Tally through 1965, and Owen remains one of Haggard's close associates. But after Haggard's third single, "(All My Friends Are Gonna Be) Strangers," hit the C&W Top Ten, he was signed by Capitol.

Haggard formed his own backing group, the Strangers, with whom he began touring an average of about 200 nights a year. (The Strangers released their first album of instrumentals in 1970.) After Haggard's first marriage ended in divorce, he married Buck Owens' ex-wife, singer Bonnie Owens. He had previously recorded with her for Tally, but their duet career began in earnest with their first joint Capitol LP, *Just Between the Two of Us*, in 1965. They shared hit records, tours, and awards until their divorce in 1978. (A few years later, Owens returned to touring and recording as a backup singer with Haggard.)

In 1966 "Swinging Doors" and "The Bottle Let Me Down" hit the Top Five on the country chart, and later in the year "The Fugitive" became his first country #1, as he was voted the Academy of Country Music's Top Male Vocalist of the Year. He has amassed more than 90 country chart singles since—including 38 #1 hits—and had at least one Top Five country hit every year between 1966 and 1987. Among his biggest hits are "Mama Tried," "Sing Me Back Home," "Hungry Eyes," "It's Not Love (But It's Not Bad)," "Everybody's Had the Blues," "If We Make It Through December," "It's All in the Movies," and "Big City." Of the hundreds of songs he's written, many have become country standards (his "Today I Started Loving You Again" has been recorded by more than 400 artists). Haggard became a controversial figure during the Vietnam War era by extolling the virtues of patriotism in "The Fightin' Side of Me" and "Okie from Muskogee."

But Haggard was more a traditionalist than a hardline conservative. His many recordings—more than 65 albums since 1963—include a tribute to Western swing pioneer Bob Wills, *A Tribute to the Best Damn Fiddle Player in the World*; a gospel tribute, *A Land of Many Churches*, which included backing from the Carter Family; *I Love Dixie Blues*, a 1974 tribute to Dixieland jazz recorded in New Orleans; and *Same Train, a Different Time*, in honor of his first idol, Jimmie Rodgers. He played at the White House in 1973 for President Nixon and his family, and later for the Reagans at their California ranch. His music was part of the Apollo 16 mission to the moon, per the crew's request.

In 1978 he married one of his backup singers, Leona Williams; that marriage also ended in divorce. (Briefly married for a fourth time, he married again in the early Nineties. He has two young children with his fifth wife, and with his first, three grown children, two of whom have pursued country-music careers.) In 1981 Haggard published an autobiography (cowritten with Peggy Russell), *Sing Me Back Home*.

An occasional actor as well as singer, he appeared on TV in *The Waltons* and *Centennial*. He made his movie debut in 1968's *Killers Three* and was featured the next year in *From Nashville with Music*. In 1980 he made a cameo appearance in *Bronco Billy,* singing a duet with Clint Eastwood, "Bar Room Buddies" (#1 C&W, 1980). In addition to Bonnie Owens and Leona Williams, Haggard has also recorded duets with both George Jones and Willie Nelson.

Haggard's hits began to wind down in the late Eighties as the new "hat acts" began to monopolize the country charts. He moved from Epic to Curb and re-

leased 1990's *Blue Jungle.* After 25 years on the road, Haggard curtailed touring to an extent, spending more time on his ranch near Lake Shasta. Just after the release of his first album in four years, *Merle Haggard 1994,* Arista/Nashville issued *Mama's Hungry Eyes: A Tribute to Merle Haggard,* with tracks by Clint Black, Brooks and Dunn, Alan Jackson, Vince Gill, and Alabama, among others. Concurrently, the independent, California-based label, Hightone, released *Tulare Dust: A Songwriters' Tribute to Merle Haggard,* with contributions from Lucinda Williams, Dwight Yoakam, Joe Ely, John Doe (X), Dave Alvin (the Blasters), Billy Joe Shaver, and others.

Haircut 100

Formed 1980, Beckenham, England
Nick Heyward (b. May 20, 1961, Beckenham), voc.; Les Nemes (b. Dec. 5, 1960, Croydon, Eng.), bass; Graham Jones (b. July 8, 1961, Bridlington, Eng.), gtr.; Memphis Blair Cunningham (b. Oct. 11, 1957, New York City, N.Y.), drums; Phil Smith (b. May 1, 1959, Redbridge, Eng.), gtr.; Mark Fox (b. Feb. 13, 1958), perc., voc.
1982—*Pelican West* (Arista)   1983—(– Heyward) *Paint and Paint* (Polydor, U.K.).
Nick Heyward solo: 1983—*North of a Miracle* (Arista)   1987—*Postcards from Home*   1989—*I Love You Avenue* (Reprise)   1993—*From Monday to Sunday* (Epic).

Though it claims but one U.S. Top Forty hit, 1982's "Love Plus One," Haircut 100's name still evokes an early-Eighties wave of pretty English boys making fluffy dance pop and ingratiating bubblegum soul. Haircut 100 did enjoy greater (albeit shortlived) success in its native U.K., where the quintet's debut album, *Pelican West* (#2 U.K., 1982), spawned the hits "Favourite Shirts (Boy Meets Girl)" (#4 U.K., 1981) and "Fantastic Day" (#9 U.K., 1982) in addition to "Love Plus One" (#3, 1982). Critics praised the group for its savvy incorporation of Latin rhythms and jazz-funk textures, but scoffed at Nick Heyward's fey vocals and the band's preening image. Heyward soon decided to pursue a solo career, and percussionist Mark Fox took over lead vocals for Haircut's followup LP, *Paint and Paint,* which never reached American shores and failed to chart in England. The group split up shortly afterward. Heyward made pleasurable, disposable pop albums on his own, while drummer Memphis Blair Cunningham later played in one of the Pretenders' numerous lineups.

Bill Haley

Born July 6, 1925, Highland Park, Michigan; died February 9, 1981, Harlingen, Texas
1955—*Rock Around the Clock* (Decca)   1968—*Greatest Hits* (MCA)   1974—*Golden Hits.*

Bill Haley emerged from country music with "Rock Around the Clock," a rockabilly song that made him a teen idol. He cut his first record, "Candy Kisses," when he was 18, then hit the road for four years as a singer and guitarist with various country & western bands. In 1948 he became a disc jockey at WPWA in Chester, Pennsylvania. Calling himself the Ramblin' Yodeler, he put together a band, the Four Aces of Western Swing, to perform regularly on his radio show. With another group—first called the Down Homers, then the Saddlemen—he recorded country songs that quickly disappeared into obscurity. In 1950 they were signed to a Philadelphia label, Essex, and recorded a handful of country sides before covering Jackie Brenston's 1951 R&B hit, "Rocket 88." That record sold only 10,000 copies, but the song convinced Haley that high-energy music that kids could sing along to, clap to, and dance to—something like black R&B—would prove popular.

In 1952 he dropped his cowboy image altogether, changed the group's name to Bill Haley and His Comets, and covered another R&B hit, "Rock the Joint," which sold 75,000 copies. A Haley original, "Crazy Man Crazy," was covered by one Ralph Marterie and given extensive airplay, but Haley's own more rambunctious version was the one sought in record shops, and in 1953 it became the first rock & roll record to make the *Billboard* pop chart.

In 1954 Haley left Essex and signed with Decca under producer Milt Gabler. His first record for his new label was a song written by Jimmy DeKnight and his manager, Dave Myers, and originally recorded in 1952 by Sunny Dae: "Rock Around the Clock." It sold only moderately when first released in spring 1954, but its followup, a cover of Joe Turner's "Shake, Rattle and Roll," hit the Top Ten both in the U.K. and in the U.S., eventually selling a million copies. When "Rock Around the Clock" was rereleased in 1955 it rose to #1. The song was included on the soundtrack of *Blackboard Jungle,* a 1955 movie about juvenile delinquents, and it led viewers to identify the balding Haley as a young rebel. Throughout 1955 and 1956 he was the most popular rock & roll performer in the world, and within those two years he had 12 U.S. Top Forty records, including "See You Later Alligator," "Burn That Candle," "Dim, Dim the Lights," "Razzle-Dazzle," and "R-O-C-K."

In Britain, where authentic rock & rollers were scarcer than in America, he was even more popular: His visit there in February 1957 met with wild enthusiasm. But already his star was descending in America. High exposure (he starred in two Hollywood movies, *Rock Around the Clock* and *Don't Knock the Rock*) revealed him to be a pudgy, rather stiff, hardly rebellious family man. His last Top Forty hit was "Skinny Minnie" in 1958. While he never attempted to modernize his sound or his image, Haley continued to work as a nostalgia act, especially in Britain and Germany, where he was always treated as a star ("Rock Around the Clock" reentered the U.K. pop chart seven times, most recently in 1974). In 1969 and through the early Seventies, Bill Haley and His Comets traveled with the Rock 'n' Roll Revival Shows promoted by Richard Nader and documented in a 1973 movie, *Let the Good Times Roll.* By the time of Haley's death from a heart attack, he had sold an estimated 60 million records; "Rock Around the Clock" alone has sold over 22 million copies worldwide. He was among the first inductees into the Rock and Roll Hall of Fame, in 1986. The Comets, meanwhile, continue to perform.

Aaron Hall, Damion Hall: See Guy

Daryl Hall and John Oates
Formed 1969, Philadelphia, Pennsylvania
Daryl Hall (b. Oct. 11, 1949, Pottstown, Pa.); John Oates (b. Apr. 7, 1949, New York City, N.Y.).
1972—*Whole Oates* (Atlantic)   1973—*Abandoned Luncheonette*   1974—*War Babies*   1975—*Daryl Hall and John Oates* (RCA)   1976—*Bigger Than Both of Us*   1977—*No Goodbyes* (Atlantic); *Beauty on a Back Street* (RCA)   1978—*Along the Red Ledge; Live Time*   1979—*X-Static*   1980—*Voices* 1981—*Private Eyes*   1982—*H₂O*   1983—*Rock 'n' Soul, Part 1*   1984—*Big Bam Boom*   1985—*Live at the Apollo with David Ruffin and Eddie Kendrick* 1988—*Ooh Yeah!* (Arista)   1990—*Change of Season.* Daryl Hall solo: 1980—*Sacred Songs* (RCA)   1986— *Three Hearts in the Happy Ending Machine* 1993—*Soul Alone* (Epic).

Daryl Hall and John Oates' blend of rock and R&B kept them on the singles chart throughout the Seventies and Eighties. They are the #1 charting duo in rock & roll history. Both were raised in Philadelphia suburbs. Oates had moved there at age four from New York City, and he began playing guitar at age eight. Hall studied voice and piano. As teens, the two frequented Philadelphia ghettos, where they joined doo-wop groups. In 1967 Hall recorded a single with Kenny Gamble and the Romeos (which included future producers Gamble, Leon Huff, and Thom Bell). He met Oates later that year when his group, the Temptones, and Oates' group, the Masters, competed in a battle of the bands at Philadelphia's Adelphi Ballroom; they shared a freight elevator while escaping a gang fight. At Temple University Oates earned a degree in journalism, and Hall studied music but dropped out in his senior term.

Hall formed Gulliver, a group that recorded one LP on Elektra in 1969, and Oates joined before it disbanded. Oates then traveled to Europe, and Hall became a studio musician, singing backup for the Delfonics, the Stylistics, and the Intruders. Upon Oates' return, the two de-

Daryl Hall and John Oates

cided to team up. In 1972 they signed with Atlantic Records and released their Arif Mardin–produced debut, *Whole Oates*, a folky album that attracted little attention. Their next LP, the R&B-oriented *Abandoned Luncheonette* (also produced by Mardin), yielded "She's Gone," a flop for Hall and Oates but a #1 R&B hit for Tavares six months later. In 1974 the two recorded *War Babies*, a concept LP, with producer Todd Rundgren. A drastic departure from their earlier efforts, the LP sold 100,000 copies in the New York area. Citing a lack of hit singles and stylistic inconsistency, Atlantic dropped them, but in 1976 the rereleased version of "She's Gone" made #7.

Their RCA debut (*Daryl Hall and John Oates*) contained "Sara Smile," a #4 hit cowritten by Hall for his frequent collaborator/girlfriend Sara Allen (whose sister Janna Allen cowrote "Kiss on My List," "Private Eyes," and other Hall and Oates songs; she died of leukemia in 1993). With the release of 1976's *Bigger Than Both of Us*, the two previous albums went gold. *Bigger* eventually became their first platinum LP and contained their first #1 single, "Rich Girl."

Hall, the more prolific writer of the two, began working with Robert Fripp on a solo LP, *Sacred Songs*, which RCA refused to release until 1980. He also sang on Fripp's *Exposure*. Yet apart from the Top Twenty "It's a Laugh" from *Along the Red Ledge* and "Wait for Me" from *X-Static*, the duo hit a late-Seventies commercial slump. Hall and Oates retrenched and decided to produce their next LP themselves. The result, 1980's platinum *Voices*, returned the duo to the singles chart with a vengeance, with "How Does It Feel to Be Back" (#30), "Kiss on My List" (#1), a cover of the Righteous Brothers' "You've Lost That Loving Feeling" (#12), and "You Make My Dreams" (#5). The following year's *Private Eyes* was similarly successful; the title cut and "I Can't Go for That

(No Can Do)" were both #1, while "Did It in a Minute" went Top Ten. H_2O yielded still more hits with "Maneater" (#1), "Family Man" (#6), and "One on One" (#7). Even the two new songs included on a best-of LP, the double-platinum *Rock 'n' Soul, Part 1*, cracked the Top Ten: "Say It Isn't So" (#2, 1983) and "Adult Education" (#8, 1984). *Big Bam Boom* incorporated a marked hip-hop influence and produced Hall and Oates' sixth and last #1 hit, "Out of Touch," as well as "Method of Modern Love" (#5, 1985), "Some Things Are Better Left Unsaid" (#18, 1985), and "Possession Obsession" (#30, 1985). After a live LP recorded at Harlem's Apollo Theatre with former Temptations Eddie Kendricks (or Kendrick, as he was billed at the time) and David Ruffin, Hall and Oates took a three-year sabbatical, during which time Hall released a second solo album, *Three Hearts in the Happy Ending Machine*. Its "Dreamtime" went Top Five in 1986.

Hall and Oates resumed recording in 1988, but this third career phase was noticeably less successful. Their two albums, *Ooh Yeah!* and *Change of Season*, contained only one hit apiece: "Everything Your Heart Desires" (#3, 1988) and "So Close" (#11, 1990). As of Hall's third solo effort, 1993's glossy *Soul Alone*, the pair had no plans to record together again. Oates was working on his first solo album.

John Hall: See Orleans

Tom T. Hall
Born Thomas Hall, May 25, 1936, Olive Hill, Kentucky
1971—*In Search of a Song*   1972—*We All Got Together And. . .*; *The Storyteller*   1973—*The Rhymer and Other Five and Dimers*   1974—*For the People in the Last Hard Town*   1975—*Songs of Fox Hollow*.

If any writer understood that the key to the durable country song was in the tale told, it was Tom T. Hall, dubbed "the Storyteller." His songs placed a premium on narrative, exemplified by Hall's most popular tune, "Harper Valley P.T.A." By the time he was nine years old Hall was already writing songs. As a teenager he played guitar in a bluegrass band and eventually landed a job as a disc jockey. Upon returning from the army in 1961 he enrolled at Roanoke College in Virginia where he studied literature, while continuing to write songs. Hall met with quick acclaim; Dave Dudley, Bobby Bare, and Burl Ives cut his songs.

By 1964 Hall had moved to Nashville, where he began a recording career of his own. His first single, "I Washed My Face in the Morning Dew" (1967), hit the C&W Top Forty. The next year Hall's "Harper Valley P.T.A." (as recorded by Jeannie C. Riley) went to #1 on the pop chart, sold six million records, won Hall a

Grammy for Best Song of the Year and a Country Music Association award for Single of the Year.

Hall's most acclaimed songs of the Seventies, including "The Year That Clayton Delaney Died" and "(Old Dogs, Children and) Watermelon Wine," relate vivid, detailed stories made all the more powerful for their economy of means. In 1973 Hall had his biggest pop hit, "I Love" (#12). Hall's "I Can't Dance" was also recorded by Gram Parsons, and Leo Kottke cut the ironic "Pamela Brown."

Carrying over the literary bent of his songwriting to more traditional avenues, Hall has published a novel, *The Laughing Man of Woodmont Cove*, and an artist's guide, *The Songwriter's Handbook*, and has had several short stories anthologized.

Johnny Hallyday

Born Jean-Phillippe Smet, June 15, 1943, Paris, France
1962—*Johnny Hallyday Sings America's Rockin' Hits* (Philips).

A major rock star in Europe in the early and mid-Sixties, Johnny Hallyday made his career covering the American and British hits of the day for continental rock fans. Hallyday (who came by his English surname through an uncle, Lee Hallyday) was adopted at a young age by an aunt. He became part of Lee Hallyday's song-and-dance act, then, after picking up a guitar, set his sights on rock & roll. Billed as the French Elvis but with a style closer to Cliff Richard's, Hallyday reached his zenith in the pre-Beatlemania era, when his stage shows caused riots in France. His biggest hit was a multilingual reading of "Let's Twist Again" ("Viens Danser le Twist"), which sold a million copies in 1961. The following year saw the release of his most successful album, *Johnny Hallyday Sings America's Rockin' Hits*, which helped institutionalize cover versions as a marketing strategy overseas.

As the decade progressed, Hallyday traveled to London and Memphis to record, searching for authentic backing tracks for his revamps of hits by others. With the advent of the Beatles, Hallyday's career lost most of its momentum, but he remained a star in his homeland for several more years. By the late Sixties, young rock talent was often shipped over from England to play on Hallyday's sessions, among them Jimmy Page, Humble Pie's Steve Marriott, Peter Frampton, and Mick Jones, later of Foreigner (who wrote some songs for Hallyday). Hallyday's ex-wife, Sylvie Vartan, was also a popular singer in France in the Sixties. In 1964 she opened concerts for the Beatles at Paris' Olympic Theatre. Hallyday continues to record in French and perform throughout Europe.

Roy Hamilton

Born April 16, 1929, Leesburg, Georgia; died July 20, 1969
1956—*Roy Hamilton* (Epic); *You'll Never Walk Alone* 1962—*Mr. Rock and Soul* 1991—*Golden Classics* (Collectables).

Roy Hamilton's late-Fifties work was characterized by a blend of R&B and gospel strains that influenced Jerry Butler and the Righteous Brothers. Hamilton grew up in Jersey City, where he sang with the Searchlight Gospel Singers in 1948. Impressed by his powerful baritone, local disc jockey Bill Cook became his manager and in the early Fifties got him a contract with Epic.

Hamilton's career took off in 1954 with "You'll Never Walk Alone," which topped the R&B chart but didn't dent the pop Top 100. He became a major attraction in black nightclubs, and by 1955 he was enjoying limited crossover success with "Everybody's Got a Home" (#42) and "Without a Song" (#77). Additionally, Hamilton released "Unchained Melody." It was the best-selling R&B record of 1955, but competing cover versions by mainstream pop artists Les Baxter and Al Hibbler kept Hamilton's version from the pop chart. Hamilton had pop hits with "Don't Let Go" (#13, 1958), "Pledging My Love" (#45, 1958), "I Need Your Lovin'" (#62, 1959), "Time Marches On" (#84, 1959), and "You Can Have Her" (#12, 1961). Hamilton's career nosedived after his success early in the Sixties, despite recordings for MGM, RCA, and AGP. He died from a heart attack in 1969.

Hammer

Born Stanley Kirk Burrell, March 30, 1963, Oakland, California
As M.C. Hammer: 1988—*Feel My Power* (Bust It); *Let's Get It Started* (Capitol) 1990—*Please Hammer Don't Hurt 'Em*.
As Hammer: 1991—*Too Legit to Quit* (Capitol) 1994—*The Funky Headhunter* (Giant).

Savvy entrepreneur, showman extraordinaire, product pitchman, inspiration for both a doll and a Saturday morning cartoon, and African-American role model, M.C. Hammer appeared to be the rap incarnation of James Brown after the release of his #1 pop album, *Please Hammer Don't Hurt 'Em*. His massive success proved short-lived, however.

Growing up in the rougher precincts of Oakland, Stanley Kirk Burrell had two interests: performing and baseball. Combining them, he'd dance in the parking lot of the Oakland Coliseum, home of the baseball A's. Discovered there by the team's owner, Charlie Finley, Burrell was hired as a bat boy and soon became the team's unofficial mascot. The players nicknamed him Little Hammer because he resembled home-run king "Hammerin'"

Hank Aaron. Two players, Mike Davis and Dwayne Murphy, gave more, each investing $20,000 in Hammer's Bust It Records, started after an abortive attempt to break into pro ball and a three-year hitch in the Navy.

Hammer's first single, "Ring 'Em," sold by Hammer and his wife, became a #1 Bay Area hit. His debut album, *Feel My Power*, coproduced by Con Funk Shun producer Felton Pilate, sold 60,000 copies. Spotted in the audience at a club by a Capitol Records exec, who "didn't know who he was, but knew he was somebody," the label found out soon enough, handing Hammer a multialbum deal and a $750,000 advance. His first Capitol release, *Let's Get It Started*, a revamped version of *Power*, eventually sold two million copies.

Recorded on the back of his tour bus for less than $10,000, *Please Hammer Don't Hurt 'Em* sold more than ten million copies, holding the #1 position for a record-shattering 21 weeks. Buttressed by an elaborate, 30-member stage show, Hammer became a household word, appearing in Pepsi ads, heavy MTV rotation, and his own kids'cartoon, *Hammerman*. He also branched out, into management (Oaktown's 3.5.7), horse racing, and his own Help the Children Foundation.

This kind of success breeds controversy, and some rappers publicly "dissed" Hammer's mainstream style and extravagant clothes (billowy harem-style pants), calling him a sellout. In 1990 Rick James sued Hammer over the sampling of "Super Freak" in "U Can't Touch This" (#8, 1990). Settling out of court, James was given cowriter credit.

For *Too Legit to Quit*, Hammer dropped the "M.C." from his name and saw his audience drop with it. Selling a more-than-respectable three million copies, *Too Legit* was a disappointment, though, and a planned world tour was canceled midway. Hammer returned in 1994 with *The Funky Headhunter*, which featured the singles "It's All Good" (#14 R&B) and "Pumps and a Bump" (#26 pop, #22 R&B).

Peter Hammill: See Van Der Graaf Generator

John Hammond

Born John Paul Hammond, November 13, 1943, New York City, New York
1962—*John Hammond* (Vanguard)   1964—*Big City Blues*; *Country Blues*   1965—*So Many Roads*   1967—*Mirrors*; *I Can Tell* (Atlantic)   1968—*Sooner or Later*   1969—*Southern Fried*   1970—*The Best of John Hammond* (Vanguard); *Source Point* (Columbia)   1971—*Dustin Hoffman as Little Big Man* soundtrack   1972—*I'm Satisfied*   1973—*When I Need*; *Triumvirate* (with Michael Bloomfield and Dr. John); *Spirituals to Swing* (Vanguard)   1975—*Can't*

Beat the Kid (Capricorn); *My Spanish Album* (Coytronics)   1976—*John Hammond: Solo* (Vanguard)   1978—*Footwork*   1979—*Hot Tracks*   1980—*Mileage* (Sonet)   1982—*Frogs for Snakes* (Rounder)   1984—*John Hammond Live in Greece* (Lyra)   1988—*Nobody But You* (Flying Fish)   1992—*Got Love If You Want It* (Pointblank)   1994—*Trouble No More.*

John Hammond is a white blues singer and the son of talent scout/producer John Hammond. He studied art and sculpture in his youth and he became interested in country and Delta blues. While attending Antioch College in Yellow Springs, Ohio, Hammond learned guitar and harmonica and started singing.

His professional career began in New York in 1963, when he recorded an acoustic blues album for Vanguard. He continued to record regularly for Vanguard in the early Sixties. In late 1963 he met some musicians who were backing rockabilly singer Ronnie Hawkins in a Toronto bar. Hammond enticed the group, the Hawks (who would later become the Band), to come with him to New York. They backed Hammond until they were lured away by Bob Dylan (a discovery of Hammond's father). In the mid-Sixties his backing band included, briefly, Jimi Hendrix.

Hammond played clubs regularly in the late Sixties and many small concert venues (the Fillmores, Matrix Ballroom) as well. In 1970 he performed on the soundtrack of the Dustin Hoffman film *Little Big Man*. The following year he recorded an album with bluesman Larry Johnson for the Biograph label. In 1973 he recorded for Columbia as part of a short-lived supergroup called Triumvirate, which also included Dr. John and Mike Bloomfield. By the late Seventies he was still playing clubs and touring internationally (he released a live album recorded in Greece in 1984). While staying true to the blues, Hammond has recorded in a variety of settings, often with name backing: Robbie Robertson, Garth Hudson, and Levon Helm of the Band, and Blues Project's Mike Bloomfield (on piano) on the mid-Sixties albums *So Many Roads* and *Mirrors*; Robertson, the Band's Rick Danko, and Rolling Stone Bill Wyman on *I Can Tell*; Duane Allman on *Southern Fried*; blues pianist Roosevelt Sykes on *Footwork*; J. J. Cale and John Lee Hooker on the Grammy-nominated *Got Love If You Want It*; and Cale and blues singer Charles Brown on *Trouble No More.*

Herbie Hancock

Born April 12, 1940, Chicago, Illinois
1963—*Takin' Off* (Blue Note)   1964—*Empyrean Isles*   1965—*Inventions and Dimensions*   1966—*My Point of View*   1967—*Blow-Up* soundtrack (MGM)   1968—*Maiden Voyage* (Blue Note)   1969—*Speak Like a Child*; *The Prisoner*   1971—*Mwandishi* (Warner Bros.)   1972—*Crossing*; *Sextant*

Herbie Hancock

(Columbia) 1973—*Headhunters* 1974—*Thrust*;
Fat Albert Rotunda (Warner Bros.) 1975—*Best of*
(Columbia); *Death Wish* soundtrack; *Manchild*
1976—*Live in Japan* (Columbia/Sony import); *Hancock* (Blue Note); *Secrets* (Columbia); *Kawaida*
(DJM/ import) 1977—*Flood* (Columbia); *Herbie*
Hancock Trio; Live Under the Sky (Columbia/Sony
import); *V.S.O.P.* (Columbia) 1978—*Sunlight*; *Quintet* (Columbia, U.K.); *Tempest in the Colosseum* (Columbia/Sony import) 1979—*An Evening with*
(Columbia, U.K.); *Corea/Hancock* (Polydor); *Feets*
Don't Fail Me Now (Columbia) 1980—*Monster*
1981—*Mr. Hands* 1982—*Magic Windows*; *Light Me*
Up; *The Quartet* 1983—*Future Shock* 1984—
Sound-System 1988—*Perfect Machine* 1994—*A*
Tribute to Miles (Qwest) 1995—*Dis Is Da Drum*
(Mercury).

Keyboardist Herbie Hancock first came to prominence as
the pianist in Miles Davis' landmark mid-Sixties quintet,
a unit that went from refined postbop chamber jazz to
pioneering electric fusion. The latter spurred Hancock
on to a funk-fusion direction of his own. Once he established himself commercially, however, Hancock divided
his time between funk and his harmonically adventurous, impressionistic acoustic jazz.

Although he had studied music, Hancock was working toward a B.A. in engineering at Grinnell College. In
1963 he came to New York City and worked with jazz
trumpeter Donald Byrd, at whose instigation Hancock
recorded his first solo LP. His "Watermelon Man" was a
pop-jazz crossover hit for Mongo Santamaria. From 1963
to 1968, Hancock worked with Miles Davis; he also
recorded solo albums and played on many sessions for
Blue Note Records. After scoring Michelangelo Antonioni's film *Blow-Up*, he left Davis and began pursuing
fusion with the 1971 album *Mwandishi*.

His breakthrough came with *Headhunters*, for which
Hancock formed the band of the same name, later explaining, "Rather than work with jazz musicians who
could play funk, I worked with funk musicians who could
play jazz." That album yielded the crossover hit "Chameleon" (#42 pop, #18 R&B, 1974). *Thrust, Manchild*, and
the *Death Wish* film soundtrack also sold well, as did *Fat*
Albert Rotunda, his soundtrack to a Bill Cosby TV cartoon special. In 1976 Hancock briefly diverged from his
electric-funk course to form V.S.O.P. (Very Special One-time Performance), an acoustic jazz group with Tony
Williams, Weather Report's Wayne Shorter, bassist Ron
Carter, and trumpeter Freddie Hubbard, playing in the
early Blue Note–Miles Davis mode. They conducted a
successful tour and recorded an album, and have since
reconvened.

Shortly thereafter, Hancock converted to Nicheran
Shoshu Buddhism and two years later undertook an
acoustic-piano duo tour with Chick Corea. In 1979 *Feets*
Don't Fail Me Now was another commercial success, as
was *Monster* in 1980. In 1981 V.S.O.P. toured and
recorded as a quartet, minus Shorter and with trumpeter
Wynton Marsalis replacing Hubbard. In 1982 Hancock
produced Wynton Marsalis' Columbia Records debut;
Hancock would later tour with Wynton and brother
Branford Marsalis.

The unexpected success of *Future Shock* and its single, "Rockit" (#71, 1983) gave Hancock even greater visibility. As produced by Bill Laswell, "Rockit" incorporated
funk rhythms and hip-hop "scratching." The accompanying video (directed by Godley and Creme) won five MTV
Video Music Awards in 1984.

Hancock also established a thriving career scoring
films, including *A Soldier's Story* (1984), *Round Midnight*
(1986), *Jo Jo Dancer Your Life Is Calling* (1986), and *Colors* (1987). Hancock won an Oscar for the *Round Midnight* soundtrack.

Though he ventures outside the genre, Hancock
never leaves jazz far behind. In 1992, Hancock organized
a "Tribute to Miles [Davis]" Tour, which included Tony
Williams, Wayne Shorter, Ron Carter, and Wallis Roney.
Hancock himself continues working in a piano trio context, displaying what is perhaps the most influential
piano style among today's post-Marsalis players. In 1994
Hancock found his music back on the pop charts in the
form of a sample—Us3 used the piano vamp from Hancock's 1964 song "Cantaloupe Island" for their jazz/hip-hop hit "Cantaloop." He also won the 1994 Grammy for
Best Jazz Instrumental Performance for his collaboration
on *A Tribute to Miles*.

Happy Mondays

Formed 1980, Manchester, England
Bez (b. Mark Berry, Apr. 18, 1964, Manchester),
perc.; Paul Davis (b. Mar. 7, 1966, Manchester),
kybds.; Mark Day (b. Dec. 29, 1961, Manchester),
gtr.; Paul Ryder (b. Apr. 24, 1964, Manchester), bass;
Shaun Ryder (b. Aug. 23, 1962, Manchester), voc.;
Gary Whelan (b. Feb. 12, 1966, Manchester), drums.
1987—*Squirrel and G-Man Twenty Four Hour Party
People Plastic Face Carnt Smile (White Out)* (Factory, U.K.) 1988—*Bummed* 1989—*Madchester,
Rave On* 1990—*Pills 'n' Thrills and Bellyaches*
(Elektra) 1991—*Live* 1992—*Yes Please* 1993—
Double Easy: The U.S. Singles.

Ecstasy-drenched and spacy, Happy Mondays dominated the British clubs and charts in the late Eighties
with their definitive acid house grooves. Led by the outspoken Shaun Ryder and featuring Bez, a dancer, Happy
Mondays practically invented the U.K. rave scene (along
with the Stone Roses) and had an almost exclusively
British following until 1990, when *Pills 'n' Thrills and
Bellyaches* (#89) caught on in the States.

Formed by Ryder and his bass-playing brother, Paul,
Happy Mondays played Manchester's Hacienda Club
before signing to Factory Records. After the band toured
with New Order, Bernard Sumner produced their second
single, "Freaky Dancin'." Their debut album, *Squirrel and
G-Man. . . ,* which John Cale produced in ten days, included the singles "Tart Tart" and "24 Hour Party People"
and established the acid house sound—bass- and drum-heavy extended dance mixes with touches of Sixties
psychedelia and Seventies R&B.

When Elektra released their second album, 1988's
Bummed, in the U.S. in 1989, it stiffed. Among other
problems, the band seemed too stoned to play their first
stateside gig. But fueled by the infectious "Step On" (#57,
1991), *Pills 'n' Thrills and Bellyaches* broke out in clubs.
The album also featured a tribute to their Sixties idol,
"Donovan" (the Ryder brothers later became romantically linked with the singer's daughters Astrella and
Oriel). A live album followed. Produced by Chris Frantz
and Tina Weymouth, *Yes Please,* along with "Cut 'Em
Loose Bruce," again hit in clubs and on modern-music
radio, but not with mainstream listeners. In 1993 the
band split up; Shaun Ryder formed a new band, Black
Grape.

Hardcore

In the early Eighties punk rock reappeared on the U.S.
West Coast in a louder, faster form known as hardcore.
Characterized by despairing, often nihilistic lyrics
screamed from a chaotic din of rapidly changing guitar
chords, it was a peculiarly American middle-class version of its artier cousin. Hardcore audiences had ex-
changed traditional punk's fashion statements (safety
pins, spiked hair, and black leather jackets) for cruder
new ones (tattoos, buzz cuts, and combat boots). And
whereas punk and new-wave fans had introduced the
pogo dance, hardcore kids originated slam dancing, or
moshing, in which members of the mostly white and
male audiences would form small pits in front of bands
and smash into one another as the music played. In addition, stage diving by audience members into the mosh
pit was a common occurrence.

Two West Coast proto-hardcore bands were the Los
Angeles–based Germs and Black Flag, each of which
formed in the late Seventies as the first wave of New York
and U.K. punk had begun to wane. Those bands' debut
albums—*GI* and *Damaged,* respectively—provided the
foundation upon which budding hardcore bands would
build. In Southern California alone, new bands popped
up like acne on a hardcore kid's face, including Agent Orange, Circle Jerks, and Fear. In San Francisco the highly
political Dead Kennedys, which formed in 1978, also provided important early inspiration, particularly for the
genre's more left-leaning adherents.

Black Flag, through its constant touring and formation of the influential DIY label SST, sparked hardcore
scenes across the country, including New York City
(Kraut, Heart Attack, early Beastie Boys), Washington,
D.C. (Minor Threat, Bad Brains), Minneapolis (Hüsker Dü,
early Replacements), Austin (the Dicks, Big Boys), and
Vancouver (Subhumans, D.O.A.). As shaved heads provided a visual invitation for a less-than-desirable constituency of white supremacist types, however, the
generally progressive hardcore scene started breaking
down. As early as 1981 the Dead Kennedys had recorded
"Nazi Punks Fuck Off" to distance "real" hardcore skinheads from the undesirable ones. By mid-decade, hardcore had begun to play itself out, splintering into thrash
and speed metal.

Tim Hardin

Born December 23, 1941, Eugene, Oregon; died December 29, 1980, Los Angeles, California
1966—*Tim Hardin I* (MGM) 1967—*Tim Hardin II*
1968—*Tim Hardin III Live in Concert* (Verve)
1969—*Tim Hardin IV; Suite for Susan Moore and
Damion—We Are—One, One, All in One* (Columbia)
1970—*The Best of Tim Hardin* (Verve) 1971—*Bird
on a Wire* (Columbia) 1973—*Painted Head; Archetypes* (MGM); *Nine* (Antilles) 1981—*Reason to Believe: The Best of Tim Hardin* (Polydor)
1994—*Hang On to a Dream: The Verve Recordings*
(Polygram Chronicles).

Singer/songwriter Tim Hardin came to prominence during the folk-blues revival in the early Sixties. He enjoyed
critical acclaim for his smoky voice but had little com-

mercial success on his own; others recorded his songs "If I Were a Carpenter" and "Reason to Believe."

Hardin traced his lineage back to the Nineteenth-century Western outlaw John Wesley Hardin. He quit high school in 1959 and joined the Marines for two years, then enrolled in the American Academy of Dramatic Art in New York, but dropped out after a week. He moved to Cambridge, Massachusetts, and began performing in the folk clubs around Harvard.

Hardin's first tapes were recorded in 1962 but weren't released until 1967, as his second album. He returned to New York in 1963 and became an influential figure in Greenwich Village folk circles, blending strains of folk, blues, and jazz and playing with a group when most folkies were strictly soloists. He began to receive national attention in 1966, the year he performed at the Newport Folk Festival, and *Tim Hardin I* picked up critical accolades. About this time, Bob Dylan named him the country's greatest living songwriter.

His songs included "If I Were a Carpenter" (covered by Johnny Cash and June Carter, Bobby Darin, the Four Tops, Bob Seger, and Robert Plant, among others), "Reason to Believe" (covered by Peter, Paul and Mary and Rod Stewart), and "Misty Roses." In the mid-Sixties he was a regular attraction on the college campus circuits both in the U.S. and in Europe. By the late Sixties, Hardin had settled in Woodstock, New York, and curtailed his performances. In 1969 he enjoyed his only Top Fifty single with Bobby Darin's "Simple Song of Freedom." Hardin's *Bird on a Wire* LP used other writers' material; its studio band included future members of East-West folk-fusion band Oregon and jazz rockers Weather Report.

In 1974 Hardin moved to southern England with his family and played regularly in English clubs. After a year, he moved back to Los Angeles. His death in his L.A. apartment at age 39 was attributed to a heroin overdose.

John Wesley Harding

Born Wesley Harding Stace, October 22, 1965, Hastings, England
1988—*It Happened One Night* (Demon, U.K.)
1989—*God Made Me Do It: The Christmas EP* (Sire)
1990—*Here Comes the Groom* 1991—*The Name Above the Title* 1992—*Why We Fight*.

John Wesley Harding took his stage name from Bob Dylan's 1968 album, but critics more often compare the handsome singer/songwriter to such Dylan heirs as Elvis Costello and Billy Bragg, punk and postpunk artists who combine trenchant wit and melodic savvy with folk rock's confessional style.

The son of two musically inclined schoolteachers—his mother had been an opera singer, his father, a jazz pianist—Harding sang and played guitar in pubs as a teenager, then pursued a Ph.D. in political and social theory at Cambridge University before deciding to make music his career in 1988. He quickly landed a deal with the U.K. label Demon Records and released the live album *It Happened One Night* (its title, like *The Name Above the Title* and *Why We Fight*, an homage to director Frank Capra) before signing to Sire. While his Sire debut LP—which featured members of Costello's band, the Attractions—drew praise for its catchy tunes and literate lyrics and spawned a successful video for the single "The Devil in Me," some detractors accused the singer of wearing his influences on his sleeve. To date, Harding, who married San Francisco–based disc jockey Denise Sullivan in 1992, has maintained a loyal cult following, promoting his records with solo acoustic performances.

Roy Harper

Born June 12, 1941, Manchester, England
1969—*Folkjokeopus* (World Pacific) 1970—*Flat Baroque and Berserk* (Harvest) 1971—*Stormcock* 1973—*Life Mask* 1974—*Valentine; Flashes from the Archives of Oblivion* 1975—*When an Old Cricketer Leaves the Crease* 1977—*One of Those Days in England* 1978—*Roy Harper 1970–75* 1980—*Unknown Soldier* (Harvest) 1985—*Whatever Happened to Jugula* (PVC) 1991—*Once* (Awareness/I.R.S.) 1994—*Unhinged* (Griffin Music).

Folksinger, songwriter, and guitarist Roy Harper is best known to American rock fans as the subject of Led Zeppelin's "Hats Off to (Roy) Harper," from its third LP. But in folk circles, and particularly in England, Harper is well known for his eccentric songs.

At age 15 he quit school and after a while joined the Royal Air Force. In an attempt to obtain a discharge, Harper pretended to be mentally ill; following his 1959 discharge he was committed to a mental institution. After his release 15 weeks later he wrote poems and songs in the streets of Blackpool. In 1964 he moved to London, and a year later began performing in clubs, part of a circle that included Jimmy Page, John Paul Jones, and Ronnie Lane. He also performed frequently in London's Hyde Park.

Harper recorded his first LP, *The Sophisticated Beggar*, for a British indie label. Beginning in 1971 with *Stormcock*, Jimmy Page began appearing on Harper's LPs. Among other musicians who have backed Harper are Pink Floyd's David Gilmour, Paul and Linda McCartney, and drummer Bill Bruford. In 1971 Harper was hospitalized with a strange illness he claims to have contracted while giving a lamb mouth-to-mouth resuscitation (actually, it was a rare congenital circulatory disorder known as multiple pulmonary arteriovenous fistula). In 1972 Harper made his film debut in the British *Made*.

Those unfamiliar with Harper's solo work have probably heard his voice: He sang lead on Pink Floyd's "Have a Cigar" from 1975's *Wish You Were Here*. He continues to tour and record in Europe, although since 1980 only four of his many records have been released in the States. *The Unknown Soldier* (1980) included "You," a duet with Kate Bush, who later appeared on Harper's LP *Once* and covered his song "Another Day."

Harper's Bizarre

Formed 1963, San Francisco, California
Ted Templeman (b. Oct. 24, 1944), lead voc.; Dick
Scoppettone (b. July 5, 1945), voc., gtr.; Eddie James
(b. Santa Cruz, Calif.), voc., gtr.; Dick Yount (b. Jan.
9, 1943, Santa Cruz, Calif.), voc., bass, gtr., drums.
1966—(+ John Peterson [b. Jan. 8, 1945, San Fran-
cisco], voc., drums)   1967—*Feelin' Groovy* (Warner
Bros.); *Anything Goes*   1968—*The Secret Life of
Harper's Bizarre*   1969—*Harper's Bizarre 4*   1970—
Best of Harper's Bizarre*   1976—*As Time Goes By
(Forest Bay).

A pop-rock group from prepsychedelic San Francisco, Harper's Bizarre had one big hit with Paul Simon's "The 59th Street Bridge Song (Feelin' Groovy)" (#13, 1967), a tune that Simon had originally offered to the Cyrkle. The group began by playing surf music in local bars, calling itself the Tikis. As such, they made their first records in the mid-Sixties for San Francisco–based Autumn Records. When Autumn went under, the Tikis became Harper's Bizarre in 1966, picked up John Peterson from another Autumn band, the Beau Brummels, and got signed to Warner Bros. Having by this time abandoned surf music for pop rock, they cut *Feelin' Groovy* with arrangements by Leon Russell. Specializing in five-part harmonies, the group revived several standards, like Cole Porter's "Anything Goes" (#43, 1967), Glenn Miller's "Chattanooga Choo Choo" (#45, 1967), and Johnny Horton's "Battle of New Orleans" (#95, 1968).

Harper's Bizarre disbanded in 1970 after recording four albums for Warner Bros. Lead singer Ted Templeman stayed on with the label and became one of its top in-house A&R men and producers (Van Morrison, the Doobie Brothers, and Van Halen, among others). Templeman also produced a 1974 album by the re-formed Beau Brummels, which included his old Harper's Bizarre mate, John Peterson.

Slim Harpo

Born James Moore, January 11, 1924, Lobdell,
Louisiana; died January 31, 1970, Baton Rouge,
Louisiana
1965—*A Long Drink of the Blues* (Stateside, U.K.)
1976—*Blues Hangover* (Flyright)   1980—*Got Love
If You Want It*   1989—*The Best of Slim Harpo*
(Rhino).

Slim Harpo was a blues singer, songwriter, guitarist, and harp player who wrote "I'm a King Bee," an early Rolling Stones showpiece. One of at least four children, Harpo grew up in Port Allen, Louisiana. His parents died while he was still a child, and he quit school to support his siblings. At age 18 he moved to New Orleans to work as a longshoreman, and later he went to Baton Rouge to work as a contractor. In the early Forties he played bars and clubs as Harmonica Slim.

Harpo met guitarist Lightnin' Slim, with whom he toured and performed (Lightnin' appeared on "Rainin' in My Heart" and "I'm a King Bee") over the next 20 years. He eventually owned his own trucking business but continued to work in clubs, often with Lightnin' Slim. He had a hit in 1961 with "Rainin' in My Heart" (#34) and in 1966 with the sly, sexual "Baby, Scratch My Back" (#16 pop, #1 R&B). He toured rock clubs through the late Sixties. Harpo died of a heart attack.

The Harptones

Formed 1953, New York City, New York
Best-known lineup: William "Willie" Winfield
(b. Aug. 24, 1929), lead tenor voc.; William "Bill"
Dempsey, second tenor voc.; Bill "Dicey" Galloway,
baritone voc.; Bill Brown (b. 1936; d. 1956), bass
voc.; Nicky Clark (b. 1943), tenor; Raoul Cita (b. Feb.
11, 1928), voc., piano.
1954—(– Galloway; + Jimmy Beckum, tenor voc.)
1956—(Numerous personnel changes follow)
1982—*Love Needs the Harptones* (Ambient Sound)
1987—*The Harptones, Featuring Willie Winfield,
vol. 1* (Relic); *The Harptones, Featuring Willie Win-
field, vol. 2*.

A unique jazz-influenced New York vocal group that enjoyed limited success in the Fifties and early Sixties, the Harptones cracked the pop market only with "What Will I Tell My Heart" (#96, 1961). Nonetheless, the group is familiar to oldies fans as the singers of such doo-wop classics as "My Memories of You" and "Life Is But a Dream."

Formed on the streetcorners of Harlem as the Harps, they changed their name to avoid a conflict with another group. In 1953 they were first featured on one of Alan Freed's revues in Cleveland, and they began recording for the New York–based Bruce label. Led by founder/lead vocalist Willie Winfield and Raoul Cita, the group's organizer, arranger, composer, and pianist, they specialized in slow, romantic songs. Their first R&B hit for Bruce was "A Sunday Kind of Love." By 1954, a year after their first record, they had changed both lineup and label with "Life Is But a Dream" on Paradise. Among the labels the group recorded for in the next decade were Rama Records ("The Masquerade Is Over"), Andrea ("What Is Your Decision"), Tip Top ("My Memories of You"), Gee ("Cry Like I Cried"), Warwick ("Laughing on the Outside"), Companion ("What Will I Tell My Heart"), and others.

The group disbanded in 1964. Winfield became a funeral director, occasionally reviving the name with new associates for local club work. In 1970 Winfield and Cita regrouped the Harptones for a rock revival show. In 1981 they recorded *Love Needs the Harptones*; the liner notes claimed that the group had rehearsed weekly for 28 years.

Don "Sugarcane" Harris/Don and Dewey

Don Harris: born June 18, 1938, Pasadena, California
N.A.—*Keep On Driving* (Musidisc)   1970—*Fiddler on the Rock* (Polydor); *Sugarcane* (Epic)   1973—*Cup Full of Dreams*; *Sugarcane's Got the Blues* (BASF).
Don and Dewey (with Dewey Terry): N.A.—*Don & Dewey* (Specialty); *They're Rockin' Till Midnight.*

He plays guitar, harmonica, and piano, but R&B veteran Don "Sugarcane" Harris is best known for his blues-rock electric violin. As half of the Fifties duo Don and Dewey, Harris cowrote "Farmer John" (covered by Neil Young on his *Ragged Glory*) and "Big Boy Pete." The pair cowrote its best-known song, "I'm Leaving It All Up to You." Harris went on to play with Johnny Otis, Little Richard, Frank Zappa, John Mayall, and Tupelo Chain Sex (with Dewey Terry).

The son of carnival performers, Harris studied classical violin with L. C. Robinson from 1944 to 1954. In the mid-Fifties he graduated from Manual Arts High School in Los Angeles. He formed the Squires in 1956, and they played local bars for many months until Harris teamed with Dewey Terry to form Don and Dewey.

They recorded for Specialty Records in the late Fifties and toured the West Coast as part of the Johnny Otis show. Otis nicknamed Harris "Sugarcane," reportedly in reference to his reputation as a ladies' man. Harris later recorded with Otis' band for Epic in 1969 (*Cuttin' Up*) and toured with his show before he and Dewey tried a comeback in the early Seventies. (They toured the U.S. and Europe together and recorded for MPS.) After his original pairing with Dewey had disintegrated in the early Sixties, Harris worked with Little Richard, touring the U.S. and Europe and recording with him.

In 1970 Harris hooked up with Frank Zappa, with whom he recorded, most notably on *Hot Rats* and *Weasels Ripped My Flesh,* which featured Harris' vocals as well as his violin playing. Zappa has said that Don and Dewey's single "Soul Motion" b/w "Stretchin'Out" on Rush Records was one of the all-time great R&B records. Both sides featured Harris' kinetic electric-violin work.

Harris also toured and recorded with John Mayall in 1970 and 1971, working concurrently throughout as an occasional solo act in L.A. clubs. In 1970 he began his solo recording career. Plagued by drug addiction, Harris' career suffered.

Terry also remained active in music, producing and playing on some of Harris' albums, playing with Johnny Otis, and releasing a single solo album. As of the early Nineties, Terry (who plays guitar, bass, and piano) has toured with a trio doing Don and Dewey material.

Emmylou Harris

Born April 2, 1947, Birmingham, Alabama
1970—*Gliding Bird* (Jubilee)   1975—*Pieces of the Sky* (Reprise)   1976—*Elite Hotel*   1977—*Luxury Liner* (Warner Bros.)   1978—*Quarter Moon in a Ten-Cent Town; Profile: The Best of Emmylou Harris* 1979—*Blue Kentucky Girl*   1980—*Roses in the Snow; Light of the Stable*   1981—*Evangeline* 1982—*Cimarron*   1983—*White Shoes*   1984—*Profile: The Best of Emmylou Harris, vol. 2*   1985—*The Ballad of Sally Rose*   1986—*Thirteen*   1987—*Angel Band; Trio* (with Dolly Parton and Linda Ronstadt); *Bluebird* (Reprise)   1990—*Duets; Brand New Dance* 1992—*At the Ryman*   1993—*Cowgirl's Prayer* (Asylum)   1994—*Songs of the West* (Warner Bros.).

During the Seventies Emmylou Harris' clear, plaintive soprano made her a country hitmaker, and the neotraditionalist arrangements on her records appealed to rock and folk fans as well. A prolific performer, Harris has continued to garner attention and praise for her work, which has been enriched by superb supporting and collaborating musicians and has included covers of material by writers ranging from Gram Parsons to Bruce Springsteen to Lucinda Williams.

Harris grew up in a Virginia suburb of Washington. In high school she was a cheerleader, beauty pageant queen, and class valedictorian and played alto sax in the marching band. In 1965 she enrolled at the University of North Carolina in Greensboro and played there with a folk duo, but moved to Greenwich Village a year and a half later, where she played clubs and sat in with Jerry Jeff Walker and David Bromberg. She also recorded an unsuccessful album for the small Jubilee label. In 1970, after a short time in Nashville, she returned to her parents' house in Washington, D.C., where she eventually found a band and began gigging locally.

After one D.C. club performance, Harris met the Flying Burrito Brothers; very impressed by her voice, they recommended her to ex-member Gram Parsons [see entry], who was looking for a female duet partner for his upcoming debut solo recording. Parsons became a huge influence on Harris, introducing her to the music of such classic country greats as the Louvin Brothers. The two

Emmylou Harris

collaborated (on two Parsons albums and a Fallen Angels tour) until Parsons' overdose in September 1973. Devastated by Parsons' death, she later wrote a song about him, "Boulder to Birmingham," and over the years kept his music alive by recording his songs.

Harris subsequently formed a new group, including some former Parsons sidemen, and signed with Warner Bros. On 1975's *Pieces of the Sky,* she was backed by Elvis Presley's former sidemen Ron Tutt, James Burton, and Glen D. Hardin. Harris' touring group, dubbed the Hot Band, included songwriter Rodney Crowell [see entry] on guitar and harmony vocals, bassist Emory Gordy Jr., and pedal steel guitarist Hank DeVito. Guitarist Albert Lee and mandolinist/guitarist Ricky Skaggs [see entry] also played with Harris.

In 1975 her remake of the Louvin Brothers' "If I Could Only Win Your Love" topped the country chart; subsequent C&W hits included "Together Again" (#1, 1976), "One of These Days" (#3, 1976), "Sweet Dreams" (#1, 1976), "(You Never Can Tell) C'est la Vie" (#6, 1977), "Making Believe" (#8, 1977), and "To Daddy" (#3, 1977). *Elite Hotel* (1976) and *Luxury Liner* (1977) also attracted some rock fans, and she appeared in studio footage for the Band's 1976 documentary *The Last Waltz,* singing Robbie Robertson's "Evangeline." In 1980 she teamed with Roy Orbison for "That Lovin' You Feelin' Again," a #55 pop single that year.

In 1977 Harris married producer Brian Ahern, who had played a large role in shaping her early hits (Ahern's other credits included Anne Murray and Crowell). She began focusing on pure country material, and *Blue Kentucky Girl* won a Grammy for Best Country Vocal Performance, Female. There were more C&W hits: "Two More Bottles of Wine" (#1, 1978), a cover of the Drifters' "Save the Last Dance for Me" (#4, 1979), and "Blue Kentucky Girl" (#6, 1979).

By 1982 Harris had eight gold albums. The early Eighties also brought numerous top country singles: "Beneath Still Waters" (#1, 1980), "Wayfaring Stranger" (#7, 1980), a cover of the Chordettes' "Mister Sandman" (#10, 1981), a duet with Don Williams, "If I Needed You" (#3, 1981), "Tennessee Rose" (#9, 1982), "Born to Run" (#3, 1982), "(Lost His Love) On Our Last Date" (#1, 1983), "I'm Movin' On" (#5, 1983), "In My Dreams" (#9, 1984), and "Pledging My Love" (#9, 1984).

Harris' marriage to Ahern ended in 1983, and she relocated to Nashville. In 1985 she released *The Ballad of Sally Rose,* a loosely autobiographical "country opera," to great acclaim. Harris cowrote and coproduced the album with her second husband, the Grammy-winning songwriter Paul Kennerley. In 1987 Harris' long-anticipated collaboration with Dolly Parton and Linda Ronstadt (who had both appeared on *Sally Rose*) finally came to fruition with *Trio.* It went platinum, reached #6 on the pop chart, and yielded C&W smashes with a version of the Teddy Bears' hit "To Know Him Is to Love Him" (#1, 1987), "Telling Me Lies" (#3, 1987), "Those Memories of You" (#5, 1987), and "Wildflowers" (#6, 1988).

Harris' other 1988 C&W hits included "We Believe in Happy Endings" (#1), with Earl Thomas Conley, and "Heartbreak Hill" (#8). In 1990 she had a #24 pop album, a compilation of previously released *Duets* pairing her with everyone from Gram Parsons to George Jones and Willie Nelson. She then replaced her longtime Hot Band with an acoustic aggregation, the Nash Ramblers, with whom she has recorded since. In 1992 Harris recorded *At the Ryman* live at the Grand Ole Opry's venerable auditorium. Her 1993 album, *Cowgirl's Prayer,* only reached #34 on the country charts but was a critical favorite.

Wynonie Harris
Born August 24, 1915, Omaha, Nebraska; died June 14, 1969, Los Angeles, California
N.A.—*Good Rockin' Blues* (King); *Good Rockin' Tonight; Party After Hours* (Aladdin) 1993—*Women, Whiskey & Fish Tails* (Ace) 1994—*Bloodshot Eyes (Best of)* (Rhino).

Wynonie Harris was a big-band blues shouter whose style was a major influence on early rock & roll. Harris dropped out of Creighton University in Omaha and began working as a comedian and dancer in the Thirties. After teaching himself to play the drums, in the late Thirties and early Forties he led his own local combo. When he moved to Los Angeles in the early Forties, he quit drumming and worked as a club emcee for a while; he also appeared as a dancer in the film *Hit Parade of 1943.*

In 1944 Harris became a vocalist with Lucky Millinder's band, with whom he cut his first records that year for Decca (and, a few years later, for King Records) and toured major ballrooms throughout America. He continued recording with jazz bands in the mid-Forties (Jack McVea, Oscar Pettiford, Illinois Jacquet, and others). He also worked with Johnny Otis, who influenced him toward a pop-tinged R&B style. While recording for King Records, Harris had his biggest successes with "Good Morning Judge," "Lovin' Machine," "All She Wants to Do Is Rock," and his mid-Fifties British hit, "Bloodshot Eyes." Harris also covered Roy Brown's "Good Rockin' Tonight," later an Elvis Presley hit. He toured widely throughout the late Forties with such traveling bands as the Lionel Hampton orchestra, Dud Bascomb, and Big Joe Turner.

Harris continued club work, often as part of package shows, into the early Fifties, cutting records for Cincinnati-based King Records and New York's Apollo label. In the mid-Fifties he opened a cafe in Brooklyn and in 1963 went to Los Angeles and did the same. He was working as a bartender when he died of cancer at age 54. Harris had attempted several comebacks in the interim. In the early Sixties he recorded for Atco and Roulette in New York and for Chicago-based Cadet. For one of his last public performances, in 1967, he played Harlem's venerable Apollo Theatre.

George Harrison

Born February 25, 1943, Liverpool, England
1968—*Wonderwall Music* (Apple)   1969—*Electronic Sounds* (Zapple)   1970—*All Things Must Pass* (Apple)   1972—*Concert for Bangla Desh* 1973—*Living in the Material World*   1974—*Dark Horse*   1975—*Extra Texture (Read All About It)* 1976—*33⅓* (Dark Horse); *The Best of George Harrison* (Capitol)   1979—*George Harrison* (Dark Horse)   1981—*Somewhere in England*   1982— *Gone Troppo*   1987—*Cloud Nine*   1989—*Best of Dark Horse 1976–1989*   1992—*Live in Japan*.

George Harrison played lead guitar and wrote occasional songs for the Beatles; he also was the group's only convert to Eastern religion. Since the Beatles broke up [see entry], he has had an uneven solo career.

Born into a working-class family, Harrison attended Dovedale Primary School, three years behind John Lennon. In 1954 he entered Liverpool Institute, a grade behind Paul McCartney. In 1956, at the height of Britain's skiffle craze, Harrison formed his first group, the Rebels. He started jamming occasionally with his new acquaintance Paul McCartney, and in 1958 McCartney introduced him to John Lennon; soon all three were playing in the Quarrymen, who later became the Silver Beetles and then the Beatles.

Besides playing lead guitar, Harrison sang backup vocals and an occasional lead ("Roll Over Beethoven," "If I Needed Someone," "I'm Happy Just to Dance with You") in the Beatles. In the mid-Sixties he was one of the first rock musicians to experiment with Indian and Far Eastern instruments; he studied with Bengali master sitarist Ravi Shankar. Harrison first played sitar on 1965's "Norwegian Wood" and later on "Within You Without You," "The Inner Light," and other songs.

Harrison wrote songs as early as 1963 ("Don't Bother Me"), but it was difficult for him to get the group to record his material, one of the problems that led to the Beatles' breakup. Harrison's compositions include "I Need You," "You Like Me Too Much," "Taxman," "Love You To," "Piggies," "Savoy Truffle," "While My Guitar Gently Weeps," "Here Comes the Sun," and "Something" (#3, 1969), the only Harrison song to become a hit single for the Beatles.

After the Beatles officially disbanded in early 1970, Harrison continued his solo career, which he'd begun in November 1968 with the electronic sound collage soundtrack *Wonderwall Music.* In November 1970 he released his three-record set *All Things Must Pass* (#1), produced by Phil Spector, which included the #1 hit single "My Sweet Lord." (A 1976 lawsuit successfully established that Harrison "unknowingly" plagiarized the song's melodic structure from an early-Sixties hit by the Chiffons, "He's So Fine.") In late summer 1971 Harrison sponsored and hosted two benefit concerts at Madison Square Garden for the people of Bangladesh. With guests including Ringo Starr, Eric Clapton, Leon Russell, and Bob Dylan, the concerts, the documentary film, and the Grammy-winning three-record set, *Concert for Bangla Desh,* were a resounding success, although funds raised by the proceeds were impounded during a nine-year audit of Apple by the IRS. (In 1981 a check for $8.8 million was finally sent through UNICEF; $2 million had been sent in 1972 before the audit began.) Harrison's song about the plight of the refugees, "Bangla Desh," hit the pop Top 25 in late 1971. *Living in the Material World* produced a #1 hit in 1973, "Give Me Love (Give Me Peace on Earth)."

In 1974 Harrison formed his own Dark Horse Records (with distribution via Warner Bros.), releasing a gold album of the same name late in the year (the title track of which hit #15 as a single) and touring America to support it. The sales of *Extra Texture (Read All About It)* were disappointing, a trend that continued unabated with *33⅓* and *George Harrison.* A tribute to the slain Lennon, "All Those Years Ago," went #2 in 1981. Starr and Paul and Linda McCartney also appear on the record. *Gone Troppo* was a commercial flop, and Harrison stopped recording for several years, to concentrate on gardening, auto-racing, and other pursuits.

Harrison began producing albums in the late Sixties by Apple Records protégés Jackie Lomax, Billy Preston, and Badfinger; he also participated in sessions by artists signed to his Dark Horse label in the mid-Seventies. He has been regularly involved with members of the Monty Python comedy group axis as executive producer of film projects, including *The Life of Brian* and *Time Bandits*. Harrison also appeared in the Beatles parody TV film, *All You Need Is Cash*. In 1979 he privately published an autobiography, *I Me Mine* (a mass market edition was published in 1982).

Harrison ended a five-year hiatus from recording with *Cloud Nine* (#8, 1987), which went platinum and yielded the Number One hit single "Got My Mind Set On You" (a cover of an oldie recorded by one Rudy Clark). The album, produced by Jeff Lynne of Electric Light Orchestra, spawned a Top 25 hit in "When We Was Fab," an evocation of the Beatles' cello-driven "I Am the Walrus" sound, which had been so influential on ELO. Harrison went on to join Lynne in the Traveling Wilburys [see entry]. In 1992, with his old friend Eric Clapton, Harrison embarked on his first tour in 18 years; that April Harrison played his first-ever U.K. solo concert (which also served to raise awareness of the Maharishi Mahesh Yogi's new Natural Law Party, then seeking seats in British Parliament).

He met his first wife, model Pattie Boyd (born March 17, 1945), in early 1964 on the set of the Beatles film *A Hard Day's Night* (in which she briefly appeared). They were married on January 21, 1966, but their marriage began coming apart a few years later, and they separated and eventually divorced in 1977. Boyd later married guitarist Eric Clapton and was the subject of Clapton's "Layla." Harrison married Olivia Arias in England in September 1978, a month after their son, Dhani, was born.

Jerry Harrison: See Talking Heads

Wilbert Harrison

Born January 6, 1929, Charlotte, North Carolina; died October 26, 1994, Spencer, North Carolina
1962—*Battle of the Giants* (Joy); *Kansas City* (Sphere)   1969—*Let's Work Together* (Sue)   1971—*Wilbert Harrison* (Buddah)   1989—*Classic R&B Hits* (Grudge)   1992—*Kansas City* (Relic).

Jump-blues singer Wilbert Harrison had two major pop hits a decade apart: "Kansas City" in 1959 and "Let's Work Together" in 1969. Harrison began recording in 1951 with "This Woman of Mine" on Rockin'. He recorded for DeLuxe and Savoy without notable success. In 1959 Fury Records released "Kansas City," a version of Leiber and Stoller's "K.C. Lovin'" (written in 1952 and first recorded by Little Willie Littlefield) that went to #1. The song was later recorded by the Beatles.

Harrison recorded through the Sixties for numerous labels (Seahorn, Neptune, Doc, Port, Vest) until "Let's

Work Together," (originally titled "Let's Stick Together"), on Sue, went to #32; it was later covered by Canned Heat, Roxy Music's Bryan Ferry, Dwight Yoakam, and the Kentucky HeadHunters. "My Heart Is Yours," on SSS International, went to #98 in 1971, and he recorded through the Seventies for Buddah, Hotline, Brunswick, and Wet Soul. For much of his career, Harrison—unable to afford sidemen—performed live as a one-man band. He released several albums in the past two decades, virtually all now out of print. He died of a stroke at age 65.

Deborah Harry: See Blondie

Grant Hart: See Hüsker Dü

Mickey Hart: See Grateful Dead

John Hartford

Born December 30, 1937, New York City, New York
1967—*Looks at Life* (RCA); *Earthwords and Music*   1968—*The Love Album; Housing Project; Gentle on My Mind and Other Originals*   1969—*John Hartford*   1970—*Iron Mountain Depot*   1971—*Aero-Plain* (Warner Bros.)   1972—*Morning Bugle*   1975—*Tennessee Jubilee* (Flying Fish)   1976—*Mark Twang; Nobody Knows What You Do*   1977—*Dillard, Hartford, Dillard* (with Doug and Rod Dillard); *All in the Name of Love*   1978—*Heading Down into the Mystery Below*   1979—*Slumberin' on the Cumberland*   1981—*You and Me at Home; Catalogue*   1984—*Gum Tree Canoe*   1987—*Me Oh My, How the Time Does Fly: A John Hartford Anthology*   1989—*Down on the River*   1991—*Hartford and Hartford*   1992—*Cadillac Rag* (Small Dog a Barkin')   1993—*Goin' Back to Dixie*   1994—*Walls We Bounce Off.*

Singer, songwriter, and banjoist Hartford wrote "Gentle on My Mind" for Glen Campbell and has recorded many folk-oriented solo albums.

Best known for his banjo work but also adept at guitar and fiddle, Hartford was raised in St. Louis, where his father was a doctor and his mother a painter. He studied art at Washington University in St. Louis, and before moving to Nashville in the mid-Sixties he worked as a sign painter, a commercial artist, a riverboat deckhand, and a disc jockey. His session work slowly picked up, and by the end of the Sixties he had participated in the Byrds' *Sweetheart of the Rodeo*. Hartford continued doing studio gigs through the early Seventies. In 1966 he signed with RCA, for which he eventually recorded eight albums.

But his biggest success came as a writer, notably "Gentle on My Mind," which, in addition to Campbell's

Grammy-winning hit, has been covered more than 200 times and has sold over 15 million copies internationally. It was originally a minor country hit for Hartford in 1967. Among his other compositions are "California Earthquake" and "Natural to Be Gone."

Hartford had his most extensive exposure in the late Sixties as a regular on the *Smothers Brothers Comedy Hour*, which was followed by a stint on Glen Campbell's show. At the start of the Seventies he hosted his own syndicated show, *Something Else*. He switched from RCA to Warner Bros. in mid-1971, releasing his debut for the label, the David Bromberg–produced *Aero-Plain* (featuring guitarist Norman Blake, dobro player Tut Taylor, and fiddler Vassar Clements). Then he switched to the small Flying Fish label, and 1976's *Mark Twang* won a Grammy in the ethnic-traditional category. He performs year-round, usually as a one-man band. He has also toured with Glen Campbell.

Dan Hartman

Born circa 1951, Harrisburg, Pennsylvania; died March 22, 1994, Westport, Connecticut
1976—*Images* (Blue Sky)   1978—*Instant Replay*
1979—*Relight My Fire*   1984—*I Can Dream About You* (MCA)   1989—*New Green/Clear Blue* (Private Music).

After playing bass with Edgar Winter during his peak years in the mid-Seventies, multi-instrumentalist Dan Hartman embarked upon a modestly successful solo career highlighted by dance-oriented singles like "Instant Replay" (#29, 1978) and "I Can Dream About You" (#6, 1984). He was most successful, however, as a producer and owner of a Westport, Connecticut, recording studio known as the Schoolhouse.

Hartman joined Winter as bassist in early 1972 and stayed with him until 1976 [see entry]. He wrote Winter's platinum single "Free Ride." Following his stint with Winter, Hartman began a solo career for Blue Sky. Despite a handful of hits (1979's "Instant Replay," 1984's "We Are the Young," and 1985's "Second Nature" were his other Top Forty entries), he rarely toured, preferring to operate the Schoolhouse, where acts such as Foghat, .38 Special, Muddy Waters, Rick Derringer, and both the Winter brothers recorded. He also produced Tina Turner, Paul Young, Jimmy Somerville, and Holly Johnson.

In the Eighties Hartman branched out into writing and producing material for films. Among his credits: *Fletch*, *Krush Groove*, *Bull Durham*, *Down and Out in Beverly Hills*, *Ruthless People*, and *Rocky IV*. The last–named produced "Living in America" (#4, 1986), James Brown's second-highest–charting single ever. At the time of his death, from a brain tumor at age 43, Hartman was working on a new album of dance music.

PJ Harvey

Formed July 1991, Yeovil, England
PJ Harvey (b. Polly Jean Harvey, Oct. 9, 1969, Yeovil), voc., gtr.; Rob Ellis (b. Feb. 13, 1962, Bristol, Eng.), drums; Stephen Vaughan (b. June 22, 1962, Wolverhampton, Eng.), bass.
1992—*Dry* (Island)   1993—*Rid of Me*; *4-Track Demos* (– Ellis; – Vaughan)   1995—*To Bring You My Love*.

Led by the talented guitarist, songwriter, and singer Polly Jean Harvey, the postpunk power trio PJ Harvey came from small-town England in 1991 and took London by storm with its raw, dynamic rock and Harvey's evocative/provocative female-centric lyrics. Harvey formed the band with two friends in Yeovil and recorded its debut for less than $5,000. After creating a buzz in London and two chart-topping singles, PJ Harvey released *Dry* on the U.K. indie label Too Pure (Island Records released the album in the U.S.). In hypnotic tunes like "Dress," "Happy and Bleeding," and "Sheela-Na-Gig," Harvey sang about discovering, reviling, and reveling in her body. The tomboyish Harvey's discomfort with her femininity fueled her lyrics and image. *Dry*'s album cover features the androgynous artist skinny and barechested.

Harvey, who grew up on a sheep farm, quickly developed a reputation for being a publicity-shy recluse and reportedly had a near nervous breakdown in 1992, after playing the mammoth Reading Festival. Recovered, she took her career in hand and chose iconoclastic Chicago-based producer Steve Albini to produce the band's second album. *Rid of Me* sounded appropriately noisy and difficult. Harvey's lyrics mocked efforts to control her sexuality and art, taunting lovers on "Rid of Me" and "Legs" and declaring her stature over cock-rockers on "50 Ft. Queenie." Press-friendly now, Harvey disappointed many fans by denouncing feminism in interviews, although listeners found consolation in lyrics that seemed to contradict her stance. Harvey turned down a chance to play 1993's Lollapalooza. Her own American tour revealed a confident performer who was adding touches of a campy glam to her trademark austere appearance.

The tour also indicated that Harvey was having trouble with her band, and in August 1993, Ellis departed. The demos for *Rid of Me*, released as *4-Track Demos*, verified criticism that Albini had buried Harvey's powerful vocals and barely touched the range of her aural ideas. The album included several new tracks, including the irresistible "Reeling."

Harvey completely dispensed with her band for 1995's *To Bring You My Love* (#40), a bluesy collection of songs that she coproduced with Flood (U2) and guitarist John Parish. Bassist Mick Harvey (ex–Birthday Party)

PJ Harvey

Young's *Dreamhouse* and Terry Riley's *In C*, both pathfinding works of the minimalist movement. Another template for Hassell was Miles Davis' *On the Corner*, a pioneer Seventies mix of electronics and sensual funk.

Traveling to India in 1972, Hassell studied with vocalist Pandit Pran Nath and laid the groundwork for the "primitive/futurist" sounds that graced *Vernal Equinox*. Incorporating technologically modified trumpet, raga, and the Afro-Brazilian percussion of Nana Vasconcelos, the debut, along with 1979's *Earthquake Island*, blueprinted his approach. Collaborations with Brian Eno (*Possible Musics/Fourth World Volume One* and *Dream Theory in Malaya/Fourth World Volume Two*) and the Daniel Lanois–produced *Aka-Darbari-Java/Magic Realism* found Hassell in the vanguard of world music in the early Eighties and paved the way for such developments in the rock mainstream as David Byrne and Eno's *My Life in the Bush of Ghosts*. Concurrently, the Jon Hassell Concert Group began touring.

As the decade progressed, Hassell's projects expanded to include a 1987 commission to compose for the Kronos Quartet and a concert with Farafina, an ensemble from Burkina Faso. *City: Works of Fiction* was Hassell at his most ambitious—synthesizer, guitar, and his own trumpet atop a polyrhythmic base.

and guitarist Joe Gore were among the guests who played on the critically acclaimed album.

Jon Hassell

Born March 22, 1937, Memphis, Tennessee
1977—*Vernal Equinox* (Lovely)   1979—*Earthquake Island* (Tomato)   1980—*Possible Musics/Fourth World Volume One* (with Brian Eno) (Editions EG) 1981—*Dream Theory in Malaya/Fourth World Volume Two*   1983—*Aka-Darbari-Java/Magic Realism* 1986—*Power Spot* (ECM)   1987—*Surgeon of the Night Sky Restores Dead Things by the Power of Sound* (Capitol)   1989—*Flash of the Spirit* 1990— *City: Works of Fiction* (Opal)   1991—*Nouvelles Polyphonies Corses* (PolyGram).

Trumpeter and theoretician of what he terms "Fourth World Music"—a combination of first and third world sensibilities—Jon Hassell builds on the austere legacy of minimalist composers and jazz's cool school to create an ambient fusion of high technology and indigenous "primitive" music.

Taking degrees at the Eastman School of Music and Catholic University, Hassell studied with Karlheinz Stockhausen and, in the late Sixties, played on La Monte

Juliana Hatfield/Blake Babies

Born July 27, 1967, Wiscasset, Maine
Blake Babies, formed 1986, Boston, Massachusetts (Hatfield, voc., bass; John Strohm [b. March 23, 1967, Bloomington, Ind.], voc., gtr.; Freda Boner [b. Sept. 3, 1967, Nashville, Tenn.], drums): 1989— *Earwig* (Mammoth)   1990—*Sunburn*   1991—*Rosy Jack World* EP.
Juliana Hatfield solo: 1992—*Hey Babe* (Mammoth) 1993—*Become What You Are* (Mammoth/Atlantic) 1995—*Only Everything* (Atlantic).

With her sweet-voiced singing juxtaposed against assertive guitar playing and introspective songwriting, Juliana Hatfield garnered attention on the college rock scene, first with the band Blake Babies, and even more so as a solo artist.

One of three children of a physician father and a *Boston Globe* fashion editor mother, Hatfield, deeply affected at age 11 by her parents' divorce, later drew on memories of adolescent unhappiness for her lyrics. Starting piano lessons from her mother at age six, Hatfield played Police and Rush covers in a high school group called the Squids before gravitating toward the sound of the Velvet Underground and X. As a voice major at Boston's Berklee College of Music, she met guitarist John Strohm and drummer Freda Boner. Switching to bass, she joined them to found Blake Babies, whose six-

Juliana Hatfield

year career and three recordings established them as college-radio stars. Seeking a harder sound, Hatfield departed in 1990; Strohm and Boner formed the band Antenna. Strohm later formed Velo-Deluxe. In 1990, Hatfield contributed lyrics to the debut album of former Bangles singer Susanna Hoffs; she also sang and played on the Lemonheads' *It's a Shame About Ray*. (Her complicated romantic relationship with Lemonheads singer Evan Dando became fodder for alt-rock gossip columns.)

Dando and John Wesley Harding appeared on Hatfield's own solo debut, the critically acclaimed *Hey Babe,* which showcased Hatfield's return to playing guitar. In 1992 she formed the Juliana Hatfield Three with bassist Dean Fisher and ex–Bullet LaVolta drummer Todd Philips; with songs about self-mutilation, anorexia, and familial tension set to pop melodies and heavy guitar, *Become What You Are* gave voice to blank-generation tension. With the entertainment media fascinated by Hatfield (1992 photo layouts in *Sassy* and *Vogue*), the singer also revealed a penchant for confessional, confrontational statements, asserting in interviews that she was still a virgin at age 25 and that women are genetically determined to be lesser guitarists than men.

Donny Hathaway

Born October 1, 1945, Chicago, Illinois; died January 13, 1979, New York City, New York
1970—*Everything Is Everything* (Atco)   1971—
Donny Hathaway   1972—Donny Hathaway Live;
Roberta Flack and Donny Hathaway (with Roberta
Flack) (Atlantic); *Come Back Charleston Blue* soundtrack (Atco)   1973—*Extension of a Man* (Atlantic)   1978—*The Best of Donny Hathaway* (Atco) 1979—*Roberta Flack Featuring Donny Hathaway* (with Roberta Flack) (Atlantic)   1980—*Donny Hathaway in Performance   1990—Donny Hathaway Collection.*

A singer, songwriter, and keyboardist best known for his duets with Roberta Flack, Donny Hathaway fused R&B, gospel, jazz, classical, and rock strains in a modestly successful solo career. He was raised in St. Louis by his grandmother, Martha Pitts, a professional gospel singer. From the age of three Hathaway accompanied her on tours, billed as the Nation's Youngest Gospel Singer. He attended Howard University in Washington, D.C., on a fine-arts scholarship. One classmate was Roberta Flack, and in the early Seventies, shortly after Flack started her solo career, the two began singing together. Their hits included Carole King's "You've Got a Friend" (#29, 1971) and "Where Is the Love" (#5, 1972), which established them as a duo. *Roberta Flack and Donny Hathaway* was a gold album, but due to personal problems both the partnership and Hathaway's solo career were put on hold for several years. When they reunited in 1978, they had their biggest hit, the gold single "The Closer I Get to You" (#2, 1978). Hathaway was working on *Roberta Flack Featuring Donny Hathaway* when he died after falling from his 15th-floor hotel room in the Essex House. (The police called it suicide; close friends refused to believe it.) The LP, released posthumously, hit #25 and went gold; a single, "You Are My Heaven," reached #47.

At the time of his death, Hathaway had released five solo albums in addition to his discs with Flack. He had recorded briefly for Curtom Records with June Conquest as June and Donnie, and got his first solo contract with Atlantic in 1970 under the patronage of King Curtis. Hathaway enjoyed R&B chart success in the early Seventies with singles like "The Ghetto, Part 1" (#23 R&B, 1970), "Little Ghetto Boy" (#25 R&B, 1972), "Giving Up" (#21 R&B, 1972), "I Love You More Than You'll Ever Know" (#20 R&B, 1972), and "Love, Love, Love" (#16 R&B, 1973). Concurrently, Hathaway worked as a producer and composer for others, including Aretha Franklin, Jerry Butler, and the Staple Singers. He also did freelance production work for Chess, Uni, Kapp, and Stax, and served as arranger for Curtom Records and band director for the Impressions. Quincy Jones hired Hathaway to score the 1972 film *Come Back Charleston Blue*. He also sang the theme song for the television series *Maude*. By the mid-Seventies he had formed his own independent production company. Hathaway's daughter Lalah came out with her debut album in 1990.

Havana 3 A.M.: See the Clash

Richie Havens

Born January 21, 1941, Brooklyn, New York
1965—*Richie Havens Record* (Douglas)   1966—
Electric Havens   1967—*Mixed Bag* (Verve)   1968—
Something Else Again   1969—*Richard D. Havens
1983*   1970—*Stonehenge* (Stormy Forest)   1971—
Alarm Clock; *"The Great Blind Degree"*   1972—
Richie Havens on Stage   1973—*Richie Havens
Portfolio*   1974—*Mixed Bag II* (Polydor)   1976—
The End of the Beginning (A&M)   1977—*Mirage*
1979—*Connections* (Elektra/Asylum)   1987—*Simple
Things* (RBI); *Richie Havens Sings the Beatles
and Dylan* (Rykodisc); *Collection*   1991—*Now*
(Solar/Epic)   1993—*Résumé: The Best of Richie
Havens* (Rhino)   1994—*Cuts to the Chase* (Forward).

Richie Havens, a black folksinger with a percussive,
strummed guitar style, enjoyed his greatest popularity
during the late Sixties. He was born and raised in the
Bedford-Stuyvesant ghetto, the eldest of nine children in
a family headed by a pianist father. As a youth, he sang
for spare change on streetcorners. By age 14 he was
singing with the McCrea Gospel Singers in Brooklyn,
and three years later he dropped out of high school to
pursue a music career. He worked his way into Greenwich Village folk circles in the early Sixties.

After recording two albums for the Douglas
International–Transatlantic label, Havens started touring clubs throughout the U.S. in 1967, and he became a
familiar act on the outdoor festival circuit, playing at the
Newport Folk Festival (1966), the Monterey Jazz Festival
(1967), the Miami Pop Festival (1968), the Isle of Wight
Festival (1969), and Woodstock (1969). Despite such
massive exposure, Havens never really transformed his
concert audiences into record consumers. Signed to
Verve in 1966, he jumped from there to MGM, A&M,
Elektra, and others.

His repertoire has featured songs by Lennon-
McCartney, Van Morrison, Bob Dylan, and James Taylor.
His only chart success was with his cover of George Harrison's "Here Comes the Sun" (#16, 1971). Havens continued to be a reliable club and concert performer
throughout the Seventies. In the late Seventies he conducted extensive tours of the Middle East and Europe;
around the same time he released his 15th album, and
first for Elektra, *Connections,* in 1979. As an actor, his film
credits include *Catch My Soul* (1974) and Richard Pryor's
Greased Lightning (1977). He was also featured in the
1972 stage presentation of the Who's *Tommy.*

Throughout the Eighties and Nineties, Havens'
slightly hoarse voice became familiar to television viewers through the dozens of commercial jingles he sang, for
everything from Amtrak, to McDonald's, to Cotton Incorporated. In 1990 he cofounded the Natural Guard, a national organization that helps children learn to protect
the environment.

Dale Hawkins

Born August 22, 1938, Goldmine, Louisiana
1958—*Susie Q* (Chess)   1969—*L.A., Memphis and
Tyler, Texas* (Bell)   1976—*Dale Hawkins* (Chess).

A rockabilly original, singer, guitarist, and bandleader
Dale Hawkins was an important influence on such later
rockers as John Fogerty, whose Creedence Clearwater
Revival had a #11 hit in 1968 with Hawkins' "Suzie Q."
Hawkins signed with Chess in the mid-Fifties and recorded for its Checker subsidiary for the next several
years. He enjoyed his most rewarding year in 1957, when
"Suzie Q" climbed to #27 on the pop chart. Hawkins followed up with more modest releases like "La Do-Dada"
(#32, 1958), "A House, a Car and a Wedding Ring" (#88,
1958), "Class Cutter Yeah Yeah" (#52, 1959), and uncharted singles like "My Babe" and "Liza Jane." James
Burton (who claims to have been coauthor of "Suzie Q"),
Scotty Moore (of Elvis Presley's band), and Roy
Buchanan were among the guitarists in Hawkins' band.

After touring the U.S. several times, Hawkins left
Chess in 1961 and in the next few years recorded, with
little impact on the market, for such labels as Tilt, Zonk,
Atlantic, Roulette, and ABC-Paramount. By the mid-
Sixties he was living in Tyler, Texas, and producing pop
hits by the Five Americans ("Western Union") and Bruce
Channel ("Hey Baby"). At the close of the Sixties
Hawkins revitalized his recording career with an album
recorded in Nashville with Box Tops producer Dan Penn.
In the Seventies, he produced Rio Grande.

Edwin Hawkins Singers

Formed 1967, Oakland, California
1969—*Let Us Go into the House of the Lord* (Pavillion); *Oh Happy Day* (Buddah); *More Happy Days*
1971—*Children (Get Together)*   1972—*I'd Like to
Teach the World to Sing*   1973—*New World*
1974—*Live*   1983—*Mass Choir* (Mercury)   1985—
The Best of the Edwin Hawkins Singers (Savoy)
1989—*Imagine Heaven* (Lection)   1990—*Music and
Arts Seminar Chicago Mass Choir*   1991—*Face to
Face* (Lection/PolyGram)   1992—*Oh Happy Day Reunion* (Intersound).

The Edwin Hawkins Singers had one of the most successful gospel pop hits ever in 1969 with "Oh Happy
Day" (#4) and returned to the Top Ten the following year
backing Melanie on "Lay Down (Candles in the Rain)"
(#6). The group's arranger, director, and pianist, Edwin
Hawkins (born August 1943, Oakland), was a student at

Berkeley in 1967 when he and an associate, Betty Watson, organized the large choir to represent their Oakland church, the Ephesian Church of God in Christ, at a Pentecostal Youth Congress in Washington, D.C. The group was originally called the Northern California State Youth Choir.

By 1969 the group was 46 members strong and backed by keyboards, drums, and electric bass. To help raise money to finance a trip to the National Youth Congress in Cleveland that year, they recorded an album in a San Francisco church on an old two-track stereo machine. It included a fiery reading of the gospel standard "Oh Happy Day," which a local disc jockey started airing. By the spring of 1969 the single was a Top Ten hit; Buddah picked up the LP, *Let Us Go into the House of the Lord*, for national distribution.

Featured on the album was vocalist Dorothy Morrison, who was born in Longview, Texas, in 1945, and who went on to some prominence as a solo gospel artist in her own right, including an appearance at the 1969 Big Sur Folk Festival. Other featured soloists in the Hawkins group included Elaine Kelly ("To My Father's House") and Margarette Branch ("I'm Going Through").

After contributing to Melanie's hit and touring Europe in 1970, the group quickly faded from prominence, partly because the personnel kept changing, and keeping such a large retinue active proved prohibitively expensive. But they remained a respected gospel force, especially in the Bay Area, for several years. Edwin Hawkins remains active as a gospel musician.

Ronnie Hawkins

Born January 10, 1935, Fayetteville, Arkansas
1963—*The Best of Ronnie Hawkins* (Roulette)
1970—*Ronnie Hawkins* (Cotillion)   1971—*The Hawk*   1972—*Rock and Roll Resurrection* (Monument)   1974—*The Giant of Rock 'n' Roll*   1990—*Best of Ronnie Hawkins and the Hawks* (Rhino).

A 40-year veteran of roadhouse rock & roll, Ronnie Hawkins is best known as the man who assembled the Band. He formed his first group in 1952 while attending the University of Arkansas and shortly thereafter cut his first record, a cover of an Eddy Arnold tune, for a local label. In the mid-Fifties, before moving to Memphis, he played piano behind Carl Perkins and Conway Twitty.

After a stint in the army, Hawkins went to Canada for the first time in 1958. For the next four years he alternated between club work there and one-nighter tours of Southern honky-tonks. In that period, he met the four Canadians and one American who later became known as the Band [see entry] (Levon Helm, like Hawkins, was a transplanted Arkansan). They joined his band, the Hawks, and accompanied him on his auto tours through the South and Canada before leaving him to back John

Hammond Jr. in 1964. (A year later they became Bob Dylan's backing band, and by 1968 they were on their own.) Among other onetime Hawks were guitarists Roy Buchanan, Duane Allman, and Dominic Troiano.

Hawkins recorded extensively for the Roulette label in the late Fifties and early Sixties. In 1959 he enjoyed two American chart hits, "Mary Lou" (#26) and "Forty Days" (#45). But rockabilly was on its way out by the time Hawkins got his recording career under way. In 1962 he settled in Toronto and became proprietor and featured attraction at the Hawk's Nest Bar. His records were hits in Canada, especially his 1963 recording of Bo Diddley's "Who Do You Love."

By the mid-Sixties Hawkins was recording for his own Hawk label in Canada. He performed regularly on the rock ballroom circuit in the late Sixties, and in 1969 he signed with Atlantic/Cotillion. *Ronnie Hawkins* was recorded in Alabama with the Muscle Shoals Rhythm Section, and it produced his last American chart single, "Down in the Alley" (#75, 1970).

In 1976 Hawkins appeared at the Band's farewell concert, documented in Martin Scorsese's film *The Last Waltz*. He continues to perform in clubs and had a cameo role in Michael Cimino's 1981 film *Heaven's Gate;* he also appeared as Bob Dylan in Dylan's *Renaldo and Clara*. In addition to his large farm and several other businesses in Canada, Hawkins hosted a television series called *Honky Tonk*.

Screamin' Jay Hawkins

Born Jalacy Hawkins, July 18, 1929, Cleveland, Ohio
1957—*At Home with* (Epic)   1961—*I Put a Spell on You*   1970—*Screamin' Jay Hawkins* (Philips)   1990—*Voodoo Jive: The Best of Screamin' Jay Hawkins* (Rhino)   1991—*Cow Fingers and Mosquito Pie* (Legacy)   1993—*Stone Crazy* (Bizarre/Rhino).

A show-biz eccentric, Screamin' Jay Hawkins was known more for his flamboyant dress and onstage shenanigans than for his singing or piano and sax playing. Hawkins was orphaned in infancy and raised by a foster family. He took piano lessons as a child and by his early teen years was performing for tips in neighborhood bars. He was a Golden Gloves champion in 1943; he continued boxing through the close of the decade and in 1949 won the middleweight championship of Alaska. He began his music career in 1952, working as a pianist and singer with a band led by guitarist Tiny Grimes, with whom he toured and recorded in the early Fifties, and he recorded with the Leroy Kirkland Band in 1954. He also toured U.S. clubs that year with Fats Domino's revue.

In 1955 Hawkins began his solo career. Adopting the "Screamin'" moniker to fit his unrestrained, rocking R&B, he started working clubs, earning a reputation for energetic showmanship that bordered on lunacy; as part of Alan Freed's package tours, Hawkins would be carried offstage in a flaming coffin.

His recorded efforts had far less impact. Aside from a few exceptional recordings like "I Put a Spell on You" (1956), "Alligator Wine" (1958), and "Feast of the Mau Mau" (1967), his records have virtually been ignored. Nonetheless he has recorded extensively over the years for numerous labels, including Okeh, Mercury, Roulette, Decca, and RCA.

In the early Sixties Hawkins lived, performed, and recorded mainly in Hawaii and England, returning to the continental U.S. in mid-decade to play the club circuit. In the early Seventies he worked out of New York City, frequently performing at the Apollo Theatre in Harlem. In the mid-Seventies he toured Europe extensively with the Rhythm and Blues Roots of Rock & Roll troupe. Hawkins remains active playing club dates. In 1982 Hawkins opened U.S. shows for Nick Lowe; ten years later, he was doing his campy act—coffin and all—on TV talk shows, to promote Rhino's *Voodoo Jive* set, and the newly recorded *Stone Crazy*, which found him sounding as energetically bizarre as ever. He has appeared in rock films, notably *Mister Rock 'n' Roll* (1957) and *American Hot Wax* (1978), as well as *Mystery Train* (1989).

Hawkwind/Hawklords

Formed 1969, London, England
Original members (as Group X/Hawkwind Zoo):
Terry Ollis, drums; Nik Turner (b. Oxford, Eng.), sax, voc., flute; Dave Brock (b. Isleworth, Eng.), gtr., voc., synth.; Dikmik (b. Richmond, Eng.), electronics, kybds.; John Harrison, bass; Mick Slattery, gtr. (over 40 personnel changes followed; the major ones are listed below).
1970—(– Slattery; + Huw Lloyd Langton, gtr.)
1972—*Hawkwind* (United Artists) (– Langton; – Harrison; + Dave Anderson, bass; + Robert Calvert [b. Pretoria, S.A.; d. 1988]; + Del Dettmar, electronics); *In Search of Space* (– Anderson; – Ollis; + Ian Kilmister, a.k.a. Lemmy [b. Dec. 24, 1945, Stoke-on-Trent, Eng.], gtr.); *Doremi Fasol Latido* 1973— *Space Ritual/Alive in Liverpool and London* (– Dikmik) 1974—(– Calvert; + Alan Powell, drums) *Hall of the Mountain Grill* 1975— (– Dettmar; – Kilmister; + Paul Rudolph, gtr.; + Simon House, violin, Mellotron, kybds.) *Warrior on the Edge of Time* (Atco) (+ Calvert) 1976— *Roadhawks* (United Artists, U.K.); *Astounding Sounds—Amazing Music* (Charisma, U.K.); *Masters of the Universe* (United Artists, U.K.) 1977—*Quark Strangeness and Charm* (Sire) 1978—(– Turner; – Powell; – Rudolph; – House) *Hawklords 25 Years On* (Charisma, U.K.) (+ Harvey Bainbridge, bass; – Calvert) (group disbands) 1979—*PXR 5*
(Charisma) (group re-forms) 1980—*Repeat Performance* (U.K.); *Live '79* (Bronze, U.K.); *Levitation* (U.K.) 1987—*Live Chronicles* (Profile) 1989—*The Xenon Codex* 1990—*Space Bandits* (Roadrunner) 1991—*Palace Springs* 1992—*Out & Intake* (Griffin); *Hawklords Live*; *California Brainstorm* (Iloki); *The Psychedelic Warlords* (Cleopatra) 1993—*Lord of Light* 1994—*It Is the Business of the Future to be Dangerous* (Griffin).

An English psychedelic rock band, Hawkwind (later Hawklords) has been a cult act since its inception, touring and often playing for free (one of its most memorable appearances was outside the gates of the Isle of Wight Festival in 1970). The group was originally called Group X, then Hawkwind Zoo, then Hawkwind, and its first public performance—a ten-minute set at All Saints Hall in Notting Hill Gate—attracted a booking agent. United Artists signed Hawkwind in November 1969.

With the 1972 addition of South African–born lyricist (and sometimes vocalist) Robert Calvert, the group's material improved. That year the quasi-psychedelic *In Search of Space* sold over 100,000 copies in Britain alone. Part of a live 1972 concert was taped, and from it sprang the prepunk heavy-metal "Silver Machine," a #3 British hit. Hawkwind's most successful album ever was the double LP *Space Ritual*, which cracked the English Top Ten in 1973. That year the band's hit-bound single "Urban Guerilla" was pulled from distribution by UA because of a coincidental outbreak of terrorist bombings in London.

The group toured the U.S. for the first time in late 1973, with a revue including a seminude dancer, Stacia. They made a couple of subsequent trips to the States in 1974 to support *Hall of the Mountain Grill*, but late in the year Indiana police impounded all of the group's equipment, claiming it owed $8,000 in back taxes, and Hawkwind returned to England.

Undaunted, by spring 1975 they were back in America for their fourth tour, to support *Warrior on the Edge of Time*. Bassist Ian "Lemmy" Kilmister was arrested by Canadian customs officials for possession of amphetamine sulphate (or cocaine; sources vary) and jailed. Not wishing to jeopardize yet another U.S. tour, the band fired him; he later formed the heavy-metal band Motörhead [see entry]. The flip side of the 1975 single "Kings of Speed" is Lemmy's "Motörhead."

Hawkwind played to much acclaim at the Reading Festival in August 1975; soon thereafter longtime collaborator science-fiction author Michael Moorcock released *New World's Fair* with instrumental backing from the band. Moorcock and coauthor Michael Butterworth featured the group in their 1976 novel, *The Time of the Hawklords* (which inspired the group's name change a few years later).

With lyricist Calvert back in the fold (during his mid-decade absence he released two solo albums: *Captain Lockheed and the Starfighters* [1974] and *Lucky Lief and the Longships* [1975], the latter produced by Brian Eno), the group reshuffled its lineup once again and by 1978 (after a brief tenure as the Sonic Assassins) had changed names to Hawklords, around the same time that Simon House (with Hawkwind since April 1974) left to join David Bowie's band. With longtime linchpin Brock (who by the late Seventies had a ten-acre farm in Devon) still dominating the band, they continued with moderate English success through the end of the Seventies.

By that point, the group had developed such a loyal cult that they were often compared to the Grateful Dead. Following an ill-fated tenure with RCA in the early Eighties, the group all but disappeared on this side of the Atlantic. Ironically, they were playing large festivals and arenas at home and all over Europe, including many free and benefit shows. Some long-departed members, including Lemmy, reunited for a tour in the early Eighties. They returned for a short concert tour of the U.S. in 1989, and *Space Bandits* received an unusual amount of media attention here. In 1990 the group added a female singer, Bridget Wishart.

As of the Nineties, the group's output (over 30 albums in the U.K.) has been widely anthologized. Nik Turner is working as a solo artist. Robert Calvert died of a heart attack in 1988, shortly before one of the group's many reunions. Dave Brock has remained the constant throughout the group's many personnel shifts.

Isaac Hayes

Born August 6, 1938, Covington, Tennessee
1967—*Presenting Isaac Hayes* (Enterprise)   1969—
***Hot Buttered Soul*   1970—*The Isaac Hayes Movement; To Be Continued*   1971—*Shaft* soundtrack;**
Black Moses*   1973—*Joy; Live at the Sahara Tahoe
1975—*Chocolate Chip* (HBS); *Disco Connection*
1976—*Groove-a-thon; Juicy Fruit (Disco Freak)*
1977—*A Man and a Woman* (with Dionne Warwick);
***New Horizon* (Polydor)   1978—*Hotbed* (Stax)**
1979—*Don't Let Go* (Polydor); *Royal Rappin's* (with Millie Jackson)   1980—*And Once Again*   1981—
Lifetime Thing*   1986—*U Turn* (Columbia); *Best of Isaac Hayes, vol. 1* (Stax); *Best of Isaac Hayes, vol. 2
1988—*Love Attack* (Columbia)   1991—*Greatest Hit Singles* (Stax)   1995—*Branded* (Pointblank); *Movement—Raw & Refined.*

As a songwriter, arranger, producer, pianist, and vocalist for Stax-Volt Records in the Sixties and early Seventies, Isaac Hayes played an essential part in the making of Memphis soul, and in the early Seventies he laid the groundwork for disco. Hayes has since been credited as

the "Original Rapper," although his influence was first evident in the sexy, seductive bedroom rapping of Barry White and Marvin Gaye.

Hayes was raised by his sharecropper grandparents, and by the age of five was singing in church. By his teens he and his grandparents had moved to Memphis, where he learned to play sax and piano. He began singing in local clubs with his own band, Sir Isaac and the Doo-Dads, and cut his first records for local labels in 1962. Around the same time, he started playing sax with the Mar-Keys, and his association with the group led to studio work with Stax Records that turned into a formal relationship in 1964, when he was hired to play on Otis Redding sessions.

In the mid-Sixties Hayes became more active as keyboardist in the Stax house band, and at Stax he developed a songwriting partnership with lyricist David Porter. Among their more than 200 collaborations were such hits as "Soul Man" and "Hold On, I'm Coming" for Sam and Dave; "B-A-B-Y" for Carla Thomas; and "I Had a Dream" for Johnnie Taylor.

Hayes began making his own Stax records in 1967, but made his reputation as a performer in 1969, when he recorded *Hot Buttered Soul*. With long songs (there were only four cuts on the whole album) and elaborate arrangements, the album hit #8 on the pop chart and went gold.

Hayes' biggest commercial triumph came in 1971, when he scored the Gordon Parks film *Shaft*. The double-album soundtrack won an Academy Award (making Hayes the first African-American composer so honored) as it yielded "The Theme from *Shaft*," which, with its insistent hi-hats, wah-wah guitars, and intoned monologue, hit #1 on the pop chart in 1971, went platinum, won a Grammy, and made Hayes an international superstar. Hayes' later appearance at the Grammy Awards telecast—swathed in silver and chains, bathed in clouds of smoke, and surrounded by beautiful women—was a showstopper. His other pop hits include covers of Burt Bacharach's "Walk On By" (#30 pop, #13 R&B, 1969), Jimmy Webb's "By the Time I Get to Phoenix" (#37 pop and R&B, 1969), and "Never Can Say Goodbye" (#22 pop, #5 R&B, 1971), all on Stax's Enterprise subsidiary. Hayes' early-Seventies concerts featured a 20-piece orchestra, the Isaac Hayes Connection, and Hayes himself, wearing tights, cape, gold chains around his bare chest, and dark glasses fronting his shaved head. One performance was documented in the film *Wattstax* (1973).

In 1975, after fighting with Stax over royalties, he signed with ABC Records, setting up his own Hot Buttered Soul (HBS) subsidiary. His first ABC album went gold, but subsequent efforts were ignored in the disco market. In 1976, the bottom fell out of Hayes' career. Six million dollars in debt, he moved from Memphis to Atlanta. In 1978 Wallace Johnson, cofounder of the Holiday

Inn chain, became his manager, but by 1980 Johnson was suing Hayes for breach of contract.

In the meantime, however, Hayes was taking steps toward a comeback. In 1977 he recorded a double set, *A Man and a Woman*, with Dionne Warwick, and he cowrote Warwick's 1979 Top Twenty pop hit "Déjà Vu." On his own on the Polydor label, he returned to the charts with "Zeke the Freak" (#19 R&B, 1978), "Don't Let Go" (#21 pop, #11 R&B, 1979), and "Do You Wanna Make Love" (#30 R&B, 1979). His duet album with Millie Jackson, *Royal Rappin's* (1979), was popular on the soul chart. His most recent Top Ten R&B hit was 1986's "Ike's Rap," an antidrug song. In 1994 he signed with Virgin Records' Pointblank label. In 1995 Hayes released his first new recordings in over six years.

He began his acting career in 1974 with *Truck Turner*, a black exploitation film that he also produced and scored. Among his other feature-film credits are *It Seemed Like a Good Idea at the Time* (1975), *Escape from New York* (1981), *I'm Gonna Git You Sucka* (1988), *Robin Hood: Men in Tights* (1993), *Posse* (1993), and *It Could Happen to You* (1994). He has also appeared in several made-for-television films and guest-starred on *The Rockford Files*, *Miami Vice*, and *The A-Team*.

Under the official name Nene Katey Ocansey I, Hayes is a member of the Royal Family of Noyami Mantse of the Kabiawe Division of the Ada Traditional Area in Ghana. As an African king, he has worked on improving the Ghanian economy (he is an honorary chief in Nigeria as well). Hayes continues to act, compose, and record; he also lectures on humanitarian issues both here and in Africa.

Ofra Haza

Born November 19, 1959, Tel Aviv, Israel
1987—*Fifty Gates of Wisdom* (Shanachie)   1988—
Shaday* (Sire)   1989—*Desert Wind*   1992—*Kirya
(EastWest).

A striking Sephardic beauty whose voice has drawn comparisons to both Barbra Streisand and legendary Middle Eastern vocalist Om Khalsoum, Ofra Haza was born to Yemenite Jewish parents in Hatikva, Tel Aviv's hardscrabble ghetto for immigrant Jews from Arab lands. At age 12 she joined the Hatikva theater troupe, with which she recorded (winning Israeli music awards for some albums). After serving two compulsory years in the Israeli army, Haza began her own recording career in 1979 and quickly became a top Israeli pop singer—whose records also sold well in neighboring Arab lands. In 1983 she won second prize in the annual Eurovision Song Contest.

In 1985 Haza returned to her roots by recording *Yemenite Songs*, a collection of ancient melodies she'd learned from her mother, with traditional instrumenta-

tion and lyrics from the Sixteenth-Century poetry of Yemenite-Jewish rabbi Shalom Shabazi. The album became a surprise world-beat hit in England, where Haza's voice was sampled from the track "Im Nin'alu" by Coldcut, for its hit 12-inch remix of rappers Eric B. and Rakim's "Paid in Full."

Haza's voice was also sampled by M/A/R/R/S in its international dance hit "Pump Up the Volume," only months before she released her first major-label U.S. album *Shaday* (#130, 1989), a mix of Middle Eastern–inflected dance tracks and conventional Western pop ballads. Its souped-up version of "Im Nin'alu" became a minor U.S. dance hit (and a Top Twenty pop hit in the U.K.). *Kirya* (1992) was produced by Don Was of Was (Not Was) and featured a guest vocal by Iggy Pop on one track. In 1992 Haza also recorded the single "Temple of Love" with British goth band Sisters of Mercy.

Lee Hazlewood

Born Barton Lee Hazlewood, July 9, 1929, Mannford, Oklahoma
1966—*Lee Hazlewood Sings Friday's Child* (Reprise)
1968—*Nancy and Lee* (with Nancy Sinatra); *Nancy and Lee Again* (with Nancy Sinatra) (RCA)   1973—
***Poet, Fool or Bum* (Capitol).**

Lee Hazlewood's long career includes work as a songwriter, a record producer, and a singer (most notably in duets with Nancy Sinatra). He was raised in Port Arthur, Texas, and attended Southern Methodist University before being drafted to fight in Korea. Upon his discharge in 1953 he became a country disc jockey in Phoenix. By 1955 he was writing songs and producing an occasional recording session. His major success of the period was Sanford Clark's 1956 hit "The Fool," which he wrote and produced and which sold 800,000 copies. (The song was also a modest hit when covered by the Gallahads that year.)

In 1957 Hazlewood moved to Philadelphia and cofounded Jamie Records (Dick Clark was one of the partners), which he used to launch the career of guitarist Duane Eddy. Over three and a half years, he produced, among others, "Rebel Rouser," "Yep!," and "Forty Miles of Bad Road." In the early Sixties Hazlewood had a hand in running such minor labels as Trey, East-West, and Gregmark; in 1965 he produced several hits for Dino, Desi and Billy. He relased Gram Parsons' International Submarine Band's album, *Safe at Home*, on his LHI label in 1968.

Hazlewood is best known to the public for his work with Nancy Sinatra. Besides producing her hits "These Boots Are Made for Walkin'" (#1, 1966) and "Sugar Town" (#5, 1966), Hazlewood dueted with her on "Jackson" (#14, 1967), "Summer Wine" (#49, 1967), "Lady Bird" (#20, 1967), and "Some Velvet Morning" (#26, 1968). By the close of the Sixties Hazlewood was living in Stockholm,

Sweden, and alternating between periods of virtual retirement and occasional solo activity in Europe. He was reportedly living in Hamburg, Germany, in the early Nineties; in 1995 he resurfaced to perform live with Nancy Sinatra in the U.S.

Head, Hands and Feet
Formed 1970, England
Albert Lee (b. Dec. 21, 1943, Leominster, Eng.), gtr., kybds.; Tony Colton (b. Feb. 11, 1942, Tunbridge Wells, Eng.), voc.; Ray Smith (b. July 9, 1943, London, Eng.), gtr.; Chas Hodges (b. Nov. 11, 1943, London), bass; Pete Gavin (b. Sep. 9, 1946, London), drums; Mike O'Neil, kybds.
1971—*Head, Hands and Feet* (Capitol) (– O'Neil)
1972—*Tracks* 1973—*Old Soldiers Never Die* (Atco).

Head, Hands and Feet was a conglomeration of British rock studio veterans. Most notable among their ranks was guitarist Albert Lee, who went on to play in Emmylou Harris' Hot Band and Eric Clapton's backup band, and to record solo. The group was cofounded by Tony Colton (who had previously written U.K. hits for such groups as the Merseybeats and the Tremeloes) and Ray Smith in 1970, after the two had played together informally for about nine years. Originally called Poet and the One Man Band, they adopted the name Head, Hands and Feet in late 1969 and stayed together until December 1972. Tony Colton had previous experience as a producer, with credits including Atomic Rooster, Yes, and Richard Harris.

Their initial efforts were impaired by management and record company problems. Their first U.S. disc, the two-record set *Head, Hands and Feet,* was released in late 1971, at which time they played just one West Coast performance. Neither it nor the Capitol followup, *Tracks,* aroused much more than idle curiosity, however. *Old Soldiers Never Die,* perhaps their most consistent effort, might have established them as a major act, but the members were quickly losing interest in their band as studio work beckoned.

Jeff Healey Band
Formed 1985, Toronto, Canada
Jeff Healey (b. Norman Jeffrey Healey, Mar. 25, 1966, Toronto), gtr., voc.; Joe Rockman (b. Joseph Rockman, Jan. 1, 1957, Toronto), bass; Tom Stephen (b. Thomas Stephen, Feb. 2, 1955, St. John, New Brunswick, Can.), drums.
1988—*See the Light* (Arista) 1990—*Hell to Pay*
1992—*Feel This* 1995—*Cover to Cover.*

Having lost his sight to retinoblastoma (eye cancer) as an infant, blues-rock guitarist Jeff Healey developed an unconventional lap-top technique that involves using all five fingers for effects and bending strings with his thumb to hit unusual notes. Healey received his first guitar at the age of three and cut his teeth on country licks. After attending the School for the Blind in Brantford, he registered at a local high school, where he played guitar and trumpet in jazz and concert bands and helped organize a blues-based group called Blue Directions. In 1985 a friend convinced legendary guitarist Albert Collins to let the 19-year-old Healey join him onstage during a Toronto club gig. Impressed, Collins invited the young musician to play with him and guitarist Stevie Ray Vaughan a few nights later. Healey was soon in hot demand for bar appearances.

Needing a band, Healey tapped local drummer Tom Stephen and Stephen's friend, bassist Joe Rockman. The Jeff Healey Band toured Canada for two years before signing with Arista Records in New York. Arista chose veteran Jimmy Iovine to produce the group's first album, just as Iovine was putting together the soundtrack for a film that featured a bar band whose guitarist was blind and played the instrument on his lap. This coincidence was even more uncanny than it might have seemed: The screenwriter for *Road House,* a film starring Patrick Swayze, had conceived the character after seeing Healey perform. The Canadian trio got the movie gig, and 1988's *See the Light* (#22) went platinum, yielding the #5 single "Angel Eyes" in 1989. Despite guest appearances by Mark Knopfler, George Harrison, and Jeff Lynne, 1990's *Hell to Pay* (#27) didn't fare as well. *Feel This* only reached #174, and in 1995 the band released an album of covers.

Health and Happiness Show: See the Bongos

Heart
Formed 1970, Seattle, Washington
Ann Wilson (b. June 19, 1950, San Diego, Calif.), voc., gtr., flute; Nancy Wilson (b. Mar. 16, 1954, San Francisco, Calif.), voc., gtr., mandolin; Roger Fisher (b. 1950), gtr.; Howard Leese (b. June 13, 1951), kybds., synth., gtr.; Michael Derosier, drums; Steve Fossen, bass.
1976—*Dreamboat Annie* (Mushroom) 1977—*Little Queen* (Portrait) 1978—*Magazine* (Mushroom); Dog and Butterfly* (Portrait) 1980—*Bebe Le' Strange* (Epic); *Greatest Hits Live* 1981— (– Derosier; – Fossen) 1982—(+ Mark Andes [b. Feb. 19, 1948, Philadelphia, Pa.], bass; + Denny Carmassi, drums) *Private Audition* 1983—*Passionworks* 1985—*Heart* (Capitol) 1987—*Bad Animals* 1990—*Brigade* 1991—*Rock the House Live!* 1993—(– Andes; – Carmassi) *Desire Walks On* 1994—*Heart: 20 Years of Rock & Roll* CD-ROM.

Heart: Mark Andes, Ann Wilson, Nancy Wilson, Denny
Carmassi, Howard Leese

The Lovemongers (A. Wilson; N. Wilson; + Sue
Ennis voc., gtr., kybds.; + Frank Cox, voc., gtr.,
mand., kybds.): 1992—*Battle of Evermore* EP (Capitol)   1995—*Road Back Home*.

Hard-rock band Heart, led by singer Ann Wilson and featuring her sister Nancy on guitar, sold millions of records in the late Seventies. All but written off by 1985, they then engineered a comeback that saw them surpass their initial success.

The Wilson sisters grew up in Southern California and Taiwan before their Marine Corps captain father retired to the Seattle suburbs. After attending college they returned to Seattle, with Nancy working as a folksinger and Ann joining an all-male local group in 1970 called Heart. (The group was formed in 1963 by Steve Fossen and Roger and Mike Fisher as the Army. They later changed the name to White Heart, shortened to Heart in 1974.) Upon joining, Ann became lead guitarist Roger Fisher's girlfriend, and when Nancy joined in 1974, she became involved with Fisher's brother Mike, who by then had retired from the stage to become the group's soundman.

After many one-nighters in the Vancouver area, in 1975 they attracted the attention of Canada's Mushroom label, run by Shelly Siegel. He had them cut *Dreamboat Annie,* which upon release in Canada sold 30,000 copies. In the U.S. Siegel released it first in Seattle, where it quickly sold another 25,000. With two hit singles— "Crazy on You" (#35, 1976) and "Magic Man" (#9, 1976)— the album eventually sold over one million copies.

By early 1977 the Wilson sisters had switched to CBS' subsidiary Portrait, a move that resulted in a prolonged legal fight with Siegel. In retaliation he released the partly completed *Magazine* at the same time Portrait released *Little Queen.* A Seattle court ruled that Mushroom had to recall *Magazine* so that the Wilsons could remix several tracks and redo vocals before rereleasing

the disc. (The Wilsons had wanted the album taken off the market completely.)

Little Queen, with the hit "Barracuda" (#11, 1977), became Heart's second million-seller; *Magazine* and the double-platinum *Dog and Butterfly* followed suit in 1978. During sessions for *Bebe Le' Strange,* the Wilson-Fisher liaisons ended. Roger Fisher formed his own band in the Seattle area. Howard Leese and Nancy took up the guitar slack, and Nancy Wilson's childhood friend Sue Ennis helped out on song collaborations. The group hit the road for a 77-city tour to support *Bebe,* then returned to make *Private Audition* with new bassist Mark Andes (Spirit, Jo Jo Gunne, Firefall) and drummer Denny Carmassi (Gamma).

That album and the following year's *Passionworks* failed to go gold, putting Heart at a career crossroads. But the group's first album for Capitol, simply titled *Heart* (#1, 1985), sold five million copies on the strength of four Top Ten hits: "What About Love?" (#10, 1985), "Never" (#4, 1985), "These Dreams" (#1, 1986), and "Nothin' at All" (#10, 1986). In June 1986 Nancy Wilson married journalist and screenwriter/director (*Fast Times at Ridgemont High, Singles*) Cameron Crowe. She made cameo appearances in both *Fast Times* and his later film, *Wild Life. Bad Animals* (#2, 1987), too, contained a chart-topper, in the power ballad "Alone," as well as "Who Will You Run To" (#7, 1987) and "There's the Girl" (#12, 1987). In 1989 Ann Wilson and Cheap Trick's Robin Zander had a #6 hit with their duet, "Surrender to Me." *Brigade* (#3, 1990) became Heart's sixth multiplatinum LP and added three more Top Twenty-five hits to its catalogue: "All I Want to Do Is Make Love to You" (#2, 1990), "I Didn't Want to Need You" (#23, 1990), and "Stranded" (#13, 1990).

Following a 1990 tour, the Wilson sisters put together an informal acoustic group called the Lovemongers with Sue Ennis and Frank Cox; a four-song EP that included a version of Led Zeppelin's "Battle of Evermore" came out in late 1992, and the quartet performed several times in the Seattle area. When Heart reemerged with *Desire Walks On* in 1993, it was without Andes and Carmassi. For the group's subsequent tour, their places were taken by bassist Fernando Saunders (b. Jan. 17, 1954, Detroit, Mich.) and drummer Denny Fongheiser (b. Apr. 21, 1959, Alameda, Calif.).

The Wilson sisters have played a key role on the Seattle music scene. Among the groups that have recorded at their Bad Animals studio are R.E.M., Pearl Jam, Alice in Chains, and Soundgarden. Heart's *Heart: 20 Years of Rock & Roll* was the first CD-ROM multimedia biography/greatest-hits package to be released.

The Heartbreakers/ Johnny Thunders
Formed 1975, New York City, New York
Johnny Thunders (b. John Anthony Genzale, July

15, 1952, New York City; d. Apr. 23, 1991, New Orleans, La.), gtr., voc.; Walter Lure (b. Apr. 22, 1949, New York City), gtr., voc.; Richard Hell (b. Richard Myers, Oct. 2, 1949, Lexington, Ky.), bass, voc.; Jerry Nolan (b. May 7, 1946, New York City; d. Jan. 14, 1992, New York City), drums.
1976—(– Hell; + Billy Rath, bass) 1977—*L.A.M.F.* (Track, U.K.) (– Nolan; + Ty Styx, drums) 1979—*Live at Max's Kansas City* (Max's Kansas City/Beggars Banquet, U.K.) 1982—*D.T.K.: Live at the Speakeasy* (Jungle, U.K.) 1984—*Live at the Lyceum Ballroom* (ABC, U.K.); *L.A.M.F. Revisited* (Jungle, U.K.).
Johnny Thunders solo: 1978—*So Alone* (Real) 1983—*New Too Much Junkie Business* (ROIR); *Diary of a Lover* (PVC) 1987—*Stations of the Cross* (ROIR).

After the original New York Dolls broke up, Johnny Thunders—who had been the Dolls' Keith Richards to David Johansen's Mick Jagger—and Jerry Nolan formed the Heartbreakers, first as a trio with former Television bassist Richard Hell, who soon left to lead his own band, the Voidoids. If the New York Dolls were a precursor to punk rock [see entry], then the Heartbreakers served as a living bridge to it—updating classic Rolling Stones–style, sneering two-guitar rock in prototypical fast-and-furious style. With Thunders' shambling, drugged-out, foul-mouthed onstage charm, and songs like "Chinese Rocks" and "Too Much Junkie Business" celebrating the heroin-junkie lifestyle, these Heartbreakers could not be confused with Tom Petty's backup band.

The Heartbreakers built a following with a year of East Coast club gigs, but drew no offers from record companies. Sex Pistols impresario Malcolm McLaren, who had been involved in the Dolls' final days, invited the Heartbreakers to tour England, where they joined the Pistols, the Clash, the Damned, and the Slits on the historic 1976 Anarchy Tour. (Jerry Nolan later claimed he and Thunders first introduced Johnny Rotten and other punks to heroin during this time.) Heralded by punk rockers who'd been inspired by the Dolls, the Heartbreakers stayed in England for over a year, recording their debut album, *L.A.M.F.* (from an obscene graffito used by the teen gangs of which Thunders and Nolan had been members). It was so poorly produced that Nolan quit the band in disgust and formed the short-lived Idols back in New York City, while former Clash drummer Terry Chimes took Nolan's place briefly before the Heartbreakers drifted apart in London.

Thunders stayed there, and in 1978 recorded a critically acclaimed solo album, *So Alone*, with backing from Sex Pistols Steve Jones and Paul Cook, Peter Perrett of the Only Ones, Thin Lizzy's Phil Lynott, and ex–Small Faces/Humble Pie guitarist Steve Marriott. The album included a rare glimpse of Thunders' tender side in the classic "You Can't Put Your Arms Around a Memory," as well as nods to his musical roots in girl-group sass ("Great Big Kiss") and surf music (an amphetamine cover of the Chantays' "Pipeline"). Thunders returned to New York in late 1978 for the first of many Heartbreakers reunion/farewell gigs, which was captured on *Live at Max's Kansas City*. In 1980 Thunders formed Gang War with former MC5 guitarist Wayne Kramer, while Lure and Rath started the Heroes with Lure's younger brother Richie (a guitarist in the late-Seventies punk band the Erasers). Thunders formed another short-lived band, Cosa Nostra, before reconvening the Heartbreakers again in 1982. By this time Lure was working as a stockbroker. In 1984, with former Generation X guitarist (and future Sigue Sigue Sputnik leader) Tony James, Thunders finally remixed *L.A.M.F.* for *Revisited*. The Heartbreakers (with Nolan) held a final New York City reunion show in 1990. A year later Thunders, just back in the U.S. from a successful tour of Japan, died of a lethal mixture of methadone and alcohol in a New Orleans hotel room. Nolan, who'd suffered from drug-related ill health for a while, died the following year.

Heaven 17
Formed 1979, Sheffield, England
Martyn Ware (b. May 19, 1956, Sheffield), synth.; Ian Craig Marsh (b. Nov. 11, 1956, Sheffield), synth.; Glenn Gregory (b. May 16, 1958, Sheffield), voc.
1982—*Heaven 17* (Arista) 1983—*The Luxury Gap* 1984—*How Men Are* 1986—*Pleasure One* (Virgin) 1988—*Teddy Bear, Duke & Psycho.*

Computer-operators-turned-synthesizer-wizards Martyn Ware and Ian Craig Marsh had worked together in the band Human League [see entry] before forming the British Electric Foundation, an experimental, dance-oriented production project that worked with a variety of singers and musicians. Heaven 17, a trio consisting of Ware, Marsh, and singer Glenn Gregory, became the best-known B.E.F. offshoot. Named after a group in Anthony Burgess' novel *A Clockwork Orange*, Heaven 17 faced the same accusations of slickness that met many techno-pop acts, but the band also won praise for its sophisticated electro-funk arrangements, and for Gregory's singing, which was judged unusually expressive for his genre.

Ware and Marsh hooked up with ex-photographer Gregory at a drama center in Sheffield. Heaven 17's first single, "(We Don't Need This) Fascist Groove Thang," was released in England in 1981; it became a minor hit there (#45), despite a BBC Radio ban induced by its title. The trio's eponymous debut album followed in 1982 and hit the U.S. charts at #68 the following year. Meanwhile, 1983's *The Luxury Gap* peaked at #4 in the U.K. In 1984

Gregory took part in the star-studded recording sessions for Band Aid's "Do They Know It's Christmas?" single. But despite *How Men Are*'s success in England (#12 U.K., 1984), a commercial foothold eluded Heaven 17 in America. In 1988, after the release of *Teddy Bear, Duke & Psycho,* Ware and Gregory focused on production projects. By this point Ware had coproduced Tina Turner's 1983 cover of Al Green's "Let's Stay Together" (#26 pop, #6 U.K.)—which featured Gregory on backing vocals—and Terence Trent D'Arby's debut album, *Introducing the Hardline According to Terence Trent D'Arby* (1987). Ware and Marsh resurrected B.E.F. at large in 1990 and produced a single for the R&B singer Lalah Hathaway in 1991. In 1994 Ware produced Erasure's LP *I Say, I Say, I Say*

Heavy D. and the Boyz
Formed 1984, Mt. Vernon, New York
Heavy D. (b. Dwight Myers, May 24, 1967, Jamaica), voc.; Eddie F. (b. Eddie Farrell, Mar. 25, 1968), DJ; G-Whiz (b. Glen Parrish, Oct. 20, 1968, New Rochelle, N.Y.), stylist; Trouble T-Roy (b. Troy Dixon, Oct. 19, 1967; d. July 15, 1990), dancer.
1987—*Living Large* (MCA)   1989—*Big Tyme* 1990—(– Trouble T-Roy)   1991—*Peaceful Journey* 1993—*Blue Funk*   1994—*Nuttin' but Love.*

At first Heavy D. seemed to be a novelty rapper, calling himself the Overweight Lover and giving his songs names like "Chunky But Funky." But his deep, amiable baritone and funky, fluid grooves, often characterized by the Teddy Riley–produced R&B-rap style New Jack Swing, won the approval of critics and serious hip-hop fans alike. In addition to Riley, the group has used a variety of well-known producers, including Erick Sermon, Marley Marl, Gang Starr's DJ Premier, and Heavy D.'s cousin Pete Rock.

Dwight Myers grew up in a middle-class, Mt. Vernon, New York, home listening to rap on the radio. While still in his teens he won $1,500 in Atlantic City, with which he and Eddie Ferrell bought a computer. He later traded it for a drum machine and started making tapes in Ferrell's basement with friends Glen Parrish and Troy Dixon. The 260-pound, 6-foot-3-inch, light-skinned Myers began calling himself Heavy D.

In 1987 Heavy D. and the Boyz released *Living Large.* Both their second album, *Big Tyme* (#19 pop, #1 R&B, 1989), and their third, *Peaceful Journey* (#21 pop, #5 R&B, 1991), sold platinum. In addition, Heavy D. wrote the theme song for the popular television show *In Living Color.* The group suffered two tragedies between *Big Tyme* and *Peaceful Journey.* In 1989 Heavy D.'s brother, Tony Myers, was gunned down. Then, while on tour in 1990, Trouble T-Roy fell from a ledge to his death during rehearsals.

Heavy D. and the Boyz: G-Whiz, Eddie F., Heavy D.

The group's string of hit singles, beginning in 1986, include "Mr. Big Stuff" (#60 R&B, 1986); "Don't You Know" (#12 R&B, 1988); "We Got Our Own Thang" (#10 R&B, 1989); "Somebody for Me" (#8 R&B, 1989); "Gyrlz, They Love Me" (#12 R&B, 1990); "Now That We Found Love" (#11 pop, #5 R&B, 1991), a rap version of Third World's #47 hit of 1979; and "Is It Good to You" (#32 pop, #13 R&B, 1991). Singles from 1993's *Blue Funk* (#40 pop, #7 R&B) were not as successful, but the Boyz came back in 1994 with the smash "Got Me Waiting" (#20 pop, #3 R&B), the first single from *Nuttin' but Love.*

Heavy Metal
The nonscientific use of the term "heavy metal" was coined by Beat novelist William Burroughs in his *Naked Lunch* and reintroduced into the pop vocabulary by Steppenwolf in their hit "Born to Be Wild" ("heavy metal thunder"). It was redefined in the Seventies by rock critic Lester Bangs in the music magazine *Creem* and subsequently overhauled by metal fans themselves by the time of its complete evolution from a hyped-up form of the blues to head-banging music for the masses.

This heavily amplified, blues-based, electric-guitar-driven rock came of age during the early Seventies in the music of bands such as Black Sabbath, Deep Purple, and the highly influential Led Zeppelin, and the most commercially successful heavy-metal act of its time, Grand Funk Railroad. The roots of metal, however, date back to the late Fifties, when North Carolina guitarist Link Wray introduced distortion in rock & roll with his instrumental "fuzz-tone" hit "Rumble" (#16, 1958). Within six years, a number of British bands, including the Animals, the Dave Clark Five, and the Kinks, began incorporating

Wray's distortion into their own music. In 1964 the Kinks' proto-metal anthem "You Really Got Me" reached #1 in Britain and #7 in the U.S.

Meanwhile a slew of young guitarists were waiting in the wings of rock & roll, ready to add their own mark to the new hard-rock sound. In 1966 a harder, updated version of the blues-influenced Yardbirds, featuring new guitarists Jeff Beck and Jimmy Page, dazzled audiences while on tour supporting the Rolling Stones. In 1967 former R&B session guitarist Jimi Hendrix made his American debut with his new band, the Experience, at the Monterey Pop Festival. And in 1968 Blue Cheer recorded what is perhaps the first bona-fide heavy-metal album, *Vincebus Eruptum,* which reached #11 primarily on the strength of its #14 single, a loud, grungy update of Eddie Cochran's 1958 #8 hit "Summertime Blues." In early 1969 Jimmy Page's new band, Led Zeppelin, released its debut album, which entered the Top Ten; within the next decade Zeppelin would become the most celebrated heavy-metal band of all time, defining many of the genre's central themes, both musical (high, soaring vocals; bombastic guitar solos; big, chunky drums; cryptic backmasking effects; and mythic lyrics) and sociological (an interest in the occult; use of symbology; theatrical stage productions).

The electric guitar is heavy metal's primary icon, and the principal gauge by which fans rate their heavy metal heroes is instrumental speed and virtuosity. The most popular metal guitarists have normally been the fastest and most innovative: Page, Hendrix, Ted Nugent, Eddie Van Halen, Angus Young, Yngwie Malmsteen. The vocalist runs a close second in importance to the guitarist, displaying dazzling range, histrionic delivery, and sex appeal: Robert Plant, Steven Tyler, David Lee Roth, Axl Rose. Although the metal arena is primarily a man's world (male-dominated bands are by far the most successful), there also have been a number of female-dominated bands, including the Runaways, Girlschool, and Vixen.

If the early Seventies was heavy metal's "golden age," the mid-Seventies was a particularly slow period. The first-generation rock audience had matured and begun listening to soft-rock bands and singer/songwriters such as James Taylor, Fleetwood Mac, Linda Ronstadt, and the Eagles. Teenagers kept metal alive in sports arenas and stadiums, embracing the cartoonish theatrics of perennial touring acts such as Kiss, Aerosmith, and Ted Nugent. By the late Seventies and early Eighties, as rock critics ignored metal and hailed punk as the new sound of rebellious youth, heavy metal was undergoing a full-scale renaissance. While the music establishment thumbed its collective nose at the genre, the real youth of America was consuming more heavy metal than ever (much more than punk), putting a succession of metal hit singles, by bands like AC/DC, Def Leppard, and Van Halen into the Top Forty.

In the Eighties, some of the more popular heavy-metal bands whose members had grown up listening to punk, new wave, and glam-punk antecedents, from the New York Dolls to Aerosmith, began playing a metal-based music with less emphasis on lengthy solos and more on punch and glamour (Mötley Crüe, Poison, Skid Row, Guns n' Roses). By the Nineties, a contingent of metal bands had upped the volume again, sped up the tempo, and adopted the apocalyptic imagery of hardcore punk (Metallica, Anthrax, Soundgarden). With this crop of bands, metal reached a new commercial peak. When the thrash-metal band Metallica's fifth album entered the charts at #1 in 1991, with a string of hits including "Enter Sandman" (#16, 1991), even the most unsympathetic critics of heavy metal could no longer ignore the music's importance to pop culture.

Bobby Hebb
Born July 26, 1941, Nashville, Tennessee
1966—*Sunny* (Philips).

Singer/songwriter Bobby Hebb is best known for the light, sentimental "Sunny" (#2, 1966). He was one of seven children of blind parents who taught him to play the guitar. At age 12 Hebb became one of the first blacks to play the Grand Ole Opry, when country legend Roy Acuff invited him to perform. In the early Sixties he moved to Chicago, graduated from a dental technician's course, and took music classes while occasionally accompanying Bo Diddley on the spoons. He studied guitar with Chet Atkins, who helped him break into show business. Hebb eventually met Sylvia Shemwell, with whom he worked as Bobby and Sylvia. He later cut such tunes as "Night Train to Memphis" and "You Broke My Heart and I Broke Your Jaw."

In 1963 Hebb's brother Hal (a member of the Marigolds) was killed in a mugging. Hebb responded with "Sunny." He was unable to sell it to publishers, but in 1966, while recording an album, he cut the song at the end of a session to use up some extra time, and it became a hit. By year's end Hebb had appeared on several major network television shows and toured the U.S. with the Beatles. (The singer claims to have recommended keyboardist Billy Preston to the Fab Four, after Ringo Starr asked him if he knew of any funky piano players.) Followup hits proved elusive, however. His last two chart appearances came before the year was out, with "A Satisfied Mind" (#39) and "Love Me" (#84).

Hebb had isolated U.K. hits like "Love Love Love" in the early Seventies on GRT Records. As the decade progressed he made occasional club appearances in America and got a reworked "Sunny" ("Sunny '76") onto the soul chart but mostly lived a quiet life in a colonial mansion in Salem, Massachusetts.

Hebb claims to have written over 3,000 songs, a third of them published—including material for Percy Sledge, Mary Wells, Marvin Gaye, Billy Preston, Herb Alpert, and Lou Rawls, whose recording of Hebb's "A Natural Man" won a Grammy in 1971. "Sunny" was widely covered as well, showing up on discs by Cher, Georgie Fame, and Gloria Lynne, among others. Hebb now lives in an artists' colony in the small Massachusetts town of Rockport.

Michael Hedges

Born December 31, 1953, Enid, Oklahoma
1981—*Breakfast in the Field* (Windham Hill)
1984—*Aerial Boundaries* 1985—*Watching My Life Go By* 1986—*Santabear's First Christmas* 1987—*Live on the Double Planet* 1988—*Strings of Steel* 1989—*The Shape of the Land* 1990—*Taproot* 1994—*Road to Return* (High Street).

Solo steel-string acoustic guitarist Michael Hedges is by far the most ferocious-sounding artist to record for Windham Hill, the pioneering "New Age" label. Hedges has the intensity—and some of the techniques—of such acclaimed rock guitarists as Eddie Van Halen.

Hedges began studying piano at age four; after growing up listening to pop and rock music (he's cited the Beatles and Jethro Tull), he took up guitar, flute, clarinet, and cello. He focused on classical guitar at the Peabody Conservatory in Baltimore, then attended Stanford's Center for Computer Research and Musical Acoustics—at both schools, studying by day and playing steel-string acoustic guitar in bars and cafes by night. Windham Hill founder Will Ackerman discovered Hedges performing at the Varsity Theater in Palo Alto. Hedges' all-instrumental debut, *Breakfast in the Field,* won raves from such jazz-rock guitar greats as Larry Coryell. Hedges' style and technique—a combination of unusual tunings, two-handed fretboard tapping, and full-chord hammer-ons and pull-offs, as opposed to the usual single-note variety—produced a harmonically rich and highly percussive sound that made his single guitar sound like a full band. *Aerial Boundaries* was nominated for a Best Instrumental Grammy; the title track was used in some TV commercials.

In 1985 Hedges introduced his vocals (in a jazzy, Joni Mitchell style), flute, synthesizer, and electric bass on the poorly received *Watching My Life Go By,* which featured guest vocals by Bobby McFerrin. That same year he recorded the soundtrack for a children's television special, *Santabear's First Christmas.* Through the late Eighties and into the Nineties with *Taproot* and *Road to Return,* Hedges continued to focus on composition and vocals in addition to his remarkable guitar play-

ing. In 1989 he contributed arranging, guitar, and background vocals to two tracks on David Crosby's *Oh Yes I Can.*

Richard Hell and the Voidoids

Formed September 1976, New York City, New York
Richard Hell (b. Richard Myers, Oct. 2, 1949, Lexington, Ky.), bass, voc.; Marc Bell (b. July 15, 1956, New York City), drums; Robert Quine (b. Dec. 30, 1942, Akron, Ohio), gtr., voc.; Ivan Julian (b. June 26, 1955, Washington, D.C.), gtr., voc.
1976—*Blank Generation* EP (Stiff) 1977—*Blank Generation* (Sire) 1978—(– Bell; + Jerry Antonius, bass, kybds.; + Frank Mauro, drums) 1980—(– Antonius; – Mauro; + Naux [b. July 20, 1951, San Jose, Calif.], gtr.; + Fred Maher, drums) 1982—*Destiny Street* (Red Star) 1984—*R.I.P.* (ROIR) 1990—*Funhunt.*
Richard Hell with the Dim Stars: 1992—*Dim Stars* (Caroline).

Richard Hell led the Voidoids, one of the most harshly uncompromising bands on New York's late-Seventies punk scene, playing songs with dissonant, jagged guitar lines and dark free-association imagery that owed something to both Captain Beefheart and the Velvet Underground. Hell had played with Johnny Thunders' Heartbreakers [see entry]; and with the Neon Boys, who later became Television [see entry]; then he formed the Voidoids to perform his own songs. They were regular attractions at punk showcase CBGB, along with Blondie, the Ramones, and Talking Heads.

Hell's 1977 debut album, *Blank Generation,* provided two anthems for the scene, the title cut and "Love Comes in Spurts." But although Hell performed frequently, he remained obscure outside New York and London. In 1979 Nick Lowe produced a single, "The Kid with the Replaceable Head."

In 1982 Hell resurfaced with a new band and an album, *Destiny Street.* (Original Voidoids guitarist Robert Quine, meanwhile, had joined Lou Reed's band for *The Blue Mask.*) Hell also began an acting career, appearing in Susan Seidelman's 1982 film *Smithereens.* Other film credits include the 1993 underground film *What About Me?*

By the mid-Eighties, Hell had seemingly put music behind him; his writing—nonfiction, fiction, and poetry—was published by a variety of magazines, and he began doing spoken-word performances. (*R.I.P.* and *Funhunt* documented early Voidoid live shows.) In 1992 Hell joined the band Dim Stars, a side project initiated by Sonic Youth's Thurston Moore and Steve Shelley with Gumball's Don Fleming. The group released a self-titled album and played a limited number of gigs.

Grammy Awards

Merle Haggard
1984 Best Country Vocal Performance, Male: "That's the Way Love Goes"

Hammer
1990 Best Music Video, Long Form: *Please Hammer Don't Hurt 'Em The Movie* (with John Oetjen and Rupert Wainwright)
1990 Best R&B Song: "U Can't Touch This" (with Rick James and Alonzo Miller)
1990 Best Rap Solo Performance: "U Can't Touch This"

John Hammond
1984 Best Traditional Blues Recording: *Blues Explosion* (with others)

Herbie Hancock
1983 Best R&B Instrumental Performance: "Rockit"
1984 Best R&B Instrumental Performance: *Sound System*
1987 Best Instrumental Composition: "Call Sheet Blues" (with Ron Carter, Billy Higgins, and Wayne Shorter)
1994 Best Jazz Instrumental Performance: *A Tribute to Miles* (with Ron Carter, Wayne Shorter, Tony Williams, and Wallace Roney)

Emmylou Harris
1976 Best Country Vocal Performance, Female: *Elite Hotel*
1979 Best Country Vocal Performance, Female: *Blue Kentucky Girl*
1980 Best Country Performance by a Duo or Group with Vocal: "That Lovin' You Feelin' Again" (with Roy Orbison)
1984 Best Country Vocal Performance, Female: "In My Dreams"
1987 Best Country Performance by a Duo or Group with Vocal: *Trio* (with Dolly Parton and Linda Ronstadt)

Emmylou Harris and the Nash Ramblers
1992 Best Country Performance by a Duo or Group with Vocal: *Emmylou Harris and the Nash Ramblers at the Ryman*

George Harrison [See also: the Beatles, the Traveling Wilburys]
1970 Best Original Score Written for a Motion Picture or TV Special: *Let It Be* (with John Lennon, Paul McCartney, and Ringo Starr)
1972 Album of the Year: *The Concert for Bangla Desh* (with others)

John Hartford
1967 Best Folk Performance: "Gentle on My Mind"
1967 Best Country & Western Song: "Gentle on My Mind"
1976 Best Ethnic or Traditional Recording: *Mark Twang*

Donny Hathaway
1972 Best Pop Vocal by a Duo, Group or Chorus: "Where Is the Love?" (with Roberta Flack)

Edwin Hawkins
1992 Best Gospel Album by a Choir or Chorus: *Edwin Hawkins Music & Arts Seminar Mass Choir—Recorded Live in Los Angeles*

Edwin Hawkins Singers
1969 Best Soul Gospel: "Oh Happy Day"
1970 Best Soul Gospel Performance: "Every Man Wants to Be Free"
1977 Best Soul Gospel Performance, Contemporary: *Wonderful!*

Isaac Hayes
1971 Best Original Score Written for a Motion Picture: *Shaft*
1971 Best Instrumental Arrangement: "Theme from *Shaft*"
1972 Best Pop Instrumental Performance by an Arranger, Composer, Orchestra and/or Choral Leader: *Black Moses*

Billie Holiday
1987 Lifetime Achievement Award

Jennifer Holliday
1982 Best R&B Vocal Performance, Female: "And I am Telling You I'm Not Going"
1985 Best Inspirational Performance: "Come Sunday"

John Lee Hooker
1989 Best Traditional Blues Recording: "I'm in the Mood" (with Bonnie Raitt)

Bruce Hornsby
1986 Best New Artist (with the Range)
1989 Best Bluegrass Recording: "The Valley Road" (with the Nitty Gritty Dirt Band)
1993 Best Pop Instrumental Performance: "Barcelona Mona" (with Branford Marsalis)

Johnny Horton
1959 Best Country & Western Performance: "The Battle of New Orleans"

Thelma Houston
1977 Best R&B Vocal Performance, Female: "Don't Leave Me This Way"

Whitney Houston
1985 Best Pop Vocal Performance, Female: "Saving All My Love for You"
1987 Best Pop Vocal Performance, Female: "I Wanna Dance with Somebody (Who Loves Me)"
1993 Record of the Year: "I Will Always Love You" (with David Foster)
1993 Album of the Year: *The Bodyguard* soundtrack (with others)
1993 Best Pop Vocal Performance, Female: "I Will Always Love You"

Helmet

Formed 1989, New York City, New York
Page Hamilton (b. May 18, 1960, Portland, Ore.),
voc., gtr.; Peter Mengede, gtr.; Henry Bogdan
(b. Feb. 4, 1961, Riverside, Calif.), bass; John Stanier
(b. Aug. 2, 1968, Baltimore, Md.), drums.
1990—*Strap It On* (Amphetamine Reptile)   1992—
***Meantime* (Interscope)   1993—(– Mengede; + Rob**
Echeverria [b. Dec. 15, 1967, New York City], gtr.)
1994—*Betty*.

With a precise, riff-heavy atonal guitar sound, Helmet falls somewhere between heavy metal and the avant-garde. Led by the clean-cut Page Hamilton—renowned for his obsession with "musical economy"—the group signed to Interscope in 1992 for a surprising million-dollar-plus contract that promised high royalty rates and nearly unheard-of creative control.

Hamilton grew up in a small town in Oregon where, in his senior year of high school, he learned to play guitar. In 1985 he moved to New York and earned a master's degree in jazz from the Manhattan School of Music. He then received an avant-noise education playing guitar for the minimalist composer Glenn Branca and in the Band of Susans. Wanting to write his own songs, Hamilton quit the Band of Susans and formed Helmet with Peter Mengede. Through *Village Voice* ads, they found John Stanier and fellow Oregonian Henry Bogdan, who had moved to New York in the Eighties and, having become disillusioned with rock, had been pursuing his painting career (he was a studio assistant for Frank Stella). Six months later came the release of the spare *Strap It On,* leading to the band's deal with Interscope.

The metalish *Meantime* (#68, 1992) followed, but it was 1994's *Betty* (#45) that expanded the group's disciplined sound by incorporating a hint of hip-hop groove; the album was produced by T-Ray, who has also worked with Cypress Hill. Rob Echeverria replaced guitarist Mengede, who was dismissed weeks before a tour in 1993 due to a strained relationship with Hamilton.

Helmet contributed songs to the soundtracks of *Judgment Night* (a 1993 collaboration with House of Pain); *The Crow* (1994), and *Johnny Mnemonic* (1995). The band made a cameo appearance in *The Jerky Boys*—performing a Black Sabbath song—with Ozzy Osbourne portraying their manager.

Jimi Hendrix

Born November 27, 1942, Seattle, Washington; died
September 18, 1970, London, England
1967—*Are You Experienced?* (Reprise)   1968—*Axis:*
Bold as Love*; *Electric Ladyland*   1969—*Smash Hits
1970—*Band of Gypsys* (Capitol)   1971—*The Cry of*
Love* (Reprise); *Rainbow Bridge*   1972—*Hendrix in
the West*   1973—*Soundtrack Recordings from the

Jimi Hendrix

***Film, Jimi Hendrix*   1975—*Crash Landing*   1976—**
Midnight Lightning*   1978—*The Essential Jimi
Hendrix*   1979—*The Essential Jimi Hendrix, vol. 2
1982—*The Jimi Hendrix Concerts*   1986—*Band of*
***Gypsys 2* (Capitol)   1988—*Radio One* (Rykodisc)**
1990—*Lifelines: The Jimi Hendrix Story* (Reprise);
Hendrix Speaks: The Jimi Hendrix Interviews
(Rhino)   1991—*Stages 1967–70* (Reprise)   1994—
***Blues* (MCA)   1995—*Voodoo Soup*.**

Jimi Hendrix was one of rock's few true originals. He was one of the most innovative and influential rock guitarists of the late Sixties and perhaps the most important electric guitarist after Charlie Christian. His influence figures prominently in the playing style of such rock guitarists as Robin Trower, Vernon Reid (Living Colour), and Stevie Ray Vaughan. A left-hander who took a right-handed Fender Stratocaster and played it upside down, Hendrix pioneered the use of the instrument as an electronic sound source—forging a trail followed by several generations of experimental rock guitarists. Rockers before Hendrix had experimented with feedback and distortion, but he turned those effects and others into a controlled, fluid vocabulary every bit as personal as the blues he began with. But while he unleashed noise— and such classic hard-rock riffs as "Purple Haze," "Foxy Lady," and "Crosstown Traffic"—with uncanny mastery, Hendrix also created such tender ballads as "The Wind Cries Mary," the oft-covered "Little Wing," and "Angel" and haunting blues recordings such as "Red House" and "Voodoo Chile." And although Hendrix did not consider himself a good singer, his vocals were nearly as wide-ranging, intimate, and evocative as his guitar playing.

Hendrix's studio craft and his virtuosity with both conventional and unconventional guitar sounds have been widely imitated, and his image as the psychedelic voodoo child conjuring uncontrollable forces is a rock archetype. His songs have inspired several tribute albums and have been recorded by a jazz group (1989's *Hendrix Project*), the Kronos String Quartet, and avant-garde flutist Robert Dick. Hendrix's musical vision had a profound effect on everyone from Sly Stone and George Clinton—and, through them, Prince—to Miles Davis. His theatrical performing style—full of unmistakably sexual undulations, and such tricks as playing the guitar behind his back (a tradition that went back at least to bluesman T-Bone Walker) and picking it with his teeth—has never quite been equaled, but in the nearly three decades since his death, pop stars from Michael Jackson (with his ever-present paramilitary jackets) to Prince have evoked Hendrix's look and style.

As a teenager, Hendrix taught himself to play guitar by listening to records by blues guitarists Muddy Waters and B. B. King and rockers such as Chuck Berry and Eddie Cochran. He played in high school bands before enlisting in the U.S. Army in 1959. Discharged after parachuting injuries in 1961, Hendrix began working under the pseudonym Jimmy James as a pickup guitarist. By 1964, when he moved to New York City, he had played behind Sam Cooke, B. B. King, Little Richard, Jackie Wilson, Ike and Tina Turner, and Wilson Pickett. In New York he played the club circuit with King Curtis, the Isley Brothers, John Hammond Jr., and Curtis Knight.

In 1965 Hendrix formed his own band, Jimmy James and the Blue Flames, to play Greenwich Village coffeehouses. Chas Chandler of the Animals took him to London in the autumn of 1966 and arranged for the creation of the Jimi Hendrix Experience, with Englishmen Noel Redding on bass and Mitch Mitchell on drums.

The Experience's first single, "Hey Joe," reached #6 on the U.K. chart early in 1967, followed shortly by "Purple Haze" and their debut album. Hendrix fast became the rage of London's pop society. Though word of the Hendrix phenomenon spread through the U.S., he was not seen in America (and no records were released) until June 1967, when, at Paul McCartney's insistence, the Experience appeared at the Monterey Pop Festival. The performance, which Hendrix climaxed by burning his guitar, was filmed for *Monterey Pop*.

Hendrix quickly became a superstar. Stories such as one reporting that the Experience was dropped from the bill of a Monkees tour at the insistence of the Daughters of the American Revolution became part of the Hendrix myth, but he considered himself a musician more than a star. Soon after the start of his second American tour, early in 1968, he renounced the extravagances of his stage act and simply performed his music. A hostile reception led him to conclude that his best music came out in the informal settings of studios and clubs, and he began construction of Electric Lady, his own studio in New York.

Hendrix was eager to experiment with musical ideas, and he jammed with John McLaughlin, Larry Coryell, and members of Traffic, among others. Miles Davis admired his inventiveness (and, in fact, planned to record with him), and Bob Dylan—whose "Like a Rolling Stone," "All Along the Watchtower," and "Drifter's Escape" Hendrix recorded—later returned the tribute by performing "All Along the Watchtower" in the Hendrix mode.

As 1968 came to a close, disagreements arose between manager Chas Chandler and comanager Michael Jeffrey; Jeffrey, who opposed Hendrix's avant-garde leanings, got the upper hand. Hendrix was also under pressure from black-power advocates to form an all-black group and play to black audiences. These problems exacerbated already existing tensions within the Experience, and early in 1969 Redding left the group to form Fat Mattress. Hendrix replaced him with an army buddy, Billy Cox. Mitchell stayed on briefly, but by August the Experience was defunct.

Hendrix appeared at the Woodstock Festival with a large informal ensemble called the Electric Sky Church, and later that year he put together the all-black Band of Gypsys—with Cox and drummer Buddy Miles (Electric Flag), with whom he had played behind Wilson Pickett. The Band of Gypsys' debut concert at New York's Fillmore East on New Year's Eve 1969 provided the recordings for the group's only album (its second album was not released until 1986). Hendrix walked offstage in the middle of their Madison Square Garden gig; when he performed again some months later it was with Mitchell and Cox, the group that recorded *Cry of Love*, Hendrix's last self-authorized album. With them he played at the Isle of Wight Festival, his last concert, in August 1970. A month later he was dead. The cause of death was given in the coroner's report as inhalation of vomit following barbiturate intoxication. Suicide was not ruled out, but evidence pointed to an accident.

In the years since his death, the Hendrix legend has lived on through various media. Randi Hansen (who appeared in the video for Devo's 1984 cover of "Are You Experienced?") became the best known of a bunch of full-time Hendrix impersonators, even re-forming the Band of Gypsys with bassist Tony Saunders and Buddy Miles—who, briefly in the late Eighties, was replaced by Mitch Mitchell. Over a dozen books have been written about Hendrix, including tomes by both Redding and Mitchell; the most authoritative bio is generally considered to be David Henderson's *'Scuse Me While I Kiss the Sky*. And virtually every note Hendrix ever allowed to be recorded has been marketed on approximately 100 albums. Of these—recordings dredged up from his years as a pickup guitarist, live concerts, and jam sessions, both bootleg and legitimate, even interviews and conversations—most attention has been given to a series produced by Alan Douglas, who recorded over 1,000 hours of Hendrix alone at the Electric Lady studio in the last year of his life. With the consent of the Hendrix estate, Douglas edited the tapes, erased some tracks, and dubbed in others, with mixed results. *Radio One* collected energetic live-in-the-studio performances by Hendrix and the Experience recorded for British radio in 1967.

In 1990 the first of several Hendrix tribute albums, *If Six Was Nine*, was released, followed by *Stone Free*. In 1991 ex–Hendrix girlfriend Kathy Etchingham, along with Eric Burdon and Mitch Mitchell and his wife Dee, began prodding Scotland Yard to reopen an investigation into Hendrix's death. England's attorney general finally agreed to the request in 1993; in early 1994 Scotland Yard announced it had found no evidence to bother pursuing the case any further. In 1993 an audiovisual exhibit of Hendrix's work called "Jimi Hendrix: On the Road Again" toured college campuses and art galleries in the U.S., to enthusiastic—and predominately young—audiences, and Paul Rodgers (Free, Bad Company, the Firm) released a Hendrix tribute album (*The Hendrix Set*, 1993) and appeared on an all-star tribute album called *Stone Free*, with Hendrix songs also covered by everyone from Eric Clapton, Jeff Beck, the Pretenders, and Buddy Guy to the Cure, Belly, PM Dawn, Ice-T, and even classical violinist Nigel Kennedy.

In 1994 24-year-old James Henrik Daniel Sundquist emerged from Sweden claiming to be the son Hendrix had sired with Eva Sundquist, during a 1969 Stockholm sojourn. Sundquist announced plans to legally challenge Hendrix's father Al as sole heir to the Jimi Hendrix estate, estimated to be worth at least $30 million. In 1993, Al—who in the mid-Seventies had begun signing away rights to portions of his son's work to various international conglomerates—claimed he'd been swindled and filed a federal lawsuit against those conglomerates, as well as various holding companies and lawyers connected to the estate.

Nona Hendryx

Born August 18, 1945, Trenton, New Jersey
1977—*Nona Hendryx* (Epic)   1983—*Nona* (RCA)
1984—*The Art of Defense*   1985—*The Heat*   1987—
***Female Trouble* (EMI)   1989—*SkinDiver* (Private**
Music).

Throughout her more than 20 years as a performer, Nona Hendryx has established herself as a versatile singer and composer with individual flair, playing girl-group pop, glam funk, hard rock, new wave, and New Age. She joined Patti LaBelle and the Bluebelles with her friend Sarah Dash when she was 16. She stayed with LaBelle and Dash through their transformation into Labelle [see entry] and their breakup in 1976. That year, on her eponymous debut, she established herself as a rocker.

Always known for her wild style, Hendryx quickly fell into New York's new-wave hipoisie, singing backup on Talking Heads' *Remain in Light*, singing on Material's 1981 club hit "Bustin' Out," and forming her own bands Zero Cool and Propaganda. *Nona* was coproduced by Material and featured a lineup including Nile Rodgers, Jamaaladeen Tacuma, and Sly Dunbar. An eclectic and impressive all-female band played on the track "Design for Living": Tina Weymouth (Talking Heads), Nancy Wilson (Heart), Valerie Simpson (Ashford and Simpson), Laurie Anderson, and Gina Schock (Go-Go's). The dance-funk album included the hits "Keep It Confidential" (#22 R&B, 1983) and "Transformation" (#40 R&B, 1983).

Many of the same personnel played on *The Art of Defense*, plus Afrika Bambaataa; the use of three percussionists and three synthesizists indicated Hendryx's interest in a fusion of rhythms and sounds. The album was again coproduced by Material. Producers Bernard Edwards and Arthur Baker brought their dance electronics skills to *The Heat*, which featured Keith Richards on the Grammy-nominated "Rock This House" and "I Sweat (Going Through the Motions)" (#28 R&B, 1984). Hendryx again pursued a mix of styles on *Female Trouble*, which yielded the single "Why Should I Cry?" (#5 R&B, 1987). She changed labels and sound for *SkinDiver*. Coproduced by Private Music founder Peter Baumann (ex–Tangerine Dream), the album was more atmospheric than her previous funk and rock work.

Hendryx has recorded and collaborated with Peter Gabriel, George Clinton, Bernie Worrell, Cameo, Mavis Staples, Bobby Brown, Prince, Garland Jeffreys, and Yoko Ono. She has written songs for Patti LaBelle, Sandra St. Victor, Naomi Campbell, and Lisa Lisa, and has produced artists, including Lisa Lisa. Her music has been used in films, including *Perfect* (1985) and *Coming to America* (1988). She has also composed for such dance companies as Alvin Ailey and Dance Theatre Workshop.

Don Henley: See the Eagles

Clarence "Frogman" Henry

Born March 19, 1937, Algiers, Louisiana
1961—*You Always Hurt the One You Love* (Argo)
1969—*Is Alive and Well and Living in New Orleans
and Still Doing His Thing* (Roulette)   1970—*Bour-
bon Street, Canal Street*   1979—*New Recordings
1983—*The Legendary Clarence "Frogman" Henry*

1994—*Ain't Got No Home: The Best of Clarence "Frogman" Henry* (MCA).

"I sing like a girl . . . I sing like a frog," claimed Clarence Henry in his rollicking 1956 Top Ten R&B hit "Ain't Got No Home." And he did—with a piercing falsetto shriek and the guttural inhaled style that earned him his nickname. Henry, who'd learned piano and trombone as a child, went on to sing and play piano with Bobby Mitchell's New Orleans R&B band in 1955 and remained a Crescent City favorite after his first hit. In 1961 he scored national pop and R&B hits with the Allen Toussaint–produced ballads "But I Do" (a.k.a. "I Don't Know Why") (by Bobby Charles) and "You Always Hurt the One You Love." His other chartmaking singles included "Lonely Street" and "On Bended Knee" (1961) and "A Little Too Much" (1962). In the late Sixties Henry appeared in a number of rock & roll revival shows, and in the early Seventies he was still a popular act in New Orleans clubs. In 1982 "Ain't Got No Home" was featured on the soundtrack of the period film *Diner.* He appears every year at the New Orleans Jazz and Heritage Festival.

Henry Cow/Fred Frith

Formed 1968, Cambridge, England
Original lineup: Fred Frith (b. Feb. 17, 1949, Heath-field, Eng.), gtr., violin, piano; Tim Hodgkinson, kybds., reeds; Chris Cutler, drums, tape effects; John Greaves, bass, piano, voc.; Geoff Leigh, reeds.
1973—*Legend* (Virgin, U.K.) 1974—*Unrest* 1975—*Desperate Straights* (with Slapp Happy); *In Praise of Learning* (with Slapp Happy) 1976—*Concerts* (Caroline, U.K.) 1978—*Western Culture* (Broadcast). Art Bears (Frith; Cutler; + Dagmar Krause): 1978—*Hopes and Fears* (Random Radar) 1979—*Winter Songs* (Recommended) 1981—*The World as It Is Today* (Re).
John Greaves/Peter Blegvad: 1977—*Kew. Rhone.* (Virgin).
Fred Frith (solo): 1974—*Guitar Solos* (Caroline) 1976—*Guitar Solos 2* 1979—*Guitar Solos 3* (Rift) 1980—*Gravity* (Ralph) 1982—*Speechless* (with Massacre) 1983—*Cheap at Half the Price* 1984—*Learn to Talk* (as Skeleton Crew) (Rift) 1986—*The Country of Blinds* (as Skeleton Crew) 1988—*The Technology of Tears* (SST) 1990—*The Top of His Head* (Crammed, Bel.); *Step Across the Border* (RecRec).

Henry Cow's determined, uncompromising eclecticism—their music spans rock, fusion, free improvisation, medieval chamber music, modern-classical, and avant-garde *musique concrète*—and committed socialist politics limited the band's following to a small, dedicated cult. Initially, the group's anticommercial leanings (it was formed the year of the Paris student riots) even kept it from a recording contract. In 1971 Henry Cow played the Glastonbury Festival (a sort of British Woodstock) en route to London to record the band's critically acclaimed debut LP. In 1973 Henry Cow scored an avant-garde British production of Shakespeare's *Tempest,* toured with the German progressive group Faust, and appeared on one side of the out-of-print *Greasy Truckers Live at Dingwall's Dance Hall* LP.

Henry Cow opened for Captain Beefheart on a European tour in 1974 and released its second LP, which included "Bittern Storm Over Ulm," a radical refraction of the Yardbirds' "Got to Hurry." Henry Cow merged in 1975 with the mutant cabaret outfit Slapp Happy (Dagmar Krause, Anthony Moore, and Peter Blegvad) for *Desperate Straights,* a collection of shorter songs, and for *In Praise of Learning,* where political lyrics were accompanied by noisy modern-classical music.

In 1978, just before *Western Culture* was released, Fred Frith, Chris Cutler, and Peter Blegvad made their first U.S. appearances in New York City. Henry Cow worked fitfully as a group until the early Eighties. Frith's various projects since have included the Art Bears with Cutler and Krause, recording dissonant art songs; Massacre, a 1983 trio with bassist Bill Laswell [see entry] and drummer Fred Maher; theater scores with John Zorn [see entry]; the Eastern European–flavored Skeleton Crew, which played what Frith called "fake folk music"; a stint in Anton Fier's Golden Palominos [see entry]; and his solo work, including free improvisations on disassembled guitars and various homemade electric instruments. On *Cheap at Half the Price,* Frith sang for the first time—typically in a peculiar high-pitched tone. Frith began releasing solo albums in 1974, some shared with fellow avant-garde guitarists such as Hans Reichel, Henry Kaiser, and Derek Bailey. By the early Nineties he was a fixture at New York City's avant-noise haven, the Knitting Factory.

Blegvad performed in New York in the early Eighties with Carla Bley [see entry], John Greaves of Henry Cow, and Arto Lindsay of DNA [see entry]; he continued to work into the Nineties, as a solo artist and on such group projects as the Golden Palominos. Moore recorded more than a half-dozen atonal poppish solo albums under the name A. or Anthony More.

The Heptones

Formed 1965, Kingston, Jamaica
Barry Llewelyn (b. 1947, Jam.); Earl Morgan (b. 1945, Jam.); Leroy Sibbles (b. 1949, Jam.).
1970—*The Heptones On Top* (Studio One); *Black Is Back* 1971—*Freedom Line*; *The Heptones and Friends, vol. 1* (Joe Gibbs) 1976—*Cool Rasta* (Tro-

jan); *Night Food* (Island)   1977—*Party Time*
1978—*In Love with You* (United Artists); *Better
Days* (Third World)   1979—*The Good Life*
(Greensleeves) (– Sibbles; + Naggu Morris [b. ca.
1951])   1981—*Street of Gold* (Park Heights)
1982—*One Step Ahead* (Sonic).

With their lilting rhythms and American-style soul harmony singing, the Heptones were the archetypical rock-
steady group. Like the "rude boys" who were their first
fans, the band members came from the Kingston slum
Trenchtown. Earl Morgan had led a previous group
called the Heptones (whose other members subsequently recorded as the Cables), and in 1965 he formed
the new vocal trio with Leroy Sibbles, formerly a welder,
and Barry Llewelyn, an auto mechanic.

    After five unsuccessful singles for Ken Lack's label,
Coxsone Dodd [see entry] released the Heptones' "Fatty
Fatty" on his Studio One label in 1966; although it was
banned from Jamaican radio because of its sexual innu-
endoes, "Fatty Fatty" was a huge hit. In Britain it was
credited to Ken Boothe (a Studio One singer who had al-
ready built a small following in the U.K.); none of the
Heptones' early British releases bore their name. The
Heptones were one of Jamaica's most popular groups of
the late Sixties, hitting with Sibbles songs like "Baby (Be
True)," "Why Must I," "Why Did You Leave," and "Cry
Baby Cry."

    They stayed with Dodd's label until 1970, by which
time rock steady was hardening into reggae. Their songs
showed reggae's influence mostly in their increasingly
political lyrics. Among their hits for producers Joe Gibbs,
Geoffrey Chung, and Harry J. were "Young, Gifted and
Black" (1970), "Hypocrites" (1971), "Freedom to the People" (1972—used as an anthem by the Jamaican People's
National Party in their successful election campaign), a
cover of Harold Melvin and the Blue Notes' "I Miss You"
(1972), and "Book of Rules" (1973)—featured in the 1979
film *Rockers*.

    In 1973 the Heptones moved to Canada for two
years, making Toronto their base for tours in the U.S. and
Great Britain. They celebrated their return to Jamaica in
1975 with the chart-topping "Country Boy," and the following year signed their first multinational contract.
Their first American-released album, *Night Food*, contained new versions of "Fatty Fatty" and "Book of Rules."
Party Time, produced by Lee Perry, emphasized the reggae sound.

    In 1979 Sibbles left the group to begin a solo career.
Morgan and Llewelyn maintained the Heptones with the
addition of Naggu Morris. They toured the U.S. in 1982,
while Sibbles toured with his own group. Throughout
the Eighties, both remained popular live draws. Sibbles
returned to Jamaica in 1992 with plans to revitalize his
recording career.

Herman's Hermits

Formed 1963, Manchester, England
Peter "Herman" Noone (b. Nov. 5, 1947, Manches-
ter), voc., piano, gtr.; Karl Green (b. July 31, 1947,
Salford, Eng.), gtr., harmonica; Keith Hopwood
(b Oct. 26, 1946, Manchester), gtr.; Derek "Lek"
Leckenby (b. May 14, 1945, Leeds, Eng.; d. June 4,
1994, Eng.), gtr.; Barry Whitwam (b. July 21, 1946,
Manchester), drums.
1965—*The Best of Herman's Hermits* (MGM)
1966—*The Best of Herman's Hermits, vol. 2* 1968—
The Best of Herman's Hermits, vol. 3.
Peter Noone and the Tremblers: 1980—*Twice
Nightly* (Johnston)   1982—*One of the Glory Boys*.
Peter Noone with Phil Ramone: 1993—*Playback*
(Noone/Ramone).

Major stars from the pop side of the British Invasion,
Herman's Hermits had 11 Top Ten hits from 1964
through 1967. By the time changing musical trends had
reduced the group to a curiosity, it had already sold over
40 million singles and albums worldwide.

    Peter Noone studied singing and acting at the Man-
chester School of Music and was featured in the early
Sixties in several plays and on BBC-TV. By 1963 he was
playing with the Heartbeats, a local Manchester group
that consisted of Karl Green, Keith Hopwood, Derek
Leckenby, and Barry Whitwam. The others claimed that
Noone, then performing under the name Peter Novak, resembled Sherman of the *Rocky and Bullwinkle* television
cartoon series; then they shortened the nickname to
Herman.

    In early 1964 they attracted the attention of U.K. pro-
ducer Mickie Most, who released the group's first single,
"I'm Into Something Good" (#13), that fall. It spent three
weeks at the top of the British chart and sold over a million copies worldwide. In 1965 the Hermits dominated
the U.S. chart, placing six singles in the Top Ten and appearing in the Connie Francis teen flick *Where the Boys
Meet the Girls*. Herman's Hermits hits (which actually
featured such British sessionmen as future Led Zeppe-
liners Jimmy Page and John Paul Jones) included "Mrs.
Brown You've Got a Lovely Daughter" (#1), "I'm Henry
the Eighth, I Am" (#1) (originally written in 1911 for a
Cockney comedian), "Can't You Hear My Heartbeat" (#2),
"Wonderful World" (#4), "Silhouettes" (#5) (originally
recorded by the Rays), "Just a Little Bit Better" (#7) (all in
1965); "Listen People" (#3), "Dandy" (#5) (written by Ray
Davies of the Kinks), "A Must to Avoid" (#8), "Leaning on
the Lamp Post" (#9) (all 1966). *The Best of Herman's Hermits* stayed on the album chart 105 weeks. Their last big
hit was "There's a Kind of Hush" (#4) b/w "No Milk
Today" (#35) in early 1967.

    By 1971 the group had disbanded amid legal battles
for royalties. The Hermits surfaced a few years later, sans

Herman, for an abortive attempt at a comeback with Buddah Records. (Noone rejoined the others briefly in 1973 for some British Invasion Revival shows.)

Initially Noone returned to acting. In 1970 he met David Bowie, who supplied him with his first British solo hit, "Oh You Pretty Thing," and played piano on the sessions. Their subsequent collaborations failed, however, as did Noone's other early-Seventies releases for Rak Records. Mid-decade, Noone spent three years hosting a mainstream British television series but quit to avoid being pigeonholed as a cabaret performer. He moved to the south of France and cut a few singles that were moderate hits there and in Belgium.

By the late Seventies Noone had taken up part-time residence in Los Angeles, where the thriving club scene induced him to try a comeback with a contemporary rock band, the Tremblers, whose members (guitarist/keyboardist Gregg Inhofer, drummer Mark Williams, guitarist Geo. Conner, and bassist Mark Browne) had played variously with the Pop, Tonio K., Barbra Streisand, and Olivia Newton-John. Their 1980 debut album, *Twice Nightly,* was the first of his records Noone had ever produced. In 1982 he released an LP entitled *One of the Glory Boys* and appeared as Frederic in the Broadway production of *The Pirates of Penzance.* Noone hosted the VH-1 program *My Generation.* Leckenby died of non-Hodgkin's lymphoma.

Kristen Hersh: See Throwing Muses/Belly

Nick Heyward: See Haircut 100

John Hiatt
Born 1952, Indianapolis, Indiana
1974—*Hangin' Around the Observatory* (Epic)
1975—*Overcoats* 1979—*Slug Line* (MCA) 1980—
***Two Bit Monsters* 1982—*All of a Sudden* (Geffen)**
1983—*Riding with the King* 1985—*Warming Up to the Ice Age* 1987—*Bring the Family* (A&M)
1988—*Slow Turning* 1990—*Stolen Moments*
1993—*Perfectly Good Guitar* 1994—*Hiatt Comes Alive at Budokan?*

Singer/songwriter John Hiatt has had his songs covered by Rick Nelson, Dave Edmunds, the Searchers, Three Dog Night, Bonnie Raitt, and others, although his solo career has been only moderately successful.

Hiatt played in various garage bands before leaving his hometown at age 18 in 1970. He was discovered in Nashville by an Epic talent scout and made two quirky albums for the label—*Hangin' Around the Observatory* and *Overcoats*—that drew critical kudos but negligible sales. Without a record contract, Hiatt spent the next few years touring folk clubs as a solo act, until signing with MCA. He released two more records, the more new-wavish *Slug Line* and *Two Bit Monsters,* and received more critical nods, but despite some touring, they failed in the marketplace. Hiatt played and sang on sessions and toured with Ry Cooder, and he appears with Cooder (singing two songs) on the soundtrack to 1981's *The Border.*

Through the first half of the Eighties, Hiatt's good-reviews/weak-sales pattern continued; meanwhile, he descended into alcoholism and suffered the suicide of his first wife. Hiatt was dumped by Geffen Records, but then got sober, remarried, and landed a new deal with A&M. He gathered Cooder, bassist Nick Lowe (who had produced some of his Geffen work), and session super-drummer Jim Keltner to record *Bring the Family*—which, with *Slow Turning* and *Stolen Moments,* would compose Hiatt's "recovery trilogy," which brought him the most glowing reviews of his career, if not much of a rise in sales. Hiatt, Cooder, Lowe, and Keltner also recorded in 1992 under the name Little Village. For *Perfectly Good Guitar,* Hiatt recruited members of such younger bands as Cracker, School of Fish, and Wire Train. Hiatt's 1994 live album was recorded with his band the Guilty Dogs.

Dan Hicks and His Hot Licks
Formed 1968, San Francisco, California
Original lineup: Dan Hicks (b. Dec. 9, 1941, Little Rock, Ark.), gtr., voc., harmonica, drums; David LaFlamme, violin; Bill Douglas, bass; Mitzy Douglas, voc.; Patti Urban, voc.
1968—(New lineup: Sherry Snow, voc.; Tina Natural [b. Christina Gancher, 1945], voc., celeste, perc.; Jimmie Bassoon, bass; Jon Weber [b. 1947], gtr.; Gary Pozzi, violin 1969—(– Bassoon; + Jaime Leopold [b. 1947, Portland, Ore.], fiddle, bass; – Pozzi; + Sid Page [b. 1947, Portland, Ore.], violin, mandolin) *Original Recordings* (Epic) (– Snow; – Gancher; – Weber; + Nicole Dukes, voc.; + Naomi Eisenberg [b. Brooklyn, N.Y.], voc., violin; + Maryanne Price [b. Providence, R.I.], voc., cornet; + Bob Scott [b. Ozarks], drums; – Dukes) 1971—
Where's the Money* (Blue Thumb) (+ John Girton [b. Burbank, Calif.], gtr.) 1972—*Strikin' It Rich* 1973—*Last Train to Hicksville . . . the Home of Happy Feet* 1991—*The Very Best of Dan Hicks and His Hot Licks* (See for Miles) 1994—*Lost in the Eighties* (Rare Prime Cuts); *At the Boarding House, 1971; Paramount Theater, 1990.
Dan Hicks solo: 1978—*It Happened One Bite* (Warner Bros.) 1988—*Mistletoe Jam* (with the Christmas Jug Band) (Relix) 1994—*Shootin' Straight* (On the Spot).

Dan Hicks writes wry, jazzy, ironic pseudo-nostalgia songs, and in the late Sixties and early Seventies he performed them with the Hot Licks, a group modeled on Django Reinhardt's quintet, and a pair of female vocalists, the Lickettes. In 1991 Hicks revived the Hot Licks name for a reunion concert.

Hicks grew up in Santa Rosa, California, started playing drums at age 11, and switched to the guitar at age 20. In his teens he played in various local folk and jazz bands, and while attending San Francisco State College he continued to drum on the side. Eventually he landed in the original Charlatans, a self-confessed amateur band, with whom he played from 1965 to 1968. During his last six months with the Charlatans, he began playing with his own group, including violinist David LaFlamme, who later formed It's a Beautiful Day [see entry].

By early 1968 Hicks' drummerless group, the Hot Licks, was signed to Epic; its only album for the label, *Original Recordings,* flopped. After a series of personnel changes, the group was signed to Blue Thumb in 1971. Their three albums for that label—*Where's the Money* (recorded live at L.A.'s Troubadour), *Strikin' It Rich,* and *Last Train to Hicksville* (their first with a drummer)—blended the Andrews Sisters, Western swing, ragtime, and jazz. Hicks became known for compositions like "How Can I Miss You (When You Won't Go Away)," "Walkin' One and Only," which was covered by Maria Muldaur, and "I Scare Myself" (recorded later by Thomas Dolby). Violinist Sid Page (who later played with Sly and the Family Stone) departed after *Last Train,* and by 1974 those particular Hot Licks were no more.

Following the group's breakup, Hicks has been sporadically active in the Bay Area as a solo artist, sometimes billed as Lonesome Dan Hicks. In early 1978 he reemerged with *It Happened One Bite.* He went on to form the Acoustic Warriors, with whom he still tours.

The Highwaymen: See Johnny Cash; Waylon Jennings; Kris Kristofferson; Willie Nelson

Jessie Hill

Born December 9, 1932, New Orleans, Louisiana
1972—*Naturally* (Blue Thumb)   1978—*Golden Classics* (Collectables).

New Orleans pianist Jessie Hill's moment of national glory came with "Ooh Poo Pah Doo—Parts I & II" (#28, 1960), the first national hit produced by Allen Toussaint. Hill wrote the song, which Toussaint orchestrated with a call-and-response format recalling Ray Charles' "What'd I Say." But Hill was unable to come up with a followup hit while recording for Minit through 1963. The closest he

came was "Whip It on Me" (#91, 1960). He then moved to Los Angeles and fell in with other New Orleans expatriates like Dr. John (who covered Hill's "Qualify" on one of his solo albums). He recorded sporadically throughout the decade, culminating in a 1970 album for Blue Thumb. In the early Seventies Hill returned to New Orleans, where he continues to perform. His songs, which include "Sweet Jelly Roll," "I Got Mine," and "Can't Get Enough," have been recorded by Ike and Tina Turner and Sonny and Cher, among others.

Hip-hop

Hip-hop, the cut-and-paste backing music for rap, is a street-derived, avant-garde art form that entered the pop consciousness with the commercial rise of rap in the early Eighties. "Rap" and "hip-hop" are used interchangeably—hip-hop, in fact, is used as much to describe rap culture (i.e., break dancing, graffiti) as to define the music.

Constructed much like a sculpture, hip-hop tracks combine "found sounds" (often digitally recorded "samples" of music, voices, or ambient noise), looped drum tracks (either natural or electronic), bass lines, guitar riffs, and turntable manipulation (which produces the music's backward, scratching, and stuttering effects). Originally inspired by early Jamaican sound-system DJs and dub producers such as U-Roy and Lee Perry—who would experiment with and talk over reggae rhythm tracks—South Bronx DJs Lovebug Starski (Kevin Smith), Kool Herc (short for Hercules), and others forged an Americanized version of the music in the early Seventies that drew more from funk sources than from reggae. The earliest recorded hip-hop appeared on songs by Grandmaster Flash ("Wheels of Steel"), Afrika Bambaataa ("Planet Rock"), and the Sugar Hill Gang ("Rapper's Delight"). As in the early days of free jazz and rock & roll, some critics initially complained that hip-hop was not music but noise.

When digital samplers became commonplace in the later Eighties, a younger generation of hip-hop producers took the form to a new level. In 1987 the Bomb Squad, the hip-hop production team behind the rap group Public Enemy, introduced a hard, dense, noisy, and highly influential sound that combined sirens and other street noise, political speeches, and music samples.

Hip-hop is like postmodern visual art: It combines bits and pieces of art and media from different eras into a nonspecific whole. Because of its acquisition of other artists' music in what some believe is a blatant violation of copyright laws, hip-hop has been under legal scrutiny and has produced a great deal of controversy. In just one of dozens of similar cases involving other groups, the rap/hip-hop group De La Soul settled out of court with the Sixties pop band the Turtles for failing to credit the group after sampling a bit from its song "You Showed Me" for their 1989 debut album, *3 Feet High and Rising.*

Robyn Hitchcock/Soft Boys

Born March 3, 1953, London, England
With the Soft Boys, formed 1976, Cambridge, Eng. (Hitchcock, voc., gtr., bass; Alan Davies, gtr.; Andy Metcalfe, bass; Otis Fagg [b. Morris Windsor], drums): 1977—*Give It to the Soft Boys* EP (Raw, U.K.) (– Davies; + Kimberley Rew [b. Eng.], gtr., voc.) 1979—*A Can of Bees* (Two Crabs, U.K.) (– Metcalfe; + Matthew Seligman, bass) 1980—*Underwater Moonlight* (Armageddon, U.K.) 1981—*Two Halves for the Price of One* 1983—*Invisible Hits* (Glass Fish/Relativity) 1993—*1976–81* (Rykodisc).
With the Egyptians, formed 1984 (Hitchcock, voc., gtr.; Andy Metcalfe, bass; Morris Windsor, drums; Roger Jackson, kybds.): 1985—*Fegmania!* (Slash); *Gotta Let This Hen Out!* (Relativity) 1986—*Exploding in Silence* EP; *Element of Light* (Glass Fish/Relativity) (– Jackson) 1988—*Globe of Frogs* (A&M) 1989—*Queen Elvis* 1991—*Perspex Island* 1993—*Respect.*
Robyn Hitchcock solo: 1981—*Black Snake Diamond Role* (Armageddon, U.K.) 1982—*Groovy Decay* (Albion, U.K.) 1984—*I Often Dream of Trains* (Glass Fish, U.K.) 1986—*Groovy Decoy* (Glass Fish/Relativity); *Invisible Hitchcock* 1990—*Eye* (Twin/Tone) 1995—*Gravy Deco (The Complete Groovy Decay/Decoy Sessions)* (Rhino); *You & Oblivion.*

Robyn Hitchcock has the heart of a singer/songwriter but the warped sensibility of a man one step ahead of or behind his time. The former Soft Boy was perhaps the definitive cult artist of the Eighties: devoutly followed but little known. Hitchcock was born in an artistic middle-class family in West London. He dropped out of art school and in 1974 moved to Cambridge, where he began performing his eccentric folk songs. He played in a number of bands, including Maureen and the Meatpackers, before forming the Soft Boys in 1976 with drummer Morris Windsor, guitarist Alan Davies, and bassist Andy Metcalfe.

After *Give It to the Soft Boys* introduced their demented progressive rock in 1977, the band fired Davies and hired Cambridge guitar wizard Kimberley Rew, later of Katrina and the Waves [see entry]. The London label Radar briefly signed the Soft Boys, but dropped them after "(I Want to Be an) Anglepoise Lamp" stiffed. *A Can of Bees* was a bizarre album whose "Human Music" introduced the folk-ballad style that would become one of Hitchcock's strengths.

The Soft Boys worked on an album that the label did not release (many of its songs were later included on

The Soft Boys: Robyn Hitchcock, Kimberley Rew, Morris Windsor, Matthew Seligman

1983's *Invisible Hits*). In 1979 the band taped an acoustic show that, with its clever covers and Hitchcock's eccentric banter, illustrated why they had a firm live following (the tape was released in 1983 via mail order). Working with a tiny budget and largely using an eight-track, the Soft Boys then recorded the masterful *Underwater Moonlight* (1980).

The Soft Boys toured the U.S. and released *Two Halves for the Price of One,* a collection of live tracks and oddities, before breaking up in 1981. Influenced by the Byrds and Syd Barrett, the Soft Boys were out of sync with the punk rock of their time, although many American bands, including R.E.M. and the Replacements, later claimed them as a major influence. In 1993 Rykodisc released a two-CD retrospective, and in January 1994 the band reunited for a show in London.

Hitchcock was still finding his voice on his first two solo albums, which he recorded with Seligman. Seligman then joined the Thompson Twins, and Hitchcock recorded *Groovy Decay* with bassist Sara Lee. (An alternative version of the album, featuring the demos with Seligman, was later released as *Groovy Decoy.*) Hitchcock retired for two years and wrote lyrics for Captain Sensible (the Damned). He returned in 1984 with the beautiful, acoustic *I Often Dream of Trains,* on which he finally sustained the combination of sensitivity and imagination that is his forte. That year the Soft Boys' first EP was rereleased as *Wading Through a Ventilator,* inspiring Hitchcock to contact Windsor and Metcalfe (who had also played with XTC and Squeeze), along with keyboardist Roger Jackson, and form the Egyptians.

The Egyptians have had a spotty career, hovering on the edges of artistic and commercial success. *Fegmania!* tracks "Egyptian Cream," "My Wife and My Dead Wife," and "The Man with the Light Bulb Head" were praised for their absurd images and narratives. With fans like R.E.M.'s Peter Buck (who has played with the Egyptians) as boosters, Hitchcock signed to A&M and scored college-radio hits with "Balloon Man" (off *Globe of Frogs*) and "So You Think You're in Love" (*Perspex Island*). Largely on the strength of live shows, he has developed a devoted audience in America (he's still largely ignored in his native England). *Respect* (1993) is dedicated to his late father; the album was recorded on the Isle of Wight, where Hitchcock sometimes makes his home. Hitchcock also paints, and many of his albums feature his artwork. By 1995, Hitchcock was no longer signed to a major label, but Rhino began reissuing all of his work on CD.

Hole

Formed 1990, Los Angeles, California
Courtney Love (b. July 9, 1964, San Francisco, Calif.), voc. gtr.; Eric Erlandson (b. Jan. 9, 1963, Los Angeles), gtr.; Jill Emery, bass; Caroline Rue, drums.
1991—*Pretty on the Inside* (Caroline)   1992— (– Emery; – Rue; + Patty Schemel [b. April 24, 1967, Seattle, Wash.], drums; + Kristen Pfaff [d. June 16, 1994], bass)   1994—*Live Through This* (Geffen) (– Pfaff; + Melissa Auf Der Maur [b. Mar. 17, 1972, Montreal, Can.], bass).

In the way that Yoko Ono can never be mentioned without the thought of John Lennon, Courtney Love will be forever tied to Nirvana's Kurt Cobain. Yet Love's confrontational stage presence with her band Hole, as well as her gut-wrenching vocals and powerful punk-pop songcraft, have made her a rock star in her own right.

Love's father, an early, minor Grateful Dead associate, and mother, a psychotherapist, divorced when she was five. As a child, she lived on a commune in New Zealand with her mother. When she was 12, she did time at an Oregon reformatory after she got caught shoplifting. Dropping in and out of college, and living off a trust fund, Love moved from place to place, working as a stripper in Japan, Alaska, and Taiwan, and hanging out with mope rockers in Liverpool, England. Back in Los Angeles, she became friendly with director Alex Cox and

scored small roles in a couple of his films, including *Sid & Nancy.*

By the time Love formed Hole with Eric Erlandson in 1990, she had already appeared as a vocalist in San Francisco in an early incarnation of Faith No More and the all-girl band Sugar Baby Doll, with Babes in Toyland's Kat Bjelland and L7's Jennifer Finch.

Hole began garnering attention on the U.S. underground via the band's incendiary live performances and two early singles, "Dicknail" and "Retard Girl." Sonic Youth's Kim Gordon and Gumball's Don Fleming coproduced the acerbic debut album, *Pretty on the Inside.* These recordings and English tours made Hole the darlings of the U.K. music press. Hole was seemingly put on hold, however, during Love's courtship with and eventual marriage to Cobain (on February 24, 1992). The band, which had been courted by several major labels, signed a lucrative contract with Nirvana's [see entry] label Geffen.

After giving birth to a daughter, Frances Bean Cobain, Love and her husband became involved in a battle with the local children's services agency over custody of the baby, due to charges in the press that Love had done heroin during her pregnancy; the couple won the right to keep their child.

In 1993 Love began recording *Live Through This* with Erlandson, Patty Schemel, and Kristen Pfaff. One week before its release, Cobain was found dead of a self-inflicted gunshot wound to the head. Amid the tragedy, the album won rave reviews. Tragedy struck again on June 16, 1994, when bassist Pfaff overdosed on heroin. Vowing to keep Hole alive, Love enlisted Canadian bassist Melissa Auf Der Maur and the band embarked on a tour, first opening for the Lemonheads, then for Nine Inch Nails. *Live Through This* (#55, 1994) made steady progress in the charts (going platinum a year later), yielding the singles "Miss World," which got modern-rock radio airplay, and "Doll Parts" (#65, 1994). The album and its singles won numerous 1994 critics' polls, including those conducted by ROLLING STONE and the *Village Voice.*

Billie Holiday

Born Eleanora Fagan, April 7, 1915, Baltimore, Maryland; died July 17, 1959, New York City, New York
1958—*Lady in Satin* (Columbia)   1959—*Last Recording* (Verve)   1972—*God Bless the Child* (Columbia)   1991—*Lady in Autumn: The Best of the Verve Years* (Verve); *The Legacy (1933–1958)* (Columbia); *The Complete Decca Recordings* (GRP).

Billie Holiday—"Lady Day"—is the preeminent female jazz vocalist. From her artistic heyday in the mid-

Thirties through the following two decades of misfortune and drug addiction, Holiday continually rewrote the rules for jazz singing. Her voice was distinguished neither by power nor by tonal beauty but by a superb, unerring ability to improvise melodic lines from the framework of standard songs; to subtly twist rhythm and expertly manipulate melody in order to personalize every song she sang. Revered for the directness and wrenching honesty of her work, Holiday relied on drama rather than sentiment to express the emotional content of her material.

Clarence Holiday, Billie's errant father, was a guitarist for Fletcher Henderson's big band. As a child Holiday did odd jobs for a local brothel in order to hear recordings of Bessie Smith and Louis Armstrong that were played there. As a child, Holiday took the surname "Billie," in emulation of her favorite movie star, Billie Dove. With her parents split up and her mother impoverished, Holiday's early adolescence turned into a nightmare when, after being raped at age ten, she was accused of being "provocative" and sent to a reformatory.

Holiday moved to New York City in the late Twenties, taking any singing jobs she could find around Harlem. Influential talent scout/producer John Hammond heard Holiday in 1933 and set up her first recording session, which included Benny Goodman as one of the supporting musicians. In 1935 Holiday began working with Teddy Wilson, Goodman's featured pianist. For Holiday's recordings Wilson would hand-pick players from the cream of the prominent big bands; it was at these sessions that Holiday developed her remarkable rapport with Count Basie's brilliant tenor saxophonist Lester Young. These Columbia recordings, which extend into the mid-Forties, are generally considered Holiday's finest work, and include such signature songs as "Miss Brown to You," "He's Funny That Way," "What a Little Moonlight Can Do," and "God Bless the Child" (which she helped compose).

Holiday joined the big band of Count Basie for one year in 1937, signing on next with white clarinetist Artie Shaw's band. Racial restrictions—Holiday wasn't allowed to enter hotels by the same entrance as the rest of the band—revolted her, and she soon quit. Holiday led her own groups until the end of her career.

Holiday's fame blossomed in 1939 during her extended engagement at New York's Cafe Society. That year she also recorded (for Commodore Records) "Strange Fruit," a signature ballad that dealt with prejudice and lynching. In 1944 Holiday left Columbia to record for Decca. During this time, Holiday's heroin addiction led to several serious legal bouts. She was imprisoned for a year and afterward was prohibited from playing New York nightclubs. Holiday's personal life was also in disarray, owing to her self-destructive attraction to abusive and manipulative men.

Although Holiday's voice was by now worn from years of drugs and drink, her Verve recordings from the Fifties capture some of her most moving and nuanced performances. By 1959 Holiday's hard living had caught up to her. On her deathbed in the New York City hospital where she was being treated for kidney disease, Holiday was arrested for heroin possession, and subsequently died.

Jennifer Holliday

Born October 19, 1960, Houston, Texas
1983—*Feel My Soul* (Geffen)   1985—*Say You Love Me*   1991—*I'm on Your Side* (Arista).

Jennifer Holliday reached the top of the pop charts via Broadway and her show-stopping performance in *Dreamgirls.* The R&B-based singer was raised in Houston by her mother, a grade school teacher. She began singing as a teenager in the Pleasant Grove Baptist Church choir. Her plans to become a lawyer were forever changed when a member of a touring production of *A Chorus Line* saw her in a Houston play and paid for her flight to New York to audition for *Your Arm's Too Short to Box with God.* Holliday got the lead.

In 1981 the singer was cast as Effie in *Dreamgirls,* the musical based loosely on the Supremes. (Ex-Supreme Mary Wilson, who maintained that the musical was emotionally if not factually true, titled her autobiography *Dreamgirl: My Life as a Supreme.*) Her performance of "And I Am Telling You I'm Not Going" (#22 pop, #1 R&B, 1982) won Holliday a Tony and a Grammy (the single appeared on the *Dreamgirls* soundtrack). Holliday became an overnight sensation: the incredible vocalist with no formal training and a downhome demeanor, the large-bodied, upstart ingenue who had walked out on director Michael Bennett (*Chorus Line*) during rehearsals for *Dreamgirls.* Geffen signed Holliday and in 1983 released *Feel My Soul* (#31), which yielded the hit "I Am Love" (#2 R&B, 1983), as well as the single "Just Let Me Wait" (#24 R&B, 1983).

In 1984 Holliday sang on the Foreigner hit "I Wanna Know What Love Is." In 1985 she returned to the stage in *Sing, Mahalia, Sing.* But *Say You Love Me,* released that year, yielded only a few minor R&B hits that failed to cross over to the pop charts. In 1986 she appeared on TV's *The Love Boat.*

Geffen dropped Holliday and Arista signed her. *I'm on Your Side* (#29 R&B, 1991) paired Holliday with established writers (Diane Warren, Angela Bofill, Narada Michael Walden) and producers (Barry Eastmond, Michael Powell) but fared little better than its predecessors, despite Holliday's much-vaunted new svelte image. The title track reached #10 on the R&B chart in 1991.

The Hollies

Formed 1962, Manchester, England

Graham Nash (b. Feb. 2, 1942, Blackpool, Eng.), gtr., voc.; Allan Clarke (b. Apr. 15, 1942, Salford, Eng.), voc.; Anthony Hicks (b. Dec. 16, 1943, Nelson, Eng.), gtr.; Donald Rathbone (b. Eng.), drums; Eric Haydock (b. Feb. 3, 1943, Manchester), bass. 1963—(– Rathbone; + Robert Elliott [b. Dec. 8, 1942, Burnley, Eng.], drums) 1965—*Here I Go Again* (Imperial); *Hear! Here!* 1966—(– Haydock; + Bernard Calvert [b. Sep. 16, 1943, Burnley, Eng.], bass) *Beat Group!; Bus Stop* 1967—*Stop Stop Stop; The Hollies' Greatest Hits; Evolution* (Epic); *Dear Eloise/King Midas in Reverse* 1968 (– Nash; + Terry Sylvester [b. Jan. 8, 1945, Liverpool, Eng.], gtr., voc.) 1969—*Words and Music by Bob Dylan; He Ain't Heavy, He's My Brother* 1970—*Moving Finger* 1971—(– Clarke; + Mikael Rikfors [b. Swed.], voc.) *Distant Light* 1972—*Romany* 1973—(– Rickfors; + Clarke) 1974—*Hollies* 1975—*Another Night* 1977—*The Hollies/Clarke, Hicks, Sylvester, Calvert, Elliott* (Epic) (– Clarke) 1978—(+ Clarke) *A Crazy Steal* 1981—(– Sylvester; – Calvert) 1983—(Group re-forms: Nash; Elliott; Hicks; Clarke) *What Goes Around . . .* (Atlantic) 1993—*30th Anniversary Collection* (EMI).

The Hollies: Bernie Calvert, Graham Nash, Tony Hicks, Allan Clarke, Bobby Elliott

After the Beatles, the Hollies were the most consistently successful singles band in Britain, and their string of hits extended into the Seventies. The group was formed by childhood friends Allan Clarke and Graham Nash, who had worked together as the Two Teens, Ricky and Dane, and the Guytones. They became the Deltas with the addition of Don Rathbone and Eric Haydock, then the Hollies after Tony Hicks joined them. Sources disagree about whether the group was named after the plant or Buddy Holly. By late 1963 they had British Top Twenty hits with covers of the Coasters' "Searchin'" and Maurice Williams and the Zodiacs' "Stay." Around this time they also wrote a book, How to Run a Beat Group.

With Clarke on lead vocals and Nash leading the harmonies, the Hollies had a string of U.K. hits that included "Just One Look," "Here I Go Again," "We're Through" (1964), "Yes I Will," "I'm Alive" (their first British #1), and "Look Through Any Window" (1965). The last was one of the several singles that entered the U.S. chart, but it wasn't until "Bus Stop" (#5) in 1966 that the group cracked the U.S. Top Ten. Over the next several months, their U.S. hits included "Stop Stop Stop" (#7, 1966), "Carrie-Anne" (#9, 1967), "On a Carousel" (#11, 1967), and "Pay You Back with Interest" (#28, 1967).

In the late Sixties the Hollies shifted to more experimental rock. The results—*Stop Stop Stop, Evolution, Dear Eloise/King Midas in Reverse*—didn't establish them as an album group. Nash, one of the group's main writers, quit in late 1968. He was reportedly upset that the band was recording an entire LP of Dylan covers (*Words and Music by Bob Dylan*) and yet had refused to record several of his own songs, including "Marrakesh Express," a hit for his next band, Crosby, Stills and Nash.

The Hollies advertised in British trade papers for Nash's replacement and found Terry Sylvester, who stayed with the group until 1981. In 1970 "He Ain't Heavy, He's My Brother" hit #7, but within a year Clarke was forced out because of personality clashes with other band members. This left Hicks the only original member. Clarke briefly pursued a solo career (*My Real Name Is 'Arold* and *Headroom*), only to rejoin the group in 1973 after his replacement, Swedish vocalist Mikael Rikfors, was fired because of his thickly accented lead vocals. Rikfors has since had a very successful career in Scandinavia; among the artists who have recorded his compositions are Cyndi Lauper, Richie Havens, and Santana.

The Hollies had their biggest U.S. hit with "Long Cool Woman (in a Black Dress)" (#2, 1972) and hit a second peak with "The Air That I Breathe" (#6, 1974). In 1977 Clarke again quit the band and released another solo LP (*I Wasn't Born Yesterday*), yet returned to the group for *A Crazy Steal*. Epic dropped the Hollies in 1979. Their last group effort was a 1980 British LP entitled *Buddy Holly,* released in conjunction with Paul McCartney's Buddy Holly Week. In 1983 Nash, Clarke, Elliott, and Hicks reformed to record *What Goes Around...*, which produced a Top Thirty version of the Supremes' "Stop! In the Name of Love." Since then, Clarke, Hicks, and Elliott have continued to tour, while 1993 saw those three plus Sylvester and original bassist Haydock record two new tracks: "Nothing Else but Love," written by Richard Marx, and Nik Kerhsaw's "The Woman I Love," a #42 hit in England. "He Ain't Heavy, He's My Brother," reissued in 1988, topped the British chart.

Buddy Holly and the Crickets

Born Charles Hardin Holley, September 7, 1936, Lubbock, Texas; died February 3, 1959, near Clear Lake, Iowa

The Crickets, formed circa 1955, Lubbock, Texas: Sonny Curtis (b. May 9, 1937, Meadow, Tex.), gtr.; Don Guess, bass; Jerry Allison (b. Aug. 31, 1939, Hillsboro, Tex.), drums. The Crickets also included, at various times, Niki Sullivan, gtr.; Larry Welborn, bass; Joe B. Mauldin, bass; Tommy Allsup, gtr.; Glen D. Hardin (b. May 18, 1939, Wellington, Tex.), piano; Jerry Naylor (b. Mar. 6, 1939, Stephenville, Tex.), voc.; Waylon Jennings (b. June 15, 1937, Littlefield, Tex.).

1957—*Chirpin' Crickets* (Brunswick)   1959—*The Buddy Holly Story* (Coral)   1963—*Reminiscing* 1964—*Showcase*   1978—*The Buddy Holly Story* soundtrack (Epic); *20 Golden Greats* (MCA)   1985— *Legend*.

Buddy Holly was a rock pioneer. He wrote his own material; used the recording studio for double-tracking and other advanced techniques; popularized the two-guitars, bass, drums lineup; and recorded a catalogue of songs that continue to be covered: "Not Fade Away," "Rave On," "That'll Be the Day," and others. His playful, mock-ingenuous singing, with slides between falsetto and regular voice and a trademark "hiccup," has been a major influence on Bob Dylan, Paul McCartney, Marshall Crenshaw, and numerous imitators. When he died in an airplane crash at 22, he had been recording rock & roll for less than two years.

Holly learned to play the piano, fiddle, and guitar at an early age. He was five when he won five dollars for singing "Down the River of Memories" at a local talent show. In the early Fifties he formed the country-oriented Western and Bop Band with high school friends Bob Montgomery and Larry Welborn. Between late 1953 and 1955 they performed on local radio station KDAV and recorded demos and garage tapes, several of which were posthumously released as *Holly in the Hills*. By 1956 (after Holly had dropped the *e* from his last name) the group's reputation on the Southwestern country circuit

Buddy Holly

led to a contract to cut country singles in Nashville for Decca. The label didn't think much of Montgomgery, who graciously bowed out, insisting that Holly accept the deal. With Sonny Curtis and Bob Guess, Holly cut "Blue Days, Black Nights" b/w "Love Me," billed as Holly and the Two Tunes. Like subsequent pure country releases ("Modern Don Juan," "Midnight Shift," and "Girl on My Mind"), it went unnoticed. One of his last recordings for the label (which Decca refused to release) was "That'll Be the Day," a song that in a later rock version became one of Holly's first hits. During this period, Holly began writing prolifically. Typical of his romantic fare was a song that began as "Cindy Lou" but was changed to "Peggy Sue" at new Cricket Jerry Allison's suggestion. ("Peggy Sue" was the future Mrs. Allison; they've since divorced.) It eventually became one of Holly's biggest hits.

Following the failed sessions with Decca, Holly and his friends returned to Lubbock. In 1956–57 Holly and drummer Allison played as a duo at the Lubbock Youth Center and shared bills with well-known stars as they passed through the area. Once they opened for a young Elvis Presley (Holly later said, "We owe it all to Elvis"), who influenced Holly's move into rock & roll.

On February 25, 1957, Holly and the newly named Crickets drove 90 miles west to producer Norman Petty's studio in Clovis, New Mexico, to cut a demo. Their rocking version of "That'll Be the Day" attracted a contract from the New York–based Coral/Brunswick label, and it rose to #1 by September. As with many of Holly's early hits, producer Petty picked up a cowriter's credit. The song's success prompted the Crickets' first national tour in late 1957. Several promoters (including those at the Apollo Theatre in New York, where Holly and his group became one of the first white acts to appear) were surprised that the group was white.

Under a contractual arrangement worked out by Petty (who quickly became Holly's manager), some discs were credited to the Crickets, while others bore only Holly's name. His first hit under the latter arrangement was "Peggy Sue" (#3, 1957), which also became one of several big hits in England, where he toured to much acclaim in 1958. "Oh, Boy!," released at year's end by the Crickets, hit #10. By 1958 Holly had reached the Top Forty with "Maybe Baby" (#17), "Think It Over" (#27), "Early in the Morning" (#32), and "Rave On" (#37).

In October 1958 Holly left Petty and the Crickets (who continued on their own), moved to Greenwich Village, and married Puerto Rico–born Maria Elena Santiago after having proposed to her on their first date. His split from Petty (who died in 1984) led to legal problems, which tied up his finances and prompted Holly to reluctantly join the Winter Dance Party Tour of the Midwest in early 1959. He also did some recording in New York; many of the tapes were later overdubbed and released posthumously. During that last tour, Holly was supported by ex-Cricket guitarist Tommy Allsup and future country superstar Waylon Jennings (whose first record, "Jolé Blon," Holly produced).

Tired of riding the bus, and in order to get his laundry done, Holly, along with a couple of the tour's other featured performers, the Big Bopper and Ritchie Valens, chartered a private plane after their Clear Lake, Iowa, show to take them to Moorhead, Minnesota. Piloted by Roger Peterson, the small Beechcraft Bonanza took off from the Mason City, Iowa, airport at about 2:00 a.m. on February 3, 1959, and crashed a few minutes later, killing all on board.

Holly's death was marked by the release of "It Doesn't Matter Anymore" (#13, 1959), which topped the English chart for six consecutive weeks. Holly left behind enough old demos and uncompleted recordings to fill several posthumous collections, of which the most extensive is *The Complete Buddy Holly Story,* a nine-record set. A 1978 feature film, *The Buddy Holly Story,* revived interest in Holly's life and career. In 1989 *Buddy,* a musical, originated in England and traveled to Broadway; as of the mid-Nineties, the show was still popular in London's West End.

The Crickets continued on as a group through 1965, with a variety of personnel revolving around Allison, Curtis, and Glen D. Hardin. This lineup had some minor U.S. success but, like Holly, the Crickets were most popular in England, where they had three early-Sixties hits—"Love's Made a Fool of You," "Don't Ever Change," and "My Little Girl"—the last of which was included in the British film *Just for Fun.* The Crickets later costarred with Lesley Gore in *The Girls on the Beach.* As the Sixties progressed, the Crickets' activities became more sporadic and included a Holly tribute album recorded with Bobby Vee. It was Vee who had filled Holly's spot on the ill-fated 1959 tour.

In 1973 Hardin left to join Elvis Presley's band (he would later join Emmylou Harris' Hot Band). Around this time the Crickets' last album was recorded with a lineup that included Allison, Curtis, and English musicians Rick Grech and Albert Lee. Curtis and Joe B. Mauldin regrouped the original Crickets in 1977 to perform in England for Buddy Holly Week (sponsored by Paul McCartney, who had just purchased the entire Holly song catalogue).

Some of the Crickets have had solo careers. In 1958 Allison released "Real Wild Child" for Coral Records (with Holly on lead guitar) under the nom de disc of Ivan. Curtis, who wrote Holly's "Rock Around with Ollie Vee," went on to write "I Fought the Law" (covered by the Bobby Fuller Four and the Clash), "Walk Right Back" (for the Everly Brothers, for whom Curtis played lead guitar off and on throughout the Sixties), and the theme song of *The Mary Tyler Moore Show.* He has made solo albums since 1958 for A&M, Mercury, Coral, Liberty, Imperial, and other labels. By the early Eighties he was still active with Elektra/Asylum, for which he released the single "The Real Buddy Holly Story" as a response to the film. Curtis maintained it was factually inaccurate.

In 1986 Holly was one of the first inductees into the Rock and Roll Hall of Fame; seven years later he was honored with his own postage stamp. Nineteen eighty-eight saw the Crickets release a new album, *Three Piece,* on Jerry Allison's Rollercoaster label. Again they played the Buddy Holly Week festival that year; McCartney joined them onstage.

Eddie Holman

Born June 3, 1946, Norfolk, Virginia
1970—*I Love You* (ABC).

R&B/soul vocalist Eddie Holman's intermittently successful career has spanned three decades. He attended the Victoria School of Music and Art in New York and studied music at Cheyney State College in Pennsylvania. His debut single was the regionally successful "Crossroads" in 1963, and he first cracked the national pop chart with "This Can't Be True" (#57) in 1966.

As the Sixties closed, Holman left Cameo for Bell Records before signing with ABC in 1969. His remake of Ruby and the Romantics' "Hey There Lonely Boy," retitled "Hey There Lonely Girl," hit #2 in 1970. Two lesser hits—"Don't Stop Now" (#48, 1970) and "Since I Don't Have You" (#95, 1970)—followed, but he did not reappear on the chart again until "This Will Be a Night to Remember" (#90) in 1977. In the early Nineties Holman was heard from again singing Christian contemporary music on his own label, Agape.

The Holy Modal Rounders
Formed 1963
Peter Stampfel (b. Oct. 29, 1938, Milwaukee, Wis.), banjo, fiddle, voc.; Steve Weber (b. June 22, 1942, Philadelphia, Pa.), gtr., voc.
1967—*Indian War Whoop* (ESP)   1968—*Holy Modal Rounders, vol. 1* (Prestige); *Holy Modal Rounders, vol. 2*   1969—*Moray Eels Eat the Holy Modal Rounders* (Elektra); *Good Taste Is Timeless* (Metro-media)   1972—*Stampfel and Weber* (Fantasy)   1976—*Alleged in Their Own Time* (Rounder)   1979—*Last Round* (Adelphi)   1981—*Goin' Nowhere Fast* (Rounder); *Have Moicy*.
Peter Stampfel: 1986—*Peter Stampfel & the Bottlecaps* (Rounder)   1989—*People's Republic of Rock 'n' Roll* (Homestead).

The Holy Modal Rounders, a loose group centering on Peter Stampfel and Steve Weber, are gonzo traditionalists who mix old folk and bluegrass tunes with their own bouncy, absurdist free associations. The Rounders' closest brush with commercial success came when their "If You Wanna Be a Bird" appeared on the *Easy Rider* soundtrack, but such songs as "Boobs a Lot" and "My Mind Capsized" kept folk rock from taking itself too seriously.

Stampfel was previously with folk groups like Mac-Grundy's Old Timey Wool Thumpers. He and Weber met in 1963 on the East Coast. They recorded albums for Prestige and then began working with the Fugs and contributed to the Fugs' first record on the Broadside label. In 1965 the groups went their separate ways; Stampfel formed the Moray Eels, and Weber revived the Rounders moniker and added other musicians for the first time (including playwright Sam Shepard, who played drums and wrote songs) for *Indian War Whoop* on ESP. They also scored Shepard's play *Operation Sidewinder*. Around the same time, the group's free-flowing lineup also briefly included Jeff "Skunk" Baxter, later with Steely Dan and the Doobie Brothers.

In the early Seventies their *Good Taste Is Timeless*, featuring "Boobs a Lot," got some FM airplay. Shortly thereafter Fantasy Records released *Stampfel and Weber*, followed in 1976 by a reunion LP, *Alleged in Their Own Time*, on Rounder Records (named in their honor). In late 1981, still folk-cult favorites, Stampfel and Weber did some East Coast dates as a duo to support *Goin' Nowhere Fast*, and Stampfel continued to appear around New York City with his group, the Bottlecaps. Stampfel now works in publishing in Manhattan and has recorded two albums.

The Honeycombs
Formed 1963, London, England
Martin Murray (b. Oct. 7, 1941, London), gtr.; Alan Ward (b. Dec. 12, 1945, Nottingham, Eng.), gtr., piano, organ; Denis D'ell (b. Denis Dalziel, Oct. 10, 1943, London), piano, gtr., harmonica, Jew's harp, voc.; John Lantree (b. Aug. 20, 1940, Newbury, Eng.), bass; Ann "Honey" Lantree (b. Aug. 28, 1943, Hayes, Eng.), drums.
1964—*Here Are the Honeycombs* (Interphon)   circa 1965—(– Murray; + Peter Pye [b. July 12, 1946, London], gtr.).

A British Invasion band, the Honeycombs were one of the first rock groups to have a female drummer. The band, originally called the Sherabons and, mistakenly, the Sherations, was formed by ex-skiffle guitarist and hairdresser Martin Murray. Ann "Honey" Lantree was a beautician working under Murray in a North London salon (which explains the "Honey" and "combs" of the group's name) who was also a drummer. Joined by three other musicians, including Honey's brother John on bass, the quintet signed with influential Sixties producer and impresario Joe Meek. In the wake of the Beatles' international success, the group's 1964 debut, "Have I the Right?" was leased to Interphon in the U.S. and hit the Top Five. It was #1 for two weeks in Britain, and its international combined sales topped one million.

The group quickly became a media staple in the U.K. and also toured France, Australia, and New Zealand. After Murray injured himself in a fall, Peter Pye replaced him. The Honeycombs had only one more chart entry in the U.S.—"I Can't Stop" (#48, 1965)—although they continued to have success in England until 1966, when Meek committed suicide.

The Honey Cone
Formed 1969, Los Angeles, California
Carolyn Willis (b. 1946, Los Angeles), voc.; Edna Wright (b. 1944, Los Angeles), voc.; Shellie Clark (b. 1943, Brooklyn, N.Y.), voc.
1990—*Greatest Hits* (HDH/Fantasy).

The Honey Cone, composed of three veteran black female R&B singers, had its biggest hit with "Want Ads" (#1, 1971). The best-known member of the original group was Carolyn Willis, formerly of the Girlfriends. Edna Wright, Darlene Love's sister, was a Raelette in several Ray Charles roadshows, a backup vocalist on hits by the Righteous Brothers and Johnny Rivers, and a solo performer with a minor 1964 hit, "A Touch of Venus." Clark had worked as an Ikette with Ike and Tina Turner and toured with Little Richard and Dusty Springfield.

The trio first sang together in 1969 as backup vocalists for Burt Bacharach on an Andy Williams TV special.

Eddie Holland signed them to Holland-Dozier-Holland's new Hot Wax label and named them. They had two minor hits that year ("While You're Out Looking for Sugar" and "Girls It Ain't Easy") before perfecting an up-beat pop-soul style similar to that of Martha and the Vandellas. In 1971 "Want Ads" (cowritten by General Johnson, a member of the Showmen and then the Chairmen of the Board), went gold and stayed at the #1 spot for one week.

Honey Cone followed up with two more tunes cowritten by Johnson—"Stick-Up" (#11, 1971) and "One Monkey Don't Stop No Show, Part 1" (#15, 1971). In 1972 they had their last Hot 100 entries with "The Day I Found Myself" (#23) and "Sittin' on a Time Bomb (Waitin' for the Hurt to Come)" (#96). By 1973 the group had disbanded and returned to independent studio work. A few years later Carolyn Willis was prominently featured on Seals and Crofts' "Get Closer."

Honeydrippers: See Robert Plant

The Hoodoo Gurus
Formed 1981, Sydney, Australia
Dave Faulkner (b. Oct. 2, 1954, Perth, Austral.), voc., gtr.; Brad Shepherd (b. Feb. 1, 1961, Sydney), gtr., voc.; Clyde Bramley, bass; James Baker, drums.
1983—*Stoneage Romeos* (A&M)   1985—(– Baker; + Mark Kingsmill [b. Dec. 4, 1956, Sydney], drums) *Mars Needs Guitars!* (Big Time)   1987—*Blow Your Cool!*   1988—(– Bramley; + Rick Grossman [b. Nov. 2, 1955, Sydney], bass)   1989—*Magnum Cum Louder* (RCA)   1991—*Kinky*   1994—*Crank* (Zoo).

Aussie pub rockers the Hoodoo Gurus build their music from the debris of American pop culture—everything from garage-band pop to science-fiction B movies. But while their unique sensibility earned them critical favor and a college-radio following, wide U.S. appeal has eluded them.

Le Hoodoo Gurus, as they were originally called, formed in a friend's living room as a five-piece band, including ex-Scientists Rod Radalj and James Baker. Singer Dave Faulkner has been the group's sole permanent member; he first came to musical infamy in 1979 with the underground hit "Television Addict" by his Perth band the Victims.

By their debut album the Hoodoos were a four-piece, with Faulkner's wacky pop songs braced by Brad Shepherd's junk-metal guitar. *Stoneage Romeos* (which was dedicated to, among others, Arnold [the Pig] Ziffel from TV's *Green Acres*) introduced the band's offbeat take in songs like "(Let's All) Turn On," "I Want You Back," "I Was a Kamikaze Pilot," and "Leilani." The album was a critical and college-radio smash Down Under and was well received in America. Shortly after its U.S. release, Mark

The Hoodoo Gurus: Dave Faulkner, Brad Shepherd, Mark Kingsmill, Rick Grossman

Kingsmill joined the band. With the first single from *Mars Needs Guitars!*, the Australian Top Twenty hit "Bittersweet," Faulkner showed a more sensitive, serious side. But on "Like Wow—Wipeout" the Hoodoo Gurus' sound was reminiscent of Sixties garage rockers, while the title track paid homage to their hankering for sci-fi kitsch.

Constant touring brought the Hoodoos to the U.S. and Europe. The Bangles helped them with one of their biggest singles, "What's My Scene," from 1987's *Blow Your Cool;* the women also sang on the album track "Good Times." On the East Coast, the band became buddies with New York's Fleshtones (who in the 1990s would release an album on Faulkner's Australian indie label). Rick Grossman, formerly of the Divinyls, joined in 1988. *Magnum Cum Louder* gave the band three alternative club hits: "Come Anytime," "Another World," and "Baby Can Dance." The album's title ironically addressed the band's reluctant pigeonholing into the college-radio market; the track "Where's That Hit?," ostensibly about baseball, is clearly autobiographical. *Kinky* featured the Hoodoo Gurus' paean to Sixties sexuality, "Miss Freelove '69," but the album failed to make a dent on the charts. Three years later, the band resurfaced with *Crank,* released several months earlier in Australia. Produced by

Ed Stasium, the hard-rocking album included guest backing vocals from ex-Bangle Vicki Peterson and New York City chanteuse Wendy Wild.

John Lee Hooker

Born August 22, 1920, Clarksdale, Mississippi
1961—*John Lee Hooker Plays and Sings the Blues* (Chess)   1962—*Folklore of John L. Hooker* (Vee Jay)   1966—*It Serves You Right* (Impulse)   1968—*Urban Blues* (Stateside)   1970—*No Friend Around* (Red Lightnin')   1971—*Coast to Coast* (United Artists); *Endless Boogie; Hooker 'n' Heat* (with Canned Heat) (Liberty); *Goin' Down Highway 51* (Specialty)   1972—*Boogie Chillun* (Fantasy); *Never Get Out of These Blues Alive*   1974—*Best of John Lee Hooker* (Crescendo); *Don't Turn Me from Your Door* (Atco)   1975—*John Lee Hooker* (New World)   1976—*Blues Before Sunrise* (Bulldog)   1978—*Live* (Lynarz); *The Cream* (Tomato)   1980—*This Is Hip* (Charly)   1981—*Hooker Alone, vol. 1* (Labor)   1982—*Hooker Alone, vol. 2*   1987—*The Best of John Lee Hooker* (GNP Crescendo)   1989—*The Healer* (Chameleon)   1991—*Mr. Lucky* (Charisma); *The Ultimate Collection 1948–1990* (Rhino)   1992—*Boom Boom* (Charisma)   1993—*John Lee Hooker on Vee-Jay 1955–1958* (Vee-Jay)   1995—*Chill Out* (Pointblank).

Blues musician John Lee Hooker helped define the post–World War II electric blues with his one-chord boogie compositions and his rhythmic electric guitar work, although his deep voice is inimitable. Hooker was one of the links between the blues and rock & roll.

Hooker was one of 11 children. He sang at church in Clarksdale, and his first musical instrument was an inner tube stretched across a barn door. In his adolescence he was taught some rudimentary guitar techniques by his stepfather, William Moore, who often performed at local fish fries, dances, and other social occasions in the late Twenties; another early influence was Blind Lemon Jefferson. In 1931 he went to Memphis, where he worked odd jobs on Beale Street. He moved to Cincinnati in 1933 and sang with gospel groups like the Big Six, the Delta Big Four, and the Fairfield Four.

Hooker moved in 1943 to Detroit, where his career eventually took root. He began recording in the late Forties. He was exclusively a singles artist for his first few very prolific years, and his first release was the eventually gold "Boogie Chillun" on the Modern label. "I'm in the Mood" sold a million in 1951, and the blues-record market was soon laden with Hooker material on myriad labels, often released under such pseudonyms as Birmingham Sam, John Lee Booker, Boogie Man, John Lee Cooker, Delta John, Johnny Lee, Texas Slim, and Johnny Williams. His only pop chart entry was with "Boom Boom" (#60, 1962), later recorded by the Animals.

In 1959 he cut his first album for Riverside Records and made his debut performance at the Newport Folk Festival. British and American rockers, including the Spencer Davis Group, the J. Geils Band, Canned Heat, and George Thorogood, have covered his songs. He toured England and Europe widely in the early Sixties and recorded and toured extensively with Britain's Groundhogs in the mid-Sixties.

By 1970 Hooker was living in Oakland, California, when he wasn't touring, and that year he teamed up with Canned Heat for *Hooker 'n' Heat* (Liberty), which made inroads on the charts in the U.S. (#73) and abroad. He was joined by Charlie Musselwhite and Van Morrison in 1972 for *Never Get Out of These Blues Alive,* which was released at about the same time Fantasy put out some previously unreleased tapes and a Galaxy release (both from 1962) on the double LP *Boogie Chillun.* Hooker continued to tour in the Seventies and Eighties, often opening for rock acts like Canned Heat and Foghat. In 1980 he appeared in *The Blues Brothers* film, and in the early Eighties he recorded solo albums.

The late Eighties brought a renewal of interest in Hooker. He sang the title role on Pete Townshend's 1989 album *The Iron Man,* based on a children's book, and joined the Rolling Stones at their Atlantic City, New Jersey, concerts that year. His album *The Healer* (#62, 1989)—with guest appearances by Carlos Santana, Robert Cray, Los Lobos, George Thorogood, Canned Heat, and others—was his biggest commercial success, spending 38 weeks on the chart and earning him his first Grammy Award for a duet with Bonnie Raitt on "I'm in the Mood." In October 1990 an all-star concert celebrating Hooker's music was held at New York's Madison Square Garden, where Hooker was joined by Raitt, Joe Cocker, Huey Lewis, Ry Cooder, Gregg Allman, Willie Dixon, and others; that year he also joined Miles Davis on the Grammy-nominated movie soundtrack *The Hot Spot* (Davis reportedly called Hooker "the funkiest man alive, buried up to his neck in mud").

In 1991 Hooker was inducted into the Rock and Roll Hall of Fame; he was nominated for another Grammy for 1991's *Mr. Lucky,* which featured tracks recorded with the Robert Cray Band, Keith Richards, Ry Cooder, Tom Waits, Van Morrison, Johnny Winter, Carlos Santana, and others. His 1992 release *Boom Boom* featured guest guitar work by ex–Fabulous Thunderbird Jimmie Vaughan and blues great Albert Collins. In early 1995 Hooker announced he would no longer tour but would continue to record until he "was in the ground," releasing *Chill Out* that year.

The Hooters

Formed 1978, Philadelphia, Pennsylvania
Rob Hyman, voc., kybds.; Eric Bazilian, voc., gtr.;

John Lilley, gtr.; Rob Miller, bass; David Uosikkinen, drums.
1983—*Amore* (Antenna)   1985—*Nervous Night* (Columbia)   1987—*One Way Home* (– Miller; + Fran Smith Jr., bass, voc.)   1989—*Zig Zag*   1993—*Out of Body* (MCA)   1994—*Greatest Hits, I* (Sony International); *Greatest Hits, II*; *The Hooters Live* (MCA International).

The Hooters burst onto the charts in the summer of 1985 with *Nervous Night* and a string of moderate hits—"And We Danced" (#21, 1985), "Day by Day" (#18, 1986), and "Where Do the Children Go" (#38, 1986)—that reflected the group's wide-ranging and diverse musical influences and loves. Blending basic rock & roll instrumentation and themes with folk instrumentation (mandolin, dulcimer, accordion, and the melodica, or "hooter," from which they took the group's name), the Hooters forged a unique sound that, since the late Eighties, has found a wider audience overseas than in the U.S.

Rob Hyman and Eric Bazilian were members of Baby Grand, a group that cut two albums for Arista in the late Seventies and included future producer Rick Chertoff. When that group broke up, Bazilian and Hyman continued writing and doing session work. They arranged for, played on, and provided backing vocals for Cyndi Lauper on her 1983 breakthrough album, *She's So Unusual,* for which Hyman cowrote the hit single "Time After Time." Shortly thereafter, the duo rounded out the group with three more members. The Hooters then released several independent singles and an album, *Amore,* which sold 100,000 copies.

Their debut for Columbia, *Nervous Night* (#12, 1985), went gold, and its followup, *One Way Home* (#27, 1987), was also certified gold, despite a lack of Top Fifty singles. By then the Hooters had won a number of music-magazine polls as best new group and best new live act but that commercial momentum didn't hold. *Zig Zag* missed the Hot 100, although a rendition of the folk classic "500 Miles," featuring Peter, Paul and Mary, who had recorded it in the early Sixties, went to #97 in 1986.

Around the world, however, it was a far different story. In England "Satellite" from *One Way Home* went to #22. It was also a hit in Germany. The group has also earned gold albums in several European countries and in Japan. Bazilian and Hyman have continued to work with a number of other artists, including Johnny Clegg and Savuka, Taj Mahal, and Sophie B. Hawkins.

Mary Hopkin

Born May 3, 1950, Pontardawe, Wales
1969—*Postcard* (Apple)   1971—*Earth Song*   1972—*Those Were the Days*   1979—*Welsh World of* (Decca); *Kidnapped*   1995—*Those Were the Days: The Best of Mary Hopkin* (Capitol).

Welsh singer Mary Hopkin was briefly an international star in the late Sixties. She began singing at age four and was soon taking voice lessons and singing in the Congregational Tabernacle Choir. Hopkin studied music, art, and English at the local grammar school and continued at Cardiff College of Music and Drama. While a student there, she earned extra money by singing in pubs. When she appeared on the BBC-TV variety show *Opportunity Knocks* in 1968, she was spotted by the model Twiggy, who told Paul McCartney about her. McCartney signed her to Apple and supervised her first sessions, which produced "Those Were the Days" (#2, 1968). The song had already been recorded by the Limeliters, who adapted it from a Russian folk song called "Darogoi Dlimmoya" (Dear for Me), first recorded in the Twenties.

Hopkin was 18 years old when her debut album, *Postcard,* was released. McCartney wrote and produced her second single, "Goodbye" (#13, 1969), which hit #2 on the British chart. She then moved on to work with producer Mickie Most. Hopkin enjoyed lesser hits in the early Seventies—including "Temma Harbour," "Que Sera, Sera (Whatever Will Be, Will Be)," "Think About Your Children" (1970), and "Knock Knock Who's There" (1972)—and toured a bit.

As an actress, in 1969 she costarred with Tommy Steele in a pantomime production of *Dick Whittington* at the London Palladium and in 1971 appeared with David Essex in *Cinderella* in Manchester. Around the same time, she married British record producer Tony Visconti and began raising their two children. Through the mid-Seventies her singing career was limited to occasional backup vocals (as Mary Visconti) for Ralph McTell, David Bowie, and Thin Lizzy. In 1976 "If You Love Me," on Visconti's Good Earth label, hit #32 on the English chart. She starred in a 1980 Christmas production of *Rock Nativity* at the Hexagon Theatre in Reading.

Around the same time she and Visconti broke up, in 1981, Hopkin returned to music. First she briefly joined a British trio, Sundance; then in 1984 she reemerged as lead singer of a group called Oasis (not to be confused with the mid-Nineties British band). Its debut album placed in the U.K. Top Twenty-five.

Lightnin' Hopkins

Born Sam Hopkins, March 15, 1912, Centerville, Texas; died January 30, 1982, Houston, Texas
1959—*Lightnin' Hopkins* (Folkways)   1965—*Down Home Blues* (Prestige)   1968—*Texas Blues Man* (Arhoolie)   1970—*Lightnin', vol. 1* (Poppy)   1972—*Double Blues* (Fantasy); *Lonesome Lightnin'* (Carnival)   1976—*All Them Blues* (DJM)   1989—*Texas Blues* (Arhoolie)   1990—*The Gold Star Sessions, vol. 1*; *The Gold Star Sessions, vol. 2*   1991—*The Complete Prestige/Bluesville Recordings* (Pres-

tige/Bluesville) 1992—*The Complete Candid Recordings of Lightnin' Hopkins and Otis Spann* (Mosaic).

The most frequently recorded traditional blues artist in history (who, paradoxically, did the bulk of his performing as an impoverished street singer), Sam "Lightnin'" Hopkins was a country-blues stylist whose career spanned more than three decades, even though he did not begin in earnest until he was nearing middle age. His solo style, with its irregular verses and voice-and-guitar call and response, has roots in the earliest blues.

Born in a small farming community, Hopkins lived virtually his entire life in the Houston area. He was one of six children (his sister and four brothers were also musicians), and at age eight he debuted on a guitarlike instrument fashioned from a cigar box and chicken wire. Subsequently his brother Joel "John Henry" Hopkins (later a well-known bluesman in his own right) taught him to play guitar. Hopkins dropped out of school to hobo through Texas, playing informally in the streets and jamming with folk legends like Blind Lemon Jefferson, whom he met in the summer of 1920. As the Thirties progressed he supported himself primarily as a farmworker, while playing for tips in Texas bars and nightspots. More than once Hopkins found himself working the Houston County Prison Farm's road gang. After drifting for several years he settled in Houston's Third Ward ghetto after World War II and then rarely left.

In 1946 Hopkins and pianist Wilson "Thunder" Smith went to Los Angeles and cut some sides for the Aladdin label. While there, he gained his Lightnin' moniker. When little came of the Aladdin sessions, he returned to Houston and, backed only by his own guitar, cut "Short Haired Woman" b/w "Big Mama Jump" in 1947 for Gold Star Records. It sold 40,000 copies, and the followup, "Baby Please Don't Go," doubled that figure, beginning two years of local success.

Over the next few years Hopkins recorded prolifically for several companies based in Houston, Los Angeles, and New York. He insisted upon being paid in cash for each studio take, thereby relinquishing his rights to his material (he rarely received royalties on his massive catalogue of work) and causing confusion in his recording legacy. (A complete Hopkins discography would include efforts for over 20 record companies.) His style and stance are represented on reissues and compilation/anthologies like Tradition's *Autobiography* and *Best*, Arhoolie's *Early Recordings*, Prestige's *Greatest Hits*, and others compiled from his hundreds of sides. Among his many compositions were "December 7, 1941," "Don't Embarrass Me, Baby," "Ball of Twine," "I'm Gonna Meet My Baby Somewhere," and "Little Antoinette."

When Texas blues fell from national favor by the mid-Fifties, Hopkins' career nosedived, though he did record and perform in Europe—usually solo, sometimes with a backing ensemble. Reduced once again to Houston street singing (perennially working the Dowling Street area), he was saved by the later folk and blues revival and was rediscovered by musicologist and author Sam Charters (*The Country Blues*), who recorded him for Folkways in 1959. That same year, he played the University of California Folk Festival, and in 1960 he appeared at Carnegie Hall in a show featuring Joan Baez and Pete Seeger. In 1961 Hopkins toured with Clifton Chenier's band and continued to play regularly at Houston nightspots like Irene's and the Sputnik Bar. Les Blank's 1969 documentary on the singer, *The Blues Accordin' to Lightnin' Hopkins,* won the Gold Hugo award at the Chicago Film Festival.

Hopkins performed at folk festivals and in rock venues in the late Sixties but was slowed by an auto crackup in 1970 that put his neck in a protective brace. Nevertheless he continued club work on and off through the Seventies. In the early Seventies he recorded for the Denver-based Tumbleweed Records. Meanwhile, tapes continued to surface on a variety of labels, and in 1972 he contributed to the soundtrack of the feature film *Sounder.* Hopkins remained sporadically active for the rest of the decade, capping his lengthy career with an appearance at Carnegie Hall in spring 1979. He did little recording in his final years but could be seen prowling the Houston streets in his black Cadillac Coupe de Ville. In 1981 he underwent surgery for cancer of the esophagus, which later proved terminal.

Nicky Hopkins
Born February 24, 1944, London, England; died September 6, 1994, Nashville, Tennessee
1966—*Revolutionary Piano* (Columbia, U.K.)
1973—*The Tin Man Was a Dreamer* 1975—*No More Changes* (Mercury).

Studio keyboardist Nicky Hopkins has been in and out of groups in Britain and the U.S. since the Sixties; Ray Davies wrote the Kinks' "Session Man" in his honor. Hopkins began playing the piano at age three and studied at the Royal Academy of Music from 1956 to 1960. He joined Screamin' Lord Sutch's Savages in 1960 and two years later moved to the Cyril Davies R&B All-Stars; the two groups included many musicians who would make their names in the British Invasion and its aftermath. Hopkins left Davies in May 1963 because of illness and began work as a session keyboardist after he emerged from the hospital 19 months later. He recorded with the Rolling Stones, the Beatles, the Who, the Small Faces, the Kinks, and other bands, and in 1968 he joined the Jeff Beck Group, which at the time included Rod Stewart and Ron Wood.

In the late Sixties he also recorded with his own

short-lived group, Sweet Thursday, which included future Cat Stevens guitarist Alun Davies and Jon Mark of the Mark-Almond Band. But after nine months in the Jeff Beck Group, Hopkins joined the Quicksilver Messenger Service in San Francisco and recorded with it on *Shady Grove.* He also recorded with Steve Miller and the Jefferson Airplane and appeared with the Airplane at the Woodstock Festival.

In the Seventies Hopkins returned to work as a sideman, touring with the Rolling Stones (he appears on "Jumpin' Jack Flash" and "Sympathy for the Devil" and the albums *Let It Bleed, Exile on Main Street,* and *Black and Blue*) in 1972 and sporadically with the Jerry Garcia Band and backing Graham Parker and others on records. His attempt at a solo career in the mid-Seventies was widely ignored. In 1979 he joined the group Night, which had a hit single that year with "Hot Summer Nights," but quit soon after. He then moved to Northern California, where he kept a low profile. He later moved to Nashville, where he died of complications from previous intestinal surgeries.

Bruce Hornsby and the Range

Formed 1984, Los Angeles, California
Bruce Hornsby (b. Bruce Randall Hornsby, Nov. 23, 1954, Richmond, Va.), voc., kybds.; David Mansfield, violin, mandolin, gtr.; George Marinelli Jr., gtr.; Joe Puerta, bass; John Molo, drums.
1986—*The Way It Is* (RCA)   1988—(- Mansfield; + Peter Harris, gtr., mandolin) *Scenes from the Southside*   1990—(- Harris) *A Night on the Town.* Bruce Hornsby solo: 1993—*Harbor Lights* (RCA).

Pianist and singer Bruce Hornsby spent years writing and playing for other artists before his own band, the Range, broke through in 1986 with "The Way It Is," an antiracism song that became a #1 pop single. Hornsby's increased visibility made his eclectic, jazz-influenced skills even more highly sought after; numerous and diverse popular acts enlisted his support, solidifying his reputation as a musician's musician. Meanwhile, Hornsby's recordings with the Range, which mixed roots-rock textures with mellow R&B overtones, continued to appeal to a core audience of adult-contemporary and album-oriented rock fans.

Raised in Williamsburg, Virginia, the lanky Hornsby played varsity basketball in high school and dreamed of a professional athletic career. His piano studies sidetracked him, though, and Hornsby wound up studying music at Boston's Berklee College and earning his degree from the University of Miami's School of Music in 1977. In 1980, with a band including his older brother, Bob, and drummer John Molo, Hornsby moved to Los Angeles. There, he and his younger brother, John, were hired as contract writers for 20th Century–Fox. (Hornsby

eventually cowrote with his two brothers the songs for his albums.) Hornsby also did session work and toured in Sheena Easton's band. By 1984, the Range's original lineup was complete and eager to be signed. At first, though, even the pushing of early supporter Huey Lewis, a big star at the time, proved futile; but then a demo of songs performed acoustically by Hornsby attracted major-label interest.

The Way It Is, fueled by the title track, reached #3 and spawned the additional hits "Mandolin Rain" (#4, 1987) and "Every Little Kiss" (#14, 1987). Subsequently, Hornsby and the Range collected a Grammy for Best New Artist. A sophomore album, 1988's *Scenes from the Southside,* reached #5 and yielded the #5 single "The Valley Road"; while 1990's *A Night On the Town* peaked at #20 and produced the #18 single "Across the River."

Meanwhile, Hornsby tickled the ivories on albums by Bob Dylan, Robbie Robertson, Bonnie Raitt, and Squeeze, among others. He wrote and played on Don Henley's 1989 hit "End of the Innocence" and toured extensively with the Grateful Dead, putting in 18 months with the band after keyboardist Brent Mydland's death in 1990. In 1993, after disbanding the Range, Hornsby released the solo album *Harbor Lights* (#46), featuring appearances by Raitt, Jerry Garcia, Phil Collins, Pat Metheny, and Branford Marsalis.

Johnny Horton

Born April 30, 1925, Los Angeles, California; died November 5, 1960, Milano, Texas
1959—*The Spectacular Johnny Horton* (Columbia) 1960—*Johnny Horton Makes History*; *Johnny Horton's Greatest Hits*   1971—*The World of Johnny Horton*   1989—*American Originals.*

Johnny Horton was one of the first country & western singers to cross over onto the pop chart. His "The Battle of New Orleans" was a #1 hit in 1959. Sources disagree about where and when Horton was born (some claim April 30, 1927, others November 30, 1929, and Tyler, Texas, is sometimes stated as his place of birth). His mother taught him to play guitar at an early age, and he later attended Seattle University, where he majored in petroleum engineering and dabbled in songwriting. After traveling around Alaska and Louisiana, he started performing in clubs and on Pasadena radio station KXLA, billed as the Singing Fisherman.

In 1951 Horton moved to Shreveport, Louisiana, where for eight years he was a star attraction on the *Louisiana Hayride* radio show. He began recording in 1951, but had little success until his move to Columbia. There his version of Jimmie Driftwood's "Battle of New Orleans" hit in 1959; it was also a hit for Lonnie Donegan in England (#2, 1959). Horton's subsequent hits included "Johnny Reb" (#54, 1959), "Sink the Bismarck" (#3, 1960), and "North to Alaska" (#4, 1960), the title song to a John Wayne film. Around 1960 Horton, an avid believer in the occult, became convinced his death was imminent. He rescheduled engagements frequently, but perhaps not often enough, for while returning home from a performance at the Skyline in Austin he was killed in a car accident. By strange coincidence, the Skyline had been the site of Hank Williams' last performance, and Horton's widow, Billy Jean, had been married to Williams as well.

Hot Chocolate

Formed 1970, London, England
Errol Brown (b. Jamaica), voc.; Patrick Olive
(b. Grenada), gtr., perc., bass; Larry Ferguson
(b. Nassau), kybds.; Harvey Hinsley (b. Mitcham,
Eng.), gtr.; Ian King, drums; Tony Wilson
(b. Trinidad), bass, voc.
1973—(– King; + Tony Connor [b. Romford, Eng.],
drums) 1974—*Cicero Park* (Big Tree) 1975—*Hot*
***Chocolate* (– Wilson) 1976—*Man to Man* 1977—**
***10 Greatest Hits* 1978—*Every 1's a Winner* (Infin-**
ity) 1979—*Going Through the Motions*
1980—*Mystery* (EMI) 1993—*Every 1's a Winner:*
The Very Best of Hot Chocolate.

This Caribbean British interracial soul band had Seventies hits with social-comment dance tunes. Their biggest one in America was "You Sexy Thing" (#3, 1976), and their "Brother Louie" (a Top Ten hit for them in England in 1973) became a #1 hit for Stories in America the same year. The London-based band got its first contract with the Beatles' Apple label, for which it released a reggae-style version of John Lennon's "Give Peace a Chance" (1970). Hot Chocolate then worked with producer Mickie Most, concentrating on singles. It established itself in the U.K. in the early Seventies with moderately successful releases like "Love Is Life" (#6 U.K., 1970) and "I Believe (in Love)" (#8 U.K., 1971). "Emma" (#3 U.K., #8 U.S., 1975) finally broke the group stateside in early 1975, followed by "Disco Queen" (#28, 1975) and "You Sexy Thing."

Errol Brown and Tony Wilson wrote most of Hot Chocolate's songs, and in the early Seventies their compositions were covered by Mary Hopkin, Peter Noone (Herman's Hermits), April Wine, and Suzi Quatro. But in 1975 Wilson left the group for a solo career (his solo debut, "I Like Your Style," came out in 1976). Hot Chocolate persevered with 1976's *Man to Man,* which expanded its considerable following in Europe. The group enjoyed moderate U.S. success with "Don't Stop It Now" (#42, 1976), "So You Win Again" (#31, 1977), "Going Through the Motions" (#53, 1979), and "Are You Getting Enough Happiness" (#65, 1982). Brown and company cracked the U.S. Top Ten again in early 1979 with "Every 1's a Winner" (#6).

Hot Chocolate remained popular in the U.K., charting with "Girl Crazy" (#7 U.K., 1982) and "It Started with a Kiss" (#5 U.K., 1982); when Brown quit for a solo career in 1987, the band broke up.

Hothouse Flowers

Formed 1986, Dublin, Ireland
Liam O'Maonlai (b. Nov. 7, 1964, Dublin), voc.,
kybds., harmonica; Fiachna O'Braonain (b. Nov. 27,
1965, Dublin), gtr.; Peter O'Toole (b. Apr. 1, 1965,
Dublin), bass, bouzouki; Jerry Fehily (b. Aug. 29,
1963, Bishops Town, Ire.), drums; Leo Barnes
(b. Oct. 5, 1965, Dublin), sax.
1988—*People* (London) 1990—*Home* 1993—
Songs from the Rain.

Hothouse Flowers has endeared itself to modern-rock fans with a rootsy, passionate pop hybrid incorporating elements of traditional Irish folk music and American blues and gospel. Singer Liam O'Maonlai and guitarist Fiachna O'Braonain met in grade school, started playing together as teenagers, and quit college in 1985 to become the Incomparable Benzini Brothers, an acclaimed street-performance act that, after the addition of a bassist, drummer, and sax player, evolved into Hothouse Flowers. In 1986 the fledgling musicians were spotted on Irish television by U2's Bono, who immediately offered them support.

The following year, Hothouse Flowers released its first single on U2's own label, Mother Records, a feat that attracted the interest of many major record companies. The band soon landed a deal with PolyGram's London label. Its 1988 debut album, *People,* reached the top of the Irish charts within a week and went to #2 in England. In America, though, *People* would only reach #88, and two subsequent albums would make even less impression. Its failure to transcend cult status in the U.S. notwithstanding, Hothouse Flowers continues to draw critical praise for its warm sound, and particularly for O'Maonlai's raw, soulful vocals, which have inspired comparisons to Van Morrison and Bruce Springsteen.

Hot Tuna

Officially split from Jefferson Airplane, 1972
Jorma Kaukonen (b. Dec. 23, 1940, Washington,
D.C.), gtr., voc.; Jack Casady (b. Apr. 13, 1944, Wash-
ington), bass.
1970—*Hot Tuna* (RCA) (+ Will Scarlet, harmonica)
1971—*First Pull Up—Then Pull Down* (+ Papa John
Creach [b. May 28, 1917, Beaver Falls, Pa.; d. Feb.
22, 1994, Los Angeles, Calif.], elec. violin; + Sammy
Piazza, drums) 1972—(– Scarlett) *Burgers* (Grunt)
1974—(– Creach) *The Phosphorescent Rat* 1975—
(– Piazza; + Bob Steeler, drums) *America's Choice*;
Yellow Fever* 1976—*Hoppkorv* 1978—*Double

Dose (+ Nick Buck, kybds.) 1979—*Final Vinyl*
1984—*Splashdown* (Relix) 1985—*Historic Hot
Tuna* 1990—(+ Michael Falzarano, gtr., mandolin,
harmonica, voc.) *Pair a Dice Found* (Epic) 1992—
Live at Sweetwater (Relix) 1993—*Live at Sweet-
water Two.*
Jorma Kaukonen solo: 1974—*Quah* (Grunt) 1979—
Jorma (RCA) 1980—*Barbeque King* 1985—*Too
Hot to Handle* (Relix); *Magic.*
**Papa John Creach solo: See Jefferson Airplane
entry.**

Jack Casady and Jorma Kaukonen, original recording
members of the Jefferson Airplane, grew up together in
northwestern Washington, D.C. After high school Kaukonen headed for the Philippines to join his relocated gov-
ernment-service parents and traveled in the Orient
before moving to San Francisco and working as a folkie.
He soon fell in with the Airplane and called his old friend
Casady, then teaching guitar in Washington. The two
stayed with the Airplane until 1972.

By then they had already started Hot Tuna (they
originally called the group Hot Shit, but RCA balked),
which was intended to operate as a satellite band. Early
on, other members of the Airplane played with Tuna, including vocalist Marty Balin and drummers Spencer Dryden and Joey Covington. The group's low-key debut was
recorded live at Berkeley's New Orleans House with harmonica player Will Scarlett and Kaukonen on acoustic
guitar. Their music eventually became loud and electric.

First Pull Up—Then Pull Down marked the arrival of
black violinist Papa John Creach. Born in Pennsylvania
in the early part of the century, Creach was 18 when his
family moved to Chicago, where he received some classical training and was briefly affiliated with the Illinois
Symphony Orchestra. By the late 1930s he had begun
two decades of touring the cocktail lounge circuit. After
settling in San Francisco in the Sixties, he became
friends with drummer Joey Covington, who recommended that Tuna get in touch with Creach. With Hot
Tuna from 1971 until 1973, Creach played concurrently
with the Airplane and launched a solo career with his
1971 self-titled Grunt/RCA debut. By the time of 1972's
Filthy, Creach had formed his own band, Zulu, which he
continued after leaving Tuna.

Hot Tuna's first album as a completely autonomous
entity was its fourth, *The Phosphorescent Rat.* The
group was a commercial oddity; despite the fact that its
mid-Seventies releases weren't big sellers, it insisted on
playing concerts of at least two hours, which necessi-
tated headliner status. In 1978 the group disbanded.

Kaukonen then resumed the solo recording career he
had started with 1974's *Quah* (produced by Casady), releasing *Jorma* in 1979. Kaukonen toured solo, while nurturing a fondness for ever-changing hair color and

tattoos. He also played briefly in a San Francisco–based
new-wave band, Vital Parts. Casady, meanwhile, materialized with white-blonde hair in a new-wave outfit of his
own, SVT. In 1984 both musicians reverted: Casady reunited with former Jefferson Airplane singers Marty
Balin and Paul Kantner in a group called KBC, while
Kaukonen, still flying solo, started playing acoustic blues
and folk again. (He later released two more albums, *Too
Hot to Handle* and the live *Magic.*) Also in 1984, Relix
Records released *Splashdown,* a Hot Tuna radio performance from 1975.

In 1983 Casady and Kaukonen staged a "temporary
reunion," playing some club dates together. The band re-
formed on a more permanent basis in 1986, adding new
member Michael Falzarano, a multi-instrumentalist and
singer, in 1990. (Falzarano had previously accompanied
Hot Tuna on its 1983 renunion gigs.) That year, a full-
fledged tour and new studio album, *Pair a Dice Found,*
followed. In 1992 Hot Tuna released *Live at Sweetwater,*
featuring guests Pete Sears (formerly of Jefferson Starship), Maria Muldaur, and the Grateful Dead's Bob Weir;
volume two followed the next year. Also in the early
Nineties, Casady toured with Paul Kantner in Jefferson
Starship: The Next Generation, while Kaukonen traveled
with Falzarano in a musical aggregation called Kau-
karano.

Son House
**Born Eddie House, March 21, 1902, Riverton, Missis-
sippi; died October 19, 1988, Detroit, Michigan
1965—*Father of the Folk Blues* (Columbia) 1973—
Son House (Arhoolie) 1979—*The Real Delta Blues*
(Blue Goose) 1991—*Delta Blues: The Original Library of Congress Sessions from Field Recordings
1941–1942* (Biograph) 1992—*Father of the Delta
Blues: The Complete 1965 Recordings* (Legacy).**

Blues vocalist and guitarist Son House—often cited as a
major influence by Muddy Waters, Robert Johnson, Bob
Dylan, and Bonnie Raitt—was one of the Mississippi
Delta bluesmen who laid the groundwork for rock & roll
in the years before World War II. House was one of the in-
stigators of the regional tendency toward biting guitar
sounds, dramatic vocals, and full-tilt rhythm sections.

House was born on a plantation and by age 15 was
delivering sermons in churches in Louisiana and Tennessee. In the early Twenties he became pastor of a Baptist church in Lyon, Mississippi. In 1927 he taught
himself to play guitar, and from then on he was a fixture
on the Delta house-party circuit. Around 1928 he worked
as part of Dr. McFadden's Medicine Show, but that career was quickly ended by a stint in the state prison at
Parchman, Mississippi. Released in 1929, he moved to
Lula, Mississippi, where he came under the tutelage of
Delta legend Charley Patton. Through Patton he

recorded his first sides for the Paramount label in 1930. House did not record again for ten years, but he was an active performer, in partnership with Willie Brown, in the rural South. In the early Forties musicologist Alan Lomax, tipped off to House's prodigious talent by Muddy Waters, recorded him for the Library of Congress (in sessions later released commercially on Arhoolie, and in 1991 on Biograph). House moved to Rochester, New York, in 1943, and from then until 1964 he played only occasionally and only locally.

Spurred by the folk-blues revival of the early Sixties, House reemerged to much acclaim, attracting a large white audience for the first time in his life. He began recording in earnest, touring the campus and coffee-house circuits, appearing at folk and blues festivals in the U.S., Canada, and Europe, and performing at rock venues. House was the subject of a 1969 film short, and he appeared in several documentaries and on television before retiring from music in 1974. He lived the rest of his years in Detroit.

The Housemartins/The Beautiful South/Beats International

The Housemartins, formed 1984, Hull, England (Paul Heaton [b. May 9, 1962, Bromborough, Eng.], voc., gtr; Stan Cullimore [b. Apr. 6, 1962, Hull], bass; Ted Key, gtr.; Hugh Whitaker, drums): 1985—(– Key; + Norman Cook [b. July 31, 1963, Brighton, Eng.], gtr. 1986—London 0 Hull 4 (Elektra) (– Whitaker; + Dave Hemingway [b. Sep. 20, 1960, Hull], drums) 1987—The People Who Grinned Themselves to Death 1988—Now That's What I Call Quite Good! (Go! Discs, U.K.).
The Beautiful South, formed 1988, Hull, England (Heaton, voc.; Hemingway, drums, voc.; Dave Rotheray [b. Feb. 9, Hull], gtr.; Sean Welch [b. Apr. 12, Enfield, Eng.], bass; Briana Corrigan [b. Antrim, Eng.], voc.; Dave Stead [b. Oct. 15, Huddesfield, Eng.], drums): 1989—Welcome to the Beautiful South (Elektra) 1990—Choke 1992—0898.
Beats International, formed 1989, Brighton, England (Cook, bass; Lindy Layton, voc.; Lester Noel, voc.; Andy Boucher, kybds.; MC Wildski, voc.): 1990—Let Them Eat Bingo (Elektra) 1991—Excursion on the Version.

When the British pop band the Housemartins dissolved in the late Eighties, three of its members went off in strikingly different musical directions. Housemartins frontman Paul Heaton and drummer Dave Hemingway formed the Beautiful South, whose juxtaposing of sweet vocals and sunny hooks with acerbic lyrics evoked the group from whose ashes it rose, while replacing the Housemartins' jangly guitar arrangements with jazzier textures. Bassist Norman Cook made a more radical de-

parture from his old group's sound by putting together the techno-dance outfit Beats International—a less surprising move than it might seem, given that Cook had DJed in clubs before and during his tenure with the Housemartins. Like the Housemartins, both the Beautiful South and Beats International enjoyed some commercial success in England, but never transcended cult status in the U.S.

Formed in 1984, the Housemartins developed a socially conscious, no-frills image and earned a reputation for scathing sarcasm. Its 1986 and 1987 albums yielded several Top Twenty pop hits, including "Caravan of Love" (#1 U.K., 1986) and "Happy Hour" (#3 U.K., 1986). After the band split up in 1988, Heaton and Hemingway maintained this basic approach while fleshing out the music somewhat. Thus, in the Beautiful South, they both sang (as did ex–Anthill Runaways vocalist Briana Corrigan), and the orchestrations were a bit more lush, often featuring keyboards. This formula generated U.K. hits like "Song for Whoever" (#2, 1989), "You Keep It All In" (#8, 1989), and "A Little Time" (#1, 1990). Meanwhile, lyricist Heaton's caustic wit continued to draw mixed reviews from critics, some of whom found him too clever—or bitter—for his own good.

Beats International, in contrast, emphasized rhythm over rhetoric. Working with a core band that included singers Lindy Layton and Lester Noel, keyboardist Andy Boucher, and rapper MC Wildski—plus guests such as Billy Bragg and the Damned's Captain Sensible—Cook produced and played bass on tracks that combined new and sampled music. In 1990 Beats scaled the British charts with the singles "Dub Be Good to Me" (#1) and "Won't Talk About It" (#9). Cook frequently works as a remixer with a variety of artists, including Aztec Camera and the Jungle Brothers.

House Music/Acid House

Created around 1981 as a musical style for Chicago's black gay culture, house music was named for the club where it began, Chicago's Warehouse. This revved-up dance music form was developed by DJ Frankie Knuckles, who mixed speedy disco beats with records of Latin, Philly, Salsoul, and African music. House combines a deep drum and bass sound with heavy reverb, tribal rhythms, and noises of the city and the jungle.

The more hypnotic acid house is a psychedelic variation on the Chicago style. When house made its way to London in the mid-Eighties, DJs there began experimenting with it, adding spaced-out grooves and samples of TV chatter and other media. Some of the so-called Chicago "white label" records got into the hands of British underground-music guru Genesis P-Orridge, whose Psychic TV and Throbbing Gristle helped lay the foundation for much of the techno-industrial music of the Eighties. P-Orridge noticed the word "acid" on the records (Chicago slang for "sampling," or "taking someone else's music"), thought it referred to LSD, and began calling the British variation "acid house." Psychic TV put out a series of acid-house albums beginning with 1988's *Jack the Tab: Acid Tablets Volume One*.

By the late Eighties, a range of English pop musicians—from indie rockers to the industrial-music fringe—began releasing acid mixes of their songs. The style returned to the American West Coast and, along with techno [see entry], spawned the rave scene of the Nineties.

The House of Love
Formed 1986, London, England
Terry Bickers (b. Sep. 6, 1965, London), gtr.; Guy Chadwick (b. Mar. 21, 1956, Hanover, Ger.), voc., gtr.; Pete Evans (b. Oct. 22, 1957, Swansea, Eng.), drums; Chris Groothuizen (b. July 8, 1965, Otahuhu, N.Z.), bass; Andrea Heukamp (b. 1965, Ger.), voc., gtr.
1987—(– Heukamp) 1988—*The House of Love* (Relativity) 1990—(– Bickers; + Simon Walker, gtr.) *The House of Love* (Fontana) 1991—*A Spy in the House of Love* (– Walker; + Simon Mawbey [b. Dec. 24, 1960, Leicester, Eng.], gtr.) 1992—*Babe Rainbow* 1993—*Audience with the Mind*.

Like their countrymen the Smiths and the Cure, the House of Love specialize in cloaking well-constructed pop songs in layers of shimmering, moody guitars. More upbeat than their predecessors, they have enjoyed some success in Britain yet retain cult status in the States.

Formed by singer/songwriter Guy Chadwick in 1986, taking their name from an Anaïs Nin novel, the original three-guitar lineup played in London pubs until its demo attracted the attention of Creation Records. In 1987 House of Love released its debut single, "Shine On." More ambitious touring led to the departure of guitarist Andrea Heukamp. They continued as a quartet, releasing their first, eponymous, album in 1988 (#156 pop, #8 U.K., 1988). The album's combination of psychedelia with contemporary guitar sounds led to their signing worldwide with Fontana. Guitarist Terry Bickers left after their second, also self-titled, album (#148, 1990). He was replaced by Simon Walker, who was himself replaced barely a year later by ex-Woodentop Simon Mawbey. In the interim an album of outtakes and B sides, *A Spy in the House of Love*, was issued. The first album of new material with this lineup was 1992's *Babe Rainbow*. By the summer of 1993, Chadwick was the House of Love's sole member; he began recording with session players for a 1995 album.

House of Pain
Formed 1990, Los Angeles, California
Everlast (b. Erik Schrody, Aug. 18, 1969, Valley Stream, N.Y.), voc.; Danny Boy (b. Daniel O'Connor, Dec. 12, 1968, Los Angeles), voc.; DJ Lethal (b. Leor DiMant, Dec. 18, 1972, Latvia), DJ.
1992—*House of Pain* (Tommy Boy) 1994—*Same as It Ever Was*.

Not merely a white rap group, House of Pain was the first Irish-American rap group. Its bios were sent out on green paper; the group's logo was a shamrock with the words "fine malt lyrics"; the group's debut album (#14, 1992) included such tracks as "Top o' the Mornin' to Ya" and "Shamrocks and Shenanigans" (#65, 1992). Everlast wore a green Boston Celtics basketball jersey in the video for House of Pain's biggest hit, "Jump Around" (#3, 1992)—which, like Kris Kross's contemporaneous hit "Jump," grafted shouted vocal hooks onto dissonant, Public Enemy–derived mixes brimming with big, bumptious beats and grating, high-pitched whistles and wheezes.

Everlast and Danny Boy first met at Taft High School in Los Angeles, where rapper Ice Cube was a student; Everlast later worked with Ice-T's Rhyme Syndicate before forming House of Pain with Danny Boy and Latvian émigré DJ Lethal. House of Pain's debut album was co-produced by DJ Muggs of hardcore Los Angeles rap group Cypress Hill.

In March 1993 Everlast was arrested at New York's Kennedy Airport for gun possession, when an unregistered (unloaded) pistol was found in his luggage. He eventually plea-bargained the charge down to a community-service sentence. The group's 1994 album, *Same as It Ever Was* (#12, 1994), included the single "On Point" (#85, 1994).

Cissy Houston
Born Emily Houston, 1933, Newark, New Jersey
1971—*Cissy Houston* (Janus) 1977—*Cissy Houston* (Private Stock) 1979—*Warning—Danger* (Columbia) 1980—*Step Aside for a Lady* 1992—*I'll Take Care of You* (with Chuck Jackson) (Shanachie).

Gospel-soul singer Cissy Houston was a member of the Sixties soul group the Sweet Inspirations and has since pursued a sporadic solo career (abetted by occasional session work) as she split her time between music and raising a family. She first sang with a family gospel group, the Drinkard Singers, which sometimes included her nieces Dionne and Dee Dee Warwick. The group was well known on the East Coast gospel circuit and recorded for RCA and Savoy.

After quitting the Drinkards, Houston established herself as a pop backup singer in New York. By 1967 she had become lead vocalist in the Sweet Inspirations. "Sweet Inspiration," a gospel-pop single, cracked the Top Twenty in early 1968, and they established further credentials with their backup work for Aretha Franklin,

Elvis Presley, Neil Diamond, Dusty Springfield, and others. Houston quit the group in 1970 and began recording solo with *Cissy Houston,* which included "Be My Baby" (#92, 1971). Houston was the first to record "Midnight Train to Georgia," which later became a hit single for Gladys Knight. She also toured as part of Dionne Warwick's backup trio, which included Dee Dee Warwick and Darlene Love. Houston devoted the next several years primarily to raising her three children, so her second solo disc was not released until 1977.

Houston has continued to be a popular backup vocalist, notably on Chaka Khan's *Chaka* (1978), Aretha Franklin's *Aretha* (1980), *Love All the Hurt Away* (1981), and *Jump to It* (1982), and Luther Vandross' *Never Too Much* (1981) and *Forever, For Always, For Love* (1982). She hosted a weekly radio broadcast from the New Hope Baptist Church in Newark and played occasional New York club dates with her then-less-famous daughter, Whitney.

Thelma Houston
Born Mississippi
1971—*Sunshower* (ABC/Dunhill)   1975—*I've Got the Music in Me* (Sheffield Labs)   1976—*Any Way You Like It* (Tamla)   1977—*The Devil in Me*; *Thelma and Jerry* (with Jerry Butler) (Motown) 1978—*Ready to Roll* (Tamla); *Two to One* (Motown) 1981—*Superstar Series, vol. 20*; *Never Gonna Be Another One* (RCA)   1983—*Thelma Houston* (MCA) 1986—*Qualifying Heat*   1990—*Throw You Down* (Reprise)   1991—*The Best of* (Motown).

Thelma Houston's dramatic quavering gospel-based delivery made her one of disco's most distinctive voices. As a youngster she sang in churches in Mississippi before her family moved to California. By the late Sixties she was working Southern California clubs, thereby attracting the attention of the Fifth Dimension's manager, Marc Gordon, who landed her a contract with ABC/Dunhill. Over the next few years, she made pop records with such producers as Jimmy Webb (the critically acclaimed *Sunshower*) and Joe Porter.

Houston's most successful effort from this period was a version of Laura Nyro's "Save the Country" (#74, 1970). Her breakthrough came via Tamla/Motown and the Gamble-Huff disco hit "Don't Leave Me This Way" (#1, 1977). Other efforts for Motown included an appearance on the soundtrack of the Motown-produced film *The Bingo Long Traveling All Stars & Motor Kings* (1976). She has also appeared in the films *Norman . . . Is That You?, Death Scream,* and *The Seventh Dwarf.* In 1977 she joined Jerry Butler for *Thelma and Jerry.* "Saturday Night, Sunday Morning" (#34 pop, #19 R&B, 1979) returned her to the chart as the disco era came to a close. Since then she's had modest success on RCA and MCA.

"You Used to Hold Me So Tight," peaking at #13 R&B in 1984, was her highest-charting record since 1976.

Whitney Houston
Born August 9, 1963, Newark, New Jersey
1985—*Whitney Houston* (Arista)   1987—*Whitney* 1990—*I'm Your Baby Tonight*   1992—*The Bodyguard* soundtrack.

As the daughter of renowned gospel and soul singer Cissy Houston and the cousin of Dionne Warwick, Whitney Houston was better connected than most young vocalists when she embarked on a recording career in the mid-Eighties. But neither genes nor industry contacts can account for the level of superstardom to which Houston quickly ascended. Blessed with a sublimely creamy, agile voice—and picture-perfect looks to boot— the singer delivered the sort of buoyant dance tunes and smooth, hummable ballads that are equally at home on the pop, R&B, and adult-contemporary charts. Critics carped that her supple singing would be better served by more soulful, less commercially ingratiating material. But where America's record-buying public was concerned, Houston became a star of the highest order, one whose appeal crossed races, cultures, and generations.

As a child, Houston sang in her family's church choir. At 15 she began performing in her mother's nightclub act. While attending Catholic high school, the lithe beauty signed with a modeling agency and posed for magazines, including *Glamour* and *Vogue.* After graduating, she continued to model and sing, backing up Lou Rawls and Chaka Khan, then at 19 was spotted by Arista president Clive Davis—who had previously steered the careers of Warwick and Houston family friend Aretha Franklin—while giving a showcase in Manhattan. Davis signed Houston and started choosing songs for her debut album, which featured duets with established stars Teddy Pendergrass and Jermaine Jackson and cost Arista an extraordinarily hefty sum of $250,000.

Released in 1985, *Whitney Houston* proved a worthwhile investment, shooting to #1 and generating the smash singles "You Give Good Love" (#3 pop, #1 R&B, 1985), "Saving All My Love for You" (#1 pop and R&B, 1985), "How Will I Know" (#1 pop and R&B, 1985), and "Greatest Love of All" (#1 pop, #3 R&B, 1986). *Whitney* solidified Houston's success, reaching #1 and spawning "I Wanna Dance with Somebody (Who Loves Me)" (#1 pop, #2 R&B, 1987), "Didn't We Almost Have It All" (#1 pop, #2 R&B, 1987), "So Emotional" (#1 pop, #5 R&B, 1987), "Where Do Broken Hearts Go" (#1 pop, #2 R&B, 1988), and "Love Will Save the Day" (#9 pop, #5 R&B, 1988). Also in 1988, Houston recorded "One Moment in Time," NBC-TV's theme song for the Summer Olympics (#5 pop). In 1989 she teamed up with Aretha Franklin

Whitney Houston

on the #5 R&B hit "It Isn't, It Wasn't, It Ain't Never Gonna Be."

In 1990 *I'm Your Baby Tonight*'s title track topped the pop and R&B charts, as did "All the Man That I Need." There were more hits in 1991—"Miracle" (#9 pop, #2 R&B), "My Name Is Not Susan" (#20 pop, #8 R&B), and "I Belong to You" (#10 R&B)—but, peaking at #3, *Baby* proved disappointing after its predecessors. Houston bounced back in a big way, though, with the 1992 film *The Bodyguard,* in which she made her acting debut (as a singing star, opposite Kevin Costner), to mixed reviews and huge box office. The movie's soundtrack—with six tracks sung by Houston—proved even more successful, hitting #1 and producing a monster single, Houston's cover of Dolly Parton's "I Will Always Love You" (1992), which remained at the top of the chart for an unprecedented 14 weeks, as well as a cover of Chaka Khan's "I'm Every Woman" (#4 pop, #5 R&B, 1993) and "I Have Nothing" (#4 pop and R&B, 1993). In 1992 Houston married singer Bobby Brown [see entry]; their first child was born the next year.

Steve Howe: See Yes

Howlin' Wolf
Born Chester Arthur Burnett, June 10, 1910, West Point, Mississippi; died January 10, 1976, Hines, Illinois
1958—*Howlin' Wolf* (Chess) 1964—*Moaning in the Moonlight* 1965—*Poor Boy* 1966—*Real Folk Blues* 1967—*More Real Blues; Evil; Live and Cookin' at Alice's Revisited* 1971—*The London Sessions* 1986—*His Greatest Sides, vol. 1* (Chess/MCA) 1987—*Cadillac Daddy: Memphis Recordings, 1952* (Rounder) 1991—*The Chess Box.*

Delta bluesman Howlin' Wolf was one of the most influential musicians of the post–World War II era, and his electric Chicago blues—featuring his deep, lupine voice—shaped rock & roll.

Chester Arthur Burnett, named after the twenty-first president, was raised on a cotton plantation in Ruleville, Mississippi, and learned guitar as a child. In the Mississippi Delta area he began studying with the rural masters, notably guitarist and vocalist Charley Patton, his biggest single influence, and his half-sister's husband, harmonica player Sonny Boy Williamson (Rice Miller).

As Howlin' Wolf, he played his first gig in the South on January 15, 1928, and throughout the Thirties frequently performed on streetcorners. He formed his first band, the House Rockers, in Memphis in 1948 with pianist Bill Johnson, lead guitarist Willie Johnson, and drummer Willie Steele. Later personnel included at various times harmonica players James Cotton and Little Junior Parker and pianist Ike Turner.

In 1951 Turner, a freelance talent scout, had Wolf record for Sam Phillips' Memphis-based Sun Records. Those masters were then leased to Chess Records, and in 1957 one of them, "Moanin' at Midnight," became his first R&B hit. In 1952 Wolf moved to Chicago, where his music was well received. Some consider the recordings he made for Chess during the Fifties and Sixties his best. Among them were the 1957 R&B hit "Sitting on Top of the World," "Spoonful," "Smokestack Lightnin'," "Little Red Rooster," "I Ain't Superstitious," "Back Door Man," "Killing Floor," and "How Many More Years." His songs, many of them written by Willie Dixon, have been covered by American and English rock acts like the Rolling Stones (with whom Wolf appeared on the *Shindig!* TV show in 1965), the Grateful Dead, the Yardbirds, Jeff Beck, the Doors, Cream, the Electric Flag, Little Feat, and Led Zeppelin.

Wolf, who stood an imposing six-three and weighed nearly 300 pounds, frequently appeared at blues and rock festivals in the late Sixties and early Seventies. His 1971 album *The London Sessions* featured backup support from Eric Clapton, Ringo Starr, Steve Winwood, Charlie Watts, and Bill Wyman. That same year Wolf received an honorary doctorate from Columbia College in Chicago. He lived the last years of his life in Chicago's crumbling South Side ghetto. He suffered several heart attacks in the early Seventies and received kidney dialysis treatment, but he continued to play occasionally; one of his last concerts was in November 1975 at the Chicago Amphitheatre with B. B. King, Bobby "Blue" Bland, and Little Milton. He entered a hospital in mid-

December and died at age 65 of complications from kidney disease. Howlin' Wolf was posthumously inducted into the Rock and Roll Hall of Fame in 1991.

The Hues Corporation

Formed 1969, Los Angeles, California
H. Ann Kelly (b. Apr. 24, 1947, Fairchild, Ala.), voc.;
St. Clair Lee (b. Bernard St. Clair Lee Calhoun Henderson, Apr. 24, 1944, San Francisco, Calif.), voc.;
Fleming Williams (b. Flint, Mich.), voc.
1974—*Freedom for the Stallion* (RCA) (– Williams;
+ Tommy Brown [b. Birmingham, Ala.], voc.);
Rockin' Soul 1975—*Love Corporation* (– Brown;
+ Karl Russell [b. Apr. 10, 1947, Columbia, Ohio],
voc.) 1977—*I Caught Your Act* (Curb); *Best of the Hues Corporation* (RCA) 1978—*Your Place or Mine* (Warner Bros.).

Disco-soul group Hues Corporation had its one big hit with "Rock the Boat" (#1, 1974), which sold over two million copies. A black vocal trio featuring two men and a woman, the Hues took its name from Howard Hughes (changing the spelling to avoid legal problems).

After working the lounge circuit, the group signed with RCA in 1973 and had a minor pop hit with the title track of its debut album, *Freedom for the Stallion*. The Corporation's big success came in mid-1974 with "Rock the Boat." Followups like "Rockin' Soul" (#18, 1974) and "Love Corporation" (#62, 1975), with Tommy Brown in place of Fleming Williams, were modest in comparison. Brown left in 1975; his spot was taken by Karl Russell.

The Hues Corporation made frequent TV appearances in the mid-Seventies and also appeared in the film *Blacula*. Longtime vocal arranger and producer Wally Holmes was still on board after the group switched to Curb Records in 1977 for *I Caught Your Act*; the LP's title track (#92, 1977) was the act's last chart appearance.

The Human League

Formed 1977, Sheffield, England
Phil Oakey (b. Oct. 2, 1955, Sheffield), voc., synth.;
Martyn Ware (b. May 19, 1956, Sheffield), synth.; Ian Craig Marsh (b. Nov. 11, 1956, Sheffield), synth.;
Philip Adrian Wright (b. June 30, 1956, Sheffield),
stage visuals.
1979—*Reproduction* (Virgin, U.K.) 1980—*Travelogue* (– Ware; – Marsh; + Ian Burden [b. Dec. 24, 1957, Sheffield], bass, synth.; + Suzanne Sulley [b. Mar. 22, 1963, Sheffield], voc.; + Joanne Catherall [b. Sep. 18, 1962, Sheffield], voc.) 1981—(+ Jo Callis [b. May 2, 1955, Glasgow, Scot.], synth.) 1982—*Dare* (A&M); *Love and Dancing* 1983—*Fascination!* 1984—*Hysteria* 1986—*Crash* 1988—*Greatest Hits* 1990—*Romantic?* 1995—*Octopus* (EastWest).
Philip Oakey with Giorgio Moroder: 1985—*Philip Oakey and Giorgio Moroder* (A&M).

Armed with synthesizers and electronic percussion, the Human League became the undisputed leader of the British electropop movement in 1982. The League topped the American chart with the million-selling "Don't You Want Me," taken from *Dare*, its third British album and first U.S. release. Led by Philip Oakey, the League had released its debut album, *Reproduction*, three years earlier. *Travelogue* followed the next year. Both critically acclaimed works featured synthesizer textures reminiscent of Kraftwerk and dark lyrics that Oakey delivered in an ominous voice reminiscent of mid-Seventies David Bowie.

Oakey felt the band's heavy reliance on prerecorded tapes in live shows was dishonest, which led to the departures of Martin Ware and Ian Marsh in 1980. The two synthesizists formed the popular Heaven 17 later that year [see entry]. Meanwhile, Oakey and remaining Human Leaguer Philip Wright recruited bassist/synthesizer player Ian Burden, two female backing singers, and synthesizist Jo Callis, former guitar-playing leader of Scotland's punk-kitsch rockers the Rezillos. Allying itself with producer Martin Rushent (the Stranglers, Buzzcocks), the Human League recorded *Dare*, which quickly brought it fame in England. Coinciding with its subsequent American success, the League toured the States, where audiences got a good taste of electropop: A drum machine kept the robotic beat.

That the group's songwriters (mainly Oakey, Callis, and Burden) were less than prolific quickly became apparent. *Love and Dancing* reprised instrumental tracks from *Dare*, while *Fascination* contained just five songs. Two of them became hits in 1983: the Motownish "Mirror Man" (#30) and "(Keep Feeling) Fascination" (#8), which mimicked the vocal arrangement style of Sly and the Family Stone. *Hysteria* introduced a gutsier sound, with Callis playing guitar and Burden thumping an actual bass. "The Lebanon," a powerful guitar-driven track about the strife in that country, was a minor hit at #64.

The following year Oakey recorded an album with disco producer Giorgio Moroder, so Human League's decision to hire modern-funk producers Jimmy Jam and Terry Lewis to helm *Crash* wasn't as surprising as it might seem. The plaintive "Human," a Jam-Lewis composition, hit #1. Curiously, rather than build on its momentum, the Human League all but disappeared until 1990. That year's "Heart Like a Wheel" from *Romantic*, was a Top Forty hit, but after that Oakey and company vanished once again. In 1994 the group recorded *Octopus*, released the next year.

Humble Pie

Formed 1969, Essex, England
Steve Marriott (b. Jan. 30, 1947, London, Eng.;
d. Apr. 20, 1991, Arkesden, Eng.), gtr., voc., kybds., harmonica; Peter Frampton (b. Apr. 22, 1950, Beck-

enham, Eng.), gtr., voc.; Greg Ridley (b. Oct. 23, 1947, Carlisle, Eng.), bass, voc.; Jerry Shirley (b. Feb. 4, 1952, Eng.), drums.
1969—*As Safe as Yesterday Is* (Immediate, U.K.); *Town and Country*   **1970**—*Humble Pie* (A&M)
1971—*Rock On*; *Performance—Rockin' the Fillmore* (– Frampton; + David "Clem" Clempson [b. Sep. 5, 1949, Eng.], gtr., voc.)   **1972**—*Smokin'*; *Lost and Found*   **1973**—*Eat It*   **1974**—*Thunder Box*   **1975**—*Street Rats* (group disbands)   **1980**—(Group reforms: Marriott; Shirley; + Bobby Tench, voc., gtr.; + Anthony Jones, bass) *On to Victory* (Atco)
1981—*Go for the Throat*   **1982**—*The Best* (A&M). Steve Marriott solo: **1976**—*Marriott* (A&M)   **1981**—*Steve Marriott*.

Early-Seventies hard-rock band Humble Pie was formed and fronted by the raspy-voiced Steve Marriott, who had left the Small Faces in 1968. He hooked up with ex-Herd guitarist Peter Frampton (whose boyish good looks had already elicited teenybopper acclaim), ex–Spooky Tooth bassist Greg Ridley, and drummer Jerry Shirley. In 1969 the group retired to Marriott's Essex cottage for months of rehearsal. Its first single, "Natural Born Boogie," hit the Top Five in the U.K. Neither the quartet's debut album, *As Safe as Yesterday Is,* nor the acoustic-oriented *Town and Country* made much of an impact in the U.S. until repackaged as *Lost and Found.*

Humble Pie toured the U.S. for the first time in late 1969 but returned home to find that the Immediate label had gone under. It found a new manager (Dee Anthony) and label (A&M), and its next LP, *Humble Pie,* featured Frampton's melodic acoustic rock. But neither it nor the gutsier *Rock On* provided an American breakthrough. Anthony sent the group to America on a frenzied tour that produced *Performance—Rockin' the Fillmore,* recorded live at New York's Fillmore East in May 1971. Loud and raucous, it went gold. Frampton left the group in late 1971 [see entry].

The loss of Frampton, combined with the outstanding sales of the rock-and-blues-oriented *Fillmore* album, prompted the group to concentrate on boogie material. *Smokin',* its first album with new guitarist Dave "Clem" Clempson, was the group's most successful, reaching #6. But shortly thereafter Humble Pie's fortunes fell, and in 1975 the members split up.

Shirley formed an L.A. group, Natural Gas, with ex-Badfinger member Joey Molland. Clempson (previously with Colosseum) joined Greenslade before he and Pie bassist Ridley teamed up with former Jeff Beck drummer Cozy Powell to form the short-lived Strange Brew. Clempson has since played with Jack Bruce, among others.

Marriott, meanwhile, led Steve Marriott's All-Stars before participating in a Small Faces reunion in 1976. By 1980 Marriott and Shirley had re-formed Humble Pie with ex–Jeff Beck vocalist Bobby Tench. Their two albums—1980's *On to Victory* and 1981's *Go for the Throat*—met with limited success. In mid-1981 the group's tour of the U.S. was interrupted when Marriott smashed his hand in a hotel door. In June, having recovered, he had to halt the tour again when he was hospitalized in Dallas with an ulcer. Once again Humble Pie disbanded, with Shirley going on to drum for the hard-rock group Fastway. At the time that Marriott died in a fire in his Sixteenth-Century cottage at age 44, he and Peter Frampton were planning to record together again.

Engelbert Humperdinck
Born Thomas Arnold George Dorsey, May 2, 1936, Madras, India
1967—*Release Me* (Parrot); *The Last Waltz*   **1968**—*A Man Without Love*   **1969**—*Engelbert*   **1970**—*We Made It Happen*; *Sweetheart*   **1971**—*Another Time, Another Place*; *Live at the Riviera Hotel, Las Vegas*   **1973**—*In Time*   **1974**—*King of Hearts*   **1976**—*After the Lovin'* (Epic)   **1978**—*Last of the Romantics*   **1979**—*This Moment in Time*   **1981**—*Don't You Love Me Anymore?*   **1983**—*You and Your Lover*   **1985**—*A Lovely Way to Spend an Evening* (Silver Eagle)   **1987**—*The New Greatest Hits of Engelbert Humperdinck* (Priority); *Remember I Love You* (White)   **1991**—*Love Is the Reason* (Critique); *Coming Home* (Decca)   **1992**—*The 25th Anniversary Album—Hello Out There* (with the Royal Philharmonic Orchestra) (Polydor)   **1993**—*Yours Until Tomorrow*   **1994**—*Quiereme Mucho.*

For over 25 years Engelbert Humperdinck has been a smooth-crooning MOR sex symbol. Like Tom Jones (with whom he once shared a manager, Gordon Mills), Humperdinck has been known to inspire legions of swooning, panty-tossing women, and, despite a paucity of recent hit singles, still commands a large, loyal following.

Arnold Dorsey spent his early childhood in India, where his father was a captain in the Royal Engineers. The family relocated to Leicester, where he finished school, learned to play the saxophone, and dreamed of fronting a big band. After a stint in the service, he began performing under the name Gerry Dorsey and recorded "I'll Never Fall in Love Again," which flopped (but was later a hit for Jones). Sidelined by a case of tuberculosis, Dorsey nearly gave up singing. By the mid-Sixties, Mills, whom Dorsey had met years before when he was a singer, had made Jones a household name. Legend has it that he suggested that Dorsey change his name to the assuredly unforgettable (though often misspelled) Engelbert Humperdinck (after the composer of *Hansel and Gretel*). Early that year Humperdinck had his first—and biggest—hit single, a cover of the Fifties C&W classic "Release Me (and Let Me Love Again)" (#4, 1967).

In the U.S. Humperdinck's subsequent efforts made respectable if not spectacular showings: "There Goes My Everything" (#20, 1967), "The Last Waltz" (#25, 1967), "Am I That Easy to Forget" (#18, 1968), "A Man Without Love" (#19, 1968), "Les Bicyclettes de Belsize" (#31, 1968), and "Winter World of Love" (#16, 1970). In the U.K., however, all but the last-named were Top Five hits. Humperdinck hosted his own television variety show in 1970 (patterned after Tom Jones' successful *This Is Tom Jones*), but it was canceled after six months. He had no more major hits in the U.S. until "After the Lovin'," which peaked at #8 in 1976. The album of the same title became the singer's last Top Twenty release here and his only platinum album.

Engelbert (he dropped the "Humperdinck" in the early Nineties), who has recorded in German, Spanish, and Italian, mounts a world tour annually and claims to have one of the biggest fan clubs in the world. His fragrance for women, Release Me, is available through the Home Shopping Channel.

Alberta Hunter

Born April 1, 1895, Memphis, Tennessee; died October 17, 1984, New York City, New York
1961—*Songs We Taught Your Mother*
(Prestige/Bluesville)   1978—*Remember My Name*
soundtrack   1980—*Amtrak Blues* (Columbia).

Alberta Hunter sang the blues for over 70 years and was one of the first black American musicians to tour the world. A spellbinding cabaret star, Hunter could be both sophisticated and sassy, winking slyly through double entendres or reducing her listeners to tears. Among her best-known recordings are "Down Hearted Blues," "A Good Man Is Hard to Find," "My Castle's Rocking," and "You Can't Tell the Difference After Dark." She began singing professionally as a teenager in Chicago. In 1921 Hunter performed and recorded with the Fletcher Henderson orchestra and made her first solo recordings. Upon moving to New York that year she began recording regularly; she recorded in 1924 with Louis Armstrong's Red Onion Jazz Babies for the Gennett label.

Hunter first performed on Broadway when she replaced Bessie Smith in the musical comedy *How Come* in 1923. By 1925 she was leading her own trio in club work and took it on subsequent national tours. In 1927, billed as "America's Foremost Brown Blues Singer," she played in England, France, and Monaco. She visited Scotland, Egypt, Greece, and the Scandinavian countries in the Thirties. Back home, Hunter appeared with Paul Robeson in a 1928 Broadway production of *Showboat* and, beginning in the early Thirties, expanded her audience through a featured spot on WABC radio's *Negro*

Achievement Hour. In the mid-Thirties she had one of her most active club periods, playing Harlem's Cotton Club and appearing at Connie's Inn with Louis Armstrong.

Hunter's recording career revitalized alongside the Depression economy, and in the mid-Thirties she recorded with the Jack Jackson Orchestra on HMV. She recorded in 1939 with the Charlie Shavers Quartet for Decca and in 1940 with the Eddie Heywood orchestra for Bluebird. She spent most of World War II with the USO touring China, Burma, India, Egypt, and Africa, including a 1945 command performance for General Dwight D. Eisenhower. She was given a meritorious service award for her contributions to the war effort.

Hunter returned to New York club work after the war and by the early Fifties was recording again. In 1957 she retired from music to work as a nurse, which she did for two decades, with only infrequent returns to performing: some sessions in 1961 and 1962 for the Prestige/Bluesville, Riverside, and Folkways labels.

In 1977, at age 82, Hunter reemerged to establish residency at the Cookery in New York's Greenwich Village. The attendant publicity prompted a Columbia contract. Her wit and style are amply demonstrated in a 1985 video, *Jazz at the Smithsonian*. She died from natural causes.

Ian Hunter

Born June 3, 1946, Shrewsbury, England
1975—*Ian Hunter* (Columbia)   1976—*All-American Alien Boy*   1977—*Overnight Angels* (Columbia, U.K.)   1979—*You're Never Alone with a Schizophrenic* (Chrysalis); *Shades of Ian Hunter* (Columbia)   1980—*Welcome to the Club* (Chrysalis) 1981—*Short Back n' Sides*   1983—*All of the Good Ones Are Taken* (Columbia)   1989—*Y U I Orta* (with Mick Ronson) (Mercury).

The former leader of Mott the Hoople [see entry], singer/songwriter Ian Hunter pursued a moderately successful solo career in the late Seventies but within a few years had faded from view.

Hunter's family settled in Blackpool but moved frequently, as Hunter's father, who worked for MI5, the British CIA, was regularly transferred. By the time Hunter was 11 he had attended 17 different schools. His family finally settled in Shrewsbury, where he played with a band called Silence that recorded an unsuccessful album. In 1962 he played harmonica in another amateur band but continued to work day jobs until 1968, when he started playing bass in Germany with Freddie "Fingers" Lee. A few months later he helped launch Mott the Hoople in England [see entry].

With its debut album in 1969, Mott the Hoople established itself as Dylan-influenced hard-rockers with

"Rock and Roll Queen" and, under the tutelage of David Bowie, became glitter-rock favorites with 1972's *All the Young Dudes* and its title single. During his last days with the group, Hunter wrote the autobiographical *Reflections of a Rock Star,* published in 1977. In late 1974 he left after being hospitalized in New Jersey for physical exhaustion.

Hunter moved to New York and made his self-titled solo debut, which featured ex-Bowie guitarist Mick Ronson, who had played in a late version of Mott. The album produced a British Top Twenty hit, "Once Bitten, Twice Shy." His next two albums were *All-American Alien Boy* and *Overnight Angels* (the latter of which Hunter later called "disgusting" and which wasn't issued in the U.S. until Columbia included it on the retrospective *Shades of Ian Hunter*).

You're Never Alone with a Schizophrenic (#35, 1979), his successful Chrysalis debut, found Mick Ronson once again producing, arranging, and touring with Hunter. By 1980 Hunter had formed his own band, including Ronson, guitarist Tom Morringello, and keyboardists George Meyer and Tom Mandell. He toured that year to promote his live *Welcome to the Club.* Mick Jones of the Clash produced *Short Back n' Sides* in 1981. Hunter has produced records, including Ellen Foley's debut album and Generation X's second LP, *Valley of the Dolls.* Hunter also wrote Barry Manilow's hit "Ships." After *All the Good Ones Are Taken,* he wasn't heard from again until 1989's *Y U I Orta,* another collaboration with Ronson. It came out months after the American band Great White scored a #5 hit with "Once Bitten, Twice Shy." Hunter put in an appearance at the April 1992 AIDS benefit concert honoring the late Freddie Mercury. He also collaborated on Mick Ronson's last LP, 1994's *Heaven and Hull* (released after Ronson's death), and participated in a Ronson tribute concert.

Ivory Joe Hunter

Born October 10, 1914, Kirbyville, Texas; died November 8, 1974, Memphis, Tennessee
1971—*The Return of Ivory Joe Hunter* (Epic); *16 of His Greatest Hits* (King); *Ivory Joe Hunter* (Everest) 1989—*I'm Coming Down with the Blues* (Home Cooking) 1994—*Since I Met You Baby: The Best of Ivory Joe Hunter* (Razor & Tie).

A pop-blues singer, pianist, and songwriter, Ivory Joe Hunter was a popular R&B figure in the Forties and Fifties, and one of the first R&B singers to interpret country songs. He started playing the piano in grade school and eventually developed a style influenced by Fats Waller. He worked as program director at KFDM radio in Beaumont, Texas, and made his first recordings in 1933 for the Library of Congress via musicologist Alan Lomax.

Hunter recorded briefly with Johnny Moore's Three Blazers for the Exclusive label. He soon started his own Ivory Records and scored his first regional hit with "Blues at Sunrise." He then left Texas in 1942 for California, where he helped form and recorded for Pacific Records ("Pretty Mama Blues"). With King Records from 1947 to 1950, his R&B hits included "Landlord Blues" and "Guess Who" in 1949, and "I Quit My Pretty Mama" in 1950. Signed to MGM, Hunter released "I Almost Lost My Mind," which hit #1 on the R&B chart and had sold a million copies by the time Pat Boone covered it in 1956. Hunter spent most of the Fifties on the R&B chart, first with such MGM releases as "I Need You So" (#2, 1950), and then, after signing with Atlantic in 1954, alongside Ray Charles and Chuck Willis.

Hunter finally reached white listeners with "Since I Met You Baby" (#12, 1956), which got him exposure on Ed Sullivan's TV show. After "Empty Arms" (1957), "Yes I Want You" (1958), and "City Lights" (1959), Hunter's popularity declined, although he continued to record. In the late Sixties he sang country as a revue member of the Grand Ole Opry in Nashville, and he tried a comeback in 1971 when he released *The Return of Ivory Joe Hunter.* In late 1974 Hunter died of cancer in a Memphis hospital. His songs have been covered by Nat King Cole, the Five Keys, and Elvis Presley, who cut "My Wish Came True" and "Ain't That Loving You, Baby."

Mississippi John Hurt

Born July 3, 1893, Teoc, Mississippi; died November 2, 1966, Grenada, Mississippi
1965—*The Best of Mississippi John Hurt* (Vanguard) 1966—*Mississippi John Hurt Today* 1968—*The Immortal Mississippi John Hurt* 1972—*Last Sessions.*

Blues singer Mississippi John Hurt was renowned for his fingerpicking and restrained phrasing. He was one of sharecroppers Isom and Mary Hurt's three children, and he lived as a sharecropper most of his life. A frequent singer in local churches, Hurt dropped out of school at age ten in 1903, by which time he'd taught himself to play a three-finger-picking style of guitar.

Most of Mississippi John Hurt's performances were for audiences in the Avalon, Mississippi, area. Heavily influenced by Jimmie Rodgers, as were many bluesmen of the era, he slowly developed an original country and Delta blues style. In 1928 he was taken to New York and Memphis to cut a few sides for Okeh Records, among them a rendition of the blues standard "Stack-O-Lee." But during the Great Depression Hurt faded back into rural anonymity until he was rediscovered, at age 70, during the early-Sixties folk-blues revival by blues enthusiast Tom Hoskins.

Hurt played at the Newport Folk Festival in 1963, 1964, and 1965, at Carnegie Hall, at rock clubs like the Cafe Au Go Go in New York, on TV's *Tonight Show* in

1963, and in the 1965 Canadian Broadcasting documentary *This Hour Has Seven Days*. He also reactivated his recording career, cutting several albums, including *Today, The Immortal Mississippi John Hurt,* and *Last Sessions,* which was recorded in a Manhattan hotel in 1966, shortly before his death from a heart attack. Hurt helped popularize such traditional material as "Candy Man Blues" and "C. C. Rider" as well as his own "Coffee Blues" and "Chicken." He was survived by his widow, Jesse, and their 14 children.

Hüsker Dü

Formed 1979, St. Paul, Minnesota
Bob Mould (b. Oct. 12, 1960, Malone, N.Y.), gtr., voc.;
Greg Norton (b. Mar. 13, 1959, Rock Island, Ill.),
bass; Grant Hart (b. Grantzberg Vernon Hart, Mar.
18, 1961, St. Paul), drums, voc.
1981—*Land Speed Record* (New Alliance)   1982—
***Everything Falls Apart* (Reflex)   1983—*Metal Circus* EP (SST)   1984—*Zen Arcade*   1985—*New Day Rising*; *Flip Your Wig*   1986—*Candy Apple Grey* (Warner Bros.)   1987—*Warehouse: Songs and Stories*   1993—*Everything Falls Apart and More* (Rhino)   1994—*The Living End* (Warner Bros.).**
Grant Hart solo: 1988—*2541* EP (SST)   1989—*Intolerance.*
Grant Hart with Nova Mob: 1991—*Admiral of the Sea* EP (Rough Trade); *The Last Days of Pompeii* 1994—*Nova Mob* (Restless).
Bob Mould solo: 1989—*Workbook* (Virgin)   1990—*Black Sheets of Rain.*
Bob Mould with Sugar: 1992—*Copper Blue* (Rykodisc)   1993—*Beaster*   1994—*File Under: Easy Listening.*

Hüsker Dü laid the groundwork for the Nineties alternative-rock boom when it became one of the first DIY-era American indie bands to land a major-label deal. The Minnesota-based power trio's influential sound expanded the parameters of punk by incorporating hummable pop melodies and introspective lyrics into a thick hardcore foundation.

Bob Mould was born to mom-and-pop grocery store owners in an upstate New York farming town near Lake Placid. In 1978 he moved to St. Paul, Minnesota, to attend Macalester College, where he took urban studies and worked part-time at a record store. It was there that he met Grant Hart, a local drummer who shared his love of punk rock, and Greg Norton, who played bass and listened to jazz. The three began rehearsing together in Norton's basement, naming themselves Hüsker Dü (Swedish for "do you remember?") after a Fifties board game.

In the early Eighties the trio signed to SST, the most respected American independent label of the Eighties, and released 1983's *Land Speed Record,* a milestone of

Hüsker Dü: Greg Norton, Grant Hart, Bob Mould

hardcore whose 17 songs clocked in at just over a meteoric 26 minutes. For the next five years, Hüsker Dü—along with Black Flag, Minutemen, R.E.M., and Twin City–peers the Replacements—toured almost constantly and released some of the most momentous albums of the postpunk era. Hüsker Dü hit its artistic peak with 1984's *Zen Arcade,* one of punk's few double-disc classics, and one of even fewer punk concept albums (it chronicled a boy's passing from adolescence into adulthood).

By 1986 the band had become plagued by internal problems, including drug use and a power struggle between songwriters Mould and Hart. On its major-label debut, *Candy Apple Grey,* Mould's lyrics had become more inward-looking than ever, while the rage in Hart's angst-laden rockers had reached boiling point. Over Warner Bros.' objections, the band followed up with a second double-disc LP, 1987's *Warehouse: Songs and Stories,* with the songwriting split down the middle. On the eve of the group's 1987 tour, Hüsker Dü's young manager, David Savoy, committed suicide.

On January 25, 1988, Bob Mould, having put down drugs and drink, quit the band to pursue a solo career as a postpunk confessional singer/songwriter. Mould's two Virgin albums took up from where his more reflective material on *Candy Apple Grey* and *Warehouse* left off. His subsequent band, Sugar, settled somewhere between the melodic roar of Hüsker Dü and his solo material. By 1995, Mould was working primarily as a solo artist. Grant Hart returned to SST for a solo album, *Intolerance,* before forming Nova Mob in 1991. Greg Norton left the music business altogether to become a chef.

Brian Hyland

Born November 12, 1943, Woodhaven, New York
1987—*Greatest Hits* (Rhino).

Brian Hyland began his lengthy and sporadically successful pop career with 1960's biggest novelty hit, "Itsy

Bitsy Teenie Weenie Yellow Polkadot Bikini," which hit the top of the chart while Hyland was still in high school. More novelty fare followed ("Lop-Sided, Overloaded and It Wiggled When I Rode It") before Hyland switched labels to ABC/Paramount, dropped his adjectival shtick in favor of pop love songs, and scored with "Let Me Belong to You" (#20, 1961).

He hit off and on through the early Sixties, his best year coming in 1962, when he released "Sealed with a Kiss" (#3), "Ginny Come Lately" (#21), and "Warmed Over Kisses (Left Over Love)" (#25). After a dry spell, Hyland returned to the chart in 1966 with "Run, Run, Look and See" (#25) and "The Joker Went Wild" (#20). In the late Sixties he recorded with slight success until he had a surprise hit in 1970 with a Del Shannon–produced remake of Curtis Mayfield's "Gypsy Woman" (#3), which found Hyland working in an uncharacteristic folk-rock mode. Subsequent attempts to revive rock and country chestnuts, like "Lonely Teardrops" (#54, 1971), proved less fruitful.

Janis Ian

Born Janis Eddy Fink, May 7, 1951, New York City, New York
1967—*Janis Ian* (Verve Forecast); *For All the Seasons of Your Mind* 1968—*The Secret Life of J. Eddy Fink* 1969—*Who Really Cares* 1971—*Present Company* (Capitol) 1974—*Stars* (Columbia) 1975—*Between the Lines*; *Aftertones* 1977—*Miracle Row* 1978—*Janis Ian* 1979—*Night Rains* 1980—*Best of Janis Ian* 1981—*Restless Eyes* 1993—*Breaking Silence* (Morgan Creek) 1995—*Revenge* (Beacon).

Singer/songwriter Janis Ian began her career at 15 with a hit about interracial romance entitled "Society's Child" in 1967. After an eight-year slump, Ian returned to pop radio in 1975 with a platinum LP and Grammy Award–winning single, "At Seventeen."

The daughter of a music teacher, Ian studied piano as a child and began writing songs when she enrolled in Manhattan's High School of Music and Art. There she changed her surname from Fink to Ian (her brother's middle name). The folk journal *Broadside* published her "Hair of Spun Gold" and invited her to perform at a hootenanny at the Village Gate. Ian soon had a contract with Elektra, but was dropped when she insisted upon recording her own material; she then signed to Verve.

In 1966 she recorded a song she had written while

Janis Ian

waiting to see her guidance counselor, "Society's Child (Baby I've Been Thinking)." It was banned by several stations and ignored by the rest until conductor Leonard

Bernstein featured Ian on his CBS-TV special "Inside Pop: The Rock Revolution," where she performed the song accompanied by the New York Philharmonic. "Society's Child" became a #14 hit in 1967.

Ian dropped out of high school in her junior year and released her first album. She recorded two more albums for Verve and gave away most of her earnings to friends and charities; management and taxes took the rest. Ian retired before she was 20. She moved to Philadelphia and married photojournalist Peter Cunningham. Her marriage lasted only a short while, and Ian returned to recording with the unsuccessful *Present Company.* She moved to California, where she lived alone and continued writing. Her next album, *Stars,* included "Jesse," a #30 hit for Roberta Flack, later covered by Joan Baez on *Diamonds and Rust.*

Ian's most commercially successful year was 1975, when she sold over $5 million worth of records. She released the platinum *Between the Lines,* which included "Watercolors" and "At Seventeen" (#3), the latter of which got her a Grammy for Best Female Vocal. Followups like *Aftertones, Miracle Row, Janis Ian,* and *Night Rains* were less popular. Following a 12-year hiatus from recording, Ian—having revealed her homosexuality—returned to the scene with *Breaking Silence,* whose subdued, folkish songs forthrightly tackled such subjects as battered wives ("His Hands"), eroticism ("Ride Me Like a Wave"), concentration camps ("Tattoo"), and Sixties nostalgia ("Guess You Had to Be There").

Ian and Sylvia

Formed 1959, Toronto, Canada
Ian Tyson (b. Sep. 25, 1933, Victoria, British Columbia, Can.); Sylvia Tyson (b. Sylvia Fricker, Sep. 19, 1940, Chatham, Ontario, Can.).
1962—*Ian and Sylvia* (Vanguard) 1963—*Four Strong Winds* 1964—*Northern Journey* 1965—*Early Morning Rain* 1966—*Play One More* 1967—*So Much for Dreaming*; *Ian and Sylvia* (Columbia) 1968—*Nashville* (Vanguard); *Full Circle*; *The Best of Ian and Sylvia* 1970—*Greatest Hits, vol. 1* 1971—*Greatest Hits, vol. 2* 1972—*You Were on My Mind* (with the Great Speckled Bird) (Columbia) 1973—*The Best of Ian and Sylvia.*
Ian Tyson solo: 1975—*Ol' Eon* (A&M) 1979—*One Jump Ahead of the Devil* (Boot) 1993—*And Stood There Amazed*; *I Outgrew the Wagon* (Vanguard) 1994—*Eighteen Inches of Rain*; *Cowboyography*; *Old Corrals & Sagebrush & Other Cowboy Culture Classics.*
Sylvia Tyson solo: 1975—*Woman's World* (Capitol).

Canadian folksingers/songwriters Ian and Sylvia were active in the folk revival of the early Sixties as performers and composers. By the late Sixties they had turned to country music.

Ian Tyson was raised on a Canadian farm, and he traveled much of western Canada working various jobs, including performing in the rodeo, until he was seriously injured at age 19. Shortly after turning 21 and enrolling in the Vancouver School of Art he started singing in clubs, sometimes as part of a group called the Sensational Stripes. Tyson graduated from art school and moved to Toronto, where he worked days as a commercial artist and, with partner Don Francks, played blues and traditional folk material. He was well known in Canadian music circles by the time he met Sylvia Fricker in 1959.

Fricker's mother was a music teacher, organist, and choir director at their church, and Fricker became involved in the Toronto folk scene after graduating from high school. Within a year of meeting, she and Tyson were performing regularly as a duo.

They moved to New York in the early Sixties and began working on the club-and-campus folk circuit. Their first album, recorded in a Masonic temple in Brooklyn, featured traditional songs; their second contained Ian Tyson's best-known song, "Four Strong Winds." Sylvia's "You Were on My Mind" (a 1965 hit for We Five) was on the duo's fourth album, *Northern Journey,* which was released around the time they were married in 1964.

As the Sixties ended the Tysons moved toward country music and briefly toured and recorded with a C&W band called Great Speckled Bird. Tyson began a solo career with a country single, "Love Can Bless the Soul of Anyone," and later became the host of a music-variety show on Canadian television. He produced Sylvia's solo debut, *Woman's World,* and she began hosting a folk-music show, *Touch the Earth,* on CBC radio. The couple divorced and went separate ways in 1975. After settling down on a ranch in the foothills of southern Alberta's Rockies, Ian Tyson began recording Canadian albums of cowboy songs, among them *Cowboyography,* which is platinum in Canada (dates above are for U.S. releases).

Ice Cube

Born O'Shea Jackson, June 15, circa 1969, Los Angeles, California
1990—*AmeriKKKa's Most Wanted* (Priority); *Kill at Will* EP 1991—*Death Certificate* 1992—*The Predator* 1994—*Lethal Injection*; *Bootlegs & B-Sides.*

When Ice Cube left the notorious L.A. rap group N.W.A in 1990, he continued writing hard-hitting gangsta rap songs that pushed buttons in the media as well as among parents, politicians, and police.

The son of strict parents (his mom was a clerk, and

his dad a groundskeeper at UCLA), South-Central Los Angeles native O'Shea Jackson found success with N.W.A [see entry] after graduating college in 1988 with a one-year degree in drafting. In 1990, he had a falling out with N.W.A's management and went solo. For his first album, Cube and his group, Da Lench Mob, enlisted Public Enemy's celebrated Bomb Squad production team, whose dense musical collages include artful uses of sampling and turntable manipulation. Released in spring 1990, *AmeriKKKa's Most Wanted* went gold in ten days and platinum in three months. A sonically forceful, lyrically vicious album, it juxtaposes a barrage of disparaging terms like "bitch" and "ho" with astute, politically charged observations of ghetto life: gang violence, black-on-black killing, abusive police, poverty, drugs, money, and sex roles.

Cube was immediately criticized by parents and officials for being a bad role model, although he took the existential position that that was not his responsibility. Even among rock critics who defended his gangsta rap for its musical *vérité* qualities, he was censured for the brutal track "You Can't Fade Me," in which the song's protagonist fantasizes aborting his girlfriend's pregnancy with a coat hanger.

AmeriKKKa's Most Wanted also introduced Cube's female collaborator, Yo Yo, who on the point-counterpoint track "It's a Man's World" offered a black woman's perspective to counter Cube's male-centric observations. (Ice Cube landed Yo Yo a reported six-figure deal with Atlantic and coproduced her 1991 debut album, *Make Way for the Motherlode*.) For all its unanswered questions and contradictions, *AmeriKKKa's Most Wanted* is considered a rap classic.

With his powerful, rhythmic baritone delivery, Ice Cube has maintained a consistently high standing among critics and fans. Still, after the *Kill at Will* EP (#34), he returned with two of his most controversial songs to date on *Death Certificate* (#2, 1991): "Black Korea," wherein he denigrates Korean market owners, and "No Vaseline," in which he antagonistically refers to N.W.A manager Jerry Heller as a "Jew." The songs led to the first condemnation of an artist in the editor's note of the music trade publication, *Billboard*. The album's single, "Steady Mobbin'," reached #30 on the R&B charts. In December 1992 Ice Cube made history again when *The Predator* debuted at #1 on both the album and R&B charts (it sold 1.5 million within a month of release). In 1994, competing with the success of his former N.W.A mate Dr. Dre, Cube's *Lethal Injection* reached #5.

Ice Cube has also appeared in movies including 1991's *Boyz N the Hood*, in which he portrayed a teenage ex-con in South-Central L.A. named Doughboy, and 1992's *Trespass*, as a thug sidekick to fellow actor/gangsta rapper Ice-T.

Ice-T

Born Tracy Marrow, circa late 1950s, Newark, New Jersey
1987—*Rhyme Pays* (Sire)   1988—*Power*   1989—*The Iceberg/Freedom of Speech . . . Just Watch What You Say*   1991—*O.G. Original Gangster*   1993—*Home Invasion* (Rhyme Syndicate/Priority); *The Classic Collection* (Rhino).
With Body Count: 1992—*Body Count* (Sire)   1994—*Born Dead* (Virgin).

Ice-T became rap's most controversial figure in 1992 after coming under fire for "Cop Killer," a song by his thrash-metal side band, Body Count. The lyrics painted a brutal picture of the strife between inner-city police and ghetto youth, and even drew criticism from then-president George Bush. At nearly every turn Ice-T has been martyred or chastised, managing to offend both the left and right with his provocative words. In the minds of his supporters, Ice-T's violent, often misogynistic tales of mayhem are more sarcastic and even humorous than cynical or gratuitous. With his blunt vocal delivery, narrative-style writing, and mesmerizing B-movie images, Ice-T was one of the earliest West Coast rappers to gain respect among the New York hip-hop set.

Tracy Marrow was raised by an aunt in Los Angeles after his parents died in an auto accident. Inspired by ghetto writer Iceberg Slim, he began penning poems while attending Crenshaw High School. At 15 he started hanging out with gang members on the streets of South-Central L.A. By 1983 he had adopted the name Ice-T (in honor of Iceberg Slim) and recorded a singsong rap called "The Coldest Rap" over a funky Jimmy Jam–Terry Lewis backing track; the song, for which he received $20, came out on the independent label Saturn. The next year Ice-T landed a regular gig at seminal L.A. rap club the Radio and was asked to appear in the movie *Breakin'* (he also appeared in its sequel).

By the time of his 1987 debut album, *Rhyme Pays*, Ice-T had started incorporating poignant stories about inner-city street life ("6 'n the Mornin'," "Squeeze the Trigger") into his heretofore mostly light, sex-obsessed repertoire. Complaining that the songs glorified sex and violence, Tipper Gore's Parents' Music Resource Center (PMRC) persuaded Sire to attach a warning sticker to the album. Meanwhile, actor/director Dennis Hopper liked Ice-T's tales enough to ask the rapper to pen the title song for his 1988 gang-culture film, *Colors*.

Power (#35 pop, #6 R&B, 1988) produced two minor hits, "High Rollers" (#76 R&B, 1989) and "I'm Your Pusher" (#13 R&B, 1988). Continuing to draw fire from cultural watchdog organizations, Ice-T teamed up with former Dead Kennedys frontman Jello Biafra, who'd had an earlier run-in with the PMRC himself, for the sarcastic kick-off track of his subsequent album, *The Ice-*

berg/Freedom of Speech . . Just Watch What You Say (#37 pop, #11 R&B, 1989). Although the album was well received, Ice-T later said he had been too preoccupied with the censorship issue. In 1991 Ice-T released his magnum opus, *O.G. Original Gangster* (#15 pop, #9 R&B), a ferocious, 24-track album that chronicled the life of a ghetto tough in songs like "Home of the Bodybag," "Straight Up Nigga," and "Lifestyles of the Rich and Infamous." *O.G.* also introduced his thrash-metal band, Body Count, on the song of the same name.

Body Count's self-titled debut album came out to little fanfare in 1992. But when a Texas police group noticed a track called "Cop Killer" on it, it threatened to boycott's Sire's parent company, Time Warner. Within a year, Ice-T became a household name. After initially supporting the artist, Time Warner eventually dropped "Cop Killer" from the album and began asking other artists under its umbrella to remove similarly objectionable items. When the company rejected the artwork for Ice-T's next solo album, *Home Invasion,* the rapper elected to be released from his seven-album contract; he left the company in January 1993 with five gold albums. (In 1993 he released *Home Invasion* [#14 pop, #9 R&B], artwork and all, on the independent label Priority.) Warner's decision to let go of Ice-T provided a chilling symbol of how intense corporate fear of rap had become in the wake of "Cop Killer."

Ice-T has appeared in several films, including *New Jack City* (1991), *Ricochet* (1991), *Trespass* (1992), and *Surviving the Game* (1994). In 1994 his autobiography, *The Ice Opinion,* was published by St. Martin's Press.

Icicle Works

Formed 1980, Liverpool, England
Robert Ian McNabb (b. Nov. 3, 1960, Liverpool), gtr., voc.; Chris Layne, bass; Chris Sharrock, drums.
1984—*Icicle Works* (Arista)   1985—*The Small Price of a Bicycle* (Chrysalis) (+ Dave Green, kybds.)
1986—*Seven Singles Deep* (Beggars Banquet, U.K.)
1987—*If You Want to Defeat Your Enemy Sing His Song* (Beggars Banquet) (– Layne; – Sharrock; + Roy Corkhill, bass; + Zak Starkey [b. Sept. 13, 1965, London, Eng.], drums)   1988—*Blind* (– Green; – Starkey; + Dave Baldwin, kybds.; + Paul Burgess, drums; + Mark Revell, gtr.)   1990—*Permanent Damage* (Epic, U.K.)   1992—*Best of Icicle Works* (Beggars Banquet, U.K.).

Playing poker-faced, neopsychedelic pop rock with jangly guitars, Icicle Works (who took their name from an obscure science-fiction novel) emerged from the same postpunk Liverpool scene that produced Echo and the Bunnymen. Icicle Works grew out of such local Liverpool bands as City Limits and Cherry Boys and scored its first U.K. hit single with "Nirvana" in 1982. The band's debut album charted in the U.S. (#40, 1984) and yielded a Top Forty pop hit in "Whisper to a Scream (Birds Fly)" (#37, 1984). The group's second album was a British hit, but failed to make the U.S. charts. In fact, Icicle Works made no further impact in the U.S., save for the news that ex-Beatle Ringo Starr's son, Zak Starkey, joined on drums for 1987's *Blind.*

Icicle Works disbanded in 1990, with bandleader Ian McNabb embarking on a solo career. He released *Truth and Beauty* on the British indie label This Way Up in early 1993 and recorded a second solo album in 1994, *Head Like a Rock,* in Los Angeles with American musicians, including Billy Talbot and Ralph Molina of Crazy Horse and legendary Meters drummer Joseph "Zigaboo" Modeliste.

Ides of March

Formed circa 1964, Berwyn, Illinois
James Peterik, lead voc., gtr., kybds., sax; Ray Herr, voc., gtr., bass; Larry Millas, gtr., organ, voc.; Bob Bergland, bass, sax; John Larson, trumpet; Chuck Somar, horn; Michael Borch, drums.
1970—*Vehicle* (Warner Bros.)   1971—*Common Bond*   1972—*World Woven* (RCA)   1973—*Midnight Oil.*

A seven-piece group with horns from the suburbs of Chicago, the Ides of March were often accused of being Blood, Sweat and Tears imitators. Their one big hit, "Vehicle" (#2, 1970), sounded like BS&T, but the Ides of March had actually formed long before Blood, Sweat and Tears (or the Ides' local contemporaries Chicago).

The group members met in elementary school and formed the band while in high school. In the next few years they all enrolled in the same college, which greatly inhibited their tour schedule. The band scored two minor 1966 hits—"You Wouldn't Listen" and "Roller Coaster"—and faded until 1970, when Peterik's "Vehicle" was released. The record had been certified gold by November 1972, but the Ides proved unable to find a followup hit.

The group left Warner Bros. for RCA, to little avail, then disbanded. A mid-Seventies attempt to regroup never got off the ground. Peterik returned to the chart over a decade later as a member of Survivor, whose single "Eye of the Tiger" hit #1 in the summer of 1982.

Billy Idol/Generation X

Born William Michael Albert Broad, November 30, 1955, Stanmore, Middlesex, England
With Generation X, formed 1976, London, England (Billy Idol, voc.; Tony James, bass, voc.; Bob Andrews, gtr., voc.; John Towe, drums): 1978—*Generation X* (Chrysalis)   1979—*Valley of the Dolls* 1981—*Kiss Me Deadly*; *Dancing With Myself* EP 1985—*The Best of Generation X.*

Billy Idol solo: 1981—*Don't Stop* EP (Chrysalis) 1982—*Billy Idol* 1983—*Rebel Yell* 1986— *Whiplash Smile* 1987—*Vital Idol* 1990—*Charmed Life* 1993—*Cyberpunk*.

From his beginnings as frontman for Generation X, Billy Idol's career has touched on trends from punk to cyberpunk. While his sincerity has sometimes been questioned, with four platinum albums—*Rebel Yell* (#6, 1983), *Whiplash Smile* (#6, 1986), *Vital Idol* (#10, 1987), and *Charmed Life* (#11, 1990)—there is no doubting his success. One of the earliest acts to embrace MTV, Idol became a network fixture in a series of sexually suggestive, bimbo-festooned videos. While widely reviled, the clips fixed Idol's sneering, leather-clad, bad-boy image and made hits of "White Wedding" (#36, 1983), "Rebel Yell" (#46, 1984), "Eyes Without a Face" (#4, 1984), "To Be a Lover" (#6, 1986), "Mony Mony 'Live'" (#1, 1987), and "Cradle of Love" (#2, 1990).

A Beatle-loving child of the Sixties, by 1976 William Broad had changed his name to Billy Idol, dyed his hair platinum blond, and begun hanging out at Malcolm McLaren's Sex boutique. He joined Chelsea, an early punk band, that year, leaving two months later with Tony James to form Generation X. Unabashedly commercial, they had a string of British hits in 1977, including "Your Generation," "Ready Steady Go," and "Wild Youth," and were the first punk band to appear on the BBC's *Top of the Pops*.

A second album, *Valley of the Dolls,* produced by Mott the Hoople's Ian Hunter, was not well received, nor was *Kiss Me Deadly*. Idol quit in 1981, but not before releasing an EP, *Dancing with Myself.*

Idol, who spent four years as a child on Long Island, moved to Greenwich Village and signed with Kiss manager Bill Aucoin. Idol put together a band with guitarist and songwriting partner Steve Stevens plus a group of local musicians and recorded an EP, *Don't Stop* (#71, 1981). Produced by Giorgio Moroder protégé Keith Forsey, it was notable for its cover of Tommy James and the Shondells' 1968 smash "Mony Mony" and a revamped version of "Dancing with Myself," a club hit. On this and subsequent albums Idol and Forsey merged punk's rebel stance with slickly produced metallic rock.

Idol's image as a lusty bad boy was maintained offstage as well. His tours were infamous for their excesses, and in 1992 Idol was accused of an attempted rape that allegedly occurred in 1985. No charges were brought. In 1990 he was seriously injured in a motorcycle accident in Los Angeles. The accident kept him from playing the part of Tom Baker in Oliver Stone's *The Doors* (1991) (he ended up playing the smaller part of Cat) and delayed the release of *Charmed Life,* his first album of new material in three years and his first without Stevens. *Charmed Life* revived Idol's career, but his rebel pose seemed

tired. After a three-year hiatus Idol returned with *Cyberpunk* (#48, 1993). Its title, videos, and accompanying computer press release caused many to claim that Idol was once again jumping on a bandwagon, this time that of a punky sci-fi Internet subculture that evolved during the late Eighties and early Nineties.

Julio Iglesias

Born Julio Jose Iglesias de la Cueva, September 23, 1943, Madrid, Spain
1980—*Hey!* (Columbia)   1981—*From a Child to a Woman*   1982—*Moments*   1983—*In Concert; Julio* 1984—*1100 Bel Air Place*   1985—*Libra*   1988—*Non-Stop*   1990—*Starry Night*   1994—*Crazy*.

From Valentino on, America's infatuation with the image of the Latin lover has refused to die. In the Eighties Julio Iglesias slipped effortlessly into the role and for a brief moment it looked as if the suave crooner would achieve in America the incredible success that he had enjoyed around the rest of the world.

The man who has sold an estimated 100 million records originally wanted to be a professional soccer player. When a near-fatal car accident ended that dream, Iglesias spent his recovery time learning how to play guitar, compose, and sing. Bowing to his father's wishes, Iglesias studied law, but music remained his love. After winning first prize at the 1968 Spanish Song Festival, where he sang his own "La Vida Sigue Igual," Iglesias was signed by Discos Columbia. The Seventies saw Iglesias becoming a major MOR star in Europe and Latin America. Often recording versions of his songs in Spanish, French, Italian, German, Portuguese, and English, Iglesias achieved near-global success.

He had his first major English-language hit in 1981

Julio Iglesias

when his version of Cole Porter's "Begin the Beguine" topped the British charts. His U.S. breakthrough came through the unlikely but immensely popular 1984 duet with Willie Nelson, "To All the Girls I've Loved Before" (#5). A duet with Diana Ross, "All of You" (#19) hit later that year. Both tracks appeared on the triple-platinum *1100 Bel Air Place.*

Iglesias' tall, dark, and handsome looks, European charm, and ultrasmooth singing endeared him to a romance-starved audience, but a noticeable difficulty with spoken English hampered his wider appeal. Despite the initial hits and adoring fans, Iglesias could not sustain his stateside recording success. He still continues to sell well (*Starry Night,* featuring his cover of Don McLean's "Vincent," went Top Forty) and has become a perennial live attraction, regularly filling houses from Radio City Music Hall to Vegas. The title track of 1994's *Crazy* was his version of the Patsy Cline standard; other tracks featured guest vocals by Dolly Parton and Art Garfunkel.

The Impressions

Formed 1957, Chicago, Illinois
Curtis Mayfield (b. June 3, 1942, Chicago), tenor voc.; Jerry Butler (b. Dec. 8, 1939, Sunflower, Miss.), baritone voc.; Arthur Brooks (b. Chattanooga, Tenn.), tenor voc.; Richard Brooks (b. Chattanooga), tenor voc.; Sam Gooden (b. Sep. 2, 1939, Chattanooga), baritone voc.
1958–59—(– Butler; + Fred Cash [b. Oct. 8, 1940, Chattanooga], voc.)   1961—(– Arthur and Richard Brooks)   1963—*The Impressions* (ABC)   1964—*The Never Ending Impressions*; *Keep On Pushing* 1965—*People Get Ready*; *Greatest Hits*   1968—*Best of the Impressions*; *We're a Winner*   1970—(– Mayfield; + Leroy Hutson, voc.)   1973—(– Hutson; + Reggie Torrian, voc.; + Ralph Johnson, voc.) 1974—*Finally Got Myself Together* (Curtom) 1976—*For Your Precious Love* (Vee-Jay); *Originals* (ABC); *The Vintage Years* (Sire)   1979—*Come to My Party* (20th Century–Fox)   c. 1980—(– Johnson; + Nate Evans, voc.)   1981—*Fan the Fire*   1989— *The Impressions' Greatest Hits* (MCA)   1992—*The Young Mods' Forgotten Story* (Curtom)   1994—*The Complete Vee-Jay Recordings* (Vee-Jay).

The Impressions' close vocal harmonies and big-band-style horn arrangements were precursors of and a major influence on Sixties soul, especially its romantic ballads. The group's original members—Sam Gooden, and brothers Richard and Arthur Brooks—were in a Tennessee group, the Roosters, and made their way to Chicago, where they hooked up with a team of songwriter/producers, Jerry Butler and Curtis Mayfield, of the Northern Jubilee Gospel Singers.

The Impressions' first hit, "For Your Precious Love"

(#11, 1958), featured Butler's lead vocals, but within the year he left the group for a solo career (although he continued to work with Mayfield). Cash, who had not been in the initial lineup, replaced Butler. After the group's next major hit, "Gypsy Woman" in 1961, the Brooks brothers dropped out, leaving the trio of Mayfield, Gooden, and Cash.

Mayfield became the Impressions' leader and, with a distinctly soft yet emotive falsetto, the group's lead vocalist. Under his guidance, the Impressions became one of the era's most popular vocal groups. Their trio vocals were also a major influence on Jamaican pop. Through the Sixties, the group had hits with Mayfield's love songs, such as "Talking About My Baby" (#14, 1964), "I'm So Proud" (#14 pop, #14 R&B, 1964), "Woman's Got Soul" (#29 pop, #9 R&B, 1965), and his gospel-tinged message songs, including "Keep On Pushin'" (#10, 1964), "People Get Ready" (#14, 1965), and "Amen" (#7, 1965). Mayfield also kept up an active career as producer, arranger, and songwriter (see solo entry); he left the Impressions in 1970.

Howard University graduate Leroy Hutson took over the group and in the early Seventies kept it on the soul chart with "Check Out Your Mind," "(Baby) Turn On to Me," and "Ain't Got Time," among others, before going solo in 1973. Cash and Gooden regrouped with Reggie Torrian and Ralph Johnson, and had a Top Twenty pop hit (#1 R&B) in 1974 with "Finally Got Myself Together," and they did the soundtrack for the blaxploitation film *Three the Hard Way.* They continued to record for various labels into the Eighties, with middling success, although a 1975 single, "First Impressions," hit the U.K. Top Twenty. In 1983 Butler and Mayfield rejoined the group for a reunion tour, and they did so periodically until Mayfield was permanently paralyzed in a 1990 stage accident.

The Incredible String Band

Formed 1965, Glasgow, Scotland
Mike Heron (b. Dec. 12, 1942), voc., gtr., assorted instruments; Robin Williamson (b. Nov. 24, 1943), voc., gtr., assorted instruments; Clive Palmer, banjo. 1966—*The Incredible String Band* (Elektra) (– Palmer)   1967—*The 5000 Spirits or the Layers of the Onion*; *The Hangman's Beautiful Daughter* (+ Christina "Licorice" McKenzie, violin, assorted instruments; + Rose Simpson, bass)   1968—*Wee Tam*; *The Big Huge*   1969—*Changing Horses* 1970—*I Looked Up*; *U*; *Be Glad for the Song Has No Ending* (Reprise)   1971—(– Simpson; + Malcolm Le Maistre, bass, voc.)   1972—*Liquid Acrobat as Regards the Air* (Elektra); *Earth Span* (Island)   1973— (– McKenzie) *No Ruinous Feud* (+ Gerald Dott, kybds., reeds)   1974—*Hard Rope and Silken Twine*

Grammy Awards

Janis Ian
1975 Best Pop Vocal Performance, Female: "At Seventeen"

Ice-T
1990 Best Rap Performance by a Duo or Group: *Back on the Block* (with others)

Julio Iglesias
1987 Best Latin Pop Performance: *Un Hombre Solo*

Indigo Girls
1989 Best Contemporary Folk Recording: *Indigo Girls*

James Ingram
1981 Best R&B Vocal Performance, Male: "One Hundred Ways"
1984 Best R&B Performance by a Duo or Group with Vocal: "Yah Mo B There" (with Michael Mc-Donald)

The Isley Brothers
1969 Best R&B Vocal Performance by a Group or Duo: "It's Your Thing"

(+ John Gilston, drums; + Graham Forbes, gtr.)
1974—*Seasons They Change.*

The Incredible String Band was a highly eclectic Scottish folk group that started in the mid-Sixties playing original songs derived not just from British traditional ballads and U.S. Appalachian tunes and blues, but from Indian ragas, Ethiopian *oud* music, calypso, Gilbert and Sullivan, and an international assortment of folk styles. Fans of their proto–world music included Led Zeppelin (Robert Plant once credited them, in a Led Zeppelin tour booklet, as an inspiration for his group's forays into British folk) and the Rolling Stones (who tried and failed to sign ISB to their Mother Earth label in the late Sixties). Though there were other shifting members of the band, ISB was essentially just two Glasgow-born songwriters, Robin Williamson and Mike Heron, who between them played a wide assortment of instruments.

Heron first played in the Edinburgh rock group Rock Bottom and the Deadbeats. Williamson played in a jug-band duo in 1965 at the Incredible Folk Club in Glasgow with Clive Palmer, who owned the club. Heron joined soon after, and the trio took its name from Palmer's club. ISB released its eponymous debut on Elektra in 1966. Afterward, Williamson and Palmer traveled in North Africa. Upon their return in late 1966, Palmer left the group, but the other two kept performing in local clubs. In November they made their first concert appearance outside Scotland, at London's Royal Albert Hall, with Tom Paxton and Judy Collins on the bill. The two American artists helped spread ISB's reputation in the U.S. (Collins later recorded Williamson's "First Girl I Loved"), and in 1967 its second LP, *The 5000 Spirits or the Layers of the Onion,* was acclaimed on both sides of the Atlantic.

A cult audience developed in the U.S., but in England ISB was a mainstay of the hippie movement. In 1967 the virtuoso multi-instrumentalist duo version of ISB recorded one more LP, *The Hangman's Beautiful Daugh-ter.* Williamson and Heron then added two women: Christina McKenzie on violin, kazoo and other instruments and Rose Simpson on bass. Their first double album together, *Wee Tam and the Big Huge* (released separately in America), was seen by some as indulgent and disappointing, and their reputation declined as the Sixties ended, though their music became increasingly ambitious. The album *U* was conceived as a loose stage show that played with a mime troupe.

In 1971 Simpson left, replaced by Malcolm Le Maistre in 1972. Gerard Dott, another multi-instrumentalist, replaced McKenzie in 1973. He had known Heron from childhood and had played in a skiffle band with Williamson and Heron. In 1971 Heron put out the solo LP *Smiling Men with Bad Reputations,* and the next year Williamson issued his own LP, *Myrrh.* The band members were drifting apart. By the time of their last show together in 1974, they had become harder-rocking after adding drummer John Gilston and guitarist Graham Forbes; both Heron and Williamson had become Scientologists. Heron did some session work and later formed Mike Heron's Reputation with ex-ISBs Gilston, Forbes, and Le Maistre. Williamson moved to L.A., formed Robin Williamson's Merry Band, and released three LPs of poetry and music and a 1981 solo album on Flying Fish Records.

Indigo Girls

Formed 1980, Decatur, Georgia; became Indigo Girls, 1983
Amy Ray (b. Apr. 12, 1964, Decatur) voc., gtr.; Emily Saliers (b. July 22, 1963, New Haven, Conn.) voc., gtr.
1986—*Indigo Girls* EP (Indigo) 1987—*Strange Fire*
1989—*Indigo Girls* (Epic) 1990—*Nomads Indians Saints* 1991—*Back on the Bus, Y'All* EP 1992—*Rites of Passage* 1994—*Swamp Ophelia.*

Blending their voices in powerful harmonies over acoustic guitars, the Indigo Girls have attained a degree of pop success rare for artists so firmly rooted in folk and women's music. Amy Ray's rough alto and moody rock songs provide an edgy balance to Emily Saliers' warm soprano and folkish compositions.

The two childhood friends began making music together while still in high school in suburban Atlanta, calling themselves Saliers and Ray. They continued to perform while attending Emory University, where they changed their name to the Indigo Girls. They released their first independent single, "Crazy Game," in 1985, followed by an EP and a full-length album before signing with Epic. They established a large enough following with their independent releases that they could maintain artistic control in their major-label deal and gather such fans as R.E.M. and the Hothouse Flowers, both of which play on the Grammy-winning, Scott Litt–produced *Indigo Girls*. Although the single "Closer to Fine" was played by MTV, VH-1, and some radio stations, constant touring, a supportive press, and devoted fans are the force behind the duo's gold and platinum record sales.

Litt produced *Nomads Indians Saints*, which featured Mary Chapin Carpenter, the Ellen James Society, drummers Kenny Aronoff and Jim Keltner, and bassist Sara Lee, and included the Grammy-nominated single "Hammer and a Nail." *Back on the Bus, Y'All* was a live EP. On *Rites of Passage*, the band experimented with rock noise and Latin and African percussion, working with producer Peter Collins, whose credits include Queensrÿche and Alice Cooper. Guests include the Roches, Jackson Browne, David Crosby, Lisa Germano, and Budgie and Martin McCarrick from Siouxsie and the Banshees. The album (#21, 1992) was nominated for a Grammy. Collins also produced 1994's *Swamp Ophelia*, which featured the duo's first totally electric song, "Touch Me Fall." In addition to including such previous guests as Germano, the Roches and Lee, *Ophelia* featured Jane Siberry, and ex–Allman Brothers pianist Chuck Leavell.

Alongside their somber spirituals, the Indigo Girls frequently sing about environmentalism, feminism, and other social issues. They have played benefits on behalf of Habitat for Humanity, the Children's Health Fund, and Humanitas, among others. Ray actively supports independent music and is the founder of the Atlanta-based Daemon Records, whose roster has included James Hall, the Ellen James Society, and Kristen Hall. In 1994 both Ray and Saliers acted in the Herbert Ross film *Boys on the Side*, starring Whoopi Goldberg, Drew Barrymore, and Mary Louise Parker.

Industrial

Using harsh digital samples, gut-thumping drum-machine beats, voice modulators, and often a heavy-metal guitar foundation, industrial music aims to sonically re-create a postindustrial society in collapse.

Pioneered in the late Seventies and early Eighties by such avant-garde bands as England's Throbbing Gristle and Cabaret Voltaire, and Germany's Einstürzende Neubauten (in English, "collapsing new buildings"), early practitioners used a combination of tape loops, oil drums, iron pipes, and other found objects to create abrasive musical statements. The New York–based producer Jim Thirlwell (a.k.a. Foetus) and Chicago band Ministry (whose Al Jourgensen has been called the "Phil Spector of industrial") brought the style to a pop audience with their cleaned-up mixes and more hook-oriented song structures.

In the late Eighties and early Nineties the form mushroomed in popularity when the music of acts like My Life with the Thrill Kill Kult, Skinny Puppy, Meat Beat Manifesto, and MC 900 Ft Jesus scored big in urban dance clubs. Industrial crossed over to a mainstream pop audience when Nine Inch Nails took the sound to the suburbs with the 1989 album *Pretty Hate Machine*.

James Ingram

Born February 17, 1952, Akron, Ohio
1983—*It's Your Night* (Qwest)   1986—*Never Felt So Good* (Warner Bros.)   1990—*It's Real*   1991—*The Power of Great Music*   1993—*Always You*.

With his smooth, deep voice and ladies' man charm, James Ingram is a true pop singles artist: In the Eighties he became a chart-topping, Grammy-winning balladeer mostly on the basis of his collaborations with such artists as Quincy Jones, Patty Austin, and Michael McDonald.

Ingram moved from Akron to Los Angeles in the mid-Seventies with the band Revelation Funk, but the group soon broke up, and he began singing demo tapes for a publishing company. Ray Charles hired Ingram to produce, play keyboards, and write songs for him. Until Quincy Jones heard one of Ingram's tapes and asked him to sing on an album, Ingram hadn't considered himself a vocalist. In 1981 Ingram won a Grammy without having released an album of his own, when he was honored for "One Hundred Ways" (#14, 1981), from Jones' *The Dude*. "Just Once" from that album went to #17. Other collaborations with Jones include "We Are the World," the film *The Color Purple*, and Michael Jackson's album *Thriller* (he cowrote "P.Y.T. [Pretty Young Thing]").

"Baby, Come to Me" (#1, 1982), from Austin's album *Every Home Should Have One*, became the theme for the soap opera *General Hospital*. Ingram's gold 1983 debut album yielded the Grammy-winning "Yah Mo B There," a duet with McDonald. Ingram performed a string of songs for soundtracks, including "How Do You Keep the Music Playing?" (#45, 1983), another duet with Austin, for *Best*

Friends; "Somewhere Out There" (#2, 1986), with Linda Ronstadt, for *An American Tail;* and "Better Way" (#66, 1987) for *Beverly Hills Cop II.* But Ingram didn't score a hit on his own until the Thom Bell–produced *It's Real,* which featured "I Don't Have the Heart" (#1, 1990).

The Ink Spots
Formed late 1920s, Indianapolis, Indiana
Members have included Jerry Daniels, gtr., voc.; Orville "Hoppy" Jones (b. Feb. 17, 1905, Chicago, Ill.; d. Oct. 18, 1944, Chicago), voc.; Charles Fuqua, gtr., voc.; Ivory "Deek" Watson, voc.
1936—(– Daniels; + Bill Kenny [b. 1915; d. Mar. 23, 1978], voc.) 1980—*The Best of the Ink Spots* (MCA).

Though the Ink Spots enjoyed their greatest popularity years before rock & roll came into being, their vocal style was a precursor to the smooth doo-wop vocal groups of the Fifties, including the Ravens, the Marcels, the Flamingos, and the Platters.

The original group was formed when Jerry Daniels, Orville Jones, Charles Fuqua, and Ivory Watson met in Indianapolis. After moving to New York City in the early Thirties, they changed their name from King, Jack and the Jesters to the Ink Spots. In 1935 they signed with RCA Victor, then Decca. Soon thereafter, lead singer Daniels left the group and was replaced by Bill Kenny. In February 1939 the Ink Spots released "If I Didn't Care," their first million-selling record. Subsequent hits included "My Prayer," "Maybe," "We Three," "Whispering Grass," "To Each His Own," and "I Don't Want to Set the World on Fire," a song that was revived in the late Eighties for Chanel commercials.

After Jones died on October 18, 1944, from what was discovered to have been a brain hemorrhage, internal dissension cast the group's future in some doubt. A flurry of personnel changes ensued, leaving Kenny the sole consistent member. Fuqua (cousin of Harvey Fuqua of the Moonglows and later Motown fame) established his own group of Ink Spots. This group toured the world and was the first black act to play in a number of venues throughout the American South. The Ink Spots had a final #1 hit with "To Each His Own" in 1946. There have been several lineups of Ink Spots through the years, but only the original lineup was inducted into the Rock and Roll Hall of Fame in 1989.

Inspiral Carpets
Formed 1986, Chadderton, England
Stephen Holt (b. Eng.), voc.; Graham Lambert (b. July 10, 1964, Oldham, Eng.), gtr.; Clint Boon (b. June 28, 1959, Oldham), organ; David Swift (b. Eng.), bass; Craig Gill (b. Dec. 5, 1971, Manchester, Eng.), drums.

Inspiral Carpets: Clint Boon, Graham Lambert, Martyn Walsh, Craig Gill, Tom Hingley

1988—(– Holt; – Swift; + Thomas Hingley [b. July 9, 1965, Oxford, Eng.], voc.; + Martyn Walsh [b. July 3, 1968, Manchester], bass) 1990—*Life* (Mute) 1991—*The Beast Inside* 1992—*Revenge of the Goldfish* 1994—*Devil Hopping.*

Inspiral Carpets emerged in the late Eighties, with Stone Roses and Happy Mondays, from Manchester, England's prerave psychedelic dance-rock scene. Inspiral Carpets were more of a throwback than other bands on the scene, with Clint Boon's reedy Farfisa organ recalling mid-Sixties garage rock, and pudding-bowl haircuts defining their look. In England the band managed to balance commercial success with independent-label credibility; in the U.S. it steadily built a core cult through albums on Mute Records (the label that had launched synth-pop bands Depeche Mode and Erasure) and live shows, where Inspiral Carpets (which recorded as live as possible in the studio) proved they could play, and blew some minds with a trippy light show.

The band's swirling, melodic neo-Sixties sound was already formed on its first single, 1987's "Plane Crash." Original vocalist Stephen Holt was replaced by Thomas Hingley, whose portentous, Jim Morrison–styled vocals evoked Ian McCulloch and Julian Cope, respectively of early Eighties Liverpool neopsychedelic bands Echo and the Bunnymen and Teardrop Explodes. Inspiral Carpets formed its own label, Cow Records, gaining notoriety for its slogan, "Cool as Fuck." The band's first album, *Life* (1990), hit #2 in the U.K.; its sophomore effort, 1991's *The Beast Inside,* did nearly as well, charting at #4 U.K. By Inspiral Carpets' third album, *Revenge of the Goldfish* (#17 U.K., 1992), Graham Lambert's guitar—often surflike in its reverb—had taken on near-equal footing with Boon's organ.

The Intruders

Formed 1960, Philadelphia, Pennsylvania
Phil Terry (b. Nov. 1, 1943, Philadelphia), voc.;
Robert "Big Sonny" Edwards (b. Feb. 22, 1942,
Philadelphia), voc.; Samuel "Little Sonny" Brown,
voc.; Eugene "Bird" Daughtry (b. Oct. 29, 1939, Kinston, N.C.), voc.
1968—*Cowboys to Girls* (Gamble)   1969—*Intruders Greatest Hits*   1973—*Save the Children.*

This vocal quartet was an early project for the production team of Kenny Gamble and Leon Huff. The group's members sang around Philadelphia in the early Sixties and recorded one single for the local Gowen Records in 1961. Three years later they met Leon Huff, who produced their single "All the Time" on Musicor Records. By 1966 Huff had teamed with Kenny Gamble to form Gamble Records, and the Intruders became the company's first signing.

The Intruders' first chart single, "(We'll Be) United" (#14 R&B), started a hot streak in 1966. "Devil with an Angel's Smile" hit #26 R&B, also in 1966. "Together" (#9 R&B; later a huge hit for Tierra), "Baby, I'm Lonely" (#9 R&B), and "A Love That's Real" (#35 R&B) in 1967 built the Intruders' and the Gamble and Huff team's national reputation.

The next year was the Intruders' peak, with the million-selling "Cowboys to Girls" (#6 pop, #1 R&B). "Love Is Like a Baseball Game" (#26 pop, #4 R&B, 1968) and "Slow Drag" (#12 R&B, 1969) followed. Gamble and Huff gave them "Sad Girl" (#14 R&B) in 1970 and "When We Get Married" (#8 R&B) and "(Win, Place or Show) She's a Winner" (#12 R&B) in 1972. The Intruders' "I'll Always Love My Mama" (#36 pop, #6 R&B, 1973) was a disco mainstay and a perennial Mother's Day favorite.

In 1975 the Intruders broke up. But in 1984, Eugene Daughtry, who'd been working as a truck driver, assembled a new group with his brother Fred, cousin Al Miller, and Lee Williams. A 1984 single, "Who Do You Love?," made the singles chart in England (#65).

INXS

Formed 1977, Sydney, Australia
Garry Gary Beers (b. June 22, 1957, Sydney), bass;
Michael Hutchence (b. Jan. 22, 1960, Sydney), voc.;
Andrew Farriss (b. Mar. 27, 1959, Perth, Austral.),
kybds., gtr.; Jon Farriss (b. Aug. 10, 1961, Perth),
drums; Tim Farriss (b. Aug. 16, 1957, Perth), gtr.;
Kirk Pengilly (b. July 4, 1958, Sydney), gtr., sax, voc.
1980—*INXS* (Deluxe, Austral.)   1981—*Underneath the Colours*   1983—*Shabooh Shoobah* (Atco);

INXS: Tim Farriss, Michael Hutchence, Jon Farriss, Garry Gary Beers, Kirk Pengilly, Andrew Farris

Dekadance EP   1984—*The Swing*   1985—*Listen Like Thieves* (Atlantic)   1987—*Kick*   1990—*X* 1991—*Live Baby Live*   1992—*Welcome to Wherever You Are*   1993—*Full Moon, Dirty Hearts.*

Years before it became fashionable for white artists to mix guitar rock textures with hip-hop beats, INXS emerged from Down Under with a danceable funk-rock fusion that would make the band international stars by the mid-Eighties. Adding to the group's commercial appeal was the charisma of its lead singer, Michael Hutchence, who combined Jaggeresque posturing with looks evoking a lankier Jim Morrison.

INXS began as a family act, originally calling itself the Farriss Brothers. While still in high school, Andrew Farriss and Hutchence—who would become INXS's primary composer and lyricist, respectively—joined forces in a band that also included Garry Beers; around the same time, Tim Farriss and Kirk Pengilly were playing in groups together. The five got together with drummer Jon Farriss in 1977, completing the lineup that would officially become INXS two years later (after Jon graduated high school). At that point, the group relocated from Perth, where Jon went to school, back to Sydney, and began playing pubs in and around the Australian capital. Gigs in other parts of the country followed, leading to an Australasian record contract.

The band soon set its sights on an American audience, signing with Atco Records and embarking on an extensive U.S. tour in support of 1983's *Shabooh Shoobah*. Later that year a studio session with noted funk producer Nile Rodgers resulted in the groove-ridden single "Original Sin," which approached the Top Forty and showed up again on 1984's *The Swing*. But INXS's real breakthrough came with 1985's *Listen Like Thieves*, which went to #11 and produced the #5 single "What You Need" the following year. *Kick* sent the Aussies into the pop stratosphere, peaking at #3 and yielding four hit singles: the #1 smash "Need You Tonight" and, in 1988, "Devil Inside" (#2), "New Sensation" (#3), and "Never Tear Us Apart" (#7). In the wake of such success, 1990's *X* was, relatively, a mild disappointment, peaking at #5 but spawning just one Top Ten single, "Suicide Blonde" (#9).

INXS nonetheless remained extremely popular, selling out London's Wembley Stadium in 1991 and releasing a live album and video, *Live Baby Live*, while Hutchence remained visible by dating bubblegum singer/actress Kylie Minogue and supermodel Helena Christensen. *Welcome to Wherever You Are* got positive reviews for its sonic adventurousness but was again only moderately successful, producing an AOR radio hit with "Beautiful Girl" (#46) in 1993. Later that year, INXS released its tenth album, *Full Moon, Dirty Hearts* (#53), which featured Chrissie Hynde (duetting with Hutchence on the title track) and Ray Charles. In 1994 INXS departed from Atlantic and joined PolyGram. In mid-1995 Hutchence was working on a solo album, and the band would subsequently begin recording a new album.

Iron Butterfly

Formed 1966, San Diego, California
Doug Ingle (b. Sep. 9, 1946, Omaha, Neb.), kybds., voc.; Ron Bushy (b. Sep. 23, 1945, Washington, D.C.), drums, voc.; Jerry Penrod (b. San Diego), bass; Darryl DeLoach (b. San Diego), voc.; Danny Weis (b. San Diego), gtr.
1968—*Heavy* (Atco) (– Penrod; – DeLoach; – Weis; + Lee Dorman [b. Sep. 19, 1945, St. Louis, Mo.], bass, gtr., piano; + Erik Braunn [b. Aug. 11, 1950, Boston, Mass.], gtr., voc.); *In-A-Gadda-Da-Vida* 1969—*Ball* (– Braunn) 1970—*Live* (+ Mike Pinera [b. Sep. 29, 1948, Tampa, Fla.], gtr., voc.; + Larry "Rhino" Reinhardt [b. July 7, 1948, Fla.], gtr.) 1971—*The Best of Iron Butterfly/Evolution*; *Metamorphosis* (group disbands) 1974—(Group re-forms: Braunn; Bushy; + Phil Kramer [b. July 12, 1952, Youngstown, Ohio], bass; + Howard Reitzes [b. Mar. 22, 1951, Southgate, Calif.], kybds., gtr.) 1975—*Sun and Steel* (MCA);

Scorching Beauty 1993—**(Group re-forms: Bushy; Pinera; Dorman; + Derek Hilland, kybds., voc.) *Light and Heavy: The Best of Iron Butterfly* (Rhino).**

Now remembered as a passing fancy of the acid-rock era, at its peak Iron Butterfly was considered a leading hard-rock band. During the group's relatively brief lifetime, it sold about seven million albums; *In-A-Gadda-Da-Vida* alone sold four million copies. The album's focal point was the 17-minute title track (featuring a 2½-minute drum solo), which was also something of a catalyst in establishing "progressive" FM radio programming.

"In-A-Gadda-Da-Vida" was written by group leader, organist, and chief vocalist Doug Ingle, whose father was a church organist. Ingle formed his first group at age 16 in San Diego, where he met drummer Ron Bushy, one of four San Diegans to accompany Ingle to Los Angeles in late 1966. In Los Angeles Iron Butterfly worked Bido Lito's and eventually moved to the Galaxy and the Whisky-a-Go-Go. By early 1967 the band had a recording contract. Its debut disc stayed on the charts for nearly a year, partly because of the national exposure the group got as an opening act for the Doors and the Jefferson Airplane. Shortly after the LP was released, three of the original members left, among them Danny Weis, later of Rhinoceros [see entry].

With new bassist Lee Dorman and guitarist Erik Braunn, Iron Butterfly recorded *In-A-Gadda-Da-Vida* ("In a Garden of Eden," some suggested), which became Atlantic's biggest seller (although the record's sales have since been eclipsed by Led Zeppelin, among others). The album stayed on the chart for 140 weeks, 81 of them in the Top Ten. An edited version of the title track hit #30. *Ball* hit #3 and went gold, but subsequent efforts failed.

In late 1969 Braunn left (and later formed Flintwhistle with Penrod and DeLoach of the original lineup; he also discovered Black Oak Arkansas). He was replaced by two guitarists, Mike Pinera (formerly of Blues Image) and Larry "Rhino" Reinhardt (who had been living with Gregg and Duane Allman). *Metamorphosis* followed, and the group broke up after its farewell performance on May 23, 1971.

During Iron Butterfly's career, all six of its albums charted; it toured the U.S. eight times and Europe as well. The group was featured in the film *Savage Seven* (along with Cream), from which came the first of several singles ("Possession" b/w "Unconscious Power"). Yet another song, "Easy Rider," was featured in the film of the same name. Pinera went on to play with Cactus and Alice Cooper. In the mid-Seventies the group was revived by Braunn and Bushy with the inconsequential *Scorching Beauty* and *Sun and Steel*. Other lineups have appeared over the years.

Iron Maiden

Formed 1976, London, England

Paul Di'anno (b. May 17, 1959, London), voc.; Steve Harris (b. Mar. 12, 1957, London), bass, voc.; Dave Murray, gtr. (b. Dec. 23, 1958, London); Doug Sampson, drums.

1979—(+ Tony Parson, gtr.)   1980—(– Parson; – Sampson; + Dennis Stratton [b. Nov. 9, 1954, London], gtr.; + Clive Burr, drums) Iron Maiden (Harvest) (– Stratton; + Adrian Smith [b. Feb. 27, 1957, London], gtr.)   1981—Killers; Maid in Japan (– Di'anno; + Bruce Dickinson [b. Paul Bruce Dickinson, Aug. 7, 1958, Worksop, Eng.], voc.)   1982—The Number of the Beast (– Burr; + Nicko McBrain [b. June 5, 1954], drums)   1983—Piece of Mind 1984—Powerslave   1985—Live After Death 1986—Somewhere in Time   1988—Seventh Son of a Seventh Son   1990—(– Smith; + Janick Gers, gtr.) No Prayer for the Dying (Epic)   1992—Fear of the Dark   1993—A Real Live One (Capitol); A Real Dead One; Live at Donnington (– Dickinson; + Blaze Bayley, voc.).

Bruce Dickinson solo: 1990—Tattooed Millionaire (Columbia)   1994—Balls to Picasso (Mercury).

Taking its name from the medieval torture device, Iron Maiden was part of England's late-Seventies crop of heavy-metal bands that avoided the stylistic diversity of the new wave in favor of exactly what had put Led Zeppelin and Black Sabbath on the map: simple guitar riffs, bone-crunching chording, and shrieking vocals.

Formed in 1976 by Steve Harris and Dave Murray, the first incarnation of Iron Maiden was inspired by the do-it-yourself punk ethos and released an EP, The Soundhouse Tapes, on its own label, Rock Hard Records. Iron Maiden, the band's 1980 major-label debut album, was pure, unadulterated screaming heavy metal. It went Top Five in Britain; the following year's Killers made #12. America, however, was slower to embrace the denim-and leather-clad group, which distinguished itself from its peers with unusually literate songs (written by Harris) full of hellish imagery ("Children of the Damned"), their themes borrowed from films ("The Number of the Beast," inspired by The Omen II) and ancient mythology ("Flight of Icarus"). Maiden was certainly one of the few bands of any genre to employ a mascot, a ten-foot rotting corpse named Eddie.

The Number of the Beast, featuring new vocalist Bruce "Air Raid Siren" Dickinson (need to know more?), topped the LP chart in Britain and initiated a streak of seven consecutive platinum or gold albums in the States, despite virtually no radio or MTV exposure. The followup, 1983's Piece of Mind, went to #14; Somewhere in Time made #11. Beginning with Seventh Son of a Seventh Son, sales began to slip. In 1990 Adrian Smith, who

came aboard in 1980, left to form A.S.A.P. with drummer Zak Starkey, son of Ringo. Janick Gers took his place in time to record No Prayer for the Dying, Maiden's last album to go gold in the States. It contained "Bring Your Daughter to the Slaughter," a song originally recorded by Dickinson alone for the Nightmare on Elm Street, Part 5 soundtrack. Dickinson's version went to #1 in the U.K.

Iron Maiden has weathered its numerous personnel changes without a hitch, but Dickinson's departure in 1993 may prove a debilitating blow. The singer, a top-rated fencer and swordsman, had already published a novel, The Adventures of Lord Iffy Boatrace, and a solo LP, Tattooed Millionaire, in 1990. His replacement was Blaze Bayley, formerly of the group Wolfsbane.

Donnie Iris: See the Jaggerz

Chris Isaak

Born June 6, 1956, Stockton, California
1985—Silvertone (Warner Bros.)   1987—Chris Isaak 1989—Heart Shaped World (Reprise)   1993—San Francisco Days   1995—Forever Blue.

Chris Isaak's pompadoured good looks are something of a throwback to the Fifties and early Sixties, and so is his music. Isaak's tender, crooning vocal style and his habit of offsetting chugging rockers with haunted ballads of isolation and heartache have invited comparisons to Elvis Presley and Roy Orbison. The singer/songwriter, who had enjoyed good reviews and an enthusiastic cult following since the mid-Eighties, scored his breakthrough hit in 1991 with "Wicked Game" (#6).

Isaak didn't embark on a musical career until after graduation from the University of the Pacific with a degree in English and communications arts. (He also boxed for a while, getting his nose broken seven times.) The singer/guitarist moved to San Francisco, where he formed Silvertone, a band that came to the attention of producer Erik Jacobsen, who helped Isaak land a solo contract with Warner Bros. Records. Isaak's 1985 debut album was named after his band, whose members have continued to back him on tour.

Despite acclaim from the press and other musicians, Isaak's moody, guitar-driven songs weren't much of a success on radio or MTV. Then in 1990, after his third album, Heart Shaped World, had been declared a flop, director David Lynch used an instrumental version of "Wicked Game" on the soundtrack to Wild at Heart. The song caught the attention of an Atlanta, Georgia, radio station music director. He tracked down Isaak's original version and, with the support of listeners, soon had it in heavy rotation. Word spread to stations across the country, and the single hit the Top Ten in early 1991. His next album, San Francisco Days, reached the Top Forty but no singles charted.

Isaak's classic handsomeness—revealed in the "Wicked Game" video—and dry sensibility have also gotten him work as an actor. After earning small parts in two Jonathan Demme films, *Married to the Mob* and *The Silence of the Lambs*, Isaak costarred in Bernardo Bertolucci's *Little Buddha*, released in 1994.

The Isley Brothers

Formed early Fifties, Cincinnati, Ohio
Rudolph Isley (b. Apr. 1, 1939), voc.; Ronald Isley (b. May 21, 1941), lead voc.; O'Kelly Isley (b. Dec. 25, 1937; d. Mar. 31, 1986, Alpine, N.J.), voc.; Vernon Isley (d. 1955), voc.
1955—(– V. Isley)   1959—*Shout* (RCA)   1962—*Twist and Shout* (Wand)   1964—*Twisting and Shouting* (United Artists)   1966—*This Old Heart of Mine* (Tamla)   1969—*It's Our Thing* (T-Neck) (+ Ernie Isley [b. Mar. 7, 1952], bass, perc., gtr.; + Marvin Isley [b. Aug. 18, 1953], bass, perc.; + Chris Jasper, kybds., synth.; + Everett Collins, drums)   1971—*In the Beginning . . . with Jimi Hendrix*   1972—*Brother, Brother, Brother*   1973—*3 + 3; Isleys' Greatest Hits*   1974—*Live It Up*   1975—*The Heat Is On*   1976—*Harvest for the World*   1977—*Go for Your Guns*   1978—*Showdown*   1979—*Winner Take All*   1980—*Go All the Way*   1981—*Grand Slam*   1983—*Between the Sheets*   1984—(– M. Isley; – E. Isley; – C. Jasper)   1985—*Masterpiece* (Warner Bros.)   1987—*Smooth Sailin'*   1989—*Spend the Night*   1990—(Ronald, Rudolph, Ernie, and Marvin Isley reunite)   1991—*The Isley Brothers Story, vol. 1: The Rockin' Years (1959–68)* (Rhino); *vol. 2: T-Neck Years (1968–85)*   1992—*Tracks of Life* (Warner Bros.).
Isley, Jasper, Isley: 1985—*Caravan of Love* (Columbia)   1987—*Different Drummer* (CBS Associated).
Chris Jasper solo: 1987—*Superbad* (CBS Associated).
Ernie Isley solo: 1990—*High Wire* (Elektra).

A Cincinnati-born family group, which by now has included two generations of Isleys, the Isley Brothers started out on the black R&B circuit and had occasional pop and AOR successes. The original members (including a fourth brother, Vernon, who died in 1955 in a bicycle accident) were encouraged to sing by their father, a professional singer, and their mother, a pianist who accompanied them when they performed in churches before Vernon's death. Tenor Ronnie Isley was soon designated lead vocalist.

While still in their teens, Ronald, Rudolph, and O'Kelly (who later dropped the O') went to New York in 1957 and over the next year recorded several unsuccessful neo–doo-wop tunes (including "The Angels Cried"). While performing at the Howard Theater in Washington,

D.C., in the summer of 1959, the group was spotted by an RCA executive, who signed the Isleys. Their debut single for the label was "Shout," written in the call-and-response gospel vocal style; it was the first and most successful of the RCA recordings produced for them by Hugo Peritti and Luigi Creatore. "Shout" reached only #47 on the pop chart but became an R&B standard (since covered by such diverse artists as Lulu, Joey Dee and the Starliters, Tom Petty, and the Blues Brothers). It eventually sold over a million copies, and the group earned enough to move the entire family from Cincinnati to New Jersey.

Although the Isleys toured widely, it wasn't until they'd left RCA in 1962 and recorded "Twist and Shout" (originally recorded by the Topnotes, later covered by the Beatles) on Wand Records that they had their next hit; it reached #17. Subsequent releases on Wand and United Artists failed to hit, and the brothers toured on the R&B circuit with their backup band, which included Jimmy James (a.k.a. Jimi Hendrix). Hendrix was with the Isleys for most of 1964 and made his first recordings with them, including several sides for Atlantic and one for the Isleys' T-Neck label ("Testify"). Some of his work with the group was released in 1971 as *In the Beginning.*

In 1965 the Isleys signed to the Motown subsidiary Tamla, but although they worked with Motown's top writing and production team, Holland-Dozier-Holland, only their first single, "This Old Heart of Mine" (#12, 1966), became a pop hit. The song hit #3 in England two years later, after the Isleys had moved there to sustain their career. In 1969 they returned home and began recording for their own label, T-Neck Records. Named after their adopted hometown of Teaneck, New Jersey, the label was a revival of a company started in the early Sixties and then abandoned. Their first release, "It's Your Thing" (#2, 1969), became their biggest pop hit, eventually selling over two million copies; it won a Grammy for Best R&B Vocal Performance. "It's Your Thing" was written and produced by the Isleys themselves, as were "I Turned You On" (#23, 1969) and "Pop That Thang" (#24, 1972).

In 1969 the Isleys added a second generation: brothers Ernest and Marvin, as well as brother-in-law Chris Jasper and nonrelative drummer Everett Collins. With Ernie's Hendrix-like guitar lines, the group often covered material by rock writers like Stephen Stills—whose "Love the One You're With" was a #18 hit in 1971 for the Isleys—Eric Burdon and War's "Spill the Wine" (#49, 1971), and Bob Dylan's "Lay Lady Lay" (#71, 1971).

"That Lady (Part I)" (#6, 1973), a two-million-selling single, made *3 + 3* a platinum album. The Isleys' next big pop hit, the gold "Fight the Power (Part I)" (#4, 1975), came from *The Heat Is On*. While the following year's *Harvest for the World* didn't produce any gold singles, it still sold over half a million copies in three days.

In the latter part of the Seventies, the Isleys adapted to the disco market. Though their pop hits ended, albums (*Go for Your Guns, Showdown, Winner Take All, Go All the Way, Grand Slam, Between the Sheets*) continued to sell gold or platinum, and they scored a number of R&B #1 hits: "The Pride" (1977), "Take Me to the Next Phase (Part 1)" (1978), "I Wanna Be with You (Part 1)" (1979), and "Don't Say Goodnight" (1980). Other R&B hits included "Between the Sheets" (#3 R&B, 1983), "Choosey Lover" (#6 R&B, 1983), "Smooth Sailin'" (#3 R&B, 1986), "Spend the Night (Ce Soir)" (#3 R&B, 1989), "One of a Kind" (#38 R&B, 1990), and "Sensitive Lover" (#24 R&B, 1992). In addition, Ronald Isley enjoyed success outside the group with a pair of duets: "Lay Your Troubles Down" (#10 R&B, 1990, with his future wife, Angela Winbush) and a remake of "This Old Heart of Mine" (#10, with Rod Stewart).

In 1984 Ernie and Marvin Isley and Chris Jasper left to form Isley, Jasper, Isley. They had a #1 R&B hit with "Caravan of Love" in 1985; the song went to #1 in the U.K. in an a cappella cover version by the Housemartins the following year. The trio's other R&B Top Twenty hits include "Look the Other Way" (1984), "Insatiable Woman" (1986), "8th Wonder of the World" (1987), and "Givin' You Back the Love" (1987). O'Kelly died of a heart attack in 1986, and not long after, Rudolph left to join the ministry. The group reunited in 1990. In 1992 the Isley Brothers were inducted into the Rock and Roll Hall of Fame. In 1994 the group won a copyright infringement suit against Michael Bolton, proving to the court's satisfaction that Bolton's hit "Love Is a Wonderful Thing" was based on their song of the same name. Bolton ignited controversy when, in commenting on the trial's outcome, he suggested that the jury had granted the Isleys a large award because they are black and he is white. The Isley Brothers were awarded 100 percent of the profits from the single and 28 percent of the profits from the album.

It's a Beautiful Day

Formed 1968, San Francisco, California
David LaFlamme (b. Apr. 5, 1941, Salt Lake City, Utah), electric violin, voc.; Linda LaFlamme, kybds.; Val Fuentes (b. Nov. 25, 1947, Chicago, Ill.), drums; Pattie Santos (b. Nov. 16, 1949, San Francisco; d. Dec. 14, 1989, Healdsburg, Calif.), voc., perc.; Hal Wagenet (b. Willits, Calif.), gtr.; Michael Holman (b. Denver, Colo.), bass.
1968—(+ Fred Webb [b. Santa Rosa, Calif.], kybds.)
1969—*It's a Beautiful Day* (Columbia)   1970—*Marrying Maiden*   1971—(– Holman; + Bill Gregory, gtr.; + Tom Fowler, bass) *Choice Quality Stuff* 1972—*Live at Carnegie Hall*   1973—
(– D. LaFlamme; + Graig Block, violin) *It's a Beautiful Day . . . Today*   1974—*1001 Nights* (group disbands)   1979—*It's a Beautiful Day.*
David LaFlamme solo: 1977—*White Bird* (Amherst) 1978—*Inside Out.*
Pattie Santos and Bud Cockrell: 1978—*New Beginnings* (A&M).

It's a Beautiful Day came to national prominence in the Seventies with its FM standard, "White Bird." The group was led by David LaFlamme, who started playing violin at age five and later played as soloist with the Utah Symphony. After serving in the army, he moved to California in 1962. Through the Sixties he performed several styles of music, including jazz with the John Handy Concert Ensemble. LaFlamme often jammed with several future members of Big Brother and the Holding Company and was part of an early version of Dan Hicks and His Hot Licks.

By the time he formed It's a Beautiful Day on a summer afternoon (hence the group name), LaFlamme was playing jazz, classical, folk, and rock. He played on a specially adapted, amplified, solid-body five-string violin (the fifth string was a low C, so the instrument's range was as wide as that of a violin and viola combined), and LaFlamme's soloing established the group as a top local draw. Three of the songs on the group's self-titled 1969 debut, including "White Bird," were penned by LaFlamme and his wife, Linda, who left the group shortly thereafter and formed the communal San Francisco band Titus' Mother. *It's a Beautiful Day* stayed on the chart for more than a year and went gold.

In 1970 the group toured England. After several personnel changes, it released *Marrying Maiden*. The LP included "Don and Dewey," a tribute to the Fifties duo of the same name, and featured Don "Sugarcane" Harris from that duo. The group disbanded in 1974 after its sixth LP, *1001 Nights*, went largely unnoticed. By that time David LaFlamme had been tossed out by the others, who allegedly felt he took a disproportionate share of royalties. Replacement Graig Block was the grandnephew of violin virtuoso Jascha Heifetz. LaFlamme later recorded two solo LPs, *White Bird* (1977) and *Inside Out* (1978). Two later band members, Bud Cockrell and David Jenkins, formed Pablo Cruise in 1973. In 1989 Pattie Santos died in a car accident.

Freddie Jackson

**Born Freddie Anthony Jackson, October 2, 1958,
New York City, New York**
**1985—*Rock Me Tonight* (Capitol)   1986—*Just Like
the First Time*   1988—*Don't Let Love Slip Away*
1990—*Do Me Again*   1992—*Time for Love*   1994—
The Greatest Hits of Freddie Jackson; *Here It Is*
(RCA)   1995—*Private Party* (FAJ/Scotti Bros.).**

Freddie Jackson was among the most successful of the
new R&B singers to follow in the wake of Luther Vandross. Along with such vocalists as James Ingram and
Alexander O'Neal, Jackson came to epitomize the "love
man"—the full-throated neoclassic soul singer whose
pleas of love and lust relied on displays of bravura technique and openhearted emotion in striking contrast to
rap.

Jackson began singing in church while growing up
in Harlem. He later held down a day job as a word
processor while singing backup vocals at night for such
established singers as Evelyn "Champagne" King and
Angela Bofill. After singing with the bands Mystic Merlin and LJE, he became so disheartened about the music
business that he quit for a year, but upon returning he
quickly came to the attention of vocalist Melba Moore.
She took Jackson on tour with her as a backup vocalist
and featured soloist, exposure that brought his long-
awaited recording contract. "Rock Me Tonight (for Old

Times Sake)" (#18 pop, #1 R&B) and "You Are My Lady"
(#12 pop, #1 R&B), from his 1985 debut album, made him
an instant star.

Jackson's first two albums went platinum, and he
became a major live act; in 1989 he headlined four nights
at Broadway's Lunt-Fontanne Theater. While pop hits tapered off, Jackson scored repeatedly on the R&B charts:
"Tasty Love" (#1, 1986) "A Little Bit More" (a duet with
Melba Moore) (#1, 1986), "Do Me Again" (#1, 1991), and
"Main Course" (#2, 1991). In 1994, in hopes of reigniting
his chart success, Jackson moved from Capitol to RCA
for *Here It Is* (#11 R&B, 1994). The next year Jackson
again switched labels and released *Private Party* (#28
R&B, 1995) on Scotti Bros.

Janet Jackson

**Born Janet Damita Jackson, May 16, 1966, Gary, In-
diana**
**1982—*Janet Jackson* (A&M)   1984—*Dream Street*
1986—*Control*   1989—*Janet Jackson's Rhythm Nation 1814*   1993—*janet.* (Virgin).**

As the baby of pop music's best-known family, Janet
Jackson could have spent her career in the shadow of
her eight siblings, particularly brother Michael. Instead,
with the help of some savvy creative and professional
advisors outside the family, Janet established herself as
the preeminent pop-funk diva of the late Eighties and

early Nineties. Her wispy voice was a pale echo of Michael's, but on Janet Jackson's albums—and in her videos and live performances, which revealed a crisp, athletic dance technique not unlike her brother's—singing wasn't the point. Janet's slamming beats, infectious hooks, and impeccable production values were perfectly suited to the breezy zeal with which she declared her social and sexual independence.

As a young child, Jackson was a tomboy who aspired to be a jockey. When she was seven, though, her father, Joseph, encouraged her to join her brothers—by then famous as the Jackson 5—in their music and variety act [see entry]. (Sister La Toya joined them for several shows in 1974; the following year, La Toya, eldest sister Rebbie, and brother Randy were all in on the act, while brother Jermaine bowed out.) Shows in Las Vegas resulted in a summer-replacement TV show in 1976 (on CBS), which led Janet to roles on the popular sitcoms *Good Times* and *Diff'rent Strokes*.

Next, Jackson secured a contract with A&M Records, and in 1982, while still managed and creatively guided by her father, she released a forgettable debut album, *Janet Jackson*. The album did yield a #6 R&B single, "Young Love." Another TV role, on the series *Fame*, followed, as did another unremarkable album, 1984's *Dream Street*, and another R&B hit, "Don't Stand Another Chance" (#9). Also in 1984, Jackson defied her family by marrying singer James DeBarge, whose R&B sibling act DeBarge was being hyped as a successor to the Jacksons. The marriage was annulled after less than a year, but the seeds of Jackson's independence from the family dynasty, and her father in particular, were firmly planted.

Then John McClain, an A&M executive and family friend, suggested that Jackson work with Jimmy Jam and Terry Lewis of the Time. Collaborating with these musicians, writers, and producers, Jackson had her breakthrough album, 1986's *Control,* which topped the pop and R&B album charts and spawned numerous hits: "What Have You Done For Me Lately" (#4 pop, #1 R&B), "Nasty" (#3 pop, #1 R&B), "When I Think of You" (#1 pop, #3 R&B), and in 1987, "Control" (#5 pop, #1 R&B), "Let's Wait Awhile" (#2 pop, #1 R&B), and "The Pleasure Principle" (#14 pop, #1 R&B). Helping fuel these singles were Jackson's highly energized, elaborately staged videos, most of which featured movie-musical-inspired choreography by Paula Abdul, who was discovered by Jackie Jackson, Abdul's boyfriend during her Los Angeles Lakers cheerleading days.

Having asserted her adulthood and self-reliance with *Control,* by 1987 Jackson had dismissed her father as manager (as other siblings had done before her) before recording *Rhythm Nation 1814. Control*'s successor dealt with larger social issues, like the need for tolerance, and found Jam and Lewis assuming more of the song-writing duties. *Rhythm Nation* hit #1 in the pop and R&B charts in 1989 and generated the smash singles "Miss You Much" (#1, pop and R&B) and, in 1990, "Rhythm Nation" (#2 pop, #1 R&B), "Escapade" (#1 pop, #1 R&B), "Alright" (#4 pop, #2 R&B), "Come Back to Me" (#2 pop, #2 R&B), "Black Cat" (#1 pop, #10 R&B), and "Love Will Never Do (Without You)" (#1 pop, #3 R&B). To promote the album, Jackson embarked on her first major tour, which matched the energy and spectacle of her videos.

In 1991 Virgin Records' owner Richard Branson lured Jackson away from A&M with a contract worth more than $30 million. Her final A&M project was a 1992 duet with Luther Vandross, "The Best Things in Life Are Free" (#10 pop, #1 R&B), recorded for the soundtrack to the film *Mo' Money.* In 1993 Jackson made her own movie debut as the heroine (opposite rapper Tupac Shakur) of director/screenwriter John Singleton's *Poetic Justice,* for which she received lukewarm reviews.

That same year, Jackson's Virgin album, *janet.,* shot to the top of the pop and R&B charts, as did the single "That's the Way Love Goes." More Top Ten singles followed, including "If" (#4 pop, #3 R&B, 1993) and "Again" (#1 pop, #7 R&B, 1994). Her new material was just as confrontational as, and more aggressively sexual than, her previous work had been; ditto for the accompanying tour, which featured Jackson in midriff-baring costumes, interacting suggestively with male dancers—indeed, more reminiscent of Madonna than of Michael. While Janet's once squeaky-clean image wasn't shattered by scandal as her brother's was, it was clear by the early Nineties that the littlest Jackson was nobody's baby, and very much her own woman.

Jermaine Jackson: See the Jackson 5

Joe Jackson

Born August 11, 1954, Portsmouth, England
1979—Look Sharp (A&M); I'm the Man   1980—Beat Crazy   1981—Joe Jackson's Jumpin' Jive   1982—Night and Day   1983—Mike's Murder soundtrack 1984—Body and Soul   1986—Big World   1987—Will Power   1988—Live 1980/86   1989—Blaze of Glory   1991—Laughter and Lust (Virgin)   1994—Night Music.

When singer Joe Jackson first emerged at the height of 1979's pop-new-wave explosion, he was frequently compared to Elvis Costello and Graham Parker. Beginning with his third album, however, Jackson shattered his "angry young man" image and released a series of credible forays into reggae and big-band jazz as well as symphonic and other idioms. As Jackson has made abundantly clear in interviews, a number of songs (including "Hit Single" and "Obvious Song"), and his controversial 1984 statement "Video Is Killing Music," he cares little for the trappings or machinations of pop stardom. Like Frank Zappa, he considers himself primarily a composer, not a rock star.

Jackson began studying violin at age 11, but after a few years he persuaded his parents to buy him a piano so that he could write songs. He later studied oboe and percussion as well. He received a scholarship to study composition at London's Royal Academy of Music from 1971 to 1974. After graduation he formed a band called Arms and Legs. While working as musical director at the Portsmouth Playboy Club, Jackson produced an LP-length demo of his songs that got him a publishing contract with Albion Music. Soon afterward A&M producer David Kershenbaum got Jackson a recording contract with his label.

Look Sharp was recorded in a week and a half. The single "Is She Really Going Out with Him?" hit #21, and the album went to #20. *I'm the Man,* released six months later, hit #22. Jackson was quickly labeled a power-pop performer, an image that was changed with the release of *Beat Crazy,* an ominous reggae-inflected LP. Jackson himself produced it, and his group was billed for the first time as the Joe Jackson Band. The LP was less commercially successful (#41), and a three-song EP that included Jackson singing Jimmy Cliff's "The Harder They Come" (available only on British import) got considerably more U.S. airplay.

Within months of the LP's release, Jackson was back in the studio working on *Jumpin' Jive,* a collection of Forties swing tunes, including some songs by Louis Jordan. A novel idea, *Jumpin' Jive* was fairly popular (#42) but yielded no hit singles, although Jackson toured the U.S. with a big band. In 1982 Jackson moved to New York to record *Night and Day,* which incorporated hints of salsa, funk, and minimalism. The sleek, jazzish "Steppin' Out" (#6) sold 250,000 copies, and the album went gold. His last Top Forty single to date was "You Can't Get What You Want (Till You Know What You Want)" (#15, 1984), from *Body and Soul.*

In 1986 Jackson recorded *Big World* over three nights before a live audience. Each subsequent album—the autobiographical *Blaze of Glory,* the instrumental *Will Power,* and the acclaimed *Laughter and Lust*—found critical favor but middling commercial success. Over time Jackson has proven more popular outside the United States, where his eclecticism, daring, and outspokenness are embraced.

Beginning with his 1983 appearance on the soundtrack for *Mike's Murder,* Jackson has scored a number of films, including *Tucker* (1988), *Queens Logic* (1990), and *Three of Hearts* (1992). He has also composed for and performed with the Tokyo Philharmonic Orchestra (*Shijin No Ie,* 1985).

Mahalia Jackson

Born October 26, 1911, New Orleans, Louisiana; died January 27, 1972, Chicago, Illinois
1963—*Bless This House* (Columbia); *Mahalia Jackson: Greatest Hits* 1968—*Sings the Best-loved Hymns of Dr. Martin Luther King* 1971—*Sings America's Favorite Hymns* 1972—*The Great Mahalia Jackson* 1976—*How I Got Over* 1991—*Gospels, Spirituals and Hymns* (Legacy/Columbia).

Mahalia Jackson is generally regarded as one of the best gospel singers ever, and is certainly the most popular. Her forceful bluesy style was greatly influenced by Ma Rainey and Bessie Smith, though Jackson never sang secular music. Aretha Franklin cites Jackson as her favorite singer.

Jackson and family regularly attended New Orleans' Mount Moriah Baptist Church. Despite her strict religious training, she heard and enjoyed New Orleans' wealth of jazz and blues. She often listened to the music of Smith and Rainey on record. In 1927 she moved to Chicago, where she worked as a domestic and a nurse. In 1935 Jackson made her recording debut after scouts for Decca Records had heard her sing at a funeral. From Decca Jackson moved to the small Apollo label, where she became a gospel legend. Her recording of "Move On Up" sold more than two million copies. In concert Jackson was known to extend it to as long as 25 minutes. Crucial to her popularity was her accompanist, pianist Mildred Falls, whom record executive John Hammond called "the greatest gospel accompanist that ever lived."

In 1954 Jackson signed to Columbia Records, where A&R director Mitch Miller used strings and choirs to back her, increasing her popularity with whites but inhibiting much of her earlier fire. At the time of her death she had a larger white than black following.

Marlon Jackson: See the Jackson 5

Michael Jackson

Born August 29, 1958, Gary, Indiana
1972—*Got to Be There* (Motown); *Ben* 1973—*Music and Me* 1975—*Forever, Michael; The Best of Michael Jackson* 1979—*Off the Wall* (Epic) 1982—*Thriller* 1987—*Bad* 1991—*Dangerous* 1995—*HIStory: Past, Present and Future, Book One.*

In the years since Michael Jackson made his first national television appearance with his brothers at the age of 11, he has evolved from a singing and dancing soul-music prodigy to the self-proclaimed but widely acknowledged "King of Pop." As a musician, he has ranged from Motown's snappy dance fare and lush ballads to techno-edged New Jack Swing to work that incorporates both funk rhythms and hard-rock guitar. At his early-Eighties zenith, still riding the crest of his best-selling album to date, *Thriller,* spotlit in his trademark red zippered jacket and single white sequined glove, he was ubiquitous. A superb businessman, Jackson has exerted unparalleled control over his career since he and his brothers (sans Jermaine) left Motown for Epic Records in 1975. As a singer, dancer, and writer, Jackson's talent is unassailable, and he created one of the most intriguing personas in popular music, at once childlike and obsessed with control.

With the passage of time, and especially since 1993, it is Jackson's personality that has dominated headlines formerly dedicated to his prodigious artistic accomplishments and humanitarian efforts. His charity work was enormous and focused always on his highly publicized and self-admitted identification with children. Infatuated with Peter Pan and E.T., Jackson seemed a kind of childlike extraterrestrial: benign (if in an eerie way), either sexless or sexually ambiguous, neither black nor white. Secluded by his celebrity, he appeared to touch down to earth only on stage or videotape; fanatically private, he generated endless gossip. In 1993 with allegations of child molestation, his career was rocked with scandal as gargantuan as his fame. Not since Shirley Temple has a child star so entranced the American public, and the massive public soul-searching the allegations against Jackson inspired were but one indication of the almost inestimable role he has played in shaping not only pop music but pop culture. Jackson returned to the tabloids in 1994 with the shocking announcement that he had wed Lisa Marie Presley, an act that led to even more speculation about his motives but that undeniably made him the son-in-law of the late Elvis Presley.

The Jackson 5's lead singer and focal point, Michael became more popular than the group as the Eighties began. He had a string of solo hits in the early Seventies ("Got to Be There," #4, 1971; "Rockin' Robin," #2, 1972; "Ben," #1, 1972) and played the Scarecrow in *The Wiz* in 1978. But it was with veteran producer Quincy Jones, whom he met while filming *The Wiz,* that Jackson began his amazing rise.

In 1979 the team's *Off the Wall* made him the first solo artist to release four Top Ten hits from a single album. "Don't Stop Till You Get Enough" (#1, 1979), "Rock with You" (#1, 1979), "Off the Wall" (#10, 1980), and "She's Out of My Life" (#10, 1980) presented the former boy wonder as a mature artist, funky enough for the dance floor and sweet enough for pop radio. In the album's wake, the Jacksons' *Triumph* sold a million copies and prompted a $5.5-million-grossing tour. Even at this early stage, Jackson and his brothers were exploring video.

In 1982 Jackson and Jones collaborated on a story-telling record of Steven Spielberg's *E.T.* The album, which was hastily withdrawn from the market due to a legal dispute, is now a prime Jackson collectable. That year, Diana Ross, one of Jackson's early mentors, scored a #10 hit with "Muscles," written and produced by Jackson. Jackson had also begun an alliance with Paul McCartney, who had written "Girlfriend" for *Off the Wall.* The two reconvened to cowrite the duet "The Girl Is Mine" (#2, 1982).

It was 1983 that marked Jackson's complete ascension. With Jones again producing, *Thriller* yielded, in addition to "The Girl Is Mine," two other hit singles by early 1983—"Billie Jean" (#1, 1983) and "Beat It" (#1, 1983) (with a guitar solo delivered gratis by Eddie Van Halen)—and went on to become the best-selling album in history, with over 45 million copies sold worldwide. Charting at #1 in every Western country, it spent a record 37 weeks at U.S. #1. The first album ever to simultaneously head the singles and albums charts for both R&B and pop, it eventually generated an unprecedented seven Top Ten singles including "P.Y.T. (Pretty Young Thing)" (#10, 1983), "Wanna Be Startin' Somethin'" (#5, 1983), "Human Nature" (#7, 1983), and "Thriller" (#4, 1983). Of its record 12 Grammy nominations, it won eight in 1983, a historic sweep.

Thriller also broke through MTV's de facto color line; where videos by black artists had rarely been shown, Michael's "Beat It," costing a then exorbitant $160,000, received extensive play. The "Thriller" video, with a voice-over by horror movie stalwart Vincent Price and state-of-the-art special effects, was directed by John Landis (*The Blues Brothers*). In May, performing solo and with his brothers on NBC's *25 Years of Motown* special, Michael popularized his distinctive Moonwalk dancestep; his "Billie Jean" was the only non-Motown song in the show. Later in 1983, while another duet with McCartney—"Say Say Say" from Paul's *Pipes of Peace*—topped the charts for six weeks, Jackson announced a $5 million sponsorship deal with Pepsi Cola.

While filming a 1984 Pepsi commercial Jackson was seriously injured when a pyrotechnic effect went awry, setting his hair on fire. The singer was hospitalized and underwent surgery for scalp burns; he later received facial laser surgery. Rumors about other reconstructive work began shortly before the release of *Thriller* and would build in coming years. Among the procedures he has been rumored to have undergone are a facelift, a purported nose surgery, and the lightening of his skin with chemicals. His autobiography admitted only to a nose job.

After receiving a Presidential Award from Ronald Reagan in June 1984, Jackson joined his brothers on a supporting tour for the Jacksons' *Victory* (from which Michael's duet with Mick Jagger, "State of Shock," reached #3). The highly publicized tour, which Jackson undertook reluctantly, was plagued by mismanagement (boxing promoter Don King was in charge, much to Jackson's displeasure, and his parents were coproducers) and internal strife (at one point, several of the Jackson brothers, their parents, and numerous other parties had retained their own lawyers). Jackson donated his revenues to children's charities. Nonetheless, the shows were considered spectacular, brimming with high-tech special effects. Jackson ended the year by receiving a star on the Hollywood Walk of Fame.

In 1985 Jackson cowrote with Lionel Richie "We Are The World," the theme song for USA for Africa, to benefit famine relief. The all-star recording reached #1. Disneyland and Disney World were chosen as sites to present "Captain Eo," a 15-minute 3D sci-fi film starring Jackson. Jackson's relationship with McCartney soured later that year as, bidding against both Paul and Yoko Ono, Jackson secured the ATV music publishing catalogue for $47.5 million. Among ATV's holdings were more than 250 Lennon/McCartney songs.

Shortly after signing a second contract with Pepsi in 1986 for $15 million, Jackson released *Bad* in 1987. Its 17-minute title track video was directed by Martin Scorsese. *Bad* generated five #1s in 1987–88: "I Just Can't Stop Loving You," "Bad," "The Way You Make Me Feel," "Man in the Mirror," and "Dirty Diana." The *Bad* Tour—over a year long—became (according to Epic Records) the biggest-grossing tour in history and one of the most expensive (Jackson's entourage included 250 people). *Bad* sold a reported 22 million copies worldwide, and Epic Records asserts it was the second-best-selling album of the Eighties, after *Thriller*. Its U.S. sales were only seven million, however.

With 1988 came Jackson's long-awaited, heavily illustrated, and brief autobiography, *Moonwalk*, in which he claimed that his father, Joseph Jackson, had hit him as a child. Generally, however, the book (edited by Jacqueline Onassis) was considered unrevealing. (A second volume of his writings, *Dancing the Dream*, was published in 1992 to less enthusiastic response.)

By the end of the Eighties, Jackson had moved from the Encino, California, family home to Neverland, an estimated $28-million, 2700-acre California ranch complete with ferris wheel, an exotic menagerie, a movie theater, and a security staff of 40. There Jackson—famous for clean living (he did not smoke, drink, or use drugs, and was rarely seen in the company of a woman)—hosted an endless series of parties for children, many of them disabled, critically ill, or underprivileged.

His popularity seemingly unassailable, Jackson signed a $28 million deal with L.A. Gear sportswear to be its spokesperson, but the idea proved a failure and Jackson was dropped after one commercial. At the start of the Nineties, however, Jackson's popularity was massive enough to land him the biggest contract awarded an entertainer up to that time. Jackson signed a $65-million deal with Sony Corporation in 1991 that promised him an unprecedented share of the profits from his next six albums, his own record label, a role in developing video software products, and a chance to star in movies. Reportedly he would receive more than $120 million an

album if each could match the sales of *Thriller*. In 1991 Jackson hosted Elizabeth Taylor's eighth wedding at Neverland.

In 1991 Jackson released *Dangerous,* which was recorded for $10 million. Coproduced by New Jack Swing creator Teddy Riley, the album featured material ("Heal the World," "Who Is It") that recalled his work with Quincy Jones, with whom he had parted ways shortly after *Bad.* Riley toughened and updated Jackson's sound, stripping off some of the studio gloss of his previous works. With the $1.2-million video for the single "Black or White," Jackson demanded that MTV and Black Entertainment Television (BET) announce him as "the King of Pop" (a fact he would later deny in a live televised interview with Oprah Winfrey). Hoping to outdistance *Bad*'s sales, he prepared for a spectacular world tour. Also in 1992, he embarked on a five-nation African tour; there, however, he was widely criticized for his aloof behavior. That same year, with his personal fortune estimated at $200 million, Jackson established the Heal the World Foundation to raise awareness of children-related issues, including abuse.

With 1993 came Jackson's crisis. The year, however, began auspiciously. Appearing in January at the NAACP Image Awards, the American Music Awards, and the preinaugural gala for President Clinton, he also reached 91 million viewers in his halftime performance at Super Bowl XXVII, the most widely viewed entertainment event in TV history. And he announced the start of a $1.25-million program to provide drug prevention and counseling services to Los Angeles children following that city's riots. In a February TV interview with a less than incisive Oprah Winfrey, he said that his increasingly pale complexion was the result of vitiligo, a skin disease, and that he was a victim of abuse at the hands of his father, Joseph. He tried to dispel such long-standing rumors as the one that he once tried to buy the bones of the Elephant Man or had slept in a hyperbaric chamber. He also said that he was dating movie actress Brooke Shields, who had been a companion during the *Thriller* period. The interview was one of the most-watched television programs in history. In March he formed Michael Jackson Productions Inc., an independent film company that would give a share of its profits to his Heal the World Foundation. In June he debuted his MJJ/Epic record label, releasing the *Free Willy* soundtrack.

Scandal erupted on August 17 when a Beverly Hills psychiatrist approached the Los Angeles Police after a 13-year-old patient claimed that Jackson had fondled him. Later specific charges, brought by the boy's father, were that Jackson had at his house sexually abused the boy earlier in the year. After the father obtained a ruling to deny Jackson contact with the son, the police raided Neverland, seizing videotapes and other possible evidence (nothing incriminating turned up). Traveling to Bangkok for the *Dangerous* Tour, Jackson denied the charges, his security consultant maintaining that the boy's father had attempted to extort $20 million to start a production company (he added that Jackson received at least 25 such extortion threats a year). With Pepsi supporting him and his retinue denying a suicide attempt, Jackson turned 35 at the end of August. Shortly thereafter Jackson canceled his second Singapore show, claiming migraine headaches.

In September Jackson's sister La Toya reported that he used to spend the night with young boys in his room. Jackson then pulled out of a deal to contribute the title track to the movie *Addams Family Values* and, after his alleged victim filed a civil suit for seduction and sex abuse, canceled the rest of the *Dangerous* Tour, maintaining that pressure from the charges had left him addicted to painkillers. Pepsi then ended its ten-year partnership with the star.

Toward the end of the year, business continued, with Sony announcing that *Dangerous* sales had topped 20 million and Jackson signing a $70-million, five-year deal with EMI Music to administer his ATV catalogue. But in December, back in the U.S., Jackson in a four-minute televised speech confronted his accusers and decried the extensive examination of his body that the police had conducted as part of their investigation.

On January 25, 1994, lawyers for Jackson and the alleged victim announced a private settlement of the boy's case for undisclosed terms. One day earlier, following a criminal investigation into Jackson's claims that the boy's father was part of an extortion plot against him, the D.A. declined to file charges. In February a Santa Barbara grand jury convened to begin hearing testimony in the case, suggesting that criminal investigation was continuing, despite the settlement of the civil case. Eventually the criminal investigation was dropped for lack of testimony. In August 1994 a statement issued by MJJ Productions verified two months of rumors that Jackson had married 26-year-old Lisa Marie Presley, who had been estranged from her husband, with whom she had two children. In June 1995 Jackson released his first solo double-CD set, *HIStory: Past, Present and Future, Book One*, consisting of 15 old and 15 new tracks. The video for the first new single, "Scream," a duet with his sister Janet (which entered the singles chart at #4), was estimated to be the most expensive in history, at $4 million.

Millie Jackson

Born 1943, Thompson, Georgia
1972—*Millie Jackson* (Spring)   1973—*It Hurts So Good*   1974—*Caught Up*   1977—*Feelin' Bitchy*
1978—*Get It Out'cha System*   1979—*A Moment's Pleasure; Royal Rappin's* (with Isaac Hayes) (Polydor); *Live and Uncensored* (Spring)   1980—*For Men Only* (Polydor); *I Had to Say It*   1981—*Just a Lil' Bit Country*   1982—*Live and Outrageous (Rated XXX)*

1986—*An Imitation of Love* (Jive)   1988—*The Tide Is Turning*   1992—*Young Man, Older Woman.*

Soul singer and songwriter Millie Jackson was internationally popular for well over a decade, thanks to live shows that interwove gritty deep-soul singing and raunchy raps. Jackson grew up in Georgia and lived with her grandfather, a preacher, until she ran away at age 14. She came to New York City and worked as a model, mostly for confession magazines. In 1964, on a bet, she jumped onstage and sang at the Palm Cafe in Harlem. For the rest of the Sixties, she worked as a singer around New York. She cut a single in 1969 for MGM but kept her day job until she signed with Spring Records in 1971.

Jackson had her first soul hit in 1972 with "A Child of God" (#22 R&B), followed by "Ask Me What You Want" (#14 R&B), and "It Hurts So Good" (#3 R&B, 1973), which was included on the soundtrack of *Cleopatra Jones*.

Her breakthrough was the 1974 album *Caught Up*, the first recording of her live act. It was a concept album on which Jackson played a wife on one side and the Other Woman on the other; it yielded a hit single, "(If Loving You Is Wrong) I Don't Want to Be Right" (#42 pop, 1974) and went gold. Both *Feelin' Bitchy* and *Get It Out-'cha System* went gold, although Jackson's language was often so blunt that she got no airplay. Jackson recorded a duet album, *Royal Rappin's*, with Isaac Hayes in 1979 and continued to play large halls and record regularly into the early Eighties, acting as her own manager and coproducer, and with her own publishing company, Double Ak-Shun Music.

Following her 1981 excursion to Nashville for *Just a Lil' Bit Country*, Jackson was absent from the recording scene for almost five years—aside from a noncharting duet with Elton John, "Act of War" (on his *To Be Continued*) until signing a new deal with Jive Records. *An Imitation of Love*, on which Jackson finally ceded production control to others, yielded a Top Ten R&B hit in "Hot! Wild! Unrestricted! Crazy Love!" But her commercial profile never again ascended to its Seventies heights. Ironically, Jackson—with her soulful vocalizing, insistence on live bands, and practiced stagecraft—found herself displaced by the rap music she'd so vividly presaged.

Randy Jackson: See Zebra

Rebbie Jackson: See the Jackson 5

Wanda Jackson

Born October 20, 1937, Maud, Oklahoma
1960—*Rockin' with Wanda* (Capitol)   1966—*Wanda Jackson Sings Country Blues*   1972—*Praise the Lord*   1974—*Country Gospel* (Word)   1979—*Great-*

est Hits (Capitol)   1990—*Rockin' in the Country: The Best of Wanda Jackson* (Rhino).

Although Jackson is known for her mid- to late-Fifties recordings as the "Queen of Rockabilly," she has since worked as a country singer and a born-again Christian gospel singer. Her father was an amateur musician, and both parents encouraged her to sing. At age 15 she had her own radio program on KLPR in Oklahoma City; the next year she began recording for Decca. She soon joined Hank Thompson's swing band and in 1956 was signed by Capitol.

None of her hits reached the Top Twenty ("Let's Have a Party," #37, 1960; "Right or Wrong," #29, 1961; and "In the Middle of a Heartache," #27, 1961), but Jackson became known for her aggressive approach, which was considered unique for the time. She has recorded in German, Dutch, and Japanese (phonetically), and frequently tours internationally. Her first hit, "Let's Have a Party," featured backing by Gene Vincent's Blue Caps. In June 1971 she and her husband "received Christ personally," and became born-again Christians. She continued performing rockabilly songs with religious themes, for Christian and secular audiences (though she refused to play nightclubs), into the mid-Eighties.

The Jackson 5/The Jacksons/The Jackson Family

Formed 1964, Gary, Indiana
Sigmund Esco (Jackie) Jackson (b. May 4, 1951, Gary), voc.; Toriano Adaryll (Tito) Jackson (b. Oct. 15, 1953, Gary), gtr., voc.; Marlon David Jackson (b. Mar. 12, 1957, Gary), voc.; Jermaine La Jaune Jackson (b. Dec. 11, 1954, Gary), voc., bass; Michael Joe Jackson (b. Aug. 29, 1958, Gary), lead voc.
1969—*I Want You Back* (also known as *Diana Ross Presents the Jackson 5*) (Motown)   1970—*ABC*; *Third Album*; *Christmas Album*   1971—*Maybe Tomorrow*   1972—*The Jackson 5's Greatest Hits* 1973—*Get It Together*   1974—*Dancing Machine* 1975—(+ Steven Randall [Randy] Jackson [b. Oct. 29, 1961, Gary], voc., kybds.)   1976—*The Jacksons* (Epic)   1977—*Motown Special* (Motown); *Anthology*; *Goin' Places* (Epic)   1978—*Destiny*   1980— *Triumph* (Epic)   1981—*Live*   1984—*Victory* 1989—*2300 Jackson Street*.
Michael Jackson solo: See entry.
Jermaine Jackson solo: 1972—*Jermaine* (Motown) 1973—*Come Into My Life*   1976—*My Name Is Jermaine*   1977—*Feel the Fire*   1978—*Frontiers* 1980—*Let's Get Serious*; *Jermaine*   1981—*I Like Your Style*   1982—*Let Me Tickle Your Fancy* 1984—*Jermaine Jackson* (Arista)   1986—*Precious Moments*   1989—*Don't Take It Personal*   1991— *You Said* (LaFace/Arista).

The Jacksons: Michael Jackson, Tito Jackson, Randy Jackson, Jackie Jackson, Marlon Jackson

Jackie Jackson solo: 1973—*Jackie Jackson* (Motown)   1989—*Be the One* (Polydor).
As the Jackson Family: Mid-Seventies—The Jackson 5; + Maureen "Rebbie" Jackson (b. May 29, 1950, Gary), voc.; + La Toya Jackson (b. May 29, 1956, Gary), voc.; + Janet Jackson (b. May 16, 1966, Gary), voc.
Marlon Jackson solo: 1987—*Baby Tonight* (Capitol). Randy Jackson solo, as Randy and the Gypsies: 1989—*Randy & the Gypsies* (A&M); as Randy Jackson's China Rain: 1991—*Bed of Nails.*
Rebbie Jackson solo: 1984—*Centipede* (Columbia) 1986—*Reaction*   1988—*R U Tuff Enuff.*
La Toya Jackson solo: 1980—*La Toya Jackson* (Polydor)   1981—*My Special Love*   1984—*Heart Don't Lie* (Private I)   1988—*You're Gonna Get Rocked.* Janet Jackson solo: See entry.

Since its national debut in 1969 with "I Want You Back," the Jackson 5 has been the most accomplished, successful black pop soul vocal group and one of the most beloved family acts in pop music. Over the group's long and unparalleled career, the Jackson brothers upheld and expanded the R&B/soul vocal traditions of their idols and mentors, evolving from a Temptations-style, closely directed vocal group to a self-contained soul/disco/pop powerhouse. The constant media focus on lead-singing prodigy Michael has overshadowed the contributions of his brothers, especially in the later phase of their career, when they each wrote and produced material on the group's two most acclaimed albums, Triumph and Destiny.

The group's father, Joseph Jackson, had been a guitarist in a group called the Falcons (not to be confused with the group of "You're So Fine" fame) with his brother and three other men. Shortly after Joseph married Katherine Scruse their quickly growing family forced him to give up his musical ambitions. Although he worked as a crane operator, he maintained an interest in music, often playing his electric guitar in the house. Katherine often led the children in singing songs, especially harmony-rich country & western standards, which she loved.

Beginning in the early Sixties Tito, Jermaine, and Jackie performed around Gary, Indiana, as the Jackson Family; around 1964 Michael and Marlon joined, and the group became the Jackson 5. Popular in their hometown, in 1968 they cut one unsuccessful single, "Big Boy" b/w "You've Changed." By then the group (which included keyboardist Ronnie Rancifer and drummer Johnny Jackson [no relation]) had been opening shows for such R&B stars as Sam and Dave, the Isley Brothers, the O'Jays, Gladys Knight and the Pips, James Brown, and the Temptations. On weekends, they traveled by van throughout the Midwest, venturing as far from home as Phoenix and Washington, D.C. Though numerous Motown performers knew of and worked with the young group, it was probably Bobby Taylor of the Vancouvers and Gladys Knight (not Diana Ross, as label publicity later claimed) who brought them to Berry Gordy Jr.'s attention. Although Gordy did not attend their Motown audition, it was filmed, and within months, the Jackson 5 were signed to the label.

Although Motown would remain a force in black music for several more years, historically speaking, the Jackson 5 were perhaps the last act to benefit from the label's all-encompassing approach to talent development. Newly relocated to Los Angeles, Motown no longer kept a staff of choreographers, etiquette teachers, and coaches. Instead, Berry Gordy entrusted much of the Jackson 5's early training to one of his most recent hirings, Suzanne de Passe. The boys and their father were moved to L.A., where they boys lived with Diana Ross or Berry Gordy. Even from this early point, friction between Gordy and Joseph Jackson over the handling of the Jackson 5 was evident, although Joseph remained, at least nominally, their manager.

In January 1970 "I Want You Back" hit #1 and sold over two million copies, becoming the first of a string of 13 Top Twenty singles for Motown, including "ABC" (#1, 1970), "The Love You Save" (#1, 1970), "I'll Be There" (#1, 1970, their biggest seller), "Mama's Pearl" (#2, 1971), "Never Can Say Goodbye" (#2, 1971), "Maybe Tomorrow" (#20, 1971), "Sugar Daddy" (#10, 1971), "Little Bitty Pretty One" (#13, 1972), "Lookin' Through the Windows" (#16, 1972), "Corner of the Sky" (#18, 1972), "Dancing Machine" (#2, 1974), and "I Am Love" (#15, 1975). Many of the group's Motown hits were written by "The Corporation" (Freddie Perren, Fonce Mizell, Deke Richards, and

Berry Gordy). The Jackson 5 toured frequently, always tutored and supervised by the Motown staff.

In 1972 the group received a commendation from Congress for its "contributions to American youth." Throughout the Seventies and Eighties, the Jacksons and their family (which included three sisters: Rebbie, La Toya, and Janet) were considered ideal role models. Prompted by Motown, the national media regularly touted the family's strong religious beliefs (mother Katherine and several of the children, including Michael, were devout Jehovah's Witnesses) and work ethic. In fact, the family was often erroneously depicted as having arisen from the ghetto, a PR fabrication that infuriated the Jackson parents. The Jackson 5 voiced their animated likenesses for a Saturday morning cartoon series in 1971, and beginning in 1976 all nine siblings starred in *The Jacksons,* a CBS musical-variety program. During that time, the entire clan also appeared in Las Vegas shows that featured the Jackson 5 (sometimes 6 with the inclusion of youngest brother Randy) and their three sisters. Like many young singing acts, the Jacksons had witnessed a decline in record sales through the mid-Seventies. They began to outgrow the teen-idol market, and through the decade all of the brothers, except Michael and Randy, married early. While dance music was beginning to dominate black music, Motown stubbornly held the Jackson 5 to its old formula rather than move in the direction of "Dancing Machine," for example. Both Joseph and the Jackson brothers believed they would benefit by writing and producing their own records, something Gordy and Motown were notoriously reluctant to permit. In fact, Joseph had overseen the construction of a state-of-the-art recording studio at the family home in Encino, California, to encourage his sons to become more creatively independent.

Like many other Motown artists, the Jackson 5 left the label over artistic control. When the group announced its departure in 1975, the label sued for breach of contract. The $20-million suit was eventually settled in 1980, with the Jacksons paying $600,000 ($100,000 in cash and $500,000 in "other items") and the label retaining all rights to the name the Jackson 5. The move also brought the family's first public rift, as Jermaine refused to leave Motown with his brothers. In 1973 he married Berry Gordy Jr.'s daughter Hazel Joy in what was then claimed to be one of the most lavish weddings in the history of Hollywood. It was also viewed by some to be the merger of record-business dynasties, but given Joseph Jackson and Berry Gordy's long-running mutual dislike, it never was.

Like Jackie (who released a quickly forgotten LP in 1973) and Michael (whose solo career is recounted in his entry), Jermaine had also tested the waters as a solo act. Although Michael continually overshadowed his siblings, in the group's early years, Jermaine was successfully promoted as a teen idol. His *Jermaine* (#27, 1972) spun off a Top Ten remake of Shep and the Limelites' "Daddy's Home." Subsequent releases on his father-in-law's label did not fare nearly as well until 1980's *Let's Get Serious* (#6 pop, #1 R&B), with its #9 pop, #1 R&B title track. For the next couple of years, Jermaine's singles made solid showings on the R&B charts (1980's "You're Supposed to Keep Your Love for Me" and "Little Girl, Don't You Worry," 1981's "You Like Me, Don't You" and "I'm Just Too Shy") but returned to the pop Top Twenty with "Let Me Tickle Your Fancy" (#18 pop, #5 R&B, 1982). Shortly thereafter, with the blessings of his father-in-law and with Hazel functioning as his manager, Jermaine moved to Arista, where his eponymously titled 1984 label debut became his first Top Twenty LP since 1980 and an R&B #1. Boosted by a string of stylishly crafted videos, "Dynamite" (#15 pop, #8 R&B, 1984) and "Do What You Do" (#13 pop, #14 R&B, 1984) pushed the album to gold. However, Jermaine's later efforts—including a duet with Pia Zadora (with whom he also performed)—flopped, and *Don't Take It Personal,* like his second, third, and fourth Motown albums, did not enter the Top 100. In 1987 Jermaine and Hazel divorced.

Meanwhile, back in March 1976, the remaining five Jackson brothers changed their name to the Jacksons and signed with Epic. Kenny Gamble and Leon Huff produced their first two Epic LPs, *The Jacksons* (featuring "Enjoy Yourself" [#6 pop, #2 R&B, 1976] and "Show You the Way to Go" [#28 pop, #6 R&B, 1977]) and *Goin' Places* (#63, 1977), neither of which the Jackson brothers believed suited them. They began writing their own material, beginning with *Destiny,* which contained "Shake Your Body (Down to the Ground)"; within a few years they were producing most of their own material as well. Except for four singles that failed to crack the Top Forty, the Jacksons picked up the streak where they'd left off and the hits kept coming: "Blame It on the Boogie" (#54 pop, #3 R&B, 1979), "Shake Your Body (Down to the Ground)" (#7 pop, #3 R&B, 1979), "Lovely One" (#12 pop, #2 R&B, 1980), "Heartbreak Hotel" (sometimes titled "This Place Hotel" and not to be confused with the Elvis Presley hit of the same name) (#22 pop, #2 R&B, 1980). In light of Michael's preeminence, many historians overlook the songwriting contributions of the other brothers, each of whom cowrote at least one of the hits above.

Through 1979 and 1980 Michael's *Off the Wall* dominated the charts. The Jacksons' *Triumph* (#10 pop, #1 R&B, 1980) sold a million copies and prompted a 39-city tour that grossed $5.5 million. Then, as always, the Jacksons' live shows garnered outstanding reviews. They were among the first acts to incorporate lavish special effects, and with *Triumph*'s "Can You Feel It," video pioneers of sorts. Although the song was not a hit, a special video produced for it was used to open their concerts. A live LP, *Jacksons Live* (#30 pop, #10 R&B, 1981), documented this period.

Through 1981 and most of 1982 the Jacksons kept a low profile, although with Michael moving increasingly outside his father's managerial control, Joseph turned his attention again to the Jackson sisters, overseeing the production of La Toya's and Janet's first albums. Neither was hugely successful, although each had a share of R&B charting singles: La Toya, with "Stay the Night" (#31 R&B, 1981) and "Bet'cha Gonna Need My Lovin'" (#22 R&B, 1983), and Janet with "Young Love" (#6 R&B, 1982) and "Say You Do" (#15 R&B, 1983). For Janet, greater success would come only after she declared her artistic independence from her father with *Control* in 1986 [see entry]. During this time, Joseph also encouraged his eldest, Rebbie, who had married a fellow Jehovah's Witness and seemed an unlikely entertainer, to record. "Centipede" (#24 pop, #4 R&B, 1984) and "Plaything" (#8 R&B, 1988) were her biggest hits. Subsequent singles, including a 1986 duet with Cheap Trick's Robin Zander ("You Send the Rain Away") and rapper Melle Mel ("R U Tuff Enuff") were quickly forgotten.

The years 1983 and 1984 marked a turning point for all the Jacksons, and beginning with the six brothers' reunion at the *Motown 25* television special taping, the family would dominate the charts and the news for the next 18 months. Interestingly, it was after the brothers' reunion—their first appearance with Jermaine since the 1974 Las Vegas show, after which he announced his decision to stay behind with Motown—that Michael dazzled the audience with his performance of his first single off *Thriller,* "Billie Jean," and unveiled his Moonwalk dance step. Critics agree that was a pivotal moment in Jackson's career, as indeed it was. But it also marked the beginning of the end for the Jackson brothers. By most credible accounts, it was Jermaine, who was always Joseph's favorite son and the most aggressive of the siblings, who pushed hardest for a continuation of the reunion and what would become the Victory Tour. Although the brothers had severed all business ties with Joseph, he and their mother, along with boxing promoter Don King, produced the tour. By the time it opened in Kansas City, on July 6, 1984, the enterprise was awash in so much controversy that Michael pledged all of his proceeds to charity. Nevertheless, the tour became the most widely covered and largest-grossing tour of its time. Given *Thriller*'s massive success, few were surprised to learn that the Victory Tour and album (#4 pop, #3 R&B, 1984) would be Michael's swansong with the group. But Marlon announced his decision to leave once the tour ended as well. His "Don't Go" (#2 R&B, 1987) from *Baby Tonight* is his biggest solo hit. Although *Victory* sold over two million copies, it spawned just one Top Ten hit, "State of Shock" (#3, 1984), a duet between Michael and Mick Jagger. It would be the Jacksons' last Top Ten pop hit.

Ironically, the family's decline began following a 24-month period between January 1983 and December 1984 when Michael had six Top Ten (including two #1s) solo hits, Jermaine had two Top Twenty pop hits, and Rebbie, Janet, and La Toya were near-constant presences on the R&B chart. But the personal and public turmoil that has marked the family was just beginning. Janet eloped with singer James DeBarge while the rest of the family was traveling with the Victory Tour; La Toya, then Michael, moved out of the family home. For La Toya, whose early ambivalence toward her career is apparent, record sales remain elusive in the United States, although she performed throughout the rest of the world. In the wake of her two appearances in *Playboy* magazine (the first of which, in 1989, became one of the magazine's best-selling issues), her international best-seller 1991's *La Toya: Growing Up in the Jackson Family* (in which she accused her father of child abuse), and her marriage to controversial manager Jack Gordon, La Toya became a figure of controversy both inside and outside the family. While her parents and several siblings have been vociferously critical of her, others, including Michael, have pledged their support. Obscured in the public outcry over her book was the fact that in the French edition of her autobiography, Katherine Jackson had written of Joseph hitting the children and having extramarital affairs; these passages were deleted from the later U.S. edition. And while several Jackson family members protested the right of any Jackson to reveal family secrets, before and after La Toya's book, several other siblings and even Joseph had floated proposals for their own version of the family saga; only Katherine and Michael (whose *Moonwalk* also alluded to physical abuse) found takers. La Toya last appeared publicly with her brothers (except Jermaine) as part of USA for Africa.

Other Jacksons made headlines as well. In 1980 Katherine Jackson (accompanied by Janet and Randy) attacked one of Joseph's secretaries in his office with a blunt instrument. No charges were filed. Jermaine's marriage to Hazel Gordy ended, as did Jackie's to his wife Enid (who later accused him of physically attacking her and won a court order barring him from her home); Jackie and Enid divorced in 1986. Randy, who had been nearly killed in a late-Seventies car accident that severely damaged his legs, was charged with physically abusing his wife and his infant daughter in 1991. He pleaded no contest to one battery charge and was to have entered a rehabilitation program. In 1994 Tito's ex-wife Delores, or Dee Dee, whom he had married in 1972 and with whom he had three children, drowned in a friend's swimming pool.

In the summer of 1989, the Jacksons—by then a quartet of Jackie, Jermaine, Tito, and Randy—released *2300 Jackson Street* (the address of their Gary, Indiana, childhood home) nearly five years after *Victory.* It peaked at a disappointing #59, and its autobiographical title track, which reunited the brothers with Michael and Janet, and a number of nieces and nephews, did not chart. In 1991 Jermaine released "Word to the Badd," a clear attack on Michael, which made headlines but did not become a hit.

The family's plans to open a Jackson family museum in Las Vegas and their mismanaged Jackson Family Honors tribute were overshadowed by the then-pending child-abuse allegations against Michael. The Family Honors program, which aired in February 1994, was plagued by slow ticket sales, allegations of financial improprieties, and a final show that was deemed lackluster. By all indications, with the exception of Michael's and Janet's spectacular careers, the Jackson family's dominance as an entertainment dynasty seems to be approaching an end. Unfortunately, their long-held public status as role models and exemplars of conservative family values has also been damaged irrevocably (oddly, in no small part because of the highly rated, family-controlled 1992 made-for-TV account of their early years, which depicted Joseph as violent and demanding). Despite all that has occurred in recent years, the Jackson family remains unique in the annals of pop-music history, a phenomenal success story that will surely continue to unfold for years to come.

Mick Jagger: See the Rolling Stones

The Jaggerz/Donnie Iris

Formed 1965, Pittsburgh, Pennsylvania
Donald Iris (b. Dominic Ierace, 1943, Ellwood City, Pa.), gtr., voc.; Ben Faiella (b. Beaver Falls, Pa.), gtr., bass; Thom Davies (b. Duquesne, Pa.), kybds., trumpet; James Ross (b. Aliquippa, Pa.), bass, trombone; William Maybray, bass; James Pugliano, drums.
1969—*Introducing the Jaggerz* (Gamble) 1970—*We Went to Different Schools Together* (Kama Sutra) 1971—(– Iris) 1975—*Come Again* (Wooden Nickel). Donnie Iris solo: 1980—*Back on the Streets* (MCA) 1981—*King Cool* 1982—*The High and the Mighty* 1983—*Fortune 410* 1985—*No Muss . . . No Fuss* (HME).

Led by frontman/lead vocalist Donnie Iris (credited on the LPs as D. Ierace), the Jaggerz had a #2 1970 single with the million-selling "The Rapper." Their debut 45, "Baby I Love You," with William Maybray on lead vocals, was a flop. The next year they signed to Kama Sutra and recorded *We Went to Different Schools Together,* which contained "The Rapper." Two subsequent singles, "I Call My Baby Candy" and "What a Bummer," never even reached the Top Seventy. By then Iris had left the band to pursue a solo career. The group continued without him and recorded an LP in 1975 for Wooden Nickel Records, but with no success.

Iris worked in a Pittsburgh recording studio and then joined Wild Cherry, which had a platinum single in 1976 with "Play That Funky Music." With ex–Wild Cherry keyboardist Mark Avsec, Iris began composing. Around 1979 he recorded *Back on the Streets* for a Cleveland label, Midwest National. He then formed his own band. MCA later released the LP nationally, and in 1980 Iris' "Ah! Leah!" went to #29. In 1981 Iris, with his band the Cruisers, released *King Cool*. It produced two Top Forty hits, with "Love Is Like a Rock" and "My Girl." Iris still continues to tour and often performs "The Rapper" in his shows. Jimmy Ross, meanwhile, still performs on the oldies circuit as a member of the Skyliners ("Since I Don't Have You").

The Jam/Paul Weller/Style Council

The Jam, formed 1973, Woking, England (Paul Weller [b. May 25, 1958, Woking], gtr., voc.; Bruce Foxton [b. Sep. 1, 1955, Eng.], bass, voc.; Rick Buckler [b. Dec. 6, 1955, Woking], drums, voc.): 1977—*In the City* (Polydor); *This Is the Modern World* 1979—*All Mod Cons; Setting Sons* 1980—*Sound Affects* 1981—*Absolute Beginners* 1982—*The Gift; Dig the New Breed* 1983—*Snap!* 1991—*Greatest Hits*.
Style Council, formed 1983, England (Weller; + Mick Talbot, kybds.; + Dee C. Lee, voc.): 1983—*Introducing the Style Council* EP (Polydor) 1984—*My Ever Changing Moods* (Geffen) 1985—*Internationalists* 1986—*Home & Abroad* 1987—*The Cost of Loving* (Polydor) 1988—*Confessions of a Pop Group* 1989—*The Singular Adventures of the Style Council (Greatest Hits, vol. 1)*.
Paul Weller solo: 1992—*Paul Weller* (Go! Discs/London) 1994—*Wild Wood*.

First with the Jam, then with Style Council and as a solo artist, songwriter/guitarist Paul Weller mined a range of pop styles, from the Jam's punk-colored Mod and Merseybeat, through the Style Council's white soul, to his Nineties excursions into folk and psychedelia. While Weller and his groups have enjoyed immense popularity in the U.K., here in the U.S., Weller's work has found a small if devoted following at best.

Though they first came to prominence in London's 1976 punk-rock explosion, the Jam shared only a high-speed, stripped-down approach with its contemporaries. The trio's clothes, haircuts, and tunes reflected an obsession with the mid-Sixties Mod style, and some termed the band the new Who. Although Paul Weller's gruffly accented vocals and his earnest songs never broke through to American audiences, the Jam became consistent hitmakers in Britain.

The Jam: Rick Buckler, Paul Weller, Bruce Foxton

Weller, attending Sheerwater Secondary Modern School in Woking, had originally formed a folk duo with guitarist Steve Brooks in 1972. They later formed the Jam with guitarist Dave Waller and drummer Rick Buckler. Waller and Brooks quit in 1974, and bassist Bruce Foxton joined. With Weller's father as manager, they worked on Sixties R&B and Mod-rock covers and some originals; in 1976 they made a successful London debut at the 100 Club's first punk extravaganza. Their debut album was a British hit, yielding a Top Forty U.K. single in the title tune (from which the Sex Pistols later used a riff for their "Holiday in the Sun"). *Modern World* followed the same format, but the album was so harshly criticized by the British music press that the highly sensitive Weller nearly broke up the band. That year the Jam also released soul covers of "Back in My Arms Again" and "Sweet Soul Music."

Just before the well-received *All Mod Cons*, the group released three successful U.K. singles: "News of the World" (#27), a cover of the Kinks' "David Watts" (#25), and "Down in the Tube Station at Midnight" (#15), which revealed a new political commitment. "Tube Station," a protest against Britain's anti-immigrant "Paki-bashing" phenomenon, was banned by the BBC. *Setting Sons* was a decline-of-the-Empire/class-conflict concept album and yielded the British hit "Eton Rifles" (#3, 1979); it also included "Heatwave." *Sound Affects* was the Jam's biggest commercial success to date, with a #1 British hit in "Start!" and another minor U.K. hit in the acoustic ballad "That's Entertainment."

The Jam continued making inroads on the American market with *The Gift*, which yielded the Motownish "Town Called Malice." Both *Cons* and *Sons* went gold in

England. In 1980 Weller appeared on Peter Gabriel's third solo LP. In October 1982 he announced that the group was breaking up: "It really dawned on me how secure the situation was, the fact that we could go on for the next ten years making records, getting bigger and bigger. . . . That frightened me because I realized we were going to end up . . . like the rest of them." Nonetheless, the group's English fans never gave up, and their last single, "Beat Surrender," came on the chart there at #1 in 1982.

Weller quickly released his first post-Jam efforts as leader of Style Council in 1983. Officially only a duo with Weller and Mick Talbot, Style Council was a bold experiment that Weller later admitted was not entirely successful. Working with a number of guest artists, including Curtis Mayfield, Style Council was conceived as an American Sixties-style soul unit with a political point of view. Critics were mixed on how well that goal was met, but U.K. fans were unanimous in their support. Between 1983 and 1988, the group had seven U.K. Top Ten hits: "Speak Like a Child" and "Long Hot Summer" (1983), "My Ever Changing Moods," "Groovin' (You're the Best Thing)" b/w "Big Boss Groove," and "Shout to the Top" (1984), "Walls Come Tumbling Down!" (1985), and "It Didn't Matter" (1987). In contrast, here in the States, the Style Council placed only one Top Thirty single, "My Ever Changing Moods" (#29, 1984), and only the album of the same name made the Hot 100, at #56, also in 1984. Facing declining interest, the Style Council disbanded in 1990. In 1986 Weller married fellow Style Council member Dee C. Lee, and later cowrote and coproduced her group Slam Slam's 1991 album *Free Your Feelings*.

Weller reemerged with the Paul Weller Movement in early 1991. He has since released two critically well-received solo albums.

Elmore James
Born Elmore Brooks, January 27, 1918, Richland, Mississippi; died May 24, 1963, Chicago, Illinois
1966—*Blues Masters, vol. 1* (Blue Horizon)   1969—*Whose Muddy Shoes* (Chess)   1970—*Tough* (Blue Horizon)   1971—*The Sky Is Crying* (Sphere Sound); *I Need You*   1973—*Street Talkin'* (Muse)   1976—*Anthology of the Blues: Legend of Elmore James* (Kent); *Anthology of the Blues: Resurrection of Elmore James*   1982—*Red Hot Blues* (Quicksilver)   1989—*The Complete Fire and Enjoy Sessions Part I* (Collectables); *The Complete Fire and Enjoy Sessions Part II*; *The Complete Fire and Enjoy Sessions Part III*; *The Complete Fire and Enjoy Sessions Part IV*   1992—*The Complete Elmore James Story* (Capricorn); *Elmore James—King of the Slide Guitar: The Fire/Fury/Enjoy Recordings*   1994—*The Classic Early Recordings, 1951–1956* (Atomic Beat).

One of the most influential postwar urban-blues guitarists, Elmore James was the one Chicago bluesman perhaps most responsible for shaping the styles of slide-guitar playing that translated from blues to rock. His anthems, like "It Hurts Me Too," "Dust My Broom" (by Robert Johnson), "Shake Your Money Maker," and "The Sky Is Crying," have been covered by Eric Clapton, Fleetwood Mac, John Mayall, Savoy Brown, George Thorogood, and others. His influence can most directly be heard in the slide-guitar work of Duane Allman and the Rolling Stones' Brian Jones.

James began picking on a homemade lard-can guitar as a child. By the late Thirties he was working Mississippi taverns with blues legends Robert Johnson and Sonny Boy Williamson (Rice Miller). Between 1943 and 1945 he served in the navy. He began recording in 1951 for the Trumpet label in Jackson, Mississippi. He later moved to Chicago but continued to perform in the South and parts of the Midwest.

It was when he began recording in Chicago that James became one of the first and foremost modernizers of the Delta blues tradition. In 1963, while visiting the home of his cousin Homesick James, a bluesman with whom he'd performed in the Forties, Elmore James suffered a fatal heart attack. His stylistic influence can be traced to bluesmen like J. B. Hutto, B. B. King, Freddie King, Jimmy Reed, and Hound Dog Taylor, as well as rockers like Jimi Hendrix and Johnny Winter. His son, Elmore James Jr., is also a musician.

Etta James
Born Jamesetta Hawkins, January 25, 1938, Los Angeles, California
1961—*At Last* (Cadet); *Second Time Around*   1963—*Etta James*; *Top Ten*; *Rocks the House*   1965—*Queen of Soul*   1967—*Call My Name*   1968—*Tell Mama*   1970—*Sings Funk*   1971—*Losers Weepers*; *Peaches* (Chess)   1972—*Miss Etta James* (Crown); *Best of Etta James*; *Twist with Etta James*; *Golden Decade* (Chess)   1973—*Etta James*   1974—*Come a Little Closer*   1975—*Etta Is Better Than Evah!*   1978—*Deep in the Night* (Warner Bros.)   1986—*Blues in the Night, vol. 1: The Early Show* (Fantasy); *The Late Show*   1988—*The Sweetest Peaches: The Chess Years, vol. 1 (1960–66)* (Chess/MCA); *The Sweetest Peaches: The Chess Years, vol. 2 (1967–1975)*; *Seven Year Itch* (Island)   1989—*The Gospel Soul of Etta James* (Arrival)   1990—*Stickin' to My Guns* (Elektra)   1992—*The Right Time* (Elektra)   1994—*Mystery Lady: Songs of Billie Holiday* (Private Music); *Live from San Francisco* (On the Spot).

Soul singer Etta James survived a decade-long heroin addiction to forge a career that has seen her turn out well over a dozen hits and was still going strong with concert appearances into the Nineties. James was in her early teens and singing with a vocal trio called the Peaches when legendary R&B bandleader Johnny Otis discovered her. At Otis' Los Angeles home, he and Etta cowrote her first hit, "Roll with Me, Henry," an answer to Hank Ballard and the Midnighters' off-color "Work with Me, Annie." Under the title "The Wallflower," "Henry" became a #2 R&B hit in 1955. That year Georgia Gibbs had a #1 pop hit with a mild cover of the tune called "Dance with Me, Henry." Later, James' version was retitled "Dance with Me, Henry."

Through the mid-Fifties James became a mainstay of Otis' revue and scored another R&B hit with "Good Rockin' Daddy" (#12, 1955). In 1960 she moved from Modern to Chess Records' Argo subsidiary, and the R&B hits began coming again: "All I Could Do Was Cry" (#2), "My Dearest Darling" (#5), and a duet as Etta and Harvey (with Harvey Fuqua of Harvey and the Moonglows) entitled "If I Can't Have You" (#52 pop, #6 R&B). She also sang background vocals on Chuck Berry's "Almost Grown" and "Back in the U.S.A."

James continued making R&B hits through the early Sixties. In 1961 she had more Top Ten R&B hits with "At Last" (#2) and "Trust in Me" (#4), and in 1962 with "Something's Got a Hold on Me" (#4) and "Stop the Wedding" (#6). In 1963 she hit the pop chart with "Pushover" (#25 pop, #7 R&B), as well as "Pay Back" (#78), "Two Sides to Every Story" (#63), and "Would It Make Any Difference to You" (#64); 1964 brought "Baby, What You Want Me to Do?" (#82) and "Loving You More Every Day" (#65).

In the Sixties she developed a heroin addiction that lasted through 1974 and kept her much of the time in L.A.'s Tarzana Psychiatric Hospital. Still, she hit big with "Tell Mama" (#23 pop, #10 R&B, 1967), "Losers Weepers" (#26 R&B, 1970), and "I've Found a Love" (#31 R&B, 1972). Though she has not had any major hit records since, James has remained a popular concert performer. She played the Montreux Jazz Festival in 1977 and opened some dates for the Rolling Stones' 1978 U.S. tour. *Seven Year Itch* was produced by keyboardist Barry Beckett, house keyboardist at Alabama's legendary Muscle Shoals studio, where James had recorded such Sixties R&B hits as "I'd Rather Go Blind." She returned to Muscle Shoals to record *The Right Time*, which reunited her with Jerry Wexler (the longtime Aretha Franklin producer, who'd worked on James' *Deep in the Night* album) and included a duet with Steve Winwood; shortly after the album's release, James was inducted into the Rock and Roll Hall of Fame. She also won the 1994 Best Jazz Vocal Performance Grammy for *Mystery Lady*.

Rick James
Born James Johnson, February 1, 1948, Buffalo, New York

1978—*Come Get It* (Gordy)   1979—*Bustin' Out of L Seven; Fire It Up*   1980—*Garden of Love*   1981— *Street Songs*   1982—*Throwin' Down*   1983—*Cold Blooded*   1984—*Reflections*   1985—*Glow*   1986— *The Flag; Greatest Hits*   1988—*Wonderful* (Reprise)   1994—*Bustin' Out: The Very Best of Rick James* (Motown).

Singer, songwriter, keyboardist, and guitarist Rick James emerged in the late Seventies with an energetic blend of blatant come-ons and dance music he calls "punk funk." James, whose mother ran numbers and whose father deserted the family, attended and was expelled from five different schools before leaving Buffalo at 15 to join the U.S. Naval Reserves. Soon after, he went AWOL and ended up in Toronto, where, as Ricky Matthews, he formed and fronted a band called the Mynah Birds, which included Neil Young and Bruce Palmer (later of Buffalo Springfield) and Goldy McJohn (of Steppenwolf). They were signed to Motown and recorded, but nothing was released, and the group soon disbanded. James then worked as a sideman, playing bass with several groups through the Seventies, with only minimal success.

In 1978 James re-signed with Motown, this time as a songwriter and producer. That year his solo debut, *Come Get It,* sold a million copies, and "You and I" was a hit (#13 pop, #1 R&B). Subsequent singles—"Mary Jane" (#41 pop, #3 R&B, 1978), "Bustin' Out" (#6 pop, #8 R&B, 1979), "High on Your Love Suite" (#12 R&B, 1979), "Love Gun" (#13 R&B, 1979), "Big Time" (#17 R&B, 1980), "Give It to Me Baby" (#40 pop, #1 R&B, 1981), "Super Freak (Part 1)" (#16 pop, #3 R&B, 1981)—have propelled each of his releases, including the uncharacteristically ballad-laden *Garden of Love,* onto the pop chart.

James' stage image—long corn-rowed and beaded hair, elaborate sequined costumes and instruments— and his bass-heavy music have prompted comparisons with Sly Stone and George Clinton's Parliament/ Funkadelic. James has also produced Teena Marie, the Temptations ("Standing on the Top"), and Carl Carlton.

Beginning around 1983, James' career entered a slump, and although he remained a formidable presence on the R&B chart, none of his releases made the pop Top Thirty. His R&B Top Twenty singles include "Dance wit' Me (Part 1)" and "Hard to Get" (1982); "Cold Blooded" (#1 R&B), "U Bring the Freak Out," and a duet with Smokey Robinson, "Ebony Eyes" (1983); "17" (1984); "Can't Stop" and "Glow" (1985); and "Sweet Sexy Thing" (1986). In 1983 he unveiled the Mary Jane Girls, a trio of sexy singers he produced and wrote for. While he had a #7 hit with his "In My House" for the Mary Jane Girls and produced comedian Eddie Murphy's debut album and #2 hit single "Party All the Time," James' own releases began to fall by the wayside. A #1 R&B song featuring rapper Roxanne Shanté, "Loosey's Rap," failed to make the pop chart at all in 1988, but James' sound returned to the pop chart via M.C. Hammer's "U Can't Touch This," a 1990 megahit that featured "Super Freak" and prompted James to sue Hammer. After the case was settled out of court, James received cowriting credit.

James made the news again in 1991 after he and a female companion were arrested and charged with two instances of physically abusing women who refused to join them in group sex. James, who admitted he was a cocaine addict and that the attacks occurred during drug binges, was later convicted of assaulting one of the women. As part of a plea-bargain agreement with prosecutors, he pled no contest to the second charge and was sentenced to five years, four months in prison. In a press release issued to coincide with the release of *Bustin' Out,* James commented on the positive aspects of his drug rehabilitation and prison experience, admitting that he had been a drug addict for over 35 years. He also claimed to have written an autobiography, tentatively entitled *Memoirs of a Superfreak.*

Tommy James and the Shondells

Formed 1960, Niles, Michigan
Original Shondells unknown. Lineup in 1965:
Tommy James (b. Thomas Gregory Jackson, Apr. 29, 1947, Dayton, Ohio), voc.; Ronald Rosman (b. Feb. 28, 1945), kybds.; Michael Vale (b. July 17, 1949), bass; Vincent Pietropaoli, drums; George Magura, sax, bass, organ.
1965—(– Pietropaoli; – Magura; + Peter Lucia [b. Feb. 2, 1947], drums; + Eddie Gray [b. Feb. 27, 1948], gtr.) 1966—*Hanky Panky* (Roulette) 1968—*Mony Mony* 1969—*Crimson and Clover*; *The Best of Tommy James and the Shondells* 1989—*Anthology* (Rhino).
Tommy James solo: 1976—*In Touch* (Fantasy) 1977—*Midnight Rider* 1980—*Three Times in Love* (Millennium) 1991—*Tommy James: The Solo Years (1970–1981).*

Tommy James and the Shondells were one of the most consistently successful American pop groups of the late Sixties. Group leader and singer James taught himself to play guitar at age nine; four years later he formed the Shondells. The group played locally, and in 1963 recorded a Jeff Barry–Ellie Greenwich song, "Hanky Panky," as a favor for a local disc jockey. In late 1965 a Pittsburgh DJ began playing it, and more than 20,000 copies were sold within a few days. After its national release on Roulette in 1966, it hit #1 and sold a million copies, whereupon James formed a new group of Shondells.

Between 1966 and 1970, when the Shondells disbanded, the group amassed 13 other Top Forty hits, among them "I Think We're Alone Now" (#3, 1967), "Mi-

rage" (#10, 1967), "Mony Mony" (#3, 1968), "Crimson and Clover" (#1, 1969), "Sweet Cherry Wine" (#7, 1969), and "Crystal Blue Persuasion" (#2, 1969). With "Crimson and Clover" (the group's biggest seller at 5½ million) the Shondells' sound became more psychedelic than bubblegum; James began producing as well. After the group disbanded, James returned to his home in upstate New York for several months (partly to recuperate from a drug problem) before reemerging in 1970 to produce Alive and Kicking's hit version of his "Tighter, Tighter." He had a #4 hit the following year with "Draggin' the Line." The Shondells, meanwhile, materialized that year as a new group called Hog Heaven; it released one LP on Roulette.

James' subsequent singles failed to crack the Top Thirty, and solo LPs like *Midnight Rider* (produced by Jeff Barry) never hit. He returned to the chart in 1980, however, with "Three Times in Love" (#19). By that time it was estimated James had sold over 30 million records. Although the Eighties brought him no more hits, covers of Tommy James and the Shondells songs seemed to be everywhere. Joan Jett took "Crimson and Clover" to #7 in 1982, and in 1987 Billy Idol's version of "Mony Mony" replaced teen singer Tiffany's "I Think We're Alone Now" as the #1 record in the country.

The James Gang

Formed 1967, Cleveland, Ohio
Jim Fox, drums; Tom Kriss, bass; Glen Schwartz, gtr. 1969—(– Schwartz; + Joe Walsh [b. Nov. 20, 1947, Wichita, Kan.], gtr., voc.) *Yer Album* (ABC) (– Kriss; + Dale Peters, bass) 1970—*James Gang Rides Again* 1971—*Thirds*; *Live in Concert* (– Walsh; + Dominic Troiano, gtr.; + Roy Kenner, voc.) 1972—*Straight Shooter*; *Passin' Through* 1973—*Best of the James Gang* (– Troiano; + Tommy Bolin [b. 1951, Sioux City, Iowa; d. Dec. 4, 1976, Miami, Fla.], gtr.); *Bang* (Atco); *Gold Record* (ABC) 1974—*Miami* (Atco) (– Bolin; – Kenner; group disbands) 1975—(Group re-forms: Fox; Peters; + Richard Shack, gtr.; + Bubba Keith, gtr., voc.) *Newborn* 1976—*Jesse Come Home.*

The James Gang was a favorite American hard-rock band during the early Seventies. Founded by drummer Jim Fox, who had played in Cleveland bands since age 14, the group earned a word-of-mouth reputation throughout the Midwest. Glen Schwartz (who left to join Pacific Gas and Electric) was replaced by future Eagle Joe Walsh [see entry], the group's best musician and star attraction. Pete Townshend, a friend of the Gang, arranged for it to open for the Who in Europe in 1971.

Despite a career-long lack of hit singles, the trio's second, third, and fourth LPs all went gold, and it continued to be a major concert draw around the world for a while after Walsh's departure to form Barnstorm. His replacement, Dominic Troiano, left in 1973 to join the

Guess Who, and Walsh recommended Tommy Bolin for the part. But Bolin (who had worked with Billy Cobham) contributed to only two LPs—*Miami* and *Bang* (originally titled *James Gang Bang*)—before joining Deep Purple. Vocalist Roy Kenner soon left as well, and in 1974 the group temporarily disbanded, only to re-form a year later with Bubba Keith and Richard Shack. The James Gang never recaptured its early momentum and disbanded for good in 1976.

Jan and Dean

Jan Berry, born April 3, 1941, Los Angeles, California; Dean Torrence, born March 10, 1941, Los Angeles
1963—*Jan and Dean Take Linda Surfin'* (Liberty); *Surf City and Other Swingin' Cities* 1963—*Drag City* 1964—*The Little Old Lady from Pasadena* 1965—*Golden Hits, vol. 2*; *Command Performance/Live in Person* 1966—*Golden Hits, vol. 3* 1971—*Legendary Masters* (United Artists) 1974—*Gotta Take That One Last Ride* 1982—*One Summer Night/Live* (Rhino).

Between their 1958 debut single, "Jennie Lee," and Jan Berry's near-fatal car crash in April 1966, Jan and Dean were the premier surf music duo, charting 13 Top Thirty singles and selling over ten million records worldwide.

The two were friends and football teammates at Emerson Junior High in Los Angeles. They formed a group, the Barons, with drummer Sandy Nelson ("Teen Beat," "Let There Be Drums") and future Beach Boy Bruce Johnston. With a singer named Arnie Ginsburg, they recorded a #8 hit for Arwin Records entitled "Jennie Lee," written about a local stripper. Torrence, who sang lead, was serving in the National Guard when the contracts were signed, so the single was credited to Jan and Arnie.

Once Torrence returned, he and Berry resumed their partnership, Ginsburg joined the army, and Arwin dropped them. Herb Alpert and Lou Adler became their managers and produced "Baby Talk" (#10, 1959) for their small Dore label. Five Top 100 entries on the Dore and Challenge labels preceded the pair's signing with Liberty in 1961. After three minor hits, in 1963 they recorded their only #1, "Surf City," a song cowritten by their friend Brian Wilson. The Beach Boys leader also contributed vocals and worked with Jan and Dean on their debut LP, *Jan and Dean Take Linda Surfin'*; Torrence, uncredited, later sang lead on the Beach Boys' 1996 smash "Barbara Ann." The Beach Boys and Jan and Dean often appeared on each other's records until their record companies objected.

Berry did the bulk of the duo's songwriting, including the soundtrack for a 1964 Fabian beach movie entitled *Ride the Wild Surf*. The pair hosted *The T.A.M.I. Show* that same year. Both continued their educations full-time (Torrence was a premed and then an architecture student at UCLA; Berry an art and design student at USC) until they were convinced of their musical success. Their hits included "Heart and Soul" (#25, 1961), "Linda" (#28, 1963), "Honolulu Lulu" (#11, 1963), "Drag City" (#10, 1964), "Dead Man's Curve" (#8, 1964), "The Little Old Lady (from Pasadena)" (#3, 1964), "Ride the Wild Surf" (#16, 1964), "Sidewalk Surfin'" (#25, 1964), "You Really Know How to Hurt a Guy" (#27, 1965), "I Found a Girl" (#30, 1965), and "Popsicle" (#21, 1966).

But by the mid-Sixties, their friendship had become strained to the point where they considered breaking up. In April 12, 1966, Berry crashed his Corvette into a parked truck at 65 m.p.h. on L.A.'s Whittier Boulevard. His three passengers were killed, and he sustained brain damage so severe that it wasn't until 1973 that he was able to remember an entire song lyric. He is still partially paralyzed and suffers speech difficulties. During the years of recovery, he regularly recorded demos for Lou Adler as therapy. Meanwhile, Torrence recorded a solo album, *Save for a Rainy Day* (which Berry was furious about), and became head of Kitty Hawk Graphics in Hollywood. Between then and 1981 he won design awards (and one Grammy) for his album covers (among his clients were the Nitty Gritty Dirt Band, the Beach Boys, Nilsson, Steve Martin, Linda Ronstadt, and of course, Jan and Dean). Berry also recorded on his own, issuing "Mother Earth" and "Don't You Just Know It" in 1972 on his old friend Lou Adler's Ode label.

The pair made a premature and unsuccessful comeback appearance in 1973, but by 1977 they were again performing live on occasion. A television movie account of their lives entitled *Dead Man's Curve* aired in 1978 on ABC-TV and renewed interest in Jan and Dean. In 1982 Jan and Dean released *One Summer Night—Live*. They appeared on the *Back to the Beach* soundtrack. The duo still makes limited public appearances.

Jane's Addiction/Porno for Pyros

Formed 1986, Los Angeles, California
Perry Farrell (b. Perry Bernstein, Mar. 29, 1959, Queens, N.Y.), voc.; Eric Avery (b. Apr. 25, 1965, Los Angeles), bass; David Navarro (b. June 6, 1967, Santa Monica, Calif.), gtr.; Steve Perkins (b. Sep. 13, 1967, Los Angeles), drums.
1987—*Jane's Addiction* (Triple X) 1988—*Nothing's Shocking* (Warner Bros.) 1990—*Ritual de lo Habitual*.
Porno for Pyros, formed 1992, Los Angeles (Farrell; Perkins; + Peter DiStefano [b. Jul. 10, 1965, Los Angeles], gtr.; Martyn Le Noble [b. Apr. 14, 1969, Vlaardingen, Netherlands], bass): 1993—*Porno for Pyros* (Warner Bros.).

Led by the flamboyant, outspoken Perry Farrell, Jane's Addiction blended elements of art rock, punk, and metal into an ambitious musical juxtaposition of sublime beauty and utter decadence. The group broke up during its peak of popularity in 1991, just after its appearances on the first Lollapalooza tour (which Farrell organized). Farrell continued chasing his muse in Porno for Pyros.

Perry Bernstein spent the early part of his life working for his jeweler father in New York City's diamond district. When he was still a child, his mother committed suicide. (Farrell alluded to this later, on "Then She Did . . ." from *Ritual de lo Habitual,* singing to a friend who has died of an overdose, "Will you say hello to my ma? . . . She was an artist, just as you were.") After her death, the Bernsteins moved to Woodmere, Long Island, and then to Miami.

Bernstein attended college briefly in Oceanside, California, but quit after having a nervous breakdown. He then started lip synching and doing exotic dancing in a Newport Beach nightclub, taking the stage name Perry Farrell by adopting his brother's first name as his last (making a pun on *peripheral*). In 1981 he started the gothlike Psi Com, which released an indie-label EP before breaking up in 1985.

A year later Farrell formed Jane's Addiction, which he named after a prostitute friend who introduced him to bandmates Eric Avery and David Navarro. Farrell, reputedly a control freak, became notorious in L.A.'s arty rock scene. Sporting day-glo girdles or black vinyl bodysuits, heavy mascara, and neon dreadlocks, he stalked stages singing in his high, mannered voice while the members of his band churned out a foreboding sound often compared to Led Zeppelin's. After the band released a self-titled live album on L.A.'s Triple X Records, a major-label bidding war ensued. Warner Bros. won, putting out *Nothing's Shocking* the following year.

In 1990, on the strength of a catchy single and video ("Been Caught Stealing"), *Ritual de lo Habitual* skyrocketed up the charts, peaking at #19. The album made the news when some record chains refused to carry it because of its cover art (it featured Farrell's own nude sculptures). At the band's request, Warners issued the album to some stores in a plain white cover with only the First Amendment printed on it.

Farrell remained in the limelight throughout 1991 when he brought his idea of an alternative-rock traveling circus to life with Lollapalooza, was busted on drug charges in Santa Monica, and brought Jane's Addiction to a close. In 1992 he and drummer Perkins formed Porno for Pyros, which put out its self-titled debut album to cool reception the following year. Navarro and Avery formed the short-lived Deconstruction in 1993 (and released a self-titled album in 1994) before Navarro left to join the Red Hot Chili Peppers.

Japan
Formed 1974, London, England
David Sylvian (b. David Batt, Feb. 23, 1958, London), voc., gtr.; **Steve Jansen (b. Steve Batt, Dec. 1, 1959, London), drums; Richard Barbieri (b. Nov. 30, 1958), kybds.; Mick Karn (b. Anthony Michaelides, July 24, 1958, London), sax; Rob Dean, gtr.**
1978—Adolescent Sex (Hansa, Ger.); Obscure Alternatives 1979—Quiet Life 1980—Gentlemen Take Polaroids (Virgin) 1981—(– Dean) Tin Drum; Assemblage (Hansa, Ger.) 1983—Oil on Canvas (Virgin) 1984—Exorcising Ghosts 1989—A Souvenir from Japan (Hansa, Ger.).
Mick Karn solo: 1982—Titles (Virgin) 1987—Dreams of Reason Produce Monsters 1993—Bestial Cluster (CMP).
Rain Tree Crow: 1991—Rain Tree Crow (Virgin).
David Sylvian solo: 1984—Brilliant Trees (Virgin) 1985—Alchemy—An Index of Possibilities (Virgin, U.K.) 1986—Gone to Earth (Virgin) 1987—Secrets of the Beehive 1988—Plight & Premonition (with Holger Czukay) (Venture) 1989—Weatherbox (Virgin); Flux + Mutability (with Czukay) (Venture) 1993—The First Day (with Robert Fripp) (Virgin).

Precursors of England's short-lived New Romantic movement, London's Japan mixed glam theatrics and synthesizer pop with influences as diverse as Erik Satie and Motown to achieve success in the Far East, notoriety at home, and indifference in the United States.

With his brother Steve on drums, David Sylvian led the quartet, which signed with German label Ariola-Hansa in 1977. Sylvian's Bryan Ferry–style vocals and the band's pop-star glamour marked them as an alternative to punk; their following was largest among Japanese listeners. With industry legend Simon Napier Bell as manager, they switched to Virgin, and their English audience grew. Sylvian began collaborating with Yellow Magic Orchestra's Ryuichi Sakamoto [see entry]; their albums continued to reflect a sometimes baffling stylistic variety, although they gained U.K. Top Twenty hits with "Quiet Life," "Ghosts," and a cover of Smokey Robinson's "I Second That Emotion."

Tension between Sylvian and bassist Mick Karn caused Japan's breakup in 1982, but its principal members continued recording. Karn alternated between music and sculpture, collaborations, session work (Midge Ure, Gary Numan, Robert Palmer), and releasing solo albums before Japan's 1991 reunion (this time, they dubbed themselves Rain Tree Crow). Sylvian's sound departed further from Japan's; either solo or with Robert Fripp or Can alumnus Holger Czukay, his work verged on New Age ambience. He also eschewed the theatricality that was his former band's trademark.

Jason and the Scorchers
Formed 1981, Nashville, Tennessee
Jason Ringenberg (b. Nov. 22, 1958, Kewanee, Ill.), voc., gtr., harmonica; Warner Hodges (b. June 4,

1959, Wurtzburg, Ger.), gtr., voc.; Jeff Johnson
(b. Dec. 31, 1959, Nashville), bass; Perry Baggs
(b. Mar. 22, 1962, Nashville), drums, voc.
1982—*Reckless Country Soul* EP (Praxis)   1983—
Fervor EP   1985—*Lost & Found* (EMI America)
1986—*Still Standing* (+ Andy York [b. July 28, 1961,
Wichita, Kan.], gtr.; + Ken Fox [b. Feb. 16, 1961,
Toronto, Ont., Can.], bass)   1989—*Thunder and Fire*
(A&M)   1992—*Essential Jason and the Scorchers,
vol. 1: Are You Ready for the Country* (EMI)   1995—
A Blazing Grace (Mammoth).
Jason Ringenberg solo: 1992—*One Foot in the
Honky Tonk* (Liberty).

Jason and the Scorchers was one of the hottest live acts
among the mid-Eighties cow-punk bands. Unlike the
majority of groups on the updated country-rock scene,
however, Jason and company actually came from
Nashville, not the West Coast.

Raised on his parents' Sheffield, Illinois, hog farm,
Jason Ringenberg sang and played guitar in a number of
bluegrass, folk, and country bands during his teens. In
1981 he moved to Nashville, where he met his fellow
Scorchers. The following year the group recorded its first
EP as Jason and the Nashville Scorchers, and toured
with R.E.M. While on the road, Ringenberg and R.E.M.
singer Michael Stipe collaborated on *Fervor's* "Both
Sides of the Line," and Stipe sang backup vocals on the
EP's "Hot Nights in Georgia." The song that most identi-
fied the Scorchers' oeuvre, perhaps, was *Fervor's*
Ramones-meets-Southern-rock update of Bob Dylan's
"Absolutely Sweet Marie."

Jason and the Scorchers' subsequent albums moved
closer to country rock, with Ringenberg's ballads becoming more heartfelt and Hodges' guitar work more
Stoneslike. Two later cover songs that further crystallized
the band's sound were "Lost Highway" (from *Lost &
Found*) and "19th Nervous Breakdown" (*Still Standing*).
The band's guitar attack was beefed up for *Thunder and
Fire* (1989) with the addition of Andy York. A grueling
1990 U.S. tour opening for Dylan hammered the nail in
the band's coffin, however. Hodges, York, and Fox joined
Del Lord Eric Ambel's Roscoe's Gang, and Ringenberg
attempted a career as a solo country artist, releasing *One
Foot in the Honky Tonk*. After EMI issued *Essential
Jason and the Scorchers, vol. 1,* consisting of the out-of-
print *Fervor* and *Lost & Found,* along with some B-sides,
the original members regrouped and began performing
again. In 1994 the band returned to the studio to record
an album, *A Blazing Grace*, released the next year.

Jay and the Americans
Formed 1961, Brooklyn, New York
**John "Jay" Traynor, lead voc.; Kenny Vance
(b. Kenny Rosenberg, Dec. 9. 1943), voc.; Sandy
Deane (b. Sandy Yaguda, Jan. 30, 1943), voc.; Howie**
Kane (b. Howard Kirshenbaum, June 6, 1942), voc.
1962—(+ Marty Sanders [b. Feb. 28, 1941], voc.;
– Traynor; + Jay Black [b. David Blatt, Nov. 2, 1941],
lead voc.)   1986—*All-Time Greatest Hits* (Rhino).

Jay and the Americans were a clean-cut vocal group
whose Sixties hits included four Top Ten entries. The
group's first hit, the Leiber and Stoller–produced "She
Cried" (#5, 1962), featured the original Jay, John Traynor,
on lead vocals. That year, he left the group, and guitarist
Marty Sanders invited his songwriting partner David
Blatt to audition. Blatt adopted the moniker Jay, and the
reconstituted group had its first hit with "Only in America" (#25, 1963). The song was originally recorded by the
Drifters, but when the group's label decided not to release it, their vocals were erased, and Jay and the Amer-
icans' were added to the original tracks. The following
year Jay and the Americans hit #3 with "Come a Little Bit
Closer," and in 1965 the grandiose "Cara Mia" hit #4.
This, their best-remembered hit, was revived in the
Netherlands in 1980 and reached #1.

In 1965 they released an uptempo cover of "Some
Enchanted Evening" (#13) and Neil Diamond's first hit as
a songwriter, "Sunday and Me" (#18). It was not until
1969 that they again hit the Top Ten, this time with the
million-selling cover of the Drifters' 1960 hit "This Magic
Moment" (#6).

The group stopped recording in 1970 after hitting
the Top Twenty for the last time with "Walking in the
Rain" (#19). A contractual dispute with United Artists
over publishing rights kept it from recording for a number of years. Jay Black kept the name alive by touring
throughout the Seventies and into the Eighties with rock
nostalgia shows. As a solo artist he recorded an album in
1975 and later had a minor European hit with "Love Is in
the Air" (John Paul Young covered it in the U.S.). Future
Steely Dan founders Donald Fagen and Walter Becker
were part of the group's backup band in the early Seventies, and in 1970 Kenny Vance produced their soundtrack
album for *You Got to Walk It Like You Talk It.* Vance also
worked as a solo artist, recording his debut album in
1975. Sanders pursued writing, and Deane went into producing. "Looking for an Echo," a nostalgic tribute to doo-
wop, was recorded with an ad hoc group that included
several Americans and ex-Rascal Eddie Brigati.

Jazz
Jazz has long been considered by many to be America's
most important and original contribution to world culture. It is music that depends primarily on improvisation
and reflects a long tradition of changing ideas of structure, freedom, and swing. The first music known as jazz
was the New Orleans style (later known as Dixieland), in
which a small group would improvise collectively on a
well-known tune. No one in particular carried melody or
harmony, but everyone was aware of them. In the Twen-

ties trumpeter Louis Armstrong and others began to separate soloists from accompaniment, each permitted different degrees of freedom—an idea that ruled jazz for the next few decades, through the harmonic and rhythmic revolutions of the big bands of the Thirties swing era (Duke Ellington, Fletcher Henderson, Benny Goodman), be-bop in the late Forties (Charlie Parker, Dizzy Gillespie), and "cool" and hard bop and modal playing in the Fifties (Miles Davis, Thelonius Monk).

In the Sixties John Coltrane began to work on a fusion of Eastern and Western improvisation, while Ornette Coleman, Cecil Taylor, and others reconsidered collective improvisation in the light of new ideas about rhythm and harmonic freedom. Rockers toyed with jazz in the late Sixties, and Miles Davis tried a version of jazz rock, later simply termed "fusion," that spawned such Seventies practitioners as Weather Report, the Mahavishnu Orchestra, Return to Forever, and Al DiMeola. Pure jazz, meanwhile, grew ever more eclectic in terms of structure and style, with bands like the Art Ensemble of Chicago and Air drawing on music from ragtime to Indian raga.

In the Eighties and early Nineties such "young lions" as brothers Wynton and Branford Marsalis and pianist/vocalist Harry Connick Jr. were highly successful with neotraditional jazz, and with the advent of CDs, major reissue projects at record labels made older jazz accessible to a newer audience. Jazz continued to cross-pollinate with other forms: New York "punk" avant-gardists like the Lounge Lizards and John Zorn drew inspiration and attitude from rock and film scores; more sophisticated New Age listeners found the meditative works of jazz pianists such as Keith Jarrett palatable; world music incorporated jazz elements; and mainstream pop stars such as Joni Mitchell and Sting sometimes recorded with jazz players. Miles Davis began an alliance with jazz and rap that found expression later in albums by Guru, Digable Planets, and others.

Jazz Crusaders: See the Crusaders

Jazzy Jeff and the Fresh Prince

Formed 1986, Philadelphia, Pennsylvania
Fresh Prince (b. Willard Smith, Sep. 25, 1969, Philadelphia), voc.; Jazzy Jeff (b. Jeff Townes, Jan. 22, 1965, Philadelphia), DJ.
1987—*Rock the House* (Jive/RCA) 1988—*He's the D.J., I'm the Rapper* 1989—*And in This Corner . . .* 1991—*Homebase* 1993—*Code Red*.

With his clean-cut image and playful, lighthearted approach to rapping, Will "Fresh Prince" Smith had little trouble winning over a multiracial mainstream audience—or parlaying that mass appeal into a successful TV sitcom *The Fresh Prince of Bel-Air*.

Townes, who began spinning records at parties when he was only ten, met Smith in 1986. The two joined forces immediately, although their professional future was soon threatened, when Smith graduated high school with a full scholarship to attend the prestigious Massachusetts Institute of Technology. The rapper chose a recording career over MIT, though, and he and Townes released their debut album, *Rock the House*, in 1987. Their breakthrough came the following year, with the double LP *He's the D.J., I'm the Rapper*, one of the first rap albums to go double platinum. This sophomore effort contained the #12 pop (#10 R&B) hit "Parents Just Don't Understand," a teenager's lament about shopping with Mom.

The duo had its biggest hit with "Summertime," a wistful ode to good times in the 'hood that went to #4. It was the first single from *Homebase*, which was released in 1991—the year after the *Fresh Prince* TV show premiered, casting Smith as a Philadelphia homeboy sent to live with wealthy Bel-Air relatives. That show's popularity, as well as Smith's 1993 feature role in the film version of John Guare's dramatic play *Six Degrees of Separation*, seemed to threaten the rapper's musical partnership with Townes. The duo released the commercially disappointing *Code Red* (#64) in 1993. In 1995 Smith teamed with Martin Lawrence in the cop/buddy movie *Bad Boys*.

Blind Lemon Jefferson

Born circa July 1897, Couchman, Texas; died circa December 1930, Chicago, Illinois
1968—*Master of the Blues, vol. 1* (Biograph) 1969—*Blind Lemon Jefferson 1926–1929* 1971—*Master of the Blues, vol. 2* 1971—*Black Snake Moan* (Milestone) 1974—*Blind Lemon Jefferson* 1988—*King of the Country Blues* (Yazoo).

One of the first country bluesmen of the Twenties, perhaps the most influential, and surely the most commercially popular, singer/guitarist Blind Lemon Jefferson (Lemon was his given first name) influenced other bluesmen like Lightnin' Hopkins, Big Joe Williams, Robert Pete Williams, T-Bone Walker, and B. B. King.

Blind from birth, Jefferson began performing in his early teens in streets and at parties and picnics. He was as much a "songster"—with a repertoire spanning blues, shouts, moans, field hollers, breakdowns, ballads, religious hymns, prison songs, and work songs—as a bluesman. As a teenager he worked throughout Texas, then hoboed through the South and Southwest, from Georgia to St. Louis, into the early Twenties, although Dallas was always his home base. Around 1925 he was signed to Paramount Records, for which he recorded his own distinctive, haunting country blues under his own name and religious songs under the pseudonym Deacon L. J.

Bates. His blues recordings were among the best-selling "race" records of the 1925–30 era.

Jefferson reportedly suffered a heart attack in 1930 in Chicago and was left on the streets to die of exposure just before Christmas. His best-remembered tunes include "Black Snake Moan," "See That My Grave Is Kept Clean," "Long Lonesome Blues," and "Booger Rooger Blues," in which he coined the term "booger rooger" (for a wild party), which later became "boogie-woogie." A 1970 biography, *Blind Lemon Jefferson,* by Bob Groom, was published by Blues World.

The Jefferson Airplane/Jefferson Starship/Starship

Jefferson Airplane, formed early 1965, San Francisco, California (Marty Balin [b. Martyn Jerel Buchwald, Jan. 30, 1943, Cincinnati, Ohio], voc.; Paul Kantner [b. Mar. 12, 1941, San Francisco], gtr., voc.; Jorma Kaukonen [b. Dec. 23, 1940, Washington, D.C.], gtr., voc.; Signe Anderson [b. Sep. 15, 1941, Seattle, Wash.], voc.; Bob Harvey, bass; Skip Spence [b. Apr. 18, 1946, Ontario, Can.], drums): 1965— (– Harvey; + Jack Casady [b. Apr. 13, 1944, Washington, D.C.], bass) 1966—*Jefferson Airplane Takes Off* (RCA) (– Anderson; + Grace Slick [b. Grace Barnett Wing, Oct. 30, 1939, Chicago, Ill.], kybds., voc.; – Spence; + Spencer Dryden [b. Apr. 7, 1943, New York City, N.Y.], drums) 1967—*Surrealistic Pillow; After Bathing at Baxter's* 1968— *Crown of Creation* 1969—*Bless Its Pointed Little Head; Volunteers* 1970—*The Worst of the Jefferson Airplane* (– Dryden; + Joey Covington, drums) 1971—(– Balin; + Papa John Creach [b. May 28, 1917, Beaver Falls, Pa.; d. Feb. 22, 1994, Los Angeles, Calif.], fiddle) *Bark* (Grunt) 1972—(– Covington; + John Barbata, drums) *Long John Silver* (+ David Freiberg [b. Aug. 24, 1938, Boston, Mass.], voc., bass, gtr., kybds.; – Kaukonen; – Casady) 1973—*Thirty Seconds over Winterland* 1974— *Early Flight* 1977—*Flight Log* 1987—*2400 Fulton Street—An Anthology* (RCA) 1990—*White Rabbit and Other Hits* 1992—*Jefferson Airplane Loves You.* As Jefferson Starship: 1974—(Slick; Barbata; Freiberg; Creach; Kantner; + Peter Kangaroo [b. Peter Kaukonen], bass; + Craig Chaquico [b. Sep. 26, 1954, Sacramento, Calif.], gtr.; – P. Kaukonen; + Pete Sears [b. Eng.], bass) *Dragon Fly* 1975— (+ Balin) *Red Octopus* (– Creach) 1976—*Spitfire* 1978—*Earth* (– Slick; – Balin) 1979—*Jefferson Starship Gold* (+ Mickey Thomas [b. Cairo, Ga.], voc.; – Barbata; + Aynsley Dunbar [b. Jan. 10, 1946, Liverpool, Eng.], drums); *Freedom at Point Zero* 1981—(+ Slick) *Modern Times* 1982—*Winds of Change* (– Dunbar; + Don Baldwin, drums) 1984—

Jefferson Airplane: Paul Kantner, Grace Slick, Spencer Dryden, Marty Balin, Jorma Kaukonen, Jack Casady

Nuclear Furniture (– Kantner; – Freiberg). As Starship: 1985—*Knee Deep in the Hoopla* (– Sears) 1987—*No Protection* (Grunt) 1988— (– Slick) 1989—*Love Among the Cannibals* (RCA) 1990—(+ Brett Bloomfield, bass; + Mark Morgan, kybds.) (group disbands) 1991—*Greatest Hits (Ten Years and Change, 1979–1991)* (RCA). Jefferson Airplane re-forms: 1989—(The 1966–74 lineup: Kantner; Balin; Slick; Casady; Kaukonen) *Jefferson Airplane* (Epic). As Jefferson Starship ("the Next Generation"): 1992—(Kantner; Casady; Creach; + Tim Gorman, kybds., voc.; + Prairie Prince [b. May 7, 1950, Charlotte, N.C.], drums, perc.; + Mark "Slick" Aguilar, gtr., voc.; + Darby Gould [b. ca. 1965], voc.) 1994— (+ Balin; – Creach) 1995—(+ Slick) *Deep Space/Virgin Sky* (Intersound). Paul Kantner solo: 1970—*Blows Against the Empire* (credited to Paul Kantner/Jefferson Starship) (RCA) 1983—*The Planet Earth Rock and Roll Orchestra.* Paul Kantner and Grace Slick: 1971—*Sunfighter* (Grunt). Kantner, Slick, David Freiberg: 1973—*Baron Von Tollbooth and the Chrome Nun* (Grunt). Grace Slick solo: 1974—*Manhole* (Grunt) 1980— *Dreams* (RCA) 1981—*Welcome to the Wrecking Ball* 1984—*Software.* Grace Slick and the Great Society: 1970—*Collector's Item from the San Francisco Scene* (Columbia). Marty Balin solo: 1973—*Bodacious DF* (RCA) 1980—*Rock Justice* (EMI) 1981—*Balin* 1983— *Lucky* 1990—*Balince—A Collection* (Rhino) 1991—*Better Generation* (GWE).

Mickey Thomas solo: 1971—*As Long As You Love Me* (MCA) 1981—*Alive Alone* (Elektra).
Craig Chaquico solo: 1993—*Acoustic Highway* (Higher Octave) 1994—*Acoustic Planet.*
Papa John Creach solo: 1971—*Papa John Creach* (Grunt) 1972—*Filthy* 1974—*Playing My Fiddle for You* (with Zulu) 1975—*I'm the Fiddle Man* (with Midnight Sun) (Buddah) 1976—*Rock Father* 1992—*Papa Blues* (Bee Bump).
KBC Band: formed 1985 (Kantner; Balin; Jack Casady; + Mark "Slick" Aguilar, gtr.; + Barry Lowenthal, drums; + Tim Gorman, kybds., voc.; + Keith Crossan, sax.): 1986—*KBC Band* (Arista).

Through myriad personnel shifts, including the 1984 departure of founder/guiding light Paul Kantner, several name changes, and its metamorphosis from a group of hippie revolutionaries to MOR pop powerhouse—and back again—the Jefferson Airplane/Starship franchise proved one of the most durable and volatile in rock.

At the start, the Jefferson Airplane not only epitomized the burgeoning Haight-Ashbury culture but also provided its soundtrack. The Airplane established a psychedelic unity with communal vocal harmonies and a synthesis of elements from folk, pop, jazz, blues, and rock. That band got started in 1965 when Marty Balin, formerly with the acoustic group the Town Criers, met Paul Kantner at the Drinking Gourd, a San Francisco club. They were first a folk-rock group, rounded out by Jorma Kaukonen, Skip Spence, Signe Anderson, and Bob Harvey, though Harvey was soon replaced by Jack Casady. Their first major show was on August 13, christening the Matrix Club, which later became the outlet for new S.F. bands. RCA signed them late in the year, and *Jefferson Airplane Takes Off* came out in September 1966 and went gold.

Just before the LP came out, in the summer of 1966, Signe Anderson left to have a baby and was replaced by former model Grace Slick. Slick had been a member of the Great Society, a group formed in 1965. The Great Society, which included Grace's husband at the time, Jerry Slick, and her brother-in-law Darby, had completed two LPs for Columbia, which weren't released until after Slick became a star with the Airplane. Spence left the Airplane to form Moby Grape and was replaced by a former jazz drummer, Spencer Dryden, completing the Airplane's most inventive lineup.

Slick's vocals were stronger and more expressive than Anderson's; she later claimed that she always tried to imitate the yowl of the lead guitar. She contributed two former Great Society songs to *Surrealistic Pillow*— "Somebody to Love" (by Grace, Darby, and Jerry Slick) and Darby's "White Rabbit" (which was banned in some areas as a drug song)—both of which became Top Ten singles, and the album (#3, 1967) sold half a million

copies. *After Bathing at Baxter's* included a nine-minute psychedelic jam-collage, "Spayre Change," and occasioned the group's first battle with RCA over obscene language: The word "shit" was deleted from the lyric sheet. *Baxter's* had no hit singles and didn't sell well, but the Airplane recouped with the gold *Crown of Creation* (#6, 1968), which included Slick's "Lather" and David Crosby's "Triad," a song about a *ménage à trois* that had been rejected by Crosby's current group, the Byrds.

The band's ego conflicts were already beginning, however, as Slick stole media attention from Balin (the band's founder) and the songwriting became increasingly divergent. Live, Slick and Balin traded vocals in battles that became increasingly feverish, and the volatile sound of the band in concert was captured on *Bless Its Pointed Little Head.* By the time the sextet recorded 1969's *Volunteers,* the Airplane's contract allowed it total "artistic control," which meant that the "Up against the wall, motherfuckers" chorus of "We Can Be Together" appeared intact. The Airplane performed at the Woodstock and Altamont festivals, but then had its second major shakeup. Dryden left in 1970 to join the New Riders of the Purple Sage (replaced by Joey Covington), and the band stopped touring when Slick became pregnant by Kantner. Anxious to perform, Kaukonen and Casady formed Hot Tuna (originally Hot Shit), which later seceded from the Airplane [see entry], although, like most band members, they would return.

In the meantime, Kantner and the housebound Slick recorded *Blows Against the Empire.* Billed as Paul Kantner and Jefferson Starship (the debut of the name), the LP featured Jerry Garcia, David Crosby, Graham Nash, and other friends. It became the first musical work nominated for the science-fiction writers' Hugo Award. At the same time, a greatest-hits package entitled *The Worst of the Jefferson Airplane* was released. On January 25, 1971, Slick and Kantner's baby girl, China, was born; and that spring, Balin, who had nothing to do with *Blows* and contributed only one cowritten composition to *Volunteers,* left. He formed a short-lived band, Bodacious D.F.

In August the Airplane formed their own label, Grunt, distributed by RCA. The band's reunited effort, *Bark* (#11, 1971), saw them with Covington and all of Hot Tuna, including violinist Papa John Creach, who had first performed with Hot Tuna at a Winterland show in 1970. The band had grown apart, though, and Hot Tuna and Kantner-Slick were each writing for their own offshoot projects. In December 1971 Slick and Kantner released *Sunfighter* under both their names, with baby China as cover girl. (China grew up to become an MTV VJ and an actor.)

In July 1972 this version of the Airplane recorded its last studio LP, *Long John Silver* (#20), with some drumming from ex-Turtle John Barbata. In August 1972 at a free concert in New York's Central Park, the band introduced ex–Quicksilver Messenger Service bassist, keyboardist, and vocalist David Freiberg to the ranks. The Airplane unofficially retired at that point. By that September Casady and Kaukonen had decided to go full-time with Hot Tuna, though they appeared on the live LP *Thirty Seconds over Winterland,* which came out in April 1973. Slick, Kantner, and Freiberg recorded *Baron Von Tollbooth and the Chrome Nun,* one of the band's least popular efforts. Slick's equally disappointing solo debut, *Manhole,* appeared in January 1974. Her drinking problem had become serious, and the band was hoping that the Tuna players would return. They did not.

Finally in February 1974, Slick and Kantner formed the Jefferson Starship (no strict relation to the group on *Blows*), with Freiberg, Creach, Barbata, and 19-year-old lead guitarist Craig Chaquico. Chaquico had played with the Grunt band Steelwind with his high school English teacher Jack Traylor and on Slick and Kantner collaborative LPs beginning with *Sunfighter.* The new group also included Peter Kangaroo (Jorma's brother), though in June he was replaced by Pete Sears, a British sessionman who played on Rod Stewart's records and had been a member of Copperhead. On *Dragon Fly* (#11, 1974), Balin made a guest appearance on his and Kantner's song "Caroline." The LP went gold.

Balin tentatively rejoined the band in January 1975, and the group's next big breakthrough came with *Red Octopus,* their first #1 LP, hitting that position several times during the year and selling four million copies. Balin's ballad "Miracles" was a #3 single. They were more popular than ever, but in Slick's opinion the music had become bland and corporate, and her rivalry with Balin had not diminished. Their followup LP, 1976's *Spitfire,* went #3 and platinum, their first album to do so. But after the successful *Earth* (also platinum) in 1978, both Slick and Balin left.

By then Slick and Kantner's romance had ended; in November 1976, she married the band's 24-year-old lighting director, Skip Johnson. Slick's alcoholism forced her to quit the band in the middle of a European tour, leading to a crowd riot in Germany when she did not appear. Her solo albums were neither great critical nor commercial successes, although throughout the years, her distinctive singing style never changed. In 1980 Balin produced a rock opera entitled *Rock Justice* in San Francisco. Balin did a solo LP of MOR love songs and in 1981 had a hit single with "Hearts (#8)."

With its two lead singers gone, the group's future again seemed in question, but in 1979 singer Mickey Thomas, best known as lead vocalist on the Elvin Bishop hit "Fooled Around and Fell in Love," joined, and Barbata was replaced by Aynsley Dunbar, a former Frank Zappa and David Bowie sideman who had just left Journey. The new lineup's *Freedom at Point Zero* (#10, 1979) went

gold. The group's momentum ground to a halt in 1980 after Kantner suffered a brain hemorrhage that, despite its severity, left no permanent damage. The next year came *Modern Times,* which featured Slick on one track; she rejoined the band in February 1981, and the Jefferson Starship again ascended with a string of Top Forty hits: "Be My Lady" (#28, 1982), "Winds of Change" (#38, 1983), and "No Way Out" (#23, 1984).

Professing his disdain for the group's more commercial direction, Kantner left in 1984, taking with him the "Jefferson" of its name. Then known simply as Starship, the group enjoyed even greater commercial success. From the platinum #7 *Knee Deep in the Hoopla* came "We Built This City" (#1, 1985), "Sara" (#1, 1986), and "Tomorrow Doesn't Matter Tonight" (#26, 1986). *No Protection* included the group's third #1 hit, 1987's "Nothing's Gonna Stop Us Now," and "It's Not Over ('Til It's Over)" (#9, 1987), which was later adopted as the theme song of Major League Baseball. The last Top Forty single, "It's Not Enough," appeared in 1989. The core trio of Thomas, Chaquico, and Baldwin, abetted by Brett Bloomfield and Mark Morgan, attempted to keep the ship aloft, but in 1990, they called it quits. Thomas formed yet another group, Starship with Mickey Thomas, whose only links to the original dynasty were himself and latecomer Bloomfield.

In the meantime, in 1989, Kantner, Slick, Balin, Casady, and Kaukonen revived the early Jefferson Airplane lineup and released *Jefferson Airplane* (#85, 1989). Before that, Kantner, Balin, and Casady formed the KBC Band; its self-titled LP went to #75 in 1986. With Starship now disbanded, Kantner reclaimed the Jefferson Starship moniker and put together a new lineup in 1991, which included Airplane/Starship stalwarts Casady and Creach as well as Tim Gorman (who had worked with the Who and the Jefferson Airplane), ex-Tube Prairie Prince, ex-KBC member Slick Aguilar, and lead singer Darby Gould, whom Kantner discovered fronting her band World Entertainment War. The next year, Balin joined. This group, dubbed by Kantner "Jefferson Starship—The Next Generation," toured in the early Nineties to positive reviews. With Slick guesting on several songs, the band recorded the live *Deep Space/Virgin Sky,* which consisted of new material as well as "covers" of classic Airplane and Starship tracks.

Garland Jeffreys

Born circa 1944, Brooklyn, New York
1969—*Grinder's Switch Featuring Garland Jeffreys* (Vanguard)   1973—*Garland Jeffreys* (Atlantic)
1977—*Ghost Writer* (A&M)   1978—*One-Eyed Jack*
1979—*American Boy and Girl*   1981—*Escape Artist* (Epic); *Rock and Roll Adult*   1983—*Guts for Love*
1991—*Don't Call Me Buckwheat* (RCA).

Garland Jeffreys' urban-romantic lyrics and tough-edged rock & roll have gained him a large critical following, though little commercial success in the U.S. Jeffreys, who is part black, part white, and part Puerto Rican, endured growing up mulatto in Sheepshead Bay, Brooklyn. He attended Syracuse University, in part because it was football hero Jim Brown's alma mater. There he befriended Lou Reed and upon graduating in 1965 spent a short while in Florence, Italy, studying Renaissance art. After briefly attending New York's Institute of Fine Arts, he began writing and singing songs.

By 1966 Jeffreys was performing solo in the Manhattan club the Balloon Farm, which also featured musicians such as Reed, John Cale, and Eric Burdon. Jeffreys made his living waiting tables and playing in several small-time bands—Train, Mandoor Beekman, and Romeo—before joining with the Buffalo-area group Raven to form Grinder's Switch in 1969. The band cut only one LP, *Grinder's Switch Featuring Garland Jeffreys*, before breaking up in 1970. Jeffreys resumed his solo career, playing Manhattan clubs and signing with Atlantic in 1973.

His self-titled debut, part of which was recorded in Jamaica, was released that March, and a nonalbum single entitled "Wild in the Streets" became an FM anthem. Critics applauded Jeffreys' emotive voice and tense music, but the single flopped. Frustrated, Jeffreys retired for a while, then returned in 1975 with a single on Arista, "The Disco Kid." Following tours with Jimmy Cliff and Toots and the Maytals, Jeffreys re-signed with A&M in late 1976 and released *Ghost Writer* the next year. That album was praised for its romantic lyrics and Jeffreys' unique vocals, but neither it nor its two followups sold well.

Jeffreys left A&M after 1979's *American Boy and Girl.* The samba "Matadoor" went Top Ten in several European countries, winning him a new U.S. deal with Epic, which released *Escape Artist* in 1981. The album included a cover of "96 Tears" and was well received. Jeffreys toured, backed by the Rumour, resulting in a live LP out in late 1981 called *Rock and Roll Adult.* Following the less-well-received *Guts for Love,* Jeffreys essentially disappeared from the recording scene for nearly eight years. His most recent album to date, *Don't Call Me Buckwheat,* is a critically acclaimed examination of racial issues.

Jellybean

Born John Benitez, November 7, 1957, New York City, New York
1984—*Wotupski!?!* (EMI America)   1987—*Just Visiting This Planet* (Chrysalis)   1988—*Jellybean Rocks the House!*   1991—*Spillin' the Beans* (Atlantic).

Jellybean Benitez was one of the first club DJs to successfully break into remixing and song production. Linked with Madonna, both romantically and professionally, he has remixed her music, along with records for Daryl Hall and John Oates, Whitney Houston, and David Bowie. His success remixing songs for the dance floor and producing albums showcasing new talent has had far-reaching influence, from the C+C Music Factory to the work of latterday British techno remixers such as Leftfield and Stetsasonic.

Born John Benitez in New York's South Bronx, he got his nickname from his sister, who teased him, asking, "Know what I mean, Jellybean?" In 1973 he scored his first job, DJing at an uptown club, Charlie's. Within a year, he was one of the most in-demand spinners in New York, working at clubs including Studio 54, Xenon, and the Fun House.

To keep things interesting on the dance floor, Jellybean began to experiment, adding percussion tracks onto songs, splicing elements from one record onto another. Moving into the studio seemed the next logical step. Here he had total control of a song, adding and subtracting elements as he saw fit. One of his first successes was a stripped-down, pumped-up version of Irene Cara's 1983 hit, "Flashdance (What a Feeling)." Soon he was remixing songs for Billy Joel ("Tell Her About It"), Paul McCartney and Michael Jackson ("Say, Say, Say"), and the Pointer Sisters ("Automatic").

He met Madonna at one of his Fun House dates, when she shared the same bill with Run-D.M.C., who were making their debut. She hired him to remix "Holiday," her first dance hit, and Benitez produced "Borderline," "The Gambler," and "Crazy for You." Their relationship lasted until just after the release of *Like a Virgin* (1984).

Jellybean's next step was to produce albums featuring vocalists he discovered, using his name to bring them attention. *Wotupski!?!,* a five-song mini-album, featured an unreleased Madonna song, "Sidewalk Talk" (#18, 1985). Subsequent albums produced hits for Elisa Fiorillo ("Who Found Who" [#16, 1987]) and Steven Dante ("Real Thing" [#82 pop, #49 R&B, 1987]). He has also produced or remixed songs for established artists, including Jocelyn Brown and Stacy Lattisaw, and has produced film soundtracks, including *Spaceballs* (1987), *The Principal* (1987), *Carlito's Way* (1993), and *The Shadow* (1994).

Waylon Jennings

Born June 15, 1937, Littlefield, Texas
1969—*Waylon Jennings* (Vocalion)   1970—*The Best of Waylon Jennings* (RCA); *Singer of Sad Songs* 1971—*The Taker/Tulsa* 1972—*Ladies Love Outlaws* 1973—*Honky Tonk Heroes* 1974—*Only*

Waylon Jennings

Daddy That'll Walk the Line; *The Ramblin' Man*
1975—*Dreamin' My Dreams* 1976—*Are You Ready
for the Country* 1977—*Ol' Waylon* 1978—*Waylon
and Willie* (with Willie Nelson) 1979—*Waylon Jennings' Greatest Hits* 1980—*Music Man* 1981—
Leather and Lace (with Jessi Colter) 1982—*Black
on Black*; *WWII* (with Willie Nelson) 1983—*It's
Only Rock & Roll* 1986—*Will the Wolf Survive*
(MCA) 1987—*A Man Called Hoss* 1988—*Full Circle* 1989—*New Classic Waylon*; *The Eagle* (Epic)
1992—*Too Dumb for New York City, Too Ugly for
L.A.* 1993—*The RCA Years—Only Daddy That'll
Walk the Line* (RCA) 1994—*Waymore's Blues*
(Epic).
**With Willie Nelson, Johnny Cash, and Kris Kristof-
ferson:** 1985—*Highwayman* (Columbia); *Despera-
does Waiting for a Train* 1987—*They Killed Him*
(Mercury) 1990—*Highwayman 2* 1995—*The Road
Goes On Forever* (Liberty).

Waylon Jennings, along with Willie Nelson, was one of
the founding fathers of the rougher, so-called outlaw
country movement that championed honky-tonk country over the string-laden Nashville style. At age 12, Jennings became one of the youngest disc jockeys in radio,
working at a Texas country station. At 22, he moved to
Lubbock, where he continued to work as a DJ and then
teamed up with Buddy Holly, who asked him to join his
touring band on bass. He toured with Holly in 1959, and

Holly produced Jennings' first solo single, "Jolé Blon," on
Brunswick Records. Jennings was booked on the charter
plane flight in which Holly was killed, but gave his seat
to the Big Bopper.

In 1963 Jennings formed his own group, the Waylors,
and played a brand of folk country, recording for Trend,
J.D.'s (part of Vocalion), Ramco, and A&M. He was signed
to RCA by Chet Atkins in 1965, began to play mainstream country, and had a hit with his version of
"MacArthur Park" in 1969, which won Jennings his first
Grammy. But in the early Seventies, with albums like
Ladies Love Outlaws, Jennings began to develop a more
rebellious style, with a rockier edge, and he was booked
into rock venues. The 1976 album *Wanted: The Outlaws*,
featuring Waylon, Willie Nelson, Tompall Glaser and Jennings' wife, Jessi Colter, was the first country LP to be
certified platinum. *Ol' Waylon*, the first platinum record
by a solo country artist, contained the #1 C&W hit "Luckenbach, Texas." Jennings' duets with Willie Nelson also
produced the hits "Good Hearted Woman" and his second Grammy winner, "Mamas Don't Let Your Babies
Grow Up to Be Cowboys" (1978). Both "Luckenbach,
Texas" and "Good Hearted Woman" crossed over to #25
on the pop charts. His *Greatest Hits* (1979) sold over four
million copies (C&W's first quadruple-platinum album)
and included the #1 country hit "Amanda." (By the early
Eighties, Jennings had to his credit five platinum LPs
and four platinum and eight gold singles.)

In 1985 Jennings joined Nelson, Johnny Cash, and
Kris Kristofferson as the Highwaymen, who have over
the years released several albums. A move to MCA and
producer Jimmy Bowen expanded Jennings' musical
range, exemplified by his cover of Los Lobos' "Will the
Wolf Survive" (#5, 1986). Jennings had triple-bypass
heart surgery in 1988 (Johnny Cash recuperated from his
own heart surgery in a room across the hall). He moved
to Epic Records in 1990; in 1991 his song "The Eagle" became an unofficial anthem for the troops of Operation
Desert Storm. Jennings' 1994 LP, *Waymore's Blues*, was
produced by Don Was (B-52's, Bonnie Raitt, Willie Nelson).

The Jesus and Mary Chain

Formed 1984, East Kilbride, Scotland
William Reid (b. Oct. 28, ca. 1958, Glasgow, Scot.),
gtr., voc.; Jim Reid (b. Dec. 29, ca. 1961, Glasgow),
gtr., voc.; Douglas Hart, bass; Murray Dalglish,
drums.
1984—(– Dalglish; + Bobby Gillespie, drums)
1985—*Psychocandy* (Reprise) (– Gillespie; + John
Moore [b. Dec. 23, 1964, Eng.], drums) 1987—*Darklands* (Warner Bros.) 1988—*Barbed Wire Kisses*
1989—(– Moore) *Automatic* (+ Richard Thomas,
drums; – Hart) 1992—*Honey's Dead* (Def American) 1994—(– Thomas; + Ben Lurie, bass, gtr.;

The Jesus and Mary Chain: Ben Lurie, Jim Reid, William Reid

+ Steve Monti, drums) *Stoned & Dethroned* (American).

With pretty pop melodies buried deep in feedback and grindingly distorted guitars, the Jesus and Mary Chain became darlings of the mid-Eighties British press and a college-radio cult hit in the United States. Their melancholy noise made them one of the most distinctive of the Velvet Underground's many musical progeny and paved the way for critically acclaimed early-Nineties noise-guitar bands such as My Bloody Valentine.

Shortly after forming the band just outside Glasgow, Scotland, the Reid brothers moved Jesus and Mary Chain to London to record their first single, "Upside Down." In late 1984 came the first in a series of drummer changes (the drummers were mostly used for live shows only, not for the albums). Bobby Gillespie, vocalist with another Scottish band, Primal Scream, replaced Dalglish on drums—which consisted of banging out simple time on a snare drum and one tom-tom, much like the Velvet Underground's Maureen Tucker. Jesus and Mary Chain's early work was fast, thrashing postpunk, delivered in furious 20-minute sets that sometimes ended with audiences violently annoyed by the brevity of the set, the loud feedback, and/or the Reids' singing with their backs to the crowd. In fall 1985 the band recorded the first of its slow, throbbing noise-pop classics, "Just Like Honey," which was built on the classic Phil Spector drumbeat from "Be My Baby." Gillespie returned to Primal Scream a month before *Psychocandy* was released to enormous critical acclaim in both England and America. The *Darklands* album was followed by a North Amer-

ican tour during which Jim Reid was arrested for assaulting a male fan, who had been heckling him during a performance. (Reid was later acquitted by a Toronto court.) In early 1992 the group was banned from the British television show *Top of the Pops* over the lyrics to its single "Reverence," which included such lines as "I wanna die just like Jesus Christ/I wanna die just like J.F.K." That summer the band played the U.S. on the second annual Lollapalooza Tour. *Stoned & Dethroned* (1994) proved a departure for the Reid brothers, with its soft, acoustic sound; the album's first single, "Sometimes Always," featured Mazzy Star's Hope Sandoval.

Jesus Jones

Formed 1988, London, England
Mike Edwards (b. June 22, 1964, London), voc., gtr.; Jerry De Borg (b. Oct. 30, 1963, London), gtr.; Barry D (b. Iain Baker, Sep. 29, 1965, Surrey, Eng.), kybds.; Al Jaworski (b. Jan. 31, 1966, Plymouth, Eng.), bass; Gen (b. Simon Matthews, Apr. 23, 1964, Wiltshire, Eng.), drums.
1989—*Liquidizer* (SBK) 1991—*Doubt* 1993—*Perverse*.

Mixing post–new-wave pop rock with liberal doses of sampling and dance rhythms, Jesus Jones scored a huge 1991 hit with "Right Here, Right Now," a song that marveled at the end of the Soviet empire and was used as a campaign theme by presidential candidate Bill Clinton before he adopted Fleetwood Mac's "Don't Stop."

Mike Edwards, Jerry De Borg, Al Jaworski, and Gen had been together in a London band called Camouflage. While vacationing in Spain in 1988, they renamed themselves Jesus Jones, reportedly because they were Brits—"Joneses"—surrounded by people named "Jesus." Iain "Barry D" Baker then joined, and he and Edwards began working on getting new sounds with digital sampling synthesizers. Influenced by rap, alternative rock, and England's prerave acid-house scene, Jesus Jones recorded its debut album in late 1988. It produced a U.K. hit in "Info Freako" (#42, 1989), which failed to chart in America but got some college-radio play. In February 1990 Jesus Jones became one of the first British bands to perform in Romania after the fall of that country's oppressive Ceaușescu regime. *Doubt* (#25, 1991) topped America's alternative-rock charts and yielded big hit singles in "Right Here, Right Now" (#2, 1991) and "Real, Real, Real" (#4, 1991). *Perverse* (#59, 1993), however, failed to make much of a splash.

Jethro Tull

Formed 1967, Blackpool, England
Ian Anderson (b. Aug. 10, 1947, Edinburgh, Scot.),

voc., flute, gtr.; Mick Abrahams (b. Apr. 7, 1943, Luton, Eng.), gtr.; Glenn Cornick (b. Apr. 24, 1947, Barrow-in-Furness, Eng.), bass; Clive Bunker (b. Dec. 12, 1946, Blackpool), drums. 1968—(– Abrahams; + Martin Barre [b. Nov. 17, 1946], gtr.) 1969—*This Was* (Reprise); *Stand Up* 1970—*Benefit* (+ John Evan [b. Mar. 28, 1948], kybds.) 1971—(– Cornick; + Jeffrey Hammond-Hammond [b. July 30, 1946], bass) *Aqualung* (– Bunker; + Barriemore Barlow [b. Sep. 10, 1949], drums) 1972—*Thick as a Brick*; *Living in the Past* (Chrysalis) 1973—*A Passion Play* 1974—*War Child* 1975—*Minstrel in the Gallery* 1976—*M.U./The Best of Jethro Tull* (– Hammond-Hammond; + John Glascock [b. 1953; d. Nov. 17, 1979, London, Eng.], bass; + David Palmer, kybds.); *Too Old to Rock 'n' Roll* 1977—*Songs from the Wood*; *Repeat: Best of, vol. 2* 1978—*Heavy Horses*; *Burstin' Out* (Live) (– Glascock; + Tony Williams, bass) 1979—*Stormwatch* (– Williams; – Evan; – Barlow; + Eddie Jobson [b. Apr. 28, 1955, Eng.], kybds., violin; + Dave Pegg [b. Nov. 2, 1947, Birmingham, Eng.], bass; + Mark Craney [b. Los Angeles, Calif.], drums) 1980—*A* 1981—(– Craney; – Jobson; + Gerry Conway, drums; + Peter-John Vettese, kybds.) 1982—*The Broadsword and the Beast* 1984—*Under Wraps* (– Conway) 1985—*Original Masters (Best of Jethro Tull)* 1987—*Crest of a Knave* (– Vettese; + Conway, drums; + Doane Perry, drums) 1988—*20 Years of Jethro Tull* 1989—*Rock Island* (– Conway; + Martin Allcock, kybds.; + Vettese, kybds.) 1991—*Catfish Rising* (– Vettese; – Allcock; + Andy Giddings, gtr.; + John "Rabbit" Bundrick, kybds.; + Foss Patterson, kybds.; + Matt Pegg, bass; – Giddings; – Bundrick; – Patterson; + Dave Mattacks, drums) 1992—*A Little Light Music* 1993—*The Best of Jethro Tull*. Ian Anderson solo: 1995—*Twelve Dances with God* (Angel).

Named for no apparent reason after an Eighteenth-century British agronomist who invented the machine drill for sowing seed, Jethro Tull has been one of the most commercially successful and eccentric progressive-rock bands. In 1988, two decades after its founding, the band won a Grammy for Best Hard Rock/Metal Performance, Vocal or Instrumental, for *Crest of a Knave*.

Jethro Tull began as a blues-based band with some jazz and classical influences and was initially proclaimed by the British press in 1968 as "the new Cream." By the early Seventies, it had expanded into a full-blown classical-jazz-rock-progressive band, and in the late Seventies it turned toward folkish, mostly acoustic rock, all the while selling millions of albums and selling out worldwide tours.

Jethro Tull's driving force is Ian Anderson. With his shaggy mane, full beard, and penchant for traditional tartan-plaid attire, Anderson acquired a reputation as a mad Faginesque character with his Olde English imagery and such stage antics as playing the flute or harmonica while hopping up and down on one leg. (He confessed to ROLLING STONE in 1993 that he had only recently learned the correct fingerings.)

Anderson moved to Blackpool as a child and met the future members of Jethro Tull in school. In the mid-Sixties he and members of both early and later Jethro Tull lineups formed the John Evan Band, which played in northern England with middling success. In late 1967 the band regrouped as Jethro Tull, adding guitarist Mick Abrahams and drummer Clive Bunker, and Anderson taught himself the flute.

The band had its first big success at the 1968 Sunbury Jazz and Blues Festival in England. Tull recorded its debut, *This Was,* that summer, and by autumn it was high on the LP chart in England. The album was released in the U.S. in 1969, and though it sold only moderately, critics hailed the band. That year the British music weekly *Melody Maker* made Jethro Tull its #2 Band of the Year, after the Beatles (the Rolling Stones were third). Abrahams left after the first LP (Black Sabbath's Tony Iommi briefly replaced him) to form Blodwyn Pig [see entry] and later the Mick Abrahams Band.

Jethro Tull's first U.S. tour in 1969 paved the way for the chart success of *Stand Up* (#20), on which Martin Barre replaced Abrahams. One of the more popular numbers on that album was an Anderson flute instrumental based on a Bach "Bourée." (*This Was* had featured Rahsaan Roland Kirk's "Serenade to a Cuckoo"; Anderson had acquired his trademark flute effects—singing through the flute and flutter-tonguing—from Kirk.) Tull's next LP, *Benefit* (#11, 1970), went gold in the U.S., and the group began selling out 20,000-seat arenas. Cornick left to form Wild Turkey and was replaced by Jeffrey Hammond-Hammond, a childhood buddy of Anderson's who'd been mentioned in several Tull tunes ("A Song for Jeffrey," "Jeffrey Goes to Leicester Square," "For Michael Collins, Jeffrey and Me").

By far the band's most successful record in the United States, *Aqualung* (#7, 1971) was an antichurch/pro-God concept album, which eventually sold over five million copies worldwide, yielding FM standards like "Cross-Eyed Mary," "Hymn 43," and "Locomotive Breath." Then Bunker left to form the abortive Jude with ex–Procol Harum Robin Trower, ex–Stone the Crows Jim Dewar, and Frankie Miller. His replacement was Barriemore Barlow, whose superlative technique was put to good use on *Thick as a Brick,* another concept album in which one song stretched over two sides in a themes-and-variations suite, a vague protest against Life Itself. The album reached #1 in the U.S. and went gold. *A Pas-*

Grammy Awards

Janet Jackson
1989 Best Music Video, Long Form: *Rhythm Nation 1814* (with others)
1993 Best Rhythm & Blues Song: "That's the Way Love Goes" (with James Harris III and Terry Lewis)

Mahalia Jackson
1961 Best Gospel or Other Religious Recording: "Every Time I Feel the Spirit"
1962 Best Gospel or Other Religious Recording: *Great Songs of Love and Faith*
1971 Lifetime Achievement Award
1976 Best Soul Gospel Performance: *How I Got Over*

Michael Jackson
1979 Best R&B Vocal Performance, Male: "Don't Stop Till You Get Enough"
1983 Album of the Year: *Thriller* (with Quincy Jones)
1983 Best New Rhythm & Blues Song: "Billie Jean"
1983 Best Pop Vocal Performance, Male: *Thriller*
1983 Best R&B Vocal Performance, Male: "Billie Jean"
1983 Best Recording for Children: *E.T. the Extra-Terrestrial*
1983 Best Rock Vocal Performance, Male: "Beat It"
1983 Producer of the Year, Non-classical (with Quincy Jones)
1983 Record of the Year: "Beat It" (with Quincy Jones)
1984 Best Video Album: *Making Michael Jackson's Thriller*
1985 Song of the Year: "We Are the World" (with Lionel Richie)
1989 Best Music Video, Short Form: "Leave Me Alone" (with others)
1993 Grammy Legend Award

Etta James
1994 Best Jazz Vocal Performance: *Mystery Lady (Songs of Billie Holiday)*

Rick James
1990 Best R&B Song: "U Can't Touch This" (with M.C. Hammer and Alonzo Miller)

Jazzy Jeff and Fresh Prince
1988 Best Rap Performance: "Parents Just Don't Understand"
1991 Best Rap Performance by a Duo or Group: "Summertime"

Waylon Jennings
1969 Best Country Performance by a Duo or Group: "MacArthur Park" (with the Kimberleys)
1978 Best Country Vocal Performance by a Duo or Group: "Mamas Don't Let Your Babies Grow Up to Be Cowboys" (with Willie Nelson)

Jethro Tull
1988 Best Hard Rock/Metal Performance, Vocal or Instrumental: *Crest of a Knave*

Jimmy Jam and Terry Lewis
1986 Producer(s) of the Year, Non-classical
1993 Producer(s) of the Year, Non-classical
1993 Best Rhythm & Blues Song: "That's the Way Love Goes" (with Janet Jackson)

Billy Joel
1978 Record of the Year: "Just the Way You Are" (with Phil Ramone)
1978 Song of the Year: "Just the Way You Are"
1979 Album of the Year: *52nd Street* (with Phil Ramone)
1979 Best Pop Vocal Performance, Male: *52nd Street*
1980 Best Rock Vocal Performance, Male: *Glass Houses*
1991 Grammy Legend Award

Elton John
1986 Best Pop Performance by a Duo or Group with Vocal: "That's What Friends Are For" (with Gladys Knight, Dionne Warwick, and Stevie Wonder)
1991 Best Instrumental Composition: "Basque"
1994 Best Male Pop Vocal Performance: "Can You Feel the Love Tonight"

George Jones
1980 Best Country Vocal Performance, Male: "He Stopped Loving Her Today"

Quincy Jones
1963 Best Instrumental Arrangement: "I Can't Stop Loving You"
1969 Best Instrumental Jazz Performance, Large Group or Soloist with Large Group: "Walking in Space"
1971 Best Pop Instrumental Performance: *Smackwater Jack*
1973 Best Instrumental Arrangement: "Summer in the City"
1978 Best Instrumental Arrangement: "Main Title (*The Wiz*)" (original soundtrack with Robert Freedman)
1980 Best Instrumental Arrangement: "Dinorah, Dinorah" (with Jerry Hey)
1981 Best R&B Performance by a Duo or Group with Vocal: *The Dude*
1981 Best Cast Show Album: *Lena Horne: The Lady and Her Music, Live on Broadway*
1981 Producer of the Year
1981 Best Arrangement on an Instrumental Recording: "Velas" (with Johnny Mandel)
1981 Best Instrumental Arrangement Accompanying Vocals: "Ai No Corrida" (with Jerry Hey)
1983 Album of the Year: *Thriller* (with Michael Jackson)
1983 Producer of the Year, Non-classical (with Michael Jackson)
1983 Record of the Year: "Beat It" (with Michael Jackson)
1984 Best Arrangement on an Instrumental: "Grace (Gymnastics Theme)" (with Jeremy Lubbock)
1985 Best Music Video, Short

Form: "We Are the World—The Video Event" (with Tom Trbovich and USA for Africa)
1985 Best Pop Performance by a Duo or Group with Vocal: "We Are the World" (with USA for Africa)
1985 Record of the Year: "We Are the World" (with USA for Africa)
1989 Trustees Award
1990 Album of the Year: *Back on the Block*
1990 Best Arrangement on an Instrumental: "Birdland" (with Jerry Hey, Ian Prince, and Rod Temperton)
1990 Best Instrumental Arrangement Accompanying Vocal(s): "The Places You Find Love" (with Glen Ballard, Jerry Hey, and Clif Magness)
1990 Best Jazz Fusion Performance: "Birdland"
1990 Best Rap Performance by a Duo or Group: "Back on the Block" (with others)
1990 Producer of the Year, Non-classical
1991 Grammy Legend Award
1993 Best Large Jazz Ensemble Performance: *Miles and Quincy Live at Montreaux* (with Miles Davis)

Rickie Lee Jones
1979 Best New Artist
1989 Best Jazz Vocal Performance, Duo or Group: "Makin' Whoopee" (with Dr. John)

Tom Jones
1965 Best New Artist

The Judds
1984 Best Country Performance by a Duo or Group with Vocal: "Mama He's Crazy"
1985 Best Country Performance by a Duo or Group with Vocal: *Why Not Me*
1986 Best Country Performance by a Duo or Group with Vocal: "Grandpa (Tell Me 'bout the Good Old Days)"
1988 Best Country Performance by a Duo or Group with Vocal: "Give a Little Love"
1991 Best Country Performance by a Duo or Group with Vocal: "Love Can Build a Bridge"

Naomi Judd (The Judds)
1991 Best Country Song: "Love Can Build a Bridge" (with John Jarvis and Paul Overstreet)

---

sion *Play* (#1, 1973) followed the same format but was even more elaborate; critics soundly thrashed Anderson for his indulgence, resulting in his permanent mistrust of the music press and a two-year touring layoff.

However, the heavily orchestrated *War Child* (#2, 1974) became Tull's next gold LP (the *Living in the Past* compilation, with a hit in its title tune, had also gone gold) and yielded a #12 hit single in "Bungle in the Jungle." *Minstrel in the Gallery*, Tull's first extended flirtation with Elizabethan folk ideas, went gold, and *M.U.* went platinum. Hammond-Hammond then left, replaced by John Glascock. In the title cut of *Too Old to Rock 'n' Roll* (#14, 1976), Anderson turned ironic self-deprecation into self-glorification. *Songs from the Wood* (#8, 1977), with its minor hit single, "The Whistler," was Tull's deepest exploration into acoustic folk (Anderson had just produced an LP for Steeleye Span, too). The band's next two albums continued to merge the rustic with Anderson's tortuously intricate classical/jazz/rock thematics.

During 1978 Glascock's health deteriorated, and he was replaced by Tony Williams. Glascock died in 1979 after undergoing heart surgery, and his replacement was former Fairport Convention member Dave Pegg. Before *A* Anderson revamped the band to include ex–Roxy Music Eddie Jobson and Mark Craney. The tour supporting *A* was documented and incorporated into the long-form video *Slipstream*. Beginning with *The Broadsword and the Beast* (#19, 1982), Anderson cowrote material with Peter-John Vettese, who had also worked with him on his solo album, *Walk into Light*. The following year's *Under Wraps* continued to evince the group's new keyboard-dominated sound and, by Tull standards, was a flop, topping at #76, making it the group's lowest-charting album of new material ever.

In 1984 a throat problem forced Anderson to give up singing for the next three years. By then he had established a profitable business raising salmon in Scotland. The first album he recorded after that involuntary hiatus was *Crest of a Knave*, the group's first gold album since *Stormwatch*, and the recipient of the first ever Best Hard Rock/Metal Performance Grammy. Many observers felt that given the competition (which included Metallica and AC/DC) and the ill-fitting category, this was one of the more ridiculous awards in Grammy history. Jethro Tull hit the road, but *Rock Island* stalled at #56, and even a return to a more blues-influenced sound could not pull *Catfish Rising* past #88. Interestingly, in the U.K. that album debuted at #1 on both the heavy-metal and folk/roots charts. *A Little Light Music*, a live recording of a stripped-down Tull consisting of only Anderson, Barre, Dave Pegg, and Dave Mattacks on drums, went only to #150.

A silver-anniversary world tour ran from early 1993 to mid-1994. Once it ended, Anderson began work on an album for EMI's classical division, and Martin Barre released his first solo album. Although Jethro Tull is not the commercial force it once was, its catalogue yields sales of one million copies worldwide annually, and its best-known songs are staples of AOR and classic-rock radio.

The Jets

Formed 1984, Minneapolis, Minnesota
Leroy Wolfgramm (b. July 19, 1965, Tonga), gtr.,
voc.; Eddie Wolfgramm (b. Aug. 14, 1966, Torrance,
Calif.), kybds., voc., sax, drums; Eugene Wolfgramm
(b. Sep. 24, 1967, Samoa), voc., perc.; Rudy Wolfgramm (b. Mar. 1, 1969, Salt Lake City, Utah),
drums, voc.; Haini Wolfgramm (b. Jan. 25, 1968, San
Francisco, Calif.), voc.; Kathi Wolfgramm (b. Sep. 6,
1970, San Diego, Calif.), voc., kybds.; Elizabeth
Wolfgramm (b. Aug. 19, 1972, Salt Lake City), voc.;
Moana Wolfgramm (b. Oct. 13, 1973, Salt Lake City),
kybds., perc., voc.

1986—*The Jets* (MCA); *Christmas with the Jets*
1987—*Magic* 1989—*Believe* 1990—*Best of the
Jets.*

Pop music's only bubblegum-funk family band to trace
its roots to the South Pacific island kingdom of Tonga,
the Jets were composed of only some of the 14 Wolfgramm children, whose Mormon parents moved from
Tonga to California, then Salt Lake City, followed by Minneapolis. Leroy Wolfgramm joined some uncles in a mid-
Seventies club act, then formed Quasar in 1978 with his
mother, Vake, and some of his sisters, performing a Poly-
nesian-cabaret act in midwestern restaurants. When a
Minneapolis hotel where the band was booked went
bankrupt, the Wolfgramms settled in that city. Quasar
became the Jets, eight Wolfgramms strong, who in 1984
caught the eye of Don Powell, a former Motown manager
who'd worked with the Jackson family and who paid for
a demo that landed the Jets a record deal.

The group's self-titled debut (#21, 1986) included
"Crush on You" (#3, 1986), "You Got It All" (#3, 1986), and
"Private Number" (#47, 1986). "Cross My Broken Heart"
(#7, 1987), from the soundtrack of the Eddie Murphy
movie *Beverly Hills Cop II*, also appeared on *Magic* (#35,
1987), as did the hits "I Do You" (#20, 1987), "Make It
Real" (#4, 1988), and "Rocket 2 U" (#6, 1988). Eugene left
the group and, as Gene Hunt, formed the dance-pop duo
Boys Club with Joe Pasquale; their sole, self-titled album
(#93, 1988) yielded one hit, "I Remember Holding You"
(#8, 1988). The Jets' star, meanwhile, began falling: *Believe* (#107, 1989) produced only minor hits in "You Better
Dance" (#59, 1989) and "The Same Love" (#87, 1989).

In February 1992 the Jets—who had performed at
the White House, at the 1987 World Series, and for the
king of Tonga—filed for bankruptcy, with Powell claiming the group owed him over half a million dollars. The
Jets disputed the amount and, after being dropped by
MCA, began touring midwestern clubs again in late 1992.

Joan Jett

Born September 22, 1960, Philadelphia,
Pennsylvania

1981—*Bad Reputation* (Boardwalk); *I Love Rock 'n'
Roll* 1983—*Album* (Blackheart/MCA) 1984—*Glo-
rious Results of a Misspent Youth* 1986—*Good
Music* 1988—*Up Your Alley* 1990—*The Hit List*
(Blackheart/Epic) 1991—*Notorious* 1994—*Pure
and Simple* (Warner Bros.).

Singer/guitarist Joan Jett was one of the most surprising
success stories of the early Eighties. The latterday leader
of the much-maligned all-female teenage hard-rock
group the Runaways [see entry], Jett could barely get a
U.S. deal for her first solo album at the beginning of 1981.
One year later her second solo LP had a #1 single and
went Top Five and platinum.

Jett's family moved to Baltimore when she was in
grade school and to Southern California when she was
14. That Christmas she got her first guitar. Her initial and
continuing inspiration was the British early-Seventies
glitter-pop music of T. Rex, Gary Glitter, Slade, David
Bowie, and Suzi Quatro, whose tough stance Jett has
most closely emulated. At 15 she met producer Kim
Fowley at Hollywood's Starwood Club and became part
of his group the Runaways. The band gave its last show
New Year's Eve 1978 in San Francisco.

In the spring of 1979 Jett was in England trying to
get a solo project going. While there she cut three songs
with ex–Sex Pistols Paul Cook and Steve Jones, two of
which came out as a single in Holland only. Back in L.A.
Jett produced the debut album by local punks the Germs
and acted in a movie based on the Runaways (with ac-
tresses playing the rest of the band) called *We're All
Crazy Now* (its title taken from the Slade song). The
movie was never released, but while working on it Jett
met Kenny Laguna (producer of Jonathan Richman, Greg
Kihn, and the Steve Gibbons Band) and Ritchie Cordell
(bubblegum legend who cowrote Tommy James and the
Shondells' "I Think We're Alone Now" and "Mony Mony").

Jett spent six weeks in the hospital suffering from
pneumonia and a heart-valve infection. She then assembled a solo debut, with Laguna and Cordell producing,
using the Jones-Cook British tracks plus guest musicians Sean Tyla and Blondie's Clem Burke and Frank Infante. As *Joan Jett*, the album came out in Europe only. It
was rejected by every major and minor label in the U.S.,
and finally Laguna put out the LP himself. After much
positive U.S. press, the album was picked up by Boardwalk in January 1981 and renamed *Bad Reputation*. But
it didn't sell.

After a year of touring with her band, the Black-
hearts, Jett's second LP, even harder-rocking than the
first, came out in December 1981, including a version of
"Little Drummer Boy" on the pre-Christmas editions. It
immediately bolted up the chart, aided by a remake of a
B side by the Arrows, the pop-heavy-metal single "I Love
Rock 'n' Roll," which hit #1 in early 1982. Jett reached

the Top Twenty twice more that year with a pair of covers, Tommy James' "Crimson and Clover" (#7) and Gary Glitter's "Do You Wanna Touch Me (Oh Yeah)" (#20).

The singer/guitarist's popularity has been sporadic ever since. The followup to *I Love Rock 'n' Roll* went gold but contained only the Top Forty "Fake Friends"; by the time of 1988's *Up Your Alley*, Jett's career appeared all but finished. The previous year, her foray into film (*Light of Day*, the story of a struggling rock & roll band, starring Michael J. Fox) had fared poorly at the box office, and even her version of the title song, penned by Bruce Springsteen, failed to break the Top Thirty. But the platinum *Up Your Alley* put Jett's gritty, unadorned hard rock back on the chart, with "I Hate Myself for Loving You" (#8, 1988) and "Little Liar" (#19, 1988). Then came another dry spell, broken only by yet another cover tune: AC/DC's vengeful "Dirty Deeds" (#36, 1990).

In 1992, Jett left Epic Records for Warner Bros. At a time when she was verging on becoming a punk anachronism, she was frequently cited as an archetype of the riot grrrl movement of women-led bands. Kathleen Hanna of Bikini Kill cowrote three songs on Jett's 1994 LP, *Pure and Simple*.

Jimmy Jam and Terry Lewis
Jimmy Jam (b. James Harris III, June 6, 1959, Minneapolis, Minn.), kybds.; Terry Lewis (b. Nov. 24, 1956, Omaha, Neb.), bass.

One of the most successful writing-and-producing teams of the Eighties, Jimmy Jam and Terry Lewis turned Janet Jackson into a multiplatinum megastar and created a long string of R&B, dance, and pop hits for a variety of artists.

Jam and Lewis, who'd been close since meeting at a Minneapolis high school in the early Seventies, had been the nucleus of Flyte Tyme, the band that became the Time when Prince came along. After a year in the Time, Jam and Lewis started Flyte Tyme Productions, to write and produce for other acts. In March 1983, while the Time was touring with Prince, Jam and Lewis went to Atlanta between Time tour dates to produce half of an album (*On the Rise*) for the S.O.S. Band. A freak snowstorm hit, and Jam and Lewis missed a flight to the next Time show. Prince fined and fired them. However, they landed a smash R&B hit with one *On the Rise* track, "Just Be Good to Me" (#55 pop, #2 R&B, 1983). Through 1983 and 1984 they fashioned similar black-chart/dance-club hits for Gladys Knight, Thelma Houston, Patti Austin, Cheryl Lynn, and Klymaxx and produced most of the album *Change of Heart* for Change, and Cherrelle's *Fragile* (which included "I Didn't Mean to Turn You On," a #2 hit in 1986 for Robert Palmer). The Jam-Lewis sound—lushly Spectorian, sleekly high-tech, elegantly funky—was already crystallized.

Jam and Lewis teamed with Janet Jackson in 1985. Their first collaboration, *Control* (#1, 1986), yielded the 1986 hit singles "Nasty" (#3 pop, #1 R&B), "What Have You Done for Me Lately" (#4 pop, #1 R&B), "When I Think of You" (#1 pop, #3 R&B), and in 1987, "Control" (#5 pop, #1 R&B), "Pleasure Principle" (#14 pop, #1 R&B), and "Let's Wait Awhile" (#2 pop, #1 R&B). In 1986 *Control* earned Jam and Lewis Grammys for Producer of the Year. The team scored more hits in 1986 with the Human League's "Human" (#1 pop, #3 R&B) and "Tender Love" (#10 pop, #4 R&B) by the Force M.D.'s; then came more black-chart hits for Cherrelle and Alexander O'Neal (who had been the original singer in Flyte Tyme); in 1987 they had a #3 R&B hit with "Keep Your Eye on Me" by Herb Alpert. The duo even worked with Pia Zadora. Jam, Lewis, and Jackson reunited for 1989's *Rhythm Nation*, a monster hit that surpassed *Control* in sales.

In 1991 they launched their own Perspective label through A&M Records. Its first release, *The Evolution of Gospel* by the 40-member Minneapolis choir Sounds of Blackness, won a 1992 Grammy; its next release, *Meant to Be Mint* by R&B vocal group Mint Condition, earned a gold record for the #6 single "Breaking My Heart (Pretty Brown Eyes)." Flyte Tyme conquered the R&B and pop charts with Karyn White's 1991 *Ritual of Love* album, which yielded the #1 single "Romantic." (White, who married Lewis in 1990, said the album was all about their relationship.) Though Janet Jackson changed labels from A&M to Virgin, she stayed with Jam and Lewis for her 1993 album, *janet.*, which entered the charts at #1 and yielded a chart-topping single in the jazzy, laid-back "That's the Way Love Goes."

The Jive Five
Formed 1959, Brooklyn, New York
Original lineup: Eugene Pitt, voc.; Thurman "Billy" Prophet, voc.; Richard Harris, voc.; Norman Johnson, voc.; Jerome Hanna (d. ca. 1962), voc.
1962—(– Harris)   1971—(Group re-forms: Pitt;
+ Casey Spencer, voc.; + Richard Fisher, voc.;
+ Webster Harris, voc.; + Johnny Watson, voc.)
1979—(Group re-forms: Pitt; Spencer; Harris;
+ Beatrice Best, voc.)   1982—(– Spencer; – Harris;
+ Herbert Pitt, voc.; + Frank Pitt, voc.) *Here We Are!* (Ambient Sound).

This doo-wop vocal group had a #1 R&B (#3 pop) hit in 1961 with the melodramatic saga of teen angst "My True Story," featuring the impassioned lead vocals of its writer, Eugene Pitt. The Jive Five followed with the R&B Top Thirty "These Golden Rings" (1962), and later made the doo-wop to soul transition with "I'm a Happy Man" (#26 R&B, 1965). Its followup, "Bench in the Park," sold poorly, and their only other successes were minor, with "Sugar" in 1968 and "I Want You to Be My Baby" in 1970.

They briefly renamed themselves the Jyve Fyve, then in 1975, Ebony, Ivory and the Jades, but saw no change in their fortunes. In 1982 they regrouped to record (along with other long-unrecorded New York–area doo-wop groups) for the Ambient Sound label. As of the Nineties the group was still active on the nostalgia circuit.

Jobriath

Born Jobriath Boone, circa 1949, California
1973—*Jobriath* (Elektra); *Creatures of the Street*.

Jobriath tried to cash in on the glitter-rock trend and turned out to be one of the most costly and least successful hypes in rock history. Elektra Records reportedly paid up to $500,000 (some say $300,000) to sign the unknown singer. Jobriath's manager, Jerry Brandt, claimed to have discovered him by overhearing a demo that Columbia Records was about to pass up. Brandt, who had previously run New York's Electric Circus and managed Carly Simon, supposedly tracked down the 24-year-old Jobriath in L.A. The singer's only prior professional credit was starring as Woof in the L.A. and New York productions of *Hair*. Other facts about his past are vague.

After Jobriath and Brandt cinched the Elektra deal, they secured a 43- by 41-foot Times Square billboard of the star nearly nude (a reproduction of the LP jacket) and set up what they claimed was a $200,000 stage debut at the Paris Opera House. The show featured the singer doing mime in an eight-foot-high Lucite cube, which later turned into a 40-foot phallic symbol/Empire State Building; Jobriath played King Kong. All this got ample media attention, aided by the singer constantly referring to himself in interviews as "a true fairy"—at least giving him historical importance as one of the few openly gay rock "stars." But it didn't help sell any records; neither did Jobriath's Jaggeresque vocals. After a second album, he vanished.

Jodeci

Formed 1988, Charlotte, North Carolina
K-Ci (b. Cedric Hailey, Sep. 2, 1969, Charlotte), voc.;
Jo-Jo (b. Joel Hailey, June 10, 1971, Charlotte), voc.;
Devante Swing (b. Donald DeGrate, Sep. 29, 1969, Newport News, Va.), voc.; Mr. Dalvin (b. Dalvin DeGrate, July 23, 1971, Newport News), voc.
1991—*Forever My Lady* (Uptown) 1993—*Diary of a Mad Band*.

Jodeci helped lead the first wave of romantically inclined R&B vocal groups who wed neo–doo-wop harmonies to Nineties dance rhythms. While at first overshadowed on the pop charts by Boyz II Men and Color Me Badd, Jodeci was enormously popular with black audiences when all three groups emerged in 1991. The group finally claimed a Top Ten pop crossover of its own two years later.

The Hailey and DeGrate brothers met while singing

Jobriath

in different Charlotte, North Carolina, church choirs. Taking their group name from a combination of three members' stage names, Jodeci landed a record deal after singing for executives at MCA's Uptown black pop label. The group's debut album, *Forever My Lady* (#18 pop, #1 R&B, 1991), sold more than two million copies, yielding hits in "Stay" (#41 pop, #1 R&B, 1991) and the title track (#25 pop, #1 R&B, 1991), which was cowritten and coproduced by Al B. Sure! DeVante Swing reciprocated by cowriting and coproducing Sure!'s album *Private Times . . . and the Whole 9.*

In April 1993 K-Ci and DeVante Swing turned themselves in to police in Teaneck, New Jersey, where they were arraigned on charges of aggravated sexual contact and weapons possession (the charges were still unresolved as of mid-1995). Four months later "Lately," from Jodeci's appearance in early 1993 on *Uptown MTV Unplugged*, rose to #4 on the pop charts (#1 R&B). Success followed with the release later that year of *Diary of a Mad Band* (#3 pop, #1 R&B), which featured the singles "Cry for You" (#15 pop, #1 R&B, 1993) and "Feenin'" (#25 pop, #2 R&B, 1994).

Billy Joel

Born May 9, 1949, Hicksville, New York
1972—*Cold Spring Harbor* (Family/Philips) 1973—*Piano Man* (Columbia) 1974—*Streetlife Serenade* 1976—*Turnstiles* 1977—*The Stranger* 1978—*52nd Street* 1980—*Glass Houses* 1981—*Songs in the Attic* 1982—*The Nylon Curtain* 1983—*An Innocent Man* 1985—*Greatest Hits: Volume I & Vol-*

Beginning as a quintessential confessional singer/songwriter, Billy Joel has gone on to render consistently well-crafted pop. Classically trained, he combines rock attitude with musicianly professionalism. Whether taking the form of rock & roll, new wave, hard-edged dance fare, Sixties nostalgia, or political statement, his songs are marked by a melodicism derived ultimately from Tin Pan Alley and Paul McCartney. His forte is the romantic ballad epitomized by his signature tune, "Just the Way You Are."

Raised in a middle-class Hicksville, Long Island, family, Joel ran with a leather-jacketed street gang as a teenager. He also boxed for three years, breaking his nose in the process. In the late Sixties he joined the Long Island band the Hassles, which released two meager-selling records on United Artists. He then formed a hard-rock duo, Attila, with Hassles drummer Jonathan Small; Small's wife, Elizabeth, would later wed Joel. Attila's only album also failed. Taking up commercial songwriting, Joel signed with Family Productions in 1971. His solo debut, *Cold Spring Harbor,* demonstrated both his fondness for his native Long Island and the somber side of his singing/songwriting approach, but because the tapes were inadvertently sped up slightly in production, Joel's voice sounded nasal and unnatural.

Legal and managerial woes precluded an immediate followup, and for six months Joel performed in West Coast piano bars under the name "Bill Martin." These experiences informed his breakthrough, *Piano Man,* yielding hits in the Top Thirty title track, the Top 100 "Travelin' Prayer" and "Worse Comes to Worst." His third solo album, another respectable seller, featured "The Entertainer" (#34, 1974). *Turnstiles* came next, and although "New York State of Mind" eventually became a standard, Joel's career appeared to be in a holding pattern. Then came *The Stranger,* and a string of hit singles: 1977's "Just the Way You Are" (#3) and 1978's "Movin' Out (Anthony's Song)" (#17), "She's Always a Woman" (#17), and "Only the Good Die Young" (#24). "Just the Way You Are," written for his first wife and manager, Elizabeth, won two Grammy Awards in 1978.

More hits followed—from 1978's *52nd Street,* "My Life" (#3, 1978), "Big Shot" (#14, 1979), and "Honesty" (#24, 1979); from 1980's *Glass Houses,* "It's Still Rock and Roll to Me" (#1, 1980) and "You May Be Right" (#7, 1980)—and in 1979, Joel appeared at the Havana Jam Concert in Cuba. In 1981 he released *Songs in the Attic,* a live collection of pre-*Stranger* material; later that year "Say Goodbye to Hollywood" (also recorded in the Seventies by Ronnie Spector) became a hit. Despite the hits, Joel remained in his most vociferous critics' eyes "a lightweight"; Joel responded publicly by tea-

ring up critical reviews onstage during his concerts.

Critically and musically, the tide seemed to turn for Joel with the socially conscious *The Nylon Curtain,* which showcased his musical skill and pop traditionalist's gift for song structure. That, along with his perseverance and industry, began winning critical converts (in 1992, Joel was inducted into the Songwriters Hall of Fame). Featuring "Pressure" (#20, 1982), "Allentown" (#17, 1982), a Reagan-era unemployment lament, and "Goodnight Saigon" (#56, 1983), about Vietnam vets, *The Nylon Curtain* went to #7. The multiplatinum *An Innocent Man,* a stylistic homage to Sixties AM-radio pop, offered "Tell Her About It" (#1, 1983), "An Innocent Man" (#10, 1983), "The Longest Time" (#14, 1984), "Keeping the Faith" (#18, 1985), and the #3 single, "Uptown Girl" (1983), a Four Seasons–esque Valentine for Christie Brinkley, the model whom Joel would marry in 1985 (the couple divorced in 1994). After a seven-night run at Madison Square Garden in 1984, he released *Greatest Hits: Volume I & Volume II,* his seventh consecutive Top Ten album.

The Bridge (1986) found him duetting, on "Baby Grand," with Ray Charles, for whom Joel's and Brinkley's daughter, Alexa Ray, was named. The next year Joel toured the Soviet Union; the live *Концерт* documented the concerts. In 1989 *Storm Front* and its first single, "We Didn't Start the Fire," charted simultaneously at #1; its centerpiece ballad, "Shameless," became a hit for Garth Brooks two years later, and its supporting tour saw Yankee Stadium hosting its first rock concert. By this time, Joel had reorganized his band, found new management, and, for longtime producer Phil Ramone, substituted Foreigner guitarist Mick Jones.

With 1993's *River of Dreams,* which entered the chart at #1, Joel's lyrical content, oftentimes topical and acerbic, revealed a more philosophical outlook. With a cover painting by Brinkley, and employing producer Danny Kortchmar (known for his work with James Taylor and Don Henley), *River* featured Leslie West (ex-Mountain) on guitar. The album's title track reached #3 and "All About Soul," with guest vocals by Color Me Badd, peaked at #29.

Joel's career has been marked by tumultuous business moves—his 1972 relinquishing of publishing rights to Family Productions, his legal battles with his first wife and former manager, and a $90-million lawsuit Joel filed against ex-manager and former brother-in-law Frank Weber in 1989 alleging fraud and misappropriation of funds (in 1990 he was awarded $2 million and, in a twist, by 1994 Joel was paying Weber $550,000 and forgiving $600,000 Weber still owed). In September 1992 Joel filed another $90-million lawsuit, this time against former lawyer Allen Grubman, charging fraud, malpractice, and breach of contract (in October 1993 Joel and Grubman announced that litigation had ceased; no news of a financial settlement followed). And not stopping, Joel also sued his onetime tour manager, Rick London (his first wife's brother-in-law); Joel then dropped the suit in early 1995. Deeply suspicious of the music business, Joel has fought for lower concert ticket prices and attacked ticket scalping; he has contributed extensively to philanthropic causes.

Unlike that of many pop legends, Joel's work has been perceived as progressing over the years, moving steadily from the purely personal, some would argue sophomoric, concerns of his earliest work to embrace a wider range of styles and subjects. As bard of everyday suburban dream and disappointment, he has achieved a singular voice and status.

David Johansen/Buster Poindexter
Born January 9, 1950, Staten Island, New York
1978—David Johansen (Blue Sky)   1979—In Style
1981—Here Comes the Night   1982—Live It Up
1984—Sweet Revenge (Passport)   1990—Crucial
Music: The David Johansen Collection (CBS Special
Projects)   1993—The David Johansen Group Live
(Epic)   1995—From Pumps to Pompadour: The
David Johansen Story (Rhino).
As Buster Poindexter: 1987—Buster Poindexter
(RCA)   1989—Buster Goes Berserk   1994—Buster's
Happy Hour (Forward/Rhino).

A rock & roll chameleon, David Johansen moved from the protopunk leader of the New York Dolls [see entry] to a sincere, soulful solo singer to Buster Poindexter, an ultrasmooth lounge singer. Like the Dolls', his solo albums garnered much critical acclaim but few financial rewards; only as Poindexter was he able to gain popular acclaim.

Growing up, Johansen played in many local bands (including the Vagabond Missionaries and Fast Eddie and the Electric Japs) before forming the Dolls in late 1971. He was the Dolls' rubber-faced, loose-jointed lead singer, a self-mocking showman. In 1975, just as the downtown New York music scene was gathering steam, the Dolls fell apart, and Johansen didn't enter a recording studio again until late 1977, when he recorded his debut solo LP. Dolls guitarist Syl Sylvain toured with Johansen to support the LP, which included several songs the two had written while they were still in the Dolls. *David Johansen* attempted to bring the Dolls' spirit to the masses ("Funky But Chic"). The album bombed commercially (selling only about 68,000 copies), but critics raved about the songwriting and Johansen's streamlined, but still raw, soulful rock.

Johansen's next two solo LPs saw him making some musical compromises to try to reach the mass audience. *In Style*, with its thicker, Motown-influenced sound (the Four Tops' Levi Stubbs is one of Johansen's early fa-

Buster Poindexter (a.k.a. David Johansen)

vorites), solidified Johansen as a critics' pet but sold only a bit better than the debut. *Here Comes the Night* (#160, 1981) tried a more overt commercial turn, but despite a tour opening for then-hitmaker Pat Benatar, the album still didn't spark much consumer interest. Since all along Johansen had been known for his top-notch live shows, he tried to recoup in 1982 by releasing his first live record, *Live It Up* (#148, 1982). The single, an Animals medley featuring "We Gotta Get Out of This Place," "It's My Life," and "Don't Bring Me Down," was a minor hit. That year, Johansen appeared at Shea Stadium, opening for the Clash and the Who.

Sweet Revenge was a last-ditch attempt at commercial success, with Johansen rapping and singing over a synthesized dance beat. Its failure caused him to rethink his career, and in 1984 he emerged as the tuxedoed Buster Poindexter (also the name of his music publishing company), playing piano bars with a repertoire that included Tiny Bradshaw and Joe Liggins songs.

Originally a trio, Poindexter's band expanded into the Banshees of Blue, with additional backup singers, guitars, and horns. The first Buster Poindexter album (#90, 1988) included a high-energy cover of the 1984 soca hit "Hot Hot Hot" (#45, 1988). Buster's success helped Johansen, who had been a member of the Ridiculous Theatrical Company before joining the Dolls, in his side career as an actor. He was cast in *Married to the*

Mob (1988) and *Scrooged* (1988); as Buster, he appeared on *Saturday Night Live* and the *Tonight Show*. In fall of 1994 Johansen hosted the show *Buster's Happy Hour* on VH-1.

Elton John

Born Reginald Kenneth Dwight, March 25, 1947, Pinner, England
1970—*Elton John* (Uni)   1971—*Tumbleweed Connection*; *Friends* (Paramount); *11-17-70* (Uni); *Madman Across the Water*   1972—*Honky Chateau*   1973—*Don't Shoot Me I'm Only the Piano Player* (MCA); *Goodbye Yellow Brick Road*   1974—*Caribou*; *Greatest Hits*   1975—*Captain Fantastic and the Brown Dirt Cowboy*; *Rock of the Westies*; *Empty Sky*   1976—*Here and There*; *Blue Moves* (MCA/Rocket)   1977—*Greatest Hits, vol. 2* (MCA)   1978—*A Single Man*   1979—*The Thom Bell Sessions EP*; *Victim of Love*   1980—*21 at 33*   1981—*The Fox* (Geffen)   1982—*Jump Up!*   1983—*Too Low for Zero*   1984—*Breaking Hearts*   1985—*Ice on Fire*   1986—*Leather Jackets*   1987—*Live in Australia* (MCA); *Greatest Hits, vol. 3, 1979–1987* (Geffen)   1988—*Reg Strikes Back* (MCA)   1989—*Sleeping with the Past*   1990—*To Be Continued*   1992—*The One*; *Greatest Hits 1976–86*; *Rare Masters* (Polydor)   1993—*Duets* (MCA)   1995—*Made in England* (Rocket/Island).

For most of the Seventies, Elton John and lyricist Bernie Taupin were a virtual hit factory, with 25 singles in the Top Forty, 16 in the Top Ten, and six #1 hits; 15 of the 19 albums released in the United States during that time went gold or platinum. In the Eighties their fortunes declined only slightly; ultimately achieving more than three dozen Top Forty hits, they have become the most successful songwriting team since John Lennon and Paul McCartney. John's rich tenor and gospel-chorded piano, boosted by aggressive string arrangements, established a musical formula, while he reveled in an extravagant public image. At the start of the Nineties John confessed the personal costs of that extravagance—drug abuse, depression, bulimia—and revealed as well his impressive struggles to regain control. Since the late Eighties, he has been deeply involved in the fight against AIDS. And while his critical stature has varied over the years, his melodic gifts have proved undeniable. He was inducted into the Rock and Roll Hall of Fame in 1994.

As Reginald Dwight, John won a piano scholarship to the Royal Academy of Music at 11. Six years later he left school for show business. By day he ran errands for a music publishing company; he divided evenings between a group, Bluesology, and solo gigs at a London hotel bar. Bluesology was then working as a backup band for visiting American soul singers such as Major

Elton John

Lance and Patti LaBelle and the Bluebelles. In 1966 British R&B singer Long John Baldry hired Bluesology as his band (in 1971 Elton coproduced an album of Baldry's).

Responding to an ad in a music trade weekly, Dwight auditioned for Liberty Records with his hotel repertoire. The scouts liked his performance but not his material. (Liberty wasn't his only audition; he was also rejected by King Crimson and Gentle Giant.) Lyricist Bernie Taupin (born May 22, 1950, Sleaford, England) had also replied to the Liberty ad, and one of the scouts gave Dwight a stack of Taupin lyrics. Six months later the two met. By then Dwight was calling himself Elton John, after John Baldry and Bluesology saxophonist Elton Dean. (Some years later he made Elton Hercules John his legal name; Hercules was a childhood nickname.) John and Taupin took their songs to music publisher Dick James, who hired them as house writers for ten pounds (about $25) a week, and whose Dick James Music owned all John-Taupin compositions until 1975.

Taupin would write lyrics all day, sometimes a song an hour, and deliver a bundle to John every few weeks. Without changing a word, and only rarely consulting Taupin, John would fit tunes to the phrases. Arrangements were left to studio producers. For two years they wrote easy-listening tunes for James to peddle to singers; on the side John recorded current hits for budget labels like Music for Pleasure and Marble Arch.

On the advice of another music publisher, Steve Brown, John and Taupin started writing rockier songs for John to record. The first was a single, "I've Been Loving You" (1968), produced by Caleb Quaye, former Bluesology guitarist. In 1969, with Quaye, drummer Roger Pope, and bassist Tony Murray, John recorded another single, "Lady Samantha," and an album, *Empty Sky.* The records didn't sell, and John and Taupin enlisted Gus Dudgeon to produce a followup with Paul Buckmaster as arranger. (Brown continued to advise John until 1976; Dudgeon produced his records through *Blue Moves,* and sporadically in the mid-Eighties.) *Elton John* established the formula for subsequent albums: gospel-chorded rockers and poignant ballads.

Uni (later MCA) released *Elton John* (withholding *Empty Sky* until 1975), and John made his historical American debut at the Troubadour in Los Angeles in August 1970, backed by ex–Spencer Davis Group members drummer Nigel Olsson and bassist Dee Murray (Murray would play with John off and on until his death in 1992). Kicking over his piano bench Jerry Lee Lewis style and performing handstands on the keyboards, John left the critics raving. "Your Song" (#8, 1970) carried the album to the American Top Ten. *Tumbleweed Connection,* with extensive FM airplay, sold even faster. By the middle of 1971, two more albums had been released: a live set taped from a WPLJ-FM New York radio broadcast on November 17, 1970, and the soundtrack to *Friends,* written three years before. Despite John's public repudiation of it, *Friends* went gold. Elton John was the first act since the Beatles to have four albums in the American Top Ten simultaneously. *Madman Across the Water* (#8) came out in October 1971, and before the year was over a Bernie Taupin recitation-and-music album, *Taupin,* was on the market.

Honky Chateau was the first album credited to the Elton John group: John, Olsson, Murray, and guitarist Davey Johnstone. And with the 1972 release of "Rocket Man" (#6), John began to dominate the Top Ten. In 1973 "Crocodile Rock" was his first #1; "Daniel" and "Goodbye Yellow Brick Road" reached #2. Then came the tidal wave: in 1974 "Bennie and the Jets" (#1), "Don't Let the Sun Go Down on Me" (#2), "The Bitch Is Back" (#4); in 1975 a cover of Lennon-McCartney's "Lucy in the Sky with Diamonds" (#1), "Philadelphia Freedom" (#1), "Someone Saved My Life Tonight" (#4), and "Island Girl" (#1). *Honky Chateau* was the first of eight #1 albums, the most successful being *Goodbye Yellow Brick Road,* which held the #1 spot for eight weeks in late 1973, and a 1974 greatest-hits compilation that held fast at #1 for ten weeks.

In 1973 John formed his own MCA-distributed label and signed acts—notably Neil Sedaka ("Bad Blood," on which he sang background vocals) and Kiki Dee (with whom he recorded "Don't Go Breaking My Heart" [#1, 1976])—in which he took personal interest. Instead of immediately releasing his own records on Rocket, he opted for $8 million offered by MCA. When the contract was signed in 1974, MCA reportedly took out a $25-million insurance policy on John's life.

That same year, Elton John joined John Lennon in the studio on Lennon's "Whatever Gets You thru the Night," then recorded "Lucy in the Sky with Diamonds" with "Dr. Winston O'Boogie" (Lennon) on guitar. Dr. O'Boogie joined Elton John at Madison Square Garden, Thanksgiving Day 1974, to sing both tunes plus "I Saw Her Standing There." It was Lennon's last appearance on any stage, and came out on an EP released after his death.

In the mid-Seventies John's concerts filled arenas and stadiums worldwide. He was the hottest act in rock & roll. And his extravagances, including a $40,000 collection of custom-designed and determinedly ridiculous eyeglasses and an array of equally outrageous stagewear, seemed positively charming.

After *Captain Fantastic* (1975), the first album ever to enter the charts at #1, John overhauled his band: Johnstone and Ray Cooper were retained, Quaye and Roger Pope returned, and the new bassist was Kenny Passarelli (formerly of Joe Walsh's Barnstorm). James Newton-Howard joined to arrange in the studio and to play keyboards. John introduced the lineup before a crowd of 75,000 in London's Wembley Stadium in the summer of 1975, then recorded *Rock of the Westies;* also that year, he was honored with a star on Hollywood's Walk of Fame. And John appeared as the Pinball Wizard in the Ken Russell film of the Who's *Tommy.* But John's frenetic recording pace had slowed markedly, and he performed less often. A live album, *Here and There,* had been recorded in 1974. John's biggest hit in 1976 was the #1 Kiki Dee duet. A single from the downbeat *Blue Moves* (#3, 1976), "Sorry Seems to Be the Hardest Word," reached #6.

In November 1977 John announced he was retiring from performing. After publishing a book of his poems— *The One Who Writes the Words for Elton John*—in 1976, Taupin began collaborating with others. John secluded himself in any of his three mansions, appearing publicly only to cheer the Watford Football Club, an English soccer team that he later bought. Some speculated that John's retreat from stardom was prompted by negative reaction to his 1976 admission in ROLLING STONE of his bisexuality.

A Single Man employed a new lyricist, Gary Osborne, but featured no Top Twenty singles. In 1979, accompanied by Ray Cooper, John became the first Western pop star to tour the Soviet Union, then mounted a two-man comeback tour of the U.S. in small halls. John returned to the singles chart with "Mama Can't Buy You Love" (#9, 1979), a song from an EP recorded in 1977 with Philadelphia soul producer Thom Bell. A new album, *Victim of Love,* failed to sustain the rally, and by 1980 John and Taupin had reunited to write songs for *21 at 33* and *The Fox.* (Taupin put out a solo album, *He Who Rides the Tiger.*) A single, "Little Jeannie," reached #3. An estimated 400,000 fans turned out for a free concert in New York's Central Park in August, later broadcast on Home Box Office. Olsson and Murray were back in the band, and John had just signed a new recording contract. His second Geffen LP—*Jump Up!*—contained "Empty Garden (Hey Hey Johnny)," his tribute to John Lennon, which he performed at his sold-out Madison Square Garden show in August 1982. He was joined on stage by Yoko Ono and Sean Ono Lennon, Elton John's godchild.

In 1983 with a version of "I Guess That's Why They Call It the Blues" (#4), featuring Stevie Wonder on harmonica, Elton had his biggest hit since 1980—and while he wouldn't match his Seventies success, he would continue to place in the Top Ten throughout the Eighties, with "Sad Songs (Say So Much)" (#5, 1984), "Nikita" (#7, 1986), an orchestral version of "Candle in the Wind" (#6, 1987), and "I Don't Wanna Go On with You Like That" (#2, 1988). His highest-charting single was a collaboration with Dionne Warwick, Gladys Knight, and Stevie Wonder, "That's What Friends Are For" (#1, 1985). Credited to "Dionne and Friends," the song raised funds for AIDS research. His albums continued to sell, but of the six released in the latter half of the Eighties only *Reg Strikes Back* (#16, 1988) placed in the Top Twenty.

And the Eighties were years of personal upheaval for John. In 1984 he surprised many by marrying studio engineer Renate Blauel; while the marriage lasted four years, John later maintained that he had realized that he was gay before he married. In 1986 he lost his voice while touring Australia and shortly thereafter underwent throat surgery. John continued prolifically recording, but years of cocaine and alcohol abuse, initiated in earnest around the time of *Rock of the Westies'* 1975 release, were beginning to take their toll. In 1988 he performed five sell-out shows at New York's Madison Square Garden, his final concert breaking the Grateful Dead's career record of 25 sell-out Garden appearances. But that year also marked the end of an era: Netting over $20 million, 2000 items of John's memorabilia were auctioned off at Sotheby's in London, as John bade symbolic farewell to his excessive, theatrical persona. (Among the items withheld from the auction were the tens of thousands of records John had been carefully collecting and cataloguing throughout his life.) In later interviews, he deemed 1989 the worst period of his life, comparing his mental and physical deterioration to Elvis Presley's last years.

Around that time, he was deeply affected by the plight of Ryan White, an Indiana teenager with AIDS. Along with Michael Jackson, John befriended and supported the boy until White's death in 1990. Confronted by his then-lover, John checked into a Chicago hospital in 1990 to combat his drug abuse and bulimia. In recovery, he lost weight and underwent hair replacement and subsequently took up residence in Atlanta, Georgia. In 1992 he established the Elton John AIDS Foundation, in-

tending to direct 90 percent of the funds it raised to direct care, 10 percent to AIDS prevention education. He also announced his intention to donate all future royalties from sales of his singles (beginning with "The One") in the U.S. and U.K. to AIDS research. That year, he released the #8 album *The One*, his highest-charting release since 1976's *Blue Moves*, and John and Taupin signed a music-publishing deal with Warner/Chappell Music—an estimated $39-million, 12-year agreement—that would give them the largest cash advance in music-publishing history.

In 1992, at the Freddie Mercury Memorial and AIDS Benefit concert at Wembley Stadium, John duetted with Axl Rose on Queen's "Bohemian Rhapsody," a reconciling gesture, given Rose's previously homophobic reputation. He also released *Duets*, a collaboration with 15 artists ranging from Tammy Wynette to RuPaul.

Unbeknownst to many fans, John has written and/or performed on countless tracks by other artists. He has played piano on records by Rick Astley, Kevin Ayers, Jon Bon Jovi, Jackson Browne ("Redneck Friend"), Bob Dylan, George Harrison, the Hollies ("He Ain't Heavy, He's My Brother"), Ringo Starr, and Rod Stewart. Among the many records to which he contributed backing vocals are Tom Jones' "Delilah" and "Daughter of Darkness," Olivia Newton-John's "The Rumour," and "Dyin' Ain't Much of a Livin'" from *Young Guns II*. With the Nineties, John was renewed personally and professionally. John's contributions to 1994's *The Lion King* soundtrack were nominated for both Grammy and Oscar awards. Of the songs nominated, "Can You Feel the Love Tonight" won the Grammy for Best Male Pop Vocal Performance, as well as an Oscar for Best Original Song. In 1995 John moved to Island Records and released *Made in England* (#13, 1995), which featured the hit single "Believe" (#13, 1995).

Little Willie John

Born William J. Woods, November 15, 1937, Cullendale, Arkansas; died May 27, 1968, Walla Walla, Washington
1956—*Fever* (King)   1970—*Free at Last*   1977—*Little Willie John 1953–1962*.

Little Willie John was part of the same revolutionary generation of gospel-trained soul singers that yielded Sam Cooke, James Brown, and Jackie Wilson. He was 18 when he had his first hit, "All Around the World," and 23 when he made his biggest hit, "Sleep" (#13, 1960). John stood just over five feet (which, combined with his youthfulness, earned him his nickname) and had a voice that was stronger and rougher than Wilson's or Cooke's, and richer and more wide-ranging than Brown's. He was first discovered at a Detroit talent show in 1951 by Johnny Otis, though King Records' Syd Nathan ignored

Otis' recommendation and instead signed Hank Ballard, who'd performed at the same show.

For the next few years John occasionally sang with the Duke Ellington and Count Basie orchestras and toured with R&B saxophonist Paul Williams' combo before King finally signed him. He first dented the R&B chart with the Joe Turner–ish big-band rock of "All Around the World." John was the first artist to record the R&B standard "Fever." His version hit the Top Thirty, but two years later Peggy Lee's went to #8. The song has since been recorded countless times, including charting versions by the McCoys (1965) and Rita Coolidge (1973). Madonna covered it on *Erotica* in 1992. Through the late Fifties he scored other R&B hits with "Talk to Me, Talk to Me," "Let Them Talk" (both ballads), and the James Brown–inspired "Heartbreak." Only "Talk to Me, Talk to Me" and "Sleep" made the pop Top Twenty. In 1966, by which time his hits had run out, Little Willie John was convicted of manslaughter and sent to prison in Walla Walla, Washington, where he died of a heart attack. Though he is an overlooked figure, his significance is perhaps best indicated by the title of an album by fellow King Records artist James Brown: *Thinking of Little Willie John and a Few Nice Things*.

Johnny and the Hurricanes

Formed 1950s, Toledo, Ohio
Johnny Paris (b. 1940, Walbridge, Ohio), sax; Paul Tesluk (b. 1941), organ; David Yorko (b. 1941), gtr.; Lionel "Butch" Mattice (b. 1941), bass; Don Staczek, drums.
1960—*Johnny and the Hurricanes* (Warwick); *Stormsville*; *Big Sound* (Big Top)   1965—*Live at the Star Club, Hamburg* (Atila)   1973—*Remember . . .* (United Artists).

Immortalized in the Kinks song "One of the Survivors" (on *Preservation Act 1*), Johnny and the Hurricanes had two highly charged Top Forty instrumental hits featuring Johnny Paris' roaring tenor sax and Paul Tesluk's Hammond chord organ: "Crossfire" (#23, 1959) and the million-selling "Red River Rock" (based on the traditional "Red River Valley"), which made #5 the same year. At that time the Hurricanes were all in their teens and were playing at park bandstands in their hometown of Toledo. They toured America and Britain, where "Red River Rock" had reached #3. They had some followup hits, "Reveille Rock" (1959), "Beatnik Fly," and "Rocking Goose" (1960), but soon developed managerial problems. Their last hits were "Down Yonder" in 1960 and "Ja-Da" in 1961. The band underwent several personnel changes, leaving only Paris; in the meantime, their managers had taken credit for writing the band's hits.

The Hurricanes went to Hamburg, Germany, in the early Sixties, where they played a short engagement, often appearing with the Beatles. In 1965 Paris formed his own label, Atila, and released the *Live at the Star Club* album, hoping to profit from the association with the by-now-famous Beatles. But by 1967 the band was popular only in Europe. During the mid-Seventies, Paris and the Hurricanes played Toledo bars with no recording contract.

Linton Kwesi Johnson

Born 1952, Chapelton, Jamaica
1978—*Dread Beat an' Blood* (Virgin Front Line) 1979—*Forces of Victory* (Mango)   1980—*Bass Culture*   1981—*LKJ in Dub*   1984—*Making History* 1985—*Linton Kwesi Johnson Live*   1986—*In Concert with the Dub Band* (Shanachie)   1990—*Tings an' Times*.

A Jamaican-English intellectual and poet, Linton Kwesi Johnson has earned critical respect and cult-level sales. His songs assault racism with protest verses in Jamaican patois, sung/spoken in a distinctive, deep voice to rock-solid reggae accompaniment.

Living in England since 1963, Johnson has been inspired by the black American scholar W. E. B. Du Bois. He was associated with the Youth League of the British Black Panther Party and, while studying for a sociology degree, he started to give poetry readings backed by a group of drummers called Rasta Love (he claims to write with a reggae beat in his head).

His first album, *Dread Beat an' Blood*, was the soundtrack to a film about Britain's Jamaican immigrants; the message of the music was in keeping with London's Rock Against Racism movement and Brixton's racial turmoil in the late 1970s. *Forces of Victory* yielded minor underground hits in "Reality Poem" and "Sonny's Lettah," while *LKJ in Dub* was predominantly instrumental. While he continued to record throughout the Eighties, Johnson regarded himself primarily as a political activist, working for Race Today, a black political organization, and writing on black affairs for academic and political publications. Between 1985 and 1988 he retired from performing, although his writing, its social consciousness paralleling that of Gil Scott-Heron, continued to influence such poets as Michael Smith and Mutabaruka.

Johnson reactivated his musical career with 1990's studio album, *Tings an' Times;* by this juncture he had become acknowledged, at least in critical circles, as not only a reggae pioneer but a forerunner of the urban poetry of rap.

Robert Johnson

Born May 8, 1911, Hazelhurst, Mississippi; died August 16, 1938, Greenwood, Mississippi
1961—*King of the Delta Blues Singers* (Columbia)

1970—*King of the Delta Blues Singers vol. 2*
1990—*Robert Johnson: The Complete Recordings.*

Though a street singer whose repertoire was not limited to the blues, Robert Johnson is among the first and most influential Delta bluesmen, despite his having recorded only 29 songs before dying at the age of 27. He is credited with writing blues standards like "Dust My Broom" (which Elmore James made into a postwar electric-blues anthem), "Sweet Home Chicago," "Ramblin' on My Mind," "Crossroads" (covered by Cream), "Love in Vain" and "Stop Breaking Down" (covered by the Rolling Stones), and "Terraplane Blues" (covered by Captain Beefheart and His Magic Band on *Mirror Man*). Equally important, Johnson's persona and his songs introduced a musical and lyrical vocabulary that are the basis of the modern blues and blues-based rock.

Little was known of Johnson's life until Peter Guralnick set out to discover what truth he could about the bluesman; his *Searching for Robert Johnson* (1988) stands as the closest thing to a definitive biography. Johnson was born to Mrs. Julia Dodds, the product of her extramarital relationship with Noah Johnson. As a young boy he lived with his mother and baby sister in a number of homes, including that of a Charles Spencer, who kept two mistresses, one of whom was Johnson's mother, and their children. Johnson's mother left him in Spencer's care until, at age seven or so, Johnson was deemed too disobedient and was returned to his mother and his new stepfather, Willie "Dusty" Willis. He lived with them in Robinsonville, 40 miles south of Memphis, until young manhood.

He began playing Jew's harp, then harmonica. Sometime in his teens he began using the surname of Johnson. Poor eyesight and lack of interest in education led him to quit school. Sometime in the late Twenties, he picked up the guitar. He was influenced by pioneering Delta bluesmen like Charley Patton and Willie Brown, as well as any number of journeyman musicians he met.

In 1929, at age 17, he married Virginia Travis; she died and their first baby died during childbirth in April 1930. Shortly thereafter Johnson met Son House, who would become an important influence on the young bluesman. It was then that Johnson decided to leave behind the sharecropping life he seemed destined for and take to the road. He returned to his birthplace, and there met his mentor, Ike Zinneman, an obscure bluesman. Also in Hazelhurst, he married Calletta Craft, a woman who reportedly worshiped him and allowed him the freedom of spending days and nights in Zinneman's company. The darker, more occult aspects of the Johnson legend first appear here. Supposedly, Zinneman learned the blues while playing his guitar while sitting atop tombstones. Johnson began writing down his songs and when not picking cotton, he performed locally in juke joints or on the courthouse steps. Sometime in the early Thirties, he left his birthplace for the Mississippi Delta. His wife suffered a breakdown and returned to her home; she died a few years later.

After a brief return to Robinsonville, he settled in Helena, Arkansas, where he met and played with Robert Nighthawk, Elmore James, Honeyboy Edwards, Howlin' Wolf, Calvin Frazier, Memphis Slim, Johnny Shines, Sonny Boy Williamson II, Hacksaw Harney—a virtual who's who of early rural blues. It was at this time that he took up with Estella Coleman and unofficially adopted her son Robert Lockwood Jr., who was to become a respected bluesman himself. Johnson toured up and down the Mississippi, as far north as New York and Canada. It also was during this time that his stature grew, and he became protective and jealous of his playing style. His repertoire included blues standards, his own compositions, and even such popular tunes of the day as "Yes, Sir, That's My Baby" and "Tumbling Tumbleweeds."

Johnson was always attractive to women; as his prowess grew, he was the object of jealousy, from fellow musicians and jilted boyfriends and husbands. He often claimed that he learned to play guitar from the Devil himself, and many of his recordings evince a haunting, otherworldly inspiration. Over the years, he became erratic, often moody, but always ambitious. For years he had wanted to record, and on November 23, 1936, he finally did. The first song he recorded was "Terraplane Blues." It became a best-selling hit for Vocalion, a Columbia Records specialty label. Over the course of three sessions that November, Johnson recorded what is perhaps the most influential single artists' catalogue in rock and blues history: "Kindhearted Woman Blues," "I Believe I'll Dust My Broom," "Sweet Home Chicago," "Rambling on My Mind," "When You've Got a Friend," "Come On in My Kitchen," "Phonograph Blues," "Blues," "They're Red Hot," "Dead Shrimp Blues" (never issued), "Cross Road Blues," "Walking Blues," "Last Fair Deal Gone Down," "Preaching Blues (Up Jumped the Devil)," "If I Had Possession Over Judgment Day," "Stones in My Passway," "I'm a Steady Rollin' Man," "From Four Till Late," "Hellhound on My Trail," "Little Queen of Spades," "Malted Milk," "Drunken Hearted Man," "Me and the Devil Blues," "Stop Breakin' Down," "Traveling Riverside Blues," "Honeymoon Blues," "Love in Vain," and "Milkcow's Calf Blues."

In August 1938 Johnson played the last show of his life. While playing at a roadhouse, he attempted to rekindle a relationship with the owner's wife. Sonny Boy Williamson, who was with him, cautioned him not to drink from an open whiskey bottle he was offered. Johnson refused to heed his warning, and three days later died of strychnine poisoning and pneumonia. He was buried in an unmarked grave.

Despite his comparatively small number of recordings, Johnson has a paramount place in blues history, and, though he played acoustically, was a strong influence on such electric bluesmen as Muddy Waters, Elmore James, Johnny Shines, Robert Jr. Lockwood, and Robert Nighthawk. There were rumors that Johnson had played electric guitar. Just after his death, producer/manager John Hammond, organizing his first landmark Spirituals to Swing concert, wanted Johnson to perform; unable to locate the late Delta bluesman, Hammond settled for Big Bill Broonzy.

To the surprise of the record industry, 1990's *Robert Johnson: The Complete Recordings,* sold over half a million copies and was certified platinum. Over half a century after Johnson's death, the CD package received a Grammy for Best Historical Recording.

Jo Jo Gunne

Formed 1971, Los Angeles, California
Jay Ferguson (b. May 10, 1947, Burbank, Calif.),
voc., kybds.; Mark Andes (b. Feb. 19, 1948, Philadel-
phia, Pa.), bass; Matt Andes (b. Calif.), gtr.; Curley
Smith (b. Jan. 31, 1952, Wolf Point, Mont.), drums.
1972—*Jo Jo Gunne* **(Asylum) (– Mark Andes;**
+ Jimmy Randell [b. Feb. 14, 1949, Dallas, Tex.],
bass) 1973—*Bite Down Hard; Jumping the Gunne*
(– Matt Andes) 1974—(+ Star Donaldson, gtr.;
– Donaldson; + John Staehely [b. Jan. 25, 1952,
Austin, Tex.], gtr.) *So . . . Where's the Show?*
Jay Ferguson solo: 1976—*All Alone in the End Zone*
(Asylum) 1977—*Thunder Island* **1979—***Real Life*
Ain't This Way **1982—***White Noise* **(Capitol).**

Jay Ferguson and Mark Andes, formerly of Spirit [see entry], left that band in January 1971 to form the straight-ahead rock band Jo Jo Gunne. Rounded out with Mark's brother on guitar and drummer Curley Smith, the band took its name from a Chuck Berry song. *Jo Jo Gunne* gave the quartet a #27 hit with "Run Run Run." Mark Andes soon left to go solo—leaving Ferguson as the main songwriter—and was replaced in November 1972 by Jimmy Randell, who'd previously played in various Texas bands.

The group recorded two more low-selling records before Matt Andes left in 1973, replaced by San Francisco guitarist Star Donaldson, who was soon replaced by John Staehely (who had played in a short-lived post–Ferguson/Andes edition of Spirit, and also worked with Smith in a Texas band called Pumpkin). The new band lasted only one LP, *So . . . Where's the Show?,* before splitting up in 1974. The Andes brothers joined yet another re-formed Spirit in 1976 (later in 1976, Mark hit it big with Firefall, and in the Eighties, with Heart [see entries]). Ferguson went on to become a solo artist with *All Alone in the End Zone* and the successful single "Thunder Island" (#9, 1978).

George Jones

Born George Glenn Jones, September 12, 1931,
Saratoga, Texas
1960—*George Jones Sings* **(Mercury);** *Country*
Church Time **1961—***Country and Western Hits*
1964—*George Jones Salutes Hank Williams* **1965—**
George Jones & Gene Pitney **(with Gene Pitney)**
(Musicor); *The Race Is On* **(United Artists) 1969—**
I'll Share My World with You **(Musicor) 1971—***We*
Go Together **(with Tammy Wynette) (Epic) 1980—**
My Very Special Guests **1981—***I Am What I Am;*
Still the Same Ole Me **1982—***A Taste of Yester-*
day's Wine **(with Merle Haggard) 1991—***Along*
Came Jones **(MCA);** *The Best of George Jones*
1955–1967 **(Rhino) 1992—***Walls Can Fall* **(MCA)**
1993—*High-Tech Redneck* **1994—***Cup of Loneli-*
ness: The Classic Mercury Years **(Mercury);** *The Es-*
sential George Jones **(Epic Legacy);** *The Bradley*
Barn Sessions **(MCA) 1995—***One* **(with Tammy**
Wynette).

George Jones is the king of country singers and a highly acclaimed songwriter. His straightforward aversion to trends and his dark but romantic persona have served him well, through nearly five decades of recordings, a highly publicized marriage to and divorce from singer Tammy Wynette, and bouts with addictions and poor health. Though he dominated country radio from the late Fifties into the Eighties, his Nineties recordings barely get airplay. He remains, however, the preeminent country stylist, and is acknowledged as such by critics and young country stars alike.

Jones grew up the eighth child in a poor Texas family, his father an alcoholic laborer, his mother a church pianist. He came to music early, singing at nine, playing guitar at 11, and writing his first song at 12. Jones ran away from home at age 14; in 1947 he was hired by the duo Eddie and Pearl. A regular radio spot gave Jones his first glimmer of fame and also got him his first endearing nickname: "Possum," so dubbed by a disc jockey for Jones' close-set eyes and turned-up nose. By 18 Jones already had a wife, a child, and a broken marriage behind him.

After three years in the Marine Corps, Jones returned to Texas to start his musical career in earnest. He again gained attention while singing on the radio. A Houston producer, H. W. "Pappy" Daily, signed Jones to the Starday label; there, Jones had his first C&W hits, including "Why Baby Why" (# 4, 1955), "You Gotta Be My Baby" (#7, 1956), and "Just One More" (#3, 1956). After Starday merged with the national Mercury label in 1957, Jones began cutting the classic singles that made him famous, among them 1959's "White Lightning," Jones' first C&W #1 and his only pop hit (#73). Other hits from this period include "Who Shot Sam" (#7, 1959), "The Window Up Above" (#2, 1960), and "Tender Years" (#1, 1961).

Jones' long string of country hits includes "She Thinks I Still Care" (#1, 1962), "You Comb Her Hair" (#5, 1963), "The Race Is On" (#3, 1964), "We Must Have Been Out of Our Minds" (a duet with Melba Montgomery) (#3, 1963), "Walk Through This World with Me" (#1, 1967), "A Good Year for the Roses" (#2, 1970), "The Grand Tour" (#1, 1974), "He Stopped Loving Her Today" (#1, 1980), and "Yesterday's Wine" (with Merle Haggard) (#1, 1982). In addition to these and other major sellers were dozens of Top Twenty hits. In all, Jones has found himself on the C&W chart—as a solo artist or in duet settings—over 150 times.

But Jones' phenomenal success as an artist ran neck and neck with his increasingly erratic behavior. Jones' excessive drinking, and later drug abuse, caused him to consistently miss shows (giving him the new nickname "No Show Jones"), shirk recording sessions, and behave violently toward wives and friends. In 1969 Jones married country superstar Tammy Wynette. Though their four-year marriage was stormy (Jones was accused of beating her and threatening her with a rifle), the two had chart success together during and after the marriage: "We're Gonna Hold On" (#1, 1973), "Golden Ring" (#1, 1976), "Near You" (#1, 1976), and "Two Story House" (#2, 1980).

Jones turned over a new leaf in his recording career and personal life during the Eighties. Eschewing the overproduced sound that had been cluttering his work, Jones returned to his honky-tonk roots. He sought help for substance abuse, amended his no-show habits, and established a stable fourth marriage. His 1992 single "I Don't Need Your Rockin' Chair" (#34 C&W), from the gold *Wells Can Fall*, featured ten contemporary country hitmakers, including Garth Brooks, Clint Black, Alan Jackson, and Travis Tritt. In 1994 Jones recorded *The Bradley Barn Sessions*, a series of duets with performers ranging from Trisha Yearwood to Keith Richards to Mark Knopfler. That fall, Jones underwent triple bypass surgery; upon recovery, he returned to the studio to record *One*, an album of duets with Wynette. The two began performing concerts together again for the first time in 17 years.

Grace Jones

Born May 19, 1952, Spanishtown, Jamaica
1977—*Portfolio* (Island) 1978—*Fame* 1979—*Muse*
1980—*Warm Leatherette* 1981—*Nightclubbing*
1982—*Living My Life* 1985—*Slave to the Rhythm*
(Manhattan) 1986—*Island Life* (Island); *Inside*
Story* (Manhattan) 1989—*Bulletproof Heart* (Capi-
tol) 1993—*Sex Drive* (Island).

Grace Jones, the provocative six-foot model-turned-disco-singer, was first mainly a cult artist of the New

Grace Jones

York gay dance clubs. There she developed a reputation as much for her archly stylish look and S&M-tinged theatrical stage show (she'd enter on a motorcycle and dance with body builders) as for her monotone singing. In 1980, when she followed the dance-club trend to emphasize rock disco, her music won more broad-based support and critical respect.

Jones grew up in Jamaica, where her father was a clergyman and influential in local politics (as was his father before him). She moved with her family to Syracuse, New York, when she was 12, and, after attending college, traveled to Manhattan to work for the Wilhelmina Modeling Agency. After a stint of acting, appearing in the film *Gordon's War*, she was far more successful as a model in Paris, posing for the covers of *Vogue, Der Stern,* and *Elle*. Jones wanted to be a singer, and while in France did some recording.

In 1977 Jones landed a record deal with Island, with disco mixer Tom Moulton as her producer, and recorded "I Need a Man," a big dance hit that summer. She had other disco hits with "La Vie en Rose" and "Do or Die." Her first three albums catered mainly to the urban dance crowd, receiving little critical attention, but that changed when she began to cover more rock-oriented material on *Warm Leatherette*. Produced by Chris Blackwell, the album included versions of the Pretenders' "Private Lives," Roxy Music's "Love Is the Drug," and Tom Petty's "Breakdown." The Sly Dunbar/Robbie Shakespeare–produced *Nightclubbing* (#32), in 1981, with a David Bowie/Iggy Pop–penned title track, had her biggest R&B single (#5) with "Pull Up to the Bumper" and was voted album of the year by England's *New Musical Express*.

"Nipple to the Bottle" (#17 R&B, 1982) helped *Living*

My Life reach #69 in 1983, and Jones scored two more R&B Top Twenty singles: "Slave to the Rhythm" (#20 R&B, 1985) from the Trevor Horn–produced album of the same title, and "I'm Not Perfect (But I'm Perfect for You)" (#9 R&B, 1986) from *Inside Story* (which Jones coproduced with Nile Rodgers). Jonathan Elia and Clivillés and Cole (better known for their C+C Music Factory) produced *Bulletproof Heart,* but none of her albums since *Nightclubbing* has entered the U.S. Top Forty.

Not surprisingly, Jones has made some memorable film appearances, in *Conan the Destroyer, A View to a Kill,* and *Boomerang.* She has also produced several acclaimed videos, including the Grammy-nominated 1983 long-form program *A One Man Show. Sex Drive* marked her return to her original label, Island. The title track was a #1 hit on the dance chart.

Howard Jones

Born John Howard Jones, February 23, 1955, Southampton, England
1984—*Human's Lib* (Elektra)   1985—*Dream Into Action*   1986—*Action Replay EP*   1986—*One to One*   1989—*Cross That Line*   1992—*In the Running*   1993—*The Best of Howard Jones.*

With his endearing pop sensibility and canny ear for a melodic hook, Howard Jones was responsible for some of the warmest and most accessible technopop of the mid-Eighties. Unlike a lot of his modern rock peers, Jones wrote lyrics that were often as buoyant as his music, revealing humanist ideals and encouraging positive action and self-esteem. As ROLLING STONE observed, this child of the Sixties was "called everything . . . from a synthesized Gilbert O'Sullivan to a high-tech hippie." The strength of his best songs was hard to deny, though, and his feel-good lyricism—which didn't preclude the occasional bittersweet lament—inspired many devoted fans.

Jones began playing piano at the age of seven. As a teenager in Canada (his parents traveled a lot), he played organ in a progressive-rock outfit called Warrior. Jones later studied at the Royal Northern School of Music in Manchester, England, but found the proclassical, antipop bias there oppressive. After dropping out, he gave piano lessons and ran a produce-delivery business with his wife while continuing to perform in clubs. He played in several funk and jazz bands after leaving school, but what finally attracted a record company executive's attention was his one-man show, which featured a drum machine, a sequencer, and polyphonic keyboards. Supplementing the act was a mime named Jed Hoile, who would tour with Jones for years to come.

In the early Eighties Jones signed to WEA in Europe and Elektra in the U.S. His 1984 debut album, *Human's Lib* (#59 U.S., #1 U.K.), did well in England and on Ameri-

can college radio, thanks to catchy numbers like "New Song" (#3 U.K., 1983) and "What Is Love" (#2 U.K., 1983). The singer made a bigger splash with *Dream Into Action,* which went to #10 in the States and yielded the lithe, rhythmic single "Things Can Only Get Better" (#5). Jones' most successful song to date was "No One to Blame," a wistful ballad from his 1986 EP *Action Replay.* Produced by Phil Collins, "Blame" peaked at #4.

In the Running (1992) was more organic in its musical approach than Jones's previous five releases had been, emphasizing the singer's piano work. The tour supporting the album featured a single percussionist accompanying Jones on piano. *In the Running* sold poorly, though, suggesting that in spite of his classical training and diverse musical experience, Jones seems destined to forever be associated with heavily synthesized pop.

Quincy Jones

Born March 14, 1933, Chicago, Illinois
1961—*The Quintessence* (MCA/Impulse)   1969—*Walking in Space* (A&M)   1970—*Gula Matari*   1971—*Smackwater Jack*   1973—*You've Got It Bad, Girl*   1974—*Body Heat*   1975—*Mellow Madness*   1976—*I Heard That!*   1977—*Roots*   1978—*Sounds and Stuff Like That*   1981—*The Dude*   1982—*Q; The Best*   1989—*Compact Jazz: Quincy Jones* (Philips/PolyGram); *Back on the Block* (Qwest)   1993—*Miles & Quincy Live at Montreux* (with Miles Davis) (Warner Bros.).

One of the most prolific and successful figures in contemporary pop, Quincy Jones began as a jazz and soul trumpeter, became a bandleader overseas, and returned to America to carve out a long and still-prospering career as a composer, arranger, and producer. Jones' best-known and best-selling work may have been with Michael Jackson, but he has worked for hundreds of other successful acts, including Herb Alpert, Louis Armstrong, LaVern Baker, Glen Campbell, Ray Charles, Jose Feliciano, Roberta Flack, Aretha Franklin, Herbie Hancock, B. B. King, Little Richard, Manhattan Transfer, Johnny Mathis, Frank Sinatra, Billy Preston, Paul Simon, Ringo Starr, George Benson, Bill Withers, James Ingram, the Brothers Johnson, and the Jacksons. Jones has also had a successful career recording under his own name and has scored over 35 films and composed about a dozen TV-show themes. As of 1995, he had been nominated for 76 Grammy Awards (the most for any artist) and won 27. And, as one of the first blacks to score films and hold record company executive posts, Jones has helped advance the status of African-Americans in the music business.

Jones moved with his family at an early age to Seattle, where he began studying trumpet while in grade school. At 14 he met Ray Charles, and the two formed a band that began playing Seattle soul clubs. While working with Charles, he became an arranger. At age 15 he joined Lionel Hampton's big band and was all set to embark on a European tour when the vibraphonist's wife demanded he be kept off the tour so he could attend school.

Within a year Jones had won a scholarship to Boston's Berklee School of Music, where he took ten classes a day and earned money by playing in strip joints at night. Word of the young trumpeter's skills got out through the jazz grapevine, and at 17 he was invited to New York by jazz bassist Oscar Pettiford to write two arrangements for an album. Jones received $17 per arrangement. He stayed in New York, relishing the opportunity to hang out with Charlie Parker, Thelonious Monk, and Miles Davis. He began playing at recording sessions and at Manhattan jazz clubs and eventually rejoined Hampton's orchestra for a European tour. Jones also toured Europe with Dizzy Gillespie. In the mid-Fifties he made Paris his home.

In Paris he became music director for Barclay Records and was staff composer/arranger for Harry Arnold's Swedish All-Stars of Stockholm. He also studied classical composition with Nadia Boulanger, who had once taught Igor Stravinsky. Through the Fifties Jones won awards in Europe for his arranging and composing. According to his bio, in the mid-Fifties Jones became the first popular conductor-arranger to record with a Fender bass; if true, that's a good indication of the way Jones has always kept his ears as open to pop and R&B as to the more sophisticated sounds of jazz. Toward the end of the decade he began leading an 18-piece big band, which was a financial failure. He returned to the States in 1961, $100,000 in debt.

In New York Jones became a vice president at Mercury Records, making him one of the first blacks to hold such a post. There he produced, arranged, and played on hundreds of sessions, as well as producing ten gold records for Lesley Gore, including "It's My Party," "Judy's Turn to Cry," and "You Don't Own Me." He won his first Grammy awards in 1963 for his arrangement of the Count Basie Orchestra's recording of "I Can't Stop Loving You," and in the mid-Sixties arranged Frank Sinatra's classic "Fly Me to the Moon." He stayed with Mercury from 1961 to 1968, and also recorded albums of his own.

In 1965 Jones scored his first film, Sidney Lumet's *The Pawnbroker*. He went on to score or write theme songs for *Mirage, The Slender Thread, Walk Don't Run, In the Heat of the Night, A Dandy in Aspic, In Cold Blood, Enter Laughing, For Love of Ivy,* and *Bob and Carol and Ted and Alice*. Jones received Oscar nominations for his *In Cold Blood* score and for "The Eyes of Love" from *Banning* (1967) and "For the Love of Ivy" (1969). He won an Academy Award for his score for *In the Heat of the Night*. He also composed theme music for TV shows, including *Ironside, The Bill Cosby Show, Sanford and Son,* and PBS's *Rebop,* and has received several Emmy awards.

In 1969 Jones signed with A&M Records and began a solo recording career in earnest. *Walking in Space* (#56, 1969) and *Smackwater Jack* (#56, 1971) won Grammys. In 1971 Jones scored the music for the Academy Awards show. By that time he had been married for several years to Peggy Lipton, star of TV's *The Mod Squad*. The couple later divorced. In 1973 he collaborated on Aretha Franklin's *Hey Now Hey* LP and won a Grammy for his single "Summer in the City" (which failed to make the pop chart) from *You've Got It Bad, Girl*. In 1974 his *Body Heat* album made the pop Top Ten and went gold. Later that year he was hospitalized for the first of two severe neural aneurysms.

Jones returned in 1976 with the first of his many protégés, the Brothers Johnson, who had performed on Jones' *Mellow Madness*. He produced and arranged their platinum debut LP, *Look Out for #1*. In 1977 Jones won an Emmy for his score for the TV miniseries *Roots,* and he scored the 1978 film *The Wiz*. It was while working on *The Wiz* that Jones met Michael Jackson. The following year Jones produced and arranged Jackson's multimillion-selling *Off the Wall*.

Jones continued his producing/arranging successes in the early Eighties with Chaka Khan and Rufus, George Benson, and James Ingram. He released another of his hit albums, *The Dude* (#10), in 1981; it was his biggest hit since *Body Heat,* remaining on the chart for over a year and yielding a Top Thirty single in a version of Chaz Jankel's "Ai No Corrida." In 1981 Jones produced another Ingram hit, "One Hundred Ways" ("Just Once" had been the first), and won five Grammy awards, including one for *The Dude*. A compilation album of his solo work, entitled *Q,* was released, and Jones went on to produce Donna Summer's self-titled album that year, as well as Michael Jackson's megahit, *Thriller* (Jones also produced Jackson's 1987 album *Bad*).

Through the Eighties, Jones moved into film and television production, coproducing Steven Spielberg's 1985 adaptation of Alice Walker's novel *The Color Purple*. After the 1985 Grammy awards gala, Jones oversaw the arrangement and production of "We Are the World," the anthem of USA for Africa. His album *Back on the Block* (#9, 1989) found Jones anticipating the Nineties "jazz-rap" trend, bringing together such jazz stars as Dizzy Gillespie, Miles Davis, Ella Fitzgerald, and Sarah Vaughan, with rappers Ice-T, Big Daddy Kane, and Melle Mel. The album, which also featured Ray Charles, won a Best Album Grammy in 1990—the same year Jones also won a Grammy Legend Award and saw the theatrical release of his film biography, *Listen Up: The Lives of Quincy Jones*.

In 1991 Jones became executive producer of the hit

NBC-TV comedy show *Fresh Prince of Bel-Air,* a vehicle for rapper Will Smith of DJ Jazzy Jeff and the Fresh Prince. Two years later, he launched the glossy hip-hop magazine *Vibe* and released *Miles and Quincy Live at Montreux*—a document of Miles Davis' final recording, for which Jones conducted the lush Gil Evans charts Davis had first recorded in the late Fifties.

Rickie Lee Jones

Born November 8, 1954, Chicago, Illinois
1979—*Rickie Lee Jones* (Warner Bros.)   1981—
***Pirates   1983—Girl at Her Volcano* EP   1984—**
***The Magazine   1989—Flying Cowboys* (Geffen)**
1991—*Pop Pop   1993—Traffic from Paradise.*

Though Rickie Lee Jones's music is an eccentric mixture of R&B, Beat jazz, and folk, her debut album made her an instant star. The LP quickly went platinum, bolstered by the single "Chuck E's in Love." It would be her only hit single, but Jones kept a solid cult following into the early Nineties.

Jones grew up in Phoenix, Arizona, Olympia, Washington, and various cities in California. In 1973, at age 19, she went to Los Angeles, where she worked as a waitress and eventually began performing in small clubs. Much of her act consisted of rhythmic "spoken word" monologues. This Beat influence was also a crucial part of her later music and led to her friendship with singer/songwriter Tom Waits. (Jones is pictured on the back of Waits' 1978 *Blue Valentine* LP, and sang a Waits song on the *King of Comedy* soundtrack.)

Jones attracted the interest of Warner Bros. Records in late 1978, when her early manager Nick Mathe sent the company a four-song demo she had originally cut under the auspices of A&M. In addition, friend Ivan Ulz sang the song "Easy Money" over the phone to Little Feat's Lowell George, who, after visiting Jones, recorded her song for his *Thanks I'll Eat It Here* solo LP. All this intrigued Warners staff producer Ted Templeman and A&R man Lenny Waronker, who signed her. The latter coproduced her debut with Russ Titleman.

Released in April 1979, "Chuck E's in Love" rose to #4. On the album, Jones' voice ranged from a faint moan to a sexy, full-throated roar. Some critics praised her unique song structures with their jazz and show-tune shadings, plus her lyrical "visions," filled with colorful low-down characters. Others saw her as a pseudo-bohemian. Jones bridled at being frequently compared to Joni Mitchell, citing Laura Nyro and Van Morrison as prime influences.

Her 1981 followup, *Pirates* (#5), used longer and more complex songs about death and transfiguration; it went gold. *Girl at Her Volcano* was a ten-inch EP; all but one song were ballad covers. *The Magazine* (#44, 1984) and *Flying Cowboys* (#39, 1989)—the latter produced by

Steely Dan's Walter Becker and featuring collaborations with the Scottish band Blue Nile—both sold respectably. The Don Was–produced *Pop Pop* (#121)—with jazzmen Charlie Haden and Joe Henderson supporting Jones as she crooned all ballad covers, ranging from Twenties Tin Pan Alley to Jimi Hendrix and Jefferson Airplane—did not fare so well. Jones duetted with John Mellencamp on "Between a Laugh and a Tear" on his 1985 *Scarecrow* album, and in 1989 with Dr. John on the Grammy-winning "Makin' Whoopee," from his *In a Sentimental Mood*. *Traffic from Paradise* featured a cover of David Bowie's "Rebel Rebel," and such guests as David Hidalgo of Los Lobos, Lyle Lovett, ex–Stray Cat Brian Setzer, and acoustic guitar virtuoso Leo Kottke (whose album *Peculiaroso* Jones produced).

Tom Jones

Born Thomas Jones Woodward, June 7, 1940,
Pontypridd, Wales
1965—*It's Not Unusual* (Parrot)   1967—*Thirteen*
Smash Hits   1968—The Tom Jones Fever Zone
1969—*Help Yourself; Tom Jones Live!; This Is Tom*
Jones   1970—Tom; I (Who Have Nothing)   1971—
She's a Lady   1972—Close Up   1973—The Body
and Soul of   1976—Say You'll Stay Until Tomorrow
(Epic)   .1977—*What a Night   1980—The Greatest*
***Hits* (London)   1981—*Darlin'* (Mercury)   1985—**
Tender Loving Care   1988—Things That Matter
Most to Me; Move Closer* (Jive)   1994—*The Lead
and How to Swing It* (Interscope)   1995—*The Com-
***plete Tom Jones* (Deram).**

With his long, lean, muscular frame, his dark, rough-hewn good looks, and his sexy moves, even in his fifties, Jones remains what female fans call "a hunk." After a career encompassing Sixties pop followed by Seventies conquests of country and Las Vegas, Jones made a surprising late-Eighties comeback, spearheaded by covers of Prince's "Kiss" (#13, 1987) and EMF's "Unbelievable."

The son of a coal miner, he grew up in a home that had no bath and began singing in church as a child. As a teenager he had problems with drinking and delinquency. By age 16 he had married and was working odd jobs, from carpentry and glove-cutting to construction. A part-time pub singer, he later taught himself drums and played with various local bands before adopting the stage name Tommy Scott and forming the Senators. By 1963 the group had become a popular local attraction, and the following year fellow Welshman Gordon Mills became his manager.

In 1964 Woodward changed his surname to Jones, after the success of the film *Tom Jones,* and with Mills went to London, where Jones signed to Decca. After one single flopped, Jones requested a new Mills number, "It's Not Unusual," which had originally been intended for

Sandie Shaw. Jones' brassy version was #1 in Britain and Top Ten in America in 1965; later that year came the million-selling followup, the Bacharach-David theme from the film *What's New Pussycat?*. In 1967 Jones' version of Porter Wagoner's country tune "Green, Green Grass of Home" (#11) was an international hit. Other hit singles from this period include "Delilah," "Love Me Tonight," and "I'll Never Fall in Love Again" (1969), "Daughter of Darkness," "I (Who Have Nothing)," "Without Love (There Is Nothing)," (1970), and "She's a Lady" (1971).

But more than a pop star, Jones was a phenomenon. Nineteen sixty-nine saw four of his albums go gold and the debut of his highly rated U.S. television variety series, *This Is Tom Jones*. Among the highlights of the show's two-year run was Jones and guest Janis Joplin bumping and grinding through a duet, much of which was shot from the waist up. Jones' reputation as a sex symbol was further enhanced by a well-publicized affair with the Supremes' Mary Wilson. (As of this writing, Jones is still wed to his first wife and is a grandfather.) Though the hits waned, Jones remained a top draw live, where female fans pelted him with room keys and panties, a form of tribute Jones claims to have tired of.

While critics have been less than kind to Jones, he has counted among his admirers Elvis Presley and Paul McCartney, who wrote "The Long and Winding Road" especially for him. His original fans, it seems, never went away, and with "Kiss," "Unbelievable," and a 1993 #1 U.K. hit with the Beatles' "All You Need Is Love," a new, younger audience embraced him as well. His well-received musical series, *The Right Time*, on VH-1 and guest shots on several TV shows, including *The Simpsons*, further fueled the early-Nineties Tom Jones "revival." The well-received *The Lead and How to Swing It* featured tracks produced by Trevor Horn, Teddy Riley, and Jeff Lynne, among others.

Janis Joplin

Born January 19, 1943, Port Arthur, Texas; died October 4, 1970, Hollywood, California
With Big Brother and the Holding Company: 1967—
Big Brother and the Holding Company **(Mainstream)**
1968—*Cheap Thrills* (Columbia).
Janis Joplin solo: 1969—*I Got Dem Ol' Kozmic Blues Again Mama!* (Columbia) 1971—*Pearl* 1972—*In Concert* 1973—*Greatest Hits* 1974—*Janis* soundtrack 1980—*Anthology* 1982—*Farewell Song* 1993—*Janis* (Sony).

Singer Janis Joplin was perhaps the premier white blues singer of the Sixties, and certainly one of the biggest female stars of her time. Even before her death, her tough blues-mama image only barely covered her vulnerability. The publicity concerning her sex life and problems with alcohol and drugs made her something of a legend. In re-

Janis Joplin

cent years periodic attempts to recast her life and work within the context of feminism have met with mixed results, and of her deceased contemporaries (Hendrix, Jim Morrison, et al.), she is perhaps the least well known to younger audiences.

Born into a comfortable middle-class family, Joplin was a loner by her early teens, developing a taste for blues and folk music; soon she retreated into poetry and painting. She ran away from home at age 17 and began singing in clubs in Houston and Austin, Texas, to earn money to finance a trip to California. By 1965 she was singing folk and blues in bars in San Francisco and Venice, California, had dropped out of several colleges, and was drawing unemployment checks. She returned to Austin in 1966 to sing in a country & western band, but within a few months a friend of San Francisco impresario Chet Helms told her about a new band, Big Brother and the Holding Company, that needed a singer in San Francisco. She returned to California and joined Big Brother [see entry].

Joplin and Big Brother stopped the show at the 1967 Monterey Pop Festival; Albert Grossman agreed to manage them, and Joplin was on her way to becoming a superstar. After a fairly successful first LP with Big Brother, Columbia Records signed the unit, and *Cheap Thrills*, with the hit single "Piece of My Heart" (#12, 1968) became a gold #1 album. Within a year Joplin had come to overshadow her backing band, and she left Big Brother (though she appears, uncredited, on a few tracks on the group's 1971 *Be a Brother* LP), taking only guitarist Sam Andrew with her to form the Kozmic Blues Band.

Joplin toured constantly and made television appearances as a guest with Dick Cavett, Tom Jones, and Ed Sullivan. Finally the *Kozmic Blues* LP appeared, with gutsy blues-rock tracks like "Try (Just a Little Bit Harder)." During this time she became increasingly involved with alcohol and drugs, eventually succumbing to heroin addiction. Yet her life seemed to be taking a turn for the better with the recording of *Pearl*. She was engaged to be married and was pleased with the Full Tilt Boogie Band she'd formed for the *Pearl* album (Pearl was her nickname). On October 4, 1970, her body was found in her room at Hollywood's Landmark Hotel, face down with fresh puncture marks in her arm. The death was ruled an accidental heroin overdose.

The posthumous *Pearl* LP (#1, 1971) yielded her #1 hit version of former lover Kris Kristofferson's "Me and Bobby McGee" and was released with one track, "Buried Alive in the Blues," missing the vocals Joplin didn't live to complete. Several more posthumous collections have been released, as well as the 1974 documentary *Janis*. The 1979 film *The Rose*, starring Bette Midler, was a thinly veiled account of Joplin's career. She has since been the subject of several biographies, including *Love, Janis,* penned by her psychotherapist sister Laura.

Louis Jordan

Born Louis Thomas Jordan, July 8, 1908, Brinkley, Arkansas; died February 4, 1975, Los Angeles, California
1975—*The Best of Louis Jordan* (MCA)   1980—*I Believe in Music* (Classic Jazz)   1992—*Just Say Moe! Mo' of the Best of Louis Jordan* (Rhino).

It's impossible to overstate Louis Jordan's importance to popular music, particularly rock & roll. In his vocal approach, song structures, and lyrics, Jordan was the direct link between rhythm & blues and rock & roll. B. B. King, Ray Charles, and Chuck Berry, among other artists, are specific in their admiration for Jordan, claiming him as an important model for their own music; all have also recorded his songs.

Jordan learned saxophone as a youth in Arkansas. He later toured with the famed Rabbit Foot Minstrels revue, in which he played behind such blues legends as Bessie Smith, Ma Rainey, and Ida Cox. Moving to New York in the mid-Thirties, Jordan, by now an accomplished jazz alto saxophonist, worked with Clarence Williams and Louis Armstrong before hooking up with drummer Chick Webb's swing band. In addition to playing sax in the horn section, Jordan began singing with the band, mainly on such blues and novelty songs as "Gee, but You're Swell" and "Rusty Hinge."

In 1938 Jordan started his own small group, the Elks Rendez-Vous Band, named for the club where they were playing a long-term engagement. Jordan signed with a major label, Decca, and in 1939 changed the name of the group to the Tympany Five.

From 1941 to 1949 Jordan had a series of hit records that defined his humorous, bluesy, and always musical approach, including "Knock Me a Kiss," "I'm Gonna Move to the Outskirts of Town," "What's the Use of Gettin' Sober (When You're Gonna Get Drunk Again)," "Five Guys Named Moe," "Is You Is or Is You Ain't My Baby," "Caldonia," "Beware," "Choo Choo Cha Boogie," "Saturday Night Fish Fry," and "Let the Good Times Roll." These songs are classic models of "jump style" rhythm & blues; their arrangements drawing from swing and blues, their rocking rhythms pointing toward a new music that was just around the corner. During this period, Jordan performed his songs in a series of short comic films that can be seen as precursors of music videos.

Jordan's hits continued into the early Fifties, "Ain't Nobody Here but Us Chickens," "Run Joe," "Early in the Morning," and "School Days" among them. By this time Jordan was not only the most popular figure in the burgeoning R&B market, but also the most influential.

Jordan's importance to rock & roll was made clear by Jordan's Decca producer Milt Gabler. When later producing seminal records by Bill Haley and His Comets, Gabler claims he fashioned their sound purely after Jordan's earlier sides, particularly in the treatment of the guitars and horns.

Jordan left Decca in 1954, and his popularity almost immediately began to diminish. Jordan recorded and toured heavily throughout the Fifties and Sixties, but rock & roll, the music he had helped bring into the world, supplanted his sophisticated, smoother style.

Jordan died in 1975 from heart failure, but his music wasn't forgotten. Joe Jackson's 1981 *Jumpin' Jive* paid tribute to Jordan in its song selections and arrangements. In the early Nineties, *Five Guys Named Moe*, a revue based on Jordan's music, ran on London's West End and New York's Broadway.

Journey

Formed 1973, San Francisco, California
Neal Schon (b. Feb. 27, 1954, San Mateo, Calif.), voc., gtr.; Ross Valory (b. 1950, San Francisco), bass; Gregg Rolie (b. June 17, 1947), voc., kybds.; Prairie Prince (b. May 7, 1950, Charlotte, N.C.), drums; George Tickner, gtr.
1974—(– Prince; + Aynsley Dunbar [b. 1946, Liverpool, Eng.], drums)   1975—*Journey* (Columbia) (– Tickner)   1976—*Look into the Future*   1977—*Next* (+ Robert Fleischman, voc.); – Fleischman; + Steve Perry [b. 1949, Hanford, Calif.], voc.)
1978—*Infinity* (– Dunbar; + Steve Smith [b. Boston, Mass.], drums)   1979—*Evolution*; *In the Beginning* 1980—*Departure*   1981—(– Rolie; + Jonathan Cain,

Journey: Jonathan Cain, Steve Perry, Neal Schon, Ross Valory, Steve Smith

kybds.) *Captured*; *Escape*   1983—*Frontiers*
1986—(– Smith; – Valory) *Raised on Radio*   1988—
Greatest Hits   1992—*Time*[3].
Steve Perry solo: 1984—*Street Talk* (Columbia)
1994—*For the Love of Strange Medicine.*
Neal Schon (with Jan Hammer): 1981—*Untold Passion* (Columbia)   1983—*Here to Stay.*
Jonathan Cain solo: 1994—*Back to the Innocence* (Interscope).

Between its 1975 debut as a predominantly instrumental progressive-rock group and their first platinum LP in 1978, Journey underwent format changes that led to its emergence as one of the top American hard-pop bands. Gregg Rolie had cofounded Santana with Carlos Santana and had sung lead on several Santana tunes, including "Evil Ways" and "Black Magic Woman." Neal Schon joined Santana after its second LP, *Abraxas,* when he was 17. The two left Santana in 1972 [see entry]. Rolie and his father opened a restaurant in Seattle, while Schon jammed with other Bay Area musicians.

Former Santana road manager Walter Herbert brought Schon and Rolie together again with ex–Steve Miller bassist Ross Valory, who, along with George Tickner, had played in Frumious Bandersnatch, a Bay Area group Herbert managed. In an impromptu contest on San Francisco station KSAN-FM, listeners were asked to name the band; the winning name was Journey. The group played its first shows with Prairie Prince, then drummer with the Tubes. When he decided to stay with the Tubes, British journeyman Aynsley Dunbar, whose earlier associations included John Mayall, Jeff Beck, Bonzo Dog Band, Mothers of Invention, Lou Reed, and David Bowie, joined. Within a year of its 1974 New Year's Eve debut at San Francisco's Winterland, the group had been signed to Columbia. Following Journey's debut LP,

on which Rolie did most of the singing, Tickner, tired of touring, left the band. The group's next two albums sold moderately. Herbert, convinced the group needed a lead singer, hired Robert Fleischman. Meanwhile, Steve Perry, a drummer/singer, had contacted the group several times asking to join. Due to a series of serendipitous events—Perry was recommended to Herbert by a Columbia executive around the time Herbert had decided to fire Fleischman—Perry was in. With *Infinity* (#21, 1978), their fourth LP and the first with Perry, Journey became a top group, as moderately successful singles ("Wheel in the Sky," "Lights") and constant touring made *Infinity* the group's first platinum LP; it eventually sold three million copies.

In September 1978, soon after *Infinity*'s success, Dunbar was dismissed from the group for what Herbert termed "incompatibility of the first order." In April 1980 Journey's Nightmare Productions charged that Dunbar had been overpaid more than $60,000 in advances. In May 1980 Nightmare Productions (in which the band members and Herbert owned stock) was sued for $3.25 million by Dunbar, who claimed that he had been "squeezed out" of the group just when the earnings were increasing and sued for breach of contract, non-payment of royalties, and other charges.

Meanwhile, Dunbar (who joined Jefferson Starship) was replaced by Steve Smith, formerly Journey's drum roadie, who had studied at the Berklee School of Music and played with Focus and Jean-Luc Ponty. "Lovin', Touchin', Squeezin' " from *Evolution* (#20, 1979) was Journey's first Top Thirty hit; earlier that year "Just the Same Way" had been a moderate success.

In 1980 "Anyway You Want It" from *Departure* (#8, 1980) hit #23. *Departure* became Journey's third consecutive multiplatinum album. Columbia repackaged material from the first three (pre-Perry) LPs as *In the Beginning.* After *Departure,* Rolie tired of touring and left. He was replaced by ex-Babys keyboardist Jonathan Cain, who cowrote Journey's 1981 #4 ballad hit, "Who's Crying Now." In 1981 Schon recorded an LP entitled *Untold Passion* with keyboardist Jan Hammer. *Escape* became the group's first #1 LP. It sold seven million copies and spawned two other Top Ten hits: "Open Arms" and "Don't Stop Believin'." All of the Perry LPs have been certified platinum, and in late 1982 the group became the first rock band to inspire a video game, Journey—Escape.

Like many other mainstream hard-rock outfits, Journey made the transition to video, and their post-1983 albums continued to sell in the millions. Bolstered by a string of Top Twenty hits that included "Separate Ways (Worlds Apart)" (#8, 1983), "Faithfully" (#12, 1983), "Only the Young" (#9, 1985)," "Be Good to Yourself" (#9, 1986), "Suzanne" (#17, 1986), "Girl Can't Help It" (#17, 1986), and "I'll Be Alright Without You" (#14, 1987), *Frontiers,*

Raised on Radio, and *Greatest Hits* sold over ten million copies combined. Steve Perry also launched a successful side solo career and had a #3 hit with 1984's "Oh Sherrie" from his double-platinum *Street Talk* (#12).

The group ended when Schon and Cain left in 1989 to join Cain's ex-Babys bandmate John Waite in Bad English [see the Babys entry]; in 1991 Valory and Rolie joined the Storm. The group's last album to date, the box set *Time³,* however, peaked at #90. In late 1993 Journey, minus Perry, reunited at a Bay Area concert honoring Herbert. In 1994 Perry had a hit album with *For the Love of Strange Medicine* (#15, 1994) and a top single, "You Better Wait" (#6, 1994).

Joy of Cooking

Formed 1967, Berkeley, California
Terry Garthwaite (b. July 11, 1938, Berkeley), gtr.;
Toni Brown (b. Nov. 16, 1938, Madison, Wis.), voc.,
piano; Ron Wilson (b. Feb. 5, 1933, San Diego,
Calif.), congas; Fritz Kasten (b. Oct. 19, Des Moines,
Iowa), drums; David Garthwaite (b. Calif.), bass.
1970—*Joy of Cooking* (Capitol) (– D. Garthwaite;
+ Jeff Neighbor [b. Mar. 19, 1942, Grand Coulee,
Wash.], bass) 1970—*Closer to the Ground* 1972—
Castles* (– Brown) 1990—*Retro Rock #3: The Best
***of Joy of Cooking* (Capitol).**

Joy of Cooking was one of the first rock bands led by women. Though the group lasted over five years, it had only one hit, "Brownsville," from its debut, and a small cult following. Terry Garthwaite began singing and playing guitar in junior high school and made her television debut at 14. A graduate of UC at Berkeley, she met Toni Brown, a creative writing graduate of Bennington, and together with Garthwaite's brother David and Ron Wilson and Fritz Kasten, they formed Joy of Cooking, a folk-rock group. Four years later they signed a record deal with Capitol, and "Mockingbird" became an FM staple. After their third LP, Brown left the group, and Garthwaite formed a larger band, which toured and recorded an album that was never released because of contractual problems.

In 1973, Brown and Garthwaite recorded an album entitled *Cross Country.* They have each recorded solo albums and were reunited in 1977 for *The Joy,* which received positive critical reaction but garnered few sales. They have since disbanded; Garthwaite has toured and recorded solo.

Joy Division/New Order

Joy Division, formed 1976, Manchester, England
(Ian Curtis [b. July 15, 1956, Macclesfield, Eng.;
d. May 18, 1980, Macclesfield], voc.; Bernard Sumner
[b. Bernard Albrecht, Jan. 4, 1956], gtr.; Peter Hook
[b. Feb. 13, 1956, Salford, Eng.], bass; Stephen Mor-
ris [b. Oct. 28, 1957, Macclesfield], drums): 1979—
Unknown Pleasures* (Factory, U.K.) 1980—*Closer
1981—*Still.*
New Order, formed 1980, Manchester (Hook; Sum-
ner; Morris; + Gillian Gilbert [b. Jan. 27, 1961, Man-
chester] kybds.): 1981—*Movement* (Factory, U.K.)
1983—*1981–1982*; *Power, Corruption and Lies*
1985—*Low-life* (Qwest) 1986—*Brotherhood*
1987—*Substance* 1989—*Technique* 1993—*Re-*
public* 1995—*(The Best of) New Order.
Electronic (Sumner; + Johnny Marr [b. John Maher,
Manchester], gtr.; + Neil Tennant [b. Neil Francis
Tennant, July 10, 1954], voc.): 1991—*Electronic*
(Warner Bros.).
Revenge (Hook; + David Hicks, gtr.; + Chris Jones,
kybds.; + Ashley Taylor, drums; + David Potts,
bass): 1990—*One True Passion* (Capitol).

Until the death of singer Ian Curtis in 1980, Joy Division was one of Britain's most admired and promising post-punk bands. New Order built on that promise, with 1983's "Blue Monday" forging an influential alliance of new-wave and dance music. Joy Division's Velvet Underground–derived drone and Curtis' matter-of-fact, gloomy lyrics scored significant club hits with "She's Lost Control," "Transmission," and "Love Will Tear Us Apart," a British hit single (#13 U.K., 1980).

Formed by Hook and Sumner after they saw the Sex Pistols play in Manchester on June 4, 1976, the group took shape after Curtis responded to a "seeking singer" ad posted by the two at the local Virgin record store. Morris joined on drums the following year. The band, naming itself Joy Division after Nazi military prostitute compounds, released a four-song EP, *Ideal for Living,* by year's end.

In April 1978, the band generated a buzz when they performed at a Stiff Records battle of the bands. After turning down deals with Britain's RCA and Radar labels, the group recorded their first album, *Unknown Pleasures,* with producer Martin Hannent. They chose Manchester independent Factory Records to release the album, which was an immediate success in the U.K.

The next year saw the band's acclaim grow as they toured England and Europe. In March they returned to the studio to record their second album, *Closer.* Curtis, who was responsible for much of the group's dark vision, suffered from epileptic grand mal seizures—occasionally while performing onstage. Having attempted suicide in the past, Curtis hanged himself on May 18, 1980, just before the release of *Closer* (Joy Division's most commercially successful album) and the group's first U.S. tour. A collection of demos, outtakes, and live performances, *Still,* was released in 1981.

The remaining members regrouped as New Order and added Morris' girlfriend Gillian Gilbert on keyboards. Like Joy Division, New Order has eschewed publicity, with no band photos on album covers, and played low-key, unemotional concerts. The group's sound—a brighter but still moody version of Joy Division, with Sumner's monotonal yet plaintive vocals at the center—gained it club hits with "Everything's Gone Green" (1981) and "Temptation" (1982).

"Blue Monday" (1983) was New Order's breakthrough. Released only as a 12-inch single, it matched the band's usual emotional chill to a propulsive dance track and reached #5 on the *Billboard* dance chart, selling over three million copies worldwide. Sessions with dance producer Arthur Baker followed, producing "Confusion" (1983), another dance-floor favorite, which hit #71 R&B.

The band left Factory Records in 1985, signing with Quincy Jones' new Qwest label. Although *Low-life* (#94, 1985) and *Brotherhood* (#117, 1986) were their first American chart albums, sales were disappointing. *Substance* (#36, 1987), *Technique* (#32, 1989), and the hit single "True Faith" (#32, 1987) turned things around, but the band members turned their backs on stardom, releasing only the British World Cup Soccer theme "World in Motion . . ." (#1 U.K., 1990) before unofficially parting ways to pursue solo projects.

Sumner had the greatest success, teaming with ex-Smiths guitarist Johnny Marr and Pet Shop Boy Neil Tennant on "Getting Away with It" (#38, 1990), featured on *Electronic* (#109, 1991). Bassist Peter Hook's solo project, Revenge, released *One True Passion* (#190, 1990), while Morris and Gilbert wrote British TV themes, eventually releasing an album as the Other Two.

New Order re-formed in 1993, releasing *Republic* (#11), followed by a successful tour of the U.S. The band members were rumored to be at odds with each other, however, by the release of a 1995 anthology.

Judas Priest

Formed 1969, Birmingham, England
Kenneth "K. K." Downing (b. Oct. 27, 1951, West Midlands, Eng.), gtr.; Ian Hill (b. Jan. 20, 1952, West Midlands), bass.
1971—(+ Rob Halford [b. Aug. 25, 1951, Birmingham], voc.; + John Hinch, drums)   1974—(+ Glenn Tipton (b. Oct. 25, 1949, West Midlands), gtr.; – Hinch; + Alan Moore, drums) *Rocka Rolla* (Gull) 1976—*Sad Wings of Destiny*   1977—(– Moore; + Simon Phillips, drums) *Sin After Sin* (Columbia) 1978—(– Phillips; + Les Binks, drums) *Stained Class* 1979—*Hell Bent for Leather*; *Unleashed in the East* (– Binks; + Dave Holland, drums)   1980—*British Steel*   1981—*Point of Entry*   1982—*Screaming for Vengeance*   1984—*Defenders of the Faith*   1986— *Turbo*   1987—*Priest . . . Live*   1988—*Ram It Down*

Judas Priest: Ian Hill, K. K. Downing, Rob Halford, Glenn Tipton, Dave Holland

1989—(– Holland; + Scott Travis, drums) *Painkiller* 1992—(– Halford; – Travis)   1993—*Metalworks '73–'93.*

Judas Priest, a leather-clad heavy-metal band, was formed by guitarist K. K. Downing and bassist Ian Hill. In 1971 frontman Rob Halford joined (he'd previously worked in theatrical lighting), having met Hill, whom his sister was then dating (and later married). The band didn't get a contract until 1974, just after guitarist Glenn Tipton joined. Its first LP was released that year, but both it and the 1976 followup, *Sad Wings of Destiny*, sold marginally.

The band began to develop a following in England, and in 1977 Priest signed with Columbia, which released *Sin After Sin*. Produced by ex–Deep Purple bassist Roger Glover, *Sin* featured guest drummer Simon Phillips and an unlikely heavy-metal version of Joan Baez's "Diamonds and Rust" similar in style to Nazareth's 1973 treatment of Joni Mitchell's "This Flight Tonight." The group's songs, highlighted by Tipton and Downing's dual lead guitar attack, were catchier and shorter than most other early-Seventies heavy metal, anticipating late-decade acts like Def Leppard.

Stained Class featured new drummer Les Binks, replaced with ex-Trapeze member Dave Holland after Priest's live-in-Japan *Unleashed in the East* record. The live LP included a version of Fleetwood Mac's "Green Manalishi." Over the years Judas Priest became increasingly known for its extravagant live show, which featured Halford, in his trademark S&M gear, thundering onstage on a Harley Davidson motorcycle. The band's seventh album, 1980's *British Steel*, was its first U.S. Top Forty entry and a heavy-metal landmark. Concise songs like "Living After Midnight" and "Breaking the Law" mated metal aggression with new-wave melodicism. Both went Top Twenty in Britain.

The 1981 followup, *Point of Entry*, failed to build on the band's momentum, but *Screaming for Vengeance* broke Judas Priest in a big way stateside and gave the group its closest thing to an American hit single, "You've Got Another Thing Comin'" (#67, 1982). The song's stylish video showed Priest performing on a laser-lit stage while a conservative business type outfitted in a trenchcoat and bowler hat appears to be fleeing some unseen, sinister force. At the clip's end, Tipton and Downing's guitars explode—as does the character's head.

Vengeance, *Defenders of the Faith*, and *Turbo* all went platinum, and Priest's mid-Eighties success spurred sales of its earlier albums. Through 1990's *Painkiller*, all but the group's second live LP, released in 1987, had sold more than 500,000 copies apiece. By the late Eighties, however, other, younger metal bands began to make inroads on Priest's audience.

In 1986 Judas Priest became the unwitting object of controversy when the parents of two Reno, Nevada, teenagers sued both the group and Columbia Records for $6.2 million, claiming a song on 1978's *Stained Class* contained subliminal messages that drove their sons to shoot themselves in 1985. One died instantly; the other lived, but overdosed fatally on methadone three years later. A judge dismissed the charges in 1990. The gold *Painkiller* came out shortly thereafter.

It proved to be the band's final album with Halford. The singer, who'd relocated to Arizona in the early Eighties, abruptly quit Judas Priest in December 1992 to form his own band, Fight. (Scott Travis, Priest's drummer since 1990, went with him.) It was an acrimonious split. After tending to the *Metalworks '73–'93* CD and video compilation, remaining members Downing, Tipton, and Hill began scouting around for a new singer, stating that they fully intended to carry on as Judas Priest.

The Judds/Wynonna

Formed 1983, Nashville, Tennessee
Naomi Judd (b. Diana Judd, Jan. 11, 1946, Ashland, Ky.), voc.; Wynonna Judd (b. Christina Ciminella, May 30, 1964, Ashland), voc., gtr.
1984—The Judds: Wynonna & Naomi (Curb/RCA); Why Not Me 1985—Rockin' with the Rhythm 1987—Heart Land; Christmas Time with the Judds 1988—Greatest Hits 1989—River of Time 1990—Love Can Build a Bridge 1990—Collector's Series 1991—Greatest Hits, vol. 2.
Wynonna Judd solo: 1992—Wynonna (Curb/MCA) 1993—Tell Me Why.

After rising to fame in the mid-Eighties, the Judds remained the most beloved mother-daughter act in country music—in any mass-appeal musical genre, in fact—until chronic hepatitis forced Wynonna Judd's

mom Naomi to retire in 1991. Though Naomi's age-defying beauty earned much media attention, it was Wynonna's rich, authoritative lead vocals (Naomi usually sang harmony) and her equally confident way with ballads and rootsy rockers that gave the duo musical cachet and enabled the younger Judd to embark on a successful solo career in the early Nineties.

Naomi married at 17, and at 18 gave birth to Christina Ciminella, who later changed her name to Wynonna. (The choice was inspired by a reference in the song "Route 66.") The family moved to Los Angeles in 1968; two years later Naomi left Wynonna's father, who had by then fathered a second daughter, Ashley (later a successful actress). Eventually, mother and children relocated to Morrill, Kentucky, where as Naomi struggled to make ends meet, Wynonna discovered the guitar. The Judds then moved back to California; there Naomi earned a nursing degree and spent her off-hours singing with Wynonna. In 1979 they were in the Nashville suburb of Franklin, and Naomi wound up nursing the daughter of a prominent C&W producer, Brent Maher, when the girl was injured in a car accident. After her recovery, Naomi gave Maher a demo tape that she and Wynonna had made; impressed, Maher passed it on to executives at RCA Records' Nashville division, who signed the duo.

Over the next few years, the Judds consistently took their smooth harmonies and old-fashioned but unsentimental songs to the top of the C&W chart. Their #1 C&W singles included "Mama He's Crazy" (1984), "Why Not Me" (1984), "Girls Night Out" (1985), "Love Is Alive" (1985), "Have Mercy" (1985), "Grandpa (Tell Me 'Bout the Good Old Days)" (1986), "Rockin' with the Rhythm of the Rain" (1986), "Cry Myself to Sleep" (1986), "I Know Where I'm Going" (1987), "Maybe Your Baby's Got the Blues" (1987), "Turn It Loose" (1988), and "Change of Heart" (1988). Other C&W hits included a remake of "Don't Be Cruel" (#10, 1987), "Give a Little Love" (#2, 1988), and "One Hundred and Two" (#6, 1991). In addition, the Judds garnered five Grammy Awards, for best country vocal duet.

After an emotional (and thoroughly publicized) farewell tour in 1991, Wynonna began working on her solo debut. *Wynonna* (1992) won critical raves, topped the C&W chart, and produced three #1 country singles: "She Is His Only Need," "I Saw the Light," and "No One Else on Earth," as well as the #4 single "My Strongest Weakness." *Wynonna* also became a #4 pop album. In 1993 Wynonna joined forces with tour-mate and fellow crossover star Clint Black for the single "A Bad Goodbye" (#43 pop, #2 C&W, 1993). Also in 1993, Wynonna released her second solo album, *Tell Me Why* (#5 pop, #1 C&W, 1993), and Naomi published a best-selling memoir, *Love Can Build a Bridge*, which was made into a highly rated TV movie in 1995. Wynonna then reunited with her mother, whose illness was in remission, for a nationally televised performance at the 1994 Super Bowl, during halftime. Later that year, Wynonna announced she was pregnant with her first child by her Nashville businessman boyfriend.

The Jungle Brothers

Formed 1986, Brooklyn, New York
Mike G (b. Michael Small, May 13, 1969, New York City, N.Y.), voc.; Afrika Baby Bambaataa (b. Nathaniel Hall, June 22, 1970, New York City), voc.; Sammy B (b. Samuel Burwell, Dec. 9, 1967, New York City), DJ.
1988—*Straight Out the Jungle* (Idlers/Warlock)
1989—*Done by the Forces of Nature* (Warner Bros.)
1993—(+ Torture [b. Colin Bobb, Oct. 18, 1974, Guyana], voc.) *J. Beez Wit the Remedy.*

The Jungle Brothers opened the doors to the Nineties jazz-rap trend by blending horns and scat vocals into their early raw, lilting hip-hop style. Often sporting bright African colors, psychedelic beads, and wire-rimmed shades, the group was part of the late-Eighties neo-hippie rap collective known as the Native Tongues, along with De La Soul and Queen Latifah.

While attending high school in Brooklyn, Michael Small began a rap group in 1986 with Harlemites Nathaniel Hall and Samuel Burwell. An early demo tape of their music made it into the hands of influential DJ Red Alert, of the New York City radio station WRKS-FM, who helped the JBs land a deal with the independent rap label Idlers Records. The group's first single, "Jim Browski," was popular among the city's hip-hop underground, but it was the B side, "I'll House You," a blend of rap and the "house" dance music style, that really turned heads.

The Jungle Brothers signed with Warner Bros. in 1989 and released *Done by the Forces of Nature* (#46 R&B, 1989). They spent the next few years producing such artists as Fishbone and A Tribe Called Quest, and contributed a song to the soundtrack of *Living Large*, a film in which they appeared. Funksters Bootsy Collins, Gary "Mudbone" Cooper, and Bernie Worrell collaborated on the 1993 album *J. Beez Wit the Remedy* (#52 R&B), as did outrageous new JB member Torture. The group's music remains influential and critically praised, though commercial success continues to elude them.

K

Tonio K.

Born Steve Krikorian, July 4, 1950, California
1979—*Life in the Foodchain* (Full Moon/Epic)
1980—*Amerika* (Arista)   1983—*La Bomba* (Capitol)
1986—*Romeo Unchained* (A&M)   1988—*Notes from
the Lost Civilization*.

Los Angeles singer/songwriter Tonio K. distinguished himself from his colleagues with his sardonic, self-consciously literate lyrics and high-velocity rock & roll. K. purposely kept his background a mystery. In his first Arista press bio he described himself as an "American Negro musician, born in New Orleans in 1900" (a line K. admitted that he took from Louis Armstrong's biography in a dictionary). In fact, he was from a white middle-class San Joaquin Valley family. In 1972 he joined a latterday version of Buddy Holly's group, the Crickets, and played bass with them for three years. When the Crickets disbanded, Krikorian turned to songwriting and a solo career, taking his pseudonym from the protagonist of Thomas Mann's short story "Tonio Kröger."

Eagles manager Irving Azoff hailed K. as a "brilliant lyricist," promoted him as a new Bob Dylan, and signed him to Full Moon, a subsidiary of Epic. His debut album was well received by the music press but aroused little public interest. In 1979 he signed with Arista, but his first album for his new label lost him his support from the critics, who found his arrogance, intellectual conceit

(lyrics in German and Greek), and belligerence too much to take. (To this encyclopedia's researcher, K. insisted that he was just joking.) K.'s 1983 LP featured an antinuclear remake of Ritchie Valens' "La Bamba" called "La Bomba."

Generally a critics' favorite over the years, Tonio K.'s albums continue to garner raves though not great sales. He has found more financial success as a writer or cowriter of hits recorded by others, including Vanessa Williams (with Brian McKnight; "Love Is"), Bonnie Raitt ("You"), and Arc Angels ("Too Many Ways to Fall"). His songs have also been recorded by Charlie Sexton, the Pointer Sisters, the Runaways, T Bone Burnett, and Aaron Neville.

Kaleidoscope

Formed 1966, Berkeley, California
Fenrus Epp (a.k.a. Max Buda, Templeton Parceley,
Connie Crill), violin, kybds.; John Vidican, perc.;
Solomon Feldthouse (b. Turkey), gtr., voc., strings;
David Lindley (b. 1944, San Marino, Calif.), violin,
gtr., voc.; Chris Darrow, gtr., voc., fiddle.
1967—*Side Trips* (Epic)   1968—*A Beacon from Mars*
(– Darrow; – Vidican; + Stuart Brotman, bass;
+ Paul Lagos, drums)   1969—*Kaleidoscope*   1970—
(– Brotman; + Ron Johnson, bass; + Jeff Kaplan
[d. 1970], gtr., voc.) *Bernice* (Columbia) (– Feldthouse;
– Crill; + Richard Aplan, flute) (group disbands)

1975—(Group re-forms: Feldthouse; Brotman; Lagos; Crill; Darrow)   1976—*When Scopes Collide* (Pacific Arts)   1988—*Greetings from Kartoonista . . . We Ain't Dead Yet* (Gifthorse/Curb) 1991—*Egyptian Candy: A Collection* (Legacy). David Lindley solo: 1981—*El Rayo-X* (Elektra) 1982—*Win This Record!*   1988—*Very Greasy.*

Kaleidoscope was known in the late Sixties for eclectic albums that drew from bluegrass, blues, Cajun music, Middle Eastern music, and acid rock, using various exotic instruments (e.g., saz, oud). Today it is remembered primarily as being the band David Lindley led before he hooked up with Jackson Browne. In the Eighties Lindley also recorded solo LPs.

Despite a noteworthy appearance at the 1968 Newport Folk Festival and a live act that included flamenco and belly dancers, Kaleidoscope's early albums, *Side Trips* and *Beacon from Mars,* were ignored. Shortly after the 1970 drug-related death of guitarist Jeff Kaplan, a recent recruit, the band broke up, although Chris Darrow, Paul Lagos, Stuart Brotman, Solomon Feldthouse, and Connie Crill reunited in 1975 to record *When Scopes Collide,* with only minor contributions from Lindley (under the name DeParis Letante) and in 1988 for *Greetings from Kartoonista.*

Darrow recorded solo albums for United Artists and other labels after leaving Kaleidoscope, including one with members of British folk-rockers Fairport Convention. "Max Buda" made a guest appearance on Darrow's 1979 LP, *Fretless.*

Kansas

Formed 1970, Topeka, Kansas
Kerry Livgren (b. Sep. 18, 1949, Kan.), gtr., kybds., synth.; Steve Walsh (b. 1951, St. Joseph, Mo.), kybds., synth., voc.; Robby Steinhardt (b. 1951, Miss.), violin, voc.; Richard Williams (b. 1951, Kan.), gtr.; Phil Ehart (b. 1951, Kan.), drums; Dave Hope (b. Oct. 7, 1949, Kan.), bass.
1974—*Kansas* (Kirshner)   1975—*Masque; Song for America*   1976—*Leftoverture*   1977—*Point of Know Return*   1978—*Two for the Show*   1979—*Monolith*   1980—*Audio-Visions*   1981—(– Walsh; + John Elefante [b. 1958, Levittown, N.Y.], voc., kybds.)   1982—*Vinyl Confessions*   1983—*Drastic Measures* (CBS Associated) (Group disbands) 1984—*The Best of Kansas*   1986—(Group re-forms: Walsh; Ehart; Williams; + Steve Morse [b. July 28, 1954, Hamilton, Ohio], gtr.; + Billy Greer, bass) *Power* (MCA)   1988—*In the Spirit of Things* 1994—*The Kansas Box Set* (Legacy)   1995—*Freaks of Nature* (Intersound International); *Kansas* (Epic). Steve Walsh solo: 1979—*Schemer-Dreamer* (Kirshner).

Although Kansas' ornate and complex rock has been dismissed by critics as a pastiche of early-Seventies British progressive rock, some of its albums have sold in the millions. For years the band labored through the Midwest, playing clubs and bars, its odd mix of Anglophilia and boogie falling on mostly bewildered ears. The members met while attending high school in Topeka, and after playing in various local groups, Kerry Livgren, Phil Ehart, and Dave Hope formed the first edition of Kansas in 1970. A year later they changed their name to White Clover and added Robby Steinhardt, a classically trained violinist who had played with orchestras in Europe when his father, chairman of the music history department at the University of Kansas, was there on sabbatical. The group went through numerous personnel changes before Ehart, seeking new ideas, went to England in 1972. On his return four months later, he revived White Clover with Hope, Steinhardt, Richard Williams, and Steve Walsh; Livgren, who became the group's main songwriter, joined soon after, and they reverted to the name Kansas.

The sextet's first album initially sold about 100,000 copies, but constant touring built its following, and Kansas' second and third LPs each sold about 250,000. *Leftoverture* (#5, 1976), which featured "Carry On Wayward Son" (#11, 1977), sold over three million copies. Nineteen seventy-seven's *Point of Know Return* (#4) went triple platinum, garnering two hit singles—"Point of Know Return" (#28) and "Dust in the Wind" (#6). *Two for the Show* (#32, 1978), a live album, is also platinum, and *Monolith* (#10, 1979) (Kansas' first self-produced venture) and *Audio-Visions* (#26, 1980) are gold.

In 1980 schisms began to form within the group. Livgren and then Hope became born-again Christians. Livgren cut a solo album, *Seeds of Change,* in 1980, as Walsh had the previous year with *Schemer-Dreamer.* Walsh also sang on ex-Genesis Steve Hackett's solo album, *Please Don't Touch.* By the end of 1981 Walsh had left the group to form a hard-rock quartet called Streets. *Vinyl Confessions,* the first Kansas LP to feature his replacement, John Elefante, went Top Twenty and delivered a #17 hit with "Play the Game Tonight." But after one more studio album, *Drastic Measures* (1983), the group disbanded. Livgren and Elefante both went on to find considerable success in contemporary Christian music, the former as an artist, the latter as a producer.

In 1986 Ehart, Williams, and Walsh re-grouped, adding the brilliant jazz-fusion guitarist Steve Morse (Dixie Dregs, Steve Morse Band) and bassist Billy Greer, who'd played with Walsh in Streets. Neither of that group's two LPs, *Streets* (1983) and *Crimes in Mind* (1985), had sold well. The revamped Kansas' first album, *Power,* produced the group's fourth, and last, Top Twenty hit, "All I Wanted." However, 1988's *In the Spirit of Things* did not find a receptive audience. *Freaks of Nature*, their next studio effort, appeared seven years later.

Paul Kantner: See Jefferson Airplane

Mick Karn: See Japan

Kasenetz-Katz: See 1910 Fruitgum Company

Katrina and the Waves
Formed 1981, England
Katrina Leskanich (b. 1960, Topeka, Kansas), voc., gtr.; Kimberley Rew (b. Eng.), gtr.; Vince de la Cruz (b. U.S.), bass; Alex Cooper (b. Eng.), drums.
1985—*Katrina and the Waves* (Capitol)   1986—*Waves*   1989—*Break of Hearts* (SBK).

This Anglo-American pop-rock band, which worked four years for its "overnight success," was led by Katrina Leskanich. The daughter of a U.S. Air Force colonel, Leskanich grew up on military bases in Nebraska, Germany, Holland, and England, where she stayed as a teenager after her father threw her out of the house for saying she wanted to be a rock star. She bagged groceries and washed dishes while pursuing her dream, finally hooking up in 1981 with ex–Soft Boys guitarist Kimberley Rew, drummer Alex Cooper (who'd attended Cambridge University with Rew), and American-born bassist Vince de la Cruz (whose father was an air force instructor, and who had met Leskanich through an English church choir directed by his mother). They called themselves Katrina and the Waves (Rew and Cooper had had a band called the Waves in the mid-Seventies).

With its polished pop-rock songs and normal attire, the band did not fit in with England's postpunk new-wave scene. Still, it managed to record a few independent-label singles in England and two albums for Attic Records of Canada, where the band had gigged before signing with Capitol Records. *Katrina and the Waves* (#25, 1985) showcased Leskanich's powerful, confident vocals and Rew's crafty guitar work and songwriting. It produced an instant smash hit in the exuberant "Walking on Sunshine" (#9, 1985), which had nothing to do with the Eddy Grant funk tune of the same name. The debut album also yielded a hit in "Do You Want Crying" (#37, 1985), and included "Going Down to Liverpool" (originally on one of the earlier Canadian albums), which was covered by the Bangles.

Waves (#49, 1986) was a critical and commercial disappointment that spawned only a minor hit single in "Is That It?" (#70, 1986). Capitol dropped the band, which retreated to England when no other offers were forth-

coming. The group wrote some 200 songs, recorded some of them on its own, and eventually saw them released by SBK as *Break of Hearts* (#122, 1989), which yielded a Top Twenty hit in "That's the Way" (#16, 1989). As of spring 1994, Rew had participated in a Soft Boys reunion show in England, and Katrina and the Waves' future was uncertain.

Eric Kaz
Born 1946, Brooklyn, New York
1972—*If You're Lonely* (Atlantic)   1974—*Cul-de-Sac*
1978—*Fuller/Kaz* (Columbia).

A sometime member of the Blues Magoos and American Flyer, Eric Kaz is best known as a songwriter. His morose, romantic heartbreak songs—including "Love Has No Pride," cowritten with Libby Titus—have been covered by Linda Ronstadt, Randy Meisner, Bonnie Raitt, Rita Coolidge, Tom Rush, Lynn Anderson, Tracy Nelson, and Peter Yarrow.

Kaz grew up in a musical family but was unenthusiastic about music lessons. He left his Brooklyn home before graduating from high school and moved to Greenwich Village, where he played in numerous folk and rock groups in the mid-Sixties. He recorded an album with Happy and Artie Traum in a group called the Children of Paradise before joining the Blues Magoos in 1970. After two years the Magoos broke up [see entry].

Kaz wrote and performed soundtracks for two early Brian DePalma movies (*Greetings*, 1968; *Hi Mom*, 1970) before signing a solo contract with Atlantic in 1972. But his singing was not as popular as his songs, and his albums served largely as demos for other singers. Tracy Nelson was one of the first to cover Kaz compositions extensively. Bonnie Raitt was the first to do "Love Has No Pride," but it was Linda Ronstadt's rendition that became a minor hit in 1973. (Kaz has accompanied both Raitt and Ronstadt in the studio.) In 1975 he joined the middleweight supergroup American Flyer (with ex–Blood, Sweat and Tears Steve Katz, ex–Velvet Underground Doug Yule, and ex–Pure Prairie League Craig Fuller), which recorded two albums for United Artists before disbanding.

Kaz has since continued a successful career as a songwriter. Among his credits are cowriting Randy Meisner's "Hearts on Fire" (#19, 1981), Don Johnson's "Heartbeat" (#5, 1986), Michael Bolton's "That's What Love Is All About" (#19, 1987), and George Strait's "I Cross My Heart" (#1 C&W, 1992).

KC and the Sunshine Band/KC
Formed 1973, Florida
Harry Wayne Casey (b. Jan. 31, 1951, Hialeah, Fla.), voc., kybds.; Richard Finch (b. Jan. 25, 1954, Indianapolis, Ind.), bass; Jerome Smith (b. June 18,

1953, Miami, Fla.), gtr.; Robert Johnson (b. Mar. 21, 1953, Miami, Fla.), drums; Fermin Coytisolo (b. Dec. 31, 1951, Havana, Cuba), congas; Ronnie Smith (b. 1952, Hialeah, Fla.), trumpet; Denvil Liptrot, sax; James Weaver, trumpet; Charles Williams (b. Nov. 18, 1954, Rockingham, N.C.), trombone.
1974—*Do It Good* (T.K.) 1975—*The Sound of Sunshine* (a.k.a. *The Sunshine Band*) 1976—*Part 3*; *KC and the Sunshine Band* 1977—*I Like to Do It* (President) 1978—*Who Do Ya (Love)* (T.K.) 1979—*Do You Wanna Go Party?* 1980—*Greatest Hits* 1981—*The Painter* (Epic) 1982—*All in a Night's Work* 1989—*The Best of KC and the Sunshine Band* (Rhino) 1993—*Oh Yeah* (ZYX). KC solo: 1984—*KC Ten* (Meca).

KC and the Sunshine Band were the most successful promulgators of the boisterous, tropically funky dance music known as the Miami Sound. The Sunshine Band originated in the T.K. Studios in Hialeah, Florida, near Miami. H. W. Casey, a former record retailer, began working in 1973 for Tone Distributors, where he met Richard Finch, a Miami session bassist hired by T.K. as an engineer. The two formed a songwriting partnership and recorded as KC and the Sunshine Junkanoo Band. (Junkanoo is a percussion-oriented pop from the Bahama Islands, characterized by a liberal mix of horns, whistles, and vocal chants.) Their first record, "Blow Your Whistle," reached #27 on the R&B chart in 1973, and its followup (as KC and the Sunshine Band), "Sound Your Funky Horn," went to #21 early the next year, persuading T.K. to release an album.

Do It Good was a hit in Europe, and the single "Queen of Clubs" went to #7 on the British chart in 1974 (not placing on the American chart until its reissue two years later) when KC and the Sunshine Band toured the U.K. Casey and Finch wrote, arranged, and produced "Rock Your Baby," a #1 hit for George McCrae (who had sung on *Do It Good*) on both pop and R&B charts in 1974, which sold a reported 11 million copies worldwide. The following year KC and the Sunshine Band struck gold with "Get Down Tonight" (#1 pop and R&B).

KC and the Sunshine Band—now expanded to nine members, all black except for Casey and Finch—ruled the charts and the dance floors for the next three years. "That's the Way (I Like It)" and "(Shake, Shake, Shake) Shake Your Booty" reached #1 on the pop chart in 1975 and 1976, respectively. The Sunshine Band became the first act to score four #1 pop singles in one 12-month period since the Beatles in 1964. Three of these were #1 R&B as well. The band's string of hit singles continued with "I'm Your Boogie Man" (#1 pop, #3 R&B, 1977) and "Keep It Comin' Love" (#2 pop, #1 R&B, 1977).

It looked as if the group had come to the end of the string in 1978 with the minor hits "Boogie Shoes" and "It's the Same Old Song," but in 1979 KC and company returned with "Do You Wanna Go Party" (#8 R&B), "Please Don't Go" (#1 pop), and "Yes, I'm Ready," the last featuring the vocals of Teri De Sario (#2 pop, #20 R&B). In 1984, after Casey recovered from a serious 1982 car crash, he hit the Top Twenty again with "Give It Up," which went to #1 in the U.K. Casey and Finch were also involved in hitmaking—as songwriters, producers, or both—for Betty Wright (her Grammy-winning "Where Is the Love"), Jimmy "Bo" Horne, Fire (the female vocal group that backed the Sunshine Band on "That's the Way"), and Leif Garrett.

In the early Nineties KC revamped his act, releasing a new album and making numerous television and concert appearances, both here and in Europe, where the group always had a strong following.

Ernie K-Doe

Born Ernest Kador Jr., February 22, 1936, New Orleans, Louisiana
N.A.—*Ernie K-Doe* (Janus); *Mother-in-Law* (Minit) 1990—*Ain't No Shame in My Game* (Syla) 1993—*I'm Cocky But I'm Good.*

With his national chart-topper "Mother-in-Law," Ernie K-Doe was one of the young black singers whose jaunty beat and rollicking good humor popularized New Orleans R&B in the early Sixties. Raised by an aunt in New Orleans, Kador was heavily influenced by gospel. By the time he was 15 he had become a member of the Golden Chain Jubilee Singers and the Zion Travellers. He made his first recording when he was in Chicago visiting his mother in 1953. It was never released. He went on to sing with the Moonglows and the Flamingos, and two years later Kador returned to New Orleans, where he made a name for himself with a vocal group called the Blue Diamonds. By then he had legally changed his name to K-Doe.

An outgoing showman, K-Doe made the Blue Diamonds a favorite act in the Crescent City. After recording with them for Savoy, he cut his first solo record, "Do Baby Do," for Specialty in 1956. He also recorded for Herald before "Hello My Lover," a single for Minit, became a regional hit in 1959. His next hit was "Mother-in-Law," a novelty song produced by Allen Toussaint. The record went to #1 on both the pop and R&B charts in 1961.

He followed "Mother-in-Law" with a handful of singles for Minit, the most successful of which were "Te-Ta-Te-Ta-Ta" (#53 pop, #21 R&B, 1961) and "I Cried My Last Tear" (#69, 1961). He later recorded for Duke, placing "Later for Tomorrow" at #37 on the R&B chart in 1967, and subsequently for Janus. Toussaint produced a couple of K-Doe albums in the early Seventies. Into the Nineties, he remained active on the New Orleans club circuit and appeared regularly at Delta region music festivals.

Keith

Born James Barry Keefer, Philadelphia, Pennsylvania
1967—*Keith* (Mercury); *98.6/Ain't Gonna Lie*
1968—*Out of Crank* 1969—*The Adventures of Keith* (RCA).

James Barry Keefer changed his name to Keith and recorded the single "Ain't Gonna Lie," which failed to crack the Top Thirty. But his next 45, "98.6," made it all the way to #7 in 1967 and earned him praise from John Lennon in a chance encounter at a London urinal. Five more singles and four albums went nowhere, however.

In 1969 Uncle Sam cut short Keefer's career. In the middle of a tour he was picked up for draft evasion, inducted into the army, and stationed in New Jersey for one year. After his hitch ended he recorded for Frank Zappa's DiscReet Records and also sang on Zappa's 1973 tour. As of the mid-Eighties Keefer was still involved in music, playing Los Angeles clubs when not tending bar.

Paul Kelly

Born Paul Maurice Kelly, January 13, 1955, Adelaide, Australia
1987—*Gossip* (A&M) 1988—*Under the Sun*
1989—*So Much Water So Close to Home* 1992—*Comedy* (Doctor Dream) 1994—*Wanted Man* (Vanguard).

Paul Kelly has been known to a (relatively small) American audience since 1987, but in his native Australia, this literate songwriter (*So Much Water So Close to Home* takes its title from a Raymond Carver story) has been working since 1977.

Kelly started out as a folksinger, playing Adelaide coffeeshops in the mid-Seventies. He moved to Melbourne in 1977 and became part of that city's pub scene. He played solo and with the bands High Rise Bombers, the Dots (who released two albums), and, finally, the Coloured Girls. The last of these, taken from a lyric in Lou Reed's "Walk on the Wild Side" were signed by A&M for American distribution. For America the name was changed to Paul Kelly and the Messengers in deference to racial sensitivities; the group (Michael Armiger, bass; Michael Barclay, drums; Pedro Bull, keyboards; Steve Connolly, guitar; and Chris Coyne, sax) adopted that name in Australia by 1989. A&M released the Australian double LP *Gossip* in the States as a single album. It mixed writerly craftsmanship with punk passion and was met with critical raves but low sales. Even production by Scott Litt (R.E.M.), brought in for *So Much Water,*

could not change matters, and A&M dropped Kelly in 1989. He moved to the States and spent the next three years looking for a U.S. deal. In 1992 he was signed by the independent Doctor Dream label, released *Comedy,* then moved to Vanguard for 1994's *Wanted Man.*

Eddie Kendricks: See the Temptations

Chris Kenner

Born December 25, 1929, Kenner, Louisiana; died January 25, 1976
1963—*Land of a Thousand Dances* (Atlantic).

New Orleans vocalist Chris Kenner had a hit single in 1961 with "I Like It Like That." But in the record business—and especially the New Orleans music community in which he was active from the Fifties—he was best known for writing songs that were hits for Fats Domino, Wilson Pickett, and the Dave Clark Five.

Kenner started his career as a singer with a gospel quartet, the New Orleans Harmonizing Four, in the early Fifties and made his first records for the Baton and Imperial labels in 1957. His "Sick and Tired" on Imperial was cut that year, but Fats Domino's cover made #22 in 1958. Kenner remained a local figure, recording for labels like Pontchartrain, until he teamed up with Allen Toussaint, producer for Minit Records' Instant label. "I Like It Like That," their first collaboration, went to #2 on both the R&B and pop charts in 1961. The song returned to the Top Ten four years later in a cover version by the Dave Clark Five. Kenner's classic "Land of 1000 Dances"—which in his 1963 rendition made it to #77—was a #6 hit for Wilson Pickett in 1966 and a #30 hit for Cannibal and the Headhunters in 1965. Two other acts, the Three Midniters and Electric Indian, had modest hits with the song. Kenner's 1964 recording of "Something You Got" was a huge success in New Orleans.

Alcoholism plagued Kenner throughout his life, which hit a low with his 1968 conviction for statutory rape. He continued to record with Instant until 1969 and died seven years later of a heart attack.

Kentucky Colonels

Formed 1961, California
Clarence White (b. June 7, 1944, Lewiston, Maine; d. July 14, 1973, Palmdale, Calif.), gtr., voc.; Billy Ray Lathum (b. Jan. 12, 1938), banjo; Roland White (b. Apr. 23, 1938, Madawaska, Maine), mandolin, voc.; Roger Bush, bass; LeRoy Mack, dobro; Bobby Sloane, fiddle.
1963—*New Sounds of Bluegrass America* (Briar)
1964—*Appalachian Swing!* (World Pacific) 1965—(– Sloane; – C. White) 1973—(+ C. White; – C.

White) 1974—(+ Clarence White) *Kentucky Colonels* (Rounder) 1975—*Livin' in the Past* (+ Scotty Stoneman, voc., fiddle); *The Kentucky Colonels with Scotty Stoneman* 1978—*Kentucky Colonels 1966* 1979—*Kentucky Colonels 1965–1967* 1980—*Clarence White and the Kentucky Colonels* 1984—*On Stage* 1991—*Long Journey Home* (Vanguard).

A seminal bluegrass band, the Kentucky Colonels featured brothers, mandolinist Roland White and guitarist Clarence White, who later went on to fame in the last edition of the Byrds. The Maine-born White brothers had been playing country music since 1954 as the Country Boys (with brother Eric on bass). In 1961 Roger Bush replaced Eric White, and the Kentucky Colonels was formed. The group established itself at folk festivals and throughout the national bluegrass circuit; it performed twice on Andy Griffith's TV show. The group's 1964 masterpiece, *Appalachian Swing!*, was reissued by Rounder in 1993.

In 1965 Clarence White left the group, turning his attention to the electric guitar and quickly becoming a top Los Angeles sessionman. White joined the Byrds in 1968 [see entry], staying until the group split up in 1973. Roland White unsuccessfully attempted to revive the Kentucky Colonels after Clarence's departure; Roland later worked with Bill Monroe and Lester Flatt and, in the Seventies, Country Gazette.

Following the Byrds' demise, the Kentucky Colonels regrouped with Clarence White for occasional shows. After one of these 1973 performances, in Southern California, Clarence White was killed by a drunk driver while loading his equipment into a van. Roland White has continued to perform on the folk and bluegrass circuit with various aggregations of players.

The Kentucky HeadHunters
Formed 1986, Edmonton, Kentucky
Greg Martin (b. Mar. 31, 1953, Louisville, Ky.), gtr.; Ricky Lee Phelps (b. ca. 1954, Cardwell, Mo.), voc.; Doug Phelps (b. ca. 1960, Cardwell, Mo.), bass, voc.; Richard Young (b. Jan. 27, 1955, Glasgow, Ky.), gtr., voc.; Fred Young (b. Sep. 8, 1958, Glasgow, Ky.), drums.
1989—*Pickin' On Nashville* (Mercury) 1991—*Electric Barnyard* (- R. L. Phelps; – Doug Phelps; + Anthony Kenny [b. Mar. 8, 1959, Glasgow, Ky.], bass; + Mark S. Orr [b. Nov. 16, 1948, Charlotte, Mich.], voc.) 1993—*Rave On!!* 1994—*That'll Work* (with Johnnie Johnson) (Elektra Nonesuch).
Brother Phelps, formed 1992 (R. L. Phelps, voc.; D. Phelps, gtr., voc.): 1993—*Let Go* (Asylum) 1995—*Anyway the Wind Blows.*

The Kentucky HeadHunters (the name comes from Muddy Waters' Fifties band the Headchoppers) play a brand of guitar-based country rock they call "hillbilly speed metal." The HeadHunters arose from the ashes of a popular but ill-fated Kentucky bar band, Itchy Brother, which was set to sign with Led Zeppelin's Swan Song label in 1980 when John Bonham's death scuttled talks.

Signed to Mercury Records on the basis of a homemade tape (released, with two additional songs, as *Pickin' On Nashville*), their first single, a metallic cover of Bill Monroe's "Walk Softly on This Heart of Mine," gave notice they were not your usual country band. It barely broke the Top Thirty, and their next single, "Dumas Walker," only reached #26 C&W, but the album turned gold faster than any other country debut, eventually selling almost two million copies and earning the band a Grammy for Best Country Performance by Duo or a Group with Vocal.

Electric Barnyard (#29) proved the HeadHunters were no fluke, going gold in one week, supported by the band's near-constant touring (270 dates in one year). The Phelps brothers left the band to pursue a more traditional sound just before the band recorded its third album. They signed with Elektra/Asylum and began recording as Brother Phelps. The HeadHunters persevered, bringing back former Itchy Brothers Orr and Kennedy and recording *Rave On!!*. They also collaborated with legendary barrelhouse piano player Johnnie Johnson (Muddy Waters, Chuck Berry) on the 1994 album *That'll Work.*

Doug Kershaw
Born January 24, 1936, Teil Ridge, Louisiana
1969—*The Cajun Way* (Warner Bros.) 1970—*Spanish Moss* 1971—*Doug Kershaw* 1972—*Swamp Grass; Devil's Elbow* 1973—*Douglas James Kershaw* 1974—*Mama Kershaw's Boy* 1975—*Alive and Pickin'* 1976—*The Ragin' Cajun* 1977—*Flip Flop Fly* 1978—*Louisiana Man* 1979—*Louisiana Cajun Country* (Starflite) 1989—*The Best of Doug Kershaw* (Warner Bros.).

Doug Kershaw is America's best-known Cajun fiddler, though his traditional bayou sound has always been a bit too exotic to secure him a major country or rock audience. Kershaw was born on a tiny island in the Gulf of Mexico in a poor French-speaking community and didn't learn English until after he turned eight. His father was an alligator hunter who shot himself through the head when Doug was just seven. The family soon relocated to Lake Arthur, Louisiana, where Doug went to school and practiced on his older brother's fiddle, which he'd first fooled with at age five; he has since taught himself 28 other instruments.

Kershaw played his first date at age eight, at a local

bar called the Bucket of Blood, with his mother accompanying him on guitar. He graduated from McNeese State University with a degree in mathematics, and then with two of his brothers he formed the Continental Playboys.

Kershaw was writing by the time he left the bayou at age 18 to try to record in Nashville. Billed as Rusty and Doug, Kershaw and his 16-year-old brother Rusty recorded for Hickory Records and became regulars on the Grand Ole Opry by 1957. After a stint in the army, in 1960 Kershaw penned his best-known piece, "Louisiana Man," which went to #10 on the country & western chart the next year and became a country standard. Also in 1961 the two hit the C&W list with "Diggy Liggy Lo" (#14), but he and his brother had no followup, and they soon broke up.

It wasn't until the later Sixties that Kershaw got beyond his regional reputation. With the help of producer Buddy Killen, he got a contract with Warner Bros., which led to 1969's *The Cajun Way*. His appearance on *The Johnny Cash Show* that summer (on the same program as Bob Dylan) attracted national attention and brought him to the rock circuit.

Kershaw was offered a cameo acting role in the "psychedelic western" movie *Zachariah*, and also appeared in *Medicine Ball Caravan* (a rock tour film), *We Have Come for Your Daughters*, and 1978's *Days of Heaven*. He continues to tour and record.

Chaka Khan

Born Yvette Marie Stevens, March 23, 1953, Great Lakes, Illinois
1978—*Chaka* (Warner Bros.)   1980—*Naughty*
1981—*What 'Cha Gonna Do for Me*   1982—*Echoes of an Era* (Elektra-Musician); *Chaka Khan* (Warner Bros.)   1984—*I Feel for You*   1986—*Destiny*
1988—*CK*   1989—*Life Is a Dance/The Remix Project*
1992—*The Woman I Am*.
With Rufus: 1973—*Rufus* (ABC)   1974—*Rags to Rufus*; *Rufu-sized*   1975—*Rufus Featuring Chaka Khan*   1977—*Ask Rufus*   1978—*Street Player*
1979—*Numbers*; *Masterjam* (MCA)   1981—*Party 'Til You're Broke*; *Camouflage*   1983—*Live—Stompin' at the Savoy* (Warner Bros.).

Chaka Khan, lead singer for Rufus and later a solo act, grew up on Chicago's South Side. At age 11 she formed her first band, the Crystalettes, which played the Chicago area. She was also very active at school and became president of the Black Students Union at age 16. At the time she was also a member of the Afro-Arts Theater, which toured briefly with Mary Wells. A few years later, when Khan was working on the Black Panthers' breakfast program, she took her African name, Chaka, which means "fire."

In 1969 Khan quit school and worked with a band called Lyfe and then the Babysitters, doing endless sets of dance music. In 1972 she teamed up with Kevin Murphy (ex–American Breed) and Andre Fisher to form Rufus. The band went on to earn six gold or platinum LPs before Khan went solo in 1978. Her first album, *Chaka*, was produced by Arif Mardin and featured members of the Average White Band and Rufus guitarist Tony Maiden. It went gold and contained Ashford and Simpson's "I'm Every Woman" (#21, and a 1993 hit for Whitney Houston).

While under contract to do two more LPs with Rufus, with whom she traded barbs in the press, Khan continued to record solo LPs and tour with her own band. In 1979 she did some backup vocals on Ry Cooder's *Bop Till You Drop*, and in 1982 she recorded live with Rufus at New York's Savoy Theater. She also collaborated with Lenny White, Chick Corea, Freddie Hubbard, Joe Henderson, and Stanley Clarke on an album of jazz standards, *Echoes of an Era*.

Khan's pop career was revived by *I Feel for You* (#14, 1984), which went platinum and yielded a #3 pop hit in the title track, an obscure song written by Prince, from his second album. Khan's version mixed in rapping by Melle Mel of Grandmaster Flash and the Furious Five, rap-style turntable-scratching effects, and harmonica flourishes by Stevie Wonder. The track won Khan a Grammy for Best Female R&B Vocal. While she continued to score R&B hits, Khan's subsequent efforts fared disappointingly on the pop charts: *Destiny* reached #67, and *CK* only #125. After that album, Khan moved to Europe, splitting time between homes in England and West Germany. She sang backing vocals on Steve Winwood's hit "Higher Love." In 1990 she won a Grammy for her duet with Ray Charles, "I'll Be Good to You." Khan's sister Taka Boom is also a singer, with a recording career of her own; Khan's daughter Milini is a member of the group Pretty in Pink.

Kid Creole and the Coconuts/Dr. Buzzard's Original Savannah Band

Dr. Buzzard's Original Savannah Band, formed 1974, New York City, New York (August Darnell [b. Thomas August Darnell Browder, Aug. 12, 1950, Bronx, N.Y.], voc., bass, gtr.; "Sugar-Coated" Andy Hernandez [a.k.a. Coati Mundi, b. Jan. 3, 1953, New York City], vibraphone, voc.; Stony Browder Jr. [b. 1949, Bronx, N.Y.], gtr., kybds.; Cory Daye [b. Apr. 25, 1952, Bronx, N.Y.], voc.; Mickey Sevilla [b. 1953, Puerto Rico], drums): 1976—*Dr. Buzzard's Original Savannah Band* (RCA)   1978—*Dr. Buzzard's Original Savannah Band Meets King Penett*   1980—*James Monroe H.S. Presents Dr. Buzzard's Original Savannah Band Goes to Washington* (Elektra).

Kid Creole (a.k.a. August Darnell)

Kid Creole and the Coconuts, formed 1980, New York City (Original lineup, Darnell; Hernandez; Fonda Rae, voc.; Lourdes Cotto, voc.; Brooksie Wells, voc.; Franz Krauns, gtr.; Andrew Lloyd, perc.; Winston Grennan, drums; Peter Schott, kybds.): 1980—*Off the Coast of Me* (Ze/Antilles) 1981— *Fresh Fruit in Foreign Places* (Sire) 1982—*Wise Guy* 1983—*Doppelganger* 1985—*In Praise of Older Women and Other Crimes* (Sire) 1987— *I, Too, Have Seen the Woods* 1990—*Private Waters in the Great Divide* (Columbia) 1991—*You Shoulda Told Me You Were . . .* 1992—*Kid Creole Redux* (Sire).

August Darnell's career has been marked by a mixture of different sounds he called "mulatto music," a combination of Latin, Caribbean, and disco rhythms with big band, swing, and pop show tunes.

The Bronx-born child of a Dominican father and French-Canadian mother, in 1965 Darnell formed the rock band the In-Laws with his brother, Stony Browder Jr. By 1976 they had formed Dr. Buzzard's Original Savannah Band, enlisting Browder's girlfriend, Cory Daye, as vocalist. That year "Whispering/Cherchez la Femme/ Se Si Bon," became a hit in New York discos, eventually reached #27 pop and #31 R&B. Later albums had trouble finding success on increasing segmented radio playlists; by 1980 the Savannah Band had all but collapsed.

Darnell originally envisioned Kid Creole and the Coconuts as a side project while Browder put together a new Savannah Band. He had produced albums for Machine and James Chance and signed a deal with Ze Records in 1980. Taking Hernandez along as cocomposer and arranger, Darnell saw Kid Creole as modern America, embodying all races and cultures. He also insisted the band be small enough to tour, something the string- and horn-laden Savannah Band could not. Onstage, band members assumed fictitious identities, sported costumes, and were part of a choreographed and elaborately produced show.

The Coconuts' debut album, *Off the Coast of Me*, and its followup, *Fresh Fruit in Foreign Places* (#180, 1981), told the story of Mimi, a tale conceived along the lines of a Latin/Caribbean *Odyssey*, with the music reflecting each stop of the story's travels. With former Savannah Band member Gichy Dan providing rapping narratives, the band performed the albums' material at New York's Public Theater.

Signs of fracture surfaced with *Wise Guy* (#145, 1982). Originally conceived as a Darnell solo project, it became a Coconuts album at the request of Warner Bros. executives. The album gave the Coconuts their only U.S. chart single, "I'm a Wonderful Thing, Baby" (#44 R&B, 1982). Kid Creole albums became Darnell albums in all but name, with the Coconuts a loose amalgamation of musicians and singers.

More popular in England, where the Coconuts had three Top Ten hits in 1982 ("I'm a Wonderful Thing, Baby," #4, "Stool Pigeon," #7, "Annie, I'm Not Your Daddy," #2), Darnell began to tour Europe extensively, appearing at the Montreux Jazz Festival and performing for the United Nations in Geneva. In the States, the Coconuts were seen in the 1984 movie *Against All Odds* and provided the music for the Francis Ford Coppola segment of *New York Stories* (1989).

Darnell recorded three more albums for Sire before he moved the Coconuts to Columbia Records in 1990. Their Columbia debut, *Private Waters in the Great Divide*, featured "The Sex of It," a song written and produced for the band by Prince.

Kid Frost

**Born Arturo Molina Jr., May 31, 1962, Los Angeles, California
1990—*Hispanic Causing Panic* (Virgin) 1992—*East Side Story*.**

Kid Frost uses hip-hop to raise Chicano consciousness, rapping in Spanish and English about life in East Los Angeles. The son of a musically minded career military man, Arturo Molina was raised on bases in Guam and Germany. Exposed to Latin music at home, he began playing guitar, keyboards, and drums. When his family returned to East L.A., he discovered the rough urban life he documents in his songs.

Kid Frost made a critical splash with his debut, *Hispanic Causing Panic* (#67 pop, #45 R&B, 1990), whose anthemic single "La Raza" (#42, 1990) heralded a new era of Latin rap. On the track "Come Together," Frost rapped about the importance of uniting rather than fighting. He practiced what he preached by founding Latin Alliance, a coalition of Hispanic rappers, in 1989. The 1991 Virgin album *Latin Alliance* featured Frost and Cuban-born Mellow Man Ace rapping with War on "Low Rider."

East Side Story (#73 pop, #54 R&B, 1992) paints blunt pictures of urban life. The single "No Sunshine," an update of the classic Bill Withers tune, was featured as the chilling backdrop to *American Me*, Edward James Olmos' film about prison life. The album includes cameos by Main Source and Boo-Yaa T.R.I.B.E. Frost follows up his messages by playing benefits for Rock the Vote and supporting antigang activities. In 1992 he rapped on "City of Fallen Angels," a record raising funds for relief efforts after the L.A. riots.

Kid 'n Play

Formed circa 1988, East Elmhurst, Queens, New York
Kid (b. Christopher Reid, Apr. 5, 1964, Bronx, N.Y.), voc.; Play (b. Christopher Martin, July 10, 1962, Queens, N.Y.), voc.
1988—*2 Hype* (Select)   1990—*Kid 'n Play's Funhouse*   1991—*Face the Nation*.

Kid 'n Play, best known for their rap and dance performances in the *House Party* movies of the early Nineties, represent hip-hop's wholesome, middle-class, television-friendly image in much the same way as Jazzy Jeff and the Fresh Prince. With his freckles and seven-inch-high vertical hairstyle, Kid, the son of a black social worker father and white teacher mother, is one of the most recognizable faces of rap; his sidekick Play, child of an ex-con-turned-minister father and church secretary mother, sports a cleaner-cut look with his neatly trimmed mustache and wacky, self-designed clothes.

Formed in the same Queens neighborhood that spawned turntable king Eric B., of Eric B. and Rakim, as well as rap producer Hurby "Luv Bug" Azor, the duo's early singles provided an upbeat alternative to New York City's harder-edged hip-hop. Their first hit, "Rollin' with Kid 'n Play" (#11 R&B, 1989), was fun and catchy. The duo followed up with several moderate hits including "2 Hype" (#46 R&B, 1989), "Fun House (The House We Dance In)" (#27 R&B, 1990), and "Ain't Gonna Hurt Nobody" (#51 pop, #26 R&B, 1991).

After *2 Hype*, with its expanded palette of go-go and house styles, sold nearly a million copies, hitting the Top Ten on the R&B albums chart, the success threatened Kid 'n Play's street credibility; they were accused in some circles of selling out. The group's complete crossover into the pop mainstream came in 1990 when they appeared in Reginald and Warrington Hudlin's surprise hit movie *House Party* with a performance that drew comparisons to Abbott and Costello. As of 1994 Kid 'n Play had returned to the silver screen three times, in *House Party 2* (1991), *Class Act* (1992), and *House Party 3* (1994), and starred in their own Saturday morning cartoon series, *Kid 'n Play*.

Johnny Kidd and the Pirates

Formed 1959, England
Best known and longest-lived lineup: Johnny Kidd (b. Frederick Heath, Dec. 23, 1939, London, Eng.; d. Oct. 7, 1966, Eng.), voc.; Mick Green, gtr.; Johnny Spence, bass; Frank Farley, drums.
1978—*Best of Johnny Kidd and the Pirates* (EMI); *Out of Their Skulls* (Warner Bros.)   1979—*Skull Wars*.

Singer Johnny Kidd is best remembered as coauthor of the rock classic "Shakin' All Over," a tune covered by many bands, including the Guess Who and the Who. Although Kidd and the Pirates never gained a commercial foothold in the United States, in his homeland Kidd is revered, and his band, the Pirates, is recognized as one of the first hard-rocking bands England produced before 1962 and a prototype for the heavy-metal guitar trios it predated by nearly a decade.

Kidd and the Pirates were primarily a singles and live concert act. Onstage, Kidd wore black leather and an eyepatch. Their first hit was Kidd's 1959 "Please Don't Touch," which hit #25 on the U.K. singles chart. A year later "Shakin' All Over," epitomizing Kidd's intense, Gene Vincent–inspired hard-rockabilly approach, was a #1 U.K. hit. "You Got What It Takes" (#25) and "Restless" (#22) were other 1960 successes, but the band didn't hit again until 1963's "I'll Never Get Over You," which went to #4. "Hungry for Love," which got as high as #20 that year, was the band's last commercial gasp, as the Merseybeat explosion put it permanently out of the limelight.

In April 1966 Kidd, depressed over his declining fortunes, disbanded the group, only to return a month later with a new lineup that included Nick Simper (later of Deep Purple). That fall Kidd died in a car crash. Ten years later, in 1976, Mick Green (who'd played with Billy J. Kramer and the Dakotas and the Cliff Bennett Band) re-formed the original Pirates with Spence and Farley. This revived lineup stayed together and recorded four U.K. albums before they broke up in 1982. By then Green was a well-established guitar hero.

Greg Kihn Band/Greg Kihn

Formed 1975, Berkeley, California
Original lineup: Greg Kihn (b. 1952, Baltimore, Md.),
voc., gtr.; Robbie Dunbar, gtr.; Larry Lynch, drums,
voc.; Steve Wright, bass, voc.
1976—*Greg Kihn* (Beserkley) (– Dunbar; + Dave
Carpender, lead gtr.)   1977—*Greg Kihn Again*
1978—*Next of Kihn*   1979—*With the Naked Eye*
1980—*Glass House Rock* (+ Gary Phillips, kybds.)
1981—*Rockihnroll*   1982—*Kihntinued* (– Carpender; + Greg Douglass, lead gtr.)   1983—*Kihnspiracy*
1984—*Kihntagious* (EMI Beserkley)   1985—*Citizen
Kihn* (EMI)   1986—*Love and Rock and Roll*   1989—
Unkihntrollable (Rhino)   1993—*Kihn of Hearts*;
Kihnsolidation: The Best of Greg Kihn (Rhino)
1994—*Mutiny* (Clean Cuts).

Greg Kihn's band—a power-pop outfit influenced by
the Yardbirds, the Beau Brummels, and Bruce Springsteen, among others—began as one of the four original acts on the Beserkley label of Berkeley, California.
Kihn first came to Berkeley from Baltimore in late
1974 and wound up contributing two solo songs to
the 1975 anthology *Beserkley Chartbusters, vol. 1*. He
also did backup vocals on Jonathan Richman's "Roadrunner."

At the time, Kihn used Earth Quake as his support
band, and his first album in 1976 featured guitarist Robbie Dunbar from that group (Dunbar's brother Tommy
was in the Rubinoos, another Beserkley act), plus bassist
Steve Wright and drummer Larry Lynch. Kihn kept
Wright and Lynch and added Dave Carpender to replace
Dunbar in early 1976. The band's second album was
harder rocking than the first and included a reworking of
Springsteen's "For You"; Springsteen later adapted the
arrangement for his own live shows.

The band's next few albums began to sell (about
125,000 copies each), and it built a following in the Bay
Area. But Kihn never developed more than a cult follow-
ing until *Rockihnroll's* "The Breakup Song (They Don't
Write 'Em)" reached #15 in 1981. Keyboardist Gary
Phillips, who joined in time for that album, had previ-
ously worked in Earth Quake and Copperhead, with ex-
Quicksilver guitarist John Cipollina.

"Jeopardy" and its popular video brought Kihn to the
Top Five in 1983 and pushed *Kihnspiracy* to #15. *Kihntagious* peaked at #121 the following year. His last hit was
"Lucky" (#30) in 1985. While Kihn has not repeated that
chart success, he has continued to release a number of
albums, both under his name and with the group. He
writes and edits a fan newsletter called *Rocklife* and has
written a number of screenplays and novels, including
The Real Reason English Rock Stars Love America,
which Kihn plans to serialize on the Internet. The critically acclaimed *Mutiny* featured Kihn in an acoustic setting, performing songs by Elliott Murphy, the Temptations, and Bob Dylan, among others.

Killing Joke

Formed 1978, London, England
Jaz Coleman (b. Feb. 26, 1960, Cheltenham, Eng.),
voc., kybds.; Geordie (b. K. Walker, Dec. 18, 1958,
Newcastle-upon-Tyne, Eng.), gtr.; Youth (b. Martin
Glover, Dec. 27, 1960, Africa), bass; Paul Ferguson
(b. Mar. 31, 1958, High Wycombe, Eng.), drums.
1980—*Killing Joke* (EG)   1981—*What's This
For . . . !*   1982—*Revelations; Ha! Killing Joke
Live EP* (– Geordie; – Youth; + Paul Raven, bass)
1983—*Fire Dances*   1985—*Night Time*   1987—
Brighter Than a Thousand Suns   1988—*Outside the
Gate* (– Ferguson; + Geordie, gtr.; + Martin Atkins
[b. Aug. 3, 1959, Coventry, Eng.], drums)   1990—
Extremities, Dirt, & Various Repressed Emotions
(Noise/RCA)   1994—*Pandemonium* (Big Life/Zoo).

Known for its loud, energetic stage performances—with
frontman Jaz Coleman wearing warpaint on his face and
shaking maniacally—England's Killing Joke initially
tried to bridge the seemingly disparate styles of punk
rock and disco with a big dance beat and noisy, abrasive
guitars. In this regard the band was similar to Public
Image Ltd., and in fact in its late-Eighties incarnation
Killing Joke included ex-PiL drummer Martin Atkins. The
band was also known for sometimes savage lyrics and
often sardonic and controversial record-sleeve art and
posters. Killing Joke was banned from performing a
Glasgow, Scotland, gig after a 1980 concert poster depicted Pope Pius XII appearing to bless two columns of
Nazi brownshirts.

Jaz Coleman, reportedly of Egyptian descent, first
began working with ex–Matt Stagger Band drummer
Paul Ferguson; Youth, who had played with the Rage at
the seminal London punk club the Vortex, and guitarist
Geordie soon joined. Their first single, "Wardance," found
careening punkish energy and stomping metallic mass
colliding over a martial rhythm. Legendary British radio
DJ John Peel, who was so impressed by "Wardance" he
said it had to be someone famous recording under an assumed name, gave it intense play. The walloping tribal
rhythms of such early Killing Joke singles as "Psyche"
and "Follow the Leader" actually landed the group on
Billboard's disco chart.

Coleman's occult obsessions led the band to disinte-
grate after its third album; he fled to Iceland in anticipation of the Apocalypse. Youth followed, then returned to
England to work with Ferguson on a new band called
Brilliant. But then Ferguson went to Iceland too, taking
new bassist Paul Raven with him. The revamped Killing
Joke returned to England and recorded more conventional albums, lacking the ominous power of its earlier

work. Geordie rejoined for the *Extremities* album, a return to noisy avant-dance form. After a four-year hiatus, Killing Joke came back as a three piece—Coleman, Geordie, and original bassist Youth—releasing the harshly metallic album *Pandemonium*. In fall 1994 the trio embarked on a world tour.

Albert King

Born Albert Nelson, April 25, 1923, Indianola, Mississippi; died December 21, 1992, Memphis, Tennessee
1962—*The Big Blues* (King) 1967—*Born Under a Bad Sign* (Stax) 1968—*King of the Blues Guitar* (Atlantic) 1972—*I'll Play the Blues for You* (Stax) 1975—*Truckload of Lovin'* (Utopia) 1977—*The Pinch* (Stax) 1979—*Chronicle; New Orleans Heat* (Tomato) 1982—*Albert King Masterworks* (Atlantic/Deluxe) 1986—*The Best of Albert King* (Stax/Fantasy) 1989—*Let's Have a Natural Ball* (Modern Blues) 1990—*Wednesday Night in San Francisco (Live at the Fillmore)* (Stax/Fantasy); *Thursday Night in San Francisco (Live at the Fillmore).*

Albert King's mammoth physical presence—he weighed more than 250 pounds and stood six-feet-four—was reflected in his harsh, imposing vocals and biting, influential blues style. He bought his first guitar for $1.25 sometime around 1931 (he later played a left-handed Gibson Flying V), and his first inspiration was T-Bone Walker. For a long while he had to work nonmusic jobs to survive (including bulldozer operator and mechanic), but in the late Forties King settled in Osceola, Arkansas, and worked local gigs with In the Groove Boys. He then migrated North, where he played drums for Jimmy Reed and also sang and played guitar on his own singles, including "Lonesome in My Bedroom" and "Bad Luck Blues" for Parrot in 1953.

King then moved to St. Louis and formed another band, but he didn't record again until 1959, when he signed to the local Bobbin label. He worked for several small companies in the early Sixties, including King Records, which released his 1961 hit "Don't Throw Your Love on Me Too Strong" (#14 R&B). But King's real break came in 1966, when he signed to Stax. Using the label's famed Memphis sidemen, he cut some of his best-known works, including "Laundromat Blues" (1966) and his album *Born Under a Bad Sign*, made with Booker T. and the MG's in 1967. King began to break through to white audiences: He appeared on the first Fillmore East show on March 8, 1968, with Tim Buckley and Big Brother and the Holding Company, and also played at the hall's closing concerts on June 27, 1971. (A live album, *Live Wire/Blues Power*, had been recorded at Fillmore West.)

In November 1969 King played with the St. Louis Symphony Orchestra, forming what was termed "an 87-piece blues band." Over the years his songs have been covered by Free, John Mayall, the Electric Flag, and others. He toured more than ever in the Seventies, though he left Stax in 1974. King signed to Utopia in 1976 and to Tomato in 1978, charting some minor R&B singles. In 1990 he made a guest appearance on guitarist Gary Moore's *Still Got the Blues,* and he continued to perform until his death from a heart attack at age 69. At King's funeral, Joe Walsh—just one of many six-string disciples—paid tribute with a slide-guitar rendition of "Amazing Grace."

B. B. King

Born Riley B. King, September 16, 1925, Indianola, Mississippi
1965—*Live at the Regal* (ABC) 1968—*B. B. King Story* (Blue Horizon) 1969—*B. B. King Story, vol. 2; Live and Well* (Bluesway/Dunhill); *Completely Well* 1970—*Indianola Mississippi Seeds* (ABC) 1971—*Live in Cook County Jail; Live at the Regal* 1973—*The Best of B. B. King* 1974—*Together for the First Time . . . Live* (with Bobby "Blue" Bland) (MCA) 1975—*Lucille Talks Back* (ABC) 1976—*B. B. King Anthology; Together Again . . . Live* (with Bobby "Blue" Bland) (MCA) 1977—*Kingsize* (ABC); *Lucille* 1978—*Midnight Believer* 1979—*Take It Home* 1981—*There Must Be a Better World Somewhere* (MCA) 1983—*Blues 'n' Jazz* 1985—*Six Silver Strings* 1986—*The Best of B. B. King, vol. 1* (Flair) 1989—*King of the Blues* 1990—*Live at San Quentin* 1991—*There Is Always One More Time; Live at the Apollo* (GRP) 1993—*Blues Summit* (MCA).

B. B. King is universally recognized as the leading exponent of modern blues. Playing his trademark Gibson guitar, which he refers to affectionately as Lucille, King's voicelike string bends and left-hand vibrato have influenced numerous rock guitarists, including Eric Clapton, Mike Bloomfield, and David Gilmour of Pink Floyd, as well as modern blues players such as Buddy Guy.

King (who is not related to the late blues guitar great Albert King, although both were born in Indianola, Mississippi) picked cotton as a youth, for which he earned as little as 35¢ per 100 pounds. In the Forties he played on the streets of Indianola before moving on to perform professionally in Memphis around 1949. As a young musician he studied recordings by both blues and jazz guitarists, including T-Bone Walker, Charlie Christian, and Django Reinhardt. During his first years in Memphis he lived with his cousin, bluesman Bukka White.

In the early Fifties King was a disc jockey on Memphis black station WDIA, where he was dubbed the

B. B. King

gold *Together for the First Time . . . Live* (1974) and *Together Again . . . Live* (1976). Stevie Wonder produced King's "To Know You Is to Love You." In 1982 King recorded a live album with the Crusaders.

King's tours have taken him to Russia (1979), South America (1980), and dozens of prisons. His concern for prisoners led him, along with attorney F. Lee Bailey, to establish the Foundation for the Advancement of Inmate Rehabilitation and Recreation in 1972. Nineteen-eighty marked the publication of Charles Sawyer's authorized biography, *The Arrival of B. B. King.* In 1981 *There Must Be a Better World Somewhere* won a Grammy Award; he won another in 1990 for *Live at San Quentin.* He was inducted into the Blues Foundation Hall of Fame in 1984 and the Rock and Roll Hall of Fame in 1987. In 1989 he sang and played with U2 on "When Love Comes to Town," from *Rattle and Hum.* In May 1991 he opened B. B. King's Blues Club in Memphis. For *Blues Summit,* King was joined by such fellow bluesmen as John Lee Hooker, Lowell Fulson, and Robert Cray.

King once said he aspired to be an "ambassador of the blues," the way Louis Armstrong had been considered America's "jazz ambassador to the world," and by the Nineties he seemed to have attained just that iconic status: He joined younger pop, country, rock, and rap stars in the prorecycling video "Yakety Yak (Take It Back)," and on the album *Simpsons Sing the Blues* from the hit animated TV series, and he continued to keep the blues before mainstream audiences of all stripes through frequent appearances on late-night TV talk shows.

Ben E. King
Born Benjamin Earl Nelson, September 23, 1938, Henderson, North Carolina
1961—*Spanish Harlem* (Atco)   1964—*Ben E. King's Greatest Hits* (Atlantic)   1975—*Supernatural Thing; Ben E. King Story*   1976—*I Had a Love*   1977—*Benny and Us* (with the Average White Band) (Atco)   1978—*Let Me Live in Your Life* (Atlantic)   1981—*Street Tough*   1987—*The Ultimate Collection: Ben E. King*   1993—*Anthology* (Atlantic/Atco).

Ben E. King's smooth tenor earned him a reputation as a romantic R&B singer for a career that has spanned more than 40 years. He hit a commercial peak as lead vocalist for the late-period Drifters and as a solo artist in the early Sixties. King sang in church choirs in North Carolina, and when his family moved to Harlem he formed his first group while attending James Fenimore Cooper Junior High. It was called the Four B's, as all members' names started with B. In the mid-Fifties King tried out unsuccessfully for the Moonglows, but by 1956 he had joined a professional band, the Five Crowns, whose manager supposedly found the 18-year-old King through a chance

"Beale Street Blues Boy." Eventually, Blues Boy was shortened to B. B., and the nickname stuck. The radio show and performances in Memphis with friends Johnny Ace and Bobby "Blue" Bland built King's strong local reputation.

One of his first recordings, "Three O'Clock Blues" (#1 R&B), for the RPM label, was a national success in 1951, landing King bookings at major black venues like Harlem's Apollo and Washington, D.C.'s Howard. During the Fifties King was a consistent record seller and concert attraction. In 1956 he played 342 one-nighters. He had recorded for the small black-oriented labels Kent, Crown, and Blue Horizon before signing with ABC Records in 1961.

King's *Live at the Regal* is considered one of the definitive blues albums. The mid-Sixties blues revival introduced him to white audiences, and by 1966 he was appearing regularly on rock concert circuits and receiving airplay on progressive rock radio. He continued to have hits on the R&B chart ("Paying the Cost to Be the Boss," #10 R&B, 1968) and always maintained a solid black following. *Live and Well,* produced by Bill Szymczyk (who later produced the Eagles), was a notable album, featuring "Why I Sing the Blues" (#13 R&B, 1969) and King's only pop Top Twenty single, "The Thrill Is Gone" (#15 pop, #3 R&B, 1970).

In the Seventies King also recorded albums with longtime friend and onetime chauffeur Bobby Bland: the meeting. King toured with the band, which included Bobby Hendricks, who left to become lead singer for the Drifters in 1957.

The Five Crowns made 11 records between 1952 and 1958, none of them hits, but in 1959 the Drifters' manager, George Treadwell (who owned the name but was deserted by the original band), thought the Crowns were good enough to become his "new Drifters." The new group immediately hit it big with "There Goes My Baby" (#2 pop, #1 R&B, 1959), sung and cowritten by King, and reputedly the first R&B hit to use strings. King sang lead on two other gold singles for the band (all produced by Leiber and Stoller), including their biggest pop smash and only #1, "Save the Last Dance for Me" (1960). He also sang on the standard "This Magic Moment" (#16 pop, #4 R&B, 1960).

In midwinter 1960 King went solo and had a #10 pop, #15 R&B hit in 1961 (supervised by Phil Spector) with "Spanish Harlem," a song Spector wrote with Jerry Leiber. King followed it with another Top Ten the same year, the stark self-penned "Stand by Me" (#4 pop, #10 R&B). In 1962 he hit with "Don't Play That Song" (#11 pop, #2 R&B). After that King fared better on the R&B chart than the pop chart, though his 1963 hit "I (Who Have Nothing)" (#29 pop, #16 R&B) became a top seller for Tom Jones in 1970. By the end of 1963 King's career had slowed; though he often played in Europe, he was largely out of the spotlight until 1975, when he re-signed with his old label, Atlantic, and had an immediate hit with "Supernatural Thing, Part 1" (#5). In 1977 he collaborated with longtime admirers the Average White Band on *Benny and Us* (with two R&B Top Thirty hits, "Get It Up" and "A Star in the Ghetto"), while continuing with several solo hits, including 1980's "Music Trance" (#29 R&B).

King's career was revived in 1986 when "Stand by Me" became a Top Ten hit a second time after it was featured in the Rob Reiner film of the same name, costarring teenage actor River Phoenix. Another song of King's—a remake of the Monotones' "Book of Love," recorded with Bo Diddley and Doug Lazy—made it into a movie, 1991's *The Book of Love.*

Carole King
Born Carole Klein, February 9, 1940, Brooklyn, New York
1968—*Now That Everything's Been Said* (with the City) (Ode) 1970—*Carole King: Writer* 1971—*Tapestry; Music* 1972—*Rhymes and Reasons* 1973—*Fantasy* 1974—*Wrap Around Joy* 1975—*Really Rosie* 1976—*Thoroughbred* 1977—*Simple Things* (Capitol) 1978—*Welcome Home* (Avatar); *Her Greatest Hits* (Ode) 1979—*Touch the Sky* (Capitol) 1980—*Pearls: Songs of Goffin and King*

1982—*One to One* (Atlantic) 1983—*Speeding Time* 1989—*City Streets* (Capitol) 1993—*Colour of Your Dreams* (King's X/Rhythm Safari) 1994—*Carole King: In Concert.*

Singer/songwriter Carole King has had two outstanding careers. Throughout the Sixties she was one of pop's most prolific songwriters, writing the music to songs such as "Will You Love Me Tomorrow?" and "Up on the Roof," with most lyrics by her first husband, Gerry Goffin. Then in 1971 her multimillion-selling *Tapestry* helped inaugurate the Seventies' singer/songwriter style.

King began playing piano at age four; in high school she started her first band, the Co-sines. While attending Queens College in 1958 she met Gerry Goffin, and the two became cowriters. King had written some early singles like "Goin' Wild" and "Baby Sittin,'" but they went nowhere. Neil Sedaka had a hit dedicated to her in October 1959 called "Oh! Carol," but her reply song, "Oh! Neil," stiffed. In 1961 she and Goffin cowrote "Will You Love Me Tomorrow?," a #1 hit for the Shirelles, and the song has been covered countless times since. The two young writers, like Sedaka, Cynthia Weil, and Barry Mann, wrote their songs for Don Kirshner and Al Nevins' Aldon Music in Brill Building cubicles. They wrote over 100 hits in countless styles, including "Wasn't Born to Follow" (the Byrds), "Chains" (the Cookies), "Don't Bring Me Down" (the Animals), and "I'm into Something Good" (Herman's Hermits). In 1962 the King-Goffin team wrote, arranged, conducted, and produced the song "The Loco-Motion" for their 17-year-old baby-sitter, Little Eva (Boyd) [see entry], and it went #1 that summer. That year King made a brief foray into solo recording, but her only hit single at the time was "It Might As Well Rain Until September" (#22). In the mid-Sixties Goffin, King, and columnist Al Aronowitz tried to launch their own label, Tomorrow Records. It failed, but one band they produced, the Myddle Class, included bass player Charles Larkey, who became King's second husband after she divorced Goffin and moved to L.A. with her two children, Sherry and Louise (who launched a recording career of her own at age 19 in 1979 with *Kid Blue*).

In 1968 King formed a group called the City with Larkey and guitarist Danny Kortchmar, who had both previously played on three Fugs albums. They also knew each other from the New York club circuit, where the Myddle Class had played with Kortchmar's band the Flying Machine, which also included vocalist James Taylor. The City never toured because of King's stage fright, though they did make one unsuccessful LP on Ode records, *Now That Everything's Been Said.* The LP later yielded hits for Blood, Sweat and Tears ("Hi-De-Ho") and James Taylor ("You've Got a Friend," which also appeared on King's *Tapestry*). Taylor encouraged King to write her own lyrics and finally record solo again, result-

Evelyn "Champagne" King 543

ing in 1970's *Writer,* with a backup band that included
Kortchmar and others (who later recorded two Atlantic
albums under the name Jo Mama). King toured with Jo
Mama and Taylor, and they all worked on the 1971 critical and commercial windfall, *Tapestry,* which had two
top singles ("It's Too Late," #1, 1971; "So Far Away," #14,
1971), went #1, stayed on the chart for nearly six years,
and sold over 15 million copies.

King's early-Seventies LPs went gold and Top Ten
(*Music* and *Wrap Around Joy* both hit #1), and in late
1974 she had a #2 hit with "Jazzman" from *Wrap Around
Joy.* In 1975 King wrote the music for a children's program, *Really Rosie,* and began to write with Goffin again.
She switched to Capitol Records in late 1976, and her
first album for the new label, *Simple Things,* went gold.
She began touring with a band called Navarro, introduced to her by Dan Fogelberg, and married her collaborator at the time, Rick Evers, who died of a heroin
overdose in 1978.

By then her albums were selling modestly, though
she did better with her 1980 *Pearls* LP, which featured
King's versions of some of her best-known Sixties collaborations with Goffin, such as "One Fine Day" (#12,
1980) and "Hey Girl." King hasn't had a Top Forty hit
since, but she still tours and records regularly. In 1989
Eric Clapton guested on the title single from *City Streets.*
Her 1993 album *Colour of Your Dreams* was released on
her own King's X label and included Guns n' Roses guitarist Slash on the track "Hold Out for Love." For *Carole
King: In Concert* the 1990 Rock and Roll Hall of Fame inductee was supported by an eight-piece band that included her daughter Sherry Goffin on background
vocals. In 1994 King made her Broadway acting debut
when she took over Petula Clark's role in *Bloodbrothers.*

Earl King

**Born Earl Silas Johnson, February 7, 1934, New Or-
leans, Louisiana**
**1978—*New Orleans Rock 'n' Roll* (Sonet); *Earl King*
(Vivid)   1986—*Glazed* (with Roomful of Blues)
(Black Top)   1990—*Sexual Telepathy*   1994—*Hard
River to Cross.***

Along with Robert Parker, Irma Thomas, and Lee Dorsey,
Earl King is one of New Orleans' major R&B singers.
King's father was a blues pianist who died when King
was a child. He started his career as a gospel singer
around 1950 and learned to play guitar and sing the
blues a few years later. He sang with pianist Huey
"Piano" Smith until 1953, when he recorded his first solo
work for Savoy under the name Earl Johnson. In 1954
King was signed by Art Rupe to Specialty Records and
had a regional hit that year with "A Mother's Love."

His touring group was then called Earl King and the
Kings (they also recorded separately for Specialty), but in

1955 King signed with Johnny Vincent's new Ace label.
He immediately scored his biggest hit, "Those Lonely,
Lonely Nights." It sold 250,000 copies without ever entering the national chart. The song, a two-chord slow
ballad, was a major influence on all future Louisiana
swamp rock, paving the way for people like Dr. John,
who later covered King's "Let's Make a Better World" on
Desitively Bonnaroo. Later that year "Don't Take It So
Hard" went to #13 on the R&B chart.

King had some local hits in 1958, like "Well-O Well-O
Well-O Baby." He worked for Rex Records in 1959 with
then staff sessionman Mac Rebennack (later known as
Dr. John). That year he also sold 80,000 copies of "Everybody Has to Cry Sometime" under the pseudonym
Handsome Earl. His first release for Imperial in 1960 was
the savage "Come On," later covered by Jimi Hendrix,
and his biggest hit for the label was a #17 R&B hit in
1962, "Always a First Time." King's witty "Trick Bag"
(an archetypal piece of New Orleans funk later covered
by Robert Palmer) was later redone by the Meters in
1976 with King sitting in. In the mid-Sixties he worked
as a session musician for Motown, where he recorded
several unreleased sides. He then returned to New Orleans, where he played with Professor Longhair, cutting
one of the Professor's best-known songs, "Big Chief."
King recorded for many obscure labels in the Sixties
while also continuing on the New Orleans scene as a
songwriter (for the Dixie Cups, Lee Dorsey, the Meters,
Fats Domino, and Professor Longhair, among others) and
producer.

During the Seventies and early Eighties he per-
formed almost every year at the New Orleans Jazz and
Heritage Festival. In 1986 *Glazed* was nominated for the
Best Contemporary Blues Recording Grammy.

Evelyn "Champagne" King

Born June 29, 1960, Bronx, New York
**1977—*Smooth Talk* (RCA)   1979—*Music Box*
1980—*Call on Me*   1981—*I'm in Love*   1982—*Get
Loose*   1983—*Face to Face*   1985—*Long Time
Coming* (RCA)   1988—*Flirt* (EMI Manhattan)
1989—*Girl Next Door* (EMI America).**

Pop-soul singer Evelyn "Champagne" King was 17 when
she hit it big with the single "Shame" (#9 pop, #7 R&B), a
sexy song that was part of disco's domination of the
charts in 1978. The publicity fable goes that King, who
grew up in Philadelphia, was working nights as a cleaning lady at Philadelphia International Studios when staff
producer Theodore Life overheard her quietly crooning
Sam Cooke's "A Change Is Gonna Come." He immediately offered to produce her, resulting in 1977's *Smooth
Talk* LP (#14, 1978), which included "Shame" and "I Don't
Know If It's Right" (#23 pop, #7 R&B). The album and
both singles went gold, as did her next album, *Music*

Box. In 1981 King had her first #1 R&B hit with "I'm in Love" (#40 pop), followed by a second R&B #1, "Love Come Down" (#17 pop). Her other R&B hit singles include "Betcha She Don't Love You" (#2 R&B, 1982), "Shake Down" (#12 R&B, 1984), "Your Personal Touch" (#9 R&B, 1985), "Flirt" (#3 R&B, 1988), "Kisses Don't Lie" (#17 R&B, 1988), and "Hold On to What You've Got" (#8 R&B, 1988). She continues to tour the U.S., Europe, and Japan.

Freddie King

Born Freddie Christian, September 3, 1934, Gilmer, Texas; died December 28, 1976, Dallas, Texas
1970—*My Feeling for the Blues* (Cotillion)   1971— *Gettin' Ready . . .* (Shelter)   1972—*Texas Cannonball* (A&M)   1973—*Woman Across the River* (Shelter)   1974—*Burglar* (RSO)   1975—*The Best of Freddie King* (Shelter); *Larger Than Life* (RSO)   1976—*Best of Freddie King* (Island)   1977—*Original Hits* (Starday/King); *(1934–1976)* (RSO)   1989—*Just Pickin'* (Modern Blues).

Freddie King, a pioneering modern blues guitarist, was a major influence on rock guitarists, especially in the British blues boom of the Sixties. Growing up in Texas, King heard the recordings of Arthur Crudup, Big Bill Broonzy, Blind Lemon Jefferson, and Lightnin' Hopkins, but he later described his guitar style as a cross between Muddy Waters, T-Bone Walker, and B. B. King (no relation)—a mixture of country and urban blues. When he was 16, his family moved to Chicago, where he would sneak into blues clubs to jam with Muddy Waters' band. He also played with Memphis Slim, LaVern Baker, Willie Dixon, and others before recording his first solo record in 1956.

In 1960 King joined the Federal label and had several big R&B hits, including "Hideaway" and "Have You Ever Loved a Woman?" (later covered on *Layla* by Eric Clapton, a longtime admirer). Federal released 77 songs by King, including 30 instrumentals, in the next six years. But by 1966 King was without a contract, living as a semiobscure legend in Texas.

Meanwhile, his songs were being covered in England by bands like Chicken Shack and John Mayall, and he eventually took advantage of the blues revival, playing some shows in the U.K. In 1968 that led to a contract with Cotillion and two albums produced by King Curtis. He then signed to Leon Russell's Shelter label, released three albums and did enough full-time concert-hall touring to earn him a more mainstream white rock audience—the largest following of his career. In 1974 King switched to RSO and cut *Burglar* in England with help from Eric Clapton; he followed it up with *Larger Than Life* in 1975. The next year, three days after a Christmas-night show in Dallas, King died of heart failure, a blood-clot, and internal bleeding from ulcers.

Jonathan King

Born Kenneth King, December 6, 1944, London, England

While little known in the U.S. outside of his wistful pop ballad "Everyone's Gone to the Moon" (#17, 1965), Jonathan King has maintained a high profile in England as a recording artist, songwriter, record-label executive, newspaper columnist, and radio and TV host. "Everyone's Gone to the Moon" hit the chart while King was still a student at Cambridge University. He was fascinated with the business end of music, however, and soon went to work in A&R for Decca Records. King discovered Genesis, naming the group and producing its first album; in 1971 he produced the Bay City Rollers' first U.K. smash, "Keep On Dancing"; and the following year he founded his own record company, UK Records, which launched the career of 10cc.

In the Seventies King scored a number of British bubblegum and novelty hits, using jokey pseudonyms like Weathermen (a name Phil Ochs suggested), Bubblerock, 100 Ton and a Feather, and Father Abraphart and the Smurps. One of his biggest records was a tongue-in-cheek heavy-metal version of the Archies' "Sugar, Sugar," in 1971, recorded under the name Sakkarin. King also enjoyed hits under his own name, among them "Una Paloma Blanca," a gold record in 1975.

King's label wound down in the U.S. and in England in 1978. He went back to work for Decca (U.K.) for one year and later hosted a radio talk show on New York's WMCA and wrote a novel, *Bible Two*, published in England in 1982. Since 1980, when he manned a regular program for BBC Radio, *A King in New York*, King has been a fixture on British radio and TV. He still materializes occasionally on the chart too: His minor 1979 hit "Gloria" became a gold #2 U.S. hit for Laura Branigan in 1982.

King Crimson

Formed 1969, England
Robert Fripp (b. May 16, 1946, Wimbourne, Eng.), gtr., Mellotron; Greg Lake (b. Nov. 10, 1948, Bournemouth, Eng.), bass, voc.; Ian McDonald (b. June 25, 1946, London, Eng.), kybds., sax, flute, voc.; Michael Giles (b. 1942, Bournemouth, Eng.), drums; Pete Sinfield (b. Eng.), lyrics, lightshow.
1969—*In the Court of the Crimson King* (Atlantic) (– McDonald; – Giles; – Lake)   1970—*In the Wake of Poseidon* (+ Gordon Haskell [b. Eng.], voc., bass; + Andrew McCulloch [b. Eng.], drums; + Mel Collins [b. Eng.], sax, flute, Mellotron)   1971—*Lizard* (– Haskell; – McCulloch; + Boz Burrell [b. Raymond Burrell, ca. 1946, Lincoln, Eng.], voc., bass; + Ian Wallace [b. Sept. 29, 1946, Bury, Eng.], drums; – Sinfield)   1972—*Islands*; *Earthbound* (Editions, U.K.) (– Burrell; – Wallace; – Collins; + Bill Bruford

[b. May 17, 1948, London, Eng.], drums; + Jamie Muir [b. Eng.], perc.; + John Wetton [b. July 12, 1949, Derby, Eng.], bass, voc.; + David Cross [b. 1948, Plymouth, Eng.], violin, kybds.; + Robert Palmer-Jones [b. Eng.], lyrics) 1973—*Larks' Tongues in Aspic* (Atlantic) (– Muir) 1974—*Starless and Bible Black*; *Red* (– Cross) (group disbands) 1975—*USA* 1981—(Group re-forms: Fripp; Bruford; + Adrian Belew [b. Robert Steven Belew, Dec. 23, 1949, Covington, Ky.], gtr., voc.; + Tony Levin [b. Anthony Levin, June 6, 1946, Boston, Mass.], bass) *Discipline* (Warner Bros.) 1982—*Beat* 1984—*Three of a Perfect Pair* (group disbands) 1991—*Frame by Frame* (EG/Caroline) 1992—*The Great Deceiver* 1994— (Group re-forms: Fripp; Bruford; Levin; + Pat Mastelotto, drums; + Trey Gunn, gtr., bass) *VROOOM EP* (Discipline) 1995—*Thrak* (Virgin).

The eerie, portentous sound of early King Crimson set the tone of British art rock. But by the time the group's Mellotron-heavy sound and psychedelic lyrics had turned into lucrative clichés, leader Robert Fripp had long since shifted the group's style toward music that was far more eccentric, complex, and dissonant.

The original Crimson's roots went back to 1967, when the Bournemouth trio Giles, Giles and Fripp began making whimsical pop, which resulted in one British-only album in 1968 called *The Cheerful Insanity of Giles, Giles and Fripp*. (For a short time Judy Dyble, early Fairport Convention vocalist, also sang with them.) The band broke up in November 1968, and while bassist Peter Giles went on to become a solicitor's clerk, Fripp and drummer Mike Giles formed Crimson with ex-Gods bassist Greg Lake and their old associate Ian McDonald, who introduced them to lyricist Pete Sinfield. Sinfield also worked the band's psychedelic light show.

Crimson made its debut at the London Speakeasy on April 9, 1969, and on July 5 the group played to 650,000 people at the Rolling Stones' free Hyde Park concert. In October *In the Court of the Crimson King*, with music by McDonald and Fripp, was released, and endorsed by Pete Townshend as "an uncanny masterpiece." But the group soon began an endless series of personnel changes, with only Fripp remaining through it all. On the band's debut U.S. tour Giles and McDonald left, the latter in a band-control squabble. The two recorded a Crimson soundalike album, *McDonald and Giles*, in 1970. During the sessions for Crimson's second album, Greg Lake also left, to form Emerson, Lake and Palmer [see entry]. He'd met Emerson, then with the Nice, during Crimson's disastrous U.S. tour. Crimson might have ended there if Fripp had accepted offers to replace Pete Banks in Yes or to join Aynsley Dunbar in Blue Whale. Instead he brought in Gordon Haskell to complete the vocals on the second album (Elton John had also tried out), got old friend Pete

Giles for a brief stint on bass, persuaded brother Mike to do "guest drumming," and pulled in some other friends, including future member Mel Collins, to finish it up. Fripp's guitar style was already distinctive; he used classical-guitar technique to create angular, sustained, screaming phrases on his Gibson, and he usually performed seated.

In late 1970 Fripp formed a new Crimson with Collins, Haskell, Sinfield, and drummer Andrew McCulloch (later of Greenslade). Jon Anderson of Yes did a guest vocal on the resulting *Lizard*. Two days after the album was finished, the band fell apart.

One vocalist who tried out for the next Crimson was Roxy Music's Bryan Ferry, but Fripp opted for singer Boz Burrell, whom he taught to play bass. The band, rounded out by Collins and drummer Ian Wallace, recorded the subdued *Islands* in 1971 and, like the first group, fell apart on its U.S. tour. (Burrell later joined Bad Company [see entry].) Even the long-standing Pete Sinfield left this time; he recorded a solo LP and produced the debut Roxy Music album. The *Islands*-period band did manage to release a poorly recorded live document of its U.S. tour, *Earthbound*, released in the U.K. only.

Fripp emerged in 1972 with his most forward-looking and brashest Crimson, including Bill Bruford (who left the far more successful Yes to join), John Wetton (of Family), new lyricist Robert Palmer-Jones, David Cross, and Jamie Muir (who left for a Buddhist monastery after *Larks' Tongues in Aspic*). This lineup specialized in brainy, gothic metal and jagged, dissonant free improvisation, and drew critical comparisons to Captain Beefheart's Magic Band and, thanks to Cross' electric violin, the Mahavishnu Orchestra. Cross also left after the followup, *Starless and Bible Black*, but he did play with the band up through its last tour, culminating in a final show in New York's Central Park on July 1, 1974. A live LP from that date and *Red*, recorded with Cross as a "guest" member in late summer 1974, were both released after the disbanding. Ian MacDonald was about to rejoin the band and did play on *Red* (he later joined Foreigner in 1976).

But as artistically successful as *Red* was, Fripp came to hate the entire art-rock movement (which was at its commercial peak), along with the mechanics of the music business itself (which he termed "vampiric"), so he officially ended the band on September 28, 1974. On October 18, 1974, Fripp stated (prematurely, it turned out): "King Crimson is completely over. For ever and ever."

Fripp decided to work as a "small, mobile, intelligent, self-sufficient unit," in contrast to the overgrown "dinosaur" bands he'd come to loathe. [See Robert Fripp solo entry.] Using the echo-delay tape system devised by Brian Eno for *No Pussyfooting*, which he dubbed "Frippertronics," Fripp played solo concerts, slowly building minimalist chords with the notes on tape. He produced and played on Daryl Hall's *Sacred Songs* and two albums by the Roches, and added guitar lines to albums by Eno, David Bowie, Peter Gabriel, Talking Heads, and Blondie. In 1980 he returned to group performing with the short-lived League of Gentlemen (the name of one of Fripp's earliest amateur bands), which also featured former XTC keyboardist Barry Andrews, and which added a danceable rock beat to Fripp's intricate, repeating guitar lines; League bassist Sara Lee went on to join Gang of Four.

In 1981 Fripp revived King Crimson as a quartet that he had been planning to call Discipline, including session bassist Tony Levin (who had toured with Peter Gabriel), guitarist Adrian Belew (ex-Zappa, ex-Bowie, ex–Talking Heads), and Bruford. The new band drew on minimalism, African and Far Eastern polyrhythms, and the angularity of the final Crimson of the Seventies. The group toured the U.S. and Europe to wide acclaim, but disbanded after recording its third album, *Three of a Perfect Pair.*

In 1994 Fripp—after recording and touring the previous year with ex-Japan vocalist David Sylvian—announced yet another reformation of King Crimson. Calling the new lineup a double trio, he enlisted two drummers, Bruford and David Sylvian's drummer Pat Mastelotto (ex–Mr. Mister). Also in the band: Belew, Levin, and Chapman Stick (a 12-string instrument combining elements of bass and guitar) player Trey Gunn (who'd been a student in one of Fripp's "Guitar Craft" seminars, and had played on the 1991 album *Kneeling at the Shrine* by Fripp's band Sunday All Over the World). This lineup recorded an EP, *VROOOM,* on the independent Discipline Records, and released 1995's *Thrak* on Virgin. A tour followed.

King Curtis
Born Curtis Ousley, February 7, 1934, Fort Worth, Texas; died August 13, 1971, New York City, New York
1967—*Live at Small's Paradise* (Atco)   1968—*Best of King Curtis; Blues at Montreux* (Atlantic)
1971—*Live at Fillmore West* (Atco)   1988—*Soul Twist* (Collectables)   1989—*The Best of King Curtis*   1994—*Instant Soul: The Legendary King Curtis* (Razor & Tie).

Saxophonist King Curtis, a definitive R&B session soloist and bandleader (of the Kingpins), was a favorite of pop, rock, soul, and jazz performers, especially after his famous tenor sax solo on the Coasters' 1957 hit "Yakety-Yak." An adopted child, Curtis was first influenced by fellow southwesterners T-Bone Walker and Buster Smith, plus such jazz saxophonists as Lester Young and Louis Jordan. He got his first sax at age 12, played in several

high school bands, and turned down several college scholarships to tour with Lionel Hampton's band.

Curtis arrived in New York in 1952 and was discovered by a record company scout who found him session work. He went on to back more than 125 performers, including the Shirelles, Wilson Pickett, Sam and Dave, Eric Clapton, the Allman Brothers, and Delaney and Bonnie. In addition, Curtis made his own records, beginning in the late Fifties. "Soul Twist," on the small Enjoy label, topped the R&B chart (#17 pop, 1962). He later signed with Capitol and then in 1965 with Atco. His first release for that label was an instrumental version of "Spanish Harlem."

Curtis played on several of Aretha Franklin's records, including "Bridge over Troubled Water," and was appointed her musical director just before he died. (He assembled the band that graced a number of her most famous records: Richard Tee, Cornell Dupree, Jerry Jemmott, and Bernard Purdie.) The saxophonist also produced or coproduced albums by Roberta Flack, Delaney and Bonnie, Donny Hathaway, Freddie King, and Sam Moore of Sam and Dave. He was stabbed to death during an argument outside his home on New York's West 86th Street.

King Floyd
Born February 13, 1945, New Orleans, Louisiana
1971—*King Floyd* (Cotillion)   1975—*Well Done* (Chimneyville)   1977—*Body English.*

Soul-funk singer King Floyd began his career at age 12 in New Orleans. He began recording for the local Uptown label in 1964, and two years later he moved to Pulsar, where he enjoyed further regional success. By the time he released his biggest hit, the self-penned slow and sassy (with reggae overtones) "Groove Me" (#6, 1971), he was working under the guidance of another New Orleans veteran, Wardell Quezergue, at the Malaco studios in Jackson, Mississippi. He made other isolated appearances on the pop chart in the early Seventies with songs like "Baby Let Me Kiss You" (#29, 1971) and "Woman Don't Go Astray" (#53, 1972). Floyd remains active in New Orleans and does session work.

The Kingsmen
Formed 1958, Portland, Oregon
Lynn Easton, voc., sax; Jack Ely, gtr., voc.; Mike Mitchell, lead gtr.; Bob Nordby, gtr., bass.
1962—(+ Don Gallucci, organ)   1963—(– Ely; – Nordby; + Gary Abbott, drums; + Norm Sundholm, bass) *The Kingsmen in Person* (Wand)   1964—*The Kingsmen, vol. 2*   1965—*The Kingsmen, vol. 3*; *The Kingsmen on Campus*   1966—*15 Great Hits*   1985—*The Best of the Kingsmen* (Rhino).

Grammy Awards

KC and the Sunshine Band
1978 Album of the Year: *Saturday Night Fever* (with others)

Harry Wayne Casey (KC and the Sunshine Band)
1975 Best R&B Song: "Where Is the Love" (with others)
1978 Album of the Year: *Saturday Night Fever* (as producer, with others)

Kentucky HeadHunters
1990 Best Country Performance by a Duo or Group with Vocal: *Pickin' On Nashville*

Chaka Khan
1974 Best R&B Performance by a Duo, Group or Chorus: "Tell Me Something Good" (with Rufus)
1983 Best R&B Performance by a Duo or Group with Vocal: "Ain't Nobody" (with Rufus)
1983 Best R&B Vocal Performance, Female: *Chaka Khan*
1983 Best Vocal Arrangement for Two or More Voices: "Be Bop Medley" (with Arif Mardin)
1984 Best R&B Vocal Performance, Female: "I Feel for You"
1990 Best R&B Performance by a Duo or Group with Vocal: "I'll Be Good to You" (with Ray Charles)
1992 Best R&B Vocal Performance, Female: *The Woman I Am*

B. B. King
1970 Best R&B Vocal Performance, Male: "The Thrill Is Gone"
1981 Best Ethnic or Traditional Recording: *There Must Be a Better*

World Somewhere
1983 Best Traditional Blues Recording: *Blues 'n' Jazz*
1985 Best Traditional Blues Recording: "My Guitar Sings the Blues"
1987 Lifetime Achievement Award
1990 Best Traditional Blues Recording: *Live at San Quentin*
1991 Best Traditional Blues Album: *Live at the Apollo*
1993 Best Traditional Blues Album: *Blues Summit*

Carole King
1971 Record of the Year: "It's Too Late"
1971 Album of the Year: *Tapestry*
1971 Best Pop Vocal Performance, Female: *Tapestry*
1971 Song of the Year: "You've Got a Friend"

King Curtis
1969 Best R&B Instrumental Performance: "Games People Play"

Kingston Trio
1958 Best Country & Western Performance: "Tom Dooley"
1959 Best Performance, Folk: *The Kingston Trio at Large*

Gladys Knight
1986 Best Pop Performance by a Duo or Group with Vocal: "That's What Friends Are For" (with Elton John, Dionne Warwick, and Stevie Wonder)

Gladys Knight and the Pips
1973 Best Pop Vocal Performance by a Duo, Group or Chorus: "Neither One of Us (Wants to Be the First to Say Goodbye)"
1973 Best R&B Vocal Performance by a Duo, Group or Chorus: "Midnight Train to Georgia"
1988 Best R&B Vocal Performance by a Duo or Group with Vocal: "Love Overboard"

Kool and the Gang
1978 Album of the Year: *Saturday Night Fever* (with others)

Kool Moe Dee
1990 Best Rap Performance by a Duo or Group: "Back on the Block" (with others)

Alison Krauss
1990 Best Bluegrass Recording: *I've Got That Old Feeling*
1992 Best Bluegrass Album (with Union Station): *Every Time You Say Goodbye*
1994 Best Southern Gospel, Country Gospel or Bluegrass Gospel Album (with the Cox Family): *I Know Who Holds Tomorrow*

Kris Kristofferson
1971 Best Country Song: "Help Me Make It Through the Night"
1973 Best Country Vocal Performance by a Duo or Group: "From the Bottle to the Bottom" (with Rita Coolidge)
1975 Best Country Vocal Performance by a Duo or Group: "Lover Please" (with Rita Coolidge)

The Northwest was a particularly fertile breeding ground for raunchy rock & roll groups in the early Sixties. Paul Revere and the Raiders became the most successful, but the most famous song—indeed one of the best-known and most notorious songs in the history of rock & roll—was "Louie Louie." Though the Raiders cut their version in 1963, it was the Kingsmen who had the hit.

"Louie Louie," first recorded by its composer, Richard Berry, in 1956, is marked by a three-chord progression simple enough to endear it to every last garage band. The Kingsmen's version (#2, 1963), recorded for $50, stood out thanks to cofounder Jack Ely, who garbled his words to the extent that no one knew exactly what he was singing; by educated guesses it was obscene enough to be banned by many radio stations and to spark an FCC investigation. The Kingsmen, however, always maintained that they had said nothing lewd. The story behind the song was chronicled in a 1993 book, *Louie Louie,* by Dave Marsh.

Two more hits followed—"Money" (#16, 1964) and "The Jolly Green Giant" (#4, 1965)—before the band retired in 1967. Guitarist Mike Mitchell formed another Kingsmen group. They signed a contract with Capitol in 1973, but nothing came of it. As of the mid-Nineties, Mitchell's version of the Kingsmen continued to perform.

Kingston Trio

Formed 1957, San Francisco, California
Bob Shane (b. Feb. 1, 1934, Hilo, Hawaii); Nick Reynolds (b. July 27, 1933, San Diego, Calif.); Dave Guard (b. Nov. 19, 1934, Honolulu, Hawaii; d. Mar. 22, 1991, Rollinsford, N.H.).
1958—*The Kingston Trio* (Capitol)   1959—*From the Hungry i; The Kingston Trio at Large; Here We Go Again!*   1960—*Sold Out; String Along; Stereo Concert*   1961—*Make Way!; Goin' Places; Close-up* (– Guard; + John Stewart [b. Sep. 5, 1939, San Diego, Calif.])   1962—*College Concert; Best of the Kingston Trio; Something Special; New Frontier*   1963—*The Kingston Trio #16; Sunny Side!*   1964—*Time to Think; Back in Town*   1965—*Best of the Kingston Trio, vol. 2*   1967—(– Stewart; – Reynolds)   1973—("New Kingston Trio": Shane; + Roger Gamble; + George Grove)   1990—*Capitol Collectors Series.*

The Kingston Trio was a clean-cut, more commercial alternative to the left-tinged folksingers of the late Fifties. Inspired by Woody Guthrie and the Weavers, the trio scored its only #1 hit in 1958 with "Tom Dooley," a song based on a Nineteenth-Century folk tune, "Tom Dula." Until the emergence of Peter, Paul and Mary, Nick Reynolds, Bob Shane, and Dave Guard were the country's preeminent folksingers: Five of their first six albums reached #1, and every one of the trio's first 17 LPs, through 1963, made the Top Twenty.

In 1961 John Stewart replaced Guard, who went on to form the Whiskeyhill Singers. The group attempted to broaden its repertoire from traditional American and English folk songs to include contemporary protest songs, such as its 1962 single "Where Have All the Flowers Gone" (#21). Nevertheless, the Kingston Trio's popularity waned, and by 1967 both Reynolds and Stewart had left (the latter for a solo career [see entry]). They were replaced by Roger Gamble and George Grove in 1973, when Shane re-formed the group as the New Kingston Trio and began touring again. A 1982 PBS TV special hosted by Tom Smothers brought together all six Kingston Trio members for the first time.

King's X

Formed 1980, Springfield, Missouri
Jerry Gaskill (b. Dec. 27, 1957, Bridgeton, N.J.), drums; Doug Pinnick (b. Sep. 3, 1950, Joliet, Ill.), bass, voc.; Ty Tabor (b. Sep. 17, 1961, Jackson, Mo.), gtr. voc.
1988—*Out of the Silent Planet* (Megaforce)   1989—*Gretchen Goes to Nebraska*   1990—*Faith Hope Love by King's X*   1992—*King's X* (Atlantic)   1994—*Dogman.*

Seeing themselves more as a band of Christians than as a Christian-rock band, the biracial King's X (bassist/vocalist Doug Pinnick is black) laces powerful pop-laden heavy metal with spiritual messages.

All three members had previously been involved in Christian music: Doug Pinnick and Jerry Gaskill met playing in the popular Christian-rock group Petra and later backed Christian rocker Phil Keaggy; Ty Tabor played bluegrass in his family's band. Tybor met Gaskill at Springfield's Evangel College, and in 1980 they formed the Edge. (A fourth member, Dan McCollom, was recruited but left the band early on.)

After touring for five years, they moved to Houston, lured by promises of financial backing. That deal collapsed, but the band met Sam Taylor (formerly with ZZ Top's management), who produced them, managed them, and rechristened them King's X, after a band he liked in high school.

Their first two albums, *Out of the Silent Planet* and *Gretchen Goes to Nebraska,* went nowhere, even though critics and other musicians took note of their structurally complex songs and tight harmonies. *Faith Hope Love by King's X* (#85, 1990), powered by the single "It's Love," finally brought the band into the Top 100. In 1991 they contributed "Junior's Gone Wild" to the *Bill and Ted's Bogus Journey* soundtrack. The next year they released their first major-label album, the self-titled *King's X* (#138), which proved to be a commercial disappointment. In 1994 King's X played the Woodstock Festival and released a new album, *Dogman,* which peaked at #88.

The Kinks

Formed 1963, London, England
Ray Davies (b. June 21, 1944, London), gtr., voc.; Dave Davies (b. Feb. 3, 1947, London), gtr., voc.; Mick Avory (b. Feb. 15, 1944, London), drums; Pete Quaife (b. Dec. 27, 1943, Tavistock, Eng.), bass.
1964—*You Really Got Me* (Reprise)   1965—*Kinks-Size; Kinda Kinks*   1966—*Kinks Kingdom; The Kinks Kontroversy; The Kinks Greatest Hits!; Face to Face*   1967—*Live at the Kelvin Hall*   1968—*Something Else*   1969—(The Kinks Are) The Village Green Preservation Society* (– Quaife; + John Dalton, bass); *Arthur, or the Decline and Fall of the British Empire*   1970—*Lola Versus Powerman and the Moneygoround, Part One*   1971—(+ John

The Kinks: (top) Dave Davies, Mick Avory, (bottom) Peter Quaife, Ray Davies

Gosling, kybds.) *Muswell Hillbillies* (RCA) 1972— *The Kinks Kronikles* (Reprise); *Everybody's in Show-Biz* (RCA) 1973—*Preservation Act 1* 1974— *Preservation Act 2* 1975—*Soap Opera*; *Schoolboys in Disgrace* 1976—(– Dalton; + Andy Pyle, bass) 1977—*Sleepwalker* (Arista) 1978—*Misfits* (– Pyle; – Gosling; + Jim Rodford [b. July 7, 1945, St. Alban's, Eng.], bass, voc.; + Gordon Edwards, kybds.; – Edwards) 1979—*Low Budget* (+ Ian Gibbons, kybds., voc.) 1980—*One for the Road* 1981—*Give the People What They Want* 1983— *State of Confusion* 1984—(– Avory; + Bob Henrit [b. May 2, 1945, Eng.], drums) *Word of Mouth* 1986—*Come Dancing with the Kinks*; *Think Visual* (MCA) 1988—*Live: The Road* (– Gibbons) 1989— *U.K. Jive* (+ Mark Haley, kybds.) 1993—*Phobia* (Columbia) 1995—*Tired of Waiting for You* (Rhino); *To the Bone* (Konk, U.K.).

The Kinks were part of the British Invasion, and their early hits, "You Really Got Me" and "All Day and All of the Night," paved the way for the power chords of the next decade's hard rock. But most of leader Ray Davies' songs have been chronicles of the beleaguered British middle class, scenarios for rock theater, and tales of show-business survival. After their first burst of popularity, the Kinks became a cult band in the mid-Seventies until, buoyed by the new wave's rediscovery of the Davies catalogue, they returned to arenas in the Eighties.

Ray Davies was attending art school in England when he joined his younger brother Dave's band, the Ravens, in 1963. In short order Ray had taken over the group—renamed the Kinks—retaining bassist Pete Quaife and recruiting Mick Avory to play drums. With this lineup they released a pair of unsuccessful singles before recording "You Really Got Me," a #1 hit in England that reached #7 in the U.S. in 1964. The following year "All Day and All of the Night" and "Tired of Waiting for You" both reached the Top Ten in the U.S. and set a pattern for future releases of alternating tough rockers ("Who'll Be the Next in Line") and ballads ("Set Me Free").

In 1966 the Kinks released two singles of pointed satire, "A Well Respected Man" and "Dedicated Follower of Fashion," indicating the personal turn Ray Davies' songs were taking. Their next album, *The Kinks Kontroversy*, though containing another hard-rock 45, "Till the End of the Day," was increasingly introspective, with songs like "I'm on an Island." Also that year, an appearance on the American TV show *Hullabaloo* resulted in a problem with the American Federation of Musicians that wasn't resolved until 1969 and prevented the group from touring the U.S. for some time "Sunny Afternoon" (#14, 1966) from *Face to Face* was their last hit of that period.

During their years of U.S. exile, Ray Davies became increasingly introspective; he later composed the first of many concept albums, *(The Kinks Are) The Village Green Preservation Society* (1969), an LP of nostalgia for all the quaint English customs (such as virginity) that all other bands were rebelling against. Dave Davies, who had been writing the occasional song for the Kinks almost from the beginning, had a "solo" hit in England with "Death of a Clown," actually a Kinks song that he wrote and sang. More of Dave's singles followed ("Susannah's Still Alive," "Lincoln County"), none of which repeated the success of "Clown." A planned solo album was recorded, but released in drips and drabs years later on collections. The Kinks' next LP, *Arthur, or the Decline and Fall of the British Empire*, was, with the Who's *Tommy*, an early rock opera, written for a British TV show that never aired. The Kinks' next concept album, *Lola Versus Powerman and the Moneygoround, Part One* (#35, 1970), was built around the story of trying to get a hit record. "Lola," undoubtedly the first rock hit about a transvestite, reached #9.

The group then left Reprise for RCA, continuing to work on concept pieces, once again without hits. Nevertheless it acquired a reputation as a cheerfully boozy live band; Kinks performances were known for messy musicianship and onstage arguments between Ray and Dave Davies, while Ray clowned with limp wrists and sprayed beer at the audience. This was chronicled on *Everybody's in Show-Biz*, a double album split between Ray Davies' first road songs and a loose live set.

Concept albums became soundtracks for theatrical presentations starring the Kinks in the next years. *Preservation Acts 1* and *2, Soap Opera,* and *Schoolboys in Disgrace* were all composed for the stage, complete with extra horn players and singers. For all of the elaborate shows, though, the albums weren't selling.

The Kinks left RCA and concept albums behind in 1976. They finally scored a hit in 1978 with "A Rock 'n' Roll Fantasy" (#30, 1978), off *Misfits. Low Budget* (#11, 1979), aided by another successful 45, "(Wish I Could Fly Like) Superman" (#41, 1979), became the Kinks' first gold record since the Reprise greatest-hits collection of their early singles.

In the meantime, new groups began rediscovering the Kinks' catalogue, notably Van Halen ("You Really Got Me") and the Pretenders ("Stop Your Sobbing"). The group, which had tightened up considerably onstage with the addition of former Argent bassist Jim Rodford in 1978, responded with *One for the Road* (#14, 1980), a double live album that was accompanied by one of the first full-length rock videos. It too went gold, as did *Give the People What They Want* (#15, 1981).

Over the years, Ray Davies has also produced two albums by Claire Hamill (for his ill-fated Konk Records), worked with Tom Robinson, and scored the films *The Virgin Soldiers* and *Percy.* Dave Davies finally came out with a solo album on RCA, *AFLI-3603,* in 1980 and another in 1981, *Glamour;* both featured Dave on most of the instruments and achieved modest success.

The Kinks' third wind continued with *State of Confusion* (#12, 1983), which gave the group its first Top Ten hit since "Lola": the delightfully nostalgic "Come Dancing" (#6, 1983). A wistful ballad, "Don't Forget to Dance," cracked the Top Thirty later in the year. Other mid-Eighties activities included *Return to Waterloo* (1985), a film Ray Davies wrote and directed, incorporating Kinks music; and Ray having a daughter, Natalie, with Chrissie Hynde of the Pretenders in 1983. The relationship ended the following year.

Beginning with *Word of Mouth,* the Kinks once again fell on hard times. None of the band's subsequent albums, on Arista, MCA, and Columbia, sold well. But the Kinks, with ex-Argent drummer Bob Henrit in place of Avory, continued touring. In 1990 the band was inducted into the Rock and Roll Hall of Fame, and in 1993 the group undertook its first U.S. tour in more than three years to promote *Phobia.* The album's first single, "Hatred (A Duet)," poked fun at the longstanding antagonism between Ray and Dave Davies that has led both brothers to quit the band on more than one occasion. The Kinks' 1995 U.K.-only release, *To the Bone,* was a live-in-the-studio rerecording of many of the band's hits. In 1994 Viking U.K. published Ray Davies' *X-Ray: The Unauthorized Autobiography.*

Kiss

Formed 1972, New York City, New York
Gene Simmons (b. Gene Klein, Aug. 25, 1949, Haifa, Israel), voc., bass; **Paul Stanley** (b. Stanley Eisen, Jan. 20, 1952, Queens, N.Y.), gtr., voc.; **Peter Criss** (b. Peter Crisscoula, Dec. 20, 1947, Brooklyn, N.Y.), drums, voc.; **Ace Frehley** (b. Paul Frehley, Apr. 27, 1951, Bronx, N.Y.), gtr.
1974—*Kiss* (Casablanca); *Hotter Than Hell* **1975**—*Dressed to Kill; Alive* **1976**—*Destroyer; Kiss—The Originals; Rock and Roll Over* **1977**—*Love Gun; Alive II* **1978**—*Double Platinum* **1979**—*Dynasty* **1980**—*Unmasked* (– Criss; + Eric Carr [b. July 12, 1950, Brooklyn, N.Y.; d. Nov. 24, 1991, New York City], drums) **1981**—*Music from "The Elder"* **1982**—(– Frehley; + Vinnie Vincent, gtr.) *Creatures of the Night* (Mercury) **1983**—*Lick It Up* **1984**—(– Vincent; + Mark St. John, gtr.) *Animalize* **1985**—(– St. John; + Bruce Kulick, gtr.) *Asylum* **1987**—*Crazy Nights* **1988**—*Smashes, Thrashes and Hits* **1989**—*Hot in the Shade* **1991**—(– Carr; + Eric Singer, drums) **1992**—*Revenge* **1993**—*Alive III.*
Paul Stanley solo: 1978—*Paul Stanley* (Casablanca).
Gene Simmons solo: 1978—*Gene Simmons* (Casablanca).
Ace Frehley solo: 1978—*Ace Frehley* (Casablanca) **1987**—*Frehley's Comet* (Megaforce) **1988**—*Live + 1* **1988**—*Second Sighting* **1989**—*Trouble Walkin'.*
Peter Criss solo: 1978—*Peter Criss* (Casablanca) **1993**—*Criss* (Tony Nicole Tony).

Kiss may have been one of the biggest-selling acts of the Seventies, but it will always be known, above all else, as the band without a face. Until 1983, when the group removed its distinctive makeup, the four members' faces supposedly had never been photographed (although pictures of them applying their makeup for an early photo session ran in *Creem* magazine in the early Eighties). Theatrics and basic hard rock have been Kiss' main calling card. The quartet formed in the heyday of glitter and rock theater, and it set out to define, at first, evil cartoon-character personas, highlighted by Gene Simmons' bass-playing, fire-breathing, (stage) blood-spewing ghoul.

The group was founded by Simmons and Stanley, who met in a band in 1970. They found Criss through his ad in ROLLING STONE. After rehearsing as a trio, the group took out an ad in the *Village Voice* for a guitarist with "flash and balls" and discovered Ace Frehley. At the time, they were all working dead-end jobs, with the exception of Simmons, who taught at P.S. 75 in Manhattan. Their visual image and game plan were in place from the start. After a few New York City shows, Kiss met independent television director Bill Aucoin, who helped the group get a deal with Casablanca Records.

Kiss: Gene Simmons, Paul Stanley, Peter Criss, Ace Frehley

The critics hissed at the anonymous heavy-metal thud rock on the band's first three albums and howled at its mock-threatening image. Nonetheless, Kiss hit it off with its fans (the Kiss Army) from the very start. After some hard financial times (an entire 1975 tour was reportedly financed on Aucoin's American Express card), the band took off with *Alive* (#9, 1975), which contained the Top Twenty anthem "Rock and Roll All Nite."

In 1976 the band's sound and image shifted toward not necessarily softer but certainly more commercial fare, beginning with Criss' ballad "Beth" (#7, 1976), a million-seller that he wrote for his wife, Lydia. Accordingly, Kiss' audience grew from mostly male adolescent heavy-metal fans to include more teenyboppers. As the group racked up more and more platinum records—six between 1976 and 1979—it became increasingly less threatening. Young fans were frequently photographed wearing the makeup of their favorite Kiss member.

On June 28, 1977, Marvel Comics published a Kiss comic book. The red ink used supposedly contained a small amount of blood from the band members themselves. It sold over 400,000 copies. In the fall of 1978, NBC broadcast a feature-length animated special entitled *Kiss Meets the Phantom of the Park*, and Marvel issued a second Kiss comic. But the group's popularity was beginning to wane. Four simultaneously released solo LPs sold poorly—Frehley's was most popular—although the group had several hit singles, including the disco-metal oddity "I Was Made for Loving You" (#16, 1979). In 1980 Criss left for a solo career. He was replaced by Eric Carr, who drummed into the Nineties and died of cancer at age 41. The group then briefly changed its image, abandoning the comic-book characters for a New Romantic–influenced look. *The Elder*, an overambitious concept album, featured songs cowritten by Lou Reed and was the group's first album not to go gold. Kiss

quickly reverted to its ghoul makeup and primitive hard-rock music, but *Creatures of the Night*, too, failed to sell 500,000 copies.

What to do? Change image again. *Lick It Up* (#24, 1983) depicted the group (now with Vinnie Vincent in place of Frehley) without its makeup and sparked a commercial resurgence. All of the group's albums since have gone either gold or platinum. By the early Nineties, Kiss had sold more than 70 million albums. And as proof that in rock & roll anyone can become a legend if they stick around long enough, 1994 saw the release of *Kiss My Ass*, on which artists as diverse as Garth Brooks, Lenny Kravitz, and Anthrax recorded their favorite Kiss songs as tribute to the band critics loved to hate.

Klaatu

Formed 1973, Toronto, Canada
John Woloschuk, bass; Terry Draper, drums; Dee Long, gtr.
1976—Klaatu (Capitol)   1977—Hope   1978—Sir Army Suit   1980—Endangered Species.

Klaatu was a so-called mystery group that in 1977 briefly benefited from a record-company-fueled rumor that its members were in fact the Beatles. Capitol (also the Beatles' label) claimed to be unaware of the band members' true identities, all the while stressing *Klaatu*'s musical similarities to *Magical Mystery Tour* and *Sgt. Pepper's* in press releases.

The band's debut LP came out in August 1976, but the real hype didn't begin until February 1977, when Steve Smith, a reporter for the *Providence Journal*, wrote an article citing the "Paul is dead"–style allusions to the Beatles, concluding that one or all of them were involved in Klaatu. Capitol sent the article all around, soon after other newspapers and radio stations picked up on the pseudo-mystery, and the band's album leaped into the Top Forty. Later, one of its songs, "Calling Occupants of Interplanetary Craft," was a hit for the Carpenters. Research by more skeptical reporters revealed that Klaatu was in fact studio musicians from Toronto.

In September 1977 Klaatu released its second album; although a spokesman said the four weren't the Beatles and hadn't meant to pretend they were, they still never formally revealed their identities. Their anonymity eventually backfired, though (ROLLING STONE declared the group "hype of the year"), and after another three albums (the last one issued in Canada only) Klaatu broke up in 1981. Ironically, guitarist Dee Long went on to work at England's AIR London studios, cofounded by Beatles producer George Martin. "I thought everybody was nuts to think we had anything to do with the Beatles," he told ROLLING STONE in the mid-Eighties.

The KLF/The Orb

**The KLF, formed 1987, England (Bill Drummond
[b. William Butterworth, Apr. 29, 1953, S.A.], synth.,
samplers; Jimmy Cauty [b. ca. 1954, Eng.], gtr.):
1990—*Chill Out* (Wax Trax!)   1991—*The White
Room* (Arista).
The Orb, formed 1990, England (Cauty, gtr.; "Dr."
Alex Paterson, synth., samplers): 1990—*Adventures
Beyond the Ultraworld* (Big Life, U.K.) (– Cauty;
+ Kristian "Thrash" Weston, gtr., synth., samplers,
perc.)   1992—*The Aubrey Mixes: The Ultraworld
Excursions*; *U.F. Orb* (Big Life)   1993—*Live 93* (Is-
land/Red)   1994—*Pomme Fritz*   1995—*Orbus Ter-
rarum*.**

Britain's mysterious, mischievous KLF made post–hip-
hop, rave-influenced, psychedelic trance-dance music
that one critic described as "dance music for the home."
Its name stood for "Kopyright Liberation Front"; the
group's stated mission was to see if sampling would
hold up in a court of law.

Bill Drummond had played in the new-wave band
Big in Japan (with Holly Johnson, later of Frankie Goes to
Hollywood); ran Liverpool's Zoo Records and managed
its two top acts, Echo and the Bunnymen and Teardrop
Explodes; and was an A&R executive with WEA Records
when he signed ex–Zodiac Mindwarp guitarist Jimmy
Cauty's band, Brilliant (whose only album flopped).
Drummond and Cauty recorded dance singles under the
names Disco 2000, Space, and Justified Ancients of Mu
Mu—often shortened to "Jams." The Jams album *1987
(What the Fuck's Going On)* drew a quick lawsuit from
Abba, whose "Dancing Queen" was heavily sampled on
it (as were the Beatles, Led Zeppelin, and others). It was
immediately recalled, and reissued—with all unauthorized samples edited out—as an extended single, "The
Jams 45 Edits EP." (Authorized samples were used in the
followup single, "Who Killed the Jams?")

As the Timelords, Drummond and Cauty combined a
hip-hop version of Gary Glitter's "Rock and Roll Part 2"
with the theme of the popular British science-fiction TV
show *Dr. Who*; the resulting "Doctoring the Tardis"
topped the U.K. chart in 1988. Cauty and Drummond
then became KLF and recorded *Chill Out,* which reflected the near–New Age work Cauty had begun doing
with the Orb—an "ambient house" variant on the KLF's
electro-dance pastiches, which Cauty had formed with
ex–Killing Joke roadie/EG Records A&R exec/London
club DJ "Dr." Alex Paterson. Cauty left the Orb after its
debut album, *Adventures Beyond the Ultraworld,* which
yielded international dance hits in "Perpetual Dawn" and
"Little Fluffy Clouds." The Orb's *Aubrey Mixes* featured
guest guitar by Steve Hillage of Gong, to whose hippie-
era space rock the Orb's ethereal work was often compared. In 1994 Paterson and Kristian "Thrash" Weston,

Cauty's replacement, with King Crimson guitarist Robert
Fripp and German producer Thomas Fehlmann, recorded
as F.F.W.D.

Back with the KLF, Drummond and Cauty scored an
international dance hit with "What Time Is Love?" (#57,
1991) from the group's first U.S. album, *The White Room*
(#39, 1991). It also contained the smash pop hit "3 A.M.
Eternal" (#5, 1991), which was accompanied by a music
video showing the group clad in robes and hoods, moving in formation as if enacting some strange cultish ritual. In 1992 the KLF had another hit with "Justified and
Ancient," a surreal feature for country music queen
Tammy Wynette, who gamely wore a skintight turquoise
mermaid dress for the video. The song reached #11 on
the pop charts—higher than Wynette's 1968 classic
"Stand by Your Man."

Drummond and Cauty broke up the KLF in late 1992
but continued working as conceptual pranksters "The K
Foundation." In 1993 they announced that they'd
recorded a "world anthem"—"Que Sera Sera," redone as
"K Sera Sera" with the Red Army Choir—but refused to
release it until world peace was achieved.

The Knack

**Formed 1978, Los Angeles, California
Doug Fieger (b. Aug. 20, Detroit, Mich.), gtr., voc.;
Berton Averre (b. Dec. 13, Van Nuys, Calif.), gtr.;
Bruce Gary (b. Apr. 7, 1952, Burbank, Calif.), drums;
Prescott Niles (b. May 2, New York City, N.Y.), bass.
1979—*Get the Knack* (Capitol)   1980—*. . . but the
Little Girls Understand*   1981—*Round Trip* (group
disbands)   1991—(Group re-forms: Fieger; Averre;
Niles; + Billy Ward, drums) *Serious Fun* (Charisma).**

In the summer of 1979 the Knack enjoyed one of the
biggest commercial debuts in rock history. Its first
album, recorded in 11 days for a mere $18,000, went gold
in 13 days, platinum in seven weeks, and eventually sold
five million copies worldwide. The single "My Sharona"
sold ten million copies. However, the group quickly suffered an equally intense backlash. With its Beatleslike
packaging (the back cover of *Get the Knack* imitated *A
Hard Day's Night*), plus what critics saw as contrived
pop innocence and sexist lyrics, the band members were
labeled cynical fakes—an accusation heightened by
their refusal to do interviews. In the wake of the Knack's
success scores of "innocent pop" L.A. bands were
signed. A "Knuke the Knack" movement arose in the
more radical quarters of the very same L.A. club scene
where the band had begun.

Though the group's publicity tried to present it as
having no past, the two main songwriters, Doug Fieger
and Berton Averre, knew each other for many years.
Fieger met Averre in California when he moved there
from Detroit in 1971 with his band Sky, which made two

LPs for RCA. During the mid-Seventies the two began writing together, and all four future members of the Knack did backup and session work. After working abroad, Fieger moved back to L.A., where he, Averre, and Bruce Gary teamed up with Prescott Niles to form the Knack in May 1978.

They played frequently on the Southern California club scene, and by December of that year they had 13 record companies bidding on them. Capitol won out, and the Knack's debut, produced by Mike Chapman (who did many of the successful pop–new-wave LPs of that year, including Blondie), was released in June 1979 with the #1 single "My Sharona." The critical backlash and the lack of individual image caught up with the Knack commercially, though, and its followup album sold a comparatively disappointing 600,000 copies. The band members began to argue constantly—they got a new manager and used producer Jack Douglas for their third LP, *Round Trip* (#93, 1981), but despite a sudden availability to the press, they couldn't shake their hype reputation, and following an unsuccessful tour in 1981 they disbanded.

Averre, Gary, and Niles continued as the Game briefly before going on to back up others: Gary drummed behind Bob Dylan, Jack Bruce, and Bette Midler; Averre, too, played with the Divine Miss M., while Niles toured with Josie ("Johnny, Are You Queer?") Cotton. They regrouped again in the mid-Eighties as the Front, with actor Steven Bauer on vocals. Fieger, meanwhile, founded Doug Fieger's Taking Chances, which went nowhere. In 1987 Niles, Averre, and a newly sober Fieger got back together, with drummer Bill Ward. A 1991 album, *Serious Fun,* did not chart, and the Knack members went their separate ways again. Fieger, in addition to playing a small role on the hit TV series *Roseanne,* recorded a solo album produced by Don Was, and as of 1994 was shopping for a record label. In 1994 the Knack began touring again after "My Sharona" found a new audience through its inclusion in the *Reality Bites* soundtrack.

The Knickerbockers
Formed 1964, Bergenfield, New Jersey
Buddy Randell, voc., sax; Jimmy Walker, drums, voc.; John Charles, bass; Beau Charles, gtr.
1966—*Lies* (Challenge).

The Knickerbockers had their one and only major U.S. hit in 1966 with a Beatleslike raver called "Lies" (#20). The band formed in 1964 as the Castle Kings, featuring Buddy Randell from the Royal Teens (who cowrote the #3 1958 novelty hit "Short Shorts"). After being discovered by producer Jerry Fuller, a songwriter for Ricky Nelson, and later the Union Gap, they changed their name, inspired by Knickerbocker Avenue in their hometown of Bergenfield, New Jersey. The band tried to follow up "Lies" with "One Track Mind," but it only made it to #46, and the Knickerbockers soon fizzled. Thereafter Walker became one of the Righteous Brothers for a while, replacing Bill Medley. He then launched an unsuccessful solo career, as did Buddy Randell.

Gladys Knight and the Pips
Formed 1952, Atlanta, Georgia
Gladys Knight (b. May 28, 1944, Atlanta), voc.; Merald "Bubba" Knight (b. Sep. 4, 1942, Atlanta), voc.; Brenda Knight, voc.; William Guest (b. June 2, 1941, Atlanta), voc.; Elenor Guest, voc.
1957—(– B. Knight; – E. Guest; + Edward Patten [b. Aug. 2, 1939, Atlanta], voc.; + Langston George, voc.) 1962—(– George) 1970—*Greatest Hits* (Soul) 1971—*If I Were Your Woman* 1972—*Neither One of Us* 1973—*Imagination* (Buddah) 1974—*Anthology* (Motown); *Claudine* (Buddah); *I Feel a Song* 1975—*2nd Anniversary; The Best of Gladys Knight and the Pips* 1976—*Gladys Knight and the Pips' Greatest Hits* 1980—*About Love* (Columbia) 1982—*Touch* 1983—*Visions* 1985—*Life* 1987—*All Our Love* (MCA) 1990—*Soul Survivors: The Best of Gladys Knight and the Pips* (Rhino). Gladys Knight solo: 1991—*Good Woman* (MCA) 1994—*Just for You.*

Gladys Knight and the Pips rose to prominence on the Motown label in the late Sixties, but their popularity peaked after they moved to Buddah in 1973. Gladys Knight and the Pips are a family, all born in Atlanta, where Gladys' parents sang in church choirs. As a child, Gladys herself sang with the Mount Mariah Baptist Church choir and toured southern churches with the Morris Brown Choir before she was five. At seven she won a grand prize on the *Ted Mack Amateur Hour,* which led to several TV appearances. The Pips were formed in 1952 at Gladys' older brother Merald's birthday party, when, to entertain the family, Gladys arranged an impromptu singing group, including Merald, sister Brenda, and cousins William and Elenor Guest. Cousin James Woods urged them to go pro; they adopted his nickname, "Pip."

They toured nationally with Jackie Wilson and Sam Cooke before Gladys was 13, but their 1957 recording debut with Brunswick went nowhere; Elenor and Brenda left to get married, and were replaced by cousin Edward Patten and Langston George. This configuration, with Gladys' grainy alto still up front, recorded its first R&B Top Twenty hit in 1961, the Johnny Otis–penned "Every Beat of My Heart." George left after two more singles ("Letter Full of Tears" went Top Five), and the group became a quartet.

The group faltered in the early Sixties. In 1962

Gladys Knight and the Pips: Edward Patten, Merald (Bubba) Knight, William Guest, Gladys Knight

Gladys had a baby, and the Pips did studio backups; even after they reunited they were still known only to R&B fans. They had no connection to the mass audience until the mid-Sixties, when they were a guest act on the Motown touring revue. Signed to Motown, their cover of "I Heard It Through the Grapevine" became a #2 smash in 1967. They also scored with "The End of the Road," "Friendship Train," and "If I Were Your Woman."

Just as "Neither One of Us" was mounting the chart, the group decided to leave Motown in 1973, citing lack of label support. Their first LP for Buddah, *Imagination*, made the move worthwhile. It was their biggest seller, going gold and yielding three gold singles: "Midnight Train to Georgia" (#1, 1973), "I've Got to Use My Imagination" (#4, 1974), and "Best Thing That Ever Happened to Me" (#3, 1974). In 1973 the group won two Grammys: Best Pop Vocal Performance by a Duo, Group or Chorus for "Neither One of Us" and Best R&B Vocal Performance by a Duo, Group or Chorus for "Midnight Train to Georgia." Motown continued to release albums by the group after it had left; the group claims it has never received royalties from these or "Neither One of Us."

The hits continued with "The Way We Were"/"Try to Remember" (#11, 1975), and they did the movie soundtrack to *Claudine* with Curtis Mayfield in 1974, which included the single "On and On" (#5, 1974). Gladys made her acting debut in 1976 in a film with the unlikely subject of love set among the Alaskan oil pipelines, called

Pipe Dreams; in 1985 she also costarred in the short-lived TV series *Charlie and Co.* In 1977, because of legal proceedings involving the band's attempted switch of labels to Columbia, plus an old unsettled suit by Motown, Gladys was not allowed to record with the Pips on LP for three years (though they did sing together live).

In the meantime, the group's popularity waned. Gladys recorded a solo LP, and the Pips did two albums for Casablanca, finally reuniting in 1980 on Columbia with *About Love*, produced by Ashford and Simpson, yielding the #3 R&B hit "Landlord." *Visions* also had a hit single, "Save the Overtime (for Me)" (#66 pop, #1 R&B, 1983) and "You're Number One (In My Book)" (#5 R&B, 1983). "Love Overboard" (#13 pop, #1 R&B, 1987), from *All Our Love* (#39, 1987), won the group a Grammy in 1988 for Best R&B Vocal Performance by a Duo or Group with Vocal. Another single from that album, "Lovin' on Next to Nothin'" went to #3 R&B the following year.

Gladys Knight's *Good Woman* (#45 pop, #1 R&B, 1991) featured many songs Knight wrote. In the accompanying press release, the group was described as "suspended." Knight's solo hits include "It's Gonna Take All Our Love" (#29 R&B, 1988), "License to Kill" (from the James Bond film) (#69 R&B, 1989), "Men" (#2 R&B, 1991), and "Where Would I Be" (#66 R&B, 1992). She also won a Grammy in 1986 for the AIDS-benefit record "That's What Friends Are For," which she recorded with Dionne Warwick, Stevie Wonder, and Elton John.

Mark Knopfler: See Dire Straits

Kool and the Gang
Formed 1964, Jersey City, New Jersey
Robert "Kool" Bell (b. Oct. 8, 1950, Youngstown, Ohio), voc., bass; Ronald Bell (b. Nov. 1, 1951, Youngstown, Ohio), tenor sax; Dennis "Dee Tee" Thomas (b. Feb. 9, 1951, Jersey City), sax, flute; Claydes Smith (b. Sep. 6, 1948, Jersey City), lead gtr.; Robert "Spike" Mickens (b. Jersey City), trumpet; Rickey Westfield (b. Jersey City), kybds.; George "Funky" Brown (b. Jan. 5, 1949, Jersey City), drums.
1971—*Live at the Sex Machine* (De-Lite); *The Best of Kool and the Gang*; *Music Is the Message* 1972— *Live at P.J.'s*; *Good Times* 1973—*Wild and Peaceful*; *Kool Jazz* 1974—*Light of Worlds* 1975—*Kool and the Gang Greatest Hits!*; *Spirit of the Boogie* 1976—(+ Clifford Adams [b. Oct. 8, 1952, N.J.], trombone) *Love and Understanding*; *Open Sesame* 1977—*The Force* (– Westfield) 1978—*Kool and the Gang Spin Their Top Hits*; *Everybody's Dancin'* 1979—(+ James "J. T." Taylor [b. Aug. 16, 1953, S.C.], voc.) *Ladies Night* 1980—*Celebrate!* (+ Curtis Williams [b. Dec. 11, 1962, Buffalo, N.Y.], kybds.;

+ Michael Ray [b. Dec. 24, 1962, N.J.], trumpet)
1981—*Something Special*   1982—*As One*   1983—*In the Heart*   1984—*Emergency*   1986—*Forever* (Mercury)   1988—*Everything's Kool and the Gang: Greatest Hits and More*   1989—(– J. T. Taylor; + Skip Martin, voc.; + Odeon Mays, voc.; + Gary Brown, voc.) *Sweat*   1993—*The Best of Kool and the Gang, 1969–1976*; *Unite* (JRS).
J. T. Taylor solo: 1989—*Master of the Game* (MCA)   1991—*Feel the Need*   1993—*Baby, I'm Back*.

In the Seventies and Eighties Kool and the Gang enjoyed many platinum hits with their horn-driven funky dance and pop music, but they started out in the mid-Sixties playing jazz. They began as the Jazziacs, formed while they were all attending Lincoln High School in Jersey City (except guitarist Smith). Leader Robert "Kool" Bell's father used to room with Thelonious Monk, whose music, along with Miles Davis' and John Coltrane's, offered early influences, as did Pharoah Sanders and Leon Thomas, who sometimes showed up at the band's local jam sessions. The group went through several name changes, including the Soul Town Review and the New Dimensions, before becoming Kool and the Gang in 1968. They shifted to more accessible funk R&B, and their eponymous debut single in 1969 reached #19 on the R&B chart.

Kool and the Gang's sound—designed by the group's musical director, Ronald Bell—was highlighted by chunky guitar fills, staccato horn blasts, and group "party" vocal chants. Several modest dance hits, like "Funky Man" (#16 R&B, 1970) and "Love the Life You Live" (#31 R&B, 1972), led to their massive breakthrough in 1973 with three top singles on one gold album, *Wild and Peaceful,* including "Funky Stuff" (#29 pop, #5 R&B, 1973), "Jungle Boogie" (#4 pop, 1974; #2 R&B, 1973), and "Hollywood Swinging" (#6, 1974). Other hit singles include "Higher Plane" (#1 R&B, 1974), "Rhyme Tyme People" (#3 R&B, 1974), "Spirit of the Boogie" (#1 R&B, 1975), "Caribbean Festival" (#8 R&B, 1975), "Love and Understanding (Come Together)" (#8 R&B, 1976), and "Open Sesame—Part 1" (#6 R&B, 1976). Their dance style anticipated disco, but they were temporarily shoved in the background by the trend, though they got a minor pop hit with "Open Sesame," which appeared on the next year's *Saturday Night Fever* soundtrack. Some of their music in the mid-Seventies reflected their "spiritual phase"—several members are devout Muslims. In the late Eighties Ronald Bell changed his name to Khalis Bayyan, and Robert Bell became Amir Bayyan.

In 1978 the band got new management and a full-fledged lead singer who could handle ballads. Tenor James "J. T." Taylor (no relation to the pop-folk singer) fronted the band on 1979's *Ladies Night,* and with the help of coproducer Eumir Deodato, it hit the pop Top Ten (#1 R&B) with the title track. The single went gold, the album, platinum. In 1980 Kool and the Gang released "Too Hot" (#5 pop, #3 R&B, 1980), and "Celebration" (#1 pop, #1 R&B, 1980), which went platinum and became a theme song for the return of the U.S. hostages from Iran, not to mention a standard of wedding bands everywhere. The *Celebrate!* LP also went platinum, as did *Something Special,* yielding the hits "Take My Heart (You Can Have It If You Want It)" (#17 pop, #1 R&B, 1981), "Steppin' Out" (#12 R&B, 1982), "Get Down on It" (#10 pop, #4 R&B, 1982), "Big Fun" (#21 pop, #6 R&B, 1982), and "Let's Go Dancin' (Ooh La, La, La)" (#30 pop, #7 R&B, 1982).

Kool and the Gang's popularity continued through the Eighties, but among their biggest hits—"Joanna" (#29, 1983) and "Tonight" (#13 pop, #7 R&B, 1984) from *In the Heart* and "Fresh" (#9 pop, #1 R&B, 1984), "Cherish" (#2 pop, #1 R&B, 1985), and "Emergency" (#18 pop, #7 R&B, 1985) from the platinum *Emergency*—were several softer ballads. Other hits include "Victory" (#10 pop, #2 R&B, 1986), "Stone Love" (#10 pop, #4 R&B, 1987), and "Holiday" (#9 R&B, 1987). Taylor left the group in 1989 and released his solo debut that year. He scored a hit single with "All I Want Is Forever," a #2 R&B duet with Regina Belle.

The group's first album without Taylor, *Sweat,* did not make a great commercial impression, peaking on the R&B albums chart at #52. The group's more recent singles include "Rags to Riches" (#38 R&B, 1988), "Raindrops" (#27 R&B, 1989), and "Never Give Up" (#74 R&B, 1989).

Kool Moe Dee

Born Mohandas DeWese, August 8, New York City, New York
1986—*Kool Moe Dee* (Jive)   1987—*How Ya Like Me Now*   1989—*Knowledge Is King*   1990—*African Pride* EP   1991—*Funke Funke Wisdom*   1993—*Greatest Hits*.

Kool Moe Dee is one of rap's more eloquent practitioners of braggadocio. Having discovered the joys of making rhymes via Dr. Seuss' *The Grinch Who Stole Christmas* and heavyweight champ Muhammad Ali's boasting, the young Mohandas DeWese was poised to join New York City's burgeoning late-Seventies rap scene. When the Treacherous Three, a rap trio he belonged to, split up, he continued on his own, releasing the musically spare *Kool Moe Dee.* The album became an instant classic of rap's so-called old school style and contained the minor pop hit "Go See the Doctor" (#89, 1987). The title track of the platinum-selling *How Ya Like Me Now* put Kool Moe Dee into a blistering feud with L.L. Cool J (he claimed Cool J ripped off his style). A temporary truce was called in 1990 when the two shook hands backstage at Harlem's

Apollo Theatre. "How Ya Like Me Now" reached #22 on the R&B chart in late 1987, but it took 1988's "Wild, Wild West" (#4 R&B) to get Kool Moe Dee into the Top Ten. His *Funke Funke Wisdom* was a critical disappointment, though it spawned the single "How Kool Can One Blackman Be?" (#49 R&B, 1991). In 1992 the IRS auctioned Kool Moe Dee's Mercedes-Benz for $20,300, the proceeds to be credited toward the $180,000 in back taxes he owed. In 1993 a greatest-hits album was released, and the next year the Treacherous Three reunited for some old school shows.

Al Kooper
Born February 5, 1944, Brooklyn, New York
1969—*I Stand Alone* (Columbia); *You Never Know Who Your Friends Are*   1970—*Kooper Session* (with Shuggie Otis); *Easy Does It*   1971—*Landlord* soundtrack (United Artists); *New York City* (Columbia)   1972—*A Possible Projection of the Future/Childhood's End; Naked Songs*   1975—*Unclaimed Freight—Al's Big Deal*   1976—*Act Like Nothing's Wrong* (United Artists)   1982—*Championship Wrestling* (Columbia)   1994—*Rekooperation* (MusicMasters)   1995—*Soul of a Man: Al Kooper Live.*
With Mike Bloomfield and Stephen Stills: 1968—*Super Session* (Columbia).
With Mike Bloomfield: 1969—*The Live Adventures of Mike Bloomfield and Al Kooper* (Columbia).

Al Kooper played a major role in the blues rock of the Sixties. He originated what has become commonly known as the "Dylanesque organ" with his work on *Highway 61 Revisited,* he helped popularize the blues with the Blues Project, and he put together Blood, Sweat and Tears, which began the big-band jazz-rock trend that influenced bands like Chicago. He also discovered Lynyrd Skynyrd and the Tubes.

Kooper, who prefers to play piano or guitar, turned professional at age 15 when he joined the Royal Teens after they had a #3 hit in 1958 with "Short Shorts." He left the band in the late Fifties, turned to writing and session work, and studied for a year at the University of Bridgeport. In 1965 he cowrote a #1 hit for Gary Lewis and the Playboys, "This Diamond Ring." That same year producer Tom Wilson gave Kooper a job playing organ on Dylan's single "Like a Rolling Stone" and later on *Highway 61 Revisited.* Kooper also backed Dylan at his 1965 Newport Folk Festival appearance and worked on *Blonde on Blonde* and, later, *New Morning.*

In 1965 Kooper and Steve Katz formed the Blues Project, and in 1967 they founded Blood, Sweat and Tears [see entries]. Kooper picked the band members and produced their 1968 debut, *Child Is Father to the Man,* but he left before the band's big commercial success, to

Al Kooper

work as a Columbia staff producer and record several collaborative LPs. The first was 1968's *Super Session* with guitarists Mike Bloomfield (whom he met during the Dylan sessions) and Stephen Stills. That album became one of the year's best sellers. Kooper again collaborated with Bloomfield in 1969 for a live LP. He went on to record several solo albums, which received less attention than his collaborations or the albums he'd done session work on, which included the Rolling Stones' *Let It Bleed* and Jimi Hendrix's *Electric Ladyland.*

By the Seventies Kooper had become known more as a producer than as a musician. He produced the first three Lynyrd Skynyrd records, the Tubes' 1975 debut, and Nils Lofgren's *Cry Tough.* In 1976 he cut his first solo LP in three years and published an autobiography, *Backstage Passes.* On St. Patrick's Day 1981 he performed in New York City in a Blues Project reunion, and later that year he toured with Bob Dylan. Kooper celebrated his 50th birthday with a Bottom Line show in 1994, a year that saw the release of his first album in 12 years, *Rekooperation.* In between he toured as part of Joe Walsh's band in 1991, played keyboards on a 1990 Byrds session, produced the 1991 LP *Scapegoats* by Green on Red, and scored a short-lived TV series, *Crime Story.* Kooper coproduced and contributed a track to the 1995 tribute album *For the Love of Harry: Everybody Sings Nilsson.*

Alexis Korner
Born Alexis Koerner, April 19, 1928, Paris, France; died January 1, 1984, London, England

1969—*Alexis Korner's All Stars Blues Incorporated* (Transatlantic) 1970—*The New Church* (Metronome) 1972—*Accidentally Born in New Orleans* (Warner Bros.); *Bootleg Him!* 1974—*Snape Live on Tour* (Brain) 1975—*Get Off My Cloud* (Columbia) 1978—*Just Easy* (Intercord) 1979—*Me* (Jeton).

Alexis Korner is better known for the musicians he discovered than for the music they made in his bands. His group Blues Incorporated, formed in 1961, was a major factor in the Sixties blues revival in England and America.

Educated throughout Europe, Korner was already 34 years old and a veteran of a dozen years in jazz and skiffle groups when he formed Blues Inc. with Charlie Watts (later a Rolling Stone), Cyril Davies, and Dick Heckstall-Smith (later of John Mayall's Bluesbreakers and Colosseum). Among the dozens of musicians to woodshed with Blues Incorporated before Korner broke up the group in 1967 were Mick Jagger; Cream's Ginger Baker and Jack Bruce; Hughie Flint (later with Mayall, then McGuinness-Flint); Danny Thompson, John Renbourn, and Terry Cox (all future Pentangle); Graham Bond; and Long John Baldry. Between Blues Incorporated and his next band, New Church, with Danish singer Peter Thorup, Korner worked with pre–Led Zeppelin Robert Plant, Humble Pie's Steve Marriott, and Andy Fraser, who later formed Free with an assist from Korner that included suggesting the group's name and arranging for its debut performance.

New Church had a sizable European following, but it wasn't until 1971 and CCS (the Collective Consciousness Society), a 25-member-plus group assembled by noted British pop producer Mickie Most and fronted by Korner and Thorup, that he had his first chart entry, at the age of 43: "Whole Lotta Love." That same year Korner appeared on B. B. King's *In London* LP, Korner's first American record. He and Thorup toured the U.S. the next year, opening for King Crimson. By tour's end Mel Collins, Ian Wallace, and Boz Burrell (later of Bad Company) had quit Crimson and formed Snape with Korner and Thorup. They recorded the album *Accidentally Born in New Orleans* around the same time that *Bootleg Him!*, a retrospective of Korner's work, was finally released in America.

In England Korner had his own popular BBC Radio 1 program. At the time of his death from lung cancer, he was working on a 13-part TV series chronicling the history of rock & roll.

Leo Kottke

Born September 11, 1945, Athens, Georgia
1969—*Twelve String Blues* (Oblivion) 1970—*Circle 'Round the Sun* (Symposium) 1971—*Mudlark*

Leo Kottke

(Capitol) 1972—*Six and Twelve-String Guitar* (Takoma); *Greenhouse* (Capitol) 1973—*My Feet Are Smiling*; *Ice Water* 1974—*Dreams and All That Stuff* 1975—*Chewing Pine* 1976—*Leo Kottke 1971–1976—Did You Hear Me?*; *Leo Kottke* (Chrysalis) 1978—*Burnt Lips* 1979—*Balance* 1980—*Live in Europe* 1982—*Guitar Music* 1983—*Time Step* 1986—*A Shout Towards Noon* (Private Music) 1988—*Regards from Chuck Pink* 1989—*My Father's Face* 1990—*That's What* 1991—*Great Big Boy*; *Essential Leo Kottke* (Chrysalis) 1993—*Peculiaroso* (Private Music).

Leo Kottke's propulsive fingerpicked guitar instrumentals and (to a lesser extent) his gallows-humor lyrics have garnered him a solid cult following. He grew up in 12 different states and tried playing violin and trombone. While he was living in Muskogee, Oklahoma, a cherry bomb planted by a neighborhood kid in a bush exploded, permanently impairing young Kottke's hearing in his left ear. Later, during a brief stint in the Naval Reserve, his right ear was damaged by firing practice. After the navy Kottke went to St. Cloud State College in Minnesota, but after three years he dropped out and began hitchhiking around and practicing the guitar, which he'd been playing since he was 11.

Kottke's first LP, *Twelve String Blues*, was a 1969 set at the Scholar Coffee House in Minneapolis. He sent tapes to guitarist John Fahey, who signed him to his own Takoma label and introduced him to manager/producer Denny Bruce (who had played drums for the early Mothers of Invention). Kottke's one album for Takoma, *Six and Twelve-String Guitar*, was a collection of solo instrumentals that eventually sold 400,000 copies; in its liner notes, Kottke described his voice as "geese farts on a muggy day." He signed with Capitol and put out six albums, using bass and drums as studio backup and introducing his vocals, which weren't so bad. He appeared on the soundtrack of Terence Malick's 1978 film *Days of Heaven*. *Guitar Music* was his first all-instrumental LP since his Takoma album; *Time Step* was produced by T Bone Burnett and included guest vocals by Emmylou Harris. Kottke continues to tour as a soloist, and in 1993 released *Peculiaroso*, produced by Rickie Lee Jones.

Kraftwerk

Formed 1970, Dusseldorf, West Germany
Ralf Hutter (b. 1946, Krefeld, Ger.), voc., electronics;
Florian Schneider (b. 1947, Dusseldorf), voc., elec-
tronics; Klaus Dinger; Thomas Homann.
1971—*Highrail* (Philips, Ger.) (– Dinger; – Homann)
1972—*Var; Kraftwerk* (Vertigo, U.K.)   1973—*Ralf*
***and Florian*   1974—(+ Klaus Roeder, violin, gtr.;**
+ Wolfgang Flur, electronic perc.) *Autobahn*
1975—(– Roeder; + Karl Bartos, electronic perc.)
Radio-Activity* (Capitol)   1977—*Trans-Europe Ex-
press*   1978—*The Man-Machine*   1981—*Computer
***World* (Warner Bros.)   1986—*Electric Cafe* (EMI)**
1990—(– Flur; + Fritz Hijbert, electronic perc.)
1991—*The Mix* (Elektra).

Kraftwerk's robotic, repetitive all-electronic music in the mid-Seventies influenced virtually every synthesizer band that came in its wake, with both the German group's sound and its ironic man-machine imagery. In 1970, Ralf Hutter and Florian Schneider, who had met studying classical music at Dusseldorf Conservatory, founded Kling-Klang Studio, where they produced two German albums. The first, *Tone Float*, was recorded when the group was called Organization, and it was heavily influenced by Pink Floyd and Tangerine Dream. Hutter and Schneider left Organization, took the name Kraftwerk ("power plant"), and began experimenting with integrating mechanized sounds from everyday life into music. After *Ralf and Florian* (not released in the U.S. until 1975), they added Klaus Roeder and Wolfgang Flur.

The German band had immediate success with its first U.S. release, *Autobahn*, which went Top Five. The requisite hit was an edited version of the 22-minute minimalist title track about a monotonous journey along the famed German-Austrian superhighway.

Kraftwerk's next two LPs were paeans to such other modern-world wonders as the radio (*Radio-Activity*) and the train (*Trans-Europe Express*). David Bowie cited the band as an influence for his *Low* and *"Heroes"* albums. There is some evidence that Bowie's "V-2 Schneider" is a tribute to the band. Kraftwerk confirmed its cold conceptualist image with "Trans-Europe Express" and "Showroom Dummies," both of which became late-Seventies disco hits. In 1977 the group toured the U.S. playing electronic instruments and dressed in mannequin outfits. The band members later threatened to tour by sending over electronic dummies of themselves while they rested at home.

Man-Machine featured more accessible music, but then Kraftwerk disappeared for three years, not emerging until 1981 with the pop-oriented *Computer World*. The album stayed on the U.S. chart for 42 weeks and produced a #1 U.K. single, "Computer Love" b/w "The Model." Meanwhile, the "Trans-Europe Express" melody made its way into rap, on Afrika Bambaataa's "Planet Rock." Since 1986's *Electric Cafe*, Kraftwerk has kept a low profile, releasing only a best-of, *The Mix*, and playing but a handful of live shows.

Billy J. Kramer and the Dakotas

Formed 1963, Liverpool, England
Billy J. Kramer (b. William Howard Ashton, Aug. 19,
1943, Bootle, Eng.), voc.; Tony Mansfield (b. May 28,
1943, Salford, Eng.), drums; Mike Maxfield (b. Feb.
23, 1944, Manchester, Eng.), gtr.; Robin Macdonald
(b. July 18, 1943, Nairn, Scot.), gtr.; Raymond Jones
(b. Oct. 20, 1939, Oldham, Eng.), bass.
1964—*Little Children* (Imperial)   N.A.—*The Best of*
***Billy J. Kramer and the Dakotas* (Capitol).**

Billy J. Kramer was the type of crooner who dominated the British pop chart until the Beatles changed the rules. But he owed his fleeting fame largely to the Beatles: He shared their manager, Brian Epstein; their label, EMI-Parlophone; and their producer, George Martin. And two of his biggest hits were written by John Lennon and Paul McCartney.

Liverpudlian William Ashton had already adopted his stage name, Billy J. Kramer, by 1963, when he and his group, the Coasters, were spotted by Brian Epstein. Epstein set Kramer up with a Manchester combo, the Dakotas, and the Beatles' songwriters, John Lennon and Paul McCartney. "Do You Want to Know a Secret?" was his first success, in 1963, followed by "Bad to Me," a hit on both sides of the Atlantic (#9 U.S.). (Kramer later recalled how he'd learned "Do You Want to Know a Secret?" from a crude demo tape John Lennon had recorded in a bathroom.) The singer's biggest non–Lennon/McCartney number was "Little Children" (#7, 1964). His last hit came in 1965, with "Trains and Boats and Planes" (#47, 1965). Soon after, Brian Epstein began devoting more and more attention to the Beatles, and the Dakotas split up. Kramer continued performing on the cabaret circuit until the mid-Seventies, when he unsuccessfully attempted a comeback. Between 1973 and 1983 he released 11 singles on seven different U.K.

labels. In 1984 Kramer relocated to Long Island, and he continues to perform on the oldies circuit.

Alison Krauss

Born July 23, 1971, Champaign, Illinois
1987—*Too Late to Cry* (Rounder)   1989—*Two Highways* (with Union Station)   1990—*I've Got That Old Feeling*   1992—*Every Time You Say Goodbye* (with Union Station)   1994—*I Know Who Holds Tomorrow* (with the Cox Family)   1995—*Now That I've Found You: A Collection.*

Blessed with an angelic voice and virtuosic fiddling skills, youthful bluegrass propagator Alison Krauss has already accrued more honors than most artists receive in a lifetiMaine By age 22, she had won two Grammys, been inducted into the Grand Ole Opry, and recorded with some of the best-known artists in country music. She also boasts noteworthy record production skills, and fronts Union Station, an acclaimed bluegrass outfit.

Krauss displayed her musical aptitude at an early age. When she was five she started taking classical violin lessons in her hometown of Champaign, Illinois, and became the state fiddling champion at age 11. The next year she discovered bluegrass, and at 14 joined Union Station, a local bluegrass band. That year the group, billed as Alison Krauss and Union Station, mesmerized a throng at the Newport Folk Festival, which garnered the young fiddler a recording contract with Rounder Records. Her first solo effort, *Too Late to Cry,* was augmented by bluegrass legends Jerry Douglas (dobro), Sam Bush (mandolin), and Tony Trischka (banjo).

Two years later, Krauss' bandleading skills were showcased on *Two Highways,* her first album with Union Station. *I've Got That Old Feeling,* a solo effort, won Krauss her first Grammy for Best Bluegrass Album. In July 1993 she was the first bluegrass artist in 29 years to join the Grand Ole Opry, and that year she was named Female Vocalist of the Year by the International Bluegrass Music Association (IBMA), which also awarded her its Album of the Year for *Every Time You Say Goodbye.*

In 1994 she produced and collaborated on the Cox Family's bluegrass/gospel album *I Know Who Holds Tomorrow,* for which she won another Grammy. She also has played on sessions with such diverse artists as Vince Gill, Michael McDonald, Dolly Parton, and Phish. In classic bluegrass style, Krauss continues to combine influences, melding the traditional with the new, thus solidifying her niche as one of the foremost ambassadors of the genre.

Lenny Kravitz

Born Leonard Albert Kravitz, May 26, 1964, New York City, New York

Lenny Kravitz

1989—*Let Love Rule* (Virgin)   1991—*Mama Said*   1993—*Are You Gonna Go My Way.*

Lenny Kravitz survived the ridicule of being called "Mr. (Lisa) Bonet" and the scorn of critics who accused him of being a derivative neohippie to forge a fairly successful career making anachronistic, soul-inflected Sixties-style rock for the Nineties.

The only child of white TV news producer Sy Kravitz and black actress Roxie Roker (of TV's *The Jeffersons*), Kravitz spent the first ten years of his life in Manhattan, then moved with his family to Los Angeles, where his first musical experience came in the California Boys Choir. He taught himself guitar, bass, piano, and drums. Kravitz attended the exclusive Beverly Hills High School (classmates included Saul Hudson, later Slash, and Maria McKee), where he adopted the David Bowie–inspired, wild-party persona "Romeo Blue." In 1985 Kravitz met actress Lisa Bonet of TV's *The Cosby Show.* They were married in 1987 and had one daughter, Zoe, before separating in 1991; their divorce became final two years later.

Let Love Rule displayed Kravitz's voice, which sounded uncannily like Elvis Costello's, and his retro-rock style, which sounded uncannily like all sorts of people—the Beatles, Bob Dylan, Jimi Hendrix. While reviews were mixed, the album sold fairly well (#61, 1989), and the title track reached #89 in 1990.

In 1990 Kravitz shared writing and producing chores with Madonna on her "Justify My Love." A year later Prince discovery Ingrid Chavez (who costarred in his *Graffiti Bridge*) sued, claiming she had cowritten the song with Kravitz. He admitted to having worked with Chavez, but maintained that they had agreed to keep her role in writing the song "private." The matter was eventually settled out of court. The rhythm track, meanwhile, had been sampled from a Public Enemy song.

In January 1991, as tensions in the Persian Gulf mounted, Kravitz hastily recorded an all-star cover of John Lennon's "Give Peace a Chance" (#54), with guitar work by Slash and vocal and video appearances by over two dozen artists, including Yoko Ono, Sean Lennon, Bonnie Raitt, Peter Gabriel, Run-D.M.C., L.L. Cool J, and the Red Hot Chili Peppers.

Mama Said sold better than its predecessor (#39, 1991), with the polished Curtis Mayfield–style "It Ain't Over Til It's Over" hitting #2. In 1993 Kravitz released *Are You Gonna Go My Way* (#12). The hard-rocking, extremely Hendrixian title track was nominated for two 1994 Grammys.

Kris Kross

Formed 1991, Atlanta, Georgia
Chris Kelly (b. Aug. 11, 1978, Englewood, N.J.), voc.;
Chris Smith (b. Jan. 10, 1979, Atlanta), voc.
1992—*Totally Krossed Out* (Ruffhouse/Columbia)
1993—*Da Bomb*.

Wearing their clothes backward and rapping in prepubescent squeaks, Kris Kross is a teenybopper, hip-hop sensation. The two Chrises were discovered by producer Jermaine Dupri while shopping at an Atlanta mall. He groomed and coached them for a year—dressing them in baggy, backward gear—and wrote songs for their multiplatinum debut, *Totally Krossed Out* (#1 pop, #1 R&B, 1992). The duo called themselves Mack Daddy (Kelly) and Daddy Mack (Smith) and rapped about missing the school bus and sneaking into clubs. Propelled by the multiplatinum single "Jump" (#1, 1992), which sampled the Jackson 5's "I Want You Back," and "Warm It Up" (#13, 1993), Kris Kross became international stars. They toured Europe opening for Michael Jackson and appeared in the film *Who's the Man?*, as well as on a score of TV shows.

By their second album, the boys' voices had begun to deepen, and they accordingly tried to evince a more hard-core attitude, rapping like young gangstas. Whereas Dupri wrote their debut, Kelly contributed some lyrics on *Da Bomb* (#13 pop, #2 R&B, 1993). Several songs featured dancehall rhythms, with reggae-rapper Supercat guesting on "Alright" (#19 pop, #8 R&B, 1993). That single and "I'm Real" (#84 pop, #45 R&B, 1993) garnered some chart success.

Kris Kristofferson

Born June 22, 1937, Brownsville, Texas
1970—*Kristofferson* (Monument)   1971—*Me and*

***Bobby McGee*; *Cisco Pete* (Columbia); *The Silver-Tongued Devil and I* (Monument)   1972—*Josie*; *Border Lord*; *Jesus Was a Capricorn*   1973—*Why Me?*   1974—*Spooky Lady's Sideshow*   1975— *Who's to Bless and Who's to Blame*   1976—*Surreal Thing*; *A Star Is Born* soundtrack (Columbia) 1977—*Songs of Kristofferson*   1978—*Easter Island* 1979—*Shake Hands with the Devil*   1980—*Help Me Make It Through the Night*; *To the Bone*   1981— *Nobody Loves Anybody Anymore*   1986—*Repossessed*   1990—*Third World Warrior* (Mercury) 1991—*Singer/Songwriter* (Columbia Legacy).**
With Rita Coolidge: 1973—*Full Moon* (A&M) 1974—*Breakaway* (Monument)   1978—*Natural Act* (A&M).
With Willie Nelson: 1984—*Music from SongWriter* soundtrack (Columbia); *How Do You Feel About Foolin' Around*.
With Willie Nelson, Johnny Cash, and Waylon Jennings: 1985—*Highwayman* (Columbia); *Desperadoes Waiting for a Train*   1987—*They Killed Him* (Mercury)   1990—*Highwayman 2*   1995—*The Road Goes On Forever* (Liberty).

Kris Kristofferson finished out the Seventies as a movie star, but several of his songs—"Sunday Morning Coming Down," "Me and Bobby McGee," and "Help Me Make It Through the Night"—have become country-rock standards. In the early Seventies, their boozy romanticism helped define "outlaw" country. After receiving a Ph.D. from Pomona College, Kristofferson went to Oxford University on a Rhodes scholarship in 1958. He first wanted to be a novelist, but he was also writing songs; he changed his name to Kris Carson and was signed by Tommy Steele's manager. In 1960, he joined the army, but five years later, when he was about to accept a job teaching English at West Point, he decided instead to invest all his time in songwriting once again, encouraged by a meeting with his idol, Johnny Cash. He moved to Nashville in 1965 and tried to pitch his songs while working as a night janitor at the Columbia studios, cleaning ashtrays at the same time Bob Dylan was recording *Blonde on Blonde* there. (Billy Swan, Kristofferson's future guitarist, later worked the same job.)

His break finally came in 1969, when Johnny Cash gave Kristofferson's song "Me and Bobby McGee" to Roger Miller, who made it a hit on the country charts. Kristofferson appeared on Cash's TV show, and Cash had a hit with "Sunday Morning" in 1969. In March 1971 Janis Joplin's version of "Bobby McGee" went to #1, and about same time Sammi Smith had a #8 pop hit with "Help Me Make It Through the Night." Kristofferson's own recording debut was released in June 1970. His commercial potential caught up to his critical success on 1971's *The Silver-Tongued Devil and I*, which went gold. The next year's *Border Lord* was panned, and from then on his recording career declined. Meanwhile, he made his film debut in 1972's *Cisco Pike* and two years later appeared in *Pat Garrett and Billy the Kid,* a film in which his second wife, Rita Coolidge, also appeared. They were married in 1973; they had met two years earlier. From there, Kristofferson established himself as an actor in *Alice Doesn't Live Here Anymore* (1974) and in *The Sailor Who Fell from Grace with the Sea* (1976), *Semi-Tough* (1971), *Convoy* (1978), and a remake of *A Star Is Born* (1976) with Barbra Streisand.

Kristofferson had a 20-year drinking problem, which he finally kicked in the late Seventies. He continued to tour and record throughout it all, though with much less commercial success. He did some joint shows and records with Coolidge until their marriage dissolved in December 1979. Since 1980 Kristofferson has appeared in well over a dozen films, including features such as *Heaven's Gate* (1980), *Rollover* (1981), *Trouble in Mind* (1985), and 1984's *SongWriter,* in which he costarred with fellow "outlaw" Willie Nelson. He has also costarred in numerous made-for-TV movies and mini-series. In 1994 he costarred in *Sodbusters.*

Kristofferson is known for his outspoken leftist political views, which, he claims, led to his break from his longtime label, Columbia, in the late Eighties. To date, all of his major country hits have been collaborative efforts with Nelson, Johnny Cash, and Waylon Jennings: 1985's "Highwayman" (#1 C&W) and "Desperadoes Waiting for a Train" (#15 C&W) and 1990's "Silver Stallion" (#25 C&W).

KRS-One: See Boogie Down Productions

Fela Anikulapo Kuti

Born Fela Ransome Kuti, October 15, 1938, Abeokuta, Nigeria
1971—*Fela with Ginger Baker Live* (with Ginger Baker) (Makossa)   1974—*Shakara*   1975—*Question Jam Answer; Roforofo Fight; Mr. Follow-Follow* (Phonodisc)   1976—*Kalakuta Show* (Makossa)   1977—*Upside Down* (London); *Zombie* (Mercury)   1979—*Coffin for Head of State* (Makossa); *V.I.P.: Vagabonds in Power*   1980—*Fela and Roy Ayers: Music of Many Colors* (Phonodisc 1986)   1981—*Black President* (Arista, U.K.); *Original Sufferhead* (Capitol); *Expensive Shit* (Makossa)   1982—*Unnecessary Begging; Alagbon Close*   1983—*Perambulator* (Lagos International)   1984—*Live in Amsterdam* (EMI, Fr.)   1985—*Army Arrangement* (Celluloid); *Shuffering and Shmiling; No Agreement*   1987—*Teacher Don't Teach Me Nonsense* (Mercury)

1988—*I Go Shout Plenty*   1989—*Beasts of No Nation* (Shanachie)   1990—*Odoo*   1992—*Black Man's Cry: Classic Fela.*

Fela Anikulapo Kuti is the leading exponent—and perhaps the originator—of afro-beat, an urban West African dance-while-you-protest style that modernized traditional Yoruba music (call-and-response chanting over polyrhythmic drumming) with repeated R&B-style horn figures and funk-styled guitar chords. Keyboardist, saxophonist, vocalist, composer, and bandleader, he is also one of the most politically outspoken figures in international pop.

Fela Kuti is the son of Funmilayo Kuti, a woman well known in Nigeria as a feminist and labor organizer; she exerted early and lasting influence on Fela, although his youthful interests were more musical than political. In 1959 he went to England to study at the Trinity College of Music, and he began playing piano in jazz, R&B, and rock bands with African, British, and American musicians, among them Ginger Baker of Cream. He also took up the alto saxophone.

Returning to Nigeria in the mid-Sixties, he formed a band that was successful enough to afford a move en masse to the U.S. in 1969. Alternating between New York and Los Angeles, the band made virtually no impression on American audiences, but influenced by American black militants, Fela returned to Nigeria in 1970 with new ideas about the role of the musician in political change.

He formed a new band, Africa 70 (also spelled Afrika 70), an ensemble of 20 instrumentalists, singers, and dancers, and began making albums that showed the influences of James Brown and Sly and the Family Stone. He set up a communal estate for the band and their families on the outskirts of Lagos, eventually building a hospital and a recording studio on its grounds (the latter with the help of Ginger Baker, who lived in Nigeria for much of the Seventies). The site became a meeting place for West African radical artists, writers, and activists and the object of harassment by Nigeria's military junta. Fela's songs were highly critical of government corruption, police brutality, and the greed of foreign investors. Nigerian hits (most of his releases) such as "Zombie" and "Monkey Banana" openly mocked the authorities.

After Fela and associates were jailed and beaten by police on a number of occasions, he declared his property the independent Kalakuta Republic. On February 18, 1977, presumably in reaction to that act of treason, 1000 armed soldiers attacked Kalakuta. In a full day of fighting, Kalakutans were raped, wounded, or arrested. Fela's mother was killed, and the settlement was burned. After being released from jail, Fela and his followers exiled themselves to Ghana for a year. There he changed his middle name from Ransome to the tribal Anikulapo and, in a related ceremony, married his 27 female singers and dancers, giving him 28 wives.

On his return to Nigeria, Fela rebuilt Kalakuta but was banned from giving concerts, which previously had drawn as many as 100,000 fans to a single performance. So, for the first time since 1970, he took his show abroad, traveling through Germany, Italy, and France with his entourage of 70. Back in Nigeria in 1979, he formed a political party, Movement of the People, and ran for the presidency of Nigeria that year until banned from the campaign by election authorities. In 1983 Fela's band, now known as Egypt 80, was joined for an African tour by American jazz trumpeter Lester Bowie, of the Art Ensemble of Chicago (he plays on *Perambulator*).

Fela had promised to run again for Nigeria's presidency in 1983, but a military government returned to power that year, and in September 1984, as he was about to depart for an international tour, Fela was arrested at Lagos Airport, and sentenced to five years in jail for currency smuggling. During his incarceration, New York avant-funk bassist and producer Bill Laswell (Material, Time Zone) finished production of material that became *Army Arrangement,* bringing in P-Funk keyboardist Bernie Worrell and other musicians to play over Fela's tapes. Meanwhile, Amnesty International took up Fela's cause, and after another change in Nigeria's government, worldwide publicity led to Fela's release in July 1985. He was immediately flown to appear at the final show of Amnesty International's Conspiracy of Hope tour in New Jersey. There, looking frail, he played piano with Rubén Blades and percussion with the Neville Brothers.

A year later, a much stronger Fela and Egypt 80 finally toured the U.S., to sizable audiences and great critical acclaim; they returned in 1989 with reggae singer Jimmy Cliff and African reggae star Lucky Dube. In March 1993 Fela was jailed once again in Lagos, on a murder charge stemming from the beating death of a worker at Fela's home The charge was eventually dropped.

Jim Kweskin Jug Band
Formed 1963
Jim Kweskin (b. July 18, 1940, Stamford, Conn.), gtr., voc.; Bill Keith, pedal steel gtr., banjo; Mel Lyman, harmonica; Fritz Richmond, jug, washtub bass; Richard Greene, fiddle; Maria D'Amato Muldaur (b. Sep. 12, 1943, New York City, N.Y.), voc., kazoo, tambourine; Geoff Muldaur, gtr., voc.
1968—*Best of Jim Kweskin Jug Band* (Vanguard)
1970—*Greatest Hits*.

The Jim Kweskin Jug Band was a slaphappy answer to the earnestness of the "folk revival" as typified by Peter, Paul and Mary. The members rarely wrote their own material but specialized in uncovering folk, blues, jazz, and novelty tunes of the past and remaking them in their raucous acoustic style. Kweskin was merely the nominal leader of the ever-shifting aggregation; Geoff Muldaur was more likely to be heard on lead vocal and guitar. Maria D'Amato, who would later wed Muldaur and have a successful duo and solo career under her married name, also sang and played fiddle, although the latter instrument would eventually be manned by future Blues Project/Seatrain virtuoso Richard Greene. Fritz Richmond blew jug and became a virtuoso on washtub bass.

One of the later additions to the band was harmonica player Mel Lyman. Lyman, a self-styled prophet and authoritarian religious leader, split up the group in 1967, with Kweskin becoming a disciple and the others going on to either solo careers or oblivion. Kweskin's solo work includes *Jim Kweskin's America* (1971), *Jim Kweskin Lives Again* (1978), and *Swing on a Star* (1980).

L

Patti LaBelle

Born Patricia Louise Holt, October 4, 1944, Philadelphia, Pennsylvania
1977—*Patti LaBelle* (Columbia)   1979—*It's Alright with Me*   1980—*Released*   1981—*Best of Patti LaBelle*   1983—*I'm in Love Again* (Philadelphia International)   1986—*The Winner in You* (MCA)   1989—*Be Yourself*   1990—*This Christmas*   1991—*Burnin'*   1992—*Live!*   1994—*Gems.*

Following the 1976 breakup of Labelle, the group she'd founded 15 years before, Patti LaBelle embarked on a solo career. Managed by her husband, Armstead Edwards, it took her nearly a decade to achieve massive success; during that time she established herself as a soul diva noteworthy for her three-and-a-half-octave contralto and theatrical stage presence.

Her self-titled debut featuring the kind of sassy funk and yearning ballads she'd been singing for years, LaBelle continued releasing credible albums while initiating an acting career. In 1982 she costarred with Al Green in the Broadway revival of *Your Arm's Too Short to Box with God* and then went on to play a blues singer in the movie *A Soldier's Story* and star in the Truman Capote/Harold Arlen musical *House of Flowers*. On television, she appeared in the Emmy-winning *Motown Salutes the Apollo* and *Sisters in the Name of Love* as well as the sitcoms *A Different World* and *Out All Night*.

On her albums, she became known primarily for duets with performers ranging from her ex-Labelle bandmates Nona Hendryx and Sarah Dash to Gladys Knight, Michael Bolton, Bobby Womack, and Grover Washington Jr. "New Attitude," from the *Beverly Hills Cop* soundtrack, gained her a #17 hit in 1985; her biggest success came with *Winner in You* and its duet with ex–Doobie Brother Michael McDonald, "On My Own" (#1, 1986).

Winning a Grammy for 1991's best R&B Female Vocal Performance for *Burnin'*, LaBelle lists among her many awards the Martin Luther King Lifetime Achievement Award and the Ebony Achievement Award; twice she has been the recipient of the NAACP Entertainer of the Year Award. Her appearance in the 1985 Live Aid telecast underscored her charitable interests: She serves as spokeswoman for the National Cancer Institute and national chairwoman of the Black Health Research Foundation.

Labelle

Formed as Patti LaBelle and the Blue Belles, 1961, Philadelphia, Pennsylvania
Patti LaBelle (b. Patricia Louise Holt, Oct. 4, 1944, Philadelphia), voc.; Nona Hendryx (b. Aug. 18, 1945, Trenton, N.J.), voc.; Sarah Dash (b. May 24, 1942, Trenton, N.J.), voc.; Cindy Birdsong (b. Dec. 15, 1939, Camden, N.J.), voc.

1967—(– Birdsong) *Dreamer* (Atlantic)   1971—
(Group renamed Labelle) *Labelle* (Warner Bros.);
Gonna Take a Miracle (with Laura Nyro) (Columbia)
1972—*Moonshadow* (Warner Bros.)   1973—*Pressure
Cookin'* (RCA)   1974—*Nightbirds* (Epic)   1975—
Phoenix   1976—*Chameleon.*
Patti LaBelle solo: See entry.
Nona Hendryx solo: See entry.
Sarah Dash solo: 1979—*Sarah Dash* (Kirshner)
1985—*You're All I Need* (Capitol).

In their 16 years together, Labelle developed from a fairly
conventional Sixties girl group—complete with sequined gowns, bouffants, and polished choreography—
into a band with a unique space-queen look, an idealistic
political consciousness, and an individual gospel-tinged
funky rock & roll sound. They began as Patti LaBelle and
the Blue Belles, bringing together LaBelle and Cindy
Birdsong from the Ordettes with Nona Hendryx and
Sarah Dash from the Del Capris. Their 1962 single "I Sold
My Heart to the Junkman" became a #15 hit, followed by
versions of "Danny Boy" (#76, 1964) and "You'll Never
Walk Alone" (#34, 1964).

The Blue Belles became a trio in 1967 when Birdsong left to replace Florence Ballard in the Supremes
[see entry]. Although they were hugely popular at the
Apollo Theatre and on the soul circuit, they were mismanaged. In 1970 Britisher Vicki Wickham (who knew
Labelle from their mid-Sixties appearance on the English TV show *Ready Steady Go,* which she produced)
became their manager, revamping their image and
leading them toward more contemporary rock. She also
encouraged Hendryx to contribute more of her own
songs.

In 1971, after Wickham rechristened the group Labelle, it released an eponymous debut on Warner Bros.
and toured the U.S. with the Who. That same year they
collaborated with Laura Nyro on *Gonna Take a Miracle,* a
collection of Fifties and Sixties soul and doo-wop remakes. In 1973 Labelle, at a headline Bottom Line show,
joined the glitter trend, debuting their soon-to-be-famous lamé space cadet suits. In 1974 they became the
first black act ever to play New York's Metropolitan
Opera House; there they introduced what was to become their only million-selling hit, "Lady Marmalade"
(#1, 1975), a shouter about a Creole hooker. The single,
written by Bob Crewe, Allen Toussaint, and Kenny Nolan,
highlighted their *Nightbirds* LP, produced by Toussaint
in New Orleans.

Since Hendryx and Patti LaBelle had basic musical
differences, Labelle broke up in 1976; both pursued solo
careers [see entries]. Sarah Dash played small clubs and
began recording solo albums in 1979. She continues to
work as a background singer for various artists, including Keith Richards, the Rolling Stones, LaBelle, and

Labelle: Nona Hendryx, Patti LaBelle, Sarah Dash

Hendryx. The three were reunited on "Release Yourself"
from LaBelle's 1991 solo album *Burnin'.*

Ladysmith Black Mambazo

Formed 1964, Ladysmith, South Africa
Joseph Shabalala (b. Aug. 28, 1940, S.A.), voc.;
Headman Shabalala (b. Oct. 9, 1945, S.A.; d. Dec. 11,
1991, S.A.), voc.; Jockey Shabalala (b. Nov. 4, 1944,
S.A.), voc.; Ben Shabalala (b. Nov. 30, 1957, S.A.),
voc.; Albert Mazibuko (b. Apr. 16, 1948, S.A.), voc.;
Abednego Mazibuko (b. Mar. 12, 1954, S.A.), voc.;
Russel Mthembu (b. Mar. 12, 1947, S.A.), voc.; Inos
Phungula (b. Mar. 31, 1945, S.A.), voc.; Jabulani
Dubazana (b. Apr. 25, 1954, S.A.), voc.; Geophrey
Mdletshe (b. Jan. 23, 1960, S.A.), voc.
1984—*Induku Zethu* (Shanachie)   1985—*Ulwandle
Oluncgwele*   1986—*Inala*   1987—*Shaka Zulu*
(Warner Bros.)   1988—*Umthombo Wamanzi*
(Shanachie); *Journey of Dreams* (Warner Bros.)
1989—*How the Leopard Got His Spots* (with Danny
Glover) (Windham Hill)   1990—*Classic Tracks*
(Shanachie); *Two Worlds One Heart* (Warner Bros.)
1991—(– H. Shabalala)   1992—*Best of Ladysmith
Black Mambazo* (Shanachie)   1994—*Liph' Iquiniso*;
Gift of the Tortoise (Warner Bros.).

Through their participation in Paul Simon's 1986 *Graceland* album and 1987 tour, Ladysmith Black Mambazo
became the most well-known African group in the Western world. Before then, they spent two decades becoming one of the best-selling groups in South Africa.
Formed by Joseph Shabalala with his family and friends
in the town of Ladysmith, LBM is a Zulu *mbube* choir
who sing a rhythmic a cappella music alternately called
mbaqanga, Isicathamiya, or "township jive." Isicathamiya was born in the mines of South Africa, where

black laborers, living in camps far from home, developed a style of competitive singing and dancing to pass the time. The workers brought the contests, called *Cothoza Mfana*, back to the townships with them.

Joseph went to Durban and sang in bands before returning to Ladysmith to form his own group, with his brothers Headman and Jockey Shabalala (Ben joined later) and his cousins Albert and Abednigo Mazibuko. Soon Ladysmith Black Mambazo were the champions of Cothoza Mfana. They got their first recording contract in 1970 and have released 28 albums in South Africa, some of which Shanachie rereleased in America (U.S. release dates are listed in discography above). LBM sang on two of *Graceland*'s tracks, "Diamonds on the Soles of Her Shoes" and "Homeless," and subsequently toured with Simon, also appearing with him on a Showtime TV special and *Saturday Night Live*.

This fame garnered the group their own deal with Warner. Their 1987 album, *Shaka Zulu*, produced by Simon and sung partially in English, won a Grammy. *Journey of Dreams* includes a Simon-arranged version of "Amazing Grace." *How the Leopard Got His Spots* is a Rudyard Kipling tale narrated by Danny Glover. On *Two Worlds One Heart*, the group collaborated with George Clinton.

Ladysmith also contributed songs to the soundtracks for *Coming to America* and *A Dry White Season*, played on harpist Andreas Vollenweider's album *Book of Roses*, appeared in Michael Jackson's *Moonwalker* video, have been regular guests on *Sesame Street*, and appeared in an award-winning 7-Up commercial. In 1992 the band toured South Africa with Simon; the following year they performed as the chorus in *The Song of Jacob Zulu*, a Steppenwolf Theatre Company production that played on Broadway at New York's Plymouth Theatre. The music won a Drama Desk Award.

Ladysmith Black Mambazo's world fame did not protect them from the brutal injustices of their homeland's political system, however. In December 1991 Headman Shabalala was shot along a highway near Durban; a white security guard was convicted of manslaughter. Joseph Shabalala has made plans to construct an academy of music at Colenso in South Africa, to teach traditional South African culture.

Greg Lake: See Emerson, Lake and Palmer

Major Lance

Born April 4, 1941, Chicago, Illinois; died September 3, 1994, Decatur, Georgia
1963—*The Monkey Time* (Okeh)   1976—*Um, Um, Um, Um, Um, Um/The Best of Major Lance* (Epic) 1977—*Live at the Torch* (Contempo)   1978—*Now Arriving* (Tamla)   1995—*Everybody Loves a Good Time! The Best of Major Lance* (Legacy).

With Curtis Mayfield writing his material and Carl Davis producing, soul vocalist Major Lance enjoyed many hits in the early Sixties and helped establish what became known as the Chicago soul sound, along with the Impressions, Jerry Butler, Gene Chandler, and others. Lance had spent some time as a professional boxer, and he recorded for Mercury before meeting Mayfield and signing with Okeh, Columbia's revitalized "race" label. After hearing the song "The Monkey Time," which Mayfield had written for Lance, Okeh president Carl Davis hired Mayfield as staff producer and Lance as a singer.

Mayfield and Lance's first release, "Delilah" (1962), was a flop. But the followup, "The Monkey Time," shot to #8 in September 1963 and helped kick off a dance trend called the Monkey. The song's orchestral sound (arranged by Johnny Pate) was adapted by Okeh as a "Chicago style" and can be heard on Mayfield's later recordings with the Impressions. Lance's highest-charting pop hit, "Um, Um, Um, Um, Um, Um," hit #5 in February 1964 (the song was also the first major English hit for Wayne Fontana and the Mindbenders the same year).

Although Lance's pop hits ceased soon after, he had several minor R&B chart successes through 1970. He switched to Carl Davis' Dakar Records in 1968 and then to Mayfield's Curtom label. In 1972 Lance recorded for Volt, and in 1974 he signed to Playboy Records, where he re-recorded "Um, Um, Um . . ." with little success. In 1982 eight of Lance's songs were included on the Epic compilation *Okeh Soul;* before its release Lance had emerged from a prison stay, on a 1978 cocaine-selling conviction. He died of heart disease at age 55 in 1994.

Mark Lanegan: See Screaming Trees

k. d. lang

Born Kathryn Dawn Lang, November 2, 1961, Consort, Alberta, Canada
1984—*A Truly Western Experience* (Bumstead)
1987—*Angel with a Lariat* (Sire)   1988—*Shadowland*   1989—*Absolute Torch and Twang*   1992—*Ingénue*   1994—*Even Cowgirls Get the Blues* soundtrack.

Because of her androgynous aesthetic, outspoken political views, and proud lesbianism, k. d. lang has frequently been attacked by conservatives, but she's come out smelling like a rose. The "cowgirl from Calgary" has claimed three Grammys, including Best Female Pop Vocalist in 1992.

Despite her initial campy approach to country & western music—she used to perform in rhinestone-studded garb and cat-eye glasses—lang is an authentic country girl, raised in an isolated rural town. She began singing at age five, and by her teen years was performing at weddings. She grew up listening to classical music and rock, discovering country when she played a Patsy Cline–type character in a play at Red Deer College. In 1982 she answered an ad in an Edmonton newspaper placed by a Western swing band. She and the band, the Reclines, toured Canada for two years.

Her first album was released by an Edmonton indie, to little notice. It was her live shows, where lang could

out-kitsch Minnie Pearl and out-emote Barbra Streisand, that drew the attention of Sire Records head Seymour Stein. Once signed, lang's more serious side came across, and she toned down her crazy stage act. *Angel with a Lariat,* recorded with the Reclines and produced by Dave Edmunds, was accordingly rocking.

In 1987 lang did a remake of "Crying" with Roy Orbison. Although the single sold 50,000 copies in the U.S., radio play eluded lang, who was considered too weird for country stations and too country for rock stations. Perhaps to prove her authenticity, *Shadowland* (1988) paid homage to the genre's leading ladies. The album was produced by former Cline mentor Owen Bradley and included guest appearances by Loretta Lynn, Kitty Wells, and Brenda Lee. On 1989's *Absolute Torch and Twang,* lang mixed her crooning (particularly on the magnificent "Pullin' Back the Reins") and honky-tonk sides ("Three Days"). The album won her a 1989 Grammy for Best Country Vocal Performance, Female.

In 1990 lang filmed a commercial for the "Meat Stinks" campaign of the People for Ethical Treatment of Animals. Although the spot never aired, *Entertainment Tonight* ran a story on it. Stations in the cattle-producing Midwest boycotted lang (not that they had played her music much before), her mother was swamped with hate mail, and the sign honoring her in her hometown was defaced with the words "Eat Beef Dyke." Lang's career proved surprisingly immune to such controversies: *Ingénue*'s smoldering pop went platinum and garnered lang one Grammy (for the track "Constant Craving") and five nominations.

Interviewed for the gay magazine *The Advocate* in 1992, lang, who had been out to anyone paying attention since she was a teen, officially proclaimed her homosexuality. Far from ruining her career, the announcement seemed to fan the fires of media interest: In 1993 *New York* magazine dubbed her the icon of "Lesbian Chic," and in photographer Herb Ritts' sendup of a Norman Rockwell illustration, a *Vanity Fair* cover showed her reclining in a barber's chair, clutching and pretending to be shaved by scantily clad model Cindy Crawford. That year lang wrote the soundtrack for *Even Cowgirls Get the Blues.* She starred in the 1991 Percy Adlon film *Salmonberries* and has stated that she plans to continue pursuing an acting career.

Daniel Lanois

Born September 19, 1951, Hull, Quebec, Canada
1989—*Acadie* (Opal/Warner Bros.)   1993—*For the Beauty of Wynona* (Warner Bros.).

Called "the most important record producer to emerge in the Eighties" by ROLLING STONE, Daniel Lanois has drawn kudos for his work with U2, Peter Gabriel, and Bob Dylan. Like his sometime collaborator Brian Eno, Lanois has experiments came to commercial fruition when Eno was tapped to produce an album for U2. For that effort, 1984's *The Unforgettable Fire*, Eno enlisted Lanois as coproducer. The results impressed another pop star, Peter Gabriel, who asked Lanois to coproduce his soundtrack to the 1984 film *Birdy*. Gabriel and Lanois again shared production credit for 1986's *So* and 1992's *Us*, Gabriel's most successful albums. Lanois continued to work with U2 as well, coproducing 1987's *The Joshua Tree* with Eno and serving as principal producer for 1991's *Achtung Baby*, which earned him another Grammy. In addition, Lanois earned praise for coproducing with Robbie Robertson the singer's eponymous solo debut in 1987, and, in 1989, for his work at the boards on Bob Dylan's *Oh Mercy* and the Neville Brothers' *Yellow Moon*.

In 1989 Lanois released *Acadie*, his debut as a singer/songwriter. The album was received enthusiastically by critics, as was its 1993 successor, *For the Beauty of Wynona*. So far, though, the quirky radiance of Lanois' songs hasn't proved as accessible to pop fans as the work of his celebrated clients.

L.A. Reid and Babyface
Formed 1984, Cincinnati, Ohio
Antonio "L.A." Reid (b. June 7, 1957, Cincinnati), drums; Kenneth "Babyface" Edmonds (b. Apr. 10, ca. 1959, Indianapolis, Ind.), voc., gtr., kybds.
Babyface: 1987—*Lovers* (Solar/Epic)   1989—*Tender Lover*   1993—*For the Cool in You*.

L.A. and Babyface are one of the most successful production and songwriting teams in R&B history; they have crafted softly funky black pop songs into #1 hits for other artists. The two met while playing in the Cincinnati R&B/funk band the Deele, where Edmonds played guitar and sang and Reid played drums. The Deele released three albums: 1983's *Street Beat*, featuring "Body Talk"; *Material Thangz*, the pair's debut as producers; and the gold *Eyes of a Stranger*, which featured the hit "Two Occasions" (#4 pop, #10 R&B, 1987).

L.A., named for the Dodgers cap he wears, and Babyface, nicknamed by Bootsy Collins for his youthful appearance, began writing songs and producing singles that soon helped define New Jack (and Jill) Swing. Often assisted by songwriter Daryl Simmons and Deele bassist Kayo, they have worked with TLC, Paula Abdul, Pebbles (Reid's wife), Karyn White, Damian Dame, the Boys, Johnny Gill, Sheena Easton, the Jacksons, Bobby Brown, Whitney Houston, Boyz II Men, and the Whispers. In 1989 the pair moved to Atlanta—helping to make that city "the southern Motown"—and formed a record company, LaFace, which has released such artists as Damian Dame and TLC. L.A. and Babyface won two Grammys in 1992 as producers and songwriters of Boyz II Men's "End of the Road." They won their third Grammy in 1994 as

Daniel Lanois

shown a flair for delicate, atmospheric touches, both in producing material for other musicians and in his own projects as a composer and recording artist. Stressing emotional vibrancy over the technical aspects of making albums, Lanois has recorded in such unlikely settings as castles and dairy barns in his efforts to elicit honest, spontaneous performances. The results of this visceral approach have ranged from the soaring intensity of his Grammy-winning coproduction (with Eno) of U2's *The Joshua Tree* to the moody, understated passion of Lanois' solo efforts.

Lanois' French-Canadian parents were both musically inclined: His mother sang, and his father (and grandfather) played fiddle. When they separated in 1963, Lanois moved with his mother to a suburb of English-speaking Hamilton, Ontario, where he learned to play guitar and began playing gigs with various Canadian artists. In 1970 Lanois set up a home studio with his brother Robert; ten years later, after working with numerous local musicians, they opened Grant Avenue Studio in Hamilton.

Lanois' break came in 1979 when Eno, who was beginning to break ground with his starkly dreamy "ambient music," did some recording at his studio. The chemistry between Eno and Lanois in their instrumental producers (with others) for Whitney Houston's soundtrack album for *The Bodyguard*.

Babyface's solo debut *Lovers* introduced his silky, romantic approach with "I Love You Babe" (#8 R&B, 1987). The double-platinum *Tender Lover* (#14, 1989) featured "It's No Crime" (#7 pop, #1 R&B, 1989), "Tender Lover" (#14 pop, #1 R&B, 1989), "My Kinda Girl" (#30 pop, #3 R&B, 1990), and "Whip Appeal" (#6 pop, #2 R&B, 1990). The second half consisted entirely of ballads he wrote. On *For the Cool in You* (#16 pop, #2 R&B, 1993), Babyface, who was having creative differences with Reid, made a big push for his own career. Yet the album spawned only two hit singles: "Never Keeping Secrets" (#15 pop, #3 R&B, 1993) and "When Can I See You" (#4, 1994). Babyface also won two 1994 Grammys for Best Male R&B Vocal Performance and Best R&B Song.

Bill Laswell/Material

Bill Laswell (b. Feb. 12, 1955, Salem, Ill.): 1983— ***Baselines*** **(Celluloid/Elektra Musician) 1988—***Hear No Evil* **(Venture/Virgin).**
With Material, formed 1979, New York City, N.Y. (Laswell, bass; Michael Beinhorn, kybds.; Fred Maher, drums): 1979—*Temporary Music 1* **EP (Zu) 1981—***Temporary Music 2* **EP (Red Music, U.K.);** ***Busting Out*** **EP (Ze-Island);** ***Memory Serves*** **(Celluloid/Elektra Musician) 1982—(– Maher; + Nicky Skopelitis [b. Jan. 19, 1960, New York City], gtr.)** ***One Down*** **1986—***Red Tracks* **(Red) 1989— (– Beinhorn)** ***Seven Souls*** **(Virgin) 1991—***The Third Power* **(Axiom) 1994—***Hallucination Engine.* **With Praxis: 1984—***Praxis* **EP (Celluloid) 1992—** ***Transmutation*** **(Axiom).**

Bassist and producer Bill Laswell is a rampant musical cross-pollinator and conceptualist, forging new directions for the fusion of jazz, rock, and funk in and outside his main project, Material. Laswell grew up in Detroit, where he played in funk bands. He moved to New York in 1978 and formed Material, originally to back Daevid Allen (Gong) on a U.S. tour. The group soon became a floating vehicle for musical experimentation.

The original incarnation of Material was based on the rhythm section of Laswell, Michael Beinhorn, and Fred Maher. They recorded a few EPs, including the club single "Busting Out" with Nona Hendryx [see entry] singing, and the album *Memory Serves,* which featured Sonny Sharrock, Fred Frith, George Lewis, and Henry Threadgill. Minus Maher but plus guitarist Nicky Skopelitis, Material recorded the funky *One Down,* again featuring Hendryx and Frith as well as Archie Shepp, Nile Rodgers, Oliver Lake, and Whitney Houston. *Red Tracks* compiled the *Temporary Music* EPs. Beinhorn departed, going on to produce such artists as Soundgarden.

On *Seven Souls,* Material explored Arabic music, featuring guests Fahiem Dandan, Simon Shaheen, and L. Shankar, as well as beat author William Burroughs. Laswell produced rather than played on *The Third Power,* which featured Bootsy Collins, the Jungle Brothers, Bernie Worrell, Sly Dunbar, and Robbie Shakespeare (Laswell produced Sly and Robbie's solo albums). On *Hallucination Engine* Material explored ambient music; the single "Mantra" was remixed by British ambient artists the Orb. Laswell's collaborators included Wayne Shorter, Shaheen, Worrell, Collins, Dunbar, Burroughs, and Shankar.

Laswell's work outside Material has been equally varied and fruitful. In 1982 he formed Massacre with Frith and Maher, releasing the album *Killing Time.* That year he also played bass on Laurie Anderson's "Mr. Heartbreak." Laswell's first solo album features key players of the Downtown New York music scene of the Eighties, including cowriter Beinhorn, Martin Bisi, Ronald Shannon Jackson, Ralph Carney, and Daniel Ponce. The album was released by Celluloid, a label Laswell helped form and run.

In 1983 Laswell cowrote and produced Herbie Hancock's hit "Rockit" and won a Grammy for a track on Hancock's following album, *Sound-System.* In 1984 Laswell produced the single "World Destruction," featuring Afrika Bambaataa and Johnny Lydon. Calling himself Praxis, Laswell experimented with hip-hop and a drum machine on a 1984 EP, and played with Bootsy Collins and guitarist Buckethead on a 1992 album. His 1988 solo album *Hear No Evil* features violinist Shankar and Skopelitis. Laswell has played with numerous other acts, including the Golden Palominos, Last Exit, Brian Eno, David Byrne, Peter Gabriel, Fab Five Freddy, John Zorn, and Peter Brötzmann. He has produced artists including Mick Jagger, Yellowman, Motörhead, Iggy Pop, and the Ramones.

In 1988 Laswell formed Axiom Records in a partnership with Island Records. There he has continued to be a postmodern Renaissance man, releasing (out-of-this-) world music, experimental jazz, and mutant rock. In 1990 he established Greenpoint Studio. He traveled to the remote village of Jajouka, Morocco, in 1991 to record Bachir Attar and the Master Musicians of Jajouka, released on Axiom as *Apocalypse Across the Sky* (1992).

Stacy Lattisaw

Born November 25, 1966, Washington, D.C.
1979—*Young and in Love* **(Cotillion) 1980—***Let Me Be Your Angel* **1981—***With You* **1982—***Sneakin' Out* **1983—***Sixteen* **(Cotillion) 1984—***Perfect Combination* **(with Johnny Gill) (Motown) 1986—** ***Take Me All the Way*** **1988—***Personal Attention* **1989—***What You Need.*

Singer Stacy Lattisaw was only 13 when she scored an international disco hit with "Dynamite" in 1980 (#8 R&B). Her mother encouraged her to go into singing, and she made her debut at ten at a high school homecoming. After many local appearances, she won a spot opening for Ramsey Lewis at a National Park Service show in Washington, D.C., for a crowd of 30,000. The show's organizer, Al Dale, sent a tape of her performance to Frederick Knight, head of T.K. Records, who offered Lattisaw a contract and wrote "Ring My Bell" for her. Lattisaw's family lawyer, acting as manager, rejected the contract, and the song wound up a #1 pop, #1 R&B hit for Anita Ward in 1979. But the lawyer introduced Lattisaw to Cotillion president Henry Allen, who signed her.

Shortly before his death, Van McCoy produced Lattisaw's debut LP, which went nowhere. Her second LP, *Let Me Be Your Angel,* produced by Narada Michael Walden, with songs by Walden and lyricist Bunny Hull, had two hits, "Dynamite," and the title track (#21 pop, #8 R&B). She supported it by playing shows with the Jacksons, the Spinners, Smokey Robinson, and the Manhattans. In 1981 she released *With You,* again produced by Walden, yielding the remake of "Love on a Two Way Street" (#26 pop, #2 R&B 1981), originally a hit for the Moments in 1970. In 1984 she released an album of duets with Johnny Gill, a childhood friend; in 1990 she had a #1 R&B hit with Gill: "Where Do We Go from Here." In addition, Lattisaw has had seven other Top Twenty R&B hits.

Cyndi Lauper

Born Cynthia Anne Stephanie Lauper, June 22, 1953, New York City, New York
1983—*She's So Unusual* (Portrait)   1986—*True Colors*   1989—*A Night to Remember* (Epic)   1993—*Hat Full of Stars*   1994—*12 Deadly Cyns and Then Some* (Epic, U.K.).

With her little-girl voice, thrift-store style, and art-school training, Cyndi Lauper was one of the earliest female icons to make use of MTV's influence and become a pop star. Her debut album was the first in history by a woman to have four Top Five singles; led by "Girls Just Want to Have Fun," it also won her the unlikely title of "Woman of the Year" from *Ms.* magazine.

Lauper was raised in Brooklyn and Queens by her waitress mother, a life she paid homage to when her mother starred in the video for "Girls." After dropping out of high school and spending a few years "finding herself," Lauper sang for cover bands on Long Island. She ruined her voice and sought training from Katherine Agresta, an opera singer and rock & roll vocal coach. She then spent four years singing and writing songs for Blue Angel, a rootsy rock band whose strong New York following never translated into sales for their eponymous 1980 Polydor album.

Lauper filed for bankruptcy after Blue Angel split, and for a while sang in a Japanese restaurant dressed like a geisha until her manager and boyfriend David Wolff landed her a deal with the CBS imprint Portrait. *She's So Unusual* (#4, 1983) became an international hit, eventually selling more than five million records in the U.S. alone, led by "Girls" (#2, 1983), "All Through the Night" (#5, 1984), "She Bop" (#3, 1984), and "Time After Time" (#1). The album, produced by Rick Chertoff and featuring Rob Hyman and Eric Bazilian of the Philadelphia band the Hooters [see entry], won Lauper a Grammy and put the singer on the brink of superstardom. On *The Tonight Show,* the rainbow-haired singer with the Betty Boop voice claimed that professional wrestler Captain Lou Albano was her mentor and had taught her the key to fame: politeness, etiquette, and grooming.

Lauper was never able to match the success of her debut, although 1986's *True Colors'* title track went to #1 and featured "Change of Heart" (#3, 1986) and a cover of Marvin Gaye's "What's Going On" (#12, 1987). In 1985 she had a #10 hit with "The Goonies 'R' Good Enough," from the film *The Goonies.* (Lauper's own ventures into acting have proved ill-fated: One movie never made it out of the studio, and 1988's *Vibes* and 1993's *Life with Mikey* flopped.)

A Night to Remember was trashed by critics and stalled at #37 on the pop charts; it contained one hit, "I Drove All Night" (#6, 1989). In 1990 she ended her personal and professional relationship with Wolff; the following year she married actor David Thornton, with Little Richard presiding.

She returned in 1993 with *Hat Full of Stars* (#112), reasserting control over her career (coproducing and cowriting all tracks) and proving to critics that she had grown with the times. The album deals with such issues as racism, backstreet abortions, and incest; collaborators include Mary Chapin Carpenter, Junior Vasquez, and her old friends the Hooters. The album faltered commercially, however, yielding no hit singles.

In 1994 Lauper made a comeback of sorts in the U.K. with the British-only release of the anthology *12 Deadly Cyns and Then Some,* which reached #2, and a remix of "Girls Just Want to Have Fun," which topped the singles chart. The album was slated for issue in the U.S. in 1995.

Leadbelly

Born Huddie Ledbetter, circa 1885, Mooringsport, Louisiana; died December 6, 1949, New York City, New York
1953—*Leadbelly's Last Sessions, vol. 1* (Folkways); *Leadbelly's Last Sessions, vol. 2*   1968—*Leadbelly Sings Folk Songs*   1969—*Leadbelly* (Capitol)   1973—*Leadbelly* (Fantasy)   1989—*Alabama Bound* (RCA); *Bourgeois Blues* (Collectables)   1991—*King of the Twelve-String Guitar* (Legacy); *Midnight Spe-*

cial (Rounder); *Gwine Dig a Hole to Put the Devil In*; *Let It Shine on Me.*

Leadbelly, the self-styled "king of the 12-string guitar," was one of the modern world's prime links to rural traditions. He helped inspire the folk and blues revivals of the Fifties and Sixties. Leadbelly grew up in Louisiana and Texas, where his family moved when he was five. He was eight when he started playing the Cajun accordion (windjammer). According to Leadbelly, at age seven he broke up arguments between his parents by hitting his father in the head with a poker and threatening him with a shotgun. Traveling around in his early teens, the singer picked up music that dated back to slave days, and by the time he was 17 he was playing guitar—first an eight-string and then the 12-string. At 18 he was forced to leave his home after he impregnated the same girl twice without marrying her. He went to West Texas to pick cotton and began playing with his friend and mentor Blind Lemon Jefferson in Dallas.

But Leadbelly's troubles followed him, and he spent a year in prison on the Harrison County chain gang for assaulting a woman. He escaped and adopted the name Walter Boyd. When he was 33 he shot and killed a man in an argument over a woman, and on June 7, 1918, he received a 30-year sentence; five years later, however, Leadbelly wrote a song begging Texas governor Pat Neff for a pardon; in 1925 Neff complied. Leadbelly's hollering style reflected his hard years in prison, and it wasn't long before he was back behind bars—for attempted murder—at Louisiana's Angola penitentiary. It was there that folklorists John A. and Alan Lomax discovered him in 1933 while recording music for the Library of Congress. The Lomaxes recorded the incarcerated Leadbelly singing an updated version of the song that had charmed Pat Neff. This time Governor O. K. Allen heard it and, likewise, let Leadbelly out of prison, in 1934.

Upon his release, the Lomaxes brought him to New York. They published a book about him in 1936, and he recorded his best-known songs: "The Rock Island Line," "The Midnight Special," and "Goodnight Irene." Whether Leadbelly wrote, adapted, or simply remembered the songs and copyrighted them for himself is unknown, though it is certain that he was the first to bring them to the public. In 1939 Leadbelly landed in jail yet again (New York's Rikers Island) and served two years for assault. But all of this only enhanced his legend. While in New York he played with Pete Seeger, Woody Guthrie, and Sonny Terry and later toured the East Coast.

Ironically, six months after the singer died of Lou Gehrig's disease in 1949, his "Goodnight Irene" became a folk hit for the Weavers. There were many repackagings of his work in the late Sixties to early Seventies, and in 1976 a film about his life, directed by Gordon Parks, was released.

Led Zeppelin

Formed 1968, England
Jimmy Page (b. James Patrick Page, Jan. 9, 1944, Heston, Eng.), gtr.; John Paul Jones (b. John Baldwin, Jan. 3, 1946, Sidcup, Eng.), bass; Robert Plant (b. Aug. 20, 1948, Bromwich, Eng.), voc.; John "Bonzo" Bonham (b. John Henry Bonham, May 31, 1948, Redditch, Eng.; d. Sep. 25, 1980, Windsor, Eng.), drums.
1969—*Led Zeppelin* (Atlantic); *Led Zeppelin II*
1970—*Led Zeppelin III*   1971—*Untitled* (known as the Runes album or *Zoso* or *Led Zeppelin IV*)
1973—*Houses of the Holy*   1975—*Physical Graffiti* (Swan Song)   1976—*Presence*; *The Song Remains the Same*   1979—*In Through the Out Door*   1980— (– Bonham)   1982—*Coda*   1990—*Led Zeppelin* (Atlantic)   1992—*Remasters*   1993—*Led Zeppelin—Boxed Set 2*; *Led Zeppelin—The Complete Studio Recordings*.

It wasn't just Led Zeppelin's thunderous volume, sledgehammer beat, and edge-of-mayhem arrangements that made it the most influential and successful heavy-metal pioneers, it was their finesse. Like its ancestors the Yardbirds, Led Zeppelin used a guitar style that drew heavily on the blues, and its early repertoire included remakes of songs by bluesmen Howlin' Wolf, Albert King, and Willie Dixon (who later won a sizable settlement from the band in a suit in which he alleged copyright infringement; see his entry for details). But what Jimmy Page brought to the band was a unique understanding of the guitar and the recording studio as electronic instruments, and of rock as sculptured noise; like Jimi Hendrix, Page had a reason for every bit of distortion, feedback, reverberation, and out-and-out noise that he incorporated—and few of the many bands that try to imitate Led Zeppelin can make the same claim.

Page and Robert Plant were grounded also in British folk music and fascinated by mythology, Middle Earth fantasy, and the occult, as became increasingly evident from the band's later albums (the fourth LP's title is composed of four runic characters). A song that builds from a folk-baroque acoustic setting to screaming heavy metal, "Stairway to Heaven," fittingly became the best-known Led Zeppelin song and a staple of FM airplay, although like most of the group's "hits," it was never released as a single. Though critically derided more often than not, Led Zeppelin was unquestionably one of the most enduring bands in rock history, selling over 50 million records.

When the Yardbirds fell apart in the summer of 1968 [see entry], Page was left with rights to the group's name and a string of concert obligations. He enlisted John Paul Jones, who had done session work with the Rolling Stones, Herman's Hermits, Lulu, Dusty Springfield, and

Led Zeppelin: Jimmy Page, John Bonham, Robert Plant,
John Paul Jones

Shirley Bassey. Page and Jones had first met, jammed together, and discussed forming a group when both were hired to back Donovan on his *Hurdy Gurdy Man* LP. Page had hoped to complete the group with drummer B. J. Wilson of Procol Harum and singer Terry Reid. Neither was available, but Reid recommended Plant, who in turn suggested John Bonham, drummer for his old Birmingham group, Band of Joy. The four first played together as the session group behind P. J. Proby on his *Three Week Hero*. In October 1968 they embarked on a tour of Scandinavia under the name the New Yardbirds. Upon their return to England they recorded their debut album in 30 hours.

Adopting the name Led Zeppelin (allegedly coined by Keith Moon), they toured the U.S. in early 1969 opening for Vanilla Fudge. Their first album was released in February; within two months it had reached *Billboard*'s Top Ten. *Led Zeppelin II* reached #1 two months after its release, and since then every album of new material has gone platinum; five of the group's LPs reached #1. After touring almost incessantly during its first two years together, Zeppelin began limiting its appearances to alternating years. The band's 1973 U.S. tour broke box-office records (many of which had been set by the Beatles) throughout the country, and by 1975 its immense ticket and album sales had made Led Zeppelin the most popular rock & roll group in the world. In 1974 the quartet established its own label, Swan Song. The label's first release was the band's *Physical Graffiti* (#1, 1975), its first double-album set, which sold four million copies.

On August 4, 1975, Plant and his family were seriously injured in a car crash while vacationing on the Greek island of Rhodes. As a result, the group toured even less frequently. That and speculation among fans that supernatural forces may have come into play (Plant believed in psychic phenomena, and Page, whose interest in the occult was well known, once resided in Boleskine House, the former home of infamous satanist Aleister Crowley) also heightened the Zeppelin mystique.

In 1976 Led Zeppelin released *Presence*, a four-million seller. The group had just embarked on its U.S. tour when Plant's six-year-old son Karac died suddenly of a viral infection. The remainder of the tour was canceled, and the group took off the next year and a half. In late 1978 they began work on *In Through the Out Door*, the band's last group effort. They had completed a brief European tour and were beginning to rehearse for another U.S. tour when, on September 25, 1980, Bonham died at Page's home of what was described as asphyxiation; he had inhaled his own vomit after having excessively consumed alcohol and fallen asleep. On December 4, 1980, Page, Plant, and Jones released a cryptic statement to the effect that they could no longer continue as they were. Soon thereafter it was rumored that Plant and Page were going to form a band called XYZ (ex–Yes and Zeppelin) with Alan White and Chris Squire of Yes; the group never materialized. In 1982 the group released *Coda* (#6, 1982), a collection of early recordings and outtakes.

Plant and Page each pursued solo careers [see entries]. Jones released a soundtrack album, *Scream for Help*, in 1986, and has worked in production. The band has reunited three times: once in 1985 at Live Aid (with Phil Collins and Tony Thompson on drums), and in May 1988, Plant, Page, and Jones performed with Bonham's son Jason on drums at the Atlantic Records 40th-anniversary celebration at New York City's Madison Square Garden. They also played at Jason Bonham's wedding and at the band's 1995 induction into the Rock and Roll Hall of Fame. Led Zeppelin's concert movie *The Song Remains the Same* (originally released in 1976) is still a staple of midnight shows around the country, and Zeppelin tunes like "Stairway to Heaven," "Kashmir," "Communication Breakdown," "Whole Lotta Love," and "No Quarter" are still in heavy rotation on classic-rock radio playlists. In 1990 a St. Petersburg, Florida, station kicked off its all-Zeppelin format by playing "Stairway to Heaven" for 24 hours straight. (Less than two weeks later, the station had expanded its playlist to include Pink Floyd.)

As of summer 1994 there were rumors that the surviving three might reunite for a tour, though not under the name Led Zeppelin, and that fall Page and Plant participated in the *No Quarter* album [see solo entries]. Jones, who was not invited to join them, was by then working and touring with Diamanda Galás, with whom he recorded 1994's *The Sporting Life.*

Albert Lee

Born December 21, 1943, Leominster, England
1979—*Hiding* (A&M)   1982—*Albert Lee*   1986—
Speechless* (MCA)   1987—*Gagged but Not Bound.

British guitarist Albert Lee has earned a strong reputation as a sideman for Jackson Browne, Dave Edmunds, Joan Armatrading, Joe Cocker, Eric Clapton, Emmylou Harris, Rodney Crowell, and others. Beyond his adaptability, he is one of the few English guitarists more interested in country music than in blues. Lee began playing piano at age seven, emulating Jerry Lee Lewis. But by 16 he had switched to guitar. In 1964 he joined Chris Farlowe's backup group, the Thunderbirds, which also included Carl Palmer. The Thunderbirds were a popular R&B outfit in England, and Jimmy Page and Steve Howe have cited Lee's work as an early influence. In 1968 the band dissolved. Lee joined Country Fever and later formed the country-influenced Heads, Hands and Feet [see entry]. After three albums, that band folded, and Lee went on to play on Jerry Lee Lewis' *The Session* LP.

In 1973 Lee joined Rick Grech with the Crickets, still singing Buddy Holly's tunes; a year later he was in Los Angeles doing session work, including a stint with Don Everly. He joined Joe Cocker for his 1974 tour of Australia and New Zealand, and A&M offered Lee a solo contract in 1975. Before he got around to finishing an album, though, Lee joined Emmylou Harris' Hot Band. He stayed in Harris' band for two years and left in 1978 to finally record his solo album but continued to play on Harris' records as well.

Instead of touring to support his own album, Lee took to the road in 1979 as part of Eric Clapton's band. He played on Clapton's live LP *Just One Night* (1980) and on his studio albums *Another Ticket* (1981) and *Money and Cigarettes* (1983). Between tours with Clapton he finished a second solo album. He has also toured with the Everly Brothers, among others.

Alvin Lee: See Ten Years After

Arthur Lee: See Love

Brenda Lee

Born Brenda Mae Tarpley, December 11, 1944, Atlanta, Georgia
1960—*Brenda Lee* (Decca); *This Is . . . Brenda*
1961—*Emotions*; *All the Way*   1962—*Sincerely*;
Brenda, That's All*   1963—*All Alone Am I*; *Let Me Sing*   1965—*Too Many Rivers*   1966—*10 Golden Years*   1975—*Brenda Lee Now* (MCA)   1976—*L.A. Sessions*   1980—*Take Me Back*; *Even Better*   1991—*The Brenda Lee Anthology, vol. 1 1956–1961*; *The Brenda Lee Anthology, vol. 2 1962–1980.

Singer Brenda Lee's five-decade-spanning recording career began when she was only 12; by 16, her single "Rockin' Around the Christmas Tree" (#14, 1960) had become an international hit. By age seven Lee was singing on radio and TV shows in Atlanta. Her father died when she was eight, and her income helped support the family. In 1956 she met Red Foley's manager, Dub Albritten. He booked her on shows with Foley, which led to national TV exposure. On July 30 of that year Lee entered a Nashville studio with Owen Bradley (producer of Patsy Cline and later Loretta Lynn) and recorded "Rockin' Around the Christmas Tree." Lee soon toured Europe, where, to appease French promoters who had thought she was an adult, Albritten spread the rumor that she was a 32-year-old midget.

Back in the U.S., Lee next recorded some of her biggest hits: "Sweet Nothings" (#4, 1960), "I'm Sorry" (#1, 1960), "I Want to Be Wanted" (#1, 1960), and many other early-Sixties Top Tens. She soon became known as "Little Miss Dynamite," and by the time she was 21 she had cut 256 sides for Decca Records.

In the Seventies Lee's hits were on the country chart rather than the pop chart. She scored with "If This Is Our Last Time" (#30 C&W, 1971), "Nobody Wins" (#3 C&W, 1973), and three Top Tens in 1974. She continues to record country hits while also doing a syndicated Nashville interview show. Lee had a small acting role in *Smokey and the Bandit 2* and sang the title song of Neil Simon's *Only When I Laugh*. In 1988 she joined Loretta Lynn and Kitty Wells as guests on k. d. lang's *Shadowland* album, produced by Owen Bradley.

Among Lee's many honors is the National Academy of Recording Arts and Sciences (the organization that awards the Grammy) Governors Award for 1984. Her lifetime record sales are estimated at over 100 million copies.

Dickey Lee

Born Dick Lipscomb, September 21, 1941, Memphis, Tennessee
1962—*The Tale of Patches* (Smash)   1965—*Dickey Lee Sings Laurie and the Girl from Peyton Place* (TCF Hall).

Perhaps best known for the melodramatic "Patches," Dickey Lee was also one of the very few Sun Records rockabilly artists to attend college after having released several records. Lee signed with Sun in 1957 and had a minor local hit with a version of "Good Lovin'." He attended Memphis State University, then in the early Sixties went on to write, produce, and record with Jack Clement for Hallway Records in Beaumont, Alabama.

Lee moved to Nashville in 1962 and established himself as a writer of country songs. He made a name for himself that year with "Patches," which hit #6 on the chart. Though primarily a songwriter, he continued to record, hitting with "I Saw Linda Yesterday" (#14, 1963) and "Laurie (Strange Things Happen)" (#14, 1965). The latter, in which the singer dates a girl who, it turns out, had died exactly one year earlier, ranks as one of the more bizarre, morbid tales woven by a pop song. He later had four Top Ten country hits—"9,999,999 Tears," "Angels, Roses, and Rain," "Rocky," and "Never Ending Song of Love"—and penned eight more songs that went to the top of the country chart. Kenny Rogers, Glen Campbell, Brenda Lee, Emmylou Harris, Reba McEntire, Merle Haggard, Elvis Presley, and George Jones (both Presley and Jones recorded his "She Thinks I Still Care"), and many other country stars have recorded Lee's songs. He continues to perform, both for country audiences and at rock-oldies shows.

Peggy Lee

**Born Norma Deloris Egstrom, May 6, 1920,
Jamestown, North Dakota
1957—The Man I Love (Capitol)   1969—Is That All
There Is?   1980—The Best of Peggy Lee (MCA)
1990—Capitol Collectors Series: The Early Years;
The Peggy Lee Songbook: There'll Be Another
Spring (Musicmasters).**

Peggy Lee's subdued singing style, which embraces jazz, blues, Latin, swing, and pop, first came to public attention in her work with the Benny Goodman orchestra, especially in 1943, when she released the hit "Why Don't You Do Right?" Lee's mother died when she was four, and she began working on a farm by 11 and singing professionally at 14, first at a Fargo, North Dakota, radio station and later at a Palm Springs hotel, where she met Goodman.

After her hit with Goodman's band, she married the group's guitarist, David Barbour, and retired for several years to have a child before she and Barbour began writing new material together, with Lee usually providing the lyrics. Lee was one of the forerunners of the rock trend that encouraged singers to write their own material, and with Barbour she wrote, among others, "I Don't Know Enough About You," "Mañana," and "It's a Good Day." She has also collaborated with Sonny Burke, Duke Ellington, Quincy Jones, Johnny Mandel, and Dave Grusin. The Lee hit most covered by rock performers is "Fever" (#8, 1958).

She was one of the first old-guard performers to recognize the Beatles' talents, and as a "reward" Paul Mc-

Cartney later wrote "Let's Love" for her, which became the title of her Atlantic debut in 1974. She had one of her biggest hits with Leiber and Stoller's "Is That All There Is?" (#11, 1969), arranged by Randy Newman.

Lee appeared in three films, making her debut in 1951's *Mr. Music,* followed by a remake of *The Jazz Singer* with Danny Thomas (1953), and *Pete Kelly's Blues* (1955), for which she was nominated for an Academy Award. In 1955 she cowrote songs and voiced the character Peg in Disney's animated feature film *Lady and the Tramp.* She also cowrote with Victor Young and sang the title song of the film *Johnny Guitar* and wrote the words and music to the title song of *Tom Thumb.*

Although she has suffered bouts of poor health, she continues to perform. In 1983 she mounted a short-lived one-woman Broadway show entitled *Peg.* Her autobiography, *Miss Peggy Lee,* was published in 1989, and was a best-seller in the U.K. She has received numerous awards throughout her career, and was a founding artist of the John F. Kennedy Center for the Performing Arts. In 1994 she received the Society of Singers' Lifetime Achievement Award.

The Left Banke

**Formed 1965, New York City, New York
Steve Martin, voc.; Tom Finn, bass; Jeff Winfield,
gtr.; George Cameron, drums; Michael Brown
(b. Michael Lookofsky, Apr. 25, 1949, Brooklyn, N.Y.),
organ, piano, harpsichord.
1967—Walk Away Renee/Pretty Ballerina (Smash)
(– Winfield; + Rick Brand, gtr.; – Brown)   1969—
The Left Banke Too   1986—Strangers on a Train
(Camerica)   1992—There's Gonna Be a Storm: The
Complete Recordings, 1966–1969 (Mercury).**

Left Banke leader Michael Brown began studying piano and harpsichord when he was eight. At 16 he wrote "Walk Away Renee." Two years later, in 1966, his band, the Left Banke, released the song as its first single, and it became a #5 hit. The followup, "Pretty Ballerina" (#15, 1967), was similar to "Renee" in its classical-tinged melody, choirboy vocals, and strings-and-harpsichord accompaniment (then dubbed baroque rock). After composing the bulk of the material for the Left Banke's debut LP and a second album, Brown left the group. The Left Banke continued unsuccessfully without him, breaking up in 1969.

Brown's next band, Montage, was not particularly successful, and he then formed Stories with vocalist Ian Lloyd but left before their big 1973 hit, "Brother Louie" (written by members of Hot Chocolate). Brown then worked for a while as an A&R man for Mercury Records.

In 1976 he formed the Beckies, who lasted long enough to record a single LP for Sire. Since then Brown has remained mostly out of sight, surfacing briefly as a sideman with New York singer Lisa Burns. "Walk Away Renee" was covered by the Four Tops in 1968 and was once again a smash. Martin, Finn, and Cameron regrouped without Brown in 1978 for an album released eight years later on the independent Camerica label, *Strangers on a Train*.

Lemonheads

Formed 1986, Boston, Massachusetts
Evan Dando (b. Mar. 4, 1967, Boston), voc., gtr., drums; Ben Deily, voc., gtr., drums; Jesse Peretz, bass.
1986—*Laughing All the Way to the Cleaners* EP (Huh-Bag) (+ Doug Trachten, drums) 1987—*Hate Your Friends* (Taang!) (– Trachten; + John Strohm, drums) 1988—*Creator* 1989—*Create Your Friends* (– Strohm); *Lick* (– Deily; – Peretz; + David William Ryan [b. Oct. 20, 1964, Ind.], drums) 1990—*Lovey* (Atlantic) 1991—*Favorite Spanish Dishes* (+ Juliana Hatfield [b. July 2, 1967, Wiscasset, Me.], bass) 1992—*It's a Shame About Ray* (– Hatfield; + Nick Dalton [b. Nov. 14, 1964, Austral.], bass) 1993—*Come On Feel the Lemonheads*.

Lemonheads started out as a democratic pop-punk band in the style of Hüsker Dü and the Replacements, but evolved into a vehicle for singer/songwriter Evan Dando's catchy postpunk pop songs. By the early Nineties, Dando's music, together with his cover-boy good looks, had won the band a succession of magazine spreads. Born in the Summer of Love to progressive parents—his mother had been a model, his father an attorney—Evan Dando grew up just north of Boston. Between his parents, two sisters, and a brother, the music around the house ranged from Steely Dan and Motown to Neil Young and Black Sabbath. When he was 12, Dando's parents split up, and he shut down emotionally. He became fascinated by Charles Manson, and years before Guns n' Roses sparked controversy by covering a Manson song, Lemonheads included the mass murderer's ballad, "Home," on *Creator*.

While still in high school, Dando and friends Ben Deily and Jesse Peretz (son of *New Republic* editor-in-chief Martin Peretz) formed the Whelps. Before recording the first EP, the group became Lemonheads, named for the popular Midwestern candy. At the time, Dando played drums. On the strength of its initial EP, Lemonheads signed with the independent Taang! label and put out *Hate Your Friends*, *Creator*, and *Lick*. But a power struggle began to erode the Dando–Deily relationship, resulting in a temporary breakup during which Dando played with Juliana Hatfield's [see entry] Blake Babies. When Dando rejoined on guitar, Deily departed.

The group signed with Atlantic after its cover of Suzanne Vega's "Luka" became popular on college radio.

Lemonheads: Nic Dalton, Evan Dando, Dave Ryan

By that time, Lemonheads had became Dando's band. Their first successful album for the major label was *It's a Shame About Ray* (#68), on which Hatfield repaid Dando by filling in on bass (one-time roommates, the two were rumored to be romantically involved, though both denied it). After the group's cover of Simon and Garfunkel's "Mrs. Robinson" became an MTV hit, Atlantic reissued *It's a Shame . . .* with that song on it. Like much of the band's work, *Come On Feel the Lemonheads* (#56, 1993)—notable for a guest appearance by former Flying Burrito Brothers pedal steel guitarist Sneaky Pete Kleinow—garnered more press coverage (particularly after Dando spoke openly about his drug use and was frequently seen with Courtney Love) than sales. In 1994 Dando began touring acoustically with English pianist, drummer, singer, and songwriter Epic Soundtracks (Swell Maps, Jacobites, These Immortal Souls), with whom he'd collaborated in songwriting.

The Lemon Pipers

Formed circa 1967, Oxford, Ohio
R. G. Nave (b. 1945), organ, tambourine; Ivan Browne (b. 1947), voc., gtr.; Bill Bartlett (b. 1946, South Harrow, Eng.), lead gtr.; Steve Walmsley (b. 1949, New Zealand), bass; Bill Albaugh (b. 1948), drums.

1968—*Green Tambourine* (Buddah); *Jungle Marmalade*.

The Lemon Pipers combined bubblegum and mild psychedelia for a #1 hit in early 1968, "Green Tambourine." Subsequent hits released later that year included "Rice Is Nice" (#46) and "Jelly Jungle (of Orange Marmalade)" (#51). By year's end the group had disbanded. Bill Bartlett later led Ram Jam, which had a Top Twenty hit in 1977, "Black Betty."

John Lennon and Yoko Ono

John Lennon, born John Winston Lennon, October 9, 1940, Liverpool, England; died December 8, 1980, New York City, N.Y.; Yoko Ono, born February 18, 1933, Tokyo, Japan.
John Lennon and Yoko Ono: 1968—*Unfinished Music No. 1: Two Virgins* (Apple) 1969—*Unfinished Music No. 2: Life with the Lions* (Zapple); *Wedding Album* (Apple); *Live Peace in Toronto, 1969* (with the Plastic Ono Band) 1972—*Some Time in New York City* 1980—*Double Fantasy* (Geffen) 1984—*Milk and Honey* (Polydor)
John Lennon solo: 1970—*John Lennon/Plastic Ono Band* (Apple) 1971—*Imagine* 1973—*Mind Games* 1974—*Walls and Bridges* 1975—*Rock 'n' Roll*; *Shaved Fish* 1982—*The John Lennon Collection* (Geffen) 1986—*John Lennon Live in New York City* (Capitol/EMI); *Menlove Avenue* (Capitol) 1988—*Imagine: John Lennon* 1990—*Lennon* (EMI).
Yoko Ono solo: 1970—*Yoko Ono/Plastic Ono Band* (Apple) 1971—*Fly* 1973—*Approximately Infinite Universe*; *Feeling the Space* 1981—*Season of Glass* (Geffen) 1983—*It's Alright* (Polydor) 1985—*Starpeace* 1992—*Onobox* (Rykodisc); *Walking on Thin Ice* 1994—*New York Rock* original cast recording (Capitol).

John Lennon was the Beatles' most committed rock & roller, their social conscience, and their slyest verbal wit. After the group's breakup, he and his second wife, Yoko Ono, carried on intertwined solo careers. Ono's early albums presaged the elastic, screechy vocal style of late-Seventies new wavers like the B-52's and Lene Lovich. L7 and Babes in Toyland have also been influenced by and benefitted from Ono's attitudinal, emotionally trailblazing work. Lennon strove to break taboos and to be ruthlessly, publicly honest. When he was murdered on December 8, 1980, he and Ono seemed on the verge of a new, more optimistic phase. In the years since Lennon's death, many critics and music historians have revised their view of Ono to recognize her contributions as a pioneering woman rock musician and avant-garde artist.

Like the other three Beatles, Lennon was born to a working-class family in Liverpool. His parents, Julia and

Yoko Ono and John Lennon

Fred, separated before he was two (Lennon saw his father only twice in the next 20 years), and Lennon went to live with his mother's sister, Mimi Smith; when Lennon was 17 his mother was killed by a bus. He attended Liverpool's Dovedale Primary School and later the Quarry Bank High School, which supplied the name for his first band, a skiffle group called the Quarrymen, which he started in 1955. In the summer of 1956 he met Paul McCartney, and they began writing songs together and forming groups, the last of which was the Beatles [see entry]. In 1994 a tape of John and the Quarrymen performing two songs, made July 6, 1957, the day he met McCartney, came to light. Recorded by Bob Molyneux, then a member of the church's youth club, it was auctioned at Sotheby's that September, fetching $122,900 from EMI. On the tape Lennon sings "Puttin' on the Style," then a #1 hit for skiffle king Lonnie Donegan, and "Baby Let's Play House," the Arthur "Hard Rock" Gunter song that had been recorded by Elvis Presley and a line of which ("I'd rather see you dead, little girl, than to be with another man") Lennon later used in the Beatles' "Run for Your Life."

Just before the Beatles' official breakup in 1970 (Lennon had wanted to quit the band earlier), Lennon began his solo career, more than half of which consisted of collaborations with Ono.

Ono was raised in Tokyo by her wealthy Japanese banking family. She was an excellent student (in 1952 she became the first woman admitted to study philosophy at Japan's Gakushuin University) and moved to the U.S. in 1953 to study at Sarah Lawrence College. After dropping out, she became involved in the Fluxus movement, led by New York avant-garde conceptual artists including George Maciunas, La Monte Young, Diane Wakoski, and Walter De Maria. During the early Sixties

Ono's works (many of which were conceptual pieces, some involving audience participation) were exhibited and/or performed at the Village Gate, Carnegie Recital Hall, and numerous New York galleries. In the mid-Sixties she lectured at Wesleyan College and had exhibitions in Japan and London, where she met Lennon in 1966 at the Indica Gallery.

The two began corresponding, and in September 1967 Lennon sponsored Ono's "Half Wind Show" at London's Lisson Gallery. In May 1968 Ono visited Lennon at his home in Weybridge, and that night they recorded the tapes that would later be released as *Two Virgins*. (The nude cover shots, taken by Lennon with an automatic camera, were photographed then as well.) Lennon soon separated from his wife, Cynthia (with whom he had one child, Julian, in 1964); they were divorced that November. Lennon and Ono became constant companions.

Frustrated by his role with the Beatles, Lennon, with Ono, got a chance to explore avant-garde art, music, and film. While he regarded his relationship with Ono as the most important thing in his life, the couple's inseparability and Ono's influence over Lennon would be a source of great tension among the Beatles, then in their last days.

Three days after Lennon's divorce, he and Ono released *Two Virgins*, which, because of the full frontal nude photos of the couple on the jacket, was the subject of much controversy; the LP was shipped in a plain brown wrapper. On March 20, 1969, Lennon and Ono were married in Gibraltar; for their honeymoon, they held their first "Bed-in for Peace," in the presidential suite of the Amsterdam Hilton. The peace movement was the first of several political causes the couple would take up over the years, but it was the one that generated the most publicity. On April 22, Lennon changed his middle name from Winston to Ono. In May they attempted to continue their bed-in in the United States, but when U.S. authorities forbade them to enter the country because of their arrest on drug charges in October 1968, the bed-in resumed in Montreal. That May, in their suite at the Queen Elizabeth Hotel, they recorded "Give Peace a Chance"; background chanters included Timothy Leary, Tommy Smothers, and numerous Hare Krishnas. Soon afterward "The Ballad of John and Yoko" (#8, 1969) was released under the Beatles name, though only Lennon and McCartney appear on the record.

In September Lennon, Ono, and the Plastic Ono Band (which included Eric Clapton, Alan White, and Klaus Voormann) performed live in Toronto at a Rock 'n' Roll Revival show. The appearance, which was later released as *Live Peace in Toronto, 1969*, was Lennon's first performance before a live concert audience in three years. Less than a month later he announced to the Beatles that he was quitting the group, but it was agreed among them that no public announcement would be made until after pending lawsuits involving Apple and

manager Allen Klein were resolved. In October the Plastic Ono Band released "Cold Turkey" (#30, 1969), which the Beatles had declined to record, and the next month Lennon returned his M.B.E. medal to the Queen. In a letter to the Queen, Lennon cited Britain's involvement in Biafra and support of the U.S. in Vietnam and—jokingly—"Cold Turkey"'s poor chart showing as reasons for the return.

The Lennons continued their peace campaign with speeches to the press; "War Is Over! If You Want It" billboards erected on December 15 in 12 cities around the world, including New York, Hollywood, London, and Toronto; and plans for a peace festival in Toronto. While the festival plans deteriorated, Lennon turned his attention to recording "Instant Karma!," which was produced by Phil Spector, who was then also editing hours of tapes into the album that would be the Beatles' last official release, *Let It Be*. In late February 1970 Lennon disavowed any connection with the Peace Festival and the event was abandoned. In April McCartney—in a move that Lennon felt was an act of betrayal—announced his departure from the Beatles and released his solo LP. From this point on (if not earlier), Ono replaced McCartney as Lennon's main collaborator. The Beatles were no more.

At the time, much attention was focused on Ono's alleged role in the band's end. An *Esquire* magazine piece racistly entitled "John Rennon's Excrusive Gloupie" was an extreme example of the decidedly anti-woman, anti-Asian backlash against Ono that she and Lennon would endure for years to come. As Ono told Lennon biographer Jon Wiener in a late 1983 interview for his book *Come Together: John Lennon in His Time*, "When John I were first together he got lots of threatening letters: 'That Oriental will slit your throat while you're sleeping.' The Western hero had been seized by an Eastern demon."

In late 1970 Lennon and Ono released their *Plastic Ono Band* solo LPs. Generally, Ono's Seventies LPs were regarded as highly adventurous avant-garde works, and were thus never as popular as Lennon's. His contained "Mother," which, along with other songs, was his most personal and, some felt, disturbing work—the direct result of his and Ono's primal scream therapy with Dr. Arthur Janov. In March 1971 "Power to the People" hit #11, and that September Lennon's solo LP *Imagine* was released; it went to #1 a month later. By late 1971 Lennon and Ono had resumed their political activities, drawn to leftist political figures like Abbie Hoffman and Jerry Rubin. Their involvement was reflected on *Some Time in New York City* (recorded with Elephant's Memory [see entry]), which included Lennon's most overtly political releases (his and Ono's "Woman Is the Nigger of the World" and Ono's "Sisters, O Sisters"). The album sold poorly, reaching only #48.

Over the next two years Lennon released *Mind*

Games (#9) and *Walls and Bridges* (#1), which yielded his only solo #1 hit, "Whatever Gets You thru the Night," recorded with Elton John. On November 28, 1974, Lennon made his last public appearance, at John's Madison Square Garden concert. The two performed three songs: "Whatever Gets You thru the Night," "I Saw Her Standing There," and "Lucy in the Sky with Diamonds," released on an EP after Lennon's death. Next came *Rock 'n' Roll*, a collection of Lennon's versions of Fifties and early-Sixties rock classics like "Be-Bop-a-Lula." The release was preceded by a bootleg copy, produced by Morris Levy, over which Lennon successfully sued Levy. *Rock 'n' Roll* (#6, 1975) would be Lennon's last solo release during his lifetime except for *Shaved Fish*, a greatest-hits compilation.

Meanwhile, Lennon's energies were increasingly directed toward his legal battle with the U.S. Immigration Department, which sought his deportation on the grounds of his previous drug arrest and involvement with the American radical left. On October 7, 1975, the U.S. court of appeals overturned the deportation order; in 1976 Lennon received permanent resident status. On October 9, 1975, Lennon's 35th birthday, Ono gave birth to Sean Ono Lennon. Beginning in 1975, Lennon devoted his full attention to his new son and his marriage, which had survived an 18-month separation from October 1973 to March 1975. For the next five years, he lived at home in nearly total seclusion, taking care of Sean while Ono ran the couple's financial affairs. Not until the publication of a full-page newspaper ad in May 1979 explaining his and Ono's activities did Lennon even hint at a possible return to recording.

In September 1980 he and Ono signed a contract with the newly formed Geffen Records, and on November 15 they released *Double Fantasy* (#1, 1980). A series of revealing interviews were published, "(Just Like) Starting Over" hit #1, and there was talk of a possible world tour.

But on December 8, 1980, Lennon, returning with Ono to their Dakota apartment on New York City's Upper West Side, was shot seven times by Mark David Chapman, a 25-year-old drifter and Beatles fan to whom Lennon had given an autograph a few hours earlier. Lennon was pronounced dead on arrival at Roosevelt Hospital. At Ono's request, on December 14 a ten-minute silent vigil was held at 2:00 p.m. EST in which millions around the world participated. Lennon's remains were cremated in Hartsdale, New York. At the time of his death, Lennon was holding in hand a tape of Ono's "Walking on Thin Ice."

Two other singles from *Double Fantasy* were hits: "Woman" (#2, 1981) and "Watching the Wheels" (#10, 1981). *Double Fantasy* won a Grammy for Album of the Year (1981). Three months after the murder, Ono released *Season of Glass* (#49), an LP that deals with Lennon's death (his cracked and bloodstained eyeglasses are shown on the front jacket), although many of the songs were written before his shooting. *Season of Glass* is the best known of Ono's solo LPs; it was the first to receive attention outside avant-garde and critical circles.

In 1982 Ono left Geffen for Polydor, where she released *It's Alright, Milk and Honey* (which featured six songs by Ono and six by Lennon) (#11, 1984), and *Starpeace*. During the Starpeace Tour Ono performed behind the Iron Curtain, in Budapest, Hungary, but the tour was not as warmly received elsewhere. None of these albums was particularly successful commercially, but in the wake of renewed appreciation for Ono's work, Rykodisc issued the six-CD box set *Onobox* in 1992 (*Walking on Thin Ice* is a compilation from that). In 1984 a number of artists, including Rosanne Cash, Harry Nilsson, Elvis Costello, Roberta Flack, and Sean Lennon (in his recording debut) participated in *Every Man Has a Woman Who Loves Him*, a collection of Ono songs. Following a 1989 retrospective at New York's Whitney Museum, Ono's work found a new audience and has since been shown continuously throughout the world. In 1994 she wrote a rock opera entitled *New York Rock*, which ran Off-Broadway for two weeks to largely positive reviews. Clearly autobiographical, the play was a love story that ends in a murder, and featured songs from every phase of her recording career.

In addition to pursuing her own projects, Ono has maintained careful watch over the Lennon legacy. In the mid-Eighties she opened the Lennon archives to Andrew Solt and David Wolper for their 1988 film biography *Imagine* (which was accompanied by a coffee-table photo book of the same title). Coming as it did just a few months after the publication of Albert Goldman's scurrilous *The Lives of John Lennon*, some observers saw *Imagine* as a piece of spin control. In fact, however, it had been in the works for over five years by then. Ono's decision not to sue Goldman (she stated that her lawyers warned that legal action would only bring more attention to the discredited tome) was in itself controversial. Paul McCartney urged a public boycott of the Goldman book, which was almost universally reviled. Shortly after its publication, Sean asked to study abroad, and Ono accompanied him to Geneva, where they took up residence for a few years. On September 30, 1988, a week before *Imagine*'s release, John Lennon received his star on the Hollywood Walk of Fame. It is located near the Capitol Records building.

On March 21, 1984, Ono, Sean Lennon, and Julian Lennon were present as New York City mayor Ed Koch officially opened Strawberry Fields, a triangular section of Central Park dedicated to his memory and filled with plants, rocks, and other objects that Ono had solicited from heads of state around the world. The day before, March 20, marked the couple's 15th wedding anniversary.

Julian Lennon

Born John Charles Julian Lennon, April 8, 1963, Liverpool, England
1984—*Valotte* (Atlantic) 1986—*The Secret Value of Daydreaming* 1989—*Mr. Jordan* 1991—*Help Yourself.*

John Lennon's only child by his first wife, Cynthia Twist, Julian Lennon already had a small niche in rock history (Paul McCartney wrote "Hey Jude" about him) before he released *Valotte,* the debut album that was his major hit. While growing up, Julian wasn't particularly close to John, who divorced Cynthia in 1968 and then relocated to New York City with Yoko Ono. Despite his father's wealth, Julian lived a typical middle-class life with his mother. Clearly, however, the younger Lennon's musical sensibilities were shaped by his father's music and that of the Beatles, as well as Steely Dan and the Police. After his father was murdered in December 1980, Lennon spent some time haunting London nightclubs before deciding to put his long-harbored musical ambitions to the test.

He hooked up with Atlantic Records and veteran producer Phil Ramone (Billy Joel, Paul Simon). In 1985 *Valotte* (named for the French chateau where it was recorded) yielded the hit singles "Valotte" (#9) and "Too Late for Goodbyes" (#5). Critics and listeners noted Lennon's uncanny physical and vocal resemblance to his father, but they also praised the young songwriter and multi-instrumentalist (guitar, keyboards, percussion) for his moodily insinuating melodies. Unfortunately, 1986's *The Secret Value of Daydreaming* wasn't as well received, and 1989's *Mr. Jordan* and 1991's *Help Yourself* were all but ignored.

Annie Lennox: See Eurythmics

Let's Active

Formed 1981, Winston-Salem, North Carolina
Mitch Easter (b. Nov. 15, 1954, Winston-Salem), gtr., voc.; Faye Hunter (b. Sep. 13, 1953, Winston-Salem), bass, voc.; Sara Romweber (b. Feb. 13, 1964, Ind.), drums.
1983—*Afoot* EP (I.R.S.) 1984—*Cypress* (– Romweber; + Eric Marshall [b. 1962, Winston-Salem], drums; + Angie Carlson [b. Sep. 13, 1960, Minn.], voc., gtr., kybds.) 1986—*Big Plans for Everybody* (– Hunter; + John Heames [b. 1965, Winston-Salem], bass) 1988—*Every Dog Has His Day.*

Let's Active was the Beatles-esque brainchild of Eighties producer du jour and multi-instrumentalist Mitch Easter, whose claim to fame was the production of R.E.M.'s first two albums. Easter and a changing cast of musicians helped define the jangle pop sound of the early Eighties.

Born and raised in Winston-Salem, North Carolina, Easter began feeling alienated from the local music scene during the Seventies, when Southern rock became the main staple; Easter had always been more interested in the studio-crafted sound of Sixties British pop. As a teenager he played with future dB's [see entry] Peter Holsapple and Chris Stamey, simulating the sound of bands like the Nazz and Move. During the punk invasion of the late Seventies, Easter opened a recording studio in his mom's garage called Mitch's Drive-In Studio; among his first big customers were Pylon, the dB's, and R.E.M. While working with those bands, he formed Let's Active as a casual side project with Faye Hunter—his girlfriend since high school—and fellow N.C. music scenester Sara Romweber. Two weeks later the trio opened for R.E.M. Initial reaction to Let's Active's jangly, bubblegum-pop sound was mixed: Some critics appreciated Easter's finely crafted pop, while others were put off by his "chronic cuteness," comparing Let's Active to the Monkees.

Between 1984 and 1986, Let's Active increasingly became a vehicle for Easter's studio indulgence. On *Big Plans for Everybody,* Easter's songwriting showed an emotional depth that heretofore had not been heard. The band became a looser aggregation, with different musicians joining in for tours. After 1988's *Every Dog Has His Day,* Easter retreated to his studio again, producing only the work of other artists. Though Easter never officially disbanded Let's Active, he began touring with another group, Velvet Crush, in 1994.

The Lettermen

Formed 1958, Los Angeles, California
Most popular lineup: Tony Butala (b. Nov. 20, 1940, Sharon, Pa.), voc.; Bob Engemann (b. Feb. 19, 1936, Highland Park, Mich.), voc.; Jim Pike (b. Nov. 6, 1938, St. Louis, Mo.), voc.
1966—*The Best of the Lettermen* (Capitol) 1967—*The Lettermen!!! . . . and "Live!"* (– Engemann; + Gary Pike); *Goin' Out of My Head* 1969—*Hurt So Bad* (– J. Pike; + Doug Curran; numerous personnel changes follow) 1974—*All-Time Greatest Hits* 1981—(Lineup: Butala; Donovan Scott Tea, voc.; Mark Preston, voc.; Donnie Pike, voc.) 1986—(Lineup: Butala; D. Pike; Tea; Robert Poynton, voc.).

The Lettermen have been harmonizing pop songs for more than 35 years. Personnel have changed, their repertoire has been revamped with the times, and their hits are long behind them, but they continue. Original members Tony Butala, Bob Engemann, and Jim Pike all had a measure of music-business experience, in guises ranging from the Mitchell Boys Choir to Stan Kenton, when they formed the Lettermen in 1960. They were hired by George Burns and Jack Benny to open their live shows.

A brief tenure with Warner Bros. Records followed before the Lettermen signed with Capitol in 1961. Their first single for the label, "The Way You Look Tonight," went gold; in 1962 "When I Fall in Love" and "Come Back Silly Girl" were Top Twenty hits. Their albums of that period always made the Top 100; four were certified gold. They have grossed over $25 million in sales for Capitol Records. As tastes in music changed, the Lettermen adapted their smooth voices to the latest trend: folk revival when they started out, electric guitars in the mid-Sixties, even disco and new wave in later years.

In 1968 they went through their first shift in personnel. Engemann was replaced by Gary Pike (Jim's brother) without affecting their hitmaking abilities; they scored one of their biggest that year with a medley of "Goin' Out of My Head" and "Can't Take My Eyes Off of You." "Hurt So Bad" (#12, 1969) was their last gold record, though the trio continued releasing records on Capitol throughout the Seventies. The Lettermen also branched into commercials, earning a Golden Globe Award for a Pan Am ad. In 1982 they left Capitol for the Applause label. While the group has not charted an LP since 1974 (though they continue to record), they still tour the world and remain a top live act.

Level 42
Formed 1980, London, England
Mark King (b. Oct. 20, 1958, Cowes, Eng.), bass, voc.; Phil Gould (b. Feb. 28, 1957, Hong Kong), drums; Boon Gould (b. Roland Gould, Mar. 4, 1955, Shanklin, Eng.), gtr.; Mike Lindup (b. Mar. 17, 1959, London), kybds., voc.
1981—Level 42 (Polydor)   1982—The Pursuit of Accidents   1983—Standing in the Light   1984—True Colours   1985—A Physical Presence; World Machine   1987—Running in the Family   1988—(- P. Gould; - B. Gould; + Alan Murphy [b. 1954; d. Oct. 19, 1989], gtr.; + Gary Husband, drums, voc.) Staring at the Sun   1989—(- Murphy) Level Best   1991—(+ Allan Holdsworth, gtr.)   1992—Guaranteed (RCA).

Level 42 play a mild fusion funk that they presented as pop in the mid-Eighties. Mark King and the Gould brothers were friends on the Isle of Wight. They moved to London in 1978 and two years later formed Level 42, picking up Mike Lindup. King had previously been a drummer but bowed to Phil Gould's superior skills on that instrument and became the band's bassist. His thumb-slapping style has since become one of the band's main attractions.

Level 42 was influenced by early-Seventies jazz-rock fusion. Their first albums were largely instrumental, until King gave in to commercial pressure and began to sing. Their early records, which sold well in the U.K., alter-

nately flopped or were not released in the U.S. The band didn't score an international hit until 1986, when they deliberately toned down their chops and turned up the pop on World Machine (#18, 1986) and "Something About You" (#7, 1986). They followed that success with Running in the Family (#23, 1987) and its single "Lessons in Love" (#12, 1987). They opened Madonna's tour in the summer of 1987 and headlined a tour on their own.

The Gould brothers left the band in fall 1987, and Level 42 has never fully replaced them. Temporary guitarist Alan Murphy died of AIDS in 1989. King has played on albums by M, Nik Kershaw, Midge Ure, and others, and has remixed tracks for Robert Palmer.

Levert
Formed 1982, Cleveland, Ohio
Gerald Levert (b. July 13, 1966), voc.; Sean Levert (b. Sep. 28, 1968), voc.; Marc Gordon (b. Sep. 8, 1964), kybds., voc.
1986—Bloodline (Atlantic)   1987—The Big Throwdown   1988—Just Coolin'   1990—Rope a Dope Style   1993—For Real Tho'.
Gerald Levert solo: 1991—Private Line (EastWest)   1994—Groove On.
Sean Levert solo: 1995—The Other Side (Atlantic).

With keyboardist/vocalist Marc Gordon, singing brothers Gerald and Sean Levert—sons of the O'Jays' Eddie Levert Sr.—formed a trio that adapted the smooth, soulful harmonies of the O'Jays, Spinners, and other leading Seventies R&B groups to a progressively aggressive funky and hip-hop–driven musical style.

The Levert siblings hooked up with Gordon while in their mid-teens. After practicing at the Leverts' home studio, the threesome began performing in Ohio clubs. An independently released single, "I'm Still," became popular in the Baltimore–Washington, D.C., region, attracting the interest of Atlantic Records. Levert's debut album, Bloodline, yielded the #1 R&B hit "(Pop, Pop, Pop, Pop) Goes My Mind." The following year The Big Throwdown (#32 pop, #3 R&B) produced the R&B singles "Casanova" (#5 pop, #1 R&B, 1987), "My Forever Love" (#2 R&B, 1987), and "Sweet Sensation" (#4 R&B, 1988). In 1988 the band again topped the R&B singles chart with "Addicted to You," from the film soundtrack Coming to America.

Also in 1988 Gerald Levert and Gordon formed Trevel Productions, a writing and producing team that worked with artists ranging from the O'Jays and Anita Baker to Men at Large and Miki Howard, whose hit "That's What Love Is" (#4 R&B, 1988) featured Gerald on vocals. Levert's 1988 album, Just Coolin' (#79 pop, #6 R&B), was produced by Trevel and generated another #1 R&B single with the title song, featuring rapper Heavy D.

"Gotta Get the Money" reached #4. *Rope a Dope Style* (#9 R&B, 1990) spawned hits with the title track (#7 R&B, 1990), "All Season" (#4 R&B, 1990), and "Baby I'm Ready" (#1 R&B, 1991). Gerald's solo album, *Private Line*, peaked at #2 R&B and included the singles "School Me" (#3 R&B, 1992), "Can You Handle It" (#9 R&B, 1992), and "Baby Hold On to Me" (#1 R&B, 1992), the latter a duet between Gerald and his father.

Bobby Lewis
Born February 17, 1933, Indianapolis, Indiana
1961—*Tossin' and Turnin'* (Beltone).

With the booming cry "I didn't sleep at all last night!" singer Bobby Lewis opened "Tossin' and Turnin'," an R&B stomp that held the #1 position on U.S. singles chart for seven weeks in 1961. Despite another hit that year with "One Track Mind" (#9), "Tossin'" proved to be Lewis' finest moment.

Growing up in an orphanage, Lewis was playing the piano by age five. Adopted at age 12, he moved with his new family to Detroit, where he was soon featured on a morning radio show. He became a journeyman blues-boogie performer in small clubs and theaters throughout the Midwest. During the Fifties he recorded jump blues and other such material in one-shot deals for a variety of labels; none of the records went anywhere. Beltone Records signed him in 1961, and then came the hits. He continued to perform in clubs and theaters through the first half of the Sixties. United Artists signed him and eventually released two volumes of *The Best of Bobby Lewis*. Lewis semiretired in 1989 but still makes the rounds on the oldies circuit, appearing on bills with Chubby Checker, the Drifters, the Shirelles, and other acts.

Furry Lewis
Born Walter Lewis, March 6, 1893, Greenwood, Mississippi; died September 14, 1981, Memphis, Tennessee
1969—*Presenting the Country Blues* (Blue Horizon)
1970—*In Memphis* (Matchbox)   1971—*Furry Lewis* (Xtra); *& Fred McDowell* (Biograph); *Furry Lewis Band* (Folkways).

Legendary Memphis bluesman Walter "Furry" Lewis is thought by some to have been the first guitarist to play with a bottleneck, a technique later used by Robert Johnson, Bukka White, and Johnny Shines. (Earlier musicians had achieved a similar effect using a knife across the strings.) The son of a Mississippi sharecropper, Lewis moved from his birthplace to Memphis in 1899 and while still in school began playing guitar in local bands with W. C. Handy, Will Shade, and the Memphis Jug Band. He was a teen when he began performing on Beale Street.

Lewis toured the country in medicine shows and also played the jukes with Memphis Minnie and Blind Lemon Jefferson as early as 1906 and straight through the Twenties. In 1916 he lost a leg in a railroad accident; it was replaced by a wooden stump. In 1927 he and Jim Jackson auditioned for the Vocalion label in Chicago. The next year his first recordings, including "Good Looking Girl Blues," "John Henry," and "Billy Lyons and Stack O'Lee," were released.

His singing style was a kind of talking blues, but the market for that music died in the Depression, and Furry spent the next 44 years supporting himself as a street cleaner. He did some performing by night, but he didn't record again until the late Fifties, when Sam Charters recorded him for Prestige. Later recordings for Biograph, Folkways, Adelphi, and Rounder never earned enough for Lewis to quit the sanitation department. He did play many blues and folk festivals in the Sixties and Seventies and recorded with Bukka White, though his best shot at fame came in the early Seventies, when he toured with Don Nix and the Alabama State Troopers and appeared on a Leon Russell television special.

In 1975 the Rolling Stones invited him along as their opening act in Memphis, and after a meeting with him, Joni Mitchell wrote "Furry Sings the Blues," which appeared on her *Hejira* album. Lewis also appeared on *The Tonight Show* and in two films, Burt Reynolds' *W. W. and the Dixie Dance King* and *This Is Elvis*. He died of heart failure at age 88.

Gary Lewis and the Playboys
Formed 1964, Los Angeles, California
Most popular lineup: Gary Lewis (b. Gary Levitch, July 31, 1945, Los Angeles), drums, voc.; Al Ramsey (b. July 27, 1943, N.J.), gtr.; John R. West (b. July 31, 1939, Uhrichsville, Ohio), gtr.; David Walkes (b. May 12, 1943, Montgomery, Ala.), kybds.; David Costell (b. Mar. 15, 1944, Pittsburgh, Pa.), bass.
1965—*This Diamond Ring* (Liberty)   1966—*Golden Greats*   1968—*More Golden Greats*.

With seven consecutive Top Ten singles in 1965 and 1966, and over 7½ million records sold, Gary Lewis was certainly one of the most successful Hollywood offspring turned rock & roller. Lewis was drafted in 1966, and since his 1969 army discharge he has attempted several comebacks. The eldest son of comedian Jerry Lewis, Gary started playing drums at age 14; four years later he formed the Playboys. They became a regular fixture at Disneyland, and producer Snuff Garrett signed them to Liberty in 1964. With Leon Russell's arrangements and Al Kooper as cowriter, the Playboys scored a #1 hit their first time out with "This Diamond Ring."

Russell also worked on the subsequent singles: "Count Me In" (#2, 1965), "Save Your Heart for Me" (#2,

1965), "Everybody Loves a Clown" (#4, 1965), "She's Just My Style" (#3, 1966), "Sure Gonna Miss Her" (#9, 1966), and "Green Grass" (#8, 1966).

The group appeared in *A Swingin' Summer* (1965) and *Out of Sight* (1966). The Playboys' popularity had waned just slightly when Lewis was drafted, and upon his discharge he re-formed the group with other musicians. Though Lewis would score two more chart singles, he would never again have a Top Ten hit, despite an attempt to update his image from teenage pop star to "sensitive" singer/songwriter. His career was further complicated by drug problems and a divorce. Lewis performs regularly on the oldies circuit with the Playboys, who now in the Nineties consisted of Rich Spina, Billy Sullivan, John Dean, and Michael Hadak.

Huey Lewis and the News

Formed 1979, Marin County, California
Huey Lewis (b. Hugh Cregg III, July 5, 1950, New
York City, N.Y.), voc., harmonica; Chris Hayes
(b. Nov. 24, 1957, Calif.), gtr.; Mario Cipollina
(b. Nov. 10, 1954, Calif.) bass; Bill Gibson (b. Nov. 13,
1951, Calif.), drums; Sean Hopper (b. Mar. 31, 1953,
Calif.), kybds.; Johnny Colla (b. July 2, 1952, Calif.),
sax, gtr.
1980—*Huey Lewis and the News* (Chrysalis)
1982—*Picture This*   1983—*Sports*   1986—*Fore!*
1988—*Small World*   1991—*Hard at Play* (EMI)
1994—*Four Chords and Several Years Ago* (Elektra).

One of the most commercially successful American bands of the early to mid-Eighties, Huey Lewis and the News have released 17 Top Forty singles and sold over 12 million albums' worth of conservative, straightahead rock & roll. While critics derided the group for its bland predictability, fans were drawn to lead singer Huey Lewis and the band's funtime personae and their radio-friendly sound.

The group traces its roots to the Bay Area, where Lewis and future News member Sean Hopper founded a country-rock group called Clover. Contrary to popular misconception, the entire band did not back Elvis Costello on his debut album; only Hopper did. The group had a U.K. record deal, and its first single, "Chicken Funk," was produced by Nick Lowe, but neither of its albums made much of an impression. Another Clover member, John McFee, quit to join the Doobie Brothers, and the group soon disbanded. Back in California, Lewis formed American Express. Among the members were Johnny Colla, Bill Gibson, and Mario Cipollina (the brother of Quicksilver Messenger Service's John Cipollina), all of whom had formerly played in Soundhole. In 1980 the group signed with Chrysalis, which requested a name change. Later that year Huey Lewis and the News' self-titled debut LP came and went without making a nick on the chart.

Huey Lewis

Early 1982 saw the release of the group's breakthrough album, *Picture This* (#13, 1982), which took off on the strength of the Mutt Lange–penned "Do You Believe in Love" (#7, 1982), followed by "Hope You Love Me Like You Say You Do" (#36, 1982). The group's second release, the seven-million-selling *Sports* (#1, 1983), stayed on the chart over three years. Boosted by a series of tongue-in-cheek videos that showcased Lewis' moviestar good looks, this album spun off five Top Twenty hits, including four Top Tens: "Heart and Soul" (#8, 1983), "I Want a New Drug" (#6, 1984), "The Heart of Rock & Roll" (#6, 1984), and "If This Is It" (#6, 1984). Late in 1984 Lewis brought suit against Ray Parker Jr., alleging that the latter's hit "Ghostbusters" was a plagiarization of "I Want a New Drug." The case was later settled out of court. The next year brought the group's first #1 single, "The Power of Love," from the hit movie *Back to the Future*.

Three years elapsed between the release of *Sports* and *Fore!* (#1, 1986), which sold three million copies. From it came five more hits: "Stuck with You" (#1, 1986), "Hip to Be Square" (#3, 1986), Bruce Hornsby's "Jacob's Ladder" (#1, 1987), "I Know What I Like" (#9, 1987), and "Doing It All for My Baby" (#6, 1987). Around this time Lewis had helped Hornsby secure a record deal, and Lewis wrote several songs on his debut album.

The News' next release, *Small World* (#11, 1988), marked a change in direction, and while critics were not impressed, there were two hits: "Perfect World" (#3, 1988) and "Small World" (#25, 1988). *Hard at Play* (#27, 1991), was the first of the group's LPs since their debut to chart outside the Top Twenty; its only hit was "Couple Days Off" (#11, 1991). *Four Chords and Several Years Ago* (#55, 1994), a collection of R&B and rock remakes, was released in 1994. Lewis made his screen acting debut in Robert Altman's 1994 film *Short Cuts*.

Jerry Lee Lewis

**Born September 29, 1935, Ferriday, Louisiana
1958—*Jerry Lee Lewis* (Sun)   1964—*The Greatest Live Show on Earth* (Smash); *Live at the Star Club Hamburg* (Philips)   1968—*Another Place, Another Time* (Smash)   1969—*Jerry Lee Lewis' Original Golden Hits, vol. 1* (Sun); *Jerry Lee Lewis' Original Golden Hits, vol. 2*   1970—*A Taste of Country; Sunday Down South; Ole Tyme Country Music; There Must Be More to Love Than This* (Mercury)   1971—*Original Golden Hits, vol. 3* (Sun); *Monsters*   1973—*The Session* (Mercury)   1978—*Best of Jerry Lee Lewis, vol. 2*   1980—*Killer Country* (Elektra)   1982—*The Best of Jerry Lee Lewis (Featuring 39 and Holding)*   1984—*18 Original Sun Greatest Hits* (Rhino)   1985—*Milestones*   1986—*Twenty Classic Jerry Lee Lewis Hits* (Original Sound)   1987—*Rare and Rockin'* (Sun)   1989—*Rare Tracks* (Rhino); *Classic Jerry Lee Lewis* (Bear Family, Ger.)   1994—*All Killer, No Filler!* (Rhino)   1995—*Young Blood* (Sire).**

Though he had only three Top Ten hits in the first purely rock & roll phase of his career, many critics believe Jerry Lee Lewis was as talented a Fifties rocker as Sun labelmate Elvis Presley. Some also believe he could have made it just as big commercially if his piano-slamming musical style was not so relentlessly wild, his persona not so threateningly hard-edged.

Lewis' first musical influences were eclectic. His parents, who were poor, spun swing and Al Jolson records. But his earliest big influence was country star Jimmie Rodgers. In his early teens he absorbed both the softer country style of Gene Autry and the more rocking music of local black clubs, along with the gospel hymns of the local Assembly of God church. Lewis first played his aunt's piano at age eight and made his public debut in 1949 at age 14, sitting in with a local C&W band in a Ford dealership parking lot. When he was 15, Lewis went to a fundamentalist Bible school in Waxahachie, Texas, from which he was soon expelled. He has often said that rock & roll is the Devil's music.

In 1956 Lewis headed for Memphis (financed by his father) to audition for Sam Phillips' Sun Records. Phillips' assistant, Jack Clement, was impressed with Lewis' piano style but suggested he play more rock & roll, in a style similar to Elvis Presley's. (Presley had recently

Jerry Lee Lewis

switched from Sun to RCA.) Lewis' debut single, "Crazy Arms" (previously a country hit for Ray Price), did well regionally, but it was the followup, 1957's "Whole Lotta Shakin' Going On" (#3), that finally broke through. The song first sold 100,000 copies in the South; after Lewis' appearance on Steve Allen's TV show, it sold over six million copies nationally. "Great Balls of Fire" (#2, 1957) sold more than five million copies and was followed by more than a half-million in sales for "Breathless" (#7, 1958) and "High School Confidential" (#21, 1958), the title theme song of a movie in which Lewis also appeared. Both "Whole Lotta Shakin'" and "Great Balls" were in the pop, country, and R&B Top Five simultaneously; "Shakin'" at #3 pop, and #1 R&B and C&W, and "Great Balls" at #2 pop, #3 R&B, #1 C&W. Lewis' high school nickname was the "Killer," and it stuck with him as he established a reputation as a tough, rowdy performer, with a flamboyant piano style that used careening glissandos, pounding chords, and bench-toppling acrobatics.

Lewis' career slammed to a stop, though, after he married his 13-year-old third cousin, Myra Gale Brown, in December 1957. (She was his third wife; at age 16 he had wed a 17-year-old, and soon after that ended he had got caught in a shotgun marriage.) The marriage lasted 13 years, but at the time, Lewis was condemned by the church in the U.S. and hounded by the British press on a 1958 tour. His career ran dry for nearly a decade. He had a modest 1961 hit with "What'd I Say," but in 1963 he left

Sun for Smash/Mercury. He toured relentlessly, playing clubs, billing his act "the greatest show on earth." On the way, he developed a drinking problem. In 1968 he played Iago in a rock musical version of Shakespeare's *Othello* called *Catch My Soul.*

Eventually, Lewis and his producer, Jerry Kennedy, decided to abandon rock & roll for country music. In 1968 Lewis had the first of many Top Ten country hits with "Another Place, Another Time," followed by "What Made Milwaukee Famous (Made a Loser Out of Me)." Between then and the early Eighties he had more than 30 big country hits, including "To Make Love Sweeter for You" (#1 C&W, 1968), "There Must Be More to Love Than This" (#1 C&W, 1971), "Would You Take Another Chance on Me" (#1 C&W, 1971), "Chantilly Lace" (#1 C&W, 1972), "Middle Age Crazy" (#4 C&W, 1977), and "Thirty-nine and Holding" (#4 C&W, 1981). Subsequent singles were minor C&W hits, none charting higher than #43.

In 1973 Lewis released *The Session,* a return-to-rock album recorded in London with a host of top British musicians, including Peter Frampton, Alvin Lee, Klaus Voormann, and Rory Gallagher, redoing oldies. It resulted in some pop chart success with "Drinkin' Wine Spo Dee Odee," an R&B song he'd performed at his public debut in 1949. In 1978 Lewis signed with Elektra and enjoyed some FM radio play with "Rockin' My Life Away." He also continued to tour, performing all the styles of his career: rock, country, gospel, blues, spirituals, and more. In 1981 Lewis played a German concert with fellow Sun alumni Johnny Cash and Carl Perkins. The show was released as an album called *Survivors* in 1982. On June 30, 1981, Lewis was hospitalized in Memphis with hemorrhaging from a perforated stomach ulcer. After two operations, he was given a 50-50 chance of survival; four months later he was back on tour. He appeared on the 1982 Grammy Awards telecast with his cousin Mickey Gilley; another cousin is TV evangelist Jimmy Swaggart.

Lewis' personal life has been marked by tragedy and controversy. In 1973 Jerry Lee Lewis Jr., who played drums in his father's band, was killed in an automobile accident. (Lewis' brother had died when hit by a car when Jerry was two.) His other son, Steve Allen (named after the talk-show host), drowned in 1962 at age three. In September 1976 Lewis accidently shot his bassist in the chest.

In 1982 his estranged fourth wife, Jaren Gunn Lewis, also drowned in a pool under mysterious circumstances shortly before their divorce settlement. His fifth wife, Shawn Stephens Lewis, was found dead in their home 77 days after their wedding. Although investigative pieces, including one in ROLLING STONE, exposed discrepancies in Lewis' and various local law-enforcement officials' accounts of the incident and flaws in the investigation, no charges were ever brought against Lewis. Despite the presence of blood at the couple's home, on Lewis, and on his wife's body, investigators did not even test to determine whose blood it was. A private and illegal (since it was conducted out of state) autopsy, performed by the same coroner who determined that Elvis Presley had succumbed to cardiac arrhythmia, declared Shawn Lewis was determined to have died from pulmonary edema. Even after published reports established problems with the investigation, the case was not reopened. Jerry Lee Lewis remarried again, taking his sixth wife. She later gave birth to Jerry Lee Lewis III, Lewis' only surviving son (he also had a daughter with Myra).

In recent years Lewis has been plagued by serious health problems and battles with the IRS. He was treated at the Betty Ford Clinic for addiction to painkillers. His health has been poor, record sales have dropped off, and he rarely performs. He last came to public attention in 1989, when the biographical film *Great Balls of Fire,* starring Dennis Quaid as Lewis, was released. Lewis was among the first ten inductees into the Rock and Roll Hall of Fame in 1986. In 1995 Lewis returned with a new album, *Young Blood,* on Sire Records.

Linda Lewis

Born London, England
1970—*Hacienda View* (Ariola, U.K.)   1971—*Say No More* (Reprise, U.K.)   1972—*Lark* (Reprise)   1973—*Fathoms Deep*   1975—*Not a Little Girl Anymore* (Arista)   1977—*Woman Overboard.*

Singer/songwriter Linda Lewis' career was grounded by the same problems Joan Armatrading later faced: how to get an American audience to accept a black female singer who isn't an R&B artist. Though Lewis' music shows some soul influence, it is more often a bubbly combination of English folk rock with reggae and pop.

Lewis was born to Jamaican parents in the Dockland area of London's East End, and her first influence was calypso. As a preteen, she had bit acting parts in *A Hard Day's Night* and *A Taste of Honey.* At age 14 her mother took her to see John Lee Hooker, and Lewis reportedly wound up taking the stage with the old bluesman for a version of Martha and the Vandellas' "Dancing in the Streets." She left acting and school to start playing in bands, first joining Herbie Goins and the Nightmares, then her own group, White Rabbit; in 1967 she achieved some recognition in Europe with Ferris Wheel.

After two years, Lewis went solo with her own material. She toured Britain with Elton John and Family, all before releasing her 1971 album *Say No More.* Critics praised Lewis' flighty three-and-a-half-octave (some sources say five-octave) voice and pop-folky material, but the record was never released in the U.S. Her next LP, the first in America, *Lark,* was produced by her future husband Jim Cregan (who later left Family for Cockney Rebel and then Rod Stewart's band). It was followed by her first

U.K. hit, "Rock-a-Doodle-Do" (#15, 1973). In 1974 Lewis did a world tour with Cat Stevens, and in 1975 she was signed to Arista, where Clive Davis tried to improve her commercial potential by matching her with R&B producers Tony Sylvester and Bert DeCoteaux. *Not a Little Girl Anymore* yielded a #6 U.K. hit with Betty Everett's 1964 smash "It's in His Kiss (The Shoop Shoop Song)." She had another British score with "Baby I'm Yours" (#33, 1976), but she didn't release another LP until 1977's *Woman Overboard*, produced by Cregan, Allen Toussaint, and Cat Stevens. The album didn't click in the U.S., and she soon lost her recording contract, although she released another LP in the U.K. before dropping from sight.

Ramsey Lewis

Born May 27, 1935, Chicago, Illinois
1964—*Barefoot Sunday Blues* (Cadet)   1965—*The In Crowd*   1966—*Hang On Ramsey!*; *Wade in the Water*   1968—*Ramsey Lewis Trio*   1973—*Ramsey Lewis' Newly Recorded All-Time, Non-Stop Golden Hits* (Columbia)   1975—*Sun Goddess*   1977—*Tequila Mockingbird*   1978—*Legacy*   1982—*Reunion*   1984—*The Two of Us* (with Nancy Wilson)   1987—*Keys to the City*   1988—*Classic Encounter*   1989—*Urban Renewal*; *We Meet Again* (with Billy Taylor)   1992—*Ivory Pyramid* (GRP)   1993—*Sky Islands*.

Keyboardist Ramsey Lewis has had much commercial success with pop-jazz instrumentals, particularly in the mid-Sixties, when his remakes of current hits—Dobie Gray's "The 'In' Crowd," the McCoys' "Hang On Sloopy"—went Top Twenty. Releasing consistently well-crafted albums, Lewis has maintained a solid midlevel career.

Lewis studied classical piano at the Chicago College of Music and De Paul University. He began playing professionally at age 16 with the Clefs, a group that included bassist Eldee Young and drummer Isaac Red Holt, with whom he formed the Ramsey Lewis Trio in 1956. In 1965 the Trio won a Grammy for "The 'In' Crowd" (#5, 1965) ("Hang On Sloopy," #11, 1965, won a Grammy in 1973 after being rereleased on *Golden Hits*). Besides the Trio's albums, Lewis also played with Max Roach, Sonny Stitt, and Clark Terry. In 1965 the Trio broke up. His former sidemen founded Young-Holt Unlimited and scored a #3 hit with "Soulful Strut" in 1969. In 1966 Lewis' new trio (Cleveland Eaton on bass and drummer Maurice White, later of Earth, Wind and Fire) quickly scored another hit with "Wade in the Water" (#19) and Lewis received another Grammy for "Hold It Right There."

Lewis enjoyed much success through the mid-Seventies, and his *Sun Goddess* (#12, 1975), produced by White, went gold. In the Eighties he explored new musical settings: *Keys to the City* juxtaposes piano with synth, *Classic Encounter* features the Philharmonica Orchestra. He also duetted with jazz pianist Billy Taylor and singer Nancy Wilson. In 1990 Lewis began cohosting a jazz radio show in Chicago. With his son Kevyn, who'd written songs for Lewis' *Urban Renewal*, he began producing music for commercials.

Smiley Lewis

Born Overton Amos Lemons, July 5, 1920, Union, Louisiana; died October 7, 1966, New Orleans, Louisiana
1970—*Shame Shame Shame* (Liberty)   1978—*I Hear You Knocking* (United Artists); *The Bells Are Ringing*.

Singer, guitarist, and pianist Smiley Lewis was a major New Orleans R&B performer, though his best songs only became pop hits for other people. His parents moved to New Orleans from his small-town birthplace when he was 11, and he began recording there in 1947 for Deluxe Records under the name Smiling Lewis. The best-loved work of this gravel-voiced singer came during his 1950–60 period, when he was produced by Dave Bartholomew, yielding such songs as "Shame Shame Shame" and two R&B hits, "The Bells Are Ringing" (#10, 1952) and "I Hear You Knocking" (#2, 1955), which featured a classic piano intro from Huey Smith. A few months later, Lewis' version of "Knocking" was eclipsed by Gale Storm's #2 pop hit cover. The song was revived 15 years later by Dave Edmunds, who made it a hit again. Another of Lewis' tunes, "One Night (of Sin)," was cleaned up and changed to "One Night (of Love)" and became a hit for Elvis Presley in 1958.

Beginning in 1961, Lewis recorded for Okeh, then Dot and Loma Records (at the last, produced by Allen Toussaint), and he worked until his death in 1966 of stomach cancer.

Gordon Lightfoot

Born November 17, 1938, Orillia, Ontario, Canada
1966—*Lightfoot* (United Artists)   1968—*The Way I Feel*; *Did She Mention My Name?*   1969—*Back Here on Earth*; *Early Lightfoot*; *Sunday Concert*   1970—*Sit Down Young Stranger* (a.k.a. *If You Could Read My Mind*) (Reprise)   1971—*Summer Side of Life*   1972—*Don Quixote*; *Old Dan's Records*   1973—*Sundown*   1974—*The Very Best of Gordon Lightfoot* (United Artists)   1975—*Cold on the Shoulder* (Reprise); *Gord's Gold*   1976—*Early Morning Rain*; *Summertime Dream* (Reprise)   1978—*Endless Wire* (Warner Bros.)   1980—*Dream Street Rose*   1982—*Shadows*   1983—*Salute*   1986—*East of Midnight*   1988—*Gord's Gold, vol. 2*   1993—*Waiting for You* (Reprise).

One of the most successful Canadian singer/songwriters, baritone Gordon Lightfoot was inspired to write his own songs by writers like Bob Dylan, Tom Paxton, and Phil Ochs in the early Sixties. Before that he played piano, worked summers in his father's laundry, and then emigrated to Los Angeles in 1958 to attend the now defunct Westlake College. There he studied orchestration but soon returned to Toronto, where he worked as an arranger and producer of commercial jingles until 1960. Encouraged by Pete Seeger and friends Ian and Sylvia, he switched to guitar and, along with his studio work, began playing folk music at local coffeehouses.

Lightfoot soon developed his own identity with countryish material, like his debut Canadian hit, "Remember Me." Ian and Sylvia added two of his folky numbers to their stage show, "For Lovin' Me" and "Early Morning Rain," and introduced Lightfoot to their manager, Albert Grossman, who promptly gave both songs to his other clients Peter, Paul and Mary. The trio made "For Lovin' Me" a #30 U.S. hit in 1965.

On his own, Lightfoot began releasing solo albums in 1966, the first six on United Artists. Each sold between 150,000 and 200,000 copies. In 1969 he switched to Reprise, and his label debut, *Sit Down Young Stranger,* sold 750,000 copies with the help of his first U.S. hit, "If You Could Read My Mind" (#5, 1971). Many other artists, including Bob Dylan, Jerry Lee Lewis, Johnny Cash, Elvis Presley, Barbra Streisand, and Judy Collins, continued to cover his songs.

Lightfoot's popularity peaked in the mid-Seventies with a #1 gold LP, *Sundown,* and its #1 title track in 1974. He hit #2 with "The Wreck of the Edmund Fitzgerald" (about an ore vessel that sank on Lake Superior), released on the *Summertime Dream* LP in May 1976. Although he didn't release a new album between 1986 and 1993, Lightfoot tours regularly and still commands a loyal following, particularly in his native Canada.

Lindisfarne

Formed 1969, Newcastle-upon-Tyne, England
Alan Hull (b. Feb. 20, 1945, Newcastle-upon-Tyne), gtr., voc.; **Rod Clements (b. Nov. 17, 1947, North Shields, Eng.),** bass, violin; **Ray Jackson (b. Dec. 12, 1948, Wallsend, Eng.),** harp, mandolin; **Simon Cowe (b. Apr. 1, 1948, Tynemouth, Eng.),** gtr.; **Ray Laidlaw (b. May 28, 1948, North Shields, Eng.),** drums.
1970—*Nicely Out of Tune* (Elektra)   **1971**—*Fog on the Tyne*   **1972**—*Dingly Dell*   **1973**—(– Clements; – Cowe; – Laidlaw; + Kenny Craddock, voc., gtr., kybds.; + Charlie Harcourt, voc., gtr.; + Tommy Duffy, voc., bass; + Paul Nichols, drums) *Lindisfarne Live* (Charisma); *Roll On, Ruby* (Elektra)   **1974**—*Happy Daze*   **1975**—*Finest Hour* (Charisma) (group disbands)   **1978**—(Original lineup re-forms) *Back*

and Fourth (Atco); *Magic in the Air* (Mercury, U.K.)
1979—*The News.*

Lindisfarne's pop folk rock was popular in England during the early Seventies, peaking in 1972 with its Top Ten U.K. album *Fog on the Tyne.* The band goes back to the mid-Sixties, when various members were playing in local Newcastle groups, including Rod Clements and Ray Laidlaw in the Downtown Faction Blues Band. All the future Lindisfarne members, except Hull, worked together as Brethren in summer 1969. With the departure of guitarist Jeff Sandler later that year, the group switched to quieter folk pop, especially after taking on folksinger/songwriter Alan Hull, who became co–lead writer with Clements in spring 1970. The band was briefly known as Alan Hull and Brethren before choosing Lindisfarne (after a small island off the Northumberland coast).

Though its debut album, *Nicely Out of Tune,* was released in the U.S., most interest was in Europe. The big British breakthrough was *Fog on the Tyne,* which was produced by Bob Johnston (who'd previously worked with Bob Dylan) and yielded the lushly melodic #5 U.K. hit "Meet Me on the Corner" (1972). Around this time, Jackson played mandolin on Rod Stewart's *Every Picture Tells a Story.* Another single, "Lady Eleanor," hit #3 in England but only #82 in the U.S., and soon the band was having trouble in the U.K. as well. *Dingly Dell* was a critical and commercial disappointment, and in 1973 Clements, Cowe, and Laidlaw left to form Jack the Lad. (Clements left Jack shortly after its mid-1974 debut.)

Hull and Jackson kept the band name, and the group became a sextet with the inclusion of Kenny Craddock (who in 1968 played with Yes drummer Alan White in Happy Magazine, and later played with Ginger Baker's Air Force and Mark-Almond) and Charlie Harcourt (formerly with Cat Mother and the All Night News Boys). Both *Roll On, Ruby* and *Happy Daze* were flops. Hull had released his first solo record, *Pipedream; Squire* came out around the time the band broke up in 1975.

The original lineup resurfaced in October 1978 with *Back and Fourth* and had its first relatively successful U.S. single, "Run for Home" (#33 U.S., #10 U.K.), but their following here never expanded. The group released several subsequent albums in England, and in 1990 had a #2 U.K. hit with a remake of "Fog on the Tyne."

David Lindley: See Kaleidoscope

Arto Lindsay: See DNA

Lipps, Inc.

Formed 1977, Minneapolis, Minnesota
Steven Greenberg (b. Oct. 24, 1950, St. Paul, Minn.),

kybds., synth., bass, drums, perc., voc.; Cynthia Johnson (b. Apr. 6, 1956, St. Paul, Minn.), voc.; David Rivkin, gtr.; Tom Riopelle, gtr.; Terry Grant, bass; Ivan Rafowitz, kybds.
1980—*Mouth to Mouth* (Casablanca); *Pucker Up.*

Lipps, Inc. (pronounced "lip-sync"), burst out of Minnesota's Twin Cities in 1980, the same year Prince began his ascent to superstardom with *Dirty Mind.* Where Prince launched a career by bridging rock, pop, and funk to form the Minneapolis Sound, Lipps, Inc., had only one big hit—the instant classic "Funkytown" (#1 pop, #2 R&B, 1980), an extended dance track that seamlessly melded percolating synth pop (complete with electronic vocals), slashing funk guitar, disco strings, and the gospelish vocals of Cynthia Johnson, over a relentless big beat.

A studio-bound unit, Lipps, Inc. was the brainchild of composer, producer, and multi-instrumentalist Steven Greenberg. Johnson had been Minnesota's Miss Black U.S.A. contestant in 1976. Aside from "Funkytown," *Mouth to Mouth* (#5, 1980) also produced a minor hit in "Rock It" (#64 pop, #85 R&B, 1980). The prompt followup album, *Pucker Up* (#63, 1980), yielded only "How Long" (#29 R&B, 1980). Lipps, Inc., scored minor hits with the subsequent singles "Hold Me Down" (#70 R&B, 1981) and "Addicted to the Night" (#78, 1983), then disbanded. Greenberg was not heard from again; Johnson kept working on the Minneapolis music scene, and as of the early Nineties was leading an all-female funk band, Kat Klub. Guitarist David Rivkin would go on to become one of Prince's sound engineers, as "David Z"; his brother Bobby was Prince's first drummer.

Mance Lipscomb
Born April 9, 1895, Navasota, Texas; died January 30, 1976, Navasota
1960—*Mance Lipscomb, Texas Sharecropper and Songster* (Arhoolie) 1964—*Mance Lipscomb, Texas Songster, vol. 2* 1966—*Mance Lipscomb, Texas Songster, vol. 3* 1968—*Mance Lipscomb, Texas Songster, vol. 4* 1970—*Mance Lipscomb, Texas Songster, vol. 5; Trouble in Mind* (Reprise).

Discovered during the early-Sixties folk-blues boom, singer, guitarist, and fiddler Mance Lipscomb is generally considered a Texas country blues great, an artistic descendant of Blind Lemon Jefferson and compatriot of Lightnin' Hopkins. Actually, though, Lipscomb was a bluesman and more: a songster and minstrel who performed ballads, reels, shouts, and breakdowns as well as blues. Though he didn't record until age 65, his influence has been noted in the work of Bob Dylan, Janis Joplin, and the Grateful Dead, among others.

Lipscomb learned to play fiddle from his father, an

emancipated slave turned professional musician, and played with him around the Navasota-Brazos area until 1911. Between shows Lipscomb taught himself guitar and worked the fields. Before 1956 he played only for small gatherings of friends and coworkers at picnics or dances. He moved to Houston in 1956, and in 1960 was discovered by Chris Strachwitz, a folk-music archivist and founder of Arhoolie Records, who brought tapes of his music to various members of the folk-blues community. Lipscomb played several folk festivals, and was recorded by Arhoolie. He continued recording and performing until 1974, when heart disease forced him to retire. He died in 1976 at age 80. Lipscomb also appeared in several documentary films: *The Blues* (1962), Les Blank's *The Blues Accordin' to Lightnin' Hopkins* (1969) and *A Well Spent Life* (1971), *Blues Like Showers of Rain* (1970), and *Out of the Blacks into the Blues* (1972).

Lisa Lisa and Cult Jam
Formed 1984, New York City, New York
Lisa Lisa (b. Lisa Velez, Jan. 15, 1967, New York City), voc.; Spanador (b. Alex Mosely, 1962, New York City), gtr.; Mike Hughes (b. 1963, New York City), drums.
1985—*Lisa Lisa & Cult Jam with Full Force* (Columbia) 1987—*Spanish Fly* 1989—*Straight to the Sky* 1991—*Straight Outta Hell's Kitchen.*
Lisa Lisa solo: 1994—*LL77* (Pendulum/ERG).

Lisa Lisa and Cult Jam come from the same New York dance-music scene that produced Madonna, but their Latin roots are authentic rather than appropriated. Lisa Velez grew up in New York City's Hell's Kitchen, the youngest of ten children. She began singing in church at age nine, and in high school was involved in musical theater. She met percussionist Mike Hughes in 1983 at the Fun House, a downtown New York club where Velez hung out because she heard Madonna was discovered there.

Hughes and Spanador had been working with the Brooklyn group and production team Full Force, which was looking for a female singer with a girlish voice for a song they had written. Taking the name Lisa Lisa, patterned after Full Force's U.T.F.O. hit "Roxanne, Roxanne," the singer and her new band and producers scored an underground dance smash with "I Wonder If I Take You Home" (#34 pop, #6 R&B, 1985). The song was first released on the 1984 *Breakdancing* compilation, then as a single in 1985. Their platinum debut album, *Lisa Lisa & Cult Jam with Full Force* (#52, 1985), featured the hit and a number of other dance tracks, including "All Cried Out" (#8 pop, #3 R&B, 1986).

Featuring a larger variety of sounds, including dance, funk, salsa, and doo-wop, the platinum *Spanish Fly* (#7, 1987) was an even bigger hit, yielding the singles "Head

Grammy Awards

Patti LaBelle
1991 Best R&B Vocal Performance, Female: *Burnin'*

Ladysmith Black Mambazo
1987 Best Traditional Folk Recording: *Shaka Zulu*

k. d. lang
1988 Best Country Vocal Collaboration: "Crying" (with Roy Orbison)
1989 Best Country Vocal Performance, Female: *Absolute Torch and Twang*
1992 Best Pop Vocal Performance, Female: "Constant Craving"

Daniel Lanois
1987 Album of the Year: *The Joshua Tree* (with Brian Eno and U2)
1992 Producer of the Year (with Brian Eno) (tie with L.A. Reid and Babyface)

L.A. Reid and Babyface
1992 Best R&B Song: "End of the Road" (with Daryl Simmons)
1992 Producer(s) of the Year (tie with Brian Eno and Daniel Lanois)
1994 Best Male R&B Vocal Performance: "When Can I See You"
1994 Best R&B Song: "I'll Make Love to You"

Cyndi Lauper
1984 Best New Artist

Peggy Lee
1969 Best Contemporary Vocal Performance, Female: "Is That All There Is?"

John Lennon [See also: the Beatles]
1966 Song of the Year: "Michelle" (with Paul McCartney)
1970 Best Original Score Written for a Motion Picture or TV Special: *Let It Be* (with George Harrison, Paul McCartney, and Ringo Starr)
1981 Album of the Year: *Double Fantasy* (with Yoko Ono)
1991 Lifetime Achievement Award

Yoko Ono
1981 Album of the Year: *Double Fantasy* (with John Lennon)

Huey Lewis and the News
1985 Best Music Video, Long Form: *Huey Lewis and the News: The Heart of Rock 'n' Roll* (with Bruce Gowers)

Jerry Lee Lewis
1986 Best Spoken Word or Nonmusical Recording: *Interviews from "the Class of '55" Recording Sessions* (with others)

Ramsey Lewis
1965 Best Instrumental Jazz Performance, Small Group or Soloist with Small Group: "The 'In' Crowd"
1966 Best R&B Group, Vocal or Instrumental: "Hold It Right There"
1973 Best R&B Instrumental Performance: "Hang On, Sloopy"

Living Colour
1989 Best Hard Rock Performance: "Cult of Personality"
1990 Best Hard Rock Performance: *Time's Up*

L.L. Cool J
1991 Best Rap Solo Performance: "Mama Said Knock You Out"

Kenny Loggins
1979 Song of the Year: "What a Fool Believes" (with Michael McDonald)
1980 Best Pop Performance, Male: "This Is It"

Los Lobos
1983 Best Mexican/American Performance: "Anselma"
1989 Best Mexican/American Performance: *La Pistola y El Corazón*

Lyle Lovett
1989 Best Country Vocal Performance, Male: *Lyle Lovett and His Large Band*
1994 Best Country Performance by a Duo or Group with Vocal: "Blues for Dixie" (with Asleep at the Wheel)
1994 Best Pop Vocal Collaboration: "Funny How Time Slips Away" (with Al Green)

Loretta Lynn
1971 Best Country Vocal Performance by a Group: "After the Fire Is Gone" (with Conway Twitty)

---

to Toe" (#1 pop, #1 R&B, 1987), "Lost in Emotion" (#1 pop, #1 R&B, 1987), "Someone to Love Me for Me" (#7 R&B, 1987), and "Everything Will B-Fine" (#9 R&B, 1988). Lisa Lisa and Cult Jam opened for David Bowie that year and toured the world as a headlining act.

The group's success began to stall with their third album, *Straight to the Sky,* which featured only the minor hit "Little Jackie Wants to Be a Star" (#29, 1989). Lisa Lisa, Cult Jam, and Full Force tried to recapture their dance/pop success by bringing in C+C Music Factory's David Cole and Robert Clivillés to produce one side of *Straight Outta Hell's Kitchen;* until then, Full Force had been the band's sole producers, songwriters, arrangers, and managers. But the album's one hit, "Let the Beat Hit 'Em" (#37 pop, #1 R&B, 1991), failed to cross over in a big way to the pop audience.

Velez subsequently parted ways with her band, producers/managers, and label. In December 1993 Pendulum/ERG released Lisa Lisa's solo debut, "Skip to My Lu" (#38 R&B); an album, *LL77,* followed in January 1994.

Velez has used her fame to try to be a positive role model for urban youth. She has participated in campaigns to increase AIDS awareness and to fight illiteracy, drug abuse, and teen suicide.

Little Anthony and the Imperials

Formed 1957, New York City, New York
Anthony Gourdine (b. Jerome Anthony Gourdine, Jan. 8, 1940, New York City), lead voc.; Ernest Wright Jr. (b. Aug. 24, 1941, Brooklyn, N.Y.), second tenor voc.; Clarence Collins (b. Mar. 17, 1941, Brooklyn, N.Y.), baritone voc.; Tracy Lord, first tenor voc.; Glouster "Nate" Rogers, bass voc.
1961—(– Lord; – Rogers; + Sammy Strain [b. Samual Strain, Dec. 9, 1941], first tenor voc.; – Gourdine; + George Kerr, lead voc.)   1963—(Group reunites: Gourdine; Strain; Wright; Collins)   1964—I'm on the Outside Lookin' In (DCP)   1965—Goin' Out of My Head (Veep)   Early 1970s—(– Wright; + Kenny Seymour, voc.)   1974—(– Seymour; + Bobby Wade, voc.) On a New Street (Avco)   1989—Best of Little Anthony and the Imperials (Rhino)   1992—(Group re-forms: Gourdine; Strain; Collins; Wright). Little Anthony solo: 1980—Daylight (MCA/Songbird).

Little Anthony and the Imperials are considered one of the best late-Fifties doo-wop groups. Their first and biggest hit was the million-selling "Tears on My Pillow" (#4, 1958). Lead singer Anthony Gourdine began his career with the Duponts, a band of Brooklyn singers who cut two singles in 1955 on the Winley and Royal Roost labels. He then formed the Chesters, who cut one song under that name in 1957 on Apollo and then were renamed the Imperials by their new label, End. The Little Anthony moniker for the then five-foot-four (he is now five-feet-ten) singer was added by Alan Freed and first turned up on later pressings of "Tears on My Pillow." The group had another hit in 1960, "Shimmy, Shimmy, Ko-ko Bop" (#24), then broke up. Little Anthony was idle until 1964, when the group re-formed minus Lord and Rogers, adding Sammy Strain. This lineup had more consistent chart success on DCP Records with "Goin' Out of My Head" (#6, 1964) (written by Teddy Randazzo, formerly of the Three Chuckles), "Hurt So Bad" (#9, 1965), and "Take Me Back" (#16, 1965).

After that the Imperials had no more major chart action but continued recording on Veep from 1966 to 1968, on United Artists (1969 to 1970), and on Avco in 1974, which yielded the #25 soul hit "I'm Falling in Love with You." Little Anthony played solo on the Las Vegas circuit in the early Seventies and, after a slow period later in the decade, became a born-again Christian. He signed a solo deal in 1980 with MCA/Songbird and released Daylight, produced by B. J. Thomas. Gourdine spent much of the Eighties and early Nineties playing supperclubs as well. Strain later joined the O'Jays, and the remaining Imperials, with a few lineup changes, continued to tour as well.

In 1992 Gourdine, Wright, Collins, and Strain reunited for a Madison Square Garden oldies show. What was supposed to have been a one-time event grew into a permanent re-formation (which Strain left the O'Jays to participate in) that officially began on Valentine's Day 1993. They continue to perform.

Little Eva

Born Eva Narcissus Boyd, June 29, 1945, Bell Haven, North Carolina
1962—Lllloco-Motion (Dimension)   1988—The Best of Little Eva (Murray Hill)   1989—Back on Track (Malibu).

Perhaps no baby-sitter in history ever got a bigger break than Eva Boyd, who, the story goes, at age 17 was baby-sitting for songwriters Carole King and Gerry Goffin. They asked her to record a tune they'd just written called "The Loco-Motion." The song borrowed its arrangement from the Marvelettes' "Please Mr. Postman." With the Cookies ("Chains") as backup singers, plus the powerhouse voice of the newly named Little Eva, the record went #1 on the pop and R&B charts in 1962. Eva had another danceable followup with "Keep Your Hands Off My Baby" (#12 pop, #6 R&B, 1962), and in 1963 she scored a Top Twenty with "Let's Turkey Trot" (#20 pop, #16 R&B), all recorded for Dimension. Eva also recorded "Swingin' on a Star" (#38, 1963), a duet with Big Dee Irwin, formerly of the Pastels.

Eva's sister Idalia also recorded with the label, earning only one minor hit, "Hoola Hooping." Eva cut a few more records for other labels, including Spring and Amy, but never re-created her original overnight success. Disenchanted with the music business, she retired in the early Seventies, but in the Nineties began performing live again on the oldies circuit.

Little Feat

Formed 1969, Los Angeles, California
Lowell George (b. 1945; d. June 29, 1979, Arlington, Va.), voc., gtr., slide gtr., harmonica; Bill Payne (b. March 12, 1949, Waco, Tex.), kybds., voc.; Richard Hayward, drums; Roy Estrada, bass, voc.
1971—Little Feat (Warner Bros.)   1972—Sailin' Shoes (– Estrada; + Kenny Gradney [b. New Orleans, La.], bass; + Paul Barrere [b. July 3, 1948, Burbank, Calif.], gtr., voc.; + Sam Clayton, congas) 1973—Dixie Chicken   1974—Feats Don't Fail Me Now   1975—The Last Record Album   1977—Time Loves a Hero   1978—Waiting for Columbus 1979—Down on the Farm (– George) (group

disbands) 1981—*Hoy-Hoy!* 1988—(Group reforms: Barrere; Payne; Hayward; Clayton; Gradney; + Craig Fuller, voc., gtr.; + Fred Tackett, gtr., trumpet) *Let It Roll* 1990—*Representing the Mambo* 1991—*Shake Me Up* (Morgan Creek) 1994—(– Fuller; + Shaun Murphy, voc.) 1995—*Ain't Had Enough Fun* (Zoo).
Lowell George solo: 1979—*Thanks I'll Eat It Here* (Warner Bros.).
Paul Barrere solo: 1983—*On My Own Two Feet* (Atlantic).

Little Feat mixed every strain of Southern music—blues, country, gospel, rockabilly, boogie, New Orleans R&B, and Memphis funk—with surreal lyrics and a sense of absurdity and professionalism that could only have come from Southern California. Despite this, Little Feat had two gold albums; the live *Waiting for Columbus* went platinum. And Little Feat enjoyed a strong cult following and became one of California's most influential bands of the Seventies.

The band was formed by Lowell George and Roy Estrada, both former Mothers of Invention; Richie Hayward, ex–Fraternity of Man (of "Don't Bogart That Joint" on the *Easy Rider* soundtrack); and classically trained pianist Bill Payne. George's bluesy vocals and slide guitar dominated the sound of the band, and his playful songwriting set its tone; although he could write conventional country-rock songs like "Willin'" (which appeared on the first two Feat albums and has been covered by Linda Ronstadt, Commander Cody, and others), he reveled in wordplay and non sequiturs. As a child, George appeared on TV's *Ted Mack's Original Amateur Hour,* playing a harmonica duet with his brother Hampton; he played flute in the Hollywood High School orchestra and, later, oboe and baritone saxophone on Frank Sinatra recording sessions. In 1965 he started a folk-rock group, the Factory, which Hayward joined after answering an ad. The Factory recorded for Uni Records. When it broke up, George became rhythm guitarist in Frank Zappa's Mothers of Invention and was with a short-lived Standells reunion before starting Little Feat.

After "Easy to Slip" from *Sailin' Shoes* failed to hit, Little Feat went through one of its many breakups, and the first (before its 1988 re-formation) to result in personnel changes. Estrada went into computer programming, though he briefly rejoined Zappa a few years later. He was replaced by two New Orleans musicians, Kenny Gradney and Sam Clayton, along with guitarist Paul Barrere.

The Little Feat of *Dixie Chicken* was slightly less raucous and more funky; the group toured with New Orleans songwriter Allen Toussaint, whose "On Your Way Down" appeared on *Dixie Chicken.* For the rest of the decade, Little Feat established itself as a touring band,

particularly on the East Coast and in the South. The group also became a mainstay of the Los Angeles music community; Payne, especially, did a lot of session work. The band kept an erratic recording schedule, partly because it was frequently breaking up, and partly because George, who had become Feat's producer, had trouble making final decisions; song titles and lyrics would often appear on album covers but not on the LPs themselves.

Beginning with *The Last Record Album,* Barrere and Payne (usually as collaborators) began to take on a larger share of the songwriting, moving the band toward jazz rock. George produced an album by the Grateful Dead (*Shakedown Street*) and announced periodically that he was working on a solo album. When *Thanks I'll Eat It Here* (originally the projected title of *Sailin' Shoes*) finally appeared in 1979, George announced Little Feat's breakup and went on tour with his own band; in the middle of the tour, he died, apparently of a heart attack. Little Feat finished *Down on the Farm* and disbanded; *Hoy-Hoy!* compiled live tracks and alternative takes.

After George's death, Hayward toured with Joan Armatrading and recorded and toured with Robert Plant. Payne returned to studio work and occasional tours, including one with James Taylor. In 1983 Barrere released a solo album and toured with his own band.

Barrere, Payne, Hayward, Gradney, and Clayton reformed Little Feat in 1988, with guitarists Fred Tackett (an L.A. sessionman who'd appeared on some earlier Feat albums) and Craig Fuller (formerly with country-rock band Pure Prairie League). *Let It Roll* (#36, 1988) went gold, *Representing the Mambo* (#45, 1990) didn't, and *Shake Me Up* reached only #126.

Little Milton

Born Milton Campbell, September 7, 1934, Inverness, Mississippi
1969—*Grits Ain't Groceries* (Checker) 1972—*Little Milton Greatest Hits* (Chess); *Walking the Back Streets* (Stax) 1974—*Golden Decade* (Phonogram); *Blues 'n' Soul* (Stax); *Montreux Festival; Tin Pan Alley* 1976—*Blues Masters* (Chess) 1983—*Age Ain't Nothin' but a Number* (MCA) 1984—*Playing for Keeps* (Malaco) 1985—*I Will Survive* 1986—*Annie Mae's Cafe* 1987—*Movin' to the Country* 1988—*Back to Back* 1990—*Too Much Pain* 1991—*Reality* 1992—*Strugglin' Lady* 1994—*I'm a Gambler.*

Veteran blues singer/guitarist Little Milton took up guitar at age 12 and at 15 left home to play with Eddie Kusick, Rice Miller (Sonny Boy Williamson), and Willie Love. In 1953 he was signed to Sun Records, where he recorded with Ike Turner (later of Ike and Tina fame). Milton soon moved on to other labels, including Meteor in 1957 and St. Louis' Bobbin, which he cofounded, in 1958.

His single "I'm a Lonely Man" caught the attention of Leonard Chess, who signed him to Checker in 1961. There he had his first real success with "So Mean to Me" (#14 R&B, 1962). In 1965 he went all the way to #1 R&B with "We're Gonna Make It," a #25 pop hit. His gospel-soulful vocals were reminiscent of Bobby Bland, yet still distinctive, earning him another top hit that year with "Who's Cheating Who" (#4 R&B, #43 pop). Some of his Checker hits were arranged by Donny Hathaway. In 1967 he had a #7 R&B hit with "Feel So Bad."

Milton had many other Checker hits (five R&B Top Twenties in 1969) before going to Memphis in 1971 to sign with Stax. He enjoyed R&B hits with that label as well, including "That's What Love Will Make You Do" (#9, 1972), and released one of his best-known singles, "Walkin' the Back Streets and Cryin'." He also performed in the 1973 film *Wattstax*.

After leaving Stax in 1976, Milton produced LPs for the Glades label in Miami and continued to tour. He experienced a career resurgence after signing to Malaco in 1984. He tours most of the year with his group, Little Milton and His Revue.

Little Richard

Born Richard Wayne Penniman, December 5, 1932, Macon, Georgia
1959—*His Biggest Hits* (Specialty); *Little Richard's Grooviest 17 Original Hits*   1965—*King of Gospel Songs* (Mercury); *Little Richard's Greatest Hits Recorded Live* (Okeh)   1975—*The Very Best of Little Richard* (United Artists)   1985—*18 Greatest Hits* (Rhino)   1990—*The Specialty Sessions* (Specialty)   1991—*The Georgia Peach*   1992—*Shake It All About* (Walt Disney).

Pounding the piano and howling lyrics in a wild falsetto, Little Richard—the so-called Quasar of Rock— became a seminal figure in the birth of rock & roll. His no-holds-barred style, mascara-coated eyelashes, and high—almost effeminate—pompadour were exotic and in many ways embodied the new music's gleeful sexuality and spirit of rebellion. In his own way—and as he is wont to exclaim to anyone in earshot—he was a king of rock & roll.

One of 12 children, Penniman grew up in a devout Seventh Day Adventist family; his two uncles and a grandfather were preachers, though his father sold bootleg whiskey. The young Penniman sang gospel and learned piano at a local church. But his parents never encouraged his musical interests, and at age 13 Penniman was ejected from their house. (In a 1982 televised interview, he claimed it was because of his homosexuality.) He moved in with a white family, Ann and Johnny Johnson, who ran Macon's Tick Tock Club. There Richard first performed.

Little Richard

In 1951 Penniman won a contract with RCA after playing at an Atlanta radio audition. His recordings during the next two years were fairly conventional jump blues, like "Every Hour" and "Get Rich Quick," neither of which made any commercial impression. In 1952 he moved to Houston, where he recorded for Don Robey's Peacock label. Initially he recorded with the backup groups the Deuces of Rhythm and the Tempo Toppers, though in 1955 he switched to fronting the Johnny Otis orchestra for four sides. He toured small black nightclubs, performing mostly blues; his rock numbers were not well received.

Down on his luck, he sent a demo tape to Art Rupe of Specialty Records in L.A., who, as luck would have it, had been looking for a hard-edged voice like Penniman's to front some New Orleans musicians. Rupe signed on "Bumps" Blackwell as the producer and, with a Crescent City rhythm section, Little Richard entered the studio on September 14, 1955. One of the songs he cut was an old between-songs filler piece called "Tutti Frutti" (with lyrics cleaned up by New Orleans writer Dorothy La Bostrie). Richard's whooping, shouting vocals, sexy-dumb lyrics, and wild piano banging on "Tutti Frutti" set the style for his future hits. The single sold to both black and white fans—over three million copies by 1968—and its influence was incalculable. Out of Richard's approximately 36 sides for Specialty, seven were gold: "Tutti Frutti" (#17), "Long Tall Sally" (#6), "Rip It Up" (#17) in 1956; "Lucille" (#21), "Jenny, Jenny" (#10), and "Keep a Knockin'" (#8) in 1957; and "Good Golly, Miss Molly" (#10, 1958). Penniman also appeared in three early rock & roll movies: *Don't Knock the Rock, The Girl Can't Help It* (both 1956), and *Mister Rock 'n' Roll* (1957).

But in 1957, at the height of his success, Little Richard suddenly quit his rock career after a tour of Australia. He claimed that a vision of the apocalypse came to him in a dream, and that he saw his own damnation. In his authorized biography he tells a story of a plane flight during which the overheated engines appeared in the darkness of night to be on fire. He prayed to God and promised that if the plane landed safely he would change his ways. A few days later while performing outdoors he caught a glimpse of the Russian satellite *Sputnik,* and days after that, a plane he was scheduled to have flown in crashed. Interpreting these incidents as divine signs that he should change his ways, Richard entered Oakwood College in Huntsville, Alabama, where he received a B.A. and was ordained a minister in the Seventh Day Adventist Church. Specialty tried to keep his conversion a secret, issuing the hit "Keep a Knockin'," pieced together from half-finished sessions.

Little Richard did not return to rock until 1964. After a failed attempt to gain a major audience on the evangelical circuit with his gospel recordings, he tried to resurrect his rock following with the anachronistic and unsuccessful "Bama Lama Bama Loo" on Specialty in 1964. The world was already switching its attention to the newer sounds of the Beatles. (Ironically, Little Richard was one of Paul McCartney's idols.) Through the years, Little Richard mounted many unsuccessful comeback attempts on Vee Jay, Modern, Okeh, and Brunswick.

His best shot came in the early Seventies, when he got a contract with Reprise and recorded three R&B/rock LPs—*The Rill Thing, King of Rock 'n' Roll,* and *Second Coming*—which garnered some fair critical notices and led to some recording sessions with Delaney and Bonnie and Canned Heat. He also performed at the Toronto Pop Festival, coverage of which is included in D. A. Pennebaker's documentary of the event, *Keep On Rockin'* (a.k.a. *Toronto Pop, 1970*) (1972). Richard did some late-night talk shows and club dates during the early Seventies, but by the decade's close he was again stressing his attachment to the church, preaching and singing gospel, and renouncing rock & roll, drugs, and his own homosexuality (he has alluded to having reformed to heterosexuality).

Nineteen-eighty-four saw the publication of *The Life and Times of Little Richard,* an authorized biography by Charles White. Incredibly frank, the book got plenty of attention for its juicy anecdotes (including a threesome with a stripper and Buddy Holly, and a mid-Seventies bout with drug addiction) and guilt-ridden accounts of his battle to tame his sexuality. "Homosexuality is contagious," he is quoted as saying. "It's not something you're born with." The book ends with a chapter-long sermon from Richard. He shares the copyright with Charles White and his longtime manager Robert "Bumps" Blackwell.

But one can never count Little Richard out of the spotlight for long, and in 1985 he launched a formidable comeback with a featured role in the hit *Down and Out in Beverly Hills.* He made guest appearances on such popular television series as *Miami Vice, Martin,* and *Full House* and has been a pitchman in commercials for a number of companies, including Taco Bell, McDonald's, and Charlie perfume. He contributed backing vocals to the U2–B. B. King hit "When Love Comes to Town," and duetted with Elton John on the latter's *Duets* and with Tanya Tucker on *Rhythm, Country & Blues* ("Somethin' Else").

In a development that surely would surprise his first-generation fans, Little Richard has had his greatest latterday recording success with a new generation: their grandchildren. After recording a rock-rap version of "Itsy Bitsy Spider" for the all-star Pediatric AIDS Foundation benefit album *For Our Children,* Richard recorded *Shake It All About.* It included children's standards, such as "On Top of Old Smokey," and his own "Keep a Knockin'" (complete with him yelling "Shut up!" to his background chorus of kids). He also appears on *Kermit Unpigged* (1994) and in Shelley Duvall's award-winning children's video, *Mother Goose Rock 'n' Rhyme.*

Little Richard was among the first ten inductees into the Rock and Roll Hall of Fame in 1986. In 1993 he received a Lifetime Achievement Award from the National Academy of Recordings Arts and Sciences. He performed at Bill Clinton's presidential inaugural in 1993. In his hometown of Macon he has been honored with a street bearing his name, Little Richard Penniman Boulevard.

Little River Band

Formed 1975, Melbourne, Australia
Beeb Birtles (b. Holland), gtr.; Graham Goble (b. 1944, Austral.), gtr.; Glenn Shorrock (b. Eng.), lead voc.; Roger McLachlan (b. New Zealand), bass; Derek Pellicci (b. Eng.), drums; Rick Formosa (b. Italy), gtr.
1975—*Little River Band* (Harvest) 1976—*After Hours* 1977—(– Formosa; – McLachlan; + David Briggs, gtr., voc.; + George McArdale, bass) *Diamantina Cocktail* 1978—*Sleeper Catcher* 1979—*First Under the Wire* (– McArdale) 1980—*Backstage Pass* (+ Wayne Nelson, voc., bass) 1981—*Time Exposure* 1982—(– Briggs; + Steve Housden, gtr.) 1982—(– Shorrock; + John Farnham [b. Eng.], voc.) 1983—*The Net* 1985—(– Pellicci; + Steven Prestwich, drums; + David Hirschfelder, kybds.) *Playing to Win* 1986—*No Reins* 1988—(– Farnham; – Hirschfelder; – Prestwich; + Shorrock; + Pellicci) 1988—*Monsoon* (MCA) 1990—*Get Lucky* (MCA/Curb) 1991—*Worldwide Love* (Curb) 1994—*Reminiscing—the 20th Anniversary Collection* (Rhino) (+ Peter Beckett, gtr.; + Tony Sciuto, gtr.).

Australia's Little River Band has enjoyed numerous hits in America with its vocal-harmony country pop. The band began in 1975 from the ashes of a CSN&Y-type group called Mississippi. Though LRB formed in Australia, only Graham Goble was born there. Glenn Shorrock, born in England, moved to Australia as a teenager and was part of one of the country's most successful Sixties teenybop bands, the Twilights (their big local competition was the Easybeats). At the same time, Beeb Birtles played in the successful Aussie band Zoot, which used to dress entirely in pink. Rick Formosa was invited to join the Edgar Winter band at 16, but his parents made him turn down the offer.

In 1972 Shorrock moved back to England, joined the classical-rock band Espranto, and later did studio sessions with Cliff Richard. There, in 1975, he met Birtles, Goble, and Pellicci, who'd just broken up Mississippi. The four agreed to form a new band (taking their name from a road sign) back in Melbourne, eventually with McLachlan (bass) and Formosa (guitar). They signed with Capitol and in 1976 released their eponymous debut, which included the #28 U.S. hit "It's a Long Way There." Before the first U.S. tour that same year, Formosa and McLachlan left.

The band's next American record was a "best of" from two Australian LPs. Titled *Diamantina Cocktail,* it included the breakthrough hit "Help Is On Its Way" (#14, 1977). LRB also scored big with "Reminiscing" (#3, 1978) and "Lady" (#10, 1979). In late 1979 "Lonesome Loser" (#6, 1979) and "Cool Change" (#10, 1979) drove the fifth U.S. LP, *First Under the Wire,* platinum. McArdale left after a 1979 U.S. tour, gave away all his money, and moved into Australia's Blue Mountains for a three-year Bible study course.

In 1980 the band released a double live album, then added American bassist Wayne Nelson. The band scored another Top Ten single in 1981 with "Take It Easy on Me" from *Time Exposure,* produced by George Martin. Other hits from that album were "Night Owls" (#6) and "Man on Your Mind" (#14).

Briggs left, then Shorrock pursued a solo career. John Farnham, a singer from Adelaide, replaced Shorrock, and numerous personnel changes followed. Farnham left for a very successful solo career in Australia, then Shorrock returned. Working again with Boylan, they recorded their first MCA LP, *Monsoon.* As of 1995 three of their LPs are platinum and two others gold.

Little Walter

Born Marion Walter Jacobs, May 1, 1930, Marksville, Louisiana; died February 15, 1968, Chicago, Illinois
1963—*The Best of Little Walter* (Chess)   1969— *Hate to See You Go*   1972—*Blues Boss Harmonica* 1974—*Confessin' the Blues*   1986—*Blues World of Little Walter* (Delmark)   1990—*The Best of Little Walter, vol. 2* (Chess)   1993—*The Essential Little Walter.*

Whether or not Little Walter was actually the first person to amplify the harmonica, as has been claimed, he was a pioneer in using the microphone to bring out the moaning, echoing, and hornlike sounds that are basic to modern blues harmonica. Walter Jacobs began playing the harmonica as a child in the South, and he attracted the attention of Muddy Waters, with whom he often recorded and toured in the late Fifties. When the blues scene centralized in Chicago and went electric in the Fifties, with Waters as one of its stars, Walter moved North. He joined Waters' band and started releasing his own records. The instrumental "Juke" was a #1 R&B hit in 1952, one of the biggest hits of any Delta-Chicago bluesman.

Throughout the Fifties Little Walter placed records in the R&B Top Ten: "Sad Hours," "Blues with a Feeling," "Mean Old World," "You Better Watch Yourself," "You're So Fine," "Key to the Highway," and his other #1 record, "My Babe." He toured with the Aces, formerly Junior Wells' band, breaking out of the blues circuit to play Harlem's Apollo and other large venues. And though he never made the pop chart, his reputation and influence were widespread, especially in England, where a generation of harmonica players learned from his records and from his disciple Cyril Davies. Walter, who possessed a volcanic temper and a fondness for drink, died from head injuries suffered in a Chicago streetfight.

Living Colour

Formed 1983, Brooklyn, New York
William Calhoun (b. July 22, 1964, Brooklyn), drums; Corey Glover (b. Nov. 6, 1964, Brooklyn), voc.; Vernon Reid (b. Aug. 22, 1958, London, Eng.), gtr.; Muzz Skillings (b. Manuel Skillings, Jan. 6, 1960, Queens, N.Y.), bass.
1988—*Vivid* (Epic)   1990—*Time's Up*   1992— (– Skillings; + Doug Wimbish [b. Sep. 22, 1956, Hartford, Conn.], bass)   1991—*Biscuits* EP   1993— *Stain.*

A black band playing rock, Living Colour used the platform of rock stardom to advocate a political agenda of self-reliance and self-knowledge. As spearheads of New York's Black Rock Coalition, they put their philosophy into action, advancing the cause of other African-American rock bands. Their energetic, rhythmically complex, and harmonically sophisticated music—which draws equally from Jimi Hendrix, Led Zeppelin, and post–*Bitches Brew* Miles Davis—was accessible enough to yield charting singles, including "Cult of Personality" (#13, 1989) and "Glamour Boys" (#31, 1989).

Vernon Reid had already gained fame as a guitarist in Ronald Shannon Jackson's Decoding Society and De-funkt before he formed Living Colour in 1983 (the group's name is taken from the old NBC preprogram announce-

Living Colour: Doug Wimbish, Vernon Reid, Corey Glover, William Calhoun

ment, "The following program is brought to you in . . ."). Originally a side project with a revolving cast of musicians, the lineup solidified in 1985 when Corey Glover, who met Reid in 1982, rejoined the band after acting in *Platoon*. Black Rock Coalition events brought Reid in contact with Berklee College of Music graduate Calhoun and Skillings, who had played with Harry Belafonte.

Mick Jagger heard Living Colour at CBGB in 1987 and offered to finance a demo. The two songs he produced, "Which Way to America?" and "Glamour Boys," helped garner the band a contract with Epic, and appeared, remixed, on their debut, *Vivid* (#6, 1988). While critically lauded, the album languished until the video for "Cult" appeared on MTV. The politically charged single became a gold record and earned the group an MTV Video Music Award for Best New Artist.

The band opened for the Stones on 1989's Steel Wheels Tour, and Reid played on Keith Richards' *Talk Is Cheap*. This activity did not detract from Living Colour. *Time's Up* (#13, 1990), which includes guests Little Richard, Mick Jagger, and Queen Latifah, received an even better critical reception than their debut, and, like *Vivid*, won the Best Hard Rock Performance Grammy.

Tensions began to rise in 1991. With no new album forthcoming, Epic released *Biscuits* (#110, 1991), an EP of outtakes, live performances, and covers. Reid and Glover played in a side project, Nightshade, and in early 1992 Skillings left the band. He was replaced by Sugarhill ses-

sion bassist and George Clinton veteran Doug Wimbish. The new band coproduced *Stain* (#26, 1993), which focused less on political issues and more on interpersonal relationships in such songs as "Bi" and "Mind Your Own Business." In early 1995 the band announced it had broken up.

L. L. Cool J

Born James Todd Smith, August 16, 1968, Queens, New York
1985—*Radio* (Def Jam/Columbia)   1987—*Bigger and Deffer*   1989—*Walking with a Panther*   1990—*Mama Said Knock You Out*   1993—*14 Shots to the Dome*.

Ever since he had his first hit single at age 16, L. L. Cool J has been one of rap's brightest artists, propelled both by his willingness to stay street and his desire to be a pop icon. L. L.'s parents divorced when he was four, and he was raised by his grandparents in Queens. He began rapping when he was nine; his grandfather bought him a DJ system when he was 11. He made tapes in his basement, which he sent to record companies, including Def Jam, then being formed by Rick Rubin and Russell Simmons. In 1984 "I Need a Beat" became Def Jam's first release; it sold 100,000 copies, and L. L. dropped out of high school.

Radio (#6 R&B, 1985) was the first Def Jam album. The platinum disc was considered groundbreaking for L. L.'s arrangement of raps into song structures, with verses and choruses. The album included the anthem "I Can't Live Without My Radio" (#15 R&B, 1985), which L. L. performed during his cameo in the movie *Krush Groove*. *Bigger and Deffer* (#3, 1987), produced by L. L. and the L.A. Posse, lived up to its title, going double platinum with the singles "I Need Love" (#14 pop, #1 R&B, 1987) and "I'm Bad" (#4 R&B, 1987). The former, a ballad, clinched L. L.'s image as a heartthrob. His name stands for Ladies Love Cool James; *Playgirl* magazine named him one of the ten sexiest men in rock.

In 1988 L. L. had a minor hit with "Going Back to Cali" (#31 pop, #12 R&B) from the *Less than Zero* soundtrack. He headlined a Def Jam tour and played a Just Say No Foundation antidrug concert at Radio City Music Hall. Some rap fans felt L. L. sold out on *Walking with a Panther* (#6 pop, #1 R&B, 1989), which yielded the single "I'm That Type of Guy" (#15 pop, #7 R&B, 1989). He was booed at an Apollo show; L. L. himself has said he was out of touch with the rap constituency at that time.

He came back swinging with the Grammy-winning *Mama Said Knock You Out* (#16 pop, #2 R&B, 1990), a tough, compelling album coproduced with Marley Marl that is L. L.'s biggest-selling record to date. L. L.'s comeback was kicked off by "The Boomin' System" (#48 pop, #6 R&B, 1990), followed by "Around the Way Girl" (#9,

1990) and "Mama Said Knock You Out" (#17 pop, #12 R&B, 1991). In May 1991 he was the first rap artist to perform on MTV's *Unplugged* (with M.C. Lyte and De La Soul appearing as well). On *14 Shots to the Dome* (#5 pop, #1 R&B, 1993), L. L. seemed confused about his strategy again; he stuck with the past by working with Marl but tried to update his credibility with some gangsta poses. None of the album's four singles made it into the Top Twenty.

Aiming for an impact outside the rap world, L. L. appeared in the films *The Hard Way* (1991) and *Toys* (1992) and performed at the 1993 presidential inauguration. In addition, concerned with children's welfare, he taped a radio commercial for a "Stay in School" literacy campaign and founded Youth Enterprises, a program for urban youth, for whom he plans to eventually establish Camp Cool J.

Richard Lloyd: See Television

Nils Lofgren

Born 1952, Chicago, Illinois
With Grin: 1971—*Grin* (Spindizzy)   1972—*1 + 1*; *All Out*   1973—*Gone Crazy* (A&M)   1985—*Best of Grin* (Epic).
Nils Lofgren solo: 1975—*Nils Lofgren* (A&M) 1976—*Cry Tough*   1977—*I Came to Dance*; *Night After Night*   1979—*Nils*   1981—*Night Fades Away* (Backstreet)   1983—*Wonderland*   1985—*Flip* (Columbia); *The Best of Nils Lofgren* (A&M)   1989— *Classics Volume 13*   1991—*Silver Lining* (Rykodisc) 1992—*Crooked Line*.

Pop-rock singer, songwriter, and guitarist Nils Lofgren was the leader of Grin and later led his own bands before joining Bruce Springsteen's E Street Band in the Eighties. Lofgren moved with his parents to Maryland, near Washington, D.C., as a child, and there he began playing accordion at age five and studied jazz and classical music before turning to rock at 15. He formed Grin in 1969 with bassist Bob Gordon and drummer Bob Berberich (later adding younger brother Tom on second guitar). The group's local reputation attracted Neil Young and Danny Whitten of Crazy Horse, whom Nils met while they were touring through Maryland. At age 17 Lofgren played piano and sang on Young's 1970 LP *After the Gold Rush*, and the next year he did a guest spot on Crazy Horse's debut LP, to which he also contributed two songs.

Instead of staying with Young or Crazy Horse, Lofgren used the credits to help him get a record contract for Grin. The trio signed to Spindizzy (a Columbia subsidiary), and its 1971 debut was critically praised for its tuneful ballads and tight melodic rockers, as was the fol-

lowup, *1 + 1,* which included "White Lies." The single never passed #75, though, and Grin's tours failed to attract large audiences. In 1973 Young again asked Lofgren to take time out from Grin to join him for the *Tonight's the Night* Tour. Lofgren agreed and later played on the 1975 album of the same name. In 1973 Grin signed with A&M, but *Gone Crazy* was not well received. That and the group's financial problems caused it to disband in mid-1974. Later that year, when Mick Taylor left the Stones, Lofgren was briefly rumored as a replacement.

Lofgren signed with A&M and debuted in 1975 with the acclaimed *Nils Lofgren*. In 1976 he followed it with *Cry Tough,* produced by Al Kooper. He began to build a following, largely on the strength of live shows, captured on a promotional-only live LP entitled *Back It Up!!* and later on a less-well-received double live set, *Night After Night. Nils* included three songs Lofgren had cowritten with Lou Reed. (A different three written by the two appear on Reed's *The Bells* LP.) In 1980 Lofgren signed with Backstreet Records, which issued *Night Fades Away.*

After joining Neil Young for his 1983 *Trans* Tour, Lofgren replaced Little Steven Van Zandt in Bruce Springsteen's E Street Band in 1984, staying until Springsteen stopped working with that group in 1991. Springsteen made a guest appearance on Lofgren's *Silver Lining* (#153, 1991), which was recorded for the tiny independent Towebell label, and picked up for distribution by a bigger indie, Rykodisc.

Kenny Loggins

Born January 7, 1948, Everett, Washington
1977—*Celebrate Me Home* (Columbia)   1978— *Nightwatch*   1979—*Keep the Fire*   1980—*Alive* 1982—*High Adventure*   1985—*Vox Humana* 1988—*Back to Avalon*   1991—*Leap of Faith* 1993—*Outside: From the Redwoods*   1994—*Return to Pooh Corner*.

Singer/songwriter Kenny Loggins has been successful both as half of the duo Loggins and Messina and later as a solo artist. He began playing guitar while in the seventh grade of a parochial school in California. His father was a traveling salesman, and the family had lived in Detroit and Seattle before settling in Alhambra, California. In college Loggins joined a folk group, but by the late Sixties he had turned to rock, first in Gator Creek, which recorded for Mercury, and then in Second Helping, on Viva Records. In 1969 he left Second Helping and worked for $100 a week as a songwriter for ABC Records' publishing outlet, Wingate Music. Around this time, he toured with the remnants of the Electric Prunes.

Back in Los Angeles Loggins met Jim Ibbotson of the Nitty Gritty Dirt Band. Ibbotson and the band decided to record four of Loggins' songs on its *Uncle Charlie and His Dog Teddy*; one of them, "House at Pooh Corner," was a minor hit. In 1970 Don Ellis, an A&R staffer at Columbia (who was also a close family friend), introduced Loggins to Jim Messina, who was looking for acts to produce. Clive Davis signed Loggins to the label, and the singer spent the year working up material with Messina, leading to their informal joint debut. Their union wound up lasting five years, yielding seven successful albums before the split in late 1976. [see entry].

By 1977 Loggins had released his solo debut, the platinum *Celebrate Me Home*. His solo music continued in the same pop-rock style as Loggins and Messina's, and it netted him tremendous success on his second LP, 1978's *Nightwatch*, which also sold over one million copies and included the #5 single "Whenever I Call You 'Friend'" (cowritten with Melissa Manchester and featuring a vocal by Stevie Nicks). Loggins' equally successful *Keep the Fire* boasted "This Is It" (#11, 1979). Loggins cowrote the Doobie Brothers' 1979 hit "What a Fool Believes."

He had a hit in 1980 with "I'm Alright" (#7), the theme song from the movie comedy *Caddyshack*. More hits from other films followed through the Eighties: "Footloose" (#1, 1984) and "I'm Free (Heaven Help the Man)" (#22, 1984), from *Footloose*; "Danger Zone" (#2, 1986), from *Top Gun*; "Meet Me Halfway" (#11, 1987), from *Over the Top*; and "Nobody's Fool" (#8, 1988), from *Caddyshack II*. For 1991's gold *Leap of Faith* and *Return to Pooh Corner*, the singer/songwriter drew heavily on his personal life; the former addressed his divorce from his wife Eva, while the latter contained songs and lullabies he'd sung to his four children.

Loggins and Messina

Kenny Loggins, born January 7, 1948, Everett, Washington; Jim Messina, born December 5, 1947, Maywood, California
1972—*Sittin' In* (Columbia); *Loggins and Messina*
1973—*Full Sail*   1974—*On Stage*; *Motherlode*
1975—*So Fine*   1976—*Native Sons*; *The Best of Friends*   1977—*Finale*   1980—*Best of Loggins and Messina*.
Kenny Loggins solo: See entry.
Jim Messina solo: 1979—*Oasis* (Columbia)   1981—*Messina* (Warner Bros.)

The highly successful Loggins and Messina partnership began by accident. Ex–Poco and Buffalo Springfield guitarist Jim Messina agreed to produce Kenny Loggins' solo album, but during the recording sessions the two discovered their styles complemented each another and decided to form a band, which scored a string of country-pop hits.

Messina was raised in Harlingen, Texas, and began

playing guitar at age five. He was 12 when his parents moved back to California. After graduating high school in 1965, Messina began doing studio work at Harmony Recorders Audio Sound, Wally Heider, and Sunset Sound, where in late 1967 he met the Buffalo Springfield while that group was recording its second LP, *Buffalo Springfield Again*. He wound up producing and playing bass on the group's final LP, *Last Time Around*, and then formed Poco with fellow ex-Springfield Richie Furay. After two years and three albums, he left Poco in November 1970 to become an independent producer for Columbia; his first project was to be Kenny Loggins.

Their live debut at the Troubadour in Los Angeles was billed as the Kenny Loggins Band with Jim Messina. On Loggins and Messina's 1972 debut album, Messina was billed as *Sittin' In*. The debut album took a slow climb up the chart but eventually went platinum, aided by one of its tunes, "Danny's Song," which became a Top Ten hit for Anne Murray. It also included the light Caribbean-pop FM radio favorite "Vahevala."

The duo's second LP was its first equal billing and gave Loggins and Messina the hit singles "Your Mama Don't Dance" (#4, 1972) and "Thinking of You" (#18, 1973). The album went platinum, as did the followup, *Full Sail*. Although generally dismissed by critics, Loggins and Messina continued to sell more gold and platinum records. Their reworking of Fifties hits, *So Fine*, sold disappointingly, and even though their final and seventh LP, *Native Sons*, went gold, they broke up in November 1976. A best-of (*The Best of Friends*) and a second live LP (*Finale*) were released after the split. Loggins, who went on to a hugely popular solo career [see entry], claims his and Messina's partnership was an informal union (each was contracted separately to Columbia), and they always thought each LP would be their last together. Messina's solo efforts met with far less acclaim that did his ex-partner's. In 1989 he rejoined Poco for the successful reunion album *Legacy*.

Jackie Lomax

Born May 10, 1944, Liverpool, England
1969—*Is This What You Want?* (Apple)   1971—*Home Is in My Head* (Warner Bros.)   1972—*Three*   1976—*Livin' for Lovin'* (Capitol)   1977—*Did You Ever Have That Feeling?*

Jackie Lomax is a well-traveled British singer. He began playing blues-tinged rock at age 16, and his second group, the Undertakers, played Hamburg at the same time as the Beatles. Lomax signed with Beatles manager Brian Epstein, who formed a new band around him called the Lomax Alliance. After Epstein died, Lomax became the first to sign with the Beatles' Apple Records. A single, "Sour Milk Sea," written and produced by George Harrison, was released in 1968, and *Is This What You*

Want? was produced by Harrison and featured Eric Clapton, Ringo Starr, and Paul McCartney.

Because Apple's business accounts were not complete, no one knows how the album sold, although some say as many as 50,000 copies. After playing a short while with the band Heavy Jelly (which got started by planting a fake review in a London magazine for a show it had never done), Lomax, disillusioned with life in England, moved to Woodstock, New York, in 1970.

After two more solo albums, *Home Is in My Head* and *Three*, Lomax returned to England in 1974 and joined Badger—previously a semiprogressive band headed by ex-Yes keyboardist Tony Kaye. Allen Toussaint produced one disappointing album, *White Lady*, and then, after a disastrous London debut, the band broke up. Lomax moved to Los Angeles, where he eventually got another solo contract with Capitol in 1975. His first LP for the label, *Livin' for Lovin'*, came out in late 1975. A 1977 followup, *Did You Ever Have That Feeling?*, also failed to click, and he lost his contract. He continues to perform as of the 1990s.

Lone Justice

Formed 1983, Los Angeles, California
Maria McKee (b. Aug. 17, 1964, Los Angeles), voc., gtr.; Ryan Hedgecock (b. Feb. 27, 1961, Los Angeles), gtr., voc.; Marvin Etzioni (b. Apr. 18, 1956, New York City, N.Y.), bass, voc.; Don Heffington (b. Dec. 20, 1950, Los Angeles), drums.
1985—*Lone Justice* (Geffen) 1986—(– Etzioni; – Heffington; + Shayne Fontayne, gtr.; + Gregg Sutton, bass; + Rudy Richman, drums; + Bruce Brody [b. Dec. 11, 1950], kybds.) *Shelter* (– Hedgecock).
Maria McKee solo: 1989—*Maria McKee* (Geffen) 1993—*You Gotta Sin to Get Saved*.
Marvin Etzioni solo: 1992—*The Mandolin Man* (Restless) 1993—*Bone*.
Ryan Hedgecock solo: 1992—*Echo Park* (Yellow Moon, U.K.).

An exponent of Los Angeles' thriving early-Eighties club scene, Lone Justice won critical kudos—and the admiration of some of rock's biggest names—with its self-titled 1985 debut album. Produced by Jimmy Iovine, the songs on *Lone Justice* folded country and gospel inflections into spirited, rootsy rock arrangements. Singer Maria McKee's mighty soprano is texturally evocative of such greats as Aretha Franklin, Janis Joplin, and Dolly Parton, and her authoritative delivery inspired comparisons to other rock and soul luminaries—among them Springsteen and Bob Dylan, who were both Lone Justice fans. So were Tom Petty, who lent the group a song for its first album, and U2, whose 1985 tour featured Lone Justice as an opening act.

The band was formed by McKee and Hedgecock, who initially began performing as an acoustic duo. Once the rhythm section was added, the band went electric, began attracting attention on the L.A. club circuit, and signed a deal with Geffen. Though *Lone Justice* garnered raves, it proved a commercial disappointment. Dissension grew within the band, particularly after Iovine, who had become the group's manager, downplayed the other members' contributions in favor of McKee's. By the second album, 1986's *Shelter*, there was an all-new lineup, save for McKee and, on acoustic guitar, Hedgecock, who left soon after the LP's release. The title ballad almost hit the Top Forty (#47), but by then the band had thrown in the towel.

McKee continued working with keyboardist Bruce Brody and released an eponymous solo debut in 1989, on which Brody, Robbie Robertson, Richard Thompson, and Marc Ribot participated as musicians and/or songwriters. (Most of the album's songs were written or cowritten by McKee, who had contributed or collaborated on a fair amount of Lone Justice's material.) For her second album, McKee reunited with Lone Justice's original rhythm section and enlisted Jayhawks guitarists/vocalists Mark Olson and Gary Louris.

As for the other members of Lone Justice, Etzioni released a pair of solo albums; Hedgecock recorded the LP *Echo Park* for a British label and formed Parlour James with Amy Allison (the daughter of Mose Allison), and Heffington contributed drums to recordings by the Jayhawks, Victoria Williams, and Tammy Rogers. Fontayne joined Springsteen's band in 1992.

Long Ryders

Formed 1982, Los Angeles, California
Sid Griffin (b. Sep. 18, 1955, Louisville, Ky.), gtr. and other stringed instruments, voc.; Stephen McCarthy (b. Feb. 12, 1958, Richmond, Va.), gtr., voc.; Greg Sowders (b. Mar. 17, 1960, La Jolla, Calif.), drums; Tom Stevens (b. Sept. 17, 1956, Elkhart, Ind.), bass.
1983—*10-5-60* EP (PVC) 1984—*Native Sons* (Frontier) 1985—*State of Our Union* (Island) 1987—*Two Fisted Tales* 1989—*Metallic B.O.* cassette (Long Ryders Fan Club).

Blending punk attitude with late-Sixties country-rock instrumentation, the Long Ryders were principal exponents of the mid-Eighties L.A. underground pop style known as cowpunk. Leader Sid Griffin left his native Kentucky for Los Angeles after reading about punk rock in a magazine. Inspired by his hero, the late Gram Parsons, he also wound up rediscovering the country music of his youth. In 1982 he formed Long Ryders with fellow displaced Southerner Stephen McCarthy. After a disappointing first EP, the band released the well-received *Native Sons* (featuring guest vocals by ex-Byrd Gene Clark). Long Ryders' Island output sold poorly and received lukewarm critical response. Unhappy with the way the label had promoted them, the band members called it quits after 1987's *Two Fisted Tales*.

Griffin, who relocated to London, eventually formed another country-rock band, the Coal Porters. McCarthy, moving back to his native Richmond, Virginia, teamed up with ex-members of the Silos, Dream Syndicate, and House of Freaks and formed the off-the-cuff outfit Gutterball, which released two albums. Both Griffin and McCarthy contributed to a Gram Parsons tribute album, *Conmemorativo*, released in 1993 on Rhino; nearly a decade earlier, Griffin authored *Gram Parsons: A Musical Biography*, published by a small press in 1985.

Loose Ends

Formed circa 1981, London, England
Carl McIntosh, bass, gtr., voc.; Jane Eugene, voc.;
Steve Nichol, trumpet, kybds.
1984—*A Little Spice* (Virgin, U.K.) 1985—*So Where Are You* 1986—*Zagora* 1988—*The Real Chuckeeboo* (MCA) 1990—(– Eugene; – Nichol; + Linda Carriere, voc.; + Sunay Suleyman, kybds.) *Look How Long*.

During its heyday in the latter half of the Eighties, the British trio Loose Ends enjoyed success in two separate capacities: first, as a pop-funk outfit whose catchy output did well on the American R&B charts; then as songwriter/producers and remixers for other R&B acts. Trumpeter and keyboardist Steve Nichol was already a working studio musician, with the Jam's album *The Gift* among his credits, when he met singer Jane Eugene at the Guildhall School of Music and Drama. The two hooked up with Carl McIntosh, a session bassist who also sang and played guitar, to complete Loose Ends' lineup, and were signed by Virgin Records' U.K. division in the early Eighties. (Their recordings would be distributed in the U.S. by MCA.)

After becoming a fixture on England's funk scene with a couple of danceable singles, the band released its debut album, *A Little Spice* (#46 U.K., 1984), in 1984; the album reached #46 in the States upon release the following year. Also in 1985, Loose Ends hit the top of the R&B singles chart with "Hangin' on a String (Contemplating)," a track featured on its second LP, *So Where Are You* (#13 U.K.). Over the next few years, the group continued making albums and scored R&B smashes like "Slow Down" (#1, 1986) and "Watching You" (#2, 1988). Meanwhile, its members wrote and produced material for pop-soul artists like Juliet Roberts, Five Star, and Cheryl Lynn, and also worked as remixers. In 1990 a new incarnation of Loose Ends, in which Eugene and Nichol were replaced by Linda Carriere and Sunay Suleyman, released the #10 R&B single "Don't Be a Fool," followed by the LP *Look How Long* (#124 pop, #28 R&B). The album generated a moderate R&B hit, "Cheap Talk" (#28, 1991).

Lords of the New Church: See the Dead Boys

Los Bravos

Formed 1965, Spain
Michael Kogel (b. Apr. 25, 1945, Berlin, Ger.), lead voc., gtr.; Manuel Fernandez (b. Sep. 29, 1943, Seville, Spain), kybds.; Miguel Vicens Danus (b. June 21, 1944, Palma de Mallorca, Spain), bass; Pablo Sanllehi, a.k.a. Pablo Gomez (b. Nov. 5, 1943, Barcelona, Spain), drums; Antonio Martinez (b. Oct. 3, 1945, Madrid, Spain), gtr.
1966—*Black Is Black* (Press).

Los Bravos became the first Spanish rock band to have an international hit single when "Black Is Black" reached #4 in 1966. A combination of local bands Mike and the Runaways (which had several hits in Spain during the early Sixties) and Los Sonor, they were signed to British Decca after Decca's Spanish representative sent one of the group's singles to producer Ivor Raymonde. Though Los Bravos never matched the sales of "Black Is Black," "Going Nowhere" and "Bring a Little Lovin'" were minor successes in 1966 and 1968 respectively, and "I Don't Care" climbed to #16 on the British chart in 1966. By the end of the decade their popularity was confined to Spain. In 1972 Kogel had a minor hit single, "Louisiana," under the name Mike Kennedy.

Los Lobos

Formed 1973, East Los Angeles, California
Cesar Rosas (b. Sep. 26, 1954, Los Angeles), gtr., voc.; David Hidalgo (b. Oct. 6, 1954, Los Angeles), voc., gtr., accordion, violin, banjo, piano, perc.; Luis "Louie" Perez (b. Jan. 29, 1953, Los Angeles), drums, voc., gtr., perc.; Conrad R. Lozano (b. Mar. 21, 1951, Los Angeles), bass, guitarron, voc.
1978—*Los Lobos del Este de Los Angeles: Just Another Band from East L.A.* (New Vista) 1983—*. . . And a Time to Dance* EP (Slash) 1984—(+ Steve Berlin [b. Sep. 14, 1955, Philadelphia, Pa.], sax, flute, kybds., harmonica, melodica) *How Will the Wolf Survive?* 1987—*La Bamba* soundtrack; *By the Light of the Moon* 1988—*La Pistola y El Corazón* 1990—*The Neighborhood* 1992—*Kiko* 1993—*Just Another Band from East L.A.: A Collection*.

For two decades Los Lobos have been exploring the artistic and commercial possibilities of American biculturalism, moving back and forth between their Chicano roots and their love of American rock. Although the band first gained fame as part of the early-Eighties roots-rock revival, they don't so much strip music down as mix it up, playing norteño, blues, country, Tex-Mex, ballads, folk, and rock.

Los Lobos: David Hidalgo, Louie Perez, Steve Berlin,
Conrad Lozano, Cesar Rosas

Cesar Rosas, Conrad Lozano, David Hidalgo, and
Louie Perez have known one another since they were
adolescents in East Los Angeles. They formed Los Lobos
(Spanish for "the Wolves") to play weddings and bars in
their neighborhood. Although they had previously
played in rock and Top Forty bands, together, they decided to experiment with acoustic folk instruments and
explore their Mexican heritage, playing norteño and conjunto music on instruments including the guitarrón and
bajo sexto. Los Lobos got their first full-time gig in 1978,
playing at a Mexican restaurant in Orange County. That
year they also released their debut album, *Just Another
Band from East L.A.*

Eventually, Los Lobos' experimentation led them
back to electric instruments. They played one of their
last acoustic shows opening for Public Image Ltd. at the
Olympic Auditorium in L.A. in 1980, where they were
booed by the audience. Nonetheless inspired by punk's
energy, Hidalgo and Perez began writing songs and
playing Hollywood clubs. The Blasters became fans and
urged Slash to sign Los Lobos.

. . . *And a Time to Dance* was produced by T Bone
Burnett and Blasters saxman Steve Berlin. Its divergent
collection of dance songs included the 70-year-old Mexican Revolution song "Anselma," which won a Grammy
in 1983 for best Mexican/American Performance. Berlin
joined Los Lobos for *Will the Wolf Survive?*, a much-
praised album whose title track later became a country
hit for Waylon Jennings. On *By the Light of the Moon*,
coproduced by Burnett, Los Lobos wrote political songs
about life in the barrio.

In 1987 Los Lobos recorded several Ritchie Valens
songs for the *La Bamba* soundtrack (#1, 1987). Though
the success of the title track (#1, 1987) and "Come On,
Let's Go" (#21, 1987) suddenly lifted Los Lobos out of
their bar band, critics' fave status, they took a noncom-

mercial detour with *La Pistola y El Corazón,* featuring
the traditional Mexican music they had played throughout the Seventies.

On *The Neighborhood,* they returned to more rocking material, working with John Hiatt, the Band's Levon
Helm, and drummer Jim Keltner. The album's title paid
homage to the deep connections the band still feels to
East L.A. In 1991 Hidalgo and Perez wrote songs with
the Band for that group's reunion album. The material inspired *Kiko,* an evocative, avant-Latin pop album produced by Mitchell Froom. In 1993 Slash released a
20-year anniversary retrospective of Los Lobos songs;
Just Another Band from East L.A.: A Collection includes
material from the band's debut LP, rare B sides, and live
tracks, as well as the band's hits.

Los Lobos have been guests on albums by Ry
Cooder, Elvis Costello, Fabulous Thunderbirds, Roomful
of Blues, and Paul Simon. Their music has been used in
the films *Eating Raoul, The Mambo Kings, Alamo Bay,*
and *Chan Is Missing.*

John D. Loudermilk
**Born March 31, 1934, Durham, North Carolina
1966—*John D. Loudermilk Sings a Bizarre Collection of the Most Unusual Songs* (RCA)   1967—*Suburban Attitudes*   1968—*Country Love Songs*
1969—*The Open Mind of John Loudermilk*   1971—
Volume 1—Elloree (Warner Bros.)   1973—*Best of
John D. Loudermilk* (RCA)   1975—*Encores*   1978—
Just Passing Through (A&M).**

Though he's made recordings of his own, John D. Loudermilk is generally known as the writer of "Tobacco Road"
and hits for George Hamilton IV, Eddie Cochran, Paul Revere and the Raiders, Anne Murray, and many others.

Growing up in Durham, Loudermilk first played a
multitude of instruments with a Salvation Army band.
When he was 13, he already had his own local radio
show (under the name Johnny Dee). His big break came
a few years later when, while working as a staff musician
for local TV station WTVD, he performed his own "A Rose
and a Baby Ruth" on the air. It was heard by a freshman
at the University of North Carolina, George Hamilton IV,
who recorded it and sold a million copies. (Hamilton also
had a Top Ten country hit with Loudermilk's "Abilene" in
1963.) In 1957 Loudermilk's "Sittin' in the Balcony" became the first hit for Eddie Cochran (#18; Loudermilk's
version, recorded as Johnny Dee, hit #38 the same
month), and in 1959 a song he wrote with Marijohm
Wilkin, "Waterloo," became a million-seller for Stonewall
Jackson. Under the name Johnny Dee, he released
"Three Stars," a tribute to Ritchie Valens, Buddy Holly,
and the Big Bopper.

Most of Loudermilk's songs had a country feel, but
he also had a solid rock and pop sense, as in his "Indian

Reservation," a #1 hit for Paul Revere and the Raiders in 1971. Among his many songwriting credits are the Everly Brothers' "Ebony Eyes" and Sue Thompson's "Sad Movies (Make Me Cry)." Two more of his songs, "Break My Mind" and "Bad News," became standards. Loudermilk himself recorded with only minor success for RC in the early Sixties and for Warner Bros. in the Seventies. More recently he has been studying ethnomusicology.

Lounge Lizards

Formed 1979, New York City, New York
John Lurie (b. Dec. 14, 1952, Minneapolis, Minn.),
sax; Evan Lurie (b. Sep. 28, 1954), piano; Arto Lind-
say (b. May 28, 1953, Richmond, Va.), gtr.; Anton
Fier (b. June 20, 1956, Cleveland, Ohio), drums;
Steve Piccolo, bass.
1981—*The Lounge Lizards* (EG)   1983—(– Lindsay;
– Piccolo; – Fier; + Peter Zummo, trombone; + Tony
Garnier, bass; + Doug E. Bowne, drums) *Lounge*
***Lizards—Live at the Drunken Boat* (Europa)**
1984—(– Zummo; – Garnier; + Roy Nathanson, sax;
+ Curtis Fowlkes, trombone; + Marc Ribot, gtr.,
trumpet; + Erik Sanko [b. Sep. 27, 1963, New York
City], bass)   1985—*Live 79/81 ROIR Sessions* cas-
sette (ROIR)   1986—*Live in Tokyo—Big Heart* (Is-
land)   1987—(+ E. J. Rodriguez, perc.) *No Pain for*
***Cakes*   1989— *Voice of Chunk* (Lagarto)   1991—**
(– Evan Lurie; – Nathanson; – Fowlkes; – Ribot;
– Rodriguez; – Sanko; – Bowne; + Michael Blake
[b. Montreal, Can.], sax; + Steven Bernstein [b. Oct.
8, 1961, Washington, D.C.], trumpet, cornet; + Jane
Scarpantoni [b. Oct. 4, 1960, Nyack, N.Y.], cello;
+ Bryan Carrott, vibes, marimba, tympani;
+ Michele Navazio [b. Mar. 10, 1960, Elgin, Ill.], gtr.;
+ Billy Martin [b. Oct. 3, 1963, New York City], perc.;
+ Oren Bloedow, bass; + G. Calvin Weston [b. June
6, 1959, Philadelphia, Pa.], drums) *Lounge Lizards—*
Berlin 1991 Part 1* (Verabra, Ger.)   1992—*Lounge
***Lizards—Live in Berlin 1991, Vol. II*   1993—(– Car-**
rott; – Bloedow; + Sanko; + Dave Tronzo [b. Dec. 13,
1957, Rochester, N.Y.], slide gtr.; + Danny Blume,
gtr.; + John Medeski, piano, organ).
With Teo Macero and London Philharmonic Orches-
tra: 1984—*Fusion* (Europa).
John Lurie solo: 1986—*Stranger Than Paradise/The*
***Resurrection of Albert Ayler* (Enigma)   1987—**
***Down by Law/Variety* (Intuition/Capitol)   1989—**
***Mystery Train* (RCA).**
John Lurie National Orchestra: 1993—*Men with*
***Sticks* (Crammed Disc).**
Evan Lurie solo: 1990—*Selling Water by the Side of*
***the River* (Island).**

The Lounge Lizards became a hip Downtown New York band in the Eighties by playing "fake jazz," music based more on the feel of jazz than the structures. The group started as a one-time gig playing songs John Lurie had written for a movie. Their punk-lounge act went over big, though, and the Lizards have taken themselves and their music increasingly seriously over the years.

The initial band, featuring brothers John and Evan Lurie, noise guitarist Arto Lindsay, former Feelies drummer Anton Fier, and bassist Steve Piccolo, was half a rock band. That lineup played on the Lizards' debut and the ROIR live cassette released in 1985, with guitarists Dana Vlcek and Danny Rosen playing on some tracks on the latter. Lindsay and Fier left, to form Ambitious Lovers and Golden Palominos respectively, and the Lizards replaced them with more conventional jazz players. The group became popular in Europe, where it recorded several live albums and where several of its albums were released before American labels caught on.

Island signed the Lizards in 1986. Lurie's vocals were featured for the first time on *No Pain for Cakes*. After two albums, Lurie became frustrated with the record company and released *Voice of Chunk* on his own label, via mail order, with ads placed in magazines and on TV. The venture lost money, and that lineup of the group broke up soon after. Lurie re-formed the Lizards for more tours and the Berlin live albums. The Lounge Lizards continued to be popular in New York and Europe into the mid-Nineties.

John Lurie has also been a successful artist outside the Lizards. He performed solo at Carnegie Hall in 1980 and in 1982 was a featured soloist with the Quebec Symphony Orchestra. In 1991 he composed string quartets for the Kronos Quartet and in 1992 composed and performed a string quartet for the Balanescu Quartet. In 1991/92 he toured Europe with the John Lurie National Orchestra. He has composed and recorded several soundtracks for filmmaker Jim Jarmusch, including *Stranger Than Paradise* (the album includes a composition for the Albert Ayler dance company), *Down by Law* (the soundtrack is backed with *Variety,* the score for a Bette Gordon film), and *Mystery Train*; other Lounge Lizards also played on these albums. In addition, Lurie acted in *Stranger Than Paradise*; *Down by Law*; *Wild at Heart*; *Paris, Texas*; and *The Last Temptation of Christ.* From 1990 to 1992 he created a pilot for a cable television series, *Fishing with John,* on which he took guests to unique fishing spots—for example, taking Tom Waits to Jamaica and Dennis Hopper to Thailand.

Evan Lurie released solo albums in Belgium in 1985 and 1989. On *Selling Water by the Side of the River* he is joined by a violinist and a bandoneon player.

Darlene Love

Born Darlene Wright, July 26, 1938, Los Angeles,
California
1984—*Live* (Rhino)   1988—*Paint Another Picture*

(Columbia)   1992—*The Best of Darlene Love* (Abkco); *Bringing It Home* (with Lani Groves) (Shanachie).

As one of Phil Spector's hand-picked early-Sixties girl-group singers, Darlene Love sang some lead vocals with the Crystals and Bob B. Soxx and the Blue Jeans, and also had hits under her own name.

Darlene Wright started singing in 1958 with an L.A. vocal group called the Blossoms. (Her sister Edna later sang with the Honey Cone [see entry], which hit big in 1971 with the #1 "Want Ads.") The Blossoms recorded without success as a foursome for Capitol Records between 1958 and 1960, and then as a trio for Challenge and Okeh. They also did backup singing on the L.A. session circuit, supporting Bobby "Boris" Pickett ("Monster Mash"), James Darren ("Goodbye Cruel World"), Bobby Day ("Rockin' Robin"), and many others.

When Love came to Spector's attention, he had her and the Blossoms sing "He's a Rebel," which went to #1 in 1962. The producer had originally intended the Gene Pitney composition for the Crystals, and in fact put *their* name on the record, though they didn't sing a note. Love also sang lead on "He's Sure the Boy I Love" (#11, 1963), also falsely credited to the Crystals, and in the short-lived vocal trio Bob B. Soxx and the Blue Jeans, who had a hit with "Zip-A-Dee Doo-Dah" (#8 pop, #7 R&B, 1963) from the Walt Disney movie *Song of the South.* All of these recordings were on Spector's Philles label.

Love went on to record six Philles singles under her own name, including "Wait till My Bobby Gets Home" (#26, 1963), "(Today I Met) The Boy I'm Gonna Marry" (#39, 1963), and "A Fine Fine Boy" (#53, 1963). She also appears on Phil Spector's classic Christmas album. Love continued to sing with the Blossoms throughout the Sixties. They were regulars on *Shindig* and toured with Elvis Presley in the early Seventies. Love then sang backup for Dionne Warwick for ten years, beginning in 1971.

In the Eighties the singer branched out into acting, appearing in the *Lethal Weapon* films and the Broadway show *Leader of the Pack.* She also recorded two solo albums. Long respected as one of the top vocalists in pop music, Love finally received long-overdue recognition in 1993, when a show based on her career, *Portrait of a Singer,* opened in January at New York City's Bottom Line club. Love performed weekly in the long-running show.

Monie Love

Born Simone Johnson, July 2, 1970, London, England
1990—*Down to Earth* (Warner Bros.)   1993—*In a Word or 2.*

Born in England but partially raised in Brooklyn, rapper Monie Love has bridged musical and geographical gaps with help from influential friends the world over. She began rapping at 14, when she set her poems to music. Love had her first success in London's dance clubs with her second single, "Grandpa's Party," a tribute to Afrika Bambaataa. In 1988 she met stateside Bambaataa boosters the Jungle Brothers, becoming their European road manager. (She raps on their second album.) Later that year she came to New York and joined the Native Tongues group of rappers, whose ranks include De La Soul and Queen Latifah.

Love first came to fame in the U.S. rapping with Latifah on "Ladies First," the track from Latifah's debut album that heralded a new wave of "womanist" hip-hop artists. She also guested on the single "Buddy" from De La Soul's groundbreaking *3 Feet High and Rising.* Her own albums have fused rap with house music, to somewhat mixed results. Three tracks on *Down to Earth,* including the singles "It's a Shame (My Sister)" (#26 pop, #8 R&B, 1991), a remake of the Spinners' 1970 hit, and "Monie in the Middle," were produced by the Fine Young Cannibals' Andy Cox and David Steele, while the Jungle Brothers' Afrika Baby Bambaataa produced six songs. The album reflected the positive political consciousness and psychedelic sense of humor of the Native Tongues school.

In between albums, Love had her first baby, and the featured cut off 1993's *In a Word or 2* (#75 R&B) was "Born 2 B.R.E.E.D." (#56 R&B). It and one other track were produced by Prince. The album challenged the conservative "family values" agenda articulated the previous year by Vice President Dan Quayle and offered words of encouragement to young blacks. The track "Bullets Carry No Names" was cowritten by Ice-T.

Love/Arthur Lee

Formed 1965, Los Angeles, California
Arthur Lee (b. 1945, Memphis, Tenn.), gtr., voc.; Bryan MacLean (b. 1947, Los Angeles), gtr., voc.; John Echols (b. 1945, Memphis, Tenn.), lead gtr.; Ken Forssi (b. 1943, Cleveland, Ohio), bass; Don Conka, drums.
1965—(– Conka; + Alban "Snoopy" Pfisterer [b. 1947, Switz.], drums)   1966—*Love* (Elektra) (+ Michael Stuart, drums; + Tjay Cantrelli, horns; Pfisterer switches to kybds.)   1967—*Da Capo* (– Pfisterer; – Cantrelli)   1968—*Forever Changes* (– MacLean; – Echols; – Forssi; – Stuart; + Frank Fayad, bass; + George Suranovitch, drums; + Jay Donnellan, gtr.)   1969—*Four Sail*; *Out Here* (Blue Thumb) (– Donnellan; + Gary Rowles, gtr.)   1970— *False Start*   1974—(Group re-forms: Lee; + Melvan Whittington, lead gtr.; + John Sterling, rhythm gtr.; + Sherwood Akuna, bass; + Joe Blocker, drums; + Herman McCormick, congas) *Reel to Real* (RSO)

1975—(Group disbands; periodic reunions follow)
1980—*Best of Love* (Rhino).

Love, headed by singer/guitarist Arthur Lee, was a seminal Sixties L.A. band, emerging from the Sunset Strip at the same time as the Byrds, Buffalo Springfield, the Doors, and the Mamas and the Papas. The group started out playing a Byrds-influenced folk rock but later covered many styles, including bluesy R&B, pop, and hard rock. Arthur Lee still performs on the club circuit, and through the years has periodically re-formed Love, with various personnel, to tour.

Lee moved from his Memphis birthplace to L.A. with his family when he was five. By age 17 he was playing in local bands, including Arthur Lee and the LAGs (styled after Booker T. and the MG's). The band, which included later Love member John Echols, cut one single for Capitol, an instrumental, "The Ninth Wave." Love was formed with unknown musicians: MacLean had been a roadie for the Byrds, and Forssi had played with the Surfaris after their hits faded. Lee originally called the group the Grassroots, but changed the name, since it was already taken by another soon-to-be-well-known band.

Love's first album was hailed by critics as a classic in the new folk-rock style and sold 150,000 copies. Its 1966 single "My Little Red Book" (penned by Burt Bacharach and Hal David) was a minor hit. The band's second album, *Da Capo*, featured some topically druggy lyrics, jazz touches, and a few personnel changes. The album was another groundbreaker, featuring one of the first side-long cuts in rock, the 20-minute-long "Revelation." The album also included the Top Forty hit "7 and 7 Is." *Forever Changes*, however, is considered by many to be Love's best, its answer to *Sgt. Pepper*, with orchestral touches, including horn and string arrangements, and a psychedelic feel that influenced many of the early-Eighties neopsychedelic British bands, such as the Monochrome Set, the Teardrop Explodes, and Echo and the Bunnymen.

In 1968 Lee reorganized the group (members of the first edition later claimed excessive drug use had driven the band apart; MacLean later said he nearly overdosed on heroin, then joined a Christian ministry and suffered a nervous breakdown) and hired a new band of three, plus four sessionmen to help out in the studio on *Four Sail* and *Out Here*; he briefly renamed himself Arthurly. Love next toured England (the band seldom left L.A.), and Lee recorded a full LP with Jimi Hendrix. The album was buried in legal problems, though one track, "The Everlasting First," turned up on *False Start* in 1970. In 1971 Lee dismissed his band.

Lee was supposed to have recorded a solo album for Columbia, but his debut wound up on A&M in 1972, the hard-rocking *Vindicator*, credited to Arthur Lee and Band Aid. Like later Love LPs, the record didn't sell well.

In 1973 he planned to make another solo album with Paul Rothchild's new Buffalo Records, but the label folded before the LP was released. In 1974 Lee came back on RSO with an all-new Love, but the music disappointed many and included three remakes of old Love cuts. His next effort was a solo EP in 1977 on Da Capo Records. In 1979 he toured locally with MacLean (whose sister Maria McKee would emerge in the Eighties with the country-rock band Lone Justice) and another incarnation of Love, and in 1980 Rhino Records put out *Best of Love*, a compilation of Sixties tunes. In 1981 the label issued a new Arthur Lee solo LP, his first in seven years. In 1994 Lee, backed by members of the New York–area punk band Das Damen, toured clubs under the Love banner, to ecstatic reaction from audiences and critics, who urged reappraisal of his oeuvre as the missing link between the Byrds and the Doors.

Love and Rockets: See Bauhaus

Loverboy

Formed 1979, Calgary, Alberta, Canada
Paul Dean (b. Feb. 19, 1946, Can.), gtr.; Mike Reno, voc.; Doug Johnson, kybds.; Matt Frenette, drums; Scott Smith, bass.
1980—*Loverboy* (Columbia)   **1981**—*Get Lucky*
1983—*Keep It Up*   **1985**—*Lovin' Every Minute of It*
1987—*Wildside*   **1988**—(Group disbands)   **1989**—
Big Ones   **1993**—(Group re-forms: Dean; Reno; Johnson; Frenette; Smith).
Paul Dean solo: 1989—*Hard Core* (Columbia).

Paul Dean had been involved with 13 unsuccessful Canadian bands (including Streetheart) before meeting Mike Reno, himself a veteran of many groups, having recorded with Moxy. They teamed up originally to work as a studio-based duo a la Steely Dan. But when record-company interest hinged on their forming a band, they held auditions. Doug Johnson, Matt Frenette, and Scott Smith were chosen, and the quintet was named Loverboy (Coverboy was also under consideration). Their modernized, new-wave–tinged hard rock became the surprise hit of 1981 as, buoyed by the group's incessant touring, their self-titled debut album went double platinum and hatched two successful singles: "Turn Me Loose" (#35, 1981) and "The Kid Is Hot Tonite" (#55, 1981). Their second album, *Get Lucky*, featured the hits "Working for the Weekend" (#29, 1981) and "When It's Over" (#26, 1982), and went multiplatinum, as did 1983's *Keep It Up*. In 1984 lead singer Reno had a hit with "Almost Paradise . . . Love Theme from *Footloose*," a duet with Ann Wilson of Heart (#7). *Lovin' Every Minute of It*, the band's last platinum effort to date, featured the Top Ten singles "Lovin' Every Minute of It" and "This Could

Be the Night." *Wildside* didn't reach the Top Forty, and *Big Ones* just scraped in at #189. The group disbanded in spring 1988, but after playing together in what was to have been a one-time-only appearance, Loverboy regrouped. A fall 1993 tour with the re-formed April Wine was followed by an 80-date U.S. tour in summer 1994.

Lyle Lovett

Born November 1, 1957, Klein, Texas
1986—*Lyle Lovett* (MCA/Curb)   1988—*Pontiac*
1989—*Lyle Lovett and His Large Band*   1992—
***Joshua Judges Ruth*   1994—*I Love Everybody*.**

Lyle Lovett's songs coolly confront the cynical, sometimes violent and misogynistic side of romance. Originally marketed as a country singer (and garnering a number of C&W hits), Lovett has taken his increasingly eclectic, sly music (and increasingly pronounced Eraserhead-style pompadour) well beyond Nashville to a wider audience and an acting career.

Born in a small town that has become a large Houston suburb, Lovett attended Texas A&M University in the mid-Seventies. He started performing at coffeehouses and continued to play in Europe, where he traveled while a graduate student. Originally doing covers, he later wrote his own songs because he felt he "was never a good enough singer to do Merle Haggard."

His career did not take off until he returned to the States in 1984. Nanci Griffith (whom Lovett met in college when he interviewed her for the school paper) covered his "If I Were the Woman You Wanted" on *Once in a Very Blue Moon* in 1984. He sang on that album and her next, *Last of the True Believers*; Lacy J. Dalton recorded his "Closing Time." Through singer Guy Clark (a Lovett idol), MCA's Tony Brown received a demo of Lovett's songs in 1984; Brown signed Lovett and produced his first three albums. While ostensibly a country album, *Lyle Lovett* features undercurrents of folk, rock, and jazz. Despite its lack of standard Nashville fare, the LP yielded four C&W hits: "Farther Down the Line" (#21 C&W, 1986), "Cowboy Man" (#10 C&W, 1986), "God Will" (#18 C&W, 1987), and "Why I Don't Know" (#15 C&W, 1987).

Lovett's subsequent albums became progressively more eclectic. The bluesy *Pontiac* (#117 pop, #12 C&W, 1988) included "Give Back My Heart" (#13 C&W, 1987), "She's No Lady" (#17 C&W, 1988), and "I Loved You Yesterday" (#24 C&W, 1988), and Lovett toured Europe backed by only his guitar and a cellist. With *Lyle Lovett and His Large Band*, he did a 180-degree turn, augmenting his sound with horns and strings. The tuxedoed singer pictured on the cover showed just how far Lovett had moved from country, and the music matched his new urbane image, with jazzy arrangements and snatches of standards. A #10 C&W album, *Large Band* lacked hit singles ("I Married Her Just Because She

Lyle Lovett

Looks Like You" reached only #45 C&W), but brought Lovett to the attention of pop audiences (#62 pop) and contained his gender-bending version of Tammy Wynette's "Stand by Your Man," later used to great effect in the 1992 film *The Crying Game*.

Joshua Judges Ruth (#57 1992), which didn't make the country charts, was recorded in Los Angeles with Little Feat producer George Massenburg, taking Lovett farther afield. The songs added heavy doses of gospel and pop, and Lovett became a featured artist on VH-1. Los Angeles seems to have agreed with Lovett: He has acted in two Robert Altman films, *The Player* (1992) and *Short Cuts* (1993), and married actress Julia Roberts in 1993 (the couple announced its breakup in 1995). In 1994 Lovett released *I Love Everybody* (#26).

Lene Lovich

Born Lili Marlene Premilovich, March 30, 1949, Detroit, Michigan
1979—*Stateless* (Stiff/Epic)   1980—*Flex*   1981—
New Toy* EP   1982—*No Man's Land*   1990—*March
(Pathfinder).

Though she has had hit singles in England and Europe, Lene Lovich has yet to reach the American singles chart. Her new-wave-era Slavic-milkmaid getup and ululating vocals were distinctive, to say the least, and they fit the oddball lyrics and pop hooks devised by Lovich and cowriter Les Chappell.

Lovich was born in Detroit and moved to England when she was 13. After studying sculpture at London's Central School of Art, she took part in experimental theater, worked as a go-go dancer, played all manner of music, and became interested in dream images (inspiring her to visit Salvador Dali). In 1975 she and Chappell joined the soul-funk band the Diversions, with whom she recorded an album for Polydor that was never released. While still with the group, Lovich recorded the Lovich-Chappell composition "Happy Christmas." In 1978 author and disc jockey Charlie Gillett introduced Lovich to Stiff Records' president, Dave Robinson. A few months later Stiff issued her version of Tommy James and the Shondells' "I Think We're Alone Now" and put her on the Be Stiff Tour '78 with Rachel Sweet, the Records, Wreckless Eric, Mickey Jupp, and Jona Lewie.

After American record companies refused her debut LP (as well as those by most other Be Stiff artists), the tour came to New York. Epic Records got interested, and in summer 1979, almost a year after its release in the U.K., *Stateless* came out in the U.S. In England, "Lucky Number" and "Say When" (written by James O'Neill of Fingerprintz) had become hit records, as did "Bird Song," the first single off *Flex*, released in 1980. "New Toy," the title track of Lovich's six-song mini-LP of 1981, was another British success that failed to crack the U.S. charts, although it was a rock-disco favorite; its writer, Thomas Dolby, subsequently started a successful solo career. In 1982 she found herself without a record label.

In addition to her records, Lovich also costarred with Herman Brood and Nina Hagen in the 1979 film *Cha-Cha*, in the lead of a French television film *Rock*, and in the title role of the 1983 London stage play *Mata Hari* (which she cowrote).

Since the mid-Eighties Lovich has been actively involved in the animal-rights movement, and in 1988 she received from People for the Ethical Treatment of Animals (PETA) its Humanitarian Award. She wrote and recorded "Rage" with Erasure; it appears on the animal-rights benefit album *Tame Yourself.* She has written for opera (*The Collector,* with Cerrone) and recorded Peter Hammil and Judge Smith's opera, *Fall of the House of Usher.* Shortly after the release of her last album to date, *March,* her label folded. She is currently writing a novel and continues to write and record with husband Les Chappell. They have two daughters.

The Lovin' Spoonful

Formed 1965, New York City, New York
John Sebastian (b. Mar. 17, 1944, New York City), gtr., autoharp, harmonica, lead voc.; Steve Boone (b. Sep. 23, 1943, Camp Lejeune, N.C.), bass; Zal Yanovsky (b. Dec. 19, 1944, Toronto, Ontario, Can.),
lead gtr., voc.; Joe Butler (b. Jan. 19, 1943, New York City), drums.
1965—Do You Believe in Magic (Kama Sutra)
1966—Daydream; Hums of the Lovin' Spoonful
1967—The Best of the Lovin' Spoonful (- Yanovsky; + Jerry Yester, gtr.)   1968—Everything Playing (- Sebastian)   1990—Anthology (Rhino).

Electrified jug band the Lovin' Spoonful had two years as New York's leading folk rockers. Its sound was dubbed "good time music," and when the good times stopped in 1967 after publicity about the arrest of Steve Boone and Zal Yanovsky for drugs, so did the quartet's hits.

John Sebastian and Yanovsky founded the Spoonful; they had been members of the Mugwumps with future Mamas and Papas Cass Elliot and Denny Doherty (as immortalized in the Mamas and Papas' "Creeque Alley"). The group's first single, Sebastian's "Do You Believe in Magic," went Top Ten in 1965, as did its followup, "You Didn't Have to Be So Nice," in early 1966. More hits followed in 1966 and 1967: "Daydream" (#2), "Did You Ever Have to Make Up Your Mind?" (#2), "Summer in the City" (the Spoonful's lone #1), "Rain on the Roof" (#10), "Darling Be Home Soon" (#15), "Nashville Cats" (#8), and "Six O'Clock" (#18). During its peak period, the Spoonful made three albums and also provided the soundtracks to Francis Ford Coppola's *You're a Big Boy Now* and Woody Allen's *What's Up, Tiger Lily?*

But that ended after Boone and Yanovsky reportedly set up someone they knew in a drug bust in May 1966. Apparently, both Boone and Yanovsky were arrested in Berkeley, California, for possession of marijuana, and in exchange for the police department not prosecuting, the two introduced an undercover narcotic agent to an acquaintance who purchased drugs, resulting in the acquaintance's arrest. The ensuing publicity created a public outcry calling for a boycott of their records and concerts. Yanovsky left the group in June 1967. He was replaced by Jerry Yester, the former producer of the Association, which included his brother Jim Yester. Though the hits didn't stop altogether ("She Is Still a Mystery," #27, 1967), the Spoonful's popularity was waning. After one LP without Yanovsky, *Everything Playing,* Sebastian, who wrote and sang most of the songs, left to start his solo career [see entry].

The group broke up in 1968. Butler formed a new Lovin' Spoonful and put out an album, *Revelation: Revolution '69,* with no success. The drummer then took up acting, appearing in several Broadway plays (*Hair, Mahogany*) and films (*Born to Win, One Trick Pony*), and also worked as a Hollywood sound editor and sound-effects man. Yester recorded *Farewell Aldebaran* with his wife, Judy Henske (coproduced by Yanovsky), and formed the band Rosebud, which made one album. He has continued to work as a producer, credited on Tom Waits' first album. Yanovsky returned to Canada and opened a restaurant in Kingston, Ontario, Chez Piggy, while Boone ran a recording studio on a 135-foot houseboat that he docked in Baltimore's Inner Harbor. Little Feat, Bonnie Raitt, Emmylou Harris, and Ricky Skaggs all recorded there, but in 1977, it sank.

The original Lovin' Spoonful reunited in 1980 to perform "Do You Believe in Magic" in Paul Simon's film *One Trick Pony*. Since 1991, Boone, Butler, and Yester have been touring as the Lovin' Spoonful, with drummer John Marrella and keyboardist/guitarist Lena Yester, Jerry's daughter.

Nick Lowe

Born March 25, 1949, Woodbridge, England
1978—*Pure Pop for Now People* (Columbia)   1979—
Labour of Lust*   1982—*Nick the Knife*   1983—*The
Abominable Showman*   1984—*Nick Lowe and His
Cowboy Outfit*   1985—*The Rose of England
1988—*Pinker and Prouder Than Previous*   1989—
Basher: The Best of Nick Lowe*   1990—*Party of One
(Reprise)   1994—*The Impossible Bird* (Upstart).
With Little Village (Lowe; John Hiatt; Jim Keltner;
Ry Cooder): 1992—*Little Village* (Reprise).

After more than five years with pub-rockers Brinsley Schwarz, Nick Lowe began writing more openly sardonic pop songs while performing with Rockpile and producing. The son of a Royal Air Force officer, Lowe grew up in England and the Middle East. His first band, Kippington Lodge, eventually became Brinsley Schwarz [see entry], for which Lowe did much of the songwriting.

When Brinsley Schwarz broke up in 1975, Lowe began releasing singles under a variety of names, honing his broad ironic streak and his unapologetic talent for lifting other people's hooks. For "Bay City Rollers, We Love You" and "Rollers Show," Lowe recorded as the Tartan Horde ("Rollers Show" later turned up on *Pure Pop*). "Let's Go to the Disco" was supposedly by the Disco Bros. In 1976 Lowe launched Stiff Records with "So It Goes" b/w "Heart of the City"; he also recorded "I Love My Label." In the next year, working as staff producer, he oversaw records by Elvis Costello (*My Aim Is True, This Year's Model, Armed Forces, Get Happy!!*), Mickey Jupp (whose "Switchboard Susan" Lowe covered on *Labour of Lust*), the Damned, Wreckless Eric, and Alberto y Los Trios Paranoias, as well as two records of his own. These included the EP *Bowi* (an "answer" to David Bowie's LP *Low*), which featured a version of Sandy Posey's "Born a Woman," and "Marie Provost," later on *Pure Pop*.

In late 1977 Lowe and Costello left Stiff to join label cofounder Jake Riviera's new venture, Radar Records. He had his first British hit with "(I Love the Sound of) Breaking Glass," which was included on that year's LP *Pure Pop* (*Jesus of Cool* in the U.K.). *Labour of Lust*, though billed as a solo album, was really the work of Rockpile [see entry]. It yielded Lowe's only American Top Forty single, "Cruel to Be Kind" (#12, 1979). He also had a charting single with "I Knew the Bride (When She Used to Rock and Roll)" (#77, 1985), with backing from Huey Lewis and the News.

Lowe remained an active producer, working on a number of Costello's albums, several LPs by Graham Parker and the Rumour (including *Howlin' Wind*), one by Dr. Feelgood, and the Pretenders' debut single, "Stop Your Sobbing," in addition to his then-wife Carlene Carter's *Musical Shapes* and *Blue Nun*, and a session with her stepfather, Johnny Cash, who performed Lowe's "Without Love" (off *Labour of Lust*). (In 1994 Cash also recorded Lowe's "The Beast in Me.")

In 1981 Rockpile disbanded, and Lowe resumed his solo career, releasing *Nick the Knife* and returning to the road with a band alternately known as the Chaps and Noise to Go that included former Rumour guitarist Martin Belmont, ex–Ace/Squeeze pianist Paul Carrack (for whom Lowe produced a solo album), and Lowe playing rhythm guitar instead of bass. Among Lowe's Eighties production credits are two later Costello albums (*Trust* and *Blood and Chocolate*, which he coproduced), the Fabulous Thunderbirds' *T-Bird Rhythm*, and John Hiatt's *Riding with the King*. In 1990 he and Carter, who had married on August 18, 1979, divorced.

During the late Eighties Lowe suffered from what he described as a deep depression for about two years. He has also suffered from alcoholism. Feeling overlooked and unable to see a future for the music he loved, he considered retiring from music. Riviera and Costello urged him to get back to work. He worked with Hiatt on his *Bring the Family* (1987), and out of that project grew Little Village, a band made up of Lowe, Hiatt, Jim Keltner, and Ry Cooder, whose self-titled album came out in 1992. Also around that time Lowe began working in Costello's band and undertook a solo acoustic tour in England. In 1990 old cohort Dave Edmunds (with whom Lowe has had an up-and-down relationship through the years) produced Lowe's *Party of One*, which included the amusing single "All Men Are Liars." In 1994 Lowe played bass on Costello's *Brutal Youth* and released the critically acclaimed, country-tinged *The Impossible Bird*.

While Lowe's commercial success has been negligible of late, his "(What's So Funny 'Bout) Peace, Love and Understanding" netted him a million dollars in publishing royalties when a cover of the song appeared on the soundtrack of *The Bodyguard*.

L7

Formed 1985, Los Angeles, California
Suzi Gardner (b. Aug. 1, 1960, Altus, Okla.), gtr.,

L7: Donita Sparks, Suzi Gardner, Jennifer Finch, Dee Plakas

voc.; Jennifer Finch (b. Aug. 5, 1966, Los Angeles), bass, voc.; Donita Sparks (b. Apr. 8, 1963, Chicago, Ill.), gtr., voc.; Roy Koutsky, drums.
1987—*L7* (Epitaph)   1990—(– Koutsky, + Demetra "Dee" Plakas [b. Nov. 9, 1960, Chicago, Ill.], drums) *Smell the Magic* EP (Sub Pop)   1992—*Bricks Are Heavy* (Slash)   1994—*Hungry for Stink.*

L7 bring a sense of outrage and outrageousness to the normally muddied world of grunge. Although the four women despise being identified by sex, they were nonetheless leaders in the early-Nineties resurgence of women rockers. The band helped found Rock for Choice, an organization that hosts fund-raising concerts to support the cause of reproductive rights. In 1992 L7 seemed to challenge the masculine clichés of rock quite literally when Sparks pulled a tampon from her vagina and threw it into the crowd at England's mammoth Reading Festival.

L7 (the name comes from the slang for "square") built their following through independent releases and frequent tours of Europe and the States. They went through a series of drummers, some of them male, before settling on Plakas. A single for Sub Pop's singles club and an EP for the label, with the catchy, anthemic "Shove," made them one of Hollywood's hottest underground bands. *Bricks Are Heavy,* featuring the popular alternative track "Pretend We're Dead," was produced by Butch Vig on the heels of his success with Nirvana's *Nevermind.* In 1994, L7 performed in the John Waters film *Serial Mom* and won more fans via Lollapalooza appearances and the release of their highly praised album *Hungry for Stink.*

Lulu

Born Marie McDonald McLaughlin Lawrie, November 3, 1948, Lennox Castle, Glasgow, Scotland
1967—*To Sir with Love* (Epic)   1971—*New Routes* (Atco)   1979—*Don't Take Love for Granted* (Rocket)
1981—*Lulu* (Alfa)   1993—*Independence* (SBK)
1994—*From Crayons to Perfume: The Best of Lulu* (Rhino).

At age 18 Lulu recorded "To Sir with Love," the title theme from the movie in which she costarred with Sidney Poitier. It quickly went to #1 in the U.S., becoming the first hit by an artist from the U.K. to hit the top of the U.S. chart without ever entering the British chart. This success led her to much work on TV and on the cabaret circuit. Before recording this pop ballad, however, she and her band, the Luvvers, had hit the British Top Ten with a cover of the Isley Brothers' hit "Shout." (Lulu's version hit #94 in the U.S. Top 100 in 1964 and #96 as a reissue in 1967 at the height of her U.S. popularity.)

Marie Lawrie made her show-business debut at age nine singing at Bridgeton Public Hall and soon began appearing regularly with a local accordion band. At age 14 she began singing weekend gigs in Glasgow clubs and by 15 was a regular in that area with her group the Glen Eagles. In 1964 her group was renamed Lulu and the Luvvers and hit the chart with "Shout."

In 1966 Lulu went solo, and in 1967 she hit the British Top Ten again with Neil Diamond's "The Boat That I Row." That year her performance in *To Sir with Love* garnered raves. In the late Sixties Lulu worked as both a TV personality and a recording artist, and in 1969 she married Bee Gee Maurice Gibb (they divorced in 1973). In 1970 at Muscle Shoals, with the production team of Jerry Wexler, Tom Dowd, and Arif Mardin, she recorded *New Routes,* from which sprang the U.S. Top Thirty hit "Oh Me, Oh My, I'm a Fool for You, Baby."

In the early Seventies Lulu toured throughout the world, headlining in such places as Las Vegas and Berlin, and had her own prime-time BBC-TV weekly music series. She was absent from the U.K. chart until 1974, when she again hit the Top Ten with the David Bowie–arranged cover of his "The Man Who Sold the World," and from the U.S. chart until 1981, when she hit with "I Could Never Miss You (More Than I Do)" (#18) and "If I Were You" (#44). Except for a remake of "Shout," a U.K. Top Ten hit in 1986, she did not record again until 1993's *Independence,* a dance-oriented work. The title cut was a U.K. Top Twenty hit and a dance hit here. Other successful singles include a duet with Bobby Womack, "I'm Back for More," and a U.K. #1 cover of Dan Hartman's "Relight My Fire." She has also begun writing songs; she cowrote Tina Turner's "I Don't Wanna Fight."

Lydia Lunch

Born June 2, 1959, Rochester, New York
1980—*Queen of Siam* (Ze)   1981—*Eight-Eyed Spy*
(Fetish); *Pre–Teenage Jesus* EP (Ze); *13.13* (Ruby)
1982—*The Agony Is the Ecstacy* EP (with the Birth-
day Party) (4AD)   1985—*The Uncensored Lydia
Lunch* cassette (Widowspeak)   1987—*Honeymoon
in Red* (with Rowland S. Howard)   1988—*Stinkfist*
EP (with Clint Ruin); *The Crumb* EP (with Thurston
Moore)   1989—*Naked in Garden Hills* (with Harry
Crews); *Drowning in Limbo*   1991—*Shotgun Wed-
ding* (with Rowland S. Howard) (Triple X)   1993—
Crimes Against Nature.

At 16, Lydia Lunch was one of New York's first "no wave"
artists with her band Teenage Jesus and the Jerks. Working with a variety of bassists, Lunch (vocals and
guitar)—alternately shrieking and chanting in a monotone—and Bradly Field (drum [sic]) recorded two singles
(later collected on a 12-inch), four cuts for Brian Eno's No
New York compilation, and an EP (pre– Teenage Jesus)
featuring original member James Chance (then Siegfried)
[see James Chance entry] on saxophone before he left
the band to form the Contortions. A side project of the
period was Beirut Slump, whose lone 45 included some-
time-Jerk Jim Sclavunos on bass and filmmaker Vivienne
Dick on violin. Lunch also starred in three of Dick's
super-8mm movies, as well as in Beth and Scott B's
Black Box, The Offenders, and in 1982, Vortex (which debuted at the New York Film Festival).

In 1980 Lunch left "no wave" behind and recorded
Queen of Siam with the aid of ex–Contortions/John Cale
bassist George Scott (a.k.a. Jack Ruby), saxophonist Pat
Irwin, ex-Voidoid and Teenage Jesus producer Robert
Quine on guitar, and big-band arranger Billy Ver Planck,
the composer of the theme to *The Flintstones.* Concurrently, Lunch, Scott, Irwin, Sclavunos (on drums), and
guitarist Michael Paumgardhen started the bluesy 8
Eyed Spy. Scott's death of a heroin overdose in 1980 kept
8 Eyed Spy from making a full studio LP, though a combination of live performances and studio work with Irwin
on bass filled a posthumous cassette and an album.

With the end of 8 Eyed Spy, Irwin concentrated on
his instrumental group, the Raybeats (he later became a
touring member of the B-52's), while Sclavunos and
Paumgardhen joined Lunch's Devil Dogs. But turnover
in personnel and a repertoire of cover songs kept that
group from recording. Instead, Lunch moved to California and started 13.13. The lineup of the group was fluid
(one version included three members of early L.A. punk
rockers the Weirdos). In 1982 Lunch appeared on an EP,
The Agony Is the Ecstacy, with the Birthday Party. Also
that year Lunch collaborated with X's Exene Cervenka
on a book of poetry entitled *Adulterers Anonymous.* The
mid-Eighties saw Lunch concentrating more on her

highly confrontational spoken-word performances. She
founded Widowspeak Productions in 1984 to release her
own and others' work. Lunch also began a collaboration
with notorious underground filmmaker Richard Kern,
starring in such films as *The Right Side of My Brain* (with
Henry Rollins) and *Fingered.*

Other collaborations were musical: She recorded
two albums with ex–Birthday Party guitarist Rowland S.
Howard, 1987's *Honeymoon in Red* and 1991's *Shotgun
Wedding*, and a 1988 EP, *Stinkfist*, with Jim Thirlwell,
a.k.a. Foetus, a.k.a. Clint Ruin. Also in 1988 she formed
the combo Harry Crews with Sonic Youth bassist/vocal-
ist Kim Gordon and recorded *The Crumb* with Sonic
Youth guitarist Thurston Moore. Lunch taught a visiting
artists workshop for the San Francisco Art Institute's
performance/video department in 1993. That year Triple
X released a three-CD box set, *Crimes Against Nature*, of
Lunch's spoken-word performances.

John Lurie: See Lounge Lizards

Luscious Jackson: See the Beastie Boys

Lush

Formed 1988, London, England
Miki Berenyi (b. Mar. 18, 1967, London), gtr., voc.;
Meriel Barham, voc.; Emma Anderson (b. June 10,
1967, London), gtr.; Christopher Acland (b. Sep. 7,
1966, Lancaster, Eng.), drums; Steve Rippon, bass.
1989—(– Barham) *Scar* EP (4AD)   1990—*Mad Love*
EP; *Sweetness and Light* EP; *Gala* (– Rippon; + Phil
King [b. Apr. 29, 1960, London], bass)   1992—
Spooky   1994—*Split.*

Lush came up in the late-Eighties London clique of self-
consciously arty bands known as "shoegazers." The
movement's so-called dream-pop sound is characterized by light, airy melodies buried deep within walls of
feedback-drenched guitar. The quartet was formed at
North London Polytechnic by literature majors Miki
Berenyi, Christopher Acland, original bassist Steve Rippon, Meriel Barham (who went on to join another
shoegazing band, Pale Saints), and Emma Anderson.
Lush became an instant hit on the city's club scene, attracting like-minded fans such as Robin Guthrie of the
Cocteau Twins, who produced some of the group's first
singles. *Gala* combined the group's EPs for the American
audience. Guthrie returned for Lush's 1992 album,
Spooky, which was criticized for showing off his dazzling
production work more than the band's actual sound. The
album still reached the U.K. Top Twenty and topped the
nation's independent chart. Lush got a big push stateside in 1992 when it opened the Lollapalooza Tour.

Frankie Lymon and the Teenagers

Formed 1955, New York City, New York
Frankie Lymon (b. Sep. 30, 1942, New York City; d. Feb. 28, 1968), lead voc.; Sherman Garnes (b. June 8, 1940, New York City; d. 1978), bass voc.; Joe Negroni (b. Sep. 9, 1940, New York City; d. 1977), baritone voc.; Herman Santiago (b. Feb. 18, 1941, New York City), first tenor voc,; Jimmy Merchant (b. Feb. 10, 1940, New York City), second tenor voc.
1956—*The Teenagers Featuring Frankie Lymon* (Gee) 1986—*Frankie Lymon and the Teenagers: For Collectors Only* (Murray Hill) 1989—*Best of Frankie Lymon and the Teenagers* (Rhino) 1994—*Frankie Lymon and the Teenagers: Complete Recordings* (Bear Family, Ger.).

When he was 13, Frankie Lymon had a #1 R&B record (#6 pop and #1 U.K.) with "Why Do Fools Fall in Love?" At 18 his career was over; eight years later he died of a heroin overdose. He was the first young black teen idol and an inspiration to countless young singers, including Ronnie Spector, Garland Jeffreys, Marvin Gaye, Michael Jackson, and Diana Ross, whose cover of "Fools" was a Top Ten hit in 1981. Over 25 years after his death, the two surviving Teenagers, Herman Santiago and Jimmy Merchant, made music-business and legal history when a federal court recognized them as the authors of the song and awarded them back royalties estimated in the millions.

The rags-to-riches-to-rags story began in New York City, where Lymon and the Teenagers were school friends who sang on street corners. The Teenagers were originally a quartet, known first as the Ermines, then as the Coupe de Villes. They discovered Lymon, who had sung in his father's gospel group, the Harlemaires, and he joined the group, which then became the Premiers. In 1955 Richard Barrett of the Valentines heard them perform on a streetcorner outside his window and arranged for the group to be signed by the record label his group recorded for, Gee. Label executives were impressed by the group with Santiago singing lead, but when it came time to record a song Santiago and Merchant cowrote, "Why Do Fools Fall in Love?," Lymon stepped in, since Santiago had a cold. The song, credited to Lymon and producer George Goldner, was their first record. By then they were known as Frankie Lymon and the Teenagers.

Lymon's boyish soprano became the group's trademark, and the group's clean-cut, innocent image was embraced by the public and the record industry at a time when Congress was beginning to investigate payola. Smiling and neatly attired in letter sweaters and loose, sharply creased trousers, Frankie Lymon and the Teenagers were a crossover smash. "Fools" was one of four Top Twenty R&B songs off the Teenagers' debut album; the others were "I Promise to Remember" (#10,

1956), "I Want You to Be My Girl" (#13 pop, #3 R&B, 1956), and "The ABC's of Love" (#14 R&B, 1956). The LP also included "I'm Not a Juvenile Delinquent," which the group sang in the 1956 Alan Freed film *Rock, Rock, Rock.* A year later, after appearing in another Freed movie, *Mr. Rock and Roll,* and making a successful tour of the U.K., Lymon left the group for a solo career.

The Teenagers continued without him, with a string of less charismatic lead singers, but nothing hit. After reuniting with Lymon briefly in 1965, the group called it quits for many years. By then Lymon, too, had fallen on hard times, mostly due to his worsening drug addiction. His first 45, "Goody Goody," was a modest hit (#20 pop, 1957); subsequent records were outright flops. A comeback attempt in 1960 with Bobby Day's "Little Bitty Pretty One" hit #58. His handlers had tried a number of new stylistic approaches for Lymon, whose natural change in voice was less appealing. But Lymon's problems ran much deeper. In the Sixties he was arrested for drug possession and claimed in an *Ebony* magazine profile to have been a pimp at the height of the Teenagers' success. He had left the army, married a schoolteacher named Emira Eagle, and was playing the lounge at an Augusta, Georgia, Howard Johnson's when he got a brief job in New York City. Just a few days after returning to his hometown he was found dead of a heroin overdose. In the Seventies Garnes died of a heart attack, and Negroni passed away after a cerebral hemorrhage. Merchant became a cab driver.

In 1981, to commemorate the silver anniversary of "Fools," Santiago and Merchant recruited Pearl McKinnon and Eric Ward. There were a few more personnel changes in the revived Teenagers. The latest edition includes Jimmy Castor [see entry], who understudied for Frankie Lymon at the group's height, and Tony Sal (ex–Ronnie and the Daytonas and the Jimmy Castor Bunch), and New York City oldies radio disc jockey Bobby Jay.

In the meantime, "Why Do Fools Fall in Love?" had proven its durability, becoming a hit record again for the Happenings in 1967, being featured on the hit *American Graffiti* soundtrack, and being covered many times. In 1984 Frankie Lymon's widow filed for a renewal of Frankie's copyright on the song, only to discover that it had become the property of Morris Levy. A lawsuit was then filed in federal court, charging that Levy and Goldner had fraudulently represented themselves as the coauthors of a song written by Frankie Lymon. With millions in back royalties at stake, Levy recalled a woman who had contacted him several years before, claiming she had been married to Lymon in the Sixties, Elizabeth Waters (who, it was later discovered, was legally married to another man when she married Lymon). Levy also tracked down another woman who claimed to have been married to Lymon, Zola Taylor, a former singer of the Platters. (She could produce no wedding license for the nuptials, which allegedly occurred in Tijuana.) It was later revealed that Levy had promised both women financial compensation in return for their disputing Emira Lymon's claim of widowhood, and it worked. Waters won the case around the same time Levy was sentenced to ten years in federal prison for extortion in another case. An appellate court reversed the decision, deeming Emira to be Lymon's legal widow.

But the twists and turns did not end there. Merchant and Santiago pressed their own case, claiming they were the true authors of the song and, thus, the rightful recipients of any royalties due. Although their case appeared weakened by the years that had elapsed, in 1992 a federal court proclaimed Jimmy Merchant and Herman Santiago—not Lymon, Goldner, or Levy, by then all deceased—the song's authors and rightful copyright owners. The two Teenagers had successfully argued that they were tricked out of the royalties, then intimidated (through a 1969 death threat) into silence. In most such cases, the plaintiffs never see justice; at best, royalties are awarded going back the previous three years. For Merchant and Santiago, though, the judge ruled in their favor and went even further, awarding royalties back to 1969.

Barbara Lynn

Born Barbara Lynn Ozen, January 16, 1942, Beaumont, Texas
1976—*Here Is Barbara Lynn* (Oval)   1988—*You Don't Have to Go* (Ichiban)   1993—*You'll Lose a Good Thing* (Sounds of the Fifties, Neth.)   1994—*So Good* (Bullseye Blues).

Barbara Lynn is an East Texas R&B singer (and left-handed guitar player) with a bluesy voice and a casual, low-key style. Her first and biggest hit, the New Orleans–style standard "You'll Lose a Good Thing" (#8 pop, #1 R&B, 1962), was written by the 16-year-old Lynn as a poem. She was discovered singing blues in Louisiana clubs by musician/arranger Huey P. Meaux, who subsequently produced all her records. Most of her early hits—including "You're Gonna Need Me" (#13 R&B, 1963) and "It's Better to Have It" (#26 R&B, 1965)—were recorded in Cosimo Matassa's New Orleans studio but were released by Philadelphia-based Jamie Records.

In 1966 Lynn signed to Meaux's Tribe label, but recorded no hits. In 1968 she went to Atlantic, hitting with "This Is the Thanks I Get" (#39 R&B, 1968) and "(Until Then) I'll Suffer" (#31 R&B, 1971). The Rolling Stones covered her "Oh! Baby (We Got a Good Thing Goin')" on *Rolling Stones Now!* Recording-wise, little was heard from Lynn through the Eighties except for a single LP from Ichiban. Six years later *So Good* was released to critical acclaim.

Loretta Lynn

Born Loretta Webb, April 14, 1935, Butcher Hollow, Kentucky
1966—*Don't Come Home a Drinkin'* (Decca)   1968—*Greatest Hits*   1970—*Coal Miner's Daughter*   1971—*Lead Me On* (with Conway Twitty)   1974—*Greatest Hits, vol. 2* (MCA)   1975—*Back to the Country; Home; When the Tingle Becomes a Chill*   1976—*Somebody Somewhere*   1977—*I Remember Patsy; Out of My Head and Back in My Bed*   1978—*We've Come a Long Way Baby*   1980—*Loretta; Lookin' Good*   1981—*Two's a Party* (with Conway Twitty)   1982—*I Lie; Making Love from Memory*   1983—*Lyin' Cheatin' Woman Chasin' Honky Tonkin' Whiskey Drinkin' You*   1985—*Just a Woman*   1988—*Who Was That Stranger*   1991—*The Country Music Hall of Fame: Loretta Lynn*   1994—*Honky Tonk Girl* (Decca/MCA).

Country singer and songwriter Loretta Lynn grew up in the remote, poverty-stricken town of Butcher Hollow, Kentucky. Named after Loretta Young, Lynn didn't do much singing in her early youth. Instead, after one month of dating, she was married at age 13 to Moony (Moonshine) Lynn (he was 19), who took her 3000 miles away to Custer, Washington, where he worked in logging camps. Lynn became a mother at 14 and had four children in her first four years of marriage; she was a grandmother at 32. Besides taking care of the kids, taking in other people's laundry, and occasionally making extra money by picking strawberries with migrant workers, Lynn began writing songs on her Sears Roebuck guitar. Her husband encouraged her to go public and became her manager, lining up shows at local bars and clubs. At age 18 Lynn cut a record for the California Zero label, "Honky Tonk Girl," which she and Moony promoted themselves by visiting radio stations around the country. They worked their way to Nashville, and the song eventually became a #14 country & western hit.

Once in Nashville, Lynn persuaded Ott Devine, manager of the Grand Ole Opry, to book her, and she first appeared there in October 1960. An appearance with Buck Owens led to a contract with Decca (now MCA), for which she's made over 30 records over a period of 20 years. Her first Decca hit, produced by Owen Bradley in 1962, was called "Success" (#6 C&W). Since then she has had 16 #1 C&W hits, including the standard "Don't Come Home a Drinkin' (With Lovin' on Your Mind)" (1966), "Fist City" (1968), "Woman of the World (Leave My World Alone)" (1969), and the autobiographical "Coal Miner's Daughter" (1970). Also in 1970 she began touring regularly with Conway Twitty, with whom she had a number of #1 C&W hits, including 1971's "After the Fire Is Gone" and "Lead Me On," followed by "Louisiana Woman, Mississippi Man" (1973), "As Soon As I Hang Up the Phone"

(1974), and "Feelins'" (1975). Lynn was the first woman ever to win the Entertainer of the Year Award from the Country Music Association, in 1972. Her self-penned controversial hit "The Pill" (#70 pop, #5 C&W, 1975) was seen by some as a down-home feminist classic, while "One's on the Way" (#1 C&W, 1971) celebrated motherhood.

In 1976 Lynn (with *New York Times* reporter George Vecsey) wrote her autobiography, *Coal Miner's Daughter,* and it became one of the ten biggest-selling books of that year.

Her later hits included the C&W #1 singles "Rated 'X'" (1972), "Love Is the Foundation" (1973), "Trouble in Paradise" (1974), "Somebody Somewhere (Don't Know What He's Missin' Tonight)" (1976), "She's Got You" (1977), "Out of My Head and Back in My Bed" (1977), as well as other C&W Top Twenty hits, such as "When the Tingle Becomes a Chill" (1975), "We've Come a Long Way, Baby" and "I Can't Feel You Anymore" (1979), and "I Lie" (1982).

In 1980 a movie based on Lynn's autobiography came out starring Sissy Spacek, to much acclaim. (Spacek, who sang Lynn's songs in the film, won the Best Actress Oscar for her performance.) Lynn herself has dabbled in acting, making guest appearances on *Fantasy Island* and *The Dukes of Hazzard,* as well as *The Muppet Show.* She remains one of country music's most popular and well-loved stars.

Lynyrd Skynyrd

Formed 1966, Jacksonville, Florida
Ronnie Van Zant (b. Jan. 15, 1949; d. Oct. 20, 1977, Gillsburg, Miss.), voc.; Gary Rossington, gtr.; Allen Collins (b. ca. 1952; d. Jan. 23, 1990, Jacksonville), gtr.; Billy Powell, kybds.; Leon Wilkeson, bass; Bob Burns, drums.
1973—(+ Ed King, gtr.) *Pronounced Leh-Nerd Skin-Nerd* (MCA)   1974—*Second Helping* (– Burns; + Artimus Pyle [b. Spartanburg, S.C.], drums)   1975— (– King) *Nuthin' Fancy*   1976—*Gimme Back My Bullets* (+ Steve Gaines [b. Seneca, Mo.; d. Oct. 20, 1977, Gillsburg, Miss.], gtr.); *One More from the Road*   1977—*Street Survivors* (– Van Zant; – Gaines) (Group disbands)   1978—*Skynyrd's First . . . And Last*   1979—*Gold and Platinum* 1987—*Legend*   1988—*Southern by the Grace of God/Lynyrd Skynyrd Tribute Tour—1987*   1991— (Group re-forms: Rossington; Pyle; Wilkeson; King; Powell; + Johnny Van Zant, voc.; + Dale Krantz-Rossington, voc.; + Randall Hall, gtr.; + Custer, drums) *Lynyrd Skynyrd 1991* (Atlantic)   1993—*The Last Rebel*   1994—*Endangered Species* (Capricorn). Johnny Van-Zant solo: 1980—*No More Dirty Deals* (Polydor)   1981—*Round Two*   1982—*The Last of*

Lynyrd Skynyrd: Leon Wilkeson, Allen Collins, Ronnie Van Zant, Gary Rossington, Artimus Pyle, Steve Gaines, Billy Powell

the Wild Ones   1985—*Van-Zant* (Geffen)   1990— *Brickyard Road* (Atlantic).

Lynyrd Skynyrd was the most critically lauded and commercially successful of the Allman Brothers–influenced Southern bands. When it first rose to prominence in 1973, the group epitomized regional pride that stressed cocky, boisterous hard rock, as opposed to the Allmans' open-ended blues. When the band broke up in 1977 after a plane crash killed Ronnie Van Zant and newcomers Steve and Cassie Gaines, Southern rock suffered a tremendous loss.

The nucleus of what would become Lynyrd Skynyrd first met in high school in their hometown, Jacksonville, Florida. Van Zant, Allen Collins, and Gary Rossington formed the band My Backyard in 1965, eventually joined by Leon Wilkeson and Billy Powell. Their later name immortalized a gym teacher, Leonard Skinner, who was known to punish students who had long hair.

The band, with original drummer Bob Burns, was playing in Atlanta at a bar called Funocchio's in 1972, when it was spotted by Al Kooper, who was on a tour with Badfinger and also scouting bands for MCA's new Sounds of the South label. Kooper signed Skynyrd and produced its 1973 debut, *Pronounced Leh-Nerd Skin-Nerd,* adding session guitarist Ed King (late of Strawberry Alarm Clock). The group's initial hook was its three-guitar attack, topping the Allmans' trademark two-guitar leads. Skynyrd first got major FM airplay with the long "Free Bird," written as a tribute to Duane Allman, which eventually became an anthem for Skynyrd fans and—when revived, without lyrics, by the Rossington-Collins Band in 1980—a tribute to Van Zant.

The band hooked up with the Who's *Quadrophenia* Tour in 1973 and began to acquire a reputation as a live act. Its 1974 followup LP, the multiplatinum *Second Helping,* also produced by Kooper, reached #12. It included another instant Southern standard, "Sweet Home

Alabama" (#8, 1974), a reply to Neil Young's "Alabama" and "Southern Man." But Van Zant often wore a Neil Young T-shirt, and Young later offered the band several songs to record, though they never made it to vinyl.

In December 1974 Artimus Pyle joined as replacement for Burns; King quit a month later. The band's third record went to #9, but 1976's *Gimme Back My Bullets,* produced by Tom Dowd, sold somewhat less. Skynyrd regrouped in October 1976 with the double live *One More from the Road* (recorded at Atlanta's Fox Theater), which went to #9, sold triple platinum, and featured new third guitarist Steve Gaines, plus a trio of female backup singers, including Gaines' sister Cassie. The band became one of the biggest U.S. concert draws.

Street Survivors, its sixth LP, was released three days before the plane crash of October 20, 1977. Skynyrd was traveling in a privately chartered plane between shows in Greenville, South Carolina, and Baton Rouge, Louisiana, when it crashed just outside Gillsburg, Mississippi, killing the three members. The rest escaped with injuries. Fuel shortage was a possible cause of the crash, although by the next year a lawsuit filed against the airplane company faulted the plane's personnel and its mechanical integrity. Ironically, the cover of the band's last LP pictured the members standing in flames and included an order form for a "Lynyrd Skynyrd survival kit." There was also a Van Zant composition about death called "That Smell." The LP cover was changed shortly after the accident, and the album (#5, 1977) went on to become one of Skynyrd's biggest sellers. The next year *Skynyrd's First . . . and Last* was re-leased, consisting of previously unavailable early band recordings from 1970 to 1972 (the band had planned on releasing it before the accident). It went platinum, and in 1980 MCA released a best-of called *Gold and Platinum.*

That same year a new band emerged from Lynyrd Skynyrd's ashes. The Rossington-Collins Band [see entry] featured four of the surviving members plus female lead singer Dale Krantz. Artimus Pyle, meanwhile, began touring with his Artimus Pyle Band in 1982.

In 1986 tragedy struck again when Allen Collins crashed his car, killing his girlfriend and leaving him paralyzed from the waist down. Four years later he died of respiratory failure due to pneumonia at age 37. To mark the tenth anniversary of the fatal plane crash, in 1987 Rossington, Powell, Wilkeson, and King put Lynyrd Skynyrd back together, along with guitarist Randall Hall and Johnny Van Zant on lead vocals. The younger brother of Ronnie and Donnie (.38 Special) was a marginally successful solo artist (hyphenating his last name during this period), releasing five albums from 1980 through 1990. Dale Krantz, by then Dale Krantz-Rossington, sang backup for the Skynyrd tour. The revamped lineup embarked on a 32-date reunion tour, which was chronicled on the following year's double live album, *Southern by the Grace of God/Lynyrd Skynyrd Tribute Tour—1987.*

In 1991 the same group (with varying drummers) began recording again. The Nineties albums carried on Skynyrd's musical tradition and were well received.

M

Kirsty MacColl

Born October 10, 1959, London, England
1981—*Desperate Character* (Polydor)   1989—*Kite*
(Charisma)   1991—*Electric Landlady*   1993—*Ti-*
tanic Days* (I.R.S.)   1994—*Galore*.

Kirsty MacColl's simultaneously witty and affecting songs and crystalline voice won her a large following in Britain, where "There's a Guy Works Down the Chip Shop Swears He's Elvis" (#14 U.K., 1981) and "Walking Down Madison" (#23 U.K., 1991) were Top Forty hits. American listeners have mostly heard Kirsty's vocals on records by the Rolling Stones, the Smiths, Talking Heads, and Van Morrison. Her duet with the Pogues' Shane Mc-Gowan, "Fairytale of New York" (#2 U.K., 1987), was one of the most successful Christmas singles ever released in Britain.

The daughter of English folk-music legend Ewan MacColl (who, among other things, wrote "The First Time Ever I Saw Your Face"), Kirsty signed with Stiff Records at age 16. Her 1979 debut single, "They Don't Know," failed to make a dent but became a hit (#8 U.S., 1984; #2 U.K., 1983) for Tracey Ullman in 1984. "Chip Shop" and *Desperate Character* (1981) showcased her talent as a rueful *pasticheur*, deftly mixing country, rock-abilly, and pop influences. A second album recorded for Polydor in 1983 was rejected and never released.

In 1984 she married producer Steve Lillywhite (Sim-ple Minds, Rolling Stones, U2, Talking Heads). Their first collaboration was a cover of Billy Bragg's "A New Eng-land" (#7 U.K., 1985). Lillywhite produced MacColl's first American releases, *Kite* (1989) and *Electric Landlady* (1991). Collaborating with guitarists Johnny Marr (the Smiths), Mark E. Nevin (Fairground Attraction), and Mar-shall Crenshaw, the albums reflect her social concerns, attacking Margaret Thatcher, shallow pop stars, and the dichotomy between rich and poor. (She also contributed a song to the *Red Hot + Blue* AIDS benefit album and hosted an environmental special on the BBC.) Musically the songs range from dance and rap inflections ("Walk-ing Down Madison") to samba ("My Affair") and include cover versions (the Kinks' "Days" [#12 U.K., 1989]) and original takes on Sixties pop (her "He Never Mentioned Love"). MacColl's 1993 album, *Titanic Days*, featured "Can't Stop Killing You" and "Angel," which received U.S. modern-rock-radio airplay. As of the mid-Nineties, Mac-Coll and Lillywhite had split.

Lonnie Mack

Born Lonnie McIntosh, July 18, 1941, Harrison, Indi-
ana
1963—*The Wham of That Memphis Man!* (Frater-
nity)   1969—*Glad I'm in the Band* (Elektra); *What-*
ever's Right*   1971—*The Hills of Indiana*
1977—*Home at Last* (Capitol); *Lonnie Mack and*

Pismo 1985—*Strike Like Lightning* (Alligator) 1986—*Second Sight* 1988—*Roadhouses & Dance Halls* (Epic) 1990—*Live! Attack of the Killer V* (Alligator).

A pioneering rock & roller, Lonnie Mack used the whammy bar of his Gibson Flying V to achieve an enormously influential rockabilly sound. Learning guitar at age five, he attended closely to Chet Atkins' and Merle Travis' thumb-and-finger-picking approach. Les Paul was also an early idol, and Mack's guitar was the highlight of his first group, Lonnie and the Twilighters, as well as the subsequent Troy Seals Band, for which he played lead.

Going solo in 1961, Mack released an instrumental version of Chuck Berry's "Memphis" that charted at #5. Feeding his guitar through a Leslie cabinet usually employed by organists, he trademarked his distinctive "twangy" sound. A followup, "Wham!," entered the Top Thirty, and a debut album, *The Wham of That Memphis Man!*, became a roots classic. While overshadowed by his playing, Mack's R&B-influenced singing also drew notice.

An occasional session player for James Brown, Freddie King, and most notably the Doors (*Morrison Hotel*), Mack put out three albums on Elektra at the turn of the decade. *Glad I'm in the Band, Whatever's Right,* and the country-inflected *The Hills of Indiana* were more critical than commercial successes, and in 1971, having assumed cult status among musicians, Mack retreated for six years. Surfacing in 1977 with *Lonnie Mack and Pismo* and the acoustic-driven *Home at Last,* he returned to strength with 1985's *Strike Like Lightning,* produced by longtime fan Stevie Ray Vaughan.

Second Sight, Roadhouses & Dance Halls, and *Live! Attack of the Killer V* confirmed his comeback. Concentrating on blues and the country and gospel roots that formed him, his later work displays, with renewed vitality, his rich vibrato guitar tone.

Madness

Formed 1978, London, England
Lee Thompson (b. Oct. 5, 1957, London), sax; Chris Foreman (b. Aug. 8, 1958, London), gtr.; Mike Barson (b. Apr. 21, 1958, London), kybds.; Dan Woodgate (b. Oct. 19, 1960, London), drums; Mark Bedford (b. Aug. 24, 1961, London), bass; Graham "Suggs" McPherson (b. Jan. 13, 1961, Hastings, Eng.), voc.; Chas Smash (b. Cathal Smythe, Jan. 14, 1959), emcee, steps, trumpet.
1979—*One Step Beyond* (Stiff) 1980—*Absolutely* 1983—*Madness* (Geffen) (– Barson) 1984—*Keep Moving* 1985—*Mad Not Mad* 1986—(Group disbands) 1988—(Group re-forms as the Madness: Foreman; Thompson; Smythe; McPherson; + Jerry Dammers [b. Gerald Dankin, May 22, 1954, India], kybds.; + Steve Nieve, kybds.; + Bruce Thomas, bass).

Madness first came to prominence in 1978, along with the Specials, in the forefront of Great Britain's ska revival. (Ska was a prereggae Jamaican dance rhythm popular in the Sixties.) In time Madness became a vaudevillian pop group, matching its self-proclaimed "nutty sound" to soul, R&B, and music-hall music as well as ska and becoming a top singles band in Britain. Lee Thompson, Mike Barson, and Chris Foreman had been together since 1976 in the band Morris and the Minors. As group membership varied, Chas Smash and future Madness manager John Hassler auditioned as replacements without success; by 1978 Graham McPherson, Dan Woodgate, and Mark Bedford had all joined the group, now known as the Invaders. That year they changed their name to Madness, after a favorite Prince Buster ska song.

In 1979 the Specials' 2-Tone label released "The Prince," dedicated to Prince Buster. When it reached #16 on the British chart, Madness signed with Stiff. Chas Smash joined as emcee and dancer, and Madness recorded *One Step Beyond.* The title cut became a Top Ten British single, and the album stayed in the British Top 75 for most of a year, peaking at #7. *Absolutely,* with the single "Baggy Trousers" (a Madness trademark onstage) peaked at #3 U.K., as Madness began to broaden its style, becoming spokesmen for Cockney youth. Other U.K. Top Ten singles from that period included "My Girl," "Work Rest and Play," "Embarrassment," "The Return of the Los Palmas Seven," "Grey Day," and "Shut Up."

In 1981 Madness made a film about starting a group, *Take It or Leave It,* playing themselves. The British album *7* included two more U.K. hits, "It Must Be Love" and "Cardiac Arrest," and Madness' first #1 British single, "House of Fun," which brought the LP to #1 as well. Through late 1983 the group's further Top Ten U.K. singles were "Driving in My Car" (1982), "Our House" (1982), "Tomorrow's (Just Another Day)" (1983), "Wings of a Dove" (1983), and "The Sun and the Rain" (1983).

But U.S. response to Madness was confined to concert audiences. *Rise and Fall* and *Complete Madness,* the latter a greatest-hits collection released simultaneously with a videocassette, were not released on a U.S. label, although they were best sellers in Britain and Europe. Despite the popularity of *Madness* (#41, 1983), which included a number of previous British hits from 1981–82, here in the U.S. the group slid back into obscurity. From that album, Madness saw its only U.S. Top Ten hit with "Our House" (#7, 1983). Despite a handful of lively and amusing videos, including "House of Fun," and another minor hit, "It Must Be Love" (#33, 1983), Madness' next album, *Keep Moving,* peaked at #109.

At home, however, Madness continued its winning streak with several more hits, among them "Michael Caine" (#11, 1984), "Yesterday's Men" (#18, 1985), and "(Waiting for) the Ghost Train" (#18, 1986). In the fall of 1986 the group disbanded, although several members returned as the Madness with an unsuccessful album, *The Madness*, that was not released here and was largely ignored at home. Its single, "I Pronounce You," was a minor U.K. hit, then that group broke up as well. Thompson and Foreman continued for one album as the Nutty Boys. Woodgate later joined Voice of the Beehive. McPherson went into management, and Smyth became an A&R man for Go! Discs Records. In 1994 the group gave a nod to the American Woodstock when it reunited for "Madstock," in London's Finsbury Park. At that time they stated that they had no plans to re-form permanently.

Madonna

Madonna

Born Madonna Louise Veronica Ciccone, August 16, 1958, Bay City, Michigan
**1983—*Madonna* (Sire)   1984—*Like a Virgin*
1986—*True Blue*   1987—*Who's That Girl*; *You Can Dance*   1989—*Like a Prayer*   1990—*I'm Breathless*; The Immaculate Collection*   1992—*Erotica* (Maverick)   1994—*Bedtime Stories.***

Madonna is the most media-savvy American pop star since Bob Dylan and the most consistently controversial since Elvis Presley. In the minds of her supporters, her sassy approach to dance music and in-your-face videos gave feminism a much-needed makeover throughout the Eighties, smashing sexual boundaries, redefining the nature of eroticism, and challenging social and religious mores. To her detractors, she merely reinforced the notion of "woman as plaything," turning the clock back on conventional feminism two decades. One thing is rarely disputed: At nearly every turn, she has maintained firm control over her career and image.

Born in Bay City, Michigan, Madonna Ciccone was one of six children. Her mother died when Madonna was six, leaving her father, a Chrysler/General Dynamics engineer, to raise the family. She began studying dance at 14 and, after graduating high school in 1976, continued her dance studies at the University of Michigan in Ann Arbor. She moved to New York City in 1978, where she studied briefly with the Alvin Ailey dance troupe.

Her first crack at pop music came when a boyfriend let her sing and play drums in his band the Breakfast Club. While in the band, she landed a brief job as backup singer and dancer with disco star Patrick ("Born to Be Alive") Hernandez. In 1981 she quit the Breakfast Club and started writing songs with a former boyfriend from her college years, Steven Bray. The two gained attention in the trendy New York club Danceteria, where the DJ,

Mark Kamins, played her tapes; it was Kamins who took Madonna's demo to Sire Records and produced her first club hit, 1982's "Everybody." After a 12-inch single, "Burning Up" b/w "Physical Attraction," hit #3 on the dance charts in early 1983, she began recording her first album with the high-profile DJ John "Jellybean" Benitez [see Jellybean entry], with whom she became romantically involved. A few months later Sire released her self-titled debut, which peaked at #8. It spawned "Holiday," a single that crossed over from nightclubs to radio, eventually topping out at #16 on the pop charts by the following year.

Madonna enlisted manager Freddie DeMann, who had guided Michael Jackson from the Jacksons' late-Seventies slump through *Thriller*. DeMann soon had Madonna making history with a couple of titillating videos. In March 1984 "Borderline" (#10), with its video celebrating interracial love, was released; it was followed by "Lucky Star" (#4), whose video offered provocative glimpses of the star's navel. Public opinion was and would remain split. Most critics initially dismissed Madonna as a prefab disco prima donna offering style over substance; a few, however, saw something different and hailed her as a strong new female voice, BOY TOY belt and all.

In late 1984 the Nile Rodgers–produced *Like a Virgin*, with its #1 title song, shot to the Top Ten upon its release; it eventually sold more than seven million copies. Doubtless inspired by her undisputable videogenic presence, DeMann had negotiated movie deals for Madonna (before her stardom, she had already acted in the low-budget indie film *A Certain Sacrifice*), landing her a small part as a nightclub singer in *Vision Quest* and the title role in *Desperately Seeking Susan*. Throughout 1985 Madonna was ubiquitous, appearing in both movies, with hit songs on three albums. By March "Crazy for You" (#1), from the *Vision Quest* soundtrack, and "Material Girl" (#2), from *Like a Virgin,* were in the Top Five simultaneously. Her other hits were *Virgin*'s "Angel" (#5) and "Dress You Up" (#5), and the club smash "Into the Groove," from the *Susan* soundtrack. Her Virgin Tour was the hot ticket during the first half of the year.

In 1986 Madonna married actor Sean Penn, with whom she appeared in the critical and commercial flop *Shanghai Surprise.* Then she hit the pop world with a musical left hook: "Papa Don't Preach" (#1), the initial single from *True Blue* (#1), drew criticism with its message that young unwed women should keep their babies. As the lyrical content of Madonna's songs deepened, critical acceptance of her began to grow. Her subsequent 1986 hits were "True Blue" (#3) and "Open Your Heart" (#1), followed in 1987 by "La Isla Bonita" (#4). Another ill-advised acting venture, 1987's *Who's That Girl,* was tied in to an album of the same name, which included the hit title song (#1) and "Causing a Commotion" (#2). Madonna took time off the following year to split with Penn and appear in David Mamet's Broadway production, *Speed-the-Plow.*

She returned to music in 1989 with *Like a Prayer,* and the title song's video—complete with burning crosses and an eroticized black Jesus—launched Madonna's biggest and costliest controversy yet. Released in March, it was censured by the Vatican and the public response prompted Pepsi to cancel the singer's lucrative endorsement deal. The ordeal made Madonna a worldwide phenomenon. *Like a Prayer* spawned four other Top Twenty hits: "Express Yourself" (#2), "Cherish" (#2), "Oh Father" (#20), and "Keep It Together" (#8).

Madonna hit her megastar stride in 1990 when she appeared as Breathless Mahoney with then-boyfriend Warren Beatty in *Dick Tracy;* its soundtrack, *I'm Breathless,* bore hits in "Hanky Panky" (#10) and the nonmovie song "Vogue" (#1), which honored and revived the popular gay dance craze. In 1991 she scored hits with "Rescue Me" (#9) and "Justify My Love" (#1); the video for the latter fanned the flames of controversy yet again. She then oversaw the film *Truth or Dare,* a documentary of her Blond Ambition Tour dressed up to look like D. A. Pennebaker's Dylan movie, *Don't Look Back.* Madonna also became one of the first pop stars to speak out about AIDS and help raise money for research.

The singer affirmed her business acumen in 1992 when she signed a multimillion-dollar deal with Time Warner, guaranteeing release of all albums, films, and books under her Maverick production corporation. Her first Maverick project was a highly controversial 128-page coffee-table photo book, *Sex,* which had Madonna posing nude and wearing S&M gear. *Sex* was followed by the album *Erotica,* which peaked at #2 and produced Top Five hits in 1992: the title track and "Deeper and Deeper." "Bad Girl" and "Rain" were both Top Forty hits in 1993. By then Maverick was releasing work by other artists, including hip-hop chanteuse Me'Shell NdegéOcello, and Madonna embarked on her worldwide Girlie Show Tour, which drew a mixed critical reaction. An appearance on *The Late Show with David Letterman* returned Madonna to the headlines in spring 1994, when, using an abundance of profanities, she engaged in a verbal sparring match with the comedian. She also returned to the pop chart that year with the #2 single "I'll Remember," from the 1994 film *With Honors.* Her late 1994 album, *Bedtime Stories* (#3), presented a fairly traditional R&B sound and yielded the hit singles "Secret" (#4, 1994) and "Take a Bow" (#1, 1995).

Magazine

Formed 1977, Manchester, England
Howard Devoto, voc.; John McGeoch, gtr., sax; Dave Formula, kybds.; Barry Adamson (b. June 1, 1958, Manchester), bass; Martin Jackson, drums.
1978—*Real Life* (Virgin) (– Jackson; + John Doyle, drums) 1979—*Secondhand Daylight* (– McGeoch; + Robin Simon, gtr.) 1980—*The Correct Use of Soap; Play* 1981—*Magic, Murder and the Weather* (I.R.S.) 1982—*After the Fact* 1987—*Rays and Hail, 1978–1981* (Virgin).
Howard Devoto solo: 1983—*Jerky Versions of the Dream* (I.R.S.).
Luxuria (Devoto and Noko): 1988—*Unanswerable Lust* (Beggars Banquet) 1990—*Beast Box.*
Visage, formed 1978 (Steve Strange [b. Steve Harrington, May 28, 1959, Wales], voc.; Midge Ure [b. James Ure, Oct. 10, 1953, Glasgow, Scotland], gtr.; Billy Currie [b. Apr. 1, 1952], violin; Formula, kybds.; McGeoch, gtr.; Adamson, bass; Rusty Egan [b. Sep. 19, 1957], drums): 1980—*Visage* (Polydor) 1982—*The Anvil* 1983—*Fade to Grey—The Singles Collection* 1984—*Beat Boy.*
Barry Adamson solo: 1989—*Moss Side Story* (Mute) 1991—*Delusion* soundtrack 1992—*Soul Murder* 1993—*The Negro Inside Me.*

Howard Devoto formed Magazine after leaving seminal Manchester punk band the Buzzcocks. The band first came to prominence with a critically acclaimed British hit single, "Shot by Both Sides," which shared its guitar line with a Buzzcocks tune, "Lipstick" (both cowritten by Devoto and Buzzcock Pete Shelley). From there, though, the band's sound became more chilly and ponderous, rounding off its punky edges with Dave Formula's adept art-rockish keyboard hooks and fills. The second album was much smoother than the first, and *Soap* was an extremely polished bid for a wider commercial market, something the band might have actually earned had it not broken up after recording only one more LP. Devoto's solo *Jerky Versions of the Dream* offered up a more idiosyncratic musical outlook; his later project, Luxuria, verged on pretension.

Formula, McGeoch and Adamson participated in Visage, the new romantic band formed by vocalist Steve Strange. Although Visage had four U.K. Top Twenty hits ("Fade to Grey," "Mind of a Toy," "Damned Don't Cry," and "Night Train"), most of the members had commitments elsewhere. McGeogh went on to play with Siouxsie and the Banshees. Midge Ure and Billy Currie were in Ultravox [see entry]. Adamson joined Nick Cave's Bad Seeds [see the Birthday Party entry], but left in 1987 to record three "faux soundtracks"—modern takes on John Barry and Bernard Herrmann—for movies that exist only in his imagination. He also contributed music to the theatrical films *Delusion* (1990) and *Gas Food Lodging* (1992).

Taj Mahal
Born Henry Saint Clair Fredericks, May 17, 1942, New York City, New York
1967—*Taj Mahal* (Columbia)   1969—*The Natch'l Blues*; *Giant Step/De Ole Folks at Home*   1971— *The Real Thing*; *Happy Just to Be Like I Am*   1972—*Recycling the Blues (and Other Related Stuff)*   1973—*Oooh So Good 'n' Blues*   1974—*Mo' Roots*   1975—*Music Keeps Me Together*   1976—*Satisfied 'n' Tickled Too*   1977—*Music Fuh Ya' (Musica Para Tu)* (Warner Bros.); *Brothers*   1978—*Evolution (the Most Recent)*   1979—*Taj Mahal and International Rhythm Band Live* (Crystal Clear)   1980—*Taj Mahal and International Rhythm Band* (Magnet); *Going Home* (Columbia)   1981—*The Best of Taj Mahal*; *Live* (Magnet)   1986—*Taj* (Gramavision)   1988—*Shake Sugaree* (Music for Little People)   1991—*Mule Bone* (Gramavision); *Like Never Before* (Private Music)   1993—*Dancin' the Blues*.

Taj Mahal began developing his archival interest in the roots of black American and Caribbean music while studying at the University of Massachusetts in the early Sixties. His family had moved to Springfield, Massachusetts, from Brooklyn when he was young; although his parents were musical (his father a noted jazz arranger and pianist), young Fredericks first sought a college degree in animal husbandry. At the same time, he became a member of the Pioneer Valley Folklore Society and studied the ethnomusicology of rural black styles.

After receiving his B.A., he played blues in Boston folk clubs before moving to Santa Monica, California, and

in 1965, forming a blues rock band with Ry Cooder and future Spirit drummer Ed Cassidy called the Rising Sons. They signed with Columbia but broke up before recording. Columbia offered the singer—whose moniker, "Taj Mahal," had appeared to him in a dream—a solo deal, and his debut, introducing guitarist Jesse Ed Davis, was released in early 1967. His early albums, including *Giant Step/De Ole Folks at Home* and *The Real Thing*, were blues records laced with ragtime. On later albums he explored calypso and reggae. Live, he's worked solo, accompanying himself with piano, guitar, bass, and harmonica, and he's also appeared with bigger bands; one featured four tubas, another included steel drums. The Pointer Sisters backed him up on some recordings in their early days.

Mahal penned the music for the 1972 film *Sounder* (in which he had a small acting role); he has since written scores for *Sounder II* and *Brothers*, as well as for television shows and for 1991's Broadway production of *Mule Bone* by Langston Hughes and Zora Neale Hurston. In 1974 he played bass with the short-lived Great American Music Band, with David Grisman and violinist Richard Greene. He continued to record and perform throughout the Eighties and into the Nineties; his 1991 album *Like Never Before* featured appearances by Dr. John, the Pointer Sisters, Daryl Hall, and John Oates.

Mahavishnu Orchestra/John McLaughlin
Formed 1971, New York City, New York
Original lineup: John McLaughlin (b. Jan. 4, 1942, Yorkshire, Eng.), gtr.; Rick Laird (b. Feb. 5, 1941, Dublin, Ire.), bass; Jerry Goodman, violin; Billy Cobham (b. May 16, 1944, Panama), drums; Jan Hammer (b. Apr. 17, 1948, Prague, Czech.), kybds.
1972—*The Inner Mounting Flame* (Columbia)   1973—*Birds of Fire*; *Between Nothingness and Eternity*   1974—*Apocalypse*   1975—*Visions of the Emerald Beyond*   1976—*Inner Worlds*   1980—*Best of the Mahavishnu Orchestra*.
John McLaughlin solo: 1969—*Extrapolation* (Verve)   1970—*Devotion* (Douglas)   1972—*My Goal's Beyond*   1973—*Love, Devotion, Surrender* (with Carlos Santana) (Columbia); *Johnny McLaughlin, Electric Guitarist*   1979—*One Truth Band*   1980— *The Best of John McLaughlin*   1981—*Belo Horizonte* (Warner); *Friday Night in San Francisco* (with Al DiMeola and Paco DeLucia) (Columbia)   1982— *Music Spoken Here* (Warner)   1985—*Mahavishnu*   1987—*Adventures in Radioland* (Verve)   1990— *Mediterranean Concerto* (ECM)   1992—*Live at the Royal Festival Hall*   1993—*Time Remembered:*

Plays Bill Evans (Verve) 1994—*Free Spirits Featuring John McLaughlin: Tokyo Live.*

The original Mahavishnu Orchestra was the apotheosis of the career of guitar virtuoso John McLaughlin. Before its formation in 1971, McLaughlin made his name in England with numerous local blues bands, notably the groups of Graham Bond and Brian Auger. He moved to America in the late Sixties and became a guitarist in demand, recording six albums between 1969 and 1971, split between the early jazz-rock fusions of Miles Davis and Tony Williams' Lifetime.

In the meantime, having recorded *Extrapolation* with jazz musicians in England, McLaughlin cut his second solo LP, *Devotion,* with Jimi Hendrix's Band of Gypsys rhythm section: drummer Buddy Miles and bassist Billy Cox and Lifetime organist Larry Young. McLaughlin recruited rock studio drummer Billy Cobham (who had played with the progressive horn-laden band Dreams and with Davis) and violinist Jerry Goodman (a veteran of the classical-influenced Flock) for his third solo album, 1972's *My Goal's Beyond,* which also featured an Indian tabla player, Badal Roy. Next he founded the Mahavishnu Orchestra by adding European jazz-oriented players Rick Laird (one-time bassist with Buddy Rich) and keyboardist Jan Hammer (who had played with Elvin Jones and Sarah Vaughan). Mahavishnu was a name given him by his guru, Sri Chinmoy, and for a time the guitarist billed himself as Mahavishnu John McLaughlin. To Miles Davis' fusion of jazz and rock, McLaughlin added his own synthesis of East and West, mixing the stop-and-start melodies and rhythms of Indian ragas with the force of rock and the improvisational options of jazz. The Mahavishnu Orchestra was an immediate sensation, opening a whole new era of jazz-rock fusion, although even those players that could match McLaughlin's speed couldn't approach his lyricism. The Mahavishnu Orchestra's second album, *Birds of Fire* (#14, 1973), hit the Top Twenty. But conflicts within the group—especially over composer credit, most of which was claimed by McLaughlin—broke up the first Mahavishnu Orchestra after their third album, a live recording.

McLaughlin recorded *Love, Devotion, Surrender* (#14, 1973) with fellow Sri Chinmoy disciple Devadip Carlos Santana and retained the Mahavishnu Orchestra name for a variety of groups, including one with drummer Narada Michael Walden (later a successful R&B producer and songwriter) and keyboardist Gayle Moran (later of Return to Forever). *Apocalypse* (#43, 1974) involved the London Symphony Orchestra and former Beatles producer George Martin. None of the later Mahavishnu orchestras got the same commercial and critical response as the first one.

In 1976 McLaughlin renounced Sri Chinmoy and gave up both the name Mahavishnu and the group name Mahavishnu Orchestra. He formed an acoustic group, Shakti (a form of yoga involving worldly pleasures), with which he recorded three albums that were even closer in style to Indian ragas than the Orchestra had been. After a collaboration with ex–Return to Forever guitarist Al DiMeola, he formed a new electric group, the One Truth Band, with which he recorded and toured. McLaughlin then moved from New York to Paris, and he has continued to record with European musicians.

The other original Orchestra members have continued to record and perform. Laird played around New York with numerous jazz and rock groups, before devoting himself to photography; after a 1974 collaboration with Hammer, *Like Children,* Goodman apparently dropped out of the music business, resurfacing in the late Eighties as a New Age artist. Hammer has recorded frequently on his own, with Jeff Beck, and in 1982 with Journey's Neal Schon; he has his own Red Gate Studio. Hammer's "*Miami Vice* Theme" was a major hit single (#1, 1985). And Cobham has recorded and performed with a new jazz-rock band nearly every year, also touring with Grateful Dead guitarist Bob Weir's Bobby and the Midnites.

From 1984 to 1986 McLaughlin reformed the Mahavishnu Orchestra with an entirely different lineup, including drummer Danny Gottlieb, keyboardist Mitch Foreman, and saxophonist Bill Evans, who had previously worked with Miles Davis.

Although never entirely forsaking electric music, McLaughlin tended thereafter to concentrate on the acoustic guitar. During the late Eighties he occasionally toured as a duo with virtuoso bassist Jonas Hellborg, and then formed a trio with percussionist Trilok Gurtu and bassist Kai Eckhardt. McLaughlin also performed orchestral works (*Mediterranean Concerto*) and appeared on the soundtrack of the 1986 jazz film *Round Midnight.*

McLaughlin performed with Miles Davis as part of a 1991 Davis career retrospective that took place just months before the trumpeter's death (McLaughlin had earlier guested on Davis' *You're Under Arrest* and *Aura*). In 1993 McLaughlin collaborated with a European classical guitar quintet to produce a tribute to the late jazz pianist and composer Bill Evans, an important influence for McLaughlin. The next year McLaughlin—back on electric guitar—teamed up with organist Joey DeFrancesco and drummer Dennis Chambers to form the Free Spirits band.

Mahogany Rush

Formed 1971, Montreal, Canada
Original lineup: Frank Marino (b. Aug. 22, 1954, Del Rio, Tex.), gtr., voc.; Paul Harwood (b. Feb. 30, 1939, Quebec, Can.), bass; Jimmy Ayoub (b. Dec. 7, 1941, Honolulu, Hawaii), drums.

1971—*Maxoom* (Kot'ai)   1973—*Child of the Novelty*
(20th Century-Fox)   1975—*Strange Universe*
1976—*Mahogany Rush IV* (Columbia)   1977—*World
Anthem*   1978—*Mahogany Rush Live*   1979—*Tales
of the Unexpected*   1980—*What's Next*   1987—*Full
Circle* (Maze)   1989—*Frank Marino and Mahogany
Rush: Double Live*   Ca. 1991—(Lineup: Marino;
Vince Marino, gtr.; Peter Dowse, bass; Timm Biery,
drums)   1993—*From the Hip* (Vision).
Frank Marino solo: 1981—*The Power of Rock 'n' Roll*
(CBS)   1982—*Juggernaut* (Columbia).

The long-running supernatural explanation of how guitarist Frank Marino came by his flashy, effects-laden
playing style entered into rock legend because it was
patently absurd. Today it ranks as an untruth that refuses to die, despite Marino's many vehement denials.
For the record, then, here's the gist of the old story. Allegedly, a teenaged Marino was in a Montreal hospital
recovering from either illness, drug overdose, or an auto
accident when he lapsed into a deep coma. Upon awakening several days later, Marino claimed he'd been
visited by the spirit of Jimi Hendrix. Although a
nonmusician (some sources say drummer and guitar
player), Marino picked up the guitar and began playing a
lot like Jerry Garcia and Hendrix. In recent years, Marino
has disavowed the story altogether.

Whatever happened, Marino, then just 17, found a
bassist and drummer, and Mahogany Rush was born.
The recorded evidence of *Maxoom* (rereleased in the
mid-Seventies by 20th Century-Fox) shows a competent
heavy-metal guitarist with an intense Hendrix fetish.
Marino slowed the pace a bit for *Novelty,* which concentrated more on actual songs, and has since diversified his
guitar style a bit in a jazz-rock fusion direction. For years,
Marino endured critical barbs and moderate records
sales (though 1983's "Strange Dreams" got some AOR
airplay) at best. Through the Eighties, however, he continued to tour and record intermittently for small labels,
all the while building a cult among the burgeoning metal
contingent.

The Main Ingredient

**Formed early Sixties as the Poets, New York City,
New York**
**Enrique Antonio "Tony" Silvester (b. Oct. 7, 1941,
Colón, Panama), voc.; Luther Simmons Jr. (b. Sep. 9,
1942, New York City), voc.; Don McPherson (b. July
9, 1941, Indianapolis, Ind.; d. July 4, 1971), voc.;
+ Cuba Gooding (b. Apr. 27, 1944, New York City),
voc.**
Ca. 1965—(- Gooding)   1970—*The Main Ingredient
L.T.D.* (RCA)   1971—(- McPherson; + Gooding)
Tasteful Soul; Black Seeds   1972—*Bitter Sweet*
(RCA)   1973—*Afrodisiac; Greatest Hits* (+ Carl

Tompkins [b. Petersburg, Va.], voc.; – Silvester)
1974—*Euphrates River*   1975—*Rolling Down a
Mountainside*   1976—*Spinning Around; Shame on
the World* (group disbands)   1977—*Music Maximus*
1980—(Group re-forms: Silvester; Simmons; Good-
ing) *Ready for Love*   1981—*I Only Have Eyes for
You*   1986—(Group re-forms: Gooding; Silvester;
+ Jerome Jackson).
Cuba Gooding solo: 1978—*The First Cuba Gooding
Album* (Motown)   1979—*Love Dancer.*

In 1971 the Main Ingredient was a smooth black vocal
trio on the rise. After years of struggle, it had placed three
singles in a row on the R&B chart—"You've Been My Inspiration" (#25, 1970), "I'm So Proud" (#13, 1970), and
"Spinning Around" (#7, 1971)—when lead singer Don
McPherson died of leukemia. With his replacement,
Cuba Gooding (who had been in the group in the Sixties
but quit to attend college), the group went on to its
greatest success.

McPherson, Luther Simmons Jr., Gooding, and Tony
Silvester formed the Poets in the early Sixties and were
signed to Mike Stoller and Jerry Leiber's Red Bird label in
1965. Their one chart record for that label was "Merry
Christmas Baby." In 1967 they left Red Bird for RCA, renaming themselves the Insiders. But their luck did not
improve until they changed their name again. "You've
Been My Inspiration" followed soon after.

After McPherson's death, the Main Ingredient
moved toward pop. "Black Seeds Keep On Growing" was
another R&B hit, reaching #15 in 1971, after which the
trio finally had its first pop hit, "Everybody Plays the
Fool" (#3 pop, #2 R&B, 1972). (In 1993 the song was covered by Aaron Neville.) More pop hits followed in 1974—
"Just Don't Want to Be Lonely" (#10 pop, #8 R&B) and
"Happiness Is Just Around the Bend" (#35 pop, #7
R&B)—as well as four more Top Forty R&B records before the Main Ingredient broke up in 1976: "You've Got to
Take It" (#18) and "You Can Call Me Rover" (#34) in 1973,
and "Rolling Down a Mountainside" (#7) and "Shame on
the World" (#20) in 1975. Gooding's brief solo career
proved disappointing. Silvester, however, became a successful producer of artists including Sister Sledge, Ben E.
King, and Bette Midler. Luther became a stockbroker. In
1980 a reunion as the Main Ingredient featuring Cuba
Gooding yielded the R&B chart single "Think Positive"
(#69). Nineteen-eighty-six's "Do Me Right" also peaked
at #69 R&B. They continued to record into the Nineties.
Cuba Gooding's son, Cuba Gooding Jr., became a successful actor whose credits include *Boyz N the Hood.*

Yngwie Malmsteen

Born June 30, 1963, Stockholm, Sweden
1984—*Yngwie Malmsteen's Rising Force* (Polydor);
Marching Out   1986—*Trilogy* (Mercury)   1988—

Odyssey (Polydor)   1989—**Trial by Fire: Live in Leningrad**   1990—**Eclipse**   1992—**Fire and Ice** (Elektra).

A flashy guitarist whose sound combines Ritchie Blackmore and Paganini, Yngwie Malmsteen is best known for his speed and technical facility. A guitar player since he was eight, in the early Eighties the Swedish-born Malmsteen sent a demo tape to *Guitar Player* editor Mike Varney. Varney paid for Malmsteen to fly to the U.S. and hooked him up with the L.A. metal band Steeler. They recorded one album in 1983 before Malmsteen moved on to Alcatrazz, a band fronted by former Rainbow lead singer Graham Bonnet. Enticed by a solo deal with Polydor, Malmsteen left Alcatrazz after two albums.

On *Rising Force* (#60, 1985) his solo debut, Malmsteen was supported by former Jethro Tull drummer Barriemore Barlow. *Marching Out* (#52, 1985) was the first appearance by his band, Rising Force. Malmsteen was seriously injured in a car accident in 1987 and did not record again until the next year. The resulting album, *Odyssey* (#40, 1988), with former Rainbow singer Joe Lynn Turner, was his most successful album to date and seemed to secure him a place in the pantheon of guitar heroes. He followed up with a live album, *Trial by Fire: Live in Leningrad* (#128, 1989). It was roundly criticized for self-indulgence, and matters were not helped by Turner's departure that year. *Eclipse* (#112, 1990) continued his slide in popularity; a move to Elektra for *Fire and Ice* (#121, 1992) did not brighten his fortunes.

Malo

Formed 1971, San Francisco, California
Original lineup: Jorge Santana (b. June 13, 1954, Jalisco, Mex.), gtr.; Arcelio Garcia Jr. (b. May 7, 1946, Manati, P.R.), voc., perc.; Abel Zarate (b. Dec. 2, 1952, Manila, Philippines), gtr., voc.; Roy Murray, trumpet, trombone, flute, sax; Pablo Tellez (b. July 2, 1951, Granada, Nicaragua), bass; Rich Spremich (b. July 2, 1951, San Francisco), drums; Richard Kermode (b. Oct. 5, 1946, Lovell, Wyo.), kybds.; Luis Gasca (b. Mar. 23, 1940, Houston, Tex.), trumpet, flugelhorn.
1972—Malo (Warner Bros.); Dos   1973—Evolution 1974—Ascension.

Like Carlos Santana, brother Jorge formed his own Latin-rock band, Malo (Spanish for "bad"). Reinforcing the Santana connection, two of Carlos' percussionists, Coke Escovedo and Victor Pontoja, guested on Malo's debut LP, which spent a number of weeks in the Top Fifteen and yielded the band's one hit, "Suavecito" (#18, 1972).

Many of Malo's members were veterans of the San Francisco scene, either with rock bands or with Latin bands from the Mission District. Richard Kermode and Luis Gasca had played together in Janis Joplin's Kozmic

Blues Band; Gasca's jazz credentials include stints with Count Basie, Woody Herman, and Mongo Santamaria. *Dos* and *Evolution* both had minor success on the album chart; *Ascension* fared worse, and the band broke up. Gasca has recorded pop-jazz albums for Fantasy Records.

The Mamas and the Papas

Formed 1965, New York City, New York
John Phillips (b. Aug. 30, 1935, Parris Island, S.C.), voc., gtr.; Dennis Doherty (b. Nov. 29, 1941, Halifax, Nova Scotia, Can.), voc.; Michelle Phillips (b. Holly Michelle Gilliam, Apr. 6, 1944, Long Beach, Calif.), voc.; Cass Elliot (b. Sep. 19, 1943, Baltimore, Md.; d. July 29, 1974, London, Eng.), voc.
1966—If You Can Believe Your Eyes and Ears (Dunhill); The Mamas and the Papas   1967—Deliver 1968—Farewell to the First Golden Era; The Papas and the Mamas (group disbands)   1969—16 of Their Greatest Hits   1971—(Group re-forms) People Like Us (group disbands)   1973—Golden Hits 1981—(Group re-forms: J. Phillips; Doherty; + Mackenzie Phillips, voc.; + Elaine "Spanky" McFarlane [b. June 19, 1942, Peoria, Ill.], voc.).

Although the Mamas and the Papas made their commercial impact with airy California folk pop and were on the scene as Los Angeles went psychedelic, they were a product of the Greenwich Village folk community. John Phillips had been active in New York since 1957; he had previously attended George Washington University and, for three months, the U.S. Naval Academy. In 1962 he met and married Holly Michelle Gilliam, who had come to New York to be a model; she began singing with his group, the Journeymen.

Denny Doherty had been a member of the Halifax Three, which, after two albums for Epic, included future Lovin' Spoonful member Zal Yanovsky. Doherty and Yanovsky joined Cass Elliot and her first husband, Jim Hendricks, to form Cass Elliot and the Big Three. The group changed its name to the Mugwumps and went electric, with Art Stokes on drums and John Sebastian on harmonica. The Mugwumps recorded one album—not released until 1967—and broke up. Sebastian and Yanovsky formed the Lovin' Spoonful, Elliot fronted a jazz trio, and Doherty joined John and Michelle Phillips as the New Journeymen.

To rehearse, the New Journeymen went to St. Thomas in the Virgin Islands; Elliot joined them and worked on the island as a waitress, then moved to California with her husband. The New Journeymen relocated to California, where they stayed with Elliot and Hendricks, and Elliot officially joined the group. They recorded backing vocals for a Barry McGuire record, then got their own contract as the Mamas and the Papas.

The Mamas and the Papas: John Phillips, Cass Elliot, Denny Doherty, Michelle Phillips

In 1966 and 1967 they had six Top Five hits—"California Dreamin'" (#4), "Monday, Monday" (#1), "I Saw Her Again" (#5), "Words of Love" (#5), and "Dedicated to the One I Love" (#2) in 1966, and the autobiographical "Creeque Alley" (#5) in 1967—and four gold albums. John Phillips also wrote a signature song of the flower-power era, "San Francisco (Be Sure to Wear Flowers in Your Hair)" (#4, 1967), which was recorded by Scott McKenzie, an ex-Journeyman. The quartet also appeared at the 1967 Monterey Pop Festival, which Phillips helped finance.

By 1968, though, the group was falling apart and decided to disband. John and Michelle Phillips had marital problems; John Phillips made a solo LP, *The Wolf King of L.A.*, and then coproduced (with Lou Adler) Robert Altman's 1970 film *Brewster McCloud*. Michelle Phillips appeared in *The Last Movie* with Dennis Hopper, to whom she was later married for eight days. In addition to the Phillipses' divorce (1970), the band had other legal problems. Dunhill and band members sued each other for breach of contract (excluding Elliot, who continued to record for the label on her own) and fraudulent withholding of royalties, respectively. In 1971 the group made what it later admitted was a poor reunion album, *People Like Us*. Cass Elliot continued her solo career until her death from choking in 1974.

Doherty recorded two solo albums but with little success. Michelle Phillips' acting career began to pick up with films like *Dillinger* and Ken Russell's 1976 movie bio of Rudolph Valentino, in which she costarred with Rudolf Nureyev. In 1977 she recorded a solo LP for A&M, *Victim of Romance*. She found greater fame on TV, as a cast member of the popular evening soap *Knots Landing*.

John Phillips had become idle by the mid-Seventies, reportedly living off his $100,000-a-year royalties from songs like "California Dreamin'." By 1975 he had stopped work altogether. He was arrested by federal narcotics agents on July 31, 1980. Phillips' eight-year, $15,000-fine sentence was reduced to 30 days. Phillips cleaned up, as did his daughter, actress Mackenzie Phillips (*One Day at a Time*). The two appeared on numerous television programs and lectured around the country. The pair also decided to revive the Mamas and the Papas. Phillips contacted Doherty (who by then was hosting a popular television show in Nova Scotia) and filled out the new foursome with Elaine "Spanky" McFarlane, from Spanky and Our Gang [see entry]. Phillips cowrote the Beach Boys' 1988 #1 smash "Kokomo." John and Michelle Phillips are the parents of singer Chynna Phillips of Wilson Phillips [see entry].

Melissa Manchester

Born February 15, 1951, Bronx, New York
1973—*Home to Myself* (Bell); *Bright Eyes* 1975—*Melissa* (Arista) 1976—*Help Is On the Way*; *Better Days and Happy Endings* 1977—*"Singing . . ."* 1978—*Don't Cry Out Loud* 1979—*Melissa Manchester* 1980—*For the Working Girl* 1982—*Hey Ricky* 1983—*Greatest Hits*; *Emergency* 1985—*Mathematics* (MCA) 1989—*Tribute* (Mika) 1994—*If My Heart Had Wings* (Atlantic).

Melissa Manchester is a singer and sometime songwriter in the Peter Allen/Carole Bayer Sager/Barry Manilow MOR axis. Coming from a musical family (her father is a bassoonist with the Metropolitan Opera), Manchester began singing jingles at age 15. She attended the High School of Performing Arts in the late Sixties while working as a staff writer at Chappell Music. Upon graduation she entered New York University and enrolled in a songwriting seminar taught by Paul Simon. She then played clubs in Manhattan, where she was discovered by Bette Midler and her accompanist, Barry Manilow. They hired her as a backup singer (Harlette) in 1971.

Six months later Manchester got a record contract of her own. Her 1973 debut, *Home to Myself,* featured many songs cowritten by Carole Bayer Sager. In 1975 her third LP, *Melissa,* yielded her first hit, "Midnight Blue" (#6). She didn't have a really big followup until her version of Peter Allen/Carole Bayer Sager's song "Don't Cry Out

Loud," which went to #10 in 1979. She cowrote Kenny Loggins' smash duet with Stevie Nicks, "Whenever I Call You 'Friend.'"

In 1980 Manchester became the first performer to have recorded two of the movie themes nominated for an Academy Award, "Ice Castles" and "The Promise." In 1982 she had her biggest hit with "You Should Hear How She Talks About You" (#5) from *Hey Ricky,* which netted her the Grammy for Best Female Vocal Performance. Through the Eighties Manchester recorded sporadically. Her *Tribute* is a collection of standards, such as "Over the Rainbow" and "La Vie en Rose." She has branched into acting, appearing in Bette Midler's film *For the Boys* and portraying the title character's mother in the television series *Blossom.*

Mandrill

Formed 1968, New York City, New York
Original lineup: Lou Wilson (b. Panama), trumpet, congas, voc.; Ric Wilson (b. Panama), sax, voc.; Carlos Wilson (b. Panama), trombone, flute, gtr., perc., voc.; Omar Mesa (b. Havana, Cuba), gtr., voc.; Bundie Cenac (b. St. Lucia, W. Indies), bass, voc.; Claude Cave, kybds., vibraphone, voc.; Charlie Padro, drums, voc.
1971—*Mandrill* (Polydor) (– Cenac; + Fudgie Kae, bass) 1972—*Mandrill Is* (– Padro; + Neftali Santiago, drums) 1973—*Composite Truth; Just Outside of Town* (– Mesa; + Doug Rodrigues, gtr.) 1974— *Mandrilland* 1975—*Best of Mandrill* (– Kae; + Brian Allsop, bass, voc.; – Santiago; + Andre Locke [b. Brooklyn, N.Y.], drums, voc.; – Rodrigues; + Tommy Trujillo, gtr., voc.); *Solid* (United Artists) (+ Wilfredo Wilson [b. Panama], voc., perc.); *Beast from the East* 1977—(W. Wilson switches to bass; – Locke; + Santiago, drums; – Allsop; – Trujillo; + Juaquin Jessup, gtr., perc., voc.) *We Are One* (Arista) 1978—(– Santiago; – Jessup; + David Conley [b. Dec. 27, 1953, Newark, N.J.], bass) *New Worlds* 1980—*Getting in the Mood* 1988—*The Best of Mandrill* (Polydor).

Emerging from the tough Bedford-Stuyvesant area of Brooklyn, Mandrill played a mixed urban brew encompassing elements of Santana-tinged Latin rock, Chambers Brothers–style soul, and horn-driven rock. The band was founded by the four Wilson brothers, all of whom spent their childhoods in Panama. After spending various amounts of time at college (Ric got a medical degree from Harvard), Ric, Lou, and Carlos began jamming together with other musicians, eventually settling on the seven-member lineup. Its debut LP became a big breakout on rock FM radio as well as black stations, aided by the eponymous title song, selling 150,000 copies in the New York area alone. The band's biggest hits were on the R&B chart, peaking with 1973's "Fencewalk" at #19. Also that year, Mandrill played with Duke Ellington at the Newport Jazz Festival. Altogether, Mandrill recorded five albums for Polydor, but in January 1975 the group switched to United Artists, moved to L.A., and went through some major personnel changes, all the while retaining the three Wilsons and original member Cave.

For *Beast from the East,* the youngest and fourth Wilson brother, Wilfredo, joined the fold as singer/percussionist. The band did well on concert tours, but still did not break big, and in 1977 it switched to Arista after contributing to the soundtrack of Muhammad Ali's film biography, *The Greatest.* Mandrill's biggest hit for Arista was "Too Late" (#37 R&B, 1978).

Chuck Mangione

Born November 29, 1940, Rochester, New York
1962—*Recuerdo* (Jazzland) 1970—*Friends and Love . . . A Chuck Mangione Concert* (Mercury) 1971—*Together* 1972—*The Chuck Mangione Quartet; Alive!* 1973—*Land of Make Believe* 1975— *Chase the Clouds Away* (A&M) 1976—*Bellavia; Main Squeeze* 1977—*Feels So Good* 1978—*Children of Sanchez* 1979—*An Evening of Magic: Chuck Mangione Live at the Hollywood Bowl* 1980—*Fun and Games* 1981—*Tarantella* 1982— *Love Notes* (Columbia) 1983—*Journey to a Rainbow* 1984—*Disguise* 1986—*Save Tonight for Me* 1988—*Eyes of the Veiled Temptress.*

By selling a million copies of his instrumental "Feels So Good" in 1978, fluegelhornist Chuck Mangione established himself as a pop-jazz star. While never recapturing that late-Seventies peak, he has remained commercially credible even as purists continue to decry his abandonment of his traditional jazz roots.

Mangione grew up in a musical family, and big jazz names passing through Rochester were entertained and fed in the Mangione household. He took up piano at age eight, trumpet two years later. In 1960 with his brother Gap on piano he formed the Jazz Brothers quintet. After they disbanded in 1965, he performed with Art Blakey and the Jazz Messengers and in trumpeter Maynard Ferguson's band.

Recording on his own, Mangione moved away from jazz's complexities to write and arrange instrumentals for a small group, often backed by strings or full orchestra. He recorded the *Friends and Love* double album with the Rochester Philharmonic. He won his first Grammy (Best Instrumental Composition, 1976) for "Bellavia." *Feels So Good* went gold in February 1978; by April of that year it was platinum, and it eventually sold more than two million copies. "Chase the Clouds Away" was played as background music by ABC-TV during telecasts of the 1976 Olympics. In 1980 Mangione was commissioned by ABC Sports to write music for the Winter Olympics (which made up *Fun and Games*), and his Olympic music won an Emmy that year for Music Composition/Direction. Mangione won another Grammy (Best Pop Instrumental Performance, 1978) for *Children of Sanchez*, a score for a film based on the Oscar Lewis book. In December 1980 Mangione held a massive benefit concert in his hometown for victims of a recent earthquake in Italy; Dizzy Gillespie, Chick Corea, and Steve Gadd were among those present.

Switching to CBS in 1982, Mangione began working with such outside producers as Eumir Deodato and Thom Bell in the mid-Eighties. His albums, beginning to employ synthesizers but otherwise still featuring melodic pop jazz, continued to sell respectably, and he toured often, occasionally appearing in concert with symphony orchestras. In the late Eighties he reunited with the Jazz Brothers for an American tour.

The Manhattans
Formed 1961, Jersey City, New Jersey
George "Smitty" Smith (d. 1971), lead voc.; Winfred "Blue" Lovett (b. Nov. 16, 1943, N.J.), bass voc.; Edward "Sonny" Bivins (b. Jan. 15, 1942, N.J.), tenor voc.; Kenneth Kelley (b. Jan. 9, 1943, N.J.), second tenor voc.; Richard Taylor (d. Dec. 7, 1987), baritone voc.
1966—*Dedicated* (Carnival)   1967—*For You and Yours*   1968— *With These Hands* (King/Deluxe) 1969—*Million to One*   1970—(+ Gerald Alston [b. Nov. 8, 1942], tenor voc.)   1971—(– Smith) 1972—*There's No Me Without You* (Columbia) 1974—*That's How Much I Love You*   1976—*The Manhattans*   1977—*It Feels So Good* (– Taylor) 1978—*There's No Good in Goodbye*   1979—*Love Talk*   1980—*After Midnight*   1981—*Black Tie*; Follow Your Heart* (Solid Smoke)   1983—*Forever by Your Side* (Columbia)   1985—*Too Hot to Stop It* 1988—(– Alston; + Roger Harris, voc.)   1993— (Group re-forms: Alston; Lovett; others)   1994— *Back to Basics* (Valley Vue).

Steadfast practitioners of a suave soul-ballad harmony style rooted in doo-wop, anchored by the recitations of "Blue" Lovett, the Manhattans have never maintained mass popularity despite a long string of hits.

Winfred Lovett and Kenneth Kelley had sung in rival Jersey City doo-wop groups; Richard Taylor met Edward Bivins during an Air Force hitch in Germany in the late Fifties. Returning to the New York area, Taylor and Bivins united with Lovett, Kelley, and Smith to form Ronnie and the Manhattans, who recorded several unsuccessful singles, one for Bobby Robinson's Enjoy Records. The Manhattans finally got their break when Barbara Brown, a singer with Joe Evans' Newark-based Carnival Records,

retired from recording; she recommended the Manhattans to Evans, who caught them at Harlem's Apollo Theatre and signed them.

After several unsuccessful singles, the group hit big in 1965 with Lovett's tune "I Wanna Be (Your Everything)," which sold 500,000 copies and made the R&B Top Twenty. (Bivins and Taylor also write songs for the group.) In the next two years the Manhattans followed with a string of transitional doo-wop/soul hits like "Searchin' for My Baby," "Follow Your Heart," "Baby I Need You," and "Can I," all of which made the R&B Top Thirty. In 1968 the group signed with King subsidiary Deluxe, for which it had only minor successes like "If My Heart Could Speak" and "From Atlanta to Goodbye."

In 1971 the group was dealt a seemingly crushing blow when Smith died of spinal meningitis. However, a replacement, Gerald Alston, was discovered in North Carolina, and with a signing to Columbia in 1972 the Manhattans continued to release romantic soul hits. Among those that made the R&B Top Ten were "There's No Me Without You" (1973), "Don't Take Your Love from Me" (1974), "Hurt" (1975), the R&B and pop #1 "Kiss and Say Goodbye" (1976), "I Kinda Miss You" (1976), "It Feels So Good (to Be Loved So Bad)" (1977), "Am I Losing You" (1978) (the only one that did not enter the pop chart), and "Shining Star" (#5 pop, #4 R&B, 1980). By then the Manhattans had been together nearly 20 years. Taylor left in 1977 to pursue his religious interests; he converted to Islam. Alston enjoyed a solo career but returned to the group for its 1993 reunion to commemorate its 30th anniversary.

Alston and Lovett form the core of the group, which still records and performs. Regina Belle, who has since gone on to a successful solo career, performed with the group in the mid-Eighties.

The Manhattan Transfer
Formed 1969, New York City, New York
Tim Hauser (b. ca. 1940, Troy, N.Y.), voc., gtr., banjo; Pat Rosalia, tambourine, voc.; Erin Dickens, gtr., tambourine, voc.; Gene Pistilli, gtr., voc.; Marty Nelson, gtr., clarinet, piano.
Sometime after 1969—(– Rosalia; – Dickens; – Nelson; – Pistilli)   1972—(+ Alan Paul [b. ca. 1949, Newark, N.J.), voc.; + Janis Siegel [b. ca. 1953, Brooklyn, N.Y.], voc.; + Laurel Masse [b. ca. 1954], voc.)   1975—*Jukin'* (Capitol, recorded before 1972 with original lineup); *The Manhattan Transfer* (Atlantic)   1976—*Coming Out*   1978—*Pastiche*; *Live* 1979—(– Masse; + Cheryl Bentyne [b. Mount Vernon, Wash.], voc.)   1980—*Extensions*   1981— *Mecca for Moderns*; *The Best of the Manhattan Transfer*   1983—*Bodies and Souls*   1984—*Bop Doowopp*   1985—*Vocalese*   1987—*Live*; *Brasil* 1991—*The Off-Beat of Avenues* (Columbia)   1992—

The Christmas Album; Anthology (Rhino) 1994—
Tonin' (Atlantic).
Janis Siegel solo: 1982—*Experiment in White* (Atlantic) 1987—*At Home* 1989—*Short Stories* (with Fred Hersch).

The Manhattan Transfer is a four-part vocal harmony group that began as a nostalgia group and has since recorded and performed in an array of styles including swing, doo-wop, jazz scat, Latin, and pop. Unlike many pop groups, however, Manhattan Transfer's eclectic approach has served them well: The group has won ten Grammy Awards, is a perennial winner of annual jazz polls, and is a strong concert draw around the world.

Manhattan Transfer first formed in 1969 as a Jim Kweskin Jug Band–style good-time group and signed to Capitol. It took its name from a novel by John Dos Passos about New York in the Twenties. The quartet soon broke up, though, and the only remaining member was Tim Hauser. (Also in that early incarnation was Gene Pistilli, who had written "Sunday Will Never Be the Same" with Terry Cashman for Spanky and Our Gang.)

The new Manhattan Transfer formed in 1972, and soon became popular on New York's cabaret circuit. Hauser had sung in doo-wop groups as a youth, around 1958 with the Criterions in high school and later with the Viscounts, who had a hit with "Harlem Nocturne." Later he played in a folk band with Jim Croce. Alan Paul was a child actor who had appeared in road companies of *Oliver* and *Grease,* in movies (*The Pawnbroker*), and in TV commercials. Janis Siegel had recorded with the Young Generation, a group produced by Leiber and Stoller and at one time groomed to be the next Shangri-Las, and in a folk group called Laurel Canyon. With fourth member Laurel Masse they released their Atlantic debut in 1975 (containing "Operator," a #22 hit) and immediately got a summer network TV replacement series, which lasted three weeks in August. But even with the nostalgia trend of the time, the band didn't sell in this country, though it had a #1 hit in England and France with "Chanson d'Amour."

In 1979, after being injured in an automobile accident, Masse left and was replaced by Cheryl Bentyne, daughter of a swing musician. The band had begun to modernize its look—shifting from tuxedos to a new wave/Deco combination—and broadened its audience with the release of *Extensions,* from which "Twilight Zone/Twilight Tone" became a modest hit (#30, 1980). That album also included the group's version of "Birdland," for which it was awarded its first Grammy. In mid-1981 the Manhattan Transfer had a Top Ten hit with a remake of the old Ad Libs song "Boy from New York City." That song won a Grammy for Best Pop Performance by a Duo or Group with Vocal, while "Until I Met You (Corner Pocket)" from the same album got the

Grammy for Best Jazz Vocal Performance, Duo or Group. The following year, Manhattan Transfer's version of "Route 66" won another Grammy, and the year after that "Why Not!" continued the streak. In late 1983 "Spice of Life," from *Bodies and Souls,* hit #40. Although conventional hit singles are rare for this group, their work is a staple of easy-listening and jazz radio formats.

With Jon Hendricks, of the team Lambert, Hendricks, and Ross, the group essayed the jazz vocal style known as vocalese, where lyrics are added to what were originally instrumental jazz pieces. The resulting *Vocalese* garnered 12 Grammy nominations (only Michael Jackson's *Thriller* got more) and won two (the group got one and the album's arrangers got the other). The next album, *Brasil,* which featured songs by Gilberto Gil and Milton Nascimento, among others, was awarded the Grammy for Best Pop Performance by a Duo or Group with Vocal.

With *The Off-Beat of Avenues,* the quartet moved to Columbia Records, and for the first time, wrote or cowrote and produced most of the work. After releasing a Christmas album, the group returned to Atlantic Records.

Barry Manilow
Born Barry Alan Pinkus, June 17, 1946, Brooklyn, New York
1972—*Barry Manilow* (Bell) 1973—*Barry Manilow II* 1975—*Tryin' to Get the Feeling* (Arista) 1977—*This One's for You; Barry Manilow Live* 1978—*Even Now* 1979—*Barry Manilow's Greatest Hits; One Voice* 1980—*Barry* 1981—*If I Should Love Again* 1982—*Oh, Julie!; Here Comes the Night* 1983—*Greatest Hits, vol. 2* 1984—*2:00 A.M. Paradise Cafe* 1985—*The Manilow Collections—Twenty Classic Hits; Manilow* (RCA) 1987—*Swing Street* (Arista) 1989—*Barry Manilow* 1990—*Live on Broadway; Because It's Christmas* 1991—*Showstoppers* 1992—*The Complete Collection and Then Some . . .* 1994—*Singing with the Big Bands.*

Pop singer/songwriter Barry Manilow has sold over 50 million records worldwide. In 1977 his unabashedly romantic (verging on mawkish) pop gave him five albums on the charts simultaneously, a record surpassed only by Frank Sinatra and Johnny Mathis. He has since focused his attention on a wide range of genres, including Broadway show tunes and traditional jazz.

When Manilow was seven, he picked up his first instrument, accordion. He later attended New York College of Music and the Juilliard School. He also worked in the CBS mailroom, and there, at 18, he met a director who encouraged him to do some musical arranging. Soon after, Manilow wrote an Off-Broadway musical adaptation of *The Drunkard,* which had a long run. In 1967 he became musical director of the CBS-TV series *Callback* and later did conducting and arranging for Ed Sullivan productions. He also played in a cabaret act duo, and in spring 1972, while filling in as house pianist at New York's Continental Baths, he met Bette Midler and soon became her musical director, arranger, and pianist. He coproduced and arranged her 1972 Grammy-winning debut and her 1973 followup. During this time he wrote commercial jingles for Dr. Pepper, Band-Aids, and State Farm Insurance, among others (contrary to popular opinion, he did not write, although he sang, McDonald's "You Deserve a Break Today").

Manilow landed a solo deal with Bell (later Arista) in 1972 but first toured with Midler as featured performer before releasing his debut LP in 1972 and doing his own road show in 1974. His second LP came out in 1973, and in only nine weeks his cover of "Mandy" went to #1 in January of 1975. Hits like "Could It Be Magic" (#6, 1975), "It's a Miracle" (#12, 1975), Bruce Johnston's "I Write the Songs" (#1, 1976), and "Tryin' to Get the Feeling Again" (#10, 1976) followed. His debut album went platinum, and over the years a dozen more followed suit, including the multiplatinum *Barry Manilow Live, Even Now,* and *Greatest Hits.* His regular coproducer was ex-Archie Ron Dante up until his tenth LP in 1981.

Manilow won an Emmy for one of his TV specials, a special Tony for a Broadway concert, and a 1978 Grammy. In 1980 he produced Dionne Warwick's platinum comeback LP, which contained the hit "I'll Never Love This Way Again." In early 1982 he hit the Top Twenty with "The Old Songs" and later had a lesser hit with a remake of the Four Seasons' "Let's Hang On." He continued scoring gold albums through the Eighties. *2:00 A.M. Paradise Cafe* (#28, 1984) and *Swing Street* found Manilow moving from schmaltzy pop to a more jazz-oriented sound (he was joined on the albums by such singers and musicians as Mel Torme, Sarah Vaughan, and Gerry Mulligan).

In 1984 Manilow scored music to words by the great lyricist Johnny Mercer, for the song "When October Goes." Mercer's widow had found a trunk full of unpublished lyrics and offered them to Manilow. Manilow eventually scored and produced an album full of Mercer lyrics 1991's *With My Lover Beside Me,* sung by Nancy Wilson. That same year saw Manilow release *Showstoppers,* a collection of Broadway show tunes on which he was joined by such stage singers as Barbara Cook, Michael Crawford, and Hinton Battle. In 1988 Manilow produced a song, "Perfect Isn't Easy," featuring Midler's voice, for the Disney movie *Oliver and Company.* In 1993 he announced that *Barry Manilow's Copacabana—The Musical* would premiere in London in 1994—when he made his film scoring debut for the animated feature *Thumbelina.* His autobiography, *Sweet Life: Adventures on the Way to Paradise,* was published in 1987.

Aimee Mann: See 'Til Tuesday

Manfred Mann

Formed 1964, England
Manfred Mann (b. Michael Lubowitz, Oct. 21, 1940, Johannesburg, S.A.), kybds.; Paul Jones (b. Paul Pond, Feb. 24, 1942, Portsmouth, Eng.), voc., harmonica; Mike Hugg (b. Aug. 11, 1942, Andover, Eng.), drums; Michael Vickers (b. Apr. 18, 1941, Southampton, Eng.), gtr.; Tom McGuinness (b. Dec. 2, 1941, London, Eng.), bass.
1964—*The Manfred Mann Album* (Ascot); *The Five Faces of Manfred Mann; Mann Made* 1965—*My Little Red Book of Winners* (– Vickers; + Jack Bruce [b. May 14, 1943, Lanarkshire, Scot.], bass) *Mann Made Hits* 1966—*Pretty Flamingo* (United Artists); *Greatest Hits* (Capitol) (– Bruce; – Jones) 1967—*Up the Junction* (Fontana) (+ Klaus Voormann [b. Apr. 29, 1942, Berlin, Ger.], bass; + Michael D'Abo [b. 1944, Bethworth, Eng.], voc., gtr., flute) 1968—*The Mighty Quinn* (Mercury).
Manfred Mann's Earth Band, formed 1971, England (Mann; + Mick Rogers, voc., gtr.; + Colin Pattenden, bass; + Chris Slade, drums): 1972—*Manfred Mann's Earth Band* (Polydor); *Glorified, Magnified* 1973—*Get Your Rocks Off* (a.k.a. *Messin'*) 1974—*Solar Fire; The Good Earth* (Warner Bros.) 1975—*Nightingales and Bombers* (+ Chris Thompson, gtr., voc.; + Dave Flett, gtr.; + Pat King, bass; – Flett; + Steve Waller, gtr.; – Waller; + John Lingwood, drums) 1976—*The Roaring Silence* 1977—*Watch* 1979—*Angel Station* 1980—*Chance* 1984—*Somewhere in Afrika* (Arista) 1991—*Plains Music* (Rhythm Safari/Priority) 1992—*The Best of Manfred Mann: The Definitive Collection* (EMI).
Michael D'Abo solo: 1970—*D'Abo* (MCA) 1972—*Down at Rachel's Place* (A&M) 1974—*Broken Rainbows* 1976—*Smith and D'Abo* (with Mike Smith) (Columbia, U.K.).

Although led by two trained musicians who shared a measure of disdain for pop music, Manfred Mann scored an impressive 16 British hit singles during the Sixties, many of which were American successes as well, including the #1 record "Do Wah Diddy Diddy" in 1964. Mann himself later moved into jazz-rock and AOR.

Manfred Mann and Mike Hugg formed the eight-man Mann-Hugg Blues Brothers in 1962, playing blues and jazz. The following year they pared the group down to a quintet with a new name, Manfred Mann. At this point, they turned to pop-oriented rock & roll. Their first two singles ("Why Should We Not?" and "Cock-A-Hoop") were not especially successful, but their third, "5-4-3-2-1" (#5 U.K., 1964), became their first hit, its popularity aided by its adoption as the theme song of the British rock television program *Ready Steady Go* (Manfred Mann's "Hubble Bubble Toil and Trouble" became the show's theme song later on). The hits came rapidly after that: "Do Wah Diddy Diddy" (#1, 1964), "Come Tomorrow" (#50, 1965), and "Pretty Flamingo" (#29, 1966).

In 1965 Vickers quit the band and was replaced briefly by Jack Bruce, who left six months later to form Cream. Bruce was replaced by *Revolver* jacket artist Klaus Voormann. Later Paul Jones quit as well to concentrate on acting and a solo recording career. He had two British hits, "High Time" and "I've Been a Bad Bad Boy," from the 1967 film *Privilege*, in which he starred, playing a pop idol. He was replaced by Mike D'Abo.

Fluctuating personnel had less discernible effect on the group's continued chart success than its leader's growing ambivalence. British hits those years included "Semi-Detached Suburban Mr. James," "Ha! Ha! Said the Clown," "My Name Is Jack," and their international hit cover of Bob Dylan's "The Mighty Quinn" (#10, 1968). After scoring the film *Up the Junction* in 1967, Mann and Hugg broke up the band and formed the more ambitious Manfred Mann's Chapter Three, complete with a five-man horn section, while McGuinness joined ex–John Mayall drummer Hughie Flint to form McGuinness Flint. Chapter Three recorded a pair of albums (*Chapter Three*, 1969; *Chapter Three, Volume 2*, 1970) before Mann and Hugg parted company, Hugg to compose soundtracks (some believe he alone was responsible for *Up the Junction*) and Mann to launch Manfred Mann's Earth Band.

The Earth Band was designed to show off the group's virtuosity in a heavy-rock format. Upon its formation in 1971, the group toured extensively, building an audience until in 1977 its version of Bruce Springsteen's "Blinded by the Light" became a #1 single. In 1973 the Earth Band had a British hit with "Joybringer," based on a tune from Gustav Holst's *The Planets*. In five more years of recording, Mann and company were not able to repeat the feat, even when they tried another Springsteen composition, "Spirit in the Night," although it did go to #40. *Somewhere in Afrika* (#40, 1984) was the highest-charting of Mann's U.S.-released albums since the gold *The Roaring Silence* (#10, 1976). "Runner" (#22, 1984) from *Somewhere* was Mann's last hit in the U.S.

Onetime lead singer Michael D'Abo, who sang lead on "Mighty Quinn," pursued an uneven solo career. He was far more successful as a songwriter; among his compositions are "Build Me Up Buttercup" (cowritten with Tony McCaulay and recorded by the Foundations) and "Handbags and Gladrags" (Rod Stewart). *Smith and D'Abo* is a collaborative effort with former Dave Clark Five lead singer Mike Smith: His daughter, Olivia d'Abo, is an actress. She played Kevin Arnold's older sister on *The Wonder Years*.

Phil Manzanera: See Roxy Music

Teena Marie
Born Mary Christine Brockert, March 5, 1956, Santa Monica, California
1979—*Wild and Peaceful* (Gordy)   1980—*Lady T; Irons in the Fire*   1981—*It Must Be Magic*   1983—*Robbery* (Epic)   1984—*Starchild*   1986—*Emerald City*   1988—*Naked to the World*   1990—*Ivory*.

Before Mariah Carey and Lisa Stansfield hit the R&B chart in the early Nineties, Teena Marie distinguished herself as a white singer worthy of the support of such soul music icons as Rick James and Motown Records. Granted, when Motown released Marie's debut album (on its Gordy label), the record company suspiciously saw fit not to put her photo on the cover. But in 1985, when Marie's single "Lovergirl" hit #4 on the pop chart (and #9 on R&B), an accompanying video got enough airplay to ensure that the attractive singer's face—which, in fact, could have been mistaken for that of a light-skinned black woman—was as accessible as her lithely soulful voice and sultry, jazz-tinged funk-pop songs.

One of six children born to music-loving parents, Mary Christine Brockert began singing professionally at the age of eight, performing at weddings (including that of one of Jerry Lewis' sons) and appearing on TV commercials, using her nickname from early on. Teena Marie also started writing songs on the family piano. Following a year at Santa Monica College, where she studied English, the singer was tapped by Motown chairman Berry Gordy for a TV project that was eventually shelved. Gordy signed her in 1977, though, and shortly thereafter, James overheard her singing in a recording studio and decided to produce her first album, *Wild and Peaceful*, which spawned the R&B hit "I'm a Sucker for Your Love" (#8, 1979). Marie continued her associations with James and Gordy for the next couple of years, touring with the former (and coyly evading speculations that they were lovers) and yielding successful R&B singles like "I Need Your Lovin'" (#9, 1980) and "Square Biz" (#3, 1981) for the latter.

In 1981, the year her fourth Motown album was released, Marie sued the company for nonpayment of royalties. She was freed from her contract and awarded a cash settlement. The singer was picked up by Epic Records; her second Epic album, *Starchild*, included "Lovergirl," her only Top Twenty pop single to date. On the R&B chart Marie remained a viable presence into the late Eighties, scoring the hits "Ooo La La La" (#1, 1988) and "Work It" (#10, 1988).

Mark-Almond Band
Formed 1970, London, England
Jon Mark (b. Cornwall, Eng.), gtrs., voc., perc.;
Johnny Almond (b. July 20, 1946, Enfield, Eng.),

voc., sax, flute, vibes, congas, oboe; Rodger Sutton (b. Eng.), bass, cello; Tommy Eyre (b. Sheffield, Eng.), piano, organ, gtr.
1971—*Mark-Almond* (Blue Thumb) (+ Dannie Richmond, perc.)   1972—*Mark-Almond 2* (+ Ken Craddock, kybds.; + Colin Gibson, bass); *Rising* (Columbia) 1973—(– Craddock; – Gibson) *Mark-Almond 73* (– Sutton; – Eyre; + Geoff Condon, horns; + Alun Davies, gtr.; + Wolfgang Melz, bass; + Bobby Torres, perc.) (group disbands)   1975— (Mark and Almond reunite)   1976—*To the Heart* (ABC)   1978—*Other People's Rooms* (A&M).

In 1970 Jon Mark and Johnny Almond, two longtime British sessionmen, left John Mayall's Bluesbreakers to form a band that combined mellow jazz and folk.

Before joining Mayall, Mark had coproduced Marianne Faithfull's early albums with Mick Jagger, and later spent two years writing for Faithfull and accompanying her on the road. He also toured with folksinger Alun Davies (later guitarist for Cat Stevens), and from there the two formed a short-lived band called Sweet Thursday, with Nicky Hopkins, Brian Odgers, and Harvey Burns. Though their sole LP on Tetragrammaton was released the day the company folded, "Gilbert Street" became an FM hit in the U.S.

Almond had worked in Zoot Money's Big Roll Band, the Alan Price Set, and his own Johnny Almond's Music Machine, which recorded two solo LPs for Deram in England. Both he and Mark joined Mayall in 1969 (they appear on *Turning Point*), but after a second LP with Mayall, *Empty Rooms,* the two formed the Mark-Almond Band with Tommy Eyre (who'd backed Joe Cocker, Juicy Lucy, and Aynsley Dunbar) and Roger Sutton, formerly of Jody Grind. The Mark-Almond Band's debut contained the FM hit "The City," an 11-minute jam. An audience began to grow, especially for the group's tours, which featured long instrumental forays. With their second LP, Mark and Almond added guest drummer Dannie Richmond, who'd long been associated with jazz bassist Charles Mingus. Mark-Almond was briefly a seven-piece band for its *73* album, before disbanding. Mark lost a finger in an accident that year, but came out with a solo LP, *Songs for a Friend,* in 1975.

Later that year he and Almond reunited to record *To the Heart.* They still hadn't found a major audience, but they got another deal on A&M in 1978, resulting in *Other People's Rooms,* which included a new version of "The City." They really were no longer a group (the album was recorded with all studio musicians besides the two principals) and called it quits for good soon after.

The Mar-Keys
Formed 1957, Memphis, Tennessee
Original lineup: Terry Johnson, drums; Steve Crop-per (b. Oct. 21, 1941, Willow Springs, Mo.), gtr.; Donald "Duck" Dunn (b. Nov. 24, 1941, Memphis), bass; Jerry Lee "Smoochie" Smith, piano; Charles Axton, sax; Don Nix (b. Sep. 27, 1941, Memphis), sax; Wayne Jackson, trumpet; Charlie Freeman (b. Memphis), gtr.
1961—*Mar-Keys* (Atlantic)   1965—*The Great Memphis Sound.*

Though they had just one Top Ten single, the Mar-Keys were among those most responsible for the development of the Memphis sound of the Sixties, the hallmark of the influential Stax-Volt label. Guitarist Steve Cropper formed the band in 1957, when he was just 16, as a quartet. By the early Sixties they had added horns and keyboards and were backing up Satellite Records (later Stax-Volt) soul stars Rufus and Carla Thomas. They also began releasing their own singles and albums of instrumentals, scoring a Top Ten hit and a gold record in 1961 with their first 45, "Last Night." In later years, after much shifting of personnel, the name Mar-Keys was quietly retired, but various bandmembers remained active. Cropper and Dunn had many hits as half of Booker T. and the MG's [see entry]. Onetime Mar-Key Don Nix went on to a modestly successful solo career and also played with Delaney and Bonnie and Leon Russell, while Jackson and latterday members Andrew Love and Floyd Newman joined the Memphis Horns, and Freeman, the Dixie Flyers.

Marky Mark and the Funky Bunch
Formed 1991, Boston, Massachusetts
Marky Mark (b. Mark Wahlberg, June 5, 1971, Dorchester, Mass.), voc.; Scott Ross (b. Apr. 6, 1969, Boston), dancer; Hector Barrons (b. May 14, 1967, Boston), dancer; Terry Yancy (b. Sep. 11, 1969, Boston), DJ.
1991—*Music for the People* (Interscope)   1992— *You Gotta Believe.*

The younger brother of New Kid on the Block Donnie Wahlberg, Marky Mark was, after Vanilla Ice, rap's second white poster boy. It wasn't long, though, before his rapping was overshadowed by his penchant for violence and for going shirtless to show off his muscular physique.

Marky had a rough upbringing in the working-class Dorchester section of Boston. He discovered hip-hop in the late Eighties, and, between doing jail time for knocking an Asian-American unconscious for his beer in 1988 and a 1990 arrest for assault, he began weight-lifting, taught himself to rap, and practiced break dancing with his brother Donnie.

In 1990 Marky recorded a demo with his brother, and just a year later, he and the Funky Bunch emerged with

"Good Vibrations." The record incorporated and credited an old disco hit by Loleatta Holloway (who was featured in the video between shots of Marky lifting weights and rolling around in bed with a pretty girl) and hit #1 in 1991. Its followup, "Wildside" (#10, 1991), was based on and credited Lou Reed's classic "Walk on the Wild Side." Marky's debut album, *Music for the People* (#21, 1991), went platinum. After his rise to fame, publicity got out about his previous violent racial incidents with black and Asian-American youths. Anti-defamation groups protested, forcing Marky to tape antiracism public service announcements.

By the end of 1992 Marky's pumped-up pectorals were omnipresent in magazines and on billboards, through his endorsement of fashion designer Calvin Klein's underwear. But *You Gotta Believe* (#67, 1992) fell quickly off the charts, yielding only one minor hit single in the title track (#49, 1992).

In August 1992 Marky and a bodyguard were charged with assaulting a man at a Dorchester tennis court (the case was eventually dismissed by the court). A year later, at a party in the Hollywood Hills, Marky allegedly got into a shouting match with Madonna's entourage, punching a talent scout for her Maverick label in the nose. No charges were filed. In October 1993 Marky released his home video workout tape. Billed as Mark Wahlberg, the singer costarred in the 1995 film *The Basketball Diaries*.

Bob Marley and the Wailers

The Wailers, formed 1963, Jamaica (Bob Marley [b. Robert Nesta Marley, Apr. 6, 1945, St. Ann's Parish, Jam.; d. May 11, 1981, Miami, Fla.], voc., gtr.; Peter Tosh [b. Winston Hubert MacIntosh, Oct. 9, 1944, Westmoreland, Jam.; d. Sept. 11, 1987, Barbican, St. Andrew, Jam.], voc., gtr.; Bunny Livingstone [b. Neville O'Reilly Livingstone, Apr. 10, 1947, Kingston, Jam.], voc., perc.; Junior Braithwaite, voc.; Beverly Kelso, voc.): 1965—(– Braithwaite; – Kelso) 1969—(+ Aston Francis "Family Man" Barrett [b. Nov. 22, 1946, Kingston, Jam.], bass; + Carlton Lloyd "Carly" Barrett [b. Dec. 17, 1950, Kingston, Jam.; d. April 17, 1987, Kingston, Jam.], drums) 1973—*Catch a Fire* (Island) (+ Earl "Wire" Lindo [b. Jan. 7, 1953, Kingston, Jam.], kybds.); *Burnin'* (– Tosh; – Livingstone).
As Bob Marley and the Wailers: 1974—(+ Bernard "Touter" Harvey [b. Jam.], kybds.; + Al Anderson [b. Montclair, N.J.], gtr.; + the I-Threes [Rita Marley, Marcia Griffiths, Judy Mowatt, all b. Jam.], voc.; + Alvin "Seeco" Patterson [b. Jamaica], perc.; + Tyrone Downie [b. Jam.], kybds.; + Julian "Junior" Marvin [b. U.S.], gtr.; + Lee Jaffe, harmonica) *Natty Dread* (Island) (– Marvin; – Jaffe; – Lindo; + Earl

Bob Marley

"Chinna" Smith, gtr.) 1975—*Live* (– Downie; + Donald Kinsey [b. May 12, 1953, Gary, Ind.]) 1976—*Rastaman Vibration* (– Kinsey; – Smith; – Harvey; – Anderson; + Marvin; + Downie) 1977—*Exodus* (– Downie) 1978—*Kaya* (+ Lindo; + Anderson; + Downie); *Babylon by Bus* 1979—*Survival* 1980—*Uprising* 1983—*Confrontation* 1984—*Legend* 1991—*Talkin' Blues* (Tuff Gong) 1992—*Songs of Freedom* (Island) 1995—*Natural Mystic*.

Tremendously popular in their native Jamaica, where Bob Marley was regarded as a national hero, the Wailers were also reggae music's most effective international emissaries. Marley's songs of determination, rebellion, and faith found an audience all over the world.

Marley left his rural home for the slums of Kingston at age 14. When he was 17, Jimmy Cliff [see entry] introduced him to Leslie Kong, who produced Marley's first single, "Judge Not," and several other obscure sides. In 1963, with the guidance of Jamaican pop veteran Joe Higgs, Marley formed the Wailers, a vocal quintet, with Peter Tosh, Bunny Livingston, Junior Braithwaite, and Beverly Kelso. Their first single for producer Coxsone Dodd, "Simmer Down," was one of the biggest Jamaican hits of 1964, and the Wailers remained on Dodd's Studio One and Coxsone labels for three years, hitting with "Love and Affection."

When Braithwaite and Kelso left the group around 1965, the Wailers continued as a trio, Marley, Tosh, and Livingston trading leads. In spite of the popularity of singles like "Rude Boy," the artists received few or no royalties, and in 1966 they disbanded. Marley spent most of the following year working in a factory in Newark, Delaware (where his mother had moved in 1963). Upon his return to Jamaica, the Wailers reunited and recorded, with little success, for Dodd and other producers. During this period, the Wailers devoted themselves to the religious sect of Rastafari.

In 1969 they began their three-year association with Lee "Scratch" Perry [see entry], who directed them to play their own instruments and expanded their lineup to include Aston and Carlton Barrett, formerly the rhythm section of Perry's studio band, the Upsetters. Some of the records they made with Perry, such as "Trenchtown Rock," were locally very popular, but so precarious was the Jamaican record industry that the group seemed no closer than before to establishing steady careers. They formed an independent record company, Tuff Gong, in 1971, but the venture foundered when Livingston was jailed and Marley got caught in a contract commitment to American pop singer Johnny Nash [see entry], who took him to Sweden to write a film score (and later had moderate hits with two Marley compositions, "Guava Jelly" and "Stir It Up").

In 1972 Chris Blackwell—who had released "Judge Not" in England in 1963—signed the Wailers to Island Records and advanced them the money to record themselves in Jamaica. Catch a Fire, their first album marketed outside Jamaica, featured several uncredited performances such as Muscle Shoals' guitarist Wayne Perkins playing lead on "Concrete Jungle" and "Stir It Up." (They continued to release Jamaica-only singles on Tuff Gong.) Their recognition abroad was abetted by Eric Clapton's hit version of "I Shot the Sheriff," a song from their second Island album. They made their first overseas tour in 1973, but before the end of the year, Tosh and Livingstone (who later adopted the surname Wailer) left for solo careers [see entries].

Marley expanded the instrumental section of the group and brought in a female vocal trio, the I-Threes, which included his wife, Rita. Now called Bob Marley and the Wailers, they toured Europe, Africa, and the Americas, building especially strong followings in the U.K., Scandinavia, and Africa. They had U.K. Top Forty hits with "No Woman No Cry" (1975), "Exodus" (1977), "Waiting in Vain" (1977), and "Satisfy My Soul" (1978); and British Top Ten hits with "Jamming" (1977), "Punky Reggae Party" (1977), and "Is This Love" (1978).

In the U.S., only "Roots, Rock, Reggae" made the pop chart (#51, 1976), while "Could You Be Loved" placed on the R&B chart (#56, 1980), but the group attracted an ever-larger audience: Rastaman Vibration went to #8 pop and Exodus reached #20. In Jamaica the Wailers reached unprecedented levels of popularity and influence, and Marley's pronouncements on public issues were accorded the attention usually reserved for political or religious leaders. In 1976 he was wounded in a murder attempt.

A 1980 tour of the U.S. was canceled when Marley collapsed while jogging in New York's Central Park. It was discovered that he had developed brain, lung, and liver cancer; it killed him eight months later. In 1987 both Peter Tosh and longtime Marley drummer Carlton Barrett were murdered in Jamaica in separate incidents. Rita Marley continues to tour, record, and run the Tuff Gong studios and record company.

Marley was a pioneer not only because he single-handedly brought reggae to the world, but because his passionate, socially observant music has become a yardstick against which all reggae will forever be measured.

Ziggy Marley and the Melody Makers

Formed 1979, Kingston, Jamaica
David "Ziggy" Marley (b. Oct. 17, 1968, Kingston), voc., gtr.; Stephen Marley (b. April 20, 1972, Wilmington, Del.), voc., perc.; Cedella Marley (b. Aug. 23, 1967, Kingston), voc.; Sharon Marley Prendergast (b. Nov. 23, 1964, Kingston, Jam.), voc.
1985—Play the Game Right (EMI America)   1986—Hey World!   1988—The Best of Ziggy Marley and The Melody Makers; Conscious Party (Virgin) 1989—One Bright Day   1991—Jahmekya   1993—Joy and Blues.

As the eldest son of international reggae stars Bob and Rita Marley, Ziggy Marley was a natural choice to fill the vacuum left by his father's death in 1981. Burdened with the double expectations of carrying on reggae's traditions and Rastafarian proselytizing while expanding the music to a new, younger audience, after a rocky start he has generally succeeded, receiving Grammy Awards for both Conscious Party and One Bright Day.

Taught guitar and drums by his father, Marley started sitting in on the Wailers recording sessions from age ten; in 1979 an already ailing Bob Marley brought Ziggy, along with sister Cedella, brother Stephen, and half-sister Sharon, into the studio to record a single, "Children Playing in the Streets." Called the Melody Makers, the group started playing at family events, gaining notice with an appearance at their father's state funeral in 1981.

Signed by EMI America, the band recorded two albums that veered toward the pop side of reggae. This, combined with Ziggy's preternatural resemblance, both physically and vocally, to his father, caused him to be dubbed, derisively, "Marley lite." Low sales, and the fact that EMI wanted to market Ziggy as a solo act, moved the band to Virgin Records.

The changes on Conscious Party (#42, 1988) went deeper than a new label. Recorded for the first time outside Kingston, with new producers (Talking Heads'

Chris Frantz and Tina Weymouth), the album was well received both commercially and critically, yielding the hit "Tomorrow People" (#39, 1988). *One Bright Day* (#18, 1989) continued this growth, while *Jahmekya* (#19, 1991) and *Joy and Blues* (#178 pop, #75 R&B, 1993) added modern dancehall and rock sounds to the mix.

Ziggy has continued the Marley tradition of political activism, becoming a Goodwill Youth Ambassador for the United Nations and winning an NAACP Image Award. He also started the Ghetto Youth United record label in Kingston to record the next generation of reggae music. In 1994 the band switched labels to Elektra.

Chris Mars: See the Replacements

Branford Marsalis
Born August 26, 1960, New Orleans, Louisiana
1984—*Scenes in the City* (Columbia)   1986—*Royal Garden Blues*; *Romances for Saxophone*   1987—*Renaissance*   1988—*Random Abstract*   1989—*Trio Jeepy*   1990—*Crazy People Music*; *Music from Mo' Better Blues*   1991—*The Beautyful Ones Are Not Yet Born*   1992—*I Heard You Twice the First Time*   1993—*Bloomington*   1994—*Buckshot LeFonque*.

Where his trumpet-playing younger brother Wynton Marsalis [see entry] represented a strict allegiance to the orthodoxies of the jazz tradition, saxophonist Branford Marsalis openly embraced pop culture while simultaneously maintaining a reputation as a serious jazz musician.

Marsalis grew up in New Orleans; his father Ellis is a renowned jazz educator and pianist. As teenagers Branford and Wynton played together in funk bands; while Wynton later disavowed these early experiences, Branford never lost his youthful taste for R&B and rock music. Becoming more committed to jazz, Branford enrolled in Boston's Berklee College of Music. After short stints with the Lionel Hampton Orchestra and Clark Terry's band, Branford joined Wynton in drummer Art Blakey's Jazz Messengers. Starting out on alto saxophone but soon switching to tenor sax, Marsalis was quickly recognized as one of the most proficient of the new traditionalists—young players who were reinvestigating the hard-bop and modal-jazz styles of the Sixties.

In 1981 Branford joined Wynton's band and subsequently appeared on his first five recordings, playing both tenor and soprano saxophones. Four years later Branford shocked the jazz world by leaving Wynton's band (by then the most popular in jazz) to record and tour with Sting. From that point on, Marsalis had few qualms crossing the boundaries of musical genre and celebrity. With Sting Marsalis recorded *The Dream of the Blue Turtles* (1985) and . . . *Nothing Like the Sun* (1987);

he also appeared in Sting's rock documentary *Bring On the Night.*

Marsalis started his own quartet in 1986, playing uncompromising jazz much as he had in Wynton's band. Like Wynton, Branford has also made classical recordings. Another Marsalis brother, Delfeayo (a trumpet player), produces most of Branford's records.

Outside projects would find him all over the pop-music map: guesting on records by Public Enemy, the Grateful Dead, the Neville Brothers, Tina Turner, and Bruce Hornsby. In 1994 Marsalis continued his exploration of musical genres with *Buckshot LeFonque*, a hip-hop project with Gang Starr's DJ Premier, whom Marsalis had worked with on the soundtrack for Spike Lee's *Mo' Better Blues.*

As an actor, Marsalis can be seen in the films *School Daze* and *Throw Momma from the Train.* In 1992 Marsalis became the musical director for *The Tonight Show* and second banana for host Jay Leno, instantly making him the most widely recognized living jazz musician in the world. He left the show in early 1995, citing personal and family matters, for an indefinite leave of absence.

Wynton Marsalis
Born October 18, 1961, New Orleans, Louisiana
1982—*Wynton Marsalis* (Columbia)   1983—*Think of One*   1984—*Hot House Flowers*   1985—*Black Codes (from the Underground)*   1986—*J Mood*   1987—*Marsalis Standard Time, vol. 1*   1988—*Live at Blues Alley*   1989—*The Majesty of the Blues*; *Crescent City Christmas Card*   1990—*The Resolution of Romance*   1991—*Intimacy Calling*; *Soul Gestures in Southern Blue: Vol. 1 Thick in the South*; *Vol. 2 Uptown Ruler*; *Vol. 3 Levee Low Moan*   1992—*Blue Interlude*   1993—*Citi Movement.*

Wynton Marsalis is the single most important figure in the current-day jazz renaissance. Marsalis galvanized a stagnant musical scene in the early Eighties with his spectacular trumpet playing and has since doggedly championed America's cultural commitment to jazz while instigating a whole new generation to return to the music.

Marsalis hails from a family steeped in jazz [see Branford Marsalis entry]. By his early teenage years Marsalis already showed prodigious talent on the trumpet. While studying classical music at school—he was a featured guest soloist with the New Orleans Philharmonic at 14—Marsalis also played funk gigs with Branford and concurrently became interested in jazz. In the summer of 1979 Marsalis accepted an invitation to attend the Berkshire Music Center at Tanglewood; that fall he was awarded a full scholarship to New York's Juilliard

School of Music. By the summer of 1980 Marsalis was already sitting in with drummer Art Blakey's Jazz Messengers. Over the next two years he would play in Blakey's band and in Herbie Hancock's V.S.O.P. quartet.

His jazz and classical credentials already in order at age 20, Marsalis was given major-label contracts to record in both genres. Marsalis formed his own quartet including Branford on saxophones, playing modal hard bop in a style associated with Miles Davis' groups of the mid-Sixties. Brashly opinionated, Marsalis took any opportunity to slam the commerciality of electric fusion—as well as pop—exalting instead the purity of acoustic jazz. Marsalis' musical prowess and sartorial splendor excited a large crop of younger jazzmen who sprang up unexpectedly in the mid-Eighties.

The combination of Marsalis' undeniable talent, his virulent outspokenness, and the full support of his powerful record company made him a star overnight. He won jazz and classical Grammys in 1983 (he has won ten altogether); his albums and performances garnered popular support hitherto unknown for a jazz musician. After Branford left his band in 1985, Wynton began delving deeper into the jazz tradition. Greater echoes of Louis Armstrong and Duke Ellington were to be heard in Marsalis' work; by *The Majesty of the Blues* (1989) Marsalis was consciously exploring his New Orleans roots, mixing earthy preswing jazz with modernistic elements derived from John Coltrane and Miles Davis. *Blue Interlude* and *Citi Movement* found him successfully experimenting with long-form compositions.

In 1988 Marsalis helped develop the jazz program at Lincoln Center and was appointed its artistic director. In the early Nineties Marsalis became interested in scoring for dance; he has since collaborated with noted choreographers Garth Fagan and Peter Martins. Marsalis remains an indefatigable performer/recording artist and a tireless supporter of jazz music.

Marshall Tucker Band

Formed 1971, Spartanburg, South Carolina
Toy Caldwell (b. 1948; d. Feb. 23, 1994, Moore, S.C.), lead gtr., steel gtr., voc.; George McCorkle, rhythm gtr.; Doug Gray (b. May 2, 1948, Spartanburg), lead voc.; Paul Riddle, drums; Jerry Eubanks (b. Mar. 9, 1950, Spartanburg), alto sax, flute, organ, piano, voc.; Tommy Caldwell (b. 1950; d. Apr. 28, 1980, Spartanburg), bass, voc.
1973—*The Marshall Tucker Band* (Capricorn)
1974—*A New Life; Where We All Belong* 1975—*Searchin' for a Rainbow* 1976—*Long Hard Ride* 1977—*Carolina Dreams* 1978—*Together Forever; Greatest Hits* 1979—*Running Like the Wind* (Warner Bros.) 1980—*Tenth* (– Tommy Caldwell; + Franklin Wilkie, bass) 1981—*Dedicated* 1982—*Tuckerized* 1983—*Just Us* (– Toy Caldwell; – Riddle; – McCorkle; – Wilkie; + Rusty Milner [b. June 2, 1958, Spartanburg], gtr.; + Tim Lawter [b. Dec. 10, 1958, Spartanburg], bass, gtr.) 1988—*Still Holdin' On* (Mercury) 1990—*Southern Spirit* (Cabin Fever Music) 1992—*Still Smokin'* 1993—*Walk Outside the Lines.*
Toy Caldwell solo: 1992—*Toy Caldwell* (Cabin Fever Music).

The Marshall Tucker Band tempered Southern rock with pop, country, ballad, and even MOR "jazz" influences. The band centered on the Caldwell brothers, who like all the original bandmembers were born and grew up in Spartanburg, South Carolina. As a teen, Toy Caldwell first worked in a rock & roll outfit, the Rants, which included George McCorkle on rhythm guitar. At the same time, brother Tommy played with Doug Gray in the New Generation. Both groups toured the club circuit until 1966, when they were all drafted into the army. After their discharge four years later, Toy wrote "Can't You See," which later became the Marshall Tucker Band's first U.S. single and a Top Five country hit for Waylon Jennings in 1976. But first he formed the Toy Factory, with Gray and Jerry Eubanks, a band that lasted almost two years, until 1971, when McCorkle, Paul Riddle, and Tommy Caldwell joined to form the Marshall Tucker Band, named after the piano tuner who owned their rehearsal hall.

Their self-titled debut was released in March 1973, and they were openers on the Allman Brothers' tour; by 1974 they were headliners. The band's songs received much FM airplay, especially "Take the Highway," "24 Hours at a Time," and "Fire on the Mountain." MTB's debut went gold, followed by five other gold records and one platinum—*Carolina Dreams*—which included "Heard It in a Love Song" (#14, 1977). On January 20, 1977, the band, along with Sea Level, played at the inauguration of President Jimmy Carter. In 1979 the group signed to Warner Bros. for *Running Like the Wind*.

On April 28, 1980, Tommy Caldwell died from injuries sustained in an automobile accident six days earlier. Only a month earlier, another brother, Tim, had died in a car accident. The band's LP in memory of Tommy, released one year later, was called *Dedicated*. Franklin Wilkie, who'd played with Toy and McCorkle in the Rants, took over on bass. He had also played in the Toy Factory, but instead of joining the initial Marshall Tucker played for six years with Garfeel Ruff, which recorded two albums for Capitol.

In 1983 Toy Caldwell, McCorkle, and Riddle, weary of the road, sold their interest in the group to Gray and Eubanks. Along with guitarist Rusty Milner and bassist Tim Lawter, both Spartanburg natives, they have continued to tour and record with a succession of musicians. As of 1994 Marshall Tucker also included guitarist Ronald

Radford (b. May 5, 1957, Spartanburg), drummer Gary Guzzardo (b. Mar. 13, 1956, Rockford, Ill.), and keyboardist Paul Thompson (b. Dec. 12, 1956, Chattanooga, Tenn.). Its *Still Smokin'* and *Walk Outside the Lines* LPs showed the band leaning more in a country direction, with several singles making the country Top 100. On February 23, 1994, Toy Caldwell died in his sleep at age 45, two years after having released a solo album.

Martha and the Vandellas/Martha Reeves

Formed 1962, Detroit, Michigan
Martha Reeves (b. July 18, 1941, Detroit), lead voc.;
Annette Beard, voc.; Rosalind Ashford (b. Sep. 2, 1943, Detroit), voc.
1963—*Come and Get These Memories* (Gordy); *Heat Wave* (– Beard; + Betty Kelly [b. Sep. 16, 1944, Detroit], voc.) 1965—*Dance Party* 1966—*Martha & the Vandellas Greatest Hits*; *Watchout!* 1967—*Martha and the Vandellas Live!* (– Kelly; + Lois Reeves, voc.) 1968—*Ridin' High* 1969—(– Ashford; + Sandra Tilley [d. 1981], voc.) *Sugar n' Spice* 1970—*Natural Resources* 1972—*Black Magic* 1974—*Martha Reeves & the Vandellas Anthology* 1980—*Martha Reeves & the Vandellas: Motown Superstar Series, vol. 11* (Motown) 1986—*Martha Reeves & the Vandellas: Compact Command Performance* 1993—*Martha Reeves & the Vandellas/Live Wire!: The Singles, 1962–1972*; *Martha Reeves & the Vandellas: Motown Legends.*
Martha Reeves solo: 1974—*Martha Reeves: Produced by Richard Perry* (MCA) 1976—*The Rest of My Life* (Arista) 1978—*We Meet Again* (Fantasy) 1980—*Gotta Keep Moving* 1986—*Martha Reeves: The Collection* (Object Enterprises, Eur.).

Driven by Martha Reeves' soulful, brassy lead vocals, the Vandellas became Motown's earthier, more aggressive "girl group" alternative to the Supremes. Their biggest hits, like "Dancing in the Street" and "Heat Wave," are among the most popular dance records of the Sixties.

Reeves, Annette Beard, and Rosalind Ashford sang as the Del-Phis in high school and cut one single on Check-Mate Records, a subsidiary of Chess. Reeves had also sung professionally under the stage name Martha LaVaille. In 1961 Reeves got a job at Motown in the A&R department as secretary to Motown A&R director William "Mickey" Stevenson. One day Motown head Berry Gordy Jr. needed background singers in short order for a session; Reeves and her friends were called in. They sang behind Marvin Gaye on "Stubborn Kind of Fellow" and "Hitch Hike" before recording "I'll Have to Let Him Go" as Martha and the Vandellas, taking their new name from Detroit's

Van Dyke Street and Reeves' favorite singer, Della Reese.

Their first hit, a beat ballad called "Come and Get These Memories" (#29 pop, #6 R&B, 1963), was followed by two explosive Holland-Dozier-Holland dance records: "Heat Wave" (#4 pop, #1 R&B, 1963) and "Quicksand" (#8, 1963). After being turned down by Kim Weston, "Dancing in the Street" (cowritten by Weston's husband, Mickey Stevenson, and Marvin Gaye) was given to Martha and the Vandellas; they turned it into their biggest hit (#2, 1964). Their other big hits included "Nowhere to Run" (#8 pop, #5 R&B, 1965) and "I'm Ready for Love" (#9 pop, #2 R&B, 1966). "Jimmy Mack" (#10 pop, #1 R&B, 1967) and "Honey Chile" (#11 pop, #5 R&B, 1967) were the last Holland-Dozier-Holland compositions they recorded, and were their last big hits.

By 1967 the group was billed as Martha Reeves and the Vandellas. Beard retired in 1963 and was replaced by former Velvelette Betty Kelly; when Kelly left four years later, Reeves' younger sister Lois took her place. Ashford quit the group in 1969 and was replaced by another ex-Velvelette, Sandra Tilley (who had also been one of the Orlons of "South Street" fame). Tilley died during surgery for a brain tumor in 1981. The group broke up in 1973 after giving a farewell performance on December 21, 1972, at Detroit's Cobo Hall. Lois Reeves went on to work with Al Green.

As recounted in her 1994 autobiography, *Dancing in the Street* (cowritten with Mark Bego), Reeves believed that her group's success was undermined by Motown and Berry Gordy Jr.'s obsession with the Supremes. For example, "Jimmy Mack" was held back from release for two years because it sounded too much like the Supremes' then-current singles. The Vandellas and the Supremes' rivalry extended beyond the charts; between Diana Ross and Reeves, it was sometimes personal. A strong personality, Reeves clashed with Gordy, often demanding answers to business questions most other Motown artists didn't ask until years after they left the label. Struggling to maintain a hectic schedule of recording and performing, Reeves became addicted to a range of psychoactive prescription drugs, exacerbating emotional problems that culminated in at least two nervous breakdowns and a period of institutionalization. She has lived drug-free since 1977. In 1989 she, Beard, and Ashford sued Motown for back royalties.

In 1974 Reeves signed with MCA. Her solo debut, produced by Richard Perry, contained a minor hit in "Power of Love." Although that album and her subsequent solo releases have been critically acclaimed, she never attained the success she had enjoyed with the Vandellas. She continues to tour and record; sometimes the Vandellas consist of her sisters Lois and Delphine. On special occasions, she performs with Beard and Ashford.

John Martyn

Born 1948, Glasgow, Scotland
1968—*London Conversation* (Island); *The Tumbler*
1970—*Stormbringer*; *The Road to Ruin*   1971—
Bless the Weather   1973—*Solid Air*; *Inside Out*
1974—*Sunday's Child*   1975—*Live at Leeds*
1977—*So Far, So Good*; *One World*   1980—*Grace
and Danger* (Antilles)   1981—*Glorious Fool* (Duke)
1982—*Well Kept Secret*   1983—*Philentropy* (Body
Swerve)   1984—*Sapphire* (Island)   1986—*Piece by
Piece*; *Foundations*; *BBC Radio I Live in Concert*
(BBC Prod., U.K.)   1990—*The Apprentice* (Off Beat)
1991—*Cooltide*   1993—*No Little Boy* (Mesa Blue
Moon); *Couldn't Love You More*   1994—*Sweet Little Mysteries: The Island Anthology* (Island).

Though never a commercial success, John Martyn's eccentric brand of folk—elliptical songwriting, intimately
bluesy singing, heavily jazz-flavored music—has held
steady appeal for critics and fans. Signed as Island's first
white solo artist, Martyn, as early as 1968's *The Tumbler*,
caused something of a stir in British folk circles by working with jazz reedman Harold McNair. *Bless the Weather*
fully extended the jazz tendencies, while *Inside Out* and
Solid Air (its title track a eulogy for Martyn's friend musician Nick Drake) found him using hypnotically repeated
melodies and echoplexed acoustic guitar. With his wife,
Beverly, Martyn produced two other jazz-inflected discs,
Stormbringer and *The Road to Ruin*.

One World introduced a new ethno-eclecticism;
Martyn had spent time in Jamaica with reggae producers Lee Perry and Jack Ruby. In 1980, after a three-year
absence due to substance abuse, Martyn delivered a
critical breakthrough with *Grace and Danger*, featuring
the percussion, vocals, and production of longtime fan
Phil Collins. *Glorious Fool*, *Well Kept Secret*, the live *Philentropy*, and *Sapphire* (its relative ebullience a tribute to
Martyn's new marriage) continued the progression;
traces of folk influence remained, but his sound now had
greater mainstream pull. In the late Eighties Martyn's alcohol problems resurfaced; he reemerged strongly, however, with *The Apprentice* and *Cooltide*. He began
recording for U.S. independent Mesa Blue Moon in 1993.

The Marvelettes

Formed 1960, Inkster, Michigan
Gladys Horton (b. 1944), voc.; Katherine Anderson
(b. 1944), voc.; Georgia Dobbins (a.k.a. Georgeanna,
a.k.a. Tillman, b. 1944; d. Jan. 6, 1980, Detroit,
Mich.), voc.; Juanita Cowart (b. 1944), voc.; Wanda
Young (b. 1944), voc.
1961—*Please Mr. Postman* (Tamla); *The Marvelettes
Sing*; *Playboy*   1963—(– Dobbins; – Cowart) *Mar-
velous Marvelettes*   1966—*Marvelettes Greatest
Hits*   1967—*Marvelettes*   1968—*Sophisticated
Soul*   Ca. 1969—(– Horton; + Anne Bogan, voc.;
– Young)   1969—*In Full Bloom*   1970—*Return of
the Marvelettes*   1975—*Anthology* (Motown)
1986—*Compact Command Performances*   1993—
Deliver: The Singles: 1961–1971.

Among Motown's female vocal groups, the Marvelettes
were the only one whose early sound was pure girl
group: girlish and sweet as opposed to sophisticated
(like the Supremes) or soulful (like Martha Reeves and
the Vandellas). The original Marvelettes were founded by
Gladys Horton, a 15-year-old high school student who,
together with four girlfriends from Inkster High School,
decided to enter a school talent contest. The acts that
placed first through third were allowed to audition for
Motown talent scouts; the Marvels, as they were then
called, came in fourth (though members have since
claimed first). Nonetheless, they did audition for a Motown scout, who advised them to develop original material. Dobbins rewrote "Please Mr. Postman," a song a
neighbor named William Garrett (who happened to be a
mail carrier) gave her. "Postman"—which features Marvin Gaye on drums—has the distinction of being not
only the Marvelettes' debut recording and their first and
biggest hit, but also Motown's first #1 pop record. The
song stayed on the chart for almost six months.

The next year proved their most successful, with
"Playboy" (#7 pop, #4 R&B), "Beechwood 4-5789" (#17
pop, #7 R&B), "Someday, Someway" (#9 R&B), and
"Strange I Know" (#10 R&B). "Too Many Fish in the Sea"
(#25 pop, #15 R&B), "I'll Keep Holding On" (#11 R&B),
and "Danger Heartbreak Dead Ahead" (#11 R&B) were
their 1965 hits. In 1963 both Dobbins and Cowart quit
the group due to the strain of touring. Florence Ballard
of the Supremes occasionally subbed on tours. Thereafter, the Marvelettes continued as a trio.

Many Motown historians assert that the Marvelettes
were not as well promoted as some of the label's other
female acts, specifically the Supremes and the Vandellas.
Ironically, in 1963 the trio refused to record a Holland-
Dozier-Holland song entitled "Baby Love." When
recorded by the Supremes, "Baby Love" turned out to be
one of 1964's biggest hits, one of Motown's best sellers,
and the first of that group's string of a dozen #1 hits.

Over the next two years, the Marvelettes, with
Wanda Young Rogers (she'd married Miracle Bobby
Rogers; they've since divorced), regained the pop chart
with three of Smokey Robinson's most notable productions: "Don't Mess with Bill" (#7 pop, #3 R&B, 1966), "The
Hunter Gets Captured by the Game" (#13 pop, #2 R&B,
1967), and "My Baby Must Be a Magician" (#17 pop,
1968; #8 R&B, 1967). Robinson's "Here I Am Baby" (#14
R&B, 1968) and Ashford and Simpson's "Destination:
Anywhere" (#28 R&B) marked the end of the Marvelettes' most lucrative years. Interestingly, while most

Motown groups duplicated their success in the U.K., the Marvelettes had just one Top Twenty hit there, Van McCoy's airy ballad, "When You're Young and in Love." By this time Horton (who along with Young had been a lead singer) had left, and the numerous personnel changes that followed reduced the group to nothing more than a name.

In 1980 Dobbins, who had married the Contours' Billy Gordon, died in her mother's Detroit home of sickle-cell anemia. Wanda Young Rogers has continued to work on and off with lineups of the Marvelettes, and several members have recorded for the British Motorcity label.

Richard Marx

Born Richard Noel Marx, September 16, 1963, Chicago, Illinois
1987—*Richard Marx* (EMI Manhattan)   1989—*Repeat Offender*   1991—*Rush Street* (Capitol) 1994—*Paid Vacation*.

The son of a jingle-composing father and a jingle-singing mother, it was perhaps inevitable that Richard Marx would create Seventies-style hook-filled pop. With his good looks, nice-guy image, and gift for catchy melodies, Marx became a sizeable MTV star in the late Eighties.

After accompanying his parents to recording studios, Marx began singing on commercial jingles himself at age five. As a teenager he began writing songs, and at age 18, through a series of acquaintances, he managed to get a demo to Lionel Richie, then a member of the Commodores. Richie encouraged Marx to come to Los Angeles; there he sang backup on such Richie solo hits as "All Night Long (All Night)" and "Running with the Night" and wrote songs with Kenny Rogers ("What About Me") and for Chicago. After writing a song for *Staying Alive*, the John Travolta sequel to *Saturday Night Fever*, he met the female lead, Cynthia Rhodes (best known for her dancing in Toto's "Rosanna" video), whom he would marry in 1989.

After five years of trying, Marx finally landed a deal of his own and promptly produced an eponymous double-platinum debut album (#8, 1987) that yielded four hit singles: the Eagleslike "Don't Mean Nothing" (#3, 1987), with slide guitar from ex-Eagle Joe Walsh; "Should've Known Better" (#3, 1987), with backing vocals by ex-Tube Fee Waybill and ex-Eagle Timothy B. Schmit; "Endless Summer Nights" (#2, 1988); and "Hold On to the Nights" (#1, 1988). The triple-platinum *Repeat Offender* produced such hits as "Satisfied" (#1, 1989), "Right Here Waiting" (#1, 1989), "Angelia" (#4, 1989), "Too Late to Say Goodbye" (#12, 1990), and "Children of the Night" (#13, 1990). The last celebrated, and raised some funds for, the Los Angeles organization of the same name, which aided teen prostitutes and runaway children.

Rush Street (#35, 1991) was promoted with a publicity stunt tour in which Marx played five coast-to-coast concerts—at airports in Baltimore, New York, Cleveland, Chicago, and Los Angeles—in 24 hours; its hit singles included "Keep Coming Back" (#12, 1991), "Hazard" (#9, 1992), and "Take This Heart" (#20, 1992). He returned in 1994 with *Paid Vacation* (#37, 1994).

Dave Mason

Born May 10, 1946, Worcester, England
1970—*Alone Together* (Blue Thumb)   1971—*Dave Mason and Cass Elliot* (with Cass Elliot)   1972—*Headkeeper; Dave Mason Is Alive!*   1973—*It's Like You Never Left* (Columbia); *The Best of Dave Mason* (Blue Thumb); *Dave Mason* (Columbia)   1975—*Split Coconut*   1976—*Certified Live*   1977—*Let It Flow* 1978—*Mariposa de Oro*   1980—*Old Crest on a New Wave*   1988—*Two Hearts* (MCA/Voyager).

Singer, songwriter, and guitarist Dave Mason has gone from being an integral early member of the acclaimed British jazz-pop band Traffic, to a top-selling solo act, to performing beer commercials when his solo albums were faltering, to a latterday member of Fleetwood Mac.

By the mid-Sixties, Mason was working in a band with drummer Jim Capaldi. In 1967 the pair met Steve Winwood, and they formed Traffic [see entry]. Mason's songwriting gave the band its first big commercial successes in the U.K. with "Hole in My Shoe," "You Can All Join In," and "Feelin' Alright" (later a Top Forty hit for Joe Cocker). However, Mason's pop-rock sensibility clashed with Winwood's jazz/blues leanings, and Mason was in and out of the band frequently, finally leaving for good in late 1968. He coproduced (with Jim Miller) the debut LP by Family [see entry], *Music in a Doll's House*, then formed a short-lived band with Capaldi, Traffic reedman Chris Wood, and keyboardist Wynder K. Frog.

Having met seminal country-rocker Gram Parsons while touring with Traffic, Mason went to Los Angeles. There, Parsons introduced him to Delaney and Bonnie Bramlett, and he joined their Friends tour of 1969, much of which was shared with Eric Clapton and Blind Faith (which included Winwood). Back in L.A., Mason recorded *Alone Together* (#22, 1970) with Capaldi, Leon Russell, Rita Coolidge, Delaney and Bonnie, and others. The LP stayed on the album chart over six months and went gold. The opening track, "Only You Know and I Know," was a #42 single for Mason in 1970; Delaney and Bonnie's version hit #20. Mason toured the U.S. much of the year, taking time off in June to play a London show with Clapton's Derek and the Dominos at their Lyceum debut.

In the summer of 1970 Mason renewed an old acquaintance with Mama Cass Elliot, forming a duo act that debuted at L.A.'s Hollywood Bowl that September, and recording a poorly received LP together. When the partnership dissolved, Mason briefly returned to England to guest with Traffic for a tour that resulted in the live LP *Welcome to the Canteen,* and he played on George Harrison's *All Things Must Pass.*

From that point on, Mason's solo career was erratic, though many of his subsequent LPs sold well. *Headkeeper* was half new material, half live renditions of earlier songs, while *Is Alive* was all of the latter. *Best of* furthered the apparent holding pattern, though *It's Like You Never Left* (#50, 1973), with support from Graham Nash and Stevie Wonder, and later albums saw Mason recoup somewhat. *Dave Mason* (#25, 1974) and *Split Coconut* (#27, 1975) were the two highest-charting albums here after his solo debut. He had his biggest solo hit in 1977, when "We Just Disagree," from *Let It Flow* (#37, 1977) reached #12. By late 1981 Mason could be heard singing radio commercials for Miller Beer.

Since 1983 he has continued to tour with his band, but his chart success has been spotty at best. In early 1994 it was announced that he had joined Fleetwood Mac [see entry]; he toured with the band that summer.

Nick Mason: See Pink Floyd

Material: See Bill Laswell

Material Issue
Formed July 4, 1986, Chicago, Illinois
Jim Ellison (b. Apr. 18, 1966, Chicago), gtr., voc.; Ted Ansani (b. Nov. 9, 1967, Chicago), bass; Mike Zelenko (b. Nov. 12, 1967, Chicago), drums.
1987—*Material Issue* EP (Big Block/Landmind)
1991—*International Pop Overthrow* (Mercury)
1992—*Destination Universe*   1994—*Freak City Soundtrack.*

Material Issue is a power-pop trio that follows in the tradition of such Northern Illinois pop-rock bands as Shoes and Cheap Trick; songwriter Jim Ellison was actually an early member of Green, Material Issue's first two records were coproduced by Shoes' member Jeff Murphy, and Cheap Trick guitarist Rick Nielsen plays on *Freak City Soundtrack.*

The group formed when Ellison and Ted Ansani were students in Chicago; they found Mike Zelenko through a "musician wanted" ad. Material Issue first distinguished itself from other punk-rock guitar bands on its self-released debut EP by singing earnest melodies with Beatlesish harmonies. In 1989 the trio recorded a single that got commercial airplay in Chicago, and the attendance at its energetic shows grew notable. They recorded *International Pop Overthrow* before they signed to Mercury; the company then released it. Mate-

rial Issue's major-label debut was a paean to girls, girls, girls; its 14 songs included the modern-rock tracks "Valerie Loves Me" and "Diane." The video for the former got frequent play, and the album dented the Top 100.

Destination Universe followed the successful formula. The track "What Girls Want" was an alternative hit that crossed over to album-rock radio and some Top Forty stations. *Freak City Soundtrack* was produced by Mike Chapman (Blondie, the Sweet), and included a cameo by Guns n' Roses guitarist Gilby Clarke. Such tracks as "Kim the Waitress" featured the same infectious, guitar-driven pop and girl idolizations for which Material Issue had become known.

Johnny Mathis
Born John Royce Mathis, September 30, 1935, San Francisco, California
1957—*Warm* (Columbia)   1958—*Merry Christmas*; *Swing Softly*; *Open Fire, Two Guitars*   1959—*Heavenly*; *Faithfully*   1963—*Johnny's Newest Hits* 1975—*Feelings*   1978—*You Light Up My Life*; *That's What Friends Are For* (with Deniece Williams)   1981—*The First 25 Years—The Silver Anniversary Album*   1984—*Johnny Mathis Live* 1986—*The Hollywood Musicals*   1993—*How Do You Keep the Music Playing?*; *The Music of Johnny Mathis: A Personal Collection.*

Johnny Mathis' smooth ballad singing and distinctive, nasal tenor voice have made him, by some people's figures, the second most consistently charted album artist in popular music, just after Frank Sinatra. He is said to have become one of America's first black millionaires. His *Greatest Hits* album from 1958 spent 490 weeks— nine and a half years—on the chart.

Mathis' parents worked as domestics for a San Francisco millionaire. At 13 he took professional opera lessons, though his early goal was to become a physical education teacher. (In 1956, while attending San Francisco State College, he was invited to the Olympic track trials held in Berkeley.) Singing in a jam session at San Francisco's 440 Club, Mathis was discovered by Columbia Records executive George Avakian, who sent him to New York to record. His first recordings were jazz-influenced, but Columbia A&R head Mitch Miller told him to switch to pop ballads.

His first hit came just one year later in July 1957, "Wonderful Wonderful" (#14), followed by "It's Not for Me to Say" (#5) and his big #1 in November, "Chances Are." Most of Mathis' big hits, including "The Twelfth of Never" (#9, 1957), "Misty" (#12, 1959), and "What Will Mary Say" (#9, 1963), were in the late Fifties and early Sixties, though his albums sold consistently well thereafter (always at least 250,000 copies, as he covered whatever MOR songs were hits at the time). He recaptured younger ears and hearts with his 1978 duet with Deniece Williams, "Too Much, Too Little, Too Late," which soared to #1 on both R&B and pop charts (he and Williams also recorded "Without Us," used as the theme for the TV show *Family Ties*). He made some unsuccessful stabs at rock and postdisco dance recordings before returning to his trademark romantic pop balladry in the late Eighties. The compilation *A Personal Collection* included a Mathis duet with Barbra Streisand, who had long cited him as a favorite and chief influence, on a medley from *West Side Story*.

Into the Nineties, Mathis was still headlining Atlantic City and Las Vegas resorts—even selling out three shows at New York's Carnegie Hall in October 1993—entrancing sell-out crowds of middle-aged people, many of whom had shared their first kiss, or conceived their children, to the (recorded) sound of his voice.

Kathy Mattea

Born Kathleen Alice Mattea, June 21, 1959, South Charleston, West Virginia
1984—*Kathy Mattea* (Mercury)   1985—*From My Heart*   1986—*Walk the Way the Wind Blows* 1987—*Untasted Honey*   1989—*Willow in the Wind* 1990—*A Collection of Hits*   1991—*Time Passes By* 1992—*Lonesome Standard Time*   1993—*Good News*   1994—*Walking Away a Winner.*

Kathy Mattea, with a solid grounding in folk, bluegrass, blues, and other country genres, has worked her way steadily up the Nashville ladder, starting as a tour guide at the Country Music Hall of Fame and rising to win the Country Music Association's Female Vocalist of the Year in 1989 and 1990.

Mattea grew up in an accomplished working-class family in Cross Lanes, West Virginia. After playing in the bluegrass band Pennsboro while in college, Mattea decided to pursue a career in music instead of science and moved to Nashville. In 1983 she signed to Mercury and had her first big country hit three years later with Nanci Griffith's "Love at the Five & Dime" (#3 C&W, 1986). Among her many subsequent C&W hits are "Goin' Gone" (#1, 1987), "Eighteen Wheels and a Dozen Roses" (#1, 1988), "Untold Stories" (#4, 1988), "Where've You Been" (#10, 1989) (a 1990 Grammy-winner written by her husband, Jon Vezner), and "Standing Knee Deep in a River (Dying of Thirst)" (#19, 1993). After her Grammy and CMA successes, Mattea stepped off the commercial path and released the introspective, Celtic-influenced *Time Passes By* (#9 C&W, 1991), but returned to mainstream country with *Lonesome Standard Time* (#41 C&W, 1992), which fared less well commercially.

After recording *Lonesome Standard Time*, Mattea experienced health problems and underwent surgery on her vocal cords. Though not an overtly political artist, at

Kathy Mattea

the 1992 CMA Awards, she spoke out against the association's refusal to support the wearing of red AIDS ribbons. Her next release was the Christmas album *Good News* (1993), followed by 1994's *Walking Away a Winner*.

Iain Matthews

Born Ian Matthew MacDonald, June 16, 1946, Lincolnshire, England
1970—*Matthews Southern Comfort* (Uni); *Second Spring* (Decca); *Later That Same Year* (MCA); *If You Saw Thro' My Eyes* (Vertigo); *Tigers Will Survive* 1973—*Valley Hi* (Elektra)   1974—*Some Days You Eat the Bear . . . and Some Days the Bear Eats You*; *Journeys from Gospel Oak* (Mooncrest)   1976—*Go for Broke* (Columbia)   1977—*Hit and Run*   1978— *Stealin' Home* (Mushroom)   1979—*Siamese Friends* 1980—*Spot of Interference* (RSO)   1988—*Walking a Changing Line* (Windham Hill)   1990—*Pure and Crooked Gold* (Gold Castle)   1992—*Best of Matthews Southern Comfort* (MCA)   1993—*The Soul of Many Places* (Elektra); *The Skeleton Keys* (Mesa Blue Moon)   1994—*The Dark Ride* (Watermelon).*
With Hamilton Pool: 1995—*Return to Zero* (Watermelon).*

A founding member of the seminal British folk-rock band Fairport Convention [see entry], Matthews (who used his middle name for a surname to avoid confusion with King Crimson's Ian McDonald, and in the past has spelled it *Ian*) left that band in 1969 after its second LP to form his own group, Matthews Southern Comfort, which hit with a cover of Joni Mitchell's "Woodstock" (#23 U.S., #1 U.K., 1971). In addition to Matthews' songwriting, vocals, and guitar, Matthews Southern Comfort also featured the pedal-steel guitar of Gordon Huntley, who went on to play on Rod Stewart's solo album *Never a Dull Moment*. Matthews left Southern Comfort in late 1970 for a solo career; in 1972 he formed Plainsong, which recorded *In Search of Amelia Earhart* (Elektra) before disbanding. He moved to California and continued recording solo albums.

Despite the Fairport association, Matthews did not consider himself a folkie; his first band, Pyramid, was a surf group. He did record *Siamese Friends,* an album of traditional music, but most of Matthews' efforts have been country-flavored pop suited to his high tenor voice. He had a pop hit in 1979 with "Shake It" (#13). In the late Seventies Matthews moved to Seattle, Washington, where he formed the band Hi-Fi with David Surkamp, former vocalist with St. Louis progressive-rockers Pavlov's Dog. Hi-Fi released a live EP (*Hi-Fi Demonstration Record*) for First American-SP&S. He worked as a talent scout for Island Music and Windham Hill from 1983 to 1988. Now a resident of Austin, Texas, Matthews remains as active and eclectic as ever: *The Skeleton Keys* was his first album to contain all-original material; he regrouped Plainsong for 1992's *Dark Side of the Room;* and in 1988 the singer/guitarist recorded *Walking a Changing Line—The Songs of Jules Shear*, Windham Hill's first all-vocal album. In the mid-Nineties Matthews appeared as part of the Austin-based trio Hamilton Pool, which also included singer/songwriters Michael Fracasso and Mark Hallman.

John Mayall/John Mayall's Bluesbreakers

John Mayall, born November 29, 1933, Macclesfield, England
The Bluesbreakers, formed 1963, London, England: Mayall, kybds., harmonica, voc., gtr.; Davy Graham, gtr.; John McVie (b. Nov. 26, 1945, London, Eng.), bass; Peter Ward, drums; – Graham; + Bernie Watson, gtr.
1964—(+ Hughie Flint, drums; – Watson; + Roger Dean, gtr.) **1965**—*John Mayall Plays John Mayall* (Decca, U.K.) (– Dean; + Eric Clapton [b. Mar. 30, 1945, Ripley, Eng.], gtr.; – Clapton; + various musicians on gtr., including Peter Green [b. Peter Greenbaum, Oct. 29, 1946, London, Eng.], gtr.; – McVie; + Jack Bruce [b. May 14, 1943, Glasgow, Scot.]; + Clapton; – Bruce; + McVie) **1966**—*Bluesbreak-*

John Mayall

ers—John Mayall with Eric Clapton (London) (– Clapton; – Flint; + Aynsley Dunbar [b. Jan. 10, 1946, Lancaster, Eng.], drums) **1967**—*A Hard Road* (– Dunbar; + Mick Fleetwood [b. June 24, 1947, Redruth, Eng.], drums; – Fleetwood; – Green; + Mick Taylor [b. Jan. 17, 1948, Welwyn Garden City, Eng.]; + Keef Hartley [b. Mar. 8, 1944, Preston, Eng.], drums; + Chris Mercer, sax; + Rip Kant, sax; – Kant); *Crusade; The Blues Alone* (+ Henry Lowther, trumpet; + Dick Heckstall-Smith [b. Sep. 26, 1934, Ludlow, Eng.], sax; – McVie; + Paul Williams, bass; – Williams; + Keith Tillman, bass) **1968**—*Diary of a Band, vol. 1; Diary of a Band, vol. 2* (– Tillman; + Andy Fraser [b. Aug. 7, 1952, London, Eng.], bass; – Fraser; + Tony Reeves, bass; – Hartley); *Bare Wires* (+ Jon Hiseman [b. June 21, 1944, London, Eng.], drums; – Mercer; – Lowther; – Hiseman; – Heckstall-Smith; + Colin Allen, drums; – Reeves; + Steve Thompson, bass); *Blues from Laurel Canyon* **1969**—(– Taylor; – Allen; + Jon Mark [b. Cornwall, Eng.], gtr.; + Johnny Almond [b. July 20, 1946, Enfield, Eng.], sax) *Looking Back; Turning Point* **1970**—*Empty Rooms* (Polydor) (– Mark; – Almond; + Harvey Mandel [b. Mar. 11, 1945, Detroit,

Mich.], gtr.; – Thompson; + Alex Dmochowski, bass; – Dmochowski; + Larry Taylor, bass; + Don "Sugarcane" Harris [b. June 18, 1938, Pasadena, Calif.], violin); *USA Union* 1971—(+ Clapton; + M. Taylor; + Hartley) *Back to the Roots* (– Clapton; – M. Taylor; – Hartley); *Thru the Years* (London) (– Mandel; – D. Harris; + Jimmy McCulloch [b. 1953, Glasgow, Scot.; d. Sep. 27, 1979, London], gtr.); *Memories* (Polydor) (– McCulloch; + Freddy Robinson, gtr.; + Blue Mitchell, trumpet; + Ron Selico, bass; + Clifford Solomon, saxes; – Selico; + Hartley) 1972—*Jazz-Blues Fusion* (+ Victor Gaskin, bass; + Fred Jackson, baritone and tenor saxes; + Charles Owens, tenor and soprano flutes; + Ernie Watts, tenor sax; – Solomon; + Red Holloway, flute, saxes); *Moving On* 1973—*The Best of John Mayall* (+ D. Harris; – Jackson; – Owens; – Watts); *Ten Years Are Gone* 1975—(– Mitchell; – Robinson; + Hightide Harris, bass, gtr.; – D. Harris; – Hartley; + Randy Resnick, gtr.; + Soko Richardson, drums) *The Latest Edition* (– H. Harris; – Resnick; + L. Taylor; – Holloway; + D. Harris; + Dee McKinnie [b. 1950], voc.; + Rick Vito [b. Oct. 13, 1949, Darby, Pa.], gtr.; + Jay Spell, kybds.); *New Year, New Band, New Company* (Blue Thumb); *Notice to Appear* 1976—*A Banquet in Blues* (ABC) 1977—(– McKinnie; – S. Richardson; – Vito; – D. Harris; + R. Holloway; + Gary Rowles, gtr.; + Frank Wilson, drums; + Warren Bryant, perc.; + Pepper Watkins, voc.; + Patty Smith, voc.) *Lots of People* (– Holloway; – Rowles; – Spell; – L. Taylor; – Wilson; – Bryant; – Watkins; – P. Smith; + James Quill Smith, gtr.; + Steve Thompson, bass; + S. Richardson, drums); *A Hard Core Package* 1978—*The Last of the British Blues* (group disbands; *Bottom Line* features nonband musicians) 1979—*Bottom Line* (DJM) (+ J. Smith; + Vito; + Chris Cameron, piano, clavinet; + Christian Mostert, soprano and tenor saxes, flutes; + Angus Thomas, bass; + Ruben Alvarez, drums; + Maggie Parker, voc.); *No More Interviews* 1980—(– Vito; – Cameron; – Mostert; – Thomas; – Alvarez; + Kevin McCormick, bass; + S. Richardson, drums) *Road Show Blues* Ca. 1981—(– McCormick; – J. Smith; – S. Richardson; – Parker; + Don McMinn, gtr.; + Bobby Manuel, gtr.; + Jeff Davis, bass; + Mike Gardner, drums) 1982—(Bluesbreakers reunion lineup: Mayall; McVie; Mick Taylor; Colin Allen) (Group disbands) Ca. 1984—(Lineup: Mayall; Coco Montoya, gtr.; Kal David, gtr.; Willie McNeil, drums; Walter Trout, gtr.; Bobby Haynes, bass) 1985—(– David; – McNeil; + Joe Yuele, drums) 1986—*Behind the Iron Curtain* (GNP Crescendo) 1987—*The Power of the Blues* (Entente, Ger.) 1988—*Chicago Line* (Island); *Archives to Eighties: Featuring Eric Clapton and Mick Taylor* (Polydor);

Primal Solos (PolyGram) 1990—(– Haynes; +Freebo, bass; – Trout) *A Sense of Place* (Island) 1991—(– Freebo; + Rick Cortes, bass) 1992—*John Mayall: London Blues, 1964–1969* (Polygram); *John Mayall: Room to Move, 1969–1974* 1993—*Wake Up Call* (Silvertone) 1994—*The 1982 Reunion Concert* (featuring 1982 lineup) (One Way); *Cross Country Blues* (featuring lineup of 1980 and 1984) (– Montoya; + Buddy Whittington, gtr.) 1995—*Spinning Coin* (Silvertone).

The father of the British blues movement, John Mayall has also been its hardiest perennial, taking the phrase "back to the roots" with more dogged seriousness than most. He's been one of the most famous talent scouts in rock music, having discovered many musicians—Eric Clapton, Mick Taylor, Jack Bruce, Keef Hartley, Aynsley Dunbar, Jon Mark, John Almond, Jon Hiseman, Peter Green, Mick Fleetwood, and John McVie—who went on to significant careers of their own. He was also something of an iconoclast: He formed his first band when he was nearly 30, and in the late Sixties, when hyperamplification was the rage, Mayall veered toward a subdued acoustic sound. As of the mid-Nineties, despite having passed age 60, Mayall continues to tour and record; early 1995 saw the release of his fortieth album.

Mayall began playing guitar and ukulele at age 12; by 14 he was playing boogie-woogie piano as well. After graduating Manchester Junior School of Art in 1949, he worked briefly as a window dresser. In 1955 he formed his first group, the Powerhouse Four. At age 18 Mayall entered the British army; upon his discharge he returned to art school. After graduating art school in 1959 he became a successful typographer and graphic artist (he later designed many of his album covers). In 1962 he formed the Blues Syndicate; he moved to London in 1963.

John Mayall and the Bluesbreakers' debut LP was recorded live in December 1964 and originally released only in England. By the time of the second Bluesbreakers LP (the first released in the U.S.) Mayall had been playing music for nearly 20 years. In 1965 Clapton was on guitar, and Jack Bruce had replaced McVie. Decca dropped the group, and around this time Mayall recorded a single, "I'm Your Witchdoctor" (produced by Jimmy Page), for Immediate. Clapton had left the group shortly before, and McVie returned in 1966 to join Green on guitar and Hughie Flint (later with McGuinness Flint) on drums. In the meantime, *Bluesbreakers, with Eric Clapton* became Mayall's first major hit. Green, McVie, and Mick Fleetwood left after 1967 to form Fleetwood Mac, and Mick Taylor (later of the Rolling Stones) came in on guitar that year; at age 16 bassist Andy Fraser (later with Free) joined in 1968; in the early Seventies guitarists Harvey Mandel (later with Canned Heat, among others); in the

Eighties Rick Vito (later of Fleetwood Mac). In addition, many other musicians have rehearsed, performed, or recorded with Mayall without officially becoming part of any of his numerous lineups. Mayall never seemed perturbed by the many personnel changes; in fact he often encouraged his musicians to leave for greater fame and wealth.

Virtually all of Mayall's albums of this period were critically acclaimed and, for blues records, commercially successful as well. *Bluesbreakers—John Mayall with Eric Clapton* and *A Hard Road* were Top Ten albums in the U.K. *Crusade,* another U.K. Top Ten LP, introduced 18-year-old Mick Taylor, drummer Keef Hartley (who, like Mayall, had an intense interest in Native American culture), and horn arrangements played by noted British jazz-rock sessionmen like Chris Mercer and Dick Heckstall-Smith. On *Blues Alone* Mayall played all the instruments except drums (handled again by Hartley). *Bare Wires* (#3 U.K.) made a transition from blues to progressive jazz rock; Heckstall-Smith and Hiseman left after this album to form the jazz-rock band Colosseum. It was the first Mayall album to enter the U.S. albums chart, peaking at #59.

After he had become known in the U.S., Mayall bought a house in the Los Angeles area and recorded *Blues from Laurel Canyon* (#68, 1969), a subdued record featuring local musicians like Canned Heat bassist Larry Taylor. *The Turning Point* (#32, 1969), Mayall's only gold LP, was all acoustic, with no drums; it featured Jon Mark's acoustic rhythm guitar and Johnny Almond's reed arsenal, and included one of Mayall's most popular tunes, "Room to Move." Mayall hit a commercial peak stateside with *Diary of a Band,* a two-volume collection of recordings by previous Bluesbreaker lineups. It was followed by his highest-charting album to date, *USA Union* (#22, 1970), which included future Mayall stalwarts Larry Taylor, Harvey Mandel, and Don "Sugarcane" Harris. Like a number of Mayall's band members, these three would drift in and out of the lineup for years to come. *Back to the Roots* (#52, 1971) featured a onetime lineup that included Mayall's latest band plus Mick Taylor, Eric Clapton, Johnny Almond, and Keef Hartley. (In 1988 Mayall, who was never satisfied with the sound of this album, discovered, restored, and remixed the original tapes, rerecording most of the drum parts with then-current Bluesbreaker drummer Joe Yuele and his own vocal and instrumental tracks. The result, *Archives to Eighties,* contains 13 of *Back to the Roots'* 18 tracks and is considered not only a successful restoration but one of Mayall's most important Eighties releases.)

Mayall shifted focus for *Jazz-Blues Fusion* (#64, 1972), which featured jazz trumpeter Blue Mitchell. Mitchell, as well as tenor saxophonist Ernie Watts and an extensive horn and reeds section appeared on *Moving On.* Mayall's music, with the exception of "Room to Move," got little airplay even during his early-Seventies heyday. By the mid-Seventies, Mayall's star had faded somewhat, as had his voice—hence the addition of female singer Dee McKinnie on *New Year, New Band, New Company. Notice to Appear,* produced by New Orleans songwriter Allen Toussaint, won little success commercially or critically. *A Banquet in Blues* and *Lots of People* continued this trend. Still, Mayall kept recording. He lost virtually everything he owned, including the original artwork for some of his album covers, which he designed, and a priceless collection of pornography (some dating back to the Victorian era), when his California home was destroyed by fire in 1979. That year also saw the dissolution of the current Bluesbreakers lineup. Mayall then recorded *The Bottom Line,* essentially a solo album that featured Cornell Dupree, Steve Jordan, Paul Shaffer, Michael and Randy Brecker, Lee Ritenour, Jeff Porcaro, and Cheryl Lynn among its many guest musicians. Both it and *No More Interviews* (the first album to feature Mayall's wife, singer/songwriter Maggie Parker, on vocals—they married in 1982) represented a return to form.

In early 1982 Mayall, McVie, and Taylor staged a Bluesbreakers reunion, playing a short series of dates in America and Australia. A live album of the reunion concerts was recorded, but not released due to lack of record-company interest. It finally saw the light of day in 1994 under the title *The 1982 Reunion Concert.*

Following *Road Show Blues,* Mayall ceased recording for the next five years, devoting his time to live performances in and around California. In 1984 Mayall assembled the core of one of his most stable lineups, featuring guitarist Coco Montoya (who would remain for a decade) and bassist Bobby Haynes. His next live release, *Behind the Iron Curtain,* neither returned him to the charts nor incited great critical enthusiasm. Yet he retained a following strong enough to support several tours of the U.S. and Europe and, unlike many blues purists of his generation, survived to catch the next blues-revival wave in the late Eighties. By the early Nineties Mayall seemed to have come full circle: His 1993 album *Wake Up Call,* which features guest artists Albert Collins, Mick Taylor, Mavis Staples, and Buddy Guy, was one of five nominated for Best Contemporary Blues Album.

Curtis Mayfield

Born June 3, 1942, Chicago, Illinois
1970—*Curtis* (Curtom)   1971—*Curtis Live; Roots*
1972—*Superfly*   1973—*His Early Years with the Impressions* (ABC)   1974—*Sweet Exorcist* (Curtom)
1975—*America Today*   1976—*Give, Get, Take and Have*   1977—*Never Say You Can't Survive*   1978—*Do It All Night*   1979—*Heartbeat* (RSO)   1980—*Something to Believe In*   1981—*Love Is the Place*

Curtis Mayfield

(Boardwalk) 1982—*Honesty* 1985—*We Come in Peace with a Message of Love* (CRC) 1990—*Take It to the Streets* (Curtom); *Live in Europe.*

Curtis Mayfield was a driving force in black music from the early Sixties through the mid-Seventies, as a singer, writer, producer, and label owner. Mayfield began singing with gospel groups such as the Northern Jubilee Singers, who were part of his grandmother's Traveling Soul Spiritualist Church. He met lifelong friend and collaborator Jerry Butler at a gospel function, and they went on to form the Impressions, a rhythm & blues vocal group, in 1957 [see entry]. In 1958 they, along with Sam Gooden and Richard and Arthur Brooks, recorded "For Your Precious Love" on Vee Jay Records. Butler's cool baritone dominated the record, and he left to pursue a solo career. Mayfield and Butler teamed up again in 1960, with Butler singing and Mayfield writing and playing guitar on "He Will Break Your Heart" (#7 pop, #1 R&B). A re-formed Impressions with Mayfield, Gooden, and Fred Cash signed with ABC-Paramount and scored with Mayfield's flamenco-sounding "Gypsy Woman" (#20 pop, #2 R&B).

Mayfield then entered a prolific period during which his writing and singing would come to define the Chicago sound, which rivaled Motown in the early and mid-Sixties. With the Impressions, Mayfield produced, wrote, and sang lead on numerous hits; some included uplifting civil rights movement messages. "It's All Right" (#4 pop, #1 R&B) in 1963; "I'm So Proud" (#14), "Keep On Pushing" (#10), and "Amen" (#7 pop, #17 R&B) in 1964; "People Get Ready" (#14 pop, #3 R&B) in 1965; and "We're a Winner" (#14 pop, #1 R&B) in 1968 reflect the quality of Mayfield's work.

Meanwhile, as the staff producer for Columbia-distributed Okeh Records, Mayfield wrote memorable music for Major Lance—"The Monkey Time" (#8 pop, #4 R&B) and "Um, Um, Um, Um, Um, Um" (#5)—and for Gene Chandler: "Just Be True" (#19) and "Nothing Can Stop Me" (#18 pop, #3 R&B). On his own Windy C and Mayfield labels he produced hits with the Five Stairsteps and Cubie, "World of Fantasy" (#12 R&B), and the Fascinations, "Girls Are Out to Get You" (#13 R&B), respectively.

In the late Sixties Mayfield started his third company, Curtom, this one distributed by Buddah Records. During the Seventies Curtom moved from Buddah to Warner Bros. to RSO Records for distribution. In 1970 Mayfield also made a major career move, leaving the Impressions to go solo, though he continued to direct the group's career through the Seventies.

Solo albums—*Curtis* (#19), *Curtis/Live!* (#21), and *Roots* (#40) all sold well, establishing Mayfield as a solo performer. But it was his soundtrack to the blaxploitation film *Superfly* that is generally considered his masterpiece—an eerie yet danceable blend of Mayfield's knowing falsetto with Latin percussion and predisco rhythm guitars. The four-million-selling album (#1, 1972) included two gold singles, "Superfly" (#8 pop, #5 R&B) and "Freddie's Dead" (#4 pop, #2 R&B); it also sold a million copies as a tape. It foreshadowed Mayfield's continued involvement with film in the Seventies. He scored *Claudine,* writing Gladys Knight and the Pips' single "On and On" in 1974; *Let's Do It Again,* which featured the Staple Singers on the title song in 1975; and *Sparkle* with Aretha Franklin in 1976. Two years later Mayfield and Franklin would team again for *Almighty Fire.* In 1977 Mayfield would both score and act in the low-budget prison drama *Short Eyes,* a critical success.

As a solo artist, Mayfield continued to score through the Seventies, with "Future Shock" (#11 R&B, 1973), "If I Were Only a Child Again" (#22 R&B, 1973), "Can't Say Nothin'" (#16 R&B, 1973), "Kung Fu" (#3 R&B, 1974), "So In Love" (#9 R&B, 1975), "Only You Babe" (#8 R&B, 1976), and two duets with Linda Clifford: "Between You Baby and Me" (#14 R&B, 1979) and "Love's Sweet Sensation" (#34 R&B, 1980).

In 1980 Mayfield, who by then had moved with his family (including six children) from Chicago to Atlanta, signed with Boardwalk Records and enjoyed a popular album and singles with *Love Is the Place* and "She Don't Let Nobody (But Me)" (#15 R&B) and "Toot 'n' Toot 'n' Toot" (#2 R&B). Mayfield rejoined the Impressions for a 1983 reunion tour. Mayfield's recording career hit a wall when Boardwalk went bankrupt, but he formed his own CRC label to release 1985's *We Come in Peace with a Message of Love,* which went unnoticed, as did his two 1990 albums for the revived Curtom label (distributed by Atlanta's Ichiban.) Mayfield continued touring, however, and was especially popular in England, where the band the Blow Monkeys recorded a duet with him in 1987, "(Celebrate) The Day After You."

In 1990 Mayfield scored the dud movie *Return of Superfly;* the music was released on an album, *Superfly 1990,* on which Mayfield collaborated with rapper Ice-T—one of several Nineties stars, such as Arrested Development and Lenny Kravitz, to cite Mayfield's influence. On August 14, 1990, while Mayfield was performing an outdoor concert in Brooklyn, New York, a lighting rig fell atop him, leaving him permanently paralyzed from the neck down. Mayfield and the Impressions were subsequently inducted into the Rock and Roll Hall of Fame, and a lavish and emotional tribute was paid to Mayfield at the 1994 Grammy Awards gala. Ironically, just a few months earlier Mayfield and Jerry Butler had joined Sam Moore of Sam and Dave, Felix Cavaliere of the Rascals, the estates of the late Mary Wells and Jackie Wilson, and dozens of other acts, as plaintiffs in a $7 billion class action lawsuit, accusing major American record labels of defrauding musicians of their health insurance, pensions, and other benefits, by systematically underreporting their earnings to the American Federation of Radio and Television Artists (AFTRA), whom the suit also accused of failing to protect the artists' interests.

In 1994 Shanachie Records released an all-star Mayfield tribute album entitled *People Get Ready,* which featured Delbert McClinton, Jerry Butler, Bunny Wailer, and Huey Lewis and the News. Another tribute, *A Tribute to Curtis Mayfield,* included Eric Clapton, Elton John, Bruce Springsteen, Gladys Knight, and Jerry Butler, among others. The enduring appeal of Mayfield's songs is evidenced in the wide range of artists who have recorded them: Deniece Williams ("I'm So Proud"), UB40 ("I Gotta Keep Moving"), David Allan Coe ("For Your Precious Love"), Rod Stewart and Jeff Beck ("People Get Ready"), and En Vogue ("Giving Him Something He Can Feel").

Paul McCartney

Born James Paul McCartney, June 18, 1942, Liverpool, England
1970—*McCartney* (Apple)   1971—*Ram* (with Linda McCartney)   1980—*McCartney II* (Columbia) 1982—*Tug of War*   1983—*Pipes of Peace*   1984— *Give My Regards to Broad Street*   1986—*Press to Play* (Capitol)   1987—*All the Best!*   1989—*Flowers in the Dirt*   1990—*Tripping the Live Fantastic; Tripping the Live Fantastic—Highlights!*   1991— *Unplugged;* CHOBA B CCCP—*The Russian Album; Liverpool Oratorio* (EMI Classics)   1993—*Off the Ground; Paul Is Live.*
Wings: 1971—(+ Linda McCartney [b. Linda Louise Eastman, Sep. 24, 1942, Scarsdale, N.Y.], kybds., voc.; + Denny Laine [b. Brian Hines, Oct. 29, 1944,

Paul McCartney

Eng.], gtr., kybds., voc.; + Denny Seiwell, drums) *Wild Life* (Apple)   1972—(+ Henry McCullough [b. Scotland], gtr.)   1973—*Red Rose Speedway* (– McCullough; – Seiwell); *Band on the Run* 1974—(+ Jimmy McCulloch [b. 1953, Glasgow, Scot.; d. Sep. 27, 1979, London, Eng.], gtr.; + Geoff Britton, drums; – Britton; + Joe English [b. Feb. 7, 1949, Rochester, N.Y.], drums)   1975—*Venus and Mars* (Capitol)   1976—*Wings at the Speed of Sound; Wings over America* (– English; – McCulloch)   1978—*London Town; Wings Greatest* (+ Steve Holly, drums; + Laurence Juber, gtr., voc.) 1979—*Back to the Egg* (Columbia).

Paul McCartney's gift for light pop songwriting has made him the most commercially successful ex-Beatle. He answered his critics in 1976 with the single "Silly Love Songs," one of many post-Beatles hits. If, as some critics maintain, his solo work hasn't measured up to the standards of his collaborations with Lennon, McCartney has still shown a consistent talent for writing songs that are tuneful and popular. McCartney was also the only ex-Beatle to form a permanent working band; Wings, which he led from 1971 to 1981, recorded for more years than the Beatles.

McCartney's father, James, led the Jim Mac Jazz Band in the Twenties. A few months after his mother Mary died of breast cancer in 1956, Paul bought his first guitar and learned to play. In June 1956 he met Lennon and asked to join his band, the Quarrymen; McCartney's rendition of Eddie Cochran's "Twenty Flight Rock" at a subsequent audition won him entry. In 1963 McCartney met Jane Asher, to whom he addressed many of his best-known love songs, and on Christmas Day 1967, at a McCartney family party, he announced his engagement. But by July 1968 the engagement was off. Soon after he met American photographer Linda Eastman, whom he married on March 12, 1969.

In April 1970, only two weeks before the scheduled release of the Beatles' *Let It Be*, McCartney released his first solo album—a one-man-studio-band LP recorded in Campbelltown, England, in late 1969. *McCartney* (#1, 1970) had a pronounced homemade quality; it was spare and sounded almost unfinished, but it also contained "Maybe I'm Amazed," which became an international hit and McCartney's first post-Beatles pop standard (the Beatles had only recently disbanded as the tune became a hit). The winsome homespun-ditty motif continued with *Ram* (#2, 1971), credited to Paul and Linda McCartney. McCartney's softer direction inspired Lennon's "How Do You Sleep?"—a vicious, thinly veiled attack on McCartney. Meanwhile *Ram* yielded "Uncle Albert/Admiral Halsey," which made #1 in America. "Another Day" (#5) was a nonalbum single in 1971.

Later in 1971 McCartney formed Wings, which was intended as a recording and touring outfit. Along with Linda, Wings featured American session drummer Denny Seiwell and ex–Moody Blues guitarist Denny Laine. Wings' *Wild Life*, with Linda McCartney on keyboards and backup vocals, sold only moderately, failing to yield a hit single. In 1972 ex–Grease Band guitarist Henry McCullough joined. McCartney spent 1972 releasing several singles, including "Give Ireland Back to the Irish" (#16 U.K.) (rush-released after the January 1972 "Bloody Sunday" incident in which British soldiers killed 13 Irish civilians in Londonderry, Ireland; the song was banned by the BBC), "Mary Had a Little Lamb" (#9, U.K., #28 U.S.) (yes, the nursery rhyme), and the hard-rocking "Hi Hi Hi." Only the last was a major U.S. hit, going to #10 in 1973.

Red Rose Speedway (#1, 1973), the next Wings album, yielded a #1 hit single in the U.S. with the heavily orchestrated ballad "My Love." Also in 1973, McCartney was arrested and then released on a drug charge, and he did his own television special, which received mixed reviews in both the U.S. and the U.K. Later Wings made its first tour of Britain, and recorded the title theme song for the James Bond film *Live and Let Die*, which went to #2 in the U.S. Laine released a solo LP, *Ahh Laine*.

After Wings' U.K. tour, Seiwell and Henry McCullough left the group. Denny Laine accompanied Paul and Linda to Nigeria to record *Band on the Run*. While each of the previous Wings albums had ended up going gold, *Band on the Run* (#1, 1974) went platinum in short order

and yielded two Top Ten hit singles—"Helen Wheels" (#10, 1973) and "Jet" (#7, 1974)—and the bouncy mini-suite title track (#11, 1974). It also included McCartney's answer to Lennon's "How Do You Sleep?" in "Let Me Roll It," and featured a cover photo of McCartney accompanied by such celebrities as film actors James Coburn and Christopher Lee.

McCartney formed a new Wings, recruiting guitarist James McCulloch from Thunderclap Newman and Stone the Crows, and drummer Geoff Britton, a British karate expert. They recorded "Junior's Farm" (#3, 1974) in Nashville in 1974, and later that year went to New Orleans (where they found new drummer Joe English) to record *Venus and Mars,* which yielded several hit singles (including the #1 "Listen to What the Man Said") and went platinum.

At the Speed of Sound found McCartney giving his bandmembers a chance to compose and sing much of the material, but McCartney's own contributions were almost all hits. Two went gold: "Silly Love Songs" (#1, 1976) and "Let 'Em In" (#3, 1976). Shortly after the album's release, Wings completed a world tour that had begun in Britain on September 9, 1975, and ended on October 21, 1976. The *Over America* triple-record live album was recorded on that tour.

In 1977 McCartney, under the pseudonym Percy Thrillington, recorded an obscure all-instrumental version of *Ram* and produced Denny Laine's *Holly Days,* a solo album of Buddy Holly songs. A live "Maybe I'm Amazed" hit #10 in 1977. That year saw the release of the McCartney-Laine "Mull of Kintyre," based on a Scottish folk song, which became the first single ever to sell two million copies in Britain. It was McCartney's first British #1 single since he'd left the Beatles. Later that year, under the name Susie and the Red Stripes, McCartney and Wings had another minor hit single in the reggae-inflected "Seaside Woman."

After *London Town*, which yielded another #1, "With a Little Luck," Jimmy McCulloch departed for the reformed Small Faces. *Back to the Egg* yielded two Top Forty hits—"Getting Closer" (#20, 1979) and "Arrow Through Me" (#29, 1979) and sold unspectacularly. In January 1980 McCartney was arrested for possession of marijuana in Tokyo at the beginning of a Japanese tour, jailed for ten days, then freed and not prosecuted. Soon after, he and Wings embarked on a British tour, after which drummer English left. McCartney then organized all-star benefit concerts for the people of Kampuchea and released *McCartney II* (#3, 1980), his first one-man-band album since his solo debut. It contained the #1 hit "Coming Up."

In April 1981 Denny Laine announced he was leaving Wings, the reason being McCartney's reluctance to tour because of the death threats he was receiving in the wake of John Lennon's murder. McCartney continued with the well-received *Tug of War*—a solo album featuring a host of guest performers (Laine, ex-Beatle Ringo Starr, Beatles producer George Martin, and most notably Stevie Wonder, who sang with McCartney on the #1 hit single "Ebony and Ivory"). *Tug* also yielded a #10 hit in "Take It Away." McCartney sang on Michael Jackson's "The Girl Is Mine," a Top Ten hit in 1983. Jackson returned the favor by singing on *Pipes of Peace*'s "Say Say Say," which topped the chart later that same year.

Embittered by the 1967 sale of publishing rights to his and John Lennon's Beatles songs to British film producer Lew Grade—a sale made while the Beatles were in India with Maharishi Mahesh Yogi—McCartney has invested extensively in pop-song copyrights over the years. Among his holdings are the entire Buddy Holly catalogue, "On Wisconsin," and "Autumn Leaves." However, shortly after "Say Say Say" was a hit, McCartney advised Michael Jackson to invest in music publishing—and Jackson later bought the Northern Songs catalogue, which included all of the Beatles songs McCartney had written with Lennon. McCartney never hid his anger at the move, especially when Jackson began licensing Beatles tunes for television commercials (such as "Revolution," used in a late-Eighties Nike sneaker ad). McCartney later told *Musician* magazine "complications with Yoko" (whose son Sean was a close friend of Jackson's) had prevented him from making a competitive bid for his own songs.

In 1984 McCartney made a dramatic feature film, *Give My Regards to Broad Street*, set within London's music industry, which was roundly panned by critics. Its soundtrack (#21, 1984) consisted largely of rerecorded Beatles and McCartney hits; the album went gold, and one new track, the ballad "No More Lonely Nights," became a #6 pop hit. He scored a #7 pop hit in 1985 with the theme song to the comedy film *Spies Like Us*. *Press to Play* (#30, 1986) found McCartney collaborating with ex-10cc Eric Stewart; the album's only hit was "Press" (#21, 1986). In 1988, as a sort of *Glasnost* gesture, McCartney released an album of rock oldies exclusively on the Soviet Melodiya label, under the title Снова в СССР ("Back in the USSR," roughly translated). For *Flowers in the Dirt* (#21, 1989) McCartney collaborated on some songs with Elvis Costello (McCartney also cowrote and played on a couple of tracks on Costello's *Spike*, including "Veronica"). The album yielded a hit in "My Brave Face" (#25, 1989), but McCartney was reportedly quite disappointed that the album failed to chart higher, despite a 1989 world tour (with a band featuring ex-Pretenders guitarist Robbie McIntosh and ex–Average White Band bassist Hamish Stuart) that was documented on *Tripping the Live Fantastic* (#26, 1990).

In early 1991 McCartney became one of the first major artists to release an album from his appearance on MTV's *Unplugged* acoustic showcase; *Unplugged (The Official Bootleg)* hit #14. Later that year McCartney released Снова в СССР in the U.S. (where it only reached #109 on the pop albums chart) and unveiled his first classical work, *Liverpool Oratorio* (#177, 1991), which failed to impress classical critics. McCartney returned to pop with *Off the Ground*, on which he again collaborated with Costello; the album entered the chart at #17 but dropped quickly and failed to yield a hit single. In April 1993 McCartney was joined onstage by Starr for "Hey Jude" at an all-star Earth Day concert in Los Angeles.

Delbert McClinton

Born November 4, 1940, Lubbock, Texas
1972—*Delbert and Glen* (Clean)   1973—*Subject to Change*   1975—*Victim of Life's Circumstances* (ABC)   1976—*Genuine Cowhide*   1977—*Love Rustler*   1978—*Second Wind* (Capricorn); *Very Early Delbert McClinton* (Le Cam)   1979—*Keeper of the Flame* (Capricorn)   1980—*The Jealous Kind* (Capitol)   1981—*Plain from the Heart*   1989—*Live from Austin* (Alligator)   1990—*I'm with You* (Curb)   1991—*Best of Delbert McClinton*   1992—*Never Been Rocked Enough*   1993—*Delbert McClinton*   1994—*Honky Tonkin' Blues* (MCA).

Delbert McClinton has been singing R&B, blues, rockabilly, and country for 35 years, starting on the Texas honky-tonk circuit. In the late Fifties McClinton's Straitjackets were the house band and one of the few white acts at Jacks, a Fort Worth club where they backed up Howlin' Wolf, Lightnin' Hopkins, and Big Joe Turner. McClinton's first record, a cover of Sonny Boy Williamson's "Wake Up Baby," released in 1960, was the first white single played on Fort Worth's KNOK.

Inspired by bluesman Jimmy Reed, McClinton switched from guitar to harmonica, and in the early Sixties, when he toured England with Bruce Channel (he'd played on Channel's #1 1962 hit "Hey Baby"), he taught some harp licks to John Lennon, who was playing in a then-unknown opening act, the Beatles. In 1964 and 1965 he had a group called the Ron Dels, who were shunted around to three labels, though one song ("If You Really Want Me To, I'll Go") did reach the Hot 100 in 1965.

McClinton spent the late Sixties on the local Texas bar circuit, until he and Glen Clark formed Delbert and Glen, a duo that cut two LPs for Atlantic's Clean subsidiary in 1972 and 1973. He didn't get a solo contract until 1975, and his subsequent albums on ABC won critical kudos but sold poorly. In 1978 he recorded two discs for Capricorn just before the label folded; his composition "Two More Bottles of Wine" later became a #1 country hit for Emmylou Harris, and the Blues Brothers recorded his "B Movie Boxcar Blues." His next record, *The Jealous Kind*, recorded with some Muscle Shoals musicians, turned his luck around, earning McClinton his own Top Forty hit, "Giving It Up for Your Love" (#8, 1980).

Since then, McClinton has retained a strong following and released several more albums. In 1991 he won a Grammy for his duet with Bonnie Raitt, "Good Man, Good Woman," and in 1993 another duet, with Tanya Tucker, entitled "Tell Me About It," was nominated for Best Country Vocal Collaboration. His *Live from Austin* was also nominated for a Best Contemporary Blues Grammy.

Marilyn McCoo and Billy Davis Jr.: See the Fifth Dimension

Van McCoy

Born January 6, 1944, Washington, D.C.; died July 6, 1979, Englewood, New Jersey
1975—*Disco Baby* (Avco)   1976—*The Hustle* (H&L)
1978—*My Favorite Fantasy* (MCA)   1979—*Lonely Dancer; Sweet Rhythm* (H&L).

Throughout the Sixties and Seventies, Van McCoy was primarily a songwriter and producer for artists such as Aretha Franklin, Gladys Knight and the Pips, Peaches and Herb, and Melba Moore. He had one of disco's biggest hits with his own 1975 instrumental single "The Hustle" (#1 pop, #1 R&B).

McCoy studied piano from age four, and a year later he and his older brother Norman, a violinist, began performing at Washington teas as the McCoy Brothers. He wrote his first song at age 12, and while studying psychology at Howard University he began singing with the Starlighters, a group that cut a few locally released records. During his second year at Howard, he moved to Philadelphia and started a record label with his uncle.

McCoy then began writing and producing hits for Ruby and the Romantics, Gladys Knight, Barbara Lewis, and others. He recorded an album on Columbia, then in 1968 formed his own record production and music publishing company with Joe Cobb. In 1973 he and Charles Kipps established White House Productions, renamed McCoy-Kipps Productions in 1976. Other popular singles by McCoy include "Change with the Times" (#46 pop, #6 R&B, 1975) and "Party" (#69 pop, #20 R&B, 1976). He died of a heart attack in 1979.

Ian McCulloch: See Echo and the Bunnymen

Michael McDonald

Born February 12, 1952, St. Louis, Missouri
1982—*If That's What It Takes* (Warner Bros.)

1985—*No Lookin' Back*   1990—*Take It to Heart* (Reprise)   1993—*Blink of an Eye*.

In the latter half of the Seventies, as singer and keyboardist for the Doobie Brothers [see entry], onetime Steely Dan [see entry] member Michael McDonald helped redefine the sound of what had once been a straight-ahead rock & roll band. McDonald's soulful, falsetto-happy vocals and gospel-influenced instrumental technique guided the Doobies into mellow R&B territory. After that group disbanded in 1980, the singer/songwriter embarked on a solo career that took him even further in that direction. On his own, and in duets with several leading R&B artists, McDonald established a smooth, light, jazz-inflected style that appealed to fans of adult contemporary music. He also garnered a few major pop singles and earned the respect of critics and the R&B community.

Just before the Doobies' breakup, McDonald sang backup on one of Christopher Cross' big hits, 1980's "Ride Like the Wind" (#2). McDonald released his first solo album, *If That's What It Takes*, two years later. The album went to #6 and spawned the single "I Keep Forgettin' (Every Time You're Near)" (#4 pop, #7 R&B, 1982). The following year he teamed up with James Ingram on "Yah Mo B There" (#19 pop, #5 R&B, 1984). *No Lookin' Back* featured a slightly harder-edged sound than its predecessor. The album peaked at #45, and its title track went to #34, both in 1985.

In 1986 another duet with a contemporary soul icon proved McDonald's biggest hit to date: "On My Own," a lovelorn ballad that paired him with Patti LaBelle, was a #1 smash. McDonald entered the Top Ten again later that year, with "Sweet Freedom" (#7), the theme song for the film comedy *Running Scared*. McDonald didn't release another studio album until 1990, though, and that effort, *Take It to Heart*, only made it to #110. In 1992 the singer enjoyed a slight commercial rebound, and a considerable artistic coup, when Aretha Franklin featured him on her 1992 R&B hit, "Ever Changing Times" (#19). Also that year, McDonald reconciled with the driving forces behind Steely Dan, Donald Fagen and Walter Becker, in the New York Rock and Soul Revue, a recording and touring collective that also included Boz Scaggs, Phoebe Snow, and Chuck Brown. In 1993 McDonald released his fourth solo album, *Blink of an Eye*, a commercial flop.

Mississippi Fred McDowell

Born January 12, 1904, Rossville, Tennessee; died July 3, 1972, Memphis, Tennessee
1969—*I Don't Play No Rock 'n' Roll* (Capitol)
1972—*Mississippi Fred McDowell 1904–1972* (Just Sunshine)   1973—*Keep Your Lamp Trimmed and Burning* (Arhoolie)   1989—*Shake 'Em On Down*

(Tomato) 1993—*The Train I Ride* (New Rose) 1995—*Live at the Mayfair Hotel* (American).

Although Mississippi Fred McDowell didn't make his first recording until the age of 55, he proved to be among the most influential of blues singer/guitarists on rock & roll, particularly with singer/guitarist Bonnie Raitt, who brought him on her early tours and recorded his songs. McDowell made dozens of records, but is probably best known as the composer of "You Got to Move," covered by the Rolling Stones on *Sticky Fingers.*

McDowell taught himself the guitar as a teenager and played locally in Tennessee while working as a farmer. In 1926 he moved to Memphis to become a professional musician, which he gave up for farming again in 1940, when he relocated to Como, Mississippi. His recording career began in 1959, at which point he began devoting more and more time to music. He made records, frequently with his wife, Annie Mae, and played at all the major folk and blues festivals of the Sixties. With the increased attention paid by rock & rollers to bluesmen, he appeared at a number of rock festivals as well. In addition to his many records, McDowell was captured in nearly a half-dozen films, including *The Blues Maker* (1968) and *Fred McDowell* (1969). He died of abdominal ulcers.

Reba McEntire

Born March 28, 1955, McAlster, Oklahoma
1980—*Feel the Fire* (Mercury) 1981—*Heart to Heart* 1982—*Unlimited* 1983—*Behind the Scenes* 1984—*Just a Little Love* 1985—*The Best of Reba McEntire; Have I Got a Deal for You* (MCA) 1986—*Whoever's in New England; What Am I Gonna Do About You; Reba Nell McEntire* (Mercury) 1987—*The Last One to Know* (MCA); *Reba McEntire's Greatest Hits; Merry Christmas to You* 1988—*Reba* 1989—*Sweet Sixteen; Reba Live* 1990—*Rumor Has It* 1991—*For My Broken Heart* 1992—*It's Your Call* 1993—*Greatest Hits, vol. 2* 1994—*Read My Mind.*

A feisty redhead with a thick Oklahoma accent, Reba McEntire parlayed a strong, pure voice and a penchant for singing songs about ordinary women—and the extraordinary demands that life places on them—into country-music superstardom. McEntire's unaffected, strikingly emotional delivery invited a few comparisons to her idol Patsy Cline. Like Cline, McEntire made news outside the C&W arena as the result of a plane crash: In 1991 eight members of her band were killed when a twin-engine jet bound for a show in Texas slammed into the side of a mountain. (The musicians were Jim Hammon, Paula Kaye Evans, Michael Thomas, Terry Jackson, Joey Cigainero, Tony Saputo, and Chris Austin, as well as band manager Kirk Cappello.) The tragedy occurred the same year that McEntire released *For My Broken Heart,* her most consistently grim album (and one of her biggest commercial successes).

McEntire's father was a steer roper on the rodeo circuit. During high school, the singer competed at rodeos, as a barrel racer, and played nightclubs with her siblings as the Singing McEntires. She eventually went to college and planned to become a teacher, but a gig singing the national anthem at the National Rodeo Finals resulted in a contract with Mercury Records. Her first Top Ten C&W hit came in 1980—four years after signing—with "(You Lift Me) Up to Heaven" (#8). A steady stream of country hits followed: "Today All Over Again" (#5, 1981), "I'm Not That Lonely Yet" (#3, 1982), "Can't Even Get the Blues" (#1, 1982), "You're the First Time I've Thought About Leaving" (#1, 1983), "Why Do We Want (What We Know We Can't Have)" (#7, 1983), and "Just a Little Love" (#5, 1984).

But it was in the latter half of the Eighties, after she switched to MCA Records, that McEntire's star really rose. Her string of Top Three C&W albums began with 1986's *Whoever's in New England* (#1), and continued with *What Am I Gonna Do About You* (#1, 1986), *Greatest Hits* (#2, 1987), *The Last One to Know* (#3, 1987), *Reba* (#1, 1988), *Sweet Sixteen* (#1, 1989), *Reba Live* (#2, 1989), *Rumor Has It* (#2, 1990), *For My Broken Heart* (#3, 1991), *It's Your Call* (#1, 1992), and *Greatest Hits, vol. 2* (#2, 1993). McEntire racked up an equally impressive list of hit country singles, including "How Blue" (#1, 1984), "Somebody Should Leave" (#1, 1985), "Have I Got a Deal for You" (#6, 1985), "Only in My Mind" (#5, 1985), "Whoever's in New England" (#1, 1986), "Little Rock" (#1, 1986), "What Am I Gonna Do About You" (#1, 1986), "Let the Music Lift You Up" (#4, 1987), "One Promise Too Late" (#1, 1987), "The Last One to Know" (#1, 1987), "Love Will Find Its Way to You" (#1, 1988), a cover of Jo Stafford's 1947 classic "Sunday Kind of Love" (#5, 1988), "I Know How He Feels" (#1, 1988), "New Fool at an Old Game" (#1, 1988), "Cathy's Clown" (#1, 1989), " 'Til Love Comes Again" (#4, 1989), "Little Girl" (#7, 1989), "Walk On" (#2, 1990), "You Lie" (#1, 1990), "Rumor Has It" (#3, 1990), "Fancy" (#8, 1991), "Fallin' Out of Love" (#2, 1991), "For My Broken Heart" (#1, 1991), "Is There Life Out There" (#1, 1992), "The Greatest Man I Never Knew" (#3, 1992), and "Take It Back" (#5, 1992).

In 1994 McEntire published her autobiography, *Reba: My Story* (written with Tom Carter), which spent 15 weeks on the *New York Times* best-seller list. That same year, her album *Read My Mind* reached #2 on the country charts.

McFadden and Whitehead

Gene McFadden, born 1948, Philadelphia, Pennsylvania; John Whitehead, born 1948, Philadelphia, Pennsylvania.

1979—*McFadden and Whitehead* (Philadelphia International) **1980**—*I Heard It in a Love Song.*
John Whitehead solo: **1988**—*I Need Money Bad* (Mercury).

Gene McFadden and John Whitehead are prolific songwriters who contributed greatly to the success of Kenny Gamble and Leon Huff's Philadelphia International Records. The duo's career began when both belonged to a vocal group called the Epsilons. They worked with many of the Stax stars, including Otis Redding, and sang background vocals on Arthur Conley's "Sweet Soul Music." Later the group's name was changed to Talk of the Town. Frustrated by their lack of success as performers, McFadden and Whitehead turned to songwriting. During their tenure as staff writers for PIR, they wrote "Bad Luck," "Where Are All My Friends," and "Wake Up Everybody" for Harold Melvin and the Blue Notes (all with arranger Vic Carstarphen); "Back Stabbers" (Whitehead with Gamble and Huff) for the O'Jays; and "I'll Always Love My Mama" (Whitehead, Carstarphen, Huff) for the Intruders.

In 1979 they recorded one of that summer's most popular singles, "Ain't No Stoppin' Us Now" (#13 pop, #1 R&B). In the early Eighties the duo produced records for Teddy Pendergrass, Melba Moore, and others. Each took a turn at recording solo albums. Whitehead was convicted in the Eighties of tax evasion. His minor R&B hit was "I Need Money Bad" in 1988.

Bobby McFerrin

Born March 11, 1950, New York City, New York
1982—*Bobby McFerrin* (Elektra Musician) **1984**—*The Voice* **1986**—*Spontaneous Inventions* (Blue Note) **1988**—*Simple Pleasures* (EMI Manhattan) **1990**—*Medicine Music* **1992**—*Hush* (with Yo-Yo Ma) (Sony Masterworks); *Play* (with Chick Corea) (Blue Note).

A human one-man band, vocalist Bobby McFerrin is one of the unique talents in the history of America's performing arts. McFerrin has developed a virtuosic ability to vocally produce musical sounds and tones that can replicate virtually any instrument—a miracle of technique and musical knowledge balanced by a zany wit and nerve.

Both of McFerrin's parents were opera singers; his father dubbed Sidney Poitier's singing in the 1959 film version of *Porgy and Bess*. McFerrin studied piano rather than voice, attending Juilliard and Sacramento State College. He had been playing piano for University of Utah dance workshops when he decided to change musical direction. While singing in journeyman bands, McFerrin came to the attention of noted jazz vocalist Jon Hendricks, who recruited him for his own group. McFerrin's next break came when comedian Bill Cosby caught him performing with Hendricks' group in a San Francisco club. Cosby got McFerrin booked at the prestigious Playboy Jazz Festival in 1980. After his triumphant appearance at the 1981 Kool Jazz Festival in New York, McFerrin was signed by Elektra.

McFerrin had no intention of being a traditional jazz singer. He performed alone, using his multitextured voice while rhythmically beating his body to simulate full-band accompaniment. Standard jazz fare was also avoided; McFerrin took on James Brown's "I Feel Good," the Beatles' "Blackbird," Cream's "Sunshine of Your Love," and funky tunes like his original "I'm My Own Walkman"; all manner of classical, jazz, and pop strains would routinely arise during his free-form performances.

In 1988 McFerrin had a fluke hit single with "Don't Worry Be Happy" (#1) a Reagan-era piece of gloss with a video that helped to cement McFerrin's lovable-madcap image. By the late Eighties McFerrin was ubiquitous—recording with jazz musicians (Chick Corea) and classical players (Yo-Yo Ma) and singing *The Cosby Show* theme and on TV commercials. In 1993 he was a featured performer at the White House jazz picnic, a sure sign of his mainstream appeal.

MC5

Formed 1965, Lincoln Park, Michigan
Rob Tyner (b. Robert Derminer, Dec. 12, 1944; d. Sep. 17, 1991, Royal Oak, Mich.), voc.; Wayne Kramer (b. Apr. 30, 1948, Detroit, Mich.), gtr.; Fred "Sonic" Smith (b. W.Va.; d. Nov. 4, 1994, Detroit, Mich.), gtr.; Michael Davis, bass; Dennis Thompson, drums.
1969—*Kick Out the Jams* (Elektra) **1970**—*Back in the USA* (Atlantic) **1971**—*High Time* **1983**—*Babes in Arms* cassette (ROIR).

Some called the MC5 (for "Motor City Five," after their home base) the first Seventies band of the Sixties. The group's loud, hard, fast sound and violently antiestablishment ideology almost precisely prefigured much of punk rock. There was, however, one crucial difference: the MC5 truly believed in the power of rock & roll to change the world.

The band first formed in high school and came to prominence in 1967–68 as the figureheads (or "house band") of John Sinclair's radical White Panther Party. At concerts and happenings they caused a sensation by wearing American flags and screaming revolutionary slogans laced with profanities. In 1968 the MC5 went with Sinclair to Chicago to play while the Democratic Convention was underway. Its debut LP (#30, 1969), recorded live in 1968, captured the band in typical raw, revved-up, radical form, and embroiled Elektra Records

The MC5: Fred "Sonic" Smith, Michael Davis, Dennis Thompson, Wayne Kramer, Rob Tyner

in controversy over the title tune's loud-and-clear shout "Kick out the jams, motherfuckers!" Some stores refused to stock the album; in response, the MC5 took out strongly worded ads in underground papers and, to Elektra's further distress, plastered one offending store's windows with Elektra stationery on which was scrawled, "Fuck you." Elektra and the MC5 parted company shortly thereafter, but not before the band had cut another version of "Kick Out the Jams," with "brothers and sisters" substituted for the offending expletive. (It was available as a single and on some subsequent issues of the album, against the band's wishes.)

When Sinclair went to jail on a marijuana charge, the MC5 was left with neither a manager nor a label. Atlantic signed the group, and its debut was produced by rock critic Jon Landau. *Back in the USA* was hailed by critics as one of the greatest hard-rock albums of all time. Record sales were almost nil, however, and never improved. Dropped by Atlantic, the band went to England but soon fell apart, with Michael Davis and Dennis Thompson the first to leave.

Thereafter, Rob Tyner had modest success as a songwriter and photographer; he died of a heart attack in 1991. Davis was last heard from in an Ann Arbor band called Destroy All Monsters, with ex-Stooge Ron Ashton; Thompson struggled with abortive solo ventures; and Smith formed a late-Seventies band, Sonics Rendezvous, that toured Europe with Iggy Pop and recorded one single. He married Patti Smith in 1980 in Detroit, where he died in 1994 from heart failure. Kramer, after pleading guilty to a cocaine-dealing charge and spending two years in prison, returned to music. He formed a short partnership with ex–New York Doll and ex-Heartbreaker Johnny Thunders (Gang War), was featured guitarist with Motor City funksters Was (Not Was) (Kramer played the psychedelic guitar on their single "Wheel Me Out"), released two singles, and led his own band, Air Raid. In

1995 he released a solo album, *The Hard Stuff,* on the punk indie label Epitaph. Guests included members of such alt-rock bands as the Muffs and Bad Religion.

The MC5's first two LPs were reissued in England in 1977 to meet the popular demand of the first punk wave, and Elektra quietly restored *Kick Out the Jams* to its U.S. catalogue in the early Eighties. A 1983 release, *Babes in Arms,* contained MC5 rarities.

Kate and Anna McGarrigle

Kate McGarrigle, born 1946, Montreal, Canada; Anna McGarrigle, born 1944, Montreal
1976—*Kate and Anna McGarrigle* (Warner Bros.) 1977—*Dancer with Bruised Knees*   1978—*Pronto Monto*   1981—*French Record* (Hannibal)   1983— *Love Over and Over* (Polydor)   1990—*Heartbeats Accelerating* (Private Music).

The McGarrigle sisters' songs bring together a wide range of folk and pop styles, from Stephen Foster parlor songs to Celtic traditional songs to Cajun fiddling to gospel to pop standards. Although their wry, generally unsentimental songs have been best-known in the U.S. as covers (by Linda Ronstadt, Maria Muldaur, and others), they have had hits in Canada and Europe, especially with songs recorded in French.

The McGarrigles grew up in Montreal and are bilingual. In the mid-Sixties they were half of the Mountain City Four, whose other members (Chaim Tannenbaum and Dane Lanken) continue to perform and record with them. While Anna was studying at Montreal's Ecole des Beaux Arts and Kate was attending McGill University, the National Film Board of Canada commissioned the Mountain City Four to score a film, *Helicopter Canada.*

Kate performed around New York in the Sixties, sometimes as a duo with Roma Baran (who later produced Laurie Anderson), and both sisters wrote songs. Anna's first effort, "Heart Like a Wheel," was used in the soundtrack of *Play It As It Lays* and became the title tune of a multimillion-selling Linda Ronstadt album; Ronstadt has also covered Kate's "Mendocino" and "You Tell Me That I'm Falling Down." Maria Muldaur covered Kate's "The Work Song" and Anna's "Cool River."

Kate married New York singer/songwriter Loudon Wainwright III, and her song "Come a Long Way" appeared on Wainwright's *Attempted Moustache,* which also included Kate's backup vocals; Kate and Anna both sang on Wainwright's *Unrequited.* Shortly after the birth of their son, Rufus, the marriage broke up.

The McGarrigles' songwriting brought them a contract on their own, but their high, reedy voices and homey arrangements were not well received by U.S. radio programmers despite critics' raves. The McGarrigles toured infrequently; their U.S. tour after their debut LP consisted of two weeks of Massachusetts dates. After

Pronto Monto, an attempt to make more conventional-sounding folk pop, the McGarrigles were dropped by Warner Bros. Kate appeared on an album by Albion Country Band, a Fairport Convention offshoot. The Mc-Garrigles reemerged with a Canadian best seller, *French Record,* a compilation of material in French from previous albums and new French songs. *Love Over and Over,* a return to their original style, was the occasion for a U.S. tour.

Roger McGuinn: See the Byrds

Barry McGuire
Born October 15, 1935, Oklahoma City, Oklahoma
1965—*Eve of Destruction* (Dunhill)   1966—*This Precious Time*   1968—*The World's Last Private Citizen.*

Singer/songwriter Barry McGuire's first and last hit was his debut solo record, the prototypical protest song "Eve of Destruction." The Bob Dylan–style folk-rock tune made #1 in 1965, although some stations banned it because of its pessimistic lyrics. It also inspired an answer record, "Dawn of Correction."

Before "Eve," McGuire had been with the New Christy Minstrels and had been the featured vocalist on their 1963 hit "Green Green." He was further credited with helping to launch the career of the Mamas and the Papas, for which he was thanked with a mention in "Creeque Alley." In the Seventies McGuire had his own dawn of redemption: After a decade of drug addiction, he became a born-again Christian and sold hundreds of thousands of Christian pop records. In the mid-Eighties he moved to New Zealand, but he continues to perform and record.

Maria McKee: See Lone Justice

Malcolm McLaren
Born January 22, 1946, London, England
1983—*Duck Rock* (Island)   1984—*Would Ya Like More Scratchin';* *Fans*   1985—*Swamp Thing*   1989—*Waltz Darling* (Epic)   1990—*Round the Outside! Round the Outside!* (Virgin)   1995—*Paris* (Gee Street/Island).

Whether hailed as a postmodern genius or reviled as a posturing charlatan, Malcolm McLaren is indisputably one of the postpunk era's most colorful and provocative characters.

McLaren spent the Sixties shuffling from one English art school to another before becoming entranced with the Internationale Situationist, a French Marxist/Dadaist faction that had stirred up trouble during the 1968 Paris student protests. In 1969 radical fashion designer Vivienne Westwood came into McLaren's life, setting into motion McLaren's firsthand involvement with youth culture. (Westwood and McLaren have a child, Joseph.)

By the early Seventies McLaren was operating a clothing store called Let It Rock that catered to the neo-Fifties Teddy Boy style. There he met the seminal glam-punk band, the New York Dolls [see entry], then on a British tour. He became their manager in late 1974 and relocated to New York. Setting the pattern for McLaren's future managerial endeavors, the relationship with the Dolls was short-lived. Back in London McLaren opened another clothing store, Sex, this time specializing in S&M fashion. Picking from the store's rebellious, underclass clientele, McLaren set about forming the Sex Pistols [see entry], a prefab band that would help play out his anarchist fantasies. McLaren's brilliant manipulation of rival record companies and the media, as well as the band itself, is the stuff of legend.

After the Pistols' breakup following their disastrous 1978 U.S. tour, McLaren devised Bow Wow Wow [see entry], centering on 14-year-old singer Annabella. Again quick fame—owing much to McLaren's incredible feel for outrageous publicity—and brisk British sales were followed by a hasty breakup. Although McLaren fostered the early careers of both Adam Ant [see entry] and Boy George [see Culture Club entry], bowing out before either reached fame, he never aligned himself fully with another group or singer again.

For his next project McLaren began merging indigenous music from around the world with contemporary black dance music, transforming himself into a brilliant synthesist in the eyes of some or a cultural imperialist to others. *Duck Rock* features "Buffalo Girls" (# 9 U.K., 1982) and "Double Dutch" (#3 U.K., 1983), unique pastiches that draw together hip-hop, southern folk music, and African tribal rhythms. *Fans* was even more outrageous, combining rap and hip-hop with opera fragments, as in the single "Madam Butterfly" (#13 U.K., 1984). *Waltz Darling,* credited to Malcolm McLaren and the Bootzilla Orchestra, found Bootsy Collins and Jeff Beck working alongside a symphony orchestra for another skewed mélange of high-, mid-, and low-brow culture.

With visions of subverting the film world, McLaren spent four unproductive years in Hollywood. He tried to develop projects with Steven Spielberg and had a highly publicized affair with actress/model Lauren Hutton. By the early Nineties McLaren had quit California. McLaren's 1995 album, *Paris,* was recorded in the city for which it was named.

John McLaughlin: See Mahavishnu Orchestra

Don McLean
Born October 2, 1945, New Rochelle, New York
1970—*Tapestry* (United Artists)   1971—*American*

Pie 1972—*Don McLean* 1973—*Playin' Favorites* 1974—*Homeless Brother* 1976—*Solo* 1977—*Prime Time* (Arista) 1980—*Chain Lightning* (Millennium) 1981—*Believers* 1983—*Dominion* 1986—*Greatest Hits Then & Now* (Capitol) 1987—*Love Tracks* 1990—*For the Memories, vols. 1 & 2* (Gold Castle) 1992—*Classics* (Curb).

Though he had occasional subsequent hits, singer/songwriter Don McLean is chiefly remembered for his #1 single of 1972, "American Pie," an 8½-minute saga inspired by the death of Buddy Holly. The song propelled his second album to #1 and obscured McLean's folksinging past and future for many years.

Before his sudden fame, McLean had earned a small following for his work with Pete Seeger on the sloop *Clearwater*, which sailed up and down the Hudson River on ecology campaigns. Perry Como turned one of the songs from McLean's debut album, "And I Love You So," into an international hit, and songwriters Norman Gimbel and Charles Fox made McLean the subject of "Killing Me Softly with His Song," Roberta Flack's Grammy Award–winning single of 1973. But even as *American Pie* yielded a second hit, the ballad "Vincent" (#12), McLean's smash success proved unrepeatable, and he spent a period of several years refusing to play "American Pie" and letting his career wind down.

McLean's albums for his new label, Millennium, started selling, and in 1981 he had a few hits: a remake of Roy Orbison's "Crying" (#5), his own "Castles in the Air" (#36), and "Since I Don't Have You" (#23). The rest of the decade found McLean bouncing from one style to another: *Dominion* was recorded live with an orchestra and rock backing band; *Greatest Hits Then & Now* was half new songs, half rerecorded best-of material; *Love Tracks* was a straight-ahead country album; and *For the Memories* included covers of songs by composers ranging from Irving Berlin, George Gershwin, and Cole Porter to Hank Williams, Willie Nelson, and Leiber and Stoller.

Grant McLennan: See the Go-Betweens

MC Lyte
Born Lana Moorer, October 11, 1971, Queens, New York
1988—*Lyte as a Rock* (First Priority/Atlantic) 1989—*Eyes on This* 1991—*Act Like You Know* 1993—*Ain't No Other*.

MC Lyte is one of rap's steadiest-hitting and most respected female stars, known for her street-smart sensibility. Lyte grew up in Brooklyn, where she began rapping at age 12. When she was 16, her father started First Priority records and released Lyte's debut single, "I

Cram to Understand U (Sam)," a clever rap about a boyfriend whose "other woman" turns out be crack. The family act continued when Lyte's brothers Milk and Gizmo of Audio Two produced *Lyte as a Rock*. The narrative songs with minimal beats included "10% Dis" and "Paper Thin."

Lyte continued to write songs that were strong on content on *Eyes on This,* including the singles "Cha Cha Cha," "Cappuccino," and "Stop, Look, Listen." "I'm Not Having It" was used in a TV commercial about AIDS, an issue Lyte has frequently spoken out about. In 1990 she became the first rapper to play Carnegie Hall when she performed at an AIDS benefit. She has recorded public service announcements for Musicians for Life and visited schools for the Stop the Violence movement.

On *Act Like You Know* Lyte called in a variety of producers to add new touches of soul and R&B to her sound. The single "When in Love" (#14 R&B, 1991) was produced by Wolf and Epic, who had created huge hits for Bell Biv DeVoe. The album also included the rap hits "Poor Georgie" (#83 pop, #11 R&B, 1992) and "Eyes Are the Soul" (#84 R&B, 1992). Lyte fans protested that the rapper had softened her tough, street style, and after *Act Like You Know* was only mildly popular compared to gangsta rap's gangbuster sales, Lyte went "hard" again on *Ain't No Other* (#90 pop, #16 R&B, 1993). The album opens with a bragging boost from KRS-One and features the single "Ruffneck" (#35 pop, #10 R&B, 1993) produced by Wreckx-N-Effect, a paean to criminally minded homeboys. The album also includes "Steady Fucking," a biting response to disses made by Roxanne Shanté. The album purposely avoided message songs; Lyte told interviewers she thought her audience was tired of hearing preaching and teaching.

MC Lyte started a management company in the early Nineties, Duke Da Moon, with fellow female rappers Lin Que and Kink Easy, both of whom perform on "Hard Copy" from *Ain't No Other.*

James McMurtry
Born March 18, 1962, Fort Worth, Texas
1989—*Too Long in the Wasteland* (Columbia) 1992—*Candyland* 1995—*Where'd You Hide the Body?*

The son of noted novelist and screenwriter Larry McMurtry, singer/songwriter James McMurtry has drawn praise for his own terse, gritty character sketches. The elder McMurtry gave his son his first guitar when he was seven: James' mother—an English professor who divorced his father while James was a toddler—taught him his first chords. Later, as a student at the University of Arizona, James McMurtry began playing and singing at a local cafe.

He eventually returned to Texas, where he tended bar in San Antonio while continuing to perform. Then his father, who was scripting a film called *Falling from Grace,* passed a copy of McMurtry's demo tape on to the movie's director and star, John Mellencamp. Impressed by McMurtry's rootsy folk-rock songs, Mellencamp helped the young singer land a record contract and co-produced his 1989 debut album, *Too Long in the Wasteland,* with Michael Wanchic, a member of Mellencamp's band. McMurtry also appeared on the soundtrack to *Falling from Grace,* as part of a group called Buzzin' Cousins, whose other members were Mellencamp, John Prine, Joe Ely, and Dwight Yoakam. (The Cousins contributed the track "Sweet Suzanne.") In 1992 McMurtry released *Candyland,* produced by Wanchic, with Mellencamp as executive producer.

Ian McNabb: See Icicle Works

Big Jay McNeely

Born Cecil James McNeely, April 29, 1927, Los Angeles, California
1956—*Big "J" in 3-D* (Federal)   1963—*Big Jay McNeely Live at Cisco's* (Warner Bros.); *Big Jay McNeely Selections* (Savoy)   1989—*Swingin' Cuts* (Collectables)   1993—*Live at Birdland 1957.*

One of the original honking rock & roll tenor saxophonists, Big Jay McNeely was famed for his playing-on-his-back acrobatics and his raw, hard-swinging playing, both of which influenced subsequent rock guitarists, such as Dick Dale and Jimi Hendrix. Billed as the King of the Honkers, McNeely had his first hits in 1949, with "Deacon's Hop" (#1 R&B) and "Wild Wig" (#12 R&B). His best-known composition is "There Is Something on Your Mind," a #5 R&B hit (#44 pop) in 1959 when sung by his own band's vocalist, Haywood "Little Sonny" Warner; New Orleans singer Bobby Marchan had an even bigger hit with "There's Something on Your Mind, Part 2" the next year (#1 R&B, #31 pop). The song has since been recorded by Gene Vincent, King Curtis, B. B. King, and Etta James.

McNeely retired from music for 20 years, during which time he worked for the post office in Los Angeles. He returned to performing in 1983, and, unlike many of his contemporaries, is doing very well. He continues to tour and to record with blues and rockabilly bands, mostly in Europe and Australia. According to Jim Dawson, the author of *Nervous Man Nervous: Big Jay McNeely and the Rise of the Honking Tenor Sax,* McNeely earned more from performing in the Nineties than at any other time in his career.

Clyde McPhatter: See the Drifters

Ralph McTell

Born December 3, 1944, Farnborough, England
1971—*You Well-Meaning Brought Me Here* (Paramount/ABC)   1972—*Not Till Tomorrow* (Reprise)   1973—*Easy*   1975—*Streets* (Warner Bros.)   1976—*Right Side Up*   1977—*Ralph, Albert, Sydney; Maginot Waltz*   1978—*Ralph McTell* (Pickwick)   1979—*Live* (Fantasy); *Slide Away the Screen* (Warner Bros.).

British folkie Ralph McTell learned the guitar, went to street-sing in Europe, came back home, and a couple of years later wrote and recorded "Streets of London." "Streets" was a cult success upon its first release, only somewhat expanding his limited English audience. Warner Bros. added strings and a female chorus to it in 1975, and it went to #1 on the British chart.

McTell responded to the acclaim with his first concert tour and another first: a band that included Maddy Prior of Steeleye Span on backing vocals. The tune was never a chart success in the U.S., though it was well enough known to give McTell something of a following. His *You Well-Meaning* was especially well received by critics.

In 1980 McTell appeared at a Christmas benefit show in London with Donovan. His name surfaced again in early 1982, when Scotland Yard raided British independent record label/store Rough Trade to seize several thousand copies of a single by British punk band Anti-Nowhere League, the B side of which was an obscene cover version of "Streets of London." More recently McTell has worked in children's television. He continues to tour and record, although his work has not been released in the United States since the Eighties.

Christine McVie; John McVie: See Fleetwood Mac

Meat Loaf

Born Marvin Lee Aday, September 27, 1947, Dallas, Texas
1971—*Stoney and Meat Loaf* (Rare Earth)   1977—*Bat Out of Hell* (Cleveland International)   1981—*Dead Ringer*   1983—*Midnight at the Lost and Found*   1984—*Hits Out of Hell; Bad Attitude*   1986—*Blind Before I Stop*   1987—*Meat Loaf Live*   1993—*Bat Out of Hell II: Back into Hell* (MCA).

Bat Out of Hell made Meat Loaf rock's first 250-pound-plus superstar since Leslie West. One of the biggest-selling LPs of the Seventies, *Bat* eventually sold seven million copies in the U.S. Within a few years Meat Loaf had all but disappeared from the U.S. music scene, only to reemerge in 1993 with an album more successful than *Bat*.

It's unclear exactly when and how Marvin Lee Aday became Meat Loaf, but by 1966, when he moved from his native Texas to California, he'd formed a band alternately known as Meat Loaf Soul and Popcorn Blizzard, which, until its breakup in 1969, had opened shows for the Who, Iggy Pop and the Stooges, Johnny and Edgar Winter, and Ted Nugent. He then auditioned for and got a part in a West Coast production of *Hair* and traveled with the show to the East Coast and then to Detroit, where he hooked up with a singer named Stoney to record the unsuccessful LP *Stoney and Meat Loaf*—rereleased in 1979 as *Meat Loaf (Featuring Stoney)*. Meat Loaf went to New York to appear in the Off-Broadway gospel musical *Rainbow in New York* in 1973, and then successfully auditioned for *More Than You Deserve*, written by Jim Steinman.

Steinman, a New Yorker who'd spent his early teen years in California, had studied classical piano. Later he wrote a play called *Dream Engine* in New York. Meanwhile, Meat Loaf had played Eddie in the hugely successful cult film *The Rocky Horror Picture Show* and sung lead vocals on one side of Ted Nugent's platinum LP *Free for All*.

After meeting at *More Than You Deserve* auditions, Meat Loaf and Steinman toured with the National Lampoon Road Show; then Steinman wrote a musical called *Never Land* (a Peter Pan update), from which would come much of the material for *Bat Out of Hell*. (*Never Land* was produced in 1977 at Washington's Kennedy Center.) Meat Loaf and Steinman rehearsed for a full year before Todd Rundgren, an early supporter of the project, agreed to produce them.

At first, *Bat*, with its highly theatrical, bombastically orchestrated teen drama, sold well only in New York and Cleveland. Then Meat Loaf hit the road with a seven-piece band that included singer Karla DeVito in the role Ellen Foley had played on the LP's "Paradise by the Dashboard Light" (which also included a cameo by New York Yankees former shortstop and announcer Phil Rizzuto). The LP was platinum by the end of the year, with the hit singles "Paradise by the Dashboard Light" (#39), "Two Out of Three Ain't Bad" (#11), and "You Took the Words Right Out of My Mouth" (#39).

Meat Loaf appeared in the films *Americathon* (1979) and *Roadie* (1980). In 1981 Steinman released his own Rundgren-produced solo LP, *Bad for Good*. Still the world awaited *Bat*'s sequel. Stories circulated that Meat Loaf had been coaxed to sing *Bad for Good* but couldn't or wouldn't because of a variety of physical and emotional problems. Finally, toward the end of 1981, *Dead Ringer* was released to meager response. Meanwhile, Steinman initiated lawsuits against Epic and Meat Loaf. *Midnight at the Lost and Found* had no Steinman mate-

rial and included a few songs cowritten by "M. Lee Aday." Meat Loaf eventually declared bankruptcy and underwent physical and psychological therapy to get his voice back. He somehow managed to keep making records, which went virtually unnoticed in the U.S., though he remained a concert draw in England.

In 1993 Meat Loaf—back with Steinman—reemerged with *Bat Out of Hell II: Back into Hell*, unabashedly picking up, in sound and story, right where "Mr. Loaf" (as the *New York Times* called him) had left off with *Bat Out of Hell*. The comeback album sold even faster than the original, entering the chart at #25 and eventually hitting #1, selling ten million copies within three months worldwide, and yielding a hit single in "I'd Do Anything for Love (But I Won't Do That)". In January 1994 that song won Meat Loaf his first Grammy, in the category of Best Solo Rock Vocal Performance. Meat Loaf also mounted a Broadway/arena-rock tour reminiscent of days of yore, with his entrance heralded by bombastic power chords interrupting a string quartet, which opened the shows playing a medley of his early hits.

Meat Puppets

Formed 1980, Phoenix, Arizona
Curt Kirkwood (b. Jan. 10, 1959, Amarillo, Tex.), gtr., voc.; Cris Kirkwood (b. Oct. 22, 1960, Amarillo), bass, voc.; Derrick Bostrom (b. June 23, 1960, Phoenix), drums.
1981—*In a Car* EP (World Imitation)   1982—*Meat Puppets* (SST)   1983—*Meat Puppets II*   1985—*Up on the Sun*   1986—*Out My Way* EP   1987—*Mirage; Huevos*   1989—*Monsters*   1990—*No Strings Attached*   1991—*Forbidden Places* (London)   1994—*Too High to Die*.

Meat Puppets started out as an engagingly incompetent, country-tinged thrash trio. By its third full-length album, however, the band had developed a signature sound that pitted the deconstructionist attitude of American hardcore against the carefree spirit of the Grateful Dead.

Brothers Curt and Cris Kirkwood grew up in Phoenix, Arizona, where they attended a Jesuit prep school and played in various mainstream-oriented rock bands. Not interested in continuing their educations, the two formed Meat Puppets along with local drummer Derrick Bostrom. In the beginning the group was so intent on playing a rough and spontaneous style of music that they refused even to rehearse.

In 1981 the Puppets released *In a Car*, a seven-inch EP of ear-splitting avant-rock boasting five songs in five minutes. The trio's irreverence so impressed Black Flag guitarist Greg Ginn that he signed the Puppets to his SST label and released the band's noisy, experimental debut LP later the following year.

The Kirkwoods took a radically different approach on *Meat Puppets II*, delivering a set of ragged, out-of-tune country-punk songs that hinted at their future, desert-breeze-style sound. Growing more professional with each subsequent release, the psychedelic/country/punk/folk on *Up on the Sun* came out to flattering reviews in 1985.

In 1990, on the strength of *Huevos* and *Monsters,* as well as Curt Kirkwood's continually improving Jerry Garcia–style fretwork, the band signed to London Records, releasing *Forbidden Places* the next year. (*No Strings Attached* is a retrospective of Meat Puppets' SST work.) The Meat Puppets guested on Nirvana's December 1993 *Unplugged* performance; the resulting CD featured three Meat Puppet songs.

Megadeth
Formed 1983, Los Angeles, California
Dave Mustaine (b. Sep. 13, 1961, La Mesa, Calif.), gtr., voc.; David Ellefson (b. Nov. 12, 1964, Minn.), bass; Chris Poland, gtr.; Gars Samuelson, drums. 1985—*Killing Is My Business . . . and Business Is Good* (Combat)   1986—*Peace Sells . . . But Who's Buying?* (Capitol) (– Poland; – Samuelson; + Jeff Young, gtr.; + Chuck Behler, drums)   1988—*So Far, So Good . . . So What?* (– Young; – Behler; + Marty Friedman [b. Dec. 8, 1962, Washington, D.C.], gtr.; + Nick Menza [b. July 23, 1964, Ger.], drums) 1990—*Rust in Peace*   1992—*Countdown to Extinction*   1994—*Youthanasia.*

When guitarist Dave Mustaine was booted out of Metallica early in its career, he formed Megadeth, which continued his former group's thrash-metal style with even more speed and intensity.

Mustaine was seven when his parents divorced, and his family wound up living in poverty in the Southern California suburbs. During his teens, Mustaine's mother was often away, leaving him with his sisters and their abusive spouses; he told a journalist that a brother-in-law once punched him in the face for listening to Judas Priest. Mustaine's revenge was to join a heavy-metal band, and in 1981 he became a founding member of Metallica [see entry], from which he was fired two years later in a power struggle over leadership and allegations of his drug use. Mustaine, who is notorious for his outspokenness and mood swings, formed Megadeth that same year with Minnesota native Dave Ellefson.

Mustaine and Ellefson hoped to create a jazz-oriented progressive strain of heavy metal based on chops as much as emotional aggression. Megadeth's first album, *Killing Is My Business . . . and Business Is Good,* succeeded in that regard and garnered mainly positive reviews, even from critics normally hostile to

Megadeth: Nick Menza, Dave Mustaine, Marty Friedman, David Ellefson

heavy metal. Mustaine's drug use, meanwhile, deepened with his discovery of heroin. Still, the band's subsequent albums, *Peace Sells . . . But Who's Buying?* and *So Far, So Good . . . So What?* (#28, 1988), continued in the band's celebrated lightning-speed, chops-heavy style.

In 1990 Mustaine was arrested for impaired driving and went into a 12-step program for his drug and alcohol problems; he has since remained clean and sober. The same year, Megadeth released *Rust in Peace,* which reached #23. Mustaine's former band, meanwhile, paved the way for thrash-metal when its self-titled album of 1991 skyrocketed to the top of the charts; Megadeth followed in Metallica's footsteps the next year with *Countdown to Extinction,* which went to #2.

Mustaine's newfound sobriety hasn't kept the guitarist from getting into trouble: In 1993 Megadeth was dumped from its opening spot on Aerosmith's tour when that group tired of Mustaine's misbehavior. According to Aerosmith's Joe Perry, "Dave Mustaine just wasn't happy, and we don't want to tour with anyone who isn't having a good time." Megadeth returned in 1994 with *Youthanasia* (the album's press release was written by novelist Dean Koontz), which debuted at #4.

The Mekons
Formed May 1977, Leeds, England
**Jon Langford (b. Oct. 11, 1957, Newport, S. Wales), voc., gtr., drums; Tom Greenhalgh (b. Nov. 4, 1956, Stockholm, Swed.), voc., gtr.
1979—*The Quality of Mercy Is Not Strnen* (Virgin, U.K.)   1980—*The Mekons* (Red Rhino, U.K.)   1982—*It Falleth Like Gentle Rain from Heaven—The Mekons Story* (CNT, U.K.)   1983—*The English Dancing Master* EP 1985—(+ Sally Timms [b. Nov.**

The Mekons: Sally Timms, Jon Langford, Susie Honeyman, Tom Greenhalgh

29, 1959, Leeds], voc.; + Susie Honeyman, violin)
Fear and Whiskey (Sin, U.K.)   1986—*Crime and Punishment* EP; *The Edge of the World*; *Slightly South of the Border* EP   1987—*Honky Tonkin'* (Twin/Tone)   1988—*So Good It Hurts*   1989—*Original Sin*; *The Mekons Rock 'n' Roll* (A&M)   1990—*F.U.N. '90* EP; *New York* (ROIR)   1991—*The Curse of the Mekons* (Blast First, U.K.)   1992—*Wicked Midnite* EP (Loud)   1993—*I ❤ Mekons* (¼ Stick)   1994—*Retreat from Memphis.*

Intensely independent, idealistic yet cynical, the Mekons are one of the longest-lasting combos of the British punk era. Their music has gone from dissonant, minimal art punk, to danceable, dub-heavy electronics, to ragged country, sensitive folk, and anthemic rock & roll. A post-punk cottage industry—and favorite among rock critics—the Mekons never attained more than a cult following. The group's bad luck with record labels and staunchly leftist politics are legendary.

Tom Greenhalgh and Jon Langford were Leeds art students when the Sex Pistols came through town in 1976. Inspired by the group's amateurish playing, Greenhalgh, who knew only two chords, formed the Mekons (named for a green-headed alien in a Fifties comic strip *Dan Dare, Space Pilot of the Future*). Within months, future guitarist Jon Langford joined on drums.

After a single, "Never Been in a Riot" (a witty reply to the Clash's "White Riot"), the band signed with Virgin and released *The Quality of Mercy Is Not Strnen,* a humorous, intelligent, but utterly inept collection of noisy punk. In a move that would repeat itself throughout the Mekons' career, Virgin dropped the band midway through recording of their second album. When some of the members bowed out, the group developed a revolv-

ing-door membership, with Greenhalgh and Langford the only constants.

The band released *Devils Rats and Piggies a Special Message from Godzilla* (later known simply as *The Mekons*) on the U.K. independent label Red Rhino. After a 1980 European tour and two subsequent New Year's Eve shows in New York City with hometown friends Gang of Four, the Mekons nearly called it quits. (Langford formed a side band, Three Johns, which put out 13 albums over the next seven years.) In 1982 the group compiled a hodgepodge of old and new material for *The Mekons Story,* released on yet another U.K. indie, CNT. With renewed vigor, they returned to the studio and recorded the country-tinged *The English Dancing Master.*

In the two years that lapsed between albums, Sally Timms, a Leeds native who had sung with the band in the past, joined, followed by ex-Rumour drummer Steve Goulding, bassist Lu Knee (a.k.a. Lu Edmonds), and classically trained violinist Susie Honeyman. In 1985 the group released the celebrated *Fear and Whiskey* (issued in the U.S. in 1989 as *Original Sin*). By then, the Mekons had evolved a distinct, though highly eclectic sound. Their mid- to late-Eighties Sin and Twin/Tone albums were generally well received, but the Mekons became most loved for their raucous live shows.

In 1989 the Mekons signed with A&M and released their most critically acclaimed album, *The Mekons Rock 'n' Roll,* a collection of heartfelt rockers with a healthy dose of skepticism. But more major-label troubles were around the corner. After the bizarre, sparse, dance-oriented *F.U.N. 90*—which contained a crude recording of the late rock critic Lester Bangs singing behind a dub-heavy track—the Mekons asked to be released from A&M, citing insufficient financial support. A&M said no, then refused to release the group's followup album. The company eventually backed down and returned the rights of the Mekons' tapes. In 1991 the aptly named *The Curse of the Mekons* appeared on U.K. label Blast First.

More problems arose in 1992 when a WEA subsidiary, Loud Records, signed the Mekons but promptly suffered financial troubles, which led to their sitting on the group's next album, a collection of Mekons-style love songs called *I ❤ Mekons,* for nearly a year. The group finally released the record on the independent ¼ Stick label in 1993; the following year they put out *Retreat from Memphis.*

Throughout their career, the Mekons' core membership of Langford and Greenhalgh (and later Timms and Honeyman) has been joined by a host of musicians, including founding members Kevin Lycett (guitar) and Mark White (vocals), ex–Pretty Thing Dick Taylor (guitar), Brendan Crocker (guitar), Rico Bell (accordion), and Sarah Corina (bass).

Grammy Awards

Madonna
1991 Best Music Video, Long Form: *Madonna: Blonde Ambition World Tour Live* (with others)

The Mamas and the Papas
1966 Best Contemporary Rock & Roll Group Performance, Vocal or Instrumental: "Monday, Monday"

Melissa Manchester
1982 Best Pop Vocal Performance, Female: "You Should Hear How She Talks About You"

Chuck Mangione
1976 Best Instrumental Composition: "Bellavia"
1978 Best Pop Instrumental Performance: *The Children of Sanchez*

The Manhattans
1980 Best R&B Performance by a Duo or Group, Vocal: "Shining Star"

Manhattan Transfer
1980 Best Jazz Fusion Performance, Vocal or Instrumental: "Birdland"
1981 Best Jazz Vocal Performance, Duo or Group: "Until I Met You (Corner Pocket)"
1981 Best Pop Performance by a Duo or Group with Vocal: "Boy from New York City"
1982 Best Jazz Vocal Performance, Duo or Group: "Route 66"
1983 Best Jazz Vocal Performance, Duo or Group: "Why Not!"
1985 Best Jazz Vocal Performance, Duo or Group: *Vocalese*
1988 Best Pop Performance by a Duo or Group with Vocal: *Brasil*
1991 Best Contemporary Jazz Performance: "Sassy"

Janis Siegel (Manhattan Transfer)
1980 Best Arrangement for Voices: "Birdland"

Barry Manilow
1978 Best Pop Vocal Performance, Male: "Copacabana (at the Copa)"

Ziggy Marley
1988 Best Reggae Recording: *Conscious Party* (with the Melody Makers)
1989 Best Reggae Recording: *One Bright Day* (with the Melody Makers)

Branford Marsalis
1992 Best Jazz Instrumental Performance, Individual or Group: *I Heard You Twice the First Time*
1993 Best Pop Instrumental Performance: "Barcelona Mona" (with Bruce Hornsby)

Wynton Marsalis
1983 Best Classical Performance, Instrumental Soloist or Soloists (with Orchestra): *Haydn: Concerto for Trumpet Orchestra in E-Flat Major / L. Mozart: Concerto for Trumpet and Orchestra in D Major / Hummel: Concerto for Trumpet and Orchestra in E-Flat Major*
1983 Best Jazz Instrumental Performance, Soloist: *Think of One*
1984 Best Classical Performance, Instrumental Soloist or Soloists (with Orchestra): *Wynton Marsalis—Edita Gruberova—Handel, Purcell, Torelli, Fasch, Molter*
1984 Best Jazz Instrumental Performance, Soloist: *Hot House Flowers*
1985 Best Jazz Instrumental Performance, Group: *Black Codes (from the Underground)*
1985 Best Jazz Instrumental Performance, Soloist: *Black Codes (from the Underground)*
1986 Best Jazz Instrumental Performance, Group: *J Mood*
1987 Best Jazz Instrumental Performance, Group: *Marsalis Standard Time, vol. 1*

Kathy Mattea
1990 Best Country Vocal Performance, Female: "Where've You Been"
1993 Best Southern Gospel, Country Gospel or Bluegrass Gospel Album: *Good News*

Paul McCartney [See also: the Beatles]
1966 Best Contemporary (Rock & Roll) Solo Vocal Performance, Male or Female: "Eleanor Rigby"
1966 Song of the Year: "Michelle" (with John Lennon)
1970 Best Original Score Written for a Motion Picture or Television Special: *Let It Be* (with George Harrison, John Lennon, and Ringo Starr)
1971 Best Arrangement Accompanying Vocalist(s): "Uncle Albert/Admiral Halsey"
1974 Best Pop Vocal Performance by a Duo, Group or Chorus: "Band on the Run"
1979 Best Rock Instrumental Performance: "Rockestra Theme"
1990 Lifetime Achievement Award Paul McCartney and Wings

Delbert McClinton
1991 Best Rock Performance by a Duo or Group with Vocal: "Good Man, Good Woman" (with Bonnie Raitt)

Michael McDonald [See also: the Doobie Brothers]
1979 Song of the Year: "What a Fool Believes" (with Kenny Loggins)
1979 Best Arrangement Accompanying Vocalist(s): "What a Fool Believes"
1984 Best R&B Performance by a Duo or Group with Vocal: "Yah Mo B There" (with James Ingram)

Reba McEntire
1986 Best Country Vocal Performance, Female: "Whoever's in New England"
1993 Best Country Vocal Collaboration: "Does He Love You" (with Linda Davis)

Bobby McFerrin
1985 Best Jazz Vocal Performance, Male: "Another Night in Tunisia" (with Jon Hendricks)
1985 Best Vocal Arrangement for Two or More Voices: "Another Night in Tunisia" (with Cheryl Bentyne)
1986 Best Jazz Vocal Performance, Male: "'Round Midnight"
1987 Best Jazz Vocal Performance, Male: "What Is This Thing Called Love"
1987 Best Recording for Children: *The Elephant's Child* (with Tom Bradshaw, Jack Nicholson, and Mark Sottnick)
1988 Best Jazz Vocal Performance, Male: "Brothers"
1988 Best Pop Vocal Performance, Male: "Don't Worry, Be Happy"
1988 Record of the Year: "Don't Worry, Be Happy" (with Linda Goldstein)
1988 Song of the Year: "Don't Worry, Be Happy"
1992 Best Jazz Vocal Performance: "'Round Midnight" (note: a different version from the one honored in 1986)

Meat Loaf
1993 Best Rock Vocal Performance, Solo: "I'd Do Anything for Love (but I Won't Do That)"

John Mellencamp
1982 Best Rock Vocal Performance, Male: "Hurts So Good"

Men at Work
1982 Best New Artist

Metallica
1989 Best Metal Performance: "One"
1990 Best Metal Performance: "Stone Cold Crazy"
1991 Best Metal Performance with Vocal: *Metallica*

Pat Metheny
1992 Best Contemporary Jazz Performance, Instrumental: *Secret Story*

Pat Metheny Group
1982 Best Jazz Fusion Performance, Vocal or Instrumental: *Offramp*
1983 Best Jazz Fusion Performance, Vocal or Instrumental: *Travels*
1984 Best Jazz Fusion Performance, Vocal or Instrumental: *First Circle*
1987 Best Jazz Fusion Performance, Vocal or Instrumental: *Still Life (Talking)*
1989 Best Jazz Fusion Performance: *Letter from Home*
1990 Best Instrumental Composition: "Change of Heart"
1993 Best Contemporary Jazz Performance, Instrumental: *The Road to You*

MFSB
1974 Best R&B Instrumental Performance: "TSOP (The Sound of Philadelphia)"
1978 Album of the Year: *Saturday Night Fever* (with others)

George Michael
1987 Best R&B Performance by a Duo or Group with Vocal: "I Knew You Were Waiting (for Me)" (with Aretha Franklin)
1988 Album of the Year: *Faith*

Bette Midler
1973 Best New Artist
1980 Best Pop Vocal Performance: "The Rose"
1989 Record of the Year: "Wind Beneath My Wings" (with Arif Mardin)

The Mighty Clouds of Joy
1978 Best Soul Gospel Performance, Traditional: *Live and Direct*
1979 Best Soul Gospel Performance, Traditional: *Changing Times*
1991 Best Traditional Soul Gospel Album: *Pray for Me*

Stephanie Mills
1980 Best R&B Vocal Performance, Female: "Never Knew Love Like This Before"

Terry Bozzio (Missing Persons)
1989 Best Rock Instrumental Performance: *Jeff Beck's Guitar Shop with Terry Bozzio and Tony Hymas* (with Jeff Beck and Tony Hymas)

Joni Mitchell
1969 Best Folk Performance: *Clouds*
1974 Best Arrangement Accompanying Vocalists: "Down to You" (with Tom Scott)

Bill Monroe
1988 Best Bluegrass Recording, Vocal or Instrumental: *Southern Flavor*

Anne Murray
1974 Best Country Vocal Performance, Female: *Love Song*
1978 Best Pop Vocal Performance, Female: "You Needed Me"
1980 Best Country Vocal Performance, Female: "Can I Have This Dance"
1983 Best Country Vocal Performance, Female: "A Little Good News"

Mel and Tim

Formed mid-Sixties, St. Louis, Missouri
Mel Harden, voc.; Tim McPherson, voc.
1970—*Good Guys Only Win in the Movies* (Bamboo);
***Mel and Tim* (Stax)   1972—*Starting All Over Again*.**

Cousins Mel Harden and Tim McPherson are best
known for their three hit singles: "Backfield in Motion"
(1969), "Good Guys Only Win in the Movies" (1970), and
"Starting All Over Again" (1972). "Backfield" (#10 pop, #3
R&B) was written by McPherson and produced by
singer Gene Chandler for his own Bamboo Records.
"Movies" (#17 R&B) was also on Chandler's label. After
solving some contractual difficulties, Mel and Tim left
Bamboo and recorded at the Muscle Shoals studio in Al-
abama. In 1972 they cut Phillip Mitchell's "Starting All
Over Again," which was leased to Memphis' Stax
Records, becoming a Top Twenty pop hit (#4 R&B).

Melanie

**Born Melanie Safka, February 3, 1947, Queens, New
York**
**1969—*Born to Be* (Buddah); *Melanie*   1970—*Can-
dles in the Rain*; *Leftover Wine*   1971—*The Good
Book*; *Gather Me* (Neighborhood)   1972—*Four
Sides of Melanie* (Buddah); *Stoneground Words*
(Neighborhood)   1973—*At Carnegie Hall*   1974—
Madrugada; *As I See It Now*   1975—*Sunset and
Other Beginnings*   1976—*Photograph* (Atlantic)
1978—*Phonogenic—Not Just Another Pretty Face*
(Midsong)   1979—*Ballroom Streets* (RCA)   1982—
Arabesque (Blanche)   1985—*Am I Real or What*
(Amherst)   1990—*The Best of Melanie* (Rhino)
1991—*Precious Cargo* (Precious Cargo)   1993—
Freedom Knows My Name (Lonestar)   1994—*Silver*.**

Singer/songwriter Melanie caught the last upsurge of
hippie innocence in songs like "Lay Down (Candles in
the Rain)" and "Beautiful People." While she sold over 22
million records around the world, her childlike demeanor,
cracked voice, and naive lyrics made her a novelty act
before her time.

Melanie Safka's family moved to Boston and then to
Long Branch, New Jersey, when she was a teenager.
After high school she studied at the American Academy
of Dramatic Arts. Soon after she signed a song publishing agreement with her future producer and husband,
Peter Schekeryk. In 1967 she won a recording contract
with Columbia Records, which released her single
"Beautiful People." When the record did not sell, Columbia dropped her and she returned to the local folk clubs
until 1969, when a single from her *Born to Be*, "What
Have They Done to My Song, Ma," hit in France.

In August 1969 Melanie appeared at Woodstock,
which inspired her to write "Lay Down (Candles in the
Rain)." Released in spring 1970, it became a #6 single,

and the *Candles in the Rain* LP went gold. From then on
it became a ritual for her loyal fans to light candles at her
shows. In summer 1970 "Peace Will Come (According
to Plan)" hit #32, and she made a live album, *Leftover
Wine*. That fall, the New Seekers had a smash hit with
their version of "What Have They Done to My Song, Ma."

In 1971 Melanie and her husband formed their own
record company, Neighborhood, and the singer immediately had her biggest success, the #1 "Brand New Key,"
which sold over three million copies. Another single off
the LP, "Ring the Living Bell," hit the Top Forty. *Gather
Me* went gold. That same year, she performed and toured
the world as a spokesperson for UNICEF.

After that, her records stopped selling, and in 1975
Neighborhood folded. She was signed by Atlantic
Records, and her label debut, *Photograph*, was coproduced by company president Ahmet Ertegun and Schekeryk. In 1978 she recorded for Midsong, and the next
year released *Ballroom Streets* on RCA. She kept making
a succession of albums on various small labels into the
Nineties, and in August 1994, the mother of three children, she performed at the gathering at the original
Woodstock festival site.

John Mellencamp

Born October 7, 1951, Seymour, Indiana
1976—*Chestnut Street Incident* (Mainman/MCA)
1978—*A Biography* (Riva)   1979—*John Cougar*
**1980—*Nothin' Matters and What If It Did*   1982—
American Fool   1983—*Uh-huh*   1985—*Scarecrow*
1987—*The Lonesome Jubilee* (Mercury)   1989—*Big
Daddy*   1991—*Whenever We Wanted*   1993—
Human Wheels   1994—*Dance Naked*.**

Singer/songwriter John Mellencamp became one of
1982's biggest stars when his fifth LP, *American Fool*,
went to #1, sold over five million copies, and yielded two
hit singles, "Hurts So Good" (#2) and "Jack and Diane"
(#1). Each of his subsequent albums has been certified
platinum. More important, perhaps, has been Mellencamp's evolution from a Springsteen-style hard-rock
stylist into what one critic called a "renaissance rocker."
From *American Fool* on, Mellencamp's critical stock rose
with his record sales.

Mellencamp was born with a form of spina bifida, a
potentially crippling neural tube defect that required
surgery and a lengthy hospitalization. Coddled by his
mother and encouraged by his father to excel, Mellencamp grew into a self-proclaimed rebel. At 17 he eloped
with his pregnant girlfriend, Priscilla Esterline, and
began attending community college and working a series of blue-collar jobs. At age 14 Mellencamp had
started his first band, and he had written a number of
songs before he moved to New York City at age 24 to
begin a music career. There he met David Bowie's manager, Tony DeFries, who christened Mellencamp Johnny

Cougar, helped him get what has been reported as a $1-million deal with Mainman, and oversaw the recording of his debut, *Chestnut Street Incident*. The LP, which consisted of cover tunes, failed to hit, and MCA dropped Mellencamp, who, it has been reported, was not even aware that he had "adopted" the Cougar stage name until he saw his album cover. That and several other early experiences in the music business no doubt contributed to the sometimes jaundiced view of show business that Mellencamp has expressed repeatedly through the years.

Four years later he signed (to his dismay, as John Cougar) with Riva Records and, working with Rod Stewart's manager, Billy Gaff, recorded two more LPs, the latter of which, *John Cougar* (#64, 1979), contained "I Need a Lover," a radio hit for Pat Benatar and a #28 hit for Mellencamp. In addition, Mellencamp's version went to #1 in Australia. *Nothin' Matters* (#37, 1980), produced by Steve Cropper, sold 900,000 copies and contained the hits "This Time" (#27, 1980) and "Ain't Even Done with the Night" (#17, 1981). Cougar divorced his first wife, with whom he had one daughter, in 1981, and that year married Vicky Granucci. They had two children, also girls.

Two years later came Mellencamp's commercial breakthrough, *American Fool* (#1, 1982). The videos for its hit singles—the Grammy-winning "Hurts So Good" (#2, 1982), "Jack and Diane" (#1, 1982), and "Hand to Hold On To" (#19, 1982)—quickly became MTV staples, and Cougar toured as an opening act for Heart. The next year's *Uh-Huh* (#9, 1983) (credited to John Cougar Mellencamp) came out with *American Fool* still on the charts and included "Crumblin' Down" (#9, 1983), "Pink Houses" (#8, 1983), and "Authority Song" (#15, 1984). That year Mellencamp embarked on his first headlining tour. With *Scarecrow* (#2, 1985) Mellencamp stayed the hard-rock course, producing another string of hits: "Lonely Ol' Night" (#6, 1985), "Small Town" (#6, 1985), "R.O.C.K. in the U.S.A." (#2, 1986), "Rain on the Scarecrow" (#21, 1986), and "Rumbleseat" (#28, 1986). In 1985 Mellencamp, with Willie Nelson and Neil Young, was a co-organizer of Farm Aid. He appeared at Farm Aid concerts I through VI. Over the years, he has given concerts to call attention to the American farmer's plight, and in 1987 he testified before a congressional subcommittee. He has also been an outspoken critic of beer- and cigarette-company sponsorship of concert tours and refuses to allow his music to be used in commercials.

Mellencamp's style took a dramatic turn with *The Lonesome Jubilee* (#6, 1987), which blended traditional American folk instrumentation (for example, Lisa Germano's violin, accordions) in a number of songs that lamented rather than celebrated contemporary Middle America. Its hits were "Paper in Fire" (#9, 1987), "Cherry Bomb" (#8, 1987), and "Check It Out" (#14, 1988). His next albums, more deeply introspective in some ways, each sold about a million copies, but the hits were fewer and farther between than in previous years. *Big Daddy*

(#7, 1989) included the somewhat cynical semiautobiographical "Pop Singer" (#15, 1989), and *Whenever We Wanted* (#17, 1991)—his first album to be released under the name John Mellencamp—featured "Get a Leg Up" (#14, 1991) and "Again Tonight" (#36, 1992). The "Get a Leg Up" video featured model Elaine Irwin, who became his third wife. In 1994 they had a son. *Human Wheels* (#7, 1993) yielded no major hit singles. *Dance Naked* (#13, 1994) featured the #3 hit cover of Van Morrison's "Wild Nights," a duet with singer/bassist Me'Shell NdegéOcello. Mellencamp's plans to embark on a large 1994 North American tour were scuttled after he was diagnosed with a heart condition. Although initial reports described Mellencamp's problem as an arterial blockage, he later admitted that he had suffered a heart attack.

Mellencamp has produced all of his own albums, as well as Mitch Ryder's *Never Kick a Sleeping Dog* (1983), James McMurtry's *Too Long in the Wasteland* (1989), and the soundtrack from *Falling from Grace* (1992), his acting and directorial debut. Written by James McMurtry's father, Larry McMurtry (*Lonesome Dove*), *Falling from Grace* garnered mixed reviews, but some praised Mellencamp's direction. In the past decade Mellencamp has also exhibited his paintings throughout the country, including in the "Twice Gifted" show. His work also appears in the book *Musicians as Artists*.

Harold Melvin and the Blue Notes

Formed 1955, Philadelphia, Pennsylvania
Harold Melvin (b. June 25, 1939, Philadelphia), voc.; Bernard Wilson, voc.; Jesse Gillis Jr., voc.; Franklin Peaker, voc.; Roosevelt Brodie, voc.
Ca. 1960—(Melvin; Wilson; + John Atkins, voc.; + Lawrence Brown, voc.) 1970—(– Atkins; + Teddy Pendergrass [b. Mar. 26, 1950, Philadelphia], voc.; + Lloyd Parks, voc.) 1972—*Harold Melvin and the Blue Notes* (Philadelphia International) 1973—*I Miss You; Black and Blue* (– Parks; + Jerry Cummings, voc.) 1975—*To Be True; Wake Up Everybody* 1976—(– Pendergrass; + David Ebo, voc.) *All Their Greatest Hits* 1977—*Reaching for the World* (ABC) (+ Dwight Johnson, bass/baritone voc.; + Bill Spratley, baritone voc.) 1980—*The Blue Album* (Source) 1981—*All Things Happen in Time* (MCA) Ca. 1993—(Lineup: Melvin; Spratley; Johnson; + Rufus Thorne, tenor voc.; + Anthony Quarterman, lead voc.).

Although formed in 1955, this Philadelphia-based vocal group did not attain widespread popularity until the mid-Seventies, with Teddy Pendergrass as lead singer. Harold Melvin founded the Blue Notes as a doo-wop group with three other singers and Bernard Wilson, who handled the group's choreography. Wilson also provided stage movements for other local groups like the Delfonics, Brenda and the Tabulations, and the O'Jays.

These Blue Notes recorded their first single, "If You Love Me," for Josie, but disbanded soon after, leaving Melvin and Wilson to regroup with new lead John Atkins and Lawrence Brown. After years in the Sixties on the chitlin' circuit, they were signed to the William Morris Agency on the recommendation of Martha Reeves. They frequently appeared in supper clubs in Las Vegas, Lake Tahoe, Reno, and Miami Beach and were known for their trademark "tie and tails" look.

In 1970 Pendergrass replaced Atkins as lead singer. (He had briefly been the group's drummer.) The next year the group signed with Kenny Gamble and Leon Huff's Philadelphia International Records and soon became one of the first groups associated with the Sound of Philadelphia. During this period, Lloyd Parks joined, making the group a quintet.

From 1972 until Pendergrass left in 1976 to pursue a solo career [see entry], Harold Melvin and the Blue Notes had three #1 R&B singles: "If You Don't Know Me by Now" (#3 pop, 1972), "The Love I Lost" (#7 pop, 1973), and "Wake Up Everybody" (#12 pop, 1976). Other hits included "I Miss You" (#58 pop, #7 R&B, 1972), "Satisfaction Guaranteed" (#58 pop, #6 R&B, 1974), "Where Are All My Friends" (#8 R&B, 1974), "Bad Luck" (#15 pop, #4 R&B, 1975), "Tell the World How I Feel About 'Cha Baby" (#7 R&B, 1976), and "Hope That We Can Be Together Soon" (#42) (featuring Sharon Paige) in 1975.

Following Pendergrass' departure for a hugely successful solo career, Melvin brought in lead singer David Ebo, and the group signed to ABC. Although the Blue Notes' label debut, "Reaching for the World," hit #6 on the R&B chart, subsequent releases failed to match their mid-Seventies success. In 1979 they switched to Source Records, where "Prayin'" was a moderate R&B hit (#18). Their last charting single was 1984's "I Really Love You." The group continues to tour.

Memphis Slim

Born Peter Chatman, September 3, 1915, Memphis, Tennessee; died February 24, 1988, Paris, France
1973—Legacy of the Blues (GNP Crescendo)
1975—Rock Me Baby (Black Lion)   1976—Chicago Boogie   1978—Boogie Woogie (Festival)   1993—Memphis Slim at the Gate of Horn (Vee-Jay).

Blues singer and barrelhouse pianist Memphis Slim was perhaps the first bluesman to leave America for Europe and become a star there. He also composed "Every Day (I Have the Blues)," which became a big-band standard when sung by Joe Williams with Count Basie's orchestra.

Having taught himself the piano, and having learned from such Memphis greats as Speckled Red and Roosevelt Sykes, Slim went to Chicago in 1939, where he met Big Bill Broonzy. Broonzy told Slim that he had talent

but lacked an original style, but by 1940 Slim had become Broonzy's accompanist, a job he held until the late Forties. Slim led his own groups as a singer/pianist on the late-Forties blues circuit, and had a minor R&B hit in the early Fifties with his own "Beer Drinkin' Woman." With the folk boom of the late Fifties and early Sixties, Slim's popularity was renewed, and he played for large white audiences for the first time. His band at that time included the Chicago bassist/composer Willie Dixon. In 1959 Slim earned a standing ovation at the Newport Folk Festival, and then shared a bill at New York City's Village Gate with Pete Seeger. At this time, he recorded for Folkways; he now has dozens of albums out on many labels.

In 1960 Memphis Slim first toured Europe and was well enough received that he went back again in 1962, doing especially well at his French debut. After an Israeli tour in 1963, he made Paris his home. He became a celebrity, a star performer at major music halls in England and all over the Continent, and an often-seen face on French TV. His later recordings failed to recapture the raw energy of his classic Fifties small-group recordings. Memphis Slim recorded with a number of British, American, and European jazz and rock musicians, including Alexis Korner (touring England in the early Sixties on occasion with Korner and Cyril Davies), and Alex Harvey before he died of kidney failure in 1988.

Men at Work

Formed 1979, Melbourne, Australia
Colin Hay (b. June 29, 1953, Scot.), voc., gtr.; Ron Strykert (b. Aug. 18, 1957, Austral.), gtr., voc.; Jerry Speiser (b. Austral.), drums, voc.; Greg Ham (b. Sep. 27, 1953, Austral.), sax, flute, voc., kybds.; John Rees (b. Austral.), bass, voc.
1982—Business as Usual (Columbia)   1983—Cargo 1984—(– Speiser; – Rees)   1985—Two Hearts. Colin Hay solo: 1987—Looking for Jack (Columbia) 1990—Wayfaring Sons (MCA).

Australia's Men at Work was one of the most successful rock groups of 1982 and won that year's Grammy for Best New Artist. Its debut LP, Business as Usual, broke the Monkees' 1966 record for the longest run at #1 for a debut LP (15 weeks) and included two #1 singles, "Who Can It Be Now?" and "Down Under."

Colin Hay, the group's lead singer and main songwriter, moved with his family to Australia from Scotland at age 14. The group, several members of which had played together in other aggregations, became a regular Australian pub band, first gaining a following at the Cricketer's Arms Hotel bar. By the time Men at Work was signed by Australian Columbia, it had a national following and was the highest-paid unrecorded band in the country. The band's debut LP, when released in its homeland, stayed at #1 for ten weeks, beating the record previously held by Split Enz's *True Colours*. In the U.S., *Business as Usual* sold five million copies and spent nearly two years on the album chart. In its videos for "Who Can It Be Now?" and the exotic "Down Under," the band established a zany persona right out of *A Hard Day's Night,* while Hay's reedy voice drew comparisons to Sting.

Cargo, issued in April 1983, had been finished since the previous summer, but was held for release because of the debut's phenomenal success. It debuted in the Top Thirty with *Business* still in the Top Five, and within weeks both albums were in the Top Ten. Men at Work's second effort was also enormously successful, going double platinum and spawning the hits "Overkill" (#3, 1983), "It's a Mistake" (#6, 1983), and "Dr. Heckyll and Mr. Jive" (#28, 1983).

But while their records were scaling the charts, Men at Work were at one another's throats, arguing over management and songwriting. Drummer Jerry Speiser and bassist John Rees left in 1984. In 1985, following the release of the gold *Two Hearts,* Hay, guitarist Ron Strykert, and keyboardist/saxophonist Greg Ham called it quits. Hay released two solo albums, but by then American audiences had lost interest.

Natalie Merchant: See 10,000 Maniacs

The Merseybeats

Formed 1963, Liverpool, England
Tony Crane, gtr., voc.; Aaron Williams, gtr., voc.; Bill Kinsley, bass, voc.; John Banks, drums.
1964—*The Merseybeats* (Fontana) (– Kinsley; + John Gustafson, bass); *England's Best Sellers* (Arc Int'l).

Taking their name from the label given to Liverpool's British Invasion bands, the Merseybeats first scored U.K. hits with ballads, starting with covers of the Shirelles' "It's Love That Really Counts" (#24, 1963) and Dusty Springfield's "Wishin' and Hopin'" (#13, 1964). Their next, and biggest, British hit came with Peter Lee Stirling's "I Think of You" (#5, 1964), followed by "Don't Turn Around" (#13, 1964), and "Last Night" (#40, 1964).

In 1964 they were joined by bassist John Gustafson (later briefly with Roxy Music) from another local hit-making unit, the Big Three. They broke up in 1966, but Tony Crane and Billy Kinsley continued as the Merseys, scoring their biggest hit with "Sorrow" (#4, 1966, U.K.), later covered by David Bowie. After a few more English hits, "I Love You, Yes I Do" (#22, 1965) and "I Stand Accused" (#38, 1966), the Merseys broke up. Crane continues to tour in England with a new lineup.

Metallica

Formed 1981, California
James Alan Hetfield (b. Aug. 3, 1963, Los Angeles, Calif.), gtr., voc.; Ron McGovney, bass; Dave Mustaine (b. Sep. 13, 1961, La Mesa, Calif.), gtr.; Lars Ulrich (b. Dec. 16, 1963, Gentoss, Copenhagen, Den.), drums.
1983—(– Mustaine; – McGovney; + Kirk Hammett [b. Nov. 18, 1962, San Francisco, Calif.], gtr.; + Clifford Lee Burton [b. Feb. 10, 1962; d. Sep. 27, 1986, Swed.]; bass) *Kill 'Em All* (Megaforce)   1984—*Ride the Lightning*   1985—*Whiplash* EP (Elektra) 1986—*Master of Puppets* (– Burton; + Jason Newsted [b. Mar. 4, 1963, Battle Creek, Mich.], bass) 1987—*The $5.98 E.P. Garage Days Re-Revisited* EP 1988—*. . . And Justice for All*   1991—*Metallica* 1993—*Live Shit: Binge & Purge.*

In the Eighties—when heavy metal was dominated by big hair and small ideas—Metallica's dense blend of brains and brawn gave the genre a much-needed charge. By 1991 fans had responded to Metallica's message in droves, buying six million copies of the group's fifth full-length album and elevating its previous LPs to platinum. In the process, grim-faced guitarist/singer James Hetfield became not only a hero for the nation's largest fraternity of misfits—suburban metalheads—but also a critically respected songwriter and bandleader.

Hetfield and Lars Ulrich came from different worlds to form Metallica in the Los Angeles suburbs in 1981. Hetfield, whose father was a trucking company owner and mother a light opera singer, was raised in a strict Christian Science home; Ulrich, a recently transplanted Dane, had intended to become a professional tennis player like his father, Torben Ulrich. What the two teenagers shared was an interest in the gritty music of U.K. hard rockers Motörhead. Adding guitarist Dave Mustaine and bassist Ron McGovney, the band started writing songs and recording demo tapes. Metallica's lineup solidified in 1983 when Bay Area guitarist Kirk Hammett replaced Mustaine (who was booted out for his excessive substance abuse and went on to form Megadeth [see entry]) and bassist Cliff Burton moved into McGovney's slot.

After gaining a solid cult following among fans who could not identify with contemporary pretty-boy pop-metal combos such as Van Halen and Bon Jovi, Metallica became known for its sophisticated, often complex song structures and serious lyrics that reflected teen obsessions with anger, despair, fear, and death. In sharp contrast to those of other death-obsessed metal bands, Metallica's lyrics pose deeper questions about justice and retribution, drug addiction, mental illness, and political violence. The group's debut album, *Kill 'Em All,* is an anarchic catharsis of gloom, with songs like "No Remorse" decrying the insanity of war, and "Seek and Destroy" looking at mindless street violence. On subsequent albums the subject matter teetered between the political (. . . And Justice for All) and the personal (Metallica).

In 1986 Metallica's tour bus skidded off an icy road in Sweden, killing bassist Burton. The surviving members took some time off before regrouping with ex–Flotsam and Jetsam bassist Jason Newsted. Newsted's more solid playing style brought a thicker, tighter sound, which contributed to the group's massive success in the late Eighties and early Nineties. On August 8, 1992, the band experienced another tragedy when their pyrotechnics went awry during an ill-fated performance with Guns n' Roses (it was the same night of Gn'R's notorious riot show) at Montreal's Olympic Stadium; Hetfield wound up walking into a wall of flames and suffering serious burns, but recovered fully.

Metallica had developed its following without the benefit of radio play, so it came as a bit of a surprise when Master of Puppets reached #29 in 1986. The followup EP, Garage Days Re-Revisited (a collection of covers of songs by various punk and metal bands including Killing Joke and the Misfits), made it to #28. Metallica's first Top Ten album was . . . And Justice for All, which reached #6 in 1988 with its single, "One," breaking into the Top Forty at #35. Its striking video included clips from the 1971 antiwar film of Dalton Trumbo's Johnny Got His Gun, the tale of a quadriplegic, faceless World War I veteran. After a three-year hiatus, the much-anticipated Metallica entered the charts at #1. The album contained a string of hits, including "Enter Sandman" (#16), "The Unforgiven" (#35), and "Nothing Else Matters" (#34). Their live album, Live Shit (#26, 1993), was recorded in 1993 at three shows in Mexico City.

The Meters

Formed 1967, New Orleans, Louisiana
Art Neville (b. Arthur Lanon Neville, Dec. 17, 1937, New Orleans), kybds., voc.; Leo Nocentelli, gtr., voc.; Joseph "Zigaboo" Modeliste, drums, voc.; George Porter Jr., bass, voc.
1969—The Meters (Josie) 1970—Look-Ka Py Py; Struttin' 1972—Cabbage Alley (Reprise) 1974— Rejuvenation; Cissy Strut (Island) 1975—(+ Cyril Neville [b. Oct. 10, 1948, New Orleans], perc., voc.) Fire on the Bayou (Reprise) 1976—Trick Bag 1977—New Directions (Warner Bros.) 1990— (Group re-forms: A. Neville; Nocentelli; Porter; + Russell Batiste, drums) Good Old Funky Music (Rounder) 1991—Funky Miracle (Charly) 1992— The Meters Jam; Uptown Rulers: The Meters Live on the Queen Mary (Rhino) 1995—(- Nocentelli; + Brian Stoltz, gtr.) Funkify Your Life: The Meters Anthology.

The Meters were better known—and better paid—as New Orleans' finest backup band than as a self-contained feature act. Their lean, peppery R&B gave a funky flavor to recordings by out-of-towners like Paul McCartney and Labelle; but on their own, their rhythms were too tricky, their vocals too understated, and their sound altogether too spare to reach a broad audience.

When Art Neville formed the group in 1967, he had been a prominent musician in New Orleans for almost 15 years. He was still in high school when, leading the Hawketts, he cut the 1954 Chess single "Mardi Gras Mambo," which made them a popular regional act, and which is still pressed every year for Mardi Gras. He had put out a handful of regional hits as a soloist—"Cha Dooky Doo" and "Ooh-Whee Baby" on Specialty in the late Fifties, and "All These Things" on Instant in 1962— before he formed Art Neville and the Sounds with his brothers Charles and Aaron as singers, along with guitarist Leo Nocentelli, bassist George Porter, and drummer Ziggy Modeliste around 1966. They played local clubs until producer Allen Toussaint and his business partner Marshall Sehorn hired the group, minus Charles and Aaron, to be house rhythm section for their Sansu Enterprises in 1968. As such, they backed Lee Dorsey, Chris Kenner, Earl King, Betty Harris, and Toussaint himself on stage and in the studio in the late Sixties and early Seventies.

Concurrently, the quartet performed on its own as the Meters. Their popularity was not limited to New Orleans, and their hits—mostly dance instrumentals—included "Sophisticated Cissy" (#34 pop, #7 R&B, 1969), "Cissy Strut" (#23 pop, #4 R&B, 1969), "Look-Ka Py Py" (#11 R&B, 1969), and "Chicken Strut" (#11 R&B, 1970).

In 1972 they signed with Reprise Records, retaining Toussaint as their producer and Sehorn as manager. The major label did not bring about a commercial breakthrough—in fact, the moderate hits gave way to minor hits—but the Meters were widely heard, if not recognized, on albums by Dr. John, Robert Palmer, Jess Roden, Labelle, King Biscuit Boy, and Paul McCartney and Wings. They backed Dr. John on tours in 1973 and King Biscuit Boy in 1974, and opened shows for the Rolling Stones on their 1975 American and 1976 European tours.

In 1975 the Meters joined George and Amos Landry—members of a Mardi Gras ceremonial "black Indian tribe," the Wild Tchoupitoulas, and uncle and cousin to Neville—in recording The Wild Tchoupitoulas (Island, 1976). Aaron, Charles, Art, and Cyril Neville contributed vocals to the sessions, reuniting the Neville Sounds for the occasion. Shortly before that album's release, Cyril joined the Meters. A year later, the group cut ties with Toussaint and Sehorn, complaining that it was denied artistic control. For New Directions the Meters teamed with San Francisco producer Dave Rubinson, but that album was not to their satisfaction either, and in 1977, when Toussaint and Sehorn claimed the Meters name, they broke up. Art and Cyril joined Aaron and Charles as the Neville Brothers [see entry]. The others found freelance work in New Orleans. Modeliste drummed for Keith Richards and Ron Wood on their New Barbarians tour in 1979.

The Meters re-formed in 1990 with drummer Russell Batiste taking over for Modeliste, who had moved to Los Angeles and become a session player. In 1994 founding member Nocentelli left the band, reportedly because of disagreements with Art Neville over whether or not the band should be compensated for samples lifted from their back catalogue by contemporary hip-hop groups. Brian Stoltz, who replaced Nocentelli, had played with the Neville Brothers Band. The Meters continue to tour. Rhino released a two-CD compilation of the group's early Josie and Warner Bros. sides, *Funkify Your Life*.

Pat Metheny

Born August 12, 1955, Lee's Summit, Missouri
1975—Bright Size Life (ECM)   1977—Watercolors
1978—Pat Metheny Group   1979—American
Garage; New Chautauqua   1980—80/81   1981—As
Falls Wichita, So Falls Wichita Falls (with Lyle
Mays)   1982—Offramp   1983—Travels   1984—Re-
joicing (with Charlie Haden and Billy Higgins); First
Circle; ECM Works   1985—The Falcon and the
Snowman soundtrack (EMI America)   1986—Song
X (with Ornette Coleman) (Geffen)   1987—Still Life
(Talking)   1988—ECM Works II (ECM)   1989—Let-
ter from Home (Geffen)   1990—Question and An-
swer (with Dave Holland and Roy Haynes)
1992—Secret Story   1993—The Road to You:
Recorded Live in Europe   1994—Zero Tolerance for
Silence   1995—We Live Here.

Practically overnight in the late 1970s, Pat Metheny became one of the most influential voices in contemporary jazz guitar. His chiming guitar work, rooted in bop but tinged with country and occasional rock overtones, insistent yet ethereal, signaled a visionary talent on the instrument.

Metheny began seriously delving into jazz music and the guitar at age 14; within two years he was working professionally in Kansas City. After a stint at the University of Miami, Metheny was invited by vibist and bandleader Gary Burton—who had heard him earlier at a Wichita jazz festival—to teach at Boston's Berklee College of Music, the premier jazz school. Metheny then joined Burton's band, at times playing an electric 12-string guitar—an almost unheard of instrument in jazz.

After playing with Burton, Metheny put together his own group including keyboardist Lyle Mays, a mainstay of Metheny's bands ever since. Before the band recorded 1978's *Pat Metheny Group*, Metheny had already re-

leased *Bright Size Life* (1975) and *Watercolors* (1977). On the latter two albums, he was accompanied by drummer Bob Moses and bassist Jaco Pastorius, whom he'd met in Miami in the mid-Seventies. Pastorius and Metheny also toured together in 1979 as part of Joni Mitchell's band (some of those performances were recorded for Mitchell's live album, *Shadows and Light*).

With the success of *New Chautauqua* (#44, 1979), *American Garage* (#53, 1979), and *As Falls Wichita, So Falls Wichita Falls* (#50, 1981), Metheny made deeper inroads into the pop market and became the most influential jazz guitar stylist since John McLaughlin. Although his own group used the instrumentation of a typical rock group, employing electric bass and keyboards (including synthesizers), Metheney kept his hand in more traditional jazz contexts. The album *80/81* found him recording with two Ornette Coleman sidemen, bassist Charlie Haden and tenor saxophonist Dewey Redman; 1984's *Rejoicing* was a trio session with Haden and drummer Billy Higgins; *Question and Answer* (1990) featured bassist Dave Holland and drummer Roy Haynes. In 1986 Metheny shared a recording with one of his heroes, Ornette Coleman, on the highly praised collaboration, *Song X*.

Metheny scored John Schlesinger's 1985 film, *The Falcon and the Snowman*, featuring "This Is Not America" (#32, 1985), cocomposed and sung by David Bowie. *Still Life (Talking)* (#86, 1987), Metheny's first album for Geffen, went gold. By the mid-Eighties, Metheny had become seriously interested in both advanced technology—experimenting widely with guitar effects and synthesizers—and world music. He began exploring Brazilian and African music and expanded his groups to include percussionists and a singer. Metheny also guested on recordings by Brazilian singer/songwriter Milton Nascimento. In the early Nineties, Metheny toured and recorded with saxophonist Joshua Redman. Despite changes in format and sound, Metheny's acclaim and popularity have remained consistent.

MFSB

Formed early Seventies, Philadelphia, Pennsylvania
1973—MFSB (Philadelphia International); MFSB:
Love Is the Message   1974—TSOP (TSOP)   1975—
Universal Love (Philadelphia International)   1976—
Philadelphia Freedom; Summertime   1977—The
End of Phase I   1978—MFSB and Gamble Huff Or-
chestra (TSOP)   1980—Mysteries of the World.

MFSB (Mother, Father, Sister, Brother) was the nickname for the crew of studio musicians who played on most of the Sound of Philadelphia records released by Kenny Gamble and Leon Huff's Philadelphia International Records in the early Seventies. Many of these musicians appeared on Cliff Nobles' popular dance tune, "The

Horse" (#2 pop and R&B), in 1968. Under the MFSB name they had a #1 pop and R&B single, "TSOP (The Sound of Philadelphia)," in 1974. For many years, that Kenny Gamble–Leon Huff composition was the theme for the syndicated music show *Soul Train*. Many MFSB members also appeared on Salsoul Orchestra recordings. Although personnel changed frequently in the later years, musicians on its most popular early LPs included Ron Kersey and Kenny Gamble (keyboards); Norman Harris, Roland Chambers, Bobby Eli (guitars); Lenny Pakula (organ); Zach Zachery (sax); Ronnie Baker (bass); Vince Montana (vibes); Earl Young (drums); Larry Washington (percussion); and Don Renaldo (conductor).

Miami Sound Machine: See Gloria Estefan

George Michael

Born Georgios Kyriacos Panayiotou, June 25, 1963, London, England
1987—*Faith* (Columbia)   1990—*Listen Without Prejudice Vol. 1*   1993—*Five Live* EP (Hollywood).

Few could have guessed that the transition from teeny-bopper idol to serious singer/songwriter would go as smoothly as it did for George Michael, who became famous as half of the pop duo Wham! [see entry] before ascending to pop superstardom with his solo debut, *Faith*. Whereas in Wham! Michael used his cherubic good looks and uncanny knack for a melodic hook to create ingratiating but disposable pop, his solo work reveals an earnest effort to achieve deeper musical and emotional resonance. Despite his radiant ballads and insidious dance tracks, some still view him as a self-conscious purveyor of blue-eyed soul. His future as a recording artist is questionable, however, in light of a 1994 court decision upholding Michael's contract with Sony, for which the singer has vowed never to record again.

Michael's first post-Wham! outing was "I Knew You Were Waiting (for Me)," a duet with Aretha Franklin that hit #1 in 1987 and earned Michael and Franklin a Grammy for Best R&B Performance by a Duo. Shortly afterward, Michael released the funky first single off *Faith*, "I Want Your Sex," which, bolstered by a sexy video, quickly soared to #2. The album would eventually spin off four #1 hits: "Faith" (1987), the shimmering "Father Figure" (1988), the romantic ballad "One More Try" (1988), and "Monkey" (1988). "Kissing a Fool" and "Heaven Help Me" each hit #5 (the latter in 1989), further boosting the eight-million-selling *Faith*, 1988's best-selling album and Grammy-winning Album of the Year.

Meanwhile, Michael continued, in his videos and media appearances, to cultivate a sex-symbol image, albeit a more rugged—leather, chin stubble, sneer—mature one than he had nurtured in Wham! But with the release of his second solo effort, *Listen Without Prejudice Vol. 1*, in 1990, Michael surprised fans and industry insiders by shunning the press and saying he wouldn't make videos. The album peaked at #2 nonetheless, and there was a chart-topping hit, the somber "Praying for Time" (#1, 1990). The danceable second single, "Freedom"—whose lyrics spelled out Michael's decision to abandon his rock-star persona—went to #8 (1990) and was made into a video, albeit without Michael's presence. (Instead, a bevy of supermodels appeared lip-syncing his vocals.) In late 1991 Michael was back on the charts with a #1 version of Elton John's "Don't Let the Sun Go Down on Me," recorded live with John.

A year later Michael announced that he would take legal action to terminate his contract with Sony Music—the corporation that took over his label, Columbia Records. He charged that Sony, still wishing to package Michael as a sex symbol, lacked respect for his artistic expression and that it only halfheartedly supported his projects benefiting the AIDS cause, among them his duet with Elton John and his four-track contribution to a compilation album called *Red Hot + Dance*. In 1993 Sony grudgingly granted Hollywood Records permission to release *Five Live*, an EP of two cover songs performed by Michael on his 1991–92 tour and three from his appearance at the Freddie Mercury tribute concert in 1992, during which he sang Queen songs with surviving members of the band. All proceeds from the record went to the Phoenix Trust, an AIDS charity set up in Mercury's memory.

In June 1994 a London court rejected Michael's claim that his contract with Sony amounted to "restraint of trade" and upheld the $12-million contract the singer had signed with the company in 1988. At the time, Michael owed the label six more albums on a contract that could run to 2003. Two months later, Michael filed an appeal of the verdict. As the legal battle continued, Michael was unable to release new product. Under a special arrangement, Michael's "Jesus for a Child" aired just once in England as part of an annual appeal to raise funds for needy children. After hearing the six-minute song, listeners pledged $32,000 to the charity.

Lee Michaels

Born November 24, 1945, Los Angeles, California
1968—*Carnival of Life* (A&M)   1969—*Recital; Lee Michaels*   1970—*Barrel*   1971—*5th*   1972—*Life; Space and First Takes*   1973—*Nice Day for Something* (Columbia)   1974—*Tailface*   1975—*Saturn Rings* (ABC)   1992—*The Lee Michaels Collection* (Rhino).

Screaming himself hoarse, pounding his overamped Hammond organ, and backed only by an enormous drummer called Frosty, Lee Michaels made his name as one of the original hard-rockers—and surely the first, perhaps the only one, to play hard rock on a keyboard rather than a guitar. His 1971 hit "Do You Know What I Mean?" stands as the classic example of Michaels' unique sound.

Though he concentrated on this heavy-keyboard approach during much of his career, Michaels could also play sax, accordion, trombone, and guitar. He'd started out as a lounge pianist in Fresno, California, in the mid-Sixties, with aspirations to be a jazz/blues horn player. Instead he joined his first band, the Sentinels, in 1965 (John Barbata, later with the Turtles and Jefferson Starship, was the drummer). He and Barbata then joined a Bay Area band led by Joel Scott Hill, but Michaels left to pursue his own sound, inspired by a Jefferson Airplane show. He assembled a five-piece band named for himself and recorded his debut LP.

After another change of heart—and much experimentation with organs and amplifiers—Michaels dismissed his band. Though the public responded favorably to his one-man-band debut, *Recital,* his greatest success resulted from collaborations with Frosty (Bartholomew Eugene Smith-Frost). About six and a half hours' worth of jamming resulted in *Lee Michaels,* his most successful LP until then. Michaels and Frosty toured as a duo, selling out major halls across the U.S. The third LP yielded "Heighty Hi" and a cover of the blues standard "Stormy Monday," both of which received substantial FM-radio airplay. Frosty then left to form his own band, Sweathog.

Michaels kept at it and had his only hits in 1971 with "Do You Know What I Mean?" (#6) and "Can I Get a Witness?" (#39); the album on which they appeared, *5th,* went Top Twenty. *Space and First Takes* featured drummer Keith Knudsen, who later left Michaels to join the Doobie Brothers, at which point Michaels retired for an extended holiday in Hawaii to "sit under a tree." He reunited with Frosty for *Tailface,* but with his successes apparently behind him, Michaels again retired after *Saturn Rings.* In 1982 he told ROLLING STONE of a planned comeback with a new LP, *Absolute Lee,* to come out on his own Squish label (it never materialized).

Mickey and Sylvia

Formed 1954

Mickey Baker (b. McHouston Baker, October 15, 1925, Louisville, Ky.), gtr., voc.; Sylvia Robinson (b. Sylvia Vanderpool, March 6, 1936, New York City, N.Y.), voc., gtr.

1989—Love Is Strange and Other Hits (RCA).

In 1954 Mickey Baker, a blues guitarist who had recorded as a solo act, met vocalist Sylvia Vanderpool. He gave her guitar lessons, and from this evolved a partnership that in 1956 produced the million-selling hit "Love Is Strange" (#11 pop, #2 R&B). The pair had two more hits—"There Oughta Be a Law" (#46 pop, #15 R&B, 1957) and "Baby You're So Fine" (#52 pop, #27 R&B, 1961)—before breaking up in 1961 when Mickey moved to Europe. (They came back together briefly in 1965 to perform a few gigs.) Later Mickey wrote several guitar instruction books, including the best-seller *Jazz Guitar.*

In 1956 Sylvia had married Joe Robinson, and more than a decade later the couple founded All Platinum Records and All Platinum Studios. As a producer, Sylvia's credits range from the 1961 Ike and Tina Turner hit "It's Gonna Work Out Fine" (on which she also played guitar) to the Moments' 1970 gold single "Love on a Two-Way Street" (which she cowrote) and Shirley (and Company)'s 1976 disco hit "Shame, Shame, Shame" (which she wrote).

In 1973 Sylvia returned to the chart with "Pillow Talk" (#3 pop, #1 R&B) on her own Vibration label and continued to hit the R&B chart through 1978, notably with "Sweet Stuff" (#16, 1974) and "Automatic Lover" (#43, 1978). In the late Seventies Sylvia revived the ailing All Platinum label by renaming it Sugarhill and putting together a group of rap vocalists, the Sugar Hill Gang [see entry], which had a smash hit with "Rapper's Delight" (#26 pop, #4 R&B, 1979). She went on to sign and produce other top rap acts like Grandmaster Flash and the Furious Five and Funky Four Plus One.

Bette Midler

Born December 1, 1945, Honolulu, Hawaii
1972—The Divine Miss M (Atlantic)   1973—Bette Midler   1974—Songs for the New Depression 1977—Broken Blossom; Live at Last   1979—Thighs and Whispers; The Rose soundtrack   1980—Divine Madness   1983—No Frills   1985—Mud Will Be Flung Tonight!   1989—Beaches soundtrack 1990—Some People's Lives   1991—For the Boys soundtrack   1993—Experience the Divine; Gypsy soundtrack.

Early on, singer Bette Midler's sexpot camp image—trash with flash—proved as important to her success as her singing. Over the next 20 years, Midler survived several career setbacks, but she turned in a series of acclaimed film performances and returned to the top of the charts in 1989 with "Wind Beneath My Wings." While most of her biggest recent hits tend toward MOR-ish sentimentality, her record-breaking 1993 concert tour proved that the Divine Miss M had lost none of her humor or charm. She is, as one critic wrote, "Sophie Tucker, Ethel Merman, and Judy Garland rolled into one furiously energetic package."

Midler was raised in Hawaii. From an early age, she took an interest in acting (her mother named her after Bette Davis), and in high school Midler worked in theater and sang in a female folk trio called the Pieridine Three. In 1965 she had a bit part as a missionary's wife in the film *Hawaii*, after which she left for Los Angeles and then later moved to New York. There (in between odd jobs like go-go dancing in a New Jersey bar), Midler got parts in several Tom Eyen Off-Broadway productions, followed by a three-year run in Broadway's *Fiddler on the Roof*, where she eventually moved from the chorus to the featured part of Tzeitel. In 1971 she played the double role of Mrs. Walker and the Acid Queen in the Seattle Opera Association's production of *Tommy*.

Around 1970 Midler decided to concentrate on singing and was soon performing at the Continental Baths, a gay men's club in New York City. She developed her campy comedy routines and a broad musical repertoire that included Andrews Sisters takeoffs, blues, show tunes, and Sixties girl-group numbers. Her piano accompanist was Barry Manilow. She quickly became a cult item and soon an aboveground sensation on major TV talk shows. Her debut, *The Divine Miss M*, went gold and won her the Grammy for Best New Artist. She appeared on the cover of *Newsweek* and had a #8 hit with a remake of the Andrews Sisters' "Boogie Woogie Bugle Boy" in 1973.

But sales after the second LP dropped off sharply, though she always retained a loyal concert following. In 1979 she starred in *The Rose*, loosely based on the life of Janis Joplin. Midler was nominated for an Oscar. The soundtrack LP went platinum in 1980, aided by the Top Ten title song. Later in the year, a Midler concert film and soundtrack entitled *Divine Madness* were released. Her humorous memoirs of her first world tour, *A View from a Broad*, hit the best-seller list that year. Her next literary effort was a children's book entitled *The Saga of Baby Divine*, which was published in 1983.

Midler's career slump began in 1982 with her next feature film, the ironically titled *Jinxed*. A critical and commercial bomb, the comedy was released amid rampant rumors of disagreements between Midler and her costars and director. Her reputation was damaged, seemingly irreparably, and she suffered a nervous breakdown. In later interviews she openly discussed that painful period as one of heavy drinking and deep depression. In 1984, after a brief courtship, she married Martin von Haselberg, a commodities trader and performance artist who was part of a duo known as the Kipper Kids. (They have since had a daughter, Sophie.) Soon thereafter Midler began to turn her career around with a series of comedies for the Walt Disney Studio–Touchstone Pictures: *Down and Out in Beverly Hills* and *Ruthless People* (1986), *Outrageous Fortune* (1987), and *Big Business* (1988), in which she and Lily Tomlin each played dual roles as two sets of twin sisters. She returned to drama with *Beaches*, a sentimental paean to women's friendship that spawned a multiplatinum, #2 soundtrack

album and the #1, Grammy-winning single "Wind Beneath My Wings."

Midler costarred with Woody Allen in *Scenes from a Mall* (1991), and later that year starred in *Stella*. In 1991 another multiplatinum album, *Some People's Lives*, produced the #2, Grammy-awarded ballad "From a Distance." An ambiguous song with allusions to God watching over humankind and how peaceful our world appears from up there, it got a lot of play during the Gulf War. She received her second Oscar nomination for *For the Boys*, a musical that follows a U.S.O. entertainer and her partner (played by James Caan) through three wars. The movie was not a commercial success but garnered favorable reviews, and the soundtrack went gold. The film was in the news again when comedienne Martha Raye charged that details of the film's story line were derived from an outline of Raye's own life story, a treatment for which Raye claimed that Midler had seen. The charges were dismissed on February 23, 1994, because the judge ruled there was no basis for the suit.

In 1992 Midler won an Emmy for singing several sentimental songs to Johnny Carson on one of the last *Tonight Show* broadcasts, including one she'd written entitled "Dear Mr. Carson," described as "a love letter from America's women." Midler's 1993 tour, Experience the Divine, showed her in top form. She delivered an over-the-top reading of Mama Rose in a made-for-television version of *Gypsy* that same year.

Midnight Oil

Formed 1976, Sydney, Australia
Peter Garrett (b. Sydney), voc.; Rob Hirst (b. Sydney), drums, voc.; Jim Moginie (b. Sydney), gtr., kybds.; Martin Rotsey (b. Sydney), gtr.; Andrew "Bear" James, bass.
1978—*Midnight Oil* (Powderworks, Austral.)
1979—*Head Injuries* 1980—(– James; + Peter Gifford, bass) *Bird Noises* EP 1981—*Place Without a Postcard* 1983—*10, 9, 8, 7, 6, 5, 4, 3, 2, 1* (Columbia) 1984—*Red Sails in the Sunset* 1985—*Species Deceases* EP 1987—*Diesel and Dust* 1990—(– Gifford; + Dwayne "Bones" Hillman [b. N.Z.], bass) *Blue Sky Mining* 1992—*Scream in Blue Live* 1993—*Earth and Sun and Moon*.

Midnight Oil holds the distinction of being the only known rock band whose lead singer ran for a seat in the Australian senate (in 1984, on a Nuclear Disarmament Party ticket). In fact, frontman Peter Garrett—he of the shaved head and somewhat forbidding stature—and his bandmates have never been shy about sharing their social and political convictions. Such concerns have often been at the fore of the Oils' lean, driving guitar rock, whether they're addressing the evils of nationalism gone amok or the dangers of dissing Mother Nature. Moreover, the band's dedication to political and environmental causes has extended beyond its songs; having formed alliances with organizations ranging from Greenpeace to the Tibet Council, Midnight Oil has endorsed these projects—through benefit concerts and general outspokenness—with an ardor that's made the efforts of many other socially conscious artists pale in comparison.

Drummer Rob Hirst and guitarists Martin Rotsey and Jim Moginie first played together as the Farm, touring Sydney's northern coast, before recruiting Garrett, then a law student, through a newspaper ad in the mid-Seventies. (Garrett received his degree in 1977 but never practiced.) In 1976, adding bassist Andrew "Bear" James to the lineup, the band became Midnight Oil and quickly developed an avid following for its live shows. Record companies were unsure of Garrett's market potential, however, and after numerous rejections, the Oils formed their own independent label, Powderworks (the group's indie releases were later reissued by Columbia in the U.S.). The band promoted its eponymous debut album (recorded in ten days) with concerts benefitting Greenpeace, the anti–uranium mining movement, and Save the Whales. A second album, *Head Injuries*, went gold in Australia.

Midnight Oil's star rose further, domestically at least, with its major-label debut album, *10, 9, 8, 7, 6, 5, 4, 3, 2, 1*, which remained in the Australian Top Forty for two years. Meanwhile, the Oils continued to work benefit concerts into their hectic touring schedule, including several on behalf of nuclear disarmament. The Oils finally enjoyed their international breakthrough when 1987's *Diesel and Dust* reached #21 in the U.S. and yielded the #17 pop single "Beds Are Burning," an angry wake-up call about the plight of aboriginal Australians—a prominent theme on the album, and in the band's work at large—and their biggest hit to date.

Blue Sky Mining followed its predecessor to the upper reaches of the American LP chart (#20), but its most successful single, "Blue Sky Mine," peaked at #47. Shortly after its release, the Oils staged a concert outside the Exxon Building in Manhattan, to express their disgust over the *Exxon Valdez* oil spill in Alaska. (A video of the performance, *Black Rain Falls*, was released to raise funds for Greenpeace.) A subsequent live album, *Scream in Blue Live* (#141, 1992), and a studio effort, *Earth and Sun and Moon* (#49, 1993), proved commercially disappointing.

Mighty Clouds of Joy
Formed late 1950s, Los Angeles, California
Joe Ligon (b. Troy, Ala.), voc.; Johnny Martin (b. Los Angeles; d. 1987), voc.; Elmo Franklin (b. Fla.), voc.; Ermant Franklin, voc.; Richard Wallace (b. Ga.), voc.; Leon Polk, voc.; Jimmy Jones, voc.

1962—*Live at the Music Hall* (Peacock) 1964—*Presenting: The Untouchables* 1966—*Sing Songs of Rev. Julius Cheeks and the Nightingales* 1968—*Live! At the Apollo* 1972—*A Bright Side* 1973—*Best of Mighty Clouds of Joy* 1974—*It's Time* (ABC/Dunhill) 1975—*Kickin'* (ABC) 1977—*Truth Is the Power* 1978—*Live and Direct; The Very Best of the Mighty Clouds of Joy* 1979—*Changing Times* (Epic) Ca. early 1980s—(+ Paul Beasly, voc.) 1980—*Cloudburst* (Myrrh) 1982—*Request Line* (ABC); *Miracle Man* (Myrrh); *Mighty Clouds Alive* 1983—*Sing and Shout* 1987—(– Beasly; – Martin; + various others, including Wilbert Williams, voc.) *Catching On* (Word) 1989—*Night Song* 1991—*Pray for Me* 1993—*Memory Lane (Best of)* 1994—(Lineup: Ligon; Wallace; Michael McCowin; Williams).

One of the top young modern gospel vocal units, and one of the very few to attempt a pop/soul crossover, the Mighty Clouds of Joy have earned three Grammy awards. They first got together in high school in Los Angeles; later Paul Beasly joined them from the Gospel Keynotes. They have shared stages with Earth, Wind and Fire, the Rolling Stones, the Reverend James Cleveland, Paul Simon, Marvin Gaye, Aretha Franklin, and Andrae Crouch.

Lead singer Joe Ligon was heavily influenced by the gritty, grunting style of the Reverend Julius Cheeks of the Sensational Nightingales, as was Wilson Pickett. Toward the end of their Peacock label days, critics began comparing the Clouds' high harmony sound to that of Curtis Mayfield and the Impressions, although overall their approach was rawer. Throughout their long career, the Mighty Clouds have worked with a number of pop producers. The Grammy-winning *Changing Times* was produced by Frank Wilson, whose earlier writing and production credits at Motown included the Supremes' "Up the Ladder to the Roof" and the Jackson Five. Wilson later produced *Night Song*. In 1980 they moved to ABC's Christian-oriented Myrrh label, and *Cloudburst* was produced by Earth, Wind, and Fire's Al McKay. Freddie Perren, another Motown producer/writer, was responsible for *Sing and Shout*. In 1987 Johnny Martin died. The group continues to tour extensively and record. They performed with Paul Simon during his 1993 monthlong series of shows in New York City.

The Mighty Diamonds
Formed 1973, Kingston, Jamaica
Donald "Tabby" Shaw (b. Oct. 7, 1955, Kingston), lead voc.; Lloyd "Judge" Ferguson (b. Aug. 28, 1949, Kingston), harmony voc.; Fitzroy "Bunny" Simpson (b. May 10, 1951, Kingston), harmony voc.
1976—*Right Time* (Virgin) 1977—*Ice on Fire*

1978—*Planet Earth*; *Stand Up* (Channel One)
1979—*Deeper Roots* (Front Line/Virgin Int'l)
1980—*Tell Me What's Wrong* (J&J)   1981—*Indestructible* (Alligator)   1982—*Reggae Street* (Shanachie)   1988—*Get Ready* (Rohit); *Never Get Weary* (Live & Learn)   1989—*Ready for the World* (Shamar)   1993—*Paint It Red* (Ras Records)
1994—*Speak the Truth*.

One of the young reggae vocal trios modeled on the original Wailers, the Heptones, and others of the late Sixties and early Seventies, the Mighty Diamonds became one of the most popular reggae groups of the second generation by setting their incisive, militant lyrics in close soft-toned harmonies and languorous rhythms.

They had their first hit in Jamaica in 1974 with "Shame and Pride." Two more hits that year showed the range of their material: "Jah Jah Bless the Dreadlocks" was based on Rastafarian chants, while "Let's Put It All Together" was a reggae version of the Stylistics' hit. (American soul music has been an essential element of virtually every Diamonds song.)

By the end of 1975, Jamaican hits like "Right Time," "Have Mercy," and "I Need a Roof" had been picked up by reggae fans in England, and in 1976 the group was signed to Virgin Records, which released their first album in the U.K. and the U.S. later that year. The year 1976 saw the Diamonds' first visit to America, when they toured with Toots and the Maytals. They made a name for themselves as entertaining showmen with their comic stage patter and occasional soul ballads.

But in spite of their Americanisms (*Ice on Fire* was produced by New Orleans R&B veterans Allen Toussaint and Marshall Sehorn), they were no more able to break into the American pop market than their Jamaican compatriots. In Jamaica, on the other hand, they continued to score big hits—"Tamarind Farm" in 1979 and "Wise Son" (#1) in 1980. "Pass the Kouchie," a hymn to marijuana, was banned by the Jamaican government, but when released as "Pass the Knowledge," it also went to #1 (1981). (Another version of this song, "Pass the Dutchie," was a hit for Musical Youth in late 1982.)

Although styles gave way to dancehall in the late Eighties, the Mighty Diamonds remained steadfast reggae traditionalists and a popular draw on the reggae concert circuit.

Mike + the Mechanics: See Genesis

Amos Milburn

Born April 1, 1927, Houston, Texas; died January 3, 1980, Houston
N.A.—*Amos Milburn* (Blues Spectrum)   1963—*The Return of the Blues Boss* (Motown).

Amos Milburn was one of rhythm & blues' most consistent-selling vocalists from the mid-Forties into the Fifties. He signed with Los Angeles–based Aladdin Records in 1946 and the next year had a million-seller with "Chicken Shack Boogie." Subsequently, Milburn would top the R&B chart with songs about alcohol: "Bad Bad Whiskey" (#1 R&B, 1950), "One Scotch, One Bourbon, One Beer" (#2 R&B, 1953), "Thinking and Drinking" (#8, 1952), and "Let Me Go Home, Whiskey" (#3, 1953). "One Scotch" was revived by George Thorogood and the Destroyers in the late Seventies. Milburn recorded for various labels, including Motown and Ace, until a stroke in the late Sixties left him partially paralyzed.

Buddy Miles

Born September 5, 1946, Omaha, Nebraska
With the Buddy Miles Express: 1968—*Expressway to Your Skull* (Mercury)   1969—*Electric Church*   1994—*Hell and Back* (Rykodisc).
With the Buddy Miles Band: 1970—*Them Changes*; *We Got to Live Together*   1971—*Message to the People*; *Live*   1972—*Carlos Santana and Buddy Miles Live* (with Carlos Santana) (Columbia).
Solo: 1973—*Chapter VII* (Columbia); *Booger Bear*   1974—*All the Faces of Buddy Miles*   1975—*More Miles Per Gallon* (Casablanca)   1976—*Bicentennial Gathering of the Tribes* (with Dickie Betts).
With the Buddy Miles Regiment: 1981—*Sneak Attack* (Atlantic).
With the California Raisins: 1987—*The California Raisins Sings the Hit Songs* (Priority)   1988—*Sweet, Delicious & Marvelous*; *Christmas with the California Raisins*.
With Hardware: 1994—*Third Eye Open* (Rykodisc).

Buddy Miles' long and interesting career spans over four decades and includes stints as a Jimi Hendrix sideman and band member as well as a lead vocal spot in the popular Claymation "group," the California Raisins. Though best known as a singer/drummer, he also plays guitar a la Hendrix, left-handed and upside down.

By the time he was 12 he was drumming in his father's jazz group the Bebops. Approximately three years later, he began working with a number of groups, including the Delfonics, the Ink Spots, and Ruby and the Romantics. He also had played on the session that produced the Jaynetts' 1963 hit "Sally Go 'Round the Roses." Miles was playing in Wilson Pickett's backup band in 1967 when guitarist Mike Bloomfield spotted him at a Brooklyn Murray the K show and invited him to join the Electric Flag [see entry]. Miles appears on that group's *A Long Time Comin'* (1968), *The Electric Flag* (1969), and *The Band Kept Playing* (1974).

In 1968 Miles formed his Buddy Miles Express from the ruins of the Electric Flag; the Express (which featured guitarist Jim McCarty, later with Cactus) peppered Miles' mélange of hard rock and soul with brassy horn charts. Then and since, Miles played drums on many other artists' records, including an early John McLaughlin album, *Devotion*, Jimi Hendrix's *Electric Ladyland*, and Muddy Waters' *Fathers and Sons*. Over the years he recorded two albums with Carlos Santana (1972's *Miles/Santana Live* and 1987's *Freedom*).

The Express came to a halt when Miles joined Hendrix and bassist Billy Cox in what was probably the first black rock group, Hendrix's Band of Gypsys. The brief alliance produced the acclaimed *Band of Gypsys*, a live album recorded on New Year's Eve 1969. It included versions of Miles' "Them Changes" and "We Gotta Live Together." Just ten months later Hendrix died in London, and Miles re-formed the Buddy Miles Express, which included Cox. It was this group that had the minor hit with "Them Changes."

Though Miles would remain prodigiously active for some time, it was his last fling at the pop charts under his own name. In 1974 he joined the reunited Electric Flag for a comeback that dissolved before the end of the year. Beginning in 1978, he served a jail term for grand theft; he had left famous tailor Nudie's store without paying for some merchandise. He was also convicted of auto theft. He formed a band at both the California Institution for Men at Chino and San Quentin.

It seemed that Miles' career was all but finished. But shortly after his release from prison in 1985, he recorded "I Heard It Through the Grapevine" for a producer friend. The track found its way to an advertising firm then "casting" the voices for its California Raisins commercials. Miles went on to voice the "lead" Claymation Raisin for the Cleo-winning series and sang on the dried fruits' three LPs, including the platinum *The California Raisins Sing the Hit Songs*, produced by Ross Vanelli. In 1992 Miles formed his latest group, Hardware, a trio that includes guitarist Steve Salas and bass player Bootsy Collins.

Steve Miller Band

Formed 1966, San Francisco, California
Steve Miller (b. Oct. 5, 1943, Milwaukee, Wis.), gtr., voc.; James "Curly" Cooke, gtr., voc.; Lonnie Turner (b. Feb. 24, 1947, Berkeley, Calif.), bass; Tim Davis, drums.
1967—(+ Boz Scaggs [b. June 8, 1944, Ohio], gtr., voc.; + Jim Peterman, kybds., voc.; – Cooke)
1968—*Children of the Future*; *Sailor* (Capitol) (– Scaggs; – Peterman; + Ben Sidran, kybds.)
1969—*Brave New World*; *Your Saving Grace* (– Turner; – Sidran; + Bobby Winkelman, gtr., bass, voc.) 1970—*Number 5* 1971—(– Davis; – Winkelman; + Ross Valory [b. 1950, San Francisco], bass;

+ Jack King, drums; + Dickie Thompson, kybds.; + Gerald Johnson, bass) *Rock Love* 1972—(– Valory; + Sidran; + Roger Clark, perc.) *Recall the Beginning . . . A Journey from Eden*; *Anthology* (– Johnson) 1973—(+ Turner; – Jack King; + John King, drums) *The Joker* (– John King; – Sidran) 1976—(+ Gary Mallaber [b. Oct. 11, 1946, Buffalo, N.Y.], drums) *Fly Like an Eagle* 1977—(+ Byron Allred; + David Denny, gtr.; + Greg Douglas, gtr.) *Book of Dreams* 1978—*Greatest Hits* 1981— (– Denny; – Douglas; + Johnson) *Circle of Love* (+ Kenny Lee Lewis, gtr.; + John Massaro, gtr.) 1982—*Abracadabra* 1983—*Live* 1984—*Italian X-Rays* 1986—*Living in the 20th Century* 1988—*Born 2B Blue* 1993—*Wide River* (Polydor) 1994—*Steve Miller Band Box Set* (Capitol).

In his long career, Steve Miller has gone from being one of the first young white West Coast blues-rockers to being one of the biggest-selling pop-rock artists of the late Seventies and early Eighties. Although his record sales have slowed considerably since (his new LPs, that is), this deliberately enigmatic figure continues to be a huge draw on the concert trail.

Miller's father was a music-loving pathologist who often brought home guests like Charles Mingus and T-Bone Walker. At age four Steve met guitarist Les Paul, who taught him some chords and later let him sit in on some Les Paul–Mary Ford studio sessions. At age 12 Miller formed his first blues band, the Marksmen Combo. The band stayed together for five years, and included Boz Scaggs, who played off and on with Miller later on and has had a prominent career of his own.

At the University of Wisconsin, Miller led one of the first blues-rock bands in town, the Ardells, which included Scaggs, pianist Ben Sidran, and future Cheap Trick manager Ken Adamany. The group later evolved into the Fabulous Knight Trains. Miller left college to go to Denmark, where he studied literature at the University of Copenhagen. He soon grew disillusioned with academia, however, and moved to Chicago, where his interest in blues was rekindled both by the classic black city-blues artists on the South Side and by the new generation of young white blues players that included Mike Bloomfield, Elvin Bishop, and Paul Butterfield. He formed a short-lived band with Barry Goldberg (who went on to join Bloomfield in the Electric Flag), the Goldberg-Miller Blues Band.

In 1966 Miller moved to San Francisco and formed the Steve Miller Blues Band with guitarist James "Curly" Cooke, bassist Lonnie Turner, and drummer Tim Davis. The quartet became a local favorite, playing many free outdoor shows; it also backed Chuck Berry on a live album recorded in 1967 at the Fillmore and contributed three tunes to the soundtrack of the film *Revolution*.

After playing the Monterey Pop Festival in 1967, Miller was approached by Capitol Records. He helped change the economics of rock music by holding out for what was at the time a record-breaking advance payment for a debut LP and a sizable royalty rate. The band's first LP *Children of the Future*, was recorded in England, with Glyn Johns and the band coproducing. It became an almost instant staple of progressive FM radio, although it failed to yield a hit single. The second LP, *Sailor* (#24, 1968), contained "Livin' in the USA," which grazed the Top Fifty and remains a rock-radio classic. By that time the band had dropped the Blues from its name.

Miller's audience expanded with his next several albums: *Brave New World* (#22, 1969), *Your Saving Grace* (#38, 1969), *Number 5* (#23, 1975), and *Rock Love* (#82, 1971). None of these albums produced hit singles, although many of Miller's album tracks continued to get heavy exposure on FM radio, especially "Brave New World," "Space Cowboy," and "My Dark Hour" (on which Paul McCartney plays bass credited under his pseudonym Phil Ramon).

In early 1972 Miller broke his neck in an auto accident, but it wasn't diagnosed until several weeks later. He then developed hepatitis, which sidelined him through early 1973. Meanwhile, the *Anthology* collection was selling well (it eventually went gold in 1977). Miller kept writing tunes while convalescing, and in 1973 *The Joker* (#2) revealed a new Steve Miller. The sound was slick and bouncy; the LP's title song was a #1 single in the U.S. and went gold; the album went platinum. Instead of rushing to capitalize on his breakthrough success, Miller took three years to deliver a followup. *Fly Like an Eagle* (#3, 1976), consolidated his newfound popular success. It stayed on the chart for nearly two years. The title tune made #2 on the singles chart and also went gold; "Rock 'n Me" was a #1 single; and "Take the Money and Run" was a #11 single; the LP and its title track even made the Top Twenty on the R&B chart. To date it has sold more than four million copies.

Book of Dreams (#2, 1977), like *Eagle*, passed the platinum mark (eventually three million copies) and contained three hits: "Jet Airliner" (#8), "Swingtown" (#17), and "Jungle Love" (#23). Those and other Miller favorites appeared on *Greatest Hits*, which has sold six million copies.

In 1978 Miller took a break and moved to a farm in Oregon, where he built a 24-track studio. He did not release another record until *Circle of Love* in 1981, which contained "Heart like a Wheel" (#24, 1981) (not the Anna McGarrigle song popularized by Linda Ronstadt) and a bizarre side-long track titled "Macho City." The album merely went gold, prompting predictions that Miller's commercial years were behind him. But 1982's *Abracadabra* gave him his third #1 in the title track. And 1988's *Born 2B Blue*, which found Miller performing jazz

standards with Ben Sidran, vibraphonist Milt Jackson, and saxophonist Phil Woods, represented a clear departure from the pop market. While it did not sell, critics were impressed.

Although no more hits have been forthcoming, Miller continues to sell some million copies a year of his greatest hits, which can be heard on classic-rock radio almost as frequently as the time and temperature. With the release of *Wide River* in 1993, the 50-year-old Miller undertook a 50-city tour, during which he played mainly to audiences less than half his age.

Milli Vanilli

Formed 1988, Munich, Germany
Fabrice Morvan (b. May 14, 1966, Guadeloupe), alleged voc.; Rob Pilatus (b. June 8, 1965, Ger.), alleged voc.
1989—*Girl You Know It's True* (Arista)   1990—*The Remix Album*.
As Rob & Fab: 1993—*Rob & Fab* (Taj).

Milli Vanilli's first hit was titled "Girl You Know It's True" (#2, 1989), but by 1990 the Grammy Award–winning duo became synonymous with all that is fake in pop. Not only were they accused of lip synching their #1 hits— "Baby Don't Forget My Number," "Blame It on the Rain," and "Girl I'm Gonna Miss You" (all 1989)—on television and onstage, but they confessed to not having sung a note on their records, either. The startling admission resulted in broken careers, a suicide attempt, over 25 lawsuits, an embarrassed Grammy Award committee, and a deeply chagrined record label.

The story begins when the German-born Pilatus, an out-of-work break dancer and model, met Fabrice Morvan, a Parisian gymnast, in a Los Angeles disco in 1984. The two frustrated singers returned to Europe to begin a career. Their initial attempt at stardom, a 1986 German release, flopped. Looking for work, they showed up at producer Frankie Farian's Munich studio. Farian, best known for his work with Boney M., had just recorded a song, "Girl You Know It's True" (originally recorded by an American band, Numarx), with a musically accomplished but unattractive band. Rob and Fab were pliable, photogenic, but musically untalented. Offering the duo $4,000 each plus royalties, Farian christened them Milli Vanilli, variously described as being Turkish for "positive energy," the name of a Berlin disco, or an homage to British synth-pop band Scritti Politti.

Decked out in bulge-revealing bicycle shorts and shoulder-length dreadlocks, Morvan and Pilatus danced and mouthed the song on European TV, working it into an international hit that crossed the Atlantic when Clive Davis picked up the song for his Arista label. An album, *Girl You Know It's True* (#1, 1989), was quickly recorded.

The Milli Vanilli scam began to unravel after Charles

Shaw, a U.S. Army veteran who was the actual singer, went public with his story in late 1989. After months of denials, Pilatus, who wanted more money and a chance to sing, confirmed that his and Morvan's sole contribution to Milli Vanilli was visual.

The Grammy committee was the first to respond, rescinding the band's Best New Artist Grammy in November. Twenty-seven lawsuits were then filed, charging Arista Records, its parent BMG, and various concert promoters with fraud. The suits were settled in a Chicago court by a decision granting anyone with proof of purchase a rebate of up to three dollars. More than 80,000 claims have been filed.

On November 30, 1991, despondent over his career and the breakup of a romance, Pilatus attempted suicide in Los Angeles. Farian released an album by the "Real Milli Vanilli" in 1991, but without Rob and Fab's visual appeal, it stiffed. Pilatus and Morvan recorded an album, *Rob & Fab,* but lacking Farian's musical gloss, it, too, failed.

Stephanie Mills

Born March 22, 1957, Brooklyn, New York
1973—*Movin' in the Right Direction* (Paramount)
1976—*For the First Time* (Motown)   1979—*What Cha Gonna Do with My Lovin'* (20th Century)
1980—*Sweet Sensation*   1981—*Stephanie*   1982—*Tantalizingly Hot* (Casablanca)   1983—*Merciless*
1984—*I've Got the Cure*   1985—*Stephanie Mills* (MCA)   1987—*If I Were Your Woman*   1992—*Something Real.*

Stephanie Mills was still a teenager when her starring role in the original Broadway production of *The Wiz* catapulted her to fame and paved the way for a recording career that would find Mills' bubbly, lyric soprano gracing several popular R&B singles. Like many R&B artists, the petite Mills got her start singing in church, at Baptist services in Brooklyn. At only nine years old, she won the prestigious talent competition at Harlem's Apollo Theatre. Appearances with the Isley Brothers and the Spinners followed, as did an album on Paramount Records and a role in the Broadway play *Maggie Flynn.*

In 1975 Mills won the part of Dorothy in the all-black musical theater adaptation of *The Wizard Of Oz.* The show was a smash, and Motown Records founder Berry Gordy Jr. took an interest in its star. (Ironically, Gordy's most famous protégée, Diana Ross, usurped the role of Dorothy in the film version of *The Wiz.*) Mills' Motown debut, *For the First Time,* was produced and written by noted hitmakers Burt Bacharach and Hal David. Nonetheless, it proved a commercial disappointment, and Motown dropped Mills. The young singer bounced right back, though, signing with 20th Century Records and, in 1979, enjoying her first R&B hit, "What Cha Gonna Do with My Lovin'" (#8). The following year Mills scored an even bigger R&B single, the #3 "Sweet Sensation," and landed a #6 pop hit with "I Never Knew Love Like This Before" (#12, R&B). In 1981 Mills again reached #3 on the R&B chart with "Two Hearts," a duet with Teddy Pendergrass.

After switching over to Casablanca Records, Mills generated just one Top Ten R&B single between 1982 and 1985, "The Medicine Song" (#8). Meanwhile, her 1980 marriage to Shalamar's Jeffrey Daniels—the first of three marriages for Mills—quickly soured. The latter half of the decade brought an improvement: Mills topped the R&B singles chart in 1986 with "I Have Learned to Respect the Power Of Love," and repeated this achievement twice the next year, with "I Feel Good All Over" and "(You're Puttin') A Rush on Me." Another song, "Secret Lady," reached #7. In the early Nineties Mills became Dorothy again in a touring company of *The Wiz.* In 1992 she released *Something Real,* which yielded one moderately successful R&B single, "All Day, All Night" (#20, 1993).

Garnet Mimms and the Enchanters

Formed 1963, Philadelphia, Pennsylvania
Garnet Mimms (b. Garrett Mimms, Nov. 26, 1937, Ashland, W.Va.), voc.; Sam Bell (b. Philadelphia), voc.; Charles Boyer (b. N.C.), voc.; Zola Pearnell (b. Philadelphia), voc.
1963—*Cry Baby* (United Artists)   1964—(– the Enchanters) *As Long as I Have You*   1966—*I'll Take Good Care of You*   1973—*Remember* EP   1977—*Garnet Mimms Has It All* (Arista).

Five of the songs Garnet Mimms recorded are better known through the versions by his fan Janis Joplin: "Cry Baby," "My Baby," "Try (Just a Little Bit Harder)," "Piece of My Heart," and "Get It While You Can." In 1962 Mimms was a promising but unsuccessful singer who had recently abandoned his R&B group, the Gainors. The Enchanters were ex-Gainor Sam Bell and Charles Boyer and Zola Pearnell, the latter two veteran gospel singers and songwriters. Philadelphia producer Jerry Ragavoy gave them their 1963 million-selling hit, "Cry Baby" (#4 pop, #1 R&B), a gritty James Brown–styled gospel-soul frenzy featuring Mimms screaming the title phrase over and over. The tune was written by Ragavoy (a.k.a. Norman Meade) and producer Bert Berns (a.k.a. Bert Russell), a co-owner of Bang. With the exception of "Maybe" (by Richard Barrett), Ragavoy cowrote the other three songs covered by Joplin as well.

Within a year, Mimms and the Enchanters (which were in fact an ever-changing roster of female session singers that at times included Dionne and Dee Dee Warwick and Cissy Houston) had three more hits: "For Your Precious Love" (#26, 1963), "Baby Don't You Weep" (#30,

1963), and "A Quiet Place" (#78, 1964). In 1964 Ragavoy split Mimms from the Enchanters. The latter went more or less ignored, but Mimms himself had hits with "Tell Me Baby" (#69), "One Girl" (#67), and "Look Away" (#73) (later covered by Manfred Mann and the Spencer Davis Group) in 1964; "A Little Bit of Soap" (#95, 1965) and "I'll Take Good Care of You" (#30 pop, #15 R&B) in 1966.

For the next several years Mimms continued to record, with spotty success. A 1974 project with members of the group Brass Construction went nowhere. In 1977 Mimms, backed by his new group, the Truckin' Co., had a minor hit in both the U.S. and the U.K. with "What It Is" from the album *Garnet Mimms Has It All*. He has since become a born-again Christian. Howard Tate, who had been one of the Gainors, had a hit with "Get It While You Can," one of Mimms' unsuccessful singles.

The Mindbenders: See Wayne Fontana and the Mindbenders

Ministry

Formed 1981, Chicago, Illinois
Al Jourgensen (a.k.a. Hypo Luxa, b. Allen Jourgensen, Oct. 9, 1958, Havana, Cuba), voc., gtr.; Lamont Welton, bass; Stevo, drums.
1981—*Cold Life* EP (Wax Trax!)   1982—(– Lamont Welton; – Stevo; + Stephen George, drums)   1983— *With Sympathy* (Arista)   1986—(– George) *Twitch* (Sire) (+ Paul Barker [a.k.a. Hermes Pan, b. Feb. 8, 1950, Palo Alto, Calif.], bass, programming; + William Rieflin [b. Sep. 30, 1960, Seattle, Wash.], drums; + Roland Barker [b. June 30, 1957, Mountainview, Calif.], kybds.)   1987—*Twelve Inch Singles* (Wax Trax!)   1988—*The Land of Rape and Honey* (Sire)   1989—*A Mind Is a Terrible Thing to Taste* (+ Mike Scaccia [b. June 14, 1965, Babylon, N.Y.], gtr)   1990—*In Case You Didn't Feel Like Showing Up (Live)*   1992—*Psalm 69: The Way to Succeed and the Way to Suck Eggs.*

Ministry began as a fairly faceless dance combo derivative of the early-Eighties British synth-pop groups. But by the band's second full-length album, frontman Al Jourgensen had started pitting the abrasive sounds of such avant-industrial pioneers as Cabaret Voltaire, Einstürzende Neubauten, and Front 242 against a full-bodied guitar assault. By the early Nineties Ministry's signature art-damaged metal had sparked an ear-bleeding sensation, and Jourgensen was being hailed as the Phil Spector of industrial disco.

After discovering punk rock at a late-Seventies Ramones show, Jourgensen moved to Chicago and formed Ministry. The group put out a few singles and an EP on the local independent label Wax Trax! before signing with Arista in 1982. When the label attempted to mold

Jourgensen into an American version of England's Howard Jones, the singer/guitarist put up a fight and was dropped. Three years later a regrouped Ministry surfaced on Sire, where, in an unusual arrangement, the group was not required to submit demo tapes to keep the company abreast of its progress. After the release of *Twitch*, Jourgensen and new partner Paul Barker began perfecting Ministry's self-described "aggro" sound: angry, shouted vocals and samples over a thick wall of guitar.

Ministry's tour for its second full-length Sire album, *The Land of Rape and Honey*, featured a virtual Who's Who of abrasive alternative rock: Nine Inch Nails' Trent Reznor, Fini Tribe's Chris Connelly, Skinny Puppy's Ogre, Jesus Lizard's David Yow, former PiL/Killing Joke drummer Martin Atkins, and others. Connelly returned as guest vocalist on *A Mind Is a Terrible Thing to Taste* and the 1990 live album *In Case You Didn't Feel Like Showing Up*. Meanwhile, Jourgensen and Barker had become figureheads of a sort of Chicago/Wax Trax! musical mafia, producing offshoot projects such as Revolting Cocks (basically Ministry with Chris Connelly as lead vocalist), 1,000 Homo DJs, Acid Horse, Pailhead, Pigface and Lard, among others.

In 1992 Ministry ascended to new heights with *Psalm 69: The Way to Succeed and the Way to Suck Eggs*. The album shipped at 350,000 copies (nearly 100,000 more than any previous release) and entered the charts at #27. It received glowing reviews, even from critics who had heretofore shunned the arty industrial genre. The single "Jesus Built My Hotrod" featured guest vocals by Butthole Surfer Gibby Haynes. Ministry's newfound success was cemented when the group appeared on the 1992 Lollapalooza Tour.

Mink DeVille/Willy DeVille

Formed 1974, San Francisco, California
Willy DeVille (b. William Boray, Aug. 27, 1953, New York City, N.Y.), voc., gtr., harp; Louis X. Erlanger, gtr., voc.; Bobby Leonards, kybds.; Ruben Siguenza, bass; T. R. "Manfred" Allen, drums.
1977—*Cabretta* (Capitol)   1978—*Return to Magenta* (– Leonards; – Siguenza; – Allen)   1980—*Le Chat Bleu* (– Erlanger; + Rick Borgia, gtr.; + Kenny Margolis, accordion, kybds.; + Joey Vasta, bass; + Thommy Price, drums; + Louis Cortelezzi, horns)   1981—*Coup de Grâce* (Atlantic)   1983—*Where Angels Fear to Tread*   1985—*Sportin' Life*.
Willy DeVille solo: 1986—*Miracle* (A&M)   1990—*Victory Mixture*   1994—*Backstreets of Desire* (Forward/Rhino).

Although Mink DeVille emerged from New York's late-Seventies punk-rock scene, its music was romantic R&B. After the band appeared on the 1976 *Live from CBGB* compilation LP, it was signed by Capitol. The core of the band was formed in San Francisco, where leader Willy DeVille had traveled after a 1971 trip to London from his Lower East Side home. There he met Ruben Siguenza and Tom Allen, and the three began playing leather bars and lounges under names like Lazy Eights and Billy De-Sade and the Marquis. After reading about the Ramones and CBGB in a music magazine, the three of them formed Mink DeVille.

The band's debut LP was produced by Jack Nitzsche and was a critical success, yielding a U.K. Top Twenty hit single in "Spanish Stroll." In 1979 Willy DeVille moved to Paris to record *Le Chat Bleu*, firing most of his band in the process. When Capitol heard the tapes of the new LP—replete with accordion-backed traditional-French and Cajun-style romantic ballads—it delayed the album's U.S. release for nearly a year, prompting DeVille to sign with Atlantic.

DeVille made his Atlantic debut with *Coup de Grâce*. Both *Where Angels Fear to Tread* and *Sportin' Life* were well received here, but little known to listeners. DeVille disbanded the group after *Sportin' Life*. Like many artists before him, DeVille found a much more enthusiastic audience in France, where he lived for a while and still maintains a home.

Mark Knopfler produced *Miracle*, which included "Storybook Love," a song nominated for an Oscar after it was included in the soundtrack to *The Princess Bride*. On *Victory Mixture*, DeVille paid tribute to New Orleans, another of his several current "hometowns."

Minor Threat: See Fugazi

Minutemen/fIREHOSE

Minutemen, formed 1979, San Pedro, California (D. Boon [b. Dennes Dale Boon, Apr. 1, 1958; d. Dec. 23, 1985, Ariz.], gtr., voc.; Mike Watt [b. Dec. 20, 1957, Portsmouth, Va.], bass, voc.; George Hurley [b. Sep. 4, 1958, Brockton, Mass.], drums): 1980—Paranoid Time EP (SST) 1981—The Punch Line 1982—Bean-Spill EP (Thermidor) 1983—What Makes a Man Start Fires? (SST); Buzz or Howl Under the Influence of Heat 1984—Double Nickels on the Dime; The Politics of Time (New Alliance) 1985—Tour-Spiel EP (Reflex); My First Bells 1980–1983 cassette; Project: Mersh EP; 3-Way Tie (for Last) 1987—Ballot Result; Post-Mersh, vol. 1; Post-Mersh, vol. 2 1989—Post-Mersh, vol. 3.
fIREHOSE, formed 1986, San Pedro, California (Watt; Hurley; eD fROMOHIO [b. Ed Crawford, Jan. 26, 1962, Steubenville, Ohio], gtr., voc.): 1986—Ragin', Full-On (SST) 1987—if'n 1989—fROMOHIO 1991—flyin' the flannel (Columbia) 1992—The Live

Totem Pole EP; The Red & the Black EP 1993—Mr. Machinery Operator.
Mike Watt solo: 1995—Ball-Hog or Tugboat? (Columbia).

The Minutemen were one of the most adventurous hard-core punk bands, taking the music to places no one expected it could go—into funk, free jazz, even folk. Fiercely independent and to the far left politically, the trailblazing power trio delivered brief, angular blasts of formless music at breakneck speeds, but with a gutsy, unaffected groove.

Mike Watt and D. Boon were childhood friends in the blue-collar town of San Pedro when they formed the Reactionaries, a fairly conventional rock four-piece. With the rise of punk in the late Seventies, they renamed themselves Minutemen (for the new brevity of their songs, and the ironic right-wing reference). In honor of his hometown, Watt spray-painted "Pedro" on the body of his bass.

Minutemen were the second band (behind Black Flag) to release a record on the seminal South Bay independent punk label SST in 1980: *Paranoid Time*, an EP of short songs and freeform political rants Watt dubbed "spiels." With 1981's *The Punch Line*, Minutemen locked into their signature groove and gained a strong following on the L.A. punk scene. *Bean-Spill* is a whiplash five-song EP with a six-minute running time. The trio ventured into free-jazz territory on *What Makes a Man Start Fires?* and *Buzz or Howl*, its music and politics taking on a near-poetic elegance in tunes like "Bob Dylan Wrote Propaganda Songs" and "I Felt Like a Gringo." The 45-song *Double Nickels on the Dime* (trucker lingo for 55 mph on Interstate 10) is one of punk's few double-record sets, and stands with Hüsker Dü's *Zen Arcade* as an American punk classic.

In 1985 the Minutemen released two albums of longer, more accessible songs—*Project Mersh* (a sarcastic play on the word *commercial*) and *3-Way Tie (for Last)*—including cover versions (Steppenwolf's "Hey Lawdy Mama" and Creedence Clearwater Revival's "Have You Ever Seen the Rain") and the most structured original compositions of their career. That year, they toured behind R.E.M.

In December 1985, at the height of the trio's career, Boon died in a van accident following a gig. Watt and Hurley planned to throw in the towel, but re-formed as fIREHOSE when an enthusiastic Minutemen fan, Ed Crawford, called from Ohio and asked to step in on guitar. fIREHOSE continued in the Minutemen vein, but with longer songs and a more folky feel (courtesy of Crawford). (Watt and his wife, former Black Flag bassist Kira Roessler, also formed the part-time double-bass duo, Dos, whose two albums, *Dos* [1986] and *Numero Dos* [1989], came out on New Alliance.) After three albums, Columbia signed fIREHOSE and released *flyin' the flannel* and *The Live Totem Pole* EP. On February 12, 1994, fIREHOSE played a final, unadvertised gig before a small, devoted crowd back where the whole thing started—in downtown San Pedro. In 1995 Mike Watt, who had played with Saccharine Trust in the mid- to late-Eighties, released a solo album, *Mike Watt: Ball-Hog or Tugboat?*, featuring a large roster of alt-rock-star guests, including Henry Rollins, Evan Dando, Eddie Vedder, J Mascis, and members of Sonic Youth, the Meat Puppets, Nirvana, Soul Asylum, and Screaming Trees.

Missing Persons

Formed 1980, Los Angeles, California
Dale Bozzio (b. Dale Consalvi, Mar. 2, 1955, Boston, Mass.), voc.; Warren Cuccurullo (b. Dec. 8, 1956), gtr.; Chuck Wild, kybds.; Patrick O'Hearn (b. ca. 1956), bass; Terry Bozzio (b. Dec. 27, 1950, San Francisco, Calif.), drums.
1982—*Missing Persons* EP (Capitol); *Spring Session M* 1984—*Rhyme & Reason* 1986—*Color in Your Life* 1987—*The Best of Missing Persons*.

Missing Persons is one of several early MTV new-wave bands remembered as much for its look as its songs. The focus of attention was vocalist Dale Bozzio, a former Boston-area Playboy Bunny with a hiccupy, Lene Lovich–like voice and a futuristic camp/sci-fi look that included peekaboo plastic outfits (including Plexiglass-bowl bras) and hot-pink hair.

Terry Bozzio was playing drums with Frank Zappa when he first met Dale Consalvi, who'd come to Hollywood to pursue acting, in a Los Angeles recording studio. Though Bozzio soon after toured with U.K., the pair eventually formed Missing Persons in 1980, the year after they married. They enlisted guitarist Warren Cuccurullo and bassist Patrick O'Hearn, who had also played in Zappa's band, and Chuck Wild, a classically trained keyboardist.

Missing Persons' eponymous debut EP, recorded in 1981 and reissued by Capitol (#46, 1982), contained what would be their two biggest hits, "Words" (#42, 1982) and "Destination Unknown" (#42, 1982), which set pop-rock melodies and Dale's squeaky voice against electronic textures. Both songs were also included on the group's first and most successful album, *Spring Session M* (#17, 1982), the title an anagram for the band's name. *Rhyme & Reason* (#43, 1984) produced only a minor hit in "Give" (#67, 1984), and when *Color in Your Life* stiffed (#86, 1986, no hit singles), the group broke up, as did the Bozzios' marriage. Dale remarried twice, released one quick-vanishing solo album on Prince's Paisley Park label, and finally settled back in the Boston area to raise two children. Terry Bozzio spent three years working with Jeff Beck (he appears on the 1989 Grammy-winning *Guitar Shop* album), then gave drum clinics and classes around the world. Cuccurullo joined Duran Duran in 1990, O'Hearn made a series of successful instrumental New Age albums, and Wild wrote scores for film and TV, including the final season of the *Max Headroom* show.

Mission of Burma

Formed 1979, Boston, Massachusetts
Clint Conley (b. May 16, 1955, Indianapolis, Ind.), bass, voc.; Roger Miller (b. Feb. 24, 1952, Ann Arbor, Mich.), gtr., voc.; Martin Swope (b. June 1, 1955, Ann Arbor, Mich.), tapes; Pete Prescott (b. Oct. 26, 1957, Nantucket Island, Mass.), drums.
1981—*Signals, Calls, and Marches* EP (Ace of Hearts) 1982—*VS.* 1985—*The Horrible Truth About Burma* 1987—*Mission of Burma* EP (Taang!); *Forget* 1988—*Mission of Burma* (Rykodisc).

Mission of Burma combined the smarts of progressive and art rock with the energy of punk, virtually inventing the shimmering, noisy but melodic wall-of-guitar sound adopted by such postpunk bands as Hüsker Dü. The band remained relatively unknown outside the Northeast during its early-Eighties heyday and split up before making its biggest impact on American independent rock.

The classically trained Roger Miller grew up in Ann Arbor, Michigan, where he would often go see his favorite local bands, the Stooges and MC5. By 1978 he had tired of the Detroit-area music scene and moved to Boston. There he joined Clint Conley in Moving Parts, which splintered into Mission of Burma, with local drummer Pete Prescott and Martin Swope, a Michigan friend of Miller's who created the band's behind-the-scenes tape effects. The first of Burma's legendary, loud gigs was in February of 1979.

Mission of Burma's debut recording was the tuneful single of 1980, "Academy Fight Song," which became a postpunk classic (R.E.M. covered it in 1989). *Signals, Calls, and Marches* contained another postpunk staple, "That's When I Reach for My Revolver." Burma hit its artistic peak on the 1982 LP *VS.* The title of the posthumous live album, *The Horrible Truth About Burma*, refers to Miller's increasing problem with tinnitus, a hearing disorder that forced Burma into early retirement in 1983. (The Taang! releases include outtakes, and the Rykodisc collection combines the first two albums with selected live and unreleased tracks.)

Miller continued making music but focused on quieter solo projects as well as his and Swope's experimental band, Birdsongs of the Mesozoic. Prescott formed Volcano Suns, and Conley dropped out of music.

Mr. Big

Formed 1988, Los Angeles, California
Eric Martin (b. Oct. 10, 1960, Long Island, N.Y.), voc.;
Paul Gilbert (b. Nov. 6, 1966, Pittsburgh, Pa.), gtr.;
Billy Sheehan (b. Mar. 19, 1953, Buffalo, N.Y.), bass;
Pat Torpey (b. Dec. 13, 1959), drums.
1989—*Mr. Big* (Atlantic)   1991—*Lean into It*
1993—*Bump Ahead*.

This hard-rock band (not to be confused with the minor Seventies British disco-pop outfit of the same name) scored a chart-topping 1991 pop hit with "To Be with You," a romantic ballad much softer and sweeter than anything else in its repertoire. Mr. Big was otherwise known for guitarist Paul Gilbert and bassist Billy Sheehan sometimes using power drills fitted with picks to play their instruments onstage. Japan's Makita Corp. power drill company sponsored Mr. Big's 1993 tour of Japan. (Gilbert once got his drill caught in his hair, an incident that later prompted him to remark, "Spinal Tap wish they'd thought of that.")

Sheehan had been an acclaimed bassist with Buffalo-based hard-rock band Talas, and with David Lee Roth, before forming Mr. Big (named after a song by Free, one of several Seventies British blues-rock bands that had inspired him); Gilbert came from speed-metal band Racer X; Pat Torpey had drummed with Impellitteri, Ted Nugent, and Robert Plant; and Eric Martin had recorded three teen-pop solo albums and led the Eric Martin Band in the early Eighties. Mr. Big's debut album (#46, 1989) yielded no hit singles; neither did *Lean into It* (#15, 1991), until a Lincoln, Nebraska, DJ began playing "To Be with You" enough to make it a local hit. Other stations followed suit, and the song entered the Hot 100 chart at #78 in December 1991, and rose to #1, where it stayed for three weeks. Commercially, the band hasn't made a dent since.

Joni Mitchell

Born Roberta Joan Anderson, November 7, 1943,
Fort MacLeod, Canada
1968—*Joni Mitchell* (Reprise)   1969—*Clouds*
1970—*Ladies of the Canyon*   1971—*Blue*   1972—
***For the Roses* (Asylum)   1974—*Court and Spark*;**
Miles of Aisles*   1975—*The Hissing of Summer
Lawns*   1976—*Hejira*   1977—*Don Juan's Reckless
Daughter*   1979—*Mingus*   1980—*Shadows and
***Light*   1982—*Wild Things Run Fast* (Geffen)**
1985—*Dog Eat Dog*   1988—*Chalk Mark in a Rain-*
storm*   1991—*Night Ride Home*   1994—*Turbulent
***Indigo*.**

One of the most respected singer/songwriters in rock, Joni Mitchell is also one of its most daring and uncompromising innovators. Her career has ranged from late-

Joni Mitchell

Sixties and early-Seventies popularity with confessional folk-pop songs to her current cult status via a series of jazz-inflected works that presaged the multicultural and world-music experiments of Paul Simon, Peter Gabriel, and Sting by more than a decade. Through the Eighties and Nineties, Mitchell's influence could be seen in a range of artists, from contemporary confessional singer/songwriters to Prince. Robert Plant and Jimmy Page are among her most ardent fans. Several of Mitchell's early compositions became famous in versions recorded by others—Crosby, Stills and Nash's "Woodstock," for example—but her own ululating vocals and open-tuned guitar inspired numerous imitators. In more recent years her smoke-burnished voice and distinctive delivery can be heard in the work of younger female jazz-influenced singers, including Rickie Lee Jones.

An only child, Roberta Anderson grew up in Saskatoon, Canada. At age nine she was stricken with polio. Defying doctors' predictions that she would never walk again, she recovered after spending nights in the children's ward singing at the top of her lungs. Throughout her childhood, she was involved in art and music. She taught herself to play guitar from a Pete Seeger instruction book. When she enrolled at the Alberta College of Art in Calgary, she took a ukulele with her to college and began playing folk music. She soon moved to Toronto, where she began performing on the local folk scene, and in 1965 married folksinger Chuck Mitchell. They moved together to Detroit a year later, where they soon separated and divorced. Chuck Mitchell continues to perform.

Mitchell became a critical sensation on Detroit's folk scene, and her notices led to a series of successful engagements in New York City. There, in 1967, she was signed by Reprise Records. In late 1968 Judy Collins had a smash hit with Mitchell's "Both Sides Now." (In 1991 Carly Simon turned the song's lyrics into a children's book.) Collins also recorded Mitchell's "Michael from Mountains" on her *Wildflowers* album; the British folk-rock band Fairport Convention recorded Mitchell's "Eastern Rain"; and Tom Rush recorded "The Circle Game." Thanks to this indirect success, Mitchell's debut LP sold fairly well. *Clouds* (#31, 1969) sold better. *Ladies of the Canyon* (#27, 1970) went platinum and yielded a minor hit single: "Big Yellow Taxi."

Mitchell's next platinum album was the critically acclaimed *Blue* (#15, 1971), which featured "Carey," "My Old Man," and "The Last Time I Saw Richard." It also included help from musician friends, including James Taylor (purportedly the subject of "Blue" and, from *For the Roses*, "See You Sometime"). *For the Roses* (#11, 1972) went gold and contained another minor hit single, "You Turn Me On (I'm a Radio)." The highest-charting album of Mitchell's long career remains *Court and Spark* (#2, 1974), with the hit single "Help Me" (#7, 1974). By this time her sound had grown from simple, unadorned acoustic guitar and voice into a sophisticated continental-pop blend. *Court and Spark* predicted Mitchell's future direction with its version of Annie Ross's jazz-jive "Twisted," Mitchell's first recorded cover.

For the live *Miles of Aisles* (#2, 1974) album, Mitchell was accompanied by the jazz-fusion band L.A. Express (including Tom Scott). *The Hissing of Summer Lawns* (#4, 1975) was a complex, esoteric avant-garde experiment that fared poorly critically. ROLLING STONE named it that year's worst album. Nonetheless, it was a commercial hit, and years later critical opinion has been revised somewhat to acknowledge its bold experiments ("The Jungle Line" was one of the first pop records to use Burundi drums) and Mitchell's cooler but no less cutting observations ("The Boho Dance"). *Hejira* (#13, 1976), though smoother and more spare instrumentally, was another commercial success that baffled many critics. To a greater degree than any of her previous works, this album tackled issues of commitment and freedom from a uniquely feminine perspective. In 1976 Mitchell appeared at the Band's San Francisco farewell concert and in the filmed documentary of that event, *The Last Waltz*.

In light of her previous two albums, the double-album *Don Juan's Reckless Daughter* (#25, 1977) was a logical if mysterious next step. Some critics felt that her lyrics had grown more convoluted and vague, a reaction to Mitchell's movement toward song structures far more ambitious and rich than the straight singer/songwriter confessional mode. Contrary to the then prevailing view, *Don Juan's Reckless Daughter* was not all wild experimentation; in fact, half of its tracks might have worked on any previous Mitchell album. But with jazz musicians

Larry Carlton and Wayne Shorter, augmented by a group of Latin percussionists (including Airto), Mitchell scouted new musical territory in "The Tenth World" and the side-long "Paprika Plains." Although perhaps indirectly, *Don Juan* led to Mitchell's most daring and most controversial project, with jazz bassist and composer Charles Mingus. Then dying of Lou Gehrig's disease (amyotrophic lateral sclerosis), Mingus invited Mitchell to collaborate with him. She set lyrics to some of the last melodies Mingus wrote, composed the rest of the material herself, and released *Mingus* not long after the bassist's death. It received mixed reviews but went to #17, an incredibly high chart position for a jazz album and a testament to Mitchell's fans' enduring interest in her work. The live album *Shadows and Light* (#38, 1980), which featured a band including Jaco Pastorius of Weather Report and jazz-rock guitarist Pat Metheny and the a cappella vocal group the Persuasions, also met mixed reviews.

Years later, Mitchell repeatedly and adamantly expressed no regrets about the rocky course she set. "I would do it all over again in a minute for the musical education," she told ROLLING STONE. In 1982 Mitchell released her first album for Geffen, *Wild Things Run Fast* (#25, 1982), a more pop-oriented album. Her cover of Elvis Presley's "(You're So Square) Baby I Don't Care" (#47, 1982) was her first charting single since a live version of "Big Yellow Taxi" from *Miles of Aisles* in 1974. That year she married her bassist, Larry Klein. (They separated just before she started recording *Turbulent Indigo*.)

With *Dog Eat Dog* (#63, 1985), Mitchell's work emphasized social commentary rather than personal introspection. Coproduced by Thomas Dolby, the album featured appearances by Michael McDonald ("Good Friends") and actor Rod Steiger (as a money-grubbing evangelist on "Tax Free"). *Chalk Mark in a Rainstorm* (#45, 1988)—with a guest roster that included Peter Gabriel ("My Secret Place"), Willie Nelson, and Tom Petty and Billy Idol ("Dancing Clown")—was hailed by some critics as a return to form. Others, however, felt that it was bland and soft. The greatest acclaim of the last decade's work was reserved for *Night Ride Home* (#41, 1991), an album of clearly accessible albeit sophisticated jazz-tinged pop. Three years later, *Turbulent Indigo* (#47, 1994) was released to glowing critical response. While promoting that album, she disclosed that she was suffering from postpolio syndrome, a neurological condition related to her childhood bout with the disease.

Throughout the Eighties Mitchell all but abandoned the concert stage. Her hastily arranged acoustic set at the 1986 Amnesty International (she was a last-minute substitute for Pete Townshend) was cut short when the crowd, obviously unfamiliar with her work, booed her.

Mitchell has produced or coproduced each of her albums since her debut (which was produced by David Crosby). A painter and photographer, she also created the art for each of her album covers. Her artwork has been exhibited throughout the world.

Willie Mitchell

Born January 3, 1928, Ashland, Mississippi
1968—*Willie Mitchell Live* (Hi); *Soul Serenade*; *Solid Soul* 1969—*On Top* 1970—*Robbin's Nest* 1971—*Hold It* 1973—*The Many Moods of Willie Mitchell* 1977—*Best of Willie Mitchell* 1986—*Willie Mitchell: That Driving Beat.*

Although he reached the R&B Top Forty repeatedly during the Sixties as a bandleader, Willie Mitchell really made his mark in the music business as vice president of Hi Records, where he helped fashion modern Memphis soul.

Mitchell studied trumpet in high school and performed in dance bands before forming his first group in 1954. By the end of the decade that group had become the house band at the Home of the Blues label, where it also began recording its own instrumentals. Mitchell became a well-known studio musician and arranger; he worked with Charlie Rich, the Bill Black Combo, and Ace Cannon, among others. Mitchell signed with Hi in 1961, and started slowly with "20-75" and "Percolatin'" in 1964, before scoring his first R&B hit in 1965, "Buster Browne" (#29). It was followed by the R&B hits "Bad Eye" (#23, 1966), "Soul Serenade" (#10, 1968), "Prayer Meetin'" (#23, 1968), "30-60-90" (#31, 1969), and "My Babe" (#37, 1969). Mitchell began producing singers, including O. V. Wright, Syl Johnson, and Otis Clay. But he never stopped playing; that's his trumpet solo on B. J. Thomas's breakthrough hit, "Raindrops Keep Falling on My Head."

After the death of Hi president Joe Cuoghi around 1964, Mitchell took on more production and administrative duties for the label, and in 1969 he abandoned what remained of his own recording career to produce his discovery, Al Green. Mitchell's first two 1970 hits as a producer were Green's "I Can't Get Next to You" and Ann Peebles' "Part Time Love." Through the decade, his success was uninterrupted. He oversaw all the recordings that placed Al Green high among the most influential singers of the Seventies and produced others in the soul style they pioneered, including Ann Peebles' "I Can't Stand the Rain."

He worked with Al Green again in the Eighties, on *He Is the Light* and *Going Away*. Among the many artists he has produced are Ike and Tina Turner, Rufus Thomas, Bobby Bland, and Paul Butterfield. In 1994 he opened his Willie Mitchell's Rhythm & Blues Club, on Beale Street, in Memphis. (The same location previously housed Jerry Lee Lewis' the Spot.)

Moby

Born Richard Melville Hall, September 11, 1965, Darien, Connecticut
1992—*Moby* (Instinct); *Ambient* 1993—*Early Underground*; *Move* EP (Elektra) 1995—*Everything Is Wrong*.

Often tagged the king of techno—as well as the first face of techno—Moby is notable among the hordes of anonymous DJs merely because he has stepped out from behind his turntable to seek the attention typically awarded only to rock stars. Yet his music—a symphonic combination of wailing disco beats, punk rock speed, and anthemic lyrics—withstands the focus. Conveniently, Richard Melville Hall's nickname, given to him as a child (in reference to his great-great granduncle Herman Melville's Moby Dick), fits perfectly with the pseudonyms of other techno artists such as Aphex Twin, the Orb, and the Prodigy. But Moby's devout spirituality, veganism, and abstinence from alcohol and drugs are a departure from the typically bacchanalian rave scene.

Moby grew up in Darien, Connecticut, where, while in high school, he formed his first band, the Vatican Commandos, a hardcore punk outfit for which he played guitar. After dropping out of college (where he studied religion and philosophy), he moved to New York City and started hanging out in dance clubs and DJing. By 1990 he had released some singles and EPs for the underground dance label Instinct, including "Go," which set the *Twin Peaks* TV show theme to a frantic dance beat and went to #10 in the U.K. in 1991. This led to some remix projects (Michael Jackson, Depeche Mode, Pet Shop Boys, Brian Eno, and the B-52's) and a record deal with Elektra.

With the release of 1995's *Everything Is Wrong* Moby stretched the techno sound; the album contains the expected high-BPM tracks but also features a bluesy punk song ("What Love") and the metallish "All That I Need." For the album's release party, Moby actually performed some of the songs on acoustic guitar.

Moby Grape

Formed 1966, San Francisco, California
Skip Spence (b. Apr. 18, 1946, Windsor, Ont., Can.), gtr.; Peter Lewis (b. July 15, 1945, Los Angeles, Calif.), gtr.; Jerry Miller (b. July 10, 1943, Tacoma, Wash.), gtr.; Bob Mosley (b. Dec. 4, 1942, Paradise Valley, Calif.), bass; Don Stevenson (b. Oct. 15, 1942, Seattle, Wash.), drums.
1967—*Moby Grape* (Columbia) 1968—*Wow* (– Spence) 1969—*Moby Grape '69*; *Truly Fine Citizen* 1971—*20 Granite Creek* (Reprise) 1978—*Live Grape* (Escape) 1983—*Moby Grape '83* (San Francisco Sound) 1993—*Vintage: The Best of Moby Grape* (Columbia Legacy).

As the Melvilles, and later, the Legendary Grape (Miller; Lewis; Mosley; Stevenson; + Dan Abernathy, gtr.; + Kirt Tuttle, drums): 1990—*The Legendary Grape* cassette (Herman).
Skip Spence solo: 1969—*Oar* (Columbia).
Bob Mosley solo: 1972—*Bob Mosley* (Reprise) 1989—*Live at Indigo Ranch* (as Mosley Grape) (San Francisco Sound).
Jerry Miller solo: 1993—*Now I See* cassette (Herman).

Of the many groups to emerge from San Francisco in the late Sixties, Moby Grape stood out as the band that most preferred structured songs to free-form jamming and the one that mixed L.A. folk rock with San Francisco's standard psychedelia. But it was never able to capitalize on its potential, partly because of hype from Columbia Records that threatened to bury its debut album. Moby Grape grew out of a Northern California group, the Frantics, that included Jerry Miller, Bob Mosley, and Don Stevenson. Mosley met Peter Lewis (son of actress Loretta Young), who had recently abandoned Peter and the Wolves for solo work; Skip Spence was a guitarist who had played drums with the Jefferson Airplane and cowritten several songs ("My Best Friend," "Blues from an Airplane") that appeared on their early albums.

Released in June 1967, *Moby Grape* became infamous at once when Columbia chose to release eight of its 13 cuts simultaneously on 45s, confusing radio DJs. Only the frenetic "Omaha" charted. The record also came with a poster of the band and a front cover photograph that featured Stevenson with his middle finger extended (later airbrushed). Amid the furor, the group's music was virtually ignored.

Its second album, *Wow*, was similarly derailed by gimmickry; it contained a track that could be played only at 78 rpm and a "bonus" LP, *Grape Jam*, that included Al Kooper and Mike Bloomfield. Moby Grape then disbanded but re-formed as a quartet soon after, without Spence, and commemorated the event with *Moby Grape '69*. This set a pattern of breakup, reformation, album, breakup that continues till this day. Because the members are legally forbidden from using the name Moby Grape, over the years they've come up with such imaginative permutations as Maby Grope, Mosley Grape, the Melvilles (as in Herman Melville, author of *Moby Dick*), and the Legendary Grape.

Absent from these reunions has been Spence, a diagnosed paranoid-schizophrenic who showed signs of mental illness during the group's original run. He once broke into Stevenson's room, claiming voices had told him the drummer was possessed by the devil; by 1968 he'd been committed to New York City's Bellevue Hospital. Now a resident of a residential-care house in San Jose, California, Spence contributed a song, "All My Life I Love You," to a 1991 album that Miller, Stevenson, Mosley, Lewis, and two new musicians recorded first under the name the Melvilles, which was later changed to the Legendary Grape. This Nineties version of Moby Grape opened shows for another reunited California band, the Doobie Brothers (whom Spence allegedly named). In 1993 Spence joined the others on stage for a Bay Area show. That year's release of a CD retrospective, *Vintage*, brought this now-revered group more attention than it ever received during its lifetime.

Modern English

Formed 1979, Colchester, England
Robbie Grey, voc., gtr.; Gary McDowell, gtr., voc.; Stephen Walker, kybds.; Mick Conroy, bass, gtr., voc.; Richard Brown, drums.
1980—*Mesh and Lace* (4AD) 1983—*After the Snow* (Sire) 1984—*Ricochet Days* (- Walker; - Brown; + Aaron Davidson, kybds., gtr., voc.) 1986—*Stop Start* 1990—*Pillow Lips* (TVT).

This British postpunk pop-rock band scored a minor MTV-era hit with "I Melt with You" (#78, 1983), a mix of pounding drums, jangling guitars, and a prominent synthesizer riff, which was much more upbeat and romantic than the songs on Modern English's bleak, Joy Division–inspired debut album. The single was from *After the Snow* (#70, 1983), which was in fact the band's best-selling album. Modern English's only subsequent U.S. chart entry was "Hands Across the Sea" (#91, 1984) from *Ricochet Days* (#93, 1984). *Stop Start* failed to crack the Top 100 of the albums chart, as did *Pillow Lips*, recorded after a four-year hiatus; the band then split apart for good.

Molly Hatchet

Formed 1975, Jacksonville, Florida
Dave Hlubek (b. 1952, Jacksonville), gtr.; Duane Roland (b. Dec. 3, 1952, Jeffersonville, Ind.), gtr.; Steve Holland (b. 1954, Dothan, Ala.), gtr.; Danny Joe Brown (b. 1951, Jacksonville), voc.; Banner Thomas, bass; Bruce Crump, drums.
1978—*Molly Hatchet* (Epic) 1979—*Flirtin' with Disaster* 1980—*Beatin' the Odds* (- Brown; + Jimmy Farrar [b. La Grange, Ga.], voc.) 1981—*Take No Prisoners* (- Farrar; + Brown) 1982—(- Thomas; - Crump; + Barry Borden [b. May 12, 1954, Atlanta, Ga.], drums; + Riff West [b. Apr. 3, 1950, Orlando, Fla.], bass) 1983—*No Guts . . . No Glory* 1984—*The Deed Is Done* 1985—*Double Trouble Live* 1990—*Greatest Hits*.
Danny Joe Brown solo: 1981—*Danny Joe Brown and the Danny Joe Brown Band* (Epic).

Molly Hatchet is a guitar-heavy Southern-blues-boogie and heavy-metal band from Jacksonville, home of Lynyrd Skynyrd, Grinderswitch, Blackfoot, and .38 Special. Ronnie Van Zant, lead singer of Lynyrd Skynyrd, planned to produce Hatchet shortly after it formed, but died in a 1977 plane crash.

The group's debut LP went platinum; the second, double platinum. All the while, Molly Hatchet (its name is from Hatchet Molly, a legendary southern prostitute who allegedly lured men to her lair, where she castrated and mutilated them) toured as steadily as any working band, often playing more than 250 dates per year. The group also established an image as gun-toting, hard-drinking rowdies. Worn out from the road, vocalist Danny Joe Brown left in early 1980; the following year he released a solo LP. Along with new vocalist Jimmy Farrar, Molly Hatchet added a horn section (from Tower of Power) for the first time on *Take No Prisoners*. Farrar then left for a solo career, and Brown rejoined. The group's 1985 live album featured a version of Lynyrd Skynyrd's "Free Bird," in tribute to their original mentor.

The Moments/Ray, Goodman and Brown

The Moments, formed mid-Sixties, Hackensack, N.J. (Mark Greene, lead voc.; John Morgan, voc.; Richie Horsely, voc.): 1969—(– Greene; – Horsely; + William Brown [b. June 30, 1946, Perth Amboy, N.J.], voc.; + Al Goodman [b. Mar. 31, 1947, Jackson, Miss.], voc.; – Morgan; + Johnny Moore, voc.) 1970—(– Moore; + Harry Ray [b. Dec. 15, 1946, Hackensack; d. Oct. 1, 1992], voc.) 1984—The Moments' Greatest Hits (Chess/MCA).
As Ray, Goodman and Brown: 1980—Ray, Goodman and Brown (Polydor); Ray, Goodman & Brown II.

The Moments were a trio that recorded numerous hits for New Jersey–based All Platinum Records' Stang label. The original Moments, featuring Mark Greene's falsetto, charted with "Not on the Outside" (#57 pop, #13 R&B) in 1968. After a series of personnel changes, a new group of Moments—Billy Brown, Al Goodman, and Johnny Morgan—had a million-selling single with "Love on a Two-Way Street" (#3 pop, #1 R&B) in 1970.

After Harry Ray replaced Morgan, the group maintained its popularity with black audiences. The Moments had another big hit with 1974's "Sexy Mama" (#17 pop, #3 R&B). A legal battle with All Platinum (owned by Joe and Sylvia Robinson, she of Mickey and Sylvia fame) in the mid-Seventies left them idle for 2½ years. They resurfaced in 1979 as Ray, Goodman and Brown on the Polydor label in the late Seventies and had a hit with "Special Lady" (#5 pop, #1 R&B, 1980), "Happy Anniversary" (#16 R&B, 1980), and "Take It to the Limit" (#8 R&B,

1989). The also provided backing vocals for a pair of Millie Jackson LPs. Ray died of a stroke in 1992.

Eddie Money

Born Edward Mahoney, March 21, 1949, Brooklyn, New York
1977—Eddie Money (Columbia) 1978—Life for the Taking 1980—Playing for Keeps 1982—No Control 1983—Where's the Party? 1986—Can't Hold Back 1988—Nothing to Lose 1989—Greatest Hits: Sound of Money 1991—Right Here 1992—Unplug It In EP.

Eddie Money is a rough-voiced rock singer whose self-titled debut album contained two hit singles, "Baby, Hold On" (#11, 1978) and "Two Tickets to Paradise" (#22, 1978). The son of a New York City policeman, Edward Mahoney seemed destined to follow in his father's footsteps, and he attended the New York Police Academy. But at night he moonlighted in a rock & roll band as Eddie Money. Deciding he loved rock more than police work, the singer quit the academy and moved to Berkeley, California, where he sang at Bay Area bars. Promoter Bill Graham signed on as Money's manager and negotiated his contract with Columbia Records.

A familiar face in the early days of MTV, Money maintained a low profile for about three years before releasing *Can't Hold Back*; during that time he was working to overcome a drug problem. That album became the biggest of his career, going platinum on the strength of a #4 duet with Ronnie Spector, "Take Me Home Tonight." He has continued with fairly consistent success through the past 15 years. His other Top Thirty hits include "Maybe I'm a Fool" (#22, 1979), "Think I'm in Love" (#16, 1982), "I Wanna Go Back" (#14, 1987), "Endless Nights" (#21, 1987), "Walk on Water" (#9, 1988), "The Love in Your Eyes" (#24, 1989), and "Peace in Our Time" (#11, 1990).

The Monkees

Formed 1965, Los Angeles, California
David Jones (b. Dec. 30, 1945, Manchester, Eng.), voc.; Michael Nesmith (b. Dec. 30, 1942, Houston, Tex.), gtr., voc.; Peter Tork (b. Feb. 13, 1944, Washington, D.C.), bass, voc.; Mickey Dolenz (b. Mar. 8, 1945, Tarzana, Calif.), drums, voc.
1966—The Monkees (Colgems) 1967—More of the Monkees; Headquarters; Pisces, Aquarius, Capricorn & Jones Ltd. 1968—The Birds, the Bees and the Monkees; Head soundtrack 1969—(– Tork) Instant Replay (group disbands) 1976—The Monkees Greatest Hits (Arista) 1986—(Group re-forms: Jones; Dolenz; Tork) Then and Now . . . The Best of the Monkees 1987—Pool It! (Rhino).

The Monkees: Peter Tork, Mickey Dolenz, Davy Jones, Mike Nesmith

The Monkees were the first, and perhaps the best, of the prefabricated Sixties and Seventies pop groups (e.g., the Partridge Family, the Archies). Manufactured by TV executives to capitalize on the success of the Beatles, they were hard to take seriously. But thanks in large part to the songwriting of Neil Diamond, Tommy Boyce and Bobby Hart, and their own Mike Nesmith, the Monkees made some exceptionally good pop records, such as "I'm a Believer," "(I'm Not Your) Steppin' Stone," and "Pleasant Valley Sunday."

Davy Jones had been a stage actor and a race-horse jockey in Britain; Mickey Dolenz, whose father had starred in several films, became a child actor at age ten in various TV shows (including NBC's *Circus Boy*) under the name Mickey Braddock; Michael Nesmith [see entry] and Peter Tork had worked as musicians before becoming Monkees. The group was formed for a TV comedy series dreamed up by Columbia Pictures executives, specifically inspired by the Beatles' film *A Hard Day's Night*. Some 500 candidates auditioned for the show in fall 1965; among those rejected were Stephen Stills and Danny Hutton (who went on to Three Dog Night). The Monkees were chosen for their personalities and photogenic capacities, not for musical ability.

In the beginning, they sang but did not play any instruments (leaving that to L.A. studio players), and on the TV show they only mimed playing as they lip synched. The show first aired in September 1966 and became an immediate success. That same year, their debut LP went gold and yielded three Top Twenty gold singles: "I'm a Believer" (by Neil Diamond), "Last Train to Clarksville," and "(I'm Not Your) Steppin' Stone." The first two hit #1.

The "nonmusician" members frantically learned instruments so they could tour and at least appear competent. They succeeded at this, though they certainly couldn't reproduce the studio sound live. With hordes of screaming teens attending every show, though, it didn't matter much anyway. This, combined with Colgems' (a Don Kirshner company) refusal to reveal the truth about the Monkees' lack of playing ability, rankled Nesmith in particular. After intergroup arguments about what to do, Nesmith told a 1967 New York press conference, "There comes a time when you have to draw the line as a man. We're being passed off as something we aren't. We all play instruments, but we didn't on any of our records. Furthermore, our record company doesn't want us to and won't let us." *Look* magazine ran the story, prompting a heated meeting between group members and Screen Gems, in which Nesmith nearly came to blows with an executive when told he could be legally suspended from the band. Eventually the band got its wish, and the hits kept on coming: Diamond's "A Little Bit Me, a Little Bit You" (#2), Gerry Goffin and Carole King's "Pleasant Valley Sunday" (#3), and John Stewart's "Daydream Believer" (#1) in 1967; "Valleri" (#3) in 1968. The LPs *Headquarters, Pisces, Aquarius. . .*, and *Birds, Bees . . .* all went gold.

The group staged successful worldwide tours in 1967 and 1968. In 1967 in London, Dolenz brought Jimi Hendrix to the band's attention, and the Monkees invited him to open their summer U.S. tour. The group's audience didn't know what to make of Hendrix, still unknown in America at the time, and booed him; he quit the tour after two weeks.

The TV show was canceled in late 1968, after which Tork left, while the other three continued for another year and a half. The Monkees' 1968 film *Head*, written by series producer Bob Rafelson and Jack Nicholson, initially struck most as a surrealistic extension of the television show's wacky humor. Featuring cameo appearances by Victor Mature, Annette Funicello, Sonny Liston, and Frank Zappa, and some of the group's more adventurous music, *Head* was a box-office flop. Twenty-five years later, however, it stands as a pioneering effort in long-form music video and a sharp, sad commentary on the Monkees, the times, and the entertainment industry.

Nesmith went on to have a fairly prolific and successful career as a country-rock songwriter ("Different Drum," a 1968 hit for Linda Ronstadt's group the Stone Poneys), singer, and producer, and an early rock-video maker (*Popclips*); Jones and Dolenz reunited with Boyce and Hart for a 1976 LP. Tork and his band the New Monks conducted small-scale tours in the early Eighties.

In 1986 the group enjoyed a major revival of popularity that pulled six of their old LPs onto the chart (the band's catalog was reissued on CD by Rhino in the Nineties). MTV rebroadcast the television series, beginning in March 1987. A new anthology, *Then and Now,* went platinum, and "That Was Then, This Is Now," one of three new tracks recorded by Jones, Dolenz, and Tork, hit #20. The trio toured that summer and came out with a new album, *Pool It!,* the following year. Nesmith had no interest in becoming a Monkee again but did join the other three onstage in July 1989, one day before the group was awarded a star on Hollywood's Walk of Fame. Both Jones, who tours tirelessly on his own, and Dolenz, a successful producer of commercials, wrote books about their experiences as Monkees. Dolenz's *I'm a Believer* (written with Mark Bego) was published in 1994.

Monks of Doom: See Camper Van Beethoven

Bill Monroe
Born September 13, 1911, Rosine, Kentucky
1962—*Bluegrass Ramble* (MCA) 1963—*Bluegrass Special* 1965—*Bluegrass Instrumentals* 1969— *Voice from On High* 1970—*Kentucky Bluegrass* 1972—*Uncle Pen* 1973—*Bean Blossom* 1984—*Columbia Historic Edition* (Columbia) 1986—*Stars of the Bluegrass Hall of Fame* (MCA) 1987—*Bluegrass '87* 1988—*Southern Flavor* 1989—*Live at the Opry—Celebrating 50 Years at the Grand Ole Opry* 1991—*Cryin' Holy unto the Lord*; *Mule Skinner Blues* (RCA) 1994—*The Music of Bill Monroe, 936-1994* (MCA).

Few practitioners of American music have had as profound an impact on their particular idiom as Bill Monroe, "the father of bluegrass." With a career spanning six decades, he is almost singlehandedly responsible for amalgamating elements of blues, gospel, jazz, country, and Celtic folk into the string-driven hybrid we now call bluegrass, named after Monroe's seminal group, the Blue Grass Boys.

The youngest of eight children, Monroe grew up in rural Kentucky and was exposed to music at an early age. His mother sang and played several instruments, while his uncle was a talented fiddler. Because his older brothers already played fiddle and guitar, the nine-year-old Bill decided to take up the mandolin.

When he was 18, Bill moved to East Chicago, Indiana, where he began paying his musical dues. Five years later, he joined his brother Charlie in Charlotte, North Carolina, where they became popular purveyors of traditional blues. Beginning in 1936, the Monroe Brothers recorded 60 songs for RCA, which showcased their mandolin/guitar configuration and their intertwining vocal harmonies. Two years later the duo split, and Bill formed the Kentuckians, soon renamed the Blue Grass Boys in honor of Monroe's beloved "blue grass state" of Kentucky.

In October 1939 Monroe and his group joined the Grand Ole Opry in Nashville and toured with the Opry's road show. Meanwhile, the Blue Grass Boys became a veritable revolving door for Monroe's talented musical apprentices. (Over 100 musicians have claimed membership in the ensemble over the years.) In 1946 Monroe assembled his most legendary cast of Blue Grass Boys: Lester Flatt (guitar and vocals), Earl Scruggs (banjo), Chubby Wise (fiddle), and Howard Watts (bass). It was with this stellar outfit that Monroe would perfect the classic bluegrass sound: high vocal harmonies, extemporaneous mandolin licks, solidly rhythmic guitar and banjo, sinewy fiddle bursts, and jazzy bass runs. The quintet recorded such classic Monroe originals as "Kentucky Waltz" (#3 C&W, 1946), "Footprints in the Snow" (#5 C&W, 1946), "Blue Moon of Kentucky" (1947) (covered in 1955 by Elvis Presley), and "Wicked Path of Sin" (#13 C&W, 1948). When Flatt and Scruggs departed in late 1948, Monroe continued his chart success. All told, Monroe had nine Top Thirty country hits between 1946 and 1959.

Monroe was elected to the Country Music Hall of Fame in 1970, but did not rest on his laurels. The 1986 album *Stars of the Bluegrass Hall of Fame* features Monroe with some famous protégés: Ralph Stanley, Mac Wiseman, and the Seldom Scene, among others. That same year the U.S. Senate passed a resolution that recognized Monroe's "many contributions to American culture," and in 1988 *Southern Flavor* won the first-ever Grammy for bluegrass music. Monroe also received the Academy of Recording Arts and Sciences' Lifetime Achievement Award in 1993. The following year he was showcased in *High Lonesome,* a critically acclaimed film documentary chronicling the history of bluegrass music. In his eighties, Monroe continues to perform regularly.

Montrose
Formed 1974, California
Ronnie Montrose (b. Colo.), gtr.; Sammy Hagar (b. Oct. 13, 1947, Monterey, Calif.), voc.; Bill Church, bass; Denny Carmassi, drums.
1973—*Montrose* (Warner Bros.) 1974—(– Church; + Alan Fitzgerald, bass, kybds.) *Paper Money* 1975—(– Hagar; + Bob James, voc.; + Jim Alcivar, kybds.) *Warner Bros. Presents Montrose* 1976— (+ Randy Jo Hobbs, bass) *Jump on It* (group disbands) 1987—(Group re-forms: Montrose; + Johnny Edwards, voc.; + James Kottack, drums; + Glen Letsch, bass) *Mean* (Enigma) 1994—*Music From Here* (Fearless Urge).
Ronnie Montrose solo: 1978—*Open Fire* (Warner Bros.) 1983—*Territory* 1988—*The Speed of Sound* 1990—*The Diva Station* 1991—*Mutatis Mutandis* (I.R.S.).

With Gamma: 1979—*Gamma 1* (Elektra)   1980—*Gamma 2*   1982—*Gamma 3*   1992—*The Best of Gamma* (GNP Crescendo).

Ronnie Montrose's heavy-metal power bands seem at odds with the delicate acoustic and restrained electric guitar he lent to Van Morrison's *Tupelo Honey* and *St. Dominic's Preview* LPs. After playing in local bands in Colorado, Montrose went to California around 1970. There he played on sessions for Beaver and Krause, the Beau Brummels, Gary Wright, Kathi McDonald, and Dan Hartman, as well as Morrison. In 1972 he played with Boz Scaggs before joining the Edgar Winter Band, and in 1973 Montrose turned down an offer to be Mott the Hoople's lead guitarist and then formed his own band.

Montrose's debut album, despite no singles, went platinum. Lead vocalist Sammy Hagar [see entry] left after Montrose's second LP for a solo career; by 1978 ex-Montrose members Church, Fitzgerald, and Carmassi were with Hagar. Carmassi later joined Heart, Coverdale/Page, and Ted Nugent. In the early Eighties Montrose was leading another band, Gamma, which released three albums before breaking up. He then briefly revived Montrose, which released *Mean* in 1987, before reverting to solo work again. Among the lineup for *Mean* were future Kingdom Come drummer James Kottak and future Foreigner singer Johnny Edwards. Montrose the group was dissolved again, and Ronnie Montrose continued to record solo. His more recent work tends toward jazz rock.

The Moody Blues

Formed 1964, Birmingham, England
Denny Laine (b. Brian Hines, Oct. 29, 1944, Jersey, Eng.), gtr., voc.; **Mike Pinder** (b. Dec. 27, 1941, Birmingham), kybds., voc.; **Ray Thomas** (b. Dec. 29, 1941, Stourport-on-Severn, Eng.), flute, voc.; **Clint Warwick** (b. Clinton Eccles, June 25, 1939, Birmingham), bass; **Graeme Edge** (b. Mar. 30, 1941, Rochester, Eng.), drums.
1965—*Go Now—Moody Blues #1* (London)   1966—*The Magnificent Moodies* (Decca, U.K.) (– Warwick; – Laine; + Justin Hayward [b. David Justin Hayward, Oct. 14, 1946, Swindon, Eng.], gtr., voc.; + John Lodge [b. July 20, 1945, Birmingham], bass, voc.) *Days of Future Passed* (Deram)   1968—*In Search of the Lost Chord*   1969—*On the Threshold of a Dream; To Our Children's Children's Children* (Threshold)   1970—*A Question of Balance; In the Beginning* (Deram)   1971—*Every Good Boy Deserves Favour* (Threshold)   1972—*Seventh Sojourn*   1974—*This Is the Moody Blues*   1977—*The Moody Blues Caught Live + 5* (London)   1978—*Octave* (– Pinder; + Patrick Moraz [b. June 24, 1948, Morges, Switz.], kybds.)   1981—*Long Distance Voy-*

The Moody Blues: Justin Hayward, Ray Thomas, Patrick Moraz, Graeme Edge, John Lodge

ager (Threshold)   1983—*The Present*   1985—*Voices in the Sky/The Best of the Moody Blues*   1986—*The Other Side of Life*   1988—*Sur la Mer* (Polydor)   1989—*Legend of a Band: Greatest Hits 1967–1988)* (Threshold)   1991—*Keys of the Kingdom* (Polydor)   1992—(– Moraz)   1993—*A Night at Red Rocks with the Colorado Symphony Orchestra*   1994—*Time Travellers*.
Justin Hayward solo: 1977—*Songwriter* (Deram)   1980—*Night Flight*   1985—*Moving Mountains* (Threshold)   1989—*Classic Blue*.
John Lodge solo: 1977—*Natural Avenue* (London).
Hayward and Lodge: 1975—*Blue Jays* (Threshold).
Graeme Edge Band featuring Adrian Gurvitz: 1975—*Kick Off Your Muddy Boots* (Threshold)   1977—*Paradise Ballroom* (London).
Ray Thomas solo: 1975—*From Mighty Oaks* (Threshold)   1976—*Hopes Wishes and Dreams*.
Mike Pinder solo: 1976—*The Promise* (Threshold)   1993—*Off the Shelf* (One Step)   1995—*Among the Stars*.

Though their first hit single, "Go Now" (#10, 1965), was a classic Merseybeat ballad, the Moody Blues were best known as one of rock's first classical-pomp groups. Since then, the Moodys have made regular forays back onto the hit-singles chart and remain a perennial arena-filling live attraction. Beginning their fourth decade (with the core quartet of Ray Thomas, Justin Hayward, John Lodge, and Graeme Edge intact since 1967), the Moody Blues have proved impervious to the long-prevalent critical view that their music is bombastic and pretentious. The Moody Blues were among the first groups to make extensive use of the Mellotron and the flute. Their early psychedelic-influenced works were highly evocative, and their sometimes obtuse lyrics (as in "Nights in White Satin") have been thought by fans to possess a deeper meaning.

All the band members had worked in various local Birmingham blues and R&B bands: Ray Thomas and Mike Pinder with the rockabilly-inspired El Riot and the Rebels (who often opened for the Beatles in England in the mid-Sixties) and later the R&B-style Krew Cats, who were popular in Hamburg, Germany. Meanwhile, Denny Laine was fronting Denny Laine and the Diplomats (which included future Electric Light Orchestra drummer Bev Bevan), and Graeme Edge had been in a series of groups, the most recent being Gerry Levene and the Avengers (which included future ELO/Move leader Roy Wood). Clint Warwick had belonged to the Rainbows. A number of misconceptions regarding the group's name have endured, but they chose Moody Blues to have the word "Blues" in it and because Mike Pinder's favorite song was Duke Ellington's "Mood Indigo."

Initially a blues-influenced band, the Moody Blues began playing in spring 1964, by which time Laine and Pinder were writing songs while at the same time the group was performing a catalogue of Motown, James Brown, and American blues songs. The group also backed a long list of American blues musicians on their U.K. tours, including Little Walter Jacobs and Sonny Boy Williamson (Rice Miller). Their second single, "Go Now," was a cover of a little-known R&B song. It went to #1 in the U.K. and #10 in the U.S. Subsequent singles did not fare as well, and the group was living near poverty. Warwick tired of the situation and left; Laine followed months later. Laine would later join Paul McCartney's Wings. John Lodge, who'd played with Thomas in bands before the Moody Blues, replaced Laine. When Eric Burdon, who had collected a bag of letters in response to an ad he'd placed to find musicians for a new Animals lineup, invited Thomas to pore through them, the first he chose was from Justin Hayward. Hayward had worked in a number of bands and just recorded a solo single, produced by Lonnie Donegan, that went nowhere. That September he was hired.

The Moody Blues signed a new recording contract, with Deram, and after a few more unnoticed singles, at the behest of the label, the group was to record a rock version of Dvorak's Symphony No. 9. Were it not for their purchase of a Mellotron (a keyboard instrument that reproduces the sounds of violins, flutes, choirs, etc., through tapes) in 1967, the Moody Blues might never have been heard from again. But with the Mellotron (and, occasionally, actual orchestras) providing grandiose symphonic accompaniment, the Moodies' material had changed to cosmic lyrics set to heavily orchestrated pop tunes and extended suites. The week's studio time Deram granted them for the Dvorak project was used instead to record Days of Future Passed. With the Hayward-penned hit single "Tuesday Afternoon" (#24, 1968), the platinum Days of Future Passed went to #27 in the U.K. (where "Nights in White Satin" was the hit single) and #3 in the U.S., where it remained on the chart over two years. That LP—credited as having been recorded with a group of musicians billed as the (nonexistent) London Festival Orchestra—kept returning to the album chart as late as 1973. Hayward's "Nights in White Satin" has had an interesting chart history, hitting #19 in 1967 in the U.K., then returning to the chart two more times in the next dozen years (#9 U.K., 1972; #14 U.K., 1979). Here in the U.S., "Nights" was not a hit until 1972, when it reached #2.

Though the Moody Blues concentrated on writing musically ambitious and lyrically profound songs, they were still capable of turning out crowd-pleasing singles, such as "Question" (#21, 1970), "The Story in Your Eyes" (#23, 1971), "Isn't Life Strange?" (#29, 1972), "I'm Just a Singer (In a Rock and Roll Band)" (#12, 1973). Their albums of this period all went gold: In Search of the Lost Chord (#23, 1968), On the Threshold of a Dream (#20, 1969), To Our Children's Children's Children (#14, 1970), A Question of Balance (#3, 1970), Every Good Boy Deserves Favour (#2, 1971), and Seventh Sojourn (#1, 1972). In addition to their widely played hit singles, the Moody Blues also had an album-track catalogue of songs that received heavy exposure on FM radio: "The Story in Your Eyes," "Ride My See Saw," "Higher and Higher," and "Legend of a Mind." In 1969 the band established its own Threshold label, a Decca subsidiary.

After Seventh Sojourn, the Moody Blues took a lengthy sabbatical, during which time all five members pursued solo and collaborative projects. Graeme Edge recorded two albums with guitarist, keyboardist, and vocalist Adrian Gurvitz; Lodge and Hayward recorded Blue Jays, a sort of Moody Blues continuation, then put out records individually; Thomas issued From Mighty Oaks; and Pinder followed with The Promise. In the late Eighties Hayward's Classic Blue found him singing "MacArthur Park" and "Stairway to Heaven," among other hits, with backing by the London Symphony Orchestra. Of his non-Moody efforts, only Blue Jays was a Top Thirty album.

In 1978 the Moody Blues regrouped for the platinum Octave (#13) (which included "Steppin' in a Slide Zone," #39, 1978), though on a subsequent U.S. tour Pinder was replaced by ex-Refugee, ex-Yes keyboardist Patrick Moraz. Pinder has since continued to compose and record, although his releases have been rare. With Moraz, the band recorded Voyager, which hit #1 and boasted the hit singles "Gemini Dream" (#12) and "The Voice" (#15). Critically regarded as outmoded, the Moody Blues soldiered on. Except for 1983's Top Thirty single "Sitting at the Wheel," the Moody Blues were absent from the singles chart until "Your Wildest Dreams" (#9, 1986), a nostalgic song accompanied by a sentimental and at times humorously self-deprecating video. The album it came from, *The Other Side of Life,* went to #9, and two years later, "I Know You're Out There Somewhere" (#30, 1988), from *Sur la Mer* (#38, 1988) was another hit. *Keys of the Kingdom* (#94, 1991) proved the group's lowest-charting album of new material, yet the Moody Blues were able to mount a successful tour. Around that time, Moraz left the group. In 1992 the Moody Blues celebrated the silver anniversary of *Days of Future Passed* with a tour featuring a full orchestra. A show at Colorado's majestic Red Rocks amphitheater was recorded for an album and filmed for a video documentary that was later shown on PBS.

Van Morrison

**Born August 31, 1945, Belfast, Northern Ireland
1965—*Them* (Parrot); *Them Again* 1967—*Blowin' Your Mind* (Bang) 1968—*Astral Weeks* (Warner Bros.) 1970—*Moondance; His Band and the Street Choir* 1971—*Tupelo Honey* 1972—*St. Dominic's Preview* 1973—*Hard Nose the Highway* 1974—*It's Too Late to Stop Now; Veedon Fleece; T. B. Sheets* (Bang) 1977—*This Is Where I Came In; A Period of Transition* (Warner Bros.) 1978—*Wavelength* 1979—*Into the Music* 1980—*Common One* 1982—*Beautiful Vision* 1983—*Inarticulate Speech of the Heart* 1985—*A Sense of Wonder* (Mercury); *Live at the Grand Opera House, Belfast* 1986—*No Guru, No Method, No Teacher* 1987—*Poetic Champions Compose* 1989—*Avalon Sunset* 1990—*Enlightenment; The Best of Van Morrison* (Polydor) 1991—*Bang Masters* (Epic); *Hymns to the Silence* (Polydor) 1993—*The Best of Van Morrison vol. 2; Too Long In Exile* 1994—*A Night in San Francisco* 1995—*Days Like This.*
With the Chieftains: 1988—*Irish Heartbeat* (Mercury).**

Part Celtic bard, part soul singer, and part ecstatically scatting mystical visionary, Van Morrison is a painfully introverted figure who rarely gives interviews and is often at a loss to explain his own lyrics. In the studio, he can sing like a soul man getting the spirit; onstage, however, his brilliance can be undercut by whim or temper, and he has upon occasion alienated audiences by rushing through songs and remaining aloof between them. Nonetheless, his influence among rock singer/songwriters is unrivaled by any living artist besides that other prickly legend, Bob Dylan. Echoes of Morrison's rugged literateness and his gruff, feverishly emotive vocal style can be heard in latterday icons ranging from Bruce Springsteen to Elvis Costello; while the Irish artist's own restless muse has kept him prolific and engaging into the Nineties.

Van Morrison

Morrison's mother was a singer, and his father collected classic blues and jazz records. He learned guitar, saxophone, and harmonica while in school, and was playing with Belfast blues, jazz, and rock bands by his mid-teens. At 15, he quit school, joined an R&B band called the Monarchs and toured Europe with them as saxophonist. While he was in Germany, a film director offered Morrison a role in a movie as a jazz saxophonist. The project expired, and Morrison returned to Belfast and opened an R&B club in the Maritime Hotel. He recruited some friends to form Them, which became an immediate local sensation as the club's house band.

Them recorded two singles in late 1964: "Don't Start Crying Now" (a local hit) and Big Joe Williams' "Baby Please Don't Go" (which made the British Top Ten in early 1965). After the latter's success, they moved to London and hooked up with producer Bert Berns. They recorded Berns' "Here Comes the Night," which went to #2 in the U.K. and made Top Thirty in the U.S. Them's next two singles, "Gloria" (by Morrison) and "Mystic Eyes," were minor U.S. hits; "Gloria" was later covered by the Shadows of Knight (who took the song to #10 in 1966) and Patti Smith. Them's lineup underwent constant changes, and Berns brought in sessionmen, including Jimmy Page, for their albums. After a mostly unsuccessful U.S. tour in 1966, the group returned to England. Morrison disbanded Them, which soon reformed with Ken McDowell as vocalist.

Morrison, meanwhile, grew frustrated by music-business manipulations (Them had wrongly been given a rough-kids image by their company), stopped performing, and moved back to Belfast. Bert Berns (a.k.a. B. Russell) formed Bang Records in New York. He sent Morrison a plane ticket and an invitation to record four singles for his new label. One of them, "Brown Eyed

Girl," reached #10 in the U.S. in 1967. Morrison toured America, but was again disgruntled when Berns released the other singles-demos as *Blowin' Your Mind*.

After Berns died of a sudden heart attack in December 1967, Morrison undertook an East Coast tour and wrote material for his next album. Warner Bros. president Joe Smith signed him in early 1968, and Morrison went into a New York studio that summer with numerous jazz musicians. In 48 hours he cut one of rock's least classifiable, most enduring albums, *Astral Weeks*, the first manifestation of Morrison's Irish-romantic mysticism. Though most of its cuts were meandering and impressionistic, with folky guitars over jazzy rhythms, topped by Morrison's soul-styled vocals, critics raved; the album is still considered one of Morrison's richest, most powerful efforts.

His next album, *Moondance* (#29, 1970), traded the jazz-and-strings sound of *Astral Weeks* for a horn-section R&B bounce. The title tune and "Come Running" were chart singles, the latter in 1970 (#39), the former not until late 1977. The fittingly titled "Into the Mystic" became a minor hit for Johnny Rivers, while "Caravan" became an FM radio favorite. It was the first Morrison album to chart in the Top 100, and eventually went platinum. *His Band and the Street Choir* (#32, 1970) yielded two uptempo R&B-flavored Top Forty hits in "Domino" (#9, 1970) and "Blue Money" (#23, 1971). By this time, Morrison had moved to Marin County, California, and married a woman who called herself Janet Planet.

Tupelo Honey (#27, 1971) reflected his new domestic contentment. It yielded a hit in "Wild Night" (#28) and went gold, thanks to progressive FM radio, which latched on to the lyrical title tune (featuring Modern Jazz Quartet drummer Connie Kay). *St. Dominic's Preview* (#15, 1972) included the minor hit single "Jackie Wilson Said" (#61) and contained two extended journeys into the mystic: "Listen to the Lion" and "Almost Independence Day." In 1972, Morrison guested on the John Lee Hooker–Charlie Musselwhite album *Never Get Out of These Blues Alive*.

By the time of *Hard Nose the Highway* (#27, 1973), Morrison had formed the 11-piece Caledonia Soul Orchestra, which was featured on the live LP *It's Too Late to Stop Now*. But in 1973, Morrison suddenly divorced Janet Planet, disbanded the Caledonia Soul Orchestra, and returned to Belfast for the first time since 1966. There he began writing material for *Veedon Fleece* (#53, 1974).

Morrison took three years to produce a followup. He reportedly began four different album sessions (one with jazz-funk band the Crusaders), which were never completed. By 1976 he was living in California again. Late that year he appeared in the Band's farewell concert, *The Last Waltz*. Finally in 1977 came *A Period of Transition* (#43, 1977), which featured short jazz and R&B-oriented tunes and backup by pianist Mac "Dr. John"

Rebennack. For *Wavelength* (#28, 1978), Morrison took on concert promoter Bill Graham as manager (they split in 1981); the album sold fairly well. Still, Morrison's chronic stage fright continued to plague him. At a 1979 show at New York's Palladium, he stormed off the stage midset without a word and didn't return.

The more serene *Into the Music* (#43, 1979) implied that Morrison had become a born-again Christian, and *Common One* (#73, 1980) delved more into extended mysticism. *Beautiful Vision* (#44, 1982) was more varied and concise, and it generated, as usual, sizable critical acclaim and respectable sales. It included "Cleaning Windows," which contained references to such Morrison inspirations as Leadbelly, bluesmen Blind Lemon Jefferson, Sonny Terry, Brownie McGhee, and Muddy Waters, as well as Beat author Jack Kerouac and country singer Jimmie Rodgers. *Inarticulate Speech of the Heart* (#116, 1983) offered "special thanks" to L. Ron Hubbard, inventor of Scientology.

With *A Sense of Wonder* (#61, 1985), Morrison continued his spiritual journey and drew further on literary influences, incorporating the work of a favorite poet, William Blake's "The Price of Experience," on the track "Let the Slave." Meanwhile, Morrison rediscovered his ethnic roots and wanderlust, leaving his California home to travel nomadlike through Dublin, Belfast, and London. On *No Guru, No Method, No Teacher* (#70, 1986), the singer shared this sense of rebirth, while the album's title sneered at critics who had tried to pigeonhole his religious beliefs.

Morrison delved deeper into Celtic imagery with *Poetic Champions Compose* (#90, 1987) and collaborated with Ireland's best-loved traditional band, the Chieftains, on *Irish Heartbeat* (#102, 1988). *Avalon Sunset* (#91, 1989) contained "Whenever God Shines His Light on Me," a duet with Cliff Richard that became Morrison's first British Top Twenty single since his days with Them, and "Have I Told You Lately That I Love You," which in 1993 became a #5 hit for Rod Stewart.

Morrison entered the Nineties with the nostalgia-drenched *Enlightenment* (#62, 1990), on which he recalled first becoming acquainted with rock & roll and continued to explore the links between spiritual and romantic love. These themes carried over onto the similarly acclaimed double album *Hymns to the Silence* (#99, 1991), while on *Too Long in Exile* (#29, 1993), the singer brought things full circle, covering songs by some of his heroes—including Ray Charles and Sonny Boy Williamson—and duetting with John Lee Hooker on Them's "Gloria," with enough ardor to dispel any suspicions that age had mellowed him. Hooker, in fact, turned up as a surprise guest at some of Morrison's concerts in the early 1990s. Morrison's spirited 1993 performances in San Francisco, documented on *A Night in San Francisco*, were indicative of his renewed vigor onstage.

Morrissey: See the Smiths

The Motels

Formed 1972, Berkeley, California
Original lineup: Martha Davis (b. Jan. 15, 1951, Berkeley), voc.; Dean Chamberlain, gtr.; Richard D'Andrea, bass.
1976—(– Chamberlain; – D'Andrea; + Michael Goodroe, bass; + Marty Jourard, sax., kybds.; + Brian Glascock, drums; + Jeff Jourard, gtr.)
1979—*Motels* (Capitol) (– J. Jourard; + Tim McGovern, gtr.) 1980—*Careful* (– McGovern; + Guy Perry, gtr.) 1982—*All Four One* (+ Scott Thurston, gtr., kybds.) 1983—*Little Robbers* 1985—*Shock*
1990—*No Vacancy: The Best of the Motels.*
Martha Davis solo: 1987—*Policy* (Capitol).

The Motels were one of Los Angeles' original new-wave bands and one of its most respected, though it took them a long time to capitalize commercially on either point. After a number of personnel shakeups, the Motels had their first hit single, "Only the Lonely," and first hit album, *All Four One*, ten years after their formation.

Motels singer/songwriter Martha Davis started her first band in 1972. Having married at age 15, she was by then the mother of two daughters. Over four years, they went from the name Warfield Foxes to the Motels, from a joke to a serious venture, and from Berkeley to Los Angeles. Early members Dean Chamberlain (who went on to Code Blue) and Richard D'Andrea (who later played with Gary Valentine's the Know) left the group. The next version, with Motels Marty Jourard, Michael Goodroe, Brian Glascock (brother of late Jethro Tull bassist John Glascock), and Jourard's brother Jeff, was signed to Capitol and recorded *The Motels*. Tim McGovern, once of L.A. power-poppers the Pop, replaced Jourard for *Careful* and an early version of *All Four One*. Capitol rejected the LP, McGovern left the Motels (to reappear with the Burning Sensations), and the band rerecorded the songs with studio musicians.

The gambit paid off with "Only the Lonely" (#9, 1982). Their next album, the gold *Little Robbers*, contained another #9 pop hit, "Suddenly Last Summer." *Shock*, another Top Forty album, included "Shame" (#21, 1985). Davis then discovered she had cancer, which contributed to the group's disbanding. She released a solo album in 1987, after she recovered. It contained "Don't Tell Me the Time."

Mother Love Bone: See Pearl Jam

Mothers of Invention: See Frank Zappa

Mötley Crüe

Formed 1981, Los Angeles, California
Tommy Lee (b. Thomas Lee Bass, Oct. 3, 1962, Athens, Greece), drums; Mick Mars (b. Bob Deal, Apr. 3, 1956, Huntington, Ind.), gtr., voc.; Vince Neil (b. Vince Neil Wharton, ca. 1961, Hollywood, Calif.), voc.; Nikki Sixx (b. Frank Carlton Serafino Ferranno, Dec. 11, 1958, San Jose, Calif.), bass.
1982—*Too Fast for Love* (Elektra) 1983—*Shout at the Devil* 1985—*Theatre of Pain* 1987—*Girls, Girls, Girls* 1989—*Dr. Feelgood* 1991—*Decade of Decadence—'81–'91* 1992—(– V. Neil; + John Corabi [b. Apr. 26, 1959, Philadelphia, Pa.], voc.)
1994—*Mötley Crüe.*
Vince Neil solo: 1993—*Exposed* (Elektra).

Mötley Crüe has parlayed an image of fast-living, hard-driving postadolescent reprobates and fast, pummeling songs into platinum-level heavy-metal superstardom, topping the charts with *Dr. Feelgood* (#1, 1989) and coming close with *Theatre of Pain* (#6, 1985), *Girls, Girls, Girls* (#2, 1987), and a greatest-hits collection, *Decade of Decadence—'81–'91* (#2, 1991).

Nikki Sixx was a member of locally successful Los Angeles metal band London when he decided to form his own band. Tommy Lee came aboard as drummer, and they decided to call themselves Christmas. Guitarist Mick Mars was discovered through a classified ad reading "LOUD RUDE AGGRESSIVE GUITARIST AVAILABLE." That he used the same hair dye as Sixx cemented the relationship. Vocalist Vince Neil was plucked from a Cheap Trick cover band. Mars came up with the new, strangely accented name, inadvertently becoming father to a thousand umlauts. Their eponymous, independently released debut was picked up by Elektra and retitled *Too Fast for Love* (#77, 1983).

Shout at the Devil (#17, 1983) with its canny hints of Satanism followed, but the band did not catch on in a big way until *Theatre of Pain* (#6, 1985). Fueled by a cover of Brownsville Station's anthemic "Smokin' in the Boys Room" (#16, 1985) and "Home Sweet Home" (#89, 1985), considered to be the first "power ballad" played on MTV, the album sold over two million copies.

For all the album sales, Crüe was known as a live band, playing rock versions of a Vegas review, a leering embrace of all things hedonistic, with elaborate sets and lighting, revolving drum sets, pyrotechnics, and dancing girls. *Girls, Girls, Girls* (#2, 1987) and *Dr. Feelgood* (#1, 1989) continued their streak of platinum albums, selling two million and four million copies respectively. *Decade of Decadence '81–'91* (#2, 1991) included new material, such as their misguided cover of the Sex Pistols' "Anarchy in the U.K."

Mötley Crüe lived the rock & roll lifestyle to the fullest, with celebrity marriages—Tommy Lee to *Dy-*

nasty and *Melrose Place* star Heather Locklear in 1986 (they divorced in 1994) and Nikki Sixx to former Prince protégée Vanity in 1987—drugs, and scrapes with the law. Sixx spent over a year addicted to heroin. In 1986 Neil was convicted of vehicular manslaughter, the result of a 1984 drunken accident that killed Hanoi Rocks drummer Nicholas Dingley and seriously injured two others. He served 20 days in jail, performed 200 hours of community service, and was assessed $2.6 million in damages.

In 1992 Neil was replaced by John Corabi. He filed a $5 million wrongful termination suit, which was unresolved as of late 1994. He formed the Vince Neil Band, which includes ex–Billy Idol sidekick guitarist Steve Stevens, bassist Robbie Crane, drummer Vik Foxx, and guitarist Dave Marshall, and released *Exposed* (#13, 1993).

Motörhead

Formed 1975, England
Lemmy Kilmister (b. Ian Kilmister, Dec. 24, 1945, Stoke-on-Trent, Eng.), bass, voc.; Eddie Clark, gtr.; Phil "Philthy Animal" Taylor, (b. Sep. 21, 1954, Chesterfield, Eng.) drums.
1977—Motörhead (Chiswick, U.K.) 1979—Overkill (Bronze, U.K.); Bomber 1980—Ace of Spades (Mercury) 1981—No Sleep Till Hammersmith 1982—Iron Fist (– Clark; + Brian Robertson [b. Glasgow, Scot.], gtr.) 1983—Another Perfect Day (– Robertson; – Taylor; + Phil Campbell [b. May 7, 1961, Pontypridd, Wales], gtr.; + "Wurzel" [b. Oct. 23, 1949, Cheltenham, Eng.], gtr.; + Pete Gill, drums) 1984—No Remorse (Bronze) 1986—Orgasmatron (GWR/Profile) 1987—Rock 'N' Roll 1988—No Sleep at All (Enigma) 1990—The Birthday Party (GWR) 1991—1916 (WTG) (– Gill; + Taylor; – Taylor, + Mikkey Dee [b. Oct. 31, 1963, Olundby, Swed.], drums) 1993—March or Die 1994—Bastards (Motörhead/ZYX).

Known to produce no less than 126 decibels in its live shows, England's Motörhead is easily one of the world's loudest rock & roll bands. The heavy-metal group's raunchy leather-biker image underlines its fascination with violence, as do such album titles as *Overkill, Bomber,* and *Iron Fist.* Motörhead's hard-and-fast sound prefigured the thrash and speed-metal genres of the late Eighties and Nineties, and the group was cited as an influence by Guns n' Roses (which had Motörhead open its 1992 U.S. tour) and Metallica.

Bassist/vocalist Lemmy Kilmister, formerly with progressive British rockers Hawkwind [see entry], put together Motörhead in 1975, and the group released its self-titled debut album in 1977 in the middle of the punk boom. After establishing itself on the British chart with two subsequent albums, the band recorded *Ace of Spades,* its official American debut. Motörhead has yet to make a significant dent in the American chart but is a huge concert draw in the U.K. and has steadily built a cult following in the U.S.

With the balladic title track of *1916,* Motörhead began breaking out of its trademark bludgeoning sound; the trend continued on *Bastards* (Kilmister originally intended to call the group Bastard) with "Lost in the Ozone," and "Don't Let Daddy Kiss Me," a song about incest from a little girl's point of view.

Onetime Motörhead guitarist "Fast" Eddie Clarke went on to form Fastway with ex–Humble Pie Jerry Shirley. He was briefly replaced by ex–Thin Lizzy Brian Robertson, before Wurzel and Phil Campbell (who has also variously gone by the names Wizzo, Zoom, and Wizzo von Wizzo) settled the lineup through the Eighties.

The Motors

Formed 1977, England
Nick Garvey, voc., gtr., bass; Andy McMasters, voc., kybds., bass; Bram Tchaikovsky (b. Peter Bramall), gtr., voc.; Ricky Slaughter, drums, voc.
1977—The Motors I (Virgin) 1978—Approved by the Motors (– Tchaikovsky; – Slaughter) 1980—Tenement Steps.

The Motors' two songwriters, Nick Garvey and Andy McMasters, met in Ducks Deluxe [see entry], a British pub-rock band. Garvey joined Ducks in its early stages in December 1972, after working as road manager for the Flamin' Groovies. The Scottish McMasters had been involved in rock since the mid-Sixties, playing for a while with the Stoics, which included Frankie Miller. He'd also written a successful record of children's songs. McMasters joined Ducks just before its second and final record, *Taxi to the Terminal Zone.* After the group broke up, Garvey switched from bass to guitar and formed the Snakes, while McMasters worked for a music publisher.

In early 1977 the two began collaborating on songs, soon recruiting ex-Snakes drummer Ricky Slaughter and guitarist Bram Tchaikovsky. Their debut, highlighted by Garvey and McMasters' dual lead vocals, boasted the British hit single "Dancing the Night Away." After the British success of "Airport" (from *Approved by the Motors*), Garvey and McMasters decided to fire the rest of the band and go on as a studio twosome with revolving musicians. Tchaikovsky went on to record four albums; Garvey produced his debut, 1979's *Strange Man, Changed Man,* which contained the Top Forty hit "Girl of My Dreams." The two Motors decided to forgo touring, and they released *Tenement Steps* (produced by Jimmy Iovine) in 1980. The LP featured the minor hit "Love and Loneliness," with Rockpile's Terry Williams on drums and ex-Man Martin Ace on bass.

Mott the Hoople

Formed 1968, Hereford, England
Stan Tippens (b. Eng.), lead voc.; Mick Ralphs
(b. May 31, 1944, Hereford), gtr., voc.; Overend Pete
Watts (b. May 13, 1947, Birmingham, Eng.), bass;
Dale "Buffin" Griffin (b. Oct. 24, 1948, Ross-on-Wye,
Eng.), drums; Verden Allen (b. May 26, 1944, Here-
ford), organ.
1969—(– Tippens; + Ian Hunter [b. June 3, 1946,
Shrewsbury, Eng.], piano, gtr., lead voc.) *Mott the
Hoople* (Atlantic) 1970—*Mad Shadows* 1971—
Wildlife 1972—*Brain Capers*; *Rock 'n' Roll Queen*;
All the Young Dudes (Columbia) 1973—(– Allen)
Mott (– Ralphs; + Morgan Fisher, kybds.; + Ariel
Bender, a.k.a. Luther James Grosvenor [b. Dec. 23,
1949, Evesham, Eng.], gtr.) 1974—*The Hoople*;
Mott the Hoople Live (– Bender; + Mick Ronson
[b. ca. 1946, Hull, Eng.; d. April 30, 1993, London,
Eng.], gtr.; – Hunter; – Ronson) 1975—(Name
changed to Mott: + Ray Major, gtr.; + Nigel Ben-
jamin, voc.) *Drive On* 1976—*Shouting and Point-
ing*; *Greatest Hits* 1993—*The Ballad of Mott: A
Retrospective* 1994—*Backsliding Fearlessly: The
Early Years* (Rhino).
British Lions (Watts; Griffin; Fisher; Major; + John
Fiddler, voc.): 1978—*British Lions* (RSO).

Mott the Hoople started out as an uneven hard-rock Dylanesque curiosity but ended as a glitter-age group. Mott
also gave rise to the solo career of songwriter Ian Hunter.
The group began in the late Sixties, when Mick Ralphs,
Verden Allen, Overend Pete Watts, and Dale Griffin
began playing around Hereford, England, in a group
called Silence. They got a record contract in early 1969
and went to London with vocalist Stan Tippens to record
under producer Guy Stevens, who renamed the band
Mott the Hoople after a 1967 novel by Willard Manus.
Tippens was replaced by Ian Hunter [see entry] in July.
(Tippens subsequently became the band's road manager
and later worked for the Pretenders.)

The group recorded its eponymous debut album in
August 1969, and it garnered much curious attention for
Hunter's Dylanlike rasp and the odd choice of covers,
such as Sonny Bono's "Laugh at Me." *Mad Shadows* was
moodier and poorly received, and the country-oriented
Wildlife was the quintet's worst seller yet. The latter also
featured a cover of Melanie's "Lay Down" and nine minutes of a live Little Richard interpretation (included because the band had spent $4,000 to tape a scrapped
concert album).

Mott became a big live attraction in England, even
though its records didn't sell. In July 1971 the group
caused a mini-riot at London's Albert Hall, which was a
factor in the hall management's decision to ban rock
completely. After the release of *Brain Capers*, the group
was ready to disband, when David Bowie stepped in to
give it a focused glam-rock image and a breakthrough
single.

He first offered "Suffragette City," but the band
wanted "Drive In Saturday," which Bowie refused to give
up. Luckily Mott accepted his offer of "All the Young
Dudes." Bowie produced the LP of the same name, and
Mott had a top British single with "Dudes." The song became a signature piece for glitter rock and a gay anthem
(something it took the all-straight band a while to get
used to). "All the Young Dudes" went to #37 in the U.S.

The group's followup, 1973's *Mott,* was its master-
piece—a self-produced effort, with the British hit singles
"Honaloochie Boogie" and "All the Way from Memphis."
It was also a concept album about the fight for, and mis-
trust of, success, highlighted by the autobiographical
"Ballad of Mott the Hoople." In June of 1974, Hunter's
Diary of a Rock Star was published in England.

Despite its success, the band began to fall apart.
Allen left because the group rarely recorded his songs.
Ralphs quit because he was upset by Allen's leaving and
irked that one of his songs for Mott, "Can't Get Enough,"
was beyond the singing range of either himself or
Hunter. (The song was a Top Five hit the following year
for Ralphs' next band, Bad Company [see entry].) Hunter
and company filled the guitar gap with Luther
Grosvenor—formerly with Spooky Tooth and Stealers
Wheel—who changed his name to Ariel Bender upon
joining. The *Live* album was taken from shows in London
in November 1973 and in New York in May 1974.

The band had just begun to sell well in the States
when another falling out occurred. Late in 1974 Mick
Ronson [see entry] replaced Bender. By the end of the
year, Hunter and Ronson had split together, and Mott the
Hoople was no more. Hunter had a solo deal with Columbia, but his first tour, billed as the Hunter-Ronson
Band, was a disaster, with half-filled houses and a disillusioned band. Meanwhile, Watts, Griffin, and Fisher carried on as Mott, joined by Ray Major and Nigel Benjamin.
They released two undistinguished albums, after which
Benjamin left, and the band fell apart. Undaunted, they
added a new lead singer, ex–Medicine Head John Fiddler, and continued for two years under the name British
Lion. After Allen had left Mott back in 1973, he formed
Cheeks with future Pretenders James Honeyman-Scott
and Martin Chambers. The group toured through 1976
but never recorded.

Bob Mould: See Hüsker Dü

Mountain

Formed 1969, New York City, New York
Felix Pappalardi (b. 1939, Bronx, N.Y.; d. Apr. 17,
1983, New York City), bass, voc.; Leslie West

(b. Leslie Weinstein, Oct. 22, 1945, Queens, N.Y.), gtr., voc.; N.D. Smart, drums
1969—*Leslie West—Mountain* (Leslie West solo) (Windfall) 1970—(– Smart; + Corky Laing [b. Apr. 26, 1948, Montreal, Can.], drums; + Steve Knight, organ) *Mountain Climbing* 1971—*Nantucket Sleighride; Flowers of Evil* 1972—*Mountain Live (The Road Goes On Forever)* (group disbands) 1973—*Best of Mountain* (Columbia) 1974—(Group re-forms: West; Pappalardi; + Alan Schwartzberg, drums; + Bob Mann, kybds.) *Twin Peaks* (– Schwartzberg; – Mann; + Laing); *Avalanche* (group disbands) 1985—(Group re-forms: West; Laing; + Mark Clarke, bass) 1986—*Go for Your Life* (Scotti Bros.) 1995—*Over the Top* (Columbia Legacy).
Leslie West solo: 1975—*The Great Fatsby* (Phantom) 1994—*Dodgin' the Dirt* (Blues Bureau International).

Cream pioneered the power-trio format; Mountain capitalized on it. The trio was formed in 1969 by Cream's producer, Felix Pappalardi, and 250-pound ex-Vagrant guitarist Leslie West.

The Vagrants had been Long Island legends but never could expand their appeal as had local predecessors the Young Rascals. Although the release of the Vagrants' single "Respect" preceded Aretha Franklin's, the group was buried when Franklin's rendition came out soon after. Atco turned to Pappalardi to record the group's fourth single, but it was another flop. When the fifth attempt proved no better, the band broke up.

West set to recording a solo album, produced by Pappalardi. The result, *Leslie West—Mountain,* inspired the two to form Mountain, with N. D. Smart held over from the *Mountain* LP, and the addition of Steve Knight. Mountain proved akin to a cruder, louder version of Cream. Propelled by the momentum of West's solo album and Pappalardi's production credentials, success was nearly instantaneous. The band's fourth live performance was at the Woodstock festival. Smart was then replaced by Corky Laing. Its debut album, *Mountain Climbing* (#17, 1970), went gold and yielded the #21 hit "Mississippi Queen."

Nantucket Sleighride earned the group another gold album in 1971. But the formula began to wear thin, and after one more studio album and a live LP, Pappalardi decided to return to production. Knight disappeared along the way as well, and ex-Cream bassist Jack Bruce joined what was thereafter known as West, Bruce and Laing. That group recorded three LPs for Columbia. Nineteen seventy-two's *Why Dontcha* and 1973's *Whatever Turns You On* were moderately successful. After the second LP, the group disbanded; a live LP, *Live 'n' Kickin',* followed.

In the ensuing years, West and Laing periodically resurrected the Mountain moniker, sometimes with Pappalardi (who'd suffered hearing loss from the group's thundering volume and had to semiretire from live work), sometimes not. They have also appeared in the New York metropolitan area billed as the New Mountain. West has also performed with his group, the Leslie West Band. In 1982 Laing formed the Mix, and from 1986 to 1989, he led a blues band that featured guest stars Mick Taylor and Lester Chambers. Since 1989 Laing has been vice president of A&R for PolyGram Records (Canada).

In 1983 Pappalardi was shot dead by his wife and songwriting collaborator, Gail Collins. Two years later West, Laing, and bassist Mark Clarke issued *Go for Your Life,* which featured concise hard-rocking numbers and a noticeably svelte (well, maybe not svelte) West. The guitarist pops up from time to time on shock jock Howard Stern's radio show. Mountain's silver-anniversary retrospective, *Over the Top,* was released in 1995.

The Move/Roy Wood

Formed 1966, Birmingham, England
Roy Wood (b. Ulysses Adrian Wood, Nov. 8, 1946, Birmingham), gtr., voc.; Bev Bevan (b. Nov. 25, 1944, Birmingham), drums, voc.; Carl Wayne (b. Aug. 18, 1944, Moseley, Eng.), voc.; Trevor Burton (b. Mar. 9, 1944, Aston, Eng.), gtr., voc.; Chris "Ace" Kefford (b. Dec. 10, 1946, Moseley, Eng.), bass, voc.
1968—*The Move* (Regal Zonophone, U.K.) (– Kefford; Burton switches to bass) 1969—(– Burton; + Rick Price [b. June 10, 1944, Birmingham], bass, voc.) 1970—*Shazam* (A&M) (– Wayne; + Jeff Lynne [b. Dec. 30, 1947, Birmingham], gtr., kybds., voc.) 1971—*Looking On* (Capitol) (– Price); *Message from the Country* 1972—(Group disbands, becoming Electric Light Orchestra) *Split Ends* (United Artists) 1974—*The Best of the Move* (A&M) 1979—*Shines On.*
Roy Wood solo: 1973—*Boulders* (United Artists); *Wizzard's Brew* (Harvest) 1974—*See My Baby Jive; Introducing Eddie and the Falcons* (Warner Bros.) 1975—*Mustard* (Jet) 1977—*Super Active Wizzo* (Warner Bros.) 1979—*On the Road Again.*

The Move's half-ironic pop made the group popular in Britain in the late Sixties. But it was virtually unknown in America until its final days, when its energies were concentrated on a transformation into the Electric Light Orchestra [see entry]. With Roy Wood's songwriting, the Move was a remarkably versatile group, sending pop singles to the top of the English chart while its albums featured extended forays into all manner of folk rock, heavy metal, and psychedelia.

The Move started in 1966, when five of Birmingham's top musicians left their respective cover bands for a greater challenge: Wood from Mike Sheridan and the

Nightriders; Trevor Burton from the Mayfair Set; and Carl Wayne, Bev Bevan, and Ace Kefford from Carl Wayne and the Vikings. Wood's compositions acknowledged British trends, notably the psychedelic movement, as well as classical music: The band's debut single, "Night of Fear," was based on the *1812 Overture*; it hit #2 on the U.K. chart in early 1967.

With the aid of Tony Secunda's crafty management, the Move achieved almost instant notoriety. Its stage act climaxed with ax destruction of television sets and automobiles, and a publicity mailing for a 1967 45, "Flowers in the Rain," depicted Prime Minister Harold Wilson in bed with his secretary, resulting in a lawsuit and the band's loss of royalties, which would have been considerable: The single reached #2 on the British chart.

Even within the group, the Move's image was divided. Carl Wayne was an aspiring balladeer, who eventually left the group for a cabaret and TV career; Trevor Burton and Chris Kefford were rock & rollers. Kefford quit first, not to be heard from again. Burton followed in 1969, upset by the implications of the Move's first and only English #1, the lush "Blackberry Way." He stayed active for a while as a member of the Uglys (with future ELO member Richard Tandy), the Balls (with Steve Gibbons and former Moody Blue Denny Laine, later of Wings), and in the late Seventies, the Steve Gibbons Band.

With Rick Price on bass, the Move recorded *Shazam*, six cuts in six different styles interspersed with man-on-the-street interviews. The album was calculated to combat the group's British bubblegum image. The British group Amen Corner turned the opening track, "Hello Susie," into a Top Five U.K. hit in mid-1969. Soon after *Shazam*'s release, Wayne left. His place was taken by Jeff Lynne, who had replaced Wood in the Nightriders as they were renamed the Idle Race. (The Idle Race enjoyed modest British popularity, due in part to the Wood composition "Here We Go Round the Lemon Tree.") After 1971's *Looking On*, which included the Move's sixth Top Ten British hit, a throbbingly heavy number titled "Brontosaurus," the band announced a planned metamorphosis into the Electric Light Orchestra, incorporating classical-music instrumentation such as cello and violin.

But there were to be more Move records: an adventurous LP, *Message from the Country*, and a series of commercial singles (collected on *Split Ends*). Meantime, Price had left the band; he had become superfluous once the group abandoned the stage. While the Move put out its last contract-fulfilling singles in 1971 and 1972 (including Lynne's rousing "Do Ya," a minor hit for the Move, later a much greater one for ELO), the recording of the first Electric Light Orchestra album was under way. On its release in summer 1972, the Move was finished. No sooner had ELO officially begun, however, than Wood quit, abandoning classical-rock for Fifties-influenced rock & roll. In the Seventies and Eighties he released al-

bums on his own and with his group Wizzard. Although little known in the U.S., he continued to have success at home: two Phil Spector–esque singles, "See My Baby Jive" and "Angel Fingers," topped the chart there in 1973.

Alison Moyet/Yaz

Born Genevieve Alison-Jane Moyet, June 18, 1961, Basildon, Essex, England
With Yaz (Moyet, voc.; Vince Clarke [b. July 3, 1960, South Woodford, Eng.], kybds.): 1982—*Upstairs at Eric's* (Sire)   1983—*You and Me Both.*
Alison Moyet solo: 1984—*Alf* (Columbia)   1987—*Raindancing*   1991—*Hoodoo*   1993—*Essex.*

Alison Moyet rose to fame in her native England in the early Eighties as half of the short-lived but influential techno-pop duo Yazoo (known as Yaz in the U.S.). While her partner, ex–Depeche Mode songwriter Vince Clarke, crafted electronic-based arrangements, cowriter Moyet's earthy, soulful alto lent heart to the material—as Annie Lennox's mezzo did to Eurythmics' music. Unlike Eurythmics, Yaz didn't enjoy commercial success in the U.S., though the duo's sultry, rhythmically compelling style—and particularly Moyet's voice—was admired by fans of progressive pop. When Yaz split up after *You and Me Both*, Clarke went on to form the Assembly, and later, Erasure [see entry]. Moyet, meanwhile, embarked on a solo career that garnered more widespread recognition in the U.K. than it did stateside.

As a teenager in the late Seventies Moyet was drawn to punk's energy but soon realized that her warm voice was better suited to R&B. She sang with a couple of pub bands before hooking up with Clarke. After Yaz disbanded, the singer continued offsetting synth-laden orchestration with a sensuous, bluesy vocal technique. Her solo debut, *Alf*, sold over a million copies in England alone and went Top Ten in several other countries. Nineteen-eighty-seven's *Raindancing* was also well received by fans, entering the British charts at #2.

Moyet was not satisfied with the production, promotion, or marketing of either album. After taking a few years off, the singer rebounded in 1991 with *Hoodoo*. A denser, more stylistically diverse album—and to Moyet and critics, more successful—it sold fewer copies than any of her previous efforts. *Essex* wasn't the commercial breakthrough, either, that Moyet may have hoped for, but the album did garner some very favorable reviews.

MTV/VH-1

Since it was first launched on August 1, 1981, MTV (Music TeleVision) has continued to play music video clips—song-length promotional films—(eventually mixed with other pop-culture programming) 24 hours a day, seven days a week, over nationwide cable television, with demographically diverse video jockeys, or VJs, introducing the music videos. Aimed at a 12-to-24-year-old audience that had grown up on rock music, television, and video games, MTV became, in effect, America's biggest rock radio station, setting trends, shaping tastes, and selling records (and perhaps videos) much the way that regional radio stations had in the past. It boosted record sales for artists it played (while no doubt lowering the chances of less "videogenic" artists) and is widely credited for rescuing the industry from a severe post-disco recession.

MTV was revolutionary. It not only revolutionized virtually every aspect of the music business, from promotion to concert tours, but changed the way listeners/viewers related to music and to the artists. For the first time, rock music—the everpresent "soundtrack" to adolescent life—also had a constant visual component. There had been early "visual jukeboxes"— the Panoram Soundies in the late Forties and Scopitones in the late Fifties and early Sixties. While some early rock acts made impressive and in some cases even conceptual short promotional clips for their records, the devices were never circulated widely enough to be considered a commercial force. While it is impossible to quantify the extent of video's contribution to an artist's success, it's equally impossible to imagine the work of an artist such as Madonna, Cyndi Lauper, or Michael Jackson outside the context of video. Such recent developments as the resurgence in elaborately choreographed live performances probably would not have occurred without video. It gave artists more direct and lasting control of their images and the public's perceptions of them than ever before. While some established artists fell by the wayside, others, such as ZZ Top, Robert Palmer, and Tina Turner, experienced wide-scale career revivals that perhaps would not have occurred without video. Through its merging of the visual language of advertising with the emotional power of music, MTV sold not only records but a whole new way of hearing and seeing.

Although the network's first clip was the prescient Buggles' "Video Killed the Radio Star," it didn't accomplish that fact overnight. In fact, MTV's early playlist was dominated by the sort of bands being played on album-oriented rock radio (Journey, REO Speedwagon), and the channel was often accused of racism. But MTV play also generated record sales for such visually appealing unknowns as British disco rockers Duran Duran—first of the so-called "video bands," so named because their success seemed unlikely without MTV and/or they were so visually appealing. The turning point didn't come until the spring of 1983 when Michael Jackson exploited MTV through his sensational videos for "Billie Jean" and "Beat It." These two clips not only broke MTV's unofficial color barrier, but symbiotically helped Jackson's *Thriller* album set new sales records and elevated the status of

MTV and music videos themselves. While earlier videos had gone beyond the straight performance clip, Michael Jackson's expensively produced, and in the case of "Beat It," lavishly choreographed works functioned as, and had the same production values as, a small musical. After Jackson, MTV was here to stay, and a rapidly burgeoning new industry was born. "Beat It" even spawned a music video subindustry of dancers and choreographers (two of whom, Toni Basil and Paula Abdul, would become MTV stars themselves).

Music videos, which early on had largely been simple performance clips of bands lip synching their songs, quickly grew in stylistic sophistication: Special effects got wilder, camera angles odder, rhythmic edits faster, imagery (much of it recycled from foreign films and commercials) more provocative. Often as not, alluring women were used gratuitously in an update of the hoary "sex sells" advertising maxim, and MTV was constantly accused of the sexist exploitation of women.

Heavy-metal videos, playing off the genre's larger-than-life trappings, were particular offenders. In the Eighties, MTV continued to play such videos frequently ("in heavy rotation," as MTV put it)—going beyond AOR radio to keep metal commercially viable, even helping to mainstream it. In fact, MTV's first genre-specific video show was *Headbanger's Ball*, for metalheads.

By the mid-Eighties MTV was programming more than music videos; its first venture into traditional TV programming, the game show *Remote Control*, was a hit, as was *Yo! MTV Raps*, which played a key role in popularizing rap in the late Eighties. The Nineties brought the hugely successful *Beavis and Butt-head*—two animated, moronic miscreants who poked nasty fun at MTV's videos and parodied its white-male-teen audience. MTV's news department was widely credited with revolutionizing political coverage and even helping elect President Bill Clinton, with its "Choose or Lose" reports in the 1992 campaign. By that time, MTV had gone global, with affiliate networks in Europe, Asia, Australia, and South America.

In 1985 MTV launched a sister channel, VH-1 ("Video Hits One"), playing "adult contemporary" soft-rock videos for an audience older than MTV's. MTV's success also inspired the Eighties launch of such other cable channels as Black Entertainment Television, the Nashville Network, Country Music Television, and "The Box"—a true video jukebox launched by former MTV exec Les Garland, which charged viewers to play each of their requested videos.

Mudhoney

Formed 1988, Seattle, Washington
Mark Arm (b. Feb. 21, 1962, Calif.), voc, gtr.; Dan Peters (b. Aug. 18, 1967, Seattle), drums; Steve Turner

(b. Mar. 28, 1965, Houston, Tex.), gtr.; Matt Lukin
(b. Aug. 16, 1964, Aberdeen, Wash.), bass.
1988—*Superfuzz Bigmuff* EP (Sub Pop)   **1989**—
Mudhoney   **1990**—*Boiled Beef & Rotting Teeth*
1991—*Every Good Boy Deserves Fudge*   **1992**—
Piece of Cake (Reprise)   **1993**—*Blinding Sun* EP;
Five Dollar Bob's Mock Cooter Stew EP   **1995**—*My
Brother the Cow.*

Mudhoney is one of the leading players in the early-
Nineties Seattle scene. Named for a Russ Meyer film, the
band formed after Mark Arm and Steve Turner left Green
River, the prototypical Northwest-sound band whose
members also went on to form Mother Love Bone and
Pearl Jam. They joined with Matt Lukin, who had been
fired by sludge progenitors the Melvins, and Dan Peters,
who briefly played with Nirvana and the Screaming
Trees. With their big, distorted, guitar sound (their debut
was named after an effects pedal), Seventies hard-rock
homages, and twisted, ironic take on rockism, Mudhoney's early records defined grunge. Their "Touch Me
I'm Sick" single was parodied as "Touch Me I'm Dick" in
the movie *Singles,* and the Matt Dillon character in that
film was rumored to be modeled after Arm.

Before Nirvana came along, Mudhoney was Sub
Pop's biggest-selling band. The group was especially
popular in England, where it first toured with Sonic
Youth in 1989 and was supported by influential DJ John
Peel. The members are faithful to the indie aesthetic,
recording *Every Good Boy Deserves Fudge* and *Piece of
Cake* at Conrad Uno's Egg Studio (first on eight-track,
then progressing to 16) and releasing numerous one-off
projects, including a 1989 single where they and Sonic
Youth covered each other and a similar 1994 single with
Texas singer/songwriter Jimmie Dale Gilmore. Financial
problems at Sub Pop drove the quartet to a major label.
Mudhoney refused to be serious on *Piece of Cake*; one
track featured Lukin making fart sounds.

Geoff and Maria Muldaur

Geoff Muldaur, born circa 1945; Maria Muldaur,
born Maria Grazia Rosa Domenica d'Amato, September 12, 1943, New York City, New York
Geoff Muldaur solo: **1964**—*Geoff Muldaur* (Prestige)
1965—*Sleepy Man Blues*   **1975**—*Is Having a Won-
derful Time* (Reprise)   **1976**—*Motion*   **1978**—*Geoff
Muldaur and Amos Garrett* (Flying Fish)   **1979**—
Blues Boy.
Maria Muldaur solo: **1972**—*Mud Acres* (Rounder)
1973—*Maria Muldaur* (Reprise)   **1974**—*Waitress in
the Donut Shop*   **1976**—*Sweet Harmony*   **1978**—
Southern Winds (Warner Bros.)   **1979**—*Open Your
Eyes*   **1980**—*Gospel Nights* (Takoma)   **1982**—
There Is a Love (Myrrh)   **1983**—*Sweet and Low*
(Tudor; Spindrift)   **1985**—*Transbluecency* (Uptown)

1991—*On the Sunny Side* (Music for Little People)
1993—*Louisiana Love Call* (Black Top).
Geoff and Maria Muldaur: **1969**—*Pottery Pie*
(Reprise)   **1972**—*Sweet Potatoes* (Warner Bros.).

The Muldaurs, who were married in the mid-Sixties and
divorced in 1972, both graduated from the early-Sixties
folk scene, Geoff with the Jim Kweskin Jug Band [see
entry], Maria with the Even Dozen Jug Band (which included John Sebastian, Stefan Grossman, Steve Katz,
and Joshua Rifkin) and the Kweskin band. They have
recorded solo and together, and Maria's has been by far
the most commercially successful career.

The two married while they were both with the Jim
Kweskin Jug Band. Geoff Muldaur had made a couple of
rather obscure albums that demonstrated his attraction to
folk blues, vintage jazz, gospel, and country music. Maria
D'Amato, in the meantime, had grown up in Greenwich
Village, listening to blues and big-band music. In high
school she formed an all-girl Everly Brothers–inspired
group, the Cameos, and then the Cashmeres, who were offered a recording contract that her mother forbade her to
sign because Maria was still a minor. She gravitated to the
Village folk scene with the Even Dozen Jug Band, then
joined Kweskin, where she sang the blues and Leiber and
Stoller—and married Geoff.

Their two duo LPs were eclectic and folksy to the
point of sounding homemade ("Produced by Nobody"
proclaimed the *Sweet Potatoes* sleeve), and both featured the guitar of Amos Garrett, with whom both Muldaurs would remain associated. In 1973 Geoff moved to
Woodstock and worked with Paul Butterfield's Better
Days band. Maria also took part in the soundtrack to
Steelyard Blues with Butterfield, Nick Gravenites, and
Mike Bloomfield.

Maria began her own career in 1973 with her enormously successful debut LP, which featured a wide
range of material by Dolly Parton, Dan Hicks, Dr. John,
Kate McGarrigle, and Wendy Waldman. "Midnight at the
Oasis" was a Top Ten single from the album, and the LP
eventually sold gold. Her second album featured horn
arrangements by Benny Carter and contained the hit
"I'm a Woman" (#12, 1975). The failure of her third album
to sell well, despite continuing critical acclaim, left her
disillusioned. Geoff, in the meantime, released elaborately produced solo albums on Reprise and folksier ones
on Flying Fish. Maria continued to record solo, albeit
more and more sporadically. In 1978 she guested on
Elvin Bishop's *Hog Heaven* LP. By 1980 she was a born-
again Christian, and within a year had released a gospel
album.

Through the remainder of the Eighties, Maria
recorded in a range of styles. *Transbluecency* was a critically lauded pop-jazz effort, while *Louisiana Love Call*
featured Amos Garrett as well as Charles and Aaron

Neville, Dr. John, and other New Orleans–based musicians. *On the Sunny Side* is a children's record. Maria has also acted (*Pump Boys and Dinettes; The Pirates of Penzance*).

Maria and Geoff's daughter, Jenni Muldaur, released her eponymously titled solo album, on which Geoff appears, in 1993.

Mungo Jerry

Formed 1969, London, England
Ray Dorset (b. Mar. 21, 1946, Ashford, Eng.), gtr., voc.; Colin Earl (b. May 6, 1942, Hampton Ct., Eng.), piano; Paul King (b. Jan. 9, 1948, Dagenham, Eng.), banjo, gtr., jug; Mike Cole, string bass.
1970—*Mungo Jerry* (Janus); *Memoirs of a Stockbroker; In the Summertime* (Pye)   1975—*Mungo Jerry* 1978—*Ray Dorset and Mungo Jerry* (Polydor).

Mungo Jerry was a British quartet of skiffle revivalists (skiffle was roughly the English equivalent of jug band music) that had a novelty hit in 1970 with "In the Summertime," a #3 single (#1 in England) that earned the group a gold record in the U.S and eventually sold six million copies worldwide.

Before 1970, the band had been known as the Good Earth, and if the name change helped it achieve its hit, it never did the trick again in the U.S. However, Mungo Jerry did have an impressive list of Top Forty successes in Britain: "Baby Jump," "Alright, Alright," "You Don't Have to Be in the Army to Fight the War," "Lady Rose," "Open Up," "Wild Love," and "Longlegged Woman Dressed in Black."

Michael Martin Murphey

Born March 14, 1945, Dallas, Texas
1972—*Geronimo's Cadillac* (A&M)   1973—*Cosmic Cowboy Souvenir*   1974—*Michael Murphey* (Epic) 1975—*Blue Sky Night Thunder; Swans Against the Sun*   1976—*Flowing Free Forever*   1978—*Lone Wolf*   1979—*Peaks, Valleys, Honky-Tonks and Alleys*   1982—*Michael Martin Murphey* (Liberty) 1983—*The Heart Never Lies*   1989—*Land of Enchantment* (Warner Bros.)   1990—*Cowboys Songs I* 1991—*Cowboy Christmas—Cowboy Songs II* 1992—*Cowboy Songs III—Rhymes of the Renegades*.

One of the original "cosmic cowboys" of country rock, Michael Murphey started out as one of the leaders of the late-Sixties to mid-Seventies Austin, Texas, "progressive country" music scene. Before he became a musician, Murphey had been intent on joining the Southern Baptist ministry, and had studied Greek at North Texas State University and creative writing at UCLA. After working as a staff songwriter at Screen Gems (the Monkees'

"What Am I Doing Hangin' 'Round"), for five years in the late Sixties and a brief stint with the Lewis and Clarke Expedition, Murphey began performing solo. Producer Bob Johnston signed him to A&M and produced Murphey's debut LP in Nashville.

The title tune of his debut made #37 on the singles chart and was covered by Hoyt Axton, Cher, Claire Hamill, and others. He smoothed out his style for his biggest hit, 1975's "Wildfire" (#3); others included "Carolina in the Pines" (#21, 1975) and "Renegade" (#39, 1976). In 1980 his "Cherokee Fiddle" was featured on the *Urban Cowboy* soundtrack; he also appeared in the film *Take This Job and Shove It*. Also that year Murphey wrote the screenplay for and appeared in *Hard Country*.

In 1982 he had a Top Twenty pop hit with "What's Forever For?" (#1 C&W). His other country hits include "Still Taking Chances" (#3 C&W, 1982), "Love Affairs" (#11 C&W, 1983), "Don't Count the Rainy Days" (#9 C&W, 1983), "Will It Be Love by Morning" (#7 C&W, 1984), "What She Wants" (#8 C&W, 1984), "Carolina in the Pines" (#9 C&W, 1985), "A Face in the Crowd" (a duet with Holly Dunn) (#4 C&W, 1987), "A Long Line of Love" (#1 C&W, 1987), "I'm Gonna Miss You, Girl" (#3 C&W, 1987), "Talkin' to the Wrong Man" (a duet with Murphey's son, Ryan) (#4 C&W, 1988), "From the Word Go" (#3 C&W, 1988), and "Never Givin' Up On Love" (#9 C&W, 1989), from the film *Pink Cadillac*. Among the artists who have covered Murphey's material are John Denver ("Boy from the Country"), the Nitty Gritty Dirt Band ("Cosmic Cowboy"), Kenny Rogers ("Ballad of Calico"), and Jerry Jeff Walker ("Backslider's Wine"). He continues to tour approximately 150 days a year.

Elliott Murphy

Born March 16, 1949, Garden City, New York
1973—*Aquashow* (Polydor)   1974—*Lost Generation* (RCA)   1976—*Night Lights*   1977—*Just a Story from America* (Columbia)   1981—*Affairs* (Courtesan)   1982—*Murph the Surf*   1984—*Party Girls/Broken Poets* (WEA International)   1985— *Après le Deluge* (EMIS)   1987—*Milwaukee* (New Rose)   1988—*Change Will Come*   1989—*Live Hot Point*   1990—*12*   1991—*If Poets Were King* EP 1992—*Diamonds by the Yard* (Razor & Tie); Paris/New York* (New Rose)   1993—*Unreal City* (Razor & Tie).

Singer/songwriter Elliott Murphy's 1973 debut was hailed as "the best Dylan since 1968," and over the years he has developed a following both in the U.S. and in Europe, where he now lives. Murphy was born and raised in Garden City, an upper-middle-class Long Island suburb. His father owned the Aqua Show in Queens, near the World's Fair grounds, where big-band acts like Duke Ellington would perform. He began playing guitar at age

12, and by age 13 he had formed his first band. In 1966 his group, the Rapscallions, won a New York State battle of the bands.

Murphy then moved to Europe, where he sang in the streets and, in 1971, had a bit part in Fellini's *Roma*. With his brother Matthew he traveled Europe, busking. He returned to New York City, where, during the early Seventies he was a regular in New York's Mercer Arts Center scene with the New York Dolls, Patti Smith, and others and performed with his band Elliott Murphy's Aquashow. He was discovered by critic Paul Nelson, but though *Aquashow* was widely acclaimed, commercial success eluded him in America. Some of his best-known songs, such as "Drive All Night" and "The Last of the Rock Stars," received exposure on FM radio. His only hits have been in Europe.

In 1981 Murphy formed his own label, Courtesan, and began writing short stories and a novel. Over the years his work has appeared in *Spin* and in ROLLING STONE, for which he conducted major interviews with Tom Waits and Keith Richards. His novel, *Cold and Electric*, was published in France in the late Eighties. He moved to Paris, where he now resides with his wife and son.

Murphy's work still garners critical acclaim. *Party Girls/Broken Poets*, for example, won the 1984 New York Music Award for Album of the Year despite its never having been released in the United States.

Peter Murphy: See Bauhaus

Anne Murray
Born Morna Anne Murray, June 20, 1945, Springhill, Nova Scotia, Canada
1970—*Snowbird* (Capitol)   1973—*Danny's Song* 1974—*Country; Love Song*   1976—*Keeping in Touch*   1978—*Let's Keep It That Way*   1979—*New Kind of Feeling*   1980—*Anne Murray's Greatest Hits*   1981—*Where Do You Go When You Dream* 1984—*Heart over Mind*   1986—*Something to Talk About*   1987—*Harmony; Country Hits; Songs of the Heart*   1988—*As I Am*   1989—*Anne Murray Christmas; Love Songs; Greatest Hits, vol. 2*   1990—*You Will*   1991—*Yes I Do*   1992—*Fifteen of the Best* 1993—*Croonin'*.

Anne Murray, an MOR country-pop singer, was the first female Canadian vocalist to earn a gold record in the U.S. (Joni Mitchell was second, with *Ladies of the Canyon*.) Born and raised in a coal-mining town, Murray was always interested in singing. While attending the University of New Brunswick in the mid-Sixties, she auditioned unsuccessfully for the Halifax TV show *Sing Along Jubilee*; two years later she was hired for the station's sum-

mer series. She taught physical education on Prince Edward Island but also sang in small clubs and sometimes on another Canadian show, *Let's Go*, spurred on by Brian Ahern (her first producer) and Bill Lamgstroth (who became her husband; they have two children).

In the late Sixties Murray recorded her first LP for the small Canadian label Arc, which led to a deal with Capitol of Canada. She debuted in America in mid-1970 with the gold *Snowbird* LP and single (#8), which became the first Canadian female gold 45 later in the year. Murray began to appear regularly on Glen Campbell's U.S. TV show and toured and recorded the LP *Anne Murray/Glen Campbell* with him in 1971. But she didn't have another major American hit until March 1973 and her Top Ten cover of Kenny Loggins' "Danny's Song." Other hit singles include a cover of Lennon and McCartney's "You Won't See Me" (#8, 1974), "Love Song" (#12, 1975), and "I Just Fall in Love Again" (#12, 1979).

After taking three years to raise a family, Murray came back in January 1978 with the platinum *Let's Keep It That Way*, her biggest success ever, bolstered by the #1 pop, #4 country, gold ballad "You Needed Me" and the Top Five country hit "Walk Right Back." *New Kind of Feeling* also went platinum, as did *Greatest Hits* and *Christmas Wishes*. As far as the U.S. pop singles charts go, Murray's big streak had ended, but she's found continued success in country. "A Little Good News" (#1 C&W , 1983) won her the Best Country Vocal Performance, Female, Grammy in 1983; it was also the Country Music Awards' single of the year. In 1985 her duet with Dave Loggins (of "Please Come to Boston" fame), "Nobody Loves Me Like You Do," was another #1 country hit and country-music award winner. Among her hit singles are "Just Another Woman in Love" (#1 C&W, 1984), "Time Don't Run Out on Me" (#2 C&W 1985), "I Don't Think I'm Ready for You" (#7 C&W, 1985), "Now and Forever (You and Me)" (#1 C&W 1986), "Feed This Fire" (#5 C&W, 1990), and a duet with Kenny Rogers, "If I Ever Fall in Love Again" (#28 C&W, 1989).

In her native Canada, she was named Country Female Vocalist of the Year every year from 1979 to 1986. She continues to tour and to record. She has sold an estimated 25 million albums worldwide.

The Muscle Shoals Sound Rhythm Section
Formed 1967, Florence, Alabama
Jimmy Johnson (b. 1943, Sheffield, Ala.), gtr.; Roger Hawkins (b. 1945, Mishawaka, Ind.), drums; David Hood (b. 1943, Sheffield, Ala.), bass; Barry Beckett (b. 1943, Birmingham, Ala.), kybds.

The Muscle Shoals Sound Rhythm Section has provided studio band backing on more than 500 R&B, rock & roll, country, and disco records. The quartet originated in the stable of session musicians at Rick Hall's Fame Studios in Florence, Alabama, home of the original Muscle Shoals Sound.

Jimmy Johnson began working for Hall as an engineer in 1962 and three years later returned to the guitar he had played as a teenager. Roger Hawkins had been in Johnson's group the Del-Rays and joined the Fame stable in 1965. David Hood started out at Fame as a trombonist, replacing Norbert Putnam as bassist when Putnam moved to Nashville in 1966. Barry Beckett took over the Fame keyboards from Spooner Oldham in 1967. As the Fame house band, their lineup was often expanded to include lead guitarists like Duane Allman, Chips Moman, and Eddie Hinton. They made their reputation as musicians on hits by Aretha Franklin, Wilson Pickett, Percy Sledge, Arthur Conley, Clarence Carter, and James and Bobby Purify (most of them produced by Atlantic Records' Jerry Wexler).

In 1969 Johnson, Hawkins, Hood, and Beckett left Fame to set up their own studio, Muscle Shoals Sound, in nearby Sheffield, Alabama. Since then the band has played on records by Paul Simon, the Staple Singers, Dusty Springfield, Leon Russell, Sam and Dave, Cat Stevens, Cher, Bobby Womack, King Curtis, Johnny Taylor, Bob Seger, Eddie Rabbitt, and Millie Jackson; in 1972 and 1973, Hawkins and Hood toured as part of the expanded lineup of Traffic. Rod Stewart, the Rolling Stones, and Boz Scaggs are among those who have recorded at the Muscle Shoals Sound Studios, with Johnson engineering.

Each of the four has worked as a producer: Johnson for Lynyrd Skynyrd, the Amazing Rhythm Aces, and Levon Helm; Hood for Wayne Perkins; Hawkins for Mel and Tim and Canned Heat; and Beckett for Bob Dylan, Dire Straits, Phoebe Snow, Southside Johnny and the Asbury Jukes, Joan Baez, John Prine, and Delbert McClinton. The year 1979 saw the unveiling of Muscle Shoals Sound Records.

Musical Youth
Formed circa 1979, Birmingham, England
Fred Waite, voc.; Kelvin Grant (b. 1971), gtr., voc.; Michael Grant (b. 1969), kybds., voc.; Patrick Waite (b. 1968; d. Feb. 1993, Birmingham), bass, voc.; Junior Waite (b. 1967), drums, voc.
1981—(– Fred Waite; + Dennis Seaton [b. 1967], voc.) 1982—*The Youth of Today* (MCA) 1983—*Different Style!*

The British-based pop-reggae band Musical Youth scored a memorable hit with "Pass the Dutchie" (#8, 1982), which became the biggest-selling reggae single since Johnny Nash's "I Can See Clearly Now" in 1972. The group's five members, aged 11 to 15 at the time, played their own instruments, did their own arrange-

ments, and wrote their own songs—with the exception of "Pass the Dutchie," which was based on the Jamaican reggae hit "Pass the Kutchie" by the Mighty Diamonds. "Kutchie" was Jamaican patois for marijuana; "Dutchie" was patois for pot, as in a cooking pot.

Musical Youth was originally formed at Duddeston Manor School in Birmingham by Fred Waite, formerly with the Jamaican vocal group the Techniques; he sang lead with his sons Junior and Patrick, and brothers Kelvin and Michael Grant. After Fred Waite was replaced by another teenager, Dennis Seaton, Musical Youth hit with "Pass the Dutchie," which was #1 in the U.K. *The Youth of Today* (#23, 1983) also spawned the minor hit "Heartbreaker" (#68, 1983). The same year, the group performed with Donna Summer on her hit single "Unconditional Love" (#43 pop, #9 R&B, 1983).

The followup album, *Different Style!,* was a tremendous disappointment (#144, 1983), yielding only the modest hits "She's Trouble" (#25, 1983) and "Whatcha Talking 'Bout" (#81, 1984). Musical Youth faded from view—making a sad return to the headlines a decade later. In February 1993, 24-year-old Patrick Waite—who, since 1990, had been arrested for allegedly robbing a pregnant woman at knifepoint (for which he'd served three years in prison), shoplifting, assaulting police, reckless driving, and credit card theft—collapsed and died at a friend's house, felled by a mystery virus while awaiting trial on charges of marijuana possession, possessing a knife, and threatening behavior. He'd reportedly been talking of re-forming Musical Youth at the time of his death.

My Bloody Valentine
Formed 1984, Dublin, Ireland
Kevin Patrick Shields (b. May 21, 1963, Queens, N.Y.), gtr., voc.; Colm Michael O'Ciosoig (b. Oct. 31, 1964, Dublin), drums; Dave Conway (b. Dublin), voc.; Tina (b. Dublin), kybds.
1985—*This Is Your Bloody Valentine* EP (Tycoon, Ger.) (+ Deborah Ann Googe [b. Oct. 24, 1962, Somerset, Eng.], bass) 1986—*Geek* EP (Fever); *The New Record by My Bloody Valentine* EP (Kaleidoscope Sound) 1987—*Sunny Sundae Smile* EP (Lazy); *Strawberry Wine* EP; *Ecstasy* EP (– Conway; – Tina; + Bilinda Jayne Butcher [b. Sep. 16, 1961, London, Eng.], gtr., voc.) 1988—*My Bloody Valentine Isn't Anything* (Relativity); *Feed Me with Your Kiss* EP (Creation, U.K.); *You Made Me Realise* EP 1990—*Glider* EP (Sire) 1991—*Tremelo* EP; *Loveless.*

The original My Bloody Valentine sounded nothing like the post-1988 model, which introduced a groundbreaking studio concoction of discordant guitar and effects and fragile melodies, kicking off Britain's late-Eighties dream-pop scene. After moving from New York to Ireland at age six, Kevin Shields befriended Colm O'Ciosoig, who shared his obsession with pop music. In 1984 the two formed My Bloody Valentine, named for a B movie, with singer Dave Conway. It wasn't until 1988's *Isn't Anything,* however, that MBV locked into its unusual, influential sound, equally inspired by the churning guitars of the Jesus and Mary Chain, the melodic sense of the Cocteau Twins, and the dissonance of Sonic Youth. Sire signed the band that same year, but it took a full three years for the band to complete its full-length magnum opus, *Loveless,* which cost a reported $500,000 and nearly sunk its British label (Creation). The LP only reached #24 in the U.K. and didn't chart in the States. The band's approach onstage—motionless and reserved—popularized the phrase "shoe gazers" to describe their (and those who followed in their footsteps) passive, introspective demeanor.

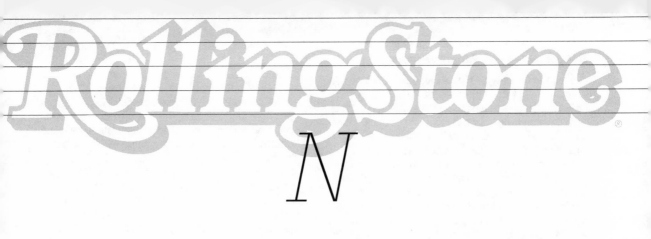

Graham Nash: See Crosby, Stills, Nash and Young; the Hollies

Johnny Nash

Born August 19, 1940, Houston, Texas
1972—*I Can See Clearly Now* (Epic)   1973—*My Merry-Go-Round*   1974—*Celebrate Life*   1979— *Let's Go Dancing*   1993—*The Reggae Collection* (Epic).

Johnny Nash was one of the first performers to bring reggae to the attention of the American public, with his #1 hit, the self-penned "I Can See Clearly Now," in 1972. He also recorded Bob Marley's first U.S. hit song in 1973 with a cover of Marley's "Stir It Up" (#12). Nash, who many believed was Jamaican, grew up in Texas and had been recording since 1957. He began singing gospel in a Baptist church and by 13 was on the Houston TV show *Matinee*, breaking the local television color bar of the time. He sang C&W as well as pop, easy-listening soul, and calypso. In 1956 Arthur Godfrey gave him a spot on his TV show, where he performed for the next seven years.

Nash began his recording career in 1957 for ABC-Paramount with "A Teenager Sings the Blues." His first chart single was "A Very Special Love" (#23, 1958), followed by "The Teen Commandments," sung with Paul Anka and George Hamilton IV (#29, 1959). In the early Sixties he recorded unsuccessfully for Warner Bros. (1962–63), Groove, and Argo (1964). Still, his compositions did well for others, like "What Kind of Love Is This," a Top Twenty hit for Joey Dee in 1962.

In the late Sixties Nash began recording at Byron Lee's studio in Jamaica and went on to build his own studio there. He formed his own labels, Joda and Jad, before hitting the chart again with the reggae "Hold Me Tight," a Top Five pop hit in 1968. Around this time he had more hits in England, including a reggae cover of Sam Cooke's "Cupid" in 1969. Nash also began to star in films, such as *Take a Giant Step*, Sweden's *Love Is Not a Game* (1974), and *Key Witness*. In 1971, living in England, he signed to Epic, leading to his "I Can See Clearly Now" peak in 1972. After 1973's "Stir It Up" (a hit in England back in 1971), Nash had no more big American hits, though he maintained his popularity in England with covers of Little Anthony and the Imperials' "Tears on My Pillow" (#1 U.K., 1975) and Sam Cooke's "(What a) Wonderful World" (#25 U.K., 1976).

Naughty by Nature

Formed 1986, East Orange, New Jersey
Treach (b. Anthony Criss, Dec. 2, 1970, East Orange), voc.; Vinnie (b. Vincent Brown, Sep. 17, 1970, East Orange), voc.; Kay Gee (b. Kier Gist, Sep. 15, 1969, East Orange), DJ.

1991—*Naughty by Nature* (Tommy Boy) 1993—*19NaughtyIII* 1995—*Poverty's Paradise.*

The rap trio Naughty by Nature came out of nowhere in summer 1991 with its massive hit "O.P.P." (#6 pop, #5 R&B), a cheating anthem for the hip-hop Nineties. Ironically, the group originally had recorded the track in 1989 but was unable to find anyone interested in releasing it until NBN met rapper Queen Latifah at a party. Latifah signed the group to her Flavor Unit Management company and brought it to Tommy Boy. "O.P.P.," with its call-and-response chorus of "Ya down wit' O.P.P.?"/"Yeah, you know me!," sold more than two million copies and was nominated for a Grammy. The key to the song's success was its juxtaposition of a rough ghetto rap by Treach (short for "the treacherous MC") with the pop pep of samples from the Jackson 5's "ABC." The song also teased the censors: Treach's rap says the title stands for "Other People's Property," but the lyrics also indicate the final P means "penis" or "pussy." The second single from *Naughty by Nature* (#16, 1991), "Ghetto Bastard," was retitled "Everything's Gonna Be Alright" for radio. Naughty by Nature also performed the single "Ghetto Anthem" from the *Juice* soundtrack.

The group returned to the top of the charts with *19NaughtyIII* (#3 pop, #1 R&B, 1993) and the single "Hip Hop Hooray" (#8 pop, #1 R&B, 1993). The song's video was directed by Spike Lee, and the group performed the hit in the movie *Who's the Man?* The album featured Vinnie's raps more than their debut had, but Treach's rhyming style continued to get lavish praise from critics and other rappers. *Poverty's Paradise* debuted at #3 pop in mid-1995.

Nazareth

Formed 1968, Dunfermline, Scotland
Dan McCafferty, voc.; Manny Charlton, gtr.; Darrel Sweet, drums; Pete Agnew, bass.
1971—*Nazareth* (Warner Bros.) 1972—*Exercises* 1973—*Razamanaz* (A&M); *Loud 'n' Proud* 1974—*Rampant* 1975—*Hair of the Dog* 1976—*Close Enough for Rock 'n' Roll*; *Play 'n' the Game* 1977—*Hot Tracks*; *Expect No Mercy* 1978—(+ Zal Cleminson [b. May 4, 1949, Glasgow, Scot.], gtr.) *No Mean City* 1980—*Malice in Wonderland* (– Cleminson) 1981—*Fool Circle* (+ Billy Rankin, gtr.; + John Locke [b. Sep. 25, 1943, Los Angeles, Cal.], kybds.); *S'Naz* 1982—*2XS* (– Locke) 1983—*Sound Elixir* (MCA) (– Rankin) 1988—*Classics* 1990—(– Charlton; + Rankin) 1993—*No Jive* (Griffin Music).
Dan McCafferty solo: 1975—*Dan McCafferty* (A&M).

Nazareth is a hard-rocking (sometimes heavy-metal) group from Scotland whose major distinguishing feature, besides its Rod Stewart–ish lead singer, Dan McCafferty, has been its penchant for inventively arranged, pile-driving versions of quieter songs by writers like Joni Mitchell, Woody Guthrie, Tim Rose, and Bob Dylan.

All of the members were born in Scotland, where they met in Dunfermline in the semipro band the Shadettes, which included McCafferty, Pete Agnew, and Darrel Sweet. When Manny Charlton joined in 1968, they changed their name to Nazareth (inspired by the first line of the Band's "The Weight") and got their first record contract in 1971. The quartet's first two LPs were generally ignored, but for 1973's *Razamanaz* it switched to A&M and got Roger Glover (ex–Deep Purple bassist) to produce. Nazareth had its first British hits that year: "Broken Down Angel" (#9) and "Bad Bad Boy" (#10). *Loud 'n' Proud* yielded a brutal version of Joni Mitchell's "This Flight Tonight," which hit big in the U.K. and got some FM airplay in the U.S. It also included a nine-minute metallic rendition of Dylan's "The Ballad of Hollis Brown." The LP established Nazareth in Europe and Canada, where it has had many gold and platinum records.

The group's only U.S. hit was "Love Hurts" (#8, 1976), the song Boudleaux Bryant wrote for the Everly Brothers, and also a hit for Jim Capaldi in England. Also that year, Nazareth reached #14 in England with "My White Bicycle," originally a psychedelia-period song from Tomorrow (a band that included future Yes guitarist Steve Howe). Vocalist McCafferty released a solo LP in 1975.

Nazareth kept its lineup intact until 1978, when it added second guitarist Zal Cleminson, who had spent five years with the Sensational Alex Harvey Band and also played on McCafferty's solo LP. He appeared only on *No Mean City* and *Malice in Wonderland*. By 1981 the group was back to a foursome, but it expanded to a sextet the following year with the additions of former Spirit keyboardist John Locke and guitarist Billy Rankin. *Malice in Wonderland* and *Fool Circle* were produced by ex–Steely Dan and Doobie Brother Jeff Baxter. (The previous five had been produced by Charlton, taking over for Glover, who had produced *Razamanaz*, *Loud 'n' Proud*, and *Rampant*.)

By the mid-Eighties, Nazareth was without a U.S. record label, but the band continued to issue albums regularly in Canada and Europe. In 1993, ten years after its last American release, Nazareth brought out *No Jive*. Once again the group was a foursome, but with Rankin in place of the talented Charlton, who'd left in 1990 to pursue production work. Long underrated by critics, Nazareth remains an unusually interesting hard-rock group.

The Nazz

Formed 1967, Philadelphia, Pennsylvania
Todd Rundgren (b. June 22, 1948, Upper Darby, Pa.),

The Nazz: Todd Rundgren, Thom Mooney, Stewkey, Carson Van Osten

gtr., voc.; **Stewkey** (b. Robert Antoni, Nov. 17, 1947, Newport, R.I.), kybds., lead voc.; **Thom Mooney** (b. Jan. 5, 1948, Altoona, Pa.), drums; **Carson G. Van Osten** (b. Sep. 24, 1946, Cinnaminson, N.J.), bass.
1968—*Nazz* (SGC) 1969—*Nazz Nazz* 1970—*Nazz 3*.

The Nazz, Todd Rundgren's first recording band, was a power-pop quartet from Philadelphia. Rundgren and Carson Van Osten came from Woody's Truck Stop (a Philly blues band), Thom Mooney was from the Munchkins, and Stewkey had previously been with Elizabeth—all local groups. The foursome made its live debut in July 1967 opening for the Doors at Philadelphia's Town Hall, and by the following February had a record contract. Its debut LP, *Nazz,* showcased Rundgren as the group's chief writer, though Stewkey handled lead vocals. The material, influenced by the Beatles and the early Who, included the hard-rocking "Open My Eyes" and "Hello It's Me," which later appeared on Rundgren's *Something/Anything* solo LP in 1972 [see entry]. The band got good press and began turning up in the teen magazines. But problems set in with its second LP, *Nazz Nazz.* There were ego conflicts (Rundgren and Mooney fought the most), and the album, originally planned as a double LP called *Fungo Bat,* was split by management into 1969's *Nazz Nazz* and 1970's *Nazz 3.* The tracks on the latter LP originally featured Rundgren's lead vocals, which were erased, with Stewkey put on instead. Before it came out, Rundgren and Van Osten quit.

Stewkey and Mooney kept a version of the Nazz going until mid-1970. Mooney then left for California and later played with the Curtis Brothers and Tattoo, with ex-Raspberry Wally Bryson. He was also in Bob Welch's power trio Paris. Van Osten became an animation artist; Rundgren became a successful producer and solo artist;

Stewkey joined a band with future Cheap Trickster Rick Nielsen called Fuse, which recorded one LP for Epic. Mooney also joined Fuse for a while but left before it became Sick Man of Europe, which later included Tom Petersson, also eventually of Cheap Trick. One bootleg disc of theirs surfaced, *Retrospective Foresight,* which included, besides some originals, several Nazz outtakes from various incarnations.

Youssou N'Dour
Born October 1, 1959, Dakar, Senegal
1986—*Nelson Mandela* (Polydor) 1987—*Inedits 84085* (Celluloid) 1988—*Immigres* (Virgin) 1989—*The Lion* 1990—*Set* 1992—*Eyes Open* (40 Acres and a Mule/Columbia) 1994—*The Guide (Wommat)* (Chaos/Columbia).

A "world beat" or "Afro-pop" pioneer, Youssou N'Dour began catching on with European and American audiences in the late Eighties with his brand of *mbalax*—traditional Senegalese percussion-based music that the singer combined with pop strings and jazz chord changes, funky horns, and Islamic-inflected vocals.

Born into a family of griots (storyteller/historians) and musicians, N'Dour grew up in cosmopolitan Dakar, listening to West African music, reggae, and R&B. In his midteens already the chief vocalist for the Star Band, Senegal's top pop outfit, he formed his own band, Etoile de Dakar, in 1979. Eventually changing their name to Le Super Etoile and becoming African superstars (N'Dour set up his own production company and opened a nightclub), the ten-piece band began performing in London and Paris in the early Eighties.

Riveted by N'Dour in concert in London in 1984, world-music enthusiast Peter Gabriel traveled to Senegal to meet him. With N'Dour appearing in 1986 on Gabriel's *So,* on Paul Simon's *Graceland,* and on a Gabriel world tour, he drew notice from Western record companies; 1986's *Nelson Mandela* introduced him to worldwide audiences. Appearing in 1988 as part of Amnesty International's Human Rights Now! Tour alongside Sting and Bruce Springsteen increased his exposure; he also recorded with Harry Belafonte and Ryuichi Sakamoto.

While some critics have accused N'Dour or his record companies of diluting the distinctively Senegalese energy of his music on *The Lion, Set,* and, to a lesser degree, *Eyes Open,* N'Dour replies that he no longer considers himself exclusively an African artist. His 1994 LP, *The Guide,* featured Branford Marsalis and Neneh Cherry as guests. Mixing social commentary and expert playing, his albums and the singer's charisma have caused some observers to speculate that N'Dour might inherit Bob Marley's position as a third-world musician with genuinely global reach.

Vince Neil: See Mötley Crüe

Nektar

Formed 1968, Germany

Derek "Mo" Moore, bass, voc.; Roy Albrighton, gtr., voc.; Alan "Taff" Freeman, kybds., voc.; Ron Howden, drums, voc.; Mick Brockett, lights and sound.

1974—*Remember the Future* (Passport)   1975—*Down to Earth*; *Recycled* (– Albrighton; + Dave Nelson [b. U.S.], gtr.)   1976—*A Tab in the Ocean*   1977—*Magic Is a Child* (Polydor).

Nektar began as a group of British expatriates living in Germany, where it developed a Hawkwind/Camel/early Genesis style of melodic semipsychedelic art rock that engendered cult interest in the U.S. during the mid-Seventies. The band's members first came to Germany in 1965, as did Deep Purple and Pink Floyd. Derek Moore and Ron Howden had met in 1964 in Tours, France, while playing in different bands. Howden joined Moore's group, the Upsetters, and the pair soon formed the Prophets. In Germany in 1965, they picked up Alan Freeman from the band MI5 and changed their name to Prophecy. Roy Albrighton (formerly with Rainbows) joined in 1968, and by late 1969 they had changed their name to Nektar. In 1970 they added Mick Brockett, officially dubbed "light musician," and added backdrop films and visual elements to complete the band's psychedelic image. (Indeed, a 1977 press release warned that epileptics should avoid Nektar's shows lest a "psychic energizer" film trigger seizures.)

The group's first LP, *Journey to the Centre of the Eye*, came out on the German Bellaphon label, in Europe only, as did the next three albums. Its U.S. debut was 1974's *Remember the Future*, a concept LP about an extraterrestrial bluebird who helps a child see the future. The group's music fit in well with art rock's commercial peak in mid-Seventies America, and the *Remember* LP became an FM staple and went Top Twenty. It was aided by a record-company decision to avoid presenting Nektar as an opening act by financing its U.S. headline tour. (This approach also proved successful for Genesis and Supertramp on their U.S. live debuts.)

Nektar moved to America around 1976. Drummer Howden began to double as lead singer, and American guitarist Dave Nelson replaced Albrighton. After *Down to Earth* (#32, 1975), the band's sales declined steadily, and Nektar eventually broke up.

Rick Nelson

Born Eric Hilliard Nelson, May 8, 1940, Teaneck, New Jersey; died December 31, 1985, DeKalb, Texas

1957—*Ricky* (Imperial)   1958—*Ricky Nelson*   1959—*Ricky Sings Again*; *Songs by Ricky*   1960—

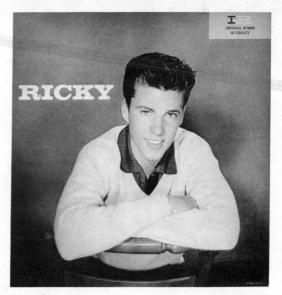

Rick Nelson

More Songs by Ricky   1961—*Ricky Is 21*   1962—*Album Seven by Rick*   1963—*Best Sellers by Ricky Nelson*; *For Your Sweet Love* (Decca)   1964—*Rick Nelson Sings "For You"*   1966—*Bright Lights & Country Music*   1967—*Country Fever* (Decca)   1968—*Another Side of Rick*   1969—*Perspective*   1970—*Rick Nelson in Concert*; *Rick Sings Nelson*   1971—*Rudy the Fifth*   1972—*Garden Party*   1974—*Windfall* (MCA)   1977—*Intakes* (Epic)   1981—*Playing to Win* (Capitol)   1986—*Memphis Sessions* (Epic)   1990—*Ricky Nelson, vol. 1: The Legendary Masters Series* (EMI)   1991—*The Best of Rick Nelson, vol. 2.*

When singer Rick Nelson was posthumously inducted into the Rock and Roll Hall of Fame in 1987, ROLLING STONE publisher and Hall of Fame cofounder Jann Wenner noted "the critical myopia that dogged [Nelson's] career." Indeed, Rick, or Ricky, as he was known early on, launched his career from a position of privilege: his family's popular weekly television series, *The Adventures of Ozzie and Harriet*. Nelson was wealthy, handsome, a household name and American teen idol long before he ever cut a record. In nearly every regard, he would seem the antithesis of the early rockers who made the music he first loved and recorded, rockabilly, and far removed from the late-Sixties environment that nurtured early country rock, of which he was at the vanguard. And yet musicians as diverse as Eric Andersen and John Fogerty, and even some of his own heroes, including Carl Perkins and Scotty Moore, admired and respected Nelson.

Nelson's father was a famous bandleader, and his mother a singer and actress who had been famous since the early Thirties. In 1949 Rick and his older brother David began playing themselves on their parents' popular radio comedy series, *The Adventures of Ozzie and Harriet,* which went to TV three years later. From his first appearance, the impish, wisecracking Rick became the most popular character. His trademark line, "I don't mess around boy," became a national catchphrase with prepubescent viewers. Not surprisingly, when Ricky began singing on the show in 1957, he had a massive audience. According to Nelson, he had no musical ambitions until after a girlfriend said she was in love with Elvis Presley. He retorted that he too was cutting a record (which he had no plans to do), and then did.

His first hit was a cover of Fats Domino's "I'm Walkin'," which went to #4 and sold a million records after Nelson performed it on TV. The flip side, "A Teenager's Romance," hit #2. Between then and 1961 he had more than two dozen pop hits, several of them double-sided, including the rockabilly "Be-Bop Baby" (#3, 1957), "Stood Up" (#2, 1958) b/w "Waitin' in School" (#18, 1958), "Believe What You Say" (#4, 1958) b/w "My Bucket's Got a Hole in It" (#12, 1958), "Lonesome Town" (#7, 1958) b/w "I Got a Feeling" (#10, 1958), "It's Late" (#9, 1959) b/w "Never Be Anyone Else but You" (#6, 1959), "Just a Little Too Much" (#9, 1959); ballads, such as "Poor Little Fool" (#1, 1958), Baker Knight's "Lonesome Town," "Sweeter Than You" (#9, 1959), "Travelin' Man," (#1, 1961), and its B side, the Gene Pitney–penned "Hello Mary Lou" (#9, 1961). Some of his early hits, including "Waitin'," "Believe What You Say," and "It's Late," were penned by Dorsey and/or Johnny Burnette. For seven years, his backup band featured James Burton, who later became Presley's lead guitarist.

Nelson had three more Top Ten hits in 1962 ("Young World," the autobiographical "Teenage Idol," and "It's Up to You"), and another in 1964, "For You." By then he had married Kris Harmon, another product of a show-business family, and become the father of his first of four children, daughter Tracy. Twins Matthew and Gunnar [see Nelson entry], and a third son, Sam, followed. As of 1964, Nelson's hitmaking days were behind him, and after the family's show was canceled in 1966, he found himself at loose ends. Late that year he appeared, costarring with Joanie Summers of "Johnny Get Angry" fame, in a little-seen, sophisticated rock satire entitled *On the Flip Side.* Nelson's fame also brought him numerous film offers, but unlike many other teen idols, he eschewed the typical teen fare for acclaimed parts in Howard Hawks' classic *Rio Bravo* (1959), which costarred John Wayne and Dean Martin, and *The Wackiest Ship in the Army* (1960), with Jack Lemmon. He continued to record (he'd signed a 20-year contract in 1963), but as he later admitted, without enthusiasm until he began recording in a style that would soon become known as country rock. On *Bright Lights & Country Music* and *Country Fever,* Nelson covered material by Doug Kershaw, Willie Nelson, Hank Williams, and Bob Dylan, as well as his own "Alone." Hanging out at the L.A. country-rock bastion the Troubadour, Nelson recruited ex-Poco bassist Randy Meisner and began forming the Stone Canyon Band, which at various times would also include Dennis Larden of Every Mother's Son; Richie Hayward, briefly on leave from Little Feat; Tom Brumley of Buck Owens' Buckaroos; and Steve Love, later with Roger McGuinn and the New Riders of the Purple Sage; and Steve Duncan, later of the Desert Rose Band. With this group, he scored a minor commercial comeback with a cover of Dylan's "She Belongs to Me" (#33, 1969). A double live album recorded at the Troubadour in 1970, *Rick Nelson in Concert,* marked a crucial turning point for Nelson. With songs by Dylan, Tim Hardin, and Eric Andersen (who supplied the liner notes), it put to rest the charge that he was a talentless teen idol and garnered unanimous rave reviews.

His next success rose out of failure. In October 1971, when Nelson and his band appeared at a rock & roll revival at New York's Madison Square Garden, the audience booed his long-hair look and new material, particularly a version of the Rolling Stones' "Honky Tonk Women." Just a few months later, on a tour of England (his first, despite having had 19 Top Forty hits there), fans, including Elton John and Cliff Richard, turned out in droves, and more important to Nelson, fully accepted his new direction. Out of these experiences, he wrote his last million-seller (his first in over a decade) and his personal anthem, "Garden Party." It hit #6 and went gold in 1972.

Nelson's followup albums didn't catch on, and by the mid-Seventies he had lost his MCA contract. He released an album on Epic in 1977, then moved to Capitol for *Playin' to Win.* For a while it was rumored that another fan, Paul McCartney, planned to produce Nelson, but nothing came of it. Partly because he so loved performing and partly due to an expensive and protracted divorce from his wife, Nelson found himself on the road an average of 250 nights a year through the late Seventies and early Eighties. When he sang in "Garden Party," "If memories are all I sang/I'd rather drive a truck," he meant it, even turning down a long-term, $1-million-dollar-plus offer (arranged by Elvis Presley's manager, Colonel Tom Parker) to play Las Vegas at a point when he was deeply in debt. In September 1984, he was invited, along with John Fogerty, the Judds, and Dave Edmunds, among others, to join in the finale of a Sun Records reunion album that featured Nelson's early idols Johnny Cash, Roy Orbison, Carl Perkins, and Jerry Lee Lewis. (The album documenting the event, *Interviews from "The Class of '55" Recording Sessions,* won a Grammy in 1986 for Best Spoken Word or Nonmusical Recording; it was Nelson's only Grammy.)

By 1985, he had assembled a new, young band: bassist Pat Woodward, drummer Ricky Intveld, keyboardist Andy Chapin (who'd worked with Steppenwolf and the Association), and lead guitarist Bobby Neal, whom Nelson had met while recording in Memphis earlier (the resulting *Memphis Sessions,* a collection of rockabilly covers, was released posthumously). That August a live documentary of Nelson was taped during a tour on which he opened for Fats Domino and was backed by the Jordanaires. He had signed a new deal with Curb/MCA and on December 26 completed recording Buddy Holly's "True Love Ways" for his upcoming album. He closed his last performance four days later with Holly's "Rave On."

On December 31, 1985, en route to a New Year's Eve show in Dallas, Texas, Nelson's burning DC-3 (which was previously owned by Jerry Lee Lewis) crashed in a field near DeKalb, Texas. Early press reports erroneously suggested that drug use, namely freebasing, might have played a role in the crash that killed Rick, his band, and his fiancée Helen Blair (the pilot and copilot survived). In fact, the National Transportation Safety Board's 1987 report determined that the fire began in a malfunctioning gas heater. Nelson was buried in Los Angeles' Forest Lawn Cemetery. In the years immediately following his death, many other artists paid tribute to him: Bob Dylan included "Lonesome Town" in his 1986 concerts, and newer artists, including Jimmie Dale Gilmore and Chris Isaak, have cited his influence.

Sandy Nelson

Born December 1, 1938, Santa Monica, California
1961—*Let There Be Drums* (Imperial)   1962—
Drums Are My Beat!; Golden Hits.

Sandy Nelson scored several hits in the late Fifties and early Sixties with his rocking guitar and drum-based instrumentals, most notably 1959's "Teen Beat" (#4). Nelson was friends with Jan and Dean, Nancy Sinatra, and Phil Spector when they were all in high school. His first band was Kip Tyler and the Flips, which at one point included future Beach Boy Bruce Johnston on piano. That band recorded for Ebb and Challenge records. Nelson later played on the Teddy Bears' gold "To Know Him Is to Love Him" (he also toured with them), and also drummed on Gene Vincent's 1959 *Crazy Times* LP before recording "Teen Beat" for the small Original Sound label. It went gold, and Nelson was quickly signed by Imperial Records, but his second hit didn't come until 1961, with "Let There Be Drums" (#7).

Just before he cut that record, Nelson lost his left foot in a car accident, but it didn't affect his drumming. He later hit with "Drums Are My Beat" (#29, 1962) and a "Teen Beat" update inventively titled "Teen Beat '65"

(#44, 1964). He continued to record, with only minor success, through the mid-Seventies.

Tracy Nelson

Born December 27, 1944, Madison, Wisconsin
1965—*Deep Are the Roots* (Prestige)   1968—*Living with the Animals* (Mercury)   1969—*Make a Joyful Noise; Mother Earth Presents Tracy Nelson Country* 1970—*Satisfied*   1971—*Bring Me Home* (Reprise) 1973—*A Poor Man's Paradise* (Columbia)   1974— Tracy Nelson* (Atlantic)   1975—*Sweet Soul Music* (MCA)   1976—*Time Is on My Side*   1978—*Homemade Songs* (Flying Fish)   1980—*Doin' It My Way* (Adelphi)   1993—*In the Here and Now* (Rounder) 1995—*I Feel So Good.*

Tracy Nelson was long considered one of the strongest female singers in rock—especially with Mother Earth during the late Sixties, when she was sometimes compared to Janis Joplin. But she soon edged away from Mother Earth's R&B gospel and began stressing country when the band moved to Nashville. One of her songs, "Down So Low," has been covered by Linda Ronstadt and many other singers.

Growing up in Wisconsin, Nelson began playing piano at age five, guitar at 13. She also sang in the church choir. She played coffeehouses while attending the University of Wisconsin and formed her first band, the Fabulous Imitations, followed by the White Trash Blues Band (no relation to Edgar Winter), which lasted two weeks. She recorded her first solo LP around this time, the blues-influenced *Deep Are the Roots,* on Prestige, with harmonica player Charlie Musselwhite and other Chicago blues musicians backing her.

In 1966 Nelson moved to San Francisco, and in July she formed Mother Earth (named after a Memphis Slim blues song). Its critically respected debut, *Living with the Animals,* included backup by Elvin Bishop and Mark Naftalin of the Paul Butterfield Blues Band. In 1969 the group moved to a farm outside Nashville, and its music became increasingly country oriented (as evidenced on *Mother Earth Presents Tracy Nelson Country*). After *Bring Me Home,* the band went through many personnel changes; the only member to stick with Nelson through them was guitarist John "Toad" Andrews. In 1973 the band (by now billed as Tracy Nelson/Mother Earth) released *A Poor Man's Paradise,* and in 1974 Nelson recorded her self-titled solo Atlantic debut. The album included a duet with Willie Nelson, "After the Fire Is Gone," which was nominated for a Grammy. In 1975 she signed with MCA, and in the late Seventies she recorded albums for the independent Flying Fish and Adelphi labels. *Homemade Songs* included a duet with Carlene Carter. Comfortable playing Nashville clubs, Nelson vanished from the recording scene for over a decade before reemerging with 1993's critically acclaimed *In the Here and Now,* recorded in Nashville with such guest artists as Musselwhite and New Orleans R&B singer Irma Thomas.

Willie Nelson

Born April 30, 1933, Abbott, Texas
1962—*... And Then I Wrote* (Liberty)   1963—*Here's Willie Nelson*   1967—*Make Way for ...* (RCA); *The Party's Over*   1968—*Texas in My Soul; Good Times* 1971—*Willie Nelson and Family; Yesterday's Wine* 1972—*The Willie Way*   1974—*Phases and Stages* (Atlantic)   1975—*What Can You Do to Me* (RCA); *Red Headed Stranger* (Columbia)   1976—*The Sound in Your Mind; Troublemaker; Wanted: The Outlaws* (with Waylon Jennings, Tompall Glaser, Jessi Colter) (RCA); *Live*   1977—*To Lefty from Willie* (Columbia)   1978—*Waylon and Willie* (with Waylon Jennings) (RCA); *Stardust* (Columbia) 1979—*Willie and Family Live; Pretty Paper;* *... Sings Kristofferson; Sweet Memories* (RCA); *One for the Road* (with Leon Russell) (Columbia) 1980—*San Antonio Rose* (with Ray Price); *Honeysuckle Rose* soundtrack   1981—*Somewhere over the Rainbow; Willie Nelson's Greatest Hits and Some That Will Be*   1982—*Always on My Mind; Poncho and Lefty* (with Merle Haggard); *Waylon and Willie: WWII* (with Waylon Jennings); *In the Jailhouse Now* (with Webb Pierce)   1983—*Tougher Than Leather; Without a Song*   1984—*City of New Orleans; Angel Eyes; Music from Songwriter* (with Kris Kristofferson); *Funny How Time Slips Away* (with Faron Young)   1985—*Half Nelson; Me and Paul; Brand on My Heart* (with Hank Snow)   1986— *Partners; The Promiseland*   1987—*Island in the Sea* 1988—*What a Wonderful World; All-Time Greatest Hits, vol. 1* (RCA)   1989—*A Horse Called Music* (Columbia)   1990—*Nite Life: Greatest Hits and Rare Tracks 1959–71* (Rhino); *Born for Trouble* (Columbia) 1991—*Who Will Buy My Memories?* (Sony Music Special Products); *Clean Shirt* (with Waylon Jennings) (Epic)   1993—*Across the Borderline* (Columbia)   1994—*Moonlight Becomes You* (Justice) 1995—*Healing Hands of Time* (Liberty); *Willie Nelson: A Classic and Unreleased Collection* (Rhino). With Johnny Cash, Waylon Jennings, and Kris Kristofferson: 1985—*Highwayman* (Columbia); *Desperadoes Waiting for a Train*   1987—*They Killed Him* (Mercury) 1990—*Highwayman 2*   1995—*The Road Goes On Forever.*

One of country & western's most popular, prolific, and distinctive singer/songwriters, Willie Nelson started out as a songwriter without much of a solo singing career and eventually became a star singer mostly covering

Willie Nelson

pop and C&W standards. His dry, wry voice and plaintive, understated delivery helped him transcend country to reach wider pop audiences. In the Seventies he spearheaded "outlaw" country—the non-Nashville alliance between "redneck" country musicians and "hippie" rock musicians—and helped establish Austin, Texas, as a country-rock capital. His grizzled face brought him film roles in *Electric Horseman, Honeysuckle Rose, Barbarossa,* and 1984's *Songwriter,* in which he costarred with Kris Kristofferson (who, a year later, would join Nelson, Johnny Cash, and Waylon Jennings on the first Highwaymen project). His problems with the Internal Revenue Service, and his leisure-time marijuana use, made him an "outlaw" for real—and a counterculture style hero to many, long after the counterculture had gone back underground.

Nelson was raised by his grandparents, and worked cotton fields until he was ten, when he began playing guitar in local German and Czech polka bands. He joined the Air Force, and later attended Baylor University in Waco, Texas. Before dropping out, he sold Bibles and encyclopedias door-to-door, worked as a disc jockey and musician, and taught Sunday school. While teaching Sunday school in Fort Worth, Nelson was also playing honky-tonk clubs on Saturday nights; when his parishioners demanded he choose between the church and music, he chose the latter. He played bars around the country, taught guitar, and wrote songs.

With the $50 he earned from his first published song, "Family Bible," Nelson went to Nashville, where songwriter Hank Cochran got him a publishing contract. Nelson wrote pop and C&W hits for many artists: "Night Life" for Rusty Draper, "Funny How Time Slips Away" for Jimmy Elledge and Johnny Tillotson, "Crazy" for Patsy Cline, "Hello Walls" for Faron Young, "Wake Me When It's Over" for Andy Williams, and "Pretty Paper" for Roy Orbison. Eventually he had a recording contract of his own, but his weathered tenor and his taste for sparse backup were considered uncommercial.

When his Nashville home burned down around 1970, Nelson moved back to Texas, continuing to record, write, and perform. In 1972 he held his first annual Fourth of July picnic with young and old rock and country musicians in Dripping Springs, Texas—an event that would soon become a local institution, with the Fourth of July named Willie Nelson Day by the Texas Senate in 1975. In Austin Nelson also began to clarify his own ideas on country music, simultaneously reclaiming traditions of honky-tonk, Western swing, and early country music and giving the songs a starker, more modern outlook. *Phases and Stages,* a concept album produced by Arif Mardin, introduced Nelson's mature style, and 1975's *Red Headed Stranger,* a "country opera," made his music a commercial success. With a hit remake of Fred Rose's "Blue Eyes Crying in the Rain" (originally recorded by Roy Acuff in the Forties), the album went gold. In 1975 Nelson shared the *Outlaws* compilation LP with Waylon Jennings, Tompall Glaser, and Jessi Colter, three other country musicians ignored by the Nashville establishment; it was the first platinum country LP.

Nelson and his band, which included his older sister Bobbie on piano, toured constantly through the Seventies and were a major concert attraction through the South and West before the rest of the country caught on. But by the end of the decade he was an established star. Nineteen-seventy-eight's *Willie and Family Live* went double platinum.

Meanwhile, Nelson's songwriting tapered off; he did an album-length tribute to Kris Kristofferson and made duet albums with George Jones, Merle Haggard, and Ray Price. The four-million-seller *Stardust,* produced by Memphis veteran Booker T. Jones, was an album of old pop standards. For *Honeysuckle Rose* Nelson wrote one new song, "On the Road Again," that became a #1 country single and a #20 pop hit. In the Eighties Nelson had multiplatinum albums with *Always on My Mind* and *Greatest Hits* while maintaining his prolific output of albums and films. The first Highwaymen collaboration with Kristofferson, Jennings, and Johnny Cash (#35, 1985) went gold—as did the 1985 *Half Nelson,* though it reached only #178 on the pop albums chart. In 1984 Nelson duetted with Julio Iglesias on the #5 pop hit "To All the Girls I've Loved Before." In 1985 he helped launch the first Farm Aid concert for America's embattled family farmers, and along with Neil Young and John Mellencamp, has helped organize each succeeding Farm Aid benefit show.

Since the early Seventies, even while performing in Las Vegas (as he did in the late Seventies), Nelson has sported his standard attire: long hair and beard, headband, jeans, T-shirt, and running shoes. The last four items were nearly the only possessions he had left after the IRS investigated him and, in 1990, slapped him with a $16.7-million bill. Nelson was forced to auction off almost all his possessions in 1991 (most of them reportedly bought by friends who vowed to return them to Nelson once he regained financial stability). To help raise desperately needed capital, Nelson sold *Who'll Buy My Memories?* (subtitled *The IRS Tapes*) direct through an 800 telephone number. Nelson and the IRS eventually agreed to a $9-million settlement, and the singer sued the accounting firm of Price Waterhouse, claiming it had mismanaged his finances. More money came in through Nelson's appearances in TV and radio ads for Taco Bell.

In 1993 Nelson recorded the acclaimed *Across the Borderline,* on which such in-demand rock pros as producer Don Was (who'd recently rescued Bonnie Raitt and the B-52's from commercial oblivion) and mixer Bob Clearmountain recorded Nelson duetting with Bonnie Raitt, Sinéad O'Connor, and Bob Dylan, on tunes by Dylan, Paul Simon, Peter Gabriel, John Hiatt, and Lyle Lovett. He followed it up with *Moonlight Becomes You,* a *Stardust*-style album of old pop standards, which began with a "hidden" track in which Nelson told listeners the album was on independent Justice Records because no major label would gamble on releasing such a record. Nelson moved to Liberty for his next recording, 1995's *Healing Hands of Time,* another set of pop standards.

Nelson

Formed 1988, Los Angeles, California
Matthew Nelson (b. Matthew Gray Nelson, Sep. 20, 1967, Los Angeles), voc., bass; Gunnar Nelson (b. Gunnar Eric Nelson, Sep. 20, 1967, Los Angeles), voc., gtr.; Brett Garsed (b. Apr. 20, 1963, Victoria, Austral.), lead gtr.; Joey Cathcart (b. June 29, 1967, San Fernando Valley, Calif.), rhythm gtr.; Paul Mirkovich (b. Mar. 20, 1963, Studio City, Calif.), kybds.; Bobby Rock (b. July 13, 1963, Houston, Tex.), drums.
1990—*After the Rain* (DGC)   1995—*Because They Can.*

While identical twin sons of the late rock star Rick Nelson Gunnar and Matthew Nelson were one of a string of successful second-generation rock acts to emerge in the late Eighties (e.g., Julian Lennon, Ziggy Marley, and Wilson Phillips), they are the only ones whose family's show-business legacy spans four generations. With their waist-length blond hair and videogenic good looks, Gunnar and Matthew were pop-star naturals, and Nelson's melodic, neo-Seventies AOR rock—echoing Boston,

Foreigner, and Heart—found a wide audience. Gunnar and Matthew grew up in a typical latterday Hollywood home, a far cry from the Fifties idyll their paternal grandparents Ozzie and Harriet Nelson depicted on their long-running TV series *The Adventures of Ozzie and Harriet*. Father Rick was always off touring, while his wife, Kris Harmon (sister of actor Mark Harmon and actress Kelly Harmon), became an alcoholic and later a drug abuser. After their parents separated bitterly in 1977 amid mutual charges of infidelity and substance abuse, the twins stayed first with their mother, then—on their 18th birthday in 1985—moved in with Rick, who'd whetted their musical appetites by taking them backstage, on tour, and to recording studios when he could. Three months later, on New Year's Eve, 1985, Rick was killed in a plane crash en route to a concert. Gunnar and Matthew had planned to accompany their father on that tour, but Rick inexplicably decided not to take them at the last minute.

Though devastated, the boys kept a previously booked engagement on TV's *Saturday Night Live* in early 1986. Stung by accusations that they were capitalizing on their father's death, the pair retreated and regrouped; Gunnar, who'd been playing drums, learned guitar so he could move out front with Matthew.

They eventually recorded demo tapes that landed a 1988 deal. Two years in the making, *After the Rain* (the title referred to their familial tribulations, which included older sister and actress Tracy Nelson's bout with Hodgkin's disease) hit #17, yielding a #1 hit single in "(Can't Live Without Your) Love and Affection," plus "After the Rain" (#6, 1990), "More Than Ever" (#14, 1991), and "Only Time Will Tell" (#28, 1991).

The Nerves: See the Beat

Michael Nesmith

Born December 30, 1942, Houston, Texas
1968—*Mike Nesmith Produces/The Wichita Train Whistle Sings* (Dot)   1970—*Magnetic South* (RCA); *Loose Salute*   1971—*Nevada Fighter*   1972—*Tantamount to Treason; And the Hits Just Keep On Coming*   1973—*Pretty Much Your Standard Ranch Stash*   1975—*The Prison* (Pacific Arts)   1976—*Best of* (RCA)   1977—*From a Radio Engine to a Photon Wing* (Island/Pacific Arts)   1978—*Live at the Palais* (Pacific Arts); *Compilation*   1979—*Infinite Rider on the Big Dogma*   1980—*Elephant Parts*   1989—*The Newer Stuff* (Rhino)   1991—*The Older Stuff: The Best of Michael Nesmith (1970-1973)*   1994—*The Garden.*

Michael Nesmith came to the Monkees as an experienced musician and continued to prosper after the group dissolved in 1969, most recently as a pioneer and

innovator in the field of video. Nesmith's mother, an ex-secretary, grew rich after inventing Liquid Paper. He grew up in Farmers Branch, Texas, just outside Dallas. When he was 20 he got a guitar as a Christmas gift upon his discharge from the Air Force. Nesmith formed local folk-country bands and played club dates, venturing farther and farther afield during the Sixties. On the way home from a Rhode Island gig, he stopped off in Memphis to do some session work with Stax/Volt Records. He then moved to Los Angeles and played the folk circuit as a solo act, until he auditioned for—and became one of—the Monkees [see entry].

In 1968 Nesmith's "Different Drum" became Linda Ronstadt's first big hit. That same year, before the Monkees broke up, he recorded an instrumental LP of his own compositions, *Wichita*. When the Monkees finally dissolved, Nesmith formed the First National Band—featuring steel guitarist Red Rhodes—and made *Magnetic South,* which yielded a hit single, "Joanne" (#21, 1970).

After *Loose Salute,* the First National Band broke up, and Nesmith—retaining Rhodes and adding bassist Johnny Meeks, who'd played with Gene Vincent's Blue Caps—formed the Second National Band. At this time, he announced plans for a trilogy of three-album sets, nine LPs in all, that would detail the past, present, and future of country & western music. However, when Jac Holzman stepped down as president of Elektra Records—with which Nesmith's Countryside label was affiliated—his replacement, David Geffen, was less receptive to the idea and shelved it.

As time went on, Nesmith's projects tended to grow more ambitious. He formed the Pacific Arts Corporation and in 1975 released the concept album *The Prison.* An enclosed book was eventually worked into a stage play/ballet. Three years later "Rio," a track from *From a Radio Engine to a Photon Wing,* was a Top Thirty hit in the U.K. and a hit in several foreign countries, thanks in large part to the innovative video clip Nesmith produced for it through his then-fledgling film company, Pacific Arts. Here in America, where the clip was rarely if ever seen, "Rio" vanished, and *From a Radio Engine* was not even among the Top 200, demonstrating the power of video. Less than three years later, Nesmith's *Elephant Parts,* a conceptual rock video that combined music, comedy, and dance, received much critical acclaim, and, in 1981, won the first Grammy ever awarded to a video. That year saw the release of his *Popclips,* a series of syndicated half-hour video programming, hosted by Howie Mandel and shown on Nickelodeon. At that point, many artists were making what would later seem primitive video clips intended for airing on foreign television and on music programs like *American Bandstand.* Warner Cable expressed interest in buying the "Popclips" name and creating all-music-video programming; Nesmith and company declined. Two years later, Warner Cable launched MTV. In the years since, Pacific Arts has been a force in music video; among the many produced there is Lionel Richie's "All Night Long." Nesmith produced the feature films *Repo Man* and *Tapeheads* as well as his own projects and videos for other artists. He is also involved in home video distribution. Reportedly a multimillionaire, Nesmith continues to record and perform sporadically.

Robbie Nevil

Born October 2, 1960, Los Angeles, California
1986—*Robbie Nevil* (EMI Manhattan)   1988—*A Place Like This* (EMI)   1991—*Day 1*.

Singer, songwriter, and guitarist Robbie Nevil had sung in Los Angeles nightclubs as a teenager, and in 1983 landed a deal as a house composer for MCA Publishing. His tunes were recorded by Eddie Kendricks, Sheena Easton, Vanity, and the Pointer Sisters, though none was a hit. After trying for several years, Nevil landed his own solo recording deal, and his debut album (#37, 1986) yielded a huge hit in the blue-eyed pop funk of "C'est la Vie" (#2 pop, #7 R&B, 1986); many listeners erroneously thought the long-haired Nevil was black (some thought he might be a member of New Orleans' Neville Brothers), until they saw him singing amidst oil derricks and fashion models on MTV. Nevil's debut album also included "Dominoes" (#14, 1986) and "Wot's It to Ya" (#10 pop, #69 R&B, 1987).

Nevil's commercial profile began slipping with *A Place Like This* (#118, 1988), which produced "Back on Holiday" (#34, 1988) and "Somebody Like You" (#63, 1989). *Day 1*—Nevil's first self-produced album, and one dominated by his guitar playing—failed to chart, and produced only minor hits in "Just Like You" (#25, 1991) and "For Your Mind" (#86, 1991).

The Neville Brothers/Aaron Neville

Formed 1977, New Orleans, Louisiana
Arthur Neville (b. Dec. 17, 1937), kybds., voc.; Charles Neville (b. 1939), saxes, perc., voc.; Aaron Neville (b. Jan. 24, 1941), voc., perc.; Cyril Neville (b. Oct. 10, 1948), perc., voc.
1978—*The Neville Brothers* (Capitol)   1981—*Fiyo on the Biyou* (A&M)   1984—*Neville-ization* (Black Top)   1985—*Live at Tipitina's* (Spindletop)   1987—*Uptown* (EMI America)   1988—*Treacherous: A History of the Neville Brothers* (Rhino)   1989—*Yellow Moon* (A&M)   1990—*Brother's Keeper*   1991—*Treacherous Too!* (Rhino)   1992—*Family Groove* (A&M)   1994—*Live on Planet Earth*.
Aaron Neville solo: 1990—*Greatest Hits* (Curb); *My Greatest Gift* (Rounder)   1991—*Tell It Like It Is* (Curb); *Warm Your Heart* (A&M)   1993—*The Grand

Tour; Aaron Neville's Soulful Christmas 1995—*The Tattooed Heart.*

By the time the four Neville brothers formed their own group in 1977, the family name had been prominent in New Orleans R&B for more than two decades. Art Neville's high school band, the Hawketts, had recorded the perennial Carnival hit "Mardi Gras Mambo" in 1954. Charles and Aaron Neville had joined the Hawketts briefly, and when Art went into the navy in 1958, Aaron inherited the group's leadership.

In 1960 Aaron had his first solo hit, "Over You" (#21 R&B), on the Minit label; his second came with "Tell It Like It Is" (#2 pop, #1 R&B) for Parlo in 1966. Art and Aaron were reunited in the Sixties, when with a three-man rhythm section they gigged in New Orleans as the Neville Sounds. In 1967 producer Allen Toussaint hired Art and the rhythm section—the future Meters [see entry]—as his house band, and the Neville Sounds broke up. Aaron resumed his solo career, recording intermittently for Instant, Safari, and Bell, but also working as a dock hand. Charles went to New York to play sax in various jazz bands; he returned to New Orleans in the early Seventies and served a three-year sentence at Angola Prison Farm for possession of two joints of marijuana.

The Nevilles got together in the studio again, this time with youngest brother Cyril, in 1975, when they backed the Wild Tchoupitoulas, a "tribe" of Mardi Gras "black Indians" led by the Nevilles' uncle, George "Big Chief Jolly" Landry. *The Wild Tchoupitoulas* was released on Island Records in 1976, and the following year, after the Meters had disbanded, the Nevilles backed Landry on stage. Soon they were performing their own sets as the Neville Brothers, a vocal group specializing in four-part harmonies. Their first album presented them as something of a disco band, however, and Capitol dropped their contract.

It was three years before they recorded their second album, after Bette Midler persuaded producer Joel Dorn to work with them and the Nevilles secured the aid of R&B veteran arranger Wardell Quezergue. The result, which featured Aaron's delicate, quavering tenor on vocal warhorses like "Mona Lisa" and "The Ten Commandments of Love," as well as New Orleans "second-line" standards like "Iko Iko," was widely praised but rarely bought, and again the Neville Brothers lost their contract. In 1982, having opened some U.S. shows for the Rolling Stones the year before, they were expected to sign with Rolling Stones Records. Instead, they recorded two live albums in New Orleans for the tiny independent Black Top and Spindletop labels. They continued to tour, carrying the feathered costumes and additional singers that transformed them into the Wild Tchoupitoulas to climax their shows.

While the Neville Brothers' recording career re-

The Neville Brothers: Cyril, Aaron, Charles, Art

mained at a commercial impasse—only *Yellow Moon* (#66, 1989) and *Brother's Keeper* (#60, 1990) made the Top 100—Aaron Neville's career as a pop balladeer was rekindled through his 1989 duet with Linda Ronstadt, "Don't Know Much," which hit #2 pop. Millions came to marvel at the incongruity of Neville's angelic falsetto voice emerging from his imposing, hugely muscled physique and rather intimidating, craggy visage. Curb and Rounder capitalized on Aaron's success with best-ofs reaching back to the early Sixties, while Ronstadt co-produced *Warm Your Heart* (#44, 1991), which included another Top Ten hit in "Everybody Plays the Fool" (#8, 1991). *The Grand Tour* (#37, 1993) yielded an "adult contemporary" hit in "Don't Take Away My Heaven," and Neville even enjoyed brief chart success with *Soulful Christmas* (#36, 1993). Aaron also won a 1994 Grammy for a vocal collaboration with Trisha Yearwood, "I Fall to Pieces."

New Age

As much of a mindset or mood as a musical genre, New Age became popular in the Eighties as an instrumental soundtrack to a broad-based but loosely defined metaphysical movement that incorporates Jungian psychology, ecological concern, and nontraditional spirituality. Varying from acoustic work to synthesized orchestration, this improvisatory 4/4 form harks back to Debussy's impressionistic attempts to find musical equivalents for natural sounds and incorporates influences ranging from jazz-rock fusion and classical minimalism to Eastern and other indigenous world music. From such critically respected efforts as Brian Eno's ambient music and the atmospheric albums of former pop and rock musicians David Sylvian, Eddie Jobson and Ryuichi Sakamoto to the easy-listening sounds of Yanni and Kitaro, New Age can be defined more accurately through its purpose than its musical components. At the very least, New Age music strives to set a mood of reflective calm; at its most

ambitious, it becomes an auditory conduit to deep meditative states.

Tony Scott's *Music for Zen Meditation* (1964), Paul Horn's *Inside the Taj Mahal* (1968), and the Paul Winter Consort's *Icarus* (1972) are antecedents for the album and record label that introduced New Age—Will Ackerman's solo guitar *In Search of the Turtle's Navel* (1976). With his wife, Anne Robinson, Ackerman founded Palo Alto, California's Windham Hill, a label that with its million-selling fifth release, George Winston's *Autumn* (1980), became known for the lushly recorded sounds that in some quarters became derided as "Muzak for yuppies." Other labels soon followed, and practitioners ranging from synthesizer players Vangelis (*Chariots of Fire*) and Jean-Michel Jarre (*Oxygene*) to acoustic musicians like pianist Liz Story and harpist Andreas Vollenweider (the first New Age Grammy winner in 1987) mainstreamed the form. In 1986 a Los Angeles radio station began New Age programming with a format entitled "The Wave."

The New Christy Minstrels
Formed 1961
1962—*The New Christy Minstrels* (Columbia)
1963—*The New Christy Minstrels in Person; Tall Tales! Legends and Nonsense; Ramblin' Featuring "Green Green"* 1964—*Today* 1966—*Greatest Hits*.

The New Christy Minstrels were an ultracommercial folk-based group that provided an early training ground for Kenny Rogers and the First Edition, John Denver, Larry Ramos, some members of the Association, actress Karen Black, future Byrd Gene Clark, Barry McGuire, and Kim Carnes.

The group was formed by Randy Sparks in 1961. He'd taken the name from the Christy Minstrels formed back in 1842 by Edwin P. Christy. The original minstrels were a vaudeville act who popularized the work of Stephen Foster until 1921, and in the later stages included Al Jolson and Eddie Cantor. The "New" Minstrels were in no way related to the originals. They wrote their own material and first hit the chart in 1963 with "Green Green" (#14), cowritten by McGuire and Sparks, "Saturday Night" (#29, 1963), and "Today" (#17, 1964). Clark was with the group at this time, when it began playing the White House and other "establishment" places.

In 1964 the New Christy Minstrels hosted their own summer television show. In 1967 their musical director at the time, Mike Settle, took three other band members—Thelma Camacho, Kenny Rogers, and Terry Williams—and formed the First Edition (according to some sources, it was Rogers who formed the group). The Minstrels continued to record, with steadily declining sales, until their breakup in the early Seventies.

New Edition
Formed circa 1981, Boston, Massachusetts
Bobby Brown (b. Bobby Bradsford Brown, Feb. 7, 1966, Boston), voc.; Michael Bivins (b. Aug. 10, 1968, Boston), voc.; Ricky Bell (b. Sep. 18, 1967, Boston), voc.; Ronnie DeVoe (b. Nov. 17, 1967, Boston), voc.; Ralph Tresvant (b. 1968, Boston), voc.
1983—*Candy Girl* (Streetwise)   1984—*New Edition* (MCA)   1985—*All for Love*   1985—*Christmas All Over the World*   1986—*Under the Blue Moon* 1988—(– Brown; + Johnny Gill [b. 1965, Washington, D.C.], voc.) *Heart Break*   1991—*Greatest Hits*.
Bobby Brown solo: See entry.
Bell Biv DeVoe: See entry.
Johnny Gill solo: 1983—*Johnny Gill* (Atlantic) 1985—*Chemistry*   1993—*Provocative* (Motown).
Ralph Tresvant solo: 1990—*Ralph Tresvant* (MCA) 1993—*It's Goin' Down*.

In the early Eighties the teenaged pop-funk outfit New Edition was dismissed as the brainchild of an ambitious writer, producer, and impresario, whose slick, bouncy songs and savvy marketing had made its members stars. By the decade's end, however, the vocal group had bred some of the most intriguing artists in contemporary R&B. New Edition's original five members met while attending junior high school in Boston's Roxbury district. They were discovered by Maurice Starr while performing in a talent show he was promoting. After Starr landed them a deal with the hip-hop label Streetwise, New Edition scored two Top Ten R&B singles in 1983, "Candy Girl" (#1) and "Is This the End" (#8). Later that year the group secured a major-label contract with MCA Records and severed ties with Starr, who went on to form New Kids on the Block.

Starr's writing and production nonetheless fueled New Edition's eponymous 1984 album, which reached #6 and spawned the hits "Cool It Now" (#4 pop, 1985; #1 R&B, 1984), "Mr. Telephone Man" (#12 pop, #1 R&B, 1985), and "Lost in Love" (#6 R&B, 1985). More successful R&B singles followed in 1985 and 1986: "Count Me Out" (#2, 1985), "A Little Bit of Love (Is All It Takes)" (#3, 1986), "With You All the Way" (#7, 1986), "Earth Angel" (#3, 1986), and "Once in a Lifetime Groove" (#10, 1986).

By now, though, the group was splintering. Bobby Brown left in 1986 to embark on a successful solo career [see entry] and was replaced by Johnny Gill, who sang on the 1988 hit "If It Isn't Love" (#7 pop, #2 R&B). Gill himself eventually went solo, as did Ralph Tresvant, whose self-titled debut album topped the R&B chart in 1990 and yielded the #1 R&B single "Sensitivity" (also a #4 pop hit). In 1991 Tresvant scored the R&B hits "Stone Cold Gentleman" (#3)—featuring Brown rapping—and "Do What I Gotta Do" (#2). In 1988 the remaining members of New Edition formed the hip-hop trio Bell Biv DeVoe [see entry]. Mutually supportive, New Edition's alumni have made appearances together in the Nineties and have discussed the possibility of reuniting on disc.

New Grass Revival: See Béla Fleck

New Jack Swing
Originated by producer Teddy Riley, New Jack Swing is a slick, highly palatable, and commercial combination of hip-hop beats and traditional R&B vocals that came to prominence in the late Eighties. Fantasy and romance dominate the style's lyrics. Among the first New Jack Swing artists were Keith Sweat ("I Want Her," 1987) and Johnny Kemp ("Just Got Paid," 1988), both produced by Riley. Later New Jack Swing artists included Riley's own group, Guy, and former New Edition members Bobby Brown (whose "My Prerogative" was a major hit in 1989) and Bell Biv DeVoe. Other producing teams embraced the lucrative genre, including L.A. and Babyface and Jimmy Jam and Terry Lewis. In 1991 Michael Jackson hired Riley to give some of the cuts on *Dangerous* a more updated sound. By the early Nineties the term New Jack Swing had become nearly obsolete in the face of an array of new artists—including Mary J. Blige, Jodeci, and Tony! Toni! Toné!—who further expanded hip-hop-based R&B.

New Kids on the Block
Formed 1985, Boston, Massachusetts
Donnie Wahlberg (b. Aug. 17, 1969, Boston), voc.; Jonathan Knight (b. Nov. 29, 1968, Worcester, Mass.), voc.; Jordan Knight (b. May 15, 1970, Worcester, Mass.), voc.; Danny Wood (b. May 14, 1969, Boston), voc.; Joe McIntyre (b. Dec. 3, 1972, Needham, Mass.), voc.

Grammy Awards

Rick Nelson
1986 Best Spoken Word or Nonmusical Recording: *Interviews from the Class of '55 Recording Sessions* (with others)

Willie Nelson
1975 Best Country Vocal Performance, Male: "Blue Eyes Crying in the Rain"
1978 Best Country Vocal Performance by a Duo or Group: "Mamas, Don't Let Your Babies Grow Up to Be Cowboys" (with Waylon Jennings)
1978 Best Country Vocal Performance, Male: "Georgia on My Mind"
1980 Best Country Song: "On the Road Again"
1982 Best Country Vocal Performance, Male: "Always on My Mind"
1990 Grammy Legend Award

Michael Nesmith
1981 Video of the Year: *Michael Nesmith in Elephant Parts*

Aaron Neville
1989 Best Pop Performance by a Duo or Group with Vocal: "Don't Know Much" (with Linda Ronstadt)
1990 Best Pop Performance by a Duo or Group with Vocal: "All My Life" (with Linda Ronstadt)
1994 Best Country Vocal Collaboration: "I Fall to Pieces" (with Trish Yearwood)

The New Christy Minstrels
1962 Best Performance by a Chorus: *Presenting the New Christy Minstrels*

Randy Newman
1984 Best Instrumental Composition: "The Natural" (tied with John Williams, "Olympic Fanfare and Theme")

Juice Newton
1982 Best Country Vocal Performance, Female: "Break It to Me Gently"

Olivia Newton-John
1973 Best Country Vocal Performance, Female: "Let Me Be There"
1974 Record of the Year: "I Honestly Love You"
1974 Best Pop Vocal Performance, Female: "I Honestly Love You"
1982 Video of the Year: *Olivia Physical*

Harry Nilsson
1969 Best Contemporary Vocal Performance, Male: "Everybody's Talkin'"
1972 Best Pop Vocal Performance, Male: "Without You"

Nine Inch Nails
1992 Best Metal Performance with Vocal: "Wish"

Nitty Gritty Dirt Band
1989 Best Bluegrass Recording: "The Valley Road" (with Bruce Hornsby)
1989 Best Country Performance by a Duo or Group with Vocal: *Will the Circle Be Unbroken, vol. 2*

Dr. Dre (N.W.A)
1993 Best Rap Solo Performance: "Let Me Ride"

1986—*New Kids on the Block* (Columbia) 1988—*Hangin' Tough* 1989—*Merry, Merry Christmas* 1990—*Step by Step*; *No More Games: The Remix Album* 1994—*Face the Music* (as NKOTB).

When composer, producer, and promoter Maurice Starr lost New Edition, the teen-soul outfit he created in the early Eighties, to a record contract dispute, the impresario resolved to create an equally successful all-white act in that band's image. Actually, New Kids on the Block eclipsed the superstardom achieved by its predecessors (as a collective unit, at least), scoring numerous smash singles and, in 1991, topping *Forbes* magazine's list of highest-paid American entertainers, over Michael Jackson and Madonna. The vocal group's R&B-flavored bubblegum pop didn't prove as popular with critics as it did with the prepubescent girls who flocked to their shows and gobbled up New Kids merchandise. After suffering some professional and legal troubles, the Kids tried to reinvent themselves as a more mature, musically ambitious act, NKOTB.

In 1984 Starr enlisted a Boston talent agency to find white singers, rappers, and dancers in the area. The agency first discovered Donnie Wahlberg, who would become the band's most outspoken and artistically confident member. (In 1991 he produced a hit album for his kid brother, Marky Mark [see entry].) Wahlberg introduced Starr to brothers Jonathan and Jordan Knight—respectively New Kids' oldest member and its falsetto-flaunting lead singer (who joined the group with braces on his teeth)—and break dancer Danny Wood, who had all been bussed to the same grade school in Roxbury, a mostly black neighborhood where Starr lived. Joe McIntyre completed the lineup of Nynuk, who became New Kids on the Block after Wahlberg wrote a song by that name for the quintet's eponymous debut album.

Originally released in 1986, *New Kids on the Block* sold poorly. But after a slow start, 1988's *Hangin'*

Tough—written, produced, and arranged by Starr—became a #1 pop album, fueled by the hits "Please Don't Go Girl" (#10, 1988) and "You Got It (The Right Stuff)" (#3, 1989). More Top Ten singles followed: "I'll Be Loving You (Forever)" (#1, 1989); "Hangin' Tough" (#1, 1989) and it's B side "Didn't I (Blow Your Mind)" (#8 1989); "Cover Girl" (#2, 1989); and "This One's for the Children" (#7, 1990). *Step by Step,* which the New Kids coproduced with Michael Jonzun and Starr, also topped the charts in 1990, generating a #1 title track and the #7 song "Tonight."

An album of remixes, released later that year, peaked at #19 in 1991. By then backlash-inducing problems had arisen: Wahlberg and McIntyre were allegedly involved in two separate brawls, in which other parties were injured. That same year Wahlberg was charged with hotel-room arson; after pleading guilty to criminal mischief, he was ordered to make public service announcements. Then a former New Kids producer sued Starr on the grounds that the boys hadn't sung on their albums, an accusation they publicly refuted. In 1992 the group resurfaced as NKOTB, with the single "If You Go Away" (#16), which didn't win over any detractors. But NKOTB's 1994 album, the Starrless *Face the Music,* fared surprisingly well with critics. The album's producers included Wahlberg, hip-hop wizard Teddy Riley, and smooth pop veteran Narada Michael Walden (Whitney Houston, Mariah Carey).

Randy Newman

Born November 28, 1944, New Orleans, Louisiana
1968—*Randy Newman* (Reprise) 1970—*12 Songs*
1971—*Live* 1972—*Sail Away* 1974—*Good Old*
***Boys* 1977—*Little Criminals* (Warner Bros.)**
1979—*Born Again; Ragtime* soundtrack (Elektra)
1983—*Trouble in Paradise* (Warner Bros.) 1984—
The Natural* soundtrack 1987—*Three Amigos
soundtrack 1988—*Land of Dreams* (Reprise)
1990—*Parenthood* soundtrack; *Avalon* soundtrack
1991—*Awakenings* soundtrack 1994—*The Paper*
soundtrack (Reprise).

Randy Newman writes mordant, ironic, concise songs with chromatic twists worthy of George Gershwin and Kurt Weill. He sings in a deep drawl and accompanies himself on piano (Fats Domino was an early hero) and often tours alone. Newman tends to write lyrics about characters bordering on the pathological: bigots, perverts, slaveship captains, ELO fans. While this practice tends to limit his pop appeal, a few of his songs have been widely covered, and he has a solid cult following. He has had one major hit single—"Short People" (#2, 1978)—and recorded other popular songs, including "The Blues" (#54, 1983) and "I Love L.A." Through the Eighties he has also established himself as a leading composer of movie soundtracks.

Randy Newman

Newman grew up in a musical family with Hollywood connections; his uncles Alfred and Lionel both scored numerous films. By age 17 Randy was staff writer for a California publishing company. One semester short of a B.A. in music from UCLA, he dropped out of school. Lenny Waronker, son of Liberty Records' president, was a close friend and later, as a staff producer for Warner Bros., helped get Newman signed to the label.

Newman's early songs were recorded by a number of performers. His friend Harry Nilsson recorded an entire album with Newman on piano, *Nilsson Sings Newman,* in 1970. Judy Collins ("I Think It's Going to Rain Today"), Peggy Lee ("Love Story"), and Three Dog Night—for whom "Mama Told Me (Not to Come)" hit #1—all enjoyed success with Newman's music.

Newman became a popular campus attraction when touring with Nilsson. His status as a cult star was affirmed by his critically praised debut, *Randy Newman,* in 1968, which featured his own complex arrangements for full orchestra, and later by 1970's *12 Songs.* He also sang "Gone Dead Train" on the 1970 soundtrack of *Performance. Randy Newman/Live* and *Sail Away* were his first commercial successes. But his audience has been limited to some degree because his songs are often colored by his ironic, pointed sense of humor, which is rarely simple and frequently misunderstood.

Good Old Boys, for example, was a concept album about the South, with the lyrics expressing the viewpoint of white southerners. Lyrics such as "We're rednecks, and we don't know our ass from a hole in the ground" made people wonder whether Newman was being satirical or sympathetic. He toured (to Atlanta and elsewhere) with a full orchestra that played his arrangements and was conducted by his uncle Emil Newman.

Little Criminals in 1977 contained Newman's first hit single, "Short People," which mocked bigotry and was taken seriously by a vocal, offended minority. "Baltimore" from that album was covered by Nina Simone. Following that album's release, Newman toured for the first time since 1974. He claimed that in the interim he'd done nothing but look at television and play with his three sons. In 1979 his *Born Again* featured guest vocals by members of the Eagles. Newman composed the soundtrack for the film *Ragtime* (the first of many soundtrack assignments) and was nominated for two Oscars (Best Song, Best Score). His 1983 album, *Trouble in Paradise,* included guest appearances by Linda Ronstadt, members of Fleetwood Mac, and Paul Simon, who sang a verse of "The Blues." That album's "I Love L.A." became something of an anthem, thanks in part to a flashy music video directed by Newman's cousin, Tim Newman (who went on to shoot popular videos for ZZ Top, among others). *Land of Dreams* (#80, 1988) spawned a minor hit in "It's Money That Matters" (#60, 1988).

New Order: See Joy Division

The New Orleans Sound

At the mouth of the Mississippi, New Orleans has stood at a crossroads where Native American, French, Spanish, English, African, Caribbean, and Latin-American cultures have mixed for over two centuries. A capital of American music at least since the Civil War, the city has shaped rhythm & blues, rock & roll, and reggae no less than its native ragtime, jazz, and Delta blues.

The barrelhouse piano of Kid Stormy Weather and Sullivan Rock, the crude but gentle vocal styles of Creole folksingers, and dances from Cuba and Trinidad were the sources from which pianist Professor Longhair forged his prototypical rock & roll in the mid-Forties. Concurrently, Dave Bartholomew assembled a band that featured many of the city's most inventive musicians and combined the loose cohesiveness of the best jazz ensembles with the "second line" syncopations and raucous brass work of Mardi Gras parade bands.

With the arrival of independent record companies such as De Luxe and Imperial, a recording industry began to flourish. Blues singer Roy Brown had the first New Orleans rock & roll hit with "Good Rockin' Tonight" in 1948, followed by Longhair admirer and Bartholomew frontman Fats Domino.

Attracted by Domino's success, independent labels like Specialty, Regal, Aladdin, Chess, and Atlantic went scouting for talent throughout the Fifties and were rewarded with hits by Lloyd Price, Guitar Slim, Shirley and

Lee, Clarence "Frogman" Henry, and Bobby Charles. Virtually every Crescent City recording was cut at studio owner/engineer Cosimo Matassa's primitive French Quarter facility with Lee Allen's Studio Band (composed of the stars of the Bartholomew band). Matassa's unadorned live-in-the-studio production and the Studio Band's fat rolling bottom and light rocking top defined the New Orleans Sound—one that Ray Charles and Little Richard, among others, went to New Orleans to capture on some of their biggest hits.

Ace Records, founded in 1955, was the first New Orleans–based label, and with Huey Smith and the Clowns, Jimmy Clanton, Frankie Ford, and Earl King, it quickly challenged the out-of-towners' supremacy. By the end of the decade, as national tastes turned to milder fare, new local labels such as Ric, Instant, Red Bird, Minit, and AFO followed Ace's lead. The most prominent young producers were Allen Toussaint and Wardell Quezergue (both Bartholomew protégés), who updated the New Orleans sound by relaxing the beat without weakening the funk; Jessie Hill, Chris Kenner, Ernie K-Doe, Irma Thomas, and the Dixie Cups kept the sound before the public in the early Sixties. By the late Sixties most of the local labels had either folded or moved to Los Angeles. Nonetheless, local talent continued to be heard nationwide via hits by Robert Parker, Aaron Neville, Lee Dorsey, and the Meters.

In the Seventies the New Orleans sound was emulated by popular artists like Dr. John, the Rolling Stones, the Band, Paul Simon, Labelle, Kool and the Gang, Paul McCartney, Parliament/Funkadelic, and later, the Clash (who booked Lee Dorsey to open for them). And within the city, the Mardi Gras and an active club scene kept old traditions alive and fostered new ones. Professor Longhair recorded several acclaimed new albums and returned to the concert circuit a few years before his death in 1980; Mardi Gras "black Indian" groups like the Wild Tchoupitoulas and the Wild Magnolias concocted a blend of ceremonial dances and R&B rhythms; and the Neville Brothers combined four-part harmonies with electric funk.

In the Eighties Aaron Neville emerged as a mainstream success, recording solo and with Linda Ronstadt. Irma Thomas experienced a revival and Fats Domino still toured, but it was with new national interest in Cajun and zydeco music (Buckwheat Zydeco, Rockin' Sidney, and Zachary Richard) that New Orleans came again to the fore. New groups like the Dirty Dozen Brass Band and the Radiators sharpened the focus on the city as did the popularity of jazz players Wynton and Branford Marsalis and revisionist crooner Harry Connick Jr. The greatest single factor in the Crescent City's importance remains its annual New Orleans Jazz and Heritage Festival, since 1970 the largest continuing showcase of roots music of every conceivable stripe.

New Riders of the Purple Sage

Formed 1969, Marin County, California
John "Marmaduke" Dawson (b. 1945, San Francisco,
Calif.), gtr., voc.; David Nelson (b. San Francisco,
Calif.), gtr., voc.; Jerry Garcia (b. Aug. 1, 1942, San
Francisco, Calif.), pedal steel gtr.; Mickey Hart
(b. ca. 1950, Long Island, N.Y.), drums; Phil Lesh
(b. Philip Chapman, Mar. 15, 1940, Berkeley, Calif.),
bass.
1970–71—(– Hart; – Lesh; + Spencer Dryden [b. Apr.
7, 1943, New York City, N.Y.], drums; + Dave Tor-
bert, bass)   1971—*New Riders of the Purple Sage*
(Columbia) (– Garcia; + Buddy Cage [b. Toronto,
Can.], pedal steel gtr.)   1972—*Powerglide*; *Gypsy
Cowboy*   1973—*Adventures of Panama Red*
1974—*Home Home on the Road* (– Torbert; + Skip
Battin [b. Feb. 2, 1934, Gallipolis, Ohio], bass); *Brujo*
1975—*Oh, What a Mighty Time*   1976—*Best of the
New Riders of the Purple Sage* (– Battin; + Stephen
Love [b. Ind.], bass); *New Riders* (MCA)   1977—
(+ Allen Kemp, gtr.) *Who Are These Guys*   1978—
Marin County Line   1982—(– Love; – Cage; + Rusty
Gauthier, gtr., violin, fiddle, mandolin, dobro)
Feelin' Alright (A&M)   1985—(– Kemp; + Gary Vo-
gensen, voc., gtr.)   1986—*Before Time Began*
(Relix)   1987—*Vintage New Riders of the Purple
Sage*   1992—*Midnight Moonlight*   1993—(– Vo-
gensen; + Evan Morgan, gtr.)   1994—(Reunion
lineup: Dawson; Nelson; Cage) *Live in Japan.*

The New Riders of the Purple Sage began as a loosely
constructed offshoot of the Grateful Dead. The group's
history dates back to spring 1969, when Dead lead guitarist Jerry Garcia first bought a pedal steel guitar and
was searching for a country band to use it in. Jams developed among Garcia and the core of the new band—
David Nelson and main songwriter John Dawson—plus
other Dead members, Mickey Hart and Phil Lesh, thus
forming the first Riders band.

Nelson and Dawson had loose connections to Dead
members dating back to 1962. Nelson first knew Garcia
and lyricist Robert Hunter from his days in the Wildwood
Boys back in art school. Nelson was also an early member of Big Brother and later the New Delhi River Band in
Marin County, California, which included Dave Torbert
and Dawson (who in 1964 had played in another Dead
progenitor, Mother McCree's Uptown Jug Champions).

Hunter and Nelson named the Riders after a 1912
novel by Zane Grey, and they became the opening band
for the Dead tours in 1970. By the time they got a contract with Columbia Records in 1971 (by then called New
Riders of the Purple Sage), former Jefferson Airplane
drummer Spencer Dryden had replaced Hart, and Torbert had taken over for Lesh. Garcia bowed out after the
debut (the Dead took up too much of his time), and in

late 1971 they added Buddy Cage on pedal steel. He'd
previously played with Ian and Sylvia's Great Speckled
Bird.

Like the Dead and Commander Cody, the Riders became associated with dope-smoking hippiedom, especially with their anthemic "Panama Red," written by
nonmember Peter Rowan. This made them a strong concert attraction, though their albums sold only moderately.
The Adventures of Panama Red was their lone LP to go
gold. The lineup was stable until February 1974, after the
live LP *Home Home on the Road,* when Torbert left to
form Kingfish with Bob Weir. Ex-Byrd Skip Battin took his
place for two LPs and then left in 1976 to join a new version of the Flying Burrito Brothers. The group then
switched to MCA and added Steve Love on bass. He'd
previously played with Roger McGuinn and Rick Nelson's Stone Canyon Band. The New Riders recorded two
LPs for MCA before they lost their contract. They continue to tour, with Dawson still at the helm, playing small
clubs across the U.S. and elsewhere. In early 1994 Nelson
formed the Dave Nelson Band. Also in 1994 the New Riders of the Purple Sage's original members Nelson, Dawson, and Buddy Cage reunited; it was the first time the
three had played together since the early Eighties.

Juice Newton

Born Judy Kay Newton, February 18, 1952, New Jersey
1975—*Juice Newton and Silver Spur* (RCA)   1976—
After the Dust Settles; *Come to Me* (Capitol)
1978—*Well Kept Secret*   1979—*Take Heart*   1981—
Juice   1982—*Quiet Lies*   1983—*Dirty Looks*
1984—*Can't Wait All Night* (RCA); *Greatest Hits*
(Capitol)   1987—*Emotion*   1988—*Old Flame*
1989—*Ain't Gonna Cry*   1990—*Greatest Country
Hits* (Curb).

Country-pop singer Juice Newton recorded five mostly
ignored albums before she suddenly hit it big in 1981
with a platinum LP and three Top Ten singles, starting
with a remake of Merrilee Rush's 1968 hit "Angel of the
Morning." Newton grew up in a Virginia seaside community and taught herself acoustic guitar at 13. She moved
to Los Gatos, California, in the late Sixties, and with
Texas-born Otha Young formed Dixie Peach. A year later,
in 1972, Newton and Young formed Silver Spur with
bassist Tom Kealey. After years of doing cover-heavy bar
gigs, the three began to concentrate on original material.

In 1975 they signed to RCA (billed as Juice Newton
and Silver Spur) and released an eponymous LP with
heavy folk-rock leanings. They did one more unsuccessful album for RCA, *After the Dust Settles,* in 1976, and
the next year signed to Capitol for *Come to Me,* produced by Elliot Mazer (who'd worked with Janis Joplin,
Neil Young, and the Band). The LP was closer to country

rock this time, and included a song given to her by Bob Seger called "Good Luck Baby Jane." Newton also did backup vocals that year on Bob Welch's solo LP *French Kiss*. In 1978 Silver Spur disbanded, and Newton went solo with *Well Kept Secret*. In 1979 she had her first country hit, "Sunshine," from *Take Heart*.

Juice was her breakthrough LP. Following the success of "Angel of the Morning" (#4), she hit with "Queen of Hearts" (#2), a rockabilly track recorded in 1979 by Dave Edmunds, both gold singles, and "The Sweetest Thing" (#7 pop, #1 C&W, 1981). The LP went platinum. Other hit singles include "Love's Been a Little Bit Hard on Me" (#7 pop, #2 C&W, 1982), "Break It to Me Gently" (#11 pop, #2 C&W, 1982), "A Little Love" (#44 pop, #64 C&W, 1984), "You Make Me Want to Make You Mine" (#1 C&W, 1985), "I'm So Hurt" (#1 C&W, 1985), "Old Flame" (#1 C&W, 1986), "Both to Each Other (Friends and Lovers)" (#1 C&W, 1986), "Cheap Love" (#9 C&W, 1986), "What Can I Do with My Heart" (#9 C&W, 1986), and "Tell Me True" (#8 C&W, 1987).

Olivia Newton-John

Born September 26, 1948, Cambridge, England
1973—*Let Me Be There* (MCA)   1975—*If You Love Me, Let Me Know*   1977—*Olivia Newton-John's Greatest Hits*   1978—*Totally Hot*   1981—*Physical* 1982—*Olivia's Greatest Hits, vol. 2*   1985—*Soul Kiss*   1988—*The Rumour*   1989—*Warm and Tender* (Geffen)   1992—*Back to Basics: The Essential Collection 1971–1992*.

Olivia Newton-John's career has mirrored the Sandra Dee-to-leather-girl transformation of her role in *Grease*—from fresh-faced pop-country singer to a sexier pop–rock & roll singer. In both guises she has had great commercial success, scoring 15 Top Ten hits. Newton-John's grandfather was Nobel Prize–winning German physicist Max Born, and her father was headmaster of Ormond College in Melbourne, Australia. Newton-John grew up in Melbourne, where in high school she formed her first band with three other girls, the Sol Four. She quit school and at age 16 won a talent contest and was sent to England. For the next two years she worked there with fellow Australian Pat Carroll (who later married Newton-John's producer John Farrar). When Carroll's visa expired, she was sent back to Australia, and Newton-John joined Don Kirshner's attempt to make a British Monkees, a short-lived band called Tomorrow (no relation to Steve Howe's first band).

She began touring with British superstar Cliff Richard and appearing regularly on his series *It's Cliff Richard*, which greatly boosted the British sales of her first single, Bob Dylan's "If Not for You" (1971), which was also a hit (#25) in America. She had other British hits with covers of George Harrison's "What Is Life" (1972) and

John Denver's "Take Me Home Country Roads" (1973). Her U.S. breakthrough came in 1973 with her first American LP, *Let Me Be There*, which went gold, aided by the gold single title track (#6), which also won her a Grammy for Best Country Vocal Performance, Female. Her next LP, *If You Love Me, Let Me Know*, went gold and included the title track gold single (#5, 1974) and a gold hit for her version of Peter Allen's "I Honestly Love You" (#1, 1974).

Newton-John moved to L.A., and her albums continued to go gold. But a number of country performers resented her presence on the country chart—with hits like "Have You Never Been Mellow" (#1 pop, #3 C&W, 1975) and "Please Mr. Please" (#3 pop, #5 C&W, 1975)—and when she won the 1974 Female Vocalist of the Year award from the Country Music Association, some members quit in protest.

Until then, Newton-John had a girl-next-door image, but that all changed in 1978 with the release of *Grease*. The film went on to become the most profitable movie musical ever made, grossing over $150 million worldwide and yielding three singles for Newton-John—"You're the One That I Want," sung with John Travolta (#1), "Summer Nights" (#5, also a Travolta duet), and "Hopelessly Devoted to You" (#3), all gold.

She and Cliff Richard hit with their 1980 duet "Suddenly" (#20), and she also appeared that year in the film fantasy *Xanadu*, which was a commercial flop. The album, however, went double platinum. Her sexier image was reinforced with *Totally Hot* and *Physical* (both platinum), the latter of which boasted three hit singles in 1982, including the #1 title single, "Physical," which topped the chart for ten weeks running. In 1983 she reunited with Travolta onscreen in *Two of a Kind;* the film was a critical and commercial failure, but its soundtrack spun off two charting singles: "Twist of Fate" (#5, 1983) and "Livin' in Desperate Times" (#31, 1984).

In 1984 she married actor Matt Lattanzi; they now have a daughter, Chloe, born in 1986. That year she opened her chain of clothing stores, Koala Blue. In the late Eighties she released her last album under her MCA contract, *The Rumour*, which did not break the U.S. Top Fifty. In 1989 she signed to Geffen, where her first release was a collection of children's songs and lullabies, *Warm and Tender*. Since the birth of her daughter, Newton-John has been active in numerous environmental-protection efforts. In the early Eighties she was honored with an Order of the British Empire (OBE). In the early Nineties she successfully underwent treatment for breast cancer.

New Wave

A virtually meaningless, highly flexible term that arose shortly after punk rock in the late Seventies, new wave was variously pop with punkish trappings—such as faster tempos, stripped-down arrangements, and alienated lyrics, like those of the Cars or Blondie—or a catch-all term for bands that emerged after 1976 and could not be categorized as pure punk, like Talking Heads or Pere Ubu.

Around 1979 there was a crop of new-wave acts whose sound and style was based on Sixties British and American rock: the Pretenders, the Romantics, the Beat, 20/20, the Records, Bram Tchaikovsky, and Nick Lowe, for example. But with a few exceptions, these acts enjoyed fleeting popularity, and with the advent of MTV, the definition of new wave took another twist, this time moving away from straight guitar-driven power pop and headlong into a cooler form of synthesizer rock. As pop movements go, this vein of new wave came and went fairly quickly, leaving little behind in terms of long-lasting influence, although, thanks to MTV, acts such as Haircut 100, Missing Persons, and Flock of Seagulls are better remembered for their looks than for their songs. As MTV began defining the mainstream, successful new-wave acts, such as the Cars, Duran Duran, and the Police, became so widely popular that they outgrew the categorization.

The New York Dolls

Formed 1971, New York City, New York
Johnny Thunders (b. John Genzale, July 15, 1952;
d. Apr. 23, 1991, New Orleans, La.), gtr.; Arthur
Kane, bass; Billy Murcia (b. 1951, New York City;
d. Nov. 6, 1972, London, Eng.), drums; Rick Rivets,
gtr.; David Johansen (b. Jan. 9, 1950, Staten Island,
N.Y.), voc.
1972—(+ Sylvain Sylvain [b. Syl Mizrahi], gtr.;
– Rivets; – Murcia; + Jerry Nolan [b. May 7, 1946,
New York City; d. Jan. 14, 1992, New York City],
drums) 1973—New York Dolls (Mercury) 1974—
Too Much Too Soon 1981—Lipstick Killers cassette
(ROIR) 1984—Red Patent Leather (Restless)
1985—Best of the New York Dolls (Mercury)
1986—Night of the Living Dolls 1993—Paris Le
Trash (Triple X) 1994—Rock 'n' Roll (Mercury).
David Johansen solo: See entry.
Johnny Thunders solo: See Heartbreakers entry.
Sylvain Sylvain solo: 1979—Sylvain Sylvain (RCA)
1981—Sylvain Sylvain and the Teardrops (with the
Teardrops).

When the New York Dolls formed in late 1971, they were not only creating some of the most passionate music of the new glitter era (and in fact defining a new New York rock style) but setting the stage for the punk movement that followed five years later.

The band members were born and grew up in various boroughs of New York City and played in local bands; several had been in Actress. In late 1971 Johnny

Thunders, Rick Rivets, Arthur Kane, and Billy Murcia began jamming, and soon they were joined by singer David Johansen. After they had replaced Rivets with Syl Sylvain, they started playing the Mercer Arts Center in Lower Manhattan, where they opened for a group called Eric Emerson's Magic Tramps. A local glitter scene of sorts developed around the group. The Dolls' music was strongly influenced by the Rolling Stones, the MC5, the Stooges, and the Velvet Underground, but was deliberately more amateurish. And their look—outrageous clothing and women's makeup—captured the outrage and threat of glitter. Despite this, their music and attitude were down to earth, and their stardom-by-self-definition stance served to keep most record companies at a distance.

During their first tour of England, Murcia died after mixing alcohol with pills; the official cause of death was suffocation. The band replaced him with Jerry Nolan, who appeared on its Todd Rundgren–produced debut. Though both the debut and its followup—which was produced by George "Shadow" Morton—were critical successes, they were commercial disasters; the group's sound and image were just too weird. After they lost their recording contract, the Dolls were briefly managed by Malcolm McLaren [see entry], who suggested that they use a communist flag as a stage backdrop. When no new record contract developed, both Nolan and Thunders left the band, and Johansen and Sylvain continued to tour with various backing musicians under the Dolls name through 1977.

Thunders and Nolan formed the Heartbreakers [see entry], and later Thunders created his own bands, one of which, Gang War, included MC5 guitarist Wayne Kramer. In 1978 Nolan and Kane played a few shows backing former Sex Pistol Sid Vicious. Johansen began his solo career in 1978 [see entry], and Sylvain stayed with Johansen's band until he quit in 1979 to start his own solo career.

Johnny Thunders died of a drug overdose in 1991. Former bandmate Jerry Nolan made his last public performance at a memorial concert for Thunders. Nolan then died shortly thereafter of a stroke at age 40.

Through the years archival Dolls material has surfaced: in 1981 ROIR released the cassette-only Lipstick Killers, a formative Dolls studio tape from 1972; Red Patent Leather documents a 1975 New York show; Night of the Living Dolls includes previously unreleased material; Paris Le Trash is another live album. In addition, there is a Mercury anthology.

The Nice

Formed 1967, London, England
Keith Emerson (b. Nov. 1, 1944, Todmorden, Eng.),
organ, piano, synth., voc.; Lee Jackson (b. Jan. 8,

1943, Newcastle-upon-Tyne, Eng.), bass, gtr., voc.; Brian "Blinky" Davison (b. May 25, 1942, Leicester, Eng.), drums; David O'List (b. Eng.), gtr., voc. 1968—*The Thoughts of Emerlist Davjack* (Immediate) (– O'List)   1969—*Ars Longa Vita Brevis*; *Nice* 1970—*Five Bridges* (Mercury); *Keith Emerson with the Nice*   1971—*Elegy*.

Besides providing the blueprint for Emerson, Lake and Palmer, the Nice was a link between the early experimentalism of late-Sixties psychedelia and classical-influenced art rock. As Keith Emerson's initial platform, its snickering desecration of the classics, along with its long instrumental interludes, helped expand the form—and pretensions—of rock.

The band began in August 1967 as a backup for English black female soul vocalist P. P. Arnold. All the members had previously played in other British groups; Emerson and Lee Jackson knew each other from the R&B aggregation Gary Farr and the T-Bones. By October the Nice had split from Arnold and released its debut single in England on manager Andrew Oldham's Immediate Records, "The Thoughts of Emerlist Davjack," also the title of its debut LP. The album's centerpiece was "Rondo," an organ raveup based on Mozart. Live, Emerson went wild on numbers like this (or on his jazzed-up version of Bob Dylan's "She Belongs to Me"), stabbing his keyboard with knives and pulling mock-masturbatory moves. Along with these antics (continued later in ELP), Emerson also wore flashy gold lamé clothes and performed stunts like burning a U.S. flag on stage at London's Royal Albert Hall during a performance of Leonard Bernstein's "America" from *West Side Story*. The Nice was subsequently banned from the hall, and Bernstein tried to stop the group from releasing its instrumental version of the song in the U.S. Partly because Emerson had become the star, guitarist David O'List left. For a few days in 1969 he replaced Mick Abrahams in Jethro Tull.

During most of the Nice's 2½-year career, it was a three-piece power trio, with Emerson establishing himself as the Hendrix of the organ. The group was popular in Europe but never sold many records in the U.S. The three were just beginning to draw some attention stateside when Emerson, playing the Fillmore West with the band, met Greg Lake while the latter was touring with King Crimson on its 1969 U.S. debut. Frustrated by the Nice's lack of success, Emerson trashed the group in early 1970 and formed ELP [see entry] with Lake and drummer Carl Palmer later that year. The Nice's last LP, *Elegy,* was released shortly after ELP's debut in 1971.

Jackson formed Jackson Heights (which recorded five LPs between 1970 and 1973), and in 1974 he and Davison teamed up with keyboardist Patrick Moraz (who was Emerson's understudy in the Nice) in an ELP-style group called Refugee. But it didn't last, and Moraz went

on to Yes and to the Moody Blues. Davison played briefly with Gong in the mid-Seventies.

Stevie Nicks: See Fleetwood Mac

Nico
Born Christa Päffgen, October 16, 1938, Cologne, Germany; died July 18, 1988, Ibiza, Spain
1968—*Chelsea Girl* (MGM/Verve)   1969—*The Marble Index* (Elektra)   1971—*Desert Shore* (Reprise) 1974—*June 1, 1974* (with Kevin Ayers, John Cale, and Brian Eno) (Island); *The End*   1981—*Drama of Exile* (Aura)   1983—*Do or Die! Nico in Europe* (ROIR)   1985—*Camera Obscura* (Beggar's Banquet, U.K.)   1988—*The Peel Sessions* (Strange Fruit, U.K.).

At one time billed as the Moon Goddess, singer Nico's gloomy, romantic music and hypnotic monotone voice were first heard in the Velvet Underground. She continued to work sporadically as a solo artist after leaving the Velvets, though a longtime heroin addiction and methadone dependency sidetracked her career.

The German-born Nico first worked as a model in Paris but got into music in the mid-Sixties through friendships with Rolling Stone Brian Jones and Stones manager Andrew Loog Oldham, for whom she cut a British single, "The Last Mile," on his Immediate label in 1965. The song was produced, cowritten, and arranged by Jimmy Page. The next year, Nico met Warhol in New York, socialized at the Factory and appeared in his film *The Chelsea Girls*. (She had played a small role in Fellini's *La Dolce Vita*.) Warhol later introduced her to Lou Reed and John Cale in the Velvet Underground. She got feature billing in the band ("the Velvet Underground and Nico"), but left after the first album. Nico's connection with the old group remained strong, though, and on her 1968 solo debut she recorded songs by Cale and Reed, as well as some by a 16-year-old named Jackson Browne, who performed with her during shows. Besides Browne, at some early shows she was accompanied by Tim Hardin and Tim Buckley. *The Marble Index* and *Desert Shore* were produced and arranged by Cale; on *The Marble Index* he played all the instruments except Nico's own droning harmonium, her trademark.

Nothing was heard from Nico for the next few years. She spent most of her time in Paris, but in early 1974 she signed with Island. She appeared in a special London concert at the Rainbow Theatre with Kevin Ayers, Cale, and Brian Eno, resulting in an album named after the date of the event, *June 1, 1974,* with Nico doing a lengthy, especially morbid version of the Doors' "The End." That song title was the name of her solo return, out later in the year, again produced by Cale. She and Island allegedly had disputes during the recording (Eno kept them from dropping her), but in 1975 they let her go.

In the later Seventies and early Eighties, Nico did periodic solo shows on the club circuit. In 1981 she released her first LP in seven years, *Drama of Exile*, which included versions of the Velvets' "I'm Waiting for the Man" and Bowie's "Heroes." She recorded what would be her last album, *Camera Obscura*, in 1985, again produced by Cale.

Leading a vagabond life, Nico floated from country to country, spending the last year of her life in Manchester, England. Reportedly, her methadone dependency had diminished and her songwriting had increased when she took her grown son, Ari (by French actor Alain Delon), on holiday to the Spanish island of Ibiza. On July 17, 1988, she had an accident on her bicycle; a cab driver found her on the side of a steep mountain road and took her to four hospitals before she was admitted. Misdiagnosed as having a sunstroke, she died there the next evening of a cerebral hemorrhage. She was cremated in Berlin, where the urn containing her ashes was buried in her mother's grave.

Night Ranger: See Damn Yankees

Willie Nile

Born Robert Noonan, June 7, 1948, Buffalo, New York
1980—*Willie Nile* (Arista)   1981—*Golden Down*
1991—*Places I Have Never Been* (Columbia)
1992—*Hard Times in America* EP (Polaris).

Singer/songwriter Willie Nile won much critical praise in 1980 for his Dylan-turned-early-Springsteen-esque folk rock. He debuted late in the game by rock standards—at age 31—after spending seven years appearing sporadically on the Greenwich Village folk scene.

Nile's grandfather had played piano with Bill "Bojangles" Robinson and Eddie Cantor. In college Nile studied and wrote poetry and got swept up in Bob Dylan's hyperverbal style of the Sixties. Late in the decade he made periodic forays to New York City to play the same clubs where Dylan began. In 1973 Nile finally moved to the Village, where he frequently played clubs like Kenny's Castaways on Bleecker Street, concentrating on folk mainly because he couldn't afford a backup band.

Tommy Flanders, ex–lead vocalist for the Blues Project, brought record company executives to Kenny's to see Nile. In 1978, with the help of a rave review from Robert Palmer in the *New York Times*, Nile got a contract with Arista. His debut, produced by Roy Halee, who had engineered the Yardbirds and Simon and Garfunkel in the Sixties, was praised for its Byrdsy guitars, its folk-melodiousness, and rocking Buddy Holly influences, plus Nile's affecting, nervous vocals (which he describes as a "curious attempt at singing"). But others found his lyrics disappointing.

Nile's early live band featured ex-Television bassist Fred Smith and former Patti Smith drummer Jay Dee Daugherty. In July the band did some stadium openers for the Who when Pete Townshend asked him to personally after hearing his debut. Nile's followup, *Golden Down*, again was much talked about in the press, and featured Daugherty, Smith, and Paul Shaffer, but did not prove a breakthrough. Nile again toured the U.S., and in 1982 he signed to Geffen, but his next album did not appear until 1991, when Columbia released *Places I Have Never Been*, on which Nile was backed by a virtual who's who of modern folk, including Roger McGuinn, Terry and Suzzy Roche, Loudon Wainwright III, and Richard Thompson. Though it failed to chart, Nile continues touring and recording. In the summer of 1992 he opened for Ringo Starr and the All-Starr Band. His first two albums have been reissued with bonus tracks by Razor & Tie Records.

Harry Nilsson

Born Harry Edward Nelson III, June 15, 1941, Brooklyn, New York; died January 15, 1994, Agoura Hills, California
1967—*The Pandemonium Shadow Show* (RCA)
1968—*Aerial Ballet*   1969—*Harry*; *Skidoo* soundtrack   1970—*Nilsson Sings Newman*; *The Point!* soundtrack   1971—*Aerial Pandemonium Ballet*; *Nilsson Schmilsson*   1972—*Son of Schmilsson*
1973—*A Little Touch of Schmilsson in the Night*
1974—*Son of Dracula* soundtrack (with Ringo Starr) (Rapple); *Pussy Cats* (with John Lennon) (RCA)
1976—*That's the Way It Is* (RCA)   1977—*Knnillssonn*   1978—*Nilsson's Greatest Music*
1988—*A Touch More Schmilsson in the Night*
1995—*Personal Best: The Harry Nilsson Anthology*.

Singer/songwriter Harry Nilsson moved to California with his family, and after graduating from a Los Angeles parochial school became a processor at a Van Nuys, California, bank. In the meantime, he learned guitar and piano. By the mid-Sixties, using the Nilsson name for his musical persona, he was writing songs, trying to sell them during the day while working nights at the bank. He sold three tunes to Phil Spector; two were recorded by the Ronettes and one by the Modern Folk Quartet. Nilsson earned extra money by singing on demos and in radio commercials, and in 1967 he signed with RCA. While Nilsson was recording his debut LP, his "Cuddly Toy" was covered by the Monkees, as his "One" would be for Three Dog Night in 1969.

Despite extravagant critical acclaim, *Shadow Show* sold poorly. However, it did bring a call from London one night: "It's John . . . John Lennon. Just want to tell you your album is great! You're great!" Later, Brian Epstein made an unsuccessful attempt to woo Nilsson from RCA to Apple. At a press conference for the launching of the Apple label, the Beatles answered "Nilsson" when asked who their favorite artist and group were.

Aerial Ballet fared better, as it included the smash hit "Everybody's Talkin'," a Fred Neil song that stayed in the U.S. Top Ten much of 1969 and was the theme song for the film Midnight Cowboy. Nilsson had written another song intended to be that film's theme, "I Guess the Lord Must Be in New York City"—a #34 hit in 1969. Harry sold fairly well, too, and Nilsson composed scores for Otto Preminger's film Skidoo (1968), for which he sang the closing credits, and the TV sitcom The Courtship of Eddie's Father (1969). Nilsson would later write and sing an original score for the animated TV movie The Point!, which yielded the #34 hit "Me and My Arrow" (a 1976 London stage production of The Point! would unite ex-Monkees Davy Jones and Mickey Dolenz). Nilsson never performed a public concert, and only rarely made televised appearances.

In 1970 Nilsson recorded an album of his friend Randy Newman's compositions. Though critically acclaimed, it sold little. The next year, though, Nilsson achieved his commercial breakthrough with Nilsson Schmilsson, which, with the #1 hit version of Badfinger's "Without You," eventually went platinum. The "Schmilsson" persona, a sort of schmaltzy alter ego, returned on subsequent LPs, like the gold Son of Schmilsson; Nilsson proudly announced that he was recording with Frank Sinatra's arranger, Gordon Jenkins. As time went on, Nilsson never quite matched Schmilsson's success. Still, several hits followed: "Coconut" (#8, 1972), "Jump into the Fire" (#27, 1972), and "Space Man" (#23, 1972).

He made the Son of Dracula (1974) film with Ringo Starr, then became Lennon's companion during the ex-Beatle's separation from his wife, Yoko Ono. During this time the two recorded Pussy Cats, an album of old rock & roll songs. Nilsson faded from the recording scene during the Eighties, straightened out, started a family, and pursued business interests, which included a Hollywood-based film distribution company. After John Lennon's murder, Nilsson became a gun-control advocate, joining the Washington, D.C.–based Coalition to Stop Handgun Violence. He made a low-key return to recording with 1988's A Touch More Schmilsson in the Night, on which he sang such pop standards as "Over the Rainbow" and "It's Only a Paper Moon." In 1993 he suffered a heart attack, which inspired him to begin writing and recording again in earnest, even though he had no contract. Just a few days after finishing a new album, and with producers Al Kooper and Danny Kapilian already working on a Nilsson tribute album, he died of heart disease at age 52, leaving behind a wife and seven children. The 1995 tribute album For the Love of Harry: Everybody Sings Nilsson featured Randy Newman, Brian Wilson, Adrian Belew, Joe Ely, and others.

Nine Inch Nails

Formed 1987, Cleveland, Ohio
Trent Reznor (b. May 17, 1965, Mercer, Pa.), voc., kybds., gtr., bass, drums, programming.
1989—Pretty Hate Machine (TVT) 1992—Broken EP (Nothing/TVT/Interscope); Fixed EP 1994—The Downward Spiral 1995—Further Down the Spiral.

Nine Inch Nails is a one-man industrial rock band whose symphonic noise and intense lyrics articulate an alienation and rage that have attracted a wide audience. The diviner of this millennarian angst is Trent Reznor, who writes, arranges, performs, and produces all of NIN's material. Reznor grew up isolated in small-town Pennsylvania, where he studied classical piano as a kid, switching to keyboards and playing in garage bands as a teen. He dropped out of Pennsylvania's Meadville College, moved to Cleveland, and recorded a self-made demo. That tape got him signed to TVT, an independent label best known for compilations of TV jingles.

Pretty Hate Machine was coproduced by Flood (Depeche Mode, U2), John Fryer (Love and Rockets, Cocteau Twins), and Adrian Sherwood and Keith LeBlanc. It yielded three college-radio hits, most notably "Head Like a Hole," whose video got extensive MTV play. Although the album vented an extremely dire, introspective outlook, it sold one million copies. This was at least in part because Reznor assembled a band that spent three years on the road promoting Pretty Hate Machine, including dazzling audiences at the 1991 Lollapalooza Tour and opening for Guns n' Roses in Europe.

NIN spent so long touring because Reznor was suing to be released from TVT, which he said didn't support him artistically or financially. Several other companies were interested in NIN, and when TVT wouldn't let Reznor go, Interscope negotiated an agreement to corelease the band. They also gave Reznor his own label, Nothing. Broken (#7, 1992) was recorded during this period in a number of locations "without the permission of The Record Label," as the liner notes say. The EP is an intensely devastated and devastating document, once again entirely masterminded by Reznor, with three tracks coproduced by Flood. NIN had Coil and Foetus's Jim Thirwell remix tracks from Broken on Fixed. Broken debuted at #7 on the pop albums chart. Reznor tested the freedom granted by his new record company on the video for "Happiness in Slavery," which showed a man being sexually tortured and ground into a pulp by a machine—a visualization of NIN's own tortured nature as a synth band venting human emotions and an apt metaphor for Reznor's feelings about the music business. This was not the first controversial NIN video: "Sin," from the first album, was refused by MTV for its images of genital piercing and gay men smearing blood on each other, while outtakes from "Down in It" were in-

Trent Reznor (a.k.a. Nine Inch Nails)

vestigated by the FBI, which suspected that they were culled from a snuff film.

Working on his next album in L.A., Reznor moved into the house where Charles Manson's followers murdered Sharon Tate. Flood again coproduced, and the album featured guitarist Adrian Belew. *The Downward Spiral* (1994), a dense, depression-filled, and uncompromising work, debuted at #2 on the charts. In the summer of 1994, NIN appeared at Woodstock '94. Reznor also produced the soundtrack for Oliver Stone's *Natural Born Killers* (1994). *Further Down the Spiral* featured remixes of NIN's 1994 album.

1910 Fruitgum Company

Formed 1968, New Jersey
Joey Levine, voc.; Bruce Shay (b. 1948), voc., gtr., perc.; Frank Jeckell, voc., gtr.; Mark Gutkowski (b. 1948), gtr.; Larry Ripley (b. 1948), horns; Rusty Oppenheimer (b. 1948), drums; Pat Karwan, gtr., voc.; Floyd Marcus, drums, voc.; Chuck Travis (b. 1946), voc., gtr.
1968—*Simon Says* (Buddah); *1, 2, 3 Red Light*
1969—*Indian Giver*.

The 1910 Fruitgum Company, like the Ohio Express (with which it shared lead singer Joey Levine), was a faceless studio assemblage formed by the Jerry Kasenetz–Jeff Katz production team for Buddah Records to record bubblegum pop. Its first hit, "Simon Says" (#4, 1968), pioneered the genre and was followed by "1, 2, 3 Red Light" (#5, 1968—later covered in concert by the

Talking Heads), "Goody Goody Gumdrops" (#37, 1968), "Indian Giver" (#5, 1969), and "Special Delivery" (#38, 1969). The group's last chart-making tune came in 1969 with "The Train" (#57). In 1968 Kasenetz and Katz merged the members with another bubblegum group, the Kasenetz-Katz Singing Orchestral Circus, which hit with "Quick Joey Small (Run Joey Run)" (#25). The 1910 Fruitgum Company disbanded in 1970.

Nirvana

Formed 1987, Aberdeen, Washington
Kurt Donald Cobain (a.k.a. Kurdt Kobain, b. Feb. 20, 1967, Hoquiam, Wash.; d. April 5, 1994, Seattle, Wash.), voc., gtr.; Krist Anthony Novoselic (a.k.a. Chris Novoselic, b. May 10, 1965, Compton, Calif.), bass; Jason Everman, guitar; Chad Channing (b. Jan. 31, 1967, Santa Rosa, Calif.), drums.
1989—*Bleach* (Sub Pop) (– Everman); *Blew* EP (Tupelo) 1990—(– Channing; + Dave Grohl [b. Jan. 14, 1969, Warren, Ohio], drums) 1991—*Nevermind* (DGC) 1992—*Incesticide* 1993—*In Utero* 1994—*MTV Unplugged in New York*.

Nirvana is widely credited with bringing the sound and spirit of late-Seventies punk rock to a mainstream pop audience. In 1992 the Seattle-based trio took the angry, nihilistic message of the Sex Pistols "Anarchy in the U.K." to #1 with its own sarcastic blueprint for frustration, "Smells Like Teen Spirit." The band's reign was tragically cut short two years later, on April 5, 1994, when leader Kurt Cobain took his life following at least one earlier suicide attempt and severe bouts with drug addiction, a chronic stomach ailment, and depression. He was 27.

Kurt Cobain and Krist Novoselic grew up in Aberdeen, Washington, a small logging town 100 miles southwest of Seattle. When Cobain was eight, his secretary mother and auto mechanic father divorced, leaving him constantly moving from one set of relatives to another. As a child he loved the Beatles, but by nine he discovered the heavier music of Led Zeppelin, Black Sabbath, and Kiss. Cobain met the 6-foot-7-inch Novoselic, son of a local hairdresser, through mutual friend Buzz Osborne of the Aberdeen band Melvins. Osborne introduced them to the hardcore punk of Black Flag and Flipper.

In 1987 Cobain and Novoselic, both of whom had long felt alienated from their working-class peers, formed Nirvana and started playing parties at the liberal Evergreen State College in nearby Olympia. The following year, Seattle independent label Sub Pop signed the band and released its first single, "Love Buzz" b/w "Big Cheese." Nirvana's debut album, *Bleach,* recorded for $606.17, came out in 1989 to kudos from the underground rock community; it sold an initial 35,000 copies, which is considerable for an indie-label release. The next year Nirvana put out another Sub Pop single, "Sliver" b/w

Nirvana: Dave Grohl, Kurt Cobain, Krist Novoselic

lenged the Cobains' parental fitness based on Love's comments in *Vanity Fair*, the couple was granted custody of the child. Amid the chaos, Nirvana released *Incesticide*, a collection of early singles and outtakes. Beginning in spring of 1993, a series of events occurred that foreshadowed the demise of Cobain and Nirvana. On May 2, the singer overdosed on heroin at his Seattle home. The following month, he was charged with domestic assault after Love summoned the police during an argument over Cobain's gun collection. On July 23, Cobain overdosed again, this time in the bathroom of a New York hotel room before a Nirvana show at the Roseland Ballroom.

On September 21, Nirvana released *In Utero*, which debuted at #1 and ultimately produced the modern-rock radio hits "Heart-Shaped Box" and "All Apologies." On January 8, 1994, Nirvana performed what would be their last American concert at the Seattle Center Arena. On February 2, the band departed for a European tour, but after a series of shows in France, Portugal, Italy, the former Yugoslavia, and Germany, decided to take a break, during which Cobain remained in Rome.

At 6:30 a.m. on March 4, Love found Cobain unconscious in the couple's room at Rome's Excelsior Hotel, the result of an overdose of the tranquilizer Rohypnol. At first it was deemed an accident, but later reports confirmed the existence of a suicide note. Cobain remained in a coma for 20 hours. When the Cobains returned to Seattle, things took a turn for the worse. On March 18, police arrived at the Cobain home again after the singer locked himself in a room with a .38-caliber revolver, threatening to kill himself. On March 30, Cobain checked into the Exodus Recovery Center in Los Angeles, but fled on April 1, after telling staff members he was going outside for a smoke. On April 8, he was found dead in a room above the garage of the couple's Seattle home, the result of a self-inflicted 20-gauge shotgun wound to his head. For weeks afterward, fans, the news media, MTV, and radio mourned his death with specials about Nirvana and the generations they inspired. In November 1994 *MTV Unplugged in New York* (#1, 1994), an album of the acoustic show taped in 1993, was released.

Following Cobain's death, Novoselic spent most of his time as an advocate for various political and social causes. Grohl started a band, the Foo Fighters, which included guitarist Pat Smear, who played on Nirvana's last tour. For the band's self-titled album, released in 1995, Grohl sang lead, played guitar, and wrote all the songs.

"Dive," and recorded six new songs (including "Smells Like Teen Spirit") with producer Butch Vig. Although opposed to major labels in principle, the band claims it shopped the songs to bigger companies in hopes of getting the message of punk to a larger audience.

A major-label bidding war ensued, with DGC ultimately offering the group a $287,000 advance (rumors had it at $750,000). With *Nevermind*, Nirvana succeeded in getting punk to the populace on a grand scale: After an initial shipment of 50,000 copies, the record kept selling, eventually bumping new albums by Michael Jackson, Garth Brooks, U2, and Hammer from the top of the chart. *Nevermind* ultimately sold ten million copies worldwide, and produced another hit, "Come As You Are" (#32, 1992).

By early 1992 the group's success was biting back. As "Smells Like Teen Spirit" continued climbing up the charts, Cobain began bemoaning the group's meteoric rise, worrying that fans were missing the point of Nirvana's antiestablishment message. Simultaneously his new relationship with Courtney Love, singer of the underground band Hole [see entry], had become a hot topic in the gossip columns. The couple married on February 24. When Love became pregnant with Cobain's child and was quoted in a *Vanity Fair* article as admitting she had used heroin during the pregnancy, news of the couple's alleged drug addiction hit the media fan. Scrutiny of the Cobain/Love affair reached a level of intensity met in the pop world only by John Lennon and Yoko Ono, or the ill-fated punk couple Sid Vicious and Nancy Spungen. On August 18, 1992, the Cobains delivered a healthy, seven-pound baby, Frances Bean. After a battle with children's services in Los Angeles, which chal-

Nitty Gritty Dirt Band

Formed 1966, Long Beach, California
Jeff Hanna (b. July 11, 1947, Detroit, Mich.), gtr., voc.; Jimmie Fadden (b. Mar. 9, 1948, Long Beach), gtr., harmonica, washtub bass, voc.; Jackson Browne (b. Oct. 9, 1948, Heidelberg, W. Ger.), gtr.,

Nitty Gritty Dirt Band: Jeff Hanna, Bob Carpenter, Jimmie Fadden, Jimmy Ibbotson

voc.; Ralph Barr (b. Boston, Mass.), gtr., clarinet, voc.; Les Thompson (b. Long Beach), bass, gtr., voc.; Bruce Kunkel (b. ca. 1948, Long Beach), gtr., violin, voc. (– Browne; + John McEuen (b. Dec. 19, 1945, Long Beach), gtr., fiddle, banjo, mandolin, voc. 1967—*Nitty Gritty Dirt Band* (Liberty); *Ricochet* 1968—(– Kunkel; + Chris Darrow, gtr., fiddle); *Rare Junk* 1969—*Alive* (– Darrow; – Barr; + Jimmy Ibbotson [b. Jan. 21, 1947, Philadelphia, Pa.], drums, kybds.) 1970—*Uncle Charlie and His Dog Teddy* 1972—*All the Good Times* (United Artists); *Will the Circle Be Unbroken* 1974—(– Thompson) *Stars and Stripes Forever* 1975—*Dream* 1976—(– Ibbotson; + John Cable, gtr., bass, voc.; + Jackie Clark, bass, gtr.) *Dirt, Silver and Gold* 1978—*The Dirt Band* (– Cable; – Clark; + Bob Carpenter [b. Dec. 26, 1946, Philadelphia, Pa.], voc., kybds., accordion; + Al Garth, violin, saxophone; + Richard Hathaway, bass; + Merle Brigante, drums) 1979—*An American Dream* 1980—(– Brigante; + Rick Schlosser, drums; – Schlosser; + Vic Mastriani, drums; + Michael Gardner, bass) *Make a Little Magic* 1981—*Jealousy* 1983—(– Garth; – Hathaway; – Mastriani; – Gardner; + Ibbotson) *Let's Go* 1984—*Plain Dirt Fashion* (Warner Bros.) 1985—*Partners, Brothers and Friends* 1986—*Twenty Years of Dirt: The Best of the Nitty Gritty Dirt Band* (Warner Bros.) 1987—(– McEuen; + Bernie Leadon [b. July 19, 1947, Minneapolis, Minn.], gtr., banjo, mandolin, voc.) *Hold On* 1988—*Workin' Band* (– Leadon); *More Great Dirt* 1989—*Will the Circle* *Be Unbroken, vol. 2* (Universal) 1990—*The Rest of the Dream* 1991—*Live-Two-Five* 1992—*Not Fade Away* (Liberty) 1994—*Acoustic.*
John McEuen solo: 1987—*John McEuen* (Warner Bros.) 1992—*String Wizards* (Vanguard) 1994—*String Wizards II.*

One of the few country-rock bands that moved from straight country folk to rock, rather than vice versa, the Nitty Gritty Dirt Band (or Dirt Band, as it was known for a time in the late Seventies and early Eighties) has delved into all sorts of musical Americana. Through the years, the group's material has gone from jug-band and novelty-string-band modes, through bluegrass and hoedowns, to country swing and country rock. Though the group has endured through many personnel changes, the core lineup of Jeff Hanna, Jimmie Fadden, and John McEuen was constant from 1966 through 1987. After that, Bob Carpenter joined; he is still with the group. Jimmy Ibbotson is another long-term member.

They were originally the Illegitimate Jug Band; Jackson Browne's short stint with the group was around this time. They joined with John McEuen's producer brother Bill and made their first LP, which yielded a modest hit single, "Buy for Me the Rain" (#45, 1967). As the band was trying to decide whether to go with rock or stay traditional, it made an appearance in the 1968 film *Paint Your Wagon* and then temporarily disbanded, though all kept busy with various musical pursuits. When the members regrouped, they recorded *Uncle Charlie*, their breakthrough LP, with the Top Ten cover of Jerry Jeff Walker's "Mr. Bojangles." Their next important project was a historic meeting with a bevy of oldtime country music stars like Roy Acuff, Earl Scruggs, Maybelle Carter, Doc Watson, Merle Travis, and Vassar Clements to record *Will the Circle Be Unbroken*. This three-album set of traditional folk and country tunes went gold and received critical raves. Over 16 years later, the group released *Will the Circle Be Unbroken, vol. 2*, which featured Johnny Cash, the Carter Family, Chet Atkins, John Denver, Emmylou Harris, Levon Helm, Roger McGuinn, Earl Scruggs, and others. That album hit #95 in mid-1989 and was their first album to chart on the pop charts since 1981. Though always popular for its lively concerts, in which band members traded myriad string and other instruments about, the Dirt Band didn't attract major attention again until 1977, when it became the first American rock group to tour the Soviet Union. The following year they arranged and later performed Steve Martin's novelty hit "King Tut" on *Saturday Night Live*. In 1980 a duet with Linda Ronstadt, "An American Dream," was a #13 hit; six months later, they had another pop hit with "Make a Little Magic," featuring Nicolette Larson. Beginning in 1983 the group had a series of 16 Top Ten C&W hits, among them the C&W Number One hits

"Long Hard Road (The Sharecropper's Dream)" (1984), "Modern Day Romance" (1985), and "Fishin' in the Dark" (1987).

In 1992 the Aspen School of Music named a scholarship in the band's honor. The following year they celebrated their silver anniversary.

Mojo Nixon

Born Neill Kirby McMillan Jr., August 2, 1957, Chapel Hill, North Carolina
Mojo Nixon and Skid Roper (Nixon, voc., gtr.; Skid Roper [b. Richard Banke, Oct. 19, 1954, National City, Calif.], washboard, perc., harmonica, mandolin): 1985—*Mojo Nixon and Skid Roper* (RBI/Enigma)   1986—*Frenzy* (Restless)   1987—*Bo-Day-Shus!!!* (Enigma)   1989—*Root Hog or Die* 1990—*Unlimited Everything* (– Roper).
Mojo Nixon solo: 1990—*Otis*   1992—*Horny Holidays.*
With Jello Biafra: 1994—*Prairie Home Invasion* (Alternative Tentacles)   1995—*Whereabouts Unknown* (Ripe & Ready).

The clown prince of postpunk roots-rock revivalists, Nixon became a cult star as an exuberant, irreverent white-trash loudmouth. Nixon's songs, which attack sanctimony and revel in lowbrow thrills, are a primitive, ferocious blend of rockabilly, blues, and R&B.

Onetime Virginia state bicycle-racing champion Kirby McMillan allegedly took a cross-country bike ride and became Mojo Nixon in New Orleans, after imbibing a concoction of green liqueurs. Nixon eventually settled in San Diego, forming a two-man band with multi-instrumentalist Skid Roper. Their debut album included "Jesus at McDonald's"; *Frenzy* featured "Stuffin' Martha's Muffin," a bawdy ode to then MTV VJ Martha Quinn. *Bo-Day-Shus!!!* expanded the Nixon-Roper cult with "Elvis Is Everywhere," in which Nixon extolled the undying spirit of Elvis Presley. *Root Hog or Die,* produced in Memphis by Jim Dickinson (Alex Chilton, Replacements), featured extra musicians and a slightly slicker sound. MTV (for which Nixon had taped some promotional spots) actually showed Nixon's video for "Debbie Gibson Is Pregnant with My Two-Headed Love Child," in which teen-pop starlet Gibson was played by actress Winona Ryder. (She costarred in the Jerry Lee Lewis biopic *Great Balls of Fire* with Nixon, who played Lewis' drummer.)

Nixon then parted company with Roper, who has recorded two countryish albums, 1989's *Trails Plowed Under* and 1991's *Lydia's Cafe,* with his band the Whirlin' Spurs. *Otis,* which included X bassist John Doe, Dash Rip Rock guitarist Bill Davis, and Del-Lords guitarist Eric Ambel, featured "Don Henley Must Die." The earnest Eagle himself did not find it funny, but the two mended

fences in July 1992, when Henley joined Nixon onstage at an Austin, Texas, club. By then Nixon had formed the Toad Liquors, with whom he recorded the Christmas album *Horny Holidays,* and had toured with ex-Blaster Dave Alvin in the Pleasure Barons. In 1993 Nixon began working with ex–Dead Kennedys frontman Jello Biafra on a "folk" album, *Prairie Home Invasion,* released on Biafra's Alternative Tentacles label in 1994.

Nova Mob: See Hüsker Dü

No Wave

Based in late-Seventies New York City, no wave grew from the crossovers between Lower Manhattan's avant-garde art and music scenes, especially punk rock. No wave was played mainly by untrained musicians who had become disenchanted with the doctrinaire conservatism of rock; they even saw punk as something that was quickly becoming institutionalized. Still, the no wavers made full use of punk's themes of nihilistic disgust, as the name indicates. The music was rough-hewn, minimal, often atonal, using noise for noise's sake.

No wave's deconstructivist tendencies were best represented by guitarist Arto Lindsay's trio DNA and the quartet Mars, while Lydia Lunch's trio Teenage Jesus and the Jerks (whose drummer played only a snare and one cymbal) perhaps best personified the genre's negativity. The Contortions were the most "musicianly" of the lot, fusing noise, free jazz, and Captain Beefheart–derived harsh guitar sonorities with a punk-paced funk rhythm.

By the Eighties, no wave was dying, and in fact it seemed to have had its short lifespan built in from its inception. Glenn Branca, onetime member of the no-wave band Theoretical Girls, went on to forge his own brand of mega-heavy-metal monumental minimalism with layered, hyper-amped guitar ensembles. One of his ensembles included Thurston Moore and Lee Ranaldo of Sonic Youth, the highly influential band that brought the dissonance and guitar textures of no wave to Nineties alternative rock.

NRBQ

Formed 1967, Miami, Florida, as the New Rhythm and Blues Quintet
Terry Adams (b. Aug. 14, 1950, Louisville, Ky.), kybds., voc., harmonica, trumpet; Joey Spampinato (b. Aug. 16, 1950, New York City, N.Y.), bass, voc.; Steve Ferguson (b. Nov. 21, 1949, Louisville, Ky.), gtr., voc.; Tom Staley (b. Mar. 3, 1950, Ft. Lauderdale, Fla.), drums; Frank Gadler (b. May 8, 1950, New York City, N.Y.), voc.
1969—*NRBQ* (Columbia)   1970—*Boppin' the Blues*

(with Carl Perkins) 1971—(+ Al Anderson [b. July 26, 1947, Windsor, Ct.], gtr., voc; – Ferguson) 1972—*Scraps* (Kama Sutra) 1973—*Workshop* (– Gadler) 1974—(+ Donn Adams [b. Jan. 16, Fleming, Ky.], trombone; + Keith Spring [b. Dec. 28, Louisville, Ky.], sax; – Staley; + Tom Ardolino [b. Jan. 12, 1955, Springfield, Mass.], drums) 1977—*All Hopped Up* (Red Rooster) 1978—*At Yankee Stadium* (Mercury) 1979—*Kick Me Hard* (Rounder/Red Rooster) 1980—*Tiddlywinks* (Rounder) 1983—*Grooves in Orbit* (Bearsville) 1985—*Tapdancin' Bats* (Rounder) 1986—*Lou & the Q* (with Capt. Lou Albano) 1986—*She Sings, They Play* (with Skeeter Davis) 1987—*God Bless Us All* 1988—*Diggin' Uncle Q* 1989—*Wild Weekend* (Virgin) 1990—*Peek-a-Boo: The Best of NRBQ, 1969–1989* (Rhino) 1992—*Stormalong* (with John Candy) (BMG Kidz); *Honest Dollar* (Rykodisc) 1993—*Stay with Me* (Columbia) 1994—*Message for the Mess Age* (Rhino/Forward) (– Anderson; + Johnny Spampinato, gtr.).

Since the late Sixties NRBQ have been playing their unique, often wacky mix of rockabilly, country, pop, jazz, and every other style of popular music, a blend the band has dubbed "omnipop." Though they've had only one charting single—"Get That Gasoline Blues" (#70, 1974)—their incessant touring, onstage unpredictability, down-to-earth humor, and intermittent releases have garnered them a dedicated cult following.

The band formed when Kentucky natives Terry Adams and Steve Ferguson met Bronx-born Joey Spampinato in Miami. While playing in a New Jersey club, they were spotted by Slim Harpo, who encouraged Steve Paul to book them into his New York club, the Scene. Their performances there drew positive press, and within the year Columbia had signed them. The band's first album—which mixed originals with covers of Eddie Cochran's "C'mon Everybody," Sun Ra's "Rocket Number 9," and Bruce Channel's "Hey! Baby"—was nearly buried by a "new Beatles" hype, and the second, a collaboration with rockabilly legend Carl Perkins, was generally misunderstood. Guitarist Al Anderson, onetime leader of the Wildweeds, a country-rock group from Connecticut, joined them in 1971 when Ferguson departed.

Vocalist Frank Gadler left after NRBQ's first Kama Sutra LP; after the second, the band took a four-year hiatus from album releases, during which Tom Ardolino replaced Frank Staley on drums. The Whole Wheat Horns—Terry Adams' brother Donn on trombone, and Keith Spring (sometimes joined by expatriate Englishman Gary Windo) on sax—became semiofficial members of the group. In 1977 they formed their own label, Red Rooster, and began producing themselves with *All Hopped Up*. It was followed by another brief stint with a

major label, Mercury, for *At Yankee Stadium*, after which NRBQ returned to Red Rooster, distributed by Rounder. Two more LPs and a reissue of *All Hopped Up* later, NRBQ signed to Bearsville, again for only one album, *Grooves in Orbit*, another critically acclaimed release that sold modestly. Another one-album major-label deal, with Virgin, produced *Wild Weekend* (NRBQ wrote lyrics for the title track, a classic early-Sixties rock instrumental by the Rebel Rousers)—the group's first album to chart (#198, 1990) since its debut had limped to #162 in 1969. *God Bless Us All, Diggin' Uncle Q*, and *Honest Dollar* were all live albums; *Stay with Me* compiled the band's early work on Columbia, while the two-volume *Peek-a-Boo* highlighted 20 years of NRBQ.

Over 25 years without commercial success has not diminished NRBQ's eclectic sound and rollicking spirit. Albums have included covers of Chipmunks songs, requests from the group's fabled Magic Box (in which they play any song the audience demands), and originals that have been recorded by other artists, including the Box Tops and the Carpenters. In 1982 alone, Adams' "Me and the Boys" was recorded by Bonnie Raitt and Dave Edmunds. Edmunds also covered Adams' "I Want You Bad." NRBQ has also backed Windo and country singer Skeeter Davis in concert and recorded *She Sings, They Play* with her in 1986; she later married Spampinato. NRBQ also recorded with its unofficial manager, professional wrestler Captain Lou Albano, before he became better known for his appearances with Cyndi Lauper. On *Stormalong*, the soundtrack of a children's cable-TV special, the group backed actor John Candy.

Adams compiled the Thelonious Monk album *Always Know* in 1979, coordinated the reissue of the Shaggs' *Philosophy of the World*, produced albums for zydeco accordionist Boozoo Chavis and ex–Chuck Berry pianist Johnnie Johnson (who was backed by NRBQ for the recording), and has toured and recorded with jazzwoman Carla Bley (who cowrote "Ida" with Adams for NRBQ's debut album). In 1993 he wrote and played music on *The Duplex Planet Radio Hour* (East Side Digital), an album of readings by David Greenberger from his periodical about senior citizens, *Duplex Planet* (Adams also backed Greenberger at occasional live readings).

Joey Spampinato was in the backing band Keith Richards assembled for the Chuck Berry film *Hail! Hail! Rock and Roll*, and in 1991 backed Eric Clapton in a series of shows at London's Royal Albert Hall. Tom Ardolino compiled *Beat of the Traps, volume 1* (Carnage Press, 1992), a vinyl-only collection of obscure vanity recordings made for people who'd answered magazine advertisements promising to "set your lyrics to our music!"

In 1991 Al Anderson quit drinking and became a staff songwriter for a Nashville publishing house; his tunes have been recorded by such country stars as Alabama,

Pam Tillis, Ricky Van Shelton, and Dennis Robbins; he's written with John Hiatt and Carlene Carter and appeared on Carter's 1993 album *Little Love Letters*. Anderson left NRBQ in 1994, following the release of *Message for the Mess Age*, to pursue a solo career. He was replaced by Spampinato's brother, Johnny, a member of the Incredible Casuals who'd filled in for Anderson in the past.

Ted Nugent/Amboy Dukes

Born December 13, 1948, Detroit, Michigan
1975—*Ted Nugent* (Epic)   1976—*Free-for-All*
1977—*Cat Scratch Fever*; *Double Live Gonzo*
1978—*Weekend Warriors*   1979—*State of Shock*
1980—*Scream Dream*   1981—*Intensities in Ten*
Cities*; *Great Gonzos! The Best of Ted Nugent
1982—*Nugent* (Atlantic)   1984—*Penetrator*
1986—*Little Miss Dangerous*   1988—*If You Can't*
***Lick 'Em . . . Lick 'Em*   1993—*Out of Control* (Epic)**
1994—*Spirit of the Wild* (Atlantic).
With the Amboy Dukes (Original lineup: Nugent; Greg Arama, bass; Steve Farmer, gtr.; Dave Palmer, drums; Andy Soloman, kybds.): 1968—*The Amboy Dukes* (Mainstream); *Journey to the Center of the Mind*   1969—*The Best of the Original Amboy Dukes*   1970—*Marriage on the Rocks/Rock Bottom* (Polydor)   1971—*Survival of the Fittest/Live* 1975—*Call of the Wild* (DiscReet); *Tooth, Fang and Claw*.
With Damn Yankees: See entry.

As the self-proclaimed Motor City Madman, guitarist Ted Nugent fashioned a sharply defined, not-so-noble savage persona, garnering him endless publicity and resulting in multiplatinum sales in the late Seventies. Through the Eighties and early Nineties, however, it became clear that his progun, prohunting (he eats everything he kills), antidrink, and antidrug positions were anything but a pose. Today he splits his time between his solo efforts, the supergroup Damn Yankees, and his various activities on the behalf of a range of conservative causes.

Growing up in Detroit, Nugent began bow-hunting at age five and playing guitar at age eight. His first band was called the Royal High Boys (1960–61), followed by the Lourdes (1962–64). By the time he was 14, he and the band had played Cobo Hall, opening for the Supremes and the Beau Brummels. The band broke up in 1965 when his family moved to Chicago. There he immediately formed the Amboy Dukes, who signed with Mainstream and released their debut that year. Though they had a local hit with "Baby Please Don't Go" in 1967, the band's only sizable success was "Journey to the Center of the Mind" (#16, 1968). It continued in various forms until 1975, recording also for Polydor and DiscReet.

When the Dukes signed with the last label in 1972,

they became known as Ted Nugent and the Amboy Dukes. Nugent tried to boost album sales with his publicity savvy, staging guitar contests against Mike Pinera (of Iron Butterfly and Blues Image), Wayne Kramer (MC5), and Mahogany Rush's Frank Marino. But things didn't begin to happen for Nugent until he signed a solo deal with Epic in 1975 and got Tom Werman as producer and Leber-Krebs as managers. In his new band, he retained bassist Rob Grange from the old Amboy Dukes. (After this, he went through periodic changes in personnel.) He continued to tour widely, and suddenly his music was getting airplay; the national press, amused by his cartoonish caveman image, began to write Nugent up. Even if many found his music to be standard heavy-metal fare, his lifelong devotion to conservation, hunting his own food, and highly quotable opinions made him good copy.

Free-for-All featured Meat Loaf on some vocals (Nugent rarely sings), but the real breakthrough was 1977's *Cat Scratch Fever*, whose double-platinum success boosted sales of the two previous LPs to two million each. Also out that year was *Double Live Gonzo* (near two million sales), followed by the platinum *Weekend Warriors*. Stern Electronics introduced a Ted Nugent pinball game. Nugent showed a slight softening of attack by covering the Beatles' "I Want to Tell You" on *State of Shock*. This gold LP ended his platinum streak. Also disappointing sales-wise was 1980's *Scream Dream*, though it contained "Wango Tango" with its cars-and-garages ("My face is a Maserati," etc.) sexual imagery; but Nugent's LPs and concerts still sold respectably.

In 1981 Nugent was backed by the D.C. Hawks (which included three brother lead guitarists, Kurt, Rick, and Verne Wagoner) for a four-axe attack. His first self-production, 1982's *Nugent*, barely grazed the chart. By that point, however, Young Ted, as he referred to himself, had reaped the rewards of having been the top-grossing tour act of 1977, 1978, and 1979. Between 1980 and 1984 he served as a Michigan County deputy sheriff and has been a featured speaker at countless gatherings of gun owners, hunters, conservationists, and law enforcement officials. Nugent is the author of *Blood Trails: The Truth About Bowhunting* and the publisher of *Ted Nugent World Bowhunters Magazine*. He is also a lifetime member of the National Rifle Association, numerous bow-hunting organizations, and several anti–drug-abuse organizations, including Drug Abuse Resistance Education (DARE). In early 1994 Midwestern Public Broadcasting Stations aired Nugent's four *Spirit of the Wild* television specials. Outspoken as ever, Nugent remarked at a Dallas gun convention, "An armed society is a polite society."

Spirit of the Wild, his first solo album in six years, included former Nugent sideman Derek St. Holmes, ex–Brownsville Station bassist Michael Lutz, and former Heart and Coverdale/Page drummer Danny Carmassi. "I

Shoot Back," "Thighraceous," and "Fred Bear, the American Hunter's Theme Song" (which sold over 100,000 copies as an independently released single) from the latest album suggest that Nugent has not mellowed with age.

Gary Numan

Born Gary Webb, March 1958, Hammersmith, England
1979—Tubeway Army (Atco); Replicas; The Pleasure Principle   1980—Telekon   1980—Dance   1982—I Assassin.

Gary Numan's synthesizer-dominated music, heavily influenced by Kraftwerk, Ultravox, and David Bowie, gave him much British success and some U.S. attention in the early Eighties. Numan joined his first band in 1977 at age 19, but he soon quit. He auditioned to be guitarist for the British band the Lasers, and after Numan became frontman, they changed their name to Tubeway Army. They were signed by Beggars Banquet (a WEA subsidiary) in early 1978. At that time, they were a standard post–Sex Pistols punk outfit, releasing two angry singles, "That's Not It" and "Bombers."

Once they entered the studio to cut their first LP, Numan discovered synthesizers. He decided to put down his guitar and make electronics the basis of Tubeway Army's sound. The rest of the band (except for bassist Paul Gardiner) hated the idea and regrouped as another punk group, Station Bombers. Numan completed the LP with Gardiner and Gary's uncle Jess Lidyard on drums. The resulting LP, Tubeway Army, was billed to Gary Numan and Tubeway Army, as was the followup, Replicas, which yielded the British #1 hit "Are 'Friends' Electric?" Besides its robot-loving lyrics, its "futurist" electronic sound had a solid dance beat, and it anticipated the electropop trend of 1981–82.

In 1979 Numan also played on and wrote songs for Robert Palmer's Clues album. Numan's The Pleasure Principle (now billed solo, without Tubeway Army) entered the U.K. chart at #1 and provided the synthesized dance-rock hit "Cars," which broke Numan in the U.S., where it hit #9. He drew a lot of attention for his elaborate pyramid-shaped live stage setup, but Americans, after some initial curiosity, didn't really appreciate his stylized look and sound, and Telekon was only modestly successful (#64). Shortly after, Numan announced his retirement from performing, although he continued to record. He became a professional pilot and, in 1981, flew around the world.

N.W.A

Formed 1986, Los Angeles, California
Ice Cube (b. O'Shea Jackson, June 15, ca. 1969, Los Angeles), voc.; M.C. Ren (b. Lorenzo Patterson, June

N.W.A: Ice Cube, Dr. Dre, Eazy-E, Yella, M.C. Ren

16), voc.; Eazy-E (b. Eric Wright, Sep. 7, 1973; d. Mar. 26, 1995, Los Angeles), voc.; Dr. Dre (b. Andre Young, Feb. 18, 1965), producer; DJ Yella (b. Antoine Carraby, Dec. 11), DJ.
1987—N.W.A and the Posse (Macola)   1989—Straight Outta Compton (Ruthless/Priority)   1990—(– Ice Cube) 100 Miles and Runnin' EP   1991—Efil4zaggin.
Eazy-E solo: 1988—Eazy-Duz-It (Ruthless/Priority)   1992—5150 Home 4 Tha Sick EP   1993—It's On (Dr. Dre) 187um Killa.
M.C. Ren solo 1992—Kizz My Black Azz EP (Ruthless/Priority)   1993—Shock of the Hour.
Dr. Dre solo: 1992—The Chronic (Death Row/Interscope).
Ice Cube solo: See entry.

With the platinum-selling Straight Outta Compton, N.W.A brought gangsta rap to the mainstream. The album was among the first to offer an insider's perspective of the violence and brutality in gang-ridden South-Central Los Angeles. With songs like "Fuck tha Police" and "Gangsta Gangsta" set in a chaotic swirl of siren and gunshot sounds, it foreshadowed such events as the 1992 L.A. riots.

In 1986 O'Shea "Ice Cube" Jackson, born and raised in a two-parent, middle-class home in South-Central—and always more interested in music and books than in gangs—met Andre "Dr. Dre" Young, who shared Cube's passion for writing rap songs. The two started writing for Eric "Eazy-E" Wright, a former drug dealer who'd started Ruthless Records with his profits; Eazy needed material for a group he'd signed to the label, HBO. When HBO rejected Cube and Dre's "Boyz-n-the-Hood," about the South-Central town of Compton, Eazy-E decided to record the song himself. Under his direction, the three started working together as Niggaz With Attitude.

After N.W.A's first collection, Cube took a year off to study drafting at the Phoenix Institute of Technology. When he returned in 1988, the group finished Eazy's solo album and started work on *Straight Outta Compton*. Released in 1989, the album sold 750,000 copies even before N.W.A embarked on a tour. In the meantime, a media storm had developed over the controversial "Fuck tha Police," resulting in a "warning letter" from the F.B.I. to the group's distributor, Priority Records. After the tour, Cube got into a financial dispute with N.W.A's manager, Jerry Heller, who Cube claimed had cheated him out of royalties. The two settled out of court in 1990, and Cube went solo [see entry]. N.W.A continued recording and selling records, but fell out of critical favor. In June 1991 the group made history again when, in the face of strong criticism from politicians and bannings from some retail chains, *Efil4zaggin* ("Niggaz 4 Life" backward) reached #1 two weeks after its release.

Members of N.W.A made the police blotter often during the early Nineties, mainly for assault charges which ended up being dismissed or settled. Dr. Dre was involved in the most notorious case when he was charged with attacking a television rap-show host in 1991; he pleaded no contest. By 1993 N.W.A's future looked doubtful, with most of the members doing solo projects. Eazy-E, who had become estranged from the other members, died in 1995 of complications due to AIDS, which had been diagnosed a month earlier when he was hospitalized for what he thought was asthma.

Aside from Ice Cube, Dr. Dre has had the most solo success: In 1993 *The Chronic* (#3 pop, #1 R&B) went triple platinum, appeared on a number of critics' year-end Top Ten lists, and spawned several hits. "Nuthin' but a 'G' Thang" (#2 pop, #1 R&B) and "Dre Day" (#8 pop, #6 R&B) introduced the rapper Snoop Doggy Dogg [see entry], who later in the year had his own hit album (produced by Dre), *Doggystyle* (#1 pop and R&B).

Laura Nyro

Born Laura Nigro, October 18, 1947, Bronx, New York
1966—More Than a New Discovery (The First Songs) (Verve)   1968—Eli and the Thirteenth Confession (Columbia)   1969—New York Tendaberry   1970—Christmas and the Beads of Sweat   1971—Gonna Take a Miracle (with Labelle)   1975—Smile   1977—Season of Lights   1978—Nested   1984—Mother's Spiritual   1989—Live at the Bottom Line (Cypress Music)   1993—Walk the Dog and Light the Light (Columbia).

Laura Nyro

Singer/songwriter Laura Nyro's dramatic gospel- and R&B-powered ballads received tremendous attention in the late Sixties and early Seventies. Though she enjoyed spectacular commercial success as a songwriter, she was and remains a critically acclaimed performer herself. Her unique, even disquieting vocal style as well as a sporadic release and touring schedule have ensured her cult status. Nonetheless, Nyro stands as one of the most important women in rock music. Her songs combined a near-religious gospel fervor, early rock & roll vocal stylings, Brill Building songcraft, and, especially later, urban jazz influences with her highly personal, evocative lyrics.

Nyro began writing songs as a young girl. Her Italian-Jewish parents were both musical; her father was a jazz trumpeter. She went to the High School of Music and Art in Manhattan and concentrated on songwriting. Her debut album, *More Than a New Discovery*, was recorded when she was just 19. Commercially, it went nowhere, but it included a number of songs that would be major hits for other artists: "Wedding Bell Blues," "Blowin' Away" (both the Fifth Dimension), "Stoney End" (Barbra Streisand), and "And When I Die" (Blood, Sweat and Tears). In 1967 she got a spot at the Monterey Pop Festival. It was her second concert appearance ever, and the audience was loudly unappreciative of her costume (one gossamer angel wing) and her soul revue (which included two black backup singers). But David Geffen, then a music agent, was sufficiently impressed by a tape of her performance to quit his job to become her manager; he soon landed her a deal with Columbia Records.

Her second album, *Eli and the Thirteenth Confession,* was produced by ex–Four Season Charlie Calello, and included "Sweet Blindness" and "Stoned Soul Picnic" (which would be hits for the Fifth Dimension) and "Eli's Comin'" (Three Dog Night). The album and its followup, *New York Tendaberry,* were critical triumphs (especially *Eli*), lavishly praised for their poetic lyrics and gospel-soul fusion. Nyro became known for her strange, intense phrasing, unexpected rhythm changes, and distinctive, wailing vocals. *New York Tendaberry* also contained her own well-known songs "Time and Love" and "Save the Country." Nyro's early work was distinguished from that of her female singer/songwriter contemporaries in several ways. It was rooted in black, urban musical genres as opposed to folk, and her lyrics, while sometimes impressionistic and obtuse, could also be explicit and challenging. "The Confession"'s "You were born a woman, not a slave" is often cited as a feminist slogan, yet the same song promises a "super ride inside my love thing," a rare sexual boast in so-called women's rock of the time.

Nyro released two more celebrated records before she retired the first time at age 24. *Christmas and the Beads of Sweat* brought together several Muscle Shoals musicians (Barry Beckett, Roger Hawkins, Eddie Hinton, and others) as well as ex-Rascals Dino Danelli and Felix Cavaliere (who coproduced the album with Arif Mardin) and Duane Allman (whose searing lead guitar work marks "Beads of Sweat"). *Gonna Take a Miracle,* credited to Nyro and Labelle, was produced by Kenny Gamble and Leon Huff. On it Nyro paid tribute to the doo-wop ("The Bells," "The Wind," "Spanish Harlem"), girl-group ("I Met Him on a Sunday"), and Motown ("Jimmy Mack," "Dancing in the Street," "Nowhere to Run") traditions that continue to exert a marked influence on her work. (*Christmas* features "Up on the Roof," and on her 1993 album, she covers the Impressions' "I'm So Proud"; she has been known for peppering her live sets with classic R&B and soul chestnuts.)

Smile (1975) received guarded praise but didn't sell, nor did *Season of Lights* (1977) or *Nested* (1978), after which she retreated to her private life again. She reemerged in 1984 with *Mother's Spiritual* (for which Todd Rundgren provided production assistance; Nyro has produced or coproduced all of her albums since *Smile*). With these records, Nyro's music took a quieter turn, as she wrote of lost love, motherhood, and a nature-oriented spirituality, a feminist worldview that would influence a number of woman singers and songwriters. The lyrics of "Mother's Spiritual" were exhibited on the walls of the Chicago Peace Museum. While Nyro kept a fairly low profile through the Eighties, she still continued to perform in smaller venues across the country, and in Europe and Asia.

Another five years passed before her next release, a live album recorded at the Bottom Line, in New York City, which Columbia refused to release. Rather than acquiesce to the label's demand for a new studio album, Nyro, who is legendary for her ambivalence toward the business of the music business, took it to a smaller label. Nineteen-ninety-three saw the release of the critically acclaimed studio album *Walk the Dog and Light the Light.*

Ric Ocasek: See the Cars

Billy Ocean
Born Leslie Sebastian Charles, January 21, 1950, Fyzabad, Trinidad, West Indies
1981—*Nights (Feel Like Getting Down)* (Epic)
1984—*Suddenly* (Jive) 1986—*Love Zone* 1988—*Tear Down These Walls.*

For four years in the late Eighties, singer Billy Ocean was a major contender on the pop charts, racking up seven Top Ten singles. Although he fit in comfortably with the new breed of "love men"—the slick, romantic R&B crooners who flourished then—Ocean's grittier approach set him apart, particularly on his funkier, uptempo hits.

Ocean's family moved from Trinidad to London when he was eight. As a young man he worked as a Savile Row tailor while singing at night. In 1976 his music career broke with the Motown-style "Love Really Hurts Without You," a major U.K. hit (#2) that reached #22 in the U.S. Eight years passed before Ocean had another significant American hit, but 1984's "Caribbean Queen (No More Love on the Run)," with its taut production and throbbing bass line, went all the way to #1. Major hits followed: "Loverboy" (#2, 1984), "Suddenly" (#4, 1984), "When the Going Gets Tough, the Tough Get Going" (#2, 1986) (which was used in the film *The Jewel of the Nile*),

"There'll Be Sad Songs (to Make You Cry)" (#1, 1986), and "Love Zone" (#10, 1986). After another #1 hit, 1988's "Get Outta My Dreams, Get into My Car," and "The Colour of Love" (#17, 1988) Ocean's streak appeared to have ended.

Phil Ochs
Born December 19, 1940, El Paso, Texas; died April 9, 1976, Far Rockaway, New York
1964—*All the News That's Fit to Sing* (Elektra)
1965—*I Ain't a'Marchin' Anymore* 1966—*Phil Ochs in Concert* 1967—*Pleasures of the Harbor* (A&M)
1968—*Tape from California* 1969—*Rehearsals for Retirement* 1970—*Greatest Hits* 1971—*Gunfight at Carnegie Hall* 1976—*Chords of Fame; Phil Ochs Sings* (Folkways) 1986—*A Toast to Those Who Are Gone* (Archives Alive) 1988—*The War Is Over: The Best of Phil Ochs* (A&M) 1989—*There but for Fortune* (Elektra); *The Broadside Tapes: 1* (Folkways)
1991—*There and Now: Live in Vancouver, 1968* (Rhino).

Folksinger/songwriter Phil Ochs was a man of contradictions: a patriotic American who came to prominence as one of the harshest establishment critics in the mid-Sixties folk-protest boom; a renowned folkie who "went electric" and rocked out some time after it had been newsworthy to do so.

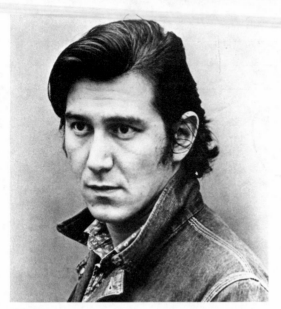

Phil Ochs

After moving to Queens, New York, with his family, Ochs followed family tradition by attending military school in Virginia. He later studied journalism at Ohio State University. He had begun writing songs, and his first musical venture was with a late-Fifties folk duo, the Singing Socialists, who became the Sundowners. Ochs then went solo, performing in Cleveland before moving to New York in 1961. Within a few years, he'd moved into Greenwich Village and the folk-protest circle that included Bob Dylan, to whom Ochs was most frequently compared.

By the time he recorded *All the News* (which featured guitar work by Danny Kalb, later of the Blues Project), Ochs had merged his literary/journalistic background with a songwriting style that was direct and abrasive. He hit his stride on *I Ain't a 'Marchin'.* The title tune and "Draft Dodger Rag" became antiwar anthems, despite a ban that prevented him from being broadcast on American radio and TV. During and after the ban, Ochs remained active in causes and protest movements. His "There but for the Fortune" was a Top Fifty hit for Joan Baez in 1965.

Harbor yielded some of Ochs' most famous tunes, such as "Outside of a Small Circle of Friends" and "The Party." After that LP's release, Ochs moved from New York to L.A., where, with top sessionmen backing him, and Van Dyke Parks producing, he recorded *Tape from California*. That LP also contained some rock & roll as well as more traditional folk tunes, such as "Joe Hill," and the antiwar anthem "War Is Over," as well as "When in Rome," an answer of sorts to Dylan's "Desolation Row."

Rehearsals and *Greatest Hits* maintained the session-men backing, to fascinating, if not especially popular, effect. The former was a bitter rocking examination of Ochs' own role as a Sixties culture hero, and saw his depression growing; the latter contained all-new material.

Gunfight saw Ochs dressed in gold lamé and backed by his L.A. sessioneers, singing his own greatest hits, as well as Merle Haggard's "Okie from Muskogee" and a medley of Elvis Presley and Buddy Holly hits; it included the audience's boos. The LP was released only in Canada. In 1973, while traveling in Africa, Ochs was the victim of a mysterious assault during which he was nearly strangled and his vocal cords were severely damaged.

During the early Seventies Ochs lived in Africa and London; he continued to perform occasionally, even though his voice had pretty much gone, and he wrote for the London periodical *Time Out*. In 1974 he was reunited with Dylan at a New York Felt Forum concert protesting the military junta in Chile; just before that event, Ochs had released the Watergate-era protest "Here's to the State of Richard Nixon." It was the last Phil Ochs record released in his lifetime. His last public appearance was at New York's Folk City on October 23, 1975. Six months later Ochs, who suffered from severe depression, hanged himself at his sister's home. The posthumous *Chords of Fame* was compiled by his brother, rock-music historian and archivist Michael Ochs.

Sinéad O'Connor

Born December 8, 1966, Dublin, Ireland
1987—*The Lion and the Cobra* (Chrysalis) 1990—*I Do Not Want What I Haven't Got* (Ensign) 1992—*Am I Not Your Girl?* (Ensign) 1994—*Universal Mother* (Chrysalis).

With her emotional delivery and confessional songs, Sinéad O'Connor has sold millions of albums. Brazenly outspoken, she was unlike any woman in pop music before her; sporting a shaven head and formless clothing, O'Connor seemed to symbolically repudiate the stereotypical female pop star's image. Spiritually inclined but anticlerical, she's startled—and at times baffled—the media and fans with her provocative statements and gestures.

The third of four children of an engineer father and a dressmaker mother, O'Connor spent a difficult childhood in conservative Dublin; she later maintained abuse by her mother (killed in a 1985 car wreck), to whom she was greatly, if ambivalently, devoted. Torn by her parents' separation when she was eight, O'Connor was expelled from Catholic schools, arrested for shoplifting, and sent to reform and boarding schools. At 15, singing Barbra Streisand's "Evergreen" at a wedding, she was discovered by Paul Byrne, the drummer for In Tua Nua, a band affiliated with U2. She cowrote In Tua Nua's first single, "Take My Hand," and began singing Dylan covers in coffeehouses. Fleeing boarding school at 16, she then studied voice and piano at Dublin's College of Music. She supported herself by waitressing and delivering "kiss-o-grams" in a French maid costume.

Moving to London in the early Eighties at the behest of Ensign Records, O'Connor collaborated with U2 guitarist the Edge on a film soundtrack (*The Captive*, 1986) while preparing her debut album. The first tapes of that project were scrapped because O'Connor despised the Celtic-derived production. She self-produced *The Lion and the Cobra* (its title taken from Psalm 91), which ranged from orchestral rock to folk to dance pop. The album sold well (#36, 1988), but with O'Connor's celebrity came controversy.

By then the mother of a son by her drummer, John Reynolds, O'Connor shocked the press by attacking U2 (calling the band's music "bombastic") and defending the IRA. She married Reynolds in 1988, but tumult continued with her firing of manager Fachtna O'Ceallaigh. The #1 *I Do Not Want What I Haven't Got* and its Prince-written single, "Nothing Compares 2 U" (#1, 1990), raised O'Connor's profile even higher. (In 1991 she alleged that Prince had physically threatened her.) Critics applauded her emotionally charged music (inspired by her separation from Reynolds), but British tabloids attacked her romance with black singer Hugh Harris and savaged her politics. Frank Sinatra assailed her refusal, at a 1990 New Jersey concert, to perform if the hall played "The Star Spangled Banner," and that same year O'Connor canceled a *Saturday Night Live* appearance in protest against what she perceived as host Andrew Dice Clay's misogyny. Nominated for four Grammy Awards, she withdrew from the competition, and in interviews aligned herself with rap rebels N.W.A and Ice-T. That year she contributed to *Red Hot + Blue*, a Cole Porter tribute album to benefit AIDS charities. (Her previous outside projects had included the B side of a single by Colourfield and vocals for 1988's *Stay Awake*, an album of Disney film music.)

O'Connor's next studio outing was a surprise, *Am I Not Your Girl?*, a collection of torch songs associated with such singers as Ella Fitzgerald and Billie Holiday. Controversy continued throughout 1992: She tore up a picture of Pope John Paul II in an appearance on *Saturday Night Live*. Two weeks later she was booed at a Bob Dylan tribute at Madison Square Garden. Also in 1992 the English rock paper *Melody Maker* reported O'Connor's imminent retirement from music; her publicist clarified that the singer was merely tired of "promoting" her career, but would in fact return to Dublin to study opera.

In 1993 O'Connor, who had appeared in a 1989 Irish film, *Hush-a-Bye Baby*, played Ophelia in *Hamlet* at Dublin's Project Arts Centre. She also toured with the WOMAD festival, organized by Peter Gabriel, with whom she was briefly romantically linked. She returned in 1994 with *Universal Mother* (#36, 1994), which mixed spoken-word political pronouncements with soft ballads and hip-hop–influenced compositions.

Odetta
Born Odetta Holmes, December 31, 1930, Birmingham, Alabama
1963—*Odetta Sings Folk Songs* (RCA)   1973—*The Essential Odetta* (Vanguard)   1987—*Movin' It On* (Rose Quartz)   1992—*At Town Hall* (Vanguard).

As a folk-blues institution, Odetta's vocal power and clarity and rich, intense singing style have long set her apart. She has made numerous recordings for various labels—none, according to critics, capturing her live impact—but most are now out of print. Odetta, influenced by Bessie Smith, went on to influence a variety of singers, including Joan Armatrading and Janis Joplin.

Upon her father's death, young Odetta Holmes assumed her stepfather's surname, Felious, and moved with her family to Los Angeles at age six. She sang in her junior high school glee club and worked as an amateur at Hollywood's Turnabout Theater around 1945. She then studied music at L.A.'s City College. In 1949 she began playing West Coast folk clubs as a singing/guitar-playing solo act. She steadily built up a reputation and through the mid- to late Fifties was touring nationwide and in Canada.

Odetta first recorded for San Francisco's Tradition label in 1956. In 1959 she married Dan Gordon. She was remarried twice, to Gary Shead in the late Sixties and to bluesman Iverson "Louisiana Red" Minter in 1977. She played the Newport Jazz Folk Festival in 1959, 1960, 1964, and 1965, and the Montreux Music Festival in Switzerland in 1976. In the early Sixties she made her first European tour and stopped off in Nigeria on the way home. Since then, she's played Japan, Australia, New Zealand, the West Indies, Morocco, and several Western European countries. Along the way, Odetta performed with Count Basie, poet/playwright Langston Hughes, Pete Seeger, Sonny Terry, ex-Basie trumpeter Buck Clayton, Bob Dylan, the Rochester Philharmonic Orchestra, and rock & roll pianist Sammy Price. She's also appeared in films—*The Last Time I Saw Paris* (1954), *Cinerama Holiday* (1955), *Sanctuary* (1960), and the TV movie *The Autobiography of Miss Jane Pittman*—as well as TV shows, playing characters or as herself, in both singing and dramatic roles.

In the mid-Seventies the Public Broadcasting System aired a documentary about her. In early 1982 Odetta appeared with Jackson Browne and others at a Santa Monica benefit show for Sing Out for Sight. Though she's never been a chart-making recording star, Odetta continues to tour, and her status has by now become legendary.

Ohio Express

Formed 1968, Mansfield, Ohio
Joey Levine, voc.; Dale Powers, gtr.; Doug Grassel, gtr.; Jim Pfayler, kybds.; Dean Kastran, bass; Tim Corwin, drums.
1968—*Beg Borrow and Steal* (Cameo); *Ohio Express* (Buddah); *Salt Water Taffy*; *Chewy Chewy*   1969—*Mercy*; *Very Best of Ohio Express*.

A studio bubblegum band like the 1910 Fruitgum Company (with which they shared producers Kasenetz-Katz and vocalist Joey Levine), the Ohio Express hit in 1968 with the million-selling "Yummy Yummy Yummy" (#4) and "Chewy Chewy" (#15). They had scored some minor success in 1967 (on Cameo Records) with "Beg Borrow and Steal" (#29) and "Try It" (#83). In late 1968 they had a minor hit with "Down at Lulu's" (#33), followed in 1969 by "Sweeter Than Sugar" (#96), "Pinch Me" (#97), "Mercy" (#30), and "Sausalito" (#86) before disbanding. Levine formed a group called Reunion.

The Ohio Players

Formed 1959, Dayton, Ohio
Best-known lineup: Billy Beck, kybds.; Clarence Satchell, saxes, flute; Jimmy "Diamond" Williams, drums, perc.; Leroy "Sugar" Bonner, gtr., voc.; Marvin Pierce, trumpet; Marshall Jones, bass; Ralph "Pee Wee" Middlebrooks, trumpet.
1968—*First Impressions* (Trip)   1969—*Observations in Time* (Capitol); *Ohio Players*   1972—*Pain* (Westbound)   1973—*Pleasure*; *Ecstasy*   1974—*Skin Tight* (Mercury); *Climax* (Westbound); *Fire* (Mercury)   1975—*Greatest Hits* (Westbound); *Honey* (Mercury); *Rattlesnake* (Westbound)   1976—*Contradiction*; *Ohio Players Gold*   1977—*Angel*; *Mr. Mean*   1978—*Jass-Ay-Lay-Dee*   1979—*Everybody Up* (Arista)   1980—*Young and Ready* (Accord)   1981—*Ouch!* (with Richard "Dimples" Fields) (Boardwalk); *Tenderness*   1984—*Graduation* (Air City)   1988—*Back* (Track).

The Ohio Players enjoyed immense popularity during the mid-Seventies with a percussive funk style influenced greatly by Sly and the Family Stone. The group was formed as Greg Webster and the Ohio Untouchables. For a time they were the backing band for the Falcons, whose lead singer was Wilson Pickett. (They can be heard on the Falcons' "I Found a Love.") The Untouchables became the Players following the recruitment of three musicians from a rival Ohio band. In 1967 they served as the studio band for Compass Records, using their free time to cut demo tapes. One of these

tapes won them a contract with Capitol Records and became *Observations in Time*.

The Players then recorded for Detroit-based Westbound Records from 1971 to 1973, gaining a #1 R&B single with "Funky Worm" (#15 pop). By the time the band signed with Mercury Records in 1974, keyboardist Junie Morrison had split for a solo career. (He later joined Parliament/Funkadelic.) The Players then embarked on a three-year run of steady hits, beginning with "Jive Turkey" (#47 pop, #6 R&B, 1974) and "Skin Tight" (#13 pop, #2 R&B, 1974) from *Skin Tight*.

The title song from the gold #1 *Fire* album went #1 on the R&B and pop charts in 1974, while "I Want to Be Free" from that same album reached #6 R&B (#44 pop, 1975). The group's luck continued as the gold #2 *Honey* yielded "Love Rollercoaster" (#1 pop and R&B, 1975), "Sweet Sticky Thing" (#33 pop, #1 R&B, 1975), and "Fopp" (#9 pop and R&B, 1976). "Who'd She Coo" in 1976 was the Players' last #1 R&B single (#18 pop); "O-H-I-O" (#45 pop, #9 R&B) in 1977 was their last big hit with Mercury. The Players cut an album for Arista Records before recording for Boardwalk Records in the early Eighties. At their peak, the Ohio Players were also renowned for their provocative album covers, featuring half-clad, often shaven-headed women in suggestive poses. More recent R&B hits include "Try a Little Tenderness" (#40, 1981) and "Let's Play (From Now On)" (#33, 1988).

Oingo Boingo

Formed 1979, Los Angeles, California
Danny Elfman (b. May 19, 1953, Los Angeles), voc.; Steve Bartek (b. Jan. 30, 1952, Garfield Heights, Ohio), gtr.; Kerry Katch, bass; Rich Gibbs, kybds.; Johnny "Vatos" Hernandez (b. Sep. 5. 1951, Los Angeles), drums; Sam Phipps (b. Oct. 1, 1953, Los Angeles), tenor sax; Leon Schneiderman (b. Jan. 25, 1954, Los Angeles), baritone sax; Dale Turner (b. July 2, 1941, Albert Lea, Minn.), trumpet, trombone.
1980—*Oingo Boingo* EP (I.R.S.)   1981—*Only a Lad* (A&M)   1982—*Nothing to Fear*   1983—*Good for Your Soul* (– Gibbs; – Katch; + John Avila [b. Jan. 14, 1957, Los Angeles], bass, voc.)   1985—*Dead Man's Party* (MCA)   1987—*BOI-NGO*   1988—*Boingo Alive*; *Skeletons in the Closet* (A&M)   1990—*Dark at the End of the Tunnel*   1991—*Best O'Boingo*   1994—*Boingo* (as Boingo) (Giant).

Extremely popular in California but never a national success, Oingo Boingo may be less significant for its own blend of high technique and quirky humor than as the training ground for frontman Danny Elfman, composer of scores for such high-profile films as *Batman* and *Dick Tracy*.

Composed of former members of a bizarre theater/comedy troupe calling itself the Mystic Knights of Oingo

Boingo, the band began as a late-Seventies new-wave outfit, notable for its horn section and for Elfman's tunes—intricately arranged oft-times comic songs that featured influences ranging from R&B to Balinese music. While drawing occasional comparisons to Frank Zappa and XTC, Oingo Boingo enjoyed neither critical acclaim nor significant sales as it recorded throughout the Eighties ("Weird Science," #45, 1985, was the group's highest-charting release). It was, however, sought after for soundtrack appearances (*Fast Times at Ridgemont High, Beverly Hills Cop, Weird Science*). Releasing his own album, *So-lo*, in 1984, Elfman continued to perform with Oingo Boingo but concentrated on television and film scores. With the music for *Pee-wee's Big Adventure* and *The Simpsons* and as chief composer for filmmaker Tim Burton (*Batman, Edward Scissorhands, The Nightmare Before Christmas*), he is one of Hollywood's most successful composers, his work reflecting the penchant for the strange and macabre that also characterizes Oingo Boingo. In 1993 the band signed its third major-label contract, with Giant Records, and shortened its name to Boingo.

The O'Jays

Formed 1958, Canton, Ohio
Bobby Massey, voc.; Walter Williams (b. Aug. 25, 1942); Eddie Levert (b. June 16, 1942), voc.; Bill Isles, voc.; William Powell (d. May 26, 1977, Canton), voc.
1965—*Comin' Through* (Imperial) (– Isles) 1967— *Soul Sounds* (Minit) 1972—(– Massey); *Greatest Hits* (Liberty); *Back Stabbers* (Philadelphia International) 1973—*In Philadelphia; Ship Ahoy* 1974— *Live in London* 1976—*Survival; Family Reunion* 1976—(– Powell; + Sammy Strain [b. Dec. 9, 1941], voc.) *Message in the Music; Travelin' at the Speed of Thought* 1977—*Collectors' Items* 1978—*So Full of Love* 1979—*Identify Yourself* 1980—*The Year 2000* (TSOP) 1982—*My Favorite Person* (Philadelphia International) 1983—*When Will I See You Again* (Epic) 1985—*Love Fever* (Philadelphia International) 1987—*Let Me Touch You* (EMI Manhattan) 1989—*Seriously* (EMI America) 1991—(– Strain; + Nathaniel Best [b. Dec. 13, 1960, N. Miami Beach, Fla.], voc.) *Emotionally Yours* 1993—*Heartbreaker.*

The O'Jays were one of the most popular black vocal groups of the Seventies, when they were in effect the voice of producers Gamble and Huff.

Eddie Levert and Walter Williams sang together as a gospel duo before forming a doo-wop group, the Mascots, with William Powell, Bobby Massey, and Bill Isles in 1958. In 1961 the Mascots made their recording debut with "Miracles" for the Wayco label. Cleveland DJ Eddie

O'Jay liked the group and gave it career advice. As a gesture of appreciation, the Mascots became the O'Jays. They cut some songs with producer Don Davis for Apollo Records before signing with Imperial and working with producer/writer H. B. Barnum. They recorded for Imperial from 1963 to 1967 and had some minor success. "Stand in for Love" (#12 R&B, 1966) was their biggest seller of the period.

In 1965 Isles left, and the group became a quartet. The O'Jays signed with Bell and had a #8 R&B hit, "I'll Be Sweeter Tomorrow," in 1967. The members were growing discouraged and contemplating retirement when Kenny Gamble and Leon Huff signed them to their Neptune label the next year. The O'Jays released four hits, including "One Night Affair" (#15 R&B, 1969) and "Looky Looky (Look at Me, Girl)" (#17 R&B, 1970). After Neptune folded in 1971, Massey quit to start producing records.

Levert, Williams, and Powell attempted self-production with a single for Saru Records, then signed with Gamble and Huff's new Columbia-distributed label, Philadelphia International. With Gamble and Huff supplying social-commentary songs, the O'Jays began an impressive string of gold and platinum records. They had eight #1 R&B singles from 1972 to 1978, including "Back Stabbers" (#3) in 1972; "Love Train" (#1) in 1973; "For the Love of Money" (#9) in 1974; "Give the People What They Want" (#45) and "I Love Music (Part 1)" (#5) in 1975; "Livin' for the Weekend" b/w "Stairway to Heaven" (#20), "Message in Our Music" (#49), and "Darlin' Darlin' Baby" (#72) in 1976; and "Use ta Be My Girl" (#4 pop, #1 R&B)) in 1978. Five of their LPs of this hot streak were certified gold; three, platinum.

In 1975 Powell was debilitated by cancer and could no longer tour. Two years later he died in the O'Jays' hometown. Sammy Strain, a member of Little Anthony and the Imperials for 12 years, replaced him. *Identify Yourself* was certified platinum in 1979.

Increasingly during this time Levert and Williams assumed a more active role in the production and writing. They continued working with Gamble and Huff through *Love Fever;* for *Let Me Touch You,* producer Thom Bell worked with Gamble and Huff. The latter album featured "Lovin' You" (#1 R&B, 1987) and "Let Me Touch You" (#5 R&B, 1987). "Have You Had Your Love Today" hit #1 on the R&B singles chart in 1989, as did "Out of My Mind" (#11 R&B) and "Serious Hold on Me" (#9 R&B), all from *Serious* (#4 R&B, 1989). In 1991 *Emotionally Yours* was certified gold; it included the hits "Keep On Lovin' Me" (#4 R&B), "Don't Let Me Down" (#2 R&B), and the Bob Dylan–penned "Emotionally Yours" (#5 R&B). In 1993 Sammy Strain returned to the re-formed Little Anthony and the Imperials [see entry] and was replaced by Nathaniel Best. That year's *Heartbreaker* was another R&B Top Ten album; its title track went to #7 R&B. Through the years the O'Jays have remained a popular headlining live act. Eddie Levert's sons Gerald and Sean sing with the hit R&B trio Levert [see entry].

Mike Oldfield

Born May 15, 1953, Reading, England
1968—*Sallyangie* (with Sally Oldfield) (Transatlantic, U.K.) **1973**—*Tubular Bells* (Virgin) **1974**—*Hergest Ridge* **1975**—*Ommadawn* **1976**—*Boxed* **1978**—*Incantations* **1979**—*Exposed*; *Platinum* **1980**—*QE 2* (Epic); *Airborn* **1982**—*Five Miles Out* **1983**—*Crises* (Blue Plate) **1984**—*Discovery*; *The Killing Fields* soundtrack (Virgin) **1985**—*The Complete Mike Oldfield* **1987**—*Islands* **1989**—*Earth Moving* **1990**—*Amarok* (Virgin, U.K.) **1991**—*Heaven's Open* **1992**—*Tubular Bells II* (Reprise).

Mike Oldfield's *Tubular Bells* was the first LP released by Virgin, and it got the new company off with a bang. It was a #1 LP in the U.K. and went gold in the U.S. It won a 1974 Grammy for Best Instrumental Composition, after being used as the theme song for *The Exorcist.*

Tubular Bells was some nine months in the making, as Oldfield played virtually all 28 instruments—mainly various guitars, basses, and keyboards—himself. The album was a more accessible reworking of ideas previously used by minimalist composers. Oldfield, however, used rock and folk motifs, layered in a controlled, ever-changing tapestry, achieving something of an artistic/commercial milestone in the arranging of a 48-minute "rock" composition.

Oldfield had launched his musical career at age 14 in an acoustic-folk duo with his sister Sally. After the duo made an album, Oldfield formed a short-lived band, Barefeet, through which he met English singer/songwriter Kevin Ayers [see entry], who had just left Soft Machine. Ayers made Oldfield the bassist (later guitarist as well) in his band, the Whole World, for 1971's *Shooting at the Moon.*

An edited version of *Tubular Bells,* known as "Mike Oldfield's Single" or "Theme from *The Exorcist,*" went to #7 in 1974, but followup LPs were unsuccessful in the U.S. Oldfield did have several more U.K. hit singles: "In Dulce Jubilo" b/w "On Horseback" (#4, 1975), "Portsmouth" (#3, 1976), "Blue Peter" (#19, 1979), and "Guilty" (#22, 1979)—the last of which saw Oldfield mating his pop-folk harmonic progressions to a disco beat, an approach furthered on the *QE 2* LP. Oldfield also recorded a disco version of composer Philip Glass's "North Star." *Islands* was a concerted effort at pop song construction, with guest vocals by Kevin Ayers, Bonnie Tyler, and ex-Family Roger Chapman.

In 1992—19 years after he'd made his mark, and 17 years after he'd arranged "Tubular Bells" for a 1975 recording by the Royal Philharmonic Orchestra—Oldfield collaborated with producer Trevor Horn (Buggles,

ABC, Art of Noise) on *Tubular Bells II,* which reached #1 on the U.K. chart.

Alexander O'Neal

Born November 15, 1953, Natchez, Mississippi
1985—*Alexander O'Neal* (Tabu/Epic) **1987**—*Hearsay* **1989**—*All Mixed Up* **1991**—*All True Man* **1993**—*Love Makes No Sense* (Tabu/A&M).

Emerging from Minneapolis' black club scene, Alexander O'Neal gained fame in the late Eighties as a soul crooner equally adept at hard-edged R&B.

In 1978 he joined Flyte Time, the neofunk outfit that included future producers Jimmy Jam and Terry Lewis [see entry]. Though O'Neal left in 1980—just as Prince discovered the band and redubbed them the Time—Jam and Lewis produced his self-titled debut. One of its singles was "Saturday Love" (1986), an R&B Top Five duet with Cherrelle that proved him a stylistic heir to Marvin Gaye and Levi Stubbs.

Hearsay, with another Cherrelle collaboration, "Never Knew Love Like This" (#28, 1988), "Fake" (#25, 1987), and a blend of rock guitar and glossy strings, followed by *All Mixed Up,* a collection of remixes, ushered in O'Neal's #3 R&B album, *All True Man* (#49 pop, 1991). *Love Makes No Sense,* with Lance Alexander and Tony Tolbert replacing Jam and Lewis as producers, found O'Neal retaining his gospel-inflected style but moving in a pop direction ("Since I've Been Lovin' You," cowritten by Michael Bolton). Drug and alcohol problems plagued him mid-decade, but O'Neal's Eighties career was a smooth progression; he achieved particular success in the U.K.

The Only Ones

Formed 1976, London, England
Peter Perrett, gtr., voc.; John Perry, gtr.; Alan Mair, bass; Mike Kellie (b. Mar. 24, 1947, Birmingham, Eng.), drums.
1978—*The Only Ones* (CBS International, U.K.) **1979**—*Even Serpents Shine*; *Special View* (Epic); *Baby's Got a Gun* **1989**—*Live* (Skyclad) **1992**—*The Immortal Story* (Columbia).

Though part of the British punk-rock explosion, the Only Ones had a traditional rock sound, evidenced in a ringing two-guitar attack reminiscent of the Byrds and in Peter Perrett's world-weary vocals and songwriting that smacked of both Lou Reed and Ray Davies. The Only Ones, in fact, had a veteran rhythm section, Mike Kellie having drummed with Spooky Tooth, Peter Frampton, and Balls, and Alan Mair having played bass with the Beatstalkers. Perrett, meanwhile, struck up a close friendship with punk progenitor Johnny Thunders, the ex–New York Doll who was backed by the Only Ones on much of his *So Alone* album and who, like Perrett, battled a heroin addiction.

The Only Ones' first single was "Lovers of Today" b/w "Peter and the Pets"; the followup, "Another Girl, Another Planet," gained international acclaim (though it failed to chart in England upon release, it hit #57 in 1992) and got considerable play in America's new-wave clubs. (In the Eighties, the song was frequently performed by the Replacements.) However, due to erratic live shows, Perrett's drug problems, and creative differences with its record label, the band was unable to consolidate an audience, despite rave reviews for its first two albums, which were condensed for U.S. release in the *Special View* Epic compilation. Penetration vocalist Pauline Murray guested on *Baby's Got a Gun,* after which the Only Ones drifted apart. In 1991, a year after the archival *Live* was released, Perrett announced that he'd kicked heroin and would re-form the band, but instead there was only the *Immortal Story* compilation from the band's first three albums.

Yoko Ono: See John Lennon and Yoko Ono

The Orb: See the KLF

Roy Orbison
Born April 23, 1936, Vernon, Texas; died December 6, 1988, Hendersonville, Tennessee
1962—*Crying* (Monument); *Greatest Hits* 1963— *Lonely and Blue* (London); *In Dreams* (Monument) 1964—*Oh Pretty Woman; More Greatest Hits* 1966—*The Very Best of Roy Orbison* 1970—*The Original Sound* (Sun) 1972—*All Time Greatest Hits* (Monument) 1977—*Regeneration* 1979—*Laminar Flow* (Elektra) 1986—*Class of '55* (with Johnny Cash, Carl Perkins, Jerry Lee Lewis) (America/Smash); *Interviews from the Class of '55 Recording Sessions* 1987—*In Dreams: The Greatest Hits* (Virgin) 1988—*For the Lonely: A Roy Orbison Anthology, 1956–1965* (Rhino); *For the Lonely: 18 Greatest Hits* 1989—*Mystery Girl* (Virgin); *Our Love Song* (CBS); *Best-Loved Standards; Rare Orbison; The Singles Collection 1965–1973* (Polydor); *The Classic Roy Orbison (1965–1968)* (Rhino); *Rare Orbison II* (CBS); *The Sun Years* (Rhino); *Roy Orbison and Friends: A Black and White Night Live* (Virgin) 1990—*The Legendary Roy Orbison* (CBS Special Products) 1992—*King of Hearts* (Virgin). With the Traveling Wilburys: See entry.

One of the original, if not the most enthusiastic, Sun Records rockabilly artists, Roy Orbison went on to become one of the most distinctive singers in popular

Roy Orbison

music. In his first peak period (1961–64), he vacillated between snarling blues rock and his mainstay, the romantic/paranoiac ballad with crescendoing falsetto and strings. With his twanging guitar and quavering belcanto tenor, Orbison scored a number of hits: "Only the Lonely" (#2, 1960), "Running Scared" (#1, 1961), "Crying" (#2, 1961), "Dream Baby" (#4, 1962), and "Oh, Pretty Woman" (#1, 1964). Orbison's brooding-loner persona was later given resonance by the personal tragedies that befell him (his wife Claudette was killed in a motorcycle accident in 1966; two of his three children died in a fire in his Nashville home in 1968).

Orbison's songwriting and his near-operatic singing have been a prominent influence on Bruce Springsteen, Chris Isaak, and k. d. lang, among others. His ostensibly placid, introverted demeanor was offset by his trademark "look": sunglasses (contrary to popular belief, he was not blind), black leather, and a slicked-back black pompadour. Despite limited success through the late Sixties and Seventies, Orbison never quit and he was in the midst of a major commercial and critical comeback when he died suddenly in 1988.

Like many other early rockers, Orbison came from country music to rock. His father played Jimmie Rodgers songs on guitar, and an uncle played the blues. By age eight, Orbison was performing on local radio shows, and while attending high school in Wink, Texas, he formed the Wink Westerners, whose repertoire consisted mainly of country and pop standards. In contrast to many early rock stars, Orbison found rock & roll relatively late in his youth, and then almost by accident. His college buddy at North Texas State College was the newly famous Pat Boone, who urged Orbison to experiment with more pop-oriented songwriting. Orbison then formed the Teen Kings from the Wink Westerners, and they recorded "Ooby Dooby." Though Orbison would later profess a greater liking at that time for slower country material than frenetic rock, the first song he sent Sun Records' Sam Phillips—the rocking "Ooby Dooby"—impressed Phillips and became Orbison's first hit in 1956 (#59). The Teen Kings soon disbanded, and Orbison remained under contract to Sun as a solo artist. But future hits eluded Orbison, who was never entirely comfortable with rockabilly and was unhappy with Phillips' direction.

Orbison then moved to Nashville, where he wrote songs for Acuff-Rose Publishing. One of his first successes was "Claudette," named for his wife, which became a hit for the Everly Brothers. Working with producer Chet Atkins, Orbison resumed his solo career, and by 1960 had signed with Monument Records. Then came the hits, starting with "Only the Lonely," a song originally written for the Everly Brothers. Subsequent hits included "Blue Angel" (#9, 1960), "I'm Hurtin'" (#27, 1961), "Candy Man" (#25, 1961), "The Crowd" (#26, 1962), "Leah" (#25, 1962), "In Dreams" (#7, 1963), "Falling" (#22, 1963), "Mean Woman Blues" (#5, 1963), "Blue Bayou" (#29, 1963, later covered by Linda Ronstadt), Willie Nelson's "Pretty Paper" (#15, 1963), "It's Over" (#9, 1964), "Goodnight" (#21, 1965), and "Ride Away" (#25, 1965). He cowrote virtually all of his hits and often produced them as well. Successful in the U.S., Orbison was also a smash in Britain, where in 1963 he toured with the Beatles. Orbison's bands during the Sixties included guitarist Bobby Goldsboro and drummer Dewey Martin (later of Buffalo Springfield).

Following his wife's death in 1966, Orbison's career went on hold. He remarried in March 1969 and later had another son. When he returned to the U.K. in 1969, the adulation was overwhelming. Even in the late Sixties, when his popularity in the U.S. was waning, he had a monthlong run at London's Talk of the Town club, and in 1975 he had a chart-topping greatest-hits compilation.

After steady but uneventful work through the Seventies, Orbison closed the decade with an opening slot on the Eagles' 1980 tour and a Grammy-winning duet with Emmylou Harris (1980's "That Lovin' You Feelin' Again") on the *Roadie* soundtrack. A 1981 comeback show in New York City was a great commercial and critical success. In 1982 "Oh, Pretty Woman" was a hit for Van Halen; it would be revived again as the title theme song of the 1990 hit film *Pretty Woman*. Orbison's comeback

began in earnest, however, when director David Lynch used the sumptuously romantic "In Dreams" in a startling scene in his film *Blue Velvet*. The next year, Orbison was inducted into the Rock and Roll Hall of Fame by Bruce Springsteen. Nineteen-eighty-seven also saw the release of *In Dreams: The Greatest Hits*, which presented newly recorded versions of Orbison's classic hits, and the taping of an all-star tribute show "A Black and White Night." Taped in Los Angeles' Coconut Grove nightclub, the tribute starred Orbison with all-star backing from Springsteen, Elvis Costello, Bonnie Raitt, k. d. lang, Jackson Browne, Jennifer Warnes, Tom Waits, and J. D. Souther.

In 1987 Orbison's duet remake of "Crying" with k.d. lang hit #42 on the country chart. A chance meeting with Bob Dylan, Tom Petty, George Harrison, and Jeff Lynne resulted in the formation of the extremely successful Traveling Wilburys [see entry]. At the same time Orbison was completing work on his next solo album, *Mystery Girl*, which included the hit Orbison-Lynne-Petty composition "You Got It" (#9, 1989), destined to become the singer's first Top Twenty hit in 25 years. While Lynne produced that track, several other artists, including T Bone Burnett (who had produced *In Dreams*), Bono, Heartbreaker Mike Campbell, and Orbison, lent production assistance on various cuts. In addition, Bono and the Edge composed "She's a Mystery to Me."

Orbison was on the brink of a major solo comeback when he died suddenly of a heart attack. The posthumously released *Mystery Girl* (#5, 1989) became the highest-charting album of his career and was eventually certified platinum. In the wake of Orbison's passing, a number of compilations and a collection of previously unreleased tracks (*King of Hearts*) were released.

Orchestral Manoeuvres in the Dark (OMD)

Formed 1978, London, England
Andy McCluskey (b. June 24, 1959, Heswall, Eng.), synth., kybds., electronics, voc.; Paul Humphreys (b. Feb. 27, 1960, London), synth., kybds., electronics, voc.; David Hughes, bass, kybds.; Malcolm Holmes, drums.
1980—*Orchestral Manoeuvres in the Dark* (Dindisc/Virgin); *Organisation* (– Hughes; + Martin Cooper, kybds., sax)   1981—*Architecture and Morality* (Virgin/Epic)   1983—*Dazzle Ships* 1984—*Junk Culture* (Virgin/A&M) (+ Neil Weir, horns; + Graham Weir, horns)   1985—*Crush* 1986—*The Pacific Age* (– N. Weir; – G. Weir) 1988—*In the Dark/The Best of OMD* (group disbands)   1991—(Group re-forms: McCluskey, synth., bass, voc.; + Nigel Ipinson [b. 1970, Eng.], kybds.; + Phil Coxon [b. 1959, Eng.], kybds.; + Abe

Jucks [b. 1971], drums) *Sugar Tax* (Virgin) 1993—*Liberator* (– Jucks; + Stuart Kershaw, drums).

One of England's longest-running and poppiest post-punk electropop bands, Orchestral Manoeuvres in the Dark was originally formed by Paul Humphreys and Andy McCluskey, two Kraftwerk fans who had first had a duo called VCL XI in 1976, then joined such little-known larger groups as Hitlers Underpantz and the Id. In 1978 they adopted the name Orchestral Manoeuvres in the Dark, recording and performing with four-track tapes they made and played back on a tape deck they called "Winston."

In June 1979 the trendy Manchester label Factory released the duo's debut single, "Electricity," a classic piece of hooky, percolating synth pop. It was a Top Forty British hit and got significant play in American new-wave clubs. Humphreys and McCluskey soon replaced their rhythm-box percussion with a live rhythm section (drummer Malcolm Holmes had been in the Id). The 1980 single "Enola Gay" (named for the plane that dropped the first atomic bomb on Japan), with a somewhat richer sound and more romantic feel than "Electricity," was a Top Ten British hit and got more play on America's burgeoning new-wave club and radio circuit.

The critically acclaimed *Architecture and Morality* barely charted in the U.S. (#144, 1982), and *Dazzle Ships* and *Junk Culture* were critically derided as overly indulgent, but OMD made a comeback with *Crush* (#38, 1985), which added the Weir brothers' horn section and yielded the group's first U.S. hit singles, "So In Love" (#26, 1985) and "Secret" (#63, 1985). OMD scored its biggest hit with "If You Leave" (#4, 1986), from the teen-romance movie *Pretty in Pink*. *The Pacific Age* (#47, 1986) yielded a hit single in "(Forever) Live and Die" (#19, 1986), and the best-of *In the Dark* (#46, 1988) produced a hit in the new track "Dreaming" (#16, 1988). The band then broke up, with Humphreys leaving McCluskey to form Listening Pool. McCluskey re-formed OMD in 1991, recording *Sugar Tax*, which failed to chart, followed by the equally unsuccessful *Liberator*.

Oregon

Formed 1970
Ralph Towner (b. Mar. 1, 1940, Chehalis, Wash.), gtr., piano, French horn; Paul McCandless (b. Mar. 24, 1947, Indiana, Pa.), oboe, bass clarinet, English horn; Glenn Moore (b. Oct. 28, 1941, Portland, Ore.), bass, piano, wooden flute; Colin Walcott (b. 1945), tablas, perc., sitar.
1973—*Music of Another Present Era* (Vanguard) 1974—*Distant Hills*; *Winter Light* 1975—*In Concert* 1976—*Oregon/Elvin Jones: Together* 1977—*Oregon/Friends* 1978—*Violin*; *Out of the Woods* (Asylum).

An offshoot of the Paul Winter Consort, for which Ralph Towner wrote "Icarus," Oregon achieved moderate commercial success with its light, organic fusion of jazz improvisation, folky arrangements, and Indian raga inflections. Often taking on a pastoral tone, the group's music was largely acoustic, with only microphones used for amplification. One factor that differentiated Oregon from other such transcontinental fusion outfits was its long-standing refusal to use lyrics or exploit "utopian" philosophies usually associated with such music.

The members went separate ways in the late Seventies to pursue various ethnomusicological studies and solo and collaborative projects. Towner has made many albums for ECM, while Walcott has worked with modern jazz trumpeter Don Cherry in a group called Codona, which also records for ECM. Oregon has since regrouped several times.

The Orioles

Formed 1946, Baltimore, Maryland
Sonny Til (b. Earlington Tilghman, Aug. 18, 1925; d. Dec. 9, 1981), lead voc.; George Nelson (d. ca. 1959), lead and baritone voc.; Alexander Sharp (d. ca. 1970s), tenor voc.; Johnny Reed, bass voc.; Tommy Gaither (d. 1950), gtr.
1950—(– Gaither; + Ralph Williams, gtr., baritone voc.) 1953—(– Nelson; + Gregory Carol, voc.; + Charlie Hayes, voc.) N.A.—*Greatest Hits* (Collectables) 1981—*Sonny Til and the Orioles Visit Manhattan Circa 1950s*.

The Orioles are cited by many rock historians as the first rhythm & blues vocal group and a harbinger of the Fifties doo-wop sound. As teens, they were known as the Vibranaires. A local saleslady/songwriter, Deborah Chessler, managed the group and landed them a spot on Arthur Godfrey's *Talent Scouts* television program in 1948. They lost but became regulars on Godfrey's national broadcast.

The group joined Natural Records in 1948, and then changed its name to the Orioles. Contrary to popular misconception, the group did not name itself for the baseball team. The Orioles made the R&B chart with several singles, including "It's Too Soon to Know" (#13 pop, #1 R&B, 1948)—the first stylistically black, or to use the industry term of the time, "race," record to place that high on the pop chart. Their later hits include "Lonely Christmas" (#8 R&B, 1949) and "Tell Me So" (#1 R&B, 1949). The latter is considered most significant because it used "a wordless falsetto doing a kind of obbligato to the lead vocal," according to critic/disc jockey Barry Hansen. This technique would later be a staple of doo-wop vocals. Other R&B hits followed: "A Kiss and a Rose" (#12 R&B, 1949), "Forgive and Forget" (#5 R&B, 1949), and "What Are You Doing New Year's Eve" (#9

Grammy Awards

Billy Ocean
1984 Best R&B Vocal Performance, Male: "Caribbean Queen (No More Love on the Run)"

Sinéad O'Connor
1990 Best Alternative Music Performance: *I Do Not Want What I Haven't Got*

Danny Elfman (Oingo Boingo)
1989 Best Instrumental Composition: "The Batman Theme"

Mike Oldfield
1974 Best Instrumental Composition: "Tubular Bells (Theme from *The Exorcist*)"

Roy Orbison [See also: Traveling Wilburys]
1980 Best Country Performance by a Duo or Group: "That Lovin' You Feelin' Again" (with Emmylou Harris)
1986 Best Spoken Word or Nonmusical Recording: *Interviews from the Class of '55 Recording Sessions* **(with others)**
1988 Best Country Vocal Collaboration: "Crying" (with k. d. lang)
1990 Best Pop Vocal Performance, Male: "Oh Pretty Woman"

Ozzy Osbourne
1993 Best Metal Performance with Vocal: "I Don't Want to Change the World"

R&B, 1949). In 1950 Gaither was killed in an automobile accident that seriously injured Nelson and Reed. "Pal of Mine" is a tribute to Gaither.

Nelson quit, and two new members made the group a quintet. This lineup recorded "Crying in the Chapel" (#11 pop, #1 R&B, 1953). It was one of the first R&B songs to cross over to the pop market, and a #3 hit for Elvis Presley in 1965. Its followup, "In the Mission of St. Augustine," was their last hit. The original Orioles disbanded in 1954, though over the years various groups have performed and recorded under the name. The year Sonny Til died, 1981, saw the release of *Sonny Til and the Orioles Visit Manhattan Circa 1950s*, which contained new versions of doo-wop oldies. By then only Reed and Williams of the original lineup were still alive. The group was inducted into the Rock and Roll Hall of Fame in 1995.

Tony Orlando and Dawn
Formed 1970, New York City, New York
Tony Orlando (b. Michael Anthony Orlando Cassavi-

tis, Apr. 3, 1944, New York City), voc.; Telma Louise Hopkins (b. Oct. 28, 1948, Louisville, Ky.), voc.; Joyce Elaine Vincent-Wilson (b. Dec. 14, 1946, Detroit, Mich.), voc.
1970—*Candida* (Bell)   **1973**—*Tuneweaving*
1974—*Prime Time*   **1975**—*Tony Orlando and Dawn/Greatest Hits* (Arista).

Tony Orlando and Dawn had many MOR hits in the early Seventies, including "Tie a Yellow Ribbon 'Round the Ole Oak Tree," the largest-selling single in 1973, which in 1981 became something of a theme song for the return of U.S. hostages from Iran. Since then the yellow ribbon has become a national symbol for any homecoming, whether from a war or a kidnapping.

At age 16 Orlando auditioned for producer Don Kirshner, who teamed him up with songwriter Carole King. Kirshner produced and King wrote Orlando's first hits, all in 1961: "Halfway to Paradise" (#39), "Bless You" (#15), and "Happy Times (Are Here to Stay)" (#82). In a short while, though, Orlando stopped singing, in part because Kirshner sold his company to Screen Gems, which was more interested in publishing than recording. For a while Orlando worked in promotion, and in 1967 he became manager of April-Blackwood Music, the publishing arm of Columbia Records.

In early 1970 Bell Records producer Hank Medress (a former member of the Tokens) asked Orlando to sing lead over a demo he had received from Telma Louise Hopkins and Joyce Elaine Vincent, a duo calling themselves Dawn. The two Detroit-based singers had previously done backup vocals for Johnnie Taylor, Edwin Starr, Freda Payne, Frijid Pink, and others. Hopkins had also been part of Isaac Hayes's Hot Buttered Soul and later sang on "Shaft." Orlando's voice was dubbed over the original, and "Candida" shot to #3 in 1970. (Supposedly, he didn't meet Dawn until after it hit.) An alternative account claims that Orlando recorded both "Candida" and its followup, "Knock Three Times" with session singers and that Hopkins and Vincent were not hired until after these were hits.

Orlando kept his day job until after their second single, "Knock Three Times," hit #1 in 1971. Then he signed with Bell, and the group (then called Dawn, featuring Tony Orlando) finally started touring in September 1971. In 1973 they returned with the #1 hit "Tie a Yellow Ribbon 'Round the Ole Oak Tree." Other hits included "Say, Has Anybody Seen My Sweet Gypsy Rose?" (#3, 1973), "Steppin' Out (Gonna Boogie Tonight)" (#7, 1974), and "He Don't Love You (Like I Love You)" (#1, 1975).

After that, their hits stopped, though they still had many concert dates and a musical variety television series that ran intermittently for two and a half years on CBS. In July 1977, during a show in Massachusetts, Orlando shocked Dawn and the audience by announcing his retirement and claiming he was giving up show business for Jesus Christ. Orlando's decision followed the death of his sister and suicide of his close friend, comedian Freddie Prinze. Orlando also had a cocaine problem and suffered from manic depression. In November 1977 he made a solo comeback, playing Las Vegas, and later signed with Casablanca, though only one chart hit, "Sweets for My Sweet" (#54, 1979), followed. He appeared on Broadway in *Barnum* in 1980. The two women worked unsuccessfully as Dawn. Hopkins later went into acting; she has appeared on television's *Bosom Buddies, Gimme a Break,* and *Family Matters.*

Beginning in the late Eighties Orlando cohosted Jerry Lewis' Labor Day Telethon to benefit the Muscular Dystrophy Association. In 1988 Orlando, Hopkins, and Vincent-Wilson briefly re-formed Dawn. In the early Nineties Orlando relocated to Branson, Missouri, where he opened the Tony Orlando Yellow Ribbon Music Theater, where he planned to perform 200 dates a year.

Orleans
Formed 1972, New York City, New York
Lance Hoppen (b. 1954, Bayshore, N.Y.), bass; Wells Kelly (d. Oct. 30, 1984, London, Eng.), organ, voc., drums; Larry Hoppen, voc., kybds., gtr.; Jerry Marotta, drums, perc.; John Hall (b. Oct. 25, 1947, Baltimore, Md.), gtr., voc.
1973—*Orleans* (ABC) 1974—*Let There Be Music* (Asylum) 1976—*Waking and Dreaming* 1977— (– Hall; – Marotta; + Bob Leinbach, kybds., voc.; + R. A. Martin, kybds., voc.) 1979—*Forever* (Infinity) 1982—*One of a Kind* (Radio/Atlantic) 1990— *Still the One* (Elektra).
John Hall solo: 1978—*John Hall* (Asylum) 1979— *Power* (Columbia) 1981—*All of the Above* (EMI America) 1983—*Search Party.*

Orleans had a few pop hits in the mid-Seventies written by leader/guitarist John Hall and his wife, Johanna. The group was founded by John Hall (among whose songwriting credits is Janis Joplin's "Half Moon"), Larry Hoppen, and Wells Kelly. Larry's brother Lance joined later in the year. Through the next year they became a popular East Coast club attraction. They signed with ABC in 1973 and cut their eponymous debut with producers Barry Beckett and Roger Hawkins at Alabama's Muscle Shoals studio.

In 1974 Orleans recorded a self-produced album at Bearsville studio, but ABC rejected it and dropped the group from the roster. Asylum picked up Orleans and released its Chuck Plotkin–produced *Let There Be Music* late in the year. "Dance with Me" (#6, 1975) was the group's first big hit. *Waking and Dreaming* contained "Still the One" (#5, 1976), which the ABC television network used as its theme song for the year.

In 1977 Hall left to begin a solo career. He signed to Elektra Records and soon became a spokesman for the anti-nuclear-power movement, playing a key role in organizing MUSE (Musicians United for Safe Energy) and writing its anthem, "Power."

Orleans continued through various personnel changes and in 1979 had a #11 hit with "Love Takes Time" from *Forever.* By this time the band had moved to MCA's Infinity label, which in 1980 went bankrupt. The group stayed together and appeared in clubs through 1981, and in 1982 released *One of a Kind.* In 1984 Wells Kelly died in London after choking on his own vomit as a result of heroin and cocaine intoxication. By the mid-Nineties, Hall had returned to perform with Orleans, including a summer 1995 tour.

Ben Orr: See the Cars

Jeffrey Osborne
Born March 9, 1948, Providence, Rhode Island
1982—*Jeffrey Osborne* (A&M) 1983—*Stay with Me Tonight* 1984—*Don't Stop* 1986—*Emotional* 1988—*One Love—One Dream* 1990—*Only Human* (Arista).

Singer/songwriter Jeffrey Osborne's soulful baritone and romantic R&B ballads were first heard in the Seventies, when he fronted the group L.T.D. and later in his highly successful solo work. He grew up, one of 12 children of an accomplished amateur trumpeter father, in New England. Learning the trumpet and then drums at an early age, Osborne played in bands throughout high school before signing on as drummer for the Greensboro, North Carolina–based L.T.D. (Love, Togeth-erness, Devotion) at age 22 in 1970. Formerly the backup band for Sam and Dave, the ten-piece horn-driven outfit encouraged Osborne's singing, and on their six albums and such hits as "Love Ballad" (#20, 1976) and "(Every Time I Turn Around) Back in Love Again" (#4, 1977), he displayed the influence of Motown, Johnny Mathis, and Sarah Vaughan.

After a decade with L.T.D., Osborne went solo, enlisting veteran jazz-rock fusion keyboardist George Duke as producer. With "On the Wings of Love," from his self-titled debut scoring #29 in 1982, Osborne blueprinted the glossy soul music approach that would become his mainstay. In 1986 his "You Should Be Mine (The Woo Woo Song)" reached #13; a year later, his Burt Bacharach–written duet with Dionne Warwick, "Love Power," became a #12 hit. Since then, while his singing style has provoked comparisons to Teddy Pendergrass and Luther Vandross, he has yet to deliver on the potential for first-rank stardom he first displayed with L.T.D.

Ozzy Osbourne

Born John Osbourne, December 3, 1948, Birmingham, England
1980—*Blizzard of Ozz* (Jet) 1981—*Diary of a Madman* 1982—*Speak of the Devil* 1983—*Bark at the Moon* (CBS Associated) 1986—*The Ultimate Sin* 1987—*Tribute* 1988—*No Rest for the Wicked* 1990—*Just Say Ozzy* 1991—*No More Tears* (Epic) 1993—*Live & Loud.*

Onetime lead singer with Black Sabbath, Ozzy Osbourne traded on his former band's legacy of loud hard rock and mystical/occult trappings, and his own propensity for grossly outrageous acts, to become one of heavy metal's best-loved and most successful frontmen [see entry]. "I'm not a musician," Osbourne once claimed, "I'm a ham." In 1981, at an L.A. meeting of Columbia Records executives, Ozzy bit the head off a live dove; a few months later he bit the head off a bat tossed to him by a fan at a Des Moines concert. (Osbourne had thought it was a rubber toy.) The latter incident resulted in the singer receiving a series of rabies shots.

Osbourne has said there was "a lot of insanity" in his family; that he'd made several suicide attempts, as early as age 14, "just to see what it would feel like"; that at one point he and Black Sabbath drummer Bill Ward took acid every day for two years; and that his last months with Black Sabbath in 1978 were "very unhappy. I got very drunk and very stoned every single day."

Osbourne's first two solo LPs went double platinum, and in 1981 "You Can't Kill Rock 'n' Roll" garnered heavy FM-AOR airplay. Osbourne was unhurt when, on March 19, 1982, near Orlando, Florida, his tour plane, which was buzzing his tour bus, crashed. Osbourne and most of his band were in the bus; Osbourne's guitarist Randy Rhoads, hairdresser Rachel Youngblood, and pilot/bus driver Andrew Aycock were all in the plane and were all killed. Rhoads was replaced within a few weeks by Brad (Night Ranger) Gillis, and the show went on. Later that year Osbourne married his manager, Sharon Arden. He also recorded a live album, *Speak of the Devil,* at the Ritz in New York. Each of his succeeding albums, except for the 1990 *Just Say Ozzy,* went at least platinum (*Bark at the Moon* and *No More Tears* went double platinum). *Tribute* (#6, 1987) included live recordings featuring Randy Rhoads, from 1981.

For Osbourne, 1986 was particularly eventful: In April he was fined several thousand dollars by the New Jersey Meadowlands after his fans trashed an arena during a concert; that summer, he made his movie debut as an antirock minister in the horror film *Trick or Treat;* and toward the end of the year, he disappeared for three weeks—eventually turning up at the Betty Ford Clinic, where he'd checked in to battle his alcoholism.

A favorite whipping boy of the religious right, Osbourne was the target of an antirock sermon delivered in early 1990 by New York City's John Cardinal O'Connor. Between 1985 and 1990, Osbourne was sued by three different sets of parents (two from Georgia, one from California), all claiming his song "Suicide Solution," from *Blizzard of Ozz,* had induced their sons to commit suicide (lamenting the death of AC/DC's Bon Scott, the song is clearly antialcohol and antisuicide). Osbourne prevailed in every suit.

In 1991 Osbourne announced his No More Tours Tour to support *No More Tears*—an alleged farewell jaunt, during which he broke a foot while jumping around onstage in Chicago, and later caused a near-riot in Irvine, California, when he invited his audience onstage (that show had been billed as a benefit to fund replacement of Randy Rhoads' graffiti-covered tombstone, which broke even once Osbourne paid damages to the venue). In October 1992 the tour brought Osbourne to San Antonio, Texas—the first time he'd played there since February 1982, when he'd been banned from the city for urinating on the Alamo (Osbourne's also been banned, for various reasons and lengths of time, from Boston, Baton Rouge, Corpus Christi, Las Vegas, and Philadelphia). Osbourne's two tour-ending shows in Costa Mesa, California, were opened by Black Sabbath, with Judas Priest's Rob Halford replacing Sabbath singer Ronnie James Dio, who refused to open for his predecessor. Osbourne did a four-song miniset with Sabbath at the final show. The tour produced the *Live & Loud* album, which earned Osbourne his first Grammy nomination, for Best Metal Performance for the track "I Don't Wanna Change the World."

Only weeks after the tour ended, Osbourne's publicists said he might indeed tour again, but not as a solo act. Alleged financial bickering scuttled subsequent negotiations for a 1993 Ozzy-Sabbath reunion tour. In spring 1994 Osbourne recorded a version of Sabbath's "Iron Man" with Irish band Therapy? for the Sabbath tribute album, *Nativity in Black.*

Osibisa

Formed 1969, London, England
Teddy Osei (b. Ghana), saxes, flute, voc.; Sol Amarfio (b. Ghana), perc.; Mac Tontoh (b. Ghana), trumpet; Robert Bailey (b. Trinidad), kybds., drums; Wendell Richardson (b. Antigua), gtr., voc.; Spartacus R. (b. Grenada), bass; Loughty Lasisi Amao (b. Nigeria), saxes.
1970—*Osibisa* (Decca) 1972—*Woyaya* 1973—*Heads* (– Amao; + Kofi Ayivor [b. Ghana], drums; – R.; + Jean Dikota Mandengue [b. Cameroon], bass; – Richardson; + Gordon Hunte [b. Guyana], gtr., voc.); *Superfly TNT* (Buddah) (– Hunte); *Happy Children* (Warner Bros.) 1974—(+ Kiki Gyan

[b. Ghana], kybds.; + Paul Golly [b. Cameroon], gtr.)
Osibirock 1975—(+ Richardson; + Mike Odumusu
[b. Lagos, Nigeria], bass) 1976—*Welcome Home*
(Antilles) (– Golly; – Gyan; – Richardson); *Ojah
Awake* 1977—(– Bailey; + Richardson); *Black
Magic Night* (group disbands) 1980—(Group re-
forms: Osei; Amarfio; Tontoh) *Mystic Nights* (Cali-
bre, U.K.).

Osibisa was by no means the first band to play a cross
between Western pop and African traditional music, but
it was the first to become more popular in the West than
in Africa. The band was made up of both African and
Caribbean musicians.

Teddy Osei's career began over a decade before he
formed Osibisa in England; in the late Fifties and early
Sixties he played sax with a highlife band, the Comets, in
Kumasi, Ghana. In 1962 he went to England on a Ghanaian government scholarship to study at the London College of Music. He led a number of bands in London,
among them Cat's Paw in the late Sixties, which included Ghanaian younger brother Mac Tontoh's longtime friend Sol Amarfio, with whom Osei recorded a film
soundtrack in London in 1969. They formed a quartet
with Nigerian drummer Remi Kabaka, until Kabaka
joined Ginger Baker's Air Force.

By 1970 West Indians Wendell Richardson and
Robert Bailey had joined, and they named themselves
with the West African Akan word for a certain dance
rhythm. Spartacus R., a West Indian, and Loughty Amao,
a West African, joined in time to record a demo tape that
BBC radio aired before record companies heard it. The
music was an original fusion of polyrhythmic African
percussion, rock guitar, keyboard riffs, and R&B-style
horn charts; songs were in Akan and in English.

After a series of London club dates, Osibisa signed
with Decca. The group's debut album, produced by Tony
Visconti, made the U.K. Top Ten and the U.S. Top Sixty. In
the next year, Osibisa toured Europe, North America, and
Africa, and in the following year traveled to the Orient
and Australia. Everywhere, the colorfully costumed band
appeared on television; in Great Britain, the BBC devoted a special to Osibisa. Its music was further spread
by the soundtrack to *Superfly TNT* and by Art Garfunkel's 1973 cover of Amarfio's "Woyaya."

By 1973, when Osibisa signed with Warner Bros., half
the original group had left. Richardson sat in for Paul
Kossoff on Free's 1973 U.S. tour, then made a solo album,
Pieces of a Jigsaw, before rejoining Osibisa in 1975. In
1976, after moving to Island Records' Antilles label, the
group had its biggest hit, "Sunshine Day" (#17 U.K.), from
Welcome Home, but the members disbanded the following year. In 1980 Osei, Amarfio, and Tontoh reunited for
Mystic Nights, made with session musicians. The group
disbanded but do perform at occasional reunion concerts.

The Osmonds/Donny Osmond/Marie Osmond

Formed 1957, Ogden, Utah
Alan Osmond (b. June 22, 1949, Ogden), voc., gtr.;
Wayne Osmond (b. Aug. 28, 1951, Ogden), voc., gtr.,
sax, banjo, bass, drums; Merrill Osmond (b. Apr. 30,
1953, Ogden), voc., bass; Jay Osmond (b. Mar. 2,
1955, Ogden), drums; Donny Osmond (b. Donald
Clark Osmond, Dec. 9, 1957, Ogden), voc., kybds.;
Marie Osmond (b. Oct. 13, 1959, Ogden), voc.;
Jimmy Osmond (b. Apr. 16, 1963, Canoga Park,
Calif.), voc., drums.
The Osmonds: 1971—*The Osmonds* (MGM); *Home-
made* 1972—*Phase-III*; *The Osmonds "Live";
Crazy Horses* 1973—*The Plan* 1974—*Love Me for
a Reason* 1975—*The Proud One; Around the World
Live in Concert* 1976—*Brainstorm* (Polydor)
1977—*The Osmonds' Greatest Hits.*
The Osmond Brothers (Alan, Wayne, Jay, and Mer-
rill): 1992—*Greatest Hits* (Curb).
Donny Osmond solo: 1971—*The Donny Osmond
Album* (MGM); *To You with Love, Donny* 1972—
Portrait of Donny; My Best to You 1973—*Alone To-
gether* 1989—*Donny Osmond* (Capitol)
1990—*Eyes Don't Lie.*
Marie Osmond solo: 1973—*Paper Roses* (MGM)
1974—*In My Little Corner of the World* 1975—
Who's Sorry Now 1977—*This Is the Way That I
Feel* 1985—*There's No Stopping Your Heart* (Curb)
1986—*I Only Wanted You* 1988—*All in Love*
1989—*Steppin' Stone* 1990—*The Best of Marie Os-
mond.*
Donny and Marie: 1973—*I'm Leaving It All Up to
You* (MGM) 1976—*Donny & Marie—Featuring
Songs from Their Television Show* (Polydor); *Donny
& Marie—New Season* 1978—*Goin' Coconuts.*

The Osmonds are the King Family of pop and country
music, and one of the longest-running family dynasties
in popular music. Between January 24, 1971, and November 6, 1978, the RIAA certified a total of 23 gold discs
recorded either by the Osmonds or by Donny and Marie
Osmond as solo acts or as a duo: five LPs and three singles by the Osmonds; four LPs and five singles by Donny;
one single by Marie; and four LPs and one single by
Donny and Marie. But their recording success, coming
as it did nearly 15 years after the group formed, proved
anything but a fluke. And although the various Osmond
family members seemed to be treading water a decade
ago, they have not only rebounded in their respective careers but carried the Osmond name in show business
into its fourth decade with their children, in the Osmond
Boys and the Osmonds Second Generation.

All of the Osmond progeny were taught music by
their parents, George and Olive, and raised in a strict

Mormon environment. They began singing religious and barbershop-quartet songs. Their big break came when in 1962 the Osmond Brothers (at the time, Alan, Jay, Merrill, and Wayne) went to Disneyland wearing identical suits and were invited to perform by the house barbershop quartet. They made their national television debut on "Disneyland After Dark," a taped musical segment shown occasionally on *Walt Disney's Wonderful World of Color*. On the recommendation of his father, Jay, Andy Williams auditioned them and invited them onto his TV variety series, where they appeared frequently from 1962 to 1971. In the mid-Sixties, the Osmonds (now with Donny) also did TV shows with Jerry Lewis and toured with Pat Boone and Phyllis Diller. By the time the boys began recording, they'd all learned to play instruments, and through diligent touring had become a mammoth MOR attraction.

Their 1971 debut LP went gold, as did Donny's million-selling debut single, "Sweet and Innocent" (#7). Earlier that year, the brothers scored a gold hit with the Jackson 5–style "One Bad Apple" (#1). Other 1971 hit singles for the Osmonds included "Double Lovin'" (#14), "I Can't Stop" (#96), and the million-selling "Yo-Yo" (#3); Donny hit gold again with "Go Away Little Girl" (#1). Their albums, for the most part, went gold as well.

The year 1972 brought more hits: Donny's "Hey Girl" b/w "I Knew You When" (#9) and the Osmonds' "Down by the Lazy River" (#4) both went gold. The Osmonds had further hits with "Hold Her Tight" (#14, 1972) and "Goin' Home" (#36, 1973). Donny hit with the singles "Puppy Love" (#3), "Why" (#13), and "Too Young" (#13) in 1972, and "The Twelfth of Never" (#8, 1973) and "A Million to One" b/w "Young Love" (#23, 1973).

At this time, Marie made her recording debut with the #1 country & western hit "Paper Roses" (#5 pop, 1973). Little Jimmy's debut LP and single, "Long Haired Lover from Liverpool," made the U.S. Top Forty in 1972 and topped the U.K. chart for six weeks. But he was most successful in Japan, where the plump nine-year-old was known affectionately as "Jimmy Boy" and later had his own television series. By the early Nineties, Jimmy had become the family's business mastermind with a financial empire built on savvy real estate investments and events production.

Marie changed her image to something a little hipper in the late Seventies and wrote a book entitled *Marie Osmond's Guide to Beauty and Dating*. In the early Eighties she and Donny were most visible doing Hawaiian Punch TV commercials. In 1978 they costarred in the film *Goin' Coconuts*. In early 1982 Donny appeared on Broadway in George M. Cohan's musical *Little Johnny Jones,* which closed on opening night. In the mid-Eighties Marie cohosted the *Ripley's Believe It or Not* TV series. She continued her success on the country charts with a number of hits including the C&W #1 singles

"Meet Me in Montana" (a duet with Dan Seals, 1985), "There's No Stopping Your Heart" (1985), and "You're Still New to Me" (a duet with Paul Davis, 1986). In the early Nineties she toured in *The Sound of Music*.

Donny headed his own production company for a number of years before returning to recording in the late Eighties. Peter Gabriel invited Osmond to record in his Bath, England, studio. Some tracks recorded there landed Osmond a deal with Capitol, and in 1988 his *Donny Osmond* (#54, 1989) spun off "Soldier of Love" (#2, 1989). Other charting singles from that album were "Sacred Emotion" (#13, 1989) and "Hold On" (#73, 1989). *Eyes Don't Lie* didn't make the Hot 100, but it contained "My Love Is a Fire" (#21, 1990). Osmond surprised many people by speaking out against the PMRC in 1985. He has continued to work in theater and appeared in *Joseph and the Amazing Technicolor Dreamcoat*.

The Osmond Brothers, sans Donny and plus Jimmy, turned to country music, with instant success. They were named *Billboard*'s top new singles group in 1992, and have since been named Branson, Missouri's group of the year. There they own, operate, and perform at the Osmond Family Theater. The family founded the Osmond Foundation for the deaf (two of the group's older brothers were born deaf). In the early Eighties the foundation was expanded and is affiliated with the Children's Miracle Network Telethon, which was cofounded by Marie and actor John Schneider and raises money for children's hospitals.

Gilbert O'Sullivan

Born Raymond O'Sullivan, December, 1, 1946, Waterford, Ireland
1972—*Himself* (MAM); *Back to Front*   1973—*I'm a Writer, Not a Fighter; A Stranger in My Own Back Yard.*

Gilbert O'Sullivan was a boyish-voiced pop singer/songwriter who burst onto the American chart in 1972 with two lilting but despairing MOR Paul McCartney-esque ballads—"Alone Again (Naturally)" (#1) and "Clair" (#2). In his early days, O'Sullivan played in a local band called Rick's Blues with future Supertramp member Richard Davies, and he had his first solo British hit in 1970 with "Nothing Rhymed" (#8). After his initial U.S. breakthrough, he enjoyed three more hits in 1973—"Out of the Question" (#17), "Get Down" (#7), and "Ooh Baby" (#25)—before dropping out of sight. He had hits in England through 1980 ("I Don't Love You, But I Think I Like You," "What's in a Kiss?"), but then vanished there as well until 1983, when he won a major lawsuit against MAM and manager Gordon Mills for back royalties.

His *Life and Rhymes* (1982) was produced by Graham Gouldman and disappeared without a trace. Six years elapsed before his next LP, *Frobisher Drive,* but neither that nor *In the Key of G* (1989) rekindled public interest. (None was released in the United States.) In late 1991 O'Sullivan was in the news again when a federal district court judge ruled that the rapper Biz Markie's unauthorized sampling of "Alone Again (Naturally)" constituted theft. This landmark case was the first to equate sampling of recorded music without the permission of the copyright owner with theft.

The Other Two: See Joy Division

Johnny Otis

Born John Veliotes, December 8, 1921, Vallejo, California
1969—*Cold Shot* (Kent)   1970—*Cuttin' Up* (Epic) 1971—*Live at Monterey; The Original Johnny Otis Show* (Savoy)   1981—*The New Johnny Otis Show* (Alligator)   1989—*The Capitol Years* (Capitol) 1993—*Spirit of the Black Territory Bands* (Johnny Otis and His Orchestra) (Arhoolie)   1995—*Too Late to Holler* (Night Train/City Hall).

As a talent scout and bandleader Johnny Otis was a central figure in the development of rhythm & blues and rock & roll in the early Fifties. Otis was born of Greek-American parents, but from his childhood he lived among blacks, and in fact, considered himself black. As he later wrote in his autobiography *Listen to the Lambs,* "I did not become black because I was attracted to Negro music. My attitude was formed long before I moved into the music field."

In his Berkeley neighborhood, Otis became interested in blues, gospel, and swing, and in his teens he became an accomplished drummer, dropping out of high school to play in the Bay Area and touring the Southwest with various swing bands. In 1941 he married his wife, Phyllis, a black woman; they had five children. By the mid-Forties Otis had his own big band, but when the big-band format lost popularity he stripped his crew down to a nine-piece group with small horn and rhythm sections, which became a standard rhythm & blues lineup. In 1945 he had his first regional hit with a version of "Harlem Nocturne." That year he also played drums on Johnny Moore's Three Blazers' hit "Drifting Blues" and discovered a group called the Royals (who would later be known as Hank Ballard and the Midnighters).

In 1948 Otis and a partner, Bardu Ali, opened a popular Watts nightclub, the Barrelhouse Club. He closed it in the early Fifties after he made a series of R&B hits featuring singers he had discovered in Los Angeles: Little Esther Phillips, Mel Walker, and the Robins, who would later become known nationally as the Coasters.

"Double Crossing Blues" (#1 R&B), "Mistrustin' Blues" (#1 R&B), "Deceivin' Blues" (#4 R&B), "Dreamin'

Blues" (#8 R&B), "Wedding Boogie" (#6 R&B), "Far Away Christmas Blues" (#4 pop, #6 R&B), and "Rockin' Blues" (#21 pop, #2 R&B) were all hits in 1950. In 1952 "Sunset to Dawn," sung by Mel Walker, was a #10 R&B hit.

From 1950 to 1954 the Johnny Otis Rhythm and Blues Caravan touring revue traveled across the U.S. with then unknown performers including Hank Ballard, Little Willie John, Big Mama Thornton, and Jackie Wilson. Otis heard Jerry Leiber and Mike Stoller's "Hound Dog," and he produced Thornton's version of it. "Every Beat of My Heart," written by Otis in the early Fifties, became Gladys Knight and the Pips' first hit in 1961, and has been covered regularly ever since.

In 1954 Otis quit the road for a DJ spot at Los Angeles' KFOX, later landing a television show in the late Fifties. But he hadn't given up music, and in 1958 he had his biggest hit with the Bo Diddley–style "Willie and the Hand Jive" (#9 pop, #5 R&B). For most of the Sixties, Otis' musical career was dormant, though he was very active in the civil rights movement and politics. His mid-Sixties book, *Listen to the Lambs,* concerned the 1965 Watts riot and also told the story of his life.

With his guitarist son Johnny Otis Jr., "Shuggie," Johnny Otis returned to recording with *Cold Shot* (1969), *Cuttin' Up* (1970), and *The Johnny Otis Show Live at Monterey* (1971), a double album reuniting his old band and singers. Otis recorded a number of early R&B artists for his Blues Spectrum label, including Louis Jordan, Charles Brown, Big Joe Turner, Eddie "Cleanhead" Vinson, Clarence "Gatemouth" Brown, and himself. In 1978 Otis became an ordained minister and founded the nondenominational Landmark Community Church in Los Angeles. He is also an accomplished painter and sculptor. As of the mid-Eighties, he was still touring the world, and his 1993 *Spirit of the Black Territory Bands* featured a Forties-style big band. He still performs in his Johnny Otis Cabaret in California and tours occasionally. He also hosts a radio show. In 1994 he was inducted into the Rock and Roll Hall of Fame.

Shuggie Otis

Born Johnny Otis Jr., November 30, 1953, Los Angeles, California
1969—*Kooper Session: Al Kooper Introduces Shuggie Otis* (Columbia)   1970—*Here Comes Shuggie Otis* (Epic)   1971—*Freedom Flight*   1975—*Inspiration Information*   N.A.—*Preston Love's Omaha Bar-B-Q* (Kent).

Johnny Otis' son Shuggie was a prodigy, playing bass professionally with a jazz band in San Diego at 12, and joining his father's band as guitarist and doing session work, playing guitar, bass, organ, piano, and harmonica by 13. *Cold Shot,* which featured Shuggie on guitar, brought him to the attention of Al Kooper, who teamed up with Shuggie for the loose jam of *Kooper Session*. The younger Otis played bass on Frank Zappa's *Hot Rats* and guitar on violinist Sugarcane Harris' first solo LP. After three more albums he retired in 1975 at age 22; in 1977 his "Strawberry Letter 23" was a Top Five hit for the Brothers Johnson. An appearance on *The New Johnny Otis Show* in 1981 was his first recording in several years, aside from session work on his father's Blues Spectrum label. He and his brother Nick, a drummer, still play in their father's band.

John Otway

Born October 2, 1952, Aylesbury, England
1977—*John Otway + Wild Willy Barrett* (Polydor, U.K.) 1978—*Deep and Meaningless* 1979—*Where Did I Go Right?* 1980—*Way and Bar*; *Deep Thought* (Stiff) 1982—*All Balls and No Willy* 1989—*The Wimp and the Wild.*

One of the great eccentric footnotes to rock history, John Otway had only one hit, his 1977 single, "(Cor Baby, That's) Really Free" (#27 U.K.). He has spent the rest of his career trying to replicate that success with a combination of constant touring in England, lunatic, hyperactive performances, and a series of ever-more-bizarre publicity stunts.

The Who's Pete Townshend signed Otway and partner Wild Willy Barrett to Track Records in 1974 and produced two flop singles. Otway was signed by Polydor during the punk explosion of 1977, even though his sound was closer to pub rock. The label suggested he recut "Cor Baby" in a more anarchic style, and Otway had "the Hit." His followup, "Geneve," a ballad recorded with an orchestra, puzzled his fans and disappeared without a trace, as did his three Polydor albums. When the label dropped him, Otway staged "Polython," a benefit concert that raised £1,500 for his former employers.

He moved on to Stiff in 1980. To promote his cover of Gene Pitney's "The Man Who Shot Liberty Valance," the label pressed three copies without Otway's vocal; he would personally visit the homes of fans who bought the instrumental versions and add the vocal "live." After two albums Stiff, too, dropped him.

Undeterred by his lack of success, Otway plowed on. He "signed" Warner Bros. as his record label in 1986, sending them a £200 advance and releasing "Jerusalem" with a counterfeit Warner label. Warners eventually released a legitimate version of the single, which sold about 50 copies.

Otway remains active (he celebrated his 2,000th show in 1993); in 1990 he wrote an autobiography, *Cor Baby, It's Really Me*. It sold more copies than any of his records.

The Outlaws

Formed 1974, Tampa, Florida
Hughie Thomasson, gtr., voc.; Billy Jones (d. Feb. 4, 1995, Spring Hill, Fla.), gtr., voc.; Henry Paul, gtr., voc.; Frank O'Keefe (d. Feb. 26, 1995), bass; Monte Yoho, drums.
1975—*The Outlaws* (Arista) 1976—*Lady in Waiting* 1977—(- O'Keefe; - Paul; + Harvey Dalton Arnold, bass; + David Dix, drums) *Hurry Sundown* 1978—(+ Freddie Salem, gtr., voc.) *Bring It Back Alive*; *Playin' to Win* 1979—(- Salem) *In the Eye of the Storm* (- Arnold; + Rick Cua, bass, voc.) 1980—*Ghost Riders in the Sky* (- Yoho) 1981— (- Jones) 1982—*Los Hombres Malo* (group disbands) *Greatest Hits of the Outlaws/High Tides Forever* 1983—(Group re-forms: Paul; Thomasson; + Chris Hicks, gtr., voc.; + Barry Borden, bass; + Jeff Howell, drums) 1986—*Soldiers of Fortune* (Pasha) (- Paul) 1993—*Hittin' the Road* (Blues Bureau International) 1994—*Diablo Canyon.*
Henry Paul Band: 1979—*Grey Ghost* (Atlantic) 1980—*Feel the Heat* 1981—*Anytime.*

Tampa's Outlaws built a solid audience by merging Eagles-style country rock and vocal harmonies (Eagles' producer Bill Szymczyk produced *Hurry Sundown*) and Allman Brothers–style twin-guitar Southern rock. The Outlaws were managed by Alan Walden, who felt it impropitious to enter a business relationship with his brother Phil, who ran Capricorn; they became Clive Davis' first Arista signing. Their name notwithstanding, the Outlaws were considerably smoother–sounding than fellow Southern rockers Molly Hatchet and .38 Special, with whom they shared an initial audience and touring circuit. The Outlaws appeared sporadically on the pop chart with "There Goes Another Love Song" (#34, 1975), two minor hits, and "(Ghost) Riders in the Sky" (#31, 1980). Henry Paul led his own band after leaving the Outlaws in 1977, but in 1983 he rejoined the group. *Ghost Riders, Bring It Back Alive*, and *Outlaws* are gold. In 1993 Paul formed Blackhawk. In 1994 the Outlaws mounted a package tour with the Marshall Tucker Band and .38 Special. Outlaws O'Keefe and Jones both died in February 1995.

Buck Owens

Born Alvis Edgar Owens Jr., August 12, 1929, Sherman, Texas
1963—*Buck Owens on the Bandstand* (Capitol); *I've Got a Tiger by the Tail* 1964—*Best of Buck Owens*; *Together Again* 1966—*Dust on Mother's Bible* 1967—*Buck Owens and His Buckaroos in Japan* 1968—*The Best of Buck Owens, vol. 2* 1972—*Too Old to Cut the Mustard* 1976—*Buck'Em!* (Warner

Bros.)   1979—*Our Old Mansion*   1981—*Love Don't Make the Bars* (Capitol)   1988—*Hot Dog!*; *Buck Owens and the Buckaroos Live at Carnegie Hall* (Country Music Foundation)   1990—*All–Time Greatest Hits, vol. 1* (Curb)   1992—*The Buck Owens Collection 1959–1990* (Rhino).

Chief purveyor, along with Merle Haggard, of the honky-tonk music dubbed the Bakersfield Sound (after his California home base), Buck Owens was a top-selling country artist in the Sixties and cohost of the country comedy television show *Hee Haw* from 1969 to 1986. Emerging from semiretirement in 1987, he gained a new audience with longtime fan and neotraditionalist Dwight Yoakam when the pair released a Top Ten country single, "The Streets of Bakersfield."

Owens nicknamed himself Buck after a favorite mule when he was just three. His farming family settled in Arizona in the Thirties. At 16, he was married and an accomplished guitarist; he moved to Bakersfield at age 21. As a session player in nearby Los Angeles, he worked with Gene Vincent, Sonny James, and Stan Freberg. He formed the Schoolhouse Playboys in 1951 and recorded rockabilly using the name "Corky Jones."

Signed to Capitol, he released under his own name the #4 hit, "Under Your Spell Again," in 1959; its success kicked off an astonishing run of 75 charting country singles that continued into the early Eighties (42 made the Top Ten; 20 reached #1). Among his #1 sellers, delivered in an appealing, almost pleading tenor voice and backed by his crack band the Buckaroos, were 1963's "Act Naturally" (covered later by the Beatles), "I've Got a Tiger by the Tail" (1965), "Waitin' in Your Welfare Line" (1966), and "Open Up Your Heart" (1966). Resisting the string-laden, pop-oriented productions of contemporary Nashville, the Buckaroos favored a rootsy style confined to drums, pedal steel, two guitars, and the occasional fiddle. Owens' 1969 version of Chuck Berry's "Johnny B. Goode" revealed his rockabilly beginnings and the populist sympathies of the Bakersfield Sound. His songs covered by artists as diverse as Ray Charles ("Crying Time") and Emmylou Harris ("Together Again"), Owens has released over 100 albums.

By his own account overexposed during his 16 years with the hugely popular but critically derided *Hee Haw*, Owens spent the latter Seventies in semiretirement. During that time he mourned the loss of Buckaroos guitarist Don Rich, who was killed in a 1974 motorcycle wreck. (Rich has drawn particular praise from Jerry Garcia.) He also concentrated on his business affairs, which included running several radio stations and a recording studio, until Dwight Yoakam contacted him in the late Eighties and encouraged him to return to active performing. The resulting new album, 1988's *Hot Dog!*, and a lavish boxed set, 1992's *The Buck Owens Collection 1959–1990*, revived general interest in Owens, a singer/composer whom musicians and true fans of modern country had always held in high esteem.

Ozark Mountain Daredevils
Formed 1971, Springfield, Missouri
John Dillon (b. Feb. 6, 1947, Stuttgart, Ark.), gtr., dulcimer, mandolin, autoharp, piano; Steve Cash (b. May 5, 1946, Springfield), voc., harmonica; Randle Chowning (b. 1950), gtr., mandolin, harmonica, voc.; Michael Granda (b. Dec. 24, 1950, St. Louis, Mo.), bass, voc.; Buddy Brayfield (b. 1951), piano; Larry Lee (b. 1947, Springfield), drums, voc., gtr., piano.
1973—*Ozark Mountain Daredevils* (A&M)   1974—*It'll Shine When It Shines*   1975—*The Car over the Lake*   1976—(– Chowning; + Rune Walle [b. Nor.], gtr., banjo) *Men from Earth*   1977—(– Brayfield; + Ruell Chapell, kybds., voc.; + Jerry Mills, mandolin; + Steve Canday, gtr., drums, voc.)   1978—*Don't Look Down*; *It's Alive*   1980—*Ozark Mountain Daredevils* (Columbia)   1983—*Best Of* (A&M)   1985—*The Lost Cabin Sessions* (Sounds Great)   1994—(Lineup: Cash; Dillon; Granda; + Bill Brown [b. Mar. 21, 1960, N.C.], gtr., voc.; + Ron Gremp [b. June 22, 1955, St. Louis], drums).

Growing out of a Springfield assemblage called Cosmic Corncob and His Amazing Mountain Daredevils, this unusually eclectic country-rock unit first came to national attention with "If You Wanna Get to Heaven" (#25, 1974). Mixing Appalachian and hillbilly string music with Southern boogie and country pop, the Ozark Mountain Daredevils released three fairly successful albums. Their 1973 eponomously titled debut went gold and peaked at #26. *It'll Shine When It Shines*, which included "Jackie Blue" (#3, 1975) was their highest-charting album, at #19.

The group's hold on the pop chart slipped after that, however. Chowning left in 1976 for a solo career. As of the mid-Nineties, Cash, Dillon, and Granda (with additional members) continue to perform throughout the United States. The group is still based in Springfield.

P

Augustus Pablo

**Born Horace Swaby, circa 1953, Kingston, Jamaica
1972—*This Is Augustus Pablo* (Kaya)   1974—*King
Tubby Meets Rockers Uptown* (Clocktower)
1975—*Ital Dub* (Trojan)   1977—*Pablo Nuh Jester*
(City Line)   1978—*East of the River Nile* (Rockers)
1979—*Original Rockers* (Greensleeves)   1980—
Rockers Meets King Tubby Inna Fire House
(Shanachie)   1982—*Earth's Rightful Ruler* (Rockers)
1983—*King David's Melody* (Alligator)   1986—*Rising Sun* (Shanachie)   1988—*Rockers Comes East*;
Eastman Dub (Greensleeves)   1989—*Rockers Story*
(Ras)   1990—*Blowing with the Wind* (Shanachie)
1991—*Pablo Meets Mr. Bassie*.**

One of the most distinguished names in reggae, dub producer, composer, arranger, and keyboardist Augustus
Pablo is equally renowned as the foremost exponent of
the melodica, which has been used by numerous reggae
artists as well as by Joe Jackson, the Clash, and Gang of
Four.

While still calling himself Horace Swaby, Pablo
taught himself piano at Kingston College School and
played the local church organ. One day he borrowed a
melodica from a girlfriend and became fascinated by it.
Bob Marley took young Swaby into his Kingston studios,
where in 1969–70 he contributed melodica lines to Lee
Perry–produced Wailers tracks such as "Sun Is Shining,"

"Kaya," and "Memphis." Pablo has also led backing
bands for Jimmy Cliff and Burning Spear and was at one
time a member of Sly Dunbar's Skin, Flesh and Bones
Band.

In 1971 producer Herman Chin-Loy gave Pablo his
nom de disc, and the following year Pablo had his first
hit single, "Java," which established his distinctive
sound: reggae rhythms supporting sinuous minor–key
melodica and organ lines and exotic modalities that
Pablo termed "Far Eastern." He claims the influence of
jazz vibraphonist Milt Jackson's "sleepy vibrato and
hang-glide sonics."

Around 1973 Pablo came under the sway of King
Tubby, who with Lee Perry was one of the first dub producers. Pablo's *King Tubby Meets Rockers Uptown* is a
landmark of dub—in which tunes are remixed almost
beyond recognition. Pablo's most formidable trait is his
unique (within dub) obsession with melody; he has
made a long–running practice of dubbing such pop
tunes as "Fiddler on the Roof" (in *East of the River Nile*'s
"Jah Light"), Rod McKuen's "Jean" (*Pablo Nuh Jester*'s
"Fat Jean"), Bill Withers' "Ain't No Sunshine" (*Original
Rockers*' "Thunder Clap"), and "Old Man River" (*This Is
Augustus Pablo*'s "Jah Rock"), as well as following standard dub practice revamping reggae hits (including
Marley's "Dem Belly Full" as "Pablo Meets Mr. Bassie,"
on the album of the same name).

Pablo's penchant for melodicism, and the near–New

Age pastoral lyricism of his arrangements, set him further and further apart from the reggae mainstream as the Eighties wore on. Only on *Rockers Comes East* did Pablo flirt with the synth-heavy computer-rhythm sound that had come to dominate dub. On his next album, 1990's *Blowing with the Wind,* he returned to his trademark plaintive riffs, mellow grooves, and melodica, string-synth, and vibraphone colorations. Pablo normally spends most of his time seeking inspiration in the remote hillsides outside Kingston; in 1985 he played a rare U.S. concert at the Kitchen in New York City, and undertook his only full-scale U.S. tour a year later.

Pablo Cruise

Formed 1973, San Francisco, California
Dave Jenkins (b. Fla.), gtr., bass, voc.; Cory Lerios (b. Calif.), kybds., voc.; Bud Cockrell (b. Miss.), bass, voc.; Steve Price (b. Calif.), drums.
1975—*Pablo Cruise* (A&M)   1976—*Life Line*
1977—*A Place in the Sun* (– Cockrell; + Bruce Day [b. Calif.], bass, voc.)   1978—*Worlds Away*   1980— *Part of the Game* (– Day; + Angelo Rossi, gtr., voc.; + John Pierce, bass, voc.)   1981—*Reflector*   1988— *Classics, Volume 26.*

An immensely successful band with a string of tunes that have become favorites on AM and FM radio and TV, Pablo Cruise exemplified the wholesome, ultra-smooth California sound. Indeed, its music has been called "music to watch sports by," and Pablo Cruise songs have been used as soundtracks for ABC's *Wide World of Sports,* CBS's *Sports Spectacular,* and NBC's *Sportsworld,* as well as for a surfing documentary called *Free Ride.* The band has also contributed to the soundtracks of the films *An Unmarried Woman* and *Dreamer.*

Pablo Cruise comes by its California heritage honestly. Dave Jenkins, Cory Lerios, and Steve Price were formerly with Stoneground, while Bud Cockrell came from It's a Beautiful Day. When Cockrell left to pursue a musical career with his wife, Pattie Santos (ex–It's a Beautiful Day), he was replaced by Bruce Day, formerly of Santana. The band first drew attention for such instrumentals as "Ocean Breeze" (from its debut LP) and "Zero to Sixty in Five" (from *Life Line*), both of which became FM radio favorites. The band's first big hit was "Whatcha Gonna Do?" (#6, 1977), but Pablo Cruise really made it with *Worlds Away,* which contained three hit singles: "Love Will Find a Way" (#6, 1978), "Don't Want to Live Without It" (#21, 1978), and "I Go to Rio" (#46, 1979). The LP sold a million copies within a year of its release, as did *A Place in the Sun.* In 1981 Pablo Cruise scored again with its final hit, "Cool Love." Jenkins went on to join ex–Creedence Clearwater Revival Stu Cook and two ex–Doobie Brothers, John McFee and Keith Knudsen, in Southern Pacific.

Jimmy Page

Born January 9, 1944, Heston, England
1982—*Death Wish II* soundtrack (Swan Song)
1988—*Outrider* (Geffen)   1993—*Coverdale/Page* (with David Coverdale)   1994—*No Quarter: Jimmy Page and Robert Plant Unledded* (with Robert Plant) (Atlantic).
With the Firm (Page, gtr.; Paul Rodgers [b. Dec. 17, 1949, Middleborough, Eng.], voc.; Chris Slade, drums; Tony Franklyn, bass): 1985—*The Firm* (Atlantic)   1986—*Mean Business.*

One of rock's most important and influential guitar players, writers, and producers, Jimmy Page has alternated between solo projects and collaborations with other superstars since the demise of Led Zeppelin [see entry] in 1980. But surpassed by new trends and technology, Page's later work has been as bound to classic rock as his legendary past accomplishments. In 1994 he finally rejoined vocalist Robert Plant to perform Led Zeppelin songs, along with new compositions, for an MTV *Unplugged* performance, entitled *Unledded,* and album, *No Quarter.*

After Zeppelin drummer John Bonham's death, Page didn't touch a guitar for nine months. His first collaborative project after that, with Yes's Chris Squire and Alan White, never made it out of the studio. His soundtrack for the film *Death Wish II* is a predominantly instrumental album (Chris Farlowe and Gordon Edwards provide vocals) that at points found him playing fitfully with synthesizers, a technological advance with which the studio wizard and blues-based axeman has had a love-hate relationship.

The 1983–84 ARMS (Action and Research in Multiple Sclerosis) tour to benefit his friend ex-Faces bassist Ronnie Lane and others afflicted with the disease brought Page to the concert stage for the first time since 1980. He also contributed to former bandmate Robert Plant's first solo album, *Pictures at 11,* in 1982.

Two years later Page founded the Firm with former Free and Bad Company vocalist Paul Rodgers. Page once referred to the band as a vehicle to show people he wasn't the drug user oft rumored. In the fall of 1984, however, he was arrested for possession of cocaine, his second offense, and his personal life continued to remain shrouded in mystery, colored by rumors of interest in the occult and a period of heroin addiction.

The Firm released two albums and toured once, to lukewarm critical and mixed fan response. Then, because he wanted to "avoid routine," Page released his first nonsoundtrack studio album, *Outrider* (#26, 1988), which features vocals by John Miles, Chris Farlowe, and Plant. A gold album, *Outrider* earned Page a Grammy nomination for best rock instrumental and sent him on his first solo tour. For his next album, Page paired up with former Deep Purple and Whitesnake vocalist David Coverdale, whose similarities to Rodgers and Plant have provoked the ex-Zep singer to call him "David Coverversion." The Page-Coverdale collaboration is a solid if somewhat generic contribution to the hard rock Page pioneered (the album peaked at #5 in 1993).

Page and Plant put their differences aside in 1994 when they reunited to record a new album, *No Quarter,* in Wales, Morocco, and London, where *Unledded,* the MTV *Unplugged* special, was taped. A mix of Led Zep and new songs, the album featured musicians from Marrakech, India, and Egypt. Page and Plant embarked on a 1995 tour to promote the album.

Robert Palmer

Born Alan Palmer, January 19, 1949, Batley, England
1974—*Sneakin' Sally Through the Alley* (Island)
1975—*Pressure Drop*   1976—*Some People Can Do
What They Like*   1978—*Double Fun*   1979—*Secrets*   1980—*Clues*   1982—*Maybe It's Live
1983—*Pride*   1985—*Riptide*   1988—*Heavy Nova*
(EMI Manhattan)   1989—*Addictions, Volume One*
(Island)   1990—*Don't Explain* (EMI)   1992—*Ridin'*
High.

During the first part of his recording career, white soul singer Robert Palmer was equally renowned for his taste in rock and R&B cover songs as for his impeccably tailored suits. By the mid-Eighties, however, Palmer had achieved mainstream stardom through a series of records that pitted his cool, understated vocals against smooth, catchy pop songs or overtly hard rockers.

Palmer spent most of his childhood on the island of Malta. Back in Britain as a teenager, he first sang in the band Mandrake Paddle Steamer, then went professional with the Alan Bown Set in 1968. The next year he joined Dada, which changed its name to Vinegar Joe, releasing three albums (*Vinegar Joe* and *Rock 'n' Roll Gypsies,* both 1972, and *Six Star General,* 1973). When the band broke up, Palmer went solo.

Sneakin' Sally Through the Alley featured backup and songs by members of Little Feat and the Meters; the title track was by Allen Toussaint. Little Feat also had a hand in *Pressure Drop,* featuring the Toots and the Maytals title cut and Palmer's own "Give Me an Inch." After making *Some People Can Do What They Like,* Palmer moved to Nassau in the Bahamas. He had his first U.S. hit with ex-Free Andy Fraser's "Every Kinda People" (#16, 1978) from *Double Fun,* followed by Moon Martin's "Bad Case of Loving You (Doctor, Doctor)" (#14, 1979) from *Secrets,* the first album Palmer produced himself.

Clues, with a band including Chris Frantz (Talking Heads) and Gary Numan, and material by Numan, found Palmer, on such cuts as "Johnny and Mary" and "Looking for Clues," moving into smooth synthesizer-driven pop.

He followed his first Top Twenty British hit, "Some Guys Have All the Luck," with *Maybe It's Live.*

Palmer's profile was raised considerably by his 1985 tenure in Power Station, a group consisting of Duran Duran's John Taylor and Andy Taylor and Chic's Tony Thompson. "Get It On" and "Some Like It Hot" (#6, 1985) saw him rocking out more than before; unwilling to tour with the band, however, he soon departed.

The sleek rock he'd debuted with Power Station fostered his breakthrough, *Riptide.* "Addicted to Love," (#1, 1986) and "I Didn't Mean to Turn You On" (#2, 1986) were guitar-powered confections with instant mainstream appeal; boosted by videos featuring deadpan elegant models mimicking the role of backup band, they established Palmer as an ironic sex symbol, an MTV-era Cary Grant.

Moving with his family to Switzerland, Palmer contributed to the film *Sweet Lies* before releasing *Heavy Nova* and its hits, "Simply Irresistible" (#2, 1988) and "Early in the Morning" (#19, 1988). Its styles ranging from bossa nova to Forties-style balladeering, the album also demonstrated Palmer's continuing eclecticism. A collaboration with UB40 on Bob Dylan's "I'll Be Your Baby Tonight" enlivened *Don't Explain,* and on *Ridin' High,* Palmer turned in a credible collection of Tin Pan Alley and cabaret standards.

Paris

Born Oscar Jackson, October 29, 1967, San Francisco, California
1990—*The Devil Made Me Do It* (Tommy Boy)
1992—*Sleeping with the Enemy* (Scarface)   1994—
***Guerrilla Funk* (Priority).**

Bay Area political rapper Paris became famous when his second album was rejected by Time Warner rap subsidiary Tommy Boy Records in the wake of the 1992 Ice-T/"Cop Killer" controversy. The album contained two objectionable songs: the cop-killing fantasy "Coffee, Donuts & Death," and "Bush Killa," which depicted the assassination of then-president George Bush. Paris chose to release the album on his own Scarface label.

Paris, who calls himself the Black Panther of Rap, founded Scarface in 1987 while still a sophomore at the University of California at Davis. A drummer, keyboard player, and economics major, he had no intention of actually becoming a rapper until he decided he wanted to get the revolutionary ideology of the Sixties Black Panther party onto the streets again. After graduating college in 1990, he spent some time with former Panther party leaders and visited Cuba, where he met Fidel Castro. The same year, Paris released his debut album, which featured songs such as "Panther Power" and "Scarface Groove." Paris' albums have been celebrated by anticensorship forces and music critics.

Mica Paris

Born Michelle Wallen, April 27, 1969, London, England
1988—*So Good* (Island)   1990—*Contribution*
1993—*Whisper a Prayer*.

A British singer of sophisticated pop soul, Mica Paris emerged as a glossy diva in the late Eighties. Actually, her origins were rootsier: Encouraged by Jamaican parents of a Pentecostal family, she began singing in church, did session work while in her teens, and performed with the Spirit of Watts gospel group.

In 1988 her jazz-inflected debut, *So Good,* sent "My One Temptation" into the British Top Ten; "Like Dreamers Do" and "Breathe Life into Me" were also U.K. hits for the chanteuse, then 19 years old. After a duet, with Will Downing, of the Roberta Flack–Donny Hathaway classic "Where Is the Love" hit #19 in the U.K., she released *Contribution,* featuring a rap by Rakim, Nile Rodgers on guitar, and material by Smokey Robinson and Prince. The album, with its urban sound more assertive than her first, again revealed impressive stylistic versatility, but its singles didn't chart as well as those on her previous effort. As with her prior albums, Paris' *Whisper a Prayer* (1993) proved to be more commercially successful in Britain than in the U.S.

Charlie Parker

Born Charles Christopher Parker, August 29, 1920,
Kansas City, Kansas; died March 12, 1955, New York
City, New York
1953—*The Greatest Jazz Concert Ever* (Fantasy)
1978—*The Complete Savoy Studio Sessions* (Savoy)
1988—*Bird: The Complete Charlie Parker on Verve*
(Verve)   1989—*The Legendary Dial Masters vols. I*
& *II* (Stash).

Alto saxophonist Charlie Parker was the most important figure in be-bop, the musical form that revolutionized jazz in the mid-Forties. Also known as "Bird" or "Yardbird" (the stories vary about how the nicknames came to be), Parker's innovative conceptions of jazz harmony and rhythm along with an incredible command of his instrument made him the most venerated musician of his time and a legend even before his untimely death at the age of 35.

Born in the right time and the right place, Parker grew up listening to the great bands and soloists who made Kansas City, Missouri, their stomping ground in the early Thirties. Hearing tenor saxophonist Lester Young with Count Basie's band inspired the precocious Parker, who had begun playing saxophone at age 11. By 17, after intensive practice, Parker had honed his skills and found work with the Kansas City band of Buster Smith, an altoist who exerted a strong influence on Parker's playing.

In 1938 and 1939 Parker spent time in New York where he got to observe advanced musicians like pianist Art Tatum and further define his burgeoning style. In 1940 Parker returned to Kansas City and joined Jay McShann's big band, with whom he did his first recordings. Parker stayed with McShann for two years, but the lure of New York City, with its coterie of forward-thinking musicians', proved too strong.

Due to a musicians' union strike that lasted for the next few years, Parker's rapid growth went undocumented. In 1943 Parker played in pianist Earl Hines' band and then the offshoot band led by Hines' singer Billy Eckstine. Both of these bands were important proto-bop bands whose players were on the cusp of jazz's next wave. During this time Parker was also attending the monumental Harlem jam sessions led by pianist Thelonious Monk and drummer Kenny Clarke, where seeds of bop's development were also being sown.

The breakthrough came in 1945 when Parker, alongside trumpeter Dizzy Gillespie—the only other player in the same virtuosic league as Parker—made a series of recordings that defined the new music including "Shaw 'Nuff," "Salt Peanuts," and "Hot House." A session under Parker's leadership soon after produced "Now's the Time," "Billie's Bounce," and "Koko." Be-bop was a whole new ball game: The harmonies were more complex, the rhythms varied and unpredictable, the tempos ultra-fast. Seemingly overnight, jazz went from dance-oriented music to art music, designed for listening only.

Parker and Gillespie, whose band had been the rage in New York, headed for California in late 1945, for what turned out to be a disastrous sojourn. Be-bop was unpopular with the West Coast public; Parker and Gillespie quarreled, and Parker slid full force into a drug problem that had plagued him since his teens. By July 1946 Parker suffered a mental collapse and was institutionalized at the Camarillo State Hospital, in California, for seven months.

On his release, Parker was again at the top of his form, cutting more brilliant sides, including "A Night in Tunisia," "Relaxing at Camarillo," "Ornithology," and "Yardbird Suite," before heading back to New York City. There he put together a first-rate band with drummer Max Roach and trumpeter Miles Davis, whose recordings for Dial are among Parker's greatest work. By this time Parker was the most acclaimed and influential jazz musician alive. Over the next few years, though, Parker's exceptional music contrasted with the downward swing of his personal life. Heroin addiction and alcoholism destroyed whatever semblance of order Parker tried to impose on his life. In 1949 Parker made a triumphant tour of Europe; in New York, a popular nightclub, Birdland, was named in his honor.

Throughout the Fifties, Parker continued making exceptional music—with his own groups, on tour with Jazz at the Philharmonic, as a solo performer, and at occasional reunions with Dizzy Gillespie, who had gone on to become a star—but his behavior had become increasingly erratic. In 1954, following the death of Parker's daughter Chan, the bottom fell out of his life. After his excessive behavior mangled an all-star performance at Birdland in early 1955, he was banned from the club. Depressed and in ill health, Parker took refuge at the New York City apartment of jazz patron Baroness Nica de Konigswarter. While watching TV there, Parker died of a hemorrhage related to pneumonia.

Graham Parker

Born November 18, 1950, East London, England
1976—*Howlin' Wind* (Mercury); *Heat Treatment*
1977—*The Pink Parker* EP; *Stick to Me*   1978—*The Parkerilla*   1979—*Squeezing Out Sparks* (Arista)
1980—*The Up Escalator*   1982—*Another Grey Area*
1983—*The Real Macaw*   1985—*Steady Nerves* (Elektra)   1988—*The Mona Lisa's Sister* (RCA)
1989—*Human Soul; Live! Alone in America*   1991—*Struck by Lightning*   1992—*Burning Questions* (Capitol)   1993—*Passion Is No Ordinary Word: The Graham Parker Anthology (1976–1991)* (Rhino)
1994—*Graham Parker's Christmas Cracker* EP (Dakota Arts)   1995—*12 Haunted Episodes* (Razor & Tie).

One of the most critically acclaimed graduates of the mid-Seventies British pub-rock scene, singer/songwriter Graham Parker was compared to Bob Dylan, Bruce Springsteen, and Elvis Costello for the best of his angry, eloquent songs. Yet the commercial success he always seemed to deserve remained, for the most part, just outside his grasp.

Until 1975, Parker lived off a succession of odd jobs—including gas-station attendant and breeder of mice and guinea pigs for a scientific institute—and fronted a number of unsuccessful London bands. He had also spent time in a cover band playing Gibraltar and Morocco in the late Sixties.

In 1975 Dave Robinson of London's fledgling independent Stiff Records label heard and liked some Parker demos, and matched him with a backing band of pub-rock veterans, the Rumour, which included guitarist Brinsley Schwarz and keyboardist Bob Andrews from the band Brinsley Schwarz (which also included Nick Lowe, who produced Parker's first few LPs), guitarist Martin Belmont from Ducks Deluxe, bassist Andrew Bodnar, and drummer Steve Goulding from Bontemps Roulez. Their first two LPs won mammoth critical acclaim but sold barely respectably in the U.S.

Parker had many run-ins with his label, Mercury, accusing it of poor distribution and promotion, resulting in

the mediocre sales (*Heat Treatment* did best, selling some 60,000 copies and peaking at #169). The poorly produced *Stick to Me* (#125, 1977)—which had to be quickly rerecorded after original tapes were mangled—met with the same results, hurt by the emergence of punk rock and Elvis Costello (to whom Parker was constantly compared despite having prefigured him), and in 1978 Parker rushed out the live *Parkerilla* LP (#149, 1978), reportedly in order to escape the Mercury contract. Parker wrote the scathing "Mercury Poisoning" about the label's alleged incompetence (in one line he refers to himself as "the best kept secret in the West"); it was released as the B side of a promotional 45 by his new label, Arista, and did not turn up on an album until the 1993 *Anthology* set.

Arista signed Parker after an intense music-industry bidding war. His first Arista LP, *Squeezing Out Sparks* (#40, 1979), stands as probably his finest artistic/commercial achievement; it made the Top Forty and sold over 200,000 copies, with such tracks as "Local Girls" and "Passion Is No Ordinary Word" garnering heavy FM radio play. Parker's star continued to rise with a live cover of the Jackson 5's "I Want You Back" (never included on an album until *Anthology*) that was widely aired on new-wave radio. But Parker was unable to consolidate that incipient success. *The Up Escalator* (#40, 1980; produced by Jimmy Iovine) and *Grey Area* (#51, 1982; produced by Jack Douglas) met with mixed response and unexceptional sales; and by then the Rumour had released a couple of LPs on their own. Various studio musicians and others, including Nicky Hopkins and Hugh McCracken, backed up Parker. Bruce Springsteen cowrote and sang on "Endless Night" on *Escalator*. Various Rumour members, meanwhile, worked with Nick Lowe and Garland Jeffreys. While Parker continued releasing critically respected albums into the Nineties, his audience did not really grow. He had a minor hit single with "Wake Up (Next to You)" (#39, 1985), but after that, only 1985's *Steady Nerves* (#57) and 1988's *The Mona Lisa's Sister* (#77) made the Top 100. *Struck by Lightning* (#131, 1991) and *Burning Questions* revealed Parker to be an artist still worthy of attention. In the mid-Nineties Parker moved to independent Razor & Tie and released the album *12 Haunted Episodes*, which was announced as his "minor-label debut."

Junior Parker

Born Herman Parker, March 3, 1927, West Memphis, Arkansas; died November 18, 1971, Blue Island, Illinois
1960—*Driving* (Duke)   1961—*Blues Consolidated*
1964—*Junior Parker* (Bluesway)   1967—*Like It Is* (Mercury)   1970—*Outside Man* (Capitol)   1972—*Blue Shadows Falling* (Groove Merchant); *Good*

Junior Parker

Things Don't Happen Everyday 1973—*You Don't Have to Be Black . . .* (People); *The Best of Junior Parker* (MCA) 1974—*Love Ain't Nothing but Business* 1976—*Love My Baby* EP (Charly, U.K.) 1978—*Legendary Sun Performers* 1992—*Junior's Blues: The Duke Recordings, vol. 1* (Duke).

A highly respected blues vocalist and harmonica player, Junior Parker may be best known as the author of Elvis Presley's 1955 classic "Mystery Train." But Parker had a long, noteworthy career of his own, which included stints with blues performers like Sonny Boy Williamson, Howlin' Wolf, B. B. King, and Johnny Ace.

Parker's career began in 1948 at a Sonny Boy Williamson show, where Parker responded to Williamson's request for a harmonica player from the audience; Parker ended up playing with Williamson for the rest of his tour and leading the band when Williamson had solo commitments. In 1949 Parker played with Howlin' Wolf and, two years later, after Wolf had temporarily retired, took over that band, which also included pianist Ike Turner and guitarist M. T. Murphy. Parker then moved to Memphis and joined the Beale Streeters, which also included B. B. King, Bobby Bland, Johnny Ace, and Rosco Gordon. In 1952 Parker formed his own band, the Blue Flames, with which he made his first recordings for Modern. He then moved to Sun Records, for which he had a massive hit, "Feelin' Good," in 1953. His second Sun release, "Mystery Train," was a minor hit; Presley had much more success with it. In 1954 Parker began a four-year association with Houston's Duke Records.

In 1953, Parker had joined the Johnny Ace Revue,

which also included Big Mama Thornton. When Ace died (losing a game of Russian roulette) in 1954, Parker took over the Revue, renaming it Blues Consolidated, and toured with it through 1961. He also toured with Bobby Bland and Joe Hinton.

Among Parker's many R&B hits were "Next Time You See Me" (#7, 1957), "Driving Wheel" (#5, 1961), "In the Dark" (#7, 1961), and "Annie Get Your Yo-Yo" (#6, 1962). Some of his better-known earlier performances were "Mother-in-Law Blues" and "Barefoot Rock." On some of these early recordings, Parker's guitarist, Pat Hare, can be heard experimenting with unusually uptempo driving rhythms and distorted solos. As late as 1971 Parker was still having minor R&B hits, like "Ain't Gon' Be No Cutting Loose" and "Drowning on Dry Land," and had recorded for Blue Rock, Minit, and Capitol. His death came after surgery for a brain tumor.

Maceo Parker

Born February 14, 1943, Kinston, North Carolina
1990—*For All the King's Men* (4th and Broadway);
***Pee Wee, Fred & Maceo* (Gramavision); *Roots Revisited* (Verve) 1991—*Mo' Roots* 1993—*Life on Planet Groove* 1994—*Southern Exposure* (RCA/Novus).**

If just for his soulful work with James Brown, saxophonist Maceo Parker's place in R&B history is secure. Parker began his musical career playing tenor saxophone in local bands in his native North Carolina; early groups in-

Maceo Parker

cluded the Junior Blue Notes, which Parker formed in elementary school with his brothers, trombonist Kellis and drummer Melvin.

In 1962 James Brown heard Melvin at a club and offered him an open invitation to join his band. Two years later, when he approached Brown to take him up on his offer, Melvin brought along Maceo, and Brown hired them both. During his tenure with Brown, Parker—who played tenor and baritone saxophones—became one of the band's chief soloists. Brown's cry, "Maceo, blow your horn," would be the prelude for Parker's funky statements.

Parker left Brown's band in 1970 and worked in a series of groups, including Maceo and the Macks, Maceo and All the King's Men, and Fred Wesley and the JBs. When Parker rejoined Brown in 1973 he switched to alto saxophone. Although Parker freelanced throughout the next 20 years with George Clinton's P-Funk conglomerations and Bootsy's Rubber Band, his main gig was with Brown. When Brown was imprisoned in 1993, Parker struck out on his own to remarkable acclaim. His first two solo recordings on Verve reached #1 on the jazz chart. Parker found that he had achieved near-legendary stature: New bands, including Deee-Lite, 10,000 Maniacs, De La Soul, and Living Colour, used him on their recordings, and rappers continually sampled his work with Brown.

Ray Parker Jr.

Born May 1, 1954, Detroit, Michigan
1978—Raydio (Arista)   1979—Rock On   1980—Two Places at the Same Time   1981—A Woman Needs Love   1982—The Other Woman; Greatest Hits 1983—Woman Out of Control   1984—Chartbusters 1985—Sex and the Single Man   1987—After Dark (Geffen)   1991—I Love You Like You Are (MCA).

First as a session guitarist/writer and currently as a performer/producer, Ray Parker has been an integral part of the Los Angeles pop music scene since the early Seventies. The group Raydio made its debut in 1978 as a vehicle for Parker's singing and writing. Although he cheerfully borrowed arrangements from Sly and the Family Stone, Free, and others, his man-about-town persona has made him a dependable hitmaker.

Parker was playing a number of instruments in elementary school before he picked up a guitar at age 12. At 16 he had appeared on a few Motown sessions. From 1969 to 1971 he played sessions for Holland-Dozier-Holland's Invictus Records. In 1972 he played on Stevie Wonder's Talking Book and accompanied Wonder on his tour with the Rolling Stones. Before forming Raydio, Parker had been active in Los Angeles as a sideman and writer. He cowrote Rufus' "You Got the Love," Barry White's "You See the Trouble with Me," and Herbie Hancock's "Keep On Doing It."

The first single from the Raydio debut, "Jack and Jill," was a major hit, reaching #5 on the R&B chart and #8 pop in 1978. By 1979 the band was known as Ray Parker Jr. and Raydio. "You Can't Change That" (#9 pop, #3 R&B, 1979) was another massive hit, making Parker one of the rare black stars of the late Seventies to receive immediate pop acceptance with each new release.

"Two Places at the Same Time" (#30 pop, #6 R&B, 1980) and the instrumental "For Those Who Like to Groove" (#14 R&B) were substantial black hits. The title cut from A Woman Needs Love (#4 pop, #1 R&B, 1981) continued Parker's crossover success. That record was recorded at Parker's Ameraycan Studios in Los Angeles, which, due to Parker's own achievements, became a popular recording site. During this period Parker produced albums by the band Brick and by singer Cheryl Lynn. The latter resulted in a Top Ten soul single, "Shake It Up Tonight." The group of musicians who backed Parker as Raydio circa 1979 were keyboardist/vocalist Arnell Carmichael, guitarist Darren Carmichael, drummer Larry Tolbert, and guitarist Charles Fearing, all old buddies of Parker's from Detroit.

By 1982's gold The Other Woman, Parker was recording as a solo act while still enjoying pop and black acceptance. With "The Other Woman," Parker moved into pop rock. He claims the idea for the song came while listening to Rick Springfield's "Jessie's Girl." That album went to #11, and Parker continued to release popular R&B singles ("Let Me Go," #3 R&B, 1982; "Bad Boy," #6 R&B, 1982); his next Top Twenty pop entry was "I Still Can't Get Over Loving You" (#12 pop and R&B, 1983).

Unquestionably Parker's biggest chart break was the 1984 #1 hit "Ghostbusters," from the popular movie of the same name. Later Huey Lewis and the News sued Parker, charging that "Ghostbusters" was essentially a rewrite of their "I Want a New Drug." The case was settled privately. Although Parker continued to release pop hits through the Eighties (including "Jamie" (#14 pop, #12 R&B, 1984), "Girls Are More Fun" (#34 pop, #21 R&B, 1985), and "I Don't Think That Man Should Sleep Alone" (#5 R&B, 1987), he also wrote and produced for other artists, including Diana Ross, Randy Hall, and New Edition (he wrote "Mr. Telephone Man"). He played on Alphonse Mouzon's The Sky's the Limit.

His only album for Geffen, After Dark, contained "I Don't Think That Man Should Sleep Alone" and "Over You" (#10 R&B, 1987), a duet with Natalie Cole. Four years later, Parker switched to MCA, for which label he released I Love You Like You Are.

Van Dyke Parks

Born January 3, 1943, Hattiesburg, Mississippi
1968—Song Cycle (Warner Bros.)   1972—Discover

America 1975—*Clang of the Yankee Reaper* 1984—*Jump!* 1989—*Tokyo Rose.*

Even by Hollywood standards, Van Dyke Parks is an oddball. His specialty—in his over three decades in the music business as songwriter, lyricist, arranger, and producer—is dense aural and verbal montages, which are most easily sampled in his lyrics for the Beach Boys' "Heroes and Villains" or "Surf's Up."

He moved with his family to Hollywood at age 13 and became a child actor while studying classical piano and composition. In the early Sixties he reportedly signed with a major studio to write soundtracks. Instead he began writing his own songs, one of which, "High Coin," has become a folk-rock standard and was covered by Bobby Vee, Harper's Bizarre, and the Charlatans (San Francisco), among others. In the mid-Sixties he produced such hits as the Mojo Men's cover of Stephen Stills' "Sit Down I Think I Love You." He played piano on Harper's Bizarre's cover of Cole Porter's "Anything Goes."

In 1966 Parks began collaborating with Brian Wilson of the Beach Boys on the never-released *Smile* LP; some of the songs appeared on later Beach Boys albums. He also produced Judy Collins, Randy Newman, Ry Cooder, Phil Ochs, Arlo Guthrie, and others, becoming something of a local L.A. legend for his mysterious, meticulous methods. His first solo LP, an ambitious and eclectic project four years in the making, earned him the reputation of "the first art-rocker."

Parks was made director of audiovisual services for Warner Bros. in 1970, a post he quit a year later. He also played keyboards on sessions with Judy Collins and with the Byrds on "5D (5th Dimension)," and in the score for Robert Altman's *Popeye,* in which he briefly appeared onscreen. His two other Seventies solo LPs showcased his love of calypso music; both featured the Esso Trinidad Steel Band. He has also scored *Goin' South* and *The Two Jakes.* Neither *Jump!,* which was centered on the fictional character of Uncle Remus, nor *Tokyo Rose,* an examination of U.S.-Japanese relations, sparked much interest. Although his records never sold very well when originally issued, they were all rereleased on CD in 1990. Parks remains an enigmatic figure.

Parliament: See George Clinton

Alan Parsons

Born 1949
Alan Parsons Project, formed 1975, London, England: 1976—*Tales of Mystery and Imagination—Edgar Allan Poe* (20th Century) 1977—*I Robot* (Arista) 1978—*Pyramid* 1979—*Eve* 1980—*The Turn of a Friendly Card* 1982—*Eye in the Sky*

1983—*The Best of the Alan Parsons Project* 1984—*Ammonia Avenue* 1985—*Vulture Culture* 1986—*Stereotomy* 1987—*Gaudi.*

Alan Parsons is mainly a producer/engineer. He worked on the Beatles' *Abbey Road* and on Paul McCartney's *Wildlife* and *Red Rose Speedway,* and he produced Al Stewart's *Time Passages.* Parsons plays keyboards and sometimes sings with his Project, which is basically a loose collection of English session players interpreting Parsons' and lyricist/manager Eric Woolfson's arty, highly synthesized and orchestrated concepts.

Vocalists on his LPs have included Arthur Brown, Steve Harley of Cockney Rebel, Allan Clarke of the Hollies, and ex-Zombie Colin Blunstone. *I Robot, Card* (about gambling obsession), and *Eye* all went platinum, and along with Parsons' other LPs have yielded an array of hits: "Games People Play" (#16, 1980), "Time" (#15, 1981), "Eye in the Sky" (#3, 1982), and "Don't Answer Me" (#15, 1984). Following the gold *Ammonia Avenue,* the group's releases have been of more interest to diehard fans than casual listeners.

Gram Parsons

Born Ingram Cecil Connor III, November 5, 1946, Winter Haven, Florida; died September 19, 1973, Yucca Valley, California
1973—*GP* (Reprise) 1974—*Grievous Angel* 1976—*Sleepless Nights* (A&M) 1979—*Gram Parsons: The Early Years 1963–1965* (Sierra/Briar) 1982—*Gram Parsons and the Fallen Angels—Live 1973* (Sierra). With the International Submarine Band: 1968—*Safe at Home* (LHI).

Georgia-bred singer/songwriter Gram Parsons brought traditional country music to the rock & roll audience. With his wracked, emotive vocals and his compelling C&W songcraft, he was a major influence on a variety of artists ranging from Emmylou Harris to Keith Richards to Elvis Costello. Though he hated the term "country rock" and the kind of music the term came to define, Parsons undoubtedly pioneered the genre, via his groups the International Submarine Band and the Flying Burrito Brothers, one album with the Byrds, and his solo recordings. Though none of the bands he started or the albums he made was ever commercially successful, he has achieved near-mythic status since his 1973 death at age 26. In the Nineties his work continues to be embraced by a new generation of artists, many of them alternative rockers, who covered his songs on a 1993 tribute album.

Ingram Cecil Connor spent most of his childhood in Waycross, Georgia. The son of a Florida citrus heiress and a Tennessee-born WWII vet, he grew up in the lap of luxury. At age nine, he learned to play the piano, but his main musical inspiration was seeing Elvis Presley perform that year at his local auditorium. By age 12 he'd begun playing guitar when his life was shattered by the suicide of his father, Coon Dog Connor.

The family moved to his maternal grandparents' mansion in Winter Haven, Florida; the next year, his mother remarried Robert Parsons, who adopted him and legally changed his name to Gram Parsons. At age 14, Parsons began playing in a succession of local rock & roll bands, as well as folk groups. In 1964 his group the Shilohs made some recordings and performed throughout the Southeast. The next year, on the day Parsons graduated from high school, his mother died of alcohol poisoning. Parsons left Florida that fall for Harvard, where he spent more time playing music than studying. After one semester, he dropped out and moved from Cambridge to the Bronx with his new group, the International Submarine Band. In 1966, with a repertoire of traditional country and R&B-tinged songs, the band played a few shows in New York, then relocated to Los Angeles after recording an unsuccessful single for Columbia. There, the band got a cameo role in Roger Corman's *The Trip* and recorded the 1968 album *Safe at Home* for a small label owned by Lee Hazlewood. Before the LP came out, however, Parsons met Chris Hillman and through him joined the Byrds [see entry]. The Byrds' *Sweetheart of the Rodeo* included two Parsons songs, "Hickory Wind" (cowritten with Bob Buchanan of the Sub Band) and "One Hundred Years from Now." (Parsons also did lead vocals on several songs that were not released until 1991, on the Byrds box set.)

After just three months in the Byrds, Parsons quit in summer 1968, refusing to join their tour of South Africa, reportedly because of his opposition to apartheid. In late 1968 he and Hillman (who also left the Byrds) formed the Flying Burrito Brothers [see entry]. He played a strong role on the Burritos' first LP, but left the band in April 1970, just before *Burrito Deluxe* came out.

In 1970 Parsons, after recovering from injuries sustained in a motorcycle accident, recorded with producer Terry Melcher some tracks that were never released. He spent the next two years indulging in the rock & roll lifestyle, including a stint at his friend Keith Richards' French villa during the recording of the Stones' *Exile on Main Street*. Parsons did not record again until his 1973 solo debut *GP,* which featured Emmylou Harris [see entry] (who'd been discovered by Hillman) and backing by Rick Grech (ex–Blind Faith); a friend from his Cambridge days, Barry Tashian (of Barry and the Remains fame); and three members of Elvis Presley's touring band, Glen D. Hardin, James Burton, and Ronnie Tutt.

Following a brief tour with his band, the Fallen Angels, Parsons returned to the studio to record *Grievous Angel*. It had just been completed when Parsons, who'd been addicted to booze and heroin, overdosed on a mix of morphine and tequila while relaxing at a favorite

desert retreat, near the Joshua Tree National Monument. He was pronounced dead after being rushed to the Yucca Valley Hospital. A few days later his coffin, en route to New Orleans for burial, was stolen by his friend and road manager Phil Kaufman and taken back to Joshua Tree and set afire. It was later revealed that Parsons had expressed a wish for a Joshua Tree cremation in the event of his death.

Parsons' legacy lived on as Emmylou Harris toured with his old band and covered and popularized his material, as did many others, including Elvis Costello on his country LP, *Almost Blue.* Costello also wrote liner notes for a 1982 British compilation of Parsons' work. Bernie Leadon's song "My Man," from the Eagles' 1974 *On the Border,* was a tribute to Parsons, and a song Richie Furay wrote about him in 1969, "Crazy Eyes," was the title track of a 1973 Poco LP. In 1979 Sierra/Briar Records released an album of early Parsons material with the Shilohs; a live recording of a Fallen Angels gig was released by the label four years later. In 1993 Rhino issued *Conmemorativo: A Tribute to Gram Parsons,* with his songs covered by the Mekons, Uncle Tupelo, Bob Mould, Peter Buck (R.E.M.), Peter Holsapple and Susan Cowsill, Steve Wynn, and others.

Dolly Parton
Born January 19, 1946, Sevierville, Tennessee
1969—*Just the Two of Us* (with Porter Wagoner) (RCA)   1970—*The Best of Dolly Parton*   1971—*Joshua*   1973—*My Tennessee Mountain Home* (RCA)   1974—*Jolene; Love Is Like a Butterfly* 1975—*Bargain Store; The Best of Dolly Parton; Dolly* 1976—*All I Can Do*   1977—*New Harvest ... First Gathering; Here You Come Again*   1978—*In the Beginning* (Monument); *Heartbreaker* (RCA)   1979—*Great Balls of Fire*   1980—*9 to 5 and Odd Jobs* 1982—*Heartbreak Express; Greatest Hits*   1983—*Burlap and Satin*   1984—*The Great Pretender; Once upon a Christmas* (with Kenny Rogers)   1987—*Trio* (with Linda Ronstadt and Emmylou Harris) (Warner Bros.); *Rainbow* (Columbia)   1989—*White Limozeen*   1991—*Eagle When She Flies*   1992—*Straight Talk* (Hollywood)   1993—*Slow Dancing with the Moon; Honky Tonk Angels* (with Loretta Lynn and Tammy Wynette)   1994—*Heartsongs* (Columbia)   1995—*The Essential Dolly Parton* (RCA).

Dolly Parton's girlish soprano and songs about oldtime virtues made her a major country star in the early Seventies. Later in that decade she wooed the pop audience and became a household name, her playful, self-deprecating comments about her blonde sex-bomb image winning hearts as her finely crafted country-pop singles yielded a succession of over 20 C&W #1 hits. Parton wrote many of her own hits, either alone or in collaboration with Bill Owens. Among the songs she has written is "I Will Always Love You," a #1 country hit for Parton in 1974 and 1982, that sold over 4 million copies in 1992 for Whitney Houston.

Parton grew up poor on a farm in Tennessee's Smoky Mountain foothills, the fourth of 12 children born to a farming couple. Her sister Stella later became a singer as well, and five other siblings have worked as professional musicians. Parton sang in church as a girl, and at age ten appeared on the Cass Walker TV show in Knoxville with members of her grade school class. She became a regular on Walker's radio show, where she performed until age 18. Parton appeared at the Grand Ole Opry at age 12, and her first single, "Puppy Love," was released by the blues-oriented Louisiana label Goldband.

One day after graduating high school in 1964 she moved to Nashville and signed with Monument. Her first day in town she met Carl Dean, whom she married two years later. Early recordings, in a rock vein, were not successful. Her big break came with "Dumb Blonde," a minor hit that peaked at #24 on the country chart. In 1967 she joined singer Porter Wagoner's syndicated country-music show, and "Miss Dolly," as she was called, became very popular with viewers. She signed to RCA, and the duo had many country hits, including "Just Someone I Used to Know" (1969) and "Daddy Was an Old Time Preacher Man" (1970). While with Wagoner, she charted over a dozen solo country & western hits, including "Joshua" (#1, 1970) and "Coat of Many Colors" (#4, 1971).

In 1974 Parton left Wagoner completely, having released *Jolene*, the title track of which became her second #1 country hit and a minor pop crossover. Other singers began to take an interest in her work. Linda Ronstadt covered "I Will Always Love You" in 1975 on *Prisoner in Disguise;* Emmylou Harris sang "Coat of Many Colors" that same year, and Maria Muldaur covered "My Tennessee Mountain Home" on her first record. The covers encouraged Parton to bring her country to the pop market, which she did with *New Harvest*. The LP was more rock oriented and included a version of "Higher and Higher." She also broke away from the country circuit to play rock clubs.

Parton's first major pop single was "Here You Come Again," which went gold and hit #3 in early 1978. The LP of the same name went platinum. She also hit the pop Top Twenty that year with "Two Doors Down." Parton had successfully crossed over; "Baby, I'm Burnin'" (#25, 1979) even had some success in discos. Other #1 C&W hits of that time include "You're the Only One" (1979), "Startin' Over Again" (1980), and "Old Flames Can't Hold a Candle to You" (1980). By 1980 Parton was a regular headliner in Las Vegas, and that year she earned an Oscar nomination for her film debut in *9 to 5* (costarring Jane Fonda and Lily Tomlin). Parton's recording of the title theme was a #1 hit in pop and country. In 1982 she costarred in *The Best Little Whorehouse in Texas* with Burt Reynolds. Her other film credits include *Rhinestone* (with Sylvester Stallone, 1984), *Steel Magnolias* (with Julia Roberts and Shirley MacLaine, 1989), *Straight Talk* (with James Woods, 1992), the made-for-television *Wild Texas Wind* (with Gary Busey, 1992), and *The Beverly Hillbillies* (1993). In 1976 she hosted a syndicated music show, *Dolly*; her 1987 prime-time variety show of the same name on ABC did not fare as well and was canceled after one season.

Immediately before the release of *Rhinestone,* Parton began a difficult period plagued by health problems. Through the Eighties she continued to score C&W #1 hits with "But You Know I Love You" (1981), "I Will Always Love You" (1982), the Bee Gees–written and –produced duet with Kenny Rogers, "Islands in the Stream" (#1, 1983), "Tennessee Homesick Blues" (1984), "Real Love" (another duet with Rogers, 1985), "Think About Love" (1985), "Why'd You Come in Here Lookin' Like That" (1989), "Yellow Roses" (1989), and "Rockin' Years" (1991), a duet with Ricky Van Shelton.

Parton's most successful album was *Trio,* a collection of traditional country songs performed with Emmylou Harris and Linda Ronstadt. It won a Grammy for Best Country Performance by a Duo or Group with Vocal in 1987. In 1993 Parton teamed up with Loretta Lynn and Tammy Wynette for *Honky Tonk Angels,* featuring the songs of such early-country singers as Patsy Cline and Kitty Wells (who appears on the title track, a hit for her back in 1952).

In 1986 Parton opened Dollywood, a Smoky Mountain theme park. She has also established the Dolly Parton Wellness and Rehabilitation Center of Sevier County Medical Center and the Dollywood Foundation, which works to lower the high school dropout rate in her home county. In 1994 she released her autobiography, *Dolly: My Life and Unfinished Business.* She has received many awards, including four Grammys and four Country Music Association awards.

The Partridge Family
Formed 1970, Los Angeles, California
David Cassidy (b. Apr. 12, 1950, New York City, N.Y.), voc., gtr.; Shirley Jones (b. Mar. 31, 1934, Charleron, Penn.), voc.
1970—The Partridge Family Album   1971—Up to Date; The Partridge Family Sound Magazine 1972—The Partridge Family Shopping Bag; The Partridge Family at Home with Their Greatest Hits 1989—The Partridge Family Lunchbox/Greatest Hits (Arista).

The Partridge Family, featuring teen idol David Cassidy, was more a marketing idea than a band. Their music was plugged on *The Partridge Family* TV series, which was about a family as traveling pop band (based loosely on the Cowsills), though only two of the actors actually sang on the group's many hit singles. The two real voices were Cassidy (who also played some guitar) and his stepmother, Shirley Jones, a veteran lead in many musicals, including *The Music Man, Carousel,* and *Oklahoma!*

Rounding out the family on the TV show were Danny Bonaduce, Brian Foster, Suzanne Crough, and ex-model Susan Dey. The show premiered on ABC on September 25, 1970, and weeks later the group's first single, "I Think I Love You," rose to #1 and went on to sell four million copies. Their debut, *The Partridge Family Album* (#4, 1970), went gold, and within 12 months, the group had two more gold LPs (eventually a total of five), both in the Top Ten. Cassidy (who played Keith Partridge) sang lead, and by 1972 he'd begun to tour and record solo as well as with "the band." Under the Partridge Family name came three more 1971 hits: "Doesn't Somebody Want to Be Wanted" (#6), "I'll Meet You Halfway" (#9), and "I Woke Up in Love This Morning" (#13). They had three more Top Forty hits, two in 1972 and then, the next year, "Looking Through the Eyes of Love" (#39).

But the Partridge Family's popularity had waned by that time, and in 1974 the show ended. Cassidy went on to a solo career [see entry]. Dey continued acting; she appeared in several films, including *Echo Park* with Tom Hulce, and became a regular on the popular television series *L.A. Law*. Bonaduce has had a checkered career, marked by run-ins with the law over drugs, several stints as a disc jockey, and a number of publicity stunts, including boxing fellow ex–teen idol Donny Osmond.

Jaco Pastorius: See Weather Report

Charley Patton
Born April 1891, Bolton, Mississippi; died April 28, 1934, Indianola, Mississippi
1988—*Founder of the Delta Blues* (Yazoo)   1991— *King of the Delta Blues*.

Gruff-voiced Charley Patton was an early Delta blues singer of mythic status. In his day the most popular bluesman in Mississippi, Patton also recorded ballads and religious and ragtime songs. His acoustic guitar technique, his bottleneck slide playing (its rhythmic complexity influenced by West African drumming), his refusal to be confined to standard 12-bar blues patterns, and the emotional intensity of his songs made him a signal figure of the Delta blues, capable of both furthering the form and transcending it.

Remaining until his death at age 43 in the Missis-

sippi Delta (the northwest corner of the state), Patton began recording for Paramount in 1929; by that time he'd already been a popular live performer to both black and white audiences for at least 15 years. "Pony Blues," "Tom Rushen Blues," and "Moon Going Down" are representative of a vast repertoire that influenced Howlin' Wolf, Big Joe Williams, and Son House. House, however, was among a sizable camp that derided Patton for "clownish" behavior, a charge refuted musically, at least, by the social consciousness evident in "Down the Dirt Road Blues" and its attack on racism and by the fervor of his religious recordings. Clearly, Patton was an outsized figure, given to his own myth making, but the thematic breadth of his songs (from tales of lust and cocaine use to political observation and finely detailed reportage) qualified him as a poetic representative of a southern rural world as complex as the one he embodied. He died in 1934 from a chronic heart condition.

Billy Paul
Born Paul Williams, December 1, 1934, Philadelphia, Pennsylvania
1970—*Ebony Woman* (Philadelphia International) 1971—*Going East*   1972—*360 Degrees of Billy Paul* 1973—*Feelin' Good at the Cadillac Club*; *War of the Gods*   1974—*Live in Europe*   1975—*Got My Head on Straight*; *When Love Is New*   1976—*Let 'Em In* 1977—*Only the Strong Survive*   1979—*First Class* 1983—*Billy Paul's Greatest Hits*   1985—*Lately* (Total Experience)   1988—*Wide Open* (Ichiban).

The success of singer Billy Paul's #1 pop and R&B hit "Me and Mrs. Jones" in 1972 helped establish Kenny Gamble and Leon Huff's then-young Philadelphia International Records and brought Paul's jazzy, unpredictable singing to its widest audience.

Paul first appeared in public at age 11, when, encouraged by friend Bill Cosby, he sang on Philadelphia radio station WPEN. As a teen, Paul had extensive musical training (Temple University, West Philadelphia Music School, Granoff Music School) and had sung with the Flamingos and the Blue Notes. He recorded as a jazz singer for Jubilee Records.

One evening in the late Sixties Paul met Gamble at Philadelphia's Cadillac Club. Paul would record for Gamble's ill-fated Neptune Records before working with him again at Philadelphia International. "Mrs. Jones," written and produced by Gamble and Huff, is regarded as one of their classic records.

Though Paul's later releases never matched "Mrs. Jones," he had several soul hits through 1980, including "Am I Black Enough for You" (#29 R&B) in 1973, "Thanks for Saving My Life" (#9 R&B) in 1974, and "Let's Make a Baby" (#18 R&B) in 1976.

Les Paul

Born Lester Polfus, January 9, 1915, Waukesha, Wisconsin

1955—*Les and Mary* (with Mary Ford) (Capitol); *The New Sound*; *Bye Bye Blues*   1956—*The Hit Makers* 1959—*Lover's Luau* (Columbia)   1965—*The Fabulous Les Paul and Mary Ford* (with Mary Ford) 1968—*Guitar Artistry* (with the Les Paul Trio); *Les Paul Now* (London)   1976—*Chester and Lester* (with Chet Atkins) (RCA)   1978—*Guitar Monsters* (with Chet Atkins)   1986—*Feedback* (with the Les Paul Trio) (Circle)   1991—*Les Paul: The Legend and the Legacy* (Capitol); *Les Paul Trio* (LaserLight) 1992—*The Best of the Capitol Masters* (with Mary Ford).

Though he had a long and successful pop-jazz career, both with and without singer Mary Ford (born Colleen Summer, July 7, 1928, Pasadena, California; died September 30, 1977), guitarist Les Paul is of paramount importance to rock & roll as the creator of the solid-body electric guitar and as a pioneer in such modern recording techniques as electronic echo and studio multitracking.

Having learned harmonica, guitar, and banjo at age 13, Paul played with midwestern semipro country & western bands. He moved to Chicago in his late teens and became a regular on WLS. He then concentrated on performing for a few years before taking over the house band at WJJD in 1934, and later became something of a hillbilly star under the pseudonym Hot Rod Red and later Rhubarb Red. He formed the Les Paul Trio—which included Chet Atkins' brother Jimmy on rhythm guitar and vocals and Ernie Newton on bass—in 1936, and with them moved to New York in 1937. They became regulars on bandleader Fred Waring's NBC radio show and stayed with Waring's Pennsylvanians orchestra for five years.

Around this time, Paul began seriously thinking about revolutionizing the guitar. He had become interested in electronics at age 12, when he built a crystal radio set. He built his first guitar pickup from ham radio headphone parts in 1934, and by 1941 he had built the first prototypical solid-body electric guitar, a four-foot wooden board with strings, pickup, and a plug, which he called the "Log," and which he still uses to test against other guitars.

Meanwhile, in New York, Paul's musical aspirations moved toward jazz. He jammed informally with such greats as Art Tatum, Louis Armstrong, Ben Webster, and others, including electric (hollow-body) guitarist Charlie Christian. Paul left Waring in 1941, spent a year as music director for two Chicago radio stations, and moved to Los Angeles. In 1942 he was drafted and worked for the Armed Forces Radio Service, playing behind Bing

Crosby, Rudy Vallee, Johnny Mercer, Kate Smith, and others. Upon his discharge in 1943 he worked as a staff musician for NBC radio in L.A. He backed Bing Crosby with his trio and toured with the Andrews Sisters. With Crosby's encouragement, Paul built his first recording studio in his L.A. garage in 1945. There he began to pioneer such now-standard recording techniques as close microphone positioning ("close-miking"), echo delay, and multitracking. In 1948 he broke his right elbow in an auto accident and had it reset at a special angle so he could still play guitar.

In the late Forties he met and married singer Mary Ford, and they began recording together—unsuccessfully at first—for Decca and Columbia. After moving to Capitol, they had a long string of hits, including "Mockin' Bird Hill" (#3, 1951), "How High the Moon" (#1, 1951), "The World Is Waiting for the Sunrise" (#3, 1951), and "Vaya Con Dios" (#1, 1953). These recordings—among the earliest multitracked pop songs—featured Ford's voice answering Paul's "talking" guitar. Paul also had some instrumental hits on his own: "Nola" (#9, 1950), "Whispering" (#7, 1951), "Tiger Rag" (#6, 1952), and "Meet Mister Callaghan" (#5, 1952). Their hits stopped in 1961; two years later Paul and Ford were divorced. Ford died of diabetes in 1977.

By that time Paul's interests had shifted to experimenting and innovating. Since they were first marketed in May 1952, Les Paul Gibsons have been known for their "hot" pickups and sustain capacity, as compared to the twangier electric guitars of Leo Fender. Paul built one model, the Les Paul Recording Guitar, in the early Fifties and used it on his own recordings, not allowing Gibson to market it until 1971.

In the early Fifties Paul built the first eight-track tape recorder, which helped pioneer multitrack recording, and he invented "sound-on-sound" recording, which has since become known as overdubbing. His other inventions include the floating bridge pickup, the electrodynamic pickup (both patented), the guitar with dual pickups, the 14-fret guitar, and various types of electronic transducers used in both guitars and recording studios.

In 1974 Paul returned to music making, and in 1977 he had a hit LP with *Chester and Lester*, with country guitarist Chet Atkins, which won a Grammy. A 1980 documentary, *The Wizard of Waukesha*, opened and closed with scenes of Les Paul in the late Seventies, still playing guitar, demonstrating his latest invention: a little box called the "Les Paulverizer," an invention that could record, play back, and allow the musician to talk to anyone onstage, and which made his guitar sound like something that had inhaled laughing gas.

Paul has remained active, recording with Al DiMeola (on the latter's *Splendido Hotel*) and Manhattan Transfer's Janis Siegel (with whom he recorded her version of

"How High the Moon" for her solo LP *Experiments in Light*). In 1988 Paul was inducted into the Rock and Roll Hall of Fame. As of the mid-Nineties, he continues to appear once a week at Fat Tuesday's in New York City, a date he's kept now for over a decade.

Paul and Paula

Paul (b. Ray Hildebrand, December 21, 1940, Joshua, Texas); Paula (b. Jill Jackson, May 20, 1942, Mc-Caney, Texas).

Personifying the clean-cut optimism of early-Sixties Kennedy-era America, Paul and Paula had a smash hit with a song about puppy love and marriage, "Hey Paula" (#1, 1963), for Philips Records.

The pair of college grads had originally gotten together to sing for a radio station's charity drive in Texas. With their matching Pembroidered sweaters, they became a popular attraction. "Hey Paula," a Ray Hildebrand ("Paul") composition, launched several other songs about romantic bliss—"Young Lovers" (#6, 1963), "First Quarrel" (#27, 1963), "Something Old, Something New" (#77, 1963), and "First Day Back at School" (#60, 1963)—but the duo quickly faded from view. Paul and Paula reunited in 1982 for a country single, "Any Way You Want Me," for Texas-based Lelam Records. The tune met with little public response.

Pavement

Formed 1989, Stockton, California
Stephen Malkmus (b. Santa Monica, Calif.), gtr., voc.; Scott Kannberg (b. Stockton), gtr., voc.; Gary Young, drums.
1991—(+ Mark Ibold [b. Cincinnati, Ohio], bass; + Bob Nastanovich [b. Rochester, N.Y.], perc., voc.)
1992—Slanted and Enchanted (Matador); Watery, Domestic EP   1993—Westing (by Musket and Sextant) (Drag City) (– Young; + Stephen West [b. Richmond, Va.], drums)   1994—Crooked Rain, Crooked Rain (Matador)   1995—Wowee Zowee!

Mixing cacophony and elegant pop, Pavement is one of the more popular of the new breed of "low-fi" bands of the Nineties. Following a DIY philosophy, the band self-financed several low-budget recordings, which displayed its altered guitar tunings, sci-fi sound effects, and distorted vocals, as well as its rudimentary pop hooks and choruses. The band's lack of an image and laidback attitude have earned them the "slacker" label.

Pavement began in 1989 when primary songwriter Stephen Malkmus and longtime friend Scott "Spiral Stairs" Kannberg distributed their own single, "Slay Tracks: (1933–1969)." The seven-inch cost them $800 and received favorable notice in the alternative press. Augmented by fellow Stocktonite Gary Young, who owned the studio where they recorded, they continued to release singles on the small Drag City label.

With the addition of Bob Nastanovich and Mark Ibold in 1991, Pavement recorded *Slanted and Enchanted,* which sold over 100,000 copies. The tuneful, oblique album appeared on many critics' year-end top ten lists. The band's early, sloppy live performances often found Young on top of the drum kit rather than behind it. In 1993 he was replaced by Stephen West.

While remaining on the independent label Matador, Pavement released the more listener-friendly *Crooked Rain, Crooked Rain* (#121, 1994). It yielded a catchy single, "Cut Your Hair," which garnered airplay on modern-rock radio.

Tom Paxton

Born October 31, 1937, Chicago, Illinois
1962—I'm the Man Who Built the Bridges (Gaslight)   1964—Ramblin' Boy (Elektra)   1965—Ain't That News   1966—Outward Bound   1967—Morning Again   1969—The Things I Notice Now   1969—Tom Paxton 6   1970—The Compleat Tom Paxton   1971—How Come the Sun (Reprise)   1972—Peace Will Come   1973—New Songs for Old Friends   1975—Something in My Life (Private Stock)   1977—New Songs from the Briar Patch (Vanguard)   1978—Heroes   1979—Up & Up (Mountain Railroad/Flying Fish)   1980—The Paxton Report   1983—Bulletin (Hogeye)   1984—Even a Gray Day (Flying Fish); The Marvellous Toy & Other Gallimaufry (Cherry Lane/Alcazar)   1986—One Million Lawyers and Other Disasters (Flying Fish); A Paxton Primer (Pax); A Folk Song Festival   1987—And Loving You (Flying Fish); Balloon-alloon-alloon (Pax)   1988—Politics (Flying Fish); A Child's Christmas (Pax)   1989—The Very Best of Tom Paxton (Flying Fish)   1990—A Car Full of Songs (Pax)   1991—Peanut Butter Pie; It Ain't Easy (Flying Fish)   1992—Suzy Is a Rocker (Sony Kids' Music).

Singer/songwriter Tom Paxton first came to prominence with his topical songs during the early-Sixties Greenwich Village folk revival along with performers like Bob Dylan, Phil Ochs, and Joan Baez. Through a career that now spans over 30 years, he has continued to release albums annually and tours the world.

Paxton was raised in Oklahoma (his parents moved there when he was ten) and studied drama at the University of Oklahoma. He began writing songs, and after graduating in 1959 with a BFA he joined the army. He later moved to New York City, where he played the folk circuit. The Gaslight Club issued his first (now out-of-print) album, but his first national major release was not until early 1964's *Ramblin' Boy*.

Paxton's albums mixed increasingly topical political

songs (like "What Did You Learn in School Today," "Talking Vietnam Pot Luck Blues," and the later "Talking Watergate") with occasional love songs (like "The Last Thing on My Mind") and children's songs. He recorded seven albums for Elektra and then switched to Reprise in 1971, when he moved to England and recorded three LPs, including *New Songs* with Ralph McTell.

Paxton's compositions are more popularly known in versions performed by others. Peter, Paul and Mary covered "Going to the Zoo" and were among the many who covered "The Last Thing on My Mind"; John Denver did "Forest Lawn" and "Whose Garden Was This?"; other songs have been covered by Judy Collins, the Kingston Trio, and the Weavers. He continues to command a loyal following, and has expanded into writing music and books for children. He has written eight children's books, published by Morrow Junior Books, and released the acclaimed children's albums *The Marvellous Toy & Other Gallimaufry, Balloon-alloon-alloon, A Child's Christmas, A Car Full of Songs, Peanut Butter Pie*, and *Suzy Is a Rocker*, most on his own Pax label. He has served as honorary chairman of the board of the World Folk Music Association and hosted the BBC Radio series *Tom Paxton's America*.

Freda Payne
Born September 19, 1945, Detroit, Michigan
1972—*The Best of Freda Payne* (Invictus)   1991—*Greatest Hits* (HDH).

Soul singer Freda Payne's greatest recording success came at Invictus Records in the early Seventies under the guidance of its owners/producers Lamont Dozier and Eddie and Brian Holland.

Payne's parents envisioned a career in the performing arts for both Freda and her sister Scherrie (who later joined a latterday version of the Supremes). Both studied voice and piano as children at the Detroit Institute of Musical Arts. Both later studied ballet. At 18 Payne moved to New York City. Her best gig in the next two years was a stint in the chorus of a Pearl Bailey show. In 1965 she was the understudy for Leslie Uggams in the Broadway musical *Hallelujah, Baby!* There she met Quincy Jones, with whom she toured. For the rest of the Sixties, she worked as a jazz singer, performing with the top big bands, including Duke Ellington's.

After Eddie Holland left Motown, he persuaded Payne to join his new label and sing pop music. In 1970 and 1971 the Holland–Dozier–Holland production team furnished Payne with some neo–Motown music, including two gold singles, "Band of Gold" (#3 pop, #20 R&B, 1970) and "Bring the Boys Home" (#12 pop, #3 R&B, 1971). The latter was one of the era's rare black anti–Vietnam songs. Other popular Payne records of the period were "Deeper and Deeper" (#24 pop, #9 R&B, 1970), "Cherish What Is Dear to You (While It's Near to You)" (#99 pop, #11 R&B, 1971), and "You Brought the Joy" (#52 pop, #21 R&B, 1971).

Subsequently she recorded for ABC and Capitol Records. In the early Eighties Payne hosted the syndicated television talk show *For You Black Woman*, and she continues to perform as a singer.

Peaches and Herb
Formed 1965
Herb Fame (b. Herbert Feemster, 1942, Washington, D.C.); Peaches: Francine Barker (b. Francine Hurd, 1947, Washington, D.C.), 1965–68 and 1969–71; Marlene Mack (b. 1945, Va.), 1968–69; Linda Green (b. Washington, D.C.), 1977 on.
1967—*Let's Fall in Love* (Date)   1968—*Greatest Hits*   1978—*2 Hot!* (Polydor)   1979—*Twice the Fire*   1980—*Worth the Wait*   1981—*Sayin' Something!*   1983—*Remember* (Columbia).

The Peaches and Herb story is a tale of three women, two careers, and one Herb. The original team of Francine Barker and Herb Fame formed in 1965 at the urging of producer Van McCoy. At the time, Barker was lead singer of a female vocal group, the Sweet Things, and Fame was a solo act on Date Records. The Sweet Things and Fame met while on tour together. McCoy suggested they form the duo, which he then produced.

The B side of their first single, "Let's Fall in Love" (#21 pop, #11 R&B), began a series of hits from 1967 to 1969 on Date: "Close Your Eyes" (#8 pop, #4 R&B), "For Your Love" (#20 pop, #10 R&B), and "Love Is Strange" (#13 pop, #16 R&B) in 1967; "United" (#46 pop, #11 R&B) in 1968; and "When He Touches Me" (#49 pop, #10 R&B) in 1969.

Marlene Mack filled in for Barker for one year, but by the time Barker returned, the duo's hits had stopped. After signing with Columbia in 1970, they suffered another dry spell and eventually quit the record business. During the Seventies, Fame was a D.C. police officer. For a time in the mid-Seventies he and Barker released singles on their own BS label in Washington. But in 1977 Fame found a new Peaches, Linda Green, and returned full-time to music. After a brief tenure with MCA Records, they signed to Polydor, where their "Shake Your Groove Thing" (#5 pop, #4 R&B, 1978) and the ballad "Reunited" (#1 pop, #1 R&B, 1979)—both from the platinum *2 Hot!* (#2 pop, #1 R&B)—were Herb's biggest hits yet. Through the early Eighties the duo released over a half dozen more charting singles, including "We've Got Love" (#44 pop, #25 R&B, 1979), "I Pledge My Love" (#19 pop, #37 R&B, 1979), and "Remember" (#35 R&B, 1983).

Pearl Harbour and the Explosions

Formed 1978, San Francisco, California
Pearl E. Gates (b. 1958, Ger.), voc.; John Stench,
drums; Hilary Stench, bass; Peter Bilt, gtr.
1979—*Pearl Harbour and the Explosions* (Warner
Bros.).
Pearl Harbour solo: 1980—*Don't Follow Me, I'm Lost
Too* (Warner Bros.).

Pearl Harbour and the Explosions were one of San Francisco's first nationally recognized new-wave bands.
Their focus was lead singer Pearl E. Gates (of American-
Filipino heritage), who started her musical career as a
dancer with the Tubes in 1976. She left the next year
with another dancer from the band, Jane Dornacker, and
formed the cabaret musical group Leila and the Snakes,
which also included John and Hilary Stench. The
Stenches and Gates then formed the Explosions with
Bilt (who was in a local cover band).

Their first single, 1979's "Drivin'," became an underground hit, and with almost no promotion sold 10,000
copies, which prompted Warner Bros. to sign them. The
band's self-titled album didn't sell, and it split in 1980.
The two Stenches went on to become part of Jorma
Kaukonen's Vital Parts, but first Hilary played awhile
with Eddie Money, and John and Bilt did a stint with the
Soul Rebels. Meanwhile, Pearl took the last name Harbour, went to London, and hooked up with Otis Watkins
(keyboardist for Shakin' Stevens) and Nigel Dixon (of the
English rockabilly band Whirlwind) and formed a group.
With their backing, Micky Gallagher (keyboardist for Ian
Dury's Blockheads) produced her debut Warners solo LP,
the rockabilly-style *Don't Follow Me, I'm Lost Too*. In
mid-1983 it was revealed that Pearl and the Clash's Paul
Simonon were married. Peter Bilt joined Romeo Void in
the early Nineties.

Pearl Jam

Formed 1990, Seattle, Washington
Jeff Ament (b. Mar. 10, Big Sandy, Mont.), bass;
Stone Gossard (b. July 20, Seattle), gtr.; Dave
Krusen, drums; Mike McCready (b. Apr. 5, Seattle),
gtr.; Eddie Vedder (b. Dec. 23, ca. 1966, Chicago,
Ill.), voc.
1991—*Ten* (Epic) (– Krusen; + Dave Abbruzzese
[b. May 17], drums)   1993—*Vs.*   1994—*Vitalogy*
(– Abbruzzese; + Jack Irons, drums).
Mother Love Bone (Ament; Gossard; + Bruce Fair-
weather, gtr.; + Andrew Wood [d. Mar. 19, 1990,
Seattle], voc.; + Greg Gilmore, drums): 1990—*Apple*
(Polydor).
Temple of the Dog (Ament; Gossard; McCready;
+ Matt Cameron [b. Nov. 28, 1962, San Diego, Calif.],
drums; + Chris Cornell [b. July 20, 1964, Seattle],
voc.): 1991—*Temple of the Dog* (A&M).

Along with Nirvana, Pearl Jam is responsible for popularizing the Seattle sound and style that came to be
known as "grunge." With their solid, guitar-heavy, Led
Zeppelin–influenced songs and the charismatic Eddie
Vedder's impassioned vocals, they leaped from obscurity
to superstardom, selling over ten million copies of their
first two albums.

Pearl Jam's roots in the Seattle scene go deep: In the
mid-Eighties Jeff Ament and Stone Gossard were members of the seminal Seattle band Green River, which split
in 1987. Half the band formed Mudhoney [see entry],
while Gossard and Ament joined singer Andrew Wood in
Mother Love Bone. One of the earliest Seattle bands to
sign with a major label, Mother Love Bone seemed on
the verge of breaking big when Wood died of a heroin
overdose in 1990. Mercury Records wanted Gossard and
Ament (with Bruce Fairweather on guitar and drummer
Greg Gilmore) to record with a new singer, but the band
declined. (Gossard, Ament, McCready, and Vedder, along
with Soundgarden's Chris Cornell and Matt Cameron,
recorded *Temple of the Dog*, #5, 1992, a memorial to
Wood, in 1990.)

Gossard and Ament, along with Seattle veteran Mike
McCready, started work on a demo tape in late 1990.
They asked former Red Hot Chili Peppers drummer Jack
Irons to join, giving him a copy of the tape. Irons was involved with his own band but passed the demo on to a
singer he knew in San Diego, Eddie Vedder. (Irons later
replaced Dave Abbruzzese in 1994.) Vedder immediately
wrote lyrics to the songs and mailed back a tape that included his vocals; he was invited up to Seattle.

With the addition of drummer Dave Krusen, the new
band was complete. They called themselves Mookie
Blaylock for the New Jersey Nets basketball player, but
changed the name to Pearl Jam, after a psychedelic con-
fection made by Vedder's half–Native American great-
grandmother, Pearl (one of several purported reasons).
(The band did not forget Blaylock: Their debut album,
Ten [#2, 1992], was named for his uniform number.) With
their Mother Love Bone connections and a growing interest in the Seattle scene, Pearl Jam was signed by Epic
Records in early 1991. Krusen left the band after the sessions for *Ten*. He was replaced by Matt Chamberlain on
tour, with Abbruzzese filling the drum chair in the fall of
1991.

The band toured extensively, headlining small halls
and opening for the Red Hot Chili Peppers, Neil Young,
and U2. They headlined the 1992 Lollapalooza Tour and
opened for Keith Richards on New Year's Eve 1992.
Vedder, Gossard, and Ament took time out to play Matt
Dillon's backing band, Citizen Dick, in the 1992 Seattle-
based movie *Singles*.

Although Pearl Jam was originally marketed as an
"alternative" band, their connection to classic rock of the
Sixties and Seventies soon became apparent. Vedder

filled in for Jim Morrison at the Doors reunion for the 1993 Rock and Roll Hall of Fame Induction Ceremonies; he also took part in concerts honoring Bob Dylan and Pete Townshend. The band backed Neil Young on "Rockin' in the Free World" at the 1993 MTV Music Video Awards.

It was also apparent that Vedder was having trouble coping with the demands of stardom: He would show up for photo sessions wearing a mask and was surly and uncommunicative in interviews. There were reports he performed drunk, and in 1993 he was arrested in New Orleans for public drunkenness and disturbing the peace after a barroom brawl. None of this detracted from the band's popularity—*Vs.* (#1, 1993), their second album, sold a record-setting 1.3 million copies in its first 13 days of release.

Pearl Jam then canceled a 1994 summer tour when, in a public dispute over service charges against Ticketmaster, it couldn't keep admission prices as low as it wanted; band members also testified against Ticketmaster before Congress. The band did not make any videos to promote *Vs.* Instead it went back into the studio and recorded its third album, *Vitalogy.* The vinyl version was released two weeks before the CD and cassette, debuting on the charts at #55—the first album to appear on *Billboard*'s album chart solely because of vinyl sales since the proliferation of the CD. Once the CD arrived in stores the album hit #1. In 1995 Pearl Jam backed Neil Young on his album *Mirror Ball.*

Ann Peebles

Born April 27, 1947, East St. Louis, Missouri
1971—*Part Time Love* (Hi)   1972—*Straight from the Heart*   1974—*I Can't Stand the Rain*   1976—*Tellin' It*   1978—*If This Is Heaven*   1992—*Full Time Love* (Bullseye Blues).

Soul singer Ann Peebles is best known for her 1973 hit "I Can't Stand the Rain," but her grainy Memphis soul singing has influenced Bonnie Raitt, among others. Peebles began performing at age eight when she joined the Peebles Choir, a gospel group founded by her great-grandfather. After graduating from high school, she started working St. Louis nightclubs. In 1969 producer Willie Mitchell signed her to his Memphis-based Hi Records, where she worked with the same session band Al Green used. Her first single, "Walk Away," hit #22, and later hits like "Part Time Love" (#7 R&B), "I Pity the Fool" (#18 R&B), and "Breaking Up Somebody's Home" (#13 R&B) sold well, particularly in the South.

"I Can't Stand the Rain" (#38 pop, #6 R&B) was written by Peebles and her husband, Don Bryant. At the time of its release John Lennon said of it, " 'Rain' is the greatest record I've heard in two years." The song has been covered by numerous performers, from rock bands to disco divas. It was later included in the film *The Commitments* (1991). Peebles continued recording through the late Seventies, after which she and her husband basically left the music business to raise their family and run a home preschool program for children. She and her husband also remained active on the Memphis gospel scene. In 1992 she returned to recording with her first record in a decade and a half, *Full Time Love.*

Teddy Pendergrass

Born March 26, 1950, Philadelphia, Pennsylvania
1977—*Teddy Pendergrass* (Philadelphia International)   1978—*Life Is a Song Worth Singing*   1979—*Teddy; Teddy Live! Coast to Coast*   1980—*TP*   1981—*It's Time for Love*   1982—*This One's for You*   1983—*Heaven Only Knows*   1984—*Greatest Hits; Love Language* (Asylum)   1985—*Workin' It Back*   1988—*Joy* (Elektra)   1990—*Truly Blessed*   1993—*A Little More Magic.*

Singer Teddy Pendergrass emerged as a major star and sex symbol after leaving Harold Melvin and the Blue Notes [see entry] in 1976, releasing four platinum albums in the late Seventies and early Eighties.

As a youngster Pendergrass was ordained a minister; he was introduced to secular music by his mother, who worked at Skioles, a big Philadelphia nightclub popular in the early Sixties. Using the club's equipment, Pendergrass taught himself to play several instruments, and by 13 he was a capable drummer. He sang with a local group in his teens, but was disillusioned when a man claiming to be James Brown's brother recorded him in a New Jersey studio, then disappeared.

At age 19 Pendergrass became the drummer for a Philadelphia band called the Cadillacs, and a year later

Teddy Pendergrass

he became the Blue Notes' drummer. During a tour of the West Indies, Blue Notes lead singer John Atkins left the group, and Pendergrass replaced him. Though in existence since 1956, the Blue Notes had their first substantial commercial success only after Pendergrass became their frontman in 1970; his shouting vocals and songs by Kenny Gamble and Leon Huff made the Blue Notes a chart staple in the mid-Seventies.

In 1976 Pendergrass quit the Blue Notes. With the release of his solo debut, he was marketed as a sex symbol and became known to his fans as Teddy Bear. "I Don't Love You Anymore" (#41 pop, #5 R&B, 1977) was the single from that platinum album. His next LP, *Life Is a Song Worth Singing,* was highlighted by the seductive "Close the Door" (#25 pop, #1 R&B, 1978), and the next summer the steamy tale continued with "Turn Off the Lights" (#48 pop, #2 R&B).

Backed by his Teddy Bear Orchestra, Pendergrass concerts were marked by intense female fan reaction. "For Women Only" concerts were instituted, with ladies given stuffed teddy bears to fondle during the show. Pendergrass' *TP* album contained another love song, "Love TKO" (#44 pop, #2 R&B, 1980), and a duet with Stephanie Mills on "Feel the Fire." They also collaborated on the single "Two Hearts" (#40 pop, #2 R&B, 1980). In 1982 "You're My Latest, My Greatest Inspiration" (#4 R&B) made the chart. Pendergrass made his film debut in *Soup for One.* He also sang one song, "Dream Girl," on the Chic-produced soundtrack.

On March 18, 1982, Pendergrass' spinal cord was severely injured when his car smashed into a highway divider outside Philadelphia. He was paralyzed from the waist down and left with only limited use of his arms. After months of physical therapy, he returned to the recording studio, and in 1984 released *Love Language,* which included his comeback hit "Hold Me" (#5 R&B, 1984), featuring vocals by Whitney Houston. Pendergrass' subsequent singles included the hits "You're My Choice (Choose Me)" (#15 R&B, 1984), "Never Felt Like Dancin'" (#21 R&B, 1985), "Love 4/2" (#6 R&B, 1986), and "Joy" (#1 R&B, 1988). He made his first live appearance after the accident at Live Aid, in 1985.

The Penguins
Formed 1954, Los Angeles, California
Cleveland Duncan (b. July 23, 1935, Los Angeles), lead voc.; Curtis Williams (b. 1935), tenor voc.; Dexter Tisby (b. 1936), voc.; Bruce Tate (b. 1935), tenor voc.
1955—(– Tate; + Randolph Jones, baritone voc.)
1957—*The Cool, Cool Penguins* (Dootone) N.A.—*Golden Classics* (Collectables) 1993—*The Authentic Golden Hits of the Penguins* (Juke Box Treasures).

After attracting a strong local following in the early Fifties, the Penguins scored a big hit with a song written either by Curtis Williams and Jesse Belvin or by Belvin alone (sources vary), "Earth Angel." The song was #8 pop, #1 R&B in 1954, and has since sold an estimated ten million copies. Unfortunately, the Crew-Cuts covered that song a year later and made it a bigger pop hit (something they'd earlier done with the Chords' "Sh-Boom").

The Penguins switched from Dootone to Mercury (they were part of a package signing engineered by manager Buck Ram that included the Platters) to Atlantic Records, never achieving followup success commensurate with their one and only hit. After making one release for Atlantic and one for Sun State Records, they returned to California nearly broke and split up. Lead singer Cleveland Duncan re-formed the band several times. In 1963 they recorded a song written for them by Frank Zappa and Ray Collins (later of the Mothers of Invention), "Memories of El Monte." When it failed to hit, Tisby and some latterday members joined the Coasters. For some 30 years the Penguins, led by sole surviving original member Duncan, have made steady appearances at Fifties revival concerts.

Michael Penn
Born August 1, 1958, New York City, New York
1989—*March* (RCA) 1992—*Free for All.*

The older brother of volatile "Brat Pack" actor Sean Penn, Michael Penn gained some fame and success in his own right with his Beatlesesque debut album *March,* which earned him the Best New Artist MTV Video Music Award (1990) and spawned a hit single in "No Myth" (#13, 1990).

Penn, who is the son of actor/director Leo Penn and actress Eileen Ryan, was born in New York's Greenwich Village and moved with his family to Los Angeles a year later. He grew up listening to the Beatles, and by junior high he had learned guitar and played in a band covering hits by David Bowie, Cream, and the Rolling Stones.

At Santa Monica High School Penn began writing what he would later call "earnest, downbeat" songs. In the early Eighties he formed a band called Doll Congress, which, despite having enough of a local following to open once for R.E.M., did not work often enough to support Penn, whose odd jobs included appearing as an extra on TV's *St. Elsewhere.* A year after he left the group, Penn performed on a 1987 episode of *Saturday Night Live* his brother Sean hosted. Penn later said the experience made him very nervous, but subsequently he hooked up with Doll Congress keyboardist Patrick Warren and began work on the songs that would make up *March.*

March garnered critical raves for its thoughtful folk pop, and, sparked by the success of the "No Myth" single and video, it sold well, too (#31, 1989). One of the most intriguing things about the album was Warren's extensive and resourceful use of the Chamberlin, an antiquated keyboard quite similar to the proto-sampling Mellotron in that each key activates a tape recording of a note played by an actual instrument (violin, flute, oboe, etc.). The album yielded another, lesser hit single in "This & That" (#53, 1990). Penn's followup album, *Free for All,* while similar in sound to *March,* reached only as high as #160 in just two weeks on the chart.

Pentangle/Bert Jansch/John Renbourn

Formed 1967, England

Bert Jansch (b. Nov. 3, 1943, Glasgow, Scot.), gtr., voc.; John Renbourn (b. Aug. 8, 1944, London, Eng.), gtr.; Jacqui McShee (b. Dec. 25, 1943, London), voc.; Danny Thompson (b. Apr. 1939, Devon, Eng.), bass; Terry Cox (b. Buckinghamshire, Eng.), drums, perc.
1968—*The Pentangle* (Reprise) 1969—*Sweet Child* 1970—*Basket of Light* 1971—*Cruel Sister*; *Reflection* 1972—*Solomon's Seal* 1973—*Pentangling* (group disbands) 1975—*Collection* 1978—*Anthology* 1983—(Group re-forms) 1985—*Open the Door* (Varrick) (– Renbourn; + Mike Piggott, gtr.; + Nigel Portman-Smith [b. Feb. 7, 1950, Sheffield, Eng.], bass) 1986—*In the Round* 1989—*A Maid That's Deep in Love* (Shanachie) 1990—(Lineup: Jansch; McShee; + Gerry Conway [b. Sep. 11, 1947, Norfolk, Eng.], drums; + Peter Kirtley [b. Sep. 26, 1945, Hebburn-on-Tyne, Eng.], gtr.) *So Early in the Spring* (Green Linnet); *Think of Tomorrow* 1992— *Early Classics* (Shanachie).
Bert Jansch solo: 1968—*Birthday Blues* (Reprise) 1969—*Stepping Stones* (Vanguard) 1970—*Jack Orion* 1971—*Rosemary Lane* (Reprise) 1973— *Moonshine* 1977—*A Rare Conundrum* (Kicking Mule) 1980—*13 Down* 1981—*Heartbreak* (Hannibal) 1990—*Sketches* (Temple) 1991—*The Ornament Tree* (Gold Castle) 1992—*The Best of Bert Jansch* (Shanachie).
John Renbourn solo: 1969—*Sir John—A Lot of Merre Englandes Musik Thynge and Ye Grene Knyghte* (Reprise) 1970—*The Lady and the Unicorn* 1972—*John Renbourn* 1972—*Faro Annie* 1976— *The Hermit* (Transatlantic, U.K.) 1979—*Black Balloon* (Kicking Mule) 1986—*The Nine Maidens* (Flying Fish) 1988—*Ship of Fools.*
John Renbourn Group: 1977—*Maid in Bedlam* (Shanachie) 1990—*The Enchanted Garden* 1991—*Live in America* (Flying Fish) 1993—*Wheel of Fortune* (with Robin Williamson).
John Renbourn with Stefan Grossman: See Stefan Grossman entry.

With the virtuoso acoustic guitarists Bert Jansch and John Renbourn, folksinger Jacqui McShee, and the jazz-based rhythm section of Danny Thompson and Terry Cox (ex–Alexis Korner Blues Band), Pentangle achieved solid cult status with a unique repertoire that included traditional English folk songs, jazz, blues, and occasional originals, all intricately arranged. It rarely used amplification until it used muted electric guitars on *Cruel Sister.* Pentangle's debut LP did fairly well on the U.K. chart; the rest achieved modest U.S. and U.K. success.

Upon their breakup in 1973, Thompson worked with Nick Drake and John Martyn, while Jansch and Renbourn reunited (they'd made a duo LP, *Bert and John,* in 1966) for tours and LPs. Renbourn had begun making solo LPs while with Pentangle, and he has over a dozen of his own records out and has recorded a number of albums with Stefan Grossman. McShee joined John Renbourn's band from 1974 to 1981. In 1983 the original lineup re-formed solely for *Open the Door,* but a newer lineup that includes cofounders Jansch and McShee continues. Danny Thompson toured with Richard Thompson in a quartet that included former Fairport Convention and Jethro Tull member Dave Pegg and Pete Zorn.

Pere Ubu

Formed 1975, Cleveland, Ohio

David Thomas, a.k.a. Crocus Behemoth (b. June 14, 1953), voc.; Tom Herman (b. April 19, 1949), gtr.; Peter Laughner (b. ca. 1953; d. June 22, 1977), gtr.; Tim Wright, bass; Allen Ravenstine (b. May 9, 1950), synth.; Scott Krauss (b. Nov. 19, 1950), drums.
1977—(– Laughner) 1978—(– Wright; + Tony Maimone [b. Sept. 27, 1952, Cleveland], bass) *The Modern Dance* (Blank); *Datapanik in the Year Zero* (Radar, U.K.); *Dub Housing* (Chrysalis) 1979—*New Picnic Time* (– Herman; + Mayo Thompson [b. Feb. 26, 1944], gtr., voc.) 1980—*The Art of Walking* (Rough Trade) 1981—*390 Degrees of Simulated Stereo* 1982—(– Krauss; + Anton Fier [b. June 20, 1956, Cleveland], drums) *The Song of the Bailing Man* 1985—*Terminal Tower: An Archival Collection* (– Thompson; – Fier; + Jim Jones [b. March 12, 1950], gtr.; + Chris Cutler [b. Jan. 4, 1947], drums; + Krauss) 1988—*The Tenement Year* (Enigma) 1989—*Cloudland* (Mercury); *One Man Drives While the Other Man Screams* (Rough Trade) (– Ravenstine; – Cutler; + Eric Drew Feldman [b. April 16, 1955], synth.) 1991—*Worlds in Collision* (Mercury) (– Feldman) 1993—*Story of My Life* (Imago).
David Thomas solo: 1981—*The Sound of the Sand and Other Songs of the Pedestrians* (Rough Trade) 1982—*Vocal Performances* EP 1983—*Variations on a Theme; Winter Comes Home* (Re Records) 1985—*More Places Forever* (Rough Trade); *Monster*

Walks the Winter Lake 1987—*Blame the Messenger.*

Pere Ubu's music is a unique mixture of control and anarchy, incorporating driving rock, synthesized "found" sounds, falling-apart song structures, and David Thomas' careening vocals and wide-eyed lyrics. Founding members Thomas and Laughner, both rock journalists (Laughner with *Creem*), named the band after the hero of *Ubu Roi*, a play by French absurdist Alfred Jarry. Ubu was part of the fertile Ohio rock scene that also fostered Tin Huey and Devo. Their first single, "30 Seconds over Tokyo" b/w "Heart of Darkness," was released independently in 1975 on Hearthan and reissued on *Datapanik.* In early 1976 the initial lineup recorded another two-sided single, "Final Solution" b/w "Cloud 149," traveled to New York City several times, and disbanded. In July they regrouped as the quintet that recorded their first three albums. Tim Wright moved to New York and joined the no-wave band DNA. In 1977 Laughner died of alcohol and drug abuse.

Though it sold only 15,000 copies in the U.S., *The Modern Dance* influenced an entire school of postpunk bands, including R.E.M., Hüsker Dü, and the Pixies. By touring the U.S. and, in 1978, England, Pere Ubu became well known on the burgeoning new-wave circuit and particularly popular in England. After their British shows, they signed with Chrysalis and released *Dub Housing,* whose dark, surreal atmosphere made it a classic underground rock album.

Herman left for solo work in 1979, making an album with some Cleveland avant-punk cohorts (*Frontier Justice*) before moving to Houston. He was replaced by Mayo Thompson, formerly of the Texas psychedelic band Red Crayola, with whom Pere Ubu recorded *The Art of*

Pere Ubu: Scott Krauss, Jim Jones, David Thomas, Tony Maimone

Walking. Ubu members also appeared on Crayola's *Soldier Talk.* Artistic and personal squabbles broke the band up again in early 1982. Maimone and Krauss formed their own group, Home and Garden.

In 1981 Thomas, an avowed Jehovah's Witness, recorded *The Sound of the Sand,* the first of two solo albums with British folk-rock guitarist Richard Thompson. He did a few solo concerts in 1982 backed only by prerecorded tapes and Tin Huey saxophonist Ralph Carney. The personnel on Thomas' 1987 album, *Blame the Messenger,* became the re-formed Pere Ubu of *The Tenement Year,* which included a two-drum lineup featuring Krauss, again, and British prog-rocker Chris Cutler, of Henry Cow and the Art Bears.

Longtime keyboardist Allen Ravenstine left Ubu after 1989's near-pop album, *Cloudland,* to become a Northwest Airlines pilot. He was replaced by Captain Beefheart sideman Eric Drew Feldman on the even more commercial-sounding *Worlds in Collision,* produced by Gil Norton (Pixies). Feldman left to join ex-Pixies leader Charles Thompson (a.k.a. Frank Black). In 1993 Pere Ubu recorded *Story of My Life,* initially titled *Johnny Rivers Live at the Whisky A Go Go,* with its most stripped-down lineup yet.

Carl Perkins

Born April 9, 1932, Tiptonville, Tennessee
1958—*Dance Album of Carl Perkins* (Sun); *Whole Lotta Shakin'* (Columbia) 1969—*Carl Perkins' Greatest Hits; Carl Perkins On Top* 1970—*Boppin' the Blues* (with NRBQ) 1973—*My Kind of Country* (Mercury) 1982—*The Survivors* (with Johnny Cash and Jerry Lee Lewis) (Columbia) 1985—*Carl Perkins* (Dot) 1986—*Original Sun Greatest Hits* (Rhino); *Up Through the Years, 1954–1957* (Bear Family, Ger.); *The Class of '55* (America) (with Johnny Cash, Roy Orbison, Jerry Lee Lewis) 1989—*Born to Rock* (Universal/MCA); *Honky Tonk Gal: Rare and Unissued Sun Masters* (Rounder) 1990—*The Million Dollar Quartet* (with Elvis Presley, Jerry Lee Lewis, and Johnny Cash) (BMG); *Classic Carl Perkins* (Bear Family, Ger.); *Jive After Five: The Best of Carl Perkins (1958–1978)* (Rhino) 1991—*The Dollie Masters: Country Boy's Dream* (Bear Family, Ger.) 1992—*Restless: The Columbia Recordings* (Columbia Legacy); *Friends, Family and Legends* (Platinum); *706 Re-Union* (with Scotty Moore) (Belle Meade) 1993—*Carl Perkins & Sons* (BMG); *Take Me Back; Disciple in Blue Suede Shoes.*

One of the architects of rock & roll, Carl Perkins is best known as the writer and original singer of the rockabilly anthem "Blue Suede Shoes" (#2, 1956). Along with Jerry Lee Lewis, Johnny Cash, and Elvis Presley, Perkins was one of the seminal rockabilly artists on Sam Phillips' Sun

Carl Perkins

label, but a series of bad breaks, followed by personal problems, undermined his solo career. Despite that, Perkins persevered, creating a body of work that has been both critically acclaimed and extremely influential on songwriters, guitar players, and singers alike.

Perkins grew up poor in a sharecropping family that picked cotton in various northwestern Tennessee fields around Tiptonville. Perkins was first put to work at age six, and it was in the fields that he first heard gospel songs. At night, he heard hillbilly country and Delta blues over the family radio. An older black field hand befriended Perkins and taught him to play guitar; by age ten Perkins was entertaining his classmates. He made his radio debut with his school band, singing "Home on the Range."

He kicked off his musical career in the mid-Forties, performing at local dances with his brothers Jay and Clayton as the Perkins Brothers Band. In 1953 drummer W. S. (Fluke) Holland joined. The next year, after hearing Presley's debut Sun single, "Blue Moon of Kentucky" (a Bill Monroe song Perkins and his group had been playing since 1949), Perkins and his brothers drove to Memphis to audition for Phillips. Shortly thereafter, they signed to the label and released Perkins' first single, "Movie Magg" (a song Perkins wrote at age 14) b/w "Turn Around." In early 1955 came "Let the Jukebox Keep on Playing" b/w "Gone Gone Gone."

Perkins' biggest hit came in late 1956. "Blue Suede Shoes" was an instant smash and made Perkins the first white country artist to cross over to the R&B chart as well. A country, pop, and R&B hit, "Blue Suede Shoes" alternated with Elvis Presley's first post-Sun single, "Heartbreak Hotel," for the top spots on national and re-

gional charts. (Shortly thereafter, Presley issued his "Blue Suede Shoes"; over time, Perkins' original sold more copies.) Perkins was at the height of his career when tragedy struck. He and his group were driving to New York City to appear on Perry Como's television program when their driver fell asleep at the wheel, causing the car to hit the back of a truck before plunging into water. The driver was killed instantly and Carl and his brother Jay were seriously injured. Although Perkins was back on the road in about a month, his brother Jay never fully recovered and was later diagnosed with a brain tumor, from which he died in 1958. Years later, Perkins admitted that he used his brother's death as a reason to drink (Clayton later committed suicide.) A quiet, self-effacing man, Perkins later observed, "I felt out of place when 'Blue Suede Shoes' was Number One. I stood on the Steel Pier in 1956 in Atlantic City . . . and the Goodyear blimp flew over with my name in big lights. And I stood there and shook and actually cried. That should have been something that would elevate a guy to say, 'Well, I've made it.' But it put fear in me."

In early 1958 Perkins moved to Columbia Records, where he recorded several more minor rockabilly hits, but by the early Sixties, he'd hit a low point. On a British tour in 1964, Perkins was surprised to learn that the Beatles admired him, and that George Harrison had taught himself to play guitar by copying Perkins' records. Perkins became friendly with the Beatles and oversaw the sessions during which they recorded five of his songs—"Matchbox," "Honey Don't," "Your True Love," "Blue Suede Shoes," and "Everybody's Trying to Be My Baby." Rick Nelson, Johnny Burnette, and Patsy Cline, among others, also covered his songs. Like many other rockabilly artists, Perkins turned to country material as the rockabilly trend died, and by 1965 he was part of Johnny Cash's touring troupe. When Cash got his national television show in 1969, Perkins became a regular guest, and he toured and recorded with Cash as well.

As a solo artist, Perkins cut some country records and recorded an album with NRBQ. After the Cash show ended, he toured as Johnny's guitarist until 1975. He then formed the C. P. Express with his sons Greg and Stan and started his own label, Suede, on which he released two albums (*The Carl Perkins Show* and *Carl Perkins Live at Austin City Limits*). In late 1978 Perkins released a basic rock & roll LP called *Ol' Blue Suede's Back*, which sold 100,000 copies in England. In 1981 he did some sessions for Paul McCartney's *Tug of War*; in early 1982, an album entitled *Survivors*, recorded live in Germany with Jerry Lee Lewis and Johnny Cash, was released. Three years later Lewis, Cash, and Orbison were reunited for *The Class of '55*, a special event that included such Perkins disciples as John Fogerty and Rick Nelson.

Through the years, Perkins has continued to record

and write. He cowrote the Judds' 1989 hit "Let Me Tell You About Love," on which he played lead guitar. In 1992 Dolly Parton had a C&W hit with a song Perkins wrote for her, "Silver and Gold." In 1992 Perkins was diagnosed with throat cancer; following treatment, he was declared cancer-free a year later. He continues to write and record. He is part owner of two Jackson, Tennessee, restaurants; one, Suede, is filled with his career memorabilia. In 1981 he founded the Carl Perkins Center for the Prevention of Child Abuse, and every year he hosts a daylong local telethon to support the center. He was inducted into the Rock and Roll Hall of Fame in 1987. David McGee wrote Perkins' official biography, *Go, Cat, Go* (1995).

Joe Perry Project: See Aerosmith

Lee "Scratch" Perry

Born Rainford Hugh Perry, circa 1940, Hanover, Jamaica
1971—*Africa Blood* (Trojan) 1976—*Super Ape* (Mango); *Roast Fish, Collie Weed and Corn Bread* (Lion of Judah) 1977—*Double Seven* (Trojan); *Return of the Super Ape* (Mango) 1979—*Cloak and Dagger* (Black Art); *Scratch on the Wire* (Island) 1980—*The Return of Pipecock Jackxon* (Black Art) 1981—*The Upsetter Collection* (Trojan) 1982— *Scratch and Co.: Chapter One* (Clocktower); *Mystic Miracle Star* (Heartbeat) 1984—*History, Mystery and Prophecy* (Mango); *Reggae Greats* 1985—*The Upsetter Box* (Trojan) 1986—*Battle of Armagideon* 1987—*Time Boom X De Devil Dead* (On-U Sound) 1988—*Satan Kicked the Bucket* (Bullwackies); *Some of the Best* (Heartbeat) 1989—*All the Hits* (Rohit); *Chicken Scratch* (Heartbeat) 1990—*Build the Ark* (Trojan); *From the Secret Laboratory* (Mango); *Message from Yard* (Rohit); *Lee Scratch Perry Meets Bullwackie in Satan's Dub* cassette (ROIR); *Version Like Rain* (Trojan) 1991—*Lord God Muzick* (Heartbeat) 1992—*The Upsetter & the Beat*; *Soundzs from the Hot Line.*
Lee Perry and Friends: 1988—*Give Me Power* (Trojan) 1989—*Open the Gate*; *Shocks of Mighty 1969-1974* (Attack) 1990—*Public Jestering.*
As Jah Lion: 1976—*Colombia Colly* (Mango).
Lee "Scratch" Perry & Mad Professor: 1989—*Mystic Warrior* (RAS); *Mystic Warrior Dub* (Ariwa).

Under many names, disc jockey, producer, record businessman, songwriter, and singer Lee Perry has been a guiding force in the development of reggae. In addition to his own trailblazing music, he has produced hits for the Wailers, Junior Byles, Max Romeo, the Heptones, Gregory Isaacs, Junior Murvin, and the Clash. Known for his bizarre behavior and stream-of-consciousness interviews, he often dons costumes and headdresses made of found objects such as feathers, toys, playing cards, and coins.

He began his career in his teens as "Little Lee Perry," a DJ for Coxsone Dodd's Downbeat Sound System. When he made his recording debut with "The Chicken Scratch" on Dodd's Studio One label in the early Sixties, he became known as Scratch Perry. For most of the Sixties, he worked at Studio One as A&R director and producer of Jamaican hits for Justin Hines, Delroy Wilson, and Shenley Dufus, among others; he also recorded his own material, such as "Trials and Crosses" and "Doctor Dick."

In 1968 Perry left Dodd and worked briefly—as producer and performer—with Joe Gibbs, Byron Lee, and Clancy Eccles. With the success of Perry's first independent release, an instrumental called "The Upsetter," he acquired another sobriquet—the Upsetter. He named his label Upsetter and his studio band the Upsetters. That same year, 1968, he had a hit with "People Funny Boy," billing himself as Lee "King" Perry. An unusually slow song for its time, "People Funny Boy" was one of the first real reggae hits. Most of Perry's late-Sixties hits, like "Clint Eastwood," "Live Injection," and "Return of Django" (#5 U.K., 1969), were instrumentals that set his spaghetti-Western–style themes in reggae as dry, spacious, and ominous as the western desert.

In 1969 Perry began working with the Wailers. During the next three years, he oversaw their transformation from a ska vocal trio into a full-fledged five-piece reggae band—with bassist Aston "Family Man" Barrett and his drummer brother Carlton from the Upsetters—that would become the most acclaimed Jamaican group in the world. "Duppy Conqueror," "Small Axe," "Kaya," and "Sun Is Shining" were some of the Wailers' songs Perry wrote. The Wailers began producing themselves for their own label in 1971 but were reunited with Perry for occasional sessions in the late Seventies.

Signed to Island in 1973, Perry and his Upsetters maintained a rocky relationship with the company on and off for several years. In 1974 he built his Black Ark Studio in the backyard of his Kingston home. Perry was one of the pioneers of the reggae instrumental studio art known as dubbing—reworking a taped track by removing some parts and exaggerating others. His use of technology such as drum machines and phase shifters gave his mixes a cutting-edge sound that had a profound influence on dub and, later, dancehall. His work in the Seventies with such toasters as U-Roy, Prince Jazzbo, I-Roy, Big Youth, and Dennis Alcapone established him in the forefront of toasters' dub; he would make hit after hit from the same rhythm track until the tape wore out. Perry recorded his own toasting under the pseudonym Jah Lion. He also recorded as Pipecock Jackson and under his own name. His most popular releases in the Seventies, "Station Underground News" and "Roast Fish and Corn Bread," were vocals.

Perry reportedly torched his studio in 1980 and began traveling. His musical output became more eccentric and experimental, though it remained highly respected by critics. He lived in Amsterdam in the mid-Eighties, and then in London. In 1990 Perry moved to Switzerland briefly before returning to Jamaica, where he continues to live and record.

The Persuasions

Formed 1962, Brooklyn, New York
Jerry Lawson (b. Jan. 23, 1944, Fort Lauderdale, Fla.), lead voc.; Jayotis Washington (b. May 12, 1941, Detroit, Mich.), tenor voc.; Joseph "Jesse" Russell (b. Sep. 25, 1939, Henderson, N.C.), tenor voc.; Herbert "Tubo" Rhoad (b. Oct. 1, 1944, Bamberg County, S.C.; d. Dec. 8, 1988), baritone voc.; Jimmy "Bro" Hayes (b. Nov. 12, 1943, Hopewell, Va.), bass voc.
1968—A Cappella (Straight)   1971—We Came to Play (Capitol)   1972—Street Corner Symphony; Spread the Word   1973—We Still Ain't Got No Band (MCA)   1974—More Than Before (A&M); I Just Want to Sing with My Friends (– Washington; + Willie Daniels, voc.)   1977—Chirpin' (Elektra) (– Daniels; + Washington)   1979—Comin' at Ya (Flying Fish)   1983—Good News (Rounder) 1986—No Frills   1988—Live at the Whispering Gallery (– Rhoad)   1994—Right Around the Corner (Bullseye Blues).

Since 1962 the Persuasions' unique brand of a cappella has made them a popular live attraction and sought-after as backup singers. Tenors Jesse Russell and Jayotis Washington, baritones Tubo Rhoad and Jerry Lawson, and nonpareil bass Jimmy Hayes started the group in Brooklyn, where all had migrated. Each had sung with gospel and secular vocal groups, and from the beginning the Persuasions have mixed doo-wop, soul, and pop into their repertoire.

The Persuasions' first recording was a single on Minit/United Artists Records in 1966. The following year they were taped at a Jersey City performance by doo-wop fan David Dashev, who got the tape to Frank Zappa, who released it as A Cappella in 1968 on his Straight Records. When Warner Bros. purchased Straight, label executives wanted to record the Persuasions with a band, but the group refused. From 1971 to 1973 the Persuasions made three records for Capitol. With MCA Records in 1973, they cut one album, We Still Ain't Got No Band. The following year Washington left the group and was replaced by Willie Daniels; Daniels left in 1977 and Washington returned that year.

Two mid-Seventies albums with A&M, More Than Before and I Just Want to Sing with My Friends, included instrumental backing and resulted in two singles making the lower end of the R&B chart: "I Really Got It Bad for You" in 1974 and "One Thing on My Mind" in 1975. From 1974 on, the Persuasions worked steadily as guest vocalists behind Stevie Wonder, Phoebe Snow, Ellen McIlwaine, Don McLean, and others. They cut the critically acclaimed Chirpin' for Elektra in 1977, with Dashev producing. After backing Joni Mitchell on a 1979–80 tour, the Persuasions were featured on her Shadows and Light live album, including the single "Why Do Fools Fall in Love?" With Rhoad's death in 1988, the group became a quartet. It was featured prominently in Spike Lee's 1990 television special "Do It A Cappella" and the accompanying album. They continue a busy touring schedule.

Pet Shop Boys

Formed August 1981, London, England
Neil Tennant (b. Neil Francis Tennant, July 10, 1954, North Shields, Eng.), voc.; Chris Lowe (b. Christopher Sean Lowe, Oct. 4, 1959, Blackpool, Eng.), kybds.
1986—Please (EMI); Disco   1987—Actually   1988— Introspective   1990—Behavior   1991—Discography   1993—Very.

Like the Monty Python comedy troupe, the duo Pet Shop Boys could have been conceived only by the English. Less a band per se than a musical vehicle for wry, cheeky commentary on pop culture, Pet Shop Boys—i.e., singer Neil Tennant and keyboardist Chris Lowe—won kudos for their clever, danceable synth pop and deadpan ballads, which were actually tender as well as irreverent.

Lowe was an architecture student and Tennant a journalist when they met in 1981 in an electronics shop and discovered they shared a passion for synthesizers and dance music. As a youth, Tennant had been active in theater and had sung and played guitar in a band called Dust; Lowe had studied piano and trombone, and had played the latter in a dance-standard band. Calling themselves Pet Shop Boys, a name taken from friends who worked in such an establishment, Tennant and Lowe began writing songs together. In 1983 Tennant, then an editor at the British pop music journal Smash Hits, hooked up with producer Bobby "O" Orlando while on business in New York. Orlando worked on an early version of the Boys' first single, "West End Girls."

In 1985 the finished mix of "West End Girls" shot to #1 in many countries, including the U.S., where Pet Shop Boys' debut album, Please, peaked at #7. Please also spawned the pop hit "Opportunities (Let's Make Lots of Money)" (#10). An album of dance remixes, Disco, followed in 1986. In 1987 Boys scored another three Top

Ten singles in America: "It's a Sin" (#9); "What Have I Done to Deserve This?" (#2), a duet between Tennant and his favorite female singer, Dusty Springfield; and a remake of "Always on My Mind" (#4).

In the summer of 1988 Pet Shop Boys released the documentary film *It Couldn't Happen Here*. After putting out another album that year, *Introspective*, the duo collaborated with Liza Minnelli in 1989 on an album called *Results*, which featured a high-tech rendition of Stephen Sondheim's "Losing My Mind." Later that year Tennant cowrote and sang on "Getting Away with It," the debut single by Electronic, a group formed by New Order's Bernard Sumner and ex-Smiths guitarist Johnny Marr.

Pet Shop Boys have continued to reap acclaim with the albums *Behavior* (#45, 1990) and *Very* (#20, 1993). In 1991, on the heels of a well-received single seguing U2's "Where the Streets Have No Name" with Frankie Valli's "Can't Take My Eyes Off of You," they released *Discography*, a singles compilation. *Very* included a remake of the Village People's "Go West," the once-triumphant song now sounding like an elegy for AIDS victims.

Pete Rock and C. L. Smooth

Formed 1984, Mount Vernon, New York
Pete Rock (b. Peter Phillips, June 21, 1970, Mount Vernon), voc.; C. L. Smooth (b. Corey Penn, Oct. 8, 1968, New Rochelle, N.Y.), DJ.
1992—*Mecca & the Soul Brother* (Elektra)   1994—*The Main Ingredient*.

Pete Rock and C. L. Smooth are rappers well respected for both their own work and Rock's production of other rap acts. The duo met in their teens in "money-earnin'" Mount Vernon, home of such hip-hop stars as Al B. Sure! and Heavy D. They began recording raps on Rock's cassette player after school, until Eddie F., the most popular local DJ and a budding producer, brought them to his 12-track. Eddie put Rock and Smooth on a remix of Johnny Gill's gold single "Rub U the Right Way," which eventually landed them their first gig outside their neighborhood, in Madison Square Garden with Gill.

Mecca & the Soul Brother was praised for its honest stories of urban romance and living and for Rock's mix of jazz, R&B, and reggae. "They Reminisce Over You (T.R.O.Y.)" (#10 R&B, 1992) was a #1 rap hit. Two years later *The Main Ingredient* peaked at #9 on the R&B chart. Rock has also produced records by Kid 'n Play, Shabba Ranks, and Heavy D.

Peter and Gordon

Formed 1963, London, England
Peter Asher (b. June 22, 1944, London), voc., gtr.;
Gordon Waller (b. June 4, 1945, Braemar, Scot.), voc., gtr.

1964—*A World Without Love* (Capitol)   1965—*Peter and Gordon*; *True Love Ways*   1966—*The Best of Peter and Gordon*   1967—*Lady Godiva*.

Peter and Gordon were an enormously successful British pop/folk team in the mid-Sixties. After their breakup, Gordon all but vanished into obscurity, but Peter Asher has kept his name in the limelight as a manager/producer of Linda Ronstadt, James Taylor, 10,000 Maniacs, and others.

Both Peter and Gordon came from upper-middle-class families and were products of private schools, the two meeting at Westminster School for Boys in London. They worked together as a campus duo, in an Everly Brothers vein, and decided to try the London club scene. Because of their school's 9:00 p.m. dorm curfew, they had to sneak over a 12-foot spiked fence to do it, which they managed successfully for around a year. Eventually they left school to concentrate on music, recording demos and making the record-company rounds.

Asher and Waller landed a contract in 1963 and within a year had their first and biggest hit, "A World Without Love," written by Paul McCartney, who at the time was courting Asher's sister Jane. The tune went to #1 in the U.S. and the U.K. in 1964.

Between 1964 and 1967 the duo had a string of U.S. hit singles that included "Nobody I Know" (#12) and "I Don't Want to See You Again" (#16) in 1964; Del Shannon's "I Go to Pieces" (#9) and Buddy Holly's "True Love Ways" (#14) in 1965; "Woman" (#14) and "Lady Godiva" (#6) in 1966; and "Knight in Rusty Armour" (#15) in 1967.

In 1968 the duo broke up, and Asher became A&R head of the Beatles' Apple label, where he signed and produced James Taylor before moving to the United States. From the early Seventies on, Asher's client roster has included Taylor, Linda Ronstadt, Carole King, Joni Mitchell, Randy Newman, and Warren Zevon, as well as such newer artists as John Wesley Harding, Iris DeMent, and Mary's Danish. In 1989 he won a Grammy for Producer of the Year for his work on Ronstadt's *Cry Like a Rainstorm, Howl Like the Wind*.

Peter, Paul and Mary

Formed 1961, New York City, New York
Peter Yarrow (b. May 31, 1938, New York City), voc., gtr.; Noel Paul Stookey (b. Nov. 30, 1937, Baltimore, Md.), voc., gtr.; Mary Travers (b. Nov. 7, 1937, Louisville, Ky.), voc.
1962—*Peter, Paul and Mary* (Warner Bros.)   1963—*Peter, Paul and Mary—Moving*; *Peter, Paul and Mary—In the Wind*   1964—*Peter, Paul and Mary in Concert*   1965—*A Song Will Rise*; *See What Tomorrow Brings*   1966—*The Peter, Paul and Mary Album*   1967—*Album 1700*   1968—*Late Again*   1969—*Peter, Paul & Mommy*   1970—*Ten Years To-*

gether 1978—*Reunion* 1986—*No Easy Walk to Freedom* (Gold Castle) 1988—*A Holiday Celebration* 1990—*Flowers and Stones* 1993—*Peter, Paul & Mommy, Too* (Warner Bros.) 1995—*Lifelines.* Peter Yarrow solo: 1972—*Peter* (Warner Bros.). Paul Stookey solo: 1971—*Paul and* (Warner Bros.). Mary Travers solo: 1971—*Mary* (Warner Bros.) 1972—*Morning Glory* 1973—*All My Choices* 1974—*Circles* 1978—*It's in Everyone of Us* (Chrysalis).

Peter, Paul and Mary became the most popular acoustic folk group of the Sixties. They were also the first to bring commercial success to Bob Dylan, by covering his "Blowin' in the Wind," a #2 hit in August 1963.

The trio met while each was working in Greenwich Village and were encouraged by manager Albert Grossman to join forces in 1961. Yarrow had had some success as a solo folk artist. After graduating in psychology from Cornell, he toured locally and appeared on the CBS special *Folk Sound U.S.A.* in May 1960. Grossman spotted Yarrow there and arranged for him to perform at the Newport Folk Festival and make a national tour. Stookey was a stand-up comic in Greenwich Village and previously had led a high school rock & roll group.

Mary Travers, who grew up in Greenwich Village, had sung in school choruses and folk groups. She sang in the chorus of a 1957 Broadway flop called *The Next President* with Mort Sahl. In 1961 she met Stookey, who encouraged her to sing again, and Grossman decided she was right to round out the trio. They rehearsed for seven months, with Milt Okun crafting their arrangements. Soon after they played a special engagement at New York's Bitter End, they signed with Warner Bros. Records.

The group's debut LP spent seven weeks at #1 in 1962, and two songs from it, "Lemon Tree" (#35) and Pete Seeger's "If I Had a Hammer" (#10) cracked the Top Forty. The latter helped bring folk and protest consciousness to the mainstream. The album remained on the Hot 100 Albums chart for three and a half years. They often toured college campuses and played at rallies. As always, they were deeply involved in the issues they sang about. They marched with Dr. Martin Luther King Jr., and in 1969 Yarrow helped organize the March on Washington.

After "Blowin' in the Wind" reached #2, the trio's cover of Dylan's "Don't Think Twice It's Alright" hit #9 in October 1963. In May of that year "Puff the Magic Dragon" (#2) stirred some controversy, since it was interpreted by some as a drug song. In fact it was just one of their many children's songs. (They released a whole LP of these in 1969 called *Peter, Paul & Mommy.*) Peter, Paul and Mary were also known for covering songs by soon-to-be-famous singer/songwriters, including John Den-

ver ("Leaving on a Jet Plane," a #1 smash in 1969) and Gordon Lightfoot ("For Lovin' Me," a Top Thirty single in 1965, and "Early Morning Rain"). Their other hit singles were "I Dig Rock and Roll Music" (#9, 1967), and "Day Is Done" (#21, 1969).

The group decided to break up in 1970 and released a best-of collection that May. It was their tenth album (out of 11) to make the Top Twenty. They pursued solo careers, with considerably less artistic and commercial success. Stookey's records (as Noel Paul Stookey) reflected his Christian religious convictions. His best-known solo song was "Wedding Song (There Is Love)" (#24, 1971), written for Yarrow's marriage. Yarrow coproduced and wrote Mary MacGregor's 1977 #1 hit "Torn Between Two Lovers." He also formed a group called the Bodyworks Band, with which he performs and records Christian-oriented music. In 1970 Yarrow was convicted of "taking immoral liberties" with a female minor; in 1981 he was granted a full presidential pardon by Jimmy Carter. Travers hosted a radio talk show for a while and later a BBC television series.

The trio reunited occasionally in the Seventies, at benefits such as the 1972 George McGovern campaign fund-raiser, which also brought back Simon and Garfunkel, and Mike Nichols and Elaine May. In 1978 they re-formed; they released a new LP and toured nationally. Their music continues to reflect contemporary political and social concerns, from "El Salvador" and apartheid ("No Easy Walk to Freedom") to AIDS ("Home Is Where the Heart Is"). They have starred in three PBS specials, including one to accompany the release of their second children's album, *Peter, Paul & Mommy, Too.*

Ray Peterson
Born April 23, 1939, Denton, Texas

A late-Fifties singer with a 4½-octave voice, Ray Peterson specialized in ballads like "The Wonder of You" (a hit for Elvis Presley in 1970) and the classic death-rock song "Tell Laura I Love Her," in which the hero dies in a stock-car race he'd entered hoping to win the $1,000 prize so he could by his girlfriend a wedding ring.

Peterson began singing while a polio patient in Warm Springs Foundation Hospital in Texas, to amuse the other patients. He started performing in local clubs and eventually moved to Los Angeles, where he was signed to RCA. His first record was 1958's "Let's Try Romance," followed by "Tail Light," a cover of the R&B standard "Fever," and the hard-rocking "Shirley Purley," none of which made the chart.

Peterson's first hit was "The Wonder of You," written by Baker Knight (#25, 1959). He followed with "Tell Laura I Love Her" (#7, 1960), the Phil Spector–produced "Corinna, Corinna" (#9, 1961), "Missing You" (#29, 1961), and "I Could Have Loved You So Well" (#57, 1962). In 1961

Peterson formed his own label, Dunes, which released all his records after and including "Corinna, Corinna," and to which he signed Curtis Lee ("Pretty Little Angel Eyes"). After some more discs for MGM failed, Peterson briefly tried a career as a country singer.

Tom Petty and the Heartbreakers

Formed 1975, Los Angeles, California
Tom Petty (b. Oct. 20, 1952, Gainesville, Fla.), voc., gtr.; Mike Campbell (b. Feb. 1, 1954, Gainesville), gtr.; Benmont Tench (b. Sep. 7, 1954, Gainesville), kybds.; Ron Blair (b. Sep. 16, 1952, Macon, Ga.), bass; Stan Lynch (b. May 21, 1955, Gainesville), drums.
1976—*Tom Petty and the Heartbreakers* (Shelter) 1978—*You're Gonna Get It*   1979—*Damn the Torpedoes* (Backstreet)   1981—*Hard Promises*   1982— (– Blair; + Howie Epstein [b. July 21, 1955], bass) *Long After Dark*   1985—*Southern Accents* (MCA); *Pack Up the Plantation*   1987—*Let Me Up (I've Had Enough)*   1991—*Into the Great Wide Open*   1993— *Greatest Hits*   1994—(– Lynch; + Steve Ferrone, drums).
Tom Petty solo: 1989—*Full Moon Fever* (MCA) 1994—*Wildflowers* (Warner Bros.).

Tom Petty

In the Seventies Tom Petty came up with a distillate of FM-radio Sixties rock—chiming Byrds guitars, Rolling Stones rhythms, and a slurred version of Bob Dylan/ Roger McGuinn vocals. First penning tales of outcasts and long-suffering lovers, he broadened his thematic range to encompass musings on his southern heritage and propagate a very American individualism. The Heartbreakers evolved into a classic rock & roll band, and Petty's invitation in the Eighties to join Dylan, Roy Orbison, George Harrison, and Jeff Lynne in the side-project supergroup the Traveling Wilburys confirmed his stature.

Petty, the son of a Florida insurance salesman, quit high school at 17 to join one of the state's top bands, Mudcrutch, with future Heartbreakers Mike Campbell and Benmont Tench. In the early Seventies they sent Petty to L.A. to seek a record contract; Denny Cordell's Shelter Records (co-owned with Leon Russell) delivered.

The group disbanded soon after moving to L.A., and while Cordell offered to record Petty solo, nothing happened until 1975, when Petty heard a demo that Campbell and Tench were working on with Ron Blair and Stan Lynch. The fivesome became the Heartbreakers, inherited Petty's Shelter contract, and released a self-titled debut in 1976. At first it sold poorly. Then the Heartbreakers toured England, opening for Nils Lofgren. Within weeks, they were headlining and the album was on the British charts. ABC (distributor of Shelter) then

rereleased "Breakdown" in the U.S., and the single cracked the Top Forty nearly a year after its initial release. Another song, the very Byrdsy "American Girl," was recorded by ex-Byrd Roger McGuinn. The band's second album boasted the singles "Listen to Her Heart" (#59, 1978) and "I Need to Know" (#41, 1978).

Just as the Heartbreakers' career was taking off, a legal battle arose when Petty tried to renegotiate his contract after MCA bought ABC Records; by mid-1979 he filed for bankruptcy. After nine months of litigation, Petty signed to Backstreet Records, a new MCA affiliate. His triumphant return, *Damn the Torpedoes,* hit #2, selling over two-and-a-half million copies, and established Petty as a star. And his singles placed higher: "Don't Do Me Like That" (#10, 1979) and "Refugee" (#15, 1980).

In 1981 Petty again got into record company trouble by challenging MCA's intention to issue *Hard Promises* with a then-high $9.98 list price. After he threatened to withhold the LP (or entitle it *$8.98*) and organized fan protest letters, the album came out at $8.98. *Hard Promises* went on to platinum status, with the #19 hit "The Waiting," yet Petty's suspicion of the business end of the music industry continued. In the Eighties, when tire manufacturer B. F. Goodrich attempted to use his "Mary's Got a Brand New Car" in a commercial, Petty filed a suit and got the ad pulled; in 1989 he refused to perform at a New Jersey gig until promoters allowed Greenpeace to set up information booths in the lobby.

In 1981 Petty gained a #3 hit in "Stop Draggin' My Heart Around," a duet with Stevie Nicks off her solo *Bella Donna,* on which the Heartbreakers also appeared, and produced Del Shannon's comeback, *Drop Down and Get Me.* In 1982 "You Got Lucky" (#20), from *Long After Dark,* reiterated the veteran strengths of the Heartbreakers, but with Ron Blair departing, they underwent the novelty of a personnel change (ex–John Hiatt sideman Howie Epstein joined on bass). Three years in the making, *Southern Accents* was hard going; frustrated during its mixing, Petty punched a wall and broke his left hand. The album, coproduced by Eurythmics' Dave Stewart, found Petty achieving a new lyrical maturity and, with "Don't Come Around Here No More," scoring a #13 hit.

In 1986 the Heartbreakers embarked upon a world tour with Dylan, and again Petty's prospects looked good, but right before the tour for 1987's *Let Me Up,* his house burned down (arson was suspected). His wife and two daughters escaped, but most of his belongings were destroyed. Respite came with the 1988 release of the Traveling Wilburys debut; and, working with former ELO founder/guitarist and fellow Wilbury Jeff Lynne, Petty released the masterful solo album *Full Moon Fever.* Its "Free Fallin'" (#7, 1989) gave him a revitalizing hit.

With most of the Heartbreakers playing on *Fever,* Petty retained band loyalty, and it paid off on *Into the Great Wide Open,* a fine collection coproduced with Lynne. In the interim Petty had released a second Wilburys album (1990's *Volume 3*) and his band had begun establishing themselves as sidemen, with Campbell working on Roy Orbison's *Mystery Girl,* cowriting Don Henley's "The Boys of Summer" and, with Lynch, contributing to Henley's *The End of the Innocence.* Meanwhile, Tench worked with such acts as U2 and Elvis Costello, and Epstein produced his girlfriend Carlene Carter's 1990 LP *I Fell in Love.*

Petty's record business controversies continued, however, with the surprise 1992 revelation that he had signed a secret $20-million, six-album deal with Warner Bros. in 1989. Reportedly he had kept the contract secret to avoid the ire of MCA, to which he owed two more albums at the time. In an unrelated dispute, in 1993 he was vindicated by the U.S. Supreme Court when it let stand a lower court's finding that Petty's "Runnin' Down a Dream" did not infringe the copyright to an earlier piece written by songwriter/plaintiff Martin Allen Fine.

A year after a #5 *Greatest Hits* album in 1993, drummer Stan Lynch, who had been working as a songwriter and/or producer with the re-formed Eagles, Leonard Cohen, Don Henley, and the Mavericks, departed the band. Petty returned in 1994 with a second solo album, the triple-platinum *Wildflowers,* which, again, featured most of the Heartbreakers.

Liz Phair

Born Elizabeth Clark Phair, April 17, 1967, New Haven, Connecticut
1993—*Exile in Guyville* (Matador)   1994—*Whip-Smart.*

Liz Phair, the in-your-face indie sweetheart, sent up "Guyville" (i.e. the male-dominated alternative music scene dubbed as such by Chicago-rockers Urge Overkill) in her double-album debut. Her *Exile in Guyville*—a loose response to the Stones' *Exile on Main Street*—drove home the point that sex has nothing to do with whether or not an artist can rock with intelligence and sexual savvy.

Raised in a wealthy suburb of Chicago, Phair studied art at Oberlin College, where she was constantly experimenting with songwriting. A friend, guitarist Chris Brokaw of the band Come, prodded Phair to make a tape of her songs, which resulted in her signing to Matador and recording *Guyville.* Her followup, *Whip-Smart* (#27, 1994), revealed itself to be a more introspective album—although her melting pot of punk, folk, and pop doesn't hide her frank, often sexual lyrics. The boldness and self-assurance Phair portrayed on her albums was not so apparent during her early concerts, however, at which Phair suffered from stage fright.

Phantom, Rocker, and Slick: See the Stray Cats

Little Esther Phillips

Born Esther Mae Jones, December 23, 1935, Galveston, Texas; died August 7, 1984, Torrance, California
1970—*Burnin'* (Atlantic)   1972—*From a Whisper to a Scream* (Kudu); *Alone Again (Naturally)*   1973—*Black Eyed Blues*   1974—*Performance*   1975—*What a Difference a Day Makes*   1976—*For All We Know; Confessin' the Blues* (Atlantic); *Capricorn Princess* (Kudu)   1977—*You've Come a Long Way Baby* (Mercury)   1978—*All About Esther*   1979—*Here's Esther . . . Are You Ready*   1986—*A Way to Say Goodbye* (Muse)   1987—*What a Difference a Day Makes* (CBS Associated)   1990—*The Best of Esther Phillips* (Columbia).

Throughout her long career, singer Esther Phillips covered blues, rhythm & blues, and jazz, each in her own earthy style. As a child in Texas, Phillips sang in churches before her family moved to Los Angeles in the late Forties. At 13 she won a talent show at Los Angeles' Barrelhouse Club, run by R&B impresario Johnny Otis. For the next three years, she recorded with Otis' orchestra as Little Esther Phillips and built a national following among black record buyers. Two duets with another Otis discovery, Mel Walker, resulted in the Top Ten R&B hits "Cupid's Boogie" (#2 R&B, 1950) and "Ring-a-Ding-Doo" (#8 R&B, 1952). As a solo singer, Phillips had a #1 R&B hit with "Double Crossing Blues" in 1950.

Because of illness, she retired in 1954 and settled in Houston. She returned to music in the early Sixties with New York's Lenox Records and in 1962 enjoyed international success with "Release Me" (#8 pop, #1 R&B), a reworking of a country hit. A 1963 duet with Big Al Downing on "You Never Miss Your Water (Until Your Well Runs Dry)" is well remembered, though it was not a hit at the time. She signed with Atlantic in the mid-Sixties and had success with a cover of the Beatles' "And I Love Her," done as "And I Love Him" (#11 R&B).

In the late Sixties Phillips' recordings suffered as she battled a heroin addiction at Synanon, a treatment center. In 1971 she signed with Kudu Records, where she cut a series of bluesy jazz albums. Her chilling interpretation of Gil Scott-Heron's antidrug "Home Is Where the Hatred Is" (#40 R&B) is considered by many to be one of her finest efforts. "I Never Found a Man (To Love Me Like You Do)" (#17 R&B) in 1972 showed that Phillips still had commercial appeal. This fact was further demonstrated by her 1975 disco hit "What a Difference a Day Makes" (#20 pop, #10 R&B, #6 U.K.). In 1981 an album on Mercury Records was produced by jazz trumpeter Benny Golson. In 1982 she duetted with Swamp Dogg on one song from his *I'm Not Selling Out, I'm Buying In.*

Plagued for years by declining health and substance-abuse problems, Phillips died of kidney and liver failure.

Phranc
Born Susan Gottlieb, August 28, 1957, Santa Monica, California
1985—*Folksinger* (Rhino)   1989—*I Enjoy Being a Girl* (Island)   1991—*Positively Phranc.*

Phranc calls herself the "all-American Jewish lesbian folksinger" and composes music in the traditional Sixties protest style of Phil Ochs, Tom Paxton, and Joan Baez. The daughter of an insurance salesman and a dental hygienist, Susan Gottlieb knew early on that she was different from her friends. By 1974 she had found refuge in the local lesbian-feminist community; the following year she changed her name to Phranc, dropped out of Venice High School, and got a buzz-cut flattop.

Musically influenced by her cantor grandfather, Phranc started singing at gay coffeehouses, and by the late Seventies discovered L.A.'s burgeoning punk-rock scene. By 1980, after playing in three punk bands, including Catholic Discipline, she had tired of the music's misogyny and Nazi iconography and written "Take Off Your Swastika" (which would show up later on 1989's *I Enjoy Being a Girl*); she played the song at a punk show one night on her acoustic guitar so members of the mosh pit could hear the words. Phranc decided then to return to folk music for good. Unlike most folkies, however, she has performed on bills with bands ranging from Dead Kennedys to Morrissey.

Phranc's unflinching treatment of her sexuality, as well as other aspects of her personal life and politics, has kept her music from gaining a wider audience. Although *Folksinger* was well received critically, it remained a cult item. In 1989 Island signed Phranc but never quite figured out how to market her. The label dropped her after the release of 1991's *Positively Phranc,* and as of 1994 she was still looking for another record deal. Meanwhile, Phranc did a series of performances in which she impersonated singer/songwriter Neil Diamond.

Bobby "Boris" Pickett
Born February 11, 1938, Somerville, Massachusetts
1962—*The Original Monster Mash* (Garpax).

Bobby "Boris" Pickett's ticket to fame was an ability to imitate monster-movie star Boris Karloff, something he put to good use on the novelty hit "Monster Mash," a #1 in 1962.

After three years in the Signal Corps in Korea, Pickett had drifted to Hollywood, where he attempted to establish himself as a comedian and actor. He appeared in 1967's *It's a Bikini World,* and later appeared in a number of television episodes (on *Bonanza, The Beverly Hillbillies, Petticoat Junction*), on television commercials, and in a few movies (*The Baby Maker*). After joining a singing group called the Cordials, he and group member Leonard Capizzi wrote "Monster Mash." Gary Paxton—Flip of Skip and Flip fame and the lead singer on the Hollywood Argyles' novelty hit "Alley Oop"—released it on his own Garpax label. There were a few less successful followups: "Monster's Holiday" (#30, 1962), "Monster Motion" (1963), and "Graduation Day" (#88, 1963). His backup group, the Crypt-Kickers, included Leon Russell and Paxton.

He continued to work as an actor and has since written screenplays, but "Monster Mash" has proven the hit that will not die. A Halloween tradition now, it was revived in 1973, and hit #3 in the U.K and #10 in the U.S. In the mid-Eighties Pickett recorded a "Monster Rap" that got some airplay. According to an interview from that period, Pickett claimed to have last performed "Monster Mash" in a Sunset Strip club backed by none other than the then-unknown Van Halen.

Wilson Pickett
Born March 18, 1941, Prattville, Alabama
1965—*In the Midnight Hour* (Atlantic)   1966—*The Exciting Wilson Pickett*   1967—*The Wicked*

Pickett; The Sound of Wilson Pickett; The Best of Wilson Pickett 1968—*I'm in Love; The Midnight Mover* 1969—*Hey Jude* 1970—*Right On* 1971—*Don't Knock My Love* 1973—*Mr. Magic Man* (RCA) 1974—*Tonight I'm My Biggest Audience; Miz Lenas Boy* 1977—*Join Me and Let's Be Free* 1978—*A Funky Situation* (Big Tree) 1979—*I Want You* (EMI) 1981—*The Right Track* 1987—*American Soul Man* (Motown) 1992—*A Man and a Half: The Best of Wilson Pickett* (Rhino/Atlantic).

Singer Wilson Pickett applied his rough, swaggering, "wicked" style to a series of stripped-down soul classics to create one of the most enduring soul legacies.

After his family migrated from Alabama to Detroit in 1955, young Pickett formed a gospel group, the Violinaires (which included Eddie Floyd and Sir Mack Rice), who were popular in local churches. In 1959 he was recruited by the R&B vocal group the Falcons. He wrote and sang lead on the Falcons' "I Found a Love" (#6 R&B, 1962). Falcons producer Robert Bateman suggested he go solo, and Pickett signed with Lloyd Price's Double L Records in 1963 and had hits with two of his songs, "If You Need Me" (#30 R&B) and "It's Too Late" (#17 R&B).

In 1964 Pickett signed with Atlantic. Following two unsuccessful singles, Atlantic executive/producer Jerry Wexler took Pickett to Memphis, where he recorded with Booker T. and the MG's. "In the Midnight Hour" (#21, 1965), credited to Pickett and guitarist/producer Steve Cropper, was a major breakthrough. Recording in a similar style with musicians in Memphis, Muscle Shoals, and Miami, Pickett had a long series of R&B hits that occasionally crossed over to pop, including "634-5789" (#13 pop, #1 R&B) and "Land of 1,000 Dances" (#6 pop, #1 R&B) in 1966; "Funky Broadway" (#8 pop, #1 R&B) in 1967; "I'm a Midnight Mover" (#6 R&B) in 1968; and the tribute record "Cole, Cooke, and Redding" (#61 pop, #4 R&B) in 1970.

Later that year he recorded in Philadelphia with the Gamble and Huff production team, scoring with "Engine Number 9" (#14 pop, #3 R&B, 1970) and "Don't Let the Green Grass Fool You" (#17 pop, #2 R&B, 1971). Pickett's last three Atlantic hits were "Don't Knock My Love" (#13 pop, #1 R&B, 1971), "Call My Name, I'll Be There" (#10 R&B, 1971), and "Fire and Water" (#24 pop, #2 R&B, 1972). In March 1971 Pickett headlined a tour of American and African musicians in Ghana. The resulting film and album, *Soul to Soul*, featured Pickett prominently.

Pickett signed to RCA Records in 1973, followed by stints with his own Wicked label, Big Tree, and EMI America, but none of his later releases proved as popular as his earlier work. He continues to tour and record, and beginning in the Eighties joined Don Covay, Joe Tex, and other Sixties soul legends in the Soul Clan. In 1991 he was inducted into the Rock and Roll Hall of Fame.

Pink Floyd

Formed 1965, London, England
Syd Barrett (b. Roger Keith Barrett, Jan. 6, 1946, Cambridge, Eng.) gtr., voc.; Richard Wright (b. July 28, 1945, London), kybds., voc.; Roger Waters (b. Sep. 6, 1944, Surrey, Eng.), bass, voc.; Nick Mason (b. Jan. 27, 1945, Birmingham, Eng.), drums.
1967—*The Piper at the Gates of Dawn* (Tower) 1968—(+ David Gilmour [b. Mar. 6, 1944, Cambridge, Eng.], gtr., voc.) *A Saucerful of Secrets* (Harvest) 1969—(– Barrett) *More* soundtrack; *Ummagumma* 1970—*Atom Heart Mother* 1971—*Meddle; Relics* 1972—*Music from La Vallee: Obscured by Clouds* soundtrack 1973—*The Dark Side of the Moon; A Nice Pair* (reissue of first two LPs) 1975—*Wish You Were Here* (Columbia) 1977—*Animals* 1979—*The Wall* 1981—*A Collection of Great Dance Songs* 1982—(– Wright) 1983—*The Final Cut; Works* (Capitol) 1984—(– Waters) 1987—(+ Wright) *A Momentary Lapse of Reason* 1988—*Delicate Sound of Thunder* 1992—*Shine On* (Columbia) 1994—*The Division Bell* 1995—*Pulse.*
Roger Waters solo: 1984—*The Pros and Cons of Hitch Hiking* (Columbia) 1987—*Radio K.A.O.S.* 1990—*The Wall—Live in Berlin* (Mercury) 1992—*Amused to Death* (Columbia).
David Gilmour solo: 1978—*David Gilmour* (Columbia) 1984—*About Face.*
Richard Wright solo: 1978—*Wet Dream* (Harvest) 1984—*Identity.*
Nick Mason solo: 1981—*Nick Mason's Fictitious Sports* (Columbia) 1985—*Profiles.*
Syd Barrett solo: See entry.

With the release of 1973's *The Dark Side of the Moon*, Pink Floyd abruptly went from a moderately successful

Pink Floyd: Rick Wright, David Gilmour, Nick Mason, Roger Waters

acid-rock band to one of pop music's biggest acts. The recording, in fact, remained on Billboard's Top 200 album chart longer than any other release in history. Along with 1979's The Wall, it established the band as purveyors of a distinctively dark vision. Experimenting with concept albums and studio technology and breaking free of conventional pop song formats, Pink Floyd prefigured the progressive rock of the Seventies and ambient music of the Eighties.

As early as 1964 Pink Floyd's original members, except Syd Barrett, were together studying architecture at London's Regent Street Polytechnic School. With Barrett, an art student who coined the name the Pink Floyd Sound after a favorite blues record by Pink Anderson and Floyd Council, they began playing R&B-based material for schoolmates. By 1967 they had developed an unmistakably psychedelic sound: long, loud suitelike compositions that touched on hard rock, blues, country, folk, electronic, and quasi-classical music. Adding a slide and light show, one of the first in British rock, they became a sensation among London's underground as a featured attraction at the UFO Club. Barrett, who was responsible for most of the band's early material, had a knack for composing singles-length bits of psychedelia, and Pink Floyd had British hits with two of them in 1967: "Arnold Layne," the tale of a transvestite (#20 U.K.), and "See Emily Play" (#6 U.K.). The latter, however, was the last U.K. hit single they would have for over a decade; space-epic titles like "Astronomy Domine" and "Interstellar Overdrive" were more typical.

In 1968 Barrett, allegedly because of an excess of LSD experimentation, began to exhibit ever more strange and erratic behavior. David Gilmour joined to help with the guitar work. Barrett appeared on only one track of Secrets, "Jugband Music," which aptly summed up his mental state: "I'm most obliged to you for making it clear/That I'm not really here." He left the band, entered a hospital, and remained in seclusion. Without Barrett to create concise psychedelic singles, the band concentrated on wider-ranging psychedelic epics.

From 1969 to 1972 Pink Floyd made several film soundtracks—the most dramatic being Zabriskie Point, in which Michelangelo Antonioni's closing sequence of explosions was complemented by Floyd's "Careful with That Axe, Eugene"—and began using in concert its "azimuth coordinated sound system," a sophisticated 360-degree P.A. With Atom Heart Mother, they topped the British chart in 1970; stateside success, however, still eluded them.

Their breakthrough came in 1973 with The Dark Side of the Moon. The themes were unremittingly bleak—alienation, paranoia, schizophrenia—and the music was at once sterile and doomy. Taped voices mumbling ominous asides (something the band had used before) surfaced at key moments. Yielding a surprise American hit

in "Money," (#13, 1973), the album went on to mammoth long-running sales success. Ultimately remaining on the Billboard Top 200 album chart for 741 weeks, Dark Side showcased the talents of Pink Floyd's chief members: Waters' lyrics, Gilmour's guitar. The two would continue to dominate the band but soon furiously contend against each other.

The group's subsequent albums explored the same territory, with Waters' songs growing ever more bitter. Wish You Were Here (#1, 1975) was dedicated to Barrett and elegized him with "Shine On You Crazy Diamond." The Wall, Waters' finest moment, topped the U.S. chart for 15 weeks, while its nihilistic hit, "Another Brick in the Wall," was banned by the BBC and in 1980 became the band's only #1 American single. Meanwhile Pink Floyd's stage shows had become increasingly elaborate. For the Dark Side and Wish tours, there were slide/light shows and animated films, plus a giant inflated jet that crashed into the stage; for Animals, huge inflated pigs hovered over the stadiums; for The Wall (due to enormous expense, performed 29 times only in New York, Los Angeles, and London) there was an actual wall built, brick by brick, across the stage, eventually obscuring the band from audience view. Shortly thereafter, Wright left, due to conflict with Waters.

With The Final Cut (#6, 1983), subtitled "a requiem for the postwar dream," Waters penned his darkest work yet. It also marked the effective end of the original Pink Floyd, with Waters bitterly departing, and Gilmour and Mason cementing their alliance.

(Two films related to the original band—minus Barrett—have been made: the documentary Pink Floyd Live At Pompeii [1971] and The Wall [1982]. The latter featured stunning animation by Gerald Scarfe—Bob Geldof starred in the live-action sequences—and illustrated music from Pink Floyd's LP of the same name. The first remains a cult movie; the second was a massive commercial success.)

In 1978, with Gilmour's David Gilmour and Wright's Wet Dream, Pink Floyd's members had started releasing solo albums. Mason had begun a sideline career as a producer in 1974 with Robert Wyatt; ultimately his very diverse roster included Gong, Carla Bley, the Damned, and Steve Hillage. Solo work continued in the Eighties: In 1984 came Waters' The Pros and Cons of Hitch Hiking, Wright's Identity, and Gilmour's About Face (with lyrical contributions by Pete Townshend). A year later Mason released Profiles. Concurrently, Gilmour played sessions with Bryan Ferry, Grace Jones, and Arcadia; in 1986 he formed David Gilmour & Friends with Bad Company's Mick Ralphs.

In 1986 Waters brought suit against Gilmour and Mason, asking the court to dissolve the trio's partnership and to block them from using the name Pink Floyd. A year later Waters lost his suit, and the other members, as

Pink Floyd, released *Momentary Lapse of Reason* (#3, 1987). As Waters put out his own *Radio K.A.O.S.*, the others launched a Pink Floyd tour that grossed nearly $30 million. (Though Wright was included on the tour and album, he wasn't legally considered an official band member but a salaried employee.) With the live *Delicate Sound of Thunder*, Gilmour, Mason, and Wright again billed themselves as Pink Floyd and went on to more successful touring, including a gig performed in Venice aboard a giant barge that was televised world-wide.

In 1990 Waters presented an all-star cast, including Sinéad O'Connor, Joni Mitchell, and Van Morrison, in a version of *The Wall* performed at the site of the Berlin Wall (chronicled in *The Wall—Live in Berlin*). Two years later he released the dour *Amused to Death*.

With Wright rejoining Gilmour and Mason as a full band member, Pink Floyd garnered immediate success with *The Division Bell* in 1994. Named after the bell in the British House of Commons that summons members to parliamentary debate, the album featured songs written by Gilmour in collaboration with his ex-journalist girlfriend Polly Samson. Two weeks after its release, *The Division Bell* shot to #1 on the album chart, and in late spring the band embarked on an elaborate tour, which attracted over five million fans. "Marooned," from *Division Bell*, won the 1994 Grammy for Best Rock Instrumental Performance.

Pulse (#1, 1995) documented the '94 tour, including a live performance of *Dark Side of the Moon* in its entirety.

Gene Pitney

Born February 17, 1941, Hartford, Connecticut
1962—*The Many Sides of Gene Pitney* (Musicor);
Only Love Can Break a Heart*   1963—*World-Wide
Winners*   1964—*Gene Pitney's Big Sixteen*; *It Hurts
***to Be in Love*   1965—*Famous Country Duets* (with**
George Jones and Melba Montgomery); *George*
Jones and Gene Pitney* (with George Jones); *Look-
***ing Through the Eyes of Love*   1966—*Big Sixteen*,**
vol. 3   1968—*Double Gold: The Best of Gene Pitney*
1969—*Sings Bacharach*   1987—*The Gene Pitney*
Anthology, 1961–1968* (Rhino)   1995—*Gene Pitney:
***The Great Recordings* (Tomato).**

Gene Pitney's long and varied career includes over 20 chart-making singles, and just as many albums, spanning rock, pop ballads, and Italian-flavored country novelties, and work and friendship with Phil Spector, the Rolling Stones, and country singer George Jones. Best known for singing pop covers, Pitney also wrote many tunes himself. His biggest hits include "Town Without Pity" (#13, 1962), "(The Man Who Shot) Liberty Valance" (#4, 1962), "Only Love Can Break a Heart" (#2, 1962), "Half Heaven—Half Heartache" (#12, 1963), "Mecca" (#12,

1963), "It Hurts to Be in Love" (#7, 1964), and "I'm Gonna Be Strong" (#9, 1964).

Pitney studied piano, guitar, and drums while at Rockville High School in Connecticut, and by the time he graduated he'd already written and published some songs. Not long after he dropped out of the University of Connecticut, he began performing as the male half of the duo Jamie and Jane, then as a singer/songwriter under the name Billy Brian. By 1961 he had written "Hello Mary Lou" for Rick Nelson. In 1962 he wrote "He's a Rebel" for the Crystals and became friends with producer Phil Spector. He also wrote for Roy Orbison and Tommy Edwards.

Yearning for a hit of his own, Pitney locked himself in a studio in 1961, played and overdubbed every instrument and multitracked his vocals. The result was his first hit, "(I Wanna) Love My Life Away" (#39, 1961). This attracted the attention of the songwriting team of Burt Bacharach and Hal David, who cowrote "Only Love Can Break a Heart," "(The Man Who Shot) Liberty Valance," and "24 Hours from Tulsa" for him. Pitney's label, Musicor, was primarily involved in country & western music, and Pitney began recording material in that vein, including an album of duets with George Jones.

In 1964 Pitney's publicist, Andrew Loog Oldham, introduced him to the Rolling Stones, whom Oldham produced. He recorded the Jagger-Richards composition "That Girl Belongs to Yesterday" and with Phil Spector sat in on one of their 1964 recording sessions. Though he was much more popular in England than in America, Pitney remained a prolific recording artist, putting out many albums per year in the mid-Sixties. At that time, in response to his tremendous popularity in Italy, he began recording albums of country tunes sung in Italian. His last U.S. chart appearance was in 1969, and he continued to hit the U.K. chart until 1974.

Since the mid-Seventies, Pitney has toured the U.S. infrequently, but continued to work elsewhere in the world. He has recorded in Italian, Spanish, and German. In 1988 a remake of "Something's Gotten Hold of My Heart," recorded with Marc Almond, went to #1 in the U.K. Five years later, Pitney finally returned to the U.S. concert stage for the first time in nearly two decades with a sold-out appearance at Carnegie Hall. Pitney divides his time between touring (largely overseas) and managing his sizable business empire, which includes the Crystal Lake Beach and Boat Club in Connecticut, where he slung hamburgers as a teen.

Pixies/The Breeders/Frank Black

Formed 1986, Boston, Massachusetts
Black Francis (b. Charles Michael Kitteridge
Thompson IV, ca. 1965, Long Beach, Calif.), gtr.,
voc.; Joey Santiago (b. June 10, 1965, Manila, Philip-

Grammy Awards

Robert Palmer
1986 Best Rock Vocal Performance, Male: "Addicted to Love"
1988 Best Rock Vocal Performance, Male: "Simply Irresistible"

Charlie Parker
1974 Best Jazz Performance by a Soloist: *First Recordings!*
1984 Lifetime Achievement Award

Ray Parker Jr.
1984 Best Pop Instrumental Performance: "Ghostbusters (Instrumental Version)"

Dolly Parton
1978 Best Country Vocal Performance, Female: *Here You Come Again*
1981 Best Country Vocal Performance, Female: "9 to 5"
1981 Best Country Song: "9 to 5"
1987 Best Country Performance by a Duo or Group with Vocal: *Trio* (with Linda Ronstadt and Emmylou Harris)

Billy Paul
1972 Best R&B Vocal Performance, Male: "Me and Mrs. Jones"

Les Paul
1976 Best Country Instrumental Performance: *Chester and Lester* (with Chet Atkins)
1983 Trustees Award

Carl Perkins
1986 Best Spoken Word or Non-Musical Recording: *Interviews*

from the Class of '55 Recording Sessions (with others)

Peter, Paul and Mary
1962 Best Folk Recording: "If I Had a Hammer"
1962 Best Performance by a Vocal Group: "If I Had a Hammer"
1963 Best Folk Recording: "Blowin' in the Wind"
1963 Best Performance by a Vocal Group: "Blowin' in the Wind"
1969 Best Recording for Children: *Peter, Paul and Mommy*

Tom Petty [See Traveling Wilburys]

Pink Floyd
1994 Best Rock Instrumental Performance: "Marooned"

Pointer Sisters
1974 Best Country Vocal Performance by a Duo or Group: "Fairytale"
1984 Best Pop Performance by a Duo or Group with Vocal: "Jump (for My Love)"
1984 Best Vocal Arrangement for Two or More Voices: "Automatic"

The Police [See also: Sting]
1980 Best Rock Instrumental Performance: "Regatta de Blanc"
1981 Best Rock Performance by a Duo or Group with Vocal: "Don't Stand So Close to Me"
1981 Best Rock Instrumental Performance: "Behind My Camel"
1983 Best Pop Performance by a

Duo or Group with Vocal: "Every Breath You Take"
1983 Best Rock Performance by a Duo or Group with Vocal: *Synchronicity*

Elvis Presley
1967 Best Sacred Performance: "How Great Thou Art"
1971 Lifetime Achievement Award
1972 Best Inspirational Performance: "He Touched Me"
1974 Best Inspirational Performance: "How Great Thou Art"

Billy Preston
1972 Album of the Year: *The Concert for Bangla Desh* (with others)
1972 Best Pop Instrumental Performance by an Instrumental Performer: "Outa-Space"

Prince
1984 Best Rock Performance by a Duo or Group with Vocal: *Purple Rain* (with the Revolution)
1984 Best New Rhythm and Blues Song: "I Feel for You"
1984 Best Album of Original Score Written for a Motion Picture or a Television Special: *Purple Rain* (with John L. Nelson and Wendy and Lisa)
1986 Best R&B Performance by a Duo or Group with Vocal: "Kiss" (with the Revolution)

John Prine
1991 Best Contemporary Folk Album: *The Missing Years*

---

pines), gtr.; Kim Deal (b. June 10, 1961, Dayton, Ohio), bass, voc.; David Lovering (b. Dec. 6, 1961, Boston), drums.
1987—*Come On Pilgrim* EP (4AD)   1988—*Surfer Rosa*   1989—*Doolittle* (Elektra)   1990—*Bossanova*   1991—*Trompe le Monde.*
The Breeders: 1990—(Deal; Tanya Donelly [b. July 14, 1966, Newport, R.I.], gtr., voc.; Josephine Wiggs [b. Brighton, Eng.], bass, cello, voc.; Shannon Doughton [a.k.a. Mike Hunt, b. Britt Walford,

Louisville, Ky.], drums) *Pod* (Elektra)   1992— (+ Kelley Deal [b. June 10, 1961, Dayton, Ohio], gtr., voc.) *Safari* EP   1993—(– Donelly; – Walford; + James Macpherson [b. June 23, 1966, Ohio], drums) *Last Splash.*
Black Francis, as Frank Black, solo: 1993—*Frank Black* (Elektra)   1994—*Teenager of the Year.*

With seductive pop melodies, distorted surf riffs, extraterrestrial lyrics, and leader Black Francis' deranged shrieks, the Pixies came off like Beach Boys on acid. Quintessential college rockers, the Pixies fared particularly well in England, where they attracted an impressive following and scored minor aboveground hits with singles such as "Monkey Gone to Heaven" and "Velouria"; in the U.S. they remained primarily critics' darlings and a major influence on such bands as Nirvana. When the quartet split up in 1992, bassist Kim Deal went on to greater success with the Breeders.

Charles Michael Kitteridge Thompson IV got his first taste of pop music making as an adolescent living in the Los Angeles suburbs and messing around with instruments in the garage. However, when his Pentecostal mother and stepfather moved the family to New England, rock & roll slipped to the back burner. It wasn't until the mid-Eighties—six months into his stint as a U-Mass exchange student in Puerto Rico—that the astronomy-obsessed Thompson gave himself a choice: He would either go to New Zealand to see Halley's comet or form a band.

In 1986 Thompson returned to Boston and recruited former college roommate Joey Santiago, who came from one of the wealthiest families in the Philippines, to play guitar. Naming themselves Pixies in Panoply, they took out a newspaper ad for a bassist interested in Hüsker Dü and Peter, Paul and Mary. Ohio native Kim Deal responded and brought along her drummer friend David Lovering. On the advice of his biological father, a biker and bar owner, Thompson adopted the stage name Black Francis.

The Pixies released their debut EP on England's arty 4AD label in 1987, and followed the next year with the full-length *Surfer Rosa*. After much domestic college-radio play and critical raves, the band signed with Elektra in 1989 and released the landmark *Doolittle*. Meanwhile the Pixies were falling apart due to a power struggle between songwriters Thompson and Deal, the latter of whom had already formed the Breeders along with Throwing Muses guitarist Tanya Donelly and released the critically acclaimed *Pod* back-to-back with the Pixies' *Bossanova*. *Trompe le Monde* continued the Pixies' space theme, but the spark was gone.

For his solo album under new pseudonym Frank Black, Thompson recruited Santiago, members of Pere Ubu, and various session players. The album found the eccentric songwriter moving closer than ever to Brian Wilson territory, even doing an appropriate cover of Wilson's *Pet Sounds*-era classic, "Hang Onto Your Ego." The Breeders' second full-length album, *Last Splash* (#33, 1994)—recorded without Donelly, who left to form Belly—was a critical smash, spawning the single "Cannonball" (#44, 1994).

Robert Plant

Born August 20, 1948, Bromwich, England
1982—*Pictures at 11* (Swan Song)   1983—*The Prin-*ciple of Moments* (Es Paranza)   1985—*Shaken 'n' Stirred*   1988—*Now and Zen*   1990—*Manic Nirvana*   1993—*Fate of Nations*.
With the Honeydrippers: 1984—*Volume One* (Es Paranza).
With Jimmy Page: 1994—*No Quarter: Jimmy Page and Robert Plant Unledded* (Atlantic).

Since Led Zeppelin's breakup, singer Robert Plant has consistently refused to rest on his laurels, instead producing a series of progressive albums that have been critical and commercial successes. In the Eighties and Nineties, he has been musically more interested in hip-hop, punk, and world musics than the heavy metal or classic rock of Zeppelin imitators. In 1994, however, after repeatedly blocking any long-term Led Zeppelin reunions, Plant joined Page to perform Led Zep songs, along with new compositions, for an MTV *Unplugged* performance, entitled *Unledded*, and an album, *No Quarter*.

Plant's first return to music after Zeppelin drummer John Bonham's death were jam sessions with a group of local R&B musicians called the Honeydrippers. He produced and wrote *Pictures at 11* (#5, 1982) with Robbie Blunt on guitar, Paul Martinez on bass, and Jezz Woodruffe on keyboards. *The Principle of Moments* (#8, 1983) was the first release by Plant's Atlantic-distributed label Es Paranza. Its music ranged from the artsy "Big Log" (#20, 1983) to the more traditional "In the Mood" (#39, 1983). In 1983 Plant went on his first solo tour.

In 1985 Plant undertook a couple of side projects: the Crawling King Snakes with Phil Collins, who recorded a cut for the *Porky's Revenge* soundtrack; and a Honeydrippers EP. The latter, which reunited Plant with Zeppelin guitarist Jimmy Page (and included Jeff Beck and Nile Rodgers), went Top Five and produced hits with the string-drenched ballad "Sea of Love" (#3, 1984) and "Rockin' at Midnight" (#25, 1985). He and Page also played live with John Paul Jones at 1985's Live Aid benefit concert. On *Shaken 'n' Stirred* (#20, 1985) Plant experimented with hip-hop motifs, synthesizers, and intricate rhythms supplied by Little Feat drummer Richie Hayward. The album was strikingly noncommercial, though it did yield the minor hit "Little by Little" (#36, 1985). Plant broke up his band after a subsequent tour. Listening to a pile of demo tapes, he discovered keyboardist Phil Johnstone, with whom he has collaborated since. Johnstone and Plant cowrote seven of the nine songs on the platinum *Now and Zen* (#6, 1988), which featured guitarist Doug Boyle, bassist Charlie Jones, and drummer Chris Blackwell. The album was widely acclaimed for its mix of old and new: "Tall Cool One" (#25, 1988) featured a solo from Page and samples of old Zeppelin songs. The track was partially a response to the Beastie Boys' heavy reliance on a sample of Led Zeppelin's "The Ocean" for their song "She's Crafty." "Tall Cool One" was later used in a Coke commercial.

Plant contributed the song "The Only One" to Page's 1988 *Outrider* album. In 1989 he recorded "Smoke on the Water" with Ian Gillan, Brian May, and Bruce Dickinson to benefit victims of a massive earthquake in Armenia. Plant worked with the same crew from *Zen* on *Manic Nirvana* (#13, 1990), which, though well received critically, went only gold. On *Fate of Nations* he "went back to the misty mountains," as he put it, playing folksy songs influenced by his rediscovery of Sixties West Coast groups like Moby Grape. Plant continued to work with Johnstone and Jones and added guitarists Kevin Scott MacMichael (Cutting Crew) and Francis Dunnery (It Bites). The album featured appearances by classical violinist Nigel Kennedy, Clannad singer Maire Brennan, and guitarist Richard Thompson. The first single was a cover of Tim Hardin's folk-rock classic "If I Were a Carpenter."

No Quarter illustrated Plant's interest in Arabic music, with two (of three) new songs recorded in Marrakech, Morocco, backed by Gnaoui musicians. Other world musicians guested on the album, including Indian ghazal singer Najma Akhtar on a new version of "The Battle of Evermore." In 1995 Plant joined Page in a tour to support the album.

The Plasmatics

Formed 1978, New York City, New York
Wendy Orleans Williams (b. 1951, New York City), voc., chainsaw, machine gun; Richard Stotts, gtr.; Chosei Funahara, bass; Wes Beech, gtr.; Stu Deutsch, drums.
1980—(– Funahara; + Jean Beauvoir, bass) 1981— *New Hope for the Wretched* (Stiff); *Beyond the Valley of 1984* (– Deutsch; – Beauvoir); *Metal Priestess* 1982—*Coup d'Etat* (Capitol).
Wendy O. Williams solo: 1984—*W.O.W.* (Passport) 1986—*Kommander of Kaos* (Gigasus) 1987—*Maggots: The Record* (Profile) 1988—*Deffest! And Baddest!* (Deffest Disc/Profile).
Jean Beauvoir solo: 1986—*Drums Along the Mohawk* (Columbia) 1988—*Jacknifed.*

The original Plasmatics were a sex-and-violence-touting heavy-metal band that debuted in the New York punk clubs in 1978. They were fronted by barely dressed ex-topless dancer Wendy O. Williams (W.O.W. for short), whose early act included smashing televisions with a sledgehammer, blowing up Cadillac Coupe de Villes, cutting guitars in half with a chainsaw, and singing.

Essentially, the band was the brainchild of manager Rod Swenson, a Yale graduate with a master's degree in fine arts. During the Seventies he came to New York, dubbed himself Captain Kink, and began producing and

The Plasmatics: Wes Beech, Jean Beauvoir, Wendy O. Williams, Richie Stotts

promoting live sex shows. One of his stars was Williams (who was raised on a farm in upstate New York and ran away at 16). After his work in porn, Swenson did videos for Patti Smith and the Ramones, which inspired him to start a band, with Williams fingering herself and demolishing things up front, backed by a guitarist (Richard Stotts) with a blue Mohawk cut who wore a nurse's uniform and sometimes a tutu, plus other visual gimmicks. The band's music was all fast and loud, and the lyrics were about murder, sex, and fast food.

The Plasmatics debuted at CBGB on July 26, 1978, and immediately got lots of media coverage for their antics. An audience began to grow, especially in England, where they stressed their connection to heavy metal. Williams kept up her stunts, as on September 12, 1980, when she jumped out of a brakeless car just before it plunged into the Hudson River. The band's debut album sold marginally, as did their followup, *Beyond the Valley of 1984*. On January 18, 1981, Williams was arrested on obscenity charges in Milwaukee. She was arrested on similar charges in Cleveland the next day. She and Swenson were also charged with resisting arrest and disorderly conduct after an altercation with the police, which landed both in a Milwaukee hospital. They later sued and lost their case. In 1982 the band signed with Capitol. Beauvoir joined Little Steven and the Disciples of Soul in 1982. Neither of his solo albums did well commercially.

Williams continues to tour and record, at times with a Plasmatics lineup. A fitness and health-food enthusiast, Williams has also pursued an acting career in film (*Reform School Girls,* 1986) and television (*McGyver,* 1990). Stotts went on to form the Richie Stotts Experience.

The Platters

Formed 1953, Los Angeles, California
Tony Williams (b. Apr. 15, 1928, Roselle, N.J.;
d. Aug. 14, 1992), lead voc.; David Lynch (b. 1929, St.
Louis, Mo.; d. Jan. 2, 1981), tenor voc.; Herbert Reed
(b. 1931, Kansas City, Mo.), bass voc.; Alex Hodge,
baritone voc.
1954—(+ Zola Taylor [b. 1934], contralto voc.)
1955—(– Hodge; + Paul Robi [b. 1931, New Orleans,
La.; d. Feb. 1, 1989], baritone voc.)   1960—*Encore of*
***Golden Hits* (Mercury) (– Williams)   1961—**
(+ Sonny Turner [b. ca. 1939, Cleveland, Ohio], lead
voc.)   1962—(– Robi; – Taylor; + Nate Nelson
[b. Apr. 10, 1932, New York City, N.Y.; d. June 1,
1984], baritone voc.; + Sandra Dawn [b. New York
City, N.Y.], contralto voc.)   1965—(Original lineup
disbands)   1986—*Anthology (1955–1967)* (Rhino)
1991—*The Very Best of the Platters* (Mercury); *The*
Magic Touch: An Anthology.

During the Platters' peak years (1955 to 1960), they were led by Tony Williams and enjoyed a series of massive crossover hits that made them the preeminent black vocal group of the time.

Original members Tony Williams, David Lynch, Alex Hodge, and Herb Reed were signed by manager Buck Ram to Federal Records in 1953. After some unsuccessful efforts, Ram replaced Hodge with Paul Robi and added Zola Taylor, who belonged to Shirley Gunter and the Queens (a group fronted by the sister of Cornel Gunter, of the Flairs and the Coasters). The Platters' seventh Federal single, "Only You," was their first regional hit. Along with another vocal group Ram managed, the Penguins, they were signed in a package deal to Mercury.

At Mercury they became one of the nation's top vocal groups and a major nightclub attraction. A new version of "Only You" (#5) along with "The Great Pretender," which hit #1 in February 1956, made 1955 a breakthrough year. In 1956 they appeared in two rock films, *The Girl Can't Help It* and *Rock Around the Clock*.

Other major hits for the Platters were "The Magic Touch" (#4 pop and R&B), "My Prayer" (#1 pop, #2 R&B), "You'll Never Know" (#11 pop, #9 R&B) in 1956; "I'm Sorry" (#23 pop, #15 R&B) in 1957; "Twilight Time" (#1 pop and R&B) and "Smoke Gets in Your Eyes" (#1 pop, #3 R&B) in 1958; and "Enchanted" (#12 pop, #9 R&B), in 1959. The Platters were very popular in England and in Australia, where virtually all of these singles were hits as well and "Smoke" went to #1.

In the summer of 1959 the group suffered a setback in popularity after the four male members were arrested in Cincinnati and accused of having had sexual relations with four female minors, among them three white girls. Although the men were acquitted, public reaction to the incident led some radio stations to pull their latest single, "Where," off the air.

The Platters' last Top Ten single was 1960's "Harbor Lights," although they had several more Top Forty singles, including "If I Didn't Care" in 1961. Williams went solo and was replaced as lead singer by Sonny Turner in 1961, but Mercury continued to release old Williams-led singles through 1964. Off the charts from 1961 to 1966, the Platters changed lineup in 1962, with Sandra Dawn replacing Taylor and Nate Nelson taking Robi's spot. At the Musicor label they had a limited comeback with "I Love You 1000 Times" (#31 pop, #6 R&B, 1966) and "With This Ring" (#14 pop, #12 R&B, 1967).

There followed wholesale personnel changes and releases on United Artists before a return to Mercury in 1974. Williams and Ram battled in court during the Seventies over the rights to the name Platters; Ram won the case. In 1989, however, the rights were returned to Robi, and in 1995 Robi's widow won back from Ram the writing and publishing interests to much of the Platters' catalogue. There have been several groups of Platters performing through the years. Zola Taylor made news in the late Eighties, when she was one of three women claiming to have been Frankie Lymon's widow. Paul Robi's daughter Franchesca leads a latterday version of the group. The Platters were inducted into the Rock and Roll Hall of Fame in 1990.

Plimsouls: See Peter Case

PMD: See EPMD

PM Dawn

Formed 1989, Jersey City, New Jersey
Prince Be, a.k.a. "the Nocturnal" (b. Attrell Cordes,
May 19, 1970, Jersey City), voc.; DJ Minutemix,
a.k.a. "J.C. the Eternal" (b. Jarrett Cordes, July 17,
1971, Jersey City), DJ.
1991—*Of the Heart, of the Soul and of the Cross:*
***The Utopian Experience* (Gee Street/Island)   1993—**
The Bliss Album . . . ? (Vibrations of Love and Anger
and the Ponderance of Life and Existence).

PM Dawn was the most pop-oriented, psychedelic, and (with Arrested Development) popular of the wave of early Nineties "alternative rap" groups. An unlikely synthesis of Brian Wilson and De La Soul—of lushly harmonized, vocal-dominated pop melodicism and exotically eclectic, flower-powered hip-hop—PM Dawn's critically acclaimed debut album *Of the Heart, of the Soul and of the Cross* found rotund, introspective vocalist and songwriter Prince Be singing (both leads and layered harmonies) as often as rapping, with equal aplomb.

Attrell and Jarrett Cordes' stepfather, a percussionist with Kool and the Gang, set Attrell's mystical course early by giving him a Donovan album. The brothers' tastes broadened through discarded 45s their garbageman uncle brought them. After graduating high school, they became Prince Be and DJ Minutemix of PM Dawn (inspired by the scripture, "in the darkest hour comes the light"). Tiny Warlock Records released their first single, "Ode to a Forgetful Mind," which found some success in England, where Gee Street Records signed the group.

PM Dawn went to London to record *Of the Heart* (#48, 1991), on which Prince Be sang "Reality Used to Be a Friend of Mine" and rapped about reincarnation in "Even After I Die"; there were also a Delta bluesslide-guitar break, a quotation from the Beatles' "Baby You're a Rich Man," and samples of Dr. John, Chick Corea, Hugh Masekela, and the Doobie Brothers. The album yielded pop hits in "Set Adrift on Memory Bliss" (#1, 1991), built on a sample of Spandau Ballet's "True," and "Paper Doll" (#28, 1992).

In January 1992 hard-core rapper KRS-One, a founder of the Stop the Violence movement, jumped onstage to attack (but not seriously harm) PM Dawn at a New York City show. It was retaliation for Prince Be's late-1991 comment to a magazine that "KRS-One says he wants to be a teacher, but a teacher of what?" Nine months later PM Dawn hit with "I'd Die Without You" (#3, 1992), a romantic ballad from the soundtrack of the Eddie Murphy movie *Boomerang. The Bliss Album . . . ?* (#30, 1993), which included Boy George's guest vocals on "More Than Likely" and a cover of the Beatles' "Norwegian Wood," produced the hit single, "Looking Through Patient Eyes" (#6, 1993).

Poco

Formed 1968, Los Angeles, California
Richie Furay (b. May 9, 1944, Yellow Springs, Ohio), gtr., voc.; Jim Messina (b. Dec. 5, 1947, Maywood, Calif.), gtr., voc.; Rusty Young (b. Feb. 23, 1946, Long Beach, Calif.), pedal steel gtr.; George Grantham (b. Nov. 20, 1947, Cordell, Okla.), drums, voc.; Randy Meisner (b. Mar. 8, 1946, Scottsbluff, Nebr.), bass, voc.
1969—*Pickin' Up the Pieces* (Epic) (– Meisner; Messina switches to bass)   1970—(+ Timothy B. Schmit [b. Oct. 30, 1947, Sacramento, Calif.], bass, voc.; Messina back to guitar) *Poco* (– Messina; + Paul Cotton [b. Feb. 26, 1943, Los Angeles], gtr., voc.)   1971—*Deliverin'; From the Inside*   1972—*A Good Feeling to Know*   1973—*Crazy Eyes* (– Furay)   1974—*Seven; Cantamos*   1975—*Head over Heels* (ABC); *The Very Best of Poco* (Epic)   1976—*Live; Rose of Cimarron* (ABC)   1977—*Indian Summer* (– Schmit; – Grantham; + Steve Chapman [b. Eng.], drums; + Charlie Harrison [b. Eng.], bass; + Kim Bullard [b. Atlanta, Ga.], kybds.)   1978—*Legend*   1980—*Under the Gun* (MCA)   1981—*Blue and Gray*   1982—*Cowboys and Englishmen; Ghost Town* (Atlantic)   1984—*Inamorata*   1989—(Original quintet re-forms) *Legacy* (RCA); *Crazy Loving: The Best of Poco 1975–1982* (MCA)   1990—*Poco: The Forgotten Trail* (Epic Legacy).

Country-rock band Poco started out in August 1968 with great commercial promise. Founders Richie Furay and Jim Messina were from Buffalo Springfield [see entry], and the L.A. country-rock scene was just beginning to peak. Rusty Young met Furay and Messina when he played pedal steel guitar on sessions for Buffalo Springfield's "Kind Woman." Young was asked to join another L.A. country-rock band, the Flying Burrito Brothers, but chose Poco. George Grantham had been a bandmate of Young's in Boenzee Cryque, a Colorado band that went to L.A., where it broke up. And Randy Meisner came from a rival Colorado band, the Poor. Furay also auditioned Gregg Allman (then with the Allman Joys) for the band, but it didn't work out.

The new band originally called itself Pogo, but Walt Kelly, the creator of the comic strip, sued, and the members changed the name to Poco. Within a month, Meisner quit (he soon joined Rick Nelson's Stone Canyon Band, then Linda Ronstadt, and then the Eagles in 1971). Several record companies considered signing Poco following its live L.A. debut in November 1968 at the Troubadour. Furay's Springfield contract with Atlantic complicated matters, but Poco was allowed to sign with Epic after the label traded Graham Nash to Atlantic (to form Crosby, Stills and Nash) in exchange for Poco.

Pickin' Up the Pieces sold over 100,000 copies. Following Meisner's departure, the band continued as a quartet until February 1970, when Tim B. Schmit (a veteran of local folk, surf, and pop groups) joined. Schmit had originally auditioned for Poco in 1968 but lost out to Meisner. This new five-member Poco recorded *Poco* and the live *Deliverin'* before Messina quit, claiming he was tired of touring. The guitarist/producer soon teamed up with Kenny Loggins.

Messina's replacement was Paul Cotton, former lead guitarist in a Buffalo Springfield–type band, the Illinois Speed Press. This lineup lasted for three LPs. In 1973, just after recording *Crazy Eyes,* Furay, frustrated with the band's poor financial prospects, left to form a quasi-supergroup, the Souther-Hillman-Furay Band, which disbanded after two LPs. He then pursued a commercially unrewarding solo career before turning his full attention to religion.

Furay's departure was expected to be fatal, but Poco's next four albums as a quartet through 1977 sold somewhat better than previous efforts. During these years, the Eagles dominated the field that Poco was expected to mine; and in 1977, after Meisner left that band,

Schmit replaced him. Drummer Grantham also quit, in January 1978.

With lone original member Young plus Cotton at the helm, the band finally hit in early 1979 with its 14th LP, *Legend* (#14). Poco now included an English rhythm section, Steve Chapman and Charlie Harrison (who'd played together eight years with Leo Sayer and Al Stewart), plus keyboardist Kim Bullard, who'd backed Crosby, Stills and Nash. The new lineup hit #17 with "Crazy Love" and then had a Top Twenty hit later that year with "Heart of the Night."

Poco's commercial success was brief, however, with subsequent albums returning to the band's previous level of sales. In 1989 the original group (with Poco's Jeff Porcaro sitting in for George Grantham on record) reformed for an album, *Legacy,* which produced two Top Forty hits: "Call It Love" (#18) and "Nothin' to Hide" (#39), the latter cowritten and produced by Poco admirer Richard Marx. The group toured in 1990 (with Steve Miller Band drummer Gary Mallaber in Grantham's place), but tensions soon arose between Furay, by then a minister in Boulder, Colorado, and the others. He soon left the group, which as of 1992 once again revolved around Young and Cotton.

The Pogues
Formed 1982, London, England
James Fearnley (b. Oct. 9, 1954, Manchester, Eng.), accordion; Jeremy "Jem" Max Finer (b. July 20, 1955, Stoke, Eng.), banjo, gtr.; Shane MacGowan (b. Shane Patrick Lysaght MacGowan, Dec. 25, 1957, Tunbridge Wells, Ire.), voc.; Andrew David Ranken (b. Nov. 13, 1953, London), drums; Cait O'Riordan, bass; Peter "Spider" Stacy (b. Dec. 14, 1958, London), whistle, voc.
1984—*Red Roses for Me* (Stiff, U.K.)   1985— (+ Philip Chevron [b. Jun. 17, 1957, Dublin, Ire.], gtr.) *Rum Sodomy & the Lash* (MCA)   1986— (– O'Riordan; + Darryl Hunt [b. May 4, 1950, Nottingham, Eng.], bass; + Terry Woods [b. Dec. 4, 1947, Dublin, Ire.], banjo) *Poguetry in Motion* EP   1988— *If I Should Fall from Grace with God* (Island) 1989—*Peace and Love*   1990—*Hell's Ditch*   1991— *Essential Pogues* (– MacGowan; + Joe Strummer [b. John Mellor, Aug. 21, 1952, Ankara, Turkey], voc.) 1993—(– Strummer) *Waiting for Herb* (Chameleon).

The musical equivalent of a pub crawl, the Pogues have staggered through a career that combines the instrumentation and tunes of traditional Irish music with the energy and attitude of punk. The band was formed in 1982 when Shane MacGowan, then a member of North London punk band the Nipple Erectors—later shortened to the Nips—saw Spider Stacy playing tin whistle in a London tube station. They hit it off and, along with Nip Jim Fearnley on guitar, began to perform traditional Irish tunes in London's streets and pubs. Calling themselves Pogue Mahone (Gaelic for "kiss my ass"), they recruited Finer, Ranken, and O'Riordan and added MacGowan's earthy, Joycean original songs to their repertoire. The sextet garnered a reputation as a drunkenly raucous live act, and in 1984 released a single, "Dark Streets of London," on their own, eponymous label. Their reputation increased when they were hired as the opening act on the Clash's 1984 tour. (Some of the Clash's political fury rubbed off, as the Pogues became vehemently anti-Thatcher.) They signed with Stiff Records that year and released *Red Roses for Me.*

Rum Sodomy & the Lash was produced by Elvis Costello, who married O'Riordan after she left the band. By then, the band had expanded to an octet. The Pogues did not record again until 1988. In the interim they appeared in Alex Cox's film *Straight to Hell* (1987) and moved to Island Records. Their initial release for the label, the Steve Lillywhite–produced *If I Should Fall from Grace with God* (#88, 1988), included the #2 U.K. hit, "Fairytale of New York," featuring singer/songwriter Kirsty MacColl [see entry]. The three Lillywhite-produced albums expanded the group's musical palette, adding Middle Eastern sounds on "Turkish Song of the Damned" from *God* and jazz stylings on *Peace and Love* (1989).

Finer and Stacy began to take on additional singing and writing chores as MacGowan's drinking (he claimed not to have spent a day completely sober since he was 14) began to interfere with his musical duties. He missed a series of 1988 U.S. dates opening for Bob Dylan, and by 1991 had become so unreliable he was asked to leave the band. He was replaced by former Clash singer Joe Strummer (who had produced 1990's *Hell's Ditch*). Strummer left in 1992, and Spider Stacy took over the vocals on 1993's *Waiting for Herb.*

In 1994 MacGowan resurfaced, performing with a new band, the Popes, for the first time on St. Patrick's Day at a London club. In 1994 the group recorded its first album, *The Snake,* filled with dark new songs by MacGowan.

Buster Poindexter: See David Johansen

The Pointer Sisters
Formed 1971, Oakland, California
Ruth Pointer (b. Mar. 19, 1946, Oakland); Anita Pointer (b. Jan. 23, 1948, Oakland); Bonnie Pointer (b. July 11, 1950, East Oakland, Calif.); June Pointer (b. Nov. 30, 1954, Oakland).
1973—*The Pointer Sisters* (Blue Thumb)   1974— *That's a Plenty; Live at the Opera House*   1975—

The Pointer Sisters: Ruth Pointer, Anita Pointer, June Pointer

Steppin' 1978—(– Bonnie) *Energy* (Planet) 1980—*Special Things* 1981—*Black and White* 1982—*So Excited* 1983—*Break Out* 1985—*Contact* (RCA) 1986—*Hot Together* 1988—*Serious Slammin'* 1989—*Greatest Hits* 1990—*Right Rhythm* (Motown) 1994—*Only Sisters Can Do That* (SBK).
Bonnie Pointer solo: 1978—*Bonnie Pointer* (Motown) 1979—*Bonnie Pointer II* 1984—*The Price Is Right* (Private).
Anita Pointer solo: 1987—*Love for What It Is* (RCA).

The Oakland-born Pointer sisters are a vocal group whose repertoire spans pop, jazz, country, and R&B, and has evoked comparisons to the Supremes and the Andrews Sisters. Their biggest hits—which didn't come until the Eighties—are soulful, high-powered pop. Both of the Pointer parents were ministers at the West Oakland Church of God. Singing in church was their only performing experience until Bonnie and June began singing in San Francisco clubs in 1969 as Pointers, a Pair. Anita joined them, and eventually San Francisco producer David Rubinson hired them as background vocalists on several records. In 1971 Bill Graham became their manager. From 1971 to 1973 the trio sang behind Elvin Bishop, Taj Mahal, Tower of Power, Dave Mason, Sylvester, Boz Scaggs, and Esther Phillips.

When the Pointers backed Elvin Bishop at Los Angeles' Whisky-a-Go-Go, Atlantic executive Jerry Wexler signed them. Two singles were cut with R&B veteran Wardell Quezergue; one, "Don't Try to Take the Fifth," was unsuccessfully released in 1972. That year, Ruth left her job as a keypunch operator to join her sisters. Rubinson helped the Pointers get out of contracts with Graham and Atlantic and signed them to ABC's Blue Thumb label.

In 1973 their self-titled debut, featuring Allen Toussaint's "Yes We Can Can" (#11 pop, #12 R&B) and Willie Dixon's "Wang Dang Doodle" (#61 pop, #24 R&B), brought national recognition. The sisters' neo-nostalgic penchant for Forties clothes, plus their wide repertoire, landed them on a number of national television variety shows. On tour they became the first black women to play Nashville's Grand Ole Opry and the first pop act to perform at San Francisco's Opera House. In 1974 PBS filmed a documentary on the Pointer family.

That year "Fairytale," written by Anita and Bonnie Pointer, went to #13 on the pop chart (#37 C&W) and won a Grammy as Best Country Single of 1974. The sisters' first two LPs went gold. The next year brought a #1 R&B hit, "How Long (Betcha' Got a Chick on the Side)" (#20 pop). But between 1975 and 1977, June suffered a nervous breakdown, the group filed a lawsuit against ABC/Blue Thumb for back royalties, Bonnie wanted to go solo, and the Pointer Sisters were still being identified (and categorized) as a nostalgia group.

In 1978 Bonnie signed a solo contract with Motown. She had top charting records there in 1978—"Free Me from My Freedom/Tie Me to a Tree (Handcuff Me)" (#58 pop, #10 R&B)—and in 1979, with "Heaven Must Have Sent You" (#11 pop, #52 R&B). She did not have another release until 1984, in part due to legal battles with Motown.

Her sisters signed with producer Richard Perry's Planet Records, where they enjoyed steady pop success. A cover of Bruce Springsteen's "Fire" (#2 pop, #14 R&B, 1979) started a string continued by Toussaint's "Happiness" (#30 pop, #20 R&B, 1979); "He's So Shy" (#3 pop, #10 R&B), and "Could I Be Dreaming" (#22 R&B) in 1980; "Slow Hand" (#2 pop, #7 R&B) in 1981; and "Should I Do It" (#13 pop), "American Music" (#16 pop, #23 R&B), and "I'm So Excited" (#30) in 1982.

The following year's Top Ten, double-platinum *Break Out* featured "Automatic" (#5, 1984), "Jump (for My Love)" (#3, 1984), a remixed version of "I'm So Excited" (#9, 1984), and "Neutron Dance" (#6, 1984). The platinum *Contact* (#24, 1985) included "Dare Me" (#11, 1985). The trio's following albums did not fare as well, and the group took time off before their releasing their 1994 SBK label debut.

Poison

Formed 1983, Harrisburg, Pennsylvania
Bret Michaels (b. Bret Michael Sychak, Mar. 15, 1963, Harrisburg), voc., gtr.; Matt Smith (b. Pa.), gtr.; Bobby Dall (b. Robert Kuy Kendall, Nov. 2, 1963, Miami, Fla.), bass, voc.; Rikki Rockett (b. Richard Ream, Aug. 8, 1961, Mechanicsburg, Pa.), drums.
1985—(– Smith; + C. C. DeVille [b. Bruce Anthony Johannesson, May 14, 1962, Brooklyn, N.Y.], gtr., voc.) 1986—*Look What the Cat Dragged In* (Enigma/Capitol) 1988—*Open Up and Say . . . Ahh!* 1990—*Flesh & Blood* 1991—*Swallow This Live* (Capitol) (– DeVille; + Richie Kotzen [b. Feb. 3,

1970, Reading, Pa.], gtr.)   1993—*Native Tongue*
(– Kotzen; + Blues Saraceno [b. Oct. 17, 1971], gtr.).

One of the most successful pop-metal groups of the late Eighties, Poison paved the way for less energetic and less glam-styled bands like Warrant and Winger. The band began in central Pennsylvania, where Bret Michaels (a diabetic, as he would reveal after Poison's rise to fame) and Rikki Rockett formed Paris with guitarist Matt Smith and bassist Bobby Dall (a licensed cosmetologist). They drove to Hollywood and became Poison. Smith was replaced by the flamboyant C. C. DeVille, a veteran of many New York and Los Angeles hard-rock bands (including Roxx Regime, which became born-again metal band Stryper after he left).

Poison's popularity on the L.A. metal-club circuit led to a record deal, and the group's debut album, *Look What the Cat Dragged In* (#3, 1986), sold three million copies, thanks to such hits as "Talk Dirty to Me" (#9, 1987), "I Want Action" (#50, 1987), and the ballad "I Won't Forget You" (#13, 1987). *Open Up and Say . . . Ahh!* (#2, 1988) yielded "Nothin' But a Good Time" (#6, 1988), "Fallen Angel" (#12, 1988), the ballad "Every Rose Has Its Thorn" (#1, 1988), and a cover of Loggins and Messina's "Your Mama Don't Dance" (#10, 1989). *Flesh & Blood* (#2, 1990) produced the hits "Unskinny Bop" (#3, 1990), "Something to Believe In" (#4, 1990), "Life Goes On" (#35, 1991), and "Ride the Wind" (#38, 1991). In late 1990 Michaels cowrote and produced his girlfriend Susie Hatton's debut album, while DeVille guested on Warrant's hit single "Cherry Pie."

Swallow This Live (#51, 1991) signaled Poison's decline. In late 1991 Michaels warned DeVille and Dall, through the metal press, to stop doing so many drugs or be fired. In 1992 DeVille was replaced by Richie Kotzen, who debuted on *Native Tongue*, which entered *Billboard*'s pop albums chart at #16 in early March 1993, but dropped off the chart three months later, yielding only the minor hit single "Stand" (#50, 1993). By year's end, Kotzen had been replaced by 21-year-old Blues Saraceno.

The Police

Formed 1977, England
Stewart Copeland (b. July 16, 1952, Alexandria, Egypt), drums; Sting (b. Gordon Sumner, Oct. 2, 1951, Newcastle, Eng.), bass, voc., sax., kybds.; Andy Summers (b. Andrew Somers, Dec. 31, 1942, Blackpool, Eng.), gtr.
1978—*Outlandos d'Amour* (A&M)   1979—*Reggatta de Blanc*   1980—*Zenyatta Mondatta*   1981—*Ghost in the Machine*   1983—*Synchronicity*   1986—*Every Breath You Take: The Singles*   1993—*Message in a Box: The Complete Recordings*   1995—*The Police Live!*

The Police: Sting, Andy Summers, Stewart Copeland

Stewart Copeland solo: 1980—*Klark Kent* EP (I.R.S.)   1985—*The Rhythmatist* (A&M).
Copeland with Animal Logic: 1989—*Animal Logic* (I.R.S.)   1991—*Animal Logic II.*
Andy Summers solo: 1987—*XYZ* (MCA)   1988—*Mysterious Barricades* (Private Music)   1989—*The Golden Wire*   1990—*Charming Snakes*   1991—*World Gone Strange.*
Summers with Robert Fripp: 1982—*I Advance Masked* (A&M)   1984—*Bewitched.*
Summers with John Etheridge: 1993—*Invisible Threads* (Mesa Blue Moon).
Sting solo: See entry.

The Police's canny, forward-looking combination of pop hooks, exotic rhythms, blond good looks, adventurous management, and good timing won the trio a mass following in America and around the world. Its distinctive sound—songs centered on Sting's bass patterns and high, wailing vocals, with Summers' atmospheric guitar, and Copeland's intricate drumming supporting and enhancing his work—was among the most influential approaches since punk. While the Police seemed at first to be a white reggae band, it later incorporated ideas from funk, minimalist, Arab, Indian, and African music. But as chief singer, songwriter, and bassist, Sting began harboring solo ambitions, which led to the band's untimely demise in 1984, following its fifth and most successful album, *Synchronicity.*

Sting, who got his nom de fame because of a yellow and black jersey he often wore as a young musician, had been a teacher, ditch digger, and civil servant and had worked with several jazz combos in Newcastle, England, including Last Exit, before he met American drummer Stewart Copeland at a local jazz club. Copeland, the son of a CIA agent, had grown up in the Middle East, attended college in California, moved to England in 1975, and joined the English progressive-rock group Curved Air [see entry].

After Curved Air broke up in 1976, Copeland formed the Police with Sting and guitarist Henri Padovani in 1977, replacing Padovani with Summers after some months of club dates. Summers had played with numerous groups since the mid-Sixties, including Eric Burdon and the Animals, the Kevin Ayers Band, the Zoot Money Big Roll Band, and Neil Sedaka; he had also studied classical guitar in California.

From the start, the Police distinguished itself by its maverick business practices. Before recording anything, the threesome portrayed a bleached-blond punk-rock band in a chewing gum TV commercial—a move that drew the scorn of Britain's punks. But in punk style, the group's first single, "Fall Out" (with Padovani), was homemade and frenzied. Released in 1978 by Illegal Records Syndicate (I.R.S.)—an independent label founded by Stewart Copeland and his brother Miles (also the group's manager)—"Fall Out" sold about 70,000 copies in the U.K.

The following year, the Police signed with A&M, negotiating a unique contract that awarded the group a higher-than-standard royalty rate instead of a large advance. The Police's next unorthodox move was to tour America before releasing any records in this country. Through Frontier Booking International (FBI)—brother Ian Copeland's agency—the band borrowed equipment, rented a van, and traveled cross-country to play club dates, sowing the seeds of a following that would make its first U.S. release, "Roxanne," a moderate hit (#32, 1979; it was already a British hit).

Both *Outlandos d'Amour* and *Reggatta de Blanc* entered the U.S. Top Thirty, while in the U.K. "Message in a Bottle" and "Walking on the Moon" went to the top of the singles chart. A 1980 world tour took the Police to Hong Kong, Thailand, India, Egypt, Greece, and Mexico—countries that rarely receive foreign entertainers. *Zenyatta Mondatta* (#5, 1980), which contained "De Do Do Do, De Da Da Da" (#10, 1980) and "Don't Stand So Close to Me" (#10, 1981), was the group's first U.S. platinum album. It was followed by a second million-seller, *Ghost in the Machine* (#2, 1981), which secured the Police among the big hitmakers of the decade with "Every Little Thing She Does Is Magic" (#3, 1981).

Meanwhile, the three musicians worked on various outside projects. Sting embarked on a film career, acting in *Quadrophenia* (1979), *Radio On* (1979), and *Brimstone and Treacle*, which he also scored (1982); and performing solo in *The Secret Policeman's Other Ball* (1982). Sum-

mers collaborated with Robert Fripp on two albums. Copeland recorded with Peter Gabriel, released a solo EP as Klark Kent, and composed the soundtrack for Francis Ford Coppola's movie *Rumble Fish* (1983).

The three regrouped for 1983's chart-topping *Synchronicity*, which spawned the monster hit "Every Breath You Take" (#1, 1983) and also produced "Synchronicity II" (#16, 1983), "King of Pain" (#3, 1983), and "Wrapped Around Your Finger" (#8, 1984). After a triumphant world tour, it was announced that the Police would take a "sabbatical" to devote time to individual pursuits; but in 1985, as Sting released a successful solo album and started touring with a new band, it became clear that the singer had no plans to reunite with Copeland and Summers.

Still, fans were hopeful when the group played together at several shows on Amnesty International's Conspiracy of Hope Tour in 1986. That year also brought a Police greatest-hits compilation that was supposed to include new tracks but didn't, largely because Sting wouldn't write any. Instead the trio included "Don't Stand So Close to Me '86," a subpar new version of the original hit, which peaked at #46. (Several remixes were intended, but a freak polo accident prevented Copeland from drumming.)

Copeland and Summers have enjoyed more modest solo success, at least commercially, than Sting [see entry]. In 1985 Copeland released *The Rhythmatist*, an album documenting his experiments collaborating with African folk percussionists. More film scores followed, as well: Oliver Stone's *Wall Street* and *Talk Radio* and numerous others. The drummer also composed themes for television series, including *The Equalizer*, and released two albums with another rock band, Animal Logic, formed with jazz bassist Stanley Clarke and singer Deborah Holland. Then, after composing *King Lear* for the San Francisco Ballet, he presented his first opera, *Holy Blood and Crescent Moon*, in 1989; a second, *Horse Opera*, followed in 1993. Summers' post-Police career, while less varied, has been distinguished by adventurous rock and fusion albums, both alone and in collaboration with such respected musicians as Fripp and British jazz guitarist John Etheridge.

Jean-Luc Ponty

Born September 29, 1942, Avranches, France
1967—*Sunday Walk* (MPS)   1968—*Electric Connection* (Pacific Jazz)   1969—*Experience*   1970—*King Kong*; *Astorama* (Far East)   1972—*Open Strings* (MPS); *Live in Montreux* (Inner City)   1973—*Ponty/Grappelli* (with Stephane Grappelli) (America)   1975—*Upon the Wings of Music* (Atlantic) 1976—*Imaginary Voyage*; *Cantaloupe Island* (Blue Note)   1977—*Aurora* (Atlantic); *Enigmatic Ocean*

1979—*Cosmic Messenger* 1980—*Civilized Evil*; *Taste for Passion* 1982—*Mystical Adventures* 1983—*Individual Choice* 1984—*Open Mind* 1985—*Fables* 1987—*The Gift of Time* (Columbia) 1989—*Storytelling* 1991—*Tchokola* (Epic) 1992—*Puss in Boots* (with Tracey Ullman) (Rabbit Ears/BMG).

Commercially successful jazz-rock-fusion violinist/composer Jean-Luc Ponty draws on both classical technique and sophisticated technology. He has played both acoustic and electric violin with Frank Zappa, the Mahavishnu Orchestra, Elton John, and his own bands. His solo records have featured both jazz stalwarts (Chick Corea and George Benson) and pop players (Ray Parker Jr. and Patrice Rushen). He has also worked on occasion with jazz violinists Stephane Grappelli and Stuff Smith.

Ponty's father, a music teacher, gave him his first violin at age three, and the boy's classical studies began at age five. Ponty left school at 13 to study violin on his own, practicing six hours a day, and at 15 entered the Conservatoire National Supérieur de Musique de Paris, graduating two years later at the head of his class. At age 18 he joined the Concerts Lamoureux Symphony Orchestra for three years. In 1964 he gave up the classics for jazz and played at the Antibes Jazz Festival the next year. He has since played several times at most of the major jazz festivals, including Newport, Montreux, and Monterey. Ponty first visited the U.S. in 1967, when he took part in a violin master class at the Monterey Jazz Festival. In 1969, after having toured Europe for three years, he moved to America to play with the George Duke Trio. He returned to Europe in 1971 and formed the Jean-Luc Ponty Experience with guitarist Philip Catherine. Before leaving America, though, he had played on Zappa's *Hot Rats* and also recorded *King Kong*, an album of Zappa compositions (because of legal problems, Zappa did not get production credit).

Back in France, Ponty met Elton John and contributed violin work to the singer's *Honky Chateau*. In 1973 he came back to America, where he spent a year with Zappa's Mothers of Invention, followed by a year with the Mahavishnu Orchestra, before forming his own band and recording a string of commercially successful jazz-rock fusion albums. From 1971 to 1979 he consistently won the violin category in *down beat*'s critics' and readers' polls.

In the Eighties Ponty began composing on synthesizers; *Fables* featured groundbreaking work on the Synclavier, an electronic keyboard that interfaces with a computer. He toured extensively, playing both a traditional Barcus-Berry open-bodied violin and a Zeta electronic model, and performed his original compositions with both the Montreal Symphony and the New Japan Philharmonic. *Tchokola* (1991), with its complex West African-based rhythms and an African band, was a marked departure from Ponty's usual sound.

Iggy Pop/Iggy Pop and the Stooges

Formed 1967, Ann Arbor, Michigan
Iggy Pop (born James Jewel Osterberg, April 21, 1947, Ypsilanti, Mich.), voc.; Ron Asheton (b. Ronald Franklin Asheton Jr., July 17, 1948, Washington, D.C.), gtr.; Dave Alexander (b. David Michael Alexander, June 3, 1947, Ann Arbor; d. Feb. 10, 1975, Detroit, Mich.), bass; Scott Asheton (b. Scott Randolph Asheton, Aug. 16, 1949, Washington), drums.
1969—*The Stooges* (Elektra) 1970—*Fun House* (– Alexander; + James Williamson [b. Birmingham, Mich.], gtr.; Ron Asheton switches to bass) 1971— (Group disbands) 1972—(Group re-forms: Pop; R. Asheton, bass; S. Asheton; Williamson) 1973— *Raw Power* (Columbia) (+ Scott Thurston, bass, kybds.) 1974—(Group disbands) 1976—*Metallic K.O.* (Skydog) 1978—*Kill City* (Bomp).
Iggy Pop solo: 1977—*The Idiot* (RCA) 1977—*Lust for Life* 1978—*TV Eye* 1979—*New Values* (Arista) 1980—*Soldier* 1981—*Party* 1982—*Zombie Birdhouse* (Animal) 1984—*Choice Cuts* (RCA) 1986— *Blah Blah Blah* (A&M) 1988—*Instinct* 1990—*Brick by Brick* (Virgin) 1993—*American Caesar*.

With his outrageous, cathartic and at times dangerous stage antics, and the relentless rock & roll that accompanied them, Iggy Pop prefigured both Seventies punk

Iggy Pop

and Nineties grunge. His persona that of the eternal misfit, saboteur of all convention, he has parlayed twisted social commentary, an affecting if limited vocal style, and unlikely survival smarts into a long career characterized by scant commercial success, sizable critical notice, and a fanatical cult.

Raised in a trailer park, James Osterberg played drums as a teen in local garage band, the Iguanas. He dropped out of the University of Michigan in 1966 and went to Chicago, where he listened to urban blues on the South Side. He returned to Detroit as Iggy Stooge and, inspired by a Doors concert, formed the Stooges. They debuted on Halloween 1967 in Ann Arbor and were appropriately frightening onstage: Iggy contorting his shirtless torso, letting out primal screams, rubbing peanut butter and raw steaks over his body, gouging his skin with broken glass, diving into the crowd, all while the Stooges played raw, basic rock. Some thought the band the embodiment and the future of rock; others were appalled that they were so unrepentantly primitive.

Elektra, the Doors' label, signed them in 1968. Their first two albums were later hailed as punk's predecessors, but at the time of their release they sold only moderately. The band went through various personnel changes following the 1970 album *Fun House*, eventually breaking up, with Iggy retiring for over a year to kick a heroin addiction. Around this time, he ran into David Bowie, who resolved to resurrect Iggy's career. Bowie regrouped some of the Stooges and produced *Raw Power*, a critical success.

A dispute with Bowie's manager Tony DeFries forced Pop and the re-formed Stooges onto the road without a manager. Through 1973, there was a return to drug addiction, and by the next year the band had imploded. Pop spent 1974–75 in Los Angeles, trying to solve assorted legal problems. He committed himself to an L.A. mental hospital and was visited by Bowie (whose "Jean Genie" on the 1973 *Aladdin Sane* is said to be about Iggy). In 1976 Bowie took Iggy with him on his European tour, after which they settled in Berlin for three years. Concurrently, Bowie produced Pop's *The Idiot* and *Lust for Life*, meditations on modern malaise that benefited from Bowie's professionalism; other albums of this period, like *Metallic K.O.* and *Kill City*, were semibootleg issues of older Stooges-era material.

In 1977 Iggy toured the U.S. with Bowie (unannounced) playing keyboards; Blondie was their opening act. Signing to Arista in the late Seventies, Pop released *New Values*, an album of trenchant rock. His other Arista work, however, suggested the beginnings of self-parody and sold dismally. Publishing his autobiography, *I Need More*, and signing with Blondie guitarist Chris Stein's Animal label in 1982, he put out another strong collection, *Zombie Birdhouse*. Yet only when "China Girl,"

cowritten by Pop and Bowie, appeared on the latter's 1983 *Let's Dance* and became a hit for Bowie did Iggy achieve a measure of financial stability and mainstream interest.

With Bowie producing and ex–Sex Pistol Steve Jones on guitar, *Blah Blah Blah* showed Pop attempting his most accessible music; peaking at #75, it fared nearly as well as *The Idiot* (#72, 1977) but alienated some of his hardcore following. Beginning in the mid-Eighties Pop began accepting character roles in movies (*Sid and Nancy, The Color of Money, Cry-Baby*); he was sought after as punk's elder statesman, even though Iggy's outrageousness by then was less a daily reality than a determined role. Married in 1984 and a proponent of at least his version of domestic bliss, Iggy reserved his animal spirits for recording. *Instinct* was Pop at his most metallic; *Brick by Brick* had him trying again for accessibility and duetting with Kate Pierson of the B-52's ("Candy"). Lauded by critics, *American Caesar* was his return to raw form, helped out with guest vocals on two tracks by one of his chief successors, Henry Rollins.

Pop

Basically any popular music that places a premium on accessibility, pop employs various means to boost both instant appeal and memorability—distinctive syncopation, novel instrumental flourishes, danceable rhythms, repeated riffs—but its signal feature is melodic emphasis. Deriving ultimately from European classical songs (themselves often folk-based) by Romantic composers like Franz Schubert, a pop approach stamped the pre-rock standards of Broadway and Tin Pan Alley. In the Fifties country-influenced performers like Buddy Holly wed assertive melody to early rock & roll's incantatory, formulaic blues elements and came up with a new kind of pop.

In the Sixties the Beatles and Motown worked pop staples (strings, celebratory lyrics, strong melodies) into rock and soul. Even in Seventies punk—generally, a sort of antipop in its rejection of the broad appeal pop strives for—artists like Elvis Costello, with his sophisticated chord structures and indelible rhymes, made pop music. And while the heavy reliance of rap on rhythm, sometimes to the exclusion of overt melody, runs counter to pop convention, its insistent rhyme, by drawing the listener in, can achieve a pop accessibility. And even a hardcore practitioner like Dr. Dre scores hits when he leavens his beats with pop hooks.

While sometimes used as an epithet to suggest glossiness, superficiality, or disposability, pop is as often an adjective as it is a noun, less a specific genre than a stylistic approach. From jazz to metal, New Age to alternative music, there are pop twists on purer forms; generally, any pop record avoids the experimental, arcane, or edgy, aiming instead, in its production, structural familiarity, and clear sentiment to reach the widest possible audience.

Pop Will Eat Itself

Formed 1986, Stourbridge, England
Graham Charles Crabb (b. Oct. 10, 1964, Sutton Coldfield, Eng.), voc.; Clinton Mansell (b. Jan 7, 1963, Coventry, Eng.), voc., gtr.; Richard March (b. Mar. 4, 1965, York, Eng.), bass, gtr.; Adam Mole (b. Apr. 8, 1962, Stourbridge), gtr., kybds.
1986—*The Poppies Say Grrr* EP (Chapter 22, U.K.); *Poppiecock* EP   1987—*The Covers* EP; *The Poppies Go Box Frenzy* (Rough Trade)   1988—*Now for a Feast*   1989—*Very Metal Noise Pollution* EP (RCA); *This Is the Day . . . This Is the Hour . . . This Is This!*   1990—*Cure for Sanity*   1992—(+ Fuzz Townshend [b. John Richard Keith Townshend, July 31, 1964, Birmingham, Eng.], drums) *The Looks or the Lifestyle*   1993—*Weird's Bar & Grill*; *16 Different Flavours of Hell*   1994—*Dos Dedos Mis Amigos* (Nothing/Interscope).

Pop Will Eat Itself: Graham Charles Crabb, Adam Mole, Clint Mansell, Fuzz Townshend, Richard March

Starting out as a fairly conventional indie-rock band, Pop Will Eat Itself evolved into a hip-hop–inspired sound-collage outfit by the late Eighties, blending everything from rap to metal to Motown. The group was a precursor to other genre-fusing U.K. combos such as Ned's Atomic Dustbin and Jesus Jones.

Graham Crabb, Clinton Mansell, Richard March, and Adam Mole came together in the mid-Eighties in England's West Midlands, playing under the names From Eden and Wild and Wondering. They switched to Pop Will Eat Itself in 1986 after seeing the phrase used as a headline in the *New Musical Express*. Inspired by U.S. rap groups Run-D.M.C., Public Enemy, and the Beastie Boys, the band switched stylistic direction on 1987's *Box Frenzy*.

In 1988 Pop Will Eat Itself signed with RCA and began work on its mainstream breakthrough album, *This Is the Day . . . This Is the Hour . . . This Is This!* Released the next year, it was followed by the group's biggest U.K. hit to date, "Touched by the Hand of Cicciolina" (#28 U.K., 1990). Though Pop Will Eat Itself never quite broke in the U.S., the band proceeded to churn out a string of U.K. hits, including "Dance of the Mad" (#32, 1990), "X Y and Zee" (#15, 1991), "92 Degrees" (#23, 1991), "Karmadrome" (#17, 1992), and "Get the Girl! Kill the Baddies!" (#9, 1993).

RCA dropped Pop Will Eat Itself during the height of the band's U.K. success. In 1993 the group signed with Infectious in the U.K. and with Nothing, the label of Nine Inch Nails' Trent Reznor, in the U.S. and released *Dos Dedos Mis Amigos* the next year.

Porno for Pyros: See Jane's Addiction

Power Station: See Duran Duran; Robert Palmer

Praxis: See Bill Laswell

Prefab Sprout

Formed 1982, England
Paddy McAloon (b. June 7, 1957, Durham, Eng.), voc., gtr.; Martin McAloon (b. Jan. 4, 1962, Durham, Eng.), bass; Wendy Smith (b. May 31, 1963, Durham, Eng.), voc., gtr.; Neil Conti (b. Feb. 12, 1959, London, Eng.), drums.
1984—*Swoon* (Kitchenware/Epic)   1985—*Two Wheels Good*   1988—*From Langley Park to Memphis*   1989—*Protest Songs*   1990—*Jordan: The Comeback* (Epic)   1992—*A Life of Surprises: The Best of Prefab Sprout.*

Singer and tunesmith Paddy McAloon, the driving force behind Prefab Sprout, has been praised as an heir to the richly melodic, tenderly lyrical tradition of pop songwriting embodied by artists like Paul McCartney, Brian Wilson, and Marvin Gaye. Although grand-scale commercial success has eluded the band, Prefab Sprout is appreciated, especially in England, for its delicate but lush postmodern pop, which incorporates subtle jazz inflections (à la Steely Dan), and for the quirky literateness of McAloon's lyrics, which have paid homage to American cultural icons such as Elvis Presley and Jesse James.

While growing up in rural England, McAloon and his brother Martin listened to records by the Beatles and the Who, and to contemporary American standards by Burt Bacharach and Jimmy Webb. In 1982 a single released independently by the siblings as Prefab Sprout, "Lions in My Own Garden (Exit Someone)," caught the attention of record store manager Keith Armstrong, who signed them to his Kitchenware Records. Then the McAloons enlisted Wendy Smith, an early fan with a breathy soprano voice, and Armstrong struck a deal with Epic Records. The band's debut album, *Swoon,* caught the attention of electropop musician/producer Thomas Dolby, who produced *Two Wheels Good* (released as *Steve McQueen* outside the U.S.), hailed by American and British critics as one of the year's best albums.

From Langley Park to Memphis produced a European pop hit with "The King of Rock 'n' Roll," which rose to #7 in the U.K. *Jordan: The Comeback* got good notices but made little impact on the charts.

Elvis Presley

Elvis Presley

Born January 8, 1935, East Tupelo, Mississippi; died August 16, 1977, Memphis, Tennessee
1956—*Elvis Presley* (RCA); *Elvis*   1957—*Elvis' Christmas Album*   1958—*Elvis' Golden Records, vol. 1*   1959—*For LP Fans Only; A Date with Elvis*   1960—*50,000,000 Elvis Fans Can't Be Wrong: Elvis' Golden Records, vol. 2; Elvis Is Back; His Hand in Mine*   1961—*Something for Everybody*   1962—*Pot Luck*   1963—*Elvis' Golden Records, vol. 3*   1965—*Elvis for Everyone!*   1967—*How Great Thou Art*   1968—*Elvis* TV special soundtrack; *Elvis' Golden Records, vol. 4*   1969—*From Elvis in Memphis; From Memphis to Vegas/From Vegas to Memphis*   1970—*Back in Memphis; That's the Way It Is; On Stage—February 1970; Elvis in Person at the International Hotel, Las Vegas, Nevada; Love Letters from Elvis; Elvis Country ("I'm 10,000 Years Old"); Elvis Sings the Wonderful World of Christmas*   1972—*Burning Love; He Touched Me; As Recorded at Madison Square Garden; Elvis Now*   1973—*Separate Ways; Aloha from Hawaii via Satellite*   1974—*Elvis—A Legendary Performer, vol. 1*   1975—*Promised Land; Today*   1976—*Elvis—A Legendary Performer, vol. 2; The Sun Sessions; From Elvis Presley Boulevard, Memphis, Tennessee*   1977—*Welcome to My World; Moody Blue; Elvis in Concert*   1978—*Elvis—A Legendary Performer, vol. 3; He Walks Beside Me*   1980—*Elvis Aron Presley*   1981—*This Is Elvis* soundtrack   1982—*Elvis: The Hillbilly Cat* (The Music Works); *Elvis: The First Live Recordings; Memories of Christmas* (RCA)   1983—*Elvis—A Legendary Performer, vol. 4*   1984—*Rocker; Elvis' Gold Records, vol. 5; Elvis—A Golden Celebration*   1985—*Reconsider Baby; A Valentine Gift for You; Always on My Mind*   1986—*Return of the Rocker*   1987—*The Complete Sun Sessions; The Number One Hits; The Top Ten Hits; The Memphis Record*   1988—*Essential Elvis; Stereo '57 (Essential Elvis, vol. 2); 50 World Wide Gold Award Hits, vol. 1, pt. 1; 50 World Wide Gold Award Hits, vol. 1, pt. 2; The Top Ten Hits; Elvis in Nashville; The Alternate Aloha*   1989—*Known Only to Him: Elvis Gospel, 1957–1971*   1990—*The Million Dollar Quartet* (with Johnny Cash, Jerry Lee Lewis, and Carl Perkins); *The Great Performances*   1991—*The Essential Elvis, vol. 3; Collector's Gold; Elvis Presley Sings Leiber and Stoller*   1992—*Elvis—The King of Rock 'n' Roll—The Complete 50's Masters*   1994—*From Nashville to Memphis: The Essential 60's Masters I.*

Simply put, Elvis Presley was the first real rock & roll star. A white southerner singing blues laced with country and country tinged with gospel, he brought together American music from both sides of the color line and performed it with a natural hip-swiveling sexuality that made him a teen idol and a role model for generations of cool rebels. He was repeatedly dismissed as vulgar, incompetent, and a bad influence, but the force of his music and his image was no mere merchandising feat. Presley signaled to mainstream culture that it was time to let go.

Presley was the son of Gladys and Vernon Presley, a sewing-machine operator and a truck driver. Elvis' twin brother, Jesse Garon, was stillborn, and Presley grew up an only child. When he was three, his father served an eight-month prison term for writing bad checks, and afterward Vernon Presley's employment was erratic, keeping the family just above the poverty level. The Presleys attended the First Assembly of God Church, and its Pentecostal services always included singing.

In 1945 Presley won second prize at the Mississippi-Alabama Fair and Dairy Show for his rendition of Red Foley's "Old Shep." The following January he received a guitar for his birthday. In 1948 the family moved to Memphis, and while attending L. C. Humes High School there, Presley spent much of his spare time hanging around the black section of town, especially on Beale Street, where bluesmen like Furry Lewis and B. B. King performed.

Upon graduation in June 1953, Presley worked at the Precision Tool Company and then drove a truck for Crown Electric. He planned to become a truck driver and had begun to wear his long hair pompadoured, the current truck-driver style. That summer he recorded "My Happiness" and "That's When Your Heartaches Begin" at the Memphis Recording Service, a sideline Sam Phillips had established in his Sun Records studios where anyone could record a ten-inch acetate for four dollars.

Presley was reportedly curious to know what he sounded like and gravely disappointed by what he heard. But he returned to the Recording Service again on January 4, 1954, and recorded "Casual Love Affair" and "I'll Never Stand in Your Way." This time he met Phillips, who called him later that spring to rerecord a song that Phillips had received on a demo, "Without You." Despite numerous takes, Presley failed miserably and at Phillips' request just began singing songs in the studio. Phillips then began to believe that he had finally found what he had been looking for: "a white man with the Negro sound and the Negro feel."

Phillips enlisted lead guitarist Scotty Moore and bassist Bill Black, both of whom were then playing country & western music in Doug Poindexter's Starlite Wranglers. Though some sources cite the date of their first meeting as July 4, 1954, the three had actually rehearsed for several months, and on July 5, 1954, they recorded three songs: "I Love You Because," "Blue Moon of Kentucky," and what would become Presley's debut, Arthur "Big Boy" Crudup's "That's All Right."

Two days later Memphis disc jockey Dewey Phillips (no relation to Sam) played the song on his Red Hot and Blue show on radio station WHBQ. Audience response was overwhelming, and that night Presley came to the studio for his first interview. Scotty Moore became Presley's manager, and "That's All Right" b/w "Blue Moon of Kentucky" became his first local hit. After playing local shows, Presley made his first—and last—appearance at the Grand Ole Opry on September 25. Legend has it that after his performance he was advised by the Opry's talent coordinator to go back to driving trucks.

By October Presley had debuted on The Louisiana Hayride, a popular radio program on which he appeared regularly through 1955. He made his television debut on a local television version of Hayride in March 1955. Meanwhile, "Good Rockin' Tonight" b/w "I Don't Care If the Sun Don't Shine" were hits in the Memphis area.

In early 1955 Moore stopped managing Presley, although he would continue to play in Presley's band for several years. Presley's new manager was Memphis disc jockey Bob Neal. Colonel Thomas Parker first entered Presley's career when he helped Neal make some tour arrangements. Presley, still considered a country act, continued to perform locally, and in April he traveled to New York City, where he auditioned unsuccessfully for Arthur Godfrey's Talent Scouts program. But on May 13 his performance in Jacksonville, Florida, started a riot, Presley's first. "Baby, Let's Play House" b/w "I'm Left, You're Right, She's Gone" was released and hit #10 on the national C&W chart in July.

That September, Presley had his first #1 country record, a version of Junior Parker's "Mystery Train" b/w "I Forgot to Remember to Forget." By this time Colonel Parker, despite Presley's agreement with Neal, had become increasingly involved in his career and negotiated RCA's purchase of Presley's contract from Sun for a then unheard-of $35,000. In addition, Presley received a $5,000 advance, with which he bought his mother a pink Cadillac. (It remains among his possessions preserved at Graceland.)

Presley became a national star in 1956. He and Parker traveled to Nashville, where Presley cut his first records for RCA (including "I Got a Woman," "Heartbreak Hotel," and "I Was the One"), and on January 28, 1956, the singer made his national television debut on the Dorsey Brothers' Stage Show, followed by six consecutive appearances. In March Parker signed Presley to a managerial agreement for which he would receive 25 percent of Presley's earnings. The contract would last through Presley's lifetime and beyond.

Presley performed on the Milton Berle, Steve Allen, and Ed Sullivan television shows. The Colonel arranged Presley's debut at the New Frontier Hotel in Las Vegas that April, but the two-week engagement was canceled after one week due to poor audience response. In August he began filming his first movie, Love Me Tender, which was released three months later and recouped its $1-million cost in three days. Elvis' hit singles that year were all certified gold; they included "Heartbreak Hotel" (#1), "I Was the One" (#19), "Blue Suede Shoes" (#20), "I Want You, I Need You, I Love You" (#1), "Hound Dog" (#1), "My Baby Left Me" (#31), "Don't Be Cruel" (#1), "Love Me Tender" (#1), "Anyway You Want Me (That's the Way I'll Be)" (#20), "Love Me" (#2), and "When My Blue Moon Turns to Gold" (#19). By early 1957 he was the idol of millions of teens and the perfect target for the wrath of critics, teachers, clergymen, and even other entertainers (including many country performers), all of whom saw his style as too suggestive; he was nicknamed Elvis the Pelvis by one writer. Presley repeatedly claimed not to understand what all the criticism was about. On January 6, when Presley made his last of three appearances on Ed Sullivan's show, he was shown only from the waist up.

In March 1957 Presley purchased Graceland, a former church that had been converted into a 23-room mansion; the next month "All Shook Up" began an eight-week run at #1. It was preceded in 1957 by "Poor Boy" (#24), "Too Much" (#1), and "Playing for Keeps" (#21). Presley's next single was his first gospel release, "(There'll Be) Peace in the Valley (for Me)"; it went to #25.

Presley was also the first rock star to cross over into films with consistent commercial, if not critical, success. His second film, *Loving You,* was released in July 1957, and "(Let Me Be Your) Teddy Bear" from its soundtrack hit #1 on the pop, country, and R&B charts, as did "All Shook Up" and "Jailhouse Rock," the title song from Presley's next movie, which featured Leiber and Stoller songs. Other hit singles from 1957 were "Loving You" (#20) and "Treat Me Nice" (#18).

That December he received his draft notice, but was granted a 60-day deferment to complete filming *King Creole,* a drama based on the novel *A Stone for Danny Fisher,* and costarring Carolyn Jones and Walter Matthau. Presley's first four feature films are considered his best. Early in the game, Presley truly intended to be taken seriously as an actor. Unfortunately, once he left the service, the choice of roles was left entirely up to Colonel Parker, and the results were rarely satisfactory, for either the audience or Presley. However, since Presley would not tour again until the early Seventies, it was through the films that most fans saw him. Despite anything that might be said of these films, that alone accounts for their massive success.

On March 24, 1958, Presley entered the army. The preceding months brought two hits: "Don't" (#1, 1958) and "I Beg of You" (#8, 1958). He took leave a few months later to be with his mother; Gladys Presley died the day after his arrival home in Memphis, on August 14, 1958. In later interviews Presley would call her death the great tragedy of his life. In the years since his death, much has been written about his relationship with his mother and her impact on his life. He was shipped to Bremerhaven, West Germany, and in January 1960 was promoted to sergeant. He was discharged in March.

Colonel Parker, meanwhile, had continued to release singles Presley had recorded before his departure, ensuring that while Elvis was gone, he would not be forgotten. And he wasn't. He scored a number of hits in absentia, including "Wear My Ring Around Your Neck" (#2, 1958), "Don'tcha Think It's Time" (#15, 1958), "Hard Headed Woman" (#1, 1958), "Don't Ask Me Why" (#25, 1958), "One Night" (#4, 1958), "I Got Stung" (#8, 1958), "(Now and Then There's) A Fool Such as I" (#2, 1959), "I Need Your Love Tonight" (#4, 1959), "A Big Hunk o' Love" (#1, 1959), and "My Wish Came True" (#12, 1959). In 1958 alone Presley earned over $2 million. Shortly after his return to civilian life in March 1960, he recorded his first stereo record, "Stuck on You" (#1), and later that month he taped a TV program with Frank Sinatra, "The Frank Sinatra–Timex Special."

In July Presley's father remarried. Vernon Presley's second wife, Davada "Dee" Stanley, and her three sons would later write *Elvis: We Love You Tender,* one of dozens of insiders' tell-all biographies that were published following his death. Also at this time, Presley gathered more closely around him the friends, employees, and hangers-on who would become known as the Memphis Mafia and would accompany him almost constantly until his death. Presley's world became increasingly insular.

G.I. Blues and *Flaming Star* were released in 1960, and "It's Now or Never" hit #1 in both the U.K. and the U.S. Presley had five #1 U.S. hits in the early Sixties: "Stuck on You," "It's Now or Never," "Are You Lonesome Tonight" (1960); "Surrender" (1961); and "Good Luck Charm" (1962). Other Top Ten singles included "I Feel So Bad" (#5, 1961), "Little Sister" (#5, 1961), "(Marie's the Name) His Latest Flame" (#4, 1961), "Can't Help Falling in Love" (#2, 1961), "She's Not You" (#5, 1962), "Return to Sender" (#2, 1962), "(You're the) Devil in Disguise" (#3, 1963), and "Bossa Nova Baby" (#8, 1963). Meanwhile, over Christmas 1960, Priscilla Beaulieu, the teenage daughter of an army officer whom Presley had met in Germany, visited Graceland. In early 1961 she moved in to live, it was said, under the supervision of Presley's father and stepmother. The press largely went along with the spin Colonel Parker put on the story, and few seemed troubled that the King of Rock & Roll shared his domain with his teenaged girlfriend.

After a live performance on March 25, 1961, at a benefit for the U.S.S. *Arizona,* Presley left the concert stage. He spent the next eight years making movies: *Wild in the Country, Blue Hawaii* (1961); *Follow That Dream, Kid Galahad, Girls! Girls! Girls!* (1962); *It Happened at the World's Fair, Fun in Acapulco* (1963); *Kissin' Cousins, Viva Las Vegas, Roustabout* (1964); *Girl Happy, Tickle Me, Harum Scarum* (1965); *Frankie and Johnny, Paradise, Hawaiian Style, Spinout* (1966); *Easy Come, Easy Go, Double Trouble, Clambake* (1967); *Stay Away Joe, Speedway, Live a Little, Love a Little* (1968); *Charro!, The Trouble with Girls (and How to Get into It), Change of Habit* (1969). With a few exceptions, the soundtrack music was indisputably poor. But by the mid-Sixties Presley was earning $1 million per movie plus a large percentage of the gross. Each of the movies had a concurrently released soundtrack LP, five of which went gold. Presley often made his displeasure with these films known to friends and associates, but Colonel Parker would not relent in his insistence that his sole client stick with a winning formula. Years later, in 1974, Parker's shortsightedness as a manager resulted in his refusing Barbra Streisand's offer to have Presley costar with her in what became a hit remake of *A Star Is Born*. Parker felt Streisand didn't deserve equal billing with Presley.

Meanwhile, the younger rock audience heard Presley disciples like the Beatles more often than they heard Presley himself. But Presley did not disappear, and he was not, like most American rockers, swept away by the British Invasion, though the Top Ten became increasingly beyond his reach, with only "Crying in the Chapel" (which he recorded in 1960), at #3 (1965), making the cut. Presley turned increasingly inward, focusing on his family. On May 1, 1967, Presley and Priscilla were wed in Las Vegas; on February 1, 1968, their only child, Lisa Marie, was born. Fearing he had been forgotten, Presley made a last-gasp bid to regain his footing. He defied Colonel Parker and followed the advice of director Steve Binder for his "comeback" television special. (Parker had wanted it to be a Christmas show.) Over the summer Presley taped the surprisingly raw, powerful *Elvis* television special that was broadcast on December 3 to high ratings. Its soundtrack reached #8. It included his first performance before an audience in over seven years (though many portions were taped without an audience). It also spun off his first Top Fifteen hit single since 1965, "If I Can Dream" (#12, 1968). With that success behind him, Presley turned to performing in Las Vegas. His month-long debut at the International Hotel in Las Vegas began on July 26, 1969, and set the course for all of Presley's future performances. His fee for the four weeks was over $1 million. Riding the crest of his comeback, Presley released a series of top singles, including "In the Ghetto" (#3, 1969), "Suspicious Minds" (#1, 1969, and his first chart-topper since early 1962), "Don't Cry Daddy" (#6, 1969), and "The Wonder of You" (#9, 1970). He toured the country annually, selling out showrooms, auditoriums, and arenas, frequently breaking box-office records. There were two on-tour documentaries released, *Elvis: That's the Way It Is* (1970) and *Elvis on Tour* (1972), the latter of which won the Golden Globe Award for Best Documentary.

Presley was honored with countless Elvis Presley Days in cities around the country, and the U.S. Jaycees named him one of the ten most outstanding young men of America in 1970. His birthplace in Tupelo was opened to the public, and on January 18, 1972, the portion of Highway 51 South that ran in front of Graceland was renamed Elvis Presley Boulevard. That October Presley had his last Top Ten hit when "Burning Love" hit #2.

Meanwhile, Presley's personal life became the sub-

ject of countless tabloid headlines. Priscilla, from whom Presley had been separated since February 1972, refused to return to Graceland, and on his birthday in 1973 he filed for divorce. Less than a week later the TV special *Elvis: Aloha from Hawaii* was broadcast via satellite to over a billion viewers in 40 countries, an indication of his international appeal, although (with the exception of three dates in Canada in 1957 and an impromptu performance while on leave in Paris in 1959) Presley never performed outside the U.S. Through it all, his records continued to sell. During his career, Presley earned 94 gold singles, three gold EPs, and over 40 gold LPs. His movies grossed over $180 million, and millions were made by the merchandising of Elvis products that ranged from T-shirts to stuffed hound dogs and bracelets, the rights to which were controlled by Colonel Parker.

Outwardly, Presley appeared to have been granted a second chance. He was more popular than ever, and the fan worship that would blossom into one of the biggest personality cults in modern history was taking hold. Offstage, however, Presley was plagued by self-doubt, poor management, and a basic dissatisfaction with his life. He repeatedly threatened to quit show business, but debts and his financial obligations to his large extended family, employees, and assorted hangers-on made that impossible. Unbeknownst to the public until mere days before his death, Presley turned to drugs. Soon after he left the army, he became increasingly wary of the public and would often rent whole movie theaters and amusement parks to visit at night. By the late Sixties he was nearly a total recluse. Among the many books written about Presley by those who knew him, Priscilla's account, *Elvis and Me*, goes so far as to suggest that he might have suffered a nervous breakdown. Although some evidence suggests that Presley may have begun taking drugs shortly after he began performing or while in the service, his abuse of prescription drugs, including barbiturates, tranquilizers, and amphetamines, increased during the last years of his life. Several painful physical conditions may have initiated this trend. Ironically, he remained devoutly spiritual, never drank alcohol, and publicly denounced the use of recreational drugs. In one of his few unplanned excursions from Graceland, he actually showed up at the White House in 1970 to meet President Richard M. Nixon and received an honorary Drug Enforcement Administration agent's badge.

Toward the end of his life, however, Presley would babble incoherently onstage and rip his pants, having grown quite obese, and on at least one occasion he collapsed onstage. Despite his clearly deteriorating health, he maintained a frantic tour schedule, because in 1973 Colonel Parker had negotiated a complex deal whereby Presley sold back to RCA the rights to many of his masters in exchange for a lump-sum payment of which only

$2.8 million came to him. Essentially, after 1973 Parker was earning nearly 50 percent commission (as opposed to the 10 percent industry standard). Worse, however, Presley was not earning any more royalties on sides recorded before 1973 although they continued to sell in the millions year after year. Presley opposed tax shelters on principle; he naively relied on his father for business advice; he gave away expensive gifts and cash heedlessly. The result, by the mid-Seventies, was impending financial disaster.

Presley's last live performance was on June 25, 1977, in Indianapolis. He was reportedly horrified at the impending publication of *Elvis: What Happened?,* the tell-all written by three of his ex-bodyguards and Memphis mafiosi that was the first printed account of his drug abuse and obsession with firearms, to name just two headline-grabbing revelations. The book came out on August 12. On August 16, 1977—the day before his next scheduled concert—Presley was discovered by his girlfriend Ginger Alden dead in his bathroom at Graceland. Although his death was at first attributed to congestive heart failure (an autopsy also revealed advanced arteriosclerosis and an enlarged liver), later investigation revealed evidence that drug abuse may have been at least part of the cause of death. Because the family was allowed to keep the official autopsy report private, speculation regarding contributing factors in Presley's death has run wild. Through the years, several insiders have insisted that he was suffering from bone cancer, to name just one unsubstantiated claim. In September 1979 Presley's private physician, Dr. George Nichopoulos, was charged by the Tennessee Board of Medical Examiners with "indiscriminately prescribing 5,300 pills and vials for Elvis in the seven months before his death." He was later acquitted.

Thousands gathered at Graceland, where Presley lay in state before he was buried in a mausoleum at Forest Hill Cemetery in Memphis. After attempts were made to break into the mausoleum, Presley's body and that of his mother were moved to the Meditation Garden behind Graceland. Nearly two years later, his father, Vernon, died and was also buried there. With Vernon dead, all of Presley's estate passed on to Lisa Marie.

Court battles over the estate ended in June 1983 after 21 months of litigation with a settlement that ended four lawsuits. One of the terms of the agreement called for Parker to turn over most of his interest in Presley's audio and visual recordings to RCA and the Presley family in return for a large monetary settlement. Lisa Marie's court-appointed guardian ad litem, Blanchard Tual, wrote in his report on Presley's financial affairs that Parker had "handled affairs not in Elvis' but in his own best interest." Priscilla Presley assumed control of the estate and through a number of business moves made the Presley estate many times more valuable than it had ever been during Elvis' lifetime. The cornerstone of the Elvis Presley Enterprises, Inc. (EPE), financial empire is the Tennessee state law Priscilla Presley pushed for that guarantees to heirs the commercial rights to a deceased celebrity's image and likeness. As a result, the name Elvis Presley is, technically speaking, a trademark, and anyone selling Presley-related memorabilia in the U.S. must pay EPE an advance fee plus a royalty on every item sold.

Claiming the funds were needed to maintain the property (the estate was valued at only $5 million in 1979, and the costs to maintain Graceland were estimated at nearly half a million dollars annually), Priscilla Presley opened Graceland to the public in fall 1982. Although it is not preserved in exactly the way Elvis Presley left it and the second floor, where his bedroom is located, remains off-limits to the public, millions have come from all over the world to pay homage to the King of Rock & Roll. At last count, 675,000 people visit Graceland annually. The Presley estate is now estimated to be worth over $100 million.

Presley's sole heir, Lisa Marie, married a fellow Scientology follower, Danny Keough, in 1988. They had two children: Danielle and Benjamin Storm. In 1993 they were divorced, and in May 1994 she married Michael Jackson. By the Nineties, over 300 books about Elvis Presley have been published in the United States alone. His enduring power as a cultural force is beyond the scope of this book but is examined in a number of works by authors including Dave Marsh, Greil Marcus, and Peter Guralnick. In 1986 Presley was among the first ten performers inducted into the Rock and Roll Hall of Fame.

Billy Preston

Born September 9, 1946, Houston, Texas
1965—*The Wildest Organ in Town* (Vee Jay)
1966—*Most Exciting Organ Ever*   1969—*That's the Way God Planned It* (Apple); *Encouraging Words*
1971—*I Wrote a Simple Song* (A&M)   1972—*Music Is My Life*   1973—*Everybody Likes Some Kind of Music*   1974—*The Kids and Me*   1975—*It's My Pleasure*   1976—*Billy Preston*   1977—*A Whole New Thing*   1980—*Late at Night* (Motown)
1981—*Billy Preston and Syreeta* (with Syreeta Wright)   1982—*Best of Billy Preston* (A&M).

Though keyboardist/vocalist Billy Preston has recorded as a solo artist since he was a teenager, he may be best known for his performances as a sideman for Little Richard, Ray Charles, the Beatles, and the Rolling Stones. Preston's family moved to Los Angeles when he was two years old. At age 12 he had a cameo part in a film about W. C. Handy, *St. Louis Blues,* playing the composer as a child. Little Richard heard him in 1962 and invited him to appear on a European tour. There, backing Richard, Preston met Sam Cooke (who signed him to his SAR label) and the Beatles. After Cooke's death Preston moved to Vee Jay records, where he cut an instrumental gospel album, *The Most Exciting Organ Ever,* his first charting record.

Preston was playing in the house band of the television show *Shindig* when Ray Charles recruited him for his band. George Harrison spotted Preston on a BBC Ray Charles special and contacted him. Subsequently he was signed to the Beatles' Apple Records, where he cut two Harrison-produced albums, *That's the Way God Planned It* (whose title cut was a minor hit) and *Encouraging Words.* Preston also became a valuable sideman for the Beatles, appearing on "Get Back" and "Let It Be." Following the Beatles' breakup, he performed on Harrison's *All Things Must Pass* and at the Bangladesh concert at Madison Square Garden in 1971.

Preston had several hits on A&M Records in the early Seventies, including the instrumental "Outa-Space" (#2 pop, #1 R&B) in 1972; "Will It Go Round in Circles" (#1 pop, #10 R&B) and "Space Race" (#4 pop, #1 R&B) in 1973; and "Nothing from Nothing" (#1 pop, #8 R&B) in 1974. Each single went gold, and "Outa-Space" won a Grammy as Best Pop Instrumental. In 1975 Preston wrote what became Joe Cocker's biggest solo hit, "You Are So Beautiful." That same year Preston was featured on the Rolling Stones' tour; he had previously recorded with them (*Goats Head Soup, It's Only Rock 'n' Roll, Sticky Fingers, Exile on Main Street*),and later appeared on *Black and Blue* and *Love You Live.*

Preston was active as a session musician through the late Seventies and into the Eighties, though his solo career declined. In 1979 he reached the Top Five with "With You I'm Born Again," a duet with Syreeta Wright on a song from the film *Fastbreak.* Preston toured with Ringo Starr in 1989 and recorded for the U.K. Motorcity label in the early Nineties, but he could not restart his career. In 1992 he pleaded no contest to charges of assault and possession of cocaine and was sentenced to prison and drug treatment, followed by house arrest and probation.

Johnny Preston
Born John Preston Courville, August 18, 1930, Port Arthur, Texas

An East Texas pop-rock singer, Johnny Preston had a #1 novelty hit in 1960 with "Running Bear," a tune inspired by a Dove Soap commercial. It was written by and featured the "oom-pah-pah" backing vocals of J. P. Richardson, also known as the "Big Bopper." The song became a hit nearly a year after Richardson's death in the February 1959 plane crash that also killed Buddy Holly and Ritchie Valens.

Before returning to obscurity, Preston had a few followup hits: "Cradle of Love" (#7, 1960), a version of Shirley and Lee's "Feel So Good" called "Feel So Fine" (#14, 1960), a cover of Little Willie John's "Leave My Kitten Alone" (#73, 1961), and "Free Me" (#97, 1961).

The Pretenders
Formed 1978, London, England
Chrissie Hynde (b. Sep. 7, 1951, Akron, Ohio), voc., gtr.; Pete Farndon (b. 1953, Hereford, Eng.; d. Apr. 14, 1983, London), bass; James Honeyman-Scott (b. Nov. 4, 1957, Hereford, Eng.; d. June 16, 1982), gtr.; Martin Chambers (b. 1952, Hereford, Eng.), drums.
1980—*The Pretenders* (Sire)   1981—*Extended Play* EP; *The Pretenders II*   1982—(– Farndon; – Honeyman-Scott)   1983—(+ Robbie McIntosh, gtr.; + Malcolm Foster, bass)   1984—*Learning to Crawl* 1986—(– Chambers; – Foster; + T. M. Stevens, bass; + Blair Cunningham, drums) *Get Close*   1987—*The Singles* (– McIntosh; – Stevens)   1990—(+ Billy Bremner [b. 1947, Scot.], gtr.; + Dominic Miller, gtr.; + John McKenzie, bass) *Packed!*   1993—(– Bremner; – Cunningham; – Miller; – McKenzie; + Chambers; + Adam Seymour, gtr.; + Andy Hobson, bass) 1994—*Last of the Independents.*

The Pretenders, originally three Englishmen and an American woman, emerged at the close of the Seventies as one of the new wave's most commercially successful groups. Their focal point was Chrissie Hynde, the band's songwriter, lead singer, and rhythm guitarist, whose tough songs and stage persona put feminist self-assertion into her own distinctive hard rock.

A single gig with an Akron band, Sat. Sun. Mat. (which included Mark Mothersbaugh, later of Devo), was Hynde's sole performing experience when, after three years of studying art at Kent State University, she left (with money earned as a waitress) for the rocker's life in London in 1974. She began writing savagely satiric reviews for *New Musical Express,* but after playing cover girl for a story on Brian Eno, she moved to France to form a band. When nothing materialized, she returned to Akron, where she joined Jack Rabbit. It broke up, and Hynde returned to France and then to England by 1976, as punk rock was burgeoning. She tried to enlist a young guitarist, Mick Jones, into her would-be group, but Jones committed himself to another new group, the Clash.

She was then hired by punk fashion entrepreneur and Sex Pistols manager Malcolm McLaren (in whose boutique, Sex, Hynde had worked when she'd first come to London) to play guitar in Masters of the Backside. After months of rehearsal, she was dismissed; the group turned into the Damned. Hynde played guitar or sang backup behind Johnny Moped, Chris Spedding, Johnny

The Pretenders: Pete Farndon, Chrissie Hynde, Martin Chambers, James Honeyman-Scott

Thunders (the New York Dolls, the Heartbreakers), and Nick Lowe. With these contacts and a growing repertoire of original songs, she recorded a demo tape. Dave Hill, founder of Real Records, became her manager and advanced her the money to audition and hire a band.

Bassist Pete Farndon had recently returned to England from Australia, where he had played for two years with a popular Aussie group, the Bushwackers. He called James Honeyman-Scott, who had toured with several bands, notably Cheeks, a group led by ex–Mott the Hoople keyboardist Verdon Allen. Honeyman-Scott joined Hynde, Farndon, and drummer Gerry Mackleduff to record two Hynde compositions—"Precious" and "The Wait"—and a 1964 number penned by Ray Davies of the Kinks, "Stop Your Sobbing." Nick Lowe pegged "Stop Your Sobbing" b/w "The Wait" for a hit and offered to produce a single, which he did in one day in fall 1978. The next day the Pretenders left for Paris for their debut gig and a week-long club engagement.

Mackleduff was replaced by Cheeks' former drummer, Martin Chambers, then working as a drummer and driving instructor in London. In January 1979 "Stop Your Sobbing" was released in Britain. Soon it was in the Top Thirty. The followup, "Kid," written by Hynde and produced by Chris Thomas, did well too. By spring the Pretenders were selling out performances all over the U.K. In May they began work on an album, with Thomas producing. The Pretenders, released worldwide in January 1980, was universally lauded. "Brass in Pocket" hit #1 in the U.K. and Australia and reached #14 in the U.S. After whipping off another single, "Talk of the Town," for the British market, Hynde brought her band stateside, where its album was rising to #9.

It took the band over a year and a half to produce a followup, although a five-song EP was released in the interim. Finally, in August 1981, Pretenders II (#10) was released to mixed reviews. It included another tune by Ray Davies, "I Go to Sleep," and Hynde showed up so fre-

quently on the Kinks tour that summer that her relationship with Ray Davies soon became public knowledge. (The two never married but had a daughter, Natalie, in 1983.) A 1981 tour of the U.S. was postponed when, in October, Chambers badly injured his hand; the eventual tour was the last time the original Pretenders played together.

Farndon was booted from the group on June 14, 1982; two days later Honeyman-Scott died of a drug overdose. Farndon himself would die of a drug overdose the following April. Surviving members Hynde and Chambers recorded the gorgeous, wistful "Back on the Chain Gang" (dedicated to Honeyman-Scott) with ex-Rockpile guitarist Billy Bremner and Big Country bassist Tony Butler; it hit #5 in 1983.

Another year passed, however, before the aptly titled Learning to Crawl, which introduced new members Robbie McIntosh and Malcolm Foster. The album (#5, 1984) went platinum and spawned hits in the raw "Middle of the Road" (#19, 1984) and "Show Me" (#28, 1984). In May 1984 Hynde married Jim Kerr, lead singer of Simple Minds; the two collaborated on a daughter but soon split up.

From 1986 to 1993, the Pretenders consisted mostly of Hynde and a succession of musicians, with spotty results. "Don't Get Me Wrong" (#10, 1986) was the group's last U.S. hit in the Eighties. McIntosh went on to play and record with Paul McCartney. For Last of the Independents, the band's first album in four years, Chambers came back on board; the newest Pretenders are Adam Seymour, formerly of the Katydids, and ex-Primitives bassist Andy Hobson. The critically acclaimed album went gold and yielded the singles "Night in My Veins" (#72, 1994) and "I'll Stand by You" (#16, 1994).

The Pretty Things

Formed 1963, Kent, England

Phil May (b. Nov. 9, 1944, Kent), voc.; Dick Taylor, gtr., bass, voc.; Brian Pendleton, gtr.; John Stax, bass, harmonica; Peter Kitley, drums (replaced by Viv Andrews, who was replaced by Viv Prince).
1965—*The Pretty Things* (Fontana, U.K.); *Get the Picture* (– Prince; + Skip Alan [b. Alan Ernest Skipper, June 11, 1948, London, Eng.], drums)   **1966**—
(– Pendleton; – Stax; + Wally Allen, bass, voc.; + John Povey [b. Aug. 20, 1944, London, Eng.], kybds., voc.)   **1967**—*We Want Your Love*; *Emotions*; *Electric Banana* (De Wolf, U.K.)   **1968**—
(– Alan; + John "Twink" Alder, drums, voc.) *More Electric Banana*   **1969**—*S.F. Sorrow* (Rare Earth); *Even More Electric Banana* (De Wolf, U.K.) (– Alder; – Taylor; + Alan; + Victor Unitt, gtr., voc.)   **1970**—*Parachute* (Rare Earth) (– Alan; – Unitt; + Peter Tolson [b. Sep. 10, 1951, Bishops Stortford, Eng.], gtr.,

voc.) 1971—(Group disbands; re-forms: + Stuart Brooks, bass; + Gordon Edwards [b. Dec. 26, 1946, Southport, Eng.], kybds., gtr.) 1973—*Freeway Madness* (Warner Bros.) 1974—*Silk Torpedo* (Swan Song) 1975—(– Brooks; + Jack Green [b. Mar. 12, 1951, Glasgow, Scot.], bass, voc.) *Savage Eye; Greatest Hits* (Philips); *Attention!* (Fontana) 1976—*The Vintage Years* (Sire) 1977—*The Singles* (Harvest, U.K.) 1978—*Live* (Jade) 1980—*Cross Talk* (Warner Bros.) 1992—*Get a Buzz: The Best of the Fontana Years* (Fontana).

The Pretty Things were a British pop-rock band that was highly regarded in the U.K. but scarcely made an impression in the U.S. The band was formed from lunchtime jam sessions at London's Sidcup Art College, where Phil May, Dick Taylor, and Keith Richards were enrolled. Taylor, after playing bass with the original Rolling Stones, switched to guitar to form the Pretty Things with May. The band's performances of material by Chuck Berry, Jimmy Reed, and Bo Diddley (they took their name from a Diddley song) were at first considered even more outrageous than the Stones', especially when their second U.K. chart single, "Don't Bring Me Down" (the first was "Rosalyn" in 1964), was banned in the U.S. in 1964 because of objectionable lyrics. Their last big U.K. hit was "Honey I Need" (#13, 1965).

But the Pretty Things took a lot longer to develop original material than the Stones, and it wasn't until 1969's *S.F. Sorrow* (based on May's short story) that the band attracted any interest in the U.S. (The album was originally released in England in 1968.) The album is one of the first "rock operas," and may have influenced Pete Townshend's writing of *Tommy.* It was a critical success, but a commercial failure, as was *Parachute,* which won ROLLING STONE's Album of the Year Award in 1971.

Meanwhile, founding member Taylor had left in November 1969, first to produce Hawkwind in 1971 and then apparently to leave the music business. Pendleton had disappeared entirely after the first few albums; the band continued despite numerous personnel changes. Bassist Jack Green, who joined in time for *Savage Eye,* had worked with T. Rex and released two solo LPs. When Pretty Things disbanded, May and Skip Alan formed Fallen Angels briefly, and other remaining members formed Metropolis. Fallen Angels released one LP. When Metropolis broke up in 1977, keyboardist Edwards briefly joined the Kinks. Since 1978 various group members have reunited, usually with May and Taylor. In 1990 one such revived lineup released a cover of Barry McGuire's "Eve of Destruction."

Alan Price
Born April 19, 1942, County Durham, England
1966—*The Price to Play* (Decca)   1967—*A Price on
His Head; The Amazing EP   1968—*The Price Is Right* (Parrot)   1970—*The World of . . .* (Decca)   1971—*Fame and Price* (with Georgie Fame) (Columbia)   1973—*O Lucky Man!* soundtrack (Warner Bros.)   1974—*Between Yesterday and Today*   1975—*Metropolitan Man* (Polydor); *Performing Price*   1976—*Shouts Across the Street*   1977—*Rainbow's End* (Jet); *Alan Price*   1978—*England My England*   1980—*Rising Sun.*

Alan Price may be best known as the organist with the original Animals [see entry], but he was performing on his own some time before founding that band and continued his career long after its demise. He formed his first group, the skiffle/blues Alan Price Combo, in 1958 while at Jarrow Grammar School and played small clubs in northeast England. This grew into the Animals, which he left in 1965. In 1966 he formed the Alan Price Set, a horn-laden band, and had some U.K. hit singles, like "I Put a Spell on You" (#9 U.K., #80 U.S.) and a cover of Randy Newman's "Simon Smith and His Amazing Dancing Bear" (#4 U.K.). He continued to record solo albums with various personnel. In the late Sixties he teamed up with Georgie Fame for a series of British stage and television appearances, leading to a television series in 1970. Together Fame and Price released an LP and a British Top Twenty single, "Rosetta."

That year, British stage and film director Lindsay Anderson commissioned Price to score his London production of *Home.* Three years later he scored Anderson's film *O Lucky Man!* and appeared in it as himself, singing songs that commented on the story. That score won Price the British Society of Film and Television Arts Award. The next year the BBC did a television documentary on him to coincide with the release of his autobiographical *Between Yesterday and Today,* and in 1975 he starred in a second film, *Alfie Darling,* for which he won the British Film Award for Most Promising New Actor. Price's last big British hit was "Jarrow Song," #6 in 1974. He rejoined the original Animals for reunion albums in 1977 and 1983. He continues to compose for film and television in his homeland, where he released solo albums through the Eighties.

Lloyd Price
Born March 9, 1934, New Orleans, Louisiana
**1972—*To the Roots and Back* (GSF)   1986—*Lloyd Price* (Specialty); *Personality Plus; Walkin' the Track*   1990—*Greatest Hits* (Curb)   1991—*Lawdy!* (Specialty)   1993—*Lloyd Price, vol. 2: Heavy Dreams.*

Singer/songwriter Lloyd Price was a major figure in the early years of New Orleans rock & roll. "Lawdy Miss Clawdy" (1952), written by Price as a commercial for a local radio station, was a #1 R&B hit. In the next two years, Price had several Top Ten R&B singles, "Oooh-Oooh-Oooh" (#5), "Restless Heart" (#8), and "Ain't It a Shame" (#7), before serving in Korea from 1954 to 1956. Upon his discharge, he relocated to Washington, D.C. There he started KRC (Kent Record Company) and recorded "Just Because." Leased to ABC-Paramount in 1957, it reached #20 pop and #4 R&B. Price soon signed to ABC and enjoyed his greatest success with "Stagger Lee" (#1 pop and R&B, 1959), a reworking of the New Orleans folk song "Stagolee."

Price's subsequent ABC recordings shifted from the rocking New Orleans style to a mainstream pop sound, as reflected by "Personality" (#2 pop, #1 R&B), "I'm Gonna Get Married" (#3 pop, #1 R&B), "Where Were You (On Our Wedding Day)" (#23), "Come into My Heart" (#2 R&B), in 1959; "Lady Luck" (#14 pop, #3 R&B) and "Question" (#9 pop, #5 R&B) in 1960. Price was an enterprising businessman during the Sixties, operating the Double L and Turntable labels and a New York nightclub called the Turntable. In 1972 he released a new album, *To the Roots and Back*. He continues to tour and is a regular on the casino and concert circuit.

Maxi Priest

Born Max Alfred Elliott, June 10, 1960, London, England
1985—*You're Safe* (Virgin, U.K.)   1986—*Intentions*
1988—*Maxi* (Virgin)   1990—*Bonafide* (Charisma)
1991—*Best of Me*   1992—*Fe Real*.

Maxi Priest is a soulful British reggae singer who in the late Eighties and early Nineties managed to win over both Jamaican musical purists and American pop radio. The son of a factory worker, Priest grew up in Southeast London. Reggae was in his genes: He is the nephew of genre pioneer Jacob Miller. Priest entered the music world through carpentry. Having built his own studio at 14, he subsequently left school and began constructing sound systems for London's Saxon International. Soon he was DJing for Saxon's mobile reggae music stations himself.

Priest's first single, "Hey Little Girl," went to #8 on the British reggae chart in 1983 and became a #1 hit in Jamaica. Virgin signed the artist and released two albums in England before Priest's U.S. debut. The record company showed marketing savvy by convincing Priest to cover Cat Stevens' "Wild World" (#25, 1988) on *Maxi*; with reggae stalwarts Sly and Robbie providing rhythms, the album also appealed to longtime reggae fans.

Priest made his first visit to reggae's home, Jamaica, for the recording of *Bonafide*. With producers including Soul II Soul, dancehall star Gussie Clarke, and Dunbar, the album covered a range of reggae styles. The single "Close to You" (#1, 1990) was Priest's biggest hit. *Best of Me* compiled Priest's singles. In 1991 the singer was fea-

tured on Shabba Ranks' "Housecall (Your Body Can't Lie to Me)" (#4 R&B) and Roberta Flack's "Set the Night to Music" (#45 R&B).

Primus

Formed 1984, San Francisco, California
Tim "Herb" Alexander (b. Apr. 10, 1965, Cherry Point, N.C.), drums; Les Claypool (b. Sep. 29, 1963, Richmond, Calif.), bass, voc.; Todd Huth (b. Mar. 13, 1963, San Leandro, Calif.), gtr.
1989—(– Huth; + Larry LaLonde [b. Sep. 12, 1968, Richmond, Calif.], gtr.) *Suck on This* (Prawn Song) 1990—*Fizzle Fry* (Caroline)   1991—*Sailing the Seas of Cheese* (Interscope)   1993—*Pork Soda*. Sausage (Claypool; Huth; Jay Lane [b. Dec. 15, 1964, San Francisco], drums):   1994—*Riddles Are Abound Tonight* (Interscope)   1995—*Tales from the Punch Bowl*.

A stark amalgam of spacy rhythms, roiling bass, angular guitar, and cartoony vocals mixed with sea chanteys, a shot of surreal humor, and a piscene obsession, Primus has become one of the leading lights of the alternative scene. The group headlined the 1993 Lollapalooza Tour and entered the charts at #7 with their fourth album, *Pork Soda* (#7, 1993).

Originally called Primate, the band was the brainchild of bassist Les Claypool (he once auditioned for Metallica and was turned down after attempting to lead them in an Isley Brothers tune), along with guitarist Todd Huth and a drum machine. Huth left in 1989, replaced by Larry LaLonde, who had played with Claypool in an earlier band, Blind Illusion. Tim Alexander was discovered through an ad.

Claypool's father lent the band $1000 in 1989 to release the live *Suck on This*. Caroline reissued the album and released their next, *Fizzle Fry*. They signed with Interscope after owner Ted Fields took them on a fishing

Primus: Tim Alexander, Les Claypool, Larry LaLonde

trip. *Sailing the Seas of Cheese,* their major-label debut, sold over 200,000 copies, and the band expanded its audience after opening for Jane's Addiction, Public Enemy, and Anthrax, and for U2 on the Zoo TV Tour, setting the foundation for the success of *Pork Soda.*

In 1994 Claypool hooked up with old bandmate guitarist Huth and drummer Jay Lane to record *Riddles Are Abound Tonight,* which includes some of their pre-Primus songs.

Prince/♀

Born Prince Rogers Nelson, June 7, 1958, Minneapolis, Minnesota
1978—*For You* (Warner Bros.) 1979—*Prince* 1980—*Dirty Mind* 1981—*Controversy* 1982—*1999* 1984—*Purple Rain* 1985—*Around the World in a Day* (Paisley Park) 1986—*Parade (Music from the Motion Picture Under the Cherry Moon)* 1987—*Sign 'O' the Times* 1988—*Lovesexy* 1989—*Batman* (Warner Bros.) 1990—*Graffiti Bridge* (Paisley Park) 1991—*Diamonds and Pearls* 1992—*The Symbol Album* 1993—*The Hits; The Hits 2; The Hits/The B-Sides* 1994—*Come* (Warner Bros.); *The Black Album; The Beautiful Experience* EP (Bellmark).

One of the most flamboyant, controversial, influential, and popular artists of the Eighties, Prince is also one of the least predictable and most mysterious, having granted only one major print interview and one stilted TV interview in his career. At a time when comparable megastars such as Michael Jackson, Madonna, and Janet Jackson were delivering an album every three years or so, Prince remained prolific to an almost self-destructive degree—and was given to wayward, self-indulgent career moves (even declaring in the 1990s a name change to an unpronounceable symbol) that could alienate even his most ardent supporters. Yet his taut, keyboard-dominated Minneapolis Sound—a rock, pop, and funk hybrid with blatantly sexual lyrics—not only influenced his fellow Minneapolis artists the Time and Janet Jackson's producers (and ex-Time members) Jimmy Jam and Terry Lewis, but also affected much Eighties dance-pop music. And Michael, Madonna, and Janet were comparable to Prince only in terms of star power; none could match the formidable breadth of his talents, which included not just singing and dancing but also composing, producing, and playing instruments (not to mention directing videos and, however ineffectively, movies). In fact, Prince played all the instruments on his first five albums and has produced himself since signing with Warner Bros. at age 21.

Under the name "Prince Rogers," Prince's father John Nelson was the leader of a Minneapolis-area jazz band, in which Prince's mother was the vocalist. Prince

Prince

started playing piano at age seven, guitar at 13, and drums at 14, all self-taught. By age 14 he was in a band called Grand Central, which later became Champagne. Four years later, a demo tape he made with engineer Chris Moon reached local businessman Owen Husney. In 1978 Husney negotiated Prince's contract with Warner Bros.

"Soft and Wet" (#92 pop, #12 R&B, 1978) from *For You* introduced his erotic approach, while "I Wanna Be Your Lover" (#11 pop, #1 R&B) and "Why You Wanna Treat Me So Bad?" (#13 R&B) from *Prince* (#22, 1979) suggested his musical range. *Dirty Mind* (#45, 1980)—a loose concept album including songs such as "Head," about oral sex, and "Sister," about incest—established Prince's libidinous image once and for all. One of its few songs that wasn't too obscene for airplay, "Uptown," went to #5 R&B, while "When You Were Mine" became Prince's most widely covered song, and a minor comeback hit for Mitch Ryder in 1983 (it was later covered by Cyndi Lauper, among others.)

Controversy (#21, 1981) had two hits, the title cut (#70 pop, #3 R&B, 1981) and "Let's Work" (#9 R&B, 1982). *Prince, Dirty Mind,* and *Controversy* all eventually went platinum. For his second album Prince had formed a racially and sexually mixed touring band that included childhood friend André (Anderson) Cymone on bass, Dez Dickerson on guitar, keyboardists Gayle Chapman and Matt Fink, and drummer Bobby "Z" Rivkin. By the *Dirty Mind* Tour, Chapman had been replaced by Lisa Coleman. In concert Prince would sometimes strip down to black bikini underpants or finish the set doing "push ups" on a brass bed.

A double album, *1999* (#9, 1982), went platinum, bolstered by the Top Ten singles "Little Red Corvette" (#6, 1983) and "Delirious" (#8, 1983) and the title track (#12, 1983). "Little Red Corvette" was also among the first videos by a black performer to be played regularly on MTV.

Prince "discovered" another Minneapolis band, the Time, whose first two albums went gold (the third went platinum); in turn, the Time supplied backup for Vanity 6, a female trio that had a club hit with "Nasty Girl" (Vanity would leave Prince's fold in 1983 to launch an unsuccessful solo career). Prince denied that he was the "Jamie Starr" who produced albums by the Time and Vanity 6. He did take both bands on tour with him, however. After the tour Dez Dickerson left Prince's band to launch an abortive solo career; he would be replaced by Wendy Melvoin.

Prince vaulted to superstardom in 1984 with *Purple Rain*, a seemingly autobiographical movie set on the Minneapolis club scene and costarring the Time and Apollonia 6 (Patricia "Apollonia" Kotero having replaced Vanity). It was an enormous hit, as was the soundtrack album, which spent 24 weeks atop the chart and sold over ten million copies, yielding hit singles in "When Doves Cry" (#1, 1984), "Let's Go Crazy" (#1, 1984), "Purple Rain" (#2, 1984), "I Would Die 4 U" (#8, 1984), and "Take Me with U" (#25, 1985). The album marked the first time in his career that Prince had recorded with, and credited, his backing band, which he named the Revolution. The opening act on Prince's 1984 tour was another of his protégées, Latin percussionist Sheila E. [see entry], the daughter of Santana percussionist Pete Escovedo, who hailed from Oakland, California, and whose album *The Glamorous Life* Prince had produced that year.

At the 1985 Grammy Awards, Prince won Best Rock Performance by a Duo or Group with Vocal for *Purple Rain* and R&B Song of the Year for "I Feel for You" (actually from *Prince*, and a hit cover for Chaka Khan in 1984). After the gala, Prince—who for all his sexual exhibitionism onstage was painfully shy offstage—declined an offer to take part in the all-star recording session for "We Are the World" (he later donated the track "4 the Tears in Your Eyes" to the *USA for Africa* album). That, and his fey demeanor at the 1985 Academy Awards show, where he won a Best Original Score Oscar for *Purple Rain,* were the first signals of Prince's personal eccentricities to his newfound mass audience. In 1985 Prince also wrote Sheena Easton's suggestive hit single "Sugar Walls," under the pseudonym "Alexander Nevermind." And Tipper Gore credited allusions to masturbation in the *Purple Rain* track "Darling Nikki" with inspiring her to form the Parents Music Resource Center and launch the Senate hearings on offensive rock lyrics, which led to the record industry's "voluntary" album-stickering policy.

Prince followed up *Purple Rain* with the psychedelic *Around the World in a Day,* which topped the chart for three straight weeks but was considered a critical and commercial disappointment. Prince reportedly had to be persuaded to release singles from it, but the album did yield hits in the Beatles-esque "Raspberry Beret" (#2, 1985) and the funky "Pop Life" (#7, 1985). Upon the album's release Prince's management announced his retirement from live performance (which would last for two years) and the opening of his own studio and record label, both named Paisley Park—after a track on the new album (which also included a spiritual epic, "The Ladder," which Prince wrote with his previously estranged father). Paisley Park recording acts included the Family (fronted by Wendy Melvoin's twin sister Susannah), Mazarati (led by Cymone's replacement, Brown Mark), Madhouse (a jazz-funk band led by Prince's sax player Eric Leeds), and Jill Jones (who'd appeared, draped around Lisa Coleman, in the "1999" video). None of them ever had a hit, although the Family's Prince-penned "Nothing Compares 2 U" would later be a massive hit for Sinéad O'Connor.

In spring 1986 Prince was back atop the pop singles chart with "Kiss," a stripped-down return to his funk roots. It would be heard (briefly) in Prince's next movie, *Under the Cherry Moon,* a romantic trifle shot on the French Riviera, with Prince replacing music video auteur Mary Lambert (Madonna's "Like a Virgin," among others) as director midway through production. The film bombed with critics and moviegoers; its soundtrack album, *Parade* (#3, 1986), yielded two minor hit singles in "Mountains" (#23, 1986) and "Anotherloverholenyohead" (#63, 1986). On July 1, 1986, Prince played an impromptu live set following the world premiere of *Cherry Moon* in Sheridan, Wyoming (where the winner of an MTV movie-premiere contest lived).

In 1987 Prince fired the Revolution (Wendy and Lisa [see entry] would go on to record as a duo, scoring a minor hit single with "Waterfall") and, retaining only Matt Fink, replaced them with a new, unnamed band featuring Sheila E. on drums. They debuted with the double-album *Sign 'O' the Times* (#6, 1987), widely hailed by critics as a return to form. It yielded hit singles in the stark title track (#3, 1987), the funky Sheena Easton duet "U Got the Look" (#2, 1987), and the poppy "I Could Never Take the Place of Your Man" (#10, 1987). Prince toured Europe with a theatrically choreographed show, but rather than touring the U.S. released a film of a concert shot in Rotterdam, Holland.

In late 1987 rumors circulated of a new Prince project, *The Black Album,* said to consist of musically and lyrically raw funk tracks; it was never officially released until late 1994, but until then it became one of the most bootlegged LPs in pop history (tapes were stolen from Warner's German pressing plant). His next official release was the mild *Lovesexy* (#11, 1988), which got lack-luster reviews and yielded only one hit, "Alphabet Street" (#8, 1988), but did prompt Prince's first U.S. tour in four years, performed on a rotating stage that Prince entered in a pink Cadillac.

In 1989 Prince had his first chart-topping album in four years with his soundtrack for director Tim Burton's big-budget *Batman* movie; "Batdance" was Prince's first #1 since "Kiss." His half-sister Lorna Nelson lost a lawsuit claiming he'd stolen her lyrics for "U Got the Look." Two months after the release of his *Batman* album, Prince—who'd already written and produced an album for Paisley Park signee Mavis Staples and undertaken productions for the Time's Morris Day and Jerome Benton and for *Batman* star (and reputed Prince paramour) Kim Basinger—released *Graffiti Bridge,* a film that seemed to be a delayed sequel to *Purple Rain,* again pitting Prince against the Time on the Minneapolis club scene. Prince's love interest was played by Ingrid Chavez, who would gain greater fame for helping Lenny Kravitz write Madonna's hit "Justify My Love" (though she'd have to sue Kravitz to get a composing credit). The movie was another critical and commercial disaster; the soundtrack album (#6, 1990) yielded the hit "Thieves in the Temple" (#6, 1990) and Tevin Campbell's Prince-penned "Round and Round" (#12, 1991).

In January 1991, at his recently opened Glam Slam nightclub in Minneapolis, Prince unveiled a new band, the New Power Generation, which would not tour the U.S. until 1993. The band included an unimpressive rapping dancer (Anthony "Tony M" Mosely), in Prince's first nod to hip-hop, which had claimed a significant share of his black pop audience, and with which he never seemed comfortable musically. The following month Prince was sued for severance pay and punitive damages by his ex-managers, Robert Cavallo, Joseph Ruffalo, and Steven Fargnoli, whom Prince had fired in 1988. Eight months later he released his fifth album in five years, *Diamonds and Pearls* (#3, 1991), which spawned Top Ten hits in the lascivious "Gett Off" (#21, 1991), "Cream" (#1, 1991), and the title track (#3, 1992). Warner Bros. made Prince a vice president when he re-signed with the label in 1992. His next album (#5, 1992) was titled after an unpronounceable merger of the male and female gender symbols; its hit singles included "7" (#8, 1992), "My Name Is Prince" (#36, 1992), and the profane "Sexy M.F." (#66, 1992). Prince produced an album for yet another protégée, Carmen Electra, and New York's Joffrey Ballet announced that it was choreographing a four-part ballet to Prince's music, called *Billboards* (it would premiere at the University of Iowa in October 1993).

In September 1993 Prince pulled the most eccentric move of his career, changing his name to the unpronounceable symbol with which he'd titled his last album. "Symbol Man," "Glyph," or "the artist formerly known as Prince"—shortened to Formerly—as he was now known, suffered widespread ridicule, followed by a business setback in February 1994, when Warner Bros. dropped its distribution deal with Paisley Park Records, effectively putting the label out of business. Two weeks later the man who used to be Prince released a new single, "The Most Beautiful Girl in the World," not on Warners but on independent Bellmark Records, which had had a huge hit the previous summer with Tag Team's "Whoomp! There It Is"; Warners said it allowed Symbol Man this "experiment," at his request but would release his future product—1994's *Come* (a compilation of old material) and the legit *Black Album.* Still bickering with Warners, Symbol Man wrote "Slave" on his cheek for a photo session; the label delayed the release of his next album until fall 1995.

John Prine

Born October 10, 1946, Maywood, Illinois
1971—*John Prine* (Atlantic)   1972—*Diamonds in the Rough*   1973—*Sweet Revenge*   1975—*Common Sense*   1976—*Prime Prine—The Best of John Prine*   1978—*Bruised Orange* (Asylum)   1979—*Pink Cadillac*   1980—*Storm Windows*   1984—*Aimless Love* (Oh Boy)   1986—*German Afternoons*   1988—*John Prine Live*   1991—*The Missing Years*   1993—*Great Days: The John Prine Anthology* (Rhino)   1995—*Lost Dogs & Mixed Blessings* (Oh Boy).

John Prine is a critically acclaimed singer/songwriter who has gone from solo acoustic folk to hard country to rockabilly to soft rock, all the while maintaining his hard-headed vision of white proletarian America.

Prine learned guitar from his father and played the Chicago coffeehouse circuit while working at the post office. With his friend and sometime production cohort Steve Goodman, Prine graduated from the Chicago folk scene. Paul Anka liked some of Prine's Hank Williams–influenced songs and was instrumental in landing him a recording contract. In 1971 Prine went to Memphis and cut his debut. That LP's most notable song may have been "Sam Stone," a bleak drug-addicted Vietnam veteran's saga, which aptly demonstrated Prine's laconic, drawling delivery.

Though his own commercial success was meager, other artists began recording his songs: the Everly Brothers did "Paradise," and both Joan Baez and Bette Midler recorded "Hello in There." *Common Sense* saw Prine shocking his folk audience by using hard-rock rhythms and a guttural singing style. *Bruised Orange,* produced by Goodman, returned Prine to the acoustic format of *Diamonds in the Rough,* while *Pink Cadillac* was an electric rockabilly album produced by Sam Phillips and his son Knox at Sun Studios.

Prine formed his own label, Oh Boy Records, in 1983. His second album for the label, the countryish *German Afternoons*, earned a Grammy Award nomination for Best Contemporary Folk Recording. After releasing his first live album in 1988, Prine won the Best Contemporary Folk Grammy for *The Missing Years*, which was produced by Howie Epstein of Tom Petty's Heartbreakers and had guest appearances by Petty, Bruce Springsteen, and Bonnie Raitt (who had been singing Prine's "Angel from Montgomery" in concert for years). Prine made his movie acting debut with a small role in John Mellencamp's 1992 *Falling from Grace*. He retains a cult following for his down-to-earth, unadorned insights.

P. J. Proby

Born James Marcus Smith, November 6, 1938, Houston, Texas
1965—*I Am P. J. Proby* (Liberty).

P. J. Proby is a Presleyesque singer who was always more popular in England than in his native America, though even there his chart appearances became increasingly rare after 1968. Proby's big break came when British TV producer Jack Good brought him to the U.K. for a Beatles special in 1964; he hit with the Good-produced "Hold Me" (#3 U.K., #70 U.S.), a frantic revival of a 1939 ballad. Before that Proby had been living in Hollywood, doing odd jobs, playing bit parts in films, and recording demos like "Jet Powers." After "Hold Me," followups failed to generate comparable success, and he switched styles; he began singing melodramatic versions of tunes from the Broadway musical *West Side Story*, for example.

Proby toured England in 1965 with Cilla Black but was expelled from the country later that year after a series of incidents in which he split his velvet trousers onstage. In 1967 his tour choreographer was Kim Fowley. That year he had his biggest U.S. hit with "Niki Hoeky" (#23). By 1968, though, Proby was bankrupt. He was lured back to England by Good in 1971 to appear in *Catch My Soul*, a rock adaptation of *Othello*. Proby also played the older Elvis Presley in the West End musical *Elvis* in 1977. After years as a steady-drawing revival act in England, Proby unexpectedly teamed up with the Dutch classical-rock band Focus in 1978 for the *Focus con Proby* LP. He's maintained a low profile since, occasionally releasing singles that generate far more curiosity than sales.

The Proclaimers

Formed 1983, Edinburgh, Scotland
Craig Reid (b. Mar. 5, 1962, Edinburgh), voc.; Charlie Reid (b. Charles Reid, Mar. 5, 1962, Edinburgh), gtr., voc.

The Proclaimers: Craig and Charlie Reid

1987—*This Is the Story* (Chrysalis)   1988—*Sunshine on Leith*   1990—*King of the Road* EP   1994—*Hit the Highway*.

As the folk-rock duo the Proclaimers, twin brothers Charlie and Craig Reid enjoyed critical acclaim, and some commercial success in the U.K., before scoring an American pop hit in 1993 with "I'm Gonna Be (500 Miles)"—a single that was originally released in 1988. While growing up in County Fife, the Scottish brothers listened to their father's collection of seminal American rock and soul records. Later the Reids became infatuated with punk and played in several bands.

As the Proclaimers they got their first break three years later, when they were invited to support the popular British band the Housemartins on tour. *This Is the Story*, a collection of sparse acoustic songs, yielded the #3 U.K. single "Letter to America." *Sunshine on Leith* found the Proclaimers working with a full band, while continuing to lend their burr-inflected vocal harmonies to songs about Scottish politics and love. The album contained the track "I'm Gonna Be (500 Miles)," which went to #11 in England and #1 in Australia. The song didn't make an impact on the U.S. pop charts, though, until it was featured on the soundtrack to the 1993 film *Benny and Joon*, after which it peaked at #3.

Procol Harum

Formed 1966, London, England
Gary Brooker (b. May 29, 1945, Eng.), piano, voc.; Keith Reid (b. ca. 1948), lyrics; Matthew Fisher (b. Mar. 7, 1946, Eng.), organ; Ray Royer (b. Oct. 8, 1945, Eng.), gtr.; Dave Knights (b. June 28, 1945, Eng.), bass; Bobby Harrison (b. June 28, 1943, Eng.), drums.

1967—(– Royer; – Harrison; + Robin Trower [b. Mar. 9, 1945, London], gtr.; + B. J. Wilson [b. Mar. 18, 1947, Eng.; d. 1989], drums) *Procol Harum* (Deram) 1968—*Shine On Brightly* (A&M)   1969—*A Salty Dog* 1970—(– Fisher; – Knights; + Chris Copping [b. Aug. 29, 1945, Eng.], bass, organ) *Home*   1971— *Broken Barricades* (– Trower; + Dave Ball [b. Mar. 30, 1950], gtr.; + Alan Cartwright [b. Oct. 10, 1945], bass)   1972—*Live in Concert* (– Ball; + Mick Grabham, gtr.)   1973—*Grand Hotel* (Chrysalis)   1974— *Exotic Birds and Fruit*   1975—*Procol Ninth* 1976—(– Cartwright; + Pete Solley, organ; Copping switches to bass)   1977—*Something Magic* (group disbands)   1991—(Group re-forms: Brooker; Trower; Fisher; Reid; + Dave Bronze, bass; + Mark Brzezicki, drums) *The Prodigal Stranger* (Zoo). Gary Brooker solo: 1979—*No More Fear of Flying* (Chrysalis)   1982—*Lead Me to the Water* (Mercury) 1984—*Echoes in the Night.* Matthew Fisher solo: 1973—*Journeys End* (RCA) 1980—*Matthew Fisher* (A&M).

With the 1967 worldwide smash "A Whiter Shade of Pale"—a combination of mystical lyrics, a somber tempo, and an organ line lifted directly from Bach's Suite No. 3 in D major—Procol Harum established itself, along with the Moody Blues, as an early British "classical rock" band. Though the band never matched that spectacular success, "A Whiter Shade of Pale" has outlasted the Summer of Love. It has sold over six million copies worldwide and has been covered in soul, jazz, and country versions.

The band—whose only other U.S. hit was an orchestrated 1972 reworking of 1967's "Conquistador"— included only one member with classical training: Matthew Fisher, who studied at the Guildhall School of Music. Procol Harum actually began as an R&B band, the Paramounts (Gary Brooker, Robin Trower, Chris Copping, and B. J. Wilson) in London's Southend section in 1963. The Paramounts made several singles, but only a cover of "Little Bitty Pretty One" achieved any local success, and they broke up in 1966.

Later that year Brooker met lyricist Keith Reid (who was always listed as a full-fledged band member on the group's albums), and they formed a band—with Fisher, Ray Royer, Dave Knights, and Bobby Harrison—to record their songs. The name Procol Harum allegedly came from the name of a friend's cat (they often jokingly referred to themselves as the "Purple Horrors"); roughly translated from Latin, it means "beyond these things." The original Procol Harum ended up recording only one single, the crucial "A Whiter Shade of Pale" (on which sessionman Bill Eyden replaced Harrison).

In the wake of the single's success (repeated to a much lesser degree in the U.K. by "Homburg" in mid-1967), Royer and Harrison were replaced by Trower and

Wilson, and this lineup recorded the first three Procol Harum albums.

In late 1969 Fisher and Knights departed (Fisher has since recorded solo albums) and were replaced by Copping. *Home* saw Trower leading the band in a harder-rocking direction. The same held true for *Broken Barricades,* but the guitarist's Jimi Hendrix–inspired hard-rock leanings were never fully integrated and seemed at odds with the band's stately pace and Reid's existential-visionary lyrics. Trower left in July 1971. He went on to form the short-lived Jude with British R&B singer Frankie Miller and then the highly successful Robin Trower Band, a Hendrixian power trio, whose 1973 debut, *Twice Removed from Yesterday,* was produced by Fisher.

With new guitarist Dave Ball, Copping concentrating on organ, and new bassist Alan Cartwright, the band recorded *Live in Concert* (#5, 1972) with the Edmonton Symphony Orchestra and the Da Camera Singers. The success of the symphonic "Conquistador" remake caused a minor resurgence in sales, on which the group failed to capitalize with *Grand Hotel* (#21, 1973), a mélange of orchestral epics and harder-rocking tunes. By the time of *Hotel,* Ball had left to form Bedlam and was replaced by ex-Cochise guitarist Mick Grabham. Two more albums, *Exotic Birds and Fruit* and *Procol Ninth,* went nowhere. After a two-year hiatus, the band tried one last time with *Something Magic*—produced by Leiber and Stoller—then broke up for good. After another two years, during which he played in the 1979 Concerts for Kampuchea, Brooker made a solo album, *No More Fear of Flying,* which was both a critical and commercial disappointment. In 1981 he played piano on Eric Clapton's LP *Another Ticket,* and in 1982 and 1984 he released two more solo records.

In 1991, two years after the death of B. J. Wilson, Brooker, Fisher, Reid, and Trower reunited to record *The Prodigal Stranger.* With Geoff Whitehorn in place of Trower, and bassist Dave Bronze and Big Country drummer Mark Brzezicki, they toured and continue to perform occasionally. Brooker has since toured with the Prague Symphony, and as of 1994 was producing and scoring an LP, *Symphonic Music of Procol Harum.*

Professor Longhair

Born Henry Roeland Byrd, December 19, 1918, Bogalusa, Louisiana; died January 30, 1980, New Orleans, Louisiana
1972—*New Orleans Piano* (Atlantic)   1975—*Rock 'n' Roll Gumbo* (Barclay)   1978—*Live on the Queen Mary* (Harvest)   1980—*Crawfish Fiesta* (Alligator) 1981—*Mardi Gras in New Orleans* (Nighthawk) 1982—*The Last Mardi Gras* (Atlantic)   1987— *Houseparty New Orleans Style* (Rounder)   1989—

New Orleans Piano (Blues Originals, vol. 2) **(Atlantic) 1993—***'Fess: The Professor Longhair Anthology* **(Rhino).**

Professor Longhair originated one of the classic styles of
rock & roll piano playing, a New Orleans potpourri—ragtime, jazz, Delta blues, zydeco, West Indian, and Afro-
Cuban dances—distilled into boogie-woogie bass lines
in the left hand and rolling arpeggios in the right. It
was the style popularized by Fats Domino, Huey
"Piano" Smith, Allen Toussaint, Dr. John, and scores of
others.

Henry Byrd first played piano when, as a boy, he discovered an abandoned upright in a New Orleans alley.
Recalling everything he'd heard while dancing for tips
outside nightclubs and behind parade bands, he taught
himself to play. It was not until he was 30, however, that
he began to work professionally as a musician; before
then he'd had stints as a prizefighter, a gambler, and a
vaudeville dancer. In 1949 he formed a quintet called
Professor Longhair and His Shuffling Hungarians, which
included Robert Parker on tenor sax and recorded four
songs—"She Ain't Got No Hair," "Mardi Gras in New Orleans," "Professor Longhair's Boogie," and "Bye Bye
Baby"—on the Star Talent label.

The following year, the Professor was signed to Mercury and rerecorded "She Ain't Got No Hair" under the
title "Baldhead," which reached #5 on *Billboard*'s R&B
chart. Longhair later recorded on over a dozen labels,
while a combination of poor health and mismanagement
kept his career from being established. He received virtually nothing for "Go to the Mardi Gras," his 1959 remake of his own "Mardi Gras in New Orleans," which
became a theme song of the annual carnival. Although
"Big Chief" was a modest hit in the Louisiana area for
him and Earl King in 1964, he soon afterward left the
music business and took up manual labor to support
himself and his family.

In 1971 Longhair was rediscovered by talent scouts
for the New Orleans Jazz and Heritage Festival; thereafter he performed at every New Orleans Festival until
his death and appeared on the 1976 live Festival album.
His comeback also took him to the Newport Folk Festival
in 1973 and to several festivals in Europe. In the last
decade of his life Atlantic released a collection of his vintage recordings, and he put out three newly recorded albums. Shortly before his death from a heart attack, he
was engaged to tour with the Clash. In 1991 he was inducted into the Rock and Roll Hall of Fame.

Progressive Rock

Generally, "progressive" denotes a form of rock music in
which electric instruments and rock-band formats are
integrated with European classical motifs and orchestrations, typically forming extended, intricate, multisec-
tional suites.

The progressive-rock movement began in Britain in
the late Sixties as an outgrowth of psychedelia's adven-
turism and owes its lyrics' frequent use of cosmic
themes to acid rock. But progressive rock is definitely a
Seventies genre, accenting a daunting instrumental virtuosity and grandiosity over earthy directness.

One of the earliest and most influential progressive-
rock albums—in an album-oriented genre—was King
Crimson's *In the Court of the Crimson King* (1969),
though that record pointed to the genre's influences,
Procol Harum and the Moody Blues (for their
churchy/symphonic classicism), and Jimi Hendrix (for
his "cosmic," highly distorted guitar style). Progressive-
rock bands of the European classical virtuoso class—of
wildly varying quality and popularity—include the Nice,
King Crimson, Gentle Giant, Yes, early Genesis, Emerson,
Lake and Palmer, Focus, Kansas, and Van der Graaf Generator.

Progressive rock is sometimes also known as "art
rock" though bands like the early Roxy Music, which
rocked hard but made full, witty use of a self-conscious,
ironic detachment that is less high-minded than Yes,
ELP, et al., are also known as art rockers, which can
cause some confusion.

Ancillary to the British/European techno-flash movement was the whimsical jazz-rock-psychedelic fusion of
Canterbury band Soft Machine, which begat a related
school of more sedate, less grandiose chamberoriented
bands that were virtuosic in a more playfully jazzy manner—the Anglo/Gallic Gong (which later went the fusion
route), Hatfield and the North, and Caravan. This form of
progressive rock has proven far less commercially successful than that of Yes, Genesis, ELP, et al.

Psychedelic Furs

Formed 1978, London, England
**Richard Butler (b. June 5, 1956, Kingston-upon-
Thames, Eng.), voc.; Tim Butler (b. Dec. 7, 1958,
Eng.), bass; Duncan Kilburn (b. Eng.), sax; Roger
Morris (b. Eng.), gtr.**
**1978—(+ John Ashton [b. Nov. 30, 1957, Eng.], gtr.)
1979—(+ Vince Ely [b. Eng.], drums) 1980—***The
Psychedelic Furs* **(Columbia) 1981—***Talk, Talk,
Talk* **(– Kilburn; – Morris) 1982—***Forever Now*
(– Ely; + Phil Calvert, drums) 1984—*Mirror Moves*
(– Calvert; + Paul Garisto, drums) 1987—*Midnight
to Midnight* **(– Garisto; + Ely; + Mars Williams, gtr.;
+ Joe McGinty, kybds.) 1988—***All of This and
Nothing* **1989—***Book of Days* **(+ Knox Chandler,
gtr., cello) 1990—(– Ely; + Don Yallech, drums)
1991—***World Outside* **(group disbands).**

Love Spit Love, formed 1991 (R. Butler; T. Butler; Richard Fortus, gtr.; Frank Ferrer, drums): 1994— *Love Spit Love* (Imago).

Though their name sounded psychedelic, the Furs' sound was very much a product of punk. Ironically, the group would become most closely associated with its very unpunklike "Pretty in Pink." The group began in early 1978 when leader, vocalist, and songwriter Richard Butler joined his younger brother Tim, Duncan Kilburn, and Roger Morris. They decided on the name because it would stand out from all the S&M-named bands of the time and pay homage to their psychedelia-era idols like the Doors, the early Stooges, and Velvet Underground.

Richard Butler had previously been an art student in college, but around his graduation he decided to pursue music, although he knew little about playing. In November 1978 John Ashton joined on second guitar, and in spring 1979 they added drummer Vince Ely. The band's early dirges (which it describes as "beautiful chaos") were played by BBC disc jockey John Peel, which led to the Furs' signing with Columbia. Their debut was produced by Steve Lillywhite and Howard Thompson, with two tracks on the U.S. version produced by Martin Hannett. Though well received, it sold only moderately, as did their 1981 followup, *Talk, Talk, Talk* (#89, 1981), despite its clearer lyrics and production (this time all by Lillywhite). The album is notable for containing the original version of "Pretty in Pink."

Despite significant MTV exposure and a high profile with college-radio audiences, the Psychedelic Furs sold only moderately here and at home. The group's third album, the gold *Forever Now* (#61, 1982), was produced by Todd Rundgren and featured brass and strings; it included the Furs' first U.S. hit, "Love My Way" (#44). *Mirror Moves* (#43, 1984) featured "Heaven," a U.K. Top Thirty single, and the group mounted a large international tour.

Around this time director John Hughes informed the group that he'd written a movie script based on "Pretty in Pink." The Psychedelic Furs' rerecorded version of the 1981 album track hit #41 and was included on the career retrospective *All of This and Nothing* (#102, 1988) and the *Pretty in Pink* soundtrack. Previous to this, the group released its highest-charting LP, *Midnight to Midnight* (#29, 1987), featuring "Heartbreak Beat," its sole Top Thirty U.S. single. Throughout the Psychedelic Furs' history, members have come and gone, with the Butler brothers and John Ashton the constants. Neither of the group's last two studio albums—*Book of Days* and *World Outside*—improved its fortunes, and in 1991 the Psychedelic Furs broke up.

Richard Butler, with brother Tim, started a new group, Love Spit Love. The group's debut album spent one week on the chart, at #195; the single, "Am I Wrong," peaked at #83 in fall 1994.

Psychedelic Rock

Also known variously as "acid rock" or the "San Francisco Sound," psychedelic music ostensibly intended to musically re-create the "trips" induced by mind-expanding drugs. Even at the height of late-Sixties antidrug hysteria and moves to ban certain songs from radio playlists because of their alleged drug references, there were lots of pyschedelic-rock hit singles: the Small Faces' "Itchycoo Park," the Moody Blues' "Tuesday Afternoon," Jimi Hendrix's "Purple Haze," the Jefferson Airplane's "White Rabbit," and Status Quo's "Pictures of Matchstick Men."

Many psychedelic bands, such as the Grateful Dead, the early Jefferson Airplane, and Quicksilver Messenger Service, came out of San Francisco and its Haight-Ashbury district, the early center of hippie activity; concurrently, Britain produced Pink Floyd. That band's music made use of electronic effects, extended forms, and popular exotica like Middle Eastern modalities and Indian raga, and introduced extended improvisation into rock, often with musically dubious results, but occasionally—as in the Grateful Dead's "Dark Star"—with enough sustained invention and group interplay to stake a legitimate claim to the rock band as jazz ensemble. (Three decades later, the Grateful Dead remains one of the few major bands still playing extended psychedelic jams in concert.)

This brand of psychedelia had some roots in the more adventurous forms of mid-Sixties American garage punk collated on albums like *Nuggets,* for example, "It's a Happening" by the Magic Mushrooms or "Incense and Peppermints" by Strawberry Alarm Clock—both more poppish and naive than later psychedelia, but ultimately no more naive and outdated than most psychedelia soon became. The 13th Floor Elevators were perhaps the most important early progenitors of psychedelic garage rock.

Nevertheless, not all Sixties and Seventies music that refers to drugs is psychedelic, and not all psychedelic music refers explicitly to drugs. Many of psychedelic music's innovations persisted through such subsequent genres as progressive rock and some forms of fusion. In the Eighties, psychedelic music inspired the sound of such alternative bands as the Dream Syndicate, Rain Parade, and the Fuzztones.

Psychic TV

Formed 1979, London, England
Genesis P-Orridge (b. Neil Megson, Feb. 22, 1950, Manchester, Eng.), voc., kybds.
1988—*Allegory and Self* (Revolver)   1990—*Towards thee Infinite Beat* (Wax Trax!); *Beyond thee Infinite*

Genesis P-Orridge of Psychic TV

Beat 1994—*Hex Sex, The Singles—Pt. 1* (Cleopatra).

Confrontational, mercurial, veering from the unlistenable to achingly pretty pop, the self-proclaimed "Temple of Psychick Youth," Psychic TV has a mission: to provide "the most important work . . . in the popular medium." Their albums, mixtures of dada, pop, and spoken word, embrace everything from side-long excursions into white noise to wispy tunes to ethnic music to found-sound collages.

It all makes sense when you discover the "collective" is led by Genesis P-Orridge, a founding member (along with Chris Carter, Cosey Fanni Tutti, and Peter Christopherson) of Throbbing Gristle. Schooled in the same situationalist thought and theories of media manipulation Malcolm McLaren used to promote the Sex Pistols, Throbbing Gristle was more a group of performance artists than a pop band in their four-year existence (1975–79). Drawing on William Burroughs and Philip K. Dick, they viewed the world as a dysfunctional, postindustrial wasteland, and their confrontational music and multimedia performances were designed to shake listeners from their acquiescence.

Psychic TV continues Throbbing Gristle's musical and media guerrilla tactics. Originally P-Orridge with Peter Christopherson, P-Orridge now insists the band is a collective with no set lineup. Some members (P-Orridge's wife, Paula Brooking, John Gosling, and Richard Daws among them) have remained through the band's numerous metamorphoses. While only a few Psy-

chic TV albums have been issued in the U.S., the band released 23 albums, one a month, on the 23rd of each month, beginning in 1982 in England (this feat put them in the *Guinness Book of World Records*). *Allegory and Self* (1988), their first American release, contains Psychic TV's 1986 British hit, "Godstar" (#67 U.K.), a pop song about Brian Jones. But soon afterward, P-Orridge changed tactics. Exposed to house music in 1989, he became enamored of the sound, dubbing it acid house, and with the albums *Towards thee Infinite Beat* and *Beyond . . .* he has moved into the realm of techno and rave, extended grooves with a noise overlay, accompanied in concert by video and slide shows.

Public Enemy

Formed 1982, Garden City, New York
Chuck D (b. Carlton Ridenhour, Aug. 1, 1960, N.Y.), voc.; Flavor Flav (b. William Drayton, Mar. 16, 1959, N.Y.), voc.; Terminator X (b. Norman Lee Rogers, Aug. 25, 1966, N.Y.), DJ; Professor Griff (b. Richard Griffin), minister of information.
1987—*Yo! Bum Rush the Show* (Def Jam)   1988—*It Takes a Nation of Millions to Hold Us Back*   1990—*Fear of a Black Planet*   1991—*Apocalypse 91 . . . The Enemy Strikes Black*   1992—*Greatest Misses*   1994—*Muse Sick-N-Hour Mess Age.* Professor Griff solo: 1990—*Pawns in the Game* (Luke Records)   1991—*Kao's II Wiz*7*Dome.* Terminator X solo: 1991—*Terminator X and the Valley of the Jeep Beets* (RAL)   1994—*Terminator X and the Godfathers of Threatt: Super Bad.*

Perhaps the most important and politically controversial group of its time, Public Enemy introduced a hard, intense, hip-hop sound and vocal delivery that changed the course of rap and influenced a generation of artists. The group's inventive production team, the Bomb Squad, tailored a unique, noisy, layered avant-garde–inspired pop sound that incorporates sirens, skittering turntable scratches, and cleverly juxtaposed musical and spoken samples. PE's songs are characterized by lead rapper Chuck D's politically charged rhymes delivered in a booming, authoritarian voice, and his sidekick/jester, Flavor Flav, who breaks in with taunts, teases, and questions.

The members of Public Enemy came together at Adelphi University on Long Island, where Carlton Ridenhour studied graphic design and worked at student radio station WBAU. There he met Hank Shocklee (future brainchild of the Bomb Squad) and Bill Stephney (future Def Jam executive), with whom he struck up a friendship, talking philosophy, politics, and hip-hop late into the night. After rapping over a track Shocklee had created, "Public Enemy No. 1," Ridenhour started appearing regularly on Stephney's radio show as Chuckie D. Def

Jam cofounder Rick Rubin heard a tape of the rap and started calling Ridenhour.

At first the rapper shunned Rubin, feeling he was too old to begin a career as an entertainer. But he eventually came up with an elaborate plan that involved Shocklee as producer, Stephney as marketer, and DJ Norman Rogers on the turntables. He recruited his Nation of Islam cohort Richard Griffin to coordinate the group's backup dancers, the Security of the First World (S1W), whose members carry fake Uzis and do stiff, martial arts moves as a parody of Motown-era dancers. Ridenhour enrolled his old friend William Drayton, who as Flavor Flav would act as a foil to Chuck D's more sober character.

Calling themselves "prophets of rage," Public Enemy released their debut album, *Yo! Bum Rush the Show,* in 1987. A more sophisticated version of early East Coast gangsta rappers like Boogie Down Productions or Schoolly D, the group at first went nearly unnoticed except by hip-hop insiders and New York critics. The second album, *It Takes a Nation of Millions to Hold Us Back,* took the pop world by storm. Reaching #42 (#1 R&B, 1988), it was immediately hailed as hip-hop's masterpiece and eventually sold a million copies. *Nation* contained the minor hit "Bring the Noise" (#56 R&B, 1988), which foreshadowed PE's knack for controversy, with Chuck D calling Black Muslim leader Louis Farrakhan a prophet. Having referred to rap as "CNN for black culture," he castigates white-controlled media in "Don't Believe the Hype" (#18 R&B, 1988).

In May 1989, just after the group did "Fight the Power" (#20 R&B, 1989), the theme song for Spike Lee's film *Do the Right Thing,* Professor Griff, who had previously made racist comments onstage, dropped a verbal bomb. In an interview with the *Washington Times,* he said Jews are responsible for "the majority of wickedness that goes on across the globe." PE leader Chuck D responded indecisively, first firing Griff, then reinstating him, then temporarily disbanding the group. When Griff then attacked his bandmates in another interview, he was dismissed permanently. Chuck D responded to the fiasco by writing "Welcome to the Terrordome" (#15 R&B, 1990), a ferociously noisy track in which the rapper asserts that "they got me like Jesus." That lyric fanned the coals of controversy yet again, with Chuck D himself being branded an anti-Semite.

PE followed with its first Top Ten album, *Fear of a Black Planet* (#10 pop, #3 R&B, 1990), which explored the nature of white racism in songs like "Burn Hollywood Burn" and "911 Is a Joke" (#15 R&B, 1990), and called on African-Americans to unite in "Brothers Gonna Work It Out" (#20 R&B, 1990) and "War at 33 1/3." Upon its release in 1991, *Apocalypse 91* shot to #4 (#1 R&B), spawning the hits "Can't Truss It" (#50 pop, #9 R&B, 1991) and "Shut Em Down" (#26 R&B, 1992). *Greatest Misses*

reached #13 (#10 R&B) in 1992 and was criticized for its unexciting remixes. The same year, Public Enemy teamed up with thrash-metal band Anthrax, with whom they had recorded a successful update of "Bring the Noise," for a joint tour. They also opened for U2's Zoo TV Tour.

PE returned in 1994 with *Muse Sick-N-Hour Mess Age,* which, like albums by other older rap artists, debuted fairly high on the charts but quickly fell in sales (#14 pop, #4 R&B, 1994).

Beginning in 1991, Flavor Flav had some run-ins with the law. He was convicted of assaulting his girlfriend and served a 20-day jail sentence. In 1993 he was charged with attempted murder when he allegedly shot at a neighbor in a domestic squabble; he chose to undergo drug rehabilitation and the charges were dropped.

Public Image Ltd. (PiL)

Formed 1978, England
John Lydon (a.k.a. Johnny Rotten, b. Jan. 31, 1956, Eng.), voc.; Keith Levene (b. Eng.), gtr., electronics; Jah Wobble (b. John Wordle, a.k.a. Dan MacArthur, Eng.), bass; Jim Walker (b. Can.), drums; Jeanette Lee, videos; Dave Crowe, business, finances.
1978—*First Issue* (Virgin, U.K.)   1979—(– Walker; + Richard Dudanski, drums; – Dudanski; + Martin Atkins [b. Aug. 3, 1959, Coventry, Eng.], drums) 1980—*Second Edition* (Island); *Paris au Printemps* (Virgin) (– Atkins; – Wobble)   1981— (– Crowe) *Flowers of Romance* (Warner Bros.) (– Lee)   1983—*Live in Tokyo* (Elektra) (– Levene) 1984—*This Is What You Want . . . This Is What You Get*   1986—*Album* (a.k.a. *Cassette,* a.k.a. *Compact Disc*)   1987—*Happy?* (Virgin)   1989—*9*   1990— *The Greatest Hits, So Far*   1992—*That What Is Not.*

Public Image arose from the ashes of the Sex Pistols, the group's original intent as much a reaction to that band as the Pistols were to Seventies rock & roll before them. Former head Pistol Johnny Rotten took his real name, John Lydon, after the last Sex Pistols show on January 14, 1978. He conceived Public Image as a group organization to create "anti–rock & roll" to embody what the more conventionally rock-rooted Pistols only sang about. Lydon teamed up with Keith Levene, who was an early member of the Clash and also a classically trained guitarist and pianist, plus novice bassist Jah Wobble and drummer Jim Walker, from the Canadian group the Furys. Their original name was Carnivorous Buttock Flies, but they quickly changed to PiL (for Public Image Ltd., the "Ltd." since they professed to see themselves as a company rather than a rock band). Financial advisor Dave Crowe was credited as a band member.

PiL made their live debut in London on Christmas Day 1978, just before their first LP, *First Issue,* came out.

It was not released in the U.S., and its slow, embittered songs got mostly negative reviews. Yet it soared to the top of the English charts. Critics caught on with 1979's *Metal Box*, initially released in England in a limited edition of 50,000 incorporating three 12-inch 45-rpm EPs squeezed into a film canister. It came out the next year in the U.S. as *Second Edition* (#171, 1980), a conventional double LP, to almost universal critical acclaim. *Second Edition* was characterized by a uniquely droning sound with prominent dublike bass, neo-psychedelic guitar from Levene, oddly danceable rhythms, and haunting echoed vocals. Levene's dissonant guitar influenced a whole range of bands, from Killing Joke and U2 to Gang of Four. The band toured the U.S. in spring 1980 with new drummer Martin Atkins. At the end of the tour in June Atkins was fired (he later recorded as Brian Brain and formed Pigface, a veritable industrial supergroup); a few weeks later Wobble was fired as well. Wobble had released two solo LPs during his time in the band, and group members charged he used some PiL backing tracks on these without permission.

Later in 1980, a live LP from the band's Paris show the previous January, called *Paris au Printemps*, was issued in Europe only. In spring 1981 *Flowers of Romance*, named for late Sex Pistol Sid Vicious' first band, was released. Atkins as drummer-for-hire played on three tracks, with Levene and Lydon handling the rest. It was a stark, mostly percussion- and vocals-oriented record with some Middle Eastern vocal influences. Its major connection to rock & roll may have been its audacity.

In May 1981 Lydon and Levene, filling in for Bow Wow Wow, played New York's Ritz. Performing behind a video screen with a hired rhythm section, with Lee on hand taping the proceedings (the images were projected onto the screen), the band jammed as Lydon and Levene taunted the sold-out crowd. They were pelted with beer bottles as a riot ensued.

In 1983, during the recording of *This Is What You Want . . .*, Levene acrimoniously left PiL. His guitar parts were erased; Levene released his version of the album independently as *Commercial Zone*. Lydon found himself with a club hit via "This Is Not a Love Song" and recruited a faceless backup band. From this point on, PiL was a *de facto* John Lydon solo project. In the recording studio, he worked with such veterans as producer/bassist Bill Laswell, guitarist Nicky Skopelitis, and drummer Tony Williams.

Enlisting producers Gary Langan on *Happy?* (#169, 1987) and Stephen Hague on *9* (#106, 1989), Lydon assembled dance music that rarely reached the bilious passion of early PiL. Backed by revolving, usually uncredited musicians, he became the type of "entertainer" he claimed to detest. Lydon reclaimed the "Rotten" moniker on *Happy?* In 1993, working with the techno production team Leftfield, he released a dance track,

"Open Up," in the U.K. His autobiography, *Rotten: No Irish—No Blacks—No Dogs* (written with Keith and Kent Zimmerman) was published in 1994.

Gary Puckett and the Union Gap

Formed 1967, San Diego, California
Gary Puckett (b. Oct. 17, 1942, Hibbing, Minn.), voc.; Dwight Bement (b. Dec. 1945, San Diego), sax; Kerry Chater (b. Aug. 7, 1945, Vancouver, Can.), bass; Gary Withem (b. Aug. 22, 1946, San Diego), piano; Paul Wheatbread (b. Feb. 8, 1946, San Diego), drums.
1968—*Woman, Woman* (Columbia); *Young Girl*; *Incredible* 1970—*Greatest Hits*.

Gary Puckett and the Union Gap had four gold pop-soul sound-alike hits within a year, beginning in late 1967 with "Woman, Woman" (#4). The band formed in January 1967 in San Diego, where all the members had gone to school. They played the local circuit as the Outcasts but then took the name Union Gap from a small town in Washington State near where Puckett grew up. The only member with prior professional experience was Paul Wheatbread, who had been a regular on Dick Clark's *Where the Action Is* and had played with the Turtles, the Mamas and the Papas, Paul Revere and the Raiders, and Otis Redding.

The Union Gap's visual gimmick was to appear in blue and gold Civil War uniforms. After "Woman, Woman" the band hit #2 with both "Young Girl" and "Lady Willpower" in 1968. Next came "Over You" (#7, 1968). "Young Girl," a British #1, became a hit (#6) a second time in England in 1974. In all, the Union Gap released four LPs plus a best-of, all produced by Jerry Fuller, author of "Young Girl," "Lady Willpower," and in 1961, Rick Nelson's #1 hit "Travelin' Man." But after 1969's "Don't Give In to Him" (#15) and "This Girl Is a Woman Now" (#9), the group's hits faded, and it disbanded in 1971.

Kerry Chater, who had written many Union Gap songs, penned tunes for Cass Elliot, Charlie Rich, and Bobby Darin. He also did backup vocals for Sonny and Cher and *The Tonight Show* and recorded two solo LPs for Warner Bros.: *Party Time Love* and *Love on a Shoestring* (1978). Puckett pursued a solo career without success. In the mid-Eighties he hit the nostalgia circuit with the Turtles in 1984 and the Monkees two years later. He still tours, writes songs with his brother David, and in 1992 released an LP in Germany, *Love Me Tonight*.

Punk Rock

Punk rock first appeared in the mid-Sixties as the aggressively amateurish, undecorous response of middle-American garage bands to the more genteel British Invasion.

This was the stuff of the *Nuggets* and *Wild Thing* compilations, tunes like ? and the Mysterians' "96 Tears" and Count Five's "Psychotic Reaction."

The punk movement that would change the face of rock, however, coalesced at anarchist artist Malcolm McLaren's Sex boutique in London a decade later in the form of the subversive, dangerous-sounding Sex Pistols. A generation of working-class British youth, disgusted with what it perceived as a corpulent, conservative, irrelevant, and institutionalized rock establishment, responded to the Pistols' cry of "Liar" and began playing by their own rules. The music was raw, abrasive, basic, and very fast, its rhythms forced and decidedly unfunky. The musicians were usually untrained and made fashion statements with severely cropped hair, black leather, and sadomasochistic bondage gear. Punk was an expression of postindustrial angst, nihilism, and revulsion; its closest antecedents were such similarly abrasive, aggressive, and minimally basic American bands as the Stooges, the MC5, and the New York Dolls.

In 1974, just before Britain's punk-rock explosion, the Ramones had emerged from New York's more arty punk scene, centered on the Bowery club CBGB, alongside Talking Heads, Patti Smith, and Television. With their stripped-down, hyperdriven remodelings of Sixties garage rock, and such apolitical songs as "Now I Wanna Sniff Some Glue" and "Beat on the Brat," they served as another inspiration to the more politically motivated British punk bands. But while the American punks didn't make an impact on mass culture until much later, in England the Pistols actually made it to the charts with the first punk antihit "Anarchy in the U.K."; the Clash had "White Riot," and the Buzzcocks had "Boredom."

Soon punk inevitably became an institution itself. It begat an acceptable corporate face in new wave, and caught on in America more through fashion advertisements and news reports than through music. The Sex Pistols broke up in 1978 at the end of their brief first and only U.S. tour; the Clash matured into an ethnic-fusion band whose politics became ever more pronounced until the band dissolved over creative differences; Buzzcocks turned to punky love songs, then broke up (only to reform and tour in the 1990s, capitalizing on the alternative-rock boom). But punk's breakdown of the "rock star" image, its skepticism of major record companies, severe weltschmerz, and introduction of female band members who shared equal footing with male counterparts had made a profound impact on post-Seventies rock. Punk had become as much a philosophy as a musical style.

By the early Eighties, punk had turned into American and British "hardcore" movements. In Southern California, an independent punk scene formed around the Long Beach–based SST record label, founded by Black Flag guitarist Greg Ginn. With bands like the Flag and Minutemen, and such non-SST groups as X and the Germs,

the scene fostered a permanent American punk-rock foundation, kicking off a DIY ("do it yourself") movement that had swept the nation by mid-decade and contributed to the rise of alternative rock in the late Eighties and early Nineties. The music was louder, harder, and faster, the politics more nihilistic than ever.

In the Nineties, as hardcore splintered into various subgenres, American punk's base shifted to the Pacific Northwest (ironically, the setting of one of the original Sixties punk-rock bands, the Sonics). Centered on the indie label Sub Pop, groups such as Mudhoney and Nirvana gave birth to a punk offshoot, grunge, that borrowed equally from Neil Young and heavy metal, and traded earlier punk fashions (shaved heads and leather) for an updated antifashion (scruffy long hair and flannel). In 1992 Nirvana became the first band to take punk's angst to the top of the chart, proving that the disaffection of mid-Seventies British youth had become epidemic.

James and Bobby Purify

James Purify, born May 12, 1944, Pensacola, Florida; Bobby Purify, born Robert Lee Dicky, September 2, 1939, Tallahassee, Florida.
1988—*100% Purified Soul* (Bell).

James and Bobby Purify's 1966 debut, "I'm Your Puppet," was laid-back soul that charmed both black and white audiences, reaching #6 pop and #5 R&B. These cousins, who had been singing together just over a year before "Puppet," had previously been members of a Florida band called the Dothan Sextet. They subsequently charted with "Shake a Tail Feather" (#25 pop, #15 R&B), "I Take What I Want" (#41 pop, #23 R&B), and "Let Love Come Between Us" (#23 pop, #18 R&B) in 1967.

In 1970 Bobby quit the act and Ben Moore became James' new partner. This duo had a hit in the mid-Seventies in the U.K. with a remake of "I'm Your Puppet," but the duo did little after 1974's "Do Your Thing" (#30 R&B).

Flora Purim

Born March 6, 1942, Rio de Janeiro, Brazil
1974—*Butterfly Dreams* (Milestone)   1975—*Stories to Tell*   1976—*Open Your Eyes, You Can Fly*   1977—*Nothing Will Be As It Was . . . Tomorrow* (Warner Bros.)   1992—*Queen of the Night* (Sound Wave)   1995—*Speed of Light* (B&W Music).
With Airto Moreira: 1985—*Humble People* (Concord/George Wein Collection)   1986—*The Magicians* (Concord Crossover)   1989—*The Sun Is Out.*
With Airto Moreira and Mickey Hart: 1989—*Dafos* (Rykodisc); *The Apocalypse Now Sessions*   1992—*Planet Drum.*
With Fourth World: 1992—*Fourth World* (Ronnie

Scott's Jazz House)   1993—*Fourth World* (B&W Music).

Singer Flora Purim grew up in a middle-class Jewish family in Rio, married Brazilian jazz percussionist Airto Moreira, and came with him to the U.S. in 1968. She worked with Moreira, Stan Getz, and others, and sang on Chick Corea's *Return to Forever* and *Light as a Feather* and Santana's *Borboletta* and *Welcome*, albums that helped introduce American audiences to Latin sounds.

Purim has a 6½-octave range and claims the childhood influence of Billie Holiday. She says that her highly developed scat-singing technique is partly attributable to language difficulties. In 1974, the same year she won *down beat*'s #1 Female Vocalist award, Purim became a music-industry cause célèbre after she was imprisoned for 18 months in Long Beach, California, for cocaine possession. She was freed in December 1975.

Her Eighties output, chiefly with Airto Moreira, David Sanborn, Mickey Hart, and the band Fourth World, continued in the jazz/Latin fusion vein. She resumed solo recording with 1993's *Queen of the Night*.

Pylon
Formed 1979, Athens, Georgia
Vanessa Briscoe Hay (b. Vanessa Briscoe, a.k.a. Vanessa Ellison, Oct. 18, 1955, Atlanta, Ga.), voc.; Randy Bewley (b. Randall Bewley, July 1955, Sarasota, Fla.), gtr.; Michael Lachowski (b. Aug. 21, 1956, Portsmouth, Va.), bass; Curtis Crowe (b. June 2, 1956, Atlanta, Ga.), drums.
1980—*Gyrate* (DB); *Pylon!!* EP (Armageddon, U.K.) 1983—*Chomp* (DB)   1988—*Hits* 1990—*Chain* (Sky).

The hardest-hitting proponents of the Athens Sound, Pylon hails from the same fertile college-town scene that produced the B-52's and R.E.M. Like an apolitical answer to England's Gang of Four, Pylon played a brutally physical, stripped-down form of funk rock, with silence and subtraction used to dramatic effect, as in dub reggae.

Pylon's members came together while studying art at the University of Georgia in Athens. Their first single, "Cool" b/w "Dub," made an immediate impact on new-wave rock-club dance floors. After *Gyrate*, which was well-received in new-wave circles, Pylon released another powerful double-A-side single, "Crazy" b/w "M-Train." *Chomp* included more college/alternative radio staples, in "Beep" and "Yo-Yo." Vanessa Briscoe (originally known as Vanessa Ellison) then married Bob Hay, who played in another Athens band, the Squalls.

Pylon disbanded by mutual agreement in 1984 (footage of the band appeared in the 1987 documentary film *Athens, Georgia: Inside/Out*). R.E.M.'s cover of "Crazy" appeared on its *Dead Letter Office*. In 1988 Pylon reunited and spent the next two years touring before recording *Chain*, which was released on the heels of the *Hits* collection, and which found the group pursuing the same old danceable, muscular minimalism.

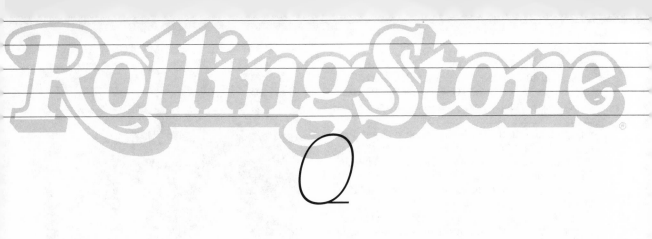

Q

Quarterflash

Formed 1980, Portland, Oregon
Rindy Ross, voc., sax; Marv Ross, voc., gtr.; Jack
Charles, voc., gtr.; Rick DiGiallonardo, kybds.; Brian
David Willis, drums; Rick Gooch, bass.
1981—*Quarterflash* (Geffen) 1983—*Take Another
Picture* 1985—*Back into Blue.*

Quarterflash debuted in 1981 with a Top Ten platinum
album and two huge pop hits, "Harden My Heart" (#3)
and "Find Another Fool" (#16). The band includes former
members of two popular Portland area bands, Seafood
Mama and Pilot.

Seafood Mama, led by the husband-and-wife team
Rindy and Marv Ross, had landed a contract with Geffen
Records and traveled to Los Angeles to record with producer John Boylan. In Portland the Rosses recruited Jack
Charles, Rick DiGiallonardo, Brian David Willis, and Rick
Gooch of Pilot to their new group. They came up with
the name, citing an Australian colloquialism, "a quarter
flash and three parts foolish." "Harden My Heart" had
been a #1 hit in the Portland area for Seafood Mama in
1980 before Quarterflash made its national hit version. A
single from *Take Another Picture*, "Take Me to Heart,"
also made the Top Twenty, in 1983, but the group broke
up two years later, only to re-form in 1990.

Suzi Quatro

Born Suzi Quatrocchio, June 3, 1950, Detroit, Michigan

1973—*Suzi Quatro* (Bell) 1974—*Quatro* 1975—
Your Mama Won't Like Me (Arista) 1977—*Aggro
Phobia* (RAK) 1978—*If You Knew Suzi* (RSO)
1980—*Greatest Hits*; *Rock Hard* (Dreamland).

Suzi Quatro was a pioneer female rocker who got a lot of
attention in her early-Seventies heyday with her leather
look and British glitter hard-pop sound. Fronting her
own band and playing hard, sexual music, she was the
prototype and idol of Joan Jett.

Born to a musical family (her father was a semipro
jazz bandleader), Quatro began playing bongos at age
eight in her father's jazz trio. Her sister Patti later played
with the all-female Fanny [see entry] for a while, and
brother Michael released several "Jam Band" LPs in the
mid-Seventies. In 1965 Suzi quit high school and formed
her first band with sisters Patti, Nancy, and Arlene, an
all-girl unit called Suzi Soul (her stage name) and the
Pleasure Seekers.

The group did some dates entertaining troops in
Vietnam, and by the end of the Sixties it had changed its
name to Cradle. Producer Mickie Most saw Cradle in
Detroit, and after the group disbanded in 1970, Suzi
Quatro took up Most's offer to come to England and sign
with his RAK Records. She wrote her own debut single,
1972's "Rolling Stone," but it didn't sell, so Most linked
her up with the highly commercial Nicky Chinn–Mike
Chapman songwriting/producing team, which gave her
a string of British hits in the bubblegum/hard-rock vein
of Slade, T. Rex, and Gary Glitter.

"Can the Can" (#1 U.K., over two million sold), "Daytona Demon" (#14 U.K.), and "48 Crash" (#3 U.K.) all hit in England in 1973, as did "Devil's Gate Drive" (#1 U.K., a million-seller) and "The Wild One" (#7 U.K.) in 1974. Quatro stressed her tough image ("She hasn't owned a dress in years," claimed her bio). Quatro tried to repeat her European triumph in the U.S. with tours in 1974 and 1975, opening for Alice Cooper. But despite heavy media coverage, commercial success was not forthcoming. "All Shook Up" and "Can the Can" were minor hits in the U.S., but during her time stateside she soon lost her British fans.

In 1977 Quatro began appearing on the hugely popular U.S. TV show *Happy Days* as the one-season semi-regular Leather Tuscadero, who fronted the hard-rock band Leather and the Suedes. She got a new record deal with RSO and released *If You Knew Suzi* (still produced by Chapman), which yielded the hit "Stumblin' In" (#4, 1979), a duet with singer Chris Norman. She signed with Chapman's label Dreamland in 1980 and had a minor U.S. hit, "Lipstick" (#51, 1981).

Quatro quit touring in 1982 to have a daughter, and in the years since she's found success in TV and on the stage: She hosted a British TV show called *Gas* in 1983; she later starred in *Annie Get Your Gun* in London's West End, and in 1991 she portrayed actress Tallulah Bankhead in a U.K. musical, *Tallulah Who?* Quatro has been married since the mid-Seventies to Len Tuckey, her longtime guitarist and a former member of the group the Nashville Teens ("Tobacco Road").

Queen

Formed 1971, England
Freddie Mercury (b. Frederick Bulsara, Sep. 5, 1946, Zanzibar; d. Nov. 24, 1991, London, Eng.), voc., piano; Brian May (b. July 19, 1947, London, Eng.), gtr.; John Deacon (b. Aug. 19, 1951, Leicester, Eng.), bass; Roger Meddows-Taylor (b. July 26, 1949, Norfolk, Eng.), drums.
1973—Queen (Elektra) 1974—Queen II; Sheer Heart Attack 1975—A Night at the Opera 1976—A Day at the Races 1977—News of the World 1978—Jazz 1979—Live Killers 1980—The Game; Flash Gordon soundtrack 1981—Greatest Hits 1982—Hot Space 1984—The Works (Capitol) 1986—A Kind of Magic 1989—The Miracle 1991—Innuendo (Hollywood) (– Mercury) 1992—Classic Queen; Live at Wembley '86; Greatest Hits; Five Live EP (with George Michael and Lisa Stansfield) 1995—Queen at the BBC.
Freddie Mercury solo: 1985—Mr. Bad Guy (Columbia) 1987—Barcelona (with Montserrat Caballe) (Hollywood) 1992—The Great Pretender.
Brian May solo: 1983—Star Fleet Project (Capitol) 1993—Back to the Light (Hollywood).

Queen: Roger Taylor, Freddie Mercury, Brian May, John Deacon

Roger Taylor solo: 1981—Fun in Space (Elektra) 1984—Strange Frontier (Capitol).

The enormously popular British band Queen epitomized pomp rock, with elaborate stage setups, smoke bombs, flashpots, lead singer Freddie Mercury's half-martial, half-coy preening onstage, and highly produced, much-overdubbed music on record. Queen can be traced back to 1967, when Brian May and Roger Taylor joined singer Tim Staffell in a group called Smile. Staffell soon left to go solo, and the remaining two Smiles teamed up with Freddie Mercury (from a group called Wreckage) and later John Deacon. They played very few gigs at the start, avoiding the club circuit and rehearsing for two years while they all remained in college. (May began work on a Ph.D. in astronomy; Taylor has a degree in biology; Deacon, a degree in electronics; and Mercury had a degree in illustration and design.) They began touring in 1973, when their debut album was released. After a second LP, the band made its U.S. tour debut opening for Mott the Hoople.

Queen's sound combined showy glam rock, heavy metal, and intricate vocal harmonies produced by multitracking Mercury's voice. May's guitar was also thickly overdubbed; *A Night at the Opera* included "God Save the Queen" rendered as a chorale of lead guitar lines. (Until 1980's *The Game*, the quartet's albums boasted that "no synthesizers" were used.) Queen's third LP, *Sheer Heart Attack*, featured "Killer Queen," its first U.S. Top Twenty hit. The LP also became its first U.S. gold.

Heavy-metal fans loved Queen (despite Freddie

Mercury's onstage pseudo-dramatics, which had more to do with his admitted influence Liza Minnelli than with Robert Plant), and the band's audience grew with its breakthrough LP, *A Night at the Opera*. It contained the six-minute gold "Bohemian Rhapsody" (#9, 1976), which featured a Mercury solo episode of "mama mia" with dozens of vocal tracks. "Bohemian Rhapsody" stayed at #1 in England for nine weeks, breaking the record Paul Anka had held since 1957 for his "Diana." The promotional video produced for it was one of the first nonperformance, conceptual rock videos.

Queen has had eight gold and six platinum records; through the mid-Eighties only its second LP and the 1980 soundtrack to the film *Flash Gordon* failed to sell so impressively. The group's U.S. Top Forty singles include "Killer Queen" (#12), 1975; "Bohemian Rhapsody" (#9), "You're My Best Friend" (#16), "Somebody to Love" (#13), 1976; "We Are the Champions" b/w "We Will Rock You" (#4), 1977; "Fat Bottomed Girls" b/w "Bicycle Race" (#24), for which the group staged an all-female nude bicycle race, 1978; "Crazy Little Thing Called Love" (#1), 1979; "Another One Bites the Dust" (#1), 1980; "Under Pressure" with David Bowie (#29), 1981; "Body Language" (#11), 1982; "Radio Ga-Ga" (#16), 1984. At first their hits were marchlike hard rock, but in the late Seventies the group began to branch out; its two biggest hits of the period were the rockabilly-style "Crazy Little Thing Called Love" and the disco-style "Another One Bites the Dust," a close relative of Chic's "Good Times," which went to #1 pop and R&B.

In 1981 Taylor released a solo album, *Fun in Space*, and later in the year the band recorded with an outsider for the first time, writing and singing with David Bowie on "Under Pressure," included on both their platinum *Greatest Hits* and *Hot Space*. One side of *Hot Space* was typically bombastic rock, while the other contained funk followups to "Another One Bites the Dust." Fans were relatively cool to *Hot Space*; it did not go platinum. Queen's next LP, *The Works* (#23, 1984), marked a return to hard-rock form. It contained the nostalgic "Radio Ga-Ga."

Queen ceased to be a commercial force in the States; its next two LPs didn't even go gold. Yet all over the world the group retained its regal status. The gold *Innuendo*, which went to #30 here, shot to #1 in Britain in early 1991. By then rumors were rampant that Mercury was ill with AIDS, something the group continually denied. That November he released a statement from his deathbed confirming the stories; just two days later he died of the disease in his London mansion at age 45.

On April 20, 1992, the surviving members of Queen were joined by a host of stars—including Elton John, Axl Rose, David Bowie, Annie Lennox, Def Leppard, and many other admirers—for a memorial concert held at Wembley Stadium that was broadcast to a worldwide audience of more than one billion. Ironically, around the time of the Wembley concert, Queen was enjoying its greatest American popularity in years, thanks to a memorable scene from the movie *Wayne's World*, in which main characters Wayne (Mike Myers) and Garth (Dana Carvey) and buddies sing along to "Bohemian Rhapsody" as it blares on the car radio. The rereleased single soared to #2.

May's second solo project came out in 1993; a posthumous Mercury solo album was released in 1992; since 1987 Roger Taylor has recorded three albums with a sideline band, the Cross.

Queen Latifah
Born Dana Owens, Newark, New Jersey, March 18, 1970
1989—*All Hail the Queen* (Tommy Boy)   1991—*Nature of a Sista'*   1993—*Black Reign* (Motown).

Queen Latifah was not the first strong female rapper, but she was the first, on the heels of Public Enemy's black nationalism and in the company of her Afrocentric Native Tongues movement, to add a pro-woman activist stance to hip-hop's agenda, clearing a space for women with her declaration of "Ladies First."

Latifah (the word is Arabic for "delicate and sensitive") grew up in middle-class East Orange, New Jersey, where she was a high school basketball star. She began her hip-hop career as a human beatbox in a group called Ladies Fresh. She then recorded tracks with her friend Mark the 45 King, who gave the demos to Fab Five Freddy, who passed them on to Tommy Boy. *All Hail the Queen* was a minor record sales-wise, but its impact was profound, primarily because of "Ladies First," a proud track in which Latifah supported girl love by rapping with Monie Love. De La Soul and KRS-One also appeared on the album. Latifah was nominated for a Grammy and named best female rapper of the year by ROLLING STONE in 1990. An informed and articulate commentator on hip-hop and youth cultures in general, La Queen became a media darling.

Latifah broke through to a larger pop audience by rapping on David Bowie's remake of "Fame" and singing with Troop and Levert on a cover of the O'Jays' "For the Love of Money" (#12 R&B, 1992) from the *New Jack City* soundtrack. On *Nature of a Sista'* she moved away from her role as rap spokesperson and into more personal, soulful arenas. She wasn't surrendering—"Latifah's Had It Up 2 Here" (#13 R&B, 1992) was the opening track—but she had had "Nuff of the Ruff Stuff." She sang on a number of tracks, used live instruments, and expanded on the house and dance rhythms she'd used on her debut, to best effect on the single "Fly Girl" (#16, 1992), which she sang with male crooners Simple Pleasure.

Latifah moved to Motown for her third and best-selling album, *Black Reign* (#15 R&B, 1994), which yielded

Grammy Awards

Queen Latifah
1994 Best Solo Rap Performance: "U.N.I.T.Y."

---

the hits "U.N.I.T.Y." (#23 pop, #7 R&B, 1994) and "Just Another Day" (#37 R&B, 1994). The album was dedicated to her brother, who had died the previous year in a motorcycle accident. (Latifah herself belongs to a cycle club.) Her increased popularity was aided by her starring role in *Living Single*. The highly rated TV sitcom has been criticized, though, for lampooning African-American lives.

Latifah has reinvested her earnings, buying a video store and starting a management and production company, Flavor Unit, whose clients include Naughty by Nature. In addition to *Living Single*, she has appeared in the films *Jungle Fever*, *Juice*, and *House Party 2* and on the TV show *The Fresh Prince of Bel-Air*. She received a 1994 Grammy for Best Rap Solo Performance for "U.N.I.T.Y."

Queensrÿche
Formed 1981, Bellevue, Washington
Chris DeGarmo (b. June 14, 1963, Wenatchee, Wash.), gtr.; Eddie Jackson (b. Jan. 29, 1961, Robstown, Tex.), bass; Scott Rockenfield (b. June 15, 1963, Seattle, Wash.), drums; Geoff Tate (b. Jan. 14, 1959, Stuttgart, Ger.), voc.; Michael Wilton (b. Feb. 23, 1962, San Francisco, Calif.), gtr.
**1983—*Queensrÿche* (EMI)   1984—*The Warning*
1986—*Rage for Order*   1988—*Operation: Mindcrime* (EMI Manhattan)   1990—*Empire* (EMI)   1991—*Operation: Livecrime*   1994—*Promised Land*.**

For almost a decade, Queensrÿche was a hard-working band whose art-metal albums won it more respect than sales. But *Empire* (#7, 1990) and its Top Ten hit single "Silent Lucidity" (#9, 1991) launched the group into international stardom. The band was formed in 1981 in the Seattle suburb Bellevue, Washington, by Chris DeGarmo and Michael Wilton. Sick of playing in cover bands, the two high school friends recruited fellow bar-band veterans Geoff Tate and Eddie Jackson. They avoided the local club scene, opting for extended rehearsals, culminating in the release of the self-financed EP *Queen of the Reich* in 1983. It sold over 20,000 copies and led to the band's signing with EMI. *Queensrÿche* (#81, 1983), the quintet's major-label debut, was an expanded version of the EP.

The Warning (#61, 1984) and *Rage for Order* (#47, 1986) were supported by tours opening for Kiss, Bon Jovi, and Metallica. *Operation: Mindcrime* (#50, 1988), a concept album depicting a nightmarish future of drugs and media manipulation, brought Queensrÿche some critical plaudits.

Empire, a more song-oriented mix of rockers and ballads, was languishing in the lower reaches of the album chart until MTV started running the video for "Silent Lucidity." The heavy exposure (at one point the video ran over 44 times a week) pushed the album to double-platinum status, with "Silent Lucidity" named *Billboard*'s most popular rock song in 1991.

The band toured extensively to support its newfound popularity, joining the Monsters of Rock Tour in 1991. Queensrÿche also released *Operation: Livecrime* (#38, 1991), an album and video recapping the elaborate stage show that accompanied the *Operation: Mindcrime* song cycle in concert. Four years after *Empire*, Queensrÿche returned with *Promised Land*, debuting at #3.

? [Question Mark] and the Mysterians
Formed 1962, Flint, Michigan
?[Question Mark] (b. 1945, Mex.), voc.; Robert Martinez, drums; Larry Borjas, gtr. Later members included Robert Balderrama (b. 1950, Mex.), gtr.; Frankie Rodriguez Jr. (b. Mar. 9, 1951, Crystal City, Tex.), kybds.; Frank Lugo (b. Mar. 15, 1947, Welasco, Tex.), bass; Edward Serrato (b. 1947, Mex.), drums.
1966—*96 Tears* (Cameo); *Action*   1985—*The Dallas Reunion Tapes: 96 Tears Forever* (ROIR).

Question Mark and the Mysterians' one song of consequence was not only a #1 hit but also epitomized a classic sound in rock & roll. The song was "96 Tears," and with its famous organ line (played on a Vox Continental, and not, as legend has it, on a Farfisa), and leader ?'s gruff vocals, it topped the chart in 1966.

The band's quick rise and fall were mirrored in the mystery surrounding it. Its leader was never photographed without sunglasses, and he legally changed his name to simply ?. (The song is credited to Rudy Martinez, though ? has refused to say whether that's his name, and he has never revealed his background. Some believe that Martinez is a name he invented to collect royalties.)

What *is* known is that most of the band members were born in Mexico and later moved to Detroit. Two original members, Robert Martinez and Larry Borjas, went into the army before the Mysterians' big success. The group became local favorites in the Detroit area, and its "96 Tears" was first cut for a small Flint, Michigan, record company. It became the most requested song on Flint's WTAC and Detroit's KCLW, leading to a national deal with Cameo Records, where it went on to sell over a million copies. Later in the year the Mysterians hit #22 with "I Need Somebody," but their followups flopped, and by 1968 they'd called it quits. Mel Schacher, later bassist with Grand Funk Railroad, played in one of the later stages of the group.

In 1981 ? made a low-level comeback with an all-new group of Mysterians. They toured and played oldies plus new material. The same year, Garland Jeffreys released a minor hit version of the old smash. ("96 Tears" had become very popular in new-wave circles in the late Seventies, seen as an early punk nugget.) Joe "King" Carrasco also performed it live in 1980 and, in fact, built his entire sound around the tinny-organ style that ? had helped pioneer.

Quicksilver Messenger Service
Formed 1965, San Francisco, California
Gary Duncan (b. Sep. 4, 1946, San Diego, Calif.), gtr., voc.; John Cipollina (b. Aug. 24, 1943, Berkeley, Calif.; d. May 29, 1989, Greenbrae, Calif.), gtr.; David Freiberg (b. Aug. 24, 1938, Boston, Mass.), bass, voc.; Greg Elmore (b. Sep. 4, 1946, San Diego), drums; Jim Murray, voc., harmonica.
1967—(– Murray)   1968—*Quicksilver Messenger Service* (Capitol)   1969—*Happy Trails* (– Duncan; + Nicky Hopkins [b. Feb. 24, 1944, London, Eng.; d. Sep. 6, 1994, Nashville, Tenn.], kybds.) *Shady Grove*   1970—(+ Duncan; + Dino Valenti [b. Chester Powers, Nov. 7, 1943, Danbury, Conn.; d. Nov. 16, 1994, Santa Rosa, Calif.], voc., gtr.) *Just for Love* (– Hopkins)   1971—(+ Mark Naftalin, piano) *What About Me* (– Cipollina; – Freiberg; + Mark Ryan, bass; – Naftalin; + Chuck Steales, organ); *Quicksilver*   1972—*Comin' Thru*   1973—*Anthology* (for next two years, band consists of Valenti, Duncan, Elmore, and a number of musicians)   1975—*Solid Silver* (group disbands)   1987—(Group re-forms: Duncan; + Sammy Piazza, drums; + W. Michael Lewis, keyboards) *Peace by Piece*   1991—*Sons of Mercury: The Best of Quicksilver Messenger Service, 1968–1975* (Rhino).

Quicksilver Messenger Service was one of the vintage acid-rock San Francisco bands of the late Sixties. Its early shows and albums (featuring the heavily tremoloed guitar work of John Cipollina, plus that of second guitarist Gary Duncan) contributed some of the best-remembered instrumental jam music of the period. But as the Sixties ended, Quicksilver's popularity waned, and it never achieved the national popularity of its San Francisco contemporaries, the Jefferson Airplane and the Grateful Dead.

The group formed in 1965 with Gary Duncan, John Cipollina (whose godfather was classical pianist Jose Iturbi), David Freiberg, Greg Elmore, and Jim Murray. Its original guitarist was to have been Dino Valenti (a Greenwich Village folksinger and, under the name "Chester A. Powers," writer of "Hey Joe" and the Young-

bloods' hit "Get Together"). But Valenti was arrested on a drug charge and jailed for 18 months.

In December 1965 the fivesome began playing the local circuit, but soon after, Murray left to study the sitar. Quicksilver recorded its debut as a quartet in December 1967, and it came out in May 1968, featuring jams like the 12-minute "The Fool." The band also provided two songs for the soundtrack of *Revolution*, out that year, and in late 1968 QMS recorded its part-live second LP, *Happy Trails*, the group's only gold album. In January 1969 Valenti got Duncan to move to New York and form a group with him; British session keyboardist Nicky Hopkins took Duncan's place and was prominently featured on *Shady Grove*.

In early 1970 Duncan returned, bringing Valenti with him. Valenti finally joined Quicksilver three years late (though his "Dino's Song" appears on the debut LP). The new sextet issued *Just for Love*, and "Fresh Air" received substantial FM airplay, helping to make the LP one of its biggest sellers (#27, 1970).

Hopkins left just before the release of *What About Me*, and some of the tracks featured his replacement, Mark Naftalin, formerly of the Paul Butterfield Blues Band. Cipollina also left around this time; he later formed Copperhead with early Quicksilverite Jim Murray. During 1971 Freiberg left. That year he was jailed for marijuana possession; in 1972 he began a 12-year hitch with Jefferson Airplane/Starship [see entry]. The remaining Quicksilver threesome—Duncan, Elmore, and Valenti—produced two more LPs, *Quicksilver* and *Comin' Thru*, with Mark Ryan (bass) and keyboardist Chuck Steales, but these sparked little public interest. Though the band didn't break up, it was virtually inactive from 1972 to 1975. That year Valenti, Duncan, and Elmore recorded *Solid Silver* with bassist Skip Olsen and keyboardist W. Michael Lewis (and with Cipollina and Freiberg making cameos). Quicksilver then disbanded.

Duncan put together another configuration in 1987 to record *Peace by Piece*, but the LP went nowhere, and Quicksilver called it a day once again. John Cipollina, whose younger brother Mario found fame in the Eighties as bassist for Huey Lewis and the News, continued to perform with a variety of bands, including the Welsh group Man and the Dinosaurs. A longtime sufferer of severe emphysema, he died in 1989 at age 45.

Quiet Riot
Formed 1975, Burbank, California
Kevin DuBrow (b. Oct. 29, 1955, Los Angeles, Calif.), voc.; Randy Rhoads (b. Dec. 6, 1956, Burbank; d. Mar. 19, 1982, Lakeland, Fla.), gtr.; Kelly Garni (b. Oct. 29, 1957, N. Hollywood, Calif.), bass; Drew Forsyth (b. May 14, 1956, Hollywood, Calif.), drums.
1977—*Quiet Riot* (CBS/Sony, Jap.) (– Garni; + Carlos Cavazo [b. July 8, 1957, Atlanta, Ga.], gtr.)   1978—

Quiet Riot II (– Rhoads; + Rudy Sarzo [b. Nov. 9, 1952, Havana, Cuba], bass; – Forsyth; + Frankie Banali [b. Nov. 14, 1953, Queens, N.Y.], drums)   1983— *Metal Health* (Pasha/CBS)   1984—*Condition Critical* (– Sarzo; + Chuck Wright, bass)   1986—*QR III* (– Wright; + Paul Shortino, voc.; + Sean McNabb, bass)   1987—(– DuBrow) *Wild Young and Crazee* (group disbands)   1988—*Quiet Riot*   1990—(Group re-forms: DuBrow; Cavazo; + Kenny Hillary, bass; + Bobby Rondinelli, drums)   1993—*The Randy Rhoads Years* (Rhino)   1995—*Down to the Bone* (Kamikaze).

Heavy-metal band Quiet Riot was a bigger attraction on the mid-Seventies Hollywood club scene than Van Halen and the Knack, yet both of them were signed to major-label recording deals before Quiet Riot. The original lineup recorded two now-out-of-print albums released only in Japan (selections from which were reissued as *The Randy Rhoads Years*) before its breakup was precipitated by the departure of guitarist Rhoads for Ozzy Os-

bourne's band. Rhoads died in a 1982 Florida plane crash a week before he was due to join the re-formed Quiet Riot in the studio.

The new Quiet Riot's first U.S. album, *Metal Health* (#1, 1983), became the highest-charting debut ever by an American metal band, thanks largely to heavy MTV play of the video for the Slade remake "Cum On Feel the Noize" (#5, 1983), in which a metalhead's bedroom exploded into a stage on which Quiet Riot was performing. The album yielded a second hit in "Bang Your Head (Metal Health)" (#31, 1983). *Condition Critical* (#15, 1984) fared worse, as did its second Slade-cover single, "Mama Weer All Crazee Now" (#51, 1984). *QR III* (#31, 1986) failed to produce a hit single.

In 1987 the band fired DuBrow, branding him an out-of-control egomaniac in an unusually harsh press release. After one eponymous album (#119, 1988), the new lineup disbanded. In 1990 DuBrow reunited with guitarist Carlos Cavazo to form Heat, which they soon renamed Quiet Riot for club tours.

Eddie Rabbitt

Born Edward Thomas, November 27, 1944, Brooklyn, New York
1975—*Eddie Rabbitt* (Elektra)   1976—*Rocky Mountain Music*   1977—*Rabbitt*   1978—*Variations*
1979—*Loveline; Best of Eddie Rabbitt*   1980—*Horizon*   1981—*Step by Step*   1982—*Radio Romance*
1983—*Greatest Hits, vol. 2* (Warner Bros.)   1984—
The Best Year of My Life*   1990—*Jersey Boy* (Capitol Nashville); *Ten Years of Greatest Hits
1991—*Classics Collection; Ten Rounds.*

After struggling on the outskirts of the Nashville country music community through much of the Seventies, Eddie Rabbitt emerged as a popular singer/songwriter in the early Eighties.

From East Orange, New Jersey, Edward Thomas migrated to Nashville in 1968 and landed a $37-a-week job as a staff writer at Hill and Range, a music publishing house. He had briefly recorded for 20th Century in 1964, without success. His big break came in 1970, when Elvis Presley recorded his "Kentucky Rain," which became Presley's 50th gold record. (In 1973 Ronnie Milsap had a #1 C&W hit with Rabbitt's "Pure Love.") Rabbitt's own singles—"Forgive and Forget," "Drinkin' My Baby (Off My Mind)," "Rocky Mountain Music," and "Two Dollars in the Jukebox"—established him with country audiences, and with his 1979 hit theme to Clint Eastwood's film *Every Which Way but Loose* he crossed over to the pop audience.

Rabbitt's hits include "Suspicious" (#13 pop, #1 C&W, 1979), "Drivin' My Life Away" (#5 pop, #1 C&W, 1980), "I Love a Rainy Night" (#1 pop, #1 C&W, 1980), "Step by Step" (#5 pop, #1 C&W, 1981), and "Someone Could Lose a Heart Tonight" (#15, 1981). Rabbitt's *Horizon* (#19, 1980) went platinum, and both "Rainy Night" and "Step" were million-selling singles. Among his other #1 C&W hits were duets with Crystal Gayle ("You and I," 1982) and Juice Newton ("Both to Each Other [Friends and Lovers]," 1986); the latter was the theme to the popular daytime soap *Days of Our Lives*. In 1983 Rabbitt's infant son was born with a rare liver disease of which he died in 1985. During that period, Rabbitt essentially put his career on hold. Rabbitt is active as a spokesperson and fundraiser for a number of children's causes.

Rabbitt returned to the C&W chart with a remake of Dion's "The Wanderer" (#1 C&W, 1988). His subsequent C&W Top Ten hits include "We Must Be Doin' Somethin' Right" (#7 C&W, 1988), "On Second Thought" (#1 C&W, 1989), and "Runnin' with the Wind" (#8 C&W, 1990).

Gerry Rafferty

Born April 16, 1947, Paisley, Scotland
1971—*Can I Have My Money Back?* (Transatlantic, U.K.)   1974—*Revisited*   1978—*City to City* (United

Artists) 1979—*Night Owl* 1980—*Snakes and Ladders* 1991—*Right Down the Line: Best of Gerry Rafferty* (EMI).

Though he had recorded a well-received 1971 solo album, it wasn't until five years after his former band, Stealers Wheel [see entry], had a hit with "Stuck in the Middle with You" that singer/songwriter Gerry Rafferty came into his own as a solo act. Previous to that, he was a member of the Fifth Column and then one half of a Scottish folk duo called the Humblebums, with Billy Connolly. He began his solo career in 1971.

In 1978 his "Baker Street" was a huge international hit—it reached #2 in the U.S.—and the LP it came from, *City to City*, went platinum and topped the album chart. It also included the #12 hit "Right Down the Line." This success came after three years of post–Stealers Wheel management and record-label problems. Rafferty, who rarely performs live and then only in England and Europe, has never repeated that degree of success, although the gold *Night Owl* contained two hits, "Days Gone Down (Still Got the Light in Your Eyes)" (#17, 1979) and "Get It Right Next Time" (#21, 1979). He produced the Proclaimers' 1987 U.K. hit "Letter from America."

Rainbow: See Ritchie Blackmore

The Raincoats
Formed 1977, London, England
Gina Birch (b. ca. 1956, Eng.), voc., bass; Ana Da Silva (b. ca. 1949, Portugal), voc., gtr.; Ross Crichton, gtr.; Nick Turner, drums.
1977—(– Crichton; – Turner; + Kate Korus, gtr.; + Richard Dudanski, drums) 1978—(– Korus; + Jeremie Frank, gtr.) 1979—(– Frank; + Vicky Aspinall [b. ca. 1956, Eng.], voc., violin, gtr., kybds.; – Dudanski; + Palmolive, drums) 1980—*The Raincoats* (Rough Trade, U.K.) (– Palmolive; + Ingrid Weiss [b. ca. 1961, Eng.], drums) 1981—*Odyshape* (– Weiss; + Dudanski; + Charles Hayward, drums, perc.; + Paddy O'Connell, bass, gtr., sax) 1983—*The Kitchen Tapes* (ROIR) 1984—*Moving* (Rough Trade, U.K.) (+ Derek Goddard, perc.) (group disbands) 1994—(Group re-forms: Da Silva; Birch; + Anne Wood, violin; + Steve Shelley [b. June 23, 1962, Midland, Mich.], drums) *The Raincoats* (Smells Like Records).

The Raincoats took a feminist approach to the "anyone can play" ethos of British punk, and in the process evolved musically—from the abrasive amateurism of their debut album, through the awkwardly graceful, folkish delicacy of *Odyshape*, to the ethno-funk inflections of *Moving*. The group also won critical acclaim for resolutely refusing to live out any of the traditional rock-woman stereotypes. Defunct for a decade, the Raincoats returned in 1994—after being invoked as an inspiration by Nirvana's Kurt Cobain—to performance and recording.

After playing their first gig in 1978, opening for the punk band Chelsea in London, the Raincoats became an all-girl group in 1979 with the addition of classically trained violinist Vicky Aspinall (the only Raincoat with any musical training) and ex-Slits drummer Palmolive. This lineup recorded the Raincoats' first single, 1979's "Fairytale in the Supermarket," and the group's crude-sounding debut album. Palmolive left to follow spiritual pursuits in India (she eventually settled in Los Angeles as a born-again Christian). She was replaced by Ingrid Weiss, who shared drumming duties on *Odyshape* with assorted males, including former Raincoat Richard Dudanski (who'd also played with Public Image Ltd.) and ex–Soft Machine Robert Wyatt. The Raincoats took a more deliberate and open-ended approach on *Odyshape;* their harmony vocals evoked traditional part- and round-singing, while Aspinall's violin recalled John Cale's viola with the Velvet Underground.

The Kitchen Tapes was recorded in 1982, on a U.S. tour. The same lineup recorded many of the same songs on *Moving*, acclaimed as the group's most confident-sounding effort yet. But the band broke up after its release. In February 1994 Cobain encouraged his band's label, DGC, to issue all three Raincoats albums in the U.S. A month later Da Silva and Birch (with Sonic Youth's Steve Shelley on drums) reunited the Raincoats for an East Coast tour of the U.S. (Ironically, they were performing in New York City the night Cobain's suicide was announced.) That summer, the Raincoats also released a self-titled EP consisting of songs broadcast live on BBC Radio 1 DJ John Peel's show in April 1994.

Bonnie Raitt
Born November 8, 1949, Los Angeles, California
1971—*Bonnie Raitt* (Warner Bros.) 1972—*Give It Up* 1973—*Takin' My Time* 1974—*Streetlights* 1975—Home Plate 1977—*Sweet Forgiveness* 1979—*The Glow* 1982—*Green Light* 1986—*Nine Lives* 1989—*Nick of Time* (Capitol) 1990—*The Bonnie Raitt Collection* (Warner Bros.) 1991—*Luck of the Draw* (Capitol) 1994—*Longing in Their Hearts*.

Singer, songwriter, and guitarist Bonnie Raitt's music incorporates blues, R&B, pop, and folk. Though her albums always sold respectably (averaging several hundred thousand copies), and she had been a headliner since the mid-Seventies, it was not until 1989's *Nick of Time* that she achieved the great success critics had been predicting since she debuted in 1971. Throughout her career, she has earned the respect of the blues legends she so admires and maintained a commitment to social activism few other artists can match.

Bonnie Raitt

The daughter of Broadway singer John Raitt (star of *Pajama Game* and *Carousel*), Bonnie Raitt started playing guitar at age 12 and was immediately attracted to the blues. In 1967 she left her L.A. home to enter Radcliffe, but she dropped out after two years and began playing the local folk and blues clubs. Dick Waterman, longtime blues aficionado and manager, signed her, and soon she was performing with Howlin' Wolf, Sippie Wallace, Mississippi Fred McDowell, and other blues legends. Her reputation in Boston and Philadelphia led to a record contract with Warner Bros.

Raitt's early albums were critically acclaimed for her singing and guitar playing (she is one of the few women who play bottleneck) as well as her choice of material, which often included blues as well as pop and folk songs. Most of Raitt's early repertoire consists of covers, and she has gone out of the way to credit her sources, often touring with them as opening acts. Her sixth album, *Sweet Forgiveness*, went gold and yielded a hit cover version of Del Shannon's "Runaway." *The Glow* (featuring her first original tunes since three on *Give It Up*) was produced by Peter Asher, but it didn't sell as well as its predecessor.

A Quaker, Raitt has played literally hundreds of benefits over the course of her career. She was a founder of M.U.S.E. (Musicians United for Safe Energy), which in September 1979 held a massive concert at Madison Square Garden, with other stars like Jackson Browne, James Taylor, and the Doobie Brothers. It was later commemorated on a three-LP set. In 1982 she released her eighth LP, *Green Light,* a harder-rocking effort aided by her backup band, the Bump Band, which included veteran keyboardist Ian MacLagan (of the Faces and the Stones); Raitt's longtime bassist and tuba-player, Freebo, remained a constant sideman through her various backup bands during this time. They toured with Raitt in mid-1982, greeted by the usual critical acclaim. Her work also appeared on the platinum 1980 *Urban Cowboy* soundtrack, with the country song "Don't It Make You Wanna Dance."

In 1983, during the recording of *Nine Lives* (#115, 1986), Raitt lost her deal with Warner Bros. Prince produced a few tracks with her, but because of scheduling conflicts, their collaboration was never completed and the tracks were never released. Instead, Raitt reemerged in 1989 on Capitol with her Don Was–produced breakthrough album *Nick of Time,* which smoothed out her rough bluesy edges yet avoided crass commercialism. It topped the charts, sold four million copies, and won a Grammy for Album of the Year (one of four won by a thunderstruck Raitt at the 1990 gala; one was for Best Traditional Blues Recording, for "In the Mood," a duet with John Lee Hooker on his album *The Healer*). The pattern held with *Luck of the Draw* (#2, 1991), another Was production, which included the hit singles "Something to Talk About" (#5, 1991) and "I Can't Make You Love Me" (#18, 1991). It sold over four million copies and netted three more Grammys, for Album of the Year, Best Female Rock Vocal Performance, and Best Pop Vocal Performance. Her former label Warner Bros. capitalized on Raitt's unprecedented high profile by releasing *Collection,* which included live duets with Sippie Wallace and John Prine.

In April 1991 Raitt married actor Michael O'Keefe. Raitt also cofounded the Rhythm and Blues Foundation, dedicated to raising awareness and money for influential musical pioneers left impoverished in their old age by unfair record deals and lack of health insurance. Raitt once again found success working with producer Don Was, as 1994's *Longing in Their Hearts* topped the charts and went platinum shortly after its release. In early 1995 Raitt became the first woman guitarist to have a guitar named for her. All her royalties from the sale of Fender's Bonnie Raitt Signature Series Strato-caster will go to programs to teach girls to play guitar.

The Ramones

Formed 1974, New York City, New York
Joey Ramone (b. Jeffrey Hyman, May 19, 1951), voc.;

The Ramones: Johnny Ramone, Joey Ramone, Marky Ramone, Dee Dee Ramone

Johnny Ramone (b. John Cummings, Oct. 8, 1951, Long Island, N.Y.), gtr.; **Dee Dee Ramone** (b. Douglas Colvin, Sep. 18, 1952, Va.), bass; **Tommy Ramone** (b. Tom Erdelyi, Jan. 29, 1952, Budapest, Hungary), drums.
1976—*Ramones* (Sire); *Ramones Leave Home*
1977—*Rocket to Russia* (– Tommy Ramone;
+ **Marky Ramone** [b. Marc Bell, July 15, 1956, New York City], drums)   1978—*Road to Ruin*   1980—
End of the Century   1981—*Pleasant Dreams*
1983—*Subterranean Jungle* (– Marky Ramone;
+ **Richie Ramone** [b. Richard Reinhardt, a.k.a. Richie Beau], drums)   1984—*Too Tough to Die*   1986—
Animal Boy   1987—*Halfway to Sanity* (– Richie Ramone; + Marky Ramone, drums)   1988—*Ramones Mania*   1989—*Brain Drain* (– Dee Dee Ramone;
+ **C. J. Ramone** [b. Christopher Joseph Ward, Oct. 8, 1965, Long Island, N.Y.], bass)   1990—*All the Stuff (And More), vol. 1*   1991—*All the Stuff (And More), vol. 2*   1992—*Loco Live; Mondo Bizarro* (Radioactive)   1994—*Acid Eaters*   1995—*Adios Amigos.*

In the mid-Seventies the Ramones shaped the sound of punk rock in New York with simple, fast songs, deadpan lyrics, no solos, and an impenetrable wall of guitar chords. Twenty years later, with virtually all of their peers either retired or having moved on to forms other than punk, Joey and Johnny Ramone, the band's core, continued adamantly to parlay the same determinedly basic sound.

The group formed in 1974, after the foursome graduated or left high school in Forest Hills, New York. The original lineup featured Joey on drums, Dee Dee sharing guitar with Johnny, and Tommy as manager, but they soon settled on their recording setup. The Ramones gravitated toward the burgeoning scene at CBGB, where their 20-minute sets of rapid-fire, under-two-and-a-half-minute songs earned them a recording contract before any of their contemporaries except Patti Smith.

In 1976 *Ramones* was a definitive punk statement, with songs like "Beat on the Brat," "Blitzkrieg Bop," and "Now I Wanna Sniff Some Glue"—14 of them, clocking in at under 30 minutes. The group traveled to England in 1976, giving the nascent British punk scene the same boost they had provided to New Yorkers. Before the year was out, *Ramones Leave Home* had been released. Then as now, the band toured almost incessantly.

With their next two singles, the group began to soften their sound slightly. "Sheena Is a Punk Rocker" and "Rockaway Beach" made explicit their debt to Sixties AM hit styles such as bubblegum and surf music, and both made the lower reaches of the Top 100. They were included on *Rocket to Russia,* which also contained the ballad "Here Today, Gone Tomorrow." At this point Tommy quit the group, preferring his behind-the-scenes activity as coproducer, "disguised" as T. Erdelyi (his real name).

His replacement was Marc Bell, henceforth dubbed Marky Ramone. He was formerly one of Richard Hell's Voidoids and before that a member of Dust, who recorded a pair of albums during the Sixties. His first LP with the Ramones, *Road to Ruin,* was their first to contain only 12 songs and their first to last longer than half an hour. Despite their glossiest production yet, featuring acoustic guitars and real solos, its two singles, "Don't Come Close" and a version of the Searchers' "Needles and Pins," failed to capture a mass audience. Neither did their starring role in Roger Corman's 1979 movie *Rock 'n' Roll High School.*

As the Eighties began, the Ramones tried working with noted pop producers Phil Spector (*End of the Century*) and 10cc's Graham Gouldman (*Pleasant Dreams*), but commercial success remained elusive. After *Subterranean Jungle,* Marky Ramone departed, to be replaced by ex-Velveteens Richie Beau. As Richie Ramone, the drummer played on four albums, before Marky returned in 1987. *Too Tough to Die,* with Eurythmic Dave Stewart producing the pop single "Howling at the Moon," recaptured some of their Seventies energy, and "Bonzo Goes to Bitburg" off *Animal Boy* offered cutting political satire, but the remainder of the Ramones' Eighties work too often found them parodying their earlier strengths.

In 1989 the Ramones gained their widest exposure with the title track to the soundtrack for Stephen King's *Pet Sematary,* but also underwent their most significant internal shift. Dee Dee departed, first to record as Dee Dee King a rap album, *Standing in the Spotlight,* and then to form the rock group Chinese Dragons. A heroin addict and substance abuser for 14 years, Dee Dee had been the Ramones' truest punk (going solo, he also joined AA); his departure signaled the end of an era, if not a style. AWOL from the Marines at the time he enlisted in the band, C. J. Ramone infused youthful energy—he was 14 years younger than Joey and Johnny—but the band's sound remained the same.

Mondo Bizarro, with a guest appearance by Living Colour guitarist Vernon Reid and songs that attacked both drugs and the PMRC's Tipper Gore, ushered the band into the Nineties, their influence by then apparent on such rowdy outfits as Guns n' Roses and the Beastie Boys. In 1994 they persevered with Acid Eaters, a tribute to Sixties idols like the Animals and Rolling Stones. With Joey sober since the start of the decade and Marky in recovery from alcoholism, they continued their relentless touring. With the release of Adios Amigos, the band hinted that it was considering calling it quits.

Rank and File
Formed 1981, New York City, New York
Chip Kinman (b. Oct. 4, 1957, Edenton, N.C.), voc., gtr., harmonica; Tony Kinman (b. Apr. 3, 1956, Quantico, Va.), voc., bass; Alejandro Escovedo (b. Jan. 10, 1951, San Antonio, Tex.), voc., gtr.; Slim Evans [b. Jim Evans], drums.
1982—Sundown (Slash) 1983—(- Escovedo; - Evans) 1984—Long Gone Dead 1987—Rank and File (Rhino).

Rank and File mixed energetic power pop with a country twang, kicking off the early-Eighties musical hybrid called cowpunk. Army-brat brothers Tony and Chip Kinman spent part of their childhoods living in North Carolina, where they were surrounded by country music. By the time they reached the West Coast in the late Seventies, the brothers had discovered punk and formed the Dils, whose politically charged "I Hate the Rich" and "Class War" are considered unsung classics of West Coast punk. In 1981, Chip Kinman teamed up with former Nuns guitarist Alejandro Escovedo in New York City to form Rank and File. (The Dils and Nuns had played together in San Francisco, and there Tony Kinman and Escovedo had performed with a looseknit group they dubbed Rank and File.) Tony joined soon after, the band dropped its rhythm section, and the three moved to Austin in 1982. There, they recruited drummer Slim Evans.

After initial cries of "sellout" from devoted Dils fans, Rank and File released Sundown to overwhelming critical praise for songs such as "Coyote," about the mistreatment of illegal aliens, and the poppy "Amanda Ruth." The Kinmans' grittier side was compared to Johnny Cash, while their harmonies were likened to the Everly Brothers. Dissension grew within the band, Escovedo and Evans left, and the Kinmans relocated to Los Angeles. Recorded with session players, Long Gone Dead received a lukewarm reception. The group's non-twangy Rhino album passed nearly unnoticed in 1987.

In 1986 Escovedo—whose extended family includes

Santana percussionist Pete Escovedo and Pete's daughter, former Prince percussionist Sheila E.—formed True Believers with his brother Javier; the band released its critically acclaimed but commercially disappointing self-titled album, produced by Memphis sessionman Jim Dickinson (Big Star, Replacements), on Rounder-EMI. Six years later Escovedo kicked off a solo career with the critical hit Gravity, followed in 1993 by Thirteen Years (both on the Austin label, Watermelon).

The Kinmans continued together as the avant-rock duo Blackbird, blending their clean harmonies and melodies with a cruder industrial sound. Between 1988 and 1993 the duo released three self-titled albums: The first two, unofficially called "the red one" and "the black one," came out on Iloki; the third, called "the orange one," was released by Scotti Brothers.

Ranking Roger: See English Beat

Shabba Ranks
Born Rexton Ralston Fernando Gordon, January 17, 1966, Saint Ann's Parish, Jamaica
1991—As Raw as Ever (Epic) 1992—Rough & Ready, Volume I; X-Tra Naked 1993—Rough & Ready, Volume II.

With his deep, gruff voice and lyrics and image based firmly in "slackness" (overt sexuality), Shabba Ranks became the biggest-selling and highest-profile star of dancehall, the reggae subgenre marked by fast rhythms and fast-talking vocals. Dancehall began in the late Sixties, is credited with anticipating and influencing rap (original Bronx rap DJ Kool Herc was an émigré from Jamaica), and gained an international audience after rap's ascendence in the late Eighties.

Like Bob Marley, Ranks emerged from Saint Ann's Parish and the Trenchtown ghetto. Influenced by such "toasters" (reggae's version of rappers) as Josey Wales and Yellowman, he began performing in Kingston in 1980 and soon was recording Jamaican hit singles with such leading record producers as King Jammy and Bobby Digital. His 1989 "Wicked in Bed" caught on with Caribbean-music fans in America and Britain, and in 1991 he was featured on Scritti Politti's cover of the Beatles' "She's a Woman," a U.K. Top Twenty hit that paved the way for a major-label deal with Epic Records. As Raw As Ever (#89 pop, #1 R&B, 1991) yielded hits in "Housecall (Your Body Can't Lie to Me)" (#37 pop, #4 R&B, 1991), a duet with reggae crooner Maxi Priest, and "The Jam" (#52 R&B, 1992), a duet with rapper KRS-One. The album won 1991's Best Reggae Grammy, making Ranks the first dancehall artist so honored. Epic then released Rough and Ready, Volume I (#78, 1992), a collection of Ranks' Jamaican hits that yielded a hit single in "Mr. Loverman" (#40 pop, #2 R&B, 1992).

X-tra Naked (#64, 1992) produced another big hit in "Slow and Sexy" (#33 pop, #4 R&B, 1992), a duet with Johnny Gill; the album also included duets with rappers Queen Latifah and Chubb Rock. Ranks then guested on Eddie Murphy's *Love's Alright* and appeared in Murphy's video for "I Was King." In December 1992, however, Ranks told a British TV show that he agreed with dancehall star Buju Banton's controversial track "Boom Bye Bye," which advocated the killing of gay men. "If you forfeit the laws of God Almighty," declared Ranks, "you deserve crucifixion." Resulting protests by gay-rights groups led *The Tonight Show* to cancel Ranks' scheduled appearance in March 1993. Ranks subsequently said he regretted his remarks and that he did not "approve of any act of violence against homosexuals or any other human beings."

Rap

Rap is a form of dance music in which vocalists—rappers—speak in rhythm and rhyme. Radio and dance-club disc jockeys, concert emcees, reggae toasters, and occasional R&B singers have talked over or chanted to music for many years, but rapping as a specialized style originated in the mid-Seventies in the discos of New York City's black neighborhoods, alongside such ghetto arts as freedom writing, break dancing, and double-dutch jump-roping.

The progenitors of rap were spinners—disco DJs who segued songs for dancers. The first notable ghetto spinners—Kool Herc, Afrika Bambaataa, Pete "DJ" Jones, and others—began working discos in the Bronx around 1974. By 1977 young admirers like Grandmaster Flash, DJ Hollywood, and Davy D were spinning at street level—in playgrounds, at parties, at gym dances—for the mostly teenaged listeners known as b–boys and fly girls, who invented the part-mime, part-acrobatics dance style called break dancing.

For their tracks, the new generation preferred James Brown, Sly and the Family Stone, Chic, and Funkadelic to newer disco hits. They experimented with turntable techniques like fast-break mixing to edit together snatches of songs; double-tracking to repeat phrases or set them out of phase; and back-spinning to elicit unexpected sounds from the grooves.

The younger spinners teamed up with rappers—Grandmaster Flash with the Furious Five, Davy D with Kurtis Blow. Initially, the role of the rapper was to keep the beat going with handclaps while the spinner changed records. Before long, rappers had developed extensive routines: lines of lyrics, slogans, double-dutch rhymes, and call-and-response exchanges with the audience. Solo rappers like Spoonie Gee extemporized much of their material, while groups like the Funky Four Plus One and Trouble Funk worked out arrangements of traded, overlapped, and unison lines.

Dancing and partying and the romantic prowess of the rapper were the dominant themes of rap, but rap also had a political thrust, recalling the work of Gil Scott-Heron and the Last Poets. Such raps as Brother D's "How We Gonna Make the Black Nation Rise?" and Grandmaster Flash and the Furious Five's "The Message" were among rap's earliest overtly political statements. Public Enemy's landmark 1988 album *It Takes a Nation of Millions to Hold Us Back,* however, set the hard-hitting tone for the political rap of the late Eighties and Nineties.

The first rap records were not made until 1979, most of them for small independent labels like Enjoy, Sugar Hill, and Clappers. Very quickly, however, rap acquired widespread popularity. The Sugarhill Gang, Fatback, and Kurtis Blow had the first national rap hits. By 1980 rap had crossed racial lines, as white acts like Ian Dury, Blondie, the Clash, and Tom Tom Club adopted rap styles into their music.

The first significant racial crossover events in rap were "Walk This Way," the 1986 collaboration of black rappers Run-D.M.C. and white rockers Aerosmith, and "(You Gotta) Fight for Your Right (to Party)," the 1987 Top Ten rap single by white rappers the Beastie Boys, whose debut album, *Licensed to Ill,* sold four million copies. In 1990 Vanilla Ice became the biggest-selling white rapper when his rap-inspired pop album, *To the Extreme,* sold eight million copies. Rap's biggest commercial crossover artist was M.C. Hammer (who later dropped the M.C.), whose 1990 dance-rap album *Please Hammer Don't Hurt 'Em* sold 15 million copies.

A number of rap subgenres appeared in the late Eighties and early Nineties. In 1986 Philly rapper Schoolly D introduced gangsta rap [see entry] with the song "PSK—What Does It Mean?" In 1989 laidback rappers De La Soul released the quirky *3 Feet High and Rising,* inadvertently spawning alternative rap. The same year, Queen Latifah (Dana Owens) inspired a generation of strong, self-confident women rappers with her debut album, *All Hail the Queen.* And in 1993 Gang Starr's Guru (Keith Elam) kicked off the jazz-rap trend when he collaborated with veteran jazzmen Donald Byrd and Courtney Pine on his first solo album, *Jazz-matazz.*

Rare Earth

Formed 1969, Detroit, Michigan
Gil Bridges, flute, saxophone, perc., voc.; Pete Rivera, drums, voc.; John Persh, bass, trombone, voc.; Rob Richards, gtr., voc.; Kenny James, kybds. 1969—*Get Ready* (Rare Earth)   1970—*Ecology* (– Richards; + Ray Monette, gtr.; – James; + Mark Olson, kybds.; + Ed Guzman [b. ca. 1944; d. July 29, 1993], perc.); *One World*   1971—*In Concert* (– Persh; + Mike Urso, bass, voc.; + Pete Hoorelbeke, drums, voc.)   1973—*Willie Remembers*; *Ma* (– Rivera)

1975—*Back to Earth* (numerous personnel changes follow)   1976—*Midnight Lady*   1977—*Rare Earth* (Prodigal)   1978—*Band Together; Grand Slam* 1993—*A Different World* (Koch Records International)   1995—*The Best of Rare Earth* (Motown).

Hard-rocking Rare Earth enjoyed several major hits with Motown Records in the early Seventies and was reportedly the first white act signed to the black-owned company. Founding members Pete Rivera, John Persh, and Gil Bridges grew up in Detroit listening to and playing Motown hits in local bars as the Sunliners. In 1969 they became Rare Earth and added three new members. With the aid of Motown session guitarist Dennis Coffey they attracted the company's attention and in 1969 were signed to a Motown subsidiary renamed Rare Earth.

The group's first album, *Get Ready* (#12), was quite successful, and the title cut, a reworking of the Temptations' hit, was a #4 single. *Ecology* and *One World* in 1970 spawned "(I Know) I'm Losing You" (#7 pop, #20 R&B, another Temptations remake), "Born to Wander" (#17 pop, #48 R&B), "I Just Want to Celebrate" (#7 pop, #30 R&B), and "Hey, Big Brother" (#19 pop, #48 R&B). Much of the group's material was produced by Motown staff producer Norman Whitfield.

Rare Earth, with Gil Bridges and Ray Monette still remaining from the early lineup, continues today. The group put out an album in 1993 and is especially popular in Germany.

The Rascals/The Young Rascals

Formed 1965, New York City, New York
Felix Cavaliere (b. Nov. 29, 1944, Pelham, N.Y.), voc., kybds.; Eddie Brigati (b. Oct. 22, 1946, New York City), voc.; Gene Cornish (b. May 14, 1945, Ottawa, Can.), gtr.; Dino Danelli (b. July 23, 1945, New York City), drums.
1966—*The Young Rascals* (Atlantic)   1967—*Collections; Groovin'*   1968—*Once upon a Dream; Time Peace: The Rascals' Greatest Hits; Freedom Suite* 1969—*See*   1970—*Search and Nearness*   1971— (– Brigati; – Cornish; + Buzzy Feiten [b. New York City], gtr.; + Robert Popwell [b. Daytona, Fla.], bass; + Ann Sutton [b. Pittsburgh, Pa.], voc.) *Peaceful World* (Columbia)   1972—*The Island of Real* 1992—*The Rascals Anthology (1965–1972)* (Rhino).
Felix Cavaliere solo: 1974—*Felix Cavaliere* (Bearsville)   1975—*Destiny*   1976—*Treasure* (Epic) 1980—*Castles in the Air*   1994—*Dreams in Motion* (Karambolage).
Eddie Brigati solo (with David Brigati): 1976— *Brigati* (Elektra).

The term "blue-eyed soul" was allegedly coined for the Rascals (although none of them had blue eyes), whose

The Rascals: Felix Cavaliere, Gene Cornish, Eddie Brigati, Dino Danelli

approximation of mid-Sixties black pop crossed the color line.

Dino Danelli began his career as a teenage jazz drummer (he played with Lionel Hampton's band) but switched to R&B while working in New Orleans, and he returned to New York to accompany such R&B acts as Little Willie John. There he met Eddie Brigati, a pickup singer on the local R&B circuit.

Felix Cavaliere had studied classical piano before becoming the only white member of the Stereos, a group based in his suburban hometown. While a student at Syracuse University, he formed a doo-wop group, the Escorts. After leaving school, Cavaliere moved to New York City, where he met Danelli, and the two migrated to Las Vegas to try their luck with a casino house band. On their return to New York, Cavaliere joined Joey Dee and the Starliters (sometimes spelled Starlighters), which included Brigati and Gene Cornish.

The Rascals came together in 1964 after Cavaliere, Brigati, and Cornish left Dee and formed a quartet with Danelli. In February 1965 they began gigging in New Jersey and on Long Island. By year's end they had changed their name to the Young Rascals (after *The Little Rascals*) and released their first Atlantic single, "I Ain't Gonna Eat Out My Heart Anymore" (#52, 1965), sung by Brigati. The group took a turn when Cavaliere sang the followup, "Good Lovin'" (#1, 1966), one of the year's biggest hits. In the following two years, the group had nine more Top Twenty hits, including "You Better Run" (#20, 1966), "(I've Been) Lonely Too Long" (#16, 1967), "Groovin'" (#1, 1967), and "A Girl Like You" (#10, 1967), most of them Cavaliere-Brigati compositions.

Established hitmakers, the group tried to get serious in 1967, dropping the "Young" from its name and the Edwardian knickers from its onstage wardrobe. With *Free-*

dom Suite, the Rascals' music took on elements of jazz, but the quartet continued to score with "How Can I Be Sure" (#4, 1967), "A Beautiful Morning" (#3, 1968), and "People Got to Be Free" (#1, 1968). Cavaliere and Brigati wrote the latter song shortly after the 1968 assassinations of Martin Luther King and Robert F. Kennedy. Though they never brandished their politics like some bands, the Rascals truly lived theirs, demanding that a black act appear on the bill at each of its concerts. The principled stand cost them dates in the South.

The Rascals never had another Top Twenty hit after "People Got to Be Free." With *Search and Nearness,* their songs made room for lengthy instrumental tracks by jazzmen like Ron Carter, Hubert Laws, and Joe Farrell. Record sales and concert attendance plummeted. In 1971 they signed to Columbia, but Brigati and Cornish left before their label debut. Filling their shoes were Buzzy Feiten (Butterfield Blues Band), fresh from sessions for Bob Dylan's *New Morning;* Robert Popwell, whose session credits included work for Dylan, Aretha Franklin, Eddie Floyd, and Tim Hardin; and Ann Sutton, who had sung with various soul and jazz groups in Philadelphia. The band broke up in the early Seventies.

Brigati recorded an album with his brother David in 1976; Cornish and Danelli started a group called Bulldog and later were part of Fotomaker with former Raspberries guitarist Wally Bryson. Feiten joined Neil Larsen in a duo in 1980. Cavaliere has continued as a solo artist and producer (Laura Nyro, Deadly Nightshade), and in 1994 released his first new album in nearly a decade and a half for producer Don Was's Karambolage label. In 1982 Danelli joined Steve Van Zandt's Little Steven and the Disciples of Soul. He, Cornish, and Cavaliere reunited in 1988 for a U.S. tour, but the following year Danelli and Cornish sued Cavaliere to prevent him from using the Rascals name. In a Solomonlike ruling, a judge allowed Cornish and Danelli to call themselves the New Rascals, and for Cavaliere to advertise himself as "formerly of the Young Rascals." In 1991 Eddie and David Brigati were featured on *The New York Rock and Soul Revue,* an allstar live album spearheaded by Steely Dan cofounder Donald Fagen.

The Raspberries/Eric Carmen

Formed 1970, Cleveland, Ohio
Eric Carmen (b. Aug. 11, 1949, Cleveland), voc., bass, gtr.; Wally Bryson (b. July 18, 1949, Gastonia, N.C.), gtr.; Jim Bonfanti (b. Dec. 17, 1948, Windber, Pa.), drums; Dave Smalley (b. July 10, 1949, Oil City, Pa.), bass, gtr.
1972—*Raspberries* (Capitol); *Fresh*   1973—*Side 3* (- Bonfanti; - Smalley; + Michael McBride, drums; + Scott McCarl, bass)   1974—*Starting Over* 1991—*Collectors Series.*

The Raspberries: Jim Bonfanti, Wally Bryson, Eric Carmen, Dave Smalley

Eric Carmen solo: 1975—*Eric Carmen* (Arista) 1977—*Boats Against the Current*   1978—*Change of Heart*   1980—*Tonight You're Mine*   1985—*Eric Carmen* (Geffen)   1988—*The Best of Eric Carmen* (Arista).

The Raspberries, with their Beatleslike harmonies, Mod-influenced suits, and power pop, seemed very out of place when they first recorded in 1972, partly because the general trend in America at the time was toward longer FM-oriented tracks.

The band formed in Cleveland in 1970 from several local groups. Jim Bonfanti had drummed on the Outsiders' 1966 hit "Time Won't Let Me." He was later in the Mods with Dave Smalley and Wally Bryson, who changed their name to the Choir. They became the most popular band in Cleveland, with a minor 1967 hit, "It's Cold Outside." Eric Carmen, who can both croon sensuously and scream rock & roll like Paul McCartney, joined the local Cyrus Erie as lead singer, and Bryson left the Choir to join Carmen's band. They recorded a few unnoticed singles for Epic; Carmen then recorded with a band called the Quick before going solo, writing and recording "Light the Way," later covered by Oliver.

At the turn of the decade, Carmen, Bryson, Bonfanti, and Smalley finally united in the Raspberries. In mid-1971 their demos attracted the attention of future producer Jimmy Ienner, who got them a contract with Capitol. Their debut LP had a raspberry-scented scratch-and-sniff sticker on the cover. The second single, "Go All The Way," hit #5 and sold more than 1.3 million copies. The second LP included "I Wanna Be with You" (#16, 1972) and "Let's Pretend" (#35, 1973). Carmen wrote and sang most of the hits, many of which (including the three listed above) were paeans to making out.

During the recording of *Side 3,* internal problems developed. Bonfanti and Smalley resisted the group's teenybopper image, and by the end of the year they'd left, forming Dynamite with two ex-members of Freeport, another Cleveland band. They were replaced by Michael McBride, who had played in Cyrus Erie with Carmen, and Scott McCarl, who had sent an audition tape to Ienner. The new foursome released its fourth and final LP, *Starting Over,* a concept album about stardom that many critics called the best LP of 1974. Although the single "Overnight Sensation (Hit Record)" reached #18, the album flopped, and the band quit in frustration.

Carmen went on to an intermittently successful solo career as a pop balladeer. His first solo LP contained three hits: "Sunrise" (#34, 1976), "Never Gonna Fall in Love Again" (#11, 1976), and "All by Myself" (#2, 1976), the last of which incorporated a Rachmaninoff melody, as did several other songs by the classically trained pianist/guitarist. Carmen had only one more Top Twenty hit over the next ten years ("Change of Heart," #19, 1978) but did compose "That's Rock 'n' Roll" (#3, 1977) and "Hey Deanie" (#7, 1977), both smashes for teen heartthrob Shaun Cassidy, and "Almost Paradise (Love Theme from *Footloose*)," a Top Ten hit for Loverboy's Mike Reno and Heart's Ann Wilson in 1984. Three years later another film, *Dirty Dancing,* gave Carmen his own hit with "Hungry Eyes" (#4, 1987). Though a followup, "Make Me Lose Control," soared to #3 the following spring, Carmen has yet to release an album of new material since 1985.

Ratt

Formed 1981, Los Angeles, California
Bobby Blotzer (b. Oct. 22, 1958), drums; Robbin Crosby, gtr.; Juan Croucier (b. Aug. 22, 1959), bass; Warren De Martini (b. Apr. 10, 1963), gtr.; Stephen Pearcy (b. July 3, 1956), voc.
1983—*Ratt* (Time Coast)   1984—*Out of the Cellar* (Atlantic)   1985—*Invasion of Your Privacy*   1986— *Dancin' Undercover*   1988—*Reach for the Sky* 1990—*Detonator*   1991—*Ratt & Roll 8191.*

One of the most popular Los Angeles metal bands, Ratt concentrated mostly on the music, a standard-issue combination of Zeppelin and Aerosmith. Four out of seven albums went platinum, with two cracking the Top Ten: *Out of the Cellar* (#7, 1984) and *Invasion of Your Privacy* (#7, 1985).

Ratt began in 1981 with friends Robbin Crosby and Stephen Pearcy. They met Warren De Martini on the club scene. After seeing drummer Bobby Blotzer on MTV, they tracked him down; Blotzer brought along Juan Croucier. Their friendship with Mötley Crüe helped them to secure a contract with Atlantic; the label signed them

after an executive saw a live show. *Out of the Cellar,* their debut for Atlantic, contained "Round and Round," the #12 hit that became an MTV staple.

Ratt remained popular for the length of its career. For 1990's *Detonator* (#23) the group collaborated with songwriter-for-hire Desmond Child. The departure of Stephen Pearcy in 1992, for the usual "artistic differences," ended Ratt's career.

Genya Ravan

Born Goldie Zelkowitz, 1942, Lodz, Poland
1972—*Genya Ravan with Baby* (Columbia)   1973— *They Love Me/They Love Me Not* (Dunhill)   1974— *Goldie Zelkowitz* (Janus)   1978—*Urban Desire* (20th Century-Fox)   1979—*And I Mean It.*

In two decades as a rock musician, Genya Ravan led one of the first self-contained all-female rock bands, sang hits for Ten Wheel Drive, and later became the first female producer hired by a major record label.

Growing up in the Jewish ghetto on New York's Lower East Side, young Goldie Zelkowitz developed an interest in R&B. She ran with a teenage gang and dropped out of high school for a musical career, which began in a Brooklyn lounge when she walked onstage and began singing with Richard Perry's band, the Escorts, which made her their lead singer. She sang their version of "Somewhere" from *West Side Story;* the record never charted nationally but made #1 in Detroit.

In 1962 she formed Goldie and the Gingerbreads, probably the first girl group in which all the women played their own instruments. They stayed together until 1969, achieving their biggest successes in England, where they eventually relocated and later toured with the Rolling Stones, the Yardbirds, Manfred Mann, and the Kinks.

In 1969 Zelkowitz changed her name to Genya Ravan and formed Ten Wheel Drive ("Morning Much Better," #74, 1970), an otherwise all-male jazz-blues band with a five-piece horn section in the mold of Blood, Sweat and Tears. She left it in 1971 to form her own band, Baby, which toured with Sly and the Family Stone and backed up Ravan on her first solo album. At that time most of her material was written by Baby's guitarist, Mitch Styles, formerly of Diamond Reo.

In 1975 Ravan became the first woman producer hired by a major label when RCA had her produce cabaret act Gretchen Cryer and Nancy Ford (who wrote the feminist musical *I'm Getting My Act Together and Taking It on the Road*) and the debut album by Rosie (who later joined the Harlettes). A little over a year later Ravan formed the short-lived Taxi. She also produced demos for CBGB owner Hilly Kristal, including the Shirts, a popular band at the club, as well as the debut LP by the Dead Boys, *Young, Loud and Snotty.* She later sang on

Blue Öyster Cult's *Mirrors* LP and did some production work with ex-Ronette Ronnie Spector. Lou Reed guested on *Urban Desire,* Ian Hunter on *And I Mean It;* both albums stuck to her hard-nosed rock vein, with many songs written by Ravan. In 1980 Ravan formed her own label, Polish Records. She appeared on *The Warriors* soundtrack.

The Ravens

Formed 1945, New York City, New York
Warren Suttles, baritone voc.; Jimmy Ricks (b. 1924; d. July 2, 1974), bass voc.; Leonard Puzey, tenor voc.; Ollie Jones, tenor voc.
1946—(– Jones; + Maithe Marshall, tenor voc.)
1950—(– Suttles; + Louis Heyward, baritone voc.; numerous personnel changes thereafter).

The Ravens were an early R&B vocal group whose material ranged from Tin Pan Alley ballads to jive to doo-wop. The group is historically significant for a number of firsts. They were one of the first vocal groups to feature a bass voice singing lead, probably the first to feature a lead falsetto tenor, and the first to add choreography to their act, making them stylistic forefathers to any of a number of male vocal groups, including the Temptations (who have included a bass-led version of "Old Man River"—the Ravens' 1946 two-million-selling hit—in their live act since the Sixties).

  Like most of their contemporaries, the Ravens began in the smooth-harmony style of the Mills Brothers. Jimmy Ricks and Warren Suttles founded the group, which recorded its first singles, including "My Sugar Is So Refined," in 1946. Shortly thereafter began the first of the group's many personnel changes, including the replacement of Ollie Jones with Maithe Marshall, whose falsetto lead became the group's trademark. Their first big hits came in 1947: "Write Me a Letter" (#24 pop, #5 R&B) and "Old Man River" (#10 R&B), which featured Ricks' bass. The next year's rendition of "White Christmas" (#9 R&B), was a major hit and laid the blueprint for the Drifters' version six years later. "I Don't Have to Ride No More" (#9 R&B) from 1950, was the group's last national hit until "Rock Me All Night Long" (#4 R&B, 1952).

  By then Marshall had been replaced by Joe Van Loan (whose brother James was a member of Billy Ward and His Dominoes). They continued to record for many years. Their 1956 lineup included three Van Loan brothers: Joe, James, and Paul. In the late Fifties Ricks sold the Ravens name, which led to countless groups performing under it through the next two decades. In the Seventies Ricks, Van Loan, and Suttles regrouped in various aggregations. Ricks, who had recorded with Benny Goodman and performed with Count Basie, never found success as a solo artist, despite recording for over a dozen labels. The other members went on to sing with other groups.

Lou Rawls

Born December 1, 1935, Chicago, Illinois
1963—*Black and Blue* (Capitol)   1966—*Lou Rawls Live; Lou Rawls Soulin'*   1967—*Too Much; That's Lou*   1968—*Feelin' Good; You're Good for Me*   1969—*The Way It Was/The Way It Is*   1971—*A Natural Man* (MGM)   1976—*All Things in Time* (Philadelphia International)   1977—*Unmistakably Lou; When You Hear Lou, You've Heard It All*   1978—*Lou Rawls Live*   1979—*Let Me Be Good to You*   1980—*Sit Down and Talk to Me*   1981—*Shades of Blue*   1983—*When the Night Comes* (Epic)   1989—*At Last* (Blue Note)   1990—*Greatest Hits* (Curb); *It's Supposed to Be Fun* (Blue Note)   1993—*Portrait of the Blues* (Manhattan); *Christmas Is the Time.*

Three-time Grammy-winning singer Lou Rawls has been a popular black MOR singer since the Fifties. He grew up on the South Side of Chicago, where he sang in church. In the mid-Fifties he was in the Los Angeles–based Pilgrim Travelers gospel group before joining the army in 1956. After returning, he toured with Sam Cooke; in 1958 Cooke and Rawls, traveling by car to a concert, were involved in an auto accident. Cooke wasn't badly hurt, but Rawls, who was initially pronounced dead, lay in a coma for five days before recovering.

  In 1959 the Travelers broke up, and Rawls began singing the blues in Los Angeles nightclubs. He also had a bit part in the popular *77 Sunset Strip* television series. For a time he was managed by Cooke, and he would later duet with Cooke on the classic "Bring It On Home to Me." Rawls signed a solo contract with Capitol Records in 1962 and recorded with moderate success until 1966, when "Love Is a Hurtin' Thing" went to #13 pop, #1 R&B. It wasn't until the mid-Sixties, with hits that mixed spoken monologues and music—like the Grammy Award–winning "Dead End Street" (#29 pop, #3 R&B, 1967)—that Rawls reached white audiences. *Lou Rawls Live* (#4, 1966) was his first of several gold albums, and during the late Sixties he appeared regularly on television variety shows and in Las Vegas nightclubs.

  In 1971 Rawls moved to MGM Records and cut the popular Grammy Award winner "A Natural Man" (#17 pop and R&B). He didn't have another major hit until he signed with Philadelphia International records in 1976. Under the guidance of producers Kenny Gamble and Leon Huff, Rawls recorded "You'll Never Find Another Love Like Mine" (#2 pop, #1 R&B) and "Groovy People" (#19 R&B) in 1976; "See You When I Git There" (#8 R&B) and "Lady Love" (#24 pop, #21 R&B) in 1977; and "Let Me Be Good to You" (#11 R&B, 1979). Rawls' only platinum album was his first under Gamble and Huff, *All Things in Time* (#7, 1976). In 1977 Rawls won another Grammy for

Best Male Rhythm & Blues Performance for *Unmistakably Lou* (#41, 1977).

Rawls subsequently became known as the voice behind Budweiser beer ads, and in fact he recorded an album entitled *When You Hear Lou, You've Heard It All,* based on that company's slogan. In the years since, the brewery has sponsored the singer's annual *Lou Rawls' Parade of Stars* telethon, which raises money for black colleges and the United Negro College Fund. As of late 1992, he had raised over $100 million.

Through the Eighties and Nineties Rawls continued to tour and record. In 1987 he released his last charting single to date, "I Wish You Belonged to Me" (#28 R&B, 1987) from *Family Reunion,* produced by Gamble and Huff. He lent his voice to three Garfield the Cat specials and the first show's soundtrack album. He has acted in several films, including *Believe in Me* (1971). The Grammy-nominated *At Last* includes guest appearances by Ray Charles and George Benson, among others. *Portrait of the Blues* (with guests Phoebe Snow, Joe Williams, and Buddy Guy, among others) and *It's Supposed to Be Fun* were coproduced by Billy Vera, though the title single of the latter was coproduced by Narada Michael Walden and Rawls.

Johnnie Ray

Born January 10, 1927, Dallas, Oregon; died February 24, 1990, Los Angeles, California
**1952—*Johnnie Ray* (Columbia)   1957—*The Big Beat*
1978—*Johnnie Ray—An American Legend.***

Though he had started to go deaf as a youngster, Johnnie Ray still managed to become one of America's most popular male vocalists of the early and mid-Fifties, with a dozen gold records. He left home for Hollywood, then ended up in Detroit in 1951. There he met blues singer LaVern Baker and her manager, Al Green (not the Memphis soul singer), who helped Ray work on his music. He was discovered by Detroit disc jockey Robin Seymour, and in 1951 he signed to Columbia's Okeh subsidiary. That year his "Whiskey and Gin" was a minor hit in the Midwest.

Ray went to New York City, where, with Mitch Miller producing and the Four Lads backing, he recorded "Cry," a #1 ballad in 1952. Because he was so emotional during his performances, Ray is frequently cited as the first popular singer to break with the cool, professional stance of earlier pop crooners like Perry Como. Among critics' nicknames for him was Prince of Wails. Through the early to mid-Fifties Ray had many pop hits, including "Please Mr. Sun," a cover of the Drifters' "Such a Night," "Just Walking in the Rain," "Yes Tonight, Josephine," and "You Don't Owe Me a Thing."

Although Ray's chart success ended in the U.S. nearly as quickly as it began, he was extremely popular in the U.K., where he made 29 chart appearances in the Top Forty, as opposed to four here, between 1952 and 1960. He also recorded three duets with Doris Day that charted there. In the following years, Ray popped up occasionally as an oldies act both on TV and in concerts. He died of liver failure. Even in death, Ray was not forgotten by his British fans: Morrissey often wore a hearing aid onstage in an unusual tribute to Ray, and the opening line of Dexy's Midnight Runners' #1 1984 hit "Come On Eileen" mentions him.

Raydio: See Ray Parker Jr.

Mac Rebennack: See Dr. John

Redbone

Formed 1968, Los Angeles, California
Lolly Vegas (b. Fresno, Calif.), gtr., lead voc.; Pat Vegas (b. Fresno), bass, voc.; Anthony Bellamy (b. Los Angeles), gtr.; Peter De Poe (a.k.a. Last Walking Bear, b. Neah Bay Reservation, Wash.), drums.
1970—*Redbone* (Epic); *Potlatch*   1971—*Message from a Drum*   1973—*Wovoka*   1974—(– De Poe; + Butch Rillera, drums) *Beaded Dreams Through Turquoise Eyes*   1975—*Come and Get Your Redbone*   1978—*Cycles* (RCA)   1994—*Redbone: Live* (Avenue/Rhino).

Redbone consisted of four Native Americans (the band's name is a derogatory Cajun slang term for half-breed) who sometimes wore traditional dress onstage and played "swamp rock" (popularized by Creedence Clearwater Revival) with some funk influences. "Come and Get Your Love," highlighted by Lolly Vegas' lead vocals, was its only major hit (#5, 1974).

The band formed in California in 1968. The members had all grown up poor in migrant camps. In the mid-Sixties brothers Pat and Lolly Vegas (the latter became Redbone's leader) played in a band on TV's *Shindig.* They also did West Coast session work, backing Odetta and John Lee Hooker, and wrote "Niki Hoeky," which became a hit for P. J. Proby (#23, 1967).

Anthony Bellamy used to play flamenco guitar at his parents' restaurant and later performed with local L.A. rock & roll bands; Peter De Poe was a ceremonial drummer on the reservation where he was born. The band united on the L.A. club circuit, got a deal with Epic, and released its debut in January 1970, including its own version of "Niki Hoeky."

Redbone's albums never sold well, and while the group did have some catchy, soulful rock tracks like 1971's "Maggie" (#45) and 1972's Top Twenty-five hit "Witch Queen of New Orleans," it later explored more traditional Indian roots music. By the late Seventies Redbone had faded. The group continues to tour, however, and in 1994 released a live album recorded in 1977.

Otis Redding

Born September 9, 1941, Dawson, Georgia; died December 10, 1967, Madison, Wisconsin
1964—*Pain in My Heart* (Atco)   1965—*The Great Otis Redding Sings Soul Ballads* (Volt); *Otis Blue/Otis Redding Sings Soul*   1966—*Complete and Unbelievable . . . The Otis Redding Dictionary of Soul; The Soul Album*   1967—*Otis Redding Live in Europe; King and Queen* (with Carla Thomas) (Stax); *History of Otis Redding* (Volt)   1968—*The Dock of the Bay; The Immortal Otis Redding* (Atco); *Otis Redding in Person at the Whisky-a-Go-Go* 1969—*Love Man*   1970—*Tell the Truth* (Atco); *Otis Redding/Jimi Hendrix Experience* (Reprise)   1982— *Otis Redding Recorded Live* (Atlantic)   1987—*The Otis Redding Story*   1992—*Remember Me* (Stax); *The Very Best of Otis Redding* (Rhino)   1993—*Good to Me: Live at the Whisky a-Go-Go, vol. 2* (Stax); *Otis! The Definitive Otis Redding* (Rhino)   1995— *The Very Best of Otis Redding, vol. 2.*

Otis Redding's grainy voice and galvanizing stage shows made him one of the greatest male soul singers of the Sixties. At the time of his death, he was making his first significant impact on the pop audience after years as a favorite among blacks.

In his youth, Redding was influenced by both Little Richard and Sam Cooke, and early in his career he was a

Otis Redding

member of Little Richard's former backing band, the Upsetters. In the late Fifties, he met Johnny Jenkins, a local guitarist, who invited him to join his group, the Pinetoppers, who were managed by Phil Walden. Feeling that he'd gone as far as he could go in Macon, Redding moved to Los Angeles in 1960. There he cut a handful of singles, including the Little Richard–esque "Gamma Lamma." Upon returning to Macon in 1961, he recorded the similar-sounding "Shout Bamalama" and garnered some local attention.

After taking odd jobs around the South, Redding worked as a chauffeur and was working again with Jenkins when the guitarist landed a contract with Atlantic. One day in October 1962, when it seemed that Jenkins' session wasn't going anywhere, Redding hastily recorded his own ballad, "These Arms of Mine." He had accompanied Jenkins to the session with the intent of getting a chance to record. By 1963 "These Arms of Mine" had become Redding's first hit. It hit #20 on the R&B chart and established Redding as a recording artist. But it was his impassioned performances on the so-called chitlin' circuit that made him, next to James Brown, the most popular black entertainer of the mid-Sixties.

Redding wrote many of his own hits, including "Mr. Pitiful" (#41 pop, #10 R&B, 1965), "Fa-Fa-Fa-Fa-Fa (Sad Song)" (#29 pop, #12 R&B, 1966), and "(Sittin' on) The Dock of the Bay" (#1 pop, #1 R&B, 1968), all cocredited to Stax session guitarist Steve Cropper; "I've Been Loving You Too Long" (#21 pop, #2 R&B, 1965), with Jerry Butler; "Respect" (#35 pop, #4 R&B, 1965), "I Can't Turn You Loose" (#11 R&B, 1965), and "My Lover's Prayer" (#61 pop, #10 R&B, 1966). He also had hits with the Rolling Stones' "Satisfaction" (#31 pop, #4 R&B, 1966) and Sam Cooke's "Shake" (#47 pop, #16 R&B, 1967). Among his LPs, *Dictionary of Soul* is considered one of the best examples of the Memphis soul sound.

Redding also played an important role in the careers of other singers. In 1967 he cut a duet album with Carla Thomas, *King and Queen,* which had a hit in "Tramp" (#26 pop, #2 R&B). Redding produced his protégé Arthur Conley's tribute "Sweet Soul Music" (#2 pop and R&B) in 1967—an adaptation of Sam Cooke's "Yeah Man"— which became a soul standard. Redding also established his own label, Jotis, and was planning to get more deeply involved in talent management, development, and production.

Redding's appearance at the Monterey Pop Festival in 1967 introduced the singer to white rock fans. His intense performance (captured in the film *Monterey Pop* and on the LP *Otis Redding/Jimi Hendrix*) was enthusiastically received. As a gesture of thanks, Redding and Steve Cropper wrote "(Sittin' on) The Dock of the Bay." It was recorded on December 6, 1967, at the end of a long session. The whistling at the end came about, Cropper claims, because Redding forgot a vocal fadeout he had rehearsed before. It would become his biggest hit, yet Redding never lived to see its release.

On December 10, 1967, his chartered plane crashed into a Wisconsin lake, killing Redding and four members of his backup band, the Bar-Kays [see entry]. In early 1968 "The Dock of the Bay" hit #1 on both the pop and R&B charts. Fourteen years later his two sons and a nephew formed their own group, called the Reddings, and covered "Dock of the Bay" (#55 pop, #21 R&B). He was inducted into the Rock and Roll Hall of Fame in 1989 by Little Richard.

Redd Kross

Formed 1978, Hawthorne, California
Greg Hetson (b. Calif.), gtr.; Jeff McDonald (b. Aug. 10, 1963, Los Angeles, Calif.), voc.; Steve McDonald (b. May 24, 1967, Los Angeles), bass; Ron Reyes (b. Calif.) drums.
1980—*Red Cross* EP (Posh Boy) 1982—(– Hetson; – Reyes) *Born Innocent* (Smoke 7) 1984—*Teen Babes from Monsanto* (Gasatanka) 1987—*Neurotica* (Big Time) 1990—*Third Eye* (Atlantic) 1993— (+ Gere Fennelly [b. Aug. 5, 1960, San Mateo, Calif.], kybds.; + Eddie Kurdziel [b. Sep. 25, 1960, Philadelphia, Pa.], gtr.; + Brian Reitzell [b. Dec. 24, 1965, Ukiah, Calif.], drums) *Phaseshifter* (This Way Up).

Like an L.A. version of the Replacements, Redd Kross are young, loud, and snotty, inhabiting a world where Kiss, the Rolling Stones, the Sex Pistols, and the Ohio Express stand as artistic equals. Through personnel changes and business setbacks, brothers Steve and Jeff McDonald have remained committed to their trash aesthetic.

The McDonalds, along with schoolmates Ron Reyes and Greg Hetson, grew up in Hawthorne, California, home of the Beach Boys. Calling themselves the Tourists (not to be confused with the British band that included future Eurythmics Annie Lennox and Dave Stewart), their first gig was opening for Black Flag, where they caught the ear of DJ, entrepreneur, and scenemaker Rodney Bingenheimer. By 1980, when they recorded an EP, they had changed their name to Red Cross (they later turned into Redd Kross after the International Red Cross threatened to sue). Hetson and Reyes then left, for Circle Jerks and Black Flag, respectively.

Using a revolving cast of L.A. alt-rock musicians (including Black Flag singer Dez Cadena), the McDonalds released *Born Innocent* and *Teen Babes from Monsanto,* the latter a collection of covers, ranging from Kiss to Charles Manson. *Neurotica* seemed ready to push them to national attention, until their label, Big Time, folded.

It took until 1990 for Redd Kross to find a new, major label and release *Third Eye.* In the interim, the McDonalds kept busy with a series of side projects, including

Tater Totz, Anarchy 6, and recording the soundtrack for the experimental Super-8 film *Desperate Teenage Lovedolls.* After *Third Eye,* Redd Kross returned to an indie label for 1993's *Phaseshifter.*

Helen Reddy

Born October 25, 1941, Melbourne, Australia
1971—*I Don't Know How to Love Him* (Capitol); Helen Reddy 1972—*I Am Woman* 1973—*Long Hard Climb* 1974—*Love Song for Jeffrey; Free and Easy* 1975—*No Way to Treat a Lady; Helen Reddy's Greatest Hits* 1976—*Music, Music* 1977—*Ear Candy; Pete's Dragon* soundtrack 1978—*We'll Sing in the Sunshine; Live in London* 1979—*Reddy* 1981—*Play Me Out* 1983—*Imagination* 1984—*Lust for Life* 1987—*Helen Reddy Greatest Hits (and More)* 1991—*Feel So Young; That's All* (Helen Reddy Inc.) 1992—*All-Time Greatest Hits* (CEMA Special Products).

Among her many hits, singer Helen Reddy will no doubt be best remembered as the composer and singer of "I Am Woman," which went to #1 in 1972 and won a Grammy. Reddy began performing at the age of four at the Tivoli Theatre in Perth, Australia, and she toured much of that country with her show-business parents. She left boarding school at age 15 to work with a road show, acting as well as singing. She eventually landed her own Australian TV show, *Helen Reddy Sings,* and in 1966 won a trip to New York in the Australian Bandstand International contest, sponsored by Philips-Mercury Records.

Reddy had little success in New York, but she did meet Jeff Wald, an agent with the William Morris talent agency, whom she married a year later. (They divorced in the early Eighties; in 1983 she married Milton Ruth.) In 1970 Wald arranged for her to perform on TV's *Tonight Show,* and within a year Reddy had her first hit, a version of "I Don't Know How to Love Him" (#13, 1971) from the rock musical *Jesus Christ Superstar.*

Reddy's other hits included "Peaceful" (#12), "Delta Dawn" (#1), and "Leave Me Alone" (#3), in 1973; "Keep On Singing" (#15), "You and Me Against the World" (#9), and "Angie Baby" (#1), in 1974; "Emotion" (#22), "Bluebird" (#35), and "Ain't No Way to Treat a Lady" (#8), in 1975; "I Can't Hear You No More" (#29) in 1976; and "You're My World" (#18) in 1977. In 1973 she had her own summer-replacement variety show on NBC, and for most of the rest of the Seventies she was a hostess on NBC's late-night rock-variety show *The Midnight Special.*

By then her run at the Top Forty had ended. She did some acting, appearing in *Airport 1975* (1974), the Disney children's film *Pete's Dragon* (1977), and *Sgt. Pepper's Lonely Hearts Club Band* (1978). She now heads her own production company and as of this writing was at work on a TV series entitled *Woman of the World*. In the mid-Seventies she served as commissioner of parks and recreation for her adopted home state of California.

Red Hot Chili Peppers

Formed 1983, Hollywood, California
Flea (b. Michael Balzary, Oct. 16, 1962, Melbourne, Austral.), bass; Jack Irons (b. July 18, 1962, Los Angeles, Calif.), drums; Anthony Kiedis (b. Nov. 1, 1962, Grand Rapids, Mich.), voc.; Hillel Slovak (b. Apr. 13, 1962, Haifa, Israel; d. June 25, 1988, Los Angeles, Calif.), gtr.
1983—(– Slovak; – Irons; + Jack Sherman, gtr.; + Cliff Martinez, drums) 1984—*The Red Hot Chili Peppers* (EMI America) 1985—(– Sherman; – Martinez; + Slovak; + Irons) *Freaky Styley* 1987—*The Uplift Mofo Party Plan* 1988—(– Slovak; – Irons; + Blackbyrd McKnight, gtr.; + D. H. Peligro, drums) 1989—(– McKnight; – Peligro; + John Frusciante [b. Mar. 5, 1970, New York City, N.Y.], gtr.; + Chad Smith [b. Oct. 25, 1962, St. Paul, Minn.], drums) *Mother's Milk* 1991—*BloodSugarSexMagik* (Warner Bros.) 1992—*What Hits!?* (EMI America) (– Frusciante; + Arik Marshall [b. Feb 13, 1967, Los Angeles, Calif.], gtr.) 1993—(– Marshall; + Jesse Tobias, gtr; – Tobias; + Dave Navarro [b. June 7, 1967, Santa Monica, Calif.], gtr.).
John Frusciante solo: 1994—*To Clara* (American).

A potent combination of L.A. skateboard cool, tattoos, thrash, and funk, the Red Hot Chili Peppers have overcome personal problems to emerge as one of the early Nineties' premier bands with 1991's *BloodSugarSexMagik* (#3) and "Under the Bridge" (#2). Their over-the-top performances and a sometimes excessive obsession with sex have inspired accusations of both sexism and criminal behavior.

After meeting at Los Angeles' Fairfax High, Flea, Slovak, and Irons, with Kiedis as MC, formed the band Anthem School. Kiedis, the son of actor and Sunset Strip personality Blackie Dammett, already had show-biz experience after playing Sylvester Stallone's son in the 1976 film *F.I.S.T.* Flea, an Australian-born, New York–raised musical prodigy, departed to join the L.A. punk band Fear, as well as act in Penelope Spheeris' *Suburbia* (1983). (He later appeared in Gus Van Sant's *My Own Private Idaho* [1992].) Irons and the Israeli-born Slovak then formed What Is This?

In 1983 the Chilis played their first show, an impromptu one-song jam at an L.A. club. The group went over well enough to be asked back (for two songs) and soon became a popular Hollywood club attraction. Their self-titled debut—with Flea, Kiedis, Cliff Martinez, and Jack Sherman (What Is This? had other contractual obligations)—was produced by Gang of Four guitarist Andy Gill. The album stiffed; Irons and Slovak returned, and the band took to the road, sometimes appearing onstage wearing only strategically placed tube socks.

Freaky Styley (1985), produced by George Clinton and with guest appearances by funk horn players Maceo Parker and Fred Wesley, improved matters musically if not commercially. More rock-oriented, *The Uplift Mofo Party Plan* (#148, 1987) sold better and contained the band's signature tune, "Party on Your Pussy."

Any optimism was shattered by the 1988 death of guitarist Hillel Slovak from a heroin overdose. Disturbed by Slovak's death and Kiedis' heroin addiction, Irons quit. An interim band with P-Funk guitarist Blackbyrd McKnight and Dead Kennedy drummer D. H. Peligro did not take hold. Kiedis recruited a Chili Peppers fan, guitarist John Frusciante, and auditions brought Chad Smith.

This version of the band recorded *Mother's Milk* (#52, 1989). With videos for "Knock Me Down" and their cover of Stevie Wonder's "Higher Ground" on MTV, it looked as if the Peppers were about to break through. The band's lifestyle came under some attack, though, with Kiedis convicted in 1989 of indecent exposure and sexual battery in an incident following a concert in Virginia. The next year during a taping of an *MTV Spring Break* special in Florida, Flea and Smith jumped offstage, with Flea grabbing a woman and carrying her on his shoulders, and Smith spanking her. The two were charged, and Flea was found guilty of battery, disorderly conduct, and solicitation to commit an unnatural and lascivious act; Smith was found guilty of battery.

The Chili Peppers' next album, *BloodSugarSexMagik*, produced by Rick Rubin, was written and recorded in a mansion the band claimed was haunted. It sold over three million copies, leading to their headlining 1992's Lollapalooza. Just before the tour, John Frusciante left the band (later releasing a solo LP) and was replaced by Arik Marshall. Marshall lasted only a year and, after many auditions and one false start with Jesse Tobias, was replaced by former Jane's Addiction guitarist Dave Navarro.

Jerry Reed

Born Jerry Hubbard, March 20, 1937, Atlanta, Georgia
1971—*When You're Hot, You're Hot* (RCA) 1972—*The Best of Jerry Reed* 1976—*Both Barrels* 1977—*East Bound and Down* 1983—*The Bird* 1985—*Collector's Series* 1986—*Lookin' at You* (Capitol).

Jerry Reed is known mostly among musicians for his fast-pickin' guitar style, and among the masses for his jokey, C&W-to-pop hits of the early Seventies. He got a record contract with Capitol in 1955 at age 18. He had been playing in bands since his early teens and had worked in a cotton mill. Initially Reed got attention as a songwriter, especially with "Crazy Legs" (which Gene Vincent recorded in 1956) and some covers by Brenda Lee.

From 1959 to 1961 Reed served in the army, and upon his release he moved to Nashville, where he had two minor hits on Columbia, "Hully Gully Guitars" and "Goodnight Irene." Reed worked primarily as a session guitarist until 1965, when he signed to RCA. Elvis Presley began to record Reed's work, giving him his first pop chart exposure with 1968's "Guitar Man" (which became Reed's nickname; it was also a hit for Reed the year before). Presley also cut Reed's "U.S. Male."

The guitarist's albums began to place on the C&W chart, and in 1970 he had his first gold single with his pop crossover debut, "Amos Moses," a swamp-rock song (#8 pop, #16 C&W). He became a household name with regular appearances on *Glen Campbell's Goodtime Hour* (1970–72). In 1971 he had a Top Ten pop and #1 C&W hit with the novelty number "When You're Hot, You're Hot," which also won a Grammy. In 1973 he again hit #1 C&W with "Lord, Mr. Ford." Reed also won critical acclaim and a Grammy for a duet LP with Chet Atkins, *Me and Jerry.* In 1982 he had a #1 C&W hit with "She Got the Goldmine (I Got the Shaft)."

He branched out into acting in the mid-Seventies with southern roles, first in 1975's *W.W. and the Dixie Dance Kings,* and then in *Gator* (1976), both with Burt Reynolds. Next he costarred in the popular Reynolds *Smokey and the Bandit* series, consisting of three feature films released between 1977 and 1983. In the meantime, Reed continued his television career, as host of *The Jerry Reed When You're Hot You're Hot Hour* (1972), as a regular on *Dean Martin Presents Music Country* (1973), playing a detective on *Nashville 99* (1977), and starring in the action-adventure series *Concrete Cowboys* (1981).

Jimmy Reed

Born September 6, 1925, Dunleith, Mississippi; died August 29, 1976, Oakland, California
1957—*I'm Jimmy Reed* (Vee-Jay)   1961—*Jimmy Reed at Carnegie Hall*   1974—*The Best of Jimmy Reed* (Crescendo)   1988—*Bright Lights, Big City* (Chameleon).

Jimmy Reed, one of the most influential blues harpists and performers, was also the composer of such standards as "Big Boss Man," "Honest I Do," "Bright Lights, Big City," and "Baby, What You Want Me to Do."

The son of a sharecropper, Reed began performing in the Chicago area in the late Forties to early Fifties, and in 1953 he signed with Vee Jay Records. His first big hit was "You Don't Have to Go" (#9 R&B) in 1955. The next year he scored with "Ain't That Lovin' You Baby" (#7 R&B). Between 1956 and 1961 he had 11 more Top

Twenty R&B hits, including "Honest I Do" (#10, 1957) and "Baby, What You Want Me to Do" (#10, 1960), both of which crossed over to Top Forty pop success.

Reed's work has been covered by many others, including Elvis Presley ("Baby, What You Want Me to Do"), Van Morrison and Them ("Bright Lights, Big City"), Pretty Things ("Big Boss Man"), the Rolling Stones, and Aretha Franklin, both of whom do versions of "Honest I Do."

He died at age 50 following an epileptic seizure. In 1988 his widow and their eight children filed a multimillion-dollar lawsuit against Arc Music, claiming that neither Reed nor his wife had sufficient education to comprehend a deal he signed in 1967, releasing all the rights to his songs for a flat fee of $10,000. As part of the settlement, both parties agreed not to divulge its terms.

Lou Reed

Born Louis Firbank, March 2, 1942, Brooklyn, New York
**1972—*Lou Reed* (RCA); *Transformer*   1973—*Berlin*   1974—*Rock 'n' Roll Animal*; *Sally Can't Dance*   1975—*Lou Reed Live*; *Metal Machine Music*   1976—*Coney Island Baby*; *Rock and Roll Heart* (Arista)   1977—*Walk on the Wild Side* (RCA)   1978—*Street Hassle* (Arista); *Live: Take No Prisoners*   1979—*The Bells*   1980—*Growing Up in Public*; *Rock and Roll Diary*   1982—*The Blue Mask* (RCA); *I Can't Stand It*   1983—*Legendary Hearts*   1984—*New Sensations*   1985—*City Lights: Classic Performances* (Arista)   1986—*Mistrial* (RCA)   1989—*New York* (Sire); *Retro* (RCA)   1992—*Magic*

Lou Reed

and Loss (Sire); *Between Thought and Expression: The Lou Reed Anthology* (RCA).
With John Cale: 1990—*Songs for Drella* (Sire).

As the lead singer and songwriter of the Velvet Underground in the late Sixties, Lou Reed was responsible for a body of work that was alienated from the optimism of the day and passionately bleak, and that remains highly influential today. He is often referred to as the godfather of punk. His solo career, which began after he left the Velvets in 1970, has been more idiosyncratic and marked by sudden turnabouts in image and sound, from self-consciously commercial product to white noise to unpredictable folk rock.

Before the formation of the Velvet Underground [see entry] in 1965, Reed grew up in Freeport, Long Island, then attended Syracuse University, studying poetry (under Delmore Schwartz, to whom Reed dedicated a song on the first Velvet Underground LP) and journalism. Reed's poems were published in *Fusion* magazine. (In 1977 he earned an award from the Coordinating Council of Literary Magazines for his poem "The Slide," and in 1992 was awarded France's Order of Arts and Letters.) After leaving Syracuse, Reed returned to New York City and worked for Pickwick Records, taking part in the studio group that recorded various Reed-penned songs, released by the Beachnuts and the Roughnecks. During this period, he met the musicians with whom he would subsequently form the Velvet Underground. With two of them he formed a band called the Primitives, which became the Warlocks and made one record.

Reed's departure from the Velvet Underground was bitter; he did not even stay to complete their fourth album, *Loaded.* He became a virtual recluse for nearly two years, until moving to England and beginning a solo career in 1971. *Transformer* (#29, 1972) was his pop breakthrough. Produced by Velvet Underground fan David Bowie, it yielded Reed's only Top Twenty hit to date, "Walk on the Wild Side," an ode to the denizens of Andy Warhol's Sixties films. With Bowie's aid, Reed made the transition to the glitter rock of the period, camping up his presumed homosexuality with bleached-blond hair and black fingernail polish. Typically, the next record, *Berlin,* was as grim in tone as *Transformer* had been playful.

Reed's recordings have continued to be unpredictable. A pair of live albums drawn from the same set of concerts (including the gold *Rock 'n' Roll Animal,* #45, 1974) featured streamlined heavy-metal versions of Velvet Underground material, while a later tour would pander to theatrics: Reed, for example, pretended to shoot up while performing the song "Heroin." *Sally Can't Dance* reached the Top Ten and was repudiated by Reed almost on release. After another live LP, he followed with *Metal Machine Music,* four sides of grating instrumental noise,

alternately considered high art worthy of RCA's classical division and a gambit to get off the label.

Reed moved to Arista in 1976 and at first made impeccably produced, harrowing music like the title cut of *Street Hassle* (#89, 1978). He then entered a relatively peaceful phase, typified by album titles like *Rock and Roll Heart* and *Growing Up in Public.* He married Sylvia Morales on Valentine's Day 1980, and his songs about the seamy side of life began to appear alongside paeans to suburban life—"I'm an average guy," he sang on *The Blue Mask.*

In the mid-Eighties Reed gained more of the spotlight when a number of postpunk bands, including R.E.M., U2, and Sonic Youth, began singing his praises and vocally claiming inspiration by the Velvet Underground. Beginning with *New Sensations* (#56, 1984) and *Mistrial* (#47, 1986), he got a second creative wind. In the three years between *Mistrial* and *New York,* he moved to Sire, where he hit an artistic plateau with *New York, Songs for Drella,* and *Magic and Loss.* A brutal song cycle about urban decay, *New York* was his first Top Forty album since *Sally Can't Dance.*

In 1989 Reed played guitar on fellow Velvet Underground drummer Maureen "Moe" Tucker's solo album, *Life in Exile After Abdication.* The same year, he reunited with another fellow VU mate, John Cale, for a work-in-progress performance of *Songs for Drella,* a pop requiem the two wrote for their late friend and mentor, Warhol, who had died three years earlier; in 1990 an album and video were released. The Velvet Underground reunited in 1993 for some well-received European dates, but again broke up bitterly before their planned U.S. performances (reportedly because Reed insisted on producing the album of the band's upcoming MTV "Unplugged" appearance, which was subsequently canceled).

Reed's 1992 album *Magic and Loss* (#80, 1992), a somber meditation on the process and pain of aging and death, inspired by the cancer deaths of two friends, was considered his most inspired work since *The Blue Mask.* The same year, RCA released a boxed set of Reed's music, *Between Thought and Expression,* which followed a 1991 book of selected Reed lyrics of the same name.

Throughout the Eighties and into the Nineties, Reed showed a newfound political activist side, appearing at the 1985 Farm Aid benefit concert and the 1986 Amnesty International Tour and contributing to the Artists United Against Apartheid *Sun City* record. In 1993 he performed at an inaugural event honoring the home state of Vice President Al Gore. Reed had also moved into acting—in the 1980 movie *One Trick Pony* and advertisements for Honda scooters, which used "Walk on the Wild Side," and Wim Wenders' 1993 film, *Faraway, So Close.*

Over the years Reed has found affinity with some of rock & roll's romantics and mythologists: Bruce Springsteen appeared uncredited on 1978's *Street Hassle,* and Reed inducted Dion into the Rock and Roll Hall of Fame; he also cowrote songs for Kiss and Nils Lofgren. Reed's sidemen have included Jack Bruce (ex-Cream) and jazz trumpeter Don Cherry; for *The Blue Mask* and *Legendary Hearts,* he toured with an acclaimed band that included ex-Voidoids Robert Quine on guitar and Fred Maher on drums, and ex–Jean-Luc Ponty bassist Fernando Saunders; and for *New York* and the *Magic and Loss* tour, he brought along R&B crooner Little Jimmy Scott as a backup vocalist. Split from his wife Sylvia by 1994, Reed was frequently in the company of avant-garde performance artist Laurie Anderson.

Martha Reeves: See Martha and the Vandellas

Reggae

Reggae was the name given in 1968 to the latest in a succession of Jamaican dance rhythms, but the term has come to refer to the various styles derived from Afro-Caribbean musics and American R&B that have flourished in Jamaica since the early Sixties.

The music popular with Jamaica's poor majority before the Forties was called *mento,* sung and played on guitars and percussion by itinerant musicians who drew from Jamaica's African heritage, from local work songs and spirituals, and from the calypso, rhumba, and merengue of neighboring islands. After World War II, music from the United States began to make an impression on Jamaicans via radio from Miami, New Orleans, and Memphis and through sound-system operators who imported the latest U.S. R&B records to play on their mobile discotheques. American R&B musicians like Louis Jordan, Roscoe Gordon, Johnny Ace, Amos Milburn, and Fats Domino dominated Jamaican popular music throughout the Forties and Fifties.

American records fell out of favor in Jamaica around 1960, and sound-system moguls like Coxsone Dodd, Duke Reid, and Prince Buster opened studios to record local talent. Kingston, Jamaica, suddenly became a recording center. Early hitmakers like Laurel Aitken, Owen Gray, Jackie Edwards, and Derrick Morgan began by imitating American R&B but rapidly developed an original sound by setting mento-style songs to R&B-style arrangements for horns, keyboards, drums, and electric guitars and bass. The odd, bouncy rhythm that crossed the R&B backbeat with the characteristically Jamaican hesitation beat became known as ska. Bands like the Skatalites, the Soul Vendors, and the Ska Kings, and singers like Stranger Cole, Eric Morris, Jimmy Cliff, Justin Hines, the Maytals, the Blues Busters, and the Wailers, made ska tremendously popular in Jamaica, particularly with the "rude boys"—the ghetto youth.

Sound systems continued to disseminate the music, giving rise to a ska offshoot called "toasting": sound-system disc jockeys would add vocal effects to the music or talk over it, reciting aphorisms and doggerel or mimicking singers and other DJs. Toasting, in turn, gave rise to "dub," the practice of manipulating playback controls to drop out or bring forward prerecorded tracks. Eventually both these styles moved from the sound systems into the studios. King Stitt and U Roy had the first toaster hits in the late Sixties and early Seventies, followed by I Roy, Big Youth, Prince Jazzbo, Dillinger, and others. Lee Perry, King Tubby, and Augustus Pablo advanced from dubbing behind toasters to recording their own "dub-wise" instrumental records.

By that time the music had gone through several stages beyond ska, roughly following the development of American R&B into the more gospel-inspired soul music of the mid-Sixties. Jamaica's heatwave of 1966 slowed ska's tempos to what became known as "rock steady"; Alton Ellis, Delroy Wilson, Ken Boothe, the Heptones, and the Paragons had hits with the relaxed, lilting rock-steady style. Rock steady was succeeded in 1968 by the looser, more upbeat "poppa-top" of the Pioneers and Desmond Dekker, and by the sparer, harder-driving reggae of the Slickers and the veteran Maytals. Reggae's distinctive sound was achieved by reversing instrumental roles: The guitar functioned mainly as a rhythm instrument, scratching chords on the offbeats, while the bass played a melodic counterpoint to the vocals; the drums provided complex cross rhythms and accents.

The ascetic, millennarian cult of Rastafari has been a presence in Jamaican music at least since the Fifties; some of the most influential ska musicians were Rastafarians, and by 1970 Rastafarianism was a crucial force in reggae. Groups like the Abyssinians, the Charmers, Burning Spear, and the revived Wailers incorporated Rastafarian ritual "burra" drumming and chanting into their music, while their lyrics quoted Rasta scripture and the mystical-political teachings of Marcus Garvey. Rasta's influence—in the ethereal sound mixes, the narcotic tempos, the esoteric language, and the Africanisms—pervaded the reggae of the Seventies.

In the second half of the decade, vocal trios like the Mighty Diamonds, Black Uhuru, and the Itals, backed by ensembles like Sly and Robbie and the Roots Radics Band, hardened the reggae beat, honed instrumental tracks to their most skeletal, and floated the result in echo, arriving at "rockers." In a parallel—sometimes overlapping—development, Dennis Brown, Sugar Minott, Gregory Isaacs, and other vocal stylists crooned more melodic, romantic songs in the "lovers' rock" mode.

While Jamaican music has had some popularity in the U.S. since the ska era, particularly as a cultural phenomenon via the late Bob Marley's Wailers, it has never found the mass enthusiasm that it has enjoyed in Europe, Africa, and South America. Millie Small, Desmond Dekker, and Jimmy Cliff have each had one U.S. Top Forty hit, but a truer indication of reggae's impact is heard in Paul Simon's "Mother and Child Reunion," Johnny Nash's "I Can See Clearly Now," the J. Geils Band's "Give It to Me," Eric Clapton's "I Shot the Sheriff," Stevie Wonder's "Master Blaster," Blondie's "The Tide Is High," and numerous other covers and originals by the Rolling Stones, Ry Cooder, Joan Armatrading, the Clash, Elvis Costello, the Police, the Specials, and the English Beat. In the Nineties reggae got a fresh boost in the U.S. when "dancehall," a rap-based offshoot, became popular in urban nightclubs. Also in the Eighties and early Nineties there were a number of major hits by artists such as Musical Youth, Ziggy Marley, Shabba Ranks, and Inner Circle.

R.E.M.

Formed 1980, Athens, Georgia
Michael Stipe (b. John Michael Stipe, Jan. 4, 1960, Decatur, Ga.), voc.; Peter Buck (b. Peter Lawrence Buck, Dec. 6, 1956, Berkeley, Calif.), gtr.; Mike Mills (b. Michael Edward Mills, Dec. 17, 1958, Orange, Calif.), bass, voc.; Bill Berry (b. William Thomas Berry, Jul. 31, 1958, Duluth, Minn.), drums.
1982—*Chronic Town* EP (I.R.S.) 1983—*Murmur* 1984—*Reckoning* 1985—*Fables of the Reconstruction* 1986—*Lifes Rich Pageant* 1987—*Document; Dead Letter Office* 1988—*Eponymous; Green* (Warner Bros.) 1991—*Out of Time* 1992—*Automatic for the People* 1994—*Monster*.

The most popular college-rock band of the Eighties, R.E.M. underwent a steady, decade-long rise from underground heroes to bona fide superstars. The quartet's arty mix of punk energy, folky instrumental textures, muffled vocals, and introspective, often oblique lyrics influenced a generation of alternative-rock bands. By the time of its $10-million, five-record deal with Warner Bros. in 1988, the band had gone from playing hole-in-the-wall pizza parlors to major arenas. In 1989 Rolling Stone named R.E.M. "America's Hippest Band."

Michael Stipe, raised by nonmusical parents in a military family that moved constantly, was an introverted child who spent much of his time hanging out with sisters Lynda and Cyndy. By 1975 he had begun reading articles about Patti Smith and the burgeoning New York punk scene and eventually bought three albums that would change his life: Smith's *Horses,* Television's *Marquee Moon,* and Wire's *Pink Flag.* While in high school in St. Louis, he joined a short-lived punk-rock cover band.

In 1978 Stipe enrolled in the art department at the University of Georgia at Athens, where he majored in painting and photography and developed an interest in surrealism and medieval manuscripts. While shopping at

R.E.M.: Bill Berry, Peter Buck, Michael Stipe, Mike Mills

the local Wuxtry record shop, he met store manager Peter Buck, a native Californian and avid pop fan who shared Stipe's interest in adventurous music. The two decided to form a band. Within a year, they connected with fellow students Bill Berry and Mike Mills, childhood friends from nearby Macon who had played together in various Southern rock groups. In April 1980 the four formed R.E.M. (named for the dream state "rapid eye movement") and began rehearsing in a converted Episcopal church. In July the group played their first out-of-state gig in Chapel Hill, North Carolina, where they met future manager and confidant, Jefferson Holt.

Though influenced by punk and the D.I.Y. aesthetic, R.E.M. developed their own energetic folk-rock style over the next year. Buck's chiming, Byrdslike guitar playing, together with Stipe's cryptic vocal style, became the group's signature sound. In 1981 they recorded a demo tape of original music at Mitch Easter's Drive-In Studio in Winston-Salem, North Carolina. Two songs from those sessions, "Radio Free Europe" and "Sitting Still," were released as a seven-inch single in July on the homegrown Hib-Tone label. The driving "Radio Free Europe" attracted positive notices, and in October the band returned to Easter's studio to record its first EP. R.E.M. signed with I.R.S. in 1982 and released *Chronic Town* to overwhelming critical praise.

The band's first full-length album, *Murmur* (#36, 1983), was an instant classic, containing everything its supporters had hoped for: more layers of ringing guitar, more passionately vague vocals, more atmospheric melodies, and more seductive pop hooks. It also included a new, tighter version of "Radio Free Europe." The group followed up with *Reckoning,* which failed to break new ground but managed to reach #27, spawning the minor hit "So. Central Rain (I'm Sorry)," and garnering favorable reviews. The group enlisted London-based folk producer Joe Boyd (Fairport Convention, Richard Thompson) for *Fables of the Reconstruction* (#28, 1985), which featured a hazy, psychedelic musical setting. *Lifes Rich Pageant* (#21, 1986) took that experiment further, but with more of a sheen, courtesy of producer Don Gehman (John Mellencamp), who encouraged Stipe to sing more clearly; its single was "Fall on Me," whose video was directed by Stipe.

Although Stipe had begun pulling out of his enigmatic shell with more intelligible vocals, his lyrics continued to confound. R.E.M.'s first major hit, "The One I Love" (#9, 1987), from the band's first Top Ten album, *Document* (#10, 1987), was a song of betrayal that was almost universally misinterpreted as a love song. Then, on the band's major-label debut, *Green* (#12, 1988), Stipe alluded to the ambiguous nature of his lyrics in "World Leader Pretend," acknowledging, "It's high time I razed the walls that I've constructed." The album's hit single, "Stand" (#6, 1988), was the simplest, most hummable song of R.E.M.'s career; the album's other single, "Pop Song 89" (#86, 1988), was a minor hit that made fun of the music business. *Dead Letter Office* (#52, 1987) is a collection of B sides and outtakes, and *Eponymous* (#44, 1988) is a greatest-hits album. R.E.M. went on a touring hiatus following *Green.*

It took three years for the band to return with the highly anticipated *Out of Time,* which rocketed to #1, went quadruple platinum, and included "Losing My Religion" (#4, 1991) and "Shiny Happy People" (#10, 1991). The video for the former was banned in Ireland for allegedly homoerotic imagery; the latter was a duet with Kate Pierson of the B-52's. *Out of Time* also featured an expanded instrumental palette of horns and mandolins. *Automatic for the People* (#2, 1992) was a somber album containing some meditations on mortality, and string arrangements by former Led Zeppelin bassist John Paul Jones. Its hits were "Drive" (#28, 1992), "Man on the Moon" (#30, 1993), and "Everybody Hurts" (#29, 1993).

During the latter part of the Eighties, R.E.M. became activists, inviting Greenpeace to set up booths at their shows and becoming involved in local Athens politics. On his own, Stipe spoke out on such issues as the environment, animal rights, and the plight of the homeless. He also ushered other artists into the public eye, including folk painter the Reverend Howard Finster, filmmaker Jim McKay (with whom he set up the film company C-00, noted for its series of public service announcements), and folksinger Vic Chesnutt. Stipe also worked with rapper KRS-One of Boogie Down Productions and Natalie Merchant of 10,000 Maniacs. Meanwhile, Buck produced music by such artists as Kevn Kinney of Drivin'

N' Cryin' and Charlie Pickett. In 1990 Buck, Berry, Mills, and singer/songwriter Warren Zevon formed a side band, Hindu Love Gods, which put out a self-titled album on Giant.

In 1994 R.E.M. returned to the fore with *Monster,* which combined rockers featuring heavily reverbed guitars (including that of Sonic Youth's Thurston Moore on one track) and distorted or almost glam-sounding vocals, as well as the band's more traditional-sounding fare. *Monster* shot to #1, though its first single, "What's the Frequency, Kenneth?" only reached #21. Soon after, the band commenced its first world tour in five years. After a few weeks, the tour was canceled in March 1995 when Berry was stricken with a brain aneurysm. Following surgery, Berry's prognosis was good, and the band continued the tour in the U.S. later in the year.

The Remains
Formed 1965, Boston, Massachusetts
Barry Tashian, gtr., voc.; Bill Briggs, kybds.; Vern Miller, bass, gtr., horns; N. D. Smart II, drums.
1967—*The Remains* (Spoonfed).

Formed by Barry Tashian along with fellow Boston University students, the Remains gained a loyal Boston following on the strength of live shows and one classic mid-Sixties garage-punk single, "Don't Look Back" (no relation to the Dylan film). In 1965 they opened local concerts by the Rolling Stones and in 1966 they opened the Beatles' U.S. tour. But after no followup hits materialized, they broke up in 1967, with various members going on to join the Flying Burrito Brothers, Kangaroo, Swallow, and Mountain. "Don't Look Back" is included on the *Nuggets* collection. Tashian briefly regrouped the band in the mid-Seventies. He has since joined Emmylou Harris' band.

Renaissance
Formed 1969, Surrey, England
Keith Relf (b. Mar. 22, 1943, London, Eng.; d. May 14, 1976, Eng.), voc., gtr.; Jim McCarty (b. July 25, 1943, Eng.), drums; Jane Relf (b. Eng.), voc.; John Hawken (b. Eng.), kybds.; Louis Cennamo, bass.
1969—*Renaissance* (Elektra) (– K. Relf; – McCarty; – Cennamo; – J. Relf; – Hawken; + Rob Hendry, gtr.; + Jon Camp, bass; + John Tout, kybds.; + Terry Sullivan, perc.; + Annie Haslam, voc.) 1972—*Prologue* (Capitol) (– Hendry; + Michael Dunford, gtr.) 1973—*Ashes Are Burning* 1974—*Turn of the Cards* (Sire) 1975—*Scheherazade and Other Stories* 1976—*Live at Carnegie Hall* 1977—*Novella* 1978—*A Song for All Seasons* 1979—*Azure d'Or* (– Sullivan; – Tout; + Peter Gosling, kybds.; + Peter Barron, drums) 1981—*Camera Camera* (I.R.S.)

1983—*Time-Line* 1990—*Tale of 1001 Nights, vol. 1*
(Sire); *Tale of 1001 Nights, vol. 2.*
Annie Haslam solo: 1977—*Annie in Wonderland*
(Sire) 1989—*Annie Haslam: Alter Ego* (Epic).
Illusion: 1977—*Out of the Mist* (Island).

Though Keith Relf and Jim McCarty founded Renaissance shortly after leaving the Yardbirds, their reign did not last long, and the incarnation that came to some prominence in the U.S. in the mid-Seventies included neither of them. In 1969 Relf and McCarty joined Relf's sister Jane and John Hawken (ex–Nashville Teens, later with Strawbs) to form an eclectic band fusing folk, jazz, and classical influences with rock. An eponymous LP on Elektra was released later in the year, but both Relf and McCarty quickly became dissatisfied with the venture. Relf and Louis Cennamo moved on to head a harder-rocking band called Armageddon. (After Relf's death the group continued and recorded for Island.)

By the group's 1972 followup, *Prologue*, all of the members had changed. The album had a pop-classical, self-consciously refined art-rock feel highlighted by John Tout's piano and Annie Haslam's clear, high-flying soprano. The lyricist was British poet Betty Thatcher, who wrote the lyrics to fit Michael Dunford's sheet music, which she would receive by mail.

Prologue got lots of U.S. FM airplay, and the group developed a strong following, particularly in New York. Before the followup, *Ashes Are Burning* (#171, 1973), Rob Hendry left and was replaced by songwriter/guitarist Dunford. With *Turn of the Cards* (#94, 1974), Renaissance switched to Sire, and its next LP, *Scheherazade* (#48, 1975), featured an entire suite complete with strings. The live LP, recorded with full orchestra on the East Coast, sold well, but the group's popularity was spotty elsewhere and nil in England. Haslam recorded the solo *Annie in Wonderland* (1977), produced by Roy Wood, formerly of the Move and the Electric Light Orchestra. In the Eighties Haslam, Camp, and Dunford (along with two new members) cut *Camera Camera* and *Time-Line* for I.R.S. Haslam still performs.

John Renbourn: See Pentangle

REO Speedwagon

Formed 1968, Champaign, Illinois
Terry Luttrell, voc.; Greg Philbin, bass; Gary
Richrath (b. Oct. 18, 1949, Peoria, Ill.), gtrs.; Neal
Doughty (b. July 29, 1946, Evanston, Ill.), kybds.;
Alan Gratzer (b. Nov. 9, 1948, Syracuse, N.Y.), drums.
1971—*REO Speedwagon* (Epic) (– Luttrell; + Kevin
Cronin [b. Oct. 6, 1951, Evanston, Ill.], voc.) 1972—
REO TWO (– Cronin; + Michael Murphy, voc.)
1973—*Ridin' the Storm Out* 1974—*Lost in a Dream*

1975—*This Time We Mean It* (– Murphy; + Cronin)
1976—*REO* (– Philbin; + Bruce Hall [b. May 3, 1953,
Champaign], bass) 1977—*You Get What You Play
For* 1978—*You Can Tune a Piano, but You Can't
Tuna Fish* 1979—*Nine Lives* 1980—*A Decade of
Rock 'n' Roll; Hi Infidelity* 1982—*Good Trouble*
1984—*Wheels Are Turnin''* 1987—*Life as We Know
It* 1988—*The Hits* (– Gratzer; + Graham Lear,
drums) 1990—(– Richrath; – Lear; + Bryan Hitt,
drums; + Dave Amato, gtr.; + Jesse Harms, kybds.)
The Earth, a Small Man, His Dog and a Chicken
1991—(– Harms) *The Second Decade of Rock & Roll.*

After more than a decade of touring and nine middling albums, this midwestern journeyman hard-pop quintet sold over seven million copies of *Hi Infidelity*. REO Speedwagon (named after a high-speed fire engine) was formed by Neal Doughty and Alan Gratzer while both were students at the University of Illinois in 1968. They became a popular local club attraction. Irving Azoff, who later managed the Eagles and Steely Dan, handled the group in the early Seventies, getting it dates opening for other popular midwestern acts like Bob Seger and Kansas. REO and Azoff severed their relationship in 1977.

Throughout the early Seventies, REO Speedwagon's records sold unspectacularly as the group continued to tour. REO went through relatively few personnel changes, the most significant being vocalist Kevin Cronin's departure in 1972 for a solo career; replacement Michael Murphy handled the singing on REO's third, fourth, and fifth LPs. Cronin then returned in 1975; his songwriting and singing would be crucial to the band's ascendance.

REO was the quintet's least successful LP, but its seventh and eighth—the live *You Get What You Play For* and *You Can Tune a Piano, But You Can't Tuna Fish*—were breakthroughs. With Cronin and Gary Richrath co-producing, REO began to develop a more distinctive sound, a mix of rock riffs and pop hooks. *Tuna* contained the band's first chart single, "Roll with the Changes" (#58, 1978), and was its first to sell a million copies. *Nine Lives* in 1979 continued in this pop-rock direction.

Hi Infidelity in 1980 was a phenomenally successful album, climbing to #1 on the *Billboard* chart three separate times. Four of its singles made the Top Forty: "Keep On Lovin' You" (#1, 1980), "Take It on the Run" (#5, 1981), "Don't Let Him Go" (#24, 1981), and "In Your Letter" (#20, 1981). The first two were heavy ballads, a style the group would rely upon from then on. *Good Trouble* (#7, 1982) was a relative disappointment, though it did contain one Top Ten single, "Keep the Fire Burnin'."

REO took a two-year sabbatical before coming out with the double platinum *Wheels Are Turnin'* (#7, 1984), which gave the band its second #1: "Can't Fight This

Feeling," a strongly melodic ballad. The band placed five more singles in the Top Twenty through 1988, but its record sales gradually slackened. When Richrath—one of the band's main writers and a fiery guitar player—left in 1990, not long after drummer Gratzer's departure, REO's ability to carry on appeared in jeopardy. But Cronin, Doughty, and Bruce Hall (a member since 1976) are still at it, with ex–Ted Nugent sideman Dave Amato on guitar and drummer Bryan Hitt, formerly of Wang Chung. In the Midwest, especially, REO can still draw crowds.

The Replacements

Formed 1980, Minneapolis, Minnesota
Paul Westerberg (b. Dec. 31, 1960, Minneapolis), voc., gtr., kybds.; Bob Stinson (b. Dec. 17, 1959, Mound, Minn.; d. Feb. 15, 1995, Minneapolis), gtr.; Tommy Stinson (b. Oct. 6, 1966, San Diego, Calif.), bass; Chris Mars (b. Apr. 26, 1961, Minneapolis), drums.
1981—*Sorry Ma, Forgot to Take Out the Trash* (Twin/Tone)   1982—*The Replacements Stink* EP   1983—*Hootenanny*   1984—*Let It Be*   1985—*The Shit Hits the Fans*; *Tim* (Sire)   1987—(– B. Stinson) *Pleased to Meet Me* (+ Slim Dunlap [b. Robert Dunlap, Aug. 14, 1951, Plainview, Minn.], gtr.)   1989— *Don't Tell a Soul*   1990—(– Mars; + Steve Foley, drums) *All Shook Down*.
Chris Mars solo: 1992—*Horseshoes and Hand Grenades* (Smash)   1993—*75% Less Fat*   1995— *Tenterhooks* (Bar/None).
Slim Dunlap solo: 1993—*The Old New Me* (Twin/Tone).
Tommy Stinson (with Bash & Pop): 1993—*Friday Night Is Killing Me* (Sire).
Paul Westerberg solo: 1993—*14 Songs* (Sire).

In the Eighties the Replacements' blend of punk guitar and pop melodies garnered critical acclaim but little commercial success. Hailing from the Minneapolis home base of acts as diverse as Hüsker Dü and Prince, the quartet was seen by its fans as generational spokesmen; Paul Westerberg's angst-ridden confessional songs cast him as a postpunk Bob Dylan.

The son of a Cadillac salesman, Westerberg was refused his high school diploma for failing to show up at graduation. After taking odd jobs as a steel mill worker and a janitor, he formed the Impediments with drummer Chris Mars, guitarist Bob Stinson, and Stinson's 12-year-old bass-playing brother, Tommy. Inspired by Westerberg's love for the Sex Pistols, the band—redubbing itself the Replacements after being banned from a club for rowdy behavior—developed a raucous, drunken stage act: Bob Stinson sometimes performed in underwear or a dress, and the set list ranged from covers of

Kiss and Cher to Westerberg's originals. Discovered by Peter Jesperson, cofounder of Twin/Tone Records, they signed with the indie label in 1980 and, gaining a following that nicknamed them the 'Mats (for "placemats"), they put out albums that progressed from the punk assault of their first two releases to the country-tinged *Hootenanny* to *Let It Be*, a collection that placed them at the forefront of alternative-rock bands.

Notorious for their alcoholic self-destructiveness and wildly uneven concerts but celebrated for Westerberg's hook-laden and painfully honest songs, the Replacements hovered on the verge of mainstream acceptance. But even their major-label signing to Sire in 1985 didn't alter their underdog status. While *Tim* and *Pleased to Meet Me* reflected the band's increasingly skillful musicianship and Westerberg's stylistic range, exhaustion began setting in. Dismissed for excessive drinking in 1987, Bob Stinson was replaced by Slim Dunlap. In 1995 Stinson was found dead in his apartment of a drug overdose; years of depression, alcoholism, and drug addiction had taken their toll.

Don't Tell a Soul delighted reviewers and produced a single that cracked the Top 100 ("I'll Be You," #51, 1989) but sold only around 300,000 copies. The band's swan song, *All Shook Down*, was a Replacements record in name only; fighting what he perceived as Westerberg's dictatorial control, Mars departed going on to release several solo albums. Steve Foley of the Minneapolis band Things Fall Down replaced him, but the album was basically a Westerberg solo project with the other Replacements employed as occasional sidemen.

Contributing to the popular soundtrack to *Singles*, a 1992 movie about the nascent Seattle music scene, Westerberg finally enjoyed a measure of success; in 1993 he released a solo debut, *14 Songs* (#44, 1993), to mixed reviews. The other Replacements also put out albums whose sound didn't depart greatly from their former band's.

The Residents

Formed 1970, San Francisco, California
1974—*Meet the Residents* (Ralph)   1976—*Third Reich n' Roll*   1977—*Fingerprince*   1978—*Not Available*; *Duck Stab/Buster & Glen*   1979— *Eskimo*; *Diskomo* EP; *Nibbles* (Virgin)   1980—*Commercial Album* (Ralph)   1981—*Mark of the Mole*   1982—*The Tunes of Two Cities*   1983—*Intermission* EP; *The Mole Show* bootleg; *Residue of the Residents*   1984—*George & James*; *Whatever Happened to Vileness Fats?*   1985—*The Census Taker* (Episode); *The Big Bubble* (Black Shroud-Ralph)   1986—*Heaven?* (Rykodisc); *Hell!*; *Stars & Hank Forever* (Ralph); *13th Anniversary Show—Live in Japan*   1987—*For Elsie* (Cryptic); *God in Three Persons*

(Rykodisc) 1988—*The Mole Show Live in Holland* (East Side Digital); *Holy Kiss of Flesh* 1989—*The King and Eye* (Enigma-Restless) 1990—*Cube-E Live in Holland* 1991—*Freak Show* (Official Product) 1992—*Our Finest Flowers* (Ralph-ESD) 1995—*Hunters, Original Soundtrack Album* (Milan). With Renaldo and the Loaf: 1983—*Title in Limbo* (Ralph).

The Residents have never identified themselves by name, nor have they ever appeared in photos without some kind of mask (usually giant eyeballs with top hats). Until 1982 they had given only one public concert, in 1976 in Berkeley, California, where they appeared wrapped in mummylike coverings and played behind an opaque screen. The Residents have made several surrealistic short films, which, like their albums, cryptically elaborate a deliberately perverse antipop vision.

About all that is known is that there are four of them, and that they emigrated from northern Louisiana to San Francisco in the early Seventies. The Residents' long-time spokesman is Jay Clem. They were named when Warner Bros. sent back an anonymous tape to "Residents" at their return address. On record they use a broad sonic palette, encompassing acoustic chamberlike instrumentation, tonal and atonal quasi jazz, electronics, noisy distortion, and intentionally whiny-nasal vocals. Until the mid-Seventies, their albums were available only on the mail-order Ralph label.

The jacket of their debut album originally featured a grotesque dadaesque parody of *Meet the Beatles*. Threatened with legal action, the Residents changed it to depict Beatle-suited figures with crawfish heads and Beatlelike names (i.e., "Paul McCrawfish," "Ringo Starrfish"). *Not Available* features modern-classical suites; *Eskimo* purports to be an Arctic cultural documentary with its otherworldly windswept sounds and native Eskimo chants; and *Commercial Album* fits 40 songs lasting one minute each (like commercials) on one LP.

In October 1982 the Residents played five shows in San Francisco and Los Angeles. Adhering to their "Theory of Obscurity," they were veiled and behind screens throughout the multimedia show, which included props and dancers enacting the "Mark of the Mole" storyline. The story became part of a Mole trilogy that included *Mark of the Mole, The Tunes of Two Cities,* and *The Residents Mole Show*. Meanwhile, the Residents and Ralph Records became embroiled in an internal conflict that led to the group's label hopping in the latter part of the decade.

The Residents issued a steady stream of albums through the Eighties, including their American Composer Series (*George & James,* a collection of George Gershwin and James Brown, and *Stars and Hank Forever,* a tribute to John Philip Sousa and Hank Williams);

God in Three Persons, an hour-long piece about sexual compulsion and violence; and *The King and Eye,* which focuses on Elvis Presley and the collapse of American pop. They spent most of 1986 touring Japan, Australia, Europe, and the United States, and in 1989 took their multimedia *Cube-E* stage show (again with dancers and props) all over the world.

The Residents issued a hodgepodge of recycled, unreleased, and live material in the Eighties: *Whatever Happened to Vileness Fats?* revives an abandoned 1972 video project, *Residue* is a rarities collection, and *Heaven?* and *Hell!* compile previously released material. *Freak Show* is a surreal musical comparison of the Residents' own strange performances with circus freak shows. In 1994 they released the album as an interactive CD-ROM.

Revenge: See Joy Division

Paul Revere and the Raiders

Formed 1960, Portland, Oregon
Paul Revere (b. Jan. 7, 1938, Harvard, Nebr.), kybds.; Mark Lindsay (b. Mar. 9, 1942, Cambridge, Idaho), voc., sax; Phil "Fang" Volk, bass; Michael "Smitty" Smith, drums; Drake Levin, gtr.
1965—*Here They Come* (Columbia) 1966—*Just Like Us!* (– Levin; + Jim "Harpo" Valley, gtr.); *Midnight Ride; The Spirit of '67* 1967—(– Volk; – Smith; – Valley; + Joe Correro Jr. [b. Nov. 19, 1946, Greenwood, Miss.], drums; + Charlie Coe [b. Nov. 19, 1944], bass; + Freddy Weller [b. Sep. 9, 1947, Ga.], gtr.) *Greatest Hits; Revolution* 1968—(– Coe; + Keith Allison, bass) 1971—*Indian Reservation* (– Correro; + Smith; + Omar Martinez, voc.; + Robert Woolley, gtr.) 1973—(– Weller) 1976—*The British Are Coming* (20th Century) (– Lindsay) 1983—*Paul Revere Rides Again* (Hitbound) 1990—*The Legend of Paul Revere.*
Mark Lindsay solo: 1970—*Arizona* (Columbia); *Silverbird* 1971—*You've Got a Friend.*

Paul Revere and the Raiders emerged from the rock & roll scene of the Northwest to become national pop successes, trading on the enormous teenybopper appeal of ponytailed lead singer Mark Lindsay. The Raiders began in 1959 as the Downbeats, a raunchy rock & roll band. Lindsay, who worked as a delivery boy at Revere's drive-in restaurant, played saxophone and sang on raucous, honking numbers like their first record, "Like, Long Hair" (1961), an independent single heard in Portland, Oregon, and nowhere else. They changed their name in mid-1962 and started wearing pseudo–Revolutionary War costumes. Columbia signed the group after hearing an unsolicited tape, and in mid-1963 the Raiders' version of "Louie Louie" was released. Though once again popular in the Northwest, their version was beaten out across America by the Kingsmen's hit. Sometime in 1964 Lindsay left the band; in early 1965 the Raiders moved to California and began to focus on a cleaner, more pop-oriented sound. Lindsay returned shortly thereafter.

"Steppin' Out" was their first national hit single (#46, 1965), aided by the band's prominence on Dick Clark's daily television rock program, *Where the Action Is.* By 1967 the group was known as Paul Revere and the Raiders featuring Mark Lindsay, which served as acknowledgment that Lindsay was cowriting most of their hits.

The group's hits during these years included "Just Like Me" (#11, 1965), "Kicks" (#4, 1966), "Hungry" (#6, 1966), "The Great Airplane Strike" (#20, 1966), "Good Thing" (#4, 1966), "Ups and Downs" (#22, 1967), and "Him or Me—What's It Gonna Be?" (#5, 1967). Despite the success, the lineup fluctuated constantly. Drake Levin was drafted in 1966 and was replaced by Jim Valley. When Levin returned from the army, he, Michael Smith, and Phil Volk formed Brotherhood, while Valley left for a solo career. Replacements included Freddy Weller (1967–73), destined for a successful solo career as a country singer, and Keith Allison (1968–75), a minor teen idol in his own right, mainly thanks to his many appearances as a regular on *Action.*

In 1969 Lindsay began to make solo records in addition to his work with the Raiders. Both enjoyed success early in the Seventies with "Arizona" (Lindsay) (#10, 1970) and "Indian Reservation" (Raiders) (#1, 1971), but little afterward. Lindsay quit the group in 1975, though he did rejoin Revere the following year to capitalize on America's bicentennial with a tour and album. Since then Lindsay has worked briefly in A&R, but mostly forged a successful career singing commercials. Revere, meanwhile, tours some 250 nights a year with a band of Raiders that as of 1991 included lead singer Omar Martinez, Ron Foos, Doug Heath, and Robert Woolley, all of whom have been with him on and off since the Seventies. In 1985 the group returned to TV on a summer series, *Rock 'N Roll Summer Action,* on ABC.

Revolting Cocks: See Ministry

Rhinoceros

Formed 1968, Los Angeles, California
John Finley, voc.; Michael Fonfara, kybds.; Danny Weis, gtr.; Alan Gerber, piano, voc.; Doug Hastings, gtr.; Jerry Penrod, bass; Billy Mundi, drums.
1968—*Rhinoceros* (Elektra)   1969—*Satin Chicken*
1970—*Better Times Are Coming.*

Rhinoceros was a manufactured "supergroup" devised by Elektra record producer Paul Rothchild in 1968. That summer Rothchild got the idea to build a group out of castoffs from proven bands, though the members he eventually settled on had not really been prime movers in the name bands they came from. Doug Hastings had briefly played in Buffalo Springfield; Billy Mundi, who'd spent time with the Los Angeles Philharmonic, had also worked for 2½ years as one of Frank Zappa's Mothers of Invention; Danny Weis and Jerry Penrod had played in the early Iron Butterfly; and Michael Fonfara had been with Jon and Lee and the Checkmates, and the Electric Flag.

Elektra initially invested $80,000 in Rhinoceros, a large sum for the time. The group's debut included "Apricot Brandy," a minor instrumental hit. Soon after the debut LP, Penrod left, briefly replaced by Weis' brother Steve, formerly the band's equipment manager. But before recording *Satin Chicken,* bassist Peter Hodgson took over. The band got only marginal public support, though, and soon Mundi, Gerber, and Hastings left. *Better Times Are Coming* was recorded with new members, but very soon afterward the band fell apart completely. Fonfara later played on Lou Reed's *Street Hassle, Sally Can't Dance, Rock and Roll Heart,* and *The Bells,* and co-produced Reed's *Growing Up in Public.*

Rhythm & Blues (R&B)

Rhythm & blues is a descriptive term that has never had a single, clear meaning. In the broadest sense, R&B denotes black pop music, but given black pop's rapid evolution and seemingly infinite capacity for innovation and reinvention, it has become a term that is often defined by whatever black musical style it is affixed to at a given point in time, rather than the other way around.

In the beginning, R&B was a euphemism with a grain of truth for black pop from the Forties to the Sixties; it replaced "race music" and gave way to soul, funk, disco, and simply "black" styles. Small rhythm & blues combos revved up Tin Pan Alley pop tunes with rhythms derived from swing jazz and vocals reflecting the blues. They linked the big-band jump blues of the Forties with early rock & roll. Early rock & roll hits were often covers by white singers of R&B hits, like Elvis Presley's version of Roy Brown's "Good Rockin' Tonight" or Bill Haley and His Comets' cleaned-up take on Big Joe Turner's "Shake, Rattle and Roll."

As black musical subgenres emerged—Motown, Stax, soul in the Sixties; disco and funk in the Seventies; rap and hip-hop in the Eighties—R&B adopted a new, albeit more traditional connotation based on its old-fashioned values. Or, as one *Billboard* writer put it, "real singers, real songs, and real musicians." In this modern context artists such as En Vogue, Boyz II Men, Anita Baker, and Luther Vandross—perhaps simply by default—would be considered R&B artists. Turner's "Shake,

Rattle, and Roll" and such latterday R&B fare as Anita Baker's "Rapture" would seem to have little in common. What they do share, and what remains a constant in the best R&B music, is the high value placed on musicianship, songcraft, and great singing.

Charlie Rich

Born December 14, 1932, Colt, Arizona; died July 25, 1995, Hammond, Louisiana
1969—*Lonely Weekends* (Sun)   1973—*Behind Closed Doors* (Epic)   1974—*There Won't Be Anymore* (RCA); *Very Special Love Songs* (Epic); *The Silver Fox*   1976—*Greatest Hits*; *Silver Linings*   1992—*Pictures and Paintings* (Sire).

One of the original Sun rockabilly artists, Charlie Rich was a country and blues singer, songwriter, and pianist. His career was fitfully successful until his MOR country and pop crossover singles "Behind Closed Doors" and "The Most Beautiful Girl" hit in 1973.

Rich grew up listening to gospel music and learned piano from his missionary Baptist mother; he also sang in the church choir. In high school he met the woman whom he married upon graduation and who later became his songwriting partner, Margaret Ann Rich. Rich played in dance bands and jazz combos, then spent a year studying music at Arkansas University in 1950.

He joined the air force in 1951, and while stationed in Oklahoma formed his own jazz unit and then a pop band, the Velvetones, which had its own local television show. Though Rich felt he should restrict music to weekends and support his family by farming, his wife pushed his musical aspirations and eventually got him signed to Sun Records. There he wrote songs and played sessions for Johnny Cash, Roy Orbison, and others. His third solo single, "Lonely Weekends," was a #22 hit in 1960.

Rich went to Mercury's Smash subsidiary in 1965, when "Mohair Sam" became his next Top Forty hit. He went to RCA in 1967, achieving a minor hit with "Big Boss Man," then went to Hi and finally Epic. At Epic Rich teamed with Nashville producer Billy Sherrill.

Things finally clicked when Rich covered Kenny O'Dell's "Behind Closed Doors," which went gold and reached #15 in 1973. Later that year "The Most Beautiful Girl" (by Sherrill, Norro Wilson, and Rory Bourke) hit #1; it too earned a gold record. The *Behind Closed Doors* LP went platinum. His subsequent Top Forty singles include "There Won't Be Anymore" (#18), "A Very Special Love Song" (#11), and "I Love My Friend" (#24) in 1974, and "Every Time You Touch Me (I Get High)" (#19, 1975). In 1978 Rich appeared in the Clint Eastwood film *Every Which Way but Loose.*

His 1992 album, *Pictures and Paintings,* showed his eclecticism, including covers of Duke Ellington's "Mood Indigo" and the gospel standard "I Feel Like Going Home." Rich died in 1995 of a blood clot in the lungs en route to Florida with his wife.

Cliff Richard

Born Harry Rodger Webb, October 14, 1940, Lucknow, India
1960—*Cliff Sings* (ABC)   1961—*Listen to Cliff*   1962—*It's Wonderful to Be Young* (Dot)   1963—*Hits from the Soundtrack of Summer Holiday* (Epic)   1964—*It's All in the Game*; *Cliff Richard in Spain*   1965—*Swinger's Paradise* soundtrack   1969—*Two a Penny* (Uni; Light)   1970—*His Land*; *Good News* (Word)   1976—*I'm Nearly Famous* (Rocket)   1977—*Every Face Tells a Story*   1978—*Green Light*   1979—*We Don't Talk Anymore* (EMI America)   1980—*I'm No Hero*   1981—*Wired for Sound*   1982—*Now You See Me, Now You Don't*   1983—*Give a Little Bit More*   1987—*Always Guaranteed* (Striped Horse)   1988—*Carols* (Word)   1989—*Songs of Life: Mission 89*   1994—*The Collection* (Razor & Tie).

Over a career that spans four decades Cliff Richard far exceeded his early billing as Britain's answer to Elvis Presley. Since his debut single, "Move It," hit #2 there in 1958, Richard has appeared on the U.K. charts over more weeks than anyone but Presley, a record he will no doubt top within the next few years. His track record in the U.S.—a relatively paltry nine Top Forty singles—doesn't even begin to hint at his massive popularity at home, where he has charted a record 107 Top Forty singles, among them 61 Top Ten hits and 13 #1s.

Harry Webb's parents were British subjects in India—his father born in Burma, his mother in India—who didn't see England until 1947. He learned guitar and sang with skiffle groups near his Herefordshire home, and formed a short-lived vocal group, the Quintones, with one other boy and three girls in 1957. He next joined the Dave Teague Skiffle Group and worked for a short time as a credit control clerk in a factory.

In 1958 he put together a backup band, the Drifters, and changed his name to Cliff Richard for the Drifters' first demo, "Lawdy Miss Clawdy." The Drifters later changed their name to the Shadows. Late that summer the group's first release, "Move It," went to #2, and after a single television appearance and a tour, British teens embraced Richard as their first homegrown rock idol. Richard followed up with two #1s, 1959's "Living Doll" and "Travellin' Light." That year he also appeared in two films, *A Serious Charge* (a.k.a. *Immoral Charge* and *A Touch of Hell*) and, the next year, *Expresso Bongo.* Later movies would include *The Young Ones* (1961), *Summer Holiday* (1963), and *Wonderful Life* (1964). Through these and a near-constant chart presence, Richard quickly became a leading teen idol, not only at home but in Australia, Germany, and elsewhere. His U.K. Top Ten hits of the period included "High Class Baby" (1958); "Travellin' Light," "Mean Streak," and "Living Doll" (1959); "Voice in the Wilderness," "Fall in Love with You," "Please Don't Tease," "Nine Times Out of Ten," and "I Love You" (1960); "Theme for a Dream," "Gee Whiz It's You," "A Girl Like You," and "When the Girl in Your Arms Is the Girl in Your Heart" (1961); "The Young Ones," "I'm Looking Out the Window" b/w "Do You Wanna Dance," "It'll Be Me," and "The Next Time" b/w "Bachelor Boy" (1962); "Summer Holiday," "Lucky Lips," "It's All in the Game," "Don't Talk to Him" (1963); "I'm the Lonely One," "Constantly," "On the Beach," "The Twelfth of Never," "I Could Easily Fall" (1964); "The Minute You're Gone," and "Wind Me Up (Let Me Go)" (1965).

The Shadows [see entry] had a few instrumental hits in England, and their hits often alternated with the recordings they made with Richard for chart positions. Meanwhile, only two of Richard's myriad early U.K. smashes made it into the U.S. Top Forty: "Living Doll" (#30, 1959) and "It's All in the Game" (#25, 1964). After that, it would be another dozen years before Richard had his next U.S. hit. At home, however, Richard was among the very few young pop artists of his generation to weather and survive the rise of what we here in America called the British Invasion. Richard's long-held cleancut image, solidified with his announcement (at a 1966 Billy Graham crusade) that he had embraced Christianity, and his widespread popularity with older listeners place Richard firmly in the British entertainment establishment. Nonetheless, fans panicked at the suggestion that he might abandon his career altogether.

As it turned out, fans worried needlessly. Richard never left the charts (in fact, his first hit of 1966 was a Mick Jagger–Keith Richards song, "Blue Turns to Grey"), and although his forays into the Top Ten became less frequent, he remained a near-constant chart presence. He began recording a series of gospel albums (*Good News, About That Man, His Land, Help It Along, Small Corners, Walking in the Light, It's a Small World, Hymns and Inspirational Songs, Carols, Songs of Life: Mission 89*) and releasing an annual Christmas single. Richard, who claims not to proselytize, also made a series of statements condemning premarital sex, drugs, and sundry attitudes and behavior associated with rock stardom. In 1968 Richard and his longtime backup group the Shadows also parted; they have reunited on several occasions in the years since.

Richard enjoyed a handful of Top Ten British singles through the late Sixties—"Visions" and "Time Drags By" (1966); "In the Country," "It's All Over," "The Day I Met Marie," and "All My Love" (1967); but his biggest hit of that era was "Congratulations," a Eurovision Song Contest contender that went to #1 in England and almost everywhere else in the world except the U.S., where it

stalled at #99. He continued to release hit singles at home, among them "Goodbye Sam, Hello Samantha" (1970) and "Power to All Our Friends" (1973).

In 1976 "Devil Woman" became a Top Ten hit in the U.S., beginning an unprecedented run of hits that included "We Don't Talk Anymore," a #1 hit in the U.K. (his tenth) that went into the U.S. Top Ten in 1979. The following year he toured America for the first time since 1963. He was also named an officer of the Order of the British Empire (like the Beatles in 1965). In 1981 Richard's autobiography, *Which One's Cliff?,* was published; he claimed not to have slept with a woman in more than 16 years and also denied that he was homosexual. Other Eighties U.S. hits included "Carrie" (#34, 1980), "Dreaming" (#10, 1980), "A Little in Love" (#17, 1981), a cover of Shep and the Limelites' "Daddy's Home" (#23, 1982), and "Suddenly" (#20, 1980), a duet with Olivia Newton-John from the film *Xanadu.*

Back at home, though, Richard remained nearly as popular as ever, and his silver show-business anniversary brought several more U.K. hits, including a duet with Phil Everly, "She Means Nothing to Me," and a six-week sold-out run at a London theater. The following year's duet with Janet Jackson, "Two to the Power of Love" (which appears on her solo album *Dream Street*) was not a hit. He has made a number of appearances on behalf of various charities, and his annual gospel concerts have become something of an institution. In 1986 he starred in the Dave Clark musical *Time*, from which he had several more U.K. hits, including the Stevie Wonder–produced "She's So Beautiful" and "Time" (#17 U.K., 1985). Also early that year he recorded a #1 U.K. version of his 1959 hit "Living Doll" with cast members of the British sitcom *The Young Ones* (named for the Richard hit of the same name); proceeds went to charity. With David Cassidy taking Richard's place in *Time* in early 1987, Richard made a stellar return to the charts with *Always Guaranteed*, boasting two U.K. Top Ten singles, "My Pretty One" and "Some People." His 1988 Christmas single, "Mistletoe and Wine," became the biggest-selling single of the year in the U.K. At year's end Richard claimed the #1 single, album, and video there. In 1989 his *Stronger* (including the Stock/Aitken/Waterman single "I Just Don't Have the Heart") joined *Always Guaranteed* as the two biggest-selling albums of Richard's career. Later that year, his duet with Van Morrison, "Whenever God Shines His Light," hit the Top Twenty, while a rerecording of "Do They Know It's Christmas" (recorded with an assemblage known as Band Aid II) went to #1.

Richard kicked off his 50th-birthday year with a series of sold-out concerts, the most ambitious of which included a full-stage re-creation of the old British TV rock show on which Richard got his first break, *Oh Boy!* He closed 1990 with the #1 U.K. Christmas song, "Saviour's

Day." His 1993 *The Album* went to #1 almost immediately. The discography above, which lists only U.S. releases, represents but a fraction of his recorded output in his homeland, where he remains one of its most beloved stars.

Keith Richards: See the Rolling Stones

Lionel Richie: See the Commodores

Jonathan Richman/Modern Lovers

Jonathan Richman, born 1951, Boston, Massachusetts
1976—*Modern Lovers* (Beserkley)   1977—*Jonathan Richman and the Modern Lovers; Rock & Roll with the Modern Lovers; Modern Lovers Live*   1979—*Back in Your Life*   1983—*Jonathan Sings!* (Sire)
1985—*Rockin' and Romance* (Twin/Tone)   1986—*It's Time for Jonathan Richman and the Modern Lovers* (Upside)   1987—*The Beserkley Years: The Best of* (Rhino)   1988—*Modern Lovers 88* (Rounder)
1989—*Jonathan Richman*   1990—*Jonathan Goes Country*   1993—*Jonathan, Te Vas A Emocionar!*
1995—*You Must Ask the Heart.*

Jonathan Richman is easily one of rock's quirkiest figures. He dreams up songs like "I'm a Little Aeroplane" or "Ice Cream Man," and croons them in a heartfelt tone of boyish wonder. Those neo-nursery rhymes are far removed from the singer, songwriter, and guitarist's early days with the original, garage-rock incarnation of the Modern Lovers, the group he formed in New England.

The Lovers—who also featured Jerry Harrison and Dave Robinson, who later joined the Talking Heads and the Cars, respectively—were inspired by the Velvet Underground and wrote songs like "Roadrunner," "Pablo Picasso," and "Hospital." But Richman's tolerance for loud music decreased, and he began to tone down the Modern Lovers; when David Robinson's drum kit was reduced to a single snare drum covered with a towel, he quit. The group also had run-ins with its record company, Warner Bros., and disbanded in 1972. Richman formed a new, completely acoustic Modern Lovers (with guitarist Leroy Radcliffe, bassist Greg "Curly" Keranen and drummer D. Sharp) and went on to cut a series of albums for the independent Beserkley label (including the 1976 release *Modern Lovers*, an anthology of Warner demos from the early Seventies).

In 1977 Richman's instrumental tune "Egyptian Reggae"—taken from *Rock & Roll with the Modern Lovers*—became a hit in England, Holland, and Germany, where he enjoys large cult followings. In 1978 Richman broke up the acoustic Modern Lovers and became a solo act. A period of self-imposed obscurity in New England was broken in 1980, when Richman began touring fairly regularly. By the early Nineties, he was living with his wife and two children in California's Sierra Nevada Mountains; in 1993 he demonstrated his growing interest in Latin culture by recording *Te Vas A Emocionar!* entirely in Spanish. Richman has yet to achieve mass acceptance. His sheer unpredictability and artistic risk-taking keep him outside the mainstream.

Andrew Ridgeley: See Wham!

Righteous Brothers

Formed 1962, Los Angeles, California
Bill Medley, b. Sep. 19, 1940, Santa Ana, Calif.;
Bobby Hatfield, b. Aug. 10, 1940, Beaver Dam, Wisc.
1964—*Right Now!* (Moonglow); *Some Blue-Eyed Soul*   1965—*You've Lost That Lovin' Feelin'* (Philles); *Just Once in My Life; Back to Back*
1966—*Soul and Inspiration* (Verve)   1967—*Greatest Hits* (Verve)   1969—*Greatest Hits, vol. 2*   1974—*Give It to the People* (Haven)   1989—*Anthology (1962–1974)* (Rhino)   1990—*Best of the Righteous Brothers* (Curb)   1991—*Reunion.*
Bill Medley solo: 1971—*A Song for You* (A&M)
1973—*Smile*   1978—*Another Beginning* (United Artists)   1980—*Sweet Thunder* (Liberty)   1982—*Right Here and Now* (Planet)   1984—*I Still Do* (RCA)   1985—*Still Hung Up on You*   1991—*Blue-Eyed Singer* (Curb).

Bill Medley and Bobby Hatfield's close-harmony ballads came to exemplify white, or so-called blue-eyed, soul. Medley and Hatfield met when both were performing with the Paramours; they broke off to form a duo in 1962. They became the Righteous Brothers reportedly after a black fan referred to them as "righteous," a popular black slang term. In 1963 they had a pop hit on Moonglow Records with "Little Latin Lupe Lu" (#49).

Phil Spector signed them to his Philles Records in 1964. There they cut "You've Lost That Lovin' Feelin'." The Barry Mann–Cynthia Weil–Spector song went to #1 pop, #3 R&B, and was successfully revived by Hall and Oates in 1980. Spector had other significant hits with the Righteous Brothers—"Unchained Melody" (#4 pop, #3 R&B, 1965), "Ebb Tide" (#5, 1965), and "Just Once in My Life" (#9, 1965)—before the duo moved to Verve Records in 1966. That year another Mann-Weil song, "(You're My) Soul and Inspiration," went to #1 pop, #13 R&B for Medley and Hatfield. In that time, the duo was also a regular act on the weekly rock TV show *Shindig!*

In 1968 they broke up, and Medley recorded solo. Hatfield kept the Righteous Brothers name and performed with Jimmy Walker. That year Medley had two minor chart singles on his own, "Brown Eyed Woman" (#43) and "Peace Brother Peace" (#48), on MGM Records.

In 1974 Medley and Hatfield reunited to record a tribute to dead rock stars, "Rock and Roll Heaven" (#3), and scored two more hits: "Give It to the People" (#20) and "Dream On" (#32). Medley then retired for five years following the 1976 murder of his first wife, Karen. The duo did appear on an *American Bandstand* anniversary television special in 1981, where they performed a substantially reworked version of "Rock and Roll Heaven" as a tribute to John Lennon. Medley signed with Planet Records in 1982 and released *Right Here and Now,* produced by Richard Perry and featuring a title track by Barry Mann and Cynthia Weil. In 1983 Medley and Hatfield toured together again, as they have continued to do on and off through the years.

The duo returned to the charts in 1990 when their "Unchained Melody" found a new audience through its inclusion in the *Ghost* soundtrack; it went platinum in rerelease. In 1987 Medley's *Dirty Dancing* duet with Jennifer Warnes, "(I've Had) The Time of My Life," won a Grammy and went to #1. In 1993 Medley recorded a new version of "(You're My) Soul and Inspiration" with singers Darlene Love, who, in 1966, had sung background vocals on the Righteous Brothers' original version of the hit. The 1990 Curb anthology was certified platinum.

Billy Lee Riley

Born October 5, 1933, Pocahontas, Arkansas
N.A—*Funk Harmonica* (Crescendo)   1977—*Billy Lee Riley* EP (Charly)   1978—*Legendary Sun Performers*; *Sun Sounds Special*   1994—*Blue Collar Blues* (Hightone).

Billy Lee Riley is perhaps among the most important of the original rockabillies, an artist whose behind-the-scenes contributions as a Sun Records sessionman and unique recorded legacy have earned him the respect of self-proclaimed fans such as Bob Dylan.

The son of a sharecropper, Riley learned to play guitar from the black farmworkers he grew up among. An adept multi-instrumentalist on guitar, harmonica, piano, and drums, Riley first recorded as a solo artist for a local Memphis label in 1955. Impressed, Sun Studios owner Sam Phillips signed Riley, and by 1955 he was playing behind labelmates Jerry Lee Lewis, Johnny Cash, Roy Orbison, Charlie Rich, and Bill Justis. With guitarist Roland Janes and drummer J. M. Van Eaton, Riley cut two rockabilly sides that were simply unlike anything anyone had ever heard before: "Red Hot" and "Flying Saucer Rock 'n' Roll." The former featured what at the time were daring lyrics ("my gal is red hot, your gal ain't doodly squat!"), while in the latter Riley breathlessly enthused about an encounter with little green men who brought "rock & roll all the way from Mars." (Both tunes were revived in 1978 by Robert Gordon and Link Wray.)

The success of "Flying Saucer" gave Riley a brief solo career—Van Eaton and Janes became the Little Green Men—but despite his good looks and wild stage moves, he was soon back in the Sun studio band. In 1962 Riley moved to Los Angeles, where he worked steadily as a session musician on recordings by Herb Alpert, Dean Martin, the Beach Boys, Rick Nelson, Pearl Bailey, and many others. By the early Seventies, he had tired of music and quit to begin his own construction and decorating business back in his native Arkansas. Word of his 1979 performance in Memphis spread through rockabilly circles worldwide, and before long Riley was back out on the road throughout Europe and England, where rockabilly commands a large, loyal following.

Although Riley released albums overseas through the years, no new material was issued here in the U.S. until 1994's *Blue Collar Blues*. The critically acclaimed collection was recorded in the old Sun studios and brought together Riley with Van Eaton and Janes, as well as saxophonist Ace Cannon.

Jeannie C. Riley

Born Jeanne Carolyn Stephenson, October 19, 1945, Anson, Texas
1968—*Harper Valley PTA* (Plantation)   1969—*Yearbooks and Yesterdays*; *Things Go Better with Love*   1991—*Here's Jeannie* (Playback).

In 1968 Jeannie C. Riley was working as a secretary in Nashville, still trying to get her career as a country singer off the ground. Everything changed when her recording of "Harper Valley PTA" hit #1 on both the pop and country charts, selling 5½ million copies globally, though in the long run it did more for its author, Tom T. Hall, than it did for Riley. She did, however, win that year's Grammy for Best Female Country Vocal Performance.

Subsequent singles—"The Girl Most Likely," "There Never Was a Time," and "Good Enough to Be Your Wife"—hit the country Top Ten, but reached only the lower regions of the pop chart. She had C&W hits through 1974. "Harper Valley PTA," on the other hand, made an impression so lasting that it inspired a film and short-lived spinoff TV series, starring Barbara Eden, 13 years after its release. The success took its toll on Riley personally, and divorce from her childhood-sweetheart husband Mickey Riley and problems with alcohol followed. In 1976 Riley reemerged, remarried to Mickey and born again. She has continued to record religious material. In 1986 she released "Return to Harper Valley."

Teddy Riley: See Guy

Terry Riley

Born June 24, 1935, Colfax, California
1966—*Reed Streams* (Mass Art)   1968—*In C* (Columbia)   1969—*Keyboard Studies* (BYG); *A Rain-*

bow in Curved Air   1971—*Church of Anthrax* (with John Cale)   1972—*Persian Surgery Dervishes* (Shandar)   1975—*Le Secret de la Vie* (Philips)   1980—*Shri Camel* (Columbia)   1982—*Descending Moonshine Dervishes* (Kuckuck)   1984—*Cadenza on the Night Plain* (with the Kronos Quartet) (Gramavision)   1986—*The Harp of New Albion* (Celestial Harmonies)   1989—*Salome Dances for Peace* (with the Kronos Quartet) (Elektra Nonesuch).

An avant-garde musician/composer who first attracted attention in prepsychedelic San Francisco, keyboardist/reedman Riley is one of the original proponents of the minimalist school of modern classical music, which includes such influential figures as Steve Reich and Philip Glass. Such music uses the layered repetition of simple modular melodies to build up a rich, hypnotic fabric of sound.

Riley worked his way through Berkeley by playing ragtime piano at a San Francisco saloon. After getting his MA in composition, he lived in Europe and toured France and Scandinavia with a floor show and various "happenings" and street theater projects. He had worked with the early minimalist La Monte Young in the Fifties and again in 1964. Riley became known for all-night concerts of live and electronic music.

Riley's best-known works include *In C* (composed in 1964, in which a large number of musicians and singers perform the same melodies in staggered sequence, to make a slowly evolving, pulsing chord), *A Rainbow in Curved Air*, and *Church of Anthrax* (the latter recorded with John Cale).

Through the Seventies, while he was on the faculty of Mills College, Riley turned from composition toward improvisation; he would use planned motifs for solo performances on electric organ with a delay-repeat system. He also studied with Indian vocalist Pandit Pran Nath. In the early Eighties his performances featured organ improvisations and Indian-influenced songs. He was also composing for string quartet (*Cadenza on the Night Plain*, for example).

The influence of the Riley/Reich/Glass school can be found in middle-period Soft Machine, Mike Oldfield's *Tubular Bells*, Robert Fripp's solo guitar performances, Talking Heads' *Remain in Light*, the work of Laurie Anderson, and much of the New Age genre. Although the above discography lists Riley's recordings, he composed but does not perform on several of them (*Keyboard Studies, Salome Dances for Peace*, and *Cadenza on the Night Plain*).

Riot Girl

Riot Girl, also spelled Riot Grrrl, was a feminist movement that rose out of the punk-rock underground in the early Nineties. The group was formed by a national network of young women who had met at college or through fanzines and bands, including some of the members of the groups Bratmobile and Bikini Kill. Riot girls gathered to discuss such issues as abuse, sexual harassment, jealousy, misogyny, patriarchal structures, lesbianism, and friendship, both in and outside the music scene. Although some of their strategies resembled consciousness-raising and other second-wave feminism tactics, riot girls associated themselves with confrontational punk rather than the introspective folk of what became "women's music." Typically, characters in a Bikini Kill song respond to incest and other abuses by screaming, "Suck my left one!"

Riot girls applied the do-it-yourself aesthetic of the underground to their own empowerment, expressing themselves through fanzines, homemade cassette tapes, and records released on independent labels like Kill Rock Stars. They wrote manifestos (sometimes on their bodies) and coined such slogans as "Resist psychic death" (a Bikini Kill song title), "Revolution girl style now," "Support girl love," and "Overthrow cock rock and idolize your girlfriend."

Riot Girl groups originally met in Olympia, Washington, and Washington, D.C. Through fanzines the loosely knit movement spread to other cities. In 1992 riot girls had their first convention, in D.C. Beginning with the teenage magazine *Sassy,* mainstream publications began to write about Riot Girl, and the movement spread. Riot Girl founders, however, complained that the press frequently misrepresented the group, often in hostile and exploitative ways. Articles frequently misused "riot girl" as a blanket term describing almost any woman in alternative rock, when many actual riot girls are not even in bands. Many grrrls henceforth refused to talk to the media, preferring to remain an underground phenomenon.

Nonetheless, the media helped introduce Riot Girl to a broader audience; the British press in particular latched onto Riot Girl as a newsworthy trend. In the U.K. the mixed-gender band Huggy Bear led the movement; in 1992 they toured England with Bikini Kill.

Minnie Riperton

Born November 8, 1947, Chicago, Illinois; died July 12, 1979, Los Angeles, California
1970—*Come to My Garden* (Janus)   1974—*Perfect Angel* (Epic)   1975—*Adventures in Paradise* 1977—*Stay in Love*   1979—*Minnie* (Capitol) 1980—*Love Lives Forever.* With Rotary Connection: 1968—*Rotary Connection* (Cadet Concept); *Aladdin*; *Peace*   1969—*Songs* 1970—*Dinner Music*   1971—*Hey Love.*

Singer Minnie Riperton's angelic five-octave voice made her one of pop's most distinctive singers. After studying opera as a child, Riperton decided she wanted a career in pop music when she reached her teens. She got a job as a receptionist at Chess Records. There she joined a vocal group called the Gems, who sang backup behind Fontella Bass, Etta James, and other Chess acts. In 1967 she sang with a black psychedelic pop band, Rotary Connection, that cut six albums. "Amen" from their 1967 debut album was an FM staple for many years, as was their version of the Rolling Stones' "Ruby Tuesday."

Riperton left the Rotary Connection in 1970 and that year recorded an unsuccessful solo album for Janus, *Come to My Garden.* She sang with Stevie Wonder's backup band Wonderlove before signing with Epic Records in 1974. *Perfect Angel,* which featured two tracks coproduced by Wonder, was her most successful album. It was certified gold and contained Wonder's "Lovin' You" (#1 pop, #3 R&B, 1975). In 1976 Riperton underwent a mastectomy and then spent much of her time as a spokeswoman for the American Cancer Society. Two years later she moved to Capitol Records, where she recorded her last album, *Minnie.* Her condition gradually worsened, and she died of cancer in Los Angeles. *Love Lives Forever* is a posthumous collection consisting of previously unreleased vocal tracks with completely new backing.

Johnny Rivers

Born John Ramistella, November 7, 1942, New York City, New York
1964—*Johnny Rivers at the Whisky-a-Go-Go* (Imperial); *Here We a-Go-Go Again!* 1965—*Meanwhile Back at the Whisky-a-Go-Go* 1966—*Johnny Rivers' Golden Hits; Changes* 1967—*Rewind* 1968—*Realization* 1969—*A Touch of Gold* 1970—*Slim Slo Slider* 1972—*L.A. Reggae* (United Artists) 1973—*Homegrown* 1974—*Last Boogie in Paris* 1978—*Outside Help* (Soul City) 1980—*Borrowed Time* (RSO) 1991—*Johnny Rivers: Anthology (1964–1977)* (Rhino).

In addition to Johnny Rivers' major achievements behind the scenes (discovering talent like the Fifth Dimension and Jimmy Webb, bringing together top studio musicians as a regular band), his own records have sold over 30 million copies. John Ramistella's family moved to Baton Rouge, Louisiana, when he was a small child. He began playing guitar at age eight, and by 13 had joined bands. On a summer trip to New York he met disc jockey Alan Freed, who changed Ramistella to Rivers and got him a contract with Gone Records. Nothing happened, though, and Rivers concentrated on songwriting in New York and L.A. One song, "I'll Make Believe," was recorded by Rick Nelson.

In 1963 Rivers landed a gig at the new Whisky-a-Go-Go on the Sunset Strip. He soon became the club's regular star attraction and, drawing a star-packed audience, made the Whisky L.A.'s hippest nightspot. Rivers' 1964 debut Imperial LP, *Johnny Rivers at the Whisky-a-Go-Go* (#12, 1964), yielded the #2 hit "Memphis." He recorded other live Whisky LPs over the years. His hits throughout the Sixties were usually covers and included "Seventh Son" (#7, 1965), a songwriting collaboration with Lou Adler entitled "Poor Side of Town" (#1, 1966), "Secret Agent Man" (#3, 1966), and two Motown covers, "Baby I Need Your Lovin'" (#3, 1967) and "The Tracks of My Tears" (#10, 1967). He covered Van Morrison's "Into the Mystic" in 1970.

In 1966 Rivers was approached by manager Marc Gordon with a group called the Hi-Fis, previously the Versatiles. Rivers liked them, renamed them the Fifth Dimension, signed them to his newly established record company, Soul City, and linked the group with his friend songwriter Jimmy Webb. Rivers played guitar on the Fifth Dimension's records and organized a regular band of studio musicians, including Hal Blaine (drums), Larry Knechtel (keyboards), and Joe Osborne (bass).

He continued to enjoy chart success as a performer in the Seventies with a remake of Huey "Piano" Smith's Fifties hit "Rockin' Pneumonia and the Boogie Woogie Flu" (#6, 1972) and the gold "Swayin' to the Music (Slow Dancin')" (#10, 1977). In 1975 he coaxed Brian Wilson out of retirement to do backups on his version of the Beach Boys' "Help Me Rhonda" (#22). Through the years, Rivers has successfully run his own song publishing business and record company, and he continues to perform.

The Rivingtons

Formed 1953, Los Angeles, California
Carl White (b. 1932; d. Jan. 7, 1980), voc.; John "Sonny" Harris (b. Tex.), voc.; Al Frazier (b. Calif.), voc.; Turner "Rocky" Wilson Jr. (b. Pensacola, Fla.), voc.

The Rivingtons were a Southern California vocal quartet of the early Sixties who hit it big twice with novelty records. They began recording as the Sharps in 1954, and among their first jobs was providing backup vocals on Paul Anka's 1956 single "I Confess," Thurston Harris' "Little Bitty Pretty One," and later, some of guitarist Duane Eddy's hits, including "Rebel Rouser."

After being rechristened the Rivingtons, the group reached the Top Fifty in the summer of 1962 with "Papa-Oom-Mow-Mow." Its successor, "Mama-Oom-Mow-Mow" failed to chart, but the following year's "The Bird's the Word" propelled them to #27 R&B. From then on, the Rivingtons were back to releasing unsuccessful though not unappreciated singles, including a reworked "Papa-Oom-Mow-Mow" in 1973.

In 1963 a Minneapolis band called the Trashmen combined "Papa-Oom-Mow-Mow" and "The Bird's the

Word" and came up with a smash, "Surfin' Bird." The Rivingtons filed suit, as they would again when the Oak Ridge Boys used the syllables "papa-oom-mow-mow" in "Elvira" in 1981.

Rob and Fab: See Milli Vanilli

Rob Base & D.J. E-Z Rock

Formed 1982, New York City, New York
Rob Base (b. Robert Ginyard, May 18, 1967, New York City), voc.; D.J. E-Z Rock (b. Rodney Bryce, June 29, 1967, New York City), DJ.
1988—*It Takes Two* (Profile)   1994—*Break of Dawn* (Funky Base).
Rob Base solo: 1989—*The Incredible Base* (Profile).

Robert Ginyard and Rodney "Skip" Bryce began their career together in Harlem in a fifth-grade rap group called Sureshot Seven. Eventually the group boiled down to the two of them, and as Rob Base & D.J. E-Z Rock they recorded a couple of singles that failed to hit. Then their track "It Takes Two" (#36 pop, #17 R&B, 1988) became a hit the summer of 1988, rising from the underground to pop radio. The song succeeded via Base's smooth, easy rap and particularly its simple yet memorable backing track; it featured samples of Lyn Collins' 1972 single "Think (About It)" and Strafe's club hit "Set It Off."

It Takes Two (#31, 1988) went platinum and included "Get on the Dance Floor" and "Joy and Pain." The latter featured vocals by young soul singer Omar Chandler and was lyrically based on an old hit by Maze, whose Frankie Beverly sued Base and E-Z Rock for copyright infringement. Base went solo for a while on the gold-selling *The Incredible Base* (#50 pop, #20 R&B, 1989). The track "Rumors" addressed several false stories circulating about Base—that he'd fathered illegitimate kids and that he'd died from smoking crack, among others. The duo reunited for 1994's *Break of Dawn*, released on their own Funky Base label.

The Robins: See the Coasters

Smokey Robinson and the Miracles/The Miracles

Formed 1957, Detroit, Michigan
William "Smokey" Robinson (b. Feb. 19, 1940, Detroit), lead voc.; Ronnie White (b. Apr. 5, 1939, Detroit), baritone voc.; Bobby Rogers (b. Feb. 19, 1940, Detroit), tenor voc.; Warren "Pete" Moore (b. Nov. 19, 1939, Detroit), bass voc.; Claudette Rogers Robinson (b. 1942), voc.
1961—*Hi, We're the Miracles* (Tamla)   1962—*Cookin' with the Miracles*; *I'll Try Something New*   1963—*The Fabulous Miracles*; *Recorded Live: On*

Smokey Robinson and the Miracles: Pete Moore, Ronnie White, Smokey Robinson, Bobby Rogers

Stage*; *Christmas with the Miracles*; *The Miracles Doin' Mickey's Monkey*   1964—(– Claudette Robinson)   1965—*Greatest Hits from the Beginning*; *Going to a Go-Go*   1966—*Away We a Go-Go*   1967—*Smokey Robinson and the Miracles Make It Happen*   1968—*Smokey Robinson and the Miracles Greatest Hits, vol. 2*; *Special Occasion*   1969—*Time Out for Smokey Robinson and the Miracles*; *Four in Blue*   1970—*What Love Has Joined Together*; *A Pocket Full of Miracles*; *The Season for Miracles*   1971—*One Dozen Roses*   1972—*Flying High Together* (– Robinson; + William Griffin [b. Aug. 15, 1950, Detroit], lead voc.)   1974—*Anthology* (Motown)   1994—*Smokey Robinson and the Miracles: The 35th Anniversary Collection*.
As the Miracles (without Robinson): 1973—*Renaissance* (Tamla)   1974—*Do It Baby!*   1975—*City of Angels*   1976—*The Power of Music*   1977—(– W. Griffin; + Donald Griffin, lead voc.) *Greatest Hits*; *Love Crazy* (Columbia); *The Miracles*.
Smokey Robinson solo: 1973—*Smokey* (Tamla)   1974—*Pure Smokey*   1975—*A Quiet Storm*   1976—*Smokey's Family Robinson*   1977—*Deep in My Soul*   1978—*Love Breeze*; *Smokin'*   1979—*Where There's Smoke*   1981—*Being with You*   1982—*Touch the Sky*   1983—*Blame It on Love and All the Great Hits*   1987—*One Heartbeat* (Motown)   1990—*Love, Smokey*   1991—*Double Good Everything* (SBK).

Soon after his debut with the Miracles, Smokey Robinson became known as one of the premier songwriter/singers in pop music. Bob Dylan called him "America's greatest living poet," and in 1987 ABC's Martin Fry sang that "Everything's good in the world tonight/When Smokey sings," and few would disagree with either. As a writer of love songs, Robinson is peerless: From the straightforward, timeless "My Girl" to the elaborately constructed, metaphor-driven "The Hunter Gets Captured by the Game," "Let Me Be the Time (on the Clock of Your Heart)," and "The Way You Do the Things You Do," he explored every aspect of romantic love. Whether making an elegant declaration of passion ("More Love"), pleading forgiveness ("Ooo Baby Baby"), or musing at love's paradoxical nature ("Ain't That Peculiar," "Choosey Beggar"), Robinson's best songs showed a rare mastery of the pop form. His delicate yet emotionally powerful falsetto is among the most romantic in pop.

Smokey Robinson made major contributions to the success of Motown, a fact acknowledged by label founder Berry Gordy Jr. when he surprised the singer with a corporate vice president title in 1961. In addition to providing the label with 27 Top Forty hits with the Miracles, he also wrote, cowrote, or produced some of Motown's biggest hits (the Temptations' "My Girl," Mary Wells' hits) as well as some of its lesser-known but more adventurous releases (like the Four Tops' "Still Water Love" and the Supremes' "Floy Joy").

Robinson founded the Miracles—all Detroit-born—while attending that city's Northern High School. As the Matadors, they played locally, usually performing Robinson originals. In 1957 they met Berry Gordy Jr. while they were auditioning for Jackie Wilson's manager. Gordy, who had written songs for Wilson, was impressed not only by their presentation but also by Smokey's prodigious songwriting. "Got a Job," an answer to the #1 hit "Get a Job" by the Silhouettes, attracted local attention in 1958. In 1959 "Bad Girl" was distributed locally by Motown and nationally by Chicago's Chess Records. It hit #93 on the pop chart and convinced Gordy to expand his fledgling record company into one that would produce and distribute its own product rather than creating records to lease to others. In 1960 "Shop Around" established both the group and the company when it went to #1 R&B, #2 pop. Its B side was the oft-covered soul ballad "Who's Lovin' You." This marked the beginning of Smokey and Gordy's relationship. According to Motown historian Nelson George, when Gordy met Smokey, the young songwriter had hundreds of finished and unfinished song lyrics in notebooks, and it was Gordy who trained him to critically weed out all but the best among them.

Throughout the Sixties, Robinson wrote songs for and produced many other Motown acts, including the Marvelettes ("Don't Mess with Bill," "The Hunter Gets Captured by the Game," and "My Baby Must Be a Magician"), Marvin Gaye ("I'll Be Doggone," with Warren Moore and Marvin Tarplin, "Ain't That Peculiar," with Moore), Mary Wells ("My Guy," "The One Who Really Loves You," and "You Beat Me to the Punch," with Ronald White), and the Temptations ("Get Ready," "Don't Look Back," and "My Girl," with White; "The Way You Do the Things You Do," with Bobby Rogers; "It's Growing," with Moore).

Though the Miracles made numerous uptempo singles such as "Mickey's Monkey" (#8 pop, #3 R&B) in 1963 and "Going to a Go-Go" (#11 pop, #2 R&B) in 1966, they are best known for their ballads, including "You've Really Got a Hold on Me" (#8 pop, #1 R&B, 1963), "Ooo Baby Baby" (#16 pop, #4 R&B, 1965), "The Tracks of My Tears" (#16 pop, #2 R&B, 1965), "More Love" (#23 pop, #5 R&B, 1967—by which time they had become Smokey Robinson and the Miracles), "I Second That Emotion" (#4 pop, #1 R&B, 1967) and "Baby, Baby Don't Cry" (#8 pop, #3 R&B, 1969). Their last big hit together was the uptempo "The Tears of a Clown," a #1 hit on both the R&B and pop charts, and in England, in 1970. A great deal of their work in these years featured Marv Tarplin on guitar; he even appeared on a few album covers as if a sixth member.

In 1972 Robinson left the group to record on his own, to spend more time with his wife, Claudette (Bobby Rogers' sister, and a Miracle until 1964, though she continued to sing on the group's records). Claudette had toured with the group until a series of miscarriages forced her off the road in the mid-Sixties. Robinson wrote "More Love" for Claudette after one of their babies was lost. Their first child, Berry William (named after Gordy), was born in 1968; their daughter Tamla (named for the label) followed. The couple divorced in 1985.

Robinson continued in his duties as a Motown vice president. He also worked frequently with Tarplin, who, after a few years with the Miracles, rejoined Robinson. *A Quiet Storm* (1975) is regarded as his best early solo album. While he was always a popular concert attraction, his record sales during the Seventies fluctuated. It wasn't until 1979's "Cruisin'" (#4 pop, #4 R&B) that Robinson again enjoyed mass success. His #1 R&B single "Being with You" (#2 pop) in 1981 continued his performing comeback, but in the ensuing years, he has placed just two more singles in the pop Top Ten (1987's "Just to See Her" and "One Heartbeat") and one LP in the Top Forty (*One Heartbeat,* which is gold). Despite rampant defections from the label through the Seventies and Eighties, Robinson did not leave Motown until 1990 (he had resigned his vice presidency there in 1988). In his 1989 autobiography, *Smokey: Inside My Life* (cowritten with David Ritz), Robinson openly discussed his marital infidelities and a mid-Eighties addiction to cocaine.

Among the artists who have covered Robinson's songs are the Beatles ("You've Really Got a Hold on Me"), the Rolling Stones ("Going to a Go-Go"), Terence Trent D'Arby ("Who's Lovin' You"), Johnny Rivers ("The Tracks of My Tears"), Blondie ("The Hunter Gets Captured by the Game"), Linda Ronstadt ("Ooo Baby Baby," "The Tracks of My Tears"), Kim Carnes ("More Love"), Rare Earth ("Get Ready"), the English Beat ("The Tears of a Clown"), Rita Coolidge ("The Way You Do the Things

Grammy Awards

Bonnie Raitt

1989 Album of the Year: *Nick of Time* (with Don Was)
1989 Best Pop Vocal Performance, Female: "Nick of Time"
1989 Best Rock Vocal Performance, Female: *Nick of Time*
1989 Best Traditional Blues Recording: "I'm in the Mood" (with John Lee Hooker)
1991 Best Pop Vocal Performance, Female: "Something to Talk About"
1991 Best Rock Performance by a Duo or Group with Vocal: "Good Man, Good Woman" (with Delbert McClinton)
1991 Best Rock Vocal Performance, Solo: *Luck of the Draw*
1994 Best Pop Album: *Longing in Their Hearts*

Shabba Ranks

1991 Best Reggae Album: *As Raw as Ever*
1992 Best Reggae Album: *X-tra Naked*

Lou Rawls

1967 Best R&B Vocal Performance, Male: "Dead End Street"
1971 Best R&B Vocal Performance, Male: "A Natural Man"
1977 Best R&B Vocal Performance, Male: *Unmistakably Lou*

Red Hot Chili Peppers

1992 Best Hard Rock Performance with Vocal: "Give It Away"

Otis Redding

1968 Best R&B Vocal Performance, Male: "(Sittin' on) The Dock of the Bay"
1968 Best R&B Song: "(Sittin' on) The Dock of the Bay" (with Steve Cropper)

Helen Reddy

1972 Best Pop Vocal Performance, Female: "I Am Woman"

Jerry Reed

1970 Best Country Instrumental Performance: *Me and Jerry* (with Chet Atkins)
1971 Best Country Vocal Performance, Male: "When You're Hot, You're Hot"
1992 Best Country Instrumental Performance: *Sneakin' Around* (with Chet Atkins)

R.E.M.

1991 Best Pop Performance by a Duo or Group with Vocal: "Losing My Religion"
1991 Best Alternative Music Album: *Out of Time*
1991 Best Music Video, Short Form: "Losing My Religion" (with Tarsem and Dave Ramser)

Charlie Rich

1974 Best Country Vocal Performance, Male: "Behind Closed Doors"

Bill Medley (Righteous Brothers)

1987 Best Pop Performance by a Duo or Group with Vocal: "(I've Had) The Time of My Life" (with Jennifer Warnes)

Jeannie C. Riley

1968 Best Country Vocal Performance, Female: "Harper Valley P.T.A."

Smokey Robinson

1987 Best R&B Vocal Performance, Male: "Just to See Her"
1990 Grammy Legend Award

Kenny Rogers

1977 Best Country Vocal Performance, Male: "Lucille"
1979 Best Country Vocal Performance, Male: "The Gambler"
1987 Best Country Vocal Performance, Duet: "Make No Mistake, She's Mine" (with Ronnie Milsap)

Rolling Stones

1986 Lifetime Achievement Award
1994 Best Rock Album: *Voodoo Lounge*
1994 Best Music Video, Short Form: "Love Is Strong" (with others)

Linda Ronstadt

1975 Best Country Performance, Female: "I Can't Help It (If I'm Still in Love with You)"
1976 Best Pop Performance, Female: *Hasten Down the Wind*
1987 Best Country Performance by a Duo or Group with Vocal: *Trio* (with Emmylou Harris and Dolly Parton)
1988 Best Mexican/American Performance: *Canciones de Mi Padre*
1989 Best Pop Performance by a Duo or Group with Vocal: "Don't Know Much" (with Aaron Neville)
1990 Best Pop Performance by a Duo or Group with Vocal: "All My Life" (with Aaron Neville)
1992 Best Tropical Latin Album: *Frenesi*
1992 Best Mexican/American Album: *Mas Canciones*

Leon Russell

1972 Album of the Year: *The Concert for Bangla Desh* (with others)

You Do"), and Luther Vandross ("Since I Lost My Baby"). He has received the Grammy's Living Legend Award and was inducted into the Rock and Roll Hall of Fame with the Miracles in 1987.

After Robinson made his final concert appearance with the group in July 1972, the Miracles continued with Billy Griffin on lead vocals. While they kept charting through 1978, only three singles attained significant chart status: "Do It Baby" (#13 pop, #14 R&B) and "Don't Cha Love It" (#4 R&B) in 1974, and their early 1976 #1 pop hit "Love Machine (Part 1)" (#5 R&B). Billy Griffin was replaced by his brother Donald, but the Miracles disbanded in the late Seventies. They have reappeared in concert and on records (most recently for the U.K. Motorcity label), sometimes including Claudette Robinson.

The Tom Robinson Band/Sector 27
Formed 1977, England
Tom Robinson (b. ca. 1951, Cambridge, Eng.), bass, voc.; Danny Kustow, gtr., voc.; Mark Ambler, organ, piano; Brian "Dolphin" Taylor, drums.
1978—*Power in the Darkness* (Harvest) (– Taylor; – Ambler; + Nick Plytas, kybds.; – Plytas; + Ian "Quince" Parker, kybds.; + Preston Heyman [b. U.S.], drums)   1979—*TRB Two* (group disbands; in late 1979 formed Sector 27: Robinson, voc., gtr.; Jo Burt, bass; Stevie B., gtr.; Derek Quinton, drums, perc.)   1980—*Sector 27* (I.R.S.) (group disbands) Tom Robinson solo: 1982—*North by Northwest* 1984—*Hope and Glory* (Geffen)   1994—*Love over Rage* (Scarface).

Singer/songwriter Tom Robinson—one of rock's few openly gay performers—was also the first successful one to musically treat his sexual preference as a political issue, as in his "Glad to Be Gay." Robinson first came to public attention during the early days of British punk in 1977. The Tom Robinson Band, like the early Clash, played rousing battle-cry rock & roll.

Robinson claimed he was first drawn to rock & roll as an angry counterpoint to his father's love of classical music. At 17 Robinson was shipped off to Finchden Manor, a home for "maladjusted boys." In his six years there he met guitarist Danny Kustow, and the two became friendly. He left for London in 1973, and there formed Cafe Society, a cabaret, folk-harmony band, with two old friends, Herewood Kaye and Raphael Doyle. Ray Davies signed them to his Konk label in 1973 and produced their one album in 1975. (Robinson and Davies had a falling out, later obliquely chronicled in "Don't Take No for an Answer" on TRB's debut.)

In 1976 Robinson left Cafe Society, and he formed the Tom Robinson Band in January 1977. In October TRB's "2-4-6-8 Motorway" went to #5 in the U.K. The band became press darlings in England, especially after

the *Rising Free* EP in early 1978, which included "Glad to Be Gay." That press attention was soon repeated in the U.S., leading to the release of the band's American debut, *Power in the Darkness*. "Glad to Be Gay" got nearly as much radio play on the big-city U.S. stations as "2-4-6-8 Motorway." Robinson also plugged Rock Against Racism on the back of the album cover and included the New York and L.A. gay switchboard numbers on the inner sleeve of the U.S. version.

The band went through some personnel changes before its second LP, which was produced by Todd Rundgren. Despite several U.S. tours, neither LP sold well. The album was poorly received in England also, and Robinson began to feel that TRB's style was no longer fresh, so he broke it up in July 1979. Earlier that year, Robinson had written a few songs with Elton John, including one for Gay Pride Week. A collaboration with Peter Gabriel, "Bully for You," appeared on *TRB Two* and was a minor hit in England.

Robinson's new band, Sector 27, appeared later in the year, influenced by the harsher wave of postpunk groups like Gang of Four, XTC, and the Cure. The band toured England and then the U.S. in summer 1980. The self-titled LP got good reviews but failed to sell, and Sector 27 fell apart. Robinson moved to Berlin, Germany, working with alternative-cabaret and theater groups. In mid-1982 he resurfaced with a solo record, *North by Northwest*. A 1983 single, "War Baby," cracked the U.K. Top Ten. Most of Robinson's subsequent releases were U.K.-only. *Hope and Glory* yielded a minor U.K. hit in a cover of Steely Dan's "Rikki Don't Lose That Number." Robinson regrouped the original TRB for the U.K. releases *Still Loving You* and the live-in-Berlin *Last Tango*, which sold unexceptionally and were dismissed by U.K. critics as nostalgia-mongering.

Robinson continued performing into the Nineties, and released *Love over Rage*, his first U.S. album in a decade. Although he still identifies himself as gay, he also publicly revealed that he has a relationship with a woman, and that together they have a young son. He is the host of *Locker Room*, a BBC Radio program about men, and still highly outspoken on a range of issues, including gay rights, AIDS, and Native Americans.

The Roches
Formed late Sixties, New York City, New York
Maggie Roche (b. Oct. 26, 1951, Detroit, Mich.), voc., gtr.; Terre Roche (b. Apr. 10, 1953, New York City), voc., gtr.
1975—*Seductive Reasoning* (Columbia)   1976— (+ Suzzy Roche [b. Sep. 29, 1956, Bronxville, N.Y.], voc., gtr.)   1979—*The Roches* (Warner Bros.) 1980—*Nurds*   1982—*Keep On Doing*   1985—*Another World*   1987—*No Trespassing* (Rhino)

1989—*Speak* (MCA)   1990—*We Three Kings*
1992—*A Dove*   1994—*Will You Be My Friend?*
(Baby Boom)   1995—*Can We Go Home Now*
(Rykodisc).

By the time their critically acclaimed debut album as a trio, *The Roches*, was released, the three Roche sisters had been singing together for some time, Maggie and Terre first as a duo, and then the trio of sisters in New York clubs. With Suzzy's sweet-and-sour voice, Terre's pliant upper register, and Maggie's near baritone, they came out of New York's folk, feminist, and bohemian traditions, mingling barbershop quartet, Irish traditional, Andrews Sisters, doo-wop, and other vocal-group styles in songs—most of them by Maggie—full of wordplays and unexpected twists. Onstage they inevitably wear an eccentric array of thrift shop clothes and sporting gear.

Maggie and Terre began singing professionally in the late Sixties. Soon Maggie dropped out of Bard College and Terre left high school so that the duo could tour. In 1970 they met Paul Simon, and in 1972 they sang backup harmonies on his *There Goes Rhymin' Simon*. Simon's lawyer got the duo a contract with Columbia, which resulted in *Seductive Reasoning*, an album that went largely unnoticed. Maggie and Terre retreated to a friend's Kung Fu temple in Hammond, Louisiana, but eventually drifted back north, performing again for the first time in June 1976 at the Women's Music Festival in Champaign, Illinois. Within a few months Suzzy, who'd been attending the State University of New York in Purchase, joined them, and they became fixtures in Greenwich Village folk clubs.

After amassing local critical raves, they recorded their trio debut LP, produced by Robert Fripp. The album sold 200,000 copies and contained "The Married Men" (later covered by Phoebe Snow) but failed to yield a hit. Terre sang on Fripp's 1979 solo LP *Exposure*, and the trio sang backup for Loudon Wainwright III's "Golfin' Blues." In 1980, augmented with the rhythm section of ex–Television bassist Fred Smith and Patti Smith drummer Jay Dee Daugherty, they recorded *Nurds*. In mid-1982 Fripp produced their third trio album, *Keep On Doing*, a primarily acoustic album that nevertheless featured members of King Crimson. *Another World* used a full rock-styled sound, but again failed to sell big numbers.

The Roches then moved to MCA, where *Speak* was another commercial failure. *We Three Kings* was a Christmas album, while *A Dove* returned to the trio's typically playful, audaciously harmonized tunes (including "The Ing Song," where the last word of every line ended in "ing"). The children's record *Will You Be My Friend?* was released independently. While restricted to a cult-sized audience, the Roches wrote and recorded music for various theater and television shows, and such films as *Crossing Delancey* and the animated feature *Land Before Time*. They also appeared on albums by the Indigo Girls, Was (Not Was), and country singer Kathy Mattea. Steven Spielberg used them to voice animated sister cockroaches, in his Nineties cartoon TV series *Tiny Toons*.

Rockabilly

Rockabilly was Elvis Presley's music, a brash, lively, unself-conscious hybrid of blues and country that became rock & roll. It emerged from Sam Phillips' Sun Studios in Memphis, where Phillips recorded small bands—slapping string bass, twanging lead guitar, acoustic rhythm guitar—with plenty of echo while singers made astonishing yelps and gulps and hiccups and stutters as they sang about girls, cars, black slacks, even little green men from outer space. Rockabilly's original manic burst of activity ended with the Fifties. Many of it leading lights—Jerry Lee Lewis, Johnny Cash, Carl Perkins—moved into country music, or into more subdued forms of rock, as did Roy Orbison. Others, such as Billy Lee Riley, Dale Hawkins, Ronnie Hawkins, and Gene Vincent, continued working, though many more languished in obscurity. Eddie Cochran died in a car accident in London in 1961.

Despite rockabilly's all too brief, colorful heyday, its sound, style, and attitude endure. Every generation of rockers has revived and rediscovered rockabilly—from Rick Nelson to Creedence Clearwater Revival to Elvis Costello to Robert Gordon with Link Wray to the Stray Cats to X to Robert Plant to Paul McCartney to Queen—and its guitar licks and high spirits inform all kinds of rock.

Rock & Roll

The term is a blues euphemism for sexual intercourse.

Rockpile

Formed 1976, London, England
Dave Edmunds (b. Apr. 15, 1944, Cardiff, Wales),
voc., gtr.; Nick Lowe (b. Mar. 25, 1949, Woodbridge,
Eng.), voc., bass; Terry Williams (b. 1948), drums;
Billy Bremner (b. 1947, Scot.), gtr., voc.
1980—*Seconds of Pleasure* (Columbia).

Though it recorded only one album under the name Rockpile, this band had made four previous U.S. tours, and its members had appeared on most solo LPs by the group's best-known members: Nick Lowe [see entry] (who specializes in ironic pop) and Dave Edmunds [see entry] (known for his revitalized rockabilly).

Ex–Love Sculpture guitarist Edmunds called his first solo album *Rockpile* (1972), and his band, which toured to support that album, was also christened Rockpile, though the only member of the more recent group was drummer Terry Williams, who'd filled in on one of Love Sculpture's U.S. tours. Williams had also played with

Rockpile: Terry Williams, Nick Lowe, Dave Edmunds, Billy Bremner

Deke Leonard and Martin Ace, whom he later joined in Man.

This initial Rockpile helped kick off England's pub-rock movement, which included other no-frills groups like Ducks Deluxe and Brinsley Schwarz. Nick Lowe of the Schwarz band met Williams and Edmunds on the pub circuit, and Edmunds produced the final Brinsley LP in 1974. On Edmunds' next solo LP, 1975's *Subtle as a Flying Mallet,* Lowe played and contributed songs.

In mid-1976 Rockpile solidified its new lineup for a brief American tour with Bad Company, rounded out by Billy Bremner, a sessionman who'd backed everyone from Duane Eddy to Lulu. The group's sets offered a furiously paced mixture of Lowe's tuneful ditties and Edmunds' more rocking outbursts. In 1980 the band's two leaders were both signed to the same label, and Rockpile released its one and only LP (#27), which included an EP of Lowe and Edmunds duetting on Everly Brothers tunes. Rockpile toured the U.S. that winter, but in February 1981 it had a bitter split. Edmunds and Lowe resumed their recording and production careers, while Williams went on to play with Dire Straits. In 1982 Bremner was a temporary replacement for the late James Honeyman-Scott in the Pretenders, but he then rejoined Edmunds' band. Most recently he has become a Nashville session musician. On his *Nick the Knife,* Lowe took a shot at Edmunds in "Stick It Where the Sun Don't Shine," but the two ended their estrangement in the late Eighties, and Edmunds produced Lowe's *Pinker and Prouder Than Previous* and *Party of One.*

Jimmie Rodgers

Born September 8, 1897, Meridian, Mississippi; died May 26, 1933, New York City, New York

1962—*Country Music Hall of Fame* (RCA)   1965—*Best of the Legendary Jimmie Rodgers*   1975—*My Rough and Rowdy Ways*   1978—*A Legendary Performer* (RCA)   1991—*First Sessions, 1927–1928* (Rounder); *The Early Years, 1928–1929*; *On the Way Up, 1929*; *Riding High, 1929–1930*; *America's Blue Yodeler, 1930–1931*; *Down the Old Road, 1931–1932*; *No Hard Times, 1932*; *Last Sessions, 1933.*

Though his recording career lasted only seven years (from 1927 until his death in 1933), Jimmie Rodgers established himself as the father of modern country music, mixing black blues with folk and traditional hillbilly country.

Rodgers first played the guitar and banjo while working as a water carrier on the M&O Railroad, where he picked up blues influences from black fellow laborers. He later worked as a brakeman until ill health forced him to quit in 1925. (He always had health problems; his mother died of TB when he was four.)

Rodgers had long been an amateur performer, but following his forced retirement he pursued music full-time, becoming a black-face performer in a medicine show. In 1926 he appeared as a yodeler and later that year formed his own band, the Jimmie Rodgers Entertainers. The group soon split. Rodgers got a solo contract with Victor Records and released "The Soldier's Sweetheart" and "Sleep Baby Sleep" in 1927, around the same time the Carter Family made its recording debut. His song "Blue Yodel" became a million-seller, making Rodgers the first country superstar. "Brakeman's Blues" also sold a million, and in 1929 he made the movie short *The Singing Brakeman;* its title became his nickname.

Even during the Depression, Rodgers' records sold well, but his health was deteriorating. Though he was critically ill and had to cancel shows, he continued to record up until his death. His final song, "Fifteen Years Ago Today," was completed the same day he hemorrhaged and lapsed into a coma. The next day he died. In 1961 Rodgers, along with Fred Rose and Hank Williams, became one of the first persons elected to the Country Music Hall of Fame.

Nile Rodgers: See Chic

Tommy Roe

Born May 9, 1942, Atlanta, Georgia
1962—*Sheila* (ABC-Paramount)   1966—*Sweet Pea* 1969—*Dizzy* (ABC); *12 in a Roe/A Collection of Tommy Roe's Greatest Hits*   1970—*We Can Make Music.*

At the peak of his career, in the late Sixties, singer/songwriter Tommy Roe could do no wrong. He had two #1 records, "Sheila" in 1962 and "Dizzy" in 1969, and also scored big with "Sweet Pea" (#8, 1966), "Hooray for Hazel" (#6, 1966), and "Jam Up and Jelly Tight" (#8, 1969). Even a version of Lloyd Price's hit from 1959, "Stagger Lee," reached the Top Thirty.

At the age of 16 Roe was living in Atlanta, leading his own group, the Satins. In 1960 he recorded one of his own songs, a bald rewrite of Buddy Holly's "Peggy Sue," called "Sheila." Two years later Roe was signed to ABC. His first single there seemed destined for failure until disc jockeys flipped over "Save Your Kisses" and found "Sheila" (in its second version), which became a huge success.

Followup records didn't fare so well. But Roe was doing much better in England, where he relocated for a while in the Sixties. He continues to perform, alternating between the oldies circuit and country shows.

Roger: See Zapp

Kenny Rogers

Born August 21, 1938, Houston, Texas
Kenny Rogers and the First Edition: 1967—*The First Edition* (Reprise); *The First Edition's Second* 1969—*The First Edition's '69*; *Ruby, Don't Take Your Love to Town* 1970—*Something's Burning*; *Tell It All Brother* 1971—*Kenny Rogers and the First Edition's Greatest Hits*; *Transition* 1972—*The Ballad of Calico*; *Backroads* (Jolly Rogers) 1973—*Monumental*; *Rollin'*.
Kenny Rogers solo: 1974—*Love Lifted Me* (United Artists) 1975—*Kenny Rogers* 1976—*Daytime Friends* 1978—*The Gambler*; *Ten Years of Gold* 1979—*Kenny* 1980—*Gideon* 1981—*Share Your Love* (Liberty); *Christmas* 1982—*Love Will Turn You Around* 1983—*We've Got Tonight*; *Eyes That See in the Dark* (RCA); *Twenty Greatest Hits* (Liberty) 1984—*What About Me?*; *Once Upon a Christmas* (with Dolly Parton) (RCA) 1985—*Heart of the Matter* 1986—*They Don't Make Them Like They Used To* 1987—*I Prefer the Moonlight* 1988—*Greatest Hits* 1989—*Something Inside So Strong* (Reprise); *Christmas in America* 1990—*Love Is Strange* 1992—*20 Great Years*; *Back Home Again* 1993—*If Only My Heart Had a Voice* (Giant).

Though usually dismissed by critics, Kenny Rogers has had nearly 30 years of success with folk pop (with the New Christy Minstrels), mild psychedelia and country rock (with the First Edition), and country-pop ballads (as a solo act).

Rogers began singing in a high school band, the Scholars, which had a regional Texas hit with "That Crazy Feeling." At the University of Houston, he joined a jazz group, the Bobby Doyle Trio, as a vocalist and recorded with it for Columbia. He then joined the New Christy Minstrels in 1966 [see entry].

The First Edition was formed by ex-Minstrels in 1967 and included Mike Settle, Mickey Jones, Terry Williams, and Thelma Camacho. The group made its debut at Ledbetter's in Los Angeles, a club owned by another ex-Minstrel, Randy Sparks. There the group was brought to the attention of musician/comedian Tommy Smothers, who put Rogers and the First Edition on his popular TV show in January 1968. This led to a Reprise contract, and the act had its first hit just a month later with the quasi-psychedelic "Just Dropped In (to See What Condition My Condition Was In)" (#5). Subsequent hits were in a more countryish vein, like "Ruby Don't Take Your Love to Town" and the Kingston Trio's "Reuben James" (#26), both in 1969. More hits followed, including the harder-rocking "Something's Burning" (#11) and the gospelish "Tell It All Brother" (#17) in 1970. From 1971 to 1973 the First Edition had its own syndicated TV show, *Rollin' on the River*.

After the breakup of the First Edition, Rogers switched to an MOR-country style and chalked up a string of big hits like "Lucille" (#5, 1977), "The Gambler" (#16, 1979), "Don't Fall in Love with a Dreamer" (a duet with Kim Carnes) (#4, 1980), Lionel Richie's "Lady" (his first #1 hit), "I Don't Need You" (#3), "Through the Years" (#13, 1982), "Love Will Turn You Around" (#13, 1982), "We've Got Tonight" (with Sheena Easton) (#6, 1983), "Islands in the Stream" (with Dolly Parton) (#1, 1983), and "What About Me?" (with Kim Carnes and James Ingram) (#15, 1984).

Between 1977 and 1979 alone Rogers sold over $100 million worth of records, and he soon became a household name. Through the mid-Eighties, Rogers' record sales cooled somewhat, although he continued to score C&W hits with "Crazy" (#1 C&W, 1984), "Morning Desire" (#1 C&W, 1985), "Tomb of the Unknown Soldier" (#1 C&W, 1986), "Twenty Years Ago" (#2 C&W, 1986), "I Prefer the Moonlight" (#2 C&W, 1987), and "The Factory" (#6 C&W, 1988), among others. *Love Will Turn You Around* and *We've Got Tonight* went gold; the Barry Gibb–produced *Eyes That See in the Dark*, *Twenty Greatest Hits*, and *What About Me?* were all certified platinum, and *Once Upon a Christmas* sold two million copies, but *Something Inside So Strong* did not even make the Top 100 albums chart.

By then Rogers had branched out into other areas with comparable success. In 1980 he began his acting career, starring in a TV movie entitled *The Gambler*, based on his 1979 hit. Since then, he has starred in four more films in the same series, in two movie-of-the-week productions as the detective MacShayne, and in the feature film *Six Pack* (1982). Since 1979 he has also starred or costarred in over a dozen television specials. He has published two books of his photography (*Kenny Rogers:*

Your Friends and Mine, 1987, and *Kenny Rogers' America,* 1986), opened a rotisserie-chicken fast-food franchise, and hosted a series of documentaries on the Old West for the Arts and Entertainment Network. He participated in USA for Africa, and with his manager, Ken Kragen, was a principal leader of the charity effort Hands Across America in 1986.

The Rolling Stones

Formed 1962, London, England
Mick Jagger (b. Michael Phillip Jagger, July 26, 1943, Dartford, Eng.), voc.; Keith Richards (b. Dec. 18, 1943, Dartford), gtr., voc.; Brian Jones (b. Lewis Brian Hopkins-Jones, Feb. 28, 1942, Cheltenham, Eng.; d. July 3, 1969, London), gtr.; Bill Wyman (b. William Perks, Oct. 24, 1936, London), bass; Charlie Watts (b. June 2, 1941, Islington, Eng.), drums.
1964—*England's Newest Hitmakers/The Rolling Stones* (London); *12 X 5* 1965—*The Rolling Stones, Now!*; *Out of Our Heads*; *December's Children* 1966—*Big Hits (High Tide and Green Grass)*; *Aftermath*; *Got Live If You Want It* 1967—*Between the Buttons*; *Flowers*; *Their Satanic Majesties Request* 1968—*Beggar's Banquet* 1969—(– Jones; + Mick Taylor [b. Jan. 17, 1948, Welwyn Garden City, Eng.], gtr.) *Through the Past Darkly*; *Let It Bleed* 1970—*Get Yer Ya-Ya's Out!* 1971—*Sticky Fingers* (Rolling Stones/Atlantic); *Hot Rocks* (London) 1972—*Exile on Main Street* (Rolling Stones/Atlantic); *More Hot Rocks: Big Hits and Fazed Cookies* (London) 1973—*Goats Head Soup* (Rolling Stones/Atlantic) 1974—*It's Only Rock 'n' Roll* 1975—*Metamorphosis* (Abkco); *Made in the Shade* (Rolling Stones/Atlantic) (– Taylor; + Ron Wood [b. June 1, 1947, Hillingdon, Eng.], gtr., voc.) 1976—*Black and Blue* 1977—*Love You Live* 1978—*Some Girls* 1980—*Emotional Rescue* 1981—*Sucking in the Seventies*; *Tattoo You* 1982—*Still Life* 1983—*Undercover* (Rolling Stones/CBS) 1984—*Rewind (1971–1984)* 1986—*Dirty Work* 1989—*Singles Collection—The London Years* (Abkco); *Steel Wheels* (Rolling Stones/CBS) 1991—*Flashpoint* 1992—(– Wyman) 1994—(+ Darryl Jones, bass) *Voodoo Lounge* (Virgin).
Mick Jagger solo: 1984—*She's the Boss* (Atlantic) 1987—*Primitive Cool* 1993—*Wandering Spirit*.
Keith Richards solo: 1988—*Talk Is Cheap* (Virgin) 1991—*Live at the Hollywood Palladium* 1992—*Main Offender*.
Bill Wyman solo: 1974—*Monkey Grip* (Rolling Stones) 1976—*Stone Alone*.
Charlie Watts Orchestra: 1986—*Live at Fulham Town Hall* (Columbia).

The Rolling Stones: Charlie Watts, Bill Wyman, Mick Taylor, Keith Richards, Mick Jagger

Charlie Watts solo: 1991—*From One Charlie* (Continuum) 1992—*A Tribute to Charlie Parker with Strings* 1993—*Warm and Tender*.
Ron Wood solo: 1974—*I've Got My Own Album to Do* (Warner Bros.) 1975—*Now Look* 1979—*Gimme Some Neck* (Columbia) 1981—*1234* 1992—*Slide on This* (Continuum).
Mick Taylor solo: 1979—*Mick Taylor* (Columbia) 1990—*Stranger in This Town* (Maze Music).
Willie and the Poor Boys (Wyman; Watts; Jimmy Page; Paul Rodgers; Kenney Jones; Andy Fairweather-Low): 1985—*Willie and the Poor Boys* (Passport) 1994—*Tear It Up* (Blind Pig).

The Rolling Stones began calling themselves the "World's Greatest Rock & Roll Band" in the late Sixties, and few disputed the claim. The Stones' music, based on Chicago blues, has continued to sound vital through the decades, and the Stones' attitude of flippant defiance has come to seem as important as their music.

In the 1964 British Invasion, they were promoted as bad boys, but what began as a gimmick has stuck as an indelible image, and not just because of incidents like Brian Jones' mysterious death in 1969 and a violent murder during their set at Altamont later that year. In their music, the Stones pioneered British rock's tone of ironic detachment and wrote about offhand brutality, sex as power, and other taboos. Mick Jagger was branded a "Lucifer" figure, thanks to songs like "Sympathy for the Devil." In the Eighties the Stones lost their dangerous aura while still seeming "bad"—they've become icons of an elegantly debauched, world-weary decadence. But Jagger remains the most self-consciously assured appropriator of black performers' up-front sexuality; Keith Richards' Chuck Berry–derived riffing defines rock rhythm guitar (not to mention rock guitar rhythm); the stalwart rhythm section, anchored by Charlie Watts, holds its own with any band's; and Jagger and Richards continue to write telling songs.

Jagger and Richards first met at Dartford Maypole County Primary School. When they ran into each other ten years later in 1960, they were both avid fans of blues and American R&B, and they found they had a mutual friend in guitarist Dick Taylor, a fellow student of Richards' at Sidcup Art School. Jagger was attending the London School of Economics and playing in Little Boy Blue and the Blue Boys, with Taylor. Richards joined the band as second guitarist; soon afterward, he was expelled from Dartford Technical College for truancy.

Meanwhile, Brian Jones had begun skipping school in Cheltenham to practice be-bop alto sax and clarinet. By the time he was 16 he had fathered two illegitimate children and run off briefly to Scandinavia, where he began playing guitar. Back in Cheltenham he joined the Ramrods, then drifted to London with his girlfriend and child. He began playing with Alexis Korner's Blues, Inc., then decided to start his own band; a want ad attracted pianist Ian Stewart (born 1938; died December 12, 1985).

As Elmo Lewis, Jones began working at the Ealing Blues Club, where he ran into a later, loosely knit version of Blues, Inc., which at the time included drummer Charlie Watts. Jagger and Richards began jamming with Blues, Inc., and while Jagger, Richards, and Jones began to practice on their own, Jagger became featured singer with Blues, Inc.

Jones, Jagger, and Richards began to share a tiny, cheap London apartment, and with drummer Tony Chapman they cut a demo tape, which was rejected by EMI. Taylor left to attend the Royal College of Art; he eventually formed the Pretty Things [see entry]. Ian Stewart's job with a chemical company kept the rest of the group from starving. By the time Taylor left, they had begun to call themselves the Rolling Stones, after a Muddy Waters song.

On July 12, 1962, the Rolling Stones—Jagger, Richards, Jones, a returned Dick Taylor on bass, and Mick Avory, later of the Kinks, on drums—played their first show at the Marquee. Avory and Taylor were replaced by Tony Chapman and Bill Wyman, from the Cliftons. Chapman didn't work out, and the band spent months recruiting a cautious Charlie Watts, who worked for an advertising agency and had left Blues, Inc., when its schedule got too busy. In January 1963 Watts completed the band.

Local entrepreneur Giorgio Gomelsky booked the Stones for his Crawdaddy Club for an eight-month, highly successful residency; he was also their unofficial manager until Andrew Loog Oldham, with financing from Eric Easton, signed them as clients. By then the Beatles were a British sensation, and Oldham decided to promote the Stones as their nasty opposites. He eased out the mild-mannered Stewart, who subsequently became a Stones roadie and frequent session and tour pianist.

In June 1963 the Stones released their first single, Chuck Berry's "Come On." After the band played on the British TV rock show *Thank Your Lucky Stars,* its producer reportedly told Oldham to get rid of "that vile-looking singer with the tire-tread lips." The single reached #21 on the British chart. The Stones also appeared at the first annual National Jazz and Blues Festival in London's borough of Richmond and in September were part of a package tour with the Everly Brothers, Bo Diddley, and Little Richard. In December 1963 the Stones' second single, "I Wanna Be Your Man" (written by John Lennon and Paul McCartney), made the British Top Fifteen. In January 1964 the Stones did their first headlining British tour, with the Ronettes, and released a version of Buddy Holly's "Not Fade Away," which made #3.

"Not Fade Away" also made the U.S. singles chart (#48). By this time the band had become a sensation in Britain, with the press gleefully reporting that band members had been seen urinating in public. In April 1964 their first album was released in the U.K., and two months later they made their first American tour. Their cover of the Bobby Womack/Valentinos song "It's All Over Now" was a British #1, their first. Their June American tour was a smashing success; in Chicago, where they'd stopped off to record the *Five by Five* EP at the Chess Records studio, riots broke out when the band tried to give a press conference. The Stones' version of the blues standard "Little Red Rooster," which had become another U.K. #1, was banned in the U.S. because of its "objectionable" lyrics.

Jagger and Richards had now begun composing their own tunes (at first using the "Nanker Phelge" pseudonym for group compositions). Their "Tell Me (You're Coming Back)" was the group's first U.S. Top Forty hit, in August. The followup, a nonoriginal, "Time Is on My Side," made #6 in November. From that point on, all but a handful of Stones hits were Jagger-Richards compositions.

In January 1965 their "The Last Time" became another U.K. #1 and cracked the U.S. Top Ten in the spring. The band's next single, "(I Can't Get No) Satisfaction," reigned at #1 for four weeks that summer and remains perhaps the most famous song in its remarkable canon. Jagger and Richards continued to write hits with increasingly sophisticated lyrics: "Get Off of My Cloud" (#1, 1965), "As Tears Go By" (#6, 1965), "19th Nervous Breakdown" (#2, 1966), "Mother's Little Helper" (#8, 1966), "Have You Seen Your Mother, Baby, Standing in the Shadow?" (#9, 1966).

Aftermath, the first Stones LP of all-original material, came out in 1966, though its impact was minimized by the simultaneous release of the Beatles' *Revolver* and Bob Dylan's *Blonde on Blonde*. The Eastern-tinged "Paint It, Black" (1966) and "Ruby Tuesday" (1967), a ballad, were both U.S. #1 hits.

In January 1967 the Stones caused another sensation when they performed "Let's Spend the Night Together" ("Ruby Tuesday"'s B side) on *The Ed Sullivan Show*. Jagger mumbled the title lines after threats of censorship (some claimed that the line was censored; others that Jagger actually sang "Let's spend some *time* together"; Jagger later said "When it came to that line, I sang mumble"). In February Jagger and Richards were arrested on drug possession charges in Britain; in May Brian Jones, too, was arrested. The heavy jail sentences they received were eventually suspended on appeal. The Stones temporarily withdrew from public appearances; Jagger and his girlfriend, singer Marianne Faithfull, went to India with the Beatles to meet the Maharishi Mahesh Yogi. Their next single release didn't appear until the fall: the #14 "Dandelion." Its B side, "We Love You" (#50), on which John Lennon and Paul McCartney sang backup vocals, was intended as a thank-you to fans.

In December came *Their Satanic Majesties Request*, the Stones' psychedelic answer record to the Beatles' *Sgt. Pepper*—and an ambitious mess. By the time the album's lone single, "She's a Rainbow" had become a #25 hit, Allen Klein was the group's manager.

May 1968 saw the release of "Jumpin' Jack Flash," a #3 hit, and a return to basic rock & roll. After five months of delay provoked by controversial album-sleeve photos, the eclectic *Beggar's Banquet* was released and was hailed by critics as the band's finest achievement. On June 9, 1969, Brian Jones, the Stones' most musically adventurous member, who had lent sitar, dulcimer, and, on "Under My Thumb," marimba to the band's sound, and who had been in Morocco recording nomadic Joujouka musicians, left the band with the explanation that "I no longer see eye-to-eye with the others over the discs we are cutting." Within a week he was replaced by ex–John Mayall guitarist Mick Taylor. Jones announced that he would form his own band, but on July 3, 1969, he was found dead in his swimming pool; the coroner's report cited "death by misadventure." Jones, beset by drug problems—and the realization that the band now belonged squarely to Jagger and Richards—had barely participated in the *Beggar's Banquet* sessions.

At an outdoor concert in London's Hyde Park a few days after Jones' death, Jagger read an excerpt from the poet Shelley and released thousands of butterflies over the park. On July 11, the day after Jones was buried, the Stones released "Honky Tonk Women," another #1, and another Stones classic.

By this time, every Stones album went gold in short order, and *Let It Bleed* (a sardonic reply to the Beatles' soon-to-be-released *Let It Be*) was no exception.

"Gimme Shelter" received constant airplay. Jones appeared on most of the album's tracks, though Taylor also made his first on-disc appearances.

After going to Australia to star in the film *Ned Kelly*, Jagger rejoined the band for the start of its hugely successful 1969 American tour, the band's first U.S. trip in three years. But the Stones' satanic image came to haunt them at a free thank-you-America concert at California's Altamont Speedway. In the darkness just in front of the stage, a young black, Meredith Hunter, was stabbed to death by members of the Hell's Angels motorcycle gang, whom the Stones—on advice of the Grateful Dead—had hired as security for the event. The incident was captured on film by the Maysles brothers in their feature-length documentary *Gimme Shelter*. Public outcry that "Sympathy for the Devil" (which they had performed earlier in the show; they were playing "Under My Thumb" when the murder occurred) had in some way incited the violence led the Stones to drop the tune from their stage shows for the next six years.

After another spell of inactivity, the *Get Yer Ya-Ya's Out!* live album was released in fall 1970 and eventually went platinum. That same year the Stones formed their own Rolling Stones Records, an Atlantic subsidiary. The band's first album for its own label, *Sticky Fingers* (#1, 1971)—which introduced their Andy Warhol–designed lips-and-lolling-tongue logo—yielded hits in "Brown Sugar" (#1, 1971) and "Wild Horses" (#28, 1971). Jagger, who had starred in Nicolas Roeg's 1970 *Performance* (the soundtrack of which contained "Memo from Turner"), married Nicaraguan fashion model Bianca Perez Morena de Macias, and the pair became international jet-set favorites. Though many interpreted Jagger's acceptance into high society as yet another sign that rock was dead, or that at least the Stones had lost their spark, *Exile on Main Street* (#1, 1972), a double album, was another critically acclaimed hit, yielding "Tumbling Dice" (#7) and "Happy" (#22). By this time the Stones were touring the U.S. once every three years; their 1972 extravaganza, like those in 1975, 1978, and 1981, was a sold-out affair.

Goats Head Soup (#1, 1973) was termed the band's worst effort since *Satanic Majesties* by critics, yet it contained hits in "Angie" (#1, 1973) and "(Doo Doo Doo Doo Doo) Heartbreaker" (#15, 1974). *It's Only Rock 'n' Roll* (#1, 1974) yielded Top Twenty hits in the title tune and a cover of the Temptations' "Ain't Too Proud to Beg." Mick Taylor left the band after that album, and after trying out scores of sessionmen (many of whom showed up on the next LP, 1976's *Black and Blue*), the Stones settled on Ron Wood, then still nominally committed to Rod Stewart and the Faces (which disbanded soon after Wood joined the Stones officially in 1976). In 1979 Richards and Wood, with Meters drummer Ziggy Modeliste and fusion bassist Stanley Clarke, toured as the New Barbarians.

Black and Blue was the Stones' fifth consecutive LP of new material to top the album chart, though it contained only one hit single, the #10 "Fool to Cry." Wyman, who had released a 1974 solo album, Monkey Grip (the first Stone to do so), recorded another, Stone Alone. Jagger guested on "I Can Feel the Fire" on Wood's solo first LP, I've Got My Own Album to Do. Wood has since recorded several more albums, and while none were commercial hits (Gimme Some Neck peaked at #45 in 1979), his work is generally well received.

The ethnic-stereotype lyrics of the title song from Some Girls (#1, 1978) provoked public protest (the last outcry had been in 1976 over Black and Blue's battered-woman advertising campaign). Aside from the disco crossover "Miss You" (#1), the music was bare-bones rock & roll—in response, some speculated, to the punk movement's claims that the band was too old and too affluent to rock anymore.

Richards and his longtime common-law wife, Anita Pallenberg, were arrested in March 1977 in Canada for heroin possession—jeopardizing the band's future—but he subsequently kicked his habit and in 1978 was given a suspended sentence.

In 1981 Tattoo You was #1 for nine weeks (1980's Emotional Rescue also went to #1) and produced the hits "Start Me Up" (#2, 1981) and "Waiting on a Friend" (#13, 1981), the latter featuring jazz great Sonny Rollins on tenor saxophone. Nineteen eighty-one's tour spawned an album, Still Life, and a movie, Let's Spend the Night Together (directed by Hal Ashby).

Through the Eighties the group became more an institution than a creative force. Neither Undercover (#4, 1983) nor Dirty Work (#4, 1986) topped the chart, as every new studio album had done in the Seventies. Each album produced only one Top Twenty hit, "Undercover of the Night" (#9, 1983) and "Harlem Shuffle" (#5, 1986), the latter a remake of a minor 1964 hit by Bob and Earl.

Jagger and Richards grew estranged from each other, and the band would not record for three years. Jagger released his first solo album, the platinum She's the Boss, in 1984. His second, 1987's Primitive Cool, didn't even break the Top Forty. Richards, who'd long declared he would never undertake a solo album (and who resented Jagger's making music outside the band), countered in 1988 with the gold Talk Is Cheap, backed up by the X-Pensive Winos: guitarist Waddy Wachtel and the rhythm section of Steve Jordan and Charley Drayton.

The two Stones sniped at each other in the press and in song: Richards' album track "You Don't Move Me" was directed at his longtime partner. Nevertheless, shortly before the Rolling Stones were inducted into the Rock and Roll Hall of Fame, in January 1989 the two traveled to Barbados to begin writing songs for a new Stones album. Steel Wheels (#3, 1989) showed the group spinning its wheels musically, and were it not for the band's first American tour in eight years, it is unlikely the LP would have sold anywhere near its two million copies. But the 50-date tour, which reportedly grossed $140 million, was an artistic triumph. As the group's fifth live album, Flashpoint (#16, 1991), demonstrated, never had the Stones sounded so cohesive onstage.

Bill Wyman cited that as a reason for his long-rumored decision to leave the group after 30 years, in late 1992. "I was quite happy to stop after that," the 56-year-old bassist told a British TV show. The announcement helped deflect attention from Wyman's love life: In 1989 he married model Mandy Smith, who was just 13½ when the two began dating. The couple divorced in 1990, the same year that Mick Jagger finally married his longtime lover, model Jerry Hall.

The early Nineties were a time for solo albums from Richards—Live at the Hollywood Palladium and Main Offender (#99, 1992)—and Jagger's Wandering Spirit (#11, 1993). Neither sold spectacularly; apparently fans are most interested in Jagger and Richards when they work together. Wood released Slide on This, his first solo album in over a decade, and Watts pursued his real love, jazz, with the Charlie Watts Quintet.

In 1994 Jagger, Richards, Watts, and Wood, along with bassist Darryl Jones (whose former credits include working with Miles Davis and Sting) released the critically well received Voodoo Lounge (#2, 1994) and embarked on a major tour that proved one of the highest-grossing of the year. Voodoo Lounge was also the group's first release under its new multimillion-dollar, three-album deal with Virgin Records, which included granting Virgin the rights to some choice albums from the Stones' back catalogue, including Exile on Main Street, Sticky Fingers, and Some Girls. Voodoo Lounge brought the Stones their first competitive Grammy, 1994's Best Rock Album.

Henry Rollins: See Black Flag

The Romantics

Formed 1977, Detroit, Michigan
Wally Palmar (b. Apr. 27, 1953, Hamtramck, Mich.), gtr., voc.; Mike Skill (b. July 16, 1952, Buffalo, N.Y.), gtr., voc.; Richard Cole, bass, voc.; Jimmy Marinos, drums, voc.
1980—The Romantics (Nemperor); National Break-out 1981—(– Skill; + Cos Canter [b. July, 25, 1954, Havana, Cuba], gtr.) Strictly Personal 1983—In Heat (– Marinos; + David Patratos, drums) 1985—Rhythm Romance (+ Skill, bass) 1989—(– Patratos; + Clem Burke [b. Nov. 24, 1955, New York City, N.Y.], drums) 1990—What I Like About You (and Other Romantic Hits) (Epic Associated).

The Romantics

With their matching suits—usually red, purple, or pink leather—and sprightly Merseybeat sound, the Romantics were one of the relatively few power-pop bands to make the national charts. They hit the Top Ten in 1983 with "Talking in Your Sleep" (#3, 1983), but are probably better known for the power-pop anthem "What I Like About You" (#49, 1980), which has been licensed for use in advertisements for, among others, Budweiser beer and Home Box Office.

Formed on Valentine's Day, 1977 (hence the name), the Romantics played East Coast clubs and later that year released "Little White Lies" b/w "I Can't Tell You Anything" on their own Spider Records. Their pop sound attracted rock critic Greg Shaw to sign them to his Bomp! label, which released "Tell It to Carrie" in 1978.

They signed with Nemperor Records in 1979, and released their eponymous debut (#61) the next year. After two more albums in the pop vein (*National Breakout*, #176, 1980; *Strictly Personal*, #182, 1981) stiffed, the Romantics mutated into a more commercial, arena-rock band on *In Heat* (#14, 1983), which contained "Talking in Your Sleep." That year, drummer Jimmy Marinos, who sang lead on "What I Like About You," left.

The Romantics soldiered on, with drummer David Patratos, then ex-Blondie Clem Burke, taking Marinos' place. In 1987 the Romantics discovered that their songs were being licensed for commercials by their managers without the band's permission. They began litigation over publishing royalties and licensing fees.

Romeo Void

Formed 1979, San Francisco, California
Debora Iyall (b. ca. 1956), voc.; Frank Zincavage, bass; Peter Woods, gtr.; Jay Derrah, drums; Ben Bossi, sax.
1980—(– Derrah; + John Stench, drums)   1981—*It's a Condition* (415) (– Stench; + Larry Carter, drums)
1982—*Never Say Never* EP; *Benefactor* (415/Columbia)   1984—*Instincts*.
Debora Iyall solo: 1986—*Strange Language* (415/Columbia).

Debora Iyall's sung-spoken songs for Romeo Void explore the empty consequences of love over a solid post-punk dance beat. The critically acclaimed band was formed in San Francisco in 1979, with most members coming from an art-school background.

Iyall, a Cowlitz Indian, wanted to become a poet as a teenager growing up in Fresno. In 1977, while studying at the San Francisco Art Institute, she sang with a Sixties-style pop revival band, the Mummers and the Poppers, and later met Frank Zincavage, a sculpture student. They formed the band with other locals Jay Derrah, Peter Woods (both from the M&Ps), and later Ben Bossi. Their debut, *It's a Condition,* featuring "Myself to Myself," received massive critical praise. Playing drums on the LP was John Stench of Pearl Harbour and the Explosions, taking over for Derrah; both were later replaced by Larry Carter. Iyall's tough, unsentimental stance on love was compared to Pretender Chrissie Hynde's, and her sexy deadpan-to-pouty voice also drew attention on the band's 1981 EP *Never Say Never,* coproduced by Ric Ocasek of the Cars. *Benefactor,* including "Never Say Never," was a dance-floor favorite. *Instincts* produced the group's only hit, "A Girl in Trouble (Is a Temporary Thing)" (#35, 1984).

Romeo Void disbanded in 1985, and Iyall released a solo album the following year. The band regrouped and performed in 1993. Iyall has also written poetry and short stories and been published in literary journals and anthologies.

The Ronettes/Ronnie Spector

Formed 1959, New York City, New York
Veronica Bennett (later Ronnie Spector, b. Aug. 10, 1943, New York City), voc.; Estelle Bennett (b. July 22, 1944, New York City), voc.; Nedra Talley (b. Jan. 27, 1946, New York City), voc.
1964—*Presenting the Fabulous Ronettes Featuring Veronica* (Philles).
Ronnie Spector solo: 1980—*Siren* (Polish)   1987—*Unfinished Business* (Columbia).

In their towering black beehive hairdos and dark eye makeup, the Ronettes were a classic mid-Sixties girl group with a sultry twist: vulnerable but tough, sexy but sweet. The Ronettes were the first bad girls of rock, a racially undefinable (the Bennetts' mother was black and Native American; their father was white) trio that became producer Phil Spector's most successful act.

All three Ronettes were related: Talley is the cousin of the two Bennett sisters. The trio began singing together as the Darling Sisters. By 1961 they had become featured dancers and vocalists at the Peppermint Lounge, performing a song-and-dance routine inspired by Hank Ballard and Chubby Checker's "The Twist." They later appeared with New York City disc jockey Murray the K's rock shows, and recorded in 1961 and 1962 for Colpix as Ronnie and the Relatives, then the Ronettes.

Spector signed them to his Philles label in 1963. Smitten with Ronnie, he attempted to sign her as a solo artist, but when the group refused to be broken up, he signed them all. Initially the trio provided background vocals for other Spector productions, including records by Darlene Love and Bob B. Soxx and the Blue Jeans. (Earlier in their career, the Ronettes backed up Little Eva, Del Shannon, Bobby Rydell, and Joey Dee, among others.) His first Wall of Sound productions for them were "Baby I Love You" and a song he cowrote with Ellie Greenwich and Jeff Barry, "Be My Baby," which in the fall of 1963 hit #2 and sold over a million copies.

The Ronettes had other, less successful hits: "Baby I Love You" (#24, 1963), "(The Best Part of) Breakin' Up" (#39, 1964), "Walking in the Rain" (#23, 1964), "Do I Love You?" (#34, 1964), "Is This What I Get for Lovin' You?" (#75, 1965), and "I Can Hear Music" (#100, 1966). In 1964 Spector began managing the group as well, and throughout the group's career Spector's possessiveness and jealousy created problems. For example, when they were set to open for the Beatles on their 1966 U.S. tour, he kept Ronnie at home and had another cousin of hers take her place on the road. By then the group was near breaking up. Talley married a New York City radio station programming director, and Estelle married producer Teddy Vann.

In 1966 Ronnie Bennett married Phil Spector. According to her autobiography, *Be My Baby,* Spector virtually held her prisoner in their Los Angeles mansion. They separated in 1973 and divorced in 1974, by which time Ronnie Spector had developed a serious drinking problem that would last several more years. Although Spector had recorded her for A&M in 1969 ("You Came, You Saw, You Conquered") and Apple in 1971 ("Try Some, Buy Some," coproduced with George Harrison), her first solo releases went unnoticed. Ronnie Spector began her long comeback with a 1973 appearance at a rock-revival show with two new Ronettes; she then released two singles on Buddah. Through the Seventies she later pursued a solo career, inspired by the fact that many notable musicians (including Billy Joel, who wrote "Say Goodbye to Hollywood" for her, and Bruce Springsteen) cited her as an influence. In 1977 Little Steven Van Zandt produced her version of "Say Goodbye to Hollywood" (with backing by the E Street Band), but it never charted. She sang on Southside Johnny's debut LP and then cut a solo album in 1980 entitled *Siren,* produced by Genya Ravan.

Ronnie Spector's biggest commercial break came in 1986 when her duet with Eddie Money, "Take Me Home Tonight," the chorus of which reprised "Be My Baby," hit #4 and became an oft-seen video. In 1986 her autobiography, *Be My Baby* (written with Vince Waldron) was published. Through the Eighties she also performed as one of the "legendary ladies of rock," along with Martha Reeves, Lesley Gore, Mary Wilson, and others.

Mick Ronson
Born circa 1946, Hull, England; died April 30, 1993, London, England
1974—*Slaughter on Tenth Avenue* (RCA)   1975—*Play Don't Worry*   1989—*Y U I ORTA* (with Ian Hunter) (Mercury)   1994—*Heaven 'n Hull* (Epic Associated).

After having played sessions with pop producer Michael Chapman and David Bowie producer Gus Dudgeon, Mick Ronson came to attention as the guitarist for Bowie's early-Seventies Spiders from Mars backing band. Upon Bowie's temporary retirement from performing in 1973, Ronson launched an unsuccessful solo career. He joined Mott the Hoople in its last days, and continued a partnership with Mott's Ian Hunter, both in the Hunter-Ronson Band and on Hunter's solo LPs. In late 1975 Ronson was a surprise member of Bob Dylan's Rolling Thunder Revue. He later went on to help produce Roger McGuinn's *Cardiff Rose* (1976), David Johansen's *In Style* (1979), and Morrisey's *Your Arsenal* (1992), as well as several Ian Hunter LPs.

In 1991, having learned he had liver cancer, the guitarist began recording a new solo album. Friends such as Hunter, David Bowie, John Mellencamp, Chrissie Hynde, and Def Leppard's Joe Elliott lent their voices to *Heaven 'n Hull,* which was released a year after Ronson's death at age 46.

Linda Ronstadt
Born July 15, 1946, Tucson, Arizona
1969—*Hand Sown . . . Home Grown* (Capitol)   1970—*Silk Purse*   1972—*Linda Ronstadt*   1973—*Don't Cry Now* (Asylum)   1974—*Different Drum* (Capitol); *Heart Like a Wheel*   1975—*Prisoner in Disguise* (Asylum)   1976—*Hasten Down the Wind*; *Greatest Hits*   1977—*Simple Dreams*   1978—*Living in the U.S.A.*   1980—*Mad Love*; *Greatest Hits, vol. 2*   1982—*Get Closer*   1983—*What's New*   1984—*Lush Life*   1986—*Sentimental Reasons*   1987—*Canciones de Mi Padre* (Elektra); *Trio* (with Dolly Parton and Emmylou Harris) (Warner Bros.)   1989—*Cry Like a Rainstorm, Howl Like the Wind* (Elektra)   1991—*Mas Canciones*   1992—*Frenesi*   1993—*Winter Light*   1995—*Feels Like Home.*

Linda Ronstadt

During a recording career spanning four decades, Linda Ronstadt has covered much of America's popular and folk music and appealed to a mass audience that, but for her, might never have heard the work of Buddy Holly, Chuck Berry, or Elvis Costello, not to mention the older pop standards and traditional Mexican songs she sang later in her career.

Ronstadt is half Mexican, half German. She grew up singing Hank Williams and Elvis Presley favorites with her siblings and Mexican folk songs with her father, who played his guitar. While in high school, Linda performed around Tucson with her brother and sister. Local guitarist Bob Kimmel invited her to go with him to L.A. She declined the invitation until after a semester at the University of Arizona, and by the end of 1964 she was in L.A., where she joined the Stone Poneys, a folk group with Kimmel and guitarist Kenny Edwards.

The trio landed a gig at the Troubadour, where promoter Herb Cohen offered Ronstadt a solo management contract. She refused the offer out of loyalty to the trio and doubts about going it alone (earlier, the three had turned down Mercury's offer to make them into a surf music group to be called the Signets). But when the Stone Poneys failed to attract further interest, they split up, and Ronstadt signed with Cohen, whom she later persuaded to manage the trio.

Cohen got the Stone Poneys a recording contract with Capitol in 1966 and hired Nick Venet to produce three albums. The first was a failed attempt to present the Poneys as a sort of Hollywood Peter, Paul and Mary. The second included one number on which L.A. session musicians backed Ronstadt—"Different Drum," written by Mike Nesmith of the Monkees—which was a Top Twenty hit in 1967. It induced Capitol to send the Stone Poneys on tour as an opening act, but Edwards soon quit. (He was reunited with Ronstadt in 1974 and was her bassist for the following five years.) Kimmel and Ronstadt stayed together for a while, using pickup musicians for another tour and recording a few tracks for the third album, but soon Kimmel dropped out, leaving Ronstadt with a contractual obligation to finish using session musicians. It sold so poorly that it wasn't until *Heart Like a Wheel* went gold seven years later that Ronstadt began to collect royalties.

Solo, Ronstadt floundered for most of the next five years. She went through a succession of managers, producers, and backup musicians (including in the last category the four original Eagles). Onstage she was often devastatingly timid, and in the studio her voice was undermined by inappropriate material and arrangements. She attracted brief notice as a country singer—playing the Grand Ole Opry in Nashville, making TV appearances on *The Johnny Cash Show* and a Glen Campbell special—and reached the Top Thirty in 1970 with "Long, Long Time" off *Silk Purse*. But by the end of 1972 she was in debt and paying commissions to two managers: Cohen (who still owned her contract) and John Boylan, her current producer. *Don't Cry Now*, her first album on Asylum (although it turned out she owed another to Capitol), was predictably bogged down unfinished in the studio.

The catalyst to Ronstadt's popularity and acclaim was Peter Asher. A former half of the British pop duo Peter and Gordon, he had gone from performing in the mid-Sixties to producing and managing. Under Asher's direction, *Don't Cry Now* was completed after a year in the works, $150,000, and three producers. Despite its flaws, the album sparked Ronstadt's career and prompted Capitol to market a collection of her early songs under the title *Different Drum*.

With Asher as producer and manager, Ronstadt made *Heart Like a Wheel*, which established her best-selling mix of oldies covers and contemporary songs. In addition to astute song choices, high standards of studio craft became Ronstadt and Asher's trademarks. Released shortly before Christmas 1974, *Heart Like a Wheel* reached #1 the following spring and eventually sold two million copies. "You're No Good" rocked to #1 on the pop singles chart while its flip side, Hank Williams' "I Can't Help It If I'm Still in Love with You," hit #2 on the country & western chart and won the 1975 Grammy Award for Best Female Country Vocal. "When Will I Be Loved" went #2 pop, #1 C&W. Although still hampered by stage fright, Ronstadt became a popular concert attraction and something of a sex symbol.

With a 1976 tour of Europe—her first outside the U.S.—she extended her popularity to the world market. *Heart Like a Wheel* was the first of 17 gold or platinum albums. She won a second Grammy in 1976. Her albums retained a California sensibility with songs by J. D. Souther and Warren Zevon, but she also expanded her repertoire to R&B (the Holland-Dozier-Holland Motown classic "Heat Wave," a couple by Smokey Robinson), show tunes (Hammerstein-Romberg's "When I Grow Too Old to Dream"), traditional folk ballads ("I Never Will Marry," "Old Paint"), reggae (Jimmy Cliff's "Many Rivers to Cross"), and even cocky rock & roll (Jagger-Richards' "Tumbling Dice"). Her hit covers of Buddy Holly ("That'll Be the Day" and "It's So Easy") brought his music to a new audience.

Ronstadt's success gave a substantial boost to other female performers. She was the first to record songs by Karla Bonoff. Maria Muldaur, Wendy Waldman, Emmylou Harris, and Dolly Parton are a few of the female singers who have harmonized with Ronstadt in the studio and onstage; and she was instrumental in the careers of Valerie Carter and Nicolette Larson. With these women, Ronstadt formed tight friendships and a sort of professional support system. (In 1987 she, Parton, and Harris released the platinum *Trio,* a project ten years in the making.)

By decade's end Ronstadt was at the height of her popularity; both *Simple Dreams* (1977) and *Living in the U.S.A.* (1978) hit #1. She was also highly visible as the constant companion of California governor Jerry Brown, with whom she shared the cover of *Time.* Ronstadt's *Mad Love* (#3, 1980) included new-wave rock. Working with a self-styled L.A. new-wave group, the Cretones, she put three songs by group member Mark Goldenberg alongside three by Elvis Costello (whose "Alison" she had covered on her previous album). The response from Ronstadt's audience was decidedly mixed, but "How Do I Make You" went Top Ten, as did a remake of Little Anthony and the Imperials' "Hurt So Bad."

Rather than return to the studio, Ronstadt tried something new—the role of Mabel in Gilbert and Sullivan's 19th-century light opera *The Pirates of Penzance.* Ronstadt performed at Central Park's Delacorte Theater in New York City through the summer of 1980 and later appeared in the film version. A subsequent attempt at opera in a production of *La Bohème* was less well-received by critics.

In 1982 she released *Get Closer* (#31), her least successful LP of new material in ten years. Ronstadt then took a stylistic right turn and crossed over to the massive "adult contemporary" (an Eighties term for "middle of the road") audience, recording three best-selling albums of pop standards, lavishly orchestrated by veteran arranger Nelson Riddle: *What's New* (#3, 1983) went double-platinum; *Lush Life* (#13, 1984) went platinum; and *Sentimental Reasons* (#46, 1986) went gold.

In 1987 Ronstadt and James Ingram topped the charts with the romantic ballad "Somewhere Out There" from the animated film *An American Tail*—and she made another commercially successful stylistic leap with the all-Spanish *Canciones de Mi Padre* ("Songs of My Father"), which went platinum though reaching only #42 on the chart. Later that year, the *Trio* album with Parton and Harris hit #6 on the chart and also went platinum (it won a Grammy for Best Country Vocal Duo/Group in 1988). *Cry Like a Rainstorm, Howl Like the Wind* (#7, 1989) went double-platinum and contained two Grammy Award–winning (for Best Pop Performance Duo/Group) ballads sung with Aaron Neville: "Don't Know Much" (#2, 1989) and "All My Life" (#11, 1990). However, two more Spanish-language albums, *Mas Canciones* and *Frenesi,* met with middling sales. Ronstadt returned to English-language recording with 1993's *Winter Light,* which she produced herself with George Massenburg (her first pop solo album in 20 years that Peter Asher did not produce).

Diana Ross

**Born March 26, 1944, Detroit, Michigan
1970—*Diana Ross* (Motown); *Everything Is Everything* 1971—*Surrender* 1972—*Lady Sings the Blues* soundtrack 1973—*Touch Me in the Morning*; *Diana and Marvin* (with Marvin Gaye); *The Last Time I Saw Him* 1975—*Mahogany* soundtrack 1976—*Diana Ross*; *Greatest Hits* 1977—*An Evening with Diana Ross*; *Baby, It's Me* 1978—*The Wiz* soundtrack; *Ross* 1979—*The Boss* 1980—*Diana*; *It's My Turn* 1981—*To Love Again*; *Why Do Fools Fall in Love?* (RCA) 1982—*Silk Electric* 1983—*Diana Ross Anthology* (Motown); *Ross* (RCA) 1984—*Swept Away* 1985—*Eaten Alive* 1987—*Red Hot Rhythm and Blues* 1989—*Workin' Overtime* (Motown) 1991—*The Force Behind the Power* 1994—*Forever Diana.***

Diana Ross' tender, cooing voice brought her to prominence as the lead singer of the Supremes in the Sixties. Upon leaving the Supremes in January 1970 [see entry], she began to establish herself as a star of records, stage, television, and screen. Through the Seventies and Eighties she showed remarkable resilience, consistently rebounding from career setbacks, and remained without question the biggest female pop star of the era.

Ross' career shift was carefully planned by Motown president Berry Gordy Jr. and was foreshadowed when in the late Sixties he changed the group's name from simply the Supremes to Diana Ross and the Supremes. By the time she did leave the group she was clearly positioned as its star. Her initial solo recordings were produced by the husband-and-wife team of Nick Ashford and Valerie Simpson. "Reach Out and Touch (Somebody's Hand)" in 1970 (#20 pop, #7 R&B) was her first solo single. Her next release, a new version of the Marvin

Gaye–Tammi Terrell hit "Ain't No Mountain High Enough" (by Ashford and Simpson), reached #1 pop and R&B. The following year, however, she faltered, releasing singles, none of which was a major hit. At that time, most of her attention was taken up with a television special and preparations for playing Billie Holiday in the first Motown film production, *Lady Sings the Blues*. The 1972 film was a commercial success, spawning a popular soundtrack of Ross singing Holiday ("Good Morning Heartache"), and garnering Ross an Oscar nomination for Best Actress.

The title songs from her next two albums, *Touch Me in the Morning* and *Last Time I Saw Him*, were both Top Twenty pop singles, the former hitting #1. In 1973 she recorded an album of duets with Marvin Gaye, *Diana and Marvin*. Her next film, *Mahogany*, directed by Berry Gordy and costarring Billy Dee Williams and Anthony Perkins, failed to match either the commercial or artistic accomplishments of *Lady*. The soundtrack, however, did have the MOR ballad "Do You Know Where You're Going To" (#1 pop, #14 R&B, 1976). Her *Diana Ross* of 1976 was highlighted by "Love Hangover," a ballad-cum-disco dance song that went #1 on both the pop and R&B charts.

As the star of Motown's misconceived film version of the Broadway musical *The Wiz*, Ross took a tremendous risk by insisting that she play the role of Dorothy. Not only was she clearly too old for the part, but the heavy-handed production (costarring Nipsey Russell, Michael Jackson, and Richard Pryor) was a critical and commercial bomb and rude awakening for Motown. Her 1977 *Baby, It's Me*, produced by Richard Perry, sold disappointingly, as did *Ross* in 1978.

She returned to Ashford and Simpson for 1979's *The Boss* (#14) and was rewarded with her best sales in years. The title song (#19 pop, #10 R&B) reestablished Ross as a pop presence. *Diana* updated her approach. Produced by Nile Rodgers and Bernard Edwards of Chic, the 1980 platinum album went to #1 R&B, #2 pop, and boasted two big singles, "Upside Down" (#1 pop, R&B) and "I'm Coming Out" (#5 pop, #6 R&B). In 1981 Ross duetted with Commodores lead singer Lionel Richie on the #1 theme from the film *Endless Love*. It was the year's most popular single, selling well over two million copies, but it proved to be her last hit for Motown.

In 1981 she ended her 20-year tenure with the company and signed with RCA Records. That fall she released her self-produced *Why Do Fools Fall in Love* (#15, platinum) and had Top Ten hits with the title cut, a remake of the Frankie Lymon and the Teenagers hit, and in 1982 with "Mirror, Mirror." In 1982 Ross released her second RCA LP, *Silk Electric*, which featured the #10 single (#4 R&B) "Muscles" (written and produced by Michael Jackson). Her next few years with RCA were fruitful: *Swept Away*, with a Top Twenty title track written and produced by Daryl Hall, went gold. "All of You," a duet with Julio Iglesias, was another hit that year. With "Missing You"—a ballad dedicated to Marvin Gaye but in the video of which Ross sang to old footage of Florence Ballard, her mother, Gaye, and Temptation Paul Williams—Ross scored her last Top Ten (#1 R&B) pop hit in 1985. *Eaten Alive*'s title track, with Michael Jackson on backing vocals, hit #10 on the R&B chart but stalled at #77 pop. Ross' biggest successes, like "Missing You," seemed to hark back to her days with Motown. In 1986 the Bee Gees–written and –produced "Chain Reaction" gave Ross a minor hit here, yet in England this affectionate re-creation of the Supremes/Holland-Dozier-Holland style went to #1. Her final RCA album, *Red Hot Rhythm and Blues*, peaked at #73 with no charting pop singles.

Ross took some time off from her career. In 1985 she married Arne Naess, a Norwegian businessman; they had two sons, Ross and Evan. She has three daughters—Rhonda, Tracee, and Chudney—born during her first marriage to entertainment manager Robert Silberstein. (In his 1994 autobiography Berry Gordy wrote of being Rhonda's true biological father.) They married in 1971 and divorced five years later. Although Ross had been romantically linked with Berry Gordy, Kiss' Gene Simmons, and record mogul David Geffen, she has remained a model of discretion and maintained a closely guarded personal life.

In early 1989 Ross left RCA and returned to Motown, where she became a corporate officer and part owner. Despite a rush of publicity and her continued strong concert-ticket sales, she could not regain a foothold on the pop charts. Neither the heavily publicized *Workin' Overtime* nor *The Force Behind the Power* got into the Top 100 albums chart. After leaving Motown, Ross began to exert greater control over her career with, some have observed, less than desirable results. As an artist and celebrity, Ross' public image was tarnished by two 1983 incidents. The first was her onstage display of temper against ex-Supreme Mary Wilson during the taping of the *Motown 25* special. Ross' reputation as a high-handed diva was already well-established, and the incident, coupled with speculation about how much of the hit play *Dreamgirls* was based on the Supremes story, only solidified that image. The second incident, in which she argued, unconvincingly, that two concerts she gave in Central Park didn't generate sufficient profits to provide her promised $250,000 donation toward a new playground proved equally embarrassing. After the first night's show was rained out, the park was heavily damaged as the crowd of 350,000 retreated from the storm. By the evening's end, 84 people had been arrested after a wild rampage in which a large number of concertgoers and others in the area surrounding the park were attacked and/or robbed. The entire incident left a bitter taste, and although Ross returned a second night to perform, she didn't deliver the funds until after Mayor Ed Koch criticized her publicly over the next five months. Unfortunately, the groundbreaking for the park coincided with the publication of Mary Wilson's *Dreamgirl: My Life as a Supreme,* which some regarded as highly critical of Ross.

In 1994 a 4-CD retrospective box set, *Forever Diana,* which Ross oversaw and delivered complete to Motown, was withdrawn from the market for poor sound quality. Earlier that year her long-awaited autobiography (which, unlike most celebrities, she insisted in writing without professional assistance), *Secrets of a Sparrow,* was published to poor reviews and disappointing sales. Through her various production companies, Ross has produced a number of television specials and made-for-TV movies, including a film biography of Josephine Baker, in which she played the title role, and 1994's *Out of Darkness,* in which she played a paranoid schizophrenic.

Regardless of her career's ups and downs, Ross' stature among her fans and her power to draw attention to her endeavors is undiminished. She will always be the "first lady of Motown," the label's biggest and perhaps most important star and one of the top entertainers of her generation.

The Rossington-Collins Band
Formed 1979, Jacksonville, Florida
Gary Rossington, gtr.; Allen Collins (b. ca. 1952; d. Jan. 23, 1990, Jacksonville), gtr.; Billy Powell, kybds.; Leon Wilkeson, bass; Barry Harwood (b. Ga.), gtr., voc.; Derek Hess, drums; Dale Krantz (b. Ind.), lead voc.
1980—*Anytime, Anyplace, Anywhere* (MCA)
1981—*This Is the Way*
The Rossington Band: 1988—*Love Your Man* (MCA).

The Rossington-Collins Band was formed by four of the five surviving members of Lynyrd Skynyrd [see entry]. Nearly two years after the 1977 plane crash that killed Skynyrd lead singer Ronnie Van Zant, guitarist Steve Gaines, and backup vocalist Cassie Gaines, Jacksonville natives Gary Rossington, Allen Collins, Billy Powell, and Leon Wilkeson—all of whom had been injured in the crash—decided to regroup. Of the surviving Skynyrds, only drummer Artimus Pyle declined to join the new band. (He went on to form his own five-piece Artimus Pyle Band in 1979 with members of the Marshall Tucker Band producing.)

Rossington-Collins solidified in late 1979. Female vocalist Dale Krantz, who sang in church gospels as a child, had played with Leon Russell in L.A. after graduating college and in 1977 joined Ronnie Van Zant's brother Donnie's .38 Special as a backup singer. Her hoarse vocals and tough persona surprised many and delighted

critics. The group also included Barry Harwood, who completed the three-guitar lineup (in the Skynyrd tradition). He also came from Jacksonville, and had done session work with Joe South and Melanie and played on three Skynyrd LPs. The last member was Derek Hess, also from Jacksonville, who had played in some local bands with Harwood.

The group's self-produced debut, *Anytime, Anyplace, Anywhere,* came out in June 1980 and went gold. Soon after the LP's release, Collins' wife, Katy, died. RCB dedicated its second album, *This Is the Way,* to her. Though the group seemed to have a promising future, it disbanded in 1983. Collins formed the Allen Collins Band with Powell, Wilkeson, Harwood, and Hess. Paralyzed in a 1986 car accident, he died in 1990. Krantz and Rossington married and started The Rossington Band in the late Eighties. In 1991 Rossington, Powell, Wilkeson, and former Lynyrd Skynyrd guitarist Ed King put together a new version of Skynyrd, with Johnny Van Zant on lead vocals. Dale Krantz sang backup.

David Lee Roth: See Van Halen

Roxette
Formed 1986, Sweden
Marie Fredriksson (b. May 30, 1958, Östra Ljungby, Swed.), voc.; Per Gessle (b. Jan. 12, 1959, Halmstad, Swed.), gtr., voc.
1986—*Pearls of Passion* (EMI, Sweden)   1988—*Look Sharp!* (EMI)   1991—*Joyride*   1992—*Tourism*   1994—*Crash! Boom! Bang!*

In the late Eighties and early Nineties, a bunch of catchy, well-executed singles made the duo Roxette Sweden's most successful musical export since Abba. Like Abba, singer Marie Fredriksson and songwriter, rhythm guitarist, and vocalist Per Gessle specialized in glossy, guilty-pleasure pop. Gessle had fronted a popular Swedish band, Gyllene Tider, and Fredriksson had embarked on a solo career before the two joined forces in the mid-Eighties. From the start, they set their sights on the English-speaking market that is essential to international stardom, writing and recording in English.

Their plan paid off in 1989, when Roxette's second album, 1988's *Look Sharp!,* made a big splash in the U.S., generating the #1 pop singles "The Look" and "Listen to Your Heart" and the #2 hit "Dangerous." In 1990 Fredriksson and Gessle again topped the singles chart with the ballad "It Must Have Been Love," featured on the soundtrack to the film *Pretty Woman.* The following year, Roxette released *Joyride,* which spawned another #1 hit with the title track; another cut, "Fading Like a Flower (Every Time You Leave)," went to #2. Also in 1991 the duo began its first worldwide tour, enlisting support from the same group of musicians who had played on their albums. But a fourth album, 1992's *Tourism,* produced no major hits. The next year, Roxette appeared on another movie soundtrack, *Super Mario Bros.,* with the song "Almost Unreal."

Roxy Music

Formed 1971, London, England
Bryan Ferry (b. Sep. 26, 1945, Washington, Eng.), voc., kybds.; Graham Simpson, bass; Brian Eno (b. Brian Peter George St. John le Baptiste de la Salle Eno, May 15, 1948, Woodbridge, Eng.), synth., treatments; Andy Mackay (b. July 23, 1946, Eng.), sax, oboe; Dexter Lloyd, drums; Roger Bunn, gtr.
1971—(– Lloyd; – Bunn; + Paul Thompson [b. May 13, 1951, Jarrow, Eng.], drums; + David O'List [b. Eng.], gtr.) 1972—(– O'List; + Phil Manzanera [b. Philip Targett-Adams, Jan. 31, 1951, London], gtr.) *Roxy Music* (Atco) (– Simpson; + Rik Kenton [b. Oct. 31, 1945, Eng.], bass; – Kenton; + John Porter, bass; – Porter; + Sal Maida, bass) 1973—*For Your Pleasure* (– Eno; + Eddie Jobson [b. Apr. 28, 1955, Billingham, Eng.], violin, synth.; – Maida; + John Gustafson, bass) 1974—*Stranded; Country Life* 1975—(– Gustafson; + John Wetton [b. 1949, Derby, Eng.], bass) *Siren* (– Wetton; + Gustafson) 1976—(– Gustafson; + Rick Wills, bass) *Viva!* 1977—*Greatest Hits* 1978—(– Jobson; + Gary Tibbs, bass; + David Skinner, kybds.; + Paul Carrack, kybds.; + Alan Spenner, bass) 1979—*Manifesto* 1980—(– Thompson; + Andy Newmark, drums; – Carrack) *Flesh + Blood* 1982—*Avalon* (Warner Bros.) 1983—*The High Road* EP 1989—*Street Life: 20 Great Hits* (Reprise) 1990—*Heart Still Beating* (Warner Bros.).
Bryan Ferry solo: 1973—*These Foolish Things* (Atlantic) 1974—*Another Time, Another Place* 1976—*Let's Stick Together* 1977—*In Your Mind* 1978—*The Bride Stripped Bare* 1985—*Boys and Girls* (Warner Bros.) 1988—*Bête Noire* (Reprise) 1993—*Taxi* 1994—*Mamouna* (Virgin).
Phil Manzanera solo: 1975—*Diamond Head* (Atco) 1978—*K-Scope* (EG-Polydor) 1982—*Primitive Guitars* (Editions EG) 1987—*Guitarissimo 75–82.*
Andy Mackay solo (with the Players): 1989—*Christmas* (Rykodisc).
Manzanera and Mackay: 1988—*Crack the Whip* (Relativity) 1989—*Up in Smoke.*
Manzanera and Quiet Sun: 1975—*Mainstream* (Antilles).
Manzanera and 801: 1976—*801 Live* (EG-Polydor).
Manzanera and John Wetton: 1987—*Wetton/Manzanera* (Geffen).

Roxy Music: Andy Mackay, Bryan Ferry, Eddie Jobson, Rick Wills, Phil Manzanera, Paul Thompson

Roxy Music defined the tone of Seventies art rock by coupling Bryan Ferry's elegant, wistful romantic irony with initially anarchic and later subdued, lush rock. The band was never as popular in America as it was in Europe, perhaps because its detachment and understatement baffled American tastes. But Ferry's witty hoping-against-hopelessness persona and Brian Eno's happy amateurism filtered into the late-Seventies new wave while Roxy Music itself was in suspension.

Ferry and bassist Graham Simpson began searching for bandmates around November 1970. Ferry, who would write almost all of Roxy's songs, is the son of a coal miner. He attended the University of Newcastle, where he studied art for three years with pop-conceptual artist Richard Hamilton. At school he sang in a more rock-oriented band, the Banshees, before joining an R&B band called the Gas Board with Simpson. He also taught art.

In January 1971 Andy Mackay joined the fledgling band; he had played oboe as a teenager with the London Symphony Orchestra and saxophone at Reading University. Mackay brought Eno with him. The earliest lineup also included classical percussionist Dexter Lloyd, who left by June, and guitarist Roger Bunn, who soon returned to session work. Drummer Paul Thompson had played with a local band, Smoke-stack, and guitarist Davy O'List had been with the Nice. O'List left after five months and was replaced by Phil Manzanera from the experimental band Quiet Sun.

Simpson decided to give up music; Roxy Music recorded its debut album with Rik Kenton, and never had a full member on bass. The group's debut album, produced by King Crimson lyricist Peter Sinfield, went Top Ten in England in 1972, and "Virginia Plain" went to #4 in Britain, where Roxy Music's Fifties-style retro-chic costumes fit in with the glam-rock fad, although its music was far more sophisticatedly primitive. In addition, Ferry's lyrics ranged from deliriously campy to acutely sensitive, and his Fifties-greaser-cum-suave-matinee-idol good looks seemed incongruous at the time. This was most apparent when Roxy Music served as opening act for Jethro Tull on a December 1972 U.S. arena tour.

The second Roxy Music album, *For Your Pleasure*, met with a similar reaction; its strangeness was popular in Britain and ignored in America. In July 1973 Eno [see entry] left for a solo career—perhaps inevitably, since he was a songwriter himself, and Roxy Music was Ferry's outlet. Ferry cut his first solo album in 1973, *These Foolish Things*. While treating Lesley Gore and Bob Dylan songs with equal camp disengagement, Ferry also showed a deep affection for pop tradition, which would continue throughout his solo career.

Teenage multi-instrumentalist Eddie Jobson, formerly with Curved Air, replaced Eno for *Stranded*, which also included writing credits for Manzanera and Mackay. With Eno gone, the music now focused on Ferry's singing rather than the band's counterpoint. *Country Life*, also released in 1974, was Roxy's first U.S. success; it went to #37, although its cover, with a glimpse of pubic hair through panties, was banned in some record stores, covered with an opaque wrapper elsewhere, and finally replaced with an inoffensive forest photo.

Roxy toured the U.S. in 1975 with bassist John Wetton, formerly of King Crimson and Family, and later with Uriah Heep, U.K., and Asia. After its most singlemindedly danceable record, *Siren*—which included Roxy's first U.S. hit single, "Love Is the Drug" (#30, 1976)—the group took what it described as an indefinite "rest," leaving the live LP *Viva!* and *Greatest Hits* in its wake.

Ferry's fourth solo album, *In Your Mind* (1977) was the occasion for a world tour with Roxy's Manzanera, Wetton, and Thompson providing backup. For his 1978 solo LP, *The Bride Stripped Bare*, Ferry recorded with Los Angeles sessionmen and several Roxy regulars. Mackay released solo albums and wrote music for the British TV series *Rock Follies*, while Manzanera recorded and toured briefly with a band called 801, featuring Eno; he also re-formed Quiet Sun for a short time and played sessions for John Cale, Eno, Nico, and others.

In 1978 Roxy Music reunited for *Manifesto*, minus Jobson, who had joined U.K.; the keyboardist later recorded with Frank Zappa and Jethro Tull. *Manifesto* (#23, 1979) (which includes "Dance Away" and "Angel Eyes") became Roxy's highest-charting U.S. album ever. The group embarked on a world tour with guest keyboardist Paul Carrack (formerly of Ace, and later with Squeeze, Nick Lowe, and Mike + the Mechanics) and two bassists, including Gary Tibbs, formerly of the Vibrators and later of Adam and the Ants. Just before that tour, Thompson broke his thumb in a motorcycle accident and left the band.

For 1980's *Flesh + Blood* Roxy Music was down to a threesome—Ferry, Manzanera, and Mackay—plus sessionmen. Though their most subdued album, it set Ferry's new (seemingly) heartfelt romantic longing against simpler but richer melodies and signaled a new direction. *Flesh + Blood* became the group's second #1 album in England (after *Stranded*) and went to #35 in the U.S. *Avalon* (#53, 1982) continued in the same vein and yielded the Top Ten British hit "More Than This." It was the group's only LP to sell a million copies in America. The next year Roxy Music toured the U.S. as an eight-piece band plus three backup singers, concurrent with a live EP called *The High Road* (which includes a version of John Lennon's "Jealous Guy," a #1 U.K. hit, shortly after the ex-Beatle's murder). As of this writing, it was the group's final road trip, with the members separating, seemingly for good. *Heart Still Beating* documents a 1982 French concert.

Given the Eighties popularity of such clearly Roxy-influenced acts as the Cars, ABC, and Duran Duran, Ferry and the band's mix of outrageous humor ("In Every Dream Home a Heartache," a love song to an inflatable doll; "Do the Strand"), tongue-in-cheek cool, and exceptional musicianship, their lack of a wider U.S. audience is baffling. Roxy's music videos, rarely seen in this country outside new-wave rock clubs, were as stylish as its album covers, and as artists' visual presentations became increasingly important, it would seem that Roxy's chance had come.

Since the breakup, Ferry's sporadic recorded output has maintained the sleek, meticulously produced sound of *Avalon*. *Boys and Girls* eventually went gold. "Kiss and Tell," a track off 1988's *Bête Noire*, became his only Top Forty U.S. hit after it was featured in the movie *Bright Lights, Big City*, starring Michael J. Fox. In 1976 Ferry had been romantically involved with *Siren*'s cover girl, model Jerry Hall; she soon left him for Mick Jagger. In 1982 he married socialite Lucy Helmore, who'd recently graced the picture sleeve of the "Avalon" 45, a #13 U.K. hit. At the time of 1993's *Taxi*, another interpretive album (produced by, of all people, Robin Trower), Ferry hinted that a Roxy Music reunion might happen, possibly around the time of the group's 25th anniversary.

Mackay and Manzanera's first post-Roxy venture was a group called the Explorers; they've also recorded as a duo and, separately, with others, such as John Wetton (Manzanera), and with an instrumental band called the Players (Mackay).

Royal Guardsmen

Formed mid-Sixties, Ocala, Florida
Billy Taylor, organ; Barry Winslow, voc., gtr.; Chris Nunley, lead voc.; Tom Richards, gtr.; Bill Balogh, gtr.; John Burdette, drums.

1967—*Snoopy vs. the Red Baron* (Laurie); *Snoopy and His Friends* 1968—*Snoopy for President.*

The comic-strip antics of Charlie Brown's pet dog inspired "Snoopy vs. the Red Baron," a #2 hit that sold three million singles for this sextet in 1966–67 and gave the group a lease on life that the members exploited to the hilt. "The Return of the Red Baron" (#15) and "Snoopy's Christmas" followed in 1967, with decreasing success. The next year, the failure of "Snoopy for President" signaled that the gimmick had run its course, and the Royal Guardsmen eventually broke up. Winslow was the Guardsman who bore the nickname Snoopy.

Royal Teens
Formed 1956, New Jersey
Bob Gaudio (b. Nov. 17, 1942, Fort Lee, N.J.), piano; Joe Villa (b. Brooklyn, N.Y.), voc.; Tom Austin (b. Fort Lee, N.J.), drums; Bill Crandall (b. Fort Lee, N.J.), sax; Bill Dalton, bass; – Crandall; + Larry Qualaino, sax; – Dalton; + Al Kooper [b. Feb. 5, 1944, Brooklyn, N.Y.], bass.

In 1958 the Royal Teens caused a brief sensation with their #3 singsong novelty, "Short Shorts." For two years they tried in vain to repeat their success with such tunes as "Big Name Button," "Harvey's Got a Girl Friend," and "Believe Me." Al Kooper, later of the Blues Project, Blood Sweat and Tears and myriad solo projects, joined a later version of the group. Pianist and "Short Shorts" coauthor Bob Gaudio would later score countless hit records as the mastermind behind the Four Seasons. In the early Eighties the "Short Shorts" melody was part of a commercial jingle for Nair depilatory cream.

David Ruffin: See the Temptations

Rufus: See Chaka Khan

The Rumour
Formed 1975, England
Bob Andrews (b. June 20, 1949), kybds.; Stephen Goulding, drums; Andrew Bodnar, bass; Brinsley Schwarz (b. Mar. 25, 1949, Woodbridge, Eng.), gtr.; Martin Belmont, gtr.
1977—*Max* (Mercury) 1979—*Frogs, Sprouts, Clogs and Krauts* (Stiff) 1980—(– Andrews) 1981—*Purity of Essence* (Hannibal).

The Rumour, five veterans of England's pub-rock scene of the early Seventies, are best known as Graham Parker's backup band on his first six LPs. But they've also recorded their own albums and backed up and produced performers other than Parker.

The Rumour were first heard from in 1976 on Parker's *Howlin' Wind*. Bob Andrews and Brinsley Schwarz came from the group Brinsley Schwarz (as did the LP's producer, Nick Lowe); Martin Belmont was originally in Ducks Deluxe; Andrew Bodnar and Stephen Goulding were the former rhythm section of Bontemps Roulez.

While working with Parker, members of the Rumour played on Lowe's *Pure Pop for Now People* and on debut LPs by Rachel Sweet and Carlene Carter (the latter produced by Andrews and Schwarz), and they recorded the albums *Max* (in reply to Fleetwood Mac's *Rumours*) and *Frogs, Sprouts, Clogs and Krauts.*

Andrews left the group in 1980, with the band continuing as a four-piece and recording *Purity of Essence*. They left Graham Parker a year later to back up Garland Jeffreys on tour (Goulding and Bodnar had played on Jeffreys' 1981 album *Escape Artist*). Belmont went on to record and tour with Nick Lowe. Bodnar has played on Parker's records since the mid-Eighties; Schwarz, too, has graced several Parker LPs.

The Runaways
Formed 1975, Los Angeles, California
Joan Jett (b. Sep. 22, 1960, Philadelphia, Pa.), gtr., voc.; Sandy West (b. 1960), drums: Micki Steele (b. June 2, 1954), bass, voc.
1975—(– Steele; + Cherie Currie [b. 1960, Los Angeles], lead voc.; + Lita Ford [b. Sep. 23, 1959, London, Eng.], gtr.; + Jackie Fox [b. 1960], bass) 1976—*The Runaways* (Mercury) 1977—*Queens of Noise* (– Fox; – Currie; + Vicki Blue, bass); *Waitin' for the Night* 1981—*Little Lost Girls* (Rhino) 1982—*Best of the Runaways.*

The Runaways were an all-female hard-rock band that suffered from hype, manipulation, and being slightly ahead of their time. Formed on the Sunset Strip in late 1975 by Kim Fowley, they were presented as five hot, tough high-school-age girls out for sex and fun (a fairly novel idea in prepunk days). But with their musical deficiencies, the stigma of Fowley-as-Svengali, and a blatantly sexual presentation—lead singer Cherie Currie wore lingerie onstage—they often seemed more like tease objects than real musicians.

The group started when Fowley met 13-year-old lyricist Kari Krome at a party. He liked her three-minute lyrics about sex, and when she suggested girls a few years older than herself to play her songs, Fowley was interested. First they got Krome's acquaintance Joan Jett and then, through some local ads, Micki Steele and Sandy West. They were going to be a threesome, but after Steele left, Lita Ford, Cherie Currie, and Jackie Fox joined. Only Ford had been in a band before.

The Runaways signed to Mercury, and their Alice

Cooper–influenced debut (with much material cowritten by Fowley and the band) came out in May 1976 to universal pans and snickers. Their only real audience was in Japan, where they earned three gold records for their debut and for *Queens of Noise* (on which Currie and Jett split lead vocals). But after some internal conflict, Currie and Fox left in mid-1977. Jett, who already did most of the writing by now, took over the lead. Vickie Blue was added on bass. Currie went on to become an actress, costarring with Jodie Foster in *Foxes* (1980), and then appearing in a succession of straight-to-video titles such as *Parasite* (1982) and *Rich Girl* (1991). She later recorded an LP with her sister Marie entitled *Messin' with the Boys.*

Waitin' for the Night did no better than its predecessors, and though the band turned in good performances as U.S. openers for the Ramones' 1978 tour, the Runaways played their last show on New Year's Eve 1978 in San Francisco. Jett felt that their last LP, *And Now the Runaways!* (out in Europe only; released in the U.S. as *Little Lost Girls* in 1981), was too heavy-metal, so at the start of 1979 she quit, and the band died. Afterward Jett took part in a B movie based loosely on the group, called *We're All Crazy Now,* after the Slade song.

Both Jett and Ford went on to successful solo careers [see entries]. Micki—now known as Michael—Steele, meanwhile, joined the poppier Bangles in 1983. Jett paid homage to her former band by reviving its "Cherry Bomb" on her 1984 album *Glorious Results of a Misspent Youth.* The following year Kim Fowley put together a new group of Runaways. After one album, 1987's *Young and Fast,* they broke up.

Todd Rundgren/Utopia

Born June 22, 1948, Upper Darby, Pennsylvania
**1970—*Runt* (Bearsville)   1971—*Runt. The Ballad of Todd Rundgren*   1972—*Something/Anything?*
1973—*A Wizard/A True Star*   1974—*Todd*   1975—*Initiation*   1976—*Faithful*   1978—*Hermit of Mink Hollow; Back to the Bars*   1981—*Healing*   1983—*The Ever Popular Tortured Artist Effect*   1985—*A Cappella* (Warner Bros.)   1989—*Nearly Human; Anthology* (Rhino)   1991—*2nd Wind* (Warner Bros.)
1993—*No World Order* (Forward/Rhino).
Utopia, formed 1974 (Rundgren, gtr., voc.; Mark "Moogy" Klingman, kybds.; Ralph Shuckett, kybds.; Roger "M. Frog" Powell, synth.; John Siegler, bass; John "Willie" Wilcox, drums; Kevin Elliman, perc.):
1974—*Todd Rundgren's Utopia* (Bearsville)   1975—*Another Live*   1976—(– Klingman; – Shuckett; – Siegler; – Elliman; + Kasim Sulton, bass)   1977—*RA; Oops, Wrong Planet*   1980—*Adventures in Utopia; Deface the Music*   1982—*Swing to the Right; Utopia* (Network)   1984—*Oblivion* (Passport)**

1985—*POV*   1989—*Anthology* (Rhino)   1993—*Utopia Redux '92: Live in Japan.*

An eclectically accomplished musician and studio virtuoso, Todd Rundgren has been recording for nearly three decades. His musical career has gone from simple pop that never brought the success some critics felt he deserved (only one gold LP, *Something/Anything?*) to the more complex progressive rock of Utopia, which did gain Rundgren a devoted cult following. Through it all, this multi-instrumentalist has maintained a prolific sideline career as a producer; he must also be regarded as a pioneer of rock video and interactive CD.

Rundgren began playing in a high school band, Money, then went on to play with Woody's Truck Stop in the mid-Sixties (a tape recording of the latter makes a brief appearance on *Something/Anything?*). In 1967 he formed the Nazz [see entry], which, contrary to then-prevailing West Coast psychedelic trends, tried to replicate the look of Swinging London in its clothes, mod haircuts, and Beatlesish pop sound. In some ways the Nazz was ahead of its time, especially in terms of Rundgren's studio facility and the band's musical sophistication. But the quartet remained a local Philadelphia phenomenon, with one minor hit single, the original version of "Hello It's Me." The Nazz broke up in 1969, at which point Rundgren formed the studio band Runt and hit the Top Twenty in 1971 with the single "We Gotta Get You a Woman."

By this time Rundgren had become associated with manager Albert Grossman, who let him produce for his new Bearsville label. By 1972 Rundgren had taken over production of Badfinger's *Straight Up* LP from George Harrison (who was involved with his Bangla Desh concerts) and had engineered the Band's *Stage Fright* and Jesse Winchester's self-titled 1971 LP, as well as produced records by the Hello People, bluesman James Cotton, the Paul Butterfield Blues Band, and Halfnelson (who later became Sparks). In 1973 he would produce the New York Dolls' debut LP, Grand Funk's *We're an American Band,* and Fanny's *Mother's Pride.*

For many, *Something/Anything?* is the high-water mark of Rundgren's solo career. On it he played nearly all the instruments, overdubbed scores of vocals, and managed to cover pop bases from Motown to Hendrix, from the Beach Boys to the Beatles. The album yielded hit singles in "I Saw the Light" (#16, 1972) and "Hello It's Me" (#5, 1973).

A Wizard, while in much the same vein, was more of a critical than a commercial success. However, Rundgren's cult following was growing. *Wizard* contained a postcard on which he asked fans to send their names to him for inclusion in a poster to be contained in his next LP. As promised, 1974's *Todd* included that poster—with some 10,000 names printed on it in tiny type.

That same year Rundgren unveiled his cosmic/symphonic progressive-rock band Utopia, which gradually expanded his following to mammoth proportions. Utopia was a more democratic band, in which Rundgren shared songwriting and lead vocals with other members (from 1977 on: Roger Powell, Kasim Sulton, and Willie Wilcox). In the mid-Seventies Utopia played bombastic suites with "cosmic" lyrics and used pyramids as a backdrop, but in the Eighties it returned to Beatles/new-wave-style pop. Despite some excellent music, the quartet never placed a single in the Top Forty or saw any of its 11 albums go gold. One of their songs, "Love Is the Answer," was a 1979 Top Ten hit for England Dan and John Ford Coley.

In 1975 Rundgren produced Gong guitarist Steve Hillage's *L*, on which Utopia played backup. A trip to the Middle East in 1978 led Rundgren to a brief flirtation with Sufism; that same year *Hermit of Mink Hollow* produced his first hit single in several years in "Can We Still Be Friends?" (a minor hit for Robert Palmer a year later). Rundgren also produced Meat Loaf's monstrously successful *Bat Out of Hell*. In 1979 alone he produced Tom Robinson's *TRB Two*, the Tubes' *Remote Control*, and Patti Smith's *Wave*, and in 1980 he produced Shaun Cassidy's *Wasp*.

By that time Rundgren had taken a strong interest in the emerging field of rock video. By 1981 he had built his own computer-video studio in Woodstock, New York, and was making technically advanced surrealistic videotapes. In 1982 Rundgren embarked on a one-man tour, playing both solo-acoustic sets and backed by taped band arrangements, with his computer-graphic videos being shown as well. He also still concentrated on production (with the Psychedelic Furs, among others) and video art.

Utopia took an indefinite sabbatical in 1985. Sulton, in addition to recording on his own, has played with Joan Jett, Hall and Oates, Patty Smyth, and Cheap Trick. Powell, designer of a shoulder-strap keyboard called the Powell Probe, now engineers software for a computer graphics firm, while Wilcox writes and produces. In 1992 the four reunited for a tour of Japan, captured on *Utopia Redux '92*.

The following year Rundgren went back out on the road as a high-tech one-man band to perform his unique new album *No World Order*. The world's first interactive music-only CD (available on Philips), it allows listeners to reshape the ten songs into an infinite number of versions. To hear the same version of a song twice, Rundgren claimed, users would have to play the disc 24 hours a day, seven days a week "well into the next millennium."

Run-D.M.C.

Formed 1981, Hollis, Queens, New York
Run (b. Joseph Simmons, Nov. 14, 1964), voc.;
D.M.C. (b. Darryl McDaniels, May 31, 1964), voc.;
Jam Master Jay (b. Jason Mizell, Jan. 21, 1965),
turntables, programming.
1984—Run-D.M.C. (Profile)   1985—*King of Rock*
1986—*Raising Hell*   1988—*Tougher Than Leather*
1990—*Back from Hell*   1991—*Together Forever:*
Greatest Hits 1983–1991*   1993—*Down with the
King.

Run-D.M.C. took hard-core hip-hop from an underground street sensation to a pop culture phenomenon. Although earlier artists, such as Grandmaster Flash and the Sugar Hill Gang, made rap's initial strides on the airwaves, it was Run-D.M.C. that introduced hats, gold chains, and untied sneakers to youth culture's most stubborn demographic group: white, male, suburban rock fans. In the process, the trio helped change the course of popular music, paving the way for rap's second generation.

The members of Run-D.M.C. grew up together in the middle-class New York neighborhood of Hollis, Queens. By the time Joey Simmons reached his teens, his older brother Russell was becoming a major figure in the burgeoning rap scene, establishing Rush Productions and later cofounding the trailblazing rap label Def Jam along with his white partner Rick Rubin. With Russell's help and encouragement, Joey and Darryl McDaniels started rapping together in the Simmons home.

Upon graduating high school in 1982, the two recruited their old basketball buddy, Jay Mizell, to back them on turntables. Run-D.M.C.'s first single was the groundbreaking 1983 anthem "It's Like That" b/w "Sucker M.C.'s" (#15 R&B); it was followed the same year by "Hard Times" b/w "Jam-Master Jay" (#11 R&B). The songs' sparse music and booming vocal delivery was informed as much by rock as by the pseudo jazz of earlier recorded rap songs. Moreover, the first single introduced Simmons and McDaniels' unconventional vocal style. Rather than trade off on the verses, they finished each other's lines. The group followed up with a string of R&B chart hits, including "Rock Box" (#22, 1984), "30 Days" (#16, 1984), "King of Rock" (#14, 1985), "You Talk Too Much" (#19, 1985), and "Can You Rock It Like This" (#19, 1985). In 1985 Run-D.M.C. starred in the movie *Krush Groove* alongside Kurtis Blow, the Fat Boys, and the Beastie Boys.

Run-D.M.C.'s third album, 1986's *Raising Hell* (#3, 1986), confirmed the group's self-professed "King of Rock" status. In one of the cleverest marketing schemes in recent memory, Rick Rubin teamed up Run-D.M.C. with then-fading pop-metal band Aerosmith for a remake of the latter's 1976 hit "Walk This Way." The song sent suburban metalheads jumping for their air guitars, as it reached #4 on *Billboard*'s pop chart (#8 R&B). Other singles from *Raising Hell* included "My Adidas" (#5,

1986), which won the group a corporate sponsorship, "You Be Illin' " (#29 pop, #12 R&B, 1986), and "It's Tricky" (#57 pop, #21 R&B, 1987).

Run-D.M.C. began its decline after 1988's *Tougher Than Leather*, putting out albums but barely making it into the Top 100. *Tougher Than Leather*, though it reached #9 on the pop albums chart, was a critical failure, and the film of the same name was a box-office bomb. *Back from Hell* was the group's first album not to go gold; by then, McDaniels and Simmons were recovering from drug and alcohol problems, as well as a rape charge (later dropped) against the latter. In 1993 Run-D.M.C. bounced back with their cleaned-up, Christian-themed seventh album, *Down with the King*, which entered the R&B chart at #1 (#7 pop).

RuPaul

Born RuPaul Andre Charles, November 17, 1960, San Diego, California
1993—*Supermodel of the World* (Tommy Boy).

Pop culture mini-phenomenon RuPaul became nearly ubiquitous in the early-Nineties entertainment media as a black drag queen singing neo-disco and propagating a philosophy that combined self-help assertiveness, a genial attack on convention, and a Warholian emphasis on marketing and self-promotion.

In the early Eighties, RuPaul was a fixture of Atlanta's art scene and sang in various comedy/cabaret/rock groups (notably RuPaul and the U-Hauls and Wee Wee Pole) until he moved to New York City in the late Eighties. There taken up by denizens of the fashionable demimonde, the six-feet-seven-inch (in heels) personality eventually signed with Tommy Boy. Off his debut album, "Supermodel (You Better Work)" was a video-channel and dance-club hit (#45 pop), and RuPaul began appearing regularly on the talk-show circuit. In 1993 his career began taking off: He recorded a duet version of Elton John's "Don't Go Breaking My Heart" for John's *Duets* album, contributed vocals to the *Addams Family Values* soundtrack, released a Christmas single ("Little Drummer Boy") from a cable television special, "RuPaul's Christmas Ball," and landed a part in the Spike Lee film *Crooklyn*. In 1995 RuPaul became the first cross-dresser to land a contract with a major cosmetics company, and his memoir, *Lettin It All Hang Out*, was published by Hyperion.

Tom Rush

Born February 8, 1941, Portsmouth, New Hampshire
1963—*Got a Mind to Ramble* (Prestige); *Blues Songs and Ballads* 1965—*Blues and Folk* (Transatlantic); *Tom Rush* (Elektra) 1966—*Take a Little Walk with Me* 1968—*The Circle Game* 1970—*Tom Rush* (Co-lumbia); *Wrong End of the Rainbow; Classic Rush* (Elektra) 1971—*Merrimack County* 1974—*Ladies Love Outlaws* 1975—*The Best of Tom Rush* (Columbia) 1982—*Tom Rush: New Year* (Night Light) 1984—*Tom Rush: Late Night Radio* 1993—*Tom Rush: Work in Progress.*

Singer and occasional songwriter Tom Rush came to prominence while working the Cambridge, Massachusetts, coffeehouse circuit (he holds a B.A. from Harvard) in the early Sixties. He was eclectic from the beginning, experimenting with blues, jazz, classical arrangements, and electric instrumentation.

Circle Game, one of pop's first concept albums, yielded Rush's two best-known performances: his own "No Regrets" and the album's title cut, written by Joni Mitchell. Rush was performing songs by Mitchell, Jackson Browne, and James Taylor before any of them were well known. Taylor has cited Rush as a prime influence on his work. *Merrimack County* presaged a two-year period of self-imposed retirement, broken only by the more commercial *Ladies Love Outlaws*. In 1980 he founded Maple Hill Productions, through which he arranged a series of concerts under the name Club 47 (after the famous Cambridge coffeehouse where Rush, Dylan, Baez, and other seminal folk artists began) to introduce modern folk artists. He also started his own mail-order record label, Night Light Recordings. He continues to write and record; he tours regularly. He is also deeply involved in a wildlife protection organization, the Wolf Fund.

Rush

Formed 1969, Toronto, Canada
Alex Lifeson (b. Alex Zivojinovich, Aug. 27, 1953, Surnie, B.C., Can.), gtr.; Geddy Lee (b. Gary Lee Weinrib, July 29, 1953, Toronto), voc., bass, gtr., kybds.; John Rutsey, drums.
1974—*Rush* (Moon/Mercury) (– Rutsey; + Neil Peart [b. Sep. 12, 1952, Hamilton, Ont., Can.], drums)
1975—*Fly by Night; Caress of Steel* 1976—*2112; All the World's a Stage* 1977—*A Farewell to Kings* 1978—*Hemispheres* 1980—*Permanent Waves* 1981—*Moving Pictures; Exit . . . Stage Left* 1982—*Signals* 1984—*Grace Under Pressure* 1985—*Power Windows* 1987—*Hold Your Fire* 1989—*A Show of Hands; Presto* (Atlantic) 1990—*Chronicles* (Mercury) 1991—*Roll the Bones* (Atlantic) 1993—*Counterparts.*

Since its 1976 breakthrough with *2112*, every one of this Canadian progressive power trio's albums has gone gold or platinum. At first critics suggested that singer Geddy Lee's high-pitched vocals, Alex Lifeson's major-chord guitar heroics, and Neil Peart's heavy but adroit drumming in usually epic-length mélanges of intricate musi-

Rush: Geddy Lee, Neil Peart, Alex Lifeson

cal structures and apocalyptic lyrics (by Peart) were highly reminiscent of vintage Yes. Rush has since won respect as an inventive thinking-man's hard-rock band. Virtuoso instrumentalists, the three regularly place high in musicians' magazines readers' polls.

Rush's initial success was based on diligent touring, as the group established itself first in Canada and the northern U.S. and gradually expanded its following despite limited airplay. The futuristic concept album *2112* (#61, 1976), now platinum, set Rush on a course of gold or platinum albums in the late Seventies. But it was with *Permanant Waves* (#4, 1980) that the trio's popularity soared. The band's eighth LP, it marked something of a departure with its shorter compositions. Rush has followed this direction ever since. The platinum *Signals* (#10, 1982) introduced a refined sound: shimmering guitar similar to that of the Police's Andy Summers, warm synthesizer backdrops, and, most notably, relatively subdued vocals from Lee, who now sang in a lower (and far more listenable) register. That remained the blueprint for Rush's music throughout the Eighties and early Nineties. Each of Rush's five albums through 1985's *Power Windows* sold at least one million copies. *Moving Pictures* (#3, 1981) sold over four million copies. And, while Rush remains the antithesis of a singles band, the shortened format of *Signals* produced an actual hit, "New World Man" (#21, 1982).

The group lowered its profile somewhat later in the decade, scaling back on touring. Yet its next five albums, from 1987's *Hold Your Fire* through 1993's *Counterparts*, went gold or platinum. *Counterparts* (#2, 1993) harked back to the group's earlier, earthier sound, with Lifeson once again the instrumental focus.

The Canadian trio has altered more than just its music over the years. Once perceived as a rather dour bunch (due largely to Peart's often weighty lyrics), Rush has long since revealed a sly sense of humor. In 1982 Lee

sang on the Top Twenty hit "Take Off" by Bob and Doug McKenzie, the Canadian-bumpkin satire by Dave Thomas and Rick Moranis of the Canada-based TV comedy show *SCTV.* Another *SCTV* character, Joe Flaherty's Count Floyd, introduced the group via video on its 1984 tour. The group often takes the stage to a prerecorded Three Stooges theme.

Jimmy Rushing

Born August 26, 1903, Oklahoma City, Oklahoma; died June 8, 1972, New York City, New York
1978—*The Essential Jimmy Rushing* (Vanguard)
1980—*Mister Five by Five* (Columbia) 1988—*The You and Me That Used to Be* (RCA).

Known as "Mr. Five by Five" for his short and wide physique, Jimmy Rushing was perhaps the best male blues-based vocalist of the swing era, during which he was a featured attraction with Count Basie's orchestra (1935–50). His tenor voice and his phrasing easily fit jazz, blues, pop, and shouting R&B.

Born to musical parents, Rushing studied violin, piano, and theory as a child, and he sang in church, school glee clubs, and opera-hall pageants. As a teenager he hoboed through the Midwest before moving to California, where he occasionally sang with Jelly Roll Morton and worked solo as a barroom singer/pianist. In the late Twenties he was with the seminal Kansas City swing band Walter Page's Blue Devils, and from 1929 to 1935 he was vocalist with another important early Kansas City big band, Bennie Moten's Kansas City Orchestra.

Rushing then worked with Count Basie, often sharing the microphone with Billie Holiday. In 1946 he recorded with Johnny Otis, and in the early Fifties he led his own septet at New York's Savoy Ballroom. He had a resurgence in popularity in the late Fifties, and in 1964 he toured Australia and Japan with Eddie Condon's All Stars. He also toured with Benny Goodman's orchestra, appeared on several TV specials, and in 1969 had a singing and acting role in the Gordon Parks film *The Learning Tree.* In 1972 he died from leukemia. Rushing was an immensely influential vocalist on generations of blues, jazz, R&B, pop, and rock singers, and his performances are available on a number of albums under both his own and Basie's names.

Leon Russell

Born Hank Wilson, April 2, 1941, Lawton, Oklahoma
1968—*Look Inside the Asylum Choir* (Smash)
1970—*Leon Russell* (A&M/Shelter) 1971—*Asylum Choir II* (Shelter); *Leon Russell and the Shelter People* 1972—*Carny* 1973—*Leon Live; Hank Wilson's Back* 1974—*Stop All That Jazz* 1975—*Will o' the

Wisp; Live in Japan   1976—*Wedding Album* (with Mary Russell) (Paradise); *Best of Leon Russell* (Shelter)   1977—*Make Love to the Music* (with Mary Russell) (Paradise)   1978—*Americana*   1979—*Willie and Leon* (with Willie Nelson) (Columbia); *Live and Love* (Paradise)   1981—*Leon Russell and New Grass Revival Live* (Warner Bros.)   1984—*Solid State* (Paradise)   1992—*Anything Can Happen* (Virgin).

Leon Russell is perhaps best known as one of the first supersessionmen, having worked for everyone from Jerry Lee Lewis and Phil Spector to Joe Cocker, Bob Dylan, and the Rolling Stones. He has also maintained a solo career as a countryish blues-gospel performer.

A multi-instrumentalist, Russell studied classical piano from ages three to 13. At 14 he learned trumpet and formed his own band in Tulsa (where he grew up) and lied about his age to land a job at a Tulsa nightclub, where he played with Ronnie Hawkins and the Hawks (who later became the Band). Soon after, Jerry Lee Lewis took Russell's band on tour. In 1958 Russell moved to Los Angeles, where he learned guitar from Rick Nelson sideman James Burton and did studio work with Dorsey Burnette, Glen Campbell, and others. Russell played on nearly all of Phil Spector's hit sessions. He also played on Bob Lind's "Elusive Butterfly," Herb Alpert's "A Taste of Honey," and the Byrds' "Mr. Tambourine Man." In the mid-Sixties he arranged some hit records by Gary Lewis and the Playboys, including the gold "This Diamond Ring." He became a close friend of Delaney and Bonnie Bramlett and in 1967 built his own studio. He appeared on the TV rock show *Shindig!* occasionally in the Shindogs band. He also played on Gene Clark's 1967 album and arranged Harper's Bizarre's 1967 *Feelin' Groovy* LP.

In 1968 Russell teamed up with guitarist Marc Benno to make the critically acclaimed but commercially unsuccessful *Asylum Choir* LP. He then went on the road with Delaney and Bonnie's Friends Tour, during which time Joe Cocker recorded Russell's "Delta Lady" at Russell's studio, where Booker T. (of MG's fame) was also working. In 1969 Russell and A&M producer Denny Cordell founded Shelter Records. The following year Russell organized the backing band for Cocker's Mad Dogs and Englishmen Tour, an event and film that eventually made him as much of a star as Cocker. When Mercury seemed reluctant to release the second Asylum Choir LP, Russell bought the master tapes and released them himself on Shelter. He played piano on Bob Dylan's "Watching the River Flow" and "When I Paint My Masterpiece" and played at George Harrison's Concert for Bangla Desh in 1971.

From then on, Russell devoted his energies to his solo career, though he toured with the Rolling Stones in the early Seventies. He also helped out his wife, singer Mary McCreary, who appeared with him on *Wedding Album* and released her own *Butterflies in Heaven* LP on Shelter in 1973. His first U.K. solo tour, in 1970, found him backed by the ex-Cocker Grease Band. That year he also played on Dave Mason's *Alone Together* LP. In fall 1970 Russell hosted a highly praised hour-long music special on public TV station WNET in New York. *Leon Russell and the Shelter People* (#17, 1971) went gold, while *Carny* (#2, 1972) also went gold on the strength of its Top Twenty single "Tight Rope." *Leon Live* also went gold, and in 1976 Russell's "This Masquerade" (as performed by George Benson) won a Grammy.

After that, Russell returned to his southwestern roots, recording and performing with Willie Nelson and leading a bluegrass band, the New Grass Revival. In recent years, Russell's recordings have been few. Bruce Hornsby produced Russell's long-awaited major-label "comeback" album, *Anything Can Happen,* which went barely noticed. He continues to tour.

Bobby Rydell

Born Robert Ridarelli, April 26, 1942, Philadelphia, Pennsylvania
1961—*Bobby's Biggest Hits* (Cameo)   1962—*Biggest Hits, vol. 2.*

In the late Fifties and early Sixties, there was a preponderance of clean-cut American boys smoothing out the threatening rock & roll beat. The most successful of these was Pat Boone, but the geographical center for this sound was Philadelphia, home of Dick Clark's *American Bandstand,* Frankie Avalon, Fabian, and Bobby Rydell.

Unlike many of the others, who were no more than pretty faces, Rydell was a genuine musician. He began playing drums at the age of six and was a nightclub attraction at seven. At nine he entered Paul Whiteman's local *Teen Club* amateur TV show and remained as a regular for three years (Whiteman shortened Ridarelli's surname to Rydell). In 1957 Rydell became the drummer for local rock & roll combo Rocco and His Saints (which also featured Frankie Avalon on trumpet), but he soon struck out on his own. Three major labels turned him down, and Rydell's first two singles for his manager Frankie Day's label flopped. He recorded three more failed singles for Cameo-Parkway.

In 1959 "Kissin' Time" became a #11 hit, launching a four-year period in which Rydell scored 19 Top Thirty smashes, including "Volare" (#4), "Sway" (#14), "Swingin' School" (#5), and "Wild One" (#2), all in 1960, and "Forget Him" (#4, 1964). Beatlemania ended his career, as presaged by the film *Bye Bye Birdie,* in which he appeared as Hugo Peabody. Although his hitmaking days were behind him, Rydell continued to perform around the world. Since 1985, he has toured with Fabian and Avalon as one of the Golden Boys of Bandstand.

Mitch Ryder and the Detroit Wheels

Formed 1965, Detroit, Michigan

Mitch Ryder (b. William Levise Jr., Feb. 26, 1945, Hamtramck, Mich.), voc.; James McCarty (b. 1947), gtr.; Joseph Cubert (b. 1947; d. 1991), gtr.; Earl Elliot (b. 1947), bass; Johnny "Bee" Badanjek (b. 1948), drums.

1966—*Jenny Take a Ride* (New Voice); *Breakout* 1967—*Sock It to Me*   1987—*Greatest Hits* (Roulette) 1989—*Rev Up: The Best of Mitch Ryder and the Detroit Wheels* (Rhino).

Mitch Ryder solo: 1967—*All Mitch Ryder Hits* (New Voice); *All the Heavy Hits* (Crewe); *What Now My Love* (Dynavoice)   1968—*Mitch Ryder Sings the Hits* (New Voice)   1969—*The Detroit Memphis Experiment* (Dot)   1978—*How I Spent My Vacation* (Seeds and Stems)   1979—*Naked but Not Dead* 1981—*Live Talkies* (Line, Ger.); *Got Change for a Million*   1982—*Smart Ass*   1983—*Never Kick a Sleeping Dog* (Riva)   1986—*In the China Shop* (Line, Ger.)   1988—*Red Blood, White Mink*   1990— *The Beautiful Toulang Sunset*   1992—*La Gash* 1994—*Rite of Passage.*

With Detroit: 1971—*Detroit* (Paramount).

Mitch Ryder is a white soul shouter from Detroit who reached his peak of popularity in the late Sixties while fronting the Detroit Wheels. His career began well before that, though. Ryder, who was born in the Polish Detroit enclave of Hamtramck and whose father sang in a big band, had sung with local combos the Tempest and the Peps before forming Billy Lee and the Rivieras. In 1965 their stage act (opening for the Dave Clark Five) caught the attention of Four Seasons producer Bob Crewe, who signed them and gave Ryder the name he became famous with (supposedly picked out of a phone book) and rechristened the Rivieras the Detroit Wheels.

Their first single combined Little Richard's "Jenny Jenny" and Chuck Willis' "C. C. Rider" into "Jenny Take a Ride," which became a #10 hit in 1966, inspiring followup medleys "Devil with a Blue Dress On" and "Good Golly Miss Molly" (#4, 1966) and "Too Many Fish in the Sea" and "Three Little Fishes" (#24, 1967). Ryder's next big hit came with the hard-rocking "Sock It to Me Baby" (#6, 1967), which was banned in some markets for allegedly being too suggestive.

At the peak of the group's success, Ryder—under the guidance of Crewe—split from the Detroit Wheels. Former Wheels Rusty Day and Jim McCarty went on to form Cactus with Tim Bogert and Carmine Appice, late of Vanilla Fudge; McCarty then joined the Rockets (with Wheels drummer Johnny Badanjek), which had a #30 hit in 1979, "Oh Well."

Ryder's first attempt at a solo career met with less success, though "What Now My Love" (#30, 1967) be-

came his sixth (and last) Top Forty hit. In 1970 he and Badanjek formed a new seven-piece group known simply as Detroit. Its one album, released in 1971, contained a classic reworking of Lou Reed and the Velvet Underground's "Rock and Roll."

By 1973 Ryder had quit music and moved to Denver. He made a comeback in the late Seventies with several albums, all containing his own songs, a few of which alluded to homosexual experiences. In 1983, two years after Bruce Springsteen helped to revive the career of his idol Gary "U.S." Bonds, longtime Ryder fan John Cougar Mellencamp produced the singer's major-label comeback, *Never Kick a Sleeping Dog.* It produced a minor hit in "When You Were Mine," written by Prince, and also contained a duet with Marianne Faithfull.

Since then Ryder has continued to tour and record, particularly in Germany, where he is revered and has released 11 albums. Ryder was in the news in 1994, when his song "Mercy," from *Rite of Passage,* was revealed to be a tribute to "suicide doctor" Dr. Jack Kevorkian. Johnny Badanjek, after a stint in the late Seventies and Eighties with the Rockets, was back with his old boss before playing with the Romantics and his own group, the Notorious Johnnies. Joseph Cubert died of liver cancer in 1991.

The Rock and Roll Hall of Fame

The Rock and Roll Hall of Fame Foundation was organized in 1983. Atlantic Records cofounder Ahmet Ertegun, along with ROLLING STONE publisher Jann S. Wenner, Sire Records head Seymour Stein, former Elektra executive vice president Bob Krasnow, music business attorney Allen Grubman, and vice president/ assistant to the chairman of Atlantic Records Noreen Woods, established an organization that would both honor the artists and preserve the history of rock & roll and related genres.

Artists who are inducted into the Rock and Roll Hall of Fame at the foundation's annual awards ceremony are chosen after a lengthy, selective process; inductees are those artists who have made, in the opinion of the selection committee, a significant, long-term or lifetime contribution to the music. The only technical requirement for qualification is that an artist must have had "a commercially released record" at least 25 years before the date of induction. Nonperforming inductees, such as record company founders and songwriters, and artists whose careers predated the rock era but whose influence is deemed significant, are also honored in different categories.

Through the years the Hall of Fame's board of directors, honorary board, nominating committee, and U.K. advisory board have included members representing virtually every record label and major music publisher, as well as representatives from a range of related fields and organizations. More than 600 music industry professionals vote from a list of nominees to choose the final inductees. Some artists are nominated several times before being inducted, and the Rock and Roll Hall of Fame's selection process has not been without its critics. Except for the eighth annual induction ceremony, which was held in Los Angeles, in January 1993, all of the inductions have taken place at the Waldorf-Astoria Hotel in New York City.

In 1995 the foundation opened the Rock and Roll Hall of Fame and Museum in Cleveland, Ohio. Designed by architect I. M. Pei, the 150,000-square-foot complex houses memorabilia, photographic and interactive sound and video exhibits, a theater, and a library. It is the first and largest public collection of rock & roll–related materials in the world.

(Asterisks in the following lists indicate inductees who have entries in this book; names of those without individual entries are followed by a brief biographical sketch.)

Early Influences/Forefathers

Louis Armstrong (b. Daniel Louis Armstrong, Aug. 4, 1901, New Orleans, La.; d. July 6, 1971, New York City, N.Y.). Inducted 1990. Trumpeter, cornetist, singer, and bandleader Louis Armstrong was the best-known jazz musician in the world. Among serious jazz historians, Armstrong is considered a virtuoso, an artist whose talent for improvisation and fabled live performances led to his being be billed as "the world's greatest trumpet player" as early as 1926. To music lovers around the world, however, Armstrong was America's first ambassador of jazz and a popular entertainer whose frequent appearances on stage, in films, on television, and on the record charts (including his #1 1964 version of "Hello Dolly") made him a household name and perhaps the biggest black entertainer of his generation.

Charlie Christian. Inducted 1990.*
Woody Guthrie. Inducted 1988.*
Howlin' Wolf. Inducted 1991.*
The Ink Spots. Inducted 1989.*
Elmore James. Inducted 1992.*
Robert Johnson. Inducted 1986.*
Louis Jordan. Inducted 1987.*
Leadbelly. Inducted 1988.*
Les Paul. Inducted 1988.*
Professor Longhair. Inducted 1992.*

Ma Rainey (b. Gertrude Melissa Nix Pridgett, Apr. 26, 1886, Columbus, Ga.; d. Dec. 22, 1939, Columbus, Ga.). Inducted 1990. Ma Rainey was among the first women blues singers and was an important influence on such later artists as Bessie Smith. Initially a singer in the minstrel tradition, Rainey began performing the blues sometime around the turn of the century. From 1923 to 1929 she recorded profusely for Paramount, including such "race" hits as "See See Rider Blues" and "Deep Moanin' Blues." She retired in 1933, following the death of her sister.

Jimmie Rodgers. Inducted 1986.*
Bessie Smith. Inducted 1989.*
The Soul Stirrers (formed early 1930s, Texas): S. R. Crain, J. J. Farley, R. H. Harris, E. A. Rundless, T. L. Brewster, Sam Cooke. Inducted 1989. The Soul Stirrers provided a crucial link between classic gospel music and modern soul. A number of established vocal-group techniques—such as having the background vocalists repeat a word or phrase and ad-libbing lyrics—were innovations pioneered by R. H. Harris. By the time the group began recording in the late Forties, the Soul Stirrers had performed around the world and for President Franklin D. Roosevelt and Winston Churchill at the White House. Among the group's best-known songs is "Peace in the Valley." The Soul Stirrers featured a number of top soul and gospel singers, including Sam Cooke [see entry], Johnnie Taylor [see entry], James Medlock, Julius Cheeks, and R. B. Robinson, who later founded the Highway QCs.

T-Bone Walker. Inducted 1987.*
Dinah Washington. Inducted 1993.*
Hank Williams. Inducted 1987.*
Jimmy Yancey (b. February 20, 1898, Chicago, Ill.; d. Sep. 17, 1951, Chicago). Inducted 1986. Blues pianist and sometimes singer Jimmy Yancey refined the technique of using the left hand to create the rhythmic accompaniment that we today recognize as boogie-woogie. Although a well-known Chicago musician from an early age, Yancey retired at age 27 to become a groundskeeper for the Chicago White Sox and did not record until 1939. Among his most popular recordings are "State Street Special," "Death Letter Blues," and "Midnight Stomp."

Nonperformers

Paul Ackerman (b. 1908, New York City, N.Y.; d. Dec. 31, 1977, Queens, N.Y.). Inducted 1995. *Billboard*'s music editor of 30 years, Paul Ackerman guided the leading music trade newsweekly's coverage of R&B, C&W, and rock & roll, pioneering rock journalism. In addition, he was the executive director of the Songwriters Hall of Fame. He retired from *Billboard* in 1973.

Dave Bartholomew. (b. Dec. 24, 1920, Edgard, La.) Inducted 1991. An architect of the New Orleans sound of the Fifties, Dave Bartholomew produced many artists, most notably Fats Domino, with whom he also frequently collaborated on songs. His father, tuba player Louis Bartholomew, encouraged his interest in music from an early age, and while still in his teens, Dave played trumpet in Fats Pichon's band on a Mississippi riverboat.

Following World War II military service, he returned to New Orleans in 1946 and started his own band, playing R&B, jazz, and standards. Bartholomew hand-picked his talent and in the late Forties signed a young pianist named Fats Domino. Bartholomew recorded regularly (his "Country Boy" sold almost 100,000 in 1949) and began producing others. In the early Fifties he worked regularly for Imperial Records, where he recorded Domino. Their first release, "The Fat Man," was the first of many Top Ten hits ("Blueberry Hill," "I'm Walkin'") for Domino.

Bartholomew also produced or arranged singles by a variety of New Orleans–based artists, including Jewel King ("3 × 7 = 21"), Lloyd Price ("Lawdy Miss Clawdy"), Shirley and Lee ("I'm Gone"), Smiley Lewis ("I Hear You Knockin'"), and Bobby Mitchell ("Try Rock and Roll"). His band also backed up Little Richard on his early recordings. Though Bartholomew continued to record on his own through the early Sixties, his reputation is primarily based on his work for others. This producer, songwriter, and arranger still leads his own big band at the New Orleans Jazz & Heritage Festival and other events.

Ralph Bass (b. May 1, 1911, Bronx, N.Y.). Inducted 1991. A prodigious producer, Ralph Bass oversaw the birth of some of rock's greatest hits (T-Bone Walker's "Call It Stormy Monday," Hank Ballard and the Midnighters' "Work with Me Annie") and signed and guided some of its greatest artists (James Brown, the Dominoes, Etta James, Little Esther Phillips, the Johnny Otis Orchestra). From 1958 through 1976 he worked for Chess Records.

Leonard Chess (b. Mar. 12, 1917, Poland; d. Oct. 16, 1969, Chicago, Ill.). Inducted 1987. Almost from its inception in 1949, Chess Records has been synonymous with Chicago-style electric blues. Leonard and his younger brother Phil recorded a virtual who's who of early blues, R&B, and proto-rock pioneers: Muddy Waters, Howlin' Wolf, Sonny Boy Williamson (Rice Miller), Etta James, Little Walter, Chuck Berry, and Gene Ammons. Phil, whose interest was jazz, recorded Ramsey Lewis and Sonny Stitt, among others.

Dick Clark (b. Nov. 30, 1929, Mount Vernon, N.Y.). Inducted 1993. As the clean-cut host of the longest-lived pop-music television series, *American Bandstand,* Clark was something of a video pioneer, bringing rock & roll into living rooms across America. From its network debut in 1957 until 1988, his *American Bandstand* not only presented virtually every important rock act of its time but functioned as an arbiter of style in every aspect of teen life, from dances to fashion. Clark hosted and/or produced a number of spinoff programs as well as producing made-for-television films (*Elvis, The Early Beatles*) and game shows (*The $20,000 Pyramid*).

Lamont Dozier [See Holland-Dozier-Holland below.]

Ahmet Ertegun (b. July 31, 1923, Istanbul, Turkey). Inducted 1987. In 1947 producer-songwriter Ahmet Ertegun cofounded Atlantic Records. With a roster that included Ruth Brown, Ray Charles, LaVern Baker, Clyde McPhatter, Ben E. King, the Drifters, the Coasters, and Chuck Willis, Atlantic quickly rose to become an R&B powerhouse. Through the years Atlantic has been home to artists such as Aretha Franklin, Led Zeppelin, Cream, the Bee Gees, Wilson Pickett, Otis Redding, Sam and Dave, Booker T. and the MG's, Crosby, Stills, Nash and Young, and the Rolling Stones, among countless others.

Leo Fender (b. Aug. 10, 1909, Buena Park, Calif.; d. Mar. 21, 1991, Fullerton, Calif.). Inducted 1992. Striking the chord heard around the world, Leo Fender perfected the electric guitar and, in doing so, became essential to the history of rock & roll. In 1948 his Fender Broadcaster became the first mass-produced solid-body electric guitar, followed by the Fender Precision. In 1950 the Broadcaster was rechristened the Telecaster. In 1954 Fender introduced the Stratocaster, the guitar of choice of Buddy Holly and Jimi Hendrix, to name just two.

Alan Freed (b. Dec. 15, 1922, Johnstown, Pa.; d. Jan. 20, 1965, Palm Springs, Calif.). Inducted 1986. Disc jockey Alan Freed was the original Pied Piper of rock & roll. Beginning in 1951 while he was spinning records in Akron, Ohio, Freed introduced primarily white teenaged listeners to black R&B, expanding its audience and helping to prompt a social revolution. Freed pioneered integrated concert bills, and his Moondog Balls, first held in Cleveland, drew not only thousands of rock-happy teens but the wrath of concerned parents and civic officials everywhere. While some artists who ended up sharing with Freed copyrights and royalties of songs he played on the radio have criticized him, there is no question that early rock & roll had no more indomitable defender than Freed: "Anyone who says rock & roll is a passing fad or a flash in the pan has rocks in his head, dad!" By 1954 Freed had moved to New York City's WINS, and before long his high profile, unsavory business associates, and apparently conflicting business interests drew him into the congressional payola investigations. Freed eventually pleaded guilty to two counts of commercial bribery in late 1962. Two years later he died.

Milt Gabler (b. May 20, 1911). Inducted 1993. Gabler was a preeminent producer of the prerock and early rock era. His credits include Louis Jordan, Lionel Hampton, Bill Haley and His Comets, the Weavers, Louis Armstrong, Billie Holiday, and Ella Fitzgerald.

Gerry Goffin (b. Feb. 11, 1939, Queens, N.Y.). Inducted 1990. With his then-wife Carole King, Gerry Goffin cowrote and/or produced a number of early rock & roll classics: the Shirelles' "Will You Love Me Tomorrow?," Bobby Vee's "Take Good Care of My Baby," Little Eva's "The Loco-motion," the Drifters' "Up on the Roof," the Animals' "Don't Bring Me Down," Aretha Franklin's

"(You Make Me Feel Like) A Natural Woman," and the Monkees' "Pleasant Valley Sunday," among many others.

Berry Gordy Jr. (b. Nov. 28, 1929, Detroit, Mich.). Inducted 1988. Songwriter, producer, and record mogul Berry Gordy Jr. founded and headed the most successful black-owned record company in history, Motown. A fairly successful songwriter (for Jackie Wilson, among others), Gordy started Motown with an $800 family loan in 1959. Within just five years he had built a roster that included not only performers such as the Supremes, the Marvelettes, the Miracles, the Temptations, the Four Tops, Marvin Gaye, Mary Wells, and Stevie Wonder but some of the most important songwriters and producers of the age, namely Smokey Robinson, Holland-Dozier-Holland, Ashford and Simpson, and Norman Whitfield. Later signings included the Commodores and Lionel Richie and the Jackson 5. Not content with hit records alone, Gordy drove Motown and its artists to conquer realms of show business formerly closed to "mere" pop stars, revolutionizing black pop stardom, and American music, forever. Gordy sold the company in 1988.

Bill Graham (b. Wolfgang Grajonca, Jan. 8, 1931, Berlin, Ger.; d. Oct. 25, 1991, near Vallejo, Calif.). Inducted 1992. Through his involvement in the San Francisco music scene of the late Sixties and control of the Fillmores East and West, promoter/manager Bill Graham revolutionized rock music in terms of both art and commerce, transforming major rock concerts from haphazard, potentially disastrous gatherings to smoothly run events. He oversaw some of the most dauntingly large and complex concert tours in history, including those by the Rolling Stones, Bob Dylan, and the Grateful Dead as well as the Amnesty International Concerts and Live Aid. In the process he became an outspoken critic of greedy artists and careless promoters (he was especially vocal in the tragic aftermath of Altamont) as well as the leading figure in merchandising. He was a co-founder of the Rock and Roll Hall of Fame. He died in a helicopter crash en route from a concert he had promoted.

Holland-Dozier-Holland. Inducted 1990. **Brian Holland** (b. Feb. 15, 1941, Detroit, Mich.). **Eddie Holland** (b. Oct. 30, 1939, Detroit). **Lamont Dozier** (b. June 16, 1941, Detroit). Songwriter-producers Brian and Eddie Holland and Lamont Dozier were key architects of the highly polished, beat-driven Motown Sound. Among their phenomenal 28 Top Ten hits from 1963 and 1966 were the Supremes' "Stop! In the Name of Love," "Where Did Our Love Go," "Baby Love," and "I Hear a Symphony"; the Four Tops' "Baby I Need Your Loving," "It's the Same Old Song," "I Can't Help Myself," and "Reach Out, I'll Be There"; and Martha and the Vandellas' "Jimmy Mack" and "Nowhere to Run." After leaving Motown in 1967, the trio founded Invictus/Hot Wax, where they produced Freda Payne, the Chairmen of the Board, and Honey Cone.

Carole King. Inducted 1990.*

Leiber and Stoller. Inducted 1987. **Jerome Leiber** (b. Apr. 25, 1933, Baltimore, Md.). **Michael Stoller** (b. Mar. 13, 1933, Belle Harbor, N.Y.). Songwriter-producers Jerry Leiber and Mike Stoller were not even 20 when they wrote their first hits, "K. C. Loving" and "Hound Dog." Through an independent production deal with Atlantic, the pair wrote and produced hits for the Coasters ("Young Blood," "Yakety Yak," "Poison Ivy," "Charlie Brown"); they wrote such Elvis Presley classics as "Loving You" and "Jailhouse Rock." Through the years they have produced a range of other groups, from the Dixie Cups and the Drifters to Peggy Lee and Procol Harum.

Sam Phillips (b. Jan. 5, 1923, Florence, Ala.). Inducted 1986. Sun Record Company owner Sam Phillips was one of the first white men to record black blues and R&B artists (among them Howlin' Wolf, B. B. King, Jackie Brenston, Rufus Thomas, Junior Parker), but his Memphis label is best known as the cradle of rockabilly. Beginning in the mid-Fifties Phillips developed a roster of artists whose cross-pollination of rhythm & blues and country & western yielded one of the wildest and most important hybrids of early rock & roll: Jerry Lee Lewis, Carl Perkins, Roy Orbison, Charlie Rich, Carl Smith, Billy Lee Riley, Johnny Cash, and of course Elvis Presley, whose contract Phillips sold to RCA in 1955 for $35,000.

Doc Pomus (b. Jerome Solon Felder, June 27, 1925, Brooklyn, N.Y.; d. Mar. 14, 1991, New York City, N.Y.). Inducted 1992. Doc Pomus began his career as a white blues singer in the Forties, but it was as a songwriter that he left an indelible mark on early rock & roll. From "Save the Last Dance for Me" and "Viva Las Vegas" (cowritten with partner Mort Shuman) to "There Must Be a Better World Somewhere" and "From the Heart," Pomus created a songwriting legacy that is unequaled.

Phil Spector. Inducted 1989.*

Jerry Wexler (b. Jan. 10, 1917, New York City, N.Y.). Inducted 1987. Producer Jerry Wexler joined Atlantic Records in 1953 and there oversaw the recording of countless classics, including Ray Charles' "What'd I Say" and Aretha Franklin's "Chain of Fools." His credits span both rock's history and its diversity to include the Drifters, Big Joe Turner, the Coasters, Dr. John, Willie Nelson, Allen Toussaint, Bob Dylan, Kim Carnes, Professor Longhair, and Delaney and Bonnie.

Lifetime Achievement

Nesuhi Ertegun (b. Istanbul, Turkey; d. Jul. 15, 1989, New York City, N.Y.). Inducted 1991. Nesuhi Ertegun had already established himself as a record producer and concert promoter before he joined his brother Ahmet and Jerry Wexler at Atlantic Records. There he focused his attention on the label's jazz roster and produced records by John Coltrane, Charles Mingus, Ornette Coleman, Bobby Short, Mabel Mercer, and Herbie Mann. He also worked with pop artists, such as Bobby Darin and Roberta Flack. In later years he headed Atlantic Records' international operations and later founded and headed WEA International before he founded EastWest Records in 1988.

John Hammond Sr. (b. Dec. 10, 1910, New York City, N.Y.; d. July 10, 1987, New York City). Inducted 1986. As a producer and talent scout John Hammond discovered and/or produced some of America's most important artists. A music journalist and later vice president of the NAACP, Hammond was a champion of racial integration; his "From Spirituals to Swing" concerts (1938–39) at Carnegie Hall were among the first to present black artists in a formal concert setting. He signed Billie Holiday, Count Basie, Lester Young, and Charlie Christian to Columbia Records and later Pete Seeger, Aretha Franklin, Bob Dylan (early on dubbed "Hammond's folly"), and Bruce Springsteen. He also oversaw Columbia's Seventies repackagings of archival recordings by Robert Johnson and Bessie Smith, among others.

Performers

The Allman Brothers. Inducted 1995.*
The Animals. Inducted 1994.*
LaVern Baker. Inducted 1991.*
Hank Ballard. Inducted 1990.*
The Band. Inducted 1994.*
The Beach Boys. Inducted 1988.*
The Beatles. Inducted 1988.*
Chuck Berry. Inducted 1986.*
Bobby "Blue" Bland. Inducted 1992.*
Booker T. and the MG's. Inducted 1992.*
James Brown. Inducted 1986.*
Ruth Brown. Inducted 1993.*
The Byrds. Inducted 1991.*
Johnny Cash. Inducted 1992.*
Ray Charles. Inducted 1986.*
The Coasters. Inducted 1987.*
Eddie Cochran. Inducted 1987.*
Sam Cooke. Inducted 1986.*
Cream. Inducted 1993.*
Creedence Clearwater Revival. Inducted 1993.*
Bobby Darin. Inducted 1990.*
Bo Diddley. Inducted 1987.*
Dion DiMucci. Inducted 1989.*
Fats Domino. Inducted 1986.*
The Doors. Inducted 1993.*
The Drifters. Inducted 1988.*
Bob Dylan. Inducted 1988.*
Duane Eddy. Inducted 1994.*
The Everly Brothers. Inducted 1986.*

The Four Seasons. Inducted 1990.*
The Four Tops. Inducted 1990.*
Aretha Franklin. Inducted 1987.*
Marvin Gaye. Inducted 1987.*
The Grateful Dead. Inducted 1994.*
Al Green. Inducted 1995.*
Bill Haley. Inducted 1987.*
The Jimi Hendrix Experience. Inducted 1992.*
Buddy Holly. Inducted 1986.*
John Lee Hooker. Inducted 1991.*
The Impressions. Inducted 1991.*
The Isley Brothers. Inducted 1992.*
Etta James. Inducted 1993.*
Elton John. Inducted 1994.*
Janis Joplin. Inducted 1995.*
B. B. King. Inducted 1987.*
The Kinks. Inducted 1990.*
Led Zeppelin. Inducted 1995.*
John Lennon. Inducted 1994.*
Jerry Lee Lewis. Inducted 1986.*
Little Richard. Inducted 1986.*
Frankie Lymon and the Teenagers. Inducted 1993.*
Bob Marley. Inducted 1994.*
Martha and the Vandellas. Inducted 1995.*
Clyde McPhatter. Inducted 1987. [See the Drifters entry.]
Van Morrison. Inducted 1993.*
Rick Nelson. Inducted 1987.*
Roy Orbison. Inducted 1987.*
The Orioles. Inducted 1995.*
Carl Perkins. Inducted 1987.*
Wilson Pickett. Inducted 1991.*
The Platters. Inducted 1990.*
Elvis Presley. Inducted 1986.*
Otis Redding. Inducted 1989.*
Jimmy Reed. Inducted 1991.*
Smokey Robinson. Inducted 1987.*
The Rolling Stones. Inducted 1989.*
Sam and Dave. Inducted 1992.*
Simon and Garfunkel. Inducted 1990.*
Sly and the Family Stone. Inducted 1993.*
Rod Stewart. Inducted 1994.*
The Supremes. Inducted 1988.*
The Temptations. Inducted 1989.*
Ike and Tina Turner. Inducted 1991.*
Big Joe Turner. Inducted 1987.*
Muddy Waters. Inducted 1987.*
The Who. Inducted 1990.*
Jackie Wilson. Inducted 1987.*
Stevie Wonder. Inducted 1989.*
The Yardbirds. Inducted 1992.*
Neil Young. Inducted 1995.*
Frank Zappa. Inducted 1995.*

S

Sade

Born Helen Folasade Adu, January 16, 1959, Ibadan, Nigeria

1985—*Diamond Life* (Portrait); *Promise*   1988— *Stronger Than Pride* (Epic)   1992—*Love Deluxe* 1994—*The Best of Sade*.

Although Sade is officially a group, for all intents and purposes vocalist Sade (pronounced *shar-day*) is Sade. Born in Nigeria, where her Nigerian father was an economics professor and her English mother a nurse, Sade Adu (her stage name) was educated in London. After studying fashion design and later modeling briefly, Sade landed a spot as backup singer with the British R&B band Pride. There she formed a writing partnership with Pride's guitarist/saxophonist Stewart Matthewman; together, backed by Pride's rhythm section, they began doing their own sets at Pride gigs. Sade's elegant, exotic look and the cool, jazz-inflected approach of her low-keyed singing immediately garnered her considerable attention. In 1983 Sade and Matthewman split from Pride along with keyboardist Andrew Hale and bassist Paul Denman and formed Sade; they got a record deal late that year.

Although Sade's 1984 U.K. debut, *Diamond Life*, with its single "Your Love Is King," quickly became a hit in Britain, the album wasn't released in the U.S. until 1985. Propelled by the bossa nova–tinged "Smooth Operator"

(#5), *Diamond Life* (#5, 1985) rose to the Top Ten; its popularity set the stage for the influx of "Quiet Storm" vocalists spearheaded by Anita Baker, among others. *Diamond Life* featured strong original material by Sade and Matthewman, including "Hang On to Your Love" and "When Am I Going to Make a Living" as well as an imaginative remake of Timmy Thomas' 1971 hit "Why Can't We Live Together." *Diamond Life* had international sales of over six million copies, becoming one of the top-selling debut recordings of the Eighties and the best-selling debut ever by a British female vocalist. In 1985 her stature as a major pop star was confirmed when Sade appeared at Wembley Stadium as part of Live Aid.

At the end of the year, *Promise* was released; the album went to #1 in the U.S., spawning the hits "The Sweetest Taboo" (#3) and "Never as Good as the First Time" (#8). Sade had a small part in the 1986 Julien Temple film *Absolute Beginners* and appears on its soundtrack.

Critics faulted 1988's *Stronger Than Pride* (#7) for musical sameness and emotional distance. Four years passed before the release of *Love Deluxe* (#3), whose brisk sales proved that Sade hadn't lost her appeal. An American tour to promote the release was also well received. *The Best of Sade* went Top Ten.

Staff Sergeant Barry Sadler

Born 1940, New Mexico; died November 5, 1989, Tennessee

1966—Ballads of the Green Berets (RCA); The "A" Team.

While recuperating from a leg wound suffered in Vietnam, Staff Sergeant Barry Sadler began writing what would become the #1 single of 1966, the patriotic novelty "The Ballad of the Green Berets." The song, inspired by Robin Moore's best-selling book *The Green Berets* (Sadler's face is on the cover of the paperback edition), was written by Moore (lyrics) and Sadler (music). The LP of the same name also went to #1 and contained such Sadler compositions as "Letter from Vietnam," "Saigon," "Trooper's Lament," and "Salute to the Nurses." Both the single and the LP were certified gold soon after their release.

Sadler wasn't heard from again until December 1978, when he was involved in a Nashville shooting incident that left local songwriter Lee Bellamy, 51, dead. The fracas was apparently over a woman; no charges were filed against Sadler. In mid-1981 Sadler was involved in another shooting incident, in Memphis, though the victim—an ex-business partner of his—wasn't killed. Sadler, in fact, justified his innocent plea by explaining, "I'm a Green Beret. If I'd shot him, he'd be dead." He wrote a series of adventure novels whose hero was a mercenary. He also established a trust fund for Vietnamese orphans.

In 1988 Sadler was shot in the head during a robbery attempt while he was entering a cab in Guatemala. Exactly what he was doing there remains a bit of a mystery. He claimed to have been there training anti-Communist contras; others have disputed that. He suffered some degree of brain damage, and as a result of the shooting was left with some paralysis as well. He died of heart failure the following year at age 49.

Doug Sahm: See Sir Douglas Quintet; Texas Tornados

Buffy Sainte-Marie

Born February 20, 1941, Saskatchewan, Canada
1964—It's My Way (Vanguard)   1965—Many a Mile 1966—Little Wheel Spin and Spin   1967—Fire, Fleet and Candlelight   1968—I'm Gonna Be a Country Girl Again   1969—Illuminations   1970—The Best of Buffy Sainte-Marie   1971—She Used to Wanna Be a Ballerina; The Best of Buffy Sainte-Marie, vol. 2   1972—Moon Shot   1973—Quiet Places   1974—Natural North American Child; Buffy (MCA)   1975—Changing Woman   1976—Sweet America (ABC)   1992—Coincidence and Likely Stories (Ensign/Chrysalis).

Born of Cree Indian parents and adopted by a white family as an infant, Buffy Sainte-Marie is the most famous Native American artist in pop music. Her unique vibratoed vocal delivery made her records something of an acquired taste. However, she is best known for the versions of her songs made hits by others artists—including "Until It's Time for You to Go," "The Universal Soldier," "Cod'ine," and "Up Where We Belong," which she cowrote—and decades of activism on behalf of Native Americans.

Sainte-Marie was discovered singing in a Boston coffeehouse by Vanguard producer Maynard Solomon. Her debut LP contained the protest song "The Universal Soldier," which became a classic of the genre, mainly through well-known cover versions by Donovan and Glen Campbell. Elvis Presley had a Top Forty hit in 1972 (#5, U.K.) with her "Until It's Time for You to Go." Though she began as a solo folksinger, Sainte-Marie infused rock, classical, orchestral, and Native American styles into her albums. *She Used to Wanna Be a Ballerina* featured backing from Ry Cooder and Neil Young and Crazy Horse.

Sainte-Marie, later married arranger, composer, and producer Jack Nitzsche, with whom she cowrote (with Will Jennings) "Up Where We Belong," a #1 1982 hit for Joe Cocker and Jennifer Warnes. From 1976 to 1981 she was a familiar face to viewers of *Sesame Street*. Following *Sweet America*, Sainte-Marie did not record again for another 15 years until *Coincidence and Likely Stories*. During that time, she continued working on behalf of Native Americans, giving benefit concerts, speaking, and founding the Nihewan Foundation for Native North American scholarships. She acted in the 1994 film *The Broken Circle*.

The Saints

Formed 1975, Brisbane, Australia
Chris Bailey, voc., gtr.; Ed Kuepper, gtr.; Kym Bradshaw, bass; Ivor Hay, drums.
1977—(– Bradshaw; + Alisdair Ward, bass) (I'm) Stranded (Sire)   1978—Eternally Yours (– Kuepper) 1987—(– Ward; – Hay; + Archie Larizza, bass; + Baz Francis, gtr.; + Iain Shedden, drums; + Joe Chiofalo, kybds.) All Fools Day (TVT)   1988—Prodigal Son.

The first Australian punk band to gain renown in Britain and the U.S., the Saints are best remembered for their debut single, a frantic buzz-saw of sound, "(I'm) Stranded."

Formed by Chris Bailey, the Saints recorded "Stranded" on their own label in 1976. After a rave review in the British music weekly *Sounds*, they were signed by EMI. Lead guitarist Ed Kuepper left in 1978 (he later formed the Laughing Clowns), and the band's focus changed to a more traditional, R&B-inflected rock & roll. In 1979 the Saints broke up, but Bailey kept the name, releasing several albums as the Saints and two solo records on French and British labels.

The original Saints, minus Kuepper, re-formed in 1984. In 1987 Bailey fired the band again. That year, recording with a new lineup, the Saints had their first American release (*All Fools Day*) in nine years. In 1990 Kuepper formed the Aints to protest Bailey's continuing use of the Saints name and material. Kuepper has also released numerous solo albums.

Ryuichi Sakamoto

Born January 17, 1952, Tokyo, Japan
1978—*Thousand Knives of Asia* (Denon)   1980—*B–2 Unit* (Alfa-Island)   1981—*Left Handed Dream* (Epic) 1983—*Merry Christmas Mr. Lawrence* soundtrack (MCA)   1985—*Esperanto* (Midi, Jap.); *Futurista* 1986—*Media Bahn Live*; *Illustrated Musical Encyclopedia*   1986—*Piano One* (Private Music)   1988— *No Boundaries* (Columbia); *Neo Geo* (Epic); *The Last Emperor* soundtrack (with David Byrne and Cong Su) (Virgin Movie Music)   1989—*Playing the Orchestra Live* (Virgin)   1989—*Gruppo Musicale* 1990—*Beauty*; *The Handmaid's Tale* soundtrack (GNP Crescendo)   1991—*Peachboy* (Windham Hill) 1992—*Heartbeat* (Virgin); *High Heels* soundtrack (Antilles)   1994—*Sweet Revenge* (Elektra).

Ryuichi Sakamoto emerged in the Eighties with "Neo Geo," a high-tech style of world music that fuses Asian and Western classical elements with other global sounds. Founder of Yellow Magic Orchestra, a techno-pop trio, the composer, producer, and actor went on to make influential film scores and pop works.

Taking up piano at age three, Sakamoto played in jazz bands in high school; his cosmopolitan upbringing exposed him to Beethoven, the Beatles, and John Cage, as well as to the films of Pier Paolo Pasolini and Jean-Luc Godard. After studying electronic music at the University of Art of Tokyo, he founded Yellow Magic Orchestra in 1978. Their single "Computer Game (Theme from *The Invaders*)," became a 1980 Top 20 U.K. hit; with two Japanese Top Ten albums, the trio, known for a robotic theatricality indebted to Kraftwerk, were hugely popular at home.

During Y.M.O.'s five-year career Sakamoto released two solo albums; his subsequent work took a genre-crossing approach. Characterized by perfectionist zeal (*Illustrated Musical Encyclopedia*, with Thomas Dolby, took 20 months to record), his output features diverse guests (Iggy Pop, Bootsy Collins, and Tony Williams on *Neo Geo*) and wide range (with David Sylvian and Ingrid Chavez, 1992's *Heartbeat* incorporates Russian rap, New York dance music, and African rhythms).

Acting with David Bowie in *Merry Christmas Mr. Lawrence*, Sakamoto also penned its score; his collaboration with David Byrne and Chinese musician Cong Su on *The Last Emperor* earned an Oscar. Sakamoto's other

Ryuichi Sakamoto

projects include music for performance artist Molissa Fenley (*Esperanto*); the score for Pedro Almadovar's *High Heels*; a piece for the 1992 Olympics; and *Beauty*, an album featuring his English-singing debut and contributions by Brian Wilson, Robbie Robertson, Arto Lindsay, Youssou N'Dour, and his wife, Akiko Yano. Sakamoto's 1994 album, *Sweet Revenge*, featured guests Holly Johnson (Frankie Goes to Hollywood) and Roddy Frame (Aztec Camera).

Salt-n-Pepa

Formed 1985, Queens, New York
Cheryl "Salt" James (b. Mar. 8, ca. 1964, Brooklyn, N.Y.), voc.; Sandy "Pepa" Denton (b. Nov. 9, ca. 1961, Kingston, Jamaica), voc.; Pamela Greene, DJ. 1986—*Hot, Cool and Vicious* (Next Plateau)   1988— (– Greene; + Deidre "Dee Dee" "Spinderella" Roper [b. Aug. 3, New York City, N.Y.], DJ) *A Salt with a Deadly Pepa*   1990—*Blacks' Magic*   1991—*A Blitz of Salt-n-Pepa Hits*   1993—*Very Necessary* (Next Plateau/London).

Salt-n-Pepa was one of the first rap groups to cross over to the pop charts and one of the few in which the rappers and their DJ were women. As of 1995, they were the only female rappers to have three platinum albums. Cheryl "Salt" James and Sandy "Pepa" Denton were working at Sears when coworker Hurby "Luv Bug" Azor (James' boyfriend) asked them to rap on a project for his audio production class at New York City's Center for Media Arts. The song, "The Show Stoppa," was an answer to

Doug E. Fresh and Slick Rick's "The Show." It was released as a single by Pop Art Records, credited to the band Super Nature, and became a minor hit, reaching #46 on the R&B charts.

Now calling themselves Salt-n-Pepa, after a line in "The Show Stoppa," the duo signed with the rap independent Next Plateau. Azor, who became their manager, produced *Hot, Cool and Vicious* and is credited on the album with writing all the songs, although the rappers have said they contributed lyrics. Three of the album's singles, "Chick on the Side," "My Mike Sounds Nice," and "Tramp," all charted moderately on the R&B charts. But then Cameron Paul, a DJ at San Francisco station KMEL, remixed "Push It" (the flipside of "Tramp"); after its release, it peaked on the pop charts at #19 in 1988. "Push It" was nominated for a Grammy in 1988, but Salt-n-Pepa and other rappers boycotted the ceremony when the rap awards were not presented in the telecast. In June that year the group played "Freedomfest: Nelson Mandela's 70th Birthday Celebration" at London's Wembley Stadium.

Azor again produced *A Salt with a Deadly Pepa*, a solid if not earthshaking followup. The album includes "Shake Your Thang," a reworking of the Isley Brothers' "It's Your Thang" (performed with D.C. go-go band EU) and a cover of "Twist and Shout," as well as "Get Up Everybody (Get Up)" and a remix of "Let the Rhythm Run," their contribution to the *Colors* soundtrack. Unfortunately, plans to record with Joan Jett, à la Run–D.M.C. and Aerosmith's collaboration, didn't pan out. *A Blitz of Salt-n-Pepa Hits* featured dance remixes of the band's hits.

Blacks' Magic (#38 pop, #15 R&B, 1990) was a huge success for Salt-n-Pepa artistically and commercially. The group, which had been accused by some rap fans of selling out, paid tribute to Afrocentricity in the album's title and cover art. Alongside Azor and guest producer Steevee-O, Salt produced or coproduced four tracks, and DJ Spinderella produced one. One Salt cut, "Expression" (#26, 1990), went gold before it even entered the Hot 100, thanks to eight weeks at the top of the rap chart. The album also included the hit "Let's Talk About Sex" (#13, 1991), which Salt-n-Pepa rerecorded in 1993 as "Let's Talk About AIDS" for a campaign to educate women about safe sex. That year the band played at the President Clinton's Inaugural Youth Ball, where they met their fan Chelsea Clinton.

Salt-n-Pepa had been having increasing disagreements with Next Plateau and Azor, with whom James was no longer romantically linked. The group demanded larger financial and creative roles in their career and, over Azor's objections, signed with London/PolyGram. Salt-n-Pepa then set much of the creative direction on the popular *Very Necessary* (#4 pop, #6 R&B, 1993), which showcased the women as sophisticated but tough rap divas. On songs like "Shoop" (#4 pop, #3 R&B,

1993) and "Whatta Man" (#3 pop and R&B, 1994), which featured En Vogue on the chorus, the group reveled in their sexuality. The album ends with a public service announcement about AIDS performed by a group of young actors from Boston.

Salt and Pepa both have film deals. The group performed the song "Start Me Up" in 1992's *Stay Tuned* (the soundtrack was released by Morgan Creek) and Salt also starred in *Who's the Man?* the next year. In 1995 Salt-n-Pepa were awarded the Best Rap Performance Grammy for "None of Your Business" (#32 pop, #57 R&B, 1994).

Sam and Dave

Samuel Moore, b. Oct. 12, 1935, Miami, Fla.; David Prater, b. May 9, 1937, Ocilla, Ga.; d. Apr. 9, 1988, Ga.
1966—*Sam and Dave* (Roulette); *Hold On I'm Comin'* (Stax); *Double Dynamite* 1967—*Soul Man* 1968— *I Thank You* (Atlantic) 1969—*The Best of Sam and Dave* 1975—*Back Atcha* (United Artists).

Sam Moore and Dave Prater's string of soul and pop hits made them the Sixties' most successful black vocal duo. Both had grown up singing in church, and each was a regular solo performer in southern clubs before they met in 1961 at Miami's King of Hearts club: Moore was emceeing an amateur-night show, and when Prater forgot the words to a Jackie Wilson song, "Doggin' Around," Moore coached him the rest of the way. The pair became a popular club attraction in the Miami area and soon signed to Roulette. They moved to Atlantic in 1965, though executive Jerry Wexler arranged for their records to be recorded at and released by Stax Records. At Stax Sam and Dave quickly became the favorite foils of the production/songwriting team of Isaac Hayes and David Porter. Their first single, "You Don't Know Like I Know" (#7 R&B), in 1966, began a string of high-powered soul hits. Later in 1966 "Hold On! I'm Comin'" went to #1 on the R&B chart (#21 pop), while "Said I Wasn't Gonna Tell Nobody" (#8 R&B) and "You Got Me Hummin'" (#7 R&B) rounded out a successful year. In 1967 Sam and Dave (nicknamed "Double Dynamite") gained their widest exposure with "When Something Is Wrong with My Baby" (#2 R&B) and the epochal "Soul Man" (#2 pop, #1 R&B). The next year they scored their last major hit, "I Thank You" (#9 pop, #4 R&B).

The duo's frantic live show was one of pop music's most exciting, yet offstage Moore and Prater barely spoke to each other. After breaking up in 1970, they reunited several times. In 1979 the Blues Brothers' success with "Soul Man" rekindled interest in them, and the duo received bookings at many clubs nationwide. But they split up for good after a New Year's Eve 1981 show at San Francisco's Old Waldorf. Prater then took to the road with another Sam: vocalist Sam Daniels.

In a 1983 interview with the *Los Angeles Herald Examiner,* Moore admitted that he had been a drug addict for 12 years and that the main reason for his feud with his ex-partner was that he'd "lost respect" for him after Prater shot his own wife during a 1968 domestic dispute. Prater escaped prosecution in that instance, but in 1987 he was arrested for selling crack to an undercover cop and sentenced to three years' probation. He died the following year in a car accident. Moore contributed vocals to Bruce Springsteen's *Human Touch* LP in 1992, the same year Sam and Dave were inducted into the Rock and Roll Hall of Fame.

Richie Sambora: See Bon Jovi

Joe Sample: See the Crusaders

Sam the Sham and the Pharaohs

Formed early 1960s, Texas
Sam the Sham (b. Domingo Samudio, 1940, Dallas, Tex.), voc., organ; David Martin, bass; Ray Stinnet, gtr.; Jerry Patterson, drums; Butch Gibson, sax.
1965—*Wooly Bully* (MGM)   1966—*Li'l Red Riding Hood*   1970—*Sam, Hard and Heavy* (Atlantic) 1985—*Pharaohization: The Best of Sam the Sham and the Pharaohs* (Rhino).

Sam the Sham and his turban-clad Pharaohs achieved brief but massive success in the mid-Sixties with their rollicking Tex-Mex rock & roll. Following the moderately successful independent single "Haunted House," Sam the Sham moved to MGM, where he hit it big with his second record, "Wooly Bully." It sold three million copies in 1965, rising to #2.

For the next two years the Pharaohs continued to rack up hit singles: "Juju Hand" (#22, 1965), "Ring Dang Doo" (#33, 1965), the million-selling "Li'l Red Riding Hood" (#2, 1966), and its followup, "The Hair on My Chinny Chin-Chin" (#22, 1966), among them. In 1967 Sam broke up the band and went solo, reverting to his given name, Domingo Samudio.

Though his years of stardom may be behind him, he did win a Grammy Award in 1970 for his liner notes to the LP *Sam, Hard and Heavy,* which featured the work of a session guitarist named Duane Allman. Samudio resurfaced in 1982, providing two original songs, sung in Spanish, to the soundtrack of *The Border.* Later on he became a street preacher in Memphis. "Wooly Bully," still a bar-band standard, was covered in 1981 by Joan Jett.

David Sanborn

Born July 30, 1945, Tampa, Florida
1975—*Taking Off* (Warner Bros.)   1976—*David Sanborn*   1977—*David Sanborn Band*   1978—*Heart to*

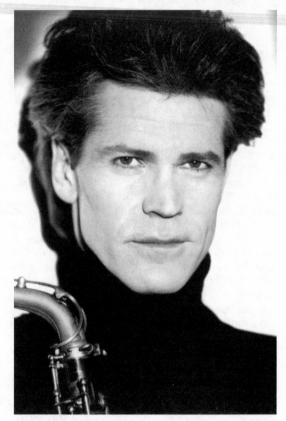

David Sanborn

Heart   1980—*Hideaway*   1981—*Voyeur*   1982—*As We Speak*   1983—*Backstreet*   1984—*Let It Speak, Love and Happiness; Straight to the Heart*   1987—*A Change of Heart*   1988—*Close-Up* (Reprise) 1991—*Another Hand* (Elektra)   1992—*Upfront* 1994—*Hearsay.*

Alto saxophonist David Sanborn has one of the most recognizable instrumental voices in pop music. As a child Sanborn suffered from polio and breathing ailments, neither of which averted his early interest in the saxophone. After moving to St. Louis, the teenaged Sanborn began playing with local R&B and jazz musicians.

In 1967 Sanborn joined the Paul Butterfield Blues Band; Sanborn played with the group at Woodstock and can be heard on *In My Own Dream, The Resurrection of Pigboy Crabshaw,* and *Live.* Leaving Butterfield, Sanborn played in the bands of a number of top musicians, including Stevie Wonder, joining him for the 1972 Rolling Stones tour for which Wonder was an opening act. (Sanborn can also be heard on Wonder's *Talking Book.*)

When Sanborn went freelance, he became the author of the ubiquitous saxophone sound of the Seventies. His classic work on James Taylor's "How Sweet It Is to Be

Loved by You" and David Bowie's "Young Americans" exemplifies the mixture of Hank Crawford–influenced R&B finesse and bold, rock-oriented grit that has become Sanborn's calling card. Sanborn can also be heard on recordings by the Eagles, Bruce Springsteen, Paul Simon, and the Rolling Stones.

Sanborn's own recording career began in 1975 and has thrived since. (He has four gold records, one platinum, and five Grammy awards.) From 1988 to 1990, Sanborn hosted the innovative television show *Night Music,* which presented a widely eclectic blend of artists.

More recently Sanborn gained greater respect among the jazz and avant-garde music community: his *Another Hand* (1991) featured noted jazzmen Bill Frisell and Charlie Haden; Sanborn also recorded with avant-garde saxophonist Tim Berne. Sanborn remains in the public eye through his frequent guest appearances with Paul Shaffer's band on *The Late Show With David Letterman.*

Santana/Carlos Santana

Formed 1967, San Francisco, California
Original lineup: Carlos Santana (b. July 20, 1947, Autlán de Navarro, Mex.), gtr., voc., perc.; Gregg Rolie (b. June 17, 1947, Seattle, Wash.), kybds., voc.; David Brown (b. Feb. 15, 1947, N.Y.), bass; Michael Shrieve (b. July 6, 1949, San Francisco), drums; Mike Carabello (b. Nov. 18, 1947, San Francisco), perc.; José Chepito Areas (b. July 25, 1946, León, Nicaragua), perc.
1969—*Santana* (Columbia)   1970—*Abraxas* 1971—(+ Neal Schon [b. Feb. 27, 1954]; + Coke Escovedo [b. Thomas Escovedo, Apr. 30, 1941, Calif.; d. July 13, 1985, Calif.], perc.) *Santana III* (– Brown; + Tom Rutley, bass)   1972—*Caravanserai*   1973— *Welcome*   1974—*Greatest Hits; Borboletta*   1976— *Amigos; Festival*   1977—*Moonflower*   1978—*Inner Secrets*   1979—*Marathon*   1981—*Zebop!*   1983— *Shangó*   1985—*Beyond Appearances*   1987—*Freedom*   1988—*Viva Santana!*   1990—*Spirits Dancing in the Flesh*   1991—*Lotus.*
Carlos Santana solo: 1972—*Carlos Santana with Buddy Miles Live* (Columbia)   1973—*Love, Devotion, Surrender* (with John McLaughlin)   1974—*Illuminations* (with Turiya Alice Coltrane) 1979—*Oneness; Silver Dreams—Golden Reality* 1980—*The Swing of Delight*   1983—*Havana Moon* 1987—*Blues for Salvador*   1992—*Milagro* (Polydor) 1993—*Sacred Fire—Live in South America*   1994— *Brothers* (Island).

Through a long, erratic career laden with personnel changes, the group Santana has maintained popularity and critical respect with what was in the beginning an innovative fusion of rock, fiery Afro-Latin polyrhythms, and contrasting cool, low-key vocals. In time, group leader/guitarist Carlos Santana was drawn to jazz-rock fusion and worked outside the band with John McLaughlin, Stanley Clarke, and others. Though the mid-Seventies saw Santana becoming involved in spiritual mysticism (he affixed "Devadip" before his name), by the decade's end the band was back in hard-driving rhythmic form and chalked up several hit dance singles. The group continued to perform off and on into the Nineties; in 1994, Santana appeared at Woodstock '94, one of three acts that had performed at the original '69 festival that were asked to return to the 25th anniversary concert.

The band evolved in San Francisco's Latin district from jam sessions between Santana, David Brown, and Gregg Rolie. With original drummer Rod Harper and rhythm guitarist Tom Frazer, they became the Santana Blues Band. Though the soft-spoken Santana felt uncomfortable as leader, he lent his name to the group because the local musicians union required that each band have a designated leader. The group's 1968 debut at San Francisco's Fillmore West (by which time it had become known simply as Santana) won it a standing ovation; through its local popularity, it won a spot in the lineup at Woodstock, where it stopped the show. The instrumental "Soul Sacrifice," featuring Michael Shrieve's drum solo, is one of the high points of the *Woodstock* soundtrack album.

Santana's overwhelming success at the festival led to a deal with Columbia, and within a few weeks of its late-summer 1969 release its debut LP was #4 and eventually went double platinum. That album's "Evil Ways" was a Top Ten single in early 1970. *Abraxas,* released later that year, sold four million copies and lodged at #1 on the album chart for six weeks; *Santana III,* the first to feature 16-year-old second guitarist Neal Schon, topped the chart for five weeks in late 1971. *Abraxas* yielded hits such as "Black Magic Woman" (#4, 1970), previously recorded by Fleetwood Mac, and veteran salsa bandleader Tito Puente's "Oye Como Va" (#13, 1971), while *Santana III* contained "Everybody's Everything" (#12, 1971) and "No One to Depend On" (#36, 1972). *Caravanserai* went platinum; *Welcome,* gold. Both LPs saw Santana's music stretching out into jazzier directions, and the band's personnel changed considerably with every album. Neal Schon and keyboardist Gregg Rolie went on to found Journey; Shrieve played various sessions, including Stomu Yamashta's *Go* series, and formed Automatic Man and, later, Novo Combo.

In 1972 Carlos Santana made his first recording outside the band, a live album with Buddy Miles. Though dismissed by critics, it too sold well, eventually going platinum. The fusion supersession *Love, Devotion, Surrender* found the guitarist playing with John McLaughlin, Jan Hammer, and Billy Cobham of the Mahavishnu Orchestra; Stanley Clarke of Return to Forever; and Larry Young of the Tony Williams Lifetime.

In 1974 Santana collaborated with Alice Coltrane and ex–Miles Davis jazz bassist David Holland, among others, for the string-dominated *Illuminations*; it didn't sell as well as *Love, Devotion, Surrender,* which had gone gold.

Borboletta featured contributions from Clarke and Brazilian musicians Airto Moreira and Flora Purim. *Lotus* stands out in Santana's mid-Seventies period; the three-record set was released in Japan in 1974 but unavailable in America until 1991. By the late Seventies Santana had tightened up his band into a funkier direction, and enjoyed a hit single with a cover of the Zombies' mid-Sixties hit "She's Not There" (#27, 1977), featuring singer Greg Walker. After two more jazz-fusion solo LPs, *Oneness* and *The Swing of Delight*—the latter featuring such fusion stars and former Miles Davis sidemen as Herbie Hancock, Tony Williams, Ron Carter, and Weather Report reedman Wayne Shorter—the Santana band's *Zebop!* became a big seller on the strength of "Winning" (#17, 1981), written by ex-Argent guitarist Russ Ballard; the following year's *Shangó* added another Top Twenty hit, "Hold On," with a lead vocal by Alex Ligertwood. *Havana Moon* featured guests Willie Nelson and the Texas blues band the Fabulous Thunderbirds.

Santana appeared at Live Aid in 1985. To celebrate its 20th anniversary the next year, the band played a special San Francisco performance that featured all previous Santana members. *Freedom* reunited Carlos Santana with Buddy Miles, who contributed vocals. The title track of Carlos Santana's eighth solo recording, *Blues for Salvador,* won a 1987 Grammy for Best Rock Instrumental Performance. An acclaimed career retrospective box set, *Viva Santana!,* was released in 1988. Carlos Santana hooked up with Miles Davis/Weather Report saxophonist Wayne Shorter for a 1988 summer tour.

Spirits Dancing in the Flesh (1990) featured guest appearances by Bobby Womack and Living Colour guitarist Vernon Reid, who played on "Jin-Go-Lo-Ba," a reworking of "Jingo," a Santana favorite from the first album. In 1992, after a 20-year association with Columbia Records, Santana moved to PolyGram, appearing first on Polydor, then on Island. *Sacred Fire—Live in South America* attested to the band's tremendous popularity in Latin America. Carlos Santana announced plans in 1993 to start his own specialty label, Guts and Grace, to release jazz and world music and selections from his extensive private collection of live performance recordings, including artists as diverse as Jimi Hendrix, Marvin Gaye, Bob Marley, and Stevie Ray Vaughan.

Joe Satriani
Born July 15, 1957, Carle Place, New York
1984—*Joe Satriani* EP (Rubina)   1986—*Not of This
Earth* (Relativity)   1987—*Surfing with the Alien
1988—*Dreaming #11* EP   1989—*Flying in a Blue*
Dream*   1992—*The Extremist*   1993—*Time Machine.

A rock guitarist of dazzling technical proficiency, Joe Satriani spent years as a relatively unknown working musician before a tour with Mick Jagger heightened interest in his own recording career. Satriani, who also played piano and drums while growing up, became fascinated with the guitar after listening to Jimi Hendrix, whose death inspired the young musician to devote himself to music. Satriani practiced along to blues and classic-rock records and learned some theory in school. He quickly became proficient enough to teach the instrument; among his early students was Steve Vai, now a fellow guitar hero. Satriani also played in bands and took lessons with the influential be-bop jazz pianist Lennie Tristano.

After a stint with a pop band called the Squares, Satriani made his recording debut, in 1984, with a self-titled instrumental EP. A couple of instrumental albums followed, selling respectably for their genre. In the late Eighties, after Satriani had toured alone and with Greg Kihn, a tip from Vai landed him on the road with Jagger. The exposure helped propel to platinum status Satriani's album *Surfing with the Alien* (#29, 1987), which became the first instrumental LP to enter the Top Forty since 1980. Satriani's 1989 effort, *Flying in a Blue Dream,* reached #23; 1992's *The Extremist* shot to #22. In 1993 Satriani released the double-CD *Time Machine,* a collection of out-of-print and previously unreleased recordings and new tracks.

Savoy Brown
Formed 1966, London, England
Kim Simmonds, gtr., voc.; Bruce Portius, voc.; Martin Stone, gtr.; Ray Chappell, bass; Leo Mannings, drums; Bob Hall, kybds.
1967—*Shake Down* (Decca, U.K.)   1968—(– Portius; – Chappell; – Mannings; + Chris Youlden, voc.; + "Lonesome" Dave Peverett [b. 1950, Eng.], gtr.; + Rivers Jobe, bass; + Roger Earl [b. 1949, Eng.], drums) *Getting to the Point* (Parrot)   1969—(– Hall; – Jobe; + Tony Stevens [b. Sep. 12, 1949, Eng.], bass) *Blue Matter; A Step Further*   1970—*Raw Sienna* (– Youlden); *Looking In*   1971—(– Peverett; – Stevens; – Earl; + Paul Raymond, kybds.; + Dave Walker, voc.; + Dave Bidwell, drums; + Andy Pyle, bass; – Pyle; + Andy Silvester, bass) *Street Corner Talking*   1972—*Hellbound Train* (– Silvester; + Pyle; – Walker); *Lion's Share* (– Bidwell; + Jackie Lynton, voc.; + Ron Berg, drums)   1973—*Jack the Toad*   1974—(– Berg; – Raymond; – Lynton; + Eric Dillon, drums; + Stan Webb, gtr., voc.; + Miller Anderson, gtr., voc.; + Jimmy Leverton, bass) *Boogie

Brothers (London)   1975—(– Webb; – Dillon; – Anderson; + Ian Ellis, bass; + Tom Farnell, drums)
Wire Fire   1976—*Skin 'n' Bone*   1978—*Savage Return*   1981—*Rock 'N' Roll Warriors* (Town House) (undocumented personnel changes may have occurred after this point)   1983—*Live in Central Park* (Relix)   1984—*Slow Train*   1988—*Make Me Sweat* (GNP Crescendo)   1989—*Kings of Boogie*   1990—*Live and Kickin'*   1993—*The Savoy Brown Collection* (Deram, U.K.)   1994—*Let It Ride* (Viceroy).

This workmanlike blues-rock band became a favorite with American audiences while never achieving widespread popularity at home in Britain. Though Savoy Brown never had a hit single, its albums sold respectably, thanks to dogged touring. The only constant in the band's membership was guitarist Kim Simmonds, who ruled the group with an iron hand and hired and fired members regularly.

Savoy Brown was formed originally as the Savoy Brown Blues Band. In 1968 drummer Bill Bruford (Yes, King Crimson, U.K.) joined them for about a week before moving on to Yes. As the British blues boom wound down in the early Seventies, Savoy Brown edged toward a more hard-rock boogie style. Around this time, it also began to concentrate almost exclusively on the U.S., where Simmonds later relocated. In 1971 Dave Peverett, Roger Earl, and Tony Stevens left the band to form another rock-boogie outfit, Foghat [see entry]. Over the years, Simmonds re-formed the band, drawing on personnel from such British blues bands as Chicken Shack (Dave Walker, Paul Raymond, Andy Silvester, Dave Bidwell, Stan Webb) and the Keef Hartley Band (Miller Anderson).

In 1973 Simmonds announced that Savoy Brown was no more, but the following year he formed yet another version. This group was also known (parenthetically) as the Boogie Brothers, and lasted for only one album. Simmonds continues to tour and record with Savoy Brown.

Leo Sayer

Born Gerard Hugh Sayer, May 21, 1948, Shoreham-by-Sea, England
1973—*Silverbird* (Warner Bros.)   1974—*Just a Boy*
1975—*Another Year*   1976—*Endless Flight*   1977—
Thunder in My Heart   1978—*Leo Sayer*   1979—*The Very Best of Leo Sayer*; *Here*   1980—*Living in a Fantasy*; *World Radio*   1993—*Leo Sayer: All the Best* (Chrysalis).

Singer/songwriter Leo Sayer has enjoyed sporadic American success, and at one point, in 1977, he had three Top Forty singles and a platinum album.

While attending Worthington Art College, Sayer formed his first band, Terraplane Blues. He later moved

to London and headed a group called Patches. Sayer then began writing songs with David Courtney. Courtney linked the group with singer/actor Adam Faith, who became its manager. After Patches' debut single sold only 55 copies, Sayer decided to go solo. Faith's wife, Jackie, renamed him Leo, thinking he looked like a lion.

Faith and Courtney produced the debut Sayer LP, *Silverbird*, at Roger Daltrey's studio in Sussex, with Sayer writing the words and Courtney the music. Daltrey liked their songs so much he recorded his debut solo with all material written by the two unknowns, making their "Giving It All Away" a #5 British hit in early 1973. *Silverbird* came out a short time later, and in keeping with the glitter trend, the cover featured Sayer in a Pierrot clown costume (which he also wore live). The LP established Sayer as a big British star in his own right and yielded the #2 English hit "The Show Must Go On."

For *Just a Boy*, Sayer gave up the clown image, which had been ridiculed in the U.S. The album became a British gold LP and featured his first U.S. hit single, "Long Tall Glasses" (#9, 1975). He split with Courtney, who wanted to go solo (he later reunited with Sayer for *Here*). On *Another Year* Sayer wrote the songs with Frank Farrell. The single "Moonlighting" went to #2 in the U.K. but was ignored in the U.S.

Sayer next linked up with Richard Perry, who suggested more covers and new songwriting alliances for 1976's *Endless Flight*. *Flight* was Sayer's platinum U.S. breakthrough and yielded three hit singles: "You Make Me Feel Like Dancing" (#1, 1976), "When I Need You" (#1, 1977), and "How Much Love" (#17, 1977). *Thunder in My Heart* went gold in the U.K. but flopped in the U.S. Soon his British audience dwindled as well. Though Sayer produced some respectable surface pop in this period, he did not return to the U.S. chart until late 1980, with a #2 cover of Bobby Vee's "More Than I Can Say." He enjoyed several more hits in the U.K. and even had his own television series there, but by decade's end, he had no record deal. His 1990 U.K. "comeback" album, *Cool Touch*, failed to restore his career.

Boz Scaggs

Born William Royce Scaggs, June 8, 1944, Ohio
1965—*Boz* (Polydor, U.K.)   1969—*Boz Scaggs* (Atlantic)   1971—*Moments* (Columbia); *Boz Scaggs and His Band*   1972—*My Time*   1974—*Slow Dancer*   1976—*Silk Degrees*   1977—*Down Two, Then Left*   1980—*Middle Man*; *Hits!*   1988—*Other Roads*   1994—*Some Change* (Virgin).

After over a decade of trying to make it as a solo act, singer/songwriter Boz Scaggs hit with a five-million-seller, *Silk Degrees*.

Scaggs grew up in Oklahoma and Texas, and while at St. Mark's Preparatory School in Dallas he met Steve Miller. He joined Miller's band, the Marksmen, as lead vocalist while Miller taught him guitar. Scaggs followed Miller to the University of Wisconsin, where they played together in a blues-rock band known as the Ardells or the Fabulous Knight Trains. Returning to Texas in 1963, Scaggs joined an R&B band, the Wigs. The next year, Scaggs and two of the Wigs—John Andrews and Bob Arthur—went to England. Finding little success, they broke up (most of the Wigs eventually forming Mother Earth), while Scaggs roved Europe as a street singer, recording his debut LP in Stockholm. He returned to the U.S. in 1967 and moved to San Francisco. There he reunited with Steve Miller for two albums with the Steve Miller Band: *Children of the Future* and *Sailor*.

Jann Wenner, editor and publisher of ROLLING STONE, helped arrange for Scaggs' U.S. solo debut with Atlantic, *Boz Scaggs*. It was released to some critical acclaim but almost no sales. The album gained most of its fame from the tune "Loan Me a Dime," which featured a memorable Duane Allman guitar solo; bluesman Fenton Robinson later successfully sued for composer credit on the song. Scaggs' second and third U.S. LPs were produced by Glyn Johns. On *My Time* he dispensed with a backing band in favor of studio musicians. Also at this time his vocals began to show more of a soul influence. This became even more pronounced on *Slow Dancer*, produced by ex-Motown producer Johnny Bristol, which was again critically hailed but not commercially successful.

Then came 1976's *Silk Degrees*, with its #3 hit, "Lowdown," and other smashes like "Lido Shuffle" (#11, 1977). His studio band for much of the Seventies included the nucleus of what became Toto. Though Scaggs has never quite matched that success, *Middle Man* yielded minor hits with "Breakdown Dead Ahead" (#15, 1980) and "Jo Jo" (#17, 1980). Scaggs also appeared on the soundtrack of the film *Urban Cowboy* (1980). In San Francisco Scaggs became known for his annual black-tie concerts on New Year's Eve.

Scaggs' 1994 Virgin Records debut, *Some Change*, was his second album in 14 years. The preceding release, *Other Roads* (#47, 1988), yielded the hit "Heart of Mine" (#35, 1988). During the mid-Eighties he opened a nightclub in San Francisco, Slim's, and, except for the 1988 album, didn't fully begin to return to music until he appeared as part of Donald Fagen's New York Rock and Soul Revue in 1991. *Some Change* (#91, 1994) was produced by former Beach Boys drummer and Bonnie Raitt band member Ricky Fataar.

Scandal: See Patty Smyth

Scarface: See the Geto Boys

Michael (or Michel) Schenker: See Scorpions; UFO

Schoolly D
Born Jesse B. Weaver, June 22, 1966, Philadelphia, Pennsylvania
1986—*Schoolly D* (Schoolly D)   1987—*Saturday Night—the Album; The Adventures of Schoolly D* (Rykodisc)   1988—*Smoke Some Kill* (Jive)   1989—*Am I Black Enough for You?* 1991—*How a Black Man Feels* (Capitol)   1994—*Welcome to America* (Ruffhouse/Columbia).

On his first album, Schoolly D pioneered gangsta rap with his chilling, unsentimental descriptions of urban violence. His eponymously titled debut featured "PSK—What Does It Mean?," a song about the Philly gang Parkside Killers, as well as the anthem "I Don't Like Rock 'n' Roll." He released his first two albums himself, then signed with Jive, which rereleased *Saturday Night. The Adventures of Schoolly D* is a selection of tracks from the rapper's first albums with a bonus track.

Schoolly D's early work was embraced by critics for its raw, journalistic outlook on what would become such familiar gangsta themes as sex and violence. The musical settings were provided by DJ Code Money. On *Am I Black Enough for You?*, the rapper tackled the issues of black nationalism and pride. His 1994 release, *Welcome to America*, featured Schoolly D backed by a band, including veteran session player and coproducer Mike Tyler and ex-Urge Overkill bassist Chuck Treece. The album also introduced rapper Cheese.

Klaus Schulze: See Tangerine Dream

Scorpions
Formed 1971, Hanover, Germany
Lothar Heimberg, bass; Klaus Meine (b. May, 25, 1948, Hanover), voc.; Jurgen Rosenthal, drums; Michel Schenker (b. Jan. 10, 1955, Savstedt, Ger.), gtr.; Rudolf Schenker (b. Aug. 31, 1948, Hildesheim, Ger.), gtr.
1972—*Lonesome Crow* (Brain)   1973—(- Rosenthal; - Heimberg; - M. Schenker; + Francis Buchholz [b. Jan. 19, 1950], bass; + Wolfgang Dziony, drums; + Ulrich Roth, gtr.)   1974—*Fly to the Rainbow* (RCA)   1976—(- Dziony; + Rudy Lenners, drums) *In Trance; Virgin Killer*   1977—(- Lenners; + Herman Rarebell [b. Nov. 18, 1949, Lubeck, Ger.], drums) *Taken by Force*   1978—*Tokyo Tapes* (- Roth; + Matthias Jabs [b. Oct. 25, 1955, Hanover], gtr.; + M. Schenker; - Jabs; + Jabs)   1979—*Lovedrive*

(Mercury); *Best of Scorpions* (RCA) (– M. Schenker) 1980—*Animal Magnetism* (Mercury) 1982—*Blackout* 1984—*Love at First Sting; Best of Scorpions, vol. 2* (RCA) 1985—*World Wide Live* (Mercury) 1988—*Savage Amusement* 1989—*Best of Rockers 'n' Ballads* 1990—*Crazy World* 1992—(– Buchholz; + Ralph Rieckermann [b. Aug. 8, Lubeck, Ger.], bass) 1993—*Face the Heat.*

The most popular rock band to come out of Germany, Scorpions broke out as a leading heavy-metal band in the mid-Eighties, with three Top Ten LPs: *Blackout* (#10, 1982), *Love at First Sting* (#6, 1984), and *Savage Amusement* (#5, 1988). Originally formed in 1965 as a pop band by Rudolf Schenker, they broke up and re-formed in 1971 as a hard-rock outfit, featuring Rudolf's brother Michel on guitar. After the 1972 debut, *Lonesome Crow,* Michel left to join UFO (changing the spelling of his name to Michael in the process). Scorpions' five albums for RCA, while popular in Europe, did not crack the American charts, partly, the band later contended, because the label prohibited them from touring stateside. (Ironically, Scorpions' forte is live performance, as was later evinced in their appearances at the US Festival in 1985 and as part of 1990's Monsters of Rock Tour.)

Matters changed with *Lovedrive* (#55, 1979), their first record for Mercury and the first to chart in the U.S. With Michael Schenker back on guitar, the band seemed to come alive. But Schenker left again, unable to keep up with the band's brutal touring schedule, and young Matthias Jabs (who had been hired before Michael returned, then fired, then rehired), took his place. Michael has since led the Michael Schenker Group, and worked with groups named the McAuley Schenker Group and Schenker/McAuley.

Blackout (#10, 1982), Scorpions' first album to go platinum, contained their first modestly successful single, "No One Like You" (#65, 1982), followed in 1984 with "Rock You Like a Hurricane" (#25) from the double-platinum *Love at First Sting* (#6). In 1988 Scorpions toured the Soviet Union, the first heavy metal band to do so. They returned in 1989, with Bon Jovi and Ozzy Osbourne, for the Moscow Music Peace Festival. A ballad, "Wind of Change" (#4, 1991), written about their Russian experiences, included on 1990's *Crazy World* (#21), was released in a Russian version and won the group an audience with then–Soviet premier Mikhail Gorbachev.

The band confronted the problems arising from Germany's reunification in the songs "Alien Nation," "Unholy Alliance," and "Ship of Fools" on 1993's *Face the Heat* (#24).

Tom Scott

Born May 19, 1948, Los Angeles, California
1967—*Honeysuckle Breeze* (Impulse) 1968—*Rural* Still Life 1971—*Great Scott* (A&M) 1974—*Tom Scott and the L.A. Express* (Ode) 1975—*Tom Cat; New York Connection* 1977—*Blow It Out* (Columbia) 1978—*Intimate Strangers* 1979—*Street Beat* 1980—*The Best of Tom Scott* 1981—*Apple Juice* 1982—*Desire* (Elektra Musician) 1987—*Streamlines* (GRP) 1988—*Flashpoint* (with Eric Gale, others) 1990—*Them Changes* 1991—*Keep This Love Alive* 1992—*Born Again* (with Randy Brecker, Kenny Kirkland, others) 1994—*Reed My Lips; Night Creatures.*

Though he has been known in jazz circles since the late Sixties, saxophonist Tom Scott didn't become widely recognized in pop until the mid-Seventies for studio work with Carole King, Joni Mitchell, Steely Dan, Blondie ("Rapture"), Paul McCartney, Barbra Streisand, and countless others.

Scott's mother was a classical pianist and his father a film and television theme composer (of, among many others, the themes to *The Twilight Zone* and *Dragnet*). At eight he took up the clarinet, but switched to baritone sax in junior high. He left college after one semester in 1966 and started playing the L.A. clubs with Don Ellis' band and then Roger Kellaway's quartet. His work with Oliver Nelson's band led to a contract with Impulse, which released his first solo album, *Honeysuckle Breeze.* He recorded another LP for Impulse, 1968's *Rural Still Life,* and then two for Flying Dutchman. He also did sessions, playing on *Phil Ochs Greatest Hits* in 1970, and began composing TV scores, first for *Dan August* in 1969. (He later wrote the themes for *Starsky and Hutch, The Streets of San Francisco, Family Ties,* and many more. He has also done movie scores for *Stir Crazy, Neighbors, Soul Man* and others.)

In 1971 Scott got a contract with A&M, and on his first LP for the label, *Great Scott,* he did a version of Joni Mitchell's "Woodstock" that so impressed Mitchell that she invited him to play on her *For the Roses* (1972). After that LP, Scott began to develop a band, an informal, ever-shifting group that became the L.A. Express, a pop-jazz band. Ode Records released *Tom Scott and the L.A. Express,* which got more attention than usual, especially after he was featured on Carole King's tour and soloed on her 1974 #2 single "Jazzman."

A new Express played on Joni Mitchell's *Court and Spark* and on her live *Miles of Aisles.* Scott disbanded the L.A. Express in the mid-Seventies. He later toured with George Harrison and Ravi Shankar and added sax to Wings' hit "Listen to What the Man Said." In 1978 Scott recorded an album with Billy Cobham, Alphonso Johnson, and Steve Kahn called *Alivemutherfoya.* He has also recorded as part of the New York Connection (with Eric Gale, Richard Tee, and Bob James).

In 1987 Scott signed to GRP, for which he released a

series of respected albums and led the GRP All-Star Big Band, which tours and records. He was musical director for the ill-fated *The Pat Sajak Show. Reed My Lips* (1994) featured such heavyweight players as Grover Washington Jr., Eric Gale, and Robben Ford.

Gil Scott-Heron

Born April 1, 1949, Chicago, Illinois
1978—*Secrets* (Arista); *The Mind of Gil Scott-Heron* 1980—*1980*; *Real Eyes* 1981—*Reflections* 1982— *Moving Target* 1984—*The Best of Gil Scott-Heron* 1993—*Spirits* (TVT).
With Brian Jackson: 1972—*Small Talk at 125th and Lenox* (Flying Dutchman); *Free Will* 1973—*Pieces of a Man* 1974—*The Revolution Will Not Be Televised*; *The First Minute of a New Day* (Arista); *Winter in America* (Strata/East) 1975—*From South Africa to South Carolina* (Arista) 1976—*It's Your World* 1977—*Bridges*.

Writer-turned-singer Gil Scott-Heron stresses his literate, politically conscious lyrics as much as his funk and jazz-based music. His ouevre has been cited as an influence on some schools of rap as well as on the burgeoning spoken-word movement of the 1990s.

Scott-Heron's mother was a librarian (his father, a pro soccer player), and Scott-Heron wrote detective stories as an early teen. At 19 he published his first novel, *The Vulture*, followed by a book of rap verse called *Small Talk at 125th and Lenox* and a second novel, *The Nigger Factory.* Scott-Heron believed he could reach more people through music, so he began to collaborate with a friend from Pennsylvania's Lincoln University, Brian Jackson. Each played piano, and at first Jackson wrote music to Scott-Heron's words, but soon they began to collaborate on the music.

The two cut three LPs for Flying Dutchman, first a mostly verbal version of his verse, *Small Talk . . .* , followed by two more musical albums, *Pieces of a Man,* which included the militant poem "The Revolution Will Not Be Televised" (also popularized by Labelle on its *Pressure Cookin'* LP), and *Free Will.* In 1974 the two became the first signing to the new Arista label, releasing *The First Minute of a New Day.* It was also the debut of Scott-Heron and Jackson's jazzy backup group, the Midnight Band.

The followup, 1975's *From South Africa to South Carolina,* included the R&B hit "Johannesburg" (#29 R&B, 1975). Scott-Heron began writing on his own, without Jackson, in the late Seventies. His first single after going solo, "Angel Dust," reached #15 on the R&B charts in 1978.

Over the years Scott-Heron's music generally has gotten good reviews, though some critics have said his lyrics tend to be didactic. He appeared at the antinuclear MUSE benefit at Madison Square Garden in September 1979, where he performed his own atomic warning, "We Almost Lost Detroit." He also recorded "Shut 'Um Down" (#68 R&B, 1980) on the same subject.

In 1985 Scott-Heron was featured on the all-star antiapartheid record *Sun City* and continued touring with his own band, the Amnesia Express. By then, the influence of Scott-Heron's work had begun to surface in rap. Public Enemy's 1991 "1 Million Bottlebags" updated Scott-Heron's 1974 "The Bottle." But although his work is regarded as a precursor of rap, Scott-Heron didn't jump on the bandwagon. "It's something that's aimed at the kids," Scott-Heron said. "I have kids, so I listen to it. But I would say it's not aimed at me. I still listen to the jazz station." Though he toured throughout the Eighties, Scott-Heron ended a ten-year hiatus from recording new material with 1993's *Spirits.*

Screaming Trees

Formed 1984, Ellensburg, Washington
Mark Lanegan (b. Nov. 25, 1964, Ellensburg), voc.; Van Conner (b. Mar. 17, 1967, Apple Valley, Calif.), bass; Gary Lee Conner (b. Aug. 22, 1962, Ft. Irwin, Calif.), gtr.; Mark Pickerel, drums.
1985—*Other Worlds* EP (Velvetone) 1986—*Clairvoyance* 1987—*Even If and Especially When* (SST) 1988—*Invisible Lantern* 1989—*Buzz Factory*; *Changes Come* double EP (Sub Pop); *Something About Today* EP (Epic) 1991—*Uncle Anesthesia*; *Anthology* (SST) (– Pickerel; + Barrett Martin [b. Apr. 14, 1967, Olympia, Wash.], drums) 1992— *Sweet Oblivion* (Epic) 1993—*Time Is of the Essence* EP.

Screaming Trees are a psychedelic-tinged postpunk band from the rural Pacific Northwest formed by 300-pound brothers Van and Gary Lee Conner. Sons of video store owners in Ellensburg, Washington, the Conners formed Screaming Trees along with friend Mark Lanegan out of a collective love of both hard rock and punk. The group's SST output is rawer and grungier than its Epic releases, although its Doorslike groove has remained a constant.

The Trees have a reputation for boozing and fighting, often breaking up and regrouping over the years. Each member has done side projects: Lanegan has recorded for Sub Pop two singer/songwriter albums, *The Winding Sheet* (1990) and *Whiskey for the Holy Ghost* (1994); Lee Conner formed the Purple Outside in 1990 and put out *Mystery Lane* on New Alliance; and Van Conner (who went on hiatus in 1991 to tour with Dinosaur Jr) formed Solomon Grundy, which released a self-titled album on New Alliance in 1990.

In 1990 the Trees signed with Epic. By the end of 1992, following the massive success of fellow Washingtonians Nirvana and Pearl Jam, the Trees' second full-length Epic release, *Sweet Oblivion,* began to garner a fair amount of mainstream exposure via MTV's "grunge-mania." The band also gained new listeners via their appearance on the platinum soundtrack to Cameron Crowe's 1992 film *Singles.*

Seal

Born Sealhenry Samuel, February 19, 1963, London, England
**1991—*Seal* (Sire)   1994—*Seal.*

Though his first recording success came through England's house-music scene, Seal's critically acclaimed debut album presented him as a somewhat mystically inclined singer/songwriter mixing elements of folk, soul, pop, and rock. The son of Nigerian and Brazilian parents who separated when he was a toddler, Sealhenry Samuel got an architecture degree, designed leather clothes, and worked in electrical engineering and other odd jobs before he began singing in London pubs. A funk band called Push invited him along on a tour of Japan, after which he joined a blues band in Thailand, then spent several months traveling alone through India.

Seal returned to England and happened to meet house/techno producer Adamski, on whose U.K. dance hit "Killer" (#1 U.K., 1990) Seal wrote lyrics and sang. That led to a deal for Seal himself, whose debut album was produced by ex-Buggle Trevor Horn (ABC, Art of Noise). *Seal* (#24, 1991) yielded a Top Ten pop hit in "Crazy" (#7, 1991), the video for which showed off Seal's distinctive facial scars (the result of an allergic reaction). The rerecorded "Killer" was only a minor hit (#100, 1991). Seal taped a 1992 environmental-awareness public service spot for MTV with labelmate Madonna, a big fan of his, and in 1993 he joined Jeff Beck on "Manic Depression," for the Jimi Hendrix all-star tribute album *Stone Free.* The next year Seal released his second album, again self-titled and produced by Trevor Horn. It peaked at #20, spawning the #21 single "Prayer for the Dying."

Sea Level: See the Allman Brothers Band

Seals and Crofts

Formed 1969, California
Jim Seals (b. Oct. 17, 1941, Sidney, Tex.), gtr., sax, fiddle, voc.; Dash Crofts (b. Darrell Crofts, Aug. 14, 1940, Cisco, Tex.), drums, voc., mandolin, kybds., gtr.
1970—*Seals and Crofts* (TA); *Down Home*   1971—*Year of Sunday* (Warner Bros.)   1972—*Summer Breeze*   1973—*Diamond Girl*   1974—*Unborn Child*   1975—*I'll Play for You*; *Greatest Hits*   1976—*Get Closer*; *Sudan Village*   1977—*One on One*   1978—*Takin' It Easy*   1979—*The Seals and Crofts Collection* (K-Tel)   1980—*The Longest Road* (Warner Bros.).

Jim Seals and Dash Crofts were a commercially successful soft-rock pop duo through the Seventies. Both were born in small Texas towns and met when Crofts was a teenage drummer for a local band. Seals joined a group called Dean Beard and the Crew Cuts; later Crofts came aboard that outfit, and to make a long, complicated story short, by mid-1958 both were touring with the Champs [see entry], then riding the success of their huge #1 Latin-rock instrumental hit "Tequila." The pair later moved to Los Angeles, where both worked as session musicians and tried to make a go of their own recording careers. In 1965 Seals and Crofts (who spent two years in the service, then returned to the Champs upon being discharged in 1964), left the Champs. Two groups, the Mushrooms and the Dawnbreakers, failed. But out of the latter, first Crofts (who married fellow Dawnbreaker Billie Lee Day) and then Seals were introduced to the Baha'i faith.

In 1969 Seals and Crofts decided to try as a duo. They signed to Talent Associates and released two largely ignored LPs before signing to Warner Bros. in 1971. Their first album for their new label also bombed, but their second, *Summer Breeze,* went to #7 in 1972 on the strength of its #6 title tune and "Hummingbird" (#20, 1972). *Diamond Girl* (#4, 1973) spun off two more hits, "Diamond Girl" (#6, 1973) and "We May Never Pass This Way (Again)" (#21, 1973). Seals and Crofts, though devout followers of their chosen faith, did not proselytize directly, but they insisted on a clause in their contracts stating that they be given time after each concert to speak to interested fans about Baha'i. Crofts' wife's sister wrote a poem after viewing a documentary on abortion. Seals wrote the music, and in 1974 the duo released "Unborn Child," an antiabortion song written from the fetus' point of view ("Momma, don't!"). Seals and Crofts, ignoring Warner Bros.' advice, also chose to title the album *Unborn Child* (#14, 1974). A critical and commercial flop, "Unborn Child" rose only as high as #66 and prompted prochoice demonstrations at many of their shows.

Over a year later they returned with "I'll Play for You" (#18, 1975), from *I'll Play for You* (#30, 1975). The following year's *Get Closer* (#37, 1976), featuring "Get Closer" (#6, 1976), was Seals and Crofts' last Top Forty LP. Carolyn Willis, formerly of Bob B. Soxx and the Blue Jeans and Honey Cone, was featured on that album and its live followup, *Sudan Village* (#73, 1976). The pair sang music for a Robby Benson film, *One on One,* from which "My Fair Share" went to #28 in 1977. *Takin' It Easy* (#78, 1978) included their last Top Twenty single, "You're the Love" (#18, 1878). Their final studio effort, *The Longest Road,* didn't even crack the album chart; Chick Corea and Stanley Clarke guest on it.

Warner Bros. dropped the duo soon after that, but by then, as both have indicated in recent years, it didn't really matter to them. Except for a short 1991–92 reunion tour and a number of appearances together at Baha'i-related gatherings, the two have not played together. Crofts lived in Mexico, then Australia, then Nashville. Seals has lived on a coffee farm in Costa Rica since 1980. Dan Seals, Jimmy's younger brother, recorded in the Seventies as half of England Dan and John Ford Coley. More recently, he has had a string of country hit singles.

The Searchers

Formed 1961, Liverpool, England
John McNally (b. Aug. 30, 1941, Liverpool), gtr., voc.; Mike Pender (b. Michael Prendergast, Mar. 3, 1942, Liverpool), gtr., voc.; Tony Jackson (b. July 16, 1940, Liverpool), bass, voc.; Chris Curtis (b. Aug. 26, 1942, Oldham, Eng.), drums, voc.
1964—Meet the Searchers (Kapp); Hear! Hear! (Mercury); This Is Us (Kapp) (– Jackson; + Frank Allen [b. Dec. 14, 1943, Hayes, Eng.], bass, voc.) 1965—The New Searchers LP; The Searchers No. 4 1966—(– Curtis; + John Blunt [b. Mar. 28, 1947, London, Eng.], drums) 1968—(– Blunt; + Billy Adamson, drums, voc.) 1972—Second Take (RCA) 1980—The Searchers (Sire) 1981—Love's Melodies 1985—(– Pender; + Spencer James, gtr., voc.) 1988—Greatest Hits (Rhino).

The Searchers were one of the best of the Liverpool pop bands to emerge in the wake of the Beatles. Their sound matched their clean-cut looks: pretty, gentle, with perfect close-harmony vocals and ringing guitar lines that presaged the Byrds.

The Searchers, originally formed to back up British singer Johnny Sandon, took their name from the John Ford–John Wayne film. They went to Hamburg, Germany, to play the Star Club after the Beatles' success there, and then returned to Liverpool. A&R man Tony Hatch offered them a recording contract after they had established a residency at Liverpool's Iron Door club. Their first U.K. hit came in 1963 with their cover of the Drifters' "Sweets for My Sweet." "Needles and Pins," written by Sonny Bono and Jack Nitzsche, was #1 in Britain in 1964 (#13 U.S.); it eventually sold over a million copies.

The Searchers toured America, Australia, and New Zealand that year. Their only subsequent U.S. Top Twenty hits were "Don't Throw Your Love Away" (#16, 1964) and "Love Potion Number 9" (#3, 1965). In Britain their Top Twenty success continued through 1965, with "Sugar and Spice" (1963); "Someday We're Gonna Love Again," "When You Walk in the Room," "What Have They Done to the Rain" (1964); and "Goodbye My Love" and "He's Got No Love" (1965). They then became stalwart club and cabaret performers for many years before resurfacing on Sire in 1979. In the wake of new wave, both The Searchers and Love's Melodies sounded entirely contemporary (containing songs by Tom Petty, Will Birch and John Wicks of the Records, and Alex Chilton) and elicited glowing reviews. Neither sold well, however, and the group returned to the touring circuit. Cofounder Pender left in 1985 to form his own live act, Mike Pender's Searchers.

John Sebastian

Born March 17, 1944, New York City, New York
1970—John B. Sebastian (MGM); John Sebastian Live 1971—Cheapo Cheapo Productions Presents the Real Live John Sebastian (Reprise); The Four of Us 1974—The Tarzana Kid 1976—Welcome Back 1989—The Best of John Sebastian (Rhino) 1993—Tar Beach (Shanachie).

John Sebastian's solo career took off almost immediately after the breaking up of his old group, the Lovin' Spoonful [see entry]. He appeared in an unscheduled set at Woodstock and captured the audience with songs like "I Had a Dream" and a persona that was the epitome of the tie-dyed hippie.

John B. Sebastian, his first solo album, featured "I Had a Dream," as well as a remake of the Spoonful's "You're a Big Boy Now," and though it produced no hit singles, it went to #20 and became the best-selling album of Sebastian's solo career. Cheapo-Cheapo Productions Presents the Real Live John Sebastian was meant to counter an unauthorized live set released and quickly deleted by his old label, MGM, and it relied largely on previously recorded material. Sebastian worked with Little Feat's Lowell George on Tarzana Kid (which included their joint composition "Face of Appalachia"). Sebastian's fortunes were temporarily reversed with his first hit single in close to ten years, "Welcome Back" (#1, 1976), the title song of the TV show Welcome Back, Kotter, which outsold the Spoonful's best-selling single by nearly two-to-one and was the second-best-selling single of 1976.

Though Sebastian then vanished from the recording scene for over 15 years, he remained active: touring, both solo and as opening act or accompanist to acts as diverse as NRBQ, Sha Na Na, Tom Petty, Graham Parker, Willie Dixon, and Les Paul; appearing on TV shows and writing music for the Care Bears show; and writing a children's book, J.B.'s Harmonica. Sebastian declined to take part in a 1992 Lovin' Spoonful reunion. In 1994 he formed the J-Band, a jug band, which appeared on Garrison Keillor's popular radio show, The Prairie Home Companion.

Jon Secada

Born Juan Secada, October 4, 1963, Havana, Cuba
1992—Jon Secada (SBK)   1994—Heart, Soul & a
Voice.

Jon Secada's debut album, released in both English and Spanish, charted in the Top Twenty, a victory both for the artist and for the Latin sound he mainstreamed, a mixture of romantic ballads and dance pop. Secada emigrated from Cuba with his parents as a child and grew up in Hialeah, Florida, where he later worked in his family's diner before earning a master's degree in jazz at the University of Miami. There he met two future members of Gloria Estefan and the Miami Sound Machine. Shopping his Stevie Wonder–influenced material to Gloria's husband and manager, Emilio, he broke into the music business by cowriting six songs for Gloria's *Into the Light*, including two 1991 #1 hits, "Coming Out of the Dark" and "Can't Forget You."

After touring with Estefan as backup vocalist, he released his first album. While his label, SBK, planned that he record only in English, he convinced the company to release two songs in Spanish. When both hit #1 on the Latin charts, he redid the entire album in a Spanish version, *Otro Día Mas Sin Verte*; it went on to win a Grammy for Best Latin Pop Album in 1992. *Jon Secada* (#15, 1992), with its four Top Forty singles, "Just Another Day," "Do You Believe in Us," "Angel," and "I'm Free," sold four million copies worldwide; all four were Latin #1 hits as well.

Neil Sedaka

Born March 13, 1939, Brooklyn, New York
1962—Neil Sedaka Sings His Greatest Hits (RCA)
1974—Sedaka's Back (MCA/Rocket)   1975—The
Hungry Years   1976—Steppin' Out   1977—A Song
(Elektra)   1980—In the Pocket   1981—Now
1986—Me and My Friends (Polydor)   1991—All-
Time Greatest Hits (RCA).

Neil Sedaka began in the late Fifties as a writer of hit songs, became a hitmaking performer himself, then returned to songwriting until the early Seventies, when Elton John helped him resume a singing career that briefly propelled him back into the spotlight.

As a teenager, Sedaka was selected by Arthur Rubinstein to play on a show on New York City's classical music station, WQXR. By that time he had become strongly attracted to popular music as well, and he began writing songs at age 13 to lyrics by his high school friend Howard Greenfield. He formed a backing band, the Tokens [see entry], which later had a hit of its own, "The Lion Sleeps Tonight."

While on a two-year scholarship to the Juilliard School in New York City, Sedaka sold his first tune, "Stupid Cupid," a hit for Connie Francis in 1958, as was his "Where the Boys Are" (which Francis sang in the hit teen movie of the same title) in 1961. He also sold Sedaka-Greenfield songs to Jerry Wexler at Atlantic Records, who placed them with R&B singer LaVern Baker and Clyde McPhatter. On the advice of Doc Pomus, Sedaka signed up with Al Nevins and Don Kirshner's Aldon Publishing. They felt Sedaka's own high-pitched voice was worth consideration and got him signed with RCA as a singer. In 1959 he had two hits, "The Diary" (#14) and "I Go Ape" (#42). More Sedaka-Greenfield hits followed: "Oh! Carol" (#9) in 1959; "Stairway to Heaven" (#9) in 1960; "Calendar Girl" (#4), "Little Devil" (#11), and "Happy Birthday, Sweet Sixteen" (#6) in 1961; "Breaking Up Is Hard to Do" (#1) and "Next Door to an Angel" (#5) in 1962. Sedaka also played a part in music-video history, with the film for "Calendar Girl" today counted among the first conceptual promotional clips.

Sedaka's performing career slowed in 1963. However, through the Sixties and early Seventies he and Greenfield continued to write hits for others, including the Fifth Dimension's "Workin' on a Groovy Thing," Tom Jones' "Puppet Man," and Davy Jones's "Rainy Jane." Greenfield, in the meantime, had also found success collaborating with Carole King; together they wrote "Crying in the Rain" for the Everly Brothers. Sedaka and Greenfield split up in 1973, after Sedaka had begun a performing comeback in England. After Sedaka made three LPs in Britain with Graham Gouldman of 10cc coproducing, Elton John helped him get back onto the U.S. chart, first by reissuing cuts from the three British LPs on one U.S. package (*Sedaka's Back*), then by having him record for his Rocket label. *Sedaka's Back* (#23, 1974) and *The Hungry Years* (#16, 1975) both went gold. "Laughter in the Rain" was a #1 hit for Sedaka in 1974, and his "Love Will Keep Us Together" (cowritten with Greenfield) was a #1 smash for the Captain and Tennille, winning a 1975 Grammy as Record of the Year.

Sedaka's second recording streak culminated with the #1 hit, "Bad Blood" (1975), which featured John on backing vocals; a bluesy reworking of "Breaking Up Is Hard to Do" (#8, 1976); and "Love in the Shadows" (#16, 1976). Since then Sedaka and Greenfield have collaborated regularly, and Sedaka has become a successful MOR ballad singer and has made numerous TV and concert appearances. In 1980 he and his daughter Dara recorded "Should've Never Let You Go," which reached #19 on the pop chart.

The Seeds

Formed 1965, Los Angeles, California
Sky Saxon (b. Richard Marsh), voc.; Jan Savage, gtr.;
Daryl Hooper, kybds.; Rick Andridge, drums.
1966—The Seeds (GNP Crescendo); Web of Sound
1967—Future   1968—Raw and Alive: Merlin's
Music Box   1969—A Full Spoon of Seedy Blues

1977—*Fallin' Off the Edge*   **1993**—*Travel with Your Mind.*

On the cusp of the early-to-mid-Sixties garage-rock boom and the mid-to-late-Sixties flower-power era came the Seeds. Their Top Forty hit of 1967, "Pushin' Too Hard," matched their scruffy looks with a nasty, threatening drive and ominous lyrics. This product of the L.A. teen scene had a few more minor hits—"Mr. Farmer," "Can't Seem to Make You Mine," and "Thousand Shadows"—later that year; all were very much in the vein of "Pushin'," though their sound gradually became more psychedelic. The group disbanded soon after.

Lead singer Sky Saxon attempted several comebacks fronting a number of bands, then wasn't heard from until ROLLING STONE magazine tracked him down at home in Kailua, Hawaii, in the mid-Eighties. There he claimed to be living with two common-law wives and five kids, and praying to dogs, since, as he explained, "God is dog spelled backwards." Jan Savage joined the Los Angeles Police Department.

Pete Seeger

Born May 3, 1919, New York City, New York
1941—*Talking Union and Other Union Songs* (Folkways)   **1943**—*Songs of the Civil War, vol. 1*
1950—*Darling Corey*   **1951**—*Lonesome Valley*
1953—*American Folksongs for Children*   **1955**—*Bantu Choral Folk Songs*   **1957–62**—*American Favorite Ballads, vols. 1 to 5*   **1958**—*Pete Seeger and Sonny Terry at Carnegie Hall* (with Sonny Terry)
1960—*Pete Seeger with Memphis Slim and Willie Dixon at the Village Gate* (with Memphis Slim and Willie Dixon)   **1960**—*American History in Ballad and Song, vol. 1*   **1961**—*American History in Ballad and Song, vol. 2*   **1963**—*We Shall Overcome* (Columbia)   **1964**—*Songs of Struggle and Protest, 1930–1950* (Folkways)   **1965**—*WNEW's Songs of Selma*   **1966**—*Dangerous Songs?* (Columbia)
1967—*Pete Seeger Sings Woody Guthrie* (Folkways); *Pete Seeger's Greatest Hits* (Columbia); *Waist Deep in the Big Muddy and Other Love Songs*
1969—*Young vs. Old*   **1972**—*The World of Pete Seeger*   **1975**—*Pete Seeger and Arlo Guthrie in Concert Together* (with Arlo Guthrie) (Warner Bros.)
1978—*The Essential Pete Seeger* (Vanguard)
1982—*Precious Friend: Arlo Guthrie and Pete Seeger* (with Arlo Guthrie) (Warner Bros.)   **1989**—*We Shall Overcome: The Complete Carnegie Hall Concert* (Columbia)   **1990**—*Children's Concert at Town Hall.*

Pete Seeger has been a major folk-music figure for longer than many current folksingers' parents have been alive. He is unquestionably the foremost folk archivist and popularizer of American folk music. From his pop-folk successes with the Weavers in the late Forties, through the Fifties, when he was blacklisted by the government, through the Sixties, when he became a cultural hero through his outspoken commitment to the antiwar and civil rights struggles, until now, Seeger has remained an indomitable, resourceful, and charming performer. He wrote a number of folk standards—including "If I Had a Hammer" (with Lee Hays) and "Where Have All the Flowers Gone?"—and has preserved and given exposure to thousands of other songs.

Seeger's interest in music began early. His father was a musicologist, and his mother a violin teacher; both were on the faculty of the Juilliard School of Music. He had learned banjo, ukulele, and guitar by his teens, when he developed an interest in America's folk-music legacy at age 16, after attending a folk festival in North Carolina. He began working with noted folk archivist and field recorder Alan Lomax before traveling around the country as a hobo, absorbing rural music. He attended Harvard University and served in the army in World War II. In the Forties Seeger became a friend and singing associate of Woody Guthrie before forming the Weavers, an enormously popular folk quartet that popularized such folk chestnuts as "On Top of Old Smokey" and Leadbelly's "Goodnight Irene" [see entry].

In the Fifties Seeger's sympathies with humanitarian socialism led him to be blacklisted by the House Un-American Activities Committee; still Seeger continued to perform wherever he could. He recorded for Folkways and signed with John Hammond and Columbia Records in the early Sixties. As always, Seeger did more than just perform. A gifted storyteller and music historian, he brought to his audiences not just the songs, but the stories of the people who wrote and first sang them. In his 1993 autobiography, *Where Have All the Flowers Gone*, for example, Seeger writes of "Wimoweh": "Please don't sing it the way the American pop record had it: 'In the jungle . . . , etc.' This trivializes a song of great historical importance."

With the arrival of the Vietnam War protests, Seeger was rediscovered by a younger audience. In 1965 the Byrds had a #1 hit with Seeger's "Turn! Turn! Turn!," a Biblical passage set to music. From the mid-Seventies on, Seeger has worked regularly with Woody Guthrie's son Arlo. He has crusaded for ecology with the sloop *Clearwater*, giving concerts along the Hudson River. Seeger has toured and sung around the world. His music instructional books and records inspired generations of self-taught musicians and folksingers (including Joni Mitchell).

Seeger's sister Peggy is also an accomplished folk musician and songwriter. In addition to her feminist anthem "Gonna Be an Engineer," Peggy also wrote with her husband Ewan MacColl. In the Fifties she moved to

England, where she joined a folk group called the Ramblers, with Alan Lomax, Shirley Collins, and Ewan MacColl (father of singer Kirsty and writer of "The First Time Ever I Saw Your Face"). A British citizen, Peggy Seeger continues to tour and record.

Bob Seger

Born May 6, 1945, Dearborn, Michigan
1969—*Ramblin' Gamblin' Man* (Capitol); *Noah*
1970—*Mongrel*   1971—*Brand New Morning*
1972—*Smokin' O.P.'s* (Palladium)   1973—*Back in '72*   1974—*Seven*   1975—*Beautiful Loser* (Capitol)
1976—*Live Bullet*; *Night Moves*   1978—*Stranger in Town*   1980—*Against the Wind*   1981—*Nine Tonight*   1982—*The Distance*   1986—*Like a Rock*
1991—*The Fire Inside*   1994—*Greatest Hits*.

For years, singer/songwriter Bob Seger remained a local Michigan rock hero. His music brought together Detroit's two legacies—hard rock and soul—while a series of bad breaks denied him the nationwide audience critics thought his hard-driving workingman's rock deserved. But he came into his own in 1976 with the gold *Live Bullet* and platinum *Night Moves* LPs.

Seger's father had been a big-band leader who quit music to work in a factory, then left the family when Seger was 12, leaving the boy to live in near-poverty with his mother and brother. (His father died in a fire in 1968.) In 1961 Seger led a three-piece band, the Decibels, then joined another local Michigan band, the Town Criers, before going on to Doug Brown's Omens. Seger recorded "East Side Story" with members of the Town Criers and the Omens; the tune had previously been a failure for the Underdogs, which included Michael and Suzi Quatro and future Eagle Glenn Frey, but Seger's version was a local hit in 1966. He later produced Frey's first solo single, "Such a Lonely Child."

In the late Sixties Seger had strong followings in the Midwest and Florida as well as more big local hits, such as "Persecution Smith," "Ramblin' Gamblin' Man," and most notably, "Heavy Music," which had begun climbing the national chart before dropping when Seger's record company, Cameo, folded. He also recorded an answer record to Staff Sergeant Barry Sadler's "The Ballad of the Green Berets"—"Ballad of the Yellow Beret"—for Are You Kidding Me Records in 1966, but when legal action was threatened, the label withdrew the 45.

Seger signed with Capitol in 1969. Despite having his first national hit in early 1969 with a rereleased "Ramblin' Gamblin' Man" (#17), he left music later that year to go back to college. By 1970, though, he was back on the road with a group called Teegarden and Van Winkle, a partnership resulting in 1972's *Smokin' O.P.'s*, his first for his own label, Palladium. *Back in '72*, partly recorded at Muscle Shoals and including J. J. Cale backing on some

Bob Seger

cuts, was yet another commercial failure, as was *Seven*, which yielded the failed single "Get Out of Denver" (later covered by Dave Edmunds).

After Seger moved back to Capitol, things slowly began to click with *Beautiful Loser*, which introduced Seger's own backup unit, the Silver Bullet Band (Drew Abbott, guitar; Robyn Robbins, keyboards; Alto Reed, sax; Chris Campbell, bass; Charlie Allen Martin, drums), and included another local Detroit hit, "Katmandu." The *Live Bullet* double album, recorded in Detroit, stayed on the U.S. chart for over three years and eventually went quadruple platinum.

The five-million-seller *Night Moves* established Seger on ballads (the hit title tune, #8, 1977; "Mainstreet," #24, 1977) as well as hard rock ("Rock and Roll Never Forgets," #41, 1977). *Stranger in Town* yielded four major hits: "Still the Same" (#4), "Hollywood Nights" (#12), and "We've Got Tonite" (#13) in 1978, and "Old Time Rock & Roll" (#28) in 1979. By the time of the four-million-selling *Against the Wind* (1980), Seger's only #1 LP, his singles had become almost exclusively ballads: "Fire Lake" (#6), "Against the Wind" (#5), and "You'll Accomp'ny Me" (#14). Only "Horizontal Bop" (#42), from that album, was uptempo. The singer's second live LP, *Nine Tonight*, became his fifth consecutive multiplatinum release.

But beginning with 1982's *The Distance*, Seger's sales began to taper off (his taking three- and five-year sabbaticals between records certainly was a factor), although that album and the two to follow, *Like a Rock* and *The Fire Inside*, each sold a million copies. *The Distance* also signaled the gradual revamping of the Silver Bullet

Band. Guitarist Drew Abbott quit in anger after Seger began using session musicians such as pianist Roy Bittan from Bruce Springsteen's E Street band and guitarist Waddy Wachtel. The band has shed members ever since, with only bassist Chris Campbell remaining. Former Grand Funk keyboardist Craig Frost came aboard in 1980 and on *Like a Rock* cowrote two songs with Seger, who also provided a home, briefly, to ex-GFR drummer Don Brewer.

Seger contributed the song "Understanding" to the soundtrack of the film *Teachers* in 1984; it went Top Twenty. "Shakedown," from 1987's *Beverly Hills Cop II*, topped the chart. The Keith Forsey tune had been offered first to Seger's pal Glenn Frey, but he contracted laryngitis and couldn't record it. *The Fire Inside* (1991), coproduced by Don Was, gave Seger only one hit, "Real Love" (#24). *Greatest Hits* charted at #8 in 1995.

The Seldom Scene

Formed 1971, Arlington, Virginia
John Duffy (b. Mar. 4, 1934, Washington, D.C.), mandolin; Mike Auldridge (b. Dec. 30, 1938, Washington), dobro; Ben Eldridge (b. Aug. 15, 1938, Va.), banjo; John Starling (b. Mar. 26, 1940, Durham, N.C.), gtr., voc.; Tom Gray, bass.
1972—*Act One* (Rebel)   1973—*Act Two*; *Act Three*
1974—*Old Train*   1975—*Recorded Live at the Cellar Door*   1976—*The New Seldom Scene Album*
1977—(– Starling; + Phil Rosenthal, gtr., voc.)
1978—*Baptizing*   1979—*Act Four* (Sugar Hill)
1981—*After Midnight*   1983— . . . *At the Scene*
1986—(– Rosenthal; – Gray; + Lou Reid, gtr., voc.; + T. Michael Coleman [b. Jan. 13, 1951, Leaksville, N.C.]; bass, voc.) *The Best of the Seldom Scene, vol. 1* (Rebel)   1988—*A Change of Scenery* (Sugar Hill)
1990—*Scenic Roots*   1992—*Scene 20: 20th Anniversary Concert* (– Reid; + Starling; – Starling)   1994—*Like We Used to Be* (+ Moondi Klein [b. Mar. 13, 1963, Port Jefferson, N.Y.], gtr., voc.).

For over 20 years the Seldom Scene has been a major proponent of "new grass," a genre that combines the instrumentation and style of bluegrass with material most often performed by rock and/or folk performers. Founded by John Duffy, "the father of modern bluegrass," the Seldom Scene's unique approach has enabled them to balance tradition and innovation without alienating advocates of either camp. The Seldom Scene's newgrass roots come honestly: Both Duffy and original bass player Tom Gray were members of the first progressive bluegrass outfit, the Country Gentlemen, formed in 1957. Like the Scene, they covered contemporary country, pop, and folk tunes in addition to bluegrass standards.

The Seldom Scene has recorded with some of the biggest names in contemporary country music, and has simultaneously acquired a reputation as a powerful, spontaneous live ensemble. Guest fiddler Ricky Skaggs graces *Act Three*, and *The New Seldom Scene Album* features Linda Ronstadt on vocals. *Old Train* includes both Skaggs and Ronstadt, as the band runs through their trademark concoction of traditional and new material. *Scene 20* chronicles two nights of performance at the Birchmere club in Alexandria, Virginia, where the band has been honing its onstage skills every Thursday night since its inception. Completely free of overdubs, this album includes all eight Seldom Scene members up to that point, and Emmylou Harris contributes lead vocals to the bittersweet "Satan's Jeweled Crown."

In 1994 the Seldom Scene released *Like We Used to Be*, which featured a return to the lineup by guitarist/vocalist John Starling, who departed again before the album was released. Taking his place was Moondi Klein, who moved to Washington, D.C., in 1984, harboring aspirations of joining the Seldom Scene, of which he had been enamored since discovering bluegrass music at age 14. By mid-1995 it was rumored that the group had decided to discontinue touring.

The Selecter

Formed 1979, Coventry, England
Noel Davies, gtr.; Charley Anderson, bass; Pauline Black, voc.; Charley "H" Bembridge, drums; Compton Amanor, gtr.; Arthur "Gaps" Hendrickson, voc.; Desmond Brown, kybds.
1980—*Too Much Pressure* (Chrysalis)   1981—*Celebrate the Bullet* (group disbands)   1992—*Out in the Streets* (Triple X) (group re-forms: Davies; Black; + Perry Melius, drums; + Martin Stewart, kybds.; + Nick Welsh, bass)   1993—*Madness* EP   1994—*The Happy Album*.

Along with the Specials, Madness, and the English Beat, the Selecter was one of the main bands in the ska-influenced two-tone trend that broke big in England in 1979. Like the other bands in this "movement," the Selecter used the old Mod two-tone fashion style as a visual aid. Its music was an upbeat blend of ska (quicker and less brooding than reggae, which also influenced the group's music), rock, and soul, with socially conscious lyrics, backed up by the band's own racially and sexually integrated personnel.

Like the Specials, the members of the Selecter all hailed from the industrial city of Coventry, about 80 miles northwest of London. Noel Davies had written a song called "The Selecter" that he tried to sell to various companies, without success. Davies and the Specials financed their own label, 2-Tone, and issued a single, "Gangsters" b/w "The Selecter," with Davies playing

The Selecter: Charley Anderson, Noel Davis, Charley Bembridge, Compton Amanor, Pauline Black, Desmond Brown, Arthur "Gaps" Hendrickson

guitar. The single went British Top Ten in 1979, and Davies formed a band.

Charley Anderson, Charley Bembridge, Arthur Hendrickson, and Compton Amanor had been playing in the Coventry roots-reggae band Hard Top 22; the band was completed with Pauline Black and Desmond Brown, who were working in another local rock-reggae outfit. Their 2-Tone label went on to become England's most successful independent record company since Stiff, and the band's 1980 debut, *Too Much Pressure,* came out in America on Chrysalis. Highlighted by Black's lead vocals, the sound was fast-paced and politically charged. It was the rage for a short while in England (the single "Three Minute Hero" went Top Ten there), but it did not go over in America despite positive press and a strong summer tour. In 1981 the Selecter released a second album, *Celebrate the Bullet,* and was featured in the film and soundtrack that year to *Dance Craze,* chronicling all the 2-Tone bands, but broke up in late 1981.

Black released a British single, "Pirates of the Airwaves," that year, but soon left the music business to concentrate on acting, appearing on the British children's show *Hold Tight.* In 1992 she again joined forces with Davies in a re-formed Selecter, featuring members of 2-Tone–style band Bad Manners. They began touring again after the release of *Out in the Streets* (1992), a greatest-hits collection, and returned to the studio in 1993 to record *Madness* with ska legend Prince Buster.

Erick Sermon: See EPMD

Brian Setzer Orchestra: See the Stray Cats

The Sex Pistols

Formed 1975, London, England
Johnny Rotten (b. John Lydon, Jan. 31, 1956, London), voc.; Steve Jones (b. Sep. 3, 1955, London), gtr.; Glen Matlock (b. London), bass; Paul Cook (b. July 20, 1956, London), drums.
1977—(– Matlock; + Sid Vicious [b. John Simon Ritchie, May 10, 1957, London; d. Feb. 2, 1979, New York City, N.Y.], bass) *Never Mind the Bollocks Here's the Sex Pistols* (Warner Bros.)   1979—*The Great Rock 'n' Roll Swindle* (Virgin).

Unabashedly crude, intensely emotional, calculated either to exhilarate or to offend, the Sex Pistols' music and stance were in direct opposition to the star trappings and complacency that they felt had rendered rock & roll irrelevant to the common bloke. Apparently, they were not alone. Over the course of their short, turbulent existence, they released a single studio album that changed if not the history of rock, at least its course. While the Sex Pistols were not the first punk rockers (that distinction probably goes to the Stooges), they were the most widely known and, at least to appearances, the most threatening. *Never Mind the Bollocks Here's the Sex Pistols* unquestionably ranks as one of the most important rock & roll records ever, its sound a raw, snarling, yet mesmerizing rejection of and challenge to not only rock & roll music and culture but a modern world that offered, as Rotten sang in "God Save the Queen," "no future." Whether the Sex Pistols were simply a sophisticated hype run amok or the true voice of their generation has been widely debated, yet, oddly, neither matters nor explains how they came to spark and personify one of the few truly critical moments in pop culture—the rise of punk.

The Sex Pistols were the brainchild of young entrepreneur Malcolm McLaren [see entry]. The owner of a London clothes boutique, Sex, which specialized in "anti-fashion," McLaren had conceived the idea of a rock & roll act that would challenge every established notion of propriety when, in 1975, he found himself managing the New York Dolls in their final months as a group. A part-time employee of Sex, Glen Matlock played bass with Paul Cook and Steve Jones; he let McLaren know they were looking for a singer. McLaren approached 19-year-old John Lydon, whom he had seen hanging around the jukebox at Sex and who was known mainly for his rudeness.

Lydon had never sung before, but he accepted the invitation and thoroughly impressed the others with his scabrous charisma. McLaren had found his act; he named the group the Sex Pistols. Allegedly, Lydon's disregard for personal hygiene prompted Jones to dub him Johnny Rotten. Ten minutes into their first gig at a suburban art school dance on November 6, 1975, the school's social programmer unplugged their amplifiers. In the early months of 1976, McLaren's carefully cultivated word-of-mouth about the Sex Pistols made them leaders of the nascent punk movement. Their gigs inspired the formation of the Clash, Buzzcocks, X-Ray Spex, Joy Division, Siouxsie and the Banshees, and countless other rebel groups in the second half of the Seventies.

The press and record industry ignored the Sex Pistols at first, but by the end of the summer the uproar—both acclamatory and denunciatory—was too loud to be ignored. In November EMI outbid Polydor with a recording contract worth £40,000. The Sex Pistols' first single, "Anarchy in the U.K.," was released in December. That month the band used the word "fucker" in a nationally televised interview; the consequent outrage led promoters and local authorities to cancel all but five of the dates scheduled on the group's national tour and EMI to withdraw "Anarchy in the U.K."—#38 on the U.K. chart in January 1977—from circulation and to terminate its contract with the Sex Pistols.

In March Matlock left to form the Rich Kids and was replaced by John Ritchie, a previously nonmusical friend of Rotten, who named him Sid Vicious. That same month A&M signed up the Pistols for £150,000; just a week later the company fired them for a balance payment of £75,000. In May Virgin signed the Pistols and released their second record, "God Save the Queen," in time to spite the queen's Silver Jubilee that June. The song was immediately banned from airplay in England. Nonetheless it was a top-selling single (cited as a blank at the #2 position on official charts, listed as #1 on independent charts).

When no hall in Britain would book the Sex Pistols, they went abroad—to the Continent in July and to the U.S. in December, by which time their album had been released. In America they found themselves the object of a little adulation, considerable hostility, but mostly uncomprehending curiosity, which turned to scoffing when the Pistols made only halfhearted attempts to live up to their reputation for savagery. Rotten was characteristically critical of the sensationalism and opportunism that had been attached to the Sex Pistols (for which he blamed McLaren), and on January 14, 1978, immediately after a concert in San Francisco, he announced the breakup of the group. *The Great Rock 'n' Roll Swindle* was a film directed by Julien Temple that included early footage of the group. Jones and Cook remained active in the punk movement and formed the Professionals; Jones materialized in the mid-Eighties in Chequered Past, which included former Blondie rhythm section Nigel Harrison and Clem Burke, Tony Sales, and singer Michael des Barres. Vicious initiated a solo career, which ended when he was imprisoned in New York on charges of stabbing his girlfriend Nancy Spungen to death in their Chelsea Hotel room. He died of a heroin overdose while out on bail before he could be tried.

Dismissing the Sex Pistols as "a farce" and reverting to his given name, Lydon formed Public Image, Ltd. [see entry]. In 1986 the surviving members of the group and Vicious' mother won a lawsuit against McLaren, charging he had tied up their royalties in two management companies. The plaintiffs were later awarded approximately $1.44 million. That same year, the critically acclaimed Alex Cox film *Sid and Nancy* was released. Nancy Spungen's mother wrote a book entitled *And I Don't Want to Live This Life*, in which she recounted her daughter's lifelong emotional and psychological problems and presented a surprisingly sympathetic view of her relationship with Vicious.

Charlie Sexton/Arc Angels

Born August 11, 1968, San Antonio, Texas
1985—*Pictures for Pleasure* (MCA)   1989—*Charlie Sexton*   1995—*Under the Wishing Tree* (with the Charlie Sexton Sextet).
With Arc Angels (Sexton, gtr., voc.; Chris Layton [b. Nov. 16, 1955, Corpus Christi, Tex.], drums; Tommy Shannon [b. Apr. 18, 1948, Tucson, Ariz.], bass; Doyle Bramhall II [b. Dec. 24, 1968, Dallas, Tex.], gtr., voc.): 1992—*Arc Angels* (DGC).

Charlie Sexton's precocious guitar skills earned him a record contract at the age of 15, but it was his high cheekbones and skinny, vaguely androgynous sensuality that won the singer and musician heavy rotation on MTV two years later, when his 1985 debut album and single hit the pop chart. Alas, a teen idol's reign is usually short-lived, and in the early Nineties, after a disappointing sophomore effort, Sexton resurfaced as one-fourth of Arc Angels, a roots-rock outfit that made a bid for the sort of artistic credibility that he had aspired to as a child prodigy. By 1994 the Arc Angels had disbanded, and Sexton formed the Charlie Sexton Sextet for his 1995 album *Under the Wishing Tree*.

Sexton's prodigious behavior began when he picked up a guitar at the age of four, encouraged by his blues-and-rockabilly-loving mother. (Younger brother Will fronts the band Will and the Kill.) By the time he was ten the fledgling musician was sitting in on club gigs around Austin, Texas; about a year later he met Joe Ely, who enlisted him for a six-week tour. Sexton then played in various other bands before being signed by MCA Records. Session work with Keith Richards and Ron Wood, Bob Dylan, and Don Henley followed before the teenager's first album, *Pictures for Pleasure*, was released and shot to #15, also spawning the #17 single "Beat's So Lonely." Sexton's low, throaty vocals and buoyantly disposable hard-rock songs evoked shades of Billy Idol. As for Sexton, his self-titled second album peaked at #104, then quickly disappeared.

In 1990, while working on material for a comeback

effort at the Austin Rehearsal Complex (ARC), Sexton encountered drummer Chris Layton and bassist Tommy Shannon, the rhythm section of Stevie Ray Vaughan's band Double Trouble, and singer/guitarist Doyle Bramhall II, the son of drummer Doyle Bramhall who had played with Vaughan's brother Jimmie in the Fabulous Thunderbirds. The musicians clicked immediately, and became the group Arc Angels shortly afterward, following Stevie Ray's death in a 1990 helicopter crash. Their eponymous 1992 debut album was predictably a gritty, bluesy, album-rock-oriented affair, and was produced by Little Steven Van Zandt, *Arc Angels* (#126, 1992) garnered critical acclaim, if not commercial success. After the group broke up, Sexton collaborated with songwriter Tonio K. on material for *Under the Wishing Tree.*

The Shadows
Formed 1958 as the Drifters, London, England
Hank B. Marvin (b. Oct. 28, 1941, Newcastle, Eng.), gtr., voc.; Bruce Welch [b. Nov. 2, 1941, Bognor Regis, Eng.], gtr., voc.; Ian Samwell, bass; Terry Smart, drums; Ken Payne, gtr.
Before 1962—(– Samwell; + Jet Harris [b. July 6, 1939], bass; – Smart; + Tony Meehan [b. Mar. 2, 1942, London], drums; – Meehan; + Brian Bennett [b. Feb. 9, 1940, London], drums)   1962—*The Shadows* (Columbia, U.K.) (– Harris; – Bennett; + "Licorice" Locking, bass)   1963—*Greatest Hits* (– Locking; + John Rostill [b. June 16, 1942, Birmingham, Eng.; d. Nov. 26, 1973], bass)   1965—*More Hits*   1968—(– Welch; + Adam Hawkshaw, gtr., voc.)   1972—(– Hawkshaw; + Welch; + John Farrar, bass, gtr., voc.)   1973—*Specs Appeal* (EMI) 1976—*Rarities*   1977—*The Best of the Shadows*; 20 Golden Greats.

While still backing British teen idol Cliff Richard in the late Fifties, the Shadows began to branch out into a successful instrumental-rock career of their own, which made ever-bespectacled lead guitarist Hank B. Marvin one of the most influential British rock guitarists.

Marvin, whose twanging guitar leads were the group's hallmark, took up banjo and guitar as a youth, and by 14 he and schoolmate Bruce Welch were playing together in skiffle groups. They moved to London's Soho section, and after a few months of living in poverty, they joined Richard's touring band, which already included Terry Smart and Ian Samwell (the latter wrote Richard's first hit, "Move It").

The group was originally called the Drifters, but changed its name to the Shadows to avoid confusion with the American vocal group. They stayed with Richard through 1968, despite their own long string of hits. They appeared with Richard in films like *Expresso Bongo, The Young Ones, Summer Holiday,* and *Finders Keepers,* and despite several personnel changes, they always maintained their trademark sound. Their first single, 1959's "Feelin' Fine," wasn't a hit, but their fourth, 1960's "Apache," was a long-running #1 in the U.K. In 1981, it was revived in a rap-funk version by the Sugar Hill Gang.

Most of their 20-plus followup hits—"F.B.I.," "Kon Tiki," "Atlantis," "Frightened City" (1961); "Shindig" (1963); "Don't Make My Baby Blue" (1965)—were instrumentals and were mainly U.K. successes, including 13 Top Ten hits. In 1962 Tony Meehan and Jet Harris performed as a duo, and they had three 1963 hits in Britain: "Diamonds" (#1), "Scarlet O'Hara" (#2), and "Applejack" (#4). After Harris was involved in a car crash, Meehan returned to songwriting and production work.

Welch finally quit in 1968, precipitating the first of several Shadows breakups. Within two years, though, he and Marvin were back together with Bennett and Australian guitarist John Farrar. They recorded two LPs as Marvin, Welch and Farrar. Ex-bassist Rostill had gone on to play with Tom Jones, to record a few solo singles, and to write tunes for Engelbert Humperdinck, the Family Dogg, and others, and was fatally electrocuted by his guitar in 1973.

Meanwhile, the Shadows had split up again in 1969—when Welch fell ill—and they re-formed several times through the Seventies. The title of 1973's *Specs Appeal* referred to Marvin's glasses. In 1977 the *20 Golden Greats* album was #1 in Britain, and the Shadows re-formed again to tour by popular demand. They have regrouped several times over the years. In 1986 Marvin appeared on a remake of "Living Doll" that Cliff Richard recorded with the cast of the popular British comedy *The Young Ones.*

Bennett, Welch, Farrar, and Marvin have done session and production work; Welch has worked with Cliff Richard and Farrar with Olivia Newton-John; Meehan has become a successful producer and arranger. As recently as the mid-Eighties, the group has placed an album in the U.K. Top Ten. In 1983 the group received the Ivor Novello award for its contribution to British music. In 1990 Bennett retired from the Shadows. Marvin pursued solo projects; Welch became a musical advisor to the long-running West End show *Buddy,* about the life of Buddy Holly. Welch and Marvin have had a prickly relationship over the years. Most recently Bennett and Marvin toured with their sons.

The Shaggs
Formed circa 1969, Fremont, New Hampshire
Betty Wiggin (b. Fremont, N.H.), voc., gtr.; Dorothy Wiggin (b. Fremont), gtr.; Helen Wiggin (b. Fremont), drums.
1969—*Philosophy of the World* (Third World)

1982—*Shaggs' Own Thing* (Red Rooster) 1988—
The Shaggs (Rounder).

The Shaggs' *Philosophy of the World* was one of the most curious collectors' records of the Seventies.

Dorothy Wiggin was the group's songwriter; she and her two sisters played the music; their father paid for the studio time, for which they traveled from their New Hampshire home to Boston. By most standards, the Shaggs were horrible, but their utter originality and boundless enthusiasm were undeniable. Their record became a valued item in the homes of such personages as NRBQ's Terry Adams. Adams arranged for the album's reissue in 1980 on NRBQ's Red Rooster label (distributed by Rounder), increasing the Shaggs' cult by leaps and bounds and whetting the appetite for more Shaggs, in the form of *Shaggs' Own Thing* and its followup, *The Shaggs.*

Shai

Formed 1990, Washington, D.C.
Garfield A. Bright (b. Oct. 21, 1969, Nashville,
Tenn.), voc.; Marc Gay (b. Jan. 21, 1969, Miami, Fla.),
voc.; Carl Martin (b. Aug. 29, 1970, Lafayette, La.),
voc.; Darnell Van Rensalier (b. May 17, 1970, Patter-
son, N.J.), voc.
1992—*If I Ever Fall in Love* (Gasoline Alley/MCA)
1993—*Right Back at Cha.*

Shai's pure vocal harmonies and a sweetly sentimental love song—"If I Ever Fall in Love" (#2 pop and R&B, 1992)—made them an overnight success. The four-part harmony group was formed by fraternity members at Howard University, who were influenced by Jodeci, Boyz II Men, and Color Me Badd.

After being turned down by several record company executives unimpressed by their live a cappella auditions, Shai (Egyptian for "personification of destiny") recorded a demo of the Martin-penned "If I Ever Fall in Love." Shortly after Shai won a demo-tape contest sponsored by the Washington, D.C., radio station WPGC, the song became a local favorite; once it was distributed to WPGC's sister stations across the country, it became a hit. Shai signed with MCA affiliate Gasoline Alley and rushed into the studio to record their first album, which they wrote and produced themselves. In 1993 *If I Ever Fall in Love* (#6 pop, #3 R&B) went double platinum and featured two more hits, the ballad "Comforter" (#10 pop, #4 R&B) and "Baby I'm Yours" (#10 pop, #19 R&B). The group's second album, *Right Back at Cha* (#127 pop, #42 R&B, 1994), was basically a remix and live album.

Shakespear's Sister: See
Bananarama

Shalamar

Formed 1977, Los Angeles, California
Jeffrey Daniels (b. Aug. 24, 1957, Los Angeles), voc.;
Jody Watley (b. Jan. 30, 1959, Chicago, Ill.), voc.;
Howard Hewett (b. Oct. 1, 1957, Akron, Ohio.), voc.
1978—*Disco Gardens* (Solar) 1979—*Big Fun*
1981—*Three for Love; Go for It* 1982—*Friends*
1983—*The Look* 1984—*Heart Break* (– Daniels;
– Watley; + Delisa Davis, voc.; + Micki Free, voc.)
1985—(– Hewett; + Sidney Justin, voc.) 1987—*Cir-*
cumstantial Evidence* 1990—*Wake Up.*
Howard Hewett solo: 1986—*I Commit to Love* (Elek-
tra) 1988—*Forever and Ever* 1990—*Howard*
Hewett* 1995—*It's Time* (Caliber).

This good-looking vocal trio were black teen idols of the late Seventies and early Eighties, and each pursued a successful solo career after leaving the group. The original Shalamar was made up of several Los Angeles session singers convened in 1977 by concert promoter Dick Griffey to record a medley of Motown dance hits, "Uptown Festival" (#25 pop, #10 R&B, 1977). With producer Leon Sylvers III, they had a dance hit with "Take That to the Bank" (#11 R&B, 1978), a lively number that was the model for other hits on Griffey's new Solar ("Sound of Los Angeles Records") label.

For a touring group, Griffey recruited Jeffrey Daniels and Jody Watley, two dancers from *Soul Train*, the television show produced by his friend and sometime business partner Don Cornelius. Howard Hewett joined after the original third member, Gerald Brown, left. "The Second Time Around" (#8 pop, #1 R&B, 1979) established them as stars; they followed up with "Right in the Socket" (#22 R&B, 1980), "Full of Fire" (#24 R&B, 1980), and "Make That Move" (#6 R&B, 1981).

Adding to their teen appeal was a real-life love triangle between Daniels, Watley, and singer Stephanie Mills. The two Shalamar singers had been childhood sweethearts, but after meeting Mills in New York, Daniels married the Broadway star; less than a year later, they were divorced—all of which was dramatically reported in teen magazines. In 1981 Shalamar released "This Is for the Lover in You" (#17 R&B, 1981) and "Sweeter as the Days Go By" (#19 R&B, 1981). The group's last two big hits were "Dead Giveaway" (#22 pop, #10 R&B, 1983) and "Dancing in the Sheets" (#17 pop, #18 R&B, 1984), the latter from the hit movie *Footloose* soundtrack.

After that, Watley left to pursue her solo ambitions [see entry]. Daniels also quit the group. He moved to England, where he hosted that country's version of *Soul Train;* he also appeared in the West End production of *Starlight Express.* Hewett, the remaining member of the most successful lineup, left in 1985. His R&B hits singles include "I'm for Real" (#2 R&B, 1986), "Stay" (#8 R&B, 1986), "I Commit to Love" (#12 R&B, 1987), "Strange Relationship" (#9, 1988), and "Show Me" (#2 R&B, 1990). In 1989 he married actress Nia Peeples. The new version of Shalamar placed a number of singles on the R&B chart, including "Games" (#11 R&B, 1987).

Sha Na Na

Formed 1968, New York City, New York
Original lineup: Johnny Contardo, voc.; Scott Powell, voc; Frederick Dennis "Denny" Greene, voc.; Don York, voc.; Bruce Clarke, bass; John "Jocko" Marcellino, drums; Ritchie Joffe, voc.; Elliot Cahn, gtr.; Henry Gross, gtr.; Chris Donald, gtr.; Screamin' Scott Simon, piano, bass; John "Bowser" Baumann, piano, voc.; Lennie Baker (b. Apr. 18, 1946, Whitman, Mass.), sax.
1969—*Rock & Roll Is Here to Stay* (Kama Sutra) 1971—*Sha Na Na* 1972—*The Night Is Still Young* 1973—*The Golden Age of Rock 'n' Roll*; *From the Streets of New York* 1974—*Hot Sox* 1975—*Sha Na Now* 1976—*Best of Sha Na Na* 1990—*34th & Vine* (Gold Castle) 1993—*The Sha Na Na 25th Anniversary Collection* (Laurie).

Sha Na Na were forerunners of the Fifties revival craze that eventually spawned television shows like *Happy Days* and the movie *Grease*. They began while students at Columbia University, making frequent appearances at the Fillmore East. Their big break was a booking at the Woodstock festival in 1969. The band's humor, choreography, and Fifties costuming caught on, and though never particularly successful on record, Sha Na Na became a popular live attraction, first on the rock & roll circuit, later in nightclubs. Their popularity reached unprecedented heights starting in 1977, when they began a syndicated TV show, which ran until 1981 and was shown around the world. They also appeared in the movie *Grease* (1978).

Over the years, personnel has been fluid, the most notable change being the departure of original guitarist Henry Gross in 1970 for a solo career, which was highlighted by the 1976 hit single "Shannon." Jon "Bowser" Bauman went into television, cohosting a local Los Angeles morning show in the Eighties. Screamin' Scott Simon cowrote "Sandy," which became a hit for John Travolta from the *Grease* soundtrack. Simon has also released solo albums. In the Seventies Donny York wrote "Rock & Roll Hall of Fame," which is planned to be used as a theme song when the Rock and Roll Hall of Fame's awards ceremonies are broadcast in the future.

As of 1994 Sha Na Na—with Jocko Marcellino, Donny York, Lennie Baker, and Screamin' Scott from the original lineup—was still performing approximately 100 dates a year around the world, including an appearance at the Woodstock '69 Reunion in Bethel, New York, and the year before that, a two-week stint in the entertainment capital of the heartland, Branson, Missouri. Latter-day members include Reggie De Leon, an actor and choreographer who appeared in *Stayin' Alive*, among other films; Chico Ryan, who had belonged to the Happenings and later toured with the Comets; Rob MacKenzie; Jimmy Wall; and Lisa, the group's first "greaserette."

The Shangri-Las

Formed 1964, Queens, New York
Mary Ann Ganser (d. 1971, N.Y.), voc.; Marge Ganser, voc.; Liz (Betty) Weiss, voc.; Mary Weiss, voc.
1964—*Leader of the Pack* (Red Bird) 1965—*Shangri-Las '65* 1966—*I Can Never Go Home Anymore*; *Golden Hits* (Mercury) 1976—*Remember (Walking in the Sand)* EP (Charly, U.K.).

Of the early-Sixties girl vocal groups who rose meteorically to fame and disappeared nearly as quickly, one of the few white units was the Shangri-Las: two sets of sisters (the Gansers were twins) who first started singing together at Andrew Jackson High School in Queens. Their stock in trade was the teen-angst-ridden minimelodramas written for them by writer/producer George "Shadow" Morton, sometimes abetted by Jeff Barry and Ellie Greenwich.

In early 1964 they attracted the attention of Morton, who got the new Red Bird label (for which he was a producer) off the ground with the first Shangri-Las hit, his "Remember (Walkin' in the Sand)" (#5, 1964). A few months later, they recorded the motorcycle-gang melodrama "Leader of the Pack"—a typically showy Morton production complete with sound effects and talk-over sections—which was #1. A death-rock classic, "Leader of the Pack" showcased Mary Weiss' emotional, often overwrought delivery, which so perfectly suited the stories of teen runaways, parental death, and good teens gone bad that followed. Their other hits included "Maybe" (#91) and "Give Him a Great Big Kiss" (#18) in 1964; "Out in the Streets" (#53), "Give Us Your Blessings" (#29), "Right Now and Not Later" (#99), and "I Can Never Go Home Anymore" (#6) in 1965; and "Long Live Our Love" (#33), "He Cried" (#65, a remake of Jay and the Americans' "She Cried"), and "Past, Present and Future" (#59) in 1966.

The group, despite several in-and-out personnel shifts (Liz left early on, and the group remained a trio), was a top concert attraction in the U.S. and the U.K. in those years. But by the late Sixties a morass of legal entanglements, poor chart showings, and a low royalty rate on their biggest hits conspired to bring the Shangri-Las to an end. All four married. Mary Ann Ganser died of encephalitis in 1971.

Del Shannon

Born Charles Westover, December 30, 1939,
Coopersville, Michigan; died February 8, 1990,
Santa Clarita, California
1961—*Runaway* (Big Top)   1963—*Little Town Flirt*
1965—*Handy Man* (Amy); *Sings Hank Williams*;
1,661 Seconds   1966—*This Is My Bag* (Liberty);
Total Commitment   1967—*Best of Del Shannon*
(Dot)   1968—*Further Adventures of Charles West-*
over   1970—*Del Shannon Sings* (Post)   1973—*Live*
in England (United Artists); *Best of Del Shannon*
(Polydor)   1975—*Vintage Years* (Sire)   1981—*Drop*
Down and Get Me (Elektra)   1990—*Greatest Hits*
(Bug/Rhino)   1991—*Rock On!* (Gone Gator/MCA).

With hit songs like "Runaway" and "Hats Off to Larry,"
Del Shannon was one of the few early rockers who wrote
his own material and held his own through the British
Invasion. Shannon was 14 when he learned guitar and
began performing in school shows. After graduating
high school, he took his stage name from those of a
friend (Mark Shannon) and his boss's car (a Cadillac
Coupe de Ville). In early 1960 a Grand Rapids area disc
jockey passed live tapes of Shannon on to manager/
publishers Harry Balk and Irving Micahnik, who then
signed Shannon to Detroit's Big Top label. Big Top sent
him to New York to record, but not much came of it.

On a second trip to New York, Shannon recorded
"Runaway," which—with its galloping beat, Max
Crook's proto-synthesizer Musitron solo, and Shannon's
nearly hiccuping falsetto vocals—went to #1 in 1961. He
followed up with "Hats Off to Larry" (#5), "So Long Baby"
(#28), and "Hey! Little Girl" (#38) in 1961; and "Little
Town Flirt" (#12) in 1962. He first toured England in 1962
and the next year met the Beatles there. His version of
Lennon-McCartney's "From Me to You" made Shannon
the first American to cover a Beatles tune.

In 1963 Shannon had legal problems with Balk and
Micahnik, and the action instituted that year dragged on
for the next decade. Still, he had more hits with "Keep
Searchin' (We'll Follow the Sun)" (#9, 1964) and "Stranger
in Town" (#30) in 1965. That year Peter and Gordon
recorded Shannon's "I Go to Pieces." In 1966 Shannon
signed to Liberty, where producer Snuff Garrett and
arranger Leon Russell tried to mold him into a teen idol.
When Tommy Boyce asked Shannon to record "Action,"
the theme for the TV rock show *Where the Action Is*,
Shannon turned him down and gave the song instead to
Freddy Cannon. The *Total Commitment* LP, belying its
title, was almost all covers. In England in 1967, Shannon
recorded an album with Andrew Loog Oldham called
Home and Away (Nicky Hopkins and John Paul Jones
played on it).

With his career on the wane, Shannon left Liberty in
1969 and concentrated on production work. He arranged

Del Shannon

Smith's 1969 hit "Baby It's You" and produced Brian Hyland's 1970 hit "Gypsy Woman." In England he recorded
tracks with Jeff Lynne of the Electric Light Orchestra (including "Cry Baby Cry"). In 1974 Dave Edmunds produced Shannon's "And the Music Plays On." The next
year, Shannon signed to Island and released a cover of
the Zombies hit "Tell Her No." During 1976 and 1977,
Shannon suffered from alcoholism, but beginning in 1979
he returned to music. He recorded material under the
production supervision of longtime fan Tom Petty, with
Petty's band the Heartbreakers backing him. The album
included "Sea of Love," which hit #33 in early 1982.

Through the remainder of the decade Shannon continued to perform, although he was financially secure. He
was reportedly suffering from severe depression when
he committed suicide in 1990 by shooting himself in the
head. A year later, his wife filed suit against the makers
of Prozac, the antidepressant drug Shannon was taking,
claiming that its use contributed to his death.

Roxanne Shanté

Born Lolita Shanté Gooden, March 8, 1970, New
York City, New York
1989—*Bad Sister* (Cold Chillin')   1992—*The Bitch Is*
Back (Livin' Large).

Roxanne Shanté was one of the first women to directly
challenge sexism in rap. At age 14 she recorded "Roxanne's Revenge" (#22 R&B, 1985), an answer to the popular U.T.F.O. song "Roxanne, Roxanne," which dissed
women who ignored the band's advances. "Revenge,"
produced by Shanté's neighbor in the Queensbridge
projects, Marley Marl, became an underground hit even
before it was pressed to vinyl and kicked off a slew of answer records. U.T.F.O. themselves tried to clarify their

position by recording with a woman they dubbed "the Real Roxanne." The group also forced Marl and Shanté to rerecord "Revenge," which sampled an original U.T.F.O. riff. Ultimately, Shanté's tough, street-smart style bested all other Roxannes.

Shanté followed her success with more Marl-produced singles. "Queen of Rox (Shanté Rox On)" was her summation of the "perils of Roxanne," while the lyrics to "Have a Nice Day" and "Go On Girl" were written by Big Daddy Kane. In 1988 she recorded "Loosey's Rap" (#1 R&B, 1988) with Rick James. Shanté toured extensively, then had a baby. She finally recorded an album in 1989; *Bad Sister* (#52 R&B, 1989) showed Shanté was a formidable, tough rapper with a dirty mouth; tracks like "Knockin' Hiney" and "Feelin' Kinda Horny" followed the tradition of her hero, Millie Jackson. On her second album Shanté dropped the name Roxanne. *The Bitch Is Back* (#82 R&B, 1992) featured a variety of producers, including Kool G Rap, the Large Professor, and Grandmaster Flash, but failed to make much of a commercial impact.

Feargal Sharkey: See the Undertones

Jules Shear
Born March 7, 1952, Pittsburgh, Pennsylvania
1983—*Watch Dog* (EMI America); *Jules EP* 1985—*The Eternal Return* 1987—*Demo-itis* (Enigma) 1989—*The Third Party* (I.R.S.) 1992—*The Great Puzzle* (Polydor) 1993—*Horse of a Different Color: The Jules Shear Collection 1976–1989* (Razor & Tie) 1994—*Healing Bones* (Polydor).
With Funky Kings: 1976—*Funky Kings* (Arista).
With Jules and the Polar Bears: 1978—*Got No Breeding* (Columbia) 1979—*Fenetiks*.
With Reckless Sleepers: 1988—*Big Boss Sounds* (I.R.S.).

A prolific songwriter and recording artist, Jules Shear is widely respected by critics and musicians for his glowing melodies and wry, insightful lyrics. Both with bands and on his own, Shear has produced smart, graceful music that has inspired comparisons to guitar pop heroes from the Byrds to Elvis Costello. Commercial success has nonetheless eluded the singer, whose songs have thus far only become pop hits as covered by other artists: Cyndi Lauper took his "All Through the Night" to #5 in 1984, and in 1986 the Bangles reached #29 with another wistful Shear ballad, "If She Knew What She Wants."

Shear began writing songs as a teenager, and his career epiphany came while he was visiting music clubs during a trip to Los Angeles after his junior year of college. Rather than return to school, he lingered in the city, and in 1976 formed the band Funky Kings with two older minstrels, Jack Tempchin and Richard Stekol. The trio released one album before Shear left to form Jules and the Polar Bears, whose buoyant rock was showcased on two albums that received excellent reviews.

Shear disbanded the Polar Bears in 1980 and relocated to Boston, where he embarked on a solo career, releasing several acclaimed albums. In 1986 Shear formed the band Reckless Sleepers with the Cars' guitarist Elliot Easton and two studio veterans. The band quickly split up, due to Shear's dissatisfaction with its hard-rock approach, but reemerged minus Easton (and plus sessions guitarist Jimmy Vivino) in 1988, with *Big Boss Sounds*. Shear went his own way again for 1989's *The Third Party*, which set his Dylanesque vocals against stark guitar work by the Church's Marty Willson-Piper. Shear's wife, Pal Shazar, contributed vocals to the title track of his 1992 solo effort, *The Great Puzzle*, which he recorded in Woodstock, New York, where he had moved from Boston. Shear also helped conceive MTV's popular *Unplugged* series, which he hosted from 1989 until 1991.

Pete Shelley: See the Buzzcocks

Shep and the Limelites
Formed 1961, Queens, New York
James "Shep" Sheppard (b. ca. 1936, Queens; d. Jan. 24, 1970, Long Island, N.Y.), voc.; Clarence Bassett, voc.; Charles Baskerville, voc.

As lead singer of the Heartbeats, James Sheppard wrote and recorded "A Thousand Miles Away," which, though it only hit #5 on the R&B chart and #53 on the pop chart, remains one of the best-remembered doo-wop ballads of the era. The group was also notable among its doo-wop contemporaries for being a trio, as opposed to the more common quartet and quintet lineups.

In 1961 he formed Shep and the Limelites and hit big with "Daddy's Home" (#2 pop, #4 R&B). Over the next year and a half, they hit the Hot 100 with five more entries, but none went higher than #42. The songs formed a song cycle, detailing the ongoing relationship and lives of the characters in the first hit. And so it was followed by "Three Steps from the Altar," "Our Anniversary," "What Did Daddy Do," and "Remember Baby." The group disbanded after a final single in 1967, "I'm a Hurting Inside."

Sheppard was found dead in 1970 in his automobile on the Long Island Expressway after having been robbed and beaten. In 1982, with "A Thousand Miles Away" featured on the soundtrack of *Diner*, Sheppard's Limelites played some doo-wop revival concerts at places like the Bottom Line in New York City.

Bobby Sherman

Born July 18, 1943, Santa Monica, California
1969—*Bobby Sherman* (Metromedia) 1970—*Here Comes Bobby*; *With Love, Bobby* 1971—*Portrait of Bobby*; *Getting Together* 1972—*Bobby Sherman's Greatest Hits* 1991—*The Very Best of Bobby Sherman* (Restless); *The Bobby Sherman Christmas Album.*

Bobby Sherman was a teenybopper heartthrob who had talent. Besides singing and acting, Sherman also played guitar, piano, trumpet, trombone, French horn, drums, and sitar. He'd begun performing in school, but rather than going into show business, he first entered college in California to major in psychology. He later told an interviewer, "I gave up psychology because I realized I was a schizo and belonged in show business with the rest of them." Actually he was disovered by an agent and cast in the television series *Shindig!*, where he was a regular from 1964 to 1966. Sherman began writing tunes and making record company rounds, eventually getting some work as a record producer, but none of his early singles clicked.

After *Shindig!* was canceled, Sherman went on to star in the ABC series *Here Come the Brides*. His first hit was 1969's "Little Woman," which made #3 and earned a gold record, and the hits kept coming: "La La La (If I Had You)" (#9, 1969), "Easy Come, Easy Go" (#9, 1970), "Hey, Mister Sun" (#24, 1970), "Julie, Do Ya Love Me" (#5, 1970), "Cried Like a Baby" (#16, 1971), and "The Drum" (#29, 1971). After that, Sherman's record sales fell off. His last bubblegum single was 1972's "Together Again," a tie-in to a failed *Partridge Family* spinoff series. Before and since, Sherman made a number of television guest appearances, on *The Monkees, Love Boat, Emergency, Fantasy Island, Lobo, Murder, She Wrote,* and *The Mod Squad.* He was also in the 1983 film *Get Crazy.*

Sherman's ex-wife married his *Brides* costar David Soul in the Seventies. Sherman is now an emergency training officer for the Los Angeles Police Department. He is also a composer and television producer.

Shinehead

Born Edmund Carl Aiken, April 10, 1962, London, England
1986—*Rough and Rugged* (African Love Music) 1988—*Unity* (Elektra) 1990—*The Real Rock* 1992—*Sidewalk University.*

Shinehead was one of the first artists to fuse reggae and rap styles. He grew up in Jamaica and moved to the Bronx as a teen. After his mom gave him a microphone, he quit college to pursue his love of music. He began toasting in 1982 with the Downbeat International mobile sound system and was a member of the early-Eighties African Love Soundsystem. Shinehead's first single was a reggae version of Michael Jackson's "Billie Jean," released in 1984.

Shinehead's debut album was issued on producer Claude Evans' label, African Love Music. It introduced the roots-rock rapper's unique and often wacky style. The track "Who the Cap Fits," based on a Bob Marley tune, was picked up by New York radio stations and became an underground hit. Elektra signed Shinehead and released *Unity,* which includes remixes of some tracks from *Rough and Rugged.* Run-D.M.C.'s Jam Master Jay produced three cuts. The title track, based on the Beatles' "Come Together," calls for rappers to join together and stop dissing each other. The album features Jamaican session band Roots Radics.

On *The Real Rock,* Shinehead shows off his knack for mimicry and odd inspiration with versions of songs by Sly and the Family Stone, Frank Sinatra, and the Everly Brothers. Shinehead continued to offer positive messages, and with his band No Offense Crew, had a strong live following. On *Sidewalk University* Shinehead covers Sting, Paul McCartney, and Stevie Wonder. The single "Try My Love" was a modest hit. In the summer of 1993 Shinehead headlined the Reggae Sunsplash Tour.

The Shirelles

Formed 1958, Passaic, New Jersey
Shirley Owens Alston (b. June 10, 1941, Passaic), lead voc.; Addie "Micki" Harris (b. Jan. 22, 1940, Passaic; d. June 10, 1982, Los Angeles, Calif.), voc.; Doris Coley Kenner (b. Aug. 2, 1941, Passaic), voc.; Beverly Lee (b. Aug. 3, 1941, Passaic), voc.
1961—*Tonight's the Night* (Scepter); *The Shirelles Sing* 1962—*Baby It's You; Greatest Hits* 1964—*Foolish Little Girl* 1972—*The Shirelles* (RCA) 1986—*Anthology* (Rhino) 1995—*The World's Greatest Girl Group.*

One of the first of the late-Fifties and early-Sixties girl groups and among the few to write their own hits, the Shirelles were also one of the most lasting. The four girls began singing together at school shows and parties. A classmate, Mary Jane (Greenberg), heard them singing one of their compositions, "I Met Him on a Sunday." Mary Jane convinced them to bring the song to her mother, Florence, who was in the music business. The Shirelles auditioned in Florence Greenberg's living room and were signed to Greenberg's Tiara label. In early 1958, "I Met Him on a Sunday" had garnered so much airplay that Decca Records bought it; it was on the pop chart for over two months, reaching #49. Greenberg formed her own independent Scepter Records, and in 1959 she released the Shirelles' cover of the "5" Royales' "Dedicated to the One I Love." Without a national distributor, the disc reached only #83 on the pop chart. In 1960 the Shirelles scored with "Tonight's the Night" (#39 pop, #14 R&B), a song cowritten by lead vocalist Shirley Owens and produced by her cowriter, Luther Dixon, formerly of the Four Buddies.

Within a year, the Shirelles had their first #1 pop hit (#2 R&B) with the Carole King–Gerry Goffin composition "Will You Love Me Tomorrow?" Scepter rereleased "Dedicated to the One I Love," and it joined "Will You" in the Top Ten for a while early in 1961.

The Shirelles became regulars on disc jockey Murray the K's Brooklyn all-star rock shows. In mid-1961 "Mama Said" (by Dixon and W. Denson) reached #4 pop, #2 R&B, and early in 1962 "Baby It's You" (by Burt Bacharach, Hal David, and Barney Williams) went to #8 pop, #3 R&B. A few months later, "Soldier Boy," a first take recorded initially as album filler, became their second #1 pop single (#3 R&B) and their biggest seller. Then Dixon (who had cowritten "Soldier Boy") left Scepter, precipitating the Shirelles' decline, although their first post-Dixon single, "Foolish Little Girl," went to #4 pop, #9 R&B in 1963.

In 1963 the Beatles covered the Shirelles' "Baby It's You" and "Boys" on their first U.K. LP. The Shirelles continued to perform and record, finally breaking up in the late Sixties, then re-forming, sometimes with different members, in the early Seventies to play revival concerts. Their later career was no doubt stymied by a contractual provision that prohibited any member who left the group from ever using the Shirelles name.

In 1994, at a Rhythm and Blues Foundation awards ceremony, the three surviving members sang together for the first time in 19 years. Addie Harris had died in 1982 of a heart attack. Shortly thereafter, all three members expressed interest in rejoining the original lineup.

Shirley and Lee/Shirley and Company

Shirley Goodman (b. Shirley Pixley, June 19, 1936, New Orleans, La.), voc.; Leonard Lee (b. June 29, 1935; d. Oct. 23, 1976, New Orleans), voc.
Shirley and Lee: 1960—*Let the Good Times Roll* (Warwick)   1990—*Shirley and Lee* (EMI).
Shirley and Company: 1975—*Shame, Shame, Shame* (Vibration).

Shirley and Lee, who recorded "Let the Good Times Roll" in 1956, were known as "the sweethearts of the blues." Many of their records were supposed to tell the continuing story of their on-again, off-again romance. Long after the duo had gone separate ways and had stopped making New Orleans R&B hits, Shirley resurfaced in 1975 with the disco hit "Shame, Shame, Shame" (#12 pop, #1 R&B).

Shirley Goodman and Leonard Lee were discovered by New Orleans studio owner Cosimo Matassa when 30 local children, including Shirley and Lee, collected nick-

els to make a two-dollar demo record of "I'm Gone" at Matassa's studio. Matassa dispatched Eddie Mesner of Aladdin Records to track down the teenaged Shirley and Lee, and they rerecorded "I'm Gone" with ace New Orleans producer Dave Bartholomew. The tune was a #2 R&B hit in 1952. Their love-story songs were minor early-Fifties R&B hits, but the big hit was "Let the Good Times Roll," a #2 R&B hit that also did well on the pop chart (#20) in 1956 and eventually sold over a million copies. Despite Shirley's unique quavery soprano, the duo didn't catch on with white audiences—and their only followup was "I Feel Good" (#38 pop, #5 R&B, 1956).

In 1960 they began recording for Warwick and had three Top 100 hits, including a 1960 remake of "Let the Good Times Roll" (#48). They split up in 1963, and Shirley briefly worked with West Coast singer Jesse Hill (of "Ooh Poo Pah Doo" fame) as Shirley and Jesse. She later did sessions for New Orleans–based performers like Harold Battiste and Dr. John. Lee recorded a few singles as Leonard Lee for Imperial and Broadside in the mid-Sixties. In 1972 the pair reunited for one of Richard Nader's Rock & Roll Revival shows.

In 1975 Shirley teamed up with an anonymous crew of studio musicians to record the smash hit "Shame, Shame, Shame," one of the first disco songs. It was cowritten and produced by Sylvia Robinson of Mickey and Sylvia.

Michelle Shocked
Born Michelle Johnston, February 24, 1962, Dallas, Texas
1986—*The Texas Campfire Tapes* (Cooking Vinyl/Mercury)   1988—*Short Sharp Shocked* (Mercury)   1989—*Captain Swing*   1992—*Arkansas Traveler*   1994—*Kind-Hearted Woman* (self-released).

Michelle Shocked's music is as unique and well-traveled as its bohemian author: a downhome hobo and squatter whose albums have shown her adept at bluegrass, rock, punk, soul, and country. Shocked grew up on various army bases until she was 14, when her stepfather retired to the small East Texas town of Gilmer. She ran away from home at 16, and in 1979 moved to Dallas to live with her father, a hippie-ish schoolteacher who had introduced Shocked to music in previous summers by taking her to bluegrass festivals and back-porch picking sessions.

Shocked attended the University of Texas in Austin for a couple years, but quit and moved to San Francisco, where she became involved in hardcore punk and squatter activism. After returning to Austin in 1983, her mother, a fundamentalist Mormon, had Shocked committed to a psychiatric hospital for a month, until the insurance ran out. Homeless, Shocked was institutionalized again and jailed a few times for political protests; during one of these experiences she decided to change her name. She lived in New York in the mid-Eighties, becoming active in the squatter and "antifolk" movements of Manhattan's Lower East Side. After Ronald Reagan was re-elected in 1984, Shocked moved to Amsterdam, although the experience of being raped in Europe ruptured her expatriate dreams.

In May 1986 she returned to Texas and volunteered at the Kerrville Folk Festival. Pete Lawrence, an English producer and label owner, overheard her playing for friends around a campfire and recorded Shocked on a Sony Walkman. He released the recording, crickets chirping in the background and all, and *The Texas Campfire Tapes* went to #1 on the U.K. indie chart. The avowed anarchist suddenly had multinational corporations offering her six-figure contracts; Shocked reputedly turned down a percentage of Polygram's advance offer in a bid for artistic control.

She had to fight for that control, however. When the label sent her to Dwight Yoakam producer Pete Anderson to produce her first album, Shocked read him a protest statement before she would proceed. He eventually convinced her of his integrity, and in two weeks they recorded *Short Sharp Shocked*, a brilliantly catchy album that got critical raves and some radio play with "When I Grow Up" and "Anchorage." The album showed Shocked was not just a folky but a skilled songwriter with serious rock and pop potential (as well as the ability to play hardcore, on one track with punk band M.D.C.). With an ode to slain graffiti artist Michael Stewart and a cover featuring a photo of Shocked in the stranglehold of a San Francisco riot police officer, Shocked also got her political say.

Anderson returned to produce *Captain Swing*, but the album, which was R&B-oriented, was less well-received. Some critics knocked Shocked for shying away from politics, although the album was named after a 19th-century term for industrial sabotage, and the first track was "God Is a Real Estate Developer."

On *Arkansas Traveler* Shocked indulged her wanderlust, recording different tracks in different cities with favorite artists, including Pops Staples, Levon Helm, Red Clay Ramblers, Taj Mahal, Don Was, Hothouse Flowers, Uncle Tupelo, Clarence "Gatemouth" Brown, Doc Watson, and Alison Krauss. She said the album completed a trilogy of tributes to her influences: Texas songwriters and honky-tonk on *Short Sharp Shocked*, jump blues and swing on *Captain Swing*, and fiddle tunes on *Arkansas Traveler*. The album included her own compositions as well as versions of classic minstrel songs and a Woody Guthrie tune. Her attempt to make a political comment on minstrelsy's role in American music by posing in blackface on the album cover, however, was stopped by her record company.

Stating in 1993 that "I am taking responsibility for my own creativity," Shocked began making moves to leave Mercury. Early the next year, she fired her manager and sued the label for failing to honor the creative control clause of her contract. She then recorded and self-released the album *Kind-Hearted Woman*, which was only available for sale at her performances.

Wayne Shorter: See Weather Report

Shriekback
Formed 1981, London, England
Dave Allen (b. Dec. 23, 1955, Cambria, Eng.) bass; Barry Andrews (b. Sep. 12, 1956, Lambeth, Eng.) voc., kybds.; Martyn Barker (b. Sep. 9, 1959, Merseyside, Eng.), drums; Carl Marsh, gtr., voc.
1982—*Tench* EP (Y America)   1983—*Care* (Warner Bros.)   1984—*Jam Science* (Arista, U.K.)   1985—*Oil and Gold* (Island) (– Marsh; + Mike Cozzi [b. Nov. 27, 1960, Usk, Wales], gtr.)   1986—*Big Night Music* (– Allen; + Doug Wimbish [b. Sep. 22, 1956, Hartford, Conn.], bass)   1988—*Go Bang!*   1989—(Group disbands)   1990—*The Dancing Years*   1992—(Group re-forms: Allen; Andrews; Barker; Cozzi) *Sacred City* (World Domination)   1994—(– Allen).

With the pedigree of Gang of Four bassist Dave Allen and XTC [see entries] singer/keyboard player Barry Andrews, Shriekback play smart, tuneful funk. But with a career marred by personnel and record company problems, the band has never gathered the momentum necessary for stardom.

Andrews and Allen joined forces when they found themselves without bands in summer 1981. Adding guitarist/vocalist Carl Marsh and a drum machine, they recorded *Tench* for the independent Y America label in 1982. With Martyn Barker aboard on drums, next year's *Care* (#188) was picked up by Warner Bros., which quickly dropped them. The band's next album, 1984's *Jam Science*, was released by Arista in Europe and the U.K. only. It was notable for its slicker sound, buttressed by synthesized strings and female backing vocals. Next on Island Records, Shriekback's *Oil and Gold*, released in America, had a harsher, rockier sound; although it contained the club favorite "Nemesis," the album did not chart, and Marsh left after its release. He was briefly replaced by former Voidoid Ivan Julian. Following the release of the dark, piano-based *Big Night Music* (#145, 1987), Dave Allen left to form King Swamp, leaving Andrews the lone original member. Doug Wimbish, later of Living Colour, took his place, while Mike Cozzi took on guitar chores. This band appears on the playful, kinetic *Go Bang!* (#169, 1988).

Shriekback disbanded in 1989. Drummer Martyn Barker joined Allen in King Swamp, while Andrews formed Illuminati. Soon after, Allen went on to start Low Pop Suicide. Then, in 1992, Shriekback reunited, with Allen joining Andrews and Barker, and released *Sacred City* on Allen's World Domination label. Busy with the label, upon which he released his first solo album, *The Elastic Purejoy*, Allen departed Shriekback in 1994. The band carried on, however, touring Europe and attempting to sign to a new label.

Sigue Sigue Sputnik

Formed 1982, London, England
Tony James (b. ca. 1956), bass; Neal X (b. Neal Whitmore ca. 1962), gtr.; Martin Degville (b. ca. 1957), voc.; Ray Mayhew (b. ca. 1965), drums; Chris Kavanagh (b. ca. 1964), drums; Yana Ya Ya, kybds.
1986—*Flaunt It* (Manhattan)   1989—*Dress for Excess* (EMI)   1990—*The First Generation* (Jungle, U.K.).

Sigue Sigue Sputnik was more a tweak of hype than an actual band. After Billy Idol [see entry] abandoned Generation X for a solo career, Gen X bassist Tony James gathered a group of men who looked the part of a punk glam band but didn't play instruments. Sigue Sigue Sputnik (the name of a Russian street gang, it means "Burn Burn Satellite") played its first gig in 1985. The group's flamboyance immediately attracted an avalanche of media attention and record company interest. They signed with EMI for a reported $6 million, although that figure was undoubtedly just part of the hype.

In 1986 SSS released "Love Missile F1-11," a single whose collage of sounds was produced by Giorgio Moroder. It went straight to the top of the British chart. Moroder also produced *Flaunt It*, the first album to contain advertisements between tracks. Not surprisingly, SSS's music failed to live up to its attention-grabbing tactics. A massive press backlash soon followed, fueled by the band's unabashed crassness, and tabloids played up violence at SSS shows: Mayhew was actually charged with injuring fans at one gig. The group's recording a single with pop hitmakers Stock, Aitken and Waterman didn't help their credibility.

Dress for Excess came with the credo "This time it's music," but few people were convinced or interested. *The First Generation* includes old demo tracks and three new songs; it was released in the U.S. in 1991 as a ROIR cassette. Sigue Sigue Sputnik split; James joined the Sisters of Mercy [see entry], while Kavanagh went on to Big Audio Dynamite [see entry].

The Silos

Formed 1985, New York City, New York
Bob Rupe (b. Sep. 16, 1956, Mich.), gtr., voc.; Walter Salas-Humara (b. June 21, 1961, New York City),
gtr., voc.; Mary Rowell (b. Sep. 6, 1958, Newport, Vt.), violin.
1985—*About Her Steps* (Record Collect)   1987—*Cuba*   1990—(– Rowell) *The Silos* (RCA)   1991—(– Rupe; + Rowell)   1992—*Hasta La Victoria* (Normal Records, Ger.)   1994—*Susan Across the Ocean* (Watermelon).
Walter Salas-Humara solo: 1988—*Lagartija* (Record Collect).
Walter Salas-Humara with the Setters: 1993—*The Setters* (Million Miles, Ger.).

The Silos were created by Walter Salas-Humara and Bob Rupe, and included violinist Mary Rowell and a revolving group of backing musicians. The group's rough-hewn, unaffected, but catchy take on folk-rock made them critical favorites in the mid-Eighties. Recording and distributing their first two albums themselves, the Silos evinced a commercial independence and a stripped-down aesthetic that blazed the trail for later "alternative" bands.

In the early Eighties Salas-Humara led the Vulgar Boatmen in Gainesville, Florida, while Rupe was part of Ft. Lauderdale's Bobs. Although they knew each other in Florida, they did not form the Silos until they had separately moved to New York within six months of each other.

To help secure gigs for their band, Salas-Humara and Rupe recorded *About Her Steps*, pressing 1,000 copies on their own Record Collect label. The album was reviewed both in the States and the U.K., garnering comparisons to the Velvet Underground, the Byrds, and R.E.M. In 1989 RCA signed the band; by the time their major-label debut was released in 1990, their A&R person had left the label, the album languished, and the group was eventually dropped.

Salas-Humara and Rupe parted ways in 1991. Salas-Humara kept the Silos name, continuing to perform and record with Rowell and assorted musicians; Rupe played briefly with Gutterball, appearing on the group's eponymously titled album in 1993. Rupe played bass for Cracker on their 1994 tour. In addition to recording the solo effort *Lagartija*, Salas-Humara joined Austin, Texas, residents Alejandro Escovedo (Rank & File, True Believers) and Mike Hall (Wild Seeds) in a side project called the Setters, issuing a self-titled album.

Carly Simon

Born June 25, 1945, New York City, New York
1971—*Carly Simon* (Elektra); *Anticipation*   1972—*No Secrets*   1973—*Hotcakes*   1974—*Playing Possum*   1975—*Best of Carly Simon*   1976—*Another Passenger*   1978—*Boys in the Trees*   1979—*Spy*   1980—*Come Upstairs*   1981—*Torch* (Warner Bros.)   1983—*Hello Big Man*   1985—*Spoiled Girl*   1986—

Singer, songwriter, and composer Carly Simon was born into an affluent, musical family. Her father, a cofounder of Simon and Schuster publishers, played classical piano in his spare time; one sister, Lucy, is a folksinger and composer; another, Joanna, is an opera singer.

She left Sarah Lawrence College to work as a folk duo with Lucy. They played New York City clubs as the Simon Sisters, breaking up when Lucy got married. The Simon Sisters cut an LP for Kapp and had a minor hit in 1964 with "Winken, Blinken and Nod." Carly continued as a solo act and in 1966 began recording material for her solo debut album with sessionmen including Robbie Robertson, Rick Danko, and Richard Manuel of the Band, Al Kooper, and Mike Bloomfield. One of the tracks to be included was a version of Eric Von Schmidt's "Baby Let Me Follow You Down," with lyrics rewritten for Simon by Bob Dylan. After the project was abandoned, Simon kept a low profile for the rest of the decade.

She reemerged in 1970 with a single from her debut LP, "That's the Way I've Always Heard It Should Be" (#10, 1971), one of many songwriting collaborations with film critic Jacob Brackman. In late 1971 the title cut of her second LP, *Anticipation* (produced by ex-Yardbird Paul Samwell-Smith), was a #13 hit, and the album was also a best seller, helping her to win that year's Best New Artist Grammy. Her later hits included the mammoth smash "You're So Vain" (#1, 1972), allegedly inspired by and sung to either Warren Beatty or Mick Jagger (who appears on it as a backup vocalist). *No Secrets* (#1, 1972) went gold later that year; it is her most successful album to date.

On November 3, 1972, she married James Taylor, and in 1974 their duet cover of "Mockingbird" hit #5; the album it came from, *Hotcakes,* went gold. *Playing Possum* would be her last Top Ten album for a few years. Among her Top Thirty hits of the mid-Seventies were "The Right Thing to Do" (1973) and "Haven't Got Time for the Pain" (1974). Simon came back strongly in 1977, with the theme song from the James Bond movie *The Spy Who Loved Me*, "Nobody Does It Better," which went to #2, and next year's "You Belong to Me" (#6), which she cowrote with Michael McDonald. *Boys in the Trees,* from which "You Belong" came, was the last Top Ten and first platinum album of her career. She and Taylor's duet of the Everly Brothers' hit "Devoted to You" went to #36, and her biggest singles of the time were "Jesse" (#11, 1980) and "Why" (#10 U.K., 1982).

With the Eighties Simon changed direction, record-ing 1981's *Torch,* her first collection of pop standards, featuring songs by Hoagy Carmichael, Rodgers and Hart, and others. (*My Romance,* from 1990, is the second such LP.) That year she also filed for divorce from Taylor (it was finalized in 1983); they have two children. Simon's legendary stage fright, which had caused her to cancel a tour in support of *Come Upstairs,* and a series of interesting but less than stellar singles (such as "Tired of Being Blonde") followed.

Simon's efforts as a composer for film paid off immediately, however, as "Coming Around Again" (from the 1987 film *Heartburn*) became a Top Twenty single and "Let the River Run" (from 1989's *Working Girl*) garnered Simon an Oscar for Best Original Song. Around this time, she also surmounted her stage fright with a live concert on Martha's Vineyard, which was filmed for a popular HBO special, "Carly in Concert—Coming Around Again," and recorded for her gold 1988 LP *Greatest Hits Live*. She also composed music for the film *Postcards from the Edge,* including "You Are the Love of My Life." In 1993 Simon's opera for young people, *Romulus Hunt,* debuted at the Metropolitan Opera and the Kennedy Center for the Performing Arts. She has also written four children's books: *Amy the Dancing Bear, The Boy of the Bells, The Fisherman's Song,* and *The Nighttime Chauffeur.* As of the mid-Nineties she is said to be at work on her first novel for adults.

Paul Simon

After the 1970 breakup of Simon and Garfunkel [see entry], Paul Simon went on to confirm his stature as a first-rate songwriter and performer. His terse, exquisitely crafted songs have drawn on early rock & roll (particularly doo-wop), reggae, salsa, jazz, gospel, blues, New Orleans, and African and South American musics, in some cases presaging the conscious blending of world music into mainstream pop by over a decade. In an unassuming, distinctive tenor, Simon has sung of matters personal and universal with attitudes ranging from the whimsical to the reverent. Simon stands apart from most folk-based singer/songwriters of his generation in that he has created a wide-ranging body of work in which the purely musical vocabulary—of style, instrumentation, and sounds—is as evocative and as expressive as his lyrics.

Simon had recorded solo in England between Simon and Garfunkel's first and second albums. On his first album after their breakup, *Paul Simon* (#4, 1972), he began working from a broader stylistic palette and playing with such celebrated artists as jazz violinist Stephane Grappelli. The first single, "Mother and Child Reunion" (#4, 1972) was cut in Jamaica, and "Me and Julio Down by the Schoolyard" (#22, 1972) showed a clear urban Latin influence. Although Simon had ventured outside the classic folk-rock idioms with Garfunkel ("Cecilia," "El Condor Pasa"), as a solo artist he pursued these new directions in earnest while returning to such as American genres as gospel on *There Goes Rhymin' Simon* (#2, 1973); "Loves Me Like a Rock" (#2) featured the venerable Dixie Hummingbirds on backup. That album also included "Kodachrome" (#2, 1973) and went on to sell two million copies. The next year's *Live Rhymin'* (#33, 1974) featured the Dixie Hummingbirds and the Peruvian folk group Urubamba.

Despite their sometimes rocky relationship, Simon and Garfunkel never completely severed ties. They performed at a George McGovern fund-raiser in 1972 and Garfunkel was a frequent guest at Simon's concerts. In 1975 they collaborated on their first record since 1970's *Bridge over Troubled Water,* the single "My Little Town" (#9), which turned up on both Garfunkel's *Breakaway* and Simon's *Still Crazy After All These Years* (#1, 1975). The latter, purportedly about the dissolution of Simon's first marriage, generated the hits "Gone at Last" (#23) (a duet with Phoebe Snow) and "50 Ways to Leave Your Lover" (#1), and won a Grammy for Best Album of 1975.

Next Simon played a small nonsinging part in Woody Allen's *Annie Hall* in 1977 and started working in television, hosting *Saturday Night Live* and his own special. His *Greatest Hits* (#18, 1977) yielded the 1977 #5 hit "Slip Slidin' Away." In 1980 Simon starred in *One Trick Pony,* for which he wrote the screenplay and soundtrack. The story of a journeyman rock & roller, *Pony* received mixed reviews and flopped at the box office, although the salsa-influenced "Late in the Evening" became a #6 hit. In 1981 Simon reunited with Garfunkel again in Central Park; the concert was documented on a live album.

A year later, the pair toured together, intending to collaborate in the studio. When those plans fell through, Simon released *Hearts and Bones* (#35, 1983), the least commercially and critically successful work of his career to date. Including a collaboration with composer Philip Glass, the album failed commercially, and with the end of his second marriage, to actress Carrie Fisher, Simon reached a personal and professional low point.

Seeking inspiration, Simon traveled to South Africa in 1985 to explore its indigenous music, which he had been studying. After participating in the recording of "We Are the World," the all-star anthem for the USA for Africa hunger relief project, he began recording in Jo-hannesburg. He emerged with *Graceland,* a dazzling collection influenced by South African dance music and featuring the vocal group Ladysmith Black Mambazo (for whom he'd later produce two albums), the Everly Brothers, and Los Lobos. *Graceland* scored #3 in 1987—a whimsical single, "You Can Call Me Al," reached #44 (and #23 in rerelease in 1987)—and won a 1986 Grammy for Album of the Year.

Recording in South Africa caused Simon to be blacklisted by the United Nations and the African National Congress (ANC) and to be picketed in concert by antiapartheid protestors. To his credit, Simon spoke at public gatherings, where he addressed his critics face to face and defended his actions, insisting that his motives in breaking the boycott on recording in South Africa were musical, not political. The UN and the ANC dropped their bans in early 1987 after Simon wrote the UN pledging to abide by the terms of their South African boycott. Simon then released a best-selling home video of the Graceland concert in Zimbabwe.

In 1990 *The Rhythm of the Saints,* incorporating strains of West African, Brazilian, and zydeco music, reached #4, and Simon and Garfunkel were inducted into the Rock and Roll Hall of Fame. The next year, Simon hosted a free Central Park concert (at which Garfunkel was pointedly asked not to appear) that drew an estimated 750,000 people. In 1992 Simon married Edie Brickell [see entry], then the lead singer for the New Bohemians; he coproduced his wife's first solo album in 1994.

Simon performed a series of 21 concerts at the Paramount in New York City in the fall of 1993. A retrospective of his career, the concert event also included a reunion with Garfunkel. Over the years, Simon's charitable and social work has involved fund-raising for Amazonian rain forest preservation, New York's homeless, and South African children. For his humanitarian efforts, the United Negro College Fund accorded him its highest honor in 1989.

Simon and Garfunkel

Formed 1962, New York City, New York
Paul Simon (b. Oct. 13, 1941, Newark, N.J.), gtr., voc.; Arthur Garfunkel (b. Nov. 5, 1941, New York City), voc.
1964—Wednesday Morning, 3 A.M. (Columbia) 1966—Sounds of Silence; Parsley, Sage, Rosemary and Thyme 1968—Bookends; The Graduate soundtrack 1970—Bridge over Troubled Water 1972—Greatest Hits 1982—The Concert in Central Park.

When they were in the sixth grade together in Forest Hills, New York, Paul Simon and Art Garfunkel found they could harmonize. The first songs they sang together were doo-wop hits, but soon they were singing their

Art Garfunkel and Paul Simon

own songs. One of those was "Hey, Schoolgirl," which the duo recorded in 1957. An agent of Big Records present at the session signed them on the spot. Calling themselves Tom and Jerry ("Tom Graph" and "Jerry Landis"), they had a Top Fifty hit with "Hey, Schoolgirl" and appeared on *American Bandstand*. Garfunkel estimates the record sold 150,000 copies. When a few followups flopped, Tom and Jerry split up.

When they met again in 1962, Garfunkel was studying architecture after trying to record as Arty Garr, and Simon was studying English literature but devoting most of his time to writing and selling his songs. In 1964 Simon, who had just dropped out of law school and quit his job as a song peddler for a music publishing company, took one of his originals to Columbia Records producer Tom Wilson. Wilson bought the song and signed the duo.

Wednesday Morning, 3 A.M.—a set that combined traditional folk songs with Simon's originals and Dylan anthems like "The Times They Are A-Changin'," performed only by the two singers accompanied by Simon's acoustic guitar—was lost in the glut of early Dylan imitations. Simon went to work the folk circuit in London, where in May 1965 he recorded a solo album. Several months later, he was performing around England and the Continent when he received the news that one of the songs on *Wednesday Morning*—"Sounds of Silence"—was the #1 single in the United States.

It was not quite the song Simon and Garfunkel had recorded. Wilson (who had played a part in electrifying Dylan's music) had added electric guitars, bass and drums to the original track. The remixed single was at

the vanguard of "folk rock." Simon returned to hit the college circuit with Garfunkel and to record a second duo album. Along with the redubbed "Sounds of Silence," the album of that name comprised folk-rock remakes of many of the songs from Simon's U.K. solo album. The production was elaborate, an appropriate setting for Simon's self-consciously poetic songs, and Simon and Garfunkel turned out to be acceptable to both teenagers (who found them relevant) and adults (who found them intelligent). In 1966 they placed four singles and three albums in the Top Thirty (the revived *Wednesday Morning, Sounds of Silence*, and *Parsley, Sage, Rosemary and Thyme*). "Homeward Bound" (#5), "I Am a Rock" (#3), and *Parsley, Sage* reached the Top Five.

Simon was not a prolific writer—most of the material on the first three Simon and Garfunkel albums had been composed between 1962 and 1965—and once *Parsley, Sage* was completed, the duo's output slowed considerably. They released only two singles in 1967: "At the Zoo" (#16) and "Fakin' It" (#23). Simon was developing the more colloquial, less literary style he would bring to his later solo work; the first sign of it was the elliptical "Mrs. Robinson," composed for the soundtrack of *The Graduate*. The film and the soundtrack album were followed within two months by *Bookends*; "Mrs. Robinson" hit #1 in June, *Bookends* soon afterward.

Simon and Garfunkel produced *Bookends* with engineer Roy Halee, who had worked on every Simon and Garfunkel session. (With *Parsley, Sage*, Halee had taken a major role in the arranging; it was Columbia's first album recorded on eight tracks.) "The Boxer" (#7), Simon and Garfunkel's only release in 1969, was Columbia's first song recorded on 16 tracks.

Bridge over Troubled Water took almost two years to make, as the duo began to pursue their individual projects. They often worked separately in the studio, and as their music became more complex they performed less often on stage; their only appearance in 1969 was on their own network television special. Around this period, Garfunkel's acting career began with a role in *Catch-22*. Soon after the record's release, Simon and Garfunkel staged a brief but very successful tour, which quieted rumors about a breakup, but by the time Garfunkel's second movie, *Carnal Knowledge*, and Simon's 1972 solo album came out, it was clear that their individual solo careers were taking precedence [see entries].

According to Simon, following a last show at the Forest Hills Tennis Stadium, the two did not speak for years. They left their joint career at its peak, though in recent years both have said that their initial intention was not to break up permanently but just to take a break from each other. After reaching #1 in spring 1970, *Bridge over Troubled Water* rode the charts for over a year and a half (spending ten weeks at the top), eventually selling over 13 million copies worldwide. The LP yielded four hit singles—the title song (a #1 hit, the biggest seller of their career), "Cecilia" (#4), "The Boxer" (#7), and "El Condor Pasa" (#18)—and won six Grammys. In 1977 it was given the British Britannia Award as Best International Pop Album of the past 25 years, and the title song received the equivalent award as a single. To date the duo has sold over 20 million albums in the United States alone.

Since 1970 the Forest Hills classmates have gotten together on a few notable occasions. The first was a benefit concert for presidential candidate George McGovern at Madison Square Garden, New York, in June 1972. (That occasion also saw the reunions of Peter, Paul and Mary and the comedy team of Mike Nichols and Elaine May.) In 1975 Simon and Garfunkel had a Top Ten hit single with "My Little Town," a song Simon wrote for Garfunkel and sang with him, which appeared on solo LPs by both. Garfunkel joined Simon to perform a selection of their old hits on Simon's 1977 television special, and the two got together again the next year in a studio with James Taylor to record a trio rendition of Sam Cooke's "(What a) Wonderful World." On September 19, 1981, Simon and Garfunkel gave a free concert for an estimated 500,000 fans in New York's Central Park, and in 1982, a double album, *The Concert in Central Park,* went platinum, peaking at #6. They embarked on an extended tour and began recording what was to have been a new Simon and Garfunkel album. Unable to resolve their creative differences, the two abandoned the project, and the material was released on the Paul Simon solo LP *Hearts and Bones.*

In the years since, the pair has reunited on several occasions. They performed several shows for charitable causes in the early Nineties, and in 1993 a smash 21-date sold-out run at the Paramount Theater in New York City, followed by a tour of the Far East. Though, technically speaking, these shows were not Simon and Garfunkel concerts (they performed together only in the first and last of the show's four segments; the balance was dedicated to Simon's solo work), fans seemed to feel otherwise. Whether for its exquisite craftsmanship or for its place as a musical-cultural touchstone, or both, the music Simon and Garfunkel created and recorded seems destined to endure. The two were inducted into the Rock and Roll Hall of Fame in 1990.

Nina Simone

Born Eunice Waymon, February 21, 1933, Tryon, North Carolina
1961—*Nina at Newport* (Colpix)   1965—*I Put a Spell on You* (Philips)   1967—*Silk and Soul* (RCA) 1969—*'Nuff Said*   1970—*Black Gold* (RCA); *The Best of Nina Simone*   1971—*Here Comes the Sun* 1972—*Emergency Ward; It Is Finished*   1978—*Baltimore* (CTI)   1982—*Fodder on My Wings* (Poly-
Gram)   1987—*Let It Be Me* (Verve)   1988—*Don't Let Me Be Misunderstood* (Mercury)   1990—*Live* (Zeta)   1991—*The Blues* (Novus/RCA)   1993—*A Single Woman* (Elektra).

Singer Nina Simone's music has gone from gospel to jazz to pop to R&B and blues to a raging black protest that moved her off the supper-club circuit and into political rallies and soul concerts. Known since the late Fifties as the "High Priestess of Soul," she enjoyed a renaissance in her sixth decade with the publication of her autobiography and the exposure given her music in a popular American film. Taking her stage name from French actress Simone Signoret, she epitomizes the soul diva.

Simone began singing in church and taught herself piano and organ by the time she was seven. She took classical keyboard lessons and attended New York's Juilliard School of Music, then began playing East Coast clubs and concerts. Her first hit was a 1959 gold record of Gershwin's "I Loves You, Porgy."

In the Sixties she moved toward R&B, recording Screamin' Jay Hawkins' "I Put a Spell on You" and "Don't Let Me Be Misunderstood" (a subsequent hit for the Animals). This led to sizable popularity in England, where she had hits with "Ain't Got No—I Got Life" (from *Hair*) in 1968 and the Bee Gees' "To Love Somebody" in 1969.

By then she had become a black-power activist (her first protest song, "Mississippi Goddam," mourned the death of slain civil rights leader Medgar Evers) and politically oriented tracks like "Four Women" (on an out-of-print Philips album) alienated her white audience. She became even more intense and unpredictable in concert, and despite continuing critical acclaim, she gradually lost her commercial standing. Financially, she fell upon hard times, and she divorced her manager/husband (her first marriage had also failed). In 1974, Simone quit the music business.

Leaving the States, Simone took up residence in Switzerland, Liberia, Barbados, France, and the U.K. in the mid-Seventies. By 1978, however, she had returned to music, releasing *Baltimore* and touring the U.S. again. While the early Eighties were a fallow period, Simone experienced a comeback in 1987 when a television commercial for Chanel No. 5 perfume used her early recording, "My Baby Just Cares for Me." Her candid 1991 autobiography, *I Put a Spell on You,* and an appearance on Pete Townshend's *Iron Man* boosted her revival. In 1993, with her music featured in the film *Point of No Return* and with a new studio album, *A Single Woman,* Simone gained a new audience for her fiercely elegant fare.

Simple Minds

Formed 1978, Glasgow, Scotland
Jim Kerr (b. July 9, 1959, Glasgow), voc.; Charlie Burchill (b. Nov. 27, 1959, Glasgow), gtr., kybds.;

Duncan Barnwell, gtr.; Mick McNeil (b. July 20, 1958, Glasgow), kybds.; Tony Donald, bass; Brian McGee, drums.
1978—(– Barnwell; – Donald; + Derek Forbes [b. June 22, 1956, Glasgow], bass)   1979—*Life in a Day* (Zoom, U.K.)   1980—*Real to Real Cacophony*; *Empires and Dance* (– McGee; + Kenny Hyslop [b. Feb. 14, 1951, Helensburgh, Scot.], drums; – Hyslop; + Mike Ogletree, drums)   1981—*Sons and Fascination/Sister Feelings Call* (Virgin, U.K.) 1982—*New Gold Dream (81-82-83-84)* (A&M); *Themes for Great Cities* (Stiff) (– Ogletree; + Mel Gaynor [b. May 29, 1959, Glasgow], drums); *Celebration* (Virgin)   1984—*Sparkle in the Rain* (A&M) (– Forbes; + John Giblin, bass; + Robin Clark, voc.; + Sue Hadjopoulos, perc.)   1985—*Once Upon a Time*   1987—*Simple Minds Live: In the City of Light*   1989—*Street Fighting Years* (– Clark; – Hadjopoulos; – McNeil; + Peter Vitesse, kybds.)   1991—*Real Life*   1993—*Glittering Prize* (– Vitesse) 1995—*Good News from the Next World* (Virgin).

Scotland's Simple Minds found some success in the latter half of the Eighties with a synth-based, epic-pop sound. The band grew out of the Glasgow punk outfit Johnny and the Self-Abusers, which included childhood buddies Jim Kerr and Charlie Burchill. Simple Minds began playing an ambitious postpunk art rock, influenced by Roxy Music and David Bowie and veering from pop songs (*Life in a Day*) to harsher, more experimental sounds (*Real to Real Cacophony*), to cool, aloof Eurodisco (*Empires and Dance*).

While Simple Minds became critical favorites with the British music press, the band did not attract a significant U.S. following until *New Gold Dream*, which had a warmer musical feel and more positive lyrics, including much religious imagery. It became the group's first American chart album (#69, 1983) and included "Promised You a Miracle" (the only track on which second drummer Kenny Hyslop ever played), which got frequent play on college radio and in rock discos. The videos for that track, and for "Someone Somewhere in Summertime," also got played on MTV.

Sparkle in the Rain (#64, 1984) united Simple Minds with U2 producer Steve Lillywhite, but failed to spawn a U.S. chart single. The band toured with the Pretenders, and in June 1984, Kerr married Pretender Chrissie Hynde in New York's Central Park. They had a daughter, Yasmin, in 1985, before divorcing a few years later. Simple Minds finally achieved their long-predicted U.S. breakthrough with "Don't You (Forget About Me)" (#1, 1985), from the soundtrack of *The Breakfast Club*. The song was written by producer/composer Keith Forsey (*Flashdance*, Billy Idol) and Steve Schiff; Bryan Ferry had turned down the song, and Simple Minds were originally against the idea of recording or releasing it. "Don't You" did not appear on the album *Once Upon a Time* (#10, 1985), which yielded hits of its own in "Alive & Kicking" (#3, 1985), "Sanctify Yourself" (#14, 1986), and "All the Things She Said" (#28, 1986).

Simple Minds were unable to further that commercial success with the concert album *Live: In the City of Light* (#96, 1987) and the politically oriented *Street Fighting Years* (#70, 1989). *Real Life* (#74, 1991) returned to the grand-scale sound and more personal lyrics and spawned a modest U.S. hit single in "See the Lights" (#40, 1991). Kerr married British actress Patsy Kensit in 1992. The band's 1993 effort, *Glittering Prize*, was a commercial bomb.

Simply Red

Formed 1982, England
Mick Hucknall (b. Michael James Hucknall, June 8, 1960, Manchester, Eng.), voc.
1985—(+ Sylvan Richardson, gtr.; + Fritz McIntyre [b. Sep. 2, 1956, Birmingham, Eng.], kybds.; + Tony Bowers [b. Oct. 31, 1952], bass; + Chris Joyce [b. Oct. 11, 1957, Manchester], drums; + Tim Kellett [b. July 23, 1964, Knaresborough, Eng.], horns, kybds.) *Picture Book* (Elektra)   1987—*Men and Women*   1989—(– Richardson; + Aziz Ibrahim, gtr.; + Ian Kirkham, sax) *A New Flame*   1991—(– Ibrahim; + Heitor T.P. [b. Brazil], gtr.) *Stars* (EastWest).

One of several mellow, blue-eyed soul acts from the U.K., Simply Red distinguished itself from the lot by virtue of its lead singer, Mick Hucknall. In addition to his striking physical appearance—a shock of red curls atop an ugly-cute face evoking a young Mickey Rooney—Hucknall boasted a shivery, keening countertenor that drew the attention, and praise, of critics. For some, however, Hucknall's distinctive voice couldn't compensate for the often effete arrangements that characterized Simply Red's hybrid of R&B and adult-contemporary pop.

As a working-class Manchester lad, Hucknall led a punk-influenced band called the Frantic Elevators in the late Seventies and early Eighties. Then, yearning to play the pop and soul music that was closer to his heart, the singer put together the short-lived first incarnation of Simply Red. Once that lineup dissolved, Hucknall recruited bassist Tony Bowers, drummer Chris Joyce, and trumpeter/synth player Tim Kellett from another Manchester band, Durutti Column. Adding gospel pianist Fritz McIntyre, Hucknall finally secured the band he wanted. In 1985, Simply Red signed to Elektra, releasing that year their first single, "Money$ Too Tight to Mention" (#13 U.K.), and debut album, *Picture Book* (featuring classically trained guitarist Sylvan Richardson, who joined the band after the single's release). It wasn't until 1986, though, that *Book*'s kickoff single, a wistful ballad called "Holding Back the Years," shot to #2 in England— and #1 in the U.S.

Simply Red was received less enthusiastically by American fans over the next few years. (In the U.K., the album *Men And Women* reached #2, and two 1987 singles, "The Right Thing" and a cover of Cole Porter's "Ev'ry Time We Say Goodbye," hit #11.) The group rebounded in 1989, though, with a remake of Harold Melvin and the Blue Notes' "If You Don't Know Me by Now" (#1 U.S., #2 U.K.). A fourth album, *Stars,* topped the British chart, but stalled at #76 in the U.S.

Frank Sinatra

Born Francis Albert Sinatra, December 12, 1915, Hoboken, New Jersey
1954—*Songs for Young Lovers* (Capitol)   1955—*In the Wee Small Hours*   1956—*Songs for Swingin' Lovers!*   1957—*Where Are You?*   1958—*Come Fly with Me; Only the Lonely*   1959—*Come Dance with Me*   1960—*Nice 'n' Easy*   1961—*Ring-a-Ding Ding!* (Reprise)   1962—*Sinatra-Basie*   1965—*September of My Years; Sinatra—A Man and His Music*   1966—*Sinatra at the Sands; That's Life*   1967—*Francis Albert Sinatra and Antonio Carlos Jobim; Francis A. Sinatra and Edward K. Ellington*   1968—*Frank Sinatra's Greatest Hits*   1969—*My Way*   1972—*Frank Sinatra's Greatest Hits, vol. 2*   1973—*Ol' Blue Eyes Is Back*   1974—*Sinatra—The Main Event Live*   1980—*Trilogy: Past, Present, Future*   1981—*She Shot Me Down*   1982—*The Dorsey/Sinatra Sessions 1940–1942* (RCA)   1984—*L.A. Is My Lady*   1988—*Tommy Dorsey/Frank Sinatra, All-Time Greatest Hits, vol. 1*   1990—*The Capitol Years* (Capitol); *The Reprise Collection* (Reprise)   1993—*The Columbia Years* (Columbia); *Frank Sinatra Duets* (Capitol)   1994—*Duets II.*

Indisputably the Twentieth Century's greatest singer of popular song, baritone Frank Sinatra was influenced by Bing Crosby's crooning, but by learning from trombonist Tommy Dorsey's breath control and blues singer Billie Holiday's rhythmic swing, he mainstreamed the concept of singing colloquially, treating lyrics as personal statements and handling melodies with the ease of a jazz improviser. His best work is standards—Cole Porter, Irving Berlin, Jerome Kern, and the Gershwins—but Sinatra, despite his 1957 denunciation of rock & roll as degenerate, has recorded songs by the likes of Stevie Wonder, George Harrison, Jimmy Webb, and Billy Joel. Not only did his freely interpretive approach pave the way for the idiosyncrasies of rock singing, but with his character a mix of tough-guy cool and romantic vulnerability, he became the first true pop idol, a superstar who through his music established a persona audiences found compelling and true.

Sinatra, an only child of a family with Sicilian roots, grew up in Hoboken and sang in the glee club of Demarest High School. His break came in 1937, when he and three instrumentalists, billed as the Hoboken Four, won on the *Major Bowes Original Amateur Hour.* After some touring, the group disbanded.

Harry James signed Sinatra to sing with his orchestra, and on July 13, 1939, two weeks after his debut as a big-band vocalist at the Hippodrome Theatre in Baltimore, Sinatra cut his first disc, "From the Bottom of My Heart," with the orchestra. Of the ten sides he recorded with them, the biggest seller, "All or Nothing at All," sold just over 8,000 copies upon release. In 1943 it was rereleased and became the first of Sinatra's many million-sellers, hitting #2 on the chart.

In 1940 Tommy Dorsey's lead singer, Jack Leonard, quit and Sinatra began a two-year stay with the trombonist. During those years, the band consistently hit the Top Ten (15 entries in 1940–41, including their first, the #1 hit "I'll Never Smile Again"). His radio work with Dorsey was the springboard for Sinatra's solo career. During the war years, Sinatra, married at the time to his childhood sweetheart Nancy, sang love songs to his mostly female audiences, notably on Lucky Strike's *Hit Parade* and at New York's original Paramount Theatre. Between 1943 and 1946 he had 17 Top Ten chart singles, and earned the sobriquets "The Voice" and "The Sultan of Swoon." With the GIs back in the U.S., public taste shifted away from these songs, and Sinatra's popularity waned. At Columbia, producer Mitch Miller burdened Sinatra with novelty songs (washboard accompaniment on one, barking dogs on another), and his sales slipped to an average of 30,000 per record. In the early Fifties, he was dropped by Columbia and by his talent agent and lost his MGM motion picture contract. To regain his popularity, he begged to be cast as Maggio in the film *From Here to Eternity.* His first nonsinging role, it won him a 1953 Oscar and a return to the limelight. (His film debut had been with the Tommy Dorsey Orchestra in 1941's *Las Vegas Nights.*)

The fledgling Capitol Records signed him in 1953 and, with ex-Dorsey trombonist and arranger Nelson Riddle, Sinatra moved into the next phase of his recording career with a new emphasis: saloon ballads and sophisticated swing tunes. With Capitol, he concentrated on albums, although he again charted in the singles Top Ten, notably with "Young at Heart" (#2, 1954), "Learnin' the Blues" (#1, 1955), "Hey! Jealous Lover" (#3, 1956), "All the Way" (#2, 1957), and "Witchcraft" (#6, 1958). His best albums of the period were arranged by Riddle, Billy May, or Gordon Jenkins.

Through the early Fifties, during which he was married to film actress Ava Gardner, having left Nancy in 1950, Sinatra became a movie star. He won especially high praise for his portrayal of a drug addict in *The Man with the Golden Arm* (1955). Beginning in 1959, two years after he divorced Gardner, his singles failed to hit the Top Thirty, and in 1961 Sinatra left Capitol to establish his own company, Reprise. (In 1963 he sold Reprise to Warner Bros. and became a vice president and consultant of Warner Bros. Picture Corp.)

Sinatra decided to try again to become a Top Forty singles artist. "The Second Time Around" hit #50 in 1961; subsequent releases charted lower. But in the mid-Sixties he recouped. He was the triumphant headliner of the final evening of the 1965 Newport Jazz Festival in a 20-song set accompanied by Count Basie's orchestra, conducted by Quincy Jones. His 1965 Thanksgiving TV special, "Frank Sinatra: A Man and His Music," a review of his 25-year career, won an Emmy and set the precedent for numerous other TV specials, including one each in the four next years. That year, he also picked up a Grammy Lifetime Achievement Award. In 1966–67 he charted three of his biggest hits in the Top Ten: "Strangers in the Night" (#1, 1966), "That's Life" (#4, 1966), and a duet with daughter Nancy, "Somethin' Stupid" (#1, 1967).

In the Sixties he made his Las Vegas debut at the Sands and continued for years as a main attraction at Caesars Palace. Leader of the notorious "Rat Pack," including Sammy Davis Jr., Dean Martin, Peter Lawford, and Joey Bishop, he came to epitomize the hard-drinking, blonde-chasing swinger; a stout Democrat who'd named his son after Franklin D. Roosevelt, he also strongly supported John F. Kennedy's presidential bid. Married from 1966 to 1968 to actress Mia Farrow, he began reconciling with youth culture, covering, with indifferent success, songs by younger writers. In 1968 he recorded "My Way," a French song to which Paul Anka wrote new English lyrics. A modest U.S. hit (#27), it was an overwhelming smash in the U.K., staying in the Top Fifty an unprecedented 122 weeks. (Sex Pistol Sid Vicious later recorded a sarcastic version.)

In 1970 Sinatra announced his retirement and was honored with a gala farewell on June 13, 1971, at the Los Angeles Music Center. He reversed that decision in 1973 with the release of *Ol' Blue Eyes Is Back,* a TV special of the same name, and a performance at the Nixon White House (over the years, Sinatra's politics had become markedly conservative; in 1985, he would produce Ronald Reagan's inaugural gala). In 1974 he mounted an eight-city, 13-date sold-out U.S. tour and performed in Japan and Australia. In Australia he again aggravated the paparazzi with his antijournalist harangues: Through the years he has referred to the males as parasites, and the females as everything from "a buck-and-a-half hooker" to "two-dollar broads." Married to Zeppo Marx's widow, Barbara, in 1976, however, he appeared somewhat to mellow. In the mid-Seventies Sinatra's career slowed down, but in mid-1980, after a five-year record-ing hiatus, he released *Trilogy,* which included a version of "Theme from New York, New York" (#32) that the city fervently adopted.

In the Eighties Sinatra continued to perform sold-out concerts in major halls, to star in movies and TV specials, and to spark controversy for his business and political associations. (His 1972 appearances before the House Select Committee on Crime investigating criminal infiltration into horseracing were front-page news.) With 1981's *She Shot Me Down* and 1984's *L.A. Is My Lady,* he appeared to have ended his recording career.

In 1993, however, he enjoyed a renaissance, with *Duets* debuting at #2. Featuring top singers—among them Aretha Franklin, Bono, Tony Bennett, Liza Minnelli, and Luther Vandross (some recording their parts via telephone)—it gained Sinatra new young fans. Still touring, with the aid of TelePrompTers, at 78, he collapsed onstage in Virginia in 1994 but soon recovered; days earlier, when presented a special "Legend" award at the Grammy Awards ceremony—with an over-the-top intro by Bono—he had waxed so emotional that his own handlers requested that television cameras cut away from his acceptance speech. Rumors abounded about Sinatra's health, but he insisted on resuming his tour. By year's end, the sequel *Duets II* was issued, featuring Chrissie Hynde, Linda Ronstadt, and Willie Nelson, among others.

A 1983 honoree at the Kennedy Center Honors, Sinatra has been involved for many years in charitable work, particularly in fund-raising for multiple sclerosis, for chronically ill children, and for awareness of child abuse.

Nancy Sinatra

Born June 8, 1940, Jersey City, New Jersey
1966—*Boots* (Reprise)   1968—*Nancy and Lee* (with Lee Hazlewood)   1970—*Greatest Hits*   1972—*Nancy and Lee—Encore* (RCA)   1987—*Boots: Nancy Sinatra's All-Time Hits (1966–1970)* (with Lee Hazlewood) (Rhino)   1989—*Fairy Tales and Fantasies: The Best of Nancy & Lee* (with Lee Hazlewood) 1995—*One More Time* (Cougar).

Frank Sinatra's daughter Nancy had several late-Sixties hits, including "These Boots Are Made for Walkin'" and "How Does That Grab You, Darlin'?" At an early age Nancy Sinatra began studying dance, acting, singing, and piano. She made her national TV debut in 1960, in a Timex special featuring her father and Elvis Presley, in his first television appearance since leaving the army. She dropped out of the University of Southern California in 1960 after marrying singer/actor Tommy Sands and did not resume her career until they divorced in 1965.

Her first few singles, "Like I Do," "Tonight You Belong to Me," and "Think of Me," were hits in England, Europe, and South Africa, but were ignored in the U.S. Then in

1966 came the #1 hit and million-selling "These Boots." She followed it up with the gold "Sugar Town" b/w "Summer Wine" (#5). In 1967 Nancy Sinatra's country & western duet with singer, songwriter, and producer Lee Hazlewood, "Jackson" (#14), sold well, as did her title tune from the James Bond film *You Only Live Twice* (#44). That year she also earned her third gold record for the #1 duet with her father, "Somethin' Stupid."

She appeared on TV rock shows like *Hullabaloo* and *American Bandstand* and acted in episodes of TV series like *The Virginian* and *Burke's Law.* She also appeared in films: *For Those Who Think Young, Get Yourself a College Girl, Bikini Party in a Haunted House,* and *Last of the Secret Agents*; she played herself in *The Oscar* and the Elvis Presley film *Speedway.* In 1968 she made the first of two albums with Hazlewood, and a year later had her last chart singles, retiring from show business soon after. In 1985, she authored a loving tribute to her father, *Sinatra, My Father.* She returned to the limelight in 1995, with a new C&W–flavored album, *One More Time,* concert appearances, and a revealing spread in *Playboy.*

Siouxsie and the Banshees

Formed September 1976, London, England
Siouxsie Sioux (b. Susan Dallion, May 27, 1958, London), voc.; Sid Vicious (b. John Simon Ritchie, May 10, 1957, London; d. Feb. 2, 1979, New York City, N.Y.), drums; Steve Severin (b. Sep. 25, 1959, London), bass; Marco Pirroni (b. Apr. 27, 1959, London), gtr.
1977—(– Vicious; – Pirroni; + Kenny Morris, drums; + Peter Fenton, gtr; – Fenton; + John McKay, gtr.)
1978—*The Scream* (Polydor)   1979—*Join Hands* (– Morris; + Budgie [b. Aug. 21, St. Helens, Eng.], drums; – McKay; + Robert Smith [b. Apr. 21, 1959, Blackpool, Eng.], gtr.)   1980—(– Smith; + John McGeoch, gtr.) *Kaleidoscope* (PVC)   1981—*Juju; Once Upon a Time/The Singles   1982—A Kiss in the Dreamhouse* (Polydor)   1983—(– McGeoch; + Smith, gtr.) *Nocturne* (Geffen)   1984—*Hyaena* (– Smith; + John Valentine Carruthers, gtr.)   1986—*Tinderbox   1987—Through the Looking Glass* (– Carruthers; + Jon Klein [b. May 9, Bristol, Eng.], gtr.; + Martin McCarrick [b. July 29, London], cello, kybds.)   1988—*Peepshow   1991—The Peel Sessions* (Strange Fruit/Dutch East India Trading); *Superstition* (Geffen)   1995—*The Rapture.*

As leader of Siouxsie and the Banshees, Siouxsie Sioux has gone from punk-rock fan to seminal punk rocker to an elder stateswoman. Outlasting most of their contempories, the Banshees have moved from an abrasive, art-punk sound into the mainstream, gaining a Top Forty hit with 1991's "Kiss Them for Me" (#23).

The Banshees grew out of the Bromley Contingent, a group of Sex Pistols fans; Sid Vicious, later a Pistol himself, played drums for their debut performance (which consisted of just one song, an elongated version of "The Lord's Prayer") at the 100 Club's 1976 punk festival. By the time their debut single, "Hong Kong Garden," and the album *The Scream* came out, only Siouxsie and Steve Severin remained from the original lineup (Marco Pirroni went on to join Adam and the Ants). Cure leader Robert Smith joined the band for a 1979 tour, and former Sex Pistol guitarist Steve Jones helped out on *Kaleidoscope*; Magazine's John McGeoch joined the band shortly before its first American tour in 1980. After appearing on two albums (*Juju* and *A Kiss in the Dreamhouse*), McGeoch left in 1982. Smith rejoined the Banshees for a live album, *Nocturne,* and in the studio for *Hyaena* (#157, 1984).

With Smith on board, the band's musical palette widened, adding symphonic elements and a cover of the Beatles' "Dear Prudence" (#3 U.K., 1983). But he found playing in two bands wearying and left in 1984. Sioux broke her kneecap onstage in 1985, and the band lay low the remainder of the year. It returned with new guitarist John Valentine Carruthers and *Tinderbox* (#88, 1986), the group's first U.S. Top 100 album. Carruthers left after *Through the Looking Glass* (#188, 1987), an album of cover versions.

Peepshow (#68, 1988), with new members Jon Klein (ex-Specimen) and Martin McCarrick, moved the Banshees in the direction of a techno/dance groove, giving the band its first U.S. chart single: "Peek-a-Boo" (#53, 1988). In 1991 the Banshees were invited by Perry Farrell to perform at the first-ever Lollapalooza. Released in conjuction with the tour, *Superstition* (#65) was the Banshees' best-selling album. Siouxsie, along with her husband, drummer Budgie, also sporadically recorded and toured as the Creatures from 1981 to 1990.

Sir Douglas Quintet/Doug Sahm

Formed 1964, California
Original lineup: Doug Sahm (b. Nov. 6, 1941, San Antonio, Tex.), gtr., voc.; Augie Meyers (b. May 31, 1940, San Antonio), kybds.; Francisco Moran (b. Aug. 13, 1946), sax; Harvey Kagan (b. Apr. 18, 1946), bass; Johnny Perez (b. Nov. 8, 1942), drums.
1965—*Best of Sir Douglas Quintet* (Tribe)   1968—*Honkey Blues* (Smash)   1969—*Mendocino   1970—Together After Five; 1 + 1 + 1 = 4* (Philips)   1971—*The Return of Doug Saldaña   1981—Border Wave* (Takoma)   1994—(Group re-forms: Doug Sahm, gtr., voc.; Meyers, kybds., voc.; Shawn Sahm, gtr.; John Jorgenson, gtr.; Speedy Sparks, bass; Neal Walker, bass; Doug Clifford, drums; Shandon Sahm, drums) *Day Dreaming at Midnight* (Elektra).
Doug Sahm solo: 1973—*Doug Sahm and Band* (At-

lantic); *Texas Tornado*; *Rough Edges* (Mercury) 1974—*Groovers Paradise* (Warner Bros.)   1976— *Texas Rock for Country Rollers* (ABC/Dot)   1980— *Hell of a Spell* (Takoma)   1988—*Juke Box Music* (Antone's)   1994—*The Last Real Texas Blues Band*.

"Mendocino" and "She's About a Mover" were Doug Sahm and the Sir Douglas Quintet's commercial peaks, but they were only part of Sahm's long, varied career. Sahm grew up around San Antonio, Texas, where he absorbed the strains of music that would show up in his bands: country, blues, Western swing, jazz, and the polkas of Mexican conjunto bands. He began performing (as Little Doug Sahm) at age six, playing steel guitar. When rock & roll arrived in the mid-Fifties, he started forming his own bands and had hits around San Antonio while still in high school.

In 1960 Sahm moved to California and continued to have local hits. In 1964, as the British Invasion got under way, he called his newest band (featuring Augie Meyers on Vox organ) the Sir Douglas Quintet. "She's About a Mover," featuring a recurring organ line reminiscent of conjunto accordion, went into the Top Twenty, spurring a short wave of Tex-Mex hits (by Sam the Sham and ? and the Mysterians). "The Rains Came" reached the Top Twenty in 1966.

With the blues revival and psychedelia, a shifting Quintet played loose-limbed blues around San Francisco; Meyer rejoined in 1968 and the group cut its last big hit, "Mendocino" (#27, 1969); at one point the band included saxophonist Martin Fierro, who went on to form the short-lived San Francisco jazz-rock group Shades of Joy. The Quintet's albums grew more experimental and spacier, and didn't sell.

Sahm returned to Texas in 1971 to cut an album of San Antonio barroom honky-tonk, then he temporarily gave up the Sir Douglas monicker. His first solo album featured Dr. John, conjunto accordionist Flaco Jimenez, jazz saxophonist David "Fathead" Newman, and Bob Dylan, who wrote the country-flavored "Wallflower" for Sahm. Mercury capitalized on Sahm's expected stardom with *Rough Edges,* a collection of Quintet outtakes, but Doug Sahm and Band never caught on.

Sahm continued to record through the Seventies under his own name, as the Sir Douglas Band (1973), and as Sir Douglas and the Texas Tornados (1976) with his mixture of Texans, Mexicans, and Californians. *Groovers Paradise* featured Creedence Clearwater's rhythm section, Stu Cook and Doug Clifford. In the late Seventies Sahm was part of the "cosmic cowboy" scene in Austin. Meanwhile, new-wave bands—particularly Elvis Costello and the Attractions—were rediscovering the organ-pumping sound of Tex-Mex. As the Eighties began, Sahm resurrected the Quintet with Meyer and Perez to make *Border Wave,* and he toured with them in

a band that also included his son, Shawn, on guitar. The Quintet periodically re-formed throughout the Eighties, and in 1990 Sahm brought back the Texas Tornados [see entry] name for a critically acclaimed collaboration with Meyers, Jimenez, and country star Freddie Fender. Sahm re-formed the Quintet yet again in 1994, reuniting with Meyers and ex-Creedence drummer Clifford and using his sons Shawn (who cowrote three songs with his dad for *Day Dreaming at Midnight*) and Shandon, who was already drumming with the Texas hard-rock band Pariah. In 1994 Sahm's blues chops were featured on the live album *The Last Real Texas Blues Band.*

Sir Mix-a-Lot

Born Anthony Ray, August 12, 1963, Seattle, Washington
1987—*Swass* (Nastymix)   1989—*Seminar*   1992— *Mack Daddy* (Rhyme Cartel/Def American)   1994— *Chief Boot Knocka* (Rhyme Cartel/American).

The first rap star to emerge from Seattle, Anthony Ray got the nickname "Sir Mix-a-Lot" in the early Eighties, while DJing at an inner-city boy's club in his hometown's Central District ghetto. His first rap single, "Square Dance Rap," attracted nationwide attention in 1985. His debut album, *Swass* (#82 pop, #20 R&B, 1988),

Sir Mix-a-Lot

contained his first pop hit, "Posse on Broadway" (#70 pop, #44 R&B, 1988); the album sold a million copies in two years. Sir Mix-a-Lot then toured with Public Enemy, whose influence was reflected on *Seminar* (#67 pop, #25 R&B, 1989), which eventually went gold.

His first release on Def American, *Mack Daddy* (#9 pop, #19 R&B, 1992), produced the Grammy-winning, two-million-selling hit "Baby Got Back" (#1 pop, #27 R&B, 1992), a sincerely lusty homage to large female derrieres. Although the Black Entertainment Television cable channel refused to play the video, MTV aired it. Sir Mix-a-Lot answered claims of misogyny by saying the song was actually an attack on the unrealistic beauty standards set by anorexic fashion models. In the summer of 1993 Sir Mix-a-Lot executive-produced *Seattle: The Dark Side,* a sampler of rap and R&B acts from his hometown, including one of his backing vocalists, E-Dawg (born Michael Johnson, January 4, 1972, Seattle). Sir Mix-a-Lot also joined Seattle grunge rockers Mudhoney on "Freak Mama," for the soundtrack of *Judgment Night.*

Sister Sledge

Formed late Fifties, Philadelphia, Pennsylvania
Joni Sledge (b. 1957), voc.; Kathie Sledge (b. 1959), voc.; Kim Sledge (b. 1958), voc.; Debra Sledge (b. 1955), voc.
1975—*Circle of Love* (Atco)   1979—*We Are Family* (Cotillion)   1980—*Love Somebody Today*   1981— *All American Girls*   1983—*Bet Cha Say That to All the Girls*   1985—*When the Boys Meet the Girls* (Atlantic)   1992—*The Best of Sister Sledge (1973-1985).*

This vocal quartet of Philadelphia-born sisters enjoyed considerable success as the Seventies ended.

The Sledge sisters made their performing debut at Philadelphia's Second Macedonia Church in the late Fifties. Their parents had both been entertainers, and their grandmother, Viola Williams, was an opera singer. Before they attended elementary school, the four girls entertained at parties as "Mrs. Williams' Grandchildren."

In 1971 they recorded "Time Will Tell" for the Money label. It was produced by Marty Bryant and the band Slim and the Boys, the team behind the Stylistics' first hit. While attending college they worked as background singers on several Kenny Gamble and Leon Huff productions, and in 1973 they were signed to Atlantic Records. All four have since graduated from Temple University.

From 1973 to 1978, Sister Sledge recorded in New York and Philadelphia without any significant success. It wasn't until the gold *We Are Family* in 1979, written and produced by Nile Rodgers and Bernard Edwards of Chic, that they became a chart presence. "He's the Greatest

Dancer" (#9 pop, #1 R&B) and "We Are Family" (#2 pop, #1 R&B) were dance hits. The latter became the theme song of the Pittsburgh Pirates, the 1979 baseball champions, and later the anthem of gays marching on Washington, D.C., that year. In 1981 (the year they began producing their own records) the quartet recorded "He's Just a Runaway," a tribute to the late Bob Marley. The next year, Sister Sledge had a hit with a cover of the Mary Wells oldie "My Guy." Although the group had no further pop hits in the U.S., they had a #1 U.K. hit, "Frankie," in 1985. After that, Kathy sought a solo career and found some success in Europe in the early Nineties.

Sisters of Mercy

Formed 1980, Leeds, England
Andrew Eldritch (b. Andrew Taylor, May 15, 1959, Ely, Eng.), voc.; Ben Gunn (b. Benjamin Matthews), gtr.; Craig Adams (b. Apr. 4, 1962, Leeds), bass; Gary Marx (b. Mark Pearman), gtr.
1982—*Alice* EP (Brain Eater)   1983—*The Reptile House* EP   1984—(– Gunn; + Wayne Hussey [b. Jerry Lovelock, May 26, 1958, Bristol, Eng.], gtr.) *Body and Soul* EP (Merciful Release)   1985—*First and Last and Always* (Elektra)   1987—(– Hussey; – Adams; – Marx; + Patricia Morrison, bass) *Floodland*   1990—(– Morrison; + Tony James [b. ca. 1956], bass; + Andreas Bruhn [b. Nov. 5, 1967, Hamburg, Ger.], gtr.; + Tim Bricheno [b. July 6, 1963, Huddersfield, Eng.], gtr.) *Vision Thing*   1992—*Some Girls Wander by Mistake* (Mute) (– James; – Bruhn; – Bricheno).*

Sisters of Mercy, progenitors of England's "goth," or "gothic," postpunk subgenre, play a darkly psychedelic, danceable music that feasts on what bandleader Andrew Eldritch considers the "corpse of rock & roll." Sisters were formed by Eldritch and Gary Marx as a studio project: a metal band with a drum machine, Doktor Avalanche. After one year and one single released on their Merciful Release label, the Sisters (named after an order of nuns) added Ben Gunn and Craig Adams so they could play live shows. Gunn left the band after its first U.S. tour, in 1983, and was replaced by former Dead or Alive guitarist Wayne Hussey.

After a string of singles and EPs established a strong Sisters following in England, WEA signed the band worldwide. By this time, Sisters had added dance and pop elements to their heavy sound, and *First and Last and Always,* produced by Dave Allen (the Cure), reached the U.K. Top Twenty. The band was having internal problems, however, and Marx left to form the group Ghost Dance. In typically macabre fashion, the Sisters played a June 1985 concert dubbed "Altamont: A Festival of Remembrance." Shortly afterward, Hussey and Adams left to form the Mission (U.K.). Eldritch, who had been having health problems, moved to Hamburg. Embroiled in a legal fight with his former bandmates, he released the EP *Gift* in 1986 under the name Sisterhood, partly to pre-empt Hussey and Adams from using that name. *Gift* featured tape collages, a cameo by American Alan Vega (Suicide), and another American, ex–Gun Club bassist Patricia Morrison.

Morrison remained Eldritch's sole collaborator on *Floodland,* whose single "This Corrosion" became popular among American alternative rockers. Meat Loaf collaborator Jim Steinman produced two album tracks. Morrison left, and Eldritch replaced her with the controversial Tony James, former Generation X bassist and Sigue Sigue Sputnik mastermind. The Sisters continued their transatlantic success with *Vision Thing,* a powerful and pointed commentary on life under Bush and Thatcher. The album, featuring new members Andreas Bruhn and Tim Bricheno and guest appearances by John Perry (Only Ones), yielded the singles "Vision Thing" and "More." In summer 1991 the Sisters, joined by ex-B.A.D. keyboardist Dan Donovan, led a tour with Public Enemy, Gang of Four, Warrior Soul, and Young Black Teenagers. As of winter 1994, Eldritch was Sisters of Mercy's sole member.

Ricky Skaggs

Born July 18, 1954, Cordell, Kentucky
1979—*Sweet Temptation* (Sugar Hill)   1980—*Family & Friends*   1981—*Waitin' for the Sun to Shine* (Epic)   1982—*Highways & Heartaches*   1983—*Don't Cheat in Our Hometown*   1984—*Country Boy* 1985—*Favorite Country Songs; Live in London* 1986—*Love's Gonna Get Ya!*   1988—*Comin' Home to Stay*   1989—*Kentucky Thunder*   1991—*My Father's Son*   1993—*Super Hits.*

He considers himself a bluegrass player, but it would be impossible to imagine new traditionalist country music without Ricky Skaggs. His work with Emmylou Harris was instrumental in bringing country music back from the slick, overproduced sound that dominated Nashville in the Seventies. As a solo artist, Skaggs has had 18 Top Ten C&W singles, with ten reaching #1, and two #2, including "Uncle Pen" (#1, 1984), the first bluegrass recording to top the country charts since 1963. Skaggs has scored eight C&W Top Twenty albums, including three #1s (*Highways & Heartaches* [#61 pop, 1982], *Don't Cheat in Our Hometown,* and *Country Boy* [#180 pop, 1984]). A virtuoso multi-instrumentalist (on guitar, mandolin, banjo, and fiddle), he became a member of the Grand Ole Opry in 1982, at the time the youngest performer ever to receive that honor.

Born into a musical family (his construction worker father played church meeting halls, and his mother was a gospel singer and songwriter), Skaggs taught himself

mandolin at age five. He also made his first public appearance that year, playing "Ruby" at a Bill Monroe concert. By the late Sixties, he started performing with Keith Whitley. When bluegrass legend Ralph Stanley was late for a show in 1970, the promoter asked Skaggs and Whitley, who were in the audience, to fill in. Stanley, who walked in while they were playing, was sufficiently impressed to add them to his band.

Tired of life on the road, Skaggs quit in 1972 and moved to Washington, D.C., where he worked for the Virginia Electric and Power company until 1974, when he joined the Country Gentlemen. He played with J. D. Crowe & the New South before forming his own band, Boone Creek, in 1975. He met Emmylou Harris at a party, and when Rodney Crowell left her Hot Band in 1978, she asked Skaggs to replace him. He played on her albums *Blue Kentucky Girl* (1979) and *Light of the Stable* (1980), and was musical director and arranger for *Roses in the Snow* (1980). Skaggs recorded two solo albums, *Sweet Temptation* (1979) and *Family & Friends* (1980), for Sugar Hill, a small North Carolina label, moved to Nashville in 1980 and signed to Epic, which released *Waitin' for the Sun to Shine* (#77 pop, #5 C&W, 1981), which proved there was still an audience for traditional country music. Subsequent albums add some rock touches but never stray far from Skaggs' country roots.

In 1981 Skaggs married Sharon White, one half of the Whites. They recorded a #10 C&W duet in 1987, "Love Can't Ever Get Any Better Than This." He has also duetted with Ray Charles on "Friendship" (1984) and performed with and produced albums for the Bellamy Brothers, Johnny Cash, Rodney Crowell, Exile, Dolly Parton, and Jesse Winchester. In 1994, as "hat acts" flourished in Nashville, Skaggs' contract with Epic ended; he continued to perform at bluegrass concerts and festivals.

The Skatalites

Formed 1963, Kingston, Jamaica
Don Drummond (d. May 6, 1969), trombone; Rico Rodriguez, trombone; Baba Brooks, trumpet; Johnny "Dizzy" Moore, fluegelhorn, trumpet; Raymond Harper, trumpet; Bobby Ellis, trumpet; Lester Sterling, alto sax; Karl Bryan, alto sax; Roland Alphonso, tenor sax; Tommy McCook, trumpet, tenor sax; Ernest Ranglin, gtr.; Jah Jerry (b. Jerome Hines), gtr.; Lloyd Brevette, bass; Jackie Mittoo (d. 1988), kybds.; Theophilus Beckford, kybds.; Gladstone Anderson, kybds.; Lloyd Nibbs, bass, perc.; Drumbago, drums; Hugh Malcolm, drums. 1963—*Ska Authentic* (Studio One)   1975—*Legendary Skatalites* (Top Ranking)   1977—*African Roots* (United Artists)   1984—*Scattered Lights* (Alligator)   1986—*Stretching Out* cassette (ROIR) 1993—*Skavoovee* (Shanachie)   1994—*Hi-Bop Ska.*

From 1963 to 1967 the Skatalites played on nearly every session recorded in Jamaica. Leader Don Drummond virtually invented ska, and the ranks of his band were filled with stars of that and later eras. The band was a major inspiration for the British two-tone movement in the late Seventies.

Drummond was a music teacher at a Catholic boys' school in West Kingston when he formed his band; some members had been his students. With varying numbers according to the demands of the session, they recorded for all of the Jamaican producers, but especially for Coxsone Dodd at his Studio One, and they backed Eric Morris, the Charms, Justin Hines, Derrick Morgan, the Maytals, the Wailers, and the Heptones. They issued instrumental records from their sessions as well, scoring Jamaican hits with "Ball o' Fire," "Independent Anniversary Ska," "Confucius," and "Dick Tracy."

One of the first Jamaican acts signed to Island Records and marketed in the U.K., they made the British Top Forty with "Guns of Navarone" in 1967. They also recorded, in various aggregations, as the Don Drummond All Stars, Roland Al and the Soul Brothers, Tommy McCook and the Supersonics, the Baba Brooks Band, the Karl Bryan Orchestra, Jackie Mittoo and the Soul Vendors, Drumbago's All Stars, Sir Coxsone's All Stars, and Roland Alphonso's Alley Cats.

By 1967 the Skatalites were no longer recording under that name, although most of the members were active in Jamaican music until the Eighties. Some moved to England, where, like Ernest Ranglin, they maintained careers as session musicians or, like Rico Rodriguez, they began making solo records. Drummond, who had won international jazz trombonist awards, died in 1969 after years of steadily worsening mental illness. In 1975 Tommy McCook, Roland Alphonso, Lloyd Nibbs, and Lester Sterling briefly reunited as the Skatalites under Lloyd Brevette's leadership.

The punky ska played by 2-Tone bands like the Specials and Madness in the late Seventies and early Eighties revived interest in the Skatalites. Rico Rodriguez played on the Specials debut album in 1979 (they also covered "Navarone" in concert). In 1988 the group, now led by Tommy McCook, toured the U.S. *Skavoovee* was released in 1993, supported by a tour that featured latter-day 2-Tone–style bands Special Beat, the Selecter (which had just re-formed), and the New York City–based Toasters.

Skid Row
Formed 1986, New Jersey
Matt Fallon, voc.; Dave "Snake" Sabo, gtr.; Scotti Hill, gtr.; Rachel Bolan, bass; Rob Affuso, drums.
1987—(– Fallon; + Sebastian Bach [b. Sebastian Bierk, April 3, 1968, Bahamas], voc.)   1989—*Skid* *Row* (Atlantic)   1991—*Slave to the Grind*   1992—*B-Sides Ourselves* EP   1995—*Subhuman Race*.

New Jersey–based hard-rock band Skid Row included Bon Jovi's original guitarist, Dave "Snake" Sabo. That connection came in handy when Bon Jovi's management signed Skid Row and offered it the opening-act slot on Bon Jovi's 1989 U.S. tour—where audiences discovered the wild, anything-goes stage persona of pretty-boy frontman Sebastian Bach. Bach would later publicly criticize Jon Bon Jovi for taking a chunk of Skid Row's publishing royalties in exchange for his early support.

The band's debut album (#6, 1989) sold four million copies, thanks to the Bon Jovi connection, heavy MTV play of the video for the anthemic "Youth Gone Wild," and the unexpected success of the singles "18 and Life" (#4, 1989) and the power ballad "I Remember You" (#6, 1989). Skid Row also contributed a cover of the Sex Pistols' "Holidays in the Sun" to the 1989 metal all-star album *Stairway to Heaven, Highway to Hell.*

Bach then began courting controversy in earnest. At a December 27, 1989, concert in Springfield, Massachusetts, he was hit in the head with a bottle thrown by a fan. Bach hurled the bottle back into the crowd—hitting an innocent girl in the face—then leaped into the throng and pummeled someone who may or may not have tossed the bottle. Bach faced four assault charges and one count of mayhem. He did no jail time but spent three years on probation and paid an undisclosed settlement to the girl he had injured, as well as giving her a personal apology (she'd also endured the taunts of schoolmates angry that she'd "made trouble" for Bach).

About the same time, Bach was pictured in a metal magazine wearing a T-shirt that read "AIDS kills fags dead" (a parody of an insecticide slogan). Asked by MTV News about the shirt, Bach laughingly said, "I do not condone, comprehend, or understand homosexuality in any way, shape, form, or size." In the face of mounting public outrage, Bach stated that he had friends who were gay and that he disapproved of gay bashing.

Slave to the Grind took a harder-edged and punkier approach than the first album and yielded no hit singles. Though it entered the chart at #1, the album fell before too long and sold only a quarter the copies of its predecessor. The five-song EP *B-Sides Ourselves* included Skid Row's covers of Jimi Hendrix's "Little Wing" and the Ramones' "Psycho Therapy."

The Skids: See Big Country

Skiffle
The name for England's equivalent of America's late-Fifties folk revival, which involved enthusiastic amateur performances of old novelty songs, New Orleans jazz,

and jug-band music, was skiffle. Lonnie Donegan was skiffle's major hitmaker ("Rock Island Line"), but the impact of the craze was that it encouraged amateur musicians to start playing and performing. Countless British Sixties rockers, including John Lennon and George Harrison of the Beatles, got started in skiffle bands.

Skinny Puppy
Formed 1983, Vancouver, Canada
Nivek Ogre (b. Kevin Ogilvie, Dec. 5, 1962, Can.), voc.; cEVIN Key (a.k.a. Kevin Crompton, b. Feb. 13, 1961, Can.), perc.
1984—*Remission* EP (Nettwerk, Can.) 1985—*Bites* 1986—*Mind: The Perpetual Intercourse* (Capitol) (+ Dwayne Goettel [b. Feb. 1, 1964, Can.; d. Aug. 23, 1995, Edmonton, Can.], kybds.) 1987—*Cleanse Fold and Manipulate* 1988—*VIVIsectVI* 1989— Rabies 1990—*Too Dark Park*; Twelve Inch Anthology* 1992—*Last Rights* 1993—*Back & Forth 2* 1995—(– Ogre).

Borrowing from pioneering U.K. electronic and industrial bands Cabaret Voltaire and Throbbing Gristle, Skinny Puppy's musical palette includes dance beats and distorted vocals, tape manipulation, and other abrasive, avant-industrial sounds. Kevin Ogilvie and former Images in Vogue member Kevin Crompton formed the group amid Vancouver's thriving early-Eighties punk scene. On its first recordings, the duo mainly attempted to re-create the sounds of its industrial-music influences. However, by the time keyboardist/sampler Dwayne Goettel joined the group permanently for 1987's *Cleanse Fold and Manipulate*, Skinny Puppy had developed its own sound, based on the ominous, minor-key themes of goth, the electronic techniques of industrial, and a passionate antivivisectionist agenda in the lyrics. In 1989 Ministry's Al Jourgensen added guitar, vocals, and his signature production sound to *Rabies*.

Key released an album of sparse, atmospheric music with the Legendary Pink Dots' Edward Ka-Spel in 1987 under the name Tear Garden. In 1990 he and longtime friend Alan Nelson recorded a more rock-oriented album as Hilt. Skinny Puppy signed to American Recordings in 1993. The group began working on an album that was not yet finished as of mid-1995, when Ogre quit, and Gottel later died from a heroin overdose.

Slade
Formed 1968, Wolverhampton, England
Noddy Holder (b. Neville Holder, June 15, 1950, Walshall, Eng.), gtr., voc.; Dave Hill (b. Apr. 4, 1952, Fleet Castle, Eng.), gtr.; Jimmy Lea (b. June 14, 1952, Wolverhampton), bass, piano; Don Powell (b. Sep. 10, 1950, Bilston, Eng.), drums
1969—*Beginnings* (Fontana) 1970—*Play It Loud*
(Cotillion) 1972—*Slade Alive* (Polydor); Slayed? 1973—*Sladest* (Reprise) 1974—*Old, New, Borrowed and Blue* (Polydor); Stomp Your Hands, Clap Your Feet* (Warner Bros.) 1975—*In Flame* 1977— Whatever Happened to Slade?* (Polydor, U.K.) 1984—*Keep Your Hands Off My Power Supply* (CBS) 1985—*Rogues Gallery.*

Distinguished by Noddy Holder's harsh screaming, a crudely thunderous rhythm section, and song titles that recast the English language ("Gudbuy T'Jane," "Cum On Feel the Noize," "Skweeze Me Pleeze Me"), Slade breathed life into early-Seventies hard rock. Within a decade, the group's influence could be seen in newer artists, including Quiet Riot (whose first hit was a cover of "Cum On Feel the Noize" and who later covered "Mama Weer All Crazee Now"), Joan Jett, and any number of glitter-influenced rockers.

Hailing from Wolverhampton, an industrial city near Birmingham, the quartet started as the In Betweens. They changed their name to Ambrose Slade and were spotted one night by Chas Chandler, the former Animal and former manager/producer of Jimi Hendrix. Chandler dropped the Ambrose and became the group's manager and producer, giving them their first British hit in 1971, a cover of Little Richard's "Get Down and Get with It," followed by the #1 record "Coz I Luv You."

The key to Slade's primitive attack was Chandler's live-in-the-studio production. Appearing onstage at first with closely cropped haircuts, blue jeans, suspenders, and construction boots—trademarks of England's working-class skinhead movement—Slade was as noisy as the Who and generated an unrestrained "Slademania." Fans stomped, clapped, rushed the stage, fainted, and tossed bras and panties onstage. Slade gradually switched its visual image, becoming one of rock's most gaudily outfitted groups. The four rockers dressed in the unlikely combination of silver sci-fi gear and high-fashion platform boots.

Their hits from this period included "Take Me Bak 'Ome" (#1 U.K., 1972), "Mama Weer All Crazee Now" (#1 U.K., 1972), "Gudbuy T'Jane" (#2 U.K., 1972), and "Cum On Feel the Noize" (#1 U.K., 1973), which were generally ignored in the U.S. In 1974 Slade starred in the film *Flame*, in which the members appeared as rock stars on the way to the top. At the same time, Slade's popularity was slipping, with decreasing sales of albums such as *Slade in Flame*, which underlined the group's maturing hard-rock style. Slade carried on, seemingly unable to regain the momentum of their peak period, when they sold more than ten million records worldwide. In 1981 the group had a British hit with "Lock Up Your Daughters," then in 1983, on the heels of the Quiet Riot hit cover, the group rebounded in the U.K. with "My Oh My," which went to #2. "Run Runaway," from *Keep Your Hands Off*

Slayer: Tom Araya, Paul Bostaph,
Kerry King, Jeff Hanneman

My Power Supply, became Slade's highest-charting single in the U.S., topping at #20. After a few more moderately successful releases in their homeland, Slade split up. Holder produced the female metal band Girlschool's 1983 album, *Play Dirty.*

Slayer

Formed 1982, Los Angeles, California
Tom Araya (b. June 6, 1961, Chile), bass, voc.; Jeff Hanneman (b. Jan. 31, 1964, Los Angeles), gtr.; Kerry King (b. June 3, 1964, Huntington Park, Calif.), gtr.; Dave Lombardo (b. Feb. 16, 1965), drums. 1983—*Show No Mercy* (Metal Blade)   1985—*Hell Awaits*   1986—*Reign in Blood* (Def Jam)   1988— *South of Heaven*   1990—*Seasons in the Abyss* (Def American)   1991—*Decade of Aggression Live* 1992—(– Lombardo; + Paul Bostaph [b. Mar. 4, 1965, Hayward, Calif.], drums)   1994—*Divine Intervention* (American).

If Slayer did not exist, the tabloid press would invent them: Loud, aggressive, and violent, their songs touch on sadism, Satanism, Nazi death camps, and serial killers. Their music was prominently featured in 1987's troubled-teen film *River's Edge.* A 1988 concert in New York's Felt Forum had to be stopped when fans rampaged, tearing up seats and pelting the stage with debris. And all five teens featured on the "Kids Who Kill" edition of *Geraldo* cited Slayer as one of their favorite bands.

Slayer began in 1982 as part of Los Angeles' Huntington Beach head-banging scene. Originally a cover band, by 1983 they had written "Aggressive Perfector," which appeared on Metal Blade Records' *Metal Mas-*

sacre III compilation. Metal Blade also released their next two albums, *Show No Mercy* and *Hell Awaits.* Their brutal songs and malevolent obsessions increased their local reputation, but they were unable to garner national attention until Rick Rubin signed them to his Def Jam label in 1986. Slayer became something of a cause célébrè that year when Columbia (Def Jam's distributor) refused to release *Reign in Blood,* citing references to Joseph Mengele in "Angel of Death," among other offenses. Geffen quickly picked up the album, which became the band's first to chart, peaking at #94. Starting with their followup, *South of Heaven* (#57, 1988), bassist/vocalist Tom Araya became the main songwriter, and Slayer's music and subject matter turned slightly more mainstream, with riffs and melodies replacing drones and the lyrics avoiding Satan for more earthbound subjects: "Death Skin Mask" from *Seasons in the Abyss* (#40, 1990) was inspired by serial killer Ed Gein.

In 1991 Slayer celebrated its first ten years together by releasing *Decade of Aggression Live* (#55) and holding down one-third of the Clash of the Titans Tour along with Megadeth and Anthrax. The band returned in 1994 with *Divine Intervention* (#8).

Percy Sledge

Born November 25, 1940, Leighton, Alabama
1966—*When a Man Loves a Woman* (Atlantic); *Warm and Tender Soul*   1967—*The Percy Sledge Way*   1968—*Take Time to Know Her*   1969—*The Best of Percy Sledge*   1974—*I'll Be Your Everything* (Capricorn)   1987—*When a Man Loves a Woman (The Ultimate Collection)* (Atlantic)   1992—*It Tears

Me Up: The Best of Percy Sledge   1995—*Blue Night* (Pointblank/Virgin).

In the mid-Sixties singer Percy Sledge was performing throughout Mississippi and Alabama as a member of the Esquires Combo. His career took a dramatic turn for the better in 1966, when he quit to go solo and scored a #1 pop and R&B hit with his debut single, "When a Man Loves a Woman." Sledge remained a popular singer through the end of the decade, working in the same intense balladeering style of "When a Man."

His successes included "Warm and Tender Love" (#17 pop, #5 R&B) and "It Tears Me Up" (#20 pop, #7 R&B) in 1966; "Out of Left Field" (#25 R&B) in 1967; "Sudden Stop" (#41 R&B) in 1968; "Any Day Now" (#35 R&B) in 1969; and especially "Take Time to Know Her" (#11 pop, #6 R&B, 1968). Sledge's career stalled in the Seventies, save for a brief resurgence with the R&B hits "Sunshine" (#89 R&B, 1973) and "I'll Be Your Everything" (#15 R&B, 1974).

Sledge's career faded somewhat after that, although he continued to tour the U.S., Japan, and the U.K. through the rest of that decade and into the Eighties. The use of "When a Man Loves a Woman" in the 1987 hit film *Platoon* sparked a resurgence for Sledge, and that year the song was rereleased in the U.K., where it went to #2. In 1989 he won the Rhythm and Blues Foundation's Career Achievement Award. He continues to perform, playing over 100 dates a year. As of the mid-Nineties, he lives in Baton Rouge, Louisiana. In 1994 he was sentenced to five years' probation afer being convicted of tax evasion.

Grace Slick: See the Jefferson Airplane

Slick Rick

Born Ricky Walters, January 14, 1965, London, England
1989—*The Great Adventures of Slick Rick* (Def Jam) 1991—*The Ruler's Back*   1994—*Behind Bars*.

Sporting a black patch over an eye blinded by broken glass as a youth, Slick Rick epitomized a pregangsta version of ghetto cool that made him a million-selling star but also proved his downfall when a jail term derailed his career. Ricky Walters moved to the Bronx as a teenager and attended New York's prestigious High School of Music and Art. As MC Ricky D. he joined with human beatbox Doug E. Fresh and the Get Fresh Crew [see entry]; his singsong voice with its odd accent was featured on their 1985 hit "La-Di-Da-Di" b/w "The Show."

Splitting from Fresh, Walters hooked up with rap impresario Russell Simmons and disappeared for three years, amid much rumor. He reemerged with the phenomenal *The Great Adventures of Slick Rick* (#31 pop, #1 R&B, 1989), which went on to sell more than a million copies. The album, produced by Jam Master Jay, Hank Shocklee, Eric Sadler, and Walters, featured "Teenage Love" (#16 R&B, 1988), "Children's Story" (#5 R&B, 1989), and the infamous misogynist rap "Treat Her Like a Prostitute." Rick was also featured on Al B. Sure!'s single "If I'm Not Your Lover" (#2 R&B, 1989).

On July 3, 1990, Walters was arrested for shooting his cousin, who had allegedly embezzled money from him, and another passenger in his cousin's car. In 1991 he was given a three-to-ten-year sentence for attempted murder. While out on bail before sentencing, Walters recorded *The Ruler's Back* (#29 pop, #18 R&B, 1991), a powerfully ominous record. While in a work-release program, he released *Behind Bars* (#51 pop, #11 R&B, 1994).

The Slits

Formed 1976, London, England
Ari Up, voc.; Kate Korus, gtr.; Suzi Gutsy, bass; Palmolive, drums.
1977—(– Korus; – Gutsy; + Tessa Pollit, bass; + Viv Albertine, gtr.)   1978—(– Palmolive; + Budgie [b. Aug. 21, St. Helens, Eng.], drums)   1979—*Cut* (Island/Antilles).

British punk rock's first all-female band of any consequence, the Slits knew nothing about how to play their instruments yet began jamming together anyway—just like many of their male counterparts. Before the band had played a gig, bassist Suzi Gutsy left to join Flicks and guitarist Kate Korus left to form the Modettes (whose "White Mice" was a club favorite and whose cover of the Stones' "Paint It Black" was a minor U.K. hit [#42, 1980]). The Slits made their stage debut in London, opening for the Clash, in March 1977 with new guitarist Viv Albertine and bassist Tessa Pollit, both from Flowers of Romance, Sid Vicious' pre–Sex Pistols backing band.

Lead singer Ari Up ("Ari" was reportedly short for her given first name, Ariana) was 14 years old at the time of the first Slits show, so the band's ability to perform was somewhat limited. Still, the Slits opened for the Clash on its 1977 "White Riot" tour. The Slits did not get a record deal until 1979, by which time original drummer Palmolive had left to help form the Raincoats [see entry], and the Slits had evolved into a white-reggae group. With guest drummer Budgie (formerly with Big in Japan and soon to join Siouxsie and the Banshees) and reggae producer Dennis Bovell, the Slits recorded their only major-label album (assorted bootlegs have also been released), the dub-influenced *Cut;* new-wave rock discos in the U.S. gave some play to the frolicsome track "Typical Girls." Demonstrating the neo-tribalism they were affecting at the time, the three Slits wore nothing but thongs and mud for the *Cut* album cover photo. For a subsequent U.S. tour, Budgie was replaced by Bruce Smith, of British avant-jazz-rock band the Pop Group, and the band was filled out by British avant-gardist Steve Beresford, on keyboards, trumpet, and miscellaneous toy instruments. The Slits broke up at the end of 1981.

Philip (P. F.) Sloan

Born 1946, Los Angeles, California
1965—*Songs of Our Time* (Dunhill)   1966—*12 More*
***Times*   1968—*Measure of Pleasure* (Atco)   1972—**
Raised on Records* (Epic, U.K.)   1993—*P. F. Sloan
***Anthology* (One Way).**
With the Fantastic Baggies: N.A.—*Tell 'Em I'm*
***Surfin'* (Imperial).**

Though he had his own career as a Dylan-styled singer/songwriter, P. F. Sloan is best known for his songwriting, particularly Barry McGuire's 1965 smash "Eve of Destruction." Before "Eve," Sloan and his partner Steve Barri had written surf-rock hits and even recorded a few of them disguised as the Fantastic Baggies on the album *Tell 'Em I'm Surfin'.*

In the years that followed, Sloan and Barri worked extensively with the Grass Roots, provided the Turtles with a hit record, "You Baby," and wrote songs for the Searchers, Herman's Hermits, and many others. Because of the groups he was involved with, Sloan's work tended to be dismissed—a situation addressed by Jimmy Webb in his song "P. F. Sloan." Barri remains active as a pop-rock producer. Shortly before his death, ex–Washington Square Bruce Jay Paskow produced an album for Sloan and played guitar in the band that backed the singer for a showcase performance in Los Angeles in late 1993. As of mid-1995, that album is yet to be released.

Sly and Robbie

Formed 1975, Kingston, Jamaica
Sly "Drumbar" Dunbar (b. Lowell Fillmore Dunbar,
May 10, 1952, Kingston), drums; Robbie "Bass-
peare" Shakespeare (b. Sep. 27, 1953, Kingston),
bass.
1981—*Sly and Robbie Present Taxi* (Mango); *60s,*
70s, 80s*   1982—*Sly-Go-Ville*   1983—*Crucial Reg-
gae Driven by Sly and Robbie*   1985—*A Dub Expe-
***rience*; *Reggae Greats*; *Language Barrier* (Island)**
1987—*Rhythm Killers*   1988—*The Summit* (RAS)
1989—*Silent Assassin* (Island)   1990—*Two*
***Rhythms Clash* (RAS).**

Sly Dunbar and Robbie Shakespeare began their careers as teenaged session musicians. They teamed up to become one of Jamaica's most celebrated rhythm sections and continued their partnership as bandleaders, producers, and record businessmen.

Dunbar started out in the Yardbrooms, a reggae band of the late Sixties that nurtured several of Jamaica's leading instrumentalists. In the early Seventies Dunbar was with Skin, Flesh and Bones, who recorded their own records and backed various singers.

Shakespeare studied with Aston "Family Man" Barrett (bassist with the Upsetters, who went on to join the Wailers) and played sessions for Burning Spear, Bunny Wailer, and others. He first played with Dunbar behind Peter Tosh in 1975, and the following year—after Dunbar had returned from touring the U.K. with the Mighty Diamonds—the two formed the Revolutionaires, a leading dub band of the Seventies. Concurrently until 1979, Dunbar and Shakespeare led Peter Tosh's band, Word, Sound and Power, in the studio and on tours of North America and Europe. Their sound exemplified the "rockers' riddims" of late-Seventies reggae. (Shakespeare played a cameo role in *Rockers,* the 1977 film inspired by that sound.)

In 1978 they set up their own record company, Taxi Productions, formed the Taxi All-Stars from the ashes of the Revolutionaires and Word, Sound and Power, and began working as producers. Taxi's first release was Black Uhuru's "Observe Life." It was followed by numerous albums for Black Uhuru, for established artists like Gregory Isaacs, Max Romeo, Prince Far-I, and Dennis Brown, and for such newer acts as the Tamlins, the Wailing Souls, Jimmy Riley, and General Echo. Their immediately recognizable sound is marked by Robbie's thundering in-the-pocket bass and Sly's innovative use of synthesized drums. In addition, Sly and Robbie (as they are invariably billed) issued their own duo and solo recordings on Taxi. In 1980 they entered into a worldwide distribution agreement with Island Records. Their early Eighties U.S. releases are anthologies of Taxi artists. In the early Eighties they worked with such reggae veterans as Jimmy Cliff, Desmond Dekker, and the Paragons and regularly took their "riddims" on the road with Black Uhuru. They have also worked with artists not usually associated with reggae: Ian Dury, Joan Armatrading, Grace Jones, Manu Dibango, Robert Palmer, and Joe Cocker. Bob Dylan used them as the rhythm section on his 1983 album *Infidels;* Mick Jagger employed them for his 1985 solo debut, *She's the Boss.*

On their own, Sly and Robbie hooked up with avant-funk bassist/producer Bill Laswell for 1985's *Language Barrier,* featuring guest appearances by Afrika Bambaataa and Bob Dylan. Laswell also produced *Rhythm Killers,* which included contributions from Bootsy Collins and dancehall star Shinehead. Collaborating with rappers KRS-One, Queen Latifah, and Young MC, Sly and Robbie produced the dub-rap hybrid *Silent Assassin.* Sly and Robbie also produced Maxi Priest's 1988 U.K. #5 hit "Wild World" (a cover of the Cat Stevens song) and Chaka Demus and Pliers 1993 Top Ten U.K. single "Tease Me."

Sly and the Family Stone

Formed 1967, San Francisco, California
Original lineup: Sly Stone (b. Sylvester Stewart,
Mar. 15, 1944, Dallas, Tex.), gtr., kybds., voc.; Freddie Stone (b. Fred Stewart, June 5, 1946, Dallas),
gtr., voc.; Larry Graham Jr. (b. Aug. 14, 1946, Beaumont, Tex.), bass, voc.; Cynthia Robinson (b. Jan.
12, 1946, Sacramento, Calif.), trumpet; Greg Errico
(b. Sep. 1, 1946, San Francisco), drums; Rosie Stone
(b. Mar. 21, 1945, Vallejo, Calif.), piano; Jerry Martini (b. Oct. 1, 1943, Colo.), sax.
1967—*A Whole New Thing* (Epic) 1968—*Dance to
the Music*; *Life* 1969—*Stand!* 1970—*Greatest
Hits* 1971—*There's a Riot Goin' On* 1973—*Fresh*
1974—*Small Talk* 1975—*High Energy* (reissue of *A
Whole New Thing* and *Dance to the Music*); *High on
You* 1976—*Heard Ya Missed Me, Well I'm Back*
1979—*Ten Years Too Soon; Back on the Right Track*
(Warner Bros.) 1983—*Ain't but the One Way*.

In the late Sixties Sly and the Family Stone fused black
rhythms and a psychedelic sensibility into a new
pop/soul/rock hybrid that drew both white and black audiences. The Family Stone's music predated disco and
inspired the many black self-contained bands that
emerged in the Seventies; along with James Brown, the
Family Stone virtually invented Seventies funk, and their
impact has proven lasting and widespread. Motown producer Norman Whitfield, for example, patterned that
label's forays into harder-driving, socially relevant material (such as the Temptations' "Run Away Child, Running
Wild" and "Ball of Confusion") on Sly's work. The pioneering precedent of Sly Stone's racial, sexual, and stylistic mix had an undeniably major influence on Prince
and Rick James in the Eighties, and the male-female
vocal interplay of Human League's "(Keep Feeling) Fascination," for example, can be traced back to any of a
number of the group's hits. In the Nineties he was paid
homage by Earth, Wind and Fire on their *Heritage* album,
and with a hit cover of "Everyday People" by rap group
Arrested Development.

Sylvester Stewart's family moved from Texas to the
San Francisco area in the Fifties. At age four, he began
singing gospel music, and at age 16 he made a local hit,
"Long Time Away." Stewart studied trumpet, music theory, and composition at Vallejo Junior College and while
in school became active on the Bay Area music scene.
With his brother, Fred, he formed several short-lived
groups, like the Stewart Bros. He was a disc jockey at
soul station KSOL, and at Autumn Records he produced
records by the Beau Brummels, Bobby Freeman, the
Mojo Men, and Grace Slick's first band, the Great Society.
He later worked for KDIA.

In 1966 Sly formed a short-lived group called the
Stoners, which included female trumpeter Cynthia

Robinson. With her he started his next band, Sly and the
Family Stone. Sly, Robinson and Fred Stewart were
joined by Larry Graham Jr., Greg Errico, and Jerry Martini, all of whom had studied music and worked in numerous amateur groups. Rosie Stone joined the group
soon after. Working around the Bay Area in 1967, this
multiracial band made a strong impression. They
recorded their debut single, "I Ain't Got Nobody" b/w "I
Can't Turn You Loose," on the local Loadstone label.

The Family Stone's debut LP, *A Whole New Thing*,
flopped. Its followup, *Dance to the Music*, included the
hit title cut (#8 pop, #9 R&B, 1968). *Life* sold fewer copies
than their previous albums, but their next release, a
double-sided single, "Everyday People" b/w "Sing a Simple Song," was #1 on both the R&B and pop charts in
1968. *Stand!* mixed hard-edged politics with the Family's ecstatic dance music. It rose to #13 on the pop chart
in 1969, and contained Sly standards like the title song,
"Don't Call Me Nigger Whitey," "Sex Machine," "Somebody's Watching You," and "I Want to Take You Higher"
(#38 pop, 1970, #24 R&B, 1969). Fiery versions of "Dance
to the Music" and "Higher," heard on the Woodstock
soundtrack album, established them as one of the finest
live bands of the late Sixties.

Singles like "Hot Fun in the Summertime" (#2 pop, #3
R&B, 1969) and "Thank You Falettinme Be Mice Elf Agin"
b/w "Everybody Is a Star" (#1 pop and R&B, 1970), were
the band's commercial peak, and the success of *Greatest
Hits* (#2, 1970) reflected their immense popularity. The
smooth post–doo-wop/pop/soul of "Hot Fun" and the
eerie funk of "Thank You" demonstrated the band's considerable range. By this time, *Stand!* had been on the
charts over 80 weeks, and most of the Family's Top Ten
singles had gone gold, as had most of their post–*Dance
to the Music* LPs. Jazz trumpeter Miles Davis, who'd
been flummoxing critics with electrified "fusion" albums,
did it again when he named Sly Stone and Jimi Hendrix
as his favorite musicians.

After 1970 Sly became somewhat notorious for arriving late or missing concerts, and it was generally known
that he was suffering from drug problems. The group's
turning point came in 1971, when *There's a Riot Goin'
On* went to #1. Its darkly understated sound, violent imagery, and controversial militant stance were a sharp
contrast to the optimism of earlier works. From that
album came "Family Affair" (#1 pop and R&B, 1971), Sly's
last across-the-board hit.

By 1972 the Family Stone were growing restless. Key
members Larry Graham and drummer Greg Errico left
and were replaced by Rusty Allen and Andy Newmark.
(Graham then formed Graham Central Station and later
had success as a solo pop balladeer [see entry].) From
Fresh, "If You Want Me to Stay" (#12 pop, #3 R&B, 1973)
did fairly well, and a blues version of "Que Sera Sera" got
some airplay, particularly when rumors of a romance be-

tween Sly and Doris Day emerged. *Small Talk* fared moderately well. It took advertising of Sly's public wedding ceremony to Kathy Silva at Madison Square Garden in 1974 to sell it out. "I Get High on You" (#3 R&B, 1975) did respectably, but subsequent albums failed.

Meanwhile, disco had emerged, and in 1979 Epic issued *Ten Years Too Soon,* a compilation album on which the quirky original rhythm tracks were erased and a disco beat dubbed in. By the mid-Seventies, stories of drug problems and arrests were part of the Sly Stone legacy. By 1979 he was with Warner Bros., attempting to make the comeback many observers felt would be as natural as James Brown's, given the current interest in and popularity of funk. In 1981, having been cited as a major influence by George Clinton, he appeared on Funkadelic's *Electric Spanking of War Babies.* He toured with Clinton's P-Funk All-Stars, on his own, and with Bobby Womack in the early Eighties. In 1983 Sly was arrested for cocaine possession; he entered a rehabilitation program a year later.

In 1986 Stone guested on ex-Time guitarist Jesse Johnson's minor hit "Crazay," which led to a deal with A&M Records. A 1987 single, "Eek-a-Bo-Static," failed to chart; that same year Stone dueted with ex-Motel Martha Davis on "Love & Affection," for the soundtrack of the movie *Soul Man.* Sly's stalled-out career stopped dead for a time when he was jailed in 1987 for cocaine possession. As of early 1995, Sly was signed to Avenue Records and said to be working on a new album.

Small Faces/Faces
**Small Faces, formed 1965, London, England
(Steve Marriott [b. Jan. 30, 1947, London; d. Apr. 20, 1991, Arkesden, Eng.], gtr., voc.; Jimmy Winston [b. James Langwith, Apr. 20, 1945, Eng.], kybds.; Ronnie Lane [b. Apr. 1, 1946, London], bass; Kenney Jones [b. Sep. 16, 1948, London], drums): 1965—
(– Winston; + Ian McLagan [b. May 12, 1945, Hounslown, Eng.], kybds.) 1966—Small Faces (Decca, U.K.) 1967—From the Beginning; There Are but Four Small Faces (Immediate) 1968—Ogden's Nut Gone Flake (– Marriott) 1969—The Autumn Stone (Immediate, U.K.) (name changed to Faces; new personnel, see below) 1970—In Memoriam 1975—The Vintage Years (Sire) 1976—(Small Faces re-form: Marriott; Jones; McLagan; + Rick Wills, bass; + Joe Brown, gtr.) Playmates (Atlantic) 1978—(– Brown; + Jimmy McCulloch [b. 1953, Glasgow, Scot.; d. Sep. 27, 1979, London], gtr.; group disbands) 78 in the Shade 1992—All or Nothing (Sony).
Faces, formed 1969, London, England (Lane; McLagan; Jones; + Rod Stewart [b. Jan. 10, 1945, Lon-**

Small Faces: Steve Marriott, Jimmy Winston, Kenney Jones, Ronnie Lane

**don], voc.; + Ron Wood [b. June 1, 1947, Hillingdon, Eng.], gtr., voc.): 1970—First Step (Warner Bros.) 1971—Long Player; A Nod Is as Good as a Wink to a Blind Horse 1973—Ooh La La (– Lane; + Tetsu Yamauchi [b. Oct. 21, 1947, Fukuoka, Jap.], bass) 1974—Coast to Coast: Overture and Beginnings (Mercury) 1975—(– Stewart) 1976—(– Wood; group disbands) 1978—Snakes and Ladders: The Best of the Faces (Warner Bros.).
Ronnie Lane solo: 1974—Anymore for Anymore (with Slim Chance) (GM) 1975—Ronnie Lane's Slim Chance (with Slim Chance) (A&M) 1976—One for the Road (Island, U.K.); Mahoney's Last Stand (with Ron Wood) (Atco) 1977—Rough Mix (with Pete Townshend) (MCA) 1980—See Me (Gem, U.K.).
Ian McLagan solo: 1979—Troublemaker (Mercury) 981—Bump in the Night.**

The Small Faces got their name for two reasons: They were small, under five feet six inches tall, and they were "faces," as in the Who's "I'm the Face," a declaration of Mod-era hipness. When the Small Faces first hit the British singles charts in 1965 with "Whatcha Gonna Do About It?" (recorded six weeks after their formation), they were seen by British youth as East London's answer to West London's Who. Led by Steve Marriott, the Small Faces became as big an attraction in Britain for their Mod clothing as for their basic, raw R&B-inspired music.

Marriott, a former child actor, formed the band with Ronnie Lane, who had already played with several local bands and was writing his own tunes. McLagan was recruited when original keyboardist Jimmy Winston left immediately after the Faces' first hit single. Rounding out the lineup was drummer Kenney Jones, who had studied drums but had never played with a professional band. Though Marriott later said that he could barely play guitar at the time, he and Lane began writing songs together. After attracting a following with fevered London club performances and the success of their first single, the Small Faces were signed to Andrew Loog Oldham's Immediate label and appeared frequently in the U.K. Top Ten for the next few years with 1966's "Sha La La La Lee," "Hey Girl," "All or Nothing," and "My Mind's Eye"; 1967's "Itchycoo Park" and "Tin Soldier"; and 1968's "Lazy Sunday." The only one of their early hits to gain any attention in America was "Itchycoo Park" (#16, 1967), a piece of psychedelia that featured one of the earliest uses of studio "phase-shifting" production.

By 1968, the band was becoming frustrated with its image as a singles band. That changed somewhat in 1968, when they released the concept album *Ogden's Nut Gone Flake*. Still, internal tensions grew, and in 1969 Marriott left to form Humble Pie [see entry]. It seemed a crucial blow at the time, but with the addition of ex–Jeff Beck Group members Rod Stewart and Ronnie Wood the Faces were Small no more. (Literally. Each of the two new members stood a head taller than the remaining, formerly Small, Faces.) The original Small Faces band later reunited, minus Lane and with the addition of Jimmy McCulloch and Rick Wills.

From 1969 to 1975 the Faces worked in the lucrative shadow of Stewart's solo career [see entry]. Loose and boozy onstage and good-timey on record, the Faces made several arena-circuit U.S. tours playing material from Stewart's solo albums as well as the hits he sang with the group—"Stay with Me" (#17, 1971) and "Cindy Incidentally" (#48, 1973)—while enjoying as wild a lifestyle as possible.

In 1973 Ronnie Lane, an original Small Face, quit and was replaced by ex-Free bassist Tetsu Yamauchi. Lane then started a traveling rock circus, complete with jugglers and fire eaters, called the Passing Show, and recorded four albums with Slim Chance; he also made *Rough Mix* with Pete Townshend of the Who in 1977. In the late Seventies Lane was debilitated by multiple sclerosis.

Meanwhile the Faces were slowly dissolving. Wood officially joined the Rolling Stones in 1976 (after having played on their 1975 tour), and McLagan regularly participated in Stones tours and such projects as the New Barbarians; he also records solo albums and has become a sought-after session hand. He moved to Austin, Texas, in the 1990s, and became active in that city's music scene. Jones, who reunited with the original Small Faces in 1977–78, officially replaced Keith Moon in the Who in 1979. He later formed the Law with Paul Rodgers in the early Nineties. Lane moved to the United States. In 1983 he appeared at the ARMS (Artists for Research into Multiple Sclerosis) concerts, which featured Ronnie Wood,

Charlie Watts, Jeff Beck, Jimmy Page, Steve Winwood, and others. Marriott died in a fire in his home. At the time of his death, he was discussing the possible re-formation of Humble Pie.

Smashing Pumpkins
Formed 1989, Chicago, Illinois
Billy Corgan (b. Mar. 17, 1967, Chicago), gtr. voc.; James Iha (b. Mar. 26, 1968, Elk Grove, Ill.), gtr.; D'arcy Wretzky (b. May 1, 1968, South Haven, Mich.), bass; Jimmy Chamberlain (b. June 10, 1964, Joliet, Ill.), drums.
1991—*Gish* (Caroline)   1993—*Siamese Dream* (Virgin)   1994—*Pisces Iscariot*.

Smashing Pumpkins' music is distinguished from most other grunge rock in its incorporation of the high production values, ornate arrangements, and melodicism of such Seventies bands as Boston and ELO.

Corgan, whose father is a guitarist, grew up in a Chicago suburb and moved to Florida at age 19 as leader of a goth band, the Marked. Returning home, he formed Smashing Pumpkins, at first simply a duo (D'arcy, Corgan, and a drum machine). A local-label single, "I Am One," led to the release of "Tristessa" on Sub Pop; in 1991, the band's debut album, with Butch Vig producing, became a college-radio favorite, eventually selling more than 350,000 copies (and going gold in 1994). The major-label followup fared even better, debuting at #10 in 1993 and making the group alternative-rock stars.

Emphasizing both the virtuosic interplay of Corgan and Jimmy Chamberlain and Corgan's confessional lyrics, the Pumpkins employed Mellotron and strings and multiple guitar parts on *Siamese Dream* and continued to edge closer to progressive rock than to punk or grunge. *Pisces Iscariot* (#4, 1994), a compiliation of earlier recordings, was the Pumpkins' version of Nirvana's *Incesticide*.

Bessie Smith
Born April 15, 1894, Chattanooga, Tennessee; died September 26, 1937, Clarksdale, Mississippi
1970—*Any Woman's Blues*   1971—*The World's Greatest Blues Singer* (Columbia); *Empty Bed Blues*; *The Empress*   1972—*Nobody's Blues But Mine*   1989—*Bessie Smith—The Collection*   1991—*The Complete Recordings, vol. 1; The Complete Recordings, vol. 2*   1992—*The Complete Recordings, vol. 3*   1993—*The Complete Recordings, vol. 4.*

Bessie Smith is generally considered the greatest and most influential American woman blues singer. She was also the preeminent black performer of her time, a singer, dancer, and actress whose later performances (in which she was billed as the Queen of All Torch Singers) revealed a stylistic versatility that promised continued success in other genres, including swing. It is, however, her blues recordings upon which her legend rests and her influence has spread, speaking powerfully, eloquently of satisfaction and defeat, hope and despair.

Smith came by her intimate acquaintance with hard times honestly. One of seven children born to a poor family, she had seen both her parents and two siblings buried before she reached the age of nine. Like many poor black youngsters of her time, she saw little opportunity, and at age 16 she joined her older brother Clarence in the Moses Stokes Company, one of many traveling vaudeville-type shows popular then. It was while working with this show that Smith first met her mentor and stylistic predecessor, Gertrude "Ma" Rainey. While the literature is rich with accounts of Rainey kidnaping Smith or the pair's alleged rivalry, in fact they were friends.

Smith left the Stokes company within a year of joining and began to perform as a solo act or with any of a number of other touring groups. After working a successful duo act with singer Hazel Greene, Smith began pursuing her solo career in earnest. Details of her life during World War I are sketchy. It is known that she married Earl Love; she later claimed he died in the war. In the early Twenties she moved north, to Philadelphia, where she married Jack Gee in June 1923. Around that same time Columbia Records released her first and most successful record, "Gulf Coast Blues" b/w "Down Hearted Blues." Selling over 780,000 copies within six months, the record launched not only Smith but Columbia's soon burgeoning "race" records division.

For the rest of the decade Smith toured the country, often in a luxurious, custom-designed railway car. Smith was feisty yet insecure, and her private life was as passionate and tumultuous as some of her darker recordings. Smith had a violent temper and an appetite for extramarital liaisons (with men and women) and liquor. Chris Albertson's acclaimed biography *Bessie* retells dozens of anecdotes, including one of her beating her husband's mistress unconscious on a Harlem street. Yet her stubborn independence served her well; once in North Carolina when she learned that a group of Ku Klux Klansmen were standing outside her show tent and beginning to pull up stakes, she charged outside and shouted, "You just pick up them sheets and run!" And they did.

Smith recorded 160 songs for Columbia, many of which she wrote or cowrote. Among the musicians she recorded with were Louis Armstrong, who joined her on the 1925 classic "Saint Louis Blues," and Fletcher Henderson. In 1929 she starred and sang in a 17-minute short film entitled "St. Louis Blues," in which she played a woman wronged by a two-timing lover. It is the only extant footage of Smith. That same year, the stock market crash and the rise of "talkies" sent the black vaudeville circuit reeling. The show business milieu in which Smith had thrived was dying, Columbia reduced her recording fee from $200 a side to $125. By 1931 she had no recording contract at all.

Smith revamped her style and her repertoire, trading her traditional feathered and beaded costumes for elegantly understated gowns and pearls. Contemporary standards, like "Tea for Two" and "Smoke Gets in Your Eyes," were part of her show. She had last recorded in 1933, but in 1937 there were plans for new recording sessions and talk of her appearing in a film. Smith seemed on the verge of a commercial comeback when she was critically injured in a Mississippi car accident. Erroneous reports that Smith died because she was refused treatment at a white hospital endured for decades, thanks in part to popular works of literature, such as Edward Albee's play *The Death of Bessie Smith* and various writings about Smith and her music. In fact, Smith was severely injured when the car in which she was riding hit a parked truck on a darkened road. Her injuries included a nearly severed arm and internal damage to the chest and head. Despite being transported to the local black hospital, where her arm was amputated and she received a transfusion, Smith died within hours. Smith's funeral was among the most lavish and well-attended of its time. In Philadelphia an estimated 10,000 mourners paid tribute to the singer as she lay in state; 7,000 stood outside as her gold-trimmed metallic, velvet-lined coffin was placed in the hearse. Despite her costly funeral, Smith's grave remained unmarked for over 30 years. Janis Joplin and Juanita Green, a woman who had worked for Smith, paid for the stone, which was unveiled in August 1970. It read: "The Greatest Blues Singer in the World Will Never Stop Singing."

Curt Smith: See Tears for Fears

Huey "Piano" Smith

Born January 26, 1934, New Orleans, Louisiana
1959—*Havin' a Good Time* (Ace)   1961—*For Dancing*   1962—*'Twas The Night Before Christmas*   1963—*Rock 'n' Roll Revival*   1978—*Rockin' Pneumonia*.

New Orleans R&B pianist Huey Smith, together with his vocal group, the Clowns, recorded some of the R&B classics of the Fifties. Smith began playing professionally at age 15 with Guitar Slim. In the early Fifties, after a stint with Earl King, he played sessions for Lloyd Price, Smiley Lewis, and Little Richard. Meanwhile, he began writing songs and recording for Savoy. A weak singer, he was unsuccessful as a soloist. Consequently, he recruited the

Clowns, originally Junior Gordon, Dave Dixon, and Roland Cook. When he signed with Ace they included Bobby Marchan, "Scarface" John Williams, and James Black. They had their first hit: "Rockin' Pneumonia and the Boogie Woogie Flu" (#52 pop, #9 R&B, 1957). A gold record, it was followed by the even bigger "Don't You Just Know It" (#9 pop, #4 R&B, 1958), with Gerri Hall, Eugene Francis, and Billy Roosevelt singing behind Marchan.

Famous for their stage shenanigans and comic dancing, Smith and the Clowns were a popular live attraction throughout the U.S., but they had no more big hits after "Don't You Just Know It." Possibly their best known record is one not credited to the group: Frankie Ford's 1959 hit "Sea Cruise," with Ford's vocal over a Clowns backup. The Clowns' own "Don't You Know Yockomo" reached #56 pop in 1959 before Marchan left the Clowns—to be replaced by Curley Moore—and Smith moved to Imperial. He returned to Ace with "Pop-Eye" (#51 pop, 1962) before the Clowns broke up.

Smith continued to work through the rest of the decade, but his success was local at best. He formed his own label, Pity-Pat, and recorded as the Hueys and Shindig Smith and the Soulshakers. In the early Seventies, he retired from show business to become a Jehovah's Witness.

Kendra Smith: See the Dream Syndicate

Patti Smith
Born December 31, 1946, Chicago, Illinois
1975—*Horses* (Arista)   1976—*Radio Ethiopia*
1978—*Easter*   1979—*Wave*   1988—*Dream of Life*.

In the early Seventies, painter-turned-poet and sometime playwright (*Cowboy Mouth,* with Sam Shepard) Patti Smith began to set her poems to the electric guitar backup of erstwhile rock writer Lenny Kaye. By the end of the decade, she had proved remarkably influential, releasing what may be the first punk-rock record (the independent 1974 single "Hey Joe" b/w "Piss Factory") and claiming the rock-musician-as-shaman role previously reserved by males. After a nine-year hiatus, Smith returned to recording with the 1988 album *Dream of Life,* the work of a more mellow but still rebellious songwriter.

Smith, who grew up in Pittman, New Jersey, first began performing her poetry backed by Kaye and pianist Richard Sohl in 1971. Along with Television, she helped put New York's punk-rock landmark CBGB on the map. As her music grew toward rock & roll, she enlisted Ivan Kral on guitar and Jay Dee Daugherty on drums. This lineup recorded *Horses* (#47, 1975), produced by John Cale, an original mixture of exhortatory rock & roll ("Glo-

ria," "Land of 1000 Dances"), Smith's poetry, vocal mannerisms inspired by Mick Jagger and Jim Morrison, and the band's energetically rudimentary playing. Aerosmith producer Jack Douglas oversaw the Patti Smith Group's second album, *Radio Ethiopia* (#122, 1976), and the result was a more bombastic guitar-heavy record, tempered by the title cut, the height of Smith's improvised free rock.

A fall from a Florida stage hospitalized Smith with neck injuries in early 1977, during which time she wrote her fourth book of poetry, *Babel* (*Seventh Heaven, Witt,* and *Kodak* preceding it). When she was able to perform again, the result was her first Top Twenty LP, *Easter* (#20, 1978), produced by Jimmy Iovine, and her only hit single, "Because the Night" (#13, 1978), written by Bruce Springsteen and revised by Smith. She then began her withdrawal from rock & roll—*Wave* (#18, 1979) was overtly religious. Soon after its release, Smith moved to Detroit to live with her new husband, ex-MC5 guitarist Fred "Sonic" Smith, and except for rare local appearances, dropped out of the music scene altogether. She and Smith, who died in late 1994, had two children together.

After the breakup of the Patti Smith Group, Sohl remained close to Smith, and Daugherty played with a variety of people, from folkies like the Roches and Willie Nile, to Tom Verlaine, the Waterboys, and the Church. Ivan Kral put in a stint with Iggy Pop (on the LP *Soldier*). Kaye led several bands, beginning with the Lenny Kaye Connection, and produced such artists as Suzanne Vega.

In 1988 Smith's comeback album, *Dream of Life* (#65), featured her husband (who coproduced the album with Iovine), Daugherty, and Sohl. Its songs included a call to arms, "People Have the Power," which got some radio airplay, as well as lullabies for her children. Smith did not tour behind the album, but five years later, on a hot summer night in 1993, she made a rare appearance at Central Park's Summerstage, reading her poetry (including "Piss Factory") and singing a few songs a capella. She dedicated her performance to two close friends who'd recently died, photographer Robert Mapplethorpe and Richard Sohl. In 1994 Norton published a book of Smith's poetry, *Early Work: 1970–1979.* The following year Smith reportedly planned to return to the studio to record a new album.

The Smithereens
Formed March 1980, Carteret, New Jersey
Jim Babjak (b. Nov. 17, 1957, Salzburg, Aus.), gtr.;
Dennis Diken (b. Feb. 25, 1957, Belleville, N.J.),
drums; Pat DiNizio (b. Oct. 12, 1955, Plainfield, N.J.),
gtr., voc.; Mike Mesaros (b. Dec. 11, 1957, Trenton,
N.J.), bass.
1980—*Girls About Town* EP (D-Tone)   1983—
Beauty and Sadness* EP (Little Ricky)   1987—*The

Grammy Awards

Sade
1985 Best New Artist
1993 Best R&B Performance by a Duo or Group with Vocal: "No Ordinary Love"

Ryuichi Sakamoto
1988 Best Album of Original Instrumental Background Score Written for a Motion Picture or Television: *The Last Emperor* (with David Byrne and Cong Su)

Salt-n-Pepa
1994 Best Rap Performance by a Duo or Group: "None of Your Business"

Sam and Dave
1967 Best R&B Group Performance, Vocal or Instrumental (Two or More): "Soul Man"

David Sanborn
1981 Best R&B Instrumental Performance: "All I Need Is You"
1985 Best Jazz Fusion Performance, Vocal or Instrumental: *Straight to the Heart*
1986 Best Jazz Fusion Performance, Vocal or Instrumental: *Double Vision* (with Bob James)
1987 Best R&B Instrumental Performance (Orchestra, Group or Soloist): "Chicago Song"
1988 Best Pop Instrumental Performance (Orchestra, Group or Soloist): *Close-Up*

Carlos Santana (Santana)
1988 Best Rock Instrumental Performance (Orchestra, Group, or Soloist): *Blues for Salvador*

Leo Sayer
1977 Best R&B Song: "You Make Me Feel Like Dancing" (with Vini Poncia)

Boz Scaggs
1976 Best R&B Song: "Lowdown" (with David Paich)

Tom Scott
1974 Best Arrangement Accompanying Vocalists: "Down to You" (with Joni Mitchell)

Jon Secada
1992 Best Latin Pop Album: *Otro Dia Mas Sin Verte*

Pete Seeger
1993 Lifetime Achievement Award

Bob Seger and the Silver Bullet Band
1980 Best Rock Performance by a Duo or Group with Vocal: "Against the Wind"

Howard Hewett (Shalamar)
1985 Best Album of Original Score Written for a Motion Picture or Television Special: *Beverly Hills Cop* (with others)

Carly Simon
1971 Best New Artist of the Year
1989 Best Song Written Specifically for a Motion Picture or Television: "Let the River Run" (from the motion picture *Working Girl*)

Paul Simon
1968 Best Original Score Written for a Motion Picture or a Television Special: *The Graduate* (with Dave Grusin)
1968 Best Contemporary Pop Performance, Vocal, Duo or Group: "Mrs. Robinson" (with Art Garfunkel)
1968 Record of the Year: "Mrs. Robinson" (with Roy Halee and Art Garfunkel)
1970 Record of the Year: "Bridge over Troubled Water" (with Roy Halee and Art Garfunkel)
1970 Album of the Year: *Bridge over Troubled Water* (with Roy Halee and Art Garfunkel)
1970 Best Arrangement Accompanying Vocalist(s): "Bridge over Troubled Water" (with others)

1970 Best Contemporary Song: "Bridge over Troubled Water"
1970 Record of the Year: "Bridge over Troubled Water" (with Roy Halee and Art Garfunkel)
1970 Song of the Year: "Bridge over Troubled Water"
1975 Album of the Year: *Still Crazy After All These Years* (with Phil Ramone) (two Grammys: one as producer, one as performer)
1975 Best Pop Vocal Performance, Male: "Still Crazy After All These Years"
1986 Album of the Year: *Graceland*

Simon and Garfunkel
1968 Best Contemporary Pop Performance, Vocal, Duo or Group: "Mrs. Robinson"
1968 Record of the Year: "Mrs. Robinson" (with Roy Halee)
1970 Record of the Year: "Bridge over Troubled Water" (with Roy Halee)
1970 Album of the Year: *Bridge over Troubled Water* (with Roy Halee)

Frank Sinatra
1959 Album of the Year: *Come Dance with Me*
1959 Best Vocal Performance, Male: *Come Dance with Me*
1965 Lifetime Achievement Award
1965 Album of the Year: *September of My Years*
1965 Best Vocal Performance, Male: "It Was a Very Good Year"
1966 Album of the Year: *Sinatra: A Man and His Music*
1966 Best Vocal Performance, Male: "Strangers in the Night"
1966 Record of the Year: "Strangers in the Night" (with Jimmy Bowen)
1979 Trustees Award
1994 Grammy Legend Award

Sir Mix-a-Lot
1992 Best Rap Solo Performance: "Baby Got Back"

Ricky Skaggs
1984 Best Country Instrumental Performance: "Wheel Hoss"
1986 Best Country Instrumental Performance (Orchestra, Group, or Soloist): "Raisin' the Dickens"
1991 Best Country Vocal Collaboration: "Restless" (with Steve Wariner and Vince Gill)

Bessie Smith
1989 Lifetime Achievement Award

Dave Pirner (Soul Asylum)
1993 Best Rock Song: "Runaway Train"

Soul II Soul
1989 Best R&B Performance by a Duo or Group with Vocal: "Back to Life" (featuring Caron Wheeler)
1989 Best R&B Instrumental Performance: "African Dance"

Soundgarden
1994 Best Hard Rock Performance: "Black Hole Sun"
1994 Best Metal Performance: "Spoonman"

Joe South
1969 Song of the Year: "Games People Play"
1969 Best Contemporary Song: "Games People Play"

Rick Springfield
1981 Best Rock Vocal Performance, Male: "Jessie's Girl"

Bruce Springsteen
1984 Best Rock Vocal Performance, Male: "Dancing in the Dark"
1987 Best Rock Vocal Performance, Solo: *Tunnel of Love*
1994 Song of the Year: "Streets of Philadelphia"
1994 Best Male Rock Vocal Performance: "Streets of Philadelphia"
1994 Best Rock Song: "Streets of Philadelphia"
1994 Best Song Written Specifically for a Motion Picture or for Television: "Streets of Philadelphia"

Pop Staples (The Staples)
1994 Best Contemporary Blues Album: *Father Father*

Ringo Starr [See also: the Beatles]
1970 Best Original Score Written for a Motion Picture or TV Special: *Let It Be* (with John Lennon, Paul McCartney, and George Harrison)
1972 Album of the Year: *The Concert for Bangla Desh* (with others)

Steel Pulse
1986 Best Reggae Recording: *Babylon the Bandit*

Sting [See also: the Police]
1983 Song of the Year: "Every Breath You Take"
1983 Best Rock Instrumental Performance: "Brimstone and Treacle"
1986 Best Music Video, Long Form: *Bring On the Night* (with Michael Apted)
1987 Best Pop Vocal Performance, Male: *Bring on the Night*
1991 Best Rock Song: "Soul Cages"
1993 Best Pop Vocal Performance, Male: "If I Ever Lose My Faith in You"

1993 Best Music Video, Long Form: *Ten Summoner's Tales* (with Doug Nichol and Julie Fong)

Stone Temple Pilots
1993 Best Hard Rock Performance with Vocal: "Plush"

Barbra Streisand
1963 Album of the Year: *The Barbra Streisand Album*
1963 Best Vocal Performance, Female: *The Barbra Streisand Album*
1964 Best Vocal Performance, Female: *People*
1965 Best Vocal Performance, Female: *My Name Is Barbra*
1977 Best Pop Vocal Performance, Female: "Love Theme from *A Star Is Born* (Evergreen)"
1977 Song of the Year: "Love Theme from *A Star Is Born* (Evergreen)" (with Paul Williams)
1980 Best Pop Performance by a Duo or Group with Vocal: "Guilty" (with Barry Gibb)
1986 Best Pop Vocal Performance, Female: *The Broadway Album*
1992 Grammy Legend Award

Barrett Strong
1972 Best R&B Song: "Papa Was a Rolling Stone" (with Norman Whitfield)

Donna Summer
1978 Best R&B Vocal Performance, Female: "Last Dance"
1979 Best Rock Vocal Performance, Female: "Hot Stuff"
1983 Best Inspirational Performance: "He's a Rebel"
1984 Best Inspirational Performance: "Forgive Me"

Smithereens Live EP (Restless); *Especially for You* (Enigma) 1988—*Green Thoughts* 1989—*11* (Capitol) 1991—*Blow Up* 1994—*A Date with the Smithereens* (RCA) 1995—*Blown to Smithereens: Best of the Smithereens* (Capitol).

The Smithereens' brand of hard-edged pop songs are reminiscent of the Sixties British Invasion, but the mor-

dant sensibility of singer/songwriter Pat DiNizio gives the band a decidedly modern point of view. The band was formed in 1980 when DiNizio answered an ad placed in a music paper by high school friends Babjak, Diken, and Mesaros. They released an EP that year, *Girls About Town*, containing three originals and a cover of the Beach Boys' "Girl Don't Tell Me." Neither that record nor a 1983 release, *Beauty and Sadness*, helped the

Smithereens get signed, so they supported themselves playing covers and backing oldie acts the Beau Brummels and Otis Blackwell.

In 1985 DiNizio sent a tape to Enigma Records. The tape, with only the band's name and DiNizio's name and phone number to identify it, fell into the hands of Scott Vanderbilt, who had become a fan while a college DJ. He signed the band to Enigma and in 1987 released *Especially for You* (#51), with guest appearances by Marshall Crenshaw (under the name Jerome Jerome) and Suzanne Vega. Its single, "Blood and Roses," was featured in a grade-B slasher film, *Dangerously Close;* the film's production company financed a video, which gained airplay on MTV.

The Smithereens toured extensively; the work paid off with *11* (#41, 1989), their most commercially successful album, and "A Girl Like You" (#38, 1989), the band's only Top Forty single. In 1994 the Smithereens moved to RCA for *A Date with the Smithereens*. The album reunited the band with producer Don Dixon (who had produced the group's first two albums) and featured Lou Reed's guitar playing on two songs.

The Smiths/Morrissey

Formed 1982, Manchester, England
Morrissey (b. Stephen Patrick Morrissey, May 22, 1959, Manchester), voc.; Johnny Marr (b. John Maher, Oct. 31, 1963, Manchester), gtr.; Mike Joyce (b. June 1, 1963, Manchester), drums; Andy Rourke (b. 1963, Manchester), bass.
1984—The Smiths (Sire); Hatful of Hollow (Rough Trade, U.K.) 1985—Meat Is Murder (Sire) (+ Craig Gannon, gtr.) 1986—The Queen Is Dead 1987— (– Gannon) Louder Than Bombs; Strangeways, Here We Come 1988—Rank 1992—Best . . . I (Sire/Reprise); Best . . . II 1995—"Singles" (Reprise).
Morrissey: 1988—Viva Hate (Sire/Reprise) 1990— Bona Drag 1991—Kill Uncle 1992—Your Arsenal 1994—Vauxhall and I 1995—World of Morrissey.

Articulate, broodingly charismatic frontman Morrissey and supple guitarist Johnny Marr made the Smiths one of the Eighties' most significant English bands. An avowed celibate whose lyrics disclosed a sexually ambiguous point of view, Morrissey was given to controversy, whether advocating animal rights or trashing Margaret Thatcher and disco. The band's trancelike guitar-based music angrily rebutted such British synthesizer pop as the Human League and Thompson Twins.

Son of a hospital porter and a librarian, Morrissey first expressed himself by writing; unemployed in the late Seventies, he wrote a book on James Dean and another on the New York Dolls, whose English fan club he headed. He also played briefly in a band called the Nose-

Morrissey (originally of the Smiths)

bleeds. Veteran of such groups as Sister Ray and Freaky Party, Marr approached Morrissey to form a band. The pair eventually enlisted drummer Mike Joyce and bassist Andy Rourke for an eponymous debut that, on U.K. indie label Rough Trade (on Sire in the U.S.), entered the British chart at #2. An earlier single, "Hand in Glove," was recorded with Morrissey's favorite female singer, Sixties British pop idol Sandie Shaw, and scored #27 in the U.K. This coup, along with *The Smiths'* "Heaven Knows I'm Miserable Now" (#10 U.K., 1984) established the band.

The meteoric rise continued with *Meat Is Murder* debuting at #1 on the British charts; the group also caused a stir via Morrissey's stage presence, the singer wearing a garland of gladioli in tribute to Oscar Wilde, a hearing aid in homage to Fifties balladeer Johnnie Ray, and a ducktail haircut patterned after English rocker Billy Fury. Some critics sniped that the group's lyrics referred to child molesting, and Morrissey offended others with sharp comments about the Band Aid benefit. His champions, though, hailed his oblique, angst-driven songs as latterday examples of Ray Davies–styled social commentary. With ex–Aztec Camera guitarist Craig Gannon added, 1986's *The Queen Is Dead* (#2 U.K.) fared handsomely, but a disappointing U.S. tour showed that the Smiths had yet to penetrate the American mainstream. Later that year Johnny Marr was involved in a serious car wreck; during his recuperation, Gannon was fired. A single, "Sheila Take a Bow," became a Top Ten

U.K. hit in mid-1987, but later that year, with Marr deeming their musical approach exhausted, the Smiths disbanded. *Strangeways, Here We Come* and the live *Rank* were released posthumously.

Despite his prolific output—*Viva Hate, Bona Drag, Kill Uncle, Your Arsenal,* and *Vauxhall and I*—Morrissey's solo career hasn't quite matched his success with the Smiths, although the singer has attracted a rabid cult following in the U.S. Besides playing sessions with Bryan Ferry, Talking Heads, the Pet Shop Boys, and Billy Bragg, Marr served for a while with the Pretenders, the The, and Electronic. Rourke and Joyce played with the Adult Net before backing up Sinéad O'Connor; Joyce eventually joined the re-formed Buzzcocks.

Patty Smyth/Scandal

Born June 26, 1957, New York City, New York
1987—*Never Enough* (Columbia)   1992—*Patty Smyth* (MCA).
With Scandal, formed 1982, New York City (Smyth, voc.; Zack Smith [b. Westport, Conn.], gtr.; Ivan Elias, bass; Benji King, kybds.; Frankie LaRocka, drums): 1982—*Scandal* EP (Columbia)   1984—*The Warrior.*

Patty Smyth rose to fame as the lead singer of Scandal, a hard-pop outfit that proved the perfect vehicle for Smyth's husky, agile voice and her sexy tough-girl image. While the band's career was short-lived, Smyth re-emerged in the Nineties as a successful solo artist. The daughter of a Greenwich Village club-owner mother, Smyth grew up in New York City, and in her teens fronted a band called Patty and the Planets. Supporting herself as a waitress, she hooked up in 1982 with guitarist Zack Smith, Scandal's founder and principal songwriter.

With the support of such singles as "Goodbye to You" (#65, 1982) and "Love's Got a Line on You" (#59, 1983), *Scandal* became the best-selling EP in Columbia Records' history. Smith left the band after its release, but not before cowriting material (with Smyth writing lyrics) for a followup album, *The Warrior* (#17, 1984), which yielded a #7 pop hit with its title track. Scandal split up not long after: Drummer Frankie LaRocka became head of A&R at Epic Records. Smyth married punk pioneer Richard Hell. The two had a daughter and later divorced.

In 1987 came Smyth's solo debut, *Never Enough* (#66, 1987), but it wasn't until five years later that, after moving to MCA, the singer re-emerged in the Top Ten with "Sometimes Love Just Ain't Enough," a #2 duet with Don Henley featured on her self-titled gold 1992 album.

Snap!

Formed c. 1989, Pittsburgh, Pennsylvania
Turbo B. (b. Durron Maurice Butler, Apr. 30, 1967, Pittsburgh), voc.; Penny Ford (b. Nov. 6, 1964, Cincinnati, Ohio), voc.; Jackie Harris (b. Jacqueline Arlissa Harris, Pittsburgh), voc.
1990—*World Power* (Arista)   1992—(– Ford; + Thea Austin, voc.) *The Madman's Return.*
Penny Ford solo: 1993—*Penny Ford* (Columbia).

Created as the project of two German producers, the dance-pop collective Snap! climbed the American chart in 1990 with "The Power," a fierce, relentless track that proved as successful on Top Forty radio as it did in clubs. Like the more visible C+C Music Factory, Snap! was an early Nineties success story manufactured by behind-the-scenes studio wizards but distinguished equally by the sizzling contributions of a succession of female vocalists.

Around 1989, the Frankfurt-based production team (Luca) Anzilotti and (Michael) Münzing recruited American rapper Turbo B. and soul singer Penny Ford, who had previously been a member of the S.O.S. Band. Crediting themselves as Benito Benites and John "Virgo" Garrett III, Anzilotti and Münzing recorded "The Power," featuring Turbo B. and Ford as Snap!, for Germany's Logic Records. (Turbo B.'s cousin, singer Jackie Harris, was also credited as a member of Snap!, and filled in for Ford on some early media appearances.) Picked up by Arista in 1990, the single topped the British chart and went almost as far in the U.S. (#2 pop, #4 R&B). Five additional Top Ten hits followed in England, with Ford singing on all of them. Ford then opted for a solo career, so Thea Austin took her place on Snap!'s 1992 sophomore effort, *The Madman's Return.* The album's first single, "Colour of Love," flopped, at which point Turbo B. quit the group, citing creative frustration. But a second single, "Rhythm Is a Dancer," reached #5 on the American pop chart.

Niki Harris, formerly a backup singer for Madonna, replaced Austin for Snap!'s next single, "Exterminate," which entered the U.K. Top Five in 1993. That same year, Penny Ford released a self-titled album on Columbia, while Anzilotti and Münzing began work on a third Snap! album with Harris.

Snoop Doggy Dogg

Born Calvin Broadus, October 20, 1972, Long Beach, California
1993—*Doggystyle* (Death Row/Interscope)

Rapper Snoop Doggy Dogg, with his lazy drawl and gangster persona, has become one of the most commercially successful and controversial artists in all of rap. Debuting in 1992 as a collaborator on Dr. Dre's 1992 multiplatinum *The Chronic,* Snoop Dogg followed soon after with the release of *Doggystyle,* which set a new record as the biggest-selling rap album.

Calvin Broadus (nicknamed Snoop by his mother) was born and raised on the tough streets of Long Beach,

California. Shortly after graduating from high school, Snoop was arrested on a cocaine charge; he spent the next three years in and out of jail. In 1990 Snoop began to record underground tapes with a friend, rapper Warren G, who subsequently gave a cassette to his brother, N.W.A's Dr. Dre. Dre was impressed with what he heard, and Dre and Snoop began working together on the single "Deep Cover" for a movie of the same name. By the time Dre started recording *The Chronic,* Snoop was his right-hand man, performing on more than half of the album. Buoyed by the acclaim received for his contributions, Snoop entered the studio to record his own album for Dre's Death Row Records. The result, *Doggystyle,* was one of the most anticipated rap records in history. It entered the *Billboard* chart at #1 the first week of its release (the first debut album ever to do so).

Despite his success, however, Snoop has failed to avoid trouble with the law. In 1993 he was arrested in connection with the murder of a man who the rapper alleges had been stalking him. Together with his bodyguard, who is reported to have fired the gun that killed the man in 1993, Snoop was arraigned to stand trial in Los Angeles. As of mid-1995, Snoop's case had yet to reach trial. In the meantime, the 1994 soundtrack *Murder Was the Case* (#1), from the short film directed by Dr. Dre, featured three Snoop songs, including the title track.

Phoebe Snow

Born Phoebe Laub, July 17, 1952, New York City, New York
1974—*Phoebe Snow* (Shelter/A&M)   1976—*Second Childhood* (Columbia); *It Looks Like Snow*   1977—*Never Letting Go*; *Against the Grain*   1981—*Rock Away* (Mirage); *The Best of Phoebe Snow* (Columbia)   1989—*Something Real* (Elektra).

With her supple contralto voice and melismatic jazz-scat abilities, Phoebe Snow burst onto the music scene with an impressive debut LP on Leon Russell's Shelter label that yielded the Top Five single "Poetry Man."

She had moved with her family from New York to Teaneck, New Jersey, at age three and did not take up music seriously until the late Sixties. A shy performer, she began to play Greenwich Village clubs in the early Seventies, singing blues, jazz, and torch songs, as well as folk and pop. After her debut LP, she toured with Paul Simon and sang with him on his hit gospel-style single "Gone at Last." Her second LP, *Second Childhood* (#13, 1976), included "Two Fisted Love," one of several Snow album tracks that weren't hits per se but were frequently played on FM radio. Her first two albums have been certified gold.

Shortly after the birth of her profoundly autistic daughter Valerie in 1975, Snow entered a period of personal and professional turmoil. A single parent through divorce, Snow, against the advice of doctors, brought her daughter home to live, and she has cared for her ever since. Meanwhile, her recording career suffered from a lack of hits. Her albums, however, still found a less impressive though loyal audience. Ironically, her voice is probably one of the most-often heard on radio and television, thanks to a series of commercials for Bloomingdale's, Stouffer's, Salon Selectives, and General Electric. In the early Nineties, she performed and recorded with Donald Fagen's Rock and Soul Revue. In 1994 she appeared at Woodstock in a gospel group with Mavis Staples, Thelma Houston, and CeCe Peniston.

Social Distortion

Formed 1979, Fullerton, California
Mike Ness (b. Apr. 3, 1962, Stoneham, Mass.), voc., gtr.; Dennis Danell (b. June 24, 1961, Tacoma, Wash.), gtr.; Brent Liles, bass; Derrick O'Brien, drums, voc.
1983—*Mommy's Little Monster* (13th Floor)   1988— (– Liles; – O'Brien; + Chris Reece [b. July 25, San Francisco, Calif.], drums; + John Maurer [b. July 14, Lynnwood, Calif.], bass) *Prison Bound* (Restless) 1990—*Social Distortion* (Epic); *Story of My Life . . . and Other Stories* EP   1992—*Somewhere Between Heaven and Hell.*

Social Distortion are suburban punk rockers who survived both their genre's burnout and their leader's drug addiction to find belated major-label success. The band was founded by Mike Ness and Dennis Danell, two Orange County schoolmates who had been inspired by the punk scene in nearby Los Angeles. They released their first single, "1945," in 1982. The following album, *Mommy's Little Monster,* introduced Social Distortion's rootsy punk, influenced equally by the Clash and the Rolling Stones. Song titles like "I Just Want to Give You the Creeps" demonstrated their rebels-without-a-cause attitude.

Ness in particular styled himself an outlaw. He was kicked out of his home at 15, subsequently living in shooting galleries, flophouses, and jail. His heroin addiction, fighting, and other self-destructive acts—he fancied himself a sort of Sid Vicious—split the band. Ness and Danell found a new rhythm section, however, and in 1985 Ness quit taking drugs and alcohol. A tour documentary recorded that year, *Another State of Mind,* captured Social Distortion still in its wild, sordid period.

On the country-influenced *Prison Bound,* Ness reflected on his past. Social Distortion returned to a more punk sound on their eponymous Epic debut, including a hard-rocking version of the Johnny Cash hit "Ring of Fire." The album sold more than 250,000 copies and landed the long-laboring underground band on MTV and a tour with Neil Young. *Somewhere Between Heaven and Hell* was another solid album with a country feel, but despite the alternative hit "Bad Luck," it failed to sell much better than its predecessor.

Soft Boys: See Robyn Hitchcock

Soft Cell/Marc Almond

Formed 1980, Leeds, England
Marc Almond (b. Peter Marc Almond, July 9, 1959, Southport, Eng.), voc.; David Ball (b. May 3, 1959, Blackpool, Eng.), synth.
1981—*Non-Stop Erotic Cabaret* (Sire)   1982—*Non-Stop Ecstatic Dancing*   1983—*The Art of Falling Apart; Soul Inside* EP   1984—*This Last Night in Sodom*   1991—*Tenement Symphony; Memorabilia: The Singles* (Mercury).
Marc Almond solo: 1988—*The Stars We Are* (Some Bizarre/Capitol)   1990—*Enchanted.*

Singer Marc Almond and synthesizer player David Ball were hardly the first pop musicians to join forces while attending art school. Still, as the technopop duo Soft Cell, they set something of a precedent by adapting a cult soul classic into a cheeky electronic dirge—then having their version of the song, Gloria Jones' "Tainted Love," become 1981's best-selling British single, as well as a #8 pop hit in the U.S. the next year. Their mutual fascination with the U.K. soul scene brought British art students Almond and Ball together, first as collaborators on theatrical music—with Almond writing lyrics to accompany Ball's instrumentals—then as Soft Cell. The band's early shows featured striking visual accompaniment, eventually attracting the attention of a quirky label called Some Bizarre. Released in 1981, the duo's debut single, "Memorabilia," failed to chart; later that year, though, "Tainted Love" generated instant success. Numerous Top Ten singles followed in England, many of them sleazily sensual and all of them distinguished by Almond's rather affected (and often pitch-shy) tenor and Ball's moody synth colorings. By 1983, however, Almond and Ball had decided to part company professionally; Soft Cell's final album, the aptly titled *This Last Night in Sodom,* was released the next year.

By this point, Almond had already formed another band, Marc and the Mambas, which in 1983 released two U.K. albums both mixing covers with electro-soul originals, both generally perceived as excessive. In 1984 the singer formed Marc Almond and the Willing Sinners, whose two albums and one EP were stylistically evocative of the Mambas' efforts (and of Soft Cell, for that matter) but somewhat better received. In the late Eighties Almond put out a few solo albums, including a Jacques Brel tribute. His first American release was 1988's *The Stars We Are* (#144, 1989), with the minor hit single

"Tears Run Rings" (#67, 1989), followed in 1990 by *Enchanted.*

Soft Machine/Robert Wyatt

Formed 1966, Canterbury, England
Mike Ratledge, kybds.; Robert Wyatt (b. Robert Ellidge, Bristol, Eng.), drums, voc.; Kevin Ayers (b. Aug. 16, 1945, Herne Bay, Eng.), gtr., voc., bass; Daevid Allen (b. Austral.), gtr., voc.
1967—(– Allen; + Larry Nolan [b. Calif.], gtr.; – Nolan)   1968—*The Soft Machine* (Probe) (– Ayers; + Hugh Hopper, bass, gtr.) *Volume 2* (Columbia)
1970—(+ Elton Dean, sax; + Marc Charig, trumpet; + Nick Evans, trombone; + Lyn Dobson, flute, sax; + Rob Spall, violin; – Evans) *Third*   1971—(– Charig; – Dobson; – Spall) *Fourth*   1972—(– Wyatt; + Phil Howard, drums; – Howard; + John Marshall, drums) *Fifth*   1973—(– Dean; + Karl Jenkins, sax, kybds.) *Sixth* (– Hopper; + Roy Babbington, bass) *Seventh*   1975—(+ Allan Holdsworth [b. Eng.], gtr.) *Bundles* (Harvest) (– Holdsworth)   1976—(– Ratledge; + John Etheridge, gtr.; + Alan Wakeman, sax) *Softs*
1977—*Triple Echo*   1978—(– Babbington; + Steve Cook, bass) *Alive and Well in Paris*   1980—(– Etheridge; – Cook; + Jack Bruce [b. May 14, 1943, Glasgow, Scot.], bass, voc.; + Dick Morisey, sax; + Alan Parker, gtr.)   1981—*Land of Cockayne* (EMI)
1984—(Group re-forms: Jenkins; Marshall; + Ray Warleigh, sax; + Dave Macrae, kybds.)   1988—*Live at the Proms 1970* (Reckless, U.K.)   1990—*The Peel Sessions* (Strange Fruit, U.K.)   1991—*As If . . .* (Elite, U.K.).
Robert Wyatt solo: 1974—*Rock Bottom* (Virgin)
1975—*Ruth Is Stranger Than Richard*   1981—*Nothing Can Stop Us* (Rough Trade)   1985—*Old Rottenhat* (Gramavision)   1990—*Compilation*
1992—*Dondestan*   1993—*Mid-Eighties* (Rhino)
1994—*Giving Back a Bit—A Little History Of* (Virgin, U.K.).

The original Canterbury progressive British rock band (along with Caravan, Gong, Hatfield and the North, National Health, Henry Cow), Soft Machine lasted through seemingly endless personnel changes to become one of Britain's most durable progressive-fusion units. Actually, the original Canterbury band was the Wilde Flowers, who got together at Canterbury's Simon Langton School, where Mike Ratledge, Hugh Hopper, Robert Wyatt, and Caravan's David Sinclair were schoolmates. The Wilde Flowers existed in varying lineups from 1963 to 1965, usually gathering at the home of Wyatt's mother, a writer and disc jockey who introduced her son to modern jazz. (One writer later described a car ride with Wyatt in which he whistled Charlie Parker's "Donna Lee" solo note for note.) Wyatt enrolled in the Canterbury College of Art but dropped out to travel in Europe. There he met beatnik/hippie and fellow avant-gardist Daevid Allen. Hopper soon joined them. Upon their return to Canterbury, they opened up the Wilde Flowers' jazz rock to include more free-form experimentations and "pataphysics," a sort of winsome absurdity derived from French playwright Alfred Jarry.

Ratledge came back to Canterbury next from Oxford University; Hopper went with Sinclair, Pye Hastings, and Richard Coughlan to form another version of the Wilde Flowers, which quickly became Caravan. Ratledge formed Soft Machine with Wyatt, Kevin Ayers, and Allen; they got the name from the William Burroughs novel. After some rehearsal, Soft Machine went to London and played with Pink Floyd at the psychedelic UFO club. At this point guitarist Andy Summers (later with the Police) occasionally played with them. In London they met producer Kim Fowley, with whom they recorded two songs, "Feelin' Reelin' Squealin'" and "Love Makes Sweet Music" (reissued on *At the Beginning*); Jimi Hendrix, who was recording "Hey Joe" in the same studio, played some rhythm guitar. The records made little impact in England, and Soft Machine went back to France, settling in St. Tropez, where they soon attracted much notoriety as the center of "happenings" surrounding Alan Zion's production of the Picasso play *Desir Attrape par la Queue.* When they finally returned to Britain late in 1967, Allen had visa problems; he went back to Paris and later founded Gong [see entry]. Soft Machine played some shows as a trio and opened Hendrix's 1968 U.S. tour (Wyatt painted a suit and tie on his bare torso on that tour). In New York they recorded their debut LP with producer Tom Wilson.

After the tour and recording sessions, Soft Machine temporarily disbanded. Ayers went to Ibiza, then Majorca, to write before forming his own band, the Whole World; Ratledge went to London; and Wyatt stayed in the U.S. The record company pressured Wyatt to reassemble the group. Ayers was replaced by Hopper. The new band recorded *Volume Two,* less a concept album than a stream-of-consciousness LP, with 17 tracks bleeding into each other over two sides and jazz influences ranging from cocktail to avant-garde. Toward the end of a long U.K. tour, they added a horn section from Keith Tippett's Centipede Orchestra for *Third,* a double LP of four side-long compositions (including Wyatt's magnum opus, "Moon in June"), which again won heavy critical acclaim but sold only moderately.

In 1971 Wyatt began to grow disenchanted with Soft Machine, as the band became more and more formulaic. He left after recording *Fourth* and formed Matching Mole, which recorded two LPs. He went on to have a critically respected career as a solo performer, and was preparing to embark on a Matching Mole reunion when he fell from a fourth-story window. He was left paralyzed from the waist down. With Ratledge's fuzz organ the sole sonic link with the band's past, and Wyatt apparently taking the band's verbal wit with him, Soft Machine gradually devolved into just another jazz-rock fusion band, recruiting members from such British units as Nucleus (whence came John Jenkins and Karl Marshall). Hopper went on to record solo concept LPs like *1984,* to form a band called Isotope, and to work with reedman Elton Dean in Soft Heap. Ayers maintained a respectable solo-singer/songwriter career of his own [see entry]. Marshall and Babbington have returned to the jazz and jazz-rock scenes. Ratledge quit Soft Machine in 1976 (replaced by Rick Wakeman's brother Alan), leaving the band with no original members. Jenkins and Marshall continued through the late Eighties and early Nineties with a lineup that was still critically respected.

In the meantime Robert Wyatt continued a solo career that has made him a long-established cult artist. His first solo album released after the fall, *Rock Bottom,* was produced by Pink Floyd's Nick Mason; it earned him the prestigious French Prix Charles Cros in 1974. Despite being wheelchair-bound, Wyatt continued to tour and to travel, and he has collaborated with a wide range of artists from Everything But the Girl's Ben Watt to Ryuichi Sakamoto. Wyatt has had two U.K. chart singles during his long solo career: a cover of the Monkees' "I'm a Believer" (#29 U.K., 1974) and a rendition of Elvis Costello's antiwar "Shipbuilding" (#35 U.K., 1983). Wyatt's later material, which is clearly political, also includes old folk and protest songs. In the early Eighties he recorded the antilynching "Strange Fruit" (first popularized by Billie Holiday) and "Caimenera" (better known as "Guantanamera").

Sonic Youth

Formed 1981, New York City, New York
Kim Gordon (b. Apr. 28, 1953, Rochester, N.Y.), voc., bass; Lee Ranaldo (b. Feb. 3, 1956, Glen Cove, N.Y.), voc., gtr.; Thurston Moore (b. July 25, 1958, Coral Gables, Fla.), voc., gtr.; Richard Edson, drums.
1982—*Sonic Youth* EP (Neutral) (– Edson; + Bob Bert, drums)   1983—*Confusion Is Sex; Kill Yr. Idols* EP (Zensor)   1984—*Sonic Death: Sonic Youth Live* (Ecstatic Peace)   1985—*Bad Moon Rising* (Homestead); *Death Valley 69* EP (– Bert; + Steve Shelley [b. June 23, 1962, Midland, Mich.], drums)   1986—*Evol* (SST)   1987—*Sister*   1988—*Master Dik* EP; *Daydream Nation* (Blast First/Enigma)   1990—*Goo* (DGC)   1992—*Dirty*   1994—*Experimental Jet Set, Trash and No Star*   1995—*Made in USA* soundtrack (Rhino).
As Ciccone Youth: 1988—*The Whitey Album* (Blast First).
Thurston Moore solo: 1995—*Psychic Hearts* (DGC).

Sonic Youth: Lee Ranaldo, Steve Shelley, Kim Gordon, Thurston Moore

Sonic Youth is the avatar of noisy, underground guitar rock. After making the transition from uncompromising avant-rockers in the early Eighties to indie guitar-pop trailblazers by decade's end, the group became the alternative music world's brightest beacon. In the Nineties, Sonic Youth's sound continued to influence younger bands, the most famous evidence being in the grungy, sometimes discordant riffs of Nirvana's "Smells Like Teen Spirit."

In the late Seventies Thurston Moore, raised in Bethel, Connecticut, and Lee Ranaldo, of New York's Long Island, hit Manhattan just in time for the end of punk rock and its avant-garde cousin, no wave. The two became acquainted while performing with downtown guitar-orchestra composer Glenn Branca, whose extended works featured several guitars playing highly textured, dissonant music. In 1981 the two formed Sonic Youth with bassist/art-school graduate Kim Gordon (who would marry Moore) and drummer Richard Edson (who later pursued acting and starred in such films as *Stranger Than Paradise* and *Do the Right Thing*). The band went through several drummers before locking in with Steve Shelley in 1986.

Sonic Youth's first recordings, released on Branca's Neutral label, mainly consisted of feedback and ringing harmonics, with Gordon or Moore intoning about death, urban decay, and other dreary, no-wave–inspired topics. Moore and Ranaldo became known for propping up a dozen or so guitars behind the band during perfor-

mances, each tuned unconventionally and some containing objects such as screwdrivers and drumsticks jammed between the strings and fretboards.

With 1985's *Bad Moon Rising*, Sonic Youth hit on a direction that incorporated swirling, Branca-style guitar textures into more traditional pop-based song structures. Critical responses were generally positive, and major labels began knocking at the band's door. But Sonic Youth held out for three more full-length indie-label albums, including the double-length classic *Daydream Nation*, while perfecting its art-pop recipe. (In the meantime they did a tongue-in-cheek tribute to Madonna under the pseudonym Ciccone Youth.)

In 1990 the group's major-label debut, *Goo* (#96), cemented Sonic Youth's stature in the music world and led to an arena tour opening for Neil Young. The move was incongruous but not altogether inappropriate, since both acts worshiped feedback and distortion. (It was also consistent with Sonic Youth's ironic sense of humor.) By the release of *Dirty* (#83, 1992), the former avant-noise-makers were being hailed as the messiahs of modern rock; even *Vanity Fair* profiled Gordon and anointed her the "godmother . . . of alternative rock." In 1994 Sonic Youth released their most popular LP to date, *Experimental Jet Set, Trash and No Star*, which peaked on the album charts at #34. Later that year, Gordon and Moore had a daughter. *Made in USA* was a Sonic Youth–composed soundtrack for a 1986 film. In 1995 Moore released the self-produced solo album *Psychic Hearts*.

Sonny and Cher

Salvatore Bono, born February 16, 1935, Detroit, Michigan; Cherilyn Sarkasian LaPier, born May 20, 1946, El Centro, California.
1965—*Look at Us* (Atco)   1966—*The Wondrous World of Sonny and Cher*   1967—*In Case You're in Love; Good Times; The Best of Sonny and Cher* 1971—*Sonny & Cher Live* (Kapp)   1972—*All I Ever Need Is You*   1973—*Live in Las Vegas, vol. 2* (MCA); *Mama Was a Rock and Roll Singer, Papa Used to Write All Her Songs*   1974—*Greatest Hits* 1986—*At Their Best* (Pair)   1991—*The Beat Goes On—The Best of Sonny & Cher* (Atlantic)   1993—*I Got You Babe: Rhino Special Editions* (Rhino). Sonny Bono solo: 1967—*Inner Views* (Atco). Cher solo: See entry.

Sonny and Cher were a husband-and-wife team who enjoyed a brief period of success as wildly garbed hippie-ish pop singers, followed by a slightly longer stretch when their Vegas-style singing and standup comedy found favor with a nationwide TV audience. The partnership ended in divorce, and Cher went on to a solo career as singer, actress, garishly gowned celebrity, and fitness guru, while Sonny Bono went into politics.

Bono spent years trying to break into the music business as a songwriter. He'd started writing songs at age seven, and at 12 appeared on the popular music show *Peter Potter's Hit Parade*. In 1957 he placed "High School Dance" on the B side of Larry Williams' "Bony Moronie." When Sonny's tune reached #90 in its own right, he became a staff producer at Specialty, where he also began recording under the name Don Christy. He had no particular success until 1964, when "Needles and Pins," which he cowrote with Jack Nitzsche, became a big hit for the Searchers. By this time, Sonny was working for Phil Spector as a writer and backup vocalist. In 1963 he met Cher when she was singing backup on some of Spector's sessions.

They married in 1964 and made a couple of unsuccessful singles under various names (Caesar and Cleo) for Vault and Reprise before signing to Atco in 1965. Their first chart entry was the million-seller "I Got You Babe" (#1, 1965). Then came "Baby Don't Go" (#8, 1965), "The Beat Goes On" (#6, 1967), and "solo" hits like Sonny's "Laugh at Me" (#10, 1965) and Cher's "All I Really Wanna Do" (#15, 1965), "Bang Bang (My Baby Shot Me Down)" (#2, 1966), and "You Better Sit Down Kids" (#9, 1967). With the exception of Bob Dylan's "All I Really Wanna Do," Bono wrote and produced all of these records. The pair also made two movies: *Good Times* (1967) and *Chastity* (1969, written by Sonny, starring Cher, named for their daughter). The pop hits slowed at the end of the Sixties.

Produced by Snuff Garrett, Sonny and Cher bounced back in 1971–72 with a pair of Top Ten hits: "All I Ever Need Is You" (#7, 1971) and "A Cowboy's Work Is Never Done" (#8, 1972). These and a series of successful appearances in Las Vegas and on countless television variety shows led to the TV series—*The Sonny and Cher Comedy Hour* (1971–74) and *The Sonny and Cher Show* (1976–77)—that made them household names. At that time, however, their marriage was breaking up. During and after the split, both tried solo careers and had solo TV shows. The duo performed their last show as husband and wife at the Houston Astrodome in 1974; they divorced in June 1975. Cher would be the more successful of the two [see entry], however, and Sonny soon abandoned show business.

Beginning in 1983 Bono operated a Los Angeles restaurant for several years before moving to Palm Springs, where he opened another restaurant and made a successful bid for the mayor's office in 1988. He has made occasional forays into performing, costarring in John Waters' *Hairspray* (1988) and making guest appearances on television programs (*The Love Boat, Fantasy Island*).

In 1987 Sonny and Cher reunited to perform "I Got You Babe" on *Late Night with David Letterman,* after which Bono seemed visibly moved. In 1991 he wrote *And the Beat Goes On,* which became a regional best-seller in a few markets. In the book Bono alleged that Cher neglected their daughter Chastity, and he painted his ex-wife as a cold, calculating careerist. In 1992 Bono, who'd never bothered to register to vote until 1988, made an unsuccessful run for the U.S. Senate. Two years later Bono was elected to the U.S. House of Representatives.

S.O.S. Band

Formed 1977, Atlanta, Georgia
Mary Davis (b. Savannah, Ga.), voc., kybds.; Jason "TC" Bryant, kybds., voc.; Bruno Speight, gtr., voc.; Billy Ellis, flute; Willie "Sonny" Killebrew, sax; John Simpson, bass, voc.; James Earl Jones III, drums.
1980—*S.O.S.* (Tabu/Columbia) (+ Abdul Raoof, trumpet, voc.)   1981—*Too* (– Jones; + Jerome "JT" Thomas, drums)   1982—*S.O.S. III*   1983—*On the Rise*   1984—*Just the Way You Like It*   1986—*Sands of Time* (– Davis; + Penny Ford [b. Nov. 6, 1964, Cincinnati, Ohio], voc.)   1987—*Diamonds in the Raw*   1988—*The Way You Like It* (CBS Special Prod.)   1991—*One of Many Nights* (A&M).

An Atlanta-based pop-funk outfit, the S.O.S. ("Sounds of Success") Band, with its eponymously named debut album (#12, 1980), spawned the massive late-disco smash "Take Your Time (Do It Right) Part 1" (#3 pop, #1 R&B, 1980), and a lesser dance hit in "S.O.S." (#20 R&B, 1980). But the group's next two albums failed to crack the pop chart; *III*, however, yielded a moderate dance hit in "High Hopes" (#25 R&B, 1982), which was the S.O.S. Band's first collaboration with the writing-producing team of Jimmy Jam and Terry Lewis, then still members of the Prince spinoff band, the Time.

In March 1983 Jam and Lewis—during a few days off from a tour by Prince and the Time—flew to Atlanta to produce some S.O.S. Band tracks. Snowed in by a freak storm, the pair missed their next tour date and were promptly fired by Prince. But one of the tracks they were producing, "Just Be Good to Me" (#55 pop, #2 R&B, 1983), reasserted S.O.S. Band's pop status, and codified Jam and Lewis' cool, plush, Chiclike sound. They produced half of *On the Rise* (#47, 1983), which also yielded "Tell Me If You Still Care" (#65 pop, #5 R&B, 1983) and "For Your Love" (#34 R&B, 1984), and worked on the group's next two albums. *Just the Way You Like It* (#60, 1984) produced hits in the title track (#60 pop, #6 R&B, 1984) and "No One's Gonna Love You" (#15 R&B, 1984); *Sands of Time* (#44, 1986) contained "The Finest" (#44 pop, #2 R&B, 1986) and "Borrowed Love" (#14 R&B, 1986).

In 1986 Jam and Lewis moved on, and Mary Davis left to launch a solo career. Her first album, *Separate Ways* (#82 R&B, 1990), spawned the single "Don't Wear It

Out" (#19 R&B, 1990). Davis was replaced by Penny Ford for *Diamonds in the Raw,* which failed to chart pop but produced the R&B hit "I'm Still Missing Your Love" (#7 R&B, 1989). Though the album didn't chart at all, 1991's *One of Many Nights* yielded the R&B hit "Sometimes I Wonder" (#12 R&B, 1991).

Soul

A merger of gospel-charged singing, secular subject matter, and funk rhythms, soul grew out of Fifties rhythm & blues, spurred by Ray Charles' eclectic, decidedly secular late-Fifties hits. In soul's mid-Sixties heyday, there were distinctive regional styles: gritty, gospelly shouting over a stripped-down backup in Memphis (Otis Redding, Sam and Dave, Wilson Pickett); smoothly orchestrated pop soul in Chicago (the Impressions, Jerry Butler); architectonic, dramatic mini-epics at Motown in Detroit (Marvin Gaye, the Temptations, Smokey Robinson, the Supremes); and a little of them all in New York (Aretha Franklin).

There's no clear division between late-Sixties soul and the black pop that followed it; but at some point, music for dancing (funk, later disco) and music for listening (pop ballads) moved decisively apart.

"Soul" was also a black slang term for authenticity and sincerity, but after it moved into the mainstream vocabulary in the late Sixties the term became diluted and, eventually, unhip.

Soul Asylum

Formed 1981, Minneapolis, Minnesota
Dave Pirner (b. Apr. 16, 1964, Green Bay, Wis.), voc., gtr.; Dan Murphy (b. July 12, 1962, Duluth, Minn.), voc., gtr.; Karl Mueller (b. Minneapolis, July 27, 1963), voc., bass; Grant Young (b. Jan. 5, 1964, Iowa City, Iowa), drums.
1984—*Say What You Will, Clarence . . . Karl Sold the Truck* (Twin/Tone) 1986—*Made to Be Broken; Time's Incinerator* cassette; *While You Were Out* 1988—*Hang Time* (Twin/Tone–A&M) 1989—*Clam Dip & Other Delights* EP (Twin/Tone) 1990—*Soul Asylum and the Horse They Rode In On* (Twin/Tone–A&M) 1993—*Grave Dancers Union* (Columbia) 1994—(– Young) 1995—(+ Sterling Campbell, drums) *Let Your Dim Light Shine.*

Soul Asylum began as a thrashy punk band in the style of hometown peers the Replacements and Hüsker Dü. The group's tireless blend of punk energy, jazzy rhythms, country shadings, and solid songwriting earned it the tag "best live band in America."

In 1981 roommates Karl Mueller and Dan Murphy, 18 and 19 respectively, formed Loud Fast Rules with 17-year-old drummer Dave Pirner. Within three years Pirner had moved to the front, and the group changed its name

to Soul Asylum. After the lo-fi *Say What You Will,* produced by Hüsker Dü's Bob Mould, the band locked into its signature song style: loud, anthemic musings on the lives of young misfits.

For the next four years Soul Asylum slogged it out on the independent label Twin/Tone, touring constantly and releasing generally well-received albums. In 1988 the group's Twin/Tone deal was picked up by Herb Alpert's A&M Records; the following year the cover of its EP *Clam Dip & Other Delights* featured a sendup of Alpert's own 1965 Tijuana Brass album *Whipped Cream & Other Delights.* The joke seemed to elicit bad karma for Soul Asylum: Its A&M albums sold poorly even though they were among the group's strongest. After a shakeup at A&M, 1990's *And the Horse They Rode In On* stiffed so badly the band members almost decided to call it quits. Meanwhile Columbia struck a deal with A&M whereby it could release Soul Asylum's next album, and in 1993 the group came back with its biggest success to date. *Grave Dancers Union* (#11) was both a critical and commercial smash, selling a million copies and scoring a #5 hit with "Runaway Train." By 1993 Pirner had begun showing up in the gossip columns because of his relationship with actress Winona Ryder, with whom he appeared in the "Generation X" film *Reality Bites.* Soul Asylum slowed down the tempos on the more acoustic-sounding *Let Your Dim Light Shine* (#6, 1995), which featured the #20 hit "Misery."

Soul Survivors

Formed 1966, New York City, New York
Kenneth Jeremiah, voc.; Richard Ingui, voc.; Charles Ingui, voc.; Paul Venturini, organ; Edward Leonetti, gtr.; Joey Forigone, drums.

Kenneth Jeremiah and the Ingui brothers were a New York vocal trio, the Dedications, until meeting Paul Venturini, Edward Leonetti, and Joey Forigone. They changed their name to the Soul Survivors and relocated to Philadelphia, where they hooked up with Gamble and Huff, who wrote and produced "Expressway to Your Heart." It became a Top Five hit on both the pop and R&B charts in 1967, but turned out to be their last success. When it was discovered that the group was white, R&B airplay slowed. When their next two singles failed, pop radio lost interest as well. The band broke up a few years later and a 1974 comeback proved unsuccessful. Jeremiah later became part of Shirley and Company of "Shame Shame Shame" fame.

Soul II Soul

Formed 1982, London, England
Jazzie B. (b. Beresford Romeo, Jan. 6, 1963, London), DJ, voc.; Daddae (b. Philip Harvey, Feb. 28, 1964, London), misc.; Nellee Hooper, programming; Caron

Wheeler (b. Jan. 19, 1963, London), voc.; Simon Law, kybds.
1989—*Keep On Movin'* (Virgin) 1990—(– Wheeler; – Law) *Vol. II 1990—A New Decade* 1992—(– Hooper; + William Mowat [b. May 27, 1954, Stamford, Eng.], kybds.; + Rick Clarke [b. Aug. 17, 1960, London], voc.; + Luis Jordam, perc.; + Kofi Kari Kari [b. Sep. 11, 1962, London], voc.) *Volume III Just Right* 1994—(– Jordam; + Sonya Alphonse [b. Jan. 3, 1975, Wimbledon, Eng.], voc.; + Melissa Bell [b. Mar. 5, 1964, London], voc.; + Vannessa Simon [b. Dec. 7, 1969, Huddersfield, Eng.], backing voc.; + Michael Garnette [b. June 1, 1963, London], kybds.; + Fluxy [b. Oct. 18, 1963, London], drums; + Enyonam Esi Gbesemete [b. Dec. 21, 1969, Ghana], backing voc.; + Julia Payne [b. Apr. 16, 1963, London], backing voc.; + Ingrid Webster [b. May 14, 1964, S. A.], backing voc.; + Damel Carayol [b. Nov. 13, 1956, Gambia], backing voc.; + Lamya Al-Maghairy [b. Oct. 30, 1968, Mombasa, Kenya], voc.; + Mafia [b. Aug. 10, 1962, London], bass).

Soul II Soul took its slow-grooving fusion of reggae, soul, and rap, music fused in the clubs of London, and internationalized it with a string of hits and a Garveyite ideology. Leader Jazzie B. has described the group as more of a concept than a band; Soul II Soul is at once an amorphous collective and Jazzie B.'s solo project. Jazzie B., whose parents are from Antigua, grew up in North London and began working in sound studios at age 11. He and childhood friend Philip "Daddae" Harvey started Soul II Soul as a mobile sound system playing reggae clubs and warehouse parties. At one party in 1985, Soul II Soul rented equipment to Nellee Hooper, formerly of Bristol hip-hop group the Wild Bunch and then Massive Attack. The two fought that night but soon were working together.

Soul II Soul defined late-Eighties British club music, and its reputation increased when Jazzie B. and other band associates DJed on a British pirate radio station. After a couple of singles failed to hit, Soul II Soul finally struck it big with "Keep On Movin'" (#11 pop, #1 R&B, 1989), a #5 U.K. hit that also found a mass audience in the U.S. The single kicked off the album *Keep On Movin'* (#14 pop, #1 R&B, 1989), called *Club Classics Vol. One* in England, where it was #1. The single and its followup, "Back to Life (However Do You Want Me)" (#4 pop, #1 R&B, 1989), both platinum hits, featured the vocals of longtime studio singer Caron Wheeler. She soon had a falling-out with Soul II Soul and left to pursue a solo career. On the album's third single, "Jazzie's Groove" (#6 R&B, 1989), Jazzie B. articulated his positivist, Afrocentric philosophy: "A happy face, a thumpin' and lovin' bass, for a thumpin' and lovin' race." The album won two Grammys.

Soul II Soul continued to grow into an umbrella for a number of enterprises, including a studio, a fashion line, boutiques, and in 1991, the label Funki Dred, originally a joint venture with Motown but now an independent company. In 1990 Hooper and Jazzie B. coproduced Sinéad O'Connor's hit "Nothing Compares 2 U"; they also produced the Chimes, Neneh Cherry, Maxi Priest, and Fine Young Cannibals. As in the past, they used an assortment of singers on *Vol. II 1990—A New Decade* (#21 pop, #14 R&B, 1990), including Victoria Wilson-James on "A Dream's a Dream" (#19 R&B, 1990) and Kym Mazelle on "Missing You" (#29 R&B, 1990) and "Get a Life" (#54 pop, #5 R&B, 1990). The album's assortment of musicians included rapper Fab 5 Freddie and saxophonist Courtney Pine. A world tour for the album featured a fashion show and a 15-piece band. Jazzie B.'s back was injured in a seven-car pileup while on the road in Illinois, however, and Soul II Soul canceled the rest of its American shows.

Wheeler returned to sing on *Volume III Just Right*, although the album mostly featured male vocalists. "Joy" (#14 R&B, 1992) was sung by Richie Stephens, while Kofi Kari Kari sang "Move Me No Mountain" (#33 R&B, 1992). By 1994, a whole new crew of musicians had joined Soul II Soul.

Soundgarden

Formed 1984, Seattle, Washington
Matt Cameron (b. Nov. 28, 1962, San Diego, Calif.), drums; Chris Cornell (b. July 20, 1964, Seattle), voc.; Kim Thayil (b. Sep. 4, 1960, Seattle), gtr.; Hiro Yamamoto (b. Apr. 13, 1961), bass.
1987—*Screaming Life* EP (Sub Pop) 1988—*Fopp* EP 1988—*Ultramega OK* (SST) 1989—*Louder Than Love* (A&M) (– Yamamoto; + Jason Everman [b. Aug. 16, 1967], bass) 1990—(– Everman; + Ben Shepherd [b. Hunter Shepherd, Sep. 20, 1968, Okinawa, Jap.], bass) 1991—*Badmotorfinger* 1994—*Superunknown*.

One of the first bands to come out of the Seattle grunge scene (and one of the earliest to sign with Sub Pop Records), Soundgarden parlayed gloomy metal riffs, surrealistic psychedelia, and punk into platinum beginning with *Badmotorfinger* (#39, 1991).

After graduating high school in Illinois in 1981, musicians Kim Thayil and Hiro Yamamoto, as well as fanzine editor (and later Sub Pop founder) Bruce Pavitt, moved to Olympia, Washington, where they planned to attend college. When this did not pan out, the three each ended up in Seattle, attracted by its nascent music scene. After playing in cover bands, Yamamoto joined his roommate and sometime drummer Chris Cornell in his new band. Thayil signed on, and they called themselves Soundgarden after a noisy pipe sculpture in a Seattle park.

The addition of drummer Scott Sundquist in 1985 (he was replaced by Matt Cameron in 1986) freed Cornell to front the band. After contributing two songs to a local compilation, they signed with the new Sub Pop label. Their two EPs, *Screaming Life* (1987) and *Fopp* (1988), attracted major-label interest. But the band decided to stay true to their indie roots, signing to SST for their debut album *Ultramega OK.*

For *Louder Than Love* (#108, 1990), the band signed with A&M. The higher profile of a major label increased sales and helped the band garner a Grammy nomination. Yamamoto left the band in late 1989 to go back to school (in 1994 he joined Truly) and was replaced by Jason Everman, who had previously played with Nirvana. Everman was soon replaced by Hunter "Ben" Shepherd in early 1990.

Badmotorfinger sales were helped by "Outshined" being chosen as an MTV "Buzz Clip" and a spot opening for Guns n' Roses on the Lose Your Illusion Tour (they were invited by Axl Rose, a longtime fan). In 1991 Cornell and Cameron, along with members of Pearl Jam, were part of Temple of the Dog, a tribute to the late Mother Love Bone singer Andrew Wood. Shepherd and Cameron released *Hater* in 1993. Nineteen ninety-four's *Superunknown*, debuting at #1, emphasized Cornell's emotional lyrical content and the band's stylistic flourishes. In 1995 the band won two Grammys for the album's "Black Hole Sun" (Best Hard Rock Performance) and "Spoonman" (Best Metal Performance).

The Soup Dragons

Formed March 31, 1985, Belshill, Scotland
Sean Dickson (b. Mar. 21, 1967, Glasgow, Scot.), voc.; Jim McCulloch (b. May 19, 1966, Glasgow), gtr.; Sushil Dade (b. July 15, 1966, Glasgow), bass; Paul Quinn, drums.
1987—*Hang Ten!* (Sire)   1988—*This Is Our Art* 1990—*Lovegod* (Big Life/Mercury)   1992—*Hotwired* 1994—(– McCulloch; – Dade; – Quinn) *Hydrophonic* (Raw TV/Mercury).

The Soup Dragons formed in the mid-Eighties as a punk-pop band, but it was a danceable rendition of the Rolling Stones' "I'm Free" (the B side of "Get Off of My Cloud") that brought the Scottish band its first chart success. Taking their name from characters on an English cartoon series, the Dragons spent their first few years together recording edgy rock albums on their own label, Raw TV. In the late Eighties the band was picked up by Sire/Warner Bros. Around the same time, U.K. bands like the Stone Roses and Happy Mondays were making the Manchester Sound, a fusion of psychedelic guitar textures and funky rhythms, big on the British charts. Whether by savvy or by coincidence, the Dragons' third album, 1990's *Lovegod,* was also in this vein; it included

the "I'm Free" cover, which featured a reggae-rap sequence—performed by Jamaican artist Junior Reid—and a gospel choir. The song peaked at #79 on the American pop chart, but became a big dance-club hit, earning the group MTV airplay. A subsequent album, 1992's *Hotwired,* featured the singles "Divine Thing" (#35, 1992) and "Pleasure" (#69, 1992). While Sean Dickson was working on the songs for *Hydrophonic,* his bandmates quit. He continued, recording the album with various artists including Bootsy Collins.

Joe South

Born Joe Souther, February 28, 1940, Atlanta, Georgia
1968—*Introspect* (Capitol)   1969—*Don't It Make You Want to Go Home; Joe South; Games People Play*   1970—*Joe South's Greatest Hits, vol. 1* 1971—*So the Seeds Are Growing*   1972—*A Look Inside*   1975—*Midnight Rainbows* (Island)   1990— *The Best of Joe South* (Rhino)   1992—*Best of Joe South* (CEMA).

Joe South was a successful sessionman who went on to become a hit songwriter and performer, crossing over from country to pop in the early Seventies. At age 11, South got his first guitar, and a year later he was appearing regularly on Atlanta country music station WGST. In 1957 he joined the band of Pete Drake, the famed country pedal steel guitar player, and in the early Sixties he recorded some unsuccessful solo singles, including "Purple People Eater Meets the Witch Doctor." He also worked for a while as a country disc jockey.

South became a regular session guitarist in Nashville and Muscle Shoals, backing up country artists such as Marty Robbins and Eddy Arnold, in addition to Bob Dylan and Aretha Franklin. He appears on Simon and Garfunkel's "Sounds of Silence." South had also begun to do some songwriting, and in the mid-Sixties he wrote hits for the Tams ("Untie Me"), Billy Joe Royal ("Down in the Boondocks"), and early Deep Purple ("Hush"). By 1968, South was recording his own material.

Introspect sold marginally, but when other performers began to cover "Games People Play," Capitol reissued the song as a single, which went gold, as did the 1969 album of the same name. The song also won a Grammy as Song of the Year. *So the Seeds Are Growing* included his 1970 hit "Walk a Mile in My Shoes" (#12). His "Rose Garden" became an international country and pop hit for Lynn Anderson (#3, 1971).

In 1971 South took time off, in part to recuperate from a hectic schedule and also because of the suicide of his brother Tommy. He lived awhile in the jungles of Maui, Hawaii, and did not record again until 1975, when *Midnight Rainbows* was released. A difficult personality, South did not perform for years. In 1994 he played a show in London called "the American South," where he was showcased along with Allen Toussaint, Guy Clark, Dan Penn, and Vic Chesnutt. "Games People Play" was again a hit in Europe by Jamaican reggae group Inner Circle. Having overcome past problems with a drug dependence, South is now in the music publishing business, as well as working toward reviving his career.

Southside Johnny and the Asbury Jukes

Formed 1974, Asbury Park, New Jersey
Southside Johnny (b. John Lyon, Dec. 4, 1948, Neptune, N.J.), voc., harmonica; Billy Rush (b. Aug. 26, 1952), gtr.; Kevin Kavanaugh (b. Aug. 27, 1951), kybds., voc.; Al Berger (b. Nov. 8, 1949), bass, voc.; Kenny Pentifallo (b. Dec. 30, 1940), drums; Carlo Novi (b. Aug. 7, 1949, Mexico City, Mex.), tenor sax; Eddie Manion (b. Feb. 28, 1952), baritone sax; Tony Palligrosi (b. May 9, 1954), trumpet; Ricky Gazda (b. June 18, 1952), trumpet; Richie "La Bamba" Rosenberg, trombone.
1976—I Don't Want to Go Home (Epic)   1977—This Time It's for Real (– Pentifallo; – Novi)   1978—Hearts of Stone (+ Steve Becker, drums; + Joe Gramalin, gtr.)   1979—The Jukes (Mercury); Having a Party with Southside Johnny (Epic)   1980—Love Is a Sacrifice (Mercury) (– Berger; + Gene Bacia, bass)   1981—Live/Reach Up and Touch the Sky   1983—Trash It Up! (Mirage)   1984—In the Heat   1986—At Least We Got Shoes (Atlantic)   1992—The Best of Southside Johnny (Epic).
Southside Johnny solo: 1988—Slow Dance (Cypress)   1991—Better Days (Impact).

Southside Johnny and the Asbury Jukes were an R&B-influenced rock band that graduated from the Asbury Park bar-band scene soon after Bruce Springsteen's massive success.

Johnny Lyon, Springsteen, and Springsteen guitarist Miami Steve Van Zandt played together in the late Sixties in Asbury Park bands like the Sundance Blues Band and Dr. Zoom and the Sonic Boom. Lyon got his nickname because he liked blues from the South Side of Chicago. After migrating to Richmond, Virginia, with a band called Studio B, Lyon returned to Asbury Park and formed a duo with Van Zandt called Southside Johnny and the Kid, which became the Bank Street Blues Band with keyboardist Kevin Kavanaugh. In 1974 Van Zandt left again to go on the road with the Dovells (of "Bristol Stomp" fame), whose backing band also included bassist Al Berger. Lyon then joined the Blackberry Booze Band, which included drummer Kenny Pentifallo. With the addition of a horn section, they became the Asbury Jukes. Van Zandt briefly rejoined them before moving on to Springsteen's band.

The Jukes became mainstays at Asbury Park's top barroom, the Stone Pony. After Springsteen's successful 1975 U.S. and European tours, Van Zandt became the Jukes' manager/producer and landed them a recording contract. Their debut LP, which included two Springsteen tunes and guest appearances by Ronnie Spector and Lee Dorsey, sold well. *This Time* featured more Van Zandt and Springsteen tunes and included guest shots by members of the Coasters, the Drifters, and the Five Satins. Their third LP, with guest appearances by Van Zandt and E Street Band drummer Max Weinberg, still contained many Van Zandt and Springsteen titles. On their self-titled fourth LP, the Jukes declared their independence from the Springsteen imprimatur by writing all their own material (Lyon and Rush were the main composers). *The Jukes* went to #48, becoming the highest-charting album of their career. While their albums began to sell less well, they remained a successful touring unit for several more years. Lyon's solo debut, *Better Days* (#96, 1991), reunited him with Van Zandt.

In the summer of 1994 Southside Johnny and the Jukes performed with Bruce Springsteen, Jon Bon Jovi, and others at the 20th-anniversary celebration for the Stone Pony in Asbury Park.

Bob B. Soxx and the Blue Jeans

Formed 1963, New York City, New York
Bob B. Soxx (b. Robert Sheen), voc.; Darlene Love, (b. Darlene Wright), voc.; Fanita James, voc.
1963—Zip-A-Dee Doo-Dah (Philles).

Out of Phil Spector's Wall of Sound stable came vocal group Bob B. Soxx and the Blue Jeans in 1963, with their only big hit a revamped swinging version of "Zip-A-Dee Doo-Dah" (#8), a tune from the Disney film *Song of the South*. The LP also included covers of tunes like "This Land Is Your Land," "Let the Good Times Roll," and "The White Cliffs of Dover."

Spector had been initially attracted to Robert Sheen (a.k.a. Bob B. Soxx) because his voice reminded him of Clyde McPhatter's. All of the Blue Jeans had been singing since their early teens, and Darlene Love and Fanita James were both members of another Spector group, the Blossoms. Though it only had three chart hits, the group was a mainstay of the rock-concert circuit between 1963 and 1965. Darlene Love [see entry] went on to have some hits of her own for Spector. James was a backup vocalist for Tom Jones in the early Seventies and continued to lead a group of Blossoms through the Eighties as well.

Spandau Ballet

Formed 1979, London, England
Tony Hadley (b. June 2, 1960, London), voc., kybds.;
Gary Kemp (b. Oct. 16, 1960, London), gtr., kybds.;

Martin Kemp (b. Oct. 10, 1961, London), bass; Steve Norman (b. Mar. 25, 1960, London), gtr., sax, perc.; John Keeble (b. July 6, 1959, London), drums.
1981—*Journeys to Glory* (Chrysalis) 1982—*Diamond* 1983—*True* 1984—*Parade* 1985—*The Singles Collection* 1986—*Through the Barricades* (Epic) 1991—*Best of Spandau Ballet* (Chrysalis, U.K.).

British dance-pop band Spandau Ballet was a product of the same fashion-conscious New Romantic scene that produced Duran Duran and Visage, among others. Spandau began as a kilt-clad synth-disco outfit, playing in a handful of ultratrendy London clubs, where genteel kids put off by punk's abrasiveness paraded around in outrageously ornate and fanciful clothes (as opposed to punk's outrageously ugly wear and ghoulish style). Spandau Ballet's reputation built so quickly that Island Records chief Chris Blackwell reportedly offered the group a contract the first time he met them, at a London party. The group refused his offer, instead forming its own Reformation label (later licensing its recordings to Chrysalis).

The group's first U.K. hits, "To Cut a Long Story Short" (#5 U.K., 1980) and "Musclebound" (#10 U.K., 1981), also got much play in U.S. rock clubs, and especially in the New York dance clubs that proliferated in the early Eighties. Late 1981 saw Spandau introduce more musical urgency into its postdisco mix, with the soul-inflected "Chant No. 1 (I Don't Need This Pressure On)" (#3 U.K., 1981), which also got heavy U.S. club play.

In 1983 Spandau Ballet surprised critics who'd been dismissing the group as shallow, unmusical fops with its first U.S. chart album, *True* (#19, 1983)—and its title single (#4, 1983)—a soulful ballad with the sound and feel of a pop standard. Indeed, nearly a decade later, psychedelic rappers PM Dawn made a sample of "True" the centerpiece of its chart-topping pop hit "Set Adrift on Memory Bliss." *True* also yielded hits in "Gold" (#29, 1983) and "Communication" (#59, 1983), but *Parade* (#50, 1984) just spawned the minor hit "Only When You Leave" (#34, 1984).

No more hits followed, and in 1985 Spandau sued Chrysalis, claiming ineffective promotion had killed its commercial chances in the U.S. The Kemp brothers launched acting careers, to great acclaim, playing real-life British gangsters the Kray twins in the 1990 film *The Krays,* signaling Spandau Ballet's demise later that year. In 1992 Gary Kemp appeared in the film *The Bodyguard,* playing the role of Whitney Houston's manager; the next year, he was featured on the hit U.S. cable-TV comedy series *The Larry Sanders Show.*

The Spaniels
Formed 1952, Gary, Indiana
James "Pookie" Hudson, lead voc.; Gerald Gregory, bass voc.; Opal Courtney Jr., baritone voc.; Ernest Warren, tenor voc.; Willis C. Jackson, tenor voc. 1955—(– Courtney; + Cal Carter, voc.; – Carter; + James Cochran, baritone voc.; – Warren; – Hudson; – Jackson; + Donald Porter, tenor voc.; + Carl Rainge, lead voc.) 1956—*Goodnight, It's Time to Go* (Vee Jay) Ca. 1960—(Lineup: Hudson; Warren; Gregory; + Bill Carey, voc.; + Andy McGruder, voc.; numerous personnel changes follow) 1993—*The Spaniels—Goodnite Sweetheart, Goodnite* (Vee Jay); *40th Anniversary* (JLJ).

A mid-Fifties doo-wop vocal group, the Spaniels had several big R&B hits but never crossed over into pop-chart success.

They began as street singers in the Gary, Indiana, ghetto, and attracted the attention of local disc jockey Vivian Carter, who became their manager and with James Bracken formed Vee Jay Records to release their material. The Spaniels' first single was "Baby, It's You," a Top Ten R&B hit in 1953, which established both the band and Vee Jay Records (whose roster would later include Jimmy Reed and Jerry Butler, among others). In early 1954, their "Goodnite Sweetheart, Goodnite" was a #5 R&B hit (covered on the pop chart by the McGuire Sisters); in 1973 it was used as the closing theme for the film *American Graffiti.* The Spaniels became a top live attraction on the national R&B circuit, but they had undergone many personnel changes beginning in 1955. Through it all, though, the group continued to chart, notably with "You Painted Pictures" (#13 R&B, 1955) and "Everyone's Laughing" (#69 pop, #13 R&B, 1957). The Spaniels began fading in the late Fifties, and shortly after "I Know" (#23 R&B, 1960), they broke up again. In 1969 "Pookie" re-formed the Spaniels. They toured the revival circuit and in 1970 released the Spaniels' last charting single, "Fairy Tales," on Lloyd Price's Calla label (#45 R&B). As recently as 1993, Hudson and Gerald Gregory continued leading the Spaniels. In 1991 the Smithsonian Institution's Rhythm & Blues Foundation bestowed upon the group its lifetime achievement award.

Spanky and Our Gang
Formed 1966, Chicago, Illinois
Elaine "Spanky" McFarlane (b. June 19, 1942, Peoria, Ill.), voc.; Malcolm Hale (b. May 17, 1941, Butte, Mont.; d. 1968), gtr., voc.; Kenny Hodges (b. Jacksonville, Fla.), gtr., voc., bass; Nigel Pickering (b. June 15, 1929, Pontiac, Mich.), bass, gtr., voc.; Lefty Baker (b. Eustace Britchforth, Roanoke, Va.), gtr., banjo, voc.; John Seiter (b. Aug. 17, 1944, St. Louis, Mo.), drums, voc.
1967—*Spanky and Our Gang* (Mercury) 1968—*Like to Get to Know You; Without Rhyme or Reason*

(– Hale) 1969—*Spanky's Greatest Hit(s); Live*
1975—*Change* (Epic).

Along with the Mamas and the Papas, Spanky and Our
Gang were part of the late-Sixties folk/pop vocal-group
movement, with major pop hits like "Sunday Will Never
Be the Same" (#9, 1967), "Lazy Day" (#14, 1967), and "Like
to Get to Know You" (#17, 1968). In 1982 Spanky joined
the re-formed Mamas and the Papas.

Elaine "Spanky" McFarlane had met Mama Cass Elliot in the early Sixties and then joined "an electric
comedy-jug band," the New Wine Singers, which included Malcolm Hale. Spanky met Nigel Pickering,
Kenny Hodges, and Lefty Baker while vacationing in
Florida. As a quartet they debuted at the Mother Blues
club and were an immediate success; they were signed
by Chicago-based Mercury Records. Malcolm Hale and
John Seiter then joined. They took their name from the
Our Gang (a.k.a. *Little Rascals*) films.

The Gang began racking up a string of soft-
rock/folk-pop hits like "Sunday Will Never Be the Same,"
"Making Every Minute Count" (#31), and "Lazy Day" in
1967; "Like to Get to Know You" and "Sunday Mornin'"
(#30) in 1968. They were often featured on network TV
variety shows, though in 1969 their ghetto-conscious-
ness protest song "Give a Damn" was banned on many
radio stations. That song was later used in a widely aired
public service announcement campaign.

Though Hale had died of cirrhosis in 1968 during the
mixing of *Without Rhyme or Reason,* they retained the
rest of the original lineup until the hits stopped in 1970.

In 1975 McFarlane and Pickering re-formed the band
with three new members, playing Texas bars until 1980;
McFarlane also appeared on Roger McGuinn's solo
debut album. Then came the Mamas and the Papas reunion, with McFarlane even being called "Mama
Spanky" by the rest of the group. Their initial concert
tour was a success, and McFarlane later worked with a
new Spanky and Our Gang lineup.

Sparks

Formed 1971, Los Angeles, California
Ron Mael (b. Aug. 12, 1950, Culver City, Calif.),
kybds.; Russell Mael (b. Oct. 5, 1955, Santa Monica,
Calif.), voc.; Earle Mankey, gtr.; Jim Mankey, bass;
Harley Feinstein, drums.
1972—*Sparks* (Bearsville); *A Woofer in Tweeter's*
Clothing 1974—(– E. Mankey; – J. Mankey; – Fein-
stein; + Martin Gordon, bass; + Adrian Fisher, gtr.;
+ Norman "Dinky" Diamond, drums) *Kimono My*
House (Island) (– Gordon; – Fisher; + Ian Hampton,
bass; + Trevor White, gtr.); *Propaganda* 1975—*In-*
discreet 1976—(– Diamond; – Hampton; – White;
+ Sal Maida, bass; + Jeff Salen, gtr.; + Hilly
Michaels, drums) *Big Beat* (Columbia) 1977—

(– Maida; – Salen; – Michaels) *Introducing Sparks*
1979—*Number One in Heaven* (Elektra) 1981—
(+ David Kendrick, drums; + Leslie Bohem, bass;
+ Bob Haag, gtr.) *Whomp That Sucker* (Why-Fi/RCA)
1982—*Angst in My Pants* (Atlantic) 1983—*Sparks*
in Outer Space 1984—*Pulling Rabbits Out of a Hat*
1986—(+ John Thomas, kybds.) *Music That You Can*
Dance To (Curb/MCA) 1988—(– Kendrick;
– Bohem; – Haag) *Interior Design* (Fine Art/Rhino)
1991—*Profile: The Ultimate Sparks Collection*
(Rhino) 1994—*Gratuitous Sax and Senseless Vio-*
lins (Logic/BMG, U.K.).

Sparks' arch combination of witty lyrics with ever-
changing pop styles has long perplexed and enticed critics and audiences. Essentially the band is an outlet for
the eclectic, eccentric Mael brothers, whose twisted
tastes may have been set when they modeled for clothing catalogues as children. The Maels formed the band
Halfnelson in the early Seventies with friends from
UCLA. Halfnelson caught the ear of Todd Rundgren, who
got the band signed to Albert Grossman's Bearsville
label and produced their first album.

When the eponymously titled disc failed to sell, the
band's manager urged Halfnelson to change its name,
and the retitled album was rereleased. The single "Wonder Girl" almost made the Hot 100 (#112, 1972). Sparks'
quirky, overwrought art pop fared little better commercially with their second album, now a cult classic. The
Maels relocated to England, where they had found some
success on tour, leaving the rest of the band behind;
Earle Mankey went on to become a producer and
recording artist, while brother Jim helped form Concrete
Blonde.

With the assistance of a new band and producer
Muff Winwood (Steve's brother), Russell's quavering
falsetto and Ron's odd lyrics found phenomenal acceptance in England, beginning with 1974's *Kimono My*
House (#4 U.K.). Their image—Ron's stiff, nerdy demeanor and signature mustache juxtaposed to Russell's
curly mane and beaming androgyny—appealed to
British teens. Sparks landed nine U.K. chart hits, starting
with "This Town Ain't Big Enough for Both of Us" (#2,
1974), "Amateur Hour" (#7, 1974), and "Never Turn Your
Back on Mother Earth" (#13, 1974). After another Top Ten
U.K. album, *Propaganda* (#9, 1974), they began to falter
the next year on the Tony Visconti–produced *Indiscreet*
(#18 U.K.). In 1976 they returned to the U.S. and recorded
Big Beat with various players, including Tuff Darts guitarist Jeff Salen. They sang two songs from the album in
the film *Rollercoaster.* On the ironically titled *Introducing*
Sparks, the Maels recorded with L.A. session players.

Seeking a change, Sparks got Giorgio Moroder to
produce *Number One in Heaven.* Although critics derided the band for going disco, the album's dance-synth

pop returned the duo to the British charts with three hits, "The Number One Song in Heaven" (#14 U.K., 1979), "Beat the Clock" (#10 U.K., 1979), and "Tryouts for the Human Race" (#45 U.K., 1979). Sparks recorded *Terminal Jive* with Moroder protégé Harold Faltermeyer; although it was never released in the U.S., the album yielded "When I'm with You," a mega-seller in France. Sparks adopted the band Bates Motel for its next few albums; Moroder associate and Queen engineer Mack produced 1981's *Whomp That Sucker*. The band divided its time between L.A. and Belgium, where it recorded the self-produced *Sparks in Outer Space*. The album features Sparks fan and Go-Go Jane Wiedlin on two songs, including "Cool Places" (#49, 1983), Sparks' biggest American hit.

After a string of albums that failed to hit in Europe or the U.S., the Maels built a home studio in L.A., where they recorded 1988's *Interior Design*. They also wrote the music for a film by Hong Kong director Tsui Hark. In late 1994 Sparks returned—performing in London and releasing the U.K. album *Gratuitous Sax and Senseless Violins*.

The Specials/Fun Boy Three

Formed 1977, Coventry, England
Jerry Dammers (b. Gerald Dankin, May 22, 1954, India), kybds.; Sir Horace Gentleman (b. Horace Panter), bass; Lynval Golding (b. July 24, 1951, Coventry), gtr.; Roddy Radiation (b. Roddy Byers), gtr.; Terry Hall (b. Mar. 19, 1959, Coventry), voc.; Neville Staples, voc., perc.; John Bradbury, drums.
1979—The Specials (Chrysalis) 1980—The Special AKA Live EP (2-Tone, U.K.); More Specials 1981—(Group disbands; group re-forms as the Special AKA: Dammers; Bradbury; + Rhoda Dakar, voc.; + Egidio Newton, voc.; + Stan Campbell, voc.; + John Shipley, gtr.; + Gary McManus, bass) 1984—In the Studio 1991—The Singles Collection 1994—(Group re-forms: Staples; Byers; Golding; Panter; + Mark Adams, kybds.; + Aitch Bembridge, drums; + Adam Birch, trombone, trumpet).
Fun Boy Three (Hall; Staples; Golding): 1982—The Fun Boy Three (Chrysalis) 1983—Waiting 1984—The Best of Fun Boy Three.

The Specials were the prime movers behind England's short-lived two-tone movement of 1979–81, which also included Madness, the Selecter, and the English Beat. (The original fans often sported two-tone clothes and the band was racially mixed, ergo the title of the "movement.")

Coming together from mid-1977 to early 1978 in Coventry, the Specials initially played both fast punk and slower roots reggae. But they were unable to bring the two sounds together into a recognizable package, so they reoriented themselves toward ska, an upbeat precursor to reggae that was fashionable in England among Mods and skinheads in the mid-Sixties.

By early 1979, after a 1978 tour with the Clash, the Specials had cut an independent single, "Gangsters," but for its B side they used a cut by another struggling band, the Selecter. Pressed on the band's 2-Tone label, the single soared to #6 on the British charts. That led to a distribution deal with Chrysalis in June 1979. Soon their 2-Tone label gave British hits to a whole movement of bands—the Selecter, the Beat, and Madness—making it for a while the most successful independent English label since Stiff.

The Specials' debut LP, out in the U.S. in early 1980, was produced by Elvis Costello. Like that of most neo-ska bands, the music was danceable and charged with antiracist sentiment. Most of the music was by leader Jerry Dammers, but it also included the 1967 ska anthem "A Message to You Rudy" (#10 U.K., 1979). The Specials were stars in England, where "Too Much Too Young," a song advocating contraception from their U.K. EP, went to #1. Their other U.K. Top Ten hits were "Rat Race," "Stereotype," and "Do Nothing" (1980). In America, however, the group made little impression, except with critics. Their followup LP confused even the few fans they had here. Released in late 1980, *More Specials* had elements of cocktail jazz, cabaret theatricality, odd pop, and not much ska. In 1981 the Specials, along with several other 2-Tone groups, were featured in a concert movie entitled *Dance Craze*, which was released in the U.K. The 2-Tone label soon fell apart, with the Beat, the Selecter, and Madness all going to other companies. But the Specials hit a poignant high point in England in the summer of 1981 when they released "Ghost Town." It was inspired by the unemployment and racial tensions in England, and its release coincided with black-white riots in Brixton and Liverpool. (Black guitarist Golding was himself a victim of a racial attack, having his throat slashed and requiring 27 stitches.) The single went #1 in England, although it was banned from airplay by the BBC.

Soon after that, though, in October, the band fell apart after vocalists Hall and Staples plus Golding quit to form Fun Boy Three. While that group made no chart impression here in the U.S., the trio had a string of Top Twenty U.K. pop hits, including "The Lunatics (Have Taken Over the Asylum)" (1981); "The Telephone Always Rings" and "Summertime" (1982); and two Top Ten U.K. singles with Bananarama: "Tunnel of Love" and "Our Lips Are Sealed" (which Hall cowrote with Go-Go Jane Wiedlin) (both 1983). Fun Boy Three also appeared on Bananarama's "It Ain't What You Do, It's the Way That You Do It" (#4 U.K., 1982). Fun Boy Three disbanded in 1983, with Hall going on to form Colourfield and, in 1990, Terry, Blair and Anouchka. Most recently he worked with

Dave Stewart in Vegas and released a solo album in the U.K.

Roddy Byers fronted a rockabilly group called Roddy Radiation and the Tearjerkers. Panter later joined General Public. Dammers and Bradbury re-formed as the Special AKA, with a new lineup in late 1981. It was this group—which included Stan Campbell of the Selecter—that recorded "Racist Friend" and "Nelson Mandela," a 1984 #9 hit in the U.K. In 1986 Dammers formed Artists Against Apartheid. Dammers would become a key organizer of the Nelson Mandela's Seventieth Birthday Party concerts in 1988. Later Bradbury, along with Golding and Staples, joined the Special Beat, which was made up of ex-Specials and ex–(English) Beat members. A new version of the Specials, with four original members, toured in 1994 and announced plans to record a new album.

Phil Spector/The Teddy Bears

Born December 25, 1940, Bronx, New York
The Teddy Bears, formed 1958, Los Angeles, Calif.
(Spector, voc.; Marshall Leib, voc.; Annette Kleinbard [a.k.a. Bard], voc.; Harvey Goldstein, voc.;
– Goldstein): 1959—*The Teddy Bears Sing!*
(Imperial).
Phil Spector as producer: 1963—*A Christmas Gift for You* (Philles) 1977—*Phil Spector's Greatest Hits* (Warner Bros.) 1991—*Back to Mono* (Abkco).

Over three decades since its heyday, Phil Spector's Wall of Sound still stands as a milestone in recording history. It changed the course of pop-record producing and produced some of rock's best-loved music. Spector raised pop production's ambition and sophistication by overdubbing scores of musicians—five or six guitars, three or four pianos, and an army of percussion, including multiple drum kits, castanets, tambourines, bells and timpani—to create a massive roar. Spector called it "a Wagnerian approach to rock & roll: little symphonies for the kids."

Spector was raised in the Bronx but moved with his mother to Los Angeles at age 12 after his father committed suicide. He began learning guitar and piano while at Fairfax High School, and at 16 played with local jazz combos. In high school, Spector met Marshall Leib, and in 1957 the two began writing songs. In early 1958, another friend, Annette Bard, joined them to form the trio the Teddy Bears. Spector's choice of a group name was supposedly inspired by Elvis Presley's hit "(Let Me Be Your) Teddy Bear." In short order they had a Top Ten U.S. and U.K. hit with Spector's first production, "To Know Him Is to Love Him," taken from the inscription on Spector's father's gravestone ("To Know Him Was to Love Him"). The Teddy Bears appeared on national television, but when Spector disagreed with the record company on the group's next release, he moved them to Imperial.

There they cut a few singles and *The Teddy Bears Sing!*, which flopped, and soon broke up.

In the fall of 1960 Bard suffered severe facial injuries in a car accident. After recovering, she changed her name to Carol Connors and has written or cowritten a number of hit records, including Billy Preston and Syreeta Wright's "With You I'm Born Again" and "Gonna Fly Now," the theme from the first *Rocky* film. Other films for which she has written music include *Sophie's Choice* and *Rocky III*. Leib became a musician and producer, for, among others, the Everly Brothers. He has also supervised music for a number of feature films.

Spector then enrolled in UCLA, and also worked as a part-time court stenographer. He dropped out and moved back to New York, where he hoped to become a U.N. interpreter in French. But he soon returned to L.A., where he decided to reenter the record business. The 18-year-old Spector approached independent producers Lester Sill and Lee Hazlewood and persuaded them to take him under their wing. At this time, he formed another group, the Spectors Three, but after several flops, they disbanded and Spector concentrated on producing.

In 1960 Sill and Hazlewood sent Spector to New York, where he worked with hitmakers Jerry Leiber and Mike Stoller. With Leiber he cowrote "Spanish Harlem," a mammoth 1961 hit for Ben E. King. Spector also played the guitar break in the Drifters' "On Broadway." He became staff producer for Dunes Records and produced Ray Peterson's "Corinna, Corinna," a Top Ten hit. By this time he was also a freelance producer and A&R man at Atlantic Records as well as an independent producer. He produced Gene Pitney's "Every Breath I Take" and Curtis Lee's "Pretty Little Angel Eyes." Back on the West Coast, the Paris Sisters' "I Love How You Love Me" and the Ducanes' "Little Did I Know" followed. The youthful Spector was becoming an industry sensation.

While these late-1961 hits were still on the charts, Spector returned to New York and with Sill formed Philles (from Phil and Les) Records. He began recording a girl group called the Crystals, who hit in early 1962 with "There's No Other (Like My Baby)." Their next Spector-produced hit, "Uptown," was an even bigger success; and then came "He Hit Me (and It Felt Like a Kiss)," which was banned in some markets because of its lyrics, and the million-selling "He's a Rebel." Spector bought out Sill's part of Philles in late 1962.

At 21, Spector was a millionaire. He began recording on the West Coast, where he crafted his Wall of Sound in earnest, using such sessionmen as guitarists Glen Campbell, Sonny Bono, and Barney Kessel, pianist Leon Russell, and drummer Hal Blaine. Within three years, Spector had 20 consecutive smash hits, including the Crystals' "Da Doo Ron Ron," "Then He Kissed Me," and "He's Sure the Boy I Love"; the Ronettes' "Be My Baby," "Baby, I Love You," "(The Best Part of) Breakin' Up," and

"Walking in the Rain"; Darlene Love's "(Today I Met) the Boy I'm Gonna Marry" and "Wait 'Til My Bobby Gets Home"; and Bob B. Soxx and the Blue Jeans' "Zip-a-Dee Doo-Dah." The Righteous Brothers' "You've Lost That Lovin' Feelin'" sold over two million copies. In 1963 Spector made a Christmas album, featuring Darlene Love's "Christmas (Baby Please Come Home)" and the Crystals' "Santa Claus Is Coming to Town." (The album has been reissued for several Christmas seasons.) In a 1964 piece Tom Wolfe profiled Spector, dubbing him "the first tycoon of teen."

By this time, however, Spector had made more enemies than friends in the record business. In 1966 came the turning point, with Ike and Tina Turner's "River Deep—Mountain High." Spector considered it his greatest production to date, but it became a hit only in England. Embittered, Spector went into seclusion for two years, during which time reports of strange, near-psychotic behavior on his part filtered out of his 23-room Hollywood mansion: Spector allegedly mentally abused his wife, Ronnie (formerly of the Ronettes); Spector carried a gun. Except for a cameo appearance as a dope pusher in the film *Easy Rider* and some hits for Sonny Charles and the Checkmates Ltd.—"Love Is All I Have to Give," "Black Pearl," and "Proud Mary" (the latter employed some 300 musicians) he remained inactive through the late Sixties.

In 1969 Spector was brought in to do a remix on the Beatles' *Let It Be*. He proved he could adapt to more minimal arrangements with Lennon's *Imagine,* which he coproduced, and he returned to the Wall of Sound style for George Harrison's *All Things Must Pass* LP. In 1971, Spector oversaw production of Harrison's *The Concert for Bangla Desh* and produced the studio sides of John Lennon and Yoko Ono's *Some Time in New York City.* In 1973 he formed Warner-Spector Records with Warner Bros., but little came of the association. In 1974 and 1975 he survived two near-fatal auto accidents, and in late 1975 formed Spector International, which found Spector working with Cher, Dion, Harry Nilsson, Darlene Love, and Spector's latest "discovery," Jerri Bo Keno, still using L.A.'s Gold Star Studios, where he'd made his classics.

Spector's last major productions were Leonard Cohen's *Death of a Ladies' Man* (1977) and the Ramones' *End of the Century* (1980). He was inducted into the Rock and Roll Hall of Fame in 1989.

Ronnie Spector: See the Ronettes

Chris Spedding
Born June 17, 1944, Sheffield, England
1970—*Backwood Progression* (Harvest, U.K.)
1972—*The Only Lick I Know* 1976—*Chris Spedding* (RAK) 1977—*Hurt* 1979—*Guitar Graffiti*

1980—*I'm Not Like Everybody Else* 1982—*Friday 13th (Live in NYC)* (Gem) 1986—*Enemy Within* (New Rose, Fr.) 1990—*Cafe Days* (Mobile Fidelity Sound Lab) 1991—*Motorbikin': The Best of Chris Spedding* (EMI, U.K.).

Chris Spedding is one of the most widely experienced session guitarists in rock. He first learned violin as a youngster, but by his early teens gave it up for guitar. He joined a hometown band, the Vulcans, in the late Fifties, went with them to London, and then joined a country band that toured U.S. Army bases for three years. In 1964 he spent a year on the ship *Himalaya* entertaining passengers; upon his return to London, he worked with ex-Animal Alan Price and ex–Manfred Mann vocalist Paul Jones.

In 1967 he formed Battered Ornaments with Pete Brown, through whom Spedding met ex-Cream bassist Jack Bruce (for whom Brown wrote lyrics). When Battered Ornaments disbanded in 1969, Spedding took his first session job on Bruce's *Songs for a Tailor* LP. He then briefly worked with Ian Carr's jazz-fusion band Nucleus and has since played fusion with Keith Tippett, Mike Westbrook, and Mike Gibbs.

For the next few years, Spedding became one of Britain's busiest session guitarists, working with Lulu, Gilbert O'Sullivan, Dusty Springfield, David Essex, Donovan (he wrote string arrangements on Donovan's *Cosmic Wheels* LP), and John Cale, among many more. During this period he recorded two solo LPs.

In 1972 Spedding and ex-Free bassist Andy Fraser formed the hard-rock band Sharks (which included session bassist Busta Jones, who went on to play with Brian Eno, Talking Heads, and Gang of Four). They made two albums, then broke up in 1974; Spedding worked with Jones on Eno's 1974 *Here Come the Warm Jets.* In 1975 Spedding joined session bassist Dave Cochran and ex–Yes/King Crimson drummer Bill Bruford to form the backing band Trigger for British folk-rock singer/songwriter Roy Harper. Trigger backed Harper on what many consider his best album, *HQ* (reissued as *When an Old Cricketer Leaves the Crease* in the U.S.), and on a 1975 U.K. tour, then disbanded. Spedding then teamed with British pop producer Mickie Most for his next solo album. Spedding's eponymous 1976 solo album yielded the Top Ten U.K. hit "Motorbikin'," and included "Guitar Jamboree," in which Spedding imitated just about every famous rock guitarist in rapid succession. During the Seventies, Spedding reportedly turned down an offer to join the Rolling Stones.

Spedding also played sessions with Roxy Music singer Bryan Ferry (on *Let's Stick Together* and *In Your Mind*) and British punk band the Vibrators. He also reportedly played power chords for the first Sex Pistols singles. In 1979 Spedding teamed up with ex–Tuff Darts singer Robert Gordon. In 1980 he played with the New York band the Necessaries, and in 1981 formed a New York trio with Busta Jones and drummer David Van Tieghem, who had worked with minimalist composer Steve Reich and Brian Eno, among others.

Through the Eighties and early Nineties, he continued doing session work for, among others, Marc Almond (ex–Soft Cell), Marianne Faithfull, Nina Hagen, and Laurie Anderson. He duetted with Chrissie Hynde on the Otis Blackwell tribute album *Brace Yourself.* He has also worked as a record producer, journalist (as music editor of *Details* magazine), and soundtrack composer. He appears in Paul McCartney's *Give My Regards to Broad Street* as a band member.

Speed Metal: See Thrash

Spinal Tap
Formed 1967, London, England (1978, Los Angeles, California)
David St. Hubbins (b. Michael McKean, Oct. 17, 1947, New York City, N.Y.), gtr., voc.; Nigel Tufnel (b. Christopher Guest, Feb. 5, 1948, New York City), gtr., voc.; Derek Smalls (b. Harry Shearer, Dec. 23, 1943, Los Angeles), bass, voc.; various drummers.
1984—*This Is Spinal Tap* (Polydor)   1992—*Break Like the Wind* (MCA).

Probably the funniest inside joke in rock history, Spinal Tap was an ambitious dead-on parody of heavy metal's clichés and excesses, put on by skilled comic actors who wrote and played their own songs and were big enough fans of the music to satirize it—however brutally—with knowing affection. Indeed, the butts of the joke embraced Spinal Tap, who were invited to take part in such all-star hard-rock projects as the 1986 Hear-N-Aid benefit single, and the 1992 London tribute concert to Queen's Freddie Mercury.

Spinal Tap's principals were old friends and veteran satirists. Harry Shearer and Michael McKean had been in the early Seventies comedy troupe the Credibility Gap; McKean starred as Lenny in the TV show *Laverne and Shirley,* and Shearer was in the 1984–85 cast of TV's *Saturday Night Live.* Also in that cast, Christopher Guest (a schoolmate of McKean's at New York University) had written for the humor magazine *National Lampoon* and won an Emmy for his writing on a Lily Tomlin TV special. Spinal Tap, performing "Rock and Roll Nightmare," debuted in a 1978 ABC-TV comedy special, *The TV Show,* on which Guest, McKean, and Shearer worked with director Rob Reiner. They all began seeking funds for a full-length Spinal Tap film, which took some six years to make.

This Is Spinal Tap was directed in semi-improvised form by Reiner (who appeared in the film as director Marty DiBergi, an obvious takeoff on Martin Scorsese, director of *The Last Waltz*) as a mock-rockumentary on a disastrous Tap tour of the U.S. Guest, McKean, and Shearer skewered all aspects of the rock biz and fomented a long and detailed history of "the loudest band in England," all of whose drummers were cursed to die bizarre, mysterious deaths. Their repertoire featured the near-Kiss of "Tonight I'm Gonna Rock You Tonight," the virtual Jethro Tull of "Stonehenge" (complete with dancing dwarf Druids), and "Big Bottom," an ode to the female derriere on which Tufnel and St. Hubbins played bass while Smalls played a *double-necked* bass. Along the way, Tap also spoofed the sounds of the British Invasion ("Gimme Some Money") and psychedelic pop ("[Listen to the] Flower People"), as well as such rock & roll "institutions" as the meddling girlfriend, the sociopathic manager, and the obsequious PR man (played by bandleader Paul Shaffer). Indeed, the film was so sharply understated that some naive moviegoers actually believed they were watching a real film about a real group.

Despite universally glowing reviews and an instant, diehard cult, neither *This Is Spinal Tap* nor its soundtrack album (#121, 1984) was a commercial smash. Still, the movie inspired a book (1984's *Inside Spinal Tap* by Peter Occhiogrosso) and—after Guest and Shearer did stints in the cast of *Saturday Night Live*—an eventual sequels of sorts. *Break Like the Wind* (#61, 1992)—with guests Cher, Jeff Beck, Joe Satriani, and Slash of Guns n' Roses, and such tracks as "Rainy Day Sun," "The Majesty of Rock," and "Bitch School" (its video got MTV airplay)—was followed by the TV special "A Spinal Tap Reunion," which mixed concert footage (shot before an adoring London audience) and testimonials by such guest stars as Martin Short, Kenny Rogers, Mel Torme, and Guest's wife, Jamie Lee Curtis.

Spin Doctors
Formed 1988, New York City, New York
Aaron Comess (b. Apr. 24, 1968, Ariz.), drums; Chris Barron (b. Christopher Barron Gross, Feb. 5, 1968, Hawaii), voc.; Mark Burton White (b. July 7, 1962, N.Y.), bass; Eric Schenkman (b. Dec. 12, 1963, Mass.), gtr.
1991—*Up for Grabs* EP (Epic); *Pocket Full of Kryptonite*   1992—*Homebelly Groove*   1994—*Turn It Upside Down* (– Schenkman; + Anthony Krizan [b. Aug. 25, 1965, Plainfield, N.J.], gtr.).

Although Spin Doctors are one of a group of early-Nineties bands who play improvisational rootsy rock in the tradition of the Grateful Dead, the Doctors first found commercial success with a pop single. Singer/songwriter Chris Barron formed the band Trucking Company in 1989 with Eric Schenkman and John Popper, a friend from high school in Princeton, New Jersey. Popper left to form Blues Traveler, and Barron and Schenkman formed Spin Doctors with fellow New School classmate Aaron Comess. They then recruited Mark White, who had played with Comess in the band Spade. Spin Doctors' first show was at a Columbia University frat house.

The band gigged constantly in the New York area, often playing three sets a night or opening for kindred spirits Blues Traveler. They developed a strong following that soon attracted record company interest. In 1991 Epic signed Spin Doctors and promoted the band on the basis of their shows; the first record was a live EP. *Pocket Full of Kryptonite* (#4, 1992) was released in the summer of 1991, but didn't take off until a year later, when radio stations and then MTV began playing "Little Miss Can't Be Wrong," a catchy if somewhat misogynist single. (Barron frequently apologized live for the line, "Been a whole lot easier since the bitch left town.")

Spin Doctors continued to tour constantly, including playing the HORDE (Horizon of Rock Developing Everywhere) Tour with Blues Traveler, Phish, and Widespread Panic—bands whose hippie-ish energy, extended jams, and untiring gigging led them to be dubbed "the living Dead." Shows are so crucial to the Spin Doctors' reputation that they encourage concert bootlegs. *Homebelly Groove* is a live album comprising the Doctors' deleted first EP plus extended versions of songs from *Kryptonite*. *Turn It Upside Down* (#28, 1994), the band's second studio release, was a disappointment both critically and commerically, with no Top Forty singles.

The Spinners

Formed 1957, Detroit, Michigan
Bobbie Smith (b. Apr. 10), tenor voc.; Pervis Jackson (b. May 16), bass voc.; Henry Fambrough (b. May 10), baritone voc.; Billy Henderson (b. Aug. 9), tenor-baritone voc.; George W. Dixon, tenor voc.
1962—(- Dixon; + Edgar "Chico" Edwards, tenor voc.)   1967—The Original Spinners (Motown) (- Edwards; + G. C. Cameron, tenor voc.)   1972— (- Cameron; + Phillipe Wynne [b. April 3, 1941; d. July 13, 1984, Oakland, Calif.], tenor voc.) 1973—Spinners (Atlantic)   1974—Mighty Love; New and Improved Spinners   1975—Pick of the Litter; Spinners Live!   1976—Happiness Is Being with the Detroit Spinners   1977—Yesterday, Today and Tomorrow (- Wynne; + John Edwards [b. St. Louis, Mo.], tenor voc.) Spinners/8   1978—The Best of the Spinners; From Here to Eternally   1979—Dancin' and Lovin'   1980—Love Trippin'   1981—Superstar Series, vol. 9 (Motown); Labor of Love (Atlantic); Can't Shake This Feeling   1983—Grand Slam 1989—Down to Business (Volt)   1991—One of a

Kind Love Affair—The Anthology (Atlantic)   1993— *The Very Best of the Spinners* (Rhino).

The Spinners started as the Domingoes, a group of Ferndale (Detroit) High School students. Around 1961 singer/producer Harvey Fuqua discovered them and began recording the quintet, now rechristened the Spinners, on Tri-Phi Records, the label he cofounded with his wife, Berry Gordy's sister, Gwen. The first Spinners single, "That's What Girls Are Made For" (#27 pop, #5 R&B, 1961), featured Bobbie Smith singing lead in a style similar to Fuqua's (not Fuqua himself, as is often reported). The group released a series of singles that didn't click, and a few years later, when Tri-Phi merged with Motown, the Spinners moved to the larger company.

The group was, in some historians' opinion, overlooked at Motown. Although the group had some hits there—"I'll Always Love You" (#8 R&B) in 1965, "Truly Yours" (#16 R&B) in 1966, "We'll Have It Made (#20 R&B) in 1971, and the Stevie-Wonder-produced-and-penned "It's a Shame" (#14 pop, #4 R&B) in 1970—the company never considered them a major act. G. C. Cameron was lead singer for much of the late Sixties, and Edwards had left. In 1972 the Spinners moved to Atlantic Records and were teamed with Philadelphia producer Thom Bell. Newcomer Phillipe Wynne, who had previously worked in a band with Catfish and Bootsy Collins, was now handling most of the lead vocals, and from 1972 to 1979 the Spinners' close-harmony ballads regularly topped the R&B and pop charts. Their hits included "I'll Be Around" (#3 pop, #1 R&B) and "Could It Be I'm Falling in Love" (#4 pop, #1 R&B), 1972; "One of a Kind (Love Affair)" (#11 pop, #1 R&B) and "Ghetto Child" (#4 R&B), 1973; "Mighty Love, Part 1" (#20 pop, #1 R&B), "I'm Coming Home" (#18 pop, #13 R&B), and, with Dionne Warwick, "Then Came You" (#1 pop, #2 R&B), 1974; "Sadie" (#7 R&B) and "They Just Can't Stop It (the Games People Play)" (#5 pop, #1 R&B), 1975; "Wake Up Susan" (#11 R&B) and "The Rubberband Man" (#2 pop, #1 R&B), 1976; "You're Throwing a Good Love Away" (#5 R&B), 1977; and "If You Wanna Do a Dance" (#17 R&B), 1978. During this time, the Spinners earned five gold albums: *Spinners* (#14, 1973), *Mighty Love* (#16, 1974), *New and Improved* (#9, 1974), *Pick of the Litter* (#8, 1975), and *Happiness Is Being with the Detroit Spinners* (#25, 1976). They were also extremely popular in the U.K., where they were known as the Detroit Spinners to avoid confusion with a British group called the Spinners.

In 1977 Wynne left for a solo career (he also toured with Parliament-Funkadelic) and was replaced by John Edwards. Wynne released several solo albums and had a minor hit with "Wait 'til Tomorrow" in 1983. Wynne died onstage of a heart attack; he was 43.

In 1979 the Spinners returned to the charts with a medley-style remake of the Four Seasons' "Working My

Way Back to You" (#2 pop, #6 R&B, #1 U.K.). Their "Cupid medley"—"Cupid/I've Loved You for a Long Time"—was another big hit (#4 pop, #5 R&B, 1980). Subsequent singles hit the R&B chart but none moved into the Top Twenty. These include "Now That You're Mine Again" and "I Just Want to Fall in Love" (1980); "Yesterday Once More/Nothing Remains the Same," "Long Live Soul Music," "You Go Your Way (I'll Go Mine)" (which was produced by James Mtume and Reggie Lucas), and "Love Connection (Raise the Window Down)" (1981); "Magic in the Moonlight" and "Funny How Time Slips Away" (1982); and "Right or Wrong," at #22 R&B (1984), the group's highest-charting single since 1980's "Cupid" medley. As of the mid-Nineties, the group continues to tour and record with the same lineup intact since 1977.

Spirit

Formed 1967, Los Angeles, California
Randy California (b. Randy Craig Wolfe, Feb. 20, 1951, Los Angeles), gtr., voc.; Jay Ferguson (b. John Arden Ferguson, May 10, 1947, Burbank, Calif.), gtr., kybds., voc.; John Locke (b. Sep. 25, 1943, Los Angeles), kybds., voc.; Mark Andes (b. Feb. 19, 1948, Philadelphia, Pa.), bass, voc.; Ed Cassidy (b. May 4, 1924, Chicago, Ill.), drums.
1968—Spirit (Ode); The Family That Plays Together 1969—Clear Spirit 1970—The Twelve Dreams of Dr. Sardonicus (Epic) (– Ferguson; – Andes; – California; + Chris Staehely [b. Tex.], gtr., voc.; + Al Staehely [b. Tex.], bass, voc.) 1971—Feedback 1973—The Best of Spirit 1974—(Group re-forms: California; Cassidy; + Barry Keene, bass) 1975—Spirit of '76 (Mercury) (+ Locke) 1976—Son of Spirit (+ Mark Andes; + Matt Andes, gtr.); Farther Along 1977—Future Games (A Magical Kahauna Dream) (– Locke; – Mark Andes; – Matt Andes; + Larry Knight, bass) 1978—Live (Potato) 1981—Journey to Potatoland (Beggars Banquet/Rhino) 1984—Spirit of '84 (Mercury) 1989—Rapture in the Chambers (I.R.S.) 1990—Tent of Miracles (Caroline) 1991—Time Circle 1968–1972 (Epic Legacy); Chronicles (WERC).
Randy California solo: 1972—Kaptain Kopter & the (Fabulous Twirlybirds) (Epic).

Though they did have one hit single, "I Got a Line on You," Spirit were known primarily for their albums: an ambitious, eclectic blend of hard rock, blues, country folk, and prefusion jazz.

Shaven-headed drummer Ed Cassidy met Randy California while he was dating the latter's mother (whom he later married) when Randy was 13. He joined Randy's band, the Red Roosters, which had been formed in 1965 and featured most of the original Spirit lineup. Previously Cassidy had drummed for jazzmen Thelonious Monk, Art

Pepper, Cannonball Adderley, and Gerry Mulligan on the West Coast in the mid-Fifties, and in the early Sixties had formed his own New Jazz Trio. In 1965 he joined Rising Sons with Ry Cooder and Taj Mahal, but was forced to leave the group after injuring his hand during a drum solo.

John Locke, who claimed to be a direct descendant of the British philosopher of the same name, first encountered Cassidy in the New Jazz Trio. At UCLA, he later met Mark Andes and Jay Ferguson, who had grown up together in the San Fernando Valley. Andes' band, the Marksmen, had played sessions with Bobby "Boris" Pickett, among others. Ferguson had met California while with a bluegrass band, the Oat Hill Stump Straddlers. In 1965 Cassidy joined California, Ferguson, and Andes in the Red Roosters, but they broke up in 1966.

In New York City, Cassidy and California played in sessions and joined numerous bands. Meanwhile, Ferguson formed Western Union with Mark and his brother Matt Andes; the band gained some local popularity before Mark Andes left to briefly join Canned Heat. In late 1966 Cassidy and California returned to the state of California and, with Locke, formed Spirits Rebellious (the name taken from a Kahlil Gibran book), which with the addition of Ferguson and Mark Andes became Spirit.

Their LPs rarely sold better than moderately well, but Spirit were critically well received. Their biggest success critically and commercially was The Twelve Dreams of Dr. Sardonicus, the last LP by the original lineup. In mid-1971 Andes and Ferguson left to form Jo Jo Gunne [see entry], with Cassidy and Locke bringing in the Staehely brothers from Texas. After recording Feedback, however, the two original members quit, leaving the Staehelys to take their own "Spirit" on the road.

Randy California then went to England, where he played sessions with British art-rocker Peter Hammill of Van der Graaf Generator. In late 1971 he began experiencing health problems (a concussion from falling off a horse, and a nervous breakdown), which sidelined him until 1972, when he released a solo LP, Kaptain Kopter & the (Fabulous Twirlybirds). When California and Cassidy re-formed Spirit in 1974, Chris Staehely went to Jo Jo Gunne.

In 1975 the group played some West Coast reunion dates with Mark Andes, who'd left Jo Jo Gunne and would go on to join Firefall and, later, Heart. Ferguson, in the meantime, had hits on his own ("Thunder Island") and became an active West Coast sessionman and producer. Spirit continued recording and touring. A 1983 reunion resulted in Spirit of '84. The group, with Cassidy and California at the helm, has reunited in various configurations over the years. Cassidy, who is now over 70 years of age, has written and published Ed Cassidy's Musicians' Survival/Resource Manual (which he sells through ads in music magazines such as Goldmine). He has also lectured and given drum seminars.

Split Enz/Tim Finn

Formed 1972, Auckland, New Zealand
Tim Finn (b. June 25, 1952, Te Awamutu, N.Z.), voc., piano; Phil Judd, voc., gtr., mandolin; Eddie Rayner, kybds., Wally Wilkinson, gtr., Jonathan Michael Chunn, bass; Emlyn Crowther, drums; Noel Crombie, perc., spoons.
1975—*Mental Notes* (Mushroom, Austral.) 1976—*Second Thoughts* 1977—(– Judd; + Neil Finn [b. May 27, 1958, Te Awamutu, N.Z.], gtr., voc.; – Chunn; – Crowther; + Nigel Griggs [b. Aug. 18, 1949], bass; + Robert Gillie, sax; + Malcolm Green [b. Jan. 25, 1953], drums) *Dizrythmia* (+ Judd; – Judd; – Gillie) 1979—*Frenzy* (– Wilkinson) 1980—*True Colours* (A&M); *Beginning of the Enz* 1981—(– Green) *Waiata* 1982—*Time and Tide* (– Green) 1984—*Conflicting Emotions* 1987—*History Never Repeats: The Best of Split Enz.*
Tim Finn solo: 1983—*Escapade* (Oz/A&M) 1986—*Big Canoe* (Virgin) 1989—*Tim Finn* (Capitol) 1993—*Before and After.*

When the New Zealand band Split Enz began playing in the mid-Seventies, they had a lot of trouble being taken seriously because of their weird appearance, complete with glaring clownlike costumes and hairdos that made them look like parrots. Their music was an eclectic artpop amalgam with innovative song structures swinging from ballads to cabaret to heavy pop. They later reemerged with neo-Beatles pop songs and well-made video clips to gain a larger audience. Ultimately, however, Neil Finn (later joined by Tim) found a broader audience with his more orthodox pop rock in Crowded House [see entry].

The band went to Australia in 1975 as a seven-piece outfit and recorded its debut, *Mental Notes,* there in May and June; it was released only in Australia. They came to the attention of Roxy Music's Phil Manzanera, who produced *Second Thoughts* in England, which was mostly new versions of material from the first record. England became their home base, and they went through many personnel changes, including the loss of major songwriter Phil Judd. (The other writer was Tim Finn.) Their records sold well only in Australia. In 1976 they made an attempt to reach Americans with a brief tour, including a date at New York's Bottom Line, opening for Henny Youngman. In January 1977 Chrysalis released their debut U.S. LP, a compilation under the title *Mental Notes.* A year later, Judd briefly rejoined, but he left again, and was replaced by Tim Finn's brother Neil, but the group soon lost their contract. Judd went on to start his own band, the Swingers.

With Tim Finn in charge, the group made itself more accessible. They groomed themselves as a pop band, performing Beatles-influenced songs that, like 10cc's, masked droll undertones with winsome melodies. The band broadened its Australian following and returned to the U.S. market with *True Colours* in 1980; new anti-counterfeiting technology allowed the record to be pressed in laser-etched vinyl with rainbow patterns. "I Got You" gave the band its first taste of U.S. airplay; the single was #1 in Australia for ten weeks, and the album sold 200,000 copies there.

Split Enz had made rock videos in its early, more eccentric form, and with the advent of cablecast rock video in the early Eighties they got wide exposure for clips based on their newer songs. Even so, their albums sold fewer copies with each release, despite containing pop gems such as "History Never Repeats." The group disbanded in 1985, reuniting four years later in New Zealand. In 1985 Tim Finn married actress Greta Scacchi and, after a less than stellar solo career, joined his brother Neil's Crowded House in 1991, only to depart two years later.

Spooky Tooth

Formed 1967, England
Mike Harrison (b. Sep. 3, 1945, Carlisle, Eng.), voc., kybds.; Gary Wright (b. Apr. 26, 1943, Creskill, N.J.), kybds., voc.; Luther Grosvenor (a.k.a. Ariel Bender, b. Dec. 23, 1949, Evesham, Eng.), gtr.; Greg Ridley (b. Oct. 23, 1947, Cumberland, Eng.), bass; Mike Kellie (b. Mar. 24, 1947, Birmingham, Eng.), drums.
1968—*It's All About . . .* (Island; reissued in U.S. in 1970 as *Tobacco Road*) 1969—*Spooky Two* (– Ridley; + Andy Leigh, bass); *Ceremony* 1970—(– Wright; + Henry McCullough, gtr.; + Chris Stainton, kybds.; + Alan Spenner, bass) *The Last Puff* 1972—(– Kellie; – McCullough; – Stainton; – Spenner; – Grosvenor; + Mick Jones [b. Dec. 27, 1944, London, Eng.], gtr.; + Chris Stewart, bass; + Bryson Graham, drums) *You Broke My Heart So I Busted Your Jaw* 1973—*Witness* 1974—(– Harrison; – Stewart; + Mike Patto [b. Sep. 22, 1942; d. Mar. 4, 1979, Eng.], kybds., voc.; + Val Burke, bass, voc.) *The Mirror* 1976—*That Was Only Yesterday* (A&M).

Though they never had a hit single or a best-selling LP, Spooky Tooth remained a bastion of Britain's hard-rock scene. Founding member Gary Wright had several hits after leaving the band.

Mike Harrison had worked as a clerk before joining the VIPs, which became the group Art in the mid-Sixties, with Mike Kellie. Wright [see entry] had been a child actor and a psychology student in New Jersey before attending college in Berlin. Spooky Tooth's first two albums, produced by Jimmy Miller, sold respectably in the U.K.; U.S. bassist Greg Ridley left for Humble Pie after the second and was replaced by Andy Leigh for *Ceremony.*

Wright brought in French electronic-music pioneer Pierre Henry to add processed *musique concrète* overdubs. Wright then left to form the short-lived Wonderwheel and reemerged a few years later on his own. Harrison brought in Henry McCullough, Chris Stainton, and Alan Spenner from Joe Cocker's Grease Band for *Last Puff.* Grosvenor left after that LP, later to join Stealers Wheel and Mott the Hoople, and Spooky Tooth entered suspended animation, with Harrison pursuing a short solo career with an LP, *Smokestack Lightning.*

Wright and Harrison re-formed the band in 1972, with future Foreigner guitarist Mick Jones. Their next two albums sold fairly well, especially *You Broke My Heart So I Busted Your Jaw.* Harrison left again to pursue a solo career in 1973; in 1974 Spooky Tooth re-formed yet again, with Mike Patto on vocals and keyboards. (He would work with a few more bands before dying of throat cancer in 1979.) They broke up for good a year later. Kellie, who in 1970 had briefly played with the British supergroup Balls (which also included Denny Laine and Steve Gibbons), resurfaced in the late Seventies with the Only Ones.

Dusty Springfield

Born Mary O'Brien, April 16, 1939, London, England
1964—*The Dusty Springfield Album* (Philips)
1966—*You Don't Have to Say You Love Me*; *Golden Hits*   1967—*Look of Love*   1968—*Stay Awhile* (Mercury)   1969—*Dusty in Memphis* (Atlantic) 1970—*A Brand New Me*   1971—*For You, Love, Dusty* (Philips)   1973—*Cameo* (Dunhill)   1978—*It Begins Again* (United Artists)   1979—*Living Without Your Love*   1982—*White Heat* (Casablanca) 1990—*Reputation*   1995—*A Very Fine Love* (Columbia).

Dusty Springfield's husky voice made her one of Britain's best-selling pop-rock singers in the Sixties. She and her brother Tom began harmonizing with radio hits as children. She briefly recorded with the Lana Sisters, then she and her brother Tom formed a folk trio, the Springfields, with Tim Field. The group, a British equivalent of Peter, Paul and Mary, had U.K. chart hits in 1962–63 with "Island of Dreams" and "Say I Won't Be There," and hit the American Top Twenty in 1962 with "Silver Threads and Golden Needles." That year, Field quit, replaced by Mike Hurst (who later produced Cat Stevens), before the trio disbanded. Tom found success as a songwriter for the Seekers, among others.

Springfield continued on her own, and in late 1963 had a British Top Ten hit with "I Only Want to Be with You," which went to #12 in the U.S. in early 1964 and eventually went gold. The tune has since been covered by many other performers. That song was Springfield's first flirtation with Motown-style soul, a sound to which

she would often return. She toured the world and had British hits through 1964–65 with Bacharach-David's "I Just Don't Know What to Do with Myself" and "Wishin' and Hopin'," and with Goffin-King's "Some of Your Lovin'" and "Goin' Back." In 1966 "You Don't Have to Say You Love Me" was #1 in the U.K. and #4 in the U.S. She continued to tour extensively and made TV appearances with Tom Jones and Engelbert Humperdinck and on *The Ed Sullivan Show.* In 1969, with producers Jerry Wexler, Arif Mardin, and Tom Dowd, she recorded *Dusty in Memphis,* which yielded the Top Ten international hit single "Son of a Preacher Man." In 1970 she moved back toward pop with *Brand New Me,* which contained "Land of Make Believe," "Silly Silly Fool," and the title cut. In England her popularity declined, though "How Can I Be Sure," a cover of the Rascals hit, was a 1970 Top Forty hit there. By then she had scored 17 U.K. and ten U.S. hit singles.

Between 1971 and 1978 Springfield lived reclusively in America and did not record, except for some backup vocals on Anne Murray's *Together* LP. In 1978 Springfield recorded two comeback albums on the West Coast. The first, *Begins Again,* produced by Roy Thomas Baker (of Queen and Cars fame), fared poorly both critically and commercially; the second, *Living Without Your Love,* produced by David Wolfert, did slightly better. She had a minor 1979 U.K. hit with "Baby Blue," and the following fall she played some New York club dates, her first in eight years.

Springfield's big commercial comeback occurred in 1987, a quarter century after "Silver Threads and Golden Needles," when fan/Pet Shop Boy Neil Tennant invited her to sing on his duo's "What Have I Done to Deserve This?" An international smash, the song hit #2 in the U.S. and in the U.K. She was also featured on the *Scandal* soundtrack, with "Nothing Has Been Proved," and in 1990 *Reputation* was a Top Twenty U.K. album. Springfield recorded her 1995 album in Nashville.

Rick Springfield

Born August 23, 1949, Sydney, Australia
1972—*Beginnings* (Capitol)   1974—*Comic Book Heroes* (Columbia)   1976—*Wait for the Night* (Chelsea)   1981—*Working Class Dog* (RCA) 1982—*Success Hasn't Spoiled Me Yet*   1983—*Living in Oz*   1984—*Hard to Hold* soundtrack; *Beautiful Feelings* (Mercury)   1985—*Tao* (RCA)   1988—*Rock of Life*   1989—*Rick Springfield's Greatest Hits.*

Rick Springfield first became a household name as an actor, playing Dr. Noah Drake on the television soap opera *General Hospital.* In 1981 he became a platinum-selling recording star as well with the #1 single "Jessie's Girl."

Springfield grew up in both Australia and England. He got his first guitar at 13 and formed several bands. He performed his first original material with Zoot, which became a top teen idol band in Australia with a #1 hit, "Speak to the Sky." His remake of "Speak to the Sky" reached the Top Fifteen that year in America. His U.S. label, Capitol, promoted Springfield as a teen star, which got him lots of fanzine coverage but kept him from being taken seriously; his next album, *Comic Book Heroes,* also flopped. Legal tangles kept Springfield out of circulation for two years, after which he signed to the small Chelsea label and released *Wait for the Night.* In 1974 he had been originally cast as lead in *The Buddy Holly Story,* but the role went to Gary Busey.

He made guest appearances on *The Six Million Dollar Man* and *Wonder Woman* while still making demos, and in early 1980 signed with RCA. *Working Class Dog,* which contained "Jessie's Girl," was released as Springfield became a regular on *General Hospital.* The album went platinum, as did *Success Hasn't Spoiled Me Yet,* with "I've Done Everything for You" (#8, 1981) and "Don't Talk to Strangers" (#2, 1982), and *Living in Oz* (#12, with the 1983 Top Ten "Affair of the Heart" and Top Twenty "Human Touch").

Springfield starred in the critically lambasted *Hard to Hold,* and the Top Twenty platinum album of the same title included Springfield's last Top Ten hit, "Love Somebody." While his subsequent singles (including "Bruce," about his being mistaken for Bruce Springsteen) all charted in the 20s, fans lost interest. With the exception of "I've Done Everything for You" (written by Sammy Hagar), Springfield wrote all of his own songs.

Bruce Springsteen

Born September 23, 1949, Freehold, New Jersey
1973—*Greetings from Asbury Park, N.J.* (Columbia);
The Wild, the Innocent and the E Street Shuffle
1975—*Born to Run* 1978—*Darkness on the Edge of*
***Town* 1980—*The River* 1982—*Nebraska* 1984—**
***Born in the U.S.A.* 1986—*Live, 1975–1985* 1987—**
Tunnel of Love* 1992—*Human Touch*; *Lucky Town
1995—*Greatest Hits.*

Bruce Springsteen is a rock & roll working-class hero: a plain-spoken visionary. He is a fervent and sincere romantic whose insights into everyday lives—especially in America's small-town, working-class heartland—have earned comparisons to John Steinbeck and Woody Guthrie. His belief in rock's mythic past and its potential revitalized pop music and made Springsteen a superstar in the 1980s.

Springsteen, of Irish-Italian ancestry, grew up in Freehold, New Jersey, the son of a bus driver and a secretary. He took up the guitar when he was 13 and joined the Castiles a year later. In 1966 the Castiles recorded (but never released) two songs cowritten by Springsteen, and they worked their way up to a string of dates

Bruce Springsteen

at New York City's Cafe Wha in 1967. During the summer after his graduation from high school, Springsteen was working with Earth, a Cream-style power trio, and hanging out in Asbury Park, New Jersey. He entered Ocean County Community College in the fall, but dropped out when a New York producer promised him a contract; he never saw the producer again.

While in college, he had formed a group with some local musicians, including drummer Vini "Mad Dog" Lopez and keyboardist Danny Federici. Called Child, then Steel Mill, the group worked the Atlantic coast down to Virginia. In summer 1969 Steel Mill visited California (where Springsteen's parents had moved); club dates in San Francisco led to a show at Bill Graham's Fillmore and a contract offer from Graham's Fillmore Records, which Steel Mill turned down because the advance was too small. The band returned East, and was joined by an old friend of Springsteen's, Miami Steve Van Zandt, on bass.

Springsteen disbanded Steel Mill in early 1971, intending to put together a band with a brass section and several singers. Meanwhile, he formed Dr. Zoom and the Sonic Boom, which played only three dates. Eventually, the Bruce Springsteen Band was formed with Lopez, Federici, Van Zandt (on guitar), pianist and guitarist David Sancious, bassist Garry Tallent, and a four-piece brass section. After the group's first show, the brass section was dropped and Clarence Clemons, a football-player-turned-tenor-saxophonist (a knee injury aborted his pro career), joined the band. The group didn't last; by autumn 1971 Springsteen was working solo.

Springsteen had auditioned for Laurel Canyon Productions, a.k.a. Mike Appel and Jim Cretecos, who had written a hit for the Partridge Family and produced an album by Sir Lord Baltimore. In May 1972 Springsteen signed a long-term management contract and an agreement giving Laurel Canyon exclusive rights to his songs. Royalty rates effective for five albums were set at a low 3 percent of retail price.

Appel arranged for his new client to audition for John Hammond, who had signed Dylan to Columbia; after hearing Springsteen sing in his office, Hammond set up a showcase for CBS executives at the Gaslight in New York City and supervised a demo session. In June 1972 Columbia president Clive Davis signed a ten-album contract with Appel that gave Laurel Canyon about a 9 percent royalty.

Within the month, Springsteen completed *Greetings from Asbury Park, N.J.* Some of Springsteen's word-crammed songs were set to acoustic singer/songwriter backup, and some to the R&B-inflected rock of the reconstituted Bruce Springsteen Band. Released in January 1973 and touted as one more "new Dylan" effort, *Greetings* initially sold about 25,000 copies, largely to Jersey Shore fans. Springsteen and the band toured the Northeast, playing extended sets that earned him followings in Boston and Philadelphia. A string of dates opening for Chicago, which limited his sets to a half-hour, convinced Springsteen not to open for other bands.

With his second album, *The Wild, The Innocent and the E Street Shuffle,* Springsteen and his band integrated lyrics and instrumental passages into long romantic narratives; the average track was over seven minutes. The album sold as poorly as its predecessor, and Springsteen decided to concentrate on his stage show. Replacing Lopez with Ernest "Boom" Carter on drums, he tightened up what became the E Street Band, hired expensive light and sound crews, and rehearsed them to theatrical precision. He made up elaborate stories, often involving band members, to introduce his songs, dramatized the songs as he sang them, and capped his sets with fervently rendered oldies.

In spring 1974 critic Jon Landau saw Springsteen opening for Bonnie Raitt in Cambridge, Massachusetts, and wrote in the *Real Paper,* "I saw rock & roll's future and its name is Bruce Springsteen." Columbia used the quotation in an ad campaign, and rave reviews of Springsteen concerts and belated notices of *The Wild* began showing up in print. By November 1974 the album had sold 150,000 copies. Springsteen and a revamped E Street Band (pianist Roy Bittan and drummer Max Weinberg replaced Sancious and Carter, who had formed their own fusion group, Tone; Van Zandt joined as second guitarist) were bogged down by an ambitious third album. Landau, who had been visiting the studio with suggestions, became coproducer with Springsteen and Appel (he would later become the singer's man-

ager). Far from toning down Springsteen's histrionics, Landau inflated them with dramatic arrangements. While the album was being mastered, Springsteen wanted to scrap it in favor of a concert album. But that plan was dropped, and in October 1975 *Born to Run* (#3, 1975) was released.

Advance sales put the album on the chart a week before its release date, and it made the Top Ten shortly afterward. Within the month, it hit #3—and gold—while "Born to Run" (#23, 1975) became Springsteen's first hit single. Springsteen embarked on his first national tour. *Time* and *Newsweek* simultaneously ran cover stories on him. Yet Springsteen was still a cult figure—the album didn't stay on the charts long. In spring of 1976 an independent auditor's report called Appel's management "unconscionable exploitation." And when Appel refused permission for Landau to produce the next album, Springsteen sued his manager in July 1976, alleging fraud, undue influence, and breach of trust. Appel's countersuit asked for an injunction to bar Springsteen from working with Landau, which the court granted. Springsteen rejected the producer Appel chose, and the injunction prevented Springsteen from recording until May 1977. An out-of-court settlement gave Springsteen rights to his songs and he was allowed to work with Landau, while his Columbia contract was upgraded. Appel reportedly received a lump sum settlement.

During the legal imbroglio, Springsteen toured and E Streeters did session work: Bittan worked with David Bowie and Meat Loaf; Van Zandt produced the debut album by Southside Johnny and the Asbury Jukes, *I Don't Want to Go Home,* which featured several Springsteen compositions. Other Springsteen songs provided hits for the Hollies ("Sandy"), Manfred Mann ("Blinded by the Light," a #1 single in 1977), Robert Gordon ("Fire," later a smash for the Pointer Sisters), and Patti Smith ("Because the Night," to which she contributed some lyrics). And Springsteen continued to write new songs, several of which were chosen for *Darkness on the Edge of Town* (#5, 1978).

Darkness was a dire and powerful album that reflected the troubled period Springsteen had just endured. On tracks like "Badlands," "Promised Land," "Adam Raised a Cain," and the title track, Springsteen sang with choked emotion about working-class problems and the hopes that keep Americans going. The album proved his depth to critics, although it failed to deliver on crossover hopes, yielding only the minor single "Prove It All Night" (#33, 1978).

Work on *The River* began in April 1979 and went on for a year and a half. Springsteen appeared on stage only twice in that period, at the Musicians United for Safe Energy (MUSE) antinuclear benefit concerts in New York, which were filmed as *No Nukes.* Meanwhile, Dave Marsh's best-selling *Born to Run: The Bruce Springsteen*

Story was released, spreading the Springsteen legend out in book length (it was released again in a revised edition, followed by a second Marsh volume, *Glory Days: Bruce Springsteen in the 1980's*, which was published in 1987).

Coproduced by Springsteen, Landau, and Van Zandt, the double album *The River* (#1, 1980) sold over two million copies. A single, "Hungry Heart" (#5, 1980), was Springsteen's first Top Ten hit, followed by "Fade Away" (#20, 1981). *The River* was notable for its shorter, verse-chorus songs that were essentially short stories or character sketches ("Wreck on the Highway," "Independence Day," "Point Blank," "The River"). These four songs especially revealed a sense of resignation, of Springsteen's characters learning to live with what they cannot change.

On the eve of *The River*'s release in October 1980, Springsteen kicked off a tour that crisscrossed the United States twice and took him to over 20 European cities; every one of his four-hour shows was sold out. In the fall, he played six benefit concerts in Los Angeles for Vietnam War veterans. In 1981 Springsteen persuaded Gary "U.S." Bonds (whose "Quarter to Three" was a favorite Springsteen encore) to return to recording, on an album produced by Van Zandt that included Springsteen material. Members of the E Street Band played sessions for Garland Jeffreys, Joan Armatrading, Ian Hunter, and others. Van Zandt continued producing Southside Johnny and the Asbury Jukes, and Bittan produced an album for rock singer Jimmy Mack.

In 1982 Springsteen made *Nebraska* (#3, 1982), a stark album recorded (initially as demo tapes) on a four-track machine at home. With its tales of losers, desperadoes, and dreamers, the album was Springsteen's folk-song commentary on the social problems of America in the Age of Reagan, and on the nihilism bred by alienation.

After *Nebraska*'s deliberately noncommercial statement, Springsteen decided to head in the other direction and try to bring his message to a mass audience. With the simple, declarative songs on *Born in the U.S.A.* (#1, 1984), Springsteen became a megastar. The album yielded a string of singles—"Dancing in the Dark" (#2, 1984), "Cover Me" (#7, 1984), "Born in the U.S.A." (#9, 1984), "I'm on Fire" (#6, 1985), "Glory Days" (#5, 1985), "I'm Goin' Down" (#9, 1985), and "My Hometown" (#6, 1985)—and was in the Top Ten for more than two years. Springsteen made his first videos for the album's singles, including "Dancing in the Dark," directed by Brian De-Palma (the single later won a Grammy). Although on *Born in the U.S.A.*, Springsteen continued to look at the dark side of the American dream, he simplified sentiments and packaged them in an album featuring a U.S. flag on the cover. Not surprisingly, many fans took "Born in the U.S.A." as an upbeat patriotic anthem, although the song was actually about the dead ends hit by a Viet-

nam vet. Ronald Reagan himself, during the 1984 presidential campaign, tried to coopt Springsteen's vision as his own in one speech. Springsteen attempted to counteract such misinterpretations by meeting with labor, environmental, and civil rights activists in towns he played and mentioning their efforts on stage. Springsteen has always played numerous benefits; in 1985 he sang on USA for Africa's "We Are the World" and Van Zandt's antiapartheid project "Sun City." But the *Born in the U.S.A.* concerts themselves fueled the spectacle of Springsteen's success, with fans waving American flags in sold-out stadiums. The previously scrawny, modest Springsteen had joined the country's mania for pumping iron, and his marathon concerts began to resemble athletic events. Nineteen-eighty-five's constant touring (with Nils Lofgren replacing Van Zandt, who went on to pursue a solo career [see entry], and Patti Scialfa added on vocals) took him to the Far East and Australia for the first time.

The 40-song live album package *Live/1975–1985* (#1, 1986) was released partly to counter the flood of bootlegs that had been traded among fans for years. It featured his cover of Edwin Starr's "War" (#8, 1986), a song whose critique he explicitly aimed in concerts at Reagan's militarism.

In 1984 Springsteen met model/actress Julianne Phillips, and the couple married in May 1985. On *Tunnel of Love* (#1, 1987) Springsteen recorded some of his most personal songs—including the Grammy-winning "Tunnel of Love" (#9, 1987), "Brilliant Disguise" (#5, 1987), and "One Step Up" (#13, 1988)—in which he detailed love unraveling. The songs proved to be painfully honest. While he was headlining the 1988 Amnesty International Human Rights Now! Tour, tabloids began reporting that Springsteen and Scialfa were having an affair. In August 1988 Phillips filed for divorce. The couple divorced the next year, and Springsteen married Scialfa in 1991. They moved to Los Angeles and eventually had three children, Evan James, Jessica Rae, and Sam Ryan.

Springsteen was apparently rethinking his life in general during this period. On the *Tunnel of Love* tour he had tried to shake up the E Street Band's live habits by repositioning them on stage. Still, the large group no longer seemed to be the correct vehicle for his music, and in November 1989 he told them he no longer needed them. During this period Springsteen was also sued by two former roadies for back pay.

After half a decade's absence Springsteen returned with the simultaneous release of two albums, *Human Touch* (#2, 1992) (coproduced by Bittan, the only E Street Band member on the albums) and *Lucky Town* (#3, 1992). The albums entered the charts at their peak positions, but merely went platinum as opposed to the multiplatinum of his previous three albums. (All of his albums have sold platinum.) Springsteen wasn't aiming for the huge success of *Born in the U.S.A.*, but the pop songs of *Human Touch*, which he painstakingly had written over several years, received mixed reviews: Critics generally preferred *Lucky Town*'s ruminations on parenting and adulthood, which revealed new possibilities for a more mature Springsteen.

Springsteen performed on a television program for the first time in 1992, appearing on *Saturday Night Live*. On tour, he recruited a new, younger band, but he hadn't quite freed himself from his old, overstated stadium style, and the shows seemed somewhat out of step with the album's more mature tone. For the first time in 15 years, Springsteen played to empty seats. In 1993 Scialfa released her first solo album, *Rumble Doll*, to general critical praise. That year Springsteen wrote and recorded "Streets of Philadelphia" (#9, 1994) for the Jonathan Demme film *Philadelphia;* the song won an Academy Award and four Grammys. *Greatest Hits,* which debuted at #1 on the charts, contained four previously unreleased songs.

Squeeze

Formed 1974, London, England
Chris Difford (b. Apr. 11, 1954, London), gtr., voc.;
Glenn Tilbrook (b. Aug. 31, 1957, London), gtr., voc.;
Julian "Jools" Holland, kybds., voc.; Harry Kakoulli, bass; Gilson Lavis (b. June 27, 1951, Bedford, Eng.), drums.
1978—*U.K. Squeeze* (A&M)   1979—(- Kakoulli; + John Bentley [b. Apr. 16, 1951, London], bass) *Cool for Cats*; *6 Squeeze Songs Crammed into One Ten-inch Record* EP   1980—*Argybargy*   1981—(- Holland; + Paul Carrack [b. Apr. 1951, Sheffield, Eng.], kybds., voc.) *East Side Story*   1982—(- Carrack; + Don Snow [b. Jan. 13, 1957, Kenya], kybds., voc.) *Sweets from a Stranger* (group disbands)   1983— *Singles 45's and Under*   1985—(Group re-forms: Difford; Tilbrook; Holland; Lavis; + Keith Wilkinson [b. Sep. 24, 1954, Southfield, Eng.], bass, voc.) *Cosi Fan Tutti Frutti* (+ Andy Metcalfe, kybds.)   1987— *Babylon and On*   1989—*Frank*   1990—(- Holland; + Matt Irving, kybds., accordion) *A Round and a Bout* (I.R.S); (- Irving; - Metcalfe)   1991—*Play* 1993—(- Lavis; + Carrack; + Pete Thomas [b. Aug. 9], drums) *Some Fantastic Place* (A&M).
Difford and Tillbrook: 1984—*Difford & Tillbrook* (A&M).
Jools Holland: 1981—*Jools Holland and His Million-aires* (I.R.S.)   1984—*Jools Holland Meets Rock'a' Boogie Billy*   1990—*World of His Own*   1991—*The Full Compliment*   1993—*The A–Z of the Piano*.
Paul Carrack solo: See Ace entry.

Though they had garnered some critical acclaim and a few minor commercial successes in the late Seventies, Squeeze appeared to have broken through in 1981 with *East Side Story*, which yielded a minor U.S. single in "Tempted" and was one of the most highly praised albums of the year. Despite that auspicious beginning (and a Top Twenty hit in 1987 with "Hourglass"), the group's commercial fortunes never improved. Bafflingly, while none of their LPs cracked the Top Thirty here, a 1983 "greatest hits" has been certified platinum.

Chris Difford and Glenn Tilbrook had been writing and performing together since 1973, and claim to have written over 1000 songs to date. Difford writing the lyrics, Tilbrook the music, the pair created a body of smart, poppish, but ultimately sophisticated songs and have often been described as this generation's Lennon and McCartney. The group was initially formed as Squeeze, but affixed a "U.K." to avoid confusion with a preexisting American band called Tight Squeeze; when the latter disbanded, they went back to Squeeze.

The title tune from *Cool for Cats,* featuring Chris Difford's eccentric throaty vocals, was a #2 U.K. hit and achieved some dance-floor success in the U.S.; "Up the Junction" from the same LP fared similarly. *Argybargy* yielded "Pulling Mussels (from a Shell)," "Another Nail in My Heart," and "If I Didn't Love You," none hits but all frequently played in new-wave clubs and on new-wave-format radio.

In late 1980 Holland left to form his own band, the Millionaires. He was replaced by Paul Carrack, formerly of Ace; he'd sung Ace's hit "How Long," which Squeeze included in its live concerts, and sang "Tempted," from the Elvis Costello–coproduced *East Side Story.* Carrack left to join Carlene Carter's band, then to work with her husband Nick Lowe's Noise to Go. He was replaced by ex-Sincero Don Snow for *Sweets,* another well-received LP, which yielded FM staples in "Black Coffee in Bed" and "I Can't Hold On." Difford became involved in England's antinuclear movement and wrote what he called the band's "first protest song," "Apple Tree," which was to be included on *Sweets* but, for unknown reasons, was not. That year Difford also cowrote "Boy with a Problem" with Elvis Costello for Costello's *Imperial Bedroom* (Tilbrook had appeared on Costello's *Trust* earlier), and Squeeze played its first Madison Square Garden concert. In the fall of 1982 the group broke up.

Difford and Tilbrook continued to collaborate, and released one eponymously titled album before re-forming the band with Holland, Lavis, and Keith Wilkinson. The resulting *Cosi Fan Tutti Frutti,* another critical hit, topped at #57, and *Babylon and On,* which contained "Hourglass" and "853-5937," stopped at #36. The next two albums were not even in the Top 100. In the meantime, Holland, something of a personality, had hosted a U.K. music show from 1982 to 1987, then hosted NBC's *Sunday Night,* a unique and respected music performance series not unlike the later *MTV Unplugged.* In

England, he has hosted film documentaries, written and starred in a U.K. sitcom about Martians, and hosted the BBC's *Juke Box Jury* and *Later with Jools Holland*. In 1993, between solo work and a stint with Mike + the Mechanics, Carrack returned to the group for *Some Fantastic Place*, which peaked at #182 and produced the single "Everything in the World."

Billy Squier

Born May 12, 1950, Wellesley Hills, Massachusetts
1980—*The Tale of the Tape* (Capitol)   1981—*Don't Say No*   1982—*Emotions in Motion*   1984—*Signs of Life*   1986—*Enough Is Enough*   1989—*Hear & Now*   1991—*Creatures of Habit*   1993—*Tell the Truth*   1995—*The Best of Billy Squier: 16 Strokes.*

After more than a decade of performing, heavy-metal guitarist Billy Squier hit it big in 1981 with "The Stroke" and enjoyed a few years of multiplatinum albums.

Squier grew up in an affluent Boston suburb, and after graduating high school he moved to New York City, where he and several friends formed Magic Terry and the Universe. Squier later returned to the Boston area, where he studied at the Berklee School of Music, planning to become a music teacher. But he soon returned to New York where in 1973 he joined the pop group the Sidewinders (he does not appear on their LP). Next he joined Piper, but after two LPs (*Piper* and *Can't Wait*) the group disbanded, and Squier began a solo career.

After his lackluster *The Tale of the Tape* (#169, 1980), Squier came back strong with a #5 LP (*Don't Say No*) and the Top Twenty "The Stroke." The album also included "My Kinda Lover" (#45, 1981) and "In the Dark" (#35, 1981) and was eventually certified triple platinum. The next year's *Emotions in Motion* included "Everybody Wants You" (#32, 1982); it sold over two million copies, boosted by heavy rotation on MTV. Much to Squier's chagrin, he was embraced as something of a teen idol, an image that was blatantly (even embarrassingly) exploited in the video for "Rock Me Tonite" (#15, 1984). That song, from Squier's last platinum album, *Signs of Life* (#11, 1984), was also his last Top Forty single to date.

Subsequent albums failed to hit: *Enough Is Enough* and *Hear & Now* went Top Seventy, while *Creatures of Habit* didn't cross into the Hot 100. He continues to tour and record.

Lisa Stansfield

Born April 11, 1966, Rochdale, England
1989—*Affection* (Arista)   1991—*Real Love*.

Lisa Stansfield topped the pop and R&B charts internationally in the early Nineties, a rare feat for a white soul singer from a small town in England. Stansfield started singing in her early teens. Although she had no formal training, she plied her skill arduously at talent contests and social clubs. In the early Eighties she presented the British children's television program *Razzamatazz*. In 1983 she formed the group Blue Zone with former schoolmates Andy Morris and Ian Devaney (her boyfriend). The trio released several singles and the album *Big Thing* but never broke out of the Manchester club circuit.

In 1989 the British production team Coldcut recorded "People Hold On" with Blue Zone, and the single went to the U.K. Top Twenty. Arista signed Stansfield as a solo artist, with Morris and Devaney as her composers, musicians, and producers. The platinum *Affection* (#9 pop, #5 R&B, 1990) became an international hit, with the singles "This Is the Right Time" (#21 pop, #13 R&B, 1990), "All Around the World" (#3 pop, #1 R&B, 1990), and "You Can't Deny It" (#14 pop, #1 R&B, 1990). Stansfield broke a color and ocean barrier by topping the U.S. R&B charts three times. In England she won Best British Female Artist at the BRIT awards in 1991, although she angered organizers by using the show to speak out against the Gulf War.

For *Real Love* (#43 pop, #18 R&B, 1991), Stansfield cut off her trademark spitcurl and presented herself as a more serious, mature artist. The singles "Change" (#27, 1991), "All Woman" (#1 R&B, 1992), and "A Little More Love" (#30 R&B, 1992) fared better with R&B and adult contemporary audiences than with the pop market. In 1992 she recorded a new version of "All Around the World" with one of her influences, Barry White. Stansfield sang Cole Porter's "Down in the Depths" for the AIDS benefit album *Red Hot + Blue*.

The Staples

Formed 1953, Chicago, Illinois
Roebuck "Pops" Staples (b. Dec. 2, 1915, Winona, Miss.), voc., gtr.; Mavis Staples (b. 1940, Chicago), voc.; Cleo Staples (b. 1934, Miss.), voc.; Pervis Staples (b. 1935, Miss.), voc.
Mid-1960s—(+ Yvonne Staples [b. 1939, Chicago], voc.)   1968—*Soul Folk in Action* (Stax); *We'll Get Over*   1971—(– P. Staples) *This Time Around*; *Heavy Makes You Happy*   1972—*Bealtitude: Respect Yourself*   1973—*Be What You Are*   1974—*City in the Sky*   1975—*The Best of the Staple Singers*; *Great Day* (Milestone)   1976—*Pass It On* (Warner Bros.)   1977—*Family Tree*   1978—*Unlock Your Mind*   1984—*Turning Point* (Private I)   1985—*Chronicle* (Fantasy)   1985—*Are You Ready* (Private I)   1991—*Freedom Highway* (Columbia Legacy)   1992—*The Staple Singers* (Stax).
Mavis Staples solo: 1969—*Mavis Staples* (Stax)   1976—*Only for the Lonely*   1977—*A Piece of the Action* (Curtom)   1979—*Oh, What a Feeling*

(Warner Bros.)   1989—*Time Waits for No One* (Paisley Park)   1993—*The Voice.*
Pops Staples solo: 1992—*Peace to the Neighborhood* (Pointblank/Charisma)   1994—*Father Father.*

First as gospel singers and then as a soul-pop group, the Staples family has maintained a strong following and had several pop and soul hits, usually fronted by Mavis Staples' breathy vocals.

The Staples family goes back to Mississippi, where as a young man Roebuck Staples played guitar and sang in local choirs. In the mid-Thirties, he and his wife, Oceola, traveled up the Mississippi River to Chicago in search of work, like many of his contemporaries. The Staples had three daughters and a son, each of whom sang from an early age. They put together a family gospel act (which, until the mid-Sixties, included all but the youngest daughter, Yvonne) and by the mid-Fifties were considered one of the finest vocal groups in the field. The group made its first recording in the early Fifties, for Pop Staples' own label, "These Are They" b/w "Faith and Grace," which they sold at concerts. In 1953 they recorded for United, and three years later for Vee Jay, both Chicago labels, without success.

In the early Sixties the Staples made their first pop (secular) recordings for Epic, but had no commercial success, although 1967's "Why" snuck onto the pop chart in the Nineties, and a version of Buffalo Springfield's "For What It's Worth" also charted later that year. Everything changed after they signed to Stax in 1968. Their new material continued to reflect the Staples' commitment to making secular music with a message, but not until 1972's gold *Bealtitude: Respect Yourself* did they make the approach commercial. The Staples' first secular hit was "Heavy Makes You Happy" (#27 pop, #6 R&B, 1971); and their next two hits, "Respect Yourself" (#12 pop, #2 R&B, 1971) and "I'll Take You There" (#1 pop and R&B, 1972), went gold. "If You're Ready (Come Go with Me)" was a #1 R&B hit in 1973. The Staples had succeeded in meshing Memphis soul shuffles with their own messages, and might have continued to release crossover hits were it not for Stax's mid-Seventies decline and eventual closing.

Curtis Mayfield's Curtom label was their next home, and in 1974 the Staples had a #1 pop and R&B hit with his "Let's Do It Again" and a #4 R&B hit with "New Orleans," both from the film *Let's Do It Again.* Mayfield also produced two of Mavis' solo albums. A couple of years later, at Warner Bros., the group changed its name to "the Staples" and released two R&B Top Twenty singles: "Love Me, Love Me, Love Me" (#11 R&B, 1976) and "Unlock Your Mind" (#16 R&B, 1978). None of their singles charted again until 1984, when three, including a cover of Talking Heads' "Slippery People," appeared. Their last R&B Top Forty single was a 1985 version of "Are You

Ready?" The group appeared in 1971's *Soul to Soul,* a documentary of a concert in Ghana, and in *Wattstax* (1973) and *The Last Waltz* (1978).

Mavis Staples also recorded solo, but without comparable success, in part because her own career was frequently suspended due to group obligations. In 1987 Prince signed her to his Paisley Park label, for which she recorded *Time Waits for No One,* which he coproduced with Al Bell (who had worked with the Staples at Stax). She opened for Prince on the overseas leg of his 1990 tour and appeared on his *Graffiti Bridge.* In addition, she has appeared on records by a range of artists, including Aretha Franklin (*One Lord, One Faith, One Baptism*), John Mayall, Ray Charles, Kenny Loggins, Marty Stuart, and Prince. Pops, who has also released solo albums, appears on Mavis' *The Voice.* His 1994 album, *Father Father,* won that year's Grammy for Best Contemporary Blues Album.

Edwin Starr

Born Charles Hatcher, January 21, 1942, Nashville, Tennessee
1968—*Soul Master* (Gordy)   1969—*25 Miles; Just We Two*   1970—*War & Peace*   1971—*Involved* 1974—*Hell Up in Harlem* soundtrack (Tamla) 1976—*Free to Be Myself* (Granite)   1977—*Edwin Starr* (GTO)   1978—*Clean* (20th Century–Fox) 1979—*Happy Radio*   1981—*The Best of Edwin Starr.*

Singer/songwriter Edwin Starr's rough, powerful voice has made him a memorable but erratic hitmaker since the mid-Sixties, though he is best known in the United States for his 1970 #1 protest song "War."

Starr sang in high school and began his professional career on Ric-Tic Records, a Detroit-based label that copied the sound of its crosstown rival, Motown, in many of its releases. On Ric-Tic, Starr had hits with his own "Agent Double-O-Soul" (#21 pop, #8 R&B, 1965) and "Stop Her on Sight (S.O.S.)" (#9 R&B, 1966). In 1968 Ric-Tic was purchased by Motown. The gritty Starr-penned "Twenty-five Miles" (#6 pop and R&B, 1969) is regarded as a soul classic. "I'm Still a Strugglin' Man" (#27 R&B) was the followup.

With producer Norman Whitfield, Starr had success in 1970 with two social commentary songs, "War" (#1 pop, #3 R&B)—originally intended for the Temptations but deemed too controversial for them—and "Stop the War Now" (#26 pop, #5 R&B). The next year brought "Funky Music Sho Nuff Turns Me On" (#6 R&B). During the late Seventies, Starr recorded for 20th Century–Fox Records. His most successful singles of the period were "H.A.P.P.Y. Radio" (#79 pop, #28 R&B, 1979) and "Contact" (#65 pop, #13 R&B, 1979). In 1982 he cut a comical commentary song, "Tired of It," for Montage Records.

Around 1983 Starr moved to England, where, like many other Sixties singers, he found a receptive audience. In fact, "H.A.P.P.Y. Radio" and "Contact" had been Top Ten hits there. He has since participated in the Ferry Aid single, "Let It Be" (1987), and recorded with Stock/Aitken/Waterman ("Whatever Makes Our Love Grow"). "It Ain't Fair" reached #56 there in 1985. As of the late Eighties, Starr was living in a country manor outside Birmingham. He also owns a rehearsal studio and cafe in Birmingham. He has continued to tour and record.

Ringo Starr

Born Richard Starkey Jr., July 7, 1940, Liverpool, England
1970—*Sentimental Journey* (Apple); *Beaucoups of Blues* 1973—*Ringo* 1974—*Goodnight Vienna* 1975—*Blast from Your Past* 1976—*Ringo's Rotogravure* (Atlantic) 1977—*Ringo the 4th* 1978—*Bad Boy* 1981—*Stop and Smell the Roses* (Boardwalk) 1983—*Old Wave* (RCA, Can.) 1989—*Starr Struck: Best of Ringo Starr, vol. 2 (1976–1983)* (Rhino) 1990—*Ringo Starr and His All-Starr Band* (Rykodisc) 1992—*Time Takes Time* (Private Music); *Ringo Starr and His All-Starr Band, vol. 2: Live from Montreux* (Rykodisc).

While some accused Ringo Starr of being a clumsy drummer, many more agreed with George Harrison's assessment: "Ringo's the best backbeat in the business." And while many in the wake of the Beatles' breakup predicted that Starr would be the one without a solo career, he proved them wrong. Not only has he released several LPs (the first came out before the Beatles disbanded) and hit singles, but he's also the only Beatle to establish a film-acting career for himself outside the band's mid-Sixties movies.

Young Richard Starkey's parents had divorced when he was three, and he was raised by his mother and stepfather, a Liverpool house painter his mother married eight years later. By the time he was 13, he'd been in and out of the hospital several times with pleurisy, and once, at age six, with appendicitis. After leaving the hospital in 1955, too old to return to school, he became a messenger boy for British Railways. In 1959, while working as an apprentice engineer, he got his first drum set as a Christmas present, and he joined the Ed Clayton Skiffle Group soon after. By 1961, he was playing drums in Rory Storme's Hurricanes. It was while on tour with that band in Hamburg, Germany, in 1961 that he met John Lennon, Paul McCartney, and George Harrison. A year later, when drummer Pete Best was ousted from the Beatles, Starr agreed to join them. The Ringo stage name came from his penchant for wearing lots of rings.

Beginning with "Boys" on the Beatles' first British album, Starr was given the occasional lead vocal, usually on covers of country tunes such as Carl Perkins' "Honey Don't" and "Matchbox" and Buck Owens' "Act Naturally." Later he sang the lead on "Yellow Submarine" and "With a Little Help from My Friends," songs written for him by Lennon and McCartney. *The Beatles* (the so-called White Album) in 1968 featured Starr's first songwriting credit, "Don't Pass Me By." After appearing in three films with the Beatles, in 1967 Starr made his solo film debut playing a Mexican gardener in the film of Terry Southern's *Candy*. He appeared in *The Magic Christian* (1969, also from a Southern book); in 1970 he costarred with David Essex in *That'll Be the Day;* in 1973 he documented the success of glitter-rock star T. Rex by directing *Born to Boogie;* in 1975 he costarred again with Essex in *Stardust;* and in 1981 he starred in the moderately successful U.S. feature *Caveman* (in April of that year he married his *Caveman* costar Barbara Bach; it was his second marriage).

Starr's solo recording career began in 1970, just before the Beatles' breakup, with *Sentimental Journey* (#22, 1970), a collection of Tin Pan Alley standards (allegedly to please his mother) produced by George Martin, with a different arranger for each track. *Beaucoups of Blues* (#65, 1970), released later that year, was a country-music collaboration with guitarist Pete Drake and other Nashville sessionmen. It fared better than its predecessor, but failed to yield a hit. In 1971 Starr appeared on Lennon's *Plastic Ono Band* and Harrison's *All Things Must Pass* LPs, and recorded two hit singles, the hard-rocking "It Don't Come Easy" (#4) and "Back Off Boogaloo" (#9).

Starr appeared at Harrison's Concerts for Bangla Desh and in 1972 sat in on Peter Frampton's *Wind of Change* LP. In 1973 he recorded *Ringo* (#2, 1973), with Richard Perry producing. The LP included three Top Ten singles—"Photograph" (#1), "You're Sixteen" (#1), and "Oh My My" (#5)—and featured songs and playing by the other Beatles; Lennon contributed "I'm the Greatest," McCartney "Six O'Clock," and Harrison "Sunshine Life for Me." *Goodnight Vienna* (#8, 1974) yielded hit singles in Hoyt Axton's "No No Song" (#3) and "Only You" (#6). *Blast from Your Past*, a greatest-hits package, went to #30 in 1975.

While comanaging a furniture-designing business with his brother in London, Starr in 1975 started his own label, Ring O' Records, and signed to Atlantic. Compared to his previous solo success, his albums for his new label made little impression; *Ringo's Rotogravure*, despite guest appearances by Lennon, McCartney, Eric Clapton, and Peter Frampton, stopped at #28 with one Top Thirty single, "Dose of Rock 'n' Roll," and *Ringo the 4th*, at #162, was a flop. *Bad Boy* (#129, 1978) continued the downward spiral.

Starr remained a familiar presence, though. In 1976

he played at the Band's San Francisco farewell concert and appeared in the film of the event, *The Last Waltz*. In 1977 he contributed to an LP by British skiffle pioneer Lonnie Donegan. In late 1981 Starr had a Top Forty hit with "Wrack My Brain," from *Stop and Smell the Roses* (#98, 1981), a tune written and produced by George Harrison. None of his subsequent albums has come near the Top 100.

Old Wave was not released in the U.S. or the U.K., and during this time Starr suffered from myriad problems, foremost among them alcoholism and drug abuse, for which both he and his wife Barbara sought treatment in 1988. At one point earlier, Starr's drinking had gotten so bad that he went to court to block the release of material he had recorded in 1987. In the meantime Starr became a star of the kiddie set in his portrayal of the miniature conductor and narrator of the acclaimed PBS series *Shining Time Station*, between 1989 and 1991. (Starr had first narrated the British series *Thomas the Tank Engine and Friends* back in 1984.)

Starr has since formed several celebrity configurations of his All-Starr Band. The first, in 1989, featured Levon Helm, Joe Walsh, Clarence Clemons, Rick Danko, and Billy Preston, and Dr. John. A 1992 lineup included Ringo's son Zak on drums, Walsh, Timothy B. Schmit, Dave Edmunds, Nils Lofgren, and Todd Rundgren. The 1992 release of *Time Takes Time*, coinciding with the silver anniversary of *Sgt. Pepper's Lonely Hearts Club Band*, brought a new flush of publicity for Starr, who often made it amply clear to interviewers that he did not wish to talk about the Beatles.

Though Starr has had little success as a recording artist in the Eighties and Nineties, he is never long out of view. He appeared in Paul McCartney's *Give My Regards to Broad Street* (1984), a television production of *Alice in Wonderland* (1985), with Zak on the Artists United Against Apartheid album and video (1985), with ex-bandmate Harrison in the video for "When We Was Fab" (1988), and as himself on *The Simpsons* (1990). In 1994 Starr's first wife, Maureen Cox Starkey Tigrett, died of cancer.

Status Quo

Formed 1962, London, England
Francis Rossi (b. May 29, 1949, London), gtr., voc.; Richard Parfitt (b. Rick Harrison, Oct. 12, 1948, Woking, Eng.), gtr., voc.; Alan Lancaster (b. Feb. 7, 1949, London), bass; John Coghlan (b. Sep. 19, 1946, London), drums; Roy Lynes, organ.
1968—*Messages from the Status Quo* (Cadet Concept); *Spare Parts* (Pye, U.K.) 1969—*Status Quotation* (Marble Arch, U.K.) 1970—*Ma Kelly's Greasy Spoon* (Pye, U.K.) (– Lynes) 1971—*Dog of Two Heads* 1972—*Best of Status Quo* 1973—*Pile Dri-*

ver (A&M) 1974—*Hello*; *Quo* 1975—*On the Level* 1976—*Status Quo* (Vertigo, U.K.); *Blue for You* 1977—*Live* (Capitol); *Pictures of Matchstick Men* (Hallmark); *Rockin' All Over the World* (Capitol) 1978—*If You Can't Stand the Heat . . .* (Vertigo, U.K.) 1979—*In My Chair* (Mode, Fr.); *Whatever You Want* (Vertigo, U.K.); *Mean Girl* (Mode, Fr.); *Just for the Record* (Pye, U.K.) 1980—*Just Supposin'* (Vertigo, U.K.); *Gold Bars* 1981—*Never Too Late* (– Coghlan; + Pete Kircher, drums) 1982—*Rock 'n' Roll*; *1 + 9 + 8 + 2* 1983—*To Be or Not to Be*; *Back to Back* (– Lancaster; group re-forms: Rossi; Parfitt; + John Edwards, bass, + Jeff Rich, drums; + Andy Bown, kybds.) 1986—*In the Army Now* 1988—*Ain't Complaining* 1991—*Rock 'til You Drop.*

Britain's longest-running hard-rock boogie band, Status Quo have actually had only one U.K. #1 single, "Down Down" in late 1974, and one U.S. hit single, the psychedelic-pop classic "Pictures of Matchstick Men" in 1968 (#12; also a Top Ten U.K. hit).

They began playing together as the Spectres while still schoolmates, and in 1966 recorded two singles for Pye Records. In 1967 they became Traffic Jam, releasing another single, then Status Quo. By 1970 they'd dropped their high-harmony pop style for heavy-metal boogie, and their albums became consistent big sellers in the U.K., though never in the U.S., which they toured several times in the Seventies.

In England Status Quo released four albums that entered the U.K. chart at #1. Among their 45 U.K. charting singles are the Top Five hits "Caroline" (1973), "Rockin' All Over the World" (1977), "Whatever You Want" (1979), "What You're Proposing" (1980), "Marguerita Time" (1983), "In the Army Now" (1986), "Burning Bridges (On and Off and On Again)" (1988), and "The Anniversary Waltz—Part 1" (1990). This longevity and tenacity have made them legends at home, sort of the Cliff Richard of heavy metal: predictable and safe. Despite the expected rounds of personnel changes, the band has remained commercially viable. In a 1993 *Q* magazine interview with Rossi and Parfitt, the pair revealed their unpretentious and very un-rock-star-like charm. Rossi said, "So what if we're boring and only do three chords? There's no point in getting hung up about it," and "As far as I know, our lyrics mean nothing."

Stealers Wheel

Formed 1972, London, England
Gerry Rafferty (b. Apr. 16, 1947, Paisley, Scot.), gtr., voc.; Joe Egan (b. Scot.), kybds., voc.; Rab Noakes, gtr.; Ian Campbell, bass; Roger Brown, drums, voc. 1973—(– Noakes; – Campbell; – Brown; + Paul Pilnick, gtr.; + Tony Williams, bass; + Rod Coombes, drums) *Stealers Wheel* (A&M) 1974—(– Pilnick;*

– Williams; – Coombes; + Gary Taylor, bass; + Joe Jammer, gtr.; + Andrew Steele, drums) *Ferguslie Park*   1975—(+ Bernie Holland, gtr.; + Dave Wintour, bass) *Right or Wrong*   1976—*Stuck in the Middle with You.*

One of the most critically respected pop groups of the mid-Seventies, Stealers Wheel were so ridden with internal turmoil they were never able to capitalize on their one big hit, "Stuck in the Middle with You," from their Leiber-Stoller–produced debut LP, which made #6 in the U.K. and #2 in the U.S. in 1973.

Gerry Rafferty formed the original Stealers Wheel, which never recorded. The band regrouped with Rafferty, Joe Egan, and guitarist Paul Pilnick (formerly of Liverpool band the Big Three; Pilnick later worked with Badger) and drummer Rod Coombes, later of the Strawbs. Stealers Wheel's eponymously titled debut included "Stuck in the Middle with You" and went to #50 in the U.S., but Rafferty had quit before it was released, and only rejoined the band after it had become a hit.

Leiber and Stoller produced *Ferguslie Park*—for which the band included ex–Spooky Tooth guitarist Luther Grosvenor, who would go on to Mott the Hoople—and though the album was again critically acclaimed, it yielded only a Top Thirty U.S. single in "Star" and sold poorly. Rafferty and Egan, the obvious nucleus of Stealers Wheel, fell out with Leiber and Stoller before recording a third LP. Mentor Williams produced *Right or Wrong,* but its release was held up for 18 months because of managerial problems, and by the time it came out the public had apparently forgotten Stealers Wheel. Rafferty and Egan were reportedly no longer speaking to each other after the LP's release. Rafferty went on to have a briefly spectacular solo career [see entry], while Egan continued to record as well. In 1993 "Stuck in the Middle with You" was resurrected when it was featured in the Quentin Tarantino film *Reservoir Dogs.*

Tommy Steele
Born Thomas Hicks, December 17, 1936, London, England

Tommy Steele, England's first rock & roll star, was a teenaged merchant seaman when a young entrepreneur from New Zealand, John Kennedy, spotted him strumming a guitar and singing in a club in London's Soho district. Kennedy became Steele's manager and began intensively promoting the youngster as a British Elvis Presley. By early 1957, Steele had had a few top chart hits and was a big-selling teen idol in Britain and much of Europe. His U.K. Top Fifteen hits included "Rock with the Caveman" (1956); "Singing the Blues" (1957); "Nairobi" and "Come On Let's Go" (1958); "Little White Bull" (1959); and "What a Mouth" (1960).

Within a year or so of his first hits, however, Steele became dissatisfied with his image and began studying dance and acting. This led to theatrical roles in London's West End (including stints with the Old Vic company). In the early Sixties Steele starred in a British hit musical, *Half a Sixpence,* which went to Broadway with similar success and yielded a top-selling soundtrack album. Steele continued acting in musical comedies (*Finian's Rainbow, Where's Jack,* and *Singin' in the Rain*).

Steeleye Span
Formed 1969, England
Ashley Hutchings (b. Jan. 1945, London, Eng.), bass; Maddy Prior (b. Aug. 14, 1947, Blackpool, Eng.), voc.; Tim Hart (b. Jan. 9, 1948, Lincoln, Eng.), gtr., voc., dulcimer; Gay Woods, voc., concertina; Terry Woods, gtr.
1970—*Hark! The Village Wait* (Chrysalis) (– G. Woods; – T. Woods; + Martin Carthy, gtr.; + Peter Knight, fiddle, mandolin, voc.)   1971— *Please to See the King; Ten Man Mop* (– Hutchings) 1972—(– Carthy; + Rick Kemp [b. Nov. 15, 1941, Little Handford, Eng.], bass, voc.; + Bob Johnson, lead gtr., voc.) *Below the Salt*   1973—*Parcel of Rogues* 1974—(+ Nigel Pegrum, drums) *Now We Are Six* 1975—*Commoner's Crown; All Around My Hat* 1976—*Rocket Cottage*   1977—(+ John Kirkpatrick, voc., accordion; + Carthy) *Storm Force 10; Original Masters*   1978—*Live at Last* (– Knight; – Johnson; group disbands)   1980—(Group re-forms: Prior; Hart; Kemp; Johnson; Pegrum; Knight) *Sails of Silver* (Takoma)   1986—*Back In Line* (Shanachie) 1989—*Tempted and Tried; Portfolio*   1992— *Tonight's the Night, Live.*

Steeleye Span were formed with the idea of introducing electric instruments to traditional British folk music— updating mainly Seventeenth- and Eighteenth-Century works found in the journals of the English Folk Dance and Song Society.

Founder Ashley Hutchings, formerly bassist for tradrockers Fairport Convention, left that band after their *Liege and Lief.* Hutchings sought out more purely history-obsessed musicians and came up with two teams: Maddy Prior and Tim Hart (who had performed locally in St. Albans, England, and recorded three traditional albums) plus Gay and Terry Woods (a married couple who were part of the folk-rock group Sweeney's Men). The new fivesome took their name from a character in the Lincolnshire ballad "Horkston Grange" and recorded *Hark! The Village Wait* in 1970. A few months later the Woodses left, and Hart brought in Martin Carthy, another folk-scene regular, and Peter Knight.

The new lineup recorded two LPs in 1971, *Please to See the King* and *Ten Man Mop,* which included more amplification on their all-traditional pieces. They began to attract attention, especially for Maddy Prior's vocals. The group were appearing in a play written for them called *Carunna*, by Keith Dewhurst, when Hutchings lost confidence in the project and, in 1971, left to form the very traditional Albion Country Band; Carthy also left. Their replacements were the more rock-oriented Rick Kemp (who had worked with Mike Chapman and spent a week once in King Crimson) and Bob Johnson (who had played in a folk duo with Knight).

This lineup gave Steeleye their first real success. *Below the Salt* in 1972 was their U.S. debut and the Latin a cappella song "Gaudete" became a British hit in 1973. By now, Hart, Carthy, and Prior were doing solo work. In 1973 the band released *Parcel of Rogues,* with its first drummer, ex-Gnidgrolog member Nigel Pegrum. He joined full-time in 1974, making them a six-piece band, inspiring the title of their next LP, *Now We Are Six,* produced by Jethro Tull's Ian Anderson. The band members now began to write their own songs and settings for traditional lyrics. Their popularity increased in the U.K. with the gold hit single "Thomas the Rhymer." The LP also featured David Bowie playing sax on "To Know Him Is to Love Him." *Commoner's Crown* in 1975 featured actor Peter Sellers playing ukulele on "New York Girls," and the even more commercial *All Around My Hat* gave them a big British hit with the title track, and also their first U.S. charting. A cult began to grow in America, drawn to the band's live show, which featured Prior's nimble jigs. In 1976 Prior recorded the album *Silly Sisters* with traditional singer June Tabor, and the two toured England. That solo outlet was indicative of the band's splintering, though. After *Rocket Cottage* failed to sell even in England, Knight and Johnson produced a duo album, *The King of Elfland's Daughter.*

In 1977, with the newly rejoined Carthy and John Kirkpatrick, Knight and Johnson announced their departure, but first the band gave a farewell concert on March 7, 1978, captured on *Live at Last.* The group has gotten back together several times since, and the band resurfaced with the most popular lineup—Prior and Hart plus Johnson, Kemp, Knight, and Pegrum, on *Sails of Silver.* Prior released another solo LP, *Year,* in 1994.

Steel Pulse
Formed 1975, Birmingham, England
Selwyn "Bumbo" Brown (b. June 4, 1958, London, Eng.), kybds., voc.; David Hinds (b. June 15, 1956, Birmingham), gtr., voc.; Stephen "Grizzly" Nisbett (b. Mar. 15, 1948, Nevis, West Indies), drums.
1978—Handsworth Revolution (Mango) 1979—Tribute to the Martyrs 1980—Reggae Fever 1982—True Democracy (Elektra) 1983—Earth Crisis 1984—Reggae Greats (Mango) 1986—Babylon the Bandit (Elektra) 1988—State of Emergency
(MCA) 1991—Victims 1992—Rastafari Centennial 1994—Vex.

Steel Pulse was one of the prime movers in the movement that cross-fertilized reggae rhythms with punk's energy. David Hinds and Selwyn Brown were inspired to start Steel Pulse by listening to Bob Marley and the Wailers' *Catch a Fire.* By 1976, with punk in full swing, the group began to play punk venues such as Manchester's Electric Circus and the Hope and Anchor in London.

Though originally a traditional sounding reggae unit, the band experimented with lusher production after moving to Elektra in 1982. While Steel Pulse's loose-limbed grooves and Brown's soaring vocals caught most listener's ears, Steel Pulse's politics have played a large part of its career. The group was among the early leaders of the Rock Against Racism movement in the late Seventies; in the late Eighties, Hinds joined a million-dollar class-action suit against the New York City Taxi and Limousine Commission after repeatedly being ignored by New York's cab drivers. Steel Pulse's radicalism has not lost it admirers; the band's 1986 album *Babylon the Bandit* won the Best Reggae Album Grammy, and the live *Rastafari Centennial* was nominated for the award in 1992.

Steely Dan
Formed 1972, Los Angeles, California
Walter Becker (b. Feb. 20, 1950, Queens, N.Y.), bass, gtr., voc.; Donald Fagen (b. Jan. 10, 1948, Passaic, N.J.), kybds., voc.; Denny Dias, gtr.; Jim Hodder (d. June 5, 1990), drums.
1971—You Gotta Walk It Like You Talk It soundtrack (Spark) 1972—(+ David Palmer, kybds., voc.; + Jeffrey "Skunk" Baxter [b. Dec. 13, 1948, Washington, D.C.], gtr.) Can't Buy a Thrill (ABC) 1973—(– Palmer) Countdown to Ecstasy 1974—(– Hodder; + Michael McDonald [b. Feb. 12, 1952, St. Louis, Mo.], voc., kybds.; + Jeff Porcaro [b. Apr. 1, 1954, Calif.; d. Aug. 5, 1992, Holden Hills, Calif.], drums) Pretzel Logic 1975—(– Baxter; + various sessionmen, including Elliot Randall, gtr.; Larry Carlton, gtr.; David Paich and Michael Omartian, kybds.; Wilton Felder, bass; Victor Feldman, perc., kybds.) Katy Lied (– McDonald) 1976—(– Porcaro; + sessionmen) The Royal Scam 1977—Aja 1978—Greatest Hits 1979—(– Dias; + sessionmen) 1980—Gaucho (MCA) 1982—Steely Dan Gold 1993—Citizen Steely Dan 1972–1980.
Donald Fagen solo: 1982—The Nightfly (Warner Bros.) 1993—Kamakiriad (Reprise).
With the New York Rock and Soul Revue: 1991—Live at the Beacon (Giant).
Walter Becker solo: 1994—11 Tracks of Whack (Giant).

Less a band than a concept, Steely Dan was one of the most advanced, successful, and mysterious pop units of the Seventies. Combining pop hooks with jazz harmonies, complicated time changes and cryptic, often highly ironic lyrics, the band sounded like no one else. Because of the perfectionism of founders Donald Fagen and Walter Becker, the outfit rarely toured, and toward the end was composed almost entirely of session musicians, while Becker and Fagen began to play less and less on their own albums. Producer Gary Katz became Steely Dan's "third member," as much because of Becker and Fagen's insistence on pristine sound quality as for Katz's role in forming the band. With Becker and Fagen fronting a version of Steely Dan that toured to great success in 1993, they proved that their long-lived cult was very much alive.

Meeting in 1967 at Bard College in upstate New York, Becker and Fagen played in amateur bands, ranging from jazz to rock to pop to progressive rock. One—Bad Rock Group—included future comedian Chevy Chase on drums. Becker and Fagen began composing together and toured from 1970 to 1971 as backing musicians for Jay and the Americans under the pseudonyms Tristan Fabriani (Fagen) and Gustav Mahler (Becker). They also wrote and recorded the album *You Gotta Walk It Like You Talk It,* produced by Kenny Vance of Jay and the Americans. They tried unsuccessfully to start a Long Island band with guitarist Denny Dias, then moved to New York City to sell their tunes to publishers, but had little success aside from placing "I Mean to Shine" on a Barbra Streisand album. They did, however, meet independent producer Gary Katz, who enlisted them at ABC/Dunhill Records in L.A. as staff songwriters as a stipulation to accepting his own contract as a staff producer. It was Katz who hatched the idea for what would become Steely Dan. Steely Dan was the name of a dildo in William Burroughs' *Naked Lunch.*

Steely Dan's debut, *Can't Buy a Thrill* (#17, 1972), yielded two hit singles, "Do It Again" (#6, 1972) and, featuring guitarist Elliot Randall, "Reeling in the Years" (#11, 1973). Hailed by critics, the album sold well. Put off by a singles-oriented audience, as well as inadequate rehearsals, Becker, Fagen, and Katz considered Steely Dan's first tour a total disaster. *Countdown to Ecstasy* (#35, 1973) contained no hit singles.

On their next effort, Steely Dan were joined by singer/keyboardist Michael McDonald, who sang mostly backup vocals. *Pretzel Logic* (#8, 1974) featured "Rikki Don't Lose That Number" (#4, 1974) and more pronounced jazz leanings; the opening of "Rikki" was a nod to hard-bop pianist Horace Silver, and "Parker's Band" saluted be-bop giant Charlie Parker. In 1974 Steely Dan went on their last tour. Hodder resumed session work; Baxter and then McDonald joined the Doobie Brothers [see entry]; though Dias continued to work with Becker

and Fagen for some time, he also returned to playing sessions. Becker and Fagen amassed enormous debts by spending lengthy spells in the studio with high-priced sessionmen. *Katy Lied* (#13, 1975), the first Steely Dan LP by Becker and Fagen plus session players, contained a single that inched into the Top Forty, "Black Friday" (#37, 1975), and featured a solo on "Dr. Wu" by jazz alto saxophonist Phil Woods. The DBX noise-reduction system used to enhance the sound malfunctioned, and the album's sleeve contained a lengthy explanation of the technology used from Becker, Fagen, and Katz; still, it sounded cleaner than most contemporary releases. A scheduled tour was scrapped during rehearsals.

The Royal Scam, like most Steely Dan albums, sold well (#15, 1976) and presented some of Becker/Fagen's most mordant lyrics. The seven-song *Aja* (#3, 1977), which included FM favorites like "Peg" (#11, 1977) and "Deacon Blues" (#19, 1978), played by such expert sidemen as the Crusaders, Wayne Shorter, and Lee Ritenour, went Top Five within three weeks of its release and became the band's first platinum album.

In 1978 jazz bandleader Woody Herman's Thundering Herd Big Band recorded five Becker-Fagen songs, selected by and under the supervision of the duo. A subsequent contractual dispute with MCA (which had absorbed ABC Records) delayed the release of *Gaucho* (#9, 1980), which yielded "Hey Nineteen" (#10, 1980) and featured guitar work by Mark Knopfler and Rick Derringer. Its B side was Steely Dan's only live recording, "Bodhisattva," from the 1974 tour. Also in 1978, Steely Dan's contribution to the movie *FM,* "FM (No Static at All)" (#22), was that soundtrack's highlight. In 1980 Becker suffered a broken leg and other injuries when a car hit him while he was walking in Manhattan.

The following year Becker and Fagen announced that they would go separate ways, though their management denied it would be a permanent separation. In 1982 *Gaucho* won a Grammy for Best Engineered Album, as had *Aja* in 1978. Such passion for sonic detail paid off when, during the Eighties and the advent of CDs, Steely Dan's highly crafted catalogue steadily sold. Fagen released his solo *The Nightfly* in 1982 to stellar reviews, then waited until 1993 for the Becker-produced *Kamakiriad.* During that time, Becker produced such artists as Rickie Lee Jones and China Crisis and handled production work for New Age label Windham Hill and jazz label Triloka. After his girlfriend died from an overdose (her mother tried to sue Becker, claiming that he had fostered the young woman's drug problem), Becker overcame his own substance-abuse problems. In the early Nineties, Becker and Fagen appeared in concert with the New York Rock and Soul Revue alongside Boz Scaggs, Phoebe Snow, and Michael McDonald, documenting the gigs on 1991's *Live at the Beacon.*

In 1993, nearly two decades since their last concert,

Becker and Fagen headed an 11-piece version of Steely Dan that reprised their works in a U.S. tour. Also that year, Becker began working on an album of his own, *11 Tracks of Whack,* which was released in 1994.

Jim Steinman: See Meat Loaf

Steppenwolf

Formed 1967, Los Angeles, California
John Kay (b. Joachim F. Krauledat, Apr. 12, 1944, Tilsit, Germany), gtr., voc.; Michael Monarch (b. July 5, 1950, Los Angeles), gtr.; Goldy McJohn (b. John Goadsby, May 2, 1945), organ; Rushton Moreve (b. ca. 1948, Los Angeles; d. July 1, 1981, Los Angeles), bass; Jerry Edmonton (b. Jerry Mc-Crohan, Oct. 24, 1946, Can.; d. Nov. 28, 1993, near Santa Ynez, Calif.), drums.
1968—(– Moreve; + John Russell Morgan, bass) *Steppenwolf* **(Dunhill);** *Steppenwolf the Second* **1969—***Early Steppenwolf* **(– Monarch; – Morgan; + Larry Byrom [b. Dec. 27, 1948, U.S.], gtr.; + Nick St. Nicholas [b. Klaus Karl Kassbaum, Sep. 28, 1943, Plön, Ger.], bass)** *Steppenwolf at Your Birthday Party* **(– St. Nicholas; + George Biondi [b. Sep. 3, 1945, Brooklyn, N.Y.], bass);** *Monster* **1970—***Steppenwolf Live;* *Steppenwolf 7* **1971—***Steppenwolf Gold/Their Greatest Hits* **(– Byrom; + Kent Henry, gtr.);** *For Ladies Only* **1972—***Rest in Peace* **(group disbands) 1973—***16 Greatest Hits* **1974—(Group re-forms: Kay; Edmonton; McJohn; Biondi; + Bobby Cochran [b. Minn.], gtr.)** *Slow Flux* **(Epic) 1975— (– McJohn; + Andy Chapin [d. Dec. 31, 1985, DeKalb, Tex.], kybds.; – Chapin; + Wayne Cook, kybds.)** *Hour of the Wolf* **(Epic) (group disbands) 1976—***Skullduggery* **1977—***Reborn to Be Wild* **1980—(Kay re-forms Steppenwolf as John Kay and Steppenwolf with all new members) 1981—***John Kay and Steppenwolf Live in London* **(Mercury, Austral.) 1982—***Wolftracks* **(Allegiance) 1984—***Paradox* **(Attic, Can.) 1987—***Rock & Roll Rebels* **(Qwil) 1990—***Rise and Shine* **(I.R.S.) 1991—***Born to Be Wild—A Retrospective* **(MCA) 1994—***Live at 25* **(ERA).**
John Kay solo: 1972—*Forgotten Songs and Unsung Heroes* **(Dunhill) 1973—***My Sportin' Life* **1978— ***All in Good Time* **(Mercury) 1987—***Lone Steppenwolf.*

Though tangentially identified with late-Sixties West Coast psychedelia, Steppenwolf's music was uncompromising hard rock, and the term "heavy metal" was popularized in their first hit, "Born to Be Wild."

Leader John Kay, never seen without sunglasses, in part because he has been legally blind since childhood, escaped from East Germany to West Germany with his war-widowed mother in 1948. Ten years later he emigrated to Canada with his mother and stepfather. A gym teacher who could not pronounce "Joachim" informally rechristened him John; several years later he adopted the Kay surname. In 1963 Kay and his family moved to Buffalo, New York, then to Santa Monica, California, where Kay fell into the burgeoning folk-rock scene and appeared on his first record playing harmonica on a song called "The Frog." He played around the country as a folk singer, and in New York met Jerry Edmonton, of a popular Canadian group called the Sparrows, a group that included Bruce Palmer, who was later replaced by the bass player from Neil Young and Rick James' group the Mynah Birds, Nick St. Nicholas. In 1965 Kay joined the Sparrows, followed by another ex–Mynah Bird, Goldy McJohn.

The group toured and recorded (including an early version of Hoyt Axton's "The Pusher") without success and eventually broke up. In 1968 ABC-Dunhill producer Gabriel Mekler encouraged Kay to re-form the group and offered them studio time to make demos. Jerry Edmonton's brother Dennis (a.k.a. Mars Bonfire) offered the group a song he'd written for his solo album, "Born to Be Wild." Opposed to reviving the Sparrow name, the group went with Mekler's suggestion, inspired by the Hermann Hesse novel he had just read: Steppenwolf.

Steppenwolf's hard rock won them favor with local audiences, and *Steppenwolf* (#6, 1968) yielded "Born to Be Wild" (#2, 1968). *The Second* yielded another massive hit single in "Magic Carpet Ride" (#3, 1968), and around the same time, "Born to Be Wild" and "The Pusher" were featured in the film *Easy Rider,* more or less solidifying Steppenwolf's enduring identification as a biker band. *At Your Birthday Party* (#7, 1969) continued the streak with "Rock Me" (from the film *Candy*) (#10, 1969). *Early Steppenwolf* (#29, 1969) consisted of older Steppenwolf demos.

Despite the tough image—in addition to his sunglasses, Kay was never seen in anything but tight black leather pants—that song gave them, Steppenwolf (which by 1969 included two members whose families had escaped postwar Germany) were an unabashedly political band. Contrary to a popular rumor, Kay did not run for a Los Angeles city council seat or any other elective post. However, he was always regarded as a highly articulate and thoughtful spokesperson for his political beliefs, most clearly articulated on the critically blasted 1969 concept work *Monster* (#17, 1970). From this album came two singles: "Move Over" (#31, 1969) and the title track (#39, 1970). *Steppenwolf Live* (#7, 1970) contained the group's next-to-last Top Forty single, "Hey Lawdy Mama" (#35, 1970). Although the big hits stopped coming, Steppenwolf remained a popular live act here and abroad, and their later albums—*Steppenwolf 7* (#19, 1970), *Steppenwolf Gold/Their Greatest Hits* (#24, 1971), and *For Ladies Only* (#54, 1971)—fared respectably, despite a lack of focus and a series of personnel changes. In early 1972, the band announced its first breakup. McJohn formed a group called Damian, and later Manbeast. Edmonton worked with a band called Seven. By the first breakup, Kay had already formed the John Kay Band and recorded his first solo album, *Forgotten Songs and Unsung Heroes.* He had a minor hit single in 1972 with "I'm Movin' On."

Lack of success with their individual projects brought Kay, Edmonton, and McJohn, along with latter-day member George Biondi and Bobby Cochran (nephew of Eddie Cochran, he had worked with the Flying Burrito Brothers and Bob Weir) back together for *Slow Flux* (#47, 1974), which included "Straight Shootin' Woman" (#29, 1974), the group's last Top Forty single. McJohn departed soon after, and Andy Chapin (who would die in the plane crash that killed Rick Nelson) replaced him. When Chapin declined to go on the road, he was replaced by Wayne Cook. This lineup recorded *Hour of the Wolf,* the first album of new material in the group's history not to reach the Hot 100. Dispirited, Steppenwolf broke up again in 1976.

Kay continued with a solo career, but reassumed leadership of new Steppenwolf lineup in 1980. In the years between 1976 and 1980 several former members had toured with unprofessional bogus versions of the group (Kay and Edmonton owned the name). Since then John Kay and Steppenwolf have recorded regularly and toured North America, Europe, and the Far East. The group appeared at Farm Aid II and III. In 1989 Kay moved to Tennessee, where he now lives. In 1994 he published his autobiography, cowritten with John Einarson, *Magic Carpet Ride: The Autobiography of John Kay and Steppenwolf.*

Most former members of Steppenwolf have remained in the music business. McJohn continues to perform in and around Seattle; St. Nicholas runs a management company and performs Christian rock; Michael Monarch formed Detective and is now part of a country songwriting duo, Stevens and Monarch; Larry Byrom is a country sessionman. Rushton Moreve died in a car accident. Edmonton, who married the widow of former Steppenwolf member Andy Chapin, was himself killed in a car accident near Santa Ynez, California.

Stetsasonic

Formed 1981, Brooklyn, New York
Daddy-O (b. Glenn Bolton, Feb. 20, 1961, Brooklyn), voc.; Delite (b. Martin Wright, Nov. 5, 1959, Queens, N.Y.), voc.; Fruitkwan (b. Bobby Simmons, May 7, 1967, Brooklyn), voc.; Wise (b. Leonard Roman, Aug. 20, 1965, Brooklyn), voc., mixer; Prince Paul (b. Paul Houston, Apr. 2, 1967, Long Island, N.Y.), mixer; DBC (b. Marvin Nemley, June 22, 1959), kybds., drums, turntable.

1986—*On Fire* (Tommy Boy)   1988—*Sally* EP; *In Full Gear*   1991—*Blood, Sweat & No Tears.*

Calling itself "the one and only hip-hop band and the future of soul music," the six-piece Stetsasonic was an ambitious rap group boasting multiple vocalists, live drums, keyboards, and two full-time mixers. Rappers Daddy-O and Delite formed the Stetson Brothers, named for the Stetson hat company, in 1982, and began performing at seminal New York hip-hop clubs. By 1984 they'd recruited Wise, Prince Paul, Fruitkwan, and DBC, changed the name to Stetsasonic, and begun work on 1986's *On Fire.* It took two years for the group to follow up with the critically acclaimed *In Full Gear,* which contained its sole hit single, "Sally" (#25 R&B, 1988). Stetsasonic hit its creative peak with *Blood, Sweat & No Tears,* but broke up shortly after its release. Leader Daddy-O continued producing (he mixed a song for rockers Sonic Youth) and released a solo album, *You Can Be a Daddy, but Never a Daddy-O,* in 1993. Prince Paul went to work as producer of De La Soul during recording of that group's 1989 debut.

Cat Stevens

Born Steven Demetri Georgiou, July 21, 1947, London, England
1967—*Matthew and Son* (Deram)   1968—*New Masters*   1970—*World of Cat Stevens* (Decca); *Mona Bone Jakon* (A&M); *Cats Cradle* (London)   1971—*Tea for the Tillerman* (A&M); *Teaser and the Firecat* 1972—*Very Young and Early Songs* (Deram); *Catch Bull at Four* (A&M)   1973—*Foreigner*   1974—*Buddah and the Chocolate Box*   1975—*Numbers; Greatest Hits*   1977—*Izitso*   1978—*Back to Earth* 1984—*Footsteps in the Dark—Greatest Hits, vol. 2* 1988—*Classics, Volume 24.*

Cat Stevens was one of the most successful singer/songwriters of the first half of the Seventies, and several of his soft, romantic, and sometimes mystical singles were Top Ten hits. After eight gold albums in a row, his star began to fade, and in the late Seventies, following a near-drowning, he converted to Islam, changed his name to Yusef Islam, and dropped out of music.

The son of a Greek father and Swedish mother, Stevens spent his early youth developing a love of Greek folk songs and dances. By the time he entered secondary school, he had also taken an interest in rock & roll and English and American folk music. While attending Hammersmith College in the mid-Sixties, he began writing his own songs and performing solo.

In 1966 independent producer Mike Hurst (formerly with the Springfields) produced Stevens' first U.K. hit single, "I Love My Dog." In 1967 "Matthew and Son" went to #2 on the British chart. Meanwhile, Stevens' tunes

Cat Stevens

were British hits for other performers as well. P. P. Arnold hit with "The First Cut Is the Deepest" (later covered by Rod Stewart), the Tremeloes with "Here Comes My Baby." Stevens toured England and Europe, becoming something of a teen idol, and shared bills with Jimi Hendrix and Engelbert Humperdinck, among others.

But Stevens became disenchanted with what he considered the shallowness of his ventures. After his 1968 hit "I'm Gonna Get Me a Gun" (#6 U.K.), he tried to work ambitious classical arrangements into his tunes, to his producers' chagrin. Stevens' career then came to a standstill when he contracted a near-fatal case of tuberculosis in late 1968 and was confined to a hospital for a year. He took that time to work on his new material, which was unveiled on *Mona Bone Jakon,* a critical success that yielded a British hit single in "Lady D'Arbanville" (#8 U.K., 1970) (purportedly about the actress Patti D'Arbanville). The muted accompaniment was by flutist Peter Gabriel (who would soon find his own fame in Genesis), percussionist Harvey Burns, and perennial Stevens collaborator guitarist Alun Davies.

Stevens' next album, *Tea for the Tillerman,* hit the U.S. Top Ten and stayed on the charts for well over a year, yielding the hit "Wild World." Stevens was now a highly successful concert performer as well. The next album was another hit; *Teaser and the Firecat* went to #3, then gold, and contained the hits "Morning Has Broken" (#6), "Peace Train" (#7), and "Moon Shadow" (#30). Though *Catch Bull at Four* and *Foreigner* were also certified gold, they yielded no big hits. At that time, unbeknownst to many of his fans, Stevens was living in Brazil, donating much of his earnings to charities such as UNESCO. With *Buddah and the Chocolate Box,* featuring

"Oh Very Young" (#10), and *Numbers,* Stevens' sales dropped off.

In 1975 Stevens began studying the Koran and later converted to the Moslem religion and changed his name. In late 1981 he announced, "I'm no longer seeking applause and fame," and auctioned off all his material possessions, including his gold records. By then he had married Fouzia Ali; as of the late Eighties, they had five children, and he was running a Moslem school outside London. In 1987 10,000 Maniacs covered "Peace Train," and the following year Maxi Priest hit the U.K. Top Ten with a version of "Wild World." What might have grown into a Stevens revival, however, was nipped in 1989, after the former singer stated that *The Satanic Verses* author Salman Rushdie deserved to be killed for blaspheming the Moslem faith. Since then, American radio stations have observed an airplay boycott of his material; 10,000 Maniacs removed "Peace Train" from later pressings of the album it first appeared on.

Al Stewart

Born September 5, 1945, Glasgow, Scotland
1967—*Bedsitter Images* (Columbia, U.K.)   1969—
***Love Chronicles* (Epic)   1970—*Zero She Flies* (Columbia, U.K.)   1972—*Orange*   1974—*Past, Present and Future* (Janus)   1975—*Modern Times*   1976—**
***The Year of the Cat*   1978—*Time Passages* (Arista)**
1980—*24 Carrots*   1981—*Indian Summer Live*
1984—*Russians and Americans* (Passport)   1988—
Last Days of the Century* (Enigma)   1992—*Rhymes in Rooms* (Mesa)   1994—*Famous Last Words.

British folk-rocker Al Stewart sold many records in the late Seventies with a sound influenced by mid-period Dylan and some distinctive name-dropping lyrics that focused on historical themes from Napoleonic invasions to Nostradamus.

Stewart, who moved to London with his widowed mother when he was three, first played in rock bands in Bournemouth beginning at age 16. He bought his first guitar from future Police-man Andy Summers and got his first guitar lessons from Robert Fripp. But after hearing Bob Dylan, he started performing his own softer compositions at small London folk clubs in the mid-Sixties. Of his first four albums, Columbia allowed only one to be released in the U.S., 1969's *Love Chronicles.* It featured Jimmy Page on guitar and was voted Folk Album of the Year by *Melody Maker*; it contained a lengthy confessional, explicit (including the word *fucking*) song about women Stewart had known.

Stewart signed with Janus Records in 1974 and released *Past, Present and Future.* Unlike his four previous LPs (which he's since repudiated), this record traded first-person love songs for historical sagas and received his first American FM airplay.

Modern Times improved the style with catchier melodies and harder-rocking music, helping it to reach the U.S. Top Thirty. His breakthrough came in late 1976 with *The Year of the Cat*. The title single became a Top Ten hit, and the LP went platinum. Stewart then switched to Arista, sparking a complicated lawsuit.

Time Passages, produced by Alan Parsons, like its predecessor, was Top Ten and platinum. Despite two more Top Thirty singles, "Song on the Radio" (1979) and "Midnight Rocks" (1980), subsequent LPs were commercial disappointments. Through the Eighties, he released just two more albums, though he toured intermittently and apparently devoted a great deal of time to collecting wine (he has received numerous awards for this). He began touring again in 1988; *Rhymes in Rooms* is a live recording from these shows.

Billy Stewart

Born March 24, 1937, Washington, D.C.; died January, 17, 1970, North Carolina
1982—*The Greatest* (Chess)　1988—*One More Time*.

Billy Stewart qualifies as a unique entry in that he is rock's only high-powered scat man (hence his nickname "Motormouth"), using his outrageous trill to rip the stuffing out of such standards as "Summertime," "Secret Love," and "Every Day I Have the Blues" (#74, 1967).

Son of a piano teacher who had her own gospel group, the Stewart Gospel Singers (Billy was a member during his late teens), he won an amateur contest in Washington with a rendition of "Summertime." This led to club bookings and later to his discovery by Bo Diddley, with whose band he played for two years. Meanwhile he cut his first single, "Billy's Blues (Parts I and 2)," and later sang with the Rainbows, who included in their quartet Don Covay.

Stewart then signed with the Okeh label; in 1961 he returned to Chess, and in 1966 he hit the Top 100 (his sixth entry) with the scorching version of George Gershwin's "Summertime" (#10), from *Porgy and Bess*, followed that same year by his equally dynamic cover of Fain and Webster's "Secret Love" (#29). Four years later, he and two members of his band were killed when their car plunged into the Neuse River in North Carolina.

Dave Stewart: See Eurythmics

John Stewart

Born September 5, 1939, San Diego, California
1968—*Signals Through the Glass* (Capitol)　1969—*California Bloodlines*　1970—*Willard*　1971—*The Lonesome Picker Rides Again* (Warner Bros.)　1972—*Sunstorm*　1973—*Cannons in the Rain* (RCA)　1974—*Phoenix Concerts Live*　1975—*Wingless An-* *gels*　1977—*Fire in the Wind* (RSO)　1979—*Bombs Away Dream Babies*　1980—*Dream Babies Go Hollywood*; *In Concert* (RCA); *Forgotten Songs*　1984—*Centennial* (Homecoming)　1986—*Secret Tapes '86*　1985—*The Last Campaign*　1987—*Trio Years* (with Nick Reynolds); *Punch the Big Guy* (Shanachie)　1991—*Neon Beach, Live 1990* (Homecoming); *Deep in the Noon*　1992—*Bullets in the Hour Glass* (Shanachie)　1993—*Chilly Winds* (Folk Era); *John Stewart: American Originals* (Capitol)　1994—*Johnny's Time Machine* (Shanachie).**

Despite a fairly successful solo career, singer/songwriter John Stewart is probably best remembered as the composer of the Monkees' hit "Daydream Believer" and as a member of the Kingston Trio.

At Pomona College in the mid-Fifties, Frank Zappa taught Stewart the chords to "Streets of Laredo." Stewart went on to form a garage-rock band, the Furies, which recorded a single in the late Fifties. Two of Stewart's tunes had been recorded by the Kingston Trio, and when the trio's manager, Frank Werber, told Stewart he was looking for a similar act to sign, Stewart formed the Cumberland Three, which included his former glee-club teacher, Gil Robbins. In July 1961 Stewart replaced Dave Guard in the Kingston Trio, staying on as a salaried member until 1967. Before leaving, Stewart had tried unsuccessfully to form a band with John Phillips (later of the Mamas and the Papas) and Scott McKenzie. He had also formed a short-lived duo with John Denver before either had gained any fame.

Nineteen-sixty-seven's "Daydream Believer" spurred Stewart on to a solo career. His debut LP flopped commercially, but *Bloodlines*, recorded in Nashville, received some critical acclaim and fared slightly better.

Despite his general lack of commercial success, Stewart has maintained pockets of loyal cultists around the country, especially in Phoenix, where his live LP was recorded in 1974. He finally had some success in 1979 with *Bombs Away Dream Babies*, produced by Lindsey Buckingham and featuring Stevie Nicks on backing vocals on the hit single "Gold," which went to #5 in the U.S. Stewart's subsequent Top Forty singles were "Midnight Wind" (#28, 1979), which also featured Buckingham and Nicks, and "Lost Her in the Sun" (#34, 1980). Stewart continues to write, record, and perform. He founded his own label, Homecoming. *Trio Years* features new versions of Kingston Trio songs.

Rod Stewart

Born January 10, 1945, London, England
1969—*The Rod Stewart Album* (Mercury)　1970—*Gasoline Alley*　1971—*Every Picture Tells a Story*　1972—*Never a Dull Moment*　1973—*Sing It Again Rod*　1974—*Smiler*　1975—*Atlantic Crossing*

(Warner Bros.) 1976—*A Night on the Town; The Best of Rod Stewart* (Mercury) 1977—*The Best of Rod Stewart, vol. 2; Foot Loose and Fancy Free* (Warner Bros.) 1978—*Blondes Have More Fun* 1979—*Greatest Hits* 1980—*Foolish Behaviour* 1981—*Tonight I'm Yours* 1982—*Absolutely Live* 1983—*Body Wishes* 1984—*Camouflage* 1986—*Rod Stewart* 1988—*Out of Order* 1989—*Storyteller: The Complete Anthology: 1964–1990* 1990—*Downtown Train: Selections from the Storyteller Anthology* 1991—*Vagabond Heart* 1992—*The Mercury Anthology* (Polydor) 1993—*Unplugged . . . and Seated* (Warner Bros.) 1995—*A Spanner in the Works.*

Gritty-voiced singer and sometime songwriter Rod Stewart earned the tag "vocals extraordinaire" during his first stint with the Jeff Beck Group and maintained it during his subsequent tenure with the Faces and his commercially much more successful solo career. After earning initial critical acclaim for his unerring choice of cover material, Stewart in the late Seventies became known as a jet-setting bon vivant and bottled-blond sex symbol, always a stellar live performer but often indulging in self-parody on his albums. While his later work failed to live up to his early awesome promise, his self-mocking charm and sheer singing skill have survived. In 1994 he was inducted into the Rock and Roll Hall of Fame.

The son of a Scottish shopkeeper, Stewart was born and raised in London but considers himself a Scot. By the time he left secondary school, he longed to be a soccer player. He erected fences and dug graves until he signed as an apprentice to a pro team. But after a year of bench-warming and odd jobs, Stewart took up with bohemian folksinger Wizz Jones. Jones supposedly taught Stewart guitar and banjo, and the two performed on Continental streetcorners until they were arrested for vagrancy in Spain and deported to England in 1963. In London Stewart began hanging out at R&B clubs. He played harmonica with Jimmy Powell and the Five Dimensions, then joined the Hoochie Coochie Men. That group (with Stewart and Long John Baldry sharing vocals) lasted a year, during which time Stewart moonlighted as a session musician and recorded a single, "Good Morning Little Schoolgirl." His stylish apparel earned him the nickname "Rod the Mod."

Baldry disbanded the Hoochie Coochie Men in 1965 to form Steampacket with Brian Auger and Julie Driscoll and again called on Stewart to share the vocals. Stewart left the group in 1966 following a dispute with Baldry, although in 1971 he and Elton John coproduced Baldry's *It Ain't Easy*. He joined Shotgun Express, which included future Fleetwood Mac guitarist Peter Green and drummer Mick Fleetwood. Modeled after Steampacket, the Express couldn't shake that group's shadow and broke up within a year.

In 1967 Jeff Beck enlisted Stewart as vocalist for the Jeff Beck Group [see entry]. Beck was especially popular in America, where the new group first toured in 1968. Petrified by the first-night audience at New York's Fillmore East, Stewart sang the opening number from backstage. *Truth* (1968) and *Beck-Ola* (1969) established Stewart as a vocal stylist, and his tenure with Beck taught him to phrase his sandpaper voice around the lead instrument.

In 1969 while still with Beck, Stewart signed a contract with Mercury. His solo debut, *The Rod Stewart Album* (#139, 1969) (originally titled *An Old Raincoat Won't Ever Let You Down*), was recorded with Mick Waller and Ron Wood of the Jeff Beck Group plus Small Faces keyboardist Ian McLagan and guitarist Martin Quittenton. Stewart's material was a grab bag of gentle folk songs, bawdy drinking songs, a taste of soul, and a couple of barrelhouse rockers. The album sold modestly—Jeff Beck Group fans considered it too subdued—but critics were impressed by Stewart's five original songs.

Planning to form a new band with Stewart and the Vanilla Fudge's Tim Bogert and Carmine Appice, Beck disbanded his group. That project finally materialized in 1972, long after Stewart and his buddy Wood had joined the Small Faces, soon redubbed the Faces [see entry]. Stewart spent the next seven years dividing his time between that band and a solo career, recording a Faces album for each of his own.

In 1970 the Faces recorded *First Step,* Stewart recorded *Gasoline Alley* (#27, 1970), and together they toured the United States twice. In the studio with the Faces, Stewart was but one of a quintet of equals merrily banging out rock & roll. On his own, he was different; the moody *Gasoline Alley* amplified his reputation as a singer and storyteller. When *Every Picture Tells a Story* came out in June 1971, the response was swift and strong. In October, the album went to #1 in America and Britain simultaneously, the first record to do so. Its first single, "Maggie May," a Stewart-Quittenton song, was the second record to do the same. Before "Maggie May" had faded, Stewart followed up with a gritty version of the Temptations' "(I Know) I'm Losing You" (#24, 1971). *Never a Dull Moment* (#2, 1972), with his own "You Wear It Well" (#13, 1972), was also a hit.

With two gold albums, Stewart's role in the Faces became strained. Their records were never as popular as Stewart's, and more than the occasional gig was undermined by the group's sodden sloppiness. Bassist Ronnie Lane quit in 1973, to be replaced by Tetsu Yamauchi, and legal battles were waged between Mercury and Warners (with whom Stewart had signed a new solo contract) over control of the Faces. While court proceedings kept him out of the studio, Mercury released a greatest-hits compilation, *Sing It Again Rod*. The next year, the disputing companies jointly issued *Coast to Coast: Overture and Beginnings,* a live album billed under "Rod Stewart/Faces Live." Late in 1974, Mercury released *Smiler* (#13, 1974), Stewart's last album for the label.

Stewart hired veteran American producer Tom Dowd and Muscle Shoals session musicians to record his Warner Bros. debut, *Atlantic Crossing* (#9, 1975). In 1975 he moved to Los Angeles to escape British income taxes and was soon the toast of the Beverly Hills celebrity set. His romance with Swedish movie starlet Britt Ekland (which ended in 1977 with a $15-million palimony suit, settled out of court) added juice to her autobiography, *True Britt,* and made him a gossip-column staple. It was the first of his liaisons with glamorous blondes. In 1979 he married Alana Hamilton, former wife of George Hamilton IV, and with her had two children; later he lived for six years with model Kelly Emberg, who also bore him a child (after the relationship ended, Emberg demanded $25 million in palimony). In 1990 he married model Rachel Hunter; they have two children.

Stewart retained Dowd and the American studio musicians for the double-platinum *A Night on the Town* (#2, 1976), his first effort to outsell *Every Picture,* largely on the strength of the biggest single of 1976, "Tonight's the Night (Gonna Be Alright)," which topped the U.S. chart for eight weeks. That year the Royal Navy adopted Stewart's cover of the Sutherland Brothers' "Sailing" as its unofficial anthem; the following year, two other singles, Cat Stevens' "The First Cut Is the Deepest" (#21, 1977) and "The Killing of Georgie (Part I & II)" (#30, 1977), about a gay friend's murder, made Stewart a star in the previously indifferent international market.

The Faces had by now fallen apart, and Wood was a full-fledged Rolling Stone. Stewart formed a new, American touring band. The hits kept coming: raunchy rockers like "Hot Legs" (#28, 1978), romantic ballads like "You're in My Heart (The Final Acclaim)" (#4, 1977), and even a #1 disco hit with "Da Ya Think I'm Sexy?" (1979). That song was damned by critics as Stewart's ultimate fall from his earlier grace; Stewart has continued to donate its royalties to UNICEF (upward of $1 million), and in the Nineties himself admitted to its tastelessness.

Of his Eighties albums, *Foolish Behaviour, Tonight I'm Yours,* and *Out of Order* all went platinum, and Stewart released Top Ten singles throughout the decade, among them "Passion" (#5, 1980), "Infatuation" (#6, 1984), "My Heart Can't Tell You No" (#4, 1988), and "Downtown Train" (#3, 1989). By and large critics continued to assail him but conceded the merit of such occasional efforts as his 1985 collaboration with Jeff Beck on the Impressions' "People Get Ready," from Beck's *Flash.*

In 1986 Stewart and a re-formed Faces gathered for a one-off performance at a London benefit for Faces' bassist Ronnie Lane, a victim of multiple sclerosis. *Out of Order* (1988), coproduced by Chic's Bernard Edwards and former Duran Duran guitarist Andy Taylor, was better received than much of his Eighties output, boosting a revival in Stewart's critical reputation that blossomed with the 1990 career overview, *Storyteller.* In 1993 Stewart put out *Unplugged . . . and Seated,* which went on to sell five million copies worldwide. *A Spanner in the Works* (#35, 1995) continued Stewart's more acoustic musical approach.

Stephen Stills: See Buffalo Springfield; Crosby, Stills, Nash and Young

Sting
Born Gordon Matthew Sumner, October 2, 1951, Newcastle, England
1985—*The Dream of the Blue Turtles* (A&M) 1986—*Bring On the Night* 1987—. . . *Nothing Like the Sun* 1988—*Nada Como el Sol* EP 1991—*The Soul Cages* 1993—*Ten Summoner's Tales*; Demolition Man soundtrack 1994—*Fields of Gold: The Best of Sting.*

Having achieved stardom as singer, bassist, and principal songwriter for the Police [see entry], Sting dissolved that band at the peak of its career in the mid-Eighties. Sting's solo career is characterized by a restless yen to experiment and, by pop standards, take risks. He has sought to push the canny musicianship and affinity for exotic musical styles that distinguished his former group in directions that a trio could never have considered. Consequently, some have lamented the absence of the Police's striking economy, just as they've found Sting's literary and historical references pretentious. To his admirers, though, Sting's post-Police projects have ensured his place among the most articulate and intuitive rock musicians of his generation.

For his first solo effort, *The Dream of the Blue Turtles* (#2, 1985), Sting enlisted a group of young jazz musicians, including saxophonist Branford Marsalis and Weather Report drummer Omar Hakim. The album was widely viewed as a reclamation of the musical turf Sting had covered while playing in jazz ensembles during his youth. But *Turtles* also drew on elements of classical music, funk, and perhaps most predictably, reggae. Moreover, the hit songs "If You Love Somebody Set Them Free" (#3, 1985) and "Fortress Around Your Heart" (#8, 1985) were as pop-savvy as any Police singles. The 1986 concert album and documentary *Bring On the Night* featured the players that Sting had assembled for *Turtles* offering live renditions of his new songs, as well as fresh takes on a few Police favorites.

... *Nothing Like the Sun* (#9, 1987), released shortly after Sting's mother died and dedicated to her, featured a revised, expanded lineup of musicians dominated by Marsalis' saxophone. As on *Turtles,* Sting often played guitar rather than his primary instrument, bass. A moody album full of dense, delicate orchestration, *Sun* spawned only one Top Ten single, the atypically funky "We'll Be Together" (#7, 1987). (The album fared well in South America, though, thanks in part to its various Latin-flavored instrumental touches; hence the EP *Nada Como el Sol,* featuring tracks from *Sun* rendered in Spanish.)

The Soul Cages, inspired by Sting's father's death, was darker still, full of haunted ballads, religious imagery, and traditional English folk flourishes that embellished a newly spare foundation provided by guitarist Dominic Miller, keyboardist David Sancious, drummer Vinnie Colaiuta, and Sting on bass. Again, an anomaly proved the one big hit: the upbeat "All This Time" went to #5. (On that single's strength, the album peaked at #2.) Sting unexpectedly shifted gears for 1993's breezy, buoyant *Ten Summoner's Tales* (#2), which featured the same core of musicians who had appeared on *Cages.* The album went double platinum, yielding the hits "If I Ever Lose My Faith in You" (#17, 1993) (which also won a Grammy) and "Fields of Gold" (#23, 1993). That same year, Sting shared a #1 megahit single with Bryan Adams and Rod Stewart, via "All for Love," from the film *The Three Musketeers.* An anthology, *Fields of Gold,* was released in 1994, featuring two previously unreleased tracks.

Equally unpredictable outside the studio, Sting supplemented his numerous film appearances (including *Dune, Stormy Monday,* and *Plenty*) in 1989 by starring in a Broadway revival of *The Threepenny Opera;* four years later he opened a series of stadium shows for the Grateful Dead. What's remained constant is his devotion to human-rights and environmental issues. In the late Eighties he not only toured with other stars to benefit Amnesty International but helped establish the Rainforest Foundation, and he has since crusaded to raise funds and awareness on behalf of the preservation of this endangered Brazilian territory.

The Stone Roses

Formed 1985, Manchester, England
Ian George Brown (b. Feb. 20, 1963, Manchester), voc.; John Thomas Squire (b. Nov. 24, 1962, Manchester), gtr.; Andy Couzens, gtr.; Pete Garner, bass; Reni (b. Alan John Wren, Apr. 10, 1964, Manchester), drums.
1987—(– Couzens; – Garner; + Mani [b. Gary Michael Mountfield, Nov. 16, 1962, Manchester], bass) 1989—*The Stone Roses* (Silvertone) 1994—*The Second Coming* (Geffen) 1995—(– Reni) *The Complete Stone Roses* (Silverton).

An overnight success in England, the Stone Roses went from playing small clubs in the mid-Eighties to massive stadiums by decade's end, with their faces appearing all over the U.K. music papers. The quartet received little more than cursory attention in the U.S., and that primarily for their role as the most celebrated combo of Manchester's mid-Eighties psychedelic rave scene. The Roses' blend of Byrdslike chiming guitars with an updated, Smiths-style pop sensibility garnered critical acclaim, although by 1990 legal problems had set them back temporarily. After winning freedom from their original label, Silvertone, the Roses landed a reported $4-million deal with Geffen in the U.S., finally returning at the end of 1994 with *Second Coming.*

Ian Brown, an idealistic blend of beatnik, hippie, anarchist, and punk rocker, came together with self-taught painter John Squire in the early Eighties. The two formed a punk band called the Patrol, which became the Stone Roses in 1985. After a couple of singles, the Roses teamed up with producer John Leckie, who helped shape their signature psychedelic pop sound. The group signed with Silvertone in 1988 and put out a single, "Elephant Stone," which reached #8 on the U.K. charts in March 1990. Following the release of their debut album, *The Stone Roses* (#86 U.S., 1989; #19 U.K., 1990), the band had a string of U.K. hits, including "What the World Is Waiting For/Fool's Gold" (#8, 1989), "Made of Stone" (#20, 1990), "She Bangs the Drums" (#34, 1990), "One Love" (#4, 1990), "I Wanna Be Adored" (#20, 1991), "Waterfall" (#27, 1992), and "I Am the Resurrection" (#33, 1992).

In 1990 members of the band vandalized the offices of Silvertone after the label reissued old material without their permission. The case got major attention in the U.K. press. The Roses were back in court later that year when they tried to leave Silvertone for Geffen; the group won the case but lost some career momentum. Their 1994 comeback album, *Second Coming,* lived up to its name via its treatment by the U.K. media, though failed to garner great commercial success in the U.S.

Stone Temple Pilots

Formed 1987 as Mighty Joe Young, San Diego, California
Weiland (b. Scott Weiland, Oct. 27, 1967, Santa Cruz, Calif.), voc.; Dean DeLeo (b. Aug. 23, 1961, N.J.), gtr.; Robert DeLeo (b. Feb. 2, 1966, N.J.), bass; Eric Kretz (b. June 7, 1966, Santa Cruz), drums.
1992—*Core* (Atlantic) 1994—*Purple.*

In the wake of the success of the Seattle Sound, Stone Temple Pilots emerged in the early Nineties with a hard-rock approach that drew heavily on the influence of earlier guitar bands from Led Zeppelin to Blue Cheer. With their debut, *Core,* going platinum shortly after its release, they stirred controversy with "Sex Type Thing," a single about date rape and a stylistic approach that some critics felt drew too heavily on Pearl Jam's.

Having met at a Black Flag concert in the late Eighties, singer Weiland and guitarist Robert DeLeo founded Mighty Joe Young to purvey a sound combining heavy-metal–derived guitar with punk brashness; they changed the group's name to Shirley Temple's Pussy before deciding on Stone Temple Pilots. Signing to Atlantic and making the triple-platinum *Core* (#3, 1993) with producer Brendan O'Brien (the Black Crowes, the Red Hot Chili Peppers), they soon gained heavy MTV exposure and, while decrying the "grunge" label, found themselves in the same sales league as Nirvana and Pearl Jam. The single "Plush," which hit #9 on the modern-rock tracks chart, continued their commercial ascension. Their followup album, *Purple,* debuted at #1 and also went triple platinum.

Stone the Crows

Formed 1969, Glasgow, Scotland
Maggie Bell (b. Jan. 12, 1945, Scot.), voc.; Les Harvey (b. ca. 1947; d. May 3, 1972, Swansea, Wales), gtr.; Jon McGinnis, kybds.; Jim Dewar (b. Oct. 12, 1946), bass; Colin Allen, drums.
1970—*Stone the Crows* (Polydor); *Ode to John Law* 1971—(– Dewar; – McGinnis; + Steve Thompson, bass; + Ronnie Leahy, kybds.) *Teenage Licks* 1972—(+ Jimmy McCulloch [b. 1953, Glasgow; d. Sep. 27, 1979, London, Eng.], gtr.) '*Ontinuous Performance.*
Maggie Bell solo: 1973—*Queen of the Night* (Atlantic)   1975—*Suicide Sal* (Swan Song).

A Scottish-English soul band, Stone the Crows (the name comes from a Scottish curse meaning "the hell with it") is perhaps most significant for introducing Maggie Bell, a blues singer in the style of Janis Joplin, who went on to a solo career.

Young Maggie Bell had gotten onstage to sing in Glasgow with Alex Harvey (who in the early Seventies led the Sensational Alex Harvey Band), earning two pounds. Harvey introduced her to his brother Les, who was leading the Kinning Park Ramblers. Within a few years Bell and Les Harvey were leading Power, which played clubs and U.S. Army bases in Europe. When Led Zeppelin manager Peter Grant discovered them, he renamed them Stone the Crows. Their first two albums were critically acclaimed but sold few copies.

Jim Dewar eventually left to join ex–Procol Harum guitarist Robin Trower, and Steve Thompson was recruited from John Mayall; with *Teenage Licks* the band seemed on the verge of success. In 1972 Bell won Britain's Top Girl Singer Award for the first of many times, but that year also saw Les Harvey electrocuted by a microphone wire during a show at Swansea University.

Jimmy McCulloch came in to finish the sessions for '*Ontinuous,* but the band soon broke up. McCulloch later joined Paul McCartney's Wings and, after that, the reformed Small Faces; he died of undetermined causes. Bell released several solo LPs. She also did a lot of session work, including Rod Stewart's *Every Picture Tells a Story.* Colin Allen went on to join Focus.

The Stooges: See Iggy Pop

Stories

Formed 1972, New York City, New York
Michael Brown (b. Michael Lookofsky, Apr. 25, 1949, Brooklyn, N.Y.), kybds., voc.; Steve Love, gtr., voc.; Ian Lloyd (b. Ian Buoncocglio, 1947, Seattle, Wash.), bass, voc., kybds.; Bryan Madey, drums, voc.
1972—*Stories* (Kama Sutra)   1973—(– Brown; + Kenny Aaronson [b. Apr. 14, 1952, Brooklyn, N.Y.], bass; + Ken Bichel [b. 1945, Detroit, Mich.], kybds.) *About Us; Traveling Underground*   1974— (– Madey; + Rick Ranno, drums).

Formed by ex–Left Banke mentor Michael Brown, Stories had a #1 hit in 1973 with "Brother Louie." The tune was written by Errol Brown and Tony Wilson of British soul group Hot Chocolate, who released a competing version of it in 1973.

Brown left before the completion of their second LP to become the guiding spirit, writer, and producer of the Beckies (though he never actually performed with them). Bassist Kenny Aaronson went on to work with Hall and Oates, Leslie West, Rick Derringer, Billy Squier, and the supergroup Hagar, Schon, Aaronson, Shrieve. Lloyd pursued a solo career. During a session for one of his albums, musician Mick Jones met fellow sessionman Ian MacDonald, and the pair went on to form Foreigner. Lloyd has since appeared on albums by Foreigner, Peter Frampton, and others. Madey joined the Earl Slick band, and his replacement, Rick Ranno, was later in the group Starz.

The Strangeloves

Formed 1965, Brooklyn, New York
Richard Gottehrer, voc.; Robert Feldman, voc.; Jerry Goldstein, voc.
1965—*I Want Candy* (Bang).

The Strangeloves' big hit was 1965's "I Want Candy" (#11). The song was treated to some bizarre versions in the early Eighties by Lydia Lunch's 8 Eyed Spy and Bow Wow Wow. The Strangeloves were originally a studio-based writer-production trio and even worked on some outside projects while they were recording their own band. Before they'd taken their name and become a group, they worked for the Angels (creating "My

Boyfriend's Back") and the McCoys ("Hang On Sloopy").

Posing as brothers Miles, Niles, and Giles Strange, the three used fake Australian accents and actually convinced everyone they met that they indeed hailed from Down Under. They had two Top Forty followups, "Night Time" (#30, 1966) and "Cara-Lin" (#39, 1965). After 1966 the band broke up, and each member went back to full-time producing (Goldstein for War, among others). Richard Gottehrer became a partner in Sire Records in 1970, and along with the two other original Strangeloves recorded unsuccessfully for the label under the name the Strange Brothers Show. In 1976 he produced the debut Blondie LP and in 1981 he coproduced the Go-Go's' first album. Feldman worked with, among others, Jay and the Americans and Johnny Mathis.

The Stranglers

Formed September 1974, Guildford, England
Jet Black (b. Brian Duffy, Aug. 26, 1958, Ilford, Eng.), drums; Jean-Jacques Burnel (b. Feb. 21, 1952, London, Eng.), bass; Hugh Cornwell (b. Aug. 28, 1949, London), gtr., voc.; Dave Greenfield (b. Mar. 29, 1949, Brighton, Eng.), kybds.
1977—IV Rattus Norvegicus (A&M); No More Heroes
1978—Black and White   1979—The Raven (United Artists, U.K.)   1980—IV Rattus Norvegicus (I.R.S.)
1981—The Meninblack (EMI America); La Folie
1982—Feline (Epic)   1984—Aural Sculpture
1986—Dreamtime   1988—All Live and All of the Night   1990—10 (– Cornwell; + John Ellis [b. June 1, 1952, London], gtr.; + Paul Roberts [b. Dec. 31, 1959, London], voc.)   1991—Greatest Hits 1977–1990   1993—(– Black; + Tikake Tobe, drums) Stranglers in the Night (Viceroy).
Hugh Cornwell solo: 1988—Wolf (Virgin).

Armed with a nasty misogynist temperament and an aggressive musical attack, the Stranglers are usually classified as a punk band, even though their keyboard-heavy sound—and birthdates—have more in common with rock's previous generation. While never popular in the States, they were hugely successful in the U.K. with 15 Top Forty hits (seven in the Top Ten), including "Peaches" b/w "Go Buddy Go" (#8 U.K., 1977) and "Golden Brown" (#2 U.K., 1982).

Their background was unusual for a punk band: The band was formed in 1974 as the Guildford Stranglers by Hugh Cornwell, a science teacher; Jet Black, an ice cream salesman and sometimes jazz drummer; and Jean-Jacques Burnel, an English-born son of French immigrants and a history graduate. In 1975, calling themselves a "soft-rock group," the trio placed an ad in Melody Maker that was answered by Dave Greenfield. After a year of club dates the band, now simply Stranglers, got its break opening for Patti Smith at Lon-

don's Roundhouse, followed by a national tour. The exposure led to their signing with United Artists in Britain and A&M in the States.

While Greenfield's swirling keyboards and Cornwell's portentous vocals on IV Rattus Norvegicus (#4 U.K., 1977) (the biological name for the Norway rat, the band mascot) and No More Heroes (#8 U.K., 1977) left critics comparing the band to the Doors, their attitude placed them squarely in the punk camp: "Peaches" was banned by the BBC for offensive lyrics, and the Greater London Council pulled the plug on a 1977 show when Cornwell appeared on stage in a "Fuck" T-shirt. The entire band was arrested in Nice, France, for inciting a riot when a 1980 concert was canceled.

Failing to make a commercial dent in the U.S., the Stranglers were dropped by A&M after Black and White. Their lack of a U.S. label caused The Raven, a #4 U.K. hit, to go unreleased stateside until 1986. In 1983, after abortive contracts with two other labels, they signed with Epic. Attempts to soften their sound culminated in Dreamtime (#172, 1987), their only U.S. chart album.

Cornwell left the band after 10 and has yet to resurface (although he did record Wolf, a 1988 solo set, while still in the band). Except for a greatest-hits collection in 1991, nothing was heard from the Stranglers until 1993, when Burnel and Greenfield anchored a new lineup on Stranglers in the Night and hit the comeback trail. In 1995 the Stranglers' publishing company sued British alt-rock band Elastica for plagiarism; the matter was settled out of court.

The Strawberry Alarm Clock

Formed 1967, Santa Barbara, California
Ed King, gtr., voc.; Lee Freeman, gtr., bass, horns, drums, voc.; Mark Weitz, kybds.; Gary Lovetro, bass, voc.; George Bunnel, bass, special effects; Randy Seol, drums, voc.
1967—Incense and Peppermints (Uni)   1968—(– Lovetro) Wake Up, It's Tomorrow; The World in a Sea Shell   1969—(– Seol; – Bunnel; + Jimmy Pitman, gtr., voc.; + Gene Gunnels, drums) Good Morning Starshine (Uni)   1970—The Best of the Strawberry Alarm Clock (– Pitman; – Weitz; + Paul Marshall, gtr., voc.)   1971—Changes (Vocalion).

This early psychedelic rock band surfaced in 1967 with the #1 hit and flower-power anthem "Incense and Peppermints." Though it would fade quickly from view, the band was renowned for its psychedelic stage show (drummer Randy Seol played bongos with his hands on fire) and for the presence of two bassists. Guitarist Ed King later resurfaced with Lynyrd Skynyrd.

The group's roots go back to King's early surf-rock group, the Irridescents. Seol broke up his group the Goldtones to join King, Mike Luciano, and Gene Gunnels, and they named themselves Thee Sixpence. They signed to All American Records, where they released "In the Building" b/w "Hey Joe" in spring 1966. Subsequent releases faded quickly. Following a major lineup shift the group learned that there were two other bands using variations of the "sixpence" name, so in March 1967 the Strawberry Alarm Clock was born.

The singer on the group's biggest hit was not even a band member, but one Greg Munford, the teenage singer of Shapes of Sound and later Crystal Circus. "Incense and Peppermints" was the B side of "The Birdman of Alkatrash," and by the time it was released in April 1967 the group had moved to Uni. Various business problems plagued the band; for example, "Incense and Peppermints" writer Ed King was not properly credited or compensated. Seven months later, the song was at #1 and the album *Incense and Peppermints* on its way to #11. Commercially speaking, it was the group's finest hour, and although another Top Forty hit followed—"Tomorrow" (#23, 1968)—the Strawberry Alarm Clock wound down. Their version of "Good Morning Starshine," from the hit musical *Hair*, was beaten on the charts by a simultaneously released rendition by Oliver. With new member Paul Marshall, King began exploring what is now called southern rock. The group appeared in Russ Meyer's *Beyond the Valley of the Dolls* (1970), and by late 1971 had disbanded. Shortly before that, however, King met Ronnie Van Zant of Lynyrd Skynyrd. In early 1973 King joined the southern-rock band, first as a bassist then as third lead guitarist.

In the summer of 1982 Lee Freeman happened to spot an ad for Strawberry Alarm Clock at an L.A. nightclub; intrigued, he went in and discovered the ad was a fake, designed to draw in original Alarm Clock members for a reunion. Freeman told ROLLING STONE he planned to assemble most of the original personnel, which he eventually did. This lineup—which included Freeman and King (by then having left Lynyrd Skynyrd and doing session work)—rerecorded "Incense and Peppermints" for a K-Tel album. Freeman then led a lineup of new musicians as the Strawberry Alarm Clock during the Eighties.

The Strawbs

Formed as Strawberry Hill Boys, 1967, Leicester, England
Dave Cousins (b. Jan 7, 1945), voc., gtr., banjo, dulcimer; Tony Hooper, gtr., voc.; Arthur Phillips, mandolin.
1968—(– Phillips; + Ron Chesterman, bass; + Sandy Denny [b. Jan. 6, 1947, Wimbledon, Eng.; d. Apr. 21, 1978, London, Eng.], voc.) 1969—(– Chesterman; – Denny; + Rick Wakeman [b. May 18, 1949, London, Eng.], kybds.; + John Ford [b. July 1, 1948, London], bass, voc.; + Richard Hudson [b. May 9, 1948, Lon-
don], drums) *Strawbs* (A&M) 1970—(+ Claire Deniz, cello) *Dragonfly* (– Deniz); *Just a Collection of Antiques and Curios* 1971—*From the Witchwood* 1972—*Grave New World* (– Hooper; – Wakeman; + Dave Lambert [b. Mar. 8, 1949, Hounslow, Eng.], gtr.; + Blue Weaver [b. Mar. 11, 1947, Cardiff, Wales], kybds.) 1973—*Bursting at the Seams*; *All Our Own Work* (Hallmark) 1974—(– Ford; – Hudson; – Weaver; + John Hawken, kybds.; + Chas Cronk, bass; + Rod Coombes, drums) *Hero and Heroine* (A&M); *By Choice* 1975—*Ghosts* (– Hawken; + John Mealing, kybds.; + Robert Kirby, kybds.); *Nomadness* 1976—*Deep Cuts* (Oyster) 1977—*Burning for You* 1978—(– Coombes; + Tony Fernandez, drums) *Deadlines* (Arista); *Best of the Strawbs* (A&M) 1989—(Group re-forms: Cousins; Hooper; Hudson; + others) *Don't Say Goodbye* 1985—*Sandy Denny and the Strawbs* (Hannibal).

Through a long career laden with personnel changes, the Strawbs have kept in touch with both their British folk roots and the Seventies progressive-rock movement. Dave Cousins, the band's main songwriter, and Tony Hooper formed the Strawberry Hill Boys (named for the London district where they rehearsed) in 1967, singing traditional British and American folk music, then recorded with Sandy Denny (who went on to Fairport Convention) before becoming the Strawbs with the addition of Richard Hudson and John Ford, from Velvet Opera. Their debut LP won great acclaim in British folk circles, but the second, which saw them turning to a keyboard-dominated progressive sound (Nicky Hopkins guested on it), left them between audiences.

Royal Academy of Music graduate Rick Wakeman's classical arpeggios took the band decisively away from folk and into progressive rock. Wakeman left in 1971 to join Yes. His replacement was Blue Weaver, who had played with Andy Fairweather-Low's Amen Corner and, with Dave Mason, had had a minor solo career under the name Wynder K. Frogg. Shortly after Wakeman's departure, internal disagreements between Cousins and Hudson and Ford led to Cousins' temporary departure, placing the band in limbo in late 1971. Cousins recorded a solo LP, *Two Weeks Last Summer;* Strawbs then regrouped and had their first British hit singles with "Lay Down" in 1972, and in 1973 with Hudson-Ford's "Part of the Union."

After a traumatic 1973 U.S. tour, Hudson and Ford left to work as a team, with three LPs and a 1974 U.S. tour. Weaver also left, and Cousins recruited John Hawken (from Nashville Teens, Vinegar Joe, and Renaissance), Chas Cronk, and Rod Coombes (of Stealers Wheel). At this time the band's audience base shifted from the U.K. to the U.S. Though they never became a truly major American attraction, they toured the U.S.

constantly and hardly ever played the U.K. After mid-dling success with a series of progressively more commercial late-Seventies LPs, the group disbanded. Hudson, Hooper, and Cousins reunited in the late Eighties.

The Stray Cats

Formed 1979, Massapequa, New York
Brian Setzer (b. 1959), gtr., voc.; Slim Jim Phantom (b. Jim McDonell, 1961), drums; Lee Rocker (b. Lee Drucker, 1961), string bass, voc.
1981—*Stray Cats* (Arista, U.K.)   1982—*Gonna Ball*; *Built for Speed* (EMI America)   1983—*Rant 'n' Rave with the Stray Cats*   1986—*Rock Therapy*   1989—*Blast Off*   1991—*Let's Go Faster* (Jordan)   1992—*Choo Choo Hot Fish* (JRS/Great Pyramid).
Phantom, Rocker, and Slick: 1985—*Phantom, Rocker & Slick* (EMI America)   1986—*Cover Girl*.
Brian Setzer solo: 1986—*The Knife Feels Like Justice* (EMI America)   1988—*Live Nude Guitars* (EMI Manhattan).
Brian Setzer Orchestra: 1994—*The Brian Setzer Orchestra* (Hollywood).

The Stray Cats' cartoonish version of classic Fifties rockabilly proved one of the surprise successes of 1982. The group was formed in a suburban Long Island, New York, town by Brian Setzer (an ex-member of the Bloodless Pharaohs), Slim Jim Phantom, and Lee Rocker. After playing the Long Island club circuit for several months, the group moved to London with their manager in the summer of 1980.

Although New Romanticism and new wave dominated the British scene, the Stray Cats soon became a popular club act. The group signed with Arista U.K., and Dave Edmunds produced their debut single, "Runaway Boys." Released in England in November 1980, "Runaway Boys" hit the British Top Ten, as did their two subsequent singles, "Stray Cat Strut" and "Rock This Town." The Stray Cats opened three dates on the Rolling Stones' 1981 North American tour; by that time their debut LP had become a top-selling import in the U.S. Their second LP, *Gonna Ball,* was not as well received as their debut, and by 1982 there were management problems as well. Nonetheless, the group signed to EMI America, which released their U.S. debut, *Built for Speed,* containing material from the two British albums. Within months, the Stray Cats' "Rock This Town" and "Stray Cat Strut" videos were in heavy rotation on MTV; "Rock This Town" was a Top Ten hit and the album sold over 2 million copies.

Rant 'n' Rave (#14, 1983) was a more moderate hit, yielding chart singles in "Sexy + 17" (#5, 1983) and "I Won't Stand in Your Way" (#35, 1983). The band then broke up (success "went to our heads," Setzer later said).

Lee Rocker and Slim Jim Phantom (by now married to actress Britt Ekland) joined ex–David Bowie guitarist Earl Slick to form Phantom, Rocker, and Slick, releasing two albums and appearing in a 1985 Carl Perkins tribute show organized by Edmunds. Setzer released two solo albums, *The Knife Feels Like Justice* and *Live Nude Guitars.* He also played Eddie Cochran (at the request of Cochran's mother) in the 1987 Ritchie Valens biopic, *La Bamba.* The original Stray Cats re-formed in 1986 for two U.S. albums, neither of which cracked the Top 100, and two more albums on small, independent labels. Setzer reemerged in 1994 with *The Brian Setzer Orchestra,* leading a 16-piece swing orchestra, playing big-band arrangements of rock, rockabilly, and pop standards.

Barbra Streisand

Born Barbara Joan Streisand, April 24, 1942, New York City, New York
1963—*The Barbra Streisand Album* (Columbia); *The Second Barbra Streisand Album*   1964—*The Third Album; Funny Girl* soundtrack (Capitol); *People* (Columbia)   1966—*Je M'appelle Barbra*   1967—*Simply Streisand*   1969—*What About Today?*   1970—*Barbra Streisand's Greatest Hits*   1971—*Stoney End; Barbra Joan Streisand*   1974—*The Way We Were*   1976—*A Star Is Born*   1977—*Streisand Superman*   1980—*Guilty*   1981—*Memories*   1985—*The Broadway Album*   1991—*Just for the Record*   1994—*The Concert.*

The top-selling female artist in history, Barbra Streisand has seen more than 30 of her 50 albums achieve gold status; she has sold 52 million albums in the U.S. alone, featuring for the most part the music of Broadway and its derivatives. And with 15 films to her credit (as of 1994), she has become emblematic of the consummate entertainer, heir to a show business tradition whose emphasis on sophistication and professionalism hark back to the prerock era. Both for her remarkable singing technique and as consistent champion of classic American popular song, Streisand stands as one of contemporary music's most significant performers.

Born in Brooklyn, Streisand moved to Manhattan following high school graduation to pursue acting. She began concentrating on singing at the start of the Sixties, first in gay clubs and then in Greenwich Village's Bon Soir club. Debuting on Broadway in *I Can Get It for You Wholesale,* she was signed to Columbia; two weeks after her self-titled Grammy-winning album was released in 1963, she was America's best-selling female singer, and her next seven albums entered the Top Five. Starring in 1350 performances as Fanny Brice in *Funny Girl* consolidated her fame; in 1968 the Hollywood version, Streisand's first film role, earned her an Oscar. A death threat she received as she was about to perform a

1967 concert in Central Park contributed to an increasing anxiety about singing in public, causing her to retire from concert appearances for more than 20 years.

All of Streisand's Sixties albums were hugely popular (nine of them charting in the Top Ten); all highlighted Tin Pan Alley fare. In the Seventies she attempted, with uneven results, the songs of younger writers (Jimmy Webb, Laura Nyro); her first rock & roll album, 1971's *Stoney End* (#10), drew praise, but critics questioned her other work in this vein. In 1977 she teamed with Bee Gee Barry Gibb on *Streisand Superman* (#3); her hitmaking power remained intact ("You Don't Bring Me Flowers" with Neil Diamond, #1, 1978; "No More Tears [Enough Is Enough]" with Donna Summer, #1, 1979).

Streisand continued to make movies—*Hello, Dolly!, The Way We Were, A Star Is Born, The Prince of Tides* (which she also directed), among the more popular—and in 1983, with *Yentl*, an adaptation of a story by Isaac Bashevis Singer, became the first woman to cowrite, direct, produce, and star in a film of her own.

In 1987 she founded the Barbra Streisand Foundation to support liberal political causes, following up on political involvement that had placed her on Richard Nixon's Enemies List and had drawn her back to live performance for "One Voice," a 1986 Democratic Party fundraiser. Among other examples of her philanthropy are the Streisand Chair in Cardiology at UCLA and the Streisand Chair on Intimacy and Sexuality at USC; she has also been outspoken in support of gay and women's rights and environmentalism.

Her pop icon status assured in the Nineties, Streisand was the beneficiary of a tribute of sorts: On *Saturday Night Live*, Mike Myers in drag played Linda Richman, host of the fictional talk show *Coffee Talk*, who, as a prototypical Long Island Streisand fan, gushed at every mention of the singer's name. In 1992 Streisand surprised viewers and *Coffee Talk* guests Madonna and Roseanne Arnold with an unbilled walk-on.

In 1994, with two New Year's performances at the Las Vegas MGM Grand Hotel's Grand Garden, Streisand returned for her first paid concerts in 22 years. With nine metal detectors in place to assuage the performer's concern for personal safety, the highly successful shows previewed her first-ever major tour later that year. The highlights of her Madison Square Garden performances were documented on *The Concert* (#10, 1994).

Barrett Strong

Born February 5, 1941, Mississippi
1975—*Stronghold* (Capitol)   1976—*Live and Love*.

Barrett Strong's career as a singer/songwriter began on a very promising note in 1961 with "Money," one of Motown founder Berry Gordy's first hits (#23 pop, #2 R&B).

It was covered by a wide variety of acts, from the Beatles to the Flying Lizards.

Strong is the cousin of Nolan Strong, of the Detroit vocal group the Diablos. Shortly after "Money," Strong joined Gordy's fledgling recording empire as a performer and a songwriter. But Strong's singing career was soon overshadowed by his songwriting duties, and after 1961 the label released no more of his singles. As a Motown staff writer, he collaborated with Norman Whitfield on some of the songs that revolutionized Motown's sound in the late Sixties and early Seventies: "I Wish It Would Rain," "Ball of Confusion (That's What the World Is Today)," "Papa Was a Rolling Stone," "Just My Imagination (Running Away with Me)," and "Psychedelic Shack," among others, for the Temptations; "Smiling Faces Sometimes" for the Undisputed Truth; and "War" for Edwin Starr. Among Strong's other songwriting credits is "I Heard It Through the Grapevine," "The End of Our Road," and "How Can I Forget."

In the mid-Seventies, he tried unsuccessfully to revive his singing career, first on Capitol Records. He works as a writer and arranger. He appeared on the 1992 album *In Their Own Words*, which featured a number of other singer-songwriters.

Stryper

Formed 1983, Orange County, California
Oz Fox (b. Richard Martinez, June 18, 1961, Whittier, Calif.), gtr.; Tim Gaines (b. Tim Hagelganz, Dec. 14, 1963, Ore.), bass; Michael Sweet (b. July 4, 1963, Whittier), voc.; Robert Sweet (b. Mar. 21, 1960, Whittier), drums.
1984—*The Yellow and Black Attack!* (Enigma) 1985—*Soldiers Under Command*   1986—*To Hell with the Devil*   1988—*In God We Trust*   1990—*Against the Law*   1991—*Can't Stop the Rock: The Stryper Collection, 1984–1991* (Hollywood).

Although their motives have been attacked by both rock critics and evangelist Jimmy Swaggart, Stryper is one of the most successful Christian rock bands, spreading the Word with a slick heavy-metal sound and ending concerts by tossing Bibles into the audience. Their most popular album, *To Hell with the Devil* (#32, 1986), briefly made them platinum-level rock stars.

Brothers Robert and Michael Sweet, inspired by Jimmy Swaggart's evangelical show, were born again in 1975. Robert decided to form a band after seeing Van Halen and being impressed by the show but distressed by the message. In 1983, with his brother on vocals, he recruited bassist Tim Gaines and guitarist Oz Fox. Calling themselves Roxx Regime, they played clubs in Orange County, California, and submitted a demo to Enigma Records. The Sweets' mother persuaded them to perform overtly Christian material, and they changed their name to Stryper after a passage in Isaiah, "With His stripes we are healed." A 1984 mini-LP, *The Yellow and Black Attack!* (named for their trademark yellow-and-black-striped outfits) was followed in 1985 by the gold album *Soldiers Under Command* (#84).

The band reached its commercial peak with the platinum *To Hell with the Devil*. (*Yellow and Black Attack!* was reissued with two extra tracks in 1986, reaching #103). A slickly produced amalgam of evangelism, power chords, and high-pitched vocals, it reached beyond the narrow Christian audience, yielding a Top Forty hit, "Honestly" (#23, 1987).

In God We Trust (#32, 1988), a blatant attempt to court pop audiences, was a relative disappointment, reaching only gold status; following 1990's *Against the Law* (#39), the band changed labels, lost the striped outfits, and was back on more typical, secular heavy-metal ground.

Stuff

Formed 1976, New York City, New York
Gordon Edwards, bass; Steve Gadd, drums; Richard Tee (b. Nov. 24, 1943, Brooklyn, N.Y.; d. July 21, 1993, New York City), kybds.; Cornell Dupree, gtr.; Chris Parker, drums; Eric Gale (d. May 25, 1994, Baja California, Mex.), gtr.
1977—*Stuff* (Warner Bros.); *More Stuff*   1979—*Stuff It*   1980—*Live in New York*   1981—*Best Stuff*.
Richard Tee solo: 1978—*Strokin'* (CBS)   1980—*Natural Ingredients*   1985—*Bottom Line* (King).
Eric Gale solo: 1975—*Negril* (Columbia)   1977—*Ginseng Woman; Multiplication*   1979—*Part of You*.
Cornell Dupree solo: 1975—*Teasin'* (Atlantic)   1988—*Who It Is* (Antilles/New Direction)   1991—*Can't Get Through* (Amazing).
Steve Gadd solo: 1984—*Gadd About* (Pro Jazz).

Stuff was an aggregation of top New York studio musicians who performed at West Side clubs, especially Mikell's, before recording several albums for Warner Bros. Gordon Edwards, the driving force behind Stuff, had a group of session players, Encyclopedia of Soul, on and off for ten years before forming Stuff. In 1975 he appeared on two Grammy Award–winning records, Paul Simon's *Still Crazy After All These Years* and Van McCoy's "The Hustle." Stuff backed Joe Cocker on *Stingray* in 1976, and most of Stuff appeared in Paul Simon's film *One Trick Pony*.

Cornell Dupree was part of King Curtis and His King Pins. Richard Tee was a gospel-based keyboardist who worked at Motown in the Sixties and met Dupree in Curtis' band. Chris Parker made a reputation with Paul Butterfield's Better Days. Steve Gadd has appeared in every context, from pop to funk to jazz.

Stuff's members split up to perform in other group projects in the early Eighties. Edwards revived Encyclopedia of Soul in 1981 and performed in a number of New York City clubs. Gadd recorded with countless other singers and musicians, including Frank Sinatra, Barbra Streisand, David Sanborn, and Chick Corea. Gale performed on albums by Frank Sinatra, Aretha Franklin, and many, many other artists. Gadd also formed the Gadd Gang, which included Tee and Dupree. Tee wrote *Mama, I Want to Sing,* which ran for eight years Off-Broadway. He also formed various aggregations and toured, in addition to his session recording activities, which included work on albums by Billy Joel, David Bowie, Diana Ross, and Peter Gabriel.

Tee died of prostate cancer at age 49; Gale of lung cancer at age 55.

Style Council: See the Jam

The Stylistics

Formed 1968, Philadelphia, Pennsylvania
Russell Thompkins Jr. (b. Mar. 21, 1951, Philadelphia), lead voc.; Airrion Love (b. Aug. 8, 1949, Philadelphia), tenor voc.; James Smith (b. June 16, 1950, New York City, N.Y.), bass voc.; Herbie Murrell (b. Apr. 27, 1949, Lane, S.C.), baritone voc.; James Dunn (b. Feb. 4, 1950, Philadelphia), baritone voc.
1971—*The Stylistics* (Avco)   1972—*Round 2: The Stylistics*   1973—*Rockin' Roll Baby*   1974—*Let's Put It All Together; Heavy*   1975—*The Best of the Stylistics; Thank You Baby; You Are Beautiful*   1976—*Fabulous* (H&L); *Wonder Woman*   1978—(– Dunn)   1979—*Love Spell* (Mercury)   1980—*Hurry Up This Way Again* (TSOP)   1986—*All Time Classics* (Amherst); *The Best of the Stylistics (1972–1974); The Best of the Stylistics, vol. 2; Greatest Love Hits*   1992—*Stylistics Christmas; Love Talk.*

Led by Russell Thompkins, the Stylistics were leading practitioners of the lush "Philadelphia sound" of the mid-Seventies. They came together in 1968, a union of two Philadelphia vocal groups. Herbie Murrell and James Dunn came from the Percussions; Thompkins, Airrion Love, and James Smith joined from the Monarchs. Robert Douglas, a member of their backing band Slim and the Boys, and road manager Marty Bryant wrote "You're a Big Girl Now" for the Stylistics. It began as a hit on the small Sebring Records in the Philadelphia area before being picked up by Avco Records and hitting the national R&B chart at #7.

Philadelphia producer/writer Thom Bell then took control of the Stylistics' music. Collaborating with songwriter Linda Creed (born circa 1949; died April 10, 1986), Bell created "Stop, Look, Listen (to Your Heart)" (#39 pop,

#6 R&B) and "You Are Everything"(#9 pop, #10 R&B) in 1971; "Betcha By Golly, Wow" (#3 pop, #2 R&B), "People Make the World Go Round" (#25 pop, #6 R&B), and "I'm Stone in Love with You" (#10 pop, #4 R&B) in 1972; "Break Up to Make Up" (#5 pop and R&B), and "Rockin' Roll Baby" (#14 pop, #13 R&B) in 1973; and "You Make Me Feel Brand New" (#2 pop, #5 R&B) in 1974.

After the Stylistics' relationship with Bell ended, it began working with other producers, including Van McCoy [see entry], but the group's record sales in America declined. They remained popular in Europe both on record and in nightclubs throughout the Seventies. Among their U.K. hits were three Top Five singles: "Sing Baby Sing" and "Na Na Is the Saddest Word" (1975), and "Can't Help Falling in Love" (1976). "Can't Give You Anything (But My Love)" (#51 pop, #18 R&B) went to #1 in the U.K. during the summer of 1975.

The group signed to Philadelphia International Records in 1980. By then, Dunn had quit due to health problems and was not replaced, and within a year Smith had left as well. The group remains active as a trio.

Styx

Formed 1963, Chicago, Illinois
James Young, gtr., voc.; John Curulewski, gtr.; Dennis DeYoung (b. Feb. 18, 1947, Chicago), kybds., voc.; Chuck Panozzo, bass, voc.; John Panozzo, drums.
1972—*Styx* (Wooden Nickel)   1973—*Styx II*; *The Serpent Is Rising*   1974—*Man of Miracles*   1975—*Equinox* (A&M) (– Curulewski; + Tommy Shaw [b. Sep. 11, 1953, Montgomery, Ala., gtr., voc.)   1976—*Crystal Ball*   1977—*The Grand Illusion*   1978—*Pieces of Eight*   1979—*Cornerstone*   1981—*Paradise Theater*   1983—*Kilroy Was Here*   1984—(Group disbands) *Caught in the Act—Live*   1990—(Group re-forms: DeYoung; Young; C. Panozzo; J. Panozzo; + Glen Burtnik, gtr., voc.) *Edge of the Century*   1995—*Styx Greatest Hits.*
Dennis DeYoung solo: 1984—*Desert Moon* (A&M)   1986—*Back to the World*   1988—*Boomchild.*
Tommy Shaw solo: 1984—*Girls with Guns* (A&M)   1985—*What If.*

One of the leading exemplars of the FM radio–oriented hard pop known as "pomp rock," Styx also claim the distinction of having been named (in a 1979 Gallup poll) the most popular rock band among American fans aged 13 to 18. At the height of its commercial powers, Styx released a string of five platinum albums, including the #1 triple-platinum *Paradise Theater* (1981).

Twins Chuck and John Panozzo, along with Dennis DeYoung and Tom Nardini, worked the Chicago-area bar circuit from 1963 until 1969, when Nardini left the group and the Panozzos and DeYoung entered Chicago State

University. There they met John Curulewski, with whom they formed TW4. James Young joined a year later, and they changed their name to Styx (after the river that flows through Hades in Greek mythology).

After incessant touring, their national break came in 1975 with the #6 single "Lady," featuring the blaring vocal triads that are a Styx trademark. From 1977 until their breakup in 1984, every one of their releases sold platinum or better: *The Grand Illusion* (#6, 1977, three million sold), *Pieces of Eight* (#6, 1978, three million sold), *Cornerstone* (#2, 1979, two million sold), *Paradise Theatre*, and *Kilroy Was Here* (#3, 1983, one million sold). Their concerts were invariably sold out. Their hit singles included "Come Sail Away" (#8, 1977); "Fooling Yourself (the Angry Young Man)" (#29) and "Blue Collar Man (Long Nights)" (#21), 1978; "Babe" (#1, 1979); and "The Best of Times" (#3) and "Too Much Time on My Hands" (#9), 1981.

In 1983 the group toured 3000-seat halls with a theatrical presentation of *Kilroy Was Here*, an anticensorship concept album that included the hit singles "Mr. Roboto" (#3) and "Don't Let It End" (#6). In 1984 the group members went their separate ways for a while. DeYoung and Shaw, who had written most of Styx's music, each embarked on initially auspicious solo careers. DeYoung's *Desert Moon* (#29, 1984) featured the #10 title single, while Shaw's *Girls with Guns* (#50, 1984) had a #33 title track. Subsequent releases were not as successful, and in 1990 Shaw joined Ted Nugent's Damn Yankees [see entry].

Four members of Styx, with newcomer Glen Burtnik, released the comeback *Edge of the Century* in the fall of 1990. Its "Show Me the Way" (#3, 1990) became something of a theme song during the Gulf War, and "Love at First Sight" was a Top Thirty single later that spring. In 1995 DeYoung played Pilate in the Broadway revival of *Jesus Christ Superstar*.

Sugar: See Hüsker Dü

The Sugarcubes/Björk

Formed 1986, Reykjavík, Iceland
Björk Gudmundsdóttir (b. Nov. 21, 1965, Reykjavík), voc.; Einar Örn Benediktsson (b. Oct. 29, 1962, Copenhagen, Den.), voc., trumpet; Thór Eldon Jonsson (b. June 2, 1962, Reykjavík), gtr.; Einar Mellax, kybds.; Bragi Ólafsson (b. Aug. 11, 1962, Reykjavík), bass; Sigtryggur "Siggi" Baldursson (b. Oct. 2, 1962, Stavanger, Nor.), drums.
1988—*Life's Too Good* (Elektra) (– Mellax; + Margret "Magga" Ornolfsdottir [b. Nov. 21, 1967, Reykjavík], kybds.)   1989—*Here Today, Tomorrow, Next Week!*   1992—*Stick Around for Joy.*
Björk solo: 1993—*Debut* (Elektra)   1995—*Post.*

The biggest rock band to emerge from Iceland, the Sugarcubes drew notice for their offbeat songs and singer Björk Gudmundsdóttir, an elfin womanchild with a powerful, keening voice. Björk, whose stepfather had been in an Icelandic rock band, recorded her first album at age 11, and later joined Theyr, a legendary Icelandic hardrock band whose drummer was Siggi Baldursson. Einar Örn Benediktsson launched Gramm Records, and with Bragi Ólafsson formed punk band Purrkur Pillnikk, whose debut EP reached Iceland's Top Twenty in 1981. In 1982 Theyr recorded with Jaz Coleman and Youth of British punk band Killing Joke (who'd suddenly turned up in Iceland fearful of an impending apocalypse), while Purrkur Pillnikk toured with British punk band the Fall (which had done some recording in Iceland, where it had a strong cult following).

In 1984 Björk, Einar, Siggi, and keyboardist Einar Mellax formed KUKL (Icelandic for "witch"), an atonal, theatrical rock band that toured Europe and released some singles on a label run by the British anarchic-punk band Crass. KUKL became the Sugarcubes, which formed the company Bad Taste (encompassing record label, art gallery, bookstore, publishing house, and radio station). *Life's Too Good* (#54, 1988) got rave reviews in England and the U.S., where MTV aired the video for the hypnotic, incantatory "Birthday."

In 1989 Björk's ex-husband Thór (with whom she has a son) married new keyboardist Magga Ornolfsdottir, while Bragi and Örn also were wed (the first openly gay marriage in rock history). *Here Today, Tomorrow, Next Week!* (#70, 1989), with fussier arrangements featuring strings and horns, was panned by critics. Björk and Baldursson then worked on *Gling Glo,* a Bad Taste album of jazzed-up Fifties Icelandic pop songs. The Sugarcubes played for French President François Mitterrand during a 1991 summit meeting in Reykjavík, before recording *Stick Around for Joy* (#95, 1992). A year later Björk ventured outside the Sugarcubes to record her first U.S. solo album, *Debut* (#61, 1993), with producer/composer Nellee Hooper of British soul/jazz collective Soul II Soul. It yielded the single "Human Behavior," which reached #2 on the modern-rock charts. In mid-1995 Björk released *Post,* which, in addition to Hooper, features such contributors as Tricky, Graham Massey, and Eumir Deodato (of *2001* fame).

The Sugar Hill Gang

Formed 1977, New York City, New York
Master Gee (b. Guy O'Brien, 1963, New York City),
voc.; Wonder Mike (b. Michael Wright, 1958, Engle-
wood, N.J.), voc.; Big Bank Hank (b. Henry Jackson,
1958, Bronx, N.Y.), voc.
1979—*Rapper's Delight* (Sugarhill)   1981—*The 8th*
Wonder.

Before the Sugar Hill Gang's "Rapper's Delight," rap was confined to the clubs and house parties in the New York City area. Following the record's release in the summer of 1979, rap became part of the pop music vocabulary.

In 1979 Sylvia and Joe Robinson's independent label All Platinum was awash in lawsuits and losing money; the husband-and-wife team (Sylvia had been a hitmaking singer as half of Mickey and Sylvia [see entry] and as a soloist) expected to quit the record business. At a party for her sister in Harlem, she heard guests chanting rhymes over the instrumental breaks in disco records. Using her son Joey as talent scout, she rounded up three youngsters from the New York area to rap over a rhythm track adapted from Chic's "Good Times" and chartered a new label, Sugarhill, to carry the record, "Rapper's Delight."

According to Sugarhill, the record sold two million copies in America. It placed #4 R&B in the U.S., made the Top Five in the U.K., Israel, and South Africa, among other countries, and went to #1 in Canada. It proved to be the Sugar Hill Gang's only big hit, although "8th Wonder" (#15 R&B, 1981) and "Lover in You" were chart singles. The group, with some personnel changes, continues to perform.

Suicide

Formed 1972, New York City, New York
Alan Vega, voc.; Martin Rev, kybds., perc.
1977—*Suicide* (Red Star)   1978—*24 Minutes Over*
***Brussels* (Bronze, U.K.)   1981—*½ Alive* cassette**
(ROIR)   1986—*Ghost Riders* cassette   1989—*A*
Way of Life* (Wax Trax!)   1992—*Suicide: Why Be
***Blue* (Brake Out/Enemy).**
As Alan Vega and Martin Rev: 1980—*Suicide* (Ze).
Alan Vega solo: 1980—*Alan Vega* (Ze/PVC)   1981—
Collision Drive* (Ze/Celluloid)   1983—*Saturn Strip
(Ze/Elektra)   1985—*Just a Million Dreams*
1989—*Vega* (Celluloid, Fr.)   1990—*Deuce Avenue*
(Musidisc, Fr.).
Martin Rev solo: 1980—*Martin Rev* EP (Infidelity)
1985—*Clouds of Glory* (New Rose, Fr.).

When artist/sculptor Alan Vega and keyboardist Martin Rev began performing at New York's Mercer Arts Center (then home to the New York Dolls), they were ahead of their time. Suicide based its music on Rev's repetitive wall-of-noise keyboards and pneumatic rhythm machines, with Vega's Presleyish vocals providing a link to rock & roll tradition. But Vega also brought a form of performance art onstage. He hit himself in the face with his microphone, he whispered and screamed, he strode into the audience seeking to incite involvement or confrontation. Some found Suicide fascinating; others thought them brilliant and important; more seemed to enjoy them as some sort of joke; and most simply hated them.

Suicide opened for the Clash and Elvis Costello on 1978 British tours, where audiences regularly flung beer bottles at the stage and a few fights broke out. On a live-in-Brussels flexi-disc, one can hear audience members grabbing the microphone from the stage and passing it around, hurling epithets at the band the whole time. In 1980 the Cars' Ric Ocasek revealed himself as Suicide's most famous fan. The Cars' *Candy-O* includes a direct allusion to Suicide in "Shoo-Be-Doo." Ocasek got Suicide to open the Cars' 1980 U.S. tour (in L.A. Suicide nearly caused riots, and the concert promoters unsuccessfully tried to have them taken off the bill), included Suicide on a Cars-hosted *Midnight Special,* and produced Suicide's 1980 Ze album. The duo broke up around 1981.

Rev released a solo instrumental EP for Infidelity Records in 1980, and Vega has recorded a series of solo albums, including the Ocasek-produced *Saturn Strip* for Elektra. The two got back together again, with Ocasek producing, for 1988's *A Way of Life,* and to record and tour in 1992.

Donna Summer

Born Donna Gaines, December 31, 1948, Boston, Massachusetts
1975—*Love to Love You* (Oasis)   1976—*A Love Trilogy*; *The Four Seasons of Love*   1977—*I Remember Yesterday* (Casablanca); *Once upon a Time*   1978—*Live and More*   1979—*Bad Girls*; *On the Radio: Greatest Hits*   1980—*The Wanderer* (Geffen); *Walk Away—Collector's Edition* (Casablanca)   1982—*Donna Summer* (Geffen)   1983—*She Works Hard for the Money* (Mercury)   1984—*Cats Without Claws* (Geffen)   1987—*All Systems Go*   1989—*Another Place and Time*   1991—*Mistaken Identity* (Atlantic)   1993—*Anthology* (Polygram).

Donna Summer was the biggest star to emerge from the mid-Seventies disco explosion and went on to pursue a successful pop career. She sang in Boston churches as a child, occasionally as a lead vocalist. In 1967, she made her professional debut at Boston's Psychedelic Supermarket. Later that year, at age 18, she landed a role in the Munich, Germany, production of *Hair.* While in Germany, she married Austrian actor Helmut Sommer, later divorcing him but keeping the Anglicized surname. For a time she sang in a Vienna Folk Opera version of *Porgy and Bess.* Working as a backup singer at Munich's Musicland Studios, Summer met producers Giorgio Moroder and Pete Bellotte. Together the trio created a string of European pop hits for Moroder's Oasis label. In 1975 Moroder licensed Oasis to America's Casablanca Records.

The orgasmic 17-minute "Love to Love You Baby" first became a major disco hit in 1975, and by year's end had crossed over to pop and R&B charts as well (#2 pop, #3 R&B). Many thought Summer would be a typical one-

Donna Summer

hit disco act, but Moroder, Bellotte and Casablanca president Neil Bogart were determined to give her hits and longevity. Her *Love Trilogy* solidified her disco following, while *The Four Seasons of Love* and "Spring Affair" (#47 pop, #24 R&B, 1976) expanded her pop audience. With 1977's *I Remember Yesterday,* Moroder expanded the music's stylistic range. The album yielded the influential synthesizer pop hit "I Feel Love" (#6 pop, #9 R&B). For the disco fairy-tale concept album *Once upon a Time* Summer contributed lyrics to most of the material. The *Live and More* album in 1978 provided Summer with her first pop #1, a cover of Jimmy Webb's "MacArthur Park." That year she also appeared in the disco film *Thank God It's Friday.* "Last Dance" from the soundtrack album won two Grammy Awards—one for Summer, one for songwriter Paul Jabara—and an Oscar for Jabara. *Bad Girls* broke down any lingering critical resistance to Summer. The rocking title track (#1 pop and R&B, 1979) and "Hot Stuff" (#1 pop, #3 R&B, 1979) made her popular with disco, pop, and rock fans. That year, Barbra Streisand duetted with Summer on "No More Tears (Enough Is Enough)" (#1 pop, #20 R&B). Two other crossover hits rounded out Summer's biggest year: "Heaven Knows" (#4 pop, #10 R&B) and "Dim All the Lights" (#2 pop, #13 R&B).

But success also brought problems. In 1980 she sued her manager, Joyce Bogart, and husband Neil for $10 million for mismanagement. She was thus able to end her Casablanca contract and to sign with Geffen Records. *The Wanderer* was her first Geffen release, the title track becoming a strong-selling single (#3 pop, #13 R&B, 1980), although the album didn't live up to sales expectations. *The Wanderer* also included Summer's first born-again Christian message song, "I Believe in Jesus." It was around this time that rumors began circulating that Summer had said the emerging AIDS epidemic was God's revenge on homosexuals for living a blasphemous lifestyle; Summer later denied the rumors, but her large audience of gays dwindled. In 1980 she married Bruce Sudano, lead singer of Brooklyn Dreams, with whom she had recorded "Heaven Knows"; they named their daughter Brook Lyn.

Donna Summer was released in 1982. The Quincy Jones–produced album was a replacement for an LP Giorgio Moroder had produced but Geffen Records had rejected. A track from that unreleased album appears on the *Fast Times at Ridgemont High* soundtrack. She then had her biggest hit album since *Bad Girls* with *She Works Hard for the Money* (#9, 1983), which yielded a massive hit single in the title track (#3, 1983), a video for which was played heavily on MTV. The album also contained a more modest hit in the reggaeish "Unconditional Love" (#43, 1983), with backing vocals by Britain's Musical Youth. *Cats Without Claws* (#40, 1984) contained a cover of the Drifters classic "There Goes My Baby" (#21, 1984); the track "Forgive Me" earned Summer her fourth Grammy, for Best Inspirational Vocal.

While *All Systems Go* went nowhere (#122, 1987), yielding only a minor hit single in "Dinner with Gershwin" (#48, 1987), *Another Place and Time* (#53, 1989) was produced by the British team of Stock, Aitken, and Waterman, who'd had synth-driven dance hits with Bananarama and Dead or Alive. They brought Summer back to the Top Ten singles chart with "This Time I Know It's for Real" (#7, 1989). As of 1995 she has earned 11 gold and two platinum singles, and eight gold and three platinum albums.

Andy Summers: See the Police

The Sundays

Formed 1988, London, England
Harriet Wheeler (b. June 26, 1963, Maidenhead, Eng.), voc.; David Gavurin (b. Apr. 3, 1963, London), gtr.; Paul Brindley (b. Nov. 6, 1963, Nottingham, Eng.), bass; Patrick Hannan (b, Mar. 4, 1966, Lymington, Eng.), drums.
1990—*Reading, Writing and Arithmetic* (DGC)
1992—*Blind.*

The Sundays were perhaps the most pop-oriented of a school of like-sounding British alternative-rock contemporaries (among them Lush and Curve) that featured waifish women's voices piping fatalistic lullabies over chiming guitars. The Sundays' best-known song, the wistful college-radio hit "Here's Where the Story Ends" from *Reading, Writing and Arithmetic* (#39, 1990), had the melancholy lyrics and jangly guitar sound of seminal mope rockers the Smiths, while Harriet Wheeler's delicate, airy soprano recalled the masters of ethereal "shoegazer" rock, the Cocteau Twins.

The Sundays emerged in 1988 and scored a U.K. hit with their first single, "Can't Be Sure" (#45 U.K., 1989). Wheeler had previously sung with a little-known London band called Jim Jiminee; she and Gavurin had been romantically involved for several years before forming the Sundays. While *Reading . . .* won the band "Best New Foreign Band" honors in a ROLLING STONE critics poll, the Sundays fared worse commercially with *Blind* (#103, 1992), which included a cover of the Rolling Stones' "Wild Horses."

Sun Ra

Born Herman Blount, May 22, 1914, Birmingham, Alabama; died May 30, 1993, Birmingham
1956—*Jazz by Sun Ra* (Delmark); *Super-Sonic Jazz* (Saturn)   1958—*Jazz in Silhouette*   1959—*Sun Ra and His Solar Arkestra Visit Planet Earth*; *We Travel the Spaceways*   1963—*Sonic Tones for Mental Therapy*   1964—*Other Planes of There*   1980—*Sunrise in Different Dimensions* (Hat Hut)   1987—*Reflections in Blue* (Black Saint)   1989—*Out There a Minute* (Blast First); *Blue Delight* (A&M)   1990—*Purple Night*   1991—*Mayan Temples* (Black Saint)   1992—*Destination Unknown* (Enja).

With his spangly costumes, circus-style multimedia concerts, otherworldly cosmology, and surreal marriage of heady avant-gardism with funky tent-show gospel, Sun Ra was one of the most unusual, colorful, and self-determined visionaries in modern popular music. With Miles Davis, he was one of the few authentic jazz figures to exert a wide, discernible influence not just on jazz artists (most explicitly the Art Ensemble of Chicago), but on rock and R&B acts too, among them George Clinton, NRBQ, Pink Floyd, and Sonic Youth (for whom Ra opened at New York's Central Park, July 4, 1992). Composer, arranger, bandleader, keyboardist, and philosopher, Ra pioneered the use of electronics, Afro-percussive polyrhythms, and collective free improvisation within bigband jazz. Perhaps the first "alternative" artist, he also documented his work through roughly 100 self-produced albums for his El Saturn Research label (many of which are now out of print).

Ra, who claimed to have been born on Saturn and sent to Earth as "an ambassador of the Creator of the Omniverse," was first known on Earth as Herman Blount. Reportedly a musical prodigy, he could instantly play a piano his parents bought for his tenth birthday (or "arrival day" as Ra would call it). Blount studied music in high school under renowned teacher and bandleader John Tuggle "Fess" Whatley and majored in music education at Alabama A&M University. After graduating in the mid-Thirties, he led the college band on tour, then played piano in a variety of little-known southern and midwestern territory bands—sometimes under the name Sonny Lee—and allegedly backed such blues singers as Wynonie Harris on occasion. By the mid-Forties he had settled in Chicago, playing piano in the band led by his idol, seminal swing arranger Fletcher Henderson; he also worked at Chicago's popular Club DeLisa, arranging scores for floorshows and visiting singers.

Sometime around 1948 Sonny Blount changed the name on his passport to "Le Sony'r Ra" and proclaimed himself "Sun Ra, cosmic messenger." Going against the be-bop–combo grain, Ra—though generally regarded as eccentric—slowly built his "Arkestra," attracting a core of talented, dedicated players, some of whom (tenor saxophonist John Gilmore, baritone saxophonist Pat Patrick, and alto saxophonist Marshall Allen) remained with him for decades. The first Arkestras merged Monk's off-center be-bop, Ellington's exotic tonal palette, and authoritative world-music elements from Africa, the Caribbean, the Middle East, and the Orient.

In the early Sixties the members moved to New York, where Ornette Coleman, Cecil Taylor, and Albert Ayler were forging the "free jazz" revolution. Ra's controlled use of dissonance, silence, and free-form techniques set him firmly in the jazz avant-garde. From the mid-Sixties on, Ra's cult following grew, especially in Europe, as he placed a heavier accent on electronic keyboards (including Moog synthesizer), massed African percussion, and the pageantry of dancers, film projections, and light shows.

The 1974 death of Duke Ellington seemed to inspire Ra to pepper his shows with punk-paced renditions of the classic Ellington and Fletcher Henderson big-band charts of his youth, presaging by several years the rediscovery of tradition by younger avant-garde jazz artists and making his concerts more accessible. By the Eighties Sun Ra was no longer a leading-edge innovator, but a colorful elder statesman who toured incessantly, often playing rock venues. His final arranging triumph may have been in orchestrating a crowd-pleasing magical mystery tour through jazz history and beyond, from throbbing tribal percussion and roiling full-band noise, to rollicking swing and galvanic neo-gospel chants about outer space.

Despite his declining health, Ra continued performing, albeit in a wheelchair and then playing only skeletal piano. After suffering a third stroke in late 1992, Ra let his band tour without him; he returned to his birthplace, where he succumbed to mounting physical complications eight days after his seventy-ninth "arrival day." Under Gilmore's leadership, the band vowed to keep playing Ra's music.

Supertramp

Formed 1969, England

Roger Hodgson (b. Mar. 21, 1950, London, Eng.), gtr., voc., bass; Richard Davies (b. July 22, 1944, Eng.), kybds., voc.; Richard Palmer, gtr.; Bob Miller, drums.

**1970—*Supertramp* (A&M) (– Palmer; – Miller; + Dave Winthrop [b. Nov. 27, 1948, N.J.], sax; + Frank Farrell [b. Birmingham, Eng.], bass; + Kevin Currie [b. Liverpool, Eng.], drums)   1971—*Indelibly Stamped*   1973—*Extremes* soundtrack (Deram) 1974—(– Winthrop; – Farrell; – Currie; + John Anthony Helliwell [b. Feb. 15, 1945, Todmorden, Eng.], sax; + Dougie Thomson [b. Mar. 24, 1951, Glasgow, Scot.], bass; + Bob C. Benberg, drums) *Crime of the Century* (A&M)   1975—*Crisis? What Crisis?* 1977—*Even in the Quietest Moments*   1979— *Breakfast in America*   1980—*Paris*   1982— *". . . famous last words . . ."*   1983—(– Hodgson) 1985—*Brother Where You Bound*   1987—*Free As a Bird; Classics, Volume 9*   1991—*The Very Best of Supertramp.*
Roger Hodgson solo: 1984—*In the Eye of the Storm* (A&M)   1987—*Hai Hai.***

Supertramp began as the wish fulfillment of a millionaire rock fan. By the late Seventies, the group's blend of keyboard-heavy progressive rock and immaculate pop had given them several hit singles and a few platinum LPs. In the late Sixties, Dutch millionaire Stanley August Miesegaes heard Rick Davies in a band called the Joint. When that band broke up, Miesegaes offered to bankroll a band if Davies would handle the music. Davies placed classified ads in London newspapers for a band. The first response was from Roger Hodgson, who was to split songwriting and singing with Davies in Supertramp, the name they took from W. H. Davies' 1938 book, *The Autobiography of a Supertramp*. Drummer Bob Miller suffered a nervous breakdown after their first LP's release; he was replaced by Kevin Currie for the next, but like the first, it flopped.

After a disastrous tour, the band (except Davies and Hodgson) broke up. Davies and Hodgson recruited Bob Benberg from pub rockers Bees Make Honey, and John Helliwell and Dougie Thomson from the Alan Bown Set, and A&M sent them to a rehearsal retreat at a Seventeenth-century farm. Their next LP, *Crime of the Century,* was the subject of a massive advertising/promotional campaign and went to #1 in the U.K. but didn't take off commercially in the U.S., though it did sow the seeds of a cult following.

In 1975 the singles "Dreamer" and "Bloody Well Right" from *Crime* achieved some chart success in both the U.K. and the U.S. Supertramp toured the U.S. as headliners, with A&M giving away most of the tickets. *Crisis?*

failed to yield a hit single, but was heavily played on progressive FM radio and solidified the band's audience base, as did *Even in the Quietest Moments* (#16, 1977), which included "Give a Little Bit" (#15, 1977). Their breakthrough was *Breakfast in America,* a #1 worldwide LP, which eventually sold over four million copies in the U.S. and contained hit singles in "The Logical Song" (#6), "Goodbye Stranger" (#15), and "Take the Long Way Home" (#10). The *Paris* live double LP hit #8; and *". . . famous last words . . ."* included another hit, "It's Raining Again" (#11, 1982). In early 1983 Hodgson announced he was leaving the group for a solo career. His first solo release, *In the Eye of the Storm* (#46, 1984), contained his only charting single, "Had a Dream (Sleeping with the Enemy)" (#48, 1984). His subsequent work was not as well received.

The group's next album, *Brother Where You Bound* (#21, 1985), contained Supertramp's last charting single, "Cannonball" (#28, 1985). Late in 1985 Supertramp embarked on a six-month tour of the United States. Hodgson briefly rejoined the group to promote the U.K. Top Ten compilation *The Autobiography of Supertramp.* Nineteen-eighty-seven's *Free As a Bird* missed the Top 100 by one and included a dance hit, "I'm Begging You."

The Supremes/Diana Ross and the Supremes

Formed 1959, Detroit, Michigan
As the Primettes (Diana Ross [b. Mar. 26, 1944, Detroit], voc.; Florence Ballard [b. June 30, 1943, Detroit; d. Feb. 22, 1976, Detroit], voc.; Mary Wilson [b. Mar. 6, 1944, Greeneville, Miss.], voc.; Betty McGlown, voc.): 1960—(– McGlown; + Barbara Martin, voc.).
As the Supremes: 1963—(– Martin) *Meet the Supremes* (Motown) 1964—*A Little Bit of Liverpool; Where Did Our Love Go* 1965—*Sing Country and Western and Pop; More Hits by the Supremes; We Remember Sam Cooke; At the Copa; Merry Christmas* 1966—*I Hear a Symphony; Supremes A Go-Go* 1967—*Sing Holland-Dozier-Holland; Sing Rodgers and Hart.*
As Diana Ross and the Supremes: 1967—*Greatest Hits, vol. 1* (Motown); *Greatest Hits, vol. 2* (– Ballard; + Cindy Birdsong [b. Dec. 15, 1939, Camden, N.J.], voc.) 1968—*Reflections; Love Child; Sing and Perform "Funny Girl"; Live at the Talk of the Town; Join the Temptations* (with the Temptations); *TCB* (with the Temptations) 1969—*Let the Sunshine In; Together* (with the Temptations); *Cream of the Crop; On Broadway* (with the Temptations); *Greatest Hits, vol. 3* 1970—*Farewell* 1974—*Anthology* 1986—*25th Anniversary.*
As the Supremes (or the "new" Supremes): 1969—

The Supremes: Diana Ross, Mary Wilson, Cindy Birdsong

(– Ross; + Jean Terrell [b. Nov. 26, c. 1944, Tex.], voc.) 1970—*Right On* (Motown); *The Magnificent 7* (with the Four Tops); *New Ways . . . But Love Stays* 1971—*The Return of the Magnificent Seven* (with the Four Tops); *Touch; Dynamite* (with the Four Tops) 1972—*Floy Joy* (– Birdsong; + Lynda Laurence, voc.); *The Supremes Produced and Arranged by Jimmy Webb* 1974—(– Terrell; + Scherrie Payne [b. Nov. 14, 1944], voc.; – Laurence; + Birdsong) 1975—*The Supremes* 1976—(– Birdsong; + Susaye Greene, voc.) *High Energy; Mary, Scherrie & Susaye* 1978—*At Their Best.*
Mary Wilson solo: 1979—*Mary Wilson* (Motown).
Scherrie and Susaye: 1979—*Partners* (Motown).
Diana Ross: See entry.

With 12 #1 pop singles, numerous gold recordings, sold-out concerts, and regular television appearances, the Supremes were not only the most commercially successful female group of the Sixties but among the top five top pop/rock/soul acts of that decade. Diana Ross, Mary Wilson, and Florence Ballard composed Motown's flagship group, Berry Gordy Jr.'s black-pop music crossover dream come true that paved the way from rock radio hits and package bus tours to Las Vegas showrooms and Royal Command Performances. At the height of the civil rights movement, they were also embraced by the world as symbols of black achievement and black womanhood. Fronted by Diana Ross during their peak years, they epitomized Holland-Dozier-Holland's classic Motown sound and the label's sophisticated style. Unlike other girl groups, the Supremes had a mature, glamorous demeanor that appealed equally to teens and adults. Beautiful, musically versatile, and unique, the original Supremes were America's sweethearts, setting standards and records that no one has yet equalled.

Diana Ross, Mary Wilson, and Florence Ballard met while living in Detroit's Brewster housing project. They began singing together in their teens and in their early years were a quartet, abetted by Betty McGlown and then Barbara Martin. Ballard was the most enthusiastic about pursuing a music career. While still in high school, she and the others became friendly with members of the Primes, a male vocal trio that included future founding Temptations Eddie Kendricks and Paul Williams. That group's manager formed the three girls, along with Williams' girlfriend, McGlown, into a "sister" group and dubbed them the Primettes. Of the three, Ballard, whose soulful style was closer to Aretha Franklin's than Ross', was originally considered the lead singer, although Ross and Wilson both sang lead. They became known locally, and through Ross came to know Smokey Robinson, who arranged their first audition for Gordy. Not yet out of high school, the Primettes were deemed too young to be signed, but they continued to hang around Hitsville, where they met other performers and contributed the occasional background vocal to records by other artists, including Mary Wells. In the meantime, they cut a single record for another local label, Lupine. Finally, in January 1961, Gordy signed the group to Motown and suggested that they change their name. Ballard suggested the Supremes.

Gordy groomed all his groups but paid special attention to the Supremes. Years later both Ross and Wilson, like several other Motown acts, would claim that Motown PR exaggerated their alleged impoverished upbringings and state that they had come to the label with their own coordinated stage costumes and choreography (masterminded by Temptation Paul Williams). The girls received instruction in dance, etiquette, and singing and were closely chaperoned. Although rumors of a romance between Gordy and Ross have endured over the years, neither has ever specifically confirmed or denied them until recently. The fact remains that Gordy was especially protective of the group and provided them with support not always offered to all his other acts.

Despite the attention, the group released nine singles that were either moderately successful (such as "Let Me Go the Right Way" and "When the Lovelight Starts Shining Through His Eyes") or flops before the Holland-Dozier-Holland team hit on the dramatic, seductive formula that showcased Ross' distinctive vocal style. Their tenth release, "Where Did Our Love Go," became their first #1 hit in summer 1964, selling over two million copies and starting a streak that resulted in two more chart-topping singles before year's end: "Baby Love" and "Come See About Me."

The Supremes' big singles of 1965 were "Stop! In the Name of Love" (#1 pop, #2 R&B), "Back in My Arms Again" (#1 pop and R&B), and "I Hear a Symphony" (#1 pop, #2 R&B). "You Can't Hurry Love" and "You Keep Me Hangin' On" were #1 on both the pop and R&B charts in 1966. "Love Is Here and Now You're Gone" (#1 pop and R&B), "The Happening" (#1 pop, #12 R&B), and "Reflections" (#2 pop, #4 R&B) hit in 1967. During that period the group averaged at least one national television appearance or major concert a week. The Supremes were regular guests not only on such popular pop shows as *Shindig!* and *Hullabaloo*, but also on mainstream programs, such as Ed Sullivan's, *The Tonight Show, The Hollywood Palace*, and countless other variety programs.

Early on, Gordy decided that the group's major television appearances would feature their latest hit and a Broadway show tune or standard. They soon became steady headliners at top Vegas venues and supperclubs around the world, including the Copacabana and London's Talk of the Town, and other top Motown acts followed suit. They recorded in several foreign languages and drew huge audiences wherever they appeared. They were also important symbols of black success. As such, they were often seen at Democratic political fundraisers, for President Lyndon Johnson, among others, and were specially invited to attend the funeral of Dr. Martin Luther King Jr. in 1968.

Although the individual group members insisted they were a team, there was no denying that the public saw Ross as the star. Gordy, who had set his sights on moving Motown to Los Angeles and becoming a movie mogul, laid plans for Ross's eventual solo career. In 1967 "Reflections" was the first single credited to Diana Ross and the Supremes. By then years of relentless touring and recording had taken their toll. Although both Ross and Wilson always credited Ballard with having founded the group, both later revealed in their respective autobiographies that Ballard's unpredictability, mood swings, and excessive drinking were threatening the group's future. In their and Gordy's defense, Ballard had missed several concert dates and become careless about her appearance and performance. Further, she was embittered by the attention being lavished on Ross, and finally in 1967 either quit or was asked to leave the group. Although until recently Ballard was portrayed as a victim of Gordy and Ross's ambitions, her story was much more complicated. She left Motown and turned management of her career over to her husband, whose sole experience in the area consisted of being Gordy's chauffeur.

Contrary to popular misconception, Ballard did not leave Motown penniless; rather, she was given approximately $160,000 but was cheated out of it by her own attorney (who was later disbarred). She recorded an album for ABC that, to date, has not been released, and her two singles releases ("It Doesn't Matter How I Say It" b/w "Goin' Out of My Head" and "Love Ain't Love" b/w "Forever Faithful," both in 1968) failed to chart. Within a few short years Ballard had three daughters and an unstable marriage and was suffering from depression, alcoholism, and myriad health problems, including high blood pressure. She lost her home and for a while was separated from her husband and receiving aid for dependent children. Despite a few public appearances, including one that was part of President Richard Nixon's inaugural festivities, she basically gave up singing. Nine years after leaving Motown, she died of cardiac arrest in Detroit at 32. Both Ross and Wilson attended the funeral, presided over by Aretha Franklin's father, the Reverend C. L. Franklin. Among her pallbearers were the Four Tops.

Ballard had been replaced by a former member of Patti LaBelle and the Blue Belles, Cindy Birdsong. By that point, Holland-Dozier-Holland had left Motown, and while the Supremes continued to have hits with material recorded before the production team's departure, there were signs that their smooth sophistication was becoming passé. "Love Child" (#1 pop, #2 R&B), an uncharacteristically bold song about illegitimacy, was the Supremes' biggest hit of 1968. They continued in the same vein with another slice of ghetto life, "I'm Livin' in Shame" (#10 pop, #8 R&B, 1969). These records were also significant for being the first on which Ross sang with anonymous background singers rather than Birdsong and Wilson. Others included the relatively less popular "The Composer" and "No Matter What Sign You Are." Their other big hits were group duets with the Temptations, with whom they costarred in two highly rated television specials, "T.C.B." (1968) and "G.I.T. on Broadway" (1969). These spun off hit albums and a string of popular singles, including "I'm Gonna Make You Love Me" and "I'll Try Something New."

By early 1969 Ross' future departure was widely rumored, and that November Motown issued the official press release. Speculation about who would replace her focused on Syreeta Wright, but Gordy gave the spot to boxer Ernie Terrell's sister, Jean Terrell, whom he'd signed to a solo contract earlier. The year ended with "Someday We'll Be Together" (#1 pop and R&B), a record that featured only one Supreme, Ross. In January 1970 Ross made her farewell appearance at the Frontier Hotel in Las Vegas. The event was documented on the live album *Farewell*.

Although Ross went on as a hugely successful solo act [see entry] her initial efforts were bested on the charts by the so-called "new" Supremes' first releases. Terrell was a stronger, earthier singer, and 1970 brought two Frank Wilson–produced hits: "Up the Ladder to the Roof" (#10 pop, #5 R&B) and "Stoned Love" (#7 pop, #1 R&B). Along with the Four Tops, this new lineup recorded three albums and hit with a powerful version of "River Deep—Mountain High" (#14 pop, #7 R&B, 1970). The progressive psychedelic blues "Nathan Jones" (#16 pop, #8 R&B) was the group's sole hit in 1971. The Smokey Robinson–written and –produced "Floy Joy" (#16 pop, #5 R&B) was considered their best effort of 1972.

By then the Supremes were not the only Motown act to suffer from the company's lack of support. Unlike early Motown artists, however, the newer Supremes, including Terrell, bristled at Gordy's authority, and early on (Wilson claims as early as January 1970) he lost interest in the group. Through a series of producers, among them Jimmy Webb and Stevie Wonder (1973's "Bad Weather") and personnel changes that left Wilson the only original and consistent member, the group struggled against Motown's, and eventually the public's, indifference. The later versions of the group didn't suffer from a lack of talent: Lynda Laurence and Susaye Greene had both been members of Stevie Wonder's group Wonderlove; Greene was a proven songwriter who would later cowrite "I Can't Help It" for Michael Jackson's *Off the Wall*. Scherrie Payne, sister of Freda, had sung with Holland-Dozier-Holland's group Glass House and was considered a technically gifted vocalist. In 1976 the Greene-Wilson-Payne lineup released the Supremes' last Top Forty single, "I'm Gonna Let My Heart Do the Walking." Wilson, who became the group's leader, decided to pursue a solo career, and the last version of the Supremes gave their final farewell performance in London in 1977. Payne and Greene continued briefly as a duo. Birdsong worked as a secretary at Motown, then attempted a solo career. She has since become intensely religious. Terrell and Laurence both retired to marry. They, along with Payne, have performed together in recent years as "Supremes."

Rumors that the hit Broadway play *Dreamgirls* was based on the Supremes' story were confirmed with the 1986 publication of Mary Wilson's best-selling autobiography *Dreamgirl: My Life as a Supreme* (cowritten with Arghus Juilliard and Patricia Romanowski). Aside from Ross, Wilson remains the best-known ex-Supreme, and she also authored a sequel recounting the latterday Supremes, her abusive marriage, and ongoing legal disputes with Motown, *Supreme Faith* (with Romanowski) in 1990. The only attempt at a Supremes reunion of Ross, Wilson, and Birdsong occurred at the taping of *Motown 25* in 1983 and ended in embarrassment when Ross pushed Wilson's microphone away from her face. Though the segment was not aired, it was widely reported and seemed to confirm the old image of Ross as the pushy leader. Despite Wilson's protests to the contrary, her depiction of Ross further damaged whatever relationship the two might have had.

In 1988, when the Supremes were inducted into the Rock and Roll Hall of Fame, Ross declined to attend, leaving Wilson and Ballard's youngest daughter, Lisa, to accept on behalf of the group. Although Wilson's solo records have not been successful, she continues to perform around the world. In January 1991 Wilson was injured and the youngest of her three children, Pedro Ferrer, was killed when she fell asleep while driving. In the wake of that accident, she and Ross were rumored to have reconciled.

Surface

Formed 1983, West Orange, New Jersey
David Townsend (b. May 17, 1954, Englewood,
Calif.), gtr., kybds., voc.; David "Pic" Conley (b. Dec.
27, 1953, Newark, N.J.), bass, sax, perc., kybds.,
flute, voc. ; Karen Copeland (d. Dec. 5, 1988, N.J.),
voc.
1984—(– Copeland; + Bernard Jackson [b. July 11,
1959, Stamford, Conn.], voc.)   1987—Surface (Co-
lumbia)   1988—2nd Wave   1990—3 Deep   1991—
The Best of Surface . . . A Nice Time 4 Lovin'
1994—(– Jackson; – Townsend; + Eric "G. Riff"
Moore [b. Aug. 23, 1971, Irvington, N.J.], voc.;
+ Everett "Jam" Benton [b. Sep. 6, 1969, Buffalo,
N.Y.], kybds., voc.).

Surface is a soul group that has scored several hits with its R&B ballads and smooth dance grooves. The band was formed by David Townsend, son of producer/songwriter Ed Townsend and a former member of the Isley Brothers band, and David Conley, who had played with the Seventies funk band Mandrill, with Karen Copeland on vocals. That version of Surface released two singles with mild success. Townsend and Conley then began working with singer and songwriter Bernard Jackson. Surface wrote songs for artists including New Edition, Isaac Hayes, the Jets, Sister Sledge, and Gwen Guthrie and began to record its own material.

Surface's eponymous debut yielded a few hits: "Happy" (#20 pop, #2 R&B, 1987), "Lately" (#8 R&B, 1987), and "Let's Try Again" (#22 R&B, 1987). They avoided sophomore jinx on 2nd Wave, which included "Shower Me with Your Love" (#5 pop, #1, R&B, 1989). They continued to hit with the R&B market on 3 Deep, which included "All I Want Is You" (#8 R&B, 1991), featuring backing vocals by Regina Belle, "Never Gonna Let You Down" (#17 pop, 24 R&B, 1991), and "You're the One" (#35 R&B, 1991).

Townsend and Conley produced Jermaine Jackson's hit "Don't Take It Personal" and Aretha Franklin's Grammy-nominated album What You See Is What You Sweat. As of winter 1994 the band had split their talents. Jackson was forming a new group and was signed to Arista, Townsend was working A&R for a record label,

and Conley was managing and producing bands including Tu Luce. Conley was also planning to resurface with a new band lineup, including singer Eric Moore.

The Surfaris

Formed 1962, Glendora, California
Pat Connolly (b. 1947), voc., bass; Jim Fuller
(b. 1947), gtr.; Bob Berryhill (b. 1947), gtr.; Ron Wilson (b. 1945; d. May 1989), drums; Jim Pash
(b. 1949), sax, clarinet, gtr.
1963—Wipe Out (Dot); The Surfaris Play Wipe Out
and Others   1964—Hit City 64   Ca. 1966—
(– Berryhill; – Connolly; – Fuller)   1981—Punkline
(N.A).

The Surfaris rode the wave of the early-Sixties surf music boom, often appearing at Southern California teen dances and beach parties with surf outfits like the Crossfires, who later became the Turtles. The Surfaris had only one big hit record, the 1963 instrumental "Wipe Out," which contained one of rock's first and most influential drum solos. The single hit #2 in 1963 and recharted at #16 in 1966.

It would be the group's only major hit and began life as a throwaway B side, recorded in two quick takes. But while "Wipe Out" would prove to be the Surfaris' ticket to fame, it was also a subject of contention for them. Their debut album, Wipe Out, they discovered, contained only two Surfaris tracks: "Wipe Out," and its A side, "Surfer Joe." The rest of the album was recorded by the Challengers, so it was that group, and not the Surfaris, who received royalties, although it was the Surfaris' hit title track that sold it. Then another Los Angeles group sued the Surfaris, claiming that they were the original and rightful Surfaris. Once all this dust settled, the group began recording again, but there were no further charting singles after "Point Panic" (#49, 1963).

After surf music went out of vogue, the Surfaris followed to the folk-rock trend without success. By the mid-Sixties, the group was basically disbanded, though Jim Pash kept lineups working for years. The group reformed on several occasions through the Seventies and in 1981 recorded a new album. Bob Berryhill and Pash have become born-again Christians; Ron Wilson died in poverty; Jim Fuller briefly joined the Seeds. Pash led a group that recorded music for the short-lived New Gidget television series in 1986.

"Wipe Out" has been revived countless times, in films (Back to the Beach, 1987), commercials (Stri-Dex, Wendy's), and on record (by Herbie Hancock, Dweezil Zappa, and Scorpions drummer Herman Rarebell, among many others). In the summer of 1987 the Beach Boys and the Fat Boys had a #12 hit with their remake of the immortal surf classic.

Surf Music

A Southern Californian genre of the early Sixties, surf rock celebrated not just catching the perfect wave but such carefree adolescent phenomena as the sun, beach parties, girls, and hot rods.

Surf music had two strains, vocal and instrumental. Jan and Dean started surf vocal music off in 1959 with their hit "Baby Talk" and followed with such genre classics as "Surf City" and "Dead Man's Curve," all featuring their trademark high harmony vocals and bouncy denatured Chuck Berry guitar riffs. The Beach Boys came along soon after, scored a series of mammoth national hits, and soon eclipsed Jan and Dean in both popularity and significance.

Instrumental surf music featured throbbing tribal tom-tom tattoos and trebly, metallic, twanging guitar riffs: the Ventures' "Walk Don't Run," the Duals' "Stick Shift," Dick Dale and the Del-tones' "Misirlou." Thanks in large part to the prolific Ventures, instrumental surf rock has proven one of rock's most influential subgenres. Surf rock's influence can be heard in the music of Blondie, the Go-Go's, the Raybeats, Reverend Horton Heat, the Cramps, Shadowy Men on a Shadowy Planet, and many other musicians, including U2's the Edge. It made a splash again on the soundtrack to *Pulp Fiction* (1994), which included a song by Dick Dale.

Sutherland Brothers and Quiver

Formed 1973, London, England
Iain Sutherland, gtr., voc., kybds.; Gavin Sutherland, gtr., bass, voc.; Peter Wood (d. Dec. 1993, N.Y.), kybds.; Tim Renwick, gtr.; Willie Wilson, drums; Bruce Thomas, bass.
1973—*Dream Kid* (Island/Columbia)   1974—*Beat of the Street* (- Thomas)   1975—*Lifeboat* (Island) (- Wood); *Reach for the Sky* (Columbia)   1976— *Sailing*; *Slipstream*   1977—(- Renwick) *Down to Earth*   1978—(Group disbands).
The Sutherland Brothers: 1979—*When the Night Comes Down* (Columbia).

The Sutherland Brothers had made two folk-rock LPs for Island in the early Seventies: *Sutherland Bros. Band* and *Lifeboat* (the latter not to be confused with the U.K. *Lifeboat* compilation). Quiver had made two of their own rock albums for Warner Bros.: *Quiver* and *Gone in the Morning.* The two groups merged and, despite some critical admiration, had only one hit single, "(I Don't Want to Love You But) You Got Me Anyway," which went to #48 in the U.S. in 1973 and got the band a spot opening for Elton John's U.S. tour that year.

Little happened for them after that until 1975, when Rod Stewart, a longtime admirer of the Sutherlands' songwriting, had a massive U.K. hit with their "Sailing." This sparked some interest in the group's next LP, *Reach*

for the Sky, which yielded the U.K. Top Ten single "Arms of Mary." When *Slipstream* failed to achieve any commercial success, guitarist Tim Renwick (who had played on David Bowie's "Space Oddity") quit halfway through the *Down to Earth* sessions, with ex–Procol Harum Mick Grabham filling in on some tracks. After the rest of Quiver quit, the Sutherlands carried on for one more album.

Thomas went on to join Elvis Costello and the Attractions; Wilson and Renwick have had lucrative careers as sessionmen. Iain Sutherland has continued to write and record. He had two solo albums in the early Eighties, and his songs have been covered by Paul Young, Merle Haggard, and the Everly Brothers, among others. His brother Gavin recorded one solo album in the early Eighties and has been successful as a writer on the subject of whaling. He published a book entitled *The Whaling Years.* Peter Wood, another ex–group member who did well with session work, died in New York of undetermined causes.

Swamp Dogg

Born Jerry Williams Jr., July 12, 1942, Portsmouth, Virginia
1970—*Total Destruction to Your Mind* (Canyon) 1971—*Rat On!* (Elektra)   1972—*Cuffed, Collared and Tagged* (Cream)   1973—*Gag a Maggot* (Stone Dogg)   1974—*Have You Heard This Story?* (Island) 1976—*Swamp Dogg's Greatest Hits* (Stone Dogg) 1977—*Finally Caught Up with Myself* (Musicor); *An Opportunity . . . Not a Bargain!*   1981—*I'm Not Selling Out, I'm Buying In!* (Takoma)   1982—*Best of Swamp Dogg* (Solid Smoke)   1989—*I Called for a Rope and They Threw Me a Rock* (S.D.E.G.)   1991— *Surfin' in Harlem* (Volt).

Singer, songwriter, and producer Swamp Dogg has had a varied career, during which his work has resulted in hits for other artists but rarely for himself. Recording at first as "Little Jerry," Jerry Williams began in the Fifties as a soul singer. By the middle of the next decade, he had scored a couple of minor hits, "I'm a Lover Man" and "Baby You're My Everything." In 1970 he became chief producer for Wally Roker's Canyon Records, where he was encouraged to stretch out musically, and therefore became Swamp Dogg. Under that name, he released *Total Destruction to Your Mind,* a psychedelically eccentric soul album influenced by Sly and the Family Stone and the Mothers of Invention.

"Mama's Baby, Daddy's Maybe" was a minor hit (#33 R&B, 1970), and Swamp Dogg began incorporating touches of bayou style, à la Tony Joe White. Williams then signed with Elektra, but *Rat On!* was a commercial and artistic failure. In 1972 he moved to Cream Records and released *Cuffed, Collared and Tagged,* which included a

Swamp Dogg (a.k.a. Jerry Williams)

tribute to Sly Stone called "If It Hadn't Been for Sly" and the John Prine song "Sam Stone." Soon after the album's release, Cream went out of business.

As a producer, Jerry Williams fared better. He wrote Gene Pitney's 1968 hit "She's a Heartbreaker," produced the Commodores' first single, "I Keep On Dancing" while an Atlantic staff member, and produced Doris Duke's Top Ten soul hit, "I'm the Other Woman to the Other Woman," in 1970. In 1971 his song "She's All I Got" was a Top Forty pop hit for Freddy North and a #1 country song for Johnny Paycheck. Williams also had soul hits sung by Z. Z. Hill, Irma Thomas, and Charlie Whitehead.

Still Swamp Dogg struggled, although he released several records through the Seventies. In the late Eighties he formed the S.D.E.G. label and management company, which had a measure of success with the rappers M.C. Breed & DFC, whose self-titled album made the R&B Top Forty. Dogg continues to release his own material as well.

Billy Swan
Born May 12, 1944, Cape Girardeau, Missouri
1971—*I Can Help* (Monument)   1975—*Rock 'n' Roll Moon* (Columbia)   1976—*Billy Swan*   1977—*Four*
1978—*You're OK, I'm OK* (A&M)   1978—*Billy Swan at His Best* (Monument).

Billy Swan, a Nashville journeyman, emerged seemingly from nowhere with one of 1974's biggest hits, the strolling organ-heavy "I Can Help." A #1 hit on both the

pop and country charts, "I Can Help" differed almost completely from Swan's usual output, which leaned toward rockabilly.

Swan had his first success when his song "Lover Please," which he had written at age 16 for his band Mirt Mirley and the Rhythm Steppers, became a nationwide hit in 1962 for Clyde McPhatter. Swan lived off that song's royalties for a time, then moved to Nashville at age 21, where his pursuit of a music career led him to replace Kris Kristofferson as janitor at Columbia's Nashville studios. Within a few years Swan was producing Tony Joe White's first three LPs (including White's hit "Polk Salad Annie"). He also lived for a time in Elvis Presley's uncle's house; in fact, after Presley covered "I Can Help," he gave Swan a pair of his socks.

In 1970 Swan played in Kristofferson's band at the Isle of Wight Festival, and in 1973 he worked with comic country singer Kinky Friedman; in 1975 the latter covered "Lover Please" (as did Kristofferson). After the international success of "I Can Help," Swan's debut album yielded a minor U.K. hit in a cover of Otis Blackwell's "Don't Be Cruel." *Rock 'n' Roll Moon,* another critically acclaimed album, contained another minor hit in "Everything's the Same." It was Swan's last pop success, but through 1975 and 1976 he embarked on successful worldwide tours, playing with Nashville session stars like Kenny Buttrey and Charlie McCoy in Paris in 1975, and with Willie Nelson in Britain in 1976. In 1986 he joined with Randy Meisner (ex-Poco and Eagles) and former Bread member James Griffin in Black Tie. The group released *When the Night Falls.*

Keith Sweat
Born July 22, 1961, New York City, New York
1987—*Make It Last Forever* (Vintertainment/ Elektra)   1990—*I'll Give All My Love to You*
1991—*Keep It Comin'* (Elektra)   1994—*Get Up on It.*

With his good looks and romantic singing style propelled by hard rhythmic tracks, Keith Sweat helped revitalize R&B in the late Eighties.

Sweat was born in Harlem, the third of five children, and grew up in projects a few blocks from the Apollo Theatre. He joined his first group at age 15, then became the frontman for Jamilah. After graduating from City College, he worked on Wall Street as a brokerage assistant. He continued to shop his demo around and eventually signed with manager Vincent Davis' Vintertainment label.

Sweat's first single, "I Want Her" (#1 R&B, 1987), produced by Teddy Riley, was the first major New Jack Swing hit, fusing soul and hip-hop. The album, *Make It Last Forever* (#15 pop, 1988; #1 R&B, 1987) was coproduced by Riley and went multiplatinum. It included the singles "Something Just Ain't Right" (#3 R&B, 1988) and

Keith Sweat

"Make It Last Forever" (#2 R&B, 1988), a duet with Jacci McGhee. Sweat continued his pop crossover success on *I'll Give All My Love to You* (#6 pop, #1 R&B, 1990), yielding the hits "Make You Sweat" (#14 pop, #1 R&B, 1990), "I'll Give All My Love to You" (#7 pop, #1 R&B, 1990), and "Merry Go Round" (#2 R&B, 1990), a ballad.

Sweat split from Davis and released *Keep It Comin'* (#19, 1991). The album featured cameos by L. L. Cool J, on "Keep It Comin'" (#17 pop, #1 R&B, 1991), and the Gap Band's Charlie Wilson, as well as the single "Your Love—Part 2" (#4 R&B, 1991). In 1992 Sweat formed Keia Records, a label featuring new R&B and rap acts, that is distributed by Elektra and based in New York and Atlanta. His 1994 album, *Get Up on It* (#8 pop, #1 R&B), yielded such singles as the title track (#69 pop, #12 R&B, 1994), "When I Give My Love" (#93 pop, #21 R&B, 1994), and "How Do You Like It?" (#48 pop, #9 R&B, 1994).

Matthew Sweet
Born Sidney Matthew Sweet, October 6, 1964, Lincoln, Nebraska
**1986—*Inside* (Columbia)   1989—*Earth* (A&M)
1991—*Girlfriend* (Zoo)   1993—*Altered Beast*
1995—*100% Fun*.**

Matthew Sweet's career has been a kind of Cook's Tour of postpunk rock, ranging from Athens, Georgia, to New York City to Los Angeles, with *Girlfriend* (#100, 1992), a pristine *Revolver*-meets-Neil-Young amalgam, finally bringing him to the public's attention.

Sweet, a musician in high school, attended the University of Georgia in Athens in 1983 because he was attracted by its music scene. He met Lynda Stipe (sister of R.E.M.'s Michael) there and joined her band, Oh-OK, playing on their Mitch Easter–produced EP, *Furthermore What* (1983). With Oh-OK drummer David Pierce, Sweet formed Buzz of Delight and wrote and produced *Sound Castles* (1984). This EP and a tape of unreleased songs produced by Don Dixon caught the attention of Columbia Records, which brought Sweet to New York and signed him to a solo deal. Settling up North, Sweet recorded *Inside*, playing most of the instruments, backed by a drum machine, and augmented with cameos by Aimee Mann ('Til Tuesday), Chris Stamey (dB's), Fred Maher, and Anton Fier. With Fier, Sweet played on the Golden Palominos' *Blast of Silence* (1986), cowriting one song, "Something Becomes Nothing."

Maher coproduced Sweet's next album, *Earth*, with the Blasters' Dave Alvin. Again it was mostly Sweet, with guest appearances by New York guitarists Richard Lloyd (Television) and Robert Quine (Richard Hell, Lou Reed) and singer Kate Pierson (B-52's). Like *Inside*, it generated massive critical admiration but scant sales. Recorded during the breakup of his marriage in 1990, *Girlfriend* (originally titled *Nothing Lasts*) was delayed when Sweet was dropped by A&M. Sweet was about to give up on shopping the tape when Zoo—which had passed on the album—signed him after its president heard the demo playing in a staffer's office. The album marked the first time Sweet had recorded with a "live" band. Its success (over 400,000 copies sold) allowed Sweet to take on other projects, playing on Lloyd Cole's 1990 European solo tour and coproducing Velvet Crush's debut, *In the Presence of Greatness* (1991).

Moving to L.A. in 1992, Sweet used producer Richard Dashut (Fleetwood Mac, Lindsey Buckingham) with Quine and Lloyd, joined by guitarist Ivan Julian, pianist Nicky Hopkins, and drummers Pete Thomas (Elvis Costello), Mick Fleetwood, and Jody Stephens (Big Star) for *Altered Beast* (#75, 1993). Sweet's 1995 release, *100% Fun* (#65), again featured guitarists Lloyd and Quine and was produced by Brendan O'Brien.

Rachel Sweet
Born 1963, Akron, Ohio
1979—*Fool Around* (Stiff/Columbia)   1980—*Protect the Innocent* (Columbia)   1981—*. . . And Then He Kissed Me*   1982—*Blame It on Love*   1992—*Fool Around: The Best of Rachel Sweet* (Rhino).

Rachel Sweet was 18 when rock fans first heard her on Stiff Records' *Akron Compilation*, with a big, twangy voice that elicited comparisons to Linda Ronstadt and Brenda Lee. Sweet had begun performing at age five, when she won first prize at an Akron talent contest with a rendition of "I Am a Pretty Little Dutch Girl." She went on to perform in summer stock theater, in TV commercials, and in club shows with Mickey Rooney and Bill Cosby. At age 11, she cut a minor country & western hit single for Derrick Records in Nashville. A few years later, producer Liam Sternberg (a friend of Sweet's father) asked her to sing on a demo of his songs, which he sent to Stiff. Sweet was attending Firestone High School in Akron when "Who Does Lisa Like?" became a minor hit in England and New York City. A cover of Carla Thomas' "B-A-B-Y," from Sweet's debut album, also generated some attention, as did her segments in the 1979 Be Stiff tour and her own tour backed by British band Fingerprintz.

With her second album. Sweet parted ways with Sternberg and Stiff, and has since been searching for a major pop hit. She reached the Top Fifty with "Everlasting Love," a duet with teen idol Rex Smith; it appeared on . . . *And Then He Kissed Me.* Sweet herself wrote and produced the album *Blame It on Love* and in 1982 she worked on a 3D horror film, *Rock 'n' Roll Hotel.* In 1988 she sang the title song of John Waters' *Hairspray.* She has since appeared on the Comedy Channel and voices the animated Barbie.

Sweet

Formed 1968, London, England
Brian Connolly (b. Oct. 5, 1948, Middlesex, Eng.), voc.; Mick Tucker (b. July 17, 1948, Middlesex), voc., drums; Andy Scott (b. July 30, 1949, Wexham, Wales), gtr., kybds., voc.; Steve Priest (b. Feb. 23, 1950, Middlesex), bass, voc., harmonica.
1971—*Funny How Sweet Co-Co Can Be* (RCA) 1972—*Biggest Hits* 1973—*Sweet* (Bell) 1974— *Sweet Fanny Adams* (RCA) 1975—*Desolation Boulevard* (Capitol); *Strung Up* (RCA) 1976—*Give Us a Wink* (Capitol) 1977—*Off the Record* 1978— *Level Headed* (– Connolly; + Gary Moberley, kybds.); *The Sweet* (Camden) 1979—*A Cut Above the Rest* 1980—*Water's Edge* (Capitol) 1982— *Identity Crisis* (Polydor, U.K.) 1990—*Live at the Marquee* (Maze) 1992—*The Best of Sweet* (Capitol).

One of the leading British hard-rock/bubblegum bands in the Chinnichap stable of British writer/producers Nicky Chinn and Mike Chapman, Sweet had hits in the U.K. and later in America as well. The band was originally formed by Brian Connolly and Mick Tucker as Wainwright's Gentlemen in 1968. As Sweet, they recorded four unsuccessful singles that flopped before Chinnichap took over in 1971. Their U.K. hits that year in-

cluded "Co-Co" and "Funny Funny." In 1972 came "Poppa Joe," "Little Willy" (also Top Ten in America in 1973), and "Wig Wam Bam"; and in 1973, "Blockbuster," "Hell Raiser," and "Ballroom Blitz" (Top Ten in the U.S. two years later).

By 1973, the blatant nature of many of Sweet's lyrics and overt stage antics led some British clubs to ban the group. They subsequently tried to abandon their bubblegum image and parted unamicably from Chinnichap. They went on to hit in 1976 in both the U.K. and the U.S. with the Top Ten single "Fox on the Run," but they didn't really change their sound until 1978's *Level Headed* (#52), which yielded the worldwide smash "Love Is Like Oxygen" (#8). A followup entitled "California Nights" was a modest U.S. hit but their last here. Things were not going so well in the U.K. either, and after the disappointment of *Water's Edge,* the group disbanded.

Sweet has returned in various incarnations with different lineups. A club remix of their hits entitled "It's It's the Sweet Mix" was a U.K. hit in 1985, prompting another re-formation, but it was short-lived. Scott toured in the late Eighties with the group Paddy Goes to Holyhead. Scott and Tucker re-formed the group for *Live at the Marquee.* Connolly is reportedly suffering from a muscular illness.

The Sweet Inspirations

Formed 1950s as the Drinkard Sisters, Newark, New Jersey
Emily "Cissy" Houston, voc.; Sylvia Shemwell (b. Sylvia Guions), voc.; Judy Clay (b. Judy Guions), voc.; Dede Warwick, voc.; Dionne Warwick (b. Marie Dionne Warwick, Dec. 12, 1940, East Orange, N.J.), voc.
Ca. mid-1960s—(– Dionne Warwick; – Dede Warwick; – Clay; + Estelle Brown, voc.; + Myrna Smith, voc.) 1968—*Sweet Inspirations* (Atlantic); *What the World Needs Now Is Love* 1970—(– Houston).

The Sweet Inspirations trace their beginnings back to the Drinkard Sisters, with Cissy Houston and her nieces Dionne and Dede Warwick, along with the Guions sisters, Judy (later Judy Clay) and Sylvia. They recorded gospel music for RCA before the group disbanded, leaving Houston and Sylvia to round out the group with two new members.

This quartet became renowned throughout the record industry for its fine backing work on hundreds of records, including some by Ronnie Hawkins, William Bell, Solomon Burke, Neil Diamond, Dusty Springfield, and Wilson Pickett. They were featured prominently on some of Aretha Franklin's best work. Atlantic Records' Jerry Wexler dubbed them the Sweet Inspirations, and led by Cissy, the group recorded two critically acclaimed albums in 1968 and had a hit single with "Sweet Inspiration" (#18 pop, #5 R&B).

The group continued doing backup work, most notably on Elvis Presley's 1969 hit "Suspicious Minds." They toured with him into the mid-Seventies. In 1970 Houston left to join Darlene Love and Dede Warwick as backup singers for Dionne Warwick [see entry]. The remaining trio continued working, touring with Elvis, and after his death, briefly with Rick Nelson. Former Sweet Inspiration Myrna Smith cowrote the bulk of the material on Beach Boy Carl Wilson's eponymous 1981 solo album.

The Swingin' Blue Jeans

Formed 1958, Liverpool, England
Original lineup: Ray Ennis (b. May 26, 1942, Liverpool), gtr., voc.; Ray Ellis (b. Mar. 8, 1942, Liverpool), gtr.; Les Braid (b. Sep. 15, 1941, Liverpool), bass; Norman Kuhlke (b. June 12, 1942, Liverpool), drums; Paul Moss (b. Liverpool).
N.A.—(– Moss)   1964—(+ Terry Sylvester [b. Jan. 8, 1945, Liverpool], gtr., voc.) *Hippy Hippy Shake* (Imperial); *Shaking Time* (Llectrola)   1965—*Hey Hey Hey Hey*   1968—(– Sylvester)   1973—(Group re-forms)   1993—*Hippy Hippy Shake: The Definitive Collection* (EMI Legends).

In 1963, just as England's Merseybeat sound was coming together, the Swingin' Blue Jeans emerged with one of the wildest rock raveups of the era, a cover of Chan Romero's "Hippy Hippy Shake." It went to #2 in the U.K. and #24 here. The next year, the group's cover of Little Richard's "Good Golly Miss Molly" hit #11, and a version of the Betty Everett hit "You're No Good" (a hit for Linda Ronstadt over a decade later) made it to #3. Though they continued to record and perform, and even re-formed in the early Seventies, no further successes came. Terry Sylvester later joined the Hollies, replacing Graham Nash. Through the early Nineties a version of the group has continued to tour.

Swing Out Sister

Formed c. 1986, Manchester, England
Corinne Drewery (b. Sep. 21, 1959, Eng.), voc.; Andy Connell, kybds.; Martin Jackson, drums.
1987—*It's Better to Travel* (Mercury)   1988— (– Jackson)   1989—*Kaleidoscope World* (Fontana/Mercury)   1992—*Get in Touch with Yourself* (Fontana).

This British dance-pop band scored right out of the box with its first single, "Breakout" (#6, 1987), a sprightly and melodic showcase for Corinne Drewery's bright vocals. The song's video gently mocked Drewery's background as a fashion designer. Andy Connell had played with Manchester-based avant-fusion band A Certain Ratio, while Martin Jackson had drummed with such bands as Magazine. Jackson left after the #1 U.K. LP *It's Better to Travel* (#40, 1987), which yielded a lesser hit in "Twilight World" (#31, 1987); he contributed drum programming to *Kaleidoscope World* (#61, 1989), which spawned the single "Waiting Game" (#86, 1989). *Get in Touch with Yourself* (#113, 1992) yielded the minor hit single "Am I the Same Girl" (#45, 1992).

David Sylvian: See Japan

Tackhead

Formed 1987, London, England
Keith LeBlanc, drums, perc., kybds.; Doug Wimbish, bass; Skip McDonald, gtr.; Bernard Fowler, voc.; Gary Clail, voc.; Adrian Sherwood, producer.
1990—*Friendly As a Hand Grenade* (TVT); *Strange Things* (SBK).
As Keith LeBlanc: 1986—*Major Malfunction* (World) 1989—*Stranger Than Fiction* (Nettwerk).
As Gary Clail's Tackhead Sound System: 1987—*Tackhead Tape Time* (Nettwerk).
As Gary Clail & On-U Sound System: 1989—*End of the Century Party* (On-U Sound).
As Gary Clail: 1991—*The Emotional Hooligan* (Perfecto).
As Little Axe: 1995—*The Wolf That House Built* (Okeh).

An umbrella techno-dance group, Tackhead was put together in the mid-Eighties when members of the Sugarhill house band—Keith LeBlanc, Doug Wimbish, and Skip McDonald—joined British dub producer Adrian Sherwood's On-U Sound label. British vocalist Gary Clail joined soon afterward, his lyrics giving the group a political bent; Clail was later replaced by vocalist Bernard Fowler. Tackhead's sound is characterized by highly experimental mixes of samples, harsh beats, funky instrumentals, spaced-out dub tracks, found sounds, tangled raps, and sung vocals. The group's groundbreaking single, "The Game," was released in 1987 and mixed heavy-metal guitar with a dance beat and samples from a sporting event.

In the early Eighties core Sugarhill members (future members of Tackhead) first came together in Bristol, Connecticut, to back rap groups such as the Sugar Hill Gang [see entry] on such records as "Rapper's Delight." The group's first full-length album, *Major Malfunction*, came out under LeBlanc's name, as did a 1983 12-inch dance single, "No Sell Out." Featuring samples of Malcolm X speeches over a spare hip-hop track, "No Sell Out" was released to great interest among the hip-hop community. The group began using the Tackhead moniker on 1987's *Tackhead Tape Time*. Tackhead and its unfixed membership continue to record in various forms into the Nineties.

Take 6

Formed 1987, Huntsville, Alabama
Alvin Chea (b. Nov. 2, 1967, San Francisco, Calif.), voc.; Mervyn Warren, voc.; David Thomas (b. Oct. 23, 1966, Brooklyn, N.Y.), voc.; Cedric Dent (b. Sep. 24, 1962, Detroit, Mich.), voc.; Claude V. McKnight III (b. Oct. 2, 1962, Brooklyn), voc.; Mark Kibble (b. April 7, 1964, Bronx, N.Y.), voc.
1988—*Take 6* (Reprise)   1990—*So Much 2 Say*

1991—(– Warren; + Joel Kibble [b. May 16, 1971, Buffalo, N.Y.], voc.) *He Is Christmas* 1994—*Join the Band.*

Take 6 is an a cappella gospel group that achieved surprising critical and commercial success with their sophisticated jazz-based arrangements. The group formed in the early Eighties at Oakwood College, a Seventh Day Adventist school. Mark Kibble joined when he heard a quartet singing in a bathroom and added his own improvisation; as the group's primary arranger, he expanded their sound from barbershop quartet to big band, with voices imitating instruments. He also brought in sixth member Mervyn Warren. Originally called Alliance, Take 6 changed their name in 1987 (the same year they signed to Reprise) when they discovered another band with that name.

Their first album contains old spirituals and compositions by Kibble and Warren. *Take 6,* featuring "Spread Love," won two Grammys and went gold. *So Much 2 Say* (#72 pop, #22 R&B, 1990) features a larger array of original compositions penned by additional band members. The added variety includes instruments—everyone in the group also plays, and Dent and Warren have done graduate work in music theory—and hip-hop and Latin rhythms. Their second album also went gold and won a Grammy. In 1990 Take 6 performed with k. d. lang in the film *Dick Tracy* singing "Ridin' the Rails."

Warren left the band in 1991; he had composed TV theme songs along the way, including the one for *Murphy Brown,* which Take 6 sang. He was replaced by Mark's brother Joel. *He Is Christmas,* which also won a Grammy, is a collection of carols. Take 6 has recorded with Dianne Reeves, Quincy Jones, Joe Sample, Johnny Mathis, and Smokey Robinson. The group's 1994 recording, *Join the Band* (#86 pop, #17 R&B), featured such artists as Ray Charles, Stevie Wonder, Queen Latifah, and Herbie Hancock.

Talking Heads

Formed 1975, New York City, New York
David Byrne (b. May 14, 1952, Dumbarton, Scot.), voc., gtr.; Tina Weymouth (b. Nov. 22, 1950, Coronado, Calif.), bass, synth.; Chris Frantz (b. May 8, 1951, Ft. Campbell, Ky.), drums; Jerry Harrison (b. Feb. 21, 1949, Milwaukee, Wis.), kybds., gtr.
1977—*77* (Sire) 1978—*More Songs About Buildings and Food* 1979—*Fear of Music* 1980—*Remain in Light* 1982—*The Name of This Band Is Talking Heads* 1983—*Speaking in Tongues* 1984—*Stop Making Sense* 1985—*Little Creatures* 1986—*True Stories* 1988—*Naked* 1992—*Popular Favorites 1976–1992: Sand in the Vaseline.*
Tom Tom Club (Weymouth; Frantz; + others): 1981—*Tom Tom Club* (Sire) 1983—*Close to the*

Talking Heads: Tina Weymouth, Jerry Harrison, Chris Frantz, David Byrne

Bone 1989—*Boom Boom Chi Boom Boom* 1992—*Dark Sneak Love Action.*
Jerry Harrison solo: 1981—*The Red and the Black* (Sire) 1988—*Casual Gods* 1990—*Walk on Water.*
David Byrne solo: See entry.

Talking Heads was a band of smart, self-conscious white musicians intrigued by the rhythms and spirit of black music. They drew on funk, classical minimalism, and African rock to create some of the most adventurous, original, and danceable music to emerge from new wave—a movement Talking Heads outlasted and transcended in their accomplishment and influence.

David Byrne and Chris Frantz met at the Rhode Island School of Design, where they were part of a quintet called, variously, the Artistics and the Autistics. With Tina Weymouth, Frantz's girlfriend, they shared an apartment in New York and formed Talking Heads as a trio in 1975; they played their first shows at CBGB that June. Their music was never conventional punk rock; it was more delicate and contrapuntal, and their early sets included covers of the 1910 Fruitgum Company. Jerry Harrison, a Harvard alumnus who had been a Modern Lover with Jonathan Richman until 1974 and had also backed Elliott Murphy, completed the band in 1977.

Talking Heads toured Europe with the Ramones before recording their first album, and once it was released they began constant touring of the U.S. and Europe. Their first album contained "Psycho Killer," which typecast them as eccentrics, an impression confirmed by Byrne's nervous, wild-eyed stage presence. The album reached the Top 100, and every subsequent album reached the U.S. Top Forty.

With *More Songs About Buildings and Food,* Talking Heads began a four-year relationship with producer Brian Eno, an experimentalist who toyed with electronically altered sounds and shared their growing interest in

Arabian and African music. *More Songs* included a cover of Al Green's "Take Me to the River," which was the band's first hit (#26, 1978). *Fear of Music* (#21, 1979) was a denser, more ominous record, but its followup, *Remain in Light* (#19, 1980), was an almost complete shift in tone—it used rhythm tracks improvised by Eno and the band in the studio that were layered with vocals and solos, a mixture of African communalism and Western technology (an approach signaled by "I Zimbra," the opening track on *Fear of Music*).

After *Remain in Light,* Talking Heads toured the world with an expanded band: keyboardist Bernie Worrell of Parliament/Funkadelic, guitarist Adrian Belew (who had played with Frank Zappa and David Bowie), bassist Busta Cherry Jones, percussionist Steven Scales, and singers Nona Hendryx (formerly of Labelle) and Dollette McDonald.

Band members then turned to solo projects. Byrne has explored electronics, performance art, and world music and scored music for films and the stage [see entry]; Harrison made *The Red and the Black*; and Frantz and Weymouth recorded as the Tom Tom Club, scoring a major disco hit with "Genius of Love," which made the album go platinum. In 1982 the Heads ended their association with Eno; they released a compilation of live performances by all versions of the band and toured the U.S. and Europe as an eight-piece group.

Speaking in Tongues, the first album of new Heads songs in three years, was released in 1983. It was their highest-charting album ever (#15, 1983) and yielded their biggest hit single, "Burning Down the House" (#9, 1983). They toured with an expanded band including Alex Weir, a guitarist with the Brothers Johnson. The tour was documented in the acclaimed movie *Stop Making Sense,* directed by Jonathan Demme. The soundtrack (#41, 1984) spent nearly two years on the pop album chart.

The Heads returned to their core lineup, and simpler song forms, on *Little Creatures* (#20, 1985), which included the Cajun-flavored single "Road to Nowhere" and "Stay Up Late," a sardonic commentary on parenting (which Frantz and Weymouth, by then married, were doing). That album, like its predecessor, went platinum (the only two to do so). In 1986 Byrne directed the feature film *True Stories* (#17), a seemingly sincere look at small-town American eccentrics; the soundtrack album, on which Talking Heads performed straightforward versions of songs sung by various characters in the film, yielded a hit single in "Wild Wild Life" (#25, 1986).

Naked (#19, 1988), produced in Paris by Steve Lillywhite (U2, Simple Minds) and reggae/world-beat keyboardist/producer Wally Badarou, featured guest performances by assorted African and Caribbean musicians living in Paris. After producing the hit album *Conscious Party* for Ziggy Marley and the Melody Makers, Weymouth and Frantz got Byrne, Harrison, and Lou Reed

to guest on Tom Tom Club's *Boom Boom Chi Boom Boom,* for a version of the Velvet Underground's "Femme Fatale." In 1990 Tom Tom Club and Harrison's band Casual Gods (which included Alex Weir) toured the U.S. with the Ramones and ex-Blondie singer Deborah Harry.

The long-rumored dissolution of Talking Heads was made official, sort of, in December 1991—when Byrne told the *Los Angeles Times* the band was finished. A month later Harrison, Weymouth, and Frantz issued a statement of their disappointment, adding that "Talking Heads *was* a great band." The band's final four new tracks were released as part of the *Popular Favorites* box-set retrospective.

Tangerine Dream

Formed 1967, Germany
Edgar Froese (b. June 6, 1944, Tilsit, Ger.), synth., kybds., gtr.; Klaus Schulze (b. Aug. 4, 1947, Ger.), synth., kybds.; Konrad Schnitzler, flute.
1970—*Electronic Meditation* (Ohr)   1971— (– Schulze; – Schnitzler; + Christopher Franke [b. Apr. 6, 1953, Berlin, Ger.], synth.; + Steve Shroyder, organ) *Alpha Centauri*   1972—(+ Peter Baumann, synth., kybds., flute) *Zeit* (– Shroyder); *Atem* 1974—*Phaedra* (Virgin)   1975—*Rubycon*; *Live* 1976—*Atem Alpha Centauri*; *Richocet*; *Stratosfear* 1977—*Sorcerer* soundtrack (MCA)   1978—(– Baumann; + Steve Jollife, flute; + Klaus Kreiger, drums) *Cyclone* (Virgin)   1979—*Force Majeure* (+ Johannes Schmoelling, synth., kybds.)   1980—*Tamgram*   1981—*Thief* soundtrack   1982—*Exit* (Elektra)   1984—*Poland* (Relativity)   1985— (– Schmoelling; + Paul Haslinger, kybds.) *Le Parc* 1986—*Legend* (MCA)   1987—*Tyger*   1988— (– Franke; + Ralf Wadephal, kybds.) *Optical Race* (Private Music)   1989—*Lily on the Beach*   1990— *Melrose*   1992—*Rockoon*   1994—*Turn of the Tides* (Miramar)   1995—*Tyranny of Beauty.*

This German ensemble, its lineup constantly shifting, has been responsible for introducing some of the spaciest exploratory synthesizer music. Though many critics have dismissed them as mere self-absorbed postpsychedelic electro-doodlers, others have praised them as sonic painters. Not only did they build up a tenacious European cult following in the Seventies, but they can be seen as precursors both of New Age and ambient-techno music.

They started out as a rock band featuring Edgar Froese (a classical music student, as was Christopher Franke), but as they became increasingly enamored of far-flung improvisations, they abandoned guitars and drums in favor of an almost completely electronic keyboard/synthesizer setup that produced echoing, droning atmospheres rather than conventional songs. Original member Klaus Schulze went on to a career of his own, in much the same musical vein, and mainstay Froese came even further to the fore.

In 1974 the group gained attention by playing a concert at Rheims cathedral in France, at which some 6000 fans tried to jam into the 2000-capacity church to hear Tangerine Dream's always-improvised and often arrhythmic, protoplasmic electronics. The next year they went to Britain for the first time, again playing cathedrals wherever possible. The tour was sold out, and featured Michael Hoenig replacing Baumann, who was busy working on his first solo album, *Romance '76*. By that time, Froese had recorded his first solo outing, *Aqua*. Among his other works are *Epsilon in Malaysian Pale, Electronic Dreams, Ages, Macula Transfer, Stunt Man, Pinnacles,* and *Kamikaze 1989*. Baumann later founded the Private Music label.

In the mid-Seventies, as they introduced vocals and lyrics (on *Cyclone*) and otherwise continued to gather fans familiar with Pink Floyd and Yes, Tangerine Dream achieved some degree of cult success in the U.S., though never on the scale they enjoyed in England and Europe. Baumann left to pursue a solo career, releasing *Repeat Repeat* in 1982, the title cut of which was a minor hit in dance clubs. At the start of the Eighties, Tangerine Dream became the first Western band to play East Berlin; they also began experimenting with sampling techniques. Key member Christopher Franke left in 1988 to pursue a solo career, composing film soundtracks and New Age music (*Pacific Coast Highway, The London Concert, New Music for Films*). As a duo, Tangerine Dream soldiered on.

Tavares

Formed circa 1959, New Bedford, Massachusetts
Ralph Tavares (b. Dec. 10, 1948); Arthur "Pooch" Tavares (b. Nov. 12, 1946); Feliciano "Butch" Tavares (b. May 18, 1953); Perry Lee "Tiny" Tavares (b. Oct. 24, 1954); Antone "Chubby" Tavares (b. June 2, 1947).
1974—*Check It Out* (Capitol); *Hard Core Poetry* 1975—*In the City* 1976—*Sky High!* 1977—*Love Storm; The Best of Tavares* 1978—*Future Bound* 1979—*Madam Butterfly* 1980—*Supercharged; Love Uprising* 1981—*Loveline* 1982—*New Directions* (RCA) 1993—*The Best of Tavares* (Capitol).

Throughout the Seventies, the harmonizing Tavares brothers had several R&B and disco hit singles. Their hit version of Hall and Oates' "She's Gone" paved the way for that duo's later success.

The group's grandparents were from the Cape Verde Islands (a Portuguese province in the Atlantic Ocean), and as children the five brothers learned to sing island folk songs and doo-wop favorites from their older brother, John. In 1963 they turned pro as Chubby and the Turnpikes, playing clubs throughout New England. By the time they signed with Capitol in 1973, they had changed their group name to Tavares. Tavares' first album was produced by Johnny Bristol, the second two by the Brian Potter–Dennis Lambert team. The group had hits with two ballads, "Check It Out" (#35 pop, #5 R&B, 1973) and "She's Gone" (#50 pop, #1 R&B, 1974). Ex–Motown producer Freddie Perren took over on *Sky High!*, and the group had the first of a string of pop-disco hits, which include "It Only Takes a Minute" (#10 pop, #1 R&B, 1975), "Heaven Must Be Missing an Angel" (#15 pop, #3 R&B, 1976), and "Whodunit" (#22 pop, #1 R&B, 1977). Major public exposure came when their "More Than a Woman" (#32 pop, #36 R&B) was included on the multimillion-selling *Saturday Night Fever* soundtrack album.

After that, the group had a higher profile on the concert circuit and on the R&B charts than with pop audiences. Their later hits included "Bad Times" (#10 R&B, 1979), "A Penny for Your Thoughts" (#16 R&B, 1982), "Deeper in Love" (#10 R&B, 1983), and "Words and Music" (#29 R&B, 1983).

James Taylor

Born March 12, 1948, Boston, Massachusetts
1966—*James Taylor* (Apple)   1970—*Sweet Baby James* (Warner Bros.)   1971—*James Taylor and the Original Flying Machine, 1967* (Euphoria 2); *Mud Slide Slim and the Blue Horizon* (Warner Bros.) 1972—*One Man Dog*   1974—*Walking Man*   1975— *Gorilla*   1976—*In the Pocket; Greatest Hits* 1977—*J. T.* (Columbia)   1979—*Flag*   1981—*Dad Loves His Work*   1985—*That's Why I'm Here* 1988—*Never Die Young*   1991—*New Moon Shine* 1993—*James Taylor Live*   1994—*Best Live.*

James Taylor was the archetypal "sensitive" singer/songwriter of the Seventies. His songs, especially his early ones, were tales of inner torment delivered in low-key tunes featuring Taylor's understated tenor and his intricate acoustic guitar accompaniments that drew on folk and jazz. Taylor came across as relaxed, personable, and open; he was imitated by a horde of would-be confessionalists, although his best songs were as artful as they were emotional. They weren't folk songs; they were pop compositions with folk's dynamics, and in them Taylor put across more bitterness and resignation than reassurance. As he continued to record, Taylor split his albums between cover singles that were hits ("Handy Man," "You've Got a Friend") and his own songs, maturing into a laid-back artist with a large and devoted following of baby boomers.

Born into a wealthy family, Taylor grew up in Boston. The family subsequently lived in Chapel Hill, North Carolina, where James' father became dean of the medical school of the University of North Carolina, and on Martha's Vineyard off the coast of Cape Cod. Everyone in the family was musical; James initially played the cello. His older brother Alex introduced him to folk and country music, and James soon took up the guitar. When he was 15, summering on Martha's Vineyard, he met another budding guitarist, Danny Kortchmar. Taylor attended high school at a private academy outside Boston. Lonely away from his family, he took off a term in his junior year to return to Chapel Hill, where he played local gigs with Alex's rock band. In 1965 he committed himself to a mental institution—McLean Psychiatric Hospital in Belmont, Massachusetts—to which his sister Kate and brother Livingston would later be admitted. There he began writing songs.

After ten months, he discharged himself and went to New York City, where Kortchmar was putting together the Flying Machine. The group played Greenwich Village coffeehouses and recorded two Taylor originals, "Night Owl" and "Brighten Your Night with My Day," in early 1967 before breaking up. Their demo tape was released as an album after Taylor became popular. One reason for the group's breakup was Taylor's addiction to heroin. In early 1968 he went to England, and in London he recorded a tape of his material and sent it to Peter Asher. As an A&R man for the Beatles' Apple Records, Asher encouraged Paul McCartney to sign him. In mid-1968 Taylor recorded his debut album in London; Asher produced and McCartney and George Harrison sat in on one cut. The LP attracted little attention, and Taylor, still hooked on heroin at the end of the year, returned to America and signed himself into another mental institution. During Taylor's five-month stay, with Apple in disarray, Asher—who became Taylor's producer and manager—negotiated a contract between Taylor and Warner Bros. Before Taylor was released, his solo stage debut at L.A.'s Troubadour had been arranged. From there he went to the Newport Folk Festival, where he met Joni Mitchell (she sang on *Mud Slide Slim*, and he played guitar on her autobiographical *Blue*).

Taylor and Asher rounded up Kortchmar, bassist Lee Sklar, drummer Russ Kunkel, and pianist Carole King to back him on his second album. *Sweet Baby James* attracted little initial attention. Eventually, however, "Fire and Rain" reached #3. *Sweet Baby James* reached the Top Ten in November 1970 and stayed on the LP chart into 1972. Taylor's Apple debut was rereleased, entering the charts in October with the single "Carolina in My Mind." Taylor appeared on a March 1971 cover of *Time* magazine, which hailed his ascent to stardom as a turn toward maturity and restraint in pop music, but at the same time publicized his drug abuse and other skeletons in his and his family's closet. The article also alluded to a possible dynasty of Taylor-made pop stars. Livingston

Taylor had launched his singing and songwriting career before his older brother had become famous, but Alex and Kate, while unquestionably musical, found less success.

Within two months of its release, *Mud Slide Slim* was the nation's #2 album. Taylor's version of Carole King's "You've Got a Friend" hit #1 in 1971, the same year that King's version came out on *Tapestry*. That year Taylor costarred with Dennis Wilson of the Beach Boys in the film *Two-Lane Blacktop*.

Then, almost as suddenly as he had emerged into public attention, he retreated from it. Except for a few benefit concerts for George McGovern's 1972 presidential campaign, Taylor did not perform for another three years. He married Carly Simon in November 1972. Taylor continued to make and sell albums, but he didn't score a Top Ten single between "You've Got a Friend" and a cover of Marvin Gaye's "How Sweet It Is" in 1975. ("Mockingbird," a duet, was released by Simon in 1974.) *One Man Dog* (#4, 1973) contained "Don't Let Me Be Lonely Tonight" (#14, 1973); *Walking Man* (#13, 1974) boasted no hit singles.

A month-long tour in 1974 signaled Taylor's reemergence. He returned to the charts with *Gorilla* (#6, 1975). Taylor's cover of "How Sweet It Is (To Be Loved by You)" hit #5 in 1975. *J. T.* (#4, 1977), including a Top Five cover of the Jimmy Jones–Otis Blackwell "Handy Man," was Taylor's first release on Columbia. *Greatest Hits* (#23, 1977), for which he rerecorded "Carolina in My Mind" and "Something in the Way She Moves," fulfilled his obligations to Warners; he signed Columbia's lucrative contract before *Hits* was released. *J. T.* also marked Asher's return as producer.

Taylor's albums since *J. T.* have not quite repeated its success—*Flag* and *Dad Loves His Work* both hit #10—but they have sold consistently. In 1978 he joined Paul Simon and Art Garfunkel on a Top Twenty cover of Sam Cooke's "Wonderful World," released by Garfunkel. In 1979 he wrote a couple of songs for a Broadway musical, *Working. Flag* yielded a Top Thirty hit with Taylor's typically understated cover of the Brill Building classic "Up on the Roof." Taylor continued to support a variety of causes with benefit concerts. He campaigned for Jimmy Carter in 1976 and for John Anderson in 1980; in 1979 he participated in the MUSE antinuclear rally concerts at Madison Square Garden and appeared in the concert film *No Nukes*.

Taylor's 1981 album, *Dad Loves His Work,* yielded a hit single duet with J. D. Souther, "Her Town Too" (#11), released amid rumors that his marriage to Simon was ending. In 1982 Simon sued Taylor for divorce. Taylor spent 1982–85 touring the globe, with a band featuring Little Feat's Bill Payne on piano. *That's Why I'm Here* (#34, 1985), with guests including Joni Mitchell, Don Henley, and Graham Nash, yielded only a minor hit single in a cover of Buddy Holly's "Everyday" (#61, 1985). In December 1985 Taylor wed for the second time, to Kathryn Walker. He continued touring extensively between albums.

Johnnie Taylor

Born May 5, 1938, Crawsfordsville, Arkansas
1968—*Wanted: One Soul Singer* (Stax)   1969—*Who's Makin' Love*; *Raw Blues*; *The Johnnie Taylor Philosophy Continues*   1970—*Johnnie Taylor's Greatest Hits*   1971—*One Step Beyond*   1973—*Taylored in Silk*   1974—*Super Taylor*   1976—*Eargasm* (Columbia)   1977—*Rated Extraordinaire*; *Chronicle—The 20 Greatest Hits* (Stax)   1978—*Ever Ready* (Columbia); *Disco 9000*; *The Johnnie Taylor Chronicle* (Stax); *Reflections* (RCA)   1985—*This Is Your Night* (Malaco)   1988—*In Control*   1990—*Crazy for You*; *Little Bluebird* (Stax)   1991—*I Know It's Wrong, But I . . . Just Can't Do Right* (Malaco)   1992—*The Best of Johnnie Taylor . . . on Malaco, vol. 1*   1994—*Real Love.*

Johnnie Taylor's gritty soul vocals made him a steady mid-Sixties hitmaker and gave him one mammoth disco hit in 1976. Taylor made his recording debut with a Vee Jay doo-wop group, the Five Echoes, in 1955. In 1957 he became lead singer of the Soul Stirrers, replacing Sam Cooke in the influential gospel quintet. After leaving the Soul Stirrers in 1963, Taylor signed with Cooke's SAR label. Although he abandoned gospel music, songs like "Rome (Wasn't Built in a Day)" reflected his deep religious roots.

Taylor hit his commercial stride after signing with Stax in 1965. Two 1966 releases, "I Had a Dream" (#19 R&B) and "I Got to Love Somebody's Baby" (#15 R&B), were minor hits. With "Who's Making Love" (#5 pop, #1 R&B) in 1968, Taylor replaced the late Otis Redding as Stax's leading male singer. "Take Care of Your Homework" (#20 pop, #2 R&B), "Testify (I Wanna)" (#4 R&B), "I Could Never Be President" (#10 R&B), and "Love Bones" (#4 R&B) in 1969; "Steal Away" (#3 R&B) and "I Am Somebody, Part II" (#3 R&B) in 1970; and "Jody's Got Your Girl and Gone" (#1 R&B) and "Hi-Jackin' Love" (#10 R&B) in 1971 continued the streak. "I Believe in You" (#1 R&B) and "Cheaper to Keep Her" (#15 pop, #2 R&B) were his last big hits for Stax.

By 1975 Stax was in turmoil, and its distributor, CBS, took over Taylor's contract. The next year, Taylor's "Disco Lady" (#1 pop and R&B) became the first single ever to be certified platinum. His last Top Forty pop hit was "Somebody's Gettin' It" (#33, 1976), although several of his singles appeared on the R&B chart through 1990. He still tours and records, most recently a string of well-received albums for the Malaco label.

Koko Taylor

Born Cora Walton, September 28, 1935, Memphis, Tennessee
1968—*Koko Taylor*   1975—*I Got What It Takes* (Alligator); *Southside Baby* (Black & Blue)   1978—*The Earthshaker* (Alligator)   1981—*From the Heart of a Woman*   1984—*Blues Explosion* (with others) (Atlantic)   1985—*Queen of the Blues* (Alligator)   1987—*Live from Chicago—An Audience with the Queen*   1990—*Jump for Joy*   1991—*What It Takes: The Chess Years* (Chess)   1993—*Force of Nature* (Alligator).*

A mighty-voiced urban blues singer, Koko Taylor is regarded as the contemporary Queen of the Blues. She grew up in Memphis on a sharecropper's farm. She began singing in her local church choir in her teens, but fell under the influence of the blues. At age 18 she and her husband Robert Taylor moved to Chicago, where she began performing with the Buddy Guy/Junior Wells Blues Band. In 1962 Willie Dixon discovered her and arranged for her to begin recording for Chess. He produced her million-selling hit, 1965's "Wang Dang Doodle," as well as other sides. From then through the present, she has toured the U.S. and Europe extensively.

In 1970 she appeared in the film *The Blues Is Alive and Well in Chicago,* and she played the Montreux Jazz and Blues Festival in 1972 with Muddy Waters. Taylor began recording for Alligator, a Chicago-based independent label specializing in blues, in 1974, and the following year formed her own band, the Blues Machine. She appeared as a singer in David Lynch's film *Wild at Heart* (1990). Of her seven Alligator releases to date, five were nominated for Grammy Awards, and in 1984 *Blues Explosion,* which featured Taylor and Her Blues Machine, Stevie Ray Vaughan and Double Trouble, and others won the Grammy for Best Traditional Blues Recording. As of this writing, she has received 14 W. C. Handy Awards, more than any other female blues artist.

Livingston Taylor: See James Taylor

Bram Tchaikovsky: See the Motors

Teardrop Explodes: See Julian Cope

Tears for Fears

Formed 1982, Bath, England
Roland Orzabal (b. Aug. 22, 1961, Havant, Eng.), voc., gtr.; Curt Smith (b. June 24, 1961, Bath), bass, voc.
1983—*The Hurting* (Mercury)   1985—*Songs from the Big Chair*   1989—*The Seeds of Love*   1992—*Tears Roll Down (Greatest Hits '82–'92)*   1993—

(– Smith) *Elemental* 1995—*Raoul and the Kings of Spain.*
Curt Smith solo: 1993—*Soul On Board* (Mercury).

The British pop duo Tears for Fears enjoyed their commercial breakthrough in 1985 with *Songs from the Big Chair*, an album of lush, literate songs that fused Beatle-sesque melodies with techno-savvy arrangements. Having met as troubled adolescents, band members Roland Orzabal and Curt Smith wrote and sang about the importance of emotional self-awareness and self-expression. Some critics found their songs whiny or precious, but most praised their tender craftsmanship.

Orzabal and Smith became friends while growing up in Bath. Both were from broken homes, and Smith, whose parents had divorced when he was very young, had dabbled in vandalism and petty theft as an adolescent. Orzabal turned to reading instead, and eventually introduced Smith to the writings of psychotherapist Arthur Janov, whose "primal scream" theory stressed that adult neuroses tend to stem from parental abandonment in childhood and that direct confrontation with these early feelings of loss is emotionally vital. In their late teens Orzabal and Smith formed a power pop band called Graduate, but dissolved that outfit in the early Eighties and focused on exploring Janov's theories, which had also influenced John Lennon, in a musical context.

As Tears for Fears, Orzabal and Smith—with some added help from ex–Graduate keyboardist Ian Stanley—began writing songs and arranging them for synthesizers. A demo of a song called "Pale Shelter" won them a recording contract, and in 1983 their debut album, *The Hurting*, was released, yielding three Top Five singles in the U.K. But Tears' American breakthrough came with their sophomore effort: *Songs from the Big Chair* topped the pop albums chart here, and scored two #1 singles, "Everybody Wants to Rule the World" and "Shout," as well as the #3 hit "Head over Heels."

The band took a career risk by waiting four years before releasing a followup to *Songs. The Seeds of Love* reached #8 and yielded a #2 single, "Sowing the Seeds of Love." It also provided a showcase for guest vocalist and rising R&B artist Oleta Adams, who sang backup on the track "Woman in Chains," and whose sultry vocals contributed to the new tracks' warmer feel.

Four years again passed before another Tears for Fears studio album (a hits compilation came out in 1992); and since Smith left the act in the interim, 1993's *Elemental* (#45) was essentially Roland Orzabal's solo debut. The album, which went gold, generated the single "Break It Down Again" (#25, 1993). That same year, Curt Smith released a solo album, *Soul On Board*. In 1994 Orzabal recorded another Tears for Fears LP, *Raoul and the Kings of Spain*, which was released in 1995.

Techno

Techno is a computer-generated dance-music style that mates the ubiquitous big beat of disco with the rapid-fire intensity of punk. Its artists are DJs who use turntables, digital samplers, and sequencers to combine a seemingly unlimited palette of found sounds (fragments of prerecorded songs, drumbeats, whistles, television chatter, and so forth) into extended suites of chaotic, stop-and-start dance music. The "hardness" of techno is measured by its beats per minute (or bpm). Detractors complain that techno is too repetitive, nervous, noisy, soulless, or asexual. Defenders champion its dense textures and rhythmic, trance-inducing qualities.

Developed in Detroit by Derrick May, and nurtured in the U.K. during the 1980s at all-night underground psychedelic dance parties called raves, techno made its way to the U.S. West Coast in the latter part of the decade. The music and parties were often fueled by the mildly hallucinogenic stimulant Ecstasy. Techno had reached a relatively large cult audience by the early Nineties when major labels began signing and promoting some of the music's leading lights, including 808 State, Moby, the Orb, and Messiah.

Despite the music's success, most techno artists prefer to remain fairly anonymous, DJing in the darkness of the rave milieu behind spiderwebs of wires and computer equipment, and often recording on vinyl records with plain white labels. Sometimes techno DJs perform and record the music's subtle variations (such as the atmospheric, Brian Eno–inspired subgenre "ambient," the rhythmic but spaced-out "trance" sound, or the Chicago-born, groove-oriented "house" style) under different pseudonyms (for example, Aphex Twin has also worked under the names AFX, Polygon Window, and the Dice Man).

Technotronic
Formed March 1989, Aalst, Belgium
Ya Kid K (b. Manuela Barbara Kamosi, Jan. 26, 1972, Kinshasa, Zaire), voc.; Jo Bogaert (b. Thomas de Quincy, May 5, 1956, U.S.), synthesizer; MC Eric (b. Aug. 19, 1968, Cardiff, Wales), voc.
1989—*Pump Up the Jam: The Album* (SBK).

An unlikely success story, Technotronic was a Belgian group that brought house music—the impersonal, club-oriented, electronic postdisco dance music pioneered in Chicago—where it never intended to go: to the top of the pop charts. The group included two young African women, one who rapped in English and one who spoke no English and did not even perform on the group's records.

Technotronic began when ex–philosophy teacher and aspiring record producer Jo Bogaert moved from the U.S. to Belgium in the late Eighties, aiming to infuse house music with hip-hop. He sent his "new beat" music tapes to prospective rappers, including another transplanted American, MC Eric, and a boyish-looking Zairean girl, Ya Kid K, who was with Belgian rap group Fresh Beat Productions. Ya Kid K was featured in "Pump Up the Jam," which became a hit in Europe and then the U.S. (#2, 1989) thanks in large part to its music video, in which Zairean-born fashion model Felly tried to lip sync rapid-fire lyrics in a language she did not speak. Felly was also featured on the cover of the group's album (#10, 1989), causing further confusion. All was cleared up when Ya Kid K and MC Eric took Technotronic on tour, opening shows for DJ Jazzy Jeff and the Fresh Prince, and then for Madonna on her 1990 Blond Ambition Tour. Bogaert later admitted that Felly had been hired purely to give Technotronic "an image." "Get Up! (Before the Night Is Over)" became another dance-to-pop crossover hit (#7, 1990); this time Ya Kid K, who had finally gotten her own management, was featured in the video. Ya Kid K worked with a different Belgian house-music group, Hi Tek 3, to record a solo single, "Spin That Wheel," for SBK's *Teenage Mutant Ninja Turtles* movie soundtrack. In 1992, working with Bogaert and her producer husband Jonathan Kamosi, Ya Kid K recorded the solo album *One World Nation*; it included "Move This," a song from Technotronic's debut album that was released as a single after being featured in a popular Revlon cosmetics commercial starring Cindy Crawford.

Teenage Fanclub

Formed 1989, Glasgow, Scotland
Norman Blake (b. Oct. 20, 1965, Bellshill, Scot.), gtr., voc.; Gerard Love (b. Aug. 31, 1967, Motherwell, Scot.), bass, voc.; Francis MacDonald (b. Nov. 21, 1970, Bellshill), drums; Raymond McGinley (b. Jan. 3, 1964, Glasgow), gtr., voc.
1990—(– MacDonald; + Brendan O'Hare [b. Jan. 16, 1970, Bellshill], drums) A Catholic Education (Matador) 1991—The King; Bandwagonesque (DGC) 1993—Thirteen 1994—(– O'Hare; + Paul Quinn, drums) 1995—Grand Prix.

An alternative to the histrionics of grunge, Teenage Fanclub's witty Sixties-flavored pop songs mixed with a modern guitar sound (exemplified by their 1992 Big Star sound-alike single, "The Concept") gained it a college-radio following in the U.S. and moderate success in the U.K.

Norman Blake and Raymond McGinley were leaders of Glasgow's Boy Hairdressers. They recorded one single, "Golden Shower" (1988), before breaking up, but Blake and McGinley continued working together. With fellow Hairdresser Francis MacDonald and new recruit Gerard Love they began writing new songs, recording an entire album's worth of material before performing in public. Francis MacDonald left for another project and Brendan O'Hare, a teenage fan, quit school to replace him. This version of the band recorded *A Catholic Education*. Signed by independent labels Creation in England and Matador in the States, the album emphasized guitars at the expense of songs, but caught the ear of DGC, which bought the band's U.S. contract.

The King, an album of instrumentals and covers recorded to fulfill Teenage Fanclub's contract with Matador, had a very limited release. Its first DGC album, *Bandwagonesque* (#22 U.K., 1991), produced by Gumball's Don Fleming, showcased the band's songwriting and received critical kudos. An opening slot on Nirvana's 1992 tour brought the group's crowd-pleasing, knockabout performances to a wider audience. The self-produced *Thirteen* (#14 U.K., 1993), like its predecessor, failed to chart in the U.S. *Grand Prix* was released in mid-1995.

Television

Formed 1973, New York City, New York
Tom Verlaine (b. Thomas Miller, Dec. 13, 1949, N.J.), gtr., voc.; Richard Lloyd, gtr., voc.; Richard Hell (b. Richard Myers, Oct. 2, 1949, Lexington, Ky.), bass; Billy Ficca, drums.
1975—(– Hell; + Fred Smith [b. Apr. 10, 1948, New York City], bass) 1977—Marquee Moon (Elektra) 1978—Adventure 1982—The Blow-Up cassette (ROIR) 1992—Television (Capitol).
Tom Verlaine solo: 1980—Tom Verlaine (Elektra) 1981—Dreamtime (Warner Bros.) 1982—Words from the Front 1984—Cover 1987—Flashlight (Phonogram/I.R.S.) 1990—The Wonder 1992— Warm and Cool (Rykodisc).
Richard Lloyd solo: 1980—Alchemy (Elektra) 1985—Field of Fire (Celluloid) 1987—Real Time (Celluloid/Grand Slamm).
Richard Hell solo: See entry.

Television appeared at the same time and place as punk rock—in the mid-Seventies at CBGB. But while the band's harsh attack and obvious affection for the Velvet Underground linked it to the rest of punk, Television's trademark chiming guitars and the tendency of lead guitarist (and main songwriter) Tom Verlaine and rhythm guitarist Richard Lloyd to spur each other on to long jams evoked such psychedelic-era bands as the Grateful Dead. (Verlaine cited the Rolling Stones, classical composer Maurice Ravel, and jazz musicians Miles Davis and Albert Ayler as influences.) Television had a devout following in New York City and had a major effect on British postpunk rock, but its albums were virtually ignored by the mass market.

Tom Miller (who renamed himself Verlaine after the French Symbolist poet) had dropped out of high school in Wilmington, Delaware, and had left colleges in South

Carolina and Pennsylvania before coming to New York in 1968. Richard Hell was a onetime boarding school roommate. With Billy Ficca they formed a short-lived band, the Neon Boys, in 1972. When Lloyd joined in late 1973, they became Television, and were one of the first bands to play at CBGB, along with the Patti Smith Group (Verlaine and Smith collaborated on a book of poetry, *The Night*). The first Television lineup made an independent single, "Little Johnny Jewel," but Hell soon left to form the Heartbreakers [see entry] with ex–New York Doll Johnny Thunders, and later he led the Voidoids. Dee Dee Ramone auditioned as bassist, but the gig went to Fred Smith, who had played in the original Blondie. The new lineup played frequently in New York, to critical raves.

In late 1974 Brian Eno produced the band's demo recordings (which are still unreleased). Despite a growing cult following, Television didn't release its debut album until 1977. *Marquee Moon* sold poorly, but it made many critics' ten-best lists that year. *Adventure* was softer, more reflective and restrained than the debut, and sold a bit better. In 1978 Television broke up; four years later the cassette-only live album, *The Blow-Up,* was released.

Verlaine released seven solo albums, and though he retained a faithful following, he was still more a critical than commercial success. Lloyd released three solo albums, and in the early Nineties recorded with John Doe (of X) and Matthew Sweet. In 1980 Ficca resurfaced with the Waitresses, a New York–Ohio band (led by ex–Tin Huey guitarist Chris Butler), who had a hit with "I Know What Boys Like" in 1981. Smith has played with a number of artists, including the Roches, Willie Nile, the Peregrines, and the Fleshtones, as well as in Verlaine's touring and recording bands and on Lloyd's solo work.

In 1992 Television reunited to record a self-titled album that, as usual, sold modestly but was well received by critics, who noted admiringly that the band's trademarks—brilliant guitar work, clever songwriting, and *noir*ish lyrics—were all still in evidence. The reunited band did a world tour in 1993, and though the group was dropped by Capitol, Television planned to record and tour together again in the future.

Temple of the Dog: See Pearl Jam

The Temptations/David Ruffin/Eddie Kendricks

Formed 1961, Detroit, Michigan
Otis Williams (b. Otis Miles, Oct. 30, 1949, Texarkana, Tex.), baritone voc.; Eddie Kendricks (a.k.a. Kendrick, b. Dec. 17, 1939, Union Springs, Ala.; d. Oct. 5, 1992, Birmingham, Ala.), tenor voc.; Paul Williams (b. July 2, 1939, Birmingham; d. Aug. 17, 1973, Detroit), voc.; Melvin Franklin (b. David

The Temptations: Dennis Edwards, Melvin Franklin, Damon Harris, Richard Street, Otis Williams

English, Oct. 12, 1942, Montgomery, Ala.; d. Feb. 23, 1995, Los Angeles, Calif.), bass voc.; Elbridge Bryant.
1963—(– Bryant; + David Ruffin [b. Davis Eli Ruffin, Jan. 18, 1941, Miss.; d. June 1, 1991, Philadelphia, Pa.], tenor voc.) 1964—*Meet the Temptations* (Gordy) 1965—*Temptations Sing Smokey*; *Temptin' Temptations* 1966—*Gettin' Ready*; *The Temptations' Greatest Hits* 1967—*Temptations Live!*; *With a Lot o' Soul*; *In a Mellow Mood* 1968— *The Temptations Wish It Would Rain*; *Live at the Copa* (– Ruffin; + Dennis Edwards [b. Feb. 3, 1943, Birmingham], lead voc.) 1969—*Cloud Nine*; *Puzzle People* 1970—*Psychedelic Shack*; *Live at London's Talk of the Town*; *Temptations' Greatest Hits, vol. II*; *Christmas Card* 1971—*Sky's the Limit* 1972— (– Kendricks; + Ricky Owens, voc.; – Owens; + Damon Harris [b. July 3, 1950, Baltimore, Md.], tenor voc.; – P. Williams; + Richard Street [b. Oct. 5, 1942, Detroit], tenor voc.) *Solid Rock*; *All Directions* 1973—*Masterpiece*; *Anthology* (Motown); *1990* (Gordy) 1975—*A Song for You*; *House Party* (– Harris; + Glenn Leonard [b. Washington, D.C.], tenor voc.) 1976—*Wings of Love*; *The Temptations Do the Temptations* 1977—(– Edwards; + Louis Price, lead voc.) *Hear to Tempt You* (Atlantic) 1978—*Bare Back* 1979—(– Price; + Edwards) 1980—*Power* (Gordy) 1981—*The Temptations* 1982—(+ Ruffin; + Kendricks) *Reunion* (– Ruffin; – Kendricks) 1983—*Surface Thrills* (– Leonard;

+ Ron Tyson, tenor voc.); *Back to Basics* (– Edwards; + Ali Ollie Woodson, lead voc.) 1984— *Truly for You* 1985—*Touch Me* 1986—*The Temptations' 25th Anniversary* (Motown); *To Be Continued* (Gordy) (– Woodson; + Edwards) 1987—*Together Again* (Motown) (– Edwards; + Woodson) 1989—*Special* 1990—*Solid Rock* 1991—*Milestone* 1993—*Hum Along and Dance: More of the Best (1963–1974)* (Rhino) (– Street; + Theo Peoples, voc.) 1994—*Emperors of Soul* (Motown) 1995—(– Franklin; + Ray Davis [b. Mar. 29, 1940, Sumter, S.C.], voc.).
The Temptations with the Supremes: 1968—*Diana Ross and the Supremes Join the Temptations* (Motown); *TCB* 1969—*Together*; *On Broadway.*
Eddie Kendricks solo: 1971—*All by Myself* (Tamla) 1972—*People . . . Hold On* 1973—*Eddie Kendricks* 1974—*Boogie Down*; *For You* 1975—*The Hit Man* 1976—*He's a Friend*; *Goin' Up in Smoke* 1977— *Slick* 1978—*At His Best*; *Vintage '78* (Arista) 1981—*Love Keys* (Atlantic).
David Ruffin solo: 1969—*My Whole World Ended* (Motown); *Feelin' Good* 1970—*I Am My Brother's Keeper* (with Jimmy Ruffin) (Soul) 1973—*David Ruffin* (Motown) 1974—*Me 'n' Rock 'n' Roll Are Here to Stay* 1975—*Who Am I?* 1976—*Everything's Coming Up Love* 1977—*In My Stride* 1979—*So Soon We Change* (Warner Bros.) 1980— *Gentleman Ruffin.*
David Ruffin and Eddie Kendricks: 1987—*David Ruffin and Eddie Kendricks* (RCA).
Ruffin and Kendricks with Daryl Hall and John Oates: 1985—*Live at the Apollo with David Ruffin and Eddie Kendrick* (RCA).
Dennis Edwards solo: 1984—*Don't Look Any Further* (Gordy) 1985—*Coolin' Out.*

The Temptations were the most consistently commercially successful and critically lauded male vocal group of the Sixties and the early Seventies. In their early "classic" lineup—with alternating lead singers Eddie Kendricks, David Ruffin, and Paul Williams, with Melvin Franklin, and group founder Otis Williams—the Tempts, as they were known, were simply untouchable. Through the years, the group's trademark razor-sharp choreography, finely tuned vocal harmonies, and a number of compelling lead singers (Ruffin, Kendricks, the little-known Paul Williams, and later, Dennis Edwards) made them the exemplars of the Motown style. The Temptations have been distinguished among their Motown stablemates (with the exception of the Four Tops) for their ability to move comfortably from smooth pop and standards to provocative, politically charged rock soul, from the Apollo to the Copacabana (and back). Despite personnel changes and conflicts, through countless triumphs and

setbacks, the Temptations, with Franklin, who died in early 1995, and Otis Williams at the helm, endured.

By 1982, the group had sold an estimated 22 million records worldwide. Because Motown Records has been the sole holdout among record companies in its refusal to open its books for R.I.A.A. certification, neither the Temptations nor any other Motown group with hits before the Eighties ever had an official gold or platinum record. The group's chart statistics, however, are unparalleled: Between 1964 and 1975 they had 19 Top Twenty albums, including their #1 collaboration with the Supremes (*TCB*). Over its career, the group has had 37 Top Forty singles (among them 15 Top Tens, including four at #1) and 28 R&B Top Ten LPs (including 15 at #1).

The original Temptations came together from two struggling vocal groups. Otis Williams (not to be confused with Otis Williams of Charms fame), Elbridge (a.k.a. Al, or El) Bryant, and Melvin Franklin had been in a series of Detroit groups, including Williams' Siberians and Otis Williams and the Distants. Once Franklin, the young bass singer of Detroit's Voice Masters, joined the Distants (which included future Tempt Richard Street), they recorded "Come On" for the local Northern label. Around the time that Williams decided to expand the group, Eddie Kendricks and Paul Williams (no relation to Otis), with Kell Osborne, were working around Detroit as the Primes. Originally from Birmingham, Alabama, this trio was making something of a name for itself in the Motor City. They were doing so well that their manager put together a "sister group," the Primettes, a quartet of young women, three of whom (Diane Ross, Mary Wilson, and Florence Ballard) would later be rechristened the Supremes. Eventually the Primes disbanded, but not before Otis Williams had seen them and been impressed by Kendricks' talent and Paul Williams' knack for creating great choreography.

Kendricks, Paul Williams, Otis Williams, Franklin, and Bryant formed the Elgins in 1961. Later rechristened the Temptations, this lineup recorded two flop singles for the Motown subsidiary label Miracle later that year ("Oh Mother of Mine" b/w "Romance Without Finance" and "Check Yourself" b/w "Your Wonderful Love"). In 1962 they had a #22 R&B single with "Dream Come True" (which featured Berry Gordy's then-wife Raynoma Gordy on harpsichord), but four more flops followed, including "Mind over Matter" b/w "I'll Love You Til I Die," which Berry Gordy forced them to release under the name the Pirates.

In late 1963, following his violent attack on Paul Williams, Bryant either quit or was fired. Among the singers considered as a replacement were brothers Jimmy and David Ruffin. David, who had created a big impression by jumping onstage with the Tempts unannounced and winning over the crowd, got the spot, and the Temptations' luck changed overnight. They began working with writer/producer Smokey Robinson, whose "The Way You Do the Things You Do" (#11 pop) launched an almost unbroken run of R&B and pop hits that extended into the early Seventies. Their 1965 hits included the classic "My Girl" (#1 pop and R&B), "It's Growing" (#18 pop, #3 R&B), "Since I Lost My Baby" (#17 pop, #4 R&B), "My Baby" (#13 pop, #4 R&B), and "Don't Look Back" (#13 pop, #4 R&B). The last was one of the rare A-side leads by Paul Williams, who, despite the guidance of choreographer Cholly Atkins, would remain the architect of the Temptations' style and sophisticated image.

The next year the hits continued with Robinson's "Get Ready" (#29 pop, #1 R&B), following by the hard soul of producers Norman Whitfield and Brian Holland's "Ain't Too Proud to Beg" (#13 pop, #1 R&B). The first single featured Kendricks on lead, the second Ruffin. From that point on, however, the majority of A sides would feature Ruffin, as did 1966's "Beauty's Only Skin Deep" (#3 pop, #1 R&B) and "(I Know) I'm Losing You" (#8 pop, #1 R&B). Around 1967 Whitfield had become the group's sole producer, moving them more deeply into a rougher-hewn soul style. All the while, however, the group continued to perform and record standards (including Melvin Franklin's longstanding showpiece rendition of "Old Man River"). Other hits from 1967 were "All I Need" (#8 pop, #2 R&B), "You're My Everything" (#6 pop, #3 R&B), and "(Loneliness Made Me Realize) It's You That I Need" (#14 pop, #3 R&B).

The year 1968 brought "I Wish It Would Rain" (#4 pop, #1 R&B), "I Could Never Love Another (After Loving You)" (#13 pop, #1 R&B), and "Please Return Your Love to Me" (#26 pop, #4 R&B). But the most significant event of this period was Ruffin's departure for a solo career. Always a volatile personality, Ruffin had come into the group having enjoyed some limited success as a solo artist. In part, he was dissatisfied with the fact that Motown did not promote him as an individual in the same manner that it was priming Diana Ross as a solo act. Ironically, in terms of stature and image, the Supremes would remain the Temptations' "sister group" in more ways than one. Ruffin bristled over the star treatment Ross received during the taping of the phenomenally successful Supremes-Tempts TV special *TCB* and other real and imagined business and personal issues. After Ruffin failed to show up for a concert, the four other members of the group (not Berry Gordy, as has often been reported) fired him.

Initially, Ruffin's departure was viewed as an insurmountable blow. Dennis Edwards (formerly of the Contours) may have lacked some of the vocal polish of his predecessor, but his more aggressive approach perfectly suited the new Sly Stone–influenced, psychedelic soul-rock hybrid Whitfield and the group forged. "Cloud Nine" (#6 pop, #2 R&B) was the first of a series of hits that broached social and political issues (although Motown

has long held that "Cloud Nine" contains no allusions to drugs, Gladys Knight and the Pips refused to record it for that reason), and seemed out of character given Motown's traditional conservatism. With "Cloud Nine" and the following hit singles—"Run Away Child, Running Wild" (#6 pop, #1 R&B) and "Don't Let the Joneses Get You Down" (#20 pop, #2 R&B) in 1969; "Psychedelic Shack" (#7 pop, #2 R&B) and "Ball of Confusion (That's What the World Is Today)" (#3 pop, #2 R&B) in 1970—the Tempts became one of the few Motown acts (including Marvin Gaye and Stevie Wonder) who got progressive FM radio airplay. Sandwiched between these releases were singles in the more familiar Tempts style: "I'm Gonna Make You Love Me," a duet with the Supremes recorded before Ruffin's departure (#2 pop and R&B, 1968), the Robinson ballad "I'll Try Something New" (#25 pop, #8 R&B, 1968), and the five-lead workout "I Can't Get Next to You" (#1 pop and R&B, 1969).

Nineteen-seventy-one began with the last Kendricks-led hit, "Just My Imagination (Running Away with Me)" (#1 pop and R&B), which is perhaps second only to "My Girl" as the group's most beloved song. Kendricks quit to start a fitfully successful solo career. Later that year, Paul Williams also left the group because of poor health. An alcoholic, Paul Williams had been performing with the group but with Richard Street singing his parts from behind the curtain. He remained involved with the group after his official departure, but personal demons and debt drove him to despair. Two years later he was discovered slumped in his parked car just blocks from Motown, dead, presumably from a self-inflicted gunshot wound.

With new replacements Damon Harris (ex-Vibration Ricky Owens was in and out of the group in just weeks and never recorded with them) and Richard Street (most recently of the Monitors), the Temptations continued moving away from ballads with "Superstar (Remember How You Got Where You Are)" (#18 pop, #8 R&B, 1971), "Papa Was a Rollin' Stone" (#1 pop, #5 R&B, 1972), "Masterpiece" (#7 pop, #1 R&B, 1973), "The Plastic Man" (#40 pop, #8 R&B, 1973), "Let Your Hair Down" (#27 pop, #1 R&B, 1973), and "Shakey Ground" (#32 pop, #1 R&B, 1975). While the Tempts continued to hit the R&B Top Ten regularly, their singles rarely reached the pop Top Thirty. Throughout this period, however, they maintained a consistent record as one of the rare Motown groups that sold albums.

Like many other Motown acts, the Temptations became dissatisfied with the label. Unlike most, however, the Tempts had retained the rights to their name and, by the time they left the label, had succeeded in writing and producing their own commercially overlooked but critically well received LP, *The Temptations Do the Temptations*. It would be their last effort under their original Motown contract. They moved to Atlantic, shortly before which Dennis Edwards left the group for the first of three times. With new singer Louis Price, the Tempts cut two discoish albums: *Bare Back* (coproduced by the Holland brothers) and *Hear to Tempt You*. These were unsuccessful, and with Edwards back in Price's place, the group returned to Motown at Berry Gordy's personal request. Gordy cowrote and produced their first hit single in seven years, "Power" (#43 pop, #11 R&B, 1980). The group seemed poised to reclaim its turf, but the Thom Bell–produced *The Temptations* missed the mark. Further releases were halted for the long-awaited Reunion Tour, which in 1982 brought Ruffin and Kendricks back into the fold. This seven-man lineup recorded *Reunion* (#37 pop, #2 R&B, 1982) and embarked on a minitour. The album's hit single, "Standing on the Top (Part 1)" (#66 pop, #6 R&B, 1982), was written and produced by Rick James. The reunion was a fan's dream come true, but talks to make it a permanent venture were scuttled amid intergroup tensions and problems between Kendricks and Ruffin and Motown.

By that point, each of their solo careers had peaked. Ruffin's first single, the urgent "My Whole World Ended (the Moment You Left Me)" (#9 pop, #2 R&B, 1969), was his biggest solo hit. In 1969 he had two other Top Twenty R&B singles, "I've Lost Everything I've Ever Loved" (#11) and "I'm So Glad I Feel You" (#18). Ruffin and his older brother Jimmy (best remembered for 1966's "What Becomes of the Brokenhearted") teamed up for a 1970 album that produced a minor hit in "Stand by Me."

David Ruffin soon hit hard times, however. "Walk Away from Love" (#9 pop, #1 R&B, 1975), produced by Van McCoy, was his only other Top Forty hit, though he did reach the R&B Top Ten with "Heavy Love" and "Everything's Coming Up Love" in 1976, and "Break My Heart" in 1979.

After quitting the Tempts, Kendricks moved to the West Coast and began to build a solo career with Motown, which had just relocated there. His early solo recordings (on Tamla) were R&B hits: "It's So Hard for Me to Say Goodbye" and "Can I" (1971), "Eddie's Love" and "If You Let Me" (1972), and "Girl You Need a Change of Mind" and "Darling Come Back Home" (1973). Kendricks' jump to the top of the R&B and pop charts came in 1973 with the falsetto-topped "Keep On Truckin' (Part 1)" (#1 pop and R&B), followed by "Boogie Down" (#2 pop, #1 R&B, 1974).

For the next three years Kendricks' songs were regularly in the R&B Top Ten: "Son of Sagittarius" (#28 pop, #5 R&B, 1974), "Tell Her Love Has Felt the Need" (#8 R&B, 1974), "One Tear" (#8 R&B, 1974), "Shoeshine Boy" (#18 pop, #1 R&B, 1975), "Get the Cream off the Top" (#7 R&B, 1975), "Happy" (#8 R&B, 1975), "He's a Friend" (#36 pop, #2 R&B, 1976). In 1977 he signed with Arista. His last single hit for Motown was "Intimate Friends" (#24 R&B, 1978). The move proved to be not as smooth as ex-

pected. Kendricks' only big hit for Arista was "Ain't No Smoke Without Fire" (#13 R&B, 1978), and in 1980 he signed with Atlantic.

Both his and Ruffin's careers seemed moribund. Then, in 1985 Daryl Hall and John Oates invited the two onstage for a recorded performance at the newly reopened Apollo Theatre. A Temptations medley reached the Top Twenty on the singles chart and revived interest in Kendricks and Ruffin, who later in 1985 lent their voices to the star-studded *Sun City* album by Artists United Against Apartheid. A 1987 album, *David Ruffin and Eddie Kendricks,* spawned a #14 R&B hit, "I Couldn't Believe It."

Kendricks next teamed up with yet another ex-Temptation, Dennis Edwards, for a 1990 single, "Get It While It's Hot," cowritten by Jermaine Jackson. Edwards had some solo success during one of his three hiatuses from the Tempts, including "Don't Look Any Further" (#72 pop, #2 R&B, 1984). Kendricks, Edwards, and Ruffin went on tour together; combined, they'd sung lead on virtually all the Temptations' Sixties and Seventies hits. In the late Eighties, Ruffin, Kendricks, and Edwards began touring with a successful Tribute to the Temptations package tour.

Things seemed to be looking up, but on June 1, 1991, Ruffin, long plagued by drug addiction (he'd been convicted of cocaine possession in 1988 and entered drug rehab the following year), overdosed on cocaine after visiting a crack house. He lapsed into a coma and when doctors at a Philadelphia hospital failed to revive him, he was pronounced dead. He was 50. Michael Jackson paid for Ruffin's funeral, which was presided over by the Reverend Louis Farrakhan and attended by countless celebrities, among them the surviving original Temptations (Otis Williams, Kendricks, and Franklin), who sang "My Girl." Aretha Franklin and Stevie Wonder also performed.

The following year, Kendricks died of lung cancer at age 52. Again, the surviving Tempts attended his funeral, where Franklin eulogized his former group mate. Later Bobby Womack organized two concerts to raise funds for the singer's survivors.

For the Temptations, however, the years following the reunion were marked by constant international touring and several surprise successes. Following the 1983 *Motown 25* segment in which the Tempts and their friends the Four Tops performed a battle of the bands, the two groups took the show on the road. The T'n'T Tour, as it was called, ran for over three years, including a sold-out stint on Broadway, beginning in 1983. They continued cowriting and coproducing much of their more recent material, including 1984's "Treat Her Like a Lady" (#48 pop, #2 R&B), a collaboration between Otis Williams and latterday member Ali Ollie Woodson. Other Eighties singles include "Sail Away" (#54 pop, #13 R&B,

1984), "My Love Is True (Truly for You)" (#14 R&B, 1985), "Do You Really Love Your Baby" (#14 R&B, 1985), "Lady Soul" (#47 pop, #4 R&B, 1986), "I Wonder Who She's Seeing Now" (#3 R&B, 1987), "Look What You Started" (#8 R&B, 1987), "Special" (#10 R&B, 1989), "Soul to Soul" (#12 R&B, 1990), and "The Jones'" (#41 R&B, 1991).

Williams penned his autobiography, *Temptations,* in 1988 with Patricia Romanowski. The Temptations were inducted into the Rock and Roll Hall of Fame, by Daryl Hall and John Oates, in 1989. The *Emperors of Soul* box set was among 1994's best-reviewed compilations. Franklin died of complications following a brain seizure; he had suffered from various health problems since the late Eighties. Williams continues to lead the Temptations into their fourth decade.

10cc

Formed 1972, Manchester, England
Eric Stewart (b. Jan. 20, 1945, Manchester), gtr., voc.; Lol Creme (b. Lawrence Creme, Sep. 19, 1947, Manchester), gtr., voc., kybds., bass; Graham Gouldman (b. May 10, 1946, Manchester), gtr., voc., bass, kybds.; Kevin Godley (b. Oct. 7, 1945, Manchester), drums, voc., kybds.
1973—*10cc* (UK)   1974—*Sheet Music*   1975—*The Original Soundtrack* (Mercury); *100cc* (UK)   1976—*How Dare You!* (Mercury) (– Godley; – Creme; + Paul Burgess, drums)   1977—*Deceptive Bends* (– Burgess; + Rick Fenn, voc., gtr.; + Tony O'Malley, kybds.; + Stuart Tosh, drums, voc., perc.); *10cc Live and Let Live*   1978—*Bloody Tourists*   1979—*Greatest Hits, 1972–1978*   1980—*Look Hear?* (Warner Bros.)   1991—(Group re-forms: Gouldman; Stewart; Godley; Creme)   1992—*Meanwhile* (Phonogram, U.K.)   1995—*Alive* (Creative Man); *Mirror Mirror* (Critique).
Godley and Creme: 1976—*Consequences* (Polydor, U.K.)   1985—*The History Mix, Volume I* (Polydor).
Graham Gouldman solo: 1968—*The Graham Gouldman Thing* (RCA)   1980—*Animalympics* soundtrack (A&M).

Composed of four prolific singers, players, and songwriters, 10cc won critical acclaim for its witty and melodic "art pop." The band began scoring pop hits as it moved closer to the boundary between parody and romantic pop. Graham Gouldman had played with Manchester bands like the Mockingbirds, as well as a later version of Wayne Fontana's Mindbenders. He wrote such mid-Sixties British rock hits as "For Your Love," "Heart Full of Soul," and "Evil Hearted You" (recorded by the Yardbirds); "Look Through Any Window" and "Bus Stop" (by the Hollies); and "No Milk Today" (by Herman's Hermits). He had left the Mindbenders in 1968 to go to New York City, where he worked unsuccessfully for bubblegum

producers Kasenetz and Katz and released the late-Sixties solo LP *The Graham Gouldman Thing,* which was coproduced by John Paul Jones, later of Led Zeppelin.

In 1970 he formed Hotlegs, which included Lol Creme, Kevin Godley, and Eric Stewart. Working out of Strawberry Studios in England, which Stewart partly owned, Hotlegs had a #2 U.K. hit with 1970's "Neanderthal Man." Stewart had also been in the Mindbenders with Gouldman; when Wayne Fontana left the group, Stewart became frontman. Godley and Creme had attended art school together (they designed 10cc's debut album cover) and played together in a few local bands, then played sessions at Strawberry Studios. Like Hotlegs, 10cc would be primarily a studio group (though Hotlegs did tour with the Moody Blues on the heels of its hit single). While fooling around in Strawberry Studios with the Godley-Creme song "Donna," they transformed it into a sharp-edged satire of late-Fifties teen-idol hits and had 10cc's first demo. They took the tape of "Donna" to British impresario Jonathan King; he claims he rechristened Hotlegs as 10cc (the name supposedly derives from the nine cubic centimeters of semen ejaculated by the average male). Within weeks of its 1972 release, "Donna" was at #2 on the British singles chart. In 1973 came "Rubber Bullets" (#1 U.K.) and "Dean and I" (#10 U.K.), followed by "Wall Street Shuffle" (#10 U.K., 1974), "I'm Not in Love" (#1 U.K., 1975), and "Art for Art's Sake" (#5 U.K., 1975). However, despite critical acclaim, they'd had no U.S. hit singles, though "Rubber Bullets" became a novelty sensation on FM radio.

That changed with the late-blooming American success of the lush "I'm Not in Love" (#2, 1975). In 1976 Godley and Creme left, to record together and to work on their guitar-modification device, the Gizmo (it clips on over the bridge, and using continuous-motion rotary plectrums, effects infinite sustain and string-section sounds). Stewart and Gouldman made *Deceptive Bends,* which featured "The Things We Do for Love" (#5, 1977), basically as a duo, then added several new members, including drummer/vocalist Stuart Tosh, formerly of British teenybopper hitmakers Pilot. *Live and Let Live* (#146, 1977) was more or less a flop, but *Bloody Tourists* yielded "Dreadlock Holiday" (#44, #1 U.K., 1978).

While Godley and Creme continued to record and produce promotional videos for other bands (they refuse to tour), and even had a Top Ten U.K. single in 1982 with "Wedding Bells," Stewart and Gouldman weren't heard from again until 1982's 10cc LP *10 Out of 10* (not released domestically), for which ex–Linda Ronstadt guitarist Andrew Gold [see entry] cowrote and coproduced three songs. 10cc then disbanded, and Gouldman and Gold formed the duo Wax, which had one U.S. hit, "Right Between the Eyes," in 1986. In 1987 "Bridge to Your Heart" went to #12 in England. Gouldman produced the Ramones (*Pleasant Dreams*) and Gilbert O'Sullivan. Stewart has produced other acts and worked with Paul Mc-Cartney (*Tug of War*).

Since 1980 Godley and Creme have become major video auteurs, conceiving and directing a number of popular, groundbreaking clips, including Duran Duran's "Girls on Film," Visage's "Fade to Grey," the Police's "Every Breath You Take," Herbie Hancock's "Rockit," and Elton John's "Kiss the Bride."

10,000 Maniacs

Formed 1981, Jamestown, New York
Natalie Merchant (b. Oct. 26, 1963, Jamestown),
voc.; Robert Buck (b. Aug. 1, 1958, Jamestown), gtr.;
Dennis Drew (b. Aug. 8, 1957, Buffalo, N.Y.), kybds.;
Steven Gustafson (b. Apr. 10, 1957, Madrid, Spain),
bass; Jerome Augustyniak (b. Sep. 2, 1958, Lack-
awanna, N.Y.), drums; John Lombardo (b. Sep. 30,
1952, Jamestown), gtr.
1982—*Human Conflict Number Five* EP (Christian
Burial Music)   1983—*Secrets of the I Ching*
1985—*The Wishing Chair* (Elektra) (− Lombardo)
1987—*In My Tribe*   1989—*Blind Man's Zoo*   1990—
Hope Chest: The Fredonia Recordings 1982–1983
1992—*Our Time in Eden*   1993—(− Merchant)
1994—*MTV Unplugged* (+ Lombardo; + Mary
Ramsey, voc.).
Natalie Merchant solo: 1995—*Tigerlily* (Elektra).

Without ever scoring a Top Ten hit single, 10,000 Maniacs steadily built a considerable audience, through college and alternative radio. The band's sprightly, thoughtful folk rock was dominated by Robert Buck's brightly jangling guitar, Dennis Drew's creamy Hammond organ, and Natalie Merchant's plaintive vocals and bookish, sometimes topical, lyrics. Merchant's decision to quit 10,000 Maniacs following its 1993 tour left the band's future in doubt.

Gustafson, Drew, and Buck first came together through the college scene that spread from Jamestown Community College to the State University of New York at Fredonia. The trio played under such names as Still Life and Burn Victims, then became 10,000 Maniacs (a misreading of the Sixties cult gore film title *2,000 Maniacs*). They were soon joined at small-club and party gigs by Merchant, who attended Jamestown CC. *Human Conflict Number Five* and *Secrets of the I Ching* were recorded through a sound-engineering program at SUNY Fredonia. Both records gleaned favorable reviews in the alternative press and some college-radio airplay.

By 1985, 10,000 Maniacs had landed a deal with Elektra. Its major-label debut, *The Wishing Chair*, got glowing reviews from the mainstream music press yet still sold poorly. Lombardo left after an extensive tour; he later formed a duo, John and Mary. Elektra assigned veteran Los Angeles folk-rock producer Peter Asher to over-

see the next LP. The combination worked, artistically and commercially, as *In My Tribe* (#37, 1987) yielded the band's first chart singles, "Like the Weather" (#68, 1988) and "What's the Matter Here" (#80, 1988), about child abuse, as well as a cover of Cat Stevens' "Peace Train." The last was dropped from the group's concerts after Stevens, a Moslem convert now known as Yusef Islam, voiced support for Moslem death threats issued against *Satanic Verses* author Salman Rushdie. The group's profile rose higher when it opened on tour for R.E.M.

Asher returned to produce 1989's *Blind Man's Zoo* (#13, 1989), a topical collection that spanned subjects ranging from pregnancy to the colonization of Africa; Merchant wrote "Trouble Me" (#44, 1989) for her father while he was hospitalized. *Hope Chest* (#102, 1990) reissued the band's first two releases. On *Our Time in Eden*, 10,000 Maniacs switched producers from Asher to Paul Fox (Robyn Hitchcock, XTC, the Sugarcubes), expanding its sound dramatically; James Brown hornmen Fred Wesley and Maceo Parker appear on "Few and Far Between." "These Are Days" (#66, 1992) was a minor hit single. Just after the album was completed, drummer Augustyniak was sidelined with a broken collarbone; ex–E Street Band drummer Max Weinberg sat in. Augustyniak was back on board for the group's performance at MTV's Inaugural Ball for President Bill Clinton in January 1993. In early August of that year, Merchant announced that she had "a desire for change and a need for growth," and would depart the band after its final tour, to pursue a solo career. The Maniacs continued on, adding the John and Mary duo to the group. Merchant released her debut solo album, *Tigerlily,* in mid-1995; it debuted at #13.

Ten Years After/Alvin Lee

Formed 1967, Nottingham, England
Alvin Lee (b. Dec. 19, 1944, Nottingham), gtr., voc.;
Chick Churchill (b. Jan. 2, 1949, Mold, Wales),
kybds.; Leo Lyons (b. Nov. 30, 1943, Bedfordshire,
Eng.), bass; Ric Lee (b. Oct. 20, 1945, Cannock,
Eng.), drums.
1967—*Ten Years After* (Deram)   1968—*Undead*
1969—*Stonedhenge; Ssssh*   1970—*Cricklewood*
Green; Watt   1971—*A Space in Time* (Columbia)
1972—*Alvin Lee & Co.; Rock 'n' Roll Music to the*
World   1973—*Recorded Live*   1974—*Positive Vi-*
brations   1975—*Goin' Home! Their Greatest Hits*
1976—*Anthology*   1977—*Classic Performances*
1981—*Hear Me Calling* (Decca)   1989—*About Time*
(Chrysalis)   1991—*Essential Ten Years After.*
Alvin Lee solo: 1973—*On the Road to Freedom*
(with Mylon LeFevre) (Columbia)   1974—*In Flight*
1975—*Pump Iron!*   1978—*Rocket Fuel* (with Ten
Years Later) (RSO)   1979—*Ride On* (with Ten Years

Later) 1980—*Free Fall* (Atlantic) 1986—*Detroit Diesel* (21 Records) 1992—*Zoom* (Domino) 1994—*I Hear You Rockin'* (Viceroy).

Ten Years After was a dependably hard-rocking blues-based band for many years, best remembered for the sped-up blues solos of guitarist Alvin Lee, whose supersonic version of "I'm Going Home" was a smash hit at the 1969 Woodstock Festival and in the *Woodstock* film. Alvin Lee and Leo Lyons grew up together in Nottingham. Lee was playing guitar by age 13, and Lyons began performing publicly at age 15. By the early Sixties, both were involved in blues groups. Lee performed in a John Lee Hooker show at London's Marquee; Lyons appeared at a Windsor Jazz Festival; both were also studio musicians. They got together in 1964 as Britain's Largest Sounding Trio (with Lyons on drums), which toured England and the Continent and was quite successful in Hamburg. In 1967 Ric Lee (no relation to Alvin) and Chick Churchill joined, completing what was now called Ten Years After.

Alvin Lee's speed made the band a popular concert attraction, and despite a lack of hits, their first few LPs sold well. By 1968 Ten Years After were regulars at New York's The Scene—where they jammed with Jimi Hendrix, Janis Joplin, and Larry Coryell—and at San Francisco's Fillmore West. In Woodstock's wake, the group had several Top Thirty LPs: *Ssssh* (#20, 1969), *Cricklewood Green* (#14, 1970), and *Watt* (#21, 1970). *A Space in Time* (#17, 1971) eventually went platinum. By that time the band had chalked up its first hit single, "I'd Love to Change the World," a dreamy song that made the U.S. and U.K. charts in 1971. The group followed with "Baby Won't You Let Me Rock 'n' Roll You" in 1972 and "Choo Choo Mama" in 1973, both minor hit singles.

After *Rock 'n' Roll Music to the World* (#43, 1972), the band took a break from touring. Lee built a studio in his Fifteenth-Century Berkshire home and recorded *On the Road to Freedom* with Mylon LeFevre; the album also featured guest appearances from Steve Winwood, Jim Capaldi, George Harrison (credited as Harry Georgeson), and Ron Wood. Churchill recorded a solo album, *You and Me.*

In early 1974, with the band's status in doubt, Lee organized a nine-piece band, including reedman Mel Collins and drummer Ian Wallace (both formerly with King Crimson), who played a show at London's Rainbow Theatre before Ten Years After's scheduled appearance. Lee's band was recorded on *Alvin Lee and Company.* Ten Years After did end up playing the Rainbow, and it turned out to be their last British concert. *Positive Vibrations* (#81, 1974) was the band's last album for the next 14 years, until 1989's *About Time* (#120). Later in 1974, Lee announced plans for a worldwide tour with a band featuring Collins, Wallace, and keyboardist Ronnie Leahy

and bassist Steve Thompson of Stone the Crows. Though Ten Years After seemed officially defunct, the band's management denied the split. In May 1975, Alvin Lee declared the group to be through and it was announced that Ric Lee had formed his own band. Ten Years After then regrouped for one last American tour. The band's demise has never been made official.

Lee continued to record with a series of groups, including Ten Years Later (in the late Seventies) and the Alvin Lee Band. A later quartet included Mick Taylor, Fuzzy Samuels, and Tom Compton, but their *RX-5* (which was not released in the U.S.) vanished without a trace.

Chick Churchill became a professional manager for Chrysalis Publishing. Leo Lyons produced some mid-Seventies albums by British heavy-metal band UFO. Ric Lee formed his own production company. Ten Years After occasionally tours.

Terminator X: See Public Enemy

Tammi Terrell
Born Thomasina Montgomery, January 24, 1946, Philadelphia, Pennsylvania; died March 16, 1970, Philadelphia
1967—*United* (Tamla) (with Marvin Gaye) 1968—*You're All I Need* (with Marvin Gaye) 1969—*Irresistible Tammi Terrell*; *Easy* (with Marvin Gaye) 1970—*Greatest Hits* (with Marvin Gaye).

Although Tammi Terrell began recording in 1961, her solo recordings were eclipsed by her immortal duets with Marvin Gaye. Terrell became involved in show business at an early age (her mother was an actress), but nearly gave it up to pursue her education. She was 15 when Luther Dixon discovered her at a talent show, which led to her recording her first single, "If You See Bill" for Scepter/Wand, in 1961. The following year Montgomery, as she was then known, recorded "The Voice of Experience." After studying psychology at the University of Pennsylvania, she recorded "I Cried" for James Brown's label. Shortly thereafter, she joined his revue and began what was by all accounts a stormy romantic relationship. She left Brown around 1964, married and divorced (contrary to many sources, her husband was not boxer Ernie Terrell), recorded briefly for Checker, then signed to Motown.

Toward the end of 1965 Terrell's "I Can't Believe You Love Me" made the R&B Top Thirty. After its followup, "Come On and See Me," failed to make an impression on the pop chart, she was paired with Marvin Gaye for a series of Ashford and Simpson duets: In 1967 "Ain't No Mountain High Enough" (#19 pop, #3 R&B) and "Your Precious Love" (#5 pop, #2 R&B); in 1968 "Ain't Nothing

Like the Real Thing" (#8 pop, #1 R&B), "You're All I Need to Get By" (#7 pop, #1 R&B), and "Keep On Lovin' Me Honey" (#24 pop, #11 R&B); in 1969 "Good Lovin' Ain't Easy to Come By" (#30 pop, #11 R&B) and "What You Gave Me" (#6 R&B). "If I Could Build My Whole World Around You" b/w the Gaye-penned "If This World Were Mine" (#10 pop, #27 R&B) was also released in 1967.

Terrell and Gaye, widely assumed to be lovers, were not. Gaye was married to Anna Gordy, and Terrell was romantically involved with Temptation David Ruffin in what was another tempestuous, at times violent, affair. Gaye, however, felt especially protective toward Terrell, so he was deeply affected after she collapsed in his arms onstage during a show in Virginia in 1967. She had long complained of severe migraine headaches, and following her collapse a brain tumor was diagnosed. Terrell retired from the road. Despite enduring eight operations over the next year and a half (resulting in memory problems and partial paralysis), she continued to record with Gaye. Late in his life, Gaye (who was devastated by Terrell's death) revealed that it was not Terrell but Valerie Simpson singing on most of *Easy*, including "Good Lovin' Ain't Easy to Come By" and "What You Gave Me." Before that, most believed Simpson stood in for Terrell only on the posthumously released "The Onion Song."

Sonny Terry and Brownie McGhee

Formed 1940
Teddell Saunders "Sonny" Terry (b. Oct. 24, 1911, Greensboro, Ga.; d. Mar. 11, 1986, Mineola, N.Y.), voc., harmonica; Walter Brown "Brownie" McGhee (b. Nov. 30, 1915, Knoxville, Tenn.).
1958—Brownie McGhee and Sonny Terry Sing (Smithsonian/Folkways)   1960—Just a Closer Walk with Thee (Fantasy)   1963—Live at the 2nd Fret (Bluesville); At Sugar Hill (Fantasy)   1974—Hometown Blues (Mainstream)   1978—Midnight Special (Fantasy)   1989—Sonny and Brownie (A&M) 1991—Sonny Terry and Brownie McGhee.
Brownie McGhee solo: 1958—Back Country Blues (Savoy)   1994—The Complete Brownie McGhee (Columbia Legacy).
Sonny Terry solo: 1960—Sonny's Story (Bluesville) 1963—Sonny Is King   1984—Whoopin' (Alligator) 1987—Sonny Terry (Collectables)   1991—The Folkways Years, 1944-1963 (Smithsonian/Folkways).

Sonny Terry and Brownie McGhee were southern blues musicians with church roots. They paired up in the early Forties and became a popular and influential folk-blues team, despite the fact that both suffered crippling childhood diseases.

Terry was blind, the result of separate childhood accidents in 1922 and 1927. He spent his early years playing harmonica around North Carolina, slowly achieving a wider reputation in the late Thirties, thanks to performances with Leadbelly and Blind Boy Fuller.

McGhee contracted polio at the age of four, though he made a substantial recovery that left him only with a limp. His entire family was musical, and he was performing with them by the age of eight. He quit school at 13 to become a full-time musician and had just begun his recording career when he was introduced to Sonny Terry.

They were a steady duo after that, although they worked apart extensively as well, McGhee under pseudonyms like Spider Sam, Big Tom Collins, Henry Johnson, and Blind Boy Williams. After being discovered by folk revivalists in the Fifties, notably Pete Seeger, they went on to perform in clubs, in colleges, and at jazz and blues festivals around the world. They've made dozens of records.

In the early Eighties McGhee began touring with his own band. Terry also continued a solo career, though they continued to appear as a duo despite the fact they did not get along particularly well.

Tesla

Formed 1984, Sacramento, California
Jeff Keith (b. Oct. 12, 1958, Texarkana, Ark.), voc.; Tommy Skeoch (b. Feb. 5, 1962, Santa Monica, Calif.), gtr., voc.; Frank Hannon (b. Oct. 3, 1966, Sacramento), gtr., kybds., voc.; Brian Wheat (b. Nov. 5, 1962, Sacramento), bass, voc.; Troy Luccketta (b. Oct. 5, 1959, Lodi, Calif.), drums.
1986—Mechanical Resonance (Geffen)   1989—The Great Radio Controversy   1990—Five Man Acoustical Jam   1991—Psychotic Supper   1994—Bust a Nut.

A blue-collar hard-rock band with a dressed-down, nice-guy image, Tesla was named for scientist Nikola Tesla, a historically overlooked pioneer of electricity and radio, who never got the credit Marconi and Edison did as inventors. Tesla's Frank Hannon once told a newspaper that "Tesla got shafted by the media," and in 1990 the band unsuccessfully lobbied the Smithsonian Institution to accept and display a bust of its namesake.

The band began when Hannon and Brian Wheat formed the Sacramento garage-rock group Earth Shaker, which expanded into the blues-rock band City Kidd. They became Tesla when one of their managers lent them *Man Out of Time*, a book about Nikola Tesla.

The group's polished, melodic metal style was in evidence on its debut album, *Mechanical Resonance* (#32, 1987)—named after one of scientist Tesla's pet theories—which sold a million copies despite yielding only the barely charting "Little Suzie" (#91, 1987). *The Great Radio Controversy* (#18, 1989) also went platinum, with a much bigger hit single in the power ballad "Love Song"

(#10, 1989). *Five Man Acoustical Jam* (#12, 1991)—an all-acoustic live album recorded in Philadelphia before MTV's *Unplugged* became a household word—based its title on the Five Man Electrical Band, whose 1971 #3 hit "Signs" Tesla covered (#8, 1991) on the album. A return to hard-rocking form, *Psychotic Supper* (#13, 1991) went gold without hit singles. After opening shows for the Scorpions in Europe and Metallica in Japan, Tesla toured on their own for a year. They returned to the studio to record *Bust a Nut* (#20), which was released in 1994.

Joe Tex

Born Joseph Arrington Jr., August 8, 1933, Rogers, Texas; died Joseph Arrington Hazziez, August 12, 1982, Navasota, Texas
1965—*The Best of Joe Tex* (Parrot); *Hold On to What You've Got* (Atlantic); *The New Boss* 1966—*The Love You Save* 1967—*The Best of Joe Tex* 1968—*Live and Lively; Soul Country* 1969—*Buying a Book* 1972—*I Gotcha* (Dial) 1977—*Bumps and Bruises* (Epic) 1978—*Rub Down* 1985—*The Best of Joe Tex* (Atlantic) 1988—*I Believe I'm Gonna Make It: The Best of Joe Tex, 1964–1972* (Rhino) 1991—*Greatest Hits* (Curb/CEMA) 1992—*Show Me: The Hits . . . & More* (Ichiban).

Soul singer Joe Tex recorded in a variety of styles but is best known for his dance hits. Tex first recorded for King from 1955 to 1957, and from 1958 to 1960 for Ace. He was a journeyman performer through most of the early Sixties, recording occasionally, but with no success. His first break came in 1961 when James Brown recorded his "Baby You're Right." In 1964 Tex signed to Buddy Killen's Dial Records, a Nashville soul label.

Recording at what would later become the famous Muscle Shoals studio, Tex broke through in 1965 with "Hold What You've Got" (#5 pop, #2 R&B). Through soul's mid-to-late-Sixties heyday, Tex had several big hits, including "I Want to (Do Everything for You)" (#1 R&B), "A Sweet Woman Like You" (#1 R&B), and "The Love You Save" (#10 pop, #2 R&B) in 1965; and the comedic "Skinny Legs and All" (#10 pop, #2 R&B) in 1967.

In 1972 Tex had a big hit year with the lecherous "I Gotcha" (#2 pop, #1 R&B). A year later he left Atlantic and through the Seventies recorded for numerous companies, although always under the guidance of Buddy Killen. In 1977 Tex had his last major hit, another comedy record, "Ain't Gonna Bump No More (with No Big Fat Woman)" (#12 pop, #7 R&B).

During his later years he had become a Moslem minister and in 1972 adopted the surname Hazziez. He spent most of his time on his farm and was known as a devoted Houston Oilers fan (among his last recordings was a tribute to running back Earl Campbell entitled "Do the Earl Campbell"). In 1981 Tex joined the Soul Clan reunion,

which included Wilson Pickett, Don Covay, Solomon Burke, and Ben E. King. Not long after, Tex died of a heart attack on his farm at age 49. Among the pallbearers at his funeral were Buddy Killen, Pickett, King, Covay, and Percy Mayfield.

Texas Tornados

Formed 1989, San Francisco, California
Freddy Fender (b. Baldemar Huerta, June 4, 1937, San Benito, Tex.), gtr., voc.; Augie Meyers (b. May 31, 1940, San Antonio, Tex.), kybds., voc., accordion, bajo sexto; Doug Sahm (b. Nov. 6, 1941, San Antonio), gtr., voc.; Flaco Jimenez (b. Mar. 11, 1939, San Antonio), accordion, voc.
1990—*Texas Tornados* (Reprise) 1991—*Zone of Our Own* 1992—*Hangin' On by a Thread* 1994—*The Best of the Texas Tornados*.

The Texas Tornados boasted four legendary Tex-Mex performers: Doug Sahm and Augie Meyers were in the Sir Douglas Quintet [see entry] in the Sixties, Freddy Fender [see entry] has been called "the Mexican Elvis," and Flaco Jimenez has been a star of conjunto music for several decades. The group first got together at a concert in San Francisco. Record companies were immediately interested in their mix of conjunto, country, polka, and R&B.

Texas Tornados was released in both English and Spanish versions. Although it yielded no single, it sold well and won a Grammy. *Zone of Our Own* mixed English and Spanish (two band members are Hispanic, two white) and was again successful in rock, Latin, and country circles. The title track of *Hangin' On by a Thread* was written for and about the Grateful Dead, a band the Texas Tornados have often been compared to because of their rootsy sound and intrepid career; the song featured Sahm's son Shawn on guitar. The band collaborated little on the album's tracks and has since broken up. Since the Tornados' inception, members had said they saw the group as a launching pad for the revitalization of their individual careers; however, by the end of 1994, the group had begun discussing the possibility of a reunion.

That Petrol Emotion: See the Undertones

Them

Formed 1963, Belfast, Northern Ireland
Original lineup: Billy Harrison, gtr.; Alan Henderson, bass; Ronnie Millings, drums; Eric Wrixen, kybds.; Van Morrison (b. Aug. 21, 1945, Belfast), voc., sax, harmonica; (– Wrixen; – Millings; + Jackie McAuley, kybds.; + Patrick McAuley, drums).

1965—*Angry Young Them* (Decca, U.K.); *Them* (Parrot) **1966**—*Them Again* **1972**—*Them* **1977**—*Story of Them* (London).

In the early days of singer Van Morrison's recording and performing career, he was backed by Them, a young Belfast garage band. Morrison and Them had major U.K. hits in 1965 with "Baby Please Don't Go" (#10) and "Here Comes the Night" (#2). Their U.S. hits were "Here Comes the Night" (#24) and "Mystic Eyes" (#33) in 1965; and "Gloria" (#71) in 1966. "Gloria" was beaten on the U.S. chart by the Shadows of Knight's version. Morrison toured Europe and the American West Coast with Them in 1966 (the Doors opened the West Coast shows). When Morrison returned home after the tour, he took a lot of time off before planning his next career move; after a short time, Them disbanded.

During its brief career, its personnel changed often, at various times including guitarist Jimmy Page and keyboardist Peter Bardens (who went on to form Camel). Following Morrison's departure for a solo career [see entry] and the group's first demise, various members attempted to resurrect the group with negligible success.

These Immortal Souls: See the Birthday Party

The The
Formed 1979, London, England
Matt Johnson (b. Aug. 15, 1961, London), voc., kybds.
1983—*Soul Mining* (Epic) **1986**—*Infected* **1989**—*Mind Bomb* **1992**—*Dusk* **1995**—*Hanky Panky*.

The The is the name given to bands led by Matt Johnson, a bald, mercurial, brooding singer/songwriter. While the The's sound has moved from the poppy new-wave dance tracks of *Soul Mining* to the intense bluesy ruminations of *Dusk*, the level of musicianship has remained consistent (over 300 musicians have appeared on the The albums, including Neneh Cherry, Sinéad O'Connor, and the Smiths' Johnny Marr), a testament to Johnson's uncompromising perfectionism.

Johnson was exposed to music while living above his father's pub in London's East End, which was favored by show-business types, and in nightclubs and dancehalls run by an uncle. At age 15 he was hired as tea boy for a small music publisher; by 18 he was assistant engineer at their eight-track studio. A 1979 ad he placed in the *New Musical Express* was answered by synthesist Keith Laws. They played their first gig that May, opening for Scritti Politti, and in 1980 released a single, "Controversial Subject" b/w "Black & White," for 4AD Records.

To satisfy a contractual obligation, Johnson released an album under his own name in 1981, *Burning Blue Soul*. A series of managerial wrangles led to his signing with Epic later that year. An album, *The Pornography of Despair*, was started, delayed, and subsequently abandoned. It took until 1983 for *Soul Mining* to become the The's official debut.

Illness prevented Johnson from recording another album until 1985. *Infected* (#89, 1987), accompanied by an album-length video, expanded the group's cult status. *Mind Bomb* (#138, 1989), a politically charged song cycle, was supported by the The's first tour. *Dusk* (#143, 1993) found Johnson working in a stripped-down acoustic context, reaching new audiences while touring with Depeche Mode. Johnson explored C&W roots music with *Hanky Panky*, an entire album consisting of his versions of Hank Williams songs.

They Might Be Giants
Formed 1984, Brooklyn, New York
John Flansburgh (b. May 6, 1960, Boston, Mass.), voc., gtr., drum programming; John Linnell (b. June 12, 1959, New York City, N.Y.), voc., kybds., accordion.
1986—*They Might Be Giants* (Bar/None) **1987**—*Don't Let's Start* EP **1988**—*Lincoln* (Restless/Bar/None) **1990**—*Flood* (Elektra) **1991**—*Miscellaneous T* (Restless) **1992**—*Apollo 18* (Elektra) **1993**—(+ Tony Maimone [b. Sep. 27, 1952, Cleve-

They Might Be Giants: John Linnell and John Flansburgh (with drummer Brian Doherty and bassist Tony Maimone)

land, Ohio], bass; + Brian Doherty [b. July 2, 1962, Brooklyn], drums)   1994—*John Henry*.

The two Johns who make up They Might Be Giants play songs as infectious and goofy as commercial jingles, yet made endearing by the duo's wacky wordplay and sheer irrepressibility. Theirs is a revenge of the nerds: College radio play and videos that look more geared for the Nickelodeon network than for MTV made them successful alternative artists and garnered them a major-label deal.

The Giants met as tykes in Lincoln, Massachusetts, where they were both from professional, middle-class households. They began writing songs together in high school, although it took them several years to form a band, during which time they both lacklusterly pursued higher education, and Linnell played in the Rhode Island new-wave band the Mundanes. In 1981 they moved to Brooklyn together and began recording songs with a drum machine. Naming themselves after a George C. Scott film, they played downtown Manhattan dives and devised an ingenious way to get around dependence on record companies and radio play: Their Dial-A-Song service featured 300 tunes on an answering machine; the line, which only cost a regular toll call, eventually received more than 100 calls a day.

Their 1986 debut became an alternative hit when MTV latched on to the video for "Don't Let's Start." The album showcased the duo's strange wit and coffee-fueled phantasmagoria of musical styles: Song titles include "Youth Culture Killed My Dog" and "I Hope That I Get Old Before I Die." The video for "Ana Ng," from *Lincoln* (#89, 1988), brought them even more popularity. Their major-label debut, *Flood,* continued their MTV-driven success with the single "Istanbul (Not Constantinople)," but the critics who had adored the band were less pleased with the album's polish. TMBG became particularly popular in England, where the readers of *Q* magazine voted them the best new act of 1990 (although they had been together six years at that point).

The Giants next produced *Apollo 18* (#99, 1992) themselves, once again proving their adeptness at clever gimmicks: The track "Fingertips" was programmed to include 21 refrains that pop up repeatedly when the CD is played on "random" or "shuffle" mode. Touring for the album, the duo played with a band (featuring Pere Ubu bassist Tony Maimone) for the first time. Soon after, Maimone joined as a permanent member, as did drummer Brian Doherty. The band's next album, *John Henry* (#61, 1994), yielded the single "Snail Shell," which received much college-radio airplay.

Thin Lizzy

Formed 1970, Dublin, Ireland
Philip Lynott (b. Aug. 20, 1951, Dublin; d. Jan. 4, 1986, Dublin), bass, voc.; Brian Downey (b. Jan. 27, 1951, Dublin), drums; Eric Bell (b. Sep. 3, 1947, Belfast, N. Ire.), gtr.
1971—*Thin Lizzy* (Decca)   1972—*Shades of a Blue Orphanage*   1973—*Vagabonds of the Western World* (London)   1974—(– Bell; + Gary Moore [b. Apr. 4, 1952, Belfast], gtr.; + Andy Gee, gtr.; + John Cann, gtr.; – Gee; – Cann; – Moore; + Brian Robertson [b. Sep. 12, 1956, Glasgow, Scot.], gtr.; + Scott Gorham [b. Mar. 17, 1951, Santa Monica, Calif.], gtr., voc.) *Night Life* (Mercury)   1975—*Fighting* (Vertigo)   1976—*Jailbreak*; *Johnny the Fox*   1977—*Bad Reputation* (– Robertson; + Moore; – Moore; + Robertson)   1978—*Live and Dangerous* (Warner Bros.)   1979—*Black Rose/A Rock Legend* (– Robertson; + Moore; – Moore; + Midge Ure [b. James Ure, Oct. 10, 1953, Glasgow], gtr.; – Ure; + Snowy White, gtr., voc.)   1980—*Chinatown* 1982—(– White; + John Sykes, gtr.) *Renegade* (+ Darren Wharton, kybds.)   1983—*Thunder and Lightning*   1984—'Life'—'Live*   1991—*Dedication: The Very Best of Thin Lizzy* (Polygram).
Phil Lynott solo: 1980—*Solo in Soho* (Warner Bros.).
Gary Moore solo: 1983—*Corridors of Power* (Mirage) 1984—*Victims of the Future*   1986—*Run for Cover* 1987—*Wild Frontier* (Virgin)   1989—*After the War* 1990—*Still Got the Blues* (Charisma)   1992—*After Hours*; *The Early Years* (WTG); *Dirty Fingers* (Roadrunner Revisited)   1993—*Blues Alive* (Virgin).

Fronted by Phil Lynott, a black Irishman, Thin Lizzy was a hard-nosed rock & roll band whose music was mostly distinguished by the strongly masculine-to-macho themes of Lynott's songs, which often celebrated male camaraderie and comic-book heroism. Thin Lizzy's finest hour was unquestionably 1976's *Jailbreak,* whose power chords and R&B undertones established the band as a major act in Britain and gave the group its greatest American success with the LP's single "The Boys Are Back in Town" (#12).

After being formed in Ireland by Lynott with his boyhood friend, drummer Brian Downey, Thin Lizzy relocated to England in 1971, subsequently scoring a hit single, "Whisky in a Jar" (#6 U.K., 1973). Eric Bell quit the band after the third LP, suffering exhaustion. Indifferent record sales followed until Thin Lizzy released *Jailbreak.* After that LP, the group continued to record a series of uneven albums (excepting 1978's *Live and Dangerous*) and failed to become a superstar attraction as was once predicted. Lynott, who earned the respect of the new-wave elite in 1978 by forming a spare-time group, the Greedy Bastards, with Rat Scabies of the Damned, released a solo album in 1980, *Solo in Soho,* which sold disappointingly. With Thin Lizzy, Lynott continued his thematic style of songwriting on albums like *Chinatown* and *Renegade,* which also spotlit the twin lead guitar work of Scott Gorham and new member Snowy White, Pink Floyd's ex–stage guitarist.

Through its career, Thin Lizzy released a series of hit singles in the U.K., among them "Don't Believe a Word" (#12 U.K., 1977), "Dancin' in the Moonlight (It's Caught Me in the Spotlight)" (#14 U.K., 1977), "Waiting for an Alibi" (#9 U.K., 1979), "Do Anything You Want to Do" (#14 U.K., 1979), and "Killer on the Loose" (#10 U.K., 1980). Thin Lizzy officially disbanded in 1983.

Lynott published two books of poetry, *Songs for While I'm Away* (1974) and *Philip*; he also continued to make solo LPs and recorded with a new group called Grand Slam. Among his charting singles, the most successful were "Yellow Pearl" (#14 U.K., 1981) and, with Gary Moore, "Out in the Fields" (#5 U.K., 1985). Following a drug overdose, Lynott succumbed to pneumonia and heart failure in early 1986. In May 1986 Thin Lizzy appeared at Self Aid, a Dublin concert, where Bob Geldof stood in for Lynott.

Moore also released a number of albums, as a solo artist and with his group G-Force. A leading blues artist in the U.K., Moore has also recorded with Colosseum II, the Greg Lake Band, and BBM (with Jack Bruce and Ginger Baker). His commercial breakthrough was 1990's *Still Got the Blues,* the title track of which hit #97 that year. Lynott sang on Moore's U.K. single, 1979's "Parisienne Walkways" (#8 U.K.).

3rd Bass

Formed 1988, New York City, New York
M.C. Serch (b. Michael Berrin, Queens, N.Y.), voc.; Prime Minister Pete Nice (b. Peter Nash, Feb. 5, 1967, Brooklyn, N.Y.), voc.; Daddy Rich (b. Richard Lawson, Queens), DJ.
1989—*The Cactus Album* (Def Jam)   1990—*The Cactus Revisited*   1991—*Derelicts of Dialect*.

A racially mixed rap trio, 3rd Bass was the second major rap group to emerge, after the Beastie Boys, with white, upper-middle-class members. Unlike the Beasties, however, 3rd Base took a traditional hip-hop approach, earning greater respect from its rapping peers. Both M.C. Serch (the son of a stockbroker father and an opera-singing mother) and Pete Nice had spent years absorbing the emerging hip-hop culture while hanging out with black youths, before they met at Manhattan's Latin Quarter club. Nice had hosted a rap show for Columbia University's radio station and had recorded tracks with rap producer Sam Sever (Run-D.M.C., Just-Ice).

Sever produced the majority of *The Cactus Album* (#55, 1989), with contributions by Hank Shocklee of Public Enemy's Bomb Squad and De La Soul's Prince Paul. In 1990 3rd Bass became the first rap group to release a remix album, *The Cactus Revisited*. Later that year Public Enemy associate Professor Griff, already under fire for

making anti-Semitic remarks in the *Washington Times,* reportedly verbally attacked Serch, who is Jewish, at Def Jam's New York offices.

Derelicts of Dialect (#19, 1991) included "Pop Goes the Weasel" (#29, 1991), a vitriolic attack on the commercialization of rap; the song's video clip featured ex–Black Flag frontman Henry Rollins, with a Vanilla Ice–style hairdo, being pummeled by Serch and Nice.

After a 1991 tour, 3rd Bass broke up. Serch recorded the 1992 solo album *Return of the Product,* featuring the single "Here It Comes." The following year, Nice and Rich released *You Rat Bastard* under their own names.

13th Floor Elevators: See Roky Erickson

.38 Special

Formed 1975, Jacksonville, Florida
Original lineup: Donnie Van Zant, voc.; Don Barnes, gtr., voc.; Jeff Carlisi, gtr.; Ken Lyons, bass; Jack Grondin, drums; Steve Brookins, drums.
1977—*.38 Special* (A&M)   1978—*Special Delivery* 1979—(– Lyons; + Larry Junstrom, bass, gtr.) *Rockin' into the Night*   1981—*Wild-Eyed Southern Boys*   1982—*Special Forces*   1983—*Tour de Force* 1986—*Strength in Numbers*   1987—(– Barnes; – Brookins; + Danny Chauncey, gtr.; + Max Carl, drums) *Flashback*   1989—*Rock & Roll Strategy* 1991—(– Carl; + Barnes; + Scott Hoffman, drums; + Bobby Capps, kybds.) *Bone Against Steel* (Charisma).

One of the many Southern-rock groups to take its cue from the Allman Brothers Band, .38 Special specializes in blues-based rock & roll that showcases twin lead guitarists and two drummers. Featuring lead vocalist Donnie Van Zant, brother of Lynyrd Skynyrd's Ronnie Van Zant, .38 Special altered its sound somewhat in the early Eighties to accommodate a more melodic approach. This resulted in "Hold On Loosely" (#27, 1981) and the band's first Top Ten single, "Caught Up in You," taken from *Special Forces* (#10, 1982).

The group cut two albums filled with competent Southern rock and toured extensively before racking up a hit album with *Rockin' into the Night* (#57, 1980), followed by the platinum *Wild-Eyed Southern Boys* (#18, 1981), *Special Forces,* and *Tour de Force* (#22, 1984). Subsequent albums fared respectably; *Strength in Numbers* (#17, 1986) and *Flashback* (#35, 1987) are both gold. In addition, the group had a string of hit singles, including "If I'd Been the One" (#19, 1983), "Back Where You Belong" (#20, 1984), "Teacher Teacher" (#25, 1984), "Like No Other Night" (#14, 1986), and "Second Chance" (#6, 1989).

B. J. Thomas

Born August 7, 1942, Hugo, Oklahoma
1969—*On My Way* (Scepter); *Greatest Hits, vol. 1*
1970—*Raindrops Keep Fallin' on My Head*; *Everybody's Out of Town*   1971—*Greatest Hits, vol. 2*
1972—*Billy Joe Thomas*   1975—*Reunion* (ABC)
1977—*B. J. Thomas* (MCA)   1983—*New Looks*
(Cleveland International)   1990—*B. J. Thomas
Greatest Hits* (Rhino).

For about six years, starting in 1966, B. J. Thomas had a run of hit singles, spotlighting his easy vocal style and MOR arrangements, most notable of which were the gold records "Raindrops Keep Fallin' on My Head" (#1, 1970) and "Hooked on a Feeling" (#5, 1968). Other successes of this period include "I'm So Lonesome, I Could Cry" (#8) and "Billy and Sue" (#34) in 1966; "The Eyes of a New York Woman" (#28, 1968); "I Just Can't Help Believing" (#9, 1970); "No Love at All" (#16, 1971); and "Rock and Roll Lullaby" (#15, 1972), which featured guitarist Duane Eddy and backing vocalists the Blossoms.

Before achieving fame on his own, Thomas belonged to a Houston combo, the Triumphs, which had a number of regional hits. In 1975 he returned to the #1 spot on the pop charts with the country tune "(Hey Won't You Play) Another Somebody Done Somebody Wrong Song" (also #1 C&W). This was followed by a 1977 Top Twenty cover of the Beach Boys hit "Don't Worry Baby." Thomas has spoken publicly of being an abused child (the subject of his song "Broken Toys"), and in the Seventies he became a born-again Christian. His subsequent releases veered between gospel (he has won two Dove Awards) and mainstream country. His first gospel album, 1976's *Home Where I Belong*, went platinum. His later country hits include "What Ever Happened to Old Fashioned Love" (#1 C&W, 1983), "New Looks from an Old Lover" (#1 C&W, 1983), and "The Whole World's in Love When You're Lonely" (#10 C&W, 1984). He is the recipient of five Grammy Awards.

Carla Thomas

Born 1942, Memphis, Tennessee
1961—*Gee Whiz* (Atlantic)   1966—*Comfort Me*
(Stax); *Carla*   1967—*King and Queen* (with Otis
Redding); *Queen Alone*   1969—*The Best of Carla
Thomas* (Atlantic)   1971—*Love Means* (Stax)
1986—*Chronicle* (with Rufus Thomas)   1992—*Hidden Gems.*

Before Aretha Franklin, Carla Thomas was black music's reigning Queen of Soul. Her "Gee Whiz (Look at His Eyes)" in 1961 was, in fact, the first Memphis soul record to make a national impact (#10 pop, #5 R&B); its success resulted in the foundation of Stax Records. The daughter of Memphis music veteran Rufus Thomas, Carla Thomas made her recording debut in 1960, when she duetted with her father on "Cause I Love You" while on summer vacation from college. After "Gee Whiz" succeeded, her education took a backseat to an active performing career.

Throughout the Sixties, Thomas was a star member of the Stax roster, scoring with "I'll Bring It Home to You" (#41 pop, #9 R&B) in 1962; "Let Me Be Good to You" (#62 pop, #11 R&B) and "B-A-B-Y" (#14 pop, #3 R&B) in 1966; with Otis Redding on "Tramp" (#26 pop, #2 R&B) and "Knock on Wood" (#30 pop, #8 R&B) and "I'll Always Have Faith in You" (#85 pop, #11 R&B) in 1967; and "I Like What You're Doing (to Me)" (#9 R&B) in 1969.

After Stax's demise in the mid-Seventies, Thomas stopped recording, but still performed on the club circuit. In the late Eighties she was an artist-in-residence for the Tennessee Arts Commission, where she worked with young people. She has essentially retired from recording. In 1993 she was given a Pioneer Award from the Rhythm & Blues Foundation.

David Thomas: See Pere Ubu

Mickey Thomas: See Jefferson Airplane

Rufus Thomas

Born March 26, 1917, Casey, Mississippi
1963—*Walking the Dog* (Stax); *May I Have Your
Ticket, Please?*   1970—*Funky Chicken*; *Rufus
Thomas Live/Doing the Push & Pull at P.J.'s*
1972—*Did You Hear Me?*   1973—*Crown Prince of
Dance*   1977—*If There Were No Music* (AVI); *Rufus
Thomas EP* (Hollywood, U.K.)   1986—*Chronicle*
(with Carla Thomas) (Stax)   1988—*That Woman Is
Poison* (Alligator)   1992—*Can't Get Away from
This Dog* (Stax).

Singer Rufus Thomas has been a fixture on the Memphis music scene since the Forties. He enjoyed his greatest record sales with his mid-Sixties and early-Seventies dance hits.

While Thomas was attending Memphis' Booker T. Washington High School in the Thirties, Professor Nat D. Williams, a history teacher and emcee of a talent show at the Palace Theater, selected him to become his sidekick in a comedy act. Upon graduation from high school, Thomas toured the South with the Rabbit Foot Minstrels, telling jokes, tap dancing, and singing. He performed at tent shows until 1940, when he married. Later that year, he replaced Williams as emcee at the Palace talent shows.

When he left the talent shows 11 years later, Thomas worked three other jobs—day worker at a textile plant, emcee at a local club, and DJing on WDIA, where he be-friended another popular disc jockey, B. B. King. During the early Fifties he recorded for Sam Phillips and his infant Sun Records. Thomas had his first national hit in 1953 with "Bear Cat" (#3 R&B), an answer record to Big Mama Thornton's "Hound Dog." Rufus and his daughter Carla were early stars of Stax Records. His two 1963 dance hits, "The Dog" (#22 R&B) and "Walking the Dog" (#10 pop, #5 R&B), helped establish that company. In the early Seventies, Thomas had another hot streak with "Do the Funky Chicken" (#28 pop, #5 R&B) and "(Do the) Push and Pull" (#31 pop, #1 R&B) in 1970, and "The Breakdown" (#2 R&B) in 1971. Into the Seventies, Thomas worked at WDIA. When Stax went bankrupt, Thomas recorded for a series of labels. He still tours.

Richard Thompson

**Born April 3, 1949, London, England
1972—Henry the Human Fly (Warner Bros.) 1976—
(Guitar, Vocal) (Carthage) 1981—Strict Tempo!
1983—Hand of Kindness (Hannibal) 1984—Small
Town Romance 1985—Across a Crowded Room
(Polydor) 1986—Daring Adventures 1988—Am-
nesia (Capitol) 1991—Rumor and Sigh 1993—
Watching the Dark: The History of Richard
Thompson (Rykodisc/Hannibal) 1994—Mirror Blue
(Capitol). Richard and Linda Thompson (b. Linda
Peters, Glasgow, Scot.): 1974—I Want to See the
Bright Lights Tonight (Carthage) 1975—Hokey
Pokey; Pour Down Like Silver 1977—Almost Live
(More or Less) (Island) 1978—First Light
(Carthage) 1979—Sunnyvista 1982—Shoot Out
the Lights (Hannibal).
Linda Thompson solo: 1985—One Clear Moment
(Warner Bros.).**

Richard Thompson, a founding member of the British folk-rock group Fairport Convention [see entry], left that band in 1971 for a career that in many ways fulfilled Fairport's goals: to link Celtic folk music to rock. Thompson's gallows-humored, fatalistic songs, whose outlook owes something to his Sufi-Moslem religion, are steeped in the jigs and reels and marches of British folk music, although they are often played on electric instruments.

After leaving Fairport, Thompson first sat in as a guitarist on British folk-rock albums like Mike and Lal Waterson's *Bright Phoebus*. He joined a loose aggregation of Fairport and folk-scene veterans, including drummer Dave Mattacks, singer Sandy Denny, and bassist Ashley Hutchings, under the name the Bunch to record an album of pop oldies, *Rock On*. On that album, a friend of Sandy Denny's named Linda Peters sang "The Locomotion," and she married Thompson soon afterward. Thompson also sat in on Hutchings' first solo project, *Morris On*.

Richard Thompson

In 1972 Thompson began his solo career with the brilliant, eccentric *Henry the Human Fly*, which juxtaposed Chuck Berry riffs with old-English concertinas on Thompson's original songs. Linda Peters Thompson sang a few backup vocals, but she didn't get full billing until *I Want to See the Bright Lights Tonight*, which was belatedly released in the U.S. as half of the double album *Almost Live (More or Less)*. Although Richard Thompson wrote all the duo's material (except for a song on their final album cowritten by Linda), he shared lead vocals with her on the albums they made together, and Linda's emotive mezzo-soprano was widely praised. In 1974 the Thompsons put together an electric band called Sour Grapes, with ex–Fairport guitarist Simon Nicol and a rhythm section, but after a tour opening for Traffic the group broke up. In 1974 the Thompsons converted to Sufism.

The pair toured Britain in 1975 with a band that included ex-Fairports Dave Pegg on bass and Dave Mattacks on drums, plus button accordionist John Kirkpatrick. Afterward they retreated to the English countryside to start a Sufi community. They returned in 1978 with *First Light*, which used a U.S. rhythm section. *Strict Tempo!* was an album of instrumentals on which Thompson played all the instruments except percussion (by Mattacks); it included traditional jigs, reels, polkas, and a Duke Ellington tune. He also sat in on the first solo album by David Thomas of Pere Ubu.

Sessions for *Shoot Out the Lights* were originally produced by Gerry Rafferty (Stealers Wheel, "Baker Street"); unhappy with the results, Thompson shelved the project. Producer Joe Boyd offered to produce the album for his new label, Hannibal.

Thompson toured the U.S. as an acoustic solo act before *Shoot Out the Lights* was released, where he met his future wife, concert promoter Nancy Covey. Returning to England, he asked Linda for a divorce. They toured together with a band including Nicol, Mattacks, and bassist Pete Zorn. But the tensions of a disintegrating marriage spilled over to the music, and the pair split acrimoniously. While Linda sought a solo contract, Richard recorded an album of country-and-Celtic-tinged break-up songs, *Hand of Kindness* (#186, 1983).

Linda signed with Warner Bros. in 1984 and released an album of edgy, countryish songs. It was released concurrently with Richard's *Across a Crowded Room* (#102, 1985), his first major-label release in seven years.

Richard Thompson's career has become a *succès d'estime*, earning critical raves and low sales. In 1993 Rykodisc released *Watching the Dark*, a three-CD retrospective covering Thompson's career. He's played on albums ranging from Suzanne Vega to Robert Plant. Joel Sonnier had a Top Ten C&W hit covering Thompson's "Tear Stained Letter." A tribute album, *Beat the Retreat*, featuring Bonnie Raitt, Los Lobos, R.E.M., Dinosaur Jr, and David Byrne, among other artists, covering Thompson's songs, was released in 1994.

The Thompson Twins

Formed 1977, Chesterfield, England
Tom Bailey (b. Halifax, Eng.), voc., kybds.; John Roog, gtr.; Pete Dodd, gtr.; Chris Bell, drums. 1981—*A Product of . . .* (T, U.K.)   1982—(+ Alannah Currie [b. Auckland, N.Z.], perc., sax, voc.; + Joe Leeway [b. London, Eng.], perc., voc.; + Matthew Seligman, bass) *In the Name of Love* (Arista) (– Roog; – Dodd; – Bell; – Seligman)   1983—*Side Kicks*   1984—*Into the Gap*   1985—*Here's to Future Days*   1986—(– Leeway)   1987—*Close to the Bone* 1988—*The Best of Thompson Twins: Greatest Mixes* 1989—*Big Trash* (Warner Bros./Reprise)   1991— *Queer* (Warner Bros.). Babble: 1994—*The Stone* (Reprise).

Actually a trio—at their peak, anyway—and without a Thompson among them, England's the Thompson Twins hit pay dirt with their quirkily videogenic looks and buoyant technopop tunes. Members Tom Bailey, Alannah Currie, and Joe Leeway were the perfect bunch to usher in the era of Boy George and Duran Duran. Singer, keyboardist, and chief songwriter Bailey was an aspiring classical pianist and percussionist/ singer Leeway a fledgling actor when they met in 1977, at a teachers' college in Cheshire; but Bailey formed the band's original four-man lineup without Leeway. This incarnation of the Thompson Twins—a name alluding to characters in Hergé's *Tin Tin* cartoon—toured London and released singles independently before signing with Arista

Records in 1981. After the release of their debut album, *A Product of . . .* , Bailey added Leeway, then a roadie, to the group. Bailey also recruited his girlfriend Alannah Currie, a former journalist who dabbled in music and flamboyant fashions, and ex–Soft Boys bassist Matthew Seligman.

This seven-piece edition of the Thompsons survived only one album. After *Set* (released in the U.S. as *In the Name of Love*), their manager, another school friend of Bailey and Leeway, fired everyone except those two and Currie. The newly spare Thompsons shot to #2 in the U.K., with their subsequent album, *Quick Step and Side Kick* (*Side Kicks* here). Moreover, the album and its successors, *Into the Gap* (#10, 1984) and *Here's to Future Days* (#20, 1985), spawned a chain of hits in England and America: in 1983, "Love on Your Side" (#45 U.S.; #9 U.K.), "We Are Detective" (#7 U.K.), "Hold Me Now" (#3 U.S. [1984]; #4 U.K.); in 1984, "Doctor Doctor" (#11 U.S.; #3 U.K.) and "You Take Me Up" (#44 U.S.; #2 U.K.); and in 1985, "Lay Your Hands on Me" (#6 U.S.) and "King for a Day" (#8 U.S. [1986]; #22 U.K.). In 1986 Leeway left the act; now the Twins were indeed a duo—and a couple. Bailey and Currie, who had initially kept their personal relationship a secret, had a child in 1988. Their professional collaborations proved somewhat less fruitful, their biggest hit to date being 1989's "Sugar Daddy," a #28 single in America.

In early 1994 Bailey and Currie resurfaced in a collective called Babble, whose sound was in the trance-ambient mode. It released *The Stone*, which featured engineer/programmer Keith Fernley (the group's other core member), vocalists Q. Tee and Amy St. Cyr, and computer whiz Charlie Whisker.

Big Mama Thornton

Born Willie Mae Thornton, December 11, 1926, Montgomery, Alabama; died July 25, 1984, Los Angeles, California
1966—*In Europe* (Arhoolie)   1967—*Chicago Blues* 1968—*Ball and Chain*   1969—*Stronger Than Dirt* (Mercury)   1971—*She's Back* (Backbeat)   1975— *Jail* (Vanguard); *Sassy Mama*   1978—*Mama's Pride*.

A singer/songwriter who also played harmonica and drums, Willie Mae "Big Mama" Thornton was a blueswoman who, in spanning the decades from country to city blues, carried forward the legacy of such seminal blueswomen as Bessie Smith, Ma Rainey, and Memphis Minnie. She was the originator of two songs later made famous by rock & roll superstars: "Hound Dog" (by Elvis Presley), written by Leiber and Stoller, and her own "Ball and Chain" (a hit for Janis Joplin).

Thornton was one of seven children; her father was a minister, her mother a church singer. She became interested in music at an early age and won first prize in a local talent show in her teens. From 1941 to 1948, she toured the South as a singer, dancer, and comedienne with Sammy Greene's Hot Harlem Revue. She settled in Houston, Texas, in 1948 and began recording there in 1951. In 1952 she worked with Johnny Otis' band on his Rhythm and Blues Caravan tour, and she appeared in package shows with Junior Parker and Johnny Ace during 1953 and 1954. She recorded for small labels like Kent and Baytone.

In 1965 Thornton toured England and Europe with the American Folk Blues Festival, and in 1967 she appeared at one of John Hammond's Spirituals to Swing concerts at Carnegie Hall, and appeared in the PBS documentary *Black White and Blue*. A year later she appeared at the Monterey Jazz Festival, and in 1969 she played the Newport Folk Festival and the Chicago and Ann Arbor blues festivals. In 1971 she appeared on the Dick Cavett talk show on ABC-TV and recorded material for the soundtrack of the film *Vanishing Point*. In 1974 she appeared on NBC-TV's rock show *Midnight Special,* and in 1980 she appeared on the "Blues Is a Woman" bill with such other veteran blueswomen as Sippie Wallace at the Newport Jazz Festival.

Thornton began recording her later albums with *In Europe. Chicago Blues,* featuring such blues giants as Muddy Waters and Otis Spann, is considered one of her best. *Jail* contains her versions of "Hound Dog" (originally an R&B hit for her in 1953, before Presley's version), "Ball and Chain," and "Little Red Rooster." She died of a heart attack.

George Thorogood and the Destroyers

Formed 1973, Delaware
Original lineup: George Thorogood (b. Dec. 31, 1952, Wilmington, Del.), gtr., voc.; Ron Smith, gtr.; Billy Blough, bass; Jeff Simon, drums.
1977—*George Thorogood and the Destroyers* (Rounder) 1978—*Move It On Over* 1979—*Better Than the Rest* (MCA) 1980—(– Smith; + Hank Carter, sax) *More George Thorogood and the Destroyers* (Rounder) 1982—*Bad to the Bone* (EMI America) 1985—(+ Steve Chrismar, gtr.) *Maverick* 1986—*Live* 1988—*Born to Be Bad* (EMI Manhattan) 1991—*Boogie People* (EMI) 1992—*The Baddest of George Thorogood and the Destroyers* 1993—*Haircut* 1995—*Let's Work Together Live.*

The son of a white-collar British immigrant and a onetime semipro baseball player, George Thorogood is a spirited re-creator of the driving, raucous urban slide-guitar blues pioneered by Chicago greats like Elmore James.

Thorogood did not become seriously involved with music until 1970, when he saw a show by another blues

archivist, John Paul Hammond. Thorogood went to California, where he was soon opening shows for Bonnie Raitt and bluesmen Sonny Terry and Brownie McGhee. In late 1978 Thorogood got some airplay with his raw adaptation of Hank Williams' "Move It On Over," the first single on the folk-oriented Rounder label. The album charted in the Top Forty. Although Thorogood publicly repudiated *Better Than the Rest,* a demo tape he had signed away, it also charted. In 1981 he and the Destroyers opened several dates on the Rolling Stones' U.S. tour. He and the Destroyers later played a tour of 50 consecutive dates in 50 different states over a two-month period.

Thorogood's big commercial break came in 1982 when "Bad to the Bone," with a video featuring Bo Diddley, got substantial exposure on MTV. The album of the same title went gold, Thorogood's second, and the group's next three albums—*Maverick, Live, Born to Be Bad*—did likewise, even though none charted higher than #32. In 1985 the group backed Albert Collins at Live Aid. Thorogood is known as much for his tongue-in-cheek lyrics (as in "I Drink Alone") as his bracing guitar work. With just one charting single, "Willie and the Hand Jive" (#63, 1985), and a stubborn commitment to straight-ahead blues rock, George Thorogood and the Destroyers have carved out a unique niche. While critics deride the group's now-formulaic approach and record sales have been relatively weak, the group continues to tour and to record.

Thrash/Speed Metal/Death Metal

As hardcore punk matured in Los Angeles and New York City in the early Eighties, a thicker, heavy-metal–based offshoot, thrash, popped up in the suburbs. Nurtured by teenage rock musicians raised on metal but also exposed to punk, thrash blended the ominous, half-step chord progressions of proto-metal band Black Sabbath and thudding grind of fringe metal act Motörhead with the speed and intensity of punk and hardcore such as the Sex Pistols and Black Flag. Where hardcore usually appealed to malcontent middle-class postpunk rockers, thrash offered angry young working-class headbangers a raw alternative to the standard pop-metal fare of Van Halen and Def Leppard.

Metallica introduced the sound on its 1983 debut album, *Kill 'Em All*; two years later the group's former guitarist, Dave Mustaine, forged an even faster version of thrash, called speed metal, with his new band Megadeth. On the East Coast, New York's Anthrax had switched from hardcore to thrash just before releasing its 1984 debut album, *Fistful of Metal*.

Thrash or speed metal that incorporates graphic images of death and destruction in its lyrics is usually referred to as death metal. While much of Megadeth's music could be filed under death metal, the style is typified by even more extreme bands such as Carcass, Napalm Death, Cadaver, and Morbid Angel. (Death metal with industrial rhythms is called grindcore.) Slayer's 1986 album *Reign in Blood,* on which more than 50 variations of the word "death" appear in the lyrics, is often cited as the archetypal death-metal album.

Three Dog Night

Formed 1967, Los Angeles, California
Danny Hutton (b. Sep. 10, 1942, Buncrana, Ire.), voc.; Chuck Negron (b. Charles Negron, June 8, 1942, Bronx, N.Y.), voc.; Cory Wells (b. Feb. 5, 1942, Buffalo, N.Y.), voc.; Mike Allsup (b. March 8, 1947, Modesto, Calif.), gtr.; Jimmy Greenspoon (b. Feb. 7, 1948, Los Angeles), kybds.; Joe Schermie (b. Feb. 12, Madison, Wis.), bass; Floyd Sneed (b. Nov. 22, 1943, Calgary, Can.), drums.
1968—*Three Dog Night* (Dunhill)   1969—*Suitable for Framing*; *Captured Live at the Forum*   1970—*It Ain't Easy*; *Naturally*   1971—*Golden Bisquits*; *Harmony*   1972—*Seven Separate Fools*   1973— (– Schermie; + Jack Ryland, bass; + Skip Konte, kybds.) *Around the World with Three Dog Night*; *Cyan*   1974—*Hard Labor*; *Joy to the World: Their Greatest Hits*   1975—*Coming Down Your Way* (ABC)   1976—*American Pastime* (– Ryland; – Konte; – Allsup; – Sneed; + Al Ciner, gtr.; + Denny Belfield, bass; + Ron Stockert, kybds.; – Hutton; + Jay Gruska, voc.)   1983—*The Best of Three Dog Night* (MCA); *It's a Jungle* EP (Passport)   1993— *Celebrate: The Three Dog Night Story, 1965–1975* (MCA).

In the late Sixties to early Seventies, Three Dog Night was one of the most popular bands in America, with 18 consecutive Top Twenty hits (11 of which were Top Tens, including three #1s), seven million-selling singles, and 12 gold LPs—their entire album catalogue up through 1974's *Joy to the World: Their Greatest Hits.* Although the group initially earned critical respect for its innovative interpretations and was a staple of progressive FM-radio playlists, it was later criticized as being crassly commercial. True, Three Dog Night's material was singles-oriented, soul-influenced pop rock, and almost always consisted of covers. And their success was phenomenal. In its favor, however, the group—which chose, arranged, and coproduced its records—provided exposure for such songwriters as Randy Newman, Elton John and Bernie Taupin, Harry Nilsson, Laura Nyro, Hoyt Axton, Leo Sayer, and others.

The band centered on three lead singers (Cory Wells, Danny Hutton, and Chuck Negron) with four backup musicians (Mike Allsup, Jimmy Greenspoon, Joe Scher-

mie, and Floyd Sneed). Wells knew Hutton from the mid-Sixties, when the latter produced Wells' band, the Enemys, for MGM. Hutton, born in Ireland but raised in the U.S., worked as a producer from age 18, and in 1965 he wrote, arranged, and produced as a solo the single "Roses and Rainbows" (for Hanna-Barbera Records, part of the cartoon company), which became a small hit. In the fall of that year, he auditioned unsuccessfully for the Monkees. Hutton also recorded for MGM, where he had the minor hit "Big Bright Eyes." It was Hutton who first hit on the three-vocalist-band idea, and he and Wells brought in Negron, who used to sing regularly at the Apollo and had recorded unsuccessfully with Columbia in the mid-Sixties. Negron also sang backup on one of Hutton's first singles. (Among others Hutton and Wells considered for the third-vocalist spot were Billy Joe Royal and Crazy Horse founder Danny Whitten.) The trio, renamed Redwood by Brian Wilson, cut two singles with Wilson producing: "Darlin'" and "Time to Get Alone." Neither was ever released, and "Darlin'" later became a hit for the Beach Boys. The trio then moved on to work with Van Dyke Parks, with whom they cut a few demos.

Frustrated by their lack of artistic control, Negron, Hutton, and Wells decided to expand their group to include backing musicians, and by 1968 the lineup was a firm seven-piece. Schermie had been with the Cory Wells Blues Band, which had broken up the year before. Sneed had backed Jose Feliciano, and Greenspoon had done many L.A. sessions. After some initial consultation with Van Dyke Parks and Brian Wilson, Gabriel Mekler, a Hungarian-born classical pianist, who had worked with Steppenwolf, became their producer.

Three Dog Night's 1968 debut, *Three Dog Night* (#11, 1969), contained three singles. "Nobody" gained initial interest. Its B side was an obscure Lennon-McCartney song previously recorded by Cilla Black, "It's for You." Though never a hit itself, "It's for You" showcased the group's three-part-harmony lead vocals. "Nobody" was followed by the Top Thirty cover of Otis Redding's "Try a Little Tenderness." Their big breakthrough came in 1969 with "One," a Harry Nilsson song that soared to #5, their first gold. *Suitable for Framing* (#16, 1969) gave them hits with "Easy to Be Hard" (#4, 1969) from the rock musical *Hair*; "Eli's Coming" (#10, 1969) by Laura Nyro, and "Lady Samantha," the first stateside success for Elton John and Bernie Taupin. On *It Ain't Easy* (#8, 1970), they covered Randy Newman's "Mama Told Me (Not to Come)" (#1, 1970). They later made Hoyt Axton's children's song "Joy to the World" #1 in 1971. They also gave Leo Sayer his first writing hit here by covering "The Show Must Go On" (#14, 1974). Their other hits include Russ Ballard's song for Argent, "Liar" (#7, 1971), "One Man Band" (#19, 1970), "An Old Fashioned Love Song" (#4, 1971), "Never Been to Spain" (#5, 1972), "Black and White" (#1, 1972), and B. W. Stevenson's "Shambala" (#3,

1973). The group's concerts were sold out around the world, and in 1972 they even hosted their own network television special.

By 1974, though, their commercial magic had finally waned. Their 13th LP, *Coming Down Your Way* (#70, 1975), was the first not to go gold. In addition, there was personal friction among the three singers, partly because Negron sang a disproportionate number of the hits and was viewed by the public as "the" lead singer. In 1976, after *American Pastime* (#123, 1976), Hutton was replaced by Jay Gruska, and the band got three new musicians, all former members of Rufus—Al Ciner, Denny Belfield, and Ron Stockert. In 1977 the group disbanded.

Hutton began managing punk bands in the later Seventies, including L.A.'s Fear. He also led a group called the Danny Hutton Hitters; they had a song on the *Pretty in Pink* soundtrack. Wells recorded a pair of solo albums, but only one, 1978's *Touch Me*, was released. Negron recorded a solo LP, too, in the early Eighties. In June 1981 the three original vocalists reunited, and two years later, they released their last record, an EP entitled *It's a Jungle*. Since the mid-Eighties Hutton, Wells, and Greenspoon have toured with other musicians as Three Dog Night. Allsup subsequently rejoined them. Negron is pursuing a solo career.

Throwing Muses/Belly

Formed 1980, Newport, Rhode Island
Kristin Hersh (b. Aug. 7, 1966, Atlanta, Ga.), gtr.,
voc.; Tanya Donelly (b. July 14, 1966, Newport), gtr.,
voc.; David Narcizo (b. May 6, 1966, Newport),
drums; Elaine Adamedes, bass.
1984—*Throwing Muses* EP (Throwing Muses)
1986—(– Adamedes; + Leslie Langston [b. Apr. 1,
1964, Newport], bass) *Throwing Muses* (4AD, U.K.)
1987—*Chains Changed* EP; *The Fat Skier* EP (Sire)
1988—*House Tornado* 1989—*Hunkpapa* 1991—
(– Langston; + Fred Abong, bass) *The Real Ramona*
1992—(– Donelly; – Abong; + Langston) *Red*
***Heaven* 1994—(– Langston; + Bernard Georges**
[b. Mar. 29, 1965, Gonaive, Haiti], bass) 1995—
University.
Belly, formed 1991, Providence, Rhode Island
(Donelly, gtr., voc.; Tom Gorman [b. May 20, 1966,
Buffalo, N.Y.], gtr.; Chris Gorman [b. July 29, 1967,
Buffalo], drums; Fred Abong, bass): 1993—*Star*
(Sire) (– Abong; + Gail Greenwood [b. Mar. 10, 1960,
Providence], bass) 1995—*King*.
Kristin Hersh solo: 1994—*Hips and Makers* (Sire).

Throwing Muses pioneered a dense, dreamy, guitar-based sound long before "alternative" was a musical term. Led by singer/songwriter Kristin Hersh and, to a lesser degree, her stepsister Tanya Donelly, they articulated a female vision—intense, meditative, raw—that

differed sharply from the videogenic pop of the Eighties.

The band was formed by four high school friends in Newport, Rhode Island. After a self-released EP that drew critical praise in Rhode Island and Boston, the Muses changed bassists. They were the first American band signed to London's 4AD label. Their eponymous debut and *Chains Changed* EP, both produced by Gil Norton, were released to gushing attention from the British press.

Their first American releases, however, were too oblique and discordant for tastes here, although the Muses have over the years built a devoted following. As college radio developed into a market segment, the Muses gained greater success with the more melodic *Hunkpapa*. Langston left (she joined Wolfgang Press and returned to record *Red Heaven* with the Muses) and was replaced by Fred Abong. The Muses had a breakthrough on alternative radio with "Counting Backwards" from *The Real Ramona*. Hersh toured America pregnant with her second child, her belly pushing her guitar far in front of her by the final dates.

Donelly developed a side project, the Breeders, with the Pixies' Kim Deal in 1990 [see the Pixies/Breeders entry]. She had contributed one or two songs per album during the Muses' career and, after *Ramona*, decided she needed an outlet devoted to her own tunes. She left Muses and formed Belly with the brothers Tom and Chris Gorman. The album's poppy, childlike tunes (Donelly calls the songs fairy tales), especially the MTV hit "Feed the Tree," brought Belly more commercial success than the Muses have known. Belly was nominated for a Grammy for Best New Act of 1993.

Meanwhile, although the Muses' *Red Heaven* contained several radio-friendly tunes and featured a cameo by Bob Mould (Hüsker Dü, Sugar), it did not get the same support from the record company and radio. Hersh subsequently recorded an acclaimed solo album, *Hips and Makers*, produced by Lenny Kaye. It included a cameo from R.E.M.'s Michael Stipe.

With bassist Bernard Georges and founding drummer David Narcizo, Hersh regrouped Throwing Muses in 1994 and recorded the self-produced *University*, released in early 1995.

Thunderclap Newman

Formed 1969, England
Andy Newman (b. ca. 1943, Eng.), kybds.; Jimmy
McCulloch (b. 1953, Scot.; d. Sep. 27, 1979), gtr.;
John "Speedy" Keen (b. Mar. 29, 1945, London,
Eng.), voc., drums; and later, Jim Avery (b. Eng.),
bass; Jack McCulloch (b. Scot.), drums.
1970—*Hollywood Dream* (Track).

Thunderclap Newman was a group haphazardly assembled by Pete Townshend in 1969. The group had one hit,

Grammy Awards

Take 6
1988 Best Jazz Vocal Performance, Duo or Group: "Spread Love"
1988 Best Soul Gospel Performance by a Duo or Group, Choir, or Chorus: *Take 6*
1989 Best Gospel Vocal Performance by a Duo or Group, Choir, or Chorus: "The Savior is Waiting"
1990 Best Contemporary Soul Gospel Album: *So Much 2 Say*
1991 Best Jazz Vocal Performance: *He Is Christmas*
1994 Best Contemporary Soul Gospel Album: *Join the Band*

Tavares
1978 Album of the Year: *Saturday Night Fever* (with others)

James Taylor
1971 Best Pop Vocal Performance, Male: "You've Got a Friend"
1977 Best Pop Vocal Performance, Male: "Handy Man"

Koko Taylor and the Blues Machine
1984 Best Traditional Blues Recording: *Blues Explosion* (with others)

The Temptations
1968 Best R&B Performance by a Duo or Group, Vocal or Instrumental: "Cloud Nine"
1972 Best R&B Vocal Performance by a Duo, Group, or Chorus: "Papa Was a Rollin' Stone"
1972 Best R&B Instrumental Performance: "Papa Was a Rollin' Stone"

Texas Tornados
1990 Best Mexican/American Performance: "Soy de San Luis"

B. J. Thomas
1977 Best Inspirational Performance: "Home Where I Belong"
1978 Best Inspirational Performance: *Happy Man*
1979 Best Inspirational Performance: *You Gave Me Love (When Nobody Gave Me a Prayer)*
1980 Best Gospel Performance, Contemporary or Inspirational: *The Lord's Prayer* (with others)
1981 Best Inspirational Performance: *Amazing Grace*

Peter Tosh
1987 Best Reggae Recording: *No Nuclear War*

Toto
1982 Record of the Year: "Rosanna"
1982 Album of the Year: *Toto IV*
1982 Producer of the Year (entire group)

David Paich (Toto)
1976 Best R&B Song: "Lowdown" (with Boz Scaggs)
1982 Best Instrumental Arrangement Accompanying Vocal(s): "Rosanna" (with others)
1982 Best Vocal Arrangement for Two or More Voices: "Rosanna"

Jeff Porcaro (Toto)
1982 Best Instrumental Arrangement Accompanying Vocal(s): "Rosanna" (with others)

Trammps
1978 Album of the Year: *Saturday Night Fever* (with others)

Traveling Wilburys [See also: Bob Dylan; George Harrison; Roy Orbison]
1989 Best Rock Performance by a Duo or Group with Vocal: *Traveling Wilburys Volume One*

Randy Travis
1987 Best Country Vocal Performance, Male: *Always and Forever*
1988 Best Country Vocal Performance, Male: *Old 8 × 10*

Travis Tritt
1992 Best Country Vocal Collaboration: "The Whiskey Ain't Workin'" (with Marty Stuart)

Ike and Tina Turner
1971 Best R&B Vocal Performance by a Duo or Group: "Proud Mary"

Tina Turner
1984 Best Pop Vocal Performance, Female: "What's Love Got to Do with It"
1984 Best Rock Vocal Performance, Female: "Better Be Good to Me"
1984 Record of the Year: "What's Love Got to Do with It" (with Terry Britten)
1985 Best Rock Vocal Performance, Female: "One of the Living"
1986 Best Rock Vocal Performance, Female: "Back Where You Started"
1988 Best Rock Vocal Performance, Female: *Tina Live in Europe*

Conway Twitty
1971 Best Country Vocal Performance by a Group: "After the Fire Is Gone" (with Loretta Lynn)

"Something in the Air," and then disbanded. Andy Newman was a 26-year-old eccentric, a barrelhouse jazz pianist who had previously worked as a post office engineer. Townshend first heard a tape of Newman back in 1963. Townshend ran into Jimmy McCulloch during a Who gig where 13-year-old Jimmy's Cowsill-type family opened the show. Townshend knew ex–John Mayall roadie "Speedy" Keen from the early Who days; Keen's "Armenia City in the Sky" wound up on *The Who Sell Out*. Townshend made the three members into a regular band and, as producer and bass player (under the pseudonym Bijou Drains), recorded Keen's "Something in the

Air." It went to #1 in England, got much FM airplay in America, but only hit #37. It was also used in the films *The Magic Christian* and *The Strawberry Statement*. Keen wrote the hit and most of the other material on *Hollywood Dream*.

The band toured England to support the single, with Jim Avery on bass and Jimmy McCulloch's brother Jack on drums (to free Keen for the front vocal spot), but it didn't work out and they disbanded in 1970. Keen went on to make two solo albums, *Previous Convictions* (1973, Track) and *Y'know Wot I Mean?* (1975, Island). Newman had his own solo, *Rainbow* (Track), and then briefly joined ex–Bonzo Dog Band member Roger Spear in Kinetic Wardrobe. McCulloch played with Stone the Crows (with Maggie Bell), John Mayall, and then Paul McCartney's Wings from 1975 until 1978; he died the following year.

Johnny Thunders: See the Heartbreakers

Tiffany
Born Tiffany Renee Darwish, October 2, 1971, Norwalk, California
1987—*Tiffany* (MCA)   1988—*Hold an Old Friend's Hand*   1990—*New Inside*.

Tiffany was only 16 when a couple of bubblegum-pop singles took her to the top of the charts. Actually, her 1987 self-titled debut album had been a commercial dud until her manager, George Tobin, helped dream up a marketing ploy that brought her to shopping malls everywhere—literally. Tobin, a music industry veteran, was in his North Hollywood studio producing a Smokey Robinson album when he met Tiffany. She was there making a demo tape for a local songwriter. Tiffany, who began singing in public when she was nine, had been performing with country bands until then; but when Tobin heard her thin but peppy voice, he decided she could be a hot pop commodity.

It took him three years to land his discovery a major-label contract, with MCA. When the album *Tiffany* proved an equally hard sell, Tobin and a publicist conceived "The Beautiful You: Celebrating the Good Life," a tour that brought Tiffany to teen-infested shopping malls around the country. Tiffany eventually hit #1 on the pop chart—the first album by a teenage girl to do so—as did two of its singles, "Could've Been" and a cover of Tommy James' "I Think We're Alone Now." Another cover, of the Beatles' "I Saw Her Standing There" (substituting the masculine pronoun), went to #7.

Alas, this teen queen's reign would be brief: After "All This Time" (#6, 1988), her sophomore album quickly faded, and a third album proved a total flop. Tiffany re-mained big news in 1988, though, by taking her mother to court, seeking emancipated-minor status. The settlement reached was a compromise: The singer would receive three lump-sum payments of her previous earnings over a period of several years, and while her mother remained her legal guardian, Tiffany would control her finances from then on. The same year as her last album, Tiffany was heard as the voice of Judy Jetson in the 1990 film *The Jetsons: The Movie*.

'Til Tuesday/Aimee Mann
Formed 1983, Boston, Massachusetts
Aimee Mann (b. Aug. 9, 1960, Richmond, Va.), voc., bass; Robert Holmes (b. Mar. 31, 1959, Hampton, Eng.), gtr.; Joey Pesce (b. Apr. 14, 1962, Bronx, N.Y.), kybds.; Michael Hausman (b. June 12, 1960, Philadelphia, Pa.), drums.
1985—*Voices Carry* (Epic)   1986—*Welcome Home* (– Pesce; + Clayton Scobel, gtr.; + Jon Brion, gtr.; + Michael Montes, kybds.)   1988—*Everything's Different Now*.
Aimee Mann solo: 1993—*Whatever* (Imago)   1995—*I'm with Stupid*.

'Til Tuesday is best known for its pop-rock hit "Voices Carry" (#8, 1985) and the often-aired video in which singer/bassist Aimee Mann dramatically breaks free of an abusive and controlling lover. After the band's breakup, Mann soldiered on as a critically praised solo artist.

Mann, who at age four was kidnapped by her estranged mother and taken to Europe, went to Boston to attend the Berklee School of Music. She sang with local punk band the Young Snakes, then briefly worked with future industrial-punk band Ministry. In 1983 Mann formed 'Til Tuesday with English guitarist Robert Holmes, drummer Michael Hausman, whom she'd met at Berklee and with whom she lived for a few years, and keyboardist Joey Pesce. The group won a battle-of-the-bands contest sponsored by a Boston radio station, which led to a record deal.

Mann's breakup with Hausman inspired many of the dark lost-love lyrics on *Voices Carry* (#19, 1985). After its release Mann became romantically involved with singer/songwriter Jules Shear; their romance dissolved around the time of 'Til Tuesday's second album, *Welcome Home* (#49, 1986), which spawned only minor hits in "What About Love" (#49, 1986) and "Coming Up Close" (#59, 1987). Mann later said her friendship with Elvis Costello helped her through the breakup, and Costello wrote one song with her for *Everything's Different Now*, which sold poorly (#124, 1988) and failed to produce a hit single. 'Til Tuesday broke up, and it was five years before Mann reemerged with the very Beatles-esque *Whatever*, a critically acclaimed moderate seller on which Hausman played drums. Mann's touring band included XTC guitarist Dave Gregory.

Timbuk 3

Formed 1984, Madison, Wisconsin
Pat MacDonald (b. Aug. 6, 1952, Green Bay, Wis.), voc., gtr., harmonica, bass; Barbara K. MacDonald (b. Oct. 4, 1957, Wausau, Wis.), voc., gtr., harmonica, violin, mandolin.
1986—*Greetings from Timbuk 3* (I.R.S.)   1988—*Eden Alley*   1989—*Edge of Allegiance*   1991—(+ Wally Ingram [b. Sep. 13, 1962, Beloit, Wis.], drums; + Courtney Audain [b. Feb. 4, 1960, Trinidad], bass) *Big Shot in the Dark*   1993—*Espace Ornano* (Watermelon)   1995—*A Hundred Lovers* (High Street/Windham Hill).

Timbuk 3 is perhaps best remembered as a novelty band, based on its use of a boombox as a rhythm section and its hit single "The Future's So Bright, I Gotta Wear Shades" (#19, 1986). But the MacDonalds are actually talented musicians with serious and often grim viewpoints. "Shades," for example, was about the dangers of yuppie avarice and nuclear technology. Pat and Barbara MacDonald met in Madison, Wisconsin, in 1978 and got married five years later. They moved briefly to New York City, then relocated to Austin, Texas, in 1984. Timbuk 3 got a record deal after being featured on a 1985 MTV program about Austin's thriving music scene.

Greetings from Timbuk 3 (#50, 1986), featuring "Shades," introduced the band's musical mix of rock, funk, folk, and country and Pat's often-sarcastic lyrics. Timbuk 3 toured with a boombox playing taped rhythm tracks. On *Eden Alley*, Timbuk 3 tried to establish themselves as more serious artists, avoiding novelty hits and weaving a Biblical theme through the album. *Edge of Allegiance* was coproduced by Denardo Coleman, the son of Ornette Coleman, and Jayne Cortez, and featured the satirical "National Holiday." For *Big Shot in the Dark*, the group used a human rhythm section for the first time. *Espace Ornano* was named after the Paris club where it was recorded. *A Hundred Lovers* got some radio airplay with its title track.

The Time

Formed 1981, Minneapolis, Minnesota
Morris Day (b. ca. 1958, Springfield, Ill.), voc.; Jesse Johnson (b. May 29, 1960, Rock Island, Ill.), gtr., voc.; Jimmy Jam (b. James Harris III, June 6, 1959, Minneapolis), kybds.; Monte Moir, kybds.; Terry Lewis (b. Nov. 24, 1956, Omaha, Nebr.), bass; Jellybean Johnson, drums.
1981—*The Time* (Warner Bros.)   1982—*What Time Is It?*   1983—(– Jam; – Lewis; – Moir; + Paul "St. Paul" Peterson, kybds., voc.; + Mark Cardenas, kybds.; + Jerry Hubbard, bass; + Jerome Benton, voc., perc.)   1984—*Ice Cream Castle* (group disbands)   1990—(Original lineup, + Benton, re-forms) *Pandemonium* (Paisley Park).
Morris Day solo: 1985—*Color of Success* (Warner Bros.)   1988—*Daydreaming.*

After Prince, the Time was the foremost exponent of the fun-rock hybrid "Minneapolis Sound"—providing a snappy, crowd-pleasing complement to Prince's more venturesome artistry. The Time was reportedly created by Prince, who put his old friend Morris Day, a onetime band mate in Prince's early group Grand Central, together with members of that band's chief rival on the Minneapolis scene, Flyte Tyme, which had included Jimmy Jam and Terry Lewis [see entry], Monte Moir, and Jellybean Johnson. Day, who'd been Grand Central's drummer, replaced Alexander O'Neal [see entry] as Flyte Tyme's vocalist. The Time was completed with the additions of guitarist Jesse Johnson and Lewis' half-brother Jerome Benton, who became the comic-foil valet to Day's preening-dandy frontman.

The Time's eponymous debut album (#50, 1981) was produced by Prince under the alias "Jamie Starr"; Day's flamboyant act, equal parts swagger and self-mockery, gave the group a cool-yet-comical personality that appealed especially to R&B audiences. Hit singles included "Get It Up" (#6 R&B, 1981), "Cool" (#90 pop, #7 R&B, 1982), and "777-9311" (#88 pop, #2 R&B, 1982). Opening for Prince on his *1999* tour, the Time nearly stole the show with its sharp-dressed choreography and burlesque antics. However, the band's second album, *What Time Is It?* (#26, 1982), yielded only one minor hit in "The Walk" (#24 R&B, 1982).

In March 1983 Jam and Lewis, moonlighting as freelance producers, were snowed into Atlanta by a freak blizzard while working with the S.O.S. Band. They missed a tour date with Prince, who immediately fired them. Moir left soon after. Jam and Lewis went on to become enormously successful composer/producers for Janet Jackson, among other artists; Moir wrote and produced with their Flyte Tyme Productions and on his own.

The refashioned Time continued, with a featured role in Prince's breakthrough film *Purple Rain*, which yielded hits for the Time in "Jungle Love" (#20 pop, #6 R&B, 1984) and "The Bird" (#36 pop, #33 R&B, 1985), both of which were included on the *Ice Cream Castle* album (#24, 1984), the group's first platinum effort. Day and Prince grew apart, however, during the filming of *Purple Rain* and eventually stopped speaking with each other; Day quit the band, followed by Jesse Johnson, and the Time fell apart.

Day released two solo albums, *Color of Success* (#37,

1985), which yielded "The Oak Tree" (#65, 1985), and *Daydreaming* (#41, 1988), which produced the hit "Fishnet" (#23, 1988). He also acted in the Andrew Dice Clay film *Adventures of Ford Fairlane,* and in the shortlived 1990 ABC-TV sitcom *New Attitude.* Johnson, who'd produced some tracks for Janet Jackson before Jam and Lewis made her a megastar, formed the Jesse Johnson Revue, which released three albums; *Shockadelica* (#70, 1986) featured a duet with Sly Stone on "Crazay" (#53, 1986).

In 1990 the original Time briefly reunited to appear in Prince's movie *Graffiti Bridge* and to record the album *Pandemonium* (#18, 1990), which included the hit single "Jerk Out" (#9, 1990).

Tin Machine: See David Bowie

Tiny Tim
Born Herbert Khaury, April 12, 1930, New York City, New York
1968—*God Bless Tiny Tim* (Reprise); *Tiny Tim's Second Album*   1969—*For All My Little Friends.*

With his strange voice (a trembling falsetto), unique appearance (big nose, stringy hair, and bag-man clothes), and sweet demeanor, Tiny Tim became a highly successful camp novelty artist in the late Sixties to early Seventies.

The budding singer had a strong record-collector's interest in the fluffy comedic pop of the Twenties—particularly Rudy Vallee—and he first performed these little-known oldies to mostly uninterested audiences in Greenwich Village. He accompanied himself on ukulele and used such pseudonyms as Darry Dover and Larry Love. By the mid-Sixties, he began to gather a cult audience. He played often at Steve Paul's Scene, and eventually got booked on *The Tonight Show,* where he became an instant national celebrity of sorts.

By 1968, rock audiences at places like the Fillmores East and West liked his act as much as older nightclub crowds. In spring 1968 his first LP on Reprise came out. He became a frequent guest on *Laugh-In* as well as the Carson show. On the latter, he was married to 17-year-old Victoria May Budinger (Miss Vicky, as he called her) on December 17, 1969. That program was the most widely watched *Tonight* show in the series' long history (with the possible exception of Carson's final appearance as host). Their daughter was named Tulip, after Tiny's one major hit, "Tip-Toe thru' the Tulips with Me" (#17, 1968). Tim and Miss Vicky first filed for divorce in early 1972, at which point he was out of public favor and broke. The divorce was final in 1977. He continues to perform occasionally and has released some interesting singles with titles such as "I Saw Elvis Presley Tiptoeing Through the Tulips" and "The Hicky on Your Neck." His latterday oeuvre includes a cover of AC/DC's "Highway to Hell," and he has starred on the MTV game show *Lip Service.* He continues to tour.

Toad the Wet Sprocket
Formed circa 1988, Santa Barbara, California
Glen Phillips, voc., gtr.; Todd Nichols, gtr.; Dean Dinning, bass, kybds.; Randy Guss, drums.
1989—*Bread and Circus* (Columbia)   1990—*Pale*   1991—*Fear*   1994—*Dulcinea.*

Toad the Wet Sprocket, a mellow, artsy rock band that took its name from a Monty Python skit that parodied rock news reports, holds the distinction of being the first group from Santa Barbara, California, to score a major-label record deal. Formed by schoolmates, Toad honed its chops at a local bar, playing under names like Three Young Studs and Glen before settling on the Python-inspired moniker. Eventually, a singer from the area asked the band to back him during a recording session, and as a return favor allowed the musicians to cut two of their own songs in his studio. With $650 Toad recorded eight more tracks, making complete what would become its first album.

Duped cassettes of the recording found their way into independent record stores in Santa Barbara, and soon word spread to Los Angeles, where record companies became interested in the group. After being courted by several big labels, Toad decided to sign with Columbia, which rereleased its first album, *Bread and Circus,* late in 1989. By that point the band had almost finished a second album; *Pale* was released in 1990. Columbia's investment showed no real signs of paying off, however, until 1992, when Toad's persistent touring started increasing its college-based following. It was that year that Toad's 1991 album, *Fear,* finally appeared in the *Billboard* Top 100. *Fear* itself peaked at #49, but the album generated two Top Twenty singles, "All I Want" (#15) and "Walk on the Ocean" (#18). *Dulcinea* (#34), the band's 1994 followup, yielded the Top Forty single "Fall Down" (#33, 1994).

The Tokens
Formed 1958, New York City, New York
Phil Margo (b. Apr. 1, 1942, Brooklyn, N.Y.), bass voc.; Hank Medress (b. Nov. 19, 1938, Brooklyn), first tenor voc.; Jay Siegel (b. Oct. 20, 1939, Brooklyn), lead baritone voc.; Joseph Venneri (b. 1937, Brooklyn), voc.; Mitchel Margo (b. May 25, 1947, Brooklyn), second tenor and baritone voc.
1962—*The Lion Sleeps Tonight* (RCA)   1966—*I Hear Trumpets Blow* (B.T. Puppy)   1967—*Portrait*

(Warner Bros.) 1971—*Both Sides Now* (Buddah) 1993—*Oldies Are Now* (B.T. Puppy).

The Tokens' best-known achievement was their doo-wop–like smash hit "The Lion Sleeps Tonight" (#1, 1961). The song, which is derived from a Zulu folk melody originally titled "Mbube" (which sounded like "wimoweh") was first a hit recording in the Thirties in Africa. It was popularized in the Fifties by Miriam Makeba, who sang it in Zulu, on Victor Records. This was followed by an English-language rendition by the Weavers entitled "Wimoweh." The Tokens' souped-up English version sold over three million copies.

The first version of the Tokens was formed in 1956 by Neil Sedaka and Hank Medress and included Eddie Rabkin and Cynthia Zoliton. The group broke up after recording two Sedaka–Howie Greenfield sides. Medress formed another group, with Jay Siegel, Warren Schwartz, and Fred Kalkstein two years later, but it too dissolved. Medress and Siegel then teamed up with brothers Phil and Mitch Margo. These four formed the group's best-known lineup. Their first single, on Warwick, had been "Tonight I Fell in Love," which sold 700,000 copies in the U.S. and 300,000 in Canada and Europe.

"The Lion Sleeps Tonight" proved a surprise international smash hit, but later records fell on deaf ears. Shortly after the early 1962 release of the "Lion"-like "B'wa Nina," the band members signed a production/A&R deal with Capitol. Unlike many similar vocal groups, the Tokens had played on and had a hand in producing their own records. They produced the Revlons, among others, but their biggest early production efforts were the Chiffons' "One Fine Day" and "He's So Fine." They also started their own record label, B.T. Puppy Records. Other production credits include the Happenings. Hank Medress produced another version of "Lion Sleeps" for Robert John on Atlantic, which also became a Top Ten smash in 1972. Medress also worked as a staff producer at Bell Records in the early Seventies and teamed up Dawn with Tony Orlando. He has since worked with Buster Poindexter and Dan Hill. Jay Siegel and the Margo brothers became Cross Country and recorded for Atlantic in 1973. In 1981 the best-known lineup reunited for a show at Radio City Music Hall. The group then split up again, with the Margo brothers forming one set of Tokens and Siegel another. Mitch Margo has also been successful as a manager and television producer/writer.

Although the Tokens' record sales never reached earlier levels, they were sought-after background vocalists and have performed on records by Connie Francis, Del Shannon, Bob Dylan, and Keith ("98.6"). Members of the Tokens continued to sing together on occasion, doing commercials for Pan Am ("makes the going great"), Ban, Clairol, Wendy's, Sunkist (the "Good Vibra-

tions" spots), and other products. They have continued to perform and record through the years. They appear on Paul Shaffer's 1989 LP, teaming up with Dion DiMucci, Johnny Maestro, and other early-Sixties stars for "When the Radio's On." The use of "The Lion Sleeps Tonight" in the Walt Disney animated feature *The Lion King* (1994) brought the Tokens back into the spotlight.

Tom Tom Club: See Talking Heads

Tone-Lōc
Born Anthony Terrell Smith, March 3, 1966, Los Angeles, California
1989—*Lōc-ed After Dark* (Delicious Vinyl) 1991—*Cool Hand Lōc*.

Rap's gravelly voiced hedonist Tone-Lōc (the name is short for his street "tag," Tony Loco) made rock history when his *Lōc-ed After Dark* became the first album by a black rap artist to go to #1 on the pop chart, thanks to "Wild Thing" (#2, 1989).

Anthony Terrell Smith, the youngest of three children, was raised in a middle-class section of L.A. by his mother (his father died when Lōc was 12). A flirtation with gang life (he was rumored to be a member of the Crips) ended when Lōc was sent to the prestigious Hollywood Professional School. A funk fan too impatient to learn guitar, Lōc was understandably attracted to rap. After junior college he joined a short-lived trio, Triple A. After graduation he sold foreclosed houses, programmed computers, and continued to rap.

His distinctive voice—the result of having his throat scalded by hot tea and brandy, his mother's cold cure—brought him to the attention of Delicious Vinyl in 1988. An initial single, "On Fire" b/w "I Got It Goin' On," was a local radio hit. His breakthrough came with the followup, "Wild Thing," an infectious paean to the joys of casual sex rapped over a guitar riff sampled from Van Halen's "Jamie's Cryin'" and cowritten by label-mate Young MC. (Apparently Young MC became involved after Lōc's rap was rejected by his label as being too obscene.) The song's video, made for about $400, became a staple of MTV and pushed sales to 2.5 million copies, making it one of the top singles of the Eighties. "Funky Cold Medina" (#3), written by Young MC, followed, also from the debut LP.

It would be two years before the release of Tone-Lōc's next album, *Cool Hand Lōc* (#46 R&B, 1991), which proved a disappointment. Lōc, who had publicly expressed an easygoing, almost casual attitude toward his musical career, has since pursued a respectable acting career. He appears in the films *Posse* and *Poetic Justice* and had a recurring role on TV's *Roc*. He lent his voice to the animated feature film *Bebe's Kids*.

Tones on Tail: See Bauhaus

Too $hort
Born Todd Anthony Shaw, April 28, 1966, Los Ange-
les, California
1987—*Born to Mack* (Dangerous Music) 1988—*Life
Is . . . Too $hort* (Jive) 1990—*Short Dog's in the
House* 1992—*Shorty the Pimp* 1993—*Get In
Where You Fit In* 1995—*Cocktails.*

Too $hort put Oakland, California, on the hip-hop map
with his slow, crude raps and proto-gangster image. The
middle-class Todd Shaw re-created himself as a pimp,
styled after characters in blaxploitation films and novels.
Too $hort, named as a youth for his then-short height,
has built up a chart-topping pop career from the very
bottom. He began rapping in the early Eighties, when he
sold homemade tapes on the streets of Oakland. His first
three albums were released by the independent label 75
Girls.

　　After he never got paid for them, he set up his own
label and production company in 1987. Along with Too
$hort, Dangerous Music has produced discs by Pooh
Man, Spice 1, and Ant Banks. Too $hort sold *Born to
Mack* out of his trunk, generating enough attention to
get signed by Jive; the album subsequently went gold.

　　Life Is . . . Too $hort (#37, 1989) was released amid
phony rumors that Too $hort had died; despite little air-
play, the album went platinum, as did its successor,
Short Dog's in the House (#20, 1990). The latter featured
"The Ghetto," a single based on the Seventies Donny
Hathaway hit "The Ghetto, Part One," as well as "Ain't
Nothin' But a Word to Me," a duet with Ice Cube that answered critics who would censor use of the word
"bitch," with a series of bleeps. Too $hort became known
more and more for his graphically violent and frequently
misogynist raps. He developed his mack persona further
on *Shorty the Pimp* (#6, 1992), which debuted at #6 on
the pop albums chart. *Get In Where You Fit In* (#1 R&B,
1993) debuted even higher at #4. The followup, *Cocktails* (#6 pop, #1 R&B, 1995), continued Too $hort's
commercial success.

Toots and the Maytals
Formed 1962, Kingston, Jamaica
Frederick "Toots" Hibbert (b. 1946, Maypen, Jam.),
lead voc.; Nathaniel "Jerry" Matthias (b. ca. 1945,
Jam.), harmony voc.; Ralphus "Raleigh" Gordon
(b. ca. 1945, Jam.), harmony voc.
1971—*Monkey Man* (Trojan) 1972—*From the Roots*
1973—*Funky Kingston* 1974—*In the Dark* 1975—
Funky Kingston (Island) 1976—*Reggae Got Soul*
1978—*The Maytals* (State) 1979—*The Best of
Toots and the Maytals* (Trojan); *Pass the Pipe*

Toots Hibbert

(Island) 1980—*Just Like That* 1981—*Live!*
(– Matthias; – Gordon) 1982—*Knockout* (Mango)
1984—*Reggae Greats: Toots and the Maytals*
1988—*Toots in Memphis.*

For over three decades, Toots Hibbert's exhortatory vocals and evangelistic stage delivery have charged Jamaican popular music with the fervor of American
gospel-rooted soul singers like Otis Redding, Solomon
Burke, and Wilson Pickett. Hibbert spent his first 15 years
in a small town in the Jamaican countryside; he left
home for Kingston in 1962 and formed a vocal trio with
Jerry Matthias and Raleigh Gordon.

　　Coxsone Dodd produced their first Jamaican hits—
"Hallelujah" (1963) and "Six and Seven Books of Moses"
(1963)—when they called themselves the Vikings. They
left Dodd for Prince Buster in 1964 and recorded "Little
Slea" as the V. Maytals before deciding to work as the
Maytals. In the next two years they worked mainly with
Byron Lee and his Ska-Kings band. With hits like "If You
Act This Way" (1964) and "John and James" (1965), they
became a leading group of the ska era.

　　In 1966 they won the Jamaican Song Festival prize
with Hibbert's "Bam Bam." That same year Hibbert was
jailed for possession of marijuana. After his release 12
months later, the Maytals recorded "54-46," commemorating his prison experience, for Leslie Kong's Beverley
label. Among the Maytals' other Beverley sides was "Do
the Reggay" [*sic*], the 1968 song usually credited with
coining the term "reggae."

　　By that time Kong was releasing Maytals singles in
Britain; "Monkey Man" was the first Maytals song to
chart overseas (#47 U.K., 1970) (it was covered in 1979 by
the Specials on their debut album). Following Kong's
death in 1971, the Maytals worked with his former partner Warwick Lynn and established a following.

　　The 1972 release of *The Harder They Come* introduced the Maytals to the U.S.; the film's soundtrack featured "Sweet and Dandy" and "Pressure Drop." In 1975, now known as Toots and the Maytals, they signed their first major contract with Island Records. Island released *Funky Kingston*—a collection culled from Trojan's *Funky Kingston* and *In the Dark*—which contained the Maytals' unique interpretation of John Denver's "Country Roads," in which "West Virginia" became "West Jamaica." Also in 1975 Toots and the Maytals made their first tour of the U.S., opening shows for the Who. The tour was badly planned, and the Maytals were booed off the stage at many dates. While they remained critical favorites, the Maytals could never match Bob Marley's or Peter Tosh's popularity.

Toots went solo in 1982, although he continued to tour as Toots and the Maytals. In 1988 at Memphis' Ardent recording studio he was accompanied by Sly and Robbie and producer Jim Dickinson (Alex Chilton, Replacements) and recorded a set of Stax/Volt covers, *Toots in Memphis*.

The Tornadoes

Formed 1962, London, England
George Bellamy (b. Oct. 8, 1941, Sunderland, Eng.), gtr.; Heinz Burt (b. July 24, 1942, Hargin, Ger.), gtr.; Alan Caddy (b. Feb. 2, 1940, London), gtr., violin; Clem Cattini (b. Aug. 28, 1939, London), drums; Roger Lavern (b. Roger Jackson, Nov. 11, 1938, Kidderminster, Eng.), kybds.
1963—*Telstar* (London).

The Tornadoes were assembled by British producer, songwriter, and entrepreneur Joe Meek in 1962 to back up vocalists who would sing his songs. After working with small-time singers John Leyton and Don Charles, the Tornadoes were hooked up with English teen idol Billy Fury. Later in the year, Meek, inspired by developments in the space program, composed an instrumental for the Tornadoes to record. "Telstar" (the name of the first U.S. communications satellite) became a #1 hit single and eventually sold over five million copies around the world. The group had just one other minor success, 1963's "Ride the Wind." They soon broke up. On February 3, 1967, Meek committed suicide. Of the original Tornadoes, George Bellamy and Heinz Burt pursued solo careers; Bellamy later started his own label. Only Clem Cattini, a studio drummer, remains active as a performer.

Peter Tosh

Born Winston Hubert MacIntosh, October 9, 1944, Westmoreland, Jamaica; died September 11, 1987, Barbican, St. Andrew, Jamaica
**1976—*Legalize It* (Columbia)   1977—*Equal Rights*
1978—*Bush Doctor* (Rolling Stones)   1979—*Mystic***
**Man   1981—*Wanted Dread and Alive*   1983—
Mama Africa (EMI)   1984—*Captured Live*   1987—
No Nuclear War   1988—*The Toughest* (Capitol).**

Peter Tosh first became known (in Jamaica in the early Sixties and in Europe and America in the early Seventies) as the baritone vocalist of the Wailers. Through his years with the Wailers, however, he also maintained a solo career. From 1964 to 1967 he released numerous singles on Coxsone Dodd's Studio One and Coxsone labels, variously calling himself Peter Mackingtosh, Peter MacIntosh, Peter Tosh, or—most often—Peter Touch. Among his solo recordings (which often featured Wailers Bob Marley and Bunny Livingston as backup singers) were early versions of "I'm the Toughest" and "400 Years," songs he was later to popularize beyond Jamaica.

Some 1969 sessions with Leslie Kong resulted in British releases on the Bullet and Unity labels, and in 1971 and 1972, recordings cut with Joe Gibbs were released in the U.K. on the Bullet, Punch, and Pressure Beat labels. In 1971 Tosh founded his own Jamaican label, Intel-Diplo H.I.M., on which he began issuing self-produced singles.

After Tosh left the Wailers in 1973 (complaining that because Marley attracted an undue share of attention overseas, he was relegated to the background), Intel-Diplo H.I.M. became his sole Jamaican outlet, and he leased his recordings to foreign companies for world distribution. Columbia got U.S. rights to *Legalize It*, on which Tosh proselytized for the many uses of marijuana, and *Equal Rights*, which contained his perennially popular "Stepping Razor."

In 1978 Mick Jagger and Keith Richards signed Tosh to Rolling Stones Records and sat in on *Bush Doctor*, which featured the Temptations' "(You Got to Walk and) Don't Look Back" performed as a duet by Tosh and Jagger (#81). Tosh and his Word, Sound and Power band toured America with the Stones that year, and Jagger joined Tosh on his *Saturday Night Live* appearance. He returned to the U.S. regularly. *Mama Africa* included a reggae remake of Chuck Berry's "Johnny B. Goode" (#84, 1983).

Tosh had a history of confrontation with the law. He was jailed for possession of marijuana in the mid-Sixties. In 1978, performing for a Kingston crowd of 30,000 that included the Jamaican prime minister, he smoked a "spliff" onstage and berated the prime minister for 30 minutes for not legalizing "ganja." Later that year he was arrested in his studio, taken to a police station, and beaten almost to death before he was released.

Tosh remained an outspoken figure on the reggae scene. In mid-1987 he released the antiwar album *No Nuclear War*. On September 11 three men armed with 9-mm pistols came to his home and murdered Tosh, local DJ Jeff Dixon, and Tosh's cook, "Doc" Brown. Four others, including Tosh's girlfriend, were injured. The motive was officially robbery, but speculation arose that political or personal enmities were involved. Although Dennis Lobban, a street vendor, was arrested and convicted of the murders in 1988, accusations that Tosh was executed refused to die. A 1993 documentary, *Stepping Razor—Red X* (the "red X" a reference to the mark Tosh claimed was placed after his name on government documents), dramatized these charges.

Toto
Formed 1978, Los Angeles, California
David Paich, kybds., voc.; Steve Lukather, gtr., voc.; Bobby Kimball (b. Robert Toteaux), voc.; Steve Porcaro, kybds.; David Hungate, bass; Jeff Porcaro (b. Apr. 1, 1954, Calif.; d. Aug. 5, 1992, Holden Hills, Calif.), drums.
1978—*Toto* (Columbia)   1979—*Hydra* (+ Joe Porcaro, perc.)   1981—*Turn Back*   1982—*Toto IV* 1983—(– Hungate; + Mike Porcaro, bass)   1984— (– Kimball; + Dennis "Fergie" Frederiksen, voc.) *Isolation*; *Dune* soundtrack (Polydor)   1986— (– Frederiksen; + Joseph Williams, voc.) *Fahrenheit* (Columbia); *The Seventh One*   1990—(– Williams; + Jean-Michel Byron [b. S.A.], voc.) *Past to Present 1977–1990*   1992—(– J. Porcaro; + Simon Phillips, drums)   1993—*Kingdom of Desire* (Relativity).

A studio band assembled by experienced sessionmen, Toto purvey a smooth, glossy power-pop sound that netted them several hit singles and top-selling LPs. Their debut album and the self-produced *Toto IV* were their biggest sellers.

Most of the band members had met around 1972 at Grant High School in Southern California, and they kept meeting on sessions for albums by Steely Dan, Cheap Trick, Pink Floyd, Earth, Wind and Fire, and others. In 1976 Jeff Porcaro, David Hungate, and David Paich performed on Boz Scaggs' *Silk Degrees* LP, for which Paich cowrote five songs with Scaggs, including "Lowdown" and "Lido Shuffle."

Toto's debut album sold over two million copies by 1979, during which year they also had a two-million-selling #5 single, "Hold the Line." Both *Hydra* (#37, 1979) and *Turn Back* (#41, 1981) sold moderately, but the big breakthrough came with *Toto IV*, which won the Album of the Year Grammy, sold over three million copies, and spun off the group's biggest hits: "Rosanna" (#2, 1982) (written for actress Rosanna Arquette) and "Africa" (#1, 1982), as well as "I Won't Hold You Back" (#10, 1983). The album earned five additional Grammys, including Record of the Year for "Rosanna."

Subsequent albums did not fare nearly as well; only *Isolation* and *Fahrenheit* cracked the Top Fifty. Critics derided the group's smooth professionalism, and

throughout their years with Toto, group members continued to contribute to others artists' work as studio hands, producers, and writers. They cowrote the Tubes' 1982 Top Forty hit "Talk to You Later"; Steve Porcaro cowrote Michael Jackson's "Human Nature"; and among Jeff Porcaro's last studio gigs was drumming on Bruce Springsteen's *Human Touch*. Jeff Porcaro died in 1992 of a heart attack; initial reports stated that it was prompted by an allergic reaction to garden pesticides, but the coroner determined that cocaine use was a contributing factor. Although not released until the year after Porcaro's death, *Kingdom of Desire* was the last Toto album on which he performed.

Tourists: See Eurythmics

Allen Toussaint
Born January 14, 1938, New Orleans, Louisiana
1958—*The Wild Sounds of New Orleans by Tousan* (RCA)   1971—*Toussaint* (Tiffany)   1972—*Love, Life and Faith* (Reprise)   1975—*Southern Nights* 1978—*Motion* (Warner Bros.)   1991—*The Allen Toussaint Collection* (Reprise).

Singer, pianist, songwriter, arranger, and producer Allen Toussaint was as important to the music of New Orleans in the Sixties as Dave Bartholomew had been in the Fifties. In the Seventies, musicians from the rest of the United States and abroad came to his city to record with him.

He began playing piano, emulating Professor Longhair, while in grade school. He made his professional debut with the Flamingos when he was in his early teens. In the mid-Fifties he began working as a studio keyboardist for Dave Bartholomew (he played piano on some Fats Domino sessions) and with Shirley and Lee. In 1958 he recorded his first solo album, calling himself Tousan. One of his first compositions, "Java," was a hit for Al Hirt in 1964.

When Minit Records was founded in 1960, Toussaint became the label's house songwriter, arranger, and producer for songs like Jessie Hill's "Ooh Poo Pah Doo," Ernie K-Doe's "Mother-in-Law," Chris Kenner's "I Like It Like That," Lee Dorsey's "Ya Ya," Barbara George's "I Know," and records for Aaron Neville, Irma Thomas, Clarence "Frogman" Henry, and Benny Spellman. Toussaint established himself as a hitmaker with the definitive New Orleans sound of the Sixties—jaunty dance music characterized by a dialogue of rolling piano licks and horn riffs. His regular studio band included tenor saxophonist Nat Perrilliat, baritone saxophonist Clarence Ford, guitarist Roy Montrell, bassist Peter "Chuck" Badie, and drummers John Boudreaux and James Black.

After producing records for the Instant, Fury, and AFO labels, in 1963 Toussaint went into the army. Even as a serviceman he remained a musician, forming the Stokes to record "Whipped Cream" for Instant; the song became a hit for Herb Alpert and the Tijuana Brass. Discharged from the army in 1965, Toussaint returned to Minit, but the label was sold to Liberty later that year. He and another New Orleans producer, Marshall Sehorn, then founded Sansu Enterprises, which included Marsaint Music Publishers and the Sansu, Amy, and Deesu labels.

In the second half of the Sixties, Toussaint wrote and produced hits for Lee Dorsey, Maurice Williams, Ernie K-Doe, Wilbert Harrison, and Sansu's studio band, the Meters. After Sansu opened Sea-Saint Studios in 1972, artists such as Paul Simon, Paul McCartney and Wings, Sandy Denny, and the Mighty Diamonds recorded there; Toussaint produced sessions by Dr. John, Labelle (including their 1975 bestseller, "Lady Marmalade"), Badger, John Mayall, and Joe Cocker. He was also responsible for the horn arrangements on the Band's 1972 live album, *Rock of Ages,* and the period music for the 1978 soundtrack to Louis Malle's *Pretty Baby.*

Toussaint records his own albums and appears live only occasionally, but his songs have been covered by the Rolling Stones ("Fortune Teller"), Herman's Hermits and Warren Zevon ("A Certain Girl"), Betty Wright ("Shoorah, Shoorah"), Three Dog Night ("Brickyard Blues"), Frankie Miller ("High Life"), Glen Campbell ("Southern Nights"), the Yardbirds, the Pointer Sisters ("Yes We Can Can"), Maria Muldaur, Little Feat, Boz Scaggs, Bonnie Raitt, Robert Palmer, and Ringo Starr. He has also guested on other artists' albums, among them Elvis Costello's *Spike.* He wrote the music for the mid-Eighties musical *Stagger Lee.* In 1993 and 1994 Toussaint appeared with a number of other singer/songwriters in a touring show called In Their Own Words.

Tower of Power

Formed 1968, Oakland, California
Lineup, ca. 1993: Emilio Castillo (b. Sep. 24, Detroit, Mich.), sax; Steve Kupka (b. Mar. 25), sax, English horn; Francis "Rocco" Prestia (b. Mar. 7), bass; Greg Adams, trumpet, voc., flugelhorn; Lee Thornburg, trumpet, flugelhorn; Nick Milo (b. Oct. 14), kybds.; Russ McKinnon (b. June 24), drums; Carmen Grillo (b. Aug. 8), gtr.; Tom Bowes (b. Oct. 29), voc.; David Mann (b. Aug. 8), tenor sax. Earlier members include: Lenny Williams (b. Pine Bluff, Ark.), voc.; Lenny Pickett, sax, flute, piccolo; Mic Gillette, trumpet, trombone, flugelhorn; Bruce Conte, gtr., voc.; Chester Thompson, kybds., voc.; David Garibaldi, drums; Brent Byars, congas.
1971—East Bay Grease (San Francisco)   1972—
Bump City (Warner Bros.)   1973—Tower of Power 1974—Back to Oakland   1975—Urban Renewal (– Williams; + Hubert Tubbs, voc.); In the Slot 1976—Live and in Living Color; Ain't Nothin' Stoppin' Us Now (Columbia)   1978—We Came to Play 1979—Back on the Streets   1981—Direct CD (Sheffield Labs)   1987—Power (Cypress)   1991— (+ Tom Bowes, voc.) Monster on a Leash (Epic) 1993—TOP.

This integrated Oakland-based R&B band reached its commercial peak between 1972 and 1975, when Lenny Williams sang lead on its hits "So Very Hard to Go" (1973) and "Don't Change Horses (in the Middle of a Stream)" (#26 pop, #22 R&B, 1974).

Emerging from the early Seventies Bay Area club scene, the band made its recording debut with *East Bay Grease* on Bill Graham's San Francisco Records in 1971. The next year, signed to Warner Bros., they scored with "You're Still a Young Man" (#29 pop, #24 R&B, 1974), with Rich Stevens as lead vocalist. Williams joined Tower of Power for their third album and continued fronting the band on *Back to Oakland* and *Urban Renewal.* During this period, the band had hits with "So Very Hard to Go" (#17 pop, #11 R&B) and "What Is Hip?" (#91 pop, #31 R&B). Williams left to sign with ABC as a solo; his R&B hits include "Choosing You" (#62) and "Shoo Doo Fu Fu Ooh!" (#31), both 1977. Hubert Tubbs succeeded him and sang lead on "You Ought to Be Having Fun" (#68 pop, #62 R&B) in 1976, when Tower was signed to Columbia.

Throughout the Seventies, Tower of Power's ultra-precise horn section worked as studio musicians on countless other acts' recordings. Among them were Elton John, Elvin Bishop, Santana, and Jose Feliciano. In 1983 Lenny Pickett was heard in avant-garde music concerts in New York (he now plays with the *Saturday Night Live* band) and keyboardist Chester Thompson joined Santana. The group—whose core membership of founder Emilio Castillo, Steve Kupka, and Rocco Prestia has remained intact through the years—then slid into a difficult period, as members dealt with substance-abuse problems and other pressures. They recorded the direct-to-CD Sheffield Labs album *Direct* and another, *Power,* an album that was privately financed and originally released only in Denmark. The group did not disband officially but didn't really begin to come back until after the horn section toured with Huey Lewis and the News during the mid-Eighties. (The Tower of Power horns appear on Lewis' *Picture This* and *Fore!*) Soon the rest of the group was traveling, too, joining the horns for Tower of Power midnight shows everywhere Lewis and the News played after their shows.

Although Tower of Power's more recent releases have not been hits, their live shows still draw rave reviews. The horn section often sits in with Paul Shaffer's band on *The Late Show with David Letterman,* and its latest studio credits include Phish's *Hoist* (1994) and Victoria Williams' *Loose* (1994).

Pete Townshend: See the Who

The Toys
Formed early Sixties, Jamaica, New York
June Montiero (b. July 1, 1946, Queens, N.Y.), voc.;
Barbara Harris (b. Aug. 18, 1945, Elizabeth, N.J.),
voc.; Barbara Parritt (b. Oct. 1, 1944, Wilmington,
N.C.), voc.
1966—*The Toys Sing "A Lover's Concerto" and "Attack!"* (DynoVoice).

The Toys were an R&B girl group whose big hit was "A Lover's Concerto," a refashioning of a Bach piece (#2, 1965). The three members met as teenagers at Woodrow Wilson High School in Queens, New York, and continued to sing after their graduation. In 1964 they were signed by the publishing firm Genius Inc., which teamed them with the songwriting duo Sandy Linzer and Denny Rendell. Their big single went #4 R&B, crossed over to pop, and also became a #5 hit in England. During 1965 the song sold over a million copies. The Toys appeared on television rock shows like *Shindig!* and toured with Gene Pitney. They also appeared in the film *The Girl in Daddy's Bikini.* They had a less successful hit in 1966 with "Attack" (#18). By the next year they were gone from the charts but continued to do session work separately.

Traffic
Formed 1967, England
Steve Winwood (b. May 12, 1948, Birmingham,
Eng.), voc., kybds., gtr.; Chris Wood (b. June 24,
1944, Birmingham; d. July 12, 1983, London, Eng.),
sax, flute; Dave Mason (b. May 10, 1946, Worcester,
Eng.), gtr., voc.; Jim Capaldi (b. Aug. 24, 1944, Eve-
sham, Eng.), drums, voc.
1967—*Mr. Fantasy* (United Artists) (– Mason;
+ Mason) 1968—*Traffic* (– Mason) 1969—*Last
Exit 1970—*John Barleycorn Must Die* (+ Rick**
Grech [b. Nov. 1, 1946; d. Mar. 17, 1990, Eng.], bass)
1971—(+ Jim Gordon, drums; + Reebop Kwaku
Baah [b. Konongo, Ghana; d. ca. mid-1980s], perc.;
+ Mason) *Welcome to the Canteen* (– Mason); *The
Low Spark of High-Heeled Boys (Island) (– Grech;**
– Gordon; + Roger Hawkins, drums; + David Hood,
bass) 1973—*Shoot Out at the Fantasy Factory*;
***Traffic on the Road* (– Hawkins; – Hood; + Rosco**
Gee, bass) 1974—*When the Eagle Flies* (group dis-
bands) 1975—*Heavy Traffic* (United Artists); *More

Heavy Traffic 1991—*Smiling Phases* (Island)
1994—(Group re-forms: Winwood; Capaldi) *Far from
Home (Virgin).**

The original Traffic had two phases. At first it was a winsomely psychedelic pop band that blended blues, folk, rock, and R&B and was fronted by Steve Winwood and Dave Mason. This group recorded such FM radio favorites as "Paper Sun" and "You Can All Join In." After Mason left, the band became Steve Winwood's vehicle for longer, moodier excursions that leaned closer to jazz and soul. This group was responsible for "Glad," "Freedom Rider," "Empty Pages," and "Rock & Roll Stew." Traffic was popular in both incarnations.

When the band formed in 1967, Winwood was its best-known member because of his lead vocals with the Spencer Davis Group [see entry]. Winwood left that band to found Traffic, and with friends Chris Wood, Jim Capaldi, and Dave Mason wrote and rehearsed in a cottage in the English countryside. Traffic's debut LP, *Mr. Fantasy,* contained two British hits, "Paper Sun" (#5 U.K., 1967) and "Hole in My Shoe" (#2 U.K., 1967). But conflicts between Mason's pop style and Winwood's jazz ambitions flared up and in late 1967 Mason split, first joining Delaney and Bonnie Bramlett before pursuing a solo career [see entry]. A 1968 film called *Here We Go Round the Mulberry Bush* contained some of Traffic's music, and the theme song was a minor hit.

Despite differences with Winwood, Mason helped cut *Traffic,* contributing the oft-covered "Feelin' Alright." But by 1968 he had left again. It looked like Traffic was finished in 1969, when Winwood joined Blind Faith with Eric Clapton, Ginger Baker, and Rick Grech. However, Blind Faith proved short-lived, and after a stint in Ginger Baker's Air Force in 1970 Winwood began recording his first solo album, the working title of which was *Mad Shadows.* Capaldi and Wood sat in on some sessions, and the LP became Traffic's most commercially successful album, *John Barleycorn Must Die* (#5, 1970), a gold album and a staple of "progressive" FM radio. The group then added Grech. The next year, before recording *Welcome to the Canteen,* Reebop Kwaku Baah was added on percussion. In addition, that live album featured Jim Gordon augmenting Capaldi on drums and a guest appearance by Mason. Despite the success of the gold album *The Low Spark of High-Heeled Boys* (#7, 1971), Gordon and Grech departed.

Winwood was then stricken with peritonitis, and the band was temporarily sidelined. Capaldi cut a solo album (*Oh! How We Danced*) in Muscle Shoals, Alabama, and in the process he recruited session players bassist David Hood and drummer Roger Hawkins into the band. They appeared on *Shoot Out at the Fantasy Factory* (#6, 1973) and with another Muscle Shoals musician, keyboardist Barry Beckett, on the live *Traffic on the*

Road (#29, 1973). By the sessions for *When the Eagle Flies* (#9, 1974), only the original trio of Winwood, Wood, and Capaldi plus bassist Rosco Gee were left. After that album's release, Winwood and Capaldi started their solo careers in earnest. Wood died in 1983 in his London apartment after a long illness; Grech died seven years later of kidney and liver failure precipitated by a hemorrhage. The cause of Reebop Kwaku Baah's death and its exact date could not be confirmed.

Winwood enjoyed a more successful solo career than any of his former band mates [see entry]. In 1994 he and Capaldi joined forces for what was termed a Traffic reunion (Rosco Gee performed in the touring band), and under the group name released the critically well received *Far from Home* (#33, 1994).

The Trammps

Formed mid-Sixties, Philadelphia, Pennsylvania
Lineup circa early Eighties: Earl Young, drums, bass
voc.; Jimmy Ellis, lead tenor voc.; Robert Upchurch,
baritone voc.; Stanley Wade, bass, tenor voc.;
Harold Wade, gtr., tenor voc.
1975—*Trammps* (Golden Fleece); *The Legendary*
Zing Album* (Buddah)   1976—*Where the Happy
***People Go* (Atlantic); *Disco Inferno*   1977—**
The Trammps III*   1978—*The Best of the Trammps
1979—*The Whole World's Dancing*   1980—
Slipping Out.

While the Trammps had their first recording success in 1965 with "Storm Warning," when they were known as the Volcanoes, it was not until a 1975 contract with Atlantic Records, several personnel changes, and the rise of disco that they became a celebrated recording and touring act. Their peak popularity came through the inclusion of their blazing rendition of "Disco Inferno" on the *Saturday Night Fever* soundtrack in 1977.

Basing their vocal style on that of the Coasters (a lead-and-bass vocal combination), the Trammps' earliest success under that name came on the Buddah label with a rendition of "Zing Went the Strings of My Heart" (#17 R&B), featuring Earl Young's bass vocal. Young, a top Philadelphia session musician and co-owner of the Philadelphia publishing and production company Golden Fleece (with producers Norman Harris and Ronnie Baker), brought the Trammps to that label after their Buddah contract expired. Their association with Golden Fleece yielded an early disco hit, "Love Epidemic" (#75 R&B), in 1973. In 1975 they signed on with Atlantic Records and had the first of a string of hits with the up-tempo love plea "Hooked for Life" (#70 R&B), followed by "Hold Back the Night" (#35 pop, #10 R&B, 1975), "That's Where the Happy People Go" (#27 pop, #12 R&B, 1976), and "Disco Inferno" (#11 pop, #9 R&B, 1977). That proved to be their last major hit, and as the disco phase drew to

a close, the Trammps faded from sight. In the 1990s, a re-formed Trammps began touring again.

The Traveling Wilburys

Formed 1988, Los Angeles, California
Nelson (later Spike) Wilbury (b. George Harrison,
Feb. 25, 1943, Liverpool, Eng.), gtr., voc.; Lucky
(later Boo) Wilbury (a.k.a. Bob Dylan [b. Robert
Allen Zimmerman], May 24, 1941, Duluth, Minn.),
gtr., voc.; Otis (later Clayton) Wilbury (b. Jeff Lynne,
Dec. 30, 1947, Birmingham, Eng.), gtr., voc., bass;
Charlie T. (later Muddy) Wilbury Jr. (b. Tom Petty,
Oct. 20, 1952, Gainesville, Fla.), gtr., voc.; Lefty
Wilbury (b. Roy Orbison, Apr. 23, 1936, Vernon, Tex.;
d. Dec. 6, 1988, Hendersonville, Tenn.), gtr., voc.;
Jim Keltner, drums.
1988—*Traveling Wilburys, Volume One*
(Wilbury/Warner Bros.) (– Orbison)   1990—*Vol. 3*.

With a lineup that included major figures from four decades of rock history, including three indisputable gods (Bob Dylan, George Harrison, and Roy Orbison), the Traveling Wilburys were by definition the ultimate supergroup. But their casual good humor and easy rocking style—not to mention their "posing" as a group of brothers—made them the antithesis of a supergroup.

The Traveling Wilburys' roots go back only as far as 1988 or so, when Harrison was setting to work on his next solo album with producer/Beatles fan Jeff Lynne. By chance they happened to find rehearsal space in Dylan's garage, and a series of casual jams with the garage owner, Tom Petty, and Orbison resulted in the new group. Their debut album was a double-platinum smash, going to #3 in late 1988 less on the strength of the minor hit single, "Handle with Care" (#45, 1988), than because of public interest in the principals. Orbison died suddenly of a heart attack less than one month after *Traveling Wilburys, Volume One* hit the chart. He was not replaced in the lineup. The group's second album, the playfully titled *Vol. 3* (#11, 1990), was another platinum effort, despite having no hit singles.

[See also individual members' solo entries; the Beatles; Electric Light Orchestra.]

Randy Travis

Born Randy Bruce Traywick, May 4, 1959,
Marshville, North Carolina
1982—*Randy Ray Live at the Nashville Palace*
(Paula)   1986—*Storms of Life* (Warner Bros.)
1987—*Always and Forever*   1988—*Old 8×10*
1989—*An Old Time Christmas*; *No Holdin' Back*
1990—*Heroes & Friends*   1991—*High Lonesome*
1992—*Greatest Hits, vol. 1*; *Greatest Hits, vol. 2*
1993—*Wind in the Wire*   1994—*This Is Me*.

With his warm baritone and neotraditional style, Randy Travis dominated country music in the late Eighties. In the wake of George Strait, Reba McEntire, and Ricky Skaggs, he found a ready audience for music that eschewed the crossover attempts of Seventies country in favor of an approach that recalled Travis' own influences, Hank Williams, Lefty Frizzell, and Ernest Tubb.

Encouraged by his father, a construction company owner, farmer, and sometime musician who hoped his sons would become the next Everly Brothers, Randy Traywick began performing publicly with his brother Ricky at around age ten. Randy's turbulent adolescence—drinking, drugs, and 100-mph car chases with the police—however, soon sidetracked him.

Lib Hatcher, owner of a Charlotte, North Carolina, country music club, intervened with a judge in one of Randy's court battles; given custody of the 17-year-old, she began managing him (the two married in 1991). Moving to Nashville in the early Eighties, they worked in a nightclub, Hatcher as manager, Traywick as dishwasher, cook, and occasional singer. On the tiny independent Paula Records, as Randy Ray, he released two singles, then recorded the 1982 low-budget album *Randy Ray Live at the Nashville Palace*, which he sold at gigs.

In 1985 the singer finally inked a deal with Warner Bros., changing his name to Randy Travis, after contributing the song "Prairie Rose" to the soundtrack for *Rustler's Rhapsody*, a movie starring John Wayne's son Patrick. He had also released a single, "On the Other Hand," that had reached #67 on the country chart (in rerelease it hit #1 in 1986).

With *Storms of Life* Travis became the first country performer to sell a million copies of his major-label debut within a year of its release. Joining the Grand Ole Opry and winning a Country Music Association "Horizon" Award, Travis embarked upon a remarkable run that saw him gain six #1 country hits in a row (1987's "Forever and Ever, Amen," "I Won't Need You Anymore [Always and Forever]," and "Too Gone Too Long"; 1988's "I Told You So," "Honky Tonk Moon," and "Deeper Than the Holler").

Travis, named Male Vocalist of the Year by the Country Music Association in 1988, was at the height of his career; a year later he sustained injuries in a serious car crash but came back with two #1s, "Is It Still Over?" and "It's Just a Matter of Time." *Heroes & Friends* included duets with George Jones, Tammy Wynette, B. B. King, and Roy Rogers, among others. *High Lonesome* sold dependably, but at the start of the Nineties Travis' hegemony was challenged by up-and-coming "hat acts" such as Garth Brooks and Clint Black, neotraditionalists whose style Travis had helped to popularize.

The Tremeloes

Formed 1959, Dagenham, England
Brian Poole (b. Nov. 3, 1941, Barking, Eng.), voc.; Alan Blakely (b. Apr. 1, 1942), rhythm gtr.; Alan Howard, bass; Dave Munden (b. Dec. 2, 1943), drums; Rick Westwood (b. May 7, 1943), lead gtr. 1966—(– Poole; – Howard; + Len "Chip" Hawkes [b. Nov. 2, 1946], bass) 1967—*Here Comes My Baby* (Columbia); *Even the Bad Times Are Good*; *Suddenly You Love Me* 1968—*58/68 World Explosion* 1974—*Shiner* (DJM) 1992—*The Best of the Tremeloes* (Rhino).

The Tremeloes began their career as the backup band for British vocalist Brian Poole, and with him had a number of U.K. hit records in 1963 and 1964, including the #1 single "Do You Love Me." When Poole left them in 1966, they brought in Len Hawkes and proceeded to eclipse their former front man with a trio of British Top Five hit records: "Silence Is Golden," "Even the Bad Times Are Good," and "Here Comes My Baby," all in 1967. All except the second hit the U.S. Top Twenty as well. Even when the hits stopped, the Tremeloes remained a viable nightclub attraction, and they continue to this day, though a car accident forced Hawkes to quit in 1974, and Blakely left on his own the following year. Poole and the Tremeloes are familiar sights on the nostalgia circuit.

Ralph Tresvant: See New Edition

T. Rex/Tyrannosaurus Rex/Marc Bolan

Formed 1967, England
Marc Bolan (b. Mark Feld, Sep. 30, 1948, London, Eng.; d. Sep. 16, 1977, London), voc., gtr.; Steve Peregrine Took (b. July 28, 1949; d. Oct. 27, 1980), drums, bass, piano, perc. 1968—*My People Were Fair and Had Sky in Their Hair But Now They're Content to Wear Stars on Their Brows* (Regal/Zonophone, U.K.); *Prophets,*

T. Rex: Mickey Finn and Marc Bolan

Seers and Sages, The Angels of the Ages   1969—
(– Took; + Mickey Finn [b. June 3, 1947], gtr., perc.)
Unicorn (Blue Thumb)   1970—*Beard of Stars*
(Regal/Zonophone, U.K.); *T. Rex* (Reprise)   1971—
Electric Warrior   1972—*The Slider; Tyrannosaurus
Rex (A Beginning)* (compiles first two U.K. LPs)
(A&M)   1973—*Tanx* (EMI, U.K.)   1974—*Zinc Alloy
and the Hidden Riders of Tomorrow*   1975—*Zip
Gun Boogie*   1976—*Futuristic Dragon*   1977—
Dandy in the Underworld.

With his Botticelli face and curls and whimsically glamorous image, Marc Bolan fronted T. Rex, a British group that generated a fan hysteria reminiscent of Beatlemania and produced 11 successive U.K. Top Ten hits between 1970 and 1974. Among these were "Bang a Gong (Get It On)" (#1), "Jeepster" (#2), and "Telegram Sam" (#1). But while T. Rex could not duplicate its British success in America (where its sole major hit was the Top Ten smash "Bang a Gong"), the group's heavy-guitar sound has had an enduring influence and can be heard in songs such as Love and Rockets' "I'm Alive" and in groups like the Soup Dragons.

T. Rex had its beginnings when the group—known as Tyrannosaurus Rex until the 1970 success of "Ride a White Swan"—was formed by Bolan in 1967 with Steve Peregrine Took. A well-known scene-making Mod in the early Sixties, Bolan released two singles in the mid-Sixties on Decca—"Hippy Gumbo" and "The Wizard"—which failed to establish him as a solo artist. But with the group John's Children, Bolan enjoyed two minor U.K. hits in 1967—"Desdemona" and "Go Go Girl." One year later, Tyrannosaurus Rex recorded its debut album (produced by Tony Visconti), which blended acoustic textures with such instruments as the Chinese gong and talking drums and accented Bolan's lyrics—a blend of myth, fantasy, and magic (others might say utter nonsense). As a British flower-power band, Tyrannosaurus Rex earned a sizable underground following and toured the U.S. in 1969.

The band began to achieve widespread success by embracing a full-blown rock attack on albums like *Electric Warrior* (#32, 1971) (which, like many of the group's hits, included backing vocals by Flo and Eddie). The group's highest-charting U.S. release was *The Slider* (#17, 1972). During the height of T. Rex mania in 1973, Ringo Starr directed a documentary on the group's success, *Born to Boogie.* Bolan and the group were at the forefront of the glitter movement, which was far more influential and lasting in their homeland than in the U.S. T. Rex's popularity declined shortly thereafter, and Bolan declared the group extinct in 1975, leaving his wife and exiling himself to America. He returned to England in 1976 and began living with American singer Gloria Jones. Respected by followers of the then-burgeoning

new-wave scene, Bolan brought the Damned on tour with his newly re-formed T. Rex in 1977 as a support act.

But his solo career never took off in the U.S., partly because of his haphazard personal life. "I was living in a twilight world of drugs, booze and kinky sex," he told ROLLING STONE. Bolan died in a crash on September 16, 1977, in a car driven by Jones. In 1980 Steve Peregrine Took died from choking.

A Tribe Called Quest
Formed 1988, Queens, New York
**Ali (b. Ali Shaheed Muhammad, Aug. 11, 1970,
Brooklyn, N.Y.), DJ; Phife (b. Malik Taylor, Apr. 10,
1970, Brooklyn), voc.; Q-Tip (b. Jonathan Davis, Nov.
20, 1970, New York City, N.Y.), voc.; Jarobi, voc.**
**1990—*People's Instinctive Travels and the Paths of
Rhythm* (Jive) (– Jarobi)   1991—*The Low End Theory*   1993—*Midnight Marauders.***

Following the lead of De La Soul, their friends and comrades in the "Native Tongues" rap collective, A Tribe Called Quest blazed alternative rap trails with a laid-back, witty, progressive style that paved the way for the "jazz rap" of Digable Planets and Us3.

Q-Tip, Phife, Ali, and Jarobi met at New York City's Murray Bergtraum High School for Business Careers. Q-Tip's association with De La Soul [see entry] and the Jungle Brothers and a four-song demo led to a 1989 deal with Jive Records. The singles "Description of a Fool" (1989) and "I Left My Wallet in El Segundo" (1990) were followed by their debut album, *People's Instinctive Travels* (#91, 1990), the first rap work to fuse jazz samples

A Tribe Called Quest

with hip-hop structures. A followup, *The Low End Theory* (#45, 1991), had a harder edge and extended the group's jazz leanings, featuring jazz great Ron Carter on upright bass. *Low End*'s "Scenario" was a minor hit (#57, 1991).

In between their albums, Tribe appeared on MTV's *Unplugged*; Q-Tip guest-rapped on Deee-Lite's "Groove Is in the Heart" and on Lenny Kravitz and Sean Lennon's "Give Peace a Chance"; all three Tribe members contributed to the Jungle Brothers' *Straight Out the Jungle* and to De La Soul's "Buddy." In 1993, while Tribe was recording its third album, Ali contributed extensive production work to jazz saxophonist Greg Osby's *3-D Lifestyles*. Released at the end of that year, *Midnight Marauders* (#8 pop, #1 R&B, 1993) yielded "Award Tour" (#47 pop, #27 R&B, 1993), with backing vocals by De La Soul's Trugoy the Dove.

Trinity: See Brian Auger

Travis Tritt
Born James Travis Tritt, February 9, 1963, Marietta, Georgia
1990—*Country Club* (Warner Bros.)   1991—*It's All About to Change*   1992—*T-r-o-u-b-l-e*; *A Travis Tritt Christmas (Loving Time of Year)*   1994—*Ten Feet Tall and Bulletproof*.

Travis Tritt's latterday outlaw sound has brought him nine #1 C&W singles and four Top Ten C&W multiplatinum albums that also crossed over onto the pop charts. As deeply influenced by Lynyrd Skynyrd and the Allman Brothers as by George Jones and Merle Haggard, this bewhiskered, blue-collar "son of the new South" has scrupulously avoided any identification with Nashville's neotraditional "hat acts."

The son of a hardscrabble farmer, Tritt taught himself to play guitar at age eight and wrote his first song at 14. He married at 18 and his wife discouraged his musical career. Tritt worked for a heating and air-conditioning equipment distributor. Neither job nor marriage lasted long. By 1985 Tritt was divorced and performing in Atlanta.

Playing small clubs around Georgia did little to advance his career. In 1986 he approached a hometown friend working as an Atlanta-based promotion man for Warner Bros. to help produce a demo. Warners signed him and released *Country Club* (#70 pop, #3 C&W, 1990), with its four C&W Top 40 singles: "Help Me Hold On" (#1, 1990), "I'm Gonna Be Somebody" (#2, 1990), "Put Some Drive in Your Country" (#28, 1990), and "Drift Off to Dream" (#3, 1991).

Tritt's insistence that country music must broaden its attraction and open itself to new sounds may have

annoyed some purists, but they could not deny his success. *It's All About to Change* (#22 pop, #1 C&W, 1991) featured a duet with Marty Stuart (who joined Tritt on the No Hats Tour in 1992), and the nasty kiss-off waltz "Here's a Quarter (Call Someone Who Cares)" (#2 C&W). Little Feat backed Tritt up on the raucous "Bible Belt." On *T-r-o-u-b-l-e* (#27 pop, #6 C&W, 1992) Tritt was joined by George Jones and Tanya Tucker on backing vocals ("Lord Have Mercy on the Working Man") and by Lynyrd Skynyrd's Gary Rossington (who cowrote "Blue Collar Man"). *Ten Feet Tall and Bulletproof* (#20 pop, #3 C&W, 1994) yielded the #1 C&W hit "Foolish Pride." Tritt's autobiography, with the same title as his 1994 album, was also published that year.

The Troggs
Formed 1965, Andover, England
Original lineup: Reg Presley (b. Reginald Ball, June 12, 1943, Andover), voc.; Chris Britton (b. June 21, 1945, Watford, Eng.), lead gtr.; Peter Staples (b. May 3, 1944, Andover), bass; Ronnie Bond (b. Ronald Bullis, May 4, 1943, Andover; d. Nov. 13, 1992, Andover), drums.
1966—*Wild Thing* (Fontana)   1967—*Best of the Troggs*   1968—*Love Is All Around*   1969—(Group disbands)   1972—(Group re-forms: Presley; Bond; + Richard Moore, gtr.; + Tony Murray, bass)   1976—*The Troggs* (Pye) (+ Colin Fletcher, gtr.); *The Original Troggs Tapes* (Private Stock); *Vintage Years* (Sire)   N.A.—(– Fletcher; – Moore; – Murray; + Peter Lucas, bass; + Dave Maggs, drums)   1992—*Archeology (1967–1977)* (Mercury) (– Bond); *Athens Andover* (with Peter Buck, Bill Berry, Mike Mills, Peter Holsapple, John Keane) (Rhino).

Though their popularity lasted only a short time, the Troggs were initially one of the most successful mid-Sixties British Invasion bands, most known for their five-million-selling seminal punk hit "Wild Thing" (#1, 1966). They never quit playing and continue to perform around the world.

The foursome formed in Hampshire in the mid-Sixties, taking their name from the term "troglodyte." "Wild Thing" was their debut single. The Troggs' other hits in 1966 were "With a Girl Like You" (#29) and "I Can't Control Myself" (#43).

Their roots-of-power-pop sound, featuring Reg Presley's wispy vocals, also got them a Top Ten hit with "Love Is All Around" (#7, 1968) (revived by Wet Wet Wet in the early Nineties on the *Four Weddings and a Funeral* soundtrack). Though their hits dried up at that point, they continued to tour Europe. They didn't record, though, for several years.

In 1976 Pye released *The Troggs*, which featured "Summertime," a double-entendre-laden song that also got U.S. FM airplay. That same year, Sire released *Vintage Years*, a retrospective, and Private Stock put out *The Original Troggs Tapes*, which was all new material. In 1980 there was the *Live at Max's Kansas City* album including older hits and newer songs. It garnered only cult interest. There was also a French import album in 1981 called *Black Bottom*, again with new and old material. In the early Nineties the group collaborated with members of R.E.M. for *Athens Andover*. They remain perennially popular in their homeland, where the group and ever-quotable frontman Reg Presley are frequently seen on television and heard on the countless commercials that use their biggest hits to sell everything from insurance to yogurt. In 1992 the group performed at Sting's wedding.

Robin Trower

Born March 9, 1945, London, England
1973—(Trower, gtr.; James Dewar [b. Scot.], bass, voc.; Reg Isadore [b. West Indies], drums) *Twice Removed from Yesterday* **(Chrysalis)   1974—***Bridge of Sighs*   **1975—(– Isadore; + Bill Lordan, drums)** *For Earth Below*   **1976—***Robin Trower Live!*; *Long Misty Days*   **1977—(+ Rusty Allen, bass)** *In City Dreams*   **1978—***Caravan to Midnight*   **1980— (– Allen)** *Victims of the Fury*   **1981—(– Dewar; + Jack Bruce [b. May 14, 1943, Glasgow, Scot.], bass, voc.; + Bill Lordan, drums)** *B.L.T.* **(– Lordan; + Isadore)   1982—***Truce* **(– Bruce)   1983—***Back It Up*   **1988—(+ Davey Pattison, voc.)** *Take What You Need* **(Atlantic)   1989—***No Stopping Anytime* **(Chrysalis)   1990—***In the Line of Fire* **(Atlantic) 1991—***Essential* **(Chrysalis) (+ Livingstone Brown, bass, voc.; + Mayuyu, drums)   1994—***20th Century Blues* **(V-12).**

In his early years with Procol Harum, Robin Trower's piercing, distorted guitar sound was more often than not compared to that of Eric Clapton. But on Procol's "Whiskey Train" (on *Home*) and "Song for a Dreamer" (on *Broken Barricades*) Trower exhibited a strong Jimi Hendrix influence; "Song for a Dreamer" was dedicated to Hendrix.

By the time of *Barricades*, it was obvious that Trower's hard-rocking style was at odds with Procol Harum's [see entry] classical-rock direction, and he left after that album, at first forming the abortive Jude with ex–Jethro Tull drummer Clive Bunker, ex–Stone the Crows bassist Jim Dewar, and Scottish blues singer Frankie Miller. When that venture ran aground, Trower took a year off to re-form a Hendrix-style power trio with Dewar and drummer Reg Isadore. They debuted with 1973's *Twice Removed from Yesterday* (#106, 1973), which was produced by ex-Procol Matthew Fisher.

With *Bridge of Sighs* (#7, 1974) and heavy American touring, Trower came into his own as a guitar hero with U.S. audiences. After that album, Isadore was replaced by Bill Lordan, formerly with Sly and the Family Stone. Meanwhile, Trower took some guitar lessons from another pioneer of electronically modified guitar, Robert Fripp, who had just disbanded King Crimson. *For Earth Below* (#5, 1975) and *Live!* (#10, 1976) were top-selling LPs, and through the Seventies Trower continued to ably demonstrate his love for Hendrix, usually with solid commercial results. *Long Misty Days* (#24, 1976) and *In City Dreams* (#25, 1977) were both certified gold. *Caravan to Midnight* and *Victims of the Fury* both hit the Top Forty.

In 1981 Trower began collaborating with ex–Cream bassist and singer Jack Bruce, for two well-received albums: *B.L.T.* (#37, 1981) (with drummer Bill Lordan) and *Truce* (#109, 1982) (Reg Isadore in Lordan's place). (*No Stopping Anytime* is a compilation of Trower's recordings with Bruce.) Trower has continued to tour and record, and while his more recent albums have not charted nearly as highly as those of his Seventies heyday, he remains a respected guitarist. In the early Nineties he appeared on and coproduced with Bryan Ferry two of the singer's albums, *Taxi* and *Mamouna*.

John Trudell

Born February 15, 1946, Omaha, Nebraska
1991—*AKA Grafitti Man* **(Rykodisc)   1994—***Johnny Damas and Me.*

Native American activist John Trudell writes and performs story songs informed by his political struggle.

John Trudell

Growing up on a Santee Sioux reservation, Trudell served as national spokesman for the Indians of All Tribes occupation of Alcatraz Island in 1969. As national chairman of the American Indian Movement from 1973 to 1979, he was the subject of a 17,000-page FBI file that documented his activities, including his 1979 burning of an American flag in front of the Bureau's Washington headquarters. Shortly thereafter, a fire "of suspicious origin" destroyed Trudell's house on the Shoshone Paiute Indian Reservation in Nevada, killing Trudell's three children, wife, and mother-in-law. In light of the FBI's refusal to investigate the incident, Trudell has consistently maintained government complicity in his family's death.

After publishing a book of poems, *Living in Reality*, in 1982, he began recording home-studio tapes with his friend Jackson Browne and in 1985 released a mail-order cassette with Kiowa Indian guitarist Jesse Ed Davis. Davis died soon after, but having gained notice from Bob Dylan and Kris Kristofferson, Trudell released an expanded version of that cassette as *AKA Grafitti Man* in 1991. His politically charged rock & roll earned strong reviews, and Trudell followed with 1994's *Johnny Damas and Me*.

True Believers: See Rank and File

The Tubes

Formed late Sixties, Phoenix, Arizona
Fee Waybill (b. John Waldo, Sep. 17, 1950, Omaha, Nebr.), lead voc.; Bill Spooner (b. Apr. 16, 1949, Phoenix), gtr.; Roger Steen (b. Nov. 13, 1949, Pipestone, Minn.), gtr.; Vince Welnick (b. Feb. 21, 1951, Phoenix), kybds.; Michael Cotten (b. Jan. 25, 1950, Kansas City, Mo.), kybds.; Prairie Prince (b. May 7, 1950, Charlotte, N.C.), drums; Rick Anderson (b. Aug. 1, 1947, St. Paul, Minn.), bass; Re Styles (b. Mar. 3, 1950), voc.
1975—The Tubes (A&M)   1976—Young and Rich 1977—Now   1978—What Do You Want from Live? 1979—Remote Control   1981—The Completion Backward Principle (Capitol); T.R.A.S.H. (Tubes Rarities and Smash Hits) (A&M)   1983—Outside/Inside (Capitol)   1985—Love Bomb   1992—The Best of the Tubes   Ca. 1993—(Lineup: Steen; Prince; Anderson; Waybill; + Gary Cambra, voc., kybds.; + Jennifer McFee, voc.; + Amy French, voc.).

From the mid-Seventies through the early Eighties, the Tubes' mixture of rock, theater, and satire proved more capable of achieving notoriety than sales. Despite one of the wildest stage shows in the business (verging at times on soft-core pornography) and critical acclaim for their records, their five LPs for A&M were flops (even though the first was produced by Al Kooper and the last

by Todd Rundgren). The Tubes came close to hits during this period with a pair of radio staples—the heavy-metal parody "White Punks on Dope" (featuring Waybill in the guise of Quay Lewd) and the mock-girl-group song "Don't Touch Me There."

Bill Spooner, Rick Anderson, and Vince Welnick started embryonic versions of the Tubes in their hometown of Phoenix in the late Sixties, though they wouldn't come to be known as the Tubes until they moved to San Francisco in 1972. Early performances were generally reviled, and it took the group three years to build a cult following sufficient to justify a recording contract. But as each LP became another commercial setback, the Tubes began to streamline their act, and by 1980 they were down to six, after experimenting with a propless all-music live show. Even then, when their self-conscious attempt at a hit record, "Don't Want to Wait Anymore," proved successful, the only Tubes present were Waybill and Prince. That song, along with the AOR hit "Talk to You Later," made the Tubes' Capitol debut, *The Completion Backward Principle* (#36, 1981), a big seller. Later that year, the group appeared in the movie *Xanadu*.

In 1983 "She's a Beauty" reached the Top Ten, helped by an eye-catching and provocative video that got wide play on MTV. The album it came from, *Outside/Inside* (#18, 1983), became the group's best-selling album to date. But the Tubes' luck didn't hold, and two years later, *Love Bomb* (produced by Rundgren) stalled at #87. Waybill showed up on Richard Marx's debut album, and Vince Welnick joined the Grateful Dead, replacing deceased keyboardist Brent Mydland. The group re-formed in the early Nineties, touring Europe and the U.S. in 1993.

Tanya Tucker

Born October 10, 1958, Seminole, Texas
1972—Delta Dawn (Columbia)   1973—What's Your Mama's Name   1974—Would You Lay with Me 1975—Greatest Hits; Tanya Tucker (MCA)   1976— Lovin' and Learnin'; Here's Some Love   1977— Ridin' Rainbows; You Are So Beautiful (Columbia); Tanya Tucker's Greatest Hits (MCA)   1978—TNT 1980—Tear Me Apart; Dreamlovers   1981—Should I Do It?   1982—Live   1983—The Best of Tanya Tucker; Changes (Arista)   1986—Girls Like Me (Capitol)   1987—Love Me Like You Used To 1988—Strong Enough to Bend   1989—Greatest Hits 1990—Tennessee Woman; Greatest Hits Encore 1991—Greatest Country Hits (Curb); What Do I Do with Me (Liberty)   1992—Can't Run from Yourself 1993—Greatest Hits 1990–1992 (Liberty); Soon 1995—Fire to Fire.

In the beginning, three things made Tanya Tucker a major country-pop star at age 14: a fine voice, Billy Sherrill's MOR-Nashville production, and an image as a

Tanya Tucker

pubescent sexpot. In the years since, she has weathered tabloid accounts of her private life, treatment at the Betty Ford Center in 1989, and a three-year hiatus from recording at the peak of her career to emerge as a mature and extremely popular country star.

Tucker got into music through her construction-worker father, Beau Tucker, who took her to country shows after the family had moved to Wilcox, Arizona, and then to Phoenix. At age 13, she appeared in the film *Jeremiah Johnson*. Her first country hit was 1972's "Delta Dawn," followed by two #1 C&W hits: "What's Your Mama's Name" and "Blood Red and Goin' Down." At age 16 she made the #1 C&W single "Would You Lay with Me (in a Field of Stone)" (#46 pop, 1974).

After she reached the age of consent, Tucker left Columbia and producer Billy Sherrill and signed with MCA. In the late Seventies, she briefly tried to become a rock singer, wearing red tights (for *TNT*, at #54 pop, her highest-charting album of the Seventies and Eighties and gold) and adding fuzz-tone guitars, but she soon retreated into country music. A highly publicized liaison with country-pop crooner Glen Campbell included some duet recordings, but it ended in 1981, and Tucker continued to work the country circuit on her own.

In 1983 she moved to Arista Records; it was an unhappy pairing, and Tucker did not record for three years after her initial Arista album. She signed with Capitol (later Liberty) Records in 1986 and began a comeback that eclipsed her earlier success. Her #1 C&W hits include "Just Another Love" (1986) and "I Won't Take Less Than Your Love" (1987); other hits were "Highway Robbery" (#2 C&W, 1988), "What Do I Do with Me" (#2 C&W, 1991), "Some Kind of Trouble" (#3 C&W, 1992), "If Your Heart Ain't Busy Tonight" (#4 C&W, 1992), "Two Sparrows in a Hurricane" (#2 C&W , 1992), "It's a Little Too Late" (#2 C&W, 1993), "Tell Me About It," a duet with Delbert McClinton (#4 C&W, 1993), and "Soon" (#2 C&W, 1993). *What Do I Do with Me* (#48 pop, #9 C&W, 1991) was her first platinum album and her biggest crossover success to date. *Can't Run from Yourself* (#51 pop, #12 C&W, 1992) was also certified platinum. With her father functioning as her manager again, Tucker tours heavily. She also appears on *Common Thread,* the Eagles tribute, and on *Rhythm Country & Blues,* where she duets with Little Richard on the Eddie Cochran classic "Somethin' Else," and she has recorded an as-yet-unreleased duet with Frank Sinatra, "Embraceable You." Her nonmusical business enterprises include a line of western wear, salsa, and an exercise video.

Ike and Tina Turner/Tina Turner

Ike Turner (b. Izear Luster Turner, Nov. 5, 1931, Clarksdale, Miss.), gtr., voc.; Tina Turner (b. Annie Mae Bullock, Nov. 26, 1939, Brownsville, Tenn.), voc.
1965—*Live! The Ike and Tina Turner Show* (Warner

Ike and Tina Turner

Bros.) 1969—*Outta Season* (Blue Thumb); *In Person* (Minit); *River Deep—Mountain High* (A&M); *The Hunter* (Blue Thumb) 1970—*Come Together* (Liberty); *Workin' Together* 1971—*Live at Carnegie Hall/What You Hear Is What You Get* (United Artists); *Nuff Said* 1972—*Feel Good* 1973—*Nutbush City Limits* 1976—*Very Best of* 1977—*Delilah's Power* 1985—*Get Back!* (Liberty) 1991—*Proud Mary: The Best of Ike and Tina Turner* (EMI).
Ike Turner solo: 1972—*Blues Roots* (United Artists) 1978—*I'm Tore Up* (Red Lightnin').
Tina Turner solo: 1975—*Acid Queen* (United Artists) 1979—*Rough* 1984—*Private Dancer* (Capitol) 1986—*Break Every Rule* 1988—*Tina Live in Europe* 1989—*Foreign Affair* 1991—*Simply the Best* 1993—*What's Love Got to Do with It* (Virgin) 1994—*Tina: The Collected Recordings, Sixties to Nineties* (Capitol).

Ike Turner and his wife Tina were first known for their late-Sixties and early-Seventies recordings and their soul revue. Ike Turner was also a seminal figure in the early years of rock & roll as both a performer and a talent scout, and in those days Tina was one of the most flamboyant, overtly sexual performers in rock, singing in a blues rasp and suggestively caressing her microphone. Beginning in 1976, when Tina snuck out of a hotel with just 36 cents in her pocket and left Ike, she embarked on one of the longest but ultimately most successful comebacks in rock history.

Ike Turner's career began when he formed his first group, the Top Hatters, in high school. Later this group evolved into the Kings of Rhythm, who worked Delta juke joints. In 1951 his band recorded "Rocket '88" at Sam Phillips' Sun studio in Memphis with lead vocal by saxophonist Jackie Brenston. Unfortunately Brenston and the Delta Cats, not Ike Turner and the Kings of Rhythm, got the label credit. It became a #1 R&B hit on the Chess label, and over the years it has been frequently cited as the first rock & roll record. Turner went on to become a top session guitarist, talent scout, and producer through the Fifties. The sessions he recorded with Junior Parker and Howlin' Wolf, B. B. King, Otis Rush, Roscoe Gordon, Bobby "Blue" Bland, and Johnny Ace were leased to Chess, Modern, and RPM Records.

In 1956 Turner moved to St. Louis, where he and his newly reconstituted Kings of Rhythm became a hot draw at several nightclubs. Annie Mae Bullock and her sister were regulars at one such club. Bullock repeatedly asked Turner if she could sing with his band; he said that she could but never called her to the stage. One night Bullock, who had never sung professionally but had been appearing in talent shows since childhood, simply grabbed the microphone and sang. Soon after, he changed her name to Tina. They eventually married in 1962 although, according to Tina, not for love. Ike later described their relationship as that of "buddies." They had one son together, and before that, Tina bore another son by another man.

Even though they were not yet married, they first recorded as Ike and Tina Turner in 1960 after a singer failed to appear for a session. Tina stood in for the missing singer, and the song, "A Fool in Love," became a hit in 1960 (#27 pop, #2 R&B). Ike then developed an entire revue around Tina. With nine musicians and three scantily clad female background singers called the Ikettes, the Ike and Tina Turner Revue became a major soul act. In 1961 they charted with "It's Gonna Work Out Fine" (#14 pop, #2 R&B) and "I Idolize You" (#5 R&B). The following year, "Poor Fool" (#38 pop, #4 R&B) and "Tra La La La La" (#9 R&B) were hits. From the mid-Sixties on, they were major stars in England, where artists such as the Rolling Stones were unabashed fans. In 1966 Phil Spector produced what proved to be his last Wall of Sound single, "River Deep, Mountain High." It went to #3 in England, but did so poorly in the U.S. that Spector did not produce again until 1969.

The Turners continued to make pop hits into the late Sixties. They opened for the Rolling Stones on their 1969 tour. They were especially successful into the early Seventies with steamy cover songs like "Come Together" (#57 pop, #21 R&B), "I Want to Take You Higher" (#34 pop, #25 R&B), and "Proud Mary" (#4 pop, #5 R&B), featuring Tina's "We never, ever do nothin' nice and easy" spoken intro. In 1973 "Nutbush City Limits" (written by Tina) hit #4 in England and #13 R&B and #22 pop in the U.S. Two years later Tina got her first movie role, playing the Acid Queen in one of the most memorable scenes of Ken Russell's film version of the Who's *Tommy*.

According to Tina and as she wrote in her 1986 best-selling autobiography, *I, Tina* (cowritten with Kurt Loder), her life with Ike was marked by near-constant physical and emotional abuse. By the late Sixties Ike had become deeply involved with cocaine and alcohol and was prone to violent outbursts. Tina's litany of his crimes against her include hitting her, pouring hot coffee on her face, burning her lip with a lighted cigarette, and forcing her to perform while ill and pregnant. She attempted suicide in 1968. After she snuck away from Ike in 1976, she got a few bookings but at one point was forced to live on food stamps. Two years later, her divorce from Ike was final. Ike has often indicated publicly that, while he does not deny having battered Tina, he denies that her version of events is entirely true.

Tina's comeback began in earnest in 1981, when the Rolling Stones offered her a few opening spots on their U.S. tour. Around that time she also opened some shows for Rod Stewart and toured the world. In 1983 she landed a solo deal and by year's end had a U.K. hit with her steamy cover of Al Green's "Let's Stay Together" (#26 pop; #6 U.K.). Her U.S. breakthrough came with *Private Dancer* (#3, 1984), a five-million-selling album that included "Let's Stay Together" (#26, 1984), "What's Love Got to Do with It" (#1, 1984), "Better Be Good to Me" (#5, 1984), "Private Dancer" (#7, 1985), and "Show Some Respect" (#37, 1985). Her next two singles were nonalbum songs from the Mel Gibson film *Mad Max Beyond Thunderdome* (1985), in which Tina costarred as Auntie Entity: "We Don't Need Another Hero (Thunderdome)" (#2, 1985) and "One of the Living" (#15, 1985). Tina swept the 1984 Grammys, with "What's Love Got to Do with It" winning Best Female Pop Vocal Performance and "Better Be Good to Me" taking Best Female Rock Vocal Performance. "What's Love" was also recognized as Song of the Year and Record of the Year.

Break Every Rule (#4, 1986), another platinum release, included "Typical Male" (#2, 1986), "Two People" (#30, 1986), and "What You Get Is What You See" (#13, 1987). In late 1985 she released a live duet with Bryan Adams, "It's Only Love," which went to #15. Tina, long legendary for her live shows, toured tirelessly. She has always been especially popular in Europe and in England, where *Tina Live in Europe* went to #8 as compared to #86 in the States. She duetted with Mick Jagger at Live Aid in 1985 and is a favorite of British rock stars. Her international tours broke records in many cities.

In 1989 Tina's first album of new material in over three years, *Foreign Affair* (#31, 1989), was released. Its singles included "The Best" (#15, 1989), which featured a sax solo by Edgar Winter, and Tony Joe White's "Steamy Windows" (#39, 1990). While it was not her most successful album in the U.S., it outsold *Private Dancer* in the U.K. Also in 1989 Tina celebrated her 50th birthday with a star-studded party that included Mark Knopfler (who wrote "Private Dancer"), Eric Clapton, and other admirers. Tina and Rod Stewart's remake of the Marvin Gaye–Tammi Terrell hit "It Takes Two" went to #5 in the U.K. in 1990. A year later, her greatest-hits package *Simply the Best* went to #1 in the U.K. but didn't clear the Hot 100 albums chart here. In 1992 Turner signed to Virgin. Her first single for that label, "I Don't Wanna Fight" (#9, 1993), was cowritten by Steve DuBerry and Lulu.

Around the time Tina left him, Ike Turner retired to his studio in Inglewood, California, and released two solo LPs. The studio was destroyed by fire in 1982. After 11 arrests on various charges, in 1990 Ike was convicted on several charges, including possessing and transporting cocaine, and sentenced to 18 months in jail. He was in prison when he and Tina were inducted into the Rock and Roll Hall of Fame in January 1991. In September of that year, he was released from jail and has since attempted to sell his own autobiography. Tina's book was made into a hit feature film, *What's Love Got to Do with It* (1993).

Big Joe Turner

Born May 18, 1911, Kansas City, Missouri; died November 24, 1985, Inglewood, California
1956—*The Boss of the Blues: Joe Turner Sings Kansas City Jazz* (Atlantic)   1960—*Big Joe Rides Again*   1976—*Nobody in Mind* (Pablo)   1977—*Things That I Used to Do*   1980—*The Midnight Special; The Best of Big Joe Turner*   1981—*Have No Fear Joe Turner Is Here*   1983—*Life Ain't Easy; Blues Train* (Muse)   1984—*Kansas City Here I Come* (Pablo)   1986—*Big Joe Turner Memorial Album: Rhythm & Blues Years* (Atlantic)   1987—*Big Joe Turner: Greatest Hits*   1989—*Flip, Flop & Fly* (Pablo)   1994—*Big, Bad & Blue: The Big Joe Turner Anthology* (Rhino).

Big Joe Turner is indisputably one of rock & roll's forefathers. Songwriter Doc Pomus once remarked of Turner, "Rock & roll would never have happened without him," and many historians agree. Turner was a classic old-style blues shouter whose powerful voice and often playful delivery turned jump-blues staples including "Shake, Rattle and Roll," "Honey Hush," "Sweet Sixteen," "Chains of Love," and "Flip, Flop and Fly" into stepping stones linking the blues and rock & roll. He had been singing for over 20 years when he recorded those songs in the early Fifties, and he performed until just months before his death, following years of chronic health problems, at age 74.

Turner got his start as a singing bartender in a Kansas City cabaret in the late Twenties. He was already known as one of the most powerful blues singers west of the Mississippi when he teamed up with boogie-woogie pianist Pete Johnson and became one of the originators of "blues shouting." In 1938 talent scout John Hammond brought Turner and Johnson to New York to appear at the Carnegie Hall concert that sparked the boogie-woogie craze of the late Thirties and early Forties. As their engagement at Cafe Society—a New York jazz club—extended into a four-year run, boogie-woogie bumped its way into mainstream white pop for the first time. Turner sang jazz-style slow blues with pianist Art Tatum, but he also shouted boogie-woogie fast blues with Johnson, and the propulsive rhythms and extroverted vocals of songs like "Roll 'em Pete" showed the stirrings of the rhythm & blues that became popular in the years after World War II.

In 1941 Turner went to Hollywood to appear in Duke Ellington's Jump for Joy Revue. He was based on the West Coast for most of the Forties, joined occasionally by Johnson and pianist Albert Ammons. In 1951 he returned to New York to play the Apollo Theatre with Count Basie. There he met Ahmet Ertegun and Jerry Wexler, who brought him to Atlantic Records, where Ertegun's "Chains of Love" gave him a #2 R&B hit. (Pat Boone had a #10 pop hit with the song five years later.) It was the first of a string of R&B hits on Atlantic between 1951 and 1956, each of which is a rock & roll classic: "Sweet Sixteen" (#4, 1952), "Honey Hush" (#2, 1953; reissued in 1960, it made the pop Top Sixty), "T.V. Mama" (#9, 1954, recorded in Chicago with Elmore James and his band), "Shake, Rattle and Roll" (#2, 1954, a big hit for Bill Haley later that year in a bowdlerized form), "Flip, Flop and Fly" (#3, 1955, covered by Johnnie Ray), "The Chicken and the Hawk" (#13, 1956), "Corrina, Corrina" (#3, 1956; at #41, his biggest pop hit), and "Rock a While" (#12, 1956). In addition to Ertegun's songs, his own, and his brother Lou Willie Turner's, he recorded material by Doc Pomus and Leiber and Stoller. The backing musicians on his classic Atlantic R&B sessions included, variously, King Curtis, Mickey Baker, Sam Taylor, Al Sears, Panama Francis, and Choker Campbell.

While he never had the pop success of his imitators, who often cleaned up the sexual metaphors and took some of the energy out of the songs, Turner continued to work through good times and bad. He toured Europe several times in the Fifties; and in the Sixties and Seventies he appeared and recorded with the Johnny Otis Show, Eddie "Lockjaw" Davis, Milt Jackson, Roy Eldridge, Dizzy Gillespie, and Pee Wee Crayton. In 1974 he was featured with Count Basie in *The Last of the Blue Devils,* a film about the Kansas City music scene.

Beginning in the early Eighties Turner started to suffer from diabetes and arthritis. Later in the decade heart and kidney problems often forced him to walk on crutches, then perform seated. Despite this, his voice never wavered.

The Turtles/Flo and Eddie

Formed 1963, Inglewood, California
Original lineup: Howard Kaylan (b. June 22, 1945,
New York City, N.Y.), voc.; Mark Volman (b. Apr. 19,
1944, Los Angeles, Calif.), voc., gtr., sax; Al Nichol
(b. Mar. 31, 1946, Winston-Salem, N.C.), gtr.; Chuck
Portz (b. Mar. 28, 1945, Santa Monica, Calif.), bass;
Donald Ray Murray (b. Nov. 8, 1945), drums.
1965—*It Ain't Me Babe* **(White Whale)   1966—***You*
Baby   **1967—***Happy Together;* ***The Turtles! Golden***
Hits   **1968—***The Turtles Present the Battle of the*
Bands   **1969—***Turtle Soup*   **1970—***More Golden*
Hits; ***Wooden Head***   **1975—***Happy Together Again*
(Sire)   1982—*20 Greatest Hits* **(Rhino)   1987—***The*
Best of the Turtles   **1988—***Turtle Wax: The Best of*
the Turtles, vol. 2   **1992—***Captured Live.*
Flo and Eddie (Kaylan; Volman): 1972—*Phlorescent*
Leech and Eddie **(Reprise)   1973—***Flo and Eddie*
1975—*Illegal, Immoral and Fattening* **(Columbia)**
1976—*Moving Targets*   **1982—***Rock Steady with*
Flo and Eddie **(Epiphany).**

The Turtles were a successful pop group of the Sixties dissatisfied with "mere" hit singles. Their aspirations to more profound statements broke up the band, with lead singers Mark Volman and Howard Kaylan joining Frank Zappa and then embarking on a duo career as the Phlorescent Leech (Flo) and Eddie.

The name Turtles came from White Whale Records. Before the band's signing in 1965, the L.A.-based combo had been known as the Nightriders, and later as the Crossfires. Their local singles during that time were uniformly unsuccessful. Once under contract, they were converted from a surf group (White Whale astutely noting that the trend was on the wane) to folk rock, then in vogue thanks to Bob Dylan, the Byrds, et al. Their debut single, Dylan's "It Ain't Me Babe," went Top Ten in 1965 and launched the band on a brief string of hits: "Let Me Be" (#20, 1965) and "You Baby" (#20, 1966), followed by "Grim Reaper of Love" (#81, 1966) and "Can I Get to Know You Better" (#89, 1966). Each of these showcased the group's trademark sound, a sophisticated pop rock dominated by Kaylan and Volman's distinctive vocals.

The Turtles weren't content, however, and were about to break up; but first they released "Happy Together" (#1, 1967), which proved to be their biggest hit, and one of 1967's Top Ten records. With their career reinvigorated, "She'd Rather Be with Me" (#3, 1967), "You Know What I Mean" (#12, 1967), and "She's My Girl" (#14, 1967) were followup hits. These, however, only stalled the internal dissatisfaction temporarily.

Though it included their last two hit 45s, "Elenore" (#6, 1968) and "You Showed Me" (#6, 1969), *The Turtles Present the Battle of the Bands* (#128, 1968) was an ambitious reflection of the group's desire to be more than AM radio fodder. Each song was meant to sound completely different from the others, literally as if performed by a different group. The gatefold sleeve presented the Turtles dressed in eleven guises, including the Crossfires. The next album, *Turtle Soup* (#117, 1969), was produced by the Kinks' Ray Davies when he was at his least commercial. The Turtles played the White House, at the invitation of Tricia Nixon, in May 1969.

The band split up for good in mid-1970. Their most successful LPs were *Happy Together* (#25, 1967) and *The Turtles! Golden Hits* (#7, 1967). Throughout their career, the Turtles had fluid personnel; only lead guitarist Al Nichol was with them from Crossfires to breakup. After some of the original members quit, replacements were found in ex-Leaves (who had one hit with "Hey Joe") bassist Jim Pons and drummer John Barbata. After Barbata quit the group, he drummed with Crosby, Stills, Nash and Young and the Jefferson Starship. Pons stuck with Volman and Kaylan into Zappa's band and the initial Flo and Eddie group. Other temporary Turtles included onetime Monkees producer Chip Douglas and former Spanky and Our Gang drummer John Seiter.

After fronting the Turtles through 1970, Mark Volman and Howard Kaylan, as Flo and Eddie, joined Frank Zappa. The alias was devised when White Whale forced the group into litigation while they were breaking up. The duo contributed to *Chunga's Revenge, Live at the Fillmore East, Just Another Band From L.A.* (which included the Turtles' "Happy Together"), and the *200 Motels* album and film.

After leaving Zappa in 1972, the pair began working and recording as the Phlorescent Leech and Eddie, at first a group that included bassist Jim Pons and another Zappa alumnus, drummer Aynsley Dunbar. Although they originally used the Phlorescent moniker to avoid contractual problems, the name stuck. Their shows and albums combine straight songs with devastating sendups of rock personalities, genres, and events. They lampooned Pink Floyd's *The Wall* show with "The Fence," a flimsy bamboo fence over which they tossed cheap inflatable toy animals. Another popular mid-Seventies routine turned the Village People's "In the Navy" into "In the Gasline." Over the years, no one and nothing—from Kiss to Joni Mitchell, Jim Morrison to Fleetwood Mac, *Flashdance* to the Beastie Boys—has been spared their dead-on, sometimes silly sendups and satires. As Volman once told ROLLING STONE, "We've never catered to the industry we were trying to succeed in."

They briefly gave up touring in 1976 following the accidental death of their guitarist, Philip Reed (he fell from a window, prompting some reports that his death was a suicide), and the untimely death of another close friend, Marc Bolan (T. Rex). Besides several LPs (the second produced by Bob Ezrin), they scored and contributed dialogue to an X-rated animation film called *Cheap*. They have also written columns for *Teen Beat, Creem, Phonograph Record,* and the *L.A. Free Press,* as well as hosting a syndicated radio show in the mid-Seventies and a short-lived late-night TV talk show in 1982. The pair has provided background vocals for Marc Bolan and T. Rex, Stephen Stills, John Lennon and Yoko Ono, Hoyt Axton, Keith Moon, David Cassidy, Alice Cooper, Tonio K., Blondie, the Knack, Sammy Hagar, Burton Cummings, Paul Kantner's Planet Earth Rock & Roll Orchestra, Roger McGuinn, the Psychedelic Furs, and Bruce Springsteen ("Hungry Heart").

Beginning in 1980 Flo and Eddie produced and composed a series of popular children's records for the *Strawberry Shortcake* and *Care Bears* soundtracks. Kaylan appeared in the film *Get Crazy* (1983). Beginning in 1989, the pair hosted an afternoon radio show on New York's WXRK. Their annual New Year's Eve shows at New York City's Bottom Line have been a tradition since the Seventies.

Volman and Kaylan, as Flo and Eddie, occasionally resurrect the Turtles name for shows. Beginning in the mid-Eighties the pair, with a backing band, have appeared with the Turtles, leading the Happy Together Tour, which included other Sixties acts.

Dwight Twilley

Born June 6, circa 1952, Tulsa, Oklahoma
With the Dwight Twilley Band: 1976—*Sincerely* (Shelter) 1977—*Twilley Don't Mind* (Arista).
Solo: 1979—*Twilley* 1982—*Scuba Divers* (EMI America) 1984—*Jungle*.

Dwight Twilley made a music career out of trying to fuse Elvis Presley's rockabilly with the Beatles' pop, and he never came closer than on his very first single. He and partner Phil Seymour became overnight sensations when "I'm On Fire" came out of nowhere and went Top Twenty in 1975. Following that early success, Twilley was bogged down by a split with Seymour, erratic live appearances, and myriad troubles with record companies. As the Dwight Twilley Band, Tulsa natives Twilley and Seymour laid down nearly all the parts on their two LPs, *Sincerely* and *Twilley Don't Mind.* Though they were popular with critics, neither album was a commercial success, in part because of the shaky condition of Shelter Records; for example, there was no LP to capitalize on "I'm On Fire" for over a year.

Twilley freed himself of Shelter and got into a new struggle with his next label, Arista. Following the release of *Twilley* and "Somebody to Love" some months later, Arista rejected his second solo album. After a lengthy battle, Twilley put out *Scuba Divers* on a new label, EMI, in 1982, complete with a redone version of "Somebody to Love." Twilley finally achieved some of the commercial success that had long been predicted for him with "Girls" (#16, 1984) from *Jungle* (#39, 1984). He has since written other songs, including the ballad "Why Do You Wanna Break My Heart" from *Wayne's World,* and an acclaimed children's book, *Questions from Dad: A Really Cool Way to Communicate with Kids,* which features a foreword from well-known therapist Dr. Susan Forward. The latter project led to Twilley's receiving an award from the Children's Rights Council. In early 1982, 150 of Twilley's paintings and drawings were displayed at the Museum of Rock Art in Los Angeles. He has continued to paint, and some of his work appears in the 1994 book *Musicians as Artists.*

Seymour, meanwhile, went on to an initially successful solo career, helped along by a pair of Twilley compositions, one of which, "Looking for the Magic," appeared originally on *Twilley Don't Mind.* Seymour recorded solo albums and had a #22 hit in 1981 with "Precious to Me." Seymour worked with a number of other artists, including Del Shannon. He was later a member of the Textones. In 1985 he was diagnosed with lymphoma, of which he died on August 17, 1993, in Tarzana, California; he was 41 years of age.

Twisted Sister

Formed February 14, 1973, Ho-Ho-Kus, New Jersey
Jay Jay French (b. John Segall, July 20, 1954, New York City, N.Y.), gtr.; Mark "The Animal" Mendoza (b. July 13, 1956, Long Island, N.Y.), bass; Eddie Ojeda (b. Aug. 5, 1954, Bronx, N.Y.), gtr.; Tony Petri, drums; Dee Snider (b. Mar. 15, 1955, Massapequa, N.Y.), voc.
1982—(– Petri; + A. J. Pero [b. Oct. 14, 1959, New York City], drums) *Under the Blade* (Secret) 1983—*You Can't Stop Rock and Roll* (Atlantic) 1984—*Stay Hungry* 1985—*Come Out and Play* 1987—(– Pero; + Joe Franco, drums) *Love Is for Suckers* 1994—*Live* (CMC).

Heavily made up and profoundly dumb, Twisted Sister's mix of Who and Alice Cooper moves was a textbook example of mid- to late-Seventies glitter/bar-band style. Their 15-year career might read like a thousand others were it not for a single Top Forty hit, "We're Not Gonna Take It" (#21, 1984), an early testament to the power of MTV.

Dressed in the most excessive glitter/trash styles, with highly teased hair and lavish eye makeup, Twisted Sister amassed a large following throughout the New York tristate area but little label interest. Proud that nothing, not even their name (which was lifted from a local, defunct band), could be considered original, Twisted Sister was popular enough to sell out New York City's 3400-seat Palladium in 1979. They released the independent *Under the Blade* in 1982. After an appearance on the British TV show *The Tube* that year, the group signed with Atlantic.

You Can't Stop Rock and Roll (#130, 1983) sold poorly, and Twisted Sister was relegated to second-division status until they made a splash at an English rock festival. With their reputation as a live band assured, it took the 1984 video for "We're Not Gonna Take It," with lead singer Dee Snider's mad Pierrot image and comically antiestablishment, patricidal storyline, to bring the band to the mainstream, sending the album *Stay Hungry* to #15. For a while Snider was a familiar face, as a regular guest on Howard Stern's radio program, a popular metal-magazine poster boy, and—along with Frank Zappa—a spokesman against censorship at the Senate subcommittee on communications hearings. In 1987 he wrote (with Philip Bashe) a fairly serious and well-received book of advice for teenagers entitled *Dee Snider's Teenage Survival Guide: How to Be a Legend in Your Own Lunchtime*.

Subsequent albums never matched *Stay Hungry*'s popularity, and the band called it quits in 1987. Snider formed the band Desperado, which recorded an album for Elektra that was never released. In 1992 his new band, Widowmaker, released an album called *Blood and Bullets*, which flopped.

Conway Twitty

Born Harold Lloyd Jenkins, September 1, 1933, Friars Point, Mississippi; died June 5, 1993, Springfield, Missouri
1961—*Greatest Hits* (MGM) 1970—*Hello Darlin'* (Decca) 1971—*We Only Make Believe* (with Loretta Lynn); *Fifteen Years Ago* 1979—*Very Best of Loretta and Conway* (MCA) 1982—*Southern Comfort* (Elektra) 1985—*Chasin' Rainbows* (Warner Bros.) 1987—*Borderline* (MCA) 1989—*Number Ones: The Warner Bros. Years* (Warner Bros.); *House on Old Lonesome Road* (MCA) 1990—*Crazy in Love; 25th Silver Anniversary Collection* 1993—*Final Touches*.

Like Charlie Rich, Conway Twitty began as a rockabilly singer, then moved more profitably into country and country-pop music. The lost-love sentimentality that made him a country star was manifested in his first big hit single, 1958's "It's Only Make Believe," which he cowrote.

In the Forties, under his given name, Harold Jenkins formed a country band called the Phillips County Ramblers. By the mid-Fifties, after Jenkins had finished a two-year army stint, they had changed their name to the Rockhousers and their repertoire to a harder-hitting mix of country, boogie-woogie, and R&B. In 1955 they cut demos for Sun Records in Memphis; by this time Jenkins had adopted the names of two towns he had passed through and became Conway Twitty. He had a minor rockabilly hit with "I Need Your Lovin'" (#93) in 1957 before "Make Believe" became a #1 pop smash. In 1960 Twitty followed with "Lonely Blue Boy" (#6). Twitty was now a pop star and appeared on TV shows and in college- and teen-oriented films. But by 1962 his pop star had waned.

He organized a country band in 1964, and with constant touring he built a huge following in the South and Southwest. In 1966, when he signed with Decca, he began churning out hits. In 1968 he had country #1s with "Next in Line" and "I Love You More Today," and followed in 1969 with "To See My Angel Cry." In 1970 he hit with "That's When She Started to Stop Loving Me" (#3 C&W) and one of the five best-selling country singles of the year, "Hello Darlin'" (#60 pop, #1 C&W). In 1971 he teamed with Loretta Lynn for the first of many duets, producing the #1 country hit "After the Fire Is Gone" (#56 pop). Twitty himself also hit that year with "Wonder What She'll Think About Me Leaving" (#4 C&W). In 1972 came the country hits "I Can't See Me Without You" (#4), "She Needs Someone to Hold Her" (#1), "I Can't Stop Loving You" (#1), and "(Lost Her Love) On Our Last Date"

(#1). The all-time country sales champ, his hit singles continued into the Eighties, with 12 #1s, including "Tight Fittin' Jeans" (1981), "The Clown" (1982), "Somebody's Needin' Somebody" (1984), and "Don't Call Him a Cowboy" (1985). In 1982 he opened Twitty City, a nine-acre theme park outside Nashville that became a major tourist attraction.

On June 5, 1993, Twitty collapsed and died after a performance in Branson, Missouri. The cause of death was a stomach hemorrhage.

2 Live Crew

Formed 1985, Miami, Florida
Luke Skyywalker (b. Luther Campbell, Dec. 22, 1960, Miami), voc.; Fresh Kid Ice (b. Christopher Wong-Won, May 29, Trinidad), voc.; Brother Marquis (b. Mark Ross, Apr. 2, New York City, N.Y.), voc.; Mr. Mixx (b. David Hobbs, Sep. 29, Calif.), DJ.
1986—The 2 Live Crew Is What We Are (Luke Skyywalker) 1987—Move Somethin' 1989—As Nasty As They Wanna Be; As Clean As They Wanna Be; Live in Concert (Effect) 1991—Sports Weekend (As Nasty as They Wanna Be Part II) (Luke) (– Ross; – Hobbs; + Verb [b. Larry Dobson], voc.) 1994— Back at Your Ass for the Nine-4.
Luke Featuring the 2 Live Crew: 1990—Banned in the U.S.A. (Luke/Atlantic).
Luke solo: 1993—In the Nude (Luke) 1994—Freak for Life 6996.

2 Live Crew had been making frankly salacious, but otherwise unexceptional, rap recordings for five years before gaining a national notoriety it otherwise might never have found, thanks to Florida authorities who sought to ban the group's records. 2 Live Crew's 1989 album As Nasty As They Wanna Be did, in fact, become the first recording ever declared obscene by an American court of law—even though the group had put a "parental warning" sticker on it and made an edited version, As Clean As They Wanna Be. But by March 1993 every obscenity ruling against the group had been overturned.

2 Live Crew founder Luther Campbell claimed to be raised a Catholic, as well as a devoted, community-minded family man; he defended his music as comedy— and indeed, more than any other rap act, 2 Live Crew drew on the black tradition of "blue-humored" party records by the likes of Redd Foxx and Richard Pryor, and the risqué Seventies work of proto-rapper Blowfly. His first single, "Throw the D," helped launch the booming, bass-heavy Miami Sound in 1984. A year later he formed his label Skyywalker Records (changed to Luke Records after a lawsuit from Star Wars creator George Lucas) and 2 Live Crew. The group's second album, Move Somethin', caught enough ears to make #68 on the pop chart.

But when 1989's As Nasty As They Wanna Be (#29, 1989) spawned a hit single in "Me So Horny" (#26, 1989), Jack Thompson—an evangelical Christian attorney from Coral Gables, Florida—launched the legal campaign against Campbell.

In March 1990 a Broward County, Florida, circuit court judge found probable cause that Nasty was obscene under state law; sheriff's deputies soon arrested a black record retailer in Ft. Lauderdale for selling the album (his conviction was later overturned; a retailer in Huntsville, Alabama, who was also prosecuted for selling the album was acquitted). Thompson got Florida governor Robert Martinez to say he thought the album was obscene. Luke Skyywalker Records sued the Broward County sheriff on First Amendment grounds, and the state federal court ruled that there was a prior restraint of free speech but that the LP was obscene. A week later Campbell and fellow rappers Chris Wong-Won and Mark Ross were arrested at a Hollywood, Florida, nightclub, for performing the songs on Nasty (which would sell two million copies, versus an eighth as many for its Clean version). Later in 1990 the New York–based alternative-rock band Too Much Joy, in a show of solidarity, would be arrested for coming to Hollywood, Florida, and performing covers of Nasty songs; the band was ultimately cleared by a jury that deliberated for 13 minutes and then criticized authorities for wasting its time.

Between court appeals, Campbell recorded Banned in the U.S.A. (#21, 1990), with a Bruce Springsteen–derived cover and title track (#20, 1990). Capitalizing on the legal furor, Atlantic Records distributed the album. However, 2 Live Crew canceled several fall 1990 shows, as well as a Banned in the U.S.A. pay-per-view cable TV special, for lack of demand. On the plus side, Campbell and his cohorts were acquitted of obscenity charges from their nightclub arrest, by a jury that included a 76-year-old woman unfazed by 2 Live Crew's vulgarity, and another woman who wanted to deliver the not-guilty verdict in the form of a rap.

In May 1992 the 11th U.S. Circuit Court of Appeals in Georgia reversed the Florida obscenity ruling against the Nasty album; seven months later the U.S. Supreme Court refused to hear an appeal, by which time the original 2 Live Crew had disbanded after releasing Sports Weekend (#22, 1991). Meanwhile, Campbell was in more legal trouble over 2 Live Crew's 1989 version of Roy Orbison's classic "Oh, Pretty Woman"—which Campbell and company had changed to be about "big, hairy," "bald-headed," and "two-timin'" women. Orbison's music publisher, the Nashville giant Acuff-Rose, had rebuffed Campbell's request for a license for the song, and sued him upon release of his version, claiming he'd damaged the song's value. Campbell defended his fair-use right to parody. A Nashville court's 1991 ruling against Acuff-Rose was overturned on appeal in 1992, and a year later the Supreme Court agreed to hear the case. Briefs on behalf of 2 Live Crew were filed by the producers of *Home Box Office* and political parodist Mark Russell, among others.

Meanwhile, Campbell's Luke Records struck gold in 1993 with the R&B vocal group H-Town, whose debut album, *Fever for Da Flavor* (#16, 1993), yielded a huge hit single in "Knockin' Da Boots" (#3, 1993). In early 1994 the Supreme Court ruled in favor of Campbell that the Orbison takeoff was a parody. Concurrently, Campbell announced a new 2 Live Crew and a publishing venture—an adult magazine called *Scandalous*. In June 1995, however, Campbell filed for bankruptcy after rapper M.C. Shy D obtained a lien against some of Campbell's property; Campbell owes Shy D $1.6 million in back royalties.

2Pac
Born Tupac Amaru Shakur, June 16, 1971, New York City, New York
1991—*2Pacalypse Now* (Interscope)   1993—*Strictly 4 My N.I.G.G.A.Z.*   1995—*Me Against the World*.

True to his appropriately titled 1995 chart-topping album, *Me Against the World*, rapper 2Pac has attempted to define himself as a performer amidst numerous criminal charges and convictions. The critical and commercial success of his music (as well as an acclaimed acting career) has been continually overshadowed by his legal entanglements. In the life of this gansta rapper, art and reality have become increasingly blurred.

Shakur, the son of a Black Panther member, spent a great deal of his childhood moving around the country. Just before settling, at the age of 17, in Marin County, California, Shakur dropped out of the Baltimore School of the Arts. The rapper then successfully auditioned to become a dancer and roadie for the rap group Digital Underground and simultaneously worked relentlessly on his own material. In 1991 he signed with Interscope and released the album *2Pacalypse Now* (#64 pop, #13 R&B, 1992), a musical mixture of inner-city portraiture and messages of racial strength.

Shakur also became a successful actor in the early Nineties, appearing in *Juice* (1992) and *Above the Rim* (1994) and giving a critically acclaimed performance opposite Janet Jackson in John Singleton's *Poetic Justice* (1993). Shakur's second album, *Strictly 4 My N.I.G.G.A.Z.* (#24 pop, #4 R&B, 1993), yielded the hits "I Get Around" (#11 pop, #4 R&B, 1993) and "Keep Ya Head Up" (#12 pop, #7 R&B, 1993).

Even longer than 2Pac's hit list, though, is his police blotter. In 1992 the rapper was arrested after a six-year-old California boy was killed by a stray bullet discharged during a scuffle between Shakur and two others. He was then charged in Atlanta with shooting two off-duty police officers in October 1993. Charges in both cases were dismissed. The following month Shakur and two members of his entourage were charged with sexual abuse following an incident in a New York City luxury hotel. In early 1994 he was found guilty of assault on *Menace II Society* codirector Allen Hughes and served 15 days in jail. By the end of the year, the rapper was found guilty of the sexual assault only a day after being shot by muggers in the lobby of a New York City recording studio. He was later sentenced to 4½ years in prison.

While his 1995 album *Me Against the World* (#1, 1995) headed to the top of the charts, Shakur headed for prison. Shakur has become the first artist to reach #1 on the *Billboard* charts while serving out a prison sentence.

Two Tons of Fun: See the Weather Girls

The Tymes
Formed 1959, Philadelphia, Pennsylvania
Original lineup: George Hilliard, tenor voc.; Donald Banks, bass voc.; George Williams, lead voc.; Albert Berry, tenor voc.; Norman Burnett, baritone voc.
1963—*So Much In Love* (Parkway); *The Sound of the Wonderful Tymes*   1968—*People* (Columbia)   1974—*Trustmaker* (RCA).

The Tymes didn't have their first hit until four years after they got together, when "So Much in Love" went to #1 on the pop charts, #4 R&B, on the local independent Parkway label. Using a similar sweet soul style, they had a trio of followup successes: "Wonderful! Wonderful!" (#7 pop, #23 R&B, 1963), "Somewhere" (#19, 1963), and "To Each His Own" (#78, 1964).

During the mid-Sixties, the group struggled once more, releasing flops on their own Winchester label (co-owned by Leon Huff, before his own massive success) and MGM, before rebounding in 1968 with "People" (#39 pop, #33 R&B) and in 1974 with "You Little Trustmaker" (#12 pop, #20 R&B). The latter was also a Top Twenty hit in the U.K. Beginning in the Seventies, the group saw a number of personnel changes, including the departures of Berry and Williams. A song by John and Johanna Hall entitled "Ms. Grace" peaked at #91 pop, #75 R&B here, but in December 1974 was #1 in the U.K. The group's last charting single was 1976's "It's Cool" (#68 pop, #3 R&B), but they have continued to tour.

Ian Tyson: See Ian and Sylvia

UB40

Formed 1978, Birmingham, England
Astro (b. Terence Wilson, June 24, 1957, Birming-
ham), voc.; James Brown (b. Nov. 20, 1957, Birming-
ham), drums; Ali Campbell (b. Feb. 15, 1959,
Birmingham), gtr., voc.; Robin Campbell (b. Dec. 25,
1954, Birmingham), gtr., voc.; Earl Falconer (b. Jan.
23, 1959, Birmingham), bass; Norman Hassan
(b. Jan. 26, 1958, Birmingham), perc.; Brian Travers
(b. Feb. 7, 1959, Birmingham), sax; Mickey
Virtue (b. Jan 19, 1957, Birmingham), kybds.
1980—*Signing Off* (Graduate, U.K.); *The Singles*
Album* 1981—*Present Arms* (DEP, U.K.); *Present
Arms in Dub* 1982—*UB44* 1983—*Live*; *1980–1983
(A&M); *Labour of Love* 1984—*Geffery Morgan*
1985—*The UB40 File* (Graduate, U.K.); *Baggariddim*
(DEP, U.K.); *Little Baggariddim* EP (A&M) 1986—
Rat in the Kitchen* 1987—*CCCP: Live in Moscow
1988—*UB40* 1989—*Labour of Love II* (Virgin)
1993—*Promises and Lies.*

Known in the U.S. for their reggae-inflected covers of
Neil Diamond's "Red Red Wine" (#1, 1988) and Elvis
Presley's "Can't Help Falling in Love" (#1, 1993), UB40
has had more than 30 singles on the British charts since
1980.

UB40's multiracial lineup and influences reflect their
roots in working-class Birmingham. Originally a gang of
layabouts (they took their name from the British unemployment form), they turned to music in early 1978, playing instruments bought with money awarded to
singer/guitarist Ali Campbell as compensation for injuries received in a bar fight.

Initially so bad they almost broke up, by Christmas
they were good enough for Chrissie Hynde to invite
them on a Pretenders tour. The band's quickly recorded
single "Food for Thought" reached #4 in the U.K. in 1980,
and was followed by the albums *Signing Off* (#2 U.K.,
1980) and *Present Arms* (#2 U.K., 1981), which included
their scathing anti-Thatcher anthem, "One in Ten" (#7
U.K., 1981).

Labour of Love (#14 pop, #1 U.K., 1983), an album of
reggae covers that contained "Red Red Wine" (#34 pop,
1984; #1 U.K., 1983), put them in the U.S. charts for the
first time. Albums of original material (*Geffery Morgan*
[#60, 1984], *Rat in the Kitchen* [#53, 1986], *UB40* [#44,
1988]), and an EP, *Little Baggariddim* (#40, 1985), which
included a cover of "I Got You Babe" with Chrissie Hynde
(#28, 1985), sold only respectably in the U.S. In 1988 a
Phoenix radio station added "Red Red Wine" to its
playlist; other stations followed suit, and the song had a
second life as a U.S. megahit, eventually climbing to #1,
bringing *Labour of Love* with it to #14.

Labour of Love II (#30, 1990) was another album of
covers and included "The Way You Do the Things You
Do" (originally done in 1964 by the Temptations), which

UB40

made it to #6. In 1993 the band released *Promises and Lies* (their second #1 U.K. album), with "Can't Help Falling in Love" and "Higher Ground" (#45, 1993) helping to propel it to #6 on the U.S. albums chart.

UFO

Formed 1969, England
Phil Mogg (b. 1951, London, Eng.), voc.; Mick Bolton, gtr.; Peter Way (b. London), bass; Andy Parker, drums.
1971—*UFO 1* (Beacon)   1974—(– Bolton; + several other guitarists before + Michael Schenker [b. Jan. 10, 1955, Savstedt, Ger.], gtr.) *Phenomenon* (Chrysalis)   1975—*Force It*   1976—(+ Danny Peyronel [b. 1953, Buenos Aires, Arg.], kybds.) *No Heavy Petting*   1977—(– Peyronel; + Paul Raymond, kybds.) *Lights Out*   1978—*Strangers in the Night*; *Obsessions* (– Schenker; – Raymond; + Paul Chapman, gtr.)   1979—*No Place to Run* 1980—(+ Neil Carter, gtr., kybds., voc.; – Chapman) 1981—*The Wild, the Willing, and the Innocent* 1982—*Mechanix* (– Way; + Paul Gray, bass) 1983—*Making Contact* (group disbands)   1985— (Group re-forms: Mogg; Raymond; Gray; + Jim Simpson, drums; + Atomic Tommy M., gtr.)   1986— (Group disbands)   1988—*The Best of the Rest* 1991—(Group re-forms: Mogg; Way; + Lawrence Archer, gtr.; + Clive Edwards, drums)   1992— *Essential UFO.*

This British hard-rock band has gone virtually unnoticed in its home country but gradually made inroads into the U.S. market. They were first a hit in France, Germany, and Japan; in 1972 they had a Japanese hit single with their version of Eddie Cochran's "C'mon Everybody," and they went there to record a live LP (*UFO Land in Tokyo*) released only in Japan.

In 1974 Michael Schenker came into the band from the German heavy-metal band Scorpions. Their next three albums, all produced by ex–Ten Years After Leo

Lyons for Chrysalis, saw them denting the American market, even as critics reviled them both at home and abroad. Schenker left in 1979 to form his own band, which has also released albums on Chrysalis. By early 1982, UFO had finally scored something of a hit single with "Back into My Life," and was opening shows for Ozzy Osbourne, but that success was marginal and short-lived. The group broke up in 1983. Since then it has re-formed and disbanded a couple more times.

Ugly Kid Joe

Formed 1990, Isla Vista, California
Whitfield Crane (b. Jan. 19, 1968, Palo Alto, Calif.), voc.; Klaus Eichstadt (b. Dec. 19, 1967, Redwood City, Calif.), gtr.; Roger Lahr, gtr.; Mark Davis (b. Apr. 22, 1964, Phoenix, Ariz.), drums.
1991—(+ Cordell Crockett [b. Jan. 21, 1965, Livermore, Calif.], bass) *As Ugly As They Wanna Be* EP (Mercury) (– Lahr; + Dave Fortman [b. July 11, 1967, Orlando, Fla.], gtr.)   1992—*America's Least Wanted* 1995—*Menace to Sobriety.*

A debut EP that sold platinum came as a surprise for Ugly Kid Joe as well as the band's record company: As Ugly As They Wanna Be hit #4 on the pop chart, fueled by the antilove anthem "Everything About You" (#9, 1992), also featured on the *Wayne's World* film soundtrack.

Ugly Kid Joe's boisterous hybrid of metal, funk, and thrash was born when singer Whitfield Crane and guitarist Klaus Eichstadt, childhood friends who had moved to Santa Barbara to attend school and hang out, decided to start a band. After some shuffling around, they settled on a lineup that included drummer Mark Davis, guitarist Roger Lahr, and bassist Cordell Crockett. Before Crockett joined, the group, which then called itself Suburban Alcoholic White Trash, chose its present moniker when booked to open for glam-rockers Pretty Boy Floyd. That gig was canceled, but Ugly Kid Joe continued to play local bars and made a demo that came to the attention of a Santa Barbara DJ. Impressed by the band's cheekily warped lyrics, the DJ contacted an entertainment lawyer, who in turn contacted Mercury Records. The Uglies followed their debut EP with an album, *America's Least Wanted,* which peaked at #29. *Menace to Sobriety,* a mix of speed metal and ballads, was released in mid-1995.

U.K.

Formed 1977, England
Eddie Jobson (b. Apr. 28, 1955, Billingham, Eng.), kybds., violin; John Wetton (b. July 12, 1949, Derby, Eng.), bass, voc.; Allan Holdsworth (b. Eng.), gtr.; Bill Bruford (b. May 17, 1949, Sevenoaks, Eng.), drums.
1978—*U.K.* (Polydor)   1979—(– Holdsworth; – Bruford; + Terry Bozzio [b. Dec. 27, 1950, San Francisco, Calif.], drums) *Danger Money.*

A British art-rock supergroup, U.K. drew together such respected veterans of the progressive-rock genre as Bill Bruford (Yes, King Crimson), John Wetton (King Crimson, Roxy Music, Uriah Heep), Eddie Jobson (Roxy Music), and Allan Holdsworth (Jon Hiseman's Tempest, Tony Williams' Lifetime, Gong, Soft Machine).

When U.K. was formed, Bruford and Wetton had last worked together in King Crimson; Holdsworth had played on Bruford's first solo album, which was released just before U.K.'s formation. U.K. became an immediate hit with progressive-rock fans, and their first album and U.S. tour did respectably saleswise.

As the band featured Jobson's keyboards most prominently, Holdsworth's fluid, jazzy guitar seemed like icing on the cake, and he and Bruford soon left to work together on more jazz-fusion projects. The focus shifted decisively to Jobson as the band became a trio with the addition of drummer Terry Bozzio, fresh from a stint with Frank Zappa's Mothers of Invention. U.K.'s music became simpler and heavier, as Bozzio was less inclined toward dauntingly tricky, cracklingly precise meters than Bruford was. After *Danger Money* had been on the LP charts for a while, U.K. disbanded. Jobson went on to tour with Jethro Tull [see entry]; Wetton cofounded another art-rock supergroup, Asia [see entry]; Bruford and Holdsworth continued to work together and separately. Bruford resurfaced in 1981 with the re-formed King Crimson [see entry], while Holdsworth came back in 1982 with a solo album and a brief low-level U.S. tour, and began working on an album produced by a fan, Eddie Van Halen. Bozzio cofounded Missing Persons [see entry].

James Blood Ulmer

Born February 2, 1942, St. Matthews, South Carolina
1978—*Tales of Captain Black* (Artists House)   **1980—*Are You Glad to Be in America?* (Rough Trade)   1981—*Free Lancing* (Columbia)   1982—*Black Rock*   1983—*Odyssey*   1984—*Part Time* (Rough Trade)   1986—*Live at the Caravan of Dreams* (Caravan of Dreams)   1987—*America—Do You Remember the Love?* (Blue Note)   1989—*Blues Allnight* (In & Out)   1991—*Black & Blue* (DIW)   1994—*Blues Preacher* (DIW/Columbia).**

In the early Eighties James Blood Ulmer was hailed as the most innovative guitarist of his day. Combining a background of ten years' hard road work on the R&B circuit and a grounding in "harmolodic" theory (harmony-movement-melodic) from its developer Ornette Coleman [see entry], Ulmer's sound has roots in blues, hard rock, and avant-garde jazz.

Before *Tales of Captain Black,* his first album as a leader, Ulmer served for four months as the first guitarist for Art Blakey's Jazz Messengers and recorded with jazz organist Larry Young (Khalid Yasin) and tenor saxophonist Joe Henderson; he also recorded with Coleman in a series of extensive though mostly unreleased sessions (Coleman appears on *Captain Black*).

During the Eighties Ulmer released more albums (*Are You Glad to Be in America?* introduced his Hendrix-style singing), backed by the cream of the younger jazz players, including drummer Ronald Shannon Jackson (who leads his own band, the Decoding Society) and well-regarded saxophonists Oliver Lake and David Murray. Ulmer's appeal is still largely to the jazz rather than rock audience, despite his being picked by Public Image Ltd. to open their first New York concert and being signed in the early Eighties to Columbia.

In the later part of the decade, Ulmer recorded for smaller labels (Rough Trade, Blue Note) and concentrated on live performance. In concert he usually appears as part of a highly amplified trio or quartet.

Ultravox

Formed 1973, London, England
John Foxx (b. Dennis Leigh, Chorley, Eng.), voc., synth.; Steve Shears, kybds., voc.; Billy Currie (b. Apr. 1, 1952), kybds., synth., violin; Chris Cross (b. Christopher Allen, July 14, 1952), bass; Warren Cann (b. May 20, 1952, Victoria, Can.), drums.
1977—*Ultravox!* (Island, U.K.)   1978—(– Shears; + Robin Simon, gtr.) *Systems of Romance* (Antilles)   1980—*Three into One* (Island) (– Foxx; – Simon; + Midge Ure [b. James Ure, Oct. 10, 1953, Glasgow, Scot.], gtr., voc.)   1981—*Vienna* (Chrysalis); *Rage in Eden*   1983—*Quartet*   1984—*Lament; The Collection*   1986—(– Cann; + Mark Brzezicki [b. June 21, 1957], drums)   1990—*U-Vox.*
John Foxx solo: 1981—*John Foxx* (Virgin, Can.).
Midge Ure solo: 1985—*The Gift* (Chrysalis)   1988—

Answers to Nothing 1991—*Pure* (RCA) 1993—*If I Was: The Very Best of Midge Ure* (Chrysalis). Billy Currie solo: 1988—*Transportation* (I.R.S./No Speak).

An important precursor of the early-Eighties British "electropop" movement, Ultravox was one of the first modern postpunk bands to dispense with guitars in favor of synthesizers. The band was formed by and around John Foxx, who had become interested in music while dabbling in synthesizers and tapes at school. Foxx went to London in 1974, began writing songs, and soon formed Ultravox, which had a minor British hit in 1977 with "My Sex" and made three critically acclaimed albums (the first produced by Brian Eno) before he left to pursue a solo career.

Ultravox regrouped with the addition of Midge Ure, formerly with Scottish popsters Slik and a late version of the ex–Sex Pistol Glen Matlock's Rich Kids. With a more dramatic lead singer and a slightly less foreboding sound, *Vienna* (#3 U.K., 1980) yielded a minor hit single in "Sleepwalk." Its title track hit #2 in the U.K. in 1981. Through its career, Ultravox was far more popular at home than in the U.S. In addition to *Vienna*, *Rage in Eden*, *Quartet*, *Lament*, *The Collection*, and *U-Vox* were all U.K. Top Ten albums. The group's U.K. hit singles include "All Stood Still" (#8 U.K., 1981), "Reap the Wild Wind" (#12, 1982), "Hymn" (#11, 1982), "Visions in Blue" (#15, 1983), "Lament" (#22, 1984), and "Love's Great Adventure" (#12, 1984).

Electropopper Gary Numan, among others, has often cited Ultravox's influence on his own work, and Ultravox's Billy Currie toured with Numan. *Three into One*, a compilation, followed *Systems of Romance* in 1980. *Rage in Eden* (like *Systems of Romance* and *Vienna*) was produced by Conny Plank. George Martin produced *Quartet*, which went to #61 and became Ultravox's highest-charting album in the U.S. It included the minor hit single "Reap the Wild Wind" (#71, 1983). None of their other albums, before or since, broke into the Top 100 here. The group produced *Lament*, which made little impression stateside. The group's last U.S. release of new material was *U-Vox*, which was released in the U.K. in 1986, a year before the band called it quits.

Several members have gone on to solo careers, most notably Midge Ure. He cowrote Band Aid's "Do They Know It's Christmas?" and is the musical director for the Prince's Trust concerts. His *Answers to Nothing* (#88, 1989) included "Dear God" (#95, 1989). Again, however, Ure's popularity in the U.S. gives no indication of his success in the U.K., where he had a number of charting singles, including two Top Tens: "No Regrets" (1982) and the U.K. #1 "If I Was" (1985). Billy Currie's first solo album featured guitarist Steve Howe. John Foxx released several solo albums in the Eighties, none of which was is-sued in the U.S. He has also charted a number of singles in England.

Uncle Tupelo
Formed 1987, Belleville, Illinois
Jeff Tweedy (b. Aug. 25, 1967, Belleville), voc., gtr., bass; Jay Farrar (b. Dec. 26, 1966, Belleville), voc., gtr.; Michael Heidorn, drums.
1990—*No Depression* (Rockville) 1991—*Still Feel Gone* 1992—*March 16–20, 1992* 1993—(– Heidorn; + Ken Coomer, drums; + John Stirratt, bass; + Max Johnson, banjo, fiddle, mandolin, steel gtr.) *Anodyne* (Sire).
Wilco, formed 1994 (Tweedy; Coomer; Stirratt; Johnson): 1995—*A.M.* (Reprise) (+ Jay Bennett, gtr.).
Son Volt, formed 1994 (Farrar; Heidorn; Dave Boquist, gtr., fiddle; Jim Boquist, bass): 1995—*Trace* (Warner Bros.).

Small-town Midwestern high school pals Jeff Tweedy and Jay Farrar began playing together in a band called the Primitives before forming Uncle Tupelo. Mixing noisy punk-influenced guitar and feedback with country-tinged melodic twang, Uncle Tupelo was one of the preeminent roots bands that arose in the Heartland in the wake of alternative rock.

After playing the local bar scene for three years, Uncle Tupelo signed with the indie label Rockville, which released *No Depression* in 1990; *Still Feel Gone* came out the next year, and national touring ensued. The group garnered a following via its compelling live shows, as well as among college radio listeners. The live-in-the-studio *March 16–20, 1992* included traditional C&W covers and was produced by R.E.M. guitarist Peter Buck. Uncle Tupelo then signed to Sire for the masterful *Anodyne*, which showcased Tweedy and Farrar's harmonies and put the focus on country rock, with multi-instrumentalist Max Johnson adding banjo, mandolin, fiddle, and steel guitar.

Tensions had been building between Tweedy and Farrar, however, and in June 1994 Farrar left the band. Under Tweedy's leadership, Uncle Tupelo transmogrified into Wilco. Its 1995 debut, *A.M.*, continued where *Anodyne* left off, winning critical acclaim and maintaining Uncle Tupelo's loyal following. Meanwhile, Farrar formed Son Volt with original Uncle Tupelo drummer Michael Heidorn, enlisting bassist Jim Boquist and guitarist/fiddler Dave Boquist. That group's first album, *Trace*, was released in late 1995.

The Undertones/Feargal Sharkey/That Petrol Emotion
Formed 1975, Derry, Northern Ireland
Feargal Sharkey (b. Aug. 13, 1958, Derry), voc.; John O'Neill (b. Aug. 26. 1957, Derry), gtr., voc.; Damian

The Undertones

O'Neill (b. Jan. 15, 1961, Belfast, N. Ire.), gtr., voc.;
Michael Bradley (b. Aug. 13, 1959, Derry), bass; Billy
Doherty (b. July 10, 1958, Larne, N. Ire.), drums.
1979—*The Undertones* (Sire)   1980—*Hypnotised*
1981—*Positive Touch* (EMI/Harvest)   1983—*The
Sin of Pride* (Ardeck, U.K.)   1986—*Cher o'Bowlies:
Pick of the Undertones* (EMI)   1994—*The Very Best
of the Undertones* (Rykodisc).
Feargal Sharkey solo: 1985—*Feargal Sharkey* (Vir-
gin/A&M)   1988—*Wish* (Virgin)   1991—*Songs from
the Mardi Gras* (Virgin, U.K.).
That Petrol Emotion, formed 1986 (Sean [a.k.a.
John] O'Neill; D. O'Neill; + Reámann O'Gormain
[b. June 7, 1961, Derry], gtr.; + Ciaran McLaughlin [b. Nov. 18, 1962, Derry], drums; + Steve Mack
[b. May 19, 1963, New York City, N.Y.], voc.):
1986—*Manic Pop Thrill* (Polydor)   1987—*Babble*
1988—*End of the Millennium Psychosis Blues*
(Virgin)   1990—*Chemicrazy* (– S. O'Neill)   1994—
Fireproof.

Northern Ireland's answer to the Buzzcocks of Manchester, England, the Undertones emerged from strife-torn
Northern Ireland with a rousing punk-pop sound—delivering teen angst and romance in fast, furious, catchy
songs, sung in a distinctive, high-pitched voice by Feargal Sharkey.

The Undertones' first single, "Teenage Kicks" (#31
U.K., 1978), was released on Belfast's Good Vibrations
label and received heavy radio play in England from influential DJ John Peel, who called it his favorite record of
all time. The band's critically acclaimed debut album
(#154, 1980; #13 U.K.,1979) had cover art based on the
Who's *My Generation* album. With *Hypnotised* (#6 U.K.,
1980) and *Positive Touch* (#17 U.K., 1981), the Undertones
slowed the pace and lowered the buzzsaw guitar noise;
though their well-crafted pop was praised by critics,
both albums failed to chart in the U.S. When the more

elaborately produced *Sin of Pride* (#43 U.K., 1983) failed
to produce a British hit single, the band broke up.

Sharkey formed the Assembly with keyboardist/com-
poser Vince Clarke (Depeche Mode, Yazoo) to record the
1983 U.K. hit single "Never Never" (#4), then launched a
solo career with the single "Listen to Your Father" (#23,
1984), on which he was backed by British two-tone band
Madness. He released three solo albums between 1985
and 1991, the first of which was produced by Dave Stewart of Eurythmics; his only U.S. charted single, "A Good
Heart" (#74, 1986), hit #1 in the U.K.

In 1986 John (now Sean) and Damian O'Neill (now
on bass) formed That Petrol Emotion—a critically well
received hard-rock band with some political lyrics and
funk and noise elements. The band had only moderate
chart success in the U.K. Sean O'Neill departed the band
in 1990.

Midge Ure: See Ultravox

Uriah Heep
Formed 1970, London, England
David Byron (b. Jan. 29, 1947, Essex, Eng.; d. Feb.
28, 1985), voc.; Mick Box (b. June 8, 1947, London),
gtr.; Ken Hensley (b. Aug. 24, 1945, Eng.), kybds.,
voc.; Paul Newton, bass; Alex Napier, drums.
1970—*Very 'eavy, Very 'umble* (Mercury)   1971—
(– Napier; + Keith Baker, drums) *Salisbury*
(– Baker; + Lee Kerslake, drums; + Mark Clarke
[b. July 25, 1950, Liverpool, Eng.], bass); *Look at
Yourself*   1972—(– Newton; – Clarke; + Gary Thain
[d. Mar. 19, 1976], bass) *Demons and Wizards*; *The
Magician's Birthday*   1973—*Live* (Warner Bros.);
Sweet Freedom   1974—*Wonderworld*   1975—
(– Thain; + John Wetton [b. July 12, 1949, Derby,
Eng.], bass, voc.) *Return to Fantasy*; *The Best of
Uriah Heep* (Mercury)   1976—*High and Mighty*
(Warner Bros.) (– Byron; – Wetton; + John Lawton,
voc.; + Trevor Bolder, bass)   1977—*Fire Fly*; *Inno-
cent Victim*   1978—*Fallen Angel* (– Lawton;
+ John Sloman, voc.; – Kerslake; + Chris Slade
[b. Oct. 30, 1946, drums)   1980—*Conquest* (– Hens-
ley; + Greg Dechert, kybds.)   1981—(Group dis-
bands; group re-forms: Box; Kerslake; + Bob
Daisley, bass; + Pete Goalby, voc.; + John Sinclair,
kybds.)   1982—*Abominog*   1983—*Head First*
1985—*Equator* (CBS) (– Daisley; + Bolder)   1988—
Live in Moscow (– Goalby; + Bernie Shaw, voc.;
– Sinclair; + Phil Lanzon, kybds., voc.); *Legacy*
1989—*Raging Silence*   1991—*Different World*.

"If this group makes it, I'll have to commit suicide,"
wrote one rock critic, expressing the critical consensus
on Uriah Heep. This hard-rocking, hard-working group
did indeed make it for much of the Seventies with a

blend of heavy metal and art rock that easily could have been the model for Spinal Tap.

The band's roots were in a London outfit called the Stalkers, which Mick Box joined in 1964. They were later joined by David Byron, who had sung on anonymous hit-cover albums alongside Elton John. Box and Byron then formed Spice with bassist Paul Newton of the Gods (which also included Ken Hensley, formerly with Kit and the Saracens and the Jimmy Brown Sound, and Mick Taylor, the latter going on to John Mayall and the Rolling Stones). Hensley worked briefly with Cliff Bennett's Toe Fat band, then joined Spice, who renamed themselves Uriah Heep after Charles Dickens' conniving paragon of "humility." They cut their hard-rock debut LP, then landed a regular drummer in Keith Baker.

The debut and *Salisbury* (#103, 1971), for which the band was augmented by an orchestra on some cuts, found only minor European success, though Uriah Heep was already an established concert attraction in Britain. *Look at Yourself* (#93, 1971) made the band a success in both the U.S. and the U.K., and they consolidated their status with *Demons and Wizards* (#23, 1972), *The Magician's Birthday* (#31, 1972), *Live* (#37, 1973), and *Sweet Freedom* (#33, 1973), which all went gold in Britain and America. Uriah Heep also made the singles chart with "Easy Livin'" (#39, 1972), "Sweet Lorraine" (#91, 1973), "Blind Eye" (#97, 1973), and "Stealin'" (#91, 1973).

In 1974 dissent plagued the band. Bassist Gary Thain suffered a near-fatal electric shock onstage in Dallas, Texas, and later complained that the band was inconsiderate of his physical well-being. Personal problems and drug use furthered Thain's conflicts with the rest of the band, and in early 1975 he was "invited" to leave; he died of a drug overdose a year later. He was replaced by John Wetton, formerly of Family and King Crimson, who stayed with the band for two albums before further internal squabbles resulted in the firing of David Byron in July 1976. Wetton soon left to record a solo album and eventually joined art-rock supergroups U.K. and Asia.

Hensley in the meantime had recorded two solo albums, 1973's *Proud Words on a Dusty Shelf* and 1975's *Eager to Please*. With new vocalist John Lawton and bassist Trevor Bolder, from David Bowie's Spiders from Mars band, Uriah Heep continued plowing its heavy-metal furrow for a few more albums. They were a favorite opening act and toured with Jethro Tull, Kiss, Rush, Foreigner, and other top-line arena rockers.

Through the years Uriah Heep has sustained many personnel changes. Among its former members are Chris Slade (now drummer for AC/DC), and Lee Kerslake and Bob Daisley (both members of Ozzy Osbourne's Blizzard of Ozz). Since 1986 the lineup has been stable. The group continues to tour and record, including ten sold-out shows in Moscow.

U.T.F.O.

Formed 1982, Brooklyn, New York
Kangol (b. Shawn Fequiere, Aug. 10, 1966, Brooklyn), voc.; Dr. Ice (b. Fred Reeves, Mar. 2, 1966, Brooklyn), voc.; Educated Rapper (b. Jeffrey Campbell, July 4, 1963, Eng.), voc.; Mix-master Ice (b. Maurice Bailey, Apr. 22, 1965, Brooklyn), DJ.
1985—*U.T.F.O.* (Select)   1986—*Skeezer Pleezer*   1987—*Lethal*   1989—*Doin' It!*   1990—*Bag It and Bone It* (Jive/RCA).

U.T.F.O. touched a nerve when they released their second rap single, "Roxanne, Roxanne" (#10 R&B, 1985), a dis of a girl who dared to refuse their advances. The hit, produced like all U.T.F.O. records by Full Force, set off more than 20 response singles, starting with Roxanne Shanté's [see entry] "Roxanne's Revenge" and leading to U.T.F.O.'s own answer, "The Real Roxanne," featuring rapper Joanne Martinez.

Untouchable Force Organization got its first break when they won a break-dancing contest in 1983 at Radio City Music Hall. The Flatbush boys subsequently toured Europe with Whodini (Dr. Ice's older brother is a member of that group), appeared on *The Phil Donahue Show*, and performed at a birthday party for Dustin Hoffman's daughter. *U.T.F.O.* featured both "Roxanne"s plus "Leader of the Pack" (#32 R&B, 1985) and "Fairytale Lover" (#36 R&B, 1985). The group grew musically on *Skeezer Pleezer*, although the album produced no hits, and Educated Rapper, who was battling a drug addiction, didn't perform on it. *Lethal* features a collaboration with thrash-metal band Anthrax and U.T.F.O.'s first foray into gangsta rap. After 1990's *Bag It and Bone It* bombed, U.T.F.O. split up. Kangol has produced such artists as Gerardo and Lisa Lisa, and Dr. Ice released a solo album in 1989.

Utopia: See Todd Rundgren

U2

Formed 1978, Dublin, Ireland
Bono Vox (b. Paul Hewson, May 10, 1960, Dublin), voc., gtr.; The Edge (b. David Evans, Aug. 8, 1961, Barking, Eng.), gtr., kybds., voc.; Adam Clayton (b. Mar. 13, 1960, Oxford, Eng.), bass; Larry Mullen Jr. (b. Oct. 31, 1961, Dublin), drums.
1980—*Boy* (Island)   1981—*October*   1983—*War*; *Under a Blood Red Sky* EP   1984—*The Unforgettable Fire*   1985—*Wide Awake in America* EP   1987—*The Joshua Tree*   1988—*Rattle and Hum*   1991—*Achtung Baby*   1993—*Zooropa*.

Over the course of the Eighties U2 became the most widely followed rock band in the world. The Irish rockers were influenced by punk's raw energy, but they immedi-

U2: The Edge, Larry Mullen, Bono, Adam Clayton

ately distinguished themselves from their postpunk peers with a huge, soaring sound—centered on Dave "the Edge" Evans' reverb-laden guitar playing and Paul "Bono" Hewson's sensuous vocals—and songs that tackled social and spiritual matters with an earnest, tender urgency. U2 shunned the sort of ironic expression and electronic gimmickry that were considered hip in the Eighties—until the Nineties, that is, when the band began drawing on such elements to reinvigorate and broaden its sound. U2 has maintained not only its massive popularity, but also its status as one of the most adventurous and groundbreaking acts in pop music.

The band members began rehearsing together while students at Dublin's Mount Temple High School. None was technically proficient at the beginning, but their lack of expertise mothered invention. The Edge's distinctive chordal style, for instance, stemmed largely from the guitarist's inability to play complicated leads, while bassist Adam Clayton and drummer Larry Mullen Jr. provided a rhythm section that was mostly pummeling ardor. The novice musicians quickly developed a following in Ireland and found a manager, Paul McGuinness, who has remained with them. They recorded independently before signing to Island Records in 1980.

U2's 1980 debut album, Boy, was produced by Steve Lillywhite. On it, the group earnestly explored adolescent hopes and terrors, rejecting hard rock's earthy egotism and punk's nihilism. Bono, U2's lyricist, was a practicing Christian, as were the Edge and Mullen; and on a second LP, called October (a 1981 Lillywhite production), the singer incorporated imagery evoking their faith. Boy and October generated the singles "I Will Fol-

low" and "Gloria," which got some airplay in the U.S.; both videos were heavily featured on MTV. An American club tour generated further interest, thanks to U2's extremely compelling live performances.

War cemented U2's reputation as a politically conscious band; among its themes were "the troubles" in Northern Ireland, addressed on the single "Sunday Bloody Sunday." Another single, "New Year's Day," went to #11 in England and #53 in the U.S., while War topped the British chart and hit #12 stateside. The group commemorated its 1983 tour with the live EP Under a Blood Red Sky, recorded at Red Rocks Amphitheatre in Colorado.

U2's next studio album, The Unforgettable Fire, was the first of several fruitful collaborations with producers Brian Eno and Daniel Lanois. The album generated the group's first American Top Forty single, an ode to American civil rights leader Martin Luther King Jr., called "(Pride) In the Name of Love" (#33, 1984). The album hit #12 in the U.S., and the Irishmen supported it by headlining arenas around the world. In 1985 U2 was proclaimed "band of the Eighties" by ROLLING STONE and made a historic appearance at Live Aid. The following year, the group joined Sting, Peter Gabriel, Lou Reed, and others for the Conspiracy of Hope Tour benefiting Amnesty International.

U2 entered the pop stratosphere with The Joshua Tree, a critical and commercial smash that topped the albums chart that year and spawned the #1 hits "With or Without You" and "I Still Haven't Found What I'm Looking For," as well as "Where the Streets Have No Name" (#13, 1987). The LP, which was produced by Eno and Lanois, won the group two Grammys, for Album of the Year and Best Rock Performance. In 1988 U2 wrapped up a triumphant worldwide tour by releasing Rattle and Hum, a double album that combined live tracks with new material and featured guest appearances by Bob Dylan and B. B. King. Rattle and Hum seemed bombastic to some critics; an accompanying film documentary also garnered mixed reviews. The LP nonetheless shot to #1 and produced a #3 single, "Desire" (1988).

In 1990 U2 covered Cole Porter's "Night and Day" for Red Hot + Blue, a compilation album benefiting AIDS research. The band's next LP, Achtung Baby, reached #1 and drew rave reviews. The LP marked a stylistic departure, featuring more metallic textures, funkier beats, and intimate, world-weary love songs. Hit singles included "Mysterious Ways" (#9, 1992), "One" (#10, 1992), "Even Better Than the Real Thing" (#32, 1992), and "Who's Gonna Ride Your Wild Horses" (#35, 1992). Another track, "Until the End of the World," was featured in Wim Wenders' 1991 film of the same name. Lanois, who produced Baby with support from Eno and Lillywhite, won a Grammy for his work.

In 1992 U2 embarked on its Zoo TV Tour, a flashy

Grammy Awards

U2

1987 Album of the Year: *The Joshua Tree* (with Daniel Lanois and Brian Eno)
1987 Best Rock Performance by a Duo or Group with Vocal: *The Joshua Tree*
1988 Best Rock Performance by a Duo or Group with Vocal: "Desire"
1988 Best Performance Music Video: "Where the Streets Have No Name" (with others)
1992 Best Rock Performance by a Duo or Group with Vocal: *Achtung Baby*
1993 Best Alternative Music Album: *Zooropa*
1994 Best Music Video, Long Form: *Zoo TV—Live from Sydney*

multimedia extravaganza that contrasted with the rugged simplicity of its previous shows. Bono adopted a series of wry guises—the leather-and-shades-sporting Fly, the demonic MacPhisto—that he'd use for encores and, in the Fly's case, press appearances. In 1993, as the tour wound down, the band reentered the studio and made *Zooropa,* a quirky, techno-drunk affair coproduced by Eno, the Edge, and engineer Flood. The album reached #1, but yielded only the minor hit "Stay (Faraway, So Close)" (#61, 1993), which was also on the soundtrack to Wenders' 1993 movie *Faraway, So Close.* Johnny Cash sang lead on the track "The Wanderer." In 1993 U2 renewed its contract with Island for an estimated $170 million. U2's contribution to 1995's *Batman Forever* soundtrack, "Hold Me, Thrill Me, Kiss Me, Kill Me," was a Top Twenty hit. As of mid-1995, the band was reportedly recording two albums simultaneously—a collaboration with Brian Eno of mostly instrumental music and one that the band described as a "rock & roll album."

Steve Vai

Born June 6, 1960, Carle Place, New York
1984—*Flex-Able* (Akashic); *Flex-Able Leftovers*
(Relativity)   1990—*Passion and Warfare*   1993—
***Sex & Religion*   1995—*Alien Love Secrets*.**

Guitarist Steve Vai has had a divided career: While his solo work has been hailed for its nuanced melding of jazz, rock, funk, and classical influences, he also has appeared as a hard-rock guitarslinger for hire on albums by Frank Zappa, David Lee Roth, and Whitesnake.

Like countless other Long Island kids, the 13-year-old Vai picked up a guitar and formed a band. Unlike most, however, he had as a neighbor and guitar teacher Joe Satriani [see entry]. In 1979, when Vai was just 18, Frank Zappa asked him to play lead guitar in his band. Vai appears on numerous Zappa recordings, including *Tinseltown Rebellion* (1981), *You Are What You Is* (1981), *Thing-Fish* (1984), *Them or Us* (1986), and several *Shut Up 'n Play Yer Guitar* albums, among others.

In 1984 Vai recorded his first solo album, *Flex-Able*, in his home studio. Picked up by Relativity, the record sold close to 250,000 copies without much publicity or airplay. *Flex-Able Leftovers* followed later that same year.

After a short stint in 1985 replacing Yngwie Malmsteen in Alcatrazz, Vai signed on as David Lee Roth's guitar player in 1986 and stayed with him for three years

and for two albums: *Eat 'Em and Smile* (1986) and *Skyscraper* (1987). He joined Whitesnake for one album, *Slip of the Tongue* (1989). In 1990 he released his third solo album, *Passion and Warfare* (#18). Nineteen-ninety-three's *Sex & Religion* (#48) signaled a move toward pop, with the addition of vocals and a band that included ex–Missing Persons drummer Terry Bozzio.

Ritchie Valens

Born Richard Stephen Valenzuela, May 13, 1941, Pacoima, California; died February 3, 1959, Clear Lake, Iowa
1959—*Ritchie Valens* (Del-Fi)   1960—*Ritchie Valens in Concert at Pacoima Jr. High*   1981—*The History of Ritchie Valens* (Del-Fi/Rhino)   1986—*The Best of Ritchie Valens*.

The first of several Latin rockers of the late Fifties and early Sixties (others were Chan Romero, Chris Montez, Eddie Quinteros, Sunny and the Sunglows, and Cannibal and the Headhunters), Ritchie Valens started playing guitar as a child, and at Pacoima High (near Los Angeles) he formed his own band, the Silhouettes.

In the spring of 1958 Valens signed with Del-Fi Records and later that year had a Top Fifty hit with "Come On, Let's Go," later covered by early-Sixties British teen idol Tommy Steele. In early 1959 Valens hit #2 on the chart with his two-sided single "Donna" and

"La Bamba," the latter based on a traditional Mexican wedding song. Valens appeared on nationwide TV and in package tours. On one such tour the stars' plane crashed in a snowstorm, killing Valens, Buddy Holly, and the Big Bopper. Valens was only 17. His life story was the basis of the 1987 hit film *La Bamba,* for which Los Lobos performed his music.

Van der Graaf Generator/ Peter Hammill

Formed 1967, Manchester, England
Peter Hammill (b. Nov. 5, 1948, London, Eng.), gtr., kybds., voc.; Hugh Banton, kybds.; Chris Judge Smith, drums; Keith Ellis, bass; Guy Evans, drums.
1968—(- Smith) *The Aerosol Grey Machine* (Mercury)   1969—(- Ellis; + Nic Potter, bass; + David Jackson, sax) *The Least We Can Do Is Wave* (Charisma)   1970—*H to He Who Am the Only One*   1971—(- Potter) *Pawn Hearts*   1973—*The Long Hello*   1975—*Godbluff*   1976—*Still Life; World Record*   1977—*The Quiet Zone*   1978—(+ Potter; + Graham Smith, violin) *Vital/Live.*
Peter Hammill solo: 1972—*Fools Mate* (Charisma); *Chameleon in the Shadows of Night*   1974—*The Silent Corner and the Empty Stage; In Camera*   1975—*Nadir's Big Chance* (as Rikki Nadir)   1977—*Over*   1978—*The Future Now*   1979—*PH 7*   1980—*A Black Box* (Blue Plate)   1981—*Sitting Targets*   1984—*Love Songs.*

One of the few top-rank British art-rock bands that never achieved more than cult success in America, Van der Graaf Generator constructed stately sepulchers of Gothic sound with Hugh Banton's churchy Hammond organ and Guy Evans' virtuosic drumming framing the intensely existential verse and tortured vocals of Peter Hammill. Hammill's relentlessly bleak visions were later cited by some members (e.g., Johnny Rotten) of Britain's late-Seventies punk-rock movement as their inspiration, and in fact Hammill created a "Rikki Nadir" persona for a solo album that presaged punk.

Van der Graaf Generator formed and split up and reformed several times, usually with the same core personnel, and played only one U.S. concert, in 1976 in New York. Hammill, however, has conducted several solo American tours, selling out club dates.

The band first came together at Manchester University in 1967. Founding member Chris Judge Smith gave the band its name (taken from a device that creates static electricity) but soon left, and the band broke up in late 1968. Hammill recorded material with the Van der Graaf core intended as a solo album, but when the band came back together before its release, *The Aerosol Grey Machine* was issued under Van der Graaf's aegis. Robert Fripp of King Crimson sat in on *H to He.* After the elabo-

rate *Pawn Hearts,* the band broke up again for three years, during which time Hammill pursued his solo career in earnest. Fripp sat in on *Fools Mate* (Hammill returned the favor on Fripp's *Exposure*), ex-Spirit guitarist Randy California on *Silent Corner.*

In 1975, upon the release of the protopunk *Nadir's Big Chance,* Van der Graaf re-formed again, with a sound that was tighter and more powerful than before. In 1978 Van der Graaf apparently broke up for keeps. Hammill has continued to record solo efforts, remaining a significant cult phenomenon; he toured South America with Guy Evans in 1993.

Luther Vandross

Born April 20, 1951, New York City, New York
1981—*Never Too Much* (Epic)   1982—*Forever, for Always, for Love*   1983—*Busy Body*   1985—*The Night I Fell in Love*   1986—*Give Me the Reason*   1988—*Any Love*   1989—*The Best of Luther Vandross, the Best of Love*   1991—*Power of Love*   1993—*Never Let Me Go* (LV/Epic)   1994—*Songs.*

Luther Vandross emerged from jingles and background singing to become one of the preeminent black male vocalists of the era. With the exception of his solo debut album, all of his LPs have been certified platinum or double platinum.

Vandross, whose older sister Patricia was a member of the doo-wop group the Crests, began playing piano at age three. In 1972 his song "Everybody Rejoice (A Brand New Day)" was included in the Broadway musical *The Wiz.* Throughout the Seventies, Vandross sang on numerous commercials (from ads for the U.S. Army to local Burger Kings). His singing was distinguished by his impeccable phrasing and vocal control. He first came to the attention of the pop world after his friend guitarist Carlos Alomar introduced him to David Bowie. Vandross ended up writing ("Fascination") and singing on David Bowie's *Young Americans* (1975) LP; he later toured with Bowie, then recorded and toured with Bette Midler (he appeared on her *Songs for the New Depression*).

He quickly became one of the busiest backing vocalists and arrangers in the business, recording with Ringo Starr, Carly Simon, Donna Summer, Barbra Streisand, and Chaka Khan, among others. During this time Vandross cut two little-noted albums under the name Luther, and sang on "Dance, Dance, Dance" and "Everybody Dance" for Chic. He continued his highly lucrative jingles career. Following his lead vocal appearances on "Searchin'" and "Glow of Love" (from Change's hit album *Glow of Love*), several labels expressed interest in signing Vandross as a solo act. With the encouragement of his friend Roberta Flack, he invested $25,000 of his own money in two demos: "Never Too Much" and "A House Is Not a Home."

In 1981 he signed with Epic Records, which, on the

basis of his demos, granted him full creative control, allowing him to write and produce. *Never Too Much* was a #1 R&B album and the title cut was a #1 R&B single (#33 pop); the album went platinum. Since then, each of his albums (with the exception of the #2 R&B *The Best of* and the platinum *Never Let Me Go;* #6 pop, #3 R&B) have topped the R&B albums chart. *Any Love* and *Power of Love* were also Top Ten pop albums. His other hit singles include "Bad Boy/Having a Party" (#3 R&B, 1982), "I'll Let You Slide" (#9 R&B, 1983), "Superstar/Until You Come Back to Me (That's What I'm Gonna Do)" (#5 R&B, 1984), "'Til My Baby Comes Home" (#4 R&B, 1985), "It's Over Now" (#4 R&B, 1985), "Give Me the Reason" (#3 R&B, 1986), "Stop to Love" (#1 R&B, 1986), a duet with Gregory Hines entitled "There's Nothing Better Than Love" (#1 R&B, 1987), "I Really Didn't Mean It" (#6 R&B, 1987), "Any Love" (#1 R&B, 1988), "She Won't Talk to Me" (#3 R&B, 1988), "For You to Love" (#3 R&B, 1989), "Here and Now" (#6 pop, #1 R&B, 1989), "Treat You Right" (#5 R&B, 1990), "Power of Love/Love Power" (#4 pop, #1 R&B, 1991), "Don't Wanna Be a Fool" (#9 pop, #4 R&B, 1991), "The Rush" (#6 R&B, 1991), a duet with Janet Jackson entitled "The Best Things in Life Are Free" (#10 pop, #1 R&B, 1992), "Sometimes It's Only Love" (#9 R&B, 1992), "Little Miracles (Happen Every Day)" (#62 pop, #10 R&B, 1993), "Heaven Knows" (#94 pop, #24 R&B, 1993), and "Never Let Me Go" (#31 R&B, 1993).

Throughout his career, he has continued to write and produce for other artists. He produced Aretha Franklin's *Jump to It* in 1982; the title cut and the album went to #1 on the R&B chart. He also produced Franklin's 1983 *Get It Right;* Cheryl Lynn's 1982 LP *Instant Love,* which contained their duet "If This World Were Mine," a cover of a Marvin Gaye–Tammi Terrell hit; and records for Dionne Warwick, Teddy Pendergrass, and Whitney Houston. In 1993 he made his motion picture debut in Robert Townsend's *Meteor Man.* His 1994 album *Songs* (#5 pop, #2 R&B) included his hit duet with Mariah Carey, "Endless Love," (#2, 1994).

Vangelis

Born Evangalos Odyssey Papathanassiou, March 29, 1943, Valos, Greece
1971—*The Dragon* (Charly, U.K.)   1973—*L'Apocalypse des Animeaux* (Polydor)   1974—*Earth* (Vertigo, U.K.)   1975—*Heaven and Hell* (RCA)
1976—*Albedo .39*   1977—*Spiral*   1978—*Beaubourg; Hypothesis* (Affinity); *Best of Vangelis* (RCA)   1979—*China* (Polydor)   1980—*See You Later*   1981—*The Friends of Mr. Cairo; Chariots of Fire* soundtrack   1982—*Blade Runner* soundtrack
1984—*The Bounty* soundtrack   1985—*Mask* soundtrack   1987—*Opera Sauvage; Ignacio* (Barclay)
1988—*Direct* (Arista)   1989—*Themes* (Polydor)

1991—*The City* (Atlantic)   1993—*Blade Runner* original music for soundtrack.
With Aphrodite's Child: 1968—*End of the World/Rain and Tears* (Vertigo, U.K.)   1969—*It's Five O'Clock*   1970—*Aphrodite's Child* (Mercury)   1972—*666—Apocalypse of John* (Vertigo, U.K.)   1975—*Best of Aphrodite's Child* (Mercury).
Jon and Vangelis: See Yes entry.

Vangelis was in France at the time of the 1968 student riots; unable to return to Greece, he formed a band with Demis Roussos. That band, Aphrodite's Child, released a series of unremarkable progressive-rock albums and had one European hit single with "Rain and Tears." Roussos went on to become an international MOR singing star. Vangelis turned to a solo career and began composing film scores with *L'Apocalypse des Animeaux.*

In 1974 Vangelis was rumored to be the replacement for Yes' departed keyboard whiz Rick Wakeman. Though he never did join Yes, Vangelis formed a lasting association with Yes singer Jon Anderson, and has worked with him on his solo projects. Vangelis also made albums on his own, such as *Beaubourg,* which were pastiches of electronic music and pop and jazz. Under the name Jon and Vangelis, he and Anderson had four U.K. chart entries, including two Top Ten hits: "I Hear You Now" (1980) and "I'll Find My Way Home" (1981).

In 1982 Vangelis finally made his commercial breakthrough with the score to the film *Chariots of Fire.* The movie theme was on the singles chart for 15 weeks and went as high as #6, while the score won an Oscar. The *Chariots* theme also inspired numerous sound-alikes for American TV commercials.

Vangelis has since scored a number of motion pictures, including *Blade Runner* (1982), *Missing* (1982), *The Bounty* (1984), *Bitter Moon* (1994), and *1492: Conquest of Paradise* (1992). He has also composed music for three Jacques Cousteau documentaries. In 1992 he received the Chevalier Order of Arts and Letters, one of France's most important artistic honors. The 1993 release of *Blade Runner* included never-before-released cuts featuring singers Mary Hopkin, Demis Roussos, and Don Percival.

Van Halen/David Lee Roth

Formed 1974, Pasadena, California
David Lee Roth (b. Oct. 10, 1955, Bloomington, Ind.), voc.; Edward Van Halen (b. Jan. 26, 1955, Nijmegen, Neth.), gtr., voc.; Alex Van Halen (b. May 8, 1953, Nijmegen), drums; Michael Anthony (b. June 20, 1955, Chicago, Ill.), bass.
1978—*Van Halen* (Warner Bros.)   1979—*Van Halen II*   1980—*Women and Children First*   1981—*Fair Warning*   1982—*Diver Down*   1984—*1984*   1985—(– Roth; + Sammy Hagar [b. Oct. 13, 1947, Monterey, Calif.], voc.)   1986—*5150*   1988—*OU812*   1991—

Van Halen: Alex Van Halen, David Lee Roth, Eddie
Van Halen, Michael Anthony

For Unlawful Carnal Knowledge 1993—*Van Halen,*
Live: Right Here, Right Now 1995—*Balance.*
David Lee Roth solo: 1985—*Crazy from the Heat* EP
(Warner Bros.) 1986—*Eat 'Em and Smile* 1987—
Skyscraper 1991—*A Little Ain't Enough* 1994—
Your Filthy Little Mouth (Reprise).
Sammy Hagar solo: See entry.

Since their national debut in 1978, Van Halen have become one of the most popular American heavy-metal
bands. Initially fronted by the flamboyant and ever-
quotable David Lee Roth and always featuring the highly
original guitar pyrotechnics of Eddie Van Halen, Van
Halen garnered a loyal mass following that has held fast
through Roth's 1985 departure.

The Van Halen brothers' father Jan was a freelance
saxophone and clarinet player who performed styles
ranging from big band to classical in the Netherlands.
The family arrived in Pasadena "with 15 dollars and a
piano," as Eddie once said, in 1967, and Jan washed
dishes, then played in wedding bands to support the
family. Beginning around age six both Eddie and Alex received piano lessons and extensive classical music
training, but once in America they discovered rock & roll.
Eddie learned to play drums, and Alex learned to play
guitar; eventually they traded instruments and started a
band called Mammoth. Roth, the even-then outgoing
and outrageous scion of a wealthy family and lead singer

of a rival band, Redball Jet, joined them. Michael Anthony, the bassist and lead singer of another group,
Snake, came aboard shortly thereafter. After learning that
there was already another group claiming the name
Mammoth, the group considered calling themselves Rat
Salade before deciding on Van Halen (which for many
years some believed was Roth's name).

Van Halen played the Pasadena/Santa Barbara bar
circuit for over three years. Their sets initially consisted
primarily of cover material ranging from disco to pop, but
they eventually introduced original songs and were soon
one of the most popular groups in California, regulars at
the Sunset Strip hard-rock club Gazzari's, and an opening act for Santana, Nils Lofgren, UFO, and other established acts. In 1977 Kiss' Gene Simmons spotted them in
L.A.'s Starwood club and financed a demo tape. After
seeing the group and hearing Simmons' recommendation, Warner Bros. Records' Mo Ostin and staff producer
Ted Templeman signed them. Their self-titled debut
album, which hit #19 and eventually sold over six million
copies, would prove to be the lowest-charting album of
their career to date. The debut single, a pile-driving cover
of the Kinks' 1964 hit "You Really Got Me," hit #36. The
followup, "Runnin' with the Devil," hit #84.

Roth's swaggering good looks and extroverted persona, not to mention pithy statements on the rock & roll
lifestyle he claimed then to espouse, assured press coverage. But while the mainstream media focused on Roth,
musicians and fans were riveted by Eddie Van Halen's
guitar mastery and an array of unorthodox techniques
that he developed as he taught himself to play: hammer-
ons, pull-offs, two-hand tapping, and any combination
thereof to produce his unique sound. In addition, the
guitarist was also known to build and/or meticulously
customize his instruments, using everything from sandpaper to chainsaws, to alter the timbre of his instrument
and achieve a distinct sound. Long before the group ever
recorded, Eddie became a legend among local guitarists
eager to learn the secret of his sound. Like countless guitarists before him, from Robert Johnson to Eric Clapton,
Eddie began performing with his back to the audience to
guard his technique.

Van Halen II, released as new wave began coming to
the fore, continued in the group's straight-rock style and
featured their first Top Twenty single, "Dance the Night
Away." *Women and Children First* spun off the singles
"Beautiful Girls" and "And the Cradle Will Rock," neither
of which hit, but the latter, a metal showcase, typified the
band's dense, loud, crunching style. In 1979 they
launched their second world tour, their first as a headliner. Early on, the band embraced its larger-than-life
image, and tour incidents, ranging from Roth's breaking
his nose while executing a jump to the band trashing a
dressing room after a promoter failed to comply with
their tongue-in-cheek contractual stipulation that the

backstage candy dish contain no brown M&Ms. *Fair Warning,* another multiplatinum effort, followed. *Diver Down,* which included a hit cover of Roy Orbison's "(Oh) Pretty Woman" (#12, 1982) and a Top Forty version of Martha and the Vandellas' "Dancing in the Street," became their highest-charting album to that point, peaking at #3. In 1981 Eddie married actress Valerie Bertinelli; in 1991 their son, Wolfgang, was born. In 1990 Eddie entered treatment for alcoholism.

The group's biggest album, however, was *1984,* a #2 album that continued the #1 hit "Jump" (on which Eddie played a synthesizer) as well as "I'll Wait" (#13, 1984), "Panama" (#13, 1984), and "Hot for Teacher" (#56, 1984), all songs supported by popular videos that showcased both Roth's alternately swaggering and clownish persona and Eddie's (and the rest of the group's) flashy musicianship. Shortly before its release, Eddie Van Halen had composed and played the guitar solo on Michael Jackson's "Beat It," a few bars of heavy metal that many observers believed helped the video land a spot on MTV's playlist. The loquacious Roth and the soft-spoken Eddie had long been considered one of rock's oddest couples. When in 1985 Roth released his four-song EP, *Crazy from the Heat,* and it spun off two hit singles, a cover of the Beach Boys' "California Girls" (#3, 1985) and Louis Prima's "Just a Gigolo/I Ain't Got Nobody" (#12, 1985), a breakup was widely rumored. The videos for the two songs were hugely popular, and for a time Roth was said to be working on a full-length film. When Roth delayed recording for Van Halen's seventh album, he and the three other members split. That June Sammy Hagar was named Roth's replacement.

The Hagar era began auspiciously, with the group's next three multiplatinum albums—*5150, OU812,* and *For Unlawful Carnal Knowledge* (or "F.U.C.K.," as the press release abbreviates it), hit #1. Among the hit singles from these records were "Why Can't This Be Love" (#3, 1986), "Dreams" (#22, 1986), "Love Walks In" (#22, 1986), "When It's Love" (#5, 1988), "Finish What You Started" (#13, 1988), and "Feels So Good" (#35, 1989). They headlined the Monsters of Rock Tour in 1988, and in 1991 bought the Cabo Wabo Cantina, a Cabo San Lucas, Mexico, restaurant and bar. The innovative, text-oriented 1992 video for "Right Now" didn't boost the single beyond #55, but it did win MTV's Best Video of the Year award and provided the theme for a round of Pepsi commercials shortly thereafter. Nineteen-ninety-three saw the release of their first live album, *Van Halen Live: Right Here, Right Now* (#5, 1993). *Balance* (#1, 1995) sold double-platinum nearly immediately upon release.

Throughout his tenure with Van Halen, Hagar has continued to release solo albums [see entry]. Diamond David Lee Roth's solo career yielded three platinum albums, with *Eat 'Em and Smile* and *Skyscraper* both Top Ten, featuring the hits "Yankee Rose" (#16, 1986, from

Eat) and "Just Like Paradise" (#6, 1988, from *Skyscraper*). The band for *Eat 'Em* included bassist Billy Sheehan, guitarist Steve Vai, and drummer Greg Bissonette. This lineup remained fairly steady for *Skyscraper,* but Sheehan left, and in 1989 Vai resumed his solo career. *A Little Ain't Enough,* a critical and commercial disappointment despite its Top Twenty showing, had no hit singles. In 1991 Roth fired his band and moved to New York City, where in April 1993 he was arrested while purchasing ten dollars' worth of marijuana in Washington Square Park (he received a year's probation). His most recent album, *Your Filthy Little Mouth,* continued the decline. Even commenting on his current low commercial standing, Roth remained quotable as ever and is planning to write an autobiography.

Vanilla Fudge

Formed 1966, New York City, New York
Vince Martell (b. Nov. 11, 1945, Bronx, N.Y.), gtr., voc.; Mark Stein (b. Mar. 1947, Bayonne, N.J.), kybds., voc.; Tim Bogert (b. Aug. 1944, New York City), bass, voc.; Carmine Appice (b. Dec. 15, 1946, Staten Island, N.Y.), drums, voc.
1967—*The Vanilla Fudge* (Atlantic)   1968—*The Beat Goes On; Renaissance*   1969—*Near the Beginning*   1970—*Rock 'n' Roll*   1982—*Greatest Hits*   1984—*Mystery*   1991—*Vanilla Fudge Live* (Rhino).

One of the first heavy-rock bands, Vanilla Fudge were also pioneers of the "long version." The band evolved from New York bar bands like the Pigeons and the Vagrants. The Pigeons included Tim Bogert, Mark Stein (who had played and sung on TV shows as a child and teenager, and who recorded in 1959 for Cameo Records) and eventually Vince Martell and Carmine Appice (who had been voted "most musically inclined" in high school).

They named themselves Vanilla Fudge in early 1967 and began practicing their "psychedelic-symphonic rock." They made their New York concert debut July 22, 1967, at the Village Theater with the Byrds and the Seeds. By the end of the year they had signed to Atlantic Records. Their first single was an extended version of the Supremes' "You Keep Me Hangin' On," complete with halfspeed tempo, Gothic organ, and quasi-raga guitar. The single was a Top Ten hit, and Vanilla Fudge's debut LP, which contained similarly treated versions of "Eleanor Rigby," "Ticket to Ride," "People Get Ready," and "Bang Bang," went gold.

The followup LP sold fairly well but is chiefly remembered as one of the most overreaching concept albums of all time; it purported to be a musical history of the previous 25 years, and included a 12-minute cut that, allegedly, contained the entire history of music.

Their third album was even less popular and contained nine minutes of Donovan's "Season of the Witch." The band finally broke up after their fifth, and least successful, album. Appice and Bogert went on to form heavy-metal band Cactus, and later teamed up with Jeff Beck in the Beck, Bogert and Appice power trio. Appice has since become a sought-after session drummer, and has often backed Rod Stewart, among others. In the mid-Eighties he formed his own band, King Kobra, and later, performed with Blue Murder. Stein formed Boomerang, and Martell's whereabouts were unknown until 1982, soon after the release of a greatest-hits package, when the group briefly re-formed. They broke up but came together again in 1984 to record *Mystery.* The group appeared together in 1988 at the Atlantic Records Fortieth Anniversary concert.

Dave Van Ronk

Born June 30, 1936, Brooklyn, New York
1959—*Ballads, Blues and a Spiritual* (Folkways)
1960—*Black Mountain Blues*   1962—*Inside Dave Van Ronk* (Prestige)   1963—*Folksinger*   1964—*In the Tradition; Dave Van Ronk and the Ragtime Jug Stompers* (Mercury); *Dave Van Ronk*   1967—*No Dirty Names* (Verve/Folkways)   1968—*Dave Van Ronk and the Hudson Dusters* (Verve)   1974—*Songs for Aging Children* (Cadet)   1976—*Sunday Street* (Philo)   1985—*Going Back to Brooklyn* (Reckless)   1988—*Somebody Else, Not Me*   1990—*Peter and the Wolf* (Alacazam); *Hummin' to Myself* (Gazell)   1991—*The Folkways Years, 1959–61* (Smithsonian Folkways)   1992—*Statesboro Blues* (EPM); *Let No One Deceive You: Songs of Bertolt Brecht* (with Frankie Armstrong) (Flying Fish) 1993—*Chrestomathy* (Gazell); *A Chrestomathy, vol. 1; A Chrestomathy, vol. 2.*

With his bawdy, gruff, yet tender singing style and considerable blues-archivist skills, Dave Van Ronk became one of the most respected members of New York's early-Sixties folk boom. Though he's never been a commercial success, he remains influential in folk circles as a performer, historian, and teacher.

Van Ronk grew up in a musical household, surrounded by his grandparents' collection of jazz and ragtime records. His grandfather also played ragtime piano. While in high school in Brooklyn, Van Ronk became avidly interested in traditional jazz and played with New York–area jazz groups upon graduation. After spending eight months at sea with the merchant marine, he returned to New York. Among his first gigs was one in 1957 opening for Odetta, an experience that spurred him on to an in-depth investigation of blues and folk music, resulting in his becoming an avid fan of Josh White. He began performing on the folk circuit.

In 1958 Van Ronk formed a jug band with his friend,

frequent collaborator, and fellow archivist Sam Charters and recorded an album for Lyrichord Records. By 1959 he had played folk festivals and been signed to Folkways. While his next few albums for Folkways and Prestige stuck with his folk-blues mode, in 1964 he performed at the Newport Folk Festival with a jazz-flavored jug band, and soon after the festival he formed the Ragtime Jug Stompers, again with Charters.

By this time, Van Ronk had long been a close friend of Bob Dylan, who in the early Sixties had frequently stayed at Van Ronk's Greenwich Village apartment. (In May 1974 he appeared with Dylan and others at a New York City benefit for Chilean political prisoners.) At one point early in his career, Van Ronk also turned down manager Albert Grossman's offer of a place in the trio that became Peter, Paul and Mary. He briefly formed a rock-style band, the Hudson Dusters, and tried his hand at acting, but returned to touring.

Unlike many other folk artists of his period, Van Ronk is better known as an interpreter of songs than as a writer. He was among the first to perform songs by Lightnin' Hopkins, for example, and his repertoire includes songs by writers ranging from Hoagy Carmichael and Louis Jordan to Joni Mitchell and the children's song, "Teddy Bears' Picnic." He continues to perform around the world and to teach guitar. His *Fingerpicking Folk, Blues, and Ragtime Guitar,* a six-tape instructional tutorial, is available through Stefan Grossman's Guitar Workshop.

Little Steven Van Zandt

Born Steven Van Zandt, November 22, 1950, Boston, Massachusetts
1982—*Men Without Women* (EMI)   1984—*Voice of America*   1987—*Freedom—No Compromise* (Manhattan)   1989—*Revolution.*

In the Eighties Steven Van Zandt emerged from stints with fellow New Jersey Shoreans Southside Johnny and Bruce Springsteen to become a political artist. He is best known for putting together the antiapartheid superstar album Sun City.

Van Zandt was raised in Middletown, New Jersey, where he formed his first band, the Source, in 1966. In the early Seventies he played in a number of groups, including Steel Mill and Southside Johnny's Asbury Jukes, before joining Springsteen's E Street Band as a guitarist in mid-decade. He also continued to work with Southside Johnny, writing songs for and producing the Jukes' first three albums.

In 1982 Van Zandt formed Little Steven and the Disciples of Soul, a 12-piece band including the Asbury Jukes' horn players, former Plasmatics bassist Jean Beauvoir, and ex-Rascals drummer Dino Danelli. Their first album was a solid, rootsy effort that Van Zandt pro-

Grammy Awards

Luther Vandross
1990 Best R&B Vocal Performance, Male: "Here and Now"
1991 Best R&B Vocal Performance, Male: *The Power of Love*
1991 Best Rhythm and Blues Song: "Power of Love/Love Power" (with Marcus Miller and Teddy Vann)

Van Halen
1991 Best Hard Rock Performance with Vocal: *For Unlawful Carnal Knowledge*

Vaughan Brothers
1990 Best Rock Instrumental Performance: "D/FW"
1990 Best Contemporary Blues Recording: *Family Style*

Stevie Ray Vaughan and Double Trouble
1984 Best Traditional Blues Recording: *Blues Explosion* (with others)
1989 Best Contemporary Blues Recording: *In Step*

1992 Best Rock Instrumental Performance: "Little Wing"
1992 Best Contemporary Blues Album: *The Sky Is Crying*

---

duced under his E Street nickname, "Miami Steve." By his second album, Little Steven had quit Springsteen's group, dropping the "Miami." *Voice of America* showed his newfound commitment to international politics; Black Uhuru later covered the track "Solidarity."

In 1984 Van Zandt made two visits to South Africa, and upon his return, he gathered over 50 performers, including Springsteen, Bob Dylan, Miles Davis, George Clinton, Bonnie Raitt, Lou Reed, and Bono, to form Artists United Against Apartheid. The group recorded Van Zandt's "Sun City." The song grew into an album, coproduced by Arthur Baker, a popular video, and a concert, all of which raised money for antiapartheid efforts. It also refocused public attention on the longstanding cultural boycott against South Africa, which many entertainers had broken by playing the lucrative Vegas-style resort Sun City.

Manhattan, the label that released *Sun City,* signed Van Zandt and released *Freedom—No Compromise,* on which he continued playing protest songs. Springsteen sang on "Native American," and Van Zandt duetted with Rubén Blades on "Bitter Fruit," a song about labor conditions in Central America. None of Van Zandt's solo records has sold well in the U.S., and his last record, *Revolution,* produced scarcely a ripple. In 1991 he reunited with Southside Johnny and Springsteen, producing Southside's *Better Days.* The single and video "It's Been a Long Time" featured the three Jerseyites. Van Zandt has also produced a number of other artists, including Gary "U.S." Bonds, Lone Justice, and Ronnie Spector.

Townes Van Zandt
Born John Townes Van Zandt, March 7, 1944, Fort Worth, Texas
1967—*First Album* (Poppy/Tomato)   1968—*For the Sake of the Song*   1969—*Our Mother the Mountain*   1970—*Townes Van Zandt*   1971—*Delta Momma Blues*   1972—*High, Low and Inbetween*   1973—*The Late, Great Townes Van Zandt*   1977—*Live at the Old Quarter*   1979—*Flying Shoes*   1987—*At My Window* (Sugar Hill)   1989—*Live and Obscure*   1993—*The Nashville Sessions* (Tomato)   1994—*Road Songs* (Sugar Hill); *No Deeper Blue.*

Townes Van Zandt is a Texas-based singer/songwriter who has been content to live the life of a hermetic, legendary folk artist while other performers have turned his songs into hits. Van Zandt was born into a wealthy, pedigreed Texas family. His reputation as a rambling man dates back to his childhood, when his family moved frequently. He began playing guitar at 15, after seeing Elvis on TV.

Along with fellow Texas singer/songwriter cult heroes like Guy Clark, Van Zandt began singing folk clubs and juke joints in Houston, branching out into the Southwest circuit. He developed a reputation as a wild man; many of his tunes are drinking songs. His cult following is primarily interested in his somber, poetic, introspective tunes and folksy tales. Van Zandt has frequently been called a more down-home Leonard Cohen.

Van Zandt moved to Nashville the year his first album came out. He never availed himself of that city's music biz, however, releasing his records on small, poorly distributed labels and allowing his song rights to get hung up in legal quagmires. He moved to Austin, Texas, in the late Seventies, just as he was getting his first mainstream exposure with Emmylou Harris' 1977 cover of "Pancho and Lefty," a song he wrote earlier in the decade. Six years later Merle Haggard and Willie Nelson turned the cut into a major country hit with their duet rendition. In 1981 Harris and Don Williams' cover of "If I Needed You" topped the country charts. Van Zandt's songs have also been recorded by Doc Watson and Guy Clark.

Van Zandt returned to Nashville in 1986 and began recording again. *At My Window* was his first album of new material in eight years. He was embraced by a new generation of folk-based artists. Canada's Cowboy Junkies took Van Zandt on tour with them in 1990, and

Van Zandt contributed two songs to the Junkies' 1992 album, *Black Eyed Man*. Van Zandt continues to be more interested in writing than recording, allowing his music to be released on disparate labels around the world. *Road Songs*, for example, was released in Europe almost two years before its U.S. issue.

Stevie Ray Vaughan

Born October 3, 1954, Dallas, Texas; died August 27, 1990, East Troy, Wisconsin
1983—*Texas Flood* (Epic)   1984—*Couldn't Stand the Weather*   1985—*Soul to Soul*   1986—*Live Alive* 1989—*In Step*   1991—*The Sky Is Crying*   1992—*In the Beginning*.
As the Vaughan Brothers (with Jimmy Vaughan): 1990—*Family Style* (Epic).

Before his untimely death in 1990, guitarist Stevie Ray Vaughan had become the leading figure in the blues-rock revival he spearheaded in the mid-Eighties.

Vaughan's first musical inspiration was his older brother Jimmy, a guitarist who later helped form the Fabulous Thunderbirds [see entry]. Together, the brothers immersed themselves in the work of blues guitar greats like B. B. King, Albert King, and Freddie King and early rock guitarists like Lonnie Mack (whose 1985 comeback, *Strike Like Lightning*, Vaughan would coproduce). By the time he was 14, Vaughan was already playing Dallas blues clubs with a variety of bands, including Blackbird, the Shantones, and the Epileptic Marshmallow. Dropping out of high school in 1972, Vaughan relocated to Austin, Texas, the up-and-coming musical haven where his brother had already established himself.

In Austin Vaughan formed the Nightcrawlers and then joined the Cobras for a year. Vaughan's next group was Triple Threat, which included Lou Ann Barton among its five vocalists. After three years with Triple Threat, Vaughan and Barton formed Double Trouble.

Barton left to go solo, and Double Trouble reverted to a power trio with Chris Layton on drums and Tommy Shannon, a bassist who had played with Johnny Winter's breakthrough band in the late Sixties. Vaughan's fluid Hendrix-meets-the-blues-masters guitar playing, his rough-edged vocals, and the trio's live intensity made them local legends. (*In the Beginning* captures a 1980 radio broadcast.)

By 1982 the band's considerable reputation had reached the Rolling Stones, who hired Double Trouble to perform at a private party in New York. That same year, veteran producer Jerry Wexler arranged for Vaughan's band to play the Montreux Jazz Festival—the first time an unsigned, unrecorded group had done so. David Bowie caught the performance and tapped Vaughan to play on his next album. Vaughan's gritty guitar work became one of the unexpected highlights of *Let's Dance*.

Legendary talent scout John Hammond became Vaughan's most important mentor, signing Double Trouble to Epic and acting as executive producer for the band's debut, *Texas Flood* (#38, 1983). Vaughan's raw, blues-drenched virtuosity struck a chord with a grass-roots audience. *Couldn't Stand the Weather* (#31, 1984) saw Vaughan pay explicit tribute to Jimi Hendrix with an exact cover of "Voodoo Chile (Slight Return)." In 1985 Vaughan became the first white performer to win the W. C. Handy Blues Foundation's Blues Entertainer of the Year award; that year Vaughan also added keyboardist Reese Wynans to the band.

After collapsing onstage during an English tour, Vaughan sought help to deal with his cocaine and alcohol addiction, entering a treatment center in September 1986. "Wall of Denial" on his 1989 album, *In Step* (#33), addressed his addiction and rehabilitation. In 1987 he made a rare film appearance trading guitar leads on "Pipeline" with surf-guitar king Dick Dale in *Back to the Beach*. A 1989 tour with Jeff Beck attested to Vaughan's renewed strength and continued popularity.

On leaving an East Troy, Wisconsin, theater—following an onstage guitar jam that included Eric Clapton, Jimmy Vaughan, Buddy Guy, Robert Cray, and Jeff Healey—Vaughan was killed in a helicopter crash. By then, Vaughan was firmly established as the era's premier blues-rock performer. Two posthumous releases—*Family Style* (#7, 1990), a collaboration with Jimmy Vaughan, and *The Sky Is Crying* (#10, 1991)—became Vaughan's best-selling recordings.

Bobby Vee

Born Robert Thomas Velline, April 30, 1943, Fargo, North Dakota
1961—*Bobby Vee* (Liberty)   1962—*Bobby Vee Meets the Crickets*; *Bobby Vee's Golden Greats* 1963—*The Night Has a Thousand Eyes*; *Bobby Vee Meets the Ventures*   1967—*Come Back When You Grow Up*   1972—*Robert Thomas Velline*   1975— *Very Best of Bobby Vee* (United Artists)   1990— *Bobby Vee* (EMI); *U.K. Tour '90* (Rockhouse).

One of the longest-lasting teen idols of the early Sixties, Bobby Vee got his lucky break when he and his band the Shadows filled in for the late Buddy Holly at a 1958 Mason City, Iowa, concert days after Holly had died in a plane crash. The Shadows (which included Bobby's brother Bill) then managed to get their song "Suzie Baby" recorded locally, and it became a hit. Producer Snuff Garrett signed the band to Liberty Records in 1959, releasing "Suzie Baby" (#77) nationally.

At Liberty, Vee was quickly (and literally) groomed for solo success, under Garrett's supervision. First, Garrett had Vee cover British teen-idol Adam Faith's "What Do You Want?," which flopped at #93 in the spring of

1960. But later that year a cover of the Clovers' R&B hit "Devil or Angel" hit #6 on the U.S. singles chart. "Rubber Ball" (cowritten by Gene Pitney) was a Top Ten hit in the U.S. (#6) and the U.K., and for the next few years the clean-cut Vee, in his high school letter sweater, sang sweetly of the ups and downs of sexless romance from the top of the charts with hits like "Take Good Care of My Baby" (#1) and "Run to Him" (#2) in 1961; "Punish Her" (#20) in 1962; and "The Night Has a Thousand Eyes" (#8) and "Charms" (#13) in 1963.

Vee was just as enormously popular in Britain as in America, and he toured both countries frequently. In the midst of his big-hit years, Vee cut a Buddy Holly tribute album with the Crickets, as well as one other album simply backed by Holly's onetime band. The mid-Sixties were fallow years for Vee, but he returned to the charts in 1967 with the million-selling "Come Back When You Grow Up" (#3). In 1972 he recorded an album under his real name, but it did not chart.

In the years since Vee has no further charting singles, but he continues to tour the world (including an annual trip to England, where in 1981 he was awarded a gold album for his *Singles Album*). He resides in Minnesota with his family, and has his own studio and record label, Rockhouse Records.

Suzanne Vega

Born July 11, 1959, Santa Monica, California
1985—*Suzanne Vega* (A&M)   1987—*Solitude Standing*   1990—*Days of Open Hand*   1992—*99.9 F.*

In 1987 a ballad about an abused child, "Luka," proved Suzanne Vega's unlikely ticket to pop stardom, reaching #3 on the singles chart and situating Vega, alongside Tracy Chapman, at the forefront of a new wave of thoughtful, folk-influenced female singer/songwriters.

Vega grew up in New York's Spanish Harlem, the eldest of four children. Her Puerto Rican stepfather, a writer and teacher, encouraged Vega's early interest in dance and the guitar. At the High School of Performing Arts, she studied the former and began composing on the latter; at 16 she began playing her songs at Greenwich Village coffeehouses. After graduating, Vega became a literature major at Barnard College, while continuing to perform acoustic folk at downtown clubs. In 1983, while supporting herself as a temporary receptionist, she met lawyer Ron Fierstein and musician/producer Steve Addabbo, who were starting their own music promotion company. The fledgling partners began managing Vega, and with their assistance, she landed a contract with A&M Records.

Produced by Addabbo and ex–Patti Smith guitarist Lenny Kaye, Vega's eponymous 1985 debut album established her as a critical and cult favorite in the U.S. and reached #11 on the British pop chart. The next year, Vega contributed the song "Left of Center" to the film soundtrack for *Pretty in Pink* and wrote lyrics for two tracks on Philip Glass' *Songs from Liquid Days. Solitude Standing* proved her domestic breakthrough album, shooting to #11 (and to #2 in England) with the help of "Luka."

In 1990 Vega's third album, *Days of Open Hand,* peaked at #50 and spawned no hit singles. But that same year, the U.K. sampling/remixing duo DNA added a funky rhythm track to "Tom's Diner," a song from *Solitude Standing,* and released it—without Vega's permission—as a bootleg. Vega and A&M were savvy enough to get rights to the single, which quickly became a club sensation and then a pop hit (#5 U.S.; #2 U.K.). In 1991 A&M capitalized further on this success by releasing *Tom's Album,* a collection of reworkings of the song by various artists, including R.E.M. Perhaps encouraged by this reception, Vega incorporated dance and technopop textures on her fourth album; nonetheless, *99.9 F* reached only #86.

Velvet Underground

Formed 1965, New York City, New York
Lou Reed (b. Louis Firbank, Mar. 2, 1942, Brooklyn, N.Y.), voc., gtr.; John Cale (b. Mar. 9, 1942, Cwmamman, South Wales), viola, bass, kybds., voc.; Nico (b. Christa Päffgen, Oct. 16, 1938, Cologne, Ger.; d. July 18, 1988, Ibiza, Sp.), voc.; Sterling Morrison, bass, gtr.; Maureen "Moe" Tucker, drums.
1967—*The Velvet Underground and Nico* (MGM/Verve) (– Nico)   1968—*White Light/White Heat* (– Cale; + Doug Yule, bass, voc.)   1969—*The Velvet Underground* (MGM)   1970—*Loaded* (Atlantic) (– Tucker; + Billy Yule, drums; – Reed; + Walter Powers, voc.)   1971—(– Morrison; + Willie Alexander, gtr.)   1972—*Squeeze* (Polydor) (group disbands); *Live at Max's Kansas City* (Cotillion)   1974—*1969 Live* (Mercury)   1985—*V.U.* (Verve)   1986—*Another View*   1993—(Group reforms: Cale; Reed; Morrison; Tucker) *Live MCMXCIII* (Sire)   1995—*Peel Slowly and See* (Polydor).

The Velvet Underground never sold many records, but as has often been said, it seemed that every Velvets fan went out and started a band. While their songs were constructed on the same three chords and 4/4 beat employed by most groups of the late Sixties, the Velvets were unique in their intentional crudity, in their sense of beauty in ugliness, and in their lyrics. In the age of flower power they spoke in no uncertain terms of social alienation, sexual deviancy, drug addiction, violence, and hopelessness. Both in their sound and in their words, the songs evoked the exhilaration and destructiveness of modern urban life. The group's sound and stance were of seminal importance to David Bowie, the New York Dolls,

Patti Smith, Mott the Hoople, Roxy Music, the Sex Pistols, R.E.M., Sonic Youth, and countless others of the protopunk, punk, and postpunk movements.

In 1964 John Cale [see entry] met Lou Reed [see entry] in New York City. Both had been classically trained—Cale as a violist and theorist, Reed as a pianist—but by the time of their first meeting Cale was experimenting in the avant-garde with La Monte Young and Reed was writing poems about down-and-out streetlife. Cale, Reed, Sterling Morrison, and Angus MacLise (percussionist in Young's ensemble) formed a group that played under various names—the Warlocks, the Primitives, the Falling Spikes—in galleries and at poetry readings around lower Manhattan. As the Primitives, they recorded a series of singles on Pickwick Records, for which Reed had once worked as house songwriter. In 1965 MacLise abruptly left for India (he died of malnutrition in Nepal in 1979 at the age of 41). Maureen Tucker was enlisted to take his place on a perdiem basis, which became permanent when she constructed her own drum kit out of tambourines and garbage-can lids.

On November 11, 1965, the group played their first gig as the Velvet Underground, opening for the Myddle Class at a high school dance in Summit, New Jersey. Within a few months, they had taken up residency at the Cafe Bizarre in Greenwich Village, where they met pop artist Andy Warhol. When the group was fired by the Bizarre's management for performing "Black Angel's Death Song" immediately after being told not to, Warhol invited them to perform at showings of his film series, *Cinematique Uptight,* and then employed them as the aural component of his traveling mixed-media show, the Exploding Plastic Inevitable. For the latter, he augmented their lineup with singer/actress Nico [see entry], whom he gave equal billing on the group's first album, although she sang only three songs. The album was recorded in 1966, and two singles—"I'll Be Your Mirror" b/w "All Tomorrow's Parties" and "Sunday Morning" b/w "Femme Fatale"—appeared. The album, which included Reed's "Heroin" and "Venus in Furs" (a song about sadomasochism), was not released for almost a year. It sported a Warhol cover with a peelable illustration of a banana.

The group had a falling-out with Warhol when it performed in Boston without waiting for Nico and the rest of the Inevitable troupe, who arrived late. The band then took on Steve Sesnick as their manager. Without Warhol's name and knack for generating publicity, the Velvet Underground faded from public attention. Their following was reduced further when the uncompromisingly noisy *White Light/White Heat* came out. It had been quickly recorded after a tour of mostly empty theaters. Cale, frequently in a power struggle with Reed, then quit the group. Rather than find another electric violist, the remaining members enlisted Doug Yule, who had played with a Boston folk-rock group, the Glass Menagerie. The third album, recorded in Los Angeles with Yule, was much softer than either of its predecessors, and it cost the group all but the most loyal of their following. MGM dropped them and it was some months before Atlantic signed the band.

Upon their return to New York to record in the summer of 1970, the Velvets played a month-long engagement at Max's Kansas City (with Billy Yule deputizing for Tucker, who was pregnant). These were the group's first appearances in New York since 1967, and they rekindled some interest. But soon after *Loaded* was finished, Reed, at odds with Sesnick, left the group and moved to England, where he lived for two years before reemerging as a solo performer. Although he denounced *Loaded,* claiming it was remixed after his departure (a charge Yule and Morrison denied), the album introduced "Sweet Jane" and "Rock and Roll."

With Doug Yule and Walter Powers sharing lead vocals, the group toured the East Coast before Morrison dropped out in 1971 to teach English at the University of Texas in Austin. Tucker, Yule, Powers, and Willie Alexander (later of the Boom Boom Band) recorded an album for MGM, but when MGM decided against releasing it, Tucker left. She moved to Phoenix, Arizona, then to southern Georgia, where she raised a family and in 1980 began recording solo efforts. Doug Yule retained the Velvet Underground name until 1973, recording what amounted to a solo album, *Squeeze,* which was released only in Britain.

With the success of Reed's solo career and, to lesser extents, Cale's and Nico's, the Velvet Underground generated more interest in the Seventies than it had during the group's existence. Two live albums were released: 1972's *Live at Max's Kansas City,* recorded the night of Reed's last appearance with the group, and 1974's *1969 Live,* recorded in 1969 in Texas and California.

In 1989 Cale and Reed did several performances together of a song cycle written in memory of Andy Warhol (who died in 1988); the songs were released on the 1990 album *Songs for Drella.* In June of that year, the original members of the Velvet Underground (minus Nico, who died in 1988 of head injuries sustained in a cycling accident) reunited onstage at a Warhol tribute in a small town outside Paris. The one ten-minute song they performed—"Heroin"—led to the band's re-forming three years later. With their longstanding differences seemingly resolved (particularly the battling egos of Reed and Cale), the group began rehearsals for several European shows slated for the summer of 1993. Highlights of the tour were documented on a video and album, *Live MCMXCIII.* That fall, however, the band fell apart once more, reportedly due to a spat between Cale and Reed over who would produce the group's upcoming MTV

Unplugged appearance and album. As of late 1994 the members had again gone their separate ways: Reed, Cale, and Tucker as solo artists, and Morrison, who occasionally performs with Tucker, to his gig as a Houston, Texas, tugboat skipper.

The Ventures
Formed 1959, Seattle, Washington
Bob Bogle (b. Jan. 16, 1937, Portland, Ore.), gtr., bass; Don Wilson (b. Feb. 10, 1937, Tacoma, Wash.), gtr.; Nokie Edwards (b. May 9, 1939, Okla.), gtr., bass; Howie Johnston (b. Wash.; d. 1988), drums.
1960—*Walk Don't Run* (Dolton)   1961— (– Johnston; + Mel Taylor [b. New York City, N.Y.], drums) *Another Smash!!; The Ventures; The Colorful Ventures*   1962—*Twist with the Ventures; The Ventures' Twist Party, vol. 2; Mashed Potatoes and Gravy; Going to the Ventures Dance Party!*   1963— *The Ventures Play Telstar, The Lonely Bull; "Surfing"; Let's Go!*   1964—*(The) Ventures in Space; Fabulous Ventures; Rock, Don't Run, vol. 2*   1965— *The Ventures Knock Me Out!; The Ventures on Stage; The Ventures a Go-Go; Christmas with the Ventures*   1966—*Where the Action Is; The Ventures/Batman Theme; Go with the Ventures; Wild Things!*   1967—(– Edwards; + Jerry McGee, gtr.) *Guitar Freakout; Super Psychedelics; Genius* (Sunset); *Golden Greats by the Ventures* (Liberty) 1969—(+ Johnny Durrill [b. Houston, Tex.], kybds.) *Hawaii Five-O; Swamp Rock*   1970—(– McGee; + Edwards) *More Golden Greats; The Ventures Tenth Anniversary Album*   1972—*Theme from Shaft* (United Artists); *Joy/Ventures Play the Classics*   1985—(– Edwards)   Circa 1990—(Lineup: Bogle; Taylor; McGee; Wilson)   1990—*Walk Don't Run: The Best of the Ventures* (EMI)   1991—*Greatest Hits* (Curb/CEMA).

The Ventures are one of the first, best, most lasting and influential of instrumental guitar-based rock combos (rivaled only by Britain's Shadows). Their trademark sound—driving mechanical drums, metallic guitars twanging out simple, catchy pop tunes—has filtered down through the years to gain prominence in the sounds of bands like Blondie, the B-52's, and the Go-Go's. Often classified as a surf-rock band, the Ventures actually predated surf music and lasted well beyond its early-Sixties boom. Some 35 years after their forming, they still play to receptive audiences.

Founding member Bob Bogle had started playing guitar by his teens. In his mid-teens, he supported himself by bringing wet cement to bricklayers, and he moved to Seattle to work. There he met Don Wilson, who had learned piano and trombone as a child, and bass and

guitar in the army. By mid-1959 they had begun playing in local clubs. They soon added Nokie Edwards on lead guitar (Bogle switching to bass) and Howie Johnston on drums. They sent their first demo, "Walk Don't Run," to various record labels. When nobody responded, Don Wilson's mother released it as a single on her own Blue Horizon label. It became an instant regional hit in 1960 and in late summer was picked up for distribution by Dolton Records (distributed by Liberty).

In August 1960 "Walk Don't Run" became a #2 hit. The Ventures followed it with a rock version of "Ghost Riders in the Sky," then "Perfidia," "Lullaby of the Leaves," "Diamond Head," and "2,000 Pound Bee," all of which were hits through the early and mid-Sixties.

In 1961 Johnston was hurt in an auto accident and left the group. He was replaced by Mel Taylor. The hits kept on coming, with versions of "Lonely Bull" and "I Walk the Line" in 1963 and a Top Ten surf remake of "Walk Don't Run" in 1964. For the next few years, their albums still sold and they continued to tour. In 1965 they released what was one of the first instructional records, *Play Guitar with the Ventures.*

In 1967 Edwards was replaced by Jerry McGee, who left in 1970 to record with Delaney and Bonnie Bramlett, after which Edwards returned. By that time, keyboardist Johnny Durrill had expanded the unit to a quintet, and the Ventures had delved into fuzz-tone and wah-wah guitar modification as well as blues, calypso, and Latin material.

In 1969 they hit the charts again with a version of the theme from the TV show *Hawaii Five-O* (#4). In 1981, with Bogle, Wilson, Edwards, and Taylor, they released a regional West Coast single, "Surfin' and Spyin'" (written by Go-Go Charlotte Caffey), and embarked on successful tours of the U.S. and Japan, where they had long been a star attraction. Bogle, Taylor, McGee, and Wilson are still active in the group.

Tom Verlaine: See Television

The Village People
Formed 1977, New York City, New York
Victor Willis, voc.; David Hodo (b. July 7, 1947), voc.; Felipe Rose (b. Jan. 12, 1954), voc.; Randy Jones, voc.; Glenn Hughes (b. July 18, 1950, Bronx, N.Y.), voc.; Alex Briley (b. Apr. 12, 1951), voc. 1977—*Village People* (Casablanca)   1978—*Macho Men*   1979—(– Willis; + Ray Simpson [b. Jan. 15, 1952, Bronx], voc.) *Cruisin'; Go West*   1980—*Live and Sleazy; Can't Stop the Music* (with other disco artists)   1981—*Renaissance* (RCA)   1982— (– Simpson; + Miles Jay; numerous personnel changes follow)   1984—*Sex Over the Phone*

The Village People

1988—*Greatest Hits* (Rhino)   1994—(Current lineup: Rose; Simpson; Hughes; Briley; Hodo; + Jeff Olson [b. Sep. 3, 1952, New York City], voc.).

Under the direction of disco producer Jacques Morali, this campy vocal group had massive late-Seventies pop hits with double-entendre songs like "Macho Man" and "Y.M.C.A." In 1977 Morali, with business partners Henri Belolo, lyricist Phil Hurtt, and Peter Whitehead, composed self-consciously gay-themed disco songs like "Fire Island" and "San Francisco." With actor/singer Victor Willis handling vocals, the songs became favorites of both gay and straight club audiences. Backed by Casablanca Records president Neil Bogart, Morali formed a group of singer/actors dressed as a cross section of gay stereotypes: a beefy biker, a construction worker, a policeman, an Indian chief, and a cowboy. As Tom Smucker wrote, they "were gay goofs to those who got the joke, and disco novelties to those who didn't."

With major hits like "Macho Man" (#25) in 1978 and "Y.M.C.A." (#2) in 1979, the Village People had six gold and four platinum records, sold out major concert halls, and appeared on numerous television talk shows. During their first burst of stardom, they reportedly sold over 20 million singles and 18 million albums worldwide. In 1979 Ray Simpson, Valerie Simpson's brother, replaced Willis as lead singer. By then, however, the group's 15 minutes appeared to have ended. For their 1981 release *Renaissance,* the group briefly traded in its gay outfits for a fling with a New Romantic wardrobe.

Through the Eighties the Village People were all but forgotten in the U.S., but the group maintained a large international following and performed throughout the world. After 1985's "Sex on the Phone" flopped here and barely cracked the Top Sixty in the U.K. (where "Y.M.C.A." reigned as one of that nation's top 25 best-selling records of all time), the group took a hiatus. The current lineup, which includes Simpson, four original members, and Jeff Olson, appeared, among other places, at Walt Disney World in Florida.

Gene Vincent

Born Eugene Vincent Craddock, February 11, 1935, Norfolk, Virginia; died October 12, 1971, Los Angeles, California
1957—*Bluejean Bop!* (Capitol)   1970—*I'm Back and I'm Proud* (Dandelion/Elektra); *If Only You Could See Me Today* (Kama Sutra)   1971—*The Day the World Turned Blue*   1991—*Gene Vincent (Capitol Collectors Series)* (Capitol).

One of the first American rockers, Gene Vincent began singing while in the Navy in the early Fifties. After being discharged in 1955, he performed regularly on live country music radio shows in Norfolk. In 1956 he recorded a demo of a song he and "Sheriff" Tex Davis had written—"Be-Bop-A-Lula"—and sent it to Capitol Records. Capitol heard an Elvis Presley sound-alike in his rockabilly stutter-and-hiccup style and signed him to a long-term contract. "Be-Bop-A-Lula," rerecorded by Vincent and his group, the Blue Caps (guitarists Cliff Gallup and Willie Williams, bass player Jack Neal, and drummer Dickie Harrell), in Capitol's imitation–Sam Phillips echo chamber, was a hit nationwide (#7). Vincent's looks—darker, tougher, greasier than Elvis', all blue denim and black leather—were featured in the 1956 movie *The Girl Can't Help It* and were imitated widely. Fans even affected his limp, the result of a navy motorcycle accident that forced him to wear a metal brace on one leg. For several years Gene Vincent and the Blue Caps were among the most popular rock & roll acts in America ("Lotta Lovin'" was a #13 hit in 1957).

When, by the end of the decade, the record industry began to favor cleaned-up, tuned-down pop stars, Vincent went abroad and found huge followings in Australia, Japan, and Europe, wherever "real American rockers" were in demand. He toured England with Eddie Cochran and was critically injured in the car crash that killed Cochran on April 17, 1960. Although Vincent recovered from his injuries, he was devastated by Cochran's death, and his career never regained momentum. Vincent's professional pursuits were no doubt compromised by heavy drinking, mood swings, and erratic behavior; he was married and divorced four times. For most of the Sixties he lived in England, where, playing the pub curcuit, he retained a small following of latterday Teddy boys.

A "comeback" album in 1970 failed to attract much attention. Through the years he suffered bouts of disabling pain because of his bad leg; in 1966 doctors suggested amputation, in fact. His fortunes continued to decline and, broke and despondent, he returned to

Gene Vincent and the Blue Caps

America in September 1971. A month later he tripped in his parents' home and ruptured a stomach ulcer; he died an hour later. "Be-Bop-A-Lula" had, by that time, sold nine million copies worldwide.

Visage: See Magazine

Vixen

Formed circa 1980, Los Angeles, California
Janet Gardner, voc.; Jan Kuehnemund, gtr.; Share Pedersen, bass; Roxy Petrucci, drums.
1988—*Vixen* (EMI Manhattan)   1990—*Rev It Up* (EMI).

An all-female band, Vixen worked in the Bon Jovi/Warrant pop/metal tradition. Roxy Petrucci, the drummer for Madame X, a popular L.A. metal band, formed the group in the early Eighties. Although Vixen found work playing at local clubs and military bases, it went through a number of musicians, including Steve Vai's wife, Pia Koko, on bass. The lineup solidified in 1987, and EMI signed the quartet the following year.

Vixen (#41, 1988), its gold debut, was buttressed by two Top Forty hits: "Cryin'" (#22, 1989) and "Edge of a Broken Heart" (#26, 1988), the latter written, arranged, and produced by Richard Marx. *Rev It Up* (#52, 1990) contained all original material, including the hit "How Much Love" (#44, 1990).

EMI dropped the band, and little has been heard from Vixen since, although bassist Share Pedersen turned up in 1991 on *Contraband,* an LP recorded by other hard-rock musicians, including guitarist Michael Schenker and drummer Bobby Blotzer, then of Ratt.

Volcano Sons: See Mission of Burma

W

Bunny Wailer

Born Neville O'Reilly Livingstone, April 10, 1947, Kingston, Jamaica
1976—*Blackheart Man* (Island)   1977—*Protest*
1979—*Struggle* (Solomonic)   1980—*Bunny Wailer*
Sings the Wailers* (Island); *In I Father's House
(Solomonic)   1981—*Rock 'n' Groove; Tribute to the*
Late Hon. Robert Nesta Marley, O.M.*   1982—*Hook,
Line and Sinker*   1983—*Roots, Radics, Rockers,
Reggae* (Shanachie)   1986—*Rootsman Skanking
1987— *Rule Dance Hall; Marketplace*   1988—*Liber-*
ation*   1990—*Time Will Tell: A Tribute to Bob Mar-
ley; Gumption*   1992—*Dance Massive*   1994—
Crucial! Roots Classics.

The last surviving member of the original Wailers, Bunny Livingstone—better known as Bunny Wailer—left the band less than a year after the group made its first tours of the U.K. and the U.S. His aversion to traveling was one reason for his departure. He vowed never to leave Jamaica, but in 1986 he relented, and a sold-out show at New York's Madison Square Garden kicked off a U.S. and European tour. International acclaim accrued to Bob Marley and Peter Tosh (the other original Wailers), while until the early Eighties, Bunny Wailer's following remained small even by Jamaican standards.

In his decade with the Wailers, he was considered the equal of Marley and Tosh as a singer and as a song-writer. "Let Him Go," "Who Feels It," "Jail House," and "Pass It On" are among the songs associated with him. He founded his own record company, Solomonic, in 1972, and recorded his first solo singles—"Life Line," "Bide Up," and "Arab Oil Weapon"—before quitting the Wailers in 1973. Between then and 1976, he retired from the record business and lived in the Jamaican countryside. When he resumed recording, he secured a distribution arrangement with Island Records and released *Blackheart Man* (backed by Marley, Tosh, and the Wailers band) in America and Europe.

Darker and denser than Marley's, less strident than Tosh's, Wailer's music found less acceptance from most quarters, and his records were usually not released in the U.S. Since 1980, as his music has become lighter and more upbeat, he has become a hitmaker in Jamaica. "Ballroom Floor," "Galong So," and "Collie Man" were big hits in 1981, while "Cool Runnings" topped the Jamaican charts that year and "Rock and Groove" followed suit in 1982.

In 1983 he began an association with Shanachie, the label that started releasing his LPs in the U.S. His recent albums, especially *Liberation,* have shown a new musical and political engagement, adding dancehall elements and topical lyrics. In 1990 his tribute to Bob Marley, *Time Will Tell,* won the Grammy for Best Reggae Recording; he won a second reggae Grammy for 1994's *Crucial!*

Loudon Wainwright III

Born September 5, 1946, Chapel Hill, North Carolina
1970—Album I (Atlantic)   1971—Album II   1972—
Album III (Columbia)   1973—Attempted Mustache
1975—Unrequited   1976—T Shirt (Arista)   1978—
Final Exam   1980—A Live One (Rounder)   1983—
Fame and Wealth   1985—I'm Alright   1986—More
Love Songs   1989—Therapy (Silvertone)   1992—
History (Charisma)   1993—Career Moves.

Folksinger/songwriter Loudon Wainwright III, the son of an American writer, has gained considerable critical respect and a modicum of sales for his self-lacerating humor, deadpan irony, and deliberate tastelessness, complemented by a comic, rubber-faced stage presence.

Wainwright grew up in Westchester County, New York, and Southern California, where his father was the Los Angeles bureau chief for *Life* magazine. At age 15 Wainwright began attending St. Andrew's School in Delaware (where later the film *Dead Poets Society* was filmed). There he developed an early interest in folk music. After graduation, he attended Carnegie Mellon Institute, where he studied acting and directing before dropping out in early 1967 at age 20. In 1968 Wainwright began playing the club and college circuit and attracting a following with his offbeat wit.

His first albums included just vocals and guitar and were simultaneously stark confessionals and a mockery of the whole idea, presenting Wainwright as a sort of insensitive singer/songwriter. With *Album III,* Wainwright mellowed his approach until it resembled slapstick more than anything else, and he crossed over into the pop chart with the Top Twenty single "Dead Skunk."

Attempted Mustache played things almost completely for laughs and failed to appreciably increase his sales, but *Unrequited* was received as a welcome return to form. For *T Shirt* and *Final Exam,* Wainwright was backed by a five-piece rock band called Slow Train for such tunes as "Watch Me Rock, I'm Over Thirty." In the early Seventies, Wainwright married Kate McGarrigle of the McGarrigle sisters, and he recorded her song "Come a Long Way." They were separated in 1977 and eventually divorced. They had two children.

Wainwright appeared in the Broadway play *Pump Boys and Dinettes* (1982) and had a small role in the TV series *M.A.S.H.* In 1982 he and Suzzy Roche became the parents of Lucy Roche. Three years later, he moved to England, where he is much more popular than he is in the States. Richard Thompson coproduced *I'm Alright* with Wainwright. In addition to touring and recording, Wainwright has continued his acting career, appearing in *The Slugger's Wife* (1985) and *Jacknife* (1989). In the U.K., he appeared on the BBC series *The Jasper Carrott Show* as, in the words of his bio, "the resident American wise-guy singer/songwriter." Although his commercial profile in the U.S. has remained low, he is still a critics' favorite, praised for his insightful if sometimes unusual songs. In 1994 Wainwright contributed "Man Who Couldn't Cry" to Johnny Cash's critically acclaimed LP *American Recordings.*

John Waite: See the Babys

Tom Waits

Born December 7, 1949, Pomona, California
1973—Closing Time (Asylum)   1974—The Heart of
Saturday Night   1975—Nighthawks at the Diner
1976—Small Change   1977—Foreign Affairs
1978—Blue Valentine (Elektra)   1980—Heartattack
and Vine (Asylum)   1983—Swordfishtrombones
(Island)   1985—Rain Dogs   1987—Franks Wild
Years   1988—Big Time soundtrack   1991—Night
on Earth soundtrack   1992—Bone Machine
1994—The Black Rider.

Singer/songwriter Tom Waits is a one-man Beatnik revival. He generally appears with a cap pulled over his brow, a cigarette dangling from his stubbled face, talksinging and/or mumbling jive in a cancerous growl to the accompaniment of cool saxophone jazz; he also writes romantic ballads, which have been covered by the Eagles, Rickie Lee Jones, and others.

Waits claims he was born in a moving taxi. He grew up in California, preferring Bing Crosby, Stephen Foster parlor songs, and George Gershwin. He also developed an intense admiration for, and identification with, such Beat writers as Jack Kerouac and Charles Bukowski. As a teenager, Waits was living out of a car and working as a doorman at the Los Angeles nightclub the Heritage when he decided he should be performing and began writing songs based on overheard snatches of conversation.

He first played at L.A.'s Troubadour club in 1969, and soon moved out of his car and into L.A.'s Tropicana Hotel (a favorite of visiting rock stars). Waits built up a strong cult following as an opening act. Working solo, he merged humorous Beatnik free-verse raps with his own compositions. In 1972 he signed to Elektra/Asylum Records, and his debut album was produced by ex–Lovin' Spoonful Jerry Yester. Though the album sold poorly, one of its songs, "Ol' 55," was covered by the Eagles on their *On the Border.* In 1973 Waits toured with a sax-bass-drums trio, often opening for Frank Zappa and the Mothers and usually drawing extremely adverse audience receptions. His second album, produced by Bones Howe, sold a little better than the first.

By 1975 Waits had built a small nationwide cult following and was still opening shows, but he had to cut his trio for financial reasons. Later that year, Waits and

Howe assembled a sax-led quartet and an audience to record *Nighthawks at the Diner* (#164, 1975). In 1976 he conducted American and European tours, which were mildly received. In London that year, he composed tunes for his next album, the jazzy *Small Change* (#89, 1976). *Foreign Affairs* (#113, 1977) contained his duet with Bette Midler, "I Never Talk to Strangers," and on *Blue Valentine* (#181, 1978) Waits introduced electric guitar for the first time.

Waits appeared as a honky-tonk pianist in Sylvester Stallone's film *Paradise Alley,* in 1979. By this time, he was involved with Rickie Lee Jones, whose picture appeared on the back cover of *Valentine.* They broke up in 1980. Waits wrote and recorded the title song for Ralph Waite's 1980 film about skid row, *On the Nickel,* and later recorded two songs for the 1985 documentary on Seattle street kids, *Streetwise,* as well as the soundtrack for Jim Jarmusch's 1992 film *Night on Earth.* In 1982 Waits' soundtrack for Francis Ford Coppola's *One from the Heart* featured him in a number of duets with Crystal Gayle; the soundtrack was nominated for an Academy Award. Coppola cast Waits in several of his films, including *Rumble Fish, The Cotton Club, The Outsiders,* and *Bram Stoker's Dracula* (in which Waits delivered a memorable turn as the fly-munching Renfield); he's also acted in the Jarmusch cult film *Down by Law,* the big-budget *Ironweed* with Jack Nicholson and Meryl Streep, and Robert Altman's *Short Cuts.*

Heartattack and Vine (#96, 1980), with Waits playing more electric guitar and an R&B slant to the music, was Waits' best seller since *Small Change,* which gives a good indication of his low commercial profile. Waits then forsook any pretense to accessibility, instead making increasingly harsh and eccentric music. *Swordfishtrombones* (#167, 1983) was an experimental rock work with a surreal range of noisy instrumentation; Waits described it as "a junkyard orchestral deviation," while critics compared it to both Captain Beefheart and Kurt Weill. *Rain Dogs* continued the experimental direction, with Waits often singing through a megaphone; it included "Downtown Train," later a hit for Rod Stewart (other artists covering Waits tunes have included Bruce Springsteen with "Jersey Girl," Marianne Faithfull with "Stranger Weather," Bob Seger with "Blind Love" and "New Coat of Paint," and Dion with "Heart of a Saturday Night" and "San Diego Serenade"). *Franks Wild Years* was based on songs from a musical play Waits wrote with the woman he would marry in 1988, playwright Kathleen Brennan. First staged by Chicago's Steppenwolf Company, the play was about a down-and-out lounge singer freezing to death on a park bench, reliving his life in hallucinatory fashion. *Big Time* was the soundtrack of a concert film-with-story that Waits produced himself.

In 1990 Waits won a lawsuit against snack-food giant Frito-Lay, which in 1988 had hired a Waits imper-sonator to sing a tortilla-chip radio jingle closely modeled on Waits' "Step Right Up" (from *Small Change*). Waits, who had consistently refused to perform in any commercials, won $2.5 million in damages, through a decision ultimately upheld by the U.S. Supreme Court.

The clattering *Bone Machine* won a 1992 Grammy Award for Best Alternative Music album. *The Black Rider,* with its demented Weimar-cabaret stylings, was the score from Waits' theatrical collaboration with avant-garde stage designer/director Robert Wilson and author William S. Burroughs. Waits and Wilson collaborated again on a 1993 update of *Alice in Wonderland.* Waits also guested on Bay Area postpunk/fusion band Primus' *Sailing the Seas of Cheese,* and on British composer Gavin Bryars' *Jesus' Blood Never Failed Me Yet,* an unlikely 1994 U.K. hit in which Bryars orchestrated the "found" mumbling of a hymn by a London drunkard.

Dave Wakeling: See the English Beat

Rick Wakeman: See Yes

Wendy Waldman

Born circa 1951, Los Angeles, California
1973—*Love Has Got Me* (Warner Bros.)   1974—
Gypsy Symphony*   1975—*Wendy Waldman
1976—*The Main Refrain*   1978—*Strange Company*
1982—*Which Way to Main Street* (Epic)   1983—*I Can See.*

A school of folk-pop singers developed in the early Seventies on America's West Coast that included Linda Ronstadt, Emmylou Harris, Karla Bonoff, Maria Muldaur, and Wendy Waldman. Waldman has since become better known for writing and/or producing hit records for others.

Waldman spent part of her childhood in Mexico and began performing at age 16 in L.A., first as a solo singer/guitarist and then with a local jug band. In 1969 she formed a folk-rock unit called Bryndle with guitarist Andrew Gold (who later worked with Ronstadt and then went solo) and Bonoff. They broke up a year later.

In 1973, as Waldman recorded her debut LP, Maria Muldaur sang two Waldman tunes, "Mad Mad Me" and "Vaudeville Man," on her own debut. Soon, Waldman, Ronstadt, Harris, and Muldaur were appearing on and contributing material to each other's albums. Waldman sang backup on Ronstadt's *Don't Cry Now* and *Heart Like a Wheel,* and Muldaur covered Waldman's "Gringo en Mexico" on *Waitress in the Donut Shop.* Judy Collins covered Waldman's "Pirate Ships," as did Kim Carnes and ex-Eagle Randy Meisner.

Waldman found it hard to break through commercially, perhaps because of the ironic surplus of West Coast folk-pop singers like herself. In 1978 she recorded and toured with a rock band promoting her *Strange Company* LP. On her Epic albums, she cowrote songs with Eric Kaz, and in 1983 she collaborated with Bette Midler. She also appeared as a backup singer with Linda Ronstadt.

Waldman cowrote the Nitty Gritty Dirt Band's 1987 #1 C&W hit "Fishin' in the Dark," as well as songs for Johnny Mathis, Ronstadt, Rita Coolidge, Kenny Rogers, Dan Seals, Nicolette Larson, and the Nitty Gritty Dirt Band, among others. In the Eighties she relocated to Nashville. Waldman also wrote Vanessa Williams' 1993 hit "Save the Best for Last," which she also produced. Among her other production credits are an album by the Ozark Mountain Daredevils and another by Christian artist Pam Mark Hall. In late 1994 she reunited with Bryndle, which began performing and writing together. This group released a self-titled album in 1995.

The Walker Brothers
Formed 1964, London, England
Original lineup: John Maus (b. Nov. 12, 1943, New York City, N.Y.), gtr., voc.; Scott Engel (b. Jan. 9, 1944, Hamilton, Ohio), bass, voc., gtr., kybds.; Gary Leeds (b. Sep. 3, 1944, Glendale, Calif.), drums, voc.
1965—*The Walker Brothers* (Star Club)   1966—*Portrait* (Philips)   1967—*Images* (Star Club) 1975—*Spotlight On* (Philips); *No Regrets* (GTO) 1976—*Lines*   1978—*Nite Flights*.

Though born in America, the Walker Brothers were usually thought of as a British Invasion group because they went to Britain in 1964 after failing to achieve any success in the U.S. In the U.K., pop producer/entrepreneur Jack Good hooked John Maus and Scott Engel up with ex–P. J. Proby drummer Gary Leeds and renamed them the Walker Brothers. Within a year, they had a minor British hit, "Love Her," which set their style: dramatic Spectorian arrangements featuring harmony vocals.

In late 1965 they scored their first big international pop hit with "Make It Easy on Yourself," and followed it up in 1966 with "The Sun Ain't Gonna Shine (Anymore)," their biggest American Top Forty hit. The Walkers were teen sensations in England, but aside from their singles successes they still couldn't really crack the American market. They split up after the *Images* album, with Scott Engel (still referring to himself as Scott Walker) going on to a somewhat successful solo career in the U.K. In 1975 the original Walkers, with many sessionmen aboard, reformed, but after one comeback hit in the U.K. with Tom Rush's "No Regrets," they faded from view. Several individual members enjoyed a modicum of solo fame in the U.K. As Scott Walker's solo recordings, released only in the U.K., became increasingly inaccessible, his status as a cult artist grew.

Jerry Jeff Walker
Born Ronald Clyde Crosby, March 16, 1942, Oneonta, New York
1968—*Mr. Bojangles* (Atco)   1969—*Driftin' Way of Life* (Vanguard); *Five Years Gone* (Atco)   1970— *Bein' Free*   1972—*Jerry Jeff Walker* (MCA)   1973— *Viva Terlingua*   1974—*Walker's Collectibles* 1975—*Ridin' High*   1976—*It's A Good Night for Singing*   1977—*A Man Must Carry On*   1978— *Contrary to Ordinary*; *Jerry Jeff* (Elektra)   1979— *Too Old to Change*   1980—*The Best of Jerry Jeff Walker* (MCA)   1982—*Cowjazz*   1987—*Gypsy Songman* (Tried & True/Rykodisc)   1989—*Live at Gruene Hall* (Rykodisc)   1991—*Great Gonzos* (MCA); *Navajo Rug* (Rykodisc)   1992—*Hill Country Rain* (MCA)   1993—*Viva Luckenbach!* (Rykodisc).

Though he first came to prominence with the psychedelic band Circus Maximus and has long enjoyed a moderately successful solo career as a "cosmic cowboy" in the Austin, Texas, area, Jerry Jeff Walker is best known for writing "Mr. Bojangles," a song covered by everyone from Sammy Davis Jr. to the Nitty Gritty Dirt Band. Walker became attracted to folk music in his youth, and while in his teens he began performing traditional songs in clubs and coffeehouses. He left home in 1959 and became a wandering minstrel, playing the East Coast and more often the West and Southwest and writing. He also worked with guitarist David Bromberg. In Austin, Walker met singer/songwriter Bob Bruno, and together they returned to New York and formed Circus Maximus. The band merged Walker's characteristic country folk with jazz rock and other exotica and became a favorite psychedelic attraction in the Northeast. Their one minor hit was the jazzy "The Wind," which later became a staple of progressive FM radio.

Disputes between Walker and Bruno about musical direction led to a breakup in 1968. New York radio DJ Bob Fass of WBAI-FM had taped "Mr. Bojangles" (about an old street dancer Walker had met in a New Orleans jail) during a broadcast by Walker and Bromberg; he aired the much-requested tape, and Walker secured a solo contract.

None of Walker's albums sold well despite the immense popularity of "Mr. Bojangles." Walker then moved to Austin, formed the Four-Man Deaf Cowboy Band, and recorded *Viva Terlingua* in a mobile truck parked in the middle of Luckenbach, Texas. He then formed the Lost Gonzo Band, who recorded an album of their own in 1975 and have toured and recorded with and without Walker since. Walker hosted TNN's *The Texas Connection* and continues to tour regularly.

Jr. Walker and the All Stars

Formed 1961, Detroit, Michigan
Original lineup: Jr. Walker (b. Autry DeWalt Walker
Jr., 1942, Blytheville, Ark.), sax, voc.; Vic Thomas,
kybds.; Willie Woods, gtr.; James Graves, drums.
1965—*Shotgun* (Soul)   1966—*Soul Session; Road
Runner*   1967—*Jr. Walker and the All Stars Live!*
1969—*Home Cookin'; Jr. Walker and the All Stars
Greatest Hits; Gotta Hold On to This Feeling*
1970—*A Gasssss*   1971—*Rainbow Funk; Moody Jr.*
1973—*Peace and Understanding Is Hard to Find*
1974—*Anthology*   1976—*Hot Shot; Sax Appeal;
Whopper Bopper Show Stopper*   1978—*. . . Smooth*
1979—*Back Street Boogie* (Whitfield)   1981—*Superstar Series, vol. 5* (Motown)   1983—*Blow the House
Down*   1986—*Compact Command Performances:
19 Greatest Hits.*

With his perky, bluesy tenor sax and raspy voice, Jr.
Walker was one of Motown's more idiosyncratic performers. In the Seventies, studio musicians like Tom
Scott and David Sanborn openly imitated Walker's tone
and attack.

Walker was a naturally gifted musician, and played
both piano and sax as a teen. He worked as a sideman in
the late Sixties with several R&B bands. With the original
All Stars he recorded "Shotgun" (#4 pop, #1 R&B, 1965)
and started a string of party hits that included "Do the
Boomerang" (#10 R&B) and "Shake and Fingerpop" (#7
R&B) in 1965; "How Sweet It Is (to Be Loved By You)"
(#18 pop, #3 R&B) and "I'm a Road Runner" (#20 pop, #4
R&B) in 1966; "Pucker Up Buttercup" (#3 pop, #11 R&B)
and "Come See About Me" (#24 pop, #8 R&B) in 1967;
and "Hip City, Part 2" (#7 R&B, 1965) in 1968.

With Walker singing more, he enjoyed success with
the mellow "What Does It Take (to Win Your Love)" (#4
pop, #1 R&B) and "These Eyes" (#16 pop, #3 R&B) in
1969; "Gotta Hold On to This Feeling" (#21 pop, #2 R&B)
and "Do You See My Love (for You Growing)" (#32 pop, #3
R&B) in 1970; and "Walk in the Night" (#46 pop, #10
R&B) in 1972.

Walker continued recording during the Seventies, including a stint with ex-Motown producer/writer Norman Whitfield's label, but was never as commercially
successful and re-signed with Motown in the early
Eighties. He is still active on the rock club circuit, playing his Motown hits. He played on Foreigner's big 1981
hit "Urgent."

T-Bone Walker

Born Aaron Thibeaux Walker, May 28, 1910, Linden,
Texas; died March 16, 1975, Los Angeles, California
1960—*T-Bone Blues* (Atlantic)   1969—*T-Bone
Walker* (Capitol)   1970—*Good Feelin'* (Polydor);
Well Done (Home Cooking)   1972—*Feelin' the
Blues* (B&B)   1973—*Dirty Mistreater* (Bluesway); *I
Want a Little Girl* (Delmark)   1990—*The Complete
Recordings of T-Bone Walker, 1940–1954* (Mosaic)
1991—*The Complete Imperial Recordings,
1950–1954* (EMI).

As the first bluesman to exploit the electric guitar,
T-Bone Walker stands as an exceptionally important and
influential figure. Walker was indispensable to the birth
of urban electric blues and its descendants, R&B and
rock & roll. His use of finger-vibrato and piercing elec-
tric-guitar sustain influenced scores of subsequent blues
guitarists, such as B. B. King, Freddie King, Buddy Guy,
Albert Collins, Albert King, Lowell Fulson, J. B. Hutto, and
Otis Rush. Walker's gritty chordal style on fast numbers
eventually gave birth to Chuck Berry's archetypal rock
guitar riffs.

Born to musical parents (he had a Cherokee Indian
grandmother), Aaron Thibeaux Walker moved with his
family to Dallas at age two. Through his church choir
and street-singing stepfather, Marco Washington, he became interested in music. He acquired the nickname
T-Bone early on; it was a corruption of his mother's pet
name, T-Bow, from Thibeaux. By the time he was ten,
Walker was accompanying his stepfather at drive-in soft
drink stands. Soon after he became "lead boy" for the
legendary Blind Lemon Jefferson, probably the most
popular and influential country bluesman of the Twenties. From 1920 through 1923 Walker led Jefferson down
Texas streets.

By late 1923 Walker had taught himself guitar and he
began entertaining at Dallas parties. He soon was ready
to leave home and tour Texas with Dr. Breeding's Big B
Tonic Medicine Show. In 1925 he joined blues singer Ida
Cox's road show, which toured the South. Back in Dallas
in 1929, Walker began recording acoustic country blues
as Oak Cliff T-Bone. He continued touring the South and
Southwest until 1934, when he moved to the West Coast.
A year later, he married a woman named Viola Lee, for
whom he wrote his "Viola Lee Blues" (later covered by
the Grateful Dead, among others). Over the next decade,
Walker worked with both small groups and big bands
(from Les Hite's to Fletcher Henderson's), both on the
West Coast and on tours through the Midwest and to
New York. As early as 1935 he had begun playing primitive electric guitar models, using a sprung-rhythm,
single-string lead style derived from Blind Lemon
Jefferson's acoustic picking. By the time he first recorded
as T-Bone Walker, in 1942, he was quite proficient on the
electric guitar and made an instant impression on
dozens of other bluesmen. In 1943 he had his biggest
blues hit with the immortal "Call It Stormy Monday,"
which as "Stormy Monday Blues" or just "Stormy Monday" has become one of the most frequently covered
blues songs.

Through the Forties and Fifties, Walker recorded often and toured frequently (usually with smaller groups). He appeared on TV shows from the Fifties through the Seventies, toured all over the world, played jazz and blues festivals from Monterey to Montreux, and in 1972 appeared in the French film *Jazz Odyssey*. In 1970 Walker won a Grammy for Best Ethnic/Traditional Recording with *Good Feelin'*. He became inactive in 1974, when he was hospitalized with bronchial pneumonia, which felled him a year later.

Joe Walsh

Born November 20, 1947, Wichita, Kansas
1972—Barnstorm (Dunhill)   **1973—The Smoker You Drink, the Player You Get**   **1974—So What**   **1975—You Can't Argue with a Sick Mind** (ABC)   **1978—But Seriously, Folks** (Asylum); **The Best of Joe Walsh** (ABC)   **1981—There Goes the Neighborhood** (Asylum)   **1983—You Bought It—You Name It** (Full Moon/Warner Bros.)   **1985—The Confessor**   **1987—Got Any Gum**   **1991—Ordinary Average Guy** (Pyramid/Epic)   **1992—Songs for a Dying Planet**   **1994—Look What I Did: The Joe Walsh Anthology** (MCA).

Hard-rock guitarist and songwriter Joe Walsh went solo after leaving his first band, the James Gang, in 1971, and later joined the Eagles [see entries]. He added some punch to the Eagles' sound, while his solo albums mixed spacious guitar production with offhandedly cheerful lyrics. Walsh's first solo album, which refined the hard-rock approach of the James Gang with vocal harmonies and more intricate arrangements, sold respectably. *The Smoker You Drink, the Player You Get* (#6, 1973) went gold on the strength of the #23 single "Rocky Mountain Way." *So What* (#11, 1975) featured Walsh's Barnstorm band (which had included bassist Kenny Passarelli and drummer Joe Vitale as well as former members of Stephen Stills' Manassas) on only a few cuts, with backing on the rest by J. D. Souther, Dan Fogelberg, and the Eagles.

In 1974 Walsh produced and played on Fogelberg's top-selling *Souvenirs* LP, and a year later guested on the first solo album by ex-Spirit Jay Ferguson. For the live *You Can't Argue with a Sick Mind* (#20, 1976), Walsh's band included ex–Beach Boys drummer Ricky Fataar, but by the time of its release Walsh had replaced Bernie Leadon in the Eagles, making his debut with them on *Hotel California*. Walsh continued sporadic solo work, and his platinum *But Seriously, Folks* (#8, 1978) lived up to its title and became a top seller on the strength of the deadpan "Life's Been Good" (#12, 1978), an account of rock-star decadence. In 1979 Walsh further endeared himself to critics and audiences with a semiserious campaign for the presidency. His platform included "Free gas for everyone"; his qualifications, "Has never lied to the American public." The Eagles broke up in 1982, but he rejoined them for their 1994 reunion.

Through the Eighties Walsh continued to record, although with lessening chart success with each outing. His last Top Forty single was "Life of Illusion" (#34, 1981) from *There Goes the Neighborhood* (#20, 1981). *You Bought It—You Name It* (#48, 1983) and *The Confessor* (#65, 1985) were Walsh's last solo forays into the Hot 100 to date. In 1993 Walsh embarked on his Vote for Me Tour, which, at one point, reunited him with his former James Gang bandmates. Walsh also has performed with Ringo Starr's All Starr Band.

War

Formed 1969, Long Beach, California
Harold Brown (b. Mar. 17, 1946, Long Beach), drums, perc.; Papa Dee Allen (b. Thomas Sylvester Allen, July 19, 1931, Wilmington, Del.; d. Aug. 30, 1988, Vallejo, Calif.), perc., voc.; B. B. Dickerson (b. Aug. 3, 1949, Torrance, Calif.), bass, voc.; Leroy "Lonnie" Jordan (b. Nov. 21, 1948, San Diego, Calif.), kybds., voc.; Charles Miller (b. June 2, 1939, Olathe, Kans.; d. 1980, Los Angeles, Calif.), reeds, voc.; Lee Oskar (b. Mar. 24, 1948, Copenhagen, Den.), harmonica; Howard Scott (b. Mar. 15, 1946, San Pedro, Calif.), gtr., voc.
As Eric Burdon and War: 1970—Eric Burdon Declares "War" (MGM); **The Black-Man's Burdon**   **1976—Love Is All Around** (ABC).
As War: 1971—War (United Artists); **All Day Music**   **1972—The World Is a Ghetto**   **1973—Deliver the Word**   **1974—War Live!**   **1975—Why Can't We Be Friends?**   **1976—War's Greatest Hits**   **1977—Platinum Jazz** (Blue Note); **Galaxy** (MCA)   **1978—Youngblood** soundtrack (United Artists) (+ Alice Tweed Smith, voc.)   **1979—(+ Luther Rabb, bass) The Music Band** (MCA) (– Dickerson; – Miller; + Pat Rizzo, reeds; + Ronnie Hammon, drums); **The Music Band 2**   **1982—(– Smith) Outlaw** (RCA) (– Rizzo)   **1983—Life (Is So Strange)** (– Brown)   **1984—(– Rabb; + Ricky Green, bass)**   **1987—Best of War . . . and More** (Priority)   **1988—(– Allen)**   **1989—(– Green; Jordan to bass)**   **1992—(– Oskar) Rap Declares War** (Avenue)   **1993—(+ Brown; + Tetsuya "Tex" Nakamura, harmonica; + Rae Valentine [b. Harold Rae Brown Jr.], music programmer; + Kerry Campbell, sax; + Sal Rodriguez, drums, perc., voc.; + Charles Green, sax, flute)**   **1994—Peace Sign; War Anthology 1970–1994.**

War's distinctive mix of funk, Latin, and jazz kept them on the charts through most of the Seventies.

War's roots reach back to 1962, when Harold Brown and Howard Scott cofounded a band called the Creators.

Still in high school, the two later met Leroy "Lonnie" Johnson and B. B. Dickerson, and in 1965 Charles Miller joined. Through the mid-Sixties the Creators worked various Los Angeles and West Coast clubs, opening for such acts as Ike and Tina Turner. The group came to a temporary halt when Scott was drafted, then Dickerson moved to Hawaii. The remaining group members stayed active in music, and at one point found themselves working under the name the Nightshift backing Los Angeles Rams football star Deacon Jones' ill-fated efforts as a singer. By then percussionist Papa Dee Allen, whose past credits included playing with Dizzy Gillespie, had joined, and the horn section had been expanded.

Around this time the group met Jerry Goldstein, a former member of the Strangeloves ("I Want Candy") and writer and producer for the Angels ("My Boyfriend's Back") and the McCoys ("Hang On Sloopy"). Goldstein, who, as manager, producer, and cowriter, would play a key role in War's success, also knew Eric Burdon [see entry], who was then seriously considering quitting music altogether. After Burdon heard the group, he and a friend, a young Danish harmonica player named Lee Oskar, joined them in a series of rehearsals. The Creators were rechristened War, and soon after, Dickerson returned.

The band recorded two albums with Burdon (three, if you count *Love Is All Around,* which consists of material recorded in August 1969, several months before sessions for the group's debut album). "Spill the Wine" (#3, 1970) was their biggest hit together; a followup, "They Can't Take Away Our Music," went to #50 in early 1971. War and Burdon were on tour in Europe in the fall of 1970, performing to rave reviews and sold-out halls. Suddenly, shortly after the death of Burdon's friend Jimi Hendrix, the singer abruptly abandoned the group. Left on their own, the members of War continued to tour and to fulfill their commitments.

War proved itself as a creative force in its own right with *War* (#190, 1971), but its breakthrough came later that year with *All Day Music* (#16, 1971), with its hit singles "All Day Music" (#35, 1971) and "Slippin' into Darkness" (#16 pop, #12 R&B, 1972). From that point, War rolled on through the decade with four Top Ten albums, including the #1 followup, *The World Is a Ghetto.* Their hits of the period included "The World Is a Ghetto" (#7 pop, #3 R&B, 1972), "The Cisco Kid" (#2 pop, #5 R&B, 1973), "Gypsy Man" (#8 pop, #6 R&B, 1973), "Me and Baby Brother" (#15 pop, #18 R&B, 1973), "Low Rider" (#7 pop, #1 R&B, 1975), and "Why Can't We Be Friends?" (#6 pop, #9 R&B, 1975). *Deliver the Word* (#6, 1973), *War Live!* (#13, 1974), and *Why Can't We Be Friends?* (#8, 1975) were all gold; *Greatest Hits* (#6, 1976), which included one new song, "Summer" (#7 pop, #4 R&B, 1976), was certified platinum.

Around this time the group also worked on movie

soundtracks for *Youngblood* and *The River Niger.* Three tracks for *The River Niger* soundtrack and other previously released and unreleased cuts composed *Platinum Jazz* (#23, 1977), the first and only platinum album in the history of Blue Note Records. In 1977 War moved to MCA Records, and the title cut from *Galaxy* was a disco hit (#39 pop, #5 R&B, 1978). In 1979 the group suffered its first personnel shift since 1970, when Dickerson left the group during the recording of *The Music Band.* Just two years later, Miller was the victim of a robbery, during which he was murdered. Subsequent albums had neither the commercial nor the artistic impact of their early and mid-Seventies releases, although the 1982 debut on RCA, *Outlaw,* promised something of a comeback, boasting "You Got the Power" and the title cut, but neither entered the pop Top Forty.

Beginning in the mid-Eighties, War, buffeted by more personnel changes and their audience's shift to disco, ceased recording and split with Goldstein. But they never stopped touring. They were onstage and opening with "Gypsy Man" when Allen died suddenly of a brain aneurysm; the group has retired the song from its live repertoire. Not long after Allen's passing, War reunited with Goldstein, and with several musicians (including Brown's son, Rae Valentine) augmenting the original core membership of Brown, Jordan, and Scott, War made a triumphant return to recording in 1994 with the acclaimed *Peace Sign* (which featured such guest musicians as Lee Oskar and José Feliciano) and a successful tour.

Billy Ward and His Dominoes

Formed 1950, New York City, New York
Billy Ward (b. Sep. 19, 1921, Los Angeles, Calif.), voc., piano; Clyde McPhatter (a.k.a. Clyde Ward, b. Nov. 15, 1931, Durham, N.C.; d. June 13, 1972, Teaneck, N.J.), voc.; Charlie White (b. 1930, Washington, D.C.), tenor voc.; Joe Lamont, baritone voc.; Billy Brown, bass voc.
1952—(– White; + James Van Loan, voc.; – Brown; + David McNeil, bass voc.; – McPhatter; + Jackie Wilson [b. June 9, 1934, Detroit, Mich.; d. Jan. 21, 1984, Mount Holly, N.J.], lead voc. 1953—(– McNeil; + Cliff Givens, bass voc.) Ca. mid-1950s—(– Lamont; + Milton Merle, baritone voc.) 1957—(– Wilson; + Eugene Mumford [d. 1978], lead voc.) Billy Ward and the Dominoes (Federal) 1960—(Lineup: Ward; Givens; Merle; + Monroe Powell, lead voc.; + Robbie Robinson, tenor voc.) 1993—*Sixty Minute Men: The Best of Billy Ward and His Dominoes* (Rhino).

This important, popular Fifties R&B vocal group is known primarily for having once counted among its members Clyde McPhatter and his replacement, Jackie

Wilson. Billy Ward and His Dominoes were the first black male vocal group to master both the smooth, sophisticated style of older groups such as the Ravens and the hard-rocking R&B epitomized in their celebratory, double-entendre-filled "Sixty-Minute Man" (1951) and the protosoul classic "Have Mercy Baby" (1952).

Group founder and sole stalwart Ward had begun studying music in Los Angeles as a child, and at age 14 won a national contest for his composition "Dejection," the award presented by conductor Walter Damrosch. During and after an army stint in the early Forties, Ward became a boxer, and after his discharge he moved east as sports editor and columnist for Transradio Press. He still loved music and was a vocal coach in the Carnegie Hall building. By the late Forties, Ward had his own voice teaching studio on Broadway, and eventually he got the idea to start a singing group with his students. Thus were born the Dominoes.

In 1950 the teenaged Clyde McPhatter joined as lead tenor, and in 1951 the group had three Top Ten R&B singles: "Do Something for Me" (#6 R&B), "I Am with You" (#8 R&B), and "Sixty-Minute Man" (#17 pop, #1 R&B). Historically, "Sixty-Minute Man" broke commercial barriers, for not only was it a wildly successful R&B hit despite (or because of) its ribald content, but it is considered to have been one of the first, if not the first R&B record by a black group to make the pop chart as well.

In 1952 their "Have Mercy Baby" was an R&B #1 for several weeks running. They again hit the Top Ten that year with "The Bells" (#3 R&B), "I'd Be Satisfied" (#8 R&B), and "These Foolish Things Remind Me of You" (#5 R&B), McPhatter's last single with the group. He then left to form the Drifters [see entry]. His place was taken by Jackie Wilson, who sang lead on "Rags to Riches" (#2 R&B, 1953), the group's biggest hit with him. An early 1955 switch to Decca and an emphasis on smooth pop brought the group its biggest pop hit, "St. Therese of the Roses" (#13, 1956), but Wilson departed for a solo career [see entry].

With new lead singer Eugene Mumford (previously of the Serenaders and the Larks), the group had several more pop hits, including the biggest of its career, "Star Dust" (#12, 1957), followed by "Deep Purple" (#20, 1957), both on Liberty. Their last charting single was a cover of "Jennie Lee." In 1960 Mumford left to go solo; he later sang with other groups, including versions of the Ink Spots and the Jubilee Four. The group remained popular as a concert attraction into the early Sixties.

Jennifer Warnes

Born Jennifer Jeane Warnes, March 3, 1947, Seattle, Washington
1970—*See Me* (Warner Bros.)   1971—*Jennifer*
1977—*Jennifer Warnes* (Arista)   1979—*Shot*

Through the Heart   1986—*Famous Blue Raincoat* (Cypress)   1992—*The Hunter* (Private).

A honey-voiced singer and sometime songwriter, Jennifer Warnes achieved her greatest success to date with a string of hit movie themes. Warnes' recording of "It Goes Like It Goes," from the 1979 film *Norma Rae*, won an Academy Award. In the Eighties she sang Randy Newman's "One More Hour" on the *Ragtime* soundtrack and scored #1 hits with a pair of duets: 1982's "Up Where We Belong," with Joe Cocker, from *An Officer and a Gentleman*; and 1987's "(I've Had) The Time of My Life," with former Righteous Brother Bill Medley, from *Dirty Dancing*. Each duet won an Oscar and netted a Grammy for vocal performance by a duo or group.

After appearing on *The Smothers Brothers Comedy Hour* in the late Sixties, she signed with Warner Bros. Records and released a couple of well-received albums that combined country and folk influences. Warnes also sang backup for several artists, including Leonard Cohen, whose songs she would later cover on the acclaimed *Famous Blue Raincoat*. After a sabbatical in the mid-Seventies, Warnes resurfaced on Arista with 1977's *Jennifer Warnes*, which yielded the #6 pop single "The Right Time of the Night," but movie soundtrack songs sustained her through the next decade.

Warrant

Formed 1984, Los Angeles, California
Joey Allen, gtr.; Jerry Dixon, bass; Jani Lane, voc.; Steven Sweet, drums; Erik Turner, gtr.
1989—*Dirty Rotten Filthy Stinking Rich* (Columbia)
1990—*Cherry Pie*   1992—*Dog Eat Dog*.

A prototypical "hair band," Warrant plays broad glam anthems spiced with an unabashedly cartoonish view of sex. The combination brought them two double-platinum albums—*Dirty Rotten Filthy Stinking Rich* (#10, 1989) and *Cherry Pie* (#7, 1990)—and Top Ten hit singles in "Heaven" (#2, 1989), "Cherry Pie" (#10, 1990), and "I Saw Red" (#10, 1991).

MTV put the video to "Cherry Pie" into heavy rotation and the band attracted an audience of mainly pubescent young girls. The subject matter of their songs aroused the interest of the PMRC, which prompted the band to respond with "Ode to Tipper Gore" (90 seconds of the band screaming obscenities) on *Cherry Pie*. An attempt to move beyond their teenybopper image with the Southern gothic–style video for "Uncle Tom's Cabin" (#78, 1991) and *Dog Eat Dog* (#25, 1992) met with limited success. Frontman Jani Lane quit the band, only to return a year later.

Dionne Warwick

Born Marie Dionne Warwick, December 12, 1940, East Orange, New Jersey

1962—*Presenting Dionne Warwick* (Scepter)
1965—*The Sensitive Sound of Dionne Warwick*
1966—*Here I Am*   1967—*Here Where There Is Love*;
The Windows of the World   1968—*On Stage and in
the Movies*; *Dionne Warwick's Golden Hits, Part
One*; *Valley of the Dolls*   1969—*Promises,
Promises*; *Soulful*; *Dionne Warwick's Greatest Mo-
tion Picture Hits*; *Dionne Warwick's Golden Hits,
Part Two*   1971—*The Dionne Warwicke Story*
1972—*Dionne* (Warner Bros.)   1973—*Just Being
Myself*   1975—*Then Came You*; *Track of the Cat*
1977—*A Man and a Woman* (with Isaac Hayes) (Hot
Buttered Soul); *Only Love Can Break a Heart* (Musi-
cor); *Love at First Sight* (Warner Bros.)   1979—
Dionne (Arista)   1980—*No Night So Long*
1981—*Hot! Live and Otherwise*   1982—*Friends in
Love*; *Heartbreaker*   1983—*How Many Times Can
We Say Goodbye*   1985—*Finder of Lost Loves*;
Friends   1987—*Reservations for Two*   1989—*The
Dionne Warwick Collection/Her All Time Greatest
Hits* (Rhino); *Greatest Hits, 1979–1990* (Arista)
1990—*Sings Cole Porter*   1992—*Hidden Gems: The
Best of Dionne Warwick, vol. 2* (Rhino)   1993—
Friends Can Be Lovers (Arista)   1994—*Aquarela do
Brasil.*

Since her debut in 1962, Dionne Warwick has been one of
the most successful American pop singers, particularly
in the Sixties, when her voice helped popularize the
work of songwriters Burt Bacharach and Hal David.

Warwick grew up in a family of gospel singers and
received considerable vocal training as a girl, singing
with the Drinkard Singers, a group managed by her
mother and including her sister Dee Dee. She attended
Hartt College of Music in Hartford, Connecticut, and
after singing background on some recording sessions,
she was signed to Scepter Records in 1962 to work with
the production and writing team of Bacharach and
David.

"Don't Make Me Over" (#21 pop, #5 R&B) in late 1962
was the first of many Bacharach-David compositions
Warwick would record, including "Anyone Who Had a
Heart" (#8) in 1963; "Walk On By" (#6) and "You'll Never
Get to Heaven" (#34), in 1964; "Trains and Boats and
Planes" (#22 pop, #49 R&B) and "Message to Michael"
(#8 pop, #5 R&B) in 1966; "I Say a Little Prayer" (#4 pop,
#8 R&B) and "Alfie" (#18 pop, #5 R&B) in 1967. Over the
next two years, she had four huge hits: "(Theme from)
Valley of the Dolls" (#2 pop, #13 R&B, 1968), "Do You
Know the Way to San Jose" (#10 pop, #23 R&B, 1968),
"This Girl's in Love with You" (#7 pop and R&B, 1969),
and "I'll Never Fall in Love Again" (#6 pop, #17 R&B,
1970) from the Bacharach-David musical *Promises,
Promises*. Of the above songs, only "(Theme from) Valley
of the Dolls" was not a Bacharach-David composition. In
addition, before 1971 Warwick had ten more Top Forty
hits.

In 1971 Warwick moved to Warner Bros. Records and
left Bacharach-David behind. She couldn't duplicate her
success, although she worked with a number of fine pro-
ducer/writers. *Just Being Myself* was written by the
Brian Holland and Lamont Dozier team, and *Track of the
Cat* by Thom Bell. In 1974 she had a Bell-produced hit,
"Then Came You," with the Spinners (#1 pop, #2 R&B).
"Once You Hit the Road" (#5 R&B) with Bell did well in
1975. In the early Seventies, on the advice of a numerol-
ogist, she added an "e" to her surname, but dropped it in
1975. A 1977 live album with Isaac Hayes, *A Man and a
Woman,* was well received.

In 1979 she returned to the charts with "I'll Never
Love This Way Again" (#5 pop, #18 R&B), produced by
Barry Manilow, and "Déjà Vu" (#15 pop, #25 R&B). In
1982 Bee Gee Barry Gibb coproduced and wrote songs
for Warwick's *Heartbreaker,* which hit with the title cut
(#10, 1982). Warwick's biggest hit singles of the Eighties
were all duets: with Johnny Mathis, "Friends in Love"
(#38, 1982); with Luther Vandross, "How Many Times
Can We Say Goodbye" (#27, 1983); and with Jeffrey Osborne, "Love Power" (#12, 1987). Her biggest hit of the
period, however, was "That's What Friends Are For," featuring Elton John, Gladys Knight, and Stevie Wonder.
The proceeds from the Grammy-winning #1 1985 hit
went to benefit AIDS research through AMFAR (the
American Foundation for AIDS Research). Warwick has
received four other Grammy Awards. In 1993 Warwick
was reunited with Bacharach and David for one song on
Friends Can Be Lovers ("Sunny Weather Lover"). That
album also contained a duet with her cousin Whitney
Houston, "Love Will Find a Way."

Warwick has also pursued a range of business interests outside music, including an interior design firm, a
fragrance called Dionne, the Psychic Friends Network,
and a television-production company. She is also involved in a number of humanitarian causes.

Martha Wash: See C+C Music Factory; the Weather Girls

Dinah Washington

Born Ruth Lee Jones, August 29, 1924, Tuscaloosa,
Alabama; died December 14, 1963, Detroit, Michigan
1959—*What a Difference a Day Makes!* (Mercury)
1960—*The Two of Us* (with Brook Benton)   1961—
Unforgettable   1987—*The Complete Dinah Washington on Mercury, vol. 1 1946–1949*; *The Complete
Dinah Washington on Mercury, vol. 2 1950–1952*
1988—*The Complete Dinah Washington on Mercury,
vol. 3 1952–1954*; *The Complete Dinah Washington*

on Mercury, vol. 4 1954–1956   1989—*The Complete Dinah Washington on Mercury, vol. 5 1956–1958*; *The Complete Dinah Washington on Mercury, vol. 6 1958–1960*; *The Complete Dinah Washington on Mercury, vol. 7 1961*   1993—*First Issue: The Dinah Washington Story (The Original Recordings)*.

Dinah Washington was the most popular black female singer of the Fifties; her sinuous, nasal, penetrating vocals were marvelously effective on blues, jazz, gospel, or straight pop songs. Growing up in Chicago, she gave gospel recitals on the South Side, accompanying herself on piano. At 15 she secretly entered and won an amateur contest at the Regal Theater and began appearing at local nightclubs. But in 1940 she returned to the church at the urging of Sallie Martin, a powerful figure in the gospel world who helped the young Ruth Jones polish her talent.

In 1942 she became immersed in secular music after agent Joe Glaser heard her sing. He suggested she change her name to Dinah Washington and recommended her to Lionel Hampton, with whom she sang from 1943 to 1946. Jazz writer Leonard Feather arranged for her to cut two of his songs for Keynote Records in 1943, "Evil Gal Blues" and "Salty Papa Blues," backed by Hampton's band. During the mid-Fifties Washington was known as the "Queen of the Harlem Blues," partly because of her sales consistency and partly because her style of blues was much more complex than that of Chicago-area singers. Among her Top Ten R&B hits were "Baby Get Lost" (#1 R&B, 1949); "Trouble in Mind" (#4 R&B, 1952); "What a Diff'rence a Day Makes" (#8 pop, #4 R&B, 1959); and "This Bitter Earth" (#24 pop, #1 R&B, 1960). Also in 1960 Washington cut two popular duets with Brook Benton, "Baby (You've Got What It Takes)" (#5 pop, #1 R&B) and "A Rockin' Good Way" (#7 pop, #1 R&B).

After 18 years with Mercury, Washington went to Roulette Records in 1961. She died in 1963 after consuming weight-reduction pills and alcohol. Thirty years later she was honored with a commemorative postage stamp. In 1993 she was inducted into the Rock and Roll Hall of Fame.

Grover Washington Jr.
Born December 12, 1943, Buffalo, New York
1971—*Inner City Blues* (Kudu)   1972—*All the King's Horses*   1973—*Soul Box*   1975—*Mister Magic; Feels So Good*   1976—*A Secret Place; Soul Box, vol. 2*   1977—*Live at the Bijou*   1978—*Reed Seed* (Motown)   1979—*Paradise* (Elektra); *Skylarkin'* (Motown)   1980—*Winelight* (Elektra); *Baddest* (Motown)   1981—*Come Morning* (Elektra)   1982—*The Best Is Yet to Come*   1984—*Inside Moves*   1985—*Anthology of Grover Washington*   1987—*Strawberry Moon* (Columbia)   1988—*Then

and Now*   1989—*Time Out of Mind*   1992—*Next Exit*   1994—*All My Tomorrows*.

Grover Washington Jr.'s recordings, featuring his soulful saxes backed by supple, funky grooves, have made him, since the Seventies, one of the most commercially viable pop jazzmen. Starting to play saxophone at age ten, Washington came from a musical family, his father a tenor saxophonist, his mother a choir singer, and his brother a drummer. At 16 he left home to tour with a Columbus, Ohio–based band, the Four Clefs. While in the army from 1965 to 1967, he gigged in Philadelphia with organ trios and rock bands. He also performed in New York with drummer Billy Cobham.

After playing on a number of albums in the early Seventies, Washington was signed to Kudu Records by pop-jazz mogul Creed Taylor. *Inner City Blues* introduced his fusion of jazz technique and pop melodicism; his gold *Mister Magic*, arranged by Bob James, established a style that proved successful throughout the Seventies and early Eighties. This was the first of seven Washington albums of the period to go #1 on the jazz chart and the first to go gold. His best-selling release was the platinum *Winelight*, which contained "Just the Two of Us," featuring Bill Withers' vocal.

Through the Eighties, Washington's audience became even more pop oriented; his mellow sound gained exposure on the theme songs for television's *The Cosby Show* and *Moonlighting*. A multi-instrumentalist (tenor, alto, soprano, and baritone saxophone, as well as clarinet, bass, and piano), Washington began working as a producer for the jazz group Pieces of a Dream and producing some of his own albums.

In 1992 Washington again went to #1 on the jazz chart with *Next Exit*. It contained "Summer Chill," cowritten with his son and nominated for a Best R&B Instrumental Grammy Award.

Was (Not Was)/Don Was
Formed circa 1981, Detroit, Michigan
Don Was (b. Donald Fagenson, Sep. 13, 1952, Detroit), bass; David Was (b. David Weiss, Oct. 26, 1952, Detroit), sax, flute; Sweet Pea Atkinson (b. Sep. 20, 1945, Oberlin, Ohio), voc.; Sir Harry Bowens (b. Oct. 8, 1949, Detroit), voc.; Donald Ray Mitchell (b. Apr. 12, 1957, Detroit), voc.
1981—*Was (Not Was)* (Ze/Island)   1983—*Born to Laugh at Tornadoes* (Ze/Geffen)   1988—*What Up, Dog?* (Chrysalis)   1990—*Are You Okay?*

Was (Not Was) unites two studiophiles (Don and David Was) overflowing with encyclopedic knowledge of pop music, some dyed-in-the-wool R&B singers, and an absurdly eclectic host of outside guests to implode all manner of white and black musical genres.

The Was "brothers" met as children while living in suburban Detroit. Hanging out in the "humour prison" — David Weiss' basement—the two spent their adolescence indulging their tilted sensibilities by publishing an alternative newspaper, staging outrageous school productions, and writing songs. Immersed in the local rock and soul scenes that commingled in Detroit, Weiss and Donald Fagenson also dabbled in the radical rock & roll politics of John Sinclair's White Panther Party.

Weiss, who plays saxophone and flute, left Detroit for Los Angeles. Fagenson, a bassist, stayed in Detroit eking out a living doing local session work and production; Weiss was writing jazz criticism for the *Los Angeles Herald Examiner* but felt unfulfilled musically. The two hometown buddies began a cross-country collaboration, Weiss concocting the surreal lyrics, Fagenson devising the genre-warping music. Taking their name from a word game of Fagenson's son, Was (Not Was) proceeded to collect members of Detroit's pop-rock-funk communities to help them on their first album. Among the groups represented were P-Funk, the MC5, Brownsville Station, and Wild Cherry. The resulting "Out Come the Freaks" and "Tell Me That I'm Dreaming" became dance hits.

Born to Laugh at Tornadoes (#134, 1983) upped the eclectic ante even more. Guests included Marshall Crenshaw, Mel Tormé, Mitch Ryder, Ozzy Osbourne, Kiss' Vinnie Vincent, and the Knack's Doug Fieger. Critics' darlings but poor sellers, Was (Not Was) were dropped by Geffen. Their next album didn't find them retreating from their now trademark mix-and-match collisions. *What Up, Dog?* (#43, 1988) featured Frank Sinatra Jr. on the priceless "Wedding Vows in Vegas" and an Elvis Costello writing collaboration, "Love Can Be Bad Luck." But extra attention was given to the band's own superlative R&B belters, Sir Harry Bowens and Sweet Pea Atkinson (assisted by Donald Ray Mitchell), whose impassioned vocals helped make "Walk the Dinosaur" a #7 hit in 1989.

Are You Okay? (#99, 1990) also has its share of unexpected guests (Leonard Cohen, Iggy Pop, the Roches), but the standout track was a remake of the Temptations' 1972 hit "Papa Was a Rollin' Stone" with Bowens and Atkinson singing and G Love E adding a rap that turned the song into a contemporary howl of urban pain.

By the late Eighties Don Was had established himself among the most in-demand producers in the music industry. His magic touch was best felt on Bonnie Raitt's *Nick of Time* (1989), a project that revitalized her career; he was also at the helm for her followups, *Luck of the Draw* and *Longing in Their Hearts*. Was has produced the B-52's, Iggy Pop, David Crosby, Paula Abdul, Willie Nelson, Waylon Jennings, and the Highwaymen. Production for Bob Dylan's 1990 *Under the Red Sky* was credited to David and Don Was. Don Was won the 1994 Producer of the Year Grammy.

W.A.S.P.

Formed 1984, Los Angeles, California
Blackie Lawless (b. Steve Duren, Sep. 4, 1954, Fla.), voc.; Chris Holmes, gtr.; Johnny Rod (b. Dec. 8, 1957, Mo.), bass, voc.; Randy Piper, gtr., voc.; Tony Richards, drums.
1984—*W.A.S.P.* (Capitol) 1985—*The Last Command* 1986—(– Richards; + Steve Riley, drums, voc.) *Inside the Electric Circus* 1987—(– Riley; + Glen Soderling, drums) *Live . . . In the Raw* 1989—(– Soderling; + Frank Banali, drums; + Ken Hensley, kybds.) *The Headless Children* 1991—(– Holmes; – Piper; – Riley; – Hensley; + Stet Howland [b. Aug. 14, 1960, Mass.], drums) 1992—(+ Bob Kulick, gtr.) *The Crimson Idol* (Capitol/EMI) 1994—*First Blood . . . Last Cuts: Best of W.A.S.P.*

W.A.S.P. would be just another mildly successful Los Angeles metal band if not for the attention of the Parents Music Resource Committee. At the 1985 Senate Commerce Committee Hearings they became the prime example of all that was obscene in rock, illustrated with a photo of lead singer Blackie Lawless posed with a buzz saw jutting none-too-subtly between his legs.

Lawless, a nephew of Fifties New York Yankee pitcher Ryne Duren, seemed born for this role. A member of the last-ditch version of the New York Dolls, he moved to Los Angeles in 1976. That year he joined forces with future Mötley Crüe member Nikki Sixx in Sister. He left in 1978 and roamed the L.A. scene until he formed W.A.S.P. with Chris Holmes, the husband of ex-Runaway Lita Ford.

The band became known for their club act, which included crotch rubbings and props like chainsaws, raw meat, and fake blood. Capitol signed them in 1984 but refused to distribute their initial single, "Animal (Fuck Like a Beast)." The coverage of the Senate hearings boosted the band's notoriety, pushing 1985's *The Last Command* to #49. *The Headless Children* (#48, 1989) tempered the band's usual treatment of sex and violence, becoming their most popular album. In 1991 Lawless introduced a new lineup, and the band became known as Blackie Lawless and W.A.S.P.

The Waterboys

Formed October 1981, London, England
Mike Scott (b. Dec. 14, 1958, Edinburgh, Scot.), voc., gtr., kybds.; Anthony Thistlethwaite (b. Aug. 8, 1955, Leicester, Eng.), sax, mandolin, gtr., bass; Kevin Wilkinson (b. Eng.), drums.
1983—*The Waterboys* (Ensign/Chrysalis) (+ Karl Wallinger [b. Oct. 19, 1957, Prestatyn, Wales], kybds.; + Roddy Lorimer [b. Glasgow, Scot.], trumpet) 1984—*A Pagan Place* (– Wilkinson; + Chris Whitten, drums) 1985—*This Is the Sea*

(– Wallinger; – Whitten; + Steve Wickham [b. Dublin, Ire.], fiddle; + Dave Ruffy [b. Eng.], drums; + Guy Chambers [b. Eng.], kybds.; + Marco Weissman, bass)   1986—(– Weissman; – Chambers; – Ruffy; + Trevor Hutchinson [b. Ire.], bass)   1988— (+ Colin Blakey [b. Falkirk, Scot.], flute, whistle, kybds.) *Fisherman's Blues*   1989—(+ Sharon Shannon [b. Ire.], accordion, fiddle; + Ken Blevins, drums; + Noel Bridgeman [b. Dublin, Ire.], drums)   1990—*Room to Roam* (– Wickham; – Blakey; – Shannon; – Bridgeman; – Lorimer; – Blevins)   1991—(– Thistlethwaite; – Hutchinson) *The Best of the Waterboys 1981–1991*   1994—*Dream Harder* (Geffen).

Scottish-born singer/songwriter Mike Scott is the sole constant member of the Waterboys, a group whose sound has changed from dramatic, horn- and keyboard-driven "big music" to folky Irish acoustic songs to guitar-based pop/rock. Throughout, Scott's incisive lyrics have for the most part reflected his interests in spirituality, mysticism, and Celtic poetry. Though quite successful in Britain in the mid-Eighties, the Waterboys have yet to find a large audience in the U.S.

Scott, whose mother was an English professor, grew up in a village on the coast of Scotland. In the late Seventies he started a fanzine, *Jungleland,* and began playing in punk bands. After studying English and philosophy at Edinburgh University, Scott moved to London with his band, Another Pretty Face. After it broke up, he started the Waterboys (named after a line in "The Kids" from Lou Reed's *Berlin*), recruiting multi-instrumentalist Anthony Thistlethwaite. The two played most of the instruments on 1983's *The Waterboys,* produced by Scott. Keyboardist Karl Wallinger joined for the band's next two recordings, adding his rich keyboard flavorings to Scott's majestic mood-rock. Critics began dubbing the Waterboys' sound "big music" after a song title on *The Pagan Place* (#100 U.K., 1984). *This Is the Sea* (#37 U.K., 1985) proved a fruitful collaboration between Wallinger and Scott, yielding the British hit single "The Whole of the Moon" (#26 U.K., 1985). (The song returned to #3 on the U.K. chart in 1991, upon rerelease on the #2 charting greatest-hits album.)

Wallinger left the band in 1985 to start his own group, World Party [see entry]. Scott moved from London to Ireland, where he put together a new band, mainly consisting of traditional Irish folk players. Three years later, the lilting, mostly acoustic *Fisherman's Blues* (#13 U.K., 1988) was the result of Scott's new musical environment. *Room to Roam* (#5 U.K, 1990) continued in this direction.

The early Nineties found Scott yearning to play electric guitar again. After a change in record labels, Scott relocated once more, this time to New York, without Thistlethwaite and his Irish bandmates. *Dream Harder* (#5 U.K., 1993) was recorded with an assortment of session players. It marked a return to electric music, though more stripped-down than the Waterboys' early albums.

Muddy Waters

Born McKinley Morganfield, April 4, 1915, Rolling Fork, Mississippi; died April 30, 1983, Chicago, Illinois
1958—*The Best of Muddy Waters* (Chess)   1960— *Muddy Waters at Newport, 1960*   1964—*Folk Singer*   1966—*Down on Stovall's Plantation* (Testament)   1968—*Sail On* (Chess)   1969—*Fathers and Sons*   1971—*They Call Me Muddy Waters*   1972— *The London Muddy Waters Sessions*   1973—*Can't Get No Grindin'*   1975—*The Muddy Waters Woodstock Album*   1977—*Hard Again* (Blue Sky) 1978—*I'm Ready*   1979—*Muddy "Mississippi" Waters Live*   1981—*King Bee*   1982—*Rolling Stone* (Chess); *Rare and Unissued*   1989—*Trouble No More (Singles, 1955–1959)* (Chess/MCA); *The Chess Box*   1994—*One More Mile.*

Muddy Waters was the leading exponent of Chicago blues in the Fifties. With him, the blues came up from the Delta and went electric, and his guitar licks and repertoire have fueled innumerable blues bands. Waters was the son of a farmer and, following his mother's death in 1918, was raised by his grandmother. He picked up his nickname because he fished and played regularly in a muddy creek. He learned to play harmonica, and as a teen he led a band that frequently played Mississippi Delta clubs. His singing was influenced by the style of local bluesman Son House. At 17, Waters began playing guitar by studying Robert Johnson records. In 1940 he traveled to St. Louis and in 1941 joined the Silas Green tent show as a singer and harmonica player. Sometime around 1941–42, Waters was recorded by folk archivists/researchers Alan Lomax and John Work in Mississippi for the Library of Congress.

In 1943 he moved to Chicago, where he found employment in a paper mill. The following year, Waters got an electric guitar and began performing at South Side clubs and rent parties. He cut several sides in 1946 for Columbia's Okeh subsidiary, but none was released until 1981, when they appeared on a Columbia blues reissue, *Okeh Chicago Blues.* In 1946 bluesman Sunnyland Slim helped Waters get signed to Aristocrat Records, where he cut several unsuccessful singles, and Waters continued playing clubs seven nights a week and driving a truck six days a week.

In 1948 the Chess brothers changed Aristocrat to Chess. Waters' first single on the new label was "Rollin' Stone," a major blues hit. "I Can't Be Satisfied" and "I Feel Like Going Home" from that year secured his position as a major blues performer. Most of Waters' early recordings featured him on electric guitar, Big Crawford or writer/producer Willie Dixon on bass, and occasionally Little Walter on harmonica. By 1951 he was supported by a complete band with Otis Spann on piano, Little Walter on harmonica, Jimmie Rodgers on second guitar, and Elgin Evans on drums.

"Honey Bee" in 1951; "She Moves Me" (#10 R&B) in 1952; "I'm Your Hoochie Coochie Man" (#8 R&B), "I Just Wanna Make Love to You" (#4 R&B), "I'm Ready" (#5 R&B), and "Got My Mojo Working" in 1954; and "Mannish Boy" (#9 R&B) in 1955 are all regarded as blues classics and have been recorded by numerous rock groups. During the Fifties, many of the top Chicago bluesmen passed through Waters' band, including Walter Horton, Junior Wells, Jimmie Rodgers, James Cotton, and Buddy Guy. In addition, Waters was helpful in the early stages of both Howlin' Wolf's and Chuck Berry's careers.

During his peak years as a record seller, Waters' sales were confined primarily to the Mississippi Delta, the New Orleans area, and Chicago. But his reputation and music were internationally known, as the attendance at concerts on his 1958 English tour revealed. The Rolling Stones named themselves after his song, "Rollin' Stone." After the mid-Fifties Waters never had another Top Ten R&B single, but his albums began to reach rock listeners. Into the Sixties, Waters appeared at concerts and festivals nationally, such as the 1960 Newport Jazz Festival, where *Muddy Waters at Newport* was cut. In the late Sixties and early Seventies, he recorded several albums either with rock musicians or in a rock direction, the best of which were the *London Muddy Waters Sessions* and *Fathers and Sons,* the latter with many of the players he had influenced, including Mike Bloomfield and Paul Butterfield. In 1971 Waters won the first of several Grammys with *They Call Me Muddy Waters.*

In the early Seventies Waters left Chess and sued Chess's publishing arm for back royalties. He signed with Steve Paul's Blue Sky records in 1976, the year he appeared at the Band's farewell concert. Using members of his Fifties bands and producer/guitarist Johnny Winter, Waters made three of his best-selling albums, *Hard Again, I'm Ready*, and *King Bee*. Winter and Waters frequently performed together in the Seventies and Eighties. He last performed publicly at a June 1982 Eric Clapton show. Waters died of a heart attack. In 1987 he was inducted into the Rock and Roll Hall of Fame.

Roger Waters: See Pink Floyd

Jody Watley

Born January 30, 1959, Chicago, Illinois
1987—*Jody Watley* (MCA)   1989—*Larger Than Life*;
You Wanna Dance With Me?   1991—*Affairs of the Heart*   1993—*Intimacy.*

Jody Watley

A leggy dance diva whose minimalist singing and videogenic glamour evoke a more elegant Janet Jackson, Jody Watley was awarded the 1987 Best New Artist Grammy for her eponymous solo debut, which reached #10 in 1987 and yielded two slamming dance-pop singles, "Looking for a New Love" (#2) and "Don't You Want Me" (#6). (Another track, "Some Kind of Lover," went to #10 in 1988.)

The daughter of a minister father and a mother who sang, Watley got her start in the Seventies as a dancer on TV's *Soul Train*. She and partner Jeffrey Daniels were tapped by producer Don Cornelius to form the dance band Shalamar [see entry]. Little more than a decorative backup singer at first, Watley began writing songs for the band and aspired to sing more, but she was stymied by lead singer Howard Hewett. In 1984 Watley left Shalamar and moved to England, where she modeled and did sessions singing, notably on the 1984 Band Aid single "Do They Know It's Christmas?" Back in Los Angeles, she hooked up with former Prince bassist André Cymone to cowrite several tracks for *Jody Watley*. Their partnership continued over the next two LPs with solid returns. *Larger Than Life* spawned "Real Love" (#2, 1989), "Everything" (#4, 1989), and, with Eric B. & Rakim, "Friends" (#9, 1989); *Affairs of the Heart* featured a few songs written solely by Watley. In 1990 Watley covered Cole Porter's "After You, Who?" for *Red Hot + Blue*, a tribute album benefiting AIDS research. Her next album, *Intimacy*, was her least dance-oriented to date—perhaps why it barely reached the Top 40 on the R&B charts, although it was well-received by critics.

Mike Watt: See Minutemen

Johnny "Guitar" Watson
Born February 3, 1935, Houston, Texas
1966—*Bad* (Okeh)   1967—*Two for the Price of One*
1968—*In the Fats Bag*   1973—*Gangster of Love*
(Fantasy)   1976—*I Don't Want to Be Alone,*
Stranger; Captured Live* (DJM); *Ain't That a Bitch
1977—*A Real Mother for Ya; Funk Beyond the Call*
of Duty*   1978—*Giant*   1979—*What the Hell Is This
1980—*Love Jones*   1981—*Johnny "Guitar" Watson*
and the Family Clone*   1987—*Three Hours Past
***Midnight* (Ace)   1994—*Bow Wow* (Bellmark).**

Johnny "Guitar" Watson enjoyed great popularity in the mid-Seventies with several hit singles and LPs, but his work has been known in blues circles since the Fifties. His playing style influenced Jimi Hendrix, among others, and his "Gangster of Love" was recorded by Steve Miller in 1968.

Watson's father taught him to play piano, and at age 11 his grandmother gave him his grandfather's guitar, which he taught himself to play. He moved to Los Angeles in 1950, where he began working as a sideman in various bands and recording as a solo artist for Federal Records. Among the bands he played in through the Fifties were those led by Amos Milburn, Bumps Blackwell, and Big Jay McNeely. In 1961 he began recording for King. His late-Fifties and early-Sixties hits include "Three Hours Past Midnight," "Those Lonely Lonely Nights," "Cuttin' In," and "Space Guitar," which was one of the first recorded songs to use reverb and feedback. Through the Sixties and Seventies, Watson performed around the U.S. and occasionally in Europe. In the early to mid-Sixties, he often toured with pianist/singer Larry Williams. Recording for DJM in the mid-Seventies, Watson had funk hits with "A Real Mother for Ya" (#41 pop, #5 R&B, 1977), "I Don't Wanna Be a Lone Ranger," and "It's Too Late." Later releases on A&M and Mercury were not as well received. He essentially retired in the early Eighties and performed occasionally in Europe. After meeting producer Al Bell, Watson began recording again. With the release of *Bow Wow* and a subsequent series of live appearances, Watson experienced a surprising resurgence.

Weather Girls
Formed 1982, San Francisco, California
Martha Wash (b. San Francisco), voc.; Izora Armstead (b. ca. 1943, San Francisco), voc.
1983—*Success* (Columbia)   1985—*Big Girls Don't*
Cry*   1988—*Weather Girls.
Martha Wash solo: 1993—*Martha Wash* (RCA).

Martha Wash and Izora Armstead are gospel-trained disco divas who have tried not to let their extra-large size deter them from pop stardom, whether using it to their advantage—calling themselves Two Tons of Fun—or fighting sexism and sizeism with lawsuits, as Wash has done.

Both women got their starts singing in church choirs in San Francisco. They first sang together in the gospel group N.O.W. (News of the World). In the late Seventies they became backup singers for disco sensation Sylvester and began calling themselves Two Tons of Fun, releasing a couple of albums on the Fantasy label. In 1982 Wash and Armstead teamed with producer and songwriter Paul Jabara to record the single "It's Raining Men" (#46 pop, #34 R&B, 1983). The song became a hit in dance clubs, where it was seized by gay men as an anthem, and was especially big in the U.K. Although the Weather Girls' subsequent albums were praised by critics and the duo continued to have a following, they never duplicated their initial success.

In 1990 Wash began singing commercial jingles and working with various groups. She provided the vocals on such dance hits as Black Box's "Everybody, Everybody," and C+C Music Factory's "Gonna Make You Sweat." But because these were groups run by producers who did not deem Wash photogenic, she wasn't credited on the albums and models lip-synched her part in videos. Wash sued the groups and their record companies for fraud, winning a contract with RCA as part of the Black Box settlement.

In 1991 she sang a duet with Luther Vandross, "I Who Have Nothing," on his *Power of Love* album. Wash's solo debut yielded two dance-club hits, "Carry On" and "Give It to You." To support her longtime gay following, Wash has performed numerous AIDS benefits. She rejoined the C+C Music Factory fold in 1994 [see entry], appearing that year on *Anything Goes.*

Weather Report
Formed 1970, New York City, New York
Josef Zawinul (b. July 7, 1932, Vienna, Aus.), kybds., synth.; Wayne Shorter (b. Aug. 25, 1933, Newark, N.J.), saxes; Miroslav Vitous (b. Dec. 6, 1947, Prague, Czech.), bass; Alphonse Mouzon (b. Nov. 21, 1948, Charleston, S.C.), drums; Airto Moreira (b. Aug. 5, 1941, Brazil), perc.
1971—*Weather Report* (Columbia) (– Mouzon; + Eric Gravatt, drums; – Moreira; + Dom Um Romao, perc.)   1972—*I Sing the Body Electric*   1973—*Streetnighter* (– Gravatt; + Ishmael Wilburn, drums; + Alphonso Johnson [b. Feb. 2, 1951, Philadelphia, Pa.], bass)   1974—*Mysterious Trav-*

eller (– Vitous; – Wilburn; + Alyrio Lima, drums; – Romao; + Ndugu [b. Leon Chancler], perc.) 1975—*Tale Spinnin'* (– Lima; + Chester Thompson, drums; – Ndugu) 1976—*Black Market* (– Johnson; + Jaco Pastorius [b. John Anthony Pastorius III, Dec. 1, 1951, Norristown, Pa.; d. Sep. 21, 1987, Ft. Lauderdale, Fla.], bass; – Thompson; + Alejandro Neciosup Acuna, perc.; + Manola Badrena [b. P.R.], perc., voc.) 1977—*Heavy Weather* (– Acuna; – Badrena) 1978—*Mr. Gone* (+ Peter Erskine [b. May 5, 1954, Somers Point, N.J.], drums) 1979—*8:30* 1980— *Night Passages* (– Pastorius) 1982—(– Erskine; + Victor Bailey, bass; + Jose Rossy, perc.; + Omar Hakim, drums) 1983—*Procession* 1985—*Sportin' Life* 1986—*This Is This.*

Between its inception in 1970 and its 1987 breakup, Weather Report was the premier electric jazz ensemble. Born of the Miles Davis groups of the late Sixties that also spawned many other fusion bands, Weather Report was one of the very few groups that managed to win commercial success while going its own way. The band's music had the drive of rock, the harmonic sophistication of jazz, the formal ingenuity of classical music, and hints of Brazilian, African, and Oriental traditions. The best-known Weather Report tunes, such as "Birdland," sound like electrified global carnivals.

Josef Zawinul and Wayne Shorter were the only constants of Weather Report. The first music Zawinul heard and played was the Gypsy folk music of his family; his first instrument was an accordion. At about the age of 12, when he was living in Nazi-occupied Vienna, he began studying classical piano. In the postwar years, he played jazz at U.S. Army clubs and Viennese cabarets. On the basis of a record he cut in a local studio, he was awarded a scholarship to study at the Berklee School of Music in Boston, and he arrived in the United States in 1959. Three weeks after classes began, he dropped out and went to New York City, where he met Shorter.

Shorter had been in the city since 1951, when he entered New York University to study music. After graduating, he played tenor saxophone with Horace Silver before joining Maynard Ferguson's band. Through Shorter, Zawinul began playing with Ferguson as well. Not long after that, however, Shorter moved on to Art Blakey's Jazz Messengers, where he stayed for five years. Zawinul also left Ferguson. He led Dinah Washington's band for over a year and did sessions behind Joe Williams, Yusef Lateef, Ben Webster, and a very young Aretha Franklin. He played the electric piano extensively during nine years in the Cannonball Adderley Quintet, which he joined in 1961, and for which he wrote "Mercy Mercy Mercy."

Shorter joined the Miles Davis Quintet (with keyboardist Herbie Hancock, drummer Tony Williams, and bassist Ron Carter) in 1964. Shorter's work with Davis and on a half-dozen solo albums established him as one of the outstanding saxophonists of the John Coltrane school, although he later tempered the Coltrane influence with his own lyricism. Shorter was also an outstanding composer; his "Nefertiti" (the title track of a 1967 Miles Davis Quintet album) convinced Zawinul that the two of them should join forces. Meanwhile, Davis decided to experiment with a large electrified ensemble, which Zawinul joined. Zawinul's composition "In a Silent Way" became the title track of the album, recorded in 1968. Zawinul continued to play with Adderley, but he joined the Davis aggregation again in 1969 to record the landmark *Bitches Brew,* to which Zawinul and Shorter contributed compositions.

Shorter left Davis soon after the *Bitches Brew* sessions, and Zawinul left Adderley the following year. Each recorded solo albums before forming a group to experiment with electric jazz. They recruited Czech bassist Miroslav Vitous, who had recently played on a Zawinul date. After studying classical composition at the Prague Conservatory, Vitous—like Zawinul—had come to the United States on a scholarship from the Berklee School of Music. His jazz credits included work with Stan Getz, Sonny Rollins, Art Farmer, Herbie Mann, Larry Coryell, and Miles Davis. Clive Davis of Columbia Records reportedly signed the group without even listening to its demo tape. With Brazilian percussionist Airto Moreira and drummer Alphonse Mouzon, Weather Report recorded its highly experimental debut album.

Moreira, who left Weather Report to join Chick Corea, was replaced by another Brazilian, Dom Um Romao, formerly of Sergio Mendes and Brasil '66. Mouzon joined the McCoy Tyner Quartet and was replaced in Weather Report by Tyner's drummer, Eric Gravatt. One side of 1972's *I Sing the Body Electric* was excerpted from a double live album released only in Japan. On the group's third album, *Streetnighter,* Zawinul began using synthesizers as lead instruments and sticking to a funkier beat. *Streetnighter* sold 200,000 copies, quite a number for an album of instrumentals. *Mysterious Traveller* (1974) went further toward dance music with fixed rhythms, riffs, and figures repeated in unison by the bass, saxophone, and synthesizers. *Traveller* introduced bassist Alphonso Johnson, formerly with Chuck Mangione. By *Tale Spinnin',* Johnson had taken over from Vitous.

Tale Spinnin' featured Zawinul's ARP 2600, one of the most advanced of the monophonic synthesizers. On *Black Market,* he introduced the Oberheim polyphonic, and the effect was dramatic. Weather Report's music became almost orchestral in texture. But as Zawinul's arsenal of sounds expanded, Wayne Shorter's role diminished on records, although in Weather Report's concerts he took ample solos. In 1973 Shorter made the album *Na-*

tive Dancer with Brazilian songwriter Milton Nascimento.

Black Market included one cut on which the bassist was Jaco Pastorius. Pastorius had introduced himself to Zawinul after a Weather Report concert in Miami in 1975 and given him tapes of his playing. The son of a professional drummer, he had started playing drums at age 13, before taking up the bass. He toured with Wayne Cochran's C.C. Riders for one year and played with Ira Sullivan's big band, the Baker's Dozen, for three. As a freelance bassist in New York and Boston, he worked with Paul Bley and Pat Metheny. His self-titled solo debut album was released concurrently with Black Market, which introduced his highly influential, busily contrapuntal fretless bass style. By the Heavy Weather sessions, he was a full member of the group, a contributing composer, and coproducer (with Zawinul). While devoting most of his efforts to Weather Report, Pastorius also recorded and toured with Joni Mitchell.

Heavy Weather was Weather Report's most commercially successful album. It sold over 500,000 copies—the first gold album for the group—and Zawinul's "Birdland" was given considerable airplay (a vocal rendition by the Manhattan Transfer was popular three years later).

Mr. Gone (1978) did not depart far from the rich orchestral sound of Heavy Weather, but the group no longer included a percussionist. With the addition of drummer Pete Erskine, Weather Report remained a four-piece unit for almost four years. A double album, 8:30, comprised three sides recorded at two dates at the culmination of the 1979 tour, and one side recorded in Zawinul's home studio. Pastorius left Weather Report in 1982 and formed his own band, Word of Mouth. Tragically, Pastorius' heroin addiction, alcoholism, and manic depression cut his career short; practically penniless, he died from extensive head injuries suffered during a fight outside a bar in 1987.

Procession (1983), with a new lineup, included the first Weather Report song with lyrics (sung by Janis Siegel of Manhattan Transfer). Without the creative three-way Zawinul-Shorter-Pastorius interchange, however, the Weather Report spark fizzled and in 1987 the band broke up.

Shorter formed his own touring groups, which tended toward more traditional jazz forms. Zawinul put together Weather Update, a fusion outfit that featured Erskine and guitarist Steve Khan. Shorter kept a low profile over the next few years. Apart from the heavily arranged Atlantis album and brief tours with Carlos Santana and a 1992 all-star Miles Davis tribute band, Shorter was out of the limelight. Ironically, his earlier Davis-era saxophone style and compositional technique had become the most influential sound for a new generation of jazz players. Zawinul continued his forays into neo-fusion with the Zawinul Syndicate, incorporating his continuing interest in world music.

The Weavers

Formed 1949, New York City, New York
Pete Seeger (b. May 3, 1919, New York City), gtr., banjo, voc.; Ronnie Gilbert, voc.; Fred Hellerman (b. May 13, 1927, N.Y.), voc., gtr.; Lee Hays (b. Mar. 14, 1914, Little Rock, Ark.; d. Aug. 26, 1981, N.Y.), voc., gtr.
1956—The Weavers at Carnegie Hall (Vanguard) 1957—Greatest Hits 1958—(– Seeger; + Erik Darling [b. Sep. 25, 1933], banjo) The Weavers on Tour; The Weavers at Home 1959—Traveling On with the Weavers 1961—The Weavers at Carnegie Hall, vol. 2 1962—Almanac (– Darling; + Frank Hamilton, banjo) 1963—(– Ham; + Bernie Krause, banjo) Reunion at Carnegie Hall, 1963 (group disbands) 1965—Songbook 1971—The Weavers' Greatest Hits 1980—(Group re-forms: Seeger; Hays; Hellerman; Gilbert) 1981—Together Again 1987— Weavers Classics; Reunion at Carnegie Hall, part 2 1993—The Weavers: Wasn't That a Time.

The Weavers were the most important and influential early American folk revivalists, as well as one of the most commercially successful.

The quartet came together, at first informally, in 1948. Lee Hays and Pete Seeger had both been in the Almanac Singers. The Weavers began recording in spring 1950, and with their second single, they had their first big hit: "Tzena, Tzena, Tzena" (#2) b/w Leadbelly's "Goodnight, Irene" (#1). That single alone later went on to sell over two million copies, a phenomenal number at that time. Their other hits included "So Long (It's Been Good to Know You)" and "On Top of Old Smoky." In 1952 the group was blacklisted because of some members' leftist political views and associations. They all but disappeared between 1952 and their triumphant Christmas Eve concert at Carnegie Hall in 1955.

Seeger left to go solo in 1958 after a dispute with the other members over participating in a cigarette commercial, which he opposed. He was replaced in succession by Erik Darling, Frank Hamilton, and in 1963, Bernie Krause. A 1963 reunion concert featured all seven Weavers, including Seeger.

The Weavers' legacy heavily influenced the early-Sixties folk boom. A number of popular Weavers tunes have made their way onto the pop charts and into the American folk tradition: "Kisses Sweeter Than Wine," "Wimoweh (The Lion Sleeps Tonight)," "If I Had a Hammer," "Guantanamera," and "Turn! Turn! Turn!"

The four original members were reunited in 1981 for a concert that was filmed for the documentary Wasn't That a Time. Between reunions, Seeger had gone on to an influential solo career [see entry]. Ronnie Gilbert has recorded a number of albums, including two with Holly Near (Lifeline, 1983; Singing with You, 1986) and Harp

(1985), with Arlo Guthrie and Pete Seeger. Her solo releases include *The Spirit Is Free* (1985) and *Love Will Find a Way* (1989).

Jimmy Webb

Born August 15, 1946, Elk City, Oklahoma
1968—*Jim Webb Sings Jim Webb* (Epic)   1970—
Words and Music* (Reprise)   1971—*And So On
1972—*Letters*   1974—*Land's End* (Asylum)   1977—
***El Mirage* (Atlantic)   1982—*Angel Heart*   1993—**
***Suspending Disbelief* (Elektra).**

At age 21, Jimmy Webb was a millionaire, having written such pop hits as Glen Campbell's "By the Time I Get to Phoenix" and the Fifth Dimension's "Up, Up and Away," both of which were Grammy nominees in 1967 for Best Song ("Up, Up and Away" won). Other often-covered Webb songs include "Wichita Lineman," "MacArthur Park," "Galveston," and "The Moon Is a Harsh Mistress."

The son of a Baptist minister, Webb grew up in rural Oklahoma, learning piano and organ. When he moved with his family to San Bernardino, California, in 1964, he was already writing songs. In 1966 he enrolled in San Bernardino Valley College, but dropped out shortly thereafter when his mother died. He moved to Los Angeles and began making the rounds of the record business. For a time he earned $50 a week working at one recording studio. He also worked for Motown's publishing company, Jobete Music, which in 1965 published Webb's "Honey Come Back." Singer and record executive Johnny Rivers recorded a Webb tune he liked, "By the Time I Get to Phoenix." Though Rivers didn't have a hit with it, he recommended Webb's work to the Fifth Dimension, which had a 1967 hit with "Up, Up and Away." That year Glen Campbell covered "Phoenix." After TWA airlines used "Up, Up and Away" as a commercial theme, Webb formed a company that provided jingles for Chevrolet, Doritos tortilla chips, and Hamm's beer. In 1968 the Brooklyn Bridge hit with Webb's "The Worst That Could Happen." That year Richard Harris (for whom Webb wrote the entire LPs *A Tramp Shining* and *The Yard Went On Forever*) scored a #2 pop hit with Webb's melodramatic "MacArthur Park," which was later covered by Waylon Jennings (who won a Grammy with it in 1969), Donna Summer, the Four Tops, and countless others. Glen Campbell had a gold hit with "Wichita Lineman."

Meanwhile, in 1968 Epic issued an album of Webb singing his own demos, without Webb's consent. Webb had previously made his singing debut with an obscure group called Strawberry Children in 1967, on the single "Love Years Coming." In 1969 he also composed music for the films *Tell Them Willie Boy Is Here* and *How Sweet It Is* and worked on a semiautobiographical Broadway musical, *His Own Dark City.*

Webb's solo concert debut in Los Angeles in February 1970 was poorly received, despite a capacity audience; none of his solo albums has been popular. In 1972 Webb produced a Supremes album, and in 1973 he found his hitmaking touch again, as Art Garfunkel (who called Webb "the best songwriter since Paul Simon") hit with Webb's "All I Know." Webb went on to produce Cher's *Stars* LP, an album by his sister Susan in 1975, and a failed Fifth Dimension reunion LP, *Earthbound,* in 1976. His own solo albums continued to meet with little acclaim, and he began taking three- and four-year intervals between recordings. *El Mirage* was produced by Beatles producer George Martin.

Webb continued writing for films (*Doc* and *The Last Unicorn,* among others) and television (*Amazing Stories, Tales from the Crypt,* and *Faerie Tale Theater*). He moved to New York City, but his dream of writing musicals for the theater would not be realized. Over a decade passed before he released his critically acclaimed *Suspending Disbelief,* produced by Linda Ronstadt. Two late 1993 New York tribute concerts, featuring Glen Campbell, David Crosby, the Brooklyn Bridge, Art Garfunkel, Michael Feinstein, and Nanci Griffith performing Webb's music, drew rave reviews.

Bob Weir: See the Grateful Dead

Bob Welch: See Fleetwood Mac

Junior Wells

Born Amos Blackmore, December 9, 1934, Memphis, Tennessee
**1966—*Hoodoo Man Blues* (Delmark); *On Tap; It's My Life, Baby* (Vanguard); *South Side Jam* (Delmark)
1967—*Blues Hit the Big Town*   1968—*You're Tuff Enough* (Mercury); *Junior Wells Sings at the Golden Bear* (Blue Rock)   1971—*In My Younger Days* (Red Lightning)   1993—*Better Off with the Blues* (Telarc).**
**With Buddy Guy: 1968—*Coming at You* (Vanguard)
1972—*Buddy Guy and Junior Wells Play the Blues* (Atlantic)   1973—*I Was Walking Through the Woods* (Chess)   1979—*Got to Use Your Head* (Blues Ball)   1981—*Alone and Acoustic* (Hightone)
1982—*Drinkin' TNT and Smokin' Dynamite* (Blind Pig)   1993—*Pleading the Blues* (Evidence).**

One of the more noted Chicago blues singers and harmonica players, Junior Wells was inspired by the blues harp of Sonny Boy Williamson and Little Walter Jacobs.

Wells began playing harmonica as a child, learning from his neighbor, Junior Parker. He played in the streets of nearby Memphis until, at age 12, he moved from the family farm in Marion, Arkansas, to Chicago. He got his first paying job at age 14. He was just 16 when he auditioned for Muddy Waters, and in 1952 he replaced Little Walter in Waters' band.

It was with Waters that Wells cut his first solo hit, "Hoodoo Man." Wells' other best-known hit was "Messin' with the Kid," later covered by Rory Gallagher. In 1966 Wells teamed up with guitarist Buddy Guy, a long-running touring and recording partnership that ended only recently. The pair's 1972 album together, *Play the Blues,* featured guest appearances by Eric Clapton, Dr. John, and the J. Geils Band. In the Seventies Guy and Wells opened tour dates for the Rolling Stones. In more recent years, Wells has toured with a large band. He appeared with Van Morrison on six dates of his 1993 U.S. tour.

Mary Wells

Born Mary Esther Wells, May 13, 1943, Detroit, Michigan; died July 26, 1992, Los Angeles, California
1961—*Bye Bye Baby* (Motown)   1962—*The One Who Really Loves You*   1963—*Two Lovers and Other Great Hits*; *Recorded Live on Stage*   1964—*Mary Wells' Greatest Hits*; *Together* (with Marvin Gaye); *My Guy*   1965—*Mary Wells Sings Love Songs to the Beatles* (20th Century–Fox)   1966—*The Two Sides of Mary Wells* (Atco)   1981—*In and Out of Love* (Epic)   1990—*Keeping My Mind on Love* (Motorcity, U.K.); *Mary Wells* (Quality).

Mary Wells was Motown's first big star. At age 16, she met Berry Gordy Jr.'s assistant, Robert Bateman. She had written a song she wanted Jackie Wilson to record and had Bateman introduce her to Gordy, who had been writing material for Wilson. Unable to write her song down, she sang the tune for Gordy. He signed her, and Motown released that song as her debut single, "Bye Bye Baby" (#45 pop, #8 R&B, 1960).

She teamed up with performer, writer, and producer Smokey Robinson in 1962, scoring a string of hits, including "The One Who Really Loves You" (#8 pop, #2 R&B), "You Beat Me to the Punch" (#9 pop, #1 R&B), and "Two Lovers" (#7 pop, #1 R&B) in 1962; "Laughing Boy" (#15 pop, #6 R&B), "Your Old Stand By" (#40 pop, #3 R&B), and "What's Easy for Two Is So Hard for One" b/w "You Lost the Sweetest Boy" (#22 pop, #8 R&B) in 1963. In 1964 came her biggest Motown hit, "My Guy" (#1 pop). Like her other collaborations with Robinson, it featured Wells' smooth, knowing, but coy delivery backed by the producer's understated poppish arrangement. Next came two duets with Marvin Gaye, "What's the Matter with You Baby" (#17, 1964) and "Once Upon a Time" (#19, 1964). Indisputably the "first lady of Motown," Wells was the first female singer there to adopt a glamorous stage persona. In 1964, at their request, she opened for the Beatles.

But shortly thereafter Wells made a different kind of Motown history, becoming the first of Gordy's successful artists to sue the label. In the wake of her hits, Wells, encouraged by her husband songwriter Herman Griffin, sued Motown and won, arguing that the recording contract she signed at age 17 was invalid. Her departure came at the height of her success and was an embarrassment to Gordy, who scrambled to discourage other labels from signing her. In an interesting press release to the music-trade magazines, Motown not only warned that Wells was still under contract to it but bravely predicted that the Supremes would have a #1 single with their forthcoming "Where Did Our Love Go." The rest is history.

Initially, Wells' future looked promising. She received a large contract with 20th Century–Fox, along with promises that she would also be making films, but her releases there went nowhere, and she never appeared in a film. She next signed with Atco in late 1965, where she had the 1966 hit "Dear Lover" (#51 pop, #6 R&B), but none of her subsequent releases was as successful as her Motown recordings. "Dig the Way I Feel" (#35 R&B) on Jubilee in 1969 was a minor hit. She retired from performing. In 1967 she married Cecil Womack, with whom she had three children. They divorced in 1977, and Wells began a relationship with Cecil's brother, Curtis Womack, with whom she had another child. She began performing again in the Eighties, as renewed interest in Motown created a demand.

In 1987 Wells became one of several ex-Motown artists to begin recording with Ian Levine. She had just finished an album for U.K. release, *Keeping My Mind on Love,* when she discovered she had cancer of the larynx in 1990. A two-pack-a-day smoker, Wells was financially devastated by her illness; she had no health insurance. Many of her friends, including Mary Wilson and Martha Reeves, rallied around her, and several artists, including Rod Stewart, Bruce Springsteen, Bonnie Raitt, and Diana Ross, provided financial assistance. One of Wells' last tours found her sharing the bill with ex-Temptations David Ruffin and Eddie Kendricks, each of whom died within a year of her.

Wendy and Lisa

Formed 1986, Los Angeles, California
Wendy Melvoin (b. ca. 1964, Los Angeles), gtr., voc.; Lisa Coleman (b. ca. 1960, Los Angeles), kybds.
1987—*Wendy and Lisa* (Columbia)   1989—*Fruit at the Bottom*   1990—*Eroica* (Virgin)   1991—*Re-Mix-in-a-Carnation*.

Former Prince bandmates Wendy and Lisa found a small measure of success on their own with a progressive fusion of pop musical styles. Wendy Melvoin and Lisa Coleman have known each other since infancy in L.A., where their fathers were session musicians. Melvoin grew up on jazz; Coleman studied classical piano. Coleman began working with Prince in 1979, first touring with him on the *Dirty Mind* tour. From 1984 to 1986 she and Melvoin played in his band the Revolution, where they arranged songs and string sections. In the film *Purple Rain*, their characters challenged Prince's autocracy.

When Prince broke the band up, the women decided to form their own group. They played almost all the instruments on *Wendy and Lisa* (#88, 1987) and wrote the songs with coproducer Bobby Z., the Revolution's former drummer. In 1988 they played on Joni Mitchell's *Chalk Mark in a Rainstorm*. On *Fruit at the Bottom* (#119, 1989), the duo added more instrumentalists, including Wendy's twin sister, Susannah (who had fronted the Paisley Park band, Family). By *Eroica*, the band was largely a family affair, including Wendy's brother Jonathan on percussion and Lisa's brother David on cello and sister Cole singing. *Eroica* also featured guest vocals by k. d. lang and a song by Michael Penn. The album showed that Wendy and Lisa had musically broken free of Prince; labelwise, they had also liberated themselves from Columbia's expectations of sexy pop hits. *Eroica,* though widely praised by critics for its fusion of funk, rock, jazz, dance, and pop, failed to chart.

Paul Westerberg: See the Replacements

Western Swing

One of the original forms of "fusion" music, Western swing merged country & western string bands with the horn arrangements of Dixieland and big-band jazz. The genre began when string bands like Milton Brown's Musical Brownies began adding jazz and pop standards, and even blues, to their repertoires. Onetime Brownie Bob Wills formed his Texas Playboys in the mid-Thirties. Within a few years, Wills had expanded his outfit into a bona fide big band, with a horn section as well as banjos, fiddles, guitars, and pedal steel guitars. Wills' Texas Playboys remain the best-remembered of Western swing dance bands. Its anything-goes hybridizing and its early use of the electric guitar made Western swing an important precursor of rock, and along with Western swing revivalists like Asleep at the Wheel, country singers including Merle Haggard and Willie Nelson carry on Western swing's jazz-and-country experiments.

Wham!
Formed 1982, London, England
George Michael (b. Georgios Kyriacos Panayiotou, June 25, 1963, London), voc.; Andrew Ridgeley (b. Jan. 26, 1963, Windlesham, Eng.), gtr.

1983—*Fantastic* (Innervision, U.K.) 1984—*Make It Big* (Columbia) 1986—*Music from the Edge of Heaven.*
Andrew Ridgeley solo: 1990—*Son of Albert* (Epic).
George Michael solo: See entry.

Dismissed as a contrived teenybopper act during its mid-Eighties reign on the pop charts, the duo Wham! is remembered for its cotton-candy singles, and as singer/songwriter George Michael's stepping stone to fame [see entry]. Michael met Wham!'s other half, Andrew Ridgeley, while they were schoolmates in Bushey, a suburb of London. In 1979 the two began playing together in a ska-based band, the Executive. When that group dissolved, they wrote songs, made demos, and landed a deal with Innervision Records, a fledgling British label. Wham!'s debut album, *Fantastic,* entered the U.K. chart at #1. Innervision kept most of the royalties, though, and after some legal hassles, the duo switched to Epic.

Their first Epic single, 1984's "Wake Me Up Before You Go Go," premiered at #1 in England; later that year, buoyed by a bouncy video featuring Michael and Ridgeley cavorting in sportswear, it topped the American charts. The ballad "Careless Whisper" also reached #1 in both countries, as did Wham!'s second album, *Make It Big.* The hits "Everything She Wants" (#1), "Freedom" (#3), and "I'm Your Man" (#3) followed in 1985. Meanwhile, critics speculated that Michael, as Wham!'s principal writer and producer, was destined to pursue a career independent of Ridgeley, whose car-racing and girl-chasing were more conspicuous than his musical contributions. When Wham! did split, in 1986—the year of its third album, *Music from the Edge of Heaven* (#10)—they went out, fittingly, with a bang: a sellout farewell concert before 72,000 fans at London's Wembley Stadium.

Ridgeley has found little post-Wham! musical success. His 1990 solo album, *Son of Albert* (#130, 1990) bombed in the U.S. and the U.K., producing only one minor U.K. hit, "Shake" (#58 U.K., 1990).

The Whispers
Formed 1962, Los Angeles, California
Walter Scott (b. Sep. 3, 1943, Fort Worth, Tex.), voc.; Wallace Scott (b. Sep. 3, 1943, Fort Worth), voc.; Nicholas Caldwell (b. Apr. 5, 1944, Loma Linda, Calif.), voc.; Marcus Hutson (b. Jan. 8, 1943, Los Angeles), voc.; Gordy Harmon, voc.
1972—*The Whispers' Love Story* (Janus) 1974— (– Harmon; + Leaveil Degree [b. July 31, 1948, New Orleans, La.], voc.) 1976—*One for the Money* (Soul Train) 1977—*Open Up for Love* 1978—*Headlights* (Solar) 1979—*Whisper in Your Ear; Happy Holidays to You* 1980—*The Whispers; Imagination*

1981—*This Kind of Lovin'* 1982—*The Best of the Whispers; Love Is Where You Find It* 1983—*Love for Love* 1984—*So Good* 1987—*Just Gets Better with Time* 1990—*In the Mood* (Solar/Epic); *More of the Night* (Capitol) 1991—*Somebody Loves You* (Intermedia) 1994—*Whispers Christmas* (Capitol).

In 1980, after years of minor hits, the Whispers became one of black music's most popular vocal groups, and in 1987, 25 years after it started, the group had its biggest pop hit of all time, "Rock Steady," which was written and produced by L.A. Reid and Babyface.

Twin brothers Walter and Wallace Scott formed the group in Los Angeles with Nicholas Caldwell, Marcus Hutson, and Gordy Harmon. They cut a few singles in the mid-Sixties on the Dore label before they met producer Ron Carson. He produced Whispers singles for Canyon/Soul Clock Records, including "Planets of Life," which became a staple of their live show, and their first chart singles, "The Time Will Come" (#17 R&B, 1969) and "Seems Like I Gotta Do Wrong" (#50 pop, #6 R&B, 1970). When Canyon folded, they recorded for Janus, for which they continued with a steady stream of moderate R&B Top Thirty hits, including "Your Love Is So Doggone Good" (#19 R&B, 1971) and "I Only Meant to Wet My Feet" (#27 R&B, 1972).

In 1974 they went to Philadelphia to work with producer/guitarist Norman Harris and the MFSB rhythm section. "Bingo" and "A Mother for My Children" did well. By then, Leaveil Degree had replaced Harmon. In the mid-Seventies, the band signed with Dick Griffey's Soul Train (later renamed Solar) label and began to climb in popularity, with more R&B hits: "One for the Money (Part I)" (#10 R&B, 1976) and a cover of Bread's "Make It with You" (#10 R&B, 1977). "(Olivia) Lost and Turned Out," a song about prostitution, hit #13 on the R&B chart in the summer of 1978. They followed with "And the Beat Goes On" (#19 pop, #1 R&B, 1980) and "Lady" (#28 pop, #3 R&B, 1980), from 1980's *The Whispers*, "It's a Love Thing" (#28 pop, #2 R&B) in 1981, and "Tonight" (#4 R&B) in 1983.

Their biggest hit to date is "Rock Steady" (#7 pop, #1 R&B, 1987), which pushed *Just Gets Better with Time* to platinum. Their 1980 album *The Whispers* is also platinum; *Imagination, Love Is Where You Find It*, and *More of the Night* (#8 R&B, 1990) are all gold. Among the Whispers' more recent hits are "My Heart, Your Heart" (#4 R&B, 1990), "Innocent" (#3 R&B, 1990), and "Is It Good to You" (#7 R&B, 1991).

Ian Whitcomb

Born July 10, 1941, Woking, England
1965—*You Turn Me On* (Tower) 1966—*Ian Whitcomb's Mod, Mod Music Hall* 1967—*Yellow Underground* 1968—*Sock Me Some Rock* 1970—*World Record Club—On the Pier* 1972—*Under the Ragtime Moon* (United Artists) 1973—*Hip Hooray for Neville Chamberlain* (Argo) 1976—*Crooner Tunes* (Great Northwest Music Co.) 1977—*Ian Whitcomb's Red Hot Blue Heaven* (First American); *Treasures of Tin Pan Alley* (Audiophile) 1980—*Pianomelt* (Sierra Brier) 1981—*At the Ragtime Ball* (with the Melody Makers) (Audiophile); *Instrumentals* (First American); *The Rock 'n' Roll Years* 1982—*Don't Say Goodbye, Miss Ragtime* (Stomp Off); *In Hollywood!* (First American).

Ian Whitcomb's third single, a falsetto-voiced, B-side novelty song called "You Turn Me On," became a Top Ten hit in 1965; it was banned in various American cities, partially because of the heavy breathing and sighing on the record and the title itself. The followup, "N-E-R-V-O-U-S!," was modeled on the hit, but only reached #59 on the charts, and Whitcomb's rock & roll career tailed off.

He has never stopped recording, however, making albums that span the entire history of pop music, as chronicled in his 1972 book *After the Ball—Pop Music from Rag to Rock*. Around that same time, Whitcomb produced *Great Balls of Fire* by Mae West, and Goldie Hawn's single "Pitta Patta." He later worked as a disc jockey on L.A.'s KROQ. He has also written music for films (including *Bugs Bunny Superstar*) and written a PBS documentary entitled "Tin Pan Alley." In 1994 he published an autobiographical collection of essays, *The Beckoning Fairground: Notes of a British Exile in Lotus Land*.

Barry White

Born September 12, 1944, Galveston, Texas
1973—*I've Got So Much to Give* (20th Century–Fox); *Stone Gon'* 1974—*Can't Get Enough* 1975—*Just Another Way to Say I Love You; Barry White's Greatest Hits* 1976—*Let the Music Play; Is This Whatcha Wont?* 1977—*Barry White Sings for Someone You Love* 1978—*The Man* 1979—*The Message Is Love* (Unlimited Gold); *I Love to Sing the Songs I Sing* (20th Century–Fox) 1980—*Barry White's Greatest Hits, vol. 2; Sheet Music* (Unlimited Gold) 1981—*Barry and Glodean* (with Glodean White); *Beware!* 1982—*Change* 1983—*Dedicated* 1987—*The Right Night and Barry White* (A&M) 1989—*The Man Is Back!* 1991—*Put Me in Your Mix* 1992—*Just for You* 1994—*The Icon Is Love; All-Time Greatest Hits* (Mercury).
Love Unlimited Orchestra: 1974—*Rhapsody in White* (20th Century–Fox); *Together Brothers* soundtrack; *White Gold* 1975—*Music Maestro Please* 1976—*My Sweet Summer Suite* 1978—*My Musical Bouquet* 1979—*Super Movie Themes, Just*

a *Little Bit Different*   1981—*Let 'Em Dance* (Unlimited Gold); *Welcome Aboard* (Presents Mr. Webster Lewis)   1983—*Rise*.

With his deep, husky voice, lush musical arrangements and songs that usually dealt with love, singer, songwriter, and producer Barry White—despite a somewhat chubby physique—became a sex symbol during the Seventies. White was also one of the pioneering producers in disco, often using large orchestras on his records.

White made his singing debut in a Galveston church choir at age eight. Two years later he was church organist and served as part-time choir director. At 16, White joined the Upfronts, a Los Angeles R&B band, as a singer/pianist, and two years later he helped arrange "The Harlem Shuffle," a minor hit in 1963 for Bob and Earl.

White developed his writing and production skills and in 1966 went to work as an A&R man for Mustang Records. There he discovered a female vocal trio called Love Unlimited (Diana Taylor, Linda and Glodean James, whom White later married) and produced their gold single, 1972's "Walking in the Rain with the One I Love" (#14 pop, #6 R&B) for Uni Records. In 1973 White signed with 20th Century–Fox Records and made his national recording debut with "I'm Gonna Love You Just a Little More Baby" (#3 pop, #1 R&B), "Never, Never, Gonna Give Ya Up" (#7 pop, #2 R&B), and "I've Got So Much to Give" (#32 pop, #5 R&B). Also that year he started to write for the Love Unlimited Orchestra, with which he had a string-laden instrumental disco hit, "Love's Theme" (#1 pop, #10 R&B). Love Unlimited's "Under the Influence" was also a big hit. In 1973–74 alone, White wrote, produced, or performed on records whose total sales exceeded $16 million. Among his gold records are *Rhapsody in White* by the Love Unlimited Orchestra (#8, 1974), *Can't Get Enough* (#1, 1974), "Can't Get Enough of Your Love, Babe" (#1 pop and R&B, 1974), "You're the First, the Last, My Everything" (#2 pop, #1 R&B, 1974); *Just Another Way to Say I Love You* (#17, 1975), and *Barry White's Greatest Hits* (#23, 1975). In 1977 *Barry White Sings for Someone You Love* (#8 pop) went platinum and "It's Ecstasy When You Lay Down Next to Me" (#4 pop, #1 R&B) went gold. Subsequent R&B hit singles including "Playing Your Game, Baby" (#8 R&B, 1978) and "Your Sweetness Is My Weakness" (#2 R&B, 1978).

By the late Seventies, White's appeal had begun to cool, though he had minor hits with a cover of Billy Joel's "Just the Way You Are" (#44 R&B, 1979) and in 1982 with the title track from *Change*. With wife Glodean, White released an album and two minor R&B chart singles, "Didn't We Make It Happen, Baby" (#78 R&B, 1981) and "I Want You" (#79 R&B, 1981). In the late Eighties White experienced something of a resurgence, with "Sho' You Right" (#17 R&B, 1987) and "For Your Love (I'll Do Most

Anything)" (#27 R&B, 1987), followed by "The Secret Garden (Sweet Seduction Suite)" (#31 pop, #1 R&B, 1990), which featured Al B. Sure!, James Ingram, El DeBarge, White, and Quincy Jones, from Jones' *Back on the Block*. Later hits included "I Wanna Do It Good to You" (#26 R&B, 1990), "When Will I See You Again" (#32 R&B, 1990), and "Put Me in Your Mix" (#2 R&B, 1991). He also appears on Big Daddy Kane's 1991 R&B hit "All of Me." In late 1994 White returned to the top of the charts with "Practice What You Preach" (#18 pop, #1 R&B, 1994) from his platinum *The Icon Is Love* (#20 pop, #1 R&B, 1994).

Bukka White

Born Booker T. Washington White, November 12, 1906, Houston, Mississippi; died February 26, 1977, Memphis, Tennessee
1963—*Bukka White* (Sonet)   1964—*Bukka White* (Columbia)   1965—*Sky Songs, vols. 1 and 2* (Arhoolie)   1966—*Memphis Hot Shots* (Blue Horizon)   1969—*Mississippi Blues* (Takoma)   1970—*Big Daddy* (Biograph)   1976—*Legacy of the Blues: Bukka White* (GNP Crescendo)   1994—*The Complete Bukka White* (Columbia Legacy)   1995—*1963 Isn't 1962* (Genes).

A cousin of blues guitarist B. B. King, Bukka White was, after Robert Johnson, a widely heard Delta bluesman. White's guitar playing (usually on an acoustic guitar) has influenced B. B. King and many others; his singing has influenced Richie Havens, among others.

White learned guitar as a child from his father, and at age ten began traveling up and down the Mississippi River as a musician. He also worked as a boxer and a baseball player in the Negro leagues. He began recording in Memphis in 1930 for Victor. In 1937 he recorded his first blues hit, the often-covered "Shake 'Em On Down," for Vocalion in Chicago. But before he could record a followup, he was jailed for two years in Mississippi's Parchman Farm Prison for shooting a man. He was recorded by the Library of Congress while in prison in 1939; pressure from his record company helped win him parole.

Upon his release, White recorded a dozen of his most famous sides for the Okeh label, but he found his rough-hewn country blues were out of style. He labored in obscurity until 1963, when John Fahey heard a recording of his "Aberdeen Mississippi Blues" and, with Ed Denson, tracked White down in Aberdeen, and recorded him for his own Takoma label. The 11 songs recorded then were the first Bukka had committed to tape in 24 years.

By then in his late fifties, White enjoyed a career revival and toured the U.S. and Europe, making occasional film and television appearances. He suffered ill health in the mid-Seventies and succumbed to cancer.

Karyn White

Born Karyn Lay Vonne White, October 14, 1965, Los Angeles, California
1988—*Karyn White* (Warner Bros.)   1991—*Ritual of Love*   1994—*Make Him Do Right.*

In the late Eighties Karyn White went from being an accomplished backup singer to topping the charts with her own smooth mix of R&B and pop. As a youth growing up in Los Angeles, White sang in her church choir, which her mother directed; her father was a trumpet player. She entered talent shows and beauty pageants as a teen, and quit the cheerleading squad to save her voice. She sold her first song to a record company at age 17. White fronted the L.A. group Legacy for a while and toured as a backup singer for R&B vocalist O'Bryan. She did studio session work for such artists as Julio Iglesias, the Commodores, Ray Parker Jr., Bobby Brown, and Sheena Easton, and cowrote songs for Stephanie Mills and Lace.

In 1986 White had her first hit, singing lead on keyboardist Jeff Lorber's dance hit "Facts of Love" (#27, 1986). The single led to her own deal with Warner Bros. *Karyn White* (#19, 1988) went multiplatinum, led by the L.A. Reid and Babyface–produced "The Way You Love Me" (#7, 1988), the ballad/anthem "Superwoman" (#8, 1989), and "Secret Rendezvous" (#6, 1989). On *Ritual of Love*, Jimmy Jam and Terry Lewis (White's husband) produced and cowrote most of the songs; White coproduced the album and cowrote ten of 12 tracks. The album yielded the hits "Romantic" (#1, 1991) and "The Way I Feel About You" (#12, 1991). *Make Him Do Right* hit #22 on the R&B album chart.

Tony Joe White

Born July 23, 1943, Oak Grove, Louisiana
1968—*Black and White* (Monument)   1969—*Continued*   1970—*Tony Joe*   1971—*Tony Joe White* (Warner Bros.)   1972—*The Train I'm On*   1973—*Home Made Ice Cream*   1977—*Eyes* (20th Century–Fox); *Tony Joe White*   1980—*Real Thing* (Casablanca)   1983—*Dangerous* (Columbia)   1993—*The Best of Tony Joe White* (Warner Bros.).

One of the prime practitioners of the late-Sixties country-rock style known as swamp or bayou rock, Tony Joe White was the only one who actually came from the Louisiana bayous and rose to national prominence. White began playing music at age 16 and formed Tony and the Mojos. His next band, Tony and the Twilights, went to Texas, where White remained as a solo singer/songwriter after the group disbanded. He then moved to Nashville, made the rounds of music publishers, and eventually hooked up with Billy Swan, who produced White's first three albums.

White's first two singles, "Georgia Pines" and "Watching the Trains Go By," went unnoticed. "Soul Francisco" was a big European hit in 1967, and White continued to be a major recording and performing star in Europe for the next five years (in 1972 he toured Europe with Creedence Clearwater Revival). In 1969 he hit the Top Ten with the single "Polk Salad Annie," which showcased White's deep, gruff voice and the stylized guitar technique White called "whomper stomper."

Despite frequent TV appearances, it was White's last hit in the U.S. However, several White songs were hits for other artists. Elvis Presley covered "Polk Salad Annie" (as did Tom Jones) and "I've Got a Thing About You Baby." In 1969 Dusty Springfield had a minor hit with White's "Willie and Laura Mae Jones"; and a year later Brook Benton made it to the Top Five with "A Rainy Night in Georgia." White has also done commercial work for McDonald's and Levi's. Two of his early-Nineties albums, *Closer to the Truth* and *Path of a Decent Groove*, were successful in Europe, New Zealand, and Australia. They were not released domestically.

White Lion

Formed 1983, Brooklyn, New York
Vito Bratta, gtr.; Dave Capozzi, drums; Felix Robinson, bass; Mike Tramp (b. Den.), voc.
1987—(– Robinson; – Capozzi; + James Lomenzo, bass; + Greg D'Angelo, drums) *Pride* (Atlantic)
1988—*Fight to Survive* (Grand Slam)   1989—*Big Game* (Atlantic)   1991—(– Lomenzo; – D'Angelo; + Tommy Caradonna, bass; + Jimmy DeGrasso, drums) *Mane Attraction.*

Led by Denmark native Mike Tramp, White Lion was a pretty-boy metal band distinguished by better-than-average songcraft. Their debut album, *Pride* (#11, 1987), sold over two million copies, yielding two Top Ten singles: "Wait" (#8, 1987) and "When the Children Cry" (#3, 1988).

Tramp, who moved to the U.S. after a six-album stint with the band Mabel in his native country, where he was known as the "Danish Michael Jackson," formed White Lion with Vito Bratta in 1983. They signed with Elektra in 1984. The label was unhappy with their initial effort, *Fight to Survive*, and refused to release the album. (It was released by an independent label in 1988, reaching #151.) With a new rhythm section, including Anthrax founding member Greg D'Angelo on drums, the band was picked up by Atlantic, which released *Pride* in late 1987. *Big Game* (#19, 1989) sold respectably but contained no hit singles. *Mane Attraction* (#61, 1991), recorded with yet another rhythm section, contained a cover of Golden Earring's "Radar Love." The band hasn't been heard from since.

Whitesnake

Formed 1978, Yorkshire, England

David Coverdale (b. Sep. 22, 1949, Saltburn, Eng.), voc.; Micky Moody (b. Aug. 30, 1950, Eng.), gtr.; Bernie Marsden, gtr.; Brian Johnston, kybds.; Neil Murray, bass; David Dowle, drums.

1978—(– Johnston; + Jon Lord [b. June 9, 1941, Leicester, Eng.], kybds.) 1979—(– Dowle; + Ian Paice [b. June 29, 1948, Nottingham, Eng.], drums) 1980—Ready an' Willing (Mirage); Live . . . in the Heart of the City 1981—Come an' Get It 1982—(– Marsden; – Murray; – Paice; + Mel Galley, gtr.; + Colin Hodgkinson [b. Oct. 14, 1945, Eng.], bass; + Cozy Powell [b. Dec. 29, 1947, Cirencester, Eng.], drums) 1983—(– Moody; – Hodgkinson; + John Sykes [b. July 29, 1959, Eng.], gtr.; + Murray, bass) 1984—Slide It In (Geffen) (– Lord; – Galley; + Richard Bailey, kybds.) 1985—(– Bailey; – Powell; + Don Airey, kybds.; + Aynsley Dunbar [b. 1946, Liverpool, Eng.], drums) 1987—Whitesnake (– Sykes; – Murray; – Dunbar; + Adrian Vandenburg [b. Holland], gtr.; + Vivian Campbell, gtr.; + Rudy Sarzo [b. Nov. 9, 1952, Havana, Cuba], bass; + Tommy Aldridge, drums) 1988—(– Campbell; + Steve Vai [b. June 6, 1960, Carle Place, N.Y.], gtr.) 1989—Slip of the Tongue 1994—Greatest Hits.

It wasn't just rock critics who derided Whitesnake as a Led Zeppelin rip-off—Led Zep frontman Robert Plant himself once dismissed Whitesnake vocalist and driving force David Coverdale as "David Coverversion." With his long blond hair, aristocratic English accent, and relentless sexual double-entendres, Coverdale struck many detractors as the real-life model for David St. Hubbins of mock-metal parody Spinal Tap. Coverdale often had the last laugh, however, scoring pop and metal hits and, eventually, even recording with Plant's erstwhile Led Zep cohort, guitarist Jimmy Page.

Coverdale had been with Deep Purple from 1973 to 1976 [see entry], then recorded two solo albums, *Whitesnake* and *Northwinds*; the former provided a band name when Coverdale formed his own group, recruiting members from Deep Purple and lesser-known U.K. hardrock outfits such as Juicy Lucy, Babe Ruth, and Gillan. The band released two Britain-only albums before making its U.S. debut with *Ready an' Willing* (#90, 1980), which yielded a minor hit single in "Fool for Your Loving" (#53, 1980). A steady stream of personnel changes, but no hit singles, followed for the next few years, until the band was signed to Geffen; despite the lack of a hit, *Slide It In* sold well (#40, 1984) and eventually went double platinum. The arrival of former Thin Lizzy guitarist John Sykes for that album proved crucial, as he helped to write the songs that would put Whitesnake over the top on its next album.

Whitesnake (#2, 1987), which would sell over six million copies, featured a chart-topping single in the pop-metal "Here I Go Again," and a #2 single in the power-ballad "Is This Love"; the very Zeppelinesque "Still of the Night" was a minor hit (#79, 1987). The band's fortunes were boosted by heavy MTV play of its music videos, which featured Coverdale's buxom girlfriend, B-movie actress Tawny Kitaen, whom he married in 1989. *Slip of the Tongue* (#10, 1989) was not as huge as its predecessor, but still successful; hit singles included an updated "Fool for Your Loving" (#37, 1989) and "The Deeper the Love" (#28, 1990). Three years later Coverdale had broken up with Kitaen and hooked up with Page (who had reportedly tried and failed to secure Plant) to record *Coverdale-Page* [see Jimmy Page entry]. After releasing *Greatest Hits,* Coverdale re-formed Whitesnake with Adrian Vandenburg, Rudy Sarzo (ex–Quiet Riot bassist), Denny Carmassi (drummer for Heart) and Warren De Martini (ex-Ratt guitarist) for a tour in Europe.

White Zombie

Formed 1985, New York City, New York

Rob Zombie (b. Robert Straker, 1966), voc.; Sean Yseult (b. 1966), bass; Ivan dePrume (b. Brooklyn, N.Y.), drums; John Ricci, gtr.

1987—Psycho Head Blowout EP (Silent Explosion); Soul-Crusher 1989—Make Them Die Slowly (Caroline) (– Ricci; + Jay "J." Yuenger [b. Chicago, Ill., 1967], gtr.) 1992—La Sexorcisto: Devil Music Vol. 1 (Geffen) 1993—(– dePrume; + Phil "Philo" Buerstatte [b. 1967, Madison, Wisc.], drums) 1995—(– Buerstatte; + John Tempesta, drums) Astro-Creep: 2000.

Fusing hardcore, heavy metal, and outsized theatrics, White Zombie celebrate trash culture, incorporating such elements as B-movie humor and true-crime gore. Along the lines of Alice Cooper, GWAR, and the Cramps, they are as much a concept as a band.

Moving to New York City after high school, Rob Straker met Sean Yseult at CBGB in the late Eighties. Soon living together, they formed White Zombie, taking the name from a 1932 Bela Lugosi horror film. Their self-produced EP gained them cult fame, as did their album *Soul-Crusher,* and in 1989 Bill Laswell produced *Make Them Die Slowly.*

White Zombie's major-label debut arrived amid personnel changes and notoriety. Televangelists attacked their gleefully "Satanic" lyrics; Zombie courted controversy by asking mass murderer Charles Manson for permission to use a sample of his voice (he declined, as did Vincent Price when presented with a similar request). When MTV cartoon characters Beavis and Butt-head praised *Sexorcisto,* the album entered the Top Thirty.

White Zombie reciprocated by contributing a song to the 1993 *Beavis and Butt-head Experience* album. The band returned in 1995 with a Top Ten album, *Astro-Creep: 2000* (#6, 1995).

Chris Whitley

Born Christopher Becker Whitley, August 31, 1960, Houston, Texas

1991—*Living with the Law* (Columbia) 1995—*Din of Ecstasy.*

Slide guitarist, singer, and songwriter Chris Whitley's blues-rock debut album won him critical acclaim and a coveted opening-act slot on Tom Petty and the Heartbreakers' 1991 U.S. tour. *Living with the Law* was the end product of a lot of travel and some lucky encounters with well-connected music industry people.

Whitley had a rootless upbringing, moving with his family from Houston to Dallas, Oklahoma City, and Connecticut; when he was 11 his parents divorced, and he moved with his mother to central Mexico, and then to a log cabin in Vermont. He took up guitar at age 15, inspired by Jimi Hendrix and Creedence Clearwater Revival. When he heard the acoustic-dobro song "Dallas" on Johnny Winter's debut album, Whitley got a Mississippi National steel-bodied guitar and began teaching himself bottleneck blues. Two years later he quit high school and moved to New York City, playing in parks and on streetcorners, where one listener who ran a travel agency offered to send him to Belgium. There, Whitley became a minor star, drifting from blues to record one funk-oriented album, before returning to New York, where a chance meeting with producer Daniel Lanois (U2, Peter Gabriel, Robbie Robertson) led to management and record deals. He recorded his 1991 debut album at Lanois' New Orleans mansion with the producer's Canadian associate, Malcolm Burn, producing. Four years later Whitley released *Din of Ecstasy.*

The Who

Formed 1964, London, England

Peter Dennis Blandford Townshend (b. May 19, 1945, London), gtr., voc.; Roger Harry Daltrey (b. Mar. 1, 1944, London), voc.; John Alec Entwistle (b. Oct. 9, 1944, London), bass, French horn, voc.; Keith John Moon (b. Aug. 23, 1947, London; d. Sep. 7, 1978, London), drums.

1965—*The Who Sings My Generation* (Decca) 1966—*Happy Jack* 1967—*The Who Sell Out* 1968—*Magic Bus—The Who on Tour* 1969— *Tommy* 1970—*Live at Leeds* 1971—*Who's Next; Meaty Beaty Big and Bouncy* 1973—*Quadrophenia* (MCA) 1974—*Odds and Sods* 1975—*The Who by*

The Who: Roger Daltrey, Pete Townshend, John Entwistle, Keith Moon

Numbers 1978—*Who Are You* (– Moon) 1979— *The Kids Are Alright* soundtrack; *Quadrophenia* soundtrack (Polydor) (+ Kenney Jones [b. Sep. 16, 1948, London], drums) 1981—*Face Dances* (Warner Bros.); *Hooligans* (MCA) 1982—*It's Hard* (Warner Bros.) 1983—*Who's Greatest Hits* (MCA) 1984— *Who's Last* 1985—*Who's Missing* 1987—*Two's Missing* 1988—*Who's Better, Who's Best* 1990— *Join Together* 1994—*The Who: Thirty Years of Maximum R&B* 1995—*Live at Leeds.*
Pete Townshend solo: 1972—*Who Came First* (Decca) 1977—*Rough Mix* (with Ronnie Lane) (MCA) 1980—*Empty Glass* (Atco) 1982—*All the Best Cowboys Have Chinese Eyes* 1983—*Scoop* 1985—*White City—A Novel* 1986—*Pete Townshend's Deep End Live!* 1987—*Another Scoop* 1989—*The Iron Man* 1993—*PsychoDerelict* (Atlantic).
John Entwistle solo: 1971—*Smash Your Head Against the Wall* (Decca) 1972—*Whistle Rymes* 1973—*John Entwistle's Rigor Mortis Sets In* (Track) 1975—*John Entwistle's Ox: Mad Dog* 1981—*Too Late the Hero* (Atco).
Keith Moon solo: 1975—*Two Sides of the Moon* (MCA).
Roger Daltrey solo: 1973—*Daltrey* (MCA) 1975— *Ride a Rock Horse* 1977—*One of the Boys* 1980—

McVicar soundtrack (Polydor) 1982—*Best Bits* (MCA) 1985—*Under a Raging Moon* (Atlantic) 1987—*Can't Wait to See the Movie* 1991—*The Best of Rockers and Ballads* (Polydor) 1992—*Rocks in the Head* (Atlantic) 1994—*A Celebration: The Music of Pete Townshend and the Who* (Continuum).

The Who started out as musical standard-bearers for England's Mods and also proclaimed themselves as "Maximum R&B." But their ringing power chords and explosive beat made them one of the most influential bands in rock history. The Who were godfathers of punk, pioneers of the rock opera, and among the first rock groups to integrate (rather than merely fiddle with) synthesizers. The smashed guitars and overturned (or blown-up) drum kits they left in their wake fittingly symbolized the violent passions of a turbulent band. The Who's distinctive sound was born of the couplings and collisions among Pete Townshend's alternately raging or majestic guitar playing, Keith Moon's nearly anarchic drumming style, John Entwistle's agile, thundering bass lines, and Roger Daltrey's impassioned vocals. Ever since guitarist and main songwriter Pete Townshend declared in "My Generation," "Hope I die before I get old," he has been embraced as a spokesman, a role he assumed (he claims) reluctantly. Nonetheless, for the rest of his career with the Who Townshend explored rock's philosophical topography, from the raw rebelliousness of "My Generation" and adolescent angst of "I Can't Explain," to such ambitious, emotionally rich songs as "Love Reign O'er Me."

All four band members grew up around London—Townshend, Daltrey, and Entwistle in the working-class Shepherd's Bush area. Townshend's parents were professional entertainers. He and Entwistle knew each other at school in the late Fifties and played in a Dixieland band when they were in their early teens, with Townshend on banjo and Entwistle on trumpet. They played together in a rock band, but Entwistle left in 1962 to join the Detours. That band included Daltrey, a sheet-metal worker. When the Detours needed to replace a rhythm guitarist, Entwistle suggested Townshend, and Daltrey switched from lead guitar to vocals when the original singer, Colin Dawson, left in 1963. Drummer Doug Sandom was soon replaced by Moon, who left a surf band called the Beachcombers. By early 1964 the group had changed its name to the Who. Not long afterward, the excitement inspired by Townshend's bashing his guitar out of frustration during a show ensured it would become a part of the act.

Shortly thereafter, the group came under the wing of manager Pete Meaden, who renamed them the High Numbers and gave them a better-dressed Mod image. The High Numbers released an unsuccessful single, "I'm

the Face" b/w "Zoot Suit" (both written by Meaden), then got new managers, former small-time film directors Kit Lambert and Chris Stamp. By late 1964 the quartet had become the Who again, and with Lambert and Stamp's encouragement they became an even more Mod band, with violent stage shows and a repertoire including blues, James Brown, and Motown covers, solely because their Mod audiences loved that music.

Despite the billing, the Who's original songs were anything but classic R&B. The group's demo of "I Can't Explain," with pre–Led Zeppelin Jimmy Page adding guitar, brought them to producer Shel Talmy (who had also worked with the Kinks) and got them a record deal. When "I Can't Explain" came out in January 1965, it was ignored until the band appeared on the TV show *Ready, Steady, Go.* Townshend smashed his guitar, Moon overturned his drums, and the song eventually reached #8 in Britain. "Anyway, Anyhow, Anywhere" also reached the British Top Ten, followed in November 1965 by "My Generation." It went to #2 in the U.K. but reached only #75 in the U.S. In Britain the Who had established their sound and their personae. Townshend played guitar with full-circle windmilling motions, Daltrey strutted like a bantam fighter, Entwistle (whose occasional songwriting effort revealed a macabre sense of humor) just stood there seemingly unmoved as Moon happily flailed all over his drum kit.

After the Who's fourth hit single, "Substitute" (#5 U.K., 1966), Lambert replaced Talmy as producer. Their second album, *A Quick One* (*Happy Jack* in the U.S.; #67, 1967), included a ten-minute mini-opera as the title track, shortly before the Beatles' concept album *Sgt. Pepper's Lonely Hearts Club Band.* The Who also began to make inroads in the U.S. with "Happy Jack" (#24, 1967) and a tour that included the performance filmed at the Monterey Pop Festival in June.

The Who Sell Out (#48, 1967) featured mock-advertisement songs and genuine jingles from offshore British pirate radio stations; it also contained another mini-opera, "Rael," and a Top Ten hit in England and the U.S., "I Can See for Miles." In October 1968 the band released *Magic Bus* (#39, 1968), a compilation of singles and B sides, while Townshend worked on his 90-minute rock opera, *Tommy.* The story of a deaf, dumb, and blind boy turned pinball champion/pop idol turned autocratic messianic guru was variously considered both pretentious and profound. Most important, however, *Tommy* was the first successful rock opera. The album hit #4 in the U.S., and its first single, "Pinball Wizard," went to #19. The band would perform *Tommy* a handful of times in its entirety—at London's Coliseum in 1969, at New York City's Metropolitan Opera House on June 6 and 7, 1970, and on some dates during its 1989 reunion tour. Excerpts, including "See Me, Feel Me," "Pinball Wizard," and the instrumental "Underture," were thereafter part of the

Grammy Awards

Bunny Wailer
1990 Best Reggae Recording: *Time Will Tell: A Tribute to Bob Marley*
1994 Best Reggae Album: *Crucial! Roots Classics*

Tom Waits
1992 Best Alternative Music Album: *Bone Machine*

T-Bone Walker
1970 Best Ethnic or Traditional Recording: *Good Feelin'*

Jennifer Warnes
1982 Best Pop Performance by a Duo or Group with Vocal: "Up Where We Belong" (with Joe Cocker)
1987 Best Pop Performance by a Duo or Group with Vocal: "(I've Had) The Time of My Life" (with Bill Medley)

Dionne Warwick
1968 Best Contemporary Pop Vocal Performance, Female: "Do You Know the Way to San Jose"
1970 Best Contemporary Vocal Performance, Female: "I'll Never Fall in Love Again"
1979 Best Pop Vocal Performance, Female: "I'll Never Love This Way Again"
1979 Best R&B Vocal Performance, Female: "Déjà Vu"
1986 Best Pop Performance by a Duo or Group with Vocal: "That's What Friends Are For" (with Elton John, Gladys Knight, and Stevie Wonder)

Dinah Washington
1959 Best R&B Performance: "What a Diff'rence a Day Makes"

Grover Washington Jr.
1981 Best Jazz Fusion Performance, Vocal or Instrumental: *Winelight*

Don Was (Was [Not Was])
1989 Album of the Year (as producer): *Nick of Time*
1994 Producer of the Year

Muddy Waters
1971 Best Ethnic or Traditional Recording: *They Call Me Muddy Waters*
1972 Best Ethnic or Traditional Recording: *The London Muddy Waters Sessions*
1975 Best Ethnic or Traditional Recording: *The Muddy Waters Woodstock Album*
1977 Best Ethnic or Traditional Recording: *Hard Again*
1978 Best Ethnic or Traditonal Recording: *I'm Ready*
1979 Best Ethnic or Traditional Recording: *Muddy "Mississippi" Waters Live*
1992 Lifetime Achievement Award

Jody Watley
1987 Best New Artist

Weather Report
1979 Best Jazz Fusion Performance, Vocal or Instrumental: *8:30*

Jimmy Webb
1967 Song of the Year: "Up, Up and Away"
1968 Best Arrangement Accompanying Vocalist(s): "MacArthur Park"
1985 Best Country Song: "Highwayman"

Wendy and Lisa
1984 Best Album of Original Score Written for a Motion Picture or a Television Special: *Purple Rain* (with John L. Nelson and Prince)

Deniece Williams
1986 Best Gospel Performance by a Duo or Group, Choir, or Chorus: "They Say" (with Sandi Patti)
1986 Best Soul Gospel Performance, Female: "I Surrender All"
1987 Best Gospel Performance, Female: "I Believe in You"

Hank Williams
1987 Lifetime Achievement Award
1989 Best Country Vocal Collaboration: "There's a Tear in My Beer" (with Hank Williams Jr.)

Hank Williams Jr.
1989 Best Country Vocal Collaboration: "There's a Tear in My Beer" (with Hank Williams Sr.)

Paul Williams
1977 Song of the Year: "Love Theme for *A Star Is Born* (Evergreen)" (with Barbra Streisand)
1979 Best Recording for Children: *The Muppet Movie* (with Jim Henson)

Steve Winwood
1986 Record of the Year: "Higher Love"
1986 Best Pop Vocal Performance, Male: "Higher Love"

Bill Withers
1971 Best R&B Song: "Ain't No Sunshine"
1981 Best R&B Song: "Just the Two of Us" (with others)
1987 Best R&B Song: "Lean on Me"

Stevie Wonder
1973 Album of the Year: *Innervisions* (two Grammys: one as producer, one as performer)
1973 Best Vocal Performance, Male: "You Are the Sunshine of My Life"
1973 Best R&B Song: "Superstition"
1973 Best R&B Vocal Performance, Male: "Superstition"
1974 Album of the Year: *Fulfillingness' First Finale* (two Grammys: one as producer, one as performer)
1974 Best Pop Vocal Performance, Male: *Fulfillingness' First Finale*
1974 Best R&B Song: "Living for the City"
1974 Best R&B Vocal Performance, Male: "Boogie On Reggae Woman"

live show. Troupes mounted productions of it around the world (the Who's performances had been concert versions), and Townshend oversaw a new recording of it in 1972, backed by the London Symphony and featuring Rod Stewart, Steve Winwood, Sandy Denny, Richard Burton, and others. In 1975 Ken Russell directed the controversial film version, which included Eric Clapton ("Eyesight to the Blind"), Tina Turner ("Acid Queen"), and Elton John ("Pinball Wizard"), as well as Ann-Margret, Oliver Reed, and Jack Nicholson. Moon (as the lecherous Uncle Ernie) and Daltrey (in the title role) also appeared in the film. Townshend collaborated with director Des McAnuff on a stage version of *Tommy* that arrived on Broadway in 1993.

Bits of *Tommy* turned up on *Live at Leeds* (#4, 1970), a juggernaut live set, which was followed by *Who's Next* (#4, 1971), a staple of FM rock radio. It included Townshend's first experiments with synthesizers—"Baba O'Riley," "Bargain," and "Won't Get Fooled Again," three songs that Townshend originally conceived as part of another (unfinished) rock opera entitled *Lifehouse*. (In 1995 a new version of *Live at Leeds*, which includes fourteen songs as opposed to the original's six, was released.) The compilation *Meaty Beaty Big and Bouncy* (#11, 1971) was followed two years later by the Who's second double-album rock opera, *Quadrophenia* (#2, 1973), a tribute to the tortured inner life of the Mods. It too was a hit and became a movie directed by Franc Roddam in 1979, with Sting of the Police in the role of the bellboy.

While the Who were hugely popular, *Quadrophenia* signaled that Townshend was now a generation older than the fans he had initially spoken for. While he agonized over his role as an elder statesman of rock—as he would do for years to come—the Who released *Odds and Sods* (#15, 1974), a compilation of the previous decade's outtakes. *The Who by Numbers* (#8, 1975) was the result of Townshend's self-appraisal ("However Much I Booze"); it lacked the Who's usual vigor, but yielded a hit single in "Squeeze Box" (#16, 1975). The band could dependably pack arenas wherever it went, but it took some time off the road after *By Numbers.*

The group members began pursuing individual projects. Moon released a novelty solo disc, *Two Sides of the Moon,* which featured such guests as Ringo Starr, Harry Nilsson, Dick Dale, Joe Walsh, and Flo and Eddie; Entwistle recorded solo LPs with bands called Ox (with which he toured in 1975) and Rigor Mortis, and produced four tracks on the debut album by the semipopular Fabulous Poodles.

Daltrey also recorded solo. His first two efforts are widely considered mediocre, although *Daltrey* boasted the oft-played "Hard Life/Giving It All Away," which, like the rest of the album, was composed by a then unknown named Leo Sayer and Adam Faith. While Daltrey's albums did decently, he had only one Top Forty single in the U.S., "Without Your Love," from the soundtrack of *McVicar.* The Townshend-penned "After the Fire" received substantial video exposure when released in 1985. Daltrey found considerably more success as an actor. Besides *Tommy,* he has starred in Ken Russell's over-the-top "biography" of composer Franz Liszt, *Lisztomania* (1975), and *McVicar* (1980), the true story of the famous British criminal John McVicar. In the mid-Eighties he played the double role of the Dromio twins in a PBS production of Shakespeare's *Comedy of Errors.* In recent years, he has also appeared on the London stage (*The Beggar's Opera,* 1991) and on British television ("The Little Match Girl," 1990).

In 1970 Townshend contributed four tracks to *Happy Birthday,* a privately released, limited-edition album recorded as a tribute to Townshend's guru, Meher Baba. The following year, *I Am,* a similar limited-edition Baba tribute album, was released. It contained another Townshend track, a nine-minute instrumental version of "Baba O'Riley." As both these records were heavily bootlegged, Townshend's response was to create an "official" version of both albums. The result, *Who Came First* (#69, 1972), was Townshend's first "real" solo album. It included the tracks from *Happy Birthday* and *I Am,* plus new songs, and demos of the Who tracks "Pure and Easy" and "Let's See Action." His second solo release was a collaboration with ex-Faces Ronnie Lane, *Rough Mix* (#45, 1977), which featured a number of FM/AOR radio staples: "Street in the City," "My Baby Gives It Away," and "Heart to Hang On To."

Meanwhile, punk was burgeoning in Britain, and the Sex Pistols among others were brandishing the Who's old power chords and attitude. Townshend's continuing identity crisis showed up in the title of *Who Are You* (#2, 1978), but the title song became a hit single (#14) that fall, and the album went double platinum. It was the last and highest-charting album by the original band.

The next few years brought tragedy and turmoil, and what Townshend later described as the end of the Who in the death of Keith Moon. Moon always reveled in his reputation as the madman of rock, and his outrageous stunts—onstage and off—were legend. His prodigious drinking and drug abuse (he was once paralyzed for days after accidentally ingesting an elephant tranquilizer) had begun to diminish his playing ability. In 1975 he left England for Los Angeles, where he continued to drink heavily. He returned to England and was trying to kick his alcoholism, but on September 7, 1978, Moon died of an overdose of a sedative, Heminevrin, that had been prescribed to prevent seizures induced by alcohol withdrawal. Although the group continued for another three years, each of the three surviving original members has stated repeatedly that the Who was never the same again.

In 1979 the Who oversaw a concert documentary of their early years, *The Kids Are Alright* (soundtrack, #8, 1979), and worked on the soundtrack version of *Quadrophenia* (#46, 1979), which also included a number of Mod favorites performed by the original artists (such as Booker T. and the MG's' "Green Onions" and James Brown's "Night Train"). Kenney Jones, formerly of the Small Faces, replaced Moon, and session keyboardist John "Rabbit" Bundrick began working with the Who. The new lineup toured, but tragedy struck again when 11 concertgoers were killed—trampled to death or asphyxiated—in a rush for "festival seating" spots at Cincinnati's Riverfront Coliseum on December 3, 1979. The incident occurred before the show, and the group wasn't told of it until afterward.

After 15 years with Decca/MCA, the Who signed a band contract with Warner Bros., and Townshend got a solo deal with Atco. His *Empty Glass* (#5, 1980) included the U.S. Top Ten hit "Let My Love Open the Door" and "Rough Boys," a song long believed to have been an angry reply to a punk musician who had insulted the Who during an interview. Much later, in a 1989 interview with writer Timothy White, Townshend denied that was the case, saying, "It's about homosexuality," and adding that "And I Moved" was as well. Townshend's admission of having "had a gay life" and his statement that "I know how it feels to be a woman because I *am* a woman" came as a surprise to many, including his bandmates.

In 1981 Townshend performed solo with an acoustic guitar at a benefit for Amnesty International, which was recorded as *The Secret Policeman's Ball*. His falling

asleep onstage was the first public sign of his deepening drug addiction. Since the year before, Townshend had been abusing alcohol, cocaine, and freebase cocaine mixed with heroin. He subsequently developed an addiction to Ativan, a tranquilizer he was prescribed during treatment for alcoholism. Ativan combined with freebase and heroin resulted in a highly publicized, near-fatal overdose during which he was rushed to the hospital from a London club. Townshend subsequently underwent electro-acupuncture treatment and cleaned up in 1982.

Amid all this, the revamped Who soldiered on. *Face Dances* (#4, 1981) included the hit single "You Better You Bet" (#18, 1981) and "Don't Let Go the Coat." But Townshend later called the new lineup's debut album a disappointment. One month after *Face Dances* came out, the Who's former producer/manager, Kit Lambert, died after falling down a flight of stairs: He was 45. (Pete Meaden had died three weeks before Moon, in 1978.) Townshend released the wordy *All the Best Cowboys Have Chinese Eyes* (#26, 1982), and soon followed it with the group's *It's Hard* (#8, 1982), an album Daltrey has since been quoted as saying should never have been released. It produced the group's last Top Thirty hit to date, "Athena" (#28). The Who then embarked on what they announced would be their last tour, ending with a concert in Toronto on December 17, 1982.

Although the group officially broke up in 1982, the quartet has reunited to perform several times since, appearing at Live Aid in 1985 and at a U.K. music-awards program in 1988. They celebrated the group's silver anniversary in 1989 with a 43-date U.S. tour, which included guest-star-studded performances of *Tommy* in Los Angeles and New York City, and later in London. For this tour Jones was replaced by session drummer Simon Phillips. Townshend, whose hearing was extremely damaged from years of listening to loud music through headphones, had to play standing behind a plastic baffle to block the onstage noise.

Townshend also released solo projects throughout the Eighties: *Scoop* (#35, 1983) and *Another Scoop* (#198, 1987) collect demo tapes, home recordings, and sundry tracks of historical interest to fans. *White City—A Novel* (#26, 1985) is a concept piece, the soundtrack to a long-form video of the same title, and includes "Face the Face"; *The Iron Man: The Musical by Pete Townshend* is the star-studded (Daltrey, Nina Simone, John Lee Hooker) soundtrack to Townshend's rock opera based on a children's story by poet Ted Hughes. *Deep End Live!*, released with an accompanying live video, barely scraped into the Top 100.

Townshend wrote in the liner notes to the 1994 boxset career retrospective *Thirty Years of Maximum R&B*: "I don't like the Who much." Through the years his attitude toward the group has seemed false at worst, conflicted at best. Despite Townshend's other projects and endeavors, including an editorship with book publisher Faber and Faber and publication of his collected stories, *Horse's Neck* (1985), it is the Who legacy for which he will be remembered. In 1993 the Broadway production of *Tommy* won five Tony Awards, including one for Townshend for Best Original Score. The next year saw the release of Townshend's *PsychoDerelict* (#118, 1994), a concept album that includes pieces written originally for the *Lifehouse* project. An examination of rock stardom's ravages, *PsychoDerelict* was also performed as a theater piece and filmed (it was subsequently broadcast on PBS). That year he also embarked on his first solo tour with a set list that included *PsychoDerelict* and a number of Who classics, including "Won't Get Fooled Again." In February 1994 Townshend, Daltrey, and Entwistle reunited for two Carnegie Hall concerts in celebration of Daltrey's 50th birthday. Accompanied by a 65-piece orchestra, the trio was also joined by guest stars including Sinéad O'Connor, Eddie Vedder, and Lou Reed, and the show was filmed for cable television. As of this writing, Townshend was at work on the stage version of *The Iron Man,* and Daltrey was producing a film biography of Moon.

Wilco: See Uncle Tupelo

Deniece Williams

Born June 3, 1951, Gary, Indiana
1976—*This Is Niecy* (Columbia)   1977—*Songbird*
1978—*That's What Friends Are For* (with Johnny Mathis)   1979—*When Love Comes Calling* (ARC)
1981—*My Melody*   1982—*Niecy*   1983—*I'm So Proud* (Columbia)   1984—*Let's Hear It for the Boy*
1986—*From the Beginning* (Sparrow); *So Glad I Know*   1987—*Water Under the Bridge*   1989—*As Good As It Gets*; *Special Love* (Capitol/EMI)
1991—*Lullabies to Dreamland* (Word/Epic)
1994—*Greatest Gospel Hits* (Sparrow).

As a child, Deniece Williams sang in gospel choirs, later recording for the local Chicago label, Toddlin' Town. She then turned her attention to a new career in nursing and became a "candy striper." Through a cousin's influence, Williams auditioned for and was recruited by Stevie Wonder to sing in his Wonderlove vocal group. (She toured with Wonder and can be heard on his 1972 LP *Talking Book* and 1976's *Songs in the Key of Life*.) After hearing a demo of her original songs, Earth, Wind and Fire's Maurice White signed Williams to his Kalimba Productions.

This Is Niecy, Williams' first album, spawned the hit "Free" (#25 pop, #2 R&B, 1977). Collaborating in 1978 with singer Johnny Mathis, Williams had a major hit in "Too Much, Too Little, Too Late" (#1 pop and R&B). The same year, the pair followed with a remake of the Marvin Gaye/Tammi Terrell hit "You're All I Need to Get By" (#47 pop, #10 R&B).

In 1982 Williams also scored with a remake of the Royalettes' "It's Gonna Take a Miracle" (#10 pop, #1 R&B), produced by Philly soul auteur Thomas Bell. Two years later, "Let's Hear It for the Boy," produced by George Duke and featured in the popular film *Footloose,* charted at #1 in both pop and R&B. Although it was her last pop smash, Williams continued to have R&B hits, including "Never Say Never" (#6, 1987). Williams began recording gospel albums in 1986; one of two she released that year, *So Glad I Know,* won a pair of Grammys.

Hank Williams

Born Hiram Williams, September 17, 1923, Mount Olive, Alabama; died January 1, 1953, Oak Hill, West Virginia
1976—*Hank Williams Live at the Grand Old Opry* (MGM)   1985—*Hank Williams: I Ain't Got Nothin' but Time, December 1946–August 1947* (Polydor); *Hank Williams: Lovesick Blues, August 1947–December 1948*; *Just Me and My Guitar* (Country Music Foundation)   1986—*Hank Williams: Lost Highway, December 1948–March 1949* (Polydor); *Hank Williams: I'm So Lonesome I Could Cry, March 1949–August 1949*   1987—*Hank Williams: Long Gone Lonesome Blues, August 1949–December 1950*; *Hank Williams: Hey Good Lookin', December 1950–July 1951*; *Hank Williams: Let's Turn Back the Years, July 1951–June 1952*; *Hank Williams: I Won't Be Home No More, June 1952–September 1952*
1990—*Rare Demos First to Last* (Country Music Foundation)   1991—*The Original Singles Collection* (Polydor)   1995—*Alone and Forsaken* (Mercury).

Hank Williams was perhaps the most important country & western performer of his time, and the most influential country artist in the development of rock & roll. His 36 Top Ten C&W hits—including the #1s "Lovesick Blues," "Why Don't You Love Me," "Long Gone Lonesome Blues," "Moanin' the Blues," "Cold, Cold Heart," "Hey, Good Lookin'," "Jambalaya (On the Bayou)," and "I'll Never Get Out of This World Alive"—and magnetic stage presence were instrumental in country music's rise in popularity during his lifetime. ("Kaw-Liga," "Your Cheatin' Heart," and "Take These Chains from My Heart" were posthumous #1 C&W hits in 1953.) But it is as a songwriter that Williams' influence most profoundly changed country music and touched virtually every style emanating from it, especially rock & roll. In compositions such as "I'm So Lonesome I Could Cry," for example, Williams expressed intense, personal emotions with country's traditional plainspoken directness, a then revolutionary approach that through the works of George Jones, Willie Nelson, and countless other country artists has come to define the genre. As a singer, Williams mastered a range of styles, from gospel to the prerockabilly playfulness of "Hey, Good Lookin'."

Hiram "Hank" Williams was born in a two-room sharecropper's shack in southeastern Alabama. His father was shell-shocked from World War I and committed himself to a veterans' hospital when Hank was seven, leaving Williams' mother to support him and his sister. She played organ in the local Baptist church, where Hank sang in the choir, and she bought him a guitar for $3.50. When he was 11, Williams moved in with relatives in a railroad camp and began frequenting the Saturday-night dances, where he learned about country music and moonshine. The following year, he moved with his family to the larger town of Greenville and began learning blues songs from a black street singer named Rufe "Tee-Tot" Payne. Williams played on streetcorners with Tee-Tot, sold peanuts, and shined shoes.

In 1937 the family moved to Montgomery, Alabama. Hank won an amateur contest by performing his "W.P.A. Blues," and, dubbed the Singing Kid, he secured a twice-weekly radio show on local station WSFA. Soon after, he formed the Drifting Cowboys and began playing the Alabama roadhouse circuit, with his mother as booking agent and driver.

By December 1944, Williams had played nearly every roadhouse in Alabama and had married Audrey Mae Sheppard. Two years later, he signed a songwriting contract with Nashville publishers Acuff-Rose, and he recorded in Nashville on the small Sterling label. Soon after, he got a recording contract with newly formed MGM and began his successful collaboration with producer/arranger Fred Rose. That summer (1948), Williams joined the popular KWKH country music radio program *Louisiana Hayride* in Shreveport. His records starting making the C&W charts, and he finally hit big with "Lovesick Blues," which became the #1 country record of 1949.

On June 11, 1949, Williams played at the Grand Ole Opry for the first time and received an unprecedented six encores. His fame grew along with his touring schedule of one-nighters across the country. Besides recording his bluesy C&W records, he also recorded gospel-influenced songs under the name Luke the Drifter. By 1952 his drinking had gotten out of hand, his health had deteriorated, and his marriage ended in divorce. Williams' chronic back problems had resulted in his dependence on painkillers, and in August he was fired from the Grand Ole Opry because of frequent no-shows. Four months later, at the age of 29, he died of a heart attack in the back of a Cadillac en route to a show in Canton, Ohio. (Many years later reports were issued that he actually died in a Knoxville, Tennessee, hotel room after excessive alcohol and drug consumption, but these have since been dismissed.)

After his death, Williams' records sold more than ever, and have continued to do so in the 35 years since. His oft-covered catalogue has produced hits for artists ranging from Fats Domino and John Fogerty's Blue Ridge Rangers to Ray Charles and B. J. Thomas. His son Hank Williams Jr. recorded his father's songs for the biographical film *Your Cheatin' Heart* (MGM, 1964); he has since gone on to his own extremely successful career.

Hank Williams Jr.

Born Randall Hank Williams, May 26, 1949, Shreveport, Louisiana
1964—*Your Cheatin' Heart* **soundtrack (MGM)**
1965—*Father & Son* **(with Hank Williams Sr.)**
1969—*Songs My Father Left Me*; *Live at Cobo Hall, Detroit* 1974—*Living Proof* 1976—*Hank Williams Jr. and Friends*; *Fourteen Greatest Hits* 1977—*One Night Stands* **(Elektra/Curb)**; *The New South* **(Warner Bros./Curb)** 1979—*Family Tradition* **(Elektra/Curb)**; *Whiskey Bent and Hell Bound* **(Elektra)** 1981—*Rowdy*; *The Pressure Is On* 1983—*Strong Stuff* 1984—*Major Moves* **(Warner Bros.)** 1985—*Greatest Hits, vol. 2*; *The Early Years, 1976–78*; *Five-O* **(Warner Bros./Curb)** 1986—*Montana Cafe* **(Warner Bros.)** 1987—*Hank "Live"*; *Born to Boogie* 1988—*Wild Streak*; *Standing in the Shadows* **(Polydor)** 1989—*Greatest Hits, III* **(Warner Bros.)** 1990—*Lone Wolf*; *AMERICA (The Way I See It)* 1991—*Pure Hank* 1992—*Maverick* **(Curb/Capricorn)** 1993—*Out of Left Field* 1995—*Hog Wild* **(MCG/Curb)**.

Hank Williams' son has carved out a country-rock career of his own. Young Williams was just three when his father died. He learned to play from his father's friends and associates, who included Jerry Lee Lewis, Johnny Cash, Ray Charles, and Brenda Lee. He changed his name to Hank Williams Jr., and with his mother guiding his career, made his debut at age eight in Swainsboro, Georgia. He made his first appearance at the Grand Ole Opry in 1960 and cut his first record at age 14, his father's "Long Gone Lonesome Blues." His formal concert debut came soon after, at Cobo Hall in Detroit. Williams then quit school and began touring, also appearing on TV. At 16, he became the youngest songwriter ever to earn a BMI citation; he also had a #5 C&W hit, "Standing in the Shadows" (1966). On tour, he mainly performed his father's material, with a band called the Cheatin' Hearts. His *Your Cheatin' Heart* soundtrack LP went gold. He later wrote soundtracks for *Time to Sing* and *Kelly's Heroes*. By age 25, he'd been married and divorced twice, and suffered from drug and alcohol problems.

Around 1974 Williams grew disenchanted with Nashville and with living up to his father's legacy. His association with his father endured on record as well:

Father & Son electronically created "duets" between Williams and his father, and 1969's *Songs My Father Left Me* presented the younger Williams creating melodies to songs for which his father had written lyrics before his death. Hank Williams Jr. temporarily stopped performing. On August 8, 1975, while mountain climbing in Montana, he fell 490 feet. The resulting injuries were so severe that his entire face had to be reconstructed surgically.

A year and a half later, he came back in the more rock-oriented "outlaw" mold; fellow "outlaw" Waylon Jennings produced *New South*. In 1979 Williams' autobiography, *Living Proof*, was published by Putnam; it later became a made-for-television film entitled *Living Proof: The Hank Williams, Jr., Story* (1983), starring Richard Thomas. He also recorded in the late Sixties and Seventies as Luke the Drifter Jr. (including two albums in 1969).

Although Williams has had a number of C&W hits through the years, he's a rare presence on the pop charts. In 1981 he had one of his biggest country hits with "All My Rowdy Friends (Have Settled Down)" (#1 C&W). Other hits included a cover of his father's "Honky Tonkin'" (#1 C&W, 1982), "Gonna Go Huntin' Tonight" (#4 C&W, 1983), "Man of Steel" (#3 C&W, 1984), "Attitude Adjustment" (#5 C&W, 1984), "All My Rowdy Friends Are Coming Over Tonight" (#10 C&W, 1984), "I'm for Love" (#1 C&W, 1985), "This Ain't Dallas" (#4 C&W, 1985), "Ain't Misbehavin'" (#1 C&W, 1986), "Country State of Mind" (#2 C&W, 1986), "Mind Your Own Business" (#1 C&W, 1986), "Born to Boogie" (#1 C&W, 1987), "Heaven Can't Be Found" (#4 C&W, 1987), "Young Country" (#2 C&W, 1988), "If the South Woulda Won" (#8 C&W, 1988), the Grammy-winning "There's a Tear in My Beer" (#7 C&W, 1989) (an electronically created duet and video using old tapes and footage of his father), "Finders Are Keepers" (#6 C&W, 1989), and "Good Friends, Good Whiskey, Good Lovin'" (#19 C&W, 1990). Subsequent releases have made more modest chart showings.

He wrote and performed the theme for ABC Television's *Monday Night Football* program. Of the over 60 albums he has recorded to date, five have been certified platinum: *The Pressure Is On* (#76, 1981), *Hank Williams, Jr.,'s Greatest Hits* (#107, 1982), *Greatest Hits, vol. 2* (#183 pop, #1 C&W, 1986), *Born to Boogie* (#28, 1987), and *Greatest Hits III* (#61, 1989). Williams has also charted a number of #1 C&W LPs, including his 50th album, *Five-O* (1985), and *Wild Streak* (1988).

Jerry Williams: See Swamp Dogg

Larry Williams
Born May 10, 1935, New Orleans, Louisiana; died January 2, 1980, Los Angeles, California
1978—*That Larry Williams* (Fantasy)   1988—*The*
Best of Larry Williams* (Ace)   1990—*Larry Williams: Bad Boy* (Specialty).

Larry Williams scored important hits in 1957–58 with "Short Fat Fanny" (#5 pop, #2 R&B), "Bony Moronie" (#14 pop, #9 R&B) (later covered by John Lennon on *Rock 'n' Roll*), and "Dizzy Miss Lizzy" (#69, 1958) (later covered by the Beatles). Their alliterative titles and frantic shouting performances made him a momentary rival to Little Richard.

Little Richard was the star performer of Specialty Records, the label that discovered Williams when he was playing piano on R&B sessions for performers like Lloyd Price, Roy Brown, and Percy Mayfield. Williams' first record for Specialty, a cover of Lloyd Price's "Just Because," was a flop, but was followed by his three big hits of 1957–58. When the hits stopped coming, Williams turned to record production for a time, and then teamed up with Johnny "Guitar" Watson, with whom he recorded several late-Sixties R&B hits. He was convicted of and served time for narcotics trafficking in the Sixties. His poorly received funk-oriented comeback album for Fantasy in 1978 was his last release. Two years later, he was found dead in his Los Angeles home, of a gunshot wound to his head. The verdict was suicide.

Lucinda Williams
Born January 26, 1953, Lake Charles, Louisiana
1979—*Ramblin' on My Mind* (Folkways)   1980—*Happy Woman Blues*   1988—*Lucinda Williams* (Rough Trade)   1989—*Passionate Kisses* EP 1992—*Sweet Old World* (Chameleon).

Lucinda Williams began her career interpreting country, folk, and blues standards with a cool, almost academic-sounding reverence for the music. After a second album of original songs, she seemingly vanished for eight years. In 1989 she returned with a vengeance with her highly praised singer/songwriter album, *Lucinda Williams*. Released on the hip indie label Rough Trade—better known for its roster of punk/alternative acts than for country singers—the album marked a critical turning point in Williams' career.

The daughter of a father who was a poet, college professor, and Hank Williams fan, Williams grew up listening to classic country. She was born in Louisiana, but her family relocated several times during her childhood to spots across the South, as well as Mexico City and Santiago, Chile. At 16, she discovered the writing of fellow southerner novelist Flannery O'Connor, whom she cites as a major influence on her songwriting. Williams attended college for a short time but dropped out in 1971 to devote herself to music.

Folkways signed Williams in 1978 and released her first two albums without fanfare. Between 1980 and 1988 she worked a series of odd jobs, moving in mid-decade from Austin, Texas, to Los Angeles, where she took voice lessons to learn how to sound like Joan Baez, and married and divorced Greg Sowders of the Long Ryders. Much of the biting material on her self-titled comeback album dealt with her marriage.

When Rough Trade collapsed in 1991, Williams was left again without a label. Chameleon stepped in and released her 1992 album, *Sweet Old World*, which featured an ethereal cover of the late folkie Nick Drake's "Which Will." Relocating to Austin, then Nashville, Williams kept busy into the Nineties. In 1993 she contributed a track to *Sweet Relief*, the benefit album for singer Victoria Williams (no relation), a victim of multiple sclerosis, and lent her signature cool background vocals to "Reunion" on Jimmie Dale Gilmore's *Spinning Around the Sun*. Williams' songs have also been covered by others: Patty Loveless scored a Top Ten country hit with "The Night's Too Long," and Mary Chapin Carpenter recorded a Grammy-winning version of her "Passionate Kisses." In 1994, after Chameleon Records became defunct, Williams joined Rick Rubin's American Recordings roster.

Maurice Williams and the Zodiacs
Formed 1959, Lancaster, South Carolina
Maurice Williams (b. Apr. 26, 1938), voc.; Henry Gaston, voc.; Wiley Bennett, voc.; Charles Thomas, voc.; Little Willie Morrow, voc.; Albert Hill, voc.; – Hill; – Morrow.

Maurice Williams and the Zodiacs had only one major hit, "Stay." Despite clocking in as the shortest #1 hit single in history, the song has lived up to its title, claiming a place in the Top Forty for three months in 1960 but returning in Top Twenty hit versions by Jackson Browne and the Four Seasons and covers by the Hollies and others. In 1987 it was included in the hit *Dirty Dancing* soundtrack, which also featured the Contours' "Do You Love Me," another example of the Southeast music trend called "beach music," of which Williams' group was a part.

Williams' various groups have contained countless members and worked under many names, beginning with Royal Charms. With another group called the Gladiolas, Williams recorded his "Little Darlin'," an unsuccessful single for them but a hit a couple of years later for the Diamonds. In 1959, following a business dispute, this group lost the rights to the Gladiolas name, and later Williams gathered a new group, which he christened the Zodiacs. This lineup—Henry Gaston, Wiley Bennett, Charles Thomas, and Williams—recorded "Stay" in 1960 with Gaston taking the falsetto break. In the wake of the record's success, the Zodiacs began touring with such established acts as Chuck Berry and James Brown. Sub-

sequent Williams compositions failed to make as big a commercial splash, but locally the Zodiacs were a top draw. In 1985 the group was inducted into the Beach Music Hall of Fame.

Otis Williams and His Charms
Formed 1954, Cincinnati, Ohio
Original lineup: Otis Williams (b. June 2, 1936), lead voc.; Rolland Bradley, tenor voc.; Joe Penn, baritone voc.; Richard Parker, bass voc.; Donald Peak, tenor voc.
N.A.—*Otis Williams and His Charms Sing Their All-Time Greatest Hits* (King).

The Charms began a string of Top Ten R&B hits in 1955 with their debut disc, "Hearts of Stone" (#15 pop, #1 R&B). Like many of their other hits, this was a cover version of a song originally recorded by another black vocal group (in this case, the Jewels). That year, they also scored with the Five Keys' "Ling, Ting, Tong" (#26 pop, #6 R&B) and "Two Hearts" (#9 R&B). In 1956 Williams took top billing, largely because all of the rest of the Charms were fired and replaced by a new lineup. The original Charms went ahead and recorded under that name, while Otis Williams' group continued to hit the R&B Top Ten with "Ivory Tower" (#11 pop, #5 R&B, 1956). "United," from 1957 (#5 R&B), proved the group's last major hit. Williams kept the Charms going until 1965 when he began recording solo, first on Okeh and then for Stop, where he and his group sang country-style tunes billed as Otis Williams and the Midnight Cowboys.

Paul Williams
Born September 19, 1940, Omaha, Nebraska
1970—*Someday Man* (Reprise)   1971—*Just an Old Fashioned Love Song* (A&M)   1973—*Life Goes On* 1974—*Here Comes Inspiration*; *A Little Bit of Love* 1975—*Phantom of the Paradise* soundtrack; *Ordinary Fool*; *Bugsy Malone* soundtrack   1977—*Classics*.

Singer/songwriter Paul Williams started out as a set painter and stunt man in films. In *The Loved One* in 1964, 24-year-old Williams was cast as a ten-year-old child genius. In 1965 he appeared with Marlon Brando in *The Chase*, as another punk kid. While on the set of *The Chase*, Williams first tried his hand at songwriting. He wrote songs with Biff Rose and comedy sketches for Mort Sahl before teaming up in 1967 with lyricist Roger Nichols. Together they wrote such million-selling MOR pop hits as the Carpenters' "We've Only Just Begun" (which started out as a commercial jingle for a bank) and "Rainy Days and Mondays," Helen Reddy's "You and Me Against the World," and Three Dog Night's "An Old Fashioned Love Song" and "Out in the Country."

Despite his limited voice, Williams became a successful singer in his own right and has long been a regular on the talk show and Las Vegas circuits. In 1975 Williams teamed up with lyricist Ken Ascher. A year later, he starred in the title role of the rock film *Phantom of the Paradise*, for which he wrote the soundtrack. The next year, he scored Alan Parker's child-gangster film *Bugsy Malone*. Williams also contributed songs to the Barbra Streisand–Kris Kristofferson remake of *A Star Is Born*, among them his Oscar-winning collaboration with Streisand, "Evergreen." Williams has gone on to write music for a number of other feature films, including *The End* (1978), *The Muppet Movie* (1979), *The Secret of NIMH* (1982), *Rocky IV* (1984), *Ishtar* (1987), and *The Muppet Christmas Carol* (1992).

As an actor Williams has appeared in a number of films, including the three *Smokey and the Bandit* films (1977–83), *The Doors* (1991), *A Million to Juan* (1994), and *Headless Body in Topless Bar* (1995), and on television (*Picket Fences*, the miniseries *People Like Us*).

Following years of cocaine and alcohol abuse, Williams underwent treatment. He not only completed the program but became a licensed drug rehabilitation counselor. His brother Mentor Williams is a country record producer and writer of a number of well-known songs, including "Drift Away."

The Tony Williams Lifetime

Formed 1969, New York City, New York
Tony Williams (b. Dec. 12, 1945, Chicago, Ill.), drums; John McLaughlin (b. Jan. 4, 1942, Yorkshire, Eng.), gtr.; Larry Young, organ.
1969—*Emergency* (Polydor) (+ Jack Bruce [b. May 14, 1943, Glasgow, Scot.], bass, voc.) 1970—*Turn It Over* 1971—(– McLaughlin; – Bruce; + Ted Dunbar [b. Jan. 17, 1937, Port Arthur, Tex.], gtr.; + Warren Smith [b. May 14, 1934, Chicago, Ill.], perc.; + Don Alias, perc.; + Juni Booth, bass) *Ego* (– Young; – Dunbar; – Smith; + Webster Lewis, organ; + David Horowitz, kybds.; + Tequila, gtr., voc.; + Tillmon Williams, tenor sax; + Herb Bushler, bass) 1972— *The Old Bum's Rush* (group disbands) 1975— (Group re-forms: Williams; + Allan Holdsworth, gtr.; + Alan Pasqua, kybds.; + Tony Newton, bass, voc.) 1976—*Believe It* (Columbia); *Million Dollar Legs*.
Tony Williams solo: 1979—*The Joy of Flying* (Columbia) 1986—*Foreign Intrigue* (Blue Note) 1987—*Civilization* 1988—*Angel Street* 1990— *Native Heart* 1991—*The Story of Neptune* 1992— *Tokyo Live*.

Tony Williams' shifting accents helped define the sound of the Miles Davis Quintet of the Sixties, a group Williams joined when he was 17. In 1969, after playing with Miles Davis [see entry] and on numerous Blue Note jazz sessions, he left to form one of the first jazz-rock fusion bands, the Tony Williams Lifetime, with organist Larry Young, guitarist John McLaughlin (who also worked with Davis at the time), and ex-Cream bassist Jack Bruce.

Lifetime played highly complex hard rock, presaging the late-Seventies "punk-funk-jazz" of Ornette Coleman and James Blood Ulmer, but after its first two albums the original Lifetime disbanded. Williams freelanced as a jazz drummer and tried making a more conventional funk album, *The Old Bum's Rush*, on which he sang. He joined fellow Davis Quintet veterans under Herbie Hancock's leadership in VSOP, with whom he continued to tour and to record.

In the mid-Seventies Williams organized another version of Lifetime, featuring guitarist Allan Holdsworth, formerly of Soft Machine and Gong. Like the first Lifetime, the group was critically acclaimed but its records sold poorly and it broke up again. Williams' 1979 solo LP featured both fusion players and a duet with avant-garde pianist Cecil Taylor.

In the Eighties Williams found new focus by returning to the music of his youth. He formed an acoustic jazz band whose nucleus included acclaimed pianist Mulgrew Miller and trumpeter Wallace Rooney. Williams can be heard on Wynton Marsalis' solo debut recording and also toured with a 1983 band featuring Wynton and Branford Marsalis.

Since 1986's *Foreign Intrigue*, Williams has composed the majority of the music for his own band. His expanded work "Rituals for String Quartet, Piano, Drums and Cymbals" was performed in 1990 with the Kronos Quartet. In 1992 Williams toured with his old Miles Davis bandmates, Ron Carter, Herbie Hancock, and Wayne Shorter, in a tribute to the then recently deceased Davis. Williams continues to work in a variety of groups.

Vanessa Williams

Born March 18, 1963, Buffalo, New York
1988—*The Right Stuff* (Wing/PolyGram) 1991— *The Comfort Zone* 1994—*The Sweetest Days* (Mercury).

Pop music teems with great comebacks, but few are as hard-won or as unexpected as that of singer Vanessa Williams. Raised in a predominantly white suburban New York community, Williams studied numerous musical instruments as well as classical and jazz dance as a child. She graduated high school with a Presidential Scholarship for drama.

While attending Syracuse University as a musical theater major, she entered the Miss America pageant, in hopes of gaining money and exposure. She won, becoming the first black Miss America in history, but got more exposure than she bargained for when in July 1984 sexually suggestive photographs she had posed for when she was 19 and working for a photographer surfaced in *Penthouse*. The resulting scandal cost her to the crown and, it seemed, all hopes of realizing the show-business aspirations that had brought her to the pageant in the first place.

Not long after the dust settled, however, Williams landed a few TV appearances and film roles. In 1987 she signed a deal with PolyGram's Wing Records; the following year saw the release of her well-received debut album, *The Right Stuff* (#38, 1988), which spawned "Dreamin'" (#8 pop, #1 R&B, 1989). *The Comfort Zone* (#17, 1991) was even more successful: Its Grammy-nominated third single, "Save the Best for Last," went to #1 on the pop, R&B, and adult contemporary charts, while "Running Back to You," the title track, and "Work to Do" respectively peaked at #1, #2, and #3, all R&B.

In 1993 Williams scored another pop hit with "Love Is" (#3), a duet with singer Brian McKnight that was featured on a soundtrack to the popular television show *Beverly Hills 90210*. Williams' TV-related credits also include hosting VH-1's *The Soul of VH-1*. Her charity work has ranged from taking part in an East Coast radio station's 1989 "Coats for Kids" campaign to contributing "What Child Is This" to *A Very Special Christmas 2*, an album whose proceeds benefited the Special Olympics. Her public disgrace apparently forgiven if not forgotten, Williams has earned several Grammy nominations and a pair of NAACP Image Awards. She released the 1994 album *The Sweetest Days* (#57 pop, #25 R&B, 1994), which yielded a hit single in the title track (#18 pop, #40 R&B, 1994). In 1995 she got rave reviews for her Broadway debut in *Kiss of the Spider Woman*; the same year, her "Colors of the Wind" (from *Pocahontas*) was a Top Thirty hit.

Sonny Boy Williamson

**Sonny Boy No. 1, born John Lee Williamson, March 30, 1914, Jackson, Tennessee; died June 1, 1948, Chicago, Illinois: N.A.—*Blues Classics by Sonny Boy Williamson* (Blues Classics); *Blues Classics by Sonny Boy Williamson, vol. 2*; *Blues Classics by Sonny Boy Williamson, vol. 3* 1959—*Blues in the Mississippi Night* (reissued 1990, Rykodisc).
Sonny Boy No. 2, born Aleck or Alex or Willie "Rice" Miller or Ford, December 5, 1897 or 1899 or 1909, Glendora, Mississippi; died May 25, 1965, Helena, Arkansas: 1959—*Down and Out Blues* (Chess) 1962—*Bummer Road* 1963—*Sonny Boy and Memphis Slim* (Vogue) 1964—*Sonny Boy Williamson and the Yardbirds* (with the Yardbirds) (Mercury) 1965—*This Is My Story* (Chess) 1966—*The Real Folk Blues* 1967—*More Real Folk Blues; The Origi-*** nal** (Blues Classics)   1973—*In Paris: Sonny Boy Williamson and Memphis Slim* (GNP Crescendo) 1976—*One Way Out* (MCA)   1989—*King Biscuit Time* (Arhoolie)   1992—*Goin' in Your Direction* (Trumpet)   1993—*Sonny Boy Williamson, vol. 1: 1937-1939* (EPM); *Sonny Boy Williamson, vol. 2: 1940-1942* (Alligator)   1993—*The Essential Sonny Boy Williamson* (MCA/Chess).

There were two Sonny Boy Williamsons. The first was John Lee Williamson, who recorded very little and is known mainly as a major influence on such blues-harp giants as Little Walter Jacobs and Junior Wells. The second was Rice Miller, by far the better known.

The first Sonny Boy is acknowledged as the first to play the harmonica as a lead, rather than accompanying, instrument. He is also considered an important and influential singer. Early in his career, he worked with Sleepy John Estes and Homesick James. He moved to Chicago in 1937, where he recorded "Good Morning, Little Schoolgirl" and "Sugar Mama" for RCA/Bluebird and played in a small group featuring Big Bill Broonzy. He was killed in a brutal attack and robbery.

The second Sonny Boy was the author of such blues standards as "One Way Out" (covered by the Allman Brothers Band), "Bye Bye Bird" (covered by the Moody Blues), "Help Me" (covered by Van Morrison), "Eyesight to the Blind" (covered by the Who on *Tommy*), "Fattening Frogs for Snakes," and "Don't Start Me Talkin'."

Miller—whose name, date of birth, and early life remain something of a mystery—was first noticed in the middle Thirties, when he toured under the name Little Boy Blue, playing with Robert Johnson, Elmore James, and others. He first came to prominence, still known as Rice Miller, singing and playing blues harp on the popular radio show *King Biscuit Time*, broadcast from Helena, Arkansas. Miller appropriated the name Sonny Boy Williamson after the show's sponsor asked him to pose as the original Sonny Boy Williamson. The original Sonny Boy did not care to tour the South, and surprisingly— since the two harmonica players' styles were different— the public accepted Miller as Sonny Boy. Not long after, the original Sonny Boy was murdered, leaving Miller (as many fellow musicians still referred to him) the only Sonny Boy.

Williamson, as he was now known, first recorded in 1951 for the Jackson, Mississippi, Trumpet label. His first hit was his first recording there, "Eyesight to the Blind." That year he also recorded with Elmore James and appeared on James' important version of Robert Johnson's "Dust My Broom." At this time Williamson was married to Howlin' Wolf's sister; they soon divorced and he remarried.

In 1955 Williamson moved to Chicago and began recording blues hits for Chess, backed at times by the

Muddy Waters band. His ambivalence regarding tour commitments and recording, coupled with a penchant for drinking, gambling, women, and rambling made him a difficult artist to manage. However, no one he ever recorded for ever got angry enough to stop working with him. Through 1961, Williamson recorded a number of blues hits, including "Don't Start Me Talkin'," "All My Love in Vain," "Keep It to Yourself," and "Your Funeral and My Trial."

Although by then in his sixties, Williamson never settled down. In 1963 he went to Europe, where he found an appreciative audience. He was especially popular in England, causing a sensation in his two-tone suit and bowler hat. In subsequent U.K. tours, he appeared on the British rock TV show *Ready, Steady, Go* and recorded live albums with British Invasion bands the Yardbirds and the Animals. He considered moving to England permanently but instead returned to Mississippi. He later recorded one last session for Chess, then returned to the Delta.

Shortly before his death, Williamson jammed with an early Ronnie Hawkins–led version of the Band, the Hawks, in a juke joint. All through the evening he had been spitting up blood, and some accounts attribute his death to tuberculosis. In fact, he died of a heart attack.

Chuck Willis

Born January 31, 1928, Atlanta, Georgia; died April 10, 1958, Atlanta
1971—*His Greatest Recordings* (Atlantic)   1980—*Chuck Willis—My Story* (Columbia)   1994—*Let's Jump Tonight! The Best of Chuck Willis, from 1951-'56* (Columbia Legacy).

Chuck Willis was a blues singer/songwriter best remembered as the "King of the Stroll" (although the Diamonds cashed in on the ensuing dance craze with their "The Stroll"). Oft-recorded Willis tunes include "I Feel So Bad" (Foghat, Delbert McClinton, Elvis Presley), "It's Too Late" (Buddy Holly, Otis Redding), and "Hang Up My Rock and Roll Shoes" (the Band, Jerry Lee Lewis).

As a teen, Willis was a popular R&B singer around Atlanta. A local DJ, Zenus "Daddy" Sears, took him to Columbia Records in 1952, where he cut a few minor releases for their Okeh label, including the R&B hits "My Story," a cover of Louis Jordan's "Caldonia," and "You're Still My Baby."

Willis, wearing turbans onstage—at one point he owned 54 of them—was often introduced to audiences as the "Sheik of the Shake." In 1956 Jerry Wexler signed Willis to Atlantic Records, and the next year Willis cut the blues standard "C.C. Rider" (#12 pop, #3 R&B). It was a major hit and established him as the "King of the Stroll." But within the year, Willis died from peritonitis, a complication of surgery for stomach ulcers; he was just

30. Posthumously, "What Am I Living For?" (#9 pop, #3 R&B, 1958) became his biggest crossover hit, followed by "Hang Up My Rock and Roll Shoes."

Bob Wills and His Texas Playboys

Formed 1935, Tulsa, Oklahoma
Bob Wills (b. Mar. 6, 1905, Limestone, Tex.; d. May 13, 1975, Fort Worth, Tex.), voc., fiddle.
1958—*Bob Wills and His Texas Playboys* (MCA)
1963—*Bob Wills Sings and Plays* (Liberty)   1968—*King of the Western Swing* (MCA)   1969—*The Best of Bob Wills and His Texas Playboys; Living Legend* 1971—*In Person*   1973—*The Bob Wills Anthology* (Columbia); *The Best of Bob Wills* (MCA)   1974—*For the Last Time* (United Artists)   1975—*Fathers and Sons* (Epic); *The Best of Bob Wills, vol. 2* (MCA) 1976—*Remembering . . . The Greatest Hits of Bob Wills* (Columbia); *In Concert* (Capitol)   1977—*24 Great Hits by Bob Wills and His Texas Playboys* (Polydor)   1982—*The Tiffany Transcriptions 1946 & 1947, vol. 1* (Kaleidoscope)   1984—*Best of the Tiffanys: The Tiffany Transcriptions 1946 & 1947, vol. 2; Basin Street Blues: The Tiffany Transcriptions 1946 & 1947, vol. 3   1985—You're from Texas: The Tiffany Transcriptions 1946 & 1947, vol. 4* 1986—*The Tiffany Transcriptions 1946 & 1947, vol. 5* 1987—*Sally Grodin: The Tiffany Transcriptions 1946 & 1947, vol. 7; Fiddle* (Country Music Foundation); *The Golden Era* (Columbia); *Columbia Historic Edition*   1988—*More of the Best: The Tiffany Transcriptions 1946 & 1947, vol. 8* (Kaleidoscope) 1990—*In the Mood: The Tiffany Transcriptions 1946 & 1947, vol. 9*   1991—*Anthology, 1935–1973* (Rhino).

Fiddler-bandleader Bob Wills helped change the course of country and pop music in the Thirties with his Texas Playboys, a Western swing band numbering anywhere from 13 to 18 members, who fused country & western, pop, blues, and big-band swing. This seminal unit introduced horns, drums, and electric guitars to country music.

The eldest of ten children born to a fiddle-playing father, Wills moved with his family to Memphis in 1913 and began playing fiddle and mandolin in square-dance bands. He moved to Fort Worth in 1929. A year later Wills joined the Light Crust Dough Boys with Milton Brown, and they began recording in 1932. Wills was fired from the band in 1933 for excessive drinking and personality conflicts with leader W. Lee O'Daniel. Wills left with banjoist Johnnie Lee Wills to form the Playboys, and they soon became regulars on radio broadcasts by WACO in Waco, Texas.

They moved to Tulsa, Oklahoma, and became regulars on KVOO. As Bob Wills and His Texas Playboys, they began recording for Brunswick in 1935. In the late Thirties Wills' daughter Laura Lee became lead singer with the band; she also wrote songs, and later married Texas Playboys guitarist Dick McBride. In April 1940 they recorded the million-selling "San Antonio Rose" (#11 pop, #3 C&W, 1944), which also became a million-seller for Bing Crosby. Over the years he recorded another 22 C&W Top Ten hits, including these #1 singles: "Smoke on the Water" (1945), "Stars and Stripes on Iwo Jima" (1945), "Silver Dew on the Blue Grass Tonight" (1945), "White Cross on Okinawa" (1945), "New Spanish Two Step" (1946), and "Sugar Moon" (1947). Among his other well-known songs were "Faded Love," "Cotton Eyed Joe," "Take Me Back to Tulsa," and "Time Changes Everything."

Wills maintained the Texas Playboys through the early Sixties. In 1962 his health began to deteriorate and he suffered a series of heart attacks. In 1968 he was named to the Country Music Hall of Fame. In 1973, during his last recording session, he suffered a stroke from which he never recovered, entering a coma that lasted until his death in 1975. A year later, the Texas Playboys reunited for some memorial concerts. In 1993 Asleep at the Wheel assembled a stellar cast of musicians for *A Tribute to Bob Wills and His Texas Playboys.* Among those participating were Garth Brooks, Merle Haggard, Brooks and Dunn, Willie Nelson, and several former Playboys.

Jackie Wilson

Born June 9, 1934, Detroit, Michigan; died January 21, 1984, Mount Holly, New Jersey
1960—*Jackie Sings the Blues* (Brunswick); *My Golden Favorites*; *My Golden Favorites, vol. 2*
1962—*Jackie Wilson at the Copa* 1963—*Baby Workout* 1965—*Spotlight on Jackie Wilson*
1967—*Whispers* 1972—*Jackie Wilson's Greatest Hits* 1983—*The Jackie Wilson Story* (Epic)
1994—*The Very Best of Jackie Wilson* (Rhino).

Jackie Wilson was one of the premier black vocalists and performers of the late Fifties and the Sixties. No other singer of his generation so perfectly combined James Brown's rough, sexy style and Sam Cooke's smooth, gospel-polished pop.

Wilson grew up in a rough section of Detroit. In the late Forties, he lied about his age, entered the Golden Gloves, and won in his division. He later quit at his mother's request. He had sung throughout his childhood, and after high school, he began performing in local clubs. He was discovered by Johnny Otis at a talent show in 1951. In 1953 Wilson successfully auditioned for Billy Ward and His Dominoes [see entry], replacing Clyde McPhatter, who had left and formed the Drifters. Wilson sang lead on "St. Therese of the Roses," the group's second pop Top Twenty hit, in 1956.

Jackie Wilson

Later that same year Wilson went solo, signing with Brunswick Records. His first single, the sassy " 'Reet Petite" (#62 pop, #11 R&B), written by his friend Berry Gordy Jr., appeared in 1957. In 1958 Wilson began making his mark with "To Be Loved" (#22 pop, #11 R&B) and "Lonely Teardrops" (#7 pop, #1 R&B), two more Gordy tunes. He hit his commercial stride in 1959 with "That's Why (I Love You So)" (#13 pop, #2 R&B), "I'll Be Satisfied" (#20 pop, #6 R&B), "You Better Know It" (#37 pop, #1 R&B), and "Talk That Talk" (#34 pop, #3 R&B). His success continued in 1960 with "Night" b/w "Doggin' Around" (#4 pop, #1 R&B), and "Am I the Man" b/w "Alone at Last" (#8 pop, #10 R&B). His stage show was as athletic as James Brown's, and the sexual hysteria surrounding Wilson at this time was such that his audiences were often worked up into a frenzy. In 1961 he was shot and seriously wounded by a female fan in his New York apartment. That year he hit big with "My Empty Arms" (#9 pop, #10 R&B).

With the exception of the frenzied "Baby Workout" (#5 pop, #1 R&B) in 1963, Wilson's next few years yielded few hits. Then in 1966 he was matched with veteran producer Carl Davis, with whom he scored two hits: "Whispers" (#11 pop, #5 R&B) and "(Your Love Keeps Lifting Me) Higher and Higher" (#6 pop, #1 R&B). Unfortunately, these were Wilson's last great recordings, although he continued to chart singles as a pop-style crooner through 1972. By 1975 he was playing the oldies circuit. On September 25, 1975, at a Dick Clark revue in the Latin

Casino in Cherry Hill, New Jersey, he suffered a heart attack onstage while singing "Lonely Teardrops," and was hospitalized and in a coma from which he emerged with significant brain damage. Eight years after the heart attack, Wilson died. He was inducted into the Rock and Roll Hall of Fame in 1987.

Kim Wilson: See the Fabulous Thunderbirds

Wilson Phillips

Formed 1989, Los Angeles, California
Chynna Phillips (b. Feb. 12, 1968, Los Angeles),
voc.; Carnie Wilson (b. Apr. 29, 1968, Los Angeles),
voc.; Wendy Wilson (b. Oct. 16, 1969, Los Angeles),
voc.
1990—*Wilson Phillips* (SBK)   1992—*Shadows and Light*.
Carnie and Wendy Wilson: 1993—*Hey Santa!* (SBK).

Wilson Phillips specialized in rich harmony vocals—no surprise given the group's lineage in two of the most popular pop-rock harmony units of the Sixties. Chynna Phillips is the daughter of John and Michelle Phillips of the Mamas and the Papas, and Carnie and Wendy Wilson's father is Brian Wilson, the creative genius of the Beach Boys.

Despite their musical roots, none of the three thought of becoming singers until 1986, when inspired by Band Aid, Live Aid, and USA for Africa, Chynna Phillips first conceived of having famous musicians' children record together for charity. Phillips considered Frank Zappa's daughter Moon Unit, who had scored a left-field hit with "Valley Girl," and Ione Skye, the actress daughter of folksinger Donovan, but she instead turned to her old friends, the Wilson sisters.

From their first rehearsals, the story goes, they found their voices fitting together naturally—Carnie singing low harmony, Wendy singing high parts, and Chynna in between. They decided to work as a group, and briefly considered adding the late Mamas and Papas member Cass Elliot's daughter Owen. The trio polished its sound for two years, working with producer Richard Perry and with songwriter Glenn Ballard (who'd collaborated with Michael Jackson, among others). When music-publishing giant Charles Koppelman launched his SBK Records, Wilson Phillips was among his first signings. With its easy-listening tempos and cotton-candy harmonies, the group's debut album was a massive hit (#2, 1990) that sold over five million copies and yielded three #1 singles in "Hold On," "Release Me," and "You're in Love"; "Impulsive" was another big hit (#4, 1990).

In stark contrast, *Shadows and Light* was one of 1992's biggest disappointments: While it reached #4 shortly after its June release and was certified platinum, it failed to yield a hit single. Some observers blamed the album's darker songs—"Flesh and Blood" dealt with the Wilson sisters' troubled relationship with their father, and there was a song about rape—while others blamed a more mature, glamorous image that may have alienated the group's vast teenaged audience. Wilson Phillips canceled a planned summer tour for lack of ticket sales and spent the rest of 1992 denying break-up rumors. The Wilson sisters released a Christmas album in 1993. As of 1995, however, there had been no more Wilson Phillips releases, and Phillips was in the studio recording a solo LP.

Jesse Winchester

Born May 17, 1944, Shreveport, Louisiana
1971—*Jesse Winchester* (Ampex)   1972—*Third Down, 110 to Go* (Bearsville)   1974—*Learn to Love It*   1976—*Let the Rough Side Drag*   1977—*Nothin' but a Breeze*   1978—*A Touch on the Rainy Side*   1981—*Talk Memphis*   1989—*Humor Me* (Sugar Hill).

Singer/songwriter Jesse Winchester's early albums were tales of exile from a southerner who had moved to Canada to avoid the draft. His later work, after he was granted amnesty, has leaned toward easygoing love songs, but Winchester still has a distinctive voice and a style that encompasses acoustic folk and Memphis rockabilly.

Winchester grew up in Memphis and played piano and sang with his church choir. He also learned guitar, and as a teenager he joined various unsuccessful rock bands. In 1967 he went to study in Munich, Germany, and when he found out that his draft notice had arrived at home, he went to Canada, where he's kept a residence ever since.

In 1970 Winchester met Robbie Robertson of the Band, who got him a management contract with Albert Grossman. Robertson produced and (with his bandmate Levon Helm) played on Winchester's debut LP, which included the much-covered songs "Biloxi," "The Brand New Tennessee Waltz," and "Yankee Lady." Todd Rundgren produced part of Winchester's second album (the title refers to Canadian football), and, like the debut, it garnered rave reviews.

Winchester became a Canadian citizen in 1973, and didn't tour the U.S. again until after President Carter declared amnesty for draft evaders in 1977. Since then, he has appeared regularly in U.S. clubs, both with a band and as a solo performer. Although his following has never been much more than marginal, he continues to write constantly and record sporadically.

Winger

Formed 1986, New York City, New York
Kip Winger (b. June 21, 1961, Golden, Colo.), bass, voc.; Reb Beach (b. Aug. 31, 1963, Baltimore, Md.), gtr.; Paul Taylor (b. 1960, San Francisco, Calif.), gtr., kybds.; Rod Morgenstein (b. Apr. 19, 1957, New York City), drums.
1988—*Winger* (Atlantic)   1990—*In the Heart of the Young* (- Taylor; + John Roth [b. May 5, 1967, Springfield, Ill.], gtr.)   1993—*Pull.*

Like Poison and Warrant, Winger was a popular light-metal rock group that combined poppy tunes and sex appeal. Hunky lead singer Kip Winger had studied classical piano and guitar with a Juilliard School teacher and had trained at the Joffrey Ballet School before meeting Paul Taylor while both were in Alice Cooper's mid-Eighties backing band. By 1986 they'd formed a band with drummer Rod Morgenstein, formerly with progressive-fusion band Dixie Dregs, and guitarist Reb Beach, who'd played sessions with Howard Jones, Chaka Khan, and the Bee Gees. The group originally called itself Sahara, but upon learning a Los Angeles band already had that name, became Winger.

Its debut album (#21, 1988) produced hits in "Seventeen" (#26, 1989) and "Headed for a Heartbreak" (#19, 1989). *In the Heart of the Young* (#15, 1990) had more hits in "Can't Get Enuff" (#42, 1990), "Miles Away" (#12, 1991), and "Easy Come Easy Go" (#41, 1991). Although, thanks to Kip Winger, the band was tremendously videogenic, its appeal quickly waned. Taylor left to pursue songwriting on his own; John Roth joined for *Pull,* a conscious attempt to essay lighter, more melodic songs that bombed, producing no hit singles. After that album's release, Morgenstein left to join the re-formed Dixie Dregs.

Wings: See Paul McCartney

Edgar Winter

Born December 28, 1946, Beaumont, Texas
1970—*Entrance* (Epic)   1971—*Edgar Winter's White Trash*   1972—*Roadwork; They Only Come Out at Night*   1974—*Shock Treatment*   1975—*Jasmine Nightdreams* (Blue Sky); *The Edgar Winter Group with Rick Derringer*   1976—*Together: Live* (with Johnny Winter)   1977—*Recycled*   1979—*Edgar Winter Album*   1981—*Standing on Rock*   1985—*Anthology* (Back-Trac)   1989—*Mission Earth* (Rhino)   1990—*Live in Japan* (with Rick Derringer) (Cypress)   1991—*The Edgar Winter Collection* (Rhino)   1994—*Not a Kid Anymore* (Intersound).

Vocalist/keyboardist/saxophonist Edgar Winter is Johnny Winter's younger brother. [See Johnny's entry for Edgar's early biography.] Edgar was playing in a jazz group around the time that Johnny rose suddenly to fame in the late Sixties. Edgar joined his brother's band, playing sax and keyboards, then left to pursue a solo career.

On his debut album, Winter played many instruments himself; though it was critically well received, it sold poorly. For his next two albums, he formed the jazz/R&B horn band White Trash, which became a popular concert attraction (they played the closing night of New York's Fillmore East). Winter broke the band up, however, and next formed the experimental hard-rock quartet the Edgar Winter Group, which featured bassist-vocalist Dan Hartman [see entry] and guitarist Ronnie Montrose [see entry]. Their first release was a single, "Hangin' Around," backed by an instrumental called "Frankenstein." An edited "Frankenstein" became the A side of the single; it went to #1 in the U.S. and sold platinum worldwide, as did the Edgar Winter Group's first album, *They Only Come Out at Night* (#3, 1972).

In late 1973, as "Free Ride" (#14, 1973) became another smash hit single, guitarist Rick Derringer [see entry], who'd produced *White Trash* and *They Only,* joined Winter's band, replacing Jerry Weems, who'd replaced Montrose. They became a major concert attraction, and *Shock Treatment* (#13, 1974), featuring Derringer, sold well. Winter then recorded a solo LP, *Jasmine Nightdreams* (#69, 1975), but returned to the group for the more rock-oriented *With Rick Derringer* (#124, 1975).

Edgar appears on Johnny Winter's *Johnny Winter* and *Second Winter,* Derringer's *All American Boy* and *Spring Fever,* Dan Hartman's first three solo LPs, and Bette Midler's *Songs for the New Depression.* In 1976 Edgar cut an album of oldies with brother Johnny. Except for two subsequent solo albums, he has remained fairly inactive since. His "Way Down South" appeared on the *My Cousin Vinny* soundtrack, and in 1990 he teamed up again with Derringer for a world tour that resulted in the *Live in Japan* album. In 1992 he performed with his brother Johnny at the Ritz in New York City; it was the first time the two had shared a stage in 15 years.

Johnny Winter

Born February 23, 1944, Leland, Mississippi
1968—*The Progressive Blues Experiment* (Imperial); *Johnny Winter* (Columbia)   1969—*Second Winter*   1970—*Johnny Winter And; Johnny Winter And Live*   1973—*Still Alive and Well*   1974—*Saints and Sinners; John Dawson Winter III* (Blue Sky)   1976—*Captured Live!; Together* (with Edgar Winter)   1977—*Nothin' but the Blues*   1978—*White, Hot &*

Johnny Winter, Randy Hobbs, Richard Hughes

Blue 1980—*Raisin' Cain* 1984—*Guitar Slinger* (Alligator) 1985—*Serious Business* 1986—*Third Degree* 1988—*The Winter of '88* (Voyager) 1991—*Let Me In* (Pointblank/Virgin) 1992—*Hey, Where's Your Brother?* 1993—*Scorchin' Blues* (Sony Legacy); *Johnny Winter: A Rock n' Roll Collection* 1994—*White Lightning: Live at the Dallas International Motor Speedway* (Magnum Music).
With Muddy Waters: 1977—*Hard Again* (Blue Sky) 1978—*I'm Ready* 1979—*Muddy "Mississippi" Waters Live* 1981—*King Bee.*

Johnny Winter came to fame as a much-heralded white blues guitarist and was widely popular in the Seventies with blues-based hard rock. In the late Seventies he returned even more strongly to his blues roots by backing up Muddy Waters on concert tours and some recordings. He returned from a four-year break to record a series of acclaimed blues records, among them two that were nominated for Grammy Awards.

Winter grew up in Beaumont, Texas, the son of a banjo- and saxophone-playing father and a piano-playing mother. He and his younger brother Edgar—who are both albinos—learned several instruments. The two brothers performed as an Everly Brothers–style duo and even auditioned for *Ted Mack's Original Amateur Hour* when Johnny was just 11. In their teens they formed local rock bands with names like Johnny and the Jam-mers, the Crystaliers, It and Them, and the Black Plague, playing mainly blues and rock. At age 15, with Johnny and the Jammers, Winter recorded his first record, "School Day Blues," for Dart Records in Houston. After graduating high school, Johnny enrolled in Lamar Technical College, but soon dropped out.

He hitchhiked to Louisiana, where he backed up local blues and rock musicians, and in the early Sixties he traveled to Chicago, where he frequented blues clubs. In 1962 Winter played with Mike Bloomfield and Barry Goldberg (they went on to form Electric Flag), among others. Winter eventually returned to Texas, where he played with various journeyman blues bands. After a few years of garnering local raves on the Georgia-Florida circuit, a 1968 ROLLING STONE article, in which Winter was described as a "cross-eyed albino with long fleecy hair, playing some of the gutsiest fluid blues guitar you've ever heard," brought Winter to national attention. New York club owner Steve Paul read the article and flew out to Texas to sign Winter. Paul installed him as a regular attraction at his club, the Scene, and within weeks Winter was attracting capacity audiences.

Winter's debut album for Columbia sold well; concurrent with its release came *The Progressive Blues Experiment,* an album of demo tapes Winter had been peddling around before he got signed. *Second Winter,* recorded in Nashville, won even more ecstatic raves and bigger sales than the debut. After that album, Winter assembled a new band (his previous one had been with him since his Texas journeyman days), including his brother Edgar and guitarist Rick Derringer, bassist Randy Hobbs, and drummer Randy Zehringer from the McCoys, who'd had a massive hit a few years earlier with "Hang On Sloopy." This band recorded *And,* after which Bobby Caldwell replaced Zehringer for *Live.* While both albums were successful, Winter's heavy touring schedule and mounting heroin problems forced him to retire for a time.

Winter came back in 1973 with the biggest album of his career to date, *Still Alive and Well* (#22, 1973), which featured a song Mick Jagger and Keith Richards had written for Winter, "Silver Train." Critically, it and *Saints and Sinners* (#42, 1974) are considered Winter's last great albums of his more rock-oriented period. In 1976 he worked with brother Edgar for the first time in several years on *Together* (#89, 1976); by that time, Edgar's popularity had eclipsed Johnny's. For *Nothin' but the Blues,* Winter was joined by Muddy Waters and his band, but the set received only moderate critical reaction and went largely unnoticed. Winter toured and frequently played festivals as a member of Waters' backing band, as well as touring on his own. He produced and sat in on Waters' LPs *Hard Again, I'm Ready, King Bee,* and *Live. Hard Again* and *Muddy "Mississippi" Waters Live* both won Grammy Awards.

Winter released a couple more albums before taking

four years off. Like many of his white blues-rock contemporaries, Winter suddenly found himself out of vogue. The Grammy-nominated *Guitar Slinger* marked his return but in a more blues-roots vein. It, along with *Serious Business* and *Third Degree*, were critically acclaimed. *The Winter of '88* brought Winter back toward rock & roll but nowhere near the popular success he had enjoyed in the Seventies. He remains one of the preeminent white bluesmen of his generation.

Steve Winwood

Born May 12, 1948, Birmingham, England
1971—*Winwood* (United Artists)   1977—*Steve Winwood* (Island)   1980—*Arc of a Diver*   1982—*Talking Back to the Night*   1986—*Back in the High Life* 1987—*Chronicles*   1988—*Roll with It* (Virgin) 1990—*Refugees of the Heart*   1995—*The Finer Things* (Island Chronicles).

Keyboardist/singer Steve Winwood has found his own hugely successful blend of pop and R&B after years of working with blues, pop, and experimental bands.

Winwood began playing piano as a child and picked up bass, guitar, and drums as a teenager. At 15 he was a member of his older brother Muff Winwood's jazz band, and a year later the two joined the Spencer Davis Group [see entry]. Stevie Winwood's lead vocals and insistent organ riffs gave the band hits with "Gimme Some Lovin'" and "I'm a Man." At 18, Winwood participated in a studio group, Powerhouse, that included Eric Clapton on guitar; their tracks appeared on *What's Shakin'*, an Elektra Records sampler. Winwood then went on to form Traffic [see entry], while Clapton worked with Cream. During Traffic's original on-again, off-again existence (1967–74), Winwood appeared with Clapton in the short-lived supergroup Blind Faith [see entry] and with Ginger Baker's Air Force.

In 1970 Winwood began work on a solo album to be called *Mad Shadows*, but it eventually became the reformed Traffic's *John Barleycorn Must Die*. After Traffic's *When the Eagle Flies*, Winwood worked with Japanese percussionist Stomu Yamashta and German synthesizer player Klaus Schulze in 1976, resulting in an album, *Go*, and a concert at Royal Albert Hall in London. Winwood's 1977 solo debut, which used a backup band, was a modest success.

But *Arc of a Diver* (#3, 1981), on which Winwood played all the instruments but sang lyrics written by others (including Viv Stanshall of the Bonzo Dog Band and Will Jennings), went platinum, with a Top Ten single, "While You See a Chance" (#7, 1981). *Talking Back to the Night* (#28, 1982), made with the same method, did not fare as well as its predecessor, but four years later the triple-platinum *Back in the High Life* (#3, 1986) took Winwood to the top of the chart with the Grammy-winning

"Higher Love" (#1, 1986, which featured Chaka Khan), "Freedom Overspill" (#20, 1986), and the title track (#13, 1987). It remains his most popular album to date. *Chronicles*, a best-of, included a hit in the remixed "Valerie" (#9, 1987), a song originally included on *Talking Back to the Night* that went only to #70 on its initial release.

Winwood's first album for Virgin, *Roll with It* (#1, 1988) was certified double platinum, a highly successful album with another trio of hit singles: "Roll with It" (#1, 1988), "Don't You Know What the Night Can Do?" (#6, 1988), and "Holding On" (#11, 1988). With *Refugees of the Heart* (#27, 1990) Winwood's MOR-ish formula seemed to have worn thin, although "One and Only Man" was a Top Twenty hit. In 1994 Winwood rejoined Jim Capaldi in a much-heralded Traffic reunion. *The Finer Things* is a four-CD retrospective.

Wire

Formed 1976, London, England
Colin Newman (b. Sep. 16, 1954, Salisbury, Eng.), gtr., voc.; Bruce Gilbert (b. May 18, 1946, Watford, Eng.), gtr.; Graham Lewis (b. Feb. 2, 1953, Grantham, Eng.), bass, voc.; Robert Gotobed (b. Mark Field, 1951, Leicester, Eng.), drums.
1977—*Pink Flag* (Harvest, U.K.)   1978—*Chairs Missing*   1979—*154* (Warner Bros.)   1980—*EP* (Rough Trade, U.K.)   1981—*Document and Eyewitness*   1984—*And Here It Is . . . Again . . . Wire* (Sneaky Pete)   1986—*Wire Play Pop* (Pink); *Snakedrill* EP (Mute)   1987—*The Ideal Copy*; *Ahead* EP; *The Peel Sessions* EP (Strange Fruit, U.K.)   1988—*A Bell Is a Cup Until It Is Struck* (Mute); *Kidney Bingos* EP; *Silk Skin Paws* EP 1989—*It's Beginning to and Back Again*; *The Peel Sessions Album* (Strange Fruit, U.K.); *On Returning (1977–1979)* (Restless Retro)   1990—*Manscape* (Mute); *Life in the Manscape* EP   1991—*The Drill* EP   1993—*1985–1990: The A List*.
As Wir: 1991—*The First Letter* (Mute).

Wire's art-school approach to punk set the U.K. quartet apart from its brasher contemporaries. Drawing more from avant-garde ideas about minimalism than from basic stripped-down rock & roll, Wire extracted the essential elements of pop—beat, rhythm, melody—and left it at that. The result was a deceptively simple, unemotional sound whose success rode on the tension between the group's often introspective lyrics, barked vocals, and sparse instrumentation. Despite little attention in the beginning, Wire's first three albums are among the most influential on the postpunk era, cited by Michael Stipe of R.E.M. and Robert Smith of the Cure.

Inspired by the burgeoning U.K. punk scene, and with only rudimentary knowledge of their instruments, South Londoners Colin Newman, Bruce Gilbert, Graham

Lewis, and Robert Gotobed came together while attending the same art school. After appearing on an obscure live punk compilation, the band signed with Harvest, a mostly psychedelic/progressive-rock label, in September 1977. Wire's first release, *Pink Flag*, is a crudely produced, 21-track assault of throbbing bass, distortion, and dissonance, but also includes moments of gentle pop elegance. (R.E.M. covered the obscure *Pink Flag* song "Strange" on its first Top Ten album, *Document*.)

Wire stretched out on *Chairs Missing*, with slightly longer songs, more skillful playing, and occasional keyboard brush strokes (played by producer Mike Thorne). The group expanded its sonic palette yet again on *154*, with added instrumentation and increased attention to production, resulting in a moodier, more sophisticated and textured sound. With its musical evolution complete, the band called it a day in 1980.

Had Wire stopped there, its impact on rock's future would still have been cemented. But in 1986, after five years of posthumous live releases and solo projects—Newman and Gotobed did four albums together under Newman's name; Gilbert and Lewis performed under several names, including Dome—the quartet reunited. With an updated experimental synth-pop sound, Wire began churning out a string of albums. Though 1987's *The Ideal Copy* approached the inventiveness of the first three albums, none of the others have been nearly as monumental. By 1991's *The Drill* EP, drummer Gotobed had tired of the group's continued fascination with technology, particularly drum machines. When he left, the band responded by dropping the last letter from its name.

Bill Withers

Born July 4, 1938, Slab Fork, West Virginia
**1971—*Just As I Am* (Sussex)   1972—*Still Bill*
1973—*Bill Withers Live at Carnegie Hall*   1974—
+'*Justments*   1975—*The Best of Bill Withers*;
Making Music (Columbia)   1976—*Naked & Warm*
1977—*Menagerie*; *'Bout Love*   1981—*Bill Withers'
Greatest Hits*   1985—*Watching You Watching Me*
1994—*Lean on Me: The Best of Bill Withers* (Columbia Legacy).**

Singer/songwriter Bill Withers recorded a string of understated hits that mixed folk and soul music, including his classic "Lean on Me." Withers was nearly 30 years old before he sought a career in music. He graduated high school and worked as a mechanic. In 1967 he moved to Los Angeles and, while working in an aerospace factory, began recording demos of his songs, which got no response. Withers had just learned to play guitar, but was considering giving up songwriting when he met Booker T. Jones in 1970.

Later in 1970 Jones produced and played on Withers'

debut LP *Just As I Am* (#39, 1971), using MG's Al Jackson and Donald "Duck" Dunn as well as Stephen Stills sharing guitar credits with Withers. The album contained the gold single "Ain't No Sunshine," which went to #3 in 1971 and was awarded a Grammy for Best R&B Song. That year Withers made his performing debut in Los Angeles. His followup, "Grandma's Hands" (#42 pop, #18 R&B, 1971), has since been recorded by a number of other singers.

Recorded with members of the Watts 103rd St. Rhythm Band, *Still Bill* (#4, 1972) was even more successful, containing "Lean on Me" (#1 pop and R&B, 1972), "Use Me" (#2 pop and R&B, 1972), and "Kissing My Love" (#12 R&B, 1973). The album was certified gold and remains the singer's most successful to date. Other hits included "Let Us Love" (#17 R&B, 1972) and "Friend of Mine" (#25 R&B, 1973). After two more albums for Sussex, Withers signed with Columbia in 1975, and there he recorded six LPs. *Making Music* (#81, 1975) contained "Make Love to Your Mind" (#10 R&B), and his second gold album, *Menagerie* (#39, 1977), had "Lovely Day" (#30 pop, #6 R&B). Subsequent releases were not nearly as successful as his earlier albums.

He sang on the Crusaders' *Rhapsody in Blues*, then on Grover Washington Jr.'s *Winelight* in 1980. For the latter, he cowrote and sang "Just the Two of Us" (#2 pop, #3 R&B), one of that year's most popular singles. He also recorded a single, "U.S.A." Outside of that, however, he was basically retired from recording until 1985's *Watching You Watching Me*. He still tours occasionally.

Peter Wolf: See J. Geils Band

Bobby Womack

Born March 4, 1944, Cleveland, Ohio
**1968—*Fly Me to the Moon* (Minit)   1971—*The
Womack "Live"* (Liberty); *Communication* (United
Artists)   1972—*Understanding*   1973—*Facts of
Life*; *Across 110th Street* soundtrack   1974—
Lookin' for a Love Again; *Bobby Womack's Greatest
Hits*; *I Don't Know What the World's Coming To*
1976—*Safety Zone*; *BW Goes C&W*; *Home Is Where
the Heart Is* (Columbia); *Pieces*   1979—*Roads of
Life* (Arista)   1981—*The Poet* (Beverly Glen)
1984—*The Poet II*   1985—*So Many Rivers* (MCA);
Someday We'll All Be Free (Beverly Glen)   1986—
Womagic (MCA)   1987—*The Last Soul Man*
1989—*Save the Children* (with the Womack Brothers) (Solar)   1994—*Resurrection* (Slide/Continuum).**

As a writer and performer, guitarist Bobby Womack has been one of the most important black musicians of the last 25 years, composing a number of rock and soul standards as well as such diverse songs as Janis

Bobby Womack

Joplin's "Trust Me" and George Benson's hit "Breezin'."

Womack and his four brothers—Cecil, Curtis, Harris, and Friendly Jr.—formed a gospel group, the Womack Brothers, in the late Fifties. On the gospel circuit, they met the Soul Stirrers and lead singer Sam Cooke, who later recruited Womack as guitarist for his own pop band. Cooke then signed the Womack Brothers to his Sar label, where, as the Valentinos, they cut two R&B classics, "It's All Over Now" and "Lookin' for a Love" (#8 R&B, 1962). The former would be a major hit for the Rolling Stones, the latter a hit for the J. Geils Band.

After Cooke's death and the Valentinos' breakup, Womack became a top session guitarist and has played on recordings by Aretha Franklin, King Curtis, Dusty Springfield, and Ray Charles, among others. By then he had married Cooke's widow, Barbara; they divorced in 1970. (Later his brother Cecil would marry Cooke's daughter Linda and form the writing and producing duo of Womack and Womack.) He also continued writing. His "I'm a Midnight Mover" and "I'm in Love" were hits for Wilson Pickett. Womack wrote and played acoustic guitar on Janis Joplin's "Trust Me."

Reviving his solo career in the late Sixties, Womack had a few moderate soul hits on the Minit label, but really picked up when he moved to United Artists. His solo career took off in the early Seventies with "That's the Way I Feel About 'Cha" (#27 pop, #2 R&B) in 1971; "Woman's Got to Have It" (#1 R&B) and "Harry Hippie" (#8 R&B) in 1972; and "Nobody Wants You When You're Down and Out" (#2 R&B) in 1973. Later R&B hits include a remake of "Lookin' for a Love" (#10 pop, #1 R&B, 1974),

"You're Welcome, Stop On By" (#5 R&B, 1974), "Check It Out" (#6 R&B, 1975), and "Daylight" (#5, 1976). His albums with Columbia and Arista saw Womack in a commercial decline. According to some sources, Womack, who counted Sly Stone among his closest friends, also had a drug problem. But in 1981 he announced he had cleaned up, and he made a tremendous comeback with the #1 R&B LP *The Poet* and a #3 R&B single, "If You Think You're Lonely Now." His most recent R&B hits include a duet with Patti LaBelle, "Love Has Finally Come at Last" (#3 R&B, 1984), and "I Wish He Didn't Trust Me So Much" (#2 R&B, 1985).

After that, Womack seemed to have disappeared. He appeared with Artists United Against Apartheid, duetted with Mick Jagger on the Rolling Stones' *Dirty Work* ("Going Back to Memphis"), and reunited with his brothers for *Save the Children,* but he released no new albums for nearly five years. He appeared on Paul Shaffer's *Coast to Coast* and Todd Rundgren's *Nearly Human.* After a period of personal turmoil, Womack reemerged with *Resurrection,* the first album released on Ron Wood's Slide Music label. (Womack had produced Wood's solo debut album in 1974.) It includes guest appearances by Keith Richards, Wood, Charlie Watts, Stevie Wonder, Brian May, and others.

Stevie Wonder

Born Steveland Judkins Morris, May 13, 1950, Saginaw, Michigan
1963—Little Stevie Wonder: The 12 Year Old Genius (Tamla); Tribute to Uncle Ray; The Jazz Soul of Little Stevie   1964—With a Song in My Heart   1965—At the Beach   1966—Up-Tight Everything's Alright; Down to Earth   1967—I Was Made to Love Her   1968—Greatest Hits; Alfie; For Once in My Life   1969—My Cherie Amour; Eivets Rednow   1970—Stevie Wonder Live; Signed Sealed & Delivered   1971—Where I'm Coming From; Stevie Wonder's Greatest Hits, vol. 2   1972—Music of My Mind; Talking Book   1973—Innervisions   1974—Fulfillingness' First Finale   1976—Songs in the Key of Life; Portrait (EMI)   1977—Looking Back (Motown)   1979—Journey Through the Secret Life of Plants soundtrack (Tamla)   1980—Hotter Than July   1982—Stevie Wonder's Original Musiquarium I   1984—The Woman in Red soundtrack (Motown)   1985—In Square Circle (Tamla)   1987—Characters (Motown)   1991—Music from the Movie Jungle Fever   1995—Conversation Peace.

Groomed from an early age for Motown stardom, Stevie Wonder mastered that label's distinctive fusion of pop and soul and then went on to compose far more idiosyncratic music—an ambitious hybrid of sophisticated Tin

Pan Alley chord changes and R&B energy, inflected with jazz, reggae, and African rhythms. A synthesizer and studio pioneer, he is one of the few musicians to make records on which he plays virtually all the instruments, and does so with both convincing technique and abandon. A lifelong advocate of nonviolent political change patterned after Martin Luther King Jr. and Mahatma Gandhi, Wonder epitomizes Sixties utopianism while remaining resolutely contemporary in his musical experiments.

Stevie Morris' prodigious musical talents were recognized when Ronnie White of the Miracles heard the ten-year-old boy, blind from infancy, playing the harmonica for his children, and introduced him to Berry Gordy Jr. of the Hitsville U.S.A.—soon Motown—organization. Gordy named him Little Stevie Wonder. His third single, "Fingertips (Part 2)," was a #1 pop and R&B hit eight months later. Both on records and in live shows he was featured playing harmonica, drums, piano, and organ, as well as singing—sometimes all in one number.

During his first three years in show business, Wonder was presented as an R&B screamer in the Ray Charles mold; much was made of the fact that both were blind. In 1964 he appeared on the screen in *Muscle Beach Party* and *Bikini Beach*. *Up-Tight* (#3, 1966) included the upbeat numbers "I Was Made to Love Her" (#2, 1967), "For Once in My Life" (#2, 1968), and "Shoo-Be-Doo-Be-Doo-Da-Day" (#9, 1968). The Wonder style broadened to include Bob Dylan's "Blowin' in the Wind" (#9, 1966), the optimistic "A Place in the Sun" (#9, 1968), and an instrumental version of Burt Bacharach's "Alfie." In 1969 he hit the upper reaches of the charts with the ballads "My Cherie Amour" (#4) and "Yester-Me, Yester-You, Yesterday" (#7).

As his adolescence came to an end, Wonder took charge of his career. By the time of *Signed Sealed & Delivered* (#25, 1970), he was virtually self-sufficient in the studio, serving as his own producer and arranger, playing most of the instruments himself, and writing material with his wife, Syreeta Wright [see entry]. In this phase, he scored three more hit singles: "Signed, Sealed, Delivered I'm Yours" (#3, 1970), "Heaven Help Us All" (#9, 1970), and "If You Really Love Me" (#8, 1971).

When he reached his 21st birthday in 1971, he negotiated a new contract with Motown that made him the label's first artist to win complete artistic control (also at 21 he was due the money he had made as a minor; despite earning over $30 million, he received only $1 million). While his singles upheld the company tradition of hook-happy radio fare, they distinguished themselves with such socially conscious subjects as ghetto hardship and political disenfranchisement, especially in evidence in "Living for the City" (#8, 1973). His albums, beginning with *Music of My Mind* (#21, 1972), on which he played most of the instruments, were devoted to his more exotic

Stevie Wonder

musical ideas (which incorporated gospel, rock & roll, jazz, and African and Latin American rhythms). To his panoply of instruments, he added synthesizers; played with rare invention and funk, they became the signature of his sound.

Wonder's 1972 tour of the United States with the Rolling Stones introduced him to a huge white audience, which helped make #1 hits of two singles released within the next year—"Superstition" (written for Jeff Beck) and "You Are the Sunshine of My Life"—from *Talking Book* (#3, 1972). The period was difficult personally for Wonder: In 1972 his marriage to Wright ended after only a year (later, with companion Yolanda Simmons, he had two children, as well as a third child by vocalist Melody McCulley). In 1973 injuries sustained in a serious car crash left him in a coma for four days.

In the four years and three albums following *Talking Book*, Wonder made three more #1 singles ("You Haven't Done Nothin'," "I Wish," and "Sir Duke"), sold millions of each, and received 15 Grammy Awards. *Innervisions* (#4, 1973) also included "Higher Ground" (#4, 1973) while *Fulfillingness' First Finale* (#1, 1974) yielded "Boogie On Reggae Woman" (#3, 1974). His songs were covered widely, and he was an acknowledged influence on musicians from Jeff Beck to George Benson to Bob Marley. Working with B. B. King, the Jacksons, Minnie Riperton, Rufus, and Syreeta Wright, he established himself as a major songwriter and producer. *Songs in the Key of Life* (#1, 1976) (a double album released after he had signed a $13-million contract with Motown) was a tour de force and remained at the top of the charts for 14 weeks.

Journey Through the Secret Life of Plants (#4, 1979), three years in the making, was ostensibly the soundtrack to an unreleased film of the same name; predominantly instrumental, it failed to catch on in a big way at the time, but can be seen as a precursor to New Age music. *Hotter Than July* (#3, 1980) returned to the street-dancing spirit of earlier periods (updated in contemporary idioms such as reggae and rap). It yielded "Master Blaster (Jammin')" (#5, 1980) and Wonder's plea for an international holiday in memory of Martin Luther King, "Happy Birthday." In 1982 fans still waiting for an album of new material were placated with hit singles: "That Girl" (#4), "Do I Do" (#13), a duet with Paul Mc-Cartney—"Ebony and Ivory"(#1)—and the greatest-hits package *Stevie Wonder's Original Musiquarium I* (#4, 1982).

The Eighties saw Wonder drastically curtailing studio work, but continuing to tour (by the end of the decade becoming Motown's first artist to play the Eastern Bloc). In 1982, with Bob Dylan and Jackson Browne, he played the "Peace Sunday" antinuclear rally at the Rose Bowl. In 1984 Detroit gave him the key to the city (he later considered a run for mayor of Detroit), and he played harmonica on Elton John's "I Guess That's Why They Call It the Blues." Participating in the recording of USA for Africa's "We Are the World" in 1985, he won that year's Oscar for Best Song for "I Just Called to Say I Love You" (#1, 1984), off the *Woman in Red* (#4, 1984) soundtrack. Dedicating the award to Nelson Mandela, he angered South African radio stations, which then banned all his music.

"Part-Time Lover" (#1, 1985) became the first single simultaneously to top the pop, R&B, adult contemporary, and dance/disco charts; its parent album, *In Square Circle,* reached #5 and won the Grammy for Best R&B Male Vocal Performance. Singing with Elton John and Gladys Knight on Dionne Warwick's "That's What Friends Are For" (#1, 1986) gained Wonder another hit, but, deemed relatively lightweight, neither *Characters* (#17, 1987) nor the soundtrack for Spike Lee's *Jungle Fever* (#24, 1991) were greeted with the almost universal acclaim his Seventies work had generated.

Wonder had spent the latter Eighties working on *Conversation Peace* (#16 pop, #2 R&B, 1995), which was released to rave reviews. In 1988, duets with Michael Jackson ("Get It") and Julio Iglesias ("My Love") kept Wonder's name before the public. He was inducted into the Rock and Roll Hall of Fame in 1989. His extensive humanitarian work has concentrated on AIDS awareness, anti-apartheid efforts, crusades against drunk driving and drug abuse, and fund-raising for blind and retarded children and the homeless.

Roy Wood: See the Move

World Music

The term *world music* was coined in the late Eighties as a way to pigeonhole popular or contemporary musical styles from countries other than the United States or Great Britain, and refers primarily to styles and genres outside these musical traditions. A growing curiosity about music from around the world arose during the Eighties, following the boom in interest in African music initiated by rock musicians Paul Simon, Peter Gabriel, and David Byrne.

World music is a sweeping category used to describe international styles that are neither art nor classical, nor artificially preserved folk music, but rather the living music of ordinary people. Some world music fails to fall neatly into that category; for instance, it is difficult to draw a line between "art" and "popular" in the music of such Egyptian artists as Oum Kalthoum or Mohamed Abdel Wahab. Much of the world music produced for American and British audiences is recorded in Paris, a hotspot particularly among African stars. *World beat,* another term describing popular music from around the world, also refers to music by British or American jazz and rock groups that incorporate international sounds into their own work (i.e., Poi Dog Pondering, 3 Mustaphas 3, Klezmatics, the Ukrainians).

Examples of world music styles are soukous, highlife, zouk, juju, rai, calypso, salsa, bossa nova, merengue, samba, gamelan, klezmer, and raga. Some of the better-known world music artists are Ofra Haza (Yemen and Israel), Nusrat Fateh Ali Khan (Pakistan), Najma (India), Joe Arroya (Colombia), Margareth Menezes (Brazil), Marta Sebestyen (Hungary), Ivo Papasov (Bulgaria), Boukman Eksperyans (Haiti), Cheb Khaled (Algeria), Salif Keita (Mali), Les Têtes Brûlées (Cameroon), Fela Anikulapo Kuti (Nigeria), and Ladysmith Black Mambazo (South Africa).

World Party

Formed 1986, London, England
Karl Wallinger (b. Oct. 19, 1957, Prestatyn, Wales), voc., kybds., various instr.
1986—*Private Revolution* (Chrysalis)   1990—*Goodbye Jumbo*   1991—*Thank You World* EP   1993— (+ Dave Caitlin-Birch, gtr.; + Chris Sharrock, drums) *Bang!*

Former Waterboys keyboardist Karl Wallinger formed World Party essentially as a solo act, writing and singing all of the songs, arranging and playing most of the instruments, and generally establishing the "band" as a vehicle for his singular musical vision. A true child of the Sixties, Wallinger adapted his infatuation with the

Beatles, Jimi Hendrix, and other pop geniuses of that era to fresh, often stunning melodies (accompanied by socially astute lyrics), shimmering guitar-pop textures, and buoyant, often funky rhythms. While this somewhat nostalgic formula engendered much acclaim, World Party's commercial performance generally failed to match its critical success.

Predictably, it was a desire for more creative control that led to Wallinger's decision to leave the Waterboys [see entry]—for all intents and purposes Mike Scott's band—after the release of 1985's *This Is the Sea*. In 1987 his first World Party single, the ominous, environmentally conscious "Ship of Fools," went to #27 on the singles chart, becoming the act's biggest hit to date. Its debut album, *Private Revolution,* reached #39, also in 1987. *Goodbye Jumbo* also had its share of ecological references and warnings—and featured a guest vocal by rising star Sinéad O'Connor (as well as appearances by Waterboys Steve Wickham and Anthony Thistlethwaite)—but didn't spawn a Top Forty single. The album peaked at #73. In promoting *Jumbo* Wallinger toured with two British musicians, guitarist Dave Caitlin-Birch and drummer Chris Sharrock, who became Wallinger's core support team, collaborating with him on World Party's next album. (The touring band also included synth player Max Edie and keyboardist Guy Chambers.) That album, *Bang!*, was released in 1993 and reached #2 on the U.K. chart. In the States, however, it only made #126.

Link Wray
Born May 2, 1935, Dunn, North Carolina
1960—*Link Wray and the Waymen* (Epic)   1963—
Jack the Ripper* (Swan)   1970—*Yesterday-Today
(Record Factory)   1971—*Link Wray* (Polydor)
1973—*There's Good Rockin' Tonight* (Union Pacific)
1976—*Stuck in Gear* (Virgin, U.K.)   1979—*Bullshot*
(Charisma/Visa, U.K.)   1980—*Live at the Paradiso*
1992—*Walkin' with Link* (Epic Legacy)   1993—
***Rumble! The Best of Link Wray* (Rhino)   1995—*Guitar Preacher: the Polydor Years* (Polydor).**
With Robert Gordon: 1977—*Robert Gordon with Link Wray* (Private Stock)   1978—*Fresh Fish Special.*

One of the more influential rock guitarists of the Fifties, Link Wray introduced the distorted fuzz-tone guitar sound on his million-selling single "Rumble." For that tune, Wray and his band the Waymen wanted to approximate the effect of a brawl that took place in a dancehall where they were performing. Wray punctured the speaker in his amplifier with a pencil, which added the crackling, burry fuzz-tone sound to a brooding, ominous mid-tempo riff, anticipating heavy metal by more than a decade.

Wray, who is part Native American, learned bottleneck guitar as a youth, after moving with his family to Arizona. He formed a country band in his late teens with his brothers Doug and Vernon (who sometimes sang under the name Ray Vernon), playing bars, juke joints, and brothels under the name Lucky Wray and the Lazy Pine Wranglers, later the Palomino Ranch Hands. After returning from the Korean War, where he lost a lung to tuberculosis, Wray was advised not to sing. Soon the group became a trio—Wray, Doug Wray on drums, and Shorty Horton on bass, with Vernon Wray producing and occasionally playing rhythm guitar and piano on a few tracks—the Ray Men.

Allegedly in 1954, Wray recorded "Rumble," cowritten by Wray and local DJ Milt Grant; by 1958 it had sold over a million copies, and it reached #16 that year. By that time Wray had also played on sessions backing his brother Vernon and with Fats Domino and Rick Nelson on Milt Grant's Washington, D.C., TV show. In 1959 Wray had another instrumental hit with the rockabilly-style "Raw-Hide" (#23, 1959). Several similar followups failed to hit, however, and by the mid-Sixties Wray had retired to a family farm commune in Maryland, where he built a three-track studio in a shed, playing live only occasionally in local bars. He recorded in his shed quite often, though; word has it that when his backup musicians could not afford drums, Wray had them stomp on the floor and rattle pots, pans, and beer cans instead. Many of Wray's three-track recordings were issued on the 1971 *Link Wray*, a critically acclaimed LP that sold little and was largely made possible by the acclaim Wray had garnered from rock stars like Pete Townshend of the Who, Jeff Beck, Bob Dylan, and the Kinks.

Wray followed the 1971 LP with several more unsuccessful albums. In 1977 Wray began working with singer Robert Gordon [see entry], but they parted company a year later, after recording *Fresh Fish Special*. In 1979 Wray recorded *Bullshot*, which was unspectacularly received. He has since moved to Denmark. The 1993 Rhino best-of compiles 20 tracks from the several labels for which he recorded.

Wreckx-N-Effect
Formed 1987 as Wrecks-N-Effect, New York City, New York
Miggady-Mark (b. Markell Riley, Dec. 5, 1970, New York City), DJ; A Plus (b. Aquil Davidson, Aug. 2, 1972, New York City), voc.; Brandon Mitchell (d. 1990), voc.; Keith KC (b. ca. 1967), voc.
1988—*Wrecks-N-Effect* EP (Atlantic)   1990—(– KC; – Mitchell) *Wrecks-N-Effect* (Motown)   1992—*Hard or Smooth* (Future/MCA).

Wreckx-N-Effect overcame a number of hurdles to finally land a Top Ten single. Lead rapper Keith KC left the group after their Atlantic EP stiffed. Their album debut fared little better, and Wreckx became ensnared in legal hassles with Motown. The final blow came in 1990, when rapper Brandon Mitchell was shot and killed in an argument over a woman.

The group's fortunes changed after New Jack Swing king Teddy Riley (member Markell Riley's brother) produced *Hard or Smooth* (#9, 1992) for his label Future. The video for the single "Rump Shaker" featured so many women in skimpy bikinis that MTV refused to air it, until the song went Top Five. In April 1993 Wreckx-N-Effect made the news again when the group got in a fight backstage at New York's Radio City Music Hall with the band A Tribe Called Quest. The Nation of Islam negotiated a settlement between the hip-hop groups.

Betty Wright
Born December 21, 1953, Miami, Florida
1968—*My First Time Around* (Atco) 1972—*I Love the Way You Love* (Alston) 1973—*Hard to Stop* 1974—*Danger: High Voltage* 1976—*Explosion!* 1977—*This Time for Real* 1978—*Betty Wright Live* 1979—*Betty Travelin' in the Wright Circle* 1981— *Betty Wright* (Epic) 1986—*Sevens* (First String) 1988—*Mother Wit* (Ms. B) 1989—*4U2NJOY* 1992—*The Best of Betty Wright* (Rhino).

Betty Wright's fiery soul vocals made her a strong presence on Miami's black music scene of the Seventies. She continued to make regular appearances on the R&B chart through the late Eighties.

Wright started as a gospel singer with her family group, Echoes of Joy. She turned to R&B at age 13, after being discovered singing along to Billy Stewart's "Summertime" by songwriter/producers Willie Clarke and Clarence Reid. They recorded "Paralyzed," which got some local attention. A year later, at 14, her "Girls Can't Do What the Guys Do" (#33 pop, #15 R&B) began an association with Miami's T.K. Records stable (including the Alston label) that would continue until that company's demise in the late Seventies.

Wright was 18 when her spunky late-1971 hit "Clean Up Woman" (#6 pop, #2 R&B) was certified gold. Her other hits included "Baby Sitter" (#46 pop, #6 R&B, 1972), "Let Me Be Your Lovemaker" (#10 R&B, 1973), and "Where Is the Love" (#15 R&B, 1975), which won a Grammy. In addition to cowriting many of her hits (including the three listed above), she also contributed background vocals to T.K. disco hits by KC and the Sunshine Band and Peter Brown in the Seventies.

In 1981 Wright moved to Epic; her first album there included "What Are You Going to Do with It," a collaboration between Wright and Stevie Wonder. Later that summer, she contributed the feisty rap to Richard "Dimples" Fields' "She's Got Papers on Me" that helped make

it a major black hit. Her second and last Epic album was produced by Marlon Jackson. She then recorded for the independent First String without success before starting her own Ms. B label. Her last two major R&B chart entries were "No Pain, No Gain" (#14 R&B, 1988) and "From Pain to Joy" (#39 R&B, 1989). Except for occasional performances here and in Europe, Wright has essentially retired from the music business.

Gary Wright
Born April 26, 1943, Creskill, New Jersey
1970—*Extraction* (A&M) 1971—*Foot Print* 1972— *Ring of Changes* (with Wonderwheel) 1975—*The Dream Weaver* (Warner Bros.); *Light of Smiles* 1977—*Touch and Gone* 1979—*Headin' Home* 1981—*The Right Place* 1988—*Who I Am* 1995— *First Signs of Life* (Worldly).

Gary Wright, ex–Spooky Tooth member and successful late-Seventies solo act, started out as a child actor, debuting on the *Captain Video* TV show in New York at age seven. He also appeared in TV and radio commercials and in the Broadway play *Fanny,* all the while studying piano and organ. He joined various high school rock bands, went to college to study psychology in New York and then to Berlin, Germany.

In Europe, Wright met Mike Harrison, and the two began performing together, leading to the formation of Spooky Tooth [see entry]. When Spooky Tooth temporarily disbanded in 1970, Wright turned to a solo career, forming the band Wonderwheel. His solo work attracted little attention, though, and in 1973 he returned to the reformed Spooky Tooth. When the band broke up for good in 1974, Wright again embarked on solo ventures, this time with much more success.

The mellow, synthesizer-dominated *Dream Weaver* yielded #2 hit singles in the title tune and "Love Is Alive," and the LP went platinum. No more hit singles were forthcoming, but Wright's subsequent albums won heavy airplay on FM radio. "Dream Weaver" was revived for a new generation, thanks to its inclusion in *Wayne's World.* Subsequent albums, filled with Wright's proto–New Age lyrics, proved less successful. Only *The Light of Smiles* (#23, 1977) and *The Right Place*, which featured Wright's last hit single, "Really Wanna Know You" (#16, 1981) were popular.

O. V. Wright
Born Overton Vertis Wright, October 9, 1939, Leno, Tennessee; died November 16, 1980
1965—*O. V. Wright* (Backbeat) 1966—*Nucleus of Soul* 1970—*Ace of Spades* 1971—*A Nickel and a Nail* 1973—*Memphis Unlimited* 1975—*Into Something (Can't Shake Loose)* (Hi) 1978—*The*

Bottom Line 1992—*The Soul of O. V. Wright* (Duke-Peacock).

A Memphis soul singer with a dark and moody voice, Wright never attained the level of success some critics believe he deserved. Like many soul singers, he began singing gospel in church as a child. He led a group called the Five Harmonaires, then joined such better-known assemblages as the Sunset Travellers, the Spirit of Memphis Quartet, and the Highway QC's. He and Roosevelt Jamison cowrote "That's How Strong My Love Is," which Wright recorded. His commercial frustrations began in 1965, when Otis Redding's version hit before Wright's did.

Wright did have several R&B hits of his own, including "You're Gonna Make Me Cry" (#6 R&B, 1965), "Eight Men, Four Women" (#4 R&B, 1967), "Ace of Spade" (#11 R&B, 1970), "A Nickel and a Nail" (#19 R&B, 1971), and "I'd Rather Be Blind, Crippled and Crazy" (#33 R&B, 1973). But despite high critical praise and the chilling quality of songs like "Ace of Spade," popular acclaim eluded Wright. Although he continued to record through the Seventies, he also suffered from drug abuse, which precipitated a fatal heart attack at age 41.

Richard Wright: See Pink Floyd

Syreeta Wright

Born Pittsburgh, Pennsylvania
1972—*Syreeta* (Mowest)   1974—*Stevie Wonder Presents Syreeta*   1977—*One to One* (Tamla); *Rich Love, Poor Love* (with G. C. Cameron) (Motown) 1980—*Syreeta* (Tamla)   1981—*Billy Preston and Syreeta* (with Billy Preston) (Motown)   1981—*Set My Love in Motion* (Tamla)   1983—*The Spell*.

As a performer, Syreeta Wright has had only one major hit, a duet with Billy Preston on "With You I'm Born Again" (#4) in 1980. But as a writer she contributed to a number of artists, most significantly to her ex-husband, Stevie Wonder.

She cut a single, "Can't Give Back the Love I Feel for You," in 1968. After it flopped, she worked as a Motown secretary and occasional background singer. She met Wonder and began songwriting as a result. She is the cowriter of such Wonder hits as "Signed, Sealed, Delivered" and "If You Really Love Me." Wonder produced her first two albums, *Syreeta* and *Stevie Wonder Presents Syreeta*. She married Wonder on September 14, 1970; they divorced 18 months later.

During that period, Wonder first sought and achieved artistic independence from Motown, with one result being some of the most acclaimed work of his career. Wright cowrote songs on Wonder's *Music of My Mind, The Secret Life of Plants*, and *Talking Book*. On the last

she cowrote "Blame It on the Sun" and "Lookin' for Another Pure Love." She continued recording for Motown, but with virtually no chart success until her duet with Billy Preston, "With You I'm Born Again." *The Spell*, produced by Jermaine Jackson, did not improve her fortunes, and shortly thereafter she retired from performing. In the late Eighties she began recording again for the British Motorcity label. She appeared on Broadway in a 1995 revival of *Jesus Christ Superstar* in the role of Mary Magdalene.

Tammy Wynette

Born Virginia Wynette Pugh, May 5, 1942, Red Bay, Alabama
1967—*Your Good Girl's Gonna Go Bad* (Epic) 1968—*D-I-V-O-R-C-E*   1969—*Stand by Your Man* 1970—*The First Lady*   1973—*First Songs of the First Lady*   1978—*Womanhood*   1980—*Only Lonely Sometimes*   1981—*You Brought Me Back* 1987—*Higher Ground*   1988—*Anniversary: 20 Years of Hits*   1989—*Next to You*   1990—*Heart over Mind*   1992—*Tears of Fire: The 25th Anniversary Collection*   1995—*One* (with George Jones) (MCA).

Tammy Wynette, whose incredible chart success was matched only by the tumultuous nature of her personal life, is a country music archetype. Between 1967 and 1979 Wynette had 29 Top Ten country hits—17 of which went to #1—and had already been married five times.

Tammy Wynette

Raised by her grandparents on their farm, Wynette worked the cotton fields in order to afford music lessons. At 17 she married and quickly had three children, one of whom was stricken by spinal meningitis; by 20, she was divorced.

Her dreams of becoming a professional musician put on hold, Wynette got a job as a hairdresser in Birmingham, Alabama. With the tenacity and determination that have served her well throughout her career, Wynette eventually broke into the music industry as a background singer, first on a local TV program and later on C&W singer Porter Wagoner's own TV show. Wynette began making forays into Nashville and in 1967 met producer Billy Sherrill. Their first single together, "Apartment #9" (#44 C&W, 1966), landed on the country charts; their next single, 1967's "Your Good Girl's Gonna Go Bad" became a #3 C&W hit.

Two #1 hits quickly followed: "My Elusive Dreams" (with David Houston) and "I Don't Want to Play House." Nineteen-sixty-eight saw the release of Wynette's classics "D-I-V-O-R-C-E" and "Stand by Your Man," both #1 C&W hits. "Stand by Your Man" (#19 pop) sold more than two million copies and became the biggest-selling record by a female singer in country music history. Wynette's recording persona as the long-suffering but loyal wife and mother was now established, and her subsequent hits over the next decade centered on that theme.

In 1968 Wynette married country superstar George Jones. With three #1 hits, the couple had better success as a recording duet than they did as husband and wife; Jones' drinking strained the relationship (he is said to have once chased Wynette around their house with a rifle), causing them to divorce by 1975.

Wynette's chart-topping streak continued throughout the Seventies and into the early Eighties. Meanwhile, the vicissitudes of her private life were making tabloid headlines: a relationship with Burt Reynolds, a fourth marriage that lasted 44 days, more than 17 major operations, a fifth marriage, a mysterious kidnapping attempt and beating (her assailant was never identified), a stint in 1986 at the Betty Ford Clinic to wean her from painkillers, even a minor involvement in the S&L scandal.

In 1992 Wynette was back in the national spotlight. "Justified and Ancient"—her collaboration with an eccentric English "rave" act, the KLF—became a freak hit in the U.S. and Britain, giving Wynette her biggest pop success since "Stand by Your Man." Another incident had wider ramifications. In an attempt to publicly defend her husband, presidential nominee Bill Clinton, against charges of infidelity, Hillary Clinton stated on *60 Minutes* that "I'm not sitting here like some little woman, standing by my man like Tammy Wynette." The country icon demanded a public apology and received one two days later. In 1995 Wynette recorded *One*, an album with Jones, and the two performed together for the first time in over a decade.

Steve Wynn: See the Dream Syndicate

Wynonna: See the Judds

X

Formed 1977, Los Angeles, California
John Doe (b. Feb. 25, 1953, Decatur, Ill.), bass, voc.;
Exene Cervenka (b. Christine Cervenka, Feb. 1,
1956, Chicago, Ill.), voc.; Billy Zoom, gtr.; Don J.
Bonebrake (b. Dec. 8, 1955, N. Hollywood, Calif.),
drums.
1980—*Los Angeles* (Slash)   1981—*Wild Gift*
1982—*Under the Big Black Sun* (Elektra)   1983—
More Fun in the New World*   1985—*Ain't Love
***Grand* (– Zoom; + Tony Gilkyson [b. Aug. 6, 1952,**
Los Angeles], gtr.)   1987—*See How We Are*
1988—*Live at the Whisky A Go-Go on the Fabulous*
***Sunset Strip*   1993—*Hey Zeus!* (Mercury)   1995—**
***Unclogged* (Infidelity).**
Exene Cervenka solo: 1985—*Twin Sisters* (with
Wanda Coleman) (Freeway)   1989—*Old Wives'*
***Tales* (Rhino)   1990—*Running Sacred*   1995—**
***Surface to Air Serpents* (213CD).**
John Doe solo: 1990—*Meet John Doe* (DGC)   1995—
***Kissingsohard* (Rhino/Forward).**

In 1980 X emerged from the L.A. punk scene as the most
critically lauded American band of the early decade. X
helped to vindicate the West Coast scene, which had
lagged behind New York and London's early punk and
new-wave movements. But while X's music was influenced by punk, their lyrics were more sophisticated. And
for all the speed and thrust of their playing, X claims
roots in rockabilly and oldtime country music, which
echoes in the vocal harmonies and duets of onetime
husband and wife John Doe and Exene Cervenka.

The band began in 1977, when John Doe and Billy
Zoom met through classified ads in a local publication.
Doe's family had moved all around America when he
was growing up, and he settled in L.A. in 1976. Zoom
had played guitar and sax with Gene Vincent for a while
in the Seventies and also fronted his own rockabilly
band, which had cut several songs. Cervenka, who'd
moved west from Florida, first met Doe at a poetry workshop in Venice, California, and the two soon became
lovers and bandmates. The couple, who later married,
also write all the band's lyrics. With Don Bonebrake, they
began playing at the Masque, Hollywood's seminal punk
club. A local following grew quickly, and in 1979, after
seeing a performance at the Whisky, ex-Door Ray Manzarek became their producer.

Their debut LP, *Los Angeles,* out on then-indie label
Slash Records in 1980, sold over 60,000 copies, a large
number at the time, and 1981's *Wild Gift* eventually sold
well. In L.A., they were considered superstars. Their
music touched on rockabilly, heavy metal, punk, and
country, plus a bit of the Doors with Manzarek's organ
and their sped-up version of the Doors' "Soul Kitchen."
Both records were highlighted by Cervenka and Doe's
minor-key vocal harmonies and by incisive lyrics. Both

X: Billy Zoom, John Doe, Exene Cervenka, D. J. Bonebrake

LPs topped critics' year-end best-of lists, and in 1981 the band was also featured in two concert films: Penelope Spheeris' punk documentary *The Decline . . . of Western Civilization* and *Urgh! A Music War.* In 1981 the band signed with Elektra, which released their third LP, *Under the Big Black Sun,* in July 1982.

Cervenka continued her work in poetry, doing spoken-word performances; writing a 1982 book of poetry with Lydia Lunch, *Adulturers Anonymous*; and recording a spoken-word album, *Twin Sisters,* with poet Wanda Coleman. John Doe began appearing in films, including *Border Radio* (1987), *Slamdance* (1987), *Great Balls of Fire* (1989), and *Roadside Prophets* (1992). Cervenka starred in the 1987 film *Salvation!* In the mid-Eighties, Cervenka and Doe formed the country-folk acoustic band the Knitters, which featured Blaster Dave Alvin on guitar, for one album, *Poor Little Critter in the Road* (1985), and live performances. Meanwhile, Zoom left X after 1985's *Ain't Love Grand* to start his own band; he has since quit the music business. He was replaced by Alvin for performances; by 1987's *See How We Are* (which featured the Alvin-penned "4th of July"), guitarist Tony Gilkyson had joined X. Cervenka and Doe's marital relationship had unraveled (they have since divorced), and after 1988's *Live at the Whisky A Go-Go,* the group went on extended hiatus. Cervenka and Doe, who have remained close friends, both released solo albums; Gilkyson collaborated with Cervenka on the rootsy *Old Wives' Tales* and *Running Sacred.*

In 1990 X (with Gilkyson) began performing again in L.A., and three years later released *Hey Zeus!* on a new label, Mercury, and undertook a national tour. Though critically well received, the band failed to garner much commercial success. Cervenka continued concentrating on poetry, releasing in 1995 the spoken-word album *Surface to Air Serpents* on Henry Rollins' 213CD label; Doe's second solo album, *Kissingsohard,* was issued by Rhino the same year. *Unclogged* featured live acoustic versions of 15 years' worth of X songs.

X-Ray Spex

Formed 1977, London, England
Poly Styrene (b. Marion Elliot, ca. 1962, London), voc.; Lora Logic (b. Susan Whitby, ca. 1961, London), sax; Jak Airport (b. Jack Stafford), gtr.; Paul Dean, bass; Chris Chrysler (b. B. P. Hurding), drums. 1978—(– Logic; + Rudi Thompson [b. Steven Rudan], sax) *Germ Free Adolescents* (Blue Plate/EMI) (– Rudan; + Glyn Johns, sax).

X-Ray Spex was one of the few bands in British punk rock's first wave with a memorable female vocalist, in Poly Styrene, who wore exotic clothing and braces on her teeth. Its other female member, saxophonist Lora Logic, would leave before the band made its only album, to lead her own group, Essential Logic.

X-Ray Spex's first hit was 1977's "Oh Bondage Up Yours!"—a sort of women's-lib anthem mixing anguish and wit, which opened memorably with Styrene cooing, "Some people think little girls should be seen and not heard," before screaming out the title. Subsequent singles "The Day the World Turned Dayglo" and "Identity" critiqued the conformity of consumer culture. A year after "Bondage," X-Ray Spex released its only album, *Germ Free Adolescents,* with a title single that was much more polished, melodic, and mellow than "Bondage."

Two months after the album's release, Styrene broke up the band, reportedly claiming to have suffered a nervous breakdown after seeing a UFO. She later joined the Krishna Consciousness movement; X-Ray Spex released one posthumous single, "Highly Inflammable" b/w "Warrior in Woolworths." Styrene left the music business, but returned in 1980, under her given name of Marion Elliot, with the tropically inflected solo album *Translucence.* She released the EP *Gods and Goddesses* in 1986, to little notice. X-Ray Spex reunited in fall 1991 for a "punk nostalgia night" at London's Brixton Academy, also featuring Sham 69, Chelsea, 999, U.K. Subs, and the Lurkers.

XTC

Formed 1977, Swindon, England
Andy Partridge (b. Dec. 11, 1953, Swindon), gtr., voc., synth.; Colin Moulding (b. Aug. 17, 1955, Swindon), bass, voc.; Terry Chambers (b. July 18, 1955, Swindon), drums; John Perkins (b. Eng.), kybds.
1977—(- Perkins; + Barry Andrews [b. Sep. 12, 1956, London, Eng.], kybds. 1978—*White Music* (Virgin, U.K.); *Go 2* (- Andrews; + Dave Gregory [b. Eng.], gtr., synth.) 1979—*Drums and Wires* 1980—*Black Sea* 1982—*English Settlement* (- Chambers) 1984—*Mummer* (Geffen); *Waxworks: Some Singles 1977-82*; *The Big Express* 1986—*Skylarking* 1989—*Oranges & Lemons* 1991—*Rag & Bone Buffet* 1992—*Nonsuch.*
As Dukes of Stratosphear: 1985—*25 O'Clock* EP (Virgin, U.K.) 1987—*Psonic Psunspot* (Geffen); *Chips from the Chocolate Fireball.*
Martin Newell and Andy Partridge: 1994—*The Greatest Living Englishman* (Pipeline).

Though never earning them sales success, XTC's fastidiously crafted art pop, characterized by innovative jerky rhythms and odd melodic twists, has provoked critical comparisons to the Beatles and gained them a fanatical cult.

In 1973 they were known as the Helium Kidz, a New York Dolls–type glitter band that played straight-ahead rock & roll in their bucolic hometown of Swindon, some 70 miles out of London. The group included XTC's later leader, Andy Partridge, plus second writer Colin Moulding and drummer Terry Chambers. In 1976 they became XTC and reorganized around Partridge's songs—material influenced by the Beatles, Small Faces, and Captain Beefheart.

The band then included John Perkins on keyboards, who was replaced by Barry Andrews (ex–King Crimson) before the foursome recorded their debut, *White Music.* That album, regarded at the time as part of the new-wave onslaught, was initially released in England only,

as was 1978's *Go 2*. The 1979 U.S. debut, *Drums and Wires,* featured the wry humor of "Making Plans for Nigel." By that album's release, Andrews had left; he later joined Robert Fripp's League of Gentlemen and co-founded Shriekback [see entry] with Dave Allen of Gang of Four.

In late 1980 *Black Sea* entered the U.S. Top Fifty. Echoing the elegiac Kinks, it was less frenetic than earlier XTC but featured their usual jolting rhythms and strangely perched hooks plus several songs about war. *English Settlement* got rave reviews but didn't sell in America. Faring better in England, it yielded the band's biggest success in "Senses Working Overtime" (#10 U.K., 1982). A double LP in Britain, it had four songs not included on the U.S. edition. The band began a spring U.S. tour, but having collapsed from exhaustion onstage in Paris earlier that year, Partridge then suffered a nervous breakdown in California due to intense stage fright. XTC canceled the tour; Partridge spent the next year as a virtual shut-in, and the group ceased playing live. Chambers then left, and the remaining trio decided to use session drummers from then on.

Mummer and *Big Express* received the usual fine reviews, and a breakthrough came with 1986's *Skylarking.* Produced, to Partridge's initial frustration, by Todd Rundgren, it gained XTC new American listeners when "Dear God," an agnostic anthem originally left off the album, was discovered by a college-radio DJ. *Oranges & Lemons,* 1989's #1 college-radio album of the year, featured a single that finally entered the Top 100 ("The Mayor of Simpleton," #72, 1989)—this despite Partridge's sparring with producer Paul Fox. And while a talent scout for XTC's British label at first rejected almost all of the 32 songs submitted for *Nonsuch,* the band stuck to its guns and again placed at #1 on the college charts.

Dogged by business troubles (XTC spent the last half of the Eighties in litigation, contending against a former manager) and by unwieldy record label relationships (Virgin handles them in the U.K.; in the U.S., their albums are licensed through Geffen), XTC are notorious for their discomfort with the music industry. They concentrate, instead, on the music itself. Partridge has produced for the Mission U.K., Lilac Time, and other bands and, epitomizing genial English eccentricity, as a hobby has amassed regiments of toy soldiers.

XTC has also fashioned its own alter ego in the Dukes of Stratosphear, releasing clever pseudo-psychedelia that harks back to their primary models. In 1985 the Dukes' *25 O'Clock* sold twice as well as XTC's *Big Express* (1984). *Psonic Psunspot* and the compilation *Chips from the Chocolate Fireball* continued the expert homage/spoof.

Y

"Weird Al" Yankovic

Born Alfred Matthew Yankovic, October 23, 1959, Lynwood, California
1983—*"Weird Al" Yankovic* (Rock 'n' Roll)   1984—
"Weird Al" Yankovic in 3-D*   1985—*Dare to Be Stu-
pid*   1986—*Polka Party!*   1988—*Even Worse
1989—*UHF/Original Motion Picture Soundtrack and*
Other Stuff*   1991—*Weird Al Yankovic's Greatest
***Hits*   1992—*Off the Deep End* (Scotti Bros.)   1993—**
Alapalooza.

A musical parodist in the broad, juvenile tradition of *Mad* magazine, "Weird Al" Yankovic adds his own gently satirical lyrics to current hit songs. His shaggy, hangdog appearance, affection for slapstick, and amiable willingness to do seemingly anything for a laugh made him a natural for videos. His burlesques of the form and its artistes— especially of Michael Jackson in "Eat It" (from "Beat It") (#12, 1983) and "Fat" (from "Bad") (#99, 1988)—became MTV staples.

Yankovic got his start in 1979, when he sent his "My Bologna"—a parody of the Knack's "My Sharona"—to Dr. Demento, a syndicated radio host specializing in novelty songs and curiosities. Recorded in a bathroom with only his accordion and vocal, it was popular enough with Demento's audience for Capitol (the Knack's label) to release it as a single. His next parody, "Another One Rides the Bus" (based on Queen's "Another One Bites

"Weird Al" Yankovic

the Dust"), became the most requested song in the first decade of the Dr. Demento show.

Yankovic signed with Rock 'n' Roll Records (a CBS subsidiary), which gave him not only access to better recording facilities and the production expertise of Rick Derringer, but the financial backing for the video of "Ricky" (#63, 1983). A combination parody of Toni Basil's hit single and video "Mickey" and homage to TV's *I Love Lucy*, "Ricky" was the first of a string of videos that skewered the music, its creators, and its audience, not to mention pop culture in general. While often hilariously hamfisted, Yankovic's takeoffs—such as "I Lost on Jeopardy" (#81, 1984) from *Weird Al Yankovic in 3-D* (#81, 1984), which rewrote Greg Kihn's "Jeopardy"; "Like a Surgeon" (#47, 1985), which tackled Madonna's "Like a Virgin," from *Dare to Be Stupid* (#50, 1985)—made their creator and star almost as much a rock celebrity as his targets.

In 1985 Yankovic released a video collection of his parodies, *The Compleat Al*. That same year MTV produced an occasional series starring Yankovic as the host of Al TV, wherein he spoofed current videos. In 1989 he wrote and starred in the unsuccessful movie *UHF*.

Polka Party! (#177, 1986), which relied more on music than on videos, stiffed. But its medley of rock tunes given the polka treatment inspired rumors—since denied—that Yankovic was a member of the singing Yankovic family, who have made polka and Western swing records since the Forties.

Even Worse (#27, 1988) marked Al's return to rock video, and Michael Jackson. For "Fat," a grossly, literally overinflated Yankovic donned a leather outfit that copied Jackson's on the cover and video of *Bad* down to the last buckle. Jackson not only gave his approval for Yankovic's versions, he lent the subway set used in "Bad" for the "Fat" video.

In 1992 Yankovic turned his eye on another musical trend, grunge, specifically Nirvana. "Smells Like Nirvana" (#35, 1992) took on the Seattle band's image and garbled lyrics, with the accompanying video again using the original set, this time adding cows and Dick Van Patten, while the cover of *Off the Deep End* (#17, 1992) had Yankovic replacing the swimming baby pictured on *Nevermind*, his gaze focused not on a dollar bill, but on a doughnut. He also mocked the traveling summer tour Lollapalooza with his 1993 album, *Alapalooza* (#46).

The Yardbirds

Formed 1963, London, England
Keith Relf (b. Mar. 22, 1943, London; d. May 14, 1976, Eng.), voc., harmonica; Chris Dreja (b. Nov. 11, 1946, London), gtr.; Jim McCarty (b. July 25, 1943, Liverpool, Eng.), drums; Paul Samwell-Smith (b. May 8, 1943, Eng.), bass; Anthony "Top" Topham (b. Eng.), gtr.
1963—(- Topham; + Eric Clapton [b. Mar. 30, 1945, Ripley, Eng.], lead gtr.) 1965—*For Your Love* (Epic) (- Clapton; + Jeff Beck [b. June 24, 1944, Surrey, Eng.], gtr.); *Having a Rave Up with the Yardbirds* 1966—*Over Under Sideways Down*; *The Yardbirds with Sonny Boy Williamson* (with Sonny Boy Williamson) (Mercury) (- Samwell-Smith; + Jimmy Page [b. Jan. 9, 1944, Middlesex, Eng.], bass, later lead gtr.; Dreja switches to bass; - Beck) 1967—*Little Games* (Epic); *The Yardbirds' Greatest Hits* 1968—*Live Yardbirds!* (group disbands) 1970—*The Yardbirds/Featuring Performances by Jeff Beck, Eric Clapton, Jimmy Page* 1971—*Live Yardbirds* 1986—*Greatest Hits, vol. 1 (1964–1966)* (Rhino) 1988—*Five Live Yardbirds* (1964, U.K.; reissued on Rhino) 1991—*Vol. 1: Smokestack Lightning* (Sony); *Vol. 2: Blues, Backtracks and Shapes of Things* 1992—*Little Games, Sessions and More* (EMI).

The Yardbirds virtually wrote the book on guitar-oriented blues-based rock & roll. They were a crucial link between mid-Sixties British R&B and late-Sixties psychedelia, setting the groundwork for heavy metal. This seminal band spawned three major guitar heroes—Eric Clapton, Jimmy Page, and Jeff Beck [see entries]—who, with the Yardbirds, pioneered almost every technical guitar innovation of the era, including feedback and fuzz tone.

The Yardbirds formed in June 1963 with Keith Relf, Chris Dreja, Paul Samwell-Smith, Jim McCarty, and guitarist Anthony "Top" Topham, who was replaced in October by Eric Clapton. Originally called the Most Blueswailing Yardbirds, the fivesome initially played all strict blues covers of Chess/Checker/Vee-Jay material. They began to attract a large cult audience, especially when they took over the Rolling Stones' residency at the Crawdaddy Club in Richmond. They soon toured Europe with American bluesman Sonny Boy Williamson; a joint LP under both their names was issued in 1966. (It was rereleased in 1975.)

The band's first "solo" album in America was *For Your Love* in August 1965, yielding the hit title track written by Graham Gouldman, later of 10cc. (In the U.K., their first LP was titled *Five Live Yardbirds* and was out in 1964; Rhino reissued it stateside in 1988. The band's British records had different lineups of songs, album titles, and release dates than the U.S. versions.) The Yardbirds' second U.S. LP, *Having a Rave Up*, featured Clapton on only four cuts. He quit in 1965 because he objected to the band's increased pop-commercial direction, namely "For Your Love." In order to stick with purist blues, he joined John Mayall's band. His replacement

The Yardbirds: Chris Dreja, Eric Clapton, Paul Samwell-Smith, Keith Relf, Jim McCarty

was Jeff Beck, and the band soon enjoyed two more hits by Gouldman—"Heart Full of Soul," with its prepsyche-delic guitar fuzz licks, and "Evil Hearted You," which charted in the U.K. only. In 1966 the band had two more hits—"Shapes of Things" and "Over Under Sideways Down"—but then Samwell-Smith, who had coproduced the band's records, bowed out to become a producer full-time. He has since produced artists including Carly Simon, Cat Stevens, Jethro Tull, and Beverley Craven.

His replacement on bass was Jimmy Page, who moved to lead guitar as soon as rhythm guitarist Dreja learned bass. For a brief time beginning in the summer of 1966, Page and Beck were co–lead guitarists. (Page was earlier asked to be Clapton's replacement but declined, recommending Beck instead.) This lineup lasted only until November. They can be seen in the rock-club se-quence in Michelangelo Antonioni's film *Blow Up*, wherein they perform "Stroll On" (actually a reworking of the Johnny Burnette Trio's "Train Kept A-Rollin'"). Beck had been missing many shows because of illness, and at the end of the year he suffered a full breakdown and left.

The band foundered from there. As a quartet, they put out one LP in 1967 called *Little Games*, produced by Mickie Most, but it was filled with old demos and substandard leftover tracks. It came out only in the U.S. More singles were released, but they didn't go far, and in July 1968 the band finally broke up. Relf and McCarty formed a folk duo called Together, followed by the classical-rock Renaissance [see entry] and later the heavy Armageddon, none of which was very successful. Relf died of an electric shock at home on May 14, 1976. Dreja became a photographer and shot the album-sleeve photos for the first album by Led Zeppelin [see entry], the band Jimmy Page formed first as the New Yardbirds to

meet this group's remaining contractual obligations.

Several repackagings of Yardbirds tracks were re-leased through the Eighties and Nineties. In 1971 the *Live Yardbirds* LP (recorded at New York's Anderson Theater on March 30, 1968) was issued, without the band's consent, and they quickly demanded its removal from the market. It has since become a highly valuable, oft-bootlegged collectors' item.

In 1983 McCarty, Dreja, and Samwell-Smith reunited to play the Marquee, and soon formed Box of Frogs with lead vocalist John Fiddler. That band released two al-bums, only one of which, *Box of Frogs*, was available do-mestically. In 1989 McCarty joined several other British Sixties pop-group members in the British Invasion All-Stars. Most recently he has also been successful record-ing New Age music as part of Stairway.

Trisha Yearwood

Born Patricia Lynn Yearwood, September 19, 1964, Monticello, Georgia
1991—*Trisha Yearwood* (MCA)   1992—*Hearts in Armor*   1993—*The Song Remembers When*   1995—*Thinkin' About You*.

With a gold debut album and a marketably smooth voice, Trisha Yearwood epitomized the early-Nineties Nashville artist: grounded in country tradition but reaching an au-dience raised on Seventies pop.

Moving to Nashville in 1985, Yearwood began singing demos. Garth Brooks enlisted her to sing backup on his debut and to tour with him; through Brooks, she met producer Garth Fundis, who produced *Trisha Year-wood* (#2 C&W, 1991). The album was an instant suc-cess, its singles, "She's in Love with the Boy" (#1 C&W,

1991), "Like We Never Had a Broken Heart" (#4 C&W, 1991) (which Yearwood cowrote with Brooks), and "That's What I Like About You" (#8 C&W, 1992), helping Yearwood win the Academy of Country Music's Top New Female Vocalist Award in 1992.

Featuring "Wrong Side of Memphis" (#5 C&W, 1992), "The Woman Before Me" (#4 C&W, 1992), and a duet with Don Henley, "Walkaway Joe" (#2 C&W, 1993), *Hearts in Armor* (#46 pop, #12 C&W, 1992) consolidated Yearwood's gains. In 1992 she contributed a version of Elvis Presley's hit "You're the Devil in Disguise" to the *Honeymoon in Vegas* soundtrack. By 1993 she had signed a deal with Revlon to market a perfume called Wild Heart, been featured in the movie *This Thing Called Love*, and been the subject of a biography, *Get Hot or Go Home—Trisha Yearwood: The Making of a Nashville Star* by Lisa Gubernick. *The Song Remembers When* (#40 pop, #6 C&W, 1993), with its accompanying cable-television special and singles "You Say You Will" (#12 C&W, 1993), "Down on My Knees" (#19 C&W, 1993), and the title track (#2 C&W, 1993), continued her rise. In 1993 she contributed "New Kid in Town" to the Eagles tribute, *Common Thread*; the following year she duetted with Aaron Neville on the Grammy-winning "I Fall to Pieces," for the anthology *Rhythm, Country and Blues*. Yearwood's fourth album, *Thinkin' About You* (#3 pop, #8 C&W)*, was released on Valentine's Day, 1995.

Yaz: See Alison Moyet; Erasure

Yellow Magic Orchestra: See Ryuichi Sakamoto

Yes
Formed 1968, London, England
Jon Anderson (b. Oct. 25, 1944, Accrington, Eng.), voc., perc.; Peter Banks, gtr., voc.; Tony Kaye (b. Jan. 11, 1945, Leicester, Eng.), kybds.; Chris Squire (b. Mar. 4, 1948, London), bass, voc.; Bill Bruford (b. William Scott Bruford, May 17, 1949, Sevenoaks, Eng.), drums.
1969—*Yes* (Atlantic)   1970—*Time and a Word* 1971—(– Banks; + Steve Howe [b. Apr. 8, 1947, London], gtr., voc.) *The Yes Album* (– Kaye; + Rick Wakeman [b. May 18, 1949, London], kybds.); *Fragile*   1972—*Close to the Edge* (– Bruford; + Alan White [b. June 14, 1949, Pelton, Eng.], drums) 1973—*Yessongs*; *Tales from Topographic Oceans* 1974—(– Wakeman; + Patrick Moraz [b. June 24, 1948, Morges, Switz.], kybds.) *Relayer*   1975—*Yesterdays*   1976—(– Moraz; + Wakeman) 1977—*Going for the One*   1978—*Tormato*

Yes: Bill Bruford, Rick Wakeman, Chris Squire, Jon Anderson, Steve Howe

1980—*Yesshows* (– Anderson; – Wakeman; + Trevor Horn [b. July 15, 1949, Hertfordshire, Eng.], voc.; + Geoffrey Downes [b. Eng.], kybds.); *Drama* (group disbands)   1982—*Classic Yes*   1983—(Group reforms: Anderson; Kaye; Squire; White; + Trevor Rabin [b. Jan. 13, 1954, Johannesburg, S.A.], gtr.) *90125* (Atco)   1985—*9012Live—The Solos*   1987—*Big Generator*   1990—(– Anderson)   1991—(+ Anderson; + Bruford; + Wakeman; + Howe) *Union* (Arista)   1991—*Yesyears* (Atco)   1993—(Group reforms: Anderson; Bruford; Howe) *Symphonic Music of Yes* (RCA); *The Very Best of Yes* (Atlantic) (group re-forms: Anderson; Kaye; Rabin; Squire; White) 1994—*Talk* (Victory).
Anderson, Bruford, Wakeman, Howe: 1989—*Anderson, Bruford, Wakeman, Howe* (Arista).
Jon Anderson solo: 1976—*Olias of Sunhillow* (Atlantic)   1980—*Song of Seven*   1982—*Animation* (Mercury)   1988—*In the City of Angels* (Atlantic) 1994—*Change We Must* (EMI); *Deseo* (Windham Hill).
Jon Anderson with Vangelis, as Jon and Vangelis: 1980—*Short Stories* (Mercury)   1982—*The Friends of Mr. Cairo*   1983—*Private Collection*   1984—*The Best of Jon and Vangelis*.

Steve Howe solo: 1975—*Beginnings* (Atlantic) 1979—*Steve Howe Album* 1991—*Turbulence*.
Chris Squire solo: 1975—*Fish Out of Water* (Atlantic).
Rick Wakeman solo: 1973—*The Six Wives of Henry VIII* (A&M) 1974—*Journey to the Center of the Earth* 1975—*The Myths and Legends of King Arthur; Lisztomania* soundtrack 1976—*No Earthly Connection; White Rock* 1977—*Criminal Record* 1978—*Best Known Works* 1980—*Rhapsodies*.
Bill Bruford solo: See entry.

One of the most successful progressive-rock bands of the Seventies, Yes combined virtuoso musicianship, suite-like neoclassical structures, and three-part high vocal harmonies to form an elaborate whole that critics called irrelevant high-flown indulgence—and that audiences loved. After undergoing byzantine personnel changes, they updated their sound in the mid-Eighties and enjoyed greater commercial success than ever.

Yes was formed after Jon Anderson met Chris Squire at a London music-industry bar in 1968. Anderson had spent the previous 12 years in various bands; Squire, a self-taught bassist, had been in the Syn. With guitarist Peter Banks, keyboardist Tony Kaye, and drummer Bill Bruford, they formed Yes. One of their first engagements was opening for Cream's London farewell concert in November 1968. The band won instant critical acclaim in Britain, and by the time of their debut album, which mixed originals with covers, were hailed as "the next supergroup." *Time and a Word*, which used an orchestra to flesh out intricately shifting arrangements, was somewhat less well received.

At this point, Yes had yet to break through in America, and Atlantic Records informed them that the next album might be their last. Banks left to form Flash and new guitarist Steve Howe—formerly of such bands as the Syndicate and Tomorrow—helped make *The Yes Album* (#40, 1971) their breakthrough. With continual FM airplay it went gold.

In 1971 Tony Kaye left to form Badger (he later joined Detective and then Badfinger [see entry]). His replacement, Rick Wakeman, had garnered acclaim with the Strawbs. *Fragile* (#4, 1972) consolidated the band's success. Boosted by an edited "Roundabout," released as a single (#13, 1972), the album went gold. With *Close to the Edge* (#3, 1972), Yes' ambition attained new heights. Consisting of three extended cuts, one of them the four-movement title suite, the album too went gold in short order. After recording it, Bruford left to join King Crimson [see entry] (whose leader, Robert Fripp, had once been approached to replace Peter Banks). His replacement was sessionman Alan White, who had played in John Lennon's Plastic Ono Band.

The live *Yessongs* (#12, 1973) was followed by the critically derided *Tales from Topographic Oceans* (#6, 1974). The album sold well, however, and the band continued to be a top-drawing live act. But *Tales* brought to a head conflicts between Wakeman, an extroverted meat-eating beer drinker, and the other players, who were sober vegetarians. Wakeman, openly expressing his disillusionment, soon left.

Wakeman's replacement was Patrick Moraz (like Wakeman, classically trained), of progressive-rock band Refugee, and he debuted on *Relayer* (#5, 1974), which, like *Close to the Edge*, featured an extended suite and forays into jazz fusion. With the release of *Yesterdays* (#17, 1975), a compilation including tracks from the first two (uncharted) Yes albums, the band took a year off and each member pursued solo projects.

After Yes had made a successful world tour with Moraz, Wakeman rejoined. Both *Going for the One* (#8, 1977) and *Tormato* (#10, 1978) returned to shorter, tighter song structures. But though Yes continued to sell albums and fill arenas, its days seemed numbered. Wakeman left again, followed by Anderson, who had written most of Yes' lyrics. Trevor Horn and Geoffrey Downes of the new-wave band the Buggles (who had had a hit with "Video Killed the Radio Star") debuted on *Drama* (#18, 1980). Shortly thereafter, Yes broke up.

Howe and Downes then joined with Carl Palmer of Emerson, Lake and Palmer and John Wetton to form the progressive-rock supergroup Asia [see entry], which debuted in 1982 with a massively successful album. Anderson continued to make solo albums. Squire and White planned to start a band called Cinema. But in mid-1983 Anderson, Kaye, Squire, White, and South African guitarist Trevor Rabin re-formed Yes and went on with *90125* (#5, 1983) and its #1 single, "Owner of a Lonely Heart," both to score the band's highest chart position and to redefine its sound. Largely due to producer Trevor Horn, Yes streamlined its approach, eschewing classical stylings for sonically gorgeous, crafty pop. Rabin's songwriting dominated *The Big Generator* (#15, 1987), after which Anderson quit.

By 1989 the band's personnel squabbles had reached new intensity; after a court battle over the group name, Squire, White, Rabin, and Kaye continued as the official Yes, while the warring faction of Anderson, Bruford, Wakeman, and Howe toured and recorded using their surnames. The two camps reconciled on *Union* (#15, 1991), going on to a world tour that, for all the logistical unwieldiness of its eight-player lineup, was a huge commercial success.

In 1993 Anderson, Bruford, and Howe joined the London Philharmonic in an album of symphonic versions of Yes songs. A year later, Yes—this time composed of the members who'd released *90125*—recorded *Talk* (#33, 1994).

Dwight Yoakam

Born October 23, 1956, Pikesville, Kentucky
1986—*Guitars, Cadillacs, Etc. Etc.* (Reprise)   1987—
Hillbilly Deluxe   1988—*Buenas Noches from a
Lonely Room*   1989—*Just Lookin' for a Hit*   1990—
If There Was a Way   1993—*This Time*   1995—
Dwight Live.

Honey-voiced singer/songwriter Dwight Yoakam can
glide from an insinuating croon to a country holler. He
set out to revive the honky-tonk tradition pioneered by
Merle Haggard, but his highly stylized image and sometimes self-righteous attitude have earned him the disap-
proval of Nashville's more conservative establishment.

Kentucky-born and Ohio-bred, Yoakam wrote his
first song at age ten. By the time he turned 18 he was
performing on the Ohio Valley honky-tonk circuit. After
attending schools in Ohio and California, Yoakam set out
for Nashville, where, by his account, he was rejected for
being "too country." (Nashville's *The Tennessean* reported that this rejection consisted of his being passed
over at an Opryland audition.)

Inspired by Californian Buck Owens, from Bakersfield, Yoakam relocated to neighboring Los Angeles in
1978; a year later he put together the Babylonian Cowboys. Pete Anderson, whose guitar playing, arrangements, and production have been a crucial element in
Yoakam's success, joined in 1982.

Gigging in San Fernando Valley honky-tonks,
Yoakam and his outfit eventually scored opening slots for
bands who were part of L.A.'s burgeoning roots-rock
scene, such as the Blasters and Los Lobos. In 1984
Yoakam released an EP, *Guitars, Cadillacs, Etc.,* on his
own Oak label. It helped land him a record deal with
Reprise's Nashville subsidiary, which rereleased it as an
album by adding three songs (and a second *Etc.* to its
title). Its debut single, a cover of Johnny Horton's "Honky
Tonk Man" (#3 C&W, 1986) and title track (#4 C&W, 1986)
proved that straight-ahead country music could go platinum.

A steady stream of country Top Ten singles—a cover
of the Elvis hit "Little Sister" (#7 C&W, 1987), "Little
Ways" (#8 C&W, 1987), "Please, Please Baby" (#6 C&W,
1987), and "Always Late with Your Kisses" (#9 C&W,
1988), from *Hillbilly Deluxe* (#55 pop, #1 C&W, 1987)—
did not change Yoakam's outsider status, though. His
trademark look—Fifties-style fancy embroidered jackets, skintight faded jeans, cowboy boots, and cowboy
hat—reflected Yoakam's love for the look as well as the
sound of traditional C&W. (In 1990, Yoakam invested in a
C&W clothing venture with Manuel, the western-wear
designer who got his start with legendary cowboy cou-
turier Nudie.)

Yoakam's next album, *Buenas Noches from a Lonely
Room* (#68 pop, #1 C&W, 1988), yielded the #1 C&W hits
"Streets of Bakersfield" (with Buck Owens, whom
Yoakam coaxed out of retirement) and "I Sang Dixie."
Yoakam sang duets with k. d. lang—the Flying Burrito
Brothers' "Sin City"—on *Just Lookin' for a Hit* (#68 pop,
#3 C&W, 1989), and with Patty Loveless on "Send a Mes-
sage to My Heart" (#47 C&W, 1992), on *If There Was a
Way* (#96 pop, #7 C&W, 1990). *Way* also featured the Top
Twenty C&W singles "You're the One" (#5, 1991), "Noth-
ing's Changed Here" (#15, 1991), and "It Only Hurts
When I Cry" (#6, 1992), cowritten with Roger Miller.

In the early Nineties, Yoakam tried his hand at acting, making a cameo in the cult film *Red Rock West,*
which starred Nicolas Cage, Dennis Hopper, and Lara
Flynn Boyle. He also scored the soundtrack for the 1992
film *White Sands* and contributed a version of Elvis'
"Suspicious Minds" (#35 C&W, 1992) to *Honeymoon in
Vegas* (the soundtrack album hit #4 in 1992). An ill-fated
love affair with actress Sharon Stone in 1992 resulted in
several emotionally charged compositions on Yoakam's
1993 platinum album *This Time* (#25 pop, #4 C&W, 1993).
The album yielded the hits "Ain't That Lonely Yet" (#2
C&W, 1993), which won the Grammy for Best Male
Country Performance in 1994, "A Thousand Miles from
Nowhere" (#2 C&W, 1993), "Try Not to Look So Pretty"
(#14 C&W, 1994), and "Fast as You" (#70 pop, #2 C&W,
1994).

Jesse Colin Young: See the Youngbloods

Neil Young

Born November 12, 1945, Toronto, Canada
1969—*Neil Young* (Reprise); *Everybody Knows This
Is Nowhere*   1970—*After the Gold Rush*   1972—
Harvest; Journey Through the Past   1973—*Time
Fades Away*   1974—*On the Beach*   1975—
Tonight's the Night; Zuma   1976—*Long May You
Run* (with Stephen Stills)   1977—*American Stars 'n
Bars*   1978—*Decade; Comes a Time*   1979—*Rust
Never Sleeps; Live Rust*   1980—*Hawks & Doves*
1981—*Re•ac•tor*   1982—*Trans* (Geffen)   1983—
Everybody's Rockin'   1985—*Old Ways*   1986—
Landing on Water   1987—*Life; This Note's for You*
(Reprise)   1989—*Freedom*   1990—*Ragged Glory*
1991—*Arc; Weld*   1992—*Harvest Moon*   1993—
Lucky Thirteen: Excursions into Alien Territory
(Geffen); *Unplugged* (Reprise)   1994—*Sleeps with
Angels*   1995—*Mirror Ball* (with Pearl Jam).

Singer/songwriter Neil Young is sometimes visionary,
sometimes flaky, sometimes both at once. He has maintained a large following since the early Seventies with
music in three basic styles—solo acoustic ballads, sweet
country rock, and lumbering hard rock, all topped by his

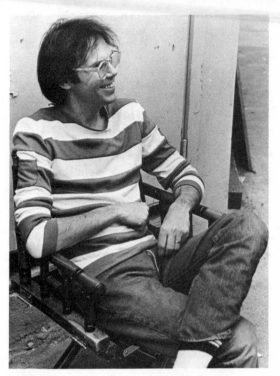

Neil Young

high voice—and he veers from one to another in unpredictable phases. His subject matter also shifts from personal confessions to allusive stories to bouncy throwaways. A dedicated primitivist, Young is constantly proving that simplicity is not always simple.

As a child, Young moved with his mother to Winnipeg, Canada, after she divorced his father, a well-known sports journalist. He played in several high school rock bands, including the Esquires, the Stardusters, and the Squires. He also began hanging out in local folk clubs, where he met Stephen Stills and Joni Mitchell. Mitchell wrote "The Circle Game" for Young after hearing his "Sugar Mountain." In the mid-Sixties Young moved to Toronto, where he began performing solo. In 1966 he and bassist Bruce Palmer joined the Mynah Birds (which included Rick James and had a deal with Motown Records); after that fizzled, he and Palmer drove to Los Angeles in Young's Pontiac hearse. Young and Palmer ran into Stills and another mutual friend, Richie Furay, out west and formed Buffalo Springfield [see entry], one of the most important of the new folk-country-rock bands, which recorded Young's "Broken Arrow," "I Am a Child," "Mr. Soul," and "Nowadays Clancy Can't Even Sing." But friction developed: Young quit the band, only to rejoin and quit again, and in May 1968, after recording three albums, the band split up.

Young acquired Joni Mitchell's manager, Elliot Roberts, and released his debut solo LP in January 1969, coproduced by Jack Nitzsche. Around the same time Young began jamming with a band called the Rockets. Renamed Crazy Horse, the band—drummer Ralph Molina, bassist Billy Talbot, and guitarist Danny Whitten—backed Young on *Everybody Knows This Is Nowhere* (#34, 1969), recorded in two weeks. The album includes three of Young's most famous songs: "Cinnamon Girl," "Down by the River," and "Cowgirl in the Sand," which, Young later said, were all written in one day while he was stricken with the flu. The album went gold (and much later, platinum), but Young decided to split his time between Crazy Horse and Crosby, Stills and Nash [see entry], which he joined in June. In March 1970 his presence was first felt on CSN&Y's *Déjà Vu*.

Young's third solo, the gold (and utterly pessimistic) *After the Gold Rush* (#8, 1970), included Crazy Horse and 17-year-old guitarist Nils Lofgren. The album yielded the single "Only Love Can Break Your Heart" (#33, 1970), and that plus the CSN&Y album put the spotlight on Young. *Harvest* (#1, 1972), with the #1 single "Heart of Gold," made the singer/songwriter a superstar.

By the release of its live album, *Four Way Street,* in spring 1971, CSN&Y had broken up. In 1972 Young made a *cinema verité* film, *Journey Through the Past;* it and its soundtrack were panned by critics. Young confused fans further with *Time Fades Away* (#22, 1973), a rough-hewn live album recorded with the Stray Gators, including Nitzsche (keyboards), Ben Keith (pedal steel guitar), Tim Drummond (bass), and John Barbata (drums). In June 1975 Young released a bleak, ragged album recorded two years earlier, *Tonight's the Night* (#25). The album's dark tone reflected Young's emotional upheaval following the drug deaths of Crazy Horse's Danny Whitten in 1972 and CSN&Y roadie Bruce Berry in 1973. In November Young released the harder-rocking *Zuma* (#25), an emotionally intense work that included the sweeping "Cortez the Killer." Crazy Horse now included Talbot, Molina, and Frank Sampedro (rhythm guitar). In 1976 Young recorded *Long May You Run* (#26) with Stills, which went gold; he and Stills embarked on a tour, but Young left halfway through.

In June 1977 Young was back on his own with the gold *American Stars 'n Bars* (#21), again a more accessible effort, with Linda Ronstadt doing backup vocals along with newcomer Nicolette Larson. *Decade* was a carefully chosen, not entirely hit-centered compilation. *Comes a Time* (#7, 1978) was folkish and went gold.

In fall 1978 Young did an arena tour called Rust Never Sleeps. He played old and new music, performing half the show by himself on piano or guitar, and the other half with Crazy Horse, amid giant mockups of microphones and speakers. Reaction to Young's seeming change in direction (although anyone paying close at-

Grammy Awards

"Weird Al" Yankovic
1984 Best Comedy Recording: "Eat It"
1988 Best Concept Music Video: "Fat" (with others)

Trisha Yearwood
1994 Best Country Vocal Collaboration: "I Fall to
Pieces" (with Aaron Neville)

Yes
1984 Best Rock Instrumental Performance: "Cinema"

Dwight Yoakam
1993 Best Country Vocal Performance, Male: "Ain't
That Lonely Yet"

Young MC
1989 Best Rap Performance: "Bust a Move"

---

tention would not have been too surprised) was swift and loud. In June 1979 he released *Rust Never Sleeps* (#8) with songs previewed on the tour, including "Out of the Blue," dedicated to Johnny Rotten and the Sex Pistols. The album also featured "Sedan Delivery" and "Powderfinger," which Young had once offered to Lynyrd Skynyrd, though they didn't record them. (Back in 1974 Skynyrd had written "Sweet Home Alabama" as an answer to Young's "Southern Man.") In November 1979 Young released the gold *Live Rust* LP (#15), culled from the fall 1978 shows and the soundtrack to a film of the tour (directed by Young) entitled *Rust Never Sleeps.*

The Eighties was a particularly strange and erratic decade for Young, even by his own unpredictable standards. Right before presidential election week 1980, he issued *Hawks & Doves* (#30), an enigmatic state-of-the-union address, with one side of odd acoustic pieces and the other of rickety country songs. Exactly one year later he released *Re•ac•tor* (#27), an all-hard-rock LP, which, despite its title, seemed to have little to do with nuclear power. In 1982 he moved to Geffen and released *Trans* (#19), which introduced what Young called "Neil 2"; he fed his voice through a computerized vocoder and sang songs like "Sample and Hold." He toured arenas as a solo performer when the album was released, singing his most-requested songs, covering "backstage" action on a large video screen, and singing along with his vocoder-ized video image on songs from *Trans.*

Young's wandering got more extreme with *Everybody's Rockin'*, a rockabilly-style album recorded and performed with a group he dubbed the Shocking Pinks, and his work started sliding down the charts. *Old Ways* was a country record with guest spots by Willie Nelson and Waylon Jennings. *Landing on Water* combined new-wave–like synthesizers with standard rock songs. And *Life* reunited Young with Crazy Horse in lackluster performances. After his disastrous relationship with Geffen—in which he was ultimately slapped with a $3-million suit for making "unrepresentative," noncommerical music—Young returned to his former label for *This Note's for You,* a horn-based R&B album recorded with a backing group called the Bluenotes. (The video for the title song attacked rockers who allowed their songs to be used in TV ads and was initially banned by MTV, although it earned the network's Video Music Award for Best Video of the Year.) In 1987, after appearing with his old cohorts in CSN at a Greenpeace benefit, Young rejoined the group briefly for the 1988 CSN&Y album, *American Dream* (#16, 1989).

Except for 1989's *Freedom,* none of Young's Eighties albums was particularly well received beyond the artist's loyal core audience, though some—such as *Trans*—had captured critics' interest. Many wrote off his Eighties period as typical Neil Young flakiness. But there were events in Young's personal life that shed light on his increased eccentricity. In 1978 his second son, Ben, was born to his wife, Pegi, with cerebral palsy (in 1972, Young's first son, Zeke, was born to his then-companion, actress Carrie Snodgress, with a milder version of the disorder). Later, in a 1992 interview with the *New York Times,* Young said his Eighties output had reflected his frustration with not being able to communicate with Ben: "*Trans* signified the end of one sound and era and the beginning of another era, where I was indecipherable and no one could understand what I was saying."

Young's extramusical activities during the Eighties were as unpredictable as the albums. In 1984, to the bewilderment of his fans, he spoke out in favor of Ronald Reagan. He also participated in the 1985 Live Aid benefit and helped organize the subsequent Farm Aid concerts. In 1986 Young and his wife started the Bridge School in San Francisco, a learning center for handicapped children with problems communicating. In 1989 a group of alternative rockers including Sonic Youth, Pixies, and Dinosaur Jr contributed to *The Bridge: A Tribute to Neil Young,* whose proceeds went to the school. (Young also organized annual benefit concerts for the school, at which a wide range of artists perform each year.)

Hailed by a new generation of postpunk musicians as the Granddaddy of Grunge, Young had a major comeback beginning in 1989 with *Freedom* (#35), his highest charter since *Trans*; he introduced its single, "Rockin' in the Free World," in an unbridled, transcendent 1989 performance on *Saturday Night Live.* Young then regrouped Crazy Horse for *Ragged Glory* (#31, 1990), a raucous, critically lauded album. With raw, feedback- and distortion-drenched hard rock, the album proved the extent of Young's influence on younger alternative-rock bands such as Dinosaur Jr and Soul Asylum. In 1991 he embraced that new generation of bands by taking noise-rockers Sonic Youth and Social Distortion on the road; the tour was documented on *Weld* (whose 35-minute instrumental companion *Arc* featured extended, noisy feedback jams). Young also began praising rap, particularly the music of Ice-T.

Harvest Moon (#16, 1992), reuniting him with members of the Stray Gators, found Young doing his sentimental acoustic/folk songs again. A sequel to *Harvest*, it was his biggest seller in 13 years. In 1992 Young appeared at the 50th birthday celebration for Bob Dylan, covering Dylan's "Just Like Tom Thumb's Blues" and "All Along the Watchtower." Released in 1993, *Lucky Thirteen* compiles Young's Geffen material, and *Unplugged* documents his live, acoustic performances following the release of *Harvest Moon*.

In 1994 Young contributed the haunting title song to Jonathan Demme's film *Philadelphia*, which was nominated for an Oscar. He also released *Sleeps with Angels* (#9, 1994), his strongest, most consistent, and critically lauded album since *Rust Never Sleeps*. After performing with Pearl Jam several times, in 1995 Young collaborated with the group on the album *Mirror Ball*, released to rave reviews in mid-1995.

Paul Young

Born January 17, 1956, Luton, England
1983—*No Parlez* (Columbia)   1985—*The Secret of Association*   1986—*Between Two Fires*   1990—*Other Voices*   1991—*From Time to Time/The Singles Collection.*

Paul Young is a handsome, blue-eyed soul singer whose massive popularity in his native England has led to the occasional pop hit in the U.S. Young was born in a North London suburb. His first group of note, Streetband, had a novelty hit in the U.K. with "Toast" in 1978. In 1979 Streetband split, and Young and other members formed the eight-piece soul band Q-Tips. The band became popular in England through frequent touring, but its eponymous 1980 album sold poorly.

Young was offered a solo contract by CBS and brought Q-Tips keyboardist Ian Kewley with him. The Royal Family band, along with backup singers the Fabulous Wealthy Tarts, accompanied Young on *No Parlez*. Lushly produced by Laurie Latham, the album was a hit in Europe. It featured a cover of Marvin Gaye's "Wherever I Lay My Hat (That's My Home)," "Come Back and Stay" (#22, 1984), and "Love of the Common People," as well as an unlikely cover of Joy Division's "Love Will Tear Us Apart."

While touring Europe and the U.S., Young strained his voice and was forced to rest. Meanwhile, the Tarts left to pursue their own careers and were replaced by George Chandler, Tony Jackson, and Jimmy Chambers; they hit with a cover of Daryl Hall's "Everytime You Go Away" (#1, 1985). The Latham-produced album included Tom Waits' "Soldier's Things" and "I'm Gonna Tear Your Playhouse Down" (#13, 1985).

Perhaps trying to balance his sex-symbol imagery, Young cowrote and coproduced (with Hugh Padgham and Kewley) *Between Two Fires*. The album yielded no hits, though. Young took an 18-month hiatus to attend to family, appearing publicly in 1988 to sing at the Nelson Mandela birthday tribute concert in Wembley. He changed direction on *Other Voices*, working with four producers (including Nile Rodgers and Peter Wolf) and such special guests as Chaka Khan, Pink Floyd guitarist David Gilmour, and Stevie Wonder (on harmonica). Young returned to the American charts by covering the old Chi-Lites tune "Oh Girl" (#8, 1990). The album also featured a version of Free's "A Little Bit of Love." Young's cover of Jimmy Ruffin's 1966 hit "What Becomes of the Brokenhearted" (#22, 1992) was featured in the movie *Fried Green Tomatoes*.

The Youngbloods/Jesse Colin Young

Formed 1965, Boston, Massachusetts
Jesse Colin Young (b. Perry Miller, Nov. 11, 1944, New York City, N.Y.), voc., bass, gtr.; Jerry Corbitt (b. Tifton, Ga.), gtr., voc.; Joe Bauer (b. Sep. 26, 1941, Memphis, Tenn.; d. 1982), drums; Banana (b. Lowell Vincent Levinger, 1946, Cambridge, Mass.), gtr., kybds.
1967—*The Youngbloods* (RCA); *Earth Music*; *Two Trips* (Mercury)   1969—*Elephant Mountain* (RCA) (– Corbitt)   1970—*The Best of the Youngbloods*; *Rock Festival* (Raccoon)   1971—*Ride the Wind*; *Sunlight* (RCA) (+ Michael Kane, bass); *Good and Dusty* (Raccoon)   1972—*High on a Ridge Top*. Jesse Colin Young solo: 1964—*The Soul of a City Boy* (Capitol); *Youngblood* (Mercury)   1972—*Together* (Raccoon)   1973—*Song for Juli* (Warner Bros.)   1974—*Light Shine*   1975—*Songbird*   1976—*On the Road*   1977—*Love on the Wing*   1978—*American Dreams* (Elektra)   1991—*The Best of Jesse Colin Young: The Solo Years* (Rhino).

The Youngbloods were a folk-rock group led by Jesse Colin Young. Though they had a jazzy, mellow West Coast sound, their roots were in Boston and New York City. Young started out playing the folk circuit in Greenwich Village, where he met Bobby Scott, a composer, singer, and pianist who had played with Bobby Darin, among others. Scott financed and produced Young's debut, *The Soul of a City Boy*. Reputedly cut in four hours, the solo LP of Young and acoustic guitar was released on Capitol in 1964. He began to play the Boston clubs and then cut *Youngblood* for Mercury, again with Scott producing, this time with a backup band including friend John Sebastian.

Inspired by the Beatles, Young decided to form a group, beginning with Massachusetts folkie Jerry Corbitt and adding Joe Bauer and Lowell "Banana" Levinger, the last being the most accomplished musician of the band. In late 1965 the new Youngbloods cut some tracks for Mercury, but these were not released until years later on *Two Trips*. Their official debut was *Youngbloods,* which included the hits "Grizzly Bear" and "Get Together," written by Dino Valenti, later a singer for Quicksilver Messenger Service. It was first a regional hit, and it didn't take off nationally until it was rereleased two years later in July 1969 after it had been used on a TV public service ad for brotherhood. In 1969 it hit #5 and went gold. RCA later renamed the first album after the single.

The band moved to Marin County, California, in late 1967. Their next two LPs were produced in New York by Felix Pappalardi before they went west. The third, *Elephant Mountain,* was overseen by Charlie Daniels. Corbitt left the band during *Elephant Mountain,* and the Youngbloods continued as a trio, signing to Warner Bros., which gave them their own label, Raccoon, in 1970. RCA began to repackage all their older work, including a "best-of" that year, also rereleasing for the third time "Darkness Darkness," previously out in August 1968 and March 1969.

The Youngbloods' first two Warners/Raccoon albums were live recordings—*Rock Festival* and *Ride the Wind*. In early 1971 they added bassist Michael Kane, freeing Young to play guitar. The band issued two more LPs—*Good and Dusty* and *High on a Ridge Top*—before disbanding in 1972. Bauer and Banana made solo albums; Corbitt had previously cut two; all of these went nowhere. Bauer, Banana, and Kane briefly united to form the band Noggins, doing one LP, *Crab Tunes,* for Raccoon in 1972. Banana also recorded as Banana and the Bunch, worked with Mimi Fariña, and taught hang gliding. Bauer succumbed to a brain tumor in 1982.

Young was the only musician to successfully carry on. *Together* had the breezy feel of the Youngbloods, again highlighted by his light, supple vocals. He has continued to tour and record. Surviving Youngblood members Banana, Corbitt, and Young reunited first in 1984–85 to tour.

Young MC
Born Marvin Young, May 10, 1967, London, England
1989—*Stone Cold Rhymin'* (Delicious Vinyl)   1991—
Brainstorm* (Capitol)   1993—*What's the Flavor?

Clean-cut, college-educated Young MC was one of the first black rappers to score a Top Ten pop hit, with 1989's "Bust a Move," a credible-sounding, yet catchy and nonthreatening, hip-hop track.

Marvin Young's parents, who'd emigrated from Jamaica to England, moved to Hollis, Queens (also home to Run-D.M.C. and L.L. Cool J), when he was two years old. He began writing songs and poems, based on fairy tales and nursery rhymes, as a child. He joined protean rap groups in high school and went to the University of Southern California, where he met Michael Ross and Matt Dike, a pair of DJ/producers who co-owned the Delicious Vinyl label. Young recorded a single for the label, "I Let 'Em Know," that found some success in the U.S. and U.K.

In 1989 Young collaborated on lyrics for Tone-Lōc's #2 pop hit "Wild Thing" (the first Top Ten pop hit by a black rapper) and its followup, "Funky Cold Medina." Still at USC, Young recorded his debut album as Young MC, *Stone Cold Rhymin'* (#9, 1989), which included the comical story rap "Principal's Office" (#33, 1989) and "Bust a Move" (#7, 1989), which won the Grammy for Best Rap Performance. Also in 1989 Young appeared on and wrote lyrics for Sly and Robbie's *Silent Assassin*.

He then tried to bolt from Delicious Vinyl, claiming, "On my album there was stuff I'd never heard before," and that the label kept him from writing soundtrack music for the Eddie Murphy movie *Another 48 Hrs*. Delicious Vinyl sued him for breach of contract. The matter was settled out of court in 1991, and Young MC released *Brainstorm* (#66, 1991) on Capitol Records. The album— full of socially responsible tracks like "Use Your Head" and "Keep It in Your Pants"—yielded only the minor hit "That's the Way Love Goes" (#54, 1991). His 1993 album, *What's the Flavor?,* flopped.

The Young Rascals: See the Rascals

Z

Robin Zander: See Cheap Trick

Zapp/Roger

Formed 1975, Hamilton, Ohio
Roger "Zapp" Troutman (b. Nov. 29, 1951, Hamilton), voc., gtr.; Lester Troutman (b. Mar. 3, 1956, Hamilton), drums; Terry Troutman (b. Apr. 7, 1961, Hamilton), bass; Larry Troutman (b. Aug. 12, 1944, Hamilton), congas.
1980—*Zapp* (Warner Bros.) 1982—*Zapp II* 1983—*Zapp III* 1985—*The New Zapp IV U* 1989—*Zapp V.*
Roger: 1981—*The Many Facets of Roger* (Warner Bros.) 1984—*The Saga Continues* 1987—*Unlimited!* 1991—*Bridging the Gap* (Reprise).
Zapp & Roger: 1993—*All the Greatest Hits* (Reprise).

Zapp had a string of post-Parliament funk hits during the Eighties, the biggest being "More Bounce to the Ounce—Part I" (#86 pop, #2 R&B, 1980). Though the group's musical foundation was funk, leader Roger Troutman often leads Zapp into light jazz or blues. The group spruces up its performances with zany costume changes and quirky vocal effects.

Roger Troutman grew up in working-class Hamilton, Ohio. As a child he remembers his parents' being unhappy during the week and happy on the weekends, when they would spend time with his aunts and uncles listening to music. Troutman associated music with hap-

piness and decided to learn to play and sing himself. He began experimenting with a vocoder, an electronic effect that makes the human voice sound robotic.

In 1975 Troutman and three brothers formed Roger and the Human Body, whose vocoderized funk became their main schtick. The group recorded an independent record, which made its way to Parliament/Funkadelic maestro George Clinton. With Clinton's help, the group landed a deal on Warner Bros., renamed themselves Zapp, and recorded their self-titled debut album with other musicians, including Bootsy Collins on guitar.

On the strength of "More Bounce to the Ounce" and "Be Alright" (#26 R&B, 1980), *Zapp* reached #19 on the pop charts in 1980 and went gold. *Zapp II* (#25, 1982) produced the hits "Doo Wah Ditty (Blow That Thing)" (#10 R&B, 1982) and "Dance Floor (Part I)" (#1 R&B, 1982). *Zapp III* (#39, 1983) spawned "I Can Make You Dance (Part I)" (#4 R&B, 1983) and "Heartbreaker" (#15 R&B, 1983). The group returned two years later with *The New Zapp IV U,* scoring a hit with "Computer Love (Part I)" (#8 R&B, 1986). But rap had taken over by mid-decade, and Zapp seemed to get lost in the shuffle; 1989's *Zapp V* charted very low at #156 (pop).

In the meantime, Troutman recorded several solo albums in the Eighties and into the Nineties, under the name Roger, and scored a big hit with 1987's "I Wanna Be Your Man" (#3 pop, #1 R&B). He also produced former Zapp backup singer Shirley Murdock's self-titled album, which included the R&B Top Ten single "Go On Without You."

In 1993 the group—renamed Zapp & Roger—charted with *All the Greatest Hits* (#39 pop, #9 R&B, 1993), which yielded the hits "Slow and Easy" (#43 pop, #18 R&B, 1993) and "Mega Medley" (#54 pop, #30 R&B, 1993). The following year, Troutman returned with *Bridging the Gap,* on which he collaborated with Scritti Politti's David Gamson.

Frank Zappa/Mothers of Invention

Born Frank Vincent Zappa, December 21, 1940, Baltimore, Maryland; died December 4, 1993, Los Angeles, California
1969—*Hot Rats* (Bizarre)   1970—*Chunga's Revenge*
1971—*200 Motels* (United Artists)   1972—*Waka Jawaka* (Bizarre)   1974—*Apostrophe (')* (DiscReet)
1975—*Bongo Fury* (with Captain Beefheart)
1976—*Zoot Allures*   1979—*Sheik Yerbouti* (Zappa); *Joe's Garage, Act I; Joe's Garage, Acts II and III*

Frank Zappa

1981—*Tinseltown Rebellion* (Barking Pumpkin); *Shut Up 'n Play Yer Guitar*   1982—*Ship Arriving Too Late to Save a Drowning Witch*   1983—*Baby Snakes*   1984—*Them or Us*   1985—*Frank Zappa Meets the Mothers of Prevention*   1986—*Jazz from Hell*   1988—*Broadway the Hard Way*   1993—*The Yellow Shark*   1995—*Civilization Phaze III.*
Mothers of Invention, formed 1964, Los Angeles (Zappa, voc., gtr., various instruments; Ray Collins, voc.; Dave Coronada, sax; Roy Estrada, bass; Jimmy Carl Black, drums; – Coronada; + Elliot Ingber, gtr.):
1966—*Freak Out!* (Verve) (– Ingber; + Bunk Gardner, sax; + Jim "Motorhead" Sherwood, gtr.; + Don Preston, kybds.; + Billy Mundi, drums)   1967—*Absolutely Free; Lumpy Gravy* (– Mundi)   1968—*We're Only in It for the Money; Cruising with Ruben & the Jets*   1969—*Uncle Meat* (Bizarre) (+ Lowell George [b. 1945; d. June 29, 1979, Arlington, Va.], gtr.; + Art Tripp III, drums)   1970—*Burnt Weeny Sandwich; Weasels Ripped My Flesh* (group disbands; group re-forms: + Ian Underwood, kybds., reeds; + Howard Kaylan [b. June 22, 1945, New York City, N.Y.], voc.; + Mark Volman [b. Apr. 19, 1944, Los Angeles], voc.; + Jim Pons, bass; + George Duke, kybds.; + Aynsley Dunbar [b. 1946, Liverpool, Eng.], drums)   1971—*Mothers Live at the Fillmore East*   1972—*Just Another Band from L.A.; The Grand Wazoo*   1973—*Over-nite Sensation* (DiscReet).

With more than 60 albums to his credit, composer, arranger, guitarist, and bandleader Frank Zappa demonstrated a mastery of pop idioms ranging from jazz to rock of every conceivable variety, penned electronic and orchestral works, parlayed controversial satire, and testified in Congress against censorship. As astute an entrepreneur as he was a musician, he was impatient with any division between popular and high art; he combined scatological humor with political wit, required of his players (Little Feat founder Lowell George, guitarists Adrian Belew and Steve Vai, and drummer Terry Bozzio among them) an intimidating skill, and displayed consistent innovation in instrumental and studio technology.

The eldest of four children of a guitar-playing government scientist, Frank Zappa moved with his family at age ten to California, eventually settling in Lancaster. Playing in school orchestras and bands, he taught himself a variety of instruments, concentrating on guitar. A collector of Fifties rock & roll and R&B singles, he also listened to modern classical composers like Stravinsky and his avowed favorite, Edgard Varèse. In high school he formed the Black-Outs and added country blues to his record collection. He met future collaborator and underground legend Don Van Vliet and allegedly christened him Captain Beefheart. In 1959 he studied music theory at Chaffey College in Alta Loma, California, dropping out after six months.

In 1960 Zappa played cocktail music in lounges and worked on his first recordings and the score for a B movie, *The World's Greatest Sinner*. He also appeared on Steve Allen's TV show, performing a "bicycle concerto" (plucking the spokes, blowing through the handlebars). In 1963 Zappa wrote a score for a Western called *Run Home Slow*, and with the money built a studio in Cucamonga, California. He befriended future Mothers Ray Collins and Jim "Motorhead" Sherwood and formed a band with Beefheart called the Soots.

Zappa was charged for conspiracy to commit pornography by the San Bernardino Vice Squad after an undercover policeman requested some sex "party" tapes: Zappa delivered tapes of faked grunting, and served ten days of a six-month jail sentence. The woman involved was bailed out of jail with royalties from "Memories of El Monte," which Zappa and Collins had written for the doo-wop group the Penguins.

In 1964 Zappa joined the Soul Giants, with Collins (vocals), Dave Coronada (sax), Roy Estrada (bass), and Jimmy Carl Black (drums). Renaming them the Muthers, then the Mothers, he moved the band onto L.A.'s proto-hippie "freak" circuit (Coronada quit, replaced by guitarist Elliot Ingber). The band played clubs for two years, mixing covers with social-protest tunes like "Who Are the Brain Police?" In early 1966 producer Tom Wilson signed them to MGM/Verve and recorded *Freak Out!* MGM, wary of the band's outrageous reputation, forced Zappa to add "of Invention" to the Mothers. Though Zappa advertised the album in underground papers and comics and earned critical respect for the album's obvious musical and lyrical distinction, it ended up losing money.

In 1966, with Ingber departing, eventually to join Captain Beefheart's Magic Band, the Mothers lineup expanded to include saxophonists Bunk Gardner and Motorhead Sherwood, keyboardist Don Preston, and drummer Billy Mundi. Released in 1967, *Absolutely Free* further satirized "straight" America with pointed tunes like "Brown Shoes Don't Make It" and "Plastic People." His montage production techniques—mingling tape edits, noise, recitative, free-form outbursts, and Varèse-like modern classical music with rock—were coming into their own. In 1967 Zappa and the Mothers also recorded *Lumpy Gravy*, with a 50-piece orchestra, including many Mothers, and *Cruising with Ruben & the Jets*, an homage to Fifties doo-wop. *We're Only in It for the Money*, a parody of the Beatles' *Sgt. Pepper*, found Zappa savaging hippie pretensions.

Billy Mundi left after *Lumpy Gravy*; by now it was apparent that the Mothers were less a band than a shifting vehicle for Zappa's art. While recording *Money*, Zappa and the group had moved to New York City's Greenwich Village, where they began a six-month residency at the Garrick Theatre. There they pioneered rock theater with a series of often-spontaneous audience-participation skits. While recording *Ruben & the Jets*, the Mothers also began recording *Uncle Meat*, a double album for a never-completed movie. It is the first example of Zappa's trademark complex-meter jazz-rock fusion.

After making *Uncle Meat*, Zappa moved the band back to L.A. and married his second wife, Gail; their four children are daughters Moon Unit and Diva and sons Dweezil and Ahmet Rodan. (Dweezil would become a solo artist in the Eighties, then form Shampoohorn with his brother in the Nineties.) In L.A. Zappa moved into movie cowboy Tom Mix's Log Cabin Ranch, where he assembled the increasingly complex *Burnt Weeny Sandwich* and *Weasels Ripped My Flesh*. By this time, the band had come to include second guitarist Lowell George and drummer Art Tripp III.

In late 1968 Zappa and manager Herb Cohen had moved to Warner/Reprise, where they formed their own Straight and Bizarre labels. Zappa recorded such acts as groupie collective the GTO's (Girls Together Outrageously, which included future best-selling author Pamela Des Barres), onetime street-singer Wild Man Fischer, Alice Cooper, and Captain Beefheart (whose *Trout Mask Replica* was one of Zappa's most memorable productions). By the time *Weasels* was released in 1970, Zappa had temporarily disbanded the Mothers because of overwhelming expenses and public apathy. Lowell George and Roy Estrada then founded Little Feat; Art Tripp III joined Beefheart (Estrada later joined Beefheart as well); Gardner and Black formed Geronimo Black.

Zappa began composing the soundtrack for *200 Motels*. He also recorded his first solo album, *Hot Rats*, a jazz-rock guitar showcase featuring Beefheart and jazz violinists Jean-Luc Ponty and Don "Sugarcane" Harris. *Hot Rats* was released to great critical acclaim in 1969, as was Ponty's *King Kong* (1970), an album of Zappa compositions (for legal reasons, Zappa's name couldn't be listed as producer and guitarist). In 1970 Zappa also performed the *200 Motels* score with Zubin Mehta and the L.A. Philharmonic at a sold-out L.A. concert. That summer, Zappa re-formed the Mothers, retaining keyboardist/reedman Ian Underwood and adding ex-Turtles Howard Kaylan and Mark Volman (singers then known as the Phlorescent Leech and Eddie) and bassist Jim Pons, jazz keyboardist George Duke, and British rock drummer Aynsley Dunbar. With this lineup and other session players, Zappa recorded *Waka Jawaka* and *Chunga's Revenge* as solo albums and the Mothers' *Live at the Fillmore East* and *Just Another Band from L.A.*

At this point, critics began accusing the Mothers of becoming a cynical, scatological joke, but Zappa displayed no discomfort in portraying two apparently contradictory personae: the raunchy inciter and the serious composer (whose stature in fact would increase over the years, and whose cult always remained intense). In 1971 the *200 Motels* film, featuring Theodore Bikel and Ringo Starr as surrogate Zappas, as well as the Mothers, was released to mixed response. In May 1971 Zappa appeared at one of the last Fillmore East concerts with John Lennon and Yoko Ono; the performance appears on Lennon/Ono's *Some Time in New York City.* As the Mothers personnel began to change more frequently, they embarked on a 1971 tour in which their equipment was destroyed in a fire at Switzerland's Montreux Casino (immortalized in opening act Deep Purple's "Smoke on the Water"), and Zappa was injured when a fan pushed him from the stage of London's Rainbow. A year later the Mothers were banned from the Royal Albert Hall for "obscenity."

The Grand Wazoo, with numerous auxiliary players, was a big-band fusion album. And in 1973 Zappa and the Mothers also recorded *Over-nite Sensation,* on which Zappa simplified his music and kept his lyrics in a scatological-humorous vein (as in "Don't Eat the Yellow Snow" [#86, 1974]). Album sales picked up. *Apostrophe (')* featured an extended jam with ex-Cream bassist Jack Bruce, as well as by-now-typical dirty jokes and satires. The 1975 *Bongo Fury* album reunited Zappa with Beefheart. The latter had fallen out with Zappa after *Trout Mask,* accusing Zappa of marketing him like "a freak."

After producing Grand Funk Railroad's *Good Singin', Good Playin'* in 1976, Zappa filed a lawsuit against Herb Cohen in 1977, and severed ties with Warner Bros., moving to Mercury two years later. There he set up Zappa Records and retired the Mothers name, calling all later groups Zappa. On the new label he released *Sheik Yerbouti* (a pun on KC and the Sunshine Band's "Shake Your Booty"), including the song "Jewish Princess," for which the B'nai B'rith Anti-Defamation League filed a complaint with the FCC against Zappa. That album also yielded a surprise hit single, "Dancin' Fool" (#45, 1979), which lampooned the disco crowd. (*Sheik* peaked at #21 on the albums chart.) *Joe's Garage, Act I,* the first installment of a three-act rock opera, included "Catholic Girls," and Zappa's penchant for barbed attacks continued to infuriate his opponents, while strengthening his own following. In 1979 Zappa released the film *Baby Snakes,* a mélange of concert footage, dressing-room slapstick, and clay-figure animation. The late-Seventies Zappa bands included guitarist Adrian Belew (who later played with Talking Heads, King Crimson, and David Bowie) and drummer Terry Bozzio (who later with his wife Dale founded Missing Persons).

In 1980 Zappa recorded a single, "I Don't Wanna Get Drafted," which Mercury refused to release, prompting him to leave the label and eventually establish his own Barking Pumpkin label.

In 1981 Zappa released his first Barking Pumpkin album, and that year, some ex-Mothers, including Jimmy Carl Black, Don Preston, and Bunk Gardner, united to form the Grandmothers. They toured and recorded, playing all-Zappa material from the Mothers' vintage late-Sixties period. That April Zappa produced and hosted a New York City concert of music by Edgard Varèse. He also released a limited-edition, mail-order-only three-album series, *Shut Up 'n Play Yer Guitar.*

Zappa parlayed stereotype satire into success once more with "Valley Girl" (#32, 1982) from the *Drowning Witch* album. The song parodied the spoiled daughters of entertainment-industry folk, specifically those in the San Bernardino Valley city of Encino, and featured inspired mimicry by then-14-year-old Moon Unit Zappa. In 1983 Zappa conducted works by Varèse and Anton Webern at San Francisco's War Memorial Opera House.

The Eighties saw Zappa consolidating his business affairs; with Gail Zappa in charge, his companies included not only Barking Pumpkin (a mail-order label, distributed by Capitol), but Honker Home Video, Barfko-Swill (for Zappa merchandise), and World's Finest Optional Entertainment Co. (to produce live shows). He also arranged with Rykodisc to rerelease his catalogue on CD. A lifelong free-speech advocate, he testified before a Senate subcommittee in 1985 and assailed the Parents' Music Resource Center (excerpts from the hearings appeared on *Frank Zappa Meets the Mothers of Prevention*); throughout the decade, he also championed voter registration drives. In 1990, at the invitation of Czechoslovakian president Václav Havel, a longtime fan, Zappa served for several months as that country's trade, tourism, and cultural liaison to the West. The following year, he considered a run for the U.S. presidency.

Artistically, the Eighties were also fertile years for Zappa. Early in the decade, the Berkeley Symphony performed his work; in 1984 conductor/composer Pierre Boulez released *Boulez Conducts Zappa/The Perfect Stranger* (#7 on the classical chart, 1984). In 1988 Zappa undertook a world tour (documented on *Broadway the Hard Way*) and won a Grammy for Best Rock Instrumental Performance for *Jazz from Hell,* an album composed on Synclavier, a highly sophisticated synthesizer that in Zappa found one of its chief devotees. Among his other late-Eighties projects were remastering his Sixties work for CD and assembling six double-CD sets of live work entitled *You Can't Do That on Stage Anymore.* In 1989 Poseidon Press published his autobiography, *The Real Frank Zappa Book.*

In 1991, in New York City on the eve of a tribute concert entitled "Zappa's Universe," Moon Unit and Dweezil Zappa announced that their father had been diagnosed with prostate cancer. A lifelong teetotaler and abstainer from drugs (Zappa, however, smoked cigarettes and drank coffee incessantly), the composer continued a rig-

Grammy Awards

Frank Zappa
1987 Best Rock Instrumental Performance (Orchestra, Group, or Soloist): *Jazz from Hell*

Zappa's Universe Rock Group Featuring Steve Vai
1993 Best Rock Instrumental Performance: "Sofa"

---

orous work schedule. In 1993 he completed a two-CD sequel to *Lumpy Gravy, Civilization Phaze III* (released in 1995), and he recorded both *The Yellow Shark*, an album of his compositions recorded by the classical group Ensemble Modern and, also with the Ensemble, an album of Varèse works tentatively entitled *The Rage and the Fury: The Music of Edgard Varèse*. Frank Zappa died on the evening of December 4, 1993, at his Los Angeles home; he was 52 years old.

Josef Zawinul: See Weather Report

Zebra
Formed 1975, New Orleans, Louisiana
Guy Gelso (b. Oct. 29, 1952, Sacramento, Calif.), drums; Felix Haneman (b. May 1, 1953, New Orleans), bass; Randy Jackson (b. Jan. 28, 1955, New Orleans), gtr., voc.
1983—*Zebra* (Atlantic)   **1984**—*No Tellin' Lies*
1987—*V.3*   **1990**—*Live.*
Randy Jackson solo: **1991**—*China Rain.*

A heavy-metal power trio centered on the songs and playing of guitarist Randy Jackson, Zebra had a hit right out of the box with their self-titled first album (#29, 1983). Jackson and Felix Haneman first played together in New Orleans in 1973. Their band, Shepherd's Bush, broke up soon thereafter, but the two decided to team up. In 1975 they met Gus Gelso playing in a quartet called Maelstrom, and three months later they formed Zebra. Friends helped them get bookings on the then-burgeoning Long Island (New York) club scene; the band moved there in 1977. They developed a following along the East Coast and were signed to Atlantic Records in 1982.

None of Zebra's later records matched the success of their debut. They tried to expand their sound on 1987's *V.3*, adding saxophonist Stan Bronstein from Elephant's Memory, to no avail. In 1991 Jackson recorded a solo album, *China Rain,* using computer technology to "play" bass and drums. He tours both with his band and as a one-man show.

Warren Zevon
Born January 24, 1947, Chicago, Illinois
1969—*Wanted—Dead or Alive* (Imperial)   **1976**—*Warren Zevon* (Asylum)   **1978**—*Excitable Boy*
1980—*Bad Luck Streak in Dancing School; Stand in the Fire*   **1982**—*The Envoy*   **1987**—*A Quiet Normal Life: The Best of Warren Zevon; Sentimental Hygiene* (Virgin)   **1989**—*Transverse City*   **1991**—*Mr. Bad Example* (Giant)   **1993**—*Learning to Flinch*
1995—*Mutineer.*

Singer/songwriter Warren Zevon's ironic tales of physical and psychological mayhem have earned him a cult following and comparisons to figures as diverse as Dorothy Parker, Raymond Chandler, Sam Peckinpah, and Martin Scorsese.

The son of Russian immigrants, Zevon grew up in Arizona and California. He studied music briefly, and after meeting Igor Stravinsky during his junior high school years, Zevon taught himself to play guitar and began writing songs. He played in local bands and at age 16 moved to New York City, then to the Bay Area. He wrote songs (including "She Quit Me Man," used in the film *Midnight Cowboy*) and released his debut LP, *Wanted—Dead or Alive.* It was poorly received, and he went to work writing jingles (for Ernest and Julio Gallo wine ads, a famous ketchup, and the Chevrolet Camaro) and as pianist and bandleader for the Everly Brothers shortly before their breakup. Over the next couple of years he continued to work with each brother separately.

In 1976 Linda Ronstadt covered Zevon's "Hasten Down the Wind" on her album of the same title. The next year two more of Zevon's songs appeared on Ronstadt's *Simple Dreams:* "Carmelita" and "Poor Poor Pitiful Me," the latter of which was a hit for Ronstadt in 1978. Zevon, who had been living in Spain, was persuaded by his friend Jackson Browne to return to the U.S. and record. Browne produced *Warren Zevon,* which was released to critical acclaim; he would produce or coproduce all of Zevon's albums through and including *A Quiet Normal Life: The Best of Warren Zevon.*

In 1978 Zevon had a #21 single with "Werewolves of London." But his career was temporarily set back by his alcoholism. He did not record for two years, and his live performances were few and erratic. His two 1980 releases, *Bad Luck Streak* and the live *Stand in the Fire,* represented something of a comeback for Zevon. He announced he had given up alcohol and he released *The Envoy,* the title track written about U.S. envoy to the Mideast Philip Habib. *Sentimental Hygiene* appeared five years later, with backing from members of R.E.M. He also recorded with three-quarters of that group under the name Hindu Love Gods in 1990.

While Zevon continues to be appreciated by critics, his sometimes edgy, satirical work eludes the mass audience. *Transverse City,* a science-fiction–inspired concept album, and *Mr. Bad Example* were not received as warmly as Zevon's earlier work. Nonetheless, as evidenced in reviews for his second live album, 1993's *Learning to Flinch,* Zevon retains his unique, original vision and remains a compelling writer and performer.

Since the early Nineties, Zevon has composed and/or performed a number of theme songs and scores for television series, including *The Drug Wars* (1990), *Tales from the Crypt* (1992), *Route 66* (1993), and *Tekwar* (1993).

The Zombies
Formed 1963, Hertfordshire, England
Colin Blunstone (b. June 24, 1945, Hatfield, Eng.), voc.; Paul Atkinson (b. Mar. 19, 1946, Cuffley, Eng.), gtr.; Rod Argent (b. June 14, 1945, St. Albans, Eng.), kybds., voc.; Hugh Grundy (b. Mar. 6, 1945, Winchester, Eng.), drums; Paul Arnold (b. Eng.), bass.
1964—(– Arnold; + Chris White [b. Mar. 7, 1943, Barnet, Eng.], bass) 1965—*Begins Here* (Decca) 1968—*Odyssey and Oracle* (Date) 1973—*Time of the Zombies* (Epic) 1985—*Live on the BBC: 1965–1967* (Rhino) 1990—*Greatest Hits* (Digital Compact Classics).

Though the Zombies had several major hits, their career was a frustrating one. Paul Atkinson, Rod Argent, and Hugh Grundy met at St. Albans School, and they soon linked up with Colin Blunstone and bassist Paul Arnold. Six months later Arnold was replaced by Chris White. After winning a rock-band contest held by a local newspaper, they got an audition with British Decca in 1964. That July, the electric-piano-centered "She's Not There" was released; it became a worldwide smash, going to #2 in America. A second single, "Leave Me Be," failed, but "Tell Her No" went Top Ten, their last hit for some time. They also contributed songs to the movie *Bunny Lake Is Missing.*

In 1967 they recorded a final LP, *Odyssey and Oracle* (the only album the band themselves approved of). But they broke up two weeks after it was completed, in December 1967. Columbia staff producer Al Kooper fought to have the album issued; when it was, in late 1968, it yielded a #3 gold hit in "Time of the Season." The band declined to re-form, although sizable sums were offered. Argent already was moving ahead on plans for his eponymous band [see entry], and most of the rest were fed up with the music business. Blunstone had first gone back to working in an insurance office, then began working as a singer under the name Neil MacArthur. With that pseudonym he had a 1970 hit with a remake of "She's Not There." He made several solo LPs under his own name for Epic, beginning in 1971 with *One Year* (produced by Argent and White). In 1978 he tried again, unsuccessfully, with *Never Even Thought* on Elton John's Rocket Records. Blunstone has since formed a group called Keats and sung on several records by the Alan Parsons Project.

Atkinson first went into programming computers but later was in A&R, working for Charisma, CBS, RCA, and MCA. Grundy also worked in Columbia A&R, but in the Eighties he was running a horse transport business near London. White cowrote songs and produced for Argent (he wrote "Hold Your Head Up"), and in the Seventies he helped discover Dire Straits. Original bassist Arnold became a doctor in Scotland. Epic released a two-record best-of, *Time of the Zombies,* in 1973.

John Zorn
Born September 2, 1953, Brooklyn, New York
1986—*The Big Gundown* (Elektra Nonesuch) 1987—*Spillane* 1989—*Spy vs. Spy: The Music of Ornette Coleman* 1990—*Naked City* 1992—*Filmworks: 1986–1990*; *John Zorn's Cobra Live at the Knitting Factory* (Knitting Factory Works).

Composer, instrumentalist, musical subversist John Zorn was the most important figure to emerge in the 1980s from New York's Downtown avant-garde music scene. Zorn became interested in jazz while briefly attending the liberal Webster College in St. Louis and began studying the alto saxophone.

By the time he returned to his hometown, New York, in 1974, Zorn had already developed his own theories of composition and improvisation incorporating ideas from traditional and avant-garde strains of jazz, classical, rock and a panoply of international aesthetics. With his whirlwind energy Zorn became the vortex of the new musical polyglot that was brewing among adventurous players on New York's Lower East Side. His hand in a multitude of projects—from be-bop tributes to obscure jazzmen to epic performances of Cobra, which applied rules of game playing to free improvisation—Zorn galvanized the scene.

While Zorn's work is generally released by independent and European labels that cater to the avant-garde, he began recording for Elektra Nonesuch in the late Eighties, beginning with *The Big Gundown,* a twisted tribute to cult film composer Ennio Morricone, and *Spillane,* which featured bluesman Albert Collins. Zorn's projects drew upon a pool of like-minded innovators, including guitarist Elliott Sharp, keyboardist Wayne Horvitz, and drummer Bobby Previte.

By the late Eighties Zorn was dividing his year between New York and Tokyo. With Fred Frith, Bill Frisell, and Joey Baron, Zorn formed the band Naked City, which touched on, among myriad musics, his new fascination

with thrash rock; Zorn's Spy vs. Spy band retransformed Ornette Coleman's music with its slamming, full-force interpretations. In September 1993, in honor of Zorn's 40th birthday, the Knitting Factory (New York's chief Downtown avant-garde music club) presented Zorn for a solid month, enabling him to cover a wide if incomplete spectrum of his musical endeavors.

ZZ Top

Formed 1970, Texas
Billy Gibbons, gtr., voc.; Dusty Hill, bass, voc.;
Frank Beard, drums.
1970—*First Album* (London)   1972—*Rio Grande Mud*   1973—*Tres Hombres*   1975—*Fandango!*
1976—*Tejas*   1977—*Best of ZZ Top*   1979—
Deguello (Warner Bros.)   1981—*El Loco*   1983—
Eliminator   1985—*Afterburner*   1990—*Recycler*
1992—*Greatest Hits*   1994—*Antenna* (RCA).

ZZ Top began as a rough-and-ready blues-rock power trio from Texas that became a huge mid-Seventies concert attraction. Their real commercial peak didn't come, however, until the Eighties, when the "Little Ol' Band from Texas" became MTV superstars and sold multiple millions of albums.

ZZ Top was built around guitarist Billy Gibbons, whose career began with the popular southwestern band Moving Sidewalks, whose "99th Floor" was a regional mid-Sixties hit. They opened one night for Jimi Hendrix, and he later mentioned Gibbons on *The Tonight Show* as one of America's best young guitarists. After Moving Sidewalks broke up, Gibbons and man-

ager/producer Bill Ham recruited Frank Beard and Dusty Hill from a Dallas band, American Blues.

Beginning with the release of *First Album* in 1970, ZZ Top has toured constantly, building a national following that has made all the band's albums gold or platinum. A year-long tour in 1976, the Worldwide Texas Tour, was one of the largest-grossing road trips in rock at the time. Onstage with the band were snakes, longhorn cattle, buffalo, cactus, and other southwestern paraphernalia. The group sold over one million tickets. They didn't record for the next three years, until 1979's *Deguello*. Though ZZ Top's only major hit singles had been *Tres Hombres'* "La Grange" (#41, 1973) and *Fandango!*'s "Tush" (#20, 1975), their albums consistently made the Top Forty.

With 1983's *Eliminator*, ZZ Top made a quantum leap from best-kept secret to massive stardom. Thanks to smartly directed video clips for such songs as "Gimme All Your Lovin'" (#37, 1983), "Sharp Dressed Man" (#56, 1983), "Legs" (#8, 1983), and "TV Dinners," Gibbons and Hill, with their long beards (ironically Beard wore only a mustache), became MTV icons, as did the cherry red 1933 Ford coupe (restored by Gibbons) that gave the album its name, and that the band drove in the videos. Thanks to this exposure, a whole new audience began buying the band's albums, and *Eliminator* (#9, 1983) sold some seven million copies, remaining on the chart for over three and a half years. "Legs" introduced a pulsating synthesizer beat into ZZ Top's crunching blues-rock riffs.

The trend continued with *Afterburner* (#4, 1985), which contained such video hits as "Rough Boy" (#22, 1985), "Sleeping Bag" (#8, 1985), "Velcro Fly" (#35, 1986), and "Stages" (#21, 1986). The album sold over three million copies. After another long world tour, ZZ Top—which had long been based in Houston—announced that, through NASA, it had booked passage as the first lounge band on the space shuttle (though the band had yet to actually fly a mission).

At the peak of its success, ZZ Top still remembered its roots, and launched a fund-raising drive to erect a Delta Blues Museum in Clarksdale, Mississippi. At a special ceremony the band unveiled the "Muddywood" guitar, made from a beam taken from the sharecropper's shack in which blues giant Muddy Waters had been raised (the groundbreaking for the museum itself was scheduled for 1995).

ZZ Top appeared to have finally tapped out the motherlode with *Recycler* (#6, 1990), which sold a relatively disappointing one million units and yielded only minor hits in "Doubleback" (#50, 1990) and "Give It Up" (#79, 1990). After Warner Bros. released *Greatest Hits*, ZZ Top left the label and signed a $30-million deal with RCA. The band's first album for the new label, *Antenna*, was named in tribute to rock radio—especially the Mexican border stations of the Fifties and Sixties that influenced the band. The album entered the chart at #14, but dropped rapidly and failed to yield a hit single. Still, even as it sat at #151 five months after its release, *Antenna* had gone platinum, proving the band still had a considerable fan base.

Appendix

Cuts from the First Edition

David Ackles

Alessi

Alpha Band

Amon Duul II

Armageddon

Peter Asher

Ashton, Gardner and Dyke

Automatic Man

Baby Huey and the Babysitters

Burt Bacharach

Jeff Barry

Dave Bartholomew

Beaver and Krause

Thom Bell

Bert Berns

The Big Three

Cilla Black

Blues Image

Elkie Brooks

Duncan Browne

Felice and Boudleaux Bryant

Cindy Bullens

The Bus Boys

Caravan

Chilliwack

Dick Clark

Clover

Colosseum and Colosseum II

Steve Cropper

Mike Curb

Tim Curry

Michael D'Abo

Clement "Coxsone" Dodd

Earth Quake

Tommy "Bubba" Facenda

Wes Farrell

The Flock

Richie Furay

Gamble and Huff

Crystal Gayle

Ellie Greenwich

Hugo and Luigi

The Jaynetts

Kasenetz-Katz

Don Kirshner

Leslie Kong

David Lindley

Magma

Barry Mann and Cynthia Weil

Moon Martin

Mike McGear

Ellen McIlwaine

Frankie Miller

Giorgio Moroder

George "Shadow" Morton

Mud

Martin Mull

Moon Mullican

Fred Neil

Jack Nitzsche

The Nutmegs

Oliver

Gary Puckett and the Union Gap

Dory Previn

The Ritchie Family

Rosie and the Originals

Jimmy Ruffin

Carole Bayer Sager

The Souther-Hillman-Furay Band

S-Z

Livingston Taylor

Johnny Tillotson

The Ultimate Spinach

Wet Willie

Jerry Wexler

A coauthor of *The* ROLLING STONE *Album Guide*, **Paul Evans** is a frequent contributor to ROLLING STONE. An Atlanta-based freelancer, he has written about Prince for *The* ROLLING STONE *Illustrated History of Rock & Roll*, third edition (Random House, 1992) and contributed to *Present Tense: Rock & Roll and Culture* (Duke University Press, 1992).

Steve Futterman is an associate editor at ROLLING STONE. His writing has appeared in ROLLING STONE, *The New Yorker*, the *New York Times*, and the *Village Voice*, among other publications.

Elysa Gardner is a frequent contributor to ROLLING STONE and wrote the introduction to *U2: The* ROLLING STONE *Files* (Hyperion, 1994). Her writing has also been published in *The New Yorker*, the *Los Angeles Times*, *Musician*, *Spin*, *Vibe*, *Mojo*, *Request*, *Entertainment Weekly*, and *Harper's Bazaar*. She lives in New York City.

Holly George-Warren is the coeditor of *The* ROLLING STONE *Album Guide* and *The* ROLLING STONE *Illustrated History of Rock & Roll*. The coauthor of *Musicians in Tune: 75 Contemporary Musicians Discuss the Creative Process* (Fireside, 1992), she has contributed to ROLLING STONE, *Option*, *Musician*, and the *New York Times*, among other publications. Her writing also appears in *Country on Compact Disk* (Grove, 1993), *Neil Young: The* ROLLING STONE *Files* (Hyperion, 1994), and *Rock She Wrote: Women Write About Rock, Pop, and Rap* (Dell, 1995). She has been the editor of Rolling Stone Press since January 1993.

Mark Kemp is the editor of *Option* magazine. His writing has appeared in a variety of publications including the *L.A. Weekly*, *San Francisco Bay Guardian*, the *Village Voice*, and ROLLING STONE. A native of North Carolina, he now lives in temperamental Los Angeles.

Evelyn McDonnell is coeditor of the anthology *Rock She Wrote: Women Write About Rock, Pop, and Rap* (Dell, 1995). She is a New York–based freelance writer whose articles have appeared in ROLLING STONE, the *Village Voice*, *Ms.*, *Interview*, *Option*, *Spin*, *Musician*, *Billboard*, and the *New York Times*.

Steven Mirkin is a New York–based freelance writer. His work has appeared in ROLLING STONE, *US*, *Entertainment Weekly*, *Spy*, *Request*, *Option*, and the *New York Times*.

Jon Pareles has written for nearly every major music publication since 1977, when his work first appeared in *Crawdaddy*. He has been music editor at *Crawdaddy*, ROLLING STONE, and the *Village Voice*. The coeditor of the first edition of the *Encyclopedia*, he is the pop music critic of the *New York Times*.

Patricia Romanowski was the editor of Rolling Stone Press from 1981 to 1983. Besides serving as the coeditor of the two editions of this *Encyclopedia*, she has cowritten 13 books, among them the national bestsellers *Dreamgirl: My Life as a Supreme* (with Mary Wilson, St. Martin's, 1986) and *La Toya: Growing Up in the Jackson Family* (with La Toya Jackson, Dutton, 1991). Other book credits include *Temptations* (with Otis Williams, G. P. Putnam's Sons, 1988) and *A Dream Is a Wish Your Heart Makes: My Story* (with Annette Funicello, Hyperion, 1994). She was editor and a coauthor of *Fresh: Hip Hop Don't Stop* (with Nelson George and others,

Random House, 1985) and *The* ROLLING STONE *Rock Almanac* (Macmillan, 1984). Her work has appeared in the *New York Times Book Review*. She lives on Long Island with her husband, author Philip Bashe, and their son, Justin.

Michael Shore is the editorial supervisor at MTV News. He's written *The* ROLLING STONE *Book of Music Video*, *Music Video: A Consumer Guide*, and *The History of American Bandstand* with Dick Clark; contributed to the first edition of *The* ROLLING STONE *Encyclopedia of Rock & Roll* and to *The* ROLLING STONE *Rock Almanac*; and written for such publications as ROLLING STONE, the *Village Voice*, *Billboard*, *Musician*, *ARTNews*, *Omni*, *American Illustrated*, *Entertainment Weekly*, and the *Soho Weekly News* (R.I.P.), where he worked from 1979 through its demise in 1982. He graduated from Fordham University in 1978.

In addition to Patricia Romanowski, Jon Pareles, and Michael Shore, contributors from the first edition of *The* ROLLING STONE *Encyclopedia of Rock & Roll* include **Ken Braun**, **Jim Farber**, **Nelson George**, **Jeff Howry**, **Ira Kaplan**, **John Milward**, and **Mitchell Schneider**.

Photo Credits

King Sunny Ade: Adam Scher; Aerosmith: Norman Seeff; American Music Club: Dennis Keeley; Babes in Toyland: Bill Phelps; The Beastie Boys: Ari Marcopoulos; Luka Bloom: Frank Ockenfels 3; Michael Bolton: Timothy White; The Bongos: EDO; Buckwheat Zydeco: Kathy Anderson; Butthole Surfers: Joseph Cultice; John Cale: Ronn Spencer Archives; Cheap Trick: Jim Houghten; Neneh Cherry: Eddie Monsoon; Leonard Cohen: Scott Newton/*Austin City Limits*; Lloyd Cole: David Sims; Albert Collins: Bill Reitzel; Julian Cope: Ed Sirrs; The Cramps: Lindsay Brice; The Cure: Paul Cox; Cypress Hill: Joseph Cultice; Terence Trent D'Arby: Chris Cuffaro; El DeBarge: F. Scott Schafer; Digable Planets: Cathrine Wessel; Dinosaur Jr: Frank Ockenfels 3; Gang Starr: Daniel Hastings; Jimmie Dale Gilmore: Scott Newton; Gipsy Kings: Bernard Matussiere; The Go-Go's: Vicki Berndt; Nanci Griffith: Rocky Schenck; Guns n' Roses: Robert John; Buddy Guy: Brad Pines; Juliana Hatfield: Andrew Catlin; Heavy D. and the Boyz: Danny Clinch; Soft Boys: Rosalind Kunath; The Hoodoo Gurus: Andrzej Liguz; Hüsker Dü: Daniel Corrigan; Julio Iglesias: Alvaro Rodriguez; Inspiral Carpets: Ian Tilton; INXS: Enrique Badulescu; Waylon Jennings: Frank Ockenfels 3; The Jesus and Mary Chain: Colin Bell; Buster Poindexter: Kate Simon; Leo Kottke: Dana Wheelock; Lenny Kravitz: Per Gustafsson; Ladysmith Black Mambazo: Rita Barros; Daniel Lanois: Kate Garner; Lemonheads: Jesse Peretz; Huey Lewis: Jeffrey Thurnher; Living Colour: Amy Guip; Los Lobos: Fredrik Nilsen; Lyle Lovett: Michael Wilson; L7: Catalina Leisenring; Madonna: Patrick DeMarchellier; Kathy Mattea: Randee St. Nicholas; John Mayall: Richard McLaurin; Megadeth: Richard Avedon; The Mekons: Michael Lavine; The Neville Brothers: Jeffrey Newberry; Trent Reznor: Joseph Cultice; Nirvana: Chris Cuffaro; Nitty Gritty Dirt Band: Butch Adams; N.W.A: Darin Pappas; Pere Ubu: Carol Kitman; Tom Petty: Robert Sebree; Primus: Andrew McNaughtan; The Proclaimers: Greg Allen; Genesis P-Orridge: Joseph Cultice; Bonnie Raitt: John Casado; R.E.M.: Keith Carter; Ryuichi Sakamoto: Mondino; David Sanborn: Lynn Goldsmith; Sir Mix-a-Lot: Karen Moskowitz; Slayer: Ken Schles; Morrissey: Dean Freeman; Sonic Youth: Enrique Badulescu; Keith Sweat: Gerhard Yurkovic; They Might Be Giants: Michael Halsband; Richard Thompson: Peter Sanders; A Tribe Called Quest: Courtesy of Zomba Recording Corporation; John Trudell: Beth Herzhaft; Tanya Tucker: Randee St. Nicholas; UB40: David Schienmann; U2: Anton Corbijn.